Assyria, Israel + Judah
The Assyrian Period   75
The Babylonian Period   60
The Persian Period   539
The Hellenistic Period 333 - 64 BCE

Periods of Israeli History

Dictionary
OF THE Old Testament
Prophets

Editors:

Mark J. Boda

J. Gordon McConville

IVP Academic

An imprint of InterVarsity Press
Downers Grove, Illinois

Inter-Varsity Press

Nottingham, England

InterVarsity Press
P.O. Box 1400, Downers Grove, IL 60515-1426, USA
World Wide Web: www.ivpress.com
Email: email@ivpress.com

Inter-Varsity Press, England
Norton Street, Nottingham NG7 3HR, England
Website: www.ivpbooks.com
Email: ivp@ivpbooks.com

InterVarsity Press® is the book-publishing division of InterVarsity Christian Fellowship/USA®, a movement of students and faculty active on campus at hundreds of universities, colleges and schools of nursing in the United States of America, and a member movement of the International Fellowship of Evangelical Students. For information about local and regional activities, visit intervarsity.org.

Inter-Varsity Press, England, is closely linked with the Universities and Colleges Christian Fellowship, a student movement connecting Christian Unions in universities and colleges throughout Great Britain, and a member movement of the International Fellowship of Evangelical Students. Website: <www.uccf.org.uk>.

All Scripture quotations, unless otherwise indicated, are the author's own translation.

Cover design: Cindy Kiple

Images: The Eternal Father in Glory with Prophets and Sibyls, from Sala dell'Udienza (1496-1500; fresco) by Pietro Perugina at Collegio del Cambio, Italy. Alinari/The Bridgeman Art Library.

USA ISBN 978-0-8308-1784-9

UK ISBN 978-1-84474-581-4

Printed in the United States of America ∞

Library of Congress Cataloging-in-Publication Data

Dictionary of the Old Testament : prophets / editors, J. Gordon McConville, Mark Boda.
p. cm.
Includes bibliographical references and index.
ISBN 978-0-8308-1784-9 (hardcover : alk. paper)
1. Bible. O.T. Prophets—Dictionaries. 2. Prophets—Dictionaries.
3. Bible. O.T.—Dictionaries. I. McConville, J. G. (J. Gordon) II. Boda, Mark J.
BS1505.55.D53 2012
224'.03—dc23

2012005240

British Library Cataloguing in Publication Data

A catalogue record for this book is available from the British Library.

P	20	19	18	17	16	15	14	13	12	11	10	9	8	7	6	5	4
Y	29	28	27	26	25	24	23	22	21	20	19	18	17	16	15		

InterVarsity Press

Project Staff

Senior Editor/Project Editor
Daniel G. Reid

Managing Editor
Allison Rieck

Copyeditor
Robert G. Maccini

Editorial &
Administrative Assistants
Rebecca Carhart
Benjamin M. McCoy
Rachel Neftzer Snavely
Elaina Whittenhall

Design
Cindy Kiple

Typesetters
Gail Munroe
Maureen Tobey
Jeanna Wiggins

Proofreaders
Adam Stevenson
Claire VanderVelde

InterVarsity Press

Publisher
Robert A. Fryling

Associate Publisher for Editorial
Andrew T. Le Peau

Associate Editorial Director
James Hoover

Production Manager
Anne Gerth

Print Coordinator
Jim Erhart

Contents

Preface

It has been both a challenge and a privilege to edit this volume on the Prophets in IVP's highly regarded series of Black Dictionaries on the Bible. The prophetic books represent a large division of the Old Testament canon and contain within them a rich variety of language, literature and ideas. For this reason, they continue to be an area of fast-moving scholarly research, attracting the attention of researchers with a wide range of interests and commitments. They have also been hugely important for theology, and in Christian interpretation have played a major part in attempts to understand the relationship between the Old and New Testaments. All this has made the editing of this volume a particularly rewarding experience.

We have been keenly aware, in approaching and undertaking the work, that some issues in interpreting the prophets are fiercely debated because matters of fundamental importance are perceived to be at stake. This might have posed an acute dilemma. Was it our task to make a case for a particular viewpoint or to try to resolve contentious issues? We believe, however, that it would have been neither possible nor desirable to do this. Instead, we have undertaken to let the volume portray a broad picture of contemporary scholarship on the Prophets. With this in mind, we are glad that we have been joined in the project by scholars from all points on the scholarly spectrum, Jewish as well as Christian.

There are several good reasons for proceeding in this way. First, it signals that we acknowledge and honor the strong commitments of all our contributors and the constituencies they represent. We sincerely hope that the volume will be read in this way, and so as a "whole offering." That is to concede that readers may find some particular article not agreeable to their way of thinking. But we hope it is implied in the range of contributions that no one viewpoint has been allowed a final word. Our contributors have respected all points of view, and all the articles are offered to our readers for their own judgment and further reflection. We think there is a balance overall, and we have no wish to present the work as a contest.

The second reason is simply that contemporary work on the Prophets is extremely varied and complex, and we think it incumbent on us to represent this in a modern dictionary on the subject. In our selection of articles, we have included, of course, articles on the prophetic books themselves, and for the purpose of this volume and series, we have followed the convention of the Christian Old Testament in including the book of Daniel. There are additional articles on the reception history of the four major prophetic books (Isaiah, Jeremiah, Ezekiel and Daniel), since reception history is a growth area in biblical study at large. And along with these stands the Book of the Twelve, since the concept of the Twelve "minor prophets" as a "book," though itself ancient, has come to prominence as an area for research in recent times. We have also included articles on aspects of prophetic language and imagery, on textual and historical topics, on prophetic genres, on hermeneutics, and on important conceptual and theological themes. And finally we have thought it essential to reflect the range of critical methodologies that are in current use. It is in this area especially (though not only here) that the fast-moving nature of research on the Prophets is evident. Though we hesitate to pick out specific articles, the list includes entries on Conversation Analysis, Performance Criticism, and Psychological and Social-Scientific approaches. These simply illustrate how the parameters of a reference work on the Prophets have changed since an earlier generation. Our contributors across the board have worked in this modern context, and we are confident that the *Dictionary* makes many fresh contributions to scholarship.

A third reason for our approach, following from the preceding, is that the collection in its range and diversity expresses the fact that our understanding of the Prophets, as of Scripture more broadly, is an unfinished work, and that interpretation inescapably involves the hearing of many voices. It is in this spirit that we present the volume to our readers.

We are grateful first to our contributors, who have worked patiently with us over a lengthy period, and responded graciously to editorial suggestion and persuasion. We have learned enormously from them. We are grateful also to Dan Reid, for his scholarly and insightful work with us as editors, as well as his judicious and tactful management of the information flow between editors and contributors, and of the project as a whole. It has been a pleasure to work with him, to say nothing of some excellent breakfasts at SBLs. We are grateful too for the expert copyediting of Robert Maccini.

Mark J. Boda
J. Gordon McConville

How to Use This Dictionary

Abbreviations
Comprehensive tables of abbreviations for general matters as well as for scholarly, biblical and ancient literature may be found on pages xiii-xxii.

Authorship of Articles
The authors of articles are indicated by their first initials and last name at the end of each article. A full list of contributors may be found on pages xxiii-xxvi, in alphabetical order of their last name. The contribution of each author is listed following their identification.

Bibliographies
A bibliography will be found at the end of each article. The bibliographies include works cited in the articles and other significant related works. Bibliographical entries are listed in alphabetical order by the author's name, and where an author has more than one work cited, they are listed by date of publication. In articles focused on the Prophetic Books, the bibliographies are divided into the categories "Commentaries" and "Studies."

Cross-References
This *Dictionary* has been extensively cross-referenced in order to aid readers in making the most of material appearing throughout the volume. Five types of cross-referencing will be found:

1. One-line entries appearing in alphabetical order throughout the *Dictionary* direct readers to articles where a topic is discussed, often as a subdivision of an article:

BABYLONIAN EXILE. *See* EXILE; ISRAELITE HISTORY.

2. An asterisk before a word in the body of an article indicates that an article by that title (or closely worded title) appears in the *Dictionary*. For example, "*covenant" directs the reader to an article entitled COVENANT. Asterisks typically are found only at the first occurrence of a word in an article. There are few cross-references to articles on prophetic books, since their presence within the *Dictionary* can be assumed.

3. A cross-reference appearing within parentheses in the body of an article directs the reader to an article by that title. For example, (*see* God) directs the reader to an article by that title.

4. Cross-references have been appended to the end of articles, immediately preceding the bibliography, to direct readers to articles significantly related to the subject:

See also DESTRUCTION; RETRIBUTION; WARFARE AND DIVINE WARFARE; WRATH.

5. Occasionally references are made to articles in the companion volumes, primarily the *Dictionary of the Old Testament: Pentateuch* (DOTP), *Dictionary of the Old Testament: Historical Books* (DOTHB) and *Dictionary of the Old Testament: Wisdom, Poetry & Writings* (DOTWPW). Others include *Dictionary of Jesus and the Gospels* (DJG), *Dictionary of Paul and His Letters* (DPL), *Dictionary of the Later New Testament and Its Developments* (DLNTD) and *Dictionary of New Testament Background* (DNTB). These references are found within the body of the text of articles. For example, a reference such as (*see* DOTP, Law) refers to the article on "Law" in the *Dictionary of the Old Testament: Pentateuch*.

Indexes
Since most of the *Dictionary* articles cover broad topics in some depth, the *Subject Index* is intended to assist readers in finding relevant information on narrower topics that might, for instance, appear in a standard Bible dictionary. For example, while there is no article entitled "Darius the Mede," the subject index might direct the reader to pages where Darius the Mede is discussed in the article on "Daniel: Book of."

A *Scripture Index* is provided to assist readers in gaining quick access to the numerous Scripture texts referred to throughout the *Dictionary*.

An *Articles Index* found at the end of the *Dictionary* allows readers to review quickly the breadth of topics covered and select the ones most apt to serve their interests or needs. Those who wish to identify the articles written by specific contributors should consult the list of contributors, where the articles are listed under the name of each contributor.

Transliteration

Hebrew has been transliterated according to the system set out on page xxii.

Abbreviations

General Abbreviations

//	parallel text	HB	Hebrew Bible
§ or §§	section or paragraph numbers	Heb	Hebrew
Akk	Akkadian	i.e.	*id est*, that is
Arab	Arabic	lit.	literally
Aram	Aramaic	masc.	masculine
c.	circa	no(s).	number(s)
cf.	*confer*, compare	NT	New Testament
chap(s).	chapter(s)	OT	Old Testament
col(s).	column(s)	*pace*	with all due respect to
contra	against	par.	parallel text(s)
d.	died	passim	in various places
DSS	Dead Sea Scrolls	pl.	plural
e.g.	*exempli gratia*, for example	r.	reigned
esp.	especially	repr.	reprint
ET	English translation	rev.	reverse (back) of a tablet
fem.	feminine	rev. ed.	revised edition
fig.	figure	sg.	singular
frg(s).	fragment(s)	v(v).	verse(s)
Gk	Greek		

Texts and Translations of the Bible

ASV	American Standard Version	NEB	New English Bible
BHQ	*Biblia Hebraica Quinta*	NET	New English Translation
BHS	*Biblia Hebraica Stuttgartensia*	NIV	New International Version
ESV	English Standard Version	NJB	New Jerusalem Bible
HCSB	Holman Christian Standard Bible	NJPS	*Tanakh: The Holy Scriptures: The*
JB	Jerusalem Bible		*New JPS Translation according to*
KJV	King James Version		*the Traditional Hebrew Text*
LXX	Septuagint	NKJV	New King James Version
MESSAGE	*The Message: The Bible in*	NLT	New Living Translation
	Contemporary Language	NRSV	New Revised Standard Version
MT	Masoretic Text	REB	Revised English Bible
NAB	New American Bible	TNIV	Today's New International Version
NASB	New American Standard Bible		

Books of the Bible

Old Testament	1-2 Kings	Is	Mic	Mk	1-2 Thess
Gen	1-2 Chron	Jer	Nahum	Lk	1-2 Tim
Ex	Ezra	Lam	Hab	Jn	Tit
Lev	Neh	Ezek	Zeph	Acts	Philem
Num	Esther	Dan	Hag	Rom	Heb
Deut	Job	Hos	Zech	1-2 Cor	Jas
Josh	Ps (Pss)	Joel	Mal	Gal	1-2 Pet
Judg	Prov	Amos		Eph	1-2-3 Jn
Ruth	Eccles	Obad	*New Testament*	Phil	Jude
1-2 Sam	Song	Jon	Mt	Col	Rev

Apocrypha

| 1-2 Esdr | 1-2 Esdras | Sir | Sirach |
| 1-4 Macc | 1-4 Maccabees | Tob | Tobit |

Old Testament Pseudepigrapha

Ahiqar	Ahiqar	4 Ezra	4 Ezra
Apoc. Ab.	Apocalypse of Abraham	Jub.	Jubilees
Apoc. Zeph.	Apocalypse of Zephaniah	Let. Aris.	Letter of Aristeas
2 Bar.	2 Baruch (Syriac Apocalypse)	Liv. Pro.	Lives of the Prophets
4 Bar.	4 Baruch (Paraleipomena Jeremiou)	Pss. Sol.	Psalms of Solomon
1 En.	1 Enoch (Ethiopic Apocalypse)	T. Sim.	Testament of Simeon

Mishnah, Talmud, and Related Literature

b.	Babylonian Talmud	Mek.	Mekilta
m.	Mishnah	Menaḥ.	Menaḥot
t.	Tosefta	Moʾed Qaṭ.	Moʾed Qatan
y.	Jerusalem Talmud	Naz.	Nazir
		Nid.	Niddah
ʾAbot	ʾAbot	Peʾah	Peʾah
ʿArak.	ʿArakin	Pesaḥ.	Pesaḥim
B. Bat.	Baba Batra	Qidd.	Qiddušin
B. Qam.	Baba Qamma	Šabb.	Šabbat
Ber.	Berakot	Sanh.	Sanhedrin
Beṣah	Beṣah	Soṭah	Soṭah
Ḥag.	Ḥagigah	Taʿan.	Taʿanit
Ḥul.	Ḥullin	Yad.	Yadayim
Mak.	Makkot	Yebam.	Yebamot
Meg.	Megillah	Yoma	Yoma (= Kippurim)

Other Rabbinic Works

ʾAbot R. Nat.	ʾAbot de Rabbi Nathan	Rab.	Rabbah (+ biblical book)
Midr.	Midrash (+ biblical book)	Sipre	Sipre
Pesiq. Rab.	Pesiqta Rabbati	S.ʿOlam Rab.	Seder ʿOlam Rabbah
Pesiq. Rab Kah.	Pesiqta de Rab Kahana	Sop.	Soperim

Dead Sea Scrolls

CD-A	Damascus Document[a]	1Q28a (1QSa)	1QRule of the Congregation
CD-B	Damascus Document[b]	1Q28b (1QSb)	1QRule of Benedictions
1QH[a]	1QHodayot[a]	1Q33 (1QM)	1QWar Scroll
1QIsa[a]	1QIsaiah[a]	1Q71 (1QDan[a])	1QDaniel[a]
1QIsa[b]	1QIsaiah[b]	1Q72 (1QDan[b])	1QDaniel[b]
1QpHab	1QPesher to Habakkuk	2Q13 (2QJer)	2QJeremiah
1QS	1QRule of the Community	2Q22 (2QapDavid?)	2QApocryphon of David?
1Q6 (1QJudg)	1QJudges	2Q26 (2QEnGiants ar)	2QBook of Giants ar
1Q7 (1QSam)	1QSamuel	3Q1 (3QEzek)	3QEzekiel
1Q9 (1QEzek)	1QEzekiel	3QLam (3Q3)	3QLamentations
1Q14 (1QpMic)	1QPesher to Micah	3Q4 (3QpIsa)	3QIsaiah Pesher
1Q15 (1QpZeph)	1QPesher to Zephaniah	4Q47 (4QJosha)	4QJoshua[a]
1Q20 (1QapGen ar)	1QGenesis Apocryphon	4Q48 (4QJosh[b])	4QJoshua[b]
1Q23 (1QEnGiants[a] ar)	1QEnoch Giants[a] ar	4Q49 (4QJudg[a])	4QJudges[a]
1Q24 (1QEnGiants[b] ar)	1QEnoch Giants[b] ar	4Q50 (4QJudg[b])	4QJudges[b]

4Q51 (4QSama)	*4QSamuela*	4Q253a (4QcommMal)	*4QCommentary on*
4Q52 (4QSamb)	*4QSamuelb*		*Malachi*
4Q53 (4QSamc)	*4QSamuelc*	4Q254 (4QcommGen C)	*4QCommentary on*
4Q54 (4QKgs)	*4QKings*		*Genesis C*
4QIsaa (4Q55)	*4QIsaiah^a*	4Q285 (4QSM)	*4QSefer ha-Milhamah*
4Q56 (4QIsa^b)	*4QIsaiah^b*	4Q378 (4QapocrJoshua^a)	*4QApocryphon of Joshua^a*
4Q57 (4QIsa^c)	*4QIsaiah^c*	4Q379 (4QapocrJoshua^b)	*4QApocryphon of Joshua^b*
4Q70 (4QJer^a)	*4QJeremiah^a*	4Q382	*4QParaphrase of Kings*
4Q71 (4QJer^b)	*4QJeremiah^b*	4Q383 (4QapocrJer^a)	*4QApocryphon of*
4Q72 (4QJer^c)	*4QJeremiah^c*		*Jeremiah^a*
4Q72a (4QJer^d)	*4QJeremiah^d*	4Q384 (4QapocrJer^b)	*4QApocryphon of*
4Q72b (4QJer^e)	*4QJeremiah^e*		*Jeremiah^b (?)*
4Q73 (4QEzek^a)	*4QEzekiel^a*	4Q385 (4QpsEzek^a)	*4QPseudo-Ezekiel^a*
4Q74 (4QEzek^b)	*4QEzekiel^b*	4Q385a (4QpsMoses^a)	*4QPseudo-Moses^a*
4Q75 (4QEzek^c)	*4QEzekiel^c*	4Q385b (4QapocrJer^c)	*4QApocryphon of*
4Q76 (4QXII^a)	*4QMinor Prophets^a*		*Jeremiah^c*
4Q77 (4QXII^b)	*4QMinor Prophets^b*	4Q385c (4QpsEzek^c)	*4QPseudo-Ezekiel^c*
4Q78 (4QXII^c)	*4QMinor Prophets^c*	4Q386 (4QpsEzek^b)	*4QPseudo-Ezekiel^b*
4Q79 (4QXII^d)	*4QMinor Prophets^d*	4Q387a (4QpsMoses^b)	*4QPseudo-Moses^b*
4Q80 (4QXII^e)	*4QMinor Prophets^e*	4Q387b (4QapocrJer^d)	*4QApocryphon of*
4Q81 (4QXII^f)	*4QMinor Prophets^f*		*Jeremiah^d*
4Q82 (4QXII^g)	*4QMinor Prophets^g*	4Q388 (4QpsEzek^d)	*4QPseudo-Ezekiel^d*
4QLam (4Q111)	*4QLamentations*	4Q388a (4QpsMoses^c)	*4QPseudo-Moses^c*
4Q112 (4QDan^a)	*4QDaniel^a*	4Q389 (4QpsMoses^d)	*4QPseudo-Moses^d*
4Q113 (4QDan^b)	*4QDaniel^b*	4Q389a (4QapocrJer^e)	*4QApocryphon of*
4Q114 (4QDan^c)	*4QDaniel^c*		*Jeremiah^e*
4Q115 (4QDan^d)	*4QDaniel^d*	4Q390 (4QpsMoses^e)	*4QPseudo-Moses^e*
4Q116 (4QDan^e)	*4QDaniel^e*	4Q391 (4QpsEzek^a)	*4QpapPseudo-Ezekiel^e*
4Q123 (4QpaleoParaJosh)	*4QParaphrase of Joshua*	4Q393	*4QCommunal Confession*
4Q160 (4QVisSam)	*4Q Vision of Samuel*	4Q397 (4QMMT^d)	*4QHalakhic Letter^d*
4Q161 (4QpIsa^a)	*4QIsaiah Pesher^a*	4Q400 (4QShirShabb^a)	*4QSongs of the Sabbath*
4Q162 (4QpIsa^b)	*4QIsaiah Pesher^b*		*Sacrifice^a*
4Q163 (4Qpap pIsa^c)	*4QIsaiah Pesher^c*	4Q401 (4QShirShabb^b)	*4QSongs of the Sabbath*
4Q164 (4QpIsa^d)	*4QIsaiah Pesher^d*		*Sacrifice^b*
4Q165 (4QpIsa^e)	*4QIsaiah Pesher^e*	4Q402 (4QShirShabb^c)	*4QSongs of the Sabbath*
4Q166 (4QpHos^a)	*4QHosea Pesher^a*		*Sacrifice^c*
4Q167 (4QpHos^b)	*4QHosea Pesher^b*	4Q403 (4QShirShabb^d)	*4QSongs of the Sabbath*
4Q168 (4QpMic?)	*4QMicah Pesher (?)*		*Sacrifice^d*
4Q169 (4QpNah)	*4QNahum Pesher*	4Q404 (4QShirShabb^e)	*4QSongs of the Sabbath*
4Q170 (4QpZeph)	*4QZephaniah Pesher*		*Sacrifice^e*
4Q174 (4QFlor)	*4QFlorilegium*	4Q405 (4QShirShabb^f)	*4QSongs of the Sabbath*
4Q177 (4QCatena A)	*4QCatena A*		*Sacrifice^f*
4QapocrLam A (4Q179)	*4QApocryphal*	4Q406 (4QShirShabb^g)	*4QSongs of the Sabbath*
	Lamentations A		*Sacrifice^g*
4Q180 (4QAgesCreat A)	*4QAges of Creation A*	4Q407 (4QShirShabb^h)	*4QSongs of the Sabbath*
4Q201 (4QEn^a ar)	*4QEnoch^a ar*		*Sacrifice^h*
4Q202 (4QEn^b ar)	*4QEnoch^b ar*	4Q481a (4QapocrElisha)	*4QApocryphon of Elisha*
4Q203 (4QEnGiants^a ar)	*4QBook of Giants^a ar*	4Q489	*4QApocalypse ar (?)*
4Q204 (4QEn^c ar)	*4QEnoch^c ar*	4Q500 (4QpapBened)	*4QBenediction*
4Q205 (4QEn^d ar)	*4QEnoch^d ar*	4QapocrLam B (4Q501)	*4QApocryphal*
4Q206 (4QEn^e ar)	*4QEnoch^e ar*		*Lamentations B*
4Q207 (4QEn^f ar)	*4QEnoch^f ar*	4Q521	*4QMessianic Apocalypse*
4Q208 (4QEnAstr^a ar)	*4QAstronomical Enoch^a ar*	4Q522 (4QapocrJosué^c?)	*4QProphecy of Joshua*
4Q209 (4QEnAstr^b ar)	*4QAstronomical Enoch^b ar*	4Q523	*4QJonathan*
4Q210 (4QEnAstr^c ar)	*4QAstronomical Enoch^c ar*	4Q530 (4QEnGiants^b ar)	*4QBook of Giants^b ar*
4Q211 (4QEnAstr^d ar)	*4QAstronomical Enoch^d ar*	4Q531 (4QEnGiants^c ar)	*4QBook of Giants^c ar*
4Q242 (4QPrNab ar)	*4QPrayer of Nabonidus ar*	4Q532 (4QEnGiants^d ar)	*4QBook of Giants^d ar*
4Q243 (4QpsDan^a ar)	*4QPseudo-Daniel^a ar*	4Q551 (4QDanSuz? ar)	*4QDaniel-Suzanna (?) ar*
4Q244 (4QpsDan^b ar)	*4QPseudo-Daniel^b ar*	4Q552	*4QFour Kingdoms^a ar*
4Q245 (4QpsDan^c ar)	*4QPseudo-Daniel^c ar*	4Q553	*4QFour Kingdoms^b ar*
4Q246	*4QAramaic Apocalypse*	5Q2 (5QKgs)	*5QKings*

5Q4 (5QAmos)	*5QAmos*	7Q2 (7QLXXEpJer)	*7QEpistle of Jeremiah*
5QLama (5Q6)	*5QLamentations*[a]	7Q4 (7QpapEn gr)	*7QEnoch*
5QLamb (5Q7)	*5QLamentations*[b]	11Q4 (11QEz)	*11QEzekiel*
5Q10 (5QpMal?)	*5QMalachi Pesher*	11Q10 (11QtgJob)	*11QTargum of Job*
5Q11 (5QS)	*5QRule of the Community*	11Q11 (11QapocrPs)	*11QApocryphal Psalms*
6Q4 (6QpapKgs)	*6QKings*	11Q13 (11Melch)	*11QMelchizedek*
6Q7 (6QpapDan)	*6QDaniel*	11Q14 (11QSM)	*11QSefer ha-Milhamah*
6Q8 (6QpapEnGiants ar)	*6QGiants ar*	11Q19 (11QT*a*)	*11QTemple*[a]
6Q9 (6Qpap apocrSam-Kgs)	*6QApocryphon on Samuel-Kings*		

Wadi Murabbaʿat

Mur 88   (XII [unopened scroll]) Scroll of Minor Prophets

Naḥal Ḥever

8Ḥev 1   (8HevXII gr) Scroll of Minor Prophets

Masada

Mas1k (MasShirShabb)   *Masada Songs of the Sabbath Sacrifice*

Classical and Early Christian Literature

Augustine
  Conf.   *Confessionum libri XIII*
  Trin.   *De Trinitate*
Cyprian
  Ep.   *Epistulae*
Eusebius
  Dem. ev.   *Demonstratio evangelica*
  Hist. eccl.   *Historia ecclesiastica*
Herodotus
  Hist.   *Historiae*
Homer
  Od.   *Odysseia (Odyssey)*
Irenaeus
  Haer.   *Adversus haereses*
Jerome
  Comm. Habac.   *Commentariorum in Habacuc libri II*
  Comm. Isa.   *Commentariorum in Isaiam libri XVIII*
  Epist.   *Epistulae*

Josephus
  Ag. Ap.   *Against Apion*
  Ant.   *Jewish Antiquities*
  J.W.   *Jewish War*
Origen
  Cels.   *Contra Celsum*
Philo
  Contempl.   *De vita contemplativa*
  Spec.   *De specialibus legibus*
Polybius
  Hist.   *Historiae*
Tertullian
  Marc.   *Adversus Marcionem*
Theodoret
  Comm. Dan.   *Commentarius in Danielem*

Periodicals, Reference Works and Serials

ÄAT	Ägypten und Altes Testament	ADOG	Abhandlungen der deutschen Orient-Gesellschaft
AB	Anchor Bible		
ABD	*Anchor Bible Dictionary*, ed. D. N. Freedman (6 vols.; New York: Doubleday, 1992)	ADPV	Abhandlungen des deutschen Palästina-Vereins
		AG	Analecta gorgiana
ABR	*Australian Biblical Review*	*AJA*	*American Journal of Archaeology*
ABRL	Anchor Bible Reference Library	*AJP*	*American Journal of Philology*
ACCS	Ancient Christian Commentary on Scripture	*AJSR*	*Association for Jewish Studies Review*
		AMD	Ancient Magic and Divination

AmUS	American University Studies	*Bib*	*Biblica*
AnBib	Analecta biblica	*BibAr*	*Bibel und Archaeologie*
ANEP	*The Ancient Near East in Pictures*	BibEnc	Biblical Encounters Series
	Relating to the Old Testament, ed. J. B.	BibH	Bible historiale
	Pritchard (Princeton, NJ: Princeton	*BibInt*	*Biblical Interpretation*
	University Press, 1954)	BibJudS	Biblical and Judaic Studies
ANES	*Ancient Near Eastern Studies*	BibOr	Biblica et orientalia
ANET	*Ancient Near Eastern Texts Relating*	BibSem	The Biblical Seminar
	to the Old Testament, ed. J. B.	BIS	Biblical Interpretation Series
	Pritchard (3rd ed., with supplement;	*BJRL*	*Bulletin of the John Rylands University*
	Princeton, NJ: Princeton University		*Library of Manchester*
	Press, 1969)	BJS	Brown Judaic Studies
ANETS	Ancient Near Eastern Texts and	BKAT	Biblischer Kommentar, Altes
	Studies		Testament
AnOr	Analecta orientalia	BLS	Bible and Literature Series
AOAT	Alter Orient und Altes Testament	*BN*	*Biblische Notizen*
AoF	*Altorientalische Forschungen*	*BOR*	*Babylonian and Oriental Record*
AOTC	Abingdon Old Testament	*BR*	*Biblical Research*
	Commentaries	BRLAJ	Brill Reference Library of Ancient
ApOTC	Apollos Old Testament Commentary		Judaism
ARM	Archives royales de Mari	*BSac*	*Bibliotheca sacra*
AS	Assyriological Studies	BSAH	Blackwell Sourcebooks in Ancient
ASTI	*Annual of the Swedish Theological*		History
	Institute	BSCS	Bible Study Commentary Series
ATA	Alttestamentliche Abhandlungen	BST	The Bible Speaks Today
ATANT	Abhandlungen zur Theologie des	BTCB	Brazos Theological Commentary on
	Alten und Neuen Testaments		the Bible
ATD	Das Alte Testament Deutsch	BTCL	Biblical and Theological Classics
AThR	*Anglican Theological Review*		Library
ATM	Altes Testament und Moderne	BTSt	Biblisch-theologische Studien
AUMSR	Andrews University Monographs:	BWANT	Beiträge zur Wissenschaft vom Alten
	Studies in Religion		und Neuen Testament
AUSS	*Andrews University Seminary Studies*	*BZ*	*Biblische Zeitschrift*
AUSTR	American University Series:	BZAW	Beihefte zur Zeitschrift für die
	Theology and Religion		alttestamentliche Wissenschaft
BA	*Biblical Archaeologist*	*CAD*	*The Assyrian Dictionary of the Oriental*
BAC	Bible in Ancient Christianity		*Institute of the University of Chicago*,
BASOR	*Bulletin of the American Schools of*		ed. E. Reiner et al. (Chicago:
	Oriental Research		Oriental Institute of the University
BBB	Bonner biblische Beiträge		of Chicago, 1956-)
BBET	Beiträge zur biblischen Exegese und	*CAH²*	*The Cambridge Ancient History*, ed.
	Theologie		J. B. Bury et al. (2nd ed.; 12 vols.;
BBR	*Bulletin for Biblical Research*		Cambridge: Cambridge University
BBRSup	Bulletin for Biblical Research		Press, 1924-1939)
	Supplements	CahRB	Cahiers de la Revue biblique
BCW	Bücherei der christlichen Welt	*CAT*	*The Cuneiform Alphabetic Texts from*
BDB	F. Brown, S. R. Driver and C. A.		*Ugarit, Ras Ibn Hani and Other Places*,
	Briggs, *A Hebrew and English Lexicon*		ed. M. Dietrich, O. Loretz and
	of the Old Testament (Oxford: Oxford		J. Sanmartín (2nd ed.; ALASP 8;
	University Press, 1907)		Münster: Ugarit Verlag, 1995)
BE	Biblische Enzyklopädie	CBC	Cambridge Bible Commentary
BEATAJ	Beiträge zur Erforschung des	CBET	Contributions to Biblical Exegesis
	Alten Testaments und des antiken		and Theology
	Judentums	*CBQ*	*Catholic Biblical Quarterly*
BETL	Bibliotheca ephemeridum	CBQMS	Catholic Biblical Quarterly
	theologicarum lovaniensium		Monograph Series
BEvT	Beiträge zur evangelischen	*CBR*	*Currents in Biblical Research*
	Theologie	CBSC	Cambridge Bible for Schools and
BFCT	Beiträge zur Förderung christlicher		Colleges
	Theologie	CC	Continental Commentaries
BHT	Beiträge zur historischen Theologie	CEB	Commentaire évangélique de la

	Bible		Grove, IL: IVP Academic, 2008)
CHANE	Culture and History of the Ancient	DSBS	Daily Study Bible Series
	Near East	*DSD*	*Dead Sea Discoveries*
ConBNT	Coniectanea biblica: New Testament	EA	El-Amarna tablets. According to
	Series		the edition of J. A. Knudtzon, *Die*
ConBOT	Coniectanea biblica: Old Testament		*el-Amarna-Tafeln* (Leipzig: Hinrichs,
	Series		1908-1915 [reprint, Aalen: Zeller,
ConJ	*Concordia Journal*		1964]). Continued in A. F. Rainey,
COS	*Context of Scripture*, ed. W. W. Hallo		*El-Amarna Tablets, 359-379* (2nd ed.;
	(3 vols.; Leiden: E. J. Brill, 1997-)		Kevelaer, 1978)
CSCD	Cambridge Studies in Christian	EBC	Everyman's Bible Commentary
	Doctrine	EBib	Études bibliques
CTA	*Corpus des tablettes en cunéiforms*	ED	Essays in Divinity
	alphabétiques découvertes à Ras	EdF	Erträge der Forschung
	Shamra-Ugarit de 1929 à 1939, ed.	*EDSS*	*The Encyclopedia of the Dead Sea*
	A. Herdner (Mission de Ras Shamra		*Scrolls*, ed. L. H. Schiffman and J. C.
	10/2; Paris: Imprimerie Nationale,		VanderKam (2 vols.; Oxford: Oxford
	1963)		University Press, 2000)
CTJ	*Calvin Theological Journal*	EH	Europäische Hochschulschriften
CTM	*Concordia Theological Monthly*	*EI*	*Eretz- Israel*
CTR	*Criswell Theological Review*	*Enc*	*Encounter*
CurBS	*Currents in Research: Biblical Studies*	EOT	Exploring the Old Testament
CurTM	*Currents in Theology and Mission*	*ErIsr*	*Eretz-Israel*
CWSSS	*Corpus of West Semitic Stamp Seals*,	EsBib	Essais bibliques
	ed. N. Avigad, rev. and compl.	*EvQ*	*Evangelical Quarterly*
	B. Sass (Jerusalem: Israel Academy	*EvT*	*Evangelische Theologie*
	of Sciences and Humanities; Israel	*ExAud*	*Ex Auditu*
	Exploration Society; Institute of	*ExpTim*	*Expository Times*
	Archaeology, Hebrew University of	FAT	Forschungen zum Alten Testament
	Jerusalem, 1997)	FBBS	Facet Books: Biblical Series
DBInt	*Dictionary of Biblical Interpretation*,	FC	Fathers of the Church
	ed. J. H. Hayes (2 vols.; Nashville:	FCB	Feminist Companion to the Bible
	Abingdon, 1999)	FCBS	Fortress Classics in Biblical Studies
DDD	*Dictionary of Deities and Demons in*	FLP	Tablets in the collections of the Free
	the Bible, ed. K. van der Toorn, B.		Library of Pennsylvania
	Becking and P. W. van der Horst	FOTL	Forms of Old Testament Literature
	(Leiden: E. J. Brill, 1995)	FRC	Family, Religion, and Culture
DDD²	*Dictionary of Deities and Demons in*	FRLANT	Forschungen zur Religion und Literatur
	the Bible, ed. K. van der Toorn, B.		des Alten und Neuen Testaments
	Becking and P. W. van der Horst	FTL	Forum theologiae linguisticae
	(rev. ed.; Leiden: E. J. Brill, 1999)	GBS	Guides to Biblical Scholarship
Did	*Didaskalia*	GPT	Growing Points in Theology
DJD	Discoveries in the Judaean Desert	GRBS	Greek, Roman, and Byzantine
DJG	*Dictionary of Jesus and the Gospels*, ed.		Studies
	J. Green and S. McKnight (Downers	GTA	Göttinger theologische Arbeiten
	Grove, IL: InterVarsity Press, 1992)	*HAL*	L. Koehler, W. Baumgartner and J. J.
DNWSI	*Dictionary of the North-West Semitic*		Stamm, *Hebräisches und aramäisches*
	Inscriptions, by J. Hoftijzer and		*Lexikon zum Alten Testament*, fascicles
	K. Jongeling (Leiden: E. J. Brill,		1-5 (3rd ed.; Leiden: E. J. Brill,
	1995)		1967-1995)
DOTHB	*Dictionary of the Old Testament:*	HALOT	L. Koehler, W. Baumgartner and
	Historical Books, ed. B. T. Arnold		J. J. Stamm, *The Hebrew and Aramaic*
	and H. G. M. Williamson (Downers		*Lexicon of the Old Testament*, trans.
	Grove, IL: InterVarsity Press, 2005)		and ed. M. E. J. Richardson (4 vols.;
DOTP	*Dictionary of the Old Testament:*		Leiden: E. J. Brill, 1994-1999)
	Pentateuch, ed. T. D. Alexander and	*HAR*	*Hebrew Annual Review*
	D. W. Baker (Downers Grove, IL:	HAT	Handbuch zum Alten Testament
	InterVarsity Press, 2003)	HBM	Hebrew Bible Monographs
DOTWPW	*Dictionary of the Old Testament:*	HBS	Herders biblische Studien
	Wisdom, Poetry and Writings, ed.	*HBT*	*Horizons in Biblical Theology*
	T. Longman III and P. Enns (Downers	HCOT	Historical Commentary on the Old

	Testament	*JPT*	*Journal of Pentecostal Theology*
HDR	Harvard Dissertations in Religion	JPTSup	Journal of Pentecostal Theology:
Hen	*Henoch*		Supplement Series
HeyM	Heythrop Monographs	*JQR*	*Jewish Quarterly Review*
HKAT	Handkommentar zum Alten	JSJSup	Supplements to the Journal for the
	Testament		Study of Judaism
HO	Handbuch der Orientalistik	JSNTSup	Journal for the Study of the New
HOTC	Holman Old Testament Commentary		Testament: Supplement Series
HSM	Harvard Semitic Monographs	*JSOT*	*Journal for the Study of the Old*
HSS	Harvard Semitic Studies		*Testament*
HTIBS	Historic Texts and Interpreters in	JSOTSup	Journal for the Study of the Old
	Biblical Scholarship		Testament: Supplement Series
HTKAT	Herders theologischer Kommentar	*JSP*	*Journal for the Study of the*
	zum Alten Testament		*Pseudepigrapha*
HTR	*Harvard Theological Review*	*JSS*	*Journal of Semitic Studies*
HUCA	*Hebrew Union College Annual*	*JTS*	*Journal of Theological Studies*
IB	*Interpreter's Bible*, ed. G. A. Buttrick (12	K	Tablets in the collections of the
	vols.; New York: Abingdon, 1951-1957)		British Museum (Kuyunjik)
IBC	Interpretation: A Bible Commentary	K&D	C. F. Keil and F. Delitzsch, *Biblical*
	for Teaching and Preaching		*Commentary on the Old Testament*,
ICC	International Critical Commentary		trans. J. Martin et al. (repr., 10 vols.;
IDB	*The Interpreter's Dictionary of the Bible*,		Peabody, MA: Hendrickson, 1996)
	ed. G. A. Buttrick (4 vols.; Nashville:	*KAI*	*Kanaanäische und aramäische*
	Abingdon, 1962)		*Inschriften*, ed. H. Donner and
IDBSup	*Interpreter's Dictionary of the Bible:*		W. Röllig (2nd ed.; 3 vols. in 1;
	Supplementary Volume, ed. K. Crim		Wiesbaden: Harrasowitz, 1966-1969)
	(Nashville: Abingdon, 1976)	*KAR*	*Keilschrifttexte aus Assur religiösen*
Int	*Interpretation*		*Inhalts*, ed. E. Ebeling (2 vols.;
IRT	Issues in Religion and Theology		Leipzig: Hinrichs, 1919-1923)
ISBE	*International Standard Bible*	KAT	Kommentar zum Alten Testament
	Encyclopedia, ed. G. W. Bromiley	KHC	Kurzer Hand-Commentar zum Alten
	(4 vols.; Grand Rapids: Eerdmans,		Testament
	1979-1988)	*KTU*	*Die keilalphabetischen Texte aus*
ISBL	Indiana Studies in Biblical		*Ugarit*, ed. M. Dietrich, O. Loretz
	Literature		and J. Sanmartín (AOAT 24/1;
ITC	International Theological		Neukirchen-Vluyn: Neukirchener
	Commentary		Verlag, 1976)
ITL	International Theological Library	LAI	Library of Ancient Israel
JANESCU	*Journal of the Ancient Near Eastern*	LCBI	Literary Currents in Biblical
	Society of Columbia University		Interpretation
JAOS	*Journal of the American Oriental Society*	LHBOTS	Library of Hebrew Bible/Old
JBL	*Journal of Biblical Literature*		Testament Studies
JBPR	*Journal of Biblical and Pneumatological*	LNTS	Library of New Testament Studies
	Research	LSTS	Library of the Second Temple Studies
JBQ	*Jewish Bible Quarterly*	MBPS	Mellen Biblical Press Series
JBR	*Journal of Bible and Religion*	MNTS	McMaster New Testament Studies
JBS	Jerusalem Biblical Studies	*MSL*	*Materialien zum sumerischen Lexikon*,
JCS	*Journal of Cuneiform Studies*		ed. B. Landsberger (17 vols.; Rome:
JerBS	Jerusalem Biblical Studies		Pontifical Biblical Institute, 1937-
JETS	*Journal of the Evangelical Theological*		1985)
	Society	*NABU*	*Nouvelles assyriologiques breves et*
JFSR	*Journal of Feminist Studies in Religion*		*utilitaires*
JHNES	Johns Hopkins Near Eastern Studies	NAC	New American Commentary
JHScr	*Journal of Hebrew Scriptures*	NCBC	New Century Bible Commentary
JJS	*Journal of Jewish Studies*	*NDBT*	*New Dictionary of Biblical Theology*, ed.
JNES	*Journal of Near Eastern Studies*		T. D. Alexander and B. S. Rosner
JNSL	*Journal of Northwest Semitic Languages*		(Downers Grove, IL: InterVarsity
JPSBC	Jewish Publication Society Bible		Press, 2000)
	Commentary	*NIB*	*The New Interpreter's Bible*, ed. L. E.
JPSTC	Jewish Publication Society Torah		Keck et al. (12 vols.; Nashville:
	Commentary		Abingdon, 1994-2002)

NIBCOT	New International Biblical Commentary: Old Testament Series
NICOT	New International Commentary on the Old Testament
NIDB	New Interpreter's Dictionary of the Bible, ed. K. D. Sakenfeld (5 vols.; Nashville: Abingdon, 2006-2009)
NIDOTTE	New International Dictionary of Old Testament Theology and Exegesis, ed. W. A. VanGemeren (5 vols.; Grand Rapids: Zondervan, 1997)
NIGTC	New International Greek Testament Commentary
NIVAC	NIV Application Commentary
NovT	Novum Testamentum
NSBT	New Studies in Biblical Theology
NTM	New Testament Monographs
NTOA	Novum Testamentum et Orbis Antiquus
NTS	New Testament Studies
NTSI	New Testament and the Scriptures of Israel
OBO	Orbis biblicus et orientalis
OBS	Oxford Bible Series
OBSt	Österreichische biblische Studien
OBT	Overtures to Biblical Theology
OCuT	Oxford Editions of Cuneiform Texts
OEANE	The Oxford Encyclopedia of Archaeology in the Near East, ed. E. M. Meyers (5 vols.; Oxford: Oxford University Press, 1997)
OIS	Oriental Institute Seminars
OLA	Orientalia lovaniensa analecta
OOTD	Outline of an Old Testament Dialogue
OPBF	Occasional Publications of the Babylonian Fund
OTE	Old Testament Essays
OTG	Old Testament Guides
OTL	Old Testament Library
OTM	Oxford Theological Monographs
OTMes	Old Testament Message
OTS	Old Testament Studies
OtSt	Oudtestamentische studiën
OTT	Old Testament Theology
OuTWP	Die Ou Testamentiese Werkgemeenskap in Suid-Afrika
PEQ	Palestine Exploration Quarterly
PFES	Publications of the Finnish Exegetical Society
PRSt	Perspectives in Religious Studies
PSB	Princeton Seminary Bulletin
PTMS	Princeton Theological Monograph Series
PTR	Princeton Theological Review
RAcc	François Thureau-Dangin, Rituels accadiens (Paris: Leroux, 1921)
RB	Revue biblique
RD	Religions and Discourse
ResQ	Restoration Quarterly
RevExp	Review and Expositor
RevistB	Revista bíblica
RevQ	Revue de Qumran
RHPR	Revue d'histoire et de philosophie religieuses
RIMA	The Royal Inscriptions of Mesopotamia, Assyrian Periods
RivBSup	Supplements to Rivista biblica
RNBC	Readings: A New Biblical Commentary
RRBS	Recent Research in Biblical Studies
RTR	Reformed Theological Review
SAA	State Archives of Assyria
SAAS	State Archives of Assyria Studies
SAIS	Studies in the Aramaic Interpretation of Scripture
SBL	Studies in Biblical Literature
SBLAB	Society of Biblical Literature Academia Biblica
SBLABS	Society of Biblical Literature Archaeology and Biblical Studies
SBLAIL	Society of Biblical Literature Ancient Israel and Its Literature
SBLANEM	Society of Biblical Literature Ancient Near East Monographs
SBLDS	Society of Biblical Literature Dissertation Series
SBLMS	Society of Biblical Literature Monograph Series
SBLRBS	Society of Biblical Literature Resources for Biblical Study
SBLSBS	Society of Biblical Literature Sources for Biblical Study
SBLSP	Society of Biblical Literature Seminar Papers
SBLSS	Society of Biblical Literature Semeia Studies
SBLSymS	Society of Biblical Literature Symposium Studies
SBLWAW	Society of Biblical Literature Writings from the Ancient World
SBLWGW	Society of Biblical Literature Writings from the Greco-Roman World
SBS	Stuttgarter Bibelstudien
SBT	Studies in Biblical Theology
SBTS	Sources for Biblical and Theological Study
ScrCon	Scripture in Context
SCRK	Studien zur christlichen Religions- und Kulturgeschichte
ScrMin	Scripta minora
SCS	Septuagint Commentary Series
SE	Studia evangelica I, II, III (= TU 73 [1959], 87 [1964], 88 [1964], etc.)
SEÅ	Svensk exegetisk årsbok
SFSHJ	South Florida Studies in the History of Judaism
SHBC	Smith & Helwys Bible Commentary
SHCANE	Studies in the History and Culture of the Ancient Near East
SHCT	Studies in the History of Christian Traditions

SHR	Studies in the History of Religions (supplement to *Numen*)	*TGUOS*	*Transactions of the Glasgow University Oriental Society*	

SHR   Studies in the History of Religions (supplement to *Numen*)

SHS   Scripture and Hermeneutics Series

SJLA   Studies in Judaism in Late Antiquity

SJOT   *Scandinavian Journal of the Old Testament*

SJT   *Scottish Journal of Theology*

SJud   Studies in Judaism

SO   Symbolae Osloenses

SOTBT   Studies in Old Testament Biblical Theology

SOTSMS   Society for Old Testament Studies Monograph Series

SPRTS   Scholars Press Reprints and Translations Series

SSN   Studia semitica neerlandica

ST   *Studia theologica*

StBT   *Studia biblica et theologica*

STDJ   Studies on the Texts of the Desert of Judah

STI   Studies in Theological Interpretation

STL   Studia theologica Lundensia

StPB   Studia post-biblica

STR   Studies in Theology and Religion

SubBi   Subsidia biblica

SUNT   Studien zur Umwelt des Neuen Testaments

SVTP   Studia in Veteris Testamenti pseudepigraphica

SWBA   The Social World of Biblical Antiquity

TA   *Tel Aviv*

TAD A   *Textbook of Aramaic Documents from Ancient Egypt*, vol. 1, *Letters*, ed. B. Porten and A. Yardeni (Jerusalem: Hebrew University, Department of the History of the Jewish People, 1986)

TAD B   *Textbook of Aramaic Documents from Ancient Egypt*, vol. 2, *Contracts*, ed. B. Porten and A. Yardeni (Jerusalem: Hebrew University, Department of the History of the Jewish People, 1989)

TAD D   *Textbook of Aramaic Documents from Ancient Egypt*, vol. 4, *Ostraca and Assorted Inscriptions*, ed. B. Porten and A. Yardeni (Jerusalem: Hebrew University, 1999)

TAPS   *Transactions of the American Philosophical Society*

TBC   Torch Bible Commentaries

TBN   Themes in Biblical Narrative

TBS   Tools for Biblical Study

TBT   *The Bible Today*

TCS   Texts from Cuneiform Sources

TDOT   *Theological Dictionary of the Old Testament*, ed. G. J. Botterweck and H. Ringgren (Grand Rapids: Eerdmans, 1974-)

TGUOS   *Transactions of the Glasgow University Oriental Society*

TH   Texte der Hethiter

ThA   Theologische Arbeiten

THAT   *Theologisches Handwörterbuch zum Alten Testament*, ed. E. Jenni, with C. Westermann (2 vols.; Munich: Kaiser; Zürich: Theologischer Verlag, 1971-1976)

Them   *Themelios*

ThEv   *Theologica evangelica*

THNTC   The Two Horizons New Testament Commentary

ThTo   *Theology Today*

TLOT   *Theological Lexicon of the Old Testament*, ed. E. Jenni, with C. Westermann (3 vols.; Peabody, MA: Hendrickson, 1997)

TLZ   *Theologische Literaturzeitung*

TOTC   Tyndale Old Testament Commentaries

TQ   *Theologische Quartalschrift*

TR   *Theological Review*

Transeu   *Transeuphratène*

TS   *Theological Studies*

TSAJ   Texte und Studien zum antiken Judentum

TSK   *Theologische Studien und Kritiken*

TThSt   Trierer theologische Studien

TTR   Tübinger theologische Reihe

TU   Texte und Untersuchungen

TUMSR   Trinity University Monograph Series in Religion

TWOT   *Theological Wordbook of the Old Testament*, ed. R. L. Harris and G. L. Archer Jr. (2 vols.; Chicago: Moody, 1980)

TynBul   *Tyndale Bulletin*

TynHS   Tyndale House Studies

UCOP   University of Cambridge Oriental Publications

UF   *Ugarit-Forschungen*

USQR   *Union Seminary Quarterly Review*

UUÅ   Uppsala universitets årsskrift

VAT   Vorderasiatische Abteilung Tontafel, Vorderasiatisches Museum, Berlin

VCSup   Supplements to Vigiliae christianae

VF   *Verkündigung und Forschung*

VT   *Vetus Testamentum*

VTSup   Vetus Testamentum Supplements

WA   D. Martin Luthers Werke, Kritische Gesamtausgabe. 72 vols. Weimar: Verlag Hermann Böhlaus Nachfolger, 1883-

WBC   Word Biblical Commentary

WBT   Word Biblical Themes

WEC   Wycliffe Exegetical Commentary

WestBC   Westminster Bible Companion

WUNT   Wissenschaftliche Untersuchungen zum Neuen Testament

WW   *Word and World*

YNER	Yale Near Eastern Researches	ZAW	*Zeitschrift für die alttestamentliche*
ZABR	*Zeitschrift für altorientalische und*		*Wissenschaft*
	biblische Rechtsgeschichte	ZDPV	*Zeitschrift des deutschen Palästina-Vereins*
ZAH	*Zeitschrift für Althebräistik*	ZTK	*Zeitschrift für Theologie und Kirche*

Transliteration of Hebrew

Consonants

א	=	ʾ	ל	=	l
ב	=	b	מ, ם	=	m
ג	=	g	נ, ן	=	n
ד	=	d	ס	=	s
ה	=	h	ע	=	ʿ
ו	=	w	פ, ף	=	p
ז	=	z	צ, ץ	=	ṣ
ח	=	ḥ	ק	=	q
ט	=	ṭ	ר	=	r
י	=	y	שׂ	=	ś
כ, ך	=	k	שׁ	=	š
			ת	=	t

Short Vowels

_	=	a
ֶ	=	e
ִ	=	i
ָ	=	o
ֻ	=	u

Very Short Vowels

ֲ	=	ă
ֱ	=	ĕ
ְ	=	ě (if vocal)
ֳ	=	ŏ

Long Vowels

(ה)ָ	=	â
ֵ	=	ê
ִי	=	î
וֹ	=	ô
וּ	=	û
ָ	=	ā
ֵ	=	ē
ֹ	=	ō

Contributors

Ahn, John, PhD. Assistant professor of Old Testament, Austin Theological Seminary, Austin, Texas: **Exile.**

Allen, Leslie C., DD. Senior Professor of Old Testament, Fuller Theological Seminary, Pasadena, California: **Jeremiah: Book of.**

Ames, Frank R., PhD. Professor of Medical Informatics, Rocky Vista University College of Osteopathic Medicine, Parker, Colorado: **Warfare and Divine Warfare.**

Arnold, Bill T., PhD. Paul S. Amos Professor of Old Testament Interpretation, Asbury Theological Seminary, Wilmore, Kentucky: **Babylon.**

Baker, David W., PhD. Professor of Old Testament and Semitic Languages, Ashland Theological Seminary, Ashland, Ohio: **Evil; Nahum, Book of.**

Barker, Joel D., PhD. Adjunct Professor of Old Testament, Heritage Theological Seminary, Cambridge, Ontario, Canada: **Day of the Lord; Rhetorical Criticism.**

Barrett, Rob, PhD. Postdoctoral Research Fellow, Georg-August-Universität, Göttingen, Germany: **Idols, Idolatry, Gods.**

Block, Daniel I., DPhil. Gunther H. Knoedler Professor of Old Testament, Wheaton College, Wheaton, Illinois: **Worship.**

Boda, Mark J., PhD. Professor of Old Testament, McMaster Divinity College, Hamilton, Ontario, Canada: **Lament, Mourning; Lamentations, Book of; Repentance; Sin, Sinners; Zephaniah, Book of.**

Brenneman, James E., PhD. President, Goshen College, Goshen, Indiana: **True and False Prophecy.**

Briggs, Richard S., PhD. Lecturer in Old Testament and Director of Biblical Studies, St. John's College, Durham University, England, United Kingdom: **Hermeneutics.**

Bruckner, James K., PhD. Professor of Old Testament, North Park Theological Seminary, Chicago, Illinois: **Habakkuk, Book of.**

Carroll R., M. Daniel, PhD. Distinguished Professor of Old Testament, Denver Seminary, Littleton, Colorado: **Ethics; Social-Scientific Approaches.**

Chisholm, Robert B., Jr., ThD. Chair and Professor of Old Testament Studies, Dallas Theological Seminary, Dallas, Texas: **Retribution.**

Cook, John A., PhD. Associate professor of Old Testament, Asbury Theological Seminary, Wilmore, Kentucky: **Hebrew Language.**

Cook, Paul M., DPhil. Affiliate Professor, Asbury Theological Seminary, Wilmore, Kentucky: **Faith; Nations.**

Dearman, J. Andrew, PhD. Professor of Old Testament, Fuller Theological Seminary, Pasadena, California: **Jeremiah: History of Interpretation.**

Dempsey, Carol J., PhD. Professor of Theology (Biblical Studies), University of Portland, Portland, Oregon: **Feminist Interpretation.**

Dempster, Stephen G., PhD. Professor of Religious Studies, Crandall University, New Brunswick, Canada: **Canon, Canonization.**

Dille, Sarah J., PhD. Independent scholar, Moorhead, Minnesota: **Women and Female Imagery.**

Duguid, Iain M., PhD. Professor of Old Testament, Grove City College, Grove City, Pennsylvania: **Ezekiel: History of Interpretation; Israel.**

Eggleston, Chad L., PhD. Assistant Professor of Religion, Huntingdon College, Montgomery, Alabama: **Wilderness, Desert.**

Evans, Craig A., PhD. Payzant Distinguished Professor of New Testament, Acadia Divinity College, Wolfville, Nova Scotia, Canada: **Dead Sea Scrolls.**

Ferris, Paul W., PhD. Professor of Hebrew Bible, Bethel University, St. Paul, Minnesota: **Prayer.**

Firth, David G., PhD. Lecturer in Old Testament and Director of Research, St. John's College, Nottingham, Nottinghamshire, England, United Kingdom: **Leadership; Messiah.**

Friebel, Kelvin G., PhD. Associate Professor of Old Testament Studies, Houghton College, Houghton, New York: **Sign Acts.**

Fuller, Russell E., PhD. Professor of Hebrew Bible, University of San Diego, San Diego, California: **Text and Textual Criticism.**

Gane, Roy E., PhD. Professor of Hebrew Bible and ancient Near Eastern languages, Andrews University, Seventh-Day Adventist Theological Seminary, Berrien Springs, Michigan: **Sacrifice and Atonement.**

Garrett, Duane A., PhD. John R. Sampey Professor of Old Testament Interpretation, The Southern Baptist Theological Seminary, Louisville, Kentucky: **Joel, Book of.**

Giles, Terry, PhD. Professor, Gannon University, Erie, Pennsylvania: **Performance Criticism.**

Glazov, Gregory Yuri, DPhil. Associate professor of biblical studies, Seton Hall University, South Orange, New Jersey: **Canonical Criticism.**

Goldingay, John, PhD. David Allan Hubbard Professor of Old Testament, Fuller Theological Seminary, Pasadena, California: **Servant of Yahweh.**

Hadjiev, Tchavdar S., DPhil. Lecturer in Old Testament Studies, Belfast Bible College, Belfast, Northern Ireland, United Kingdom: **Honor and Shame; Peace, Rest.**

Halton, J. Charles, PhD. independent scholar: **Law.**

Hayes, Elizabeth R., D.Phil. Adjunct professor of Old Testament, Fuller Theological Seminary, Pasadena, California: **Justice, Righteousness.**

Hays, Christopher B., PhD. D. Wilson Moore Assistant Professor of Ancient Near Eastern Studies, Fuller Theological Seminary, Pasadena, California: **Death.**

Hays, J. Daniel, PhD. Dean of the Pruet School of Christian Studies and Professor of Biblical Studies, Ouachita Baptist University, Arkadelphia, Arkansas: **Prophecy and Eschatology in Christian Theology.**

Heiser, Michael S., PhD. Academic Editor, Logos Bible Software, Bellingham, Washington: **Chaos; Destruction; Divine Council.**

Hilber, John W., PhD. Professor of Old Testament Grand Rapids Theological Seminary, Grand Rapids, Michigan: **Liturgy and Cult.**

Hildebrandt, Wilf, ThD. Dean of Education, Summit Pacific College, Abbotsford, British Columbia, Canada: **Spirit of Yahweh.**

Hill, Andrew E., PhD. Professor of Old Testament Studies, Wheaton College, Wheaton, Illinois: **Malachi, Book of.**

Irwin, Brian P., PhD. Associate Professor of Old Testament/Hebrew Scripture, Knox College, Toronto School of Theology, University of Toronto, Toronto, Ontario, Canada: **Social Justice.**

Jenson, Philip P., PhD. Lecturer in Old Testament, Ridley Hall, Cambridge, England, United Kingdom: **Temple.**

Johnson, Timothy J., PhD. Senior pastor, Rock Valley Chapel, Beloit, Wisconsin, and adjunct professor, Philadelphia Biblical University, Langhorne, Pennsylvania: **Apocalypticism, Apocalyptic Literature.**

Johnston, Philip S., PhD. Senior Tutor, Director of Studies in Theology and Religious Studies, Hughes Hall, University of Cambridge, Cambridge, England, United Kingdom: **Afterlife.**

Kelle, Brad E., PhD. Professor of Old Testament, Point Loma Nazarene University, San Diego, California: **Israelite History.**

Kessler, John, DTheol. Professor of Old Testament, Tyndale University College and Seminary, Toronto, Ontario, Canada: **Haggai, Book of.**

Klingbeil, Gerald A., DLitt. Research Professor of Old Testament and Ancient Near Eastern Studies, Seventh-day Adventist Theological Seminary, Andrews University, Berrien Springs, Michigan: **Animal Imagery.**

Klingbeil, Martin G., DLitt. Professor of Biblical Studies and Archaeology, Southern Adventist University, Collegedale, Tennessee: **Floral Imagery.**

Lamb, David T., DPhil. Associate Professor of Old Testament, Biblical Theological Seminary, Hatfield, Pennsylvania: **Word of God; Wrath.**

LeCureux, Jason T., PhD. Director of Old Testament Studies, Trinity Theological College, Brisbane, Queensland, Australia: **Obadiah, Book of.**

Lim, Bo H., PhD. Assistant Professor of Old Testament, Seattle Pacific University, Seattle, Washington: **Isaiah: History of Interpretation.**

Lucas, Ernest C., PhD. Vice Principal and Tutor in Biblical Studies, Bristol Baptist College, Bristol, England, United Kingdom: **Daniel: Book of.**

Lund, Jerome A., PhD. Consultant in Biblical Languages, Accordance, Kviteseid, Telemark, Norway: **Aramaic Language.**

Marlow, Hilary F., PhD. Research Associate for Cambridge Inter-faith Programme and Affiliated Lecturer in Biblical Hebrew, Faculty of Divinity, University of Cambridge, Cambridge, England, United Kingdom: **Creation Theology; Land.**

Martens, Elmer A., PhD. President Emeritus and Professor Emeritus of Old Testament, Fresno Pacific Biblical Seminary, Fresno, California: **Eschatology.**

Mason, Rex, DD. Fellow Emeritus, Regent's Park College, Oxford: **Prophecy and Tradition.**

Matthews, Victor H., PhD. Professor of Religious Studies and Dean of the College of Humanities and Public Affairs, Missouri State University, Springfield, Missouri: **Prophecy and Society.**

McConville, J. Gordon, PhD. Professor of Old Testament Theology, University of Gloucestershire, Cheltenham, England, United Kingdom: **Hosea, Book of; Micah, Book of.**

McKeown, James, PhD. Lecturer in Hebrew and Old Testament, Union Theological College Belfast, Belfast, Northern Ireland, United Kingdom: **Forgiveness.**

Meier, Samuel A., PhD. Professor of Near Eastern Languages and Cultures, The Ohio State University, Columbus, Ohio: **Angels, Messengers, Heavenly Beings.**

Millard, Alan R., MPhil. Emeritus Rankin Professor of Hebrew and Ancient Semitic Languages, University of Liverpool, Liverpool, England, United Kingdom: **Writing and Prophecy.**

Möller, Julie C., DPhil. Associate Professor of Biblical Studies, Grove City College, Grove City, Pennsylvania: **Salvation, Deliverance.**

Möller, Karl, PhD. Senior Lecturer in Theology & Religious Studies, University of Cumbria, Lancaster, England, United Kingdom: **Amos, Book of.**

Moore, Michael S., PhD. Director, Arizona Research Center for the Ancient Near East, Scottsdale, Arizona: **Divine Presence; Wealth and Poverty.**

Morgan, David M., PhD. Assistant Professor of Biblical Studies and Associate Director of the Bryan Institute, Bryan College, Dayton, Tennessee: **Remnant.**

Moyise, Steve, PhD. Professor of New Testament, University of Chichester, Chichester, England, United Kingdom: **Prophets in the New Testament.**

Oswalt, John, PhD. Visiting distinguished professor of Old Testament, Asbury Theological Seminary, Wilmore, Kentucky: **God.**

Parker, Tom C., MPhil. Director, Fuller Theological Seminary Southwest, Phoenix, Arizona: **Marriage and Divorce.**

Person, Raymond F., Jr., PhD. Professor of Religion and Chair of the Department of Philosophy and Religion, Ohio Northern University, Ada, Ohio: **Conversation Analysis.**

Peterson, Brian N., PhD. Assistant Professor of Old Testament and Hebrew Bible, Lee University, Cleveland, Tennessee: **Cosmology.**

Phinney, D. Nathan, PhD. Associate Professor of Biblical Studies, Malone University, Canton, Ohio: **Call/Commission Narratives.**

Rata, Tiberius, PhD. Professor of Old Testament Studies and Chair of Biblical Studies Department, Grace College and Theological Seminary, Winona Lake, Indiana: **Covenant.**

Redditt, Paul L., PhD. Emeritus Professor, Georgetown College, Georgetown, Kentucky: **Editorial/Redaction Criticism; Prophecy, History of.**

Routledge, Robin L., PhD. Senior Lecturer in Old Testament and Academic Dean, Mattersey Hall College, Mattersey, Nottinghamshire, England, United Kingdom: **Blessings and Curses.**

Sandy, D. Brent, PhD. Visiting Professor of New Testament, Wheaton College, Wheaton, Illinois: **Mountain Imagery.**

Schart, Aaron, PhD. Professor for Old Testament and New Testament, University Duisburg-Essen, Institute for Protestant Theology, Essen, Germany: **Twelve, Book of the: History of Interpretation.**

Shields, Martin A., PhD. Sydney, Australia: **Prophecy and Wisdom.**

Stead, Michael R., PhD. Visiting Lecturer in Old Testament, Moore Theological College, Sydney, Australia: **Intertextuality and Innerbiblical Interpretation; Visions, Prophetic.**

Stökl, Jonathan, DPhil. Researcher, University College London, London, England, United Kingdom: **Ancient Near Eastern Prophecy.**

Strawn, Brad D., PhD. Vice President for Spiritual Development and Dean of the Chapel, Southern Nazarene University, Bethany, Oklahoma: **Prophecy and Psychology.**

Strawn, Brent A., PhD. Associate Professor of Old Testament, Candler School of Theology, Emory University, Atlanta, Georgia: **Prophecy and Psychology.**

Stromberg, Jacob, DPhil. Visiting Lecturer, Duke Divinity School, Durham, North Carolina: **Formation of the Prophetic Books.**

Stuart, Douglas, PhD. Professor of Old Testament, Gordon-Conwell Theological Seminary, South Hamilton, Massachusetts: **Jonah, Book of.**

Sweeney, Marvin A., PhD. Professor of Hebrew Bible, Claremont Lincoln University and Claremont School of Theology, Claremont, California, and Professor of Tanakh, Academy for Jewish Religion California, Los Angeles, California: **Twelve, Book of the.**

Thomas, Heath A., PhD. Assistant Professor of Old Testament and Hebrew, Southeastern Baptist Theological Seminary, Wake Forest, North Carolina, and Fellow in Old Testament Studies, The Paideia Centre for Public Theology, Ancaster, Ontario, Canada: **Suffering; Zion.**

Tiemeyer, Lena-Sofia, PhD. Senior Lecturer in Hebrew Bible, University of Aberdeen, Aberdeen, Scotland, United Kingdom: **Ezekiel: Book of.**

Toffelmire, Colin M., PhD (cand.). McMaster Divinity College, Hamilton, Ontario, Canada: **Form Criticism.**

Tucker, Wade Dennis, Jr., PhD. Associate Professor of Christian Scriptures and Associate Dean of Academic Affairs, George W. Truett Theological Seminary, Baylor University, Waco, Texas: **Daniel: History of Interpretation.**

Van Dam, Cornelis, ThD. Emeritus Professor of Old Testament, Canadian Reformed Theological Seminary, Hamilton, Ontario, Canada: **Divination, Magic.**

Watts, Rikk E., PhD. Professor of New Testament, Regent College, Vancouver, British Columbia, Canada: **Exodus Imagery.**

Williamson, H. G. M., PhD,. DD. Regius Professor of Hebrew and Student of Christ Church, University of Oxford, Oxford, England, United Kingdom: **Isaiah: Book of.**

Wolters, Al, PhD. Professor Emeritus of Religion and Theology/Classical Languages, Redeemer University College, Ancaster, Ontario, Canada: **Zechariah, Book of.**

Wray Beal, Lissa M., PhD. Associate Professor of Old Testament, Providence Theological Seminary, Winnipeg, Manitoba, Canada: **Literary Approaches.**

ABRAHAMIC COVENANT. *See* COVENANT.

AFTERLIFE

Like the rest of the OT, the Prophetic Books are concerned primarily with this life rather than anything beyond it, and the prophets themselves with repentance and reform in the present life rather than judgment or recompense in an afterlife. However, the judgment that they proclaim often includes death, while they occasionally address those with an unhealthy interest in the dead. Further, a few texts portray national demise and restoration as *death and resurrection, and this paradigm is eventually extended to individual fate. Nevertheless, the relevant texts are often difficult, and their exact meaning is unclear (for detailed discussion of all texts mentioned, see Johnston 2002).

    1. Death
    2. The Dead
    3. Surviving Death

1. Death.

The Prophetic Books contain little narrative, and what there is entirely lacks the intergenerational time span of Genesis or Kings. Thus, death is seldom recorded as simply the natural end of life, as is common elsewhere in the OT (see Johnston, *DOTHB* 215–18). However, the general fragility of life and the certainty of death are noted—for example, in contrast to the permanence of God's word (Is 40:7).

At the same time, the prophetic focus on issues of life and death leads to the occasional portrayal of death as an enemy. Women will lament that "death has come up into our windows . . . to cut off our children," while the grim reaper leaves a trail of ungathered sheaves (Jer 9:21-22). Elsewhere Sheol is thought to open its mouth wide but never to be satisfied (Is 5:14; Hab 2:5). There are some parallels here to Ugaritic Mot (e.g., *KTU* 1.5.ii.3-4), though in the OT death is barely personified and never deified.

In one text Yahweh apostrophizes Sheol as destructive, toying with the idea of ransoming its victims but then declining (Hos 13:14). This tension is only resolved in the NT when the outcome is reversed through Christ's resurrection (1 Cor 15:54-55). That resolution is nevertheless foreseen in the Isaiah Apocalypse, where Yahweh will destroy the shroud and "swallow up death forever" (Is 25:7-8).

2. The Dead.

The Prophetic Books contain the only two underworld descriptions in the OT, and both are brief (these complement evocative imagery elsewhere, notably Ps 88). Isaiah 14:9-11 describes the former great king of Babylon descending to Sheol, now as weak as those whom he had conquered. Ezekiel 32:17-32 predicts the Egyptians joining the many other slain armies lying in their ethnic groups, prostrate and immobile in a vast cavern. These texts fit the typical OT portrayal of the underworld as the general human fate, devoid of meaningful existence and remote from Yahweh.

Various legal texts prohibit Israelites from contacting or venerating the dead. However, several prophetic texts indicate that such practices indeed existed, though it is impossible to establish their extent at any one period or through time. Isaiah instructs his disciples to oppose necromancers, whose future is bleak (Is 8:19-22). He also indicts drunken priests and rulers who "made a covenant with death" (Is 28:15); their practices possibly include necrotic activity, but the proposed allusions are tenuous. Another Isaianic passage condemns fertility cults, child sacrifice and *idolatry in general (Is 57:3-13), which quite plausibly included consulting or honoring the dead (Is 57:6, 9). A final text castigates those who "sit inside tombs, and . . . eat swine's flesh" (Is 65:3-4), a similar illicit combination though tantalizingly without further detail. Ezekiel's lengthy vision contrasts the pure temple of the future with the tainted previous one, defiled by royal corpses and possibly their veneration (Ezek 43:7, 9).

One possible context for honoring the dead was the *marzēăḥ*. The West Semitic root *mrzḥ* is attested in several contexts (Ebla, Ugarit, Moab, Elephantine, Phoenicia, Nabatea, Palmyra, Talmud) to indicate a social group, or its gatherings, or their location. These gatherings often involved eating and drinking and were sometimes explicitly funerary or commemorative. The Hebrew *marzēăḥ* occurs twice in the OT, once implying revelry and with no obvious link to the dead (Amos 6:7, in a variant construct form, *mirzaḥ*), and once in a funerary context, where *bēt-marzēăḥ* is usually translated "house of mourning" and contrasted with "house of [wedding] feasting" (Jer 16:5, 9). The phrase "house of mourning" without further explanation implies that this was an established custom in late preexilic times. Some scholars argue that the *marzēăḥ* necessarily involved ancestor cults, which were generally prevalent, and that other biblical references to this were later removed by orthodox redactors. However, evidence from other cultural contexts does not prove that the *mrzḥ* was primarily related to the dead. And if the Israelite version had been so related, then the posited zealous redactors would surely also have expunged the references just noted.

Two further phenomena have sometimes been associated with ancestor cults. First, *tĕrāpîm*, often translated "household gods," feature in several narratives (Gen 34; Judg 18; 1 Sam 19) and as divinatory objects in a few prophetic texts (Ezek 21:21; Hos 3:4; Zech 10:2). The *tĕrāpîm* may well have represented revered ancestors, but arguments that this necessarily indicates an active ancestor cult are tenuous. Second, religiously significant pillars (*maṣṣēbôt*) occur in several narratives, including that of sacrifice at Sinai (Ex 24:4), and again coupled with sacrifice in a prophetic text (Hos 3:4 [alongside *tĕrāpîm*]). These pillars have also been associated with ancestor veneration,

since Absalom set up a self-commemorative pillar, and the dutiful son in the Aqhat epic set up "a pillar of his ancestor" (*skn ilib* [*KTU* 1.17.i.27]). However, these arguments are equally tenuous, since Absalom lacked offspring to venerate him, and the Ugaritic text uses different terms and reflects a different socioreligious context.

3. Surviving Death.
Apart from the aspects discussed below, the Prophetic Books share the general OT perspective of Sheol as the only specified human destiny (for recent summary, see Routledge). The identity of individuals can persist in family line and name (as is emphasized by Levenson), but this is quite different from individual afterlife.

3.1. Heavenly Books. There are a few intriguing references to heavenly books in the prophets (as elsewhere). These occur with different wording in a variety of contexts and may well imply different underlying ideas. Some scholars trace the Israelite concept back to the Babylonian "tablets of destiny" or to Persian civilian registers, but these may have no relevance and at most they show religious and administrative parallels.

In an Isaianic vision, the restored community "will be holy, everyone who has been recorded for life in Jerusalem" (Is 4:3). As an alternative to the prevalent religious cynicism, Malachi offers "a book of remembrance . . . of those who revered Yahweh" (Mal 3:16). Daniel's final apocalyptic vision climaxes with the deliverance of "everyone who is found written in the book" (Dan 12:1). His earlier terrifying vision of the Ancient of Days included heavenly assizes: "The court sat in judgment and the books were opened" (Dan 7:10). And the events detailed in his lengthy final vision are recorded in a "book of truth" (Dan 10:21).

Intertestamental and NT writers understood "the book of life" as referring to postmortem fate (e.g., *1 En.* 47:3; 90:20; 108:3; *Jub.* 30:20, 22; 36:10; Lk 10:20; Phil 4:3; Heb 12:23; Rev 21:27), and this interpretation has often been read back into the OT. This approach takes the few OT references as glimpses of future hope. However, this need not be the meaning in their initial context. The record for life (Is 4:3) applies to the current life on earth, not a later one. The divine comment on those in Malachi's heavenly book, "on the day when I act

. . . I will spare them" (Mal 3:17), suggests preservation during judgment rather than life after death. Even the book of names in Daniel's final vision (Dan 12:1), though mentioned just before resurrection, concerns "your people [who] shall be delivered"—that is, who will survive the unprecedented "anguish" and presumably remain alive on earth. Similarly, the books mentioned in several psalms need imply no more than Yahweh's careful concern and provision for his people.

In Daniel's earlier vision, the opening of books in the heavenly court (Dan. 7:10) leads to the destruction of the fourth beast and the subjugation of the other three, divine judgment on current ungodly oppression as a prerequisite to the "heavenly human" and his earthly people receiving God's kingdom. The opening of the heavenly books leads here to judgment on the four beasts, not on all humans. This is a function different from that ascribed to it in later eschatology, though the development is natural. The NT recasts the various elements of Daniel's visions to describe the parousia of Christ, and the resurrection and final judgment of all humanity. The books opened in Daniel's heavenly court are one significant element in this, and thus they are the strongest OT link between heavenly books and the afterlife.

3.2. National Restoration. Two prophetic texts use the concept of renewal of human life as a metaphor for national restoration. Hosea 6:2 invites a return to Yahweh, the very one who had brought destruction on the nation: "After two days he will revive us; on the third day he will raise us up, that we may live before him." The context and language suggest healing from physical wounds and sickness; for example, "three days" occurs in Hezekiah's healing (2 Kings 20:8, though not Is 38) and in Mesopotamian medical texts.

Some scholars see a death-and-resurrection motif in Hosea 6:2. However, the text does not specify that the wounding is fatal, and both the verbs "revive" (*hyh*, Piel) and "raise up" (*qwm*, Hiphil) occur frequently and in varied contexts. J. Day (1996; 1997) notes references to death in the immediate context (Hos 5:14; 6:5), and parallels between Hosea 5—6 and Hosea 13—14. He sees death-and-resurrection motifs in Hosea 13—14, so argues that they occur also in Hosea 5—6, notably resurrection in Hosea 6:2. But Hosea's profuse images appear throughout his book, giving several themes within each chapter and numerous parallels across different chapters. Death is certainly a theme in Hosea 5—6; 13—14, but this does not determine the meaning of Hosea 6:2.

Nevertheless, there is perhaps a more profound link between wounding and death, healing and resurrection. Hosea grapples in anguish with the message of God's punishment and destruction of the nation, while still clinging to the hope of healing and restoration. Inevitably the images that he uses may fuse together, so that healing from grievous wounds and resurrection from the dead are alternate images for the renewal of a moribund nation. Hosea and his audience may have been aware of death-and-resurrection motifs, from whatever source, but they are not necessarily evident here.

In a stupendous vision Ezekiel prophesies to a valley littered with bones, which first regroup as skeletons and, on further word, return to life. The vision is immediately explained: the exiled Israelites have lost hope, but Yahweh will open their graves and repatriate them, and they will live (Ezek 37:1-14). The vision of revivified bodies clearly indicates a restored people, but it says nothing about personal resurrection, even if it was later interpreted in that way. The references to graves in Ezekiel 37:12-13 may seem to imply the latter, but they must be taken in context. Israelites normally buried their dead in rock-cut tombs or, for the poor, in shallow pits, so the equivalent for them of unburied bones coming to life would be bodies emerging from graves. In applying this vision to Israel, Ezekiel 37 first translates the imagery into a culturally relevant equivalent before giving its meaning.

Whether Ezekiel or his contemporaries had a concept of personal resurrection is irrelevant, though the prophet's cautious reply to Yahweh's opening question makes this unlikely. Resurrection could have been part of the religious backdrop, but the vision makes as much sense without it. Ezekiel proclaimed God's message of restoration after destruction, of resettlement after banishment, of national life after death. So the imagery of physical bodies being reconstituted would be a perfect illustration. Its use does not imply a prior belief in resurrection, any more than our understanding of science fiction implies a belief in any of its imaginative worlds. Ezekiel's vision uses physical reconstitution as an image of national restoration, but it says nothing determinative about individual resurrection.

3.3. Individual Resurrection. There are a few possible allusions to individual return to life outside the Prophetic Books. God's power to kill and make alive is twice asserted (Deut 32:39; 1 Sam 2:6), though neither text refers to specific individuals. The prophets Elijah (1 Kings 17:22) and Elisha (2 Kings 4:34) caused life to return, as did the latter's bones (2 Kings 13:20-21), but all these were cases of resuscitation within a few hours of death. These events, though certainly miraculous, were significantly different from resurrection of the long dead.

A clear allusion to individual return to life occurs in the famous fourth Servant Song. After being "cut off from the land of the living" and buried, the enigmatic servant will "see offspring and prolong days . . . see and be satisfied" (Is 53:10-11). There is no mention of resurrection. But the few descriptions of his new life are strongly evocative of earthly existence: offspring, days, seeing, allotted portion. So the servant apparently returns to life in some unspecified form (*see* Servant of Yahweh).

Two texts are more explicit. The Isaiah Apocalypse offers several glimpses of Yahweh's general triumph over death, most notably when he "will swallow up death forever" (Is 25:8). It then notes that the wicked dead do not rise (Is 26:14) but boldly asserts, "Your dead shall live, their corpses shall rise" (Is 26:19). The context is one of national revival and restoration, but there is more here. Both verses refer specifically to "the shades" and "the dead" (i.e., to deceased individuals), while in the latter verse the dust-dwellers will awake and sing, Yahweh's life-giving dew will fall, and the earth will disclose the shades. The imagery clearly envisages the personal resurrection from death of at least some Israelites. The application may be national, but the imagery presupposes a concept of individual resurrection.

Finally, Daniel 12:2 speaks unmistakably of personal resurrection at the climax of Daniel's final vision (Dan 10—12): "Many of those who sleep in the dust of the earth shall awake, some to everlasting life, and some to shame and everlasting contempt." This clearly is individual resurrection of both righteous and wicked. However, it may still be limited. The context focuses on Daniel's people, not all humanity, and the phrase "many of" probably means "many, but not all" (cf. *rabbîm min* elsewhere; e.g., Esther 8:17), rather than "the many" (cf. NIV: "multitudes"). In context, they are probably those who die in the final persecution, some rising to be rewarded for their resistance, others to be shamed for their collaboration. So this resurrection envisages the Jewish people, and possibly only one specific generation.

The two last texts are dated by nearly all scholars to much later than the times of their putative authors, Isaiah 24—27 as late postexilic and Daniel as second century. The theme of overcoming death forms part of the argument, since it is considered a very late development. In particular, resurrection in Daniel (as in 2 Maccabees) is interpreted as a theological response to the Antiochene persecution and Jewish martyrdom (e.g., Burkes). Thus, resurrection belief only emerged at the very end of the OT period, too late to influence other writers.

In contrast, some critical scholars propose an earlier, preexilic date for Isaiah 24—27, while conservative scholars continue to argue for the unity of Isaiah and Daniel, as respectively eighth- and sixth-century books. However, it must then be accepted that the potentially revolutionary belief in personal resurrection remained theologically unassimilated into Israelite faith. If glimpsed by Isaiah of Jerusalem and developed by Daniel in exile, the theme remained unexplored by these writers elsewhere and was ignored by successive prophets of the seventh to fifth centuries, as well as psalmists, sages and historians. To them, the concept of resurrection was unknown or incomprehensible, and their works maintain the traditional Israelite view of the unwelcome underworld. Thus, resurrection and life after death remained marginal to OT belief, whether chronologically or theologically, and awaited exploration in intertestamental literature and resolution in the NT.

See also DEATH.

BIBLIOGRAPHY. **S. L. Burkes**, *God, Self, and Death: The Shape of Religious Transformation in the Second Temple Period* (JSJSup 79; Leiden: E. J. Brill, 2003) 87-158; **J. Day,** "The Development of Belief in Life after Death in Ancient Israel," in *After the Exile: Essays in Honour of Rex Mason*, ed. J. Barton and D. J. Reimer (Macon, GA: Mercer University Press, 1996) 231-58; idem,

"Resurrection Imagery form Baal to the Book of Daniel," in *Congress Volume: Cambridge, 1995*, ed. J. A. Emerton (VTSup 66; Leiden: E. J. Brill, 1997) 125-33; **P. S. Johnston,** "Death and Afterlife," *DOTHB* 215–18; idem, *Shades of Sheol: Death and Afterlife in the Old Testament* (Downers Grove, IL: InterVarsity Press; Leicester: Apollos, 2002); **J. D. Levenson,** *Resurrection and the Restoration of Israel: The Ultimate Victory of the God of Life* (New Haven: Yale University Press, 2006); **R. L. Routledge**, "Death and Afterlife in the Old Testament," *Journal of European Baptist Studies* 9.1 (2008) 22-39.   P.S. Johnston

AMOS, BOOK OF

The book of Amos, possibly the earliest legacy of the "writing prophets," is a paradigm of the prophetic genre. It is notable especially for its powerful rhetorical language, while its most significant theological contribution to the biblical canon lies in the uncompromising censure of the social injustice prevalent in Israelite society in the eighth century BC.

1. Structure and Argument
2. Composition and Interpretation
3. Theology
4. Place in the Canon

1. Structure and Argument.

1.1. Structure. Until well into the 1980s it was common for OT scholarship to affirm that the Prophetic Books, Amos included, lack a clear structure. According to G. von Rad, "The prophetic corpus lies before us in what are, to some extent, very shapeless collections of traditional material, arranged with almost no regard for content or chronological order" (von Rad, 33). Of Amos it has been said that the book "has too little story, too little train of thought, and too little internal coherence to hold interest for more than a few verses or, at most, a chapter" (Coote, 1).

However, such views had to be thoroughly revised following detailed redaction- and rhetorical-critical investigations, with the effect that R. Gordon can now claim that "the prophetic books . . . clearly represent the work of craftsmen and rhetoricians who sought to influence not only by the content of the message but also by the literary form into which they molded it" (Gordon, 107). Similar conclusions have been reached with regard to the arrangement of Amos, but since the book features a complex array of structural devices and literary forms, no final consensus has been reached regarding its structure.

At the most basic level, Amos can be divided into three or four parts: Amos 1—2, the introduction; Amos 3—6, often labeled the "words"; Amos 7—9, the "visions." The final verses of Amos 9 sometimes are treated as a separate part that is thought to have been appended in postexilic times. However, this outline, which provides no more than a general starting point, glosses over the fact that Amos 7—9, in addition to *visions, also features a historical narrative (Amos 7:10-17), judgment speeches (Amos 8:4-14) and a *salvation oracle (Amos 9:11-15). Observations such as this led some earlier commentators to reassign (some of) those sections to other parts of the book (see, e.g., the overview of proposed solutions regarding Amos 7:10-17 in Gordis, 217-18), but B. Childs probably is correct to conclude that "the editorial shaping established no theological significance between Amos' words and visions" (Childs, 404).

In an attempt to move beyond the general tripartite outline, various proposals have been suggested. For instance, a structural function has sometimes been assigned to the hymn fragments in Amos 1:2 (if this is to be included among the hymn fragments); 4:13; 5:8-9; 9:5-6 (Koch), to the distribution and use of, in some cases, highly elaborate divine names (such as *ʾădōnāy yhwh ʾĕlōhê haṣṣĕbāʾôt* in Amos 3:13 [see Koch; Dempster]), to heptads and seven-plus-one series (Limburg) and to "telescoping n+1 patterns" (O'Connell). However, none of these proposals has won wide appeal (for further discussion, see Möller 2003, 62-88).

A far more popular approach has been to find a variety of chiastic structures in the book of Amos. This endeavor goes back to some early studies by J. de Waard and N. Tromp, who argued that Amos 5:1-17 displays a concentric arrangement. Building upon these proposals, some have attempted to extend the outer limits of this central chiasm to include wider sections of the book. Intermediate steps are represented by the works of J. Lust, who extended the boundaries to Amos 4:1—6:7, and P. Noble, who found a chiastic arrangement throughout Amos 3:9—6:14. The most far-reaching chiasms that have been suggested encompass more or less the entire book of Amos (see, e.g., Dorsey; Rottzoll). However, while the early studies by de Waard and Tromp successfully demonstrated the chiastic arrangement of Amos 5:1-17, thus making a significant contribution to the study of the book of Amos, many of the proposals for more extensive concentric structures suffer from a tendency to rely on obscure section breaks, exaggerate the level of correspondence between purportedly parallel parts, or delete or rearrange passages that sit awkwardly within the proposed arrangement (see the discussion in Möller 2003, 64-74).

Perhaps a better way forward is to pay attention to indicators of aperture and closure within the text, such as divine speech formulas and other structural markers. Based on these, it has been suggested that, in addition to the historical superscription in Amos 1:1 and the motto in Amos 1:2, the book consists of nine major units (Möller 2003, 89-103). The first of these, the introductory series of oracles against the nations in Amos 1:3—2:16, is easily identified as one of the book's major sections due to its strophic arrangement, in which each of the eight oracles not only is introduced by the divine speech formula "This is what the LORD says," but also features additional recurring elements, such as the phrase "For three sins of . . . , even for four, I will not turn back my wrath." The occurrence of a major break after Amos 2:16 is signaled by the introductory words "Hear this word the LORD has spoken against you, O people of Israel" in Amos 3:1. Similar phrases in Amos 4:1 and Amos 5:1, together with other structural indicators, such as the inclusio achieved by the use of *pāqad* ("punish") in Amos 3:2, 14 and the chiastic arrangement of Amos 5:1-17, indicate that the oracles against the nations are followed by three extended judgment speeches in Amos 3:1-15; 4:1-13; 5:1-17.

These judgment speeches give way to two extended woe oracles in Amos 5:18-27; 6:1-14, each of which is introduced by the term *hôy* ("woe"). In the visions-cum-narrative section Amos 7:1—8:3 we find another passage that is serial in nature in that each of its four visions is introduced by the words "This is what the Sovereign LORD/he showed me," a phrase that performs a similar function to the recurring divine speech formula in Amos 1:3—2:16. The two final parts are introduced by phrases that represent variations on the introductory markers employed in earlier sections of the book.

Thus, the words "hear this" mark the commencement of another judgment speech in Amos 8:4-14, while the book's conclusion in Amos 9:1-15 is opened by the phrase "I saw the LORD standing by the altar," which by its repetition of the term *rāʾâ* (Qal "see" in Amos 9:1; Hiphil "show" in Amos 7:1, 4, 7; 8:1) recalls the introductions to the earlier visions. These two final parts share some similarities in that both end in sections introduced by the eschatological formulas "in that day" (Amos 8:9, 13; 9:11) and "the days are coming" (Amos 8:11; 9:13). To summarize, this analysis suggests that the book of Amos falls into the following main parts: Amos 1:1-2; 1:3—2:16; 3:1-15; 4:1-13; 5:1-17; 5:18-27; 6:1-14; 7:1—8:3; 8:4-14; 9:1-15.

1.2. Argument. The book opens with a superscription (Amos 1:1), which briefly introduces the prophet Amos and outlines the period of his ministry with reference to the ruling kings in Israel and Judah, thus pointing to a time toward the earlier part of the eighth century BC (*see* Israelite History). The book's gloomy mood is foreshadowed in Amos 1:2, a verse perhaps best understood as the book's motto. This is followed by a series of oracles that threaten Israel's neighbors with the divine punishment for their atrocious war crimes (Amos 1:3—2:5). The series, which appears to play on the audience's nationalistic feelings, features an adroit rhetorical arrangement that moves from foreign *nations proper (Arameans, Philistines, Phoenicians) to Israel's blood relatives (Edomites, Ammonites, Moabites) before apparently settling on the sibling nation, Judah (Amos 2:4-5), whose inhabitants are accused of having rejected the divine Torah, as the prime target. However, Amos's words turn out to be a cleverly designed rhetorical trap, for his harangue eventually culminates in a judgment speech against the Israelites themselves (Amos 2:6-16). It is they who are singled out as the prime target of the divine punishment, and their inclusion in this powerful discourse suggests that the social injustice, the oppression of the poor and marginalized, that especially the upper echelons of Israel's society are guilty of is just as bad as, if indeed not worse than, the war crimes committed by their neighbors.

It has been argued that the book from this point on presents the debate between the prophet Amos and his complacent audience (see Möller 2003), who reject the prophetic message of judgment, relying instead on their cherished theological traditions (such as the *Day of the Lord [see Amos 5:18-20]). A reading of the book in its final form suggests that the debate is triggered by Amos's denunciation of Israel in the concluding part of the introductory series of oracles against the nations (Amos 2:6-16). To this the people apparently replied that they would not be punished by their God, who, after all, had elected them as his chosen people. The people's reply has to be inferred at this point, but similar responses are explicitly stated throughout (see Amos 5:14; 6:1-3; 9:10). In response to the Israelites' reliance upon their status as the chosen people, Amos, in what is the first of a series of extended judgment speeches addressed to Israel, stresses that this status, far from implying impunity from punishment, brings with it a greater level of responsibility (Amos 3:1-2).

That the book of Amos features the debate between the prophet and his audience is suggested not only by those passages that refer to the people's objections (e.g., Amos 5:14; 9:10), but also by the fact that the prophet feels compelled to reinterpret and subvert cherished theological concepts such as the *exodus tradition (Amos 2:9-10; 3:1-2; 9:7) and the Day of the Lord (Amos 5:18-20). Indeed, with regard to Amos's allusions to the exodus tradition, it can be seen that the prophet's stance becomes increasingly more radical. In Amos 2:9-10 the exodus is simply affirmed, and in Amos 3:1-2 the special responsibilities ensuing from Israel's election as God's chosen people are pointed out, while in Amos 9:7 any special status is now flatly denied. This is best understood in the context of a debate where positions have become more and more entrenched, thus demanding more drastic rhetorical measures from Amos if he is to succeed in his attempt to get his audience to face up to reality. The hymn fragments extoling God's destructive powers (Amos 4:13; 5:8-9; 9:5-6) and the acerbic criticism of Israel's religious activities (Amos 4:4-5; 5:21-23) are also best understood from the polemical perspective demanded by this dialogical context.

The judgment speeches in Amos 3:1-15; 4:1-13; 5:1-17, each of which is introduced by the phrase "Hear this word," reiterate the threat of the divine punishment, but they also represent progressive stages in the debate between the prophet and his audience. In Amos 3:1-15 the judgment is threatened at the beginning and reaffirmed at the end of the speech (Amos 3:1-2, 13-15). Its initial announcement once again features Amos's rhetorical shock tactics, for the basic meaning of the verb *pāqad* in Amos 3:2 is "to visit." In its context here, which talks about Israel's election, the natural assumption would be to take this as a friendly visit, and it is only when Amos makes the point that God is going to visit because of "all your sins" that it becomes clear that God's intention is to visit in order to punish his people. The concluding judgment section (Amos 3:13-15), which repeats the verb *pāqad* (Amos 3:14), underlines that the punishment is aimed especially at the rich, the owners of several, richly adorned houses, and that there will be no refuge anymore, since the horns of the altar, which would have guaranteed sanctuary (see Ex 21:13-14; 1 Kings 1:50; 2:28), will be cut off.

In between these framing judgment sections we find Amos arguing his case. First (Amos 3:3-8), in response to an apparent demand that he refrain from proclaiming such a terrible message, Amos employs a series of rhetorical questions to make the point that he has no other choice: "The Sovereign LORD has spoken; who can but prophesy?" He even, in another polemical twist, offers the supporting evidence of two witnesses, ironically provided by Ashdod and Egypt—described by one commentator as "experts in terms of oppression" (Rudolph, 163)—which are called upon to witness the oppression that is going on in Israel's midst (Amos 3:9-10) and that will lead to an enemy plundering the fortresses of the plunderers (Amos 3:10-11). But surely God would rescue his people from such an attack, or so the people assumed. To this objection Amos replies with heavy irony, indicating that there will be a "rescue," but only in the form of some worthless remains that merely prove that God's devastating judgment has indeed taken place (Amos 3:12). For that is the point of the remains that a shepherd might rescue from a lion's mouth: they serve as evidence that the animal truly has been torn by a wild beast (Ex 22:13; see also Gen 31:39).

The well-to-do are also the focus at the beginning of the next judgment speech (Amos 4:1-3), as Amos singles out Israel's upper-class women as an illustration of the lifestyle that Yahweh denounces. Again the oppression of the poor and needy is highlighted, together with what appears to be a drinking problem, as these "cows of Bashan," as the *women are called, are known for demanding drink from their husbands. God now even swears that they will be punished for their outrageous behavior; and the punishment is described in the most drastic of terms (Amos 4:2-3). The numerous *sacrifices and tithes that the people boast about cannot avert this punishment (Amos 4:4-5), as Amos points out, again with the help of a heavy dose of irony, as he parodies a priest's call to *worship. Whereas a priest might have encouraged the people to "go to Bethel and worship; go to Gilgal and bring your sacrifices," Amos turns this on its head when he says, "Go to Bethel and sin; go to Gilgal and sin yet more" (Amos 4:4). Once more the judgment announced at the beginning of the discourse (Amos 4:2-3) is reaffirmed at least implicitly at its end when the Israelites are called upon to prepare for a meeting with a God who is described in highly ominous terms as the one who turns dawn to darkness and treads upon the high places of the earth (Amos 4:12-13). This meeting will be necessary not least because the people had failed to respond to Yahweh's earlier acts of judgment, which had been intended to occasion their return to him (Amos 4:6-11).

The drama increases in the third judgment speech (Amos 5:1-17) when Amos suddenly laments Israel's fall (Amos 5:1-3). When read in context, the text's implication is that this is the outcome of Israel's meeting with Yahweh, which appears to have resulted in the nation's death. However, as we read on, the exhortation to seek God and live (Amos 5:4-6) indicates that it is not too late, and that the divine punishment might yet be averted. Yet the central part (Amos 5:7-13) of this chiastically arranged text underlines the existing crisis between Yahweh and Israel. God's people, who pervert justice (Amos 5:7, 10, 12), commit social crimes and live a self-complacent life (Amos 5:11), are to face the creator God, whose awesome destructive powers are once again highlighted in one of the book's hymn fragments (Amos 5:8-9). This contrast between Yahweh and his people provides the backdrop for another exhortation (Amos 5:14-15), which now admonishes the Israelites to seek good instead of *evil. If they were to do this, Yahweh might still be merciful toward at least the "remnant of Joseph."

However, the concluding part (Amos 5:16-17) suggests otherwise. Forecasting the people's wailing in response to the divine passing through their midst, it anticipates a negative outcome to Israel's meeting with their God.

The ensuing "woe oracles" in Amos 5:18-27; 6:1-14 are fitting sequels to the lament in Amos 5:16-17. Again, the transition to Amos 5:18 from the preceding verse gives the impression of Amos reacting to an implied response by his addressees. The prophet's references to Israel's meeting with God (Amos 4:12; 5:17) triggered the people's memory of the Day of the Lord tradition, which they understood to speak of a time when God would come to their rescue. Because they believed Yahweh to be with them (Amos 5:14), his arrival would be a glorious occasion, a day of light (Amos 5:18). But Amos turns the Day of the Lord tradition against them (Amos 5:18-20). That day, far from being a day of light, would turn out to be utter darkness. It would be a time of terror, as the prophet's story of a person fleeing from a lion and getting away from a bear only to be bitten by a snake illustrates. Further reasons for Amos's negative interpretation of the Day of the Lord are given in Amos 5:21-27, a passage that also explicates the consequences of that day as the people's exile "beyond Damascus." Here, as in Amos 4:4-5, the focus is on empty worship rituals together with a lack of concern for justice (Amos 5:21-24).

In the second woe oracle (Amos 6:1-14) Amos once more rebukes the people's complacency and contemptuous lifestyle, which slights "the ruin of Joseph"—that is, the ruin of the poor (Amos 6:1-7). Again Amos appears to be reacting to the audience's objections to his message of judgment. Those who trust in their military prowess, thinking that this would help them against any threat of exile, are reminded of others who had suffered military defeat despite their assumed strength (Amos 6:2-3). The ruling classes' attempt to "put off the evil day" thus only testifies to their self-delusion, and their excessive decadence and complacency pictured in Amos 6:4-6 will soon come to an end when, in another ironic twist, Israel's leaders will lead their people into exile (Amos 6:7). The remainder of this extended woe oracle sees Amos struggling to convince the Israelites that Yahweh is indeed going to punish them, that the impending judgment will be of the utmost severity

(Amos 6:8-11, 14), that their pride and complacency are abhorred by God (Amos 6:8, 13), and that the injustice they are guilty of is profoundly irrational and unnatural (Amos 6:12).

The visions in Amos 7:1—8:3, together with the embedded narrative report of Amos's clash with the priest Amaziah, which confirms the hostile attitude of Amos's audience (Amos 7:10-17), emphasize that the punishment, while not desired by Amos, will not be averted (Amos 7:8; 8:2). Twice, having become alert to the disastrous consequences of Yahweh's destructive actions in the first two visions, Amos had been successful in obviating the judgment by interceding on Israel's behalf (Amos 7:2, 5). However, in the third vision (Amos 7:7-9) he is prevented from a similar course of action by the fact that there does not appear to be a picture of devastation. In fact, it seems that the significance of the third vision is not immediately clear to the prophet, and when he eventually receives an explanation, Yahweh, before spelling out the punishment, declares that he would not spare Israel again (Amos 7:8). At this point, the visions are interrupted by the story of Amos's encounter with Amaziah (Amos 7:10-17), which appears to have been included here because Amaziah's refusal to take Amos's words as a divine message (compare Amos's "then the Lord said" in Amos 7:8 with Amaziah's "this is what Amos is saying" in Amos 7:11) illustrates the problem that Amos had been facing all along. With the priest's intervention, which is intended to silence the prophet, the debate between Amos and his audience intensifies. The placement of the fourth vision (Amos 8:1-3) after this interlude stresses that the priest's attempt had been futile: God and his prophet cannot be silenced. This vision also features the climactic announcement that "the end has come upon my people Israel" (Amos 8:2).

In another judgment speech in Amos 8:4-14 Amos revisits the exploitative practices of the rich and powerful (Amos 8:4-6) (see Wealth and Poverty), before once again focusing upon the divine judgment and its implications (Amos 8:7-14). The judgment section, which is introduced by another divine oath (Amos 8:7), returns to the notion of Yahweh's awe-inspiring cosmic power (Amos 8:9). The theme of mourning and wailing also resurfaces (Amos 8:10), but the most striking feature is the announcement of a famine, yet not a famine of food and

drink but rather of hearing the word of the Lord (Amos 8:11-13). This is poetic judgment par excellence: those who did not want to listen to Yahweh's word when Amos proclaimed it will one day hunger and thirst for it, but in vain. Their search for the life-sustaining word of Yahweh is described in vivid colors, but all their attempts will be futile (Amos 8:12).

The divine judgment that had been at the center of Amos's proclamation is depicted as finally occurring in the last, climactic vision (Amos 9:1-4), in which Amos witnesses Yahweh ordering the destruction of the temple. Its fall brings about the demise of the people, and although some may be able to make an initial escape, Yahweh will track them down wherever they hide. Now Israel's God is no longer content with his people's exile but instead is determined to destroy them (Amos 9:4). The book's final hymn fragment (Amos 9:5-6) underlines that no one could possibly escape from this God, who only has to touch the earth for it to melt and who can pour the waters of the sea out over the face of the earth. Now, in a last polemical flourish, Israel is denied special status altogether (Amos 9:7-8). Their exodus experience and election will not save them, as the sinful kingdom will be destroyed. It also becomes clear, however, that Israel's end (see Amos 8:2) entails not the total annihilation of the populace but rather the demise of Israel as a national entity, and that it is "all the sinners among [God's] people" who are the prime target of the divine judgment (Amos 9:9-10). Their identity has been revealed throughout the book in passages that talk about social injustice and hollow worship practices, but, in a fitting conclusion to the debate that Amos has been leading with his audience, the prophet emphasizes that it is the ones who had been complacent all along, thinking that "disaster will not overtake or meet us," who are most at risk.

An image of future restoration, agricultural abundance and security in the *land concludes the book (Amos 9:11-15). This envisaged future, contrary to J. Wellhausen's well-known dictum that these verses offer "roses and lavender instead of blood and iron" (Wellhausen, 96), does not mitigate, let alone negate, Amos's message of judgment. In line with a message that knows culprits and victims, hope is offered for those who are not to be counted among the sinners. From a rhetorical perspective, one might say that while the announcements of judgment provide "negative motivation" by warning the addressees not to continue with their present lifestyle, the salvation oracle in Amos 9:11-15 offers "positive motivation" by appealing to the audience's hopes and aspirations. The book eventually closes with the words "says the LORD your God," which is the only time that Yahweh is called "*your* God," thus reinforcing the emotive impact of Amos's final words, which seek to elicit a positive response from the prophet's audience.

2. Composition and Interpretation.

The foregoing analysis of Amos's argument is based on a rhetorical reading that engages with the final form of the text as it has come down to us and interprets the book without recourse to diachronic reflections on how the text might have come into being. This is in line with prominent developments in the study of the OT literature over the last thirty years, which have witnessed an increased focus on the study of the text's final form that is primarily concerned with the investigation of its structure, poetics or rhetorical nature. These developments have also left their mark on Amos studies (see, e.g., Carroll R. 1992; Möller 2003). However, alongside the exploration of these new avenues, which also include studies that approach the text from various reader-centered perspectives that pay attention to the contribution made by the reader in the generation of meaning, there is an undiminished emphasis on the investigation of Amos's composition that assumes that an adequate reading of the book must be able to relate its individual parts to their putative times of composition.

2.1. The Composition of the Book of Amos. Modern research on Amos shows the same tendencies as the scholarly investigation of the OT prophets generally. From the 1880s to the 1920s interpreters concentrated on the innovative impetus of the prophet, understood by some as an "ethical monotheist," whose task it was to announce the divine ethical imperative (Wellhausen). This stress often went hand in hand with a search for Amos's *ipsissima verba*, the very words of the prophetic genius. From the 1920s onward form and tradition critics reversed this trend when they focused on the social and institutional settings (such as the Israelite cult or certain wisdom circles) of the

speech forms used by Amos and understood the prophet largely as a transmitter of traditional theological convictions (*see* Form Criticism). What characterized these early approaches was their concern with the oral stages of the prophet's words. In contrast to this earlier emphasis, redaction criticism, which emerged in the 1960s, attends to the book's literary history and attempts to trace its stages of growth (*see* Editorial/Redaction Criticism). Contrary to their predecessors, who were interested in the prophet's *ipsissima verba*, which were deemed to be far superior to any "secondary" or "inauthentic" additions, redaction critics reject such pejorative labels and affirm the value of contributions made by later redactors in their quest to adapt the prophetic message to changed historical circumstances.

The beginnings of redaction-critical work on Amos can be traced back to W. Schmidt's 1965 article, in which he argued that several passages show the influence of a Deuteronomistic redaction. Schmidt's conclusions, which were based primarily on philological observations (i.e., on comparisons of certain phrases in Amos with the language and style of the Deuteronomists), had a significant impact on Amos studies, affecting, for instance, H. Wolff's influential presentation of the book's redactional growth. Wolff was the first to posit that behind the book of Amos lay a long history of literary growth, stretching from the eighth century BC down to postexilic times and leading to the book's six redactional layers. However, since the first three stages are thought to date either to Amos's own time or to the period immediately following his prophetic ministry, in Wolff's redaction-critical model the majority of the book is still understood in close connection with the prophet himself.

Wolff's work on the redaction history of the book of Amos, though highly influential, found few supporters as such. However, it did lead to further attempts to come to terms with the book's composition, the most notable of which has been provided by J. Jeremias, who published a series of redaction-critical studies as well as a commentary on Amos. Similarly to Wolff, he believes that the book has been continually updated in order to adapt its meaning to changed historical situations. According to Jeremias, Amos's message therefore "can be recovered only through complicated, and in many instances only hypothetical, reconstruction" (Jeremias, 5). And he maintains that the book as we now have it in the biblical canon comes from the (late) postexilic period, having undergone a long redactional process that spanned several centuries. This, in Jeremias's view, is highly significant for the book's interpretation, for "the modern exegete must deal first of all with the exilic/postexilic history of transmission of Amos' message. Any attempt to get back to earlier strata of the book, not to speak of Amos' actual words themselves, is necessarily burdened by a (variously differing) degree of uncertainty" (Jeremias, 9).

One of the most complex analyses of Amos's literary growth has been provided by D. Rottzoll, who isolates no fewer than twelve redactional layers, each of which he seeks to link to its own specific historical setting. The account of redaction-critical developments up to this point might suggest that the findings have become increasingly complex, with the number of proposed redactional layers ever increasing, but it should be noted that this is not necessarily the case. Thus, for instance, A. Park has detected only three compositional layers, all three of which, he claims, have been composed during the preexilic era. Most recently, T. Hadjiev has similarly argued for a less complex scenario, suggesting that a "repentance scroll," written in the northern kingdom, was later reworked in Judah when its message was applied to the southern kingdom. Sometime later, an independently composed "polemical scroll" was added before the resulting book was edited once more in the exilic period.

2.2. Amos and the Redaction of the Twelve. Whereas the works surveyed above agree in their assumption that the development of the book of Amos was a self-contained process, from around the mid-1980s onwards there has been a constant flow of studies that have moved beyond the boundaries of the individual Prophetic Books in an attempt to trace the redaction history of the minor prophets, or the so-called *Book of the Twelve, as a whole. Here the assumption is that the redaction history of Prophetic Books such as Amos did not develop in isolation from the other books that make up the Twelve. Instead, it has been suggested that these books were gathered together from a fairly early stage in their development, and that subsequent editors or redactors not only left

their mark on individual books, but also were engaged in redactional operations that spanned several of the books within the Twelve.

Important stages in the investigation of the redaction history of the Twelve, which cannot be traced here in any detail, include E. Bosshard's observation of structural similarities between Isaiah and the Twelve, which he interpreted as reflecting deliberate redactional efforts by the same tradents, and J. Nogalski's two-volume work, which investigates redactional catchword links and proposes that two multivolume collections (i.e., a "deuteronomic corpus," consisting of early versions of Hosea, Amos, Micah and Zephaniah, and a "Haggai-Zechariah 1—8 corpus") eventually were combined into a "Joel layer." This layer, dated to the fourth century BC, also included Nahum, Habakkuk, Joel, Obadiah and Malachi, while the subsequent addition of Zechariah 9—14 and Jonah at last completed the Twelve's redaction history.

One of the difficulties with proposals that focus on catchword links between adjacent books lies in the possibility that the order of the individual books within the Book of the Twelve may have been somewhat variable, as is indicated by a comparison of the MT with the versions found in the LXX and in 4Q76, one of the texts discovered at Qumran (*see* Dead Sea Scrolls). Indeed, it has been suggested that the order preserved in the LXX should be considered to reflect the original ordering of the Twelve, which, if correct, would seriously undermine many of the redaction-critical proposals that have been advanced in recent years. Finally, mention should be made of A. Schart's study, which is of particular interest in this context because it understands the development of the Twelve as a gradual process of revisions of the book of Amos. As envisaged by Schart, the process is thought to be far more complex than the scenarios proposed by Nogalski and others in that the development of the Book of the Twelve is supposed to have gone through multiple redactional layers.

2.3. Interpreting Amos. The redaction-critical study of Amos has made a substantial contribution to our understanding of the book. Redaction criticism represents a major advance over against earlier attempts at identifying the prophet's *ipsissima verba* in assigning a more positive role to proposed redactional additions, which are no longer regarded as inauthentic and inferior. Despite redaction criticism's interest in earlier redactional layers and the tracing of the book's development, the canonical text is generally regarded in more positive terms in that subsequent modifications of the prophetic message are understood as legitimate endeavors to relate Amos's words to changed historical circumstances. In addition to this positive outlook on the redactors' work, redaction criticism's minute attention to details has also helped to advance our understanding of Amos.

However, perceived weaknesses in redaction-critical methodology have led to the emergence of alternative approaches that concentrate on the received text of the book of Amos rather than its assumed literary development. The ostensible presence of textual inconsistencies and intertextual verbal clues that have played a major role in redaction-critical reconstructions has been questioned by some. But perhaps more importantly, it has been pointed out that redaction criticism's insistence that a proper understanding of the biblical books necessitates that readers are capable of relating individual passages to their presumed historical contexts, which in turn presupposes detailed knowledge not only of those contexts but also of redaction-critical methodology and findings, has had the effect of taking the Bible out of the hands of the laity. This, ironically, reverses the aspiration of the Reformation, whose heirs many redaction critics claim to be, for the Reformers were intent upon making it possible for Scripture to be understood apart from any overriding authority, which in their day and age would have referred to the church. Another serious problem with the redaction-critical approach is that historical interpretation of Amos's redactional layers often runs counter to the perspective demanded by the text itself, as B. Childs especially has highlighted (Childs, 408). However one believes the book to have come into being, canonically it is best read as what it purports to be: the words of the prophet Amos (Amos 1:1).

Some major commentators on Amos (e.g., F. Andersen and D. Freedman; S. Paul) have therefore largely resisted redaction-critical trends. In addition, several approaches have emerged that concentrate on Amos's final form, seeking to elucidate the book's poetics (Carroll R. 1992) or to apply a rhetorical-critical perspective (Möller 2003). In the former case, the book is subjected to a detailed literary analysis that pays close attention not only to formal textual mechanics, such as structural markers and rhetorical devices, but also to characterization and point of view in order to enable readers to enter the world of the text. When coupled with a theological hermeneutic, such an approach can help us to address questions such as how the representation of reality in the textual word of the book of Amos, including its depiction of the identities of God and his people, might draw modern readers of faith into the book's "covenantal discourse" and challenge them to respond to the divine demands and guidance for life in once again very significantly changed historical situations.

Rhetorical-critical readings (*see* Rhetorical Criticism) that apply a sociolinguistic model of interpretation and approach the prophetic literature as a form of social discourse understand the book's rhetoric in suasive terms and thus seek to explicate its "art of persuasion." Based on the classical Aristotelian conception of rhetoric and, in some cases, on the steps of rhetorical-critical analysis outlined by G. Kennedy (Kennedy, 33-38), these readings pay close attention to the rhetorical situation and the specific problem or exigency that occasioned the utterance in question. In the case of the book of Amos, it has been suggested that the presentation of the prophet struggling, and failing, to convince his eighth-century BC Israelite audience that their God would punish them for their disregard for the poor was utilized as a cautionary precedent in a subsequent Judean context, a time when Amos's successors were for their part striving to convince their fellow Judeans of the impending divine judgment should they fail to mend their ways (Möller 2003, 119-20). The rhetorical situation influences the rhetorical choices made by the speaker or writer, such as Amos's rhetoric of entrapment that was mentioned above in connection with the book's oracles against the nations.

The rhetorical situation and problem also determine the choice of rhetorical genre. In the book of Amos the judicial genre is prevalent, yet this does not necessarily reflect the author's main purpose, as has sometimes been argued (see Kennedy, 19), but might rather be indicative of the rhetorical strategy, which is yet another aspect that has attracted scrutiny by rhetorical critics. In Amos the presence of nonjudicial rhetoric (such as rhetorical questions) and the inclusion of the prophet's appeal to his audience's emotions—for instance, in the warning that the divine punishment would lead to a time of lamentation and wailing (Amos 5:1-3, 16-17; 8:10)—suggest that the overarching purpose of those presenting the prophet's debate with his Israelite audience is best described not as judicial but rather as deliberative: it is an attempt to persuade subsequent Judean readers to reexamine their own lifestyle and theological assumptions, especially regarding issues such as divine election and protection. Rhetorical critics also seek to evaluate the rhetorical effectiveness of the discourse in question, whether or to what degree the utterance is a fitting response to the exigency that prompted it. With reference to Amos, one might conclude that "at a time when, for instance, the prophet Isaiah, criticizing the Judaean elite for their social crimes and luxurious lifestyle, announced the divine judgment as a consequence of the people's wrongdoings, the book of Amos would have been a powerful means for backing up that message" (Möller 2003, 296).

The canonical approach developed by B. Childs and those following in his footsteps similarly focuses on Amos's final form (see Canonical Criticism). While acknowledging that the book is the result of complex literary developments, the stance endorsed by proponents of this approach is one in which the interpreter identifies with the perspective suggested by the text itself. Childs illustrates this with reference to the salvation oracle in Amos 9:11-15. Whereas redaction critics tend to regard this passage as a commentary on the *exile, a reality that the redactor had already experienced, in Amos 9 both the threatened *destruction and exile and the promise of the nation's subsequent restoration are in fact presented as future events. It is for this and similar reasons that Childs arrived at the conclusion, already alluded to above, that redaction-critical readings (Childs refers specifically to Wolff's approach) often run counter to the perspective demanded by the biblical text itself (Childs, 408).

It probably is fair to say that the last two decades have seen some greater awareness among Western biblical scholars of the contribution made to the study of the book of Amos by those who understand themselves as reading "from the margins" or "from below," from the perspective of marginalized groups throughout the world. These are intentionally contextual readings (although it is now more widely acknowledged and understood that any reading is determined to a large extent by the context in which it originates) that approach the biblical text out of a deep desire to redress injustices endured because of race or gender and all too frequently legitimated by the biblical interpretation of those in power. A helpful introduction to these readings that is still reasonably up-to-date has been provided by M. Carroll R., who refers to African American, Hispanic American, *feminist and womanist perspectives and looks at ideological critique of Amos, ecological readings and interpretations from Africa and Latin America (Carroll R. 2002, 53-72) (see Hermeneutics).

Some of these readings have found in Amos's "alternative imagination" an ally "that persuades the reader that ultimate power, far from being 'a monopoly of throne and temple,' remains with Amos's God" (García-Treto, 124) or "a model dissenting voice to what appears to have been the prevailing way of thinking about Israel's divine election," a voice that "criticizes the hegemonic interpretation of what it meant to be God's elect people" (Weems, 222). Others, adopting a hermeneutics of suspicion, have been critical of the way the poor are "gendered" in Amos and of the book's apparent lack of concern with the lamentable fate of poor women in eighth-century BC Israel (Sanderson). It is, however, instructive to note M. Carroll R.'s observation that "the level of suspicion argued by First World scholars does not find an echo in the Two-Thirds World" (Carroll R. 2002, 67), where the book of Amos tends to be received as an encouragement and an inspiration by liberationists committed to social change.

3. Theology.
Since the early part of the twentieth century there has been a strong tendency to regard the prophet Amos as the messenger of an inescapable and all-inclusive divine punishment. Yet this has not gone uncontested, as others have rejected what has been described as the construal of the prophet as the messenger of a nation-murdering God, maintaining that Amos's proclamation aimed at *repentance rather than the announcement of an inexorable disas-

ter. More recently, the application of sociolinguistic approaches such as rhetorical criticism and speech-act theory has gone some way toward overcoming the aforementioned dichotomy by demonstrating that prophetic judgment oracles, by their very nature, evoke the possibilities of ineluctable doom and of mercy invoked by repentance (see Möller 2001).

Discussions of Amos's theology, such as those alluded to above, have tended to focus on the theology of the prophet Amos rather than on the theological contribution made by the book bearing his name. Moreover, the understanding that Amos's theology is restricted to an unconditional announcement of divine punishment goes hand in hand with judgments regarding the inauthenticity or secondary nature of passages, such as the calls to seek God in Amos 5:4-6, 14-15 and the salvation oracle in Amos 9:11-15, which seem to contradict the prophet's categorical proclamation of judgment by offering some rays of hope. Of course, a different picture emerges once it is admitted that prophetic oracles of judgment are genuinely open to the two possibilities of ineluctable doom and of mercy invoked by repentance. In this case, glimpses of hope and salvation are no longer as incompatible and out of place as is frequently maintained.

Yet another situation arises with the focus shifting to the theology of the book of Amos, although in this case too there are at least two principal avenues along which to proceed. One is the route taken by redaction criticism, which concentrates on the gradual development of the emerging book's theology. This has been traced in a variety of ways, but the general principle is that each subsequent version needs to be understood as a theological response to the specific time of its composition or redaction. As noted above, some redaction-critical proposals envisage highly complex scenarios involving several stages in the development of the book and thus also its theology. To illustrate this with a simple example, redaction critics generally maintain that the theologies of the book's earlier versions did not include the message of hope and salvation now found in Amos 9:11-15, and that this was introduced only during the final stage of its development by exilic or postexilic redactors whose theology once again reflects and responds to the exigencies of their own situation.

Another approach to the discussion of Amos's theology is to focus on the book's final form. Although redaction criticism also eventually arrives at this, for other scholars Amos's canonical text has been the focal point throughout. From such a perspective, a "full" theological reading entails not only an awareness of the prophet's condemnation of the social injustice prevalent in Israelite society and the attendant threat of the forthcoming divine judgment; it also includes an appreciation of Amos's vision of a restored people who, at some stage in their future, will once again enjoy life in the land under the divine blessing. Other theological emphases appear in, for instance, the oracles against foreign nations (Amos 1—2), which highlight God's sovereign control over the entire world and his resolve to hold the nations accountable for their inhumane war crimes, and in the book's hymn fragments (Amos 4:13; 5:8-9; 9:5-6) with their focus on God's awesome power displayed in creation and de-creation.

As regards contemporary engagement with Amos's theology, special attention should be drawn to Latin American theologies of liberation, for which the book of Amos has been a highly inspirational text. Interpreting it out of their own concrete political, economic and social circumstances, such readings have discovered a great sense of affinity between those conditions and the world depicted in the biblical text. And this affinity has enabled liberationist interpreters to appropriate Amos's message in their desire to modify prevailing political and economic realities and construct a society characterized by solidarity with the poor and marginalized and "sacrificial service in the struggle to eradicate oppression" (Carroll R. 1992, 19).

4. Place in the Canon.

As noted above, recent redaction-critical scholarship has devoted considerable effort to the investigation of Amos's place in the Book of the Twelve, not only historically but also in terms of its literary links with other parts of the Twelve. Redaction critics have paid particular attention to literary echoes, such as that of Joel 3:16a (MT 4:16a) in Amos 1:2, which are commonly regarded as deliberate redactional linkages aimed at juxtaposing the two prophetic writings. While these observations have led to a variety of suppositions concerning the development of the book of the Twelve, they also are profitably employed in a canonical reading of the text that seeks to interpret Amos in the light of its place in the biblical canon. However, such a canonical perspective is not confined to perceived literary links but seeks also to read the entire book of Amos against the wider context provided by the canon, beginning with the Book of the Twelve but also considering, in turn, the prophetic corpus more generally, the OT as a whole and, ultimately, the full biblical canon consisting of OT and NT.

From such a canonical viewpoint, Amos's message of judgment can be fruitfully compared with, for instance, a text such as Habakkuk 1:12-17. For whereas one prophet, Amos, can readily and unproblematically announce a divine judgment in the form of an enemy invasion, Habakkuk, by raising the question of theodicy that such an enemy attack elicits, offers an intriguing canonical counterperspective. In the wider outlook afforded by the canon of the OT and regardless of how the historical relationship between the prophets and the Torah is construed, Amos is portrayed as presupposing some of the stipulations found in the Torah (see Law). Examples of this include the regulations regarding a garment taken in pledge (Ex 22:26), which are referred to in Amos 2:8, and the instructions concerning the remains of an animal mangled by wild beasts (Ex 22:13), which inform Amos's ironic statement about rescue in Amos 3:12. From a canonical viewpoint, such passages present the prophet as an interpreter and an enforcer of the divine instructions contained in the Torah. Another link between Amos and the Torah has been seen in the book's utilization of the language of the pentateuchal curses and blessings in its numerous judgment speeches and the salvation oracle in Amos 9:11-15 (see Stuart, xxxi-xlii).

Canonical links between the NT and the book of Amos are most readily perceived in the two quotations found in the book of Acts. In Acts 7:42-43 Amos 5:25-27 is interpreted as a reference to Israel's idolatry during the time in the wilderness, whereas in Acts 15:13-18 James reapplies the rebuilding of David's fallen booth (Amos 9:11-12) to God forming a new people for himself from among the Gentiles. But it would be wrong to give the impression that a canonical reading is dependent upon direct quotations. In the pages of the NT allusions to the OT abound at many different levels, beckoning us to read one in the light of the other. A general illustration of this is the ministry of Jesus, whose praxis and eschatological message about the kingdom of God evince clear links with the OT prophets. Another example concerns certain statements in the letter of James regarding the luxurious lifestyle of the rich and their oppression of the poor (Jas 2:6-7; 5:1-6), which clearly are influenced by the language of the OT prophets generally and perhaps some of Amos's speeches in particular.

See also DAY OF THE LORD; SOCIAL JUSTICE; TWELVE, BOOK OF THE.

BIBLIOGRAPHY. *Commentaries:* **F. I. Andersen and D. N. Freedman,** *Amos: A New Translation with Introduction and Commentary* (AB 24A; New York: Doubleday, 1989); **J. Jeremias,** *The Book of Amos: A Commentary,* trans. D. W. Stott (OTL; Louisville: Westminster/John Knox, 1998); **S. M. Paul,** *Amos: A Commentary on the Book of Amos* (Hermeneia; Minneapolis: Fortress, 1991); **W. Rudolph,** *Joel, Amos, Obadja, Jona* (KAT 13/2; Gütersloh: Mohn, 1971); **J. E. Sanderson,** "Amos," in *The Women's Bible Commentary,* ed. C. A. Newsom and S. H. Ringe (Louisville: Westminster/John Knox, 1992) 205-9; **D. Stuart,** *Hosea—Jonah* (WBC 31; Waco, TX: Word, 1987); **H. W. Wolff,** *Joel and Amos: A Commentary on the Books of the Prophets Joel and Amos,* trans. W. Janzen, S. D. McBride Jr. and C. A. Muenchow, ed. S. D. McBride Jr. (Hermeneia; Philadelphia: Fortress, 1977). *Studies:* **E. Bosshard,** "Beobachtungen zum Zwölfprophetenbuch," *BN* 40 (1987) 30-62; **M. D. Carroll R.,** *Contexts for Amos: Prophetic Poetics in Latin American Perspective* (JSOTSup 132; Sheffield: JSOT, 1992); idem, *Amos—The Prophet and His Oracles: Research on the Book of Amos* (Louisville: Westminster/John Knox, 2002); **B. S. Childs,** *Introduction to the Old Testament as Scripture* (Philadelphia: Fortress, 1979); **R. B. Coote,** *Amos among the Prophets: Composition and Theology* (Philadelphia: Fortress, 1981); **J. de Waard,** "The Chiastic Structure of Amos v 1-17," *VT* 27 (1977) 170-77; **S. Dempster,** "The Lord Is His Name: A Study of the Distribution of the Names and Titles of God in the Book of Amos," *RB* 98 (1991) 170-89; **D. A. Dorsey,** "Literary Architecture and Aural Structuring Techniques in Amos," *Bib* 73 (1992) 305-30; **F. O. García-Treto,** "A Reader-Response Approach to Prophetic Conflict: The Case of Amos 7.10-17," in *The New Literary Criticism and the Hebrew Bible*, ed. J. C. Exum and D. J. A. Clines (JSOTSup 143; Sheffield: JSOT, 1993) 114-24; **R. Gordis,** "The Composition and Structure of Amos," in *Poets, Prophets, and Sages: Essays in Biblical Interpretation* (Bloomington: Indiana University Press, 1971) 217-29; **R. P. Gordon,** *"The Place Is Too Small for Us": The Israelite Prophets in Recent Scholarship* (SBTS 5; Winona Lake, IN: Eisenbrauns, 1995); **T. S. Hadjiev,** *The Composition and Redaction of the Book of Amos* (BZAW 393; Berlin: de Gruyter, 2009); **G. A. Kennedy,** *New Testament Interpretation through Rhetorical Criticism* (Chapel Hill: University of North Carolina Press, 1984); **K. Koch,** "Die Rolle der hymnischen Abschnitte in der Komposition des Amos-Buches," *ZAW* 86 (1974) 504-37; **J. Limburg,** "Sevenfold Structures in the Book of Amos," *JBL* 106 (1987) 217-22; **J. Lust,** "Remarks on the Redaction of Amos V 4-6, 14-15," in *Remembering All the Way: A Collection of Old Testament Studies Published on the Occasion of the Fortieth Anniversary of the Oudtestamentisch Werkgezelschap in Nederland*, ed. B. Albrektson et al. (OtSt 21; Leiden: E. J. Brill, 1981) 129-54; **K. Möller,** "Words of (In-)evitable Certitude? Reflections on the Interpretation of Prophetic Oracles of Judgement," in *After Pentecost: Language and Biblical Interpretation*, ed. C. Bartholomew, C. Greene and K. Möller (SHS 2; Grand Rapids: Zondervan, 2001) 352-86; idem, *A Prophet in Debate: The Rhetoric of Persuasion in the Book of Amos* (JSOTSup 372; London: Sheffield Academic, 2003); **P. R. Noble,** "The Literary Structure of Amos: A Thematic Approach," *JBL* 114 (1995) 209-26; **J. D. Nogalski,** *Literary Precursors to the Book of the Twelve* (BZAW 217; Berlin: de Gruyter, 1993); idem, *Redactional Processes in the Book of the Twelve* (BZAW 218; Berlin: de Gruyter, 1993); **R. H. O'Connell,** "Telescoping N+1 Patterns in the Book of Amos," *VT* 46 (1996) 56-73; **A. W. Park,** *The Book of Amos as Composed and Read in Antiquity* (SBL 37; New York: Peter Lang, 2001); **D. U. Rottzoll,** *Studien zur Redaktion und Komposition des Amosbuchs* (BZAW 243; Berlin: de Gruyter, 1996); **A. Schart,** *Die Entstehung des Zwölfprophetenbuchs: Neubearbeitungen von Amos im Rahmen schriftenübergreifender Redaktionsprozesse* (BZAW 260; Berlin: de Gruyter, 1998); **W. H. Schmidt,** "Die deuteronomistische Redaktion des Amosbuches: Zu den theologischen Unterschieden zwischen dem Prophetenwort und seinem Sammler," *ZAW* 77 (1965) 168-93; **N. J. Tromp,** "Amos V 1-17: Towards a Stylistic and Rhetorical Analysis," in *Prophets, Worship, and Theodicy: Studies in Prophetism, Biblical Theology, and Structural and Rhetorical Analysis, and on the Place of Music in Worship*, ed. A. S. van der Woude (OtSt 23; Leiden: E. J. Brill, 1984) 56-84; **G. von Rad,** *Old Testament Theology, 2: The Theology of Israel's Prophetic Traditions*, trans. D. M. G. Stalker (Edinburgh: Oliver & Boyd, 1965); **R. J. Weems,** "Womanist Reflections on Biblical Hermeneutics," in *Black Theology: A Documentary History, 2: 1980-1992*, ed. J. H. Cone and G. S. Wilmore (Maryknoll, NY: Orbis, 1993) 216-24; **J. Wellhausen,** *Die kleinen Propheten* (4th ed.; Berlin: de Gruyter, 1963).   K. Möller

ANCIENT NEAR EASTERN PROPHECY

One of the most exciting changes in the study of prophecy in the Hebrew Bible in the last thirty years is the realization that other ancient Near Eastern cultures also knew prophecy, just as there were prophets in Israel. Not only do they know of people who occasionally were inspired to speak in a deity's name, but also there were "professional" prophets, people recognized as regularly speaking in the name of a deity. This article focuses on those individuals in the ancient Near East who were "professional" prophets and, therefore, whose social and religious role is directly comparable to that of the Israelite *nābî'*.

1. The Corpora
2. Terminology
3. Comparison of Prophecy in the Hebrew Bible and in the Ancient Near East

1. The Corpora.
Most texts come from two large archives: the royal archive from Old Babylonian Mari (eighteenth century BC) and the Neo-Assyrian state archives (seventh century BC). Some of the texts preserve oracles transmitted in letters by governors and priests to their king; other texts are administrative documents that attest to the existence of prophets even when we do not have oracular material. In addition, there are some Aramaic inscriptions from Transjordan. Prophecy as such is usually not identified in Egyptian, Ugaritic and Hittite sources, but a number of recent studies have challenged this

consensus. Recent English translations of virtually all ancient Near Eastern prophetic texts can be found in Nissinen 2003c. Some, but not all, of the texts are also available in *ANET* 449-55, 604-7.

1.1. Old Babylonian/Mari. The royal archives from Mari were found in excavations of Tell Hariri on the Euphrates in Eastern Syria close to the Syrian-Iraqi border in the first half of the twentieth century. There are about fifty administrative letters containing reports of prophetic oracles written by high officials such as governors and addressed to the king, most of them to King Zimri-Lim, but a few also to Yasmaḫ-Addu, his predecessor. The first text was published in 1950, but most texts have recently been edited by J.-M. Durand and D. Charpin. There are also other administrative texts, such as lists of expenses, which show that prophets were provided for by the royal administration. Most oracles contained in the letters are concerned with cultic provisions for various temples and military matters, and they include some criticism of the king's behavior. There are also one to two texts each from Ishchali (Ellis 1987), Uruk (van Dijk) and Kish (Dalley).

1.2. Neo-Assyrian State Archives. The Neo-Assyrian state archives have been known for over a century, and the so-called *Sammeltafeln* (tablets collecting several oracles) were first published in 1889 by A. Delattre. Despite the obvious similarities between these texts and some biblical passages, few Hebrew Bible scholars took note of them until their reedition in 1997 by S. Parpola. In addition to the two *Sammeltafeln*, there is one *adê* ("covenant")-tablet, several tablets containing a single oracle, a few letters containing quoted oracles, and administrative documents attesting to prophets, most of which are published in Nissinen 1998b.

1.3. Aramaic Inscriptions. There are three *Aramaic inscriptions with prophetic content: the Deir ʿAlla inscription (750-650 BC), the Zakkur inscription (805-775 BC) and the Amman citadel inscription (late ninth century BC).

1.3.1. Deir ʿAlla. The Deir ʿAlla inscription contains an oracle of doom by Balaam bar Beor, the *ḥ[z]h ʾlhn* ("seer of the gods"). This inscription recently has been interpreted as an indication that not all ancient Near Eastern prophecy was positive for the king (Blum; Williamson). There can be little doubt that the archival nature of ancient Near Eastern evidence for prophecy has a bias toward supportive messages, and that negative oracles were not preserved; however, they did presumably occur, as indicated by SAA 16 59, a letter to the king in which it is reported that a female slave prophesied in support of a rival pretender to the throne. The oracle preserved in the Deir ʿAlla inscription is a literary narrative creation, and in its depiction of an apocalyptic future it is more akin to Egyptian literary predictive texts such as the so-called Prophecy of Neferti than prophetic oracles preserved in Akkadian texts or in the Hebrew Bible. It also shows that the genre "predictive text" was known in Transjordan, close to Israel, in the early eighth century BC.

1.3.2. Zakkur. The Zakkur inscription is a royal inscription by King Zakkur of Hamath. In the text he thanks his god Baʿal-Šamen for rescuing him from Bar Hadad II, who had laid siege to Zakkur. According to the inscription, Baʿal-Šamen answered [*b*]*yd ḥzyn wbyd* ʿ*ddn* ("through seers and messengers") and it contains the classical "fear not" formula of salvation oracles from Neo-Assyrian and biblical texts (Nissinen 2003b). The term ʿ*ddn*, plural of ʿ*dd*, comparable to biblical Hebrew ʿ*dd* in 2 Chronicles 15:1; 28:9, is difficult to translate (Barstad 2003).

1.3.3. Amman Citadel. The Amman Citadel inscription is difficult to decipher, and so it is unclear whether it is intended as recording an oracle from Milkom or as a narrative about the beneficiary deeds of that deity. Despite the argument that if these words are Milkom's, they must be prophecy (Sasson), it is unclear whether this oracle is prophetic or was gained by more technical means (see 2.4 below the question of technical versus intuitive divination).

1.4. Corpora in Which the Existence of Prophecy Is Disputed (Egypt, Ugarit, Hittites, Ebla, Emar).

1.4.1. Egypt. For most of the twentieth century, there has been a consensus that the sociological phenomenon "prophecy" did not exist in Egypt. Instead, there are several texts that could be regarded as falling into the category "literary predictive texts" (Ellis 1989): the Prophecy of Neferti and the Admonitions of Ipu-Wer. There is also the story of Wenamun, the Egyptian official sent to Byblos to buy wood who, during his adventures, encounters prophets (Schipper). Apart from the travelogue told by Wenamun, none of these texts explicitly includes a human intermediary from a deity to a human addressee, which is one of the requirements according to the standard definition of prophecy (Weippert, 289-90; Nissinen 2004). Either, like in Neferti, the human is portrayed as a wise man who knows the future or, like in the Memphis and Karnak stelae, the deity speaks directly to the royal addressee. This led N. Shupak to come forward with her interpretation of these religious specialists as wise men (Shupak 1990; 2006, #3063).

More recently, two approaches have reassessed the use of the Egyptian texts for the study of prophecy in the Hebrew Bible and in ancient Israel. J. Hilber (2012; forthcoming) has attempted to find evidence for prophetic activity in victory inscriptions. As with Mesopotamian inscriptions, it is always possible that words ascribed to deities in inscriptions result from prophetic activity, but any other form of *divination can also be their source. The other approach regards Egyptian literary texts as appropriate comparative material to prophecy in the Hebrew Bible precisely because they are literary productions; Egyptian and biblical texts are, to a large extent, representatives of the genre "literary predictive texts" (Grabbe, 86-87; Scurlock; Weeks).

The only Egyptian text that may go back to the socioreligious phenomenon "prophecy" is *Wenamun*, the story of an Egyptian official on a rather adventurous journey to Byblos to acquire timber for the Amun-Re temple at Karnak. Everything that could go wrong on his journey does go wrong: his money is stolen, and he is even arrested. Wenamun's fortunes change only when a person referred to as *ꜥdd ꜥꜣ* appears and, while in trance, announces a divine decree to let Wenamun go. The term *ꜥdd ꜥꜣ* is extremely rare (only here and in P. Berlin 10494) and is now mostly translated as "ecstatic" because of the similarities with Aramaic *ꜥdd*. Whether or not this text is fictitious, the person who goes into ecstasy is not Egyptian, but Phoenician. Thus, if this Egyptian text is read as an example of prophecy, it should be taken not as Egyptian prophecy but rather as Levantine prophecy.

1.4.2. Ugarit. Recently, N. Wyatt suggested that an episode in the Keret epic (*KTU* 1.15 ii 17-iii 19) should be understood as a prophetic oracle. However, in that text El talks directly to Keret rather than going through an intermediary, rather like in many ancient Near Eastern dreams.

1.4.3. Hittites. It is unclear whether the Hittite term LÚ DINGIR[lim]-*ni-an-za-ma* ("ecstatic man of god") should be translated as prophet as suggested by R. Beal. The most promising context for finding out its significance is in the Second Plague Prayer by Muršili II: "Let me either see it in a dream, or let it be established through an oracle, or let an 'ecstatic man of god' declare it." G. Beckman points to 1 Samuel 28:6, where the same order (dreams, oracles, prophets) occurs, and therefore he translates the Hittite term as "prophet." This may well be justified, but the data does not provide any further information as to how these "prophets" operated, and "unfortunately no examples of their utterances survive" (Beal, 381). Additionally, the term "man of the Storm-god" occurs in Middle Hittite rituals denoting a priest who introduces the king to the deity but who does not seem to perform any divinatory functions (Taggar-Cohen, 248-70).

1.4.4. Ebla. In 1976 G. Pettinato claimed that he had found two classes of prophets in texts from twenty-fourth century BC Ebla, the *maḫḫû* and the *nabiʾutum*. In 1977 Pettinato modified this to *nabî* and *maḫḫû*, citing TM.75 G.428 and 1860. The second of the two texts was already well known to the scholarly public, as Pettinato previously had claimed that it contained reference to Sodom and Gomorrah. Pettinato later admitted that this tablet is a metallurgical text and does not contain references to Sodom and Gomorrah or prophets (Archi, 151-52). Despite this, references to prophecy at Ebla can still be found in modern scholarly literature. While it is impossible to prove that prophecy did not exist in Ebla, we can confidently say that no evidence of it, textual or otherwise, has reached us today.

1.4.5. Emar. The textual evidence for the existence of prophecy at Emar is somewhat stronger but by no means conclusive. The root *nbʾ* is attested in two professional titles, *nabû and *munabbiātu, in the following four texts: Emar 373:97', 379:11-12, 383:10' and 406:5' (Arnaud 1986; 1987). D. Fleming (1993a; 1993b; 1993c) adduced these titles, and the isolated occurrence of the *nabī ša Ḥanameš* in a text from Mari (ARM 26 216), arguing for an active etymology of Hebrew *nābîʾ*, for which he was criticized by J. Huehnergard (for Fleming's response, see Fleming 2004). Because the Mari text is often understood as referring to prophecy, Fleming and others regard the Emar occurrence as referring to prophecy too. However, it is by no means certain that this Mari text refers to prophecy; the context and the language of ARM 26 216 suggest technical divination but do not rule out the possibility of intuitive divination/prophecy. The usage of the verb *nb'* in Emar suggests the invocation of deities/ancestors, and it is therefore likely that the two related nominal forms *nabī* and **munabbiātu* are also related to ancestor worship (Stökl forthcoming b). As in the case of Ebla, it is impossible to prove that prophecy did not exist in Emar, but no evidence for its potential existence survived.

2. Terminology.
Much research has focused on understanding the professional titles used in prophetic texts from Mari and the Neo-Assyrian Empire. The title *muḫḫûm/maḫḫû* (fem. *muḫḫûtum/maḫḫûtu*) is used in both corpora. The term *āpilum* (fem. *āpiltum*) occurs only in the Mari texts, while *raggimu* (fem. *raggintu*) is used exclusively in Neo-Assyrian texts. Prophecy is one of the few religious professions in the ancient Near East that is performed by men and women and for whom the same terms are used (albeit in masculine and feminine forms). Unlike in most other religious professions, there do not appear to be any differences between male and female prophets (Stökl 2010).

2.1. *muḫḫûm/maḫḫû*. The *muḫḫûm* ("ecstatic"; Neo-Assyrian *maḫḫû*), an ecstatic cult official, is attested throughout Mesopotamian history, mostly unrelated to prophecy. Because at Mari they mostly occur in letters in which they transmit divine messages, most scholars believe that the *muḫḫûm* is a professional "prophet." However, it is unclear whether this is in fact the case. It is possible that the term refers to a specific kind of cult ecstatic, similar to, for example, the *zabbu*, close to whom the *muḫḫûm* appears in lexical lists. This in turn raises the question of what we mean when we use the term *prophet*: is it the socioreligious role or the technical term for a profession? If we mean the former, then some individual *muḫḫûm*s are prophets; but the term is not a technical one for a professional prophet.

2.2. The *āpilum* and the *raggimu*. The *āpilum* is the technical term for a prophet in the Old Babylonian period. It used to be translated as "answerer," but the better translation "spokesperson" is gaining ground (Merlo; van der Toorn 1998, 60). The Neo-Assyrian equivalent of the Old Babylonian *āpilum* is the *raggimu* ("shouter"). While it is generally assumed that they are employed in temples, it is significantly less clear than normally assumed. They are the "spokespeople" of a deity, and in the case of Mari prophecy, they often, but by no means always, speak in temples. But, as ARM 26 199 shows, royal officials send the *āpilum Lupaḫum* to a number of different temples, implying that he is working for the royal administration. It seems that some prophets, maybe even many prophets, had some form of an association with a temple, but that they were not required to have such a connection. Significantly, the same is also true for other professional diviners in the ancient Near East.

2.3. Prophecy and Gender. There is a debate on the involvement of people with third-gender in prophecy in the ancient Near East. Here, "gender" is used to describe the social role performed by people—that is, the question is whether they behave like men or women, rather than their biological sex. At Mari three religious professionals called *assinnu* are reported to be involved in prophecy. Elsewhere, particularly in texts from the first millennium, *assinnu* are described as men whom the goddess (Ishtar) had turned into women (Henshaw). The *assinnu* were cult performers who were ecstatic and danced, as did other cult "ecstatics," such as the *zabbu* and probably the *muḫḫûm*. It is argued that because the *assinnu* performed an ambiguous gender role, ambiguous gender performance is common in prophetic people, particularly in the Neo-Assyrian period (Parpola; Huffmon; Nissinen forthcoming). There is ample evidence for *assinnu* in the Neo-Assyrian period; however, they never prophesy. The Neo-Assyrian evidence for gender ambiguity consists of three peculiar spellings in SAA 9 1 (texts 1, 4, 5) that leave open the possibility that the writer may have been attempting to write ambiguous gender performance of three prophets. This is, however, extremely unclear. In my view, it is difficult to defend the thesis that gender ambiguity is well established on the basis of one tablet, which can be interpreted in various ways. While it is impossible to disprove that people with ambiguous gender were involved in prophecy, there is equally little to suggest that prophecy was a particularly prominent occupation with ambiguous gender (Stökl forthcoming a; Zsolnay).

2.4. Divination and Prophecy. Deuteronomy 13; 18 condemn divination. The study of prophecy in Mesopotamia, however, has shown that far from being opposed to technical forms of divination, prophecy is an integral part of the system of divination there; it is one of the ways in which the human king (and others) has access to information from the divine sphere (Nissinen 2000). It is therefore better to classify prophecy as one of the many forms of divination, where "divination" refers to all manner of communication with the divine with the aim of finding out the will of a deity. With this terminology, prophecy is an "intuitive" form of divination, while the reading of entrails, for example, is one of the technical forms of divination. This terminology has the benefit of explaining the similarities between various forms of divination while still allowing for differences between them (Nissinen 2010b; Grabbe, 150-51; Pongratz-Leisten).

3. Comparison of Prophecy in the Hebrew Bible and in the Ancient Near East.

3.1. Criticism of the King. One of the major features of biblical prophecy is the radically critical encounter of prophecy and king. There is no direct evidence for such meetings from anywhere in the nonbiblical material. Some of this absence can be explained by the nature of the sources: the nonbiblical sources come mostly from royal archives and royal inscriptions, while the biblical text could be classified, at least in parts, as protest literature. Royal archives are unlikely to preserve messages critical of a king in particular and human kingship in general. Some criticism of the king's actions in particular instances can be found in the Mari letters. Additionally, in a Neo-Assyrian letter (SAA 16 59) an incident is quoted in which a female slave prophesied in favor of a pretender to the throne. Though not critical toward kingship in general, this letter shows that prophecies against the king were delivered. It is only through the accident of preservation that they do not survive (Nissinen 1998a; 2003a).

3.2. Prophecies of Doom, Salvation Oracles and the Function of Prophecy/Divination. Most an-

cient Near Eastern prophecy is in support of the king, with a significant focus on legitimizing the rule of a new king (Dalley). One common form of oracle is the promise of support against enemies both without and within, similar to, for example, Isaianic promises of divine support for Judah. On the basis of such similarities, some scholars recently have argued that Israelite prophecy, as seen in Isaiah, presumably followed the same model: they mostly gave salvation oracles in favor of the king. It is true that most preserved oracles from nonbiblical sources are positive for the king and can very well be compared to salvation and victory oracles (van der Toorn 1987). However, they also knew more critical forms of oracles. E. Blum and H. Williamson have pointed to the Deir ʿAlla inscription to show that ancient Near Eastern prophets were capable of pronouncing oracles of doom as well as salvation oracles. It certainly is to be expected that prophets, just like other diviners, occasionally pronounced oracles of doom. These should not, however, be understood as oracles of unconditional doom, but rather as oracles that attempt to cause a change of behavior by warning the king that otherwise the announced catastrophe will take place (Tiemeyer). This may indicate that biblical oracles of doom should be understood as conditional as well. Interpreted in that way, Amos does not announce the destruction of the northern kingdom, but rather that it will be destroyed unless the ruling classes mend their ways. Mesopotamian omen literature is full of omens that announce the destruction of the capital, the state, the death of the king and other such catastrophes. Their purpose was to warn the addressee of the outcome if nothing was done to change the conditions. When oracles occurred that supported a rival king, as in the example given above (SAA 16 59), it appears that they could be taken as "false prophecy" (Nissinen 1996).

3.3. Cultic Prophecy. Ever since S. Mowinckel's magisterial study on Psalms, there has been the consensus that cultic prophecy existed in Israel, and most scholars find it in the ancient Near Eastern sources as well (Hilber 2005) (*see* Liturgy and Cult). With regard to the ancient Near Eastern texts, many oracles occur in temples, and the *muḫḫû/maḫḫû* (pl.) are active participants of the temple cult. Currently, the consensus view is that there was cultic prophecy in the ancient Near East. Many oracles are said to have occurred within the temple. However, if by "cultic prophecy" we mean prophecy that occurred within the temple cult, the evidence base consists of the *Eštar*-ritual texts from Old Babylonian Mari (FM 3 2 and 3), and even that is far from clear (Durand and Guichard 1997). One of the two texts stipulates that if the *muḫḫû* "go into trance" (*immaḫû*), the musicians will play a certain melody. The verb *māḫû* ("to rave") is translated there by supporters of cultic prophecy as "to prophesy" rather than with its normal meaning. The evidence for professional prophecy within the cult in the ancient Near East is very slim indeed and depends on how one translates the verb *māḫû*, either with its normal meaning or with a special meaning for this text. It appears instead that the Old Babylonian *muḫḫû* and his Neo-Assyrian counterpart fall within another class of cult ecstatics within Mesopotamian religion.

Another issue that comes up in these two texts (FM 3 2 and 3) is the connection between prophecy and music. Although the OT Prophetic Books are silent on the matter, 2 Kings 3:15 shows a clear link between prophecy and music. The question, however, is not only whether music and prophecy occur in the same text, but also whether there is some form of functional link between them. Although 2 Kings 3:15 is fairly clear on the issue, in the two texts from Mari this link is less clear. In FM 3 3 the musicians are supposed to play a ritual lament when the cult ecstatics do not go into trance. In FM 3 2 it appears that the opposite is the case: the musicians play the lament only if the ecstatic has gone into trance. Both texts breaks off immediately afterwards. This indicates that while there is temporal connection between ecstasy and music in Mari, there is no proof that music is used to induce prophetic trance.

3.4. The Literary Production of Literary Predictive and Prophetic Texts. M. de Jong argued that the Neo-Assyrian *Sammeltafeln* present us with something of an intermediate stage between the individual oracle by a prophet and literary predictive texts as found in Egypt and Mesopotamia (de Jong, 395-442). Further, since it is not always clear whether a divine utterance that is cited in Neo-Assyrian royal inscriptions and elsewhere is the result of prophecy or more technical forms of divination—that is, from a form-critical perspective they can look identical—the literary reflexes of various forms of divination become very difficult to distinguish.

At Mari the following procedure appears to have been at work: a prophet pronounces an oracle in front of a governor or an important priest, or it is reported to them and they include it in their regular report to the king. A. Schart identified Mari letters in which a governor reports two oracles to the king as an early stage in the production of literary prophetic texts. It is true that some reports combine several oracles in a larger text, but administrative letters often report several events. The Neo-Assyrian *Sammeltafeln* are a better example of the early stages adding several prophetic oracles in one physically continuous text. From the Neo-Assyrian Empire, we can see that if the oracle was deemed useful to preserve, they kept it on an individual tablet in the archive. At some point, several oracles were combined and written down on a *Sammeltafel*. It is likely that these *Sammeltafeln* were then used as source material in the composition of royal inscriptions. Indeed, the letters reporting an individual oracle are themselves already literary products and should be read as such. This does not mean that the oracles that they contain are fabricated; to the contrary, it simply means that they were written down after the fact. It is likely that similar processes took place in Israel and Judah as well (*see* Writing and Prophecy).

3.5. General Assessment. Research on ancient Near Eastern prophecy has proven to be very influential for the study of prophecy in the Hebrew Bible, particularly in providing paradigms of how prophecy was integrated into society. Prophecy was common in the ancient Near East, and therefore prophecy should no longer be regarded as confined to Israel. At the same time, there is no evidence that ancient Near Eastern prophecy ever fundamentally questioned the monarchy. Some social criticism can be found (Nissinen 2003a). Much of the difference can be explained by pointing out that the evidence for ancient Near Eastern prophecy that we have comes from royal archives, whereas in the Hebrew Bible we find also the evidence of circles that were critical of the establishment. The longer time period that the OT Prophetic Books could grow explains the lack of genres such as the prophetic novel. The similarity of the underlying socioreligious phenomenon can also be seen in the use of the expression "thus say DN" in both corpora (Nissinen 2010a). Through studying nonbiblical ancient Near Eastern prophetic texts we gain a control in our (re)constructions of prophecy in ancient Israel and Judah, and they enable modern readers to better appreciate ancient societies' views on communication with the divine (Barstad 2000).

See also DIVINATION, MAGIC; LITURGY AND CULT; PROPHECY, HISTORY OF; PROPHECY AND SOCIETY; SOCIAL-SCIENTIFIC APPROACHES; WRITING AND PROPHECY.

BIBLIOGRAPHY. A. Archi, "Further Concerning Ebla and the Bible," BA 44 (1981) 145-54; D. Arnaud, Recherches au pays d'Aštata: Emar VI, 3: Textes sumériens et accadiens: Texte (Paris: Éditions Recherche sur les civilisations, 1986); idem, Recherches au pays d'Aštata: Emar VI, 4: Textes sumériens et accadiens: Texte (Paris: Éditions Recherche sur les civilisations, 1987). H. M. Barstad, "Comparare necesse est? Ancient Israelite and Ancient Near Eastern Prophecy in a Comparative Perspective," in Prophecy in Its Ancient Near Eastern Context: Mesopotamian, Biblical, and Arabian Perspectives, ed. M. Nissinen (SBLSymS 13; Atlanta: Society of Biblical Literature, 2000) 3-11; idem, "The Prophet Oded and the Zakkur Inscription: A Case of Obscuriore Obscurum?" in Reading from Right to Left: Essays on the Hebrew Bible in Honour of David J. A. Clines, ed. J. C. Exum and H. G. M. Williamson (JSOTSup 373; London: Sheffield Academic, 2003) 25-37; R. H. Beal, "Divination and Prophecy. Anatolia," in Religions of the Ancient World: A Guide, ed. S. I. Johnston et al. (Cambridge, MA: Belknap Press, 2004) 381-82; G. M. Beckman, "Plague Prayers of Muršili II (1.60)," in Context of Scripture, 1: Canonical Compositions from the Biblical World, ed. W. W. Hallo and K. L. Younger (Leiden: E. J. Brill, 1997) 156-60; E. Blum, "Israels Prophetie im altorientalischen Kontext: Anmerkungen zu neueren religionsgeschichtlichen Thesen," in "From Ebla to Stellenbosch": Syro-Palestinian Religions and the Hebrew Bible, ed. I. Cornelius and L. Jonker (ADPV 37; Wiesbaden: Harrassowitz in Kommission, 2008) 81-115; S. Dalley, "Old Babylonian Prophecies at Uruk and Kish," in Opening the Tablet Box: Near Eastern Studies in Honor of Benjamin R. Foster, eds. S. C. Melville and A. L. Slotsky (CHANE 42; Leiden: E. J. Brill, 2010) 85-97; M. J. de Jong, Isaiah among the Ancient Near Eastern Prophets: A Comparative Study of the Earliest Stages of the Isaiah Tradition and the Neo-Assyrian Prophecies (VTSup 117; Leiden: E. J. Brill, 2007); A. Delattre, "The Oracles Given in Favour of Esarhaddon," BOR 3 (1889) 25-31; J.-M. Durand and D. Charpin, Archives épistolaires de Mari (ARM 26; Paris: Éditions Recherche sur les civilisations, 1988); J.-M. Durand and M. Guichard, "Les rituels de Mari," in Florilegium marianum III: Recueil d'études à la mémoire de Marie-Thérèse Barrelet, ed. D. Charpin and J.-M. Durand (Mémoires de N.A.B.U. 4; Paris: Société pour l'étude du Proche-Orient ancien, 1997) 19-78; M. Ellis, "The Archive of the Old Babylonian Kititum Temple and Other Texts from Ishchali," JAOS 106 (1987) 757-86; idem, "Observations on Mesopotamian Oracles and Prophetic Texts: Literary and Historiographic Considerations," JCS 41 (1989) 127-86; D. E. Fleming, "The Etymological Origins of the Hebrew nābî': The One Who Invokes God," CBQ 55 (1993a) 217-24; idem, "LÚ and MEŠ in ᴸᵘna-bi-iᵐᵉˢ and Its Mari Brethren," NABU (1993b) §4; idem, "Nābû and Munabbiātu: Two New Syrian Religious Personnel," JAOS 113 (1993c) 175-83; idem, "Prophets and Temple Personnel in the Mari Archives," in The Priests in the Prophets: The Portrayal of Priests, Prophets, and Other Religious Specialists in the Latter Prophets, ed. L. L. Grabbe and A. O. Bellis (JSOTSup 408, London: T & T Clark, 2004) 44-64; L. L. Grabbe, Priests, Prophets, Diviners, Sages: A Socio-Historical Study of Religious Specialists in Ancient Israel (Valley Forge, PA: Trinity Press International, 1995); R. A. Henshaw, Female and Male: The Cultic Personnel; The Bible and the Rest of the Ancient Near East (PTMS 31; Allison Park, PA: Pickwick, 1994); J. W. Hilber, Cultic Prophecy in the Psalms (BZAW 352; Berlin: de Gruyter, 2005); idem, "Prophetic Speech in the Egyptian Royal Cult," in On Stone and Scroll: Essays in Honour of Prof. Graham Ivor Davies, ed. J. Aitken, K. Dell and B. Mastin (BZAW 420; Berlin: de Gruyter, 2011); idem, "Royal Cultic Prophecy in Assyria, Judah, and Egypt," in "Thus Speaks Ishtar of Arbela": Prophecy in Israel, Assyria and Egypt in the Neo-Assyrian Period, ed. R. P. Gordon and H. M. Barstad (Winona Lake, IN: Eisenbrauns, forthcoming); J. Huehnergard, "On the Etymology and Meaning of Hebrew NĀBÎ'," EI 26 (1999) 88*-93*; H. B. Huffmon, "The Assinnum as Prophet: Shamans at Mari?" in Amurru 3: No-

mades et sédentaires dans le Proche-Orient ancien; Compte rendu de la XLVIe Rencontre assyriologique internationale, Paris, 10-13 juillet 2000, ed. C. Nicolle (Paris: Éditions Recherche sur les civilisations, 2004) 241-47; **P. Merlo**, *"āpilum* of Mari: A Reappraisal," *UF* 36 (2004) 323-32; **M. Nissinen**, "Falsche Prophetie in neuassyrischer und deuteronomistischer Darstellung," in *Das Deuteronomium und seine Querbeziehungen*, ed. T. Veijola (PFES 62; Helsinki: Finnische Exegetische Gesellschaft; Göttingen: Vandenhoeck & Ruprecht, 1996) 172-95; idem, "Prophecy against the King in Neo-Assyrian Sources," in *"Lasset uns Brücken bauen ...": Collected Communications to the XVth Congress of the International Organization for the Study of the Old Testament, Cambridge 1995*, ed. K.-D. Schunck and M. Augustin (BEATAJ 42; New York: Lang, 1998a) 157-70; idem, *References to Prophecy in Neo-Assyrian Sources* (SAAS 7; Helsinki: Neo-Assyrian Text Corpus Project, 1998b); idem, "The Socioreligious Role of the Neo-Assyrian Prophets," in *Prophecy in Its Ancient Near Eastern Context: Mesopotamian, Biblical, and Arabian Perspectives*, ed. M. Nissinen (SBLSymS 13; Atlanta: Society of Biblical Literature, 2000) 89-114; idem, "Das kritische Potential in der altorientalischen Prophetie," in *Propheten in Mari, Assyrien und Israel*, ed. M. Köckert and M. Nissinen (FRLANT 201; Göttingen: Vandenhoeck & Ruprecht, 2003a) 1-33; idem, "Fear Not: A Study on an Ancient Near Eastern Phrase," in *The Changing Face of Form Criticism for the Twenty-First Century*, ed. M. Sweeney and E. Ben Zvi (Grand Rapids: Eerdmans, 2003b) 122-61; idem, *Prophets and Prophecy in the Ancient Near East* (SBLWAW 12; Atlanta: Society of Biblical Literature, 2003c); idem, "What Is Prophecy? An Ancient Near Eastern Perspective," in *Inspired Speech: Prophecy in the Ancient Near East; Essays in Honour of Herbert B. Huffmon*, ed. J. Kaltner and L. Stulman (JSOTSup 378; London: T & T Clark International, 2004) 17-37; idem, "Comparing Prophetic Sources: Principles and a Text Case," in *Prophecy and Prophets in Ancient Israel: Proceedings of the Oxford Old Testament Seminar*, ed. J. Day (LHBOTS 531; London: T & T Clark, 2010a) 3-24; idem, "Prophecy and Omen Divination: Two Sides of the Same Coin," in *Divination and Interpretation of Signs in the Ancient World*, ed. A. Annus (OIS 6; Chicago: Chicago University Press, 2010b) 341-51; idem, "Gender and Prophetic Agency in

the Ancient Eastern Mediterranean," in *Prophets Male and Female: Gender and Prophecy in the Hebrew Bible, the Eastern Mediterranean and the Ancient Near East*, ed. C. L. Carvalho and J. Stökl (Atlanta: Society for Biblical Literature, forthcoming); **S. Parpola**, *Assyrian Prophecies* (SAA 9; Helsinki: Helsinki University Press, 1997); **G. Pettinato**, "The Royal Archives of Tell Mardikh-Ebla," *BA* 39 (1976) 44-52; idem, "Relation entre les royaumes d'Ebla et de Mari au III millenaire, d'après les archives royales de Tell Mardikh - Ebla," *Akkadica* 2 (1977) 20-28; **B. Pongratz-Leisten**, *Herrschaftswissen in Mesopotamien: Formen der Kommunikation zwischen Gott und König im 2. und 1. Jahrtausend v. Chr* (SAAS 10; Helsinki: Neo-Assyrian Text Corpus Project, 1999); **V. Sasson**, "The ʿAmmān Citadel Inscription as an Oracle Promising Divine Protection: Philological and Literary Comments," *PEQ* 111 (1979) 117-25; **A. Schart**, "Combining Prophetic Oracles in Mari Letters and Jeremiah 36," *JANESCU* 23 (1995) 75-93; **B. U. Schipper**, *Die Erzählung des Wenamun: Ein Literaturwerk im Spannungsfeld von Politik, Geschichte und Religion* (OBO 209; Fribourg: Academic Press; Göttingen: Vandenhoeck & Ruprecht, 2005); **J. Scurlock**, "Prophecy as a Form of Divination, Divination as a Form of Prophecy," in *Divination and Interpretation of Signs in the Ancient World*, ed. A. Annus (OIS 6; Chicago: Oriental Institute of the University of Chicago, 2010) 277-316; **N. Shupak**, "Did the Phenomenon of Biblical Prophecy Exist in Ancient Egypt?" [in Hebrew], in *Proceedings of the Tenth World Congress of Jewish Studies, Jerusalem, August 16-24, 1989: Division A, The Bible and Its World*, ed. D. Assaf (Jerusalem: World Union of Jewish Studies, 1990) 59*-64*; idem, "The Egyptian 'Prophecy': A Reconsideration," in *"Von reichlich ägyptischem Verstande": Festschrift für Waltraud Guglielmi zum 65. Geburtstag*, (eds.) K. Zibelius-Chen and H.-W. Fischer-Elfert (Philippika 11, Wiesbaden: Harrassowitz, 2006), 133-44; **J. Stökl**, "Female Prophets in the Ancient Near East," in *Prophecy and Prophets in Ancient Israel: Proceedings of the Oxford Old Testament Seminar*, ed. J. Day (LHBOTS 531; London: T & T Clark, 2010) 47-61; idem, "Gender Ambiguity in Ancient Near Eastern Prophecy? A Re-Assessment of the Data Behind a Popular Theory," in *Prophets Male and Female: Gender and Prophecy in the Hebrew Bible, the Eastern Mediterranean and the Ancient Near East*, ed. C.

L. Carvalho and J. Stökl (Atlanta: Society for Biblical Literature, forthcoming a); idem, "The מתנבאות of Ezekiel 13 Re-Considered," *JBL* (forthcoming b); **A. Taggar-Cohen,** *Hittite Priesthood* (TH 26; Heidelberg: Winter, 2006); **L.-S. Tiemeyer,** "Prophecy as a Way of Cancelling Prophecy—the Strategic Uses of Foreknowledge," *ZAW* 117 (2005) 329-50; **K. van der Toorn,** "L'oracle de victoire comme expression prophétique au Proche-Orient ancien," *RB* 94 (1987) 63-97; idem, "Old Babylonian Prophecy between the Oral and the Written," *JNSL* 24 (1998) 55-70; **J. van Dijk,** "Die Tontafeln aus dem Palast des Sînkāšid," in *XVIII. vorläufiger Bericht über die von dem Deutschen Archäologischen Institut und der Deutschen Orient-Gesellschaft aus Mitteln der Deutschen Forschungsgemeinschaft unternommenen Ausgrabungen in Uruk-Warka, Winter 1959/60,* ed. H. Lenzen (ADOG 7; Berlin: Mann, 1962) 61-62; **S. Weeks,** "Predictive and Prophetic Literature: Can *Neferti* Help Us Read the Bible?" in *Prophecy and Prophets in Ancient Israel: Proceedings of the Oxford Old Testament Seminar,* ed. J. Day (LHBOTS 531; London: T & T Clark, 2010) 25-46; **M. Weippert,** "Aspekte israelitischer Prophetie im Lichte verwandter Erscheinungen des Alten Orients," in *Ad bene et fideliter seminandum: Festgabe für Karlheinz Deller zum 21. Februar 1987,* ed. U. Magen and G. Mauer (AOAT 220; Kevelaer: Butzon & Bercker; Neukirchen-Vluyn: Neukirchener Verlag, 1988) 287-319; **H. G. M. Williamson,** "Isaiah: Prophet of Weal or Woe?" in *"Thus Speaks Ishtar of Arbela": Prophecy in Israel, Assyria and Egypt in the Neo-Assyrian Period,* ed. R. P. Gordon and H. M. Barstad (Winona Lake, IN: Eisenbrauns, forthcoming); **N. Wyatt,** "Word of Tree and Whisper of Stone: El's Oracle to King Keret (Kirta), and the Problem of the Mechanics of Its Utterance," *VT* 57 (2007) 483-510; **I. Zsolnay,** "The Misconstrued Role of the *assinnû* in Ancient Near Eastern Prophecy," in *Prophets Male and Female: Gender and Prophecy in the Hebrew Bible, the Eastern Mediterranean and the Ancient Near East,* ed. C. L. Carvalho and J. Stökl (Atlanta: Society for Biblical Literature, forthcoming).   J. Stökl

ANGELS, MESSENGERS, HEAVENLY BEINGS

The Prophetic Books are distinguished from other biblical literature in at least two ways with respect to the subject of the angelic realm. On the one hand, unlike many narrative texts in the OT, most texts in the prophets tend to ignore any direct contemporary activity of angels in human affairs. On the other hand, there are a few select texts in the prophets, specifically texts associated with later apocalyptic literature, in which contemporary angelic activity becomes not just prominent but central.

1. Defining Angelic Functions and Roles
2. Mediating God's Message
3. "Angel of the LORD"
4. Specific Supernatural Creatures
5. Physical Appearance
6. Summary

1. Defining Angelic Functions and Roles. Angelic roles widely attested in the Bible are found also in the prophets, even if there are but few examples. The protection and rescue of God's people from calamity (cf. Gen 48:16; Num 20:16; Ps 91:11-12) occurs in the case of Daniel in the lion's den (Dan 6:22) and the three young men in the blazing furnace (Dan 3:28). An extension of this role, the destruction of God's enemies (cf. 2 Sam 24:15-17; 1 Chron 21:14-27; 2 Kings 19:35), occurs when 185,000 Assyrian soldiers are slain in one night (Is 37:36) and when the population of Jerusalem is decimated in judgment (Ezek 9:1-11). The angelic praise and adoration of God (Job 38:7; Ps 29:1-2; 148:2; Neh 9:6) surfaces when seraphim extol God's holiness in Isaiah's presence (Is 6:3).

The English word *angel* does not correlate easily with any Hebrew word, for the English word unequivocally refers to a supernatural being with unspecified duties in God's service. This word, however, derives from Greek *angelos* ("messenger"), referring to an individual, human or divine, having the focused task of communicating a message long-distance from one party to another (Meier 1988). Because the Hebrew (and Aramaic) word *malʾāk* was a precise semantic counterpart to the Greek word, there are at least two fundamental shifts in meaning that complicate our reading of the activity of these supernatural creatures when they appear in the Prophetic Books.

On the one hand, the English word *angel* means less than the Hebrew term *malʾāk*. In English its reference is confined to the supernatural world, and if we apply the word to humans, we do so only metaphorically ("You are such an angel"). In contrast, one-third of all references to *mal'ākîm* in prophetic and apocalyptic books are to humans, where the term is translated not as "angel" but rather as "messenger" or "ambassador" (Is 14:32; 18:2; 30:4; 33:7; 37:9, 14; Jer 27:3; Ezek 17:15; 23:16, 40; 30:9; Nah 2:13; Hag 1:13; Mal 2:7). The Hebrew term's broad reference thus may result in ambiguity if the context does not make it clear if a human is in view (e.g., is the *mal'āk* whom God sends in Mal 1:1 a human "messenger" or a supernatural "angel"?).

The many references to human *mal'ākîm* underscore, on the other hand, how the English word *angel* also means much more than the Hebrew term *mal'āk*, for the latter narrowly focuses the activities of these human messengers: the transmission of verbal messages over a substantial distance from one party to another. Since the word *mal'āk* simply means "messenger" (general Semitic root *l'k* ["to send"]), it is clear that the primary task of a supernatural *mal'āk* in early Hebrew was to relay messages from God to humans, unlike "angels" in English, whose tasks encompass all activities that God may delegate to the members of his supernatural entourage. Thus, although cherubim and seraphim are commonly assumed in contemporary culture to be angels, it would be a misnomer in biblical Hebrew (and early Greek) to call them *mal'ākîm* (or *angeloi*) "messengers": the bizarre appearances of such creatures immediately disqualify them from ever being sent by God with a message to humans. It is only in later Hebrew and Greek (and English) that the terms *mal'āk* and *angelos*, through the natural evolution of language, extended their meaning to encompass all supernatural beings in God's employ. It is misleading to read this later, broader meaning back into the biblical text.

2. Mediating God's Message.

Given, then, the precise significance of Hebrew *mal'āk* as "messenger" (supernatural or human), it is noteworthy how rarely supernatural messengers are identified by this term in prophetic and apocalyptic books of the OT. The prophets do speak of the activity of supernatural creatures in Israel's past, such as the one that wrestled with Jacob (Hos 12:3-4; cf. Gen 32:24-32) or the one that protected Israel through the wilderness sojourn (Is 63:9; cf. Ex 23:20-23). But nearly half of all occurrences of

the word in the Prophetic Books, and most of the occurrences that refer to supernatural creatures, appear in the book of Zechariah. There the word usually refers to a supernatural creature that dialogues with this prophet in a series of night visions that reveal what God is doing among the nations and for Judah. The backbone of the first six chapters of this book (Zech 1:8—6:8) is a retelling of Zechariah's perception of, and dialogue with, a variety of supernatural creatures, some of which are explicitly identified as *mal'ākîm*. Zechariah carries on a sustained dialogue with one supernatural messenger characteristically identified in strikingly unusual Hebrew as the "angel who was speaking with me" (*hammal'āk haddōbēr bî* [Zech 1:9, 13, 14, 19; 2:3; 4:1 ,4, 5; 5:5, 10; 6:4]). This angel answers questions, asks questions, makes explanations, and dialogues with God (Zech 1:13).

This exceptional encounter between Zechariah and a supernatural messenger (*mal'āk*) from God is explicable from the very nature of the prophetic office. When information is provided about the source of their proclamations, the classical prophets are presented as receiving their messages directly from God, unmediated by any other creatures (e.g., Is 6:8; Jer 1:9; Ezek 1:1—3:11; Hos 1:2-9; Amos 7:1—8:2; Hab 2:1-2). The classical prophets had direct access to God, participating with other supernatural beings in the divine council where God's decrees originated (e.g., Is 6:1-9; Jer 23:18-22; Amos 3:7; cf. 1 Kings 22:19-23), rendering superfluous any messenger relay between God and his prophet. As time progressed, however, prophetic literature portrays the prophet gradually losing his place on the *divine council (Meier 2009, 19-62). With the rise of *apocalyptic literature, of which the book of Zechariah is a harbinger, God's message is relayed to humans indirectly by angelic intermediaries (e.g., *1 En.* 19:1; 72:1; *4 Ezra* 4:1; 5:31; *T. Levi* 2:6-9; *Apoc. Zeph.* 3:1; 11:3). Thus, in the book of Ezekiel God's voice is heard throughout, even though angels begin to provide revelation in Ezekiel 40—42. In the book of Daniel the voice of God is never heard, and it is angels who do any explaining of God's future plans for the world.

3. "Angel of the LORD."

In the same way that the Hebrew term *mal'āk* ("messenger") is limited in its appearance in the Prophetic Books, an "angel of the LORD" is also a designation that generally is not significant for the prophets, a phrase appearing only in Isaiah and Zechariah of a supernatural creature. The identical phrase, "angel of the LORD," is applied as a legitimate title for the prophet Haggai (Hag 1:13) and priests (Mal 2:7) as individuals who relay God's word to humans, so once again it is not clear that the very presence of the title indicates a peculiar and distinctive creature of exalted status. On the contrary, the OT knows of no uniquely privileged being, "*the* angel of the LORD," a perspective similar to what continues in the NT (Mt 1:20; 2:13, 19; 28:2; Lk 1:11; 2:9; Jn 5:4; Acts 5:19; 8:26; 10:3; 12:7, 23; Gal 4:14; note the interpretation of Ex 3:2 in Acts 7:30). The earliest accessible interpretation of this phrase that removes its ambiguity ("*an* angel of the LORD"? "*the* angel of the LORD"?) is the LXX, which typically translates "an angel of the Lord" whenever the phrase first occurs in a narrative (Meier, *DDD*[2] 53-59). Early Christian interpreters saw in the figure a reference to the preincarnate Christ (e.g., Eusebius, *Dem. ev.* 5.10-11 [§§235-238]; *Hist. eccl.* 1.2), a consensus later reversed by those who followed Augustine in seeing this designation as simply referring to any supernatural messenger sent from the Lord (Augustine, *Trin.* 3.22-26).

The solitary occurrence of the phrase in Isaiah (Is 37:36) is explicable in a narrative that has been introduced into the book from the Deuteronomic History (2 Kings 19:35), where a "messenger of Yahweh," supernatural or human, is otherwise a more common figure (Judg 2:1-4; 5:23; 6:11-22; 13:3-21; 2 Sam 24:16; 1 Kings 19:7; 2 Kings 1:3, 15). Zechariah is the only prophet for whom the phrase "angel of the LORD" is important, occurring six times in three contexts (Zech 1:11, 12; 3:1, 5, 6; 12:8). The LXX in two of these contexts introduces the creature as "an angel of the LORD" (Zech 3:1; 12:8)—that is, a supernatural envoy who relays God's messages to humans (Zech 3:1, 5, 6) and with whom the house of David is favorably compared (Zech 12:8; cf. 2 Sam 14:17, where David was compared to an envoy from God to render wise decisions). The third context (Zech 1:11, 12) is not entirely lucid in distinguishing the characters who speak, but if one assumes that the single angel who is identified in a number of different ways in Zechariah 1:8-14 is everywhere the same figure, one is confronted again with a supernatural

envoy from God delegated with the task of communicating to Zechariah God's message.

4. Specific Supernatural Creatures.
Names for specific angels are exceptional, corresponding to an apparent aversion at times to reveal their names to humans (Gen 32:29; Judg 13:17-18). In mustering the heavenly armies (see 4.1 below), however, God is said to call them all by name (Is 40:26), and the names of a few of God's supernatural warriors are preserved: "Pestilence" and "Plague" (Heb *deber* and *rešep* in Hab 3:5 [the latter widely attested as a deity in polytheistic cultures]; cf. "Fury, Rage, and Havoc" in Ps 78:49, identified as "a band of angels of evil" [ASV]), names associated with their particular means of devastation (whether the depictions here were intended as poetic metaphor or as a portrayal of supernatural beings is moot; it is certain that many preexilic Israelites subscribed to the latter, it is possible that many recognized the former, and for many the distinction would have been irrelevant). It is only in the last five chapters of the book of Daniel that supernatural messenger figures are explicitly provided with individual names when they cordially interact with humans in the OT. In these chapters, Gabriel functions as a revealer and interpreter (Dan 8:16; 9:21), while Michael is one of the foremost angelic princes, with a more militant role (Dan 10:13, 21; 12:1).

4.1. The Stars. The astral bodies—sun, moon, stars—are explicitly identified as God's heavenly "hosts" (Jer 8:2; cf. Deut 17:3; 2 Kings 23:5), something that humans are quite capable of seeing (Is 40:26). The connection of astral bodies with God's angelic hosts is explicit in the Bible (Is 14:12-13; cf. Josh 5:13-15; Judg 5:20; Job 38:7; Ps 148:2-3), prompting considerable later speculation as to the precise physical reality involved (Halpern; Scott) and encouraging the connection between the innumerable stars and the innumerable angels (Jer 33:22; Dan 7:10; cf. Job 25:3). The Hebrew term *ṣābā'*, translated as "host," simply means "army," with its verbal counterpart meaning "to wage war" (e.g., Is 29:7, 8; Zech 14:12), a connection that Isaiah makes explicit: "The LORD of hosts [*ṣĕbā'ôt*] is mustering a host [*ṣĕbā'*] for battle" (Is 13:4).

Thus, the divine epithet "LORD of hosts" is a portrait of God in a militant posture as he leads his angelic armies against the forces of evil, whether human or divine. This epithet is a distinctive feature of Isaiah and Jeremiah, as well as of the three postexilic books Haggai, Zechariah and Malachi. These armies/stars/supernatural beings that accompany God into battle when he confronts evil (e.g., Judg 5:20; Rev 12:3-7; 19:14, 19), who provide part of the background for the astral phenomena in prophetic elaborations of the divine warrior's march to battle in the storm (e.g., Is 13:10-13; Joel 3:11-16; Hab 3:11; cf. Josh 10:11-13), are said to employ chariots, horses and swords (Josh 5:13-15; 2 Kings 6:15-17; 1 Chron 21:16) just as God does (Hab 3:8-11). These angelic armies consequently are associated quite comfortably with supernatural chariots and horses (Zech 1:8-11; 6:1-8) and were a constant temptation for Israelites to worship (Jer 19:13; Zeph 1:5).

4.2. Classes of Supernatural Beings. Discrete categories of supernatural creatures are identified in the prophets and nowhere else in the Bible. The "Watchers" (Aram *ʿîr*; Gk *egrēgoros* ["wakeful one, vigilant one"] in Aquila and Symmachus) are mentioned only in Nebuchadnezzar's dream in Daniel 4 (Dan 4:13, 17, 23) in the Bible, although they are abundantly attested in Second Temple literature. These creatures in the Bible make decrees about human history, descend from heaven, and give orders to carry out these decrees.

Seraphim, also, are explicitly named as supernatural creatures in God's service only in the book of Isaiah (Is 6:2, 6), bearing a name that, if it is a *Qattāl* nominal pattern, could reflect the meaning "a burner, one who sets on fire." It is likely that Isaiah's vision assumes a serpentine figure, for elsewhere the same word refers to venomous snakes that inhabit the desert (Deut 8:15; Is 30:6), that fatally bit Israelites (Num 21:6), and as a remedy for which Moses made a bronze model (Num 21:8). Since there are references to the ability of these desert-dwelling creatures to fly (Is 14:29; 30:6), one is encouraged to think of the winged uraeus that appears on preexilic Hebrew seals (*CWSSS*, nos. 11, 104, 127, 194, 206, 284, 381) in imitation of Egyptian royal iconography, where such supernatural creatures could be represented with wings, hands and legs (Joines).

Cherubim are a characteristic feature of only one prophetic book, Ezekiel, where one-third of all biblical occurrences of the term are found. The only other mention of cherubim in

the prophetic corpus occurs in Hezekiah's prayer that probably was incorporated into the book of Isaiah from the book of 2 Kings (Is 37:16 // 2 Kings 19:15). This peculiar focus in Ezekiel is likely a function of Ezekiel's intimate connection with the temple, which was elaborately decorated with representations of cherubim (Ezek 41:18-20, 25; cf. 1 Kings 6:23-32; 7:29, 36; 8:6-7). Indeed, the extended verbal description of these composite creatures occupies much of the stunning introduction to the book: four wings, four faces (human, lion, bull, eagle), calves' hooves, human hands, and radiant like bronze (Ezek 1:5-12). These four creatures serve here, and often in Ezekiel's book, as bearers of God's portable throne (Ezek 1:26; 10:1) with its accompanying wheels (Ezek 1:15-21; cf. Ezek 9:3; 10:1-22; 11:22; 43:2-3). This task of supporting or transporting God is elsewhere specified as a distinctive function of cherubim (2 Sam 6:2; Ps 18:10; 80:1; 99:1; Is 37:16), reflected in the design of the ark, where the two cherubim figures with their outstretched wings were understood to form a platform above which God manifested himself (Ex 25:22; Num 7:89). The emphasis upon this activity for cherubim in the book of Ezekiel results from the prophet's new relationship to the divine council, for unlike his predecessors who participated in the council's deliberations, Ezekiel has the council come to him, so to speak, with a decision that has already been ratified (Meier 2009, 21-24).

Typically, the cherubim are portrayed in Ezekiel as a group without further specification of individual identity. However, God singles out an exceptional cherub, explicitly so identified twice (Ezek 28:14, 16) in an oracle against the king of Tyre that is rich in imagery associated with God's sacred mountain (Ezek 28:12-19). The story that unfolds is allusively told only in barest outlines, recounting the privileged status and gifts of this creature that God trusted with his most intimate access. Nevertheless, the cherub betrayed these privileges and was expelled, consumed by fire.

5. Physical Appearance.

The extended descriptions of these classes of supernatural creatures in God's service contrast with descriptions of supernatural messengers (*malʾākîm*) that are sent to humans with messages from God. The latter usually are not physically described, suggesting that there was nothing remarkable about their appearance. In fact, the term "man" commonly appears as a way of describing supernatural messengers from God: "the man Gabriel" flies to Daniel with information (Dan 9:21), one who has "the appearance of a man" is divinely commissioned to interpret a vision (Dan 8:15) or to strengthen Daniel (Dan 10:18), while one "according to the likeness of the sons of men" opens Daniel's mouth so that he can dialogue with God's envoy (Dan 10:16) (cf. Gen 18:2-22; Judg 13:3-8; Tob 5:4-6, where the terms *malʾāk/angelos* and "man" appear together to refer to the same supernatural creatures). As a result, it is not awkward for Hosea to identify Jacob's ancient wrestling partner as a *malʾāk* (Hos 12:4) even though the narrator of Gen 32:24 called this figure a "man," and the actors called him *ʾĕlōhîm* (Gen 32:28, 30). The identification "man" for superhuman envoys dispatched by God with their characteristic tasks can continue in the prophets (Ezek 9:2-3; 40:3-5; 47:3; Dan 10:5; 12:6-7).

The unremarkable human appearance of such supernatural messengers is assumed in earlier books of the Bible where they are not described, for there is nothing out of the ordinary. The nondescript character of supernatural messengers changes in the later books of the Bible, in tandem with the rise of apocalyptic literature. Physical description becomes very important in apocalyptic literature as the extraordinary appearance of even the messenger angels is underscored: although they can have human hands, legs and eyes (Ezek 40:3, 5; 47:3; Dan 10:5-6; 12:7), are described as "standing" (Heb *ʿmd* [Ezek 40:3; 43:6; Dan 8:15; 10:16; 12:5]), wearing linen clothing (Ezek 10:6-7; Dan 10:5; 12:6, 7) and girded with gold (Dan 10:5), they clearly are nonhuman, with a luminous radiance (Dan 10:6) comparable to precious stones (Dan 10:6) and bronze (Ezek 40:3; Dan 10:6), while their speech can be described as a roaring (Dan 10:6). The human response to supernatural messengers in these later contexts is generally a complete physical breakdown (Dan 8:17-18; 10:7-12, 15-19), unlike in most earlier biblical texts (e.g., Gen 16:7-13; 18:1-8; Josh 5:13-15; Judg 13:9-16; 1 Kings 19:5-8). In such portraits of supernatural messengers wings are notably absent. Instead, wings are associated only with the more bizarre creatures in God's service

that have tasks other than relaying messages to humans, such as seraphim (Is 6:2), cherubim (Ezek 1:6-25; 3:13; 10:5-21; 11:22; cf. Ex 25:20) and others (Zech 5:9).

The overt similarity of supernatural messengers to humans on so many levels proceeds from an awareness in ancient Israel that angelic creatures were understood to be made in the image of God no less than humans, and evidently more so. God addresses the divine council at creation with the cohortative "Let us make man in our image" (Gen 1:26; cf. Is 6:8), an image that was once in some fashion more congruent between God and his divine retinue in the light of Genesis 3:22 ("the man has become like one of us"). The epithet "son(s) of God" (Dan 3:25, 28; cf. Job 1:6) is one way of referring to angelic-like beings that reflects the divine image in such creatures (cf. Gen 5:3), an epithet that appears in other ancient cultures of the Near East to affirm a genetic continuity but whose mechanics Israel denied. In the same way, even the word *ʾĕlōhîm* itself, typically translated "God," can be used to identify the class of supernatural beings that includes both God and the creatures subordinate to God ("gods" [Ps 82:1, 6 KJV]; cf. the LXX translation of *ʾĕlōhîm* in Ps 8:5 as *angeloi*, and Heb 2:7, which in turn stresses the subordinate status of humans to all these). The fact that both God and angelic creatures can be subsumed together under a common noun (*ʾĕlōhîm*) that cannot apply to humans underscores the greater continuity between angels and God. A specific communicable attribute that is more characteristic of supernatural creatures than humans is connected to God's identity as "the Holy One" (2 Kings 19:22; Job 6:10; Is 5:24), for he often shares this title with angels who are called "holy ones" (Dan 4:13, 17, 23; 8:13; Zech 14:5; cf. Job 15:15; Ps 89:5-7). Both of these epithets are applied to the genus of supernatural creatures indiscriminately, unlike their restricted applicability to humans in the OT, for whom this quality is contingent and not natural: the only human who can be identified as a "son of God" is the Judean king (2 Sam 7:14; Ps 2:7), and the only human who bears the epithet "holy one" is a priest (Ps 106:16), in marked contrast to the NT, where all of redeemed humanity are distinctively identified as "sons of God" (e.g., Rom 8:14; 1 Jn 3:2) and by the substantive "holy one(s)" (e.g., Eph 1:1; Phil 4:21).

6. Summary.

For most of the Prophetic Books in the Bible, the supramundane cosmos of living creatures is an arena that attracts little attention. It is God who is everywhere at work with an immediacy of interaction with humans accompanied by sporadic references to mediate causes that are largely confined to the human realm (e.g., Is 10:5-7; Jer 25:9). Some later visionary contexts in the Bible, however, gradually expand this perception to include an increasing interest in the supernatural creatures that do God's bidding at a time that God distances himself from his people during the *exile (Ezek 8:6; 10:18-19; 11:23; cf. Dan 9:12-19; Zech 1:12). A proliferating heavenly bureaucracy gradually unfolds (cf. Dan 10:10-21) that exhibits an increasingly transcendent God at work through myriads of supernatural creatures.

See also DIVINE COUNCIL; IDOLS, IDOLATRY, GODS.

BIBLIOGRAPHY. **B. Halpern,** "The Assyrian Astronomy of Genesis 1 and the Birth of Milesian Philosophy," *ErIsr* 27 (2003) *74-*83; **V. Hirth,** *Gottes Boten im Alten Testament: Die alttestamentliche Mal'ak-Vorstellung unter besonderer Berücksichtigung des Mal'ak-Jahwe-Problems* (ThA 32; Berlin: Evangelische Verlagsanstalt, 1975); **D. Irvin,** *Mytharion: The Comparison of Tales from the Old Testament and the Ancient Near East* (AOAT 32; Neukirchen-Vluyn: Neukirchener Verlag, 1978); **K. R. Joines,** "Winged Serpents in Isaiah's Inaugural Vision," *JBL* 86 (1967) 410-15; **G. J. Marshall,** *Angels: An Indexed and Partially Annotated Bibliography of Over 4300 Scholarly Books and Articles Since the 7th Century B.C.* (Jefferson, NC: McFarland, 1999); **S. Meier,** "Angel of Yahweh," *DDD*[2] 53-59; idem, *The Messenger in the Ancient Semitic World* (HSM 45; Atlanta: Scholars Press, 1988); idem, *Themes and Transformations in Old Testament Prophecy* (Downers Grove, IL: IVP Academic, 2009); **A. Rofé,** "Israelite Belief in Angels in the Pre-Exilic Period as Evidenced by Biblical Traditions" [in Hebrew] (Ph.D. diss., Hebrew University of Jerusalem, 1969); **A. Scott,** *Origen and the Life of the Stars: A History of an Idea* (Oxford: Clarendon Press, 1991); **M. Welker,** "Angels in the Biblical Traditions: An Impressive Logic and the Imposing Problem of their Hypercomplex Reality," *ThTo* 51 (1994) 367-80.   S. A. Meier

ANGER. *See* WRATH.

ANIMAL IMAGERY

The past decades have witnessed an increasing recognition of the important interaction between human beings and animals. Environmental pressures and the tremendous changes brought on nature by human development have highlighted the importance of ecology and also resulted in an increasing number of studies dealing with biblical and ecological issues (Martens).

These are not new issues. Ancient Israelites, living in a premodern and agrarian society, recognized the importance of fauna and flora as part of creation order and, in consequence, employed a surprising quantity of animal imagery in their written documents. This article focuses upon these literary devices in the prophetic literature of the OT, including also the apocalyptic book of Daniel. All the references cannot be discussed here, but distinct categories of usage will be introduced, following a short section looking at current research on the topic and a concise introduction to the concept of metaphor and imagery. The descriptive categories used in this entry (e.g., wild, domesticated, *Mischwesen*) are based on the source domain—that is, the real-life category from which the metaphor or imagery has been taken.

1. Animal Imagery and Metaphors in Current Scholarship
2. Wild Animals and Animal Imagery
3. Domesticated Animals and Animal Imagery
4. *Mischwesen* and Animal Imagery
5. Conclusion

1. Animal Imagery and Metaphors in Current Scholarship.

Over the past decades an increasing number of studies have focused upon animal imagery in the OT (Jenni; Lucas; Schwab; Janowski, Neumann-Gorsolke and Glessmer; Dell; Riede; Strawn; Nielsen; Kuntz; Forti; Shemesh). Most of these looked at poetry or wisdom writings, where animal imagery occurs repeatedly. Some of this research studied the bigger hermeneutical issue of how animal imagery (especially linked to God) may contribute to biblical theology (Nielsen) or described the interaction between human being and animal in the OT (Riede; some chapters in Janowski, Neumann-Gorsolke and Glessmer). Connected to these endeavors has been the drive to understand metaphor theory more adequately (see Seifert, 11-85; Nwaoru; Aaron; G. A. Klingbeil 2006; M. G. Klingbeil, 115-19), recognizing both the literary and the conceptual power of these literary images. Since word pictures (including metaphors, similes, symbols) establish either consciously or subconsciously a link between disparate entities (such as a comparison), they are important communicators and are used more often in poetic texts than in prose, though not exclusively so. These verbal images are providing a view of the mental map of the user (or author), opening, beyond the literary level, vistas of worldview, theology and social realities (see de Hulster, 270).

It has been recognized that large portions of the prophetic literature of the OT are written in poetry, even though not all prophetic texts are poetic texts, but could be understood instead as a hybrid "prophetic prose," consciously utilizing both poetic and prosaic literary characteristics (Petersen, 32-33). Keeping in mind these specific literary conventions, we must pay close attention to the conceptual world of the imagery, as it reflects on the social, economic and environmental conditions of the biblical authors as well as on their theological understanding of the creator God, who was active in Israel and the world (see Creation Theology).

What kind of animal imageries did Israel's prophets use in order to communicate the word of the Lord? A careful reading of the biblical texts shows a wide gamut of both domesticated and wild animals that are used metaphorically to make distinct points. Most of these animals were familiar to the readers, and their particular characteristics easily supplemented or even carried the prophetic message in a meaningful way. Some of these animals were uncommon in Palestine (e.g., the crocodile) or even non-existent, such as the *Mischwesen* described in Daniel 7:4, 6 (a lion with eagle's wings, and a leopard with four wings).

Often, animal imagery is expressed indirectly, making use of sounds and verbal forms that characterize specific animals but without naming the animal per se. Enemies roar or growl like lions (Is 5:29, 30) while the persecuted can growl like bears or moan like doves (Is 59:11) (see Nielsen). Judgment imagery often contains references to tearing something apart (Hos 5:14; 6:1), even though the same verbal form (*trp*) is also used to describe the pred-

atory manner of degenerate leadership (Ezek 22:25; Zeph 3:3). In an attempt to make sense of the hundreds of references to animal imageries in the prophets of the OT, this article is divided into three basic sections, beginning with metaphors that use wild (undomesticated) animals, followed by a discussion of references to domesticated animals, and finally a look at *Mischwesen* (hybrid animals), which often appear in apocalyptic contexts.

2. Wild Animals and Animal Imagery.

Generic references to the beasts (either *bĕhēmâ* or *ḥayyâ*) of the field occur often and seem to indicate the natural world per se. For example, Joel 1:20 describes how nature suffers the divine judgment. Notably, the same expression reappears in Joel 2:21, denoting the restored lands. Both in creation (or re-creation) and judgment, humanity is closely linked to the animal world. Similar concepts can be found also in Jonah's narrative (Jon 3:7; 4:11) and are already foreshadowed in the creation (Gen 1—2) and flood records (Gen 6:12 mentions "all flesh" [see Stipp]).

Many times prophets use imagery of wild animals, such as lions, wolves or locusts, to indicate pending judgment (e.g., Is 5:29; 15:9; Hos 5:14; 13:7; Joel 1; Amos 4:9; 5:19; Nahum 3:15-17; Zeph 3:3; Zech 11:3). Even today, locust plagues still represent a major destructive force. The prophets used different Hebrew terms to describe the locust phenomenon (Joel 1:4 employs four different Hebrew terms, possibly suggesting a life cycle), indicating both the magnitude and immensity of the day of judgment (Simkins, 101-7; cf. Croatto). Joel's description of an overwhelming locust invasion uses a well-known phenomenon (i.e., a locust plague that people living in the Levant were familiar with) in order to graphically describe the complete military destruction that God would bring upon his wayward people (see Day of the Lord). The huge numbers and the unstoppable nature of the locust attack inform the imminent military invasion, providing it with a bone-chilling background "noise" that communicates effectively. Interestingly, Joel 1:7 employs an additional animal image, the lion, seeking to indicate utter destruction.

Other imagery of wild animals associated with judgment includes serpents (Jer 8:17; Amos 5:19), maggots and worms (Is 14:11), leopards (Jer 5:6) and eagles (Jer 48:40; 49:22). A particular characteristic of the animal applies to the divine judgment that often is brought about by human agents. Swiftness, inevitability, speed, completeness of destruction and uncountable numbers are part of the communicative purpose of employing these images. Although wild animals were part of God's creation (and thus subject to the Creator), they could not be controlled by humans and thus represented dangerous forces.

Notably, however, the biblical prophets did not always employ the same metaphor in a standardized manner. A leopard did not only indicate swift and complete destruction; it also was used to highlight the impossibility of change—after all, the spots of a leopard cannot be simply wiped off or changed (Jer 13:23). The lion metaphor did not only symbolize divinely ordained judgment (be it through direct divine intervention or outside conquest); at times, God himself is described as a lion fighting ferociously for his people and his city (Is 31:4). As with other literary devices, animal metaphors need to be read contextually and not only according to specific "typical" categories.

Frequently associated with the messianic age, savage and dangerous undomesticated animals are pictured together with helpless domesticated animals that, in a post-fall world, often represented the prey of the wild animals. Wolves graze with lambs; a leopard lies down with a goat kid; a young lion will be together with a calf yearling; bear and cow will feed together (Is 11:6, 7). The hole of the cobra and viper will no longer be dangerous to a playing child (Is 11:8). New and unexpected behavioral patterns are the characteristics of the messianic age (Is 65:25).

Sometimes people groups are compared to wild animals. Ezekiel decries the fact that prophets, instead of proclaiming God's word, tear apart the poor and the widow. Israel is as poisonous and dangerous as a scorpion (Ezek 2:6). Judah is compared to a swift female camel or donkey in heat as she follows Baal (Jer 2:23-24). Assyria and Egypt are like a bee or a fly respectively, called by God's whistle and at his disposal (Is 7:18). In both cases the insect metaphor indicates the swarming, suffocating and inescapable nature of the invading powers. Babylon's armies are compared to a slithering and hissing serpent and devouring grasshop-

pers (Jer 46:22-23), emphasizing the quick and quiet approach as well as their huge numbers that cannot be counted. Babylon's conquest of Judah is as speedy as a leopard, as fierce as wolves hunting in a pack, and as eager as an eagle swooping down to devour a meal (Hab 1:8). However, people groups can also be described as weak and powerless, as, for example, Moab, which is as helpless as a wandering bird thrown out of its nest (Is 16:2).

Desert animals, such as jackal and ostrich, are frequently mentioned when the prophets want to highlight complete desolation (Is 13:22; 34:13-14; Jer 9:10; 10:22; 49:33; 51:37). Vultures and birds of prey not only devour cadavers on the roads and deserts of Palestine but are also an indication of complete divine judgment (Is 34:15; Ezek 13:20; 32:4; 39:4-5), sometimes even with more specific indications of the direction from which they will come (Is 46:11).

Unexpected comparisons at times challenge the reader to readjust expectations. God is not only like a lion in his death pounce of judgment; he also is like a moth that causes uneasiness and discomfort that, hopefully, will result in a wake-up call of his wayward people (Hos 5:12), even though it should be noted that it may be possible that the Hebrew ʿāš used in Hosea 5:12 is a homonym referring to an "emaciating disease" (cf. the difficult translation in the LXX using tarachē), which provides a better parallel to the second member of the parallelism (Macintosh, 207-8).

Dogs generally are much-loved pets these days. However, in the biblical world they were mostly regarded as lowlife, crouching on the outskirts of society. Isaiah 56:10-11 describes Israel's leaders in a pejorative manner as dumb or greedy dogs who pay no attention to the impending doom and look only after their own interests. In Jeremiah 15:3 the dog metaphor is used in a rather distinct way and is part of a list of four means of divine destruction: sword, dogs, vultures and beasts, three of which come from the natural world. This sequence highlights the completeness of divine punishment.

Finally, a number of more exotic wild animals appear in the prophets, including stork, turtledove, swift and swallow (Jer 8:7). They all know (ydʿ) seasons and times and are obedient to the natural laws. In contrast, Israel does not know Yahweh's law—a theme that appears frequently in prophetic texts (e.g., Is 1:3 [in connection with domesticated animals]; Jer 2:8; Hos 5:4).

To summarize this section: The natural world outside of house and town is subject to God's power and order and, since creation, is intricately linked to humanity. The sounds and behaviors of wild and savage animals provide graphic images to communicate effectively the nature of the judgment that God is about to bring upon a wayward people and the nations surrounding Israel. The Day of the Lord is not only a significant theological motif; it is described in terms that must have been very real to people living close to the land and its creatures. However, judgment is not the only motif communicated through metaphors involving wild animals. Restoration, and a God who fights like a lion for his people, are part and parcel of the prophetic message as conveyed by animal imagery.

3. Domesticated Animals and Animal Imagery.
The domestication of animals marked a significant development in human society. Nomadic hunter-gatherers became herders and farmers and developed a different relation to animals. Instead of focusing primarily on food (the hunter can eat the prey only once!), domestication opened the way for secondary use, such as milk, wool, fiber, eggs and a more dependable meat supply (Borowski, 23-29; G. A. Klingbeil 2003a, 411-13; *DOTHB*, 1-20). Domesticated animals also began to impact farming (as plow animals) and changed the way people and goods traveled.

By the time the Israelite prophets preached and wrote their messages, domesticated animals had already been established in the Levant for millennia. They were a part of daily life, even in small towns and urban centers.

The image of well-fed cows from fertile Bashan is used in Amos 4:1 in comparison to the wealthy, fat, lazy, self-sufficient female elite of Samaria (similar also Amos 6:4). These elite will experience judgment, deportation and ruin. Hosea 4:16 employs a similar metaphor and compares the stubbornness of Israel to the stubbornness of a young calf.

All of the appropriate sacrificial animals were domesticated, most likely because domesticated animals provide a more reliable source for *sacrifices than wild animals. Bulls, calves, lambs, goats and doves were offered to the Lord as part of the daily *tāmîd* (i.e., the daily continuous burnt offering for the community) or in response to a specific problem or sin. The sacrificial legislation, found specifically in Leviticus 1—7, clearly correlates between social status and the particular sacrificial animal. When a priest was convicted to offer a sin offering, he was required to offer a young bull, while a leader recognizing unintentional sin had to offer a male goat. A common member of the Israelite community had to offer a female lamb or (if unable to afford one) two doves or two young pigeons (Lev 4—5). The different animals highlight the typological or symbolic function of the sacrificial system and reflect the stratification of Israelite society.

The prophets treat the *temple and its cult (including also the animal sacrifices) as a given (*see* Liturgy and Cult). However, the prophetic critique of the ritual system points beyond the sacrificial animal to the motivation and commitment of the offerer. Micah 6:6-8 is a classic locus of this important concept (on this prophetic critique, see G. A. Klingbeil 2007a, 70-80), as is Isaiah 1:11-18. This critique focused on particular religious practices and was cyclical (i.e., every new generation of prophets seems to have taken it up). It was not aimed at ritual per se; rather, *forgiveness and rightful living tended to be separate issues in the minds of ancient Israelites, and the prophets pointed their audience to this dichotomy.

The prophets are aware of (and decry) the sacrificial use of domesticated animals for idolatrous *worship (Hos 8:5-6) and compare the *idolatry and sinfulness of God's people to donkeys or horses in heat (Jer 5:8; Ezek 23:20).

The generic term "flock" (*ṣōʾn*) is often used to describe people and could refer in positive or negative contexts to Israel and Judah (Is 40:11; 63:11; Jer 13:17, 20; 23:2, 3; 25:35; Ezek 34:2, 3, 6; Zech 9:16; 10:3; 11:4-17). God is depicted as the shepherd who guides his flock and will restore a "remnant flock" (Is 63:11; Jer 31:10, 12; Ezek 34:11).

Lambs not only are prime sacrificial animals but also are used to indicate helplessness (Is 16:1 [cf. the parallel image of a young bird thrown out of its nest in Is 16:2]; Jer 12:3) or willingness (Is 53:7). Jeremiah, confronted by family opposition and persecution, feels like a lamb led to the slaughter (Jer 11:19).

Among the equids, horses and mules were animals for the elite (G. A. Klingbeil 2003a; 2003b) and could appear in a list of luxury items (Ezek 27:14). Together with chariots, they could indicate strength (Jer 17:25). The one who owned a horse (or a mule) was powerful, and many horses suggested accumulated power (Ezek 38:4, 15; Hab 1:8) and self-reliance (Is 30:16; 31:1, 3; Hos 1:7; 14:3; Hab 3:8; Zech 9:10). Reference to horses is often made in contexts of judgment (Jer 4:13; 46:4, 9; 47:3; 51:27). Those affected by judgment include the covenant people as well as other surrounding nations. In Zechariah four distinctly colored horses with riders (Zech 1:8-17) appear in the opening vision of the prophet, and together with the four horses and chariots of the last vision (Zech 6:1-8), they form an inclusio (or envelope structure) of the first part of the book. The text does not provide a clear explanation regarding the difficult-to-translate colors. They may have simply helped to distinguish the four horses from a distance. In the vision the celestial riders report back from their exploratory mission throughout the earth. The use of horses as the fastest domesticated animal, generally reserved for military or royal purposes, highlights the speedy nature of the mission and its far-reaching extent. Zechariah's audience may have immediately remembered the extended and extremely fast messenger service of the Persian period (see G. A. Klingbeil 1995).

Foreign nations often are compared to animals, though not always domesticated ones. For example, in Jeremiah 46:20 Egypt is described as a beautiful young heifer, attractive and inviting. Isaiah describes Moab's refugees as a three-year-old heifer that is skittish and fleeing (Is 15:5). In the same vein, Moab is as helpless as a wandering bird thrown out of its nest (Is 16:2).

To summarize this section: We can note both positive and negative imagery of domesticated animals throughout the prophetic corpus. God is the shepherd of the "flock" of his people Israel. The sacrificial temple cult requires domesticated animals, even though its prophetic critique reminds Israel that external form and internal motivation need to go hand in hand. Specific characteristics of domesticated animals (such as speediness, playfulness, fearfulness) are used to describe other nations. The horse imagery is often connected to mili-

tary prowess, speed and self-reliance and regularly appears in contexts of judgment.

4. *Mischwesen* and Animal Imagery.
Some animals that appear in prophetic or *apocalyptic literature could not be easily spotted in the wild. Isaiah 27:1 refers to Leviathan (*liwyātān*), a serpentine being that will be slain by the Lord "in that day/time," referring to the future *Day of the Lord, a day of divine judgment, when wrong will be set right. It is quite feasible to argue that the biblical author included here a conscious reference to an Ugaritic myth (possibly *KTU* 1.5, also known as the Baal Cycle) that was reshaped and used polemically to demonstrate Yahweh's superiority over all powers (Averbeck, 337-40). This polemic use of extrabiblical material (or concepts) can also be found in numerous other references in the OT—for example, Psalm 121:6 (G. A. Klingbeil 1997), Isaiah 24:21-23 (Barker) and Daniel 2:34-35 (G. A. Klingbeil 2007b).

The *tannîn* is another animal not easily identified. In Isaiah 27:1 (and possibly Is 51:9) it is linked to Leviathan. However, in other references it is associated with the Pharaoh of Egypt, and its description would fit a crocodile (Ezek 29:3; 32:2). The translation of the term in Ezekiel (which may be misspelled there) is not easy, as demonstrated by the LXX's rendering of "dragon" in Ezekiel 29:3. In this passage the imagery of a great battle that the Lord dominates is reminiscent of Isaiah 27:1 and Leviathan.

Hybrid beings (*Mischwesen*) occur also in the vision of Ezekiel 1 (cf. Ezek 10:14). The prophet describes these creatures as human-like (Ezek 1:5), with four faces and four wings (Ezek 1:6), the feet of a calf and gleaming like burnished bronze (Ezek 1:7). Four different faces reminded Ezekiel of a human being, a lion, an ox and an eagle (Ezek 1:10). Some elements of these living beings are reminiscent of ancient Near Eastern religious art (Keel), even though there is no exact depiction of these cherubim (cf. Ezek 10:14). The prophet struggles to find the right words (or terminology) to describe this unearthly reality that is also reflected in the grammatical variance of pronouns and verbal forms that vacillate between masculine and feminine forms (Greenberg, 44). The prophet, recognizing the strangeness of these creatures, describes them as *Mischwesen* that share characteristics from humans and known animals, all fused together. The lion's fierceness is linked to the eagle's swiftness and majesty, while the bull is chosen for its steady power and its value as a plow and transport animal (see Block, 96-98). The presence of the human face appears to be a reminder of God's creative power, as humanity was made in the "image" and "likeness" of God (Gen 1:26-27). It seems that the significance of these four faces exceeded the sum of the imagery (Block, 96), pointing to God's omnipotence and omnipresence and reminding the reader that heavenly realities, including God, are completely different from human realities.

Other *Mischwesen* occur in Daniel's vision found in Daniel 7, following the summary statement detailing the "four great beasts" (Dan 7:3). As has been noted before, their backgrounds are not necessarily Mesopotamian *Mischwesen* (Eggler). The first hybrid animal is a lion with eagle's wings (Dan 7:4), followed by a bear that was raised up on one side (Dan 7:5), a leopard with four wings (Dan 7:6) and, finally, a dreadful fourth beast (Dan 7:7) for which the prophet finds no fitting nametag. Based on the explanation given in Daniel 7:17, these four beasts represent four "kings." It should be noted that the LXX translates here *basileiai* ("kingdoms"). Many interpreters have noted the parallel nature of Daniel 2 and Daniel 7 (Collins, 297), whereby Daniel 7 recapitulates and adds to the already established historical sequence of major kingdoms found in Daniel 2. These hybrid beasts are unclean animals (Ford, 205-6), which is significant in light of the fact that the fourth beast's attack appears to be religious (Dan 7:21, 25).

Suggestions of possible sources and background for the hybrid animals in Daniel have been manifold. E. C. Lucas has discussed most of these but has noted that one should not disregard a possible OT background (cf. Hos 13:7, which contains the list of the same animals) (see Lucas 182-85). J. Eggler has suggested that the two key elements of the composite animals (e.g., the lion and the wings) should be studied separately (in terms of both their iconography and their significance in the prophecy), highlighting the importance of understanding the conceptual background of the imagery as compared to often superficial parallels taken from diverse ancient Near Eastern sources.

Other hybrid beings can be found in Zecha-riah 5:5-9, where two female figures, having wings like a stork, carry the enigmatic ʾêpâ (NRSV: "basket"), containing a woman identified as wickedness, on the wind to Shinar (i.e., Babylon). Based on Sumerian and Akkadian cognates, it has been suggested that ʾêpâ does not indicate the well-known weight or measure but rather refers to a cult room for a divine statue that was situated atop a Mesopotamian temple building (Meyers and Meyers, 295-97). The two female composite beings with stork wings carry the cult cella toward Babylon, thus purifying the land. They are not explicitly described as cherubim (which generally are masculine in the OT). One wonders about the significance of the reference to the stork, which was a migratory bird with a particularly large wingspan and associated with maternal roles. Additionally, it has been suggested that Zechariah used ḥăsîdâ because of its phonetic similarity to ḥāsîd ("the devoted, faithful") (Smith, 211). In either case, the focus is upon the action rather than upon the instruments.

5. Conclusion

As has become clear in this discussion, context is the main factor when studying the use of animal imagery in the prophets of the OT. This appears to be a truism in a dictionary focusing upon a particular genre of the OT. The use of animal imagery reminds us of the importance of this key concept. Lions are not only majestic animals associated with kings or the messianic age; they also can be symbols of divine judgment. Both familiar and unfamiliar animals are part and parcel of an important communicative strategy, taking the reader from the known (and often mundane) to the unknown, surprising and challenging word of Yahweh that reminds the careful reader (and listener) that God is the Lord of creation, in both salvation and judgment.

See also CREATION THEOLOGY; FLORAL IMAGERY; LAND; MOUNTAIN IMAGERY; WILDERNESS, DESERT.

BIBLIOGRAPHY. **D. H. Aaron,** *Biblical Ambiguities, Metaphor, Semantics, and Divine Imagery* (BRLAJ 4; Leiden: E. J. Brill, 2001); **R. Averbeck,** "Ancient Near Eastern Mythography as It Relates to Historiography in the Hebrew Bible: Genesis 3 and the Cosmic Battle," in *The Future of Biblical Archaeology: Reassessing Methodologies and Assumptions; The Proceedings of a Symposium*

August 12-14, 2001 at Trinity International University, ed. J. K. Hoffmeier and A. Millard (Grand Rapids: Eerdmans, 2004) 328-56; **W. D. Barker,** "'And Thus You Brightened the Heavens . . . ': A New Translation of KTU 1.5 i 1-8 and Its Significance for Ugaritic and Biblical Studies," *UF* 38 (2006) 41-52; **D. I. Block,** *The Book of Ezekiel: Chapters 1-24* (NICOT; Grand Rapids: Eerdmans, 1997); **O. Borowski,** *Every Living Thing: Daily Use of Animals in Ancient Israel* (Walnut Creek, CA: Altamira, 1998); **J. J. Collins,** *Daniel* (Hermeneia; Minneapolis: Fortress, 1993); **J. S. Croatto,** "Las langostas del libro de Joel a la luz de los textos de Mari," *RevistaB* 61.4 (1999) 249-60; **I. de Hulster,** *Iconographic Exegesis and Third Isaiah* (FAT 2/36; Tübingen: Mohr Siebeck, 2009); **K. J. Dell,** "The Use of Animal Imagery in the Psalms and Wisdom Literature of Ancient Israel," *SJT* 53 (2000) 275-91; **J. Eggler,** "Iconographic Motifs from Palestine/Israel and Daniel 7:2-14" (D.Litt. diss., University of Stellenbosch, 1998); **J. M. Ford,** "Jewish Law and Animal Symbolism," *JSJ* 10 (1979) 203-12; **T. L. Forti,** *Animal Imagery in the Book of Proverbs* (VTSup 118; Leiden: E. J. Brill, 2008); **M. Greenberg,** *Ezekiel 1-20: A New Translation with Introduction and Commentary* (AB 22; New York: Doubleday, 1983); **B. Janowski, U. Neumann-Gorsolke and U. Glessmer, eds.,** *Gefährten und Feinde des Menschen: Das Tier in der Lebenswelt des alten Israels* (Neukirchen-Vluyn: Neukirchener Verlag, 1993); **E. Jenni,** "Zur Semantik der hebräischen Personen-, Tier- und Dingvergleiche," *ZAH* 3 (1990) 113-66; **O. Keel,** *Jahwe-Visionen und Siegelkunst: Eine neue Deutung der Majestätsschilderungen in Jes 6, Ez 1 und 10 und Sach 4* (SBS 84/85; Stuttgart: Katholisches Bibelwerk, 1977); **G. A. Klingbeil,** "Agriculture and Animal Husbandry," *DOTHB* 1-20; idem, "*rkš* and Esther 8, 10.14: A Semantic Note," *ZAW* 107 (1995) 301-3; idem, "Sun and Moon in Psalm 121:6: Some Notes on Their Context and Meaning," in *To Understand Scriptures: Essays in Honor of William H. Shea*, ed. D. Merling (Berrien Springs, MI: Institute of Archaeology, Siegfried H. Horn Archaeological Museum, Andrews University, 1997) 33-43; idem, "Methods and Daily Life: Understanding the Use of Animals in Daily Life in a Multi-Disciplinary Framework," in *Life and Culture in the Ancient Near East*, ed. R. Averbeck et al. (Bethesda, MD: CDL, 2003a) 401-33; idem, "'Man's Other Best Friend': The Interaction of Equids and Man in Daily Life in Iron Age II Palestine as Seen in Texts, Artifacts, and Images," *UF* 35 (2003b) 259-90; idem, "Metaphors and Pragmatics: An Introduction to the Hermeneutics of Metaphors in the Epistle to the Ephesians," *BBR* 16 (2006) 273-93; idem, *Bridging the Gap: Ritual and Ritual Texts in the Bible* (BBRSup 1; Winona Lake, IN: Eisenbrauns, 2007a); idem, "'Rocking the Mountain': Text, Theology, and Mission in Daniel 2," in *"For You Have Strengthened Me": Biblical and Theological Studies in Honor of Gerhard Pfandl in Celebration of His Sixty-Fifth Birthday*, ed. M. Pröbstle, G. A. Klingbeil and M. G. Klingbeil (St. Peter am Hart: Seminar Schloss Bogenhofen, 2007b) 117-40; **M. G. Klingbeil,** "Metaphors That Travel and (Almost) Vanish: Mapping Diachronic Changes in the Intertextual Usage of the Heavenly Warrior Metaphor in Psalms 18 and 144," in *Metaphors in the Psalms*, ed. P. van Hecke and A. Labahn (BETL 231; Louvain: Peeters, 2010) 115-35; **J. K. Kuntz,** "Growling Dogs and Thirsty Deer: Uses of Animal Imagery in Psalmic Rhetoric," in *"My Words Are Lovely": Studies in the Rhetoric of the Psalms*, ed. R. L. Foster and D. M. Howard Jr. (LHBOTS 467; London: T & T Clark, 2008) 46-62; **E. C. Lucas,** "The Source of Daniel's Animal Imagery," *TynBul* 41 (1990) 161-85; **A. A. Macintosh,** *Hosea* (ICC; Edinburgh: T & T Clark, 1997); **E. A. Martens,** "Yahweh's Compassion and Ecotheology," in *Problems in Biblical Theology: Essays in Honor of Rolf Knierim*, ed. H. T. C. Sun et al. (Grand Rapids: Eerdmans, 1997) 234-48; **C. L. Meyers and E. M. Meyers,** *Haggai, Zechariah 1-8: A New Translation with Introduction and Commentary* (AB 25B; Garden City, NY: Doubleday, 1987); **K. Nielsen,** "I Am Like a Lion to Ephraim: Observations on Animal Imagery and Old Testament Theology," *ST* 61 (2007) 184-97; **E. O. Nwaoru,** *Imagery in the Prophecy of Hosea* (ÄAT 41; Wiesbaden: Harrassowitz, 1999); **D. L. Petersen,** "Rethinking the Nature of Prophetic Literature," in *Prophecy and Prophets: The Diversity of Contemporary Issues in Scholarship*, ed. Y. Gitay (SBLSS; Atlanta: Scholars Press, 1997) 23-40; **P. Riede,** *Im Spiegel der Tiere: Studien zum Verhältnis von Mensch und Tier im alten Israel* (OBO 187; Fribourg: Universitätsverlag; Göttingen: Vandenhoeck & Ruprecht, 2002); **E. Schwab,** "Die Tierbilder und Tiervergleiche des Alten Testaments: Material und Problemanzeigen," *BN* 59 (1991) 37-43; **B. Seifert,** *Metaphorisches Reden von Gott im Hoseabuch*

(FRLANT 166; Göttingen: Vandenhoeck & Ruprecht, 1996); **Y. Shemesh,** "'And Many Beasts' (Jonah 4:11): The Function and Status of Animals in the Book of Jonah," *JHScr* 10.6 (2010) <http://www.arts.ualberta.ca/JHS/Articles/article_134.pdf>; **R. A. Simkins,** *Yahweh's Activity in History and Nature in the Book of Joel* (ANETS 10; Lewiston, NY: Edwin Mellen, 1991); **R. L. Smith,** *Micah-Malachi* (WBC 32; Dallas: Word, 1984); **H.-J. Stipp,** "'Alles Fleisch hatte seinen Wandel auf der Erde verdorben' (Gen 6,12): Die Mitverantwortung der Tierwelt an der Sintflut nach der Priesterschrift," *ZAW* 111 (1999) 167-86; **B. A. Strawn,** *What Is Stronger Than a Lion? Leonine Image and Metaphor in the Hebrew Bible and the Ancient Near East* (OBO 212; Fribourg: Universitätsverlag; Göttingen: Vandenhoeck & Ruprecht, 2005). G. A. Klingbeil

APOCALYPTICISM, APOCALYPTIC LITERATURE

Within scholarship, the term *apocalypse* typically refers to a specific literary genre that employs prophecies and *visions concerning the end of time. Those literary works that conform to these standards are considered members of apocalyptic literature; the worldview or ideology associated with these books often is labeled *apocalypticism*, and the word *apocalyptic* is the adjective used to describe something that characterizes this worldview.

While the book of *Daniel stands out as the quintessential example of an apocalyptic book in the OT and is frequently, though not uniformly, considered part of the prophetic corpus, several decidedly prophetic books do exhibit clear apocalyptic characteristics, such as Isaiah, Ezekiel, Zechariah and Joel. In fact, many argue that prophecy birthed the apocalyptic phenomenon found in the Bible. Therefore, a discussion of the ideas related to apocalypse and its relationship with the prophetic corpus is essential to grasping a more complete understanding of the OT Prophetic Books and their influence.

1. Essential Definitions and Terms
2. Proposed Origins of Apocalypse
3. Theology or Function of Apocalypse
4. Early Apocalyptic in the Prophets
5. Summary

1. Essential Definitions and Terms.
1.1. Definitions.

1.1.1. Defining Apocalypse. Going back to 1832, scholars have struggled with how both to consistently define and to categorize the concept of apocalypse (J. Collins 1998, 3). The term *apocalypse* is of Greek origin, drawn from the word *apokalypsis*, which is the first word in the NT book of Revelation and typically is translated as "revelation." In some ways, the book of Revelation serves as a kind of exemplar for a book conforming to the literary genre of apocalypse, and fidelity to Revelation's literary characteristics commonly has served as a kind of litmus test to which all other potential apocalyptic candidates are measured. As a result, denoting books as apocalyptic has been more of a post-NT phenomenon. However, many works predating the book of Revelation, the vast majority of which are not found in either the Jewish or the Christian biblical canons, seem to accord with many, though not all, of Revelation's literary features, therefore leading scholars to conclude that a more precise working definition was needed. To meet that need, a study group from the Society of Biblical Literature (SBL) was charged to develop a more detailed and systematic framework for determining which books could be accurately categorized as apocalyptic. J. Collins, who was a key architect within that group and is today the most influential figure in the discipline of apocalyptic studies, noted that the group's primary effort in determining whether a book could be classified as apocalyptic was to discern "whether a group of texts share a significant cluster of traits that distinguish them from other works" (J. Collins 1998, 4). To that end, the study group produced the following working definition: "a genre of revelatory literature with a narrative framework, in which a revelation is mediated by an otherworldly being to a human recipient, disclosing a transcendent reality which is both temporal, insofar as it envisages eschatological salvation, and spatial insofar as it involves another, supernatural world" (J. Collins 1979, 9). Beyond this dense definition, the study group composed a detailed "master paradigm" that serves to unpack the definition even further (J. Collins 1979, 5-8).

1.1.2. SBL Study Group Master Paradigm. Assuming the centrality of revelation, this paradigm divides into five sections, each of which lists various characteristics that define that section. Under the first section, "manner of revelation," various mediums by which the revelation is communicated are listed as well as several features associated both with the mediator and the human recipient. The two largest sections are dedicated to the content of the revelation; one treats temporal elements such as protology, history, present salvation and the eschatological milieu, and the other addresses the spatial, otherworldly components. The fourth section briefly addresses the parenesis flowing from the mediator to the recipient of the revelation, and the concluding section lists both instructions to the recipient and the presence of a narrative conclusion.

1.1.3. Other Scholarly Approaches to Defining Apocalypse. While most in the academy tend to accept this rather comprehensive working definition, not all fully embrace it. Even after the SBL study group's groundbreaking work was completed, several lamented that it did not go far enough to clarify which books are most clearly apocalyptic, and others suggested that it went too far. Writing after the study group's work, R. Webb still referred to *apocalyptic* as a "slippery term" and offered a helpful survey of four main approaches to defining apocalyptic. First, the "traditional" approach is represented by K. Koch's work, which compiles lists of apocalyptic characteristics and compares prospective works to those characteristics (Koch, 18-35). It emphasizes the content of an apocalypse, such as that found in apocalyptic eschatology as compared with prophetic eschatology (see 1.2.4 below), but neglects important features such as history. Second, the "literary-form" approach emphasizes the literary features of an apocalypse, in particular, the simple presence of a revelation. C. Rowland's work best exemplifies this approach (Rowland 1982, 14), and it is criticized for being too inclusive because it displaces the central role of apocalyptic eschatology. Third, the "essentialist" approach of E. P. Sanders combines the traditional and the literary-form approaches by combining the place of a revelation with the content of hope for restored circumstances (Sanders, 458). It is also considered vulnerable to being overly inclusive. Fourth, Webb describes the work of the SBL group as an "eclectic" attempt to incorporate recurring traits while simultaneously elevating those traits traditionally limited to apocalypses, such as apocalyptic eschatology. One can see that integration within the paradigm itself as "revelation" is central in both its "manner" and its

"content." In the end, Collins felt that "transcendence" serves as the core characteristic of the master paradigm, defining both the literary form and the content of a prospective apocalyptic work (J. Collins 1979, 10-12). To date, despite many challenges to it, the work of the SBL study group has yet to be eclipsed and continues to serve as the benchmark for defining what the term *apocalypse* means and how it is manifested in both biblical and extrabiblical works.

1.2. Terms.

1.2.1. Apocalypticism. The term *apocalypticism* can be construed as "the ideology of a movement that shares the conceptual structure of the apocalypses" (J. Collins 1998, 3). It is generally accepted that something of an apocalyptic movement existed in the period between the second century BC and the second century AD, from which apocalyptic works abound and during which, one might say, apocalypticism flourished. Several examples emerging from this period support this notion. Apocalyptic fervor can be found in many pseudepigraphal works, such as the several books of *Enoch* and *Baruch* and various *Testaments*. Apocalyptic features also influence the deuterocanonical books, such as in Maccabees and perhaps the Wisdom of Solomon. In addition, the Qumran community that produced the Dead Sea Scrolls is widely recognized as an apocalyptic group producing several works indicating that apocalypticism defined much of the life, writings and culture of this group. Apocalyptic impulses seem to enter into the LXX as well. For example, Job is described as being resurrected in LXX Job 42:17, whereas no such mention is found in the MT of Job. Naturally, apocalyptic ideas heavily season all of the NT, not the least of which is found in Jesus' teachings in Matthew 24—25; Mark 13 and Paul's teachings (e.g., 1 Thess 4), and some even suggest that James 5 evinces apocalyptic ideas.

1.2.2. Eschatology. The term *eschatology* generally refers to the study of all matters concerning the end times, which, as seen in the SBL master paradigm, play a significant role in defining a legitimate work of apocalypse. However, a distinction is often made between prophetic eschatology and apocalyptic eschatology. P. Hanson usually is credited with making the distinction as part of his immensely important study examining the origins of apocalypses, which will be considered in greater detail below.

1.2.3. Apocalyptic Eschatology. Hanson defined the term *apocalyptic eschatology* as "a religious perspective which focuses on the prophetic announcement to the nation of the disclosure (usually esoteric in nature) to the elect of the cosmic vision of Yahweh's sovereignty—especially as it relates to his acting to deliver his faithful—which disclosure the visionaries have largely ceased to translate into the terms of plain history, real politics, and human instrumentality due to a pessimistic view of reality growing out of the bleak post-exilic conditions within which those associated with the visionaries found themselves. Those conditions seemed unsuitable to them as a context for the envisioned restoration of Yahweh's people" (Hanson 1979, 11-12).

1.2.4. Prophetic Eschatology. Hanson defined the term *prophetic eschatology* as "a religious perspective which focuses on the prophetic announcement to the nation of the divine plans for Israel and the world which the prophet has witnessed unfolding in the *divine council and which he translates into the terms of plain history, real politics, and human instrumentality; that is, the prophet interprets for the king and the people how the plans of the divine council will be effected within the context of their nation's history and the history of the world" (Hanson 1975, 11).

1.2.5. Vaticinia ex Eventu. As seen in Hanson's definitions, the one word that most readily distinguishes apocalyptic eschatology from prophetic eschatology is *history.* The prophets did not lose sight of events related to their own immediate world, whereas the practitioners of apocalypses were more concerned with the cosmic, transcendent "otherworldly" realm. Nevertheless, history plays a highly important role in apocalypses, especially as it relates to predicted events. Much of scholarship tends to accept the notion that the authors of apocalypses projected into the future certain so-called predictions about events that had already occurred in history. This practice is known as *vaticinia ex eventu.* Hanson describes this phenomenon as "retrospect" whereby the writers would "verify the visionary's insights into the sovereignty of Yahweh" (Hanson 1975, 28). Naturally, not all scholars hold to this view, complaining that such a practice would represent a kind of uncomfortable deception not in accord with the Bible's claims. The classic example of the debate between the two approaches is bound up in the dating of the book of Daniel. Most of scholarship holds to a second-century BC date despite the book's self-depiction to have been written during the time of the exile in the sixth century BC. While most would share J. Collins's view that the book of Daniel is fictive and therefore does not necessarily accurately depict actual history (J. Collins 2002, 14), others, such as E. Lucas maintain a more nuanced view, suggesting that based on literary and linguistic analyses, no final conclusion can be made concerning the dating of Daniel, and that both a second-century BC date and a sixth-century BC date could be equally substantiated while simultaneously holding to the inspiration and authority of the Bible (Lucas, 312) (*see* Daniel: Book of). Similar debates influence the dating of those specific sections of the prophets that seem to be affiliated with apocalypses, such as Isaiah 24—27, where many would not date this section to the time of Isaiah ben Amoz, preferring instead a postexilic date well over a century after Isaiah's ministry.

2. Proposed Origins of Apocalypse.

2.1. Wisdom as Source of Apocalypse. Until G. von Rad's paradigm-shattering hypothesis that apocalypses grew out of the Wisdom literature, scholarship tended to accept the notion that prophecy birthed apocalypse. Von Rad argued that unlike the prophets, the authors of apocalypses viewed history as determined and were therefore more naturally akin with the sages who produced the books contained in the Wisdom literature, such as Proverbs, Ecclesiastes and Job (von Rad 1965, 2:301-8). While the intersection of apocalypse and wisdom had been examined in the nineteenth century and early twentieth century, it was likely the massive influence of von Rad himself that forced scholarship to reconsider the theory. Von Rad argued, "The decisive factor, as I see it, is the incompatibility between apocalyptic literature's view of history and that of the prophets. The prophetic message is specifically rooted in the saving history, that is to say, it is rooted in definite election traditions. But there is no way which leads from this to the apocalyptic view of history" (von Rad 1965, 2:303). In addition to the differing views of history, von Rad argued that "knowledge based on a universal Jahwism" was an essential connection between wisdom and apocalypse (von Rad

1965, 2:308). Von Rad's later work on the Wisdom literature further developed the central place of determinism as a formative link between wisdom and apocalypse, arguing that history was subordinate to divine determination, and that determinism, even more so than eschatology, was pivotal to an apocalypse (von Rad 1972, 278). Von Rad's inability to produce a biblical book that clearly demonstrated the transition from wisdom to apocalypse contributed to scholarship's resistance to his thesis. More recent research into the apocalyptic impulses prevailing in the book of Job may provide a starting point for reengaging von Rad's view (Johnson, 170). Nevertheless, von Rad's theory stimulated further research into the possibility of wisdom being the source for apocalypse.

2.2. Mantic Wisdom as Source of Apocalypse.
Picking up where von Rad left off, H. Müller refined the theory, arguing that Mesopotamian mantic wisdom instead of Jewish wisdom was a more likely candidate as the source of apocalypse. Employing the book of Daniel as an archetype, Müller argued that Daniel 1—6 represented the kind of mantic wisdom typically affiliated with Mesopotamian sages, according nicely with Daniel's purported provenance. Müller argued the latter half of Daniel (Dan 7—12) represented the transformation from mantic wisdom into an apocalyptic ethos marked by eschatology, pseudepigraphy and special enlightenment. M. Fishbane also perceived mantic influences in Daniel. However, accepting that mantic influences can be found throughout Daniel, and in several other prophetic books such as Isaiah, Ezekiel, Jeremiah and Zechariah, Fishbane argued that the author of Daniel strategically assembled older prophecies that resulted in introducing the reader to the "mental world of the wise believers" who were able to produce "an atmosphere of confidence in the inevitability of the apocalyptic forecast" (Fishbane, 493-94). Building on Fishbane's work, paying particular attention to Zechariah 9—13, K. Larkin's study reinforces the possibility that mantic wisdom served as an important source of apocalypse. She concludes that "formal wisdom can have an influence on the production of eschatology, and this is demonstrated in Zechariah 9-13, a mantological anthology which pays respect to prophetic and historical traditions as well as to cultic traditions" (Larkin, 253).

2.3. Prophecy as Source of Apocalypse.
Returning to scholarship's traditional view that prophecy was the source of apocalypse, Hanson's influential work continues to represent one of the most accepted defenses within scholarship. Dispensing with those who argued that apocalypses emerged from either Persian Zoroastrianism or various forms of ancient Near Eastern wisdom, Hanson considered various ancient Near Eastern influences "late" and "limited in their influence to peripheral embellishments" (Hanson 1975, 7-8). Instead, Hanson argued that apocalyptic eschatology owes itself to an "unbroken development from pre-exilic and exilic prophecy." Prior to the fall of Jerusalem in 587 BC, the prophetic trajectory is described by Hanson as marked by an effort to integrate Yahweh's cosmic rule with the Jewish historical and political situation. However, after 587 BC, the Jews' barren political landscape produced a change whereby the prophets were replaced by "visionaries" who, while sharing the prophetic practice of receiving visions, began to "abdicate the other dimension of the prophetic office, the translation from prophetic into historic events" (Hanson 1975, 16). Hanson then seeks to discover biblical works that reveal this transition from prophets to visionaries, which, he asserts, is most ideally located in Isaiah 55—66. He argues that the supposed postexilic context demonstrates a more pessimistic period wherein the hope for restoration was waning, and that the "political-historical realm was overcome by evil, and was no longer a realm over which they had any control" (Hanson 1975, 26). He concludes with the following four assertions concerning the source of apocalyptic eschatology: (1) it is "solidly" in the prophetic tradition of Israel; (2) it occurred in the sixth to fifth centuries BC; (3) its essential characteristic is the "abandonment of the prophetic task of translating the vision of the divine council into historical terms"; (4) a struggle within the community in the Second Temple period existed between the visionary and the "hierocratic" elements, which refers to those of the Zadokite priesthood, which served "as the sole custodian of the central cult for the remainder of the Persian period, and was in position to mold the character of postexilic Judaism along the lines of its temple theology" (Hanson 1975, 29). Naturally, not all concur that Hanson's conclusions are definitive, and,

in particular, Hanson's central tenet of a dualist polarization existing within Judaism is frequently challenged as reductionist. While Hanson's historical reconstructions surely influence his hermeneutics and have received much-needed critical responses, his primary contribution was to reestablish the hypothesis that apocalypses emerged from prophecy. At the same time, one of his most lasting contributions to the study of apocalypses has been to identify several prophetic works under the category of "early apocalyptic" dating to the late sixth and early fifth centuries BC that represent various stages of development between prophecy and apocalyptic as a way to "escape from the harsh realities of this world which were contradicting the covenant promises" (Hanson 1975, 27). He lists several examples that will be examined below.

3. Theology or Function of Apocalypse.

3.1. Rejected and Accepted. Because of the fantastic images and seemingly unintelligible language commonly associated with apocalypses, many deride this category of biblical literature as being too dangerous to integrate into meaningful theological reflection. For some, the apparent presence of overly mythic and violent features demands that the message of apocalypses cannot be taken seriously. At the same time, heightened popular appreciation for apocalypses in nearly every generation dissuades theologians from retreating too far away. Rare is the culture where some contemporary apocalyptic discourse concerning the end of time is lacking.

3.2. Exhortation and Consolation. In seeking to address what purpose may lay behind an apocalypse, D. Hellholm offered a corollary to the SBL's working definition, adding that apocalypses were "intended for a group in crisis with the purpose of exhortation and/or consolation by means of divine authority" (Hellholm, 27). J. Collins concurs: "The illocutionary functions and consolation can generally be maintained for Jewish apocalypses" (Collins 1998, 41). A. Collins supports the notion that apocalypses were designed to bridge the gap between the transcendent world and the earthly realm by seeking to "influence both the understanding and behavior of the audience by means of divine authority" (A. Collins 1986, 7). Accordingly, in times of crisis, whatever action was pro-

moted by the writer was deemed credible because God's voice was added, thereby establishing the message as authoritative.

3.3. Resistance Literature. A. Portier-Young recently argued that the first Jewish apocalypses arose as literary forms of resistance to the prevailing empire. Because empires exerted tremendous influence over culture, dominating every facet of life, resisting this suffocating influence "required challenging not only the physical means of coercion, but also the empire's claims about knowledge and the world" (Portier-Young, xxii). Building on the work of R. Albertz, Portier-Young concentrates her study on Hellenistic apocalypses and identifies two forms of resistance to empire: resistance action and resistant discourse, the latter being capable of replacing the "logic of empire" with an "alternative vision of reality" where God's hidden power and providence are revealed (Portier-Young, 44). Therefore, as resistance literature, the Hellenistic apocalypses "asserted a threatened identity and covenant and empowered their readers for resistance" (Portier-Young, 382).

3.4. Hope in the Future. Hanson emphasizes the importance of hope in apocalypses, arguing that those who are in despair of their earthly circumstances look to the work of God's future plan as both an inspiration to endure and a source of comfort (Hanson 1987, 28). This hope and comfort are situated on the "central confessions of Yahwistic, and, especially, prophetic faith." God is just, compassionate and sovereign and will not forsake his people as he directs history towards its divine purpose where evil cannot prevail (Hanson 1987, 42, 64).

3.5. Perseverance in Suffering. Other research in apocalyptic literature suggests that a central message is that of persevering in one's faith in the midst of suffering (Johnson). Apocalypses clearly were written during times of crisis, whether during the Babylonian captivity in the sixth century BC, or under the threatening hand of Antiochus Epiphanes in the second century BC, or during the persecutions of Christians in the first century AD. In whatever context, the authors of the biblical apocalypses championed one central message: never lose faith in God, even in the midst of desperate suffering, for God will reward the faithful and punish the wicked. For example, in Daniel

12:12 the angel regards those as blessed who are able to persevere during the period when the regular burnt offerings are taken away and the time of the abomination of desolation is established. In Revelation 14:12 we read, "Here is a call for the endurance of the saints, those who keep the commandments of God and their faith in Jesus" (ESV).

4. Early Apocalyptic in the Prophets.

4.1. Early Apocalypses. If Hanson is correct that prophecy is the parent of apocalypses, then we should not be surprised to find examples of nascent apocalypses in the prophetic corpus. Hanson has pointed to several of these sections within the prophetic corpus that he labels either "proto-apocalyptic" or "early apocalypse." Having reviewed many of the most salient features associated with apocalypses, we may find it helpful to examine some of those prophetic sections in light of what scholarship has come to identify as apocalyptic.

4.2. Isaiah 24—27. *Isaiah's third set of oracles is often called the "Isaiah Apocalypse." Many have considered the overtly eschatological themes contained within these four chapters to be the primary witness to an early form of apocalypse. As noted earlier, Hanson considers this section of Isaiah to be a late sixth-century or early fifth-century BC example of "early apocalyptic." While others, such as J. Motyer (Motyer, 162) and J. Watts (Watts, 310), are less inclined to do so, arguing instead that treating these chapters as apocalyptic merely on their eschatological features is a stretch, the material does seem to lend itself to several other apocalyptic characteristics that suggest that it is indeed akin to apocalypses. The section's opening words portend the eschaton: "Behold, the LORD will empty the earth and make it desolate, and he will twist its surface and scatter its inhabitants" (Is 24:1 ESV). A global final judgment appears to be in view, which is reiterated on several occasions—for example, "Therefore the inhabitants of the earth are scorched, and few men are left" (Is 24:6 ESV). The earth itself suffers during this conflagration: "The earth is utterly broken, the earth is split apart, the earth is violently shaken" (Is 24:19 ESV). Despite this calamitous description of the end, hope continues to reside in the Lord of hosts, who will "make for all peoples a feast of rich food. . . . He will swallow up death

forever; and the Lord GOD will wipe away tears from all faces" (Is 25:6-8 ESV). Keeping with the theological motif of enduring in the midst of suffering, Isaiah declares with a hint of triumphalism, "It will be said on that day, 'Behold, this is our God; we have waited for him, that he might save us. This is the LORD; we have waited for him; let us be glad and rejoice in his salvation'" (Is 25:9 ESV). Resurrection is possibly suggested as an example of this hope: "Your dead shall live; their bodies shall rise. You who dwell in the dust, awake and sing for joy!" (Is 26:19 ESV). Symbolizing the death of evil, in God's final judgment he will punish "Leviathan the fleeing serpent, Leviathan the twisting serpent, and will slay the dragon that is in the sea" (Is 27:1 ESV). Finally, Israel will then "blossom and put forth shoots and fill the whole world with fruit," and "in that day a great trumpet will be blown, and those who were lost in the land of Assyria and those who were driven out to the land of Egypt will come and worship the LORD on the holy mountain at Jerusalem" (Is 27:6, 13 ESV). One can readily identify many apocalyptic themes in this section of Isaiah that correlate nicely with several elements listed in the SBL master paradigm such that it would be difficult not to construe Isaiah 24—27 as anything other than an early form of apocalyptic.

4.3. Ezekiel 38—39. Referring to a future invasion of Israel, this exilic prophecy identifies the mysterious Gog of Magog as a chief adversary that God will ultimately destroy. L. Allen refers to it as protoapocalyptic and cites P. Grech, who wrote that *Ezekiel was "an example of apocalyptic taking off but still touching the runway" (Allen, 210). Further confirming its apocalyptic flavor, Gog and Magog resurface in Revelation 20 at the end of Jesus' millennial reign: "And when the thousand years are ended, Satan will be released from his prison and will come out to deceive the nations that are at the four corners of the earth, Gog and Magog, to gather them for battle; their number is like the sand of the sea" (Rev 20:7-8 ESV). Allen also indicates that the Gog unit in Ezekiel "colored the prediction of the end of Antiochus Epiphanes" in Daniel 11:40-45, and then, perhaps referring to the Jewish tractate "Succos," Allen asserts that these chapters "became a firm part of Jewish eschatology in rabbinic tradition" (Allen, 210). For example, Ezekiel 38:16 states, "In the latter days I will bring you against my land, that the nations may know me, when through you, O Gog, I vindicate my holiness before their eyes" (ESV). God's sovereignty even over Gog's motivation for invading Israel demonstrates that he has complete control over historical events. The identity of Gog and Magog has perplexed scholars, and no consensus has emerged; however, the overt references to a final battle and Israel's complete restoration clearly reveal an early form of apocalypse.

4.4. Zechariah.

4.4.1. Zechariah 1—8. Even though Hanson did not consider Zechariah 1—8 to be a source of early apocalyptic, several others have seen clear apocalyptic indicators in this section and would argue that the first part of *Zechariah is an extremely important representation of protoapocalypse (Cook, 125-27). For example, in Zechariah 1:8 we are immediately introduced to Zechariah's vision of horsemen that transports us to similar images of eschatological judgment in both Zechariah 10 and Revelation 6: "I saw in the night, and behold, a man riding on a red horse! He was standing among the myrtle trees in the glen, and behind him were red sorrel, and white horses" (Zech 1:8 ESV). All four horsemen and their chariots are sent to patrol the earth in Zechariah 6. Other key apocalyptic images include the presence of Satan in Zechariah 3, lampstands in Zechariah 4, and personified "Wickedness" being judged in Zechariah 5. In addition, S. Cook considers the seemingly dualistic distinction between the present age and the coming age as a reflection of "the coming millennial era" in Zechariah 8 (Cook, 129).

4.4.2. Zechariah 9—14. Hanson argued that Zechariah 9—14 represents a protoapocalyptic work communicating oracles from the same visionary tradition found in Isaiah 55—66 (Hanson 1979, 286). With the prospect for a transformed society unlikely, Hanson argues that the writers adopted the myth of divine warrior for their apocalyptic projection of the future in order to "keep faith alive" (Hanson 1987, 115-16). This apocalyptic vision required a new creation to defeat evil and allow justice and peace to flourish (Hanson 1987, 116-17). Although apocalyptic features certainly exist in these six chapters, only in Zechariah 14 can a full-blown apocalypse be found (Smith, 285). The ultimate battle is prophesied in Zechariah 14:2-4;

"For I will gather all the nations against Jerusalem to battle. . . . Then the LORD will go out and fight against those nations. . . . On that day his feet shall stand on the Mount of Olives" (ESV). Yahweh is portrayed as coming with his "holy ones" to rescue his people, and some see this as a reference to the so-called rapture in 1 Thessalonians 4:13-17 (Zech 14:5 ESV). Ushering in the new era of peace, the final day will discover that "living waters shall flow out from Jerusalem. . . . And the LORD will be king over all the earth (Zech 14:8-9 ESV). Even the topography will be changed, as the whole land will be transformed into a plain (Zech 14:10 ESV). Jerusalem will be secured and never again have to exist in insecurity (Zech 14:10-11 ESV).

4.5. Joel 2:28—3:2. This brief passage functions as part of *Joel's second oracle that addresses how God will restore his people and subjugate their enemies. It is packed with apocalyptic imagery, including "wonders in the heavens and on the earth, blood and fire and columns of smoke" all happening "before the great and awesome day of the Lord comes" (Joel 2:30-31 ESV). Judgment defines the book, and D. Stuart recognizes that two "Days of Yahweh" exist in Joel, one directed to the timeframe of Joel, and one directed to the future. The time between the two judgments is uncertain, but a "more distant end" seems to be of great concern for the writer (Stuart, 231).

5. Summary.

While not claiming to have the final word, the SBL study group's definition of apocalypse and its accompanying master paradigm have been widely accepted as the standard for discerning whether or not a particular work could be considered an apocalypse. When one applies this to certain passages in the prophetic corpus, several embryonic forms of apocalypse represented in a variety of prophetic books can easily be identified.

The presence of so many protoapocalyptic sections testifies to the ongoing importance of investigating the relationship between apocalypse and prophecy. The numerous witnesses of this particular generic intersection have led many prominent scholars to conclude that prophecy is the most natural source for apocalypse. While much research prefers mantic wisdom as an alternative source for apocalypse, perhaps not enough attention has been given to von Rad's proposal that Jewish wisdom is the source. Research into the apocalyptic impulses woven throughout the book of Job suggests that a fresh analysis of von Rad's thesis is merited (Johnson).

Identifying the source greatly impacts one's decision regarding the social context from which apocalypse grew, which in turn influences decisions about dating, provenance and purpose. All of these naturally weigh into how one interprets apocalyptic texts. To date, prophecy is the regnant hypothesis, but enough alternatives exist to suggest that more research is required.

See also DANIEL: BOOK OF; DANIEL: HISTORY OF INTERPRETATION; ESCHATOLOGY; PROPHECY, HISTORY OF; PROPHECY AND WISDOM; VISIONS, PROPHETIC.

BIBLIOGRAPHY. **L. Allen,** *Ezekiel 20-48* (WBC 29; Nashville: Thomas Nelson, 1990); **A. Y. Collins,** "Introduction: Early Christian Apocalypticism," *Semeia* 36 (1986) 1-12; **J. J. Collins,** "Introduction: Towards the Morphology of a Genre," *Semeia* 14 (1979) 1-20; idem, *The Apocalyptic Imagination: An Introduction to Jewish Apocalyptic Literature* (2nd ed.; Grand Rapids: Eerdmans, 1998); idem, "Current Issues in the Book of Daniel," in *The Book of Daniel: Composition and Reception,* ed. J. J. Collins and P. W. Flint (2 vols.; Boston: Brill Academic, 2002) 1:1-15; **S. Cook,** *Prophecy and Apocalypticism: The Postexilic Social Setting* (Minneapolis: Fortress, 1995); **M. Fishbane,** *Biblical Interpretation in Ancient Israel* (Oxford: Clarendon, 1985); **P. Hanson,** *The Dawn of Apocalyptic: The Historical and Sociological Roots of Jewish Apocalyptic Eschatology* (rev. ed.; Philadelphia: Fortress, 1979); idem, *Old Testament Apocalyptic* (Nashville: Abingdon, 1987); **D. Hellholm,** "The Problem of Apocalyptic Genre and the Apocalypse of John," *Semeia* 36 (1986) 13-64; **T. J. Johnson,** *Now My Eye Sees You: Unveiling an Apocalyptic Job* (HBM 24; Sheffield: Sheffield Phoenix, 2009); **K. Koch,** *The Rediscovery of Apocalyptic: A Polemical Work on a Neglected Area of Biblical Studies and Its Damaging Effects on Theology and Philosophy,* trans. M. Kohl (London: SCM, 1972); **K. Larkin,** *The Eschatology of Second Zechariah: A Study of the Formation of a Mantological Wisdom Anthology* (CBET 6; Kampen: Kok Pharos, 1994); **E. Lucas,** *Daniel* (ApOTC 20; Leicester: Apollos, 2002); **J. A. Motyer,** *Isaiah: An Introduction and Commentary* (TOTC; Downers Grove, IL: InterVarsity Press, 1999); **H. P. Müller,** "Mantische Weisheit und Apokalyptik," in *Congress Volume: Uppsala 1971* (VTSup 22; Leiden: E. J. Brill, 1972) 268-93; **A. E. Portier-Young,** *Apocalypse against the Empire: Theologies of Resistance in Early Judaism* (Grand Rapids: Eerdmans, 2011); **C. Rowland,** *The Open Heaven: A Study of Apocalyptic in Judaism and Early Christianity* (New York: Crossroad, 1982); **E. P. Sanders,** "The Genre of Palestinian Jewish Apocalypses," in *Apocalypticism in the Mediterranean World and the Near East: Proceedings of the International Colloquium on Apocalypticism, Uppsala, August 12-17, 1979,* ed. D. Hellholm (Tübingen: Mohr Siebeck, 1983) 447-59; **R. Smith,** *Micah-Malachi* (WBC 32; Nashville: Thomas Nelson, 1984); **D. Stuart,** *Hosea-Jonah* (WBC 31; Waco, TX: Word, 1987); **G. von Rad,** *Old Testament Theology,* trans. D. M. G. Stalker (2 vols.; New York: Harper & Row, 1965); idem, *Wisdom in Israel,* trans. J. D. Martin (Nashville: Abingdon, 1972); **J. D. W. Watts,** *Isaiah 1-33* (WBC 24; Waco, TX: Word, 1985); **R. L. Webb,** "Apocalyptic: Observations on a Slippery Term," *JNES* 49 (1990) 115-26.   T. J. Johnson

APOCRYPHA, PROPHETIC. *See* DEAD SEA SCROLLS.

ARAMAIC LANGUAGE

In contrast to the Aramaic of the book of Ezra, which appears in official letters from the Achaemenid (Persian) period (*see* DOTHB, Aramaic Language), the Aramaic of the book of *Daniel appears in stories and visions (i.e., in literary texts) set in the Neo-Babylonian and Achaemenid periods (Dan 2:4b—7:28). The Aramaic of Daniel differs slightly from that of Ezra and, like that of Ezra, can be placed in the Achaemenid period. However, Standard Literary Aramaic, to which the Aramaic of Daniel belongs, developed from Official Aramaic and continued throughout the ancient Near East until after the Greek conquest (Kaufman, 115). Aramaic literary texts from Qumran were composed in forms of Standard Literary Aramaic, not in Palestinian Aramaic. Consequently, the Aramaic of Daniel shares some features with the Aramaic found in Qumran literary texts (*see* Dead Sea Scrolls).

The versification of the MT differs in places from that of the English translations: MT 3:31-

33 = ET 4:1-3; MT 4:1-34 = ET 4:4-37; MT 6:1 = ET 5:31; MT 6:2-29 = ET 6:1-28. Due to its technical nature, this article will be referenced according to the MT.

This article does not include a discussion of the question of an Aramaic original for Daniel 1, which purportedly was translated into Hebrew (Collins, 38). The presence of an Aramaism such as ʾăšer lāmmâ (Aram dlmh, "lest" [Dan 1:10]) does not prove translation from Aramaic to Hebrew, but it does demonstrate Aramaic influence on Hebrew.

Aramaic, a West Semitic language with a datable history of some three thousand years, served as the lingua franca for the empires of Assyria, Babylonia and Persia. According to Genesis, the patriarchs of Israel had Aramean roots. Arameans such as Balaam the son of Beor and the Aramean kingdoms of Aram-Zobah and Aram-Damascus played notable roles in the history of biblical Israel. (For a fuller discussion of Aramaic and the importance of Aramaic in the world of ancient Israel, see Lund, 50-53.)

1. Sources
2. Bilingualism in Daniel
3. Vocabulary of the Aramaic of Daniel
4. The Function of the Qere in Relation to the Kethib in the MT of Daniel
5. Orthography and Phonology of the Aramaic of Daniel
6. Morphology of the Aramaic of Daniel
7. Morphosyntactic Functions of the Verb
8. Syntax of the Aramaic of Daniel
9. Suggested Emendations for Critical Evaluation

1. Sources.

The MT and fragmentary texts from Qumran (1Q71; 1Q72; 4Q112; 4Q113; 4Q115) serve as the sources for our knowledge of the Aramaic of Daniel. 1Q71 contains fragments of Daniel 2:4-6; 1Q72 contains fragments of Daniel 3:23-31; 4Q112 contains fragments of Daniel 2:9—7:28; 4Q113 contains fragments of Daniel 5:10—7:28; 4Q115 purportedly contains fragments of Daniel 3:24-25; 4:6, 13-15; 7:16-17.

2. Bilingualism in Daniel.

The book of Daniel is written partly in Hebrew (Dan 1:1—2:4a; 8:1—12:13) and partly in Aramaic (Dan 2:4b—7:28). Rather than being due to amalgamation, a bilingual author deliberately used both languages to express change in point of view; in the Hebrew sections the author writes from an ideological internal position, while in the Aramaic section he is more detached (Arnold, 9-13). The Aramaic section, Aramaic being the language of the world, focuses on the eternal and universal rule of God over the nations (Albertz, 175-79), while the Hebrew sections, Hebrew being the language of Israel, focuses on how the stories and visions relate specifically to Israel. The use of Aramaic in Daniel lends authenticity to stories set in foreign lands (see Snell, 43).

3. Vocabulary of the Aramaic of Daniel.

Vocabulary choice in the Aramaic suggests a time of composition in the Persian period, despite the use of Greek words for musical instruments, which some herald as evidence of a Greek time period.

3.1. Greek Words. Three Greek words, all names of musical instruments, appear in the Aramaic of Daniel: qîtrôs (Qere qatrôs or qatrōs), "kithara" (Dan 3:5, 7, 10, 15); sûmĕpōnĕyâ (Dan 3:5, 15) or sîppōnĕyâ (Qere sûppōnĕyâ) "bagpipe, drum" (Dan 3:10) (see Mitchell and Joyce, 25-26); and pĕsantērîn (Dan 3:5, 10, 15) or pĕsantĕrîn, "harp" (Dan 3:7). Whereas once this was trumpeted as a clear indication of a late date of the Aramaic of Daniel, Greek influence is widely attested in the Near East already in the eighth through sixth centuries BC, so that such a claim is dubious in and of itself (Kitchen, 44-50).

3.2. Persian Words. Persian terms, specifically Old Persian terms (Kitchen, 43), to describe functionaries in Nebuchadnezzar's court appear to be substitutions for Babylonian terms and indicate composition in the Achaemenid period: ʾăhašdarpan, "satrap"; ʾădargāzar, "counselor"; gĕdābar, "treasurer"; dĕtābar, "law official"; and tiptāyēʾ (sg. form uncertain), "magistrates" (Dan 3:2). The adjective ʾazdāʾ, "certain," also appears (Dan 2:5).

3.3. Aramaic Glosses. The phrase bĕnoghāʾ, "at dawn," appears to be a gloss of bišparpārāʾ, "at dawn" (Dan 6:20). The fact that both phrases apparently occur in 4Q113 and are represented in Theodotion's LXX text would point to a very early textual development (*see* Text and Textual Criticism). J. Collins suggests that in Daniel 4:12 the phrase baʿăśab ʾarʿāʾ, "in the grass of the earth," is a gloss of bĕditʾāʾ dî bārāʾ, "in the grass of the field," since it is omitted in

Daniel 4:20, where the rest of the sentence is repeated with a slight change (Collins 210, 227). Yet, it seems strange that a gloss would be so far removed from what it glosses.

3.4. The Form dahăwān. The translation of the enigmatic feminine plural form *dahăwān* (Dan 6:19) as "diversions" offers a reasonable compromise between the contextual guesses "foods," "musical instruments," "musicians," and "dancing girls"—pleasures and amusements fit for a king. The translation "concubines" requires emendation to *lĕhēnān*.

3.5. The Form kaśdâ. The form *kaśdâ*, "Chaldean," with the sibilant *ś*, appears in the Aramaic of Daniel, whereas the form *kaldu*, "Chaldea," (< *kaśdu*), with the liquid *l*, appears in a Neo-Assyrian royal inscription, written in Standard Literary Babylonian. In Standard Literary Babylonian the combination sibilant + dental (here *ś* + *d*) becomes *l* + dental (here *l* + *d*).

3.6. The Root šdr. The root *šdr* means "to strive": *hăwā* *mištaddar lĕhaṣṣālûtēh*, "he was struggling to rescue him" (Dan 6:15). This root is cognate with later Aramaic *ʾištaddal*, "to strive, struggle," and later Hebrew *hištaddēl*, "to strive, struggle," the letters *rêš* and *lāmed* being liquids.

3.7. Complementary Verbal Roots.

3.7.1. The Root yhb. The root *yhb*, "to give," is used for the suffix conjugation, the active participle, and the imperative, while the root *ntn*, "to give," is used for the prefix conjugation and, in Ezra, the infinitive.

3.7.2. The Root ykl. The root *ykl*, "to be able," appears in the suffix conjugation, the prefix conjugation, and the active participle; the root *khl*, "to be able," appears only in the active participle.

4. The Function of the Qere in Relation to the Kethib in the MT of Daniel.

W. Morrow and E. Clarke proposed that the Qere (reading tradition) of Daniel reflects an early spoken Palestinian dialect dating to AD 200-600. S. Fassberg criticized their thesis on methodological grounds, demonstrating that they ignored relevant comparative data, the omission of which skewed their results. Fassberg dates the Qere of Daniel much earlier than do Morrow and Clarke. In fact, for one feature at least—the morphology of the middle weak participle—comparative material attests the form of the Qere of Daniel earlier than the Kethib of Daniel (Fassberg, 11). This section will present how the Qere differs from the Kethib without arguing why. Diachronic difference in dialect is not the only possible solution.

4.1. To Record Alternate Phonology.

4.1.1. The Attached Second-Person Singular Pronoun to Masculine Plural Nouns and to Prepositions. With masculine plural nouns, the Kethib records the ending -*ayik*, while the Qere reads -*āk*: *lĕʿabdayik* is written, *lĕʿabdāk* is read, "your servants" (Dan 2:4); *lĕśānēʾayik* is written, *lĕśānēʾāk* is read, "to those who hate you" (Dan 4:16). The prepositions ʿ*l* and *qdm* also exhibit this same variation: ʿ*ălayik* is written, ʿ*ălāk* is read, "concerning you" (Dan 5:14); *qādāmayik* is written, *qādāmāk* is read, "before you" (Dan 6:23).

4.1.2. The Feminine Absolute Form or Determined Masculine Singular Form of Ordinals, Gentilics, and Adjectives ending in -āy. The Kethib records the ending as -*āyāʾ*, while the Qere records it as -*āʾā*: *tĕlîtāyāʾ* over against *tĕlîtāʾâ*, "a third [kingdom]" (Dan 2:39); *rĕbîʿāyāʾ* in contrast to *rĕbîʿāʾâ*, "a fourth [kingdom]" (Dan 7:23); *kaśdāyāʾ* set against *kaśdāʾâ*, "the Chaldean king" (Dan 5:30); *pārĕsāyāʾ* versus *pārĕsāʾâ*, "[Cyrus] the Persian" (Dan 6:29); ʿ*illāyāʾ* against ʿ*illāʾâ*, "the Most High [God]" (Dan 3:26).

4.1.3. The Determined Masculine Plural Form of the Gentilic. The Kethib records the ending of the masculine plural form of gentilics as -*āyēʾ*, while the Qere records it as -*āʾê*: *kaśdāyēʾ* over against *kaśdāʾê*, "the Chaldeans" (Dan 4:4).

4.1.4. Middle Weak Active Participle Masculine Plural. The Kethib reads *zāʾăʿîn*, while the Qere reads *zāyĕʿîn*, "trembling" (Dan 5:19).

4.2. To Distinguish a Feminine Third Person Plural Morpheme in the Suffix Conjugation. The Qere preserves a distinct feminine plural morpheme -*â*, while the Kethib uses the masculine plural morpheme -*û* for both masculine and feminine: *nĕpaqû* is written, *nĕpaqâ* is read (subject ʾ*eṣbĕʿān*, "fingers"), "came out" (Dan 5:5); ʾ*etʿăqarû* is written, ʾ*etʿăqarâ* is read (referent "horns"), "they were plucked up" (Dan 7:8); *ûnĕpalû* is written, *ûnĕpalâ* is read (referent "horns"), "and they fell" (Dan 7:20).

4.3. To Record an Alternative Form of the Second-Person Singular Personal Pronoun. The Qere reads ʾ*ant* over against the Kethib, which reads ʾ*antâ*, "you" (Dan 2:29). The form ʾ*antâ* also appears in Aramaic texts from Qumran.

4.4. To Correct a Hebrew Form into an Aramaic Form.

4.4.1. The Form ʾalpîn. The Qere ʾalpîn, "thousands" (Dan 7:10), an Aramaic form, corrects the Kethib ʾalpîm, a Hebraism (the corresponding Hebrew vocalization is ʾălāpîm). However, the Masoretes did not correct the Hebrew form ʾănāšîm, "men" (Dan 4:14).

4.4.2. The Forms tîkkûl *and* tikkûl. The Qere readings tîkkûl and tikkûl, "you are able" (Dan 5:16), correct the Hebrew form tûkal twice, perhaps unnecessarily, since the Hebrew form yûkal appears in Daniel 2:10. Yet the Aramaic form yikkûl also appears (Dan 3:29). A bilingual author could mix languages.

4.5. To Correct Spelling.

4.5.1. The Form ʾeštannî. The Qere ʾeštannî, "was changed," a singular form, corrects the Kethib ʾeštannû, a plural form, to make it agree with the singular subject ṣĕlemʾanpôhî, "the visage of his face" (Dan 3:19); that is, read yôd for wāw.

4.5.2. The Form šālû. The Qere šālû, "error," corrects the Kethib šlh (meaning uncertain) (Dan 3:29); that is, read wāw for hê.

4.6. To Record a Ben Asher Reading.
The Qere ribĕbān, "myriads," records a reading of Ben Asher against the Kethib ribbĕwān (Dan 7:10).

4.7. To Delete a Superfluous Letter.
In Daniel 4:14 the Qere deletes what the Masoretes viewed as a superfluous wāw in the Kethib ʾnwš, reading ʾănāšāʾ, "[the kingdom of] men" (the same Qere/Kethib appears in Daniel 4:13 without the notation "superfluous"). Official Aramaic does have one attestation of ʾnwš, however, meaning "household" (*TAD* D 8.4:24), so it could be a legitimate Aramaic form in Daniel. In Dan. 2:39 the Qere ʾăraʿ, "lower," an absolute form, deletes the final ʾālep of the Kethib ʾarʿāʾ, a determined form (Dan 2:39).

5. Orthography and Phonology of the Aramaic of Daniel.
The orthography and phonology of the Aramaic of Daniel fit nicely into Standard Literary Aramaic, a dialect arising from the Official Aramaic of the Persian Empire. The representation of */ḏ/ by d and */ḍ/ by ʿ, the use of ś as opposed to s, dissimilation by nûn, the open final long /ā/ in the word kĕmâ as over against later kmn, and the spelling of the causative and reflexive conjugations with both h and ʾ demonstrate this.

5.1. Consonantal Representation of */ḏ/.
Extrabiblical Aramaic texts from the fifth and fourth centuries BC—the Achaemenid texts from Egypt, the legal texts from Wadi Daliyeh, and the Idumean Ostraca—almost always use zî ("of, who, which, that"), although dî also appears (*TAD* A 2.3; 2.4; B 3.4; 3.12). The Aramaic of both Daniel and Ezra use only dî. The Aramaic of Daniel uses the noun dĕhab, "gold" (Dan 2:32), in contrast to zhb, widely attested in the Aramaic texts from Egypt. However, *TAD* B 3.1:9 has the spelling dhb too. In the past, some have argued for a later dating of Biblical Aramaic based on this phenomenon, but the external evidence no longer warrants this deduction. The earliest dated document that has d instead of z dates from 483 BC: lmʾhd, "to seize" (*TAD* B 4.4:17). The form dh, "this" (*TAD* A 2.5:7), appearing in a text from Hermopolis, may be as early as the late sixth century BC.

5.2. The Consonant ʿ Represents */ḍ/.
The Aramaic of Daniel, like that of Ezra, uses ʿ to represent */ḍ/, not the chronologically earlier q preserved in the Aramaic texts from Egypt, the Samaritan papyri from Wadi Daliyeh, and the book of Jeremiah. Daniel reads ʾarʿāʾ, "the land" (Dan 2:35), as against ʾarqā, "the earth" (Jer 10:11), and ʾāʿāʾ, "wood" (Dan 5:4, 23), as opposed to ʿq.

5.3. The Consonant ś Does Not Change to s as in Later Dialects.
The Aramaic of Daniel retains the spelling with /ś/, not replacing it with s as in later dialects: śaggîʾ, "abundant" (Dan 4:9); śām (+ ṭĕʿēm), "give an order" (Dan 6:14). This feature characterizes Standard Literary Aramaic: śgyʾyn, "great" (4Q207 1, 4); śm, "set" (11Q10 XXXVIII, 5), but contrast symw, "place" (11Q10 XXI, 5); śymʾ, "be situated" (1Q20 XXII, 10).

5.4. Dissimilation by Nûn.
The progressively assimilated root ydʿ, "know," producing gemination is dissimilated by nûn: *maddaʿ > mandaʿ, "intelligence" (Dan 5:12). The root ʿll, "enter," also exhibits dissimilation by nûn in the causative suffix conjugation: hanʿēl, "brought in" (Dan 2:25). These phenomena also appear in the Aramaic documents from Egypt. With regard to the verb slq, "go up," the hapʿel infinitive of the causative conjugation substitutes nasalization for gemination (Rosenthal, §21): lĕhansāqâ, "[the king commanded] to bring [Daniel] up [from the pit]" (Dan 6:24).

5.5. Representation of Final Long /ā/.
Final long /ā/ can be represented by ʾālep or hê

without distinction, as demonstrated by *kĕtābā'* and *kĕtābâ*, "writing" (Dan 5:24, 7). Final long /ā/ is not closed with a *nûn* as in some later Aramaic dialects: *bĕ'ênā'*, "we requested" (Dan 2:23), and *rĕmênā'*, "we threw" (Dan 3:24). Compare *b'dnyn' šm'n'*, "with our ears we heard" (11Q10 XIII, 3). Contrast *kĕmâ*, "how" (Dan 3:33), with *kmn* found in the later 1Q20 XXII, 29 (1Q20 also attests *km'* [1Q20 XX, 4]).

5.6. Spelling of the Causative and Passive/Reflexive Conjugations.

5.6.1. Causative. While the Aramaic of Daniel overwhelmingly prefers to mark the causative with *h*, it also uses *'*: *hanpēq*, "[which Nebuchadnezzar] brought" (Dan 5:2); *'aṭṭarû*, "strip off [its leaves]" (Dan 4:11), < *ntr*.

5.6.2. Passive/Reflexive. While the Aramaic of Daniel allows marking of the passive/reflexive in *'*, it prefers the marking *h*: *hitgĕzeret* (4Q112: *'tg[zrt]*), "[a stone] was cut out" (Dan 2:34); *bĕhitbĕhālâ* (4Q113: *b'tbh[lh]*), "anxiously" (Dan 6:20).

5.7. Consonantal Representation of */ṯ/.

The consonant *t* represents */ṯ/: *tĕkēl*, "sheqel" (Dan 5:25, 27); *tĕqîltâ*, "you have been weighed" (Dan 5:27). By contrast, Hebrew represents this historical phoneme by *š*.

6. Morphology of the Aramaic of Daniel.

This section will include a discussion of the morphology of the pronoun, the noun, the verb, the adjective, and the adverb, with a view to better understanding the text.

6.1. Pronouns.

6.1.1. Independent Personal Pronouns. *'ănâ*, "I" (Dan 2:8); *'antâ = 'ant* (masc. sg.), "you" (Dan 2:29 [issue of Kethib versus Qere]); *hû'*, "he" (Dan 2:47); *hî'*, "she" (Dan 2:44); *'ănaḥnâ = 'ănaḥnā*, "we" (Dan 3:16-17); *'antûn* (masc. pl.), "you" (Dan 2:8); *'innûn*, "those, them" (Dan 2:44 [see demonstrative pronouns, Dan 6:25]); *'innîn* (fem. pl.), "they" (Dan 7:17); *himmôn*, "them" (Dan 2:34-35; 3:22), by contrast with Ezra, which has *himmô* (Ezra 4:10), as do the Achaemenid period Aramaic texts from Egypt. Independent personal pronouns in the third person may be used as demonstrative pronouns (see 6.1.3 below) or as the copula: *'antâ hû' rēšâ dî dahăbā'*, "you are the head of gold" (Dan 2:38); *hălā' dā' hî' bābel*, "is this not Babylon?" (Dan 4:27).

6.1.2. Suffixed Personal Pronominal Elements. These elements can be suffixed to nouns, prep-

ositions and verbs. Official Aramaic (Muraoka and Porten, 26) and the Aramaic of Ezra (Lund, 55) attest both final *mêm* and final *nûn* with pronominal elements of the second- and third-person plural; the Aramaic of Daniel according to the MT attests only the chronologically later *nûn*. 4Q112, however, attests forms in *mêm*: *mnhm*, "part of them" (Dan 2:42). Attested forms are as follows: *-ēh* as in *gišmēh*, "his body" (Dan 4:30); *-hî* after long vowels, as in *ṭiprôhî*, "his nails" (Dan 4:30); *-k* as in *'ăbûk*, "your father" (Dan 5:11), and *'ĕlāhāk*, "your God" (Dan 6:21) (the corresponding element *-kh*, in *'bwkh* and *'lhkh* found in the Qumran manuscripts of Daniel, appears to be a Hebraism); *-î* as in *mandĕ'î*, "my reason" (Dan 4:33); *-nî* with verbs, as in *lĕhôdā'utanî*, "to tell me" (Dan 2:26); *-hôn* as in *lĕhôn*, "to them" (Dan 3:14); *-hm* as in *mnhm*, "part of them" (4Q112; Dan 2:42); *-hēn* as in *bênêhēn*, "among them" (Dan 7:8 Qere); *-kôn* as in *'ĕlāhăkôn*, "your God" (Dan 2:47); *-nā'* as in *hôda'tenā'*, "you told us" (Dan 2:23). The relative pronoun *dî* immediately followed by the preposition *l* + attached personal pronoun expresses possession: *hokmĕtā' ûgĕbûrĕtā' dî lēh-hî'*, "wisdom and power are his" (Dan 2:20).

6.1.3. Demonstrative Pronouns. *dĕnâ* (masc. sg.), "this" (Dan 4:15); *dā'* (fem. sg.), "this" (Dan 4:27); *dikkēn*, "that" (Dan 2:31); *'illēn*, "these" (Dan 7:17); *'illēk*, "those" (Dan 3:12). Personal pronouns also can serve as demonstratives: *hû' ṣalmā'*, "that statue" (Dan 2:32); *malkayyā' 'innûn*, "those kings" (Dan 2:44).

6.1.4. Demonstrative Element h. What at first blush looks like a proleptic pronominal suffix attached to a preposition derives from a demonstrative element *hā* (Rosenthal, §40). Two syntagms appear: preposition with demonstrative element + determined noun, and preposition with demonstrative element + preposition with determined noun. The pseudopronominal suffixes differ in gender, the masculine being *-ēh*, and the feminine being *-ah*.

6.1.4.1. Preposition with Demonstrative Element + Determined Noun. *bēh zimnā'*, "at that very time" (Dan 3:7); *bah ša'ătā'*, "at that very moment" (Dan 4:30); *minnah malkûtâ*, "from this very kingdom" (Dan 7:24).

6.1.4.2. Preposition with Demonstrative Element + Preposition with Determined Noun. *bēh bĕlêlyā'*, "on this very night" (Dan 5:30); *bēh bĕdānîyē'l*, "in this very Daniel" (Dan 5:12).

6.1.5. Interrogative Pronouns. *man*, "who, whom"

(Dan 3:15; 4:29), *mâ,* "what" (Dan 4:32).

6.2. The Morphology of the Noun.

6.2.1. The Masculine Plural Emphatic Phoneme. The masculine plural emphatic phoneme is *-ayyāʾ,* as in *malkayyāʾ,* "kings" (Dan 2:44), and *gubrayyāʾ,* "men" (Dan 3:27), except in gentilics where the Kethib has *-ayēʾ* but the Qere has *-āʾê,* as in *kaśdāyēʾ* (Qere *kaśdāʾê*), "Chaldeans" (Dan 4:4). The plural foreign word *tiptāyēʾ,* "magistrates" (Dan 3:2-3), projects a singular absolute ending in *-ay* like gentilics (so Porten and Lund, 309; contra Rosenthal, §58).

6.2.2. The plural construct of yôm. The plural construct of *yôm,* "day," is *yômê* (Dan 5:11), not *yômāt* as in Ezra (Ezra 4:15, 19).

6.2.3. The noun raʿyôn. The noun *raʿyôn,* "thought" (Dan 2:30), with the afformative *-ôn* instead of *-ān,* reflects the influence of Hebrew on Aramaic. By contrast, Syriac, a later Aramaic dialect, attests the cognate lexeme *reʿyān.*

6.3. The Morphology of the Verb.

6.3.1. Infinitive. The *peʿal* infinitive has a *mêm* preformans, as in *lĕmiknaš,* "to gather" (Dan 3:2), while those of the derived stems do not, as in *lĕkappātā,* "to bind" (Dan 3:20), and *lĕhayĕtāyâ,* "to bring" (Dan 5:2). In the derived stems, the form ending in *-â* appears as the absolute form, while the form ending in *-ût* (or *-ut*) appears as the construct form when a pronoun is affixed: *lĕhaškāḥâ,* "to find" (Dan 6:5); *lĕšēzābûtēh,* "to rescue him" (Dan 6:15). Where a noun follows as the object (only attested once), the construct form ends in *-at*: *ʾaḥăwāyat ʾāḥîdān,* "explaining riddles" (Dan 5:12); compare *lĕhanzāqat malkîn,* "to injure kings" (Ezra 4:22).

6.3.2. Internal Passive. The internal passive characterizes the Aramaic of Daniel, which can place it in the Achaemenid period, as evidenced from the fifth-century BC Aramaic texts from Egypt (Muraoka and Porten, §30) (the texts from Hermopolis [*TAD* A 2] may date to the late sixth century BC) and from the book of Ezra (Lund, 56). However, Standard Literary Aramaic texts from Qumran also employ the internal passive: *wšbyqt ʾnh ʾbrm bdylhʾ wlʾ qtylt,* "and I Abram was spared because of her and I was not killed" (1Q20 XX, 10), which would allow for a later date. Only suffix conjugation forms are attested in Daniel.

6.3.2.1. Internal Passive of the Simple Conjugation. *ʾĕdayin lĕdānîyʾēl bĕḥezwāʾ dî lêlyāʾ rāzāh gĕlî,* "then the mystery was revealed to Daniel in a vision of the night" (Dan 2:19); *gubrayyāʾ*

ʾillēk kĕpîtû, "those men were bound" (Dan 3:21); *ûmin ʾănāšāʾ ṭerîd,* "and he [Nebuchadnezzar] was driven away from human society" (Dan 4:30; cf. 5:21); *tĕqîltâ bĕmoʾzanyāʾ,* "it has been weighed on the scale" (Dan 5:27); *ḥāzēh hăwêt ʿad dî mĕrîṭû gappayh ûnĕṭîlat min ʾarʿāʾ* . . . *ûlĕbab ʾĕnāš yĕhîb lah,* "and I was looking while its [the first beast's] wings were plucked off and it was taken up from the earth . . . and a human heart was given it" (Dan 7:4).

6.3.2.2. Internal Passive of the Causative Conjugation. *wĕhussaq dānîyēʾl min gubbāʾ,* "and Daniel was brought up from the pit" (Dan 6:24); *bēʾdayin dānîyēʾl huʿal qŏdām malkāʾ,* "then Daniel was brought before the king" (Dan 5:13); *ûkĕʿan huʿallû qādāmay hakkîmayyāʾ,* "and now the sages have been brought before me" (Dan 5:15); *wĕʿal raglayin keʾĕnāš hŏqîmat,* "and it was made to stand upon legs like a human" (Dan 7:4); *wĕhûbad gišmāh,* "and its [the beast's] body was destroyed" (Dan 7:11).

6.3.3. Prefix Conjugation of the Verb hwh. The prefix conjugation of *hwh* ("to be") takes a *lāmed* preformative to indicate third-person masculine, whether indicative, subjunctive or jussive in function: *ûmin nišbĕtāʾ dî parzĕlāʾ lehĕwēʾ bah,* "and some of the hardness of iron will be in it" (Dan 2:41); *ṭĕʿēm dî bĕkol šālṭān malkûtî lehĕwôn zāʾăʿîn wĕdāḥălîn min qŏdām ʾĕlāhēh dî dānîyēʾl,* "a decree that in all my royal dominion they should tremble and fear before the God of Daniel" (Dan 6:27); *lehĕwēʾ šĕmēh dîʾĕlāhāʾ mĕbārak,* "May the name of God be blessed" (Dan 2:20). The Aramaic texts from Egypt have *yôd,* not *lāmed,* yet Ezra too has *lāmed.* Literary texts from Qumran attest *lāmed* as well.

6.4. Morphology of the Adjective.
The patterns *kattîb, kattāb* and *kittāb* appear: *ʿattîq,* "ancient" (Dan 7:9); *šallîṭ,* "sovereign" (Dan 4:14); *qayyām,* "enduring" (Dan 6:27); *ḥiwwār,* "white" (Dan 7:9); *ʿillāy,* "highest" (Dan 3:26). Passive participles serve as adjectives: *bĕrîk,* "blessed" (Dan 3:28); *mĕsattar,* "hidden" (Dan 2:22). Some adjectives take the *-ān* affix: *ʾêmĕtān,* "terrible" (Dan 7:7), and *tinyān,* "second" (Dan 7:5).

6.5. Morphology of the Adverb.
Adverbs end in *-āt, -ût, -āʾ* and the masculine singular absolute state: *ṭĕwāt,* "[he spent the night] fasting" (Dan 6:19); *tinyānût,* "a second time" (Dan 2:7); *ʾēzēh yattîrāʾ,* "[and the furnace] was heated excessively" (Dan 3:22); *ûqĕṣap śaggîʾ,* "and he became very angry" (Dan 2:12).

7. Morphosyntactic Functions of the Verb.
From a text-linguistic point of view, the suffix conjugation is the primary verbal form of narration, while the prefix conjugation is the primary verbal form of discourse (Shepherd, 71). Morphosyntax goes further in interpreting how forms are used to express tense, aspect, and modality.

7.1. Morphosyntactic Functions of the Suffix Conjugation. The suffix conjugation primarily expresses simple past time but preserves the earlier anterior/resultative function as well (Li, 38).

7.1.1. Simple Past Function. bēʾdayin qĕrēb nĕbûkadneṣṣar, "then Nebuchadnezzar approached" (Dan 3:26).

7.1.2. Anterior/Resultative Function.

7.1.2.1. Present Anterior/Resultative Function. gubrayyāʾ ʾillēk lāʾ śāmû ʿălāk malkāʾ ṭĕʿēm, "these men have not shown proper deference to you, O king" (Dan 3:12).

7.1.2.2 Past Anterior/Resultative Function. Pluperfect subordinated to a simple past: *ûnĕbûkadneṣṣar malkāʾ šĕlaḥ lĕmiknaš laʾăḥaš darpĕnayyāʾ . . . lĕmētēʾ laḥănukkat ṣalmāʾ dî hăqēm nĕbûkadneṣṣar malkāʾ,* "And Nebuchadnezzar the king sent to gather the satraps . . . to come to the dedication of the statue that Nebuchadnezzar the king had set up" (Dan 3:2). The form *hăqēm* is anterior in time to the form *šĕlaḥ.* Present perfect or simple past subordinated to a future: *ûlēʾṣelem dahăbāʾ dî hăqēmtā lāʾ nisgud,* "and we will not worship the statue of gold that you have set up" (or "you set up") (Dan 3:18). The form *hăqēmtā* is anterior in time to the form *nisgud,* which expresses future time in this context.

7.1.3. Modal Past: Hypothetical Condition. lāʾ nĕhaškaḥ lĕdānîyēʾl dĕnâ kol ʿillāʾ lāhēn haškaḥnāʾ ʿălôhî bĕdāt ʾĕlāhēh, "We will not find any pretext against this Daniel unless we find it against him in the law of his god" (Dan 6:6). The form *haškaḥnāʾ* expresses a hypothetical condition.

7.2. Morphosyntactic Functions of the Prefix Conjugation. The prefix conjugation expresses future, general present, past imperfective and modality (Li, 98-99).

7.2.1. Prefix Conjugation to Express Simple Future. hĕwētāʾ rĕbîʿāyitāʾ malkû rĕbîʿāyāʾ tehĕwēʾ bĕʾarʿāʾ dî tišnēʾ min kol malkĕwātāʾ wĕtēʾkul kolʾarʿāʾ ûtĕdûšinnah wĕtadqinnah, "As for the fourth beast, there will be a fourth kingdom on the earth which will be different from all the kingdoms, and it will devour all the earth, and

it will trample it [the beast], and it will pulverize it [the beast]" (Dan 7:23).

7.2.2. Prefix Conjugation to Express General Present. ûlēman dî yiṣbēʾ yittĕninnah ûšĕpal ʾănāšîm yĕqîm ʿălayyah, "and to whomever he [the Most High] wishes he gives it [the kingdom of man], and the lowest of men he [the Most High] sets up over it [the kingdom of man]" (Dan 4:14).

7.2.3. Prefix Conjugation to Express Past Imperfective. ʾelep ʾalpîm yĕšammĕšûnēh wĕribbô ribbĕwān qādāmôhî yĕqûmûn, "A thousand thousands were serving him and a myriad myriads were standing before him" (Dan 7:10); *wĕʿiśbāʾ kĕtôrîn yĕʾkul ûmiṭṭal šĕmayyāʾ gišmēh yiṣṭabbaʿ,* "and he would eat grass like oxen, and his body would be drenched with the dew of heaven" (Dan 4:30).

7.2.4. Prefix Conjugation to Express Modality. wĕʾoḥŏrān lāʾ ʾîtay dî yĕhawwinnah qŏdām malkāʾ, "and there is no other who can reveal it before the king" (Dan 2:11).

7.2.5. Prefix Conjugation to Express Jussive. kĕʿan dānîyēʾl yitqĕrê ûpišrāʾ yĕhaḥăwēh, "now let Daniel be summoned and let him declare the interpretation" (Dan 5:12).

7.3. Morphosyntactic Functions of the Active Participle.
The active participle expresses present time: *yādaʿ ʾānâ dî ʿiddānāʾ ʾantûn zābĕnîn,* "I know that you are buying time" (Dan 2:8); *hûʾ gālēʾ ʿammîqātā ûmĕsattĕrātāʾ,* "he reveals the deep and the hidden" (Dan 2:22). Its use in past narration expresses the historic present, bringing readers into the past as though they were there: *bēʾdayin mitkannĕšîn ʾăḥašdarpĕnayyāʾ . . . weqāʾāmîn lāqŏbēl ṣalmāʾ . . . wĕkārôzāʾ qārēʾ,* "Then the satraps assemble . . . and stand opposite the statue . . . and the herald proclaims" (Dan 3:3-4). The formulaic use of the active participle of the verb *ʾmr* to introduce direct speech may also fit here: *ʿănô tinyānût wĕʾomrîn,* "they answered a second time and say" (Dan 2:7). The active participle also functions as a past progressive: *wĕqarnāʾ dikkēn ʿābĕdâ qĕrāb,* "and this horn was waging war" (Dan 7:21). Once, it expresses future: *wĕlāk ṭārĕdîn min ʾănāšāʾ,* "and they will drive you away from humanity" (Dan 4:22 [see 8.5 below]).

Often, the periphrastic construction, the combination of a finite form of *hwh* ("to be") and the active participle, expresses progressive action: *mĕhallēk hăwâ,* "he was walking about"

(Dan 4:26); *hăwô bā'ayin*, "[the presidents and satraps] were seeking" (Dan 6:5); *dî lehĕwōn . . . yāhăbîn lĕhôn ṭa'mā'*, "that they might be giving account to them" (Dan 6:3).

7.4. Morphosyntactic Functions of the Nonactive Participle. The passive participle functions primarily as a verbal adjective, while the t-stem participle functions as the passive counterpart to the active participle (Li, 59).

7.5. Morphosyntactic Functions of the Imperative. The imperative functions as a directive and as an optative: *ḥelmā' ûpišrēh hahăwonî*, "tell me the dream and its interpretation" (Dan 2:6); *malkā' lĕ'olmîn ḥĕyî*, "O king, may you live forever" (Dan 2:4).

7.6. Morphosyntactic Functions of the Infinitive. The infinitive can serve as the complement of a verb: *wa'ămar lĕhôbādâ lĕkol hakkîmê bābel*, "and he commanded to destroy all the sages of Babylon" (Dan 2:12). With a preposition, it can function adverbially: *ûbĕhitbĕhālâ . . . 'ăzal*, "and he went . . . hastily" (Dan 6:20). The infinitive may also appear in a temporal clause introduced by a preposition similar to Hebrew: *ûkĕmiqrĕbēh* [variant *ûbĕmiqrĕbēh*] *lĕgubbā' lĕdānîyē'l bĕqāl 'ăṣîb zĕ'îq*, "and when he approached the den, he cried out to Daniel with a sad voice" (Dan 6:21). The phrase *lā' lĕhašnāyâ* (Dan 6:9, 16) means "not for changing," that is, "immutable."

8. Syntax of the Aramaic of Daniel.

This section includes a discussion of the function of the definite article, expressions of the genitive relationship, the position of the demonstrative pronoun in relation to its nominal head, government of the verb and expression of the indefinite subject.

8.1. Function of the Definite Article. The definite article expresses determination in contrast to the absolute state, which expresses indetermination. Contrast *hêwĕtā' rĕbî'āyitā'*, "the fourth beast" (Dan 7:23), with *malkû rĕbî'āyā'*, "a fourth kingdom" (Dan 7:23).

8.2. Expressions of the Genitive Relationship. The second noun in the syntagm called by grammarians the *nomen rectum* ("governed noun") qualifies the first noun in the syntagm called by grammarians the *nomen regens* ("governing noun") in simple constructs as well as in constructions with *dî*.

8.2.1. Simple Construct.

8.2.1.1. Simple Construct with Determined nomen rectum. *wĕ'eṣbĕ'āt raglayyā'*, "the toes of

the feet" (Dan 2:42); *'ĕlāh šĕmayyā'*, "the God of heaven" (Dan 2:44); *mĕdînat bābel*, "the province of Babylon" (Dan 2:49); *'attîq yômayyā'*, "the Ancient of Days" (Dan 7:22).

8.2.1.2. Simple Construct with Indefinite nomen rectum. *malkût 'ālam*, "an everlasting kingdom" (Dan 7:27).

8.2.2. Constructions with dî. Akkadian influence on Aramaic led to the use of *dî* meaning "of" in Official Aramaic; Old Aramaic texts of the tenth through the eighth centuries BC do not use *dî* in this way.

8.2.2.1. The Syntagm Noun Determined by Definite Article + dî + Geographic Name. *bĕnê gālûtā' dî yĕhûd*, "the exiles of Yehud" (Dan 5:13); *hēkal malkûtā' dî bābel*, "the royal palace of Babylon" (Dan 4:26); *'ăbîdtā' dî mĕdînat bābel*, "the business of the province of Babylon" (Dan 2:49).

8.2.2.2. The Syntagm Noun Determined by Definite Article + dî + Noun Determined by Definite Article. *rēšā' dî dahăbā'*, "the head of gold" (Dan 2:38); *šĕbîbā' dî nûrā'*, "the flame of fire" (Dan 3:22); *passā' dî yĕdā'*, "the palm of the hand" (Dan 5:24); *lĕgubbā' dî 'aryāwātā'*, "the den of lions" (Dan 6:17); *sôpā' dî millĕtā'*, "the end of the matter" (Dan 7:28).

8.2.2.3. The Syntagm Noun Determined by Definite Article + dî + Noun Determined by Pronominal Suffix. *ûlēmā'nayyā' dî baytēh*, "the vessels of his house" (Dan 5:23).

8.2.2.4. The Syntagm Noun Determined by Proleptic Pronominal Suffix + dî + Noun Determined by Definite Article or Proper Noun. *šĕmēh dî 'ĕlāhā'*, "the name of God" (Dan 2:20); *ûbĕyômĕhôn dî malkayyā' 'innûn*, "and in the days of those kings" (Dan 2:44); *'ĕlāhēh dî dānîyē'l*, "the God of Daniel" (Dan 6:27); *wa'ăkalû qarṣêhôn dî yĕhûdāyē'*, "and they maligned the Jews"; literally, "and they ate the pieces of the Jews" (Dan 3:8).

8.2.2.5. The Syntagm Noun in Absolute Form + dî + Noun in Absolute Form. *ṣĕlem dî dĕhab*, "a statue of gold" (Dan 3:1); *ûbe'ĕsûr dî parzel ûnĕḥāš*, "and with a band of iron and bronze" (Dan 4:12); *gappîn 'arba' dî 'ôp*, "four wings of a bird" (Dan 7:6); *wĕšinnayin dî parzel lah rabrĕbān*, "and it had large teeth of iron" (Dan 7:7); *nĕhar dî nûr*, "a river of fire" (Dan 7:10).

8.2.3. Construction with lāmed. Lāmed introduces the genitive noun in the date formula: *bišnat hădâ lĕbēl'šaṣṣar* [read *lĕbēlša'ṣṣar*] *melek bābel*, "in the first year of Belshazzar king of Babylon" (Dan 7:1).

8.2.4. Constructions of the Type Noun in Construct + Preposition + Noun. běhezwî ʿim lêlyāʾ, "in visions of the night" (Dan 7:2), equivalent to běhezwê lêlyāʾ (Dan 7:7, 13); malkĕwāt tĕhôt kol šĕmayyāʾ, "the kingdoms under the whole heaven" (Dan 7:27).

8.3. Position of the Demonstrative Pronoun in Relation to Its Nominal Head.

8.3.1. Bipartite Constructions.

8.3.1.1. Nominal Head + Demonstrative Pronoun. rāzāʾ děnâ, "this mystery" (Dan 2:30); gubrayyāʾ ʾillēk, "those men" (Dan 3:12).

8.3.1.2. Demonstrative Pronoun + Nominal Head. děnâ ḥelmāʾ, "this dream [I was seeing]" (Dan 4:15, contra NRSV).

8.3.2. Tripartite Constructions.

8.3.2.1. Demonstrative Pronoun + Nominal Head + Adjective. ʾillēn ḥêwātāʾ rabrĕbātāʾ, "these great beasts" (Dan 7:17).

8.3.2.2. kl + Demonstrative Pronoun + Nominal Head. kol ʾillēn malkĕwātāʾ, "all these kingdoms" (Dan 2:44).

8.4. Government of the Verb: Marking of the Direct Object.

8.4.1. The Letter lāmed to Mark the Direct Object. Lāmed can mark the direct object, as in Official Aramaic (Muraoka and Porten, §74d), especially with persons: malkāʾ lĕdānîyēʾl rabbî, "the king exalted Daniel" (Dan 2:48); lehakkîmê bābel ʾal tĕhôbēd, "do not destroy the sages of Babylon" (Dan 2:24); ûmĕḥāt lĕṣalmāʾ, "and it [the stone] struck the statue" (Dan 2:34).

8.4.2. The Particle yāt to Mark the Direct Object. The particle yāt marks the direct object once in Daniel, the direct object being an attached personal pronoun: dî mannîtā yātĕhôn, "whom you appointed" (Dan 3:12).

8.4.3. No Marker for the Direct Object. The direct object does not need to be marked: bēlšaʾṣṣar malkāʾ ʿăbad lĕḥem rab, "Belshazzar the king made a great feast" (Dan 5:1); ûmalkāʾ ḥāzēh pas yĕdâ, "and the king was seeing the palm of the hand" (Dan 5:5); goddû ʾîlānāʾ, "cut down the tree" (Dan 4:11).

8.5. Expression of Indefinite Subject. The third-personal masculine plural of the finite verb expresses the indefinite subject: wîqārâ heʿdiyû minnēh, "and they removed glory from him" (Dan 5:20), better rendered in English as "and his glory was taken from him"; wĕlāk ṭārĕdîn min ʾănāšāʾ, "and they will drive you away from humanity" (Dan 4:22), better rendered as "you will be driven away from humanity."

9. Suggested Emendations for Critical Evaluation.

Readers should evaluate for themselves the following suggested emendations. (1) Two emendations have been offered for wĕʿal malkûtî hotqĕnat, "it was established over my kingdom" (Dan 4:33): waʾălay malkûtî hotqĕnat, "and my kingdom was restored to me," or wĕʿal malkûtî hotqĕnēt, "and I was reestablished over my kingdom." (2) Read bēlšaʾṣṣar ("Belshazzar") for bēlʾšaṣṣar in some textual witnesses of Daniel 5:1 and in Daniel 7:1 (metathesis of ʾālep and šîn). (3) Emend bĕgôʾ nidneh, "in its sheath" (Dan 7:15), to bĕgin dĕnāh, "on account of it" (Collins, 275). First, if one were to emend the text, the emendation should read bĕgôʾ dĕnāh because bĕgin is attested only in the later Jewish Palestinian Aramaic, and bĕgôʾ appears elsewhere in the language of Daniel. Second, a close parallel appears in 1Q20 II, 10, wnšmty lgw ndnhʾ, "and my breath within its sheath," which speaks in favor of not emending the text. Third, the referent in the text is rûḥî, "my spirit," which is feminine, so one might expect the form nidnah. Rosenthal prefers to vocalize the form as nĕdānah (Rosenthal, §190), deriving the lexeme from Persian nidāni.

See also DANIEL: BOOK OF; HEBREW LANGUAGE.

BIBLIOGRAPHY. R. Albertz, "The Social Setting of the Aramaic and Hebrew Book of Daniel," in *The Book of Daniel: Composition and Reception,* ed. J. Collins and P. Flint (2 vols.; VTSup 83; Leiden: E. J. Brill, 2002) 1:171-204; B. T. Arnold, "The Use of Aramaic in the Hebrew Bible: Another Look at Bilingualism in Ezra and Daniel," *JNSL* 22 (1996) 1-16; J. J. Collins, *Daniel* (Hermeneia; Minneapolis: Fortress, 1993); E. M. Cook, "Word Order in the Aramaic of Daniel," *Afroasiatic Linguistics* 9.3 (1986) 1-16; P. W. Coxon, "The Syntax of the Aramaic of Daniel," *HUCA* 48 (1977) 107-22; S. E. Fassberg, "The Origin of the *Ketib/Qere* in the Aramaic Portions of Ezra and Daniel," *VT* 39 (1989) 1-12; M. L. Folmer, *The Aramaic Language in the Achaemenid Period: A Study in Linguistic Variation* (OLA 68; Leuven: Peeters, 1995); S. A. Kaufman, "Aramaic," in *The Semitic Languages,* ed. R. Hetzron (Routledge Family Language Descriptions; New York: Routledge, 1997) 114-30; idem, "Comprehensive Aramaic Lexicon" (http://cal1.cn.huc.edu); K. Kitchen, "The Aramaic of Daniel," in *Notes on Some*

Problems in the Book of Daniel, by D. Wiseman et al. (London: Tyndale, 1965) 31-79; **T. Li,** *The Verbal System of the Aramaic of Daniel* (SAIS 8; Leiden: E. J. Brill, 2009); **J. A. Lund,** "Aramaic Language," *DOTHB* 50-60; **A. R. Millard,** "Daniel 1-6 and History," *EvQ* 49 (1977) 67-73; **T. C. Mitchell and R. Joyce,** "The Musical Instruments in Nebuchadnezzar's Orchestra," in *Notes on Some Problems in the Book of Daniel,* by D. Wiseman et al. (London: Tyndale, 1965) 19-27; **W. S. Morrow and E. G. Clarke,** "The *Ketib/ Qere* in the Aramaic Portions of Ezra and Daniel," *VT* 36 (1986) 406-22; **T. Muraoka and B. Porten,** *A Grammar of Egyptian Aramaic* (HO 32; Leiden: E. J. Brill, 1998); **S. J. Pfann,** "4Q Daniel[d] (4Q115): A Preliminary Edition with Critical Notes," *RevQ* 17 (1996) 37-71; **B. Porten and J. A. Lund,** *Aramaic Documents from Egypt: A Key-Word-in-Context Concordance* (Winona Lake, IN: Eisenbrauns, 2002); **B. Porten and A. Yardeni,** *Textbook of Aramaic Documents from Ancient Egypt* (4 vols.; Jerusalem: Hebrew University, 1986-1999); **F. Rosenthal,** *A Grammar of Biblical Aramaic* (Wiesbaden: Harrassowitz, 1968); **M. B. Shepherd,** *The Verbal System of Biblical Aramaic: A Distributional Approach* (SBL 116; New York: Peter Lang, 1995); **D. C. Snell,** "Why Is There Aramaic in the Bible?" *JSOT* 18 (1980) 32-51; **M. Sokoloff,** *The Targum of Job from Qumran Cave XI* (Ramat-Gan: Bar-Ilan University, 1974); **Z. Stefanovic,** *The Aramaic of Daniel in the Light of Old Aramaic* (JSOTSup 129; Sheffield: JSOT, 1992); **E. Ulrich,** "The Text of Daniel in the Qumran Scrolls," in *The Book of Daniel: Composition and Reception,* ed. J. Collins and P. Flint (2 vols.; VTSup 83; Leiden: E. J. Brill, 2002) 2:573-85.

J. A. Lund

ASSYRIA, ASSYRIAN PERIOD. *See* ISRAELITE HISTORY.

ATONEMENT. *See* SACRIFICE AND ATONEMENT.

B

BAAL WORSHIP. *See* Idols, Idolatry, Gods.

BABYLON

This ancient city located in southern Mesopotamia lay nearly sixty miles southwest of modern Baghdad (Klengel-Brandt, 251). Babylon sat on the banks of a canal of the Euphrates River, the Arakhtum, sometimes identified simply as the Euphrates itself. The city played a significant role in biblical times. Because of Babylon's political and cultural importance, it gave its name to the region, Babylonia, which at certain periods of history covered all of southern Mesopotamia, extending from the point near modern Baghdad where the Tigris and Euphrates rivers flow closest to each other southeastward to the marshes of the Persian Gulf.

The city and region gave rise to one of the greatest empires of preclassical antiquity. The Babylonians incorporated and expanded the culture of their third-millennium predecessors in the region, the Sumerians, and may themselves be credited with nearly countless innovations and contributions to human civilization. They left a permanent mark on history in literature, art, science and religion. The Babylonians are most notable in the Bible as the seemingly all-powerful nation used to punish ancient Israel for its failure to maintain the covenant with God. In biblical imagery, the city of Babylon itself eventually came to represent all that was evil.

1. Babylon and Babylonia in the First Millennium BC
2. Babylon and Babylonia in the Old Testament Prophets

1. Babylon and Babylonia in the First Millennium BC.

The name "Babylon" is of unknown origin and meaning, and the city itself was of little significance politically in the third millennium BC (Arnold 2004, 2, 32-33). In the first half of the second millennium, however, the city and region rose to prominence under Hammurabi's dynasty, which saw Babylon become the center of an empire for the first time. Within a few centuries, Babylon rose from relative obscurity to become the political center of all Mesopotamia and then an empire of such magnitude that it left an indelible mark on the rest of human history. Its inhabitants were largely Amorite and, later in the millennium, Kassite. A millennium later, during the biblical period, Babylonians were a mixture of these older groups together with Arameans, Chaldeans and many others. By the time of the Neo-Assyrian period, when the Israelite prophets appear on the scene, Babylon was already an ancient and venerated city, considered the cultural capital of all Mesopotamia. Its political significance was derived partly from this perception as an ancient holy city, making it an important symbol of power and prestige. Its political history during the time of the OT prophets may be summarized in two periods, the Early Neo-Babylonian (1155-625 BC) and the Neo-Babylonian (625-539 BC).

The sociopolitical history of Babylonia during the early Iron Age is complex. No single political entity or royal dynasty dominated the area, and several people groups of diverse ethnic and regional backgrounds populated Babylonia. The whole of southern Mesopotamia was characterized from the mid-twelfth century BC to approximately 800 BC by a lack of political continuity. On the other hand, the cultural history of Babylonia during this period is not as complex. Preservation of Babylonia's great literary classics continued among the scribes, while production of new literature in Akkadian continued, even after the simpler alphabetic Aramaic became available (Arnold 2004, 81-82). In general, the early Neo-Babylonian period was a time of intense interest in the past with a commitment to preserving the great literary accomplishments of Babylonia's heritage and especially the salient features of the second-millennium culture. The cultural and religious significance of Babylon was accompanied by the rise of Babylon's god, Marduk, reflected in one of the greatest literary accomplishments of the ancient world, the *Enuma Elish*. Probably composed originally in the second millennium with a different deity as its hero, the *Enuma Elish* was updated and adapted in the early Neo-Babylonian period with Marduk as the hero to reflect the significance of the city of Babylon and its god. Although routinely also known as the "Creation Epic," the composition has as its central theme the exaltation of Marduk and the justification of his supremacy at the head of the Babylonian pantheon. As such, this great literary piece reflects an era when the city of Babylon had risen politically above all other cities in southern Mesopotamia as the traditional locus of divine power in the world. At the beginning of the Iron Age, a new sense of nationalism emerged with Babylon at the center of a world empire. Theologically, this nationalism may also have reflected a significant religious innovation: the idea of Marduk not only as creator of the world but also as personally stronger than all other powers combined (Goldstein, 27-31). This exaltation of Marduk was not as exclusive as the exaltation of Yahweh in ancient Israel, but it provides an important backdrop for the ideological divide between Israel's prophets and the scribes and priests of ancient Babylonia.

The ancient Near East witnessed dramatic political changes around 1200 BC, especially in the Levant and the Mediterranean rim. The collapse of Bronze Age culture coincides with the collapse of the dominant empires of the Mediterranean world—the Hittites of Asia Minor and the Mycenaean civilization on the mainland of Greece—as well as most of the city-states in the Levant. Within a fifty-year period at the turn from the thirteenth to the twelfth centuries, nearly every city in the eastern Mediterranean world collapsed, marking the beginning of hundreds of years of political struggle and uncertainty in the region. The first causes of this political upheaval are difficult to discern, but the arrival of so-called Sea Peoples certainly contributed to the changes. Rather than mass national folk migrations, we should think of the immigration of dozens of small groups from the Aegean who likely were raiders hoping to sack royal centers (Arnold 2004, 75-77). These newcomers were one factor in the transition from Bronze Age to Iron Age around 1200 BC. Babylonia remained relatively stable at first, experiencing little direct impact from the carnage in the west. Ultimately, however, the events in the eastern Mediterranean led to the arrival of Arameans in Babylonia. Their appearance, together with other climatic and natural causes, contributed to a period of decline in Babylonia in the early first millennium. Most cities were drastically reduced in population, and the surrounding countryside gave way to pressure from new tribal groups.

The first centuries of the first millennium BC saw a resurgence of the Assyrian Empire in the north, which resulted in Assyro-Babylonian conflict as the characteristic feature of Mesopotamian history during this period. Even during periods of Assyrian dominance Babylonian culture was more influential across the ancient world, being older and perceived as more sophisticated, especially compared to the relatively provincial Assyria. Cuneiform tablets from Babylonia and Babylonian scribal expertise were coveted by Assyrian rulers, illustrating the interesting love-hate relationship that Assyria had with Babylonia during these centuries.

During its long history Babylonia frequently was ruled by newly arrived foreign elements (Amorites in the Old Babylonia period, Kassites during the Middle Bronze period and Chaldeans in the Neo-Babylonian Empire). But around the turn of the first millennium, Babylonia was ruled by a succession of several dynasties featuring native Babylonian rulers, so that the period 1158-812 BC may be called "Babylonia for the Babylonians" (Brinkman, 278). After a relatively strong dynasty known as the Second Dynasty of Isin (1158-1026 BC), Babylonia was ruled by a succession of three brief and undistinguished dynasties: the Second Sealand Dynasty, the Bazi Dynasty and the Elamite Dynasty, taking us to approximately 980 BC (Arnold 2004, 79-81). The next century and a half left few sources for reconstructing a detailed history. Both Assyria and Babylonia frequently were occupied with a common threat arriving in Mesopotamia from the west, Aramean tribal groups, which eventually would play an important political role in the region. Babylonia thus was marked by political instability, continued Aramean and Chaldean infiltrations, and the superiority of Assyrian military might to the north. After the Assyrians captured and deported Babylonian rulers in 813 BC and again in 812 BC, the region entered a period of anarchy for over a decade.

For the next two centuries a new political power, the Chaldeans in southern Babylonia, would compete with Assyria for control of the region. Chaldean tribal groups were settled in the swamps and lakes of the lower courses of the Tigris and Euphrates Rivers and were distinct culturally and ethnically from the Arameans in northern Babylonia. They adapted quickly to Babylonian culture, controlling the trade routes of the Persian Gulf area and accumulating considerable wealth, with which they paid tribute to the Assyrians, while they also grew in number and strength. Chaldeans became contenders for the Babylonian throne by the middle of the eighth century BC. The first Chaldean monarch, Eriba-Marduk, was honored in later tradition as the one who restored political stability to Babylonia in the 760s, and was capable of repairing Babylon's temples and engaging in other building activities. From the time of Nabonassar (c. 747-734 BC), ancient Babylonian scholars began keeping systematically precise records of historical events. Beginning with his reign, the Neo-Babylonian Chronicle Series provides valuable historiographic data for this period, recording outstanding events of each year (Arnold 2006). Greek astronomers recognized the Nabonassar era as a turning point in the history of science, and the term "Chaldean" came to mean "astronomer" in Hellenistic times (Rochberg-Halton, 115). Conflict with Assyria in the north continued, however, and with the rise of Tiglath-Pileser III in 745 BC, Nabonassar remained in power only by collaborating with the north while nevertheless providing enough stability for economic recovery in Babylonia.

After Nabonassar, Babylonia was weakened considerably by internal revolts. Eventually Tiglath-Pileser himself assumed the throne of Babylon, attempting to consolidate his control

of the south and becoming the first Assyrian monarch in four centuries to unite Assyria and Babylonia in a dual monarchy. This would constitute official Assyrian policy for the next century. Soon after the reign of Sargon II began in Assyria, another Chaldean, Merodach-baladan II, seized the Babylonian throne and succeeded at uniting the previously fragmented Chaldean tribes. Merodach-baladan is most notable for his ability to forge military alliances in his anti-Assyrian efforts, as he did with Babylon's neighbor to the east, Elam. He attempted to draw Hezekiah of Judah into this international coalition against Assyria, as we know from 2 Kings 20:12-19 and Isaiah 39 (see 2.2 below). As an adroit strategist, Merodach-baladan was able to rule Babylonia free of Assyrian interference for a decade (721-710 BC). Ultimately, however, the overwhelming military might of Assyria proved too much for him. In 710 BC, Sargon II of Assyria removed Merodach-baladan and resumed a dual monarchy over Assyria and Babylon. For the next century Assyrian monarchs expended considerable energy trying to control Babylonia, with varying levels of success. Sennacherib used the most aggressive tactics, resulting eventually in the devastation of Babylon, leaving it to languish without royal leadership for eight years. His son Esarhaddon abandoned this approach and resumed instead the dual monarchy, during which time Babylonia experienced gradual economic growth and moderate prosperity. Upon his death, he divided Assyria and Babylonia between his sons, Ashurbanipal and Shamash-shum-ukin respectively, as sibling kingdoms in an attempt to perpetuate peace. Tragically, however, this only resulted in civil war (652-648 BC), in which Assyria recaptured Babylon (Manasseh of Judah may have collaborated with the anti-Assyrian forces [see 2 Chron 33:11-13; Arnold 2004, 91]). Even as Babylonia lost this conflict, the vulnerability of the Assyrian Empire became apparent. While the Assyrian Empire had expended enormous resources to defeat Babylon, southern Mesopotamia itself recovered from the conflict rapidly. The Assyrian threat to Babylonian nationalism had galvanized and unified tribal groups in Babylonia in anti-Assyrian sentiment, and a foundation was thereby established for one final native Semitic empire with Babylon as its capital.

A new period of Babylonian history was inaugurated by the dynasty of Nabopolassar (625-605 BC) and his son and successor, Nebuchadnezzar II (604-562 BC). The former contributed to the defeat of the Assyrians and restored Babylon to a time of renewed grandeur unmatched since the great Hammurabi a millennium earlier. And Nebuchadnezzar's legendary pride (Dan 4:30) is not without justification, as he transformed Babylon into the greatest city of the ancient world. This is known as the Chaldean Empire or, better, the Neo-Babylonian Empire (625-539 BC). The Chaldean roots of the empire are evident for readers of the OT prophets, where "Chaldea" and "Chaldean" are frequent synonyms for "Babylon" and "Babylonia." The significance of the Neo-Babylonian Empire may be described best against the backdrop of other events in Mesopotamia during the first millennium, which was dominated by a series of imperial powers, primarily the Assyrian Empire, the Persian Empire, and later the arrival of Alexander the Great and Greek rule. For a much briefer period during the seventh and sixth centuries, Babylon rose to premier international status and enjoyed a spectacular period of strength and prosperity. The Neo-Babylonian Empire may be thought of as a mere interlude between the Assyrians and Persians, a period of extremely brief duration. Yet the grandeur of this empire, especially under Nebuchadnezzar II, and its legacy in the biblical and classical sources left an indelible mark on subsequent history, making this one of the most important and interesting periods of ancient Babylonian history.

At the death of Ashurbanipal, Nabopolassar seized the throne of Babylon and established the new dynasty. His reign was devoted to driving the Assyrian army from Babylonian soil and consolidating local rule in Babylon. After the fall of the city of Ashur, he established an alliance with his new powerful neighbors in the north, the Medes. They agreed to share power, the Medes in northern Mesopotamia, leaving Nabopolassar free in central and southern Mesopotamia, as well as in Syria. Upon Nabopolassar's death in 605 BC, the crown prince, Nebuchadnezzar, assumed the throne, having recently led Babylonian forces in an impressive victory against the Egyptians at Carchemish (Jer 46:2). The new king quickly fell heir to most of the former territories of the Assyrian

Empire. He reestablished Babylonia as the leading power in the ancient world, rivaling that of Hammurabi in strength and size. Unfortunately, Jehoiakim of Judah made the fatal mistake of believing that Egypt was the stronger of the two powers, assuming a policy for Judah that would have devastating consequences. Conflict between Jerusalem and Babylon resulted first in the siege of Jerusalem in 597 BC, duly noted in the Neo-Babylonian Chronicle Series, reflecting the strategic importance of Jerusalem among Babylon's western holdings (Arnold 2006, 417 [chronicle 5, lines rev 11-12]). A second, more devastating destruction of Judah's capital occurred in 586 BC, which constitutes a central and defining moment in biblical history. The trauma of the Babylonian destruction of Jerusalem left an unmistakable imprint on the survivors in exile and, arguably, on the very shape of the OT itself. The macrostructure of the Hebrew Bible may be said to revolve around the narration of this event as its apex; the loss of city, temple and monarchy is the conclusion of the primary history, the center point of the Latter Prophets and the Writings (Freedman, 6-7). Nebuchadnezzar's defeat of Jerusalem included deportation of Judean populations in 597, 586, 582 BC and perhaps others, marking the distinction between homeland and Diaspora, between life in the land and exile.

Culturally, ancient Israel shared many similarities with Babylon. These included a religiously dominated culture vis-à-vis today's secularizing materialism, the principle of association that governed intellectual processes, and the basic conservatism of both societies (van der Toorn, 1-9). Also like the Israelites, ancient Babylonia produced literature of high quality. The Babylonians left us hundreds of thousands of texts comprising a scribal curriculum, sometimes called a literary "canon," which was fixed probably somewhere around 1200 BC (Oppenheim, 13; Reiner, 294-95). These cultural similarities, however, only throw into bold relief the religious dissimilarities, which became the focal point of the critique of the OT prophets.

2. Babylon and Babylonia in the Old Testament Prophets.
The historical and political realities of the Iron Age led several Israelite prophets to character-

ize Babylon as the quintessential place of religious hubris and idolatry, which was considered tantamount to a refusal to worship or acknowledge the rightful place of deity. Characteristic of most of these texts is a pejorative tone typical of references elsewhere in the Bible, which includes nearly five hundred references to Babylon, the region of Babylonia or its inhabitants, counting those in both Testaments (Arnold 2004, 10). Because of its political and cultural significance beginning with Hammurabi's dynasty in the early second millennium BC, and its role later in destroying Jerusalem and deporting large numbers of Israelites, Babylon came to carry theological significance in the Bible. The prophets of Israel had especially pointed criticisms of Babylonian religion and imperialism (Vanderhooft, 115-202).

2.1. Babylon and Babylonia in Oracles "Against the Nations." Both Isaiah and Jeremiah include Babylon among their collections of oracles "against the nations" (Is 13—14; Jer 50—51). Isaiah's oracle against Babylon is the first of a series of such sermons against several nations (Is 13—23). Isaiah announces that Yahweh will use the Medes to destroy Babylon, and that the city will be completely uninhabited, abandoned forever (Is 13:17, 19-20; 14:22-23). The downfall of the king of Babylon is celebrated in terms that came to symbolize the destruction of any hostile enemy of God (Is 14:4-21). Rather than the first of a group, as in Isaiah's oracles against the nations, Jeremiah's prediction of Babylon's downfall is the climax of his collection, arranged geographically, starting with Egypt and sweeping across the Fertile Crescent west to east, culminating with Babylon (Jer 46—51 [although the LXX has a significantly different arrangement]). Jeremiah especially delights in the anticipated shame of Babylon's deity, Marduk, or simply "Bel" (Jer 50:2; 51:44). Babylon, the great conqueror of all nations will itself be conquered, and like Isaiah's prophecy, Jeremiah anticipates a day when Babylon will become an utter desolation, unfit for human occupation (Jer 50:3, 13; 51:29, 37). Indeed, Babylon will become like Sodom and Gomorrah, uninhabitable (Jer 50:39-40; cf. Is 13:19). And again like Isaiah, Jeremiah identifies the Medes as Babylon's destroyer (Jer 51:11, 28). Babylon's destruction will also mark the end of the exile; all the peoples of both northern Israel and southern Judah will be reunited at Zion by an everlasting covenant with Yahweh (Jer 50:4-5, 19). Ezekiel too has oracles against the nations (Ezek 25—32). Although Ezekiel does not single out Babylon for its own destruction, his judgment oracles concerning the nations identify Babylon as the instrument by which God punishes all the rest. King Nebuchadnezzar himself is summoned by God against Tyre and Egypt, his armies are strengthened especially against Egypt, and he will put an end to Egypt's multitudes (Ezek 30:10). Nebuchadnezzar and the Babylonians are "the most terrible of the nations" and are used by Yahweh to bring ruin upon Egypt (Ezek 30:11; cf. Ezek 26:7; 29:18-19; 30:24-25; 32:11).

In addition to Babylon's role in these oracles "against the nations," the city is the focus of many other prophetic texts, as the following list illustrates.

2.2. Isaiah. The threat to ancient Israel and Judah during the lifetime of eighth-century BC Isaiah was Assyria, not Babylon. Yet even Isaiah foresaw the danger that Babylon would present in the future, especially as narrated in Isaiah 39. Sometime around 713 BC, emissaries of Merodach-baladan II, a Chaldean prince who had seized the Babylonian throne and unified the previously fragmented tribes of Babylonia, arrived in Jerusalem to pay Hezekiah a visit (Arnold 2004, 90). The good king naively hosted the Babylonian visitors and gave them a tour of all his possessions (Is 39:2-4). But Isaiah warned that, having survived the Assyrian threat, Judah eventually would fall to descendants of these very Chaldean visitors (Is 39:5-7).

In the prophecies most often accredited to an anonymous follower of Isaiah in the sixth century BC (Is 40—55), Babylon becomes a symbol of the evil oppressor when described as a beautiful woman reduced to slavery, and the prophet celebrates her humiliation (Is 47:1-7). The long awaited return from exile in Babylonia is described as a miraculous event comparable to the crossing of the Red Sea (Is 51:9-11). The prophet's acerbic critique of idolatry clearly has Babylonian religious practices in view. The artisans who fashion such *idols will be shamed because they create a worthless and lifeless object that can neither see nor know (Is 44:9-11). The ironsmiths and carpenters who work on the Babylonian idols grow tired or hungry or cold. They foolishly take the same wood used for the idols to cook food or warm themselves by the fire, and so they are incapable of perceiving the futility of their idol making (Is 44:12-20; cf. Is 40:19-20). Similarly, the Babylonians transported humanoid images of their chief deities, Marduk and Nabu ("Bel" and "Nebo"), on beasts and cattle who grow weary carrying them (Is 46:1-2). The Babylonian deities are incapable of moving themselves or even supporting their own weight.

2.3. Jeremiah. We have more biographic information for Jeremiah than any other Israelite prophet. He lived through the period of Israel's history that prophets before him only warned about. He witnessed the premature and tragic death of King Josiah, the ignominious decade-long rule of Jehoiakim, the disastrous rule of Zedekiah, the capture and destruction of Jerusalem at the hands of the Babylonians and the exile of God's people (for historical details, see Cogan, 262-69). Jeremiah is rightly known as "the weeping prophet" (cf. Jer 9:1; Lam 2:11).

This period was characterized by bitter debate over whether Judah ought to submit to the Babylonian yoke or attempt to maintain independence, most often linked to dependence on Egypt as an ally. Jeremiah was unequivocally committed to the strategy of surrendering to Nebuchadnezzar because he believed that punishment was inevitable after the loss of Josiah and his reform agenda, and because he wanted to minimize the effects of the punishment. Jeremiah insisted instead upon accepting vassalage to Babylon as a means of survival. His message was assiduously rejected as pro-Babylonian by Jerusalem's ruling establishment, and he personally suffered for his position. Yet his message was consistent that Babylon would be used by Yahweh to punish Judah: "I am going to bring upon you a nation from far away, O house of Israel, says the LORD. It is an enduring nation, it is an ancient nation, a nation whose language you do not know, nor can you understand what they say" (Jer 5:15). The nation used as an instrument of divine wrath is a distant one of strange and incomprehensible speech, a distant and foreign nation of long duration.

At times, Jeremiah refers to Babylonia cryptically when he warns that disaster will break forth "out of the north" (Jer 1:14; 6:1, 22-23) (Arnold, *NIDB*). Seven times in Jeremiah and four times in Zechariah this ominous title is used for the geographic regions north of ancient Israel, specifically Syria and northern Mesopotamia, and by extension, Babylonia. Several topographical features of Syria-Palestine give it a decidedly north-south orientation, in particular the Mediterranean Sea to the west and the desert to the east and southeast, so that the international highways run north and south. This means that typically, enemies from Western Asia of necessity brought their armies into southern Syria-Palestine from the north, even the Babylonians and Assyrians in the extreme east and northeast. Whether or not the identity of Jeremiah's foe from the north country may be positively identified with any specific historical group has been a matter of scholarly debate, but the Babylonians clearly came to be so identified after 586 BC, and it seems reasonable to assume that even before that date, the foe from the north could be any Mesopotamian imperial power looming on the horizon (Vanderhooft, 136-49). In Jeremiah's *call narrative, evil itself is announced as imminent, about to break forth from the north against Judah (Jer 1:13-16). In Jeremiah 4—6 the prophet reveals Yahweh's plan to bring great destruction from the north against Judah. This destruction will be the result of a nation skilled with "bow and spear," a cruel nation that will show no mercy to *Zion (Jer 6:22-23; 10:22; 25:9). Ironically, at the conclusion of the book, the prophet is comforted by the knowledge that Babylon will one day encounter its own enemy from the north, the Medo-Persian forces, another great and mighty nation arriving from the north country to bring destruction and vengeance, this time against Babylon itself (Jer 50:3, 9, 41-42).

At other times, Babylon is referred to in mysterious cryptograms as a way of hiding the specific reference and therefore establishing plausible deniability but still clearly condemning the city; such is the case with "Sheshach" and "Leb-qamai" (Jer 25:26; 51:1, 41) (Arnold 2004, 10). Other designations for Babylon are not intended to be cryptic but rather illustrate the rhetorical impact that the city had on the imagination of Israel's prophets—for example, Merathaim, meaning "double rebellion," and Pekod, named for one of the prominent Aramean tribes of Babylonia, the Puqudu (Jer 50:21).

2.4. Ezekiel. Using especially acute language, Ezekiel identifies Babylon as Yahweh's instrument for punishment against the nations (Ezek 25—32) as well as against Judah itself. The prince of Jerusalem and the city's inhabitants will be caught in Yahweh's snare and brought to Babylon (Ezek 12:10-13). The prophet compares Babylon to a great eagle that came to cut off the top of an impressive cedar (Jehoiakim) and planted in its place a twig to sprout and grow (Zedekiah). But the young tree was also rebellious, so he went into exile to Babylon, where Yahweh entered into judgment with him there for treason (Ezek 17). Through the prophet Ezekiel, Yahweh even prepares a path for Babylon to come to Jerusalem to put the city to siege, with carefully marked signposts so the enemy king can find the city easily (Ezek 21:18-23). The king of Babylon has two choices, symbolized by the cities of Rabbah in Ammon and Jerusalem in Judah. Nebuchadnezzar is portrayed using divinatory practices loathsome to the Israelites—extispicy (examination of animal entrails), belomancy (shaking of arrows) and the use of idols or teraphim—to determine which city to attack. But despite the uncertainty of the Babylonians and their illegitimate practices for discerning divine will, Yahweh summons them directly to Jerusalem for punishment rather than Rabbah.

Oholibah, representing Jerusalem, lusted after male figures in wall carvings, the Babylonians dressed in their brightly colored fine clothes, and she invited them to share her bed and defiled herself with them (Ezek 23:14-18). As a result, Yahweh turned from her in disgust, as he had earlier turned from her sister, Oholah, representing Samaria, and used her erstwhile lovers, the Babylonians, "from the north" to punish her (Ezek 23:22-30).

2.5. Habakkuk. We know little of the historical circumstances of Habakkuk's ministry. For this reason, the single reference to the Chaldeans in the book (Hab 1:6) is open to interpretation, although it probably denotes the imminent arrival of the Babylonian army. The term "Chaldeans" (sometimes translated "Babylonians" [e.g., NLT]) may have been a metaphor for some other entity, and yet the description of them in Habakkuk 1:6-11 collaborates everything we know about Israelite perceptions of Babylonia during this period. Babylonia is a "fierce and impetuous nation" marching throughout the earth to take possessions at will (Hab 1:6). Justice in Babylonian society has no external constraints (Hab 1:7). Their army is terrifying, led by swift horse-drawn chariots

that come for violence and destruction (Hab 1:7-9). No realm or fortification can stop them; they are enamored with their own strength (Hab 1:10-11). What drives the prophetic message forward in this book is the conviction that Yahweh himself is arousing this fierce Babylonian army to march against Judah (Hab 1:5-6). Habakkuk is tormented by the realization that, on the one hand, Judahite society is unjust, wicked and deserving of punishment (Hab 1:2-4), and, on the other hand, God is about to use the dreaded Babylonian army as the instrument of that punishment (Hab 1:12-17). Habakkuk's ministry is focused on Yahweh's use of the Babylonians to punish the more righteous people of Judah, and he longs for the Babylonians to get their own day of judgment. From his perspective, Babylon may be compared to Sheol, for just as Sheol's appetite for the dead is insatiable, so is the greed of the Babylonian Empire for other nations (Hab 2:5, 8). The Babylonian Empire was founded on violence and iniquity (Hab 2:12). And like Isaiah, this prophet derides the idolatry of the Babylonians, who create "a teacher of lies" out of wood and then cannot understand why the image does not wake up and answer them (Hab 2:18-19). By contrast, the whole earth—presumably including the Babylonians—must learn to keep silence before Yahweh, who resides in his holy temple (Hab 2:20). This truth is enough to comfort the prophet, who is reminded of Yahweh's great salvation of old (Hab 3:2-15) and pledges to endure faithfully the traumatic circumstances of the imminent future while he waits patiently for Yahweh to bring judgment on the Babylonians (Hab 3:16-19).

2.6. Zechariah. In the vision-oracle section of Zechariah 1—6, Babylon is again the agent of divine discipline. Yet the city exceeded its divine calling and therefore is deserving of its own punishment. The superscriptions at Zechariah 1:1, 7 identify the period of Darius the Great of Persia as the time of Babylon's just punishment. The fulfillment of earlier prophetic expectations and hopes that Babylon would be punished came not at the relatively peaceful capture of Babylon by Cyrus in 539 BC, but rather with the harsher policies of Darius following Babylonian rebellions against Persia in 522 BC and 521 BC (Boda, 30-41). Zechariah thus identifies Darius as the one who fulfills the prophetic hope for Babylon's punishment.

2.7. Daniel. The role of Babylon in Daniel 1—5 is that of a ferocious human empire capable of many atrocities, yet vulnerable and ultimately doomed because of God's opposition. Nebuchadnezzar's siege of Jerusalem in 605 BC provides the backdrop for the events of Daniel 1, including the capture and deportation of Daniel and his three friends (on the historical difficulties, see Provan, Long and Longman, 381n112). The forced acculturation of the Hebrew lads, intentionally indoctrinating them as Babylonians complete with new names, symbolizes the experiences of all Jews of the Babylonian exile. The Babylonian court of Nebuchadnezzar is the setting of Daniel 2—4 and that of Belshazzar in Daniel 5. These stories of Daniel and his friends in Babylonia emphasize the results of royal opposition to God's will. No matter how powerful, intimidating or seemingly invincible, human power can quickly be reduced to insane ridicule when confronted by the truth of God's faithful witnesses. If the royal pride of Nebuchadnezzar and Belshazzar is self-destructive and temporary, this certainly is true for any number of lesser ancient kingdoms.

Babylon's rebellious pride and vulnerability are also evident in the book's sequence of four earthly kingdoms (Dan 2; 7). Rather than a collection of oracles against the nations, as in other OT prophets (e.g., Is 13—23), Daniel envisions four powerful world empires, followed by a fifth, eternal kingdom. These are not oracles against Israel's enemies, but rather visions of future empires that oppose God and oppress God's people. Babylon serves in this scenario as the prototype of human pride and rebellion, functioning in Daniel's stories and visions as the human anti-kingdom to God's coming kingdom of peace and sovereignty. Specific identity of the four world empires in Daniel 2; 7 is a moot question (i.e., Babylon/Media/Persia/Greece or Babylon/Medo-Persia/Greece/Rome), but the message is not: all earthly kingdoms, no matter how powerful, are ephemeral and prone to self-destruction. Ultimately, the Son of Man will usher in the eternal kingdom of the Ancient of Days (Dan 7:13-14), and God's people, the "saints of the Most High," will do well to wait faithfully for that great day.

See also EXILE; ISRAELITE HISTORY; NATIONS.

BIBLIOGRAPHY. **B. T. Arnold**, *Who Were the Babylonians?* (SBLABS 10; Leiden: E. J. Brill, 2004); idem, "The Neo-Babylonian Chronicle Series," in *The Ancient Near East: Historical Sources in Translation*, ed. M. Chavalas (BSAH; Oxford: Blackwell, 2006) 407-26; idem, "North Country, The," *NIDB* 4:282; **M. J. Boda**, "Terrifying the Horns: Persia and Babylon in Zechariah 1:7-6:15," *CBQ* 67 (2005) 22-41; **J. A. Brinkman**, "Foreign Relations of Babylonia from 1600 to 625 B.C.: The Documentary Evidence," *AJA* 76 (1972): 271-81; **M. Cogan**, "Into Exile: From the Assyrian Conquest of Israel to the Fall of Babylon," in *The Oxford History of the Biblical World*, ed. M. Coogan (Oxford: Oxford University Press, 1998) 242-75; **D. N. Freedman**, *The Unity of the Hebrew Bible* (Ann Arbor: University of Michigan Press, 1991); **J. Goldstein**, *Peoples of An Almighty God: Competing Religions in the Ancient World* (ABRL; New York: Doubleday, 2002); **E. Klengel-Brandt**, "Babylon," *OEANE* 1:251-56; **A. L. Oppenheim**, *Ancient Mesopotamia: Portrait of a Dead Civilization* (rev. ed.; Chicago: University of Chicago Press, 1977); **I. W. Provan, V. P. Long and T. Longman III**, *A Biblical History of Israel* (Louisville: Westminster/John Knox, 2003); **E. Reiner**, "First-Millennium Babylonian Literature," *CAH²* 3/2 (1992) 293-321; **F. Rochberg-Halton**, "New Evidence for the History of Astrology," *JNES* 43 (1984) 115-40; **D. S. Vanderhooft**, *The Neo-Babylonian Empire and Babylon in the Latter Prophets* (HSM 59; Atlanta: Scholars Press, 1999); **K. van der Toorn**, *Sin and Sanction in Israel and Mesopotamia: A Comparative Study* (SSN 22; Assen: Van Gorcum, 1985).   B. T. Arnold

BABYLONIAN EXILE. *See* EXILE; ISRAELITE HISTORY.

BABYLONIAN PERIOD. *See* BABYLON; ISRAELITE HISTORY.

BLESSINGS AND CURSES

Blessings and curses are predominantly linked to *covenant, and primarily to the covenant relationship between God and Israel. Curses, in the form of defeat and *exile, follow disobedience. However, God's purpose is to restore his people, renew the covenant and reestablish the covenant blessings, seen predominantly in material well-being and the spiritual renewal necessary for the covenant to be sustained, and also through his people to extend those blessings to all *nations and the whole earth.

1. Terminology and Usage
2. Theological Significance

1. Terminology and Usage.

1.1. Blessings. References to blessing or being blessed in the OT usually are linked with the Hebrew root *brk*, including *běrākâ* ("blessing") and *bārûk* ("blessed"). Sometimes words from this root occur in the context of blessing God (Dan 2:19-20; 3:28; 4:34; Zech 11:5; cf. Is 66:3), with the sense of offering grateful praise to God for his goodness.

More commonly, *brk* relates to blessing received from God. Within the Prophetic Books there are no direct examples of one person pronouncing a blessing on another (although cf. Is 65:16; Jer 17:7; 31:23). Another term, *'ašrê*, refers to being in a "blessed" or "happy" state (e.g., Is 32:20; 56:2; Dan 12:12; Mal 3:2). This word may be used in a secular context, and so it is not synonymous with *bārûk*, which indicates the state of one who is blessed as a result of being in receipt of God's blessing (Brown, 763-64). Nevertheless, the terms overlap in meaning, particularly in the Prophetic Books of the OT, where the reason for being "happy" is closely linked with the bestowal of divine favor.

The Assyrian king's invitation to the people of Judah to "make a blessing [*běrāka*] with me" (Is 36:16) may, because of the link between blessing and covenant, point to an agreement that is of mutual benefit (Murtonen, 174). However, as part of a speech that challenges confidence in God (Is 36:18-20) and suggests that the king of Assyria can give the *peace and prosperity elsewhere associated with God's future rule (Is 36:16; cf. Mic 4:4; Zech 3:10), it might also be a call to trust Assyria, rather than God, as the source of hope and blessing.

1.2. Curses. There are three main Hebrew roots relating to "curses," "cursing" or "being cursed" in the OT (*'rr*, *'lh*, *ql*), and their usage in the prophetic literature broadly corresponds to their usage in the OT as a whole. These are frequently mentioned alongside blessing as its antithesis (Jer 17:5-8; 20:14-15; Zech 8:13; Mal 2:2; 3:9-10). There is considerable overlap of the semantic ranges of these terms, particularly in the context of the relationship between God and human beings; and when these terms are used in the OT, Gordon questions the view that a distinction may be made between them (Gordon, 492; cf. Scharbert, *TDOT* 1:415;

Brichto, 215-18). However, although the terms may be used in the same or similar contexts and may sometimes be interchangeable, each also has its own particular function and emphasis.

The root *'rr* occurs, frequently, in the curse formula "cursed be . . . " or "let . . . be cursed," formed with the Qal passive participle, *'ārûr*, followed by the object of the curse. Although Jeremiah uses this formula in a personal context to curse the day of his birth (Jer 20:14-15), that use is exceptional in the OT, where the expression is used primarily in relation to the consequences of transgressing the requirements (specific or implied) of Israel's covenant relationship with God (Jer 11:3; 17:5; Mal 1:14). This formula plays an important part in connection with the legal requirements set out in Deuteronomy (Deut 27:15-26; 28:16-19); and it is not surprising that the expression is used most frequently by Jeremiah, who appears to have been significantly influenced by Deuteronomic theology. However, while in Deuteronomy the curse is pronounced by the Levites, and elsewhere it may be pronounced by other figures in authority (e.g., Josh 6:26; 1 Sam 14:24), in the prophetic literature the *'ārûr* formula is always put into the mouth of God, perhaps reflecting the prophets' lack of confidence in existing secular and religious institutions to uphold covenant faithfulness (e.g., Jer 23:9-11). The invocation of such a curse would have the effect of excluding offenders from the covenant community, and so both distancing the community as a whole from the offenses described and also acting as a deterrent to future disobedience.

The most frequent form of *'lh* in the prophetic literature, as in the OT as a whole, is the noun *'ālâ*; the associated verb appears only in the infinitive (Hos 4:2; 10:4), where again it is used as a noun. These terms are associated predominantly with the curse that binds participants in a treaty or covenant to the obligations demanded by their relationship, and which is invoked when the conditions of that relationship are broken. By entering into a solemn, sworn commitment, parties effectively put themselves under the curse (*'ālâ*) that accompanies that commitment; and this close identification of oath and curse is reflected in the fact that *'ālâ* is also translated "oath" (e.g., Ezek 16:59; 17:13-19; cf. Hos 10:4). There is some overlap here with the more common word for "oath", *šěbû'â*, although the terms are not synonymous, and where ʾālâ is used, the main focus continues to be less on the oath itself and more on the consequences of breaking the sworn commitment. In this context there is also a close link between ʾālâ and bĕrît ("covenant"). In Hosea 10:4 ʾālôt refers to the oaths or curses that accompany covenant making (though in this case instead of acting as a solemn bond that holds the parties together, the commitment is criticized as being without substance). Similarly, in Ezekiel 17:13 making a covenant is paralleled with putting a person under the ʾālâ that is associated with it. Conversely, breaking the covenant is equivalent to despising the ʾālâ (Ezek 16:59; 17:16, 18-19). Elsewhere, ʾālâ refers to the curse that comes on the people and the land as a result of breaking their covenant obligations to God (Is 24:6; Jer 23:10; Dan 9:11; Zech 5:3).

While ʾrr and ʾlh are set predominantly in the context of covenant, qll has a wider semantic range. It is used, for example, in the context of cursing those who are perceived to be the cause of distress (Is 8:21) or who, like Jeremiah, are viewed as a source of annoyance (Jer 15:10). However, in the prophetic literature, particularly the book of Jeremiah, qll is also linked with the divine judgment that follows the people's sin. The people will become "a curse" or "an object of cursing" (e.g., Jer 24:9; 25:18; 26:6; 42:18; 44:8, 12, 22; Zech 8:13), pointing to the severity of judgment and perhaps implying that their fate will be something that others wish on their enemies when pronouncing a curse (cf. Jer 29:22) (Brichto, 196; Mitchell, 59-60; Scharbert, *TDOT* 13:41). Although there is no specific reference to bĕrît in these verses, the related occurrence of the covenant formula "they will be my people and I will be their God" (Jer 24:6) and the frequent link between cursing and disobedience (Jer 25:8; 26:4; 42:13; 44:10), which echoes Deuteronomic theology, set this judgment too within the context of breaking covenant obligations. This further indicates the overlap in meaning of these three terms, and the use of ʾālâ rather than qĕlālâ in Jeremiah 29:18 also indicates that under some circumstances the terms may be interchangeable (this is evident too in the occurrence of all three roots in the covenant curses in Deut 27–30).

2. Theological Significance.

2.1. The Power of Words. There has been debate about whether the declaration of blessings and curses in Israel was seen, as elsewhere in the ancient Near East, as a magical formula, carrying with it the effective power to bring about the consequences described (see, e.g., the summary by Thiselton). The suggestion that this may have been an earlier understanding in the OT (Scharbert, *TDOT* 1:265; *TDOT* 2:303; *TDOT* 13:43; Westermann, 56-59) may also be questionable (Thiselton, 296); in any case, it seems widely acknowledged that in the prophetic literature, which seeks to separate true worship of Yahweh from the mechanistic practices associated with other religious systems, blessings and curses have no magical power. It is possible that by burning Jeremiah's scroll, Jehoiakim thought he could remove the implicit curse of defeat and exile by the Babylonians (Jer 36:29), and that might represent the popular theology. However, that threat of judgment received its power from God, and it seems reasonable to assume that all such blessings and curses are effective, not because of the power of the words themselves, but because God, who is the source of the declaration, will ensure that they are carried out; "In the Bible, good fortune and misfortune . . . are traceable to God, and prayers or imprecations invoking these are, even when not made explicit in the text, addressed to the Deity" (Brichto, 218; see also Mitchell, 173-76; Thiselton, 295-96). The fact that God may choose to reverse either the promises of blessing or the curses that would otherwise be expected to fall on the people (e.g., Mal 2:2; 3:9-10; cf. Jer 18:7-10) further indicates that the effective power lies with God and is not inherent within the blessings or curses themselves.

2.2. Treaty Curses. As already noted, curses in the Prophetic Books may be associated with breaking a covenant. Blessings and curses were associated with ancient Near Eastern treaties, and several studies have noted parallels between curses found in treaties, particularly from Syria and Mesopotamia from the ninth to seventh centuries BC, and imprecations within the prophetic writings (see Fensham; Hillers; Johnston). In such treaties gods of the parties involved were invoked to fulfill the curses associated with failure to comply with treaty obligations. In one such treaty, made between Nebuchadnezzar and Zedekiah, king of Judah, Zedekiah was required to swear by God (2

Chron 36:13). And, when the king of Judah broke the covenant, even though it was a political agreement and probably made under duress, God defended it and threatened judgment on Zedekiah (Ezek 17:11-21). However, the imprecations do not bind God to act in a particular way. So (as suggested by Johnston, 417), Nahum can urge defiance of the curses associated with breaking the vassal treaty with Assyria and offer assurance that God not only will protect Judah but also will bring those covenant curses back onto Assyria. This different divine response may also reflect Assyria's brutality toward its vassals and the probability that the initial treaty included the acceptance of foreign gods (2 Kings 16:10).

2.3. Blessings and Curses and God's Covenant with Israel. The link between curses and breaking covenant is particularly significant in the context of God's covenant with Israel. In the Prophetic Books, as elsewhere in the OT, God's blessing is closely associated with the physical well-being of the people, including freedom from oppression, which leads to peace and security in the *land, and material prosperity in the form of rainfall and plentiful harvests (e.g., Is 32:18-20; 65:20-25; Ezek 34:26-29; Hag 2:19; Zech 8:10-13; Mal 3:10-12). This blessing reflects God's covenant commitment to his people in the book of Deuteronomy as they prepare to enter the promised land: divine blessing, including prosperity and continued possession of the land, will follow obedience (e.g., Deut 11:13-15, 26-29; 28:1-14). However, the corollary is also true: disobeying the requirements of the covenant relationship between God and his people will bring God's curse, which will be evident in the withdrawal of divine blessing, the results of which might include drought, failing harvests, defeat by enemies and eventual expulsion from the land (e.g., Deut 11:16-17, 26-29; 28:15-44). That is the situation envisaged by the prophets. Despite continual warnings, the increasing apostasy of the people has resulted in the disasters threatened in the covenant curses befalling the nation (Jer 11:3; 23:10; Dan 9:11; Zech 5:3). Thus, Jeremiah reminds the people of the choice put before them (Jer 11:3–5) and goes on to note that their persistent failure to fulfill the requirements of their covenant relationship has resulted in God's curse, in the form of defeat and exile (Jer 11:7-8). There are also several passages that appear to depict God bringing a legal case against Israel (e.g., Jer 2:4-13; Hos 4:1-3; Mic 6:1-5; cf. Is 1:2-3; 3:13-15). These so-called covenant lawsuits may have their origins in the context of international law where a party to a treaty could be held accountable for failure to meet its covenant obligations.

Isaiah 24:5-6 also refers to a curse that follows breaking the "everlasting covenant" (*bĕrît ʿôlām*), which probably is a reference to the covenant with Noah. That covenant was made, following the flood, with all life on earth, and breaking it results in a curse that is also universal, consuming the earth. This curse echoes the devastation of the flood (Is 24:18b) and suggests a return to something like the chaos of Genesis 1:2 (cf. Jer 4:23; Zeph 1:2-4).

2.4. Future Blessings. Although sin leads to God's curse, judgment is not God's final word, and renewed obedience opens the way to God's blessing. Thus, the lack of prosperity that persisted after the return from exile will be reversed as the people renew their commitment to God by rebuilding the *temple (Hag 2:18-19; Zech 8:9-13), which was a symbol of God's presence among them and of their continuing covenant relationship with him, and by giving God his due in the form of tithes and offerings (Mal 3:10; cf. Ezek 44:30).

In other passages God's blessings appear to be associated with a more distant future age, which will follow God's direct intervention to deliver and restore his people and establish his reign. C. Westermann notes a close relationship between deliverance and the age of peace and prosperity that ensues, and divine blessing, and sees both as key elements in God's promises about the future (Westermann, 34). The blessings of that coming age are still described in terms of material well-being, including lasting peace and security under the Davidic messiah (Ezek 34:23-31; cf. Is 11:1-9), the subservience of the nations (Is 61:5), longevity (Is 65:20-22) and increased prosperity (e.g., Is 65:8-10; cf. Joel 3:18). There is also an important spiritual dimension. God's purpose is to establish a new and lasting covenant with his people (Is 61:8; Ezek 34:25; cf. Jer 31:31-34; Hos 2:16-19), and in order to enable the obedience necessary for that covenant to be maintained, the hearts of the people will be changed (Jer 31:3). In that context, material prosperity in terms of the renewed fruitfulness of what was barren desert becomes also a metaphor for the inward transformation of God's people through the pouring out of his *Spirit (Is 32:15-20; 44:3-5; cf. Ezek 36:24-30).

In this coming consummation, divine blessings are available also to non-Israelite *nations. There is tension here with the apparent subservience of the nations (e.g., Is 49:23; 60:10-16). Nevertheless, Isaiah 19:24-25 portrays Egypt and Assyria (which may be seen as representatives of warring nations formerly opposed to Israel) standing alongside Israel as equal participants in divine blessing. This is further indicated in Jeremiah 4:2, which echoes God's promises to Abraham (Gen 12:3) and to the Davidic king (Ps 72:16) and emphasizes Israel's agency. As the nations see the extent of the divine blessing received by a renewed and restored Israel, they will want to share in it and in the relationship with God that makes it possible (Zech 8:13, 20-23; cf. Is 2:2-4; 25:6-8; 56:3-8).

Future blessings are also described in terms of a new creation. The promise in Isaiah 61:8 of a *bĕrît 'ôlām* ("everlasting covenant") echoes the language of Isaiah 24:6. However, in contrast to that earlier passage, where breaking the covenant threatens to return the earth to precreation chaos, in the coming age God will reaffirm his victory over chaos and bring about both the recreation of his people (see Is 51:1-3, 9-11) and the creation of a new world order (Is 65:17-25) in which God's blessings extend to the whole earth.

See also COVENANT; PEACE, REST; RETRIBUTION; WRATH.

BIBLIOGRAPHY. **H. C. Brichto,** *The Problem of "Curse" in the Hebrew Bible* (Philadelphia: Society of Biblical Literature, 1963); **M. L. Brown,** "ברך," *NIDOTTE* 1:757-67; **F. C. Fensham,** "Common Trends in Curses of the Near Eastern Treaties and *Kudurru*-Inscriptions Compared with Maledictions of Amos and Isaiah," *ZAW* 75 (1963) 155-75; **R. P. Gordon,** "Curse, Malediction," *NIDOTTE* 4:491-93; **D. R. Hillers,** *Treaty-Curses and the Old Testament Prophets* (BibOr 16; Rome: Pontifical Bible Institute, 1964); **G. H. Johnston,** "Nahum's Rhetorical Allusions to Neo-Assyrian Treaty Curses," *BSac* 158 (2001) 415-36; **C. W. Mitchell,** *The Meaning of BRK "To Bless" in the Old Testament* (SBLDS 95; Atlanta: Scholars Press, 1987); **A. Murtonen,** "The Use and Meaning of the Words *L'barak* and *B'rakā* in the Old Testament," *VT* 9 (1959) 158-77; **J. Scharbert,** "אלה," *TDOT* 1:261-66; idem, "ארר," *TDOT* 1:405-18; idem, "ברך," *TDOT* 2:279-308; idem, "קלל," *TDOT* 13:37-44; **A. C. Thiselton,** "The Supposed Power of Words in the Biblical Writings," *JTS* 25 (1974) 281-99; **C. Westermann,** *Blessing in the Bible and the Life of the Church* (OBT; Philadelphia: Fortress, 1978).   R. L. Routledge

BURIAL. *See* DEATH.

C

CALL/COMMISSION NARRATIVES

The term *call narrative* (or *commission narrative, vocation account, Berufungsbericht*) is a form-critical term denoting a specific literary genre "in which a prophet or the prophetic tradition refers to the initiatory commission of the prophet" (Sweeney, 542). Complete call narratives appear only in the Major Prophets: Isaiah, Jeremiah and Ezekiel (Is 6:1-13; Jer 1:4-19; Ezek 1:1—3:15). Other prophetic books, including Hosea, Amos and Jonah, contain only more limited references to a call experience (Hos 1:2; Amos 7:14-15; Jon 1:2).

1. Biblical Sources
2. History of Scholarship
3. Life Setting and Tradition History

1. Biblical Sources.

Because the idea that Yahweh calls and commissions both individuals and groups for specific tasks is integral to the theological outlook of many OT writers, the motif of the call can be found throughout the OT. In addition, a number of texts that can be described as narratives of a call are generally not considered as examples of the call narrative genre proper (e.g., Abraham's call in Gen 12:1-2; Joshua's commissioning in Josh 1:1-9; Samuel's call in 1 Sam 3:1—4:1). This is an interesting state of affairs and raises important questions about how call narratives have been defined. The list of call narratives proper is made up of a group of texts that exhibit significant formal similarities. These narratives exist both inside and outside the Prophetic Books.

1.1. Call Narratives Outside the Prophetic Books. Call narratives outside the Prophetic Books that are important for understanding those within the Prophetic Books include the call of Moses (Ex 3:1—4:7), the call of Gideon (Judg 6:11-17, 36-40) and the anointing of Saul (1 Sam 9:1—10:16). In addition, the narrative of Micaiah ben Imlah's conflict with Ahab and Zedekiah in 1 Kings 22:1-28 (esp. vv. 19-23), while not properly a call narrative, has figured prominently in scholarly discussion. The description of the divine court's deliberations to which Micaiah is privy in this passage resembles the encounters in the divine throne room in Isaiah 6 and Ezekiel 1:1—3:15.

Leaving aside 1 Kings 22:1-28 as a special case, a number of similarities among these narratives are important for understanding the call narratives of the prophets. First, each contains a direct proclamation by Yahweh or his envoy to the called person announcing his special status (Ex 3:1-6; Judg 6:12; 1 Sam 9:20). Second, in each narrative the person called expresses his inadequacy for the task assigned to him. Gideon and Saul are from "insignificant" tribes and families (Judg 6:15; 1 Sam 9:21). Moses offers a series of four reasons for his inadequacy (Ex 3:11, 13; 4:1-2, 10). Third, in each narrative Yahweh responds with some reassurance. Finally, in all of them some sign is given to the called person.

1.2. Call Narratives Within the Prophetic Books.

1.2.1. Hosea, Amos and Jonah. Although none of them contains a call narrative in its fullest sense, Hosea, Amos and Jonah contain limited references to a call experience that may be contrasted with the more elaborate narratives of Isaiah, Jeremiah and Ezekiel (see Hos 1:2; Amos 7:14-15; Jon 1:2). In the book of Jonah, the prophet simply is instructed, "Arise and go to the great city Nineveh and call out unto it" (Jon 1:2). Commentators acknowledge that this call to go to Nineveh may mark the beginning of Jonah's prophetic activity, but most agree that it more likely represents not a call to the prophetic office but rather an instruction to perform a specific task. In Hosea the reference is more ambiguous: "When Yahweh began to speak with Hosea, Yahweh said to Hosea, 'Go take for yourself a wife of whoredom'" (Hos 1:2). This phrase may indicate "a reference to a dramatic call to prophetic service" (Andersen and Freedman, 45). Or, it may not be an "account of an initiation connected with a prophetic call" at all (Wolff, 13). Although the book of Amos likewise does not contain a typical call narrative, it does refer to Amos's call during the narration of his conflict with the priest Amaziah. After Amaziah accuses Amos of prophesying for money, Amos responds that he is not a *nābî'* ("prophet") or a *ben-nābî'* ("son of a prophet"), but rather is specially commissioned by Yahweh. "Yahweh took me from following the flock, and Yahweh said to me, 'Go prophesy to my people Israel'" (Amos 7:14-15).

1.2.2. Jeremiah. Though not without literary critical problems, Jeremiah's call narrative (Jer 1:4-19) is most similar to those of Moses, Gideon and Saul, but it exhibits a particularly close resemblance to Moses' narrative. Jeremiah receives a commission from Yahweh that uses strong language of selection and appointment (Jer 1:4-5). Yahweh has chosen Jeremiah from the womb and given him a special task. Like each of the earlier figures, Jeremiah offers a reason for his inadequacy: he does not know how to speak, for he is only a youth (Jer 1:6). Yahweh offers reassurance (Jer 1:7-8), promising to be with Jeremiah. It has been suggested that Yahweh's response, extending a hand and touching Jeremiah's mouth, constitutes the sign, though it is important to note that unlike the earlier narratives, no sign is explicitly promised or requested. As with Moses, Yahweh does emphasize that Jeremiah will speak his words (Jer 1:9). The commissioning component of the call narrative is joined to a series of two *visions that explain the message of destruction that Jeremiah is to proclaim (Jer 1:13-16), reassure Jeremiah that Yahweh would carry out his word (Jer 1:11) and remind him not to be afraid (Jer 1:17). These visions may be regarded as further signs to Jeremiah (Holladay, 31).

1.2.3. Isaiah. The book of Isaiah also contains a narrative of the prophet's commissioning and exhibits some features similar to other call narratives. Like Jeremiah and Ezekiel, the prophet has divine action or words associated with his mouth (Is 6:6-7). He expresses his inadequacy (Is 6:11, according to Habel), and receives reassurance (Is 6:11-13, again according to Habel). The sign, however, is absent, and on further consideration, we can see that Isaiah's expression of inadequacy has nothing to do with his task; indeed, it occurs before one is assigned to him. Moreover, the way in which the divine charge is presented is unusual. It is not really a charge at all; rather, it is a question directed to the divine council that the prophet overhears (Is 6:8). The instruction "Go" comes later (Is 6:9). M. Sweeney notes that Kaplan, Knierim, Kaiser, Wildeberger and Steck do not consider Isaiah 6 a call narrative (Sweeney, 135). To this list we can add C. Seitz, who agrees with Steck that Isaiah 6 is not an inaugural call to the prophetic office but rather a narrower commission to a specific task (Seitz, 54). Sweeney himself does believe that Isaiah 6 functions as a call narrative, even though it does not fit the expected pattern (Sweeney, 136). The decisions of all these scholars raise important questions about the definition and function of call narratives.

1.2.4. Ezekiel. Ezekiel's call narrative has also presented issues for form critics, the most significant of which is the relationship between the commissioning narrative (Ezek 2:1—3:15) and the lengthy vision that precedes it (Ezek 1:1-28). W. Zimmerli has argued persuasively on form-critical and tradition-historical grounds that the visionary material of Ezekiel 1 cannot be easily separated from the commissioning episode. The commissioning component of Ezekiel's call narrative contains some of the features common to preprophetic call narratives. Ezekiel is approached by Yahweh and is told that he is being sent by Yahweh (Ezek 2:3-5). He is given reassurances by Yahweh (Ezek 2:6) and is told that Yahweh will enable him to withstand the resistance that he will encounter (Ezek 3:7-11). However, it is very difficult to identify the element of the narrative that functions as a sign, and there is no expression of inadequacy within the traditional boundaries of the narrative. N. Habel identifies the sign as the feeding of Ezekiel with the scroll (Ezek 2:8—3:3) (Habel, 313-14). By contrast, M. Greenberg claims that no sign is either asked for or given, indicating a discontinuity with the call narratives of Moses and Gideon (Greenberg, 81).

2. History of Scholarship.

R. Kilian's 1967 article traces the history of critical scholarship on call narratives. Because the bulk of sustained work on these narratives considered as a group occurs between 1935 and 1971, the present discussion will focus on that formative period; however, it will also be important to note a few things about earlier and subsequent work.

2.1. From Calvin to Duhm. Prior to the rise of form-critical scholarship, call narratives within the Prophetic Books were understood in the main as biography, presenting in a relatively simple and direct way the lived experience of the prophet. This certainly is true of premodern commentators such as John Calvin, who reads the call narrative of Jeremiah as a report of the prophet's encounter with God, a report that then becomes instructive for understanding the call of a Christian minister (Calvin, 38). Critical scholars of the late nineteenth century, though they eschewed the premodern search for messianic texts in the prophets, shared the premodern interest in the prophets as historical personalities (Blenkinsopp, 27-28). They wanted to understand the prophets' uniqueness in the history of Israelite religion and saw their call narratives as helpful to this task (*see* Prophecy, History of). As Kilian notes, no one up to this point really had paid any attention to the form in which these call narratives appeared, mainly because they were interested in other questions (Kilian, 357). Driven by J. Herder and the romantics, the focus was on the prophetic personality, and the call narrative was seen as a way to gain insight into this personality, in particular its spirituality and *psychology.

2.2. Gunkel, Schmidt and Form Criticism. With H. Gunkel came a fuller realization of the problem of the distance between the actual lives of the prophets and their writings collected centuries afterward (Gunkel 1915, xxxviii). It is Gunkel who, in his 1915 introduction to H. Schmidt's *Die grossen Propheten* (Gunkel 1915, xlv-lxix) and then more thoroughly in his own *Die Propheten* (Gunkel 1917, 104-40), begins to examine these writings more closely by identifying genres found within them (*see* Form Criticism). But it was Schmidt himself who first applied Gunkel's methods to call narratives. He was convinced that the call narratives of Isaiah, Jeremiah and Ezekiel exhibited remarkable formal similarity. This could not be coincidence, nor could it be explained simply by arguing for a common experience. Rather, said Schmidt, it showed that there must have existed a carefully designed form that was used for the narrative presentation of these call experiences (Schmidt, 391). Although Schmidt's observation laid the groundwork for later work on call narratives, it would be years before this work would begin in earnest (Kilian, 357).

2.3. The 1960s. The fifteen years between 1956 and 1971 witnessed a proliferation of publications on the call narratives, eventually reaching a point where scholars felt the need to apologize for the presumption that anything new could be added to the discussion (Habel, 297).

2.3.1. Ernst Kutsch. In 1956, E. Kutsch, as a result of a study of the call of Gideon (Judg 6:11-24), argued that one could detect in the Gideon narrative a carefully constructed "schema" that was repeated in the Elohistic call story of Moses (Ex 3:10-12), in the call of Jeremiah (Jer 1:5-10) and in the anointing of Saul (1 Sam 10:1-7). This schema Kutsch identified simply as the preprophetic call schema (*vorprophetisches Berufungsschema*). He noted four elements of this schema: the announcement of the assignment by Yahweh; the refusal of the called person; the overcoming of the refusal by Yahweh; and a sign as proof that the assignment had come from Yahweh (Kilian, 359).

2.3.2. Walther Zimmerli. Another contribution to the discussion came at about the same time (1955) as a part of Zimmerli's commentary on Ezekiel (ET 1979). Zimmerli argued that there were in fact two distinct types of call narratives evident in the OT, either of which would have been regarded as a typical form. In addition to the form outlined by Kutsch above, "there is a second expanded type of call narrative" that Isaiah and Ezekiel employ (Zimmerli, 99). In Isaiah and Ezekiel, Yahweh's word of commissioning arises in the context of an overwhelming vision of the divine throne room. In the context of the divine court, Zimmerli notes, there is a greater distance between Yahweh and the prophet. Unlike the story of Jeremiah, which allows room for reluctance and even objection on the part of the prophet, in the narratives of Isaiah and Ezekiel there is "no room left for refusal" (Zimmerli, 99). With regard to form, Zimmerli concludes, "The differences serve to make clear that we are not dealing with a fixed formula" (Zimmerli, 99). Rather, the words of the commission from Yahweh can be combined with a vision of his throne room with "remarkable freedom;" this variation of the form arises in the ninth to eighth centuries BC (Zimmerli, 100). Zimmerli's suggestion that there may be multiple kinds of call narratives helps make sense of some of the divergences noted earlier.

2.3.3. Norman Habel. Habel published the earliest systematic study of call narratives available in English and so exerted an early influence on English-speaking scholars who did not have access to the German literature. Habel examined the call narratives of Gideon, Moses, Jeremiah, First Isaiah, Ezekiel and Second Isaiah in order to offer some conclusions about where the form originated and how it developed over time. Like Zimmerli, Habel believed that prophetic call narratives arose from a prophet's experience filtered through earlier traditions. Unlike Zimmerli, however, Habel argued for just a single type of call narrative shared among all the prophets. Moses' call narrative (itself a template for Gideon and others) is used as a paradigm that "the classical prophets . . . appropriate and develop" in order to establish "a specific link with the past history of Israel" (Habel, 316). Further, in contrast with Kutsch's four elements, Habel identified a generally consistent set of six elements that usually appear in a particular order: a divine confrontation, the introductory word, a commission, an objection, a reassurance and a sign. Although Habel's six elements often are acknowledged in contemporary discussions, his thesis that all prophetic call narratives are of a single type is not as broadly accepted.

2.3.4. Wolfgang Richter and Klaus Gouders. Two further studies from this period are important to note. First is the work of Richter, who in two detailed monographs examined the preprophetic call narratives (Gideon, Moses, Saul). Richter's preprophetic call narrative schema resembles Kutsch's; however, he adds a "description of the need" at the beginning (the Israelites are being oppressed by enemies: Egyptians, Philistines, Midianites) and a "savior formula" at the end (the called person in

each case is told that they will "save" the Israelites) (Richter, 142-67). After a thorough investigation of these narratives and a comparison with the call narratives of the Major Prophets, Richter concludes that the form of the call narrative originates during the period of the judges. The calls of Gideon and Saul represent the earliest form of this genre (Richter, 176).

The 1971 published dissertation of Gouders offers a thorough study of the call narratives of Moses and the three Major Prophets. Gouders's conclusions about the type(s) and elements of the call narrative echo those of Zimmerli. There are indeed two types of call narrative, an Isaianic type and a Jeremianic type, with Ezekiel's call narrative being a mixed form. Contrary to Richter, Gouders concludes with G. von Rad that the call narrative genre originates with the prophets, and that this genre then exerts influence on the call narratives of Moses and the judges via later redactors and/or authors (Gouders, 199-201). For Gouders, the prophets' articulation of their call is essential both to their personal identity and to their legitmation before Israel (Gouders, 244).

2.4. Contemporary Work on Call Narratives. Since the 1970s, scholarly work on call narratives as a distinct genre has diminished significantly. Instead, scholars tend to focus on call narratives as components of the biblical books of which they are a part. B. Long has advised that the best way to understand a call narrative is to investigate the relation of the unique features of each prophet's call narrative to the larger literary themes of the book (Long, 11). Examples of this approach are available in the best commentaries (e.g., Sweeney on Isaiah, Childs on Exodus) and also in exegetical articles and essays dealing with the passages in question (e.g., Wilson; Sharp). Alternatively, some studies have examined how some of the commonly expected components of the call genre can be found in other parts of the book (Jeppesen; Phinney) and what this might mean for the book's editorial history. One notable exception to the trend away from the consideration of the genre as a whole is H.-C. Schmitt's article highlighting evidence for the influence of wisdom traditions on prophetic call narratives (Schmitt, 214-15).

3. Life Setting and Tradition History.
Important questions face all form-critical dis-

cussions of call narratives. If the call narrative is a distinct genre, what is its origin? How did it develop over time? For what purpose was any given call narrative written down? What is the relationship between the call narratives found in the Prophetic Books and those found outside them? Though not exhaustive or systematic, the following discussion highlights some of the more notable attempts to answer these questions.

3.1. The Uniqueness of the Call Narrative. It has been suggested that the call narrative is sui generis; its origin is not related to any previous Israelite form or life setting, but rather is intimately connected with the rise of prophetism. As G. von Rad puts it, "The prophetic call [experience] gave rise to a new literary category, the account of a call" (von Rad, 2:54). On this view, the call narrative forms developed during the Israelite monarchy, the Isaiah form earlier (ninth to eighth centuries BC) and the Jeremiah form later (seventh century BC), and primarily served as a way to authenticate the prophet before his audience and to demonstrate that the message that the prophet spoke was from Yahweh (Gouders, 188). Call narratives "were not characteristic of the representatives of Jahwism from the very beginning" (von Rad, 2:54). The call narratives of Moses (Ex 3) and those found in the Deuteronomistic History (Gideon, Samuel) represent the tradition's later reflection on those figures in light of the experiences/narratives of the prophets of the monarchic period. Proponents of this view do not necessarily deny the experiences of these earlier figures; rather, they argue that the way those experiences are portrayed literarily is heavily influenced by the prophetic call narratives.

3.2. Development from the Commissioning Speech. Another alternative, offered by Habel, accepts the legitimating function of the call narrative but suggests that the form itself derives from court messenger practices in the ancient Near East (Habel, 317). Building on C. Westermann's work on the prophet as Yahweh's messenger, Habel cites Genesis 24:35-48, in which Abraham's servant recounts to Laban the narrative of his own commission by Abraham. This, Habel says, is an example of what must have been a typical pattern of credential presentation used by "ambassadors or messengers on a special mission," and it is this pattern that the prophets emulate (Habel, 322). In fol-

lowing the pattern, the messengers "not only spelled out the reason for their coming, but also repeated the commission ceremony from their master" (Habel, 322) Unlike von Rad, Habel believes that the prophetic call narratives "appropriate and develop the call traditions reflected in the structure of the calls of Moses and Gideon" (Habel, 316). Development runs from Moses to Ezekiel, not vice versa.

3.3. Bidirectional Canonical Influence. In his Exodus commentary B. Childs offers a kind of mediating position between the preceding two views, acknowledging that there is a complex relationship between the tradition associated with Moses and the later office of the prophet. On the one hand, Childs notes, "The tradition linked Moses' call as Yahweh's messenger with the later phenomena of classical prophetism. It recognized correctly that a new element entered with Moses which set [this later period] apart from the patriarchal period. The patriarchs received revelation in theophanies, but had no commission to transmit a message to others. Moses' call recounts the deep disruptive seizure of a man for whom neither previous faith nor personal endowment played a role in preparing him for his vocation" (Childs, 56). However, Childs continues, "It is also clear that the later prophetic office influenced the tradition of Moses' call. Particularly in the expanded form of the present text, the series of questions raised by Moses in objection to being sent echo the inner and outer struggles of the prophets of Israel" (Childs, 56). The call of Moses influences the prophets, but literary influence runs the other way as well.

3.4. Development from a Priestly Oracle of Salvation. The idea that the prophets were closely connected with the cult (*see* Liturgy and Cult) arises first with the work of S. Mowinckel, but it is H. Reventlow who asserts that the call narratives themselves are liturgical components of real cultic rituals in which cultic officials formally ordain the prophet to his office (Reventlow, 76-77). The call narratives of Ezekiel and Isaiah certainly show evidence of cultic influence, and Jeremiah comes from a priestly family; however, most today are convinced that Reventlow overestimated the connection between prophets and the cult (Blenkinsopp, 32).

3.5. The Prophet as the Vizier of Yahweh. K. Baltzer has suggested that a close form-critical cousin of the call narrative can be found in narratives recounting the appointment of Egyptian viziers, high-ranking officials in Egypt to whom the authority of the king was directly delegated (Baltzer 1975, 136-49). On this basis, he argues that the prophets understood themselves as Yahweh's viziers rather than as mere messengers. The prophet-as-messenger idea simply does not "explain the claims which men like Isaiah, Jeremiah and Ezekiel made with respect to the rank of their office" (Baltzer 1968, 570). Perhaps the best biblical analogy is in 2 Kings 18, where the Rabshakeh, clearly a Babylonian royal official, also serves as a messenger of Sennacherib.

3.6. Call Narratives and Prophetic Legitimation. Until relatively recently, one common view of the function of prophetic call narratives was that they served to legitimate the prophet as an authentic messenger of Yahweh before a skeptical audience. The conclusion was based in part on the autobiographical form of the narratives and also on evidence for resistance to the prophet's messages. However, several recent works that emphasize the function of call narratives as components of individual books rather than as examples of a larger genre have offered alternative views. B. Long, after assessing anthropological work done on intermediary figures in so-called primitive societies, questions whether call narratives ever function primarily to authenticate the messenger. And J. Robson, in his recent work on Ezekiel, suggests that Ezekiel's call narrative functions not to authenticate the prophet, but rather to portray him as an example of the obedience that Yahweh would have of all his people.

3.7. Ways Forward. When we consider the variety of challenges associated with a strictly form-critical approach to the genre as a whole, it seems that the contemporary tendency to focus on call narratives within the context of their particular books is a wise one (see Sweeney and Ben Zvi). Although certain call narratives exhibit a great deal of formal similarity with each other, and all call narratives exhibit some, it may be that there is still too much diversity to argue for a consistent literary form. Rather, we have narratives that are united by their subject matter, broadly considered, and, as Childs has suggested, by the fact that they are theologically shaped by a shared tradition.

See also DIVINE COUNCIL; FORM CRITICISM; LITURGY AND CULT; PROPHECY, HISTORY OF; VISIONS, PROPHETIC.

BIBLIOGRAPHY. **F. I. Andersen and D. N. Freedman,** *Hosea* (AB 24; Garden City, NY: Doubleday, 1980; **K. Baltzer,** "Considerations Regarding the Office and Calling of the Prophet," *HTR* 61 (1968) 567-81; idem, *Die Biographie der Propheten* (Neukirchen-Vluyn: Neukirchener Verlag, 1975); **J. Blenkinsopp,** *A History of Prophecy in Israel* (Philadelphia: Westminster, 1983); **J. Calvin,** *Commentary on the Book of the Prophet Jeremiah and Lamentations* (trans. J. Owen; Grand Rapids: Eerdmans 1950); **B. S. Childs,** *The Book of Exodus: A Critical, Theological Commentary* (OTL; Philadelphia: Westminster, 1974); **K. Gouders,** *Die prophetischen Berufungsberichte Moses, Isaias, Jeremias und Ezechiel: Auslegung, Form- und Gattungsgeschichte, zu einer Theologie der Berufung* (Bonn: Rheinische Friedrich-Wilhelms-Universität, 1971); **M. Greenberg,** *Ezekiel 1-20* (AB 22; Garden City, NY: Doubleday, 1983); **H. Gunkel,** introduction to *Die grossen Propheten,* by H. Schmidt (Göttingen: Vandenhoeck & Ruprecht, 1915) ix-lxx; idem, *Die Propheten* (Göttingen: Vandenhoeck & Ruprecht, 1917); **N. C. Habel,** "The Form and Significance of Call Narratives," *ZAW* 77 (1965) 297-323; **W. L. Holladay,** *Jeremiah 1: A Commentary on the Book of the Prophet Jeremiah Chapters 1-25* (Hermeneia; Philadelphia: Fortress, 1986); **K. Jeppesen,** "Call and Frustration: A New Understanding of Isaiah 7:21-22," *VT* 22 (1982) 145-57; **R. Kilian,** "Die Prophetischen Berufungsberichte," in *Theologie im Wandel: Festschrift zum 150-jährigen Bestehen der Katholisch-Theologischen Fakultät an der Universität Tübingen, 1817-1967* (TTR 1; Munich: Wewel, 1967) 356-76; **E. Kutsch,** "Gideons Berufung und Altarbau Jdc 6,11-24." *TLZ* 81 (1956) 75-84; **B. O. Long,** "Prophetic Authority as Social Reality," in *Canon and Authority: Essays in Old Testament Religion and Theology,* ed. B. Long and G. Coates (Philadelphia: Fortress, 1977) 3-20; **D. N. Phinney,** "The Prophetic Objection in Ezekiel 4:14 and Its Relation to Ezekiel's Call," *VT* 55 (2005) 75-88; **H. Reventlow,** *Liturgie und prophetisches Ich bei Jeremia* (Gütersloh: Mohn, 1963); **W. Richter,** *Die sogeannten vorprophetischen Berufungsberichte: Eine literaturewissenschaftliche Studie zu 1 Sam 9,1-10, 16, Ex 3f. und Ri 6,11b-17* (FRLANT 101; Göttingen: Vandenhoeck & Ruprecht, 1970); **J. Robson,** *Word and Spirit in Ezekiel* (LHBOTS

447; New York: T & T Clark, 2006); **D. Rudman,** "Is the Rabshakeh Also Among the Prophets? A Rhetorical Study of 2 Kings XVIII 17-35," *VT* 50 (2000) 100-110; **H. Schmidt,** *Die grossen Propheten* (Göttingen: Vandenhoeck & Ruprecht, 1915); **H.-C. Schmitt,** "Das sogenannte vorprophetische Berufungsschema: Zur 'geistigen Heimat' des Berufungsformulars von Ex 3,9-12; Jdc 6,11 und 1 Sam 9,1-10,16," *ZAW* 104 (1992) 202-15; **C. Seitz,** *Isaiah 1-39* (IBC; Louisville: John Knox, 1993); **C. J. Sharp,** "The Call of Jeremiah and Diaspora Politics," *JBL* 119 (2000) 421-38; **M. A. Sweeney,** *Isaiah 1-39: With an Introduction to Prophetic Literature* (FOTL 16; Grand Rapids, Eerdmans, 1996); **M. A. Sweeney and E. Ben Zvi,** eds., *The Changing Face of Form Criticism for the Twenty-First Century* (Grand Rapids: Eerdmans, 2003); **G. von Rad,** *Old Testament Theology* (trans D. Stalker; 2 vols.; Louisville: Westminster/John Knox, 1965); **R. R. Wilson,** "Prophecy in Crisis: The Call of Ezekiel," *Int* 38 (1984) 117-30; **H. W. Wolff,** *Hosea* (trans. G. Stansell; Hermeneia; Philadelphia: Fortress, 1978); **W. Zimmerli,** *Ezekiel 1: A Commentary on the Book of the Prophet Ezekiel Chapters 1-24* (trans. R. Clements; Hermeneia; Philadelphia: Fortress, 1979). D. N. Phinney

CANON, CANONIZATION

When the word *canonization* is used in common parlance, people often have in mind ecclesiastical bodies that made unilateral decisions about whether books should be included or excluded from a divinely inspired collection of books. Unfortunately, the evidence for such councils is meager in the ancient world, especially with reference to the OT. Even the terms *canon* and *canonization* used in reference to authoritative collections of books were coined long after the biblical period. Athanasius, in his Thirty-Ninth Festal Letter, is the first to use the terms to signify an explicit list of divinely authoritative books (AD 350). This has not deterred scholars from searching for such evidence, but nonetheless it is clear that the canonization process is mysteriously obscured, perhaps intentionally to emphasize the sacred authority of the documents themselves.

1. Terminology
2. Internal Evidence
3. External Evidence
4. Jewish and Christian Canonical
   Traditions

1. Terminology.

When dealing with the canonization of the prophets, it is important to clarify terms. In the Jewish tradition the "Former Prophets" refers to the historical books of Joshua, Judges, Samuel and Kings, which are matched with the "Latter Prophets," referring to the writing prophets Isaiah, Jeremiah, Ezekiel (the Major Prophets) and the *Twelve (the Minor Prophets). For the purposes of this article, the major focus will be on the canonization of the writing prophets.

2. Internal Evidence.

Even though the terms *canon* and *canonization* came into specific usage later to describe a divinely authoritative collection of books, the concept of such a list was present at a much earlier time. In fact, the inscribing of the Ten Commandments at Sinai is probably the first seminal canon in ancient Israel. Moses, viewed as the ultimate prophet in Israel (Ex 34:5-7; Num 12:6-8; Deut 34:10-12), was the person to whom the first canonical text—the ten words inscribed by the finger of God—was entrusted to be placed at the very center of community life as the will of God for the entire nation, both present and future (Ex 25:22; Deut 10:5). In fact, further divine revelations to the community came through Moses, and a prophetic institution was established as a successor to Moses so that the role of Sinai as the decisive revelation of the divine will was continued in Israel. One might even say that prophetic succession "institutionalized" or "contemporized" Sinai (Deut 18:15-22).

In stories about the prophets and in their sayings the focus is on their speech, which is viewed as divinely authoritative. The prophets are seen as visionaries and as messengers. Indeed, one of the hallmarks of prophecy is the introduction of their speech with the words "Thus says Yahweh." Young Samuel is one whose words do not fail to be fulfilled (1 Sam 3:19). A dead prophet's bones resurrect a corpse (2 Kings 13:20-21). A prophet's words resurrect a dead nation (Ezek 37:1-14). Prophetic words have power and authority; they are like a fire, a hammer that shatters rock (Jer 23:29), making the prophet trembling and drunk (Jer 23:9) and inspiring him with dread and fear before an awesome God (Amos 3:8). These words are not mere information;

rather, they "pluck up and tear down, build and plant" (Jer 1:10) and accomplish what the divine will intends (Is 55:11). That there would be an interest in inscribing the prophets' words and preserving them for future generations seems a logical step.

The first evidence of such activity is found in Isaiah, when the prophet is urged in a particularly dark period to ensure that his prophetic words will be preserved for a future generation as a witness of their truth ("Bind up the message and seal the instruction with my disciples" [Is 8:16]). Meanwhile, the prophet and his disciples are to wait patiently for the Lord to act. Later, the prophet is urged to write down a prophecy on a tablet so that the people might have it in future days "as a witness forever" (Is 30:8) (*see* Writing and Prophecy). It probably was such early texts that became the nucleus of the later book of Isaiah. Similarly, later, during Jeremiah's time, the prophet is urged to produce a scroll that contained all his prophecies and to read them to the people at worship in the *temple. The comprehensive nature of the prophecies read out to the people at one time was intended to produce *repentance and renewed commitment to God (Jer 36:1-3). The divine word on a scroll becomes separate from its human author and takes on a life of its own as the word of God. This is demonstrated in one particular example when Ezekiel is called to be a prophet during the *exile (Ezek 2:8—3:4). In a *vision, God hands him a scroll filled with the divine word for him to ingest. Here the scroll exists before the prophet has even spoken its words or his scribe had written down the words.

Moses, as the supreme prophet, came to be associated with the Torah, the first five books of the OT, in particular the last book of Deuteronomy. From early times these books, especially Deuteronomy, were regarded as the divine revelation for all generations of Israelites. When the book of Deuteronomy fell into disuse, was lost and was later recovered, its divine authority was recognized by Josiah and his courtiers, who tore their garments after hearing its words read to them, having been convicted of their nation's idolatrous ways (2 Kings 22). This text of the Torah became the basis of a renewed *covenant between the people and God and inspired a radical religious and social revolution. The divine authority of the Torah

was powerfully demonstrated. But what is important for prophecy in particular is that nearly a generation later, the same divine authority was shown for a prophetic scroll. In a text already mentioned, Jeremiah the prophet was told to make a scroll of his prophecies and read them to the people in order to produce the same effect that the Torah scroll had on an earlier generation, but the representative of the new generation, King Josiah's son, would have nothing to do with any reform (Jer 36). Instead of ripping up his garments, he tore apart the prophetic scroll and threw it into a fire in what may have been the first book-burning incident in recorded history. The moral difference between the two kings, father and son, could not have been greater. But the important point for canonization is that the prophetic text should have registered the same impact as the Torah text. Both texts thus had "canonical" authority prior to the exile of Judah. Almost in passing, it is mentioned in Jeremiah that the destroyed prophetic scroll was reproduced, with more prophecies added (Jer 36:32). This shows in some ways the indestructible character of the prophetic word. It emerged from the fire to do its own work in history.

The prophetic charism naturally led to the words of the prophet being transcribed not only as a witness to the truth of the prophecies to later generations but also as a word that transcended its first temporal historical context. Prophecy in the nature of the case represented divine revelation, and when transferred to a textual medium, it carried all the theological freight of divine authority now made permanent and transcending its original historical context. It thus had a prima facie case for canonicity. In fact, the final edition of the prophetic writings in the HB reflect this divine authority. In each of the major prophecies of Isaiah, Jeremiah and Ezekiel prominence is given to a divine call in which is emphasized the role of the prophet as a mediator of the divine will (Is 6; Jer 1; Ezek 1—3). All previous social relationships fall into the background before this new communicative task. The divine words placed in the prophetic mouth are especially conspicuous, and by the time of Ezekiel, as already mentioned, a prophetic scroll that the prophet must ingest is dramatically in focus.

When the prophetic scrolls were finally produced, the evidence suggests that their final editors saw them as having "canonical authority." The titles of their works stressed the importance of prophetic authority, divine authority communicated with specific prophetic terminology ("saw," "vision," "word of the LORD," "oracle") and generally in a historical context (during the reign of certain kings). This common terminology suggests that the prophetic scrolls were viewed as part of a collection that obviously was authoritative (Is 1:1; Jer 1:1-4; Ezek. 1:1-3; Hos 1:1; Joel 1:1; Amos 1:1; Obad 1; Jon 1:1; Mic 1:1; Nah 1:1; Hab 1:1; Zeph 1:1; Hag 1:1; Zech 1:1; Mal. 1:1).

Despite the various differences among them, there is a consistent claim to divine authority using technical terms for divine revelation. Thus, although the words are dated to a particular time and to a particular person, the person is important only inasmuch as he is a vehicle for the divine word. For example, the words of Amos are important because they are the words of God. Sometimes, particular effort is made to validate the prophetic authority, as in the dating of the prophecies, occasionally even in specific terms (e.g., "two years before the earthquake" [Amos 1:1b]). The preservation, editing and transmission of these oracles demonstrate the sacred authority of these writings and their relevance for future generations.

The use of the oracles of earlier prophets in later times shows their divine authority. For example, Micah's electrifying words to a complacent audience in Jerusalem that the temple would be destroyed and the holy city decimated are remembered a century later in Jeremiah's time, when the earlier prophecy is cited virtually verbatim (Mic 3:12; Jer 26:18). One of the later prophets, Zechariah, prophesying in the exile, clearly refers to the divine authority of earlier prophetic words. The prophets who spoke them have been long since dead, but the words that they spoke have been alive and well, bringing about judgment (Zech 1:1-6; 7:7-14). This shows clearly that in Zechariah's time the words of earlier prophets have been remembered and preserved. In the later section of Zechariah (Zech 9—14) there is much dependence on early prophetic texts, which shows their authority (cf., e.g., Zech 14:2-3 with Ezek 38—39; Zech 14:5 with Amos 1:2; Zech 14:8 with Ezek 47; Zech 14:10 with Is 2:1-5).

In particular, the writing of the revelations

of the so-called Minor Prophets on one scroll, which later became known as The Twelve, whose *terminus ad quem* would have been the early postexilic period, suggests the time when these writings were integrated into a collection with the Torah. From details such as these, D. N. Freedman argues that the Prophets were canonized during this period.

Finally, there is some evidence that suggests that canonical tradents or editors may have "stamped" these documents with a canonical "imprimatur." At the end of the Torah there is an extraordinary emphasis on Moses as the prophet par excellence, and at the end of the Prophets in certain early orderings there is an extraordinary emphasis on both Moses as the representative of the Torah and Elijah as the representative of the Prophets, suggesting that these two complexes of literature have been integrated into a whole, the Law and the Prophets, and are to be read in harmony, not in dissonance (cf. Deut 34:10-12; Mal 4:4-6). Both texts may also suggest that the age of prophetic revelation has come to an end, and that the important task is to study and observe and wait in anticipation of a future great prophetic revelation that would coincide with the appearance of Elijah, the prophet most like Moses in the OT.

3. External Evidence.

3.1. The End of Prophetic Inspiration. It is clear that after the postexilic period there was a growing awareness in some broad streams of Judaism that the age of canonical prophecy had ceased. In a number of texts that specifically deal with divine authority and sacred writings the term *prophet* is conspicuous. Josephus writes about a closed corpus of divinely inspired scriptures that is divided into three categories: law, prophets, and hymns and other books (Josephus, *Ag. Ap.*1.37-42). This corpus consists of five books of the law, thirteen books of prophets and four of a nonprophetic genre. Based on Josephus's use of Scripture in his works, it is probable that all the traditional prophetic books would have been included in the second division, plus other historical books that would have been regarded as being written under prophetic inspiration. Josephus is absolutely clear that the age of canonical revelation ceased with the last of the biblical prophets during the Persian period.

The belief that it was particularly prophetic

inspiration that produced Scripture is also attested in the NT when the entire OT revelation can be termed "all that the prophets spoke" (Lk 24:25). Similarly, the second-century AD apocryphal work *Gospel of Thomas* can describe the OT simply as the collection of "the twenty-four prophets" (*Gos. Thom.* 52). The number "twenty-four" referred to the complete number of books in the Hebrew Bible.

Josephus and other writers probably believed that prophetic inspiration could still sporadically occur, but that canonical prophets such as Isaiah, Ezekiel, Jeremiah and the Twelve were in a different category altogether. The prophetic cessation of these types of prophets is seen in a number of statements like this one from 1 Maccabees: "So they tore down the altar and stored the stones in a convenient place on the temple hill until there should come a prophet to tell what to do with them" (1 Macc 4:45b-46 [cf. 1 Macc 9:27; 14:41]). It is perhaps possible to understand these statements in a way that does not reflect the absence of the activity of prophecy, but it is certainly not a natural reading of these texts.

Signs of this belief can be seen among the rabbis of the Mishnah, where the prophets are regarded as preceding the rabbis (*m. ʾAbot* 1:1; cf. *m. Peʾah* 2:6). A reference in the Tosefta makes explicit this understanding: "When the latter prophets died, that is, Haggai, Zechariah, and Malachi, then the Holy Spirit came to an end in Israel. But even then they made them hear through an echo" (*t. Soṭah* 13:3 A, B). Other examples from rabbinic sources describe the cessation of a prophetic age: "Until then, the prophets prophesied by means of the holy spirit. From then on, give ear and listen to the words of the sages" (*S. ʿOlam Rab.* 30 [cf. *2 Bar.* 85:3; *b. Soṭah* 48b; *b. Sanh.* 11a]).

Another clear indication of the prevalence of a belief in the end of a prophetic epoch is the proliferation of pseudepigrapha. There is a virtual myriad of books written under pseudonyms, such as *Apocalypse of Adam, Apocalypse of Abraham, Apocalypse of Elijah, 1-3 Enoch, Testament of Moses, 4 Ezra, Joseph and Aseneth, Testaments of the Twelve Patriarchs*. The most reasonable explanation of the use of pseudonyms is to secure "canonical authority" for the literature by dating it to a period during the exact succession of the prophets.

But this idea of a long-lost prophetic age is also shown by important devout works that were not written pseudonymously but nonetheless lacked the important qualification. A statement in the Tosefta reads, "The books of Ben Sira and all books written thenceforward do not impart uncleanness to hands" (*t. Yad.* 2:13b). All of these texts suggest that a canonical epoch has come to an end, and literature written after this canonical epoch was not written by canonical prophets and therefore could not be part of the canon of Scripture. The assumption is that the prophetic books have long been canonized.

Among rabbinic traditions there is mention of the need by some rabbis "to store away Ezekiel." This was a serious concern because that meant that the book's canonical status was in doubt as it was to be removed from daily use and caused to perish, even though it might still be respected. In the Talmud there is mention of a famous rabbi who burned three hundred barrels of late-night oil successfully reconciling the contradictions between Ezekiel's vision of the temple and the Torah's vision of the tabernacle (*b. Šabb.* 13b). However, the problems that harmonization presented showed that the book itself was already considered canonical. Another rabbinic tradition suggests that to remove Ezekiel probably meant "to remove it from liturgical use." The story was told of a child who was reading the first chapter probably flippantly, and the fire from the heavenly vision leapt from the page and consumed him (*b. Ḥag.* 13a). Evidently, the desire for removal stemmed from a desire to avoid the danger of profanization or blasphemy. But the book's canonization was never in doubt.

Other traditions seem to confirm this. In the Mishnah (*m. Meg.* 4:10; *m. Ḥag.* 2:1) there is a note that the chariot vision should not be read by someone who is not a sage. Jerome makes reference to the following Jewish tradition: "The beginning and ending of Ezekiel, the third of the four, are involved in so great obscurity that like the commencement of Genesis they are not studied by the Hebrews until they are thirty years old" (*Epist.* 53).

3.2. The Identity of the Prophets. The book of Sirach shows clearly that by 180 BC at the latest all of the prophets were considered in the biblical canon. First, Ben Sira reflects on the biblical heritage of Jews and their biblical role models in the section commonly referred to as "In Praise of the Fathers" (Sir 44—49). He begins by providing an impressive list of heroes who are virtually household names to his audience, beginning with Adam and ending with Nehemiah. The prophets are mentioned in particular: "But they called upon the Lord, who is merciful, and stretched out their hands toward him; and immediately the Holy One heard them out of heaven, and delivered them by the ministry of Isaiah"; "They burnt the chosen city of the sanctuary, and made the streets desolate, according to the prophecy of Jeremiah"; "It was Ezekiel who saw the glorious vision, which was showed him upon the chariot of the cherubim"; "And of the twelve prophets let the memorial be blessed, and let their bones flourish again out of their place, for they comforted the people of Jacob, and delivered them by assured hope" (Sir 48:20; 49:6, 8, 10). Here it is significant that the twelve Minor Prophets are viewed as a "booked entity," placed at the end of a prophetic collection, which is preceded by the sequence of Isaiah, Jeremiah and Ezekiel.

Second, there is a direct quotation from the ending of the book of Malachi, the last prophet of the Twelve, regarding the coming of Elijah, who would "turn the heart of the father unto the son, and to restore the tribes of Jacob" (Sir 48:10). This shows that the final words of the book of the twelve Minor Prophets were there, indicating a completed collection.

Two generations later, when Ben Sira's grandson wished to translate his grandfather's book into Greek, he indicated twice that his grandfather's book was essentially an attempt to make relevant an authoritative body of literature named "the law, the prophets and the other books." He also stressed that the translation of his father's book into Greek would inevitably result in loss of the original meaning, just as was true when the Bible—the law, the prophecies and the rest of the books—was translated into Greek. Not only can a major division of the Bible be called "the prophets" or "the prophecies," but also it is apparent that these prophets have been translated into Greek by the LXX translators, since the Greek translation of Sirach was heavily indebted to the LXX.

Around the same time as Ben Sira (180 BC), the book of Tobit mentions several prophets in particular (Amos [Tob 2:6], Nahum [Tob 14:4, Codex Sinaiticus], Jonah [Tob 14:4, Codices Vaticanus and Alexandrinus]) but also speaks of the prophets as a collective entity. The dying Tobit's last words contain advice for Tobiah to flee Nineveh, where the coming judgment announced by a prophet will soon occur. But beyond the judgment there is hope, as God will restore his people once again, and the temple will be rebuilt "just as the prophets of Israel spoke" (Tob 14:5). The prophets probably are viewed together as a collective entity.

Throughout literature written during the late pre-Christian period, the prophets are so significant that they constitute part of the title for the Hebrew Bible. Thus, the biblical corpus is most frequently called "the law and the prophets." This title or a variant is found not only in the prologue to Sirach but also in the following works. In 2 Maccabees, before a major battle Judas comforts his soldiers from "the law and prophets" (2 Macc 15:9). In 4 Maccabees the writer encourages his audience with the example of the father of the famous martyrs who taught his children from "the law and the prophets" (4 Macc 18:10). At Qumran, not only were all the prophetic books used, particularly Isaiah, but also commentaries were written on some of them, and the entire scriptural corpus was named variously "books of the law . . . and the words of the prophets" (CD-A VII, 15-17) or "Moses and the prophets" (1QS I, 1-3) or the "book of Moses [and] the book[s of the pr]ophets and Davi[d]' (4Q397 14-21, 10) (see Dead Sea Scrolls). Similar titular formulae were used in the NT, with fourteen references to "the law and the prophets" (e.g., Mt 5:17; 7:12; 22:40; Lk 16:16; Jn 1:45; Acts 13:15; 24:14; Rom 3:21). Although Philo makes little reference to the prophetic writings, he does refer to an ascetic group that regularly studied a corpus of literature called "laws, oracles delivered by prophets, psalms and anything else that fostered piety" (*Contemp.* 25).

This common nomenclature for the Hebrew canon shows how significant the term *prophets* was. Clearly, there were nonprophetic books included in this category as some texts indicate, but they could be grouped together with the prophetic writings under their name.

4. Jewish and Christian Canonical Traditions.

The prophets are confined to the second division of the Hebrew Bible, with the earliest attested order based on chronology: Isaiah, Jeremiah, Ezekiel, the Twelve (Sirach). This chronological order is preserved in Jerome and is dominant in the Hebrew manuscript tradition of the Middle Ages, beginning with the Cairo Codex (AD 896) and the Aleppo Codex (AD 925).

However, a literary order is found in an early text (AD 125-150): Jeremiah, Ezekiel, Isaiah, the Twelve (*b. B. Bat.* 14b). This may be based on the decreasing size of the books, but the rabbis gave theological reasons for this order. The four literary prophets are paired with four former prophets: Joshua, Judges, Samuel, Kings. And since Kings ends on a note of judgment and Jeremiah begins on such a note, it was thought fitting to keep them together, with the remaining books producing a momentum of hope: "Let us see again. Isaiah was prior to Jeremiah and Ezekiel. Then why should not Isaiah be placed first? — Because the Book of Kings ends with a record of destruction and Jeremiah speaks throughout of destruction and Ezekiel commences with destruction and ends with consolation and Isaiah is full of consolation; therefore we put destruction next to destruction and consolation next to consolation" (*b. B. Bat.* 14b). In the later Hebrew tradition, this sequence is reflected in a series of manuscripts dated to the twelfth century AD and later, but it is not nearly as common. There is also evidence of a third sequence, reflected in a few manuscripts beginning in the twelfth century AD: Jeremiah, Isaiah, Ezekiel, the Twelve.

One important feature of the above Jewish tradition, however, is the exclusion of *Daniel from the prophetic books. It is placed uniformly in the third division of the canon, the Writings. The traditional explanation for its exclusion from the prophetic division is that it was not written until much later (165 BC), and since the prophetic division was already closed, it had to be relegated to the third division of the canon, which was not closed until the end of the first century AD. For two reasons, this view is no longer tenable. First, it cannot be determined that the third division was closed until a later time. Second, there was a tradition that Daniel was a wisdom book, and that he was an interpreter of dreams, to be distinguished from a "prophet" or "seer," titles for prophets that never were used to describe him.

However, there is another ancient Jewish tradition reflected in Josephus in which Daniel was regarded as part of the Prophets. This tradition is preserved in Christian lists beginning with Melito (AD 170), where the sequence near the end of his list is Isaiah, Jeremiah, the Twelve, Daniel, Ezekiel (Eusebius, *Hist. eccl.* 4.26.13–14). A similar order is attested by Origen (Eusebius, *Hist. eccl.* 6.25). But by far the more common order among the early Christian Greek lists is as follows: the Twelve, Isaiah, Jeremiah, Ezekiel, Daniel. Another feature of these lists is the tendency of these literary prophets to migrate toward the end of the OT. This escalates their eschatological function in anticipating and preparing the way for the coming of the Messiah as announced in the NT, but it is impossible to say whether this is a distinct Christian contribution or another pre-Christian Jewish order that early Christians adopted and adapted. At any rate, by a later period the prophets are uniformly placed at the end of the OT, and the sequence of Isaiah, Jeremiah, Lamentations, Ezekiel, Daniel and the twelve Minor Prophets has become fixed in the Christian OT. The influence of the LXX, in which Jeremiah is regarded as the author of Lamentations, has attracted the latter to Jeremiah.

See also CANONICAL CRITICISM; FORMATION OF THE PROPHETIC BOOKS; TWELVE, BOOK OF THE; WRITING AND PROPHECY.

BIBLIOGRAPHY. **D. E. Aune,** *Prophecy in Early Christianity and the Ancient Mediterranean World* (Grand Rapids: Eerdmans, 1983) 103-4; **J. Barton,** *Oracles of God: Perceptions of Ancient Prophecy in Israel after the Exile* (New York: Oxford University Press, 2007); **R. Beckwith,** *The Old Testament of the New Testament Church* (Grand Rapids: Eerdmans, 1985); **J. Blenkinsopp,** *Prophecy and Canon: A Contribution to the Study of Jewish Origins* (Notre Dame, IN: Notre Dame University Press, 1977); **P. Brandt,** *Endgestalten des Kanons: Das Arrangement der Schriften Israels in der jüdischen und christlichen Bibel* (BBB 131; Berlin: Philo, 2001); **S. Chapman,** *The Law and Prophets: A Study in Old Testament Canon Formation* (FAT 27; Tübingen: Mohr Siebeck, 2007); **J. H. Charlesworth,** *The Old Testament Pseudepigrapha,* 1: *Apocalyptic Literature and Testaments* (New York: Doubleday, 1983); **B. S. Childs,** *Introduction to the Old Testament as Scripture* (Philadelphia: Fortress, 1979); **S. G. Dempster,** "From Many Texts to One: The Formation of the Hebrew Bible," in *The World of the Aramaeans,* 1: *Biblical Studies in Honour of Paul-Eugène Dion,* ed. P. M. Michèle Daviau, J. W. Wevers and M. Weigl

(JSOTSup 324; Sheffield: Sheffield Academic, 2000) 19-56; idem, "The Prophets, the Canon and the Canonical Approach: No Empty Word," in *Canon and Biblical Interpretation*, ed. C. G. Bartholomew et al. (SHS 7; Grand Rapids: Zondervan, 2007) 293-329; **D. N. Freedman,** "The Law and the Prophets," in *Congress Volume: Bonn, 1962* (VTSup 9; Leiden: E. J. Brill, 1963) 250-65; **M. G. Kline,** "The Correlation of the Concepts of Canon and Covenant," in *New Perspectives on the Old Testament*, ed. J. B. Payne (Waco, TX: Word, 1970) 265-79; **S. Z. Leiman,** *The Canonization of Hebrew Scripture: The Talmudic and Midrashic Evidence* (2nd ed.; New Haven: Connecticut Academy of Arts and Sciences, 1991); **L. M. McDonald,** *The Formation of the Christian Biblical Canon* (rev. ed.; Peabody, MA: Hendrickson, 1995); idem, *The Biblical Canon: Its Origin, Transmission, and Authority* (3rd ed.; Peabody, MA: Hendrickson, 2007); **L. M. McDonald and J. A. Sanders,** eds., *The Canon Debate* (Peabody, MA: Hendrickson, 2002); **S. A. Meier,** *Themes and Transformations in Old Testament Prophecy* (Downers Grove, IL: InterVarsity Press, 2009); **J. Sailhamer,** *Introduction to Old Testament Theology: A Canonical Approach* (Grand Rapids: Zondervan, 1995); **O. H. Steck,** "Der Kanon des hebräischen Altens Testaments: Historische Materialen für eine ökumenische Perspektive," in *Vernunft des Glaubens: Wissenschaftliche Theologie und kirchliche Lehre; Festschrift zum 60. Geburtstag von Wolfhart Pannenberg,* ed. J. Rohls and G. Wenz (Gottingen: Vandenhoeck & Ruprecht, 1988) 231-52; **A. C. Sundberg Jr.,** "'The Old Testament of the Early Church' Revisited," in *Festschrift in Honor of Charles Speel*, ed. T. J. Sienkewicz and J. E. Betts (Monmouth, IL: Monmouth College, 1996) 88-110; **G. Tucker,** "Prophetic Superscriptions and the Growth of the Canon," in *Canon and Authority: Essays in Old Testament Religion and Theology*, ed. G. W. Coats and B. O. Long (Philadelphia: Fortress, 1977) 56-70.   S. G. Dempster

CANONICAL CRITICISM

The term *canonical criticism* denotes a family of modern biblical interpretive methods and approaches that advocate attention to the final shape and/or shaping of the canon as a remedy to the crisis in biblical theology occasioned by the distancing between historical analysis and theological reflection. To understand why its proponents defend it as the most comprehen- sive in the academy (Seitz) requires an understanding of the work of Brevard S. Childs, whose diagnosis of this crisis (Childs 1970) led to his formulation of a canonical approach (Childs 1979), and of James A. Sanders, who coined the term *canonical criticism* (Sanders 1972; 1987).

1. The Work of James A. Sanders and Brevard S. Childs
2. The Prophetic Canon
3. The Law and the Prophets
4. The Prophetic Corpus in the Masoretic Text, the Septuagint and the Christian Canon
5. The Canon, Liturgy and Mystagogy
6. Conclusion

1. The Work of James A. Sanders and Brevard S. Childs.

1.1. James A. Sanders. Sanders, a pioneer of research on ancient canons, advocates canonical criticism as a corrective to post-Enlightenment scholarship's decanonizing of Scripture. This scholarship, he argued, liberated the Bible from the pulpit but chained it to the scholar's desk. Nonetheless, as biblical scholars eventually showed the biblical texts to have originated in faith-filled study and worship, clarification of these origins required refocusing biblical interpretation around two foci: canonical process and canonical *hermeneutics.

Canonical process denotes how the canon in all its multiplicity was shaped. Since the meaning given to the whole transcends combinations of its precursors, the forces that shaped the whole must be ferreted out by canonical hermeneutics: biblical thinkers depolytheized what they learned from others, monotheized it, Yahw(eh)ized and then Israelitized it. Monotheizing nurtures the ability to affirm God as the God of death as well as of life (1 Sam 2:6), to suffer defeat, and to see God's bias for the weak, as illustrated by prophetic narratives (e.g., 1 Kings 17—19). The canon shifts the reader's focus from human-centered moralism to God-centered theology. To moralize is to focus on the self. To theologize is to focus on what God does with the sinful likes of the reader mirrored in the text. If one has to moralize, one ought to imitate God not as redeemer of one's privileged group, but rather as creator of all, and this is the mark of true as opposed to false prophets (Sanders 1977; 1987, 101, 188).

1.2. Brevard S. Childs. Childs typically begins commenting on a text by reviewing what historical-critical methodologies reveal about its historical and literary layers, and then he shows how these methodologies fail to account for the text's final shape. Since the axiom of historical-critical scholarship of prophetic literature impels its proponents to reconstruct and prioritize the original words and/or figures of the prophets, they invariably devalue whatever is secondary as homily or theology. Repudiating this axiom as uncritical, Childs advocates the final text as what its tradents intended to transmit as Scripture for future readers. Childs elucidated the many ways in which they did this for the prophetic corpus (Childs 1979). These he summarized (Childs 1978) as follows.

The original prophetic message was integrated into a larger framework that either transcends the historical doom-laden perspective of the prophet and offers hope beyond destruction, as illustrated by Amos 9:8b-15, or interprets the original message metaphorically to refer it to a different audience, as illustrated by the reconfiguration of Hosea's sign acts condemning northern Israel's adulterous *worship of Baal to condemn southern Judea's idolatrous practices as religious adultery. Rather than weakening the original messages of judgment, the prophetic oracles may either be placed within interpretive rules of faith that serve to remind the people that they stand under Moses' law, as illustrated by Malachi and its appendices, or arranged around dominant motifs illustrating the pattern or typology of God's coming rule, as exemplified by Isaiah's and Micah's oracles of judgment and salvation. Collections of original oracles may also be either cloaked in the language of a larger body of canonical literature to present their authors as divinely sent Mosaic followers, as done for Jeremiah by Deuteronomy, or detached from their original historical context, subordinated to a new one, and dehistoricized in the process to make the book as a whole address all later generations, as is the case with Deutero- and Proto-Isaiah. Alternatively, the historical oracles could be preserved but given eschatological focus by reordering and framing, as done by introducing and concluding Nahum and Habakkuk, respectively, with a hymn. Ezekiel illustrates that such refocusing is unnecessary where the eschatological framework is original.

Nonetheless, symbolic oracles may be given radically new eschatological interpretations by shifting the referent within the original oracles to a still future event, as illustrated by Zechariah's *visions and language in which references to the return from the *exile as a second exodus are reeschatologized and projected into a still future escape and redemption.

Throughout his analysis, Childs reiterates that the exegete must struggle to discern the authoritative final shape of the canon and appreciate that it derives from Israel's participation in the transmission of the divinely inspired prophetic word—that is, in tradition. To ignore this and concentrate on hypothetical reconstructions of original words, figures and events is to obscure how prophecy works and why the prophetic corpus was received by the NT.

1.3. Sanders and Childs Compared. Both Sanders and Childs focus on the canon as a corrective to post-Enlightenment decanonization of Scripture. This commonality exposes them to the anxiety that they subordinate scholarship to confessional norms. In facing this criticism, Sanders concludes that since most biblical scholars are religious, they would be more scientific by admitting instead of hiding the role of religious norms in their work. This response shields Sanders from the charge of relativism. The same obtains for his fourfold canonical hermeneutics, which, despite its left leanings, aims to establish norms for biblical interpretation. His commitments to the canonical process allow him to value all past and present canons and traditions of interpretation but, by the same token, preclude him from granting definitive authoritative status to a single final text. He judges such granting to be one of Childs's key faults (Sanders 1987, 167-69).

The fundamental difference between the two scholars is that while Sanders sees his "canonical criticism" to be in continuity with historical-critical methodology, Childs stresses the discontinuity between the latter and his "canonical approach." The gap between the two revolves around Childs's notion that the tradents of prophetic texts obscured their traces and switched the text's historical referents. This gap in turn makes many historical-critics and religious conservatives worry that he bypasses questions about Scripture's historical validation (Barr). Scholars who may yet agree with the notion that the tradents obscured their traces and switched the text's historical referents might nonetheless charge Childs with failure to explain these phenomena by reference to politics or ideology. The obscuration could, for example, be referred to the wish of the priestly and scribal representatives of the law to subordinate and domesticate the law (Blenkinsopp) or, conversely, to an attempt by the representatives of the prophets to keep the law alive and free of distortion (Brueggemann). The difference between these positions and that of Childs lies in their focal points: the former focus on history, ideology and transformation of tradition; Childs focuses on the final text (see Seitz).

2. The Prophetic Canon.

Childs noted textual linkages between prophetic books, as between Nahum and Habakkuk, and Isaiah and Micah, but his reflection on the manuscript variations of the order in these books led him to focus on the individual books and dismiss their order's significance (Childs 1979, 309-10, 434, 454). The significance of the canonical shape(s) of the prophetic corpus, especially that of the *Twelve, has, nonetheless, become a topic of interest.

A variety of literary devices has been discerned to integrate the Prophets so as to adapt their words to later audiences (see Watts and House; Nogalski and Sweeney). Textual allusions link Malachi 3:22 (the end of the Latter Prophets in the Jewish MT tradition) to Joshua 1:2, 7 (the beginning of the Former Prophets in the Jewish tradition), Zechariah 14 to Isaiah 2 and Isaiah 66 (the beginning and the end of the first book of the Latter Prophets), and Zechariah 13:9 to Hosea 2:25 and Malachi 3:3 (the beginning and the end of the Twelve in both the LXX and the MT (Nogalski 1996). Turning to the MT version of the Twelve, one may note that Hosea introduces the theme of God's patience by *intertextual links in the names of his children ("Not My People," "No Compassion") to the foundational account of Moses and God at Sinai after the incident of the golden calf and their dialogue about whose people the murmuring Israelites are and on the nature of divine compassion (Ex 33—40) (Seitz, 234). Hosea then ends with a call to repentance with which the next book, Joel, begins. Joel ends with a pronouncement of judgment against the nations, which theme is then taken up by Amos. Since Joel precedes Amos in the HB, the citation of Joel 4:16 (ET 3:16), "The LORD roars from Zion," at Amos 1:2 broadens Amos's oracle into one of universal divine judgment. The citation of the first two imperatives of Hosea 4:15 in Amos 4:4, but focusing Hosea's words on the sins of Judah, serves to prevent Judean readers from understanding Hosea's message to have been addressed only to Israel (Jeremias). The reversal in Joel 4:10 (ET 3:10) of the well-known pacific prophecy of Isaiah 2:4 // Micah 4:3 ("they shall beat their swords into plowshares") precludes mechanical readings. This, then, is the burden of the permutation of the divine formula at Exodus 34:6-7 regarding the dialectic between divine wrath and mercy, which links the "who knows whether . . . ?" of Joel 2:12-14 and Jonah 3:9, and the doxology of Micah 7:18-20, which concludes the first half of the Twelve in the MT. Given that the formula belongs to the context of Moses' intercession at Exodus 34, the recurrent and central use of this formula suggests an overarching theology of divine judgment on both the north and the south that sought (1) to affirm that God, while not being held hostage to evil, was free to forgive any who repent, and (2) to call the wise to know God's ways in preparing for the coming great *Day of the Lord (Seitz, 209). Since Joel's images of fertility, plague, drought and locust attack continue to be reinterpreted in the Twelve, interest has peaked in ascertaining how Joel, with its distinct position in the LXX and the MT, may help to identify the transcended "historical" paradigm that shaped and defined the overall outlook of each version of the Twelve (Nogalski 2000; Sweeney 2005, 189-209). The Twelve conclude with Malachi. Malachi's opposition to divorce and insistence on the covenant echo Hosea's use of the divorce metaphor to represent Israel's disrupted relationship with Yahweh. Parallel motifs in Isaiah 1 and Isaiah 65—66 serve to frame the contents of Isaiah as well (Seitz, 213).

3. The Law and the Prophets.

The Prophets are also linked to the Torah at their seams. The Torah concludes by establishing Joshua as Moses' successor as a prophet (Deut 34:9). The Former Prophets commence by establishing the Torah as the measure of prophetic genuineness (Josh 1:8-9). The Latter

Prophets conclude by enjoining the audience to remember the Torah of God's "servant" Moses, warning them of the coming of the terrible Day of the Lord, but also reassuring them of the prior coming of Elijah, with his healing ministry (Mal 3:22-24 [ET 4:4-6]). Attention to these links fosters sensitivity to linkages at lower levels. Thus, the Torah is given eschatological drive by pivotal divine prophecies: God's promise to Abraham to bless all the nations through him, and God's promise to Israel to send another prophet like Moses (Deut 18:15-18). In light of the Torah's concluding description of Moses as the "LORD's servant" who remains unrivaled in divine intimacy and saving efficacy among the prophets to date (Deut 34:10-12), neither Elijah, despite his communion with God at Horeb and ascent to heaven at death, nor Jeremiah, despite his receiving the prophetic word from the hand of God and prophesying a new covenant written on the heart, fulfills this expectation. If the *servant herald of a new *exodus announced in Isaiah 40—66 is the servant-prophet of Deuteronomy 18, evidently he is yet to come (Dempster).

Such readings suggest that the Torah and the Prophets are a joint dialogical construct of promise and fulfillment, protology and eschatology. S. B. Chapman has developed this thesis to the extent of repudiating the linear theory of canon formation that stipulates that the Law, the Prophets and the Writings developed in successive stages, tracing this theory to a rabbinic subordination of the Prophets to the Torah. Noting the way in which the Law and the Prophets are joined by presenting Moses as both covenant mediator and model prophet, and the parallelism of terms such as "law" and "word," or expressions such as "my servants the prophets," Chapman sees in such textual phenomena a coordination of two mutually interactive authorities that he identifies as the source of a (bipartite) canon and traces to the Deuteronomists. Although this approach leads him to emphasize the fluidity of the canon in its process of development from a bipartite to a tripartite form, he consciously sees himself to be working in continuity with Childs by explaining that the canon was transmitted from the start as a recognizable statement of ideals (presenting guidelines for self-indictment and search for the good of the other) rather than as a propagandistic ideology.

4. The Prophetic Corpus in the Masoretic Text, the Septuagint and the Christian Canon.

The notion that the Torah and the Prophets represent two focal points of a dialogical construct raises important questions about how the prophetic corpus was/is appropriated in the Christian and Jewish canons. The Christian canon generally orders the OT books chronologically and concludes the OT with the Prophets. This may be seen in OT lists of all the Eastern and Western church fathers from the fourth century AD onward (barring Jerome, Rufinus and Codex Vaticanus of the LXX) (see McDonald, 438-44). This allows the OT to pave way for the NT. This effect is strengthened in current Catholic and Protestant Bibles, which adapt the Masoretic order of the Prophets to conclude the OT with Malachi (McDonald, 443-44), enabling one to identify Malachi's Elijah and new servant/Moses with Matthew's John the Baptist and Christ, respectively. On the other hand, the rabbinic tradition espoused in the MT and also adopted by Jerome, Rufinus and Codices Sinaiticus and Alexandrinus (McDonald, 441-42) place the Prophets (Nebiim) between the Torah and the Writings (Ketubim), creating a structure known by acronym as the Tanak.

The conceptions behind these two different ways of ordering the Prophets in the Scriptures are evidently in need of explanation. For M. A. Sweeney, the middle position of the Prophets in the Tanak serves to explain the disruption between the Mosaic vision of Israel completing God's purposes for creation by keeping the covenant, as narrated in the Torah, and the reconstitution of that ideal by the rebuilding of the *temple and observance of the Torah in the land and world at large, as set out in the Writings. In M. A. Sweeney's reading, this lends the Tanak an antieschatological thrust vis-à-vis the eschatological thrust given to the canon in Christian bibles, which conclude the OT with the Prophets (Sweeney 1997).

Although the assumption that the Writings and therefore the Tanak serve antieschatological (i.e., priestly and theocratic) ideological interests is contentious (see Chapman, 210-40, esp. 210n6), it is instructive for reflections on the origins and shapes of the canons of the MT and of the Christian OT (chiefly in its LXX forms) and the place therein of the Prophets.

Sweeney takes the prophetic corpora of both the MT and the LXX to be ultimately concerned with the disruption and restoration of God's covenantal relation with his people. The Prophets in the MT conclude with the Twelve, in the arrangement of whose first six books Sweeney discerns the clue to the differences between the MT and LXX. In the MT these books are Hosea, Amos, Micah, Joel, Obadiah, Jonah. In the LXX they are Hosea, Joel, Amos, Obadiah, Jonah, Micah. The LXX of the Twelve, as of Jeremiah and Ezekiel, betrays a tendency to focus first on Israel and then on Judah, as if to make the former a model for the latter, and only then on the nations and on their punishment and restoration in Jerusalem. The MT, by contrast, interweaves focus on Israel and the nations and emphasizes the role of Jerusalem for both.

Sweeney infers that these structural differences relate the LXX not to Ptolemaic and Alexandrian but rather to late monarchic concerns, and the MT to later Persian ones. His reading concurs with others that judge the LXX to hold value not just as a translation of and a reordering of the final Hebrew *text (*pace* Seitz, 204n24), but as a witness of an alternate and possibly equally important parent Hebrew text (Tov, 54), implying that the development of the Hebrew text was not linear but branched, and so allowing reference to alternate "final" texts of Scripture (as Sanders and Chapman would advocate against Childs). The significance of the point here lies in Sweeney's inference that the LXX's concern with Israel and the nations fits in well with the Christian understanding of prophecy (Sweeney 2005, 188). This implies that the eschatological thrust of the LXX order of the Twelve is not simply a Christian reconfiguration of early or late Jewish conceptions but rather an adaptation of early Jewish/Israelite ones.

If the fit between the LXX shape of the Twelve and Christian conceptions of prophecy was extrapolated over wider stretches of the prophetic corpus, one could opine that the placement of the Prophets in the Christian LXX derives from Jewish traditions rather than from Christian reconfigurations thereof. In lieu of ancient manuscript testimony to corroborate this proposal, Chapman's thesis continues to offer a viable solution to the issue inasmuch as the discrepancy between the placement of the

Prophets in the LXX and the Tanak may be resolved by positing that the tripartite canon is a late development of an original bipartite construction (Trebolle Barrera).

5. The Canon, Liturgy and Mystagogy.
Recalling that the canonical approach serves to correct post-Enlightenment attempts at decanonization of the Scriptures, we may find that an alternative way of relating the Prophets to the Torah and the Writings and vice versa, versus the proeschatological or antieschatological prism offered by Sweeney, is situated in attempts to understand how the liturgy, as represented by Psalms (and the Writings), and supposedly representing priestly, theocratic concerns, serves to mediate and foster bridges between the Law and the Prophets, protology and eschatology. The prophets can speak typologically and eschatologically of a new exodus only because they presuppose the historical importance of the original exodus. As the canon uses historical events and material realities as signs of future events and divine realities, the eschatological senses are grounded on the literal and historical. But if the canon aims to bring the believer into covenant relationship with God, its aim is one with the liturgical readings of the Scriptures that aim to bring the believer into living contact with the saving divine works narrated in those Scriptures. One could then identify this mystagogic principle, grounded on the historical and literal sense, as reflecting the basic contours of Scripture's prophetic canonical shape (Hahn, 228-29).

6. Conclusion.
Despite Childs's neglect of the prophetic corpus as a whole and of its multiple versions, recent work on the Prophets, especially the Twelve, vindicates his central notion that the tradents masked their footprints and switched historical referents to turn the words of the prophets into time and space-transcending Scripture. Via Sweeney and Chapman, one could split the argument between Childs and Sanders about the unity or multiplicity of the canon and/or the importance of the synchronic as opposed to the diachronic approach by arguing with Sanders that Childs was wrong to ignore the versions, but, by arguing with

Chapman, that because the canon originates in a unified dialogical construct, of Torah and the Prophets, there is an organic connection between its original and final canonical forms whereby not every multiplicity has the same authenticity and value. As for Childs's and Sanders's argument about whether or not the historical-critical method can adequately grasp the final shape of the canon, the shift toward canon consciousness in recent work on the Prophets, because much of it is rooted in *literary-structural approaches, might initially seem to vindicate Sanders's position. Whether it does so fully, however, depends on whether or not Sanders's position, in aspiring to grasp Scripture as Scripture, as God's word, and preserve continuity with historical-critical methodology, can really escape the critique of the essential shortcomings of historical-critical methodologies in dealing with the final form of Scripture. As C. Seitz has shown, G. von Rad, a champion of historical-critical methodology who admitted that real theological interpretation of history comes into sharpest profile in the combination of sources (as when J's fall is read in the light of P's "very good"), ultimately failed to perceive in the final form of the canon anything more than a preservation of traditions whose sense could not have been the originally intended meaning (Seitz, 173). Seitz can find no other practitioner of historical-critical methodology whose work overcomes this failure (see the analogies that he draws between von Rad, Blenkinsopp and Barton [Seitz, 142-46, 172]). To grasp the prophetic canon as it is transmitted, and to read it seriously, seems to necessitate a different conception of prophecy and hermeneutics, as well as of history and time, than are available to approaches whose secular assumptions necessitate the decanonization of the Scriptures and/or whose theological assumptions, also borne by von Rad, impede engagement with the "final form" of the OT because this may contradict the voice of the NT (Seitz, 174-78).

See also CANON, CANONIZATION; EDITORIAL/REDACTION CRITICISM; FORMATION OF THE PROPHETIC BOOKS; HERMENEUTICS; INTERTEXTUALITY AND INNERBIBLICAL INTERPRETATION; LITERARY APPROACHES; TEXT AND TEXTUAL CRITICISM.

BIBLIOGRAPHY. J. Barr, "Childs' Introduction to the Old Testament as Scripture," *JSOT* 16 (1980) 12-23; **C. G. Bartholomew et al.,** eds., *Canon and Biblical Interpretation* (SHS 7; Grand Rapids: Zondervan, 2006); **J. Blenkinsopp,** *Prophecy and Canon: A Contribution to the Study of Jewish Origins* (Notre Dame, IN: University of Notre Dame Press, 1977); **W. Brueggemann,** *Hopeful Imagination: Prophetic Voices in Exile* (Philadelphia: Fortress, 1986); **S. B. Chapman,** *The Law and the Prophets: A Study in Old Testament Canon Formation* (FAT 27; Tübingen: Mohr Siebeck, 2000); **B. S. Childs,** *Biblical Theology in Crisis* (Philadelphia: Westminster, 1970); idem, "The Canonical Shape of the Prophetic Literature," *Int* 32 (1978) 46-55; idem, *Introduction to the Old Testament as Scripture* (Philadelphia: Fortress, 1979); **S. G. Dempster,** "The Prophets, the Canon and a Canonical Approach: No Empty Word," in *Canon and Biblical Interpretation*, ed. C. G. Bartholomew et al. (SHS 7; Grand Rapids: Zondervan, 2006) 293-332; **S. W. Hahn,** "Canon, Cult and Covenant: The Promise of Liturgical Hermeneutics," in *Canon and Biblical Interpretation*, ed. C. G. Bartholomew et al. (SHS 7; Grand Rapids: Zondervan, 2006) 207-35; **J. Jeremias,** "The Interrelationship between Amos and Hosea," in *Forming Prophetic Literature: Essays on Isaiah and the Twelve in Honor of John D. W. Watts*, ed. J. W. Watts and P. R. House (JSOTSup 235; Sheffield: Sheffield Academic Press, 1996) 171-86; **L. M. McDonald,** *The Biblical Canon: Its Origin, Transmission, and Authority* (Peabody, MA: Hendrickson, 2007); **L. M. McDonald and J. A. Sanders,** eds., *The Canon Debate* (Peabody, MA: Hendrickson, 2002); **J. D. Nogalski,** "Intertextuality in the Twelve," in *Forming Prophetic Literature: Essays on Isaiah and the Twelve in Honor of John D. W. Watts*, ed. J. W. Watts and P. R. House (JSOTSup 235; Sheffield: Sheffield Academic, 1996) 102-24; idem, "Joel as 'Literary Anchor' for the Book of the Twelve," in *Reading and Hearing the Book of the Twelve*, ed. J. D. Nogalski and M. A. Sweeney (SBLSymS 15; Atlanta: Society of Biblical Literature, 2000) 91-109; **J. D. Nogalski and M. A. Sweeney,** eds., *Reading and Hearing the Book of the Twelve* (SBLSymS 15; Atlanta: Society of Biblical Literature, 2000); **R. Rendtorff,** *The Canonical Hebrew Bible: A Theology of the Old Testament*, trans. D. E. Orton (TBS 7; Leiden: Deo, 2005); **J. A. Sanders,** *Torah and Canon* (Philadelphia: Fortress, 1972); idem, "Hermeneutics of True and False Prophecy," in *Canon and Authority: Essays in Old Testament Religion* *and Theology*, ed. G. W. Coats and B. O. Long (Philadelphia: Fortress, 1977) 21-41; idem, *From Sacred Story to Sacred Text: Canon as Paradigm* (Philadelphia: Fortress, 1987); **C. Seitz,** *Prophecy and Hermeneutics: Toward a New Introduction to the Prophets* (Grand Rapids: Baker Academic, 2007); **M. A. Sweeney,** "Tanak versus Old Testament: Concerning the Foundation for a Jewish Theology of the Bible," in *Problems in Biblical Theology: Essays in Honor of Rolf Knierim*, ed. H. T. C. Sun et al. (Grand Rapids: Eerdmans, 1997) 353-72; idem, *Form and Intertextuality in Prophetic and Apocalyptic Literature* (FAT 45; Tübingen: Mohr Siebeck, 2005); **E. Tov,** "The Septuagint as a Source for the Literary Analysis of Hebrew Scripture," in *Exploring the Origins of the Bible: Canon Formation in Historical, Literary, and Theological Perspective*, ed. C. A. Evans and E. Tov (Grand Rapids: Baker Academic, 2008) 31-56; **J. C. Trebolle Barrera,** "Origins of a Tripartite Old Testament Canon," in *The Canon Debate*, ed. L. M. McDonald and J. A. Sanders (Peabody, MA: Hendrickson, 2002) 128-46; **J. W. Watts and P. R. House,** *Forming Prophetic Literature: Essays on Isaiah and the Twelve in Honor of John D. W. Watts* (JSOTSup 235; Sheffield: Sheffield Academic, 1996).

G. Y. Glazov

CHAOS

In the Hebrew Bible the concept of chaos refers broadly to cosmic disorder—conditions contrary to God's design for all things. For the biblical writer, the world as humanity experiences it was set in order by God but is constantly threatened by forces in opposition to that order (Murray, 17, 21). Wisdom and poetic literature of the Hebrew Bible is replete with references to a divine struggle against chaos and death (Mabie, 41-54). This struggle often is depicted as combat between God and the primordial sea, or a monstrous dragon from that sea, which is subdued and restrained by divine power. The prophets draw upon these depictions and their themes both to identify Israel's enemies with the forces of chaos and to look forward to a time when the dragon, the chief symbol of chaos, will finally be vanquished and eradicated (Is 27:1).

1. Background to Chaos Imagery in the Prophets
2. Chaos Imagery in the Prophets

1. Background to Chaos Imagery in the Prophets.

1.1. Ancient Near East.

1.1.1. Mesopotamia. The concept of a primeval struggle between a god and a sea monster to produce an ordered world is well known in Mesopotamian literature. The principal example is that of *Enuma Elish*, a Babylonian myth wherein the chief deity of the pantheon, Marduk, defeats the sea dragon Tiamat. Having defeated Tiamat, Marduk splits her corpse in two to produce the ordered heaven and earth known to humans. A landmark study in 1895 by H. Gunkel introduced readers to the *Chaoskampf* ("struggle against chaos") motifs in this literature. Gunkel forcefully proposed that the Mesopotamian material was the source for OT texts that described a battle between Yahweh and the sea and creatures such as Leviathan (Ps 74:12-17; Is 27:1) and Rahab (Ps 89:5-14; Is 51:9). Subsequent scholarship, however, has diverted much of this discussion away from Mesopotamia toward the literature of Canaan, specifically Ugarit, since the parallels from that material are much more explicit (Tsumura). Recent scholarship has also made it clear that *Chaoskampf* should be understood as a subset of divine conflict portrayals ("theomachy") in the ancient Near East (Walton, 49).

1.1.2. Ras Shamra (Ugarit). The literature of Ugarit provides secure conceptual links to the OT description of God's struggle against the forces of chaos. The Baal Cycle features a cosmic battle between Baal (Baal-Hadad) and the sea deity Yamm (cf. Heb *yām* ["sea"]). Yamm is represented as a sea monster. One name for this chaos monster is "Tunnan" (*KTU* 1.3 iii:39-42; Heb *tannîn* ["dragon"]), called the "twisted serpent" (*bṭn ʿqltn*; Heb *nāḥāš ʿăqallātôn*) or "fleeing serpent" (*bṭn brḥ*; Heb *nāḥāš bāriaḥ*). Another is Litānu (*KTU* 1.5 i:1-3; Heb *liwyātān* ["Leviathan"]). In Ugaritic religion it is this battle that determines who will serve as the ruler of the pantheon under the supreme but distant god, El. With the help of the goddess Anat, Baal emerges victorious (*KTU* 1.16 iii:5-9; 1.2 iv:5-10), earning the titles *ʿly(n)* ("Most High"; Heb *ʿelyôn*) and *rkb ʿrpt* ("Rider/Charioteer of the Clouds"; Heb *rōkēb bāʿărābôt* and similar phrases). Baal also wins a house (a temple) of his own (*KTU* 1.3-4), and his dominion is cast as everlasting (*KTU* 1.2 iv:10). In addition to the overlap between Ugaritic Yamm

("Sea") and Hebrew *yām* ("sea"), the two languages and their literature share other terms involving water that speak of the primordial waters, such as the deity *nhr* ("River," another name of Yamm; cf. Heb *nāhār* ["river"]). Most scholars view the cosmic struggle between Baal and Yamm as pointing to kingship and temple building (the broader theomachy theme). While those outcomes are obvious, cosmological connections to the ordering of creation are also present (Fisher).

1.2. Old Testament.

1.2.1. Old Testament Wisdom Literature and Genesis 1. The OT often connects the forces of chaos with the sea (Heb *yām*). The reasoning is understandable. Terrestrial humanity would naturally view the vast, raging ocean as uncontrollable and always potentially deadly, filled with bizarre, terrifying creatures. It is therefore not surprising that a monstrous sea serpent was a common mythopoetic symbol in the ancient Near East (Mabie, 45-46; Wakeman; Kloos; Day; Watson). The clearest examples of God subduing a chaos sea monster to bring about an ordered creation are found in the OT Wisdom literature (Job 7:12; 26:12-13; 41; Ps 74:12-17; 89:5-14; 93). Other passages describe the waters at the creation of the world under control without a battle motif (Gen 1:2, 6-10; Ps 33:7-8; Prov 8:24, 27-29).

Although most scholars no longer would follow Gunkel's views of literary borrowing, many would agree that Genesis 1 is in some respects a response to Babylonian (Marduk-Tiamat) mythology. This connection would in turn suggest an exilic composition or redaction of Genesis 1 that was either contemporaneous with or a precursor to the major texts in prophetic literature that repurpose chaos imagery (see 2 below). With respect to Genesis 1:2, 6-10, *těhôm* ("the deep") is already subdued when God sets to work in ordering the heavens and earth. That is, Yahweh is already in control of the forces of chaos. Either a battle has already taken place or it is unnecessary due to the superiority of Israel's God. Nevertheless, chaos will come to an end, as the prophets forecast (Is 27:1) and the book of Revelation confirms (Rev 21:1, "the sea was no more"). Ultimately, for the OT writer, the subjugation and defeat of chaos concerns both mastery and maintenance of the created order and the celebration of the kingship of Yahweh (Levenson, 123-27; Walton, 54-63).

1.2.2. Historicization of Chaos in the Pentateuch. The motifs of the subjugation of chaos and the celebration of the kingship of Yahweh are dramatically combined in Exodus 15, the Song of Moses after the Red (Reed) Sea crossing. The description is echoed in the prophets.

In Exodus 15 the deliverance from Egypt is portrayed as divine combat between Yahweh, the "man of war" (Ex 15:3), and his foes. Even though water covered the land and the Egyptians, Exodus 15:12 declares that Yahweh stretched out his right hand, and "the earth" (*'ereṣ*) swallowed the Egyptians. The word *'ereṣ* is used in Jonah 2:6 to describe the prophet in the depths of the sea in the belly of the great fish, but it clearly points to the cosmic underworld, as the place of Jonah's lament is the land "at the roots of the mountains" where "bars" make escape impossible. At this victory, the Song of Moses celebrates Yahweh's dominion over other gods: "Who is like you, Yahweh, among the gods [*'ēlim*])?" Isaiah also casts Yahweh's mastery of the waters, creating a conduit for his children to pass to safety but violently destroying the army of Egypt, in terms of a victory over the watery chaos and its chaos monster: "Was it not you who cut Rahab in pieces, who pierced the dragon? Was it not you who dried up the sea, the waters of the great deep, who made the depths of the sea a way for the redeemed to pass over?" (Is 51:9-10). Just as the waters of chaos are subdued at creation, so Isaiah later portrays Egypt as the stifled chaos beast, Rahab (Is 30:7).

2. Chaos Imagery in the Prophets.

2.1. The Dragon and the Sea Historicized. The biblical prophets employ a range of naturalistic metaphors to denote the cosmic nature of the struggle between Yahweh, Israel and their mutual enemies (Geyer 1987; 1999). Imagery of watery chaos is part of that repertoire. The sea and the chaos monster metaphorically characterize Pharaoh and Egypt (Is 30:7; 51:9-10; Ezek 29:3; cf. Ezek 32:2). Isaiah also apparently describes *Babylon in similar terms (Is 13:5, 8) (Geyer 1987). In like manner, Isaiah forecasts that Judah will be swept away by the torrents of the flooding Euphrates, a metaphor for Assyria (Is 8:5-8).

The rationale of these literary portrayals is as much to align the enemies with cosmic disorder, the primeval state of affairs contrary to Yahweh's intentions, as it is to portray Yahweh as superior to the deities of the enemy nations. The OT writers saw the Gentile nations and their lesser gods as allotted to each other by the decision of the superior Yahweh (Deut 4:19-20; 32:8-9 [with Qumran and the LXX]) (Heiser). Opposition to and conquest of Israel, Yahweh's own nation and sacred space, was akin to chaos breaking free, if only for a moment. The gods of the nations will be permanently destroyed in the eschaton (Ps 82 [esp. vv. 6-8]) along with the chaos dragon (Is 27:1).

Egypt is specifically targeted with this language in several passages. Isaiah cleverly links the defeat of the primeval chaos monster with the events associated with the deliverance of Israel from Egypt from death at the Red/Reed Sea (Boyle): "Awake, awake, put on strength, O arm of the LORD; awake, as in days of old, the generations of long ago. Was it not you who cut Rahab in pieces, who pierced the dragon? Was it not you who dried up the sea, the waters of the great deep, who made the depths of the sea a way for the redeemed to pass over?" (Is 51:9-10).

Ezekiel also applies primeval chaos imagery to Egypt, casting Pharaoh as a great dragon (*tannîn*) that Yahweh will capture and feed to the birds of heaven (Ezek 29:1-5; 32:1-8).

Isaiah utilizes the motif of watery chaos to describe another of Israel's mortal enemies, Assyria (Is 17:12-14; cf. Is 8:5-8). Maltreatment of Israel reflects the attempt of chaos to break the bonds imposed by the God of Israel. Yahweh may loosen his restraint of these forces in an act of judgment, but that is the only rationale for foreign oppression of Israel for the prophets. Only Yahweh controls and wields chaos; it must do his bidding. The forces of chaos, restrained since creation, can neither act with impunity nor be manipulated by apostate Israel. Hence comes Isaiah's mockery of Israel's solicitation to Egypt for protection (Is 30:1-7). Pharaoh is a feckless aid because Egypt is "Rahab, who sits still" (Is 30:7 [emending the MT] (Day, *ABD* 2:228).

The prophets Jeremiah and Habakkuk utilize motifs of chaos to describe the threat of the Babylonians. In Jeremiah 51:34 Nebuchadnezzar is cast as the "dragon" (Heb *tannîn*) that swallows up Judah. In Jeremiah 51:44 the prophet tells his readers that Yahweh will punish Bel (a dragon deity in Babylonian religion) by removing from his mouth what he has swallowed. Chaos will again be subdued. Habakkuk

conveys the same message. Just as Yahweh came from the south (Teman) into Canaan—an allusion to the journey to the promised land after the defeat of Egypt at the sea (Heb *yām*)—so will God act to deliver his people from the Babylonians. To conjure the image of Egypt's decimation under the plagues before their downfall at the sea, Habakkuk portrays Yahweh moving into Canaan with an entourage that includes foreign deities as his servants, described in Habakkuk 3:5 as naturalistic forces of "pestilence" (Heb *deber*) (del Olmo Lete) and "plague" (Heb *rešep*) (Xella). Yahweh shakes the mountains as he moves (Hab 3:6), promising a violent, decisive judgment of Babylon (Hab 3:8), just as his wrath "was against the rivers [*nĕharîm*]" and his indignation "against the sea [*yām*]".

2.2. The Dragon and the Sea Eschatologized. The operative hermeneutic within the biblical canon is that all things will reach final resolution in conformity to Yahweh's original intention for them at the beginning (*Urzeit* and *Endzeit*). As such, the symbolism of primeval chaos involving the dragon and the sea feature prominently in eschatological discourse.

The eschatologization of chaos imagery is most transparent in the so-called Little Apocalypse (Is 24—27): "In that day the LORD with his hard and great and strong sword will punish Leviathan the twisting serpent, Leviathan the crooked serpent, and he will slay the dragon that is in the sea" (Is 27:1). The parallels to the Baal Cycle are explicit. The message is equally clear: Leviathan's final destruction by Yahweh will coincide with the eschatological restoration of Israel (Is 27:2). Yahweh will have a people on earth as it was intended in Eden.

This eschatological message is dramatically reiterated in Daniel 7. Scholars have long recognized that Israelite adaptation of material from the Baal Cycle illuminates much of Daniel 7 (Emerton; Collins, 286-94). The chapter begins with the stormy winds stirring up the raging sea, out of which emerge four beasts (Dan 7:1-8). That the beasts are not aquatic creatures but nevertheless come from the sea shows clearly that the reader is confronted with chaos metaphors. The divine council meets (Dan 7:9-10) in the presence of God (Ancient of Days), and the beasts are sentenced to death, one of them immediately (Dan 7:11-12). At the judgment of the chaos monsters from the sea, one "like a son of man" comes upon the clouds of heaven and is exalted to everlasting dominion and kingship by the Ancient of Days (Dan 7:13-14). Both the flow of the chapter and its major constituent elements show the familiar utilization of Canaanite mythopoetic language to exalt the supreme God of Daniel, Yahweh, over the cosmos.

The eschatological language of the prophet Daniel is also significant in that the victory over chaos is linked to a second deity figure (the "son of man") later identified with Jesus in the Gospels (Mt 26:57-68). The result is a prophetic connection of primeval victory over the forces of chaos with messianic kingship. This connection works its way into the Gospels in other ways as well, where Jesus rebukes the sea (Lk 8:22-25) and treads upon it (Mt 14:28-33; cf. Ps 89:5-10, 20-27). One may also compare Revelation 12, where Michael defeats a seven-headed dragon, identified with the devil. Another multiheaded beast rises from the sea (Rev 13:1-5) to oppose God and Christ before its final destruction (Rev 20:10). The new Eden appears where there is no more disruption from chaos—there is no more sea (Rev 21:1).

See also COSMOLOGY; DEATH.

BIBLIOGRAPHY. **M. O. Boyle**, "'In the Heart of the Sea': Fathoming the Exodus," *JNES* 63 (2004) 17-27; **J. J. Collins**, *Daniel: A Commentary on the Book of Daniel* (Hermeneia; Minneapolis: Fortress, 1993); **J. Day**, *God's Conflict with the Dragon and the Sea: Echoes of a Canaanite Myth in the Old Testament* (UCOP 35; Cambridge: Cambridge University Press, 1985); idem, "Dragon and Sea, God's Conflict With," *ABD* 2:228-32; **J. A. Emerton**, "The Origin of the Son of Man Imagery," *JTS* 9 (1958) 225-42; **L. Fisher**, "Creation at Ugarit and the Old Testament," *VT* 15 (1965) 313-24; **J. Geyer**, "Twisting Tiamat's Tail: A Mythological Interpretation of Is. XIII 5 and 8," *VT* 37 (1987) 164-79; idem, "Desolation and Cosmos," *VT* 49 (1999) 49-64; **H. Gunkel**, *Creation and Chaos in the Primeval Era and the Eschaton: A Religio-Historical Study of Genesis 1 and Revelation 12*, trans. K. Whitney (Grand Rapids: Eerdmans, 2006 [1895]); **M. S. Heiser**, "Deuteronomy 32:8 and the Sons of God," *BSac* 158 (2001) 52-74; **C. Kloos**, *Yhwh's Combat with the Sea: A Canaanite Tradition in the Religion of Ancient Israel* (Amsterdam: G. A. van Oorschot; Leiden: E. J. Brill, 1986); **J. Levenson**, *Creation and the Persistence of Evil: The Jewish Drama of Divine Omnipotence* (San Francisco: Harper & Row, 1988); **F. J. Mabie**, "Chaos and Death," *DOTWPW* 41-54; **R. Murray**, *The Cosmic Covenant: Biblical Themes of Justice, Peace, and Integrity of Creation* (London: Heythrop, 1992); **G. del Olmo Lete**, "Deber," *DDD*[2] 231-32; **D. Tsumura**, *Creation and Destruction: A Reappraisal of the Chaoskampf Theory in the Old Testament* (Winona Lake, IN: Eisenbrauns, 2005); **M. K. Wakeman**, *God's Battle with the Monster: A Study in Biblical Imagery* (Leiden: E. J. Brill, 1973); **J. H. Walton**, "Creation in Genesis 1:1-2:3 and the Ancient Near East: Order Out of Disorder after *Chaoskampf*," *CTJ* 43 (2008) 48-63; **R. S. Watson**, *Chaos Uncreated: A Reassessment of the Theme of "Chaos" in the Hebrew Bible* (BZAW 341; Berlin: de Gruyter, 2005); **P. Xella**, "Resheph," *DDD*[2] 700-703.

M. S. Heiser

CHILDBEARING. *See* WOMEN AND FEMALE IMAGERY.

COMFORT. *See* LAMENT, MOURNING.

COMPOSITION OF PROPHETIC BOOKS. *See* FORMATION OF THE PROPHETIC BOOKS.

CONFESSION. *See* PRAYER; REPENTANCE.

CONVERSATION ANALYSIS

Conversation analysis (hereafter CA) is a social-scientific method to understand how naturally occurring language works in everyday conversation and in institutional settings. CA has been used in relationship to literature, including some biblical texts.

1. History
2. Basic Observations
3. Application to Literature
4. Conversation Analysis and Jonah
5. Potential Application to Prophetic Literature

1. History.

Early forms of sociology, like most of the social sciences, were primarily interested in two areas: the major institutions that shape human society—that is, government, religion, kinship relations—and that which was understood to be abnormal. However, this emphasis has certain problems. For example, how can we know what is "deviant" behavior if we do not understand what is "normal" behavior? How can we understand major institutions if we do not understand everyday interactions? These kinds of questions led UCLA sociologists E. Goffman and H. Garfinkel to seriously question how sociology was practiced and to create the branch of sociology called "ethnomethodology," the study of the "ethnic" methods (i.e., the participants' own commonsense skills and abilities) that enable participants to produce and recognize meaningful social interaction in everyday life. In other words, even everyday life has institutional structures that should be carefully studied. Before Goffman and Garfinkel, sociologists generally assumed that they knew what was "normal," so that what was "normal" did not need to be studied, only that which was "abnormal" or institutional.

One of Goffman's and Garfinkel's doctoral students, H. Sacks, accepted their insights into the study of everyday life and applied it to everyday language. Sacks understood that social interaction was extremely dependent on language, so if all social interaction is institutionalized in some way (as Goffman and Garfinkel taught), then conversation must also be institutionalized. This line of inquiry led Sacks to assert that there must be "order at all points" in conversation, which leads to the question "Why that now?" for all aspects of talk-in-interaction, including previously unstudied items such as nonlexicals (e.g., "oh"), laughter and pauses, all of which had been dismissed by linguists as inconsequential in the assumed messiness of everyday conversation.

Upon completion of his dissertation, Sacks joined the UCLA sociology faculty. Sacks and his early doctoral students, especially E. A. Schegloff and G. Jefferson, established some of the basic observations of CA that have now significantly influenced various disciplines, especially sociology, anthropology, linguistics and communications theory.

Building upon the basic observations of CA concerning everyday conversation, later conversation analysts have studied the interrelationship between language and institutions—for example, doctor-patient interactions, courtroom speech, 911 calls and retail service encounters. These studies have demonstrated how necessary knowledge of everyday conversation is to the study of institutional talk, because institutional talk consists of adaptations of the practices of everyday conversation. Such stud-

ies of institutional talk have led to various practical insights, so that now some trained conversation analysts teach in law schools, medical schools, ESL programs and other professionally oriented disciplines.

Although the early history of CA was dominated by studies limited to English and then other Indo-European languages, the basic observations of CA have been confirmed many times with some revisions by studies in languages in many linguistic families, including but not limited to Native American languages, Aboriginal languages of Australia, various East Asian languages and Semitic languages. Therefore, the universality of the basic observations of CA for human language appears to be justified.

2. Basic Observations.

J. Heritage has expressed the four basic assumptions underlying CA as a discipline as follows:

(1) interaction is structurally organized; (2) contributions to interaction are both context-shaped and context-renewing; (3) these two properties inhere in the details of interaction so that no order of detail in conversational interaction can be dismissed a priori as disorderly, accidental or interactionally irrelevant; and (4) the study of social interaction in its details is best approached through the analysis of naturally occurring data (Heritage, 22). These methodological assumptions have led to two basic observations of CA: turn-taking and sequence organization.

2.1. Turn-taking. In their 1974 article Sacks, Schegloff and Jefferson observe the following about conversation: (1) turn-taking occurs, (2) usually only one speaker talks at a time, and (3) turns often occur with little or no gaps. These three observations, when taken together, strongly suggest that there must be some systematic way of determining when a turn at talk begins and ends and who has the floor to speak. This seminal article outlines the turn-taking system that operates in conversation so that speakers can take turns at speech with little or no gap between turns and little overlapping speech. Turns at talk are constructed in ways that enable participants to project when a turn will be completed. Turns can be allocated to the next speaker by the current speaker and, if not, then by self-selection. A hierarchical set of practices further helps the participants to proceed in the conversation in an orderly fashion or, when these practices are violated, to interpret the potential conflict. This article convincingly demonstrated how complex, flexible and efficient the structures of everyday conversation are, despite our naïve assumption about how simple everyday conversation must be.

2.2. Sequence Organization. Turns at talk often occur in sequences, such as question/answer and offer/refusal. Such sequences, called "adjacency pairs," can be characterized as follows:

> Adjacency pairs are sequences of two moves (verbal or non-verbal) that are:
> (i) adjacent or containing an insertion sequence (for example, a clarifying question between question and answer)
> (ii) produced by different individuals
> (iii) ordered as a first part and a second part
> (iv) typed, so that a particular first part has a range of second parts, those which are linguistically preferred and those which are linguistically dispreferred (Person 1996, 16).

Thus, adjacency pairs occur in two types: (1) those with preferred second parts; (2) those with dispreferred second parts. Preferred seconds are generally brief utterances given without delay and are unmitigated. In contrast, dispreferred seconds generally contain the following four characteristics: (1) a delay; (2) a preface; (3) an account for why the dispreferred response is being done; (4) a declination component, which often is indirect or mitigated. Compare the following transcription of two adjacency pairs from actual conversations (Atkinson and Drew, 58).

> Adjacency pair with preferred second (invitation/acceptance):
> A: Why don't you come up and see me some//time?
> B: I would like to.

> Adjacency pair with dispreferred second (invitation/refusal):
> A: Uh, if you'd care to come and visit a

little while this morning, I'll give you a cup of coffee.
> B: (*pause*) Well, that's awfully sweet of you. I don't think I can make it this morning,
> (*pause*) Uhm, I'm running an ad in the paper and, and, uh, I have to stay near the phone.

The preferred response is brief and, in this case, occurs even before the turn has been completed (the beginning of B's turn is represented by the slash lines // and indentation). The dispreferred response occurs after a brief pause, which is followed by a preface (in this case, "Well" and an appreciation), a mitigated refusal ("I don't think"), and an account for why B is not accepting the invitation ("stay near the phone"). Similar structures are found in other adjacency pairs in English, such as:

First part	Preferred second	Dispreferred second
Request	Acceptance	Refusal
Offer	Acceptance	Refusal
Question	Expected answer	Unexpected or no answer
Blame	Denial	Admission

Note that what is linguistically preferred (i.e., preferred within societal norms) may not be what the individual speaker of the first part wants to hear. For example, when someone blames someone else, admission of guilt may be what the individual wants to hear. However, the linguistic/societal expectation is that denial is the preferred second. Also, although the structure of adjacency pairs is universal, the content within specific adjacency pairs may differ; for example, in some cultures refusal may be the preferred response to an invitation, at least until the invitation is repeated a certain number of times.

3. Application to Literature.

Few conversation analysts have applied CA to written texts, and even fewer to literary texts, probably because of the insistence on naturally occurring data in CA in opposition to the dominance of written texts in earlier forms of linguistics that denigrated conversation as an acceptable object of study. However, J. Atkinson expresses the justification for CA study of written texts thus: "An adequate understanding of how texts are produced and responded to may remain elusive so long as the issue is pursued without making close comparative reference to how talk works" (Atkinson, 230).

Some literary scholars have found CA useful in their analyses (see the review of literature in Person 1999b, 12-14). These scholars have demonstrated that the representation of dialogue in literature follows the same set of practices found in everyday conversation. In other words, literary discourse is a form of institutional talk adapted from the set of practices found in everyday conversation.

R. F. Person has applied CA to a variety of literary texts, including Homeric epic, Shakespeare, the Bible, and modern English-language short stories and novels. He has demonstrated that despite certain limitations of its graphic medium, literature can represent to some extent all aspects of the complexity of everyday talk in interaction, including nonlexical items (such as "uh-huh"), body movement (such as gaze and gesture), silence, and prosody (such as intonation, rate of speech). Furthermore, the literary representation of everyday conversation provides structures in the literary text that guide readers as they coproduce the meaning in the "conversation" that occurs between the readers and the text (Person 1999a). In his study of the "became silent to silence" formula in Homeric epic, Person demonstrated the relationship of this formula to the surrounding narrative context and how the "became silent to silence" formula acts as a preface for dispreferred seconds and how other formulae in its narrative context often provide other characteristics of dispreferred seconds (e.g., accounts). In his study of *Wiederaufnahme* (resumptive repetition) in biblical and ancient Near Eastern literature, he demonstrated that this "literary" device appears to be an adaptation of a conversational device called "restarts," which often occurs when a speaker has regained control of the turn-at-talk. In his study of "oh" in Shakespeare, he demonstrated that the English spoken four hundred years ago during the time of Shakespeare used "oh" in all of the various sequences identified in recent CA studies as well as some analogous sequences that have not yet been identified in CA literature on "oh" in everyday conversation.

4. Conversation Analysis and Jonah.

Person's most comprehensive study of applying CA to a single piece of literature is his 1996 monograph, *In Conversation with Jonah*. After providing an introduction of CA and a rationale for applying CA to the literary representation of dialogue, he offers a commentary on the book of Jonah, demonstrating how the narrative develops in relationship to the adjacency pairs of the conversations between the characters, whether explicitly represented by the narrator or not. He then demonstrates how this knowledge of how adjacency pairs function in the narrative sequence contributes to the construction of the different narrative elements of plot, character, atmosphere and tone. For example, concerning characterization, all of the characters in the narrative, except Jonah, produce the preferred response of acceptance to divine commands; therefore, the prophet Jonah is placed in a category of himself—that is, one who engages in conflict talk. For example, concerning the satirical tone, the narrator manipulates the readers by not giving Jonah's account for his refusal in Jonah 1:3, but by referring to it later in Jonah 4:2. This delay of Jonah's account makes his actions appear more ridiculous, thereby adding to the satirization of Jonah as petty.

After providing this discussion of the various narrative elements, Person develops a reader-response approach by adapting the work of W. Iser in light of his own observations from CA concerning how conversational structures inform the narrative. Applying this approach to the Jonah narrative, he then provides another commentary, this one explicating the role of the implied reader of the narrative.

The implied reader of Person's commentary is, of course, only as competent a reader as Person himself is. Therefore, he provides a discussion of how a multitude of various historical readers have interacted with the Jonah narrative in those places where the narrator omitted dialogue (at least in the form of direct speech), where the narrator changed the order of reported events and in the identification of the satirical tone of the narrative. These actual readers are found in commentaries, sermons, creative fiction based on Jonah, children's Bible stories, rabbinic sources, and even in Person's recounting of how the narrative asserted itself on himself, requiring him to change his understanding of the interaction of the characters in the narrative world. His explication of these various readings of Jonah demonstrates once again how the basic observations of CA can be useful, this time in the history of interpretation.

5. Potential Application to Prophetic Literature.
Recent applications of CA to literature show promise for future applications of CA to literature, including prophetic literature. Person's work on the book of Jonah certainly provides a model that could be applied, in part or as a whole, to other narrative texts—for example, the biographical narratives in the book of Jeremiah or the prophetic stories in the books of Samuel and Kings.

Since most of the material in the Latter Prophets consists of prophetic oracles, a slightly different approach would be necessary. However, even what on the surface appear to be monologues in literature involve dialogues with imagined conversants or within one's own persona. Therefore, the poetic oracles could be analyzed to discern the implied adjacency pairs between the prophet and the addressee(s) in judgment oracles (e.g., Amos 9:1-5), between the prophet and God in laments (e.g., Jer 20:14-18), between the prophet and God in call narratives (e.g., Ezek 1:4—3:27), and so forth. Such an approach could lead to a better understanding of prophetic speech in general, especially if it includes comparative analyses of prophetic literature from the wider ancient Near East (see the essays in Nissinen).

See also FORM CRITICISM; RHETORICAL CRITICISM; SOCIAL-SCIENTIFIC APPROACHES.

BIBLIOGRAPHY. **J. M. Atkinson,** "Two Devices for Generating Audience Approval: A Comparative Study of Public Discourse and Texts," in *Connectedness in Sentence: Discourse and Text,* ed. K. Ehlich and H. van Riemsdijk (Tilburg Studies in Language and Literature 4; Tilburg: Tilburg University, 1983) 199-236; **J. M. Atkinson and P. Drew,** *Order in Court: The Organisation of Verbal Interaction in Judicial Settings* (London: MacMillan, 1979); **J. Heritage,** "Current Developments in Conversation Analysis," in *Conversation: An Interdisciplinary Perspective,* ed. D. Roger and P. Bull (Intercommunication 3; Philadelphia: Multilingual Matters, 1989) 21-47; **I. Hutchby and R. Woffitt,** *Conversation Analysis: Principles, Practices and Applications* (Cambridge: Polity, 2008); **M. Nissinen,** ed., *Prophecy in Its Ancient Near Eastern Context: Mesopotamian, Biblical, and Arabian Perspectives* (SBLSymS 13; Atlanta: Society of Biblical Literature, 2000); **R. F. Person Jr.,** "The 'Became Silent to Silence' Formula in Homer," *Greek, Roman, and Byzantine Studies* 36 (1995) 327-39; idem, *In Conversation with Jonah: Conversation Analysis, Literary Criticism, and the Book of Jonah* (JSOTSup 220; Sheffield: Sheffield Academic, 1996); idem, "A Reassessment of *Wiederaufnahme* from the Perspective of Conversation Analysis," *BZ* (1999a) 241-48; idem, *Structure and Meaning in Conversation and Literature* (Latham, MD: University Press of America, 1999b); idem, "'Oh' in Shakespeare: A Conversation Analytic Approach," *Journal for Historical Pragmatics* 10 (2009) 84-107; **H. Sacks, E. A. Schegloff and G. Jefferson,** "A Simplest Systematics for the Organization of Turn-Taking for Conversation," *Language* 50 (1974) 696-735.
R. F. Person Jr.

COSMOLOGY

Generally defined, cosmology is the study of the origin and structure of the cosmos/universe and how it functions. With the rise of modern archaeology over the past 150 years or so, our understanding of ancient Hebrew cosmology has become better informed. This is directly connected to the unlocking of cognate literatures from the ancient Near East (e.g., Sumerian, Akkadian, Egyptian, Ugaritic). The ubiquitous ancient Near Eastern accounts of the origins of the universe and how it operates have been covered at length in an earlier volume of this dictionary series and need not be rehearsed here (see Lucas). Naturally, when one thinks of cosmology, Genesis 1—2, Job 38—42, Proverbs 8 and Psalm 104 immediately come to mind as opposed to the prophetic corpus. However, through a close analysis of the prophetic texts one can learn a lot about their cosmological worldview (e.g., Is 45:18).

Today, due to modern science and intergalactic space probing, modern readers of the OT tend to wrestle more with competing cosmogonic perspectives (i.e., arguments about the origin of the universe), such as theistic evolution, creationism and evolution, as opposed to how the cosmos functions (perhaps with the exception of certain branches of science such as quantum physics [see Lennox]). For the OT prophets and ancient Near Eastern peoples, these concepts often were blurred due to their belief that the universe originated and functioned at the hands of the god(s). Of course, for each ancient culture one finds competing polemical accounts as to how exactly the god(s) created the universe. For example, in the Babylonian creation myth, *Enuma Elish*, Marduk creates the heavens and the earth by slaying and dividing the goddess Tiamat (*ANET* 67-68, 501-2, tablets IV, V), whereas in certain Egyptian creation accounts, such as "The Repulsing of the Dragon and Creation" (*ANET* 6-7), creative acts take place through spitting and masturbation by the chief god, Khepri (note that Egyptian creation myths vary widely). The Hebrew creation account is no less polemical when it focuses on one God, who creates both by speaking (Gen 1) and through a more "hands-on" fashioning of specific parts of his created order (e.g., Adam is fashioned [*yāṣar*] from the dust of the ground [Gen 2:7]).

One area where the prophets differed from their ancient Near Eastern counterparts was in their developing monotheistic perspective (e.g., Is 37:19; 44:6; Jer 5:7; 10:11; 14:22; 16:20; Dan 5:23) (for an overview on the rise of monotheism in ancient Israel, see Lang 1983; 1986). For the OT prophets, Yahweh alone was both creator and sovereign over that *creation (e.g., Is 37:16; 40:12, 22-28; 42:5; 44:24; 45:12, 18; 48:13; Jer 32:17; Amos 9:5-6; Jon 1:9). Moreover, by the very nature of their callings as *covenant enforcers, it was only natural for the prophets to see Yahweh working through his created order not only to reach out to a wayward nation but also as a means of indicting both them and their neighbors for sin and rebellion. From prophet to prophet one can trace how each used cosmology, not so much as a means of presenting a detailed cosmological picture per se, but rather as a way of showcasing the sovereign rule of Yahweh. Nevertheless, in many cases the prophets referenced what appears to be a three-tiered cosmos where heaven and Sheol served as polar extremes (e.g., Is 7:11; Amos 9:2). By doing such, the prophets promoted the belief that there was no place where humankind could escape from Yahweh's sovereign hand, a reality also echoed by the psalmist (Ps 139:8).

1. A Canonical Methodology.
Tracing the prophets' use of cosmology from century to century, though valid and perhaps a rewarding undertaking, would prove more cumbersome than need be, especially in light of the debates surrounding the dates of a given prophet and his work (e.g., Isaiah, Obadiah, Joel). For this reason, a canonical approach to the subject will be adopted here, even though a prophet such as Hosea or Amos may in fact predate the prophet Isaiah. In this way, one can study how a particular book/tradition viewed cosmology and used it for didactic purposes.

2. Isaiah.
The book of Isaiah has the most references to cosmology within the prophetic corpus. Arguably, this could be due in part to the possible time spanned within the book (eighth through sixth centuries BC). Isaiah refers to what can be understood as either a two-tiered (heaven and earth [Is 37:16; 42:5; 45:12, 18; 51:16; 65:17; 66:1, 22]) or an implied three-tiered cosmos (i.e., the merismus: the heavens and the lower parts of the earth, and then all that is in between on the earth itself—e.g., mountains and trees [Is 44:23]). It is the three-tiered cosmos alluded to in Isaiah 44:23 that is unique insofar as it moves away from the picture presented in Genesis. Genesis 1:1 depicts a general bipartite designation for the created cosmos: God created "the heavens and the earth" (*haššāmayim wĕʾēt hāʾāreṣ* [for a similar division, see Neh 9:6]). The phraseology in Genesis accounts only for two main parts to the cosmos, but there is other biblical evidence of a further subdividing of the earthly tier into upper and lower portions (i.e., the inhabited world and the underworld [e.g., Ex 20:4; Deut 5:8; Job 38:4-38; Ps 115:16-17; Prov 8:22-31; Amos 9:1-3; see also Ps. 135:6; Prov 3:19-20]). This tripartite designation also appears in ancient Ugarit

("The Baal Cycle" [*ANET* 132, i:40; 135, vii:45-52; 138, ii:1-20]), Egypt ("Hymn to the Nile" [*ANET* 372, xii:5]), and Babylon ("The Creation Epic" [*ANET* 67, 501-2, tablet IV lines 130-146, tablet V lines 23-60]). While many of the Prophetic Books do not address such a systematized cosmos or have any cosmological references at all for that matter (e.g., Obadiah), Isaiah tends to use a more developed picture of the cosmos than do his counterparts as a means of proving the omnipotence and transcendence of Yahweh (e.g., Is 44:23).

In Isaiah 40:22 the prophet paints a picture of God's sovereign and transcendent perspective of the earth: "It is [God] who sits above the vault/circle [*ḥûg*] of the earth, and its inhabitants are like grasshoppers; he is the one who stretches out the heavens like a veil [*dōq*] and spreads them out like a tent [*ʾōhel*] to dwell in." There are at least two ways of understanding *ḥûg hāʾāreṣ* ("circle of the earth") in this context. First, L. Koehler and W. Baumgartner suggest that *ḥûg hāʾāreṣ* comes from the belief that the earth was "conceived of as a disc" (*HALOT*² 1:295). However, *The Old Testament Hebrew-English Dictionary* sheds further light on this first definition by noting that "the reference to a circle would have been understood in ancient Near Eastern cosmology as implying a flat, disk-shaped earth, bounded by its circular horizon. Alternatively, and in keeping with some ancient cosmologies, the earth was considered to be delimited above by a hemispherical dome, which contained the 'windows' or 'floodgates of heaven,' which God would open to allow the rains, or other calamities or blessing, to fall (cf. Gen. 7:11; Isa. 24:18; Mal. 3:10)" (Lint, 2:58) (so too BDB 295; Clines, 3:169).

The context of the passage stresses, in hyperbolic terminology, the sovereignty and omnipotence of God over mere idols. Yahweh is pictured as a gargantuan being who measures the waters in the hollow of his hand (Is 40:12); the nations are mere dust before him (Is 40:15). Furthermore, the author goes on to note that the entire nation of Lebanon is insufficient as a sacrifice before him (Is 40:16). Poetically, these terrestrial objects are nothing in comparison to so great a God. In keeping with this theme, the author thus conceives of God as transcendent and dwelling above or over the vault (*ḥûg*) of the heavens (cf. Job 22:14; 26:10; Prov 8:27; Amos 9:6). Indeed, not only does the verse begin by identifying the area above the vault as the place where Yahweh dwells, but also the author uses the same participial form of the verb *yāšab* to juxtapose God's dwelling place with those who dwell on the earth far below.

In Isaiah 40:22b the author continues the description of Yahweh's power by using the poetic word pair *dōq* ("veil") and *ʾōhel* ("tent") as a metaphor for Yahweh's creative act of "spreading out" the heavens (cf. Is 42:5; 44:24; 51:13) like a veil (*dōq*) or tent (*ʾōhel*) (cf. a similar metaphor in Is 34:4). The word *dōq* generally means "thin transparent cloth" (*CBL*, 258; BDB 201; *HALOT*² 1:229; *TWOT* 1:194), which in this context can be understood to represent the sky, especially at night, when the celestial lights appear to sparkle through a thin, see-through veil. However, when it is combined poetically with *ʾōhel*, the author appears to be more focused on the "spreading out" (*māṭaḥ*) action as opposed to the former understanding (cf. Is 45:12 and alternate language in Is 48:13). J. Goldingay therefore likens Yahweh's cosmological "tent" to a Bedouin who freely spreads a pavilion anywhere and then sits in the doorway "in sheikhly dignity and authority" (Goldingay, 56). Yahweh thus presides over the cosmos while the earth rests secure (cf. Ps 27:5) (Stadelmann, 50). Interestingly, in Isaiah 40:23 the prophet furthers the cosmological language when he notes that in light of Yahweh's sovereignty the judges are reduced to "nothing" (*tōhû*) (cf. Is 40:17; 45:18; Jer 4:23), a cosmological term reminiscent of Genesis 1:2, where the earth is said to be "formless and void" (*tōhû wābōhû*).

The author of Isaiah also addresses the celestial bodies, which are naturally a part of every ancient cosmology (e.g., Is 13:10). Isaiah uses the stars (*kôkābîm*), moon (*yārēaḥ*) and sun (*šemeš*) as objects of blessing and cursing (cf. Is 30:26; 34:4). These cosmological chess pieces are also at the bidding of the sovereign Yahweh (Is 38:8; 40:26), mere objects to be disposed of in the eschaton (Is 60:19-20). Throughout the ancient Near East the sun and moon often were worshiped as gods (e.g., the Egyptian sun-god Ra; the Babylonian moon-gods Nanna, Suen [= Sîn] and Ashimbabbar; the Ugaritic moon-god Yarikh/Yarikhu [see, e.g., *KTU* 1.18 iv:9; 1.41:27]). Because of this, the author of Deuteronomy warns against the worship of these celestial bodies (Deut 4:19; 17:3). Isaiah and many of the OT prophets direct a number of their prophetic indictments against Israel for acting out what the author of Deuteronomy condemns (e.g., Is 1:13-14; 47:13; Jer 7:18; 8:2; 19:13; 32:29; 44:17-19, 25; Ezek 8:16; Dan 8:10; Amos 5:26; Zeph 1:5). King Manasseh epitomizes this detestable practice among the Israelites (see 2 Kings 21:3-5), thus drawing the ire of the biblical writers and prophets (e.g., 2 Chron 33:1-11; Jer 15:4 [note also King Hoshea's sin in 2 Kings 17:16 and Josiah's reforms in 2 Kings 23:5]). Therefore, to combat the futility of such acts, the prophets often stressed the subservient and transient nature of this cosmological level to the sovereignty of Yahweh (e.g., Is 13:10; 30:26; 34:4; 38:8 [paralleled in 2 Kings 20:10-11]; 40:26; 60:19-20; Jer 31:35; 44:25; Ezek 32:7; Joel 2:10, 31; 3:15; Amos 5:8; 8:9; Hab 3:11). It is not at all surprising that the Israelites often veered into idolatry in this area, given that most of their feasts and festivals were closely linked to seasonal cycles, especially of the moon (e.g., Num 29:6; Neh 10:33; Ezek 45:17; 46:3). Therefore, the prophets emphasized the timekeeping function of the celestial realm over and against the ancient Near Eastern perception of their deification (cf. Jer 31:35).

Closely associated with the celestial realm are meteorological phenomena such as clouds, precipitation and storms. Isaiah makes note of precipitation in a number of contexts (e.g., *bārād*, "hail" [Is 28:2]; *šeleg*, "snow" [Is 55:10]; *tal*, "dew" [Is 26:19]; *māṭār*, "rain" [Is 55:10]; *zerem*, "storm" [Is 28:2]; *rûaḥ*, "wind" [Is 7:2; 17:13]; *sûpâ, sĕʿārâ, saʿar*, "storm wind" [Is 5:28; 21:1; 29:6; 40:24; 41:16; 66:15]). Interestingly, whereas the book of Malachi addresses the cosmological perspective of precipitation falling from the "windows of heaven" (see 6 below), Isaiah makes note of these "windows" (*ʾărubbôt*) only once (Is 24:18). Isaiah instead tends to focus on these phenomena as being under the sovereign control of Yahweh to be used as a means of blessing (Is 30:23; 44:3, 14) and cursing (Is 5:6; 24:18).

As is the normal practice throughout the prophetic corpus, Isaiah references the earthly tier both in generic terms (Is 1:2; 4:2; 5:26; 6:3; 8:9; 11:4; 12:5; 14:7) and in oracles of judgment (Is 11:4; 18:3; 28:2). Inevitably, many references often stress the sovereign and omnipotent nature of Yahweh through his creative acts in forming the heavens and the earth (Is 13:13; 40:12, 22; 42:5; 44:24; 45:12, 18; 48:13; 51:13,

16). There are also references to the role that the foundations of the earthly realm play. In the book of Isaiah Yahweh is presented not only as laying the foundations of the earth (Is 51:13), but also as the one who will shake the foundations of the earth (*môsĕdê ʾāreṣ*) to their core in the *Day of the Lord (Is 24:18). The protoapocalyptic language of Isaiah 24:19-20 thus describes the feebleness of the very earth itself when Yahweh acts in judgment (cf. Is 2:19, 21; 13:13; 24:1-21; 41:5; 51:6).

The third level of the cosmos, Sheol (*šĕʾōl* [note also *taḥtiyyôt ʾāreṣ*, "the lower parts of the earth," in Is 44:23]), also sheds light on Isaiah's cosmology (see also the metaphor in Is 26:19). Sheol appears both independently and as part of poetic couplets whereby the Pit (*bôr*) is presented as synonymous (Is 14:15; 38:18). While Sheol appears in a general sense throughout Isaiah (Is 28:15; 38:10, 18; 57:9), it is the author's use of it to show Yahweh's omnipotence that dominates. A sovereign God must have the power of life and death over his subjects, and he must be able to condemn to Sheol. Throughout the book of Isaiah this is indeed the picture presented, especially in light of Isaiah 14:15-27, where Yahweh condemns the king of Babylon to a miserable existence there (see also Is 5:14; 28:18) (*see* Afterlife).

In Isaiah 14 two cosmological extremities—the heights of heaven and the depths of Sheol—are juxtaposed in metaphorical terms (see also Is 51:13). Isaiah 14:13-15 records a sequence of poetic phrases reflecting mythological concepts depicting the heights to which the king of *Babylon sought to elevate himself and the depths to which he ultimately fell. Although no one phrase can be taken to designate a particular location for Yahweh's throne or abode (i.e., is it in heaven generally speaking, or above the stars, or on the mount of the assembly, or above the clouds?), it does suggest to the reader that Yahweh's abode is viewed as existing in a place of elevation, the heavens. Interestingly, the reference to the "mountain of the assembly" (*har môʿēd*) in Isaiah 14:13 (cf. a similar usage in Ugaritic, *pḫr.mʿd*, "assembly of the gods" [*KTU* 1.2 i:14]) does have a possible cosmological connection. Ancient Near Eastern peoples sometimes understood the entire cosmos to be likened to a cosmic mountain. Much like a mountain climber, the king of Babylon is said in Isaiah 14:13 to have desired to metaphorically "ascend/scale" (*ʿālâ*) the heavens and the clouds. However, the king of Babylon fails to attain his desired outcome (for competing ancient Near Eastern interpretations of this passage, see Childs, 126; Stadelmann, 90; Watson, 394). Whatever mythological connections lie behind the text, the cosmological concepts are clear. Isaiah speaks in well-known mythological and cosmological terms to show the hubris of the king of Babylon who actually thought that he was a god who could ascend above the created order to the position of the sovereign Yahweh. Instead, he is brought to the depths of Sheol.

3. Jeremiah.
Jeremiah's polemical tirades against idols open the door for general cosmological comments relating to the creative powers of Yahweh. Jeremiah shows the sovereignty of Yahweh by noting that he alone, not the idols worshiped by Judah, has created the heavens and the earth (Jer 10:11). Much like the book of Isaiah, Jeremiah seeks to show Yahweh's sovereign purposes in judging his people through cosmological themes. For example, in Jeremiah 4:22-29 the prophet pronounces judgment upon Judah using a de-creation process whereby the organized cosmos is presented as being "formless and void" (tōhû wābōhû [Jer 4:23]), an obvious allusion to Genesis 1:2. Or consider Jeremiah's use of meteorological events such as rain (gešem, "rain"; yōreh, "spring rains"; malqôš, "latter rain") and showers (rĕbîbîm) as a means of showing Yahweh's *blessing and cursing (Jer 3:3; 5:24; 14:22). He also likens Yahweh's judgment to storm winds of various types (e.g., rûaḥ qādîm, "east wind"; sûpâ, "whirlwind"; sĕʿārâ, "storm wind"; saʿar, "storm" in general [Jer 4:13; 18:17; 23:19; 25:32; 30:23]) coming from the "four corners" (ʾarbaʿ qĕṣôt) of the cosmos (Jer 49:36).

Jeremiah draws several verbal pictures of his cosmology. He presents the wind as being held in "storehouses" (ʾôṣār), no doubt in the upper cosmological tier (Jer 10:13; 51:16). He notes that Yahweh has delimited the terrestrial seas by the sands of the shores (Jer 5:22) and has established the world by his wisdom and stretched out the heavens through his understanding (Jer 51:15). The prophet also uses a cosmological merismus in Jeremiah 31:37 in the midst of a series of rhetorical statements related to cosmological functions and realities

(Jer 31:35-37). In every case the prophet makes it clear that it is Yahweh who created and controls the universe and its functions. For example, he posits, if someone "can measure the heavens" or can search the "foundations of the earth," then Yahweh would reject his people (see also Jer 33:20-21, 25-26). Surprisingly, apart from these references to the foundations of the earth, Jeremiah makes no mention of Sheol or the Pit in his prophecies, even though he frequently speaks of the deaths of those who reject God. Instead, Jeremiah speaks only of a bipartite cosmos (Jer 32:17; cf. Jer 33:2).

Finally, Jeremiah declares that the very voice of Yahweh causes a tumult in the celestial waters (Jer 10:13; 51:16). Jeremiah's comments may come from the cosmological perspective that there existed above the dome of the heavens a "celestial ocean" (see Gen 1:6-7; Ps 148:4; also called the mabbûl mayim, "flood of water" [e.g., Gen 6:17; 7:6, 7, 10, 17; Ps 29:10]). Although the prophets move away from ancient Near Eastern creation mythology in the strictest sense of the term, the cosmological parallels here are telling. In Babylonian creation mythology the god Marduk splits the goddess Tiamat's body and uses one half of it to make a solid shell-like dome to hold back the celestial waters (ANET 67-68, 501-2, tablets IV, V). Similarly, in Egyptian cosmology, the goddess Nut is pictured with an elongated body with fingertips and toes on the ground. Her body is arched upward, being supported by the air-god Shu (ANEP 183, fig. 542). The arched-bodied Nut and halved Tiamat thus serve a similar function as the semicircular dome (ḥûg) implied here and noted above in the discussion on Isaiah.

4. Ezekiel.
Ezekiel too employs cosmological concepts in order to show the sovereignty of Yahweh. Although Ezekiel identifies the three tiers of the cosmos throughout his work, nowhere does he list them together. Perhaps the most detailed of his cosmological descriptions comes in the opening verses and chapters of his book. It is here that the reader gets a glimpse into the heavenly realm.

Ezekiel's opening vision of Yahweh's glory (kābôd) by the river Chebar highlights the heavenly level above which Yahweh dwells. This level Ezekiel calls the rāqîaʿ ("expanse" or "firmament" [Ezek 1:22, 23, 25, 26; see also Ezek

10:1]). Next to Genesis 1, which uses *rāqîaʿ* nine times, Ezekiel has the most occurrences of this particular term (see also Ps 19:2; 150:1). Within scholarly circles there still remains some debate as to what *rāqîaʿ* means both here and elsewhere. Some feel that the concept of a "solid" surface comes from a later period through the influence of translations of *rāqîaʿ*, like the Vulgate's *firmamentum* or the LXX's *stereōma* (*TWOT* 2:862). Ezekiel describes this *rāqîaʿ* as being "like the awesome eye/gleam of ice" (Ezek 1:22) but does not specifically identify its solidity. The verbal root *rqʿ* often reflects the idea of the beating or spreading out flat of a piece of metal into plates (Ex 39:3; Num 16:38-39; 2 Sam 22:43; Is 40:19; Jer 10:9) or the stamping of feet (Ezek 6:11; 25:6). However, it is also used to designate Yahweh's creative acts of spreading out "the earth or the sky like a layer" (Lint, 6:599) (see Is 42:5; 44:24), thus making a dome or the vaulted heavens which holds up the celestial waters (BDB 956). In the Mosaic tradition of Genesis 1, *rāqîaʿ* seems to be used interchangeably between the atmospheric level where birds fly and the planetary level (Gen 1:14, 17, 20) (*TWOT* 2:862). However one interprets *rāqîaʿ* elsewhere, here it seems to be a solid surface that holds up the throne of Yahweh. One could argue that this may in turn have some connection to the area above Isaiah's dome (*ḥûg*).

Ezekiel uses several atmospheric and planetary phenomena to show Yahweh's glory and sovereignty over his creation and in the context of judgment (e.g., Ezek 32:7-8). To begin with, the dreaded east wind (*rûaḥ haqqādîm* or *rûaḥ sěʿārôt*) is applied in oracles against Yahweh's people (Ezek 13:11, 13; 17:10; 19:12) and the *nations (Ezek 27:26). Furthermore, the use of cloud(s) (*ʿānān*, *ʿāb*) as metaphors for Yahweh's glory (Ezek 1:4; 10) and the hubris of the nations (Ezek 31:3, 10, 14) is also attested. Finally, the prophet warns that rain (*gešem*, *māṭar*) will be withheld as judgment upon Judah (Ezek 22:24) and will fall excessively to judge both Israel and the nations (Ezek 13:11; 38:22).

Ezekiel also references the second level of the cosmos using the terms *ʾereṣ* ("earth") and *ʾădāmâ* ("land") synonymously for the land of Israel (e.g., Ezek 6:14; 7:2, 7, 23, 27; 8:12, 17; 9:9; 11:15, 17; 12:19, 20, 22; 13:9; 14:15; 15:8; 17:13; 21:2, 3), Babylon (Ezek 1:3; 16:29; 17:4, 5) and Egypt (Ezek 20:5, 6, 9; 23:19). Cosmologically, Ezekiel does draw a distinction between the

heavens and earth at various junctures (Ezek 1:15, 19, 21; 7:21; 10:16, 19; 12:6, 12; 19:12; 28:17; 29:15; 32:4; 34:6, 28; 35:14; 39:18) and even points out the atmospheric space "between" (*bên*) these two cosmological extremes (e.g., Ezek 8:3; cf. 1 Chron 21:16; Zech 5:9); this latter example no doubt is reflective of Ezekiel's desire to show the ethereal nature of the event. On two separate occasions Ezekiel shows the power of Yahweh over the cosmos by noting that God will cause the mountains to shake (Ezek 38:20) and the earth to shine with his "glory" (Ezek 43:2).

The lower level of the earth, which houses the abode of the dead, appears frequently in select chapters of Ezekiel. Ezekiel utilizes this level as a means of showing Yahweh's sovereignty over people's destiny. Although it is only implicit that Ezekiel saw this region as a separate cosmological tier from the earthly realm, it is evident that the prophet did see a distinct difference between the two. Ezekiel uses both "Sheol" (*šěʾôl* [Ezek 31:15-17; 32:21, 27]) and "Pit" (*bôr* [Ezek 26:20; 31:14, 16; 32:18, 23-25, 29, 30]) as names for this lower region, sometimes interchangeably (Ezek 31:16). He also identifies this region as the "earth beneath" (*ʾereṣ taḥtît* [Ezek 26:20; 31:14, 16, 18]). Interestingly, much like Jonah, Ezekiel intimates that Sheol is below the great watery depths (*těhôm* [Ezek 31:15]).

5. Daniel.

Quite clearly, the author of Daniel sought to present Yahweh as sovereign by making an obvious cosmological distinction between the heavenly and the earthly realms (e.g., Dan 4:17, 25; 5:21; 7:27). However, perhaps with the exception of a few *apocalyptically nuanced references (e.g., Dan 8:10), the book of Daniel records very few direct cosmological analogies. Yahweh is presented as the "God of heaven" (*ʾĕlāh šěmayyāʾ* [Dan 2:18, 19, 37; 5:21, 23]), the "Most High" (*ʿillāyāʾ* [Dan 3:26; 4:2, 17, 24, 25, 32, 34; 5:18, 21; 7:25]), the "Highest One" (*ʿelyônîn* [Dan 7:18, 22, 25, 27]), the "Lord of Heaven" (*mārēʾ šěmayyāʾ* [Dan 5:23]), and in one instance he is even presented metaphorically as "Heaven" (*šěmayyāʾ*) itself (Dan 4:26). Also, angelic messengers are presented implicitly descending from the heavenly realms to deliver messages (Dan 4:23; 9:21-27; 10:9-21; 12:5-13). Finally, in a synonymous parallel bicolon the author of Daniel parallels the brightness of the *rāqîaʿ* and the stars (*kôkābîm*) of the heaven (Dan 12:3). The author here appears to make a direct connection between the expanse (*rāqîaʿ*) and the celestial level where the planets and luminaries reside—a very "Mosaic" concept (see 4 above).

Unlike Ezekiel and Isaiah, Daniel records no references to atmospheric phenomena apart from his visionary experience where he sees the "one like a son of man" coming in the clouds (Dan 7:13). Furthermore, the only tangential reference to Sheol is possibly Daniel 12:2, where the text reads that the righteous will arise from the dust of the ground or, more literally, from the "land of dust" (*ʾadmat ʿāpār*). However, this cryptic reference offers little insight into the cosmological thinking of the author concerning a lower tier to the cosmos.

6. The Book of the Twelve (Minor Prophets).

The Book of the Twelve, also known as the Minor Prophets, varies widely in its presentation of cosmological facets, with some books remaining completely silent on the topic (e.g., Obadiah). As with the Major Prophets, when the Minor Prophets do use cosmology within their oracles it is for the purpose of showing the sovereignty of Yahweh over his creation. No one prophet offers a complete vignette of his cosmology, but each prophet does offer a glimpse into the cosmological worldview of his day. Zechariah and Jonah, for example, present a bipartite description of the cosmos (Jon 1:9 [much like Nehemiah, Jonah includes the seas as a separate designation]; Zech 12:1 [see also comments in 4 above concerning the possibility of an area between the heavens and the earth in Zech 5:9]), whereas Amos, being the most detailed in his cosmological descriptions, presents the clearest picture of a three-tiered cosmology, especially the heavenly tier. In showing the far-reaching judgments of Yahweh, Amos puts forward the cosmological limits of Sheol, the heavens and various levels of the earthly realm as areas controlled by Yahweh (Amos 9:2-3). Moreover, in Amos 9:6 the prophet points out that it was Yahweh who built the upper chambers and the vaulted "dome" (*ʾăguddâ*, a synonym for *rāqîaʿ* [see *NIDOTTE* 3:1198]) over the earth, a similar picture noted by Isaiah.

The Minor Prophets were also instrumental in indicting the nation for covenant violations that included meteorological and cosmic disturbances. For example, the rains (*gešem*) and dew (*ṭal*) became an effective weapon in the prophetic arsenal for blessing and cursing (e.g., Hos 6:3; 13:15; Joel 2:23; Amos 4:7, 9; Nah 1:3; Zech 8:12; 10:1; 14:17-18; Mal 3:10; see also Gen 7:11; 8:2; Lev 26:19; Deut 11:13-14; 28:23-24; 1 Kings 8:35-36; 2 Kings 7:2, 19; 2 Chron 6:26; Job 5:10; Ps 78:23). Malachi 3:10 picks up on the blessings of rain and adopts the metaphor of the "windows of heaven" (*ʾărubbôt haššāmayim*) pouring forth this bounty (see also the Egyptian concept of the "doors of heaven" from the period of Thut-Mose III in *ANET* 446; cf. Ps 78:23). Interestingly, we find no other clear reference in the ancient Near East to the idea of "windows" in heaven, perhaps with the exception of the window constructed in Baal's house (see Walton, Matthews and Chavalas, 384; *ANET* 134, vi:1-10). Even though the OT authors recognized that rain came from the clouds (e.g., 1 Kings 18:44; Is 5:6; Zech 10:1), Malachi and Isaiah (see 2 above) adopt the metaphor of cosmic windows as a way of explaining the natural phenomenon. Given a geographical region so heavily reliant upon seasonal rains, there is little wonder why this particular meteorological event was an effective means of judgment.

In a similar vein, storm winds (*sûpâ*) were most often utilized in oracles of cursing (Hos 8:7; 13:15; Zech 7:13). Just as the psalmists attributed these meteorological phenomena to Yahweh (Ps 18:7-15; 29:3-9), the prophets intimate that Yahweh is to be likened to the awesome power of the thunderstorm, with its flashing arrows of fire and the roar of thunder (Jer 10:13; 25:30; 51:16; Hab 3:9-11; Zech 9:14). That is not to say that the OT prophets pictured Yahweh in a similar fashion as the Canaanites pictured their storm god Baal (see Pritchard, plates 136, 140), but rather that the natural phenomenon of the storm was an easily adapted metaphor for Yahweh's sovereign and majestic nature. As L. Stadelmann concludes, "The fundamental difference between Yahweh and Baʿal lies in the fact that Baʿal personifies the meteorological phenomena, whereas Yahweh controls them" (Stadelmann, 125).

At the terrestrial level, the Minor Prophets generally focus on Yahweh as the creator of heaven and earth (e.g., Amos 4:13; 5:8; 9:6; Jon

1:9; Nah 1:3-6; Zech 12:1), with the purpose of showing his sovereignty over his creation (e.g., Hab 3:4-6, 9-10; 3:11-15; Zeph 1:2-3). They also reference the earthly tier in general terms (e.g., Mic 7:13; Hab 2:14; Zeph 1:18; Zech 1:10-11; 4:10) but make it clear that Yahweh is, and will be, the lord of that creation (Zech 6:5; 14:9). For example, Yahweh is depicted as causing the sun and the moon to be darkened at his bidding (Joel 2:10, 15, 30; Amos 8:9; Zeph 1:15), with them standing still before his glory (Hab 3:11). Several of the Minor Prophets also note the trembling and cataclysmic changes of the heavens and the earth when Yahweh appears (Joel 2:10; 3:15; Amos 9:5; Mic 1:3-4; Hag 2:6; Zech 14:3-8).

At various points in the OT the *mountains appear to be presented as the foundations/pillars (*môsād*) that bore up the heavenly dome (cf. Job 26:10-11; 2 Sam 22:8). In Akkadian tradition this mythological mountain range was known as Mâšu (see *ANET* 88, tablet 9, col. 2). In the Minor Prophets the "roots" (*qeṣeb*) of the mountains also stretched into the third cosmological tier, the netherworld, thus offering a firm foundation for both the earth and the firmament (Jon 2:6; Mic 6:2; see also 1 Sam 2:8; 1 Chron 16:30; Job 9:6; 38:4-6; Ps 18:7, 15; 75:3; 82:5; 104:5; Prov 8:29; Is 24:18; 51:13; Jer 31:37). During the covenant indictment speech in Micah 2 the prophet uses poetic parallelism to identify the enduring qualities of the mountains as the "foundations" (*môsādîm*) of the earth, but he does not go beyond this basic connection to the underworld. The belief that the mountains in some way connected the three cosmic tiers may explain why they attracted sacred importance.

The Minor Prophets offer very little insight into the concept of Sheol and the subterranean realm of the dead. Hosea, Amos, Jonah and Habakkuk are the only ones who make any clear reference to Sheol (Hos 13:14; Amos 9:2; Jon 2:2, 6; Hab 2:5). Hosea and Habakkuk use Sheol as a metaphor for death, whereas Jonah and Amos connect it to the lower cosmological tier. Jonah, in his descent into the abyss of the sea, likens his experience to a journey into Sheol. He notes that his experience paralleled that of descending to the "roots of the mountains" (*qiṣbê hārîm* [Jon 2:6]). Although Sheol often is personified in the OT as "swallowing" people (2 Sam 22:6; Ps 18:5; 69:15; 141:7; Prov

1:12; 27:20; 30:16; Is 5:14; Hab 2:5), there is no evidence that it is to be likened to the Ugaritic god of the underworld, Mot, who does battle with his foes (Stadelmann, 168; *ANET* 138-39). Furthermore, in ancient Near Eastern thinking the path to Sheol or the underworld was at the western horizon. It was here that the shades would be taken to the netherworld by the setting sun. Although Numbers 16 suggests that Korah and his cohorts were swallowed alive into Sheol (see also Ex 15:12), the prophets do not make it clear exactly how one descends to the realm of the dead.

7. The Sacred Mountain and Divine Warrior.

Two other concepts appear throughout the prophetic corpus that shed light on prophetic cosmological perspectives: (1) the role of the sacred mountain; (2) Yahweh as the divine warrior protecting his cosmological space: the temple and Israel.

OT and ancient Near Eastern peoples viewed select mountains as sacred (e.g., Ex 3:1; 1 Kings 19:8; Ps 2:6; note also Mount Zaphon in Ugarit [see *ANET* 133, v:85] and the sacred ziggurat at Ur and the massive ziggurat Etemenanki beside Marduk's temple at Esagila in Babylon). There is no doubt that cultic rites on the mountains/high places played a dominant role in Israel, for it is against these pagan practices that the prophets spoke vociferously (e.g., Is 15:2; 36:7; Jer 7:31; 17:2-3; 19:5; Ezek 16:39; Hos 4:13; 10:8). However, the prophets did not completely jettison the sacred importance placed upon select mountains as found in both the Torah and Former Prophets (e.g., Horeb in Mal 4:4; see also Ex 3:1; 1 Kings 19:8). They tended to stress the centrality of Mount *Zion, the *temple and the city of Jerusalem in light of Yahweh's plans and purposes (e.g., Is 2:2; Mic 4:1; Zech 14:10). Therefore, it is no surprise that the OT and the Apocrypha present Mount Zion/Jerusalem as the "navel of the earth" (*ṭabbûr hā'āreṣ* [Ezek 38:12; see also Is 28:16; Ezek 5:5; *Jub.* 8:19; *1 En.* 26:1]). Ancient Near Eastern cultures such as Babylon, Assyria, Persia, Egypt and Greece equated prominent religious cities with the "center" of their nations as well (see Stadelmann, 147-53) (note also the role of Mount Gerizim in the religious life of the Samaritans [Josephus, *Ant.* 11.310; 18.85]). Paradigmatically, Isaiah and his contemporary Micah saw Mount

Zion as elevated above all the mountains in the last days as a center of Yahweh worship (Is 2:1-4; Mic 4:1-5; see also Dan 9:16, 20; 11:45; Joel 2:1; Hag 2:6-9).

The central cosmological role of Yahweh as creator and defender of his people plays out in several prophetic texts as Yahweh roars forth from Mount Zion and his temple as the divine warrior (Is 24:23; Ezek 38—39; Joel 3:9-21; Amos 1:2; Mic 2:13; Nah 1:2; Zeph 2:11-13; 3:16-17; Zech 2:13; Mal 1:4-5). Joel and Zechariah in particular make it clear that the cosmological chaos in the *Day of the Lord will be directly connected to Yahweh's defense of his land and people (e.g., Joel 2:1-17, 32; 3:16-17; Zech 12:7-9; 14:1-4). Furthermore, as the divine warrior, the sovereignty of Yahweh is also highlighted by his control of the wellspring of the cosmos, the chaotic sea (*yām*)—something common throughout the OT prophets (Is 17:12-13; 23:11; 50:2; Ezek 27:25; 32:2-3; Jon 2:4). This harks back to Genesis 1, where the sea is in need of "conquering." For the prophets, Yahweh's control and conquering of the sea shows not only his omnipotence but also his control of the primal cosmological entity. There is no question that in certain places the prophets are recalling ancient Near Eastern mythology whereby a patron deity battles the *chaos of the primordial sea (in the OT known as Rahab [e.g., Is 51:9; Hab 3:8; see also Job 9:8; 26:12; Ps 77:16-20; 89:10]). Although the imagery is reminiscent of Marduk's battle with Tiamat (Babylon) and Baal's struggle with Yam (Ugarit), the remnants of the mythological concept are subservient to the sovereignty of Israel's God (*see* Warfare and Divine Warfare).

8. Conclusion.
One of the key purposes for the prophetic use of cosmological motifs is to prove that Yahweh, as creator, is indeed sovereign over not only the cosmos but also those who inhabit it. Due to the prophetic impetus, it is also natural for this usage to focus primarily on judgment upon Israel and the nations. Throughout the prophetic corpus the prophets show that Yahweh uses his cosmos not only as a means of blessing (e.g., Jer 5:24) and judgment (e.g., Jer 3:3; 14:1-4) but also as the stage upon which Yahweh shows his omnipotence (Hab 3). For the covenant people and those dependent upon the natural order of the cosmos, such as the seasonal cycles, these motifs prove effective. For the nations and those who reject the message of the prophets, the realm of the dead—Sheol and the Pit—serve as a just, ultimate punishment for unfaithfulness and hubris, and this message resonates not only throughout NT theological thought but also in many circles even today.

See also CHAOS; CREATION THEOLOGY; DEATH; MOUNTAIN IMAGERY; ZION.

BIBLIOGRAPHY. **B. S. Childs**, *Isaiah* (OTL; Louisville: Westminster/John Knox, 2001); **D. J. A. Clines**, ed., *The Dictionary of Classical Hebrew* (8 vols.; Sheffield: Sheffield Academic, 1996); **J. C. de Moor**, *An Anthology of Religious Texts from Ugarit* (Nisaba 16; Leiden: E. J. Brill, 1987); **J. Goldingay**, *The Message of Isaiah 40-55: A Literary-Theological Commentary* (London: T & T Clark, 2005); **C. H. Gordon**, *Ugaritic Textbook: Grammar, Texts in Transliteration, Cuneiform Selections, Glossary, Indices* (AnOr 38; Rome: Pontifical Biblical Institute, 1965); **R. S. Hess**, *Israelite Religions: An Archaeological and Biblical Survey* (Grand Rapids: Baker Academic, 2007); **B. Lang**, *Monotheism and the Prophetic Minority: An Essay in Biblical History and Sociology* (SWBA 1; Sheffield: Almond, 1983); idem, "Zur Entstehung des biblischen Monotheismus," *TQ* 166 (1986) 135-42; **J. C. Lennox**, *Seven Days That Divide the World: The Beginning According to Genesis and Science* (Grand Rapids: Zondervan, 2011); **G. A. Lint**, ed., *The Complete Biblical Library: The Old Testament Hebrew-English Dictionary* (7 vols.; Springfield, MO: World Library, 1995); **E. C. Lucas**, "Cosmology," *DOTP* 130-39; **J. W. McKay**, "Helel and the Dawn Goddess: A Re-examination of the Myth in Isaiah XIV 12-15," *VT* 20 (1970) 451-64; **J. B. Pritchard**, ed., *The Ancient Near East: An Anthology of Texts and Pictures* (Princeton, NJ: Princeton University Press, 2011); **B. B. Schmidt**, "Moon," *DDD²* 585-93; **L. I. J. Stadelmann**, *The Hebrew Conception of the World: A Philological and Literary Study* (AnBib 39; Rome: Pontifical Biblical, 1970); **D. Stuart**, "Malachi," in *The Minor Prophets: Zephaniah, Haggai, Zechariah, Malachi*, ed. T. E. McComiskey (Grand Rapids: Baker, 1998) 1245-1396; **J. H. Walton**, *The Lost World of Genesis One: Ancient Cosmology and the Origins Debate* (Downers Grove, IL: InterVarsity Press, 2009); **J. H. Walton, V. H. Matthews and M. W. Chavalas**, *The IVP Bible Background Commentary: Old Testament* (Downers Grove, IL: InterVarsity

Press, 2000); **W. G. E. Watson,** "Helel," *DDD*[2] 392-94; **H. Wolf,** "dōq," *TWOT* 194-95; **I. Zatelli,** "Astrology and the Worship of the Stars in the Bible," *ZAW* 103 (1991) 86-99.

B. N. Peterson

COURT TALES. *See* DANIEL: BOOK OF.

COVENANT

The concept of covenant is fundamental in understanding biblical history, theology and the intertwining of the two. The Hebrew word translated as "covenant" is *bĕrît*, and its etymology is complex. While the word cannot be attached with confidence to any Hebrew verbal root, it seems that the word can best be related to the Akkadian word *biritu*, which means "clasp, fetter." If so, the covenant might be thought of as a bond. Another Akkadian reference is the word *birit*, meaning "between," and thus it sees the covenant as an arrangement between two or more parties. Lastly, the Akkadian word *barû* ("to see") may indicate that the word could be translated as "obligation" (see Weinfeld 1973; Kalluveettil, 7-16; McConville).

While a covenant can be a simple pact or treaty between two people (Gen 21:27; 1 Sam 18:3), God's covenants with his people are broader in focus, and generally they contain promises that God makes on behalf of his people. The concept of covenant is not unique to Israel; rather, the concept was fundamental in ancient Near Eastern cultures from the beginning of recorded time. Indeed, some OT covenants follow the structure of the Hittite suzerain-vassal treaty: preamble, historical prologue, stipulations, provision for deposit in the temple, list of witnesses, and curses/blessings (Mendenhall, 31-34; McCarthy, 37-81; Niehaus, 81-141). The concept of covenant is not late in Israel's history and theological development; it was part of religious, social, and political spheres as early as the fifteenth century BC (contra Nicholson; see Kitchen 1989, 121-32). In the OT the concept of covenant is clearly outlined in the Pentateuch. The word first appears in Genesis 6:18 in God's covenant with Noah (for a detailed description of the covenant with creation motif, see Dumbrell, 33-39). The covenants could be divided into universal, ancestral and national. The universal covenant refers to the covenant that God established with creation after the universal flood recorded in Genesis 6—9. The ancestral covenants refer to the covenants that God made with Abraham (see Williamson, *DOTP* 139-55).

The prophets speak directly about the specific covenants, or they allude to them extensively throughout their writings. This article focuses on the Abrahamic, Mosaic, Davidic and new covenants as addressed by God's servants, the prophets. The term "covenant" appears fifty-five times in the Major Prophets of the Hebrew canon (13x in Isaiah; 25x in Jeremiah; 17x in Ezekiel), seven times in Daniel, and fifteen times in the Minor Prophets. Of the occurrences in the Minor Prophets, nine times it refers to the Mosaic covenant (Hos 6:7; 8:1; Zech 9:11; 11:10; Mal 2:4, 5, 8, 10; 3:1), once to a future covenant (Hos 2:18), once to covenants that people make with each other (Hos 10:4), once to a covenant that Israel makes with Assyria and Egypt (Hos 12:1), once to a "covenant of brotherhood" that the people of Tyre did not keep (Amos 1:9), once to an alliance of Edom (Obad 1:7), and once to a covenant between a husband and a wife (Mal 2:14). However, the covenant motif appears much more often in both the Major and the Minor Prophets, especially in conjunction with the people's disobedience to the covenant stipulations as they were set forth in the Ten Commandments.

1. The Abrahamic Covenant
2. The Mosaic Covenant
3. The Davidic Covenant
4. The New Covenant

1. The Abrahamic Covenant.

1.1. Major Prophets. In the Abrahamic covenant (Gen 12; 15; 17) God promised Abraham a great name, a great nation and a great land. These promises had been partly fulfilled by the time of Moses and Joshua. But Abraham was to be more than just a recipient of divine blessing; he himself was to be a blessing to others. "Through you," God promises, "all the families of the earth will be blessed" (Gen 12:3). By the time of Joseph, God has fulfilled the first two promises to such an extent that the Egyptian Pharaoh feared the people of Israel (Ex 1). The people of Israel will inherit the promised land, but only later, during the time of Joshua. Even so, the prophets use Abraham and God's covenant with him to encourage his people. God through Isaiah exhorts his people not to fear because, after all, they are Abraham's offspring, and thus they are the recipients of God's power and presence (Is 41:8-10). Furthermore, God encourages his people to remember God's faithfulness to Abraham. Just as God blessed and multiplied Abraham, so will he bless and multiply Abraham's descendants (Is 51:1-2).

One way the concept of covenant comes to the forefront is through the use of the covenant formula, which appears in three versions with particular variants: (1) "I will be your God"; (2) "You will be my people"; (3) a combination of the first two (see Rendtorff, 13-28). Within the context of the Abrahamic covenant, the formula appears twice in Genesis 17, where God affirms to Abraham, "I will establish my covenant between me and you . . . to be God to you and to your offspring after you" (Gen 17:7). After the promise of the land, the formula is present again in the promise "I will be their God" (Gen 17:8). Before the establishment of the Mosaic covenant, God reminds his people of the covenant made with Abraham (Ex 6:2-6), and then the covenant formula reappears, "I will take you to be my people, and I will be your God" (Ex 6:7). This promise is given in the context of the land promise, which is not unique to the Abrahamic covenant and will be a recurring theme in other, subsequent covenants (McComiskey, 48-51).

1.2. The Minor Prophets (The Twelve). *Sin, judgment and restoration are the three main themes on which the Minor Prophets focus. The people's sin is particularly tied in with the failure to obey the Mosaic covenant, but the Abrahamic covenant is alluded to in the language of restoration. The restoration that most Minor Prophets speak about relating to the Abrahamic covenant is the promise of the return to the land following the judgment through *exile. In Hosea the Israelites are described as doves returning to their homes from Assyria (Hos 11:11), and in Joel the land of Judah is promised a perpetual inhabitation. Joel describes this land hyperbolically as having mountains dripping with sweet wine and hills flowing with milk (Joel 3:18-20). Obadiah employs merism to describe the totality of the land that the exiles will possess as extending from Zarephath in the north to the Negev in the south (Obad 20). In the last verse of Micah the children of Israel are identified as the descendants of Abraham and Jacob; thus, they are the recipients of God's faithfulness and steadfast love (Mic 7:20). A return to the *land is implied

at the end of Zephaniah as well when God promises to bring his people in and to gather them together (Zeph 3:20). The only occurrence of the covenant formula in the Minor Prophets occurs in Zechariah's language of restoration: "I will bring them to dwell in the midst of Jerusalem. And they shall be my people, and I will be their God, in faithfulness and in righteousness" (Zech 8:8). The presence of the promise here is important because it occurs after the return from the Babylonian exile, and thus it could have an important eschatological nuance.

2. The Mosaic Covenant.

2.1. The Major Prophets. The most prominent of the covenants is *God's covenant with Israel that was established at Sinai. When the NT makes reference to the old covenant, it refers to this covenant. It is important to note from the outset that there are many similarities between the Abrahamic and Mosaic covenants. The covenant formula "I will be your/their God and you/they will be my people" appears in both the Abrahamic and the Mosaic covenants, emphasizing the fact that what God desired was a relationship with his people (Gen 17:8; Ex 6:7). The promise of land is also prominently displayed in the Mosaic covenant, affirming that the Abrahamic covenant promises and stipulations do not cease with the Mosaic covenant; rather, they are reemphasized. God's intervention on behalf of Israel in Egypt is done in conjunction with God's promises to the patriarchs (Ex 3:7-8, 16-22; 6:4; 13:5, 11). The Ten Commandments are the first part of a three-part section of the Mosaic *law, and they represent the most important teachings of this covenant. The prophets addressed the people's keeping and breaking of this covenant by referring back to the Ten Commandments (due to his documentary presuppositions, W. Eichrodt fails to see the prophets addressing the Mosaic covenant [Eichrodt, 51-52]). The breaking of the first three commandments in particular had to do with one's relationship with God. This was repeatedly condemned by God through the prophets. In the eighth century BC God speaks through Isaiah that "their land was filled with idols" (Is 2:8) that they worshiped (Is 2:20). But Isaiah also prophesies about a time of repentance when the people will get rid of their *idols (Is 30:22; 31:7). During the ministry of Jeremiah the people were still guilty of breaking the first commandment by worshiping "carved images and foreign idols" (Jer 8:19). Even though these idols were powerless (Jer 10:5, 14), the people "polluted" the land with these "detestable idols" (Jer 16:18). Ezekiel prophesies about the people's judgment by being exiled because they worshiped idols (Ezek 6:9, 13). The situation worsened during the time of Ezekiel to such a degree that the leaders of Israel practiced idol worship even in the *temple (Ezek 8). But God promises to restore Israel by cleansing them from their idolatry. This restoration anticipates the new covenant, and it will be made possible by the giving of a new heart and by the putting of God's Spirit within them (Ezek 36:25-26). Daniel speaks in prayer of God keeping his covenant (Dan 9:4) and of God's "holy covenant" (Dan 11:28, 30, 32), which is opposed, attacked or forsaken (see also Dan 11:22, where a "prince of the covenant" is opposed).

Another important aspect of the Mosaic covenant that is repeated throughout the prophets is the sign of this covenant: the Sabbath (Ex 31:13-17). In Isaiah, those who keep the Sabbath are considered blessed (Is 56:2), they please God (Is 56:4), and will have their *sacrifices accepted on God's altar (Is 56:6-7). On the other hand, those who fail to keep the Sabbath are said to profane it (Is 56:6) and seek their own pleasure on this holy day (Is 58:13). Through the prophet Jeremiah God reminds his people not to bear a burden on the Sabbath day (Jer 17:21), but to keep it holy (Jer 17:22). Failure to keep the Sabbath holy will bring about God's judgment in the form of the destruction of Jerusalem (Jer 17:27). Ezekiel speaks of Israel's rebellion against God in terms of profaning the Sabbath (Ezek 20:13, 16, 21, 24; 22:8; 23:38) or disregarding the Sabbath (Ezek 22:26). On the other hand, Ezekiel prophesies about a future time of restoration when the Levitical priests will keep God's Sabbaths holy (Ezek 44:24). During this time people will worship during the Sabbath (Ezek 46:3), they will bring sacrifices (Ezek 46:4) and offerings (Ezek 46:12).

If the first four commandments of the Ten Commandments had to do with one's relationship with God, the last six commandments had to do with one's relationship with his parents (fifth) and neighbors (sixth through tenth). The prophets list sinful violations of these six com-

mandments throughout their works, but more emphasis is given to the first four commandments. The breaking of the sixth commandment, "You shall not kill," is addressed in language that includes words such as "blood," "bloodshed," and/or "bloodstains." Through the prophet Isaiah God indicts Israel, saying that their "hands are full of blood" (Is 1:15) or "defiled with blood" (Is 59:3). God, the faithful gardener, plants a vineyard; but instead of it yielding justice, it yields bloodshed (Is 5:7), and those who oppress others "are swift to shed innocent blood" (Is 59:7). Jeremiah uses similar language to describe the people's rebellion. They have filled the land "with the blood of innocents" (Jer 19:4), and they shed innocent blood (Jer 22:17). In Ezekiel's time the land was described as "full of bloody crimes" (Ezek 7:23) and "full of blood" (Ezek 9:9). Ezekiel 22 is devoted in its entirety as an indictment on the "city of bloodshed." Ezekiel is summoned by the Lord to judge the "bloody city" (Ezek 22:2) because of all its abominations. The city is labeled as such because it is a city "that sheds blood" (Ezek 22:3, 9), a city "that became guilty" because of the blood that it shed (Ezek 22:4), and a city whose princes "are bent on shedding blood" (Ezek 22:6). Subsequently, the cry against it is "Woe to the bloody city!" (Ezek 24:6, 9).

The seventh commandment, "You shall not commit adultery," is one that the prophets address repeatedly. Even though Israel's rebellion was couched in figurative language when they were accused of spiritual adultery (Jer 3:9; 5:7; Ezek 23:37, 43), the prophets also address the physical aspect of individuals breaking this holy commandment. Adultery is one of the sins listed in Jeremiah's famous Temple Sermon, in which he lists the sins for which the nation is guilty (Jer 7:9). The false prophets "commit adultery," the very sin they are called to condemn (Jer 23:14). In his letter to the Babylonian exiles Jeremiah affirms that adultery was one of the sins for which the people were sent into exile (Jer 29:23).

The last three commandments are the least mentioned in the Major Prophets. Jeremiah lists stealing in his Temple Sermon (Jer 7:9), and God accuses the false prophets of stealing sermons from each other (Jer 23:30). Through Isaiah God condemns the prophets who lie (Is 9:15) and the religious leaders "have made lies" their refuge (Is 28:15). Lying is also condemned in general terms, usually in connection with idolatry and bloodshed (Is 57:11; 59:3-4). In Jeremiah the scribes are described as having "a lying pen" (Jer 8:8), the people are deceiving their neighbors (Jer 9:5), and the prophets are prophesying lies (Jer 14:14; 23:14; 23:25-26, 32; 27:10, 14-16; 29:9, 21, 31). Through Ezekiel God continues to condemn the false prophets who are lying to God's people (Ezek 13:19; 21:29; 22:28).

2.2. The Minor Prophets (The Twelve). The Minor Prophets remind the people of their responsibility to keep the stipulations of the Mosaic covenant, but mostly they condemn the people for breaking the covenant. Hosea compares the people with Adam because they have "transgressed the covenant" (Hos 6:7). This transgression will bring about God's judgment (Hos 8:1). Furthermore, instead of trusting in Yahweh, the people made a covenant with Assyria and Egypt (Hos 12:1).

The people's idolatry is constantly condemned by the Minor Prophets because the people's rebellion represents a clear violation of the first three commandments, which were the backbone of the Mosaic covenant. Hosea condemns the people's manufacturing and attaching themselves to idols (Hos 4:17; 11:2), idols that generally were manufactured of gold and silver (Hos 8:4; 13:2). The people's sin is magnified in that the priests, who are supposed to be spiritual leaders, themselves have resorted to idolatry (Hos 10:5-6). Hosea mentions Baal as one of the specific idols worshiped by the people (Hos 11:2), while most prophets speak against worshiping idols in general (Mic 1:7; Hab 2:18; Zech 13:2). The people's rebellion is emphasized by the fact that the priests fell into the same types of sins (Zeph 1:4). Israel's idolatry is sometimes couched in language of spiritual adultery, with Israel accused of "whoredom" (Hos 6:10). Hosea writes that Israel "has played the whore" (Hos 2:5; 4:15; 5:3; 9:1), "a spirit of whoredom led them astray" (Hos 4:12), and they "loved a prostitute's wages" (Hos 9:1).

The people's failure to keep the Sabbath is not mentioned directly in the Minor Prophets. The Sabbath is mentioned only once by Hosea and once by Amos. In Hosea God promises to put an end to Israel's Sabbaths (Hos 2:11), while in Amos the people mention the Sabbath only in their desire for it to be over so that they might engage in deceitful business practices (Amos 8:5).

Micah addresses the fifth commandment when he lists the failure of people to honor their parents among the sins with which God describes the total corruption of the people (Mic 7:5-6). As in the Major Prophets, the Minor Prophets present the people's failure to obey the sixth commandment, prohibiting murder, in language such as "innocent blood" and "bloodshed." God uses legal language to condemn Israel. Instead of obedience to the covenant, "bloodshed follows bloodshed" (Hos 4:2), and the people "lie in wait for blood" (Mic 7:2). Israel's moral fiber had been compromised to such an extent that the men of Israel "commit adultery" (Hos 4:2), and they "go aside with prostitutes" (Hos 4:14), which is a clear violation of the seventh commandment, "You shall not commit adultery." Israel's unfaithfulness extends to the women as well: their "daughters play the whore," and their "brides commit adultery" (Hos 4:13-14). The postexilic prophet Zechariah speaks of a two-sided, flying scroll that may be a reference to the two halves of the Decalogue (Zech 5:1-4). The word "curse" employed in Zechariah 5:3 is the same employed in the Torah (Ex 20:15; Deut 5:19); thus, the curse of Zechariah's vision could be synonymous with the curse of the law.

2.3. The Priestly Covenant. A less important covenant that is first noted in the Torah is the priestly covenant or the covenant with Levi (Eichrodt, 65). Although covenant terminology is absent at the consecration of the priests (Ex 28—29; Lev 8), covenantal language is present in subsequent texts. During the Israelites' *wilderness wandering Yahweh makes a covenant of peace with Phinehas, a direct descendant of Aaron (Num 25:11-12). This is also called "a covenant of perpetual priesthood" (Num 25:13). The perpetual nature of this covenant is addressed by the book of Jeremiah, which presents the priestly covenant in the same category as the Davidic covenant (Jer 33:21-22). The postexilic prophets confirm the perpetual nature of God's covenant when Zechariah anticipates a messianic time when a priest will be on the throne of David (Zech 6:9-15). The true priest is the one to come (Leupold, 76). Furthermore, through Malachi God affirms that the covenant with Levi will stand in spite of the priests' failure to abide by its terms (Mal 2:1-9). Though distinct from the Mosaic covenant, this priestly covenant runs in parallel with the Mosaic, and it is aimed at maintaining the relationship between Yahweh and Israel (Williamson 2007, 105-6).

3. The Davidic Covenant.

3.1. The Major Prophets. Whereas the Mosaic covenant had the structure of a suzerain-vassal treaty, the Davidic covenant is a grant/royal covenant whose promises are articulated in 2 Samuel 7:8-16 (Weinfeld 1970, 184-96). The promises God made in the covenant with David include those that will find realization during David's lifetime (2 Sam 7:9-11a) and those that will find realization after David's death (2 Sam 7:11b-16). During David's lifetime the people will receive a great name (2 Sam 7:9), a great land (2 Sam 7:10) and rest (2 Sam 7:11). After David's death, God promises the people a house (2 Sam 7:11), posterity through a descendant who will always sit on the royal throne (2 Sam 7:12) and an eternal kingdom (2 Sam 7:13). Through the prophet Isaiah God promises to give the people a "Prince of Peace," who will reign from the "throne of David" (Is 9:6-7). This righteous king on whom the Spirit of God will rest is associated with David because he will come forth "from the stump of Jesse," David's father (Is 11:1-2, 10). In an oracle regarding Moab God promises that he will raise "the tent of David one who judges and seeks justice" (Is 16:5). This Davidic king is also foreshadowed in Hezekiah and is addressed by God as "the LORD, the God of David your father" (Is 38:5). The irrevocability of this covenant is understood in the language employed in Isaiah 55:3-5, where God promises to make an "everlasting covenant." Just as David experienced God's loving-kindness, so too will Israel benefit from God's acts of covenant love.

God's covenant with David is addressed by both Jeremiah and Ezekiel. Even though the language of judgment against the Davidic kings is harsh (Jer 13:13-14; 22:2-5, 30), the language of hope speaks of the certainty of the future fulfillment of the royal covenant with David. Indeed, God promises "to raise up for David a righteous branch" who will be both righteous and just (Jer 23:5-6; 33:15). The perpetual nature of the kingship is repeated forcefully in God's promise that "David shall never lack a man to sit on the throne of the house of Israel" (Jer 33:17). The fulfillment certainty of this covenant is as certain as the creation order (Jer 33:20-26). Ezekiel's harsh words for the present

shepherds of Jerusalem (Ezek 34:1-10) are contrasted with the assurance that a future Davidic shepherd, God's servant, will shepherd God's people (Ezek 34:23-24; 37:24-25) (*see* Messiah).

3.2. The Minor Prophets (the Twelve). Hosea, Amos, Micah and Zechariah envisage a future time of restoration in which the royal covenant will be fulfilled by the eternal reign of a Davidic king. During this time of restoration the people will turn back to God by seeking the Lord and "David their king" (Hos 3:5). After prophesying about judgment due to sin, Amos foretells of a time when God "will raise the booth of David that is fallen and repair its breaches" (Amos 9:11). Subsequently, the people will be restored to the former glory before God used the Assyrian and Babylonian exiles to punish his people. Micah anticipates the Davidic king who will be born in Bethlehem, will hail from the tribe of Judah (Mic 5:2), and will shepherd's God's flock "in the strength of the LORD" (Mic 5:4). The fulfillment of the royal covenant with David will bring peace and security, and God's name will be great "to the ends of the earth." Messianic prophecies couched in "servant" and "branch" terminology are similar to that of the Major Prophets. If this is the same "branch" as mentioned in Jeremiah, then he is associated with David (Jer 23:5, 33:15). Later, in Zechariah, this branch reappears as a king who will build an eschatological temple, the future domain of the Messiah (Zech 3:8-10; 6:9-15).

4. The New Covenant.

The expression "new covenant" appears only in the book of Jeremiah (31:31-34), but the concept is present in other Prophetic Books, such as Isaiah, Ezekiel, Hosea and Malachi. Isaiah anticipates the new covenant primarily through the Servant Songs (Is 42:1-9; 49:1-13; 50:4-11; 52:13—53:12). The *Servant of Yahweh, the embodiment of God's covenant, is the agent through whom God's covenant blessing will be extended to all people. God declares that this servant himself will be "a covenant for the people" (Is 42:6). The new covenant is also anticipated by Isaiah through the promise of the eternal covenant of peace (Is 54:10). This covenant will usher the period that will be characterized by the absence of divine wrath. The peace aspect of this covenant is more than just the absence of war or hostility; it also has the connotation of the sum total of covenant blessing. The Servant of Yahweh as described in Isaiah will inaugurate a new covenant that has the Davidic covenant as its basis, thus one that is linked to messianic hopes. This is an everlasting covenant associated with the person and work of the Servant of Yahweh, and will thus result in everlasting joy (Is 55:3; 61:8).

The promises of the new covenant are made explicit in Jeremiah 31:31-34, a passage that is critical to the Book of Consolation (Jer 30—33). The coming days of restoration will usher in this new covenant that Yahweh will make with his people. The language of covenant making is similar to that used with the Abrahamic covenant (Gen 15:18) and the Mosaic covenant (Ex 34:10; Deut 5:2). Even though Yahweh made covenants with people in the past, this covenant is labeled as "new" both to differentiate it from the old ones, especially the Mosaic, and also to indicate that it will have new features not included in the previous covenants (see Kaiser, 11-23). This covenant will be all encompassing since it will be made "with the house of Israel and the house of Judah" (Jer 31:31). Just as both Israel and Judah have been affected by God's judgment through exile, they will both benefit from the coming restoration available through the new covenant promises.

The fact that the new covenant will be different than the old (Mosaic) covenant can be seen from the expression "not like the covenant I made with their fathers" (Jer 31:32). The need for a new covenant is not because the form or function of the old was flawed (after all, God was its designer), but rather because of the people's failure to obey it. The people broke the old covenant even though God was their covenant-giving husband (Jer 31:32). Here the covenant breaking is apostasy, and it is analogous to adultery.

The specific stipulations of the new covenant are enumerated in Jeremiah 31:33-34. The Mosaic law was written on tablets of stone (Ex 31:18), and these stones could be broken (Ex 32:19). The law could be lost (2 Kings 22:8), burned (Jer 36:23) or drowned (Jer 51:63), but the law written on the heart is permanent. The central motif of the new covenant is the knowledge of Yahweh (Jer 31:34). This knowledge was first accomplished through the teaching of the law. Moses was instructed to teach this law to the people, and in return they were to teach it to their children (Deut 6). The prophets emphasized that knowing God meant obeying the covenant stipulations. Thus, Hosea rebuked the people for not knowing God (Hos 4:1-2), and this lack of knowledge is synonymous with the lack of knowledge of the law (Hos 4:6). What God desires is both knowledge of and love for him (Hos 6:6).

One of the greatest promises of the new covenant is that the new covenant in general, and the promise of knowing God specifically, are not restricted to a specific social class or age group. Rather, God promises, "They shall all know me, from the least of them to the greatest" (Jer 31:34). This knowledge of God is also tied in with his forgiveness of sin. "I will remember their sin no more" is the last promise of this unbreakable covenant. It is through God's forgiveness of sin that the universal knowledge of God is possible. The author of Hebrews quotes Jeremiah 31:31-34 in its entirety in Hebrews 8:8-12 to emphasize that this covenant is superior to the old covenant not merely because of better promises, but because of Christ being the mediator. Indeed, the book of Hebrews affirms Jesus' superiority over Moses, Melchizedek, the priests and the angels.

Like Jeremiah, Ezekiel emphasizes that the institution of the new covenant in the hearts of the people is possible only through the presence of God's Spirit in the people's hearts. Twice in the book of Ezekiel God promises to give the people a new heart and to put his Spirit within them (Ezek 11:19; 36:26). Only under such conditions can the people now obey God's rules and commandments (Ezek 36:27). The new covenant is instituted by Jesus at the establishment of the Lord's Supper (Luke 22:20; cf. 1 Cor. 11:25) and inaugurated on the cross. All covenants find partial/ultimate fulfillment in the life, death and resurrection of Christ, through whom we have the great name "children of God," and through whom we have forgiveness of sin and eternal life.

See also BLESSINGS AND CURSES; IDOLS, IDOLATRY, GODS; LAW; SIN, SINNERS.

BIBLIOGRAPHY. W. Brueggemann, *The Covenanted Self: Explorations in Law and Covenant* (Minneapolis: Fortress, 1999); W. J. Dumbrell, *Covenant and Creation: A Theology of the Old Testament Covenants* (BTCL; Carlisle: Paternoster, 1997); W. Eichrodt, *Theology of the Old Testament*, vol. 1, trans. J. A. Baker (OTL; Philadelphia: Westminster, 1961); W. C. Kaiser Jr. "The

Old Promise and the New Covenant: Jeremiah 31:31-34," *JETS* 15 (1972) 11-23; **P. Kalluveettil,** *Declaration and Covenant: A Comprehensive Review of Covenant Formulae from the Old Testament and the Ancient Near East* (AnBib 88; Rome: Biblical Institute, 1982); **K. A. Kitchen,** *Ancient Orient and Old Testament* (Chicago: InterVarsity Press, 1966); idem, "The Fall and Rise of Covenant, Law, and Treaty," *TynBul* 40 (1989) 118-35; **H. C. Leupold,** *Exposition of Zechariah* (Grand Rapids: Baker, 1971); **D. J. McCarthy,** *Treaty and Covenant: A Study in Form in the Ancient Oriental Documents and in the Old Testament* (AnBib 21A; Rome: Biblical Institute, 1978); **T. E. McComiskey,** *The Covenants of Promise: A Theology of the Old Testament Covenants* (Grand Rapids: Baker, 1985); **G. J. McConville,** "ברית," *NIDOTTE* 1:747-55; **G. E. Mendenhall,** *Law and Covenant in Israel and the Ancient Near East* (Pittsburgh: Biblical Colloquium, 1955); **E. W. Nicholson,** *God and His People: Covenant and Theology in the Old Testament* (Oxford: Clarendon, 1986); **J. J. Niehaus,** *God at Sinai: Covenant & Theophany in the Bible and Ancient Near East* (SOTBT; Grand Rapids: Zondervan, 1995); **T. Rata,** *The Covenant Motif in Jeremiah's Book of Comfort: Textual and Intertextual Studies of Jeremiah 30-33* (SBL 105; New York: Peter Lang, 2007); **R. Rendtorff,** *The Covenant Formula: An Exegetical and Theological Investigation,* trans. M. Kohl (OTS; Edinburgh: T & T Clark, 1998); **M. Weinfeld,** "The Covenant of Grant in the Old Testament and in the Ancient Near East," *JAOS* 90 (1970) 184-203; idem, "Covenant Terminology in the Ancient Near East and Its Influence on the West," *JAOS* 93 (1973) 190-99; **P. R. Williamson,** "Covenant," *DOTP* 139-55; idem, *Sealed with an Oath: Covenant in God's Unfolding Purpose* (NSBT 23; Downers Grove, IL: InterVarsity Press, 2007).

T. Rata

CREATION THEOLOGY

The views of G. von Rad and his contemporaries that the Israelite doctrine of creation developed late in the biblical tradition and is secondary to faith in God's saving action in history has dominated OT scholarship in the twentieth century. This perspective is misplaced, being based more on von Rad's reaction against the nature-religion ideologies of German National Socialism in the 1930s than on the Bible, but it has lingered in both academy and seminary. Von Rad draws heavily on creation texts in Isaiah 40—55 to support his thesis, but in so doing, he evokes a narrow view of what creation is and how it is depicted in the biblical texts (Marlow 2009, 60-66). In contrast, C. Westermann observes that God as Creator is not an article of faith but rather a fundamental premise running throughout the OT: "God's saving action can be an object of belief; Creation cannot" (Westermann, 71). Some scholars have stressed the importance of creation as one of the key theological themes of the OT Wisdom literature, even suggesting that the two are virtually synonymous (Perdue). However, such conflation of *wisdom and creation takes no account of the rich and diverse ways in which creation is depicted in other biblical texts such as the Prophetic Books. The language of creation is very much an integral part of the prophetic understanding rather than a "wisdom idea" introduced into the texts.

1. Creation Vocabulary
2. Cosmic Language
3. Figurative Language
4. Theological Themes
5. Some Key Texts

1. Creation Vocabulary.
The Hebrew verb *bārā'* ("to create") occurs about fifty times in the OT, almost always with God as the subject. Twenty-nine of these occur in the Prophetic Books, of which twenty-one are found in Isaiah 40—66, and a further eleven occur in the Priestly (P) texts of early Genesis (Gen 1; 5; 6). Von Rad's argument that Israelite creation theology originated in the exilic period is partly based on the view held by many scholars that both P and the later sections of Isaiah derive from the exilic or postexilic period. Although there are good reasons to support this view (see 5.2 below), the basic premise that the presence or absence of belief in God as Creator can be determined by word occurrence alone is flawed. Numerous other terms are used by the biblical prophets to denote God's creative activity, including God as the one who forms (*yāṣar*) the *mountains (Amos 4:13) and light (Is 45:7), makes (*'āśâ*) the constellations (Amos 5:8) and founds (*yāsad*) the earth (Is 48:13; Amos 9:6). These and similar terms may be brought together in a string of God's creative actions and attributes (Is 45:18; Jer 10:12; 33:2). More important are the numerous concepts, metaphors and ideas

that "support the belief in YHWH as creator, without stating it explicitly" (Paas, 60) as well as the theological themes related to God's interaction with the world that presuppose him as Creator of all that is.

2. Cosmic Language.

Cosmic themes and language form an important part of the repertoire of the prophets, and the way in which these are woven into the account of God's dealing with his people suggests that, for the prophets, the entire cosmos participates as part of God's creation in human political and social spheres. The terms "the heavens" (haššāmayim) and "the earth" (hāʾāreṣ) are employed together over sixty times. As well as featuring extensively in descriptions of the creation and its contents, particularly in Isaiah 40—55 (see 5.2 below), the earth and the heavens are appealed to as witnesses to God's indictment of his people (Is 1:2; Mic 6:1-2) and as joyful participants in God's *salvation (Is 44:23; 45:8; 49:13). Upheaval in the heavens as well as on earth is a sign of the Lord's coming (Joel 2:10; see also Nah 1:5) and of his judgment against those foreign nations that challenge his sovereignty, whether *Babylon (Is 13:9-10) or Edom (Is 34:4). Such cosmic disturbance is also the result of Israel's continued rebellion against their God, as graphically depicted in the prophet Jeremiah's *lament (Jer 4:19-26).

3. Figurative Language.

The prophets make extensive use of a wide range of metaphorical language taken from creation to describe God and his relation to his people. The book of Hosea is particularly rich in figurative language, including extensive creation imagery. God is depicted as a wild *animal—a lion (Hos 11:10; see also Is 31:4; Jer 49:19; Amos 3:8) and a bear (Hos 13:8)—such imagery stressing the Lord's supremacy and power and the need to fear him (Marlow 2009, 163-65; see also Strawn). More positively, the Lord is described as a rock, providing shelter and protection in times of trouble (Is 17:10; 26:4; 44:8; Hab 1:12), as the source of water to his people, falling like refreshing dew on Israel (Hos 6:3), and as the fountain of life to them (Joel 3:18). Such imagery for God taken from creation highlights the integral relationship between Creator and creation. As T. Fretheim notes, it "serves to temper a certain anthropocentricity in our talk about God. In fact . . . it could be said that God's transcendence is given a special lift by the use of such natural metaphors, for among other things they evoke wonder and awe in human beings" (Fretheim, 247).

4. Theological Themes.

The biblical understanding of *God as Creator is primarily concerned not with his creative act of bringing the world into being, but rather with his ongoing involvement in and with his creation. Although the unquestionable belief that the Lord alone is Creator of the world is implicit in much of the prophetic material, a number of other important theological themes concerning God's relation to his creation permeate the writings of the prophets.

4.1. Sovereignty over Creation. God's supremacy over the whole of creation is demonstrated in the prophets in a number of ways. Jeremiah describes him as a God who is near and not far off, and one who fills his creation (Jer 23:23-24). God is present in the world that he made, and his relationship to it is neither limited to the human sphere nor mediated solely through human beings (Fretheim, 172). This is demonstrated in the fact that the creation mourns to God (Jer 12:11) and God himself addresses the land directly (Jer 22:29). Both annual and diurnal rhythms are under God's control; the Lord maintains the "fixed orders" of the world—the cycles of night and day (Jer 31:35-36)—and yet is also able to disrupt them (Is 13:10; Ezek 32:7-8; Joel 3:15). When the Lord summons the creation, it responds in obedience to him (Amos 1:2; 9:5-6), often in contrast to its human inhabitants (Hos 11:1-2). The creation itself reveals something of God—his incomparable greatness and power (Is 40:25-26) and his name "the Lord of hosts" (Amos 4:13). The created world also acts as an agent of God's judgment (see 4.4 below).

4.2. Provision for Creation. An important part of the notion of God as Creator is his action in sustaining and providing for his creation. In the prophets, it is the Lord who both gives the rain, which is crucial in a land of high summer temperatures and water scarcity (Jer 10:13; Zech 10:1), and withholds it (Is 3:1, Jer 3:3). He governs the weather patterns, on which the success of agriculture depends, giving rain for seedtime and guaranteeing the harvest (Is 30:23; Jer 5:24). For Amos, the failure of the rains is an opportunity for the Israelites to turn back to God, but to no avail (Amos 4:7-8). In the postexilic prophet Haggai, the people's failure to rebuild God's house results in the heavens withholding the rain and the earth its produce (Hag 1:9-11), while Malachi urges the people to bring their tithes and offerings to God in order to guarantee the Lord's provision for them (Mal 3:10-11). As well as literal depictions, the importance of water to life in ancient Israel makes it a powerful metaphor for God's blessing on his people (Is 12:3; 41:17-18) and for their rejection of him (Jer 2:13). In Hosea's extended *marriage metaphor, which graphically portrays Israel's broken relationship with God (Hos 2), the prophet stresses that it is the Lord, not the Canaanite deities, who provides grain, wine and oil—the essential commodities of the day (Hos 2:8). It is the Lord's goodness in giving these necessities that is celebrated in the prophets' messages of hope (Jer 31:10-12; Ezek 36:28-30). Even the actions of a farmer in knowing when to sow seed and how best to harvest are attributed to the Lord's wisdom (Is 28:29).

4.3. Justice, Righteousness and World Order.
H. Schmid notes that in the ancient Near East "cosmic, political and social order find their unity under the concept of 'creation'" (Schmid, 105). The view that the king as the representative of the deity on earth is guarantor of the order of creation, which is particularly associated with the Egyptian concept of *maat*, is also important in the biblical tradition (e.g., 2 Kings 8; Ps 72). In Isaiah, this royal ideology is combined with concepts of *justice (mišpāṭ) and righteousness (ṣĕdāqâ) to denote the maintaining or breaking of creation order. Justice and righteousness are associated with the reign of an ideal king (Is 11:1-5; 32:1; see also Jer 23:5) and also with the well-being of the entire created order, not just human society (Is 11:6-9; 32:15-17). In other prophetic texts the terms "justice" and "righteousness," either individually or combined as a hendiadys or parallelism, are used to denote the well-being of creation, whether by means of God's actions in the world (Jer 9:24; Hos 2:19) or those of human beings (Jer 22:3). Where justice and righteousness are lacking, all that is good and ordered in the world comes under threat (Is 59:8-9, 14; Amos 5:6-7, 10-12).

4.4. Creation and Judgment.
In several prophetic texts the appearing of God in judgment on the earth (theophany) has a dramatic effect on the physical world. The whole creation, not just human society, is disrupted when the Lord descends from his heavenly temple (Mic 1:3-5), and his coming is accompanied by storms and clouds (Nah 1:2-5). In Habakkuk's extended theophany (Hab 3:3-15) God's glory shines forth (Hab 3:3-4), but his awesome power shakes his creation to its very core, as both the seas (Hab 3:15) and the nations (Hab 3:12) are trampled in his anger. The messages of judgment that comprise so great a part of the Prophetic Books present a inextricable link between human behavior and the moral order of creation. In Isaiah 24 the whole cosmos, heavens and earth, is disrupted (Is 24:4) and lies polluted because its inhabitants have "transgressed laws, violated the statutes, broken the everlasting covenant" (Is 24:5). The "everlasting covenant" (bĕrît ʿôlām) here may evoke, according to R. Murray, an ancient Israelite tradition of a cosmic covenant between God and the world. This *covenant, or ordering of the world (Jer 33:20-26), can be broken by human beings, whose disobedience to God and transgression of the law violate the God-given order of the world. The resultant disorders in human society, in the land and in the cosmos are the consequences of that broken covenant (Is 24:6-13).

A similar pattern can be seen in Hosea 4, where the disloyalty of God's people (Hos 4:1) has devastating effects, not just on society (Hos 4:2), but also on the wider creation (Hos 4:3). Likewise, Jeremiah highlights the connection between the foolishness and faithlessness of God's people and the well-being of creation (Jer 4:22-26; 9:12-13) and lays responsibility for this "unmaking" of creation at the feet of Judah's leaders (Jer 12:10-11) (*see* Land). Contemporary scientific understanding sees the disruption of the physical world by events such as earthquakes and volcanic eruptions as a natural and essential geological process and cautions us against adopting a simplistic approach to the relationship between sin and natural disaster. Nevertheless, the prophetic understanding of a close interconnection between human behavior and the well-being of creation is very relevant in the light of the environmental issues currently facing the planet (Marlow 2008).

4.5. Restoration of Creation.
If the prophets

make a strong causal link between disobedience to the Lord and the disruption of the physical world, a similar connection is drawn between renewal of the people's relationship with God and the restoration of creation. The prophets' vision of hope includes the wilderness blossoming in glory and splendor (Is 35:1-2; 41:18-20) and the mountains flourishing (Joel 3:18; Amos 9:13b). Agriculture is again successful, to an extent that surpasses natural expectations (Amos 9:13a). The broken cosmic covenant is reestablished. In Ezekiel this is a covenant of peace that includes the giving of rain and the restoration of fertility (Ezek 34:25), while in Hosea the covenant is with the wild animals (Hos 2:18), a covenant that results in security for God's people (Hos 2:19-20) as well as the flourishing of the earth (Hos 2:21-22). The vision of the prophet in Isaiah 11 is for a kingdom of wisdom and godliness in which justice and righteousness prevail in society (Is 11:3-5) and harmony is restored between humanity and the rest of creation (Is 11:6-9), a vision echoed at the end of the book (Is 65:25). The coming salvation of the Lord is a reason for all creation to rejoice, from shore to shore, from mountain to desert (Is 42:10-12; 44:23).

5. Some Key Texts.

Although the language of creation and theology permeates the writing of the OT prophets, a number of texts give special emphasis to the Lord as Creator and his relationship with the creation.

5.1. Creation Hymns in Amos. The three fragmentary creation hymns, or doxologies, in the book of Amos (Amos 4:13; 5:8-9; 9:5-6) have been the subject of much debate, in particular concerning their origin and purpose (Marlow 2009, 139-46). Each hymn describes God almost exclusively in terms of his creation and control of the cosmos. Each one affirms that the attributes of the Lord to which they refer are part of his essential and unalterable character—his "name"—and in each of them the Lord is depicted as the God who communicates, both to humanity and to the wider creation. Amos 4:13 comprises five phrases, the first two of which highlight the Lord's cosmic power as creator of mountains and wind, while the final two speak of his activity within the world. Sandwiched in the middle of this description of creation and Creator is the enigmatic expression "he reveals to human beings his thoughts." The central position of the phrase draws attention to the relative insignificance of humankind compared with the power and splendor of creation and with the majesty of God's presence on earth; it also highlights the fact that it is human beings to whom the Lord chooses to reveal something of himself.

The second hymn, Amos 5:5-6, expands the description of the Lord's cosmic power in Amos 4:13 to include the creation of the constellations Pleiades and Orion, and it reiterates the Lord's power over the rhythms of day and night. The third hymn, Amos 9:5-6, echoes some aspects of the second one. Its context suggests the possibility that God's power in creation might be turned against human beings who attempt to hide from his judgment (Amos 9:2-4). God's action, in the second and third hymns, of summoning the waters and pouring them out on the earth may be looking forward to a local flood yet to come or be harking back to the ancient flood tradition. Alternatively, it could signify God's ability to reverse his own acts of creation, in particular the separation of dry land from water (Gen 1:6-10). The evoking of the created world in the context of the Lord's judgment against his people suggests a moral order built into the very structure of creation.

5.2. Creator God in Isaiah 40—55. In all the material of the Prophetic Books, Isaiah 40—55, and in particular Isaiah 40—48, offers the most extensive and carefully developed understanding of God as Creator and his relationship to his creation (Fretheim, 181-94). The reasons for such an emphasis on God as Creator probably lie in the historical situation to which these prophetic oracles are addressed, toward the end of the Babylonian exile (ca. 550-540 BC). With the final conquest of Judah by the Babylonian emperor Nebuchadnezzar in 587 BC, the people of God had lost their temple and their king, much of the population was exiled in a foreign land, and doubt was cast on their status as God's chosen people (the heartache and theological questioning that this catastrophe provoked are graphically depicted in the book of Lamentations). Those in exile undoubtedly faced serious temptation to abandon their Lord and embrace Babylonian idol worship. In this context, as R. Rendtorff notes, "Faith in God the Creator was perceived and experienced as the all-embracing framework, as the fundamental, all-underlying premise for any talk about God, the world, Israel, and the individual" (Rendtorff, 107-8).

Isaiah 40—48 emphasizes the importance of God as Creator, both to offer hope that the Lord has not abandoned his people and to warn against adopting Babylonian religious practices. The extended creation oracle in Isaiah 40:12-31 follows an outpouring of hope and comfort (Is 40:1-5) and explains that God's power as Creator transcends history, in terms of both the historical events that have befallen the weak, disheartened Israelites (Is 40:27-28) and the ever-present hubris of their earthly conquerors (Is 40:21-24). The scale and the splendor of God's creative activity are stressed (Is 40:12, 26), and his might is contrasted with the impotence of human rulers (Is 40:15-17; 41:4-5) and foreign idols (Is 40:18-20). God's power as Creator is closely linked with his actions in Israel's past, in particular the exodus (Is 43:15-17), as well as with his choice of the Persian king Cyrus as the means by which salvation will come to Israel (Is 45:11-13). The understanding of God as Creator of all is also key to the restoration of Israel's sense of identity (Is 43:1-5; 44:1-3) and their calling to be a light to the nations (Is 42:5-7). The relationship between creation, redemption and salvation in Isaiah 40—55 is the subject of much discussion and is beyond the scope of this article; suffice it to note, "For Isaiah 40-55, creation is the beginning, middle, and end of God's work with the world. God originated the cosmos, has continued creative work all through the course of the world's history, and will one day bring a new heaven and new earth into being" (Fretheim, 193).

See also ANIMAL IMAGERY; COSMOLOGY; FLORAL IMAGERY; LAND; MOUNTAIN IMAGERY; WILDERNESS, DESERT.

BIBLIOGRAPHY. **T. E. Fretheim,** *God and World in the Old Testament: A Relational Theology of Creation* (Nashville: Abingdon, 2005); **H. Marlow,** *The Earth Is the Lord's: A Biblical Response to Environmental Issues* (Cambridge: Grove Books, 2008); idem, *Biblical Prophets and Contemporary Environmental Ethics: Re-reading Amos, Hosea and First Isaiah* (Oxford: Oxford University Press, 2009); **R. Murray,** *The Cosmic Covenant: Biblical Themes of Justice, Peace and the Integrity of Creation* (HeyM 7; London: Sheed & Ward, 1992); **S. Paas,** *Creation and Judgement: Creation Texts in Some Eighth Century Prophets* (OTS 47; Leiden: E. J. Brill, 2003); **L. G. Perdue,** *Wisdom and Creation: the Theology of Wisdom Literature* (Nashville: Abingdon, 1994); **R. Rendtorff,** *Canon and Theology: Overtures to an Old Testament Theology,* trans. and ed. M. Kohl (Edinburgh: T & T Clark, 1994 [1991]); **H. H. Schmid,** "Creation, Righteousness, Salvation: 'Creation Theology' and the Broad Horizon of Biblical Theology," in *Creation in the Old Testament,* ed. B. W. Anderson (IRT 6; London: SPCK, 1980 [1973]) 102-17; **B. A. Strawn,** *What Is Stronger Than a Lion? Leonine Image and Metaphor in the Hebrew Bible and the Ancient Near East* (OBO 212; Fribourg: Academic Press; Göttingen: Vandenhoeck & Ruprecht, 2005); **G. von Rad,** "The Theological Problem of the Old Testament Doctrine of Creation," in *The Problem of the Hexateuch and Other Essays,* trans. E. W. Trueman Dicken (London: SCM, 1984 [1936]) 131-43; **C. Westermann,** *Creation,* trans. J. Scullion (London: SPCK, 1974 [1971]).

H. F. Marlow

CREATOR. *See* CREATION THEOLOGY; GOD.

CULT. *See* LITURGY AND CULT.

CULTIC PROPHECY. *See* ANCIENT NEAR EASTERN PROPHECY.

CUP OF WRATH. *See* WRATH.

CURSES. *See* BLESSINGS AND CURSES.

D

DANIEL: BOOK OF

The book of Daniel has often been the center of debate. Debates about the interpretation of prophecy and historical accuracy have sometimes overshadowed the message of the book. This article outlines the structure and content of Daniel and discusses some general principles of interpretation. It then surveys the current state of the debates about historical and interpretation issues before discussing the date, authorship and composition of the book. It concludes by summarizing its message and its influence on the NT.

1. Structure and Content
2. Literary Forms and Genre
3. Historical Issues
4. Interpretation Issues
5. Date, Authorship and Composition
6. The Message of Daniel
7. Daniel and the New Testament

1. Structure and Content.

1.1. The Hebrew/Aramaic Book. Daniel 1—6 contains stories about Judean exiles in Babylon from 606/5 BC, when the Neo-Babylonian ruler Nebuchadnezzar takes captives from Jerusalem to Babylon, to shortly after the Persian capture of Babylon in 539 BC. They are written in the third person about Daniel and his friends. Daniel 7—12 contains *visions focusing on the persecution of the Jews by Antiochus IV in 167-164 BC, recounted in the first person by Daniel. The book begins in *Hebrew, but when Nebuchadnezzar's advisors begin to speak in Daniel 2:4, the language changes to *Aramaic. It changes back to Hebrew at Daniel 8:1, continuing in Hebrew until the end of the book. The linguistic division does not coincide with the division between stories and visions. This gives Daniel 7 a pivotal role in binding the two halves of the book together, especially since Daniel 2—7 has a striking chiastic structure.

(A) A dream about four earthly kingdoms and God's kingdom (Dan 2)
  (B) A story about Judeans who are faithful in the face of death (Dan 3)
    (C) A story about royal pride that is humbled (Dan 4)
    (C') A story about royal pride that is humbled (Dan 5)
  (B') A story about a Judean who is faithful in the face of death (Dan 6)
(A') A vision about four earthly kingdoms and God's kingdom (Dan 7).

The theme of this section is the faithfulness of the Judeans to God under pagan rulers. Daniel 8:1—12:8 contains the complementary theme of faithfulness under persecution. This is anticipated in the references in Daniel 7 to the persecution of "the saints of the Most High," again giving this chapter a pivotal role.

Daniel 1 provides an introduction to the whole book. It explains how Daniel and his three friends come to be in exile in the royal court in Babylon and sets the time frame (Dan 1:1, 21). Mention of Daniel's skill in visions and dreams (Dan 1:17) prepares the way for Daniel 7—12. Daniel 12:9-13 forms a conclusion to the whole book. The phrase "those who are wise will understand" (*hammaśkîlîm yābînû*) (Dan 12:10) echoes the reference to "young men skilled [*maśkîlîm*] in all wisdom, knowledge and insight [*mĕbînê*]" (Dan 1:4).

Based on this discussion, one can suggest an outline structure for the book:

1.2. The Greek Additions. The Greek text of Daniel includes passages not found in the Hebrew/Aramaic text. There is no evidence that they were ever part of it. The Prayer of Azariah and the Song of the Three Young Men are inserted between Daniel 3:23 and Daniel 3:24. These are pious embellishments of the story, giving further glory to God and underlining the divine origin of the Judeans' deliverance from the fiery furnace. The stories of Susanna and of Bel and the Dragon are separate chapters in the Greek form of the book. Susanna is not a court tale. Its central issue is not Jewish identity but rather personal morality. The others resemble court tales, but Daniel's enemies are priests and the populace of Babylon, not sages. They are polemics against idolatry. The Latin Vulgate translation of the OT included these additions, which are accepted as part of the Roman Catholic and Orthodox canons.

2. Literary Forms and Genre.

2.1. Court Tales. The stories in Daniel 1—6 fit into the context of a type of literature that was widespread, both in time and geography, in the ancient Near East. These stories about wise courtiers (sages) are called "court tales" by modern scholars. As well as the biblical stories of Joseph and Esther (the latter with its subplot about Mordecai the courtier), there is the story of Ahiqar from ancient Mesopotamia. An Aramaic version of it has been found among the documents from the Jewish colony at Elephantine (fifth century BC). Several such stories are known from ancient Egypt, the best known being the stories of Sinuhe (c. 1900 BC), Wenamun (c. 1000 BC) and Onchsheshonqy (c. 400 BC). D. Redford listed various common motifs that occur in these stories (Redford, 94-97). L. Wills extended the range of tales studied to include those told by the Greek writer Herodotus (Wills, 55-70).

Scholars have often recognized that the stories in Daniel 3 and Daniel 6 differ from the others in Daniel 1—6. W. Humphreys gave the two types the names "tales of court conflict"

(Dan 3; 6) and "tales of court contest" (Dan 2; 4; 5). J. Collins analyzed the patterns of the two types of tale (which also apply to other stories) (J. Collins 1977, 34-54). In tales of court contest the king is faced with a problem that neither he nor his sages can resolve. The hero is called in and succeeds and is elevated to high position. In tales of court conflict the hero is initially in a state of well-being. Because of some kind of conspiracy, he is endangered and condemned to death or prison. He is eventually released and restored to his position of honor, or even promoted. Daniel 1:8-16 contains a variant of the court contest pattern.

These ancient Near Eastern court tales seem to have been written for three main reasons. First, they are entertaining. They contain humor (e.g., Dan 3:1-7) and satire (e.g., the picture of the king in Dan 6 manipulated by his courtiers and trapped by his own immutable law) and were meant to be enjoyed by the readers or hearers. They express the art of the storyteller rather than simply the concerns of the historian. When, as in Daniel, the humor and satire are turned against the rulers, it gives the story a subversive edge. Second, many court tales aimed at edifying the readers. By drawing the readers or hearers to identify with the characters, good storytelling is an effective teaching method. The stories in Daniel teach theological and moral truths. Third, court tales about courtiers in the service of foreign kings encourage conquered peoples to maintain their sense of ethnic identity and worth and to take a generally positive attitude to their situation. In Daniel the issue of identity centers on faithfulness to the God of Israel. When this clashes with the demands of the ruler, the story has a subversive edge.

2.2. Visions. In Daniel 7:1-2, Daniel's experience is described both as a "dream" and a "vision." The vision accounts in Daniel 7—8 fit the pattern of dream reports in the ancient Near East identified by A. Oppenheim:

Introduction	7:1	8:1
Report of the vision	7:2-27	8:2-25
End of the vision	7:28a	8:26
Daniel's reaction	7:28b	8:27

The accounts in Daniel 9; 10–12 do not fit this pattern.

The visions of Daniel 7-8 are examples of

symbolic visions, because images and actions are seen that symbolize something else. The visions in Daniel 9; 10—12 are examples of epiphany visions, in which a supernatural being appears and conveys a message.

The individual images in symbolic visions are not like ciphers in a code, whose meaning is exhausted once the code has been broken. These symbols draw on established cultural images, ideas and stereotypes, as well as the feelings that they evoke. They have a "feel" about them that simple ciphers do not have. As a result, they evoke a "gut reaction" that goes beyond any simplistic "this is that" interpretation. It may be hard for later readers to discern these noncipher aspects of symbols because usually they are specific to the culture in which the symbols became current. The attempt to capture something of the wider significance of the symbols used has produced extensive discussion and debate about the religio-historical background of the imagery used in Daniel 7—8 (Lucas 1990).

2.3. The Literary Form of Daniel 8:23-25; 11:3-45. The form and content of these passages has no parallel in Hebrew prophecy. In 1964 A. Grayson and W. Lambert published some texts which they called "Akkadian Prophecies" and drew attention to similarities between them and Daniel 8:23-25; 11:3-45. Five core texts are now known: the Marduk Prophecy, the Šulgi Prophecy, the Dynastic Prophecy, the Uruk Prophecy, and Text A. Two other texts, Text B and LBAT 1543, have similarities with this group.

The introductions of the Marduk and Šulgi Prophecies present them as speeches by the god Marduk and the king Šulgi of Ur (c. 2094-2047 BC) respectively. The introductions of the other core texts are broken off or too damaged to make sense. All five are purported prophecies in the form of concise surveys of a series of rulers' reigns. The rulers are unnamed but are referred to as "a king/prince" or as "the king of X." Plausible correlations can be made between most of the rulers and events alluded to in the texts and known historical rulers and events. On the assumption that the texts originate from soon after the latest event that they record, they can be dated to between the twelfth (the Marduk Prophecy) and the third century (the Dynastic Prophecy) BC.

Daniel 11 has significant points of similarity

with these prophecies. There is a similarity of style, which W. Lambert characterizes as a "concise annalistic history with names censored and the verbs in the future tense" (Lambert, 9). There is a semantic similarity in the phrase "(after him) a king shall arise," which is used as a section divider in the Akkadian Prophecies. Daniel 11 lacks a regular section divider but does use a similar phrase (Dan 11:2, 3, 7, 20, 21; 12:1). The phrases "in his place shall arise" and "a king will arise" do not occur elsewhere in the Hebrew Bible, so influence from the Akkadian Prophecies is plausible. A further reason for suggesting a direct link between Daniel 11 and the Akkadian Prophecies is the lack of comparable material from elsewhere. Another similarity between Daniel and the Akkadian Prophecies is the command to seal up the book in Daniel 12:4. The Dynastic Prophecy ends with a secrecy colophon. So, E. Lucas has suggested that the form of the prophetic surveys of history in Daniel 8:23-25; 11:2-12:4 is best explained if they originated in the Babylonian Diaspora and the author was well acquainted with such Babylonian literature (Lucas 2002, 269-72). The Akkadian Prophecies have close associations with the literature of Babylonian mantic wisdom (the interpretation of omens, dreams and visions) as distinct from the didactic wisdom found in proverbs and related literature (Biggs). Daniel and his friends were skilled in Chaldean literature and wisdom (Dan 1:17-20), and in the stories it is mantic wisdom that is prominent (Lucas 2002, 56, 70). It is also notable that there is increasing recognition that Babylonian mantic wisdom influenced the development of apocalyptic literature (Lucas 2002, 311).

Since they seem to have been written after most of the events that they describe, the purpose of the Akkadian Prophecies was not to predict the course of history but rather to interpret it—in particular, to explain and to legitimate the current situation. In some cases the closing lines seem to look to the immediate future, expressing what the author hoped would happen.

2.4. Prophecy and Apocalypse. K. Koch drew attention to the variety of different definitions of *apocalyptic in use up to 1970. He stressed the need to distinguish the literary genre of apocalypse from the historical apocalyptic movement from which it arose. He also argued that a clear definition of the genre must be arrived at before attempting to understand the movement and listed what he saw as key characteristics of apocalypses. Koch's approach has been refined in two ways. P. Hanson made a distinction between apocalypse (the literary genre), apocalyptic eschatology (a religious perspective) and apocalypticism (the symbolic universe of a religio-social movement).

A seminar of the Society of Biblical Literature produced a definition of the literary genre of apocalypse based on a study of works normally classed as apocalypses from the period 250 BC to AD 250: "Apocalypse is a genre of revelatory literature with a narrative framework, in which a revelation is mediated by an otherworldly being to a human recipient, disclosing a transcendent reality which is both temporal, insofar as it envisages eschatological salvation, and spatial, insofar as it involves another, supernatural world" (J. Collins 1979, 9). The seminar also concluded that apocalypses fall into two subgenres: those with other worldly journeys and those with a review of history. The definition carries the caveat that its intention is only to mark out the boundaries of the genre and not to give a complete or adequate description of the constituent works that fall within that boundary. It covers only the constant core characteristics of apocalypses. Most apocalypses are a composite of several types of literature. This definition has found wide, but not universal, acceptance. Some scholars want to add to it a statement about the function of an apocalypse, usually along the lines that it provides consolation and encouragement to a group in a crisis situation.

Daniel 10—12 is the only section of the OT that this definition fits well. It is an apocalypse with a review of history. In both form and content the book of Daniel as a whole stands out as different from the Prophetic Books of the OT. Its eschatology is apocalyptic rather than prophetic. However, it also differs in form and content from the classic apocalypses. Overall, Daniel lies somewhere on a line of development between the Hebrew prophets and the Jewish apocalypses but appears to be closer in form and content to the apocalypses. It is perhaps best regarded as one of the earliest examples of the apocalyptic genre.

3. Historical Issues.

3.1. Daniel 1:1-2. Jeremiah 25:1 equates the fourth year of King Jehoiakim of Judah with the first year of King Nebuchadnezzar of *Babylon, whereas Daniel 1:1 has Nebuchadnezzar besieging Jerusalem in the third year of Jehoiakim. The two statements can be correlated if Jeremiah is using the Egyptian way of reckoning regnal years, with the months between a king's accession to the throne and the following New Year counted as "year one" of his reign, and Daniel is using the Babylonian system, in which this period was "year zero."

A. Millard shows that if Daniel 1:1 is based on the Babylonian system and an autumnal New Year is assumed (which may have been the case in Judah), then Jehoiakim's third year would have run into October 605 BC (Millard, 69). By then, Nebuchadnezzar had become king and might have been with the army in Syria. In any case, Nebuchadnezzar need not have been present at whatever event may be referred to in Daniel 1:1. It was quite common in the ancient Near East for the actions of subordinates to be attributed to their superiors. Therefore, some punitive action by the Babylonian forces against Jehoiakim, an Egyptian vassal, late in his third year is a possibility.

3.2. Daniel 5. For some ten years of his reign, Nabonidus was absent from Babylon, based at Teima in Arabia. According to the *Verse Account of Nabonidus* 2.20, when he went to Teima, Nabonidus "entrusted the kingship" to Belshazzar (*ANET*, 313). The use of the title "king" of Belshazzar in Daniel has been seen as mistaken and unhistorical because he seems not to have enjoyed some royal prerogatives, including the title *šarru* ("king") (Beaulieu, 185-203). A bilingual inscription on a statue discovered at Tell Fakhariyeh is relevant to this issue (Millard and Bordreuil). The statue depicts a ninth-century BC ruler of Guzan. The Assyrian text describes him as *šakin Guzani* ("governor of Guzan"), whereas the Aramaic text styles him *mlk gwzn* ("king of Guzan"). This indicates that *mlk* in Aramaic had a wider meaning, or was used more loosely, than *šarru* in Akkadian. So, the use of *malka'* in Daniel 5 is neither inaccurate nor unhistorical.

According to Akkadian sources, Belshazzar was the eldest son of Nabonidus. Why, then, is he represented as the son of Nebuchadnezzar in Daniel 5? Three answers have been proposed. First, D. Wiseman argues that Nabonidus, who was a member of Nebuchadnezzar's court, may have married one of his daughters (Wiseman 1985, 10-11). This would make Belshazzar Nebuchadnezzar's grandson. In the Semitic languages "father/son" can be used of more distant forebears/descendants. Second, a literary reason could lie behind the linking of Nebuchadnezzar and Belshazzar. The empire was at its height under the former and met its end under the latter. Third, the story in Daniel 4 was originally about Nabonidus. The application of it to Nebuchadnezzar resulted in the change of parentage for Belshazzar. This possibility is discussed below (see 3.3 below). None of these proposals is entirely convincing, and choosing between them is a matter of weighing probabilities.

3.3. Material Related to Daniel 4—5. There is a considerable scholarly consensus that Nabonidus's absence from his capital lies behind the story of Nebuchadnezzar's madness in Daniel 4. Support for this has been found in an Aramaic text discovered at Qumran, the *Prayer of Nabonidus* (4Q242 [definitive publication, J. Collins 1996]). There are points of contact with Daniel 4: a Babylonian king is afflicted for seven years, a Jewish diviner is involved, the king writes a letter to honor God, and the narrative is in the first person, with the king speaking. Some scholars see reference to a dream in another piece of the fragment, but others dispute this on good philological grounds (J. Collins 1996, 92). There are, however, notable differences between the two texts: the king's name is different, the king's affliction is different, and the Jewish diviner is not named. Collins concludes, "The fragmentary state of the document does not permit us to claim a direct literary relationship. The stories may be different developments of a common tradition" (J. Collins 1993, 218).

A fragmentary cuneiform text seems to refer to some mental disorder afflicting Nebuchadnezzar, perhaps to his neglecting and leaving Babylon, and tells of repentance for neglect of the worship of the gods. It has been suggested that the latter part of the text refers to Amel-Marduk, but Wiseman (1985, 102-3) gives good reasons for taking all of it as referring to Nebuchadnezzar.

Clearly, caution is in order regarding the consensus that Daniel 4 was originally a story about Nabonidus that has been transferred to Nebuchadnezzar, especially since very little is known from Babylonian sources about the last thirty years of Nebuchadnezzar's life.

3.4. Darius the Mede. Darius the Mede is one of the major enigmas in the book of Daniel. He is not known from any sources outside the Bible. Cyrus the Persian conquered Babylon. There has been a long and complicated debate about the issue of Darius the Mede in the book of Daniel (for a classic review of the debate up until 1934, see Rowley).

Most scholars have concluded that Darius the Mede is a literary construct, not a historical person. There are prophetic oracles about a Median conquest of Babylon (Is 13:17; 21:2; Jer 51:11, 28). The writer of Daniel, not knowing the actual course of events, assumed that the Babylonian Empire fell to the Medes before the rise of Persia. So, the narratives in Daniel 1—6 required a Median king between Belshazzar and Cyrus the Persian (Dan 6:28). Darius the Mede was created to meet this requirement. What is said about the figure of the ram in Daniel 8:3-4 raises a question mark against this. J. Montgomery comments, "The moments of the vision of the horns well represent the relation of Media and Persia in power and time" (Montgomery, 328). Commenting on the same verses, E. Heaton says, "One wonders whether the writer's knowledge of their history is quite as inaccurate as some other references to the Median kingdom suggest" (Heaton, 192).

Some have argued that "Darius the Mede" was another name for the general who captured Babylon on behalf of Cyrus. Cuneiform sources refer to him as "Ugbaru" or "Gubaru," and in classical writings he is called "Gobryas." However, it is now clear that he died not long after capturing Babylon, and that Cambyses was "king of Babylon" under his father for about a year (Grabbe 1988).

Wiseman (1956) proposed that Daniel 6:28 is the key to Darius the Mede's identity. This verse can be translated as "Daniel prospered during the reign of Darius, that is, the reign of Cyrus the Persian." This takes the *wāw* in this verse as explicative, as it clearly is in 1 Chronicles 5:26, where this kind of construction identifies Pul as being one and the same as Tiglath-pileser. Wiseman also argued that since Cyrus took over the Median Empire and had a Median mother, he could be called a Mede, even "king of the Medes." Moreover, he would have been about sixty-two when he conquered Babylon (Dan 5:31). The statement that Darius's father was Ahasuerus (Dan 9:1) is a problem, since Cyrus's father was named "Cambyses." Wiseman suggested that "Ahasuerus" might have been an old Achaemenid royal title. B. Colless supports Wiseman on literary grounds. He notes that most of the major figures in the book of Daniel have two (or more) designations. He also argues that it is very unlikely that the author was ignorant of the biblical references to Cyrus as the conqueror of Babylon (e.g., 2 Chron 36:20-23; Ezra 1:2-4; Is 45:1). As a "student of prophecy" (Dan 9:1-2), he knew that the Medes should play a part in the destruction of Babylon (e.g., Jer 51:11, 28). Cyrus was partly Median and ruled the Medes as well as the Persians. This is emphasised by giving him the alternative name "Darius the Mede." Wiseman's suggestion seems to provide a plausible answer to the enigma, but it is a case of what is possible and not what is proven.

4. Interpretation Issues.

4.1. The Four Empires and the Small Horn.
This is a hotly debated issue in the study of Daniel. The earliest evidence that we have of the interpretation of Daniel 7 is *Sibylline Oracles* 3:388-400, dating from about 140 BC. It identifies the fourth kingdom as that of Alexander and his successors. Since at least the time of Josephus (*Ant.* 10.10.4) there has been a tradition of interpretation identifying the fourth kingdom with the Roman Empire. 2 Esdras 12:11-12, written at about the same time that Josephus wrote, identifies the fourth kingdom as Rome but makes it clear that this is a break with the then accepted interpretation. The choice therefore is between the sequence Babylonian, Median, Persian, Greek and the sequence Babylonian, Medo-Persian, Greek, Roman.

The interpretation in Daniel 8 makes it clear that the ram with two horns represents the combined Medo-Persian Empire. Cyrus II (the Great) of Persia began his reign in 559 BC as a vassal of the Medes. He rebelled, and in 550 BC he defeated the Median king Astyages and incorporated Media and Persia into one empire. The goat represents the Greek Empire, and the single "conspicuous" horn is Alexander the Great. In the years 334-331 BC he won a series of victories over Darius III and became ruler of an empire stretching from Greece to India and Egypt to central Asia. At

the height of his power he died of a fever in Babylon in 323 BC, and his empire was divided among his generals. Following a period of infighting, four kingdoms emerged. Two of these were the Seleucid kingdom, which included Syria and Mesopotamia, and the Ptolemaic kingdom in Egypt. They fought for control of the area that included Judea.

4.1.1. The Small Horn. There is general agreement that the small horn in Daniel 8 symbolizes Antiochus IV, who usurped the Seleucid throne from his nephew. He became increasingly megalomaniac. From 169 BC his coins picture his head with the title *theos epiphanēs* ("god manifest"). He probably saw himself as an incarnation of the god Zeus. In 167 BC he instigated a severe persecution of the orthodox Jews, attempting to stamp out their religion. This provoked the Maccabean Revolt, and in December of 164 BC forces under Judas Maccabeus recaptured the temple and cleansed and rededicated it. Antiochus died at about this time, struck down by a sudden illness while robbing a temple in Persia. The language of Daniel 8:10 is symbolic and draws on Isaiah 14; Ezekiel 28, which speak of earlier rulers (of Assyria and Tyre) whose pride led them to have pretensions of deity. They use imagery found also in the texts from Ugarit, which tell how the god Athtar, the morning star, made a failed attempt to take over Baal's throne.

The imagery of the small horn seems to pick up on the image used in Daniel 7:8, suggesting that the horns in the two visions symbolize the same ruler. There are considerable similarities between the horns in the two visions: both arise out the second stage of a great empire, become great from small beginnings, exhibit blasphemous arrogance, persecute and prevail against the "holy ones" for a set period, and oppose God and are destroyed by God. There are also differences: one grows as an additional horn among ten, while the other grows from one of four horns; one uproots three of the previous ten horns, while the other appears without harming any of the previous four or increasing their number; the actions of the first are centered on "the holy ones of the Most High," while those of the second also include desecration of a "holy place" and halting its sacrifices; one has dominance for "a times, two times, and half a time," but the other for "two thousand three hundred evenings and mornings."

The differences are not contradictory; they are complementary views resulting from differences in focus of the two visions. In Daniel 8 the preceding rulers of the Seleucid Empire are not mentioned. Instead, it focuses on the horn's relationship to the four successor kingdoms of Alexander's empire. This prepares the way for Daniel 11, which will focus on the struggle between two of them, because the Jews get caught up in it. Meanwhile, this vision gives more details of Antiochus's dealings with the Jews, expanding on the single statement in Daniel 7:25 that he planned "to change the set times and the law."

4.1.2. The Fourth Empire as Greece. If the small horns of the two visions both refer to Antiochus, then the fourth empire in Daniel 7 must be Alexander's. Since the vision of the four beasts is a counterpart of the dream in Daniel 2, the same interpretation must apply to the kingdoms of that dream too. The main objection to the sequence Babylonian, Median, Persian, Greek has been that there was no Median Empire between the Babylonian and the Persian, and the Medes never ruled over Judea as did the other empires.

This ignores the possibility that Daniel's viewpoint is not that of a modern historian, but rather that of a Jew exiled in Babylon. The Medes never ruled the territory of Israel or Judah, but they did rule over some Israelites. The Assyrians deported many of the Israelites and settled some "in the cities of the Medes" (2 Kings 17:6; 18:11). The Judeans were interested in the plight of their northern kindred. Judean prophets uttered oracles about the return of these exiles (e.g., Jer 30—31; Ezek 37; Mic 5). The author of Daniel was aware of the prophecies of restoration in Jeremiah (Dan 9:2) and incorporates in Daniel 9 a prayer expressing the distress of Judah, the inhabitants of Jerusalem, and "all Israel, those that are near and those that are far away, in all the countries where you have driven them" (Dan 9:7).

The structure of the visions in Daniel 2; 7 means that the kingdoms are presented sequentially, but there is no reason why they should not be contemporaneous, or overlap. In fact, the Babylonian and Median Empires did overlap, and the Median Empire reached the peak of its power when Babylon's power was waning. So, the sequence in Daniel can be seen as a quite reasonable perception of history from the fall of the Assyrian Empire to an intervention by God to establish his kingdom, presented from the perspective of a Jewish exile in Babylon. During this period those Judeans and Israelites who are experiencing God's chastisement and who will, if they remain faithful, share in the ultimate kingdom, experience the power of Babylon, Media, Persia and Greece.

4.1.3. The Fourth Empire as Rome. Conservative scholars have favored this position partly because it avoided the perceived problem of the Median Empire and partly because it makes the visions in Daniel 2; 7 point to Jesus' coming. The problems raised by identifying Rome as the fourth empire are significant. First, nothing in what is said of the fourth kingdom in the vision of the image suggests it is Rome. What is said about marriage alliances in Daniel 2:43 fits well the use by the Seleucids and Ptolemies of such alliances. Their marriage alliances are prominent in Daniel 11. Second, nothing that is said about the fourth beast points specifically to Rome, whereas the description of it as "different from all the others" (repeated for emphasis [Dan 7:7, 19]) fits with the fact that Greece, under Alexander the Great, was the first nonoriental power to conquer the Near East. Third, if Rome is the fourth kingdom, one has to make a distinction between the small horns of Daniel 7 and Daniel 8. As discussed above, this is unnecessary and unlikely. Finally, if the fourth kingdom is Greece, each of the surveys of history in Daniel 2; 7; 8; 11 has the same terminus, the persecution of the Jews by Antiochus IV. Also, the statement in Daniel 8:25 that the little horn is broken "by no human hand" echoes Daniel 2:34, where a stone "cut out, not by human hand" strikes the feet of the image and destroys it. This suggests that the fourth kingdom of the image and the Greek Empire, which gave rise to Antiochus IV, the small horn, are the same.

4.2. "One Like a Son of Man" and "The Holy Ones of the Most High." In both Aramaic and Hebrew the phrase "son of man" (whether using the root *'dm* or *'nš*) denotes a human being. There is much debate about whom or what is denoted by the human figure in Daniel 7:13.

First, there are "individual" interpretations. A few have suggested a historical deliverer of the Jews such as Judas Maccabeus. The Jewish apocalypses *1 Enoch* 37—71 and *4 Ezra* 13 clearly interpret Daniel 7:13 in terms of a messianic figure (*see* Messiah). Christians have applied this to Jesus (e.g., Beasley-Murray). However, there is no Davidic messianic figure elsewhere in Daniel. The cloud imagery has led some to argue that a supernatural, angelic figure is intended, noting that elsewhere in Daniel angels have a human appearance. The figure has then usually been identified with Michael, the angelic "prince" of the Jews (e.g., J. Collins 1993, 310). However, the two figures are not explicitly linked when Michael appears later in Daniel.

Second, there are "collective" interpretations (e.g., Hartman and Di Lella). The figure represents "the [people of the] holy ones of the Most High" (Dan 7:18, 22, 25, 27). They, like the figure in the vision, receive kingship and dominion.

Finally, there are "symbolic" interpretations (e.g., Lucas 2002, 186-87). The scene in the throne room is a continuation of the vision of the beasts, and the human figure seems to stand in contrast to the beasts. They are deprived of kingship and dominion; he receives it forever. They symbolize earthly, human powers; he symbolizes the kingdom of God. He is a human figure because it was to humans made in the image of God that God gave dominion and rule over the earth (Gen 1:26-28).

The distinction between the collective and symbolic interpretations is not clear-cut. Consistency within the context of the vision favors the latter, but "the holy ones of the Most High" might be seen as the historical expression of the kingdom of God on earth. However, their identity is also a matter of debate. When the adjective *qĕdôšîm* is used as a noun in the Hebrew Bible, it nearly always refers to heavenly beings. It refers to humans in Psalm 34:9 and possibly in Deuteronomy 33:2; Psalm 16:3. For this reason, some scholars (e.g., J. Collins 1993, 316-18) conclude that "the holy ones of the Most High" refers to the angelic counterpart of Israel. They then take "the people of the holy ones of the Most High" (Dan 7:27) to refer to Israel. Against this others (e.g., Hartman and Di Lella, 89-102) argue that the small horn's actions against the "holy ones" in Daniel 7:21, 25 fit most naturally with Antiochus's actions against the Jews. They interpret Daniel 7:27 epexegetically as "the people which consists of the holy ones of the Most High" and argue that the context of Daniel 7 requires the rarer use of *qĕdôšîm* to denote humans.

4.3. The Seventy Sevens. J. Montgomery surveyed what he called "the trackless waste of assumptions and theories" that have been used by those seeking to interpret Daniel 9:24-27 in terms of "an exact chronology fitting into the history of Salvation" (Montgomery, 390-401). His discussion can be updated by those by J. Baldwin (172-78) and A. Collins (112-23). Only a few representative interpretations can be considered here.

The word for "sevens" in Daniel 9:24-27 is used in Daniel 10:2-3 to refer to "weeks," and those seeking a chronological interpretation appeal to Leviticus 25:8, in which the period of forty-nine years leading to the Jubilee Year is spoken of as "seven weeks of years." Deciding the starting point of a chronological scheme, the time of "the going out of a word to restore and build Jerusalem" (Dan 9:25), is problematic. The context of Daniel reading "the word of Yahweh to Jeremiah the prophet" (Dan 9:2) suggests strongly that this refers to one of Jeremiah's oracles. The main possibilities are the prophecy about seventy years (Jer 25:12 [605 BC]); the repeat of this in his letter to the exiles (Jer 29:10 [597 BC]); his prophecies of restoration (Jer 30:18-22; 31:38-40 [c. 587 BC]). None are commands to "restore and build Jerusalem," but Jeremiah 30:18 contains promises that Jerusalem will be "rebuilt on its mound."

Alternatives are either Artaxerxes' decree recorded in Ezra 7:12-26 (458 BC?) or Artaxerxes' warrant given to Nehemiah in Nehemiah 2:7-8 (445 BC). Only the latter clearly relates to rebuilding Jerusalem, though limited to the city wall and gates. It is arguable that had the reference been to a royal decree rather than a prophetic oracle, then a term more specific than "a word" would have been used.

Another issue is the punctuation in Daniel 9:25. The NRSV and most modern English translations follow the MT and put a semicolon or period after "seven weeks." This results in reference to an "anointed leader" coming after seven weeks, and then in Daniel 9:26 a different anointed leader being "cut off" after a further sixty-two weeks. The NIV follows Theodotion's Greek translation and the Latin Vulgate in not having this punctuation break. This allows the possibility that one and the same "anointed leader" is referred to in both verses. However, the reference to the period of seven weeks in

Daniel 9:25 is left hanging without an explanation. It seems more likely that it marks some significant event.

4.3.1. Messianic Interpretations. These take Daniel 9:25-26 to refer to a single period of sixty-nine weeks and an anointed leader who comes at the end of it. Starting from Artaxerxes' decree given to Ezra, if this is dated to 458 BC (a debatable point), then sixty-nine weeks of years leads to AD 26, a possible (though debatable) date for the beginning of Jesus' public ministry. The stopping of sacrifices and offerings after half a week (Dan 9:27) is taken to be the result of Jesus' death, with AD 30 as a possible (though debatable) date for this. The final half-week is pushed into the indefinite future.

Starting from the more likely date of Artaxerxes warrant to Nehemiah (445 BC) has the problem that the end point is AD 39. An attempt to solve this problem is made by postulating that the years are "prophetic years" of 360 days only, bringing the date down to AD 32. This is taken to be the year of Jesus' death. The whole of the final week is then postponed to the indefinite future.

There are significant problems with these interpretations. First, there is no clear interest in a messianic figure elsewhere in Daniel. Second, the most likely referent for the "word" in Daniel 9:25 is the prophecies of Jeremiah. Third, the most natural interpretation of Daniel 9:25-26 is that they refer to two different "anointed leaders," the first coming after seven weeks. Fourth, there is nothing in the text to suggest a "time chasm" either before or in the middle of the last week. A. Konkel also argues against this on the grounds that the use of masculine plural in the phrase "seventy weeks," when "weeks" normally has a feminine plural form, indicates a plurality that forms one total, unbroken, quantity. Finally, the appeal to "prophetic years" is unconvincing special pleading. Some ancient Near Eastern calendars did use thirty-day months, but they also included intercalary days to keep the calendar in step with the true year.

4.3.2. Maccabean Interpretations. These take one of Jeremiah's prophecies as the starting point and the "anointed leader" who comes after seven weeks as one of the major figures involved in the first return from exile (Cyrus, Zerubbabel, Joshua). The seven weeks (forty-nine years) can then fit the period in exile

(586/7-539/8 BC). The "anointed leader" who is "cut off" after sixty-nine weeks is taken to be Onias III, the Jewish high priest who was deposed and murdered in 171 BC. The middle of the last week then falls in 167 BC, when Antiochus IV outlawed the Jewish religion, desecrated the temple, and instigated persecution of faithful Jews. This provoked the Maccabean Revolt, and the end of the final week is taken to be the rededication of the temple by Judas in 164 BC.

The problem here is that the period between the return from exile and Onias's murder (367 years) is shorter than sixty-two "weeks" (434 years). This often is explained by assuming that the prophecy is a *vaticinium ex eventu* ("prophecy after the event"), and that the author had only a vague knowledge of the true chronology. It is, however, questionable whether Jewish writers were ignorant of the chronology of the period (Laato, 213-19).

4.3.3. A Symbolic Interpretation. In 2 Chronicles 36:19-23 Jeremiah's seventy years are understood symbolically. The period from the destruction of Jerusalem and the temple to the first return (forty-nine years) is related to the need for the land to make up its lost Sabbaths. That this is said to be fulfilled by the seventy years implies that the number is understood symbolically as ten Sabbatical cycles. Seven, seventy and ten are numbers associated with completeness (Jenson), so ten Sabbatical cycles, seventy years, is a complete period of rest. Daniel 9:24-27 may be another symbolic interpretation of Jeremiah's prophecy.

There are several verbal and thematic links between Daniel's prayer and Leviticus 26:27-45 (Fishbane, 488-89), a passage about a period of divine wrath measured in Sabbatical cycles. The idea of "weeks of years" probably arises from Leviticus 25:8, which is in a passage about Sabbatical cycles and the Jubilee Year, the time of release from slavery and debt. This provides good grounds for understanding the seventy weeks in symbolic terms involving Sabbatical cycles and Jubilees. Starting with the destruction of Jerusalem and the temple, the first seven weeks (one Jubilee cycle) lead to the first release, the initial return from exile. This foreshadows the great release after seventy weeks (ten Jubilee cycles), the end of the Antiochene persecution and the rededication of the temple. What is the significance of the sixty-nine-week period? A figure that is one less than a perfect number (such as six in 666 as the number of the beast in Rev 13:18) can symbolize the antithesis of perfection. So, it is appropriate that the climax of persecution should come after sixty-nine weeks as the prelude to the great release. This is not intended as an exact chronological scheme, though it just so happens that the first seven weeks roughly fits the period between the destruction of the temple and the first return, and the period between Onias's murder and the rededication of the temple was approximately seven years. The scheme is not chronology but rather chronography, a symbolic scheme of history that is intended to interpret major events in it, not to provide a means of predicting them. There are many examples of this in the surviving Jewish apocalypses (see Grabbe 1979). As a theological interpretation of history, the schema of seventy weeks is about judgment for a broken covenant (Sabbatical years and Jubilee Years going unobserved) but also about Yahweh as a redeemer who saves his people from slavery and oppression. This fits well with the preceding context of Daniel's prayer.

4.4. Daniel 11:40-45. Daniel 11:21-45 seems to deal with the career of Antiochus IV Epiphanes. However, Daniel 11:40-45 bears no relation to what is known of his death due to a sudden illness after an unsuccessful attempt to rob a temple in Persia.

Since Jerome, Christians have often seen an antichrist figure (or anti-God figure like Gog in Ezek. 38—39) in these verses. Indeed, some have seen this figure coming to the fore at Daniel 11:36. The weakness of this interpretation is that there is no clear change of subject signaled at Daniel 11:40 or earlier.

Most modern commentators see here evidence that Daniel 11:2-39 is a *vaticinium ex eventu*, with these verses looking to the downfall of Antiochus. This does not necessarily mean that they are a "false prediction." They make considerable use of phrases from earlier Hebrew prophets, especially Isaiah's prophecies about Assyria's downfall. This could be a way of asserting in general terms the certainty of his downfall, without being intended as a detailed prediction of how it will occur. A new slant is given to this approach if it is accepted that the author is using an existing literary form, that of the Akkadian Prophecies. As

noted above, these use the form of a quasi-prophecy to bring out the meaning of a period of history. In one case, the Uruk Prophecy, it ends with a statement of the author's hope for the future expressed in language drawn from Akkadian prayers said for or by the king (Lucas 2002, 293).

4.5. How Long? No satisfactory explanation has been suggested for the answers given to this question in Daniel 8:14; 12:11-12. The "two thousand three hundred evenings and mornings" (Dan 8:14) might refer to that number of days, or it might indicate the number of morning and evening sacrifices and thus refer to 1,150 days. It may be significant that twenty-three is one-third of sixty-nine, a significant number of weeks in Daniel 9:24-27. If so, it may symbolize a fixed period of oppression.

The suggestion that the numbers in Daniel 12:11-12 are successive attempts to "correct" the prediction of 1,150 days in Daniel 8:14 seems unlikely. As each "prediction" was proved wrong, it would have reduced confidence in the book. Their (probably symbolic) significance is now lost to us.

5. Date, Authorship and Composition.
Although most scholars favor a Maccabean date for the final form of Daniel, there are still those who argue for a sixth- or early fifth-century date.

5.1. Linguistic Issues. At the end of the nineteenth century S. R. Driver wrote, "The verdict of the language of Daniel is thus clear. The *Persian* words presuppose a period after the Persian empire had been well established: the Greek words *demand*, the Hebrew *supports*, and the Aramaic *permits*, a date *after the conquest of Palestine by Alexander the Great*" (Driver, lxiii).

Three of the musical instruments in Daniel 3 have Greek names. P. Coxon argues that in a specialized area such as music Greek influence might have been marked early on. There is evidence that Greeks had contact with the ancient Near East from the eighth century BC onwards. Coxon concludes that the presence of these words in Daniel is neutral with regard to the question of dating.

K. Kitchen argues that all the Persian loanwords in Daniel are all Old Persian words, belonging to before 300 BC. J. Collins (1993, 19) accepts that Kitchen's evidence "does weigh against the theory that the whole book originated in the second century," and that a late sixth-century date is compatible with the Persian loanwords. He thinks that a later date is more probable, allowing time for extensive linguistic borrowing.

It is now agreed that the *Aramaic used in Daniel is the Official Aramaic that was in use from about 700 BC to 200 BC. Comparisons of the Aramaic of Daniel with the material from Elephantine (fifth century BC), Samaria (fourth century BC) and Qumran (second century BC and later) suggest that Daniel's Aramaic is closer to that of the Samaritan papyri than that at Qumran (J. Collins 1993, 17).

The *Hebrew of Daniel is more like the late biblical Hebrew of Ezra, Nehemiah and Chronicles than the exilic Hebrew of Ezekiel. There are clear differences between Qumran Hebrew and the Hebrew of Daniel (J. Collins 1993, 19-23).

Overall, it is clear that Driver's claim that the linguistic evidence demands a second-century BC date is no longer valid, though it does seem to favor a late postexilic date.

5.2. Other Arguments. The claim that historical inaccuracies in the book militate against an early date has lost much of its force (see 3 above). Daniel is in the third section of the Hebrew canon (the Writings), not in the second (the Prophets). This is sometimes taken as evidence of its late date. The survey of Israel's history in Sirach 44—49 may indicate that all the books in the Prophets were accepted as Scripture by the early second century BC. However, Baldwin argues that the omission of Daniel from the Prophets is explicable on the basis of its different character rather than its late date (Baldwin, 71).

There is a growing consensus that the stories originate from the Diaspora of the Persian period. Hartman and Di Lella comment, "The many correct references to customs and terms used at the Persian court have often been noted by commentators" (Hartman and Di Lella, 13). The picture that they give of the pagan kings and their relationship to faithful Jews is too positive for stories composed in the second century BC. Two major issues of the Maccabean period are ignored: circumcision and Sabbath observance.

Rationalistic denial of the possibility of predictive prophecy may influence views of the date of Daniel's visions. For many supporters of a Maccabean date, however, the possibility of such prophecy ("Could God do it?") is not the issue. More to the point, given the detailed focus on events in the early second century BC in Daniel 7—11, is the question "Would God do it?" J. Goldingay argues that such detailed, long-range, predictive prophecy is not consistent with the picture of God revealed elsewhere in Scripture: "He does not give signs and reveal dates. His statements about the future are calls to decision now; he is not the God of prognosticators. He calls his people to naked faith and hope in him in the present, and does not generally bolster their faith with the kind of revelations that we are thinking of here. He does sometimes grant evidences to those who cannot believe without them, and thus we dare not exclude the possibility that this was the case with the book of Daniel. But the presumption is by no means in favour of this possibility" (Goldingay, 45).

There is also a literary issue. The whole of Scripture comes in the literary forms of the authors' times and cultures. Pseudonymous quasi-prophecy is a common feature of Jewish apocalypses. We should not reject it as an unworthy literary form simply because we do not understand the psychology of both author and readers involved in its use. B. Metzger comments with regard to Daniel, "Whatever idiom or mode of expression [the author] would use in ordinary speech must surely be allowed him when moved by the Holy Spirit" (Metzger, 22). It may be that he used the genre of the Akkadian Prophecies (see 2.3 above).

Evidence regarding the date of the final form of Daniel is not clear-cut. A reasoned, and reasonable, defense can be made of either an early or a late date. Acceptance of either is consonant with belief in the divine inspiration and authority of the book.

5.3. Authorship and Composition. Since the stories are written *about* Daniel, acceptance of an early date for the book does not settle the issue of authorship. The book may have been put together by the (anonymous) author of the stories or by a separate editor.

Those who accept a Maccabean date generally assume that the visions and the final form of the book come from among those called "the wise" in Daniel 11:33-35; 12:3. No convincing case has been made for identifying these with any one of the groups known to exist within the Judaism of the time. It is also generally assumed, because of the prominence of the fate of Jerusalem and the temple in the visions, that the book was compiled in Judea. However, Psalm 137; Nehemiah 1; Daniel 1:1-2; 5:23 show that Jews in the Diaspora had a passionate concern about this. What is said of "the wise" in Daniel 11:33-35 does not require them to be Judean Jews. Some of them may have gone to Judea to encourage their compatriots there, or they may have conveyed their encouragement in writing (the book of Daniel?) and expected to face suffering in the Diaspora. Lucas (2000) suggests that the origin of the book was a collection of court tales (Dan 2—6 and maybe an earlier form of Dan 1) composed in Aramaic, as that was the vernacular. These were treasured by a group of educated, upper-class Diaspora Jews who found careers in government service because they provided a vision of how to remain faithful to God in their situation. The Antiochene crisis challenged their generally positive worldview. The visions are the experience of one or more members of the group as they strove to understand what was happening. They were written in Hebrew because that seemed appropriate for more esoteric material. They were combined with the stories that formed the basis of the group's self-understanding because the apocalyptic worldview of the visions was a development from that of the stories, not a departure from it. Attributing the visions to Daniel was not an attempt to deceive people; it was an expression of the group's sense of solidarity and continuity with their past traditions.

6. The Message of Daniel.

6.1. Sovereignty: Human and Divine. Nebuchadnezzar's capture of Jerusalem and looting of the temple to take some of its vessels to the treasury of his gods (Dan 1:1) might imply the superiority of Babylon's gods. Daniel 1:2 immediately counters this. Yahweh "gave" the king of Judah and the temple into Nebuchadnezzar's power, for reasons not specified until Daniel 9. Yahweh is the supreme king, who "changes times and eras, removing kings and establishing kings" (Dan 2:21) and has a goal for history. He will "raise up a kingdom that is eternal and will not be destroyed" (Dan 2:44). Eventually Nebuchadnezzar, after his hubris in which he sees himself as the supreme king (Dan 4:30) has been broken and humbled, confesses that

Yahweh "does as he wishes with the forces of the heavens, and the inhabitants of the earth" (Dan 4:35), and, importantly, that "all his deeds are right and his ways just" (Dan 4:37).

Yahweh's rule is not arbitrary; it is morally determined. In the vision in Daniel 7:9-14 the Ancient of Days judges the earthly powers that have become subhuman, bestial, in their arrogant, self-centered exercise of sovereignty. He deprives them of their sovereignty and gives it to "one like a human being." It is in God's kingdom, under his sovereignty, that humanity reaches its full potential. Salvation history culminates in the achievement of the purpose that God had when creating the world, a world in which humans exercise sovereignty as his representatives (Gen 1:26-28). This is the significance of the "one like a son of man" receiving sovereignty in Daniel 7:13-14. Daniel 4:10-12 paints a picture of the good that human rulers can achieve. When humans image God, they have the right to rule in his name and will bring peace and wholeness to his creation. Those who recognize God's sovereignty over them are those who will allow God to rule through them. When they try to be God, they lose the right to rule, and their rule may become subhuman, bestial.

Achieving God's purpose will not be easy. God's people will experience suffering before receiving the kingdom (Dan 7:21-22). This raises the question of why God's purposes sometimes seem to be frustrated and take a long time to come to fruition (note the cry "How long?" in Dan 8:13; 12:6). A partial answer is given in Daniel 9—11. Daniel's prayer of confession and repentance makes clear that Yahweh gave Judah into the power of Nebuchadnezzar as an act of judgment, visiting on Judah the curses of the covenant that Judah had repeatedly broken. It was a moral act in which Yahweh responded to human behavior, and the prayer assumes that he will respond to confession and repentance. God gives humans a measure of freedom, and this affects the way his purposes are carried out. Daniel 11 contains both allusions to God's sovereignty (Dan 11:27, 29, 36, 45) and statements that, within limits, a human king can "do as he pleases" (Dan 11:3, 16, 36).

6.2. Faithfulness: Human and Divine. Daniel 1 also introduces the theme of faithfulness. Because God allows rulers enough freedom to become bestial, those who are committed to God sometimes suffer. As a result, they are challenged to adopt a lifestyle of faithfulness. In Daniel 1 the issue is personal integrity. Daniel makes a stand dictated by his own conscience before God in relative privacy and does it diplomatically. The Jews in Daniel 3 have to oppose idolatry openly. The conspirators in Daniel 6 target Daniel's religious practice because that seems like the best way to succeed. He could still pray to God secretly, but since his piety was common knowledge, that would have been to compromise. In each case God is faithful to the faithful Jews. In the stories the Jews are kept safe in the furnace or lions' den, and not just delivered from it, as an angel mediates God's presence to them. In the context of the whole book, the stories are not just simplistic promises of God's deliverance; they prepare the way for the references to the suffering, persecution and martyrdom of the faithful in Daniel 7—12.

The stories encourage the faithful to become involved in the pagan world with the hope of some measure of success and effective witness, even though there are risks. The visions depict a much more difficult situation. God's sovereignty means that the faithful cannot presume on what God's response will be. Belshazzar's blasphemy meets with swift retribution, while that of the small horn is allowed to continue for a considerable time before it is ended. The faithful may be delivered *from* death in a fiery furnace (Dan 3) or *through* death in the fires of persecution (Dan 12). The visions encourage the faithful to stand firm until God's purposes triumph. Those given wisdom are encouraged to use it to "give understanding to many" (Dan 11:33) and to "lead many to righteousness" (Dan 12:3). These references to "the wise" and the "many" whom they influence may allude to the Suffering Servant of Isaiah 52:13—53:12. The way to glory for the wise is faithful service despite the suffering that it brings.

God's faithfulness to those who are faithful stretches beyond death. Daniel 12:2-3 contains the only clear statement in the Hebrew Bible of belief in resurrection of the dead. Those who have suffered and died because of their faithfulness are promised resurrection to everlasting life. Those who have opposed God and persecuted them will be raised to "shame and everlasting abhorrence." To "the wise" is prom-

ised special glory, as they "will shine like the stars." The language here is allusive, and exactly what is meant by the different destinies is not made clear.

6.3. Angelology. Daniel has the most developed *angelology in the Hebrew Bible. This enables talk about God's involvement in the world while preserving God's transcendence. The struggle between heavenly beings called the "princes" of Persia, Greece and Israel (Dan 10:13, 20) expresses the idea that history has a transcendent dimension, and that there is a synergy between events in heaven and on earth. The same is true of Daniel 7, where the vision of God's throne room follows the vision of the beasts. However, the measure of sovereignty given to humans means that what happens in heaven does not totally determine what happens on earth, and vice versa.

7. Daniel and the New Testament.

There is general agreement that Daniel 7:13 lies behind Jesus' reference to himself as the Son of Man. It links his claim to bring in the kingdom of God with the completing of God's purpose in creating the world. This theological understanding of Jesus' work is expounded in Hebrews 2. The consummation of Jesus' own ministry at his parousia is expressed using the imagery of Daniel 7:13. In Daniel 7 the "one like a son of man" is associated with the suffering "holy ones," and this probably contributed to Jesus' conviction that he must face suffering.

Also related to the coming of the kingdom of God in Jesus' ministry is the saying about the stone in Luke 20:18. It alludes to Isaiah 8:14-15 and Daniel 2:34-35 and identifies Jesus with the stone that crushed the statue.

The major antichrist figure in Revelation is "the beast" that rises out of the sea and is a hybrid of the four beasts of Daniel 7 (Rev 13:1-4). It also shares features with the small horn of Daniel 7—8. The time for which it exercises authority (Rev 13:5) seems based on Daniel 12:7. Revelation reapplies the theological significance of the small horn without any attempt to treat what Daniel says of it as detailed predictions about the antichrist. The Roman Empire is portrayed as the current manifestation of the same arrogant, blasphemous, bestial exercise of human sovereignty against God and God's faithful people.

The fact that discipleship involves suffering

is a common theme in the NT. 1 Peter 4:12-14 alludes to the story in Daniel 3 in its assurance that the Spirit of God will be with those who face the "fiery ordeal" of suffering for Christ (*see* Prophets in the New Testament).

See also APOCALYPTICISM, APOCALYPTIC LITERATURE; ARAMAIC LANGUAGE; DANIEL: HISTORY OF INTERPRETATION.

BIBLIOGRAPHY. *Commentaries*: **J. G. Baldwin,** *Daniel* (TOTC; Downers Grove, IL: InterVarsity Press, 1978); **J. J. Collins,** *Daniel: A Commentary on the Book of Daniel* (Hermeneia; Minneapolis: Fortress, 1993); **S. R. Driver,** *The Book of Daniel* (CBSC; Cambridge: Cambridge University Press, 1900); **M. Fishbane,** *Biblical Interpretation in Ancient Israel* (Oxford: Clarendon Press, 1998); **L. F. Hartman and A. A. Di Lella,** *The Book of Daniel* (AB 23; Garden City, NY: Doubleday, 1978); **E. Heaton,** *The Book of Daniel* (TBC; London: SCM, 1956); **E. C. Lucas,** *Daniel* (AOTC 20; Downers Grove, IL: InterVarsity Press, 2002); **J. A. Montgomery,** *A Critical and Exegetical Commentary on the Book of Daniel* (ICC; Edinburgh: T & T Clark, 1927). *Studies*: **G. R. Beasley-Murray,** "The Interpretation of Daniel 7," *CBQ* 45 (1983) 44-58; **P.-A. Beaulieu,** *The Reign of Nabonidus, King of Babylon, 556-539 B.C.* (New Haven: Yale University Press, 1989); **R. D. Biggs,** "The Babylonian Prophecies and the Astrological Traditions of Mesopotamia," *JCS* 37 (1985) 86-90; **B. E. Colless,** "Cyrus the Persian as Darius the Mede in the Book of Daniel," *JSOT* 56 (1992) 113-26; **A. Y. Collins,** "The Influence of Daniel on the New Testament," in *Daniel: A Commentary on the Book of Daniel,* by J. Collins (Hermeneia; Minneapolis: Fortress, 1993) 90-123; **J. J. Collins,** *The Apocalyptic Vision of the Book of Daniel* (HSM 16; Missoula, MT: Scholars Press, 1977); idem, "Introduction: Towards the Morphology of a Genre," *Semeia* 14 (1979) 1-20; idem, "4QPrayer of Nabonidus Ar," in *Qumran Cave 4.XVII: Parabiblical Texts, Part 3,* by G. Brooke et al. (DJD 22; Oxford: Clarendon Press, 1996) 83-93; **P. W. Coxon,** "Greek Loan Words and Alleged Greek Loan Translations in the Book of Daniel," *TGUOS* 25 (1973) 95-121; **J. E. Goldingay,** "The Book of Daniel: Three Issues," *Them* 2 (1977) 45-49; **L. L. Grabbe,** "Chronography in Hellenistic Jewish Historiography," *SBLSP* 17 (1979) 43-68; idem, "Another Look at the *Gestalt* of 'Darius the Mede,'" *CBQ* 50 (1988) 198-213; **A. K. Grayson and W. G. Lambert,** "Akkadian Prophecies," *JCS* 18 (1964) 7-30; **P. D. Hanson,** "Apocalypticism," *IDBSup* 28-34; **W. L. Humphreys,** "A Life-Style for Diaspora: A Study of the Tales of Esther and Daniel," *JBL* 92 (1973) 211-23; **P. P. Jenson,** "Seven," *NIDOTTE* 4:35; **K. A. Kitchen,** "The Aramaic of Daniel," in *Notes on Some Problems in the Book of Daniel,* by D. Wiseman et al. (London: Tyndale, 1956) 31-79; **K. Koch,** *The Rediscovery of Apocalyptic: A Polemical Work on a Neglected Area of Biblical Studies and Its Damaging Effects on Theology and Philosophy* (trans. M. Kohl; SBT 22; London: SCM, 1972); **A. H. Konkel,** "Week," *NIDOTTE* 4:20-24; **A. Laato,** "The Seventy Yearweeks in the Book of Daniel," *ZAW* 102 (1990) 212-24; **W. G. Lambert,** *The Background of Jewish Apocalyptic* (London: Athlone, 1978); **E. C. Lucas,** "The Sources of Daniel's Animal Imagery," *TynBul* 41 (1990) 161-85; idem, "Daniel: Resolving the Enigma," *VT* 50 (2000) 66-80; **B. M. Metzger,** "Literary Forgeries and Canonical Pseudepigrapha," *JBL* 91(1972) 3-24; **A. R. Millard,** "Daniel 1-6 and History," *EvQ* 49 (1977) 67-73; **A. R. Millard and P. Bordreuil,** "A Statue from Syria with Assyrian and Aramaic Inscriptions," *BA* 45 (1982) 135-41; **A. L. Oppenheim,** "The Interpretation of Dreams in the Ancient Near East," *TAPS* 46 (1956) 179-373; **D. B. Redford,** *A Study of the Biblical Story of Joseph (Genesis 37-50)* (VTSup 20; Leiden: E. J. Brill, 1970); **H. H. Rowley,** *Darius the Mede and the Four World Empires in the Book of Daniel* (Cardiff: University of Wales Press, 1935); **L. M. Wills,** *The Jew in the Court of the Foreign King: Ancient Jewish Court Legends* (HDR 26; Minneapolis: Fortress, 1990); **D. J. Wiseman,** "Some Historical Problems in the Book of Daniel," in *Notes on Some Problems in the Book of Daniel,* by D. Wiseman et al. (London: Tyndale, 1956) 9-18; idem, *Nebuchadrezzar and Babylon* (Oxford: Oxford University Press, 1985). E. C. Lucas

DANIEL: HISTORY OF INTERPRETATION

The book of Daniel has been one of the most influential biblical books on Western culture. Citations of the book and allusions to its content can be found not only in commentaries and homiletical material, but also in political rhetoric, historical reconstructions, artistic representations and even prognostications. Despite its relative brevity (twelve chapters), it has exerted considerable influence upon those who recognize the book of Daniel as Scripture.

1. Early Jewish Tradition
2. New Testament
3. Patristic Period
4. Medieval Period
5. Reformation Period
6. Historical-Critical Study

1. Early Jewish Tradition.

1.1. Qumran. The book of Daniel as represented in the Masoretic tradition would have reached its current form some time during the reign of Antiochus Epiphanes IV (167-164 BC). Although late in development, the Daniel tradition garnered attention as an authoritative source relatively quickly within the Jewish tradition.

The apocalyptic nature of Daniel accorded well in many ways with the theology and worldview of Qumran (*see* Dead Sea Scrolls). A total of eight Daniel scrolls were discovered at Qumran, dating from the late second century BC to the middle of the first century AD. Of the remaining books in the canon, only Psalms, Deuteronomy, Isaiah, Genesis, Exodus and Leviticus appear there in greater number. Every chapter except Daniel 12 is represented among the eight fragments of Daniel (Ulrich). Daniel 12, however, is attested in 4Q174 in a midrash on the last days, suggesting that the book in its entirety was present in some form to the Dead Sea sect. Moreover, the bilingual nature of Daniel in the MT is retained in the Qumran texts, as seen most clearly in 1Q71 with the shift from Hebrew to Aramaic at Daniel 2:4b.

In addition to the eight biblical manuscripts of Daniel, there are nine nonbiblical scrolls that pertain to the book of Daniel, all written in Aramaic. In varying ways, these either relate to the story of Daniel, or Daniel functions as a primary figure in the text. For example, the *Prayer of Nabonidus* (4Q242) recounts the fate of a Babylonian king afflicted with sickness for seven years, only to recover with the aid of a Jewish exile. The relationship between the *Prayer of Nabonidus* and Daniel 4 is difficult to establish, but most likely the Qumran text represents a tradition that stands between the Babylonian accounts of Nabonidus and the account in Daniel 4. The *Pseudo-Daniel* compositions (4Q243; 4Q244; 4Q245) present Daniel before the king and his court, drawing upon the notion of Daniel as a visionary. 4Q551 arguably

alludes to a Susanna-type figure, but this connection remains speculative at best (Flint, 362).

A number of Qumran texts appropriate the language and imagery of Daniel. For example, the notion of eschatological war in the *War Scroll* (1Q33) appears to draw directly from the language of Daniel 11—12. The periodization of history, as seen in Daniel, appears frequently in Qumran texts (see 4Q180; 11QMelchizedek; Damascus Document). In 11Q13 II, 18 the writer mentions one who is "anointed by the spirit" and suggests that this person is the one about whom Daniel spoke (Dan 9:25-26). Surprisingly, there is no explicit reference to Daniel 12:3 or the notion of a resurrection as presented in Daniel 12. This is all the more striking given the significant influence of Daniel 11—12 on the scrolls, especially the *War Scroll* (1Q33) and the *Community Rule* (1QS). A possible exception to this claim is 4Q521, but whether it is a product of the Dead Sea community remains a matter of debate (J. Collins 1995, 121).

The absence in the scrolls of any allusion to Daniel 7 and, more particularly, to the "one like a son of man" in Daniel 7:13 is unexpected, particularly given the frequency with which the label "son of man" is used in subsequent Jewish and Christian texts (see 2.1 below). Although "one like a son of man" does not appear in a Qumran text, 4Q246, frequently referred to as "the son of God text," does refer to a figure who will be called "son of God" and "son of the Most High." Although some scholars contend that this figure is negative, representing one of the Seleucid kings, most aver that it represents a messianic figure. Although the prophet Daniel is not mentioned in the text, the language and themes appear derived from the book of Daniel, making 4Q246 "probably the oldest surviving interpretation" or adaptation of Daniel 7 (J. Collins 1995, 166).

1.2. Apocalypse of Zephaniah. Dated from middle of the first century BC to the end of the first century AD, *Apocalypse of Zephaniah* employs a number of explicit references to the book of Daniel. The version of Daniel in use by the author clearly had the tale of Susanna included, given that in his prayer for deliverance from distress he mentions Susanna, as well as Shadrach, Meshach and Abednego as examples of God's deliverance (*Apoc. Zeph.* 6:10). In the same chapter, using language derived from

Daniel 10:5-6, the author describes the appearance of a "great angel" that visited him (*Apoc. Zeph.* 6:11). Elsewhere the author mentions the "Book of the Living" (*Apoc. Zeph.* 3:7), similar to that envisioned in Daniel 7:10, and in his descriptions of the angelic figures, the author adopts the language of Daniel 7:10 but reconfigures the role of the "thousands of thousands" and "myriads of myriads" of angels (*Apoc. Zeph.* 4:2).

1.3. Similitudes of Enoch *and* 4 Ezra. The *Similitudes of Enoch* (*1 En.* 37—71) and *4 Ezra* (both first century AD) draw from the Daniel tradition. In *1 Enoch* 47:3 the visionary writes, "I saw the Head of Days sit down upon the throne," at which point he opened the "books of the living." The Head of Days functions as the Enochic equivalent to Daniel's Ancient of Days (Dan 7). He takes his place upon the throne, opening up the books in judgment (Dan 7:10). In *1 Enoch* 46:1 the Head of Days is described as having a head "white like wool," a description found in Daniel 7:9. Unlike the Dead Sea sect, however, those who produced the *Similitudes of Enoch* made explicit use of the "son of man" concept found in Daniel 7:13, adapting it in new ways. Following *1 Enoch* 47, and the depiction of the Head of Days opening the books of the living ones, *1 Enoch* 48 introduces the arrival of a new figure, the Son of Man, who in the *Similitudes of Enoch* resembles the figure of Wisdom in Proverbs 8, a heavenly preexistent figure, as evidenced in *1 Enoch* 48:6; 62:7. He functions as the heavenly counterpart of all the righteous on earth, and at the right time he will strike down the kings from their thrones and sit on the throne of glory to judge (*1 En.* 62:5). In the final chapter of the *Similitudes of Enoch*, however, the angel reveals to Enoch that he in fact is "the son of man born in righteousness." Whether one follows J. Collins (1993) with the claim that *1 Enoch* 70—71 is a later addition, or whether one follows Vanderkam (1992) with the assertion that these chapters suggest that Enoch has a heavenly counterpart, the more pressing point is that the figure of the Son of Man is given a more explicit identity in the subsequent Danielic traditions.

In *4 Ezra* 12:10-11 the angel instructs Ezra that the vision that he saw is "the fourth kingdom that appeared in a vision to Daniel your brother." In *4 Ezra* 13:1-3 Ezra recounts a dream he had in which "something resembling a man"

was brought up from the depths of the sea and the "man was flying with the clouds of heaven," a reference to Daniel 7. The one that resembles a man is said to be of Davidic lineage: "the Messiah whom the Most High has kept until the end of the days" (*4 Ezra* 12:32). As in *1 Enoch*, the Son of Man in *4 Ezra* is preexistent, and like the Messiah of Isaiah 11, he will be from the Davidic line. In both instances (*Similitudes of Enoch* and *4 Ezra*) the Son of Man wreaks havoc upon the wicked, exacting judgment upon the nations (Reynolds). The conjoining of these themes, heavenly savior and Davidic messiah, reflects the flexibility of the Son of Man concept in responding to the political and religious crises of the day.

1.4. Josephus. Josephus's comments on Daniel in *Jewish Antiquities* not only represent another witness to the Daniel tradition from the first century AD, but equally so suggest the prominence already attached to the book in that period. In his recapitulation of Jewish history Josephus clearly has a non-Jewish audience in mind (*Ant.* 1.10-11), but as L. Feldman has noted, Josephus appears to be addressing a Jewish audience as well (*Ant.* 1.14). In addition, some scholars (e.g., Daube) have suggested that Josephus understood or at least presented Daniel as a type of himself, a Jewish captive working under the auspices of a foreign power.

In his larger work, Josephus fails to mention prophets such as Amos and Hosea and gives only scant attention to Isaiah and Ezekiel. Perhaps somewhat surprisingly, then, Josephus provides an extensive account of Daniel, concluding that Daniel was "one of the greatest prophets" (*Ant.* 10.266). According to Josephus, the accuracy of Daniel's predictions are evidence that Daniel must have "conversed with God" about such matters (*Ant.* 10.267). To highlight the significance of the book of Daniel, even to non-Jewish rulers, Josephus includes an otherwise unknown claim that the book of Daniel was shown to Alexander the Great with regard to the prediction that the Persians would be overthrown by the Greeks (*Ant.* 11.337).

Although Josephus was recounting the history of the Jewish people, he adapted the story of Daniel for his non-Jewish audience. Josephus employs many of the characteristic features of Greco-Roman literature in his presentation of Daniel. He emphasizes Daniel's noble birth as well as his physical beauty (*Ant.* 10.186). Similar to Plato's philosopher-king, Daniel exhibits the cardinal virtues of wisdom, courage, temperance, justice and piety throughout Josephus's presentation of Daniel (Feldman, 45-46).

In several places Josephus's rendition of the Daniel narrative appears to lack the more supernatural elements found in the biblical tradition. For example, Josephus reports that the three youths were preserved in part by the providence of God, in that by requiring a vegetarian diet, God had made the bodies of the three youths too strong to be consumed by fire (*Ant.* 10.190-194). Further, Josephus omits any mention of Gabriel or other such heavenly figures, including the fourth figure in the furnace. Although such features are noticeably absent in *Jewish Antiquities,* Josephus maintains a sincere belief in divine providence, suggesting that the book of Daniel provides a strong antidote to the Epicurean belief that the universe carries on with "mechanical necessity."

Josephus clearly understood the Roman Empire to be the fourth kingdom (*Ant.* 10.276), but given his audience, he is reluctant to draw any conclusions about the future of the fourth kingdom, preferring instead to enjoin the Jewish reader to be diligent in "reading the book of Daniel" to discover the fate of that kingdom (*Ant.* 10.210). Josephus's work demonstrates already a common hermeneutical proclivity of subsequent interpreters: to "extend" the book of Daniel in an effort to interpret contemporary political, social and theological crises.

1.5. Other Sources. The Danielic influence is present in a number of other sources from this period. For example, the hymn of Moses found in *Testament of Moses* 10 draws heavily from the language and imagery of Daniel 12, developing in particular the notion of resurrection found in Daniel 12:3. In *Lives of the Prophets,* much like Josephus's *Jewish Antiquities,* the character of Daniel receives significant treatment, more so than many of the other prophets. Not surprisingly, the stories of the three youths (Dan 3) and the lions' den (Dan 6) are recounted in 3-4 Maccabees.

2. New Testament.

As with the other writings surveyed above from the first century AD, the book of Daniel exerted considerable influence upon the writers of the NT (*see* Prophets in the New Testament). An appendix in the Nestle-Aland *Novum Testamentum Graece* (27th ed.), which records both quotations and allusions, cites over two hundred references to Daniel, suggesting that the influence of Daniel on the NT is similar to that of Psalms or Isaiah (Evans, 490). Although exact quotations of Daniel are rather limited (Mt 24:30; 26:64; Mk 13:26; 16:62; Lk 21:27), frequent allusions to the language and imagery of Daniel permeate the entire NT.

2.1. The Son of Man. The influence of Daniel 7 upon NT writers, and in particular the connection between Daniel 7 and the "Son of Man" sayings in the Gospels, has generated a considerable body of literature in the last century alone. Earlier in the twentieth century, interpreters such as S. Mowinckel argued that the notion of a "son of man" figure derived from what he perceived to be a "divine Primordial Man" figure that appeared in Indo-Iranian myths. Mowinckel contended that the "son of man" concept was a Jewish adaptation of that larger ancient Near Eastern concept. Further, Mowinckel contended that "son of man" was actually understood as a title meant to identify a heavenly messiah figure that would come to earth to judge the earth.

More recent scholars (Lindars) rejected both Mowinckel's connection of the term with a divine primordial man and his contention that the phrase functioned as a title in late Jewish eschatological thought. Instead, more recent work has noted the use of the term in late Jewish literature, in particular *4 Ezra* and the *Similitudes of Enoch,* suggesting that this literature appropriates the Danielic "one like a son of man" in new ways, linking it to a reinterpreted notion of a messiah (Reynolds), and even the vindication of a messianic figure (Wright). Among the concepts posited in such texts, the "son of man" is preexistent, messianic, and responsible for the destruction of the wicked. As A. Collins has suggested, these common features imply "that the emergence of an apocalyptic 'Son of Man' need not be seen as a Christian development in response to the experience of Jesus as raised from the dead," but in fact may reinforce the notion that Jesus presupposed these same concepts in his own interpretation of Daniel 7, even as he added his own "innovative twist" to the concept (A. Collins, 90).

The phrase "son of man" is used more frequently than any other phrase to speak of Jesus in the Gospels. Worth noting is that throughout the Gospels, the phrase only appears in the speeches of Jesus (in Jn 12, the crowd quotes the earlier comment of Jesus), and while not titular in nature, the phrase was used as a means of self-designation by Jesus (Marshall). J. Dunn has sought to narrow the connection between the phrase "son of man" and the influence of Daniel 7, suggesting that when the phrase "son of man" appears alongside other terms or ideas from Daniel 7, such as "coming" and "on the clouds of heaven," then the direct influence of Daniel upon the usage of the phrase is indisputable (Dunn, 529). For example, even as the "son of man" is depicted as "coming with the clouds of heaven" in Daniel 7, so too will the "Son of Man" (Jesus) arrive in the clouds (cf. Mk 13:26; 1 Thess 4:17; Rev 1:7). The fact that the phrase itself fails to appear in later NT writings, however (with the exception of Acts 7:56; Rev 1:13; 14:14), suggests that it was not necessarily titular in nature and, moreover, did not exert a considerable influence upon the Christology of the early church (Marshall; A. Collins; Dunn).

2.2. The Abomination of Desolation.

The phrase "abomination of desolation" appears in Daniel 9:27; 11:31; 12:11, as well as 1 Maccabees 1:54, and in all four instances the desecrating actions of Antiochus IV Epiphanes are clearly in view. Within the Synoptic Gospels, the phrase is used explicitly in Mark 13:14; Matthew 24:15, with Matthew making the connection to Daniel explicit: "the desolating sacrilege standing in the holy place, as was spoken by the prophet Daniel (let the reader understand)." Given the significance of the Maccabean period in the collective memory of those in first century AD Palestine, scholars have suggested that the use of the phrase by the Gospel writers must refer to a situation analogous to the events under Antiochus, whether it be events surrounding Caligula in AD 40 or those surrounding the Jewish war in AD 66-70. The suggestion that a military leader or force appears in view is verified in Luke 21:20, where the phrase has been modified thus: "When you see Jerusalem surrounded by armies, then know that its desolation has come near." The Synoptic Gospels locate Jesus' use of the phrase within his larger eschatological discourse, as seen in Mark 13 in a manner similar to the way

in which Daniel 9:27 was used earlier in *Testament of Levi* 15:1. The idea of a desolating sacrilege also informs 2 Thessalonians 2.

2.3. The Book of Revelation.

Not surprisingly, allusions to Daniel appear throughout the book of Revelation, arguably even serving to structure the book as a whole. G. Beale has suggested that Daniel 2:28-29 has been appropriated in Revelation 1:1, but with a significant modification. In Daniel, the text mentions the things that will happen in the "latter days," but the writer of Revelation, while using the language of Daniel 2, shifts the horizon of expectation, explaining that the purpose of the book is "to show . . . what things must take place soon [*en tachei*]." Beale has noted a similar use of Daniel 2 in Revelation 4:1; 22:6b, suggesting that together with Revelation 1:1 these three texts function as a framework for the book in its entirety. The use of Danielic language at key junctures in the book is indicative of the influence that Daniel had upon the writer of Revelation throughout.

A. Collins argues that Revelation 1:9—3:22 appears to have been modeled on Daniel 10:2—12:4. Both sets of texts detail an epiphany of a heavenly being to a human. The human identifies himself and his location and then offers a rich description of the heavenly being. The human falls to the ground, only to be comforted by the heavenly being. In addition to the overall structure of this section, there are more detailed inferences, again with significant modifications. The description of the heavenly figure in Revelation 1:15 resembles that mentioned in Daniel 10:5-6. More explicitly, the writer of Revelation picks up the language of Daniel 7, referring to the "one like a son of man" in Revelation 1:13, but then he merges that figure with the Ancient of Days figure mentioned as well in Daniel 7. In Daniel the two figures are distinct entities, but in Revelation 1 the "one like a son of man" is described as having hair "white like wool," no doubt an attempt to reinforce the notion of his divine status (Rowland, 101).

The primary antagonist in the book of Revelation, referred to simply as "the beast," functions as an antichrist figure. The descriptive language of the beast employed in Revelation 13:1-10 derives from the imagery of the four beasts found in Daniel. The beast in Revelation has ten horns, as did the fourth beast in Daniel, yet the beast in Revelation has seven heads, the total number of heads of all the beasts in Daniel. Moreover, Revelation 13 explains that the beast arises from the sea, again drawing from the descriptive language in Daniel 2. In Daniel 7—8 the hubris of the fourth beast is exhibited through arrogant speech; Revelation 13 explains that the beast utters "haughty and blasphemous" speech, clearly drawing from the Daniel tradition.

3. Patristic Period.

Just as the book of Daniel exerted considerable influence upon the writers of the NT, so too did the book upon the early church fathers. Irenaeus (c. AD 130-200) alluded to Daniel throughout his work *Against Heresies*. The stone not hewn by human hands that crushes the statute in Daniel 2 is understood as a type or figure of Christ (*Haer.* 3.21.7). The same understanding of a type or figure is found in Irenaeus's reading of Daniel 3 concerning the fourth individual in the furnace, as well as his reading of Daniel 7 and the "son of man" who comes on the clouds. As J. Gammie has suggested, Irenaeus's treatment of Daniel 12:4 is most revealing in regard to his own view of Scripture. Whereas Daniel 12:4 recounts that Daniel is instructed to shut up the words and seal them "until the end of time," Irenaeus contends that this "disclosure" took place at the cross of Christ (*Haer.* 4.26.1), or, more succinctly put, the Christ event becomes the lens through which to read all of Scripture. In constructing his own millenarian eschatology, Irenaeus draws from Revelation and 2 Thessalonians as well as Daniel 9, suggesting that the antichrist would rule for three and a half years (Dan 9:27), and that at the end of the age, all the saints of the Most High would receive the kingdom of God (Dan 7:27). Unlike the interpreters who follow, however, Irenaeus did not posit dates for the "end of days."

Hippolytus (c. AD 170-236), a disciple of Irenaeus, wrote the first known Christian commentary on a book from the Hebrew Bible. In his commentary on Daniel he wedded martyrdom theology with the exegesis of Daniel in light of the persecution launched in AD 193 by Emperor Septimius Severus. In his exegesis of Daniel 3, Hippolytus explains that the three youths are a "pattern for all believing people." Despite the immediate threat of persecution,

however, Hippolytus contended that the end was not imminent. Instead, he noted that the age of the world would last six thousand years, followed by the thousand-year reign of Christ. Hippolytus argued that because Jesus came five thousand five hundred years after Adam, there remained considerable time until the arrival of the end. For Hippolytus, this view was substantiated in his understanding of the seventy weeks mentioned in Daniel 9. The birth of Jesus concluded the sixty-ninth week, but the seventieth week refers to the final days, when Elijah, Enoch and the antichrist will appear. As W. Shelton has noted, the removal of any notion of imminent return was intended to reinforce the call to martyrdom (Shelton, 110).

Due to the extensive persecution during the late second and third centuries, a number of writers made use of Daniel as a means for exhortation in a manner similar to Hippolytus. Origen's *Exhortation to Martyrdom* was written in AD 235 during the reign of Maximinus Thrax. In his *Epistles*, Cyprian responded to the expansive persecution under Decius (AD 249-251), three times employing Daniel 3. Those in prison he exhorted to have faith, the "same kind as once did Ananias, Azarias, and Misael, the illustrious youths to whom, when shut up in the furnace . . . the heat of hell could have no power" (*Ep.* 80.3). Several martyrdom stories emerged from this period, a number of them alluding to Daniel, with particular interest in Daniel 3; 6, including *The Martyrdom of Saints Montanus and Lucius* and *The Martyrdom of Bishop Fructuosus and His Deacons, Augurius and Eulogius.*

The most significant commentary from the period was that of Jerome (AD 347-419). In his treatment of Daniel he sought to refute the claims of the Neoplatonist philosopher Porphyry, who not only argued for the pseudonymity of Daniel but also suggested that the book of Daniel had been written some time after the persecution by Antiochus IV Epiphanes. Jerome himself did not jettison a historical reading of Daniel. He followed the Antiochene school of interpretation, rejecting allegorical readings (cf. Origen), preferring instead the more literal and historical reading of the text (see his rejection of Hippolytus's interpretation of Dan 9:24-27). Despite his penchant for a more "literal" reading, however, Jerome defended a christological interpretation of Daniel

2; 7, as well as a reinterpretation of Daniel 12:1-3, which he believed referred to the resurrection of the faithful following the overthrow of the antichrist.

Theodoret of Cyrus served as bishop of Cyrus, Syria, during the years AD 423-457 and was a prolific writer influenced by the Antiochene approach to interpretation. His commentary on Daniel can be dated to approximately AD 433, and according to his introduction, there were two impetuses for his writing. He explains, "Our friends required of us commentary on this author" (*Comm. Dan.* 1260). His second reason is to respond to the Jewish claim that the book of Daniel did not belong among the Prophets, but instead among the Writings. Like Jerome, Theodoret offered a christological interpretation for Daniel 2 ("the stone hewn out of a mountain"), as well as the "son of man" text in Daniel and the identification of the seventy weeks in Daniel 9. Unlike Hippolytus, however, the political affairs of the day appear to have little if any impact on the origin of the commentary or on Theodoret's interpretation. Moreover, Theodoret appears to have little interest in providing precise calculations on the "last days" based on the book of Daniel and instead understands Daniel to be a critique against world empires in light of the sovereignty of God.

4. Medieval Period.

4.1. Jewish Interpretation. Rabbinic interpretation of Daniel represented considerable diversity as well. The wisdom and piety of Daniel was frequently noted. It was said of Daniel, "If he were in one scale of the balance and all the wise men of the heathens were in the other, he would outweigh them all" (*b. Yoma* 77a). In other texts, rabbinic interpreters supplied additional details not found in the biblical story of Daniel. In both *Sanhedrin* and *Pirqe Rabbi Eliezer*, Daniel is portrayed as not only wise, but also as a eunuch (associating Is 39:7 with the events of Daniel). Other writings suggest that the huge stone that was placed in front of the lions' den was actually a stone that had been rolled from Palestine to Babylon just for this use (*Midr. Ps.* 66). And after Daniel had spent the night with 1,469 lions, he was found that morning reading the Shema (*Midr. Ps.* 66). *The Chronicles of Jerahmeel* (twelfth century) reflects the coalescing of a number of these traditions

in the recounting of the Daniel story.

Subsequent Jewish scholars produced a number of works on Daniel concerned with a more literal and exegetical rendering of the text. The apocalyptic nature of Daniel itself did push the writers in their interpretive decisions. The commentary by Rashi (AD 1040-1105) explained that the messianic prophecies were related to the fourteenth century (not his own), thereby downplaying any expectation of an immanent and cataclysmic change during his own time. Ibn Ezra (AD 1091-1167) encouraged readers to refrain from speculating about the dates associated with the prophecies of Daniel, yet he assigned some events to his own day (Dan 7) and others to the events of the second century BC (Dan 8). The last great medieval Jewish exegete of Daniel was Isaac Abravanel (AD 1437-1508). He wrote *Wells of Salvation* after the Jews had been expelled from Spain, and for Abravanel, the book of Daniel became instructive for Jews living in exile, awaiting the kingdom of God on earth.

4.2. Influence on Medieval Literature. In addition to commentaries and writings, the book of Daniel produced another genre of literature, which demonstrates most clearly the impact of this book on subsequent generations. Many of these writings reflect the Daniel tradition as appropriated in the medieval period. At least twenty-three apocryphal apocalyptic texts were generated from the fourth to eleventh centuries with Daniel as the chief figure in the book. Although these works are not a "midrash" on Daniel, they reflect the belief that the Daniel tradition remained a viable vehicle for theological discourse. A number of these writings reflect the appropriation of the Daniel tradition in light of political and social events of the day. For example, the *Syriac Apocalypse of Pseudo-Methodius* dates to the seventh century AD and is concerned primarily with the Muslim invasion of the Byzantine Empire.

More popular forms of apocalyptic thought drew from Daniel as well. Joachim of Fiore (c. 1135-1202) cited Daniel 7:27 in his discussions of the third age that will come after the defeat of the antichrist. It was also during this time that the identification of the pope as the antichrist emerged, a theme that carried over into the Reformation period in the writings of Martin Luther. Even more suggestive politically is Daniel's appropriation in the *Book of a Hundred*

Chapters. Following the death of Frederick I, prophets began to speak of a future Frederick who is to come, who will restore Germany to its glory. And in the *Book of a Hundred Chapters* the four empires of Daniel are identified as France, England, Spain and Italy, while Germany was to be the fifth and greatest empire, led by this new Frederick.

During this period Nebuchadnezzar is a frequently cited figure, particularly in regard to the notion of madness or the image of the lunatic. At times he is portrayed as the mad sinner, at other times as the unholy wild man, and yet others as the holy wild man. Such a reading of Nebuchadnezzar appears in the thirteenth-century work of Albert the Great (*Commentaria in librum Danielis*), the *Glossa ordinaria* (PL 114:282) and numerous other works of the period.

5. Reformation Period.

Martin Luther contends in his preface to the book of Daniel that the Roman Empire is the fourth kingdom. He suggests that the ten horns mentioned in Daniel refer to the ten kingdoms that emerged from the Roman Empire, including Syria, Greece, Italy, England and Germany among others, and he refers to the little horn as "Mohammed," a reference to the Turkish defeat of Greece, Egypt and parts of Asia. Although ten kingdoms emerged from the Roman Empire, Luther is quick to assert that heritage of the Roman kingdom has now been transferred to the German Empire, which shall "remain until the Last Day no matter how weak [the German empire] may be." Although Luther espoused no specific timetable for the last days, his exegesis (see below) suggests that he understood the time to be near.

Luther's hermeneutic, like that of other contemporaries, including Philip Melanchthon, George Joye and John Knox, may best be described as an "actualizing exegesis" (Firth). Although Luther's preface to Daniel addresses the narrative of the text, including the praise of Daniel as a virtuous figure, Luther connects the biblical text with more immediate historical events. In his discussion of Daniel 8; 11, Luther does mention Antiochus IV Epiphanes, instead quickly shifting to discussions of the antichrist, identifying the pope with the figure in Daniel 11. In *Heerpredigt wider dem Türken* (1529), Luther declares the Turks to be the fourth beast and implores the reader to join in the eschatological battle against the foe. Further, he interprets the wars mentioned in Daniel 11 as an allusion to events associated with Jan Huss.

John Calvin's treatment of Daniel remains much more philological. Rather than claiming that the events outlined in Daniel presaged his own era, as did Luther, Calvin asserted that the visions of Daniel pertain to events no later than that of Nero, unconvinced that the last days were imminent. Calvin contends that the seventy weeks in Daniel 9 refer to the coming of Jesus and the destruction of Jerusalem at the hands of Rome.

6. Historical-Critical Study.

With the rise of "higher criticism," a number of issues moved to the fore in discussions related to Daniel. In their commentaries on Daniel, Hugh Broughton (1596) and Hugo Grotius (1642) both dispensed with identifying the antichrist as the pope, preferring instead to recognize the fourth kingdom as Greece. Rather than understanding the book of Daniel as a road map of Western history and politics, critical scholars have wrestled with other matters, including that of genre, social setting, and sources of influence. This is not to suggest, however, that the tendency toward "actualizing exegesis" ceased with the period of the Reformation (see 6.1 below).

6.1. The Continued Use of Actualizing Exegesis. The Fifth Monarchy movement, an anti-Cromwellian movement, in the 1650s understood themselves to be the fifth kingdom mentioned in Nebuchadnezzar's dream, and William Miller (1782-1849) determined on the basis of Daniel 8:14 that the end of the world would be in 1843, subsequently recalculated to 1844. Both incidents mirror Luther's appropriation of Daniel to contemporary political, theological and ecclesial matters. In the late nineteenth century, the book of Daniel figured significantly in the dispensational movement begun by J. N. Darby (1800-1882). The dispensational approach to Scripture and theology was later "codified" in some sense with the Scofield Reference Bible, released in 1909 by Cyrus Scofield. More recently, the writings of Hal Lindsey (*The Late Great Planet Earth*) and Tim LaHaye and Jerry Jenkins (the Left Behind series) have popularized a dispensational reading of Scripture.

6.2. Dating of the Book of Daniel. During the nineteenth and twentieth centuries, the question of the date and authenticity of the book of Daniel remained a source of contention. Beginning with Bertholdt (1806), von Lengerke (1835) and Ewald (1850), historical-critical study of Daniel tested the assumptions of a sixth-century dating of the book. Critical study resulted in a near consensus view of a Maccabean date for the book in its entirety, as argued in the earlier commentaries of Bevan (1892), Driver (1900), Marti (1901) and Montgomery (1922), among others. More recent commentaries by Lacocque (1979), Goldingay (1988), J. Collins (1993), and Smith-Christopher (1996) all argue for a second-century BC dating of the book. The sixth century BC date had its proponents in the nineteenth century with writers such as Hengstenberg (1831), Pusey (1864) and Keil (1867), and despite the emerging consensus among most critical scholars for a Maccabean date, the sixth century BC date has been defended in the twentieth century by R. D. Wilson (1917), E. J. Young (1949) and Joyce Baldwin (1978), in particular.

6.3. The Definition of Apocalyptic Literature and the Book of Daniel. Scholars in the twentieth century have worked to agree upon a common set of markers that identify a text more narrowly as an apocalypse. In the 1979 issue of *Semeia*, J. Collins articulated a description of such literature that has served as the operational definition for all subsequent discussions of genre. The definition emphasized literature that is "revelatory literature within a narrative framework" mediated by an "otherworldly being," disclosing a transcendent reality. Within the larger corpus of literature deemed an apocalypse (e.g., *1 Enoch, 2 Baruch, 4 Ezra, Apocalypse of Zephaniah*), the book of Daniel, in particular Daniel 7—12, has been recognized as a "historical apocalypse," with features more nearly resembling those in the *Animal Apocalypse* and the *Apocalypse of Weeks* found in *1 Enoch*, as well as *4 Ezra* and *2 Baruch*. A considerable body of research has emerged in recent decades analyzing the connections between Daniel and the apocalyptic literature found at Qumran, as well as the larger corpus of literature from the Second Temple period (see the representative articles in Collins and Flint).

6.4. Roots of Apocalypticism. A number of studies in the last half of the twentieth century explored the roots of apocalypticism. J. Collins (1977) noted the influence of mythological themes found in Canaanite texts and their influence on the book of Daniel. Similar studies have been carried out by S. Paul and J. Walton. N. Cohn, however, has suggested that themes such as supernatural evil and resurrection, among other apocalyptic themes, are of Persian origin. S. Cook has challenged this position, arguing that such a view robs the literature of its own imaginative power, while failing to recognize that the chief influence on Daniel appears to be the prophetic corpus in the Hebrew Bible. Arguably, the tales have an anthological style, with frequent allusions to and reinterpretation of biblical texts, while the visions contain explicit references to the prophetic corpus (Dan 9).

The renewed interest in apocalyptic writings in general within the last century has led to a more refined definition of the genre and consequently a more robust discussion concerning the similarities and differences between Daniel and other apocalypses from the same general period. Abandoning the predictive claims in Daniel suggested by earlier interpreters, recent interpreters have focused instead on the historical, theological and rhetorical elements of the book, given the social milieu, and in particular the oppressive reign of Antiochus IV Epiphanes.

The history of interpretation suggests that communities of faith through the centuries have found the book of Daniel to be a fertile source for constructive theological reflection. A casual review of such a history might highlight only the more sensational or bizarre interpretations, but critical engagement with the literature reinforces the seriousness with which the people of faith took the interpretive process in light of the world around them.

See also APOCALYPTICISM, APOCALYPTIC LITERATURE; DANIEL: BOOK OF; HERMENEUTICS.

BIBLIOGRAPHY. **G. K. Beale,** *The Use of Daniel in Jewish Apocalyptic Literature and in the Revelation of St. John* (Lanham, MD: University Press of America, 1974); **K. Bracht and D. S. du Toit,** eds., *Die Geschichte der Daniel-Auslegung in Judentum, Christentum, und Islam: Studien zur Kommentierung des Danielbuches in Literatur und Kunst* (BZAW 371; New York: de Gruyter, 2007); **N. Cohn,** *Cosmos, Chaos, and the World to Come: The Ancient Roots of Apocalyptic Faith* (New

Haven: Yale University Press, 1993); **A. Y. Collins,** "The Influence of Daniel on the New Testament," in *Daniel: A Commentary on the Book of Daniel*, by J. Collins (Hermeneia; Minneapolis: Fortress, 1993) 90-123; **J. J. Collins,** *The Apocalyptic Vision of the Book of Daniel* (HSM 16; Missoula, MT: Scholars Press, 1977); idem, ed., *Apocalypse: The Morphology of a Genre* (Semeia 14; Missoula, MT: Scholars Press, 1979); idem, *Daniel: A Commentary on the Book of Daniel* (Hermeneia; Minneapolis: Fortress, 1993); idem, *The Star and the Scepter: The Messiah of the Dead Sea Scrolls and Other Ancient Literature* (New York: Doubleday, 1995); **J. J. Collins and P. W. Flint,** *The Book of Daniel: Composition and Reception* (2 vols.; VTSup 83; Leiden: E. J. Brill, 2002); **S. L. Cook,** *The Apocalyptic Literature* (Nashville: Abingdon, 2003); **D. Daube,** "Typology in Josephus," *JJS* 31 (1980) 18-36; **M. Delgado, K. Koch and E. Marsh,** *Europa, Tausendjähriges Reich und Neue Welt: Zwei Jahrtausende Geschichte und Utopie in der Rezeption des Danielbuches* (SCRK 1; Stuttgart: Kohlhammer, 2003); **L. DiTommaso,** *The Book of Daniel and the Apocryphal Daniel Literature* (SVTP 20; Leiden: E. J. Brill, 2005); **J. D. G. Dunn,** "The Danielic Son of Man in the New Testament," in *The Book of Daniel: Composition and Reception*, ed. J. J. Collins and P. W. Flint (2 vols.; VTSup 83; Leiden: E. J. Brill, 2002) 2:528-49; **El'azar ben Asher ha-Levi,** *The Chronicles of Jerahmeel* (trans. M. Gaster; BibH 6; New York: Ktav, 1971); **C. A. Evans,** "Daniel in the New Testament: Visions of God's Kingdom," in *The Book of Daniel: Composition and Reception*, ed. J. J. Collins and P. W. Flint (2 vols.; VTSup 83; Leiden: E. J. Brill, 2002) 2:490-527; **L. H. Feldman,** "Josephus' Portrait of Daniel," *Hen* 14 (1992) 37-96; **K. R. Firth,** *The Apocalyptic Tradition in Reformation Britain, 1530-1645* (Oxford: Oxford University Press, 1979); **P. W. Flint,** "The Daniel Tradition at Qumran," in *The Book of Daniel: Composition and Reception*, ed. J. J. Collins and P. W. Flint (2 vols.; VTSup 83; Leiden: E. J. Brill, 2002) 2:329-67; **J. Gammie,** "A Journey through Danielic Spaces: The Book of Daniel in the Theology and the Piety of the Christian Community," *Int* 39 (1985) 144-56; **Jerome,** *Commentary on Daniel* (trans. G. Archer; Grand Rapids: Eerdmans, 1958); **B. Lindars,** *Son of Man: A Fresh Examination of the Son of Man Sayings in the Gospels* (London: SPCK, 1983); **I. H. Marshall,** "Son of Man," *DJG* 775-81; **S. Mowinckel,** *He That Cometh: The Messiah Concept in the Old Testament and Later Judaism* (Grand Rapids: Eerdmans, 2005); **S. Paul,** "The Mesopotamian Babylonian Background of Daniel 1-6," in *The Book of Daniel: Composition and Reception*, ed. J. J. Collins and P. W. Flint (2 vols.; VTSup 83; Leiden: E. J. Brill, 2002) 1:55-68; **B. E. Reynolds,** *The Apocalyptic Son of Man in the Gospel of John* (WUNT 2/249; Tübingen: Mohr Siebeck, 2008); **C. Rowland,** *The Open Heaven: A Study of Apocalyptic in Judaism and Early Christianity* (New York: Crossroad, 1982); **W. B. Shelton,** *Martyrdom from Exegesis in Hippolytus: An Early Church Presbyter's Commentary on Daniel* (Eugene, OR: Wipf & Stock, 2008); **Theodoret of Cyrus,** *Commentary on Daniel* (trans. R. Hill; SBLWGW 7; Atlanta: Society of Biblical Literature, 2006); **E. Ulrich,** "The Text of Daniel in the Qumran Scrolls," in *The Book of Daniel: Composition and Reception*, ed. J. Collins and P. Flint (2 vols.; VTSup 83; Leiden: E. J. Brill, 2002) 2:573-85; **J. C. Vanderkam,** "Righteous One, Messiah, Chosen One, and Son of Man in 1 Enoch 37-71," in *The Messiah: Developments in Earliest Judaism and Christianity*, ed. J. H. Charlesworth (Minneapolis: Fortress, 1992) 169-91; **J. Walton,** "The Anzu Myth as Relevant Background for Daniel 7?" in *The Book of Daniel: Composition and Reception*, ed. J. J. Collins and P. W. Flint (2 vols.; VTSup 83; Leiden: E. J. Brill, 2002) 1:69-89; **N. T. Wright,** *Jesus and the Victory of God* (Minneapolis: Fortress, 1996).

W. D. Tucker Jr.

DARIUS THE MEDE. *See* DANIEL: BOOK OF.

DAUGHTER ZION. *See* ZION.

DAVIDIC COVENANT/KINGSHIP. *See* COVENANT; MESSIAH.

DAY OF THE LORD

The Day of the Lord is a significant recurring theme in the prophetic literature of the OT. At its essence, it refers to a time of Yahweh's unmistakable and powerful intervention. It appears in a variety of contexts in prophetic literature and draws together a wide array of images. The prophets employ the specter of the Day of the Lord to offer both warning and hope, announcing both disaster and *salvation. The Day of the Lord continues to engender a significant amount of scholarly discussion concerning its origins, development and essential meaning. This article explores the usage of the Day of the Lord in prophetic literature, focusing on the vocabulary that invokes this day, its origins and temporal orientation. It then explores the varied uses of the Day of the Lord across the OT Prophetic Books.

1. Foundations
2. The Day of the Lord in the Major Prophets
3. The Day of the Lord in the Minor Prophets (Book of the Twelve)
4. Reception of the Concept
5. Conclusion

1. Foundations.

1.1. Terminology. One of the most significant issues encountered when considering the Day of the Lord in prophetic literature is the determination of which passages contain this theme. To begin, there are fifteen verses in the OT that contain the exact phrase *yôm yhwh* ("Day of the LORD"): Isaiah 13:6, 9; Ezekiel 13:5; Joel 1:15; 2:1, 11, 31 (3:4 MT); 3:14 (4:14 MT); Amos 5:18, 20; Obadiah 15; Zephaniah 1:7, 14 (2x); Malachi 3:23 (4:5 MT). Some scholars, most notably Y. Hoffman, insist that a discussion of the Day of the Lord must begin with these passages alone (Hoffman, 44). He would argue that only after taking account of these explicit references is it viable to broaden the scope of the study. This perspective is appealing because it provides an easily manageable collection of texts from which to derive an understanding of the Day of the Lord.

This restrictive approach, however, faces numerous challenges. One of the most significant concerns the viability of identifying the phrase *yôm yhwh* as a discrete term that always conveys a certain idea or meaning. D. Ishai-Rosenboim points to the variety of contexts that employ "day of the Lord" language and argues that the literal meaning of the phrase is so broad that it defies easy categorization (Ishai-Rosenboim, 400). Furthermore, the number of variant phrases that invoke the context of a day characterized by a powerful intervention of Yahweh suggests that the Day of the Lord resonates more broadly than just in those fifteen passages (Nogalski, 193).

This understanding permits the consideration of a significant number of different prophetic passages that seem to invoke the Day of the Lord but employ variations on the phrase *yôm yhwh*. These variations include the insertion of a preposition into the middle of the phrase *yôm yhwh*, referring to a day of Yahweh's anger or *wrath, and the addition of other descriptors to the day (Weiss, 64-65). These variations on *yôm yhwh* widen the pool of available texts to include Isaiah 2:12; 34:8; 61:2; Jeremiah 46:10; Ezekiel 7:19; 30:3; Zephaniah 1:18; 2:2, 3; Zechariah 14:1.

It is also possible to further broaden the potential range of the Day of the Lord. Other stock phrases such as *bayyôm hahû* ("on that day") and *bayyāmîm hāhēmmâ* ("in those days") seem to function within the prophetic literature as references to Yahweh's actions or days where Yahweh's activity is imminent, suggesting that they may form part of the Day of the Lord motif complex (Nogalski, 194). The frequency of these phrases within the prophetic corpus would greatly expand the range of texts under consideration and would suggest that the Day of the Lord is a more prevalent motif in prophetic literature than generally has been admitted.

The range of terminology under discussion has significant ramifications for understanding this theme in prophetic literature. This methodological question permits no easy answer, since we should neither dilute the power of the motif by permitting overly broad criteria nor dismiss passages that evoke similar imagery on the ground of minimal lexical variance. The current trend appears to favor the consideration of a broader range of texts, acknowledging that the concept of the Day of the Lord invokes a certain sense of Yahweh's intervention into human affairs for a variety of purposes. This places the focus upon the rhetorical effect of invoking the Day of the Lord with all of its attendant imagery. Consequently, it is useful to consider variations on the phrase *yôm yhwh* that invoke similar images in order to explain the purposes and effects of Yahweh's actions on the Day of the Lord. The prophets employ an array of terms and phrases to discuss the features and results of this intervention. Thus, limiting the Day of the Lord to the specific verses that contain the phrase *yôm yhwh* is overly restrictive and diminishes the significance of this concept throughout prophetic literature.

1.2. Origins. The question of the origins of the Day of the Lord in Israelite religious expression consumes much of the energy devoted to this topic. Various references to the Day of the Lord in prophetic literature play significant roles in this discussion. S. Mowinckel is a key figure in the discussion of the origins of the Day of the Lord, which he locates in harvest celebrations and an annual festival of enthronement in which Yahweh took his place as the rightful ruler over Israel. This festival would occur at the end of the agricultural cycle, when the earth hovered on the brink of returning to chaos and only the renewed presence of Yahweh could restore prosperity and fertility (Mowinckel, 140). Consequently, this festival in which Yahweh was again symbolically enthroned as king of Israel reflected the desire for Yahweh to act restoratively to guarantee another year of prosperity and security. The Day of the Lord, in this understanding, reestablishes Yahweh's governance over Israel and pointed to his great acts as a means of cementing his position. This perspective is rooted in comparisons with practices from Babylonian and Canaanite practices that celebrate a ritual enthronement of deities (Gray, 24-25).

The evidence that Mowinckel adduces for the existence of this festival and the enthronement of Yahweh derives from the discussion of the Day of the Lord in Amos 5:18-20, which claims that the Day of the Lord will be a day of darkness rather than a day of light. Amos 5:21-24 then denounces Israel's cultic festivals for their apparently empty piety, which probably included this enthronement festival (Mowinckel, 132). Amos 5:18-20 is thus a shocking reinterpretation of the motif because its roots in the enthronement festival gave it an initial sense of the day when Yahweh would remember his *covenant and act to restore prosperity. Instead, the prophetic use of the motif in Amos introduces the idea of judgment and *destruction in Yahweh's actions.

This theory of the origins of the Day of the Lord receives significant challenges from those who question the existence of the enthronement festival and argue that it relies too much on Babylonian cultic practices (Černý, 44-45). Instead, L. Černý proposes that Day of the Lord has its origins as a day decreed by Yahweh in which Yahweh will act to shape the future of Israel. Prophetic figures took the concept and suggested that Yahweh's shaping could include negative consequences. This occurs in Amos 5:18-20, where the combination of perceived re-

ligious apostasy, political instability and foreign threat combined to render inappropriate any positive portrayals of Yahweh's intervention (Černý, 103). As the period of prophetic proclamation proceeded, the fall of Jerusalem made it appear that the Day of the Lord had already taken place, but later prophets were able to reappropriate the concept to serve the needs of the exilic and postexilic communities, where it pointed forward to describe a situation that was "international, global and universal," which ultimately marked the end of ages and announced final judgment (Černerný, 79-80).

Following Mowinckel and Černý, G. von Rad advanced another influential proposal for discussing the origin of the Day of the Lord. His hypothesis probably has garnered the most support in the discussion of the origins of the Day of the Lord and is the theory that provides the background for most of the subsequent discussion of the motif. Notably, von Rad's work offers one of the narrowest examinations of the motif, as he claims that he intends to focus on the passages that contain the phrase *yôm yhwh* (von Rad 1959, 97). Uniquely, he asserts that Amos 5:18-20, almost uniformly considered the "earliest" Day of the Lord passage, is not an appropriate place from which to begin the investigation because of the lack of surrounding context that would reveal the content of the motif. Von Rad also leaves aside Isaiah 2:12, usually considered the next earliest use of the motif because it deals generally with the results and effects of Yahweh's arrival on his day, rather than with the day itself.

For his study, von Rad focuses on four passages (Is 13; 34, Ezek 7; Joel 2) that, in his estimation, discuss the Day of the Lord in sufficiently significant detail. From a close reading of these passages, he locates the origins of the Day of the Lord in the concept of holy war with Yahweh as the divine warrior who descends to achieve victory over his enemies (*see* Warfare and Divine Warfare). Von Rad thus claims that the Day of the Lord reflects a "pure event of war," and he specifically rejects Mowinckel's enthronement hypothesis (von Rad 1959, 108). Locating the origins of the Day of the Lord in the realm of holy war permits von Rad to explain the motifs that it employs including the appearance of Yahweh, the mustering of his army, the terror that afflicts his enemies, cosmological cataclysms and the sacral element of devoting the plunder to Yahweh. These martial motifs certainly suggest that the Day of the Lord resonates with the idea of Yahweh establishing supremacy over opposing nations through military conquest (Stuart, 161).

Ultimately, von Rad concludes that the use of the Day of the Lord in prophetic literature reflects "a bold actualization of ancient Yahwistic ideas" (von Rad 1959, 105). Essentially, the prophets appropriate the idea of Yahweh coming as divine warrior and use it to warn that Yahweh could target Israel and Judah themselves, as well as offer hope that Yahweh eventually would defeat foreign oppressors.

The identification of holy war as the origin of the Day of the Lord motif is the principal point of departure for further studies, which both build from and critique this position. F. Cross tries to combine Mowinckel and von Rad's hypotheses by claiming that the Day of the Lord reflects a combination of kingship and conquest traditions: a day both of Yahweh's holy warfare and of Yahweh's enthronement (Cross, 21). Others advance competing proposals to determine the origins of the Day of the Lord, with F. Fensham agreeing with von Rad and Mowinckel that the motif originated within the prehistory of Israel but asserting instead that it ought to be linked to treaty curses for the community's own misdemeanors (Fensham, 94). Fensham specifically raises issues with von Rad's hypothesis, including questioning why the Day of the Lord can be directed against Israel and why the idea of war does not appear to be present in every mention of the concept, highlighting especially the context surrounding Amos 5:18-20, which focuses upon Israel's transgressions and empty religious festivals. This critique is especially relevant in the context of Amos because one would expect an early mention of the motif to reflect its theological underpinnings. Notably, Fensham does not dispute that militaristic motifs occur in the discussion of the Day of the Lord, but he seeks to subordinate them under the broader category of punishment for the breaking of covenant. He argues that "the Day of the Lord is a day of punishment which may not be a day of war, but a day in which certain curses took effect. . . . The Day of the Lord is a day of judgment and punishment" (Fensham, 94-95).

The emphasis on punitive aspects of the Day of the Lord makes it difficult to account for its salvific potential, which various Day of the Lord passages explore in some detail. When prophets invoke the Day of the Lord against foreign *nations, they use motifs of military defeat and responses from the natural world to characterize the totality of their destruction, since covenant curses are not applicable. When the Day of the Lord is directed against Yahweh's people, it may be possible to see elements of curses from Yahweh's covenant treaty with Israel. These include, but are not limited to, curses of military destruction. This resonance, however, is not sufficient evidence to establish that covenant curses provide the basis for the Day of the Lord as it is employed in prophetic literature (*see* Blessings and Curses).

M. Weiss directly challenges von Rad's identification of holy war as the origin of the Day of the Lord, citing the existence of numerous prophetic texts that employ the vocabulary of holy war that are not part of the corpus of passages that invoke the Day of the Lord. Essentially, this indicates that the Day of the Lord is sufficiently complex that it cannot be perfectly conflated with the idea of holy war. Significantly, this list includes Amos 5:18-20 and Isaiah 2, which are possibly the earliest mentions of the Day of the Lord, but which von Rad relegated to positions of secondary importance in his own analysis because of what he considered the insufficient depth with which they approached the subject. Instead, Weiss argues that the Day of the Lord is a more generic concept, adapting itself according to use that the different prophetic figures wished to employ. The unifying feature throughout passages that invoke the Day of the Lord is Yahweh's appearance and action; essentially, to raise the specter of the Day of the Lord is to anticipate "an actual theophany in all of its concrete incisiveness" (Weiss, 47). Weiss's work helps to demonstrate the limitations of assigning the origin of the Day of the Lord to one particular image complex; instead, he appears to allow for greater creativity on behalf of the prophets who used the Day of the Lord to evoke images of Yahweh acting in varied fashions. Interestingly, Weiss breaks with other interpreters in that he grounds his approach to the Day of the Lord in the prophetic literature, arguing that the Day of the Lord is primarily a prophetic concept that Amos helped to establish through his use of the phrase *yôm yhwh* (Weiss, 60). He maintains, however, that the phrase would have been comprehensible to Amos's audience as referring to a time of Yahweh's appearance and action. This broad approach to the concept has the advantage of being able to handle the available material in a reasonably clear and coherent manner.

Finally, Y. Hoffman argues instead that the root of Day of the Lord material is theophany, "a special and exceptional intervention in the current stream of events" that Yahweh accomplishes (Hoffman, 44). Hoffman's analysis is tightly restricted to those passages that contain the exact phrase *yôm yhwh*. He questions those studies that accord the same level of significance to passages containing the variant phrases, claiming that the proper way to proceed is to engage in a detailed philological examination of the phrase itself before moving toward an evaluation of related phrases. Hoffman takes issue with Weiss's assertion that the Day of the Lord was not a familiar concept by the time of Amos, arguing that Amos's assertion that the Day of the Lord will be a day of darkness and not light packs rhetorical punch only if there is already an assumption of what the Day of the Lord ought to entail (Hoffman, 38).

Curiously, Hoffman argues that while in Amos the concept of the Day of the Lord must have been known, the exact phrase *yôm yhwh* may not have been fixed. This actually argues against his own injunction to consider only those passages that use the exact phrase, since one could argue that other synonymous phrases are invoking the same context. What unites the Day of the Lord passages for Hoffman is this sense of it being a day when Yahweh will appear and act in a powerful or miraculous fashion. Consequently, the surrounding motifs of cosmic upheaval, war and judgment on the wicked should be expected companions to the appearance of the Day of the Lord in prophetic literature.

In summary, the preceding discussion illustrates the continuing lack of consensus concerning the origins of the Day of the Lord. Instead, there is a broad spectrum of hypotheses that strive to peer back into the murky past and describe the origins of the motif, in spite of the paucity of evidence and disagreements over which prophetic texts ought to have priority. Suggestions for the origins of the Day of the Lord include a range of sources, such as holy war traditions, theophany, enthronement festivals, enactment of covenant treaty curses, or

some combinations of these. This lack of scholarly consensus is not surprising given the difficulty of trying to trace the development of this motif through Israel's existence while only having direct evidence of its existence in a limited number of prophetic texts. This research, however, does help to elucidate various elements of the image complex evoked when the prophetic literature invokes the Day of the Lord. These include most obviously the appearance of Yahweh, which often is accompanied by descriptions of war, cosmic upheaval, judgment and destruction, the targets of the day, and its temporal proximity.

1.3. Temporal Orientation. The flexibility of the Day of the Lord motif in prophetic literature is also on display when in regard to its temporal orientation. One of the enduring questions surrounding the Day of the Lord concerns the timing of when the prophets expected it to occur. On many occasions it is evident that the future is in view, where the Day of the Lord is a prophesied day that brings either judgment or restoration. There is some room for variation in whether this future appearance of the Day of the Lord also indicates an eschatological end to history (*see* Eschatology). Imminence is a clear feature of the Day of the Lord, with numerous references emphasizing that the day is "near" or "coming" (Is 13:6; Ezek 30:3; Joel 1:15; 2:1; 3:14; Zeph 1:7, 14). The nearness of the day rhetorically heightens the power of the motif because its power looms over those against whom Yahweh directs it. The progression of the prophetic literature appears to adopt a more eschatological orientation culminating with establishment of Yahweh's reign and the cleansing of Israel and the nations in Zechariah 14, and with the promise of the return of Elijah as a harbinger of the Day of the Lord in Malachi 4.

The temporal orientation of the Day of the Lord appears to stretch beyond its future appearance. Specifically, several passages (Is 22:1-14; Jer 46:2-20; Lam 1:12; 2:22; Ezek 13:1-9) seem to refer to the Day of the Lord as a past historical event in which Yahweh exercises divine authority over the outcome. J. Everson links Isaiah 22:1-14 with Sennacherib's invasion, Jeremiah 46:2-20 with the battle of Carchemish, and Ezekiel 13:1-9 and Lamentations 1—2 with the *Babylonian capture of Jerusalem (Everson, 331). This challenges the dominant streams of interpretation that focus on the Day of the Lord as a final and decisive intervention of Yahweh into history. Interestingly, these passages describe Yahweh acting to both defeat a foreign enemy (Is 22; Jer 46) and to bring judgment upon Jerusalem and Judah (Lam 1—2; Ezek 13). This range of usage again confirms the flexibility of the Day of the Lord for prophetic proclamation. Everson correctly states that "the Day of YHWH was a powerful concept available to the prophets for their use in interpreting various momentous events—past, future or imminent" (Everson, 335). These past occurrences of the Day of the Lord emphasize its martial nature, which builds on the tradition that von Rad established, but the evidence of the temporal flexibility of the Day of the Lord is a valuable contribution to the discussion.

2. The Day of the Lord in the Major Prophets.

We now consider examples of the Day of the Lord in prophetic texts. In keeping with the foregoing discussion concerning terminology, texts that employ different phrases to invoke the Day of the Lord will be referenced here. The following discussion cannot be exhaustive, but it does provide an orientation to the flexibility and power of the Day of the Lord motif in prophetic proclamation.

2.1. Isaiah. Isaiah contains several attested references to the Day of the Lord both through the phrase *yôm yhwh* and its variants. Isaiah 2:12 refers to a *yôm layhwh ṣĕbāʾôt* ("day for the Lord Almighty"), in which Yahweh establishes his supremacy over the nations and their idols. The preceding context accuses Yahweh's people of idolatry, which he will rectify by appearing in power. The verses that follow delineate the range of those who suffer the effects of the Day of the Lord, focusing upon those who are prideful and arrogant (Is 2:12) and eventually revealing their insignificant stature in comparison to Yahweh (Is 2:22).

These verses further describe the range of those against whom Yahweh directs his day, using images drawn from nature, such as the cedars of Lebanon and the oaks of Bashan (Is 2:13-14), as well as human artisanship in the description of towers, walls and ships (Is 2:15-16). This picture of the Day of Lord emphasizes its terror and judgment against those who do not acknowledge Yahweh, making explicit reference to how they will abandon their idols

when Yahweh makes his divine presence inescapably evident (Is 2:20-21). Martial images relating to Yahweh's army or divine victory in battle are absent; rather, the appearance of Yahweh is sufficient to cause terror and panic.

Another key passage that uses the Day of the Lord occurs in Isaiah 13, which explicitly invokes the coming of the *yôm yhwh* (Is 13:6, 9). The context is an oracle against Babylon that claims that Yahweh is mustering an army to unleash destruction, bringing martial imagery to bear (Is 13:5). The Day of the Lord in this passage reflects the outpouring of Yahweh's wrath on Babylon. It combines the images of Yahweh's army with the theophanic nature of the day by pointing to the trembling and darkening of the heavenly bodies that respond to the arrival of Yahweh (Is 13:10). This resonates with core images of the Day of the Lord, where the whole cosmos responds to Yahweh's intervention with darkness and trembling (cf. Joel 2:21-32; Amos 5:18-20; Zeph 1:14-16). The responses of those against whom Yahweh directs the Day of the Lord mirror the trembling of nature, with images relating to convulsion, pain and torment.

Isaiah 22:5 also invokes the Day of the Lord by using a phrase stating that there is a day of devastation that belongs to the "Lord God of hosts" (*ʾădōnay yhwh ṣĕbāʾôt*). The martial images in the surrounding context resonate with other instances of the Day of the Lord. This passage creates the context of a people experiencing defeat because Yahweh acts against them (Is 22:6-11). It paints Judah's attempts at self-reliance as futile in the wake of Yahweh acting against the city. It also shows the flexibility of the Day of the Lord motif within a prophetic book, as some believe that it references an Assyrian invasion of Judah, adding divine sanction to a historical event.

Isaiah 34:8 follows the other references to the Day of the Lord in announcing judgment against foreign nations. It announces a "day of vengeance for Yahweh" (*yôm nāqām layhwh*), which contains numerous references to martial imagery, most notably the image of Yahweh wielding a bloodied sword (Is 34:6). The surrounding context of this chapter establishes Yahweh's supremacy over all armies and describes the responses of nature of his conquests (Is 34:1-4). Interestingly, Edom now personifies the enemy against whom Yahweh moves, rather than Babylon as in Isaiah 13. The text makes evident the destruction entailed by the Day of the Lord by describing a return to nature, where Yahweh's judgment erases all evidence of human activity (Is 34:13-15).

2.2. Jeremiah. The exact phrase *yôm yhwh* does not occur in Jeremiah, but there is at least one passage that seems invoke motifs related to the Day of the Lord. Jeremiah 46:10 refers to a day that belongs to the "Lord GOD of hosts" (*'ădōnay yhwh ṣĕbā'ôt*), while the parallel clause describes it as a *yôm nĕqāmâ* ("day of vengeance"). The context of this day again highlights its martial attributes, referring to Yahweh's sword (Jer 46:10b) and the destruction of the warriors who oppose Yahweh (Jer 46:12). The target of the Day of the Lord in this instance is Egypt, and the prophetic oracle is set against the backdrop of the Egyptian defeat at Carchemish (Jer 46:2). The reference to Yahweh's weaponry and the description of the day as a day of vengeance indicate that this passage resonates with Isaiah 34:6, where Yahweh again breaks the power of a foreign enemy and establishes supremacy. The temporal orientation of the Day of the Lord in this passage looks backward to this historical event and interprets it through the lens of Yahweh's control over nations and their armies. Associating this passage with the Day of the Lord may offer the clearest indication of the ability of this prophetic motif to address past situations as well as warn of future appearances of Yahweh.

2.3. Ezekiel. Ezekiel also employs the Day of the Lord in several different contexts to indicate the nature of Yahweh's intervention into human affairs. Ezekiel 7:19 occurs in the context of a prophetic announcement of judgment against those who profane the temple in Jerusalem, and the prophet claims that this will occur "on the day of the LORD's wrath" (*bĕyôm 'ebrat yhwh*). The prophet sets up this judgment with the announcement "Behold, the day," which introduces a lengthy list of the elements that this day contains. Martial imagery again plays an important role, as Yahweh's sword menaces the community, while Yahweh continues to reveal the depths of the divine power through the promise of plague and famine. The response of the audience, as it convulses and laments, reflects its inability to stand in the face of Yahweh's power. Ezekiel thus uses the Day of the Lord on this occasion to emphasize Yahweh's incipient judgment on the covenant community that failed to remain faithful.

Ezekiel 13:5 is set in the context of an address against false prophets who claim to have a word from Yahweh. Yahweh declares through Ezekiel that these prophets have not stood in the breaches of the wall or assembled for battle *bĕyôm yhwh* ("on the day of the LORD"). The vision of the Day of the Lord that Ezekiel constructs here sets Yahweh as an invader against a besieged city whose prophets refused to play their allotted role. Yahweh then announces judgment against the false prophets in Jerusalem through exercising divine authority over nature and bringing a destroying wind (Ezek 13:13). Here, again, the Day of the Lord targets Yahweh's own people and uses images of Yahweh's control over nature to describe the coming destruction.

Ezekiel 30 again demonstrates the flexibility of the Day of the Lord within an individual prophetic book by using this motif to announce destruction against Egypt. This chapter activates the Day of the Lord with a double reference to the nearness of the day, and then states that it is a "day for the LORD" (*yôm layhwh*) (Ezek 30:3a). The proximity of the day is a regular feature of the Day of the Lord, increasing the sense of imminence behind Yahweh's intervention. Ezekiel 30 also draws from the image world of cosmic darkness (Ezek 30:3b) and martial imagery to describe the effects of this day (Ezek 30:4). Interestingly, in this chapter Yahweh uses the Babylonians as agents of the Day of the Lord (Ezek 30:10), perhaps substituting for the heavenly army (cf. Is 13:3-6; Joel 2:10-11), but the chapter ultimately emphasizes Yahweh's authority over the activities of all the nations through a series of first-person verbs that describe Egypt's destruction (Ezek 30:13-19). The Day of the Lord that Ezekiel announces against Egypt ultimately indicates Yahweh's claim over all the nations, which learn that Yahweh is God through his inescapable intervention into their affairs.

3. The Day of the Lord in the Minor Prophets (Book of the Twelve).

A significant number of the references to the Day of the Lord derive from the Book of the *Twelve, such that the Day of the Lord can be seen as an underlying theme that helps to organize a reading of this collection (Rendtorff, 89). R. Rendtorff specially identifies a common refrain in the use of the Day of the Lord in Joel, Amos and Zephaniah, emphasizing the need to seek and return to Yahweh. Furthermore, twelve of the fifteen uses of the collocation *yôm yhwh* occur within this corpus, while there are also numerous examples of variant expressions that appear to invoke the Day of the Lord. This may substantially increase the number of texts that could be considered under the rubric of the Day of the Lord.

J. Nogalski aptly summarizes the broad sweep of the Day of the Lord in Book of the Twelve with the idea that the texts that evoke the Day of the Lord reflect an indication of Yahweh's intervention into human affairs. This intervention can be foretold or remembered (Nogalski, 196). It can also have both positive and negative effects on Israel and Judah, depending on the prophet's particular message. Yahweh's appearance and action comprise an important element of prophetic persuasion, and the Day of the Lord provides the prophets with an opportunity to emphasize Yahweh's authority and the necessity of responding appropriately.

3.1. Joel. Joel contains five references to the Day of the Lord that use the exact collocation *yôm yhwh*, spanning the length of the book (Joel 1:15; 2:1, 11, 31 [3:4 MT]; 3:14 [4:14 MT]). Joel demonstrates the range of Day of the Lord imagery by employing this concept in contexts of both woe and weal. In the first half of the book Joel 1:15 introduces the Day of the Lord into a discussion of an overwhelming locust plague and drought, suggesting that the situation faced by the audience has a divine source. Joel 2:1 and Joel 2:11 then form an inclusio around the description of Yahweh's army as it marches against Jerusalem, bringing destruction in its wake. This passage expands on the Day of the Lord by attaching descriptions of the darkness (Joel 2:2) and trembling of the heavenly bodies (Joel 2:10). These references highlight the capacity of the Day of the Lord to unleash devastation against Yahweh's own covenant people, using both natural and supernatural agents to threaten destruction.

Joel 2:12-32 reverses this picture and uses the concept of the Day of the Lord to announce the possibility of rescue thanks to Yahweh's powerful intervention. A call to return to Yahweh lays the foundations for the reversal of the Day of the Lord, where it now signifies restoration rather than destruction. This is a signifi-

cant development because it indicates that Yahweh's covenant community may have the ability to avert the Day of the Lord by responding according to the prophet's prescriptions. Joel 2:31 (3:4 MT) echoes the use of the Day of the Lord earlier in the chapter when it describes the darkening of heavenly bodies, but in this instance Yahweh offers escape from the Day of Lord for those who call upon his name.

The final occurrence of the phrase *yôm yhwh* is in Joel 3:14 (4:14 MT), and it emphasizes the way in which this prophetic book enacts a complete reversal of the sense of the Day of the Lord. This is evident in a comparison the use of the Day of the Lord in Joel 2:1-2, 10-11 and Joel 3:14-16 (4:14-16 MT). In the former passage the call goes up to sound an alarm in Zion because the day of Yahweh is near. Joel 2:10-11 then reveals that this Day of the Lord entails Yahweh leading an unstoppable army against *Zion. Meanwhile, Joel 3:14 also announces that the Day of the Lord is near, using almost the same vocabulary. In Joel 3:14-16, however, Zion is the location of Yahweh's divine activity. Following the announcement in Joel 3:14 that the Day of the Lord is near, Joel 3:16 declares that Yahweh roars from Zion, essentially rendering it impregnable by his very presence. In both instances the Day of the Lord results in a call going out from Zion, but the call in Joel 2 sounds the alarm, whereas the call in Joel 3 reinforces the complete security of Zion because the text establishes that Yahweh is Zion's guardian.

Joel also appears to invoke the Day of the Lord through variant phrases, including *bayyôm hahûʾ* ("on that day") in Joel 3:18 (4:18 MT) and *bayyāmîm hāhēmmâ* ("in those days") in Joel 2:29; 3:1 (3:2; 4:1 MT). All three passages employ these phrases in a forward-looking context where Yahweh will break into history to either judge or offer salvation to Judah and/or foreign nations. The intervention of the deity in these passages resonates with the picture of the Day of the Lord found in the explicit mentions of that day in Joel 1:15; 2:1, 11, 31; 3:14, which suggests that the Day of the Lord is also in view in these particular examples.

3.2. Amos. Amos uses the Day of Lord in the context of a prophetic threat against Israel. Amos 5:18 calls down woe on those who long for the Day of the Lord, which Amos then describes as a day of darkness, not of light (cf. Joel 2:1-2; Zeph 1:15-16). The phrase *yôm yhwh* then recurs in Amos 5:20, alongside imagery that emphasizes the gloomy nature of the day.

Two elements of use of the Day of the Lord in Amos merit special attention. First, Amos 5:18, 20 are commonly thought to be the earliest uses of the collocation *yôm yhwh* in prophetic literature, which has given them a significant role to play in discussions of the origins and development of the concept. Second, these references admirably reveal the ambiguity associated with the Day of the Lord. Amos castigates those who long for the Day of the Lord, prophesying that it will bring darkness and destruction. This may implicitly suggest that there was a stream in Israelite religious expression that expected the Day of the Lord to be a positive experience, perhaps providing rescue from enemies and oppression. Amos thus potentially introduces a new trajectory by suggesting that Yahweh's actions on the Day of the Lord could target Israel (Hoffman, 41). This widens the usefulness of the Day of the Lord motif and permits the prophets to use its rhetorical force to speak of both woe and weal for their audiences.

3.3. Obadiah. Obadiah 15 refers to the *yôm yhwh* in the context of the announcement of judgment against Edom. It locates the Day of the Lord as a day of judgment against all nations, focusing in particular on the fate of Edom. Obadiah looks to a coming Day of the Lord, referring to it as "near" (cf. Is 13:6; Ezek 30:3; Joel 1:15; 2:1; 3:14; Zeph 1:7, 14). It also shares with Joel 3:4 the idea of escape from the Day of the Lord rooted in Zion (Obad 17). Obadiah adds one unique feature to the imagery surrounding the Day of the Lord in that it portrays Judah as an agent in executing the verdict (Snyman, 85). It is clearly Yahweh's power that overthrows the offending nation, but Obadiah does provide a greater role for the people of Yahweh beyond that of passive recipients of rescue. The Day of the Lord remains a time when Yahweh intervenes into human affairs, but there is room for a creative presentation of how his involvement will occur.

3.4. Zephaniah. Zephaniah is heavily indebted to the concept of the Day of Lord. Zephaniah 1:7, 14 (2x) explicitly refer to the *yôm yhwh* in order to announce judgment against Judah. Both verses refer to the imminence of the Day of the Lord, while Zephaniah 1:14 overtly adopts a martial tone when it portrays Yahweh as a mighty warrior shouting a battle cry. Zephaniah 1:15-16 then combines theophanic and martial image worlds by describing the Day of the Lord as a day of darkness and cloud, but also a day of horn blasts against cities and their defenses.

Parallel phrases continue to provide the pictures of the Day of the Lord as a day of Yahweh's judgment against Judah and Jerusalem. Zephaniah 1:18 points to the *yôm ʿebrat yhwh* ("day of the LORD's wrath"), while Zephaniah 2:2-3 refers to the *yôm ʾap-yhwh* ("day of the LORD's anger"). Zephaniah 2:2-3 is also notable in that it explicitly calls its audience to repent and return to Yahweh in order to escape the Day of the Lord. This echoes the development of the Day of the Lord in Joel by providing an element of overt conditionality into announcements of the Day of the Lord against Israel and Judah, suggesting that a proper response can turn it aside.

Zephaniah 3 shifts perspective and points to the positive elements of the Day of the Lord. Zephaniah 3:11, 16 use *bayyôm hahûʾ* ("on that day") to point to a time when Yahweh restores Judah and Jerusalem. This chapter continues the theme of Zephaniah in using martial imagery to describe Yahweh (Zeph 3:17), but in this instance Yahweh as mighty warrior is a symbol of protection rather than condemnation. These examples denote a progression in Zephaniah's use of the Day of the Lord. It begins as a day of disaster and judgment for Judah, but perhaps through the call to repentance in Zephaniah 2:1-3 Yahweh's activities by the end of the book effectively restore and protect Judah, signifying a renewed relationship with Yahweh.

3.5. Zechariah. The final three chapters of Zechariah are replete with images that reflect the Day of the Lord. Zechariah 12:1—13:6 employs the phrase *bayyôm hahûʾ* ("on that day") ten times to describe the effects of Yahweh's intervention in human affairs (Zech 12:3, 4, 6, 8 [2x], 9, 11; 13:1, 2, 4). This intervention follows several different lines. Zechariah 12:1-9 uses this concept to indicate how Yahweh will protect Jerusalem from hostile nations, keeping it secure while he brings its enemies to destruction. Zechariah 12:10-14 shifts the focus to the house of David and Jerusalem and describes the magnitude of its weeping in the wake of the fate of the enigmatic figure whom they pierced (Zech 12:10). This probably reflecting an internal purification element to the

Day of the Lord that goes along with the external protection previously described. Zechariah 13:1-6 continues the internal focus as it describes the cleansing of house of David and Jerusalem through the removal of idolatry (Zech 13:1-2). This will happen in conjunction with Yahweh's removal of false prophecy from the community, suggesting a divinely inspired cleansing of the community's religious expression (Zech 13:3-6).

Zechariah 14:1 refers to a *yôm-bāʾ layhwh* ("day coming for Yahweh") to introduce its detailed discussion of Yahweh's appearance and Jerusalem's final fate. In the verses that follow, multiple uses of *bayyôm hahûʾ* ("on that day") reinforce the idea that this chapter focuses upon the Day of the Lord (Zech 14:4, 6, 8, 9, 13, 20, 21). The use of the Day of the Lord in Zechariah 14 proceeds along interesting trajectories. It casts the day in a martial tone, referring to a day in which Yahweh fights (Zech 14:3), but it differs even from the previous presentation of the Day of the Lord in Zechariah. As in Joel 3:14; Obadiah 15; Zechariah 12:1-8, Jerusalem is the location from which Yahweh fights on this day, but unlike those passages, Yahweh's presence in Zechariah 14 does not guarantee the inviolability of Jerusalem. Instead, Zechariah 14 announces the capture of the city and the mistreatment of half of its inhabitants before Yahweh acts to rectify the situation (Zech 14:2-3). The closest resonances to this description of the Day of the Lord derive from Joel 3:4 and Obadiah 17, which indicate the potential for there to be survivors who escape the Day of the Lord by calling on the name of Yahweh. The capture of the city seems to be a more intensive purification process than is found in Joel or Obadiah, but after this process finishes, Yahweh is able to establish Jerusalem as the seat of divine kingship.

The Day of the Lord undergoes a significant progression as it unfolds throughout this chapter. Zechariah brings out other recurrent images including the trembling of nature (Zech 14:4) and darkness (Zech 14:6). After the description of purification, the Day of the Lord in Zechariah 14 highlights the restorative elements for Jerusalem while emphasizing the destructive fate of those nations who oppose Yahweh (Zech 14:12-13) and his sovereignty over the entire world (Zech 14:9). Interestingly, Zechariah 14:14 may resonate with Obadiah 15

in that it also appears to portray the newly purified Judah as an active agent fighting alongside Yahweh on the Day of the Lord. This would reflect the sincerity of Judah's commitment to Yahweh after his actions on its behalf. The Day of the Lord concludes in this chapter with the defeat of the nations, their pilgrimage to acknowledge Yahweh's sovereignty, and the establishment of Jerusalem as a holy city devoted to Yahweh. In this way, it summarizes both the trajectories of external protection and internal purification that Zechariah evokes.

3.6. Malachi. The final verses of Malachi invoke the Day of the Lord in the context of Yahweh judging between the righteous and the wicked. The temporal outlook of these verses concerns a future judgment. Malachi uses the Day of the Lord to set up distinctions within the Judahite community, where the coming of the day promises salvation for those who obey Yahweh and devastation for those who do not. The crux of what it means to follow Yahweh is to remember the law of Moses (Mal 4:4).

The idea of the Day of the Lord is also present in Malachi 3:17; 4:1 through references to a day of Yahweh's action. Malachi 3:17 refers to the day when Yahweh acts to preserve the faithful *remnant. He refers to them as a treasured possession, which invokes echoes of the Sinai covenant (cf. Ex 19:5). Malachi 4:1 (3:19 MT) again invokes the Day of the Lord by referring to *hayyôm bāʾ* ("the day is coming"), where Yahweh's judgment takes on images of an all-consuming fire. Again, restoration is also possible for those who faithfully serve Yahweh.

Malachi 4:5 (3:23 MT) also uniquely describes the return of the prophet Elijah as a harbinger of the Day of the Lord (cf. Rev 11). This suggests an intermediate stage where the audience has the opportunity to listen to Elijah in order to experience the restorative elements of the Day of the Lord. Failure to heed Yahweh's prophet will lead to the Day of the Lord bringing judgment and devastation. Malachi echoes Joel 2:10-11 by referring to the "great and terrible" Day of the Lord. The presence of Elijah may serve a similar function to Joel's prophetic call to return to Yahweh in Joel 2:12-17. The prophetic announcement of the Day of the Lord as judgment against Judah and Jerusalem seems to function as a rhetorical appeal for the audience to heed the prophetic word and return to proper worship of Yahweh.

4. Reception of the Concept.

Here we briefly consider the Day of the Lord and its continuing impact beyond the borders of the OT. The impact of this concept spills into the NT and even into contemporary theological pursuits.

4.1. New Testament Reception. The Day of the Lord resonates across the canon and is picked up in the NT in the context of the work of Jesus Christ and the inauguration of the church. It continues to employ powerful and evocative images of cosmic upheaval and divine judgment to emphasize the overwhelming importance of this day. One of the most striking examples is found in Peter's sermon in Acts 2, which explicitly links the events of Pentecost with the prophecy of the Day of the Lord in Joel 2:28-32 (see Acts 2:14-24). This connects the beginning of the church to the prophetic concept of the Day of the Lord. Other mentions of the Day of the Lord have eschatological overtones, signifying the judgment that Jesus can bring as the resurrected Messiah (Vander Hart, 16-17). The Day of the Lord thus is inextricably linked with the work of Jesus Christ and the inauguration of his kingdom. The full weight of the Day of Lord is still anticipated, but through Jesus the NT writers see its fulfillment coming to pass (see Rom 2:5, 16; 1 Cor 1:8; Phil 1:6; 1 Thess 5:2-8; 2 Thess 1:10; 2:2; 2 Pet 3:10, 12) (*see* Prophets in the New Testament).

4.2. Recent Developments. In recent years different methodological approaches have been brought to bear on the Day of the Lord that may offer new interpretive opportunities. Two of them may be briefly considered. First, D. Kille considers Amos's use of the Day of the Lord from the perspective of Jungian *psychology, suggesting that its apparent reversal of expectations reflects strategies of communicating with an audience that is employing repression and projection to avoid dealing with the harsh realities of the Day of the Lord. The function of the reversal is to disturb the audience and to cut through any attempts to deflect the power of the prophetic proclamation (Kille, 272-76).

Second, from the perspective of global scholarship, M. Udoekpo considers the Day of the Lord in Zephaniah from a theological perspective. He challenges the lack of theological consideration in studies of source and development of the Day of the Lord and traces some links from Zephaniah's use of the Day of the Lord into the NT (see Lk 1:26-38; Rom 9:27-29; 1 Thess 4:13-18). His work is also notable for considering how the Day of the Lord speaks into the African cultural context, suggesting that it addresses the continued necessity of full commitment to Yahweh amidst a "pluri-religious and multi-cultural society" (Udoekpo, 290). Further methodological diversity may continue to add new dimensions to continued study of the Day of the Lord.

5. Conclusion.

The Day of the Lord continues to be a fruitful theme to consider in OT prophetic literature. Disputes over its terminology and origins are likely to continue, but the essence of the concept as a time in which Yahweh intervenes powerfully and effectively into the affairs of this world is well established. The Day of the Lord also admirably highlights the creativity and rhetorical power of the OT prophets as they invoke images relating to warfare, creation and chaos, and theophany in the attempt to capture the power inherent in this day. The flexibility of the Day of the Lord is also in view when the prophets can use it to castigate Israel and Judah as well as to offer salvation and rescue from the hands of their oppressors. The invocation of the Day of the Lord is a significant tool in prophetic imagery, and it helps to powerfully demonstrate Yahweh's responsive relationship with Israel and Judah. For the prophets, human affairs do not proceed unnoticed by Yahweh; indeed, the Day of the Lord provides a powerful reminder of Yahweh's presence and ability to shape events according to the divine purpose. This purpose does not cease at the conclusion of the OT, but continues to speak into the NT and contemporary contexts.

See also DESTRUCTION; ESCHATOLOGY; RETRIBUTION; SALVATION, DELIVERANCE; WARFARE AND DIVINE WARFARE; WRATH.

BIBLIOGRAPHY. **J. Barton,** "The Day of Yahweh in the Minor Prophets," in *Biblical and Near Eastern Essays: Studies in Honour of Kevin J. Cathcart,* ed. C. McCarthy and J. F. Healey (JSOTSup 375; London: T & T Clark, 2004) 68-79; **K. J. Cathcart,** "Day of Yahweh," *ABD* 2:84-85; **L. Černý,** *The Day of Yahweh and Some Relevant Problems* (Prague: Nákl. Filosofické fakulty Univ. Karlovy, 1948); **F. M. Cross Jr.,** "The Divine Warrior in Israel's Early Cult," in *Biblical Motifs: Origins and Transformations,* ed. A. Altmann (Cambridge, MA: Harvard University Press, 1966) 11-30; **F. E. Deist,** "Parallels and Reinterpretation in the Book of Joel: A Theology of Yom Yahweh?" in *Text and Context: Old Testament and Semitic Studies for F. C. Fensham,* ed. W. Claassen (JSOTSup 48; Sheffield: JSOT, 1988) 63-80; **J. A. Everson,** "The Days of Yahweh," *JBL* 93 (1974) 329-37; **F. C. Fensham,** "A Possible Origin of the Concept of the Day of the Lord," in *Biblical Essays: Proceedings of the Ninth Meeting of "Die Ou-Testamentiese Werkgemeenskap in Suid-Afrika," Held at the University of Stellenbosch, 26th-29th July 1966* (Stellenbosch: Potchefstroom Herald, 1966) 90-97; **J. Gray,** "The Day of Yahweh in Cultic Experience and Eschatological Prospect," *SEÅ* 39 (1974) 5-37; **R. H. Hiers,** "Day of the Lord," *ABD* 2:82-83; **Y. Hoffman,** "The Day of the Lord as a Concept and a Term in Prophetic Literature," *ZAW* 93 (1981) 37-50; **D. Ishai-Rosenboim,** "Is יוֹם ה' (the Day of the Lord) a Term in Biblical Language?" *Bib* 87 (2006) 395-401; **D. A. Kille,** "The Day of the Lord from Jungian Perspective," in *Psychology and the Bible: A New Way to Read the Scriptures,* 2: *From Genesis to Apocalyptic Vision,* ed. J. H. Ellens and W. G. Rollins (Westport, CT: Praeger, 2004) 267-76; **G. A. King,** "The Day of the Lord in Zephaniah," *BSac* 152 (1995) 16-32; **R. W. Klein,** "The Day of the Lord," *CTM* 39 (1968) 517-25; **P. D. Miller Jr.,** "The Divine Council and the Prophetic Call to War," *VT* 18 (1968) 100-107; idem, *The Divine Warrior in Early Israel* (HSM 5; Cambridge, MA: Harvard University Press, 1973); **S. Mowinckel,** *He That Cometh,* trans. G. W. Anderson (Oxford: Blackwell, 1956); **J. D. Nogalski,** "The Day(s) of YHWH in the Book of the Twelve," in *Thematic Threads in the Book of the Twelve,* ed. P. L. Redditt and A. Schart (BZAW 325; Berlin: de Gruyter, 2003) 192-213; **R. Rendtorff,** "How to Read the Book of the Twelve as a Theological Unity," in *Reading and Hearing the Book of the Twelve,* ed. J. D. Nogalski and M. A. Sweeney (SBLSymS 15; Atlanta: Society of Biblical Literature, 2000) 75-90; **P.-G. Schwesig,** *Die Rolle des Tag-JHWHs-Dichtungen im Dodekapropheton* (BZAW 366; Berlin: de Gruyter, 2006); **S. D. Snyman,** "Yom (YHWH) in the Book of Obadiah," in *Goldene Äpfel in silbernen Schalen: Collected Communications from the XIIIth Congress of the International Organization for the Study of the Old Testament, Leuven, 1989,* ed. K. D. Schunck and M. Augustin (BEATAJ 20; Frankfurt: Peter Lang, 1992) 81-91; **D. K. Stuart,** "The Sovereign's Day of Conquest," *BASOR* 221 (1976) 159-64; **M. U. Udoekpo,** *Re-thinking the Day of YHWH and the Restoration of Fortunes in the Prophet Zephaniah: An Exegetical and Theological Study of 1:14-18; 3:14-20* (OOTD 2; Frankfurt: Peter Lang, 2010); **M. J. Vander Hart,** "The Transition of the Old Testament Day of the Lord into the New Testament Day of the Lord Jesus Christ," *Mid-America Journal of Theology* 9 (1993) 3-25; **G. von Rad,** "The Origin of the Concept of the Day of the Lord," *JSS* 4 (1959) 97-108; idem, *Holy War in Ancient Israel,* trans. B. C. Ollenburger (Grand Rapids: Eerdmans, 1991); **M. Weiss,** "The Origin of the 'Day of the Lord,'" *HUCA* 37 (1966) 29-60.   J. D. Barker

DAY OF YAHWEH. *See* DAY OF THE LORD.

DEAD SEA SCROLLS

Among the finds at the Dead Sea are approximately 225 scrolls of Scripture (235 if the deuterocanonical books, also known as the books of the Apocrypha, are included). Every book of what in time would become the OT is represented at Qumran, at least in fragmentary form, with the exception of Esther. Three books of the OT Apocrypha are also represented (Tobit, Sirach, Letter of Jeremiah). The books of *Jubilees* and *Enoch* may have been thought of as Scripture at Qumran, given the number of copies (fifteen and twenty respectively), as well as the fact that they are quoted a few times. The Prophets play a very important role in Qumran's eschatology and community self-understanding.

1. Canonical Books of the Prophets
2. Extracanonical Books of the Prophets
3. Interpretation of the Prophets

1. Canonical Books of the Prophets.
Most of the books of the prophets are well represented at Qumran and elsewhere in the region of the Dead Sea. The Latter Prophets, especially Isaiah, are better represented than the Former Prophets. But Qumran's Former Prophets scrolls are very important as witnesses to the Hebrew text and as inspiration for some very interesting legendary and interpretive traditions.

1.1. Joshua. Fragments of two scrolls of Joshua were recovered from Cave 4 (4Q47; 4Q48). These scrolls preserve portions of Joshua 2—8; 10; 17. The text of Joshua at Qumran agrees with Josephus by saying that Joshua built an altar immediately after crossing the Jordan (see Josephus, *Ant.* 5.16-20). The Joshua text in places agrees with the LXX (in that it is shorter than the Hebrew text and sometimes shorter than the Greek) and in places agrees with the MT. It is an important witness to the text of Joshua in the period shortly before Jesus and Christian beginnings.

1.2. Judges. Fragments of three scrolls of Judges were recovered from Qumran, two from Cave 4 (4Q49; 4Q50) and one from Cave 1 (1Q6). These scrolls preserve portions of Judges 6; 8—9; 19; 21. There are indications that the Hebrew text of the Joshua scrolls is a bit shorter than that of the MT.

1.3. Samuel. Fragments of four scrolls of Samuel (in antiquity 1–2 Samuel were regarded as a single book, even if preserved as two scrolls), one in Cave 1 (1Q7) and three in Cave 4 (4Q51; 4Q52; 4Q53). Most of the text of Samuel is preserved, and in many places the Samuel scrolls of Qumran agree with the LXX. Significantly, 4Q51 preserves the equivalent of about three verses missing at the beginning of 1 Samuel 11, the account of the tyrant Nahash, who oppressed the Gadites and Reubenites. The recovered material coheres with the account of the story told by Josephus and explains why Nahash made the demands that he made. The same Samuel scroll, moreover, tells us that Goliath was only four cubits and a span in height (about 6 feet 6 inches), instead of six cubits and a span in height (about 9 feet 6 inches) as read in the MT.

1.4. Kings. Fragments of three scrolls of Kings have been recovered: a leather scroll in Cave 4 (4Q54), a leather scroll in Cave 5 (5Q2) and a papyrus scroll in Cave 6 (6Q4). These scrolls preserve portions of 1 Kings 1; 3; 7—8; 12; 22; 2 Kings 5—9. 4Q54 preserves an otherwise lost part of 1 Kings 8:16, a part of the verse not preserved in the MT or the LXX.

1.5. Isaiah. There are twenty-one Isaiah scrolls. Best known are the two well-preserved scrolls from Cave 1: 1QIsaᵃ (also known as the *Great Isaiah Scroll*) and 1QIsaᵇ. The former, which dates to the second century BC, preserves almost the entire text of Isaiah and matches the text of the MT closely. Ironically, photographs of the *Great Isaiah Scroll* taken by John Trever in 1948 (in color and in black and white) preserve the text more fully and more clearly than does

the actually scroll itself today. Other fairly well-preserved scrolls include 4Q56 and 4Q57. There are also five commentaries, or pesharim, on portions of Isaiah (4Q161; 4Q162; 4Q163; 4Q164; 4Q165). These commentaries preserve some of the text of Isaiah.

In addition to the many quotations in these commentaries, the book of Isaiah, not surprisingly, is quoted frequently in the nonbiblical scrolls, some twenty-eight times in all. More than half of these quotations appear in the *Damascus Document* (CD), an important foundational document of the Qumran community. Of these quotations, perhaps the most important is Isaiah 40:3: "A voice cries out, 'In the wilderness prepare the way of the Lord.'" The scribe understands "in the wilderness" as referring not to the location of the voice that cries out but rather to the place where the way of the Lord is prepared. This important verse is cited in 1QS VIII, 13-14 and is understood as in reference to the Qumran community, whose task in the *wilderness is to study Scripture and come to a better understanding of God's law. Indeed, the community refers to itself as "the Way," much as the early Christian movement did (see Acts 9:2; 19:9, 23; 24:22). For Christians, Isaiah's "way of the Lord" took on special meaning thanks to the preaching and baptizing of John the Baptist (see Mt 3:1-3; Mk 1:2-3; Lk 3:1-6; Jn 1:19-23), a wilderness prophet whose message and lifestyle parallel in important ways those of the men of Qumran.

1.6. Jeremiah. There are six Jeremiah scrolls, one in Cave 2 (2Q13) and five in Cave 4 (4Q70; 4Q71; 4Q72; 4Q72a; 4Q72b). Some of these scrolls (esp. 4Q71; 4Q72a) exhibit affiliation with the LXX, whose Greek text is noticeably shorter than the Hebrew text. One of the oldest biblical scrolls found at Qumran is the heavily corrected 4Q70, which dates at least as far back as 200 BC. The book of Jeremiah is cited in three nonbiblical scrolls. There are also four scrolls of (Jeremiah's) Lamentations and one small fragment of the apocryphal Letter of Jeremiah (7Q2), which in the Apocrypha serves as the sixth chapter of Baruch.

1.7. Ezekiel. There are fragments of six Ezekiel scrolls, which preserve portions of Ezekiel 1; 4—5; 7; 10—11; 16; 23—24; 35—38; 41 (1Q9; 3Q1; 4Q73; 4Q74; 4Q75; 11Q4). Ezekiel is cited five times in nonbiblical scrolls.

1.8. Minor Prophets. Eight scrolls of the Minor Prophets were found at Qumran, seven in Cave 4 (4Q76; 4Q77; 4Q78; 4Q79; 4Q80; 4Q81; 4Q82) and one in Cave 5 (5Q4). Two more were found at Naḥal Ḥever (8Ḥev 1) and Wadi Murabbaʿat (Mur 88). There are commentaries (pesharim) on Hosea (4Q166; 4Q167), Habakkuk (1QpHab), Micah (1Q14; 4Q168), Nahum (4Q169) and Zephaniah (4Q170). In addition to the many quotations of the text in these commentaries several of the Minor Prophets are cited in nonbiblical scrolls.

1.9. Daniel. Daniel apparently was viewed as a prophet at Qumran (in the MT the book of Daniel is listed among the Writings). There are eight scrolls, ranging in date from 125 BC to AD 50: two in Cave 1 (1Q71; 1Q72), five in Cave 4 (4Q112; 4Q113; 4Q114; 4Q115; 4Q116) and one in Cave 6 (6Q7). Much of the Hebrew and Aramaic text of Daniel is preserved in these scrolls. The last chapter, Daniel 12, is missing. However, Daniel 12:10 is quoted in 4Q174 IV, 3-4, where it is introduced as taken from the "book of Daniel the prophet." Also to be noted is 11Q13 II, 18, where Daniel 9:25-26 is quoted in a prophetic context.

1.10. 1 Enoch. 1 Enoch is part of the canon of Scripture in the Ethiopic Church. At Qumran some twenty scrolls of *1 Enoch,* all of them fragmentary and all of them in Aramaic (with the exception of a few small Greek fragments from Cave 7), have been recovered (1Q23; 1Q24; 2Q26; 4Q201; 4Q202; 4Q203; 4Q204; 4Q205; 4Q206; 4Q207; 4Q208; 4Q209; 4Q210; 4Q211; 4Q530; 4Q531; 4Q532; 6Q8; 7Q4). The only extensive portion of this book not attested at Qumran is the so-called Similitudes of Enoch (*1 En* 37—71), in which a messianic "son of man" figure is prominent. The quasi-scriptural status of *1 Enoch* is attested by its quotation in the NT letter of Jude (see Jude 14-15). Jesus himself may have alluded to *1 Enoch* 10:4 in Matthew 22:13.

2. Extracanonical Books of the Prophets. Scattered in OT literature are references to various writings on which presumably the authors of the books of Samuel, Kings and Chronicles drew. In 2 Samuel 1:18 we hear of a "Book of Jashar" (cf. Josh 10:13). In 1 Kings 11:41 we hear of the "Book of the Acts of Solomon." In 1 Kings 14:19 we hear of the "Book of the Chronicles of the Kings of Israel" (cf. 1 Kings 15:31; 16:5, 14, 20, 27, 33; 22:39; 2 Kings 1:18;

10:34; 13:8; passim). And in 1 Kings 14:29 we hear of the "Chronicles of the Kings of Judah" (cf. 1 Kings 15:7, 23, 31; 22:45; 2 Kings 8:23; 12:19; passim). Some of these lost writings were related to known prophets, others to unknown prophets. A number of these interesting writings are referenced in Chronicles, a work produced over a period of time, probably ranging from 500 BC to 350 BC.

The Chronicler mentions the "Chronicles of Samuel the seer," the "Chronicles of Nathan the prophet" and the "Chronicles of Gad the seer" (1 Chron 29:29). Elsewhere we hear of the "History of Nathan the prophet," the "Prophecy of Ahijah the Shilonite" and the "Visions of Iddo the seer concerning Jeroboam the son of Nebat" (2 Chron 9:29). We hear of the "Chronicles of Shemaiah the prophet and of Iddo the seer" (2 Chron 12:15). We hear of "the story of the prophet Iddo" (2 Chron 13:22). The reference to "the vision of Isaiah the prophet the son of Amoz, in the Book of the Kings of Judah and Israel" (2 Chron 32:32 [cf. Is 1:1]) may not be to the canonical book of Isaiah. Finally, we hear of "the Chronicles of the Seers" (2 Chron 33:19).

The many references to otherwise unknown writings attest the existence of a great deal of literature loosely related to what in time became canonical Scripture. These references may also have encouraged the belief that additional books of prophecy and visions could be "found," and this belief, accordingly, may well have encouraged the production of more books.

Just as there are several apocryphal works that expand on themes related to the books of Moses (to update the law, to credit various prophetic visions to Moses), so there are many apocryphal works that expand on themes related to the prophets. Again, in general the purpose of these writings, as is the case with many of the apocalypses and testaments in the Pseudepigrapha, is to have a well-known prophet of the classical period speak to current events or events sensed soon to take place. These utterances may be eschatological, but sometimes they are legal and/or cultic. Many such "prophetic" writings have been found among the DSS.

2.1. Joshua Apocrypha. A number of apocryphal texts about or attributed to Joshua have been found at Qumran. These include *4QParaphrase of Joshua* (4Q123), *4QApocryphon of Joshua* (4Q378; 4Q379) and *4QProphecy of Joshua* (4Q522).

2.2. Samuel Apocrypha. There are at least two apocryphal works related to Samuel the prophet: *4QVision of Samuel* (4Q160) and *6QApocryphon on Samuel-Kings* (6Q9). Perhaps we should also include 2Q22, which could be an apocryphon of David, and 4Q523, which could be an apocryphon concerning Jonathan.

2.3. Kings Apocrypha. There are a number of apocryphal texts related to the book of Kings and some of its principal players. Among these is *4QParaphrase of Kings* (4Q382), which may have focused on Elijah. Elisha is the focus of *4QApocryphon of Elisha* (4Q481a). Mention also should be made of *11QApocryphal Psalms* (11Q11), which seems to be focused on Solomon and his exorcistic and prophetic powers.

2.4. Jeremiah and Ezekiel Apocrypha. Several apocryphal texts feature the prophets Jeremiah and Ezekiel. These include 4Q383; 4Q384; 4Q385; 4Q385a; 4Q385b; 4Q385c; 4Q386; 4Q387a; 4Q387b; 4Q388; 4Q388a; 4Q389; 4Q389a; 4Q390; 4Q391. Of special interest are *4QApocryphon of Jeremiah^a* (4Q383) and *4QApocryphon of Jeremiah^c* (4Q385b). The latter draws on Jeremiah 40—44 and seems to portray the prophet Jeremiah as a Moses-like figure.

2.5. Daniel Apocrypha. There are several texts that appear to be part of the "Daniel series." Besides the well-known additions to Daniel (Susanna, Bel and the Dragon, Prayer of Azariah, Song of the Three Youths), preserved in the LXX, Qumran offers an *Aramaic Prayer of Nabonidus* (4Q242), an *Aramaic Vision of Daniel* (4Q243; 4Q244; 4Q245), an *Aramaic Vision of the Son of God* (4Q246), an *Aramaic Vision of the Four Kingdoms* (4Q552; 4Q553) and, possibly, an *Aramaic Vision* (4Q489). The *Aramaic Prayer of Nabonidus* is of interest because of its linkage of illness, sin, forgiveness and exorcism, which are elements found together in the teaching and activities of Jesus of Nazareth. The *Aramaic Vision of the Son of God* is quite intriguing in light of four remarkable parallels with the annunciation of the conception of Jesus (see Lk 1:32-36). It is said of Jesus and the eschatological personage envisioned in the Aramaic scroll from Qumran that each will be called "Great," "Son of God" and "Son of the Most High," and each will rule forever.

2.6. Malachi Apocryphon. 5Q10 and 5Q11 seem to be fragments of an apocryphon based on Malachi. The text is addressed to the "King of Glory." It praises God and gives thanks for his protective power against the demonic forces.

3. Interpretation of the Prophets.

Just as important as the text types attested by the Prophets scrolls of Qumran and the region of the Dead Sea are the interpretive traditions. These interpretive traditions appear in the Prophets scrolls as variants and glosses, and they appear, especially, in the formal commentaries (pesharim) and quotations in other writings.

3.1. Variants. Most variants are scribal errors, often accidental omissions (see Is 2:3, where in the *Great Isaiah Scroll* the scribe omits the phrase "the mountain of the Lord") or errors from habit (see Is 49:6, where in the *Great Isaiah Scroll* the scribe reads "tribes of Israel" instead of the correct "tribes of Jacob"). Some variants actually correct the text (and often agree with the LXX). As an example of the latter, the *Great Isaiah Scroll* correctly reads at Isaiah 53:9, "with rich men, his tomb," instead of the way it reads in the MT, "with a rich man in his deaths."

Some variants are "enrichments" of the text through the addition of words and phrases found elsewhere in the biblical text. We see a number of these examples in the *Great Isaiah Scroll*. At Isaiah 1:15b we read, "Your hands are full of blood, your fingers with iniquity." The second clause comes from Isaiah 59:3. At Isaiah 51:6 we read, "Lift up your eyes to the heavens, and look at the earth beneath, and see who created these." The third clause was borrowed from Isaiah 40:26. At Isaiah 52:12b we read, "For the Lord will go before you, and the God of Israel will be your rear guard; the God of all the earth he will be called." The third clause is derived from Isaiah 54:5 and very appropriately prepares for the Servant Song (Is 52:13—53:12) that follows. At Isaiah 7:14 the *Great Isaiah Scroll* reads, "His name shall be called Immanuel," instead of "She shall call his name Immanuel." The *Great Isaiah Scroll* reading reflects Isaiah 9:6, "His name shall be called Wonderful Counselor. . . . "

Some variants appear to be deliberate changes of the text to bring out a new meaning. A series of changes at Isaiah 6:9-10 in the *Great Isaiah Scroll* offers an interesting example. Replacing the negative particles in Isaiah 6:9 with similar-sounding conjunctions leads to this reading: "Keep on listening, *because* you may understand; keep on looking, *because* you may perceive." A slight alteration of spelling creates a new imperative in the next line of this verse and the beginning of the next: "Make the heart of this people *appalled.* Stop its ears and turn away its eyes." The *Great Isaiah Scroll* copyist drew upon Isaiah 33:15, which describes the righteous person as one "who stops his ears from hearing of murder, and shuts his eyes from looking upon evil." The idea of being appalled at evil and returning to the Lord is found elsewhere in the Prophets (see Hos 5:15—6:1) and at Qumran (see 1QHᵃ XV, 5-6). Accordingly, the alterations in Isaiah 6:9 transform Isaiah's word of judgment into an exhortation to guard against evil. This would then explain one more variant near the end of Isaiah 6:10, where we read "Let it [the people] understand in its heart" instead of "Lest it understand in its heart." The purpose of Isaiah 6:9-10 is not to pronounce a word of judgment on Israel but rather to exhort the faithful (probably the men of Qumran) to turn away from evil and to understand and so return to the Lord for healing and restoration. The variants here in the *Great Isaiah Scroll* are not misspellings; they are deliberate interpretive changes.

There are also some interesting variants in the *Great Isaiah Scroll* Servant Songs (*see* Servant of Yahweh). The Suffering Servant Song seems to read, "Just as many were astonished at you— so *I anointed* his appearance beyond anyone (else), and his form beyond that of (other) sons of men—so shall he *sprinkle* many nations *because of himself* " (with italics indicating departures from the MT). Instead of "marred," the servant is "anointed," thus suggesting that the servant is the awaited *Messiah. This interpretation is consistent with the Targum, which also identifies the servant as the Messiah (cf. the Targum of Is 52:13: "my servant, the Messiah"; Is 53:10: "they shall see the kingdom of their Messiah"). The meaning of "sprinkle" may be clarified by a passage in the *Rule of the Community* scroll: "At that time God will purify by his truth all the deeds of a man; and he will refine him more than the (other) sons of men. . . . He shall sprinkle each with a spirit of truth" (1QS IV, 20-21). The "man" whom God has refined "more than the (other) sons of men" may well be the Messiah, through whom God will "sprinkle" humanity "with a spirit of truth."

3.2. Paragraphing and Marginal Sigla. The *Great Isaiah Scroll* also exhibits some paragraphing and marginal sigla that seem to have interpretive significance. In column 43 one can observe a prominent hat-shaped siglum in the right-hand margin, right where Isaiah 52:7 begins: "How beautiful upon the mountains are the feet of him who brings good tidings . . . who says to Zion, 'Your God reigns.'" The siglum may be a combination of the Greek *paragraphos*, which is a long horizontal line (—), and a large *sāmek* (the Hebrew letter *s*), which indicates the beginning of a section (*seder*). The circle-shaped *sāmek* resting on the horizontal line gives the siglum the appearance of a derby hat. A simpler siglum (this time the horizontal line by itself) appears in the right-hand margin of column 44 separating Isaiah 52:15 and Isaiah 53:1. Paragraphing for the whole passage is Isaiah 52:7-12; 52:13-15; 53:1-8; 53:9-12.

The sigla in the MT are similar, though less pronounced. Accordingly, both the *Great Isaiah Scroll* of Qumran and the MT appear to view Isaiah 52:7-12 and the well-known Song of the Suffering Servant, Isaiah 52:13—53:12, as two related units, perhaps with Isaiah 52:7-12 introducing the song. Interestingly enough, this is how several modern commentators understand the sense of Isaiah 52—53, even though no reference is made to the *Great Isaiah Scroll.*

Even the Targum, the later Aramaic translation and paraphrase, links Isaiah 52:7 with the Song of the Suffering Servant. We see this in a change of wording in Isaiah 53:1. The Hebrew's "Who has believed our report?" becomes in the Targum "Who has believed this our good tidings?" This means that the good tidings (or gospel) announced by the prophet in Isaiah 52:7 have to do with Lord's Suffering Servant in Isaiah 53:1. And, as noted above, the Targum goes on to identify the servant as none other than the Messiah.

The linkage between Isaiah 52:7 and Isaiah 53:1 is attested in Paul and Peter, two major figures in the early church. Paul quotes the two passages side by side in Romans 10:15-16. They are linked allusively in Peter's speech to Cornelius (esp. Acts 10:36, 43). In Christian circles the linkage of these two Isaiah passages may have originated with Jesus himself, who proclaimed, "The kingdom of God is at hand . . . believe in the gospel" (Mk 1:15). Not only does he proclaim the good tidings (or gospel) in language that derives from Isaiah 40:9 and

Isaiah 52:7, but also his language reflects the way Isaiah was being paraphrased and interpreted in *Aramaic in the synagogue. In the Targum the good tidings of these passages are summed up in the words "The kingdom of your God is revealed!" Yet Jesus will later tell his disciples, in language that echoes the Song of the Suffering Servant, "The Son of Man also came not to be served but to serve, and to give his life as a ransom for many" (Mk 10:45 [cf. Is 53:8, 10, 12]). Indeed, in the Gospel of John Jesus declares that the Son of Man must be "lifted up" (Jn 12:31, 34). In saying this, he alludes to Isaiah 52:13: "Behold, my servant . . . shall be lifted up, and shall be very high." A few verses later the Johannine evangelist quotes Isaiah 53:1: "Who was believed our report?" (Jn 12:38), thus strengthening the link between Jesus the Son of Man and the Suffering Servant of Isaiah 52:13—53:12.

3.3. Pesher Interpretation. The formal commentaries, or pesharim, on the Prophets and Psalms are eschatological and semiallegorical. The writers of these commentaries believed that they lived in or very close to the "last days." They interpreted Scripture from this perspective, even claiming to possess insights denied the OT prophets themselves. This perspective is clearly expressed in the commentary on Habakkuk: "Then God told Habakkuk to write down what is going to happen to the generation to come; but when that period would be complete He did not make known to him. When it says, 'so that with ease someone can read it,' this refers to the Teacher of Righteousness to whom God made known all the mysterious revelations of his servants the prophets" (1QpHab VII, 1-5). The prophet Habakkuk did not know when his prophecy would be fulfilled, but God made this known to the Teacher of Righteousness, the authoritative teacher of the Qumran community. This teacher is the one who has fulfilled the prophetic anticipation that the day will come when "with ease someone can read" Habakkuk's prophecy and interpret it. All of the pesharim reflect this perspective.

3.3.1. Isaiah. Fragments of five commentaries on Isaiah were recovered from Cave 4. *4QIsaiah Pesher^a* (4Q161) comments on portions of Isaiah 10—11. Following the quotation of Isaiah 10:28-32, the commentary states that "this refers to the last days," in which a great battle will take place. After the quotation of Isa-

iah 10:33-34, which refers to the felling of the trees of Lebanon, the commentary predicts the coming of the Kittim (the Romans), who will fall at the hand of Israel. Isaiah 11:1-5, which foretells the sprout from the stock of Jesse, is applied, not surprisingly, to the "Branch of David," who will arise in the last days. He will rule over Israel and will be guided by the Zadokite priests. This Branch of David, of course, is none other than the Messiah. *4QIsaiah Pesher^b* (4Q162) comments on portions of Isaiah 5 and foretells coming famine and the presence in Jerusalem of "men of mockery," probably critics of the men of Qumran. *4QIsaiah Pesher^c* (4Q163) comments on portions of Isaiah 10; 14; 30. The text is quite fragmentary; very little of the commentary proper has survived. The phrases "last days" and "flattery seekers who are in Jerusalem" are read. *4QIsaiah^d* (4Q164) comments on portions of Isaiah 54. The "rubies of all your battlements" (Is 54:12a) are, we are told, in reference to the twelve priests. Only tiny fragments of *4QIsaiah^e* (4Q165) have survived. One part comments on Isaiah 40:11, "Like a shepherd he will graze his flock," which is applied to the Teacher of Righteousness.

We may have a sixth commentary on Isaiah from Cave 3, *3QIsaiah Pesher* (3Q4). All that has survived are quotations and brief comments on Isaiah 1:1 and Isaiah 1:2. The eschatological orientation is clear enough ("The interpretation concerns all the things to come"). There is also reference to the "day of judgment." There is also another fragment from Cave 4 (4Q500) that interprets Isaiah 5:1-7 (Isaiah's Song of the Vineyard) in terms of the temple establishment. But this scroll is not a commentary.

3.3.2. Hosea. Two fragmentary commentaries on Hosea were recovered from Cave 4. *4QHosea Pesher^a* (4Q166) comments on Hosea 2:6-12. Only small portions of the commentary have survived. The focus is on the punishment inflicted upon Israel during the time of the nation's exile. *4QHosea Pesher^b* (4Q167) comments on Hosea 5:13-15 and Hosea 6:7. The commentator foresees the appearance of the Lion of Wrath and the last priest.

3.3.3. Micah. Two fragmentary commentaries on Micah have been recovered: one from Cave 1, *1QMicah Pesher* (1Q14), and one from Cave 4, *4QMicah Pesher (?)* (4Q168). The fragments of *1QMichah Pesher* contain quotations of Micah 1:2-6, 9; 6:15-16. In Micah 1:5 the commentator finds reference to the Teacher of Righteousness and the "council of the Community [*yhd*]." Only two fragments of *4QMicah Pesher (?)* have been identified with confidence (frgs. 1, 3 [frgs. 2, 4 belong to *4QHosea Pesher*[b]]). *4QHosea Pesher*[b] fragment 36 might belong to *4QMicah Pesher (?)*, but only part of one word can be seen. All that can be made out is the text of Micah 4:8-12. No commentary survives.

3.3.4. Nahum. A substantial portion of a commentary found in Cave 4, *4QNahum Pesher* (4Q169), has survived. This commentary, on Nahum 1:3—3:14, is remarkable because in addition to the usual eschatological predictions and semiallegorical identifications it actually refers to recent past events that are easily recognized. The commentary interprets the theological significance of Demetrius III's attempt, with help from a number of Pharisees, to overthrow the Hasmonean ruler Alexander Jannaeus and the violent reprisals against the Pharisees. Besides Jannaeus (r. 103-76 BC), the commentary alludes to Alexander's widow, Salome Alexandra (r. 76-67 BC), and their sons Hyrcanus II and Aristobulus II (r. 67-63 BC). These events are also recounted by Josephus (see Josephus, *J.W.* 1.85-131; *Ant.* 13.320-432; 14.1-79). The Romans are identified as the "Kittim" (and they are identified by this sobriquet in other commentaries). The Seleucid ruler Demetrius III Eukerus (r. 95-88 BC) is identified by his name "Demetrius, king of Greece," probably because there was no recognized sobriquet for this figure among the men of Qumran. "Antiochus" is mentioned, whereby Antiochus IV Epiphanes probably is in view. The Pharisees are called the "Seekers-after-Smooth-Things" and "Ephraim," after the rebellious Israelite tribe. The Sadducees are called "Manasseh," after the apostate king of Judah. Alexander Jannaeus is identified as the "Lion of Wrath." The Qumran community refers to itself as "Judah." An unknown group is dubbed the "House of Peleg." We are told that they are allies of Manasseh (i.e., the Sadducees).

One of the most gripping elements of this commentary is its interpretation of Nahum 2:12b: "he [the lion] has filled his caves with prey and his dens with torn flesh." The passage is interpreted in reference to Jannaeus, the Lion of Wrath, who "hanged men up alive," a reference to the crucifixion of eight hundred Pharisees, a gruesome event described by Josephus ("While he feasted with his concubines in a conspicuous place, he ordered eight hundred of the Jews to be crucified, and slaughtered their children and wives before the eyes of the still-living wretches" [Josephus, *Ant.* 13.380]).

3.3.5. Habakkuk. The best preserved of the pesharim is the commentary on Habakkuk, *1QHabakkuk Pesher* (1QpHab). Its thirteen columns of text provide commentary on Habakkuk 1:2—2:20. Apparently, this is where the commentary originally came to an end (there are only four lines of text at the top of col. 13). Of course, one cannot be sure. Two scribes produced this scroll. The first scribe penned 1QpHab 1:1—12:13a; the second penned 1QpHab 12:13b—13:4. Perhaps there was more commentary to be penned. The first two columns are fragmentary. Most of what is lost is at the bottom of the scroll, where the scroll, rolled up and placed in a jar right-side up, is most vulnerable to moisture and rot. The last two or three lines of every column are lost.

This commentary tells us much about the community that produced it. Key players are the "Teacher of Righteousness," the "Man of the Lie," the "House of Absalom," the "Wicked Priest" and the "One Who Spouts the Lie." The commentary is eschatological, anticipating the coming of the Kittim (i.e., the Romans), judgment and the downfall of the priest of Jerusalem. The prophecy of Habakkuk is consistently understood to refer to recent events in the history of the Qumran community and to an eschatological judgment soon to take place. The "traitors" of Habakkuk 1:5 are understood to refer to the allies of the Man of the Lie, who refused to listen to the Teacher of Righteousness. The "Chaldeans" of Habakkuk 1:6 refer to the Kittim. The "wicked one" who "swallows up one more righteous than himself" of Habakkuk 1:13 refers to the House of Absalom and their partisans, who refused to support the Teacher of Righteousness when he was slandered by the Man of the Lie. The woe pronounced against the "one who multiplies what is not his own" in Habakkuk 2:6 refers to the Wicked Priest. And so it goes.

3.3.6. Zephaniah. A few small fragments of two commentaries on Zephaniah were recovered from Cave 1 (*1QZephaniah Pesher* [1Q15]) and Cave 4 (*4QZephaniah Pesher* [4Q170]). The first quotes Zephaniah 1:18b—2:2; the second quotes Zephaniah 1:12-13. Very little commentary has survived.

3.3.7. Malachi. Tiny fragments of a commentary on Malachi were found in Cave 5 (*5QMalachi Pesher* [5Q10]). All that can be made out are quotations of Malachi 1:14a and Malachi 1:14b. There is reference to the "scoffers," which supports the identification of the text as a pesher. Fragments of a text in Cave 4 (*4QCommentary on Malachi* [4Q253a]) may be another commentary on Malachi. All that is extant is a fragmentary quotation of Malachi 3:16-18 and a few words of commentary.

3.3.8. Other Interpretation. Many other scrolls quote and interpret passages from the Prophets. Only a few can be discussed here.

3.3.8.1. 4QFlorilegium (4Q174) and 4QCatena A (4Q177). The theme of this text is the last days. In 4Q174 Nathan's prophecy is quoted in part (2 Sam 7:10-11a). The word "place" is understood to refer to the temple that Solomon eventually would build (4Q174 II, 18—III, 3). The commentary goes on to quote 2 Samuel 7:11b ("I will give you rest from your enemies"), understanding it to refer to the time of the Qumran community, when the wicked, the "children of Belial," try to make the "Sons of Light" stumble (4Q174 III, 7-9). The promise to David to raise up a son (2 Sam 7:12-14) is taken in a messianic sense (4Q174 III, 10-13). Other passages from the prophets are cited, such as Isaiah 8:11; Ezekiel 37:23; Daniel 12:10. All of these passages are understood in an eschatological sense, as referring to the time of the men of Qumran. The fragmentary 4Q177 continues this eschatological theme, quoting along the way Isaiah 37:30; 32:7; Micah 2:10-11; Zechariah 3:9; Ezekiel 25:8; Hosea 5:8, as well as a number of passages from Psalms, which the men of Qumran also regarded as prophetic and eschatological.

3.3.8.2. 4Q285 and 11Q14. These overlapping texts have been called the "Rule of War" and the "War of the Messiah." They quote Isaiah 10:34—11:1 (the falling of the trees of Lebanon and the rise of the sprout from the stump of Jesse) and then offer this commentary: "[This is the] Branch of David. Then [all forces of Belial] shall be judged, [and the king of the Kittim shall stand for judgment] and the Leader of the congregation—the Bra[nch of David]— will have him put to death. [Then all Israel shall come out with timbrel]s and dancers, and

the [high] priest shall order [them to cleanse their bodies from the guilty blood of the c] orpse[s of] the Kittim" (4Q285 7, 3-6; 11Q14 1 I, 11-15). The "Branch of David" is the eschatological Messiah. The Kittim are the Romans. This remarkable passage envisions the Roman emperor (the "king of the Kittim") slain by the Messiah. After the battle the high priest organizes the cleanup, lest the land of Israel be polluted by the "guilty blood" of the slain Romans.

3.3.8.3. 1Q28b. Appendix B of the *Rule of the Community* scroll, known as *1QRule of Benedictions*, provides a series of blessings. Column 5 articulates the blessings for the "prince of the community." Throughout these blessings words and phrases from Isaiah 11 appear. The messianic prince "with righteousness" will "judge the poor, and decide with equity for the meek of the earth" (1QSb V, 21-22, quoting Is 11:4). He will judge the earth and "with the breath" of his "lips" he will "kill the wicked" (1QSb V, 24-25). Isaiah 11:4 is again quoted, though with some modification. Additional texts are cited, including Isaiah 11:5; Micah 4:13; Numbers 24:17. The last passage was widely interpreted in Jewish late antiquity in reference to the eschatological Messiah.

3.3.8.4. 4Q254. Several fragments of 4Q254 (*4QCommentary on Genesis C*) contain commentary on Jacob's deathbed blessings of his sons (Gen 49). Fragment 4 is of special interest, for it quotes part of Zechariah 4:14 ("two sons of oil") in what appears to be commentary on either the blessing of Judah (Gen 49:8-12) or the blessing of Simeon and Levi (Gen 49:5-7). This curious description, "two sons of oil," is distinctive of Zechariah and may reflect Zechariah's eschatological perspective. In later rabbinic interpretation the "two sons of oil" are understood to be the anointed high priest and anointed king, the Messiah (see *Sipre* §97 [on Lev 7:35-38]; *ʾAbot R. Nat.* A 34:4; *Num. Rab.* 14:13 [on Num 7:84]). The "two sons of oil," wherever fragment 4 should be positioned in 4Q254, probably refers to the eschatological descendants of Levi, the patriarch from whom the anointed high priest will descend, and of Judah, the patriarch from whom the anointed king, the Messiah, will descend. Accordingly, 4Q254 may well be the earliest documentation of a form of diarchic messianism, in which an anointed priest and an anointed king were expected figures who would faithfully serve God and Israel side by side. This diarchic messianism reflects Israel's kingly history and the expectations of the prophets Zechariah and Haggai. It may also have relevance for interpreting Jesus' confrontation of the temple establishment shortly after his entry into Jerusalem.

See also APOCALYPTICISM, APOCALYPTIC LITERATURE; CANON, CANONIZATION; FORMATION OF THE PROPHETIC BOOKS; MESSIAH; PROPHETS IN THE NEW TESTAMENT; TEXT AND TEXTUAL CRITICISM.

BIBLIOGRAPHY. **M. G. Abegg, P. W. Flint and E. Ulrich,** *The Dead Sea Scrolls Bible: The Oldest Known Bible Translated for the First Time into English* (San Francisco: HarperCollins, 1999); **R. Achenbach,** "The Pentateuch, the Prophets, and the Torah in the Fifth and Fourth Centuries B.C.E.," in *Judah and the Judeans in the Fourth Century B.C.E.,* ed. O. Lipschits, G. N. Knoppers and R. Albertz (Winona Lake, IN: Eisenbrauns, 2007) 253-85; **G. Brin,** "The Laws of the Prophets in the Sect of the Judaean Desert: Studies in 4Q375," *JSP* 10 (1992) 19-51, reprinted in *Qumran Questions,* ed. J. H. Charlesworth (BibSem 36; Sheffield: Sheffield Academic, 1995) 28-60; **G. J. Brooke,** "Prophecy," *EDSS* 2:694-700; idem, "4Q254 Fragments 1 and 4, and 4Q254a: Some Preliminary Comments," in *Proceedings of the Eleventh World Congress of Jewish Studies: Jerusalem, June 22-29, 1993* (Jerusalem: World Union of Jewish Studies, 1994) 185-92; idem, "Parabiblical Prophetic Narratives," in *The Dead Sea Scrolls after Fifty Years: A Comprehensive Assessment,* ed. P. W. Flint and J. C. VanderKam (2 vols.; Leiden: E. J. Brill, 1998) 1:271-301; idem, "The Rewritten Law, Prophets and Psalms: Issues for Understanding the Text of the Bible," in *The Bible as Book: The Hebrew Bible and the Judaean Desert Discoveries,* ed. E. D. Herbert and E. Tov (New Castle, DE: Oak Knoll, 2002) 31-40; idem, "The Twelve Minor Prophets and the Dead Sea Scrolls," in *Congress Volume: Leiden 2004,* ed. A. Lemaire (VTSup 109; Leiden: E. J. Brill, 2006) 19-43; **M. Broshi,** "On netinim and False Prophets," in *Solving Riddles and Untying Knots: Biblical, Epigraphic, and Semitic Studies in Honor of Jonas C. Greenfield,* ed. Z. Zevit et al. (Winona Lake, IN: Eisenbrauns, 1995) 29-37; **M. Burrows,** "Prophecy and Prophets at Qumran," in *Israel's Prophetic Heritage: Essays in Honor of James Muilenburg,* ed. B. W. Anderson and W. Harrelson (New York: Harper, 1962) 223-32; **C. A. Evans,** "1QIsaiah[a] and the Absence of Prophetic Critique at Qumran," *RevQ* 11 (1984) 537-42; idem, "'The Two Sons of Oil': Early Evidence of Messianic Interpretation of Zechariah 4:14 in 4Q254 4 2," in *The Provo International Conference on the Dead Sea Scrolls: Technological Innovations, New Texts, and Reformulated Issues,* ed. D. W. Parry and E. Ulrich (STDJ 30; Leiden: Brill, 1999) 566-75; idem, "Diarchic Messianism in the Dead Sea Scrolls and the Messianism of Jesus of Nazareth," in *The Dead Sea Scrolls: Fifty Years after Their Discovery; Proceedings of the Jerusalem Congress, July 20-25, 1997,* ed. L. H. Schiffman, E. Tov and J. C. VanderKam (Jerusalem: Israel Exploration Society and the Israel Antiquities Authority, 2000) 558-67; **A. Finkel,** "The Oracular Interpretation of the Torah and Prophets as Reflected in the Temple Scroll and Pesharim of Qumran," in *Proceedings of the Eleventh World Congress of Jewish Studies, Division A: The Bible and Its World,* ed. D. Assaf (Jerusalem: World Union of Jewish Studies, 1994) 179-84; **R. E. Fuller,** "Textual Traditions in the Book of Hosea and the Minor Prophets," in *The Madrid Qumran Congress: Proceedings of the International Congress on the Dead Sea Scrolls, Madrid, 18-21 March, 1991,* ed. J. Trebolle Barrera and L. Vegas Montaner (2 vols.; STDJ 11; Leiden: E. J. Brill, 1992) 1:247-56; idem, "4QMicah: A Small Fragment of a Manuscript of the Minor Prophets from Qumran, Cave IV," *RevQ* 16 (1993) 193-202; **F. García Martínez,** "The Text of the XII Prophets at Qumran," *OTE* 17 (2004) 103-19; **R. P. Gordon,** "The Targum to the Minor Prophets and the Dead Sea Texts: Textual and Exegetical Notes," *RevQ* 8 (1974) 425-29; **L. L. Grabbe,** "The Law, the Prophets, and the Rest: The State of the Bible in pre-Maccabean Times," *DSD* 13 (2006) 319-38; **R. Gray,** *Prophetic Figures in Late Second Temple Jewish Palestine: The Evidence from Josephus* (New York: Oxford University Press, 1993); **G. Howard,** "Lucianic Readings in a Greek Twelve Prophets Scroll from the Judaean Desert," *JQR* 62 (1971) 51-60; **A. P. Jassen,** "The Presentation of the Ancient Prophets as Lawgivers at Qumran," *JBL* 127 (2008) 307-37; **R. G. Kratz,** "Mose und die Propheten: Zur Interpretation von 4QMMT C," in *From 4QMMT to Resurrection: Mélanges qumraniens en hommage à Émile Puech,* ed. F. García Martínez, A. Steudel and E. Tigchelaar (STDJ 61; Leiden: E. J. Brill, 2006) 151-76; **A. Shemesh,** "A Note on 4Q339 'List of False Prophets,'" *RevQ*

20 (2002) 319-20; **L. A. Sinclair,** "Hebrew Text of the Qumran Micah Pesher and Textual Traditions of the Minor Prophets," *RevQ* 11 (1983) 253-63; **E. Tov,** "The Literary History of the Book of Jeremiah in the Light of Its Textual History," in *Empirical Models for Biblical Criticism,* ed. J. Tigay (Philadelphia: University of Pennsylvania Press, 1985) 211-27; idem, "The Jeremiah Scrolls from Cave 4," *RevQ* 14 (1989) 189-206; **E. Tov, R. A. Kraft and P. J. Parsons,** *The Greek Minor Prophets Scroll from Nahal Hever (8HevXIIgr) (The Seiyal Collection 1)* (DJD 8; Oxford: Clarendon Press, 1990); **E. Ulrich et al.,** eds., *Qumran Cave 4. X: The Prophets* (DJD 15; Oxford: Clarendon Press, 1997).

C. A. Evans

DEATH

As rhetoricians, the OT prophets were adept at persuasion; in their times, as today, death was the ultimate threat, and thus it was one of the most powerful images that they could invoke. At times, they offer a choice between life and death; more often still, they present a miserable death as the fate of those who reject the word of God or oppress God's people. Furthermore, the prophets preserve a number of references to beliefs and practices surrounding death that shed light on Israelite religion and culture.

1. Burial and Mourning
2. The Dead
3. The Underworld and Its Deities
4. The Rhetoric of Death

1. Burial and Mourning.
In the prophetic texts there are no descriptions of typical burials such as one finds throughout Genesis through 2 Kings (on the archaeology of burials in ancient Israel, see Bloch-Smith). Instead, one finds in prophetic warnings and threats a kind of photographic negative of proper burial, describing its opposite. It is quite clear in the prophets, as elsewhere, that the lack of proper sepulture and mourning is viewed as a terrible fate, thus the threat of having one's corpse exposed is a particularly persistent theme in Isaiah, Jeremiah and Ezekiel (e.g., Jer 19:7: "I will make them fall by the sword before their enemies. . . . I will give their dead bodies for food to the birds of the air and to the wild animals of the earth" [see section 4]). This phenomenon is known as "antiburial" and reflects actual historical practices of invading armies. It is also manifest in the burning of kings (or their remains), usually as punishment for political "rebellion" (Is 30:33; Amos 2:1). This reflects historical practices known in Egypt and Assyria and is not to be confused with cremation, which was not widely practiced in the ancient Near East.

Israelite customs of mourning and lamentation appear to have been very similar to those of Israel's neighbors, and these practices are well-attested in the prophets. A great number of Hebrew roots refer to mourning (*'bl, spd, nhh, šhh, qdr, yll, 'nh*), but a coherent picture nevertheless emerges. At the death of a prominent person, a whole family (Zech 12:12) or tribe (Num 20:29) might gather. Indeed, allowing for hyperbole and the semimythical character of certain texts, a whole nation might be said to gather (Gen 50:10; Deut 34:8; 1 Sam 25:1; 1 Kings 14:18); more likely, a maximum turnout would have included representatives from the whole nation, as the Neo-Babylonian king Nabonidus described in the case of his mother's burial. Large numbers of mourners helped to mark a successful life since lack of mourning was seen as a curse (Jer 16:4; 25:33).

Physical manifestations of mourning included a bowed posture (Ps 35:13); shaving the head or disheveling the hair (Ezek 27:31; Amos 8:9); tearing garments (Joel 2:12); donning sackcloth or other specific "mourning garments" (Jer 4:8; 6:26; Joel 1:8); and smearing ashes on the body (Jer 6:26; Job 2:8). The practices may have been intended to establish a link with the dead person by approximating the same physical appearance (i.e., low, dusty, etc.). There were certain limitations on outward expressions of mourning, however; for example, gashing flesh is portrayed as a foreign practice (Jer 49:3) and is specifically prohibited (Lev 19:28; Deut 14:1).

Vocal weeping and wailing (e.g., Jer 4:8) were central to mourning. Professional mourners seem to have been employed in some cases: "Call for the mourning women to come; send for the skilled women to come; let them quickly raise a dirge over us, so that our eyes may run down with tears" (Jer 9:16–17 [cf. Amos 5:16]). There also are other signs that lament may have been formalized, such as the reference to the *qinah* form in Ezekiel 19:14: "This is a lamentation [*qînâ*], and it shall be used as a lamentation [*qînâ*]" (see also

Ezek 27:2, 32; 28:12; 32:2, 16; Amos 5:1). The cry *hôy* (which occurs some fifty times in the prophets, including twenty-one in Isaiah) also seems to have been typical of funerary laments (see Jer 22:18; 34:5; Amos 5:16), although that original social context was forgotten in later periods. The interjection often is translated as "Ah!" "Alas!" or "Woe!"

On the one hand, there do not seem to have been great changes in the Israelites' personal mourning practices over time. On the other hand, specific public mourning festivals are reported to have arisen in specific periods to honor certain people, such as Josiah (2 Chron 35:24-25) and Jephthah's daughter (Judg 11:39-40). Zechariah 7:3-5 refers to a custom of mourning in the fifth and seventh months, almost certainly related to the destruction of Jerusalem in the fifth month.

Although the data are less than conclusive, it appears that there were some dedicated spaces for mourning and the cultic functions associated with burials. Ecclesiastes 7:2, 4 mentions a "house of mourning" (*bêt-ʾēbel*), and Judah seems to have had a specific type of venue in which funerary feasting could take place. Called a *marzēaḥ*, it is attested twice in the Bible, both in the prophets (Jer 16:5; Amos 6:7). The Jeremiah 16 passage clearly places the *marzēaḥ* in a mourning context and likely alludes to actual funerary feasts. Amos 6:7 draws on the same events but appears to be a deliberate mischaracterization of the banquets of the wealthy as funerary banquets; that is, the prophet was mocking the way in which the participants were feasting as death was approaching.

Other apparent biblical references to a *marzēaḥ* include Amos 4:1; Hosea 4:16-19; Isaiah 28:7-8. Since the *marzēaḥ* is implicitly condemned in both its biblical attestations, it may well have been viewed by Yahwistic prophets as inappropriate and as a threat to Yahweh's worship, probably because the living might seek the blessing and aid of the spirits of the dead at such an event. A similar phenomenon by a cognate name (*marziḥu*) is known from Ugarit, where it was connected to the invocation of the dead.

2. The Dead.

Corpses were thought to cultically defile anyone who touched them, according to priestly law (e.g., Num 5:2, 19:13). Among the prophets,

Ezekiel and Haggai also show awareness of defilement by dead bodies (Ezek 6:5; 44:25; Hag 2:13-14). Not surprisingly, then, the concern about corpse defilement is most likely to occur in works influenced by priestly ideas.

The OT distinguishes itself from the literature of surrounding cultures by its polemic against belief in the supernatural power of the dead. The dead, it is said, do not praise (e.g., Ps 30:10; 88:10); instead, they "go down into silence" (Ps 115:17). They know nothing (Eccles 9:5, 10) and sit in darkness (Lam 3:6). Although this polemic is not particularly widespread in the prophets, Isaiah 14:10 provides a significant example (see also Is 47:5; Jer 48:2). This sort of polemic does not necessarily mean that belief in the power of the dead was not held by many in ancient Israel; indeed, the opposite may be true (*see* Afterlife).

3. The Underworld and Its Deities.

The underworld in Israelite thought is known primarily by the name "Sheol," which appears to be a uniquely Hebraic term, the etymology of which is contested. Although it occurs sixty-five times in the Bible, its use in the prophets is surprisingly limited: it occurs only six times outside of Isaiah and Ezekiel 31—32 (Hos 13:14 [2x]; Amos 9:2; Jon 2:3 [which really is an embedded psalm]; Hab 2:5).

Death is personified quite clearly at times in the Bible. Some of these clearly allude to the West Semitic tradition of a swallowing god of death, Mot, attested most famously in the Ugaritic Baal Cycle. One of the most prominent instances is found in Isaiah 5:14 ("Sheol has enlarged its appetite and opened its mouth beyond measure"), but there are also others. Habakkuk 2:5 describes an arrogant Babylonian ruler who "makes his gullet wide like Sheol, and is as insatiable as Mot." One might also mention Hosea 13:14 ("Death, where are your plagues?"). The lament of Jeremiah 9:20, "Death has come up into our windows, it has entered our palaces, to cut off the children from the streets and the young men from the squares," is also highly reminiscent of other ancient Near Eastern cultures' fears of demonic assaults.

Despite these occurrences, it is not likely that Mot had a cult in Judah or Israel or was commonly regarded as an active divine presence. Isaiah 28:15, 18 refer to a "covenant with

Death," but this is almost universally regarded as a reference to some other deity or perhaps to a foreign nation personified. The author has argued that the Hebrew word for "death" (*mwt*) puns on the name of the Egyptian national goddess Mut, whose name probably sounded almost identical, and who was indeed seen as a guarantor of Egypt's political agreements (Hays 2010).

The underworld god Molek certainly was known to the Israelites (Lev 18:21; 20:2-5; 2 Kings 23:10; Jer 32:35; Is 57:9 [emended from *melek*, "king"]), although later copyists sometimes confused him with the Ammonite deity Milcom. Molek is repeatedly portrayed as a god who received child sacrifices (see, in addition to the above texts, Ezek 16:21; 23:37-39), but space limitations preclude a full discussion of the topic (see Heider).

Mot and Molek were not the only supernatural chthonic powers named in the prophets. Although Jewish interest in demonology would peak much later, demons appear sporadically in the OT. The Semitic plague deity Rešeph becomes a henchman in Yahweh's wrathful retinue in Habakkuk 3:5: "Before him went Pestilence, and Plague [*ršp*] followed close behind." Demons are also often portrayed seminaturalistically as wild *animals, sometimes haunting wastelands as in other ancient Near Eastern cultures (*see* Demons and Deities). Perhaps the most obvious reference is in Isaiah 34:14, to Lilith, a well-known Mesopotamian demon. The divine adversary *haśśāṭān* (Zech 3:1-2) bears mentioning, although his name was not applied to the king of the underworld until much later.

4. The Rhetoric of Death.
Many biblical texts employ imagery of life and death for rhetorical ends. Most of these fall into certain distinct categories. (1) There are psalmic laments, in which supplicants frequently describe their suffering in terms of encroaching death to impel God's action on one's behalf or to thank God for salvation already experienced (e.g., Ps 9:14; 13:3; 28:1; 30:3; 56:14; 49:15; 68:21; 86:13; 103:4; 143:7). (2) There are legal punishment clauses, where death is threatened (e.g., Lev 20:10-12). (3) There are wisdom dichotomies (or alternatives), which present a choice between death and life. This motif is likely rooted in wisdom

discourse—for example, Proverbs 12:28: "In the path of righteousness there is life, in walking its path there is no death" (cf. Prov 8:36; 13:14; 14:27). It explodes again in the prophets (and in Deuteronomistic literature) during the Neo-Assyrian period. The close of Moses' monologue in Deuteronomy 30:15-20 may be the most prominent manifestation ("I set before you life and death. . . . Choose life!"). Precisely the same sort of rhetoric manifests itself more concisely in the exhortations of the prophets, particularly by the time of the exile—for example, Jeremiah 21:8: "See, I am setting before you the way of life and the way of death" (cf. Ezek 33:11; 18:23; 18:32). One might conclude, then, that the "wisdom alternative" was taken up by the prophets, particularly after the eighth century BC. (4) There are prophetic judgment speeches. This final major type of rhetoric employing imagery of death might be characterized as "aversion therapy"—the association of certain beliefs and actions with death imagery so graphic and horrifying as to make them unappealing. This most commonly takes the form of images of corpse exposure. Leaving the corpse to the elements and to desecration was an awful fate because it denied a restful afterlife to those so exposed; it was also, of course, repulsive at a purely natural level. The repeated threats of corpse exposure may suggest a particularly strong aversion to the dead body in Judean culture; issues of cultic purity and prohibitions of contact with the dead probably were among the forces at work. "Aversion therapy" was used already by Isaiah of Jerusalem (e.g., Is 14:19: "you are cast out from your grave"), and Jeremiah and Ezekiel seize on it with special enthusiasm, becoming the exemplars of the technique (e.g., Jer 7:33; 8:1-2; 9:22; 14:16; 16:4; 19:7; 22:18; 26:23; 36:30; Ezek 6:5-7; 29:5).

It is likely that this imagery also reflects Judeans' intimate, historical familiarity with the horrors of warfare, suffered especially at the hands of the Mesopotamians. In some cases, such as Nahum 3:1-3, this is particularly clear: "Horsemen charging, flashing sword and glittering spear, piles of dead, heaps of corpses, dead bodies without end—they stumble over the bodies!" The vast destruction and carnage of the Neo-Assyrians' military campaigns first reached Israel and Judah during Isaiah's career, which suggests his work as a natural jumping-off point for that literary motif (e.g., Is 14:19-20, which probably reflects on the death of Sargon II on campaign in 705 BC).

All of these traditions draw on death's negative connotations in Israel, holding up death as an unwelcome destination and as a punishment. One could identify a fifth, "pessimistic" tradition in which death is welcomed, which stands in some tension with the aforementioned types of rhetoric. This may be seen most obviously in Job (e.g., "Why did I not perish at birth, and die as I came from the womb?" [Job 3:11]), but also in cases where prophets were suffering persecution (e.g., Moses [Num 11:15], Elijah [1 Kings 19:4], Jeremiah [Jer 20:7-18]). However, examples of that view are so uncommon as to call into question its status as a "tradition"; it is better to identify it as a reaction against tradition for the sake of shock value.

See also AFTERLIFE; DESTRUCTION.

BIBLIOGRAPHY. E. Bloch-Smith, "The Cult of the Dead in Judah: Interpreting the Material Remains," *JBL* 111 (1992a) 213-24; idem, *Judahite Burial Practices and Beliefs about the Dead* (JSOTSup 123; Sheffield: Sheffield Academic, 1992b); H. C. Brichto, "Kin, Cult, Land and Afterlife—A Biblical Complex," *HUCA* 44 (1973) 1–54; B. S. Childs, "Death and Dying in Old Testament Theology," in *Love and Death in the Ancient Near East: Essays in Honor of Marvin H. Pope*, ed. J. Marks and R. Good (Guilford, CT: Four Quarters Publishing, 1987) 89-91; R. E. Friedman and S. D. Overton, "Death and Afterlife: The Biblical Silence," in *Death, Life-after-Death, Resurrection and the World-to-Come in the Judaisms of Antiquity*, part 4 of *Judaism in Late Antiquity*, ed. A. Avery-Peck and J. Neusner (HO 55; Leiden: E. J. Brill, 2000) 35-60; R. S. Hallote, *Death, Burial, and Afterlife in the Biblical World: How the Israelites and Their Neighbors Treated the Dead* (Chicago: Ivan R. Dee, 2001); C. B. Hays, "The Covenant with Mut: A New Interpretation of Isaiah 28:1-22," *VT* 60 (2010) 212-40; idem, *Death in the Iron Age II and in First Isaiah* (Forschungen zum Alten Testament; Tübingen: Mohr Siebeck, 2011); G. C. Heider, *The Cult of Molek: A Reassessment* (JSOTSup 43; Sheffield: JSOT, 1985); W. Janzen, *Mourning Cry and Woe Oracle* (BZAW 125; Berlin: de Gruyter, 1972); P. S. Johnston, *Shades of Sheol: Death and Afterlife in the Old Testament* (Downers Grove, IL: InterVarsity Press, 2002); P. J. King and L. E. Stager, *Life in Biblical Israel* (LAI; Louisville: Westminster/John Knox, 2001); T. J. Lewis, *Cults of the Dead in Ancient Israel and Ugarit* (HSM 39; Atlanta: Scholars Press, 1989); J. Lust, "On Wizards and Prophets," in *Studies on Prophecy: A Collection of Twelve Papers* (VTSup 26; Leiden: E. J. Brill, 1974) 133-42; J. L. McLaughlin, *The Marzēaḥ in the Prophetic Literature: References and Allusions in Light of the Extra-Biblical Evidence* (VTSup 86; Leiden: E. J. Brill, 2001); G. E. Mendenhall, "From Witchcraft to Justice: Death and Afterlife in the Old Testament," in *Death and Afterlife: Perspectives on World Religions*, ed. H. Obayashi (Westport, CT: Greenwood, 1992) 67-81; H. Nutkowicz, *L'homme face à la mort au royaume de Juda: Rites, pratiques et représentations* (Paris: Cerf, 2006); S. M. Olyan, *Biblical Mourning: Ritual and Social Dimensions* (Oxford: Oxford University Press, 2004); idem, "Some Neglected Aspects of Israelite Interment Ideology," *JBL* 124 (2005) 601-16; L. Y. Rahmani, "Ancient Jerusalem's Funerary Customs and Tombs, Part Two," *BA* 44 (1981) 229-35; J. W. Ribar, "Death-Cult Practices in Ancient Palestine" (Ph.D. diss.; University of Michigan, 1973); B. B. Schmidt, *Israel's Beneficent Dead: Ancestor Cult and Necromancy in Ancient Israelite Religion and Tradition* (FAT 111; Tübingen: Mohr Siebeck, 1994); M. S. Smith and E. Bloch-Smith, "Death and Afterlife in Ugarit and Israel," *JAOS* 108 (1988) 277-84; K. Spronk, *Beatific Afterlife in Ancient Israel and in the Ancient Near East* (AOAT 219; Neukirchen-Vluyn: Neukirchener Verlag, 1986).

C. B. Hays

DECALOGUE. *See* COVENANT; LAW.

DELIVERANCE. *See* SALVATION, DELIVERANCE.

DELIVERER, GOD AS. *See* GOD.

DEPORTATION. *See* EXILE.

DESERT. *See* WILDERNESS, DESERT.

DESTRUCTION

The concept of destruction and its vivid portrayal occur frequently in the OT. At the macrolevel, the OT speaks of destruction as a divine, physical judgment, the inevitable result of wicked or unrighteous behavior on the part of both individuals and national entities. The former is the predominant focus of OT Wisdom literature (e.g., Ps 1:6; 37:38; 49:5-9; 73:18-19; 92:7; 145:20; Prov 6:12-15; 14:11) (Mabie). In the prophetic literature, language of destruction is informed by Israel's covenant relationship with Yahweh as a nation in the promised land. The Torah and the OT Historical Books describe the birth of the nation and the struggle against the hostile forces occupying the promised land, a struggle finally won in the days of David and Solomon. The ministries of the Major Prophets and the Minor Prophets took place in the years following the fracturing of Israel's monarchy, a situation that fostered religious apostasy and ill-fated alliances with enemy Gentile (non-Israelite) *nations. The prophets focused on the importance of Israel's loyalty to Yahweh as their god and separation from the pagan Gentiles. They repeatedly preached that such spiritual devotion would ensure the destruction of Israel's enemies and warned that Yahweh's election of Israel would not avert destruction for Israel if they pursued other gods. Israel's spiritual defections consequently prompted harsh language of destruction. Despite his *wrath, Yahweh also swore through the prophets to honor his *covenant with Israel by preserving a believing remnant out of the ashes. This vow was expressed in two ways: the promise of imminent destruction of the nations hostile to Israel, and a more remote future time when all the forces aligned against Yahweh and his people would be ultimately defeated, ushering in his global kingdom.

1. Vocabulary of "Destruction"
2. Preprophetic Background
3. Destruction of Yahweh's Unfaithful People
4. Destruction of Israel's National Enemies

1. Vocabulary of "Destruction."

Biblical writers use a wide range of vocabulary to speak of destruction, though some verb lemmas are most prominent: $šmd$, $'bd$, $šḥt$. Each of these lemmas appears frequently in the prophetic material. The verb $šmd$ occurs ninety times (the majority in the Hiphil stem) and basically refers to physical destruction, most often of people. God is the subject of this verb roughly 80 percent of the time (*NIDOTTE* 4:151). The lemma $'bd$ occurs even more frequently (roughly two hundred occurrences). Most of these instances are in the Qal, where the meaning is "to be destroyed" or "to be

lost." Nearly seventy of these occurrences are in the Piel (41x) and Hiphil (26x), with the meaning "to exterminate" or "to destroy" (*NIDOTTE* 1:223-24). In over two-thirds of the occurrences in Qal and Hiphil stems, and in one-third of those in the Piel stem, Yahweh is the direct or implied agent of destruction (*TLOT* 14). The verb $šḥt$ occurs about 140 times in the OT, most often in the Hiphil (96x) and Piel (39x) stems, with a semantic range including "to wipe out," "to spoil," "to ruin" and "to destroy" (*NIDOTTE* 4:92). This lemma is "anchored particularly firmly in the conceptual realm of war" because its participial form evolved into "a technical military term [that] indicates a particular division in ancient Near Eastern armies" (*TLOT* 1318).

2. Preprophetic Background.

Prior to the prophetic period, language for "destruction" in the Torah and the OT Historical Books described a holy war directed at nations hostile to his people (*see* Warfare and Divine Warfare). Yahweh assumed the role of a divine destroyer, "a supernatural envoy from God assigned the task of annihilating large numbers of people" (Meier, 240). In literary-theological terms, the strategy used to convey this idea is the supernatural personification of "destruction" language. The most obvious example is the "destroyer" (Heb $mašḥît$, a Hiphil participle of the root $šḥt$) of the firstborn in the final plague against Egypt (Ex 12:23). This passage both differentiates and identifies Yahweh and the destroyer: "For the LORD will pass through to strike the Egyptians, and when he sees the blood . . . the LORD will pass over the door and will not allow the destroyer [$mašḥît$] to enter your houses to strike you." Elsewhere in the OT the destruction is attributed to Yahweh himself (Ex 4:23: "I will kill your firstborn"; cf. Ex 11:4-5; 12:12—13:23a, 27, 29; Ps 78:51; 105:36). The imagery of Yahweh destroying the enemy of his people continued with the exodus from Egypt. Exodus 15, the song sung by Moses and the Israelites after the miraculous deliverance at the Red/Reed Sea, informs us that Yahweh is "a man of war" (Ex 15:3) who drowned the armies of Egypt, "overthrowing" (hrs) and "devouring" ($'kl$) them (Ex 15:7).

The theme of Yahweh as the warrior who destroys the enemies of his people is also prominent in Deuteronomy and the Deuteronomistic

History (Joshua through 2 Kings). These portions of the Hebrew Bible describe the outworking of Yahweh's covenant with the patriarchs to grant their descendants (Israel) the land of Canaan. God had instructed Israel through Moses to "devote to destruction" (ḥrm) certain cities and populations in the land of Canaan (Num 21:2-3; Deut 7:2; 13:15; 20:17). Joshua was charged with carrying out these instructions as well and did so (Josh 6:18-21; 8:26; 10:28-40; 11:11-21) under the command of Yahweh, who appeared in a theophany to him as "the captain of the armies of Yahweh" (Josh 5:13-15; cf. Ex 3:1-6).

In this early period, then, Yahweh was the mighty destroyer, fighting for his beloved Israel. During the prophetic period, after Israel had become unfaithful by pursing other gods, the language and motifs of destruction would be repurposed to describe the fate of Israel.

3. Destruction of Yahweh's Unfaithful People.

As Israel embarked on the task of possessing the promised land, they were warned not to violate their covenantal relationship with God: "Yahweh will send on you curses, confusion, and frustration in all that you undertake to do, until you are destroyed [šmd] and perish [ʾbd] quickly on account of the evil of your deeds, because you have forsaken me" (Deut 28:20). But both the northern kingdom of Israel (= Israel, Ephraim, Samaria) and the southern kingdom (Judah) abandoned exclusive loyalty to Yahweh. Prophets to both kingdoms denounced the spiritual infidelity, prophesying the destruction of Israel (destroyed in 722 BC by Assyria; cf. Hos 8:8) and Judah (exiled into Babylon in three waves, c. 605-586 BC; cf. Is 39:1-7; Jer 20:4-6).

3.1. Oracles against Israel. Several of the Prophetic Books devote considerable space to long rhetorical denunciations ("oracles") of Israel (Jer 1—25; Ezek 6—7; 12—24; Amos 3—6), and virtually every one of the Prophetic Books contains some indictment of God's people. "Thus says the LORD: Even so will I spoil [šḥt] the pride of Judah and the great pride of Jerusalem. This evil people, who refuse to hear my words, who stubbornly follow their own heart and have gone after other gods. . . ." (Jer 13:9-10). Ezekiel and Hosea (Ezek 6:3; 30:13; Hos 10:8) announced impending disaster for Isra-

el's apostate high places (bāmôt), altars (mizbĕḥôt), idols (gillûlîm) and images (ʾĕlîlîm), all of which would be demolished (ʾbd). Micah prophesied (Mic 5:14) that Israelite cities in which carved images (pĕsîlîm) and Asherah poles (ʾăšerîm) were found would be destroyed (šmd). In the days leading to the Babylonian captivity, Jeremiah warned that the false prophets who were telling the populace that Yahweh would protect them were liars: "For it is a lie that they are prophesying to you, with the result that you will be removed far from your land, and I will drive you out, and you will perish [ʾbd]. . . . They are prophesying falsely in my name, with the result that I will drive you out and you will perish [ʾbd], you and the prophets who are prophesying to you" (Jer 27:10, 15). The errant house of Jeroboam was "destroyed [šmd] . . . according to the word of the LORD" (1 Kings 15:29). The line of Ahab was "wiped out [šmd] according to the word of the LORD that he spoke to Elijah" (2 Kings 10:17). Elsewhere, Yahweh told his people through Jeremiah in no uncertain terms that "I have destroyed [ʾbd] my people; they did not turn from their ways" (Jer 15:7), and that "I will not pity or spare or have compassion, that I should not destroy [šḥt]" the kings, priests, prophets and inhabitants of Jerusalem (Jer 13:13-14).

3.2. Israel and "the Day of the Lord." The personal offense taken by Yahweh at Israel's apostasy is expressed in two ways. First and most frequently, the destructive judgment of Israel is described as "the day of the LORD" (see Day of the Lord). The descriptive phrase left no doubt as to what had prompted judgment and who was inflicting it. This same phrase was also used by the prophets for the apocalyptic destruction of Israel's enemies (Geyer; see 4.2 below).

The "day of the LORD" with respect to God's judgment of his people was described in several ways. Some prophets connected it to natural disasters and celestial omens. Amos warned Israel that the Day of the Lord would be "darkness, and not light" and "gloom with no brightness" (Amos 5:18, 20). The connection to natural disasters included pestilence and crop failure (Joel 2:1-11; Hag 1:5-6; 2:14-19; Mal 3:9-12). Still others described it in terms of the horror of battle, where people are forced to flee for their lives, imagery that would be literalized for many who heard the words (Is 3:18—4:1; 22:5;

157

Hos 1:4-5; Amos 2:13-16; 8:3, 9). Still more alternative language makes the destruction's association with the evil of the people clear (Ezek 7:7-12, 19; Mal 4:1, 5). The familiar description of foreign nations as instruments of punishment is also included in "day of the LORD" passages (Is 5:26-30; Hos 11:5; Amos 3:9-11) (Geyer). Some texts indicate that certain prophets believed that the Day of the Lord was very near (Ezek 7:7, 10, 12; 22:4; Joel 3:14; Zeph 1:7; Mal 3:1-2).

3.3. Supernatural Destroyers. The second expression of personal affront in regard to Israel's apostasy and impending destruction involves the personification of "destruction" language, a strategy employed previously in the defeat of Israel's enemies in Egypt and at the Red/Reed Sea. Now, however, the prophets wield it to convey a terrible message: Yahweh is personally sending supernatural agents of destruction against his people (Kapelrud). In Ezekiel 9:1-6 a group of angelic beings are commanded by Yahweh to pass through Jerusalem and slaughter everyone who was guilty of committing idolatry. None of these figures are called "destroyer," though the word is part of their commissioning (lĕmašḥît [Ezek 9:6]). At the exodus event, the destroyer's judgment on the firstborn had been described as a plague (negep [Ex 12:13]). Two other words for plagues are personified as supernatural destroyers in the Hebrew Bible: qeteb and deber (Deut 32:24; Ps 91:6; Hos 13:14) (del Olmo Lete; Wyatt). Isaiah 28:2 employs the imagery of a supernatural destroyer against Israel by warning of "a destroying tempest" (lit., "a tempest of qeteb [destruction]") sent by Yahweh against "the drunkards of Ephraim [i.e., Israel]."

4. Destruction of Israel's National Enemies.

Despite the horror of Yahweh's destruction of Israel and *exile of Judah, the prophets were quite clear that God's use of foreign *nations as instruments of his wrath should not be construed as an endorsement of those foreign nations. They would get what was coming to them as well. The "destruction" language is cast in both eschatologically imminent terms and a more remote apocalyptic judgment of the nations.

4.1. Oracles against the Nations. Destruction rhetoric aimed at Israel's historic enemies frequently comes in the form of "oracles," poetic diatribes labeled by scholars as "oracles against the nations." Several of the Prophetic Books devote considerable space to this rhetorical genre (Is 13—23; Jer 46—51; Ezek 25—32). For example, Isaiah prophesies the destruction of strongholds in Canaan, specifically Tyre (šmd [Is 23:11-12]). Ezekiel warns that destruction awaits the Ammonites, Moabite, Edomites and Philistines (šmd, 'bd, ḥrbh [Ezek 25]). Likewise targeted for destruction are the city of Tyre (šḥt, 'bd [Ezek 26:4, 17; 28:16]) and the Egyptians (šmd [Ezek 30:13; 32:12]). Zephaniah declares that Assyria will be demolished by the hand of Yahweh (šmd, 'bd [Zeph 2:13]). The book of Obadiah announces the destruction of Edom ('bd [Obad 8]). Jeremiah portends the destruction of Moab (šmd [Jer 48:8]). Amos forecasts the doom of Philistine cities ('bd [Amos 1:8]), Tyre, and Edom ('kl [Amos 1:9-12]). Jeremiah, using a wide range of vocabulary, also prophesies the destruction of Babylon. Babylon will be "destroyed" (šḥt [Jer 51:11]), "devastated" (šdd [Jer 51:55]), "broken" (šbr [Jer 28:2]) and "killed" (mwt [Jer 41:2]).

4.2. The Future Day of the Lord. All the prophets target the nations with declarations of destruction and judgment, but several go much further in prophesying a "day of the LORD" involving many or even all nations hostile to Yahweh and Israel (Jer 25:33; Ezek 30:2-5; 38:17-39:8; Joel 3:14). According to Zechariah 12:3-9; 14:12-13, "on that day" Yahweh will destroy all the nations opposed to Jerusalem. Even more audacious is the language used by Zephaniah, who proclaimed that Yahweh would destroy "all the inhabitants of the earth" (Zeph 1:7-18), a viewpoint shared by Isaiah 13:6-8.

The apex of the language of apocalyptic destruction transcends even the defeat of all the nations of the earth. Passages in Isaiah and Jeremiah insist that the Day of the Lord will involve the punishment of the cosmic powers, the host of heaven (Is 24:21), a conflict that will threaten the very fabric and order of creation itself.

The two most noteworthy passages regarding this total cosmic upheaval are Isaiah 27:1 and Jeremiah 4:23-28. Isaiah 27:1 equates "that day" with Yahweh's climactic victory over the forces of primeval chaos, personified by Leviathan, "the dragon that is in the sea." Jeremiah 4:23-28 also resorts to the description of primeval chaos. Situating the oracle in "that day" (Jer

4:9), the prophet writes, "I looked on the earth, and behold, it was without form and void [tōhû wābōhû]; and to the heavens, and they had no light." The phrase tōhû wābōhû is an explicit reference to the unformed heavens and earth in Genesis 1:2. Scholars debate when these verses in Jeremiah were penned in relation to other passages securely assigned to the apocalyptic genre, but they agree that the language is consistent with an apocalyptic outlook (Eppstein; Hayes). There could hardly be a more dramatic way to cast divine visitation.

See also CHAOS; DAY OF THE LORD; DEATH; WARFARE AND DIVINE WARFARE; WRATH.

BIBLIOGRAPHY. **V. Eppstein,** "The Day of Yahweh in Jeremiah 4:23-28," *JBL* 87 (1986) 93-97; **J. Geyer,** "Mythology and Culture in the Oracles against the Nations," *VT* 36 (1986) 129-45; **K. Hayes,** "Jeremiah IV 23: *tōhû* without *bōhû*," *VT* 47 (1997) 247-49; **A. Kapelrud,** "God as Destroyer in the Preaching of Amos and in the Ancient Near East," *JBL* 71 (1952) 33-38; **F. J. Mabie,** "Chaos and Death," *DOTWPW* 41-54; **S. Meier,** "Destroyer," *DDD*[2] 240-44; **G. del Olmo Lete,** "Deber," *DDD*[2] 231-32; **N. Wyatt,** "Qeteb," *DDD*[2] 674.   M. S. Heiser

DIRGES. *See* JEREMIAH: BOOK OF; LAMENTATIONS, BOOK OF.

DIVINATION, MAGIC

The terms *divination* and *magic* are difficult to define, and the two have some overlap. The prophets refer to divination and magic in terms of disapproval and condemnation. From the perspective of the prophetic writings, divination therefore can be said to involve the use of illicit means to seek information or direction normally hidden from humans. Magic can be understood as the attempt to influence for good or avert evil by the unlawful use of supernatural forces.

1. Divination
2. Magic
3. The Prophetic Response
4. Theological Implications

1. Divination.

The Hebrew root *qsm* denotes divination and its practitioners in general (the root *nḥš*, which also refers to divination, is not found in the prophets). The use of the Aramaic root *gzr* in Dan 2:27; 4:7 (MT 4:4); 5:7, 11 likely re-

fers to diviners in a general sense.

The cultural and religious world in which the prophets labored was saturated with divination, but Yahweh's prophets put it in a negative light. They condemned it (Is 44:25; Zech 10:2; cf. Deut 18:10), associated it with false prophecy inside Israel (Jer 27:9; 29:8; Ezek 13:6-9, 17, 23; 22:28; Mic 3:5-7, 11), essentially equated it with lies and falsehood (*šeqer* [Jer 14:14]), and contrasted its futility with the power of Yahweh's *Spirit enabling the prophet to discern justly and declare Israel's sin (Mic 3:8). However, so deeply established was the evil of divination within God's people (2 Kings 17:17; 21:6; Is 2:6), that when the prophets pictured the collapse of society, it was specifically mentioned as part of the passing scene (Is 3:1-3; Mic 3:6). Diviners were even found in postexilic Israel (Zech 10:2).

1.1. Specific Divinatory Methods.

1.1.1. Rhabdomancy. Rhabdomancy is divination by the use of wooden sticks or rods. Hosea may be referring to this practice when he articulates Yahweh's accusation: "My people consult their sticks [*ʿēṣô*], and their staffs [*maqlô*] inform them" (Hos 4:12) (Macintosh, 151-52). There is, however, no consensus on the meaning of this passage. The king of Babylon's shaking of arrows (Ezek 21:21) may be belomancy, a form of rhabdomancy, but the king's actions have also been interpreted as divination by lot.

1.1.2. Hepatoscopy. Hepatoscopy, a specialized form of extispicy, is the examination of the liver of a sacrificial animal for omens. Babylon was famous for this type of divination, and its king is pictured as practicing it (Ezek 21:21). Some have thought that King Ahaz read omens from sacrificial animals (2 Kings 16:2, 15; cf. Lev 3:3-5; Deut 18:10). The prophets make no direct reference to this form of divination within Israel.

1.1.3. Oneiromancy. Oneiromancy is divination by means of dreams. Jeremiah referred to the false prophets using dreams to convey their lies (Jer 23:25; 29:8-9; cf. Deut 13:2-5). Oneiromancy was a well-established practice in Babylon (Butler). Not surprisingly, its royal court was equipped with those who claimed to be able to interpret dreams (Dan 2:4; 4:6).

1.1.4. Teraphim. Teraphim (Heb *tĕrāpîm*) can be identified as images (*HALOT* 1795) used for divinatory purposes, but no scholarly consensus exists on their precise identity and use. Zechariah 10:2 identifies them as oracular devices that are condemned: "The teraphim utter deceit, and the diviners see deception." The king of Babylon "consulted the teraphim" (Ezek 21:26). Hosea 3:4 predicts that "the Israelites will live many days . . . without ephod and teraphim." Since the northern kingdom did not have the officially sanctioned ephod with the Urim and Thummim, this reference (and the LXX translation) may indicate that teraphim functioned as a substitute for the Urim and Thummim (cf. Judg 17:5) (Van Dam, 149-51; cf. Rofé). On the other hand, teraphim have been connected with necromancy because of their association with mediums and spiritists in Josiah's reformation (2 Kings 23:24) (Van der Toorn).

1.1.5. Astrology. Astrology as a divinatory means sought signs or omens foretelling the future in celestial phenomena. Astrology had a long history in Mesopotamia. Babylonian astrologers were characterized as those "who divide the heavens [Qere: *hōbĕrê šāmayim*], who look at the stars [*haḥōzîm bakkôkābîm*], who make known at the new moons what is coming upon you" (Is 47:13). The courts of Nebuchadnezzar and Belshazzar had at their beck and call Chaldeans (*kaśdîm* [Dan 2:2]), best known for their proficiency in astrology (Rochberg-Halton, 505). Israel was impressed by "the signs of the heavens" (Jer 10:2) and worshiped the heavenly bodies (Jer 8:2).

1.1.6. Necromancy. Necromancy is communication with the dead to understand better the past or to know the future. When Judah was threatened in the eighth century BC by Assyria, God's people inquired of the mediums (*ʾôbôt*) and spiritists (*yiddĕʿōnîm*) who consulted "the dead" (*hammētîm*) (Is 8:19; cf. Is 29:4). Necromancy may also be referred to elsewhere. The people "sit among the graves and spend the night in secret places" (Is 65:4). The suggestion that necromancy is alluded to in Isaiah 28:7-22 seems unlikely (Johnston, 158-60). Necromancy was known in Mesopotamia (Cryer, 181-83) and may also have been practiced in Syria-Palestine (Jeffers, 173-81; cf. Schmidt, 100-122, 201-20) and Egypt (see Is 19:3) (Ritner).

1.1.7. Soothsaying. Soothsaying as a divinatory practice involved predicting the future, but it is unclear exactly how or on what basis the predictions were made. Isaiah characterized Israel as rejected by God because the nation was full of soothsayers (*ʿōnĕnîm*) like the

Philistines were (Is 2:6). Jeremiah warned the people directly: "Do not to listen to your [false] prophets, diviners (*qōsĕmêkem*), your interpreters of dreams, your soothsayers (*ʿōnĕnêkem*) and sorcerers (*kaśśāpêkem*)" (Jer 27:9). Elsewhere the soothsayers were also associated with sorcery or witchcraft, *kešep* (Mic 5:12 [MT 5:11]), and *ʿōnĕnâ* sometimes is translated as "sorcerer" (Is 57:3).

2. Magic.
Most often magic is referred to with the root *kšp* ("to practice sorcery"). Although, like divination, magic and sorcery were strictly forbidden (Deut 18:10-11), these practices made deep inroads into the life of God's people and were considered an acceptable part of society. When Isaiah listed the prominent and respected people of his day, he included the "skillful magician" (*ḥăkam ḥărāšîm*) (Is 3:3 [see *HALOT* 358]) and the "expert enchanter" (*nĕbôn lāḥaš*) (Is 3:3; cf. Jer 27:9). The use of the positive attributes "skillful" and "expert" perhaps are ironic, given that Yahweh is the source of wisdom, and that Isaiah's prophecy scorns the wisdom of diviners (cf. Is 11:2; 44:25; 47:10). On the other hand, this usage may simply indicate that according to human standards, they were considered expert at their craft.

Magic and sorcery (*kĕšāpîm*) were associated with Nineveh (Nah 3:4) and especially with Babylon, the city of sorceries (*ḥăbārîm*) and magic spells (*kĕšāpîm*) (Is 47:9, 12). It is interesting to note that when Nebuchadnezzar wanted his dream recounted and explained, he called in the wise men (cf. Dan 2:12), who were identified as "magicians [*ḥarṭummîm*], conjurers [*ʾaššāpîm*], sorcerers [*mĕkaššĕpîm*] and Chaldeans [*kaśdîm*]" (Dan 2:2). Apparently, dream interpretation included dispelling or removing any evil consequences of such a dream by the use of magic (Oppenheim 2008, 218-19).

3. The Prophetic Response.
To appreciate the prophets' disapproval of divination and magic, one needs to be aware of some of the presuppositions informing these practices (Van Dam, 114-24). Divination and magic would be inconceivable without the notion that the natural world was conceived personally. The gods were in and behind the phenomena and forces of nature. There was no qualitative difference between the gods and

humans. Through divination the diviner attempted to find out the intent and desires of the gods on the assumption that they spoke through the arrangement of the sticks or rods, through the features of a liver, or by the arrangement of the stars in the heavens. The gods were also thought to communicate through dreams. One could seek an incubation dream for getting the necessary information by spending a night in a holy place such as a temple (COS 1.60:157, 159; 2.155:422-24, 428; Butler, 217-39). By collecting omens and the anomalous results (whether positive or negative) that were observed, diviners developed enormous bodies of scientific literature to be used for future reference (Oppenheim 1977, 210-12).

Because the gods were conceived as part of nature, there was always the temptation to control and manipulate the gods and the messages that were divined. However, in this worldview larger independent forces were above the gods. To counter these, both humans and gods would resort to magical incantations and spells (Kaufmann, 40-42; Van Dam, 122).

The prophetic outlook was completely different. Israel's *God is the only God. He is not part of the natural world; rather, he created it and is above it (Is 42:5; 45:18). He cannot be manipulated, for he is sovereign and in complete control. He determines the future (Is 14:24-27). There is no point in seeking omens by divination (cf. Is 47:12-15; Mic 3:6-7). Indeed, God frustrates the omens of diviners (Is 44:25). He is the one who directs the history of Israel and the nations (Is 45:1-7; Jer 32:17-23). There is no power or force above him. Therefore, to pay respects to Fortune (gad) or Destiny (měnî) is to forsake Yahweh (Is 65:11). Not surprisingly, the prophets condemned all forms of divination and magic (cf. Deut 18:10-11).

Besides the general prohibitions, the prophets also condemned specific methods of divination. Jeremiah strongly denounced dreams conjured up by false prophets to spread lies (šeqer [Jer 23:25-28; 27:9-10; 29:8-9]). Such abuse, however, did not prevent Yahweh as sovereign God from using dreams that he sent to give his revelation to Nebuchadnezzar. But, Babylon's wise men, enchanters, magicians and diviners were powerless and unable to provide the interpretation. God had to reveal that to his prophet Daniel (Dan 2; 4).

With regard to astrology, there was no need

for Israel "to be dismayed by the signs of the heavens" (Jer 10:2; cf. Jer 10:6-7, 11-13), since God created the heavenly bodies (Is 40:26; Jer 31:35; Amos 5:8). Being enamored with astrology included worshiping the heavenly bodies as astral deities, a practice that God strictly forbade (Deut 4:19). Thus, the reforming king Josiah had ordered the removal from the temple of all the vessels made for "all the host of heaven" (kōl ṣĕbāʾ haššāmāyîm) and deposed the priests who had burnt incense to "the sun, the moon and the constellations and all the host of the heaven" (2 Kings 23:4-5; cf. Deut 4:19; 17:2-7; Jer 8:1-2; Ezek 8:16). Both the northern and southern kingdoms were severely punished because of such worship (2 Kings 17:16-18; Jer 8:2; 19:13). The futility of depending on astrology is evident in Isaiah's taunting Babylon to let their astrologers come forward to save them (Is 47:13).

In opposing necromancy (cf. Deut 18:11), Isaiah tellingly asked, "When men tell you to consult mediums and spiritists, who whisper and mutter, should not a people inquire of their God? Why consult the dead on behalf of the living?" (Is 8:19). Because God is the living God, they should go to him.

When it came to the practice of magic, God served notice that he would judge his people because of it and remove sorceries from them (Mic 5:12; Mal 3:5). Also, Nineveh stood condemned in part because of its sorceries (Nah 3:1-4). To be sure, magic was ineffective (Is 47:9, 12), for God is sovereign and can overcome magic (cf. Jer 8:17). It is noteworthy that Nebuchadnezzar found God-fearing Daniel and his three friends ten times wiser and more understanding than the magicians and conjurers of his kingdom (Dan 1:20).

4. Theological Implications.
God's revelation of himself as the only God, who is above and sovereign over all creation, undergirded his prophets' prohibition of divination and magic. These were mere human attempts to get hidden information from gods of their own making and to influence the course of events. In biblical religion, the living God came to humans and revealed himself and his will. Although God forbade the seeking of divine knowledge by way of divination as practiced in the nations, God did accommodate himself to the human desire to inquire of God and permitted the use of the lot

(Prov 16:33), the Urim and Thummim (Ex 28:30; Num 27:21) and the inquiry of God through the prophets (2 Kings 3:10-20; Jer 21:2; Ezek 20:1-3) in order to determine the divine will or knowledge.

The Prophetic Books clearly distinguish prophecy from divination. It is, therefore, not helpful to characterize canonical prophecy as a type of divination, as is becoming more common today (see Kitz). False prophecy, on the other hand, is associated with divination (Heb root *qsm*) and is characterized as a human endeavor (Is 44:25; Jer 14:14; 27:9; 29:8 Ezek 13:6-9; 22:28; Mic 3:5-7, 11). The root *qsm* is never used of true prophets.

By forbidding divination, Yahweh wanted to encourage his people to rely on his word. Significantly, Isaiah told Israel to go to the living God rather than to mediums and spiritists, and he enjoined, "To the law and to the testimony! If they do not speak according to this word, it is because they have no dawn" (Is 8:20; cf. Is 45:19). The people were to turn to the word and to the prophets, who had been promised to bring that word (cf. Deut 18:15 in context). The divine word was to show the way for God's people. God esteemed the one "who is humble and contrite in spirit, and trembles at my word" (Is 66:2).

See also ANCIENT NEAR EASTERN PROPHECY.

BIBLIOGRAPHY. **S. A. L. Butler,** *Mesopotamian Conceptions of Dreams and Dream Rituals* (AOAT 258; Münster: Ugarit-Verlag, 1998); **F. H. Cryer,** *Divination in Ancient Israel and Its Near Eastern Environment: A Socio-Historical Investigation* (JSOTSup 142; Sheffield: JSOT, 1994); **A. Jeffers,** *Magic and Divination in Ancient Palestine and Syria* (SHCANE 8; Leiden: E. J. Brill, 1996); **P. S. Johnston,** *Shades of Sheol: Death and Afterlife in the Old Testament* (Downers Grove, IL: InterVarsity Press, 2003); **Y. Kaufmann,** *The Religion of Israel from Its Beginnings to the Babylonian Exile* (trans. M. Greenberg; New York: Schocken, 1972); **A. M. Kitz,** "Prophecy as Divination," *CBQ* 65 (2003) 22-42; **A. A. Macintosh,** *A Critical and Exegetical Commentary on Hosea* (ICC; Edinburgh: T & T Clark, 1997); **A. L. Oppenheim,** *Ancient Mesopotamia: Portrait of a Dead Civilization* (rev. ed., completed by E. Reiner; Chicago: University of Chicago Press, 1977); idem, *The Interpretation of Dreams in the Ancient Near East* (repr., Piscataway, NJ: Gorgias, 2008 [1956]); **R. K. Ritner,** "Necromancy in Ancient Egypt," in *Magic and Divination in the Ancient World*, ed. L. Ciraolo and J. Seidel (AMD 2; Leiden: E. J. Brill, 2002) 89-96; **F. Rochberg-Halton,** "Astrology in the Ancient Near East," *ABD* 1.504-7; **A. Rofé,** "'No *Ephod* or *Teraphim*'—*oude hierateias oude dēlōn:* Hosea 3:4 in the LXX and in the Paraphrases of the Chronicles and the *Damascus Document*," in *Sefer Moshe: The Moshe Weinfeld Jubilee Volume*, ed. C. Cohen, A. Hurvitz and S. M. Paul (Winona Lake, IN: Eisenbrauns, 2004) 135-49; **B. B. Schmidt,** *Israel's Beneficent Dead: Ancestor Cult and Necromancy in Ancient Israelite Religion and Tradition* (Winona Lake, IN: Eisenbrauns, 1996); **C. Van Dam,** *The Urim and Thummim: A Means of Revelation in Ancient Israel* (Winona Lake, IN: Eisenbrauns, 1997); **K. Van der Toorn,** "The Nature of the Biblical Teraphim in the Light of the Cuneiform Evidence," *CBQ* 52 (1990) 203-22.

C. Van Dam

DIVINE ASSEMBLY. *See* DIVINE COUNCIL.

DIVINE COUNCIL

The term *divine council* is used broadly by Hebrew Bible scholars to refer to the "heavenly host," the pantheon of divine beings who administer the affairs of the cosmos (Handy; Mullen 1980; *ABD* 2:214-17). All ancient Mediterranean cultures had some conception of a divine council. The Hebrew Bible describes a divine council under the authority of Yahweh, the God of Israel. While the divine council of Israel and its neighbors share significant features, the divine council of Israelite religion was distinct in important ways. This article briefly summarizes the more important aspects of the divine council in the Hebrew Bible and its relationship to the prophetic office (see further Heiser, *DOTWPW* 112-16; 2008).

1. Foundational Passages and Vocabulary
2. Prophets and the Divine Council
3. The Divine Council as Divine Warriors in the Prophets

1. Foundational Passages and Vocabulary.

1.1. Vocabulary for the Council. Understanding the relationship of the heavenly council and the prophets requires an acquaintance with certain key passages and vocabulary. Psalm 82 is an essential text for understanding the Israelite divine council. The psalm contains an explicit reference to a divine assembly under the authority of God (*'elōhîm*) along with a subsequent plural use of the word *ʾelōhîm* ("God, gods"): "God [*ʾelōhîm*] stands in the divine council [*baʿădat-ʾēl*]; among the gods [*ʾelōhîm*] he passes judgment" (Ps 82:1). The second occurrence of *ʾelōhîm* certainly is plural, as the preposition "in the midst of" (*bĕqereb*) precedes the term. The Trinity cannot explain this plurality, since the psalm goes on to describe how God charges the other *ʾelōhîm* with corruption and sentences them to die "like humankind." Psalm 89:5-7 also places the God of Israel "in the assembly of the holy ones" (*biqhal qĕdōšîm*) and then asks, "For who in the clouds can be compared to Yahweh? Who is like Yahweh among the sons of God [*bĕnê ʾēlîm*], a god greatly feared in the council [*sôd*] of the holy ones?" These passages clearly depict a heavenly council ("in the clouds") and not, as some scholars suggest, a council of earthly human judges. The concept of a council does not conflict with the notion that its head, Yahweh, is a triune being, nor does it impinge on monotheism, since the Israelite understanding of the council saw Yahweh as a unique, incomparable deity who was the creator of the heavenly host and its unquestioned sovereign (Heiser 2008).

1.2. Vocabulary for the Divine Abode/Throne Room. The vocabulary describing the divine abode and the council meeting place found in the Hebrew Bible corresponds very closely to vocabulary in ancient Near Eastern literature cognate to the Hebrew Bible (Clifford; Heiser, *DOTWPW* 112-16). For example, in the literature of the city-state of Ugarit, the divine council and its gods met on a cosmic mountain. The high god El dwelt on this mountain, which also was described as a well-watered garden. With his council, El issued divine decrees from his "tent" and "tent shrine" (*CTA* 1.III.26ff.). The Ugaritic god Baal, the deity who oversaw the council for El, held meetings in the "heights" of Mount Ṣapānu, governing from his palace of lapis lazuli, whose courtyard was fashioned with "paved bricks."

These descriptions are present in the Hebrew Bible with respect to Israel's God and his council. Yahweh dwells on mountains (Sinai or Zion [e.g., Ex 34:26; 1 Kings 8:10; Ps 48:1-2]). The Jerusalem *temple and *Zion are said to be located in the "heights" of the *ṣāpôn* ("the north" [Ps 48:1-2; Is 14:13]). Additionally, Mount Zion is described as a watery habitation (Is 33:20-22; Ezek 47:1-12; Joel 3:18; Zech 14:8),

much in the fashion of the garden of Eden (Gen 2:6-15), called the "garden of God," and the "holy mountain of God" in Ezekiel 28:13-16. At Sinai Moses and others saw Yahweh and feasted with him at a banquet. The account in Exodus 24 notes that under God's feet was a paved construction of "sapphire stone" (Ex 24:10). Other striking parallels include Yahweh's frequent presence in the tabernacle tent and the description of Zion as Yahweh's tent (Ps 26:8; 74:7; 1 Chron 9:23; Is 33:20). That the members of Yahweh's host are present in his abode or throne room is indicated by the presence of the heavenly host at Sinai (Deut 33:1-2; cf. Acts 7:53; Gal 3:19), the presence of "thrones" (plural) and a "court" before the enthroned Ancient of Days in Daniel 7:1-10, and divine council sessions found elsewhere (1 Kings 22:19; cf. 2 Chron 18:18). Yahweh's "location" and the presence of the council were therefore inseparable in terms of Israel's "cosmic geography," similar to our familiar conception of God and his *angels living in the same place. The throne room of God was where God held court with his servant council.

2. Prophets and the Divine Council.

2.1. The Divine Council as Witness to God's Decrees and Acts. The divine throne room is the place from which Yahweh governs the world with his heavenly council, the place where "Yahweh's decrees directing the human community and the divine world are set forth and through whom they are communicated or enacted" (Miller 2000, 426).

The most transparent example of this interaction is 1 Kings 22:13-23. The prophet Micaiah ben Imlah, summoned to prophesy about an alliance between Jehoshaphat and Ahab and the fate of their planned assault on Ramoth-gilead, tells Ahab, "I saw the LORD sitting on his throne, and all the host of heaven standing beside him on his right hand and on his left; and the LORD said, 'Who will entice Ahab, that he may go up and fall at Ramoth-gilead?'" (1 Kings 22:19-20). The narrative continues with Micaiah describing the spirits of the heavenly host deliberating with one another about how to accomplish Yahweh's decree.

The council therefore has the important role of bearing witness to God's decrees and acts. Not surprisingly, this notion is common outside the Hebrew Bible in cognate divine council descriptions (Bokovy). Amos 3 describes the Lord's intention to punish Israel. In Amos 3:7 we read that "the Lord GOD does nothing without revealing his council/counsel [*sôd*] to the prophets." This declaration is followed by two plural imperatives in Amos 3:10 ("*Proclaim* to the strongholds . . . and *say*. . .") and Amos 3:13 ("*Hear* and *testify* against the house of Jacob, declares the Lord GOD, the God of hosts"). Again Israel and Judah are not the recipient of the commands, creating the distinct possibility that the divine council is called upon to witness the judgment meted out by the Lord (Bokovy).

2.2. Prophetic Commissioning and the Divine Council: Precursors to the Classical Prophets. Broadening the conception of a prophet to someone who serves as the righteous spokesperson for God allows one to appreciate the motif of a direct divine encounter-commission in the lives of many biblical figures singled out for service to God prior to the period of the classical prophets.

The motif of a divine encounter is applied to the first man, Adam, whom God appointed as ruling steward over Eden, the well-watered garden and mountain of God (Gen 2:6-15; Ezek 28:13-16), the abode of God and his council. Proceeding from Adam, Enoch and Noah "walked with God" (Gen 5:22, 24; 6:9). The former "prophesied," according to Jude 14-15, while the latter is referred to as a "herald of righteousness" (2 Pet 2:5) who told his contemporaries of the coming flood, warning them of God's judgment (1 Pet. 3:20).

The theophanic encounters of the patriarchs are well known. Genesis 12:1-7 and Genesis 15:1-6 record God's appearance to Abraham, calling him out of paganism to father a people for God, a people who would serve as mediators between the Gentile nations and the true God. That this account was visible is suggested by the language of manifestation in Genesis 15:1 and in Acts 7:2-4, where Stephen notes that the glory of Lord "appeared" to Abraham before he journeyed to Haran. Yahweh likewise appeared to Isaac (Gen 26:1-5) and Jacob (Gen 28:10-22; 31:11-13; 32:22-32; cf. Hos 12:3-4). Later in the story of Israel, Moses was commissioned at the burning bush (Ex 3:1-15) and encountered God subsequently many times (e.g., Ex 19:16—20:21; 24:9-18; 33:7-11). The elders of Israel under Moses were commissioned directly by Yahweh (Num 11:24-25), as was Joshua (Deut 31:14-23; Josh 5:13-15). Various judges of Israel, leading up to the time of the classical prophets, also met Yahweh when they were called to ministry. The book of Judges records a dramatic appearance to Gideon (Judg 6), an event that the writer notes took place "under the terebinth at Ophrah" (Judg 6:11, 19). The reference to the terebinth is of interest, as trees often marked places where Yahweh had appeared to people such as Abraham (Gen 12:6; 13:18; 14:13; 18:1) (Nielsen, *DDD* 637, 851). The prophetess Deborah (Judg 4:4) also apparently received messages from the Lord under "the Palm of Deborah" (Judg 4:4-5). The "word" of the Lord "appeared" to Samuel, the last of Israel's judges, as a boy, "standing" before him to inform him of Eli's fate (1 Sam 3). This theophanic manifestation apparently occurred with some regularity to Samuel (1 Sam 3:20-21).

2.3. Prophetic Commissioning and the Divine Council: The Classical Prophets. The popular conception of a prophet is of someone empowered by God to foretell the future. But in fact, the forecasting of future events was an infrequent part of a prophet's ministry. To speak prophetically in the biblical sense meant simply to be a spokesperson for God, to serve as God's mouthpiece to his covenant people, Israel, and to their enemies. In biblical literature, God chose prophets and commissioned them for such ministry (*see* Call/Commission Narratives). This commissioning took the form of a direct encounter with God in connection with the divine council (Kingsbury; Nissinen).

The call of Isaiah, described in the book that bears his name, is no doubt the most familiar instance of prophetic commissioning in God's throne room (Is 6:1-9). The scene is quite reminiscent of 1 Kings 22:19-23, where Yahweh met with his council concerning the wicked King Ahab. Having decreed Ahab's death, Yahweh allows council members to suggest the means for the execution of the decree. In the case of Isaiah, after the prophet is purified for God's presence (Is 6:6-7), Yahweh asks the council, "Whom shall I send, and who will go for us?" (Is 6:8). Isaiah immediately volunteers. The reader then learns that Yahweh has already decreed that his people will be judged, but he tells the prophet to preach "until the cities lie waste . . . and the land is a desolate waste." The council appears again in Isaiah 40, though its presence is hard to detect in English translations. The council's presence is indicated primarily by the presence of plural imperatives whereby God commands an unidentified group in a context that rules out a human audience (Cross). For example, in Isaiah 40:1-2 we read, "Comfort, comfort my people, says your God." The two imperatives "comfort" are grammatically plural in Hebrew, as are the ensuing commands "Speak tenderly to Jerusalem and cry to her." To whom are these commands intended for response? The answer cannot be Jerusalem or Israel, for they are the objects of the commands. For this and other contextual reasons, many scholars argue that the divine council is the audience (Cross; Seitz). Whereas in Isaiah 6 punishment was decreed, this time Yahweh and his council pronounce deliverance from *exile.

Ezekiel likewise receives his mission directive before the throne of God. Unlike Isaiah, who was brought to the throne, this time the throne of the Lord comes to the prophet in a vision by the river Chebar (Ezek 1:1-14, 26-28; 10:1). The description utilizes vocabulary familiar to Yahweh's appearances at Sinai (Ex 19:16-18; 20:18; 24:9-11, 17; Deut 4:36) (Miller 1965) and the throne room description of the divine council meeting in Daniel (Dan 7:9-10). The enthroned Yahweh commands Ezekiel to stand and receive his commission (Ezek 2:1-3) to a defeated but still rebellious people (Ezek 2:4-7).

Like Isaiah and Ezekiel, the prophet Jeremiah was commissioned in a direct encounter with God. In Jeremiah 1 we read that at the beginning of the prophet's ministry the "word of the LORD" came to him (Jer 1:4) to appoint him a prophet. The theophany becomes even more dramatic as the passage continues, where the "word" is identified as Yahweh (Jer 1:6-7), who has come in human corporeal form, reaching out his hand to touch Jeremiah's mouth (Jer 1:9). This dramatic call legitimized Jeremiah's status as a prophet. Jeremiah 23 reveals that God judges a prophet false who has never "stood in the council of the LORD" (Jer 23:16, 18). The Lord declares of false prophets, "If they had stood in my council, then they would have proclaimed my words to my people, and they would have turned them from their evil way, and from the evil of their deeds" (Jer 23:22). The implication is clear: true prophets have appeared before the divine council, whereas false prophets have not.

3. The Divine Council as Divine Warriors in the Prophets.

Prophetic declarations of eschatological holy *war also involve the divine council (Miller 1968). The divine council (along with human warriors) forms a cosmic army on the Day of the Lord in the writings of the prophets (Is 13:1-8; Joel 3:11-12; Zech 14:1-5). This language is in turn drawing upon other material in the Hebrew Bible that casts the divine council as an army (Deut 33:1-5; 2 Kings 6:15-17; Ps 68:16-17). This context also adds nuance to the common title for Israel's God, "Lord of hosts," for "host" (ṣābāʾ) is a word used frequently in the Hebrew Bible for a military force (e.g., 2 Sam 3:23; Ps 108:12).

See also ANGELS, MESSENGERS, HEAVENLY BEINGS; CALL/COMMISSION NARRATIVES.

BIBLIOGRAPHY. **D. E. Bokovy,** "Invoking the Council as Witnesses in Amos 3:13," *JBL* 127 (2008) 37-51; **R. Clifford,** *The Cosmic Mountain in Canaan and the Old Testament* (HSM 4; Cambridge, MA: Harvard University Press, 1972); **F. M. Cross,** "The Council of Yahweh in Second Isaiah," *JNES* 12 (1953) 274-77; **L. Handy,** *Among the Host of Heaven: The Syro-Palestinian Pantheon as Bureaucracy* (Winona Lake, IN: Eisenbrauns, 1994); **M. S. Heiser,** "Divine Council," *DOTWPW* 112-16; idem, "Monotheism, Polytheism, Monolatry, or Henotheism? Toward an Assessment of Divine Plurality in the Hebrew Bible" *BBR* 18 (2008) 1-30; **E. Kingsbury,** "The Prophets and the Council of Yahweh," *JBL* 83 (1964) 279-86; **P. D. Miller,** "Fire in the Mythology of Canaan and Israel," *CBQ* 27 (1965) 256-61; idem, "The Divine Council and the Prophetic Call to War," *VT* 18 (1968) 100-107; idem, "Cosmology and World Order in the Old Testament: The Divine Council as Cosmic-Political Symbol," in *Israelite Religion and Biblical Theology: Collected Essays* (JSOTSup 267; Sheffield: Sheffield Academic, 2000), 422-44; **E. T. Mullen Jr.,** *The Divine Council in Canaanite and Early Hebrew Literature* (HSM 24; Chico, CA: Scholars Press, 1980); idem, "Divine Assembly," *ABD* 2:214-17; **K. Nielsen,** "Oak," *DDD* 637; idem, "Terebinth," *DDD* 851; **M. Nissinen,** "Prophets and the Divine Council," in *Kein Land für sich allein: Studien zum Kulturkontakt in Kanaan, Israel/Palästina und Ebirnari für Manfred Weippert zum 65. Geburtstag,* ed. U. Hübner and E. Knauf (OBO 186; Göttingen: Vandenhoeck & Ruprecht, 2002) 4-19; **C. R. Seitz,**

"The Divine Council: Temporal Transition and New Prophecy in the Book of Isaiah," *JBL* 109 (1990) 229-47.

M. S. Heiser

DIVINE PRESENCE

Each section of the Hebrew Bible alludes to the divine presence, that aspect of deity that R. Otto calls the *mysterium tremendum et fascinans* (Otto, 12-41). Whether defined as the object causing the numinous experience (Tracy, 174-76) or the numinous experience itself (Otto, 12-35), the divine presence in the Pentateuch engages a number of characters (Terrien, 63-160), while the Writings abstractly reflect on it in the lyrical (Ps 10:1; 18:1-3), lament (Lam 1:2, 21), apocalyptic (Dan 9:20) and wisdom traditions (Job 28; Prov 8). Whereas an earlier generation claims that no deity but Yahweh deliberately "hides himself" (*mistattēr* [Is 45:15]) (Miskotte, 267), contemporary readers counter that a growing mass of literary evidence, combined with a growing appreciation for the peculiarities distinguishing the methods used by historians versus theologians, nullifies such a claim (Podella, 33-70; Kutsko, 157-69; Burnett, 2). Aware of these developments, the following survey lists some of the more prominent ways in which the presence-absence polarity operates within the Prophets.

1. Imag(in)ing the Divine Presence
2. Prophetic Encounters with the Divine Presence
3. Summary

1. Imag(in)ing the Divine Presence.

Most references to "the presence" in English Bibles derive from translations of the Hebrew noun *pānîm* (*plurale tantum*), both in its nominal as well as its prepositional formulations (Simian-Yofre, 608-14). Cognate usage occurs in Ugaritic (*pnm* [*CAT* 1.2 iii 4]), Moabite (*lpny kmš*, "Chemosh's presence" [*KAI* 181:13, 18]), Akkadian (*panū* [pl.], the moon-god Sin's "presence," [*Erra Epic* 2C:15]), Aramaic (*pnh* [*DNWSI* 918]), Phoenician (*lpnm* [*KAI* 26A ii 4]), Punic (*pn bʿl*, "countenance of Baal," referring to the goddess Tannit [*KAI* 78:2]) and Qumranian Hebrew texts (*lpnwhy* [1QS 6:26), so the fact that similar parameters envelop the semantic possibilities of Hebrew *pānîm* comes as no surprise (*HAL* 887-90).

Overlapping the semantic field of Hebrew *pānîm* stands the semantic field of Hebrew *kābad* ("to honor, glorify") and its nominal derivative *kābôd* ("glory, honor") (Weinfeld, 27-37). Akkadian cognates appear in the Creation Epic to describe Marduk as greatly "honored" among the gods (*kabātu* [*Enuma Elish* 4:3, 5]), and ancient Near Eastern scribes often depict their deities (and the monarchs representing them) with crowned heads radiating fiery "auras" (Akk *melammū*). The moon-god Sin, for example, wears such an aura (*KAR* 69:22), as does the war-god Assur (*CAD* "M/2:10") and the scorpion monsters confronting Gilgamesh (*Epic of Gilgamesh* 9:44). It also appears in the Canaanite glosses from Amarna animating mayor Biridiya's complaint that Pharaoh "honors" (*kabādu*) those of his neighbors who maliciously treat him, Pharaoh's loyal servant, with contempt (EA 245:39). Similarly, Hebrew *kābôd* describes the terrifying glory and awesome majesty of Yahweh's divine presence (Weinfeld, 29).

2. Prophetic Encounters with the Divine Presence.

2.1. Moses. Following the spectacular theophanic events on Mount Sinai (Ex 20–33), Moses' face radiates a supernatural aura of its own as he descends the mountain to begin leading the Hebrews on a prolonged trek through the wilderness, an idyllic time (Ps 105; Jer 2:1-3; Hos 2:14-15) in which "prophetic revelations" (Knohl, 74) occur to him in a "tent of meeting" (*ʾōhel mōʿēd*) through "face to face" (*pānîm ʾel-pānîm*) encounters (Ex 33:11). Portrayed as the "ideal mediatorial figure" (Orlov, 184) (see Deut 18:15), Moses participates in the first of these encounters, in Exodus 33:13-20, as follows (see Seebass, 328-30):

Moses: "If I have found favor in your sight, let me know your ways, so that I may (continue to) know you."

God: "My presence [*pānay*] will walk [pl., *yēlēkû*; LXX adds 'before you']. . . ."

Moses: "If your presence [*pānêkā*] does not walk [pl., *hōlēkîm*], . . . how will it be known whether I have found favor? . . ."

God: "All right, I will do this thing you ask. . . ."

Moses: "Please, let me see your glory [*kēbōdekā*]."

God: "My goodness [*ṭûbî*] will pass before you. . . . But you cannot see my presence [*pānay*]."

Several things occur in this paradigmatic encounter, not least the prophet's demand that the wilderness trek be aborted until or unless the divine presence promises to provide it with hands-on leadership, not through angelic (or any other) mediation, but directly through "his presence" (*pānāyw* [Deut 4:37]) (Knapp, 108). All future prophetic encounters tend to refer, in varying degrees, to this paradigmatic encounter of Moses with the divine presence in the wilderness.

2.2. Samuel. Entering Canaan, the Hebrews continue following the divine presence hovering over the tabernacle (cloud by day, pillar of fire by night), but not to the indigenously Canaanite "high places" (*bāmôt*). Extending the space provided within the original "tent of meeting," the divine presence soon comes to inhabit another "place" (*māqôm*), one specially designed to house the Name (Deut 12:5-18), the "tabernacle" (*miškān* [Ex 25:9]) (Langer, 21-23; Weinfeld, 36-37), followed by the *temple (1 Kings 8:1-13) (Moore 2003, 233-37). Because of the ubiquitous temptation to *idolatry, all Hebrew cultic activity—feasting, fasting, tithing, Levitical benevolence—is carefully delimited to this firmly boundaried "place" (Deut 14:23; 15:20; 16:11; 18:7), cemented in Deuteronomy via name-dwelling formulae like those inscribed on Mesopotamian monuments (Richter, 204-6).

Unlike Moses, Samuel does not engage the divine presence visually. According to 1 Samuel 3:1, visions have become "rare" (*yāqār* [i.e., they no longer "break through," *niprāṣ*]). Instead, the primary channel for prophetic communication becomes the divine voice (1 Sam 3:1-10), thereby confirming and conforming to the polarity generally presumed throughout the prophetic corpus: northern prophets tend to receive auditions, while southern prophets tend to experience *visions (Wilson, 135-296). Later, when Samuel calls "all Israel" to a cultic ceremony at Mizpah involving communal fasting and the pouring out of water, the text explicitly locates this activity "in the presence" (1 Sam 7:6). Ascertaining by lottery the identity of the first Hebrew king, Samuel then writes down the "kingship laws" (*mišpaṭ hammělukâ*) and deposits them in a safe place "in Yahweh's presence" (*lipnê yhwh* [the ark of the covenant?]) before anointing Saul king (1 Sam 10:25; 11:15). Fleeing for their lives, David and his men eat the "bread of the Presence" (*leḥem happānîm*) at a Yahweh shrine in a small village while fleeing the wrath of this Hebrew king (1 Sam 21:6).

2.3. Elijah. Like the Mosaic "tent of meeting" and tabernacle, Solomon's temple provides another holy "place" for the divine presence to encounter the Hebrews on a regular basis. On the day of the temple's inauguration, in fact, another wilderness-like cloud appears, a nimbus so opaque that the priests in the temple cannot see well enough to perform their duties (1 Kings 8:11). When Elijah takes on the Baal priests, the divine presence descends on Mount Carmel to support him via another wilderness symbol, a column of heavenly fire (Ps 50:3). Later, a number of meteorological disturbances occur before Elijah on Mount Horeb (1 Kings 18—19) before a heavenly chariot descends to carry him off into the heavens (2 Kings 2:11) (Moore 2003, 97-102; 279-84; Tabor, 92).

2.4. Isaiah. After Israel splits into "two nations under God," Judah's predilection to divorce laissez-faire worship from *covenant ethics soon causes Yahweh to ask, "When you come to see my Presence [*lērāʾôt pānāy*], who seeks this from your hand?" (Is 1:12). The demonstrative pronoun in this question refers to the plethora of butchered animals, exotic incense and pagan rituals to which so many Judahites have addicted themselves in lieu of covenant justice (Is 1:10-17). Such behavior makes the Presence so "weary" that he soon finds himself "averting my eyes" and "closing my ears," even when his children cry and plead and scream for help (Is 1:14-15).

The call narrative in Isaiah preserves one of the clearest depictions of the Presence in the entire Bible (Is 6:1-5). Unlike the Ephraimite Samuel's prophetic encounter with the divine voice, the southern prophet Isaiah sees something (Wilson, 135-296). Unlike Moses' vision of the divine "back," the vision that Isaiah sees is of a Being so huge that just the hem of his robe "fills" (*mělēʾîm*) the temple (Is 6:1), though, as with the Mosaic theophany, the specific contours are carefully and strategically "occluded" (*yěkasseh pānāyw*) (Is 6:2 [LXX pl., *katekalypton*]) by strange winged creatures (*śěrāpîm*) whose function may be modeled after creatures and characterizations preserved in much older Canaanite texts (Day, 149-51). Isaiah's inaugural vision intertextually parallels Ezekiel's vision at the river Chebar (Ezek 1:1—2:10), but attempts to make it parallel Elijah's heavenly ascent are considerably less certain (*pace* Tabor, 92).

More convincing are the intratextual parallels generated by the oracles of comfort and renewal in Isaiah 40—55, especially those alluding to the "wilderness sojourn" in Isaiah 40—44 (Westermann, 29-41; Evans, 49). Identifying Israel as a "light to the nations" (Is 42:7), Yahweh assures his servant (Is 42:1) that the glory responsible for radiating this light is of divine origin and is available to no nation other than Israel (Is 42:8, repeated verbatim in Is 48:11). To a postexilic audience struggling to understand its newly reinforced, overtly missional identity, this evidently needs stating and restating (see, e.g., Is 58:8). Even when "thick darkness" covers the earth, Israel's light shines so brightly that it cannot be dimmed. The divine glory is simply too powerful to allow this to happen (Is 60:1-2). Having spent decades in Gentile captivity, newly freed Israel's challenge is to reflect this glory in ways that can heal the broken, enable the poor, and liberate the imprisoned (Is 61:3).

Reprising the wilderness experience, Isaiah foretells a time when Jerusalem will be cleansed by fire, after which the divine glory will become manifest through yet another cloud, this one over Mount Zion (Is 24:23). This cloud is to be protected by a "covering" described in Isaiah 4:5-6 by four synonymous terms: huppâ ("canopy"), sukkâ ("pavilion"), ṣēl ("shade") and maḥseh ("refuge") (see Evans, 48-50). Each of these nouns has roots in the bedrock of the Hebrew wilderness tradition (Frankel, 31-37; Moore 2009, 189-92), yet beyond its appearance to Judah (Is 2:19-21), the "Presence of Yahweh's terror" (pĕnê paḥad yhwh [Is 2:10]) will appear to Tyre (Is 23:18) as well as Egypt (Is 19:16-17). With these promises Isaiah broadens and redefines the character of the Presence, not only in terms of comfort and protection, but also in categories involving the use of terror and "trembling" (rāgaz [Is 64:2; cf. Jer 5:22]) (Muntingh, 157-58).

2.5. Jeremiah. Like Kings, the book of Jeremiah focuses attention on the divine assembly as a holy place to which only true prophets have access (*see* Divine Council). Whereas Micaiah ben Imlah narrates the inner workings of this assembly from the perspective of an eyewitness (1 Kings 22:15-28) (Moore 2003, 126-31), Jeremiah categorically asserts that false prophets, by definition, are charlatans without access to the divine assembly (Jer 23:16-18). The Book of Consolation (Jer 30—33) elaborates this by listing a number of divine promises, one formulated in the binary language of legal analogy: (1) as surely as the sun, moon and stars are "fixed orders" (ḥuqqot, a term used to describe "legal statutes" in Ex 12:14, 17; Ezek 44:5 [see *HAL* 333]) in the cosmos, so (2) Israel stands as a "nation in my Presence" (gôy lĕpānay, Jer 31:35-36). The conclusion to the Book of Consolation reinforces this analogy through repetition: (1) just as surely as "my covenant" establishes "day and night" as "fixed orders" (ḥuqqot), so (2) it is impossible for the Presence to reject his people or fail to restore their fortunes (Jer 33:10-25). How this will occur, exactly, is postponed until Ezekiel lays out the schematic blueprints of the new temple (Ezek 40—48), but to refugees weary of foreign laws and foreign customs, assurances like this go a long way toward aiding the process of identity reformation, not to mention the reclamation of political, socioeconomic and religious confidence. Thus, Jeremiah not only "addresses survivors for whom disaster has become a permanent reality," he also "offers grounds for reconstituting the character of the (returning Jewish) community" (O'Connor, 88).

2.6. Ezekiel and Habakkuk. Whereas Moses comes closer than most other prophets to experiencing the fullness of the divine presence, Ezekiel comes closest to feeling the full force of the divine absence. Jeremiah partially feels this absence in his *laments, especially those preserved in Jeremiah 17—20 (Diamond, 140-44), but Ezekiel experiences the shock of seeing the divine glory rise up and leave the temple (Ezek 10:18-22) (Weinfeld, 27-33). Whereas Jonah flees the divine presence for a little while (Jon 1:3, 10), Ezekiel not only watches it spectacularly arrive (Ezek 1:1-28), he also watches it spectacularly leave. Why does it leave? Because the divine presence cannot cohabit a "place" completely filled with *"idols" (Ezek 6:4-6; 14:3-7 ["idols" are always gillûlîm in Ezekiel, never ᵓĕlōhîm]). Thus, since the divine presence cannot dwell in the midst of other "presences," absence, by default, becomes the only option (Kutsko, 25-76). Nevertheless, in spite of all this, Ezekiel dares to dream of a day when the divine glory will return and bring Israel back to life like fresh water in dry desert (Ezek 43:4; 47:1-12), a day when all discourse about the returning glory will resonate with "God himself dwelling in the Temple, expressed in such a way that his transcendence is safeguarded" (Cody, 220).

That the prophets would so readily agree with Habakkuk's catchphrase ("Yahweh is in his holy temple; let all the earth keep silence before him" [Hab 2:20]) might at first glance seem more than a little incongruous. After all, many cultures view prophecy as something peripheral to the concerns of central institutions such as temple cults (Wilson, 32-42). Yet peripheral intermediaries sometimes gravitate toward the center, and this tends to cause varying degrees of ambivalence between prophets and priests. Ezekiel is a classic example of this ambivalence (Wilson, 282-86).

2.7. Haggai and Zechariah. The book of Haggai opens with pointed descriptions of the contemptuous attitudes adopted by many returned exiles with regard to the prospect of rebuilding the Jerusalem temple. Evidently, many of these refugees have come to believe that the divine glory has forever abandoned them, never to return. This would explain why so many begin to think that the temple should not be rebuilt, and that what might be rebuilt will doubtless be embarrassingly insignificant. Haggai forthrightly challenges these objections by repeatedly voicing the determination of the divine presence in their midst: "I am with you" (Hag 1:13; 2:4), and "My spirit abides among you" (Hag 2:5). The effect of these reassurances translates into an immediate increase in motivation among many of these refugees, albeit without eliminating all of their detractors (Neh 4:1-23) (Assis, 582-96).

To those who doubt the whereabouts of the divine presence, the prophet Zechariah observes in his first night vision a decision on Yahweh's behalf to "return to Jerusalem" and "build a house" (Zech 1:16). Each of the following night visions corroborates this intention. Four blacksmiths rise up to pulverize the four horns responsible for expelling Judah from the land (Zech 1:18-21). A man with a measuring line discovers so much life in the new Jerusalem that the only "wall" large enough to protect it is the glory of Yahweh himself (Zech 2:5). Should the high priest Joshua behave appropriately, Yahweh promises to grant "rights of passage" (*mahlĕkîm* [the same term as in Ezek 42:4]) inside the precincts of the new temple (Zech 3:7). Two olive trees representing the political and religious arms of Israel's new government will faithfully communicate Yahweh's in-

tentions. The terrifying side of the divine presence also makes itself known, first as a flying scroll whose mission is to "abide" in the houses of liars and thieves until they are consumed, then as a woman in a basket (named "Wickedness") who is taken to Babylon and deposited there in her own "house." Finally, four chariots pulled by four horses will continue to patrol the earth in order to "set my spirit at rest" (Zech 6:8).

3. Summary.
Powerful as it may be, the Hebrew concept of divine absence does not identically overlap the Christian concept of *deus absconditus*, especially as the latter is articulated in the writings of the medieval reformer Martin Luther. Whereas the OT concept presupposes the Deity's unwillingness to be present in the midst of other "presences" (Kutsko, 151), the NT concept presupposes the power of the presence at the cross, the only point on the Christian spatiotemporal continuum where the *deus absconditus* and the *deus revelatus* mysteriously intersect (Kattenbusch, 204). Whereas the latter grounds itself in the mystery of vicarious messianic atonement, the former grounds itself in the bond of eternal covenant (*bĕrît ʿôlām*) (Polaski, 143-45), a theological idea in which eternal abandonment is not just impossible, but inconceivable.

See also GOD; IDOLS, IDOLATRY, GODS; SPIRIT OF YAHWEH; TEMPLE; WORSHIP.

BIBLIOGRAPHY. **E. Assis,** "A Disputed Temple (Haggai 2,1-9)," *ZAW* 120 (2008) 582-96; **J. S. Burnett,** *Where Is God? Divine Absence in the Hebrew Bible* (Minneapolis: Fortress, 2010); **A. Cody,** *Ezekiel: With an Excursus on Old Testament Priesthood* (OTMes 11; Wilmington, DE: Michael Glazier, 1984); **J. Day,** "Echoes of Baal's Seven Thunders and Lightnings in Psalm 29 and Habakkuk 3:9 and the Identity of the Seraphim in Isaiah 6," *VT* 29 (1979) 143-51; **A. R. Diamond,** *The Confessions of Jeremiah in Context: Scenes of Prophetic Drama* (JSOTSup 45; Sheffield: JSOT, 1987); **C. A. Evans,** "Jesus, John, and the Dead Sea Scrolls: Assessing Typologies of Restoration," in *Christian Beginnings and the Dead Sea Scrolls*, ed. J. J. Collins and C. A. Evans (Grand Rapids: Baker Academic, 2006) 45-62; **D. Frankel,** "Two Priestly Conceptions of Guidance in the Wilderness," *JSOT* 81 (1998) 31-37; **F. Kattenbusch,** "*Deus Absconditus* bei Luther," in *Festgabe für D. Dr. Julius Kaftan zu* *seinem 70. Geburtstag* (Tübingen: Mohr, 1920) 170-214; **D. Knapp,** *Deuteronomium 4: Literarische Analyse und theologische Interpretation* (GTA 35; Göttingen: Vandenhoeck & Ruprecht, 1987); **I. Knohl,** "Two Aspects of the 'Tent of Meeting,'" in *Tehilla le-Mosheh: Biblical and Judaic Studies in Honor of Moshe Greenberg,* ed. M. Cogan (Winona Lake, IL: Eisenbrauns, 1997) 73-79; **J. F. Kutsko,** *Between Heaven and Earth: Divine Presence and Absence in the Book of Ezekiel* (BibJudS 7; Winona Lake, IN: Eisenbrauns, 2000); **G. Langer,** *Von Gott erwählt—Jerusalem: Die Rezeption von Dtn 12 im frühen Judentum* (OBSt 8; Klosterneuburg: Verlag Österreichisches Katholisches Bibelwerk, 1989); **K. H. Miskotte,** *When the Gods are Silent,* trans. J. W. Doberstein (New York: Harper & Row, 1967); **M. S. Moore,** *Faith under Pressure: A Study of Biblical Leaders in Conflict* (Siloam Springs, AR: Leafwood, 2003); idem, "Numbers," in *The Transforming Word: One-Volume Commentary on the Bible,* ed. M. A. Hamilton (Abilene, TX: Abilene Christian University Press, 2009) 185-202; **L. M. Muntingh,** "Fear of Yahweh and Fear of the Gods according to Isaiah and Qohelet," in *Studies in Isaiah,* ed. W. C. van Wyk (Pretoria West: NHW, 1980) 143-58; **K. M. O'Connor,** "The Book of Jeremiah: Reconstructing Community after Disaster," in *Character Ethics and the Old Testament: Moral Dimensions of Scripture,* ed. M. D. Carroll R. and J. E. Lapsley (Louisville: Westminster/John Knox, 2007) 81-92; **A. Orlov,** "In the Mirror of the Divine Face: The Enochic Features of the *Exagoge* of Ezekiel the Tragedian," in *The Significance of Sinai: Traditions about Sinai and Divine Revelation in Judaism and Christianity,* ed. G. J. Brooke, H. Najman and L. Stuckenbruck (TBN 12; Leiden: E. J. Brill, 2008) 183-200; **R. Otto,** *The Idea of the Holy: An Inquiry into the Non-Rational Factor in the Idea of the Divine and Its Relation to the Rational,* trans. J. W. Harvey (London: Oxford University Press, 1923); **T. Podella,** Ṣôm-*Fasten: Kollektive Trauer um den verborgenen Gott im Alten Testament* (AOAT 224; Kevelaer: Butzon & Bercker; Neukirchen-Vluyn: Neukirchener Verlag, 1989); **D. C. Polaski,** *Authorizing an End: The Isaiah Apocalypse and Intertextuality* (BIS 50; Leiden: E. J. Brill, 2000); **S. L. Richter,** *The Deuteronomistic History and the Name Theology: lᵉšakkēn šᵉmô šām in the Bible and the Ancient Near East* (BZAW 318; Berlin: de Gruyter, 2002); **H. Seebass,** "Mose in einem seiner Ausnahmegespräche mit Gott: Zu Exod 33,12-23," in *Gott und Mensch im Dialog: Festschrift für Otto Kaiser zum 80. Geburtstag,* ed. M. Witte (2 vols.; BZAW 345; Berlin: de Gruyter, 2004) 1:301-31; **H. Simian-Yofre,** "פָּנִים," *TDOT* 11:589-615; **J. D. Tabor,** "Heaven, Ascent to," *ABD* 3:91-94; **S. Terrien,** *The Elusive Presence: Toward a New Biblical Theology* (San Francisco: Harper & Row, 1978); **D. C. Tracy,** *The Analogical Imagination: Christian Theology and the Culture of Pluralism* (New York: Crossroad, 1981); **M. Weinfeld,** "כָּבוֹד," *TDOT* 7:22-38; **C. Westermann,** *Das Buch Jesaja: Kapitel 40-66* (ATD 19; Göttingen: Vandenhoeck & Ruprecht, 1981); **P. J. Williams,** "Lying Spirits Sent by God? The Case of Micaiah's Prophecy," in *The Trustworthiness of God: Perspectives on the Nature of Scripture,* ed. P. Helm and C. R. Trueman (Grand Rapids: Eerdmans, 2002) 58-66; **R. R. Wilson,** *Prophecy and Society in Ancient Israel* (Philadelphia: Fortress, 1980).   M. S. Moore

DIVINE WARFARE. *See* WARFARE AND DIVINE WARFARE.

DIVINE WARRIOR. *See* COSMOLOGY; WARFARE AND DIVINE WARFARE.

DIVORCE. *See* MARRIAGE AND DIVORCE.

DRAMA, PROPHETIC. *See* SIGN ACTS.

E

ECONOMIC JUSTICE. *See* SOCIAL JUSTICE; WEALTH AND POVERTY.

EDITORIAL/REDACTION CRITICISM

Editorial or redaction criticism is a tool of biblical study that investigates the manner in which biblical authors/editors employ and shape their sources in developing their own message. It focuses on the placement of the traditions as well as differences in perspective between redactors and their sources. First used in NT studies, it has become widely used in OT studies as well. The following discussion first describes the rise and use of redaction criticism out of previously existing methods, and then it illustrates the use of the method by scholars investigating the Major Prophets and the Minor Prophets of the Bible.

1. The Rise and Use of Redaction Criticism
2. Formulae Used by Redactors
3. Quotations, Citations, Allusions and Catchwords Used by Redactors
4. Themes, Structures and Indications of Time Used by Redactors
5. The Redaction of the Prophetic Books as Wholes
6. Conclusion

1. The Rise and Use of Redaction Criticism.

1.1. The Rise of the Method. Strictly speaking, an emphasis on oral tradition, such as that of the so-called Scandinavian school of scholars (e.g., I. Engnell, E. Nielsen, G. Widengren), is not part of redaction criticism, though the Scandinavians were important in moving OT scholarship beyond source criticism and its concentration on underlying written documents. An advance toward redaction criticism

occurred when M. Noth argued that the Pentateuch was comprised of five previously independent collections of traditions dealing with the patriarchs, the exodus, the wandering in the wilderness, the conquest and the giving of the law. Another step was the work of G. von Rad, who argued that the themes of the Pentateuch were arranged following the confession found in Deuteronomy 26:5-9. It begins with Abraham, continues with the oppression in Egypt, the exodus, and ends with the entry into Canaan (conveniently summarized in von Rad, 1:121-28). Interest in the editors or redactors of OT books had been born, and a number of scholars took up the task of studying them under the method called "tradition history" (see Rast). Those scholars also studied the reuse of earlier traditions in later passages. The term "redaction history," however, appeared in connection with the work of three NT scholars after WWII: G. Bornkamm on the Gospel of Matthew, H. Conzelmann on the Gospel of Luke, and W. Marxsen on the Gospel of Mark (Perrin, 25-39). Their work proved so insightful that OT scholars began using both their method and its name.

1.2. The Use of the Method. Redaction criticism focuses on the work of editors in texts. Although writing is quite old in the Middle East, reaching back to the ancient Phoenicians, early efforts dealt mainly with records, wills and official documents. It is probably not accidental that the "writing prophets" appeared beginning in the eighth century BC, the time when public *writing blossomed in ancient Israel (Schmid, 44). Short versions of what earlier prophets said might have been transmitted orally alongside accounts of their deeds (esp. Elijah and Elisha), but nothing like Amos or Hosea, let alone the sixty-six-chapter book of Isaiah, arose before the eighth century BC. These collections, moreover, seem to have grown over time, as source critics demonstrated long ago. The growth of the prophetic books also left a trail that can be traced by redaction critics.

How, then, do such scholars work? Simply put, they look for signs of editing/redaction, including superscriptions (e.g., "The Book of the Vision of Nahum"), incipits or introductory sentences (e.g., "In the eighth month, in the second, year of Darius, the word of the LORD came to the prophet Zechariah" [Zech 1:1]), introductory formulae (e.g., "Thus says the LORD"), concluding formulae (e.g., "says the LORD"), quotations of earlier texts (e.g. Ex 34:6-7/Num 14:18/Deut 7:10 in whole or in part in Joel 2:13; Jon 4:2; Mic 7:18; Nah 1:2-3) and allusions to earlier texts (e.g., Zech 3:10, on which the postexilic Mic 4:4 depends) (Redditt 2008b, 72). In addition, they note the arrangement of materials.

Redaction critics, thus, may well employ the results of the use of other methods (including source and *form criticism), but with the intention of determining what redactors started with and how they modified it. Redaction critics also reckon with the possibility of a series of redactors at work in a book. The books of *Isaiah and *Daniel and the Book of the *Twelve in particular seem to have undergone stages of growth over several centuries (for a summary of redactional techniques observable in the Book of the Twelve, see Redditt 2003, 12-15). The remainder of this article, then, illustrates the types of redactional indicators discerned within the Major and the Minor Prophets of the Old Testament canon and how redaction critics use those indicators.

2. Formulae Used by Redactors.

2.1. Superscripts. Many of the Prophetic Books open with a superscription—that is, a heading that divulges something about what follows, commonly the names of the putative prophet whose message is being conveyed (modern scholars do not necessarily agree that everything that follows such a superscription necessarily derived from the prophet named). They are Isaiah 1:1; Jeremiah 1:1-3; Ezekiel 1:2-3; Hosea 1:1; Joel 1:1; Amos 1:1; Obadiah 1:1a; Micah 1:1; Nahum 1:1 (which actually contains two different superscripts); Habakkuk 1:1,

Zephaniah 1:1; Malachi 1:1 (again two superscripts). Superscripts for Isaiah, Jeremiah, Ezekiel, Hosea and Amos contain material that tell the reader something about the prophet to whom the messages are being ascribed, but the others list only the name and perhaps other pertinent information. Zephaniah, for example, begins as several others do: "The word of the LORD that came to Zephaniah son of Cushi" (Zeph 1:1). The name "Cushi," however, means "Ethiopian." A reader might wonder if such a person were indeed an authentic spokesperson for Judah's God, and so, one might presume, a redactor added the Yahwistic pedigree that follows, tracing the prophet back three more generations of men whose names ended in "iah" to someone named "Hezekiah" (the eighth-century BC king of Judah?). Thus, the superscription seeks to stamp the imprimatur of Yahweh on the collection of sayings of the prophet. Sometimes the superscript contains additional information, such as an indication of the time when the prophet flourished (Is 1:1; Jer 1:1-3; Ezek 1:2-3; Hos 1:1; Amos 1:1; Mic 1:1).

E. Conrad thinks that superscripts are heavily nuanced. He calls attention to the phrase "a vision of Isaiah" (Is 1:1; cf. Obad 1, Nah 1:1), arguing that the word for "vision" in these texts designates genuine *visions of God received in the temple. The phrase "the words of [the prophet]" regarding what the prophet saw in Jeremiah 1:1; Amos 1:1, as well as the designation "things seen" in Ezekiel 1:1, mark all three as "unconventional" prophets, clueing the informed reader of distinctions that are lost in English translation (see Conrad).

The books of Isaiah, Habakkuk and Zechariah contain internal superscriptions. Isaiah 2:1 at a minimum introduces a major section of the book, and at some point in the history of the growth of the book it may have stood at the beginning. Isaiah 13:1 introduces a prediction against Babylon, and it may well serve secondarily as the beginning of a collection of sayings against foreign nations. Isaiah 15:1; 17:1; 19:1; 21:1; 22:1; 23:1 also introduce short prophecies of destruction by identifying the persons/nations condemned in the following verses, with the last chapter closing that section of the book. Habakkuk 3:1 is clearly a superscription at home in the Psalter, suggesting that the song that follows was a later addition to Habakkuk. (One should note that the word *selâ* in Hab 3:3,

9 and 13 appears nowhere else in the Hebrew Bible outside of Psalms. Likewise, the subscript in Hab 3:19 is similar to the ending of a number of Psalms.) J. Roberts, however, insists that redactionally the song follows a pattern seen elsewhere in Habakkuk of a lament followed by a song of praise, and that it reports a visionary experience (Roberts, 148-51).

2.2. Incipits. Some of the Prophetic Books, however, begin with or contain elsewhere sentences that introduce the prophet to whom the words are ascribed. Examples include Ezekiel 1:1; Haggai 1:1; 2:1, 20; Zechariah 1:1, 7; 7:1. Like superscripts, they function to begin the recorded revelation, but they are part of the narrative. A comparison of Ezekiel 1:1 with Ezekiel 1:2-3 illuminates the difference.

2.3. Introductory Formulae. Prophetic messages within a given book often open with introductory formulae, some or many of which appear to be from a redactor. Form critics long ago called attention to the phrase "thus says Yahweh," which often introduces short prophetic utterances, often but not always predictions of doom. Perhaps the most famous redactional use of this formula is in Amos 1:3, 6, 9, 11, 13; 2:1, 4, 6. Critics have long noted that the seven states condemned in Amos 1—2 follow no particular order. The text jumps back and forth geographically, and some texts are more fully developed than others. J. Jeremias suggests the following history of the traditions. The initial arrangement included the threats against Damascus (Amos 1:3-5) and Ammon (Amos 1:13-15), both traditional enemies of the northern kingdom, plus the one against Israel (Amos 2:6-16). The sayings of Amos were collected in or brought to the south, to Judah, as is shown by the mention of southern kings in the superscript (Amos 1:1). When the collection came south, a later saying against Judah (Amos 2:4-5) was included to "update" Amos for southern readers. The final version of the book appeared in the exilic or Persian period. It added oracles against Gaza (Amos 1:5-8), Tyre (Amos 1:9-10), Edom (Amos 1:11-12) and Moab (Amos 2:1-3) (Jeremias, 25). The bitter enmity expressed against Edom arose as a consequence of Edom's conduct during the final siege of Jerusalem in 586 BC (see Obad 8-14, 19-21).

2.4. Concluding Formulae. At times, given prophetic passages may conclude with a formula. Often one finds *nĕʾum-yhwh*, "declaration of Yahweh" (e.g., Jer 2:3). This formula may stand alone or be further elaborated: "declaration of the LORD of hosts" (Is 17:3), "declaration of the Lord GOD" (Jer 2:22), "declaration the LORD God of Israel" (Is 17:6). Although the formula typically marks the end of a passage, it can appear in the middle (Jer 8:12), apparently to emphasize that what the prophet is saying is uttered under the impulse of God.

The book of Isaiah offers an example of a longer concluding phrase. The sentence "For all this his anger has not turned away, and his hand is stretched out still" appears in Isaiah 5:25; 9:12, 21; 10:4 (NRSV). Despite the present separation of the first from the last three of these texts, the repeated phrase suggests that at one time all of them stood together. The rhetorical effect of the phrase was powerful, and a redactor critic might offer something like the following explanation. The sayings explained catastrophes that had befallen both northern Israel and southern Judah by charging the people with sin. The sayings also warned that more divine punishment was in the offing if the sins continued. As the text stands now, however, the original connection among the four texts has been broken by the insertion of a much older collection (Is 6:1—8:21, if not Is 9:7) and the addition of a prediction of the defeat of Israel and Judah by Assyria because of their sins (Is 10:5-19). The earlier meaning and function of four passages inadequately anticipates the coming punishment by God at the hands of Assyria.

3. Quotations, Citations, Allusions and Catchwords Used by Redactors.

3.1. Definitions. Much recent redaction criticism has focused on the use of quotations, citations, allusions and catchwords, so it will be useful to define these. Quotations are direct quotes of enough words of a source in a new document to imply use. Well-known phrases (e.g., "thus says the LORD"), therefore, do not constitute quotations, though even relatively short, but striking or characteristic turns of phrasing might well. Citations are cases where a biblical author refers to another work but does not actually quote it. Allusions are implied or indirect references by one work to another. Finally, catchwords are devices whereby an author picks up a word from one line and repeats it in a later line. In cases of alleged *intertextual borrowing, R. Schultz argues, one "should look for indications of *contextual awareness*, including *interpretive re-use*, which indicates verbal *dependence* which is conscious and purposeful" (Schultz, 32).

3.2. Quotations. One of the most important examples of quotations in the prophets is the use of Exodus 34:6-7/Numbers 14:18/Deuteronomy 7:10 in whole or in part in Joel 2:13; Jonah 4:2; Micah 7:18; Nahum 1:2-3. Each text gives the quotation the text's own particular emphasis, but the use of the confession of faith at least forms a theme within the Book of the Twelve. N. Lane, moreover, in a paper delivered at the 2008 Annual Meeting of the Society of Biblical Literature, pointed out that in the sequence of the collections in the LXX the four citations appear much closer together than they do in the MT, where they are spread out over twenty-three chapters. The LXX sequence for the first seven of the twelve is Hosea, Amos, Micah, Joel, Obadiah, Jonah and Nahum. In the LXX all four quotations appear within only ten chapters. Moreover, Joel ends (Joel 3:19-21 [MT 4:19-21]) by contrasting the futures of Edom and Judah, which is the subject matter of Obadiah, surely sufficient reason for a redactor to place Joel directly ahead of Obadiah. J. Nogalski has argued persuasively that the sequence in the MT is original (Nogalski 1993b, 48-57, 274-78), so a redaction critic might wonder if the new order for the twelve in the LXX might have been guided at least in part by a desire to highlight the quotation from Exodus.

3.3. Citations. Hosea 6:5 employs a citation. The verse speaks of the prophets (not named) whom God used to hew Israel. The reader must supply the identity of the prophets in question and the content of their message. Amos 6:5 employs another citation. There the prophet criticizes wealthy people who recline on beds of ivory, lounge on their couches, and "sing idle songs to the sound of the harp, and like David improvise on instruments of music" (NRSV). The verse draws upon David's reputation as a musician (cf. 1 Sam 18:10-11; 19:9-10).

3.4. Allusions. Two example of the use of allusions must suffice. One clear example is the prediction of a "new covenant" in Jeremiah 31:31-34. Nowhere do the verses quote anything in Exodus through Deuteronomy (the "old covenant"), but the verses draw a clear contrast between the Sinai covenant and the covenant that

God was about to make with Judah. Also, Isaiah 43:1-2 reuses both the creation and the exodus motif in promising the captives in Babylon that God would recreate them.

3.5. Catchwords. Catchwords often appear within a given saying (e.g., Is 24:4, 18- 20), and Nogalski has argued that a whole series of catchwords ties together the collections that form the Book of the Twelve (Nogalski 1993a, 20-57). A word or several words used late in a given collection will be picked up and reused early in the next. One case is the odd mention of strangers "casting lots" for Jerusalem in Obadiah 11, followed a few verses later in Jonah 1:7 by the more logical mention of sailors casting lots to discern who on board was responsible for the savage storm threatening to wreck the ship carrying the prophet (Nogalski 1993a, 33). Another case involves catchwords between the end of Micah and the opening of Nahum. Three examples must suffice. First is the use of the question "who is a god like you?" in Micah 7:18, followed by the confession four verses later in Nahum 1:2, which says: "A God jealous and avenging is Yahweh." In that same context, both Micah 7:18 and Nahum 1:8 speak of God's "passing over." Finally, Micah 7:14 speaks of "Carmel" and "Bashan," as does Nahum 1:4 as well (Nogalski 1993a, 37-39). Proof is perhaps not possible here, but certainly it appears as if the end of Micah and the beginning of Nahum were edited to fit together.

4. Themes, Structures and Indications of Time Used by Redactors.

4.1. Themes. The Book of the Twelve again offers a wealth of examples of the use of common themes. Nogalski lists four that occur repeatedly in the Book of the Twelve: (1) the day of Yahweh (e.g., Joel 2:1-11; Zech 1:2-6); (2) fertility of the land or lack thereof as the punishment of God (e.g., Joel 1:2-2:17; Hag 1:6, 10-11); (3) the fate of God's people (positively, e.g., Mal 3:10; Joel 2:14; negatively, repeatedly in Hosea through Zephaniah, e.g., Hos 4:1-3; Zeph 1:4-6); (4) theodicy (extensively through the use of the confession in Exod 34:6-7) (Nogalski 2007).

4.2. Structures. In addition to recognizing themes in shaping a work, redaction critics may also recognize structures. One favorite structure in the prophets is that of chiasmus, a pattern whereby a passage returns to its starting place. A brief schema showing how the two collections Nahum and Habakkuk fit together as a chiasmus will illustrate (Christensen):

A. Hymn of theophany (Nahum 1)
    B. Taunt song against Nineveh
      (Nahum 2—3)
        X. The problem of theodicy
          (Habakkuk 1:1—2:5)
    B'. Taunt song against the "wicked
      one" (Habakkuk 2:6-20)
A'. Hymn of theophany (Habakkuk 3)

Another device used frequently by biblical redactors in arranging prophetic texts is the sequence of doom followed by hope. K. Cuffey finds four basic sections in Micah as it stands. Each section is developed in terms of doom and hope; each doom section specifies punishment, and each hope passage contains a promise. The following outline demonstrates that structure (based on Cuffey, but with themes reflecting the reading of Micah in Redditt 2008a, 269):

Theme: Micah 1:2—2:13. Honesty and justice among the people
Doom: Micah 1:2—2:11. *Punishment* for social sins committed by the wealthy
Hope: Micah 2:12-13. *Promise* in 2:12-13: God will gather a remnant
Theme: Micah 3:1—4:8. Honesty and justice among the leaders
Doom: Micah 3:1-12. *Punishment* against rulers, prophets and priests
Hope: Micah 4:1-8. *Promise* in 4:6-7: God will gather a remnant
Theme: Micah 4:9—5:15. Punishment and redemption of Jerusalem
Doom: Micah 4:9—5:1. *Punishment* against Jerusalem
Hope: Micah 5:2-15. *Promise* in 5:7-8: God will reign over Zion
Theme: Micah 6:1-7:20. Sin and righteousness before God
Doom: Micah 6:1—7:6. *Punishment* for injustice and idolatry
Hope: Micah 7:7-20. *Promise* in 7:18: God will pardon a remnant

4.3. Dates. Haggai and Zechariah 1—8 comprise a case of redaction by date. Date formulae appear in Haggai 1:1; 1:15—2:1; 2:10, 20; Zecha-riah 1:1, 7; 7:1. All of these verses date the sayings of the two prophets between the second and fourth years of King Darius (Darius I, ruler of Babylon from 522/1 to 486 BC). Redactionally, therefore, the two prophets are made contemporaries, though neither prophet actually refers to the other. Thus, redaction critics often have concluded that one redactor produced the combined work, drawing perhaps on older reports of the prophets' preaching.

4.4. Other Indications of Time. S. De Vries studied the use of several temporal transition words or phrases: "then," "now," "(and it shall be) on that day," "in those days," " at that time," "behold days are coming," "afterwards" and "at the end of the ages." He distinguished between those that occurred as part of a passage (either originally or redactionally) and introductory transitions (as formulas for attaching material redactionally). He discovered that "then" and "now" appear exclusively as integral transitions, the phrase "behold the days are coming" belongs almost exclusively to Deuteronomistic and Jeremianic redactions, and the remaining indicators are always redactional (De Vries, 20). Thus the phrase "on that day" in texts such as Zechariah 12:3, 6, 8, serves as a redactional device to link previously separate verses.

5. The Redaction of the Prophetic Books as Wholes.

Isaiah 65:2 God spreads out his hands to a rebellious house.	Isaiah 1:2 God reared children, but they rebelled against God.
Isaiah 65:3 They are a people who provoke God.	Isaiah 1:4 The whole head is sick, utterly estranged.
Isaiah 65:3 They corrupted sacrifice in gardens.	Isaiah 1:29 Israel would blush because of the gardens that they chose.
Isaiah 65:6 God will repay into their bosom.	Isaiah 1:5 Why do the people continue to be smitten?
Isaiah 65:8 God will not destroy them all.	Isaiah 1:9 If Yahweh had not left a remnant, they would have become like Sodom.
Isaiah 65:15 God's servants will be called by a different name.	Isaiah 1:26 Jerusalem will be called the "city of righteousness."
Isaiah 66:18-20 All nations will come to God's holy mountain.	Isaiah 2:1-4 Let us go up to the mountain of Yahweh.

Table 1. Redactional Bracket of Isaiah

5.1. The Redaction of Isaiah. In the case of *Isaiah, the persona of one prophet, the eighth-century BC Isaiah, extends over the entire work, so that scholars speak of "Deutero-Isaiah" in Isaiah 40—55 and of "Trito-Isaiah" in Isaiah 56—66. Although numerous tradition bearers may have contributed to the book, their names were not preserved, so their identities are lost. Instead, the sayings of Isaiah seem to have undergone extensive redactional work, framed by a "bracket" around the whole book (see table 1) (Childs, 543-44).

5.2. The Redaction of Jeremiah. For the book of *Jeremiah, J. Rosenberg discerns a redactional pattern behind the whole work (material below based on Rosenberg, 190-91; see Redditt 2008a, 269; note that this frame applies only to Jeremiah in the MT, not in the LXX).

A. Historical head note (Jer 1:1-3)
  B. Commission (Jer 1:10)
    C. "Prophet to the nations" theme introduced (Jer 1:5-10)
      D. Doom for Israel; poetic oracles mostly (Jer 1—10)
        E. Prophet cut off from Anathoth; prose mostly (Jer 11—28)
          F. Optimistic prophecies; renewal of Israel; prose brackets a poetic center (Jer 29—31)
        E'. Prophet returns to Anathoth; prose mostly (Jer 32—45)
      D'. Doom for the nations; mostly poetic oracles (Jer 46—51)
    C'. "Prophet to the nation" theme culminates (Jer 50—51)
  B'. Prophet's concluding message (Jer 51:59-64)
A'. Historical appendix (chap. 52)

Like most such patterns, this one may be accused of being arbitrary, but there is much to commend it. In particular, it highlights the optimistic chapters in the middle of Jeremiah and handles such pairings as doom for Israel and for the nations.

5.3. The Redaction of Ezekiel. Two devices discussed above figure prominently in the redaction of *Ezekiel. The first is a series of dates found in Ezekiel 1:1-3; 3:16; 8:1; 20:1; 24:1; 26:1; 29:1, 17; 30:20; 31:1; 32:1, 17; 33:21; 40:1. These dates lend to the book the impression of being a chronological record, except that Ezekiel 29:1 and Ezekiel 29:17 are out of sequence. Ezekiel 26:1 dated the prophet's speech to the first day of a month not stated and the eleventh year of the exile of King Jehoiachin of Judah (i.e., late July 593 BC). The next date—the twelfth day, tenth month, tenth year (Ezek 29:1)—is at least ten months earlier. The third date—the first day, the first month, and the twenty-seventh year (Ezek 29:17)—is by far the latest date in the book. In Ezekiel 30:20-26, however, the date is the seventh day, the first month, the eleventh year, resuming the sequence that had obtained before the two in Ezekiel 29.

It seems clear, therefore, that a later redactor modified the chronological sequence in favor of the schema of doom against Jerusalem and Judah (Ezek 4—24), doom against foreign nations (Ezek 25—32) and hope for the future (Ezek 34—48). This schema was prefaced by Ezekiel 1—3, a report of Ezekiel's call vision, and interrupted by Ezekiel 33, a report the fall of Jerusalem predicted in Ezekiel 1—24.

5.4. The Redaction of Daniel. The first piece of evidence that a redaction critic faces in connection with *Daniel is that the book employs two different languages, *Hebrew and *Aramaic. It begins (Dan 1:1—2:4a) and ends (Dan 8:1—12:13) in Hebrew, but the middle chapters (Dan 2:4b—7:28) are in Aramaic. Critics posit two redactors of the Aramaic section, one who arranged Daniel 4—6 (Collins, 37), and a second who added Daniel 2:4b-49 plus Daniel 3 and Daniel 7. The resulting Aramaic section of Daniel exhibits a chiastic structure that most likely was deliberate.

A. A dream about four world kingdoms replaced by a fifth (Dan 2:4b-49)
  B. Three friends in a fiery furnace (Dan 3:1-30)
    C. Daniel interprets a dream for Nebuchadnezzar (Dan 4:1-37)
    C'. Daniel interprets the handwriting on the wall for Belshazzar (Dan 5:1-31)
  B'. Daniel in the lions' den (Dan 6:1-28)
A'. A vision about four world kingdoms replaced by a fifth (Dan 7:1-28)

This version probably would have had an introduction to Daniel, his friends and their circumstances, which is now lost. Possibly, however, much of what is now Daniel 1 appeared in that introduction, was translated into Hebrew and perhaps was expanded in the process (Redditt 1999, 26-27). Traces from the hand of the redactor may be found in Daniel 1:3-7; 2:6, 49; 4:8, 19; Daniel 5:12 (see Redditt 1999, 27-29).

The Hebrew chapters seem to have been added one vision at a time, but within a couple of years. The Aramaic section knows and "predicts" the coming of Antiochus IV Epiphanes, the Seleucid ruler of Palestine in the years 175-164 BC, identified as a "little horn" (cf. Dan 7:8; 8:9). Daniel 8 added his committing "the transgression that makes desolate" (Dan 8:13). That event was Antiochus's defilement of the temple in Jerusalem in late 167 BC, an event involving erecting a "desolating sacrilege" in the temple (1 Macc 1:54) and dedicating it to the Greek god Olympian Zeus (2 Macc 6:2). The final vision (Dan 10—12) becomes increasingly detailed about the events leading up to the death of Antiochus, which it actually predicts (Dan 11:44), though it has him die in Palestine, when in fact he died in Persia. The final prediction in Daniel 12:11-12 possibly was intended to assure the reader that everything had happened that needed to happen before God unveiled his own kingdom.

5.5. The Redaction of the Book of the Twelve. The example of Haggai and Zechariah 1—8 reveals that redaction critics also focus on the structure of the Book of the Twelve as one edited work. They point to the date formulae and other shared characteristics of Hosea, Joel, Amos and Zephaniah and postulate a so-called Book of the Four, comprised of two northern (Hosea, Amos) and two southern (Micah, Nahum) prophets, whose works were collected in Judah to explain the fall of Israel and warn of the impending fall of Judah. Haggai-Zechariah 1—8 seem to have been redacted together, and Nahum-Habakkuk as well (see 4.2 above). It is a predictable step, then, to attempt to write the history of the redaction of the Book of the Twelve (see esp. Nogalski 1993a; 1993b; Schart). It seems likely that Malachi was attached to Haggai/Zechariah 1—8 and joined to the Book of the Four and Nahum/Habakkuk. Joel and Obadiah, plus Jonah, were added to bring the total to twelve, always a favored number in

the OT. One of the principles for merging would have been chronology, preserved by the dates.

6. Conclusion.
Editorial/redaction criticism has come of age as a widely used method in the study of prophets since its introduction in the twentieth century. It is not always possible to distinguish it from other newer methods such as *canonical, reader and *rhetorical criticism, but it focuses on the work of the editors/redactors and their intentions, so far as those intentions may be convincingly derived from their work.

See also CANONICAL CRITICISM; FORM CRITICISM; FORMATION OF THE PROPHETIC BOOKS; INTERTEXTUALITY AND INNERBIBLICAL INTERPRETATION; RHETORICAL CRITICISM.

BIBLIOGRAPHY. **B. Childs,** *Isaiah* (OTL; Louisville: Westminster/John Knox, 2001); **D. A. Christensen,** "The Book of Nahum: A History of Interpretation," in *Forming Prophetic Literature: Essays on Isaiah and the Twelve in Honor of John D. W. Watts,* ed. J. Watts and P. House (JSOTSup 235; Sheffield: Sheffield Academic, 1996) 187-94; **J. J. Collins,** *Daniel* (Hermeneia; Minneapolis: Fortress, 1993); **E. G. Conrad,** "Forming the Twelve and Forming Canon," in *Thematic Threads in the Book of the Twelve,* ed. P. Redditt and A. Schart (BZAW 325; Berlin: de Gruyter, 2003) 96-101; **K. H. Cuffey,** "Remnant, Redactor, and Biblical Theologian," in *Reading and Hearing the Book of the Twelve,* ed. J. Nogalski and M. Sweeney (SBLSymS 15; Atlanta: Society of Biblical Literature, 2000) 185-208; **S. J. De Vries,** "Futurism in the Preexilic Minor Prophets Compared with That of the Postexilic Minor Prophets," *SBLSP* 41 (2001) 19-38; **J. Jeremias,** *The Book of Amos: A Commentary* (OTL; Louisville: Westminster/John Knox, 1998); **N. Lane,** "YHWH and the Nations: Parallels to Exodus 34:6-7 in the Twelve," paper presented at the Annual Meeting of the Society of Biblical Literature, Boston, November 21-25, 2008; **J. Nogalski,** *Literary Precursors to the Book of the Twelve* (BZAW 217; Berlin: de Gruyter, 1993a); idem, *Redactional Processes in the Book of the Twelve* (BZAW 218; Berlin: de Gruyter, 1993b); idem, "Recurring Themes in the Book of the Twelve: Creating Points of Contact for a Theological Reading," *Int* 61 (2007) 125-36; **M. Noth,** *A History of Pentateuchal Traditions,* trans. B. Anderson (Englewood Cliffs, NJ:

Prentice-Hall, 1972 [1948]); **N. Perrin,** *What Is Redaction Criticism?* (GBS; Philadelphia: Fortress, 1969); **W. E. Rast,** *Tradition History and the Old Testament* (GBS; Philadelphia: Fortress, 1972); **P. L. Redditt,** *Daniel* (NCBC; Sheffield: Sheffield Academic, 1999); idem, "The Formation of the Book of the Twelve: A Review of Research," in *Thematic Threads in the Book of the Twelve,* ed. P. Redditt and A. Schart (BZAW 325; Berlin: de Gruyter, 2003) 1-26; idem, *Introduction to the Prophets* (Grand Rapids: Eerdmans, 2008a); idem, "The King in Haggai—Zechariah 1-8 and the Book of the Twelve," in *Tradition in Transition: Haggai and Zechariah 1-8 in the Trajectory of Hebrew Theology,* ed. M. Boda and M. Floyd (London: T & T Clark, 2008b) 56-82; **J. J. M. Roberts,** *Nahum, Habakkuk, and Zephaniah: A Commentary* (OTL; Louisville: Westminster/John Knox, 1991); **J. Rosenberg,** "Jeremiah and Ezekiel," in *The Literary Guide to the Bible,* ed. R. Alter and F. Kermode (Cambridge: Harvard University Press, 1987) 184-206; **A. Schart,** *Die Entstehung des Zwölfprophetenbuchs: Neubearbeitungen von Amos im Rahmen schriftenübergreifender Redaktionsprozesse* (BZAW 260; Berlin: de Gruyter, 1998); **K. Schmid,** *Literaturgeschichte des Alten Testaments: Eine Einführung* (Darmstadt: Wissenschaftliche Buchgesellschaft, 2008); **R. L. Schultz,** "The Ties That Bind: Intertextuality, the Identification of Verbal Parallels, and Reading Strategies in the Book of the Twelve," in *Thematic Threads in the Book of the Twelve,* ed. P. Redditt and A. Schart (BZAW 325; Berlin: de Gruyter, 2003) 27-45; **O. H. Steck,** *Der Abschluss der Prophetie im Alten Testament: Ein Versuch zur frage des Vorgeschichte des Kanons* (BTSt 17; Neukirchen-Vluyn: Neukirchener Verlag, 1991); **G. von Rad,** *Old Testament Theology,* trans. D. M. G. Stalker (2 vols.; New York: Harper, 1962-1965).

P. L. Redditt

ENACTED PROPHECY. *See* PROPHECY AND SOCIETY; SIGN ACTS.

ESCHATOLOGY

Eschatology, defined as the "last things" or a distinct age beyond the present age, entails discussions about the end of history, matters of death, resurrection, judgment and the eternal state. Eschatology, from the Greek words *eschatos* ("final, last") and *logos* ("study of") has to do with the future, but chiefly the kind of future that is significantly discontinuous from the present, a future that represents the culmination of Yahweh's purposes.

This article deals primarily with expectations yet to be fulfilled, whether within history or beyond history. The OT ends on an eschatological note: "Lo, I will send you the prophet Elijah before the great and terrible day of the LORD comes. He will turn the hearts of parents to their children and the hearts of children to their parents, so that I will not come and strike the land with a curse" (Mal 4:5-6 NRSV). In this single announcement are bundled issues of time, named events, details involving certain subjects (e.g., land) and questions of interpretation (e.g., literal versus figurative, the identity of Elijah, the time of fulfillment).

The distinction between prophetic eschatology, which deals mainly with processes within history, and apocalyptic eschatology, with its crises-oriented heightened use of imagery and the final state, is only minimally helpful when considering the OT prophets (*see* Apocalypticism, Apocalyptic Literature). The eschatological topics to which prophets speak have to do with the future of *Israel, *nations, humankind and the *cosmos. For each, there are major questions of interpretation, answers to which often are determined by the larger streams/systems of interpretation. Three of these are dispensationalism (a subset of premillennialism), Reformed/covenant theology and mediating approaches.

1. Terminology and Announcement Genres
2. The Future of Israel
3. The Future of Nations
4. The Future of Humankind
5. The Future of the Cosmos
6. Conclusion: A Synoptic Theological Interpretation

1. Terminology and Announcement Genres.

Certain vocabulary is common to futuristic announcements. Two prominent phrases are "the days are coming" (*yāmîm bāʾîm* [e.g., Jer 23:5; 49:2]) and "in that day" (*bayyôm hahûʾ*). The latter expression occurs over one hundred times in the Prophetic Books (e.g., Is 19:16, 18, 19, 23, 24; Hos 2:16); fifteen of these are in Zechariah 12—14. The Hebrew phrase *bĕʾaḥărît hayyāmîm* (lit., "in after days" [Is 2:2]) has been translated "in days to come" (NRSV), "it shall come to pass in latter days" (ESV) and "in the last days" (NIV) (see Ezek 38:16; Dan 2:28; 10:14). "The day of the LORD" (*yôm yhwh*) is a significant, somewhat technical expression for future judgment as well as salvation (see Amos 5:18; Joel 1:15; 2:30-31) (*see* Day of the Lord).

Two kinds of oracles, straightforward messages from Yahweh, specifically deal with the future. One is the judgment speech, with its standardized form of accusation and announcement (e.g., Ezek 25:15-17). The second, its counterpart the *salvation oracle, can include various components: (1) an allusion to lament is part of the announcement of salvation (Is 41:17; Jer 31:2-6); (2) motivations become part of the assurance of salvation (Is 43:5; Jer 30:10-11); (3) descriptions of a state of well-being are characteristic of other forms (Jer 31:23-25) (Westermann).

Future events were envisioned through symbolic actions or sign acts. Judah's doom is announced in the breaking of a potter's jar (Jer 19:1-13; cf. Ezek 4:1-8). Israel's future reunification is foretold with the use of two sticks (Ezek 37:15-23). *Zion is a symbol of the city of God wherein are captured the prophets' hopes and ideals, so much so that D. Gowan gives to Zion a central place in OT eschatology (Gowan, 4-20).

2. The Future of Israel.

In Jeremiah alone there are more than 220 verses on the subject of the doom of *Israel and Judah (e.g., Jer 4:4-8; 6:1-8) (see Payne, 324). Starkly put, sin on the part of the people, but also and especially by the leaders, is the immediate cause for coming disaster (Is 1:2-6; Jer 2:9-13; Ezek 22:1-12). Agents responsible for destruction include armies, famine, pestilence and wild animals (Ezek 14:21). Assyria's conquest of Israel (722 BC) and Babylon's conquest of Jerusalem (586 BC) and the consequent exile represent the historical fulfillment of these threats.

But beyond the judgment is salvation, now described in glowing terms as a golden age and only partially fulfilled in the sixth century BC. The prophets tell of the dispersed exiles returning to live in the *land (Is 43:5-7; Jer 24:4-7; Ezek 11:16-21) and of a rebuilt *temple in Jerusalem to which God's glory returns (Ezek 40—48). Israel will be restored as a garden (Is 51:3;

61:11; Jer 31:12). *Worship places and practices will be restored (Jer 31:6, 10-14). A new *covenant will be established, including the gift of a new heart (Jer 31:31-34), in part because of God's determination "never to draw back from doing good to them" (Jer 32:40 NRSV) and also to insure that there will be no more defection from Yahweh (Ezek 36:26-29a). Fear will be removed because Israel's enemies will be destroyed (Jer 30:10; 46:27; Ezek 39:26; Mic 4:4). Allowing for some hyperbole, one can argue for a fulfillment within subsequent history. The exiles returned in 539 BC. Jerusalem's walls were rebuilt (Neh 6:15), and a temple was completed in 516 BC. Yet this question is asked: Have all these promises been fulfilled?

There are those who answer no. For example, there is not a Davidide on the throne (Jer 23:5-6; Ezek 34:23), nor has there been the revitalization that Ezekiel pictures (Ezek 34—48). Nations bringing tribute to Israel awaits fulfillment (Is 45:14; 61:4-11). Moreover, dispensationalists claim, Yahweh's land grant was part of an unconditional promise (Gen 17:8). Drawing on the NT mention of a millennium (Rev 20), classical dispensationalists and others posit a future time when a regathered nation of Israel will be the recipients of the glories promised (Is 60:1-22) (see Walvoord, 115-31). "Promises made here [about 'your people and your holy city' in Dan 9:24-27] are not yet realized in our time. Since God keeps His commitments, something more in terms of fulfillment can be anticipated" (Blaising and Bock, 93).

Scholars in the Reformed/covenant tradition demur. They regard the promises made to Israel in a more figurative or spiritual sense and see them fulfilled in the NT church. They object to the sharp distinction made between Israel and the church as two peoples of God. Besides, the kingdom of God is transnational. Thus, they do not hold to a national Israel as a part of God's ongoing plan. The true descendants of Abraham are not the physical offspring but rather the spiritual (Rom 9:5-8). In their view, the millennium is not a specified time period but rather is symbolic (Bavinck, 99-127; Bloesch, 87-113; Bauckham and Hart, 132-39).

A third, mediating position, akin to historical premillennialism, while affirming a single people of God, allows for a millennial era in which national Israel may play a role. While admitting the use of symbolism and wary about an overly literal interpretation of the texts, and less given to filling out details, those who hold this view nevertheless affirm that the prophet's depiction of a golden age has this-world implications for Israel (e.g., Ladd, 19-28).

The salvific scenario for Israel is not the only one portrayed. Ezekiel points to a time when the world's nations, led by Gog of Magog, will descend on Israel to destroy it. Such an event, with its strong overtones of the "last days," raises fulfillment questions. J. F. Walvoord concludes that the upheaval described by Ezekiel falls during the tribulation period prior to the millennium (Walvoord, 103-20). Noting that Revelation 19—20 draws heavily on Ezekiel, D. Block, in mediating mode, observes that for John, the revelator, Ezekiel's prophesy becomes "identified as the penultimate event in human history" (Block, 492).

2.1. Issues of Interpretation.

2.1.1. The Identity of God's People. At one level, the people of God are the people of Israel, the physical descendants of Abraham to whom God in covenant made the promises of blessing, descendants and land. However, even though an ethnic group serves as nucleus, the covenant is not confined to certain ethnicities. Egypt and Assyria become part of God's people (Is 19:24-25; cf. Is 56:6-7). Non-Israelites enter God's ministry (Is 66:18-21). In a narrow historical sense, the covenant people are Israelites; theologically speaking, the covenant people are followers of Yahweh, regardless of ethnic origin.

Does ethnic Israel figure into God's plan for the future? Jeremiah avers, "If this fixed order [sun, moon, stars and the natural environment] were ever to cease . . . , then also the offspring of Israel would cease to be a nation before me forever" (Jer 31:36). Paul, while regarding the Christ event as pivotal, continues to speak of an ethnic Israel (Rom 9—11; esp. Rom 11:15-16). Thus, to dismiss the future role of an ethnic Israel runs the risk of ignoring statements in both the OT and the NT. One needs to leave open the possibility that in God's program there is yet a future place for Israel.

2.1.2. Literal or Figurative. The view that Israel has a future role in God's program leans heavily on the language of the prophets, which pictures the prosperity and the glories that accompany the people of Israel settled in their land. This land may be figurative. Even the description in Ezekiel of a future temple and a city may be better understood as carrying the interpretation given by the prophet, "The Lord is There" (Ezek 48:35). While not taking away from the force of futuristic announcements, one must make allowance, following the Reformed/covenant viewpoint, for the prophet's use of figurative language. "Eschatological thought is an imaginative picturing of the unimaginable" (Bauckham and Hart, 138). The combination of literal and figurative language renders a defined mosaic but leaves unanswered issues of temporal sequence (Sandy).

2.1.3. God's Covenant with Israel. Those who envision an ongoing national people at the end time rely on texts about *covenant that they regard as unconditional. Among the challenges to the notion of an unconditional covenant are not only notions of what a covenant is, but also Scriptures that associate ethical behavior with the maintenance of covenant (e.g., Ezek 33:23-29; cf. Jer 7:3, 5-7). While it is true that in Jeremiah and Ezekiel the land of Israel is identified as the land promised to Abraham, Isaac and Jacob, that promise is not, for these prophets, a reason for Israel's return to the land. Rather, it is about Yahweh's compassion and reputation. It is about the nations' acknowledgment of Yahweh and his ways, and it is about the free worship of Yahweh (Martens, 339-43). Yet, since the covenant promises are large and secured by Yahweh's faithfulness, one must not discount the possibility of a future time when Israel will dwell in its own land.

3. The Future of Nations.

Prophets tell of the future of certain nations. Some prophets devote major space to the subject (Is 13—23; Jer 46—51; Ezek 25—32). Two books focus entirely on a single nation: Nahum on Assyria, and Obadiah on Edom. The devastation, destruction and demise of these nations and/or their capitals often are profiled in arresting ways (e.g., "Wild animals shall live with hyenas in Babylon . . . ; she shall never again be peopled, or inhabited for all generations" [Jer 50:39 NRSV]). Less emphasized are the reasons for such destruction, but generally, as with Babylon, judgment falls because "she has sinned against the Lord" (Jer 50:14 NRSV). Specifically, these sins are those of pride, arrogance and violence (Is 13:11; cf. Jer 48:29). Amos cites slavery, the harsh and unconscionable treatment of neighbor, treaty breaking and rudeness as reasons for Yahweh's destruction of specified nations (Amos 1:3-2:3). Moab is destroyed because of its misplaced trust in its strongholds (Jer 48:7). At least one nation is censured because of its bad treatment of God's people Israel (Ezek 25:1-7). The future for these nations is dark. Again, as illustrated by *Babylon, prophecies of apparent end-time scenarios (Is 13:6-16) merge with now historically fulfilled words (Is 13:17-22).

A principle at work is enunciated in Jeremiah when he visited the potter's house. Just as the malleability of the clay is a factor in the final product, so the response of a people plays into the nature of their future (Jer 18:1-11), as is illustrated in the book of Jonah. Destruction was decreed on Nineveh, but, given its inhabitants' repentance, God spared the city. The larger theology is that God in his grace extends pity to a nation, even to its *animals (Jon 4:11). Another key element in Yahweh's judgment on nations is a display of his glory with the intent that nations will acknowledge him (Ezek 38:23; 39:21-22).

There is good news for certain nations. The day is coming when it will be said, "Blessed be Egypt my people and Assyria the work of my hands" (Is 19:25 NRSV [cf. Jer 46:25-26]). God "will restore the fortunes of Moab in the latter days, says the LORD" (Jer 48:47 NRSV). The phrase "restoring fortunes" (šûb šĕbût) also ends oracles against Ammon (Jer 49:6) and Elam (Jer 49:39). Earlier translations (e.g., KJV) concluded that the word šĕbût derived from šbh ("to take captive") and so translated "bring again the captivity." Recent scholarly consensus is that the word šĕbût is a form of the word šûb ("to return"), and the phrase is literally "turn the turning," with the meaning "to bring about the restoration of" (Westermann, 258-61). Although some of these salvation-type promises have been fulfilled in history, others await a more end-time fulfillment, it seems.

Both punitive judgment and blessed salvation for the nations and for Israel are contained in *"day of the LORD" announcements. That day is depicted as the decisive intervention of Yahweh. Figures of speech employed are those from the cosmos (sun and moon darkened), from history (victory in war) and from society (a great convocation). One scenario is of multitudes gathered before Yahweh in the valley of decision (judgment) (Joel 3:14); the outcome is one of punishment for the nations (cf. Is 34:1-17) and for those who are proud and idolatrous (Is 2:12-22). The outcome is also salvation for some, a paradisiacal prosperity for Judah/Israel (Joel 3:18-20; cf. Is 35:1-10). The outcomes, described with an aura of finality, warrant the view that the "day of the LORD" is an especially end-time event. Yahweh will be exalted on that day, and his rulership will be recognized (Is 2:11b).

Ezekiel paints a scene in which nations will fare badly. He envisions an apparent end-time destruction of nations. A massive coalition of nations, including Magog (see Gen 10:2) and other anciently known peoples, attack a restored Israel (Ezek 38—39). There is great loss of life and a staggering pile-up of captured ammunition. Yahweh, who has incited these nations to move against Israel, intervenes in the battle. Gog, prince of Magog, and the allies are vanquished, and Israel is spared (Ezek 38:21-22). One might conclude that the nations will be annihilated, although Zechariah, if describing the same event, speaks of survivors who will become Yahweh worshipers (Zech 14:16).

A similar vision of the elimination of nations is given by Daniel in his dream of a great anthropomorphic image. As interpreted within the biblical text, this image's head of gold is Nebuchadnezzar of Babylon (Dan 2:36-38). Successive empires are represented by the arms and the chest of silver, the thighs of bronze, the legs of iron, and the feet of both iron and clay (Dan 2:32-33). The entire image is crushed and pulverized by a stone that is cut, but not by human hands, from the mountain. That stone, representing a divine agent, demolishes earth's kingdoms. An eternal kingdom, the kingdom of God, is established.

3.1. Issues of Interpretation.

3.1.1. Temporal References. Certain terminology is conventionally understood as referring to the "last days" when, alternatively, the meaning may better be rendered "in the future." A case in point is the message about nations beating their swords into plowshares (Is 2:2-4; Mic 4:1-5). Some see fulfillment in an indeterminate future or in the millennial age (see commentaries). The phrase bĕʾaḥărît hayyāmîm (lit., "after days") may mean not the "last days" but rather "whenever," which yields the sense that whenever peoples seek for a divine message and follow God's directives, warfare is no longer an option (Wolff). Perhaps one should entertain both interpretations: obedience to the will of God eliminates resorting to war and violence; in the far-off, future age nations will no longer be at war, since they have embraced God's ways.

3.1.2. Identification of Empires in Daniel's Visions. *Daniel's vision of the statue (Dan 2), the beasts (Dan 7) and the ram/goat (Dan 8) suggests a succession of empires. The Medo-Persian Empire is represented by the ram with two horns (Dan 8:20). Those who combine the meanings of two or more of these visions conclude that the dominant empires will be Babylon, Medo-Persia, Greece and Rome. Even though each has had its day in history, the theory of a revived Roman Empire in some form brings dispensationalists to suggest that a yet distant future fulfillment is to occur (Walvoord, 88-102). Those, Reformed/covenant scholars among them, who regard Greece as the final empire in the series see an already completed fulfillment of the little horn (Dan 7:8; 8:9-11) in Antiochus IV Epiphanes (175-164 BC). The mediating position is largely noncommittal about the future of nations but, like others, seizes firmly on the overriding message that nations, though powerful and even vicious, are under divine control.

As to identifications, it is prudent to follow the advice of Irenaeus of Lyons, a great theologian of the second century AD. What he said about the number of the beast (666) in Revelation 13:18 is applicable here: "It is . . . more certain, and less hazardous to await the fulfillment of the prophecy, than to be making surmises, and casting about for any names that may present themselves, inasmuch as many names can be found possessing the number mentioned; and the same question will, after all, remain unsolved" (quoted in Armerding and Gasque, 115).

Greater agreement can be expected on the significance of the stone uncut by human hands that demolishes the earthly kingdom. That stone is the Messiah, Jesus Christ, who becomes foundational for the coming kingdom. In Jesus that kingdom was inaugurated, but the world still awaits the full establishment of the kingdom of God.

4. The Future of Humankind.

Prophetic announcements that apply to humans more generically are about death, resurrection judgment, and life hereafter.

Little is said in the OT about what transpires for the individual after death. It seems that life, if it can be called such, is extremely minimized for the person who enters Sheol. Two snapshots of the shadowy existence there are given: the arrival of an Egyptian Pharaoh (Ezek 32:20-31) and a Babylonian ruler who comes to rest on a bed of maggots (Is 14:4-11). The language used is that of "sleep" (Is 14:8). Death marks a transition to a different realm. To conclude that the state of the dead is one of unconsciousness is not warranted, however, and certainly not when the evidence of the NT is adduced (Lk 16:28; Phil 1:23).

Isaiah is forthright in declaring a resurrection. "Your dead shall live, their corpses shall rise. O dwellers in the dust, awake and sing for joy! . . . The earth will give birth to those long dead" (Is 26:19 NRSV). The Suffering Servant is depicted, following a reading from Qumran, as one who will see light, a possible oblique reference to the resurrection (Is 53:11). The vision of Ezekiel about dead bones coming to life is about the communal and corporate restoration of Israel (Ezek 37:1-14), but indirectly it relates to the resurrection of the dead, in the sense of prefiguring it (Wright, 46-47). The fuller story is hinted at in Isaiah 25:8, where the Lord of hosts "will swallow up death forever" (cf. 1 Cor 15:54).

Daniel's statement is the most explicit in the OT about the resurrection: "Many of those who sleep in the dust of the earth shall awake, some to everlasting life and some to shame and everlasting contempt" (Dan 12:2 NRSV [cf. Jesus' reiteration in Jn 5:25-29]). Two destinies are envisioned, one positive and one negative. A positive description of that future is found in the pictorial of the new Jerusalem (Is 65:17-25), apparently the backdrop for John's vision (Rev 21). Negatively, it is said of those who rebelled against God that "their worm shall not die, their fire shall not be quenched" (Is 66:24 [cf. Jesus' description of Gehenna in Mk 9:48]).

The prophets assume a future judgment, for retribution is part of present and end-time reality (Is 63:1-6; Jer 25:29-33; Ezek 38-39; Hab 2:6-8; Zech 14). A major feature of the Day of the Lord is Yahweh's judging of the peoples. The upshot is safety and protection for some (Joel 3:16b-17) and dire disaster for others (Joel 3:19). The day is one of Yahweh's *wrath and *destruction (Zeph 1:14-16). That which was spoken in Ecclesiastes, "God will bring every deed into judgment, including every secret thing whether good or evil" (Eccles 12:14 NRSV) gains specificity in Daniel with the description "The court sat in judgment, and the books were opened" (Dan 7:10c NRSV). The setting for judgment is the Ancient One seated on a fiery throne (Dan 7:9).

4.1. Issues of Interpretation.

4.1.1. Body and Soul. Since details about the resurrection in the OT are sparse, large questions remain. One of these is whether the OT affirms a body-soul dichotomy, a concept of the soul separate from the body that derives from Greek philosophy and seems sometimes to be supported by the OT (e.g., Eccles 12:7). Engaging with the whole of Scripture, however, biblical scholars argue that a view of body-soul dualism is not biblically tenable (Wright, 28, 147-63; Bavinck, 31). Christian theologians affirm duality, thereby recognizing both a body and a soul-spirit dimension, but not dualism. The OT speaks of persons holistically, with body, soul and spirit, even in death.

4.1.2. How Many Resurrections? So sparse is the information from the OT that the question of the number of resurrections is moot. Drawing on NT statements about the first resurrection (Rev 20:4-5), dispensationalists traditionally posit a resurrection of the righteous at the onset of the millennium and a resurrection of the wicked at its close, as well as a final or third resurrection (Blaising and Bock, 270-83). Some in the Reformed/covenant camp distinguish two types of resurrection, spiritual and physical (see discussion in Erickson, 73-89).

5. The Future of the Cosmos.

Announcements about the future of the cosmos, the world of nature, are both negative (chaos will return) and positive (a new earth will be created) (see Cosmology). The undoing of the present order of creation is graphically depicted by Jeremiah: "I looked on the earth, and lo, it was waste and void; and to the heavens, and they had not light. I looked on the mountains, and lo, they were quaking, and all the hills moved to and fro" (Jer 4:23-24 NRSV). In this heavy pulsing poetry, all that exists apparently is annihilated before the Lord's fierce anger (Jer 4:26). Similarly, Zephaniah describes a creation that has become undone through a cosmic cataclysm in which all life, with allusions to the Genesis creation account, has been swept away (Zeph 1:2-3; cf. the seismic changes in Zech 14:3-10 and the opening lines of Is 24—27). Joel talks about signs in the heavens, blood and fire, the sun turned to darkness, and the moon to blood (Joel 2:3-31). The event, labeled a "day of the LORD," is universal in scope: "In the fire of his passion the whole earth shall be consumed; for a full, a terrible end he will make of all the inhabitants of the earth" (Zeph 1:18b NRSV). Such cosmic changes are end-time changes, though allowance must be made that "the cosmic imagery provides hyperbolic language to underline the significance of a specific historical and geographical situation" (Collins, 140).

The reasons for such drastic action are, unsurprisingly, human-related. Prior to Jeremiah's depiction of the world's dismal return to chaos, he complained that his people "are skilled in doing evil, but do not know how to do good" (Jer 4:22 NRSV [cf. Jer 4:17b, 18]). Similarly, the prophet Hosea connects the disarray in the environment to the immoral ways of a people (Hos 4:1-3). Given that gross sinful behavior brings severe detrimental effects upon the environment within history, at the eschaton extreme ubiquitous evil will bring about the total destruction of creation itself (see Creation Theology).

And yet all has not ended. Ezekiel tells of God's salvific action in an unspecified future. In barren regions trees will abound, and deserts will flourish (Ezek 36:30; cf. Is 41:18-20; 51:3; 55:12-13). Forests will be a safe place (Ezek 34:25; cf. Is 29:17). As a symbol of divine blessing, fish will teem in a river described as flowing eastward from the temple to the Dead Sea in a new topography (Ezek 47:9).

Isaiah's statement about the far-off future is forceful. "I [Yahweh] am about to do a new thing" (Is 43:19 NRSV). Isaiah describes a scene of re-creation, presumably after the undoing of the first creation. "For I am about to create new heavens and new earth; the former things shall not be remembered or come to mind" (Is 65:17 NRSV). Those things that earlier brought sorrow will be forgotten. In this new world, people aged one hundred will be considered young (Is 65:20). The natural world will also be unlike the earlier, for "the wolf and the lamb shall feed together" (Is 65:25 [cf. Is 11:6-8]). It will be a peaceable kingdom where things are made new (*see* Peace, Rest). Worship of Yahweh will be universal in this new world (Is 66:22-23). These announcements are prefaced with a brief mention of God's faithfulness (Is 65:16). It is, then, more than mere conjecture to say that God's commitment to his people is such, and the realization of his plan for humankind and the earth is such, that in the end the creation of a new heaven and earth is not only welcomed, but necessary. The whole earth will be full of the knowledge of God (Is 11:9), "drenched in God" (Wright, 102). God will be all in all.

An issue of interpretation here involves the newness of the new creation. It is natural to think of the new creation of the cosmos to be on the order of the restoration of the former cosmos, and thus a re-creation. But scholars point out that the new creation is to be conceptualized not as a restoration, or makeover, but rather as a transmutation of one order of existence into another (Bloesch, 77). That transmutation still keeps a focus on the earth, even if it is a new earth. N. T. Wright holds that this new earth is the locale of the "heaven" for which people hope (Wright, esp. 104-8, 201-5). Although his arguments incorporate the NT, the basis for his claim that the "place" of heaven is the new earth is the larger salvation story, including the OT.

6. Conclusion: A Synoptic Theological Interpretation.

God has come, he is coming, he will come (Zech 14:5b; Is 35:4) (see Moltmann). The forward movement in the prophetic announcements is unmistakable; it may even be said that the hope of God's coming defines Christianity. History is not cyclical, as in other worldviews, but instead has direction. God is engaged in that history. That history is moving toward the denouement, the Day of the Lord, the realization of the establishment of the kingdom of God. "The establishment of God's rule, his Kingdom, is the central hope of the prophets" (Ladd, 43).

A consistent theology of history is discernible whether the subject is Israel, the nations, the cosmos or the individual. Yahweh directs the course of events according to a righteous standard. Sin, whether in the form of disobedience to the covenant (Israel), or the transgression of universal ethics (the nations), or the

taint brought upon nature through human evil (the cosmos), or the insubordination to the Almighty by the individual, results in divine judgment. But the goal (telos) is not destruction but rather redemption.

In general, the prophets depict the future as a mosaic. The overall texture, often in the forms of overlays, can be identified; they contain large salvific elements. For the West, the chronology of events matter. For the East, and certainly in ancient times, the character of the event was the crucial element: the "what" was more significant than the "when." Curiosity in regard to calendaring and sequencing is understandable, but it was not the centerpiece of the prophets' speech about the future. Both Daniel (Dan 12:4, 9) and Jesus (Mk 13:32) cautioned against attempts at mapping the future.

Taken together, the large number of prophecies about Israel, the nations, humanity generally and the cosmos convey a message about a God who is sovereign, righteous and caring and whose span of concern is for the individual, for the faith community, for nations and for the world of nature. God is a God of majesty, with full detailed knowledge of the world. He knows the end from the beginning (Is 41:22). Yahweh is the universal sovereign over the natural world (Zech 10:1-2) as well as over all political structures (Dan 4:34-35; 6:25-28; 7:13-14, 23-27). The message of eschatology is a message of hope (see Bauckham and Hart; Chia; Moltmann; Polkinghorne; Sauter, 119-208; Wright).

Eschatology and *ethics are interlocked. Behaviors, whether godly or ungodly, determine the future, whether short term or ultimately (Ezek 7:9; cf. Ezek 7:27) (Miller).

In the final disposition of all things righteousness will prevail. In the last judgment God will deal fully and finally with evil, for judgment will fall on the wicked, and the world will be set right, and that on a cosmic scale. The enduring image is that because of the Messiah, "they will neither harm nor destroy on all my holy mountain; for the earth will be filled with the knowledge of the LORD as the waters cover the sea" (Is 11:9 NRSV).

See also AFTERLIFE; APOCALYPTICISM, APOCALYPTIC LITERATURE; COSMOLOGY; CREATION THEOLOGY; DAY OF THE LORD; ISRAEL; LAND; PROPHECY AND ESCHATOLOGY IN CHRISTIAN THEOLOGY; RETRIBUTION; SALVATION, DELIVERANCE; ZION.

BIBLIOGRAPHY. **C. E. Armerding and W. W. Gasque,** eds., *A Guide to Biblical Prophecy* (Peabody, MA: Hendrickson, 1989); **R. Bauckham and T. Hart,** *Hope against Hope: Christian Eschatology at the Turn of the Millennium* (Grand Rapids: Eerdmans, 1999); **H. Bavinck,** *The Last Things: Hope for This World and the Next,* ed. J. Bolt, trans. J. Vriend (Grand Rapids: Baker; Carlisle: Paternoster, 1996); **C. A. Blaising and D. L. Bock,** *Progressive Dispensationalism* (Grand Rapids: BridgePoint Books, 2000); **D. I. Block,** *The Book of Ezekiel: Chapters 25-48.* (NICOT; Grand Rapids: Erdmans, 1998); **D. G. Bloesch,** *The Last Things: Resurrection, Judgment, Glory* (Downers Grove, IL: InterVarsity Press, 2004); **R. Chia,** *Hope of the World: A Christian Vision of the Last Things* (Downers Grove, IL: IVP Academic, 2005); **M. J. Erickson,** *A Basic Guide to Eschatology: Making Sense of the Millennium* (rev. ed.; Grand Rapids: Baker, 1998); **D. E. Gowan,** *Eschatology in the Old Testament* (Philadelphia: Fortress, 1986); **D. J. Hayes,** *The Message of the Prophets: A Survey of the Prophetic and Apocalyptic Books of the Old Testament* (Grand Rapids: Zondervan, 2010) 77-90; **A. A. Hoekema,** *The Bible and the Future* (Grand Rapids: Eerdmans, 1979); **G. E. Ladd,** *The Last Things: An Eschatology for Laymen* (Grand Rapids, Eerdmans, 1978); **E. A. Martens,** "Motivations for the Promise of Israel's Restoration to the Land in Jeremiah and Ezekiel" (Ph.D. diss., Claremont Graduate School, 1972); **P. D. Miller Jr.,** *Sin and Judgment in the Prophets: A Stylistic and Theological Analysis* (SBLMS 27; Chico, CA: Scholars Press, 1982); **J. Moltmann,** *The Coming of God: Christian Eschatology,* trans. M. Kohl (Minneapolis: Fortress, 1996); **J. B. Payne,** *Encyclopedia of Biblical Prophecy: The Complete Guide to Scriptural Predictions and Their Fulfillment* (New York: Harper & Row, 1973); **J. Polkinghorne,** *The God of Hope and the End of the World* (New Haven: Yale University Press, 2002); **D. B. Sandy,** *Plowshares and Pruning Hooks: Rethinking the Language of Biblical Prophecy and Apocalyptic* (Downers Grove, IL: InterVarsity Press, 2002); **G. Sauter,** *What Dare We Hope? Reconsidering Eschatology* (Harrisburg, PA: Trinity Press International, 1999); **J. F. Walvoord,** *The Nations, Israel and the Church in Prophecy* (Grand Rapids: Academie Books, 1988); **C. Westermann,** *Prophetic Oracles of Salvation in the Old Testament,* trans. K. Crim (Louisville: Westminster/John Knox, 1991); **H. W. Wolff,** "Swords into Plowshares: Misuse of a Word of Prophecy?" in *The Meaning of Peace: Biblical Studies,* ed. P. B. Yoder and W. M. Swartley, trans. W. W. Sawatsky (Elkhart, IN: Institute of Mennonite Studies, 2001) 110-26; **N. T. Wright,** *Surprised by Hope: Rethinking Heaven, the Resurrection, and the Mission of the Church* (New York: HarperOne, 2008).

E. A. Martens

ESCHATOLOGY IN CHRISTIAN THEOLOGY. *See* PROPHECY AND ESCHATOLOGY IN CHRISTIAN THEOLOGY.

ETHICS

The prophets have long been understood as champions of social justice. Almost one hundred and fifty years ago, J. Wellhausen portrayed the eighth-century BC prophets—Isaiah, Micah, Amos, Hosea—as champions of what he called "ethical monotheism," which in his mind represented the high point of Israelite religion. From this perspective, the faith of these individuals had progressed beyond primitive tribal religion and was unencumbered with the deadening trappings of religious ritual into which belief in the God of Israel would degenerate. Relationship with God was defined by proper moral conduct. This understanding greatly influenced scholarship and, at a more popular level, advocates of the social gospel at the end of the nineteenth century and into the early decades of the twentieth. Few today set so starkly the moral demands of the prophets over against the cult, but the perception that the prophets were defenders of justice remains strong. The label "prophetic" is used across a wide spectrum of theological persuasions and in liberation theologies around the globe to refer to individuals or initiatives that act on behalf of the vulnerable. Even those who have been wary of some of the tenets of the social gospel and liberation theologies are increasingly becoming aware of the valuable contribution of this literature toward formulating ethical positions to contemporary problems.

This focus on ethics is appropriate, even if the reconstruction of prophetic faith by Wellhausen and others is overly simplistic. In both the Historical Books and the Prophetic Books prophets demonstrate broad social concern, which is grounded in the person of God, who is committed to humanity and is deeply moved by injustice and the suffering that it causes. Elijah and Elisha, for example, respond to the needs of widows (1 Kings 17:7-24; 2 Kings 4:1-7), and commitment to justice in every realm—socio-economic, judicial, political—characterizes the Prophetic Books. This emphasis marks a major difference between the biblical material and the prophetic oracles of other regions of ancient Mesopotamia. What has been recovered of those prophets has almost no mention of social concerns; instead, these oracles are concerned with military success, the maintenance of sanctuaries and their personnel, and proper attention to religious ceremonies.

The purpose of this article is to survey the variety of methodologies that have been utilized to study the ethics of the prophetic literature. Some are limited to the descriptive purpose of recovering the messages of these books. Others are committed to extracting moral teaching for those who seek to find guidance there for their moral life; descriptive results now serve prescriptive ends. Both kinds approaches are reviewed in this article.

1. Concerns of Past Research
2. Recent Studies of Prophetic Ethics
3. New Directions in Scholarship

1. Concerns of Past Research.

1.1. Theological Traditions Behind Prophetic Ethics. During the first three-quarters of the twentieth century scholarship concentrated on trying to specify the theological tradition(s) that undergirded the prophetic message. The four primary candidates were the covenant, the law, clan wisdom and creation.

The *covenant emphasis argued that the prophetic literature decried the violation of the expectations of the ancient tribal association with Yahweh. That is, according to this perspective, its ethical concerns do not reflect a new morality introduced by the prophets but rather hearken back to the historic obligations of the people before God and among themselves. Key terms, such as *mišpaṭ* ("justice"), *ṣĕdāqâ* ("righteousness") and *ḥesed* ("steadfast love, mercy"), and the many metaphors utilized in these books (especially the trope of *marriage) were defined in terms of the demands of that vertical relationship with God and their implications for community life. The prophetic exhortations and warnings were connected to the covenant blessings and curses of Leviticus 26 and Deuteronomy 28.

A second option was to claim that the prophets had in view the violation of specific *laws. Jeremiah 7:9 and Hosea 4:2 appear to allude to the Ten Commandments (Ex 20:1-17; Deut 5:6-21), and many passages seem to assume particular mandates, even if these are not cited explicitly. Examples include abuses in the legal system (Is 10:2; 29:21; Amos 5:12; Mic 3:11; Hab 1:3-4; cf. Ex 23:1-8; Deut 16:18-20), unjust acquisition of land (Is 5:8; Mic 2:1-2; cf. Lev 25), dishonesty in the market place (Amos 8:4-6; Mic 6:10-11; cf. Lev 19:35-36; Deut 25:13-16) and sexual impropriety (Amos 2:7; cf. Lev 18:8, 15, 17; 20:10-20). The Prophetic Books also repeatedly denounce both Israel's and Judah's worship of God (Is 1:10-20; 58; Jer 7:1-11; Amos 5:21-24; Zech 7; Mal 3:2-5) because it is divorced from the care of widows and orphans, the poor and aliens, all of whom are vulnerable individuals that the law demanded be cared for.

Other scholars turned to the Wisdom literature to explain prophetic ethics (*see* Prophecy and Wisdom). On the basis of form-critical studies, H. Wolff argued that in Amos the concepts of the "right" (Amos 3:10) and "justice and righteousness" (Amos 5:7, 15, 24; 6:12) find their source in clan wisdom (Prov 8:8-9; 24:26; 1:3; 2:9; 16:8). Similarly, the condemnation in Amos of false scales (Amos 8:5) and worship divorced from ethics (Amos 5:21-24) arose originally, he believed, within clan wisdom circles (Prov 11:1; 16:11; 20:23; 15:8; 21:23, 27). These insights Amos would have learned from the elders of his hometown of Tekoa and elsewhere, in contradistinction to the ways of the learned scribes and advisors of the royal court and the political acumen and protocols taught and practiced there.

A fourth approach located the moral order within *creation. This argument can go in one of two directions. The first is the conviction that the prophetic literature establishes a direct correlation between *sin and its judgment (Schmid; Fretheim): evil deeds trigger corresponding consequences in nature and history (Jer 6:19; 17:10; Ezek 7:27; 22:31; Hos 4:1-3). A second explanation appeals to a form of natural law—that is, the concept that all peoples share some common moral sensibilities perceptible within creation and human experience. This could explain, for instance, the denunciation of cruel acts of *warfare by the surrounding nations in passages often labeled by scholars as the "oracles against the nations" (Is

13—23; Jer 46—51; Ezek 25—32; Amos 1—2; Nahum; Obadiah). The assumption is that everyone, even those outside of faith in Yahweh and beyond the borders of Israel and Judah, would agree that certain behavior is reprehensible, and that those who perpetrate such atrocities should be held accountable (Barton).

Each of these four proposals has textual support, but each also has its detractors. The covenant option is a case in point. Scholars dispute the date of the emergence of this concept. Unlike those who argue for its foundational importance, some believe that covenant is a relatively late theological category, no earlier than the second half of the eighth century BC (cf. Hos 6:7; 8:1) or even later, and therefore it would have had little significance for a prophet such as Amos. This disagreement as to the date of the covenant theme has had no final resolution. The criticism of the approach that links prophetic teaching to specific laws is that the prophets primarily refer to moral principles instead of explicit legislation, hence the generalities in the language of their moral censure. On the other hand, connections to the Wisdom literature sometimes are tenuous and can match neither the quantity nor the clarity of possible links to the legal material. Finally, it is not difficult to perceive in the Prophetic Books a belief in an underlying moral framework grounded in the natural order of things, a notion that would have been shared across cultures. Although there may be disagreement concerning the connection between cause and effect, few would argue against the broader concept of a cosmic moral design.

It is more realistic to say that the ethical message of the prophets cannot be limited to any one theological tradition, and that these traditions were not as neatly distinct in content and bound to circumscribed groups of advocates as some might suppose. The prophets would have moved and spoken within a moral universe into which multiple theological emphases fed. They argued on the basis of the range of theological material available to them to communicate the divine word. These principles endure and are the framework for modern appeals to the prophetic text.

1.2. Approaches Defined by Textual Redactions. Some scholars perceive inconsistencies or diverse perspectives within the Prophetic Books instead of uniform ethical voices. These tensions, they contend, are proof that their canonical form derives from several authors at different times. Accordingly, their efforts are directed at reconstructing the ethics of the authors or redactors of the putative redactional layers delimited by various critical theories (*see* Redaction/Editorial Criticism). These diachronic approaches attempt to trace the hypothetical ethical trajectories within each book.

For example, there are studies of the book of Isaiah that limit their horizon to the ethics of "Isaiah of Jerusalem," by which is meant material that may be traced back to the eighth-century BC prophet according to critical criteria. The working assumption is that this is to be found primarily within what is commonly called "First Isaiah" (Is 1—39), while the ethical message of the rest of the book and some sections of Isaiah 1—39 are attributed to other hands (Barton). R. Coote distinguishes three layers in the book of Amos, each of which, he contends, arose within dissimilar historical settings and social circumstances. The initial stage is rooted in the historical prophet and denounces socioeconomic oppression perpetrated by Samaria's elite; the second originated in Judah in the seventh century BC and adds cultic concerns to the demand for justice; the final, postexilic layer offers a word of hope at the book's end to those who had experienced the realities of divine judgment announced in the earlier collections. Similar work has been done on other Prophetic Books.

These studies seek to give an account for the complexities of these books with a historical-literary model. They continue a long-standing emphasis of biblical scholarship on trying to retrace the development of biblical books, even as they complement that focus with attempts to ascertain the ethical teaching embedded in each stratum. These presentations of the ethical message of strands of material are only as assured as the viability of the critical theories upon which they are built. *Canonical criticism and the increasing interest in final-form studies are an expression, at least to some degree, of dissatisfaction with the subjective decisions regarding issues such as the dating of texts and the nature of the ethical discourse possible in certain contexts.

In addition, the density of the message of a book may have another explanation. Complexity is not contrary to ethical coherence, but rather can testify to the moral nuancing, the difficulties of real-life situations, and the simultaneous multiple personal and social ethical debates common to all communities. Beyond the descriptive efforts of these approaches lies the question of whether these critical reconstructions are an exercise restricted to academic circles, far removed from the competence and needs of faith communities that utilize the Prophetic Books as Scripture to inform their moral life. The growing textual sophistication that these approaches require can render problematic the feasibility of appropriating the Prophetic Books as an ethical resource. The opposite danger, of course, is to remove the biblical text and its message from any kind of historical and sociocultural setting and thus reduce its ethical teaching to disembodied, transcendent moral principles.

2. Recent Studies of Prophetic Ethics.

2.1. Social-Science and Historical Approaches.
In the past, scholars described the settings of ancient Israel in a general way, claiming simply that the prophets decried the change in the moral atmosphere wrought by the rise of the monarchy, which was said to have been accompanied by the absorption of Canaanite values, or that the woes of Israel were to be pinned on some form of nascent capitalism. More recent *social-science and historical approaches have attempted to ascertain with greater theoretical precision and more detail the socioeconomic and political contexts that sparked prophetic anger.

Sociological approaches to prophetic ethics are not new. They arose in the early twentieth century. An important landmark study was M. Weber's *Ancient Judaism* (originally published as a series of essays in 1917-1921), which attributed the criticism of the prophets to the conflict between the rural village proletariat and urban patricians generated by the establishment of the monarchy, the tension-filled transformation of the ancient tribal covenant confederation to a bureaucratic state, and the concentration of wealth and power in the cities. This dichotomy between rural and urban shaped generations of scholarly views, even as Weber's investigation of the socioeconomic power arrangements suggested in the biblical text led to an interest in probing the possible concrete dynamics that may lie behind its message. Weber, of course, was a sociologist who

ventured into the realm of the biblical scholarship of his day and incorporated its critical positions into his work.

The last three decades have witnessed a more informed application of social-science methodologies to the study of prophetic ethics. This research often goes hand in hand with positions elaborated by contemporary higher-critical scholarship about dating biblical texts (e.g., Pleins). The value of this work depends not only on the careful readings of the text, but also on how well versed biblical scholars are with the standards of the social sciences and with the specific sociological research to which they appeal. Each proposal may find a degree of resonance within the biblical material, which then gives it an aura of plausibility, so the comprehensiveness of its treatment of prophetic passages also must come into play in any evaluation of its explanatory value.

Interest has centered especially on models that might help interpreters comprehend the socioeconomic conditions and political structures condemned by the prophets (for a survey, see Houston, 18-51). These studies attempt to identify the mechanisms of oppression and the groups responsible for that state of affairs. Complicating matters for the researcher is that the world of ancient Israel and Judah, like any other, was not static. Systemic realities and their corresponding key actors would have changed as the monarchy and its policies morphed across the centuries in response to the shifting nature of the economic, political and military interactions with immediate neighbors and with the empires that cast their threatening shadows across the region.

One of the explanatory hypotheses that have been advanced is that of rent capitalism by O. Loretz and B. Lang. In rent capitalism peasants are dependent upon urban merchants and moneylenders. Diverse factors, such as inadequate rainfall, war and poor crop yields, press peasants into an inescapable cycle of debt to these city dwellers from whom they must go to acquire seed, tools and even food; circumstances at their worst result in these peasants succumbing to debt slavery and the loss of their land and facilitates the rise of latifundia (large estates) in the hands of the powerful. N. Gottwald and M. Chaney suggest that the model of the tributary state offers the best account of the prophetic message. Building on the Marxist notion of the "Asiatic mode of production," Gottwald contends that in ancient Israel rural communities were forced to give their agricultural surpluses to the central authorities—that is, the bureaucracy of the monarchy—who in turn redistributed those gains to their supporters; in time, the peasant producers also were exploited by the state to provide goods for a growing export economy, which also solely benefited the ruling class. A third proposal, by R. Simkins and W. Houston, is that ancient Israel functioned as a patronage society, in which wealthy and powerful patrons had a reciprocal relationship with their poorer clients. The latter would have expected protection and gracious provision from the former, while the patron would have counted on the loyalty of those under his care. This pattern of personal relationship, they contend, was integral to the cultural fabric of the ancient world and would have shaped attitudes and behaviors from the familial (father and the extended family) and clan and village (local head and tribe) levels to that of the monarchy (king and subjects). They judge that the OT prophets criticize violations of these arrangements, the oppression of clients by their respective patrons.

Sociological method has been used not only to reconstruct the social and economic realities of ancient Israel. It also has informed the dynamics of moral life that may be reflected in prophetic texts. A. Mein's work on Ezekiel tries to identify the various moral worlds—that is, the contexts, worldviews and religious ideologies—of the different social groups that experienced the *exile. He concentrates particularly on Jerusalem's deported elite, who would have struggled with the loss of prestige, privilege and identity as a defeated minority in a foreign setting, to explain Ezekiel's interconnection of ethical responsibilities with the stress on ritual, repentance and the vision of restoration. Another turn in the application of social science studies applies them to both biblical and modern settings. For example, G. Cuéllar utilizes diaspora research to probe Isaiah 40—55 in order to find parallels between the timely words directed at that ancient exilic community and the *corridos* songs of northern Mexico. The prophetic text offers a liberating voice to the Mexican American immigrant experiences in the United States and the crisis of identity and sociocultural marginalization common to

minority displaced peoples.

In addition to these various kinds of sociological approaches, new research into the historical backgrounds is providing more precise interpretation of the prophetic message. Archaeological findings of epigraphic and monumental evidence, along with realia from daily life, illuminate the biblical text in fresh ways. Examples abound. Activities that are condemned, such as the excesses of the *marzēaḥ* feast in Amos 6:4-7 and Jeremiah 16:5-9 (perhaps also Is 5:11-13; 28:7-8; Amos 2:7-8; 4:1), now are better understood (McLaughlin). The words of Isaiah (Bäckersten; Cohen and Westbrook) and Amos (Radine) are set against the backdrop of Assyrian foreign policy in the eighth century BC. Historical allusions within the rhetoric of the Prophetic Books surface that earlier scholarship had not noticed and provide a higher level of realism to the ethical material.

2.2. Feminist and Ideological Studies.

*Feminist approaches consider the prophetic literature to be intrinsically culturally conditioned against women. This shortcoming, it is argued, is manifest in the negative portrayals of Israel as a wayward, unfaithful wife and in the descriptions of judgment as terrible abuse perpetrated on her (note Jer 3—4; Ezek 16; 23; Hos 1—3). At the same time, the God of the prophets is portrayed as a male, a jealous and violent husband. Feminists contend that the theology of these books legitimates and perpetuates false and destructive views of women at best and physical aggression against women at worst. They are the product of a patriarchal ideology, a fact that necessarily impacts assessment of their ethics.

Feminist approaches to prophetic ethics and views on its continuing ethical relevance can be placed along a spectrum. Feminist ethicists differ on the pervasiveness of negative elements inherent to the prophetic material and, therefore, on the moral authority to be granted to it today. Some criticize the prophets for a harmful view of women (and for other matters, such as what is viewed as the indiscriminate violence of divine judgment) but still appreciate these books for their championing of the poor, the ethical critique of worship, the condemnation of the powerful, and the vision of cosmic redemption where nature and human life will be restored. These fundamental moral commitments within this literature are deemed to point the way toward a contemporary commitment to living a life of justice and ecological sensitivity in spite of the other damaging dimensions that cannot be accepted (Dempsey).

Others are not so generous in their appreciation of the Prophetic Books. They contend that the problematic language and utterly foreign underlying beliefs cannot be overcome, so the ethical authority of the prophets is disallowed. The prophetic literature does not contain the ethical compass that is needed, but it can serve as an ethical interlocutor or as a negative foil with which one can wrestle in trying to process in one's moral life the person of God and the vicissitudes of a woman's existence (O'Brien).

These approaches raise important issues, such as the character of biblical metaphors, their purpose and limitations, and the role of competing and complementary tropes. Theological convictions are being reexamined, in particular the meaning of biblical authority and the nature of God. The comprehension of patriarchy and its presence within the biblical text, along with the history of how these texts have been appropriated, have become major topics of research. Decisions on these matters determine in large measure the interpretation of contested passages and the appraisal of the value of the prophets for moral life.

Feminist approaches are perhaps the earliest example and most weighty of those within the broader movement of ideological criticism. Ideological criticism treats the biblical books as any other literature; it examines and evaluates the accuracy and view of reality that is communicated through the rhetoric of texts and then considers the morality of what the language is trying to legitimate and to inculcate in its readers. This is a hermeneutics of suspicion that questions texts and encourages resisting the literary strategies of their encoded ideologies, which can be blatantly expressed or subtly disguised as subtexts. This subversive reading "against the grain" often is done self-consciously from a certain interested position (such as feminism). Primacy is given to the reader as over against any written text, even the Bible, which many take as sacred Scripture. Whereas what it teaches is commonly taken as truth about God and ethics, ideological criticism highlights what it considers to be knotty portrayals of God's speech, actions and attitudes and the unacceptable moral things that the Bible commends or commands of those that are his people. A. Davies is troubled by what is said about the scope and methods of divine judgment in the book of Isaiah; this discomfort arises not only from the fact that some of these ideas are historically conditioned, but also from the realization that the notion of divine judgment violates the ethical convictions of many Christians today. In the end, he believes that the book of Isaiah demands trust in an incomprehensible God, one who functions with a double standard and contradicts what he demands of humans and what he judges them for. M. Gray believes that the statement "the LORD is a God of justice" (Is 30:18; cf. Is 61:8) is undermined by the book's content. Once again skepticism reigns, as the reader exposes the hidden agendas of the text. Gray juxtaposes Isaiah 1 and Isaiah 58 and, on the basis of a detailed textual analysis, concludes that the inconsistencies in the justice of God and his failures in creating a more equitable people and world can serve as the motivation for human initiatives to effect change in spite of God (Is 58:6-10). In his mind, this interpretive stance is deeply missiological.

2.3. Literary Approaches and Character Ethics. Whereas higher critical studies investigate the literary prehistory of the Prophetic Books and the ethical material of their various redactions, literary approaches concentrate on the final, or canonical, form of these books. These approaches can reflect simply an aesthetic interest in the structure and language of individual books or of its collections (such as the Book of the Twelve as a whole or combinations of books within that group). When connected to ethics, however, this focus moves beyond artistic concerns to discussions about how this literature functions in moral life (the power of these texts) and how it can be best appropriated by those who consider it to be Scripture (the question of textual method). These commitments stand in sharp contrast to ideological critiques that question the viability of the prophets for ethics.

Literary approaches have been most extensively utilized for character ethics. There are several constituent elements of character ethics: a set of traditions that offer a vision of reality and the purpose of life, a concept of the "good" to which the moral life is directed that is defined by those traditions, and a community within which that good is modeled and encouraged. In this scheme, the Bible merits first place as the fund of traditions that shapes the view of life and the world of those who embrace it as Scripture; it presents the meaning of the "good" and exhorts its readers to conform their minds, hearts and every sphere of human experience to that ideal. The believing community should serve as the place where such matters find their incarnation in moral exemplars among its members and are nurtured by the proclamation of the divine word and the practices of worship.

The majority of this kind of study in the OT has attended to narratives and the Wisdom literature, but the landscape of this research is changing. Fruitful explorations, for instance, of Jeremiah, Ezekiel, Amos and Micah, are efforts in this direction (Carroll R., 2001; Carroll R. and Lapsley; Lapsley). These readings of prophetic texts have two focal points. First, they direct careful attention to the moral life of those within these texts; they look at dimensions of the character of the prophets and other persons (their ethical values, the struggles and emotions, fears and hopes) in the crucibles of existence described there and at what ethical behavior God expected of Israel and the nations then, and thus perhaps for today. W. Janzen includes the prophetic as one of his five models of life before God in his paradigmatic approach to OT ethics. The prophets are exemplary in their exhortations to justice and holiness and in their willingness to fulfill their calling in the face of rejection and suffering.

Second, these approaches also inquire into how texts impact their readers. These are not, then, simply thorough examinations of prophetic texts as literature useful for ethics (the substance of what is presented there as applicable for modern life); they probe the power of this literature as Scripture to mold the character of the reader. W. Brueggemann is an important figure in explaining the potential influence of the "prophetic imagination" on the reader's sociopolitical understandings and commitments. Another area of interest is the kind of reader that might best be equipped to engage the text (Briggs). These approaches, therefore, appeal to philosophical hermeneutics and philosophical ethics—the mechanisms by which the text functions as a means of form-

ing a people of virtue, and the unique skills of the virtuous reader as the most appropriate interpreter of these texts for ethics.

3. New Directions in Scholarship.

This survey demonstrates that the prophetic literature is a rich resource for ethics, whether the goal is to describe the ethical thinking and moral behavior of ancient Israel (or of the authors of these books), or the purpose is to probe the Prophetic Books for contemporary ethical guidance. There are many options among scholarly approaches. Although a bit simplistic, the following categorization that is commonly used to characterize basic emphases of biblical studies helps summarize this review of approaches to ethics in the prophets: some studies focus on what is "behind" prophetic texts (traditions and literary prehistory, social-science and historical backgrounds), others on what is "in" these texts (literary studies), and still others what is "in front of" them in terms of their impact (feminism and ideological criticism, character ethics).

Each of these trajectories of scholarship will continue, but at least three new approaches deserve mention. The first is related to the shift in scholarly interest from the prehistory of OT texts to the time frame of their production, which is increasingly being assigned to the Persian period. This change in focus of the social setting of the literature affects the appreciation of the socioeconomic and political critique of the Prophetic Books. No longer do those passages serve as a window into the world of oppressive practices of, for example, eighth-century BC Israel and Judah; rather, they may have served as an indirect means for the scribes of the postexilic community, who compiled or even penned these books, to disparage life under Persian rule in Yehud with the authoritative voice of the prophets of the past. By presenting their condemnation in the mouth of the ancient spokespersons of God, they would have deflected attention from themselves, even as they made their ethical argument against the empire. This shift affects both the descriptive task of comprehending the ethical message of the prophetic literature as well as the prescriptive implications that might be drawn for contemporary life.

A second development arises from the movement to develop a theological interpretation of the OT as Christian Scripture. There is no hard-and-fast definition of what this theological interpretation actually is, and perhaps this perspective will encompass several kinds of ways of reading and interpreting biblical texts, but there are several shared commitments that are significant for the use of the prophetic literature for ethics (Carroll R., forthcoming). First, the biblical text is taken to be the authoritative word for the church. In other words, the ecclesial setting is believed to be the most appropriate place within which to do ethical readings, and the church the most suitable group for which such work is done. Ethics cannot be an academic exercise removed from the life of the church, nor can it be simply descriptive of what may lie behind the text or in its pages. Second, the focus of looking at the Bible for ethics will be on its canonical form, not on hypothetical redactional layers or the settings of its production. Research will look at how the world of the text can shape Christian faith theologically and morally instead of concentrating on questions set by modern critical agendas. Third, the OT is recognized as part of Christian Scripture, so ethical reflection necessarily will consider how the prophetic message set within that broader framework might point to the life and teaching of Jesus and connect to the rest of the NT.

The third avenue of future research is to pursue new topics of ethical relevance for the Prophetic Books. One area in which the prophetic literature is being explored more rigorously for ethical insights in the twenty-first century concerns the environment. Scholars are interfacing ecological studies with readings of prophetic texts to establish the theological bases for Christian commitment to and involvement in environmental efforts. Some scholars, who are engaged in ecological hermeneutics, such as those of the Earth Bible Project, assume in concert with ecofeminism a suspicious stance vis-à-vis the prophetic text's view of nature, questioning to what degree it is anthropocentric and perhaps counterproductive to modern sensibilities (Habel; cf. Dempsey). Others take a positive perspective about the orientation that the biblical material can empower (Marlow; Wright). Themes that are garnering attention include the interdependence of humanity and the created order, the relationship between nature and the moral order, the connection between the creation and divine blessing and judgment, and the eschatological visions of a redeemed natural order. At the very least, scholars need to be aware of the largely agrarian mindset of the biblical authors, which is quite different from their own predominantly urban elite perspective (Davis).

See also HERMENEUTICS; JUSTICE, RIGHTEOUSNESS; SOCIAL JUSTICE; WEALTH AND POVERTY.

BIBLIOGRAPHY. **O. Bäckersten,** *Isaiah's Political Message: An Appraisal of His Alleged Social Critique* (FAT 2/29; Tübingen: Mohr Siebeck, 2008); **J. Barton,** *Understanding Old Testament Ethics* (Louisville: Westminster/John Knox, 2003); **R. S. Briggs,** *The Virtuous Reader: Old Testament Narrative and Interpretive Virtue* (Grand Rapids: Baker Academic, 2010); **W. Brueggemann,** *The Prophetic Imagination* (rev. ed.; Minneapolis: Fortress, 2001); **M. D. Carroll R.,** "Seeking the Virtues among the Prophets: The Book of Amos as a Test Case," *ExAud* 17 (2001) 77-96; idem, "Failing the Vulnerable: The Prophets and Social Care," in *Transforming the World? The Gospel and Social Theology,* ed. D. Hughes and J. A. Grant (Nottingham: Apollos, 2009) 33-48; idem, "Ethics and the Old Testament," in *Hearing the Old Testament,* ed. C. Bartholomew and D. Beldman (Grand Rapids: Eerdmans, forthcoming); **M. D. Carroll R. and J. E. Lapsley,** eds., *Character Ethics and the Old Testament: Scripture and Moral Life* (Louisville: Westminster/John Knox, 2007); **M. L. Chaney,** "Bitter Bounty: The Dynamics of Political Economy Critiqued by the Eighth-Century Prophets," in *The Bible and Liberation: Political and Social Hermeneutics,* ed. N. K. Gottwald and R. Horsley (rev. ed.; Maryknoll, NY: Orbis; London: SPCK, 1993) 250-63; **R. Cohen and R. Westbrook,** eds., *Isaiah's Vision of Peace in Biblical and Modern International Relations: Swords into Plowshares* (New York: Palgrave, 2008); **R. B. Coote,** *Amos among the Prophets: Composition and Theology* (Philadelphia: Fortress, 1981); **G. L. Cuéllar,** *Voices of Marginality: Exile and Return in Second Isaiah 40-55 and the Mexican Immigrant Experience* (AUSTR 271; New York: Peter Lang, 2008); **A. Davies,** *Double Standards in Isaiah: Reevaluating Prophetic Ethics and Divine Justice* (BIS 46; Leiden: E. J. Brill, 2000); **E. W. Davies,** *Prophecy and Ethics: Isaiah and the Ethical Tradition of Israel* (JSOTSup 16; Sheffield: Sheffield Academic, 1981); **E. F. Davis,** *Scripture, Culture, and Agriculture: An Agrarian Reading of the Bible* (New York: Cambridge University Press, 2009);

C. Dempsey, *Hope amid the Ruins: The Ethics of Israel's Prophets* (St. Louis: Chalice, 2000); **T. E. Fretheim,** *God and World in the Old Testament: A Relational Theology of Creation* (Nashville: Abingdon, 2005); **H. Gossai,** *Justice, Righteousness, and the Social Critique of the Eighth-Century Prophets* (AUSTR 141; New York: Peter Lang, 1993); **N. K. Gottwald,** *The Politics of Ancient Israel* (Library of Ancient Israel; Louisville: Westminster John Knox, 2001); **M. Gray,** *Rhetoric and Social Justice in Isaiah* (LHBOTS 432; London: T & T Clark, 2006); **N. Habel,** ed., *The Earth Story in the Psalms and Prophets* (Earth Bible 4; Sheffield: Sheffield Academic, 2001); **W. J. Houston,** *Contending for Justice: Ideologies and Theologies of Social Justice in the Old Testament* (rev. ed.; London: T & T Clark, 2008); **W. Janzen,** *Old Testament Ethics: A Paradigmatic Approach* (Louisville: Westminster/John Knox, 1994); **J. Jensen,** *Ethical Dimensions of the Prophets* (Collegeville, MN: Liturgical, 2006); **K. Koch,** "Is There a Doctrine of Retribution in the Old Testament?" in *Theodicy in the Old Testament*, ed. J. L. Crenshaw (OBT; Philadelphia: Fortress, 1983) 57-87; **B. Lang,** "The Social Organization of Peasant Poverty in Biblical Israel" in idem, *Monotheism and the Prophetic Minority: An Essay in Biblical History and Sociology* (SWBA 1; Sheffield: Almond, 1983) 114-27; **J. E. Lapsley,** *Can These Bones Live? The Problem of the Moral Self in the Book of Ezekiel* (BZAW 301; Berlin: de Gruyter, 2001); **O. Loretz,** "Die prophetische Kritik des Rentenkapitalismus," *UF* 7 (1975) 271-78; **H. Marlow,** *Biblical Prophets and Contemporary Environmental Ethics* (Oxford: Oxford University Press, 2009); **J. L. McLaughlin,** *The Marzēaḥ in the Prophetic Literature: References and Allusions in Light of the Extra-Biblical Evidence* (VTSup 86; Leiden: E. J. Brill, 2001); **A. Mein,** *Ezekiel and the Ethics of Exile* (OTM; Oxford: Oxford University Press, 2001); **J. M. O'Brien,** *Challenging Prophetic Metaphor: Theology and Ideology in the Prophets* (Louisville: Westminster/ John Knox, 2008); **J. D. Pleins,** *The Social Visions of the Hebrew Bible: A Theological Introduction* (Louisville: Westminster/John Knox, 2001); **J. Radine,** *The Book of Amos in Emergent Judah* (FAT 2/45; Tübingen: Mohr Siebeck, 2010); **H. H. Schmid,** "Creation, Righteousness, and Salvation: 'Creation Theology' as the Broad Horizon of Biblical Theology," in *Creation in the Old Testament*, ed. B. W. Anderson (Issues in Religion and Theology; Philadelphia: Fortress, 1985) 102-17; **R. A. Simkins**, "Patronage and the Political Economy of Monarchic Israel," *Semeia* 87 (1999) 123-44; **M. Weber,** *Ancient Judaism*, trans. and ed. H. H. Gerth and D. Martindale (Glencoe, IL: Free Press, 1952); **H. W. Wolff,** *Amos the Prophet: The Man and His Background*, trans. F. McCurley (Philadelphia: Fortress, 1973); **C. J. H. Wright,** *Old Testament Ethics for the People of God* (Downers Grove, IL: InterVarsity Press, 2004).   M. D. Carroll R.

EVIL

Evil is one of the themes uniting the Prophetic Books with their wider biblical context. Since the ethical components of evil run counter to God's will as expressed in *creation and *covenant, it precipitates a significant area of theological interest.

1. English and Hebrew Usage
2. Lexical Discussion
3. Prophetic Usage

1. English and Hebrew Usage.

In English, "evil" has a consistently negative connotation, coming at the opposite end of the spectrum from "good." Both have a range of reference, but "evil" is used most frequently in the moral or ethical sphere, in which sense there is often an element of perverse intentionality. This element is lacking in the case of natural evil, where inanimate things or natural occurrences are injurious or harmful, or at least are not beneficial. The concept has become personified as the "Evil One," Satan himself.

A related but distinct concept is *"sin," which falls at the opposite end of the spectrum from "righteousness" (*see* Justice, Righteousness). The "evil/good" category is universal, finding a place within all worldviews, each of which has its own understanding of things that are either beneficial or harmful. On the other hand, "sin/righteousness" is context specific, unique to the particular expectations and prohibitions understood within any specific worldview. From a Judeo-Christian, biblical worldview, sin and righteousness are how one breaks or maintains the relationship with God, which is established by the covenants contained in the OT and the NT. There is, therefore, overlap but not absolute identification between the "evil/ good" and "sin/righteousness" spectra.

The most frequent Hebrew root denoting "evil" is r^{cc} and its cognates. The semantic range of the r^{cc} family in Hebrew is broader than that of English "evil." In Jeremiah 24:3, 8; 29:17 the description of figs as "bad" or "rotten" (NIV, NASB, Message) indicates that they are of such poor quality as to be unfit for human consumption. In Ezekiel 5:17; 14:15, 21 animals are designated "wild" (NIV, NRSV) or "dangerous" (HSCB) because they, like disease and war, are inimical to human flourishing, which their removal allows (Ezek 34:25). Neither use includes any moral judgment (hence the KJV's literal rendition, "evil," with its intrinsic moral connotation as noted above, is inappropriate) but rather points to aspects of their nature that do not aid human well-being. None of these examples are sin. However, uses of this Hebrew word family where aspects of human life involve moral censure or result from inappropriate human activity indicate both evil and sin. One might thus conceptualize the Hebrew understanding of evil as a larger concept within which is contained the concept of sin as a subcategory. Another Hebrew term rendered as "evil," the noun $\bar{a}wen$, has a narrower range of usage than does r^{cc}. It refers to human wrongdoing and its results, not to the inanimate realm, and so fits within the subcategory of sin.

2. Lexical Discussion.

The most common Hebrew root translated as "evil" among the English versions is r^{cc}, which within the Prophetic Books occurs as a verb twenty-four times; as the adjective ra^c, which is most commonly used substantively, fifty-nine times; and as three nouns: $r\bar{a}^c\hat{a}$, which is formally indistinguishable from a feminine adjective used substantively, one hundred fifty-six times; $r\bar{o}a^c$, thirteen times; and $m\bar{e}ra^c$, once. The NRSV in Daniel 12:4 idiosyncratically adopts the proposed emendation from the MT $d\bar{a}^cat$ ("knowledge") to $r\bar{a}^c\bar{o}t$ ("evils"), a minor change on one Hebrew consonant and an alternate reading of a vowel, vowels not having been recorded in the original transcription. Even if the emendation is correct, it adds nothing to the understanding of the semantic field of "evil."

English versions also use "evil" to translate $\bar{a}wen$, which, occurring twenty-seven times in the prophetic literature, is significant enough to receive comment in this article. Some also translate $ma^c\bar{a}l\bar{a}l$ as "evil deeds" (Jer 11:18 NRSV). The term itself appears neutral, however, usually requiring the separate adjective "evil" to provide a negative connotation, so this term will not be studied here. Neither will the ESV's redundant addition of "evil" to modify $dibb\hat{a}$ ("slander") in Ezekiel 36:3.

An analysis of what the prophets considered evil as determined through a study of these specific terms shows other instances where similar actions are recorded though without a specific identification of them as evil. Some of these cases will be mentioned as well.

3. Prophetic Usage.

3.1. Evil Actions. Evil is never systematically explained in the biblical text, but our understanding of it is aided by looking at things to which it is compared or contrasted. "Evil" (r^{cc}) is used several times as a contrasting polar opposite of "good" ($t\hat{o}b$), the former to be avoided and the latter sought (Is 7:15-16; Jer 13:23; 25:5; Amos 5:14-15). Those who reverse this order through childish naiveté show a foolish lack of understanding (Jer 4:22), while those who purposefully switch them are condemned (Is 5:20; Mic 3:2; Mal 2:17).

Within the Prophetic Books, the first occurrence of a word from the semantic field of "evil" is in the context of sin, iniquity and corruption, all three being elements of a purposeful separation by the practitioner from God (Is 1:4). This separation through sin is a common theme in the prophets (e.g., Is 3:9; Jer 16:10; 36:3; Ezek 20:44; 36:31), reflecting a rebellion against Israel's divine king (Jer 2:19; 18:10; 32:32-33; Is 65:2 ["not good"]), not listening to him (Jer 32:23) but turning instead to their own anarchic leadership (Is 47:10; Jer 7:24; 11:8; 13:10; 16:12; 18:12), to following *idols and other gods (Jer 7:30; 11:17; 35:15; 44:3, 5), or to taking part in other abominable activities (Jer 44:22; Ezek 6:9). In addition to a breach of relationship with God, "evil" can also indicate damage done to relations with other humans, through arrogance or insolence (Is 13:11), extortion and robbery ("not good" in Ezek 18:18), mistreatment of the poor and helpless (Is 32:7; Jer 5:28; Zech 7:10), perverting justice though bribery (Is 33:15; Mic 7:3), or destroying and killing (Is 33:15; 59:7; Jer 31:28; Jon 3:8). A clear example of the perversion is among Israel's shepherd-leaders, whose evil consists of reversing their expected role vis-à-vis their charges, scattering those whom they should protect (Jer 23:2). This is highlighted by a wordplay, contrasting "evil" (r^{cc}) with "shepherding" ($r^c h$) (Jer 22:22; 23:2). Wanton, evil destruction is also attributed to the visionary beasts in Daniel 7, even though the designation of "evil" is not applied to them.

This litany of wrongs does not reflect an ad hoc list of elements, but rather many of the evils noted by the prophets are counter to the standards that God previously established at creation and more specifically upon entering into a covenant relationship with Israel at Mount Sinai. In other words, the standard of the prophets as to what was evil is based mainly on material presented in the Pentateuch. Humankind, created in God's image, was to be God's co-regent in superintending and tending God's creation (Gen 1:26-28; 2:15), assisting in maintaining and furthering the "good" that characterized creation when it left God's hand (Gen 1:31). The evil condemned by the prophets runs counter to the human creation mandate, and it perverts the creational harmony between the divine, human and *animal spheres evidenced in Genesis 1—2 (e.g., Gen 2:1-4; cf. Is 56:2).

Specific expectations of God for humankind are spelled out among the covenant ordinances, and a number of the evil acts condemned by the prophets directly challenge these. Exclusive covenant allegiance of Israel to their great king, Yahweh, which is a main element in the Decalogue (Ex 20:3-6; Deut 5:7-10), is replaced by idol worship (Jer 1:16; 2:13; 11:17; 35:15). People dishonor Yahweh's special day, the Sabbath (Ex 20:8-11; Deut 5:12-15; Is 56:2). In the sphere of interpersonal relationships, people kill (Ex 20:13; Deut 5:17; Is 59:7), commit spiritual adultery (Ex 20:14; Deut 5:18; Jer 3:2; 23:10), steal (Ex 20:15; Deut 5:19; Hos 7:1) and lie (Ex 20:16; Deut 5:20; Is 59:15; Jer 9:3; Dan 11:27; Zech 8:17). They also subvert the clear commands requiring acceptable sacrifices to be unblemished (Lev 1:10; Mal 1:8).

One verse deserves particular comment in today's climate, where business or profit often is vilified. Habakkuk 2:9 bemoans those who "get evil gain" (NRSV). Gain ($besa^c$) itself is not intrinsically evil, as some would picture it. It seems originally to be a neutral construct (Kellermann, 207), with any negative connotations supplied by the context, such as in the Habakkuk passage (cf. Is 33:15; 57:17). It can also have a positive connotation (Mic 4:13). It does then seem to develop a more negative connotation in

itself, mainly due to its inappropriate acquisition or use through means such as bribes (e.g., 1 Sam 8:3), so care needs to be used in interpreting it.

Evil actions are not limited to God's covenant people. Aram (Syria), Israel's neighbor to the east, joined with them in plotting evil by attacking Judah (Is 7:5-6). The actions taken by *Babylon against Judah were designated "evil" and were punished by God (Jer 51:24, 60). Assyria, and its capital, Nineveh, also engaged in evil activity noticed by God (Jon 1:2), as did the "nations" (Zech 1:15).

The noun $\bar{a}wen$ shares part of its semantic range with r^{cc}, at times paralleling it (Is 31:2; 59:7; Jer 4:14; Ezek 11:2; Mic 2:1). It designates iniquitous worship practices such as breaking Sabbath (Is 1:13) or consulting idols (Hos 12:11 [Heb v. 12]; Zech 10:2). It also designates actions detrimental to the poor and others who are defenseless (Is 10:1-2; 32:6), those mistreated in legal contexts (Is 29:20-21), and shedding blood (Hos 6:8). Its perpetrators are either foolish (Is 32:6) or purposefully wicked (Is 59:7). Also, $\bar{a}wen$ is regularly associated with inappropriate speech (Is 58:9; Zech 10:2).

Prophets condemn many of these same evil actions even though not specifically designating them as "evil," so one must be careful not to assume that a simple word study can exhaust the topic. A lengthy representative list of many of the deeds already enumerated is found in Ezekiel 22:6-12.

3.2. Evil Results. The range of meanings of the root r^{cc} shows that it can denote a spectrum pointing to a process rather than a single event or action. A similar example of a process concept from English is "farming," which involves a myriad of discrete activities under the overarching concept of crop production and animal husbandry. A Hebrew example is the word $hatta^2t$, which can be employed to indicate a range of related concepts, depending on its context, including sin itself (Jer 31:34), the resultant guilt (Jer 17:1), punishment for sin (Zech 14:19) and a *sacrifice atoning for sin (Ezek 44:27). In any specific case, one of these meanings from across the meaning spectrum of a single word would be in mind, so it is important to understand which nuance is intended.

In the case of the root under discussion, "evil" performed by Israel and Judah results in Yahweh speaking "evil" over them (Jer 11:17); thus, a bad action yields a bad result, with both action and result described by the same term (Is 31:2; 47:10-11; Jer 18:8-11; 26:3; Ezek 6:9-10; Jon 3:10), or the bad result following negative actions specified by other terms (Jer 4:18). This bad consequence of a bad act is what T. Fretheim refers to as "the created moral order" (Fretheim, 49). This usage describing the result of an evil act is well translated as "catastrophe, disaster," reflecting the negative impact upon the recipient while avoiding any negative moral connotation of the word itself in these cases. This shows the importance of relativity or point of view, since, C. S. Lewis pointed out, a hell for humans could, at the same time, be heaven for mosquitoes (Lewis, 141). For humans, what appears harmful (bad or evil) to them could in fact be beneficial if it precipitates the cessation of unacceptable behavior. This understanding of the term is quite important theologically because on many occasions God is said to cause this "disaster" (Is 45:7; Jer 19:3, 15; 26:13; 35:17; 40:2; Ezek 14:22). A translation using "evil" in these instances, as in, for example, the KJV rendition of Amos 3:6 ("Shall there be evil in a city, and the LORD hath not done it?"), could be seen to attribute moral depravity to God. Therefore, one must use care in determining which semantic nuance of the terms best suits the situation.

Israel itself can acknowledge human culpability for "evil" consequences (Jer 26:19; Dan 9:14). There is a nexus of evil and disaster that is evident even to pagans, though not always recognized by God's prophets (Jon 1:7-8). Those who deny this connection will perish (Amos 9:10).

The misfortune is not solely the result of breach of the covenant between Israel and its God, however. Unnamed plotters threaten Moab with disaster (Jer 48:2, 16), while God promises to bring it against both Elam (Jer 49:37) and Babylon (Jer 51:2, 64).

The word 'āwen also indicates deleterious results of evil actions, the disaster of *exile (Amos 5:5), or the incursions of an army from the north (Jer 4:14).

Preferable to the suffering resulting from practicing evil is the joy derived from avoiding disaster (Is 56:2), which positive outcome is God's ultimate goal (Jer 18:8; 26:3; 29:11; 32:42; 42:10; Joel 2:13; Jon 4:2; cf. Is 55:7 ['āwen]).

See also JUSTICE, RIGHTEOUSNESS; REPENTANCE; SIN, SINNERS.

BIBLIOGRAPHY. D. W. Baker, "רעע," NI-DOTTE 3:1154-58; W. Eichrodt, Theology of the Old Testament, trans. J. A. Baker (OTL; London: SCM, 1967) 2:483-95; T. E. Fretheim, Creation Untamed: The Bible, God, and Natural Disasters (Grand Rapids: Baker Academic, 2010); A. J. Heschel, The Prophets (New York: Harper & Row, 1962); D. Kellermann, "בצע," TDOT 2:205-8; C. S. Lewis, The Problem of Pain (New York: HarperCollins, 2001); J. C. McCann Jr., "בֶּצַע," NIDOTTE 1:694-95.   D. W. Baker

EXILE

The study of the period of the biblical exile, or forced migration, is complex. This seminal period is no longer viewed simply as a monolithic period of approximately seventy years of punishment (Jer 25:11-12; 29:10; Zech 1:12; 7:5; Dan 9:2), while the *land of Judah remained dormant and in purification until its restoration. Even though there had already been a displacement and resettlement of the northern kingdom of Israel to Assyria (721 BC), the exile has been understood historically as the southern kingdom of Judah's experience of displacement and resettlement in *Babylon in the sixth century BC. The critical examination and reevaluation of this period now involves a careful study of at least three or four generations in Babylon, a *remnant community or communities back in Judah (with Mizpah replacing Jerusalem after 587 BC) dealing with parallel or even sharply different issues of survival than their Judeo-Babylonian counterparts, as well as Judean refugees in Egypt, Pathros, Ethiopia, Elam, Hamath (Elephantine) and presumably the coastlands as well (Jer 31:10; Ezek 39:6; Dan 11:30; CD) (see Israelite History).

1. Preliminary Considerations
2. The Nomenclature of "Exile"
3. Displacement
4. Resettlement and Generational Consciousness

1. Preliminary Considerations.
1.1. The Three Waves of Displacement. Historically, with three distinct waves of displacement to Babylon in 597, 587 and 582 BC, the time frame of the exile is classically marked as beginning ca. 597 BC, from the initial wave of the first generation Judeans (or Judeo-Babylonians) displaced to Babylon, until 538 BC, the brink of the first wave of the third and fourth generation Judeo-Babylonians/Persians pre-

paring for return migrations to Yehud. An alternative time frame has been suggested by R. Albertz, from 587 to 520 (or 515) BC, that is, from the destruction of the *temple in Jerusalem to the rebuilding of the (second) temple. However, such a demarcation eclipses the import of the displaced and resettled royal Davidic family, the military, the elites, and the merchants and skilled classes of peoples of 597 BC. It was these principal groups' work that established the first Judean ethnic enclave in Babylon (Ps 137; Ezek 1:1; 3:15), thereby making life less caustic for subsequent Judean forced migrants who arrived in 587 and 582 BC. Delineating the exile by temple-centered events rather than by people-centered events places undue emphasis on an edifice, as significant as it was. A more serious complication that rises with this attempt to re-date the exile is that by 520 or 515 BC the exilic period had made its way into the Achaemenid (Persian) or the return migrations period— well into the time of Darius. Outside a small circle of modern scholars focused on the temple, the scholarly consensus is that the study of the exile of Judah and the Judeans is best understood as a period under the hegemony of the Neo-Babylonians (626-539 BC: Nabopolassar [620-605 BC]; Nebuchadnezzar [605-562 BC]; Amel-Marduk [562-560 BC]; Neriglissar [560-556 BC]; Labasi-Marduk [556 BC]; Nabonidus [556-539 BC]).

1.2. Approaches to the Study of the Exilic Period. Traditionally there are three accepted and proven methods for the critical study of the exilic period: historical-archeological, literary and sociological (*see* Social-Scientific Approaches). The sociological approach, which includes historical and literary analyses, has been the catalyst for promising new thinking and insights (e.g., J. Wellhausen, D. Smith-Christopher, H. Barstad, J. Ahn). Just as history has a way of repeating itself, so also do social structures. How peoples, individually and collectively in ancient or modern times, respond to displacement and resettlement has not changed much. Examining the struggles and the rebuilding of lives in successive waves of various (im)migrants and their families reveals similar human experiences of struggle and joy. U. Segal points out that regardless of whether a migration is involuntary or voluntary, the lives of all first generation (im)migrants are laden with indescribable hardships, pains and sacrifices—with past traditions and ideals clashing under new domains. Yet the issues and concerns of each ensuing generation are noticeably different. Thus, accurately identifying those sets of social constructions and structures that confronted the Judeans will substantially aid us in better understanding the exile, or forced migrations, of the sixth century BC.

2. The Nomenclature of Exile.

2.1. Synonyms. Lexically, the most common expression for exile in Biblical Hebrew is *glh*. Yet there are at least eight additional comparable Hebrew or Aramaic terms (*bdr* [Aramaic], "scatter"; *bzr*, "scatter"; *zrh* "scatter"; *npṣ*, "spread out, scatter"; *pwṣ*, "scatter, disperse"; *dḥh* [Niphal], "be pushed"; *ndḥ* [Piel], "force out"; and *šbh* [Niphal], "be taken captive") that express both the individual and collective experience of forced migration.

2.2. Exile. Much of previous critical scholarship on the exile, from Henrich Ewald (1878) to Adolphe Lods (1950), primarily advanced Julius Wellhausen's social observation of the various classes of peoples taken into exile. Unfortunately Wellhausen's brilliant insight was reduced into one grossly generalized and uniform view of Judeans all laboring in great depression, groaning under the wrath of Yahweh. In Wellhausen's *Prolegomena to the History of Ancient Israel* (1885), followed by W. Robertson Smith (1905), the first generation of critical scholars of exile spoke of this period as the "Babylonian Captivity," the "Chaldean Vassalage" or simply the "exile," in its most painfully hopeless and damaging aspects. Much of mid- to late-nineteenth-century biblical scholarship on the exilic period was not necessarily about the period itself but focused on issues in three areas of OT study: (1) whether the Pentateuch was produced before or during/after the exile; (2) Isaiah 40—55 (or 40—66) as belonging to a distinctive author in Babylon or elsewhere; (3) the period as a monochrome background for the study of Jeremiah, Ezekiel and Deutero-Isaiah.

2.3. Exile and Restoration. However, beginning with M. Noth (1953, ET 1967) a transitional generation of exilic scholars contributed significantly to advance the study. C. Whitley (1957) and P. Ackroyd (1968) observed that the sixth century BC had been a dynamic age of intellectual movements, with Taoism in China, the Upanishads of pre-Buddhism, Hinduism in India, Zoroastrianism in Iran, the Orphic-Pythagorean tradition in Greece and the Hebrew exilic prophets in Babylon. It was noted that Israel's literature in response to the exile took on a more meaningful nature when compared with the known literature of the sixth century BC. Thus the Babylonian exile was deemed especially significant, for like the rebirth of a phoenix, there resulted out of pain and hardship a powerful and sustainable literary culture. Indeed, the period of exile was positively linked with restoration.

By 1989 D. Smith's (Smith-Christopher) path-breaking *Religion of the Landless*, a sociological approach to the subject, had demonstrated how the Judeans lived and even flourished as minorities in Babylon in spite of their traumatic experiences. And with the publication of K. van Lerberghe and A. Schoors' edited volume, *Immigration and Emigration within the Ancient Near East* (1995), a new window opened for biblical scholars dealing with *glh* as migration. Now there were invaluable studies on nonindigenous peoples (sojourners, immigrants, foreigners in general, hostages, corvée labors).

2.4. Deportation. H. Barstad's *The Myth of the Empty Land* (1996) signaled a break from scholars studying simply "exile" or "exile and restoration," and was followed by a collection of essays on the exile from the European Seminar in Historical Methodology, published as *Leading Captivity Captive* (1998). These two works reshaped the landscape of contemporary exilic scholarship. This second generation of exilic scholarship (1996-2010) charted a fresh perspective by transcending the past and proposing and advocating the construct of the "myth of the empty land." In other words, the exile never happened but was a mythopoetic construct, a literary trope or invention at best (R. Carroll, P. Davies, T. Thompson). And yet for others (B. Oded, R. Albertz) the exile was a watershed historical period, the most seminal period in Israel's history. Indeed, as Albertz poignantly noted, without the exilic experience, ancient Israel would never have arrived at full-blown monotheism, and the missional component of being "a light to the nations" would not have developed. Yet others pressed on with salient questions like: What precisely is the "exile"? Is it to be dated at 597, 587 or 582 BC? Or

should it be from 587/6 to 515 BC, or from 598/7 to 538 BC? Is establishing a time frame even necessary, since the exile endured into the Second Temple period? In short, Barstad's innovative thesis that the Judean landed gentry played an important role after the multiple "deportations" to Babylon has provided a much-needed social construct for understanding those that remained in the land after the displacements. But before expanding on Barstad's social construction, we must briefly remark on the term "deportation," which is associated with second-generation exilic scholarship.

In contemporary North American and generally Western sociological, political and jurisprudential settings, "deporting" or "deportation" is connected with "mass deportation," "undocumented peoples," or removing foreign nationals—in other words, the so-called immigration problem. When used to describe the events and the people of Judah in the sixth-century BC, this usage is alarming, even if the term is being used in a neutral sense. Biblical scholars who continue to advocate the use of "deportation" or "deported" when referring to the sixth-century Judeans are overlooking the critical contemporary issue in which "deportation" is closely tied to returning (or detaining) illegal immigrants. The proper term when referring to involuntary mass-movement of people is "displacement."

Barstad's social construction of the *remnant that remained in Judah underscores the importance of socioeconomics. Despite the fact that the king, his court, military, scribes, artisans and others were displaced and resettled in Babylon, the suggestion is that there was minimal disturbance to everyday Judean life since the Judean economy was primarily agrarian. A fully functional, undisrupted Judean society, with trade, commerce, worship and scribal activity continued. In Barstad's understanding the Chronicler's characterization that "the land was empty" is seen as a myth since the land was still populated. While there is much to be gained from Barstad's contribution, a sociological assessment of his construction raises questions beyond those pursed by B. Oded and others who have debated the notion of myth. A society experiencing a drain of its intellectuals, elites, politicians, military, traders, artisans, smiths and so forth would suffer immediate and long-term disruptions and discontinuities.

The removal or dismissal of the various functional roles represented by the displaced groups of 597 BC projects a gradually decaying, dysfunctional society after each additional displacement in 597, 587 and 582 BC. If, however, replacements or substitutes of peoples are factored in to fill the void left by the displaced groups of 597 BC (that is, from the populace of qualified or unqualified Judeans, or qualified non-Judeans from Edom, Ammon, Moab or other regions), at some point the important question of identity and ethnicity needs to enter into Barstad's social construction. Clearly by the period of the return migrations there was a rich heterogeneous society in Yehud. This was in contrast with the more ethnically monolithic and homogenous—but socioeconomically diverse communities—represented by the Judeo-Babylonians/Persians of the return.

Additionally, a series of pressing questions need to be addressed by Barstad: What does each succeeding Judahite (to distinguish them from the Judeans who involuntarily or voluntarily fled) generation look like? What were the issues and concerns of the first-, second- and third- (and possibly even the fourth-) generation Judahites who continued to populate and survive in the region, along with the Samaritans and others? Were there any similarities or differences between them and their Judeo-Babylonian generational counterparts? A social construction of the exilic period now requires a full working knowledge of each *generation unit* (a term coined and defined by the social philosopher K. Mannheim). Thus when it comes to biblical texts of the exilic period, the question is refined to, which *exilic generational text* is it? Is it a first-, transitional, second- or third-generation exilic Judeo-Babylonian text?

In fact, there were continuities and discontinuities in Judah after the displacements. But in support of Barstad's social construction, the central Judahite perspective on the exile during its seventy years was of a continuous period of judgment, punishing the children for the sins of the fathers down to the third and fourth generation (Ex 20:5; 34:7; Deut 5:9). However, from a Judeo-Babylonian point of view—clearly for the second and subsequent generations in Babylon—the outlook is quite different. That is, each generation is responsible for its own action (Jer 31:29; Ezek 18:2). In fact, for the likes of Daniel, Shadrach, Meshach, Abednego and others,

there were opportunities for upward socioeconomic movement. Herein lies the fundamental difference between the two predominant views on the period of exile, or forced migrations.

2.5. Forced Migrations. The third generation of exilic scholarship speaks of "forced migration," "displacement and resettlement" and "diaspora studies" to reframe and further advance our understanding of the exilic period. The introduction of forced-migration studies to exilic scholarship was undertaken by J. Ahn in his 2006 Yale dissertation (published in 2011 as *Exile as Forced Migrations*) and has subsequently fostered new critical reflection on the exilic, or forced-migrations, period. In parallel with "forced migration," "return migration" is the suggested corollary for reexamining issues and concerns of the postexilic period. For biblical studies the term *forced migrations* (plural) plays a role in all three recorded displacements of 597, 587 and 582 BC.

The study of forced migration takes into account theories of migration, reasons for such force and analyses of displaced peoples. It seeks to identify extrinsic factors or forces that cause involuntary movements of peoples. Forced migration produces a host of problems: urban redevelopment, population structure, redistribution policies, regional redevelopment followed by challenges to identity and ethnicity and so forth. Biblical scholars and specialists on the exilic period can benefit by reflecting on these and other issues that likely played some role in the sixth century BC.

A problem in contemporary exilic scholarship is the conjoining of the 597 and 587 BC groups due to the inability of past scholarship to discern the separate concerns of the two groups. Past studies have neglected the fact that by 587 BC Judah was already conquered and annexed by the Neo-Babylonians (597 BC). Technically, it is correct to speak of the first wave of forced migrants as exiles. But to speak of the second displacement of the 587 BC group as exiles is a misnomer. The fact that the territory of Judah was already subjugated, incorporated and recognized as a part of the expanded Neo-Babylonian Empire suggests that the event that took place in 587 BC was in fact an internal displacement of peoples from the periphery of the Babylonian empire (Judah) to the center (Babylon), not another exile.

Judah ceased to exist autonomously after Jehoiachin relinquished the throne in 597 BC. The state of Judah was reduced to a vassal status, and thus the 587 BC event was not so much a conquering or even a reconquering of Judah or Jerusalem, but a means of quelling an insurrection by destroying Judah's religious edifice as punishment and relocating its landed gentry to Babylon to serve as expendable laborers. The 582 BC event is also best understood in this way, for here we read of another group of people, including Jeremiah, crossing an international boundary and seeking asylum or refuge in Egypt (Jer 24:8; cf. Jer 26:21). Thus we rightfully turn to refugee studies to further understand the groups associated with 582 BC, which voluntarily took flight to Egypt or elsewhere.

In 2 Kings 24:4-16 we read that in the "eighth year" of Nebuchadnezzar, ten thousand people (2 Kings 24:14) were taken to Babylon. In 2 Kings 24:16, however, seven thousand able men for war and one thousand artisans and smiths were displaced. The discrepancy in these recorded numbers is further complicated by the figures presented in Jeremiah 52:28-30: In Nebuchadnezzar's "seventh year," 3,023 were displaced; in the eighteenth year, 832; in his twenty-third year, Nebuzaradan, the captain of the guard, took 745 men of Judah into forced migration.

S. Hermann says, "we must suppose that even after the fall of Jerusalem [587/6 BC], further groups of the population were sent into exile at intervals, even if we cannot see the reason for this measure or the system behind it" (Hermann, 291). Perhaps the system behind the multiple forced migrations of Judeans to Babylon was the result of careful socioeconomic planning for regional development. We can be reasonably certain, even without direct evidence, that the Neo-Babylonians must have carefully calculated the exact number of persons needed for each specific irrigation-canal project (or other building projects). The fact that Jeremiah 52:28-30 records exact figures in decreasing numbers is significant. These do not appear to be arbitrary figures since they decrease as the years progress. Although this suggests that there may have been less demand for Judean workers, it is more likely that the Babylonian irrigation infrastructure had reached its maximum capacity. The authors or redactors of Jeremiah were probably aware that in the Deuteronomistic history the figures

were larger and rounded off, but the data preserved in this text clearly denotes a clarification with statistical precision.

In contrast to the single, punctuated mass displacement policy of the Neo-Assyrians (to punish rebellions), the Neo-Babylonians most likely implemented a gradual and repeated system of displacement to maintain and then expand their central economy. Again, in contrast to the Neo-Assyrians, who practiced an expansionist policy of integrating vassal populations into subparts of their acquired empire (a very costly and economically draining enterprise), the Neo-Babylonians practiced the opposite by forcing migration for regional economic development. They brought labor forces, skilled and unskilled, as well as raw and finished material, to Babylon. The Neo-Babylonians imposed forced migration on conquered persons to work on their extensive and numerous primary, secondary and tertiary canals. This repeated systematic and calculated move would have prevented any immediate overpopulation. Such an oversupply of laborers would have had the domino effect of shortages in housing, problems with food distribution, issues with water supply as well as the risk of serious health problems.

Current scholarship recognizes three types of forced migration.

2.5.1. Derivative Forced Migration (DFM). This is a "static migration" that results from geopolitical and cartographical rearrangement. Since the Neo-Babylonians expanded and included Judah into their remapped empire when Jehoiachin relinquished his throne in 597 BC, Derivative Forced Migration best describes the first displacement to Babylon in 597 BC. This term also takes into account the Judeans that encountered an "exile-less exile." In fact, even after the additional forced migrations in 587 and 582 BC, the characteristics of Derivative Forced Migration existed.

2.5.2. Purposive Forced Migration (PFM). The varied purposes of forced migration may be attributed to profit, culture, race, religion, security, punishment or revenge. The forced migration of Judeans in 587 and 582 BC is best described as Purposive Forced Migration related to international security issues, the punishment for Zedekiah's rebellion, as well as the profit motivation to sustain regional economic growth in Babylon.

2.5.3. Responsive Forced Migration (RFM). In contrast to the first two, which are *involuntary* forced migration, Responsive Forced Migration is a *voluntary* relocation from one country to another. In response to forces of political or natural oppressions of tyranny, warfare, domestic or climate-related change, people choose to migrate voluntarily. Thus in 582 BC a group of Judeans, including Jeremiah, *voluntarily* crossed over into Egypt in response to the fear of Babylonian reprisal. This also perhaps best describes the forced migrations to the coastlands.

2.5.4. Summary. All three types of forced migration are applicable to the events of the sixth century BC and are tabulated in table 1.

	597 BC	587 BC	582 BC
Judeo-Babylonians	DFM	PFM	PFM
Judeans (in the land)	DFM	DFM	DFM
Judeo-Egyptians (and possibly coastlands)			RFM

Table 1.Types of Forced Migration and Sixth-Century Judeans

3. Displacement.

For exilic and biblical studies, the study of displacement highlights the intrinsic or internal migration issues that impact the lives of displaced peoples. Issues and concerns that arise because of forced population transfer to a new nation are manifold: (1) tensions between local and central politics; (2) clashes between cultural/traditional values and new ones; (3) struggles of socioeconomic classes; (4) challenges of preserving one's first language (Hebrew) in the immediacy of one's family or community while dealing with the language or languages of the dominant culture (e.g., Aramaic for speaking and Akkadian/Sumerian for reading or writing); (5) restrictions of food or diet; (6) issues of gender and marriage (e.g., at what generational point does intermarriage become a realistic possibility); (7) problems of raising children and grandchildren in a bifurcated or dual culture; (8) questions of partial or full acculturation or assimilation; (9) struggles to maintain religious practices, including those for the sake of social identity; (10) defining the concept of home (is it Babylon or Judah/Yehud?). These and other factors become visible upon full resettlement. And indeed, in Babylon the Judeo-Babylonians experienced the range of concerns as forced migrants or immigrants over a period epitomized as "seventy years."

Complementing the three types of forced migration (see 2.5 above) a typology of displacement has been developed.

3.1. Development-Induced Displaced Persons. In our contemporary world we see that thousands of people are displaced from their homelands or areas of habitual residence and resettled for purposes of economic development, industrialization (e.g., dam projects) or even preserving a rainforest. Nations or governmental entities carry this out in the name of eminent domain.

In the event of 597 BC, the king, his royal family, political advisers and court, as well as scribes, priests, military, and the artisans and smiths may be seen as Development-Induced Displaced Persons (DIDPs). The Neo-Babylonian government used its displaced and resettled persons for the development of its arable land and dilapidated infrastructure as well as for political control of Judah.

Moreover, from the Neo-Babylonian socioeconomic and theo-political point of view, the empire likely used this forced migration to achieve its goals of regional economic infrastructure redevelopment and urban stimulus. Ethnic enclaves were created beside the irrigation canals of Babylon, where they maintained the canals for agricultural production. Such efforts would be renewed with fresh workers arriving in 587 and 582 BC, possibly including other displacements not recorded in the OT. Sustaining ethnic enclaves requires two items for success: capital and maintaining the same ethnic group, if necessary through a program of chain migration.

From a Neo-Babylonian point of view, if the first wave of forced migrants in 597 BC had been completely ineffective, there would have been little or no need for additional displacement and resettlement of Judeans to Babylon. From a Judeo-Babylonian point of view, we must assume that the elites, including those who once ran a nation, fully recognized the purpose of their displacement and resettlement. Should they fail, there may have been severe consequences imposed on them and their children. Their local form of governance and outlook would not have been exclusive to the Judeo-Babylonian community but inclusive of those who remained in their homeland of Judah. And should a disaster strike Judah, as it did in 587 and 582 BC under the reigns of Zedekiah and Gedeliah, forced migration to Babylon would function as a means of saving lives.

3.2. Internally Displaced Persons. The category Internally Displaced Persons is internationally recognized today as referring to individuals or groups who, without crossing an internationally recognized state border, have been forced to flee their homes or regular domiciles in order to avoid violence, armed conflict, disaster or violations of human rights. The Judeans of 587 BC experienced armed conflict, violence, and human-made disaster (famine via the two- or three-year siege [cf. Deut 28:48-57]). The Babylonians forced the labor class, or the people of the land, to leave their homes and places of habitual residence. Against their will, and in violation of human rights, the Judeans were forcibly relocated within the expanded empire to Babylon. In the modern context internal displacement is recognized as occurring where large construction projects are used to forcibly relocate minority groups. This can be seen in the additional displacements of the Judeans to the irrigation canals of Babylon in 587 and 582 BC.

3.3. Refugees. In contrast to Internally Displaced Persons, refugees are people who flee against their will because of fear for their lives but cross an internationally recognized state border. So it was with those who fled after Gedaliah's murder in 582 BC: "All the soldiers, women, children and eunuchs whom Johanan brought back from Gibeon" (Jer 41:16) voluntarily fled and sought asylum in Egypt despite Jeremiah's warning not to go down to Egypt (Jer 42:19). This group crossed an international border into Egypt whereas the other 582 BC group was internally displaced to Babylon.

Profiling the group taken to Babylon in 582 BC has apparently not been attempted in exilic scholarship until now. The four fast days commemorating the catastrophe of Jerusalem in Zechariah 8:19 are: (1) the start of the siege (the tenth month: Jer 52:4), (2) the breaching of Jerusalem's wall (the fourth month: Jer 52:6-7), (3) the destruction of Jerusalem (the fifth month: Jer 52:12-13) and (4) the assassination

of Gedaliah (the seventh month: Jer 41:1-2). Gedaliah likely represented all the displaced people from the 582 BC event. Clearly his murder was traumatic. He symbolized and meant a lot to the people he represented. The biblical text speaks of the "people of the land" that remained after the initial and secondary displacements: "None remained except the poorest people of the land," and "the captain of the guard Nebuzaradan left some of the poorest of the land to be vinedressers and plowmen" (2 Kings 25:12; Jer 52:16). This offers some insight into the economic context of post-587 BC. When Ishmael son of Nethaniah, the son of Elishama, and ten men assassinate Gedaliah, the purpose was to completely disrupt and economically cut off Judah's production of wine, balm and other goods that flowed into Babylon. It was successful. Johanan and the remaining leaders took the remaining Judahites to Egypt, and eventually this group would become the Elephantine Jews in Egypt.

Because Gedaliah was pro-Deuteronomic, we can suppose that the Deuteronomic code that advocates on behalf of the poor, and especially the "foreigners," was in full practice. So rightfully, although hard work was imposed on the foreigners and the poor Judahites of the land, we ought to surmise that they were well treated, with respect and dignity, and all enjoined in the faith of Yahweh. Gedaliah is remembered as this group's ideological representative. Yet, although the displacement of this 582 BC group to Babylon is recorded, the people that make up this particular event are not recorded. Yet their children, the second generation of the 582 BC group, resurface as the ones who claim, "Let not the foreigner who has joined himself to the LORD say, 'The LORD will surely separate me from his people'" (Isa 56:3). These words would best be assigned to the second and subsequent generation of descendants of the 582 BC group. In Babylon, ironically, they continued to experience and perpetuate the stereotype of being "children of foreigners."

3.4. Summary. In summary, the Judeans of 597 BC are best described as Development-Induced Displaced Persons who experienced Derivative Forced Migration. The 587 BC Judeans displaced to Babylon are Internally Displaced Persons who experienced Purposive Forced Migration. And those taken to Babylon in 582 BC are also considered Internally Displaced Persons, having experienced Purposive Forced Migration. But those who responded and took flight by crossing into Egypt or possibly elsewhere are best seen as refugees or asylum seekers who experienced Responsive Forced Migration.

4. Resettlement and Generational Consciousness.

4.1. Resettlement. With resettlement, factoring in a complicated process of moving thousands of peoples (for modern-day cases see Ahn 2011, 62-66), individuals and families soon after begin to unpack their experience by critically reflecting on their new life—comparing and contrasting the social construction of reality of the past and their present. The social construction of reality is reflected upon in Psalm 137:1: "There, by the irrigation canals of Babylon, there we lived and wept when we remembered Zion" (Ps 137:1). However, the reality check is that it is not the first generation of forced (im)migrants that can move out, but their children (the 1.5 and second generation) and their children's children (third generation) that finally break free—moving and climbing upward on the socioeconomic ladder by "building, planting, and living" (Jer 29).

4.2. Generational Consciousness. An important new contribution to the study of the exilic or forced migrations period is "generational consciousness." Interestingly, most sociological works that trace generational issues and concerns conclude with the third generation: M. Lee Hansen's law of the third generation is that "What the son or daughter wishes to forget, the grandson or granddaughter wishes to remember." Usually by the fourth generation there is complete and full assimilation and upward integration. This three-generational consciousness is interestingly visible in prophetic literature, especially in Isaianic scholarship's designation of First-Second-Third Isaiah.

The unresolved impasse of the seventy years in exilic scholarship finds resolution when the seventy years is understood as a marker of social reflectivity—reflectivity of self-consciousness that is social in nature. It attests to a threefold Judeo-Babylonian generational consciousness. More specifically, it precisely marks three and a half generations, with each generational unit demarcated by twenty years, as the book of Numbers suggests. Thus, the generational makeup of the entire Judeo-Babylonian society

in Babylon is the first (twenty years) generation, the transitional (1.5) generation (ten years), the second generation (twenty years), and the third generation (twenty years). The period of approximately seventy years is roughly broken down as follows:

597-577 BC: First Generation Judeo-Babylonians (*twenty years*): Psalm 137

Generational description: Adult Judeans displaced and resettled to Babylon

Social issues: hardships as found in all first-generation forced migrants

597 BC: Loss of social prestige, status, being reduced to corvée work on the irrigation canals of Babylon, experiencing insults, longing to return

587 BC: Loss of children and destruction of the temple

582 BC: Dismissed by the first and second waves of migrants, hybrid identity issues

Theological motif: Communal lament

597-587/582 BC: Transitional (1.5) generation of Judeo-Babylonians (*ten years*): Jeremiah 29

Generation description: Judean adolescents/teenagers brought to Babylon (Daniel and his three friends)

Social issues: build, live, plant, marry, have children—to prosper economically

Theological motif: Golah hope in the fabric of prayer

576-556 BC: Second generation of Judeo-Babylonians (*twenty years*): Isaiah 43

Generation description: Born to the first or 1.5 generation parents in Babylon

Social issues: Assimilation through education, in-group and out-group, economic issues within the second generation between the descendants of 597, 587, 582 BC

Theological motif: New creation

555-535 BC: Third generation of Judeo-Babylonians (*twenty years*): Numbers 32

Generation description: Born to second-generation parents (first generation Judeo-Persians)

Social Issues: Defining home and what constitutes home

Theological motif: Justifying home on the other side of the Jordan

This generational demarcation helps to identify the issues and concerns of each Judeo-Babylonian generational unit. In addition, it helps place particular exilic biblical texts in their proper generational *Sitz im Leben*. This Judeo-Babylonian generational consciousness is an integral aspect of contemporary exilic scholarship.

See also BABYLON; EXODUS IMAGERY; ISRAELITE HISTORY; LAND; REMNANT; TEMPLE.

BIBLIOGRAPHY. **P. Ackroyd,** *Exile and Restoration* (OTL; Philadelphia: Westminster, 1968); **J. Ahn,** *Exile as Forced Migrations: A Sociological, Literary, and Theological Approach on the Displacement and Resettlement of the Southern Kingdom of Judah* (BZAW 417; Berlin/New York: de Gruyter, 2011); idem, ed., *The Last of Kings on Exile: Forced Migrations in 2 Kings 24-25* (Leiden: forthcoming); **J. Ahn and M. Leuchter,** eds., *The Prophets Speak on Forced Migrations: Exile in Major and Minor Cadence* (BZAW; Berlin/New York: T & T Clark, 2012); **J. Ahn and J. Middlemas,** eds., *By the Irrigation Canals of Babylon: Approaches to the Study of the Exile* (LHBOTS 526; New York/London: T & T Clark, 2012); **R. Albertz,** *Israel in Exile: The History and Literature of the Sixth Century B.C.E.* (Atlanta: Society of Biblical Literature, 2003); **H. Barstad,** *The Myth of the Empty Land: A Study in the History and Archeology of Judah during the "Exilic" Period* (SO 28; Oslo: Scandinavian University Press, 1996); **M. Coogan,** "Into Exile: From Assyrian Conquest of Israel to the Fall of Babylon," in *The Oxford History of the Biblical World*, ed. M. D. Coogan (Oxford: Oxford University Press, 1998) 242-75; **L. L. Grabbe,** ed., *Leading Captivity Captive: The 'Exile' as History and Ideology* (JSOTSup 278/ ESHM 2; Sheffield: Sheffield Academic, 1998); **M. Halvorson-Taylor,** *Enduring Exile: The Metaphorization of Exile in the Hebrew Bible* (VTSup 141; Boston/Leiden: Brill, 2011); **S. Hermann,** *A History of Israel in Old Testament Times* (Minneapolis: Fortress, 1981); **A. James,** "Questioning the Terminology and Definitions of Forced Migrations," in *The Politics of Forced Migration: A Conceptual, Operational and Legal Analysis*, ed. N. Nachmias and R. Goldstein (Baltimore: Publish America, 2004) 39-61; **E. Janssen,** *Juda in der Exilszeit: Ein Beitrag zur Frage der Entstehung des Judentums* (FRLANT 69; Göttingen: Vandenhoeck & Ruprecht, 1956); **J. Kiefer,** *Exil und Diaspora: Begrifflichkeit und Deutungen im antiken Judentum und in der Hebräischen Bibel* (ABG 19; Leipzig: Evangelische Verlagsanstalt, 2005); **R. Klein,** *Israel in Exile: A Theological Interpretation* (OBT; Philadelphia: Fortress, 1979); **K. van Lerberghe and A. Schoors,** eds., *Immigration and Emigration within the Ancient Near East: Festschrift E. Lipiński* (Leuven: Peeters, 1995); **O. Lipschits,** *The Fall and Rise of Jerusalem: Judah under Babylonian Rule* (Winona Lake, IN: Eisenbrauns, 2005); **O. Lipschits and J. Blenkinsopp,** eds., *Judah and the Judeans in the Neo-Babylonian Period* (Winona Lake, IN: Eisenbrauns, 2003); **M. Noth,** "The Jerusalem Catastrophe of 587 BC and Its Significance for Israel" in *The Laws in the Pentateuch and Other Essays* (Philadelphia: Fortress, 1967) 260-80; **B. Oded,** *Mass Deportations and Deportees in the Neo-Assyrian Empire* (Wiesbaden: Reichert, 1979); **L. Pearce,** "New Evidence for Judeans in Babylonia," in *Judah and the Judeans in the Persian Period*, ed. O. Lipschits and M. Oeming (Winona Lake, IN: Eisenbrauns, 2006) 399-411; **B. Porten,** *Archives from Elephantine: The Life of a Jewish Military Colony* (Berkley, Calif.: University of California Press, 1968); **U. A. Segal,** *A Framework for Immigration* (New York: Columbia University Press, 2002); **D. L. Smith,** *The Religion of the Landless: The Social Context of the Babylonian Exile* (Bloomington, IN: Meyer Stone, 1989); **D. L. Smith-Christopher,** *A Biblical Theology of Exile* (OBT; Minneapolis: Fortress, 2000); **M.W. Stolper,** *Entrepreneurs and Empire: The Murašû Archives, the Murašu Firm, and Persian Rule in Babylonia* (Leiden: Nederlands Historisch-Archeologisch Instituut te Istanbul, 1985); **C. C. Torrey,** *The Composition and Historical Value of Ezra-Nehemiah* (BZAW 2; Giessen: J. Ricker, 1896); **E.A. Unger,** *Babylon: Die Heilige Stadt nach der Beschreibung der Babylonier* (2 Auflage; ed. R. Borger; Berlin: deGruyter, 1970); **D. S. Vanderhooft,** *The Neo-Babylonian Empire and Babylon in the Latter Prophets* (HSM 59; Atlanta: Scholars Press, 1999); **K. van Lerberghe and A. Schoors,** eds., *Immigration and Emigration within the Ancient Near East: Festschrift E. Lipiński* (OLA 65; Leuven: Uitgeverij Peeters en Departement Oriëntalistiek, 1995); **C. F. Whitley,** *The Exilic Age* (Westport, CT: Greenwood, 1957); **R. R. Wilson,** "Forced Migration and the Formation of the Prophetic Literature," in *By the Irrigation Canals of Babylon: Approaches to the Study of the Exile*, ed. J. Ahn and J. Middlemas (LHBOTS 526; New York/London: T & T Clark, 2012); **R. Zadok,** *The Jews in Babylonia during the Chaldean and Achaemenian Periods according to the Babylonian Sources* (Haifa: University of Haifa Press, 1979).

J. Ahn

EXODUS IMAGERY

There are a number of places in the prophets where the influence of particular moments in the exodus is clearly and commonly recognized (e.g., Is 11:15-16; Jer 7:22; 34:13; Ezek 20:5, 36; Hos 2:15; 11:1; Amos 3:1; Mic 6:4; 7:14-15). These texts primarily appeal to the fundamentals of Yahweh's previously revealed character and sovereign power as the basis for Israel's present judgment and future restoration. This suggests that the exodus was widely seen as Israel's foundational and identity-shaping moment. If so, as with all such events, one then would expect it to be the prophets' presupposition and hence something that could be evoked often by a simple allusion. Furthermore, the exodus is not so much a cluster of isolated events as an interrelated narrative tapestry. An appeal to one aspect may well imply interconnections with other related themes. But allusions of this kind depend on prior knowledge. It is here, when we move beyond explicit statements to inquire what else of the exodus the prophets knew, that matters quickly become more complex and therefore controversial. Our only substantial data for comparison is the extant pentateuchal exodus narratives. But this immediately raises the question of the relative dating and sources of those pentateuchal passages under consideration and, indeed, of the Prophetic Books themselves.

Given the constraints of this article, the following working assumptions have been made. First, based on various indications in Israel's Scriptures, the exodus is taken to include those events from Yahweh's initial response to Israel's cry in Egypt up to Moses' final words on the threshold of the conquest. Second, in keeping with vast majority of recent scholarly work on this subject, a final-form canonical approach is taken here. This is not to deny the benefits of redactional and source studies of the exodus and covenant traditions or of the Prophetic Books themselves. But such matters could not reasonably be resolved in an article of this limited scope. On the positive side, it does allow us, for example, to appreciate the intertextual links across the "three" Isaiahs and the role of Hosea in leading off the Book of the Twelve. Third, in order to help the reader identify possible allusions and to avoid undue repetition, we begin with a brief recital, in narrative form, of the exodus, highlighting its various themes and motifs. The level of detail herein is in large degree the result of attempting to correlate this overview with the kinds of detail considered in the close readings undertaken in a number of the articles listed in the bibliography.

The reader is cautioned, however, that this summary is necessarily a highly compressed and artificial construct. It should not be taken to suggest that every prophet had recourse to all these particular details in this particular form. The summary is simply a guide emerging from the particular circumstances of this article. On the other hand, reading the prophets even on this somewhat artificial basis can offer, if not certainty, at least some strong indications of the extent of a given prophet's understanding of the exodus and the influence that such understanding exerted on his writings.

Finally, the sections on the individual prophets combine my own close reading of the exodus narratives and the prophets in concert with the work of others. If a particular allusion was judged convincing in respect to one prophet, it was, in keeping with my attempt to read the entire corpus with a consistent level of sensitivity, applied across the board to others.

1. Exodus Themes
2. The Major Prophets
3. Daniel
4. The Book of the Twelve
5. Conclusion

1. Exodus Themes.

The exodus begins with Yahweh showing himself to be the *covenant-keeping God who hears Israel's cry (Ex 2:24; 3:7-14; Deut 9:5) and who, in begetting, creating and carrying them, establishes his father-son relationship with his people (Ex 4:22; Deut 1:31; 32:5-6, 15-18). In bringing them out of slavery (Ex 6:13; 7:4; 12:17; Lev 26:13; Deut 5:6) to *worship him on "this mountain" (e.g., Ex 3:12; 4:23; 8:1, 20), plundering their enemies (Ex 11:1-3; 12:35-36) and giving them a land flowing with milk and honey (Ex 3:8; Deut 6:3), he became their Redeemer, Savior, Deliverer and Rock (Ex 3:8; 6:6; 13; 14:30; 15:13; 18:10-11; Deut 7:8; 9:21; 13:5; 32:4, 15-18). At the same time, through his mighty arm and outstretched hand, particularly at the Reed Sea (Ex 14—15), he shows himself to be the mighty warrior Lord over creation and the nations and their gods (Ex 12:12; 15:11; 18:11; 34:10; Num 33:4; Deut 1:30; 3:24; 4:34; 10:12;

26:18; cf. Ex 19:16). This dual aspect of merciful redeemer and judicial warrior is intended to reveal his glory, making his name known not just to Israel (Ex 6:2-8; 10:2; Deut 5:24) and the Egyptians (Ex 7:5; 9:29; 14:17-18), but also throughout the earth (Ex 9:16; 32:12). Thus, on the one hand, Egypt is humbled and the nations tremble (Ex 15:14; Deut 2:25), but on the other hand, a mixed multitude also comes up out of Egypt with the possibility of joining Israel (Ex 12:38-49).

The central moment of the exodus occurs after Yahweh's fearful and earth-shattering descent on Sinai, intended to instill fear against sin (Ex 19:16-19; 20:18-21), when he makes covenant with Israel to be their God and they his kingdom-priest people (Ex 19:6; 24; Num 9:1-14; cf. Ex 6:7). Its terms will govern their relationship with him and the land and its continued fruitfulness (e.g., Ex 6:4; 20—23; 34; Lev 1—9; 11—27; Num 5—6; 15:1-26; 18—19; 28—30; Deuteronomy). Its wisdom, along with his presence, is to serve as a witness to the nations (Deut 4:6-8). Israel is to have no other gods (Ex 20:3, 23; 23:13-32; Deut 5:7; 12:12-13). If they do, Yahweh will judge them by giving them over to their enemies (Deut 7:4; 8:19; 11:28; 32), withdrawing his presence (Deut 31:18; 32:16-20), casting them out like the nations before them (Lev 18:24; Deut 8:20) and scattering them in foreign lands (Lev 26:33, 37-39; Deut 4:27; 28:64). On the contrary, as he is holy, they are also to be holy (Lev 11:44-46; Deut 26:19). As he is just and righteous, so also they are to be, remembering that they were once oppressed as slaves in Egypt (Ex 23:2-6; Deut 16:18-20; 24:17-18; 32:4). In this context and having made the appropriate preparation (Ex 25—31; 35—39; Num 7—8), the climax of the exodus is the transfer of Yahweh's presence to the tabernacle, now a moveable Mount Sinai, to dwell among his people (Ex 33:14-16; 40:34-38; Num 9:15-23; cf. Lev 26:12).

But Yahweh's deliverance and faithful provision are met with Israel's rebellion (Ex 16—17; Num 11—20). Expressed most clearly in the adulterous incident of the golden calf (Ex 32; cf. Num 5:11-31), it is here, however, that the true nature of Yahweh's character is revealed. He is the merciful and gracious Lord, who, although by no means leaving the guilty unpunished, abounds in steadfast love and faithfulness to the thousandth generation (Ex

33:19; 34:6-7; cf. Ex 15:3; 20:6). Moses subsequently lays before Israel the two ways, life or death, now on offer from the Lord (Deut 27—32; cf. Lev 26), who can either kill and make alive, wound or heal (Ex 15:26; Deut 32:39). Envisaging the prospect of a rebellious Israel's being cursed and scattered among the nations (Deut 28:64-68; 32:19-26; cf. Lev 26:33), Moses offers, based on Yahweh's compassion, the hope that after judgment will come repentance and final restoration (Deut 30:1-10; 32:36-43; cf. Lev 26:40-45).

2. The Major Prophets.

2.1. Isaiah. No other prophetic work reflects the paradigmatic influence of exodus motifs as does Isaiah. Well-recognized in Isaiah 40—55, it has been less so in the other main sections (Is 1—39; 56—66).

2.1.1. Isaiah 1—39. Isaiah begins with both negative and positive echoes of the exodus. Yahweh's opening complaint is addressed to his rebellious "sons" (Is 1:3-7; cf. Is 29:23; 30:1-2, 9; 63:8) and reflects Moses' Deuteronomic curses and warnings, which are taken up again in Isaiah 5; 28; 30 (see also Deut 21:18-21) (Bergey; Keiser). Yet this is answered by a vision of a future exodus-like theophany over Mount *Zion (Is 4:5) to which, echoing the exodus aim that God's glory and name be known throughout the earth, many *nations will come (Is 2:1-4). Likewise, Isaiah's characteristic designation of God as the "Holy One of Israel," occurring some thirty times throughout the entire work, recalls Yahweh's "I am holy" self-revelation and provides the basis for his actions first as judge and then redeemer (e.g., Is 1:4; 5:19; 12:6; 17:7; 29:19; 37:23; 40:25; 45:11; 54:5; 60:9). In this respect, the similarly repeated references to God's righteousness and *justice are at least partly grounded in the exodus revelation and hence his expectations of the same in Israel (e.g., Is 1:12-28; 5:7-24; 9:7; 11:4-7; 28:17; 32:16-17; 42:21; 45:8, 21; 56:1; 58:2). As judge, Yahweh in an antiexodus refuses to heal (Is 6:10; cf. Ex 15:26) or show compassion (Is 9:17; cf. Is 27:11) and stretches out his mighty hand against his people (Is 1:24-25; 5:25; 8:11; 9:12-21; 10:4), who now flee from his Sinai-like earth-shattering and glorious presence (Is 2:19-21). Because they have forgotten God their "Rock" (Is 17:10), their land, full of idols (Is 2:6-8; cf. 31:7) and injustice (Is 1:4, 15-17, 21-23), will be cursed (Is

17:11). Although the vine of his planting, they have produced wild fruit (Is 5; cf. Deut 32:32-35). Adding insult to injury, Yahweh's rebellious sons now seek salvation from Egypt (Is 30:1-2; 31:6); not surprisingly, their plans will fail disastrously (Is 30:5-7; 31:1-3).

But this is not the last word. As redeemer, the Lord of the exodus will "stretch out his hand" not only over the mighty waters of Assyria (cf. Is 8:7-8), just as he had the sea of Egypt (Is 10:24-26; 30:31), but also over all the nations (Is 14:26-27; 19:16; 23:11; 26:11). Showing himself still the "Everlasting Father" and "Mighty God" (Is 9:6), he will, in the context of a restored Davidic ruler (Is 11:1-9), extend his hand a second time to effect a new exodus, this time from Assyria (Is 11:11-16) but also Egypt, so that the *remnant of his people might worship again on his holy "mountain" (Is 27:12-13). Thus, the prophet reprises the strains of the exodus Song of the Sea (Is 12:2-5; cf. Ex 15:1-2, 21), for the Lord will again have compassion on his people and restore them (Is 14:1; cf. Is 30:18-19). Correspondingly, the nations will then experience the power of his theophanic coming and raised arm (Is 30:27-32; 31:3; 33:2-3) as Yahweh hears his people's cry (Is 30:19), heals them (Is 30:26), plunders their enemies (Is 33:4, 23b-24) and reveals his glory, waters springing up in the desert, as he leads the redeemed along a "Holy Way" back to their "Rock" in Jerusalem (Is 30:29; 35:1-10). Whereas the exodus spoke of a mixed multitude coming up with Israel, in this greater new exodus there would now be a highway both for Egypt, whose cry the Lord will also hear (Is 19:20), and for Assyria, who, along with Israel, will be God's blessed and worshiping peoples (Is 19:18-24).

2.1.2. Isaiah 40—55. Although questioned by some and the nature of the language and imagery debated (is it concrete or metaphorical? [Kiesow; Barstad; Lim]), the exodus is more influential here than in any other part of the prophetic corpus (Anderson). Its presence in the prologue (Is 40:1-11), the end of the first section (Is 48:20-21) and the epilogue (Is 55:12) suggests its paradigmatic significance. Beginning with the recollection of Israel's retribution from Yahweh's (outstretched) "hand" (Is 40:2; cf., e.g., Is 1:24-25; 5:25), the scene-setting proclamation of his coming "in might" and as a shepherd to deliver his people that all nations might see his glory clearly recalls Israel's first exodus (Is 40:3-11; cf. Is 42:13; Ps 77:21; 78:52). Consequently, Yahweh's promise of his presence (Is 40:9; 52:6), declaration "I am he!" (*ʾănî hûʾ* [Is 41:4; 43:10, 13; 46:4; 48:12]), self-designation as "Redeemer," "Savior" and "Rock" (Is 41:14; 43:3, 11, 14; 44:6, 8, 24; 45:15, 21; 47:4; 48:17; 49:7, 26; 54:5, 8), concern for righteousness (Is 42:1-6, 42:21; 45:8, 21; 51:4), and declaration of compassion, everlasting love and mercy (*rḥm, ḥsd* [Is 49:10, 13, 15; 54:7-8, 10; 55:7; cf. Is 47:6]) are best understood as deriving from and evoking his exodus self-revelation (cf. Ex 3:14; Deut 32:39).

In first responding to Israel's fear and then condemning their obtuse faithlessness (Watts), the prophet appeals to Yahweh's powerful creational acts in "the former things" of the first exodus to demonstrate and provoke trust in his ability to do even a greater thing in this "new" second exodus (Is 42:9; 43:16-19; 48:6). In this respect, his vast superiority over the nations' lifeless *idols is demonstrated in part by his control over *creation, first evident in his saving acts at the exodus (Is 40:17; 44:26-27; 45:21; 46:8-9).

Yahweh comes once again as a warrior, his mighty arm ruling for him (Is 40:10-11; 42:13; 49:24-26; 50:2; 51:5), but it is not Sinai being shaken but rather entire *mountains and hills laid waste (Is 42:15). Because he loves Israel (Is 43:4; 46:3-6), he will gather their "sons and daughters," whom he created for his glory, from east and west (Is 43:1-6; cf. Deut 32:6) and bring them in glorious procession (Is 40:11; 42:16; 49:10) to the place of his *presence, now restored Zion (Is 40:2, 9; 41:27; 44:26-28; 46:13; 51:3, 11, 16-17; 52:1-2; cf. Is 4:5). As the one who dries up the deep (Is 44:27), making a path through the sea and destroying chariot and rider (Is 43:16-17), he will lead them through the waters and the fire (Is 43:1-7). In this more leisurely new exodus—they will not go out in haste—he will again be their front and rear guard, turning darkness into light before them (Is 42:16; 52:15; cf. Ex. 13:21-20; 14:19-20) and providing rivers in the desert (Is 43:19-20; 41:18-19; 48:21; 49:10-12). This predication of the future hope on the exodus is explicit both in Yahweh's reminders that his hand is not too short to save, that he can dry up the sea and open rivers in the *wilderness (Is 50:2), and in the prophet's subsequent prayer that Yahweh awaken his mighty arm by reminding him of his dividing the sea for the redeemed (Is 51:9-11).

Of particular interest is the integration of the Isaianic servant and, as we saw in Isaiah 9—11, the Davidic king in this new exodus hope. If Isaiah 51:17—52:12 describes Zion's being prepared for deliverance from Babylon, and Isaiah 54 the city's glorious restoration, then Isaiah 52:13—53:12 describes the "way" in which this new exodus deliverance takes place (Watts). Yahweh's mighty delivering "arm" is ultimately revealed to Israel and the nations (Is 53:1; cf. Is 52:10, 15) in his righteous servant's bearing of Israel's Deuteronomic exilic curse (Is 53:4-5, 11; 1:5-6; cf. Deut 28:59-61; Ceresko; on the servant as a second Moses, see Hugenberger) (see Servant of Yahweh). In the subsequent restoration of Yahweh's servants, the everlasting covenant with David is fulfilled as the nations flock to their glory (Is 54:17; 55:5; cf. Is 45:22; 52:10).

2.1.3. Isaiah 56—66. The bleaker realities of these chapters see an increasing emphasis on the ability of Redeemer-Savior Yahweh (Is 59:20; 60:16; 63:8-10) to effect his promises through his "mighty arm" (Is 59:1, 16; 60:16; 62:8; 63:1, 12; 66:14). The prophet's first evocations of the exodus appear in Yahweh's promise of a new exodus gathering not just of Israel but also foreigners (Is 56:8) and the promise of his saving presence in response to his people's cry (Is 58:9). But they are most prominent in the two warrior songs (Is 59:15b-21; 63:1-6) and especially the final complaint (Is 63:11—64:12).

The former, in bracketing the vision of a restored Jerusalem (Is 60—62), reiterate that Redeemer Yahweh's "strong arm" will effect his people's *salvation, causing the nations, as in the exodus, to fear his glory (Is 59:16, 19-20; 63:1, 4-5; cf. Is 52:13—53:1; 62:10), and his people, now reaffirmed as "priests of the LORD" (cf. Ex 19:6) to enjoy their wealth (Is 60:11-12; 61:6). Thus, the summons goes out to build up the highway upon which the holy and redeemed people will return (Is 62:10-12; cf. Is 35:1-10).

The final complaint contains the most extended appeal to the exodus in the entire work. Reflecting back on the events that brought Israel to its present desperate situation, the prophet recalls, in classic fashion, how Savior Yahweh's great compassion (*rḥm*) and steadfast love (*ḥsd*) in redeeming and carrying them (cf. Deut 1:31) were met by Israel's rebellion, causing him to become their enemy (Is 63:7-10). Urging

Yahweh to remember the days of Moses, when his strong arm divided the waters, making an eternal name for himself (Is 63:11-14), the prophet, addressing Yahweh as "Father" and "Redeemer" (Is 63:16; 64:8), prays that Yahweh again rend the heavens, come down, shake the mountains, do fearful deeds on behalf of his people, and cause the nations to tremble (Is 63:1—64:4). The whole concludes with Yahweh's promise that his hand will be with his servants (Is 66:14), so that, in keeping his exodus project, all nations will see his glory (Is 66:18-19).

2.2. Jeremiah. In Jeremiah the influence of the exodus is similarly seen from the outset, informing both Yahweh's opening complaint against his people (Jer 2:1—3:10) and the prophet's famous Temple Sermon (Jer 7:1-15). In the complaint Israel's youthful devotion to the Lord, and his faithful guiding presence through the wilderness to a fruitful *land (Jer 2:2-7a), are set in sharp contrast to the nation's present infidelities. Not least of their infidelities is their devotion to other gods (Jer 2:7b—3:10; cf. Jer 5:19; 10:1-11), whereby, as in Isaiah 5, they have become a degenerate vine (Jer 2:21; cf. Deut 32:32-33). Although Yahweh's "firstborn son" (cf. Jer 31:20), they are now "faithless children" (e.g., Jer 3:14, 22). In the sermon, which details numerous covenant infractions, the exodus emphasis on covenantal obedience rather than *sacrifice (Jer 7:22-23) reveals the folly of Israel's trust in the temple's sanctity. Their present disobedience, including especially their idolatry, is traced back to the day their ancestors came out of Egypt (Jer 7:24-26), being couched primarily in terms of transgressing the Sinai covenant (e.g., Jer 2:9; 8:8; 9:13; 11:1-12; 16:10-13; 22:9; 26:4; 32:23; 44:10, 23). Instead of their own wisdom, might or wealth, they should trust in Yahweh's revealed steadfast love and justice (Jer 9:24).

Consequently, although God had mercifully kept covenant in giving them a land flowing with milk and honey (Jer 11:5), this time he will honor its curses (Jer 11:2-4; 16:13). In contrast to the incident of the golden calf, Yahweh will not have compassion on them (Jer 13:14; cf. Ex 34:6-7), even if Moses stood before him (Jer 15:1-2). In an antiexodus they will "go out" into exile and death (Jer 21:9). Because they failed to observe the Sabbath (Jer 17:19-27), the particular mark of their being his holy people (see Ex 31:12-16), their land will now lie desolate (e.g., Jer 4:26; 6:8; 9:11, 15-16; 10:22; 22:5-6; 34:22; 44:2, 6, 22). In a reversal of the exodus, Yahweh's outstretched hand and mighty arm will again perform their wonderful deed, but now against them (Jer 21:2, 5; cf. Jer 6:12; 15:6; 21:5; 27:5-8). In resiling from their covenantal obligation, made when Yahweh had released them from slavery in Egypt, to release their slaves every seventh year, he will now "release" them to sword, pestilence and famine (Jer 34:8-22). And these will follow them even to Egypt, where, unthinkably, given Yahweh's earlier redemption (e.g. Jer 2:18, 36; cf. 2:6; 7:22, 25; 11:4, 7), they have disobediently gone in vain hope of escape (Jer 41:17—46:28). In keeping with his character revealed at the exodus, he will by no means leave them unpunished (Jer 46:28b).

But even so, this same revealed character means that the Lord will not make an end of his people (Jer 46:28a; cf. Lam 3:22, 32). He promises that there will be a new exodus that will so outshine the old that Yahweh himself will now be known by it (Jer 16:14-15; 23:6-8). The ark will no longer be remembered or needed, since Jerusalem itself will be the Lord's throne (Jer 3:16). The positive presence of the exodus is most clearly felt in the Book of Consolation (Jer 30—33) (van der Wal), set in deliberate counterpoint in the middle of many chapters of "no exodus" hopes (Jer 26—45) (Yates). Mighty Yahweh, who with outstretched arm had performed signs and wonders in Egypt, will, in keeping with his character revealed therein, again show steadfast love to the thousandth generation (Jer 32:17-21; cf. Jer 30:18; 31:3, 20; 33:11, 26; see also Jer 42:12). He will bless "their tents" (Jer 30:18), have mercy on "his beloved son" (Jer 30:18; 31:3, 20), lead the redeemed back from exile (Jer 31:7-11) and again plant them in their land, where they will be his people and he their God (Jer 30:22; 31:26-34). Taking up the earlier emphasis on their breaking covenant, Yahweh will effect a new covenant, written not on stone but rather on their hearts (Jer 31:31-32; cf. Ex 32:19; Deut 30:6). And, as in Isaiah, this new exodus is linked with the restoration of the Davidic line (Jer 30:9; 33:15-26).

In a final word of encouragement, Jeremiah declares that even if enslaving Babylon refuses to let his people go (cf. Ex 7:14; 10:3-4), their kinsman Redeemer, mentioned only here in Jeremiah (Jer 50:34), mighty Yahweh, "the Holy One," will turn his "hand" against it (Jer 51:25), intervening against its horses and chariots (Jer 50:29, 37a), plundering its houses (Jer 50:37b) and drying up its waters (Jer 50:33-38) (see Bellis). For even though Israel and Judah have filled their land with guilt before "the Holy One of Israel," he, unable to deny his exodus character, has not forsaken them (Jer 51:5).

2.3. Ezekiel. Compared to Isaiah and Jeremiah, in Ezekiel's message to the exiles the exodus plays a more limited and somewhat different role. Ezekiel shares the idea that their, and their ancestors', failure to keep the law (Ezek 5:6-7; 11:12; 16:59)—again notably their apostasy to other gods—is the covenantal cause of their desolation (Ezek 5:14-17; 7:2; 9:1-11; 14-16; cf. Ezek 33:23-29). As Yahweh had bared his arm at the exodus, so too Ezekiel will bare his arm in prophesying that God's hand was now against his people (Ezek 4:7; 6:14; 13:9; 14:9, 13; 16:27) (on Ezekiel as a new Moses, see Idestrom). Jeremiah's rebuke of Judah's whoredoms finds an extensive and intentionally shocking counterpart in Ezekiel's account of Jerusalem's lewdness (Ezek 16; cf. Hosea [see 4.1 below]). But there is also a message of hope to those dispersed among the nations (Ezek 11:16). Yahweh will, in language reminiscent of Jeremiah (Jer 30—31), regather them in a new exodus (Ezek 20:33-34; cf. Ezek 25:7, 13, 16), giving them a new heart and new spirit so that they will keep his commandments, and they will be his people and he their God (Ezek 11:16-20; 16:62), blessing their land (Ezek 36:6-12).

But there are new developments. Elements of the prophet's opening vision seem to echo the Sinai theophany (Ezek 1:4, 22; cf. Ex 19:16-18; 24:10, 15-17)—a kind of anti-Sinai presaging judgment?—and only in Ezekiel is there such an emphasis on the reversal of the high point of the exodus wherein Yahweh's presence departs from his temple (Ezek 10—12; cf. Ezek 25:3). While covenant obedience continues to lead to life and disobedience to death (Ezek 18; 33:10-20), the Exodus 34:7 tradition is modified so that the sins of the parents will be visited no longer on their children but rather upon the perpetrators themselves (Ezek 18:2-4, 20; cf. Ezek 33:10-20).

More remarkable is Ezekiel 20:5-38, the prophet's most extended engagement with the exodus. Beginning with the customary traditions of Yahweh's self-revelation and gift of a land flowing with milk and honey (Ezek 20:5-7, 15b, 19-20), Ezekiel's exodus is one of Israel's unrelenting rebellion (cf. Ezek 2:5). It begins, uniquely, with Israel's refusal to reject Egypt's gods even while in bondage (Ezek 20:7-8a; 23:8, 19-20, 27; cf. Josh 24:14)—this might partially explain the extended diatribe against Egypt (Ezek 29—32)—countered by Yahweh's commitment "for the sake of his name" to continue with their deliverance (Ezek 20:8b-10; cf. Ex 32:11-14). This initiates a threefold cycle, repeated throughout the wilderness journeying and into the land: (1) Yahweh's gift of his life-giving statutes and Sabbath as a testimony to his holiness (Ezek 20:11-12, 18-20), (2) Israel's refusal to obey, breach of Sabbath and persistent idolatry (Ezek 20:13a, 21a, 27-32), (3) Yahweh's withholding of his *wrath (Ezek 20:13b-14; 21b; cf. Ex 32:10-14; Num 14:11-20) while passing suspended sentence upon them (Ezek 20:15-16, 23-24; cf. Ex 32:34; Num 14:21-23), a sentence now meted out in the exile. The reference in Ezekiel 20:25 to God giving "bad statutes" in the exodus remains enigmatic, but it may be an ironic polemic against the people's perverse twisting of the law of the firstborn (see Ex 13:12-13) to justify their sacrificing children to Molech. If they insisted on this diametrically opposed reading, then Ezekiel would carry it through to its conclusion such that instead of intending life, Yahweh intended their devastation and death.

In another striking development and perhaps addressing the continued rebellious unbelief implied by Isaiah 40—55 (see 2.1.2 above) (Ezek 36:20, 23), Yahweh will enter into judgment even with the exiles (Ezek 20:36; cf. Ex 32:25-28, 35; Num 11:1-3, 33; 16). Bringing them back to the wilderness, he would cause them to "know" in a new "face-to-face" revelation that "I am the LORD" (cf. Ex 29:46), imposing the bond of covenant and pouring out his wrath not on the nations but instead on the rebels among them, who, he promises, will not return to the land (Ezek 20:33-38; cf. Ezek 11:21; Num 14:21-23; 20:9-12; Deut 5:4).

But for the rest, concerned, as in the exodus, for his holy name (Ezek 36:21-23, 32; cf. Ex 32:11-14), Yahweh will cleanse them (Ezek 36:21-25; cf. Ezek 16:9) and give them a new heart and spirit to follow his commands, blessing them and their land (Ezek 36:26-38; 37; cf. Ezek 34:25-31) (see Kohn). Through his "hand"

he will again display his glory, causing both Israel and the nations to know that he is "the Holy One of Israel," showing his people mercy (Ezek 39:25) and never again hiding his face from them (Ezek 39:21-29). And as in Isaiah and Jeremiah, Ezekiel's new exodus also envisages the restoration of the Davidic dynasty (Ezek 34:23-24; 37:24-25). Finally, picking up on his earlier vision of Yahweh's departing presence, this renewed relationship results not in a moveable tabernacle (Ex 25-31, 35-40) but rather in a new, fixed temple (Ezek 40—48) from which Yahweh's presence will never depart (Ezek 48:35) (Levenson).

3. Daniel.

The recollection of Yahweh's exodus self-revelation forms the basis of Daniel's prayer of confession (Dan 9). He acknowledges God's covenant faithfulness, steadfast love and merciful forgiveness (Dan 9:4, 9), confessing that Israel's transgression of Moses' law has justly led to their being cursed and driven into exile (Dan 9:5, 7, 11, 13-14). But appealing to the "Lord our God, who brought your people up out of Egypt with a mighty hand," thereby making his name great (Dan 9:15), Daniel asks on the basis of God's great mercies that he forgive, hear and act to restore his people (Dan 9:18-19).

4. The Book of the Twelve.

4.1. Hosea. Yahweh's exodus self-revelation lies at the heart of both Hosea and, to the extent that this book introduces the corpus, the Book of the Twelve (Bosman): he will not leave unpunished Israel's idolatrous recapitulation of the "adultery" of the golden calf (Hos 3:1; 8:4-6; 10:5; 11:2; 13:2; 14:8). If they had turned to him, he would have "redeemed" them, but instead they sought help from, of all places, Egypt (Hos 7:13-16). Embodying Yahweh's experience of Israel's exodus infidelities beginning at Baal-Peor (Hos 9:10; cf. Num 25:1-5), Hosea marries an adulterous wife (Hos 2; 11), whose offspring's names, "I will not have compassion" and "Not my people" (Hos 1:6, 9), declare the consequences of Israel's repudiation of the Sinai covenant (e.g., Hos 4:6; 8:1) (McKenzie notes Hosea's link between the exodus and Deuteronomy).

This judgment is played out in Hosea's ironic, *lex talionis* reversal of various exodus motifs. Having been "I am" for them, in a play on

Exodus 3:14 he will now be "not I am for you" (Hos 1:9b). Critiquing, as does Jeremiah, their misplaced trust in sacrifice (Hos 6:6), Hosea declares that because they did not reflect Yahweh's steadfast love and righteousness in their dealings with others (Hos 4:1; 6:6; 10:12), he will no longer show either to them (Hos 6:6; 10:12), and none shall deliver them from his hand (Hos 2:10). Although they are his son whom he had called from Egypt (Hos 11:1-4), because they refused his repeated invitations to come to him, he will return them to Egypt, from whence he had brought them (Hos 11:5; cf. Hos 8:13; 9:3). As he had delivered them by a prophet (Hos 12:13), he will now destroy them and send them back by the word of his prophets (Hos 12:10). Similarly, just as Yahweh, their only God and Savior since Egypt (Hos 12:9; 13:4a), had provided for them (Hos 13:5-6a), now, having grown fat and abandoned him (Hos 13:6b), they will become his prey (i.e., provision), and there will be none to save or redeem (Hos 13:6b-11). He will, in a reversal of the exodus, divest them of their rich dwellings and reduce them to living in tents again (Hos 12:9). He will neither deliver nor redeem them from either Sheol or exodus-like deathly pestilence (Hos 13:14).

Nevertheless, Hosea, echoing the language of the Sinai self-revelation, declares that Yahweh will "in steadfast love and mercy" take them as his wife again (Hos 2:19). His compassion for his son will rise within him (Hos 11:8). Because he is "the Holy One," he will not again destroy Ephraim (Hos 11:9) and will yet call them "my people" (Hos 2:1; 1:11). In a new exodus from both Egypt and Assyria (Hos 11:10-11), he will again lead them into the wilderness, where they will respond as in the days of their exodus youth (Hos 2:14). The very place where Israel first sinned through Achan (see Josh 7:1), now the Valley of Achor (ʿākôr means "sorrow" or "trouble"), would become the "gate of hope" (Hos 2:14-15; cf. Num 13:23-26), and they would again own David as their king (Hos 3:5).

4.2. Joel. Faced with the looming and dreadful *"day of the Lord," Joel likewise recalls Yahweh's merciful relenting after the incident of the golden calf, calling the people to repentance (Joel 2:1-2, 13). His hopeful question, "Who knows?" (Joel 2:14), reminds them, however, that now, as then, Yahweh's mercy is not a foregone conclusion, the Lord being free to show compassion to whom he chooses (see Ex 33:19). But as with Moses, Joel's appeal to the importance of Yahweh's reputation among the nations (Joel 2:17; cf. Ex 32:11-14) results in the Lord doing great things for his people, blessing them in the land and dwelling among them (Joel 2:18-27).

4.3. Amos. Amos too contrasts the Lord's great kindness in bringing Israel up from Egypt, guiding them through the wilderness and giving them the land (Amos 2:10) with their faithless rejection of his law (Amos 2:4). As did Jeremiah and Hosea, he rebukes Israel's misplaced trust in ritual, reminding them that God required no regular sacrificial program during the wilderness (Amos 5:25). This both relativizes sacrifice and reminds Israel that Yahweh's priorities lie in the goodness and justice that characterize him (Amos 5:10-24). Since of all the families on the earth he had known them alone, now he will punish the entire family that he brought up from Egypt (Amos 3:1-2), visiting them, Hosea-like, with pestilence after the manner of Egypt (Amos 4:9-10) and sending them into exile (Amos 5:27; cf. Deut 30:28). Anticipating Jonah, Amos employs the archetypical exodus verb "to bring up" (ʿālâ [see Ex 3:8, 17]) to challenge Israel's smug belief that being Yahweh's special people is sufficient to protect them (Amos 9:7). Nevertheless, in keeping with his character, he will "show favor" (ḥānan) to the remnant (Amos 5:15), raising again the fallen tent of David (Amos 9:11).

4.4. Jonah. The constancy and freedom of Yahweh's character also stand at the heart of the book of Jonah, but now surprisingly extended to the nations. Echoing Joel 2:14's hopeful question, "Who knows?" it is the Ninevites who repent and finding mercy (Jon 3:6-10). Yahweh's final double interrogation of Jonah's (and Israel's) bitter and parochial nationalism (Jon 4:2-9) turns on Jonah's sure knowledge of God's exodus character (Jon 4:2). The concluding message is clear: just as Yahweh freely chose to show mercy to idolatrous Israel, he is free to show compassion to repentant Nineveh (Jon 3:10; 4:10-11).

4.5. Micah. In his complaint against Israel Micah invokes Yahweh's "redemption" of Israel from the house of slavery, noting in particular his provision of leadership through Moses, Aaron and Miriam (Mic 6:4). Having announced judgment because Israel has failed to reflect God's character (Mic 6:8), Micah, in last few verses of the book, returns to the question raised by Hosea's awful announcement of Yahweh's rejection of his people (Bosman). Because of Yahweh's exodus self-revelation, judgment cannot be the last word. The God who delights in clemency will again show mercy, compassion and covenant faithfulness to his remnant people (Mic 7:18-20; cf. Ex 34:6-7). Envisioning a new exodus in which Yahweh will redeem the remnant (Mic 7:12; 4:6-7, 10; 5:3), Micah prays for a repetition of God's mighty exodus deeds whereby the nations might again be terrified (Mic 7:15-17) and their wealth devoted to him (Mic 4:13).

4.6. Nahum. References to the exodus become less frequent in the second half of the Book of the Twelve. To introduce his message to Nineveh, Nahum too returns to Yahweh's Sinai self-revelation. Declaring that the Lord is slow to anger, Nahum, in his alteration of "great in love" (Ex 34:6b) to "great in power," underlines the certain albeit delayed consequences of Nineveh's actual failure to repent: "the LORD will by no means clear the guilty" (Nah 1:3). That power is then underlined via echoes of the shattering impact upon the earth of Creator Yahweh's exodus descent (Nah 1:4-6).

4.7. Habakkuk. With the Assyrians gone, Habakkuk is now faced with the mystery of how "the Holy One," "the Rock," can use the even more wicked Babylonians to judge his people (Hab 1:12). He too reflects on Yahweh's character (Hab 3:2) and power over creation when the "Holy One" came as demonstrated in his exodus plagues (Hab 3:3-5), his shattering descent on Sinai (Hab 3:6), his defeat of Egypt at the sea, and subsequent conquest (Hab 3:6-15), but this time to find comfort in the face of Judah's impending desolation.

4.8. Haggai. On the other hand, Haggai's postexilic declaration that Creator Yahweh's presence is with Zerubbabel, Joshua and the remnant people is in accordance with his promise when he brought them, similarly small and weak, out of Egypt (Hag 2:4-5). And therefore, as in the exodus, they can expect the imminent shaking of the heavens, the earth and all nations (Hag 2:6-7a), with the nations' treasure coming into his house (Hag 2:7b-9; cf. Mic 4:13). If they purify themselves and return to him, they will no longer experience his covenant curse upon their lands (Hag 2:17).

4.9. Zechariah. Zechariah contains no specific recollection of the exodus, though the de-

mand for kindness (*hesed*) and mercy (*raḥămîm*) (Zech 7:9) appears to originate in Yahweh's revealed character. A clearer echo perhaps is the Lord's promised compassionate redemption, on the basis of "I am their God" and in answer to their cry, of the exiles from Egypt and Assyria as they pass, recalling the Reed Sea, through the sea of distress (Zech 10:6-12; cf. Zech 1:16; 8:8). After judgment and in accordance with God's covenant promise, they will again be his people and he their God (Zech 13:9), which results, as in several other prophets, in the restoration of David's house (Zech 12:7-8; cf. Zech 13:1).

4.10. Malachi. Finally, at the conclusion of the Book of the Twelve, Malachi returns to two central concerns of the exodus: Yahweh's presence and his reputation among the nations (Mal 1:11). The promised "messenger of the covenant" in Malachi 3:1 reprises the role of the exodus "angel of the LORD" (Ex 23:20). He is to prepare for Yahweh's long-delayed returning presence by calling Israel back to covenantal obedience (Mal 3:2-4), the prerequisite of being blessed in the land (see Ex 23:21-33). Having reminded Israel of their long-standing rejection of Yahweh's Sinai statutes (Mal 3:7a), Malachi calls them to remember the Sinai ordinances of Moses (Mal 4:4), lest when the Lord comes, he strike the land with a curse (Mal 4:6).

5. Conclusion.
In beginning with the canonical pentateuchal accounts of the exodus, this article assumed both its interrelated complexity and foundational nature. The extensive, diverse, sometimes specific, but more commonly allusive nature of the prophets' appeals to the exodus strongly implies a significant body of knowledge shared between themselves and their audiences. The exodus, in all its breadth of interwoven ideas and motifs, apparently is not their invention but rather is an older complex of traditions upon which they freely drew without any hint of the need either to justify that appeal or to explain its presumed content. Here was something sufficiently well known that although the prophets sometimes were very specific in drawing parallels, in many places they felt that a simple allusion would suffice. So while on the surface it might appear that concepts such as justice, righteousness and compassion are common currency, the material here suggests that at least for a number of the

prophets these norms were grounded in Yahweh's exodus self-revelation.

Even so, it is important to recognize that the prophets' individual engagement with the exodus very much reflects the needs of their particular situations. Although often sharing a range of fundamental ideas, different prophets reflect different aspects of those traditions in ways that most contribute to driving their message home. Nevertheless, even though it would still be mistaken to assume that this article's opening summary reflects what every prophet knew, there is sufficient commonality to suggest that they knew and assumed a great deal more about the exodus than perhaps was previously thought.

In terms of the exodus itself, the prophets' "theology" is essentially historical. Their fundamental assumption is that Yahweh's character and authority as creator and peerless Lord, as revealed at the exodus, remains constant. He who brought Pharaoh and the mountains low, who divided the waters and rescued his people, has lost none of his power, righteousness, compassion and faithfulness. As he had acted for the sake of his glorious name in the past, he will and can be relied upon to act again. If Israel becomes like the nations and rebels against him, his mighty hand will mete out the same justice against them as it did against the Egyptians. And the same applies to any nation that in arrogance exalts itself against him.

But it is here that the most remarkable contribution of the exodus to the prophets' message emerges: the deep and abiding conviction of a just Yahweh's overwhelming propensity to mercy and compassion—and not just to Israel, but also to the nations. As the creator of this good world, Yahweh's primary intention is to bring deliverance, life and blessing, both initially to Israel and through them to the nations. The exodus, it seems, was always intended to be cosmic in scope. Although lying outside the concerns of this essay, it seems that this is precisely the perspective taken by a later prophet, Paul of Tarsus (cf. Gal 1:15; Acts 14:27 with Jer 1:5; Is 49:1-6), in his magisterial achievement in Romans 9—11 (esp. Rom 11:25-36).

In this last respect, one must also note the frequently assumed link between the new exodus and the restoration of the Davidic kingdom. Apparently, as the solitary dating in 1 Kings 6:1 of the construction of Solomon's temple to the deliverance from Egypt suggests, a number of the prophets held the Davidic kingdom to be, finally, the ultimate realization of the exodus. It was in these early years of the Davidides that Yahweh's presence dwelled in a settled house among his blessed people and their land, and to whose glory evident in his wise and just king the nations were drawn.

See also COVENANT; EXILE; LAND; LAW; PROPHECY AND TRADITION; SALVATION, DELIVERANCE; WILDERNESS, DESERT.

BIBLIOGRAPHY. **B. W. Anderson**, "Exodus Typology in Second Isaiah," in *Israel's Prophetic Heritage: Essays in Honor of James Muilenberg*, ed. B. W. Anderson and W. Harrelson (New York: Harper, 1962) 177-95; **H. M. Barstad**, *A Way in the Wilderness: The "Second Exodus" in the Message of Second Isaiah* (Manchester, UK: University of Manchester Press, 1989); **A. O. Bellis**, "The New Exodus in Jeremiah 50:33-38," in *Imagery and Imagination in Biblical Literature: Essays in Honor of Aloysius Fitzgerald, F.S.C*, ed. L. Boadt and M. S. Smith (CBQMS 32; Washington, DC: Catholic Biblical Association, 2001) 157-68; **R. Bergey**, "The Song of Moses (Deuteronomy 32.1-43) and Isaianic Prophecies: A Case of Early Intertextuality?" *JSOT* 28 (2003) 33-54; **J. P. Bosman**, "The Paradoxical Presence of Exodus 34:6-7 in the Book of the Twelve," *Scriptura* 87 (2004) 233-43; **A. R. Ceresko**, "The Rhetorical Strategy of the Fourth Servant Song (Isaiah 52:13-53:12): Poetry and the Exodus-New Exodus," *CBQ* 56 (1994) 42-55; **Y. Hoffman**, "A North Israelite Typological Myth and a Judaean Historical Tradition: The Exodus in Hosea and Amos," *VT* 39 (1989) 169-82; **G. P. Hugenberger**, "The Servant of the Lord in the 'Servant Songs' of Isaiah," in *The Lord's Anointed: Interpretation of Old Testament Messianic Texts*, ed. P. E. Satterthwaite, R. S. Hess and G. J. Wenham (TynHS; Grand Rapids: Baker; Carlisle: Paternoster, 1995) 105-40; **R. Idestrom**, "Echoes of the Book of Exodus in Ezekiel," *JSOT* 28 (2003) 489-510; **T. A. Keiser**, "The Song of Moses: A Basis for Isaiah's Prophecy," *VT* 55 (2005) 486-500; **K. Kiesow**, *Exodustexte im Jesajabuch: Literarkritische und motivegeschichtliche Analysen* (OBO 24; Göttingen: Vandenhoeck & Ruprecht, 1979); **R. L. Kohn**, *A New Heart and a New Soul: Ezekiel, the Exile and the Torah* (JSOTSup 358; London: Sheffield Academic, 2002); **J. D. Levenson**, *Theology of the Program of Restoration of Ezekiel 40-48*

(HSM 10; Missoula, MT: Scholars Press, 1976); **B. H. Lim,** *The "Way of the Lord" in the Book of Isaiah* (LHBOTS 522; New York: T & T Clark, 2010); **J. Lust,** "Exodus 6,2-8 and Ezekiel," in *Studies in the Book of Exodus,* ed. M. Vervenne (BETL 126; Leuven: Leuven University Press, 1996) 209-24; **S. McKenzie,** "Exodus Typology in Hosea," *ResQ* 22 (1979) 100-108; **S. Paganini, C. Paganini and D. Markl,** eds., *Führe Mein Volk Heraus: Zur innerbiblischen Rezeption der Exodusthematik; Festschrift für Georg Fischer* (Frankfurt: Peter Lang, 2004); **A. Rayappan,** "Out of Egypt: Bondage and Liberation in Jeremiah," in *Führe Mein Volk Heraus: Zur innerbiblischen Rezeption der Exodusthematik; Festschrift für Georg Fischer,* ed. S. Paganini, C. Paganini and D. Markl (Frankfurt: Peter Lang, 2004) 37-53; **M. F. Rooker,** "The Use of the Old Testament in the Book of Hosea," *CTR* 7 (1993) 51-66; **A. van der Wal,** "Themes from Exodus in Jeremiah 30-31," in *Studies in the Book of Exodus,* ed. M. Vervenne (BETL 126; Leuven: Leuven University Press, 1996) 559-66; **R. E. Watts,** "Consolation or Confrontation? Isaiah 40-55 and the Delay of the New Exodus," *TynBul* 41 (1990) 31-59; **G. E. Yates,** "New Exodus and No Exodus in Jeremiah 26-45: Promise and Warning to the Exiles in Babylon," *TynBul* 57 (2006) 1-22. R. E. Watts

EXTRA-CANONICAL BOOKS OF PROPHETS. *See* DEAD SEA SCROLLS.

EZEKIEL: BOOK OF

The book of Ezekiel is set in the Jewish community in *Babylon during the sixth century BC. It is presented as the first-person account of the prophet Ezekiel, a man of priestly descent from among the first group of deportees from Judah in 593 BC (Ezek 1:1-3).

1. Historical Issues
2. Textual and Literary Issues
3. The Message of the Book of Ezekiel
4. The Book of Ezekiel in Texts from the Second Temple Period
5. Canonization of the Book of Ezekiel
6. Ideological Readings

1. Historical Issues.

1.1. Author and Prophet. It is important to distinguish between the literary persona of the prophet Ezekiel within the book of Ezekiel and the author(s) of the book itself. Although the two personae may coincide, this cannot be taken for granted. Personifications are common to all literature, although the form in which they occur differs. Sometimes entirely fictive characters are presented as historical persons, sometimes historical persons are hidden behind a screen of fiction, and sometimes personifications are made deliberately recognizable as literary fiction (de Moor, vii). This realization highlights the need to differentiate between the author of a prophetic text and the prophetic "I" within that same text. Scholarly views range from those who see a given prophetic book as based upon the sayings of a specific historical person to those who regard the prophetic literature as unhistorical presentations of prophets (Gitay). In the specific case of Ezekiel, from time to time scholars have voiced the idea of pseudepigraphy. This latter idea stems primarily from the perceived references to events during the Hellenistic era (Torrey, 83-99) and the protoapocalyptic features in Ezekiel (e.g., Feist). None of these theories has won any larger following, however. More recently, scholarship has focused on the presentation of Ezekiel as a literary character within the book bearing his name. For example, several scholars explore the ways in which the literary persona of Ezekiel is presented as a prophet and/or as a priest within the book.

1.2. Date and Compositional Growth. The book of Ezekiel in its present form is likely to be the result of several redactions, possibly reaching well into the Hellenistic era. For instance, the changes between first and third person may indicate that the book is composite in nature. Notably, Ezekiel 1:1 refers to the prophet in the first person, as does Ezekiel 1:4, while Ezekiel 1:2-3 speaks of him in the third person.

At the same time, the identification of the author of the greater part of the book of Ezekiel with a Jewish deportee in Babylon in the sixth century BC is supported by several factors. (1) The descriptions of the Babylonian exilic community in the book of Ezekiel fit the picture that can be gleaned from the meagre contemporary Neo-Babylonian sources (Mein, 59-66). (2) Based on the assumption that the chronology at least in part corresponds to topology, the language of the book of Ezekiel fits chronologically the sixth century BC, even if a later date cannot be excluded on linguistic grounds alone (Hurvitz; Rooker; Ehrensvärd).

(3) On the presupposition that the divine oracles in the book of Ezekiel at least to a certain extent reflect the experiences of the person uttering them, that person can easily be identified as one suffering posttraumatic stress disorder (PTSD) as the result of experiencing the violence of the Neo-Babylonian attacks on Jerusalem and the deprivation and humiliation of deportation (Smith-Christopher, 32-33). (4) Although parts of the book of Ezekiel contain eschatological and/or *apocalyptic imagery that is reminiscent of the imagery in texts from the Hellenistic period, it can be argued that this type of imagery was present already in texts from the Persian period. Notably, Ezekiel 38 shares features with Isaiah 24—27; 66:18-24; Haggai 2:6-7, 21-22; Joel 3:16; Zechariah 14:4, 5. It is highly unlikely that the material in Haggai is later than the Persian period, and it is debatable as to whether the other texts are as late as the Hellenistic period. (5) It is reasonable to assume that the author of the book of Ezekiel corresponds to a relatively large extent with the first-person narrator (Block 2004, 230), although that must remain a conjecture.

These factors have not prevented some scholars from detecting complex stratification in the book of Ezekiel, with dates ranging from the sixth to the third centuries BC. For instance, J. Garscha postulates three chief layers of the book of Ezekiel: (1) the original prophetic book (*VEz*), containing, but not identical to, the words of the prophet Ezekiel (500-485/460 BC); (2) the Deutero-Ezekielian reworking (*DEz*) (400-350 BC); (3) the cultic-law redaction (*SEz*) (300 BC). The key to Garscha's dating scheme is the laments over the king of Tyre (Ezek 26—28). Garscha, as well as other scholars, assumes that the content of Ezekiel 26—28 speaks about actual historical situations, and accordingly he attempts to identify these situations. Since we know that Alexander the Great destroyed Tyre in 332/331 BC, Garscha concludes that the material in Ezekiel 26—28 refers to this destruction. It follows that the recensions *VEz* and *DEz* must be older than 332 BC, and *SEz* must be younger (Garscha, 283-311; cf. Saur).

This methodology is based on the presupposition that events referred to in prophetic texts correspond directly to historical events contemporary with the author. This presupposition is, however, open for dispute. The very fact that a prophet envisions the destruction

of Tyre (Ezek 26—28) need not reflect the prophet's contemporary reality. On the contrary, such a prediction may tell us instead that the prophet wished for its destruction. We might therefore conclude that at the time of the composition of Ezekiel 26—28 Tyre was a strong city, and that an Israelite prophet wished for its downfall.

1.3. Geographical Setting. Given the probability that the greater part of the book of Ezekiel was composed by a member of the Jewish community in Babylon in the sixth century BC, a careful reading of the book will provide insight into the exiles' lives. A strong case can also be made that the ministry and the message of the book of Ezekiel cannot be adequately understood unless we take its exilic background into account (*see* Exile).

Despite the likelihood that other biblical texts were composed by the Jewish community in Babylon, the book of Ezekiel is unique in the Hebrew Bible in that it presents the ministry of the prophet as taking place in Babylon. The first-person narrator describes his daily life in the Babylonian community. He mentions, for example, the Jewish settlement of Tel-abib (Ezek 3:15), and he refers to elders (Ezek 8:1; 14:1; 20:1), which implies that the exiles had some form of self-rule. In addition, the reference to prophets in Ezekiel 13 suggests that there were prophets other than Ezekiel in the Jewish community in Babylon, and that these prophets were free to deliver their oracles in some form of public space (Mein, 66-73).

This picture of the Jewish community is corroborated by the scant extrabiblical evidence. This evidence is primarily onomastic in character—that is, texts that mention persons with names containing a theophoric element related to Yahweh, or names that are accompanied by the ethnic designation "Judahite." There are three tablets from the early Persian period with Hebrew names, another ninety texts in a private collection (the TAYN corpus) containing references to Jews living in the Babylon-Borsippa region in the sixth century BC, and the Murashu archive from Nippur with tablets dating from 454 to 404 BC. All this evidence, taken together, seems to show that the Jews in Babylon were relatively well integrated into society, although it is unlikely that they assimilated into the population around them (Grabbe, 316-17).

Despite its exilic setting, much of the book

of Ezekiel concerns Jerusalem. For example, the material in Ezekiel 8—11 depicts the removal of the *divine presence from Jerusalem, while the material in Ezekiel 40—48 envisions God's return and the subsequent rebuilding of the city. Likewise, several passages in the book appear to display knowledge of life in Jerusalem between 597 and 586 BC, a time during which the prophet Ezekiel must have already been living in Babylon (2 Kings 24:12; 2 Chron 36:10; cf. Ezek 1:1-2, which refers to the fifth year of exile [i.e., 593 BC]). The accounts in Ezekiel 8—11 portray the prophet as present, although in a vision, in Jerusalem. Ezekiel 8, for example, purportedly describes the kinds of worship that took place in the Jerusalem temple. Other passages, such as Ezekiel 12, concern the leaders of Jerusalem (Ezek 12:10). These factors have led some scholars to argue that the prophet was actually based in Judah rather than in Babylon, either during all (Herntrich) or part (Bertholet, xii-xvi) of his active prophetic ministry.

These interpretations are unconvincing for two reasons. First, it is possible that the descriptions of the rituals in the Jerusalem temple in Ezekiel 8 are influenced by the author's experiences prior to his deportation. It can be argued that the author, identified with Ezekiel the prophet and the priest, was familiar with the situation in the Jerusalem temple. Although he probably was not yet ordained as a priest (Ezek 1:1; cf. Num 4:3; 1 Chron 23:3, where thirty was the age of ordination) and therefore might not have taken an active role in the rituals, he would have known what was going on in the temple.

Second, there is no need to interpret the references to activities in Judah as evidence of actual journeys to Judah. Instead, it is preferable to accept the biblical explanation that the descriptions in Ezekiel 8—11 are based on a *visionary experience (Joyce, 6). As such, they could be a literal description of what was taking place in the temple, but also they could depict the author's opinion of the temple worship. In other words, nothing compels us to regard the descriptions in Ezekiel 8 as reflecting actual rites in the Jerusalem temple in the sixth century BC (see Liturgy and Cult). It is preferable to see them as polemical exaggerations through which the author sought to convince his audience that the destruction of the Jerusalem tem-

ple was God's justified act of punishment of the sinful people of Judah. A few scholars go further and interpret the descriptions in Ezekiel 8 as having risen from the prophet's own damaged fantasy than reflecting any reality (Halperin, 58-79).

1.4. Dependence on Earlier Biblical Texts. The book of Ezekiel is part of the longer tradition of ancient Israelite literature. It depends upon and also develops further motifs and ideas found in earlier material. In particular, there are similarities between the book of Ezekiel and the pentateuchal Priestly source (P), the texts of the Holiness School (HS) (Lev 17—26) and the book of Deuteronomy.

The book of Ezekiel shares a common literary language with the pentateuchal P source and contains material that relates to priestly concerns. The key sections are Ezekiel 3:17-21; 14:1-12; 18:1-20; 22:1-16 (Joyce, 10; Levitt Kohn, 31-75). This shared language and area of interest can be explained in different ways. If we identify the author of the book of Ezekiel with the character bearing the same name, and if we accept that this person was a priest, as indicated by Ezekiel 1:3, then it is natural to assume that such a person would not only concern himself with priestly matters but also use language associated with the priestly writing of the Pentateuch (Haran, 214). Alternatively, it is possible to distinguish between the material that does not reflect priestly concerns and the material with close ties to P. The latter material may then be explained as secondary material, added by a redactor who sought to bring the book of Ezekiel closer to its own priestly interests (see, e.g., Garscha). Of these two explanations, the former is more compelling because of its simplicity.

It is important to determine the direction of influence of the related material. In short, is the book of Ezekiel the earlier text, which P then reworks, or does P constitute a source upon which Ezekiel draws? Furthermore, to what extent did these two texts exist in their current form at the time when this influence took place? For example, the laws in Ezekiel 40—48 and some of the laws in P share a number of concerns, yet the individual laws often contradict each other. Notably, they disagree about the number of animals to be sacrificed on the same occasion, as well as the measures of the grain offering and the quantities of accompanying oil to be used.

Those scholars who advocate a preexilic origin of P naturally see P, although probably not in its current form, as the earlier source upon which the book of Ezekiel draws. M. Haran, for example, maintains that the two texts are independent manifestations of the same school, with P being the original source, while the material especially in Ezekiel 40—48 forms a freer version. Haran explains the discrepancies between the two texts by suggesting that instead of Ezekiel modifying P directly, he remembered P from his time serving in the temple before the exile. Other scholars see P as a later development of a tradition to which the book of Ezekiel belongs. W. Zimmerli, for example, argues that P drew from a general stream of priestly tradition of which the book of Ezekiel forms an earlier part (Zimmerli 1979, 52).

The mutual influence of the book of Ezekiel and P in terms of both vocabulary and concepts has theological implications for the reading of Ezekiel. For instance, the book of Ezekiel develops the priestly concept of Yahweh's glory. The P material in the Pentateuch employs the Hebrew term *kābôd* as a technical expression for God's presence. It emphasizes God's incorporeal nature (Ex 24:16-17), his potentially lethal presence (Ex 20:18; Num 16:19-21) and his association with the tabernacle (Ex 29:43; 40:34-35; Lev 9:6, 23). The theophanies in Ezekiel 1:28; 3:23; 44:4 use the same expression to denote God's graphic form. For example, Ezekiel 1:4 transforms the notion of God's manifestation in fire and cloud (cf. Ex 24:16-17) into an astonishingly anthropomorphic revelation of God's appearance. The vision accounts in Ezekiel develop the priestly notion of God's presence in the tabernacle into a picture of the mobility of God's presence, from his temple in Jerusalem (Ezek 1) to the exile (Ezek 11:22-23) and back to Jerusalem (Ezek 43:2-5) (Kutsko, 79-100).

The situation is similar when it comes to the relationship between the book of Ezekiel and HS. Is HS the later text, which depends on the book of Ezekiel, or does the book of Ezekiel depend on HS? Alternatively, do HS and the book of Ezekiel show signs of mutual literary dependence? These questions are complicated by the issue of the relationship between HS and P. Is HS an independent preexilic or postexilic source that at one point was incorporated into

P? Alternatively, are the authors of HS actually the redactors of P, with HS being composed to supplement and interact with P (Lyons, 5)?

Zimmerli's views on this matter are important. He maintains that the similarities and differences between the book of Ezekiel and HS are the result of reciprocal influence between the two growing corpora of texts. For example, while Ezekiel 17; 18; 20 depend on an early form of HS before it was incorporated into P, Leviticus 26 depends in part on the thoughts of Ezekiel 34:25-31 (Zimmerli 1979, 46-52).

More recent scholars, especially in the Anglo-American world, tend to regard the book of Ezekiel as the later text. R. Levitt Kohn, for example, maintains that the Ezekielian author(s) utilized not only P but also HS. In view of the recent trend of seeing the authors responsible for HS as the redactors of P, she argues that there is no evidence to suggest that the book of Ezekiel influenced the authors of HS. On the contrary, her word study suggests that the affinity between the book of Ezekiel and P is on the same level as that between the book of Ezekiel and HS. She therefore concludes that the Ezekielian author(s) utilized both sets of material without particular differentiation (Levitt Kohn, 85, 96-104). Likewise, M. Lyons argues that the book of Ezekiel made use of a preexisting body of material in the HS. It appeals to its authority yet also transforms it in order to develop its own argument. For example, it turns the positive and negative instructions in HS into accusations. Leviticus 18:4-5 mentions God's statutes and ordinances by which an Israelite should live. The later Ezekiel 22:7-12 contains a list of accusations, many of them alluding to laws in Leviticus 18—20, which then serve as the basis for the judgment promised in Ezekiel 22:2, 4-5, 14-15 (Lyons, 12-26).

The book of Ezekiel further contains expressions and concepts that are associated with Deuteronomy. Ezekiel 6, for example, presupposes the polemic against the high places of the Deuteronomic reform. Moreover, the material in Ezekiel 18 parallels that in Deuteronomy 12:1-4, and the verdict of stoning for a harlot in Ezekiel 16; 23 may reflect the legal material in Deuteronomy 13:10; 22:21. Some scholars therefore have suggested that the author(s) of the book of Ezekiel drew not only on P but also on D. Levitt Kohn, for example, has demonstrated that the Ezekielian author(s) appropriated the terminology of both sets of texts and created a synthesis, fitting for the new context of the community in exile (Levitt Kohn, 94-95). Along the same lines, T. Ganzel has shown that the Ezekielian author(s) had familiarity with Deuteronomy and created a new synthesis by combining the Deuteronomic language of *idolatry with the priestly concepts of impurity.

There are also links between the book of Ezekiel and the book of *Jeremiah, exemplified by the shared notion of "a new heart" (Ezek 11:19-20; 36:26-27; Jer 24:7; 31:31-34; 32:38-40). The affinity of the "new heart" in Jeremiah and Ezekiel with the idea of "circumcising the heart" in Deuteronomy 30:6 suggests that the prophetic writers depended on the Deuteronomic text. It is furthermore likely that the Ezekielian author(s) had access to the material in Jeremiah (Joyce, 39-40).

Finally, it is an open question as to what extent the book of Ezekiel and Isaiah 40—55 influence one another (*see* Isaiah: Book of). Some scholars argue that there is no awareness in Isaiah 40—55 of the teaching of the book of Ezekiel (e.g., Herrmann, 304), while other scholars maintain the opposite. Zimmerli, for example, argues that both texts share the idea of a return of the exiles to Judah accompanied by God's own return, and that both texts contain the notion that God's return to Judah is independent of Israel's repentance (Is 52:7-10; Ezek 43) (Zimmerli 1982, 113). Likewise, D. Baltzer makes a case that Ezekiel and Isaiah 40—55 share seven key concepts, and he explains these similarities by their shared origin in the time of the exile. For example, he maintains that Zion-Jerusalem and the temple stand in the foreground in both texts (Is 40:1-11; 49-55; Ezek 11:16; 20:39-44) (Baltzer, 27-48).

Despite Zimmerli's and Baltzer's arguments, there seems to be little support for the notion of direct influence between Isaiah 40—55 and Ezekiel. Instead, the differences between the two texts are more significant than their similarities. The notion of repentance differs significantly in the two textual corpora. Likewise, the two sets of texts differ widely in their respective treatment of Zion-Jerusalem and the temple. While the material in Ezekiel 40—48 assigns great importance to the temple but refrains from mentioning *Zion, the material in Isaiah 49—55 places personified Zion in the foreground yet never refers to the temple. A close connection between the various materials in Isaiah 40—55 and Ezekiel is therefore unlikely.

2. Textual and Literary Issues.

2.1. Style. The style of the book of Ezekiel is unique among the prophetic writings. First, in contrast to most other books in the Prophets, which consist primarily of short oracles written in poetry, the book of Ezekiel contains long prose narratives and extended oracular passages. Second, the prophetic persona plays a more significant role in the book of Ezekiel than what is usual in the prophetic literature, with the exception of the book of Jeremiah. The prophet Ezekiel speaks and is spoken to by God, he acts and God causes him to act. For example, all the prose narratives are presented as spoken by the prophet in the first-person singular. The book of Ezekiel opens with prophetic, rather than divine, speech: "when I was among the exiles" (Ezek 1:1), and this style continues throughout the book. Along the same lines, the oracles often are framed by statements such as "the LORD said to me." The prophet also describes his actions in the first-person singular. He describes how he eats the scroll that God gives him (Ezek 3:2), how God's spirit takes him on visionary journeys (Ezek 3:14; 8:1-3; 40:1-2) and how he discusses with God (Ezek 4:12-15). The oracular material in the book of Ezekiel also contains descriptions of the prophet's behavior. For instance, God commands Ezekiel to perform *sign acts such as acting out the siege of Jerusalem by placing a brick and an iron plate in front of him (Ezek 4:1-4) and by shaving his head (Ezek 5:1-4). This style reinforces the autobiographical mode of the book. At the same time, the prophet is dwarfed by God, for whom he speaks. The book of Ezekiel thus presents the prophet as doing and saying nothing apart from what God wants him to do.

2.2. Structure. There are different ways of viewing the structure of the book of Ezekiel. On the surface level, the chronological formulas found throughout the book, beginning with Ezekiel 1:1 and ending with Ezekiel 40:1, create thirteen literary units of varying lengths. The dating formulas are arranged roughly in chronological order, although some of the units appear out of linear order (Ezek 29:1 and Ezek 29:17). These literary units may contain more than one type of material and diversity of content (e.g. Ezek 32:17—33:20, where Ezek 32:17-32 contains an oracle against Egypt and Ezek 33:1-20 contains an oracle concerning a watchman) (Mayfield, 10-12, 182).

In regard more to content, the book of Ezekiel is commonly divided into three main sections. According to this structure, the book of Ezekiel begins with the prophet's call vision and ends with the vision of the new temple in Jerusalem.

The first section, Ezekiel 1—24, contains material that precedes the fall of Jerusalem in 587/586 BC. This section can be subdivided into three subsections, each introduced by a date. Ezekiel 1:1 opens with a date, followed by Ezekiel's first visionary journey and subsequent prophetic call (Ezek 1:1—3:15), prophetic signs and their interpretations (Ezek 3:16—5:17) and oracles of judgment (Ezek 6—7). Ezekiel 8:1 provides a new date, followed by Ezekiel's second visionary journey and accompanying oracles of judgment (Ezek 8—11), prophetic sign acts and their interpretation (Ezek 12:1-20) and oracles of judgment (Ezek 12:21—19:14). Ezekiel 20:1 contains yet another date, followed by various oracles of judgment.

The second section, Ezekiel 25—32, contains oracles against foreign nations in the same manner as, especially, Jeremiah (Jer 46—51) and Isaiah (Is 13—30). These oracles fall into two halves. The first half, in Ezekiel 25—28, contains oracles against Ammon, Moab, Edom, Philistia (Ezek 25), Tyre (Ezek 26:1—28:19) and Sidon (Ezek 28:20-23), and it ends with a brief oracle to Israel (Ezek 28:24-26). The second half, Ezekiel 29—32, consists of a collection of oracles and laments concerning Egypt.

The third section, Ezekiel 33—48, changes the tone from judgment to *salvation. This section falls into several subsections. Ezekiel 33 reports the fall of Jerusalem, and the subsequent Ezek 34—37 combines promises for the future restoration of Judah mixed in with references to the people's past *sins and judgment for its *leadership. Israel will be restored under God's leadership (Ezek 34) and cleansed from its sins and impurity (Ezek 36:16-37). Ezekiel is then taken on his third visionary journey, to the valley of the dry bones (Ezek 37:1-14), followed by an oracle of the future reunification of the northern and southern kingdoms (Ezek 37:15-28). The following material in Ezekiel 38—39 depicts the future invasion by Gog of Magog and his subsequent defeat. The final subsection, Ezekiel 40—48, features Ezekiel's fourth visionary journey. It contains detailed instructions of the future temple (Ezek 40:5—42:20), a vision within the vision of God's return to Jerusalem (Ezek 43:1-9) and his commission to the prophet to tell the people of Israel about the temple, its form and its laws, so that they can obey God (Ezek 43:10-12). The visionary tour continues in Ezekiel 43:13—46:24 with instructions concerning, among other things, the design of the altar, its dedication and prescriptions for the various offerings (Ezek 43:13-27; 45:18—46:15), rules for Levites and priests (Ezek 44:10-31), and the allotment of the land around the temple to the priestly personnel and the secular leadership (Ezek 45:1-8). The descriptions in the last two chapters change character. The prophet is led through the entrances of the temple to the land outside, which is gradually being filled with life-giving water coming from a source within the temple precincts (Ezek 47:1-12). The final material outlines the borders of Israel and the division of the *land (Ezek 47:13—48:35).

This division of the text is influenced by the perceived growth of the text. It is commonly assumed that the material in Ezekiel 1—24 was composed prior to the fall of Jerusalem in 586 BC, while the material in Ezekiel 33—48 was written afterward. Alternatively, the implied preexilic setting of the material in Ezekiel 1—24 indicates the way in which to read the text rather than its actual date of composition.

It further emphasizes the perceived distinct origin of the oracles against the *nations in Ezekiel 25—32. It is commonly held that these oracles originated independently from the rest of the book of Ezekiel (Zimmerli 1983, 4). However, given that the dating schema encompassing the entire book of Ezekiel incorporates these oracles, and given that the indirect audience of the oracles against the nations is Israel, a few scholars see them as integral to the book and largely primary in authorship (Joyce, 43).

The book of Ezekiel is punctuated at key points by three vision reports of theophanies, linked together by similar opening phrases (Ezek 1:1-3; 8:1-3; 40:1-2). These reports emphasize God's power and omnipresence and provide additional structure to the oracles in Ezekiel.

Finally, two interrelated literary motifs run alongside each other throughout the book of Ezekiel. The "watchman" motif is attested in Ezekiel 3:16b-21; 33:7-9. In both passages God appoints the prophet Ezekiel to be a watchman over the people of Israel. The first passage occurs in the beginning of the prophet's ministry leading up to the fall of Jerusalem in 586 BC, while the second one happens shortly before the news reaches the prophet that Jerusalem has been destroyed (Ezek 33:21). The motif of the prophet's muteness runs parallel to the watchman motif. It appears first in Ezekiel 3:22-27, directly following God's calling Ezekiel to be a watchman. This creates a seemingly impossible situation where Ezekiel, as the watchman, is unable to call out. The same motif reappears in Ezekiel 24:27, which predicts the end of Ezekiel's muteness, and reaches its climax in Ezekiel 33:21-22, immediately after the prophet has been informed about the fall of Jerusalem (Ezek 33:21), when his muteness is lifted (see 3 below).

2.3. Textual Criticism. The book of Ezekiel is preserved in two different textual editions: the Hebrew Masoretic Text (MT) and the Greek text of the Septuagint (LXX) (*see* Text and Textual Criticism). The latter text is a translation, probably carried out in Egypt around 150 BC (Olley, 15). The central question concerns the dating and form of the so-called Hebrew *Vorlage* of this translation, the Hebrew text upon which the Greek translation is based. In short, which of the two—the Hebrew *Vorlage* of the LXX or the Hebrew text of the MT—is the earlier text upon which the other text is based?

This discussion has significant repercussions for the dating of the final form of the book of Ezekiel. If the Hebrew *Vorlage* of the LXX is the earlier text, then the Hebrew text of the MT must be a product of the late Persian or even Hellenistic period. This conclusion is based on the following sequence of deduction. The LXX Greek translation stems from the Hellenistic period. This translation is based on an earlier Hebrew *Vorlage* of unknown date. At one point, the textual ancestor of the MT (i.e., the Hebrew text that later developed into the MT) modified this *Vorlage*. The question is when this modification took place. Although it is likely that the Hebrew *Vorlage* of the LXX is significantly older than the Hellenistic period, possibly going all the way back to the sixth cen-

tury BC, there would have been little point in modifying it before it reached the official status in the Greek translation of the LXX.

Much scholarly ink has been spilled in investigating the chronological relationship between these two editions. The scholarly debate has primarily focused on key texts in which the differences between the MT and the LXX have considerable exegetical consequences. For example, several scholars consider the MT of Ezekiel 28:11-19 to be a later, Hellenistic emendation of the Hebrew *Vorlage* of the LXX (Stordalen, 334-48). Likewise, exegetes argue that the differences between Ezekiel 7 in the MT and the LXX are best explained as the result of intentional editorial additions to the ancestor of the MT during the Hellenistic era. These additions sought to make the extant text agree with the theological notions prevalent in the Judaism of the time (Lust, 7-20).

There are strong arguments on both sides of the debate. In view of some of the arguments, it is possible that some parts of the MT stem from the Hellenistic period. Nonetheless, until we have more conclusive data at our disposal, each case needs to be considered individually.

3. The Message of the Book of Ezekiel.
The message of the book of Ezekiel walks hand in hand with its structure. Its overarching feature is the proclamation of *God's holiness, glory and power. No other book of the Bible explores God's absolute awesomeness and otherness in such lavish language. It opens with a vision account of God's overpowering presence (Ezek 1), and the reader is reminded at regular intervals of God's majesty (e.g., Ezek 8:2-5).

This notion of God as utterly holy, glorious and powerful also provides the key for understanding the theology of the book of Ezekiel pertaining to the destruction of Jerusalem in 587/586 BC. The holy God of Israel cannot tolerate sin and demands the sole devotion of his people. Since the people failed to live up to God's demands, God punished them by allowing the Neo-Babylonian armies to conquer their land and to destroy their capital city. In this sense, the book of Ezekiel is a theodicy; that is, it seeks to justify God's behavior by declaring that God's acts of punishment toward his people were the direct consequences of their sins (*see* Retribution). Moreover, the book declares that the fall of Judah was not a sign of

God's inability to care for his people. On the contrary, it affirms his power over not only Judah but also the Neo-Babylonian Empire, over which he rules and uses as a tool for punishing Judah (Ezek 4—24). Nonetheless, for the sake of his own glory, God, as the supreme ruler of the world, is willing to bring Judah back from the ashes and to resurrect them as a people again (Ezek 34—48).

God's supremacy and executive power are further elucidated through the descriptions of the prophet Ezekiel. The prophet is portrayed as God's ultimate tool, on the verge of losing his own identity. Ezekiel is a man completely overpowered by God. He behaves, speaks and even feels at the impulse of God's *Spirit, and he fulfills God's commands without pausing to question them or even to reflect about them. He internalizes God's word and, in a sense, becomes God's word through the symbolic eating of the scroll (Ezek 2:9—3:3). In this manner, the book of Ezekiel certifies that it contains only God's unadulterated speech.

In contrast to God's glory, there is nothing glorious or even good in the people of Judah. From the very beginning, Judah was deprived (Ezek 16:3b-5), and only God was in a position to save them from their natural squalor (Ezek 16:6-14). They are incorrigible, despite God's acts on their behalf (Ezek 16:15-34; cf. Ezek 20:5-26, 27-29), and thus fully deserving of punishment (Ezek 16:35-52; cf. Ezek 20:30-38). In fact, the people of Judah lack the inherent ability to do good. Left alone, they will always choose to disobey God because they have hearts of stone (Ezek 11:19; 36:26).

In this dismal situation, Judah's leaders carry most of the responsibility. The material in Ezekiel 8:10-12 portrays the elders of Judah as being involved in all kinds of "abominations" in the Jerusalem temple. Along similar lines, the critique in Ezekiel 13, directed toward members of the exilic community in Babylon, attacks male and female prophets and accuses them of neglect and of misleading the people by trapping them with false prophecies. In more general terms, the oracle in Ezekiel 22:23-31 rages about the failures of Judah's princes, priests, officials and prophets for their failure to lead Judah in correct worship of God.

At the same time, each individual in the generation leading up to the fall of Jerusalem is responsible for its destruction and the ensuing exile. The material in Ezekiel 18 repudiates the exiles' claims that their ancestors' sins would have caused their current suffering and maintains that the exiles brought their current suffering upon themselves. Ezekiel 18 thus preaches "collective responsibility" in the sense that all the individuals in Judah contributed to the fate of their nation (Joyce, 19-20, 23-26, 139).

Through the combined use of the watchman theme and the notion of Ezekiel's muteness (see 2.2 above), the book of Ezekiel creates an intricate theology of sin, repentance and punishment. God calls Ezekiel to be a watchman (Ezek 3:16-21) who is responsible for warning the people of God's pending punishment (and indirectly calling them to *repentance). If the prophet fails to convey the warning, he and the people will be punished. If, however, he fulfills his task, he will go free, regardless of whether or not the people repent. As to the people, the book of Ezekiel portrays a dichotomy between the righteous person, who repents in response to the watchman's warnings, and the persistent wicked person, who dies in any event (Tiemeyer 2005, 382-83).

Yet, there is a pervasive sense in the book of Ezekiel that the people will not repent and, as a result, that God must punish them. Just after God has assigned Ezekiel to be a watchman for Jerusalem (Ezek 3:17-21), God makes Ezekiel mute (Ezek 3:22-27). This divine act removes Ezekiel's ability to mediate between God and the people ($\bar{i}š$ $m\hat{o}k\hat{i}a\d{h}$ [Ezek 3:26]). In this manner, God hampers Ezekiel's ability to intercede and thus guarantees that God can carry out his planned punishment. It appears as if Ezekiel was actually able to speak, but he could utter only God's words and only when God chose to open his mouth. When it is too late for the people to change—that is, when God has already meted out his punishment over Jerusalem—Ezekiel is called anew to be a watchman, and his muteness is removed (Ezek 33:21-22) (Tiemeyer 2006, 207-13).

Although the people who remained in Judah until the Babylonian destruction in 587/586 BC bear the brunt of the blame, the exilic community gets its fair share of critique (e.g., Ezek 14:1-11). It is, for example, unclear whether the critique against the shepherds in Ezekiel 34:1-10 is directed against the last leaders of the kingdom of Judah or against the leaders of the exilic community in Babylon (Block 1998, 277).

God, in his anger over the sins of his people and their misdirected *worship, decides to abandon his city and his temple (Ezek 11:22-23) before meting out his punishment over them. Deprived of God's presence, Jerusalem is left vulnerable to the onslaught by God's agents, the Neo-Babylonian armies (see Block 1997, 360).

God's presence will return, however, when the divine punishment has run its course (Ezek 43:1-9). The final vision report in the book of Ezekiel describes how a new temple will be built (Ezek 40:1—43:11). This new temple comes with new regulations (Ezek 43:12—46:24) relating to the altar, the status of the Zadokite priesthood, the role of the Levites and the celebration of festivals. Surrounding the temple, and with the temple as its origin, there will be a new land (Ezek 47:1-12) with new boundaries (Ezek 47:13-23; 48:1-7, 23-29), and in its midst will be a special allotment for God (Ezek 48:8-14). There will also be a new Jerusalem (Ezek 48:30-35), the name of which will be "God is here" (Ezek 48:35).

God, in consideration of his glory and despite his people's unworthiness, chooses to re-establish his *covenant with them (Ezek 16:53-63; 36:16-30, 33-38; cf. Ezek 20:39-42). The restoration is solely dependent on God's own desire and is unrelated to any change in the people's behavior (Ezek 36:22-23). God will fully restore, indeed resurrect, the people of Israel (Ezek 37). They will be purified from their defilement (Ezek 36:25-29), at which point they will feel endless remorse and shame for their past behavior (Ezek 16:62; 36:31-32; cf. Ezek 20:43-44). God will also bring his people back from the nations among which he has scattered them (e.g., Ezek 11:14-18; 34:11-16; 36:8, 24). Back in their own land, the people will have plenty to eat and leisure to rest, as God will care for them and restore their health and strength (Ezek 34:14-16). He will make a covenant of *peace with them and ensure that they will never again be the victims of other nations (Ezek 34:25-31), and he will make them abundant and prosperous (Ezek 36:8-11). God will also give the people new hearts that have a renewed capacity and desire to follow his will (Ezek 11:19-20; 36:25-27). At the same time, God will judge those from among his people who seek to do harm to the weaker ones (Ezek 34:17-22).

God further promises his people a new shepherd/leader, called "God's servant David," whom he himself will appoint (Ezek 34:23-24; 37:24-25). Another figure, the "prince" (*nāśî'*), appears later in Ezekiel 44—46; 48. There is probably continuity between the two characters, as there is continuity between the *messianic hope in Ezekiel 1—39 (Ezek 17:1-24 [esp. vv. 22-24]; 21:30-32) and that in Ezekiel 40—48. The *nāśî'* is portrayed as a mortal cultic figure of messianic character and with a political role in the eschatological future envisioned in Ezekiel 40—48 (Levenson, 57-107).

4. The Book of Ezekiel in Texts from the Second Temple Period.

The book of Ezekiel is referred to in the Apocrypha, the Pseudepigrapha, the Dead Sea Scrolls and the NT.

4.1. The Book of Ezekiel in the Apocrypha and the Pseudepigrapha. The Apocrypha and the Pseudepigrapha refer primarily to Ezekiel 1; 10; 34; 37. The material in *1 Enoch* 14; 39; 71, for example, reuses the imagery of Ezekiel 1; 10. In addition, both the *Animal Apocalypse* of *1 Enoch* 89—90 and *Psalms of Solomon* 17 use Ezekiel as the means of advancing messianic hope. Both texts notably allude to the description of David as the shepherd in Ezekiel 34. Finally, 4 Maccabees 18 quotes Ezekiel 37:3 as part of its defense of the resurrection (Manning, 78-99).

4.2. The Book of Ezekiel in the Dead Sea Scrolls. Many of the *Dead Sea Scrolls refer to the book of Ezekiel, which suggests that it was held in high esteem in the Qumran community (Zimmerli 1979, 74-75). The *Damascus Document* (CD) and *Hodayot* (1QH^a) contain most of the allusions. For example, CD-B XIX, 33-35 alludes to the references to prophets in Ezekiel 13:9, 1QH^a XIV; XVI reuse the imagery of water and plants of Ezekiel 17; 19; 31, and the *Songs of the Sabbath Sacrifice* (Mas1k; 4Q400; 4Q401; 4Q402; 4Q403; 4Q404; 4Q405; 4Q406; Q407) draw upon the images of the throne visions in Ezekiel 1; 10. In addition, the descriptions of the temple in the *Temple Scroll* (11Q19 XXIX, 8—XLVII, 15) are dependent on the material in Ezekiel 40—48.

Although these later texts apply the text of Ezekiel to the specific conditions in the Qumran community, they are sensitive to its meaning within the context of the book of Ezekiel. This combination of extensive and careful use of Ezekiel suggests that many of the Qumran authors had a strong affinity for the book of Ezekiel. The Qumran community shared its priestly interest in the temple, the Levitical law and the priesthood, and the concern for Jerusalem and its need to be punished. There are also similarities between the Qumran community and the book of Ezekiel in terms of eschatology. For example, the Qumran community constructed its eschatology as a replay of the exile and restoration as seen through Ezekiel's eyes, and it reused many of its key themes, such as the purification of the community in the wilderness, the giving of God's Spirit, and God's return to the restored temple (Manning, 22-77).

Another group of texts expands and interprets select parts of Ezekiel. For example, the extant fragments of *4QPseudo-Ezekiel* (4Q385; 4Q385c; 4Q386; 4Q388; 4Q391), probably constituting four literary units, contain versions of passages from the book of Ezekiel. As far as scholars can tell, the author(s) of these fragments rewrote select passages from the book of Ezekiel and added to them other material. For instance, 4Q385 2-3; 4Q386 1 I; 4Q388 8, 7 attest to a reworked version of Ezekiel's vision of the valley of the dry bones (Ezek 37:1-14), and 4Q385 6 probably contains a rewritten version of Ezekiel's opening vision (Ezek 1) (see further Tromp, 70-75; Jassen, 231-34).

4.3. The Book of Ezekiel in the New Testament. Although the name of the prophet Ezekiel is nowhere mentioned in the NT, the NT evokes several key passages in the book of Ezekiel (*see* Prophets in the New Testament). The NT Epistles contain some of the clearest cases of allusions. For instance, 2 Corinthians 5:17 and Ephesians 2:3 pick up the concept of a new heart from Ezekiel 11:19-20; 36:25-27 and transform it into a motif of grace. These later texts use it as a picture of God restoring Israel and, by extension, humankind to a condition that God intended for them all along (Duguid, 157-58). Likewise, Romans 2:24 alludes to the notion of God's name having been desecrated among the nations in Ezekiel 36:22, and Romans 10:5 and Galatians 3:10-11 reuse the idea in Ezekiel 20:11 that one should live by God's laws. It is also possible to detect an oblique reference to Ezekiel 12:22, 27 in 2 Peter 3:4.

Among the Gospels, the material in John 10:11-18 alludes to the shepherd imagery in Ezekiel 34; 37:15-28. The material in Ezekiel 34 is used primarily to make a connection between Jesus and God. This passage is useful to the Evangelist in that it contrasts the bad shepherds of Israel with two good ones, God and David. The Gospel of John portrays Jesus as fulfilling all the criteria that God fulfills in Ezekiel 34. For example, like God in Ezekiel, Jesus describes the people as "my flock" and "my sheep" (e.g., Ezek 34:3, 6, 30; John 10:14, 16, 26-27), and like God in Ezekiel, Jesus will rescue the sheep (Ezek 34:7-10; John 10:12-13). Furthermore, both John and Ezekiel emphasize the relationship between sheep and shepherd, expressed through the sheep's knowledge of their shepherd (Ezek 34:27, 30, 31; John 10:3, 14, 27). In this manner, the evangelist conveys the distinct impression that Jesus is God. The evangelist also refers to Ezekiel 34 in order to liken Jesus' opponents, symbolized by the "thief" and the "hireling," to bad shepherds (John 10:8, 10, 12-13; cf. Ezek 34:3-8). In contrast, the material in Ezekiel 37 is alluded to in John in order to establish a link between Jesus and David (John 10:16; cf. Ezek 37:19, 22-24). As David is God's faithful servant, appointed by him to care for the sheep, so Jesus is God's faithful representative who fully carries out God's work (Manning, 114-24).

The parable of the true vine in John 15:1-10 is influenced by the language and imagery of the vine metaphors in Ezekiel 15:1-8; 17:1-10, 19. As in the case of John 10, by alluding to the Ezekielian material, the NT authors transform it so that it can serve new purposes. First, the target audience is changed. The vine metaphors in their original context pronounce judgment upon Jerusalem and its leaders. In contrast, John uses them to encourage the disciples to trust only in Jesus and to explain the betrayal by Judas. In this respect, John's use of Ezekiel's vine metaphors probably should be understood in the light of the conflict with Jerusalem and its rulers that is present elsewhere in John's Gospel. Second, the identity of the vine is redefined. Whereas the vine denotes the whole people of Israel in the original context, in John the branches that Jesus will take care of and prune are only those who follow his teaching (Manning, 135-49).

The book of Revelation contains the majority of the allusions to the book of Ezekiel. There is some debate as to the extent of the influence, but most scholars agree on the following set of allusions: (1) the vision of the chariot in Ezekiel 1 underlies John's vision of the heavenly throne room with the four creatures surrounding Jesus in Revelation 4:1-8; (2) the notion that the prophet is forbidden to eat the scroll in Ezekiel 2:8-9 is echoed in Revelation 5:1, 10; (3) the notion of protection from the slaughter in Ezekiel 9:1-11 reappears in Revelation 7:1-8; (4) the condemnation of the prostitute in Ezekiel 16:23 is alluded to in Revelation 17:1-6, 15-18; (5) the oracles against Tyre in Ezekiel 26—28 serve as the model for the lament over the fall of Babylon (Rome) in Revelation 18; (6) the prophecies against Gog in Ezekiel 38—39 are picked up and transformed in Revelation 19—20; (7) both Ezekiel and Revelation end with a vision of the new temple (Ezek 40—48; Rev 21—22). In particular, Revelation 22:1-2 is modeled after Ezekiel 47:1-8.

The material in Revelation depends upon yet also transforms the texts in the book of Ezekiel. We see this phenomenon clearly in the reuse of Ezekiel 38—39 in Revelation 19—20. First, there is the significant correspondence between the descriptions of the birds' banquet and how they are being invited to gorge on the corpses of the defeated army in Revelation 19:17-21 and Ezekiel 39:4, 17-20. Second, Revelation 20:7-10 and Ezekiel 38—39 share four themes: (1) the notion that the nations will attack God's people; (2) a reference to the great size of Gog's army and the worldwide recruitment to it; (3) God's direct intervention from heaven; (4) reference to "fire and sulfur." At the same time, there is a marked difference between the two texts. For instance, in Ezekiel 38:2 God commands Ezekiel to prophecy against Gog, of the land of Magog, the chief prince of Meshech and Tubal. In contrast, Revelation 20:8 treats Gog and Magog as a pair of names and portrays them as coming from all over the world rather than from one specific country. Likewise, the material in Ezekiel 38:4-6 tells how God is ultimately responsible for Gog's attack on Israel: God will turn Gog around, put hooks in his jaws, and bring him and his army forth. Revelation 20:7 changes the theological meaning of this passage drastically by introducing the character of Satan and making him responsible for deceiving Gog and Magog (Boe, 274-345).

The identification of Gog and Magog has been endlessly debated, ranging from ancient powers to modern world leaders (see the overview in Boe, 88-99). Already the Aramaic Targum to Ezekiel (Ezek 39:16) identifies Gog with Rome.

There are also some similarities between the book of Ezekiel and the NT that probably are not the result of direct influence. For example, Jesus is described as the "son of man" throughout the NT. Notably, all four Gospels use this appellation as part of Jesus' self-representation, as do Acts 7:54-57; Hebrews 2:6-9; Revelation 1:12-18; 14:14. In the OT this appellation is attested primarily in the book of Ezekiel, where God calls the prophet "son of man" more than ninety times, and where it either emphasizes his humanity or is used instead of a personal pronoun. Nonetheless, it is questionable whether the NT writers are influenced by its use in the book of Ezekiel. Instead, they more likely are indebted to the specific use in Daniel 7:13, where the expression "son of man" refers to a divine being, and to its similar use in *1 Enoch* 37—71.

It is also important to note that the NT writers never use the vision of the dry bones in Ezekiel 37 as a symbol for Jesus' resurrection or for the resurrection of believers in him, with the possible exception of John 5:25-28, which mentions the final resurrection of those who believe in Jesus (Manning, 160-65). Likewise, rabbinic Judaism never uses Ezekiel 37 as a prooftext to support the belief in a general eschatological resurrection.

5. Canonization of the Book of Ezekiel.

The book of Ezekiel was accepted into the *canon of the synagogue and church with difficulty. First, Ezekiel's claim to have seen God (Ezek 1:28) was not easily accepted. Notably, later patristic traditions sought to alleviate the situation by maintaining that Ezekiel had not seen God's essence but only his image. Second, certain regulations in the book of Ezekiel deviate from the cultic regulations as found in the Pentateuch (*b. Menaḥ.* 45a; *b. Šabb.* 13b) (see Stevenson and Glerup, xix). This lack of agreement with the pentateuchal material caused the rabbinic discussion concerning the canonical status of the book of Ezekiel to last well into the fifth century AD. The rabbis sought to determine whether the book of Ezekiel, alongside books such as Ruth, Esther and Ecclesiastes, "defiled the hands"—that is, whether it should be considered as part of the literature deemed to be inspired of God and sacred to the Jews.

6. Ideological Readings.

6.1. Feminist Readings—Ezekiel 16 and 23.
Much *feminist research on the OT has focused on the book of Ezekiel. In particular, the oracles in Ezekiel 16; 23, with their sexual and marital imagery, are key texts for those scholars who seek to highlight that many biblical texts are misogynist. These passages further stand out among those passages in the OT that contain sexual and marital metaphors because of their stark descriptions of sexual violence toward female Israel and Judah (*see* Women and Female Imagery).

The historical context of both Ezekiel 16 and Ezekiel 23 is the fall of Jerusalem to the Neo-Babylonian armies in 587/586 BC. The prophet Ezekiel is condemning the people of Judah for making politically alliances especially with Egypt (Ezek 16:26-29; 23:3) instead of trusting in God (implied by the imagery [cf. Ezek 29:16]).

The literary narratives in Ezekiel 16 and Ezekiel 23 consist of two related yet markedly different accounts. Looking more closely at Ezekiel 16, the chapter describes how God finds Jerusalem as a newborn baby, lying abandoned at the roadside, and rescues her. God "makes her flourish" (Ezek 16:7), and she matures. When God sees that she has reached sexual maturity, God takes her to him, washes her, clothes her and bedecks her with jewels (Ezek 16:8-14). Jerusalem then has sexual relations with other men and forgets her miserable youth (Ezek 16:15-34). God tries in vain to curtail her (sexual) activities (Ezek 16:27). Then, as a way of making Jerusalem pay for her sins and to vent his anger against her, God exposes her naked before her former lovers, who then stone her and hack her with their swords (Ezek 16:35-43). God promises that he will later remember his covenant with her and restore her (Ezek 16:60, 62). In response, he maintains, Jerusalem will feel shame and disgrace (Ezek 16:61, 63).

There are two ways of looking at Ezekiel 16 and Ezekiel 23. One can interpret the text in its historical setting and focus on the underlying tenor of the metaphor—that is, on Judah's political alliances and God's anger at Judah's lack of trust in his ability to preserve them. In con-

trast to the marital imagery in Hosea 1—3 and Jeremiah 2, the ultimate aim of the imagery in Ezekiel 16 and Ezekiel 23 is not to bring Jerusalem to repentance. Instead, it provides a compelling tale of Judah's depravity and God's resulting righteous wrath, told in order to justify God's destruction of Jerusalem. The people of Judah did not obey God's commandments, and therefore God had to punish them (Baumann, 145, Tiemeyer 2010) (see 6.2 below). Alternatively, one can look at the text from a literary perspective and concentrate on the vehicle of the metaphor—that is, on the interplay between the man (God) and his wife (Judah). Most feminist scholarship on Ezekiel 16 and Ezekiel 23 approaches the text from this perspective (e.g., Moughtin-Mumby, 156-205).

In general, feminist critique of the sexual and marital imagery in the OT is aimed at the expressed patriarchal ideas that are understood to be both sexist and misogynistic. As in all the surrounding cultures, a woman's sexuality was owned first by her father and then, after her marriage, by her husband. Whereas a man could have multiple sexual partners, as long as these partners were not the wives of other men, a woman was restricted to chastity while unmarried and, once married, to a sexual relationship with her husband. As to marriage, it was not a covenant between two equals, but rather one between a master and his subordinate woman. If the woman displeased her husband and/or was unfaithful to him, the husband had the legal and societal right to cast her off, to chastise her physically and to publically humiliate her. In contrast, a woman had no rights regarding a faithless husband. Feminist scholars argue that this gender inequality, inherent to the world of the OT, has rendered the sexual and marital imagery of the Bible difficult for readers today. It therefore is not the description of God and Israel as sharing a bond of intimacy and love in itself that causes problems. Problems arise, however, when one takes seriously the view of marriage presupposed by the ancient Israelite writers. Readers of the Bible need to realize that the prevalent modern view of marriage, it being a symbol of mutual love and reciprocal respect, and the ancient Israelite concept of marriage do not coincide. More specifically, readers must reject the notion that a husband had the right to physically abuse his wife in response to her unfaithfulness. In such a case, the woman's actual guilt is irrelevant, as no act of unfaithfulness justifies stripping a woman naked in public and having her stoned and hacked with swords (Ezek 16:37-40). Feminist scholars further maintain that an exegete who justifies this kind of divine behavior by appealing to God's immense love and rightfully felt jealousy is not taking the text seriously. Moreover, the notion that God, after brutally beating and publicly humiliating his wife, is graciously prepared to overlook her past faithlessness and take her back (Ezek 16:59-62) presents an image that is too close to situations of domestic violence to sit comfortably with today's readers. What woman should be urged to return to an abusive husband? Thus, the metaphor of God as Israel's husband has, for many contemporary readers, become a symbol of force and oppression.

Several nonfeminist scholars regard Ezekiel 16 as an expression of God's grace. He is prepared to love his wife unconditionally even though she, given the debt of her guilt, is totally undeserving of his affection. Moreover, many scholars see God's jealously as a reflection of the intensity of his deep love for Israel. D. Block, for example, argues that God's jealousy is an expression of his love, a love that "is fueled not by an exploitative need to dominate but by ardor for the well-being of the object" (Block 1997, 13). In the particular context of Ezekiel 16, he maintains that it presents God as a gracious savior who lavishes his favors on the helpless infant/young woman (Block 1997, 469-70). From a feminist perspective, such a reading is unacceptable for several reasons. First, it is unwarranted to detach Ezekiel 16:1-14, 60-63 from its larger context and read it as an image of God's grace. As a whole, Ezekiel 16 is like a Cinderella story gone tragically awry. One cannot look at God's rescue of infant Jerusalem and his subsequent marriage to her without also looking at his horrific punishment of her because of her sins and her subsequent life of shame. Second, such a reading betrays a view of men and women in which the man is always the active partner while the woman is simply there to be adorned and to satisfy his (sexual) needs (Ezek 16:8, 13). Jerusalem is not really valued for the qualities of her soul or her intellectual capabilities. Third, the whole "fairy tale" of God's rescue and subsequent marriage to Judah is a Lolita story of broken trust and

sexual abuse of power over a minor in his care (see Baumann, 161). It raises the question as to why God rescued the infant in the first place. His saving act of baby Judah is not depicted as part of his impartial desire to take care of her and raise her to adulthood and independence, as he becomes interested in washing off the blood that covered her as a newborn only after she has reached sexual maturity (Ezek 16:9).

The issue of intended versus unintended audience of texts containing sexual and marital metaphors complicates the reading of Ezekiel 16 and Ezekiel 23. The rhetoric of these two oracles, in their historical context, was meant for the prophet's male audience, and later for the male readership of the text, as the means of shaming them into repentance by likening them to women. Military defeat and exile had, in a sense, already emasculated them, and now they are further humiliated by being likened to women (see Kamionkowski, 58-91). From this perspective, the rhetoric of Ezekiel 16 and Ezekiel 23 must have been very powerful. For a contemporary female reader, however, it requires complicated mental gymnastics to get the message of Ezekiel 16 and Ezekiel 23 right. She needs first to imagine herself to be a man in order to then feel ashamed for being likened to a woman.

Finally, feminist scholarship points out that the use of imagery relating to prostitutes betrays the assumption that women actively choose to become prostitutes because they enjoy being sexually promiscuous (Ezek 16:23-32). The discrepancy between this fantasy and the reality is glaring. In the past as well as today, most women who become prostitutes do so because they are (1) sold, kidnapped or abandoned as children, (2) raped and thus declared unmarriageable, (3) enslaved or (4) unable to support themselves and their children in any other way. Prostitution itself is therefore yet another form of violence against woman.

6.2. Post-Holocaust Readings. Post-Holocaust theology shares certain aspects with feminist readings in that both approaches, although from different perspectives, question God's right to punish Judah. There is a strong sense among scholars who look at the biblical texts through the lens of post-Holocaust theology that the model for sin and punishment attested in the book of Ezekiel is inadequate in light of Jewish suffering. The theology of the book of

Ezekiel that states that the people of Judah, rather than God, were responsible for their death and exile because of their sins cannot be upheld in view of the suffering of the Jews in the Holocaust. It cannot be maintained that the victims are to be blamed for their own suffering (Sweeney, 128-46). As K. Darr says, "In a world where holocausts happen, we dare not follow Ezekiel when he insists that suffering, alienation and exile are God's just punishment for sin" (Darr, 114). In order to "survive" the book of Ezekiel, some scholars have opted for counterreadings. Darr, for example, reads Job as a corrective of the book of Ezekiel (Darr, 113), and L.-S. Tiemeyer reads it together with Lamentations (Tiemeyer 2010).

6.3. Psychological Readings. The prophet Ezekiel often exhibits strange behaviors and states: muteness (Ezek 3:26), visionary traveling (Ezek 1; 8—11; 37; 40—48), emotional paralysis after his wife's death (Ezek 24:15-27), pornographic language (Ezek 16; 23) and sign acts (Ezek 4:1—5:4), such as acting out of the siege of Jerusalem with the help of a tile and an iron griddle (Ezek 4:1-3), and lying on one side for 390 days (Ezek 4:4-8), to name but a few. Given such behavior, scholars have from time to time argued that Ezekiel, as a literary figure and/or as the author of the book, was a psychotic who suffered from a paranoid condition (*see* Prophecy and Psychology).

Recently D. Halperin and D. Smith-Christopher have advanced this type of research. Halperin maintains that many of the violent images, particularly against women, in the book of Ezekiel, as well as the portrayal of God as a vengeful deity, stem from the prophet's sick mind, the result of sexual abuse as a child (Halperin, 133-34). The author (i.e., the prophet Ezekiel) was a profoundly disturbed man whose ways of thinking and expressing his thoughts are dominated by a pathological loathing of female sexuality. This becomes evident primarily in his pornographic descriptions of women in Ezekiel 16; 23 (Halperin, 142-51), his behavior following his wife's death (Halperin, 176-83), and his symbolic language pertaining to pollution that fuses the terminology of ritual pollution with female sexuality, as in, for example, Ezekiel 7:20-22 (Halperin, 151-54).

From a very different angle, Smith-Christopher argues that the divine oracles in the book of Ezekiel reflect, at least in part, the actual experiences of the prophet Ezekiel, who utters them. The descriptions and theology in these oracles are directly influenced by the prophet's experiences of the violence caused by the Neo-Babylonian attacks on Jerusalem and the deprivation and humiliation of deportation. As such, we should read the book of Ezekiel as the literary creation of a man who suffers posttraumatic stress disorder (PTSD) (Smith-Christopher, 75-104).

This field of research is not uncontested. First, it rests to a very large extent on the assumption that the prophet Ezekiel, as described within the book of Ezekiel, corresponds fully with the author of the book (see 1.1 above). Second, it challenges the claim of the book of Ezekiel, which describes the prophet's behavior as the immediate result of God's power upon him. Notably, both Halperin and Smith-Christopher maintain that the book of Ezekiel tells us more about the human being Ezekiel than about God. Ezekiel was an ill man whose illness influenced his writings. In contrast, the book of Ezekiel describes the prophet as a (healthy) person whose odd behavior is the result of the power of God's Spirit over him, and who uttered God's undiluted word.

6.4. Other Readings. The vision reports in the book of Ezekiel have fascinated people outside mainstream Christianity and rabbinic Judaism. In particular, the vision report in Ezekiel 1 (alongside Gen 6:1-4) has often been connected with the so-called ancient astronaut theories, which claim that intelligent extraterrestrial beings visited earth, and that this contact triggered the development of human cultures, technologies and/or religions. J. F. Blumrich, an aeronautical engineer, is the chief proponent of these theories. He maintains that a close reading of Ezekiel 1 reveals that Ezekiel saw a spacecraft consisting of three major systems: a main body, four helicopters that support the main body, and a capsule (Blumrich, 14, fig. 1; cf. Lieb, 42-73). However, none of these theories have received much attention in peer-reviewed studies in scientific journals.

6.5. The Book of Ezekiel in Art and Literature. Most depictions of the prophet Ezekiel in art are connected to his vision reports. For example, the paintings in the Dura-Europos synagogue (a third-century BC synagogue situated between Aleppo and Baghdad on the bank of the Euphrates) depict Ezekiel's visions (Ezek 1; 8—11; 37; 40—48) (Kraeling, 355-59). Likewise, in 1518 Raphael famously painted the scene depicted in Ezekiel 1, his only motif taken from the book of Ezekiel. Allusions to the book of Ezekiel in literature tend to be limited to Ezekiel's vision reports. For instance, John Milton, in *Paradise Lost*, speaks of the "chariot of paternal deity" (book 6, line 750), the vehicle on which the Son of God travels in order to fight the rebellious angels in the celestial battle (see Lieb, 21-31). Influenced by Milton, William Blake's poetry and artwork also draw on Ezekiel 1 (Rowland).

See also EXILE; EZEKIEL: HISTORY OF INTERPRETATION; HERMENEUTICS; SIGN ACTS; TEMPLE; VISIONS, PROPHETIC.

BIBLIOGRAPHY. *Commentaries:* A. Bertholet, *Hesekiel* (HAT 1/13; Tübingen: Mohr, 1936); D. I. Block, *The Book of Ezekiel: Chapters 1-24* (NICOT; Grand Rapids: Eerdmans, 1997); idem, *The Book of Ezekiel: Chapters 25-48* (NICOT; Grand Rapids: Eerdmans, 1998); I. M. Duguid, *Ezekiel* (NIVAC; Grand Rapids: Zondervan, 1999); P. M. Joyce, *Ezekiel: A Commentary* (LHBOTS 482; London: T & T Clark, 2007); J. W. Olley, *Ezekiel: A Commentary Based on Iezekiēl in Codex Vaticanus* (SCS; Leiden: E. J. Brill, 2009); K. Stevenson and M. Glerup, eds., *Ezekiel, Daniel* (ACCS 13; Downers Grove, IL: InterVarsity Press, 2008); W. Zimmerli, *Ezekiel 1: A Commentary on the Book of the Prophet Ezekiel, Chapters 1-24*, trans. R. E. Clements, ed. F. Cross and K. Baltzer (Hermeneia; Philadelphia: Fortress, 1979); idem, *Ezekiel 2: A Commentary on the Book of the Prophet Ezekiel, Chapters 25-48*, trans. R. E. Clements, ed. F. Cross and K. Baltzer (Hermeneia; Philadelphia: Fortress, 1983). *Studies:* D. Baltzer, *Ezechiel und Deuterojesaja: Berührungen in der Heilserwartung der beiden grossen Exilspropheten* (BZAW 121; Berlin: de Gruyter, 1971); G. Baumann, *Love and Violence: Marriage as Metaphor for the Relationship between YHWH and Israel in the Prophetic Books*, trans. L. M. Maloney (Collegeville, MN: Liturgical, 2003); D. I. Block, "In Search of Theological Meaning: Ezekiel Scholarship at the Turn of the Millennium," in *Ezekiel's Hierarchical World: Wrestling with a Tiered Reality*, ed. S. L. Cook and C. L. Patton (SBLSymS 31; Leiden: E. J. Brill, 2004) 227-39; J. F. Blumrich, The Spaceships of Ezekiel (New York: Bantam, 1974); S. Boe, *Gog and Magog: Ezekiel 38-39 as Pre-Text for Revelation 19,17-21 and 20,7-10* (WUNT 2/135; Tübingen: Mohr Siebeck, 2001); K. Darr, "Ezekiel's Justifications of God: Teaching Troubling Texts," *JSOT* 55 (1992) 97-117; J. de Moor, ed., *The Elusive Prophet: The Prophet as a Historical Person, Literary Character, and Anonymous Artist* (OTS 45; Leiden: E. J. Brill, 2001); M. Ehrensvärd, "Linguistic Dating of Biblical Texts," in *Biblical Hebrew: Studies in Chronology and Typology*, ed. I. Young (JSOTSup 369; London: T & T Clark, 2003) 164-88; U. Feist, *Ezechiel: Das literarische Problem des Buches forschungsgeschichtlich betrachtet* (BWANT 7/18; Stuttgart: Kohlhammer, 1995); T. Ganzel, "Transformation of Pentateuchal Descriptions of Idolatry," in *Transforming Visions: Transformations of Text, Tradition, and Theology in Ezekiel*, ed. W. A. Tooman and M. A. Lyons (PTMS 127; Eugene, OR: Pickwick, 2010) 33-49; J. Garscha, *Studien zum Ezechielbuch: Eine redaktionskritische Untersuchung von 1-39* (EH 23/23; Frankfurt: Peter Lang, 1974); Y. Gitay, "The Projection of the Prophet: A Rhetorical Presentation of the Prophet Jeremiah," in *Prophecy and Prophets: The Diversity of Contemporary Issues in Scholarship*, ed. Y. Gitay (SBLSS; Atlanta: Scholars Press, 1997) 41-55; L. L. Grabbe, *A History of the Jews and Judaism in the Second Temple Period*, 1: *Yehud: A History of the Persian Province of Judah* (LSST 47; Edinburgh: T & T Clark, 2004); D. J. Halperin, *Seeking Ezekiel: Text and Psychology* (University Park: Pennsylvania State University Press, 1993); M. Haran, "Ezekiel, P, and the Priestly School," *VT* 58 (2008) 211-18; V. Herntrich, *Ezechielprobleme* (BZAW 61; Giessen: Töpelmann, 1933); S. Herrmann, *Die prophetischen Heilserwartungen im Alten Testament: Ursprung und Gestaltwandel* (BWANT 5; Stuttgart: Kohlhammer, 1965); A. Hurvitz, *A Linguistic Study of the Relationship between the Priestly Source and the Book of Ezekiel: A New Approach to an Old Problem* (CahRB 20; Paris: Gabalda, 1982); A. P. Jassen, *Mediating the Divine: Prophecy and Revelation in the Dead Sea Scrolls and Second Temple Judaism* (STDJ 68; Leiden: E. J. Brill, 2007); S. Kamionkowski, *Gender Reversal and Cosmic Chaos: A Study on the Book of Ezekiel* (JSOTSup 368; London: Sheffield Academic, 2003); R. Levitt Kohn, *A New Heart and a New Soul: Ezekiel, the Exile and the Torah* (JSOTSup 358; London: Sheffield Academic, 2002); C. H. Kraeling, *The Synagogue* (Excavations at Dura-Europos 8.1; New Haven: Yale University

Press, 1956); **J. F. Kutsko,** *Between Heaven and Earth: Divine Presence and Absence in the Book of Ezekiel* (BibJudS 7; Winona Lake, IN; Eisenbrauns, 2000); **J. D. Levenson,** *Theology of the Program of Restoration of Ezekiel 40-48* (HSM 10; Missoula, MT: Scholars Press, 1976); **M. Lieb,** *Children of Ezekiel: Aliens, UFOs, the Crisis of Race, and the Advent of End Time* (Durham, NC: Duke University Press, 1998); **J. Lust,** "The Use of Textual Witnesses for the Establishment of the Text," in *Ezekiel and His Book: Textual and Literary Criticism and their Interrelation,* ed. J. Lust (BETL 74; Leuven: Leuven University Press, 1986) 7-20; **M. A. Lyons,** "Transformation of Law: Ezekiel's Use of the Holiness Code (Leviticus 17-26)," in *Transforming Visions: Transformations of Text, Tradition, and Theology in Ezekiel,* ed. W. A. Tooman and M. A. Lyons (PTMS 127; Eugene, OR: Pickwick, 2010) 1-32; **G. T. Manning Jr.,** *Echoes of a Prophet: The Use of Ezekiel in the Gospel of John and in the Literature of the Second Temple Period* (JSNTSup 270; T & T Clark, 2004); **T. D. Mayfield,** *Literary Structure and Setting in Ezekiel* (FAT 2/43; Tübingen: Mohr Siebeck, 2010); **A. Mein,** *Ezekiel and the Ethics of Exile* (OTM; Oxford: Oxford University Press, 2001); **S. Moughtin-Mumby,** *Sexual and Marital Metaphors in Hosea, Jeremiah, Isaiah, and Ezekiel* (OTM; Oxford: Oxford University Press, 2008); **M. F. Rooker,** *Biblical Hebrew in Transition: The Language of the Book of Ezekiel* (JSOTSup 90; Sheffield: JSOT, 1990); **C. Rowland,** "Ezekiel's *Merkavah* in the Work of William Blake and Christian Art," in *The Book of Ezekiel and Its Influence,* ed. H. J. de Jonge and J. Tromp (Aldershot: Ashgate, 2007) 183-200; **M. Saur,** *Der Tyroszyklus des Ezechielbuches* (BZAW 386; Berlin: de Gruyter, 2008); **D. L. Smith-Christopher,** *A Biblical Theology of Exile* (OBT; Minneapolis: Fortress, 2002); **T. Stordalen,** *Echoes of Eden: Genesis 2-3 and Symbolism of the Garden in Biblical Hebrew Literature* (CBET 25; Leuven: Peeters, 2001); **M. A. Sweeney,** *Reading the Hebrew Bible after the Shoah: Engaging Holocaust Theology* (Minneapolis: Fortress, 2008) 128-46; **L.-S. Tiemeyer,** "The Watchman Metaphor in Isaiah LVI-LXVI," *VT* 55 (2005) 378-400; idem, "God's Hidden Compassion," *TynBul* 57 (2006) 191-213; idem, "To Read—or Not to Read—Ezekiel as Christian Scripture," *ExpTim* 121 (2010) 1-8; **C. C. Torrey,** *Pseudo-Ezekiel and the Original Prophecy* (New Haven: Yale University Press, 1930); **J. Tromp,** "'Can These Bones Live?' Ezekiel 37:1-14 and Eschatological Resurrection," in *The Book of Ezekiel and Its Influence,* ed. H. J. de Jonge and J. Tromp (Aldershot: Ashgate, 2007) 61-78; **W. Zimmerli,** "Jahwes Wort bei Deuterojesaja," *VT* 32 (1982) 104-24.

L.-S. Tiemeyer

EZEKIEL: HISTORY OF INTERPRETATION

From the beginning, the book of Ezekiel has offended, challenged and inspired those who would seek to interpret it. However, as cultural mores and theological views have altered over time, different aspects of the book have been deemed interesting or offensive. For example, modern readers often are offended by the prophet's graphic language and his supposed endorsement of violence against women in Ezekiel 16; 23, while being largely untroubled by the book's apparent conflicts with other canonical texts. In contrast, ancient readers were far more concerned about the latter than the former, which they dealt with by simply allegorizing the text. As with other biblical books, there has also been sustained debate in the modern period over Ezekiel's authorship and unity, both of which were largely taken for granted during the premodern period. This article traces the history of the book's interpretation from its earliest reception down to the contemporary period.

1. From the Beginning to the New Testament
2. Rabbinic and Early Christian Interpretation
3. Medieval and Reformation Interpretation
4. Modern Interpretation

1. From the Beginning to the New Testament.
The immediate impact of the prophecies of Ezekiel and of the book that bears his name is not easy to ascertain. During his own time, the prophet had the opportunity to address the elders of the people (Ezek 14:1) and crowds of fellow exiles (Ezek 33:31). Yet in those days, he was regarded by many as merely a singer of popular songs: they listened to him perform as entertainment, but had little appetite to have their lives changed by his message (Ezek 33:32). This was exactly what the Lord himself told Ezekiel would happen: had he been sent to a

foreign nation, there might have been an openness to listen, but the house of Israel would not listen to Ezekiel because their foreheads were hard and their hearts stubborn (Ezek 3:7).

However, D. Block argues that the influence of Ezekiel was largely responsible for a dramatic spiritual transformation in the hearts of the *exiles, from the moral and theological chaos of the preexilic situation to a renewal of spiritual interest and hope in the ancient promises of God (1997, 43). Certainly, the fall of Jerusalem would have dramatically validated his prophetic claims, yet it is not clear how widespread the acceptance of his message was, even among the exiles in Babylon. There was no attempt to implement his radical vision of a new Israel in a renewed land when the Judeans returned home. To be sure, some aspects of his vision, such as his design for the new *temple, would have been virtually impossible to construct, but other aspects, such has the transformation of the annual pilgrim festivals (ch. 46), would certainly have been practicable. Perhaps this legislation was not implemented because the Judeans rightly recognized that that was never intended to be its purpose. It was designed to convey the prophet's message of purification and separation from *evil through the medium of legislation, just as the same message was conveyed through the medium of architecture (40-42) and geography (47-48).

In terms of the rest of the OT, Ezekiel's writings certainly influenced the prophecies of *Zechariah, especially the passage addressing the shepherds of Israel in Ezekiel 34, which forms the background for Zechariah 11. There are plausibly also some connections with the Book of *Daniel as well, though little sign of influence on the other post-exilic writings exists. Ezekiel is only rarely mentioned in the inter-testamental period as well. Ben Sirach includes him in his list of famous Israelites (49:8), while 4 Macabbees, written in the first century AD, praises a man for being someone who "affirmed the word of Ezekiel." Josephus attributes two books to Ezekiel, which presumably refers to the so-called "Apocryphon of Ezekiel" in addition to his canonical book (*Ant.* 10.5.1). The *Dead Sea Scrolls attest to strong influence by the prophet, especially in their defense of Zadokite claims to the priesthood. The community was also interested in the opening vision of the Lord seated on his chariot-throne borne by the cherubim, and in motifs such as the marking of the foreheads of those who will be saved. They saw these people who mourned over the defilement of Jerusalem as a group like themselves – a faithful remnant of an unfaithful people (Cothenet, 1988).

The NT never quotes Ezekiel directly, though his influence is nonetheless present. Ezekiel's favorite title for himself ("son of man," in the sense of "mortal one") is picked up by Jesus, who used it to evoke the ambiguity of his mission: given its contrasting use in Ezekiel and Daniel 7, it was the perfect title for the one who came to identify with us in our humanity, but who is also the exalted Lord of heaven. The clearest influence is on the apostle John, who quotes Jesus as the Good Shepherd, the one who reflects the fulfillment of Ezekiel 34.

The influence of Ezekiel on John is also clear in the Book of Revelation (Moyise, 1995). John picks up on Ezekiel's prophecy of a final cataclysmic battle against the forces of evil, led by Gog (Rev. 20:8-9). Similarly, his vision of a New Jerusalem is clearly modeled after Ezekiel's new temple, though with striking and crucial differences, not least its name: Ezekiel's city was deliberately named "The Lord is there" rather than Jerusalem. What is more, John's city has no temple and is itself at the center of the vision, while it has gates that stand wide open to the redeemed from all nations, in contrast to Ezekiel's central temple with its towering gatehouses and high walls. Whereas Ezekiel described a temple in which no human being ever had access to the Holy of Holies, John describes a city which has itself become a giant Holy of Holies, a perfect, golden cube with God's throne at the center, offering free access to all those who have washed their robes in the blood of the Lamb (Rev. 21). In other words, John shows us Ezekiel's vision refracted through the lens of fulfillment in Christ. The temple and city that were separated in Ezekiel to preserve the temple's sanctity have now been reunited and merged in the New (and sanctified) Jerusalem, the heavenly bride of Christ. All those who were once far off from God through their sin now have open access to the throne of God's holy presence in Christ, who has become our great High Priest. Yet in keeping with Ezekiel's vision, there still exists a realm of "outside," where the unclean dwell forever, closed off from access into the realm of the holy (Rev. 22:15). Just as Ezekiel antici-pated, a time is coming when the holy will no longer be defiled by the intrusion of the pro-fane (*see* Prophets in the New Testament).

2. Rabbinic and Early Christian Interpretation.

In the rabbinic writings there is a particular fascination with the opening and closing vi-sions of Ezekiel, along with a stress on the dif-ficulty and danger of reading his words. Ac-cording to Jerome, Jews under thirty years of age were forbidden from reading the begin-ning and ending of the book, and the caution-ary tale is recorded of a child who picked up a copy of the Book of Ezekiel at his teacher's home and apprehended the true meaning of the extremely obscure and much-debated He-brew word *ḥašmal* the substance of which the divine figure appears to be comprised in Eze-kiel 1:27. Instantly, fire came out from the *ḥašmal* and incinerated him (*b. ag.* 13a). Yet a symbolic understanding of this opening vision was crucial to the survival of Judaism after the destruction of the temple in AD 70. In a situa-tion reminiscent of the Babylonian exile, they once again had to live without the sign of the Lord's presence in their midst. In this situa-tion, the *vision of the Lord seated on his *merkabâ*, or throne-chariot, became central to their thinking as a symbol of the Lord's tran-scendence and immanence with his people. Through this mobile presence, the sovereign Lord of all of the universe could still dwell with his people wherever they found themselves.

At the other end of the book, the Rabbis had problems with Ezekiel's temple vision in chap-ters 40-48. Here the chief difficulty lay in har-monizing the regulations of Ezekiel with the very different ones prescribed by Moses in the Pentateuch. For example, Ezekiel described two very similar annual festivals which were hard to align with the three different annual festivals (Passover, Weeks and Tabernacles) that had been established by Moses. One of the Rabbis, Hananiah ben Hezekiah, is said to have hidden himself away in his attic and burned three hundred barrels of oil in his lamp in his search for a reconciliation between the differ-ent laws. It was thanks to the success of his la-bors that the book of Ezekiel as a whole was saved from being excluded from the canon (*b. Shab.* 13b). Unfortunately, the fruits of his

work were not preserved and, bereft of his wis-dom, others among the Rabbis gave in to the counsel of despair, referring their pupils to a higher authority: Elijah would explain it all when he came (*b. Mena.* 45a).

It is fair to say that the Book of Ezekiel was not the primary OT text expounded in the early church, though a number of its images were popular in Christian art. Irenaeus identi-fied the four faces of the living creatures in Ezekiel 1—the lion, the man, the ox and the eagle—as representing the fourfold picture of Christ revealed in the four Gospels (*Haer.* 3.11.8). The vision of the valley of the dry bones attracted attention as a proof text for the resur-rection of the body and was explained as such by Tertullian (*De carnis resurrectione*) and Hilary of Poitiers. Origen preached a series of ser-mons on the parts of Ezekiel that were included in the liturgical calendar, expounding the prophet in allegorical terms, and apparently also wrote a commentary on larger parts of the book, which, however, has not survived. During the threatening days when Rome was under siege between 410 and 414, Jerome wrote a lengthy commentary on Ezekiel, reflecting in a letter to his friend Eustochium, "It seemed as though I was sharing the captivity of the saints." Gregory I (540-604) preached a series of ser-mons on the book during a later siege of Rome, focusing on the first and last visions of the prophet. Augustine preached two sermons against the Donatists on Ezekiel 34 and made significant use of chapters 18, 22 and 34 in his dogmatic works.

3. Medieval and Reformation Interpretation.

Much of the medieval work on Ezekiel was a re-working of earlier scholarship. Rabanus Mau-rus (c. 780-856) wrote a commentary that is es-sentially a compilation of Jerome and Gregory the Great, with a few original comments and citations of other more recent scholars. His contemporary, Haimo of Auxerre, did likewise. These works formed the foundation for the later *Glossa Ordinaria*, a monumental attempt to provide a biblical text with notes and cita-tions from the church Fathers and Jewish com-mentators, as well as pictures and diagrams. In contrast to this continuation of the pattern of allegorical exegesis, Richard of St. Victor (d. 1173) explored the literal sense of the prophet's words, especially his portrayal of the new temple, seeing it as a promise to Israel that the temple and city would eventually be rebuilt. His focus on the literal meaning of the text reflected his greater access to, and appreciation for, Jewish interpretation.

One specific passage which attracted significant interest during the medieval period was Ezekiel 44:1-3, with its description of the closed east gate of the temple. This text was used to argue that in the incarnation, Christ entered the world in the normal way (Ratramnus; *Part. Mar. 3:14*), or alternatively that since Christ was able to pass through closed doors, he came into this world without any of the pain and suffering that was normally associated with childbirth (Radbertus; *De assumptione Sanctae Mariae Virginis*). For Thomas Aquinas, Ezekiel 44 was the classic proof text for the perpetual virginity of Mary, since it clearly states that no man has passed through it but only the Lord, after which it remains shut forever (*Summa Theologica III Q.XXVIII art. 3*).

Martin Luther first engaged with Ezekiel when he was preparing his translation of the Bible into German. Strikingly, he published his translation of Ezekiel 38—39, which deal with the assault of Gog on Israel, separately from and in advance of the rest of the Bible. Luther's interest in this *apocalyptic portion came against the background of the imminent threat of invasion by the Turks, who threatened Hungary in 1527 and had advanced as far as Vienna in 1529. Luther read these chapters of Ezekiel in conjunction with Revelation 20 and identified the Muslim Turks as the personification of Gog, while the church was the true Israel that was depicted under siege in the prophecy (*LW* 45.202). The devil was stirring these enemies up in a last ditch, desperate assault on the Lord's people: together with the Pope, the Turks were Satan's last and greatest weapon against the church. Luther also took a strongly christological approach to interpreting the prophecy: for example, the throne chariot in the opening vision is "the spiritual vehicle of Christ on which he rides in this world," while the new temple in Ezekiel 40—48 pictures the kingdom of Christ surviving on the earth until its final day (*LW* 35.293).

Even though they broke with Rome, the Reformers did not completely reject medieval patterns of exegesis. Huldrich Zwingli followed

Aquinas in seeing Ezekiel 44:1-3 as a proof text for the perpetual virginity of Mary (*SW* 14.685-741). Yet he did not follow Luther in making contemporary application of Ezekiel 38—39; instead he saw it as having been completely fulfilled in the oppression of the Jews in the days of Alexander the Great. Meanwhile, John Calvin never completed a commentary on Ezekiel. Although he preached a series of sermons on Ezekiel in the 1550s, he only began to write his commentary on it at the close of his life and left it unfinished at chapter 20. His hermeneutical approach was more historical than Luther's, recognizing the context of the original readers in the Babylonian exile, while still applying their message to Christ and his church. Thus, for Calvin, the vision of the valley of dry bones was not primarily to be understood as a prophecy of the resurrection, as it was for the church Fathers, but rather as a depiction of the captivity and restoration of Israel. As such, however, it also conveyed a lesson of hope to the church and to individual Christians. Since he also did not write a commentary on Revelation, it may be that he found apocalyptic texts less appealing and immediately relevant than Luther had done.

Seventeenth century English exegetes showed more interest in Ezekiel than Calvin. The early scholar of apocalyptic, Joseph Mede (1586-1639), identified the New World as the true home of Gog. He believed that its Native American inhabitants were descended from the Scythians and would assault Europe in the last days. Meanwhile, the Puritan William Greenhill published five volumes on Ezekiel over the period 1645-1667, volumes that began as a lengthy series of expository lectures. Like much Puritan exegesis, they alternate between awareness of the original historical context and the desire for practical application that at times leads them into allegorical exposition, fastening on superficial similarities between the text and the preacher's context. In spite of that, Greenhill resisted the temptation to identify Gog as any contemporary foe; after surveying many different interpretations from the past, ranging from the Pope and the Turks all the way back to Alexander the Great, he left the identity of this enemy of the church open. He confessed that he found much of the detail about the temple in chapters 40-48 virtually incomprehensible, but asserted nonetheless that the overall message of this portion is a depiction of the Christian church and its worship under the figures and types of the old covenant. A little later in America, the eighteenth century scholar Cotton Mather was forced to interact with Joseph Mede's conjecture about the identity of Gog. He took it as a serious, though far from established, possibility, but stressed rather the positive aspect of his New England forefather's errand into the wilderness and the prospect of redemption for even this previously god-forsaken land. He drew on the image in the prophet of "the waters in Ezekiel's vision growing and rising still" to express his optimism about the future of this project to establish a new and pure community of the faith (Bercovitch, 1972).

4. Modern Interpretation.

Well into the modern period, the single authorship of Ezekiel was regarded as firmly established. S. R. Driver's comment that "the whole from beginning to end [bears] the stamp of a single mind" represents the vast majority opinion of nineteenth century scholarly opinion. However, dissenting voices started to emerge at the beginning of the Twentieth Century and received considerable impetus from the work of G. Hölscher, published in 1924. Hölscher argued that the original prophet was a poet, and using that and other criteria, asserted that a mere 144 verses out of the 1,273 that make up the book belonged to the prophet himself. The tension between poetry and prose paralleled the tension between the prophetic (poetic) persona of the prophet and his priestly (prosaic) interests. Following Wellhausen's reconstruction of Israel's history, it was believed that these belonged to separate groups from distinct historical periods, and therefore could not both have come from the same pen. Ezekiel's prophecies were also thought to contain a strong stress on "individual responsibility," which appealed to scholars as a progressive idea, but alongside that they also contained much interest in ritual and the cultus, which were thought to be regressive.

In the 1930s the idea that the book was a pseudepigraphic work from significantly after the Judean exile was popularized by C. C. Torrey. His work flowed from seeing a tension between material in the book that required a Judean location and the purported setting of the book in exile in Babylon. He argued, therefore,

that the book was written in the third century BC in Judah and was originally set in the 30th year of Manasseh, but had then been later revised to fit a new, exilic date. Other scholars picked up and adapted the idea of a Judean ministry for the prophet, either for the whole or part of his career.

By the 1950s, these speculative attempts to divide up the book and to divorce parts of it from its putative setting were losing steam. Form and tradition criticism continued to identify individual portions and strata of the book as secondary, a movement that reached its height in the work of Zimmerli. Yet these movements tended to be relatively conservative in their conclusions in the case of the Book of Ezekiel, allowing a substantial majority of the book to be the prophet's own work, with many of the later accretions coming from members of the prophet's school. Those who were critical of Zimmerli's work tended to attack the idea of a long and lingering transmission process, through otherwise unattested "schools," in favor of fewer and more substantial redactors (Clements, 1982). There have continued to be a few scholars maintaining more radical views, such as Garscha and Pohlmann, but their arguments have not generally found favor. Meanwhile, the traditional case for essential composition by a single author writing in the Babylonian exile in the sixth century BC has continued to be defended by M. Greenberg and D. Block.

In the early part of the twentieth century much of the theological interest in Ezekiel revolved around psychological questions. As was mentioned earlier, many scholars saw Ezekiel as advancing a new religious insight, "individual responsibility." Ezekiel 18 in particular was seen as the herald of something radically distinct from the views of older texts, which stressed corporate responsibility. Yet more recent scholarship has recognized the fact that this passage is more about generational responsibility than individual responsibility: the history of any generation does not simply depend on the behavior of their father's generation but on their own (Joyce, 46). *Repentance is always an option for a community, not just for an individual. So the prophet's views were not as radical as earlier imagined.

There have also been attempts to psychoanalyze the prophet and thus to account for his strange behavior (Broome; Halperin). As a result, Ezekiel has been diagnosed as having suffered extreme problems in his relationship with his mother, probably in addition to having suffered serious childhood sexual abuse (*see* Prophecy and Psychology). These too have not found much following, not least because psychoanalyzing a historical person based solely on their writings must always be a highly speculative venture, while unusual *sign acts were part and parcel of the ministry of the prophets, especially when their calling was to hostile audiences (Friebel, 1999).

Equally speculative have been the attempts to identify the vision of the divine throne-chariot of chapter 1 as an interaction between the prophet and a spacecraft. This view was first introduced by Erich von Däniken in his 1968 book, *Chariots of the Gods?*, in which he argued that many features of ancient civilizations and religions stemmed from early contacts with UFO's. Although not garnering any scholarly support, von Däniken's colorful thesis has since become a staple of science fiction and the tabloid press. Similar associations between Ezekiel's vision and spacecraft have been identified in a variety of modern cults, especially in the teachings of Elijah Muhammed, the founder of the Nation of Islam (Lieb, 1998).

Other popular writers have returned to Luther's speculative approach to identifying the actors in the final battle of Ezekiel 38-39 with modern people and nations. Hal Lindsey's bestseller, *Late Great Planet Earth* (1970), was merely the most prominent publicity vehicle for a movement, when it identified the Rosh of Ezekiel 38:2 with Russia, Meshech with Moscow and Tubal with Tobolsk. These ideas had already been put forward in the early part of the century in the notes of the dispensationalist *Scofield Reference Bible*. Lindsey developed these ideas into a complex jigsaw linking biblical names and places with current events around the world, which he then used to argue for the imminent rapture of the church and the end of the world, events that he said would certainly take place during the 1980's. In spite of the failure of his detailed timelines, he and others continue to argue in the same vein and have a large public following in fundamentalist and conservative evangelical circles.

More recently, a number of *feminist scholars have been highly critical of Ezekiel's depiction of women, especially in chapters 16 and 23. This has been described as "pornographic" and repressive to women's sexuality, as well as being likely to lead to the abuse of women by their husbands (Van Dijk Hemmes; Exum). However, no evidence has been produced to demonstrate that these chapters were ever intended to be interpreted in those ways, or that they have ever actually been used as the foundation for such conclusions. These feminist readings have more in common with allegorical exegesis, in which any superficial resemblance between text and application could be justified on the basis of the practical utility of the application. Rather than being legitimate attempts to interpret the text in its original context, these readings seek to critique and resist those ancient texts on the basis of modern Western criteria of right and wrong (Patton, 2000).

Over the past few years, there have been a growing number of academic studies of Ezekiel taking the final form of the text seriously as the source for theological reflection (*see* Canonical Criticism). Building on the work of Greenberg and Block, there has been more skepticism about the ability of modern scholarship to identify redactional layers, and a corresponding desire to treat the text more holistically. There has been a growing interest in the *rhetorical form of the book (Renz), its connection with ancient Near Eastern background materials (*see* Ancient Near Eastern Prophecy) and the interplay between the prophetic and priestly roles of Ezekiel (Odell & Strong; Patton & Cook), the concept of *retribution in Ezekiel (Duguid; Wong), and the connection between the Book of Ezekiel and *ethics (Lapsley; Mein). Meanwhile, more traditional diachronic explorations of the text have continued as well, often in fruitful dialogue with the more holistic approaches (Tuell). These diverse approaches and methods show the vitality of the field of study at this time and show promise of yet more insights from the Book of Ezekiel in the years ahead.

See also EZEKIEL: BOOK OF; FEMINIST INTERPRETATION; HERMENEUTICS; PROPHECY AND ESCHATOLOGY IN CHRISTIAN THEOLOGY.

BIBLIOGRAPHY. **S. Bercovitch,** "Cotton Mather," in *Major Writers of Early American Literature*, ed. E. Emerson (Madison: University of Wisconsin Press, 1972) 93-150; **D. I. Block,** *Ezekiel 1-24* (NICOT; Grand Rapids: Eerdmans,

1997); idem, *Ezekiel 25-48.* (NICOT; Grand Rapids: Eerdmans, 1998); **E. C. Broome,** "Ezekiel's Abnormal Personality," *JBL* 65 (1946) 277-92; **J. Calvin,** *Ezekiel I,* trans. D. Foxgrover and D. Martin (repr., Grand Rapids: Eerdmans, 1994); idem, *Ezekiel II,* trans. T. Myers (repr., Grand Rapids: Baker, 1989); idem, *Sermons sur le livre des révélations du prophète Ézéchiel chapitres 36-48,* ed. E. A. de Boer and B. Nagy (Supplementa Calviniana: Sermons inédits, 10/3; Neukirchen-Vluyn: Neukirchener Verlag, 2006); **R. E. Clements,** "The Ezekiel Tradition: Prophecy in a Time of Crisis," in *Israel's Prophetic Tradition,* ed. R. Coggins, A. Phillips and M. Knibb (Cambridge: Cambridge University Press, 1982) 119-36; **S. L. Cook and C. L. Patton,** eds., *Ezekiel's Hierarchical World: Wrestling with a Tiered Reality* (Atlanta: SBL, 2005); **E. Cothenet,** "Influence d'Ezéchiel sur la spiritualité de Qumrân," *RQ* 13 (1988) 431-439; **E. A. De Boer,** *John Calvin on the Visions of Ezekiel: Historical and Hermeneutical Studies* (Leiden: Brill, 2003); **S. R. Driver,** *An Introduction to the Literature of the Old Testament* (New York: Scribners, ⁹1913); **I. M. Duguid,** *Ezekiel and the Leaders of Israel* (SVT 56; Leiden: Brill, 1994); **J. C. Exum,** *Plotted, Shot and Painted: Cultural Representations of Biblical Women* (Sheffield: Sheffield Academic, 1996) 101-128; **K. G. Friebel,** *Jeremiah's and Ezekiel's Sign Acts: Rhetorical Non-verbal Communication* (JSOTSup 283; Sheffield: Sheffield Academic, 1999); **J. G. Galambush,** "Ezekiel, Book of," in *Dictionary of Biblical Interpretation,* ed., J. H. Hayes (Nashville, TN: Abingdon, 1999) 1.372-375; **J. Garscha,** *Studien zum Ezechielbuch* (Berne and Frankfurt: Peter Lang, 1974); **Gregory the Great,** "Homiliarum in Ezechielem Prophetam Libri Duo," *PL* 76.785-1072; **M. Greenberg,** *Ezekiel 1-20* (AB; Garden City, N.Y.: Doubleday, 1983); **W. Greenhill,** *An Exposition of Ezekiel* (repr.; Edinburgh: Banner of Truth, 1994); **D. Halperin,** *Seeking Ezekiel: Text and Psychology* (State College, PA: Pennsylvania State University, 1993); **G. Hölscher,** *Hesekiel; der Dichter und das Buch* (BZAW 39; Giessen: Töpelmann, 1924); **Jerome,** "Commentariorum in Ezechielem Prophetam Libri Quatuordecim," *PL* 25.15-490; **P. Joyce,** *Divine Initiative and Human Response in Ezekiel* (JSOTSup 51; Sheffield: JSOT, 1989); **J. K. Jue,** *Heaven Upon Earth: Joseph Mede (1586-1638) and the Legacy of Millenarianism* (Dordrecht: Springer, 2006); **J. E. Lapsley,** *Can These Bones Live? The Problem of the Moral Self in the Book of Ezekiel* (BZAW 301; Berlin: De Gruyter, 2001); **M. Lieb,** *Children of Ezekiel: Aliens, UFOs, the Crisis of Race, and the Advent of End Time* (Durham, NC: Duke University Press, 1998); **H. Lindsey,** *The Late, Great Planet Earth* (Grand Rapids: Zondervan, 1970); **M. Luther,** *Luther's Works* (55 vols.; St. Louis: Concordia; Philadelphia: Fortress, 1955-1986); **C. Mather,** *Magnalia Christi Americana* (Boston, 1702); **A. Mein,** *Ezekiel and the Ethics of Exile* (Oxford: Oxford University Press, 2002); **J. Mede,** "A Conjecture Concerning Gog and Magog in the Revelation," in *The Works of the Pious and Profoundly Learned Joseph Mede* (London, 1664) 713; **M. Odell and J. T. Strong,** eds., *The Book of Ezekiel: Theological and Anthropological Perspectives* (Atlanta: SBL, 2000); **C. L. Patton,** "'Should Our Sister Be Treated Like a Whore?': A Response to Feminist Critiques of Ezekiel 23," in *The Book of Ezekiel: Theological and Anthropological Perspectives,* ed., Odell and Strong (Atlanta: SBL, 2000) 221-38; **F. Pohlmann,** *Ezechielstudien* (BZAW 202; Berlin: De Gruyter, 1992); **Rabanus Maurus,** "Commentariorum in librum Ezechielem libri viginti," *PL* 110.493-1084; **T. Renz,** *The Rhetorical Function of the Book of Ezekiel* (Leiden: Brill, 1999); **Richard of St Victor,** "In Visionem Ezechielis," *PL* 196.527-600; **K. Stevenson and M. Glerup,** eds., *Ezekiel, Daniel* (ACCS; Downers Grove, IL: InterVarsity Press, 2008); **C. C. Torrey,** *Pseudo-Ezekiel and the Original Prophecy* (New Haven: Yale University Press, 1930); **S. S. Tuell,** *The Law of the Temple in Ezekiel 40-48* (HSM 48; Atlanta: Scholars Press, 1992); **F. van Dijk Hemmes,** "The Metaphorization of Woman in Prophetic Speech," *VT* 43 (1993) 162-70; **E. von Däniken,** *Chariots of the Gods? Unsolved Mysteries of the Past* (London: Souvenir, 1968); **K. L. Wong,** *The Idea of Retribution in the Book of Ezekiel* (SVT 87; Leiden: Brill, 2001); **W. Zimmerli,** *Ezekiel,* trans. R. E. Clements (Hermeneia; Philadelphia: Fortress, 1979); **H. Zwingli,** *Sämtliche Werke,* ed. E. Egli (Zürich: Verlag Berichthaus, 1956-59).

I. M. Duguid

F

FAITH

Faith in the OT, and particularly in the prophetic literature, usually is portrayed in terms of fidelity to *covenant obligations or to *ethical expectations as communicated by the prophet. For this reason, faith (or faithfulness) serves as the basis for the relationship between *God and the people. As the following discussion observes, the prophetic call to remain faithful to covenant obligations is applied in various directions in the prophetic literature. In addition, the prophets often were concerned to emphasize the unfailing faithfulness of Yahweh, especially within the context of historical developments.

Since much of the prophetic literature of the OT involves exhortation toward certain behavior, varying conceptions of faith can be found among the prophets instead of a uniform expectation of what faith should be. Moreover, the subject of faith is rarely addressed as an isolated topic. Rather, prophetic understandings of a faithful relationship with Yahweh usually are embedded within the prophetic messages. Thus, for example, one prophet may conceive of faith primarily as the exclusive *worship of Yahweh, while another may proclaim that the proper response of faith is fair and just behavior. In any case, the faith proclaimed by the prophets always has ethical implications for relationships among Israelites and with Yahweh.

1. Terminology
2. Expressions of Faith
3. Ahaz and Hezekiah
4. The Faithfulness of Yahweh

1. Terminology.

Several different words are used in the OT prophetic literature to express the idea of faith. Relevant terms include the verb ʾmn (Niphal, "to be reliable, faithful"; Hiphil, "to believe") and related nominal forms, such as ʾōmen ("faithfulness"), ʾāmēn ("faithfulness"), ʾĕmet ("firmness, trustworthiness") and ʾĕmûnâ ("faithfulness"). The verb bāṭaḥ ("to trust") and related nouns (biṭḥâ ["confidence"], biṭṭāḥôn ["confidence"], mibṭāḥ ["trust"]) also refer to faith or confidence in the direction of Yahweh or elsewhere. At the same time, faith is often described in terms relating to covenant obligations. The words ḥesed ("goodness, faithfulness") and ṣedeq/ṣĕdāqâ ("righteousness") are key expressions that refer to the covenant faithfulness of people or Yahweh. Many of these terms are used together to indicate that faith often is conceived within the framework of covenant obligations between the people and Yahweh, resulting in various implications for ethical behavior on the part of the people.

2. Expressions of Faith.

The concept of faith is applied in a variety of directions in the prophetic literature. The following discussion is not intended to be comprehensive, but instead provides a sample of the many different ways that faith is described in the Prophetic Books. For example, faith often is conceived in terms of the exclusive worship of Yahweh, frequently using the imagery of *marriage fidelity. The classic example of this comes from the book of Hosea, in which Israel's pursuit of Baal is compared to an unfaithful wife (Hos 2:5, 13; cf. Hos 4:12-13; Ezek 16:1-63).

One predominant theme among the early "writing" prophets is injustice and abuse, particularly in the political and social affairs of Israel and Judah. They seem especially interested in addressing the growing disparity between wealthy landowners and the poor (see Wealth and Poverty). For these prophets, such inequities come under the purview of the faith of the people. For example, Hosea offers harsh critique against the corruption and injustice among the people of Israel (Hos 7:1). In addition, the prophet hands down an indictment against Israel for lacking faithfulness (ʾĕmet), loyalty (ḥesed) and knowledge (daʿat) of God (Hos 4:1). Here, collocation of faithfulness with the covenantal concepts of loyalty and knowledge indicates that faithfulness is conceived in terms of covenantal obligations (cf. Hos 2:19-20; 6:4, 6-7). Hosea also calls for sowing righteousness (ṣĕdāqâ) and reaping loyalty, instead of plowing wickedness and reaping injustice (Hos 10:12-13) (see Justice, Righteousness). This latter example also includes trusting in its own military capability among Israel's misdeeds (cf. Is 31:1).

Many other prophets echo Hosea's concern for *social justice. In the book of Amos faith often is portrayed in terms of adhering to justice (mišpāṭ) and righteousness (ṣĕdāqâ) (Amos 5:7, 24, 6:12), particularly as they relate to the powerful elite, who "trample the head of the poor into the dust of the earth" (Amos 2:7 NRSV). For Amos, there is no virtue in observing copious festivals and offerings as long as injustice reigns among the people (Amos 5:21-24). What is more, observance of the Sabbath is seen by some only as a hindrance to conducting fraudulent business practices and oppressing the poor (Amos 8:4-6). The exhortation in Amos is to abandon evil and injustice and to seek Yahweh, in the hope that Yahweh might be gracious to a small remnant among the people of Israel (Amos 5:4-6, 14-15). Micah also condemns unfair and oppressive practices, such as bribery (Mic 3:11; 7:3) and the use of dishonest weights (Mic 6:11). There may be no clearer statement of the sort of response to Yahweh that Micah advocates than to do justice (mišpāṭ), love kindness (ḥesed), and walk humbly with God (Mic 6:8).

Isaiah joins other eighth-century BC prophets in denouncing injustice, especially among the rich and powerful of Jerusalem. Thus, he speaks out against those who "join house to house" (Is 5:8) and exploit the poor (e.g., Is 3:14-15). In one memorable example Isaiah uses a play on words to describe their injustice and unrighteousness (Is 5:7): "he waited for justice [mišpāṭ], but instead, bloodshed [miśpāḥ];

for righteousness [ṣĕdāqâ] but instead, a cry [śĕʿāqâ]!"

Zechariah explicitly recalls the admonition of earlier prophets to act with faithfulness (ʾĕmet), particularly when dealing with vulnerable members of society, such as widows, orphans and aliens (Zech 7:9-12; 8:16, 19; cf. Zech 1:4, 6). He then announces Yahweh's intent to dwell in Zion, which will be called the "city of faithfulness" (ʿîr-hāʾĕmet [Zech 8:3]).

In addition to matters of justice, sometimes faith is conceived in terms of dependency on Yahweh instead of military capability or international alliances. In the book of Isaiah, for example, King Hezekiah of Judah must trust (bāṭaḥ) Yahweh instead of other nations such as Egypt for the deliverance of Jerusalem from Assyria (Is 36:4-9, 15; 37:10; cf. Is 31:1). This same emphasis resonates in the book of Jeremiah (e.g., Jer 17:5, 7), and Jeremiah 2:36-37 seems to recall the specific circumstances regarding Hezekiah and Isaiah (cf. Jer 46:25). Likewise, Jeremiah often sets trusting in the deception of those who resist Babylon against trusting in the message of Yahweh as delivered by the prophet (Jer 13:25; 28:15; 29:31; 39:18). Along similar lines, Jeremiah's so-called Temple Sermon warns against trusting in the security of the *temple (Jer 7:4, 8, 14). According to Jeremiah, putting trust in such sources for deliverance from Babylon is misguided. Instead, Judah should trust in Yahweh, even if that means submission to Babylon (Jer 13:25). In a similar fashion, Ezekiel speaks against trusting in Egypt (Ezek 17:1-24; 29:16).

Habakkuk 2:4 is frequently cited as an explicit expression of faith in the OT, since it declares that the righteous (ṣaddîq) live by faith(fulness) (ʾĕmûnâ). This text can be interpreted in such a way that ʾĕmûnâ ("faith[fulness]") modifies either the substantive adjective "righteous" ("the righteous in their faith shall live") or the verb "live" ("the righteous shall live by their faithfulness"). In the immediate context of Habakkuk 2 the latter is more likely, as the text describes patient anticipation of a response from Yahweh. This verse is especially significant because of its influence on NT understandings of faith (cf. Rom 1:17; Gal 3:11; Heb 10:38), but there is considerable disagreement about Paul's citation of this passage. While the MT of Habakkuk 2:4 has a third-person pronoun ("his faith"), the LXX translation has a first-person pronoun ("my faithfulness"). Thus, the Hebrew text seems to refer to the faithfulness of the individual (or of the "vision" in Hab 2:3 [see Roberts, 107]), whereas the LXX speaks of "my" (i.e., God's) faithfulness (Smith, 107; Robertson, 181; Wenham, 10-17). However, in both instances of Pauline quotation of Habakkuk 2:4 (Rom 1:17; Gal 3:11) the pronoun is omitted altogether (Fitzmyer, 236-46). As J. D. G. Dunn observes, it is possible that Paul was aware of both the Hebrew and Greek textual traditions, in which case the omission of the pronoun allows for the widest possible interpretation of the text. Rather than forcing a choice between whether the text speaks of God's faithfulness or human faithfulness, Paul may very well have been deliberately ambiguous so as to embrace both traditions (Dunn, 44-46).

3. Ahaz and Hezekiah.

Special attention should be given to the portrayal of the faith of the Judean kings Ahaz and Hezekiah, since this accounts for one of the most explicit expressions of faith in the prophetic literature. According to the biblical sources (2 Kings 15:37; 16:5-9; 2 Chron 28:1-27; Is 7:1-9), Rezin the king of Aram and Pekah the king of northern Israel were pressuring Ahaz to join their coalition against Assyrian expansion. When Ahaz refused to take part, Rezin and Pekah proceeded to launch an attack against Judah. This provides the historical background for the well-known interaction between Isaiah and Ahaz in Isaiah 7:1-9. In this passage Yahweh reassures Ahaz that Rezin and Pekah will not succeed in their attack against Jerusalem, but at the same time, Yahweh exhorts Ahaz to strengthen his faith. Using a play on the verb 'mn, the prophet proceeds to tell Ahaz in Isaiah 7:9 that if he does not believe (ta'ămînû), he will not endure (tē'āmēnû). Clearly, this text indicates that Ahaz should have faith in Yahweh in the midst of these circumstances, but the precise nature of that faith is not immediately obvious.

As G. C. I. Wong observes, the faith described in Isaiah 7:9 is often viewed in connection with the sort of passivity that seems to be described in Isaiah 7:4, in which Yahweh tells Ahaz to be quiet and not to fear, among other things (Wong, 536-40). Understood one way, Ahaz should passively trust in Yahweh for deliverance rather than taking any steps toward self-defense. However, Wong argues that hiššāmēr (NRSV: "take heed") in Isaiah 7:4 can also be understood to mean "be alert" or "be on guard," which hardly necessitates passive inactivity (cf. 1 Sam 19:2; 2 Kings 6:10;). Likewise, the following word, hašqēṭ (NRSV: "be quiet"), need not refer to inaction (cf. Is 57:20; Jer 49:23).

It is possible that the faith demanded by these verses in Isaiah 7 could be understood as "leaving room for God's sovereign action, desisting from self-help" (von Rad, 130). At this point in the development of the events, however, Ahaz has not yet been given the option to capitulate to Aram or Israel, so this is an improbable interpretation of the text. It might be more plausible to suppose that this particular instance of faith in Yahweh implies that Ahaz should not turn to Assyria for help against the neighboring coalition. However, the book of Isaiah conspicuously omits that this was precisely Ahaz's course of action, at great political and economic expense (2 Kings 16:7-9). This leads Wong to conclude that the faith advocated in Isaiah 7 cannot be understood in terms of the rejection of Assyrian assistance (Wong, 540-42). Although these verses do not detail the nature of the faith that Ahaz should have, Wong proposes that the faith that Isaiah 7:4-9 promotes can be broadly conceived in terms of belief in the word of Yahweh as given by the prophet. Thus, Isaiah 7:10-13 critiques Ahaz's veneer of piety that claims not to require a sign from Yahweh while ignoring the sort of injustice and unrighteousness that the previous chapters of the book describe (cf. Is 1:14-17; 3:13-14; 5:7). As H. Wildberger observes, faith is an act of trust that includes action: "binding oneself to what is promised, obligating oneself to what is demanded, and making use of what is promised as one determines one's own course of action" (Wildberger, 645-46).

The question of Ahaz's faith is clarified by setting it alongside the portrayal of Hezekiah's faith in Isaiah 36:1—37:38. That these two kings are set forth for comparison is indicated by the numerous points of correspondence between the two third-person narratives (Ackroyd, 491-94; Conrad 1991, 38-40). Both accounts involve an imminent military threat against the city of Jerusalem; in the case of Isaiah 7, the threat comes from the Syro-Ephraimite coalition, whereas Isaiah 36—37 is set against the backdrop of the Assyrian king Sennacherib's campaign in Judah. More specifically, the scene for both encounters is set at "the end of the conduit of the upper pool on the highway to the Fuller's Field" (Is 7:3; 36:2 NRSV). This point of detail plays no particular role in either narrative, other than to link the two accounts. Moreover, the "dial of Ahaz" in Isaiah 38:8 provides explicit reference to the former king. In each narrative the king is considerably distressed at the news of the attack (Is 7:2; 37:1), which prompts the interaction with the prophet Isaiah, who says not to fear (Is 7:4; 37:6) and offers words of assurance predicting a failed invasion. Finally, both episodes feature the provision of a sign from Yahweh to confirm the prophetic word (Is 7:11, 14; 37:30; 38:7, 22).

Despite these points of continuity between the two accounts, the differences set Hezekiah's faith against that of Ahaz (Conrad 1988, 73-74). Whereas the prophet Isaiah approaches Ahaz uninvited in Isaiah 7, Hezekiah invites Yahweh's involvement through the ministry of the prophet (Is 37:1-4). Moreover, the Assyrian accusations that Hezekiah is deceiving the people (Is 36:18) and himself (Is 37:10) emphasize Hezekiah's trust in Yahweh for deliverance. To make the distinction of faith between the two kings even clearer, Isaiah 7:9 uses the play on the verb ʾmn to describe Ahaz's refusal to believe, while Isaiah 38:3 invokes a related noun (ʾĕmet) to refer to Hezekiah's faithfulness in walking before Yahweh. Thus, Ahaz's lack of faith is characterized by his refusal to accept Yahweh's offer of a sign (Is 7:11-12), whereas Hezekiah accepts signs (Is 37:30; 38:7) and even requests them (Is 38:22). The point of emphasis in both accounts is that confidence should be placed in Yahweh's promise to defend Jerusalem for David's sake rather than in foreign alliances (cf. Is 7:2, 13; 37:35). In Isaianic terms, one could say that Hezekiah's faith is a better reflection of the name "Immanuel," meaning "God with us" (Is 7:14) (Conrad 1988, 73-74).

4. The Faithfulness of Yahweh.

Finally, an important concept in the prophetic literature is the faithfulness of Yahweh, which usually is expressed with the term *hesed* (e.g., Is 54:10; 63:7; Jer 31:3). The subject of Yahweh's faithfulness often is used by the prophets as an implicit contrast with the unfaithfulness of the people. The implication is that Yahweh's faithfulness remains steadfast, while the same cannot be said of Israel and Judah (Is 40:6; Jer 2:2; Hos 4:1; 6:4). Yahweh's faithfulness sometimes is applied in two main ways within the context of Yahweh's punishment of the people. On the one hand, Yahweh's faithfulness provides the basis for his abundant mercy and his reluctance to mete out punishment (Joel 2:13; Mic 7:18); on the other hand, when Yahweh does pass judgment, it is out of his faithfulness and genuine love for his people (Is 54:8; Jer 9:24; 32:18). Thus, judgment against the people of Israel and Judah is viewed as the result of a loving God who cares enough to discipline his people.

See also COVENANT; JUSTICE, RIGHTEOUSNESS.

BIBLIOGRAPHY. **P. R. Ackroyd,** "Isaiah 36-39: Structure and Function," in *"The Place Is Too Small for Us": The Israelite Prophets in Recent Scholarship,* ed. R. P. Gordon (SBTS 5; Winona Lake, IN: Eisenbrauns, 1995) 478-94; **E. W. Conrad,** "The Royal Narratives and the Structure of the Book of Isaiah," *JSOT* 41 (1988) 67-81; idem, *Reading Isaiah* (OBT; Minneapolis: Fortress, 1991); **J. D. G. Dunn,** *Romans 1-8* (WBC 38A; Dallas: Word, 1988); **J. A. Fitzmyer,** *To Advance the Gospel: New Testament Studies* (New York: Crossroad, 1981); **J. J. M. Roberts,** *Nahum, Habakkuk, and Zephaniah* (OTL; Louisville: Westminster/John Knox, 1991); **O. P. Robertson,** *The Books of Nahum, Habakkuk, and Zephaniah* (NICOT; Grand Rapids: Eerdmans, 1990); **R. L. Smith,** *Micah-Malachi* (WBC 32; Waco, TX: Word, 1984); **G. von Rad,** *The Message of the Prophets,* trans. D. M. G. Stalker (New York: HarperCollins, 1965); **G. J. Wenham,** *Faith in the Old Testament* (Leicester: Theological Students' Fellowship, n.d.); **H. Wildberger,** *Isaiah 28-39,* trans. T. H. Trapp (CC; Minneapolis: Fortress, 2002); **G. C. I. Wong,** "Faith in the Present Form of Isaiah VII 1-17," *VT* 51 (2001) 535-47.   P. M. Cook

FALSE PROPHECY. *See* TRUE AND FALSE PROPHECY.

FATHER, GOD AS. *See* GOD.

FEMALE IMAGERY. *See* WOMEN AND FEMALE IMAGERY.

FEMALE PROPHETS. *See* PROPHECY, HISTORY OF.

FEMINIST INTERPRETATION

Within the field of biblical studies one of the more controversial approaches to the biblical text has been feminist interpretation, and yet this interpretation has yielded significant information that has challenged not only the way people hear and read the text but also how they view life. This article explores feminist interpretation in relation to the OT prophetic literature. The discussion begins with a description of feminist interpretation, followed by a thumbnail sketch of the interpretation's history and the various lenses that are part of this approach. Consideration is then given to some of the problems for feminists reading the Bible today. The second part of the discussion focuses on various themes within prophetic biblical literature that have come to the fore as a result of feminist interpretation. The last part of the discussion explores the use of metaphorical language used in the prophetic texts, with a specific focus on the book of Hosea and metaphors associated with God. Feminist interpretation has come of age and continues to be a tour de force in the biblical arena.

1. Description, History and Lenses of Feminist Interpretation, and Problems for Feminists Reading the Bible.

1.1. Description of Feminist Interpretation. From its earliest stages, feminist interpretation has been associated with a concern for the rights of all people, which included the abolition of slavery, religious freedom, civil rights, just labor conditions, and a striving for world peace. Part of the fabric of liberation theologies, feminist interpretation focuses on issues of oppression, justice and equality. K. O'Connor notes that feminist biblical interpretation emerged from a host of societal changes involving women and how women began to think about life and about themselves and their role in society, and consequently, "women began to read the Bible with feminist consciousness" (O'Connor, 11). The main enterprise of feminist interpretation is how the Bible can be a saving and liberating word for women. A feminist interpretation begins with a critique of existing patriarchal, hierarchical and unconscious forms of thought and ways of organization and advocates for alternative ways of seeing and living out life. A feminist interpretation privileges women's experiences, voices, values, concerns and differences and argues for more inclusive language and less ambiguous translations. Not all who interpret the Bible from a feminist perspective do so from a religious perspective. Some read the text as a literary or historical document, and thus the Bible's religious authority is neither a concern nor an issue. Furthermore, for many feminist interpreters, God is neither male nor female, and accordingly the use of gender-specific pronouns is avoided.

1.2. History of Feminist Interpretation. Feminist interpretation is not a phenomenon of the twentieth century. Resistance to sexism has occurred throughout history. For example, in medieval times Hildegard of Bingen and Christine de Pizan were among the earliest commentators to critique the Bible from a "woman-focused" perspective. In the eighteenth century Judith Sargent Murray, founder of schools for girls in the United States, cited a nonsexist interpretation of Genesis 2—3 to support her efforts to establish centers of learning. In the nineteenth century the women's movement influenced the development of feminist interpretation. Sojourner Truth and Anna Julia Cooper, along with Jarena Lee and Matilda Joslyn Gage, focused on the emancipatory message of the biblical text in their efforts to challenge both racism and sexism. In 1895 Elizabeth Cady Stanton and a group of women developed *The Woman's Bible,* a text that examined each book of the Bible to expose how women were treated, both positively and negatively. In the twentieth century the first wave of feminist interpretation occurred with the publications of *God's Word to Women: One Hundred Bible Studies on Women's Place in the Divine Economy* by Katherine Bushnell, *The Bible Status of Women* by Lee Anna Starr, and *All the Women of the Bible* by Edith Deen. The second wave of feminist interpretation occurred in the mid-twentieth century and was an outgrowth of the civil rights movement. Betty Friedan's book *The Feminine Mystique* (1963) marked the beginning of the second wave in the United States, along with the works of Margaret Crook (*Women and Religion*), Elsie Culver (*Women in the World of Religion*), Rosemary Radforth Ruether (*Religion and Sexism*), Letty Russell (*The Liberating Word: A Guide to Nonsexist Interpretation of the Bible*), Phyllis Trible (*God and the Rhetoric of Sexuality*), Mary Daly (*The Church and the Second Sex*), and Alice Laffey (*An Introduction to the Old Testament: A Feminist Perspective*). Perhaps the most influential feminist biblical scholar of both the twentieth and twenty-first centuries is Elisabeth Schüssler Fiorenza, whose critical thought and work have taken feminist interpretation to new heights and depths. She has developed a process of biblical interpretation characterized by a series of hermeneutical moves and turns, specifically, a hermeneutics of (1) experience, (2) domination and social location, (3) suspicion, (4) critical evaluation, (5) creative imagination, (6) re-membering and reconstruction and (6) transformative action for change (Schüssler Fiorenza, 165-90). Unlike many of her colleagues writing in this area of interpretation, Schüssler Fiorenza emphasizes the importance of going beyond gender in order to address the whole range of categories of oppression.

1.3. The Methods of Feminist Interpretation. Feminist interpretation focuses on the biblical narrative and poem as they are received as text. Feminist interpretation emphasizes reading the text as a product of its own culture, and it uses all sorts of comparative, historical data to reconstruct a picture of women's life in ancient Israel. Feminist biblical interpreters examine texts to see how women are presented or hidden in the Bible, whether or not women are named, to what extent women appear strong, virtuous, victimized or weak. Feminist biblical interpreters also attend to the images and metaphors of God and address biblical laws affecting women adversely. Postmodern feminist interpretation includes literary and sociological analyses as well as reader-response analyses. This type of interpretation considers the class and culture of many women hearing the biblical text today and calls people to conversion. One of the pioneers in a feminist postcolonial approach to the Bible, and to prophetic literature in particular, is Gale Yee, who emphasizes the need not only to study gender but also to analyze elements of class, race and power both in the text and in the interpreters.

Within the area of feminist interpretation several subcategories have emerged. Womanist interpretation draws on African American women's experience to analyze biblical texts in relation to race, ethnicity, class and gender. This area of interpretation stresses the concept of intersectionality, whereby various forms of oppression are unlocked and treated as multidimensional (for a study of the emergence of womanist scholarship and biblical interpretation and its contributions to biblical studies, see Junior). Mujerista interpretation has the survival and liberation of Latinas in North America as its goal and theological criterion. Asian American feminist interpretation views the Bible through the lens of the concerns of women of Asian heritage. Masculist interpretation shares the feminist commitment to mutuality between genders. Biblical interpretation through this lens examines, from a male perspective, the ways biblical texts construct masculinity. Other equally important feminist lens for interpretation include equal rights/liberal feminism, complementarity feminism, gynecentric/radical feminism, lesbian feminism, gender feminism, maternal feminism, relationality feminism, ecofeminism, postmodern feminism, third world/differences feminism, international feminism, religious feminism, postbiblical feminism and critical liberationist feminism (on these and other such lenses, see Schüssler Fiorenza, 60-64). Many of these dimensions of feminist interpretation and its various lenses have influenced and been used in interpreting biblical prophetic literature, especially with regard to the book of Hosea.

1.4. Problems for Feminists Reading the Bible. Among the many problems for feminists reading the Bible are the scarcity of female characters (*see* Women and Female Imagery); the androcentric fabric of the biblical text; the sexist language used in regard to people and God that markedly excludes women; texts that encourage violence against women; and the fact that the societies that produced the Bible were, for the most part, patriarchal and hierarchical. Furthermore, the history of interpretation of the Bible indicates a bias against women. Lastly, feminists are divided on the question of authority of the Bible.

2. Themes Explored in Feminist Interpretations of the Prophetic Literature.

2.1. Women and Violence. The rigor of feminist interpretation of the OT Prophet Books has yielded a rich harvest of ideas and has exposed many themes that need to be held up for ongoing critical reflection and hermeneutical assessment. One such theme is women and violence.

In her study on the topic N. Bowen discusses the metaphorical violence of a jealous husband against his wife in prophetic literature. She examines Hosea 1—3; Jeremiah 2—3; Ezekiel 16; 23 (Bowen, 186-99). What becomes clear in each of these texts is that when relationships are hierarchically structured, most often the structure causes the one deemed "superior" by society to reassert control over the "subordinate" one. This reassertion of control sometimes takes the form of physical violence, as in the case of Ezekiel 16.

2.2. War. Related to women and violence is the theme of *war. Feminist interpretation has pointed out that in the prophetic texts men are the ones who make war (e.g., Is 3:2, 25; Jer 11:22; Ezek 9:2; Hos 9:13; Joel 3:9; Amos 1:4, 13; Obad 1:9; Mic 5:5-6; Zech 10:5), and women are the spoils of war (e.g., Jer 38:22-23, Ezek 30:17-18). In times of war women are the most vulnerable, as is expressed through the images of pregnant women's wombs being ripped out (Hos 13:16; Amos 1:13) and mothers being dashed to pieces with their children (Hos 13:16). These images symbolize devastation and the annihilation of a people in general.

2.3. Marriage. Within prophetic literature feminist interpretation has given much attention to the theme of *marriage and has shown that the metaphorical covenant relationship between Israel and God is hierarchically structured and influenced by the actual cultural reality of marriage in Israel, which itself was hierarchically structured. Women are presented as sexually subordinate to men, and men are in control of women's sexual reproduction. The portrait of Israel as subordinate to God's control mirrors the cultural reality. Both of these images come together in the image of Samaria and Jerusalem as God's wife, a metaphor used throughout prophetic literature. Additionally, cities oftentimes are symbolized as an unfaithful wife who has betrayed God, the faithful husband (e.g., Ezekiel 16), and is therefore deserving of punishment, which includes a host of

violent acts, such as being stripped naked (Ezek 16:39; 23:26; Hos 2:3), public exposure, defamation and mockery (Ezek 16:37, 57; 23:10, 29; Hos 2:3, 10), mutilation (Ezek 23:25, 34), gang rape (Ezek 16:40), stoning (Ezek 16:40; 23:47) and death (Ezek 16:40; 23:10, 47). Such imagery often is understood by feminist interpreters to be pornography because it involves objectification, dominance, pain and degradation. The marriage metaphor has been linked to psychological and structural violence. When the threat of violence is used as a means to control, then such a threat becomes psychologically abusive. In a hierarchical setting, when one deemed "superior" uses force for the purpose of subordination and subjugation of one deemed "inferior," that relationship and its structures hierarchy become relationally and structurally violent. Finally, feminist interpretation has brought to the surface the structural violence inherent in the prophetic marriage metaphors in general and in the book of *Hosea in particular (see 3.2 below; for a cultural understanding of marriage in the ancient world, in biblical times and in the Bible itself, see Pressler; see also Purdue et al.; on the marriage metaphor in Isaiah, Jeremiah, Ezekiel and Hosea, see Baumann).

2.4. Patriarchy. Another theme that surfaces in feminist interpretation is patriarchy. Broadly understood, patriarchy involves systems of legal, social, economic and political relations that not only validate but also enforce the notion of male superiority and the sovereignty of males as heads of families over other dependent persons in any given household. From a feminist perspective, patriarchy violates women because it denies women the right to be autonomous. Within a patriarchal societal structure and household, women are denied the right to construct culture, to control property, to maintain bodily integrity, to formulate their own decisions and to express their own views and opinions. Patriarchy both restricts and prohibits women's participation in Israelite culture. For example, women are restricted to the margins of cultic life roles, becoming singers and mourners (Jer 9:17; Ezek 33:16). Even though some women function as prophets or in the prophetic role (e.g., Ex 15:20; Judg 4:4; 2 Kings 22:24), women were, for the most part, viewed as illegitimate and dangerous by biblical writers (e.g., Jer 7:18; Ezek 13:17-23). Specific word choice found in prophetic literature betrays Israel as a patriarchal culture. Examples include "man" and "men," "father" and "fathers," "son" and "sons," "brother" and "brothers" when the whole of a society is being inferred. Another example is the naming of people and land after the patriarchs of Israel and Judah (e.g., Is 9:8; Ezek 8:12; Hos 1:10; Amos 2:4, 6; Mic 1:5).

In one of the first introductions to the OT from a feminist perspective, A. Laffey argues that "a patriarchal culture is, by its nature, hierarchical" (Laffey, 152), a reality implied in the listing of people presented in Isaiah 24:2. Thus, one could see from the arrangement of the text references that the priest is superior to the people, the mistress to her maid, the seller to the buyer, the lender to the borrower, the creditor to the debtor, and the father to the son (e.g., Mal 1:6), as Laffey suggests (Laffey, 152). In a patriarchal-hierarchical culture, men would also be considered superior to women and children. This particular kind of culture also sets parameters around worship. Only the priests have charge of the *temple and the altar (Ezek 40:45-46), and the only animals fit for *sacrifice to God are those that are males and without blemish (Ezek 43:22, 23, 25; 45:18, 23; Mal 1:14). The only appropriate wives for priests are virgins of the stock of the house of Israel (Ezek 44:22). Other men could marry widows and divorcées, but these types of women are inappropriate for priests (Ezek 44:22). Thus, within the ranks of both men and women a patriarchal-hierarchical order existed in ancient Israel. Additionally, while all males were circumcised, women were not, and any woman who belonged to an Israelite man was subsumed under the male's circumcision. Finally, even though Israel condemned all false prophets, the prophet Ezekiel is particularly harsh on false women prophets (Ezek 13:18-23).

2.5. Harlotry. One theme that has drawn extensive comment from feminist scholars is harlotry, which involved the infidelity of Israel and the jealousy of God, particularly in the eighth century BC. This theme of harlotry is most prominent in Hosea 1—3, where, traditionally understood, the marriage between Gomer and Hosea becomes symbolic for the covenant between God and Israel. Both Israel and Gomer were unfaithful to their "spouses." This theme of harlotry also surfaces in Isaiah 1:21; Jeremiah 2—3; Ezekiel 16; 23; Micah 1:6-7. In the prophetic literature harlotry was not only about sex acts at high places, but also about spiritual whoredom that violated covenant with God. Israel sought other gods and trusted in foreign powers and often solicited protection from foreign powers instead of trusting only in God. Thus, Israel was guilty of apostasy (for a sampling of the scholarly conversation on this particular theme, see Bellis, esp. 177-90; Setel, 86-95, 157-59; Weems 1989; Ortlund, esp. 47-75). G. Yee offers an excellent analysis of the image of faithless Israel in Hosea and challenges some of the more traditional views of the image of harlotry in Hosea (see esp. Yee, 81-109.)

2.6. Menstruation. With respect to natural bodily functions, women during their menstrual cycles are considered "unclean," and men are not allowed to approach women when they are menstruating (Ezek 18:6; 22:10). Hence, a normal bodily function becomes a stigma for a woman and a cause for her being alienated by others during certain times each month.

2.7. Israel's History as Men's History. Feminist interpretation on prophetic literature has pointed out that, for the most part, Israel's history is the history of men, as is evidenced by how the prophets name their various "houses": house of Ahab (Mic 6:16), David (Is 7:2; 22:22; Jer 21:12; Zech 12:7-8; 13:1), Esau (Obad 1:18), Hazael (Amos 1:4), Isaac (Amos 7:16), Israel (e.g., Is 5:7; 46:3; 63:7; Jer 2:4; Ezek 3:1, 4; 4:3, 4; Hos 1:6; 5:1; Amos 5:3, 4, 25; 6:14; Zech 8:13), Jacob (e.g., Is 2:5, 6; 10:20; 46:3; Jer 2:4; 5:20; Ezek 20:5; Amos 3:13; 9:8; Obad 1:17, 18; Mic 2:7), Jeroboam (Amos 7:9), Joseph (Amos 5:6; Zech 10:6; Obad 1:18), Judah (e.g., Is 22:21; 37:31; Jer 3:18, 20; 5:11; Ezek 4:6; 8:17; Hos 1:7; 5:12; Zech 8:13; 10:3, 6), Levi (Zech 12:13), Nathan (Zech 12:12) and the king or kings (Jer 19:13; Hos 5:1).

2.8. Men as Israel's Exemplars. Coinciding with the theme of Israel's history as men's history is the theme of men as Israel's exemplars, another point unearthed by feminist interpretation on prophetic literature. For example, wisdom is associated with Daniel (Ezek 28:3); Jacob is God's servant (Ezek 28:25; 37:25; cf. Is 58:14; Mal 1:2); Cyrus is God's anointed one (Is 45:1); Jeremiah is the one consecrated and appointed a prophet to the nations (Jer 1:5); Hosea is the faithful one in his marriage with Gomer (Hos 1:2-9); Isaiah is the recipient of a vision of God in the temple and called to be a prophet (Is 6:1-

13); Abraham is God's friend and associated with God's promise of land to Israel (Is 41:8; cf. Is 63:16; Ezek 33:24); David is the recipient of God's covenant and is the shepherd and king of God's people (Is 55:3; Ezek 34:23-24; 37:24, 25); Joseph is the son of a patriarch, and because of that relationship he shares in God's promise not to destroy again the world by water (Is 54:9); and Moses stands renown for the exodus experience (Is 63:11-12) and as the giver of the law (Mal 4:4). Only one female exemplar is cited: Sarah (Is 51:2). Thus, Israel's self-understanding and consciousness were shaped by male figures that the prophetic biblical texts laud.

2.9. Language Used to Speak of God. Feminist interpretation of prophetic literature has also drawn attention to the language associated with and related to God. This God-language is predominantly male and reflects many of the roles assumed by males in their respective cultures and societies. For example, just as men are fathers, so God is described as "Father," as an "Everlasting Father" (Is 9:6; 63:16; cf. Jer 3:4, 19; Mal 1:6). Just as men are kings, so God is named "King" (Is 41:21; Jer 10:10; 51:57; Ezek 20:33; Zeph 3:15). Just as men are warriors, so God is depicted as a warrior (Is 13:4-5; 42:13; Jer 21:5; Ezek 21:5; Joel 2:11; Zeph 3:17; Zech 13:7-8). Just as men are bridegrooms, so God is a bridegroom (Is 62:5); Just as men are husbands, so God is a husband (Is 54:5; Jer 31:32). Furthermore, God is not only a warrior but also the Lord, the God of hosts, the commander-in-chief of the heavenly and earthly powers (Is 1:9; 44:6; Nah 2:13; Zeph 2:9; Zech 1:3; Mal 1:4). God is named after the patriarchs. Israel's God is the "Holy One of Israel" (Is 10:20; 41:16; Jer 50:29), the "God of Israel" (Is 29:23; Jer 9:15; Ezek 8:4; Zeph 2:9), the "Creator of Israel" (Is 43:15), the "Holy One of Jacob" (Is 29:23), the "Mighty One of Jacob" (Is 49:26; 60:16), the "God of Jacob" (Is 2:3; Mic 4:2), the "God of David" (Is 38:5) and the "LORD, who redeemed Abraham" (Is 29:22).

2.10. Women as Men's Possessions. Another theme that surfaces in feminist interpretation of prophetic literature is women as men's possessions. Jeremiah 14:16 makes clear that women "belonged" to men. Hosea 12:12 indicates that Jacob "bought" Leah and Rachel, his two wives, from his father-in-law, Laban. When divine judgment is cast upon Israel, the men of the day will lose their houses and fields and also their "wives," and all will be given to others (Jer 6:12; 8:10; cf. Jer 38:23). Divorce is a man's prerogative, and if a man divorces his wife, the one who sought the divorce would never again take back his former wife because she would be considered "damaged goods" (Jer 3:1; cf. Is 50:1). Only men can initiate divorce; women are not allowed to divorce their husbands. When the prophets exhort against divorce, they address the males of their day, since women are "kept" by the men (Mal 2:14-16).

2.11. Pornography. One last theme featured in feminist interpretation of prophetic literature is pornography. Here the work of T. Setel becomes foundational to the discussion of this particular theme (Setel, 86-95). Setel argues that significant congruencies exist between biblical, and especially prophetic, texts on the one hand, and modern pornographic depictions of female sexuality on the other hand. Setel notes further that in both cases objectified female sexuality is used as "a symbol of evil" (Setel, 86). A. Brenner draws on Setel's work and, referencing Setel, argues that "feminist *definitions* of pornography vary. However, most of them aggress that pornography deals with the objectification and degrading of 'woman' in a manner that makes the abuse of females acceptable or even commendable; that it restricts female sexual choice to an actual act of slavery; and that it stresses the nature and meaning of male power" (Brenner 1993, 185-86). Looking at Jeremiah 3 and Ezekiel 16 in this light, Brenner argues further that "pornography preserves and asserts male social dominion through the control of female sexuality" (Brenner 1993, 186). Brenner concludes that whether or not a historical person named "Jeremiah" was responsible for the pornographic passages attributed to him remains uncertain (Brenner 1993, 193). Brenner's final observation is this: "Whoever composed those passages perceived women and men—not to mention God—and gender relations in a certain way. That vision, that male fantasy of desire which presupposes a corresponding and complementary mystical fantasy of female desire, is pornographic" (Brenner 1993, 193 [see also Brenner 1995]).

2.12. Justice for All. While much of feminist interpretation of prophetic literature focuses on deconstruction, the other side of the spectrum is also represented with a push for a balanced reading of texts, one that takes into account not only the unpleasant, distasteful and offensive elements of and images in the text, but also the complimentary, glorious and inspirational passages of prophetic literature. For example, Micah recognizes women's vulnerability and singles out women for special mention (Mic 2:9). In Amos both women and men are accountable to God and responsible for *social justice. Just as the wayward men of Israel will suffer divine chastisement, so also Israel's women will share in this experience. Amos predicts doom for the idle, rich women who oppress the poor and crush the needy (Amos 4:1-3). Feminist interpretation also brings to the fore another dimension of God, the compassionate one, who is concerned for widows, orphans, slaves, women, sinners and the dispossessed. In Ezekiel 34:15-16 the prophet heralds God's promise to the helpless. God will feed them with justice. One last example is *Zion. A city once debased will be "the city of righteousness—redeemed by justice" (Is 1:26-27), where the needy among God's people will find refuge in "her" (Is 14:32).

3. Use and Critique of Metaphorical Language and Imagery in Prophetic Literature.

3.1. Use of Female Metaphors and Images. Feminist interpretation of prophetic literature explores the use of metaphorical language, especially when those metaphors appeal to the female gender. The main metaphor in the book of Hosea is the faithful husband and the unfaithful wife, symbolizing the covenant relationship between God (Hosea) and Israel (Gomer). This eighth-century BC metaphor allows the woman—the harlot and also the adulteress—to symbolize the practice of *idolatry (see, e.g., Hos 1:2; 2:8-13; cf. Jer 2:20, 33; 3:1-3; 11:15; Ezek 16; 43:7; Mic 1:7; Nah 3:4). In general, Micah describes an evil time in Judah when trust is no longer possible: "Guard the doors of your mouth from her who lies in your embrace" (Mic 7:5). Deutero-Isaiah's way of describing sinners in Judah is to accuse them of being "sons of a sorceress, and offspring of an adulterer and a whore" (Is 57:3). Ezekiel compares bad conduct to women who are impure and unclean on account of their menstrual cycle. Zechariah has a vision of a woman sitting on an ephah. For Zechariah, she is the personi-

fication of wickedness (Zech 5:7-8).

Elsewhere in prophetic literature the female gender is used to speak of a city, country and people. Examples of cities include Rabbah (Amos 1:14) and her daughters (Jer 49:3), Samaria (Ezek 16:46; Hos 13:16; Amos 3:9) and her daughters (Ezek 16:53, 55), Zion (Is 1:27) and her daughters (Is 1:8; Zech 2:10), Jerusalem (Is 51:17; Ezek 16) and her daughters (Mic 4:8; Zeph 3:14; Zech 9:9), Sidon (Is 23:4) and her daughters (Is 23:12), Tyre (Is 23:15) and her daughters (Ezek 26:6, 8), Sodom (Ezek 16:46, 48, 49) and her daughters (Ezek 16:53, 55, 56), daughter of Gallim (Is 10:30), daughter of Tarshish (Is 23:10), Bethlehem Ephrathah (Mic 5:2), Gaza (Amos 1:7), Rahab (Is 51:9), Gebal (Ezek 27:9) and Tehaphnehes (Ezek 30:18).

Examples of countries that are personified as women include Moab (Is 16:2), Egypt (Is 19:14; Jer 46:11, 24; Ezek 23:21), Edom (Ezek 16:57; 32:29), Elam (Ezek 32:24), Judah (Jer 3:7-8, 10), the land of the Philistines (Ezek 16:27, 57), Israel (Amos 5:2; Jer 18:13) and Babylonia (Is 47:1; Jer 50:42; Ezek 23:17; Zech 2:7). A. Laffey comments, "A woman may be understood to have much in common with a city or a country: she may be more or less valuable, more or less beautiful, large or small, a greater or lesser source of nurture, faithful or unfaithful. It is a compliment to a city or a country to personify it; it is an insult to women that cities and countries are so personified!" (Laffey, 162).

Furthermore, Israel's enemies are condemned by means of female imagery that connotes vulnerability, powerlessness and inferiority. For example, the Egyptians will be like women (Is 19:16); the Babylonians will become women (Jer 50:37; cf. Jer 51:30); the hearts of the warriors of Moab and Edom will be like the heart of a woman in labor (Jer 48:41; 49:22); and the Assyrian troops have become like women (Nah 3:13).

Two striking instances where female imagery is used to cast aspersions upon infidelity and wickedness occur in Jeremiah and Ezekiel. Unfaithful Zion is compared to a woman dressed in crimson, decked with ornaments of gold, and eyes enlarged with paint, beautified for her lovers (Jer 4:30). In Ezekiel the poet uses two harlots, Oholah and Oholibah, to describe the sordid state and wicked deeds of Jerusalem and Samaria (Ezek 23).

Divine chastisement to be meted out to Judah, Israel and their enemies is captured through the use of female imagery. Many examples have been brought to the fore by feminist interpretation. In some instances women will be deprived of conception, pregnancy and giving birth (Hos 9:11; cf. Is 23:2). Women will experience a miscarrying womb and dry breasts (Hos 9:14). Their children in their wombs will come to full term, but the women will not have enough strength to bring them forth (Is 37:3). Some children will be brought forth to die (Hos 9:16). A wife will be forsaken (Is 54:6), her skirts lifted up (Jer 13:22, 26; Nah 3:5). Women— wives, mothers, daughters—will be exiled (Jer 22:6; 38:22-23; 41:10). Even Rachel will weep because her children are no more (Jer 31:15).

Prophetic literature also uses female imagery to indicate both fertility and transformation. Jerusalem, a city once forsaken by Israel's God, will now be redeemed. Her land will be married (Is 62:4); her children will marry her (Is 62:5). Mother Jerusalem will provide breasts so that her children can suck and be satisfied from her consoling breast, and she will carry them on her arm and dandle them on her knees (Is 66:11-12).

One particular metaphor that has drawn much attention from feminist interpreters is that of Daughter Zion. C. Mandolfo's bold work deals with the construction of Daughter Zion in the prophets and presents her as finding her own voice, which she uses with clarity, force and power. C. Maier explores the use of this metaphor and its personification in relation to feminist perspectives on the body. Complementing Maier's work is that of F. W. Dobbs-Allsopp, who also explores the female personification of cities in general and Zion in particular. Finally, C. Dempsey looks at the metaphor of Jerusalem/Zion in its transformative state in Isaiah 60—62 (see also Weems 1995; Streete).

3.2. Metaphorical Language in the Book of Hosea: Traditional Feminist Interpretations and Newer Understanding. One of the Prophetic Books that has attracted substantial interpretation from a feminist perspective is Hosea. The main discussions focus on Hosea 1—3 and the husband-wife metaphor. Faithful Hosea represents God, and unfaithful Gomer represents Israel. The traditional interpretation centers on the theme of adultery on Gomer's and Israel's part, and feminist scholars take issue with the use of gendered language whereby a female

is the unfaithful one and the male is the faithful one. Hence, the marriage metaphor of Hosea 1—3 is fraught with problems (for discussion on the gendered language and the marriage metaphor in the book of Hosea, see Day; Sherwood; Bellis; Stienstra; Bird.) A. Keefe proposes alternative views to the typical understanding of Hosea 1—3. She cautions against reading the text against the background of Western androcentrism. She cogently argues that the central metaphor in the book of Hosea 1—3 is familial, not marital.

3.3. Metaphorical Language for God. One of the more thorny issues raised by feminist interpretation is the metaphorical language used to speak of *God. The metaphors range from a mother who births and protects Israel (Is 46:3-4) like a mother bear (Hos 13:8), to an abusive husband (Ezek 16) and a contrite spouse (Is 54:1-10). Whatever the metaphors for God may be, caution is needed to keep the metaphors from being taken literally. Metaphorical language for God is historically, culturally, socially, politically and theologically conditioned, oftentimes used polemically. In a recent study J. O'Brien offers a rigorous critique of the God metaphors used in prophetic literature. O'Brien's study invites further discussion, as it is both scholarly and confessional.

4. Conclusion.
Feminist interpretation of the prophetic literature enjoys a rich, deep and expanding discussion too broad and extensive to capture in a short article such as this one. Feminist interpretation has changed the way audiences read and hear the biblical text and often how people live their lives. Feminist interpretation has blazed a trail that exposes centuries of oppression and injustice endured by women. Yet, the biblical text is not without beams of a hopeful, radiant light that beckons people to continue to search for truth while working for equality and peace. Finally, new directions in feminist interpretation, including the interpretation of the Prophetic Books, are on the horizon. Forthcoming is a new series, the Wisdom Bible Commentary (Liturgical Press), which will examine each book of the Bible from a feminist perspective while incorporating voices from around the globe. Feminist interpretation has yielded much fruit, but the harvest remains plentiful and awaits new laborers from present and future generations.

See also HERMENEUTICS; HOSEA, BOOK OF; MARRIAGE AND DIVORCE; SOCIAL-SCIENTIFIC APPROACHES; WOMEN AND FEMALE IMAGERY; ZION.

BIBLIOGRAPHY. **G. Baumann,** "Prophetic Objections to YHWH as the Violent Husband of Israel: Reinterpretations of the Prophetic Marriage Metaphor in Second Isaiah (Isaiah 40-55)," in *Prophets and Daniel,* ed. A. Brenner (FCB 8; London: Sheffield Academic, 2001) 88-120; **A. O. Bellis,** *Helpmates, Harlots, Heroes: Women's Stories in the Hebrew Bible* (Louisville: Westminster/John Knox, 1994); **P. Bird,** "'To Play the Harlot': An Inquiry into an Old Testament Metaphor," in *Gender and Difference in Ancient Israel,* ed. P. L. Day (Minneapolis: Fortress, 1989) 75-94; **N. R. Bowen,** "Women, Violence, and the Bible," in *Engaging the Bible in a Gendered World: An Introduction to Feminist Biblical Interpretation in Honor of Katherine Doob Sakenfeld,* ed. L. Day and C. Pressler (Louisville: Westminster/John Knox, 2006) 186-99; **A. Brenner,** "On 'Jeremiah' and the Poetics of (Prophetic?) Pornography," in *On Gendering Texts: Female and Male Voices in the Hebrew Bible,* ed. A. Brenner and F. van Dijk-Hemmes (BIS 1; New York: E. J. Brill, 1993) 177-93; idem, "On Prophetic Propaganda and the Politics of 'Love': The Case of Jeremiah," in *A Feminist Companion to the Latter Prophets,* ed. A. Brenner (FCB 8; Sheffield: Sheffield Academic, 1995) 256-74; **J. Day,** "Hosea and the Baal Cult," *Prophecy and the Prophets in Ancient Israel: Proceedings of the Oxford Old Testament Seminar* (LHBOTS 531; London: T & T Clark, 2010) 202-24; **C. J. Dempsey,** "From Desolation to Delight: the Transformative Vision of Isaiah 60—62," In *The Desert Will Bloom: Poetic Visions of Isaiah,* ed. A. J. Everson and H. C. P. Kim (SBLAIL 4; Atlanta: Society of Biblical Literature, 2009) 217-32; **F. W. Dobbs-Allsopp,** "Daughter Zion," in *Thus Says the Lord: Essays on the Former and Latter Prophets in Honor of Robert R. Wilson,* ed. J. J. Ahn and S. L. Cook (LHBOTS 502; London: T & T Clark, 2009) 125-34; **N. Junior,** "Womanist Biblical Interpretation," in *Engaging the Bible in a Gendered World: An Introduction to Feminist Biblical Interpretation in Honor of Katherine Doob Sakenfeld,* ed. L. Day and C. Pressler (Louisville: Westminster/John Knox, 2006) 37-46; **A. A. Keefe,** *Woman's Body and the Social Body of Hosea* (JSOTSup 338; Sheffield: Sheffield Academic, 2001); **A. L. Laffey,** *An Introduction to the Old Testament: A Feminist Perspective* (Philadelphia: Fortress, 1988); **C. M. Maier,** *Daughter Zion, Mother Zion: Gender, Space, and the Sacred in Ancient Israel* (Minneapolis: Fortress, 2008); **C. R. Mandolfo,** *Daughter Zion Talks Back to the Prophets: A Dialogic Theology of the Book of Lamentations* (SBLSS 58; Atlanta: Society of Biblical Literature, 2007); **J. M. O'Brien,** *Challenging Prophetic Metaphor: Theology and Ideology in the Prophets* (Louisville: Westminster/John Knox, 2008); **K. M. O'Connor,** "The Feminist Movement Meets the Old Testament: One Woman's Perspective," in *Engaging the Bible in a Gendered World: An Introduction to Feminist Biblical Interpretation in Honor of Katherine Doob Sakenfeld,* ed. L. Day and C. Pressler (Louisville: Westminster/John Knox, 2006) 3-24; **R. C. Ortlund Jr.,** *Whoredom: God's Unfaithful Wife in Biblical Theology* (Grand Rapids: Eerdmans, 1996); **C. Pressler,** "The 'Biblical View' of Marriage," in *Engaging the Bible in a Gendered World: An Introduction to Feminist Biblical Interpretation in Honor of Katherine Doob Sakenfeld,* ed. L. Day and C. Pressler (Louisville: Westminster/John Knox, 2006) 200-11; **L. G. Purdue et al.,** *Families in Ancient Israel* (Louisville: Westminster/ John Knox, 1997); **E. Schüssler Fiorenza,** *Wisdom Ways: Introducing Feminist Biblical Interpretation* (Maryknoll, NY: Orbis, 2001); **T. D. Setel,** "Prophets and Pornography: Female Sexual Imagery in Hosea," in *Feminist Interpretations of the Bible,* ed. L. M. Russell (Philadelphia: Westminster, 1985) 86-95; **Y. Sherwood,** *The Prostitute and the Prophet: Reading Hosea in the Late Twentieth Century* (JSOTSup 212; London: T & T Clark International, 1996); **N. Stienstra,** "YHWH Is the Husband of His People: The Marriage Metaphor in the Book of Hosea," in *YHWH Is the Husband of His People: Analysis of a Biblical Metaphor with Special Reference to Tranlsation* (Kampen: Kok Pharos, 1993) 96-126; **G. C. Streete,** *The Strange Woman: Power and Sex in the Bible* (Louisville: Westminster/John Knox, 1997); **R. J. Weems,** "Gomer: Victim of Violence or Victim of Metaphor?" in *Interpretation for Liberation,* ed. K. G. Cannon and E. Schüssler Fiorenza (Semeia 47; Atlanta: Scholars Press, 1989) 87-104; idem, *Battered Love: Marriage, Sex, and Violence in the Hebrew Prophets* (Minneapolis: Fortress, 1995); **G. A. Yee,** *Poor Banished Children of Eve: Women as Evil in the Hebrew Bible* (Minneapolis: Fortress, 2003).
C. J. Dempsey

FLORAL IMAGERY

Truth in the Bible is sometimes communicated through abstract propositions, but also often, and even more frequently, through images. Prophetic literature especially abounds with imagery evoking a cognitive response that tries to explain abstract theological concepts, such as the fleeting nature of human existence in the face of God's transcendence, through metaphorical language: "The grass withers, the flower fades . . . ; surely the people are grass" (Is 40:7). These images are literary in character but refer to an absent literal reality. Literary and literal reality converge in the cognitive concept of an image that is a mediated representation of that mostly absent reality, creating a virtual reality that has been interpreted by the producer (author) and that needs to be interpreted through perception by the recipient (reader/listener). Thus, a tension between the absence of the original object and its substitution is created that establishes meaning and communicates biblical truth in a nonpropositional manner. These images can be reproduced in literature through a variety of devices, such as symbols, similes and metaphor. Metaphor is the most widely used trope in biblical literature, especially in Hebrew poetry, which in turn is the preferred literary mode of the OT prophetic literature.

The Hebrew prophets were as much poets as they were God's mouthpieces. Recent research in cognitive linguistics and its application to biblical metaphor theory demonstrates the importance of metaphor for our understanding of the Bible and the divine (see DesCamp and Sweetser; Feyaerts). Most of our theological conceptualizations of God are metaphorical in character, as they create an overlap between the unknown domain of God and the known domain of the metaphor through a set of associated commonplaces. The plant-related metaphors of God as a vineyard farmer (Is 5:1-7) or even as a tree (Hos 14:8-9) found in the prophetic literature serve as powerful interactive metaphors that create new meaning through a tension between the differing realities.

    1. Floral Imagery and Prophetic Metaphor
    2. Floral Imagery in the Prophets
    3. Floral Imagery in the Bible and Floral
       Images of the Ancient Near East
    4. Floral Imagery and Its Theological Force

1. Floral Imagery and Prophetic Metaphor.

Floral imagery—here in the sense of flora, referring to all plant life—in the OT Prophetic Books is far more than ornamental in nature and communicates important prophetic themes and theological motifs through the usage of metaphor and symbols. Prophetic metaphor often draws on plant imagery that can be linked to the prophetic engagement with *covenant theology. The covenant promises that are intrinsically connected to the physical makeup of the land often refer to its bountiful vegetation (e.g., Deut 8:7-8) and are as often contrasted through prophetic critique with the desolation of the land and its vegetation because of the disobedience of the people (e.g., Joel 1:10-12). Within this metaphorical repertoire, the usage of floral imagery serves to refer to the broad prophetic themes of judgment and restoration with a further range of related meanings.

Floral imagery can be communicated by reference to the actual plant or by using lemmas such as *prḥ* ("to sprout, bud, bloom, blossom"), *ṣmḥ* ("to sprout, spring up"), *ṣwṣ* ("to flourish, bloom") and *prḥ* ("bear fruit, be fruitful"), which in their verbal forms express the dynamic idea of extraordinary, spontaneous growth as well as the state of glorious beauty and splendor and the bearing of fruit. However, a reading of biblical imagery cannot be approached only with the help of a concordance search, since metaphors are invoked implicitly rather than explicitly. Thus, in order to identify the respective floral imagery, a much broader reading of the prophetic texts is needed that is informed and guided by an understanding of metaphor theory.

2. Floral Imagery in the Prophets.

In an attempt to organize the floral images found throughout the Prophetic Books, here they are presented according to the major themes that they develop, first within negative contexts of judgment and then within positive contexts of restoration. This is followed by miscellaneous other usages. Each section follows a rough outline of different plant groups preceded by the usages of the verbal forms.

2.1. Floral Imagery of Judgment. Isaiah is the author who employs floral imagery most frequently among the Hebrew prophets. Through verbal forms, in the context of three eschatological "in that day" sections that form part of the oracles against the nations (Is 13:1—20:6), Isaiah describes how the foreign seedlings of false religion and political realism that Israel has planted have budded and blossomed (prḥ) into grief and pain (Is 17:10-11). In an interesting application of metaphorical incongruence, Ezekiel uses two verbal forms of floral imagery to underline the certainty of the impending judgment over Judah and Jerusalem: the rod of violence is blooming (ṣwṣ) and arrogance is budding (prḥ). In Habakkuk 3:17 judgment is represented by the failing economic agricultural base of Israel, where the fig trees no longer are budding (prḥ). However, floral imagery expressed through verbal roots is more frequently found in the images of restoration.

2.1.1. Trees. The most frequent usage of floral imagery found in the Prophetic Books is linked to trees, especially trees used in Israelite agriculture and forestry (fig, olive, almond, cedar, palm, cypress, etc.). Often nations and kings are likened to trees, and judgment usually is expressed in the cutting down of a tree (Is 6:13; 9:14 [terebinth, oak, sycamore, cedar]; 14:8 [cypress, cedar]; 37:24 [cedar, cypress]; Jer 11:16 [olive]; Ezek 31:3-8 [cedar]; Dan 4:4, 11, 14; Amos 2:9 [cedar]; Zech 11:2 [cypress, cedar, oak]). Furthermore, the destruction or drying up of trees as the agricultural base for Israel's economy is used to illustrate God's judgment against his people (Is 2:13 [cedar, oak]; 9:14 [palm]; Joel 1:7 [fig]; 1:12 [fig, palm, apple, pomegranate]). The lack of fruit on the trees demonstrates Israel's lack of faithfulness toward God (Jer 8:13 [fig]; Hos 9:10 [fig]), and the beating of an olive tree in order to harvest the fruit is a metaphor for God's judgment of the nations (Is 24:13). Isaiah in particular employs tree metaphors widely, and while there are a variety of motifs expressed by them, they become the communicative strategy to transmit the important though paradoxical theological theme of judgment (the cutting down of a tree) and restoration as exemplified by the *remnant that even can point as far as the messianic restoration (the shoot that will sprout out of the stump [Is 4:2]).

2.1.2. Shrubs. Shrubs used as floral imagery for judgment are mainly centered on the word pair "briers and thorns," which communicates the pervasive entanglement with injustice (Is 9:18; 10:17; 27:4; Ezek 2:6; Mic 7:4) and the dev-astating after-effects of judgment (Is 7:23-25; 32:13; 34:13; Hos 10:8) when undesired vegetation takes over. Thorns, briers, weeds or nettles on their own communicate the same notions (Is 7:19; 33:12; Jer 4:3; Hos 2:6; 9:6; Jon 2:5; Nahum 1:10; Zeph 2:9). In the context of a polemic against Israel's *idolatry, Hosea metaphorically connects Israel's worthless oaths and empty covenants to impending judgment that will sprout like poisonous weeds (Hos 10:4). The metaphorical incongruence between God's judgment and the poisonous plants increases the impact of the imagery. The bitter juice of the wormwood shrub, sometimes used for medicinal purposes, is used to symbolize God's punishment (Jer 9:15; 23:15) and is also contrasted with the sweet fruit of righteousness (Amos 5:7; 6:12). Reeds and papyrus plants are appropriately mentioned in connection with judgment over Egypt (Is 18:2; 19:6; Ezek 29:6) and the castor-oil shrub in whose shade Jonah rests overlooking Nineveh serves as an illustration of God's judgment and grace.

2.1.3. Flowers. Flowers, especially their blossoms (ṣîṣ), in judgment imagery are most frequently connected to the concept of the temporal limitations of beauty (Is 28:1, 4; 40:6-8) and power (Nahum 1:4), usually in the face of God's judgment (Is 5:24; 18:5). The flax flower, an important resource for the ancient weaving industry, is also mentioned in contexts of judgment (Is 19:9; Hos 2:5, 9).

2.1.4. Grass. The usage of grass in prophetic imagery follows along the same lines as that of flowers, where its withering usually is an expression of God's judgment (Is 15:6; 37:27; Jer 14:5).

2.1.5. Vines. The familiar imagery of Israel as a choice vine echoes the care of God for his chosen people and highlights the contrast between his election of Israel and his rejection by Israel (Is 5:2, 5, 6; Jer 2:21), which does not bear fruit. Consequently, the wood of the vine is only good to be burned (Ezek 15:2).

2.1.6. Grain. Hosea observes the lack of sprouting grain and interprets it as a sign of God's judgment (Hos 8:7; Joel 1:10), indicating that without God's blessings, the wheat that has been sown turns into thorns (Jer 12:13).

2.1.7. Gardens. As part of the plagues cycles, Amos 4:9 makes reference to gardens that have been destroyed by blight and mildew through divine intervention so as to motivate Israel to repentance. The garden in prophetic imagery often connects to the paradise motif, and its destruction indicates the spiritual distance between Israel and its creator. The plants in this garden, as has been observed above, are mostly functional rather than ornamental and serve an economic purpose. These are the plants of the covenant promise that within the context of judgment illustrate the tangible and spiritual reversal of the blessings. The floral imagery of judgment thus drives home the point of how far Israel has removed itself from the covenant and how deeply its spiritual existence and physical subsistence have been affected by this.

2.2. Floral Imagery of Restoration. Floral imagery of restoration is frequently used in contrast to judgment imagery, sharpening the distinction between an unfaithful and faithless people and the ideal situation of what could have been otherwise. Numerically, the usages of floral imagery within the context of restoration are about half as many as those related to judgment, but interestingly, the metaphorical repertoire corresponds mostly between the two themes.

2.2.1. Verbal Forms. While, as just noted, the restoration usages of floral imagery are disproportionate to those related to judgment, verbal forms are used more frequently in restoration imagery than in judgment imagery and naturally lend themselves to the idea of restoration. Hosea, within the context of a tree metaphor representing Israel's restoration by a growing cedar and olive tree, sees the nation also blooming (*prḥ*) like a lily (or rose?) and a garden that recalls the eschatological garden motif of Eden restored (Hos 14:5, 7). The metaphor moves beyond the familiar in Hosea 14:8, where Yahweh is likened to a cypress or, more likely, a juniper (*Juniperus excelsa*), which is further qualified by the adjective *ra'ănān* ("flourishing, luxuriant, full of leaves"), denoting its superior appearance in comparison to Israel as a growing cedar and olive tree. The choice of tree for Yahweh is further underscored by its extensive usage in the construction of the *temple (e.g., 1 Kings 5:22). While the blending of metaphor is surprising and needs to be understood within the context of tree metaphors throughout the OT, it becomes clear that Israel can grow and flourish only under the protection of its divine king, Yahweh. The dynamic *ṣmḥ* ("sprout, spring up") is mainly used by Isaiah, and on an abstract level he

makes reference to new things that spring up (Is 42:9; 43:19) in the context of the description of the work of the messianic Servant of Yahweh. There is also salvation, righteousness, praise (Is 45:8; 61:11) and healing (Is 58:8; 66:14) springing up, as well as the descendants of Jacob, who will sprout like trees (Is 44:4). Further, the eschatological blossoming (*ṣwṣ*) of Israel describes the nation in terms of restoration. Finally, in a messianic vision, Ezekiel sees an individual sprouting like a horn that serves as an ancient Near Eastern symbol of strength and power. The verbal root *ṣmḥ* is related to the noun *ṣemaḥ* ("shoot" or, alternatively, "vegetation, growth"), which is used by Jeremiah, Zechariah and to a lesser extent by Isaiah and Ezekiel as a specific messianic term (Jer 33:15; Ezek 29:21; Zech 3:8; 6:12).

2.2.2. Trees. A wide variety of trees are used for the imagery of restoration, often grouped together representing the floral bounty of Israel and indicating to the modern reader the level of forestation and agricultural activity in ancient Israel. In a reversal from desolation to restoration, Isaiah foresees a reforestation of the wilderness (Is 41:19 [cedar, acacia, myrtle, olive, cypress, plane, pine]). He later picks up on the same group of conifers (Is 60:13 [cypress, plane, pine]) in describing the rebuilding of *Zion and the beautification of its sanctuary. As much as the olive tree was beaten in the context of judgment (Is 24:13), the restoration image of a remnant is found in the gleanings that are left on the olive tree after the harvest (Is 17:6). The same concept of the remnant is referred to in the stump of a terebinth or an oak (Is 6:13) from which the holy seed will arise. Palm trees figure prominently in Ezekiel's vision of the restoration of the temple (Ezek 40:16; 41:18), where they were used there as ornamental elements symbolizing life, sustenance and peace. During the postexilic restoration the prophet Haggai indicates that from the day the foundation of the temple was laid, God's blessing has returned to his people in that the fruit trees are producing again (Hag 2:19 [vine, fig, pomegranate, olive]).

2.2.3. Shoots. The shoot or branch (*ṣemaḥ*) is used as a messianic title by various Hebrew prophets. As part of the tree metaphor, the shoot first establishes the Davidic credentials of the *Messiah (Jer 23:5; 33:15), but it also conveys the concept of the remnant coming forth from the stump (Is 4:2). Zechariah combines the messianic shoot with the Servant of Yahweh title (Zech 3:8; 6:12). The shoot as *nēṣer* has similar messianic connotations (Is 11:1; cf. Dan 11:7), but also it can be extended to God's people as a whole (Is 66:21).

2.2.4. Shrubs. Among the shrubs in restoration imagery, the briers and thorns are now removed (Ezek 28:24) and replaced by more pleasant vegetation, the cypress and the myrtle tree (Is 55:13). Reeds are representative of flowing fresh water that turns the *wilderness into a garden (Is 35:7). Finally, the fragile reed that will not be broken becomes an image of God's careful restoration (Is 42:3).

2.2.5. Flowers. The crocus (narcissus?) and the lily are mentioned among the flowers within the imagery of restoration. The exact identification of the various biblical species remains a point of botanical interpretation, but both flowers blossom as a result of the restorative changes that the land is experiencing by way of divine intervention and are connected to the image of bountiful abundance in contrast with a previously waterless and dry wasteland that God is restoring (Is 35:1-2; Hos 14:5).

2.2.6. Grain and Vines. Finally, grain and vines (together with fig trees) are mentioned in Isaiah as a false promise of restoration made by Assyrian envoys who are trying to convince Hezekiah to surrender Jerusalem (Is 36:16-17).

2.3. Miscellaneous Usages of Floral Imagery. Floral imagery as denoting blessings and curses that are ultimately related to the notion of judgment and restoration are also employed in the prophetic literature of the OT. Similar to the tree imagery in Psalm 1, Jeremiah describes the person who places trust in the Lord as a tree planted by streams of water (Jer 17:7-8), whereas the person who trusts human beings instead of the Lord is likened to a shrub in the desert (Jer 17:5-6).

There are a number of usages of floral imagery within the Prophetic Books that cannot be easily grouped under the two main themes of judgment and restoration. Trees and plants are used within the literary context of a prophetic parable or riddle used by Ezekiel to prophetically sketch the final history of Judah before the exile and to confront Zedekiah with his unfaithfulness towards Nebuchadnezzar. The cedar treetop (Ezek 17:3-4) refers to Jehoiachin and the nobles of Judah. Then there is a seed that is planted by an eagle (Nebuchadnezzar) and grows into a vine (Zedekiah) that in turn stretches its roots toward a second eagle (Egypt), only to be finally uprooted (Ezek 17:5-10). The section ends in a rich messianic parable using the same floral imagery repertoire (Ezek 17:22-24) but applying it to the Messiah and his people. Nevertheless, one can also here detect the two motifs of judgment and restoration couched within the parable. Another parable is presented in Isaiah 28:24-26 that uses the image of a sowing farmer planting his field with different herbs and grains in order to demonstrate God's sovereignty in dealing with his people.

There are a also number of literal usages of plants in the Prophetic Books, such as Amos introducing himself as a sycamore dresser (Amos 7:14), the description of the pomegranate decorations of the temple that were taken away by the Babylonians during the destruction of Jerusalem (Jer 52:22-23), and the polemics against the artisans who make idols (Is 44:14; Jer 10:3). However, these literal usages of plants demonstrate the proximity of the prophetic imagery to its ancient audience as well as its usage as source domain in the process of metaphor blending.

3. Floral Imagery in the Bible and Floral Images of the Ancient Near East.

It has become apparent that floral imagery in the Hebrew prophets centers on the themes of judgment and restoration, which are intrinsically connected to covenant theology. The repertoire of imagery employed by the prophets arises from the flora of ancient Israel and the daily interaction with it through agriculture and industry. However, as outlined in the introduction, the literary usage of the imagery in most instances goes beyond a mere literal understanding of the flora, and the different plants metaphorically convey important theological motifs. The cognitive processes underlying this literary metaphor creation can be linked to iconographic images that surrounded the Hebrew prophets and influenced their choice of imagery. As an example, the widely used tree metaphor may be taken: trees are likened to nations and kings, which are cut down or dried up within judgment imagery, or sprout again, grow and bear fruit under God's restorative power.

The motif of the sacred tree is found throughout the ancient Near East, and depictions of trees appear in various contexts on a variety of media. As part of a complex image found on a storage jar at Kuntillet ʿAǧrud, stemming from the eighth century BC, there is a stylized palm tree with lotus flowers flanked by two caprids and a striding lion below. The stylized tree can be interpreted as a representation of the goddess Asherah in a context of fertility. Or there is a stamp seal of unknown provenance from the seventh century BC on which is depicted a palm tree representing the goddess Asherah flanked by two dancing worshipers. The widely used stylized sacred trees of ancient Near Eastern iconography are found mostly in contexts of fertility and adoration. However, there is a critical engagement by the Hebrew prophets with this iconographic repertoire, and Isaiah engages in polemic against the artisans who make idols (Is 44:14) and the Asherim (Is 17:8; 27:9), which most probably were cult objects with stylized tree representations of Asherah. This demonstrates how the prophets interpreted the floral imagery differently and in contrast with the cultural and religious environment in which Israel existed during the period of the Hebrew prophets.

4. Floral imagery and Its Theological Force.

Floral imagery and nature as a whole in the Hebrew prophets are always instrumental in God's redemptive interventions in history, whether in contexts of judgment or of restoration. The theological strength of metaphors that are connected to the world of nature is related to the veracity of the imagery, especially from the point of view of an ancient agrarian Israelite culture. The unknown—abstract divine concepts of covenant exemplified through judgment and restoration—is interactively illuminated through the known reality of everyday life and its constant interaction with the flora of Syro-Palestine. That there are at times surprising, even shocking, images only enhances the depth of understanding that is provided by revelation to make known the issues of salvation to humankind. These images only serve to underline the otherness of Yahweh over against the other gods of the ancient Near East, echoing the strong monotheistic message of the Hebrew prophets.

See also ANIMAL IMAGERY; LAND; WILDERNESS, DESERT.

BIBLIOGRAPHY. **B. A. Asen,** "The Garlands of Ephraim: Isaiah 28:1-6 and the Marzēaḥ," *JSOT* 71 (1996) 73-87; **A. Berlin,** *The Dynamics of Biblical Parallelism* (Bloomington: Indiana University Press, 1985); **A. Bloch,** "The Cedar and the Palm Tree: A Paired Male/Female Symbol in Hebrew and Aramaic," in *Solving Riddles and Untying Knots: Biblical, Epigraphic, and Semitic Studies in Honor of James C. Greenfield,* ed. Z. Zevit, S. Gitin and M. Sokoloff (Winona Lake, IN: Eisenbrauns, 1995) 13-17; **I. Cornelius,** "Paradise Motifs in the 'Eschatology' of the Minor Prophets and the Iconography of the Ancient Near East," *JNSL* 14 (1988) 41-83; **I. J. de Hulster,** "What Is an Image?" in *Iconography and Biblical Studies: Proceedings of the Iconography Sessions at the Joint EABS/SBL Conference, 22-26 July 2007, Vienna, Austria,* ed. I. J. de Hulster and R. Schmitt (AOAT 361; Munster: Ugarit-Verlag, 2009) 226-32; **M. T. DesCamp and E. E. Sweetser,** "Metaphors for God: Why and How Do Our Choices Matter for Humans? The Application of Contemporary Cognitive Linguistics Research to the Debate on God and Metaphor," *Pastoral Psychology* 53.3 (2005) 207-38; **K. Feyaerts,** ed., *The Bible through Metaphor and Translation: A Cognitive Semantic Perspective* (RD 15; Oxford: Peter Lang, 2003); **O. Keel,** *The Symbolism of the Biblical World: Ancient Near Eastern Iconography and the Book of Psalms,* trans. T. J. Hallet (New York: Seabury, 1978); **M. G. Klingbeil,** "Del caos al orden: Temas mitológicos en el libro de Isaías," *Theologika* 14.1 (1999) 66-85; **K. Nielsen,** *There Is Hope for a Tree: The Tree as Metaphor in Isaiah* (JSOTSup 65; Sheffield: JSOT Press, 1989); **J. M. O'Brien,** *Challenging Prophetic Metaphor: Theology and Ideology in the Prophets* (Louisville: Westminster/John Knox, 2008); **B. Oestreich,** *Metaphors and Similes for Yahweh in Hosea, 14:2-9 (1-8): A Study of Hoseanic Pictorial Language* (Friedensauer Schriftenreihe Reihe A, Theologie 1; Frankfurt: Peter Lang, 1998); **L. Ryken, J. C. Wilhoit and T. Longman III,** eds., "Flowers," *Dictionary of Biblical Imagery* (Downers Grove: InterVarsity Press, 1998) 294-96; **C. Sticher,** "'Die Gottlosen gedeihen wie Gras': Zu einigen Pflanzenmetaphern in den Psalmen; Eine kanonische Lektüre," in *Metaphors in the Psalms,* ed. P. van Hecke and A. Labahn (BETL 231; Leuven: Peeters, 2010) 115-34; **T. Stordalen,** *Echoes of Eden: Gen-*

esis 2-3 and Symbolism of the Eden Garden in Biblical Hebrew Literature (CBET 25; Leuven: Peeters, 2000); **United Bible Societies,** *Fauna and Flora of the Bible* (Helps for Translators 11; London: United Bible Societies, 1972); **J. G. Westenholz,** *Sacred Bounty Sacred Land: The Seven Species of the Land of Israel* (Jerusalem: Bible Lands Museum, 1998); **M. Zohary,** *Plants of the Bible: A Complete Handbook to All the Plants with 200 Full-Color Plates Taken in the Natural Habitat* (Cambridge: Cambridge University Press, 1982).

M. G. Klingbeil

FORCED MIGRATION. *See* Exile.

FORGIVENESS

Messages of judgment permeate the OT Prophetic Books. The prophets frequently warn their audiences about coming judgment and the *wrath of God (*see* Retribution). These prophets clearly found no joy or satisfaction in doom-laden messages (Jer 9:1). Their messages of doom and warnings of judgment make sense only in the context of the prophets' belief in the compassion and forgiveness of *God. The prophets called on the people to repent because they believed that this would lead to a gracious divine response of forgiveness and the withdrawal of the threatened judgment (Ezek 18:23). When the people failed to respond, making judgment inevitable, many of the prophets looked forward to a new beginning when Yahweh would once again reign over a cleansed and forgiven people who would acknowledge and obey him (Is 11:6-9).

In order to understand the significance of forgiveness in the Prophetic Books, we must study the vocabulary related to forgiveness. However, a study of vocabulary alone does not exhaust the subject because a message of judgment may presuppose that forgiveness is available to those who heed the message. Thus, here the introduction to the vocabulary of forgiveness will be followed by a study of the main themes relating to the prophetic understanding of forgiveness.

1. Vocabulary
2. Main Themes Relating to Forgiveness in the Prophets
3. Conclusion

1. Vocabulary.
The three main verbs that relate to the concept of forgiveness in the prophetic books (and indeed in the entire OT) are *sālaḥ* ("to forgive"), *kipper* ("to atone") and *nāśāʾ* ("to lift up, carry").

The most frequent use of the verb *sālaḥ* in prophetic literature is in the book of Jeremiah, where it occurs six times. The first two occurrences express the view that Yahweh will not forgive Israel because of the seriousness of their *sins and their refusal to *repent (Jer 5:1, 7). However, Jeremiah uses the same verb to highlight the prospect of the future restoration and forgiveness of Israel (Jer 31:34; 33:8; 36:3; 50:20). The verb also occurs once in Isaiah, where those who return to Yahweh are assured of being pardoned abundantly or freely (Is 55:7). Daniel and Amos beseech God to forgive his people (Dan 9:19; Amos 7:2). God is always the subject of this verb; it is never used in relation to humans forgiving one another.

The verb *nāśāʾ* often means "to lift up, carry." When used in relation to sin, it usually refers to bearing sin like a burden or bearing the consequences of sin (Is 53:12; Ezek 4:5-6; 44:10, 12). However, occasionally it refers to taking sin away in an act of forgiveness (Is 2:9; 33:24; Hos 1:6; 14:2; Mic 7:18).

The verb *kipper* usually means "to atone, make atonement." It refers to covering sin or blotting it out and thus is closely linked with the idea of forgiveness. Sins that are atoned for, or covered, may be forgiven so that reconciliation between the suppliant and God may take place. Isaiah's sins were "atoned for" when the burning coal from the altar touched his lips (Is 6:7). God himself will make atonement for the shameful things that Israel has done (Ezek 16:63). Ezekiel envisages a time in the future when sacrifices will be offered to make atonement (Ezek 45:15, 17). However, Jeremiah prays that God should not provide a means of atonement for those who are trying to kill him (Jer 18:23).

Although these are the three main verbs relating to forgiveness, the concept is also conveyed by the verb *ḥānan* ("to be gracious"), which often implies the idea of forgiveness (Is 30:18-19; 33:2). Furthermore, the noun "forgiveness" occurs once in Daniel 9:9, and in Isaiah 40:2 the announcement of forgiveness to the exiles includes the idea that their sins have been "paid for" (*rāṣâ*).

The experience of forgiveness is sometimes expressed using metaphorical language. Hezekiah praised God for casting all his sins behind him (Is 38:17). Dramatic language is used by Micah as he describes God subduing iniquity and casting sins into the depths of the sea (Mic 7:19).

2. Main Themes Relating to Forgiveness in the Prophets.

2.1. God Is Gracious and Forgiving.
The prophets taught that God was long-suffering and gracious and took no pleasure in the punishment of the wicked (Ezek 18:23, 30-32; Hos 11:8). In the context of a chilling forecast of disaster and judgment, Joel reassures his audience that if they repent, Yahweh will respond in mercy because "he is gracious and merciful, slow to anger, and abounding in steadfast love; and he relents over disaster" (Joel 2:12-13 ESV).

The prophet Jonah was reluctant to preach to the citizens of Nineveh because he knew that the Lord was "a gracious God and merciful, slow to anger and abounding in steadfast love, and relenting from disaster" (Jon 4:2 ESV). Since Jonah hoped that Nineveh would be destroyed, he did not want God to be gracious, and this is why he attempted to avoid the commission to preach to them.

However, this message of God's grace and mercy was understood in the context of God's intolerance of sin. The prophetic message was conditioned by an understanding of Yahweh as gracious and forgiving, but also as the holy God, who punishes sin and wrongdoing wherever he finds it. Although Israel had a special relationship with God, this did not mean that they could sin with impunity (Amos 3:2). Sin always created a barrier between Yahweh and his people (Is 59:1-2). Although Israel's God was gracious and forgiving, Israel must meet the necessary conditions in order to receive forgiveness.

Therefore, there is a tension in the prophets' message between Yahweh's mercy and his anger against sin and rebellion. This is clearly seen in Hosea's portrayal of Yahweh struggling within himself because although the nation deserved punishment, he wanted to forgive and not punish because of his great compassion for them (Hos 11:8-10; cf. Is 2:9). As M. Boda points out, "Hope therefore lies not with Israel's ability to repent but rather with Yahweh's grace in spite of Israel's apostasy" (Boda, 302).

2.2. Cultic Activity Does Not Guarantee Forgiveness.
Frequent references to sacrifices provide evidence that many people relied on them to provide atonement for their sins without giving due thought to repentance and obedience. As J. Oswalt observes, "Israel was surrounded by religions that promised automatic propitiation and blessing without commitment or ethical change" (Oswalt, 97). However, the prophets taught that deliberate sin and persistent rebellion could not be rectified through the sacrificial system (Is 1:10-20; Jer 7:21-23). Even enthusiastic cultic activity and the offering of a great number of sacrifices could not substitute for repentance and a humble submission to Yahweh's law (Amos 5:21-24; Mic 6:6-7). Thus, Hosea warned the people that even though they would come with their flocks and herds to seek Yahweh, they would not be able to find him because "he has withdrawn from them" (Hos 5:6). Instead of their altars being places of atonement and forgiveness, they had become "altars for sinning and Yahweh is not pleased with them" (Hos 8:11-13; 9:4 ESV; cf. Amos 4:4).

Jeremiah also had to deal with people who believed that their adherence to the sacrificial cult and temple was all that Yahweh required. Jeremiah's early ministry overlapped with Josiah's religious reformation, but he did not see this as the answer to the problem of the nation's guilt. Jeremiah's approach was that the reformation of the cult was an outward religious movement that could be effective only if accompanied by an inner change (Jer 3:10). The reformation conducted by Josiah failed to lead to God's forgiveness because it was not accompanied by genuine repentance and transformed behavior. Repentance at a much deeper level was required (Jer 3:21-4:4). As V. Eldridge points out, "What is in these verses is no shallow, self-centred sorrow for sin but the removal of every influence and attraction which was in competition with Yahweh for a place in his people's love (Jer 4:1)" (Eldridge 327-28). The prophets called on people to take God seriously and not to be lulled into a sense of false security by a misuse of the sacrificial system.

2.3. Forgiveness Is the Divine Prerogative.
Although the prophets emphasized the mercy of God, they also taught that forgiveness could not be assumed. Forgiveness was not the automatic response of God to certain righteous acts or meritorious behavior. Thus, Joel declares that the Lord is "gracious and merciful, slow to

anger, and abounding in steadfast love," but immediately following this affirmation he emphasizes that forgiveness cannot be taken for granted, and he asks, "Who knows whether he will turn and relent?" (Joel 2:14 ESV; cf. Amos 5:15; Zeph 2:3). Forgiveness was the divine prerogative, and human beings must humbly rely on God's mercy rather than presumptuously claim forgiveness as their right. The prophetic message that Yahweh was gracious and forgiving was not an invitation to complacency. There were conditions to be fulfilled before forgiveness could be received, and it could never be taken for granted.

The prophets' understanding of the character and nature of God convinced them that the *ethical and social implications of worshiping Yahweh could not be ignored if forgiveness was to be received. In particular, the concept of justice was high on the prophetic agenda (*see* Social Justice). As the righteous judge of all the earth, Yahweh could not condone unethical behavior. Amos establishes his understanding of Yahweh's justice by showing that it extended even to the behavior of other nations (Amos 1:1—2:3). If Yahweh punishes the nations for their war crimes, then Israel should also expect condemnation and punishment for the sinful and unethical behavior that characterized society. Yahweh looked for lives that were compatible with his just demands, and Israelite society had become an affront to his standards of righteousness and justice (Amos 5:21-24).

Isaiah calls for a personal encounter with Yahweh (Is 1:18-20). Although there has been much discussion about the exact meaning of Isaiah 1:18, J. Willis has argued convincingly that attempts to deny that it offers forgiveness to the obedient have been unsuccessful (Willis, 35-49). The passage is set in a court context, and Israel is invited to debate the issues relating to sin and judgment. The pathway to forgiveness begins with obedience. The contrast between the colors highlights the dramatic change that forgiveness can bring in making sins that are like scarlet become white as snow (Is 1:18). An obedient response to Yahweh's challenge ("Come now") would lead to the forgiveness of most deeply dyed sins and transgressions. On a practical level, Israel is offered a choice between obedience that would lead to the enjoyment of the benefits of the land and disobedience that would result in being destroyed and removed from it. Forgiveness would be possible only in the context of obedience and a restored relationship with God. Isaiah uses language that highlights God's willingness to forgive and balances it with a clear indication that this offer of forgiveness is conditional.

Thus, the prophets maintained a careful balance between their understanding of Yahweh as a merciful and gracious God and their knowledge of the majestic holy God who championed justice and would not tolerate sin. As Nahum points out, the gracious nature of God does not undermine his justice or mean that the guilty will escape punishment (Nah 1:3). God does not ignore sin. Sin cannot simply be forgiven without an adequate response (Jer 46:28). The prophets sought to convince their hearers that forgiveness was the divine prerogative, and it was to be humbly sought through obedience and faith.

2.4. Israel's Future. Did the prophets believe that Israel would be forgiven, or were they convinced that judgment and not forgiveness would be Israel's future prospect? There are some passages that suggest that forgiveness was impossible because of the nation's refusal to repent (Is 22:14).

Ezekiel pointed out that because of Israel's persistent sin and rebellion, forgiveness was unavailable to the present generation (Ezek 9:9-10). Early in his ministry Jeremiah may have believed that Israel could and would repent and be forgiven (Jer 3:12-13; 7:5-7; 26:1-3). However, later in his ministry Jeremiah became convinced that in the immediate future the nation would experience the wrath of God and not his forgiveness, and it was even pointless to pray for forgiveness (Jer 5:7; 7:16). This conclusion was based not on an unwillingness to forgive on Yahweh's part but rather on the unwillingness of Israel to repent, which the prophet realized was just as unlikely as a leopard changing its spots (Jer 13:23).

One particularly puzzling passage apparently suggests that the preaching of the prophet would make forgiveness less likely. During Isaiah's call, Yahweh instructs him to preach and to "make the heart of this people dull, and their ears heavy, and blind their eyes" (Is 6:10 ESV). This command to "make the heart of this people dull" suggests that Isaiah's ministry will make forgiveness less likely. The dull hearts are not simply the result of Israel's negative response to Yahweh's message; rather, this is part of the judgment on the nation that just as Pharaoh's heart was hardened because he was Yahweh's adversary, Israel was now out of harmony with God and in no fit condition to receive his message. G. von Rad comments that this section of Isaiah's call "sounds as if it shuts the door on everyone, and it was intended to be understood in this way" (von Rad, 2:154). This seems to indicate that forgiveness is impossible, but we must remember that in this same passage God provided atonement and forgave the prophet himself when the coal from the altar touched his lips (Is 6:7). Thus, the prophet is living proof that God is still willing to forgive the repentant and to restore individuals to harmony with himself. However, for the rebellious nation of Israel, the future promised judgment and not forgiveness.

This inevitability of immediate judgment did not deter Isaiah from a positive understanding of Yahweh's intention for the future of the nation. The name of his son Shear-jashub (Is 7:3) means "a remnant shall return." This future hope of a forgiven *remnant shines through the gloom of the predictions of judgment (Is 4:3; 10:20-21; 11:11, 16; 28:5). Hope for the future is one of the main themes in the later chapters of the book of Isaiah, where Yahweh pronounces comfort for his people because "her iniquity is pardoned" and "she has received from the LORD's hand double for all her sins" (Is 40:1-2 ESV). Forgiveness is offered freely to those who "Seek the LORD" and who "call on him." Those who "return to the LORD" will be welcomed by his "compassion," and "he will abundantly pardon" (Is 55:6-7 ESV). Central to Isaiah's message is the role of the "servant" who becomes a sacrifice and bears the iniquity of the people (Is 52:13—53:12) (*see* Servant of Yahweh). Through the undeserved suffering of the servant come peace, healing and the removal of sin (see Boda, 208).

Judgment followed by future hope and a restored relationship are also clearly presented in the book of Hosea. The names of Hosea's children are initially linked to coming judgment. However, the warning is accompanied by the promise that the meaning of the names will be reversed, and they are linked to restoration and blessing. One of the main themes of Hosea is the divorce of the unfaithful wife. However, it is the concept of "steadfast love" that is most

prominent, and there is an overwhelming hope that the faithless wife will be brought back home again (Hos 2:14-23). Hosea perceives a remarkable tension within the heart of God because God's overwhelming desire is to forgive and not punish. Thus, God states, "My heart recoils within me; my compassion grows warm and tender. I will not execute my burning anger" (Hos 11:8-9 ESV).

The concept of a new *covenant is introduced by Jeremiah as Israel's hope for the future. The concept is introduced in the context of Israel's failure. It is argued that Israel had broken the covenant made at Sinai even though it had given the nation great privileges as Yahweh's spouse (Jer 31:31-32). Israel's flirtation with heathen gods and practices had destroyed the covenant relationship with God. The concept of a new covenant was a message of hope that the relationship between God and his people could be renewed. The success of this new covenant was guaranteed because it was God's initiative, and he would ensure that it did not fail. The new covenant represented a new opportunity, a new beginning and a new start for God's people. In the past they had not turned to him with all their hearts (Jer 17:1, 9), but now the new covenant would be written upon their hearts and not merely on stone. The emphasis will be on the individual's personal knowledge of Yahweh, and he will forgive all their sins (Jer 31:34; 50:20).

Zechariah expressed hope for the future using the concept of a "cleansing fountain" (Zech 13:1). This image highlighted the prophetic faith that God's future agenda for his people was forgiveness and mercy. This unilateral provision of a cleansing fountain evoked ideas of continual effective forgiveness.

3. Conclusion.

The prophetic messages warned Israel that sin must be taken seriously. Yahweh would not ignore sin, and if it was not dealt with, it would incur his wrath and bring terrible judgment on the nation. However, Yahweh loved his people and would graciously forgive them if they turned from their evil ways. Sacrifices alone would not ensure forgiveness, and they needed to be accompanied by sincere repentance and a genuine change of behavior on the part of the worshipers. Forgiveness was always the undeserved gift of a gracious God.

See also *See also* GOD; JUSTICE, RIGHTEOUSNESS; REPENTANCE; RETRIBUTION; SACRIFICE AND ATONEMENT.

BIBLIOGRAPHY. **M. J. Boda,** *A Severe Mercy: Sin and Its Remedy in the Old Testament* (Winona Lake, IN: Eisenbrauns, 2009); **W. Brueggemann,** *Texts That Linger, Words That Explode: Listening to the Prophetic Voice* (Minneapolis: Fortress, 2000); **W. Eichrodt,** *Theology of the Old Testament* (2 vols.; London: SCM, 1967); **V. J. Eldridge,** "Jeremiah, Prophet of Judgement," *RevExp* 78 (1981) 319-30; **J. Goldingay,** *Old Testament Theology,* 2: *Israel's Faith* (Downers Grove, IL: IVP Academic; Milton Keynes: Paternoster, 2006); **J. G. McConville,** "The Judgement of God in the Old Testament," *ExAud* 20 (2004) 25-42; **J. P. J. Oliver,** "סלח," *NIDOTTE* 3:259-64; **J. N. Oswalt,** *The Book of Isaiah: Chapters 1-39* (NICOT; Grand Rapids: Eerdmans, 1986); **G. von Rad,** *Old Testament Theology,* trans. D. M. G. Stalker (2 vols.; London: SCM, 1975); **J. T. Willis,** "On the Interpretation of Isaiah 1:18," *JSOT* 25 (1983) 35-54. J. McKeown

FORM CRITICISM

Form criticism is a method used to analyze biblical literature with respect to categories of genre and social background, examining both broad categories of kinds of prophecies or stories, as well as their particular instantiation. It is possible to identify two major streams or waves of scholarship with respect to this analysis of genre (German *Gattung*) and form (German *Form*), which one might identify as classic form criticism and new form criticism. The purpose of this article is to explore the inception and evolution of form criticism as a critical method both generally and with a particular interest in form criticism of the biblical prophetic literature. This will include exploring both of these major movements of form criticism and offering some reflections on the further development of form criticism as a methodology for the examination of the prophetic literature.

This article is structured in four major sections followed by a conclusion. The first section gives a very brief overview of the history and development of form criticism (for a more detailed history of form criticism in the early and middle twentieth century, see March, 141-57; Westermann, 13-89), noting some of the major scholars who have been involved in form

critical work in the prophetic literature especially. The second section examines classic form criticism. This examination proceeds not as a history, noting the work of every important critic along the way, but instead with an eye for important elements of form criticism as a methodology. These elements include the question of originally oral subunits in prophetic literature, genre and the development of prophetic traditions, and the vitally important concept of *Sitz im Leben*. This section closes with a brief overview of those prophetic genres commonly identified by classic form criticism. The third section examines the so-called new school of form criticism. Much of what this new school offers exists as a critique of the work of the classic form critics. Consequently, the third section follows a structure similar to that of the second. The third section examines the problems related to orality and literacy, the question of historicism and the world behind the text, and the question of both literary and social contextualization with respect to genre. The fourth section include a comparison of the work of a classic form critic (H. Wolff) to that of a new form critic (E. Ben Zvi) with respect to a specific piece of prophetic literature, in this case Micah 7:1-7.

1. A Brief History of Form
2. Classic Form Criticism
3. New Form Criticism
4. A Form-Critical Exercise: Micah, Old and New
5. Conclusion

1. A Brief History of Form.

It is generally accepted that H. Gunkel was the first to propose the notion of a systematic analysis of genres in the OT, likely due to his interest in the folklore work of Jakob and Wilhelm Grimm (Tucker, 5). This is not to say that nobody before Gunkel had studied the various genres of literature found in the OT. Indeed, as M. Buss has shown, the study of genre both generally and with specific regard to the biblical literature has a very long history (Buss 1974, 1-31). What Gunkel brought to the endeavor that was unique and new was his focus on the history of Israelite literature as a history of genre development (Gunkel 2001, 33). Gunkel was very interested in examining the historical development of Israelite religion of the religious literature of ancient Israel, but since he believed that providing an accurate history of the authorship, collection and redaction of the biblical literature was impossible due to practical limitations, he suggested instead that biblical criticism should begin with an examination of the history of genres, as these represented much deeper and more fixed social realities (Gunkel 2001, 32).

Gunkel's call to the study of genres was taken up by a wide variety of biblical critics. Gunkel himself gave only sparse attention to the prophetic literature (e.g., Gunkel 1969), spending considerably more time on narrative texts (Gunkel 1901) and Psalms (Gunkel 1967). Scholars such as H. Gressmann and S. Mowinckel should be mentioned alongside Gunkel, as both studied with him personally, though Mowinckel is particularly known for his extensive work in Psalms. The very basic genres found in the prophetic literature described by Gunkel himself (Gunkel 1906, 32-33; 1969) received considerable expansions and clarification by later writers such as Gressmann (Gressmann 1910; 1929), who explored various types of oracles against foreign nations, and J. Lindblom (Lindblom 1924) and L. Köhler (Köhler 1945), who were among the first to identify the messenger speeches in the prophetic literature, particularly as indicated by the phrase "thus says Yahweh" (March, 147-48). Also of significant importance is the work of C. Westermann, who both refined and extended the work of prior form critics (see especially his extensive review of previous research, Westermann, 13-89), particularly with regard to both messenger speeches and oracles of salvation and destruction. In addition to these we should also note the work of G. Tucker in his *Form Criticism of the Old Testament* and K. Koch in his *Growth of the Biblical Tradition*.

On December 18, 1968, at the annual meeting of the Society of Biblical Literature, J. Muilenberg offered as his presidential address his paper "Form Criticism and Beyond." This paper, in which Muilenberg sounds not unlike Gunkel's own call for a move beyond literary criticism, points out the many benefits, but also the potential limitations, of the form-critical method. Muilenberg suggested that the time had come to move beyond form criticism to a new method that would examine "the structural patterns that are employed for the fashioning of a literary unit" (Muilenberg, 8). He

referred to this new method as *"rhetorical criticism" (Muilenberg, 8). Intriguingly, while this appears to be the first sign of the end of form criticism as an active methodology, Muilenberg's call to a focus on the structure of the final form of the text is only shortly thereafter found as a matter of significant concern in the work of self-identified form critics. Indeed R. Knierim's "Old Testament Form Criticism Reconsidered" moves form criticism explicitly into the realm of structuralism (e.g., Knierim, 439-40) and suggests that Muilenberg's call to move beyond form criticism is entirely unnecessary because the "way he summarizes 'rhetorical criticism' . . . could also be part of an article on the form-critical method" (Knierim, 458n91). What Knierim's paper heralds is the beginning of a new school of form criticism. This new form criticism is marked particularly by a focus on the literary text as we have it (as opposed to underlying oral precursors) and by an interest in the literary situation (*Sitz im Literatur*) as opposed to the social situation (*Sitz im Leben*) of genres. Several scholars deserve mention here. M. Sweeney's introduction to his commentary on Isaiah represents a particularly systematic presentation of the program of the new form criticism (Sweeney 1996). Sweeney's work is of particular interest with regard to *in-tertextuality and the *Sitz im Literatur* of prophetic texts. Also of great importance is the work of E. Ben Zvi, who has gone so far as to identify the "prophetic book" as a genre unto itself (Ben Zvi 2000a). Also of note is Buss's recent collection of essays, which present his "relational form criticism" (Buss 2010). For a selection of essays that represent the various concerns of the new form critics, see Sweeney and Ben Zvi.

The relationship between classic form criticism and new form criticism could be described in a variety of ways. It may indeed be legitimate to regard the new form criticism as a total inversion of Gunkel's original project (so Sudermann). Alternatively, one might regard the new form criticism as a project that, along with classic form criticism, exists within the fold of a greater continuum that we might refer to as genre criticism. In any case, whether one sees either (or both) of these schools of thought as an aberration or mutation, the fact remains that they are important methods that have been used (to greater and lesser effect) to examine the genres of the biblical literature. We turn now to a fuller examination of how each of them has attempted to go about this task.

2. Classic Form Criticism.

In order to understand form criticism as it was conceived by Gunkel and developed by his later intellectual heirs, one must take note of three essential assumptions of the method. First, the biblical literature generally, and the prophetic literature particularly, was originally an oral phenomenon (Gunkel 1969, 61). Second, there existed a long and complicated tradition of development in which the prophetic sayings were transmitted orally and then finally collected and edited into the written forms that were transmitted as the Prophetic Books. Third, both the original oral communication and the oracles as they were developed by the tradition correspond to a vitally important social situation or institution that made them first meaningful. The examination of genre in the Prophetic Books in this stream of critical thought both began with and is founded upon these assumptions, and it made use of the concepts of genre and form to describe more completely the world behind the prophetic texts and the consequent meaning of prophetic oracles.

For Gunkel, the prophet was the mouthpiece of God, a person whose life and voice were co-opted by the divine in order to present the words of God to the people. "As when a lion roars no one asks whether or not one should be frightened, but anyone feels involuntarily afraid, so everyone becomes a prophet who hears Yahweh's voice" (Gunkel 1969, 49). God speaks through the prophet, and prophecy is the only available response. This is a key element of Gunkel's conception of prophets and prophecy. Ancient prophecies were not carefully considered and highly reflective speeches or works of literature; they were spontaneous explosions, always orally delivered. Westermann suggests that Gunkel stops short of accepting an "ecstatic theory," but if this is so, it is only just so (Westermann, 24; cf. Gordon, 7). Thus, any exploration of the nature of prophecy, and of the basic types of prophecy, must necessarily begin (for Gunkel at least) with these original, oral speeches.

This conclusion is founded in part upon the various narratives that center on prophets (e.g., the narrative of Elijah and Elisha) and in part

as an extrapolation of some oral features found in the Prophetic Books. Thus, "We must try and imagine [the prophetic] sayings being uttered orally, and not as they stand on paper, if we are to understand them" (Gunkel 1969, 61). Of course, this conclusion is based on the assumption that the Prophetic Books present themselves as the utterances of a prophet to the people. Note, as an example, Ezekiel's call. He has a personal confrontation with God (Ezek 1—2), after which he is told to go and speak to the people (Ezek 3:1). Clearly, oral declaration is a significant component of Ezekiel's calling as a prophet of Yahweh.

Following Gunkel, it was taken as given that underneath the prophetic literature lay the speeches of the prophets themselves. Therefore, in Westermann's words, "One begins with that which a word in the Old Testament really is—a personal event to which speaking as well as hearing belongs; a kind of happening that moves from the person (the one speaking) to another person (the one hearing)" (Westermann, 93 [see also Tucker, xi; Zimmerli, 23; Koch, 27n2]). But for such communication between humans to be accessible and comprehensible, it was argued, it must take on a recognizable, and relatively generic, guise (Koch, 14). Therefore, these oral communications needed to be classified into groups or genres and analyzed.

The questions that necessarily follow involve the nature of the spoken prophecies. Who speaks, and to whom? What is the content of that speech? What is the structure of that speech? The answers to the first and second questions are that God speaks, through the prophet, to the people. A review of the prophetic literature then provides two broad categories of addressees: the nations and Israel/Judah. With regard to content and form, these speeches were announcements, either of judgment or of salvation (Westermann, 93-94).

From this it was suggested that prophetic speech is messenger speech. The prophets are the messengers of Yahweh. Note the formula "thus says the Lord" (*kōh ʾāmar yhwh*), which is found throughout the OT, particularly in the Former and the Latter Prophets (Tucker, 59). Not only is the *kōh ʾāmar* formula found with Yahweh as the referent, but frequently the utterance that is being reported comes from the mouth of a king through royal messengers (e.g., Ex 5:10; 1 Kings 2:30; 20:3, 5; 2 Kings 1:11; 9:18-19; 18:19, 29). Gunkel suggested that this formula indicates that the prophets saw themselves as messengers relating a message directly from Yahweh (Gunkel 1969, 67; see also Westermann, 38). If this is accurate, and the prophets saw themselves as messengers, "then there is a foundation of formulas, speech forms, and speeches which have been passed down, where one can be assured of encountering the self-understanding of the prophets and of being on solid ground" (Westermann, 39). It is, then, upon this foundation of the messenger formula that the analysis of oral prophetic forms is built.

Before we proceed, a number of elements of this project must be pointed out. Note first of all Westermann's incredibly confident tone, speaking in terms of assurance and certainty. Though not quite universal, this supreme confidence in assured results is indicative of much of the classic form-critical venture. But the point about the messenger formula raises a significant question. Why should the existence of messenger formulas suggest to us that the historic prophets thought of themselves as messengers? This characterization of them as messengers of God serves to juxtapose God's sovereign voice with the voices of earthly kings and rulers. This is particularly evident in Exodus 5, where Pharaoh's refusal to heed God's pronouncement and issuing of his own counterpronouncement lead directly to a curse from God. The message is relatively straightforward: God is powerful, and his messengers must be heeded. Although this may be indicative of a prophetic speech pattern that was generally recognized, such a conclusion is neither necessary nor assured. This could just as well be a literary trope meant for those who read the biblical texts.

As has been noted, the conception of the prophet as divine messenger serves as the foundation for the further characterization of prophetic speech patterns. The prophets were oral preachers. "Since their authority came not from men but from God, they spoke whenever and wherever they felt compelled to do so" (Tucker, 70). This is rather similar to Gunkel's conception of the prophets as ecstatic preachers, though in Tucker's description the preaching is not involuntary. Tucker's words suggest that the prophets existed as a particular social

class within Israelite society, and that their authority (if they were true prophets) was recognized (note that not all classic form critics saw prophecy as a social institution unto itself). They were known as the messengers of God, and one of the things that made them known was the use of formulaic language. Thus, Westermann critiques H. Wolff's suggestion that prophetic speech consisted of both revelation and comment by the prophet. For Westermann, all that follows the messenger formula in the original oral pronouncement must be the very word of God (Westermann, 57-58, 74-75, 95).

Eventually, of course, these pronouncements made by the prophets themselves were recorded and transmitted to later generations. For many of the classic form critics, it is here that the prophecies themselves died (Koch, 58). But this literary funeral was not immediate. Before being set down in writing, the words of the prophets enjoyed a lengthy history of oral transmission. Beginning with the now common assumption that prophetic speech was the short and direct saying of the prophet himself (e.g., the very words of Isaiah [see Mowinckel 2002, 11, 53]), it followed that those words, which Isaiah himself likely did not write down, were somehow transmitted to the next generation.

The types of prophetic literature enable the modern researcher to see a kind of continuity, a prophetic tradition. Thus, according to Tucker, "In this endeavor we are not trying to recover the ideal and hypothetical 'prophet' by means of a 'standard' prophetic genre or genres; we are looking for that continuity which should aid us in understanding each individual" (Tucker, 55). Each individual prophet stood within a tradition of prophecy, and so understanding the tradition will aid in our understanding of the individual. This is a question of what the social institution was that was connected to the prophecy, and how the prophet and the oral tradition of his prophecy were connected to that institution.

The prophets were recognizable figures with disciples who followed them and recorded and transmitted their words (see Is 8:16-18) (Tucker, 69). Zimmerli suggests that there is evidence for "a typical scene from the prophetic 'school'" to be found in the scenes where the prophet sits together with the elders or heads of house from the people (Ezek 8:1; 14:1-

11; 20:1-44; 33:31; 2 Kings 6:32) (Zimmerli, 109). Whether or not the prophets had disciples, Zimmerli's account is rather unconvincing, particularly the evidence from Ezekiel. These passages seem analogous not to some theorized prophetic school, but instead to the interactions between the prophet and the king in Isaiah and Jeremiah. These elders appear to have authority among the exiled community (they have no king now), and so they come to the prophet for counsel regarding the will of God (see Ezek 20:3, where God responds to the elders through Ezekiel).

Whether or not we can identify these so-called prophetic schools or groups of prophetic disciples from the text itself, the assumption has generally been made that the Prophetic Books themselves are a product of the gradual development of complexes, or groups, of sayings that came together and were associated with one another over the history of the tradition. "Sayings have come to form tradition complexes because they share the same catchword, have similar content, have the same addressee, or are from the same period in the prophet's work" (Mowinckel 2002, 44). For Mowinckel, the task of source, form, and tradition-historical criticism is the recovery of that which is more original, and the identification of the development of the given tradition. The entire tale must be told from beginning to end or, to put it differently, from spoken oracle (*ipsissima verba*) to final canonical literature. To do anything less is to fail in the task of tradition-historical criticism, to be like "a horse 'refusing the fence'" (Mowinckel 2002, 78). The principal role of form criticism in this task is to identify units of prophetic speech and to tie those types to social situations (*Sitz im Leben*). The critic is thus, in theory, able to distinguish those elements that are more original (down to the very words of the initial prophet) from those elements that have been added by later tradition (Mowinckel 2002, 80, 145n17). Some later critics expressed doubts regarding the recovery of the original words of the prophet and hope only for more original strata (Koch, 52).

This identification of individual units, a purely objective enterprise in Mowinckel's view, is accomplished by examining the text and identifying the various markers that generally open and close individual prophetic oracles (Mowinckel 2002, 43). In this sense, form

criticism picks up where the old higher critics leave off, taking the disparate segments identified, establishing their generic qualities and classifying them, whether as oracles of salvation or judgment (or some other genre), and then examining them in light of the social situation (in the sense of social institution) to which those prophetic genres belong.

Mowinckel (among others) suggests that the development of the tradition history serves the purpose of making the initial prophecies usable by later generations. "This trend . . . led in several cases to a transformation and a new edition of an older prophetic saying so that it also came to express the hope of restoration in the new situation" (Mowinckel 2002, 79 [so also Zimmerli, 23-24]). Thus, the design of the Prophetic Books as we have them facilitates (in some instances at least) the reactualization of the prophetic material by later generations. As we will see, the new form critics at times make similar suggestions. The hallmark of the classic approach is that Mowinckel desires to move beyond the text itself to the more original, older material as well as to the world that stands behind the theoretical reconstructions of earlier textual and oral stages in the transmission process.

This is the point at which transmission and *Sitz im Leben* meet. The primary proposed benefit of form criticism for the tradition-historical project is the identification of an ongoing social context in which a given oracle (or complex of oracles) was transmitted. "A tradition that remains alive and even has a history does so only because it is an expression of some aspect of the life of society and exercises a social function, whether in the cult, public life, or the more private life of the family. The form, together with its contents, points exactly to the social location of the tradition; the form is socially and psychologically given, the one appropriate in the particular situation" (Mowinckel 2002, 7). This is Mowickel's presentation of *Sitz im Leben*. It is not so much particular or general cultural context, but instead the social tradition or institution in which and from which the oracle takes its form. The original *Sitz im Leben* is the social situation of the original oral utterance, and all the subsequent developments within the tradition either are tied to this original *Sitz im Leben* or find their oral and literary afterlife by being appropriated into some other literary type with its own *Sitz im Leben* (Koch, 35). It is within these social situations and institutions that prophecy finds its place, and from them that the prophets have taken the structure and, to some degree, the content of their prophecies (i.e., the genre of the prophecies).

For Mowinckel in particular there is a relationship between the transmission of the prophetic tradition and the *Sitz im Leben* of the various prophetic oracles. The oracles themselves continue to exist only because some social institution is maintained in which they are recognizable and intelligible. This may be a process of adaptation, or it may indicate that a given social institution has been maintained, but in any case the oracle cannot survive without some social situation to give it context and meaning.

In contrast to this, Tucker sees the prophetic role as a social institution in and of itself. No other social institution is required to explain the maintenance and transmission of the complex of oral tradition. Thus, the *Sitz im Leben* for Tucker *is* the "prophetic role," since prophecy is a very specific institution in ancient Israel (Tucker, 76).

There is some material support for Mowinckel's views to be found in a text such as Jeremiah, as the two different extant collections (MT and LXX) suggest a set of Jeremiah material that was circulating in unarranged form, and that this material came together into two different versions of the final book. The difficulty is that while we may extrapolate something like the development of tradition that Mowickel envisions from this evidence, we simply do not have the oral complexes to which he refers, let alone specific evidence of the *ipsissima verba*. We have no record whatsoever of a set of well-known sayings or oracles that were transmitted together in some social institution or other. What is more, even though we know something of the literary history of Jeremiah (due to the Greek and Hebrew versions), we do not have similar evidence for the other biblical books. Any suggestion made regarding other books in the prophetic literature must be extrapolated based upon what we know of Jeremiah's transmission history and upon what we guess about the relationships between various oracles in a given prophetic work. Furthermore, we must make those guesses based upon other guesses about the existence and function of social institutions within ancient Israel. It is here that the enterprise begins to crumble.

The purpose of form criticism, according to Tucker, is to "relate the texts before us to the living people and institutions of ancient Israel" (Tucker, xi). As has been noted, there are problems with this view, and we will examine further difficulties below. However, it must also be noted that an important and accurate concept underlies this statement. Communicative actions—and that certainly is what texts are—do indeed have underlying social situations and institutions that have an effect upon interpretation. Communication does not occur apart from some kind of social situation. This cannot be denied. Additionally, certain fixed forms do occur both in everyday speech and in various kinds of literature. Think, for instance, of the English phrase "good morning," which functions as a simple greeting and need not indicate that a given morning is good at all. Or, with regard to literary forms, consider the clichéd introductory phrases "It was a dark and stormy night" and "Once upon a time." The question is not whether some broader context must be sought, or whether genre categories may be useful, but what context that might be and the way in which a category or categories could be useful.

In addition to the important, if problematic, concepts discussed above, classic form criticism has also produced an entire set of helpful general genre categories into which much of the prophetic literature may be said to fall. In defining genres there is a tension between too much structural definition and too little. Tucker, for instance, criticizes Westermann for his overly defined categories. There is a twofold problem. First, many prophecies that should (in Tucker's view) be included within a given genre are excluded, and second (and more important), Westermann's highly defined categories suggest some kind of "ideal or the original pattern appropriate for prophetic speech" (Tucker, 64n94). Tucker suggests instead that it is helpful to describe, in very general terms, the features and characteristics of broad types of prophecy and to allow interpreters to then explore their relationships to the various instantiations of actual prophetic oracles. What is included in the list given below, therefore, is defined in very broad strokes.

As early as Gunkel we find two basic forms of

prophetic oracle, both of them negative: accusation of the people and announcement of judgment (Westermann, 18). Westermann emphasizes that the prophets are not preachers of repentance, though some other form critics identify the oracles in this way. The prophets are principally preachers of doom (Westermann 19, 65-70). Given this, he revises Gunkel's categories and speaks in terms of oracles of destruction and oracles of salvation as the two broadest and most ubiquitous types of prophecy. There are a number of other significant prophetic forms, listed below, but judgment and salvation are the mainstays of the prophetic literature—judgment particularly so.

The following is a list of types of prophetic speech, as listed principally by March (March, 159-69). Note that in all of these the question of *Sitz im Leben* seems to be the least settled and most often disputed, obviously due to lack of evidence:

1. Prophecy of disaster—This category, in particular, and the next one (prophecy of salvation) are the most notable and important, but determining the *Sitz im Leben* for both is difficult, as is determining whether or not these are original to the prophets of Israel or borrowed from neighboring cultures.
   a. indication of situation
   b. prediction of disaster
   c. concluding characterization
2. Prophecy of salvation—This is essentially the same as the prophecy of disaster.
   a. (optional) appeal for attention
   b. indication of situation
   c. prediction of salvation (promise)
   d. concluding characterization
3. Woe oracle—This is considered a secondary type, borrowed.
   a. introduced by *hôy*
   b. participle or substantive, which indicates the subjects of the oracle
   c. second participial clause + finite verb indicating offense
   d. announcement of judgment
4. Trial speech
   a. summons to trial
   b. trial, including speeches by participants
   c. sentencing
5. *Rîb* speech, a possible subcategory of the trial speech (see Is 1; Mic 6; Jer 2)
   a. introduction, including call for hearing

   b. questioning of witnesses and statement of accusation
   c. prosecutor's speech
   d. derogatory statements regarding cult and need for compensation
   e. declaration of guilt and threat of destruction
6. Disputation speech
7. Call to repentance—This type has been disputed. Wolff suggested that any element of repentance should be considered subordinate to the associated oracle of destruction or salvation. T. Raitt identifies this form, citing twenty-nine examples, preponderantly in Jeremiah. These often occur in relation to oracles of salvation.
   a. appeal with messenger formula
   b. motivation with promise/threat

There is no doubt that classic form criticism has helped to move the study of OT prophecy forward. It has provided important reflection upon the possible oral origins of the prophetic literature, as well as questions concerned with the theoretical history and development of the prophetic texts as we have them today. The concept of *Sitz im Leben* hits upon the vitally important fact that communication occurs in context. "Still the definition of the *Sitz im Leben* remains a pressing problem in the study of prophetic speech forms" (March, 176). The problem with *Sitz im Leben* is fairly obvious: we lack evidence from which to draw in order to construct a convincing *Sitz im Leben*. It is not that there may not have been just such a phenomenon, but how could one know if it had been isolated and described accurately? In all cases we must rely only upon other literature, and we have no experience of the culture of ancient Israel directly. What is particularly striking about this problem is that uncovering the *Sitz im Leben* is one of the hallmark promises of form criticism (Deist, 583). It is difficult to avoid disillusionment with a methodology that cannot accomplish one of its chief aims. This is the situation that has led, more than anything else, to the move away from *Sitz im Leben* and toward a search for a situation in literature or book. The enterprise is, in many ways, relatively similar. It is the goal that differs markedly.

The new form critics do not depart entirely from the work of the older generation. "Rather, the limitations of the older methods are more frankly acknowledged and the desirability of a more sophisticatedly flexible approach to the biblical texts is being recognized" (Gordon, 19). We find a shift to the text, as opposed to the world behind the text. This does not negate the impulse to know more about the cultural milieu of ancient Israel and postexilic Judah. Comparative studies, as well as the narrative sections of the Latter Prophets and the tales of the Former Prophets, remind us of the flesh-and-blood prophets who inhabited the ancient Near East. Although it is perhaps impossible to truly get behind the text to the social situations and traditions in which these various prophetic figures worked, it does not follow that they did not exist or that they are merely constructs of later redactors (Gordon, 21).

As R. Gordon notes, "It would be a pity if doctrinaire dismissals of older approaches were to turn the idea of a 'paradigm shift' into a euphemism for a neologistic tyranny which, in the familiar way of some Old Testament scholarship, assumed far more about what *cannot* be known about the workings of Israelite prophecy (for example) than the evidence justifies" (Gordon, 26). This is a very good corrective to the creation of a new "orthodoxy" with regard to form and tradition. The evolution of the form-critical methodology in recent years has its own flaws, some which are even reminiscent of classic form criticism.

However, as the star of classic form criticism sets, we do see the rise of new emphases in scholarly examinations of the genre and structure of the prophetic literature, including a greater focus on final forms and the importance of the role of the redactor in the creative production of the text (Deist, 595-96; see also Knierim). In this project, which is referred to here as the new form criticism, we begin with one of the shoals upon which the classic project foundered: the basic and almost shockingly obvious truth that the prophetic literature is, in fact, literature.

3. New Form Criticism.
In the middle-to-late twentieth century, developments in philosophy, linguistics and literary theory began to challenge reigning presuppositions about how texts developed and what we can and cannot know about this process (Sweeney and Ben Zvi, 3). One of the most significant developments for the form-critical en-

terprise was a move to a focus on the whole text (Campbell, 23). One may speak now of a great diversity of form-critical approaches, making use of a variety of interdisciplinary methods. "They advance synchronic and diachronic literary analyses as well as studies of the interrelationships between text and language, text and society (and social structures), text and culture, texts and audience, and texts and other texts" (Sweeney and Ben Zvi, 5). Form criticism is now a method in progress (Sweeney and Ben Zvi, 9). One of the notable features of this movement is, of course, critical engagement with the classic form-critical project. This examination and analysis of new form criticism will mirror, therefore, section 2 above. First, we will examine the concept of an oral/literate divide and what it means that prophetic literature appears as literature. Second, we will explore the possibilities and problems involved with engaging in a world behind the text. Third, we will survey the concept of context and ask, among other things, "*Sitz im* What exactly?"

Although we may refer to a new school of form criticism, it must be noted that for some who promote and practice this new form criticism, many of the initial assumptions and goals of classic form criticism remain. The divorce between these two camps is not total, but there are some significant changes in emphasis, as E. Blum makes clear: "OT exegesis asking for the historical, intended meaning of the texts will always be dependent on 'genre investigation' in Gunkel's sense. It will be dependent on the question of the form and meaning of the individual texts in their intended reception, which is pursued with literary-critical methods" (Blum 2003, 45). Note that while Blum retains a concern for history and intention, this concern shifts to an intended readership as opposed to the oral background or the intentions of the prophet. Although many shifts and changes are involved, and although scholars such as Blum (and many others cited here) are very careful and nuanced in their examination of data, it must be emphasized that the rumors concerning the death of historical criticism have been greatly exaggerated.

As we noted above, the fact that the prophetic literature is indeed written literature must be taken into account (Floyd 2000, 111). "In fact, this feature has a substantial bearing on the social role of these books, the status of their composers and readers (as opposed to those to whom the text must be read), the social function of high literacy, the construction of language and discourse, and the role of writing as the propagation of theological/ideological viewpoints, including particular views of society and its hierarchy" (Ben Zvi 2000a, 8). Regardless of the precise origins of the prophetic literature, the only thing that we have before us are texts, and those texts represent the work of a highly literate subculture (see Writing and Prophecy). They have their own characteristics (aesthetic, epistemological, theological and otherwise) that, in the end, are the responsibility of those who collected, edited and transmitted them (Ben Zvi 2000a, 8; Campbell, 23). What is more, these texts appear to have functioned as divine revelation to these literate editors and transmitters (Ben Zvi 2000a, 12). Although it is entirely possible (perhaps even probable) that the prophetic literature was at some point an oral phenomenon, we simply have no direct evidence of this. We have only the text.

Additionally, the strong focus on orality that characterized classic form criticism is not without ideological underpinning. M. Floyd notes that for modern interpreters, the prophet acts as a kind of savage protoromanticist, and the scribe as a kind of protorationalist (Floyd 2000, 114, 119). This certainly is true of Gunkel, whose work evinces strong romanticist leanings, which often have the flavor of a kind of historical paternalism; the wise scholar observing the noble savage with amusement and grudging respect (Gunkel 1901, 1, 61). Floyd is tremendously concerned with the residual effect on biblical studies of the thinking of Wellhausen and Gunkel in this regard. He indicts these scholars for creating stereotypes of the scribe and prophet that are maintained today: "On the one hand, prophets were active in Israel's history from its primitive beginnings. They were basically oral poets or orators, not writers. . . . On the other hand, scribes became active in Israel's cultural history at a relatively late date. They were basically rationalistic intellectuals at home in academic institutions or schools" (Floyd 2000, 120 [see, likewise, Campbell, 18]). We see this in the form-critical focus on the original, the oral, as the more important. The later, written scribal work represents the death of the vibrant and culturally connected oral kernel.

What is needed here is not simply a total shift from a focus on orality to a focus on literacy in our study of prophetic literature. The problem is much more complex (see Ong). It is essentially certain that the vast majority of the population of both ancient Israel and postexilic Judah were illiterate (Ben Zvi 2000a, 5n8, 6, 10, 21n60). Given this, the prophetic literature must have been collected, edited and transmitted by a relatively small subsection of the populace with specialized skills These are Ben Zvi's famous literati, (Ben Zvi 2000a; also throughout Ben Zvi's work). But it is important not to overemphasize the divide between oral and written. Although these were written texts in their later reception, it seems very likely that they also had a significant oral life. The literati who interacted with these texts were most likely an elite class, but they also must have fulfilled some function in the community if that community were to tolerate their presence.

As K. van der Toorn suggests, these literati likely were attached in some way to the temple or religious structure, and consequently both they and, one must assume, the texts with which they worked played a role in that setting (see, e.g., Lk 4:16-19) (van der Toorn, 82). Thus, it may be helpful when reflecting on genre and form to consider the possible performative role of a text within a community. "Any given performance of a traditional power or story necessarily evokes, through specific expressions of traditional language, imagery, themes, and patterns, the larger body of stories and poems in the common store of material familiar in varying degrees to performer and audience" (Culley, 50). One of the things that this kind of thinking suggests is the possibility of "orally-derived texts," which are "traditional texts conceived largely in oral terms but still produced in writing" (Culley, 53). Think, for instance, of the manuscript of a modern sermon. Although it is written, and therefore is in a literary medium, it reflects more closely the linguistic register of a particular kind of oral communication. Thus, that a text may have apparently oral features alongside apparently literary features is not at all surprising.

Floyd suggests that "when prophecy is occasionally described as an activity that involves writing, the documents tend to function as a substitute for oral delivery rather than an alternative to it" (Floyd 2000, 103). This does not negate R. Culley's concept of an orally derived text, as indicated by Floyd's reference to Jeremiah 29:1-32; 51:59-64 suggest texts that were indeed intended to be read to the exiles. Although note also that the first letter is sent specifically to the cultural elite (Jer 29:1 [though also with the intent of being read to the people generally]), and the second letter was specifically meant to be read aloud to the people (Jer 51:61). This is an example of orality and literacy functioning side by side.

In addition to this more subtle and difficult conception of the relationship between orality and literacy, new form criticism also challenges the classic attempt to get behind the text as it stands in order to identify the more original sayings, as well as the tradition history of a given text. Instead of conceiving of the Prophetic Books as collections of relatively disparate prophetic sayings (Zimmerli, 23), new form critics begin their investigations with the assumption that these texts are coherent and have been skillfully collected, edited and transmitted.

As Ben Zvi notes, all models for understanding the nature and development of the Prophetic Books are circular to some degree. What sets his apart is that it does, in fact, have access to one indisputably external and objective fact: the existence of written prophetic books (Ben Zvi 2000a, 16). He therefore posits the prophetic book as a form of prophecy in and of itself. Ben Zvi's basic definition of "book" is "a written work that presents itself as a self-contained unit—with a clear beginning and conclusion—and shows a significant degree of textual coherence and distinctiveness" (Ben Zvi 2000a, 1n2 [see also Ben Zvi 2003, 279-80]). He further suggests that "an 'authoritative book' is one that communicates an explicit or implicit claim for social and theological/ideological authoritativeness, and was likely accepted as such by at least some substantial sector of the ancient readership and rereadership" (Ben Zvi 2003, 280). Although Ben Zvi's identifying features—a beginning, an end and a middle that stick together to some degree—may seem somewhat sparse, this is a significant step away from the assumption that the Prophetic Books were relatively haphazard collections with many internal seams and flaws. By positing a beginning-middle-end structure, Ben Zvi suggests a written text that was developed intentionally and skillfully.

These simple structural ties help to indicate a unit in which a reader can hope to find some degree of cohesion. Within this relatively loose macrostructure, Ben Zvi suggests that a prophetic book generally contains sets of readings. These readings may be roughly analogous to traditional literary subunits, and consequently their structures may in some instances be analogous to traditional form-critical genre categories. The fundamental difference is that Ben Zvi views these traditional genre categories not as representative of some earlier, oral social situation, but as intrinsically connected to the greater category of "book." Therefore, "since 'prophetic reading' is the only genre present in the body of a prophetic book, the entire body of the prophetic book is associated primarily with a single setting in life, namely, the reading of prophetic books by those able to read and reread them" (Ben Zvi 2003, 287). Such a text would, as he notes, suggests material of great value to the literate (and likely illiterate) community.

Ben Zvi emphasizes again and again that the prophetic books were "meant to be read, reread, meditated upon, again and again, to be read (and reread) to others who cannot read by themselves, and certainly not to be read once and then discarded" (Ben Zvi 2003, 280n16). This reminder is of vital importance to modern people who may not think about books or literature in these kinds of terms. There were no public libraries or bookstores with coffee shops in ancient Israel or postexilic Judah. It must be emphasized that there is a vast gap between the highly (indeed, almost universally) literate culture of the modern West and the culture in which the prophetic literature was produced. If a book was important enough to record in the manner that the scriptural texts were recorded (as opposed, say, to being written on shards of pottery, as with the Lachish letters), then almost certainly they were important enough to be reread and mused over as Ben Zvi suggests. The written form must be taken seriously indeed.

At least one of the social locations that matter, then, is that of the literate readers for whom the final form of the book presumably was intended. Given Floyd's comments regarding orality and literacy, however, it probably is necessary to also take into account (if possible) audiences to whom the text may have been read (see Neh 8, where Ezra reads from the law to all of the people). And so we see that new form criticism does indeed reconstruct the social milieu of those people who edited and preserved these books. However, this is done in relatively general terms and on the basis of what is usually considered accepted assumptions (e.g., limited literacy in the general population). But, in all of this, we must always remember that just as Gunkel's or Mowinckel's reconstructions of the original, oral, social situation of a given genre were highly theoretical, so also are present social reconstructions decidedly theoretical in nature (Kim, 96). The need for caution and humility in the face of relatively sparse evidence cannot be overemphasized.

But this focus upon the final form of the text, and upon its later reception and the social milieus involved in that process, bring to mind again the question of contextual situation. If all communication must be contextualized, both culturally and situationally, how might one speak of context in the new form criticism? Clearly, the traditional concept of *Sitz im Leben*, tied so closely as it is to the original, oral communication and to the development of the prophetic tradition, is more or less done away with. What stands in its place depends upon the already noted concept that the Prophetic Books were meant to be read, reread and meditated upon.

Here H. Kim, citing J. Crenshaw, notes that recovering the actual date or historical setting of any of the biblical books is fraught with problems, and in many cases it may be impossible apart from making significant assumptions (Kim, 93n19). Kim suggests that the way forward is R. Melugin's textually created context. Thus, we speak less of a *Sitz im Leben* and more in terms of "*Sitz im Text, Sitz im Buch, Sitz im Literati (Literatur),* and *Sitz im Reder*" (Kim, 94). I would add to this *Sitz im Kanon* or *Sitz im Kollection* (e.g., the Latter Prophets, or the Book of the Twelve). Note, for instance, the form-critical concerns that arise when Ben Zvi suggests that the Former Prophets should be read as prophetic and not historical literature (a genre distinction [Floyd 2003, 306-7]). Such a reconceptualization of contextual situation brings to the fore work on allusion and intertextuality in the prophetic literature, work which takes as significant the various points of allusion and intersection between the various components

of different corpora of literature within the prophetic corpus (see Sweeney 2005). Additionally, this suggests that the Prophetic Books need not be read in linear fashion, as is our wont in the modern world, but could better be thought of as mosaics and could be read "section by section, and searched for their tapestry-like interconnections" (Floyd 2003, 305).

Of course, one of the dangers of this kind of reading is that it may completely unhinge the text from the historical realities in which it was produced. Again, regardless of how much we wish to think the contrary, language is intimately tied to social situations, and all acts of linguistic communication are tied to some social setting or another. Kim is correct, therefore, to say that "if a text portrays life forward as well as in the present, it also portrays it backward. Otherwise, that text loses its account of history, of the past" (Kim, 95). All of the hermeneutical and historical spheres must be examined, though of course not all need be examined in every instance. Additionally, whichever context an interpreter chooses, that context (both textually and sociohistorically) must be taken into account at all times (Kim, 100).

But whichever context one might choose, when we speak of form criticism in this way—that is, as a text-centered enterprise—what we are exploring is the intersection of genre and form, of category and instance, of abstraction and text (Campbell, 23; Sweeney and Ben Zvi, 9). The search that we undertake is not for an ideal genre category, nor for an underlying situation, but rather for a heuristic tool. Genre is, then, an abstraction based on the content and structure of many individual texts. It is a way of drawing connections between various units in the hope that drawing these connections will help to elucidate the individual units in light of one another.

4. A Form-Critical Exercise: Micah, Old and New.

We turn now to an exercise that should make very clear the extraordinary practical differences between classic and new form criticism and also demonstrate the general characteristics of each endeavor. In what follows I will draw a brief comparison between H. Wolff's and E. Ben Zvi's commentaries on Micah. Both are explicitly form-critical in their approach, but as will become clear, the two methodologies are very different. These commentaries will be compared first with regard to their introductions to Micah as a prophetic work, particularly with regard to questions of genre and setting. Then they will be compared with regard to the ways these two critics analyze a specific passage of prophetic literature, Micah 7:1-7.

Wolff begins his commentary by setting the book within its historical milieu. This includes both the time of the historical prophet Micah (the neo-Assyrian era) and the time of the transmission of Micah's prophetic tradition (the neo-Babylonian era [Wolff, 1]). Wolff is certain that "Micah of Moresheth appeared in the second half of the eighth century," and that "the book contains numerous sayings that stem not from Micah but from a much later period" (Wolff, 1). The career of the prophet himself is discussed at length. Wolff, examining the book's superscription, presents comparative evidence from Kings and other ancient Near Eastern historical texts and discusses the chronology of Israel's eighth-century BC kings, all the while attempting to reconcile various elements of Micah's prophecies with the historical occurrences recorded in his various other sources (Wolff, 2-5). In the end, he assigns some material to Micah himself in the eighth century BC, and some material is assigned to various anonymous additions ranging from the seventh century BC to the postexilic period. "The historical background of all the prophecies contained in the book of Micah comprehends, therefore, a span of time of about 300 years" (Wolff, 5).

After discussing the dates of the various prophecies in Micah, Wolff goes on to examine the life of Micah himself. Wolff suggests where Micah's proclamations took place (both in Moresheth and Jerusalem), and also that Micah likely held a position of authority in Moresheth, perhaps as an elder of some kind (Wolff, 6-7). Wolff also concludes that Micah himself was active as a prophet "between 733 and 722," and that the following passages can be assigned to the prophet: Micah 1:6, 7b-13a, 14-16 (excluding the first word of v. 14); 2:1-4, 6-11; 3:1-4, 5-8, 9-12 (Wolff, 8-9). Wolff thus reconstructs both the work and the general historical milieu of the man Micah and also shows which prophecies are not original to Micah and in what historical milieu those non-Micah oracles best fit.

Compare this procedure to Ben Zvi's point of departure. While agreeing with the general consensus of earlier scholarship (including Wolff's) that much of Micah is from post-586 BC, he has no interest in attempting to determine which prophecies were written in which period (Ben Zvi 2000b, 9). "Contrary to these redaction-critical studies . . . this commentary has its starting point in the book of Micah as it stands, rather than on the putative words of the prophet Micah" (Ben Zvi 2000b, 10). Ben Zvi's setting, then, is neither the eighth century BC nor any point on Wolff's three-hundred-year continuum. Instead, he focuses on the period in which the book of Micah was likely (for Ben Zvi) to have been collected and edited into a literary whole. This is some time in the Persian II period (450-332 BC), and the social situation to which the text is connected is the temple community (Ben Zvi 2000b, 10). The people behind the production of the text are the literate elite of that community, and the book was intended as divine revelation. The genre that Ben Zvi designates is, therefore, that of a prophetic book (Ben Zvi 2000b, 8-9).

In regard to the superscription of the book and the fact that it is ascribed to the prophet Micah, these elements are, for Ben Zvi, tools to help create the text world of the book (Ben Zvi 2000b, 16). It is not that these prophecies originated with Micah himself, nor is it that these prophecies are the work of a school of later disciples who wished to emulate Micah's work. Micah is instead called upon as an authoritative, non-Jerusalemite, voice from the past who can legitimately preach the Jerusalemite theology of the *literati* (Ben Zvi 2000b, 22).

Obviously, we are in different worlds when we read these two different methodological approaches, but how are these disparate approaches applied to a particular text? In his examination of Micah 7:1-7 Wolff reads the text very closely in an attempt to determine if these words belong together as an original unit. He suggests that Micah 7:4b is a later addition, tied to Micah 7:11-12 due to the use of "day." He notes that although the admonitions and warnings of Micah 7:2-4a differ from those in Micah 7:5-6, these do constitute an original unit based on fact that in this type of lamentation a combination of different admonitions on a similar theme occurs elsewhere (Jer. 9:1-5; 12:6) (Wolff, 202-3). Thus, form-critical grounds are used to establish the connection between these verses. With regard to setting, Wolff suggests that the speaker is a prophet, though neither Micah nor a contemporary, living in the postexilic community characterized by instability and some degree of social disorder, which would have led to the lack of confidence in neighbors, officials and even family (Wolff, 204). In his discussion about the purpose of the passage Wolff notes the variation from the typical features of such a lament text. Although such texts generally include some kind of announcement of judgment or vindication, here we find only "lament upon lament" with no announcement of punishment (Wolff, 209). So we see that Wolff here compares this specific instantiation of a prophetic lament with a more general, or typical, genre category.

Ben Zvi also suggests that Micah 7:1-7 constitutes a single unit, but for entirely different reasons. This is the case because "the text strongly suggests to its intended readers" that these verses belong together (Ben Zvi 2000b, 166). With respect to setting, Ben Zvi reviews the proposals of previous scholars who suggest that this is a lament for a festival or perhaps an instance where the speaker is the king, but Ben Zvi rejects these proposals because they "clearly deal with issues that stand beyond the limits of what can be known with any reasonable degree of certainty" (Ben Zvi 2000b, 171). Since there is no explicit evidence in the text itself tying it to any given historical setting, Ben Zvi suggests that this is an intentionally dehistoricized text, meant to be reapplied by later reading communities (Ben Zvi 2000b, 171). Apart from this, the only social setting for this passage is the same as the setting for the rest of the readings in Micah (and the rest of the prophetic literature for that matter): the socially and economically elite *literati* (Ben Zvi 2000b, 172). With regard to genre, Ben Zvi does note that this is a lament of some kind, and that it is also a prophetic "reading" designed to be reread and ruminated upon (Ben Zvi 2000b, 170-71). The readers are meant to identify with the speaker and to ponder the questions of injustice that he raises.

This very brief comparison reveals both the similarities and the dramatic differences that these two versions of form criticism bring to a text. Although both work with essentially the same unit delimitation, come to similar conclusions regarding the history of the text (e.g.,

postexilic), and even assign a similar genre label to the unit (lament), their approaches to reading are drastically different. Wolff, working on very limited evidence, attempts to recreate both the general historical and social situation of the historical Micah and of the later editors responsible for Micah 7:1-7, all in the hope of providing a sense of the social situation that gave rise to these words. Ben Zvi, because the evidence is very limited, disregards the possibility of recreating the historical background of the book's creation and instead focuses on the reception of the final form by a theoretical community that would have been likely to receive, reread and recopy this text. The differences in setting have a significant impact upon how one might study this passage. On the one hand, we have the words of a prophetic figure spoken against the oppressive powers of his time, lamenting the social disorder that pits son against father; on the other hand, we have a community of socially elite *literati* (the fat cats themselves, as it were) rereading and transmitting this text to later generations.

5. Conclusion.

While it is clear that some aspects of the form-critical venture have been severely critiqued, and that there are components of the project that perhaps should be abandoned, it does not follow that a sensitive examination of genre and form is of no value in our examination of biblical prophetic literature. What is needed, above all, is that we return to a foundational dependence upon the text itself as our best source of data, and that we practice our analysis of genre categories with care and caution.

Genre categories are best understood neither as ideal structures nor as simple products of social institutions. Instead, genre should be thought of, for the biblical literature, as a general category abstracted from particular instances. Thus, we begin with particular units of prophetic texts, and in comparing these units we abstract common elements and take note of significant differences. In this way, it becomes possible to offer legitimate grounds for comparison that are drawn from the text, while yet taking seriously the fact that the resulting genre categories are abstractions. Then the use and function of a particular structure within a particular unit of text may be examined in light of both the abstracted genre and other instances of similar forms. In addition, we may also analyze the use and function of a particular text and its genre within the book or collection in which it is found, thus comparing the interplay between multiple genres.

Moving forward, this type of analysis can benefit from continued interdisciplinary interaction. By drawing on the insights of discourse analysis, sociolinguistics and various forms of literary criticism, we may hope to be able to use a variety of tools to describe those textual elements from which we might abstract genre characteristics. In all of this, however, we must take note of the many difficulties that surround this type of examination.

The tensions that exist between classic and new form criticism remind us that although questions of genre and form remain helpful (and perhaps necessary) categories, such projects must be strongly constrained by the text as we have it. Of course, as has been noted repeatedly above, context matters in communication. These texts arose in some cultural situation, whether as ecstatic oral pronouncements or as refined religious literature, and all communication is situationally conditioned to some degree. This remains a serious problem not only for the form-critical enterprise, but also for biblical interpretation in general. Despite its checkered past with regard to *Sitz im Leben*, however, form criticism is still a valuable contextual tool. We certainly should be hesitant and cautious in speaking of specific social and historical settings for which the text offers no direct evidence, but we must remember that the text itself offers us a setting. It is hoped that careful examination of the text, using tools designed for this very purpose, will help to glean information that can further our conversation with the ancient prophetic literature.

Recent critiques and advancements related to form criticism have helped, not to destroy or dismantle the form critical project, but instead to breath fresh life into it. As form critics continue to examine the text carefully and continue to reflect upon how various passages both resemble and differ from one another, form criticism continues to offer a set of tools that can be of great use. Increasing subtlety and methodological diversity have the potential to ensure that form criticism not only survives but also thrives in the discipline of biblical studies.

See also CANONICAL CRITICISM; CONVERSATION ANALYSIS; EDITORIAL/REDACTION CRITICISM; FORMATION OF THE PROPHETIC BOOKS; INTERTEXTUALITY AND INNERBIBLICAL INTERPRETATION; LITERARY APPROACHES; PERFORMANCE CRITICISM; PROPHECY AND SOCIETY; SOCIAL-SCIENTIFIC APPROACHES; WRITING AND PROPHECY.

BIBLIOGRAPHY. **E. Ben Zvi,** "Introduction: Writings, Speeches, and the Prophetic Books: Setting an Agenda," in *Writings and Speech in Israelite and Ancient Near Eastern Prophecy*, ed. E. Ben Zvi and M. H. Floyd (SBLSymS 10; Atlanta: Society of Biblical Literature, 2000a) 1-29; idem, *Micah* (FOTL 21B; Grand Rapids: Eerdmans, 2000b); idem, "The Prophetic Book: A Key Form of Prophetic Literature," in *The Changing Face of Form Criticism for the Twenty-First Century*, ed. M. A. Sweeney and E. Ben Zvi (Grand Rapids: Eerdmans, 2003) 276-97; **E. Blum,** "*Formgeschichte*—A Misleading Category? Some Critical Remarks," in *The Changing Face of Form Criticism for the Twenty-First Century*, ed. M. A. Sweeney and E. Ben Zvi (Grand Rapids: Eerdmans, 2003) 32-45; **M. J. Buss,** "The Study of Forms," in *Old Testament Form Criticism*, ed. J. H. Hayes (TUMSR; San Antonio: Trinity University Press, 1974) 1-56; idem, *The Changing Shape of Form Criticism: A Relational Approach*, ed. N. Stipe (HBM 18; Sheffield: Sheffield Phoenix, 2010); **A. F. Campbell,** "Form Criticism's Future," in *Changing Face of Form Criticism for the Twenty-First Century*, ed. M. A. Sweeney and E. Ben Zvi (Grand Rapids: Eerdmans, 2003) 15-31; **R. C. Culley,** "Orality and Writtenness in the Prophetic Texts," in *Writings and Speech in Israelite and Ancient Near Eastern Prophecy*, ed. E. Ben Zvi and M. H. Floyd (SBLSymS 10; Atlanta: Society of Biblical Literature, 2000) 45-64; **F. Deist,** "The Prophets: Are We Heading for a Paradigm Shift?" in *"The Place Is Too Small for Us": The Israelite Prophets in Recent Scholarship*, ed. R. P. Gordon (SBTS 5; Winona Lake, IN: Eisenbrauns, 1995) 582-99; **M. H. Floyd,** "'Write the Revelation!' (Hab 2:2): Re-Imagining the Cultural History of Prophecy," in *Writings and Speech in Israelite and Ancient Near Eastern Prophecy*, ed. E. Ben Zvi and M. H. Floyd (SBLSymS 10; Atlanta: Society of Biblical Literature, 2000) 103-43; idem, "Basic Trends in the Form-Critical Study of Prophetic Texts," in *The Changing Face of Form Criticism for the Twenty-First Century*, ed. M. A. Sweeney and

E. Ben Zvi (Grand Rapids: Eerdmans, 2003) 298-311; **R. P. Gordon,** "A Story of Two Paradigm Shifts," in *"The Place Is Too Small for Us": The Israelite Prophets in Recent Scholarship,* ed. R. P. Gordon (SBTS 5; Winona Lake, IN: Eisenbrauns, 1995) 3-26; **H. Gressmann,** *Der Messias,* Forschungen zur Religion und Literatur des Alten und Neuen Testaments, 43. Heft (Göttingen: Vandenhoeck & Ruprecht, 1929); **H. Gressman, H. Gunkel, M. Haller, H. Schmidt, W. Stärk, and P. Volz,** *Die Schriften des Alten Testaments in Auswahl,* 7 vols. (Göttingen: Vandenhoeck & Ruprecht, 1910); **H. Gunkel,** *The Legends of Genesis,* trans. W. H. Carruth (Chicago: Open Court Publishing, 1901); idem, *The Psalms: A Form-Critical Introduction,* trans. T. Horner (FBBS 19; Philadelphia: Fortress, 1967); idem, "The Israelite Prophecy from the Time of Amos," in *Twentieth Century Theology in the Making,* 1: *Themes of Biblical Theology,* ed. J. Pelikan (London: Fontana, 1969) 48-75; idem, "Israelite Literary History," in *Water for a Thirsty Land: Israelite Literature and Religion,* ed. K. C. Hanson (FCBS; Minneapolis: Fortress, 2001) 31-41; **H. C. P. Kim,** "Form Criticism in Dialogue with Other Criticisms: Building the Multidimensional Structures of Texts and Concepts," in *The Changing Face of Form Criticism for the Twenty-First Century,* ed. M. A. Sweeney and E. Ben Zvi (Grand Rapids: Eerdmans, 2003) 85-104; **R. Knierim,** "Old Testament Form Criticism Reconsidered," *Int* 27 (1973) 435-68; **K. Koch,** *The Growth of the Biblical Tradition: The Form-Critical Method* (New York: Macmillan, 1988); **L. Köhler,** *Kleine Lichter: 50 Bibelstellen Erklärt,* Zwingli-Bücherei, 47 (Zürich: Zwingli-Verlag, 1944); **J. Lindblom,** *Die literarische Gattung der prophetischen Literatur: Eine literargeschichtliche Untersuchung zum Alten Testament* (UUÅ 1; Uppsala: A.-b. Lundequistska Bokhandeln, 1924); **T. Longman III,** "Israelite Genres in Their Ancient Near Eastern Context," in *The Changing Face of Form Criticism for the Twenty-First Century,* ed. M. Sweeney and E. Ben Zvi (Grand Rapids: Eerdmans, 2003) 177-95; **W. E. March,** "Prophecy," in *Old Testament Form Criticism,* ed. J. Hayes (TUMSR; San Antonio: Trinity University Press, 1974) 141-77; **S. Mowinckel,** *The Psalms in Israel's Worship,* trans. D. R. Ap-Thomas (2 vols; New York: Abingdon, 1962); idem, *The Spirit and the Word: Prophecy and Tradition in Ancient Israel,* ed. K. C. Hanson (FCBS; Minneapolis: Fortress, 2002); **J. Muilenburg,** "Form

Criticism and Beyong," *JBL* 88 (1969) 1-18. **M. Nissinen,** ed., *Prophecy in Its Ancient Near Eastern Context: Mesopotamian, Biblical, and Arabian Perspectives* (SBLSymS 13; Atlanta: Society of Biblical Literature, 2000); **W. J. Ong,** *Orality and Literacy: The Technologizing of the Word* (London: Routledge, 1991); **T. Raitt,** "The Prophetic Summons to Repentance," *ZAW* 83 (1971) 30-49; **M. A. Sweeney,** *Isaiah 1-39: With an Introduction to Prophetic Literature* (FOTL 16; Grand Rapids: Eerdmans, 1996); idem, *Form and Intertextuality in Prophetic and Apocalyptic Literature* (FAT 45; Tübingen: Mohr Siebeck, 2005); **M. A. Sweeney and E. Ben Zvi,** eds., *The Changing Face of Form Criticism for the Twenty-First Century* (Grand Rapids: Eerdmans, 2003); **G. M. Tucker,** *Form Criticism of the Old Testament* (GBS; Philadelphia: Fortress, 1971); **K. van der Toorn,** *Scribal Culture and the Making of the Hebrew Bible* (Cambridge, MA: Harvard University Press, 2007); **C. Westermann,** *Basic Forms of Prophetic Speech,* trans. H. White (Louisville: Westminster/John Knox, 1991); **W. Zimmerli,** *The Fiery Throne: The Prophets and Old Testament Theology,* ed. K. C. Hanson (Minneapolis: Fortress, 2003).

C. M. Toffelmire

FORMATION OF THE PROPHETIC BOOKS

It is an axiom of most scholarship on the Prophetic Books that they are composite, that they are the product of a complex, often lengthy, process of development. Rather than being written out from scratch by a single hand, most of these books were "made," incorporating sources, sometimes rearranging these or commenting upon them to serve a fresh role in their new literary contexts. Thus, we can speak of the "formation" of prophetic literature. The importance of this topic issues from two distinct but related lines of inquiry: reconstructing the original words of the prophets behind these books and, alternatively, probing the rationale of the final form of this literature.

1. Evidence
2. Methodological Considerations
3. The Formation of a Prophetic Book
4. The Formation of the Prophetic Corpus
5. Implications

1. Evidence.
How do scholars know that the prophetic books

of the OT were made and not merely written in the sense just mentioned? The composite nature of these works is strongly suggested by two types of evidence.

1.1. Empirical Evidence. The composite nature of the prophetic books is suggested by what has been called "empirical evidence" (Carr 37-101; Tigay). We have "texts whose evolution can be documented by copies from several stages in the course of their development" (Tigay, xi). In certain cases, therefore, the earlier source (or a copy of it) has been preserved alongside the later text that incorporated it, the one depending literarily on the other. Instances of such empirical evidence have come to us from the cuneiform literature of ancient Mesopotamia (second millennium BC) and the *Dead Sea Scrolls (Second Temple period). Significantly, these two bodies of evidence frame the period within which the Prophetic Books were produced. Not surprisingly, therefore, the Bible itself preserves such evidence. Chronicles, a long recognized example of this phenomenon, rewrites its source (Genesis through 2 Kings), omitting, rearranging and adding material to create a new work with its own aims and strategies. Both the source and the rewriting have come down to us in the record.

But do we have any empirical evidence relating to the Prophetic Books themselves, evidence demonstrating that they were made in this fashion, that ultimately they are the product of many hands? A positive answer emerges from two well-known examples.

1.1.1. Jeremiah LXX/MT. The book of *Jeremiah is preserved in two different versions, the first reflected in the Masoretic Text (Jeremiah MT), and the second in the Greek translation (Jeremiah LXX). Some have regarded the differences between these two versions as the work of the Greek translator, but most would now trace the majority of these differences back to the Hebrew text used by the translator (Tov, 363-84). Supporting this are two Hebrew manuscripts of Jeremiah discovered at Qumran (4Q71; 4Q72a) that agree at several points (though not in every detail) with Jeremiah LXX against Jeremiah MT.

Many see the shorter text underlying the LXX and preserved in 4Q71 and 4Q72a as the earlier of the two versions, the other being the longer form reflected in the MT. This in turn has enabled scholars to describe an added layer

of material in version II, a layer reflected in the MT but not in the LXX. Some of these additions seem rather mundane, but others appear strategic. For example, Jeremiah MT 25:14; 27:7 are postexilic additions dealing with the punishment of Babylon after seventy years (Tov, 382-83), an issue of interpretation surfacing in several other texts related to this period (2 Chron 36; Ezra 1; Dan 9). Another such addition, likely related to the two just mentioned, is Jeremiah MT 33:14-26, a passage promising the return of Davidic rule ("a righteous branch") and a firm covenant. This addition draws from other passages in Jeremiah, combining Jeremiah 23:5-6, the promise of a true branch for David's line, with Jeremiah 29:10, the promise of return from *exile at the end of Babylon's seventy years (Schmid, 207-21). Whatever the meaning of these additions, they underscore that the two versions of Jeremiah present us with empirical evidence for the composite nature of a prophetic book.

1.1.2. Isaiah 36—39 and 2 Kings 18:13—20:19. The same may be said for Isaiah 36—39 and its parallel account in 2 Kings 18:13—20:19. Apart from a few differences, the two accounts are nearly identical, so that one likely depends on the other, one being the source and the other the borrower. For good reason, most scholars regard the 2 Kings version as the earlier of the two, the source borrowed into Isaiah 36—39 (Williamson 1994, 189-211). In this case, not only was an earlier source borrowed into Isaiah, but also it was modified in the process. To this narrative was added a psalm of Hezekiah (Is 38:9-20), which ends by expressing the hope for a return to the "house of the LORD." In connection with this hope, the "sign" given Hezekiah in 2 Kings 20:5-11 has been split in two by the Isaiah editor (Is 38:5-8, 21-22), who placed that aspect of the sign concerning the "house of the LORD" just after the reference to this at the end of the newly introduced psalm (Stromberg 2011b, 205-22). The point is that we have a copy both of the source (2 Kings 18:13—20:19) and of its reworking into Isaiah (Is 36—39). Once again, then, we have empirical evidence suggesting that the Prophetic Books were made and not simply written, that they are composite texts incorporating sources, the products of multiple hands. If this is correct, then (even without the help of such empirical evidence) we can reasonably expect to find signs within the

Prophetic Books that they were in fact made in this manner, which leads into the next point.

1.2. Inferential Evidence. The other line of evidence suggesting that the Prophetic Books had a complex history of formation may be called "inferential evidence." In this category, we do not have copies of the source text to compare with the borrowing text. Rather, through a process of "informed speculation," the composite nature of the books can be inferred from the features of the texts themselves, features explained most simply by appeal to editing of sources.

Since several examples of this type of evidence are given later (see 2 below), only one instance will be mentioned here. Jeremiah 36 narrates an incident in which Jeremiah tells his scribe to write what he dictates to him on a scroll. The scroll, a warning to the people of Judah, is then read publically, but ultimately it is destroyed. In response, Jeremiah gives another scroll to his scribe, who proceeds to write "all the words of the book that King Jehoiakim of Judah had burned in the fire; and many words similar to them were added" (Jer 36:32). Thus, the narrative tells of two stages in the scroll's development: there was an earlier, shorter version of it and also a later, longer one. Since the scroll itself is an element within the narrative looking back on the incident, the scroll and the book of Jeremiah (which contains the narrative) would have to be two separate documents. If we accept, as many have done, that some form of this scroll ultimately found its way into the book of Jeremiah (or at least that the book would have us think that it did), then it stands to reason that here the book presents itself as the product of multiple stages of literary activity, which is true even if the narrative itself is a complete fiction, a position rejected by Reimer (Reimer, 209-16). Identifying the historical level at which this claim applies is not without difficulty, but there is no reason to reject this aspect of the book's own self-presentation: it developed over time, incorporating at least one source itself expanded.

Probable though it is, this conclusion must be inferred entirely from the book's present form, so that it presents a line of evidence quite different from the empirical sort discussed above. Baruch's first scroll was totally destroyed, leaving nothing to posterity. Inferential evidence such as this remains by far the largest body of evidence that we possess for the composite nature of the Prophetic Books. Almost all copies of the sources used to make these books have been lost to history.

2. Methodological Considerations.
If for the most part all we have is evidence of the inferential sort, this raises an obvious question: how can one get at the formation of these books if all we have is the end product of this process—their present, final forms? By what means can scholars perceive depth in a text and then reconstruct a history of its development? Important here are the observations made in "redaction criticism"—that is, the study of how texts were edited in ancient Israel (*see* Editorial/Redaction Criticism). Here only some of the most important points are presented.

2.1. A Single Book or Passage with Historically Dissimilar Material. A single book may contain material whose assumed historical background differs from one passage to the next such that a single author could not have composed the whole from scratch. In this case, the historical background assumed by a passage may help distinguish it from another passage in the same book. One of the best-known examples of this comes from the book of Isaiah (Stromberg 2011a, 1-54). Some material in Isaiah 1—39 assumes an earlier period before the exile, during the ministry of the prophet Isaiah when Assyria ruled. At the same time, however, Isaiah 40—66 assumes that the Babylonian exile had taken place. Note, for example, Isaiah 64:11-12, which is not prediction or even prophecy but rather is lament—lament leading to supplication for restoration after Babylonian invasion, when the temple was destroyed ("Our holy and beautiful house . . . has been burned with fire"). Consider also Isaiah 48:20, where the people are told, "Come out of Babylon, flee from the Chaldeans." This is an imperative not a prediction, an imperative that makes sense only if spoken to a people already in exile in Babylon. Such passages, to which others could easily be added, show that the latter half of Isaiah presumes rather than predicts a postdestruction setting, making Isaiah the prophet a very unlikely author for these texts. Observations like these allow scholars to distinguish the material in terms of authorship, while enabling them to discern which of it was written earlier and which of it later.

2.2. Rough Edges in the Text. Because many biblical books (including the prophets) were not composed from scratch, but rather used preexisting sources, their literary character often includes rough edges. Many of the Prophetic Books are like a patchwork quilt, made of different pieces. Where these different pieces join, one often finds a rough edge, a disjuncture in the text better explained as the result of editing preexisting material than as wholly new composition. Scholars differ in their judgments as to what constitutes a disjuncture, and whether or not any one particular rough edge points to a composite feature of the text; but such edges exist, and the Hebrew text of the Prophetic Books abounds with them.

Take, for example, the opening verses of Ezekiel (Ezek 1:1-4), which, beginning with the first person in verse 1, shift abruptly to the third person in verses 2-3, and then without warning move back to the first person in verse 4. Also, "by the river Chebar" in verse 3 is slightly redundant, since this location is already given in verse 1. Thus, verses 2-3 usually are explained as an addition (Zimmerli, 100-101). Indeed, removing verses 2-3 produces a seamless text: "I saw visions of God . . . and I looked, and behold, a storm wind." Part of the purpose of this addition was to locate the date in verse 1 ("the fifth day of the month") in the time of Jehoiachin's exile, employing a form of title found elsewhere (e.g., Hag 1:1). Such disjunctures are often easiest to explain by positing the work of an editor, and attention to these throughout a book can yield insight into the editor's larger aims.

2.3. Differences in Style, Language or Theological Outlook. In conjunction with these first two points, one often finds differences in style, language or outlook. In the Gog oracles of Ezekiel 38—39, for example, W. A. Tooman notes several stylistic differences between this section and the rest of the book (Tooman, 65-72). While occasionally it is possible to explain such differences in terms of the strategy of a single author, this is not always the case; sometimes they do not appear to serve any particular function. When this is so, attention to editorial features of the text can often explain the shift. Thus, Tooman observes two discontinuities between Ezekiel 38—39 and the book: (1) the Gog oracles depict the restoration community in a manner "which does not correspond with its description in 33.1-37.28," for example, by

dividing the restoration into two periods; (2) the Gog oracles interrupt the connection between "the summary of restoration in 37.24-28 and its visionary depiction in chapters 40-48," a connection suggested by the fact that temple rebuilding is mentioned only in these two passages in the book (Tooman, 72-84). In the light of these discontinuities as well as the change in style, Tooman argues that the Gog oracles are a late insertion into the book, and he shows that these oracles have borrowed locutions from other biblical books (notably the Torah and the Prophets), being built up like a scriptural mosaic.

2.4. Fortschreibung. One feature of book formation in ancient Israel receiving renewed attention is known in German scholarship as *Fortschreibung.* Here a scribe or editor writes up new material in light of, and onto, the preexisting sources being used. This technique seems to have been especially important in the editing of the Prophetic Books (Kratz, 37-39). R. G. Kratz identifies at least three contexts from which such additions draw and for which they present themselves as guides to reading. (1) They can draw from the larger context of a book to which they are added (e.g. Jer MT 33:14-26 [see 1.1.1 above]). (2) Orienting themselves toward a whole book, these additions can also draw on a larger literary corpus outside that book, both to situate the book within that corpus and to supplement that larger literary context (e.g. Ezek 38—39 [see 2.3 above]). (3) Other such additions can draw from a narrow context but be oriented toward a larger strategy in the book.

Such is the case with Isaiah 7:15, which scholars have long argued is an addition reformulating the announcement of Immanuel's birth. Birth announcements in the OT are highly regular, in that where the explanation of the child's name is signaled by the conjunction *kî* ("because"), the explanation follows immediately after the announcement of his birth (so Is 8:3-4). In the case of Isaiah 7:14-17, the comment in Isaiah 7:15 breaks the pattern found everywhere else, so that it looks secondary to the original form of the sign. Strengthening this, Isaiah 7:15 appears to be a piece of *Fortschreibung,* composed by drawing on Isaiah 7:16 and Isaiah 7:22.

"For, before the lad *knows to reject the bad and*

choose the good, the land whose two kings you dread will be forsaken" (Is 7:16).

"For, everyone left in the midst of the land *will eat curds and honey*" (Is 7:22b).

The italic material in these verses is drawn together in Isaiah 7:15.

"Curds and honey he will eat until he knows to reject the bad and choose the good" (Is 7:15).

Apart from slightly different syntax in "to know" (probably necessitated by the joining of these two "pieces"), Isaiah 7:15 does not actually contain any new words. Thus, it is a model example of *Fortschreibung* that draws on its immediate context. Even so, this bit of editing should not be viewed narrowly. The same editor probably was at work in Isaiah 36—39, which shows many connections to Isaiah 7 and was also edited with respect to a "sign" given the king. All of this likely formed part of a larger strategy seeking to affirm the Davidic promise after exile (Stromberg 2011a, 107-27; 2011b, 205-28).

Paradoxically, such redaction aimed at the reader also reflects the earliest reception of the prophets, being explanation of the sources by the redactor. The broader methodological point here, however, is that by studying such allusions (or textual dependencies) scholars are able to gain further leverage on which texts came first and which came later in the process of formation.

2.5. The Cumulative Argument. The last principle to be mentioned is probably the most important: the cumulative nature of arguments about the formation of a passage or book in the prophetic literature. Although it probably is always possible to find an alternative explanation for any one of the features listed above when that feature stands alone, such an explanation becomes increasingly improbable the more such features appear in a single passage, as is the case with the examples mentioned above. When several of these features appear, a cumulative case begins to emerge wherein each adds weight to the other, so that an editorial explanation becomes the most plausible one.

3. The Formation of a Prophetic Book.

What were the motives behind and stages in the formation of a prophetic book? We can expect that each book will have had a unique history, but still there are lines of continuity to be drawn that help sketch a general picture of this process.

3.1. Motives. Before looking at the possible stages in the formation of a prophetic book, we should first consider the motives or impulses behind its production. Why, once the words of a prophet were written down, were these then made into a book receiving so much attention by the author(s) and editor(s) involved? What motivated these bookmakers?

A variety of motives are ascribed to these individuals (Childs; Clements, 217-29; Kratz, 32-48), but two features present themselves fairly consistently to the careful reader of these texts: (1) the editors of these books regarded the words that they had inherited as inspired and authoritative; (2) it was precisely this which motivated them to seek to enable that word (through editing) to speak in a new literary context and to new situations to which (it was presumed) it did speak (Stromberg 2011a, 84). Indeed, such a motive was anticipated by those first responsible for putting the prophets' words into writing, preserving these words for posterity seeing them as inspired. For example, Isaiah 8:16-18 and Isaiah 30:8-9 tie preserving the prophetic word with an anticipation of its future divine fulfillment (Kratz, 42, 45-46; Williamson 2000, 293-99). The importance for this process of putting the prophet's words in written form in the first place can scarcely be overemphasized. The prophetic word, once written, was able to become the object of studied reflection and in its new material form was able to live on beyond the prophet's own day, speaking to the circumstances of subsequent generations.

3.2. The Prophet's Message. Before the prophetic book there was the prophetic message. Any evaluation of the formation of this literature is bound to be guided by some notion of what was said by the actual prophet whose name the book bears. The problem of reconstructing the prophet's message arises above all else in connection with prophecies of *salvation and judgment, both of which are now found side by side in the Prophetic Books.

In reconstructing the preaching of the prophets, scholars have proposed different models for relating these contrasting prophecies (Köckert, Becker and Barthel; Kratz, 32-

48). At least four views are presented on the matter. (1) The prophets preached both destruction and salvation, the tension between the two arising either from different audiences addressed or from development in the prophets' thinking. (2) The prophets exhorted their audiences to *repentance, announcements of judgment scaring them into this posture, and words of salvation coaxing them into it. (3) The prophets preached inevitable judgment, the words of salvation only referring to wasted chances at restoration or being altogether secondary. (4) The prophets originally preached hope and salvation, as may be suggested by (in some cases) their close ties to the royal court. In this view, the prophecies of judgment are secondary.

The prophetic message also had a form. Many have argued their message was first and foremost oral, being short and poetic (Clements, 218-19). While this may have been the case for certain prophets in certain periods, the prophetic corpus preserves material generated over hundreds of years, over which time the content and the form of prophetic preaching were likely to have changed. Some prophecy may have focused on writing from the start (e.g., Ezekiel), some of it perhaps being purely literary with little or no connection to the message of a prophetic figure (e.g., Jonah, Malachi).

When decisions about a prophet's preaching are made the starting point in tracing the formation of a prophetic book, they inevitably determine the outcome. An alternative to this approach begins with the present form of the literature and works backwards to a conclusion. In practice, however, most scholars have oscillated between these two approaches.

3.3. From Prophet to Text. The messages of the prophets eventually were put into written form, some of them no doubt being written from the beginning (*see* Writing and Prophecy). This stage presented an opportunity to shape the prophetic message (Kratz, 39-46). Some recent work on this, looking at Assyrian prophetic texts in particular, argues against the long-held critical consensus that the prophets' message was primarily one of judgment. Noting that what a prophet said was bound up with what a prophet was, M. J. de Jong, for example, has made the case that the prophets functioned as servants of the state, of which they were, as a consequence, always supportive. It follows, then, that all of the prophetic mate-

rial announcing irrevocable judgment on the state must be secondary to the actual message preached by the prophets. Judgment entered their message when their words first received written form, judgment being read retrospectively into the earlier oracles in the light of the downfall of Israel and Judah to the Assyrians and Babylonians respectively. It remains to be seen whether such an argument persuades. The Assyrian prophecies are hardly representative of the whole phenomenon of prophecy in the ancient Near East; moreover, there is a closer analogue (the Deir ʿAlla text) that points in the opposite direction (Blum). Also, it needs to be asked whether such a view can do justice to the literary history of the Prophetic Books themselves, first-order evidence that must be dealt with in its own right.

3.4. From Text to Book. Once the prophetic message took on written form, it then was made into a book, a process that employed several editorial techniques: (1) compilation, whereby the separate oracles were gathered into a collection; (2) *Fortschreibung*, whereby new material was written in light of and onto the old (see 2.4 above); (3) juxtaposition, whereby the separate oracles sometimes were juxtaposed with each other in an effort to provide an interpretive context (as T. S. Hadjiev has argued for Amos 3:12; 9:9-10); (4) the order of preexisting material sometimes was rearranged, as with the oracles against the nations in Jeremiah that are found in the middle of the book in the LXX but at its end in the MT (Tov, 362n1). The result, at least for the Major Prophets, was a broad compositional design, summarized by some scholars in the following sequence: oracles against Israel/Judah, oracles against the nations, hope for Israel/Judah (so Isaiah, Jeremiah LXX, Ezekiel). It is everywhere evident that such editorial work aimed at producing strategies to guide the reader through the material.

The editors employing such techniques had at their disposal at least two methods for introducing their changes. They could write their addition into the margin of the scrolls (cf. 1QIs[a] XXXVIII, 21-22), or they could put the changes directly into the text when recopying the scroll (Stromberg 2011b, 143-45). At some point, major editorial work on these books ceased, and they were regarded as more or less complete. Once this occurred, the Prophetic Books entered a phase that scholars have called "transmission," wherein efforts were focused on preserving the scroll and faithfully recopying it, though even here sometimes additions of various sorts could be made (Stromberg 2011a, 99-102). The upshot of all of this is that some features of these texts owe their existence to source, others to strategy, and still others to transmission.

4. The Formation of the Prophetic Corpus.

The formation of the prophetic corpus was inseparable from the making of the books themselves, and, after a certain point, vice versa. Moreover, this formative process did not take place within a vacuum, but rather in the midst of, and as a force behind, Israel's history.

4.1. Historical Moments in the Formation of the Prophetic Corpus. With caution, we can pinpoint decisive moments in Israel's history that shaped the prophetic corpus, producing broad patterns throughout the whole. R. E. Clements describes three key moments in the process that produced the prophetic canon, outlining its effect on "prophetic eschatology" (Clements, 191-202).

First, when the northern kingdom of Israel fell to the Assyrians (722 BC), there arose a period of hope centered on Judah, a possible example being Hosea 3:5: "in the last days" the children of Israel "will seek the LORD their God and David their king."

Second, when the southern kingdom of Judah fell to the Babylonians (587 BC), there arose among the prophets a great voice of hope, leading to a reshaping and reinterpretation of the whole collection of antecedent prophecy. Thus, Hosea 3:5 will have been reread in the light of the destruction of Jerusalem as referring to an even further distant future. This destruction probably also led to the exilic prophecies of restoration in Isaiah 40—55 becoming the lens through which were read the preexilic prophecies of Isaiah 1—39 (Williamson 1994). This whole process arose out of Babylonian destruction, according to Clements, and gave the prophetic corpus a pattern of judgment followed by hope, hope for return to and restoration in the land.

Finally, of great significance to this process was the reestablishment of political and religious life in Jerusalem under Persian rule (539 BC). The actual "restoration" under the Persians fell far short of the expectations set by that great voice of hope that arose after Babylo-

nian destruction. This caused those responsible for the prophetic literature in this period to look to a more remote and transcendent future for fulfillment, a process clearly evident in, for example, the postexilic Isaiah 56—66 (Stromberg 2011b, 12-13, 74-141).

For Clements, the reinterpretation of older oracles that these events inspired took place within the formation of a canonical corpus of prophecy, a corpus that encouraged the development of a unifying frame of reference by which each of the Prophetic Books was affected. Thus, the formation of the books intersected with the formation of the prophetic canon, an important ingredient of which was the interpretive and editorial search for restoration (see Williamson 2000).

4.2. Collection and Composition. At some point the individual prophetic books were read together and in connection with this collected together into a prophetic corpus. Clements's essay raises an important question regarding this process: to what extent was composition a part of the process of collecting the individual prophetic books together?

This question can be illuminated by the Minor Prophets. Many now regard this collection as a book rather than a mere anthology, calling it the "Book of the Twelve." Not denying that this is a collection of more or less twelve books, they note that the earliest references to it indicate that it was written on a single scroll and regarded as a unity (e.g., Sir 49:10; Acts 7:42). They also note evidence suggesting that these books were intentionally arranged with respect to one another, via the repetition of certain phrases, for example (e.g., Joel 3:16 // Amos 1:2). This line of research has now reached the point where several scholars have argued that the formation of this collection entailed editorial additions seeking to bind the whole together (Wöhrle). If so, this would be a clear instance where composition belonged to the process of collecting individual prophetic books together.

Is there any evidence, however, that such a process lay behind the prophetic collection as a whole? Again, the Book of the *Twelve may suggest an answer. Scholars draw attention to the last few verses of Malachi, which come at the end of the Twelve and therefore at the end of the Prophets as a whole in the traditional Hebrew canon. These verses (Mal 4:4-6 [MT 3:22-24]) seem to be an editorial expansion corresponding to a similar addition at the end of the Pentateuch (Deut 34). Thus, just as the whole Pentateuch has been given a conclusion in Deuteronomy 34, so has the whole prophetic collection in Malachi 4:4-6. Supporting this conclusion, scholars observe a parallel set of additions at the beginning of Joshua and in Psalm 1 (Josh 1:8; Ps 1:2-3). Together, these expansions focus on the importance of the *tôrâ* ("instruction") of Moses and the return of prophecy. From this there emerges a redactional line across the whole of Scripture in whatever form it had at the time (see those cited in Wöhrle, 421-27).

In a striking manner, this redactional pattern aligns itself with the ordering of the OT books in the traditional Hebrew *canon (the Tanak: Torah [Pentateuch], Nebiim [Prophets], Ketubim [Writings]) (see table 1).

Torah	Nebiim	Ketubim
Deut 34	Josh 1:8 Mal 3:22-24	Ps 1:2-3

Table 1. Redactional Pattern of Hebrew

This, however, should not necessarily be taken to imply that the creation of the one coincided in time with that of the other; the Tanak may simply be a later reflection of the conception underlying this redaction, though one cannot rule out an early tripartite scriptural collection (note, e.g., Luke 24:44 and the prologue to Sirach [see Barrera]). However this is resolved, there is a great deal to be said for the probability of the redactional layer uncovered, and this view seems to be gaining ground in the debate. If this is correct, Malachi 4:4-6 presents us with evidence that the process of collecting the whole of the prophetic corpus entailed composition, composition oriented toward that collection, framing it in terms of eschatological expectation (cf. Clements above). This editorial work (if it is such) will have been undertaken in a period with changing notions about what a prophet was (Barton), so that, for example, Daniel (quite different from the other books and in fact excluded from the "prophets" in the Hebrew canon) was nevertheless eventually thought of as such.

5. Implications.

Two implications for the study of the Prophetic Books follow from this survey. First, if the prophetic literature had such a complex history of development, then it is no simple task to reconstruct the prophetic figures that stand behind these books. Second, much more attention needs to be given to how these books were to be read in the first place. Recent research in this area has undergone something of a sea change in how it regards the process driving the formation of this literature and, as a result, the final forms of the books that it produced (Kratz, 32-48; Stromberg 2011a, 55-94). Past scholarship tended to view these texts as the result of a series of unrelated, almost haphazard, additions, so that the books themselves received their present forms more by chance than intention. Scholars are now beginning to recognize the extent to which this process was highly deliberate, giving the prophetic literature shape and strategy, often embedded at the level of the whole book. Thus, these books, though composite, have literary strategies not discoverable by looking at the original isolated sayings of the prophets in their respective historical contexts.

See also EDITORIAL/REDACTION CRITICISM; FORM CRITICISM; INTERTEXTUALITY AND INNERBIBLICAL INTERPRETATION; PROPHECY AND TRADITION; WRITING AND PROPHECY.

BIBLIOGRAPHY. **J. T. Barrera,** "Origins of a Tripartite Old Testament Canon," in *The Canon Debate,* ed. L. M. McDonald and J. A. Sanders (Peabody, MA: Hendrickson, 2002) 128-45; **J. Barton,** *Oracles of God: Perceptions of Ancient Prophecy in Israel after the Exile* (New York: Oxford University Press, 1986); **E. Blum,** "Israels Prophetie im altorientalischen Kontext: Anmerkungen zu neueren religionsgeschichtlichen Thesen, " in *"From Ebla to Stellenbosch": Syro-Palestinian Religions and the Hebrew Bible,* ed. I. Cornelius and L. Jonker (ADPV 37; Wiesbaden: Harrassowitz, 2008) 81-115; **D. Carr,** *The Formation of the Hebrew Bible* (New York: Oxford Univeristy Press, 2011); **B. S. Childs,** "Retrospective Reading of the Old Testament Prophets," *ZAW* 108 (1996) 362-77; **R. E. Clements,** *Old Testament Prophecy: From Oracles to Canon* (Louisville: Westminster/John Knox, 1996); **M. J. de Jong,** "Biblical Prophecy—A Scribal Enterprise. The Old Testament Prophecy of Unconditional Judgement Considered as a Literary Phenomenon," *VT* 61 (2011) 39-70; **T. S. Hadjiev,** "The Context as Means of Redactional Reinterpretation in the Book of Amos," *JTS* 59 (2008) 655-68; **M. Köckert, U. Becker and J. Barthel,** "Das Problem des historischen Jesaja," in *Prophe-*

tie in Israel: Beiträge des Symposium "Das Alte Testament und die Kultur der Moderne" anlässlich des 100. Geburtstags Gerhard von Rads (1901-1971), Heidelberg, 18.-21. Oktober 2001, ed. I. Fischer, K. Schmid and H. G. M. Williamson (ATM 11; Münster: LIT Verlag, 2003) 105-36; **R. G. Kratz,** *Prophetenstudien: Kleine Schriften II* (FAT 74; Tübingen: Mohr Siebeck, 2011); **D. J. Reimer,** "Jeremiah Before the Exile?" in *In Search of Preexilic Israel: Proceedings of the Oxford Old Testament Seminar,* ed. J. Day (JSOTSup 406; London: T & T Clark International, 2004) 207-24; **K. Schmid,** *Schriftgelehrte Traditionsliteratur: Fallstudien zur innerbiblischen Schriftauslegung im Alten Testament* (FAT 77; Tübingen: Mohr Siebeck, 2011); **J. Stromberg,** *An Introduction to the Study of Isaiah* (London: T & T Clark, 2011a); idem, *Isaiah after Exile: The Author of Third Isaiah as Reader and Redactor of the Book* (OTM; Oxford: Oxford University Press, 2011b); **J. H. Tigay,** ed., *Empirical Models for Biblical Criticism* (Philadelphia: University of Pennsylvania Press, 1985);

W. A. Tooman, *Gog of Magog: Reuse of Scripture and Compositional Technique in Ezekiel 38-39* (FAT 2/52; Tübingen: Mohr Siebeck, 2011); **E. Tov,** *The Greek and Hebrew Bible: Collected Essays on the Septuagint* (VTSup 72; Leiden: E. J. Brill, 1999); **H. G. M. Williamson,** *The Book Called Isaiah: Deutero-Isaiah's Role in Composition and Redaction* (Oxford: Clarendon Press, 1994); idem, "Hope under Judgement: The Prophets of the Eighth Century BCE," *EvQ* 72 (2000) 291-306; **J. Wöhrle,** *Der Abschluss des Zwölfprophetenbuches: Buchübergreifende Redaktionsprozesse in den späten Sammlungen* (BZAW 389; Berlin: de Gruyter, 2008); **W. Zimmerli,** *Ezekiel 1: A Commentary on the Book of Ezekiel, Chapters 1-24,* trans. R. E. Clements, ed. F. M. Cross and K. Baltzer (Hermeneia; Philadelphia: Fortress, 1979).

J. Stromberg

FOUR EMPIRES. *See* DANIEL: BOOK OF.

FUTURE. *See* ESCHATOLOGY.

G

GOD

It has been asserted that God is the "center" of OT theology. If it is true of the OT as a whole, it is especially true in the prophets. Here he is not only the primary character; he is also the primary speaker, with much of the material said to have been received in verbal form directly from him. He is the one who calls Israel to account, begging, pleading, cajoling, thundering, cursing and judging. He intrudes into the historical experience of the people at every level, refusing to let them escape from him in the easy practice of ritual or in the syncretism that was always so attractive. As such, he reveals himself to Israel in a variety of roles, which we will explore below.

    1. Overview
    2. Revealer
    3. Creator
    4. The Only God
    5. Lord of History
    6. Sovereign King
    7. Covenant Partner
    8. Father
    9. Shepherd
    10. Judge
    11. Deliverer/Redeemer

1. Overview.

Much of the revelation of God in the prophets is shaped on the anvil of the geopolitical issues confronting the prophets during the period when the prophetic literature was first spoken and written. While it is true that from the biblical perspective prophetic ministry spanned the entire period of Israel's experience from Abraham to Malachi, the recorded prophetic literature covers a much shorter time span, from about 775 BC to about 425 BC (both dates being subject to decisions about the dating of the book of Joel [some wish to date the completion of the book of Daniel to 167 BC]). During that period Israel and Judah were confronted with a succession of three different "world" empires: Assyria, Babylon and Persia (*see* Israelite History). Thus, most of the prophetic utterances were made against that backdrop. In particular, these utterances addressed the question of interpreting that historical situation. What did the rise of these great powers mean for Israel's understanding of Yahweh? If Israel and Judah were conquered, did this mean that Yahweh had failed them? If not, why would he have allowed or, worse yet, caused these conquests to occur, given the favored status with Yahweh that Jacob's descendants supposedly enjoyed?

Readers of the prophetic literature, whether first-time or frequent, often share the same reaction, that the picture of Yahweh here is so negative. In fact, the widely held opinion that the God of the NT is not the same God as the one found in the OT is largely based on conclusions drawn from a reading of the prophetic books. To be sure, the reaction is not without basis. As A. Heschel famously observed a half-century ago, Yahweh is a God of pathos. He cares deeply about his people; he is jealous for them. He is neither Plato's "The Good" nor Aristotle's "Unmoved Mover." He is overjoyed when his creatures find their true potential in a wholehearted loving relationship with him, doing what they were made to do, and he is furious when they prostitute themselves in relationships that are self-serving and ultimately destructive. Two factors dictate that there will be more of the latter divine response than the former in the Prophetic Books. The first is that humans are predisposed to self-destruction. This is first described as early as Genesis 6:5. We are not neutral in regard to God; we are inclined away from him. This predisposition to serve self rather than God (in spite of a sworn covenant) was coming to its climax in Israel and Judah during the period when the prophets were writing. Yahweh could not be neutral about the patterns into which his bride was settling.

The second factor is the historic setting of international *warfare and conquest during which the prophets spoke and wrote. Destruction, bloodshed and oppression were the norms. How was this to be interpreted? Were these conditions something that existed in spite of the wishes of a mild and essentially helpless heavenly observer? Or did he directly cause them as expressions of an essentially vindictive and vengeful character? Or did he use *sinful human behaviors to accomplish what he intended to be curative outcomes? The latter is the interpretation that the prophets were inspired to give. But even here we do not see an uninvolved practitioner administering certain palliatives. Hardly! God sees his beloved unconcernedly throwing herself into an abyss, and although he intends to use that experience for ultimate redemption, he can in no way forgo his horror and fury that she would do this to herself and to him.

But this description of God in the Prophetic Books highlights an important point. These books are not intended to be read in isolation from the rest of the canon. The God of the prophets is also "the God and Father of our Lord Jesus Christ, the Father of compassion and the God of all comfort" as the apostle Paul styles him (2 Cor 1:3). This is precisely the point that the church fathers were seeking to make when they refused to give up the thirty-nine books of the OT. The NT perspective of Yahweh is part of a larger revelation, functioning as a corrective and a redressing of the balances. But in the same way, the prophetic picture corrects the sentimental understanding of God that can emerge from reading the NT alone. The thundering judge in the Prophetic Books is at the same time the beckoning savior in the NT. Both of these aspects must be held in tension if we are to have a correct understanding of the biblical God.

At the same time, it should not be thought that the NT perspective is an alien one somehow imposed as a corrective on a resistant OT. It is precisely because God loves not just his people, but all people, that he cares so deeply

for them. Jonah knew this when he tried to avoid going to Nineveh. He knew that if even the cruel Assyrians would *repent, Yahweh would be quick to *forgive them (Jon 4:2). In substantiating his statement, the prophet clearly is alluding to the expression of God's tenderness and grace found already in Exodus 34:6-7. We might think also of the divine cry of love for Israel found in Hosea 11:8-9. So also, when the postexilic Judeans were accusing Yahweh of not blessing them enough, his first utterance is not condemnation but rather a proclamation that he has always loved them (Mal 1:2). So if the dominant motif in the prophets is divine anger, it must not be allowed to blot out the reality of the underlying divine compassion.

Finally, it should be said that God is described in so many ways in the prophets that any attempt to organize these descriptions into discrete categories will involve a good deal of theological interpretation, and that will certainly be the case in this essay.

2. Revealer.

In recent years a good deal has been made of the fact that persons in other cultures around Israel spoke messages that they reported to have been received from a god (see Ancient Near Eastern Prophecy). This is especially the case at Mari, an Amorite city on the middle Euphrates dating about the middle of the second millennium BC. In particular, many of these messages include a formula such as "This is what X [the god] says." This has led some scholars to suggest that there is really nothing unique about the Israelite prophetic messages. To be sure, it is said, they are longer and more complex, but in terms of their basic idea—a spoken message received from a divine personage—they are of the same genre.

As with many other points of biblical theology, we can agree that these structural similarities clearly exist. However, that does not mean that the two literatures are the same thing, or that they are doing the same thing. In particular, they are not the same kind of revelation (if the Mari prophecies are revelations at all). Prophecies in the ancient Near East were almost entirely given to the business of predicting the future for the benefit of the prophet's patron. This sort of prophecy existed in Israel at various points, as the Bible reports (1 Kings

22:5-6). But those prophetic messages of which the biblical books of prophecy consist are of a very different order. Here prediction of the future is not the primary point; to be sure, it is essential, but it is secondary to the main point. That main point is a challenge to the moral behavior of the hearers, which moral life is clearly defined by the moral character of Yahweh as that character was defined in the covenant. This is precisely the difference between a false prophet and a true prophet in biblical terms. The true prophet conditioned his predictions of the future upon the responses of the people to these moral challenges. The false prophet confirmed the people in their faulty moral choices with unconditional promises of a rosy future (see Jer 23:16-18).

Some, however, will point out that the prophets at Mari and elsewhere in the ancient Near East did not only make predictions about the future, but also they revealed the will of the god in the same way that the Israelite prophets revealed the will of Yahweh. Again, this is misleading. Elsewhere, the will of the gods is almost entirely related to specific questions or events. To be sure, there are instances where that took place in Israel (although the reports of the incidents are frequently accompanied by prophetic retorts that this is not what the questioner should be concerned about, as in the case of King Jeroboam's wife and the prophet Ahijah [1 Kings 14:1-18]). But in the Prophetic Books the revealed will of God rarely has to do with specific events. Instead, it is regularly addressed to issues of moral character.

This emphasis on the God who speaks is at the heart of the biblical message. It is so because of the understanding of reality that prevails throughout the Bible. That understanding is grounded in the concept of transcendence. Yahweh is not continuous with the cosmos. He is discontinuous with it; he is other than it. In the opposing worldview deity is coterminous with the cosmos. Thus, to experience the cosmos is to experience deity. To know the cosmos is to know deity. In that understanding language is distinctly secondary. Immediate experience is the preferred means of knowing. This is not the case in the Bible. Since God is not the cosmos, experience of the cosmos is not, de facto, to know God. So how are the creatures to know the transcendent Creator, if they are to know him at all? It is through the means

whereby persons, who are by definition discontinuous with each other, communicate: language. Words are the means of sharing experience and knowledge across the divide. Thus, it is no accident that Yahweh speaks creation into existence. It does not emerge from his body, nor is it an effusion of his being. He is other than it.

This understanding permeates the prophetic literature. God communicates with persons in complex language. Thus, the prophets are not mere mouthpieces for God, but dialogue partners. *Form critics, insisting upon the commonality of Hebrew prophecy with prophecy elsewhere in the ancient Near East, sometimes hypothesize that the initial messages of the prophets must have been short statements that have then been expanded in the mouth of God by the prophets. But the evidence for such claims is questionable at best. Instead, the text has long, complex messages from God, which the prophets sometimes question or to which they even object. Yahweh, in revealing himself to the prophets, is modeling the kinds of relationships that he is seeking with all people. The expectation is not that the prophet's personality will be submerged into God's, or that the prophet will become merely a mouthpiece for God. Rather, the prophet is expected to be a willing partner with God, conscious of the issues and paying the price for this demanding and dynamic relationship.

The dynamics of the divine revelation are seen in the prophetic calls narrated in the text. They range from Amos's "the LORD took me" (Amos 7:15) to the markedly indirect "Whom shall I send?" of Isaiah (Is 6:8). Between these extremes are the call of Ezekiel, with its visual cues culminating in a clear command to eat a scroll whose bitter words he found strangely sweet (Ezek 3:1-3), and Jeremiah's back-and-forth dialogue concerning his suitability (Jer 1:4-10). Whatever else we may see in these accounts, we do not see any formulaic sameness. Yahweh is not communicating formulae; he is in a complex, life-and-death dialogue through the prophets with people about whose life and character he is passionately concerned. Thus, he communicated in a variety of forms and manners, given differing situations, in order to cross the uncrossable divide between the Creator and his creatures. Something of this variety is seen in the visual means of communication that God used. We can think of the decayed loincloth, the marred pot, and the broken pot in Jeremiah (Jer 13:1-7; 18:1-4; 19:10-11). Or we can see Ezekiel lying on one side and then the other for many long days (Ezek 4:4-6). Then there is the urbane Isaiah going naked for three years (Is 20:3). All of these "signs" are accompanied by words, but without the visual markers the words would be far less effective (*see* Sign Acts).

To be sure, there are some formulae used especially to mark the openings and closings of blocks of communications. The most common of these is "Thus says the LORD," which occurs more than 350 times. However, it is not simply a stock formula, as is demonstrated by the clustering of its usages. While the phrase occurs thirty-six times in Isaiah, 149 times in Jeremiah and 123 times in Ezekiel, it does not occur at all in Hosea, Joel, Jonah, Habakkuk, Zephaniah or Malachi. The absence of the phrase in these books short-circuits a possible response to its absence in Daniel, which is that Daniel is not really to be considered a prophetic book. Another formula of revelation is "the *word of the LORD" ("Hear the word of the LORD" 31x [Isaiah 4x; Jeremiah 14x; Ezekiel 10x; Hosea 1x; Amos 2x]; "The word of the LORD came" 62x [Jeremiah 10x; Ezekiel 48x; Zechariah 4x]). Daniel says that "a word went forth" in response to his *prayer, and the angelic messenger is detailed to declare it (Dan 9:23), and in Daniel 10:1 it is said that "a word was revealed" to Daniel. Isaiah also uses the same term in the context of verbal communication four times (Is 22:14; 23:1; 40:5; 53:1) Others are "the mouth of the LORD has spoken (Is 1:20; 40:5; 58:14; Jer 9:12; Mic 4:4) and the simple "the LORD spoke to me" (Is 8:5, 11; Jer 28:1; Ezek 2:2; 3:24). But these are markers, and they do not confine in any way what follows, which may range from admonition to exhortation to announcement of judgment to announcement of *salvation. This variety has been one of the confounding factors for form critics. In several cases there are no comparable forms to be found elsewhere, as is the case with most of the so-called salvation oracles in the Bible. And in others the freedom with which the prophets handle the supposed forms seems inexplicable. Critics too often have resorted to large-scale emendation in order to make the passages conform to the expected norm. All this is to say that the commu-

nication from Yahweh that the prophets claim to have received is only consistent with a complex and creative personality who wishes to communicate and not merely to make pronouncements.

3. Creator.

It is widely known that the verb "to create" (Heb *bara'*) occurs more frequently in Isaiah than in Genesis (Isaiah 21x, Genesis 11x, with seven of the eleven in Genesis referring to the creation of humanity). The majority of the occurrences in Isaiah (13x) are found in Isaiah 40—45, where the prophet is insisting that Yahweh is the only God, and that he alone knows the future. The usage of *bara'* in the OT shows that it is speaking of bringing into existence something that had never existed before or of causing something to happen that had never happened previously (cf. Num 16:20). This point is critical to Isaiah's argument. He is insisting that the gods, being part of this world, are unable to materially affect the course of things by doing something new. Since they are only personalized expressions of the psycho-socio-physical forces of the cosmos, they are captive to its cycles and cannot change those in any significant way. But the God who brought the cosmos into existence can change its patterns in any way he chooses. He can cause springs to erupt in the desert, or he can dry up the Euphrates (Is 43:19-20).

This idea was of extreme importance to the Judean exiles. In all the history of the practice of exile, we never hear of anyone going home again. This was one of the purposes of the practice: to destroy the distinctive culture of the various people groups and integrate them into the larger culture of the empire. Thus, from that point of view, it was foolish to think of being delivered from captivity and returning home with one's culture in some sense intact. If it had never happened before, it was impossible for it to happen now. Isaiah agrees with that point: the gods had never done a new thing in the past and certainly could not do a new thing in the future. But, the prophet insists, Yahweh is not a personified cosmic force. He is the one who brought the cosmos into existence, and thus he can do something that had never been done before: take his people back out of the hand of the conqueror.

The idea of God as revealer is directly associated with his role as the Creator (*see* Creation Theology). The idol worshipers were challenged to report just one time when one of their gods had specifically predicted a future event prior to its occurrence (Is 43:9; 44:7-8). The clear answer is that it had never happened. It had not happened for two reasons. First, since the gods were only the personified forces of the cosmos, they were incapable of complex speech dealing with unknown variables in keeping with the unique situation and needs of a dialogue partner. But it was not beyond Yahweh. Through the prophet, Yahweh reminded them that he had specifically predicted the *exile, when all the conventional wisdom of Israelite theology had seen that as impossible. But even more astonishing, he had predicted return from exile at the hands of a pagan ruler whom he dared to name far in advance. How could he speak in these ways? It was simply because he was not a captive of the cosmic system, but rather had created it.

The second reason why Yahweh's challenge could not be answered by the idol worshipers was that the gods were incapable of doing anything new. They could not predict what the cosmic system would do in the future except insofar as it replicated the general patterns of the past. The thunderstorm hardly knows what track it will take, except that it might "know" that it will not move from east to west in the northern hemisphere. The gods had not created the cosmos as a brand new thing, but had only ordered the chaotic matter that was eternally existent. Thus, they could hardly inform their worshipers of some new and unique thing that they would do in the future that had never happened before. They were incapable of doing such things, and furthermore, there is no way of accounting for new things, given that worldview. If events did occur that had no precedence, then some way had to be found at once to integrate them into the preexisting system and, in effect, to make them "not new," because something genuinely new would call that entire understanding of reality into question.

On the other hand, the glory of Yahweh is that as Creator he is constantly doing new things. Thus, in Isaiah 43:18, after a clear allusion to the *exodus, he tells the people to forget the former things because he is about to do something new. He was not going to replicate the exodus in this deliverance. Why should he?

He had already done that once! Clearly, the hearers were expected to remember the former things in regard to what they taught about the goodness, power and dependability of God. But when it came to freezing what he had done and how he had done it, they were to forget all that. Why are humans inclined to do those things? It is because of our inveterate need for control. The entire thought system of paganism stems from this need. If we can find ways of integrating whatever happens into what always happens, we protect ourselves from unfortunate surprises and give ourselves the illusion of control. But the Creator is not subject to our control.

Another term that Isaiah uses to speak of Yahweh as creator is "maker" (*'ōśê* [Is 17:7; 29:16; 51:13; 54:5; see also Is 45:12]). The prophet uses the term to connote the folly of the thing that has been made disputing the terms of its making with its maker, of the fact that in the end those who have endured judgment will turn back to their maker, of despair being a result of forgetting who has made us, and of the fact that God is not merely our maker but also is our husband and redeemer. Fundamental to all of these is the idea that the one who made us not only has the right to pass judgment on our behavior, but also is able to break into the endless circle of cause and effect and deliver us into a new plane of living. This is possible because Yahweh, the Creator and the Maker, is himself the ultimate cause and is not captive to any other causes.

But if the teaching of God as the Creator is especially prominent in the book of Isaiah, it is by no means missing from the other prophets. Although the term *bara'* with reference to God occurs only in Jeremiah (Jer 31:22), Amos (Amos 4:13) and Malachi (Mal 2:10), the concept of Yahweh as the sole originator of the cosmos is to be found in several of the other prophets, especially in Jeremiah. At times it is expressed in the context of diatribes against *idolatry, as in Isaiah. So Jeremiah can say that the gods who did not make the heavens and the earth will perish, whereas God made the earth, the world and the heavens by his own power and wisdom (Jer 10:10-16). The concept is also used to provide the basis for God's judgment of his people (Amos 4:12-13; 5:7-10) and his redemption of them. So, Zechariah uses Yahweh's role as creator to explain how it is that tiny Jerusalem will become "a cup of stumbling" for the surrounding *nations (Zech 12:1-2). These are possible because the Creator is necessarily the lord of history (see 5 below). It is because Yahweh is the Creator that he can turn over all the nations to his servant Nebuchadnezzar (Jer 27:5) (although Daniel does not appeal to creation, he makes a similar argument with regard to God's absolute sovereignty [see 5.2 below]). Likewise, in his prayer recorded in Jeremiah 32:17-25. Jeremiah makes creation the basis for Yahweh's lordship of history. Thus, he is able to bring about both judgment and redemption (Jer 33:2). Additional occurrences of the concept appear in Hosea, Jonah and Malachi. Hosea charged that instead of trusting their Maker, Israel was turning to fortifications and palaces (Hos 8:14). Jonah confessed to the terrified sailors that he served the God who made the sea and the land (Jon 1:9), which truly terrified them. Malachi argued that since Israel was created by the one God, the Israelites have an obligation to one another (Mal 2:10).

4. The Only God.

The idea that Yahweh is the Creator of the cosmos is directly related to the idea of his uniqueness. It would be difficult to say which of these concepts came first, however, and it may be that both sprang from the understanding that Yahweh is not a part of the cosmos, is transcendent. Clearly, there can only be one Being in the universe who is other than all other beings. In the same way, then, it is appropriate to believe that this Being is the cause of the existence of the cosmos. He is not merely the orderer of preexistent and eternal matter as is the chief god in the misnomered "creation accounts" among Israel's neighbors; rather, he brings something into existence that did not exist before. He is the only God.

As with creation, the uniqueness of Yahweh is given special prominence in Isaiah. Several times it is said that Yahweh is God, and there is no other (Is 45:5-6, 14, 18, 21-22; 46:9; see also Joel 2:27). But even when the point is not expressed this directly, there is no question of its presence. The significance of the repeated attacks against idolatry lies here. This is not to say that it would be permissible to worship other gods if they were not represented by idols; rather, it is precisely because the worship of other gods is inextricable from idolatry that it is wrong to worship them. They are not gods; they are like the sticks and stones representing them, the creations of human ingenuity. Thus, idols are an abomination (tô'ēbâ), an offense to the creation order, as is the worship of them (Is 41:24; 44:19; 66:3; Jer 13:26; 16:18; 32:32, 34; 44:22; Ezek 5:11; 6:9, 11). Ezekiel's customary reference to idols as gillûlîm ("round things"), probably a scatological term, reinforces this inference. We may *worship our Maker, or we may worship what we have made. But what we have made is not worthy of the term "god." There is only one worthy of that term. This truth is expressed in the Bible in the phrase "the living God" (as opposed to the lifeless gods). Thus, it is significant that King Darius calls Yahweh this in response to Daniel's deliverance from the lions (Dan 6:26). Another term of derision applied to the gods is šiqqûṣ, something disgusting and worthless. So Daniel sees the setting up of the šiqqûṣ šōmēm ("the abomination of desolation") in the *temple in Jerusalem as signaling the beginning of the final struggles of earth. It is a contest between the living God and the antithesis of God: something made attempting to usurp the power and prerogatives of the Maker (see also Hos 8:6; 14:3; Hab 2:18-20). In Jonah the point is made by implication: it is Yahweh who is the God of Assyria, not some other. Habakkuk (Hab 1:12) speaks of his God as the one who will not die (in contrast to the other gods, who are already dead). Zechariah predicts that the day will come when the very names of the idols will perish from the land (Zech 13:1), and ultimately the name of Yahweh will be the only divine name on the earth (Zech 14:9; so also Mal 1:11).

The transcendence of God that makes him the only God is especially underlined in the prophets by their univocal attacks on religious ritual performed on the basis of sympathetic magic. In paganism, where the gods are simply personifications of the forces of the cosmos, a fundamental doctrine is correspondence: the god is the tree, and the tree is the god. Therefore, what is done to the tree is necessarily done to the god. This becomes the whole rationale for ritual. One's attitudes toward the god and behavior in other areas of life have no bearing on the efficacy of the ritual. If the ritual is done correctly, then the links between humanity, nature and deity are intact, and the desired result is guaranteed. This is a very comfortable doctrine because it gives humans the illusion of control. It was no less attractive to the Israelites than it was to their neighbors. Yet, the prophets, from Isaiah to Malachi, are uniform in their attacks on ritual conceived in this way. This is so much the case that one even finds Amos, speaking for God, saying, in effect, "I never commanded you to offer sacrifices" (Amos 5:21-26), an obviously hyperbolic statement intended to convey the point that the people thought that *sacrifices were the end, when in fact the people themselves were the end, as seen in the command to love the Lord with their whole hearts. The faithful offering of sacrifices would be pleasing to God if that activity actually represented wholehearted devotion to God (Joel 2:15-17; Mal 3:3-4), but when it was engaged in as a means of placating God while "worshipers" kept their lives for themselves, it was deeply disgusting to God (Is 1:10-15; 65:1-5; Jer 14:12; Hos 5:6; Amos 4:4, 5; 5:21; 8:10). Since this manipulative understanding of ritual is at the heart of paganism, when the Israelites worshiped Yahweh in this way they soon fell prey to the worship of the manufactured gods of their neighbors. To this the prophets reacted with even greater violence. Ezekiel's vision of the defiled temple in Jerusalem (Ezek 8:1 – 10:22) is the most notable expression of this outrage, but it is found in many of the other prophetic writings as well (e.g., Jer 7:1-11; Hos 4:11-13; Zeph 1:4-6).

A transcendent God cannot be manipulated through earthly rituals. So how is he to be related to? The only possibilities are surrender and trust. But those are so intangible; how can we know we have done these things? The evidence, the prophets tell us, is lives that reflect the character of Yahweh. If we do what he does and act as he acts, then it is clear that we are wholly devoted to him. So Isaiah says that instead of ritualistic religion we should be practicing good and rejecting *evil by seeking justice, rebuking the oppressor, defending the fatherless and pleading for the widow (Is 1:16-17). This thought is echoed again and again (Jer 5:26-29; Ezek 22:6-12; Dan 9:10; Hos 4:1-2; Amos 5:10-15; Mic 6:6-8; Zeph 3:11-13; Zech 7:9-10; Mal 2:7-8) (see 7 below). It is as we value humans as ends and not as means that we testify to the amazing character of the biblical God. When we care for those who are incapable of returning the favor, we show that we do indeed know God, who is defined by self-denying, self-giving love.

Another way of expressing the uniqueness of God in the prophets is found primarily in the book of Isaiah. This is the title "the Holy One of Israel." The title occurs only thirty-one times in the Bible (including the one occurrence of "the Holy One of Jacob" in Isaiah), of which twenty-six are in Isaiah. It is tempting to believe that the overwhelming nature of the experience of God's holiness described in Isaiah 6 stamped itself on Isaiah's thinking in an unforgettable way. "Holiness" is a way of expressing divine otherness, and the threefold "Holy, holy, holy is the LORD of hosts" (Is 6:3) is saying that Yahweh is the only truly holy being in the universe. He alone is "Other," and thus it is that the whole earth is full of his glory and not that of any other.

5. Lord of History.

5.1. A Different Understanding of Time. One of the most remarkable features of the Israelite prophetic understanding is that human choices in the present can affect the future. This idea that the future is not merely a recycling of the past, and the present is directly related to the two concepts of Yahweh as creator and revealer. In the worldview of continuity the future is dictated by what has already happened. So the outcome of one's life is shaped by the position of the stars on the day of one's birth. Time is a never-ending cycle, coming from nowhere and going nowhere, without overall meaning or purpose. But once it is granted that there was a distinct beginning to time, that this beginning was purposive, and that this purpose can be known, progress in time becomes a real possibility. Coupled to those ideas is the idea that humans are persons in the image of God, which means that their actions are free, not compelled by continuities with forces outside of themselves. The final component that the Bible brings to this confluence of ideas is that God speaks promises in the present whose fulfillment in the future is contingent upon subsequent human choices. When all of these concepts are brought together, as they are in the Bible, a whole new way of thinking about time becomes possible.

This new way of thinking can be seen in the interchange between divine pronouncements, human choices and the eventual outcome. God can make an unequivocal statement about something bad that is going to happen in the future, something that is a result of a series of bad choices in the past. These choices were bad because they did not conform to the character and purpose of the Creator, as revealed either explicitly (as in the covenant) or implicitly (through reflection on the creation). So Jonah was detailed to inform Nineveh that in forty days time the city would be destroyed. There were no contingencies in that pronouncement; it *would* happen. However, the Assyrian people chose to repent of their bad choices, and God changed his mind, something that Jonah knew was a distinct possibility. He knew this because he knew that Yahweh's purpose is not to destroy the wicked, but rather to move them to changed behavior (Jon 3:4—4:3; see also Ezek 18:23). The same point is implicit in Jeremiah. The prophet repeatedly says that Judah has no hope of avoiding the coming exile. The sins of Manasseh had come to their full fruition, and the end was irreversible (Jer 15:4). Yet, at the same time, Jeremiah fervently called for repentance on the part of the people. The implication is clear: even at that late date, if the Judeans had responded with genuine, far-reaching repentance, the exile would not have happened.

The principle remains in effect even when the predicted bad outcome was not the result of bad choices. So Isaiah informed Hezekiah that he was going to die, and as with Assyria, there were no contingencies in the pronouncement (Is 38:1). But Hezekiah entered into a dialogue with Yahweh, reminding him of all the good choices that he had made in his life, as summed up in the claim that he had walked before Yahweh with a whole (i.e., undivided) heart. As a result, he was granted fifteen more years of life. Obviously, Hezekiah was not telling Yahweh something that he did not already know. Once again, it is divine-human dialogue that is in play, with a possible purpose of helping Hezekiah recall what was important for his own life in any future that he might have.

None of this is to say that the prophets think that human choices are never constrained, or that they know nothing of historical conditioning. It seems very probable that this is the point in the mysterious command of Yahweh to Isaiah in his call. The prophet was told to preach a message that would blind eyes, deafen ears and fatten hearts. It seems that what is being said is

that if Isaiah is faithful and preaches the full counsel of God, his own generation was so far gone that his message would only drive them farther from God. It would have to be a later generation—in fact, one after the exile—that would be in a position to hear. That understanding is supported by the prophet's words in Isaiah 8, where he seals his message and entrusts it to his disciples. All this is to say that the prophets do not consider Yahweh's lordship over history in some simplistic way. Just as the prophetic message came through a complex communicative interaction between the prophets and God, so the shaping of history was the result of such a complex historical dialogue between the Creator/Revealer and human persons whom he wished to see make the right historical choices.

5.2. Events in Time and Space under God's Control. In the ancient Near Eastern world of the prophets it was understood that when nations fought, their gods were fighting as well. Thus, geopolitical realities reflected divine realities. Whichever nation triumphed did so because its gods had triumphed over the conquered nation's gods. This undoubtedly lay behind the Israelite conviction that they could not fall to the Mesopotamian powers that were sweeping westward on their way to dominating Egypt. After all, in Israel's view, Yahweh was supreme over the other gods. In that light, he could not allow his people to be defeated. A variant on this theme appears in the Assyrian interchange with Hezekiah and his ambassadors in Isaiah 36—37. Here, the Assyrian emperor, Sennacherib, does not even invoke his gods, instead claiming in his own power to have conquered the gods of all the nations and "thrown them into the fire" (Is 37:19; see also Is 10:10-11). But the point remains the same: if a nation is defeated, it is because its gods were defeated. The one caveat that must be entered regarding this pattern has to do with some of the ancient Near Eastern laments over city destructions. In these cases, the city was understood to have been destroyed because its god or goddess had abandoned it. Thus, the god was not defeated per se, but voluntarily surrendered his or her property.

The understanding of the Hebrew prophets does not conform to any of these. The geopolitical events in Israel's world have one cause alone: the will of Yahweh. He directs the movements of nations; they are merely tools in his hand. So Assyria is merely the axe in Yahweh's hand (Is 10:15). It may think that it swings itself, but that is no more the case with Assyria than it is with a literal axe. Furthermore, the events that were taking place during the tumultuous years of 850 BC to 400 BC were not the result of self-made tyrants choosing to exalt themselves; rather, they were the outworking of a divine strategy that had been in effect from the beginning (Is 14:26-27; 46:10; 55:11; Jer 29:11). This is not to say that these nations were mere puppets conforming to some timeless blueprint that admitted of no exceptions. As noted above, Yahweh was, and is, infinitely flexible in light of good and bad human choices. But his strategy—restoring the world from the effects of human sin—is unchanging, and the actions of Assyria, Babylon and Persia were made to fit seamlessly into that divine strategy.

This point is nowhere made more clearly than in the narratives of Daniel. Nebuchadnezzar understood himself to be the ruling figure in the world and to be where he was and what he was as a result of his own superior ability and intellect. But that was not the case; it is Yahweh who makes and deposes kings and kingdoms. Nebuchadnezzar had been allowed to hold the place he did by the gracious permission of Yahweh, and unless he acknowledged that fact, he was no more than one of the cattle in the field (Dan 4:31). The fact is that "the Most High rules in the kingdom of men and gives it to whomever he chooses" (Dan 4:17, 25, 32; 5:21). This is an important insight into the prophetic understanding of the divine-human relationship: unlike the animals, humans have the capacity to recognize the gifts a good God has given them. If we do not recognize that fact, we are no better than the animals. With regard to Nebuchadnezzar, Jeremiah makes a similar point: Nebuchadnezzar is to be obeyed and his covenant with Judah is to be kept because he is Yahweh's servant, doing Yahweh's work in the world (Jer 27:6-8). Ezekiel makes a similar point: in attacking Tyre, Nebuchadnezzar is Yahweh's worker, carrying out Yahweh's judgment, and if that attack is not completely successful, he will be given Egypt in compensation (Ezek 29:18-19). So much for lofty imperial pretensions to independent action! A further example of this lordship over history as it relates to persons is found in Isaiah's references to Cyrus. This Persian emperor, undoubtedly the most powerful person

in the world of his day, is claimed in the present book to have been named 125 years before his birth and given the function of restoring exiled Israel to its homeland. For doing this, he, like Nebuchadnezzar, before him, will be given not only Egypt, but Ethiopia as well. The book goes so far as to name Cyrus as Yahweh's *mašîaḥ*, his "anointed one," for the purpose of restoring Jerusalem (Is 44:28—45:1).

One final expression of Yahweh's lordship over history is found in the oracles against the nations. Collections of the oracles appear in Isaiah, Jeremiah and Ezekiel, and the books of Nahum and Obadiah are each such an oracle, against Assyria and Edom respectively. Habakkuk 2 is an oracle against Babylon, and Zephaniah 2 is composed of brief oracles against several nations. In Zechariah there are no oracles as such, but the first three visions (Zech 1:7—2:13) make the point that Yahweh has made it so that the nations no longer pose a threat to his people. Then, in Zechariah 14, the final chapter, Yahweh uses his people to destroy the enemy nations. Finally, Amos 1 is composed of a series of judgments pronounced on various nations around Israel. All of these are a way of expressing the point that the whole world is under the lordship of Yahweh and will be held accountable for the historical choices that the nations have made. For the prophets, Yahweh is not one of the gods of the world; he is the only God, and there is no nation that can independently shape its own destiny without reference to him.

In the three Major Prophets the placement of the collections is significant. In Isaiah they appear in Isaiah 13—23, just after the section composed of Isaiah 7—12, which details the full implications of Ahaz's disastrous choice to rely on Assyria rather than the Lord for protection from Israel and Syria. In this position the oracles are showing that it is foolish to trust any of the nations of humanity because all of them are historically accountable to Yahweh, and because the only final hope that they have is in Yahweh. In Ezekiel the oracles are positioned between Ezekiel 1—24, which lead up to the destruction of Jerusalem in 586 BC, and Ezekiel 33—48, which flow from that destruction and promise the return. In this position the oracles confirm that none of the nations surrounding Judah would benefit from the destruction, and that none of the nations upon which the Judeans were tempted to rely, such as Egypt and Tyre, could be of any assistance at all. In short, Judah's destiny was not in the hands of the nations; rather, their destiny was in the hands of Judah's God. Likewise, the positioning of the oracles in Jeremiah is significant, and the different positioning in the LXX and the MT reflects that significance. In the LXX they follow Jeremiah 25, in which Jeremiah predicted the return from exile. In that chapter the prophet said that if Yahweh punished "the city that bears my name" for its misdeeds, how did the nations think that they could escape similar punishment? The issue is not geopolitical maneuvering, but rather moral responsibility to the one God of the universe. In the LXX the oracles follow that general statement as a particularization of it. In the MT the oracles appear after Jeremiah 45, after the narrative of Jerusalem's destruction and the events flowing from it. This placement likewise says that Judah's God is God of the whole world, and that if Judah is accountable to him for its actions, the rest of earth's nations are no less accountable. As such, they cannot prevent God's restoration of Judah.

6. Sovereign King.

Yahweh is not just the lord of history in the Prophetic Books; he is in fact the lord of everything. The phrase "the Lord Yahweh" (*'ădōnāy yhwh*) appears more than 250 times in the prophets, primarily in Isaiah (30x, of which eleven are "Lord Yahweh of hosts"), Jeremiah (13x, of which five are "Lord Yahweh of hosts"), Ezekiel (194x, most of which occur in announcement formulae, with either "thus says" [*kōh 'āmar*] or "declares" [*nĕ'um*]), and Amos (20x, of which one is "Lord Yahweh of hosts"). The phrase is also found at least once in Daniel, Obadiah, Micah, Zephaniah and Zechariah. With this use of the term *'ădōnāy* in conjunction with the divine name, these prophets are witnessing to their conviction that Yahweh is characterized by sovereignty. The "I Am" is indeed lord of the universe. One wonders if this combination and this understanding, especially as it occurs with such extreme frequency in Ezekiel, may be one of the reasons why *'ădōnāy* eventually came to replace *yhwh* altogether in classical Judaism. In any case, it is clear that the prophets understood Yahweh's rule to be absolute.

The prophets also refer to Yahweh as king, a concept that they share with the psalmists. So

Isaiah recognized that although Uzziah was dead, Isaiah had seen the true king, "Yahweh of hosts" (Is 6:3). Later, he was to say that in place of all the false human leaders of the nation, Yahweh was the true lawgiver, judge and king (Is 33:22). When Isaiah presents Yahweh's case against the idols, Yahweh's kingship is given prominent play (Is 43:15; 44:6, 21). Isaiah 44:6 is especially dense with theological import: "Thus says Yahweh, the King of Israel, and his Redeemer, Yahweh of hosts, 'I am the first and I am the last; and apart from me there is no God.'" Jeremiah makes a similar point when he says that Yahweh is "the true God; he is the living God and the everlasting King" (Jer 10:10). Both of these prophets, who were well aware that the pagans around them visualized their pantheons in terms of a royal court, were insisting that there is only one Being who truly qualifies as king: the one, transcendent, "I Am." Three times in Jeremiah's oracles he has "the King, whose name is Yahweh of hosts," giving a stinging command to one of the nations (Jer 46:18; 48:15; 51:57). Finally, in Zechariah and Malachi the concept appears again. Zechariah says that at the end of time Yahweh's kingship will be recognized over all the earth (Zech 14:9, 16, 17). Like Isaiah and Jeremiah, he links the idea of kingship with uniqueness: "And Yahweh will become king over all the earth. On that day Yahweh will be one and his name will be one" (Zech 14:9). Fittingly, the last reference among the prophets combines several of these kingly titles: "sacrifices to the Lord what is blemished. For I am a great King, says Yahweh of hosts, and my name is feared among the nations" (Mal 1:14).

The title "Yahweh of hosts" (*yhwh ṣĕbā'ôt*) deserves special attention in this section because of its connotations in regard to sovereign power. The "hosts" in question are heavenly armies (cf. NLT: "LORD of Heaven's Armies"). That is confirmed by the narrative in 2 Kings 6:8-23, where the Syrian army surrounding the village where Elisha was staying were themselves surrounded by horses and chariots of fire that were invisible to all but Elisha and, after prayer, his servant Gehazi (although the term itself does not appear in the narrative). An alternative form in which this appellation occurs is "Yahweh, God of hosts." This phrase occurs in the prophets thirty-one times, primarily in Isaiah, Jeremiah and Amos (once in Hosea

[Hos 12:5]). "Yahweh of hosts" occurs 216 times (Isaiah 51x [44x in Is 1—39]; Jeremiah 70x; Micah 1x; Nahum 2x; Habbakuk 1x; Zephaniah 2x; Haggai 13x; Zechariah 52x; Malachi 24x). Of these, the vast majority occur in the context of speaking ("thus says Yahweh of hosts," "declares Yahweh of hosts," "the word/words of Yahweh of hosts," etc.). It is also interesting to observe that proportionally more of the occurrences are found in the postexilic prophets than elsewhere, except for Isaiah and Jeremiah. In light of the fact that many of the occurrences in Isaiah and Jeremiah are found in those two prophets' oracles against the nations, it begins to appear that these references to Yahweh as having absolute power are especially prominent in those situations where the nation of Israel seems powerless before the other nations of the world. This might explain the complete absence of the phrase in Ezekiel, where Judah's powerlessness is not an issue.

7. Covenant Partner.

7.1. Covenant as Essential Foundation. Although the term *covenant* is not especially frequent in the Prophetic Books (61x), it is everywhere understood that the covenant with Yahweh forms the basis for Israel's relationship with him. This is especially the case with Jeremiah, as might be expected with the discovery of the Book of the Law during the temple renovations in the reign of Josiah (2 Kings 22:8). So we read, "Tell them this is what the LORD, the God of Israel, says, 'Cursed is the man who does not obey the terms of this covenant—the terms I commanded your forefathers when I brought them out of Egypt, out of the iron-smelting furnace.' I said, 'Obey me and do everything I command you, and you will be my people, and I will be your God'" (Jer 11:3-4). Ezekiel echoes this foundation when he repeats the formula "You will be my people, and I will be your God" numerous times (e.g., Ezek 11:20; 14:11), as well as the other exodus formula "Then you will know that I am Yahweh" (e.g., Ezek 6:7, 10; 7:4). But even when these more explicit references to, or reflections of, the Sinai covenant are not present, that covenant is everywhere assumed by the prophets from Amos onwards (on the permanence of covenant, see Goldingay, 182-92). So while the other nations are judged for basic inhumanity to others, Judah and Israel are judged for their failure to keep the terms of the covenant (Amos 2:4-8). Hosea can simply say that people who give sacrifices rather than love (*ḥesed*), refusing to "know God," have "broken [God's] covenant" (Hos 8:1), with the apparent expectation that his hearers will understand what covenant he is talking about. In the same way, Isaiah begins with Yahweh bringing a charge of rebellion against Israel (Is 1:2). This charge is directly related to the covenant stipulations. The people have fixated on the ceremonial aspects of the covenant (Is 1:11) while neglecting what the covenant is really seeking to produce: godliness. Thus, he charges them with having neglected the widow, the orphan and the stranger (Is 1:17). Likewise, Micah could say that God did not want rivers of oil or mountains of sacrifices, but rather justice, love and a humble walk with God. All of this presumes that the people should have known these things, and that it is fair to punish them for not having done them.

7.2. Covenant in Terms of Marriage. That the prophets saw the covenant in personal terms rather than in merely legal ones is made clear by their expressing the covenant in terms of *marriage. Hosea in Israel in the eighth century BC and Ezekiel in Judah in the sixth century BC are notable for having done this, and this spread in time and space gives some indication of how pervasive this understanding was. Evidence of this understanding is found in many of the other prophets as well. It is especially clear when we find sin being expressed in terms of prostitution (Is 57:3; Jer 3:2; 13:27; Mic 1:7). It is not merely that Yahweh's *law has been broken, but his heart as well. This divine anguish is portrayed powerfully in the cry recorded in Hosea 11:8: "How can I give you up, Ephraim?" Further evidence is found in the use of *yādaʿ* ("to know") in relation to God. It seems probable that the connotations of personal intimacy associated with this word across the span of its usage would have affected the ways in which it was understood in texts such as Isaiah 43:10; Jeremiah 2:8; Daniel 11:32; Joel 3:17. The use of the term in this way in Hosea would tend to confirm this understanding (Hos 4:1-2; 5:4).

This nuptial understanding of the covenant, especially as expressed in Ezekiel and Hosea, underlines that the basis of the covenant between Yahweh and Israel is radically different from that of the Hittite suzerainty treaties upon which the Sinai covenant is formally modeled. In the suzerainty treaty the basis was conquest. The emperor had conquered a hostile people and now imposed upon them a covenant that they could not resist if they wished to avoid national annihilation. With Israel and Yahweh the situation was vastly different, as illustrated in two different ways by Hosea and Ezekiel. In both cases, we find Yahweh offering something that he did not have to offer to someone who was in a position to offer little back but love. In Hosea's case, it is the offer to give the prostitute the legal standing and social position of a wife. In Ezekiel's case, it is assuming the parental obligation for an unwanted child. In both cases, the basis is free grace, nothing more. That Yahweh hopes in both cases to benefit from the relationship by gaining the love of the other person in no way affects the gracious basis of the covenant. And that basis is further illustrated in both cases when the partners, having initially accepted the terms, and have either been married or tacitly accepted the offer of marriage, then turn around and repudiate the husband's love. In the case of Hosea, he buys back his wife, promising to woo her again (Hos 3:1-4). In the case of Ezekiel, though the bride-to-be has gone after other lovers and has been abused by them, the guardian offers to take her back, promising an "everlasting covenant" with her (Ezek 16:60; see also Is 55:3).

If this marriage metaphor shows that grace is understood by the prophets to be both the basis and the modus operandi of the covenant, it also underlines a point that Deuteronomy makes very clear: the motivation for keeping the terms of the covenant is love, not coercion. If the imagery of sovereign and servant provides one apt metaphor for the relation between God and humans, it is by no means the only metaphor, and perhaps not always the best one. We keep the covenant not because we must or be destroyed, but because we wish to and in so doing will find our deepest fulfillment in intimacy with our Creator and Maker, our divine husband. The NT underlines the importance of this understanding when it speaks of the church as the bride of Christ (Eph 5:27; Rev 21:1) and envisions the inauguration of eternal bliss as a wedding feast (Rev 19:9).

8. Father.
Yet another way in which the prophets expressed their understanding of Yahweh was as father. It was not uncommon for the high god, such as Anu among the Sumerians or El among the Canaanites, to be referred to as the father of the gods. But here the emphasis is upon the engendering function of the father. This god sexually engendered all the others through Ki or Asherah, his wife. There is no trace of this understanding among the Hebrew prophets. The closest one comes to it is the statement in Jeremiah 31:9 that Yahweh will restore his people "because I am Israel's father and Ephraim is my firstborn son." Obviously, this is not understood in any literal sense, but rather asserts that God's care for his people is like that of a father for a firstborn son. Other occurrences use "father" in similar ways. So Isaiah 63:16 has the people saying that even if their actual father, Abraham, would disown them, Yahweh would adopt them as his own children. Isaiah 64:8 says that since Yahweh is their father, he cannot be angry with them forever. In Jeremiah 3:19 the movement is from the other direction as Yahweh protests that he thought that his people would call him "Father" and not turn aside from following him. In that vein, Ezekiel says that on the basis of their behavior, their father must have been an Amorite and their mother a Hittite (Ezek 16:3, 45). Finally, Malachi pleads with the people that since they have one Father (i.e., one Creator), they ought to think of one another in determining their course of behavior (Mal 2:10). It should also be noted here that on two occasions in Isaiah it is said that Yahweh acts like a mother (Is 49:15; 66:13).

9. Shepherd.
Although a shepherd was in the lowest social stratum in the ancient world, it was fairly common for kings to refer to themselves as the shepherds of their people. This practice was carried on in Israel as well, and the prophets frequently castigated the kings for being rapacious shepherds who ate their flock instead of caring for it (Is 56:11; Ezek 34:8-10; Zech 11:16-17). So just as Yahweh was the true king of his people, he also was the true shepherd. Interestingly, most of the occurrences where Yahweh is seen in this role are in the context of the return from exile. The flock that was scattered, in part because of the failure of its human shepherds, would have to be supernaturally regathered. So Isaiah 40:11 speaks of him carrying the lambs in his arms, and Jere-

miah 31:10 has him gathering the scattered flock. Ezekiel 34:12-22 has an extended treatment of this image, with Yahweh gathering the flock, making them lie down to rest. But it also depicts him as protecting the weaker sheep from the more aggressive ones. But a new twist is added when Yahweh, having said, "I myself will be the shepherd of my sheep" (Ezek 34:11, 15), says, "I will set up over them one shepherd, my servant David" (Ezek 34:23). That interplay seems to be continued in both Micah and Zechariah. In Micah 7:14 it appears that Yahweh is called upon to shepherd his people, but in Micah 5:4 it is the ruler to be born in Bethlehem who is depicted as the shepherd. Likewise, in Zechariah both Yahweh and the one whom he appoints are said to be the shepherd (Zech 10:3; 11:4).

10. Judge.
One of the key ways in which the prophets see God is as judge. However, the English term *judge* is much more constrained than the Hebrew one being translated. The Hebrew term *šōpēṭ* does not primarily refer to a legal officer who passes judgment in criminal cases; rather, the judge comes to establish an order in which right prevails and wrong receives its just due. To understand this, one should think of the activities of those persons designated "judges" in the biblical book of that same name. Thus, in the prophets the coming of the judge, as it is in the book of Psalms, is just as often a cause for rejoicing as it is a cause for apprehension (Is 11:4; 61:3; cf. Ps 96:11-13). If the judge will condemn the idolatry, adultery, greed, oppression and self-indulgence of his people (Ezek 7:8), he will also take vengeance upon those who have oppressed and violated his people (Ezek 35:11). He will not let the pride, greed or brutality of the oppressors go unpunished (Hab 2:2-20). The same arm that tenderly gathered the lambs is raised to smash down those who slaughtered the lambs (Is 40:10-11).

The role of the judge in establishing the divinely intended order is seen in the passage duplicated in Isaiah and Micah: "He shall judge between the nations, and shall decide disputes for many peoples; and they shall beat their swords into plowshares, and their spears into pruning hooks; nation shall not lift us sword against nation, neither shall they learn war anymore" (Is 2:4; Mic 4:3). The actions of the judge will be for the purpose of bringing about jus-

tice on the earth. But again, there is a discrepancy between the Hebrew and English words in their connotations, with the Hebrew original having much wider connotations than the English. Whereas the English term *justice* connotes fairness, legal equity and the guaranteeing of what may be considered rights, the Hebrew word *mišpaṭ* connotes much more. It connotes that cosmic order which the Creator intended (see Jer 5:4-5). The justice that Yahweh intends to bring to the earth through his servant (Is 42:1, 4) is no less than a restoration of a marred and sullied earth to its original intended state. This is by no means to diminish the importance of establishing and enforcing equity and fairness for the oppressed of earth (Is 61:8; Jer 5:28; Ezek 18:8; Amos 5:15). It is only that justice does not stop there, but only begins.

11. Deliverer/Redeemer.
While the occurrence of "Savior," "saved," "Redeemer" and "redeemed" is largely limited to Isaiah 40—63 (8x, 5x, 13x, 10x respectively), the concepts are not so limited. They are found in the first part of Isaiah (e.g., Is 1:27), in Jeremiah (Jer 14:8), Ezekiel (Ezek 36:29), Daniel (Dan 3:17), Zephaniah (Zeph 1:18), Micah (Mic 6:4) and Zechariah (Zech 10:8). The point that is made so forcefully in Isaiah is repeated in the other prophets. It was Yahweh who delivered his people into the hands of the oppressors, and therefore he was fully able to deliver them from the hands of the oppressors should he wish to do so (Is 50:1-3). And indeed he did so wish. In fact, such a deliverance is presented as a display of his "rightness" (*ṣĕdāqâ* [Is 51:8; 56:1]). Clearly, it would not be "right" for this God to leave his people in captivity, although in view of their breaking of the covenant it might be perfectly just to do so. Again, we see that Yahweh did not conceive of the covenant merely in legal terms, but rather as a vehicle for shaping the "walk" that he wished to have with his creatures (cf. Gen 17:1). But he was not going to be limited by any limitations that the vehicle might have had. He would deliver his people, not only for love (Hos 14:4), but also to demonstrate his essential nature to the world (Ezek 36:22-24).

See also DIVINE COUNCIL; DIVINE PRESENCE; FORGIVENESS; IDOLS, IDOLATRY, GODS; PRAYER; SPIRIT OF YAHWEH; WORD OF GOD; WORSHIP.

BIBLIOGRAPHY. **W. Brueggemann,** *The Prophetic Imagination* (Philadelphia: Fortress, 1978);

idem, *Hopeful Imagination: Prophetic Voices in Exile* (Philadelphia: Fortress, 1986); **M. Buber,** *The Prophetic Faith* (New York: Macmillan, 1949); **R. E. Clements,** *Prophecy and Covenant* (London: SCM, 1965); **A. Coppedge,** *Portraits of God: A Biblical Theology of Holiness* (Downers Grove, IL: InterVarsity Press, 2001); **W. Eichrodt,** *Theology of the Old Testament* (trans. J. Baker; 2 vols.; Philadelphia: Westminster, 1961-1967); **J. Goldingay,** *Old Testament Theology, 2: Israel's Faith* (Downers Grove, IL: InterVarsity Press, 2006); **D. Gowan,** *Theology of the Prophetic Books: The Death and Resurrection of Israel* (Louisville: Westminster/John Knox, 1998; **A. Heschel,** *The Prophets* (New York: Harper & Row, 1962); **W. Houston,** "What Did the Prophets Think They Were Doing? Speech Acts and Prophetic Discourse in the Old Testa-ment" *BibInt* 1 (1993) 167-88; **J. Oswalt,** *The Book of Isaiah: Chapters 1-39* (NICOT; Grand Rapids: Eerdmans, 1986); idem, *The Book of Isaiah: Chapters 40-66* (NICOT; Grand Rapids: Eerdmans, 1998); **O. Steck,** *The Prophetic Books and Their Theological Witness,* trans. J. Nogalski (St. Louis: Chalice, 2000); **G. von Rad,** *The Message of the Prophets,* trans. D. M. G. Stalker (New York: Harper & Row, 1965). J. N. Oswalt

GODS. *See* IDOLS, IDOLATRY, GODS.

GREEK OLD TESTAMENT. *See* TEXT AND TEXTUAL CRITICISM.

GUILT. *See* SIN, SINNERS.

H

HABAKKUK, BOOK OF

This article describes the current understanding of literary and stylistic features, historical contexts and canonical significance of the book of Habakkuk. It elucidates the sometimes cryptic text using rhetorical, dialogical and historical methods.

Some scholars consider the name "Habakkuk" (*hăbaqqûq*) to derive from the name of an Akkadian garden plant (Roberts, 86). The Hebrew root (*hābaq*) means "to embrace," especially as a means of keeping warm when there is no other shelter (e.g., Job 24:8; Lam 4:5). God's revelation of Judah's coming devastation was embraced by Habakkuk in faith (Hab 3:17). The embrace of God's dialogue with him became a shelter for Israel, when it appeared that every other means of shelter would be removed.

1. Theological, Literary and Historical Contexts
2. Content of Habakkuk
3. Canonical Issues

1. Theological, Literary and Historical Contexts.

1.1. Central Themes.

1.1.1. The Burden of Faith. Habakkuk 1:1 speaks of "the oracle that the prophet Habakkuk saw" (cf. Amos 1:1; Mic 1:1). "Oracle" (*maśśā'*) is closely related to the word "burden" (*maśśā'*). This oracle was given to the prophet in a *vision of dialogue with God (Hab 2:1; cf. Jer 28:10-15). The burdensome message for Jerusalem was the imminent arrival of the Babylonians, who would soon destroy the city. Habakkuk called the people not to despair, but to live by *faith (Hab 2:4b) and to share his joy in the Lord (Hab 3:18).

1.1.2. The Lord Prepares His People for Devastating Change. The Lord told Habakkuk that Judah's prosperity and autonomy would end, and that his protection would be withdrawn. The Lord promised that things would improve after the devastation if they could cling to their memory of his past faithfulness (Hab 3). They had the benefit of forewarning and the witness of a faithful and believing prophet (Hab 3:17-19).

1.1.3. A Dialogical Complaint and Response. The vision (*hāzôn*) that God commanded Habakkuk to write (Hab 2:2) included the prophet's probing questions, God's responses and a concluding psalm of trust. Habakkuk began with a complaint against local corruption but was drawn into a progressively more difficult understanding of faith. God took Habakkuk's persistent question of theodicy, "Why do you . . . ?" (Hab 1:3, 13), and made the prophet wrestle with a broader international reality.

The increasingly difficult word from the Lord caused a faith struggle for the prophet. He believed that the Lord could not tolerate wickedness, yet he noted that evil prospered. Habakkuk sought an explanation he could pass on to his audience (Hab 2:1), but none was forthcoming. By the end of the conversation he realized that the near future would lack visibly manifest reasons to believe, leaving only faith in God's promise. Without immediate material evidence of God's love, he would have to say, "Although the fields produce no food . . . yet I will rejoice in the LORD" (Hab 3:17-18).

1.1.4. Knowledge of the Glory. The words "For the earth will be filled with the knowledge of the glory of the LORD, as the waters cover the sea" are both the centerpiece of the five woes (Hab 2:12-14) and the physical center of the book. This declaration refers to God's intention to bless all the nations of the world through Israel, bringing the whole creation back to the Creator (see Ex 9:16; Num 14:21; Is 11:9).

1.2. Genres. Habakkuk contains a variety of classic biblical genres typical of the Prophetic Books, but they are used in unusual ways for surprising *rhetorical purposes. Most scholars take the combination of genres as evidence of an uncertain redaction history by the author and/or editors (*see* Editorial/Redaction Criticism). The genres include an individual *lament used in a dialogical complaint (Hab 1:1-4, 12-17); a judgment oracle (Hab 1:5-11); a complaint-response oracle (Hab 2:2-4); woe oracles given as taunts (Hab 2:6-20); and a theophanic psalm (Hab 3:1-15) combined with a psalm of trust (Hab 3:16-19). Several applications of genres stand out.

1.2.1. Lament Used in a Dialogical Complaint (Hab 1:1-4, 12-17). Habakkuk's questions of lament/complaint are also found throughout the psalms: "How long?" (Ps 6:3; 13:1-2; 79:5; 89:46); "Why do you . . . ?" (Ps 10:1; 44:23-24; 74:11). The inclusion of God's response has similarities to the book of Job. Habakkuk's and Job's questioning is presented as faithful protest (cf. Job 42:7-8). Each of them conversed directly with God (cf. Job 30:2-23, 31:6, 35). The Lord led both of them out of older theological constructs into new understandings of God's way in the world (Hab 1:5, 12-13; 2:2-6; 3:16-19; cf. Job 42:1-9).

1.2.2. Woe Oracles Given as Taunts (Hab 2:6-20). The five woes are rhetorically remarkable in their use as a promise by God. Some argue that here *hôy* is a simple exclamation (cf. Is 55:1: "Hey, everyone who thirsts" [NET]) introducing the taunts, rather than meaning "Woe!" (Roberts, 118), but the setting of captivity does befit the woe of a dirge. In context, these oracles are given before the exile, to be voiced by the future captives. "Will not all of them taunt him with ridicule and scorn, saying, 'Woe . . . '?" (Hab 2:6a). Woes usually are voiced against the people by God (e.g., Is 5:8-23), but here God's voice is democratized for all *nations and peoples (Hab 2:5b-6a). Captives do not usually taunt their persecutors, yet they will have God's voice as a prophetic weapon of hope. It is "subversive literature" (Prior, 243). Set in this literary context, it is a rhetorically brilliant and sociologically complex gift (Bruckner, 228-34, 243-48).

1.2.3. The Psalm (Hab 3). Habakkuk 3 is a complete psalm with superscription (Hab 3:1) and concluding musical instructions (Hab 3:19b). It begins with a theophanic song (Hab 3:3-15) linked to the final psalm of trust (Hab 3:16-19) by means of the prophet's first-person voice (Hab 3:2, 16). The theophany describes a physical manifestation of the presence of the Lord (Hab 3:2-15; cf. Ex 15:3-12; 19:16-19; Judg 5:4-5; Ps 18:6-19; 68:4-19), visible in the elements of his creation: sun, lightning, flood, plague and earthquake. God strides forth upon the earth as a warrior against crime, and people and the earth tremble at his power.

Some argue that Habakkuk 3 was added much later, as it is missing from DSS commentary (1QpHab). The majority think that it is part of the original MT tradition (Andersen, 259-60), confirmed in the second-century Minor Prophet scroll found at Wadi Murabbaʿat and present in the early LXX versions and in the Naḥal Ḥeber first-century Greek manuscript. The more archaic language of the chapter is in keeping with the liturgy of theophanic visions (Sweeney, 1:479; Roberts, 148-58). It is also a fitting response after the prophet's questions and God's revelation in the first two chapters (Hiebert 1986, 129-49).

1.3. Literary Style. Habakkuk's abrupt changes in speaker, subject matter, historical referent and genre make it difficult to follow. In the first chapter, God does not directly answer Habakkuk's questions, but responds to the prophet's lamenting petition with a judgment oracle for Judah (Hab 1:5-11). God does not defend his goodness, but rather complains with the people against the wicked (Hab 1:11). His most direct response comes in the second chapter, "The righteous shall live by faith" (Hab 2:4b), in the midst of the rhetorical complexity of the woes (Hab 2:6-20).

The third chapter recollects past demonstrations of the God's power. Here a theophanic psalm functions as part of the prophet's lament, longing for the days of God's more obvious presence (Hab 3:2-15). The lamenting context is established at the end of the theophany, in the first-person voice (Hab 3:16). The dialogical setting of the introduction and conclusion hold this unusual book together, and the canonical setting implies inspiration by God, even of the questioning complaint (Hab 1:1).

1.4. Historical Setting. Habakkuk was a temple musician-prophet (Hab 3:19b) (Bruce, 832), a contemporary of *Nahum, *Zephaniah and *Jeremiah, who prophesied during violent upheavals at the end of the seventh century BC. The book is a collection of oracles written during dramatic political change in Jerusalem (Hab 2:2) (see Israelite History).

The first chapter describes Jerusalem before *Babylon's defeat of Egypt at Carchemish (605 BC). The prophet's complaints focus on corrupt King Jehoiakim, who ruled Jerusalem as a vassal of Egypt (609-605 BC) and then of Babylon (605-601 BC). Jehoiakim killed innocents who opposed him, and he refused to pay poor laborers (2 Kings 23:35-37; Jer 22:13-19). Under his administration, prophets and priests committed adultery and abused authority (Jer 23:1-2, 9-11). He killed the prophet Uriah for prophesying that Jerusalem would fall (Jer 26:20-23), and he burned Jeremiah's hand-written prophecy (Jer 36).

The second chapter's five woes/taunts (Hab 2:6-20) imply Babylon's future defeat of Jerusalem. After the Babylonian king Nebuchadnezzar secured a victory at Carchemish (605 BC), he retained Jehoiakim as his vassal until 601 BC, when Jehoiakim rebelled by refusing to pay tribute. Babylon marched on Jerusalem, and in 597 BC Jerusalem surrendered. When Jehoiakim died, he was replaced by his son Jehoiachin, who was taken to Babylon with the educated and skilled population of Jerusalem. The monarchy ended with Zedekiah, propped up by Nebuchadnezzar as Judah's last king (597-586 BC). The psalm of hope in the third chapter also reflects the situation of the exiles.

2. Content of Habakkuk.

2.1. Habakkuk 1. The first chapter records two sets of prophetic questions posed to God. First, "Why do you tolerate wrongdoing?" (Hab 1:2-4). God's response is indirect: "Look, . . . I am raising up the [more wicked] Babylonians" (see Hab 1:5-11 [author's paraphrase]). The second set of questions reasserts, "Why then do you tolerate the treacherous?" (Hab 1:12-17 NIV). They rephrase, intensify and expand the original question in light of the new information given in God's response.

2.1.1. Habakkuk 1:1-4. Habakkuk wonders how long he must wait for God's help against violence (Hab 1:2). Judah's problems with corruption are addressed in three matched pairs: injustice ('āwen) and wrongful *suffering ('āmāl); *destruction (šōd) and violence (ḥāmās); strife (rîb) and conflict (mādôn). The latter two are legal terms marking the many lawsuits and legal quarrels in the courts. These six problems have four results, also presented in poetic pairs: the law is paralyzed, and justice never prevails; the wicked hem in the righteous so that justice is perverted (Hab 1:4). In a few brief words Habakkuk describes a ruined society full of crime, violence, corruption, mock legal battles and the defeat of the righteous, and he wants to know why God tolerates it.

2.1.2. Habakkuk 1:5-11. God's response rhetorically matches Habakkuk's complaint without directly answering the questions and redirects from local to international violence. God graphically describes the greater corruption and power in seven verses (Hab 1:5-11). Habakkuk: "Why do you make me look at [rᵓh] injustice? Why do you tolerate [nbṭ] wrong?" (Hab 1:3). God: "Look at [rᵓh] the nations and watch [nbṭ]" (Hab 1:5). To bring an end to Judah's corruption and violence, God would raise the cruel, impetuous Babylonians. Some translations have "the Chaldeans," a biblical name for neo-Babylonians, especially under Nebuchadnezzar's rule (see 2 Kings 25:1-13; Jer 21:4; Ezek 23:23).

The Babylonians' terrifying reputation is described in Habakkuk 1:6. They were "ruthless" (mar), galling and fierce. They were "impetuous" (māhar) and swift. The rhyming Hebrew words described an army that could rapidly change political structures. The Babylonians were feared and dreaded because they were "a law to themselves" (Hab 1:7). They would function as God's agent but would not be the permanent solution to Habakkuk's complaint about Judah's rulers.

The Babylonians' swift advance to Jerusalem is compared to wild animals: their "horses are swifter than leopards"; they are "fiercer than wolves at dusk, the cavalry gallops headlong, from afar"; they fly "like vultures swooping to devour" (Hab 1:8-9). Nebuchadnezzar demonstrated his military aggression following the battle at Carchemish (605 BC) by pursuing the defeated Egyptian army more than one hundred and fifty miles to crush them completely (Roberts, 96). Once the Babylonians had defeated both the Assyrians at Nineveh (612 BC) and the Egyptians (605 BC), no one could stop them. They could "scoff at rulers." Once they controlled trade routes, they could "laugh at all fortified cities," building earthen ramps to go over city walls.

2.1.3. Habakkuk 1:12-17. Habakkuk struggles to accept the prospect of the more wicked Babylonian rule in Jerusalem and rephrases the questions based on the new information (Hab 1:12). "Why do you tolerate the [more] treacherous [than Judah]?" (Hab 1:13 [author's paraphrase]). In Habakkuk 1:14-16 the prophet expands the question with a fishing metaphor and concludes (Hab 1:17) by again pushing the question of God's toleration of the wicked.

The intensification of Habakkuk's renewed complaint begins abruptly in response to the news of the Babylonian advent. He quotes to God what he knows about God, "You are from everlasting, my God, my Holy One," adding, "We will not die!" (Hab 1:12). The prophet refers to the eternal promises to Abraham and to David at the heart of Israel's faith (see Gen 12:1-3; 15:4-6; 17:5-8; 2 Sam 7:13, 16; 1 Kings 2:45; 9:5). He appeals to the traditional reputation of the Lord: "Your eyes are too pure to look on evil, you cannot tolerate wrong" (Hab 1:13a). This appeal sets up the questions that follow: "Why do you tolerate the treacherous [Babylonians]" and "Why are you silent while the wicked swallow up the more righteous?" (Hab 1:13b).

The heart of his objection is the enjoyment and success that the wicked find in their cruel actions (Hab 1:15b). Habakkuk offers nine objections via a metaphor. The wicked fisherman pulls the righteous up with hooks, catches them in his net, gathers them up in his dragnet, rejoices, is glad, sacrifices to his net, burns incense to his dragnet, lives in luxury, and enjoys the choicest food. The first three objections concern the wicked fisherman's abusing. The fourth and fifth concern his happiness. The sixth and seventh object to his false worship, amplifying God's observation in Habakkuk 1:11b. The last two wonder about his high standard of living.

Habakkuk ends the nine-point list with another form of his original questions (Hab 1:3, 13) that could be paraphrased, "Are you going to keep on tolerating this? If so, how long?" (Hab 1:17). This forms the primary question of the book. The answer in the second chapter will be "Yes, for a while."

2.2. Habakkuk 2. The prophet waits on the city wall to see what answer the Lord will give (Hab 2:1). The Lord tells him to write and publish two ways in the world: faith or puffed-up desire (Hab 2:2-6a). The first way is for the righteous: "The righteous will live by faith." The second way in the world, "puffed-up desire," leads to five woes from the mouths of Babylonian captives (Hab 2:6b-20). These woes form God's second response to Habakkuk's questions about the toleration of wicked people. God will act through the faithful living of the righteous and through the woes that will befall the wicked.

2.2.1. Preparing for an Answer (Hab 2:1-3). The prophet needed a more detailed response for his constituency. "I will look to see . . . what I will answer to my complaint" (Hab 2:1b [author's translation; KJV and NASB have "when I am reproved," which refers to the prophet's worry about what the people will say]). The news about the Babylonian onslaught would raise serious questions in Jerusalem (Hab 1:5b), and Habakkuk had no words of his own to offer. He had to wait (cf. Jer 42:1-7).

Habakkuk 2:2 is the only place where the Lord is introduced as the speaker (Hab 2:2a). God says, "Write down . . . make plain on tablets so a herald may run with it" (Hab 2:2). The debated meanings of "run" include the following: even one running can read it; one who reads will run in terror; one who reads will live by it; the reader's eye will run easily over it. The point is that the message may be easily understood.

The Lord's second comment (Hab 2:3) is a repetitive warning that the way of faith would require waiting for his vindication during seventy years of exile (see Jer 25:12). It "will not prove false," and "it will certainly come" (Hab 2:3). These introductory words prepared them for answers about the future of the righteous (Hab 2:4b) and the success of the wicked (Hab 2:6-20).

2.2.2. Two Ways: Faith or Puffed-up Desire (Hab 2:4-5). Habakkuk 2:4-5 is the apex of God's message to the prophet. "See, he is puffed up; his desires are not upright" (Hab 2:4a [other translations have "his soul"]). "Puffed-up" (ʿāpal [NRSV: "proud"]) is an odd expression: being swollen like a tumor or swollen with presumptive pride (see Num 14:44). It refers to the earlier invectives, "a law to themselves" (Hab 1:7) and "whose own strength is their god" (Hab 1:11). "His desires are not upright" is a fundamental response to Habakkuk's complaint (Hab 2:4a). "Desire" (nepeš, often translated as "soul") refers to "life in relation to others." The Babylonians' "desires" could be upright or not. The Lord will not take away their will to choose or examine their "desires" or ("soul").

Habakkuk 2:5 adds three descriptive details to the "way of the puffed up." Excessive wine "is treacherous," deceiving the drinker into unwarranted self-importance (cf. Hab 2:15; Is 28:7-8). Some translations use the Syriac, Qumran (1QpHab) and some Greek versions' word "wealth" (hwn) instead of the Hebrew "[the] wine" (hyyn). Many accept "wealth" in spite of the Babylonian reputation (Prior, 241). The second mark of the puffed-up is arrogance. Third, they are never "at rest" because of their greed. "Like death," the Babylonians are never satisfied.

Habakkuk 2:4b describes the way of the righteous person: "The righteous will live by their faith." "Faith" (ʾemûnâ) here refers to faithfulness, trust and steadfastness. In canonical context, "living by faith" means believing the word of the Lord given through Habakkuk (Crenshaw, 14). It means commitment to the radical faith sung of in chapter three (Hab 3:17-19).

2.2.3. The Voice of Captives (Hab 2:6-20). The five woes describe the true consequence of wicked living. Joy is not their reward, as the prophet observes (Hab 1:15). God's justice will be accomplished through the natural judgments of societies against the corrupt and violent.

In the first woe, victims of extortion will take revenge (Hab 2:6b-8). The most common form of extortion was to demand tribute in exchange for not leveling a city, as in 597 BC Jerusalem. The Babylonians carried off the treasures of the* temple and the palace. Babylon's crimes were against people as well as against the earth (Hab 2:8b).

In the second woe, history will remember acts of violence (Hab 2:9-11). Those who build security by unjust gain will be exposed to public shame (*see* Honor and Shame). Even the "wall-stones and woodwork will cry out" against them. The Babylonian crime was "the ruin of many peoples" to build "household" security, "to set his nest on high, to escape the clutches of ruin." The metaphor of the nest echoes "the vulture swooping to devour" (Hab 1:8). The distinct hissing sound of the Hebrew letter ṣ ("ts") resounds in the key words of the text: "builds gain" (bōṣēaʿ beṣaʿ), "to escape"

(lĕhinnāṣēl), "you have plotted" (yāʿaṣtā), "the ruin of" (qĕṣôt) and "woodwork" (mēʿēṣ). The creaking house will call out the shame of the ruined builder (Hab 2:11).

The third woe of the puffed-up will be the knowledge that they spent their lives for nothing. Those who build profit through bloodshed and crime will forfeit not only their lives, but also the glory of the Lord that will fill the earth (Hab 2:12-14). Babylon's crimes were perpetrated against the many cultures of the ancient East (Hab 2:5-6), but also against the Lord (Hab 2:14).

The fourth woe concerns those who entice others to drunkenness. They will succumb to the terror of trees and *animals (Hab 2:15-17). It implies a practice of inducing drunkenness and also serves as a symbol of their stripping of trees, animals, lands and cities. The Babylonians' "glory" (Hab 2:16a, 16b) in these practices will itself be covered by shame. This "glory" stands in stark contrast to the "glory of the LORD" that will "fill the earth" (Hab 2:14).

The "cup in the LORD's right hand" refers to his interceding power (see Ex 15:6; Ps 17:7; 20:6; 44:3). The tables will be turned. Babylon's cup will be "filled up," but with shame (Hab 2:5, 16a). Their acts of destruction will remain with the perpetrators as a terrifying memory.

The fifth woe of the puffed-up is futility for those who trust in lifeless created things (Hab 2:18-20). Their silent idols cannot teach or respond to their trust. This taunt is sevenfold. An idol has no value because it is made by a human, teaches lies, cannot speak, cannot come to life, cannot wake up, cannot give guidance and has no breath. The concluding expression is dramatically sarcastic: "It teaches! Look! It is gold and silver! And full of breath! Oh, there is not any in it" (Hab 2:19). By contrast, the Lord is present in the temple (*see* Divine Presence). He has created, teaches truth, is speaking, alive, awake, gives guidance, and is the one who gives the breath of life. Conversely, "silence" is for the people to keep in his presence (Hab 2:20b). No one has to call out to wake God for insight. He is already speaking.

2.3. Habakkuk 3. The third chapter is a psalm to the Lord in response to the dialogue of the first two chapters. The "I-you" dialogue with the Lord is not over. Habakkuk accepts the Lord's responses in a psalm of trust, struggling to express his deeply rooted faith in the

Lord. This psalm was sung, the last verse giving instrumental direction to the music leader (Hab 3:19). "On Shigionoth" is the (unknown) musical setting for singing (cf. Ps 7:1). Its probably derives from *šāgâ*, meaning "to stumble" or "to go astray," perhaps a reference to Habakkuk's need for God's guidance.

The structure begins with a formal refrain, perhaps an antiphonal response, "LORD, I have heard of your fame" (Hab 3:1). The song continues in three musical stanzas and a concluding bridge. Its structure is established by the word *selâ* as follows: refrain (Hab 3:2); stanza one (Hab 3:3-8); stanza two (Hab 3:9-13a); stanza three (Hab 3:13b-15); musical bridge (Hab 3:16-19). The three stanzas are introduced by half-verses that function as titles. The title of stanza one is Habakkuk 3:3a and ends with *selâ*. The lyrics follow (Hab 3:3b-8) until the second stanza title in Habakkuk 3:9 (again followed by *selâ*).

Habakkuk's song struggles to retain dearly held beliefs about God's way of power in the world. He recounts in three stanzas the Lord's reputation for visible displays on Israel's behalf. He longs for them to "be renewed" (*hayyêhû*, "let them live" [Hab 3:2]). Although the stanzas express the prophet's faith in God's past deeds, it is a subtle form of protestation. Not until the concluding bridge (Hab 3:16-19) does the prophet relinquish the plea for immediate intervention and accept the revelation of Babylon's rise given in the second chapter.

2.3.1. Renew Your Fame and Your Deeds, O Lord (Hab 3:2). The main themes of Habakkuk's song are contained in this refrain. "Your fame" (*šim‛ăkā*) is from the root meaning "heard." He "heard" that the Lord delivered Israel from Egypt and from the later assaults of the Philistines (see Josh 9:9; Is 66:19). He pleads in the third and fourth phrase that the Lord will return to this mode of operation in the world. Finally, the prophet sings for mercy to accompany the Lord's *wrathful response to sin.

2.3.2. In Days of Old God Came Forth (Hab 3:3-8). The first stanza describes the days of old when God came forth as a brilliant warrior for Israel against their enemies in lightning, plague, earthquake and storms on the waters (Hab 3:3-8). The Deuteronomic history recounts how God used earthquake (Josh 6), torrential rains (Judg 4—5), thunderstorm (1 Sam 7), wind (2 Sam 5) and a plague (2 Kings 18—

19) to rout Israel's enemies (*see* Warfare and Divine Warfare).

Teman is in southern Palestine and the Paran Mountains are on the eastern edge of the Sinai Peninsula. There, God's formation of Israel began after their deliverance from the Egyptian army at the Sea (Ex 14—15). Habakkuk 3:7 describes the distress of Cushites and Midianites, who were in distress because the Creator was present with Israel (see Num 31:7; Judg 3:10) and perhaps because of their *idolatry (*’āwen*, "distress" or "idolatry"). The three rhetorical questions of Habakkuk 3:8 sound the central theme, highlighting God's dramatic display of power. Habakkuk longs for this kind of intervention against the Babylonians.

2.3.3. He Uncovered His Bow and Arrows to Deliver Israel (Hab 3:9-13a). The second stanza (Hab 3:9-13a) declares the purpose of the Lord's wrath: to save his chosen people, who are, in this poetic parallelism, his "anointed" one (see Ex 19:6; Ps 28:8). When the Lord arrives as a bowman (see Deut 32:23; Ezek 5:16), the memories of Israel are the background of this psalmic collage (cf. Ps 77:11-20). Earth, water and fire acknowledge the Creator and act for his delivering purposes (Hab 3:10-11a).

2.3.4. You Crushed the Leader of Wickedness (Hab 3:13b-15). The third stanza describes the paradigmatic victory over Pharaoh. The "crushing of the head" of the chaos monster, Leviathan (as in Ps 74:12-14), means that the Lord establishes cosmic order and justice (see Ps 89:9-10; Job 26:12-13; Is 27:1; 51:9-10). The memory of the Lord's intervention against evil is the hope that holds Habakkuk's audience in face of impending devastation. They believe that the Lord will eventually defeat Babylon too.

2.3.5. The Fear, Faith and Joy of Habakkuk (Hab 3:16-19). The psalm concludes with Habakkuk's honest fear about the Babylonian conquest and his faithful joy in the Lord (Hab 3:16-19). The prophet finally acknowledges he has "heard" the Lord's word about Babylon's coming triumph (Hab 3:16). Although terror stricken, he accepts that the Lord will work in a different and unsettling way to accomplish his purpose (Hab 2:14) through *exile and return. He declares his unconditional allegiance no matter what the consequences.

In Habakkuk 3:17 the prophet lists the primary sources of food and agricultural commerce of the ancient East: figs, grapes, olives, produce, sheep and cattle. Even in their absence Habakkuk stalwartly resolves to be joyful (Hab 3:18-19). His emphatic confession consists of two sets of parallel statements with his confession of faith at the center: "The Sovereign LORD is my strength."

Joy is a typical theme in Hebrew psalms. Habakkuk's joy stands in contrast, however, to the usual rejoicing over God's good gifts and protection (cf. Ps 5:11-12; 13:5-6; 16:5-11; 47:1-4). Habakkuk rejoices even without them. His joy stands also in contrast to that of the Babylonians, who rejoice because they live in luxury and enjoy the choicest food (Hab 1:15-16).

Habakkuk 3 creates and maintains hope in the face of a calamitous future, providing a lasting resource for survival. It demonstrates the geography of hope in two ways: looking back by reciting the Lord's victories on Israel's behalf (cf. Deut 26:1-11; Ps 78) and by looking up at creation's wonders as a sign of the Creator's presence and power (cf. Ps 19:1-4; Is 40:12-31; 42:5-25).

3. Canonical Issues.

Habakkuk expresses many facets of Israel's rich heritage. Habakkuk 3 echoes the exodus, *wilderness wandering and entrance to the promised *land. The close dialogue with God in Habbakkuk 1 parallels the book of Jeremiah. The struggle with the prosperity of the wicked is likewise lamented in the psalms and in the wisdom of Ecclesiastes and Job. The book is a bridge to the enduring faith established in the Babylonian exile and of the Diaspora (Hab 3:16-19).

A widely discussed issue in the history of interpretation is the meaning of Habakkuk 2:4b, usually translated as "the righteous will live by his faith" (be'ĕmûnātô [RSV, NASB]). A better translation is "by their faithfulness" (cf. NIV; NET), taking the pronominal suffix in its common inclusive form and 'emûnâ in its common meaning of "faithfulness," meaning "steady trust." Another translation possibility is "by its faithfulness," referring to the word of God given to Habakkuk in the "revelation" (Hab 2:2-3) (Roberts, 105). Related to this alternate possibility is the LXX rendering, "the righteous shall live by my faith [ek pisteōs mou]"—that is, by God's faithfulness. In any case, the primary social context of "faith/faithfulness" in Hebrew is expressed as a child's trust in the faithfulness of a nursemaid to carry the child (Is 60:4 NIV: "carried"; Ruth 4:16 NIV: "cared for"). One has faith in God and in the word of revelation when one lives faithfully. The point is that when Babylon destroys Jerusalem, God's people will live by faith/faithfulness and not material measures.

When Habakkuk 2:4b is quoted in the NT, the reference points shift (Rom 1:17; Gal 3:11; Heb 10:38). All three texts are without the pronoun, having simply "by faith" (ek pisteōs), thus generalizing the source. In Romans Paul quotes "the righteous shall live by faith" as a universal message for all cultures and peoples (Rom 1:15-17; cf. Gen 15:6; Rom 4:3; Gal 3:6). He used this quotation to connect the older concept of "the righteous," referring to Jews of integrity who lived faithfully in the community before God, with the new revelation of "a righteousness from God," which is Jesus Christ, for the Gentile (Rom 3:21; cf. 1 Cor 1:30; 1 Pet 3:18; 1 Jn 2:1).

Paul returned to this quote (Gal 3:11) in order to convince Gentiles not to seek righteousness by means of the Jewish law. He explained, "Clearly no one who relies on the law is justified before God, because 'the righteous will live by faith'. . . . He redeemed us in order that the blessing given to Abraham might come to the Gentiles through Christ Jesus, so that by faith we might receive the promise of the Spirit" (Gal 3:11, 14 NIV). Paul was not setting up a dichotomy between faith as "assent" and living a life of patient trust and endurance (see Hiebert, NIB 7:643). He argued that Christ Jesus had become righteousness in place of the law. He expected Christians to assent to Christ as their righteousness by living patiently within that righteousness. The meaning of the verse remains similar, while the referent has changed.

In Hebrews 10:38 the primary referent of "faith" is persevering in difficult times, as in Habakkuk (Heb 10:25-39). The difference between the texts is the object of the faith. Habakkuk called the people to live with confidence (Hab 2:6-20) that the Babylonians would be destroyed and the Lord would appear again on the earth in power (Hab 3:1-15). The object of the NT text is the promise that God will judge the wicked and receive the forgiven upon Christ's return (Heb 10:17-19, 23).

See also BABYLON; BOOK OF THE TWELVE; EVIL; EXILE; FAITH.

BIBLIOGRAPHY. E. **Achtemeier,** *Nahum-Malachi* (IBC; Atlanta: Westminster/John Knox, 1986); **F. I. Andersen,** *Habakkuk: A New Translation with Introduction and Commentary* (AB 25; New York: Doubleday, 2001); **D. Baker,** *Nahum, Habakkuk and Zephaniah: An Introduction and Commentary* (TOTC; Downers Grove, IL: InterVarsity Press, 1988); **L. Boadt,** *Jeremiah 26-52, Habakkuk, Zephaniah, Nahum* (OTMes 10; Wilmington, DE: Michael Glazier, 1982); **W. P. Brown,** *Obadiah through Malachi* (WestBC; Louisville: Westminster/John Knox, 1996); **J. K. Bruckner,** *Jonah, Nahum, Habakkuk, Zephaniah* (NIVAC; Grand Rapids: Zondervan, 2004); **F. F. Bruce,** "Habakkuk," in *The Minor Prophets: An Exegetical and Expository Commentary,* ed. T. McComiskey (3 vols; Grand Rapids: Baker, 1992) 2.831-96; **J. Crenshaw,** "Theodicy in the Book of the Twelve," *SBLSP* 41 (2001) 1-18; **R. D. Haak,** Habakkuk (VTSup 44; Leiden: E. J. Brill, 1992); **T. Hiebert,** "The Book of Habakkuk," *NIB* 7.623-55; idem, *G-d of My Victory: The Ancient Hymn in Habakkuk 3* (HSM 38; Atlanta: Scholars Press, 1986); **R. Mason,** *Zephaniah, Habakkuk, Joel* (OTG; Sheffield: JSOT, 1994); **J. Neusner,** *Habakkuk, Jonah, Nahum and Obadiah in Talmud and Midrash: A Source Book* (SJud; Lanham, MD: University Press of America, 2007); **G. M. O'Neal,** *Interpreting Habakkuk as Scripture: An Application of the Canonical Approach of Brevard S. Childs* (SBL 9; New York: Peter Lang, 2007); **D. Prior,** *The Message of Joel, Micah and Habakkuk: Listening to the Voice of God* (BST; Downers Grove, IL: InterVarsity Press, 1999); **J. J. M. Roberts,** *Nahum, Habakkuk, and Zephaniah: A Commentary* (OTL; Louisville: Westminster/John Knox, 1991); **O. P. Robertson,** *The Books of Nahum, Habakkuk, and Zephaniah* (NICOT; Grand Rapids: Eerdmans, 1990); **R. L. Smith,** *Micah-Malachi* (WBC 32; Waco, TX: Word, 1984); **M. Sweeney,** *The Twelve Prophets* (2 vols.; Berit Olam; Collegeville, MN: Liturgical, 2000).

J. K. Bruckner

HAGGAI, BOOK OF

Haggai is second only to *Obadiah in brevity among the books of the Hebrew Bible. It contains several prophetic oracles, accompanied by precise dates and set in a chronological framework. Its principal thematic concerns are the rebuilding of Yahweh's house (Hag 1:2-15; 2:1-5), its purification (Hag 2:10-19) and future glorification (Hag 2:6-9), as well as the future of the Davidic line and the promises attached to it (Hag 2:20-23). The book provides no biographical information about Haggai, but it does manifest profound interest in his status as a prophet (Hag 1:1, 3, 12, 13; 2:1, 10), his role in the restoration of the *temple and the life of the community, and the unparalleled success that he enjoyed. Once disdained in scholarly circles as a late and inferior form of prophecy, this book has enjoyed a resurgence of interest and has been extensively examined for its value as a source regarding political, religious and societal life in Yehud in the early Persian period (522-515 BC), as well as its creative theological reflection and innovative reconfiguration of earlier Israelite traditions (Petersen; Meyers and Meyers; Wolff; Verhoef; Kessler 2002; Tollington).

1. Text, Form and Structure
2. Compositional History
3. Reading Haggai
4. Theological Vision and Message
5. Significance

1. Text, Form and Structure.

The *text of Haggai is well preserved and poses only a few significant text-critical problems. Chief among these are the reference to "the word which I covenanted with you when you came out of Egypt" in Haggai 2:5 (missing in the LXX) and the phrase "once again, in a little while" in Haggai 2:6 (LXX: "still once"). In both cases the MT is to be preferred (Barthélemy). A significant textual and translational issue occurs in Haggai 1:2a. Whereas many translations render this "the time has not come," a better translation is "it is not the time to come" (Kessler 2002, 103-4; Barthélemy, 923). The book's form is difficult to define. Unlike prophetic texts such as Isaiah and Jeremiah, it does not consist of a series of juxtaposed prose and poetic oracular and narrative materials. Rather the book consists of a series of prophetic oracles and a brief narrative redactionally arranged to chronicle Haggai's role in the Judean community's transition from disappointment and frustration to renewed hope. Some have seen the book as a "brief historical narrative" (Petersen). Others have noted a greater stress on prophecy than narrative (Floyd 2000, 261) and designated it as a "dramatized prophetic compilation" (Kessler 2002, 246; Meadowcroft,

10). The book is structured according to an A/B/A'/B' pattern. The A sections (Hag 1:1-11; 2:10-19) are characterized by reproaches against the people with prospects of hope, while the B sections (Hag 2:1-9, 20-23) focus on encouragement and promise. A brief narrative (Hag 1:12-15) intervenes between the first two A/B sections. It describes the results of the prophetic word and moves the dramatic progress of the book forward. Each of the sections is loosely structured around four elements: (1) introductory formula (Hag 1:1; 2:1, 10, 20); (2) dramatic conflict (temple in ruins, populace unconcerned [Hag 1:2]; builders discouraged [Hag 2:2-3]; pervasive impurity [Hag 2:14]; implied: Israel subject to the nations [Hag 2:21-22]); (3) divine challenge to obedience and *faith (Hag 1:4-7, 9-11; 2:4-5, 14-17); (4) declaration of promise (Hag 1:8; 2:6-9, 18-19, 21-23).

2. Compositional History.

Scholars generally see Haggai as a series of oracles set in a redactional framework (*see* Editorial/Redaction Criticism). Opinion regarding the book's date tends to favor either an early date close to the proclamation of the oracles as dated in the book (Meyers and Meyers, xliii-xlv; Kessler 2002, 31-57; Wolff, 17-19) or a far later date reflecting a lengthy period of redaction, up to one hundred years (Beuken, 184-216, 331-36; Ackroyd 1951; 1952), possibly in combination with the formulation of Zechariah 1—8 and Malachi (Sérandour 1995; 1996) or with the twelve Minor Prophets (Nogalski 1993). One way to assess these opinions is to ask when the dates were attached to the oracles, and when the framework was completed.

2.1. The Date Formulae. The oracles in Haggai are grouped around four specific days, from August to December during the "second year of Darius": (1) day 1/month 6 (Hag 1:1); (2) day 24/month 6 (Hag 1:15); (3) day 21/month 7 (Hag 2:1); (4) day 24/month 9 (Hag 2:10, 18, 20). The precision and concentration of these dates is unparalleled in the OT (although Zech 1—8 and Ezekiel display significant attention to precise dates). Certain scholars have suggested that the dates were attached to the oracles as much as one hundred years after their proclamation (Ackroyd 1951); however, several factors would indicate that these dates were attached to the oracles close to their proclamation. First, comparison of the form of the dates in Haggai to both biblical and extra-biblical material reveals a closer affinity to earlier dating practices than later ones. Second, the date formulae are not self-consistent (the order of the elements differs) and display no obvious ideological tendency, making it unlikely that they were added later for theological purposes. Third, the common Persian-period practice of compiling and dating prophetic oracles makes it unlikely that Haggai's oracles were preserved but not dated for a lengthy period (Kessler 2002, 41-51).

2.2. The Redactional Framework. If it may be affirmed that the book's dates were attached to the oracles close to the time of their proclamation, what date may be posited for the assembling of these dated oracles into the broader redactional framework present in the text as we have it? While some have argued for a date in a significantly later period, several indicators favor an earlier date: (1) the oracle predicting Zerubbabel's exaltation (Hag 2:23) is transmitted without any attenuation, suggesting that he still held office (Kessler 2002, 51-52); (2) the temple's rededication ceremony (515 BC) is not mentioned (Meyers and Meyers, xlii-xliv); (3) no attempt is made to distinguish Darius I (Hag 1:1) from Darius II (Verhoef, 10); (4) the eschatological fervor of the oracles is left largely intact (Mason, 1977) (Haggai stands in contrast to much later Persian period literature [Chronicles, Ezra-Nehemiah], which displays much less eschatological interest); (5) the date formulae are closely woven into the redactional frame (Floyd 1995, 476-79), indicating that the two should be considered together, not separately. In sum, the book as a whole may be read as reflecting the period between Haggai's proclamation and the temple's rededication (520-515 BC).

3. Reading Haggai.

3.1. Historical Context. Haggai's oracles are set in the early years of Persian rule over the former kingdom of Judah (*see* Israelite History). While a broader knowledge of Israelite history of the sixth century BC is extremely important for understanding Haggai, the following points are essential. Early in the sixth century BC Jerusalem and its temple were devastated, and a portion of the Judean population was *exiled to Babylon. Judah ceased to be a kingdom under Davidic rule, dashing earlier hopes invested in the nation and its royal house. Under the Persians, Judah was reduced to a small province (called "Yehud"), ruled by a governor and consisting of a greatly reduced territory comprising Jerusalem and its environs to a radius of about 25 km (Lipschits, 134-84; 258-71; Lemaire). A small contingent of returnees had arrived in Yehud during the reign of Cyrus the Great (ruled ca. 558-530 BC), however work on the temple was not undertaken until the reign of Darius I (ruled c. 522-486 BC). At that time, subsequent to the arrival of Zerubbabel the governor (of Davidic descent), Joshua the Zadokite priest and a contingent of exiles, Haggai reproaches the community for its neglect of the temple. Work is begun, and the temple is completed and rededicated in 515 BC (see Ezra 6:15-16).

3.2. Oracles and Framework. Several scholars maintain that the book contains two distinct perspectives: that of the prophet himself, and that of the book's editors (Beuken; Wolff; Mason 1977). Some maintain that Haggai was a nonexiled Judean (Wolff, 17) who spoke primarily to the nondeportees but whose words the editorial framework then transformed into a message designed to refute the claims of the Samaritans to the north (Beuken, 228-29, 334). Others see the prophet as addressing only the people, while the framework draws attention to the importance of Joshua and Zerubbabel (Sérandour 1996, 11), placing special emphasis on Zerubbabel, who has rebuffed the offer of Samaritan aid (Wolff, 19-20). Some view the oracles as strongly eschatological. The redactional framework, however, sought to attenuate such fervor. These approaches have been strongly criticized. First, the supposition that Haggai was a nonexiled Judean and representative of that group is highly speculative and rests entirely on inference. Second, it is doubtful that there is any allusion to Samaria at all in Haggai (see below on Hag 2:10-19). Third, distinctions between the theological perspectives of the oracles and framework are tenuous, given the difference in the types of material in the two sections (framework, consisting of names, dates, formulae concerning the reception of the prophetic word, versus oracles drawing on traditional motifs from Deuteronomistic, priestly and Zion theological streams [see Steck]). Fourth, there are several indications of linguis-

tic continuity between the two sections. For example, the epithet "LORD of hosts" (*yhwh šĕbā'ôt*) occurs in the oracles in Haggai 1:2, 5, 7; 2:7, 8, 9a, 9b, 23 and in the framework in Haggai 1:14. For a fuller discussion see Kessler 2002, 52-55. Fifth, there is a lack of consensus among scholars as to precisely which words ought to be assigned to the framework. Thus, though undoubtedly there was redactional activity whereby the original oracles of Haggai were collected and set within a broader framework reflecting specific theological concerns (e.g., to place a greater emphasis on the role of the political and religious leadership), there is not enough data available to make fine distinctions between the two (Floyd 1995, 473). One can access the "historical Haggai" only through the framework's portrait of him. While some differences in emphasis between the oracles and the framework must be acknowledged, it is more prudent to see in the book a continuity of perspectives between the oracles and framework regarding several issues facing the community during the early years of Persian rule.

3.3. Political Peace or Chaos? Scholars have debated whether the "second year of Darius" (Hag 1:1, 15; 2:10) refers to 521 or 520 BC. In 521 BC the empire was in upheaval, as Darius I, who had recently come to power, faced an orgy of revolt in various regions. Several scholars (e.g., Bickerman) saw a relationship between the shaking of the nations in Hag 2:6-9, 21-22 and the political instability in the empire. The oracle of Zerubbabel in Haggai 2:23 was thought to be an indication of a messianic movement (Waterman) that sought to gain independence and install the governor as king. This, it was argued, was why Zerubbabel suddenly disappears from view. Recent scholarship (Kessler 2002; Wolff, 74-76) has largely rejected these suggestions and views the year in question as 520 BC. Thus, Haggai's oracles were delivered in 520 BC on August 29 (Hag 1:1), September 21 (Hag 1:15), October 17 (Hag 2:1 [the seventh day of the Feast of Tabernacles]) and December 18 (Hag 2:10, 18, 20). Haggai's words regarding the coming shaking of the nations, glorification of the temple (Hag 2:6-9) and exaltation of Zerubbabel (Hag 2:20-23) should be read against the backdrop of imperial peace and stability. Thus, they reflect an ongoing hope for Yahweh's decisive intervention in history despite the stability of the Persian empire and its firm grip on Yehud (cf. Zech 1:11-12).

3.4. A Fragmented or Unified Community? Several biblical texts reveal conflict between those Judeans exiled to Babylon (the *golah*) and other groups of Yahwists, particularly those who remained in the land (Jer 24; 42—44; Ezra-Nehemiah [see Japhet]). At times the conflict concerned land tenure (see Ezek 11:14-21; 33:23-29). Can traces of such a conflict be seen in Haggai? Probably not, for two reasons. First, there is little archaeological evidence that the *golah* returnees settled in areas where the nonexiled Judeans lived (Lipschits, 237-71). Second, no clear evidence can be found in Haggai for any preference for one group over another. Zerubbabel and Joshua (Hag 1:1) are returnees, while the "people of the land" (Hag 2:4) refers to the Judean population, whether remainees or returnees (Wolff, 78-79). The reference to the "all the remnant of the people" who respond to Haggai's preaching (Hag 1:13) stresses the responsiveness of the entire community (Kessler 2002, 141-42; Tollington, 54). There is neither reference to those who do not obey nor any indication that the faithful constitute a distinct group (Hag 2:1-5; cf. Mal 3:16-18). It is also significant that Haggai makes no mention of the exile or the Diaspora. The book thus minimizes whatever fractures may have existed within Yahwism, to reinforce the theme of the success of the prophet and the dawning of a new day.

3.5. Relationship to Other Texts. Exegetes differ on whether Haggai should be read as an independent unit or as a part of a broader structure. C. Meyers and E. Meyers and J. Wöhrle see it as structurally united with Zechariah 1—8, A. Sérandour with Zechariah 1—8 and Malachi, and still others with the twelve Minor Prophets as a whole (Nogalski 1993; House). A variety of matters of form and content (especially the book's theological vision of the community and covenant) render it likely that Haggai is a distinct work containing one of the earliest Persian-period voices (Kessler 2008). As such, it should be read as a self-contained unit. Nevertheless, it is also probable that Haggai was incorporated into other emerging compilations of prophetic works, or that other texts (such as Zechariah and Malachi) may even have been written in light of it (Kessler 2002; 2008).

4. Theological Vision and Message.

Haggai was produced at a time when Israel's understanding of its institutions (monarchy, national independence, *covenant, future role among the nations) and very identity were in profound crisis. Earlier theological beliefs could have been seen as worthless, having been invalidated by recent events. Haggai affirms that the tiny community in Yehud, under foreign domination and a shadow of its former self, was nevertheless the theological heir of monarchic Israel, and that its institutions were intact, although provisionally existing in somewhat different forms. Haggai achieves this continuity between past and present through the creative reconfiguration of earlier theological ideas (called "traditions" in scholarly literature) stressing constancy in substance despite change in form. This phenomenon can be seen in the major sections of the book. In Haggai 1:1-11 the people are portrayed as self-indulgent, preferring their own comfort to concern for Yahweh's house. They view poor harvests as justifying their inactivity, making the delaying of work on the temple out to be the "wisest" choice (Kessler 2002). The prophet responds by interpreting the community's misfortunes as divine judgments—a concept deeply rooted in Deuteronomy 28; Leviticus 26; Amos 4 (see below)—designed to alert them to their sin and prod them to action. Haggai's interpretation of these events indicates that he views the Sinai covenant as still functioning, despite the people's disobedience (see Hag 2:5).

Haggai views the reconstruction of the Jerusalem temple as a profoundly important duty. This is significant since temple building is not demanded in earlier Deuteronomistic (Deuteronomy, Joshua—2 Kings) or priestly (Leviticus) traditions. In Haggai's vision, however, restoration would be incomplete without the Jerusalem temple, and he views neglect of it as evidence of disdain for Yahweh (Hag 1:3-11; cf. Deut 28:58-59). To underscore the great importance of this task, Haggai creatively applies terminology associated with extreme covenant violation in the Deuteronomistic and priestly traditions to the community's neglect of the temple (compare Hag 1:6a with Deut 28:38a; Hag 1:6b with Lev 26:26; Hag 1:9 with Deut 28:38a; Hag 1:10 with Lev 26:19-20, Deut 11:17a, 28:23-24; and Hag 1:11 with Deut 28:51). The book contains numerous allusions to other OT texts and themes, and creative configurations of them, in light of the new realities of the Persian period. In Haggai 1:12-15 the leaders and people are described as obeying the prophet's message. Their response is phrased so as to contrast it with the community that refused to heed Jeremiah (cf. Jer 43:4), indicating that the renewed community is now responding as it should have done earlier. In Haggai 2:1-5 the prophet addresses the people's disappointment at the appearance of the temple under construction. Using a traditional formula of encouragement, Haggai urges the builders to be strong (cf. Deut 31:6-7; Josh 1:6, 9) and unafraid (cf. Gen 15:1; Ex 14:13; Deut 1:21; Is 35:4) and assures them that Yahweh is with them (cf. Gen 26:24; 28:15) and will very soon intervene and glorify his house (Hag 2:6-9). Such innerbiblical allusions serve to emphasize the continuity between Haggai's hearers and earlier moments in the people's history (for further examples, see Kessler 2002, 153-57; 183-95; 218; 239-42). Haggai's stress on continuity with the past is also underscored in that he does not refer to a first or second temple, but to Yahweh's one house, which had been glorious in the past, was recently in ruins and is presently of poor appearance, but whose future will be stupendous (Hag 2:3, 9).

In Haggai 2:10-14 the prophet consults the priests on a ritual matter and uses their response to express the "impure" condition of the community (Hag 2:14). Some have seen Haggai's concern here as the people's ethical failures (Mason 1982, 144), or their wrongful inclusion of the Samaritans in the temple building (Wolff, 90-96). However, Haggai 2:10-19 more likely refers to the need for the ceremonial ritual purification of the temple (Petersen, 93; Kessler 2010) from its earlier defilement by both the people's sin (cf. Ezek 6:4-5; 9:7-9; 20:43; 22:6-16) and the Babylonian invaders (Kessler 2002, 214-15). Such practice is well known from Mesopotamian sources (Boda and Novotny; Ellis; Hurowitz, 264-69), The prophet declares the refoundation ceremony undertaken by the people on day 24/month 9 (Hag 2:10, 15, 18) to have cleared away the defilements of the past and assures them of Yahweh's blessing (Hag 2:18-19; cf. Zech 4:7).

Haggai 2:20-23 addresses the question of the future of the promise of an eternal dynasty to David (2 Sam 7:4-17) and the seeming rejection of that promise in Jer 22:24-30. In Haggai 2:6-7, 21-22 the prophet describes Yahweh's coming shaking of the heavens and the earth, which will usher in a new era of blessing. Such language evokes Yahweh's interventions in the past (Hag 2:21-22; cf. Ex 14:9; 15:1; Judg 7:22) as well as existing eschatological hopes (Hag 2:21-22; cf. Is 19:2; Ezek 38:19-21). The oracle in Haggai 2:23, using language saturated by earlier tradition, affirms that Zerubbabel, like the nation (Deut 7:6), David (1 Kings 8:16) and Jerusalem (1 Kings 11:13), has been chosen by Yahweh, and that he is truly Yahweh's servant (cf. Abraham [Gen 26:24]; Moses [Num 12:7-8]; David [2 Sam 7:5]). Furthermore, unlike Jehoiachin, whose faithlessness evoked Yahweh's rejection, and who is likened to a signet ring thrown away (Jer 22:24), Zerubbabel has been faithful and will experience future exaltation by Yahweh, who will "take" him (Hag 2:23; cf. Israel [Ex 6:7]; the Levites [Num 3:12]; David [2 Sam 7:8]), restore and exalt him like a signet recovered, leaving the promise to David intact (Kessler 2006).

5. Significance.

Despite its brevity, Haggai is a highly important book. The temple that Haggai championed played a crucial role in the life of Israel, Jesus of Nazareth and the early church (see Acts 2:46-47). The book furthermore stressed the ongoing importance of the prophetic office at a time when prophecy's relevance was questioned. The prophetic word was Yahweh's most powerful agency for effecting change. Thus, although Yahweh controlled the climatic conditions and harvests (Hag 1:2-11) and could cause upheavals in the cosmos and terrify the nations (Hag 2:6-9, 21-22), it was only his word though Haggai which was able to stir up the hearts of his recalcitrant people (Hag 1:13-14). The book's creative reconfiguration of Israel's earlier theological concepts enabled this community to adapt to the new and unforeseen conditions of life under foreign rule, affirming that, contrary to appearances, Yahweh's covenant and promises were intact, and his work of renewing his community had begun. Thus, Yahweh's people could labor in confident hope of his coming intervention for them. The promise to Zerubbabel (Hag 2:23) assured the community that the promise to David (2 Sam 7:14) had not been removed. The NT sees the ultimate fulfillment of that promise in Jesus of Nazareth, the descendant of Zerubbabel (Mt 1:12; Lk 3:27). Furthermore, Hebrews 12:25-28 views Haggai's prophecy of the shaking of the heavens and earth as referring to both to the kingdom of which the Christian community was already part and the anticipated parousia, when it would be consummated (*see* Prophets in the New Testament).

See also TWELVE, BOOK OF THE; EXILE; TEMPLE.

BIBLIOGRAPHY. *Commentaries:* J. G. Baldwin, *Haggai, Zechariah, Malachi: An Introduction and Commentary* (TOTC; London: Tyndale, 1972); M. J. Boda, *Haggai, Zechariah* (NIVAC; Grand Rapids: Zondervan, 2004); T. Meadowcroft, *Haggai* (RNBC; Sheffield: Sheffield Phoenix, 2006); C. L. Meyers, and E. M. Meyers, *Haggai, Zechariah 1–8* (AB 25B; Garden City, NY: Doubleday, 1987); D. L. Petersen, *Haggai and Zechariah 1–8* (OTL; London: SCM, 1985); P. L. Redditt, *Haggai, Zechariah, Malachi* (NCBC; Grand Rapids: Eerdmans, 1995); P. A. Verhoef, *The Books of Haggai and Malachi* (NICOT; Grand Rapids: Eerdmans, 1987); H. W. Wolff, *Haggai: A Commentary*, trans. M. Kohl (Minneapolis: Augsburg, 1988). *Studies:* P. R. Ackroyd, "Studies in the Book of Haggai," *JJS* 2 (1951) 163–76; idem, "Studies in the Book of Haggai," *JJS* 3 (1952) 1–13; D. Barthélemy, ed., *Critique textuelle de l'Ancien Testament, 3: Ezéchiel, Daniel et les 12 Prophètes* (OBO 50/3; Fribourg: Editions Universitaires; Göttingen: Vandenhoeck & Ruprecht, 1992); W. A. M. Beuken, *Haggai-Sacharja 1–8: Studien zur Überlieferungsgeschichte der frühnachexilischen Prophetie* (SSN 10; Assen: Van Gorcum, 1967); E. J. Bickerman, "En marge de l'écriture," *RB* 88 (1981) 19–23; M. J. Boda and J. Novotny, eds. *From the Foundations to the Crenellations: Essays on Temple Building in the Ancient Near East and the Hebrew Bible* (AOAT 366; Münster: Ugarit-Verlag, 2010); R. S. Ellis, *Foundation Deposits in Ancient Mesopotamia* (YNER 2, New Haven: Yale University Press, 1968); M. H. Floyd, "The Nature of the Narrative and the Evidence of Redaction in Haggai," *VT* 45 (1995) 470–90; idem, *Minor Prophets: Part 2* (FOTL 22; Grand Rapids: Eerdmans, 2000); P. R. House, *The Unity of the Twelve* (JSOTSup 97; Sheffield: Almond, 1990); V. Hurowitz, *I Have Built You an Exalted House: Temple Building in the Bible in Light of Mesopotamian and Northwest Semitic Writings* (JSOTSup 115; Sheffield: Sheffield Academic, 1992); S. J. Japhet, "The Concept of the 'Remnant' in the Restoration Period: On the Vocabulary of Self-Definition," in *From the Rivers of Babylon to the Highlands of Judah: Collected Studies on the Restoration Period*, ed. S. Japhet (Winona Lake, IN: Eisenbrauns, 2006) 432–49; J. Kessler, *The Book of Haggai: Prophecy and Society in Early Persian Yehud* (VTSup 91; Leiden: E. J. Brill, 2002); idem, "Haggai, Zerubbabel, and the Political Status of Yehud: The Signet Ring in Haggai 2:23," in *Prophets, Prophecy, and Prophetic Texts in Second Temple Judaism*, ed. M. H. Floyd and R. D. Haak (LHBOTS 427; New York: T & T Clark, 2006) 102–19; idem, "Tradition, Continuity and Covenant in the Book of Haggai: an Alternative Voice from Early Persian Yehud," in *Traditions in Transition: Haggai and Zechariah 1–8 in the Trajectory of Hebrew Theology*, ed. M. H. Floyd and M. J. Boda (LHBOTS 475; New York: T & T Clark, 2008) 1–39; idem, "Temple Building in Haggai: Variations of a Theme," in *From the Foundations to the Crenellations: Essays on Temple Building in the Ancient Near East and the Hebrew Bible*, ed. M. J. Boda and J. Novotny (AOAT 366; Münster: Ugarit-Verlag, 2010) 357-80; A. Lemaire, "Populations et territories de la Palestine à l'époque perse," *Transeu* 3 (1990) 31-74; O. Lipschits, *The Fall and Rise of Jerusalem: Judah under Babylonian Rule* (Winona Lake, IN: Eisenbrauns, 2005); R. Mason, "The Purpose of the 'Editorial Framework' of the Book of Haggai," *VT* 27 (1977) 413–21; idem, "The Prophets of the Restoration," in *Israel's Prophetic Tradition: Essays in Honour of Peter R. Ackroyd*, ed. R. Coggins, A. Philipps and M. Knibb (Cambridge: Cambridge University Press, 1982) 137–53; J. Nogalski, *Literary Precursors to the Book of the Twelve* (BZAW 217; New York: de Gruyter, 1993a); idem, *Redactional Processes in the Book of the Twelve* (BZAW 218; New York: de Gruyter, 1993b); A. Sérandour, "Réflexions à propos d'un livre récent sur Aggée-Zacharie 1–8," *Transeu* 10 (1995) 75–84; idem, "Les récits bibliques de la construction du Second Temple: Leurs enjeux," *Transeu* 11 (1996) 9–32; O. H. Steck, "Theological Streams of Tradition," in *Tradition and Theology in the Old Testament*, ed. D. Knight (Philadelphia: Fortress, 1977) 183–214; J. E. Tollington, *Tradition and Innovation in Haggai and Zechariah 1–8* (JSOTSup 150; Sheffield: Sheffield Academic, 1993); L. Waterman, "The Camouflaged Purge of Three Messianic Conspirators," *JNES* 13 (1954) 73–78; **J. Wöhrle,** "The Formation and Intention of the Haggai-Zechariah Corpus," *JHScr* 6.10 (2006) <http://www.arts.ualberta.ca/JHS/Articles/article_60.pdf>.

J. Kessler

HARLOTRY. *See* FEMINIST INTERPRETATION; WOMEN, FEMALE IMAGERY.

HEAVEN. *See* COSMOLOGY.

HEAVENLY BEINGS. *See* ANGELS, MESSENGERS, HEAVENLY BEINGS.

HEBREW LANGUAGE

There are many striking features of the Hebrew language of the Prophetic Books. These include oracular forms, both native (e.g., the accusation-threat pattern of judgment speech, woe oracles) and borrowed (e.g., funeral dirge, trial speech), typical prophetic phrases (e.g., messenger formulae such as *kôh ʾāmar yhwh* ["thus says the LORD"] and *nĕʾum yhwh* ["oracle of the LORD"]), metaphoric and parabolic speech (e.g., Ezek 16) and cryptic expressions (e.g., Is 28:10, 13). Most such features constitute distinct and independent topics in their own right (e.g., form criticism, metaphor). By contrast, the linguistic peculiarities in the Prophetic Books generally are absorbed into the critical discussion of their composition and dating. At the same time, some of the most debated issues in the translation and interpretation of the Prophetic Books revolve around questions of the poetic form of prophetic speech and the temporal orientation of prophetic passages as indicated most frequently by verbal forms. This article surveys the role of language in critical introductory discussion of the Prophetic Books and focuses in particular on the issues of poetry and temporality.

1. Poetry in the Prophetic Books
2. Language and Composition of the Prophetic Books
3. Temporal Orientation of the Prophetic Books

1. Poetry in the Prophetic Books.
The major portion of the Prophetic Books is treated as poetry, while several distinct sections clearly are prose narrative (see 2 below on individual books; on the difficulties in distinguishing prose and poetry in Biblical Hebrew in light of the lack of visual versification, see Cook, *DOTWPW* 260-67). The "prose particle count" method developed by F. Andersen and A. Forbes aims at distinguishing prose and poetry based on the density of certain grammatical words that are recognized as being common in prose narrative and infrequent in unambiguous poetic texts. F. Andersen and D. Freedman report that according to this measure, most prophetic literature is neither clearly poetic nor clearly prose but rather is "an intermediate mode" (Andersen and Freedman 1989, 145). C. Meyers and E. Meyers reflect this view when they explain that although a prose-particle count clearly identifies Haggai and Zechariah 1—8 as prose, they contain smaller units that are "clearly 'poetic'" and might be properly termed "oracular prose" (Meyers and Meyers 1987, lxvi-lxvii).

Similarly, A. Hill, using the same prose-particle procedure, identifies the book of Malachi as prose while also recognizing the "elevated" style of the oracles, evident from the numerous poetic devices employed (Hill 1998, 24, 38-39). Hill also observes that much of German scholarship has followed H. Gunkel in treating the oracles of Malachi as poetry, while British and American scholars have tended to treat them as prose (Hill 1998, 23). Unsurprisingly, then, it is easy to find differences between modern versions and translations with respect to the visual layout of prophetic passages. For example, the NRSV presents Ezekiel 30 as almost all poetry (Ezek 30:1, 5, 9, 20 are set as prose). The REB is mostly in agreement with the NRSV, except that it also sets off Ezekiel 30:7-8, 12b as prose. By contrast, the NAB and the NJB treat Ezekiel 30 as prose.

The distinction between prose and poetry in the Prophetic Books is part of, and sometimes confused with, the more crucial issue of the distinction between literary and oral. That is, a major question within compositional historical research on the Prophetic Books is which parts of these books originated as oral proclamations by the prophets and which began as literary compositions. Andersen and Freedman note that oral speech, as a general rule, is more "poetical" than literary composition (Andersen and Freedman 1980, 61). This observation, while valid, served in past generations as a justification for the assumption that all poetic prophetic texts began as oral speeches and all prose prophetic texts are the product of editorial, literary work (e.g., G. Hölscher attributed to the prophet just 144 verses of the sixteen poetic and five elevated prose sections in the book of Ezekiel). However, in recent decades this assumption has been shown to be simplistic (e.g., see Block, 1:17-23 on Ezekiel in this regard, and see Floyd on the relationship between oral and written prophecy generally). It seems groundless to assume that prophets could relate God's messages to the people only in poetic form or that redactors could compose only prose. In Jeremiah, for example, we find a mixture of more poetic and more prosaic prophetic speeches along with third-person narratives by the prophet, often attributed to the work of his scribe, Baruch (see Holladay, 11-16). The book of Ezekiel is notable for being mostly prose, but there is good reason to think that the dated "memoir" style of preserving Ezekiel's prophetic pronouncements derives from his own hand (see Block, 1:20). As new methods for distinguishing oral and literary origins of the biblical literature are developed (e.g., Polak), scholars may be in a better position to discriminate between these categories within the prophetic literature.

In any case, the Prophetic Books have in common with unambiguously poetic books, such as Psalms and Job, numerous poetic devices such as metaphor, word play and alliteration. Examples include the following: (1) word play on *qāyiṣ* ("summer fruit") and *qēṣ* ("end") in the vision in Amos 8:1-3 (see Alter, 160-61); (2) rhyme/alliteration in Isaiah 5:7: *wayĕqaw lĕmišpaṭ wĕhinnê mišpāḥ liṣdāqâ wĕhinnê ṣĕ῾āqâ* ("he hoped for justice, but look, oppression; he looked for righteousness, but look, an anguished cry"), and in Isaiah 7:9: *᾽im lō᾽ ta᾽ămînû kî lō᾽ tē᾽āmēnû* ("if you do not believe, you will not be established") (see Wildberger, 675); (3) the frequency of double-duty particles in Jeremiah, that is, the ellipsis of prepositions or other grammatical words, as in Jeremiah 3:23: *miggĕbā῾ôt hāmôn hārîm* ("from the hills, [from] the tumult of the mountains") (see Holladay, 75).

2. Language and Composition of the Prophetic Books.

Close attention to the language of the Prophetic Books has long been thought crucial to unraveling their often complex history of composition (*see* Formation of the Prophetic Books). So strong is this conviction that discussions of their language rarely take place outside of analyses of their composition history. This section surveys the linguistic features and their role in the composition history of each of the Prophetic Books.

2.1. Isaiah. The book of Isaiah is mostly poetic, containing some of the loftiest poetic passages among the Prophetic Books (esp. Is 40—55). H. Wildberger cautions, however, that differences in poetic form (meter) in the book fail to distinguish among the compositional layers in the book (Wildberger, 672). Interspersed within the poetry are several notable prose narrative passages, including the call narrative (Is 6), the narrative of the symbolic names (Is 7—8) and the narrative of Sennacherib's threat to Jerusalem (Is 36—39), which parallels (and probably derives from) the account in 2 Kings 18—20.

Differences between vocabulary and style in Isaiah 1—39 and Isaiah 40—66 are primary data for deciding the critical question of authorship of these sections. There are a few distinctive phrases, notably "the Holy One of Israel" (Is 1:4; 5:19, 24; 10:20; 12:6; 17:7; 29:19; 30:11-12, 15; 31:1; 37:23; 41:14, 16, 20; 43:3, 14; 45:11; 47:4; 48:17; 49:7; 54:5; 55:5; 60:9, 14), spread throughout the book, which some scholars point to as evidence of single author for the book (e.g., Oswalt, 20-21). However, there are numerous other phrases distinctive of Isaiah 40—66 but rare or absent in Isaiah 1—39: *bāḥar* ("to choose") in reference to God's choice of Israel or his servant (Is 14:1; 41:8-9; 43:10; 44:1-2; 48:10; 49:7); the verb *hālal* ("to praise") (Is 38:18; 41:16; 45:25; 62:9; 64:10) and the noun *tĕhillâ* ("praise") (Is 42:8, 10, 12; 43:21; 48:9; 60:6, 18; 61:3, 11; 62:7; 63:7); *kî ᾽ănîyhwh* with modifying relative clause ("because I am Yahweh who …") (Is 41:13; 43:3; 45:3; 49:23, 26; 60:16; 61:8); participle references to God as redeemer (*gā῾al*, "to redeem") (Is 41:14; 43:14; 44:6, 24; 47:4; 48:17; 49:7, 26; 54:5, 8; 59:20; 60:16; 63:16) or creator (*bārā᾽*, "to create") (Is 4:5; 40:26, 28; 41:20; 42:5; 43:1, 7, 15; 45:7-8, 12, 18; 48:7; 54:16; 57:19; 65:17-18) (see Driver 1908, 238-40). Other differences exhibited between the language of Isaiah 1—39 and Isaiah 40—66 are more difficult to quantify. S. R. Driver summarizes as follows: "There are also literary features of a more general character, which differentiate the author of c. 40-66 from Isaiah. Isaiah's style is terse and compact; the movement of his periods is stately and measured; his rhetoric is grave and restrained. In these chapters [Is 40—66] a subject is often developed at considerable length; the style is much more flowing; the rhetoric is warm and impassioned; and the prophet often bursts into lyrical strain" (Driver 1908, 240-41).

2.2. Jeremiah. The book of Jeremiah shows much more complex a mixture of prose and poetry than Isaiah. Jeremiah 1—25 contains many poetic oracles of judgment, whereas prose narrative accounts of Jeremiah's life are contained mostly in Jeremiah 26—45. Interspersed through these chapters are prose speeches that exhibit in their vocabulary and syntax a relationship with the prose speeches in the books of Deuteronomy, Samuel and Kings. Finally, Jeremiah 46—51 contains poetic oracles against the nations.

This variety of materials is widely understood to indicate a complex composition history. The relationship between the language of Jeremiah and Deuteronomy has been of particular interest, and W. Holladay concludes that there is dependency in both directions: Jeremiah borrowed from proto-Deuteronomic material while latter editors of Deuteronomy in turn borrowed from Jeremiah (Holladay, 53). Further, Holladay discusses possible borrowings of language in Jeremiah from other sources, including the pentateuchal traditions, the Historical Books, and earlier prophetic books (Holladay, 35-70). In turn, Jeremiah's language seems to have had an impact on subsequent biblical texts and writers, including Lamentations, exilic Deuteronomic editors and the later prophetic books of Ezekiel, Second and Third Isaiah, and Zechariah 1—8 (see Holladay, 80-93).

This evidence of widespread *intertextuality in Jeremiah along with disagreements about what data are relevant to drawing a linguistic profile make it difficult to state anything definite about the language of Jeremiah, thus making problematic R. Polzin's use of it as a benchmark in his typology. For instance, Holladay's excellent survey of "Jeremiah's use of language" yields nothing concrete with regard to Jeremiah's particular dialect of Hebrew (Holladay, 75-78). Most of his observations, such as double-duty particles, word plays and ambiguity, merely point to the poetic features in Jeremiah, while more particular uses, such as the pleonastic infinitive absolute for contradictory statements (Jer 4:10; 13:12; 22:10), do not constitute dialectal evidence.

2.3. Ezekiel. The book of Ezekiel is different again from both Jeremiah and Isaiah in that it is mainly prose with only a few poetic passages (e.g., Ezek 7; 17; 19). Even where there are more extended poetic sections, they are interspersed with narrative portions (e.g., the oracles against the nations in Ezek 26—32).

In like manner to the centrality of Deuteronomy in studies of intertextuality in Jeremiah, the focus in Ezekiel studies is on the relationship of its language to the Priestly writings/school. However, while Ezekiel exhibits similar concerns and vocabulary as Priestly books (e.g., Leviticus), it also shows a certain uniqueness of language. W. Zimmerli notes that Ezekiel lacks many terms and verbs found in other portions of the OT while showing a high degree of unique vocabulary (Zimmerli, 22-24). For example, frequently occurring terms for "deliverance" or "salvation" (terms from the roots *yšʿ*, *gʾl, pdh*) do not appear in Ezekiel. Similarly, key terms from Deuteronomic thought, such as *bāṭaḥ* ("to trust"), *ḥesed* ("covenant loyalty" or "lovingkindness") and *ʾāhab* ("to love") are absent from Ezekiel. Compared with Psalms, Ezekiel lacks the language of "to cry out" (*šwʿ, ṣʿq, zʿq*), and in contrast to the Priestly writings and Holiness Code (Lev 17—26), Ezekiel notably lacks terms such as *qāṭar* ("to burn incense"), *ʾiššeh* ("fire offering") and *nādar* ("to make a vow").

Against these absences, Ezekiel contains some 130 unique words. For example, the following verbs occur only in Ezekiel: Piel *btq*, "to slaughter" (Ezek 16:40); Qal *dlḥ*, "to make turbid (waters)" (Ezek 32:2, 13); Qal *ḥdr*, "to penetrate (with a sword)" (Ezek 21:19); Hophal and Pual *htl*, "to be swathed" (Ezek 16:4); Hiphil *tʿh*, "to lead astray" (Ezek 13:10) (cf. *tʿh*); Qal *khl*, "to paint (the eyes)" (Ezek 23:40); Qal *ksm*, "to trim (the hair)" (Ezek 44:20); Qal *kpn*, "to turn toward" (Ezek 17:7); Qal *nqʿ*, "to free oneself, turn away" (Ezek 23:22, 28) (cf. *yʿq*), Piel *shh*, "to sweep away" (Ezek 26:4); Qal *ʿwg*, "to bake" (Ezek 4:12); Niphal *ṣrb*, "to be scorched" (Ezek 21:3); Polel *qss*, "to pluck" (?) (Ezek 17:9); Qal *qrm*, "to cover" (Ezek 17:8); Piel *ššm*, "to lead along on a rope" (Ezek 39:2). Some of Ezekiel's unique vocabulary is used multiple times—for example: *ʾăgappîm*, "troops" (Ezek 12:14; 17:21; 38:6, 9, 22; 39:4); *ʾelgābîš*, "hail (stones)" (Ezek 13:11, 13; 38:22); *ʾattîq*, "passage, street" (?) (Ezek 41:15-16; 42:3, 5); *ḥăbōl*, "pledge" (Ezek 18:12, 16; 33:15); *ḥelʾâ*, "rust" (Ezek 24:6, 11-12); *ḥašmal*, some precious stone (?) (Ezek 1:4, 27; 8:2); *ḥittît*, "terror" (Ezek 26:17; 32:23-27, 32); *mĕkûrâ*, "(ethnic) origin" (Ezek 16:3; 21:30; 29:14); *miqsām*, "oracle" (Ezek 12:24; 13:7); *ʿagābîm*, "passions, love songs" (Ezek 23:11; 33:31-32); *ʿizzābôn*, "merchandise" (Ezek 27:12, 14, 16, 19, 22, 24, 33); *pōʾrâ*, "shoots" (Ezek 17:6; 31:5-6, 8, 12-13); *ṣammeret*, "top (of a tree)" (Ezek 17:3, 22; 31:3, 10, 14); *rĕkullâ*, "trade" (Ezek 26:12; 28:5, 16, 18); *taznût*, "harlotry" (Ezek 16:15, 20, 22, 25-26, 29, 33-34, 36; 23:7-8, 11, 14, 17-19, 29, 35, 43) (see further Zimmerli, 23).

Ezekiel's language is also notably formulaic (see Block, 1:30-39): the address *ben-ʾādām* ("son of man") occurs ninety-three times in the book and elsewhere only in Daniel 8:17; Ezekiel's favorite designation for his audience is *bêt-yiśrāʾēl* ("house of Israel")", which occurs eighty-three times in the book, accounting for over half (57 percent) of its occurrences in the Bible; the introductory formula *wayhi dĕbar yhwh ʾēlay lēʾmōr* ("the word of Yahweh came to me") occurs more than fifty times, and the messenger formula *kōh-ʾāmar ʾădōnāy yhwh* ("thus says the Lord Yahweh") occurs over one hundred times; and Ezekiel's distinctive "recognition" formula *wĕyādĕʿû kî ănî yhwh* ("then they will know that I am Yahweh") occurs, in several variations, over fifty times. Finally, Ezekiel is replete with commands to Ezekiel to engage in prophetic activities, most frequently *hinnābēʾ . . . wĕʾāmartā* ("prophesy . . . and say"), some twenty-four times.

As in the case of Jeremiah, however, it is difficult to draw clear conclusions from these data regarding the book's composition. Arguments regarding dating have drawn attention to the extent of Aramaisms in the book (see Zimmerli, 21-22), but disputes over the determination and definition of "Aramaisms" and their significance in dating biblical texts (see Eskhult; Hurvitz) make even their presence or absence in the book equivocal for questions of dialect or dating. M. Rooker has examined the language of Ezekiel in light of Polzin's typology of "Classical" and "Late" Biblical Hebrew. He concludes that the mixture of late and early

features in the book points to its language as "transitional" between the two stages (Rooker, 185-86). The central focus of Rooker's book is on the thirty-seven Late Biblical Hebrew features found in Ezekiel, which include the areas of orthography (e.g., *plene* דּוִיד [*dāwîd*] in Ezek 34:23 versus דּוִד [*dāwīd*] spelling of "David" in Ezek 34:24; 37:24-25), morphology (e.g., first-person subject pronoun *ʾănî* [169x] instead of *ʾănōkî* [only in Ezek 36:28]; third-person masculine pronoun *hēm* used in place of the feminine *hēn* [Ezek 1:5-6; 3:13; 23:47]) (for a full list, see Rooker, 182-83), and syntax (e.g., the use of the direct-object marker *ʾēt* with subjects [Ezek 10:22; 16:4; 17:21; 20:16; 29:4; 35:10; 44:3]). However, Polzin's typology has been severely criticized in recent years (e.g., Young, Rezetko and Ehrensvärd), calling for a reassessment of this and other data with regard to the stages of development of Hebrew.

2.4. Daniel. The language of the book of Daniel has received a good deal of attention, not only because of its curious bilingual Hebrew-*Aramaic character (Dan 2:4b—7:28 is written in Aramaic), but also because the language data have been central in dating the book—a debate involving issues of prophecy versus apocalyptic literature and the nature of Scripture. Over a century ago, Driver famously remarked, "The verdict of the language of Daniel is thus clear. The *Persian* words presuppose a period after the Persian empire had been well established: the Greek words *demand*, the Hebrew *supports*, and the Aramaic *permits*, a date *after the conquest of Palestine by Alexander the Great*" (Driver 1900, lxiii). Arguments for an earlier date have likewise looked to the linguistic data for support.

K. Kitchen pointed out twenty-one possible Akkadian loanwords (*ʾargĕwān*, "purple"; *ʾăšap*, "enchanter"; *ʾattûn*, "furnace"; *hēkal*, "temple"; *zîw*, "radiance"; *zākû*, "innocence"; *zĕmān*, "time"; *ḥšḥ*, "need"; *karbĕlā*, "hat"; *korsē*, "throne"; *mĕnē*, "mina"; *nĕwālû*, "dunghill"; *sĕgan*, "prefect"; *ʿiddān*, "time"; *peḥâ*, "governor"; *pehar*, "potter"; *parzel*, "iron"; *pĕrēs*, "half-shekel"; *šêzib*, "rescue"; *šĕgal*, "concubine"; *tĕlat*, "triumvir") and nineteen Persian loanwords (*ʾădargāzar*, "counselor"; *ʾazdāʾ*, "certain"; *ʾăhašdarpan*, "satrap"; *gĕdābar*, "treasurer"; *dat*, "law"; *dĕtābar*, "law official"; *habrâ*, "companion"; *haddām*, "limb"; *hamnîkâ*, "necklace"; *zan*, "kind"; *nĕbizbâ*, "present"; *nebrĕšâ*, "lamp"; *nĕdan*, "sheath"; *sĕrak*, "official"; *paṭîš*, "shirt"; *pitgām*, "message"; *rāz*, "secret"; *tiptāy*, "police chief"; *kārôz*, "herald") in the book (Kitchen, 34-35; for discussion of this list, see Collins, 18). More importantly, Kitchen observes that the administrative terms are predominantly Persian loanwords, some of which the Greek translators of the book did not understand (Kitchen, 40, 43). J. Collins notes that while not requiring a pre-Hellenistic date for the book, this fact stands over and against the view that the book wholly originated in the second century (Collins, 19).

The increased finds of Imperial Aramaic (600-200 BC) documents and the Qumran discoveries have greatly advanced the characterization of Biblical Aramaic and the Aramaic of Daniel in particular. There are relatively few linguistic (versus stylistic) differences between the Biblical Aramaic of the fifth-century BC book of Ezra and Daniel besides the preservation of the older third-person plural pronoun *himmô* in Ezra versus *himmôn* in Daniel. Collins notes that on the one hand, comparison with the fourth-century BC Samaria papyri shows the Aramaic of Daniel to be later, while on the other hand, the language appears to be older than the Qumran Aramaic in the *Genesis Apocryphon* (Collins, 16-17). Collins concludes, "The balance of probability, then, favors a date in the early Hellenistic period for the Aramaic portions of Daniel, although a precise dating on linguistic grounds is not possible" (Collins, 17).

The Hebrew of Daniel has more commonalities with Second Temple literature (e.g., Chronicles) than with exilic compositions. Driver lists twenty-five words/phrases that Daniel shares almost exclusively with the latest canonical writings: *malkût*, "kingdom" (e.g., Dan 1:1) (cf. *mamlākâ*); *miqṣat*, "some of" (Dan 1:2, 5, 15, 18) (cf. partitive *min* preposition); indirect command *ʾmr l-* versus direct speech (Dan 1:3, 18; 2:2); *parṭĕmîm*, "nobles" (Dan 1:3); *madāʿ*, "knowledge" (Dan 1:4, 17); *minnâ*, "to appoint" (Dan 1:5, 10, 11); the numeral following rather than preceding the substantive (e.g., Dan 1:5, 12); *ʾăšer lammâ*, "lest" (Dan 1:10); *ḥiyyēb*, "to incur guilt" (Dan 1:10); *gîl*, "age" (Dan 1:10); the order proper name followed by *hammelek* versus the earlier reverse order (Dan 1:21; 8:1); absence of *wayhî* ("and it was") before temporal infinitival phrases (e.g., Dan 8:8, 18); *tāmîd*, to describe the daily burnt offering versus the older *ʿôlōt tāmîd* (e.g., Dan 8:11, 12); the expres-

sion *ʿal ʿomdî* ("upon my standing") (Dan 8:18); *nibʿat*, "to be afraid" (Dan 8:17); *ʿāmad* for "to stand up" versus earlier *qûm* (e.g., Dan 11:2-4, 7); *ʾăbāl* with adversative ("but") force (Dan 10:7, 21); *ʿāṣar kōăḥ*, "to have strength" = "to be able to" (Dan 10:8, 16; 11:6); *ṣāpîr*, "he-goat" (Dan 8:5, 8, 21); *rāšam*, "to inscribe" (Dan 10:21); *heʿĕmîd*, with the sense "to appoint, establish" (Dan 11:11, 13, 14); *tōqep*, "power, force" (Dan 11:17); *bizzâ*, "prey" (Dan 11:24); *ʾappeden*, "palace" (Dan 11:45); *hizhîr*, "shine" (Dan 12:3) (Driver 1908, 506-7).

Collins concurs with Driver's judgment that the "grace and fluency" even of early Second Temple literature is absent in Daniel (Collins, 22). By contrast, the Hebrew of Daniel is characterized by numerous Aramaisms, Persian loanwords (e.g., from Driver's list above: *madāʿ*, "knowledge"; *miqṣat*, "some of"; *ṣāpîr*, "he-goat"; *rāšam*, "to inscribe"; *gîl*, "age"), and by late grammatical constructions and expressions often in common with Qumran literature (e.g., *hyh* ["to be"] with periphrastic participle in Dan 1:16; 8:5; 10:2 and about fifty times at Qumran; absence of *wayhî* ("and it was") before temporal infinitival phrases; long first-person forms in Dan 10:16 and regularly at Qumran; the late idiom *śām ʿal lēb* ["to lay upon the heart" = "to resolve"] in Dan 1:8) (see further Collins, 20-23).

Finally, the bilingualism in Daniel has been judged to be more than a stylistic curiosity, but a compositionally significant characteristic: the Aramaic stories (Dan 2—6) may have circulated independently before being incorporated into the book, to which was added an introductory narrative, possibly originally in Aramaic (Dan 1), and the vision account of Daniel 7. Perhaps somewhat later the Hebrew chapters of Daniel 8—12 were added (see Collins, 24).

2.5. The Book of the Twelve (Minor Prophets). The type of discussions in which the language of the Book of the Twelve (Minor Prophets) features varies from book to book in the collection among three main sorts: identification of "northernisms," intertextuality or dependence on other books within the canon or specifically the Book of the Twelve, or discussions of dating and composition. This last category is consistently interrelated with discussions of the first two sorts. For example, northernisms in Micah 6—7 to some scholars are indicative of northern prophetic authorship; intertextuality, if the direction of dependence can be demonstrated, is crucial in relative dating of the books in the collection as well as identifying the composition of the collection itself. The language of the Book of the Twelve is surveyed here in terms of these three types of discussion.

Northernisms, or instances of Israelian Hebrew, in the Book of the Twelve are limited to Hosea, Amos and Micah 6—7. Northernisms in Hosea are unsurprising, given that the prophet probably was a native of a northern tribe (see the extensive treatment by Yoo), while northernisms in Amos are explained by his prophesying in the north despite hailing from Tekoa in Judah. Micah 6—7 was identified as coming from the hand of a northern prophet by F. Burkitt already in 1926, and the presence of Israelian Hebrew in those chapters is thought to support his thesis. In these books/chapters, grammatical forms appear that align with Aramaic (e.g., *rōʿeh* ["desire" versus "shepherd"] in Hos 12:2; negative *ʾal* used to negate a substantive, *wăʾal rāʿ* ["and not evil"], in Amos 5:14, as in Deir ʿAlla; Hithpael used as a passive, *wĕyištammēr huqqōt ʿomrî* ["and the laws of Omri are observed"], in Mic 6:16), Phoenician (e.g., *yāsûrû* ["to rebel against"], from *srr* but vocalized as Phoenician *ô > û*, in Hos 7:14; indefinite use of demonstrative, *yôm hûʾ* ["that day"], in Mic 7:12 [cf. Heb *hayyôm hahûʾ*]), Ugaritic (e.g., third-weak root infinitive *ḥakkê* in Hos 6:9 vocalized as Ugaritic [cf. Heb *ḥakkôt*]), or a combination of these (e.g., fem. demonstrative *zô* in Hos 7:16 like Aramaic and Phoenician [cf. Heb *zōʾt*]; negative *bal* in Hos 7:2; 9:16 like Phoenician and Ugaritic; narrative use of infinitive absolute in Amos 4:5, *wĕqatter mēḥāmēs tôda* ["and burn a *toda*-offering from leaven"], like Ugaritic and Phoenician; particle of existence *ʾiš* in Mic 6:10, cognate with Ugaritic and Aramaic [cf. Heb *yēš*] [Rendsburg]). Vocabulary items also appear in these books/chapters that G. Rendsburg identifies as part of the lexicon of northern Hebrew (e.g., *ʾahab* ["love"] in Hos 8:9; *ʾarmôn* ["palace, citadel"] in, e.g., Hos 8:14; Amos 1:4; *ʾetnâ* ["price"] in Hos 2:14; *hêkāl* ["palace"] in Hos 8:14; Amos 8:3; *hēdeq* ["brier, thorn"] in Mic 7:4; *ḥēleq* ["field"] in Hos 5:7; Amos 7:4).

Intertextuality is a notable feature in several of the Minor Prophets. A. Berlin notes that Zephaniah is a "study in intertextuality" and goes on to cite parallels between Zephaniah and Genesis 1—11 (e.g., the Table of Nations in Genesis 10 and the oracles of the nations in Zephaniah 2), Deuteronomic vocabulary (e.g., the description of religious syncretism in Zephaniah 1 and the description found in 2 Kings 23), other prophetic books (e.g., *ʾāsōp ʾāsēp* ["I will sweep away"] in Zeph 1:2 and *ʾāsōp ʾăsîpēm* ["I will utterly sweep them away"] in Jer 8:13; *has mippĕnê ʾădōnāy yhwh* ["hush before the Lord GOD"] in Zeph 1:7 and *has mippănāyw* ["hush before him"] in Hab 2:20), Psalms (e.g., *ʿanwē hāʾāreṣ* ["humble of the land"] [cf. Ps 76:10]), and Wisdom literature (e.g., *ʿawlâ* ["wrong"] in Zeph 3:5, 13, which occurs only three other places in the Minor Prophets [Mic 3:10; Hab 2:12; Mal 2:6] but nine times in Job and in Prov 22:8) (Berlin, 13-17). Similarly, Obadiah shows direct dependence on Jeremiah's Edom oracle (Jer 49), and P. Raabe lists numerous other phrases in Obadiah that parallel other books in the canon (Raabe, 32). In recent decades interest has turned to intertextuality within the Book of the Twelve as a clue to the composition and redaction of the collection as whole. J. Nogalski argues that "catchwords" appear at the seams of the books (i.e., last chapter of one book and first chapter of the next book) as a literary strategy for tying the books together in the collection (Nogalski 1993a; 1993b).

The importance of the language for dating the Prophetic Books is foremost in the case of Jonah, Joel and the postexilic books of Haggai, Zechariah and Malachi. The dating of Jonah and Joel is notoriously difficult, which accounts for the use of linguistic data to narrow possibilities. For instance, J. Crenshaw notes a number of linguistic peculiarities in Joel that argue for a sixth- or fifth-century BC date for the book, including the following: late words such as *haššelaḥ* ("missile" [Joel 2:8]), *ḥûs* ("have compassion on" [Joel 2:17]), *ṣaḥanâ* ("stench" [Joel 2:20]), *sôp* ("rear" [Joel 2:20]) and first-person pronoun *ʾănî* instead of *ʾanōkî*; and late expressions such as *bêt* ("house" of the temple [e.g., Joel 1:9]) and *bĕnê-ṣiyyôn* ("sons of Zion" [Joel 2:23]) (Crenshaw, 26). At the same time, Joel exhibits intertextuality with other books of the Bible (see the list in Crenshaw, 27-28) and uncertain temporal orientation with regard to the "day of the LORD": are the events past or future (see 3 below)?

Jonah contains a number of "late" or Aramaic-based words or grammatical expressions that feature in discussions of composition date. These include *mallāḥ* ("sailor" [Jon 1:5]), *sepînâ* ("ship" [Jon 1:5]), *zaʿap* ("fury" [Jon 1:15]), *qerîʾâ* ("message" [Jon 3:2]), *ṭaʿam* ("authority" [Jon 3:7]), *ribbô* ("myriad" [Jon 4:11]), Hithpael *ʿšt* ("to intercede" [Jon 1:6]), Qal *štq* ("to calm down," used with inanimate subject [Jon 1:11]), Piel *mnh* ("to appoint" [Jon 2:1; 4:6-8]); Piel *qdm* ("to plan" [Jon 4:2]), Qal *ʿml* ("to labor over" [Jon 4:10]); words uncommonly associated with inanimate entities, such as *ḥāšab* ("to consider") with the subject "boat" (Jon 1:4), *šātaq* ("to calm down" [Jon 1:11]) and *zaʿap* ("fury" [Jon 1:15]) used of the sea, *ḥûs* ("to pity" with the object "plant" (Jon 4:10); and expressions such as *ḥātar* ("to dig") used of rowing (Jon 1:13), *ʾĕlōhê haššāmayim* ("God of the heavens" [Jon 1:9]), the order *ḥannûn wĕraḥûm* ("gracious and compassionate" [Jon 4:2]) versus *raḥum wĕḥannûn* (Ex 34:6), the *š* relative constructions (Jon 1:7, 12, 4:10) and the interchange of the prepositions *ʾel* and *ʿal* (Sasson 1990: 22-23).

The language of the postexilic prophetic books—Haggai, Zechariah, Malachi—have been subjected to an analysis within the framework of Polzin's typology Late Biblical Hebrew in an effort to sort out precisely when these books might be dated relative to the other postexilic writings—Ezra, Nehemiah, Chronicles (for summary, see Hill 1982; 1983; 1998, 395-400). Polzin's typology Late Biblical Hebrew is based on analyzing the frequency of nineteen different features within Chronicles, Ezra, Nehemiah and selections from the J and E source in the Pentateuch, the various layers of the Priestly code, the court history (2 Sam 13—1 Kings 1) and portions of the work of the Deuteronomist (i.e., framework of Deuteronomy and parts of the Deuteronomistic history) (see Polzin, 85-90). Polzin concluded that JE, the court history and the Deuteronomist are Classical Biblical Hebrew, while the Priestly code is Late Biblical Hebrew, as are Chronicles, Ezra and Nehemiah. Hill has argued that using the same set of features places the postexilic prophetic books—Haggai, Zechariah, Malachi—typologically between Classical Biblical Hebrew and Late Biblical Hebrew of the later parts of the Priestly code, which are dated to the period of Ezra and Nehemiah (c. 600-450 BC). More specifically, Hill concludes these pro-

phetic books, along with Jonah and Joel, should be dated to around 500 BC (Hill 1998, 400).

Given how late in the prophetic stream of writing these postexilic prophetic books are, it is unsurprising how much intertextuality is found in them. Meyers and Meyers discuss the numerous "correspondences" of language between Haggai and Zechariah 1—8 (Meyers and Meyers 1987, xlviii-l), and in their treatment of Zechariah 9—14 they list the numerous correspondences between those chapters and other parts of the Hebrew Bible (Meyers and Meyers 1993, 35-45). Hill's assortment of intertextual links, set out in a verse-by-verse list, shows how rich these latest of prophetic books were in their use and reuse of vocabulary from earlier parts of the canon (Hill 1998, 401-12).

Linguistic discussions of the books of Nahum and Habakkuk, apart from intertextuality within the Book of the Twelve, are largely confined to philological discussions of difficult verses, which are plentiful, or identification of Akkadian loanwords (e.g., the connection of *mĕṣurâ* in Nah 2:1 [MT 2:2] and *māṣôr* in Hab 2:1 with Akk *nāṣar* ["guard"], interpreted as "guard tower" in both cases).

The foregoing characterizations of the language of the Prophetic Books (e.g., descriptions such as "late" language and "Aramaisms") have recently become controversial, with a few scholars arguing that linguistic data cannot be reliably used to date the biblical texts either relative to one another or absolutely (e.g., Young, Rezetko and Ehrensvärd), and others responding with new assessments of the existing data (e.g., Miller-Naudé and Zevit).

3. Temporal Orientation of the Prophetic Books.

Perhaps no characteristic of Hebrew language is more troublesome for the interpretation of the Prophetic Books as the temporal contours of its verbal system. The tense-aspect-mood system of Biblical Hebrew is still not fully understood, and the switching among various verb forms in the prophetic literature, especially the poetic sections, is such that in places it defies explanation. Such problems are exacerbated in the Prophetic Books by the caricaturing of the prophets as "foretellers," which casts into further confusion the uncertainties about whether the prophets in places are making pronouncements about the past, the present, the future, or a combination of

Habakkuk	Verb + gloss	Hebrew	NRSV	REB	NAB	NJB	NJPS
1:2a	šiwwaʿtî, "I cry out"	perfect	future	noun	present	present	future
1:2b	tišmāʿ, "you hear"	imperfect	future	future	present	future	(future-implied)
1:2c	ʾezʿaq, "I cry out"	imperfect	future	present	present	present	future
1:2d	tôsîa, "you save"	imperfect	future	present	present	future	(future-implied)

Table 1. Verb Translations of Habakkuk 1:2

these. For example, J. Barton makes this stunning admission: "Nothing can really be said about the time references in Joel on the basis of the verb forms used" (Barton, 69). The variety of ways the verbs in Habakkuk 1:2 ("O LORD, how long shall I cry for help, and you will not listen? Or cry to you 'Violence!' and you will not save?" [NRSV]) have been rendered by modern translators is a good illustration of the difficulties (table 1 is based on Andersen, 103).

The difficulties evident here can be multiplied many times over. They emerge from uncertainty with the overall temporal orientation (Is he complaining of things that have happened or of things that will happen? Is he crying out, or has he cried out, or both?), the uncertain syntax (Does the initial interrogative influence the interpretation of the perfect verb that follows, or should it be treated as extending only to the vocative: "How long, LORD? I have cried out!"?), and ambiguity of meaning for some forms (Are "will not hear" and "will not save" temporal statements, or are they descriptions of God's unwillingness to respond?).

Behind such passage-specific issues stand several features of the Hebrew verbal system that feed into such ambiguities. First, tense is not encoded in the morphology of the two main verbal forms, the perfect and imperfect. Instead, these two verb forms contrast in terms of the way they portray events: either as a whole event with beginning and end point in view (perfect), or as in the process of unfolding (imperfect) (see Cook 2001; 2006). In the realm of past tense, this distinction may be analogically illustrated by the contrast between English simple past ("it flew") and past progressive ("it was flying"). Nevertheless, these two verb forms imply a "default" temporal interpretation (see Smith), such that the perfect is generally interpreted as referring to past events, and the im-

perfect refers to nonpast events. Nevertheless, crossover is possible and demonstrates their lack of explicit temporal indications—for example, 1 Samuel 1:10, "She prayed to Yhwh and she was weeping greatly" (imperfect), and Genesis 15:18, "To your descendants I hereby give this land" (perfect). Difficulties with the temporal interpretation of these forms are particularly evident in the sphere of present time, where the two forms most overlap, such as in proverbial statements (see Cook, *DOTWPW* 260-67) or in prophetic passages such as Habakkuk 1:1-2, cited above.

Second, both the perfect and imperfect forms can express both statements of fact (indicative mood) and statements of possibility (nonindicative mood). Nonindicative statements most frequently are expressions of the speaker's will (e.g., Jer 7:27: "You shall speak [irreal perfect = *waw*-consecutive perfect] to them these words"; Ezek 5:17: "And a sword I will bring [imperfect] upon you") or the expression of hypothetical or conditional/contingent events, as in this following passage: "If you are willing [imperfect] and obey [irreal perfect = *waw*-consecutive perfect], the good of the land you shall eat [imperfect]; but if you refuse [imperfect] and rebel [irreal perfect = *waw*-consecutive perfect], by the sword you shall be devoured [imperfect]" (Is 1:19-20).

The difficulties with interpreting the verbs in the Prophetic Books are well illustrated by the grammatical category "prophetic perfect," which appears already in the medieval grammatical discussions of the biblical prophets (see Rogland, 53-56). This category was developed to explain instances of the perfect(ive) verb that seem to refer to an indicative future event in prophetic literature, such as Isaiah 5:13a: "Therefore my people will go into captivity [perfect] because they lack knowledge of me" (REB). Other examples include "be full" in Isaiah 11:9, "dry up" in Isaiah 19:7 and "capture" in Jeremiah 48:41 (see Klein).

The "prophetic perfect" explanation has taken several forms, but generally grammars point to the imminency and vividness of a future event so expressed by the perfect verb (see Rogland, 53-54). If we treat this as a rhetorical device, we can see a certain analogy with the "historical present" tense found in so many languages, including English and NT Greek (e.g., Mk 15:24: "And they crucified [present tense: *staurōsin*] him"). However, as analogous as these might appear, the identification of prophetic perfects has proved uncertain. Quite a number of examples that some grammarians or commentators treat as clear cases of future events expressed by the perfect verb, other authorities interpret as past events. Thus, it is only as an ad hoc process of elimination that examples of the prophetic perfect can be identified (see Klein). On this basis, M. F. Rogland has argued that many of the passages brought forward as examples of the prophetic perfect are misidentified (Rogland, 58-113). Rather, the perfect verb is functioning with much more "normal" senses (i.e., past and perfect expressions), which senses are missed by scholars because they overlook the possibility of future perfect expressions ("this will have happened") or temporal shifts such as quoted speech or visionary narratives.

In fact, the principles that Rogland puts forward to narrowly explain the prophetic perfects are more widely explanatory of the variety of verb forms found in prophetic literature. In particular, three issues need to be taken into account: (1) the temporal (deictic) shifts occasioned by quotations and visionary passages; (2) the means available to the prophets for expressly signaling future time; (3) the conditional nature of prophetic threats as over and against the caricatured interpretations of their pronouncement as "prediction." These three issues are treated here in turn.

In *vision reports we find the prophets describing events that may be past or future, but the vision itself is present before their eyes. As a result, these static descriptions may utilize a number of different verb forms, including both perfects (especially with stative predicates) and imperfects, as well as the participle and null-copula/verbless expressions. The vision report in Habakkuk 3 is a good illustration of the variety of verb forms that may appear in such a context. The visionary portion extends from Habakkuk 3:3-15, and the mixture of various verbs (thirty-two in all) is quite diverse, yet the NRSV, NIV and NKJV translate all as past verbs, while the REB, NAB and JB mostly use present verbs, and the NASB and NLT both show a split between present verbs in Habakkuk 3:3-7 as past verbs in Habakkuk 3:8-15. Some authorities claim that the verbs should be interpreted as future on the basis that the perfect forms in the passage are "prophetic perfects" (de Regt, 92).

The alternation between imperfect and perfect verbs may be clarified by attention to characteristics of temporal immediacy in a vision report, such as in Habakkuk 3. On this basis, the passage, which begins mainly with imperfect verbs (Hab 3:3-5), is best translated with present progressive verbs, which convey the events as going on at the very moment in which they are described by the prophet. The stative perfect in Habakkuk 3:3 expresses a present state, as is typical (see Gibson, 61).

> 3:3Eloah from Teman is coming
> [imperfect],
> and the Holy One from Mount Paran.
> His glory has covered [perfect] the
> heavens,
> and his praise fills [stative perfect] the
> earth.
> 3:4His splendor is [imperfect] like a light
> —rays from his hand, and there is his
> power.
> 3:5Before him is going [imperfect]
> pestilence,
> and plague is coming [imperfect] forth
> at his feet.

The change from the dominance of the imperfect verbs in Habakkuk 3:3-5 to perfect and past narrative forms (= *waw*-consecutive imperfects) in Habakkuk 3:6-7 conveys a shift away from a temporal immediacy of the report. This shift coincides with the shift of focus on God's arrival to the earth's reaction to his arrival: only the actions of Eloah stand in narrative order expressed by past narrative verbs, underscoring that "the earth quaked" and "the nations shook" as a direct consequence of Eloah's standing and looking (Hab 3:6). The prophet's reference to himself in Habakkuk 3:7 ("I saw") underscores the distancing of himself from the visionary experience, as he is able to reflect upon his watching of the vision. The shift in verbal dominance to perfects and pasts points to a past progressive rendering of the imperfect in Habakkuk 3:7.

> 3:6He stood [perfect] and the earth quaked [past],
> he looked [perfect] and the nations shook [past],
> and the ancient mountains shuddered [past],
> the everlasting hills sank on his everlasting path.
> 3:7Under disaster I saw [perfect] the tents of Cushan,
> the curtains of the land of Midian were trembling [imperfect].

A similar alternation appears in the second half of the poem (Hab 3:8-15): the predominance of imperfect verbs coincides with a description of God's theophanic approach (Hab 3:8-9, 12), and the predominance of perfect verbs with a description of the earth's reaction (Hab 3:10-11). And in the final alternation (Hab 3:13-15) the prophet once again distances himself from the temporal immediacy of the visionary experience with perfect verbs, this time to reflect on the significance of God's arrival: he has come to save his people.

> 3:8Is it with the rivers you are angry [stative Perfect], Yahweh,
> or at the rivers (is) your anger,
> or at the sea (is) your wrath,
> that you are riding [imperfect] your horses,
> your chariots of victory;
> 3:9(that) you are brandishing [imperfect] your naked bow
> —oaths of (your) tribes, a command;
> (that) you are cleaving [imperfect] rivers in the earth?
>
> 3:10The mountains have seen you [perfect],
> are writhing [imperfect],
> a torrential downpour has passed [perfect],
> the deep has given [perfect] its voice,
> its high hand the sun has raised [perfect],
> 3:11the moon has stood [perfect] in its

> lofty abode—
> at the light of your arrows (which) are coming [imperfect],
> at the splendor of the flash of your spear.
> 3:12In fury you are marching [imperfect] on the earth,
> in wrath you are threshing [imperfect] the nations.
> 3:13You have come forth [perfect] for the salvation of your people,
> for the salvation of your anointed.
> You have crushed [perfect] the head of the wicked house
> —laying bare the foundation to the neck.
> 3:14You have pierced [perfect] with your staff the head of its warriors
> —(who) were storming [imperfect] to scatter me;
> their exultation (is) as to devour the poor in secret.
> 3:15You have trodden [perfect] in the sea with your horses
> —great foaming waters!

By contrast, the prophets sometimes cast their descriptions quite unambiguously into the future. One of the ways they do this is by using a tense-indicating copula verb. The copula "to be" verb is extremely frequent in the Bible, appearing most frequently either as a marker of past events (past narrative = waw-consecutive imperfect wayhî ["and it was"]) or future events (irreal perfect = waw-consecutive perfect wehāyâ ["and it shall be"]). About half of the occurrences of wehāyâ ("and it shall be") appear in the Prophetic Books, usually alone but sometimes in a set phrase such as "and it shall be on that day" or "and it shall be at time." The following passage from Zephaniah 1 illustrates the use of this verb to unambiguously portray the events described as happening in some future time when God takes action, as he has announced earlier in the chapter that he intends to do (I have placed the circumlocution "and it will be," as found in older translations, in parentheses and italicized the future auxiliary verb, which is the real significance of the wehāyâ form):

> 1:7Hush before the Lord GOD, for the day of the LORD is near.
> Indeed, he has prepared a sacrifice,

consecrated his guests.

[1:8](And it will be) on the day of the
   sacrifice I *will* punish [irreal perfect]the
officials and the king's sons
and all who dress themselves in foreign
   attire.

[1:9]And I *will* punish [irreal perfect] all
   who leap over the threshold on that day
—those who fill their master's house
   with violence and fraud.

[1:10](And it will be) on that day—oracle of
   the LORD
—there *will* be the sound of a cry from
   the Fish Gate,
and of a howl from the Second Quarter,
and a crash from the hills.

[1:11]Wail, inhabitants of the Mortar,
for all the traders have perished;
all who weigh out silver are cut off.

[1:12](And it will be) at that time I *will*
   search [imperfect] Jerusalem with
   lamps,
and I *will* punish [irreal perfect] the
      people who rest complacently on
      their dregs,
those who say in their hearts, "The LORD
   will not do good, nor will he do harm."

[1:13]So that their wealth becomes plunder,
   and their houses desolation.
And if they build houses, they shall not
   inhabit them;
and if they plant vineyards, they shall not
   drink wine from them.

Although the prophets had the means to describe events as unambiguously future, they
were not simple foretellers. Much more frequently the description is one of what will happen if God's people will not heed the prophetic
warning (see Jer 18:1-11). Following the passage
from Zephaniah cited above, the prophet calls
for the people to seek the Lord before the day
of the Lord comes (Zeph 2:3). For this reason,
the description in Zephaniah 1 is not simply
cast in future time using *wehāyâ*, but uses nonindicative expressions of what God intends versus indicative expressions of what will happen
(e.g., "I will punish" [Zeph 1:8, 9, 12]). These
verbs, like the copula *wehāyâ*, are irreal perfects, which makes the statements of God's action conditional threats: "If this, then that." In
other words, the entire tenor of the prophecy,
via the grammar of the Hebrew, is set not as a
forecast of future activities of God, but as a
statement of intended action that is contingent
upon the people's response.

See also ARAMAIC LANGUAGE; INTERTEXTU-
ALITY AND INNERBIBLICAL INTERPRETATION;
WRITING AND PROPHECY.

BIBLIOGRAPHY. **R. Alter,** *The Art of Biblical
Poetry* (New York: Basic Books, 1985); **F. I. An-
dersen,** *Habakkuk: A New Translation with Intro-
duction and Commentary* (AB 25; New York: Doubleday, 2001); **F. I. Andersen and A. D. Forbes,**
"'Prose Particle' Counts in the Hebrew Bible,"
in *The Word of the Lord Shall Go Forth: Essays in
Honor of David Noel Freedman in Celebration of His
Sixtieth Birthday,* ed. C. Meyers and M. O'Connor
(Winona Lake, IN: Eisenbrauns, 1983) 165-83;
F. I. Andersen and D. N. Freedman, *Hosea: A
New Translation with Introduction and Commentary* (AB 24; Garden City, NY: Doubleday, 1980);
idem, *Amos: A New Translation with Introduction
and Commentary* (AB 24A; New York: Doubleday, 1989); **J. Barton,** *Joel and Obadiah* (OTL;
Louisville: Westminster/John Knox, 2001); **A.
Berlin,** *Zephaniah: A New Translation with Introduction and Commentary* (AB 25A; New York:
Doubleday, 1994); **D. I. Block,** *The Book of Ezekiel* (2 vols.; NICOT; Grand Rapids: Eerdmans,
1997-1998); **F. C. Burkitt,** "Micah 6-7: A Northern Prophecy," *JBL* 45 (1926) 159-61; **R. P. Carroll,** *Jeremiah* (OTL; Philadelphia: Westminster,
1986); **B. S. Childs,** *Introduction to the Old Testament as Scripture* (Philadelphia: Fortress, 1979);
J. J. Collins, *Daniel* (Hermeneia; Minneapolis:
Fortress, 1993); **J. A. Cook,** "Hebrew Language," *DOTWPW* 260-67; idem, "The Hebrew
Verb: A Grammaticalization Approach," *ZAH*
14.2 (2001) 117-43; idem, "The Finite Verbal
Forms in Biblical Hebrew Do Express Aspect,"
JANES 30 (2006) 21-35; **J. L. Crenshaw,** *Joel: A
New Translation with Introduction and Commen-
tary* (AB 24C; New York: Doubleday, 1995); **L.
de Regt,** "Hebrew Verb Forms in Prose and in
Some Poetic and Prophetic Passages: Aspect,
Sequentiality, Mood and Cognitive Proximity,"
JNSL 34 (2008) 75–103; **S. R. Driver,** *The Book of
Daniel* (CBSC; Cambridge: Cambridge Univer-
sity Press, 1900); idem, *An Introduction to the Lit-
erature of the Old Testament* (ITL; New York: C.
Scribner's Sons, 1908); **M. Eskhult,** "The Importance of Loanwords for Dating Biblical Hebrew Texts," in *Biblical Hebrew: Studies in Chronology and Typology,* ed. I. Young (JSOTSup 369;
London: T & T Clark, 2003) 8-23; **M. H. Floyd,**

"Prophecy and Writing in Habakkuk 2,1-5," *ZAW* 105 (1993) 462-81; **J. C. L. Gibson,** *Davidson's Introductory Hebrew Grammar: Syntax* (4th ed.; Edinburgh: T & T Clark, 1994); **A. E. Hill,** "Dating Second Zechariah: A Linguistic Examination," *HAR* 6 (1982) 105-34; idem, "Dating the Book of Malachi: A Linguistic Reexamination," in *The Word of the Lord Shall Go Forth: Essays in Honor of David Noel Freedman in Celebration of His Sixtieth Birthday*, ed. C. Meyers and M. O'Connor (Winona Lake, IN: Eisenbrauns, 1983) 77-89; idem, *Malachi: A New Translation with Introduction and Commentary* (AB 25D; Garden City, NY: Doubleday, 1998); **W. L. Holladay,** *Jeremiah 2: A Commentary on the Book of the Prophet Jeremiah, Chapters 26-52* (Hermeneia; Minneapolis: Fortress, 1989); **G. Hölscher,** *Hesekiel, der Dichter und das Buch: Eine literarkritische Untersuchung* (BZAW 39; Giessen: Töpelmann); **A. Hurvitz,** "Hebrew and Aramaic in the Biblical Period: The Problem of 'Aramaisms' in Linguistic Research on the Hebrew Bible," in *Biblical Hebrew: Studies in Chronology and Typology*, ed. I. Young (JSOTSup 369; London: T & T Clark, 2003) 24-37; **K. A. Kitchen,** "The Aramaic of Daniel," in *Notes on Some Problems in the Book of Daniel*, ed. D. Wiseman (London: Tyndale, 1965) 31-79; **G. L. Klein,** "The 'Prophetic Perfect,'" *JNSL* 16 (1990) 45-60; **C. Meyers and E. Meyers,** *Haggai, Zechariah 1-8: A New Translation with Introduction and Commentary* (AB 25B; Garden City, NY: Doubleday, 1987); idem, *Zechariah 9-14: A New Translation with Introduction and Commentary* (AB 25C; New York: Doubleday, 1987); **C. Miller-Naudé and Z. Zevit,** eds., *Diachrony in Biblical Hebrew* (Winona Lake, IN: Eisenbrauns, forthcoming); **J. Nogalski,** *Literary Precursors to the Book of the Twelve* (BZAW 217; Berlin: de Gruyter, 1993a); idem, *Redactional Processes in the Book of the Twelve* (BZAW 218; Berlin: de Gruyter, 1993b); **J. Oswalt,** *The Book of Isaiah: Chapters 1-39* (NICOT; Grand Rapids: Eerdmans, 1986); **F. H. Polak,** "Style Is More Than the Person: Sociolinguistics, Literary Culture and the Distinction between Written and Oral Narrative," in *Biblical Hebrew: Studies in Chronology and Typology*, ed. I. Young (JSOTSup 369; London: T & T Clark, 2003) 38-103; **R. Polzin,** *Late Biblical Hebrew: Toward an Historical Typology of Biblical Hebrew Prose* (HSM 12; Missoula, MT: Scholars Press, 1976); **P. R. Raabe,** *Obadiah: A New Translation with Introduction and Commentary* (AB 24D; New York: Doubleday, 1996); **G. Rendsburg,** "A Comprehensive Guide to Israelian Hebrew: Grammar and Lexicon," *Orient* 38 (2003) 5-35; **M. F. Rogland,** *Alleged Non-Past Uses of Qatal in Classical Hebrew* (SSN 44; Assen: Van Gorcum, 2003); **M. F. Rooker,** *Biblical Hebrew in Transition: The Language of the Book of Ezekiel* (JSOTSup 90; Sheffield: Sheffield Academic, 1990); **J. M. Sasson,** *Jonah* (AB 24B; New York: Doubleday, 2000); **C. S. Smith,** "The Pragmatics and Semantics of Temporal Meaning," in *Proceedings: Texas Linguistic Forum 2004*, ed. P. Denis et al. (Somerville, MA: Cascadilla, 2006) 92-106; **L. Stulman,** *The Prose Sermons of the Book of Jeremiah: A Redescription of the Correspondences with Deuteronomistic Literature in the Light of Recent Text-Critical Research* (SBLDS 83; Atlanta: Scholars Press, 1986); **W. G. E. Watson,** *Classical Hebrew Poetry: A Guide to Its Techniques* (JSOTSup 26; Sheffield: Sheffield Academic, 1986); **H. Wildberger,** *Isaiah 28-39*, trans. T. Trapp (CC; Minneapolis: Fortress, 2002); **Y. J. Yoo,** "Israelian Hebrew in the Book of Hosea" (Ph.D. diss., Cornell University, 1999); **I. Young, R. Rezetko and M. Ehrensvärd,** *Linguistic Dating of Biblical Texts* (London: Equinox, 2008); **W. Zimmerli,** *Ezekiel 1: A Commentary on the Book of the Prophet Ezekiel, Chapters 1-24*, trans. R. Clements, F. Cross and K. Baltzer (Hermeneia; Philadelphia: Fortress, 1979). J. A. Cook

HELLENISTIC PERIOD. *See* Israelite History.

HERMENEUTICS

Hermeneutical questions arise in connection with the OT Prophetic Books in a variety of ways. As opposed to interpretive questions regarding how to interpret the specific texts (on which, see the articles on each of the Prophetic Books), hermeneutical questions concern how one evaluates the various interpretive options, and what sorts of criteria are pertinent to the wise handling of the scriptural texts. Such questions have classically considered the temporal range of prophetic prediction and the nature of prophetic fulfilment, most particularly in Christ in the NT, but also in the time of the reader. More recently, hermeneutical questions have in particular considered questions of canon and canonical setting, both internal to the prophetic corpus and in regard to the links between the prophetic canon and the rest of

Jewish and Christian Scripture, as well as questions about the social location of prophecy and reader-oriented questions regarding how the texts are appropriated today. In general, hermeneutics succeeds in bringing fresh questions to bear on the reading of the texts rather than in the offering of substantive interpretations. It is therefore rightly to be understood as one auxiliary discipline (among others) that will assist the interpreter to be well placed for proceeding to interpretive engagement with the text rather than prejudging what such engagement should look like.

1. Hermeneutical Frameworks
2. Modes of Reading the Prophetic Texts
3. Hermeneutical Approaches to the Reading of Prophetic Texts Today
4. Discerning the Prophetic Word Then and Now

1. Hermeneutical Frameworks.
How one reads scriptural texts always depends in large part on the interpretive goals one has in reading. Broadly speaking, the majority of such interpretive goals may be grouped into a limited number of overlapping categories: the historical, the literary and the theological. In this section we consider background issues in these three categories, all of which play their part in framing the interpreter's approach to the text.

1.1. Historical Interests. Questions about the historical contexts of the prophets whose words are recorded in these books are to a limited extent invited by the texts themselves. Prophetic collections (either whole books or subsections [e.g. Ezek 24]) usually begin with a sentence that orients the reader to some historical setting. Typically, this is a time period during which the word of Yahweh came to the prophet, although only about half the Minor Prophets do this. Isaiah 1:1 is a straightforward example: a reference to "the days of Uzziah, Jothan, Ahaz, and Hezekiah, kings of Judah." This time period, extending through much of the second half of the eighth century BC, serves as an indication of the historical period of Isaiah's ministry, although little of the book of *Isaiah requires specific reference to historical events for its interpretive significance. Thus, for example, Isaiah 1:7-9 reads as a text that makes sense against the putative background of the Assyrian siege of Jerusalem in 701 BC, but the text of Isaiah 1 neither compels nor requires such a reference (*see* History of Israel). Rather, the point is that Yahweh is the one who leaves survivors even in the midst of desolation, very probably in 701 BC, but in other circumstances too.

The books of *Ezekiel and *Daniel offer various ways in which a reader might construct a chart of dates against which to map individual textual units, but these markers are hardly key to the flow of the finished book in either case, and there is little interpretive gain from laying out the disordered chronology of each book. The reader of Daniel, for instance, does not seem to be expected to correlate Daniel 7:1 or Daniel 8:1 with Daniel 5, nor to find much significance in Daniel 9's location in the same time period as Daniel 6. Likewise, early readers of *Amos may have known the specific time indicated by "two years before the earthquake" (Amos 1:2), but the loss of this historical reference point to later readers does not make problematic the reading of the book of Amos. Amos 7:10-17 gives indication of some of the historical setting of the prophet Amos, and it has long been standard for critical commentaries to begin their accounts of the book with this information. Perhaps it is significant, though, that the compilers of the book of Amos evidently did not think that the reader needed to start here. A book such as *Joel is notoriously difficult to locate with reference to any dates at all; the best that interpreters can do is postulate possible dates for invasions by what are referred to as "locusts" (Joel 1:4-12; 2:25) (though it is an open question as to whether this is a reference to an invading army or actual locusts), or try to deduce information about the state of the priesthood from passing references to temple practice (Joel 2:15-17). Reading Joel for information regarding its historical setting is manifestly a reading "against the grain."

Most likely, the claim of superscriptions such as Jeremiah 1:1; 25:1; 26:1 and so forth is to emphasize that the prophetic word comes in specific places and times, and that the word of Yahweh is deeply engaged with the lived social realities of God's people (and, to a lesser though significant extent, other people). In particular, it is generally the case that prophetic texts are appropriately situated with respect to the sixth-century BC exile of the southern kingdom. Those who warn of impending *exile, or who point to exile as the grim vindication of their word, need to be read with this particular historical context in mind. Postexilic prophetic voices (found prominently in the later chapters of Isaiah as well as *Haggai-*Malachi) tend to operate with different agendas (e.g., regarding the nature of the restored people in the land). It is rare that the interpreter needs to press further than this general level of observation with regard to historical specificity.

On the other hand, it is undoubtedly true that the interpreter will be assisted by recent studies that have sought a "thicker" sociohistorical description of the phenomenon of exile itself. Thus, "exile" is today often read through the rubric of "forced migration," and this sheds considerable interpretive light on the complex issues concerning what proportion of the population was deported, who stayed behind, and how these different traditions negotiated the recombination of Israelites after the "return." Such studies of the world "behind the text" offer hermeneutical insights into the matters taken up in the text, especially those concerning matters of power, authorization, cooperation and so forth (for a compelling analysis that draws links with the situation of today's readers with respect to power, see Smith-Christopher 2002).

A further level at which historical contexts are relevant is the level at which the spoken oracle becomes the written text (*see* Writing and Prophecy). This leads more naturally to literary and canonical questions concerning the finished collections of prophetic sayings, to which we now turn.

1.2. Literary Collections. How did the spoken word of the prophet become the literary collection of oracles going under the prophet's name? The traditional answer in both Jewish and Christian understanding was that the prophets themselves were responsible for the literary compositions bearing their names. With the rise of historical consciousness in the modern world, and awareness of the significance of oral tradition in the process of transmission of the prophetic word, critical scholarship settled on a model more akin to a prophetic speaker and a literary editor who were not normally thought to be the same people. Scholarly interest initially focused on isolating historical contexts for individual oracles, but in more recent times it has broadened to include also a

concern to understand the redactor's (literary) art and the potential theological significance of the collected text (see Childs 1979, 305-10).

The texts themselves offer little indication of how the process of transmission and collection might have worked (*see* Formation of the Prophetic Books). Such clues as there are remain difficult to assess. One obvious focus of attention is the account in Jeremiah 36 relating the story of how the prophet's spoken oracles are consigned to writing by the scribe Baruch. The initial written version is burned, but a rewritten and expanded scroll (see Jer 36:32) is commissioned. In the context of the book of Jeremiah this account is intended to emphasize the enduring power of the prophetic word, lasting beyond its original oral context and even, in this very narrative, surviving King Jehoiakim's attempt to destroy the written version. Such a reading of the "plain sense" of the text of Jeremiah 36 does not, however, straightforwardly address historically oriented questions about how the spoken word is linked to its written representation. Attempts to correlate the scrolls mentioned in Jeremiah 36 with versions of the material in the finished book of Jeremiah have been inconclusive, and scholarly judgments range from those who, in a largely historicizing approach, see the historical Jeremiah's words gathered by his "colleague and friend, Baruch the scribe" (Lundbom 2004, 254; see also Lundbom 1986), through to those for whom the account of Jeremiah 36 is, as is much of the rest of the book, part of its ideologically motivated argument for receiving the text of Jeremiah as authoritative (Carroll 1986).

A possible insight into the "behind the scenes" working of the prophetic collections occurs in Isaiah 8:16, "Bind up the testimony, seal the teaching among my disciples," which some have argued indicates a reference to something like an "Isaianic school." This may then be read in conjunction with Isaiah 29:11-12, which depicts a scroll already in existence—a sealed document that can be understood only by those who grasp Isaiah's prophetic message, in contrast to uncomprehending "outsiders" (cf. Is 29:13-14). One might have here an indication of a group of Isaiah's followers who operate with a written testimony to his spoken words originating, in the first instance, with the prophet himself. Once such a collection is in existence, it then makes sense to suppose that further words could be added to it as those involved awaited the day when the scroll would be "opened" to all (or at least to the faithful in Israel) (Blenkinsopp, 1-55).

What is the hermeneutical significance of such an account? First, it should (rightly) complicate our notions of authorship with respect to ancient texts. That the eighth-century BC prophet Isaiah is present as a voice in the book of Isaiah does not amount to the claim that he "wrote the book." Historical enquiries regarding how the literary collections came about (e.g., Williamson) thus work with no hermeneutically significant category corresponding to the modern notion of authorship (Barton, *NIDB* 1:354-55). Although it is common to postulate a distinction between oral prophets and literate scribes, with the latter co-opting the oracles of the former for the purposes of centralizing and controlling the social impact of the word of Yahweh, more recent accounts have rightly challenged whether it is realistic to think of the two groups as quite so distinct (Floyd). The written prophetic text might best be understood on the analogy of a musical score awaiting performance: the function of the text is as an *aide-mémoire*, best performed/read by one who knows the content and flow of the overall text, though *in extremis* capable of being read by a literate newcomer. The literary collections thus serve as vehicles for the prophetic reenactment of the original oracles, still bearing the force of being a revelation of Yahweh (Doan and Giles). In this way, we can see that what have traditionally been called "prophetic *sign acts," such as Jeremiah's breaking a yoke or Ezekiel's lying on his side before a model of Jerusalem (Friebel 1999), are special cases of what was in fact the normal manner of representation of the prophetic: as enacted performance (see also Stacey 1990). It is an important hermeneutical point to recognize that authorship then and now is not the same phenomenon, and failure to grasp this had led to attempts to critique or to defend largely anachronistic notions of authorship in the prophetic corpus.

A relatively concise example of the complex compositional processes involved may be found in the book of Amos, which assumes a later and somewhat distinct perspective in its final verses (Amos 9:10-15, with 9:8b looking like a late insertion too). Such an addition makes sense in the context of the literary work that is the finished book, but not as part of a historical occasion on which the prophet Amos might have added such a hopeful oracle to his generally relentless pronouncement of doom and imminent judgment upon the northern kingdom. What is at stake theologically in such a literary observation will be taken up in 1.3 below.

The final sections of the *Book of the Twelve (on which, see 1.3 below) also indicate their separate literary origins by way of superscriptions saying simply "an oracle" (*maśśāʾ* [Zech 9:1, 12:1; Mal 1:1]). The resultant "books" of Zechariah and Malachi are literary creations, dependent upon spoken words at particular historical points, but now operating in a new context of reception.

A good example of the difference it makes to read a prophetic text with an ear for its literary dimensions concerns the famous question of Isaiah in 6:11: "How long, O Lord?" Isaiah is wrestling with the demanding commission to spread a prophetic message that will not be heeded, indeed to spread it with the specific intent that people will not turn. Perhaps significantly, he asks how long such a situation will endure (rather than, e.g., why he is to minister in this way). The answer is "until," followed by a series of descriptions of what must happen before arriving at the final "holy seed," which appears to be all that will be left by the time he is done. One can accept that such a divine commissioning occurred at some point in Isaiah's ministry. However, the question that confronts the reader of the literary work that is now the book of Isaiah may be put like this: does the reader now read after the "how long/until" dynamic has played out, or is the reader still reading within the period of hardening described in 6:9-10 (van Wieringen, 49)? Some have suggested that part of the achievement of the complex finished book of Isaiah is to show how this hardening works out until the new word of comfort pronounced in Isaiah 40 (e.g., Conrad 1991). The reader, on this view, is invited to reflect on how the ministry described in Isaiah 6:9-13 has its effect, without being the implied addressee of that message. It is clear that the reader of Isaiah in the context of Christian Scripture is being invited to revisit this question again in the light of Matthew 13:10-17, as well as NT citations of the text such as in Acts 28:25-27, perhaps to reflect in new ways on the questions of divine hardening and human repentance in the wake of Jesus' ministry (see Moberly 2003).

1.3. Canonical Considerations. Reading prophetic texts in their canonical setting clearly draws upon and presupposes each of the framing perspectives considered thus far: the historical and the literary. The groundbreaking analysis by B. Childs (Childs 1979) urges that a focus upon the canonical context(s) of biblical books is key to reading them "as Christian scripture" (*see* Canonical Criticism). In many ways, his analysis of the book of Isaiah is a paradigm example of what is at stake (Childs 1979, 311-38; see also Childs 2000).

Childs does not dispute that the oracles collected in the sixty-six chapters of Isaiah derive from a range of historical circumstances, not all recoverable by the attentive reader. The situation is undoubtedly more complex than the notion of "First Isaiah" (Isaiah ben Amoz, of Jerusalem [see Is 1:1]) providing Isaiah 1—39 in the eighth century BC, "Second Isaiah" writing words of comfort and hope in the exile (Is 40—55), where Jerusalem is told that her sins are paid for (i.e., the end of exile is nigh), and then "Third Isaiah" writing after the return from exile (Is 56—66). Several passages do not fit this threefold division very easily, such as Isaiah 24—27, which looks like a late *apocalyptic text. Nevertheless, the one constant in the midst of such historical reconstruction is the finished text of the book of Isaiah as we have it. Textual variations between different manuscript traditions do not complicate this point unduly. Thus, Childs suggests that what the interpreter of Scripture must do is to wrestle with the finished form of the text, allowing that it contains various historical recensions and signs of literary editing, but pressing on to ask what is at stake in the finished text's reading as it does. In the case of Isaiah: why is judgment (even if it is mitigated in many specific passages of Is 1—39) followed by comfort (Is 40—55), and then why is the great visionary sweep of Isaiah 40—55 followed by the difficult and frequently grim internal tensions of Isaiah 56—66, as evidenced by passages such as Isaiah 63:1-6; 65:13-16?

The case of Amos 9 was mentioned above. Childs's analysis of the ending of the book of Amos makes clear what is at stake in his hermeneutical approach. He argues with respect to the later additions that Amos 9:8b introduces a restriction on the judgment on Israel, which is assumed in Amos 9:9-10, and which "has to do with the ultimate purpose of God in the future of Israel. The discourse moves into the realm of eschatology (11, 13). It turns on the possibility of a new existence after the end has come" (Childs 1979, 407). While this does not soften the message of total judgment, it is important to note that the editor "transcends the perspective of the prophet himself." For Childs's own account, this suggests that we now have Yahweh's perspective in Amos 9:12b. Even if one does not go that far, it is clear that reading Amos in a canonical perspective requires a shift in focus away from the prophet Amos and the historical context of his oracles and toward the purposes for which this collection has been received and passed on for its southern audience, with lessons to learn from the fate that befell the northern kingdom.

Childs's approach to the OT books still sees them largely as independent literary identities, though he allows occasionally for canonical linkages between the books. Such linkages have been explored on a literary level in the "new canonical criticism" of Conrad (Conrad 2003). More recent canonically oriented interpretation has also asked theological questions about the canonical collection as a whole and its function within the canon.

At the most basic level, the identification of a certain collection of books as "prophetic books" or "prophets" makes a claim about their function within the canon. Christian canons tend to gather the Prophetic Books at the end of the OT, beginning with Isaiah. Jewish canons operate with the category of "former prophets" (Joshua, Judges, Samuel, Kings) and "latter prophets" (broadly the Christian subcollection but without the books of Daniel or Lamentations). For some, this category of prophets is the second of three discrete sections of the Jewish canon: Law, Prophets, Writings (as perhaps attested in Luke 24:44). In a significant study, however, J. Barton has urged that there is a strong tradition of usage (including in NT times) where "prophetic book" meant simply an inspired or authoritative book, and that the only books held in a fundamentally separate category were the five books of the Torah (Barton 1984; see also Barton 1986, 35-95). It follows that when Scripture is referred to as "the law and the prophets," this is to be read as indicating a distinction between the five books of the Torah (the law) and everything else (thus, indiscriminately, what we now call "prophetic books" and any others that followed them). This opens the way for Barton to explore a characterization of the prophetic books of Isaiah through Malachi on grounds internal to themselves: the particular functions of those texts as they might have been received in their original historical contexts (see 2 below).

Contrastingly, S. Chapman has argued that "the law and the prophets" is to be understood as a hermeneutically significant phrase implying an intentional canonical structuring. He suggests that from its earliest "proto-canonical" formation in the mid-sixth century BC, collected Scripture was always in the form of "the law (of Moses) and the words (of the prophets)," and that the development of the canon retained this fundamental theological "grammar." The "writings," on this account, eventually become a separate collection in a tripartite canon, although they emerged initially simply as part of the theological claim of the "law and the prophets" that constitutes "the fully mature witness of Israel to a dialectic that continues to be constitutive of the reality of God" (Chapman, 292). Chapman's thesis works by way of a historical reconstruction of the development of the canon. It is developed in a theological and hermeneutical direction in the work of C. Seitz, who urges that this understanding gives a stable theological center to authoritative Scripture in NT times. This is a stability based on the theological significance of the "law and prophets" framework, which may stand alongside a recognition that the development of "writings" as a separate category might still be in process at the time of Jesus. One significant hermeneutical implication of this approach concerns the role of Scripture in helping to settle what is at stake in NT times, as against accounts suggesting that it is essentially "the rule of faith" that is fundamental to the formation of the NT canon (e.g., Allert). Thus, the "prophets" play their role in theological witness to the God of Israel, known also through the Torah, and now newly revealed as the God and Father of Jesus Christ. Such an account clearly emphasizes the theological significance of the prophets in the scope of Christian Scripture overall, even if the historical basis behind some of the arguments upon which it rests may remain contested. It is

worth noting, though, that this offers a way of conceptualizing the significance of Scripture in NT times alongside the recognition that the canon may not have been closed at this point.

Both Barton and Chapman work with a model whereby any particular moment of "closure" of the prophetic canon remains historically uncertain; but there are different implications drawn (at least in part because they have different interpretive goals). In the former case, the result is that the hermeneutical significance of canonical factors in the interpretation of particular texts (in both the OT and the NT) tends to be downplayed. In the latter case, the argument is that there remains hermeneutical significance regardless of canon closure.

It is worth noting the particular oddity mentioned above concerning the placement of the book of Daniel within the Christian prophetic canon but within the "writings" of the Jewish Bible. Arguably, this can be overinterpreted as a matter of hermeneutical significance with regard to the book itself. The man Daniel was considered a prophet in NT times, as, for example, when Matthew 24:15 refers to Daniel 11:31; 12:11 with the phrase "spoken of by the prophet Daniel." One way or another, the book is therefore prophetic, regardless of its canonical location. In any case, one could not draw conclusions about either the state of the canon or the date of the book of Daniel from this angle because of the open-endedness of the various subsections of the canon in the relevant time period.

The other main topic of interest in canonically oriented studies in recent years has been the development of attention to the Book of the Twelve. The notion that such a singular "book" is appropriately taken as the corresponding unit to the book of Isaiah or Ezekiel, which are of comparable length to the Book of the Twelve and are similarly anthological in their own ways, has suggested to some that individual units of the book (the so-called Minor Prophets) should rightly be interpreted within their context in the finished collection (among many such voices, see the essays collected in Nogalski and Sweeney; Redditt and Schart). However, specific proposals for interpretive significance beyond this have proved more elusive. One suggestion has been the phenomenon of "catchword linkage," whereby a noteworthy word or phrase at the end of one prophet is taken up at the beginning of the next (such as "Yahweh roars from Zion" [Joel 3:16; Amos 1:2]), perhaps to draw attention to some broader thematic link. Another concerns the shape of the plot of the Book of the Twelve, which P. House has argued follows the arc of an Aristotelian "comic plot" that moves through the stages of sin, then down toward punishment, and then onward and upward toward redemption, with the resolution occurring in the postexilic sections of the overall book (House, 124). One of the problems in making specific claims in this area is the variation in orderings of the component texts within the Book of the Twelve in different canonical collections. Even so, the general point remains concerning the possibility of considering on a case-by-case basis what counts as the most helpful context for reading any particular one of the Minor Prophets, and whether there might be large-scale coherence alongside disconnection between separate elements. This may in turn assist the interpreter in bringing similar questions to the reading of texts in the longer books (Isaiah, Jeremiah, Ezekiel).

2. Modes of Reading the Prophetic Texts.

As with all significant texts, there are many dimensions to the hermeneutical functions of prophetic texts. This section considers some of the range of functions of the prophetic texts as they were originally received in Israel, while the next expands the focus to ways in which the texts function hermeneutically for readers today. An illuminating taxonomy of considerations relating to how the texts might have been received by NT times is offered in J. Barton's *Oracles of God*, the subtitle of which precisely delineates the matter at hand: *Perceptions of Ancient Prophecy in Israel after the Exile*. Barton proposes that there were four different ways in which such texts might have been read in NT times, which he helpfully describes as four "modes of reading" (Barton 1986, 151-53). We will in fact consider the third by way of contrasting it with the second and thus take in turn three different modes here: the ethical, the eschatological and the theological-mystical.

2.1. Halakah. Prophecy could be read as *ethical instruction (Barton 1986, 154-78). The claim is not that all prophecy is in some sense ethical, but that in some instances the prophets were understood as presenting halakah—directions on how life is to be lived before God.

Barton cites verses such as Daniel 9:10 (or 2 Macc 2:1-4) as instances of prophetic words being taken as halakah and finds this tradition extended into the NT, though only intermittently, in cases such as John 4:19, or more consistently in the later epistles (2 Tim 3:16-17 being a notable instance, as is the citation of OT prophets as moral examples in Heb 11). He further suggests that one of the reasons why prophetic texts become standards of moral appeal is in fact because they have been successful in their prediction. Since that predictive function is no longer in operation, the texts become cherished for their witness to a way of living that derives some of its moral force from the predictive capacity of the prophet.

2.2. Eschatology. A second mode of reading the Prophetic Books focuses on their eschatological dimensions: many "regarded the contemporary relevance of prophecy (on which all agreed) as consisting in their [the prophets'] foreknowledge of the present times" (Barton 1986, 179). In many ways, this captures the popular understanding of prophecy, at least in its typically modern "predictive" sense, although one senses that the ethical edge (see 2.1 above) has also begun to capture the popular imagination in the description of people such as Martin Luther King Jr. as prophetic. It is clear that at least some of the time the prophets were predicting what was to come. This understanding of prophecy is captured well in the extended hermeneutical reflection of 1 Peter 1:10-12, which J. Green has described as "the 'hermeneutical key' or, better, a theological hermeneutic of Scripture . . . a theological pattern by which to order the prophetic witness" (J. Green, 251). Two points may be made with respect to different aspects and implications of this thesis.

2.2.1. Ethics and/or Eschatology? It is sometimes said that the ethical thrust of prophetic texts is to be contrasted with the eschatological emphasis, as if they were two disjointed forms of interpretation or were readings of two fundamentally different types of text. It certainly is fair to say that by the time of the NT it is the predictive sense of OT texts that is to the fore in the appeal made to them. Thus, Amos, for example, so often cited today in broader ethical discussion, has comparatively little predictive material and is directly cited in the NT in just two instances: Amos 5:25-27 taken up in the historical review in Acts 7 (Acts 7:42-43, citing the LXX), and the celebrated case of Amos 9:11-12 informing the council of Jerusalem's decision regarding the requirements of torah obedience for Gentiles (Acts 15:16-17, again working from the LXX). The former instance is a text witnessing to Israel's *wilderness traditions, while the latter is only predictive of the outpouring of the Spirit on Gentiles at something of an interpretive stretch. Of Amos's ethical vision there is no direct citation in the NT, which perhaps should surprise twenty-first-century interpreters of Scripture more than it seems to. Isaiah, on the other hand, is repeatedly cited, particularly understood as a text speaking about what had now come to pass in Christ (*see* Prophets in the New Testament).

Nevertheless, the eschatological horizons of the prophet would have been at least in part ethical in nature. If a prophet describes the way a society must be in order to embody justice and righteousness and addresses such words to a society conspicuously lacking in these qualities, then there is a sense in which such a fundamentally ethical pronouncement looks to the future for its "fulfilment." It may be that this mixture of the ethical and the eschatological is a key aspect of what is in view in Matthew's having Jesus say that he has come not to abolish but rather to fulfill "the law and the prophets" (which equally may be a way of signaling all of Scripture, though the point would remain the same). Occasions when the prophets lift their eyes to the genuinely far horizon are often signaled in the text: "then afterward" begins the vision of Joel 2:28-32, quoted by Peter at Pentecost (see Acts 2:14-21). The more normal mode of prophetic discourse seems to presuppose that one should not press too hard the distinction between looking ahead and seeking change in the present; rather, one should think of these perspectives as two sides of the same coin.

2.2.2. Apocalyptic. A particular aspect of the above line of argument concerns the hermeneutical significance or otherwise of classifying some prophetic texts as *"apocalyptic" (from Gk *apokalypsis*, "revelation"). Although clearly there are apocalypses in the straightforward sense of texts that are revealing something, it has been widely debated as to whether there is a meaningful genre category "apocalyptic." In a strikingly influential thesis, P. Hanson argued that apocalyptic represented a kind of

"collapse of prophecy" whereby disillusioned reformers of society withdrew from active engagement with the world and retreated to a safe distance from which they could predict the end of all things and the removal, in one way or another, of the present evil age. Part of the supporting argument for this involved postulating a split in the social world that produced such postexilic texts as Third Isaiah, where a "hierocratic" party of (Zadokite) priests who had returned from exile were in conflict with "visionaries" (including, in Hanson's view, the prophet known as Second Isaiah and his followers) who had imagined a different life restored back to the land. Weary of the conflict, the apocalyptic voice arose out of the desire to see a discontinuous fresh start, on the other side of sweeping judgment. However, a range of factors has led to the demise of this thesis. First, the lack of supporting evidence for the social setting that it imagines suggests that it is at best only one possible reading of the texts rather than a compelling historical account. Second, the apocalyptic language sometimes adduced to support such a case should better be interpreted as a different style of prophetic language but with the same goals of seeking change and transformation within the present order. As one study of Daniel puts it, "An apocalypse is intended to interpret present earthly circumstances in the light of the supernatural world and the future, and to influence both the understanding and the behavior of the audience by means of divine authority" (Smith-Christopher, *NIB* 7:22).

In short, the debate about genre focuses on how far one should define the terms *apocalyptic* or *apocalypse* in terms of form or content, and clearly it will continue. A helpful summary is offered by L. DiTommaso: "Despite several problems, including a tendency to mold to its contents, the label 'apocalyptic literature' remains a common and useful if general term, although it should be restricted to instances where precise definitions are unneeded or inappropriate" (DiTommaso, 241).

In terms of hermeneutical significance, one may conclude that apocalyptic is also a form of ethically engaged prophecy, indeed the very strand characterized as "eschatological," but not thereby prejudged with respect to the temporal horizons of its content. Nevertheless, this discussion opens up with greater clarity the notion of a prophetic tradition that specifically allows for divine providence in broad terms but without the attendant expectation of Yahweh's imminent disruptive activity. The focus here would be more on divine providence. This is Barton's third "mode of reading" the prophets (Barton 1986, 214-34), although it may be noted that his examples of this mode are generally drawn from outside the OT canon.

2.3. Theological Reflection and Mysticism. A final strand within the prophetic texts as we have them is what Barton describes as the view of the prophet as "someone with special insights into theological truths" (Barton 1986, 235). This has two main elements within it. On the one hand, the prophet is one who sees how God is at work in human affairs, for which the label "theologian" might be appropriate. The record of God's dealings with Israel becomes the springboard for prophetic reflection upon the nature of God; Jeremiah 14:17-22 might be an example (and the logic of the prayer of Daniel 9 points the same way). On the other hand, the prophet is one who, whether because of particular experiences or through reflection on what has been observed, may come to speak of the nature of God in himself. Here a passage such as Ezekiel 1 is a particularly striking example, and it gave rise to a whole mystical tradition (*merkabah* [chariot] mysticism) that would go on to play a considerable role in subsequent theological and spiritual reflection. At the root of these phenomena is the simple point that the prophet is qualified to speak on behalf of God and therefore is one to whom others might look as they seek to understand God's ways in the world (and in himself).

3. Hermeneutical Approaches to the Reading of Prophetic Texts Today.

It is one thing to seek a description of the hermeneutical functions of prophetic texts as they were received in ancient (specifically, NT) times. The task before today's reader of these texts, however, opens up a whole range of hermeneutical considerations that rapidly multiply beyond the confines of their own intended functions. Hermeneutics is particularly concerned to describe and evaluate these complex transactions between texts and readers, and there are many ways of approaching this subject. We will consider a small sample of such approaches, all of which offer specific insights into what is sometimes too broadly described

as "reader-response criticism." At the most general level, reader-oriented approaches range across a whole spectrum from concerns that offer particular insight into the dynamics of the text when seen from certain points of view, through to readings that rest content with allowing the reader to remake the text in their own image without regard to how much justice is done to the text. For an example of the latter, one might cite the approach to Isaiah offered in *The Queer Bible Commentary*: "Christians have plucked [Isa 7,14-16] from any reference to Ahaz, curds, honey or the king of Aram and Israel, and applied it wholesale as a predictive-prophecy-come-true about Jesus of Nazareth. Why should we as queers not feel a similar freedom to pluck from these texts (as well as any attendant scholarship) those nuggets which may prove useful to us?" (Koch, 376). Here, however, we will focus on some approaches that do not equate embracing the reader in the hermeneutical discussion with abandoning all appeals to criteria or appropriateness to the text.

3.1. Texts as Performative Actions. We noted that prophetic texts operate across a range of functions in terms of their relationship to the world in which they are heard or read (see 2 above). The simplest way to describe the multifunctionality of such texts is in the language of "performative utterances." Prophetic texts describe some aspects of reality but also serve to bring about other aspects. Prophetic oracles are thus prime candidates for the category of "speech acts" as developed by J. Austin and J. Searle (see Briggs). In one particularly illuminating analysis of "What did the prophets think they were doing?" W. Houston uses the conceptuality of speech-act theory to explore the ways in which the prophetic act of denunciation or judgment can be seen as separable from the actual responses elicited by the prophet. In speech-act terminology, the former is an illocutionary act, taking place in the pronouncing of the words, while the latter is perlocutionary, contingent upon the real-world vagaries of human response to the oracle. "As long as the prophets' hearers understood that they were warning them, calling for repentance or whatever the particular speech act might be, and understood the content of the warning or whatever it might be, then the prophets had *done* what they set out to do, even if they had not achieved the effect they had hoped for" (Houston 1993, 177).

This perspective is also the most helpful way of making use of the traditional form-critical study of types of prophetic oracle, of which a standard account is offered by C. Westermann (1991a; 1991b), and which has been helpfully adapted to the context of assessing written prophetic texts by more recent form-critical studies (*see* Form Criticism). Thus D. Petersen suggests that "one may discern at least five basic forms of prophetic literature: divinatory chronicle, vision report, prophetic speech, legend, and prophetic historiography" (Petersen 2003, 274). Within Petersen's category of "prophetic speech" we find the more familiar range of forms of prophetic speech, corresponding more to the concerns of Westermann's account. A typical sample list includes judgment oracle (Jer 6:16-21); woe oracle (Is 10:1-4); lawsuit (Mic 1:2-7); lament (Jer 8:18—9:3); hymn (Hab 3:2-15); song (Is 5:1-2); allegory (Ezek 17:2-10); acrostic (Nah 1:2-8) (Petersen 2002, 29).

Such analyses examine how these different types of prophetic text deploy various kinds of social convention to produce certain archetypal kinds of effect. This classificatory project is, arguably, not always hermeneutically enlightening, since identifying the form in view is dependent upon judging the nature of the text under consideration in the first place, making it difficult in turn to draw conclusions about the text from its form-critical classification. Generally, it is in analyzing those oracles that do not fit comfortably into the standard classifications that form-critical insight is most helpful. (This is a special case of a general point about genre classifications: they tend to be hermeneutically illuminating mainly in cases where the standard conventions break down.) Thus, for example, one might note the way in which Amos "takes up his lament" in Amos 5:1, leading the reader to anticipate the identification of some departed person or grouping as the cause of the lament, only for the prophet to identify the "house of Israel" as the one to be reckoned "dead"—a shock to the house of Israel no doubt, and a shock that is part of the point of Amos 5:1. However, even this relatively textbook case of the benefits of form-critical classification relies on understanding the spoken word in its historical context, since as a literary creation the book of Amos is apparently intended for a southern readership who are to learn from Yahweh's ways with the northern kingdom that led up to the northern exile in 722/1 BC.

One major implication of a speech-act theory perspective on prophetic texts, however, is that the type (or form) of oracle deployed is determined by the illocution performed rather than by the perlocutionary success of otherwise of the oracle. It is the total communicative act of the prophet (and the text) that should occupy the interpreter, holding together the prophetic intention and the effect of the prophetic words in a range of possible relationships. This way of thinking allows us to make sense of the well-known conundrum of the prophet *Jonah, who precisely because he is successful turns out to be wrong: Nineveh is not overthrown, because the Ninevites heed the implicit warning in his oracle of doom (cf. Jon 3:4, 10, and the intervening narrative). Literary critic T. Eagleton enjoyed the irony thus: Jonah's words produce "a state of affairs in which the state of affairs they describe won't be the case" (Eagleton 1990: 233). As Houston points out, Jonah's illocution is successful, and the range of potential perlocutions is what is at stake in the next step of the narrative (Houston 1991).

The most thorough application of speech-act theory to explore the performative nature of prophetic OT texts is J. Adams's analysis of Isaiah. Adams argues that the central message of Isaiah 40—55 "is a *call to return or turn to Yahweh* . . . for the addressee to *forsake sin, acknowledge and confess Yahweh as God alone,* and *embrace the role of his servant*" (Adams, 91). Adams takes seriously the multidimensional performative force of the texts and avoids restricting them to flat referential puzzles in which the interpretive key is to identify the speaker, or the servant, or the historical conditions behind the text. This framework is subtle enough to account for the fulfillment of these passages in Jesus as well as their ongoing availability for self-involvement to the attentive reader today. Thus, "by participating in the prophetic function of Isa 40-55 . . . confessors return to Yahweh, forsake sin, profess him alone, and embrace the role of his servant" (Adams, 210). Those who read the text participate in its illocutionary functions and can be bound into the community envisaged by the text. There is scope for further work along these lines with other prophetic texts.

3.2. Texts as Imaginative Construals.

Although prophetic texts are only at most loosely historiographical, they do often witness to what has happened in Israel and beyond. But rather than describe them as "historical" or "witnessing" texts, it seems more appropriate to note that when their attention is turned toward such matters, it is usually in a way that casts the events in new light or offers striking (and generally Yahwistic) perspectives. The reader of the prophets is offered not so much independent access to the social realities of life in ancient Israel as a rhetorically constructed vision of what has come to pass or is happening in the wider sociopolitical world. The most helpful rubric for considering this aspect of the texts' function has been provided by the fresh and fruitful approach to reading prophetic texts offered by W. Brueggemann in a variety of works dating back to his 1978 book *The Prophetic Imagination*. In this and many other writings Brueggemann has mapped out a rich set of reading practices that navigate between acknowledging the rhetorical constructs of the texts and the critical difficulties of reconstructing the ancient history behind them. In a summary treatment he observes that imaginative remembering "is the clue to valuing the Bible as a trustworthy voice of faith while still taking seriously our best critical learning" (Brueggemann 2003, 8).

Brueggemann defines imagination as "the human capacity to picture, portray, receive, and practice the world in ways other than it appears to be at first glance when seen through a dominant, habitual, unexamined lens" (Brueggemann 1993, 13). As a mode of human knowing, it thus particularly resonates with those who read in our present situation, which may be loosely defined as "postmodern" without thereby being overcommitted to any particular philosophical articulations of the postmodern. This aspect of the reader's situation then allows fresh perception of the imaginative dimension of the prophets' works themselves. In a series of reflections on a hermeneutic that can itself be characterized as prophetic and imaginative, Brueggemann suggests that "the task of prophetic ministry is to nurture, nourish, and evoke a consciousness and perception alternative to the consciousness and perception of the dominant culture around us" (Brueggemann 1978, 13). In this initial formulation of an imaginative hermeneutic, he perhaps overemphasizes a contrast between two traditions found in the OT and possibly exaggerates the "royal tradition" as a foil to his substantive task of describing what a prophetic imagination looks like; nevertheless, his characterization makes significant points about how one's practices of reading might unlock liberating dimensions in the prophetic texts. Thus, the royal consciousness "leads people to numbness, especially to numbness about death," whereas prophetic imagination seeks "to bring people to engage their experiences of suffering to death" (Brueggemann 1978, 46). Similarly, the former "leads people to despair about the power to new life," while the latter seeks "to bring people to engage the promise of newness that is at work in our history with God" (Brueggemann 1978, 62-63). In a subsequent study he examines these themes in the three Major Prophets and makes an explicit hermeneutical move of urging a "dynamic equivalence" between the imaginative visions of these prophets and the readings of their texts required by those "who find themselves in an alienated cultural situation," for whom these texts are "a resource for hopeful imagination today" (Brueggemann 1986, 132).

Despite the enormous impact of Brueggemann's approach to the prophetic texts in terms of his showing how they might be released to speak freshly to today's world, there has been conspicuously little scholarly engagement with his notion of "prophetic imagination" (though see de Hulster 2010). Arguably, Brueggemann has performed the service of articulating a mode of approaching the text that is no longer so unusual in terms of interpreters more broadly operating within the loosely defined postmodern context noted above. Nevertheless, relatively rare discussions of "imagination and responsible reading" (Hart) or "the faithful imagination" as it operates within Christian approaches to Scripture in the postmodern world (G. Green, 187-206) are still valuable reflections on what is at stake in appealing to the imaginative construal both in and of the OT's prophetic texts, and in moving helpfully to the present interpretive horizon. There remains scope, however, for a careful integration of Brueggemann's concerns with more explicitly christological emphases in interpretation, which might probe what is at stake in seeing Israel's imaginative hopes taken up in some sense in the person of Christ.

3.3. Texts That Invite Ideological and Theological Advocacy.

Brueggemann's work highlights one of the most striking hermeneutical developments in biblical studies in recent decades: the turn away from supposedly value-free or neutral scholarship and the embrace of a "decentered" set of practices that explicitly engage with questions of the location of the reader and the ideological and theological (as well as cultural and other) perspectives that are bound up in such reading. A key moment along this trajectory was E. Schüssler Fiorenza's influential Society of Biblical Literature presidential address in 1988, in which she argued that all biblical scholarship represents an advocacy position of some kind. Much recent scholarship on the Prophetic Books embodies just such a conviction, whether undertaken from a vantage point of ideological suspicion or from a more theological perspective seeking to appropriate in some manner the claims of the text for today's reader.

Arguably, ideological/advocacy reading is one of the most prominent academic approaches to biblical texts today. It is given particularly sharp and eloquent expression in some of the essays of D. Clines, whose book *Interested Parties* (subtitled *The Ideology of Writers and Readers of the Hebrew Bible*) seeks "to uncover the ideologies that lie beneath the surface . . . especially ways in which [interpreters] either uncritically adopt the ideology of the text they are commenting on or impose the values of their own ideology upon the biblical text" (Clines, 18). Clines demonstrates, for example, how interpreters of Amos persistently elide any difference between their own hermeneutical framework and that assumed by the prophet in the text, with the result that supposedly critical interpretations are little more than contemporary paraphrases of Amos's own agenda (Clines, 76-93). On the one hand, it may be a testimony to the persuasive power of the prophetic texts that it does not seem to occur to most commentators that evaluative questions might persist after the task of explicating the prophetic message has been undertaken: Is Amos right? Does Isaiah have a point? On the other hand, such a hermeneutical step immediately requires the articulation of an alternative evaluative scheme from which to make any further judgments. Ideological critique of the OT

text, therefore, typically devolves fairly quickly on to ethics and broader (often postmodern) theory (for a good example of which, see Collins, 131-61) or else on to theological attempts to articulate what is at stake in such reading.

Theological interpretation has been a major emphasis in biblical hermeneutics in the early twenty-first century. It too can be subject to the critique offered by Clines, that it reduces to pious paraphrase or fails to probe the theological conceptuality at stake in the texts. Nevertheless, when undertaken in full awareness of such hermeneutical issues, theological interpretation of the prophetic texts offers the chance for Jewish and for Christian readers to allow these texts to play their part in witnessing to the demands of life before the God of these texts. Although certain key texts (notably Is 53) have markedly different receptions in Jewish and Christian traditions, there is much common ground between these theological perspectives. Such an awareness mitigates against some Jewish traditions that overly subsume readings of the prophets to the task of interpreting the Torah, or some Christian (notably Protestant) traditions that highlight those passages that seem to critique ritual or cultic worship (e.g., Is 1:10-20; Amos 5:21-25) as if to suggest that such matters could be downgraded in an overall understanding of the prophetic message (see Brettler, 458). Such an unnuanced "Protestant" perspective has tended to say more about the worldview of those modern interpreters who disliked priestly and legal traditions than about the views at work in the prophetic texts, which assume an overall orientation that encompasses both ritual worship and wider horizons of justice.

Studies of *justice (mišpaṭ)* and its concomitant righteousness (ṣĕdāqâ) in the prophets are one example of concerns that may bring a strong ethical edge into fruitful dialogue with wider theological perspectives about the God of Israel. This allows an ongoing task of theological articulation of the claims made both upon and on behalf of those who stand in the faith traditions that develop beyond the prophetic corpus. Such studies also indicate that one should not distinguish too sharply between ideological and theological approaches on hermeneutical grounds: they can involve the same patient weighing of interpretive frameworks and their moral and ethical commitments, even while disagreeing on the weight attached to more specifically theological claims in the text (a good example is Houston 2008, 52-98, 161-69 especially, in a study that bears the subtitle *Ideologies and Theologies of Social Justice in the Old Testament*).

3.4. Texts That Summon the Reader. A final hermeneutical approach that deserves brief mention is the appeal to the prophetic texts made in the work of one of the great hermeneuts of the twentieth century, P. Ricoeur (1913-2005). Although much of Ricoeur's hermeneutical work was kept separate from his theological convictions, he did occasionally address matters of biblical interpretation, including in his 1986 Gifford Lectures, published as *Oneself as Another* (1992), although its two biblical-theological studies were published separately from the main work (Ricoeur 1995; 1997). The first of these concerned "The Summoned Subject in the School of the Narratives of the Prophetic Vocation." In the second, a broader work primarily occupied with the question of how one should conceive of the self as a morally responsible and well-defined agent, he urged that Scripture plays the fundamental hermeneutical role of helping to constitute the self by holding it in dialogue before a wide range of biblical witnesses to the God who lies behind it and who gives it its imaginative and typological unity. This leads him to focus on the OT's prophetic call narratives because they are prime examples of the OT's "dialogic structure that confronts the words and acts of God with the response human beings give to them" (Ricoeur 1995, 263). The result is a "sent, mandated, commanded subject" (or self) who, through the call of God that comes via the conscience, models profoundly the nature of selfhood to which the reader of Scripture is called. To use one of Ricoeur's terms, the engaged reader is "refigured" through the hermeneutical dynamic of the text, and the reader's self is thereby reconstituted.

Ricoeur's work generally, and notably this aspect of it, requires some transposition to meet the demands of theological reflection on the hermeneutical frameworks that he brings to bear (see Stiver, 175-78, 234-38). However, this is a striking example where he effectively insists that prophetic call narratives perform in particular the task that in general is Scripture's function to perform: to help form readers who are invited and willing to submit themselves to the requirements of the God of the text. In short, readers are summoned by the prophetic text, and in the process they are transformed.

4. Discerning the Prophetic Word Then and Now.

We have considered the hermeneutical issues of how one approaches the texts, the modes of reading to which the texts themselves were subject in their own contexts, and then some hermeneutical dimensions of the question of how one might navigate between the texts and today's readers. In concluding, it is worth focusing on one particular issue that is central to the appropriate handling of prophecy: discernment. This question arises on a number of levels, but we will consider briefly only two "poles" of the issue: how the prophetic texts themselves speak to the question of criteria for discernment, and how one might deploy such prophetic texts discerningly today. In particular, a pressing hermeneutical question is how (or whether) one can relate the OT prophetic texts to an issue such as the contemporary environmental crisis, which is framed at least primarily in the terms of current debate rather than as a matter arising out of exegesis of the texts in the first instance. The subtitles of the two sections that follow are drawn from monographs that offer suggestive ways forward in the question of how to draw appropriately on the OT texts today.

4.1. Prophecy and Discernment. R. W. L. Moberly's *Prophecy and Discernment* is in part a response to earlier studies of "hermeneutics in true and false prophecy," such as J. Sanders's influential study under that title, which effectively locate the question of discernment in the need for time to pass in order that events may judge whether the prophetic word is proved true or not. Moberly's alternative proposal is that the prophet, who is "in essence *one who speaks for God*," must be one who has stood in the divine presence (Moberly 2006, 4, 9). However, this does not remove the basis on which one might speak for God to some unexaminable "spiritual realm" beyond the canons of critical inquiry. Whatever psychological or emotive aspects of prophetic ministry might be in place, there remains, insists Moberly, something that can be discussed and probed: "It is the content of the encounter with the divine that is determinative of its validity" (Moberly 2006, 10). The apparently "inaccessible" is rendered "accessible" by both the character of the prophet and the nature of the message, and "the visible gives access to the invisible; the moral gives critical purchase on the spiritual" (Moberly 2006, 225).

The major case study by which this thesis is established concerns Jeremiah and what Jeremiah models with regard to the core task of speaking for God. On the one hand, those whom the book of Jeremiah designates as false prophets are false because they do not speak out of their experience of the presence of God. With respect in particular to Jeremiah 23, "The absence of these prophets from YHWH's council is shown by their failure to proclaim a message whose purpose was to turn [shūv] people from evil into ways that would be more in keeping with YHWH's will and character" (Moberly 2006, 75). On the other hand, Jeremiah himself offers the example of how prophecy should work: "The all-important claim to be from God—to have stood in the divine council, to be sent, to speak YHWH's word(s)—is to speak of a divine realm that is not vacuous, for the reason that it is the prophet's lifestyle and message, whose moral character are open to scrutiny in the present, which give content to the claim about God. *The 'spiritual' nature of the prophetic message, whether or not it is from God, is determined by its 'moral' content and accompaniment*" (Moberly 2006, 81 [italics added]).

Such an approach integrates an ethical agenda with the reading of Scripture without reducing the tasks of such reading to any form of moralism. Moberly's proposal indicates that Jeremiah 28, where Hananiah predicts release from the yoke of Babylon within two years, is about prophetic conflict, but not substantively about criteria for resolving questions of discernment, which are rather in view in Jeremiah 23. A fundamental aspect of this thesis is that right discernment of the prophetic voice cannot sidestep broader questions having to do with the standing of the prophet morally and ethically before God. The prophetic texts, therefore, should not be seen as either reflecting or inviting a process whereby one might claim immediate access to the divine voice without needing to engage in careful weighing of how the divine word can be understood in dialogue with many other issues. On a hermeneutical level, this in turn suggests that those who read the OT prophetic texts must themselves engage with the same demandingly wide range of moral and ethical matters in rightly discerning how to handle the texts for their voice today.

4.2. Biblical Prophets and Contemporary Environmental Ethics. One striking example of such a need for discernment is the way in which the relevance or otherwise of OT prophetic texts to matters such as today's environmental concerns has been understood at different times. Readers inclined to feel the moral force of such matters will read the texts alert to their address of such issues, whereas it is relatively easy to demonstrate that many exegetes have not been inclined to ask such questions in their reading of the texts. A constructive proposal along these lines is put forward by H. Marlow, who uses the biblical prophets as a lens for exploring various aspects of the current environmental crisis. She is able to demonstrate that a good deal of the reception of prophetic texts in the Christian tradition has been largely inattentive to the significance of broader ecological concerns, and she sets out to recover material in the text that can "demonstrate an ethic which values all people and the whole of creation" (Marlow, 277).

A hermeneutically sophisticated project along comparable lines is E. Davis's study *Scripture, Culture, and Agriculture*, which engages intensely with both the OT and contemporary agrarian writing, notably that of W. Berry. In her chapter on the prophets Davis draws suggestive and compelling parallels between the ways in which both the OT prophets and the new agrarians trace the links between treatment of the land and wider questions of economy, greed and trust. Most telling: "Our relationship to the soil, demonstrated primarily in our practices of food production and consumption, is fundamental to every other aspect of human life" (Davis, 121). Davis traces how various prophetic texts, notably the eighth-century BC prophets, offer sharp poetic images exploring these links. Rather like the concluding oracles of the book of Amos, Davis concludes that on the topic of the future of our planet, "the Bible as a whole tends toward a tenacious but severely chastened hope" (Davis, 180).

Such approaches exemplify how today's readers might appeal responsibly to the prophetic texts in the context of contemporary issues where the voice of the God of Israel might still be discerned today.

See also: CANONICAL CRITICISM; CONVERSATION ANALYSIS; DANIEL: HISTORY OF INTERPRETATION; EDITORIAL/REDACTION CRITICISM; ETHICS; EZEKIEL: HISTORY OF INTERPRETATION; FEMINIST INTERPRETATION; FORM CRITICISM; INTERTEXTUALITY AND INNERBIBLICAL INTERPRETATION; ISAIAH: HISTORY OF INTERPRETATION; JEREMIAH: HISTORY OF INTERPRETATION; PERFORMANCE CRITICISM; PROPHECY AND ESCHATOLOGY IN CHRISTIAN THEOLOGY; PROPHETS IN THE NEW TESTAMENT; RHETORICAL CRITICISM; TWELVE, BOOK OF THE: HISTORY OF INTERPRETATION.

BIBLIOGRAPHY. **J. W. Adams,** *The Performative Nature and Function of Isaiah 40-55* (LHBOTS 448; New York: T & T Clark, 2006); **C. D. Allert,** *A High View of Scripture? The Authority of the Bible and the Formation of the New Testament Canon* (Evangelical Ressourcement; Grand Rapids: Baker Academic, 2007); **J. Barton,** "Authorship, OT," *NIDB* 1:354-55; idem, "'The Law and the Prophets': Who Are the Prophets?" *OtSt* 23 (1984) 1-18; idem, *Oracles of God: Perceptions of Ancient Prophecy in Israel after the Exile* (London: Darton, Longman & Todd, 1986); **J. Blenkinsopp,** *Opening the Sealed Book: Interpretations of the Book of Isaiah in Late Antiquity* (Grand Rapids: Eerdmans, 2006); **M. Z. Brettler,** "Nevi'im: Introduction," in *The Jewish Study Bible*, ed. A. Berlin and M. Brettler (Oxford: Oxford University Press, 2004) 451-61; **R. S. Briggs,** *Words in Action: Speech Act Theory and Biblical Interpretation; Toward a Hermeneutic of Self-involvement* (Edinburgh: T & T Clark, 2001); **W. Brueggemann,** *The Prophetic Imagination* (Philadelphia: Fortress, 1978); idem, *Hopeful Imagination: Prophetic Voices in Exile* (Philadelphia: Fortress, 1986); idem, *Texts under Negotiation: The Bible and Postmodern Imagination* (Minneapolis: Fortress, 1993); idem, *An Introduction to the Old Testament: The Canon and Christian Imagination* (Louisville: Westminster/John Knox, 2003); **R. P. Carroll,** *Jeremiah* (OTL; London: SCM, 1986); **S. B. Chapman,** *The Law and the Prophets: A Study in Old Testament Canon Formation* (FAT 27; Tübingen: Mohr Siebeck, 2000); **B. S. Childs,** *Introduction to the Old Testament as Scripture* (London: SCM, 1979); idem, *Isaiah* (OTL; Louisville: Westminster/John Knox, 2001); **D. J. A. Clines,** *Interested Parties: The Ideology of Writers and Readers of the Hebrew Bible* (JSOTSup 205; Sheffield: Sheffield Academic Press, 1995); **J. J. Collins,** *The Bible after Babel: Historical Criticism in a Postmodern Age* (Grand Rapids: Eerdmans, 2005); **E. W. Conrad,** *Reading Isaiah* (OBT; Minneapolis: Fortress, 1991); idem, *Reading the Latter Prophets: Toward a New Canonical Criticism* (JSOTSup 376; London: T & T Clark International, 2003); **E. F. Davis,** *Scripture, Culture, and Agriculture: An Agrarian Reading of the Bible* (Cambridge: Cambridge University Press, 2009); **I. J. de Hulster,** "Imagination: A Hermeneutical Tool for the Study of the Hebrew Bible," *BibInt* 18 (2010) 114-36; **L. DiTommaso,** "Apocalypses and Apocalypticism in Antiquity (Part 1)," *CBR* 5.2 (2007) 235-86; **W. Doan and T. Giles,** *Prophets, Performance, and Power: Performance Criticism of the Hebrew Bible* (New York: T & T Clark, 2005); **T. Eagleton,** "J. L. Austin and the Book of Jonah," in *The Book and the Text: The Bible and Literary Theory*, ed. R. Schwartz (Oxford: Blackwell, 1990) 231-36; **M. H. Floyd,** "'Write the Revelation!' (Hab 2:2): Re-imagining the Cultural History of Prophecy," in *Writings and Speech in Israelite and Ancient Near Eastern Prophecy*, ed. E. Ben Zvi and M. Floyd (SBLSymS 10; Atlanta: Society of Biblical Literature, 2000) 103-43; **K. G. Friebel,** *Jeremiah's and Ezekiel's Sign-Acts: Rhetorical Nonverbal Communication* (JSOTSup 283; Sheffield: Sheffield Academic, 1999); **G. Green,** *Theology, Hermeneutics, and Imagination: The Crisis of Interpretation at the End of Modernity* (Cambridge: Cambridge University Press, 2000); **J. B. Green,** *1 Peter* (THNTC; Grand Rapids: Eerdmans, 2007); **P. D. Hanson,** *The Dawn of Apocalyptic: The Historical and Sociological Roots of Jewish Apocalyptic Eschatology* (Philadelphia: Fortress, 1975); **T. Hart,** "Imagination and Responsible Reading," in *Renewing Biblical Interpretation*, ed. C. Bartholomew, C. Greene and K. Möller (SHS1; Grand Rapids: Zondervan, 2000) 307-34; **P. R. House,** *The Unity of the Twelve* (JSOTSup 90; Sheffield: Almond, 1990); **W. Houston,** "What Did the Prophets Think They Were Doing? Speech Acts and Prophetic Discourse in the Old Testament," *BibInt* 1 (1993) 167-88; idem, *Contending for Justice: Ideologies and Theologies of Social Justice in the Old Testament* (rev. ed.; JSOTSup 428; London: T & T Clark, 2008); **T. Koch,** "Isaiah," in *The Queer Bible Commentary*, ed. D. Guest et al. (London: SCM, 2006) 371-85; **J. R. Lundbom,** "Baruch, Seraiah and Expanded Colophons in the Book of Jeremiah,"

JSOT 36 (1986) 89-114; idem, *Jeremiah 21-36* (AB 21B; New York: Doubleday, 2004); **H. Marlow,** *Biblical Prophets and Contemporary Environmental Ethics: Re-Reading Amos, Hosea, and First Isaiah* (Oxford: Oxford University Press, 2009); **R. W. L. Moberly,** "'Holy, Holy, Holy': Isaiah's Vision of God," in *Holiness: Past and Present,* ed. S. C. Barton (London: T & T Clark, 2003) 122-40; idem, *Prophecy and Discernment* (CSCD 14; Cambridge: Cambridge University Press, 2006); **J. D. Nogalski and M. A. Sweeney,** eds., *Reading and Hearing the Book of the Twelve* (SBLSymS 15; Atlanta: Society of Biblical Literature, 2000); **D. L. Petersen,** *The Prophetic Literature: An Introduction* (Louisville: Westminster/John Knox, 2002); idem, "The Basic Forms of Prophetic Literature," in *The Changing Face of Form Criticism for the Twenty-First Century,* ed. M. A. Sweeney and E. Ben Zvi (Grand Rapids: Eerdmans, 2003) 269-75; **P. L. Redditt and A. Schart,** eds., *Thematic Threads in the Book of the Twelve* (BZAW 325; Berlin: de Gruyter, 2003); **P. Ricoeur,** *Oneself as Another,* trans. K. Blamey (Chicago: University of Chicago Press, 1992); idem, "The Summoned Subject in the School of the Narratives of the Prophetic Vocation," in *Figuring the Sacred: Religion, Narrative, and Imagination,* trans. D. Pellauer, ed. M. I. Wallace (Minneapolis: Fortress, 1995) 262-75; idem, "The Self in the Mirror of the Scriptures," in *The Whole and Divided Self,* ed. D. E. Aune and J. McCarthy (New York: Crossroad, 1997) 201-20; **J. A. Sanders,** "Hermeneutics in True and False Prophecy," in *Canon and Authority: Essays in Old Testament Religion and Authority,* ed. G. W. Coats and B. O. Long (Philadelphia: Fortress, 1977) 21-41; **E. Schüssler Fiorenza,** "The Ethics of Biblical Interpretation: Decentering Biblical Scholarship," *JBL* 107 (1988) 3-17; **C. R. Seitz,** *Prophecy and Hermeneutics: Towards a New Introduction to the Prophets* (Grand Rapids: Baker Academic, 2007); idem, *The Goodly Fellowship of the Prophets. The Achievement of Association in Canon Formation* (Grand Rapids: Baker Academic, 2009); **D. L. Smith-Christopher,** "The Book of Daniel," *NIB* 7:17-194; idem, *A Biblical Theology of Exile* (OBT; Minneapolis: Fortress, 2002); **D. Stacey,** *Prophetic Drama in the Old Testament* (London: Epworth, 1990); **D. R. Stiver,** *Theology after Ricoeur: New Directions in Hermeneutical Theology* (Louisville: Westminster/John Knox, 2001); **A. L. H. M. van Wieringen,** *The Implied Reader in Isaiah 6-12* (BIS 34; Leiden: E. J. Brill,

1998); **C. Westermann,** *Basic Forms of Prophetic Speech,* trans. H. White (Philadelphia: Westminster/John Knox, 1991a); idem, *Prophetic Oracles of Salvation in the Old Testament,* trans. K. Crim (Philadelphia: Westminster/John Knox, 1991b); **H. G. M. Williamson,** *The Book Called Isaiah: Deutero-Isaiah's Role in Composition and Redaction* (Oxford: Clarendon Press, 1994).

R. S. Briggs

HIGH AND LIFTED UP. *See* ISAIAH: BOOK OF.

HOLY ONE OF ISRAEL. *See* ISAIAH: BOOK OF.

HOLY SPIRIT. *See* SPIRIT OF YAHWEH.

HONOR AND SHAME

Honor and shame are important concepts in the world of ancient Israel, as is attested by their frequent mention in OT literature. Honor is an appreciation of one's own value and worth that is publicly acknowledged by others, often with the help of symbolic actions or rituals. Shame is a low estimation of oneself caused by failure to meet certain agreed social standards and by an accompanying attitude of contempt and derision. Both are very much public phenomena dependent on one's interaction with other people and the way they observe and judge a person's qualities and behavior.

   1. The Vocabulary of Honor and Shame
   2. Shame and Failure
   3. Honor and Shame in Judgment and Salvation
   4. Honor and Shame in Divine-Human Relationships
   5. The Objective and Subjective Aspects of Shame
   6. The Honor of God

1. The Vocabulary of Honor and Shame.
Biblical Hebrew has a rich vocabulary related to the concept of shame: *bwš,* usually rendered "to be ashamed" (*bûšâ, bōšet,* "shame"), although recently Y. Avrahami has argued that its basic meaning is "to be disappointed"; *klm,* "to be humiliated, to be put to shame" (*kĕlimmâ, kĕlimmût,* "insult, humiliation"); *ḥpr,* "to be ashamed"; *qlh,* "to be contemptible" (perhaps a by-form of *qll,* "to be light, small, insignificant"; *qālôn,* "shame"; *qîqālôn,* "disgrace"); *špl,* "to be low, to humiliate" (*šāpāl,* "low, humble, of little

value"; *šēpel*, "lowliness, humiliation"); *ḥrp*, "to taunt" (*ḥerpâ*, "disgrace"); *bwz*, "to show contempt" (*bûz*, *bûzâ*, "contempt"); *bzh*, "to despise, be despised" (*bizzāyôn*, "contempt"); *n'ṣ*, "to spurn, treat disrespectfully" (*ně'āṣâ*, "humiliation"); *zll*, "to despise." The most important Hebrew root connected with the idea of honor is *kbd*. The verb means "to be heavy, be weighty" and hence "to honor, to be honored," and the noun (*kābôd*) denotes "honor, reputation, glory, splendor." Other words related to this concept are *hādār*, "splendor, dignity"; *hôd*, "power, majesty"; *gā'ôn*, "eminence, pride"; *gē'ût*, "illustriousness"; *šēm*, "name, reputation"; *tip'eret*, "beauty, splendor, glory, fame"; *ṣĕbî*, "beauty, splendor"; *yĕqār*, "preciousness, honor"; *tĕhillâ*, "glory, praise."

2. Shame and Failure.

Failure is one of the basic reasons why people experience shame. In a military or judicial contest, to lose means to be ashamed, while to win is equivalent to shaming one's opponent (Mic 7:10; Zech 10:5). It is against such a background that Jeremiah's prayers that his persecutors be shamed must be understood (Jer 17:18; 20:11). In these verses to be put to shame is placed in parallel with disaster, *destruction, dismay, stumbling, not prevailing and not succeeding. The disgrace (*bwš*, *ḥpr*) of the seers in Micah 3:7 stems from their inability to elicit an answer from God—that is, their failure to perform their function as seers. In Jeremiah 8:9 the wise are put to shame (*bwš*) through the failure of their wisdom, which is unable to achieve security for the nation.

A nation experiences shame as a result of defeat in battle, loss of territory or the capture of its capital. The defeats of Israel (Jer 2:36), Egypt (Jer 46:11-12), Moab (Jer 48:1, 20, 39), Damascus (Jer 49:23), Tyre (Is 23:9) and *Babylon (Jer 51:47) are described with the help of shame terminology. J. Stiebert interprets a number of these references as reflecting an antiforeign ideology of the postexilic period that somehow sees shame connected to foreignness (Stiebert 2002, 125), but there is no basis in the texts for such a conclusion. The shame of the foreign *nations, like Israel's shame, stems from the mere fact that they have failed in battle and have shown themselves to be weak and inadequate. Natural disasters such as crop failure (Joel 1:11-12, contrast with Joel 2:23-27)

(see Simkins, 46) and drought (Jer 14:1-4) also bring shame. The reason for disgrace in this instance is probably the notion that famine is indicative of God's abandonment of his people (for a connection between abandonment and shame, see Is 54:4-7).

3. Honor and Shame in Judgment and Salvation.

Shame and judgment are tightly interconnected in prophetic literature. In Micah 2:6 "humiliation" (*kĕlimmôt*) is even used as a shorthand reference to the doom preached by the prophet (Wagner, 191, 195). Most prominent is the association of God's judgment with the shame of military defeat. In such contexts shame is used in parallel with mourning, destruction, ruin and death (Jer 9:19; 15:9; 23:40; 50:12; Ezek 7:18; Obad 10). The sneer and derision of the nations are an important element of the descriptions of such military misfortunes (Jer 46:12; 48:39; 51:51; Ezek 34:29; 36:6; Zeph 2:8) as well as of the shame experienced during the time of famine and drought (Joel 2:17) (on this, see also Simkins, 48, 51, and the criticisms of Stiebert 2002, 78-79). The fact that in social life shame functions as a sanction of unacceptable social behavior (Bechtel, 50-52, 76) also facilitates the association of Israel's shame and punishment (see the comparison with a thief in Jer 2:26).

Judgment and shame in the OT are confined predominantly to this world. Only rarely is the question of shame beyond the grave touched upon. Honor in *death was traditionally connected to the high social status of the deceased, the manner of their death and a proper burial, while lack of burial or dishonorable death brought disgrace (Is 14:18-19; Jer 22:18-19). There also may have been beliefs in the existence of places of honor and shame in the underworld (Eichrodt, 437-38). Ezekiel 32:17-31 plays on such notions to depict polemically the ultimate disgrace of Egypt in Sheol and its confinement there to spheres of uncleanness (Strong, 489-97). In Daniel 12:2 we find a radical development and transformation of such ideas. There the "shame [*ḥărāpôt*] and everlasting contempt" of those resurrected for punishment is contrasted with the "everlasting life" of the righteous and the wise (cf. Is 66:24) (*see* Afterlife).

As judgment brings disgrace, salvation leads to the removal of shame. It involves the transition from shame to joy (Is 61:7; 65:13) and entails restoration of the honor (*kbd*) of the exiles in both the sight of God and the sight of other nations (Is 43:4; Jer 30:19; Zeph 3:19). Restoration promises often include the assurance that "you shall not (again) be put to shame [*bwš*]" (Is 45:17; 49:23; 54:4; Zeph 3:11). In such places the glory (*kābôd, tipᵓeret*) of *Zion is in parallel to its vindication and deliverance and results from the end of its abandonment and the renewal of its relationship with the Lord (Is 62:1-4). Recently, J. T. Strong has suggested that the message of Ezekiel's vision of the valley of the dry bones (Ezek 37:1-14) is that through recreating Israel anew the Lord not only resurrects the nation to a new life after defeat and judgment, but also restores their honor reversing the shame of the exile, depicted in the vision as dishonorable death (Strong, 497-504).

4. Honor and Shame in Divine-Human Relationships.

4.1. Sin. In prophetic literature honor is connected to *sin in quite a surprising way. On a certain level, honor is tied to having a good reputation and is recognized as the basis of one's social position (Simkins, 49; Lemos, 228). Those of prestige, influence and wealth are called "honored men" (Is 3:5; 5:13; 23:8; Nah 3:10). However, human honor is not generally perceived in a positive light. It is seen as an expression of arrogance and independence that defies the Lord and attracts his judgment (Stiebert 2002, 88-89). The honor of Assyria's military success is depicted as an empty boast (Is 10:12-15) that eventually leads to humiliation and destruction (Is 10:16-18; see also Is 13:19; 16:14; 17:1-4; 21:16; Jer 48:18; Ezek 31:18; Dan 4:37). Similar is the fate of Ephraim, whose wreath and glorious beauty (*šĕbî tipᵓartô*), symbols of his wealth, position and honor, are cast down by the Lord (Is 28:1-5). Shebna, who attempts to gain honor for himself by his splendid grave and chariots, is humiliated and rejected as "shame [*qālôn*] to his master's house," possibly because his search for honor is seen as an expression of arrogance (Is 22:15-18). Two other sins are also closely connected with the concept of shame: reliance on human strength (Is 30:1-5) and trust in other gods (Is 42:17; 44:9, 11; 45:16; Jer 10:14; 17:13; 51:17). Both of these constitute an implicit refusal to rely on the Lord's power that leads ultimately to disappointment and failure. The Isaiah tradition makes the con-

nection between these plain by describing both Egypt and idols with the same phrase, "no profit," which underlines their ineffectiveness.

4.2. Repentance. While in judgment Israel is objectively shamed by Yahweh, internalizing this shame can lead to realization of the inherent shamefulness of sin and thus can bring about repentance. In Jeremiah 31:18-19 a feeling of shame (*bwš, klm*) at the sins of the past accompanies Ephraim's return to the Lord and is contrasted with the earlier rebuke that Judah "refused to be ashamed [*klm*]" (Jer 3:3)—that is, refused to repent of its apostasy. In Ezekiel the Israelites are called in the light of God's mercy and grace to be ashamed (*bwš, klm*) of what they had done (Ezek 36:31-32). According to Ezekiel, however, such an experience of shame (*bwš*) and humiliation (*kĕlimmâ*) ultimately will not be the prerequisite but the result of divine forgiveness and deliverance (Ezek 16:63; 39:26 [contrast *BHS*: "they will forget their shame"]). This shame probably is to be regarded as a constitutive element of true repentance stemming from the nation's realization of its own inadequacy and moral responsibility (Wagner, 192; contrast Odell and see the discussion in Stiebert 2002, 155-60). J. E. Lapsley has argued that in those passages the "gift of shame" is to be seen as a salvific act of God, part of reconstituting Israel's new moral identity based on true knowledge of God and of self (Lapsley, 142-57).

4.3. Mutual Honor. While shame signals the disruption of divine-human relationship, expression of honor is the normal way in which this relationship functions. Israel is called to honor (*kbd*) the Lord in the cult (Is 43:23; Hag 1:8; Mal 1:6) and to honor the Lord alone. To honor other gods is a grave and destructive sin (Dan 5:23). But these outer forms of expression, important as they are, are insufficient. They must reflect an appropriate inner attitude; otherwise, they are merely "honoring [*kbd*] with the lips" and become empty and meaningless (Is 29:13). Honor has, therefore, both an objective and a subjective aspect. Objectively, it is expressed in symbolic actions that proclaim publicly human appreciation of divine glory; subjectively, it has to do with an attitude of submission and adoration.

Honor is not conferred only by people of inferior social standing to a superior. A suzerain may honor his vassals (Olyan, 204-8) as a king may honor a faithful servant (Dan 2:6). In the same way, the Lord honors his people by giving them joy, prosperity and dominion over their oppressors (Is 60:9-16). The Isaianic *Servant of the Lord, who is humiliated by others, is honored (*kbd*) in the sight of the Lord (Is 49:5), and this honor is what ultimately matters (Is 50:7). In the Prophetic Books the only way for humans to receive honor is by it being granted to them by the Lord, not by earning it through their own efforts.

5. The Objective and Subjective Aspects of Shame.

There is debate as to what extent the concept of shame, which has more to do with the outer pressure from society, must be distinguished from or identified with that of guilt, which is related more to the inner pressure of an individual's conscience (Bechtel, 48-55; Stiebert 2000, 256-59). There is also disagreement whether shame is to be understood solely objectively, as a loss of status (Odell, 103), or if it includes also a subjective aspect, with feelings of unworthiness and personal shortcoming (Stiebert 2002, 93-94; Lapsley, 133-37).

Shame is clearly distinguished from guilt by the fact that it is inexorably linked to what others think of oneself. Therefore, someone may experience shame without having committed any morally objectionable acts simply because others find that person's actions unacceptable. Jeremiah, for example, complains that he has come forth from his mother's womb only to experience toil and shame (Jer 20:18 [*bōšet*])—that is, the derision of his compatriots because of his prophetic message (Jer 20:7, 10). Like Jeremiah, the Suffering Servant in Isaiah is publicly insulted and humiliated (*klm*), yet, in contrast, he claims that he will not be humiliated and put to shame (*klm, bwš*) because it is the Lord who helps him and vindicates him (Is 50:6-7). It is clear that on this occasion shame is related not to what others think of the Suffering Servant but rather to what the Lord thinks and does for him (contra Wagner, who interprets *klm* in Is 50:7 as referring to "existential destruction" [Wagner, 195]). Assurance of the Lord's coming vindication triumphs over present disgrace. This line of development reaches a climax in Isaiah 53:2-4, where public humiliation becomes in fact not something negative and repulsive but rather is endowed with new meaning and redemptive significance. Here we see the same pattern as in Isaiah 50:6-7: the apparent initial disgrace of the servant culminates in his ultimate exaltation (Is 52:13).

Shame, therefore, involves more than the fear of losing face. It is related to what one perceives to be right and wrong in the light of one's own conscience and sometimes regardless of public opinion. For this reason, Jeremiah can reproach his contemporaries that "they acted shamefully [*bwš*] . . . but were not ashamed [*bwš*]" and even "did not know how to feel humiliation [*klm*]" (Jer 6:15; 8:12). In this situation their behavior seems to have not received social reprimand, yet Jeremiah thinks that they still should experience shame because their actions are intrinsically shameful. Similar thinking probably underlines the complaint in Zephaniah 3:5 that the "unjust knows no shame [*bōšet*]" as well as the designation of Judah as a "shameless nation" in Zephaniah 2:1 (the meaning of the text is disputed). In the light of these verses, Stiebert's analysis that shame involves fundamentally a negative self-judgment in the light of an ideal that the individual holds in common with the community (Stiebert 2000, 256) seems to be correct. Due to its objective and subjective aspects, the concept of shame helps us to gain a fresh appreciation of the inherent connection between the sin of Israel and the judgment resulting from that sin. The clearest way this is achieved in the prophets is through the use of the sexual metaphor to describe both Israel's shameful behavior and the shame of Israel's punishment. Such imagery is particularly strong in Hosea, Jeremiah and Ezekiel, who portray Israel (and Judah) as an adulterous woman unfaithful to her divine husband. The metaphor of fornication and adultery is most commonly used to condemn worship of other gods and to convey the notion that idolatry is as shameful as is indecent sexual conduct (Hos 1:2; 2:2-5; 3:1; Jer 2:20-28; Ezek 16:15-25). Judgment is portrayed with the help of the image of shaming a woman by exposing her nakedness. Northern Israel (Hos 2:2, 10), Judah (Jer 13:26) and Jerusalem (Ezek 16:37), as well as Assyria (Nah 3:5) and Babylon (Is 47:3), are to suffer such fate. A number of these passages, with their vivid and shocking imagery, often are perceived as problematic by modern readers and as degrading to women (Shields, 7, 13). However, we must not lose sight of the fact that their primary aim is not to comment or give guidance on gender relations but rather to interpret aspects of Israel's relationship with God by utilizing existing cultural preconceptions about what is appropriate and inappropriate in male and female behavior. It is noteworthy that through the use of the marriage metaphor the predominantly male audience of the prophets is called to experience in relation to Yahweh a type of shame that on a purely social level is appropriate only for females.

The use of the sexual metaphor is one of the points where insights gained from anthropology might potentially be fruitful in advancing our understanding of the text. It has been pointed out that in Mediterranean societies honor and shame are closely linked with sexual relations and gender roles. A married woman who has intercourse with another man destroys the honor of her husband (Delaney, 40, 42; Giovannini, 68; see also Stone, 44, 69-126, 142-44). If the story of Hosea 1—3 is read through such a cultural lens, an important aspect of its message would be brought to light. The behavior of Gomer brings disgrace upon Hosea as Israel's *idolatry brings disgrace upon her divine husband, Yahweh. In a striking countercultural move, the prophet (and God) places his love for his wayward wife above his own honor and is determined to restore her to himself even at the expense of his own humiliation. Attractive as this reading is, it is surprising that in Hosea 1—3 there is no mention whatsoever of the theme of the husband's disgrace and honor. The focus is solely on the shamefulness and the shame experienced by Gomer/Israel.

6. The Honor of God.

The only one who has a proper and undeniable claim to honor in the prophetic literature is the Lord himself. His honor results from his holiness, creation power, dominion over the world and historic acts of judgment and *salvation (Is 6:3; 43:7; Ezek 28:22; 36:21-23; Dan 4:34), and this stands in sharp contrast to human transience and arrogance (Is 2:10-22; 40:5-8). Even the sun and the moon, here representing either the created order or, more likely, astral deities worshiped throughout the ancient world, are ashamed (ḥpr, bwš) before the manifestation of the Lord's glory (kābôd) (Is 24:23).

This raises the question of whether the Lord can be in any way dishonored or put to shame (see the survey of discussion in Stiebert 2002,

96-98). The motif of God acting out of concern to preserve his honor is encountered in a variety of OT texts (Glatt-Gilad). Historically, it is connected to the belief that the fortunes of a given nation reflect on the reputation of its god (see the shame of Bel and Merodach in Jer 50:2, and compare Jer 48:13). So the Babylonian exile causes God's name to be despised (n'ṣ) and profaned (ḥll) among the nations (Is 52:5; Ezek 36:19-21) because he is perceived to be weak and ineffective in protecting his people. It is because of concern for his name (šēm) that God refrains from total extermination of Israel after the exodus from Egypt (Ezek 20:9, 14, 22) and during the exile (Is 48:11), and it is to protect his honor that he brings back his people to their land (Ezek 36:21-23).

Unlike Israel, Yahweh cannot experience shame because of doing something shameful in and of itself or because of failing to achieve his purposes. Yet the OT seems to suggest that he can be disgraced in the eyes of the world because he has allowed himself to be so intimately associated with one nation that their humiliation may become his. By entering into a special relationship with Israel, God makes himself vulnerable and opens himself to the effects of the sins and failures of his people. This is not presented as insignificant to God: he guards his honor zealously, yet his honor is not so important as to make him disassociate from Israel completely.

The question still remains as to why it would matter to an almighty God what his reputation among the gentile nations is (Glatt-Gilad, 63-64). Within a canonical context, Yahweh's concern for his name prepares the way for the missiological stance of the NT. The Lord's acts of judgment and salvation, which reflect on his reputation, serve to make his name (šēm) known among the nations (Ezek 28:22-23; 38:23). Thus, Yahweh's concern for his honor has a revelatory dimension to it. What the nations think of Israel's God matters because he wants to be known beyond the borders of Canaan. He is not content to remain only Israel's God; he intends to be honored throughout the whole world, which he has created.

See also DEATH; EXILE; SIN.

BIBLIOGRAPHY. **Y. Avrahami**, "בוש" in the Psalms—Shame or Disappointment?" *JSOT* 34 (2010) 295-313; **L. M. Bechtel**, "Shame as a Sanction of Social Control in Biblical Israel: Judicial, Political, and Social Shaming," *JSOT* 49 (1991) 47-76; **C. Delaney,** "Seeds of Honor, Fields of Shame," in *Honor and Shame and the Unity of the Mediterranean,* ed. D. D. Gilmore (Washington, DC: American Anthropological Association, 1987) 35-48; **W. Eichrodt,** *Ezekiel* (OTL; Philadelphia: Westminster, 1970); **M. J. Giovannini,** "Female Chastity Codes in the Circum-Mediterranean: Comparative Perspectives," in *Honor and Shame and the Unity of the Mediterranean,* ed. D. D. Gilmore (Washington, DC: American Anthropological Association, 1987) 61-74; **D. A. Glatt-Gilad,** "Yahweh's Honor at Stake: A Divine Conundrum," *JSOT* 98 (2002) 63-74; **S. Kirkpatrick,** *Competing for Honor: A Social-Scientific Reading of Daniel 1-6* (BIS 74; Leiden: Brill, 2005); **T. S. Laniak,** *Shame and Honor in the Book of Esther* (SBLDS 165; Atlanta: Scholars Press, 1998); **J. E. Lapsley,** *Can These Bones Live? The Problem of the Moral Self in the Book of Ezekiel* (BZAW 301; Berlin: de Gruyter, 2000); **T. M. Lemos,** "Shame and Mutilation of Enemies in the Hebrew Bible," *JBL* 125 (2006) 225-41; **M. S. Odell,** "The Inversion of Shame and Forgiveness in Ezekiel 16:59-63," *JSOT* 56 (1992) 101-12; **S. M. Olyan,** "Honor, Shame and Covenant Relations in Ancient Israel and its Environment," *JBL* 115 (1996) 201-18; **H. Seebass,** "בּוֹשׁ," *TDOT* 2:50-60; **M. E. Shields,** "Multiple Exposures: Body Rhetoric and Gender Characterization in Ezekiel 16," *JFSR* 14 (1998) 5-18; **R. A. Simkins,** "'Return to Yahweh': Honor and Shame in Joel," *Semeia* 68 (1996) 41-54; **J. Stiebert,** "Shame and Prophecy: Approaches Past and Present," *BibInt* 8 (2000) 255-75; idem, *The Construction of Shame in the Hebrew Bible: The Prophetic Contribution* (JSOTSup 346; Sheffield: Sheffield Academic, 2002); **K. Stone,** *Sex, Honor and Power in the Deuteronomistic History* (JSOTSup 234; Sheffield: Sheffield Academic, 1996); **J. T. Strong,** "Egypt's Shameful Death and the House of Israel's Exodus from Sheol (Ezekiel 32.17-32 and 37.1-14)," *JSOT* 34 (2010) 475-504; **S. Wagner,** "כלם," *TDOT* 7:185-96. T. S. Hadjiev

HOSEA, BOOK OF

The Book of Hosea is the first, and longest, in the series of what used to be called the Minor Prophets, now more often called the Book of the Twelve. Like the book of Amos, it is set in the northern kingdom of Israel, but unlike Amos, the prophet Hosea was himself a northerner, and his prophecy is set shortly before the fall of that kingdom in 722 BC. Hosea is, in this respect, unique among the prophetic books. Its prominence among the Twelve makes it important in modern readings of the Twelve as a book. Its influence extends further than this, however, and its affinities with Deuteronomy and Jeremiah in particular are often noted. It is also significant for its powerful, imaginative use of language, especially in its portrayal of God.

1. Authorship, Date, Setting
2. Composition
3. Historical and Religious Background
4. Metaphor and Sexual Imagery in Hosea
5. Hosea's Theology in Canonical Context

1. Authorship, Date, Setting.
The prophet Hosea worked in the northern kingdom of Israel in the decades leading up to its fall at the hands of the Assyrians in 722 BC (*see* Israelite History). He was, therefore, one of the earliest prophets whose name is attached to an OT book, a little later than Amos and roughly contemporary with Isaiah of Jerusalem, and the only one (apart from Jonah) who came from the north. The mention of King Jeroboam II (ca. 786-746 BC) in the superscription (Hos 1:1) suggests that Hosea began preaching before that king's death, and the pronouncement in Hosea 1:4 of the end of the house of Jehu presupposes a setting before the death of King Zechariah, son of Jeroboam, in 745 BC, the last reigning member of that dynasty (2 Kings 15:8-12). Many of the individual sayings in the book are difficult to assign confidently to a date, as we will see below. Some of them, however, indicate a period of prosperity such as Israel enjoyed in Jeroboam's reign (e.g., Hos 2:8). The date of Jeroboam's death is disputed (753 BC, according to Stuart, 9), and so Hosea may have begun his work as early as the 750s. F. Andersen and D. Freedman think that the bulk of Hosea's work was complete by about 735 BC, since the events of the Syro-Ephraimite war (735-733 BC) are not in evidence in the book, nor indeed the fall of the northern kingdom (722 BC) (Andersen and Freedman, 37). There are sayings that are naturally taken to point to the end of the kingdom (e.g., Hos 1:4-5; 8:5-10; 11:5-7; 13:16), and some of these look beyond that end to a restoration (Hos 11:10-11; 14:4-7), but it does not follow that Hosea lived

to see it. The superscription tells that his work lasted into the reign of King Hezekiah of Judah, but since estimates of that king's accession year vary (from 727 to 715 BC), it is not certain that this implies that the prophet lived and worked up to and beyond the fall of the kingdom. It should also be noted that some commentators do not take the superscription as supplying historical evidence of this sort, but rather see it as an editorial perception of the relation of the prophet's work to the kingdom of Judah.

It is striking, indeed, that while Hosea lived and worked in the north, the superscription (Hos 1:1) names four kings of Judah and only Jeroboam among the northern kings of the same period, omitting the six last of the latter (2 Kings 15:8—17:6). Hosea certainly was interested in the kings and other rulers of Israel (e.g., Hos 5:10; 8:4; 10:3), and one passage appears to have in mind one of the royal assassinations that marked the last decades of the northern kingdom (Hos 7:3-7 [for various commentators' suggestions as to which king, see Ben Zvi 2005, 158]). Their omission suggests that the superscription reflects a time after Hosea, and the fall of the north, when the book took on significance for Judah, where, of course, it was received and preserved. Features such as these raise the question of the book's composition, to which we now turn.

2. Composition.

As with all the Prophetic Books, the book that bears Hosea's name is not identical with the words of the prophet. Both the superscription (Hos 1:1) and the third-person narrative in the remainder of Hosea 1 are presumably from the hand of someone other than Hosea. Hosea 3, in contrast, records a message from Yahweh to Hosea in his own voice. These obvious points pose the question of the process from Hosea's words to the form of the book that we possess. One factor to be observed in this connection is the several allusions to Judah (Hos 1:7; 4:15; 5:5; 8:14; 12:2) (Davies, 104-5), each making some comparison between Israel and Judah. These may simply put the two kingdoms on a par, as both deserving judgment (Hos 5:5; 8:14), or make the fate of Israel a warning to Judah (Hos 4:15), or in one case contrast the destiny of the two, indicating mercy for Judah but not for Israel (Hos 1:7). Given that the king-

dom of Judah outlived Israel by more than a century, many think that the words of Hosea underwent some expansion in the southern kingdom in order to make them relevant to that kingdom. Hosea's words of judgment on the north, as well as his words of salvation, might prove relevant to Judah too. A special case is Hosea 12:2, where the name "Judah" may even have been substituted for an original "Israel," which seems to be more suitable in the context because the verse introduces a passage about the patriarch Jacob (Davies, 104-5). The sole allusion to King David in the book (Hos 3:5) has also been regarded as a Judean addition because it was in Judah that the succession to David had been maintained since the time of Solomon's son Rehoboam. The words "and to David their king" could be an interpretation of "return to Yahweh" as implying renewed loyalty to the house of David in Jerusalem.

A second factor in assessing the relationship between author and book is the shaping of the book itself. The first block, Hosea 1—3, is unified by the theme of adultery or prostitution. Each of the three chapters is independent and deals with the topic in its own way. In Hosea 1 a narrator tells how Hosea is commanded by Yahweh to marry Gomer, "a woman of harlotries," as a sign of the unfaithfulness of Israel to Yahweh. In Hosea 2 Yahweh employs the metaphor of husband and wife to exhort Israel to turn back from her "lovers," with their false promises, and recognize him alone as the true giver of the gifts of life. And in Hosea 3, a short chapter, Hosea narrates in his own voice a different account of a command from Yahweh to marry an adulterous woman (on the identity of this woman, see 4 below). Although these three units are different in style and specific substance, they share the use of sexual figures of speech to convey their messages, and also a concept of Yahweh's action toward Israel, in which a time of judgment gives way to one of *salvation. This same movement thus characterizes Hosea 1—3 as a whole.

With Hosea 4 comes a change of style, and henceforth we hear a long series of prophetic oracles (Hos 4—14). The theme of Israel's adultery recedes, and the individual units are no longer so clearly demarcated as in Hosea 1—3. However, there are signs of careful composition in this section too. The most striking illustration of this is that although the dominant tone of the prophecies is judgment, there are two places where the message of salvation breaks through strongly: Hosea 11:8-11; 14:4-8. Since these are placed late in the collection, the latter being virtually the book's final word, it seems that this section too has been shaped in order to articulate a movement of thought similar to that in Hosea 1—3, with judgment leading in the end to salvation.

Because of the double climactic expression of Yahweh's intention to save, some scholars think of two subsections in the collection of oracles, Hosea 4—11; 12—14, with each of these building to a climax in a word of salvation (Wolff, xxix-xxxii; Jeremias 1983, 18-19). Others, however, take Hosea 4—14 as a single block (Andersen and Freedman, 52-53; Mays, 15-16; Eidevall, 9). M. Sweeney also adopts a twofold division of the book, but he defines the sections as Hosea 1:2-11; 2:1—14:8, corresponding to the words of the narrator and those of Hosea (Sweeney, 12-13). In all cases, of course, the larger blocks break down into a series of smaller units (Ben Zvi 2005, 96); and conversely, the larger blocks are interrelated.

The corollary of observations about a careful structure in the book is that the sayings of Hosea have been subject to theological shaping in its production. H. Wolff thought that Hosea himself was responsible not only for much of the content of the book but also for some of its shaping (Hos 2:2—3:5; 12—14) (Wolff, xxix, xxx-xxxi), while a group of his immediate disciples took this further. The references to Judah testify to at least two Judean expansions, the first adopting Hosea's vision of future restoration (Hos 1:7), while a later level used the downfall of the north as a warning (Hos 4:15; 5:5c; 8:14) (Wolff, xxxi-xxxii). These expansions belong within the Deuteronomic-Deuteronomistic movement spanning two centuries after Hosea's time (Wolff, xxxi). J. Jeremias, following Wolff, argued that the sayings in Hosea 4—14 were carefully composed so as to articulate Hosea's enduring theological message (Jeremias 1983). For example, between Hosea 4:16; 7:13; 13:14 a sequence is created in which Yahweh is seen to reflect on Israel's stubbornness and his own purpose to "redeem" (*pdh*), building to a climax in Hosea 13:14 (Jeremias 1996, 63). For this reason, the expansions in Judah were simply a logical extension of a process that began in Hosea's time (Jeremias 1996, 66).

For both scholars (and others, such as Davies, 30-32), the message of grace at the heart of the book (as in Hos 11:8-11; 14:4-8) could confidently be attributed to Hosea himself (Wolff, xxx; Jeremias 1983, 20).

Andersen and Freedman differ from Wolff in finding that the message about Judah is embedded in Hosea's prophecy from the start. Hosea is in this sense like Amos, himself from Judah, who addressed his prophecies to the north but could speak about Judah too (Andersen and Freedman, 191-92). There is nothing intrinsically unlikely about this, since Hosea had a strong sense of Israel's history and might well have understood that both kingdoms were heirs to it (Andersen and Freedman, 192). Equally, the reference to King David could be from Hosea just as probably as from later Judean redactors. Andersen and Freedman point out, justifiably, "We hardly know enough of Hosea's political thinking to rule out the restoration of the Davidic kingdom as an eschatological expectation" (Andersen and Freedman, 307).

Since much of the discourse of the book is by its nature capable of being dated to a variety of periods, some scholars by contrast focus not on the question of the authenticity of the prophet's words, but on the book as a product of the kingdom of Judah or later. E. Ben Zvi believes that the book originated after the exile in Persian Yehud. Geographical allusions to places in the north, for example, do not necessarily indicate a setting in the northern kingdom but rather belong to "constructions of the past," which do not require historical accuracy but merely have to comport with what is generally known and accepted (Ben Zvi 2005, 14, 18-19). This could explain the omission of several northern kings in the superscription, for example. Ben Zvi also thinks that the *exile pervades Hosea as a theme, that it functions as a purification process, and that *Israel's ideal future lies beyond such an experience (Ben Zvi 2005, 14-15). This involves reading certain texts as referring to the exile even though they do not do so explicitly (such as the return to the wilderness in Hos 2:14-15). The people of Yehud are now in that situation. Hosea was produced for the benefit of the literate elite in Yehud, both to educate and empower it as the proponents of the type of Israelite identity expressed by the book (Ben Zvi 2005, 19). The memory of Yahweh's punishment "is relived as social memory" and functions to edify and warn; it even operates (paradoxically) to assure Yehud that God will never abandon them (Ben Zvi 2005, 97-98). Ben Zvi concurs with the more conservative interpreters of Hosea that a strong theology of grace stands at the center of the book, but his perspective on the book's setting and purpose puts it in a rather different light (see also Trotter, 51-89).

The two types of approach to the book reviewed above address the distance between the setting of Hosea's life and work and the reception of the book in Judah and after the exile. There is an intrinsic difficulty in tracing with any exactness the trajectory from Hosea's words to the written page. Indeed, Jeremias thought that even the earliest composition of the prophet's sayings no longer had the original specific situation in view (Jeremias 1996, 65-66). It remains probable that the book preserves a record of the prophet's life and ministry. However, it must be acknowledged that its language is such as to preclude an explanation of it in terms of one particular historical location (on language, see further 4 below).

3. Historical and Religious Background.

3.1. Political Change. Against the background of the looming threat from Assyria, Hosea's Israel faced economic, political and religious issues. After King Jeroboam II, Israel's fortunes changed, chiefly because of the campaign by the Assyrian king Tiglath-Pileser III, or Pul, (745-728 BC), to assert Assyrian power throughout the region. Israel almost immediately became a vassal state (2 Kings 15:19-20), and around 733 BC Tiglath-Pileser annexed key cities and areas in Galilee and carried sections of the population into exile (2 Kings 15:29). This is the time of the Syro-Ephraimite war (2 Kings 16:5-9; Is 7:1-17), an abortive attempt by Israel and Syria to fight off the Assyrian advance. After this, Israel's last king, Hoshea, was a mere puppet ruling over a greatly reduced territory. The fall of the north in 722 BC, therefore, was the culmination of a sequence of events spanning two decades.

The period in Israel was also one of internal strains, symptomized by the series of short reigns and palace coups (described in 2 Kings 15:8-26). This restlessness may have arisen from royal misrule in itself, to which both Amos and Hosea testify. But it also could be related to As-

syrian pressure, as it appears to emanate from areas such as Gilead, where the Assyrian presence was first acutely felt (see, e.g., 2 Kings 15:25) (Cogan and Tadmor, 178).

The peace and prosperity of Jeroboam's time thus came to an end in political upheaval. These conditions probably explain Hosea's opposition to forming alliances with great powers (Hos 5:13; 7:11), his adverse comments on kings in general (Hos 5:10; 8:4-5; 10:1-7) and perhaps sayings such as the allusion to Gilead in Hosea 6:8. The disaster that he predicted for the kingdom was unfolding before his eyes.

3.2. Religious Issues. The political chaos had a counterpart in religious conditions. It is clear that Hosea places the *worship of Yahweh in opposition to that of Baal (as in Hos 2), and that Israel's fate is bound up with proper worship. That worship and the affairs of state were closely connected is evident from the policy of the Judean king Ahaz, who adopted Assyrian forms of worship in his bid to secure Assyrian backing for his rule (2 Kings 16:10-16).

But what kinds of alternatives are represented by Yahweh and Baal? Several factors have to be considered. First, it is not immediately obvious what the term *ba'al* refers to. It occurs seven times in the book (Hos 2:8, 13, 16, 17; 9:10; 11:2; 13:1). Of these, three are in the plural (Hos 2:13, 17; 11:2), and two refer in the singular to the god Baal (Hos 2:8; 13:1). A further singular occurrence is in Hosea 2:16, where we read "my *ba'al* " as an appellation of Yahweh that must no longer be used (but rather *'îšî*, "my husband"). In Hosea 9:10 the episode at Baal-Peor is recalled, where a god Baal apparently was localized to that place (see Num 25:3-5). The same verse has a further reference to the god Baal in the term "shame" (*bōšet*) (cf. NRSV, "a thing of shame," and this substitution of "shame" for Baal elsewhere, as in the name "Ishbosheth" for Ishbaal the son of King Saul [2 Sam. 2:12; 1 Chron. 8:33]).

These usages do not add up to a systematic portrait of the god Baal. The term *ba'al* in itself can be a proper name, as in the god Baal known at Ugarit as a major deity. This may be the best way to understand Baal in Elijah's contest with the Phoenician "prophets of Baal" in 1 Kings 18. But *ba'al* can also be a generic appellative, "lord" or "master," hence, for example, the *ba'al* of Peor. In Hosea it is possible that a major deity called "Baal" coexists with numerous localized deities bearing that name. The attribution of "my *ba'al*" to Yahweh in Hosea 2:16 may go back to a belief that Yahweh was one *ba'al* among others.

Equally, the significance of a polemic against Baal could have changed with time. Jeremias thinks that the idea of the worship of Baal in the eighth century BC had become a kind of "abstraction"; the point of Hosea's use of it may be to indict the worship of Yahweh as in some way degraded (Jeremias 1996, 88-89, 102). The question takes us into the theology of the book, to which we will return below. It also requires some attention to Hosea's rich figurative language because language and theology are inextricably related here, and sexual metaphors in particular play a key role in depicting both Israel's sin and Yahweh's judgment, love and faithfulness. We turn next, therefore, to Hosea's language.

4. Metaphor and Sexual Imagery in Hosea.
Hosea's metaphors and similes come thick and fast in some passages (on metaphor in Hosea, see Eidevall; Seifert; Morris; Moughtin-Mumby, 51-61; cf. Macintosh, lxiii). In Hosea 5:12-14 Yahweh declares, "I am like a moth [or 'maggots'] to Ephraim, and rottenness to the house of Judah" (Hos 5:12). Israel's problem is a sickness, or wound, that requires healing (Hos 5:13). And Yahweh is like a savage lion, tearing and carrying off its prey (Hos 5:14; 13:7). Yahweh can come like the showers and early rains (Hos 6:3). He is like dew (Hos 14:5), and both he and Israel are trees (Hos 14:5-8). Israel is depicted (metaphorically) as adulterers, who are then further compared to a "heated oven," in an extended simile in which the heat of the oven also expresses anger and sedition (Hos 7:4-7). Ephraim is a cake, in an image that includes the elements of both mixing and turning from the baking process to suggest different kinds of weakness (Hos 7:8-9), and also like a dove, "silly and without sense" (Hos 7:11). The devastation of Israel can be conveyed as an undoing of creation, and the land itself can be said to "mourn" (Hos 4:3). Further examples include Hosea 8:7-10; 9:10, 13, 16; 10:1, 11, 12; 12:7. In some of these cases the metaphor seems to take over and develop the idea (as with the "oven" in Hos 7:4-7). In other cases the metaphor may recur in a new way, along with the theological movement of the book. Yahweh the tearing lion is also the lion who roars at the return of his people to their home from places of judgment (Hos 11:10). And Israel, formerly cast as a dove in its senseless pursuit of impotent sources of aid, now returns from such places "like birds" and "like doves" (Hos 11:11). Most strikingly, Yahweh, who Israel is commanded in Hosea 2:16 no longer to call "my *ba'al*," but rather "my husband" (*'îšî*), is "not a man" (*lō' 'îš*) in Hosea 11:9.

Not only do metaphor and simile abound, but so also does wordplay, though usually it is lost in translation. The name "Jezreel" ("God sows") is a play on "Israel," and in Hosea 1:4 this allows Israel to be characterized by bloodshed in an allusion to the actions of Jehu against the house of Ahab (2 Kings 10). Yet Jezreel in its connotation of "sowing" can recur in a picture of people and land restored (Hos 2:21-22). The name "Ephraim" suggests fruitfulness (*pĕrî*), which is exploited for wordplay in Hosea 13:15 ("flourish," *yaprî'*) and Hosea 14:8 (where the MT has "your fruitfulness" [so the NIV]). The form "I will heal" (*'erpā'*) in Hosea 14:4 also suggests the same name. The verb *šûb* ("to turn, return"), a key term in Hosea's theology, as we will see, is the subject of a number of wordplays, not least in Hosea 14. G. Morris has identified "at least seventy" puns (collected in Morris, 148-51; cf. Macintosh, lxiv). Both metaphor and wordplay tend toward an expressive or suggestive kind of meaning and can produce ambiguity. Morris gives Hosea 10:1 as an example of this because the word *bôqēq* can mean either "fruitful" or "empty" (so the KJV), and also because *yĕšawweh* ("yields, brings forth") resembles *šāwĕ'* ("vanity"), which occurs in Hosea 10:4 (Morris, 91-92).

These general observations about language in Hosea should inform an understanding of the most prominent and well-known set of metaphors in the book: the depiction of Yahweh's relationship with Israel in sexual or marital terms (*see* Marriage and Divorce). We saw above that Hosea 1—3 affords distinct reflections on that relationship by using language drawn from the sexual sphere. The connection between Hosea's marital and sexual relationships in Hosea 1; 3 and Yahweh's love for Israel is developed in Hosea 2. In Hosea 2:2 Yahweh's repudiation of Israel as his "wife" ("She is not my wife, and I am not her husband") amounts to an affirmation that such a relationship previously existed between them, in line with the renunciations of

Hosea 1:6-9 ("not my people," "not pitied"). Hosea 2 develops Yahweh's jealousy toward Israel because of her "lovers" and moves through to a marital reconciliation (Hos 2:19-20). The correspondence between Hosea's love life and Yahweh's is made explicit in Hosea 3:1.

The way in which the sexual metaphor works is slightly elusive, however. Yahweh's initial instruction to Hosea is to "take for yourself a wife of harlotries" (ʾēšet zĕnûnîm [Hos 1:2]). This expression leaves open the question as to Gomer's actual offense. Is she a prostitute, as the root znh apparently implies, or an adulteress? The two types of offense are paired in Hosea 2:2, and the woman in Hosea 3:1 is accused of adultery. And again, has she already acquired this reputation when Hosea is told to marry her, or does she become promiscuous or unfaithful thereafter? These questions are complicated because of the well-known problem of relating Hosea 1 and Hosea 3. The woman in Hosea 3 is not identified as Gomer. Yahweh says to Hosea, "Go again, love a woman . . ." (Hos 3:1). The only sign that the text in Hosea 3:1 presupposes the narrative in Hosea 1 is the word "again," which need imply only that Hosea has been given a similar command in the past (the word "again" [Heb ʿôd] could alternatively be taken with "Yahweh said" [so the NRSV], but the point is hardly affected). Here, indeed, he is not told to "marry" the woman, but rather to "love" her. This is, of course, consistent with his being already married to her, and one can therefore suppose that the woman in Hosea 3 is indeed Gomer, and that she has left Hosea for another man, so committing "adultery," as in Hosea 3:1. Hosea is thus commanded to take back his wife in spite of her unfaithfulness to him. This scenario is presupposed by the NIV translation of Hosea 3:1: "Go, show your love to your wife again, though she is loved by another and is an adulteress," but the relationship between the two incidents is deliberately left open by the ESV, as in the Hebrew: "Go again, love a woman who is loved by another man and is an adulteress."

For reasons such as these, it probably is misguided to try to compose a narrative of the marital lives of Hosea and Gomer from the data in the book. Formally, the instructions to Hosea may be taken to entail prophetic symbolic actions, and this can mitigate the need to construct a biographical account (see Sign Acts). However, as R. Abma rightly points out,

there are obvious difficulties with disengaging the actions from Hosea's real life and relationships, since if the women are different, it would be an odd way to represent Yahweh's faithful love. In Abma's proposed solution to this dilemma the two passages can refer to the same woman as long as "Hosea 1 and 3 are not read as accounts of successive events but as parallel accounts with different accents" (Abma, 211n216). In this way, the separate incidents contribute to a powerful accusation of apostasy, in which the figurative uses of adultery and harlotry flow into each other in a sequence of images based on the underlying notion of sexual misbehavior. This conclusion is supported further by the ideas that the land has committed harlotry, and that Hosea is to take not only a "woman of harlotries" but also "children of harlotries" (Hos 1:2) (the NIV is strictly more accurate than the ESV and the NRSV in omitting the verb "have" in the latter case). Are these the same as the children whom Hosea and Gomer now have together? What makes them "children of harlotries?" The impression again is that the sexual language is applied to its purpose in a way that overflows the boundaries of the love lives of Hosea and Gomer.

In what way do the sexual metaphors relate to the sins of Israel? Not only in Hosea 1—3, but also in Hosea 4:10-14, 18; 5:3-4; 6:10; 8:9; 9:1, the topic of "harlotry" (zānâ, zĕnûnîm) recurs, supported by terms for "adultery" (nāʾap [Hos 4:13]), "cult prostitutes" (qĕdēšôt [Hos 4:14]) and "lovers" (ʾăhābîm [Hos 8:9]). This "harlotry" is closely associated with acts of worship, such as "enquiring of a thing of wood" (Hos 4:12) and sacrifice in groves of trees (Hos 4:13). Does this particular language and imagery tell us something about the nature of Israel's offense?

One common answer is to suppose that the prophet was criticizing a kind of religion in which sexual practices at sanctuaries played an important part (e.g., Wolff, 85-86; Mays, 8-12). Andersen and Freedman state it thus: "The language of [4:14b] makes it clear that promiscuity and sacrifice were part of a full-scale cult" (Andersen and Freedman, 370). The religion of Baal is thus conceived as a "fertility religion" or "fertility cult," and Baal essentially as a god who guarantees agricultural fertility. This is taken to be entailed in a Baal mythology in which the potency of the god to fertilize the earth is inseparable from his sexual potency, the earth being portrayed as a mother goddess. Such activity of the gods is then mimicked in the cult by the sympathetic magic of sexual intercourse (Wolff, 15; Andersen and Freedman, 157-58; Mays, 8-9; Jeremias 1983, 27-28). Since Israel's unfaithfulness is depicted as sexual infidelity, and Baal religion is at the same time seen to be marked by transgressive sex, the nature of Hosea's rhetorical strategy can be expressed thus: "Here metaphor and reality are almost synonymous" (Mays, 25). One result of this approach to the language is the need to make claims about the lives of the protagonists to fit it. When Gomer is subjected to such speculation, she can be characterized as doubly sinful, not only an unfaithful wife but also as a participant in the sexual rituals of the Baal cult, and thus a cult prostitute (Andersen and Freedman, 166; Mays, 26).

For many modern interpreters, this view presses the texts too hard for a kind of information that they cannot yield. One problem is that the theory that the Baal cult is a fertility religion, in the sense supposed, has been called into question because of lack of evidence and on the grounds that the supposed supporting mythology of a sexualized earth is no longer accepted as the best interpretation of the known Canaanite Baal texts (Keefe, 73-75; cf. Moughtin-Mumby, 9; Abma, 137-39). In addition, Yahweh is actually like Baal in the sense that he exercises power over the natural order. Indeed, it is part of Hosea's case that Yahweh does what the people mistakenly suppose Baal can do (Hos 2:8-9).

*Feminist readers are concerned to challenge what they see as the equation of the female with sinfulness or passivity and to show that the feminine imagery in the book cannot be reduced to a cipher for sin and unfaithfulness. S. Moughtin-Mumby opposes a "substitutionary" view of the marriage metaphor as unduly limiting the scope and suggestive power of the sexual imagery (Moughtin-Mumby, 6). A. Keefe, expressing a similar concern, focuses on Hosea 1—2 to the exclusion of Hosea 3 because she thinks that these chapters illustrate better the suggestive power of the language.

Feminist response is varied, however. In one version, feminist scholars accept the analysis in which the sexual imagery has its background in fertility religion, and thus the dualism in which the male equates with a transcendent type of religion, and the female with a type that affirms the bodily and material aspects of life. Women in goddess worship asserted their autonomy and secured the goods of life for children and family (Keefe, 62-64, citing van Dijk-Hemmes and Setel). This, however, is subject to the weakness of the postulate of the fertility cult. In another version, the female characterization of Israel in Hosea aims to undermine received symbols of identity, where woman is "other" to an Israel identified by men as male, and so is intended to induce shame (Keefe, 154, citing Leith). This faces the difficulty that restored Israel continues to be characterized as female, as in Hosea 2:16-20 (Keefe, 155). Y. Sherwood, however, also finds deconstructive force in the text in its identification of male Israel with a promiscuous woman (Sherwood, 313). She pursues a robust ideological "inversion of critical tradition" and an intention to "retrieve the female character from her 'virtual' and reflective role" (Sherwood, 255). For Keefe, this goes too far. She rejects the older feminist dilemma between "text-affirming" and "text-negating" approaches, acknowledges the liberating force of the text of Hosea in its reception history, and calls for a greater understanding of the social determinants of the text before applying a rigorously resistant reading (Keefe, 142-46).

5. Hosea's Theology in Canonical Context.

Hosea occupies a significant place in the OT canon, standing at the head of the Book of the Twelve in both the MT and the LXX (see Sweeney) (see Twelve, Book of the). The significance of this depends somewhat on how far one regards the Book of the Twelve as having thematic coherence. However, Hosea suitably occupies its prominent position because of the intense treatment that it gives to certain theological topics. It has, as we have seen, both a strong sense of Yahweh's history with Israel and a wide historical scope. With its reach back to Israel's beginnings and its capacity to be reappropriated in the later periods of Israel's history, it evinces a kind of theology of history. Its trajectory therefore corresponds to that of the Twelve, which stretches from Hosea's own northern Israelite perspective on the history of all Israel through to the situation of Persian Yehud as reflected overtly in Haggai, Zechariah and Malachi. This historical vision in Hosea is accompanied by a theological one, with its movement through sin and judgment to repentance and restoration. Theologically too, therefore, Hosea is a suitable entrée to the Twelve.

By the same tokens, however, Hosea's canonical affinities are not confined to the Twelve. The theological sequencing of *covenant making and covenant breach, followed by divine judgment, covenant renewal and restoration can be found in almost all the major literary blocks of the OT, with its pervasive paradigms of exodus, Sinai, land, loss of land, repossession of land. This pattern is mapped on to a story of the relationship between Yahweh and Israel, which begins in covenant breach (Ex 32; Jer 2) and strains forward toward renewed and better-grounded covenantal relationship, expressed in, for example, Jeremiah's concept of new covenant (Jer 31:31-34). The story takes place among and in view of the nations, which also undergo the judgment of Yahweh and, in some places, receive the hope of participating in promises made to Israel.

Hosea is noted especially for linguistic and theological affinities with Deuteronomy (Weinfeld, 366-70), which have led to a perception that Hosea exhibits theological tendencies that came to fuller definition in Deuteronomy. Central to the comparison are the ideas of the love of Yahweh for Israel (albeit developed in different language in the two books), the gift of land, the controversy with other gods, and the conditionality of covenant. Some of these affinities will be noted in what follows. It should be remembered, however, that Hosea remains distinctive in its theological expression. It does not feature a strong statement of the inclusion of the nations, for example. On the other hand, it is unsurpassed in its portrayal of the suffering love of Yahweh for his people.

5.1. Israel's Sin. The crisis that the book of Hosea addresses is predicated on the mutual relationship between Yahweh and Israel. The supreme good is the "knowledge of God" (Hos 4:1), which goes beyond the discharge of any religious duty (Hos 6:6). The absence of this in Israel is equated in Hosea 5:4 with "the spirit of harlotry" (there it is called "the knowledge of Yahweh"). It means fundamental failure, and their offense is expressed correspondingly in highly personal and emotive terms. Yahweh complains that Israel "went after her lovers and forgot me" (Hos 2:13 [cf. Hos 13:6]). The concept of Yahweh as betrayed husband is expressed with the emotional intensity of suffering, unrequited love. The motif of "forgetting" Yahweh recalls Deuteronomy 8, but in Hosea it has the added force of betrayal with other "lovers." A key relational term for Hosea is "faithful love" (*ḥesed*), which should mark relationships both within Israelite society and between the people and Yahweh. In Hosea 4:1-2 this quality is juxtaposed with "knowledge of God" but also is allied with the obligations of citizens to each other, in terms reminiscent of the Decalogue. In Hosea 6:4-6 this "faithful love" in Israel is as fleeting as the morning cloud or dew. Israel is characterized by its opposite, treachery (Hos 6:7). They habitually fail to "seek" or "return to" Yahweh (Hos 7:10), instead fleeing senselessly to any other source of help (Hos 7:11-16). There are certain echoes of the OT traditions of law, covenant and commandment, especially in Hos 8:1 (cf. Hos 6:7), but these are firmly in the context of the "first commandment," to have no other gods besides Yahweh (Ex 20:3). They may profess their allegiance to him, but their protestations of loyalty cannot mask their deep infidelity (Hos 6:7; 8:2-3). The call to *repent in Hosea 6:1-3 apparently bears no fruit, given the sequel in Hosea 6:4-6 (see Boda, 299-300). It is no accident that Hosea twice castigates the "calf" of Samaria or Beth-aven (Hos 8:5-6; 10:5-6) and thus the memory of the golden calf worshiped by Israel in the very moment of its constitution as Yahweh's people by covenant at Sinai (Ex 32), and the calf set up by King Jeroboam 1 of Israel in opposition to the worship in Solomon's temple in Jerusalem. Even the forms of Yahweh's speech reveal an anguished heart, pondering how to deal with his wayward people, showing a powerful impulse to compassion yet frustrated by their fickleness (Hos 6:4; 6:11b–7:1).

The relationship between Yahweh and Israel, with its mutual obligations, is thus the framework for Hosea's whole message. This explains both the language of intimacy used to characterize Israel's offense and the portrayal of the offense as the worship of Baal, or "the *baʿalîm.*" There is indeed a strictly religious side to their *sin, since Hosea strongly criticizes them for their vigorous sacrificing on many altars (Hos 4:13; 8:11-13; 10:1-2) and names places of false worship. This intensity of worship is highly ironic in Hosea's view, since it is precisely not what it hopes to be, "knowledge of God." Israel's sin is compounded by self-deception, and their religious practice perpetuates this in a vicious circle, such that they are deprived of "understanding" (Hos 4:10-11) and swept along by "a spirit of harlotry" (4:12). Here is an important function of the "harlotry" trope. The language and imagery drawn from the sphere of intimate personal relationships have the power to suggest the human capacity for a complete loss of bearings in the life of mind and spirit. This is the point of connection between the religious aspect of Hosea's critique and the wicked practices in which Israel engages. True "knowledge of God" would result in right practice in the various spheres of life. The closing comment of the book (Hos 14:9), probably from the hand of its final redactor, picks up acutely this important dimension of its thought.

However, it is clear that the content of Israel's sin is not confined to their life of worship and religion (for a review of the vocabulary and imagery of sin in Hosea, see Boda, 297). Israel's failure is comprehensive; they have broken their covenant with Yahweh and rebelled against his "law" (tôrâ). The paralleling of these two concepts echoes the theological structure of the Sinai covenant in the pentateuchal accounts, where laws given by Yahweh become the substance of the covenantal obligations placed upon Israel (Ex 20-23; Deut 5-26). Hosea's use of the term tôrâ is variously understood as referring to a body of law, perhaps the Mosaic *law itself (Stuart, 131), or in contrast a more general "instruction" of Yahweh given through the priests to the people (Sweeney, 86). The point is hard to decide on the basis of Hosea itself. Suffice it to say that Hosea has an understanding of Israel's commitment to Yahweh having objective expression in obligations that were mutually understood. This kind of obligation was inseparable, however, from "knowledge" (Hos 4:6), which in Hosea must be understood as "knowledge of God" (Hos 4:1). Israel's commitment to "law" was part of its close relationship with Yahweh.

The content of this "law" may be presumed to have covered a range of spheres of Israel's life. It is adumbrated in Hosea 4:2, with its echoes of the Decalogue, but there is no concern here to unfold the implications of the Decalogue in detailed elaboration of tôrâ (unlike Deut 12—26, though that elaboration is no more "legalistic" than Hosea, since Deuteronomy also looks beneath external observance to "the heart" [Deut 6:5]). Rather, the individual commandments (against false swearing, lying, killing, stealing, adultery) are prefaced by the qualities of character that the prophet seeks: truthfulness (ʾĕmet), faithful love, or "mercy" (ḥesed) and "knowledge of God." He looks for what Jesus later would call "the weightier matters of the law" (Mt 23:23): "mercy" (ḥesed) rather than *sacrifice (Hos 6:6; cf. Mt 9:13) and "righteousness" (ṣĕdāqâ), paired again with "mercy" (Hos 10:12). Hosea assumes that Israel is capable not only of knowing Yahweh's "laws," but also of understanding and assimilating them in a way that gives direction to all of life. The quality of "righteousness" meant a profound commitment to right dealing, honest relationships and the good of the society as a whole. Israel should know that their salvation could not lie in forging alliances with foreign powers, trying to pick the winner in the ever-changing political conflicts of the region. Priests, prophets and kings are guilty of self-trust (Hos 10:14) and misrule (Hos 4:4-5; 5:1, 10; 8:4; 10:3). The people as a whole are characterized as tending repeatedly to apostasy (Hos 11:2), expressed as a turning away from Yahweh, a failure to turn back to him and seek him, a turning instead to another source (Hos 7:16 has a difficult phrase, lōʾ ʿal, which may be a corruption of a text meaning "to Baal," or alternatively, "not to the Most High"). This "turning" (šûb) is a key term in the portrayal of Israel's moral character, expressing a dynamic that drives them away from Yahweh as well as the moral force required for an effective return to him.

5.2. Yahweh's Response in Judgment. This diagnosis of Israel's ills, depicted in exactly these terms (Hos 5:13; 7:1; 11:3; 14:4), goes a long way to explaining the dominant relational metaphors used in the book. Israel is rebellious at heart and has perverted a relationship that should have been grounded in love. The effects of this rebellion are profound, disrupting the close synthesis of Yahweh, people and land that Yahweh himself had put together. The judgment of Yahweh appears first as the frustration of Israel's every effort to secure their own life. As Yahweh gave the grain, wine and oil, so he will take it back (Hos 2:8-9). The land that "whored away from Yahweh" (Hos 1:2) now "mourns" (Hos 4:3), signifying drought, in a personification that expresses its failure to be the resource for life that Yahweh had intended for it. If Israel hoped for prosperity and fertility through the objects of its misplaced trust, these hopes are catastrophically dashed in images of barrenness and death (Hos 4:10; 8:7-10; 9:16-17; 10:13-15).

Undergirding Yahweh's judgment is a rendering of Israel's history with him, a particular characteristic of Hosea's prophecy. Its engagement with history forces itself immediately on the reader with its unexpected take on Jehu, who is remembered elsewhere for his extirpation of the house of Baal at Yahweh's command (2 Kings 10), a century before Hosea. Now the "house of Jehu" stands guilty of bloodshed. No doubt the tyrannies of Jeroboam and his successors, of the "house of Jehu," are primarily in view. Yet the startling invocation of the celebrated scourge of Baal, in a prophecy that targets apostasy to Baal particularly, adds to the force of the accusation.

The controversy with Baal in Hosea 2 depends on the premise that Yahweh gave Israel the *land and its bounty in the first place. Hosea knows the pentateuchal traditions of patriarchs (Hos 12:2-6), *exodus from Egypt (Hos 11:1; 13:4) and the *wilderness period (Hos 13:5), together with a theology of gift and abundance in the land. He thus evokes allusively a whole understanding of history. In the vivid picture of the patriarch Jacob, who "strove with God" and had a relationship with him, who stands to be punished for his sin yet has a chance to "return" (Hos 12:2-6), the destiny of Israel is also portrayed. The story of the exodus lies close to the surface. The images of plenty in Hosea 2:8 recall descriptions of the rich land as in Exodus 3:8, 17; Numbers 13:27; Deuteronomy 8:7-10; 11:9-12. In the pentateuchal story the promise of land comes with warnings about the dangers of abandoning Yahweh (e.g., Deut 8). In some places the danger is expressed as the worship of Baal, which can be couched in the language of "harlotry" (Ex 34:15-16 [in view of the discussion above, it is noteworthy that Israel's "sons and daughters" play the harlot here]). Hosea 2 exhibits a contention about the source of Israel's prosperity in the land. Yahweh declares that it was

he who gave "the grain, the wine and the oil" (Hos 2:8), adopting terms familiar from Deuteronomy (Deut 7:13), in a symbolic evocation of the land's full sustaining power, while Israel claims to find it in her "lovers" (Hos 2:5). When Yahweh complains that "they did not know" that he was the giver, this "not knowing" is the morally culpable sort that Hosea calls "no knowledge of God" (Hos 4:1) or "forgetting Yahweh" (Hos 2:13; 4:6; 8:13; 14:6).

Yahweh's judgment, therefore, puts this history into reverse. The retraction of the gifts (Hos 2:9) is evident in the images of drought that we have observed, as well as in starker images of destruction (Hos 10:14-15; 13:16). But beyond that, Israel will be deprived for a time of the land itself and also the *divine presence that went with it (Hos 5:15, cf. 3:4). There is deep irony in this forced removal of the very things that they had labored to keep. Similarly, as Israel delighted to make many altars, so their altars will be removed, root and branch; as their love (hesed) was as fleeting as a morning cloud or the early dew (Hos 6:4), so will they themselves become (Hos 13:3) (Morris, 59-60).

This radical separation of Israel from its land could be taken to correspond to *exile. In Hosea's terms it is expressed as a return to the "wilderness," which once lay between exodus and land (Hos 2:15), or indeed back to "Egypt" itself (Hos 8:13), in powerful images of reversal of the history of salvation. The "return to Egypt" is not meant literally; it is both a picture of the violent removal of Israel from its land and a condemnation of Israel's abortive attempt to seek political assistance from Egypt in the diplomatic posturing that led up to the overwhelming of the region by Assyria. In the paralleling of Egypt and Assyria (Hos 6:11; 9:3; 11:5) the figure of Egypt is used not only to characterize Assyria as captor and enslaver, but also to recall that "return to Egypt" (as a resource and means of life) is a forbidden route for the people that once was taken from slavery there into the freedom of service to Yahweh (Deut 17:16). In this sense, Egypt may indeed literally be Egypt, but it could stand for any nation to which Israel looked for aid in a way that compromised its allegiance to Yahweh.

This analysis expresses forcefully not only a knowledge of the history but also a theology of it. Yahweh is the one who could oversee events so as to free Israel from its subjection to a great power, but by the same token he can bring a new power to oppress them again. Egypt and Assyria are, in a sense, the same thing, powers that have their own sustaining rationale in the world, opposed to Yahweh and his project in Israel, yet ultimately under his sway and liable to be recruited to his purposes. For this reason, Babylon and Persia in their turn could take the place of Assyria, without having to be named, and thus the message of Hosea in the eighth century BC could speak again to the kingdom of Judah in the seventh century or to the people of Yehud in the sixth century and beyond. Yahweh's judgment upon Israel is an action on the stage of world history, since his purpose for Israel is ultimately a purpose for the whole world, and it is capable of reenactment in ever new forms.

5.3. Yahweh Returns to Israel in Compassion. The compendious view of history in Hosea extends to his restoration of his people. In Hosea 2:15 the Valley of Achor refers to a border town in the territory of Judah (see Josh 15:7), memorialized in the narrative of Achan, who "troubled" Israel by infringing the ḥerem—that is, by stealing the booty devoted to Yahweh and meant to be destroyed—the name "Achor" being a play on the verb ʿākar, meaning "to trouble" (Josh 7:24-26). The place of trouble now becomes a "door of hope." This typifies a movement within Hosea in which Yahweh's impulse to judge gives way to his will to save. The pattern is contained in each of the chapters of Hosea 1—3. "Jezreel" changes from a synonym for judgment to one of glorious restoration (Hos 1:5, 11); the names of the three children have their significance reversed, so that Israel is restored to its status as Yahweh's covenant people (Hos 2:21-23); and they will return to Yahweh after a period of disciplinary deprivation (Hos 3). The inclusion of "David their king" in this picture (Hos 3:5) is unique in Hosea and bespeaks a concept of history in which the kingdom of neither Israel nor Judah can fully encompass what it means to be "Israel." The memory of David as a model of faithful kingship under Yahweh belongs to Hosea's vision of the restoration of the covenant people.

Land is closely related to people in the evocation of Yahweh's relationship with Israel, and Yahweh's decision to give the land its richness is the indispensable condition for it to realize its potency. In the portrayal of Israel's sin, the land itself was said to have "whored" away from

Yahweh (Hos 1:2), and the land "mourned" as a result (Hos 4:3). The vision of Hosea takes in God, people and land in a synthesis reminiscent of the order of *creation. There is a deep connection between right worship, right acting and the capacity of the land to yield its richness. That this is not a connection that can be compelled by religious manipulation is at the heart of Hosea's caustic criticism of excessive sacrificing. Rather, it is a connection that Yahweh seeks to accomplish in his covenantal relationship with Israel. Therefore, just as the withering of the land is inextricably linked with the sin and punishment of the people, so a "covenant" with the land is part of their restoration (Hos 2:18-23). The set of metaphors with which the book closes vividly depicts Yahweh's relationship with Israel in terms of a flourishing, fruitful land (Hos 14:5-8), with a hint of the untroubled fellowship of Eden.

At the heart of the powerful reversal that lies deep in Hosea's structure is a "turning" that goes on in Yahweh himself. The inner life of Yahweh is inseparable from the story. In keeping with the pervasive relational metaphors in the book, Yahweh yearns for his people. If Israel is punished by separation from what it loves, the separation has also to be endured by Yahweh. It is a kind of love story, which can be read in Hosea 5:15—7:1. Yahweh will "go and return" to his place to wait for Israel to come back to him (Hos 5:15). Israel then declares an intention to do so, in precisely corresponding terms ("Let us go and return to Yahweh" [Hos 6:1]). Yet this utterance of both confession and trust does not lead to Yahweh's acknowledgment of their return. Rather, he expresses his frustration with them in emotive self-address: "What shall I do with you, O Ephraim? What shall I do with you, O Judah?" (Hos 6:4). And he protests about the weakness of their ḥesed, their love or loyalty, the special quality of committed relationship. They can profess their loyalty all they like, he knows from experience that they cannot sustain it. In Hosea 6:11b—7:1 Yahweh's strong desire to "restore the fortunes" of his people and "heal" them looks like a repeated movement toward them, always met by their obduracy. The story of Yahweh's love seems doomed to disappointment.

But this dynamic of despair is relieved by the remarkable double dénouement in Hosea 11; 14. Hosea 11:1-7 recalls the early stages of Yahweh's troubled relationship with Israel by casting them in the exodus from Egypt as Yahweh's beloved child, who then persists in turning from him to other gods. The discourse of Yahweh begins to move along a by now well-rehearsed path: Israel will "return to the land of Egypt" as a punishment (Hos 11:5), their prayers unheard (Hos 11:7) as in Hosea 6:1-6. But suddenly Yahweh speaks in a quite new way (Hos 11:8-9). It is a tone of passionate love that we have met before (Hos 6:11b—7:1), yet only in frustration. Now we have the most moving expression of Yahweh's own agonized dilemma, his "fierce anger" overwhelmed by his "compassion." The language is strongly emotive, beginning not with statements of intent but rather with four rhetorical questions in which Yahweh pictures to himself the impossibility of his finally destroying the child he has cared for since infancy. His heart is "overturned" within him, the moment in which the pervasive theme of "turning" is expressed in the person of Yahweh. He moves to declaration of intent: "I will not act according to my fierce anger; I will not again destroy Ephraim"—literally, "turn to destroy" (Eidevall, 179). This is a turning of a different sort. And the unexpectedness of it is crowned by the reason finally given: his deity and his holiness. "For I am God and not a man, the Holy One in your midst, and I will not come in anger" (Hos 11:9). The logic of the prophecy here seems to be turned on its head. Should not the "Holy One" come in wrath against sin? Yet here the measure of God's deity and holiness is precisely that he acts instead in compassion. This remarkable turning continues in Hosea 11:10-11. Yahweh, who like a lion had once "torn" Ephraim (5:14), now utters a lion's roar to bring his children back (Moughtin-Mumby, 56); the "dove" that had gone senselessly to Egypt and Assyria (Hos 7:11) now flies back from those places, God's people returned at last to their homes.

Hosea 12—14 repeats the familiar trajectory. Here Israel is exhorted to "return," and they speak words of fresh commitment to Yahweh. These now find acceptance with him because he declares his renewed resolve to heal and love them, in a play on the word meaning "return" ("I will heal their turnings [mĕšûbâ], for my anger has turned [šûb] away from them" [Hos 14:4]). So they do "return to live" (Hos 14:7 [some translations obscure this with "live again"]), the last act attributed to Israel in the book. In this chapter all the sin and anger are transformed in what G. Eidevall (referring to Hos 14:5-8) calls "a final magnificent reversal of all reversals" envisaging "not only a return from exile, but a return to the ideal beginning—to paradise" (Eidevall, 242). This judgment rests on the dense metaphorical language, drawn from the natural world, especially trees—even Yahweh is like an "evergreen cypress" (Hos 14:8). Trees once had been a scene of *idolatry, and they even could be objects of false worship (Hos 4:12-13). The language itself thus participates in the redemption of all things (Moughtin-Mumby, 58; Morris, 126). In its double climax in pictures of reversal, Hosea offers some of the OT's most penetrating and memorable testimonies to the faithfulness and love of God.

See also FEMINIST INTERPRETATION; MARRIAGE AND DIVORCE; TWELVE, BOOK OF THE.

BIBLIOGRAPHY. *Commentaries:* **F. I. Andersen and D. N. Freedman,** *Hosea: A New Translation with Introduction and Commentary* (AB 24; Garden City, NY: Doubleday, 1980); **J. Jeremias,** *Der Prophet Hosea* (ATD 24/1; Göttingen: Vandenhoeck & Ruprecht, 1983); **F. Landy,** *Hosea* (RNBC; Sheffield: Sheffield Academic, 1995); **A. A. Macintosh,** *A Critical and Exegetical Commentary on Hosea* (ICC; Edinburgh: T & T Clark, 1997); **J. L. Mays,** *Hosea* (OTL; London: SCM, 1969); **D. Stuart,** *Hosea—Jonah* (WBC 31; Waco, TX: Word, 1987); **M. Sweeney,** "Hosea," in *The Twelve Prophets, 1: Hosea, Joel, Amos, Obadiah, Jonah,* ed. D. W. Cotter (Berit Olam; Collegeville, MN: Liturgical, 2000) 1-144; **H. W. Wolff,** *Hosea: A Commentary on the Book of Hosea,* trans. G. Stanstell, ed. P. D. Hanson (Hermeneia; Philadelphia: Fortress, 1974). *Studies:* **R. Abma,** *Bonds of Love: Methodic Studies of Prophetic Texts with Marriage Imagery (Isaiah 50:1-3 and 54:1-10, Hosea 1-3, and Jeremiah 2-3)* (SSN 40; Assen: Van Gorcum, 1999); **E. Ben Zvi,** "Observations on the Marital Metaphor of YHWH and Israel in Its Ancient Israelite Context: General Considerations and Particular Images in Hosea 1:2," *JSOT* 28 (2004) 363-84; idem, *Hosea* (FOTL 21A/1; Grand Rapids: Eerdmans, 2005); **M. Boda,** *A Severe Mercy: Sin and Its Remedy in the Old Testament* (Siphrut 1; Winona Lake, IN: Eisenbrauns, 2009); **R. S. Chalmers,** *The Struggle of Yahweh and El for Hosea's Israel* (HBM 11; Sheffield: Sheffield Phoenix, 2008); **M. Cogan and H. Tadmor,** *II Kings: A New*

Translation with Introduction and Commentary (AB 11; Garden City, NY: Doubleday, 1988); **G. I. Davies,** *Hosea* (OTG; Sheffield: Sheffield Academic, 1993); **E. F. Davis,** *Scripture, Culture and Agriculture: An Agrarian Reading of the Bible* (Cambridge: Cambridge University Press, 2009); **G. Eidevall,** *Grapes in the Desert: Metaphors, Models and Themes in Hosea 4-14* (ConBOT 43; Stockholm: Almqvist & Wiksell, 1996); **P. Fiddes,** "The Cross of Hosea Revisited: the Meaning of Suffering in the Book of Hosea," *RevExp* 90 (1993) 175-91; **S.-H. Hong,** *The Metaphor of Illness and Healing in Hosea and Its Significance in the Socio-Economic Context of Eighth-Century Israel and Judah* (SBL 95: New York: Peter Lang, 2006); **J. Jeremias,** *Hosea und Amos: Studien zu den Anfangen des Dodekapropheton* (FAT 13; Tübingen: Mohr Siebeck, 1996); **J. P. Kakkanattu,** *God's Enduring Love in the Book of Hosea: A Synchronic and Diachronic Analysis of Hosea 11,1-11* (FAT 2/14; Tübingen: Mohr Siebeck, 2006); **A. Keefe,** *Woman's Body and the Social Body in Hosea* (JSOTSup 338; London: Sheffield Academic, 2001); **F. Landy,** *Beauty and the Enigma: And Other Essays on the Hebrew Bible* (JSOTSup 312; Sheffield: Sheffield Academic, 2001); **M. J. W. Leith,** "Verse and Reverse: The Transformation of the Woman, Israel, in Hosea 1-3," in *Gender and Difference in Ancient Israel,* ed. P. L. Day (Minneapolis: Fortress, 1989) 95-108; **H. Marlow,** *Biblical Prophets and Contemporary Environmental Ethics: Re-Reading Amos, Hosea and First Isaiah* (Oxford: Oxford University Press, 2009); **G. Morris,** *Prophecy, Poetry and Hosea* (JSOTSup 219; Sheffield: Sheffield Academic, 1996); **S. Moughtin-Mumby,** *Sexual and Marital Metaphors in Hosea, Jeremiah, Isaiah, Ezekiel* (OTM; Oxford: Oxford University Press, 2008); **B. Seifert,** *Metaphorisches Reden von Gott im Hoseabuch* (FRLANT 166; Göttingen, Vandenhoeck & Ruprecht, 1996); **T. D. Setel,** "Prophets and Pornography: Female Sexual Imagery in Hosea," in *Feminist Interpretation of the Bible,* ed. L. Russell (Philadelphia: Westminster, 1985) 86-95; **Y. Sherwood,** *The Prostitute and the Prophet: Hosea's Marriage in Literary-Theoretical Perspective* (JSOTSup 212; Sheffield: Sheffield Academic, 1996); **J. M. Trotter,** *Reading Hosea in Achaemenid Yehud* (JSOTSup 328; Sheffield: Sheffield Academic, 2001); **F. van Dijk-Hemmes,** "The Imagination of Power and the Power of Imagination: An Intertextual Analysis of Two Biblical Love Songs, the Song of Songs and Hosea 2," *JSOT* 44 (1989) 75-88; **R. Vielhauer,** *Das Werden des Buches Hosea* (BZAW 349; Berlin: de Gruyter, 2007); **M. Weinfeld,** *Deuteronomy and the Deuteronomic School* (Oxford: Clarendon Press, 1972); **G. A. Yee,** *Composition and Tradition in the Book of Hosea: A Redaction Critical Investigation* (SBLDS 102; Atlanta: Scholars Press, 1987).

J. G. McConville

I

IDOLS, IDOLATRY, GODS

The medieval rabbi Rashi quotes the *Sifre,* "As long as idolatry (exists) in the world, (God's) fierce anger (will exist) in the world" (cf. Deut 13:17). The prophets give voice to this jealous exclusivity: loyalty to Yahweh is incompatible with honoring other gods or divine images. Idolatry is the fundamental crime against Yahweh, a rejection not of some aspect of his ways for Israel but of his very place at the center of Israel's life (*see* God). The passionate prophetic struggle against idolatry is, although not present in every book, pervasive and shares significant features across the prophets, although the various books exhibit differing emphases.

*Worship of images and worship of other gods than Yahweh are conceptually distinct activities, and clarity in distinguishing them can be helpful (Greenspahn; Barton). However, the prophets generally connect both types of worship with turning away from Yahweh, and so in this article "idolatry" is used to refer to the overarching offense. It is worth noting that there are no clear examples of prophetic concern about worshiping images of Yahweh.

    1. Idolatry in Israel's History
    2. Basic Features of Idolatry in the Prophets
    3. Vocabulary
    4. Idolatry in Particular Prophetic Books

1. Idolatry in Israel's History.

It is helpful to begin with the canonical and historical settings of the prophetic texts. Canonically, Israel's religion in the OT follows a rough trajectory from unified focus on Yahweh alone under Moses in the exodus to continual struggles against idolatry and accompanying moral failures that begin in the wilderness and continue to the destructions of the northern and southern kingdoms. In the primary history, the most prominent idolatrous offenses include the golden calf at Sinai (Ex 32—34; Deut 9—10), the Baal of Peor (Num 25), the cyclic pattern outlined in Judges 2:11-23 and demonstrated throughout the book, Solomon turning to other gods (1 Kings 11), Jeroboam's golden calves (1 Kings 12:25-33) and the institution of Baal worship by Ahab and Jezebel in the northern kingdom (1 Kings 16:29-34), and Manasseh's idolatry in the southern kingdom (2 Kings 21:1-18). Focal points of struggle against idolatry in this history include Deuteronomy's programmatic focus on Yahweh alone (e.g., Deut 6:4-9), Joshua's covenant renewal (Josh 23—24), Elijah's confrontation with the prophets of Baal (1 Kings 18), and the reforms of Jehu and Josiah (2 Kings 10; 23). The postexilic restoration is portrayed as a time largely concerned with other issues than idolatry.

The canonical texts do not describe Israelite religion in neutral terms; they advocate particular beliefs and practices as normative for Israel. Historians, on the other hand, critically reconstruct the breadth of Israelite beliefs and practices based on both the biblical texts and a wide variety of other material, textual and iconographic evidence. That Israel's real-life religions were extremely varied and often failed to meet the biblical norms of orthodoxy should be unsurprising. Among historians there is a broad consensus on the major features of the history of Israel's religion (see, e.g., Hess, 347-51). Pre-Israelite Levantine religion revolved around deities such as El and Baal, who bore significant similarities to Yahweh. These gods were worshiped through institutions of temples, sacrifices and feasts not wholly unlike later Israelite practices. There are no undisputed extrabiblical texts mentioning Yahweh during Israel's premonarchic period. But from the period of the rise of the kingdoms of Israel and Judah, while strong connections continue between Israelite religion and its West Semitic background, Yahwistic religion emerges as a distinct and historically observable entity. This religion held distinctive traditions such as Yahweh's acts in the exodus, giving of the law, and taking of the land. Toward the end of the monarchic period there was a growing emphasis on Yahweh's striking intolerance of Israel's worship of other deities and use of images. The various forms of monotheism, from programmatically demanding the worship of Yahweh alone to denying the existence of other gods, likely gained prominence only in the latter period of the monarchy and the exile, respectively (Gnuse).

It is difficult to reconstruct the religious practices and ideas that came under attack by the prophets and the Prophetic Books. Scholarly positions can change quite drastically. One important example concerns fertility cults (Ackerman, *NIDB* 2:450-51). As is indicated by polemical biblical and classical texts, such ancient Near Eastern cults were long understood to be filled with sexual excess. But biblical polemics that accuse Israelites of "playing the whore" on "every high hill and under every green tree" (e.g., Jer 2:20; 3:6) should likely not be read literally to reconstruct religious practices that included sacral sexual intercourse. There is no convincing historical evidence of such. Rather, these powerful metaphors express prophetic outrage at Israelite idolatry. Beyond sexual issues, scholars have long made creative connections between the mythological dying and rising of Baal in the Baal Cycle and seasonal fertility rites. Such methods for reconstructing religious belief and practice are now questioned (Smith). In contrast to these straining reconstructions, Jeremiah 44 presents a markedly less sensational vignette of a fertility cult where worshipers of the Queen of Heaven describe their practices and its expected results: burning incense and pouring libations in order to assure adequate harvests and protection from military defeat (Jer 44:17-19).

Although the fiery prophetic critiques can be read on their own terms, contextually sensitive readers should seek to comprehend the thoughts of those practicing the criticized religions. One recent advance has been in understanding the manufacture of cult images and the rituals by which the images became embodiments of the divine. These were carefully shaped religious acts that distanced the human maker from the worshiped images (Dick). Such rituals likely lay behind Isaiah's parody of image manufacture (e.g., Is 44:9-20), which should be read as high satire rather than a portrayal with which practitioners would have agreed. Similarly, readers of the prophets should always be vigilant to the use of creative literary forms. Recent studies of Hosea 1—3, for example, suggest that the prophet may have been criticizing not a currently thriving Baal cult but oppressive socioeconomic or political policies (Kelle, 202-8).

2. Basic Features of Idolatry in the Prophets.

Although some of the Prophetic Books emphasize certain aspects of idolatry, there is much in common across them. As a starting point, it is important to note that idolatrous worship often resembled acceptable worship of Yahweh except that the object of worship was an image or other god. Common elements included such things as sacred places, bowing down and offering incense and sacrifices.

In the prophetic analyses, idolatrous worship does not usually stand alone, but rather is connected to a wide variety of moral failures, including such things as oppression of the helpless, murder and adultery (e.g., Jer 7:6, 9; Ezek 22:2-12). Most abominable to the prophets are the claims that idolatry is connected with child sacrifice (Is 57:5; Jer 7:31; 19:5; 32:35; Ezek 16:20-21; 20:31; 23:39) (Stavrakopoulou).

Idolatry is also not just a personal matter; it has social and political associations. For purposes of national prosperity and security, idolatry is juxtaposed with trusting material strength, such as wealth, military power and foreign alliances, which replace trust in Yahweh (Is 2:6-9, 12-22; Jer 2:9-19; Ezek 16:23-29; 23:7, 30).

In terms of metaphor, Israel's idolatry is often described as sexual promiscuity, adultery and unbridled lust that offends the "marriage" with Yahweh. Within the metaphor, the jealous "husband" pours out humiliation and violence upon his disloyal "wife" (Jer 13:26-27; Ezek 16; Hos 2).

Yahweh is deeply provoked by Israel's idolatry. He alone has been their God and savior, rescuing them from Egypt, caring for them in the wilderness, and bringing them into the good land. Despite this, Israel has forgotten Yahweh and his care and has instead turned to other gods. The prophets nowhere condemn idolatry by invoking laws forbidding it (e.g., Deut 5:6-10); rather, they present idolatry as an obvious and nonsensical personal offense against Israel's beneficent God.

The structure of the prophetic description of Yahweh's response to idolatry comes in three phases. First, Yahweh threatens to destroy the nation as punishment for its idolatry. Second, after the destruction has been realized against the northern and southern kingdoms, it is explained to be a result of their idolatry. In both of these phases, the powerless other gods cannot deflect Yahweh's will; the prophets mock the very idea of calling for help from wood and stone (e.g., Jer 10). In the third phase, Yahweh reestablishes Israel with a vision for a relationship marked by faithfulness and no more idolatry (Is 2:17-18; 30:22; 31:7; Ezek 11:18-20; 36:25; 37:23; Hos 2:14-23).

3. Vocabulary.

The overarching term, characteristic of Deuteronomy, for gods other than Yahweh is simply "other gods" (*ʾĕlōhîm ʾăḥērîm*). Among the prophets, this phrase occurs almost exclusively in Jeremiah (18x), but also once in Hosea (Hos 3:1). Jeremiah also uses the phrase "foreign/strange gods" (*ʾĕlōhê nēkār*) once (Jer 5:19). Generic reference to gods other than Yahweh is made with phrases such as "their gods," "the gods of the nations," "the gods of [place name]" and "the gods of the earth."

Gods are also cited by name, though there are two special cases of an ambiguity between a name and a generic (Halpern, 61-78). First, the term *baʿal* sometimes refers to the personal name of a particular deity, but also it can be a title through its root meaning of "lord" or "husband," as indicated by the definite article: "the baal." It also often appears in the plural: "the baals." This title seems to have also been associated with Yahweh, as Hosea hails the day when Yahweh will no longer be called "my Baal" (Hos 2:16). The second unusual case is *ʾăšērâ*, which can refer either to a sacred object (a pole or tree: "an asherah" or "the asherah") or to a goddess ("Asherah") who was the consort of

the high father god El in the Ugaritic myths (Hadley). Noteworthy are the ninth- or eighth-century BC inscriptions found in Kuntillet ʿAjrud and Khirbet el-Qom that refer to Yahweh and "his asherah/Asherah," the interpretation of which is contested. All four references in the prophetic literature can be interpreted as sacred objects rather than the name of the goddess (Is 17:8; 27:9; Jer 17:2; Mic 5:14).

Clearer cases of proper names for gods in the prophets appear predominantly in later prophetic writings and include "Chemosh" (Jer 48:7, 13, 46), "Tammuz" (Ezek 8:14), "Amon" (Jer 46:25; Nahum 3:8), "Apis" (Jer 46:15), "Bel" ("Lord" = Marduk/Merodach [Is 46:1; Jer 50:2; 51:44]), "Meni" and "Gad" (Is 65:11), "Marduk/Merodach" (Jer 50:2), "Milcom" (Jer 49:1, 3; Zeph 1:5), "Molech" (Is 57:9 [debated]; Jer 32:35) and "Nebo" (Is 46:1). The "Queen of Heaven" (Jer 7:18; 44:17, 18, 19, 25) likely refers to a syncretism of West Semitic Astarte and Mesopotamian Ishtar (Ackerman, *NIDB* 4:703).

The terminology for idols is widely varied and can be divided into two types: terms referring to the physical objects or their manufacture and derisive terms of ridicule. Of the first sort, the terms *pesel* and *pāsîl* relate to the verb for "carving" and refer to idols hewn from stone, clay, wood or metal. Similarly, *ṣelem* likely relates to a verb for "cutting," *ʿōṣeb* and *ʿāṣāb* to "shaping" or "fashioning," and *nesek*, *nāsîk* and *massēkâ* to "pouring" for idols made from molten metal. Debatable is *ʿēṣâ* (Hos 10:6; cf. Hos 4:12), possibly related to the word for "wood" to refer to a wooden idol.

Terms of the second type ridicule idols by naming them through demeaned objects. The term *gillûlîm* likely refers to balls of dung and is always used contemptuously (39x in Ezekiel; 1x in Jeremiah). Isaiah, Jeremiah, Ezekiel, Daniel, Hosea, Nahum and Zechariah use the term *šiqqûṣ* to refer to idols as "detested things." Indicating insufficiency and worthlessness is the term *ʾĕlîl* (10x in Is 1—39; 1x in Ezekiel; 1x in Habakkuk). The terms *hebel* and *šāwěʾ* mean, respectively, "ephemeral vanity" and "emptiness" (Jon 2:8; and a few times in Jeremiah). Finally, *šeqer* means "falsehood" (Is 44:20). Such derogatory terms are also used adjectivally in many other places to express contempt for idols.

Less common and less clear terms for idols include *tĕrāpîm* (Ezek 21:21; Hos 3:4; Zech

10:2), sometimes simply transliterated as "tera-phim" or translated as "household gods" or "idols," and *sēmel* (Ezek 8:3, 5), a term of unknown origin, found in Phoenician inscriptions and referring to a statue or idol. The term *ṣîr* seems to refer once to idols (Is 45:16) but may reflect a textual or interpretational error.

4. Idolatry in Particular Prophetic Books.
Although prophetic treatment of idolatry overlaps substantially, emphases of particular books are worth noting (see Wolff).

The book of Jeremiah describes an existential struggle for Judah's loyalty to Yahweh against the lure of other gods, with dire consequences of destruction hanging in the balance. Although the people seem to find the deities exchangeable, the prophet obviously sees them as incomparable: "My people have committed two evils: they have forsaken me, the fountain of living water, and dug out cisterns for themselves, cracked cisterns that can hold no water" (Jer 2:13 NRSV [cf. Jer 2:11]). Although the people cry out to Yahweh for help, he will not listen to their tainted voices, and their cries to other gods are useless (Jer 11:11-12). They think that the Queen of Heaven will provide for them, but such ideas only lead Yahweh, the only true God, to destroy them (Jer 44:15-30). The thrust is that the people wrongly think that Yahweh and the other gods are comparable and exchangeable. Although conflict over false prophecy is prominent in Jeremiah, this issue predominantly concerns conflicting claims to Yahweh's words, not the words of other gods (e.g. Jer 28).

Ezekiel's terminology is unusual in that the book never honors gods other than Yahweh with the label *ʾĕlōhîm* ("gods"), preferring the derogatory *gillûlîm* ("dung balls") to emphasize their disgusting impurity. This term is rarely used by other prophets and may represent Ezekiel's own creativity or something derived from his priestly tradition (Wolff, 407). This theme of impurity is prominent in his vision of increasingly abominable idolatry in the temple itself (Ezek 8) and Yahweh's threat to desecrate Judah's idolatrous altars and places of worship with corpses (Ezek 6). Ezekiel 20 describes Israel's history from Egypt to exile as filled with defiling idolatry.

Isaiah 1—39 is not focused on idolatry in particular, often subordinating it to dependence upon wealth and military power (Is 2:6-9, 12-18). This material prefers the term *ʾĕlîlîm* for idols, likely meaning "weaklings" in contrast to their purported and desired strength. This political conflict with other gods is dramatized in the narrative of Hezekiah's standoff with the Assyrians (Is 36—37 // 2 Kings 18—19). Isaiah 40—55 takes a different tack with a message of hope and power that stood in contrast to the experience of defeat and *exile: Yahweh is the unique divine power and alone announces what will happen and brings it to pass, as exemplified in the predicted exile and return (Is 41:21-29; 43:8-15; 44:6-8; 45:20-25). Yahweh is no mere national deity; he wields universal power, as demonstrated through creation (Is 40:12-26). These chapters are the high point of the prophetic exaltation of Yahweh and the complementary denial of the reality of other gods. The idol makers, idol worshipers and their idols are worthy only of ridicule, the idols being lifeless, silent and powerless (Is 40:19-20; 41:5-7; 44:9-20; 46:5-7; cf. Jer 10:2-10) (MacDonald, 29-31), something that the nations will eventually realize, causing them to turn to Yahweh (e.g. Is 45:22-24). In Isaiah 56—66 there is renewed condemnation of actual idolatrous practices (Is 57:3-13; 65:2-5, 11; 66:3, 17).

In the Book of the Twelve, Hosea reflects the oldest use of *marriage metaphors for Israel's relationship to Yahweh and sexual metaphors of adultery and prostitution for idolatry (Hos 2; 4:10-18; 5:3-7; 6:10; 7:4; 9:1). Related metaphors are used by Jeremiah, Isaiah and Ezekiel (Moughtin-Mumby). In the book of Jonah, the non-Israelite sailors and Ninevites respond to Jonah's God in light of his mighty acts on the sea and threats against the city (Jon 1:16; 3:5-9). Micah presents a striking contrast between each nation walking in the name of its own god and all nations seeking Yahweh (Mic 4:2, 5). Condemnation of idolatry sometimes extends to other nations, as in Nahum's threat against Nineveh's gods and idols (Nahum 1:14; see also Jer 48:35 against Moab, and Ezek 30:13 against Egypt). Habakkuk sees Babylon trusting its strength as a god (Hab 1:11), though their idols are worthless and lifeless compared to Yahweh (Hab 2:18-20). Zephaniah, set within the era of Josiah's reform, expresses Yahweh's intent to remove Baal, Milcom and their worshipers (Zeph 1:4-6) and looks forward to all nations bowing to Yahweh (Zeph 2:11). The explicitly postexilic prophets focus less on other gods than lack of regard for Yahweh and his temple (Hag 1:4, 9; Zech 7:5-6; Mal 3:14), though Malachi warns of other gods encroaching through marriage (Mal 2:11; cf. Ezra 9—10). Idolatry does appear briefly in Zechariah, but it is largely envisioned as disappearing from the land, with Yahweh becoming the only God over the whole earth (Zech 5:5-11; 10:2; 13:2; 14:9).

In Daniel, the struggle is not primarily against idols and other gods but rather against the godlike Babylonian and Persian kings. The kings several times assert themselves as autonomous powers or even gods (Dan 3:1-7; 4:30; 5:20-28; 6:1-9; cf. Is 14:13-14; Ezek 28:2), but they are repeatedly compelled to acknowledge Israel's God (Dan 2:47; 3:26, 28; 4:1-3, 34-37; 5:29; 6:16-27). In the vision of Daniel 11 a king asserts himself above every god, but the book ends with a promise of deliverance from the arrogant king (Dan 11:36-39; 12:1). In all of the prophets, no power can be compared with Yahweh.

See also GOD; LITURGY AND CULT; WORSHIP.

BIBLIOGRAPHY. **S. Ackerman,** "Fertility Cult," *NIDB* 2:450-51; idem, "Queen of Heaven," *NIDB* 4:703; **J. Barton,** "'The Work of Human Hands' (Ps 115:4): Idolatry in the Old Testament," *ExAud* 15 (1999) 63-72; **M. B. Dick,** "Prophetic Parodies of Making the Cult Image," in *Born in Heaven, Made on Earth: The Making of the Cult Image in the Ancient Near East,* ed. M. B. Dick (Winona Lake, IN: Eisenbrauns, 1999) 1-53; **R. Gnuse,** "The Emergence of Monotheism in Ancient Israel: A Survey of Recent Scholarship," *Religion* 29 (1999) 315-36; **F. E. Greenspahn,** "Syncretism and Idolatry in the Bible," *VT* 54 (2004) 480-94; **J. M. Hadley,** *The Cult of Asherah in Ancient Israel and Judah: Evidence for a Hebrew Goddess* (UCOP 57; Cambridge: Cambridge University Press, 2000); **B. Halpern,** "The Baal (and the Asherah) in Seventh-Century Judah: Yhwh's Retainers Retired," in *From Gods to God: The Dynamics of Iron Age Cosmologies* (FAT 63; Tübingen: Mohr Siebeck, 2009) 57-97; **R. S. Hess,** *Israelite Religions: An Archaeological and Biblical Survey* (Grand Rapids: Baker Academic, 2007); **B. E. Kelle,** "Hosea 1-3 in Twentieth-Century Scholarship," *CurBS* 7 (2009) 179-216; **N. MacDonald,** "Aniconism in the Old Testament," in *The God of Israel: Studies of an Inimitable Deity,* ed. R. P. Gordon (UCOP 64; Cambridge: Cambridge University Press, 2007) 20-34; **J. Milgrom,** "The

Nature and Extent of Idolatry in Eighth-Seventh Century Judah," *HUCA* 69 (1998) 1-13; **S. Moughtin-Mumby,** *Sexual and Marital Metaphors in Hosea, Jeremiah, Isaiah, and Ezekiel* (OTM; Oxford: Oxford University Press, 2008); **C. North,** "The Essence of Idolatry," in *Von Ugarit nach Qumran: Beiträge zur alttestamentlichen und altorientalischen Forschung,* ed. J. Hempel and L. Rost (BZAW 77; Berlin: Töpelmann, 1958) 151-60; **R. H. Pfeiffer,** "The Polemic against Idolatry in the Old Testament," *JBL* 43 (1924) 229-40; **M. S. Smith,** "Interpreting the Baal Cycle," *UF* 18 (1986) 313-39; **F. Stavrakopoulou,** *King Manasseh and Child Sacrifice: Biblical Distortions of Historical Realities* (BZAW 338; Berlin: de Gruyter, 2004); **S. Weeks,** "Man-Made Gods? Idolatry in the Old Testament," in *Idolatry: False Worship in the Bible, Early Judaism and Christianity,* ed. S. C. Barton (London: T & T Clark, 2007) 7-21; **H. W. Wolff,** "Jahwe und die Götter in der alttestamentlichen Prophetie," *EvT* 29 (1969) 397-416.

R. Barrett

IMMANUEL PROPHECY. *See* ISAIAH: BOOK OF; WOMEN AND FEMALE IMAGERY.

INNERBIBLICAL INTERPRETATION. *See* INTERTEXTUALITY AND INNERBIBLICAL INTERPRETATION.

INTERCESSION. *See* PRAYER.

INTERPRETATION. *See* HERMENEUTICS.

INTERTEXTUALITY AND INNERBIBLICAL INTERPRETATION

The term *intertextuality* refers to the ways in which the meaning of a text is shaped by its relationships with other texts. Debate continues as to whether intertextuality ought properly to address diachronic questions of historical priority and dependencies between texts, or whether it is a purely synchronic technique focused on texts (in toto) and/or readers. However, this debate between "synchronic" and "diachronic" factions fails to recognize that both are valid concerns of intertextuality. A text engages in a dialogue with other texts at the time it was written, and that same text continues to contribute to a dialogue with other texts, especially in the case of a biblical text because its meaning is shaped by the wider canon of Scripture.

Both as classically defined and presently practiced (especially in the field of biblical studies), *intertextuality* is an umbrella term that encompasses both innerbiblical interpretation and synchronic intertextuality.

1. Defining Intertextuality
2. Types of Intertextuality
3. Issues of Intertextuality in the Prophets
4. Conclusion

1. Defining Intertextuality.

The term *intertextuality* was coined by J. Kristeva in 1969 to refer to the study of the semiotic matrix within which a text's acts of signification occur. Kristeva argued that "any text is constructed of a mosaic of quotations; any text is the absorption and transformation of another" (Kristeva, 66). Kristeva's poststructuralist approach (building upon the work of postformalist M. Bakhtin, and further developed by R. Barthes) specifically refrains from asking questions about historical priority, authorial intent and influence. However, in an ironic twist of history, Kristeva's term has undergone its own intertextual transformation and has come to mean something wider than her original conception. This transformation has arisen out of the three key observations about texts that intertextuality is based upon. First, all texts are created from a "mosaic" of other texts. No text is a completely unique creation, autonomous in relation to every other text. Second, every text asserts its meaning in relation to other texts. In the terminology of Bahktin, meaning arises out of a "dialogue" between texts. Third, meaning does not reside with a bare text alone; the reader has an irreducible role to play in the production of meaning.

However, each of these three observations entails a spectrum of possibilities. Every text may well be made up of other texts, but the nature of the reuse may span everything from the mere repetition of a phrase drawn from the general web of meaning to an explicit citation. Likewise, all texts assert their meaning in dialogue with other texts, but this might be a friendly dialogue that supports and affirms or an unfriendly dialogue that seeks to overthrow another text. Similarly, the reader's role can span everything from decoding a meaning encoded by a text's original author to creating a meaning that could not have been in the contemplation of the original author. These spectra are represented in figure 1.

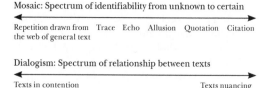

Mosaic: Spectrum of identifiability from unknown to certain

Repetition drawn from Trace Echo Allusion Quotation Citation
the web of general text

Dialogism: Spectrum of relationship between texts

Texts in contention   Texts nuancing
with each other   each other

Reader's role: Spectrum from creating meaning to decoding texts

Readers discover /   Readers decode
create meaning   the meaning of a text

Figure 1: Three Spectra

These three spectra of possibilities mean that there cannot be a single intertextual approach. Kristeva's poststructuralistic semiotic intertextuality is one, but only one, among a diversity of intertextualities. To understand this diversity, it is important to consider the range of options on each of these three spectra.

1.1. Text Creation: Texts Are a Mosaic of Quotations. R. Barthes develops Kristeva's insight that texts are a mosaic of quotations: "Any text is a new tissue of past citations. Bits of code, formulae, rhythmic models, fragments of social languages, etc., pass into the text and are redistributed within it, for there is always language before and around the text. Intertextuality, the condition of any text whatsoever, cannot, of course, be reduced to a problem of sources or influences; the intertext is a general field of anonymous formulae whose origin can scarcely ever be located; of unconscious or automatic quotations, given without quotation marks" (Barthes 1981, 39).

Although intertextuality cannot be "reduced to a problem of sources or influences," it must, as a matter of logic, include these sources and influences where they can be identified. Barthes is more interested in the "general field of anonymous formulae whose origin can scarcely ever be located" because of the implications this has for poststructuralist semiotics. However, this does not nullify the analysis of those parts of the "textual mosaic" where intertexts can be identified, albeit with greater or lesser degrees of specificity. The mosaic spectrum diagram in Figure 1 provides descriptions for a range of identifiable connections between texts:

- A *citation* is an attributed quotation (i.e., acknowledging source).
- A *quotation* is an identifiable word-for-word repetition.
- An *allusion* is a partial reuse of a sequence of words or themes.
- An *echo* is similar to an allusion, but where less identifiable elements are reused.
- A *trace* (as defined by J. Derrida) is the indication of an absence that defines a presence. Any signifier contains "traces" of other signifiers that shape its meaning.

Where a text has become part of the fabric of the web of the "general text" and/or communicative codes of a culture, there may no direct, identifiable connection with subsequent texts, notwithstanding their apparent reuse of key words or themes from that text. The spectrum above is shown with unmarked boundaries between the terms because in practice the categories blend into each other, and different scholars use different metrics for assessing and categorizing.

1.2. Text Meaning: Meaning Comes from Dialogue between Texts. M. Bakhtin described the complex relationship between texts as "dialogism." However, defining what he meant by this is no mean feat, since Bakhtin used the concept of dialogic in multiple senses. For our purposes, we should distinguish between the following:

(1) Dialogical language. All language is dialogical, in that it cannot help but assert its meaning in dialogue with a complex web of utterances which already exist.

(2) Dialogical discourse. Some discourses are dialogical, in that they require the interaction of multiple voices (i.e., polyphony) to produce meaning.

(3) Dialogical truth. Some truths are dialogical in nature. In contrast to "monological" truths, which can be reduced to a series of propositions utterable by anyone without affecting their truth value, a dialogical truth is one that cannot be stated as a single proposition or by a single voice. Instead, a dialogical truth can emerge only via the interaction of several unmerged voices (i.e., multivalency).

It should be clear from this analysis that while all texts will be dialogical in the first sense, only a subset of texts will be dialogical in the second sense, and only some truths will be dialogical in the third sense. The appropriate category (or categories) will vary, depending on the text under consideration. One cannot necessarily assume that a dialogical text entails polyphony or multivalency in every case, notwithstanding the popularity of these buzzwords in our postmodern milieu.

The meaning of a text is established in dialogue with other texts (see Dialogism in Figure 1). The greater the degree of contention with the existing "voices" in the intertextual web, the greater the potential for multivalency, as multiple meanings compete.

1.3. Hermeneutics: A Reader's Role in the Production of Meaning. An intertextual approach recognizes that a reader has an irreducible role to play in the production of meaning because the recognition and evaluation of connections between texts is a process that occurs in the mind of the reader.

Literary theorists have different explanations of the process by which readers are involved in the production of meaning. Writing from the perspective of semantic theory, U. Eco describes how "open texts" with "productive codes" are "decoded" by readers (Eco 1984; 1989). A different description of a similar process can be seen in M. Riffaterre's concept of an "ungrammaticality"—a word or phrase that, because of its awkwardness in the present context, points to another text that provides the key to its decoding and thus aids readers in the production of meaning: "The dual sign works like a pun. We will see that the pun in poetic discourse grows out of textual 'roots.' It is first apprehended as a mere ungrammaticality, until the discovery is made that there is another text in which the word is grammatical; the moment the other text is identified, the dual sign becomes significant purely because of its shape, which alone alludes to that other code" (Riffaterre, 82).

From a different perspective again is W. Iser's description of "indeterminacy" arising from "gapped texts": "The indeterminate sections or gaps of literary texts are in no way to be regarded as a defect; on the contrary, they are a basic element for the aesthetic response. . . . The reader fills in the remaining gaps. He removes them by a free play of meaning-projection, and thus by himself repairs the unformulated connections between the particular views" (Iser, 12); "The indeterminate elements of literary prose—perhaps even of all literature—represent the most important link between text and reader. It is the switch that activates the reader in using his own ideas in order to fulfil the intention of the text. . . . The meaning is conditioned by the text itself, but only in a form that allows the reader himself to bring it out" (Iser, 43).

Although there are significant differences in the approaches of Eco, Riffaterre and Iser, a common feature is that each recognizes the role of a reader in the production of meaning. What is significant to note, however, is that granting this role to the reader does not necessarily entail the conclusion that readers "create" meaning. Eco speaks of readers "decoding" a meaning in the text, and Iser speaks of a meaning "conditioned by the text" that is brought out by a reader. That is, both reader and text have an irreducible role to play in the production of meaning for "open" or "gapped" texts.

The extent of the reader's role in the production of meaning will depend on the reader's goal. If the reader's aim is to decode the meaning of a text that its author encoded for his original audience, then this leads to a diachronic approach to the text. If the aim of the reader is to discover what the text might now mean through its continuing dialogue with other texts, then this leads to a synchronic approach.

1.4. Intertextuality as Both Synchronic and Diachronic. The foregoing analysis of these three observations underpinning intertextuality indicates that it has both synchronic and diachronic dimensions. Some scholars have denied the legitimacy of this kind of approach, arguing that it is invalid to seek a point of intersection between synchronic "intertexuality" and diachronic "innerbiblical interpretation" (Eslinger). B. Sommer argues for a complete dichotomy between "innerbiblical allusion" and "intertextuality." According to Sommer, the former is diachronic in character, "asking how one composition evokes its antecedents, how one author is affected by another, and what sources a text utilizes," whereas the approach of the latter is synchronic in nature, focusing "not on the author of a text but either on the text itself (as part of a larger system) or on the reader

. . . interpret[ing] signs in the text by associating them with related signs in the reader's own mind" (Sommer 1998, 7). Sommer's categorization relies on the analysis by J. Clayton and E. Rothstein, who argue for "intertextuality" as originally framed by Kristeva and Barthes.

The problem with this approach is that it fails to recognize that the term *intertextuality* has undergone its own intertextual transformation. As P. Tull demonstrates, intertextual examinations of the Hebrew Scriptures are much broader than Sommer's two-category dichotomy allows. Many (perhaps most) biblical scholars who view their approach as "intertextual" are not poststructuralists or reader-response critics.

Instead, we must allow that intertextuality has a breadth of meaning, arising from its three key conceptual underpinnings outlined above. Intertextuality can validly encompass a hermeneutical approach that views author, text and reader as important to the interpretive process, and in which both diachronic concerns and synchronic concerns are important in coming to the meaning of a text.

2. Types of Intertextuality.
2.1. Innerbiblical Interpretation.
2.1.1. Innerbiblical Exegesis. In his landmark book *Biblical Interpretation in Ancient Israel*, M. Fishbane examines the phenomenon of innerbiblical exegesis, whereby a later biblical writer reuses, reinterprets or reapplies an earlier biblical text. Fishbane argues that the received text (the *traditum*) has been transmitted by human agents who have incorporated their own exegesis of it in the process of transmission (the *traditio*). Thus, the text as we now have it is a complex interweaving of *traditio* and *traditum*. Fishbane argues that innerbiblical exegesis arises from the interplay between two factors: a respect for an authoritative teaching and a concern to "preserve, render contemporary, or otherwise reinterpret these teachings or traditions in explicit ways for new times and circumstances" (Fishbane 1985, 8).

Fishbane detects innerbiblical exegesis on the basis of the following: (1) formal markers: technical formulae used by the scribes when they updated a text (e.g., the scribal gloss "that is, Bethel" in Gen 35:6); (2) parallel texts: a comparison of parallel texts within the MT, or between the MT and its principal versions (e.g., the changes between two law codes in Exodus and Deuteronomy, or parallel narratives in 1 Kings and 2 Chronicles); (3) text-critical analysis: evidence of redundancy, alteration or supplementation to the text, based on established historical critical judgments.

Employing postbiblical categories drawn from rabbinic exegesis, Fishbane arranges his analysis under four headings: (1) *scribal exegesis* examines the comments, clarifications and corrections added to the text in the process of scribal transmission; (2) *legal exegesis* examines the reinterpretation or extension or reapplication of preexisting legal texts; (3) *aggadic exegesis* examines the adaptation of the inherited *traditum* for the sake of new theological insights, attitudes and speculations, often drawing forth latent and unsuspected meanings from it; (4) *mantological exegesis* examines the reinterpretation of prophetic oracles. Fishbane argues that this occurs because a prophetic vision or oracle was not, or not conclusively, actualized and needed to be reinterpreted or reapplied. According to Fishbane, "the unexpected deferral of fulfillment . . . elicits reinterpretation of the *traditum*" (Fishbane 1996, 46).

Most of the examples of innerbiblical exegesis in the prophets that Fishbane discusses are either aggadic exegesis or mantological exegesis, though there are scattered examples of the other types. For example, Fishbane cites Jeremiah 17:21-22 as an example of the legal exegesis of the Mosaic Sabbath command (Fishbane 1989, 11).

Aggadic exegesis in the prophets can result in the following (all these examples are from Fishbane 1985, 292-426):

- interpretation and extension of a cultic regulation by "lemmatic deduction or inference" (e.g., the law of cultic contamination in Hag 2:11-14; cf. Lev 6:20);
- spiritualization of content (e.g., Jer 2:3 reapplies the law of sacred donations in Lev 22:14-16 to Israel as the consecrated object);
- nationalization of content (e.g., Jer 5:21-24 applies the law of the wayward son in Deut 21:18-21 to the nation of Israel);
- exegetical transformation and reappropriation (e.g., the reinterpretation of Gen 1:1-2:4 in Deutero-Isaiah);
- rhetorical inversion (e.g., Mal 1:6-2:9 ironi-

cally inverts the priestly blessing in Num 6:23-27);
- subversion of an older tradition by a new (e.g., Ezek 18:18-32; 33:12-20 supplants the idea of transgenerational punishment in Exod 34:6-7).

Mantological exegesis in the prophets can result in the following (all these examples are from Fishbane 1985, 461-521):

- Rhetorical reworking: the oracle against princes, judges, prophets and priests in Zephaniah 3:3-4 is reworked and embellished in Ezekiel 22:25-28.
- Revision: Ezekiel 29:17-20 revises an earlier word of judgment against Tyre in Ezekiel 26:7-14.
- Reapplication: "There are many striking reapplications of the prophetic words of Isaiah of Jerusalem in the later 'Isaianic' tradition. All bear on the presentiment that the words forecast by Isaiah of old are now near fulfillment, or are about to be reversed" (Fishbane 1985, 497).
- Reinterpretation: the "seventy years" of subjugation to Babylon in Jeremiah 25:9-12 is variously reinterpreted in 2 Chronicles 36:18-21; Zechariah 1:12; 7:1; Daniel 9:2.
- Mantic anthology: new prophecy created from a "prophetic patchwork" (Fishbane 1985, 493) of older prophecy. For example, Zechariah 1—6; 9—12; Daniel 7—12 are "mantological anthologies which are intended to be read together" (Fishbane 1985, 521).

Scholars since Fishbane have noted that the phenomena that he describes as innerbiblical exegesis go well beyond "exegesis" in the strict sense of the word. "Innerbiblical allusion" has been proposed as an alternate label (Eslinger), but this too is problematic (Sommer 1996b). A better encapsulating description of this type of intertextuality is "innerbiblical interpretation" (Weyde).

2.1.2. Innerbiblical Interpretation in the Prophets. Those who investigate innerbiblical interpretation use a variety of methodological approaches, but the common factor is that these approaches (like that of Fishbane) focus on the way that a later text has reused, reapplied, reinterpreted or otherwise transformed an earlier text or tradition. The following are some significant investigations of innerbiblical interpretation in the prophets.

J. Day gives a number of examples of the reuse in the prophets of the law, the creation and other primeval traditions, historical and legendary traditions, the psalms and other prophets (i.e., prophets quoting prophets).

A number of authors have investigated innerbiblical interpretation in Isaiah. Sommer examines innerbiblical allusion in Isaiah 40—66 (Sommer 1998). He finds allusions based on a large amount of shared vocabulary and word play between "earlier" texts and Isaiah 40—66. P. Willey follows an "intertextual" approach that asks many of the same questions about authorial intent, antecedent texts and the historical situation of the book of Isaiah that Sommer considers. J. Hibbard examines the intertextuality of Isaiah 24—27. He argues that these chapters form one of the latest literary layers in the book of Isaiah, and a key part of their literary strategy is the reuse and evocation of earlier texts from the Hebrew Bible.

Another rich field for research into innerbiblical interpretation has been the book of Zechariah. R. Mason examines "inner-biblical exegesis" in Zechariah 9—14, evaluating how these chapters reuse both Zechariah 1—8 and other prophets. K. Larkin evaluates and extends Fishbane's thesis that Second Zechariah is a mantological anthology. R. Nurmela examines innerbiblical interpretation in Zechariah 1—8; 9—14. M. Stead examines the intertextuality of Zechariah 1—8 (Stead 2009).

Finally, B. Levinson supplies a very helpful bibliographic essay on innerbiblical interpretation.

2.2. Synchronic Intertextuality. Synchronic intertextuality arises from the dialogical nature of texts (see, under 1 above, the second spectrum). Not only does a text enter into a dialogue with the texts extant at the time it was written, but also it continues to contribute in a dialogue with other texts. This phenomenon can be approached in two distinct ways, as follows.

2.2.1. Canonical Intertexuality. In both the Christian interpretative tradition and in rabbinic exegesis, biblical texts have their meaning shaped by the wider context of the canons of the OT and the Hebrew Bible respectively.

The exegetical motto of the Reformers was *scriptura scripturam interpretatur* ("Scripture in-

terprets Scripture"). According to the Westminster Confession, "The infallible rule of interpretation of Scripture is the Scripture itself; and therefore, when there is a question about the true and full sense of any Scripture (which is not manifold, but one), it must be searched and known by other places that speak more clearly." By this principle, an "earlier" text might have its meaning clarified and shaped by a dialogue with "later" texts – that is, shaped by a canonical intertextuality.

Similarly, Fishbane describes the exegetical practices of rabbinic midrash as being grounded on two hermeneutical assumptions: (1) the fact that all interpretation takes place within the canon and presupposes the possibility that all of its texts may be compared or in some way correlated; (2) the assumption of the omnicoherence of Scripture in all its details (Fishbane 2000, 43). These two assumptions allow two texts mutually to inform the interpretation of one another, in ways not contemplated by their respective authors.

These hermeneutical assumptions of Christianity and Judaism lead to a canonical intertextuality, where it is possible to recognize a meaning in a text unknown or unclear to its original (human) author (cf. 1 Pet 1:10-12; 2 Pet 1:19). The objective basis of this canonical meaning is the presupposition that an ultimate author (God) has given shape to the *canon, and consequently that there is an overarching coherence and meaning to the Scriptures.

When it comes to applying this kind of intertextual approach to the prophets, there are several different permutations. One variation is the work of B. Childs on *canonical criticism, which seeks to understand the meaning of a text in the wider context of Christian Scripture. Another variation, on a smaller scale, is aspects of work done on the *Book of the Twelve. Recognizing the Book of the Twelve as a discrete literary unit leads to a form of canonical intertextuality (just with a smaller "canon"), in that the meaning of an individual book within that collection comes to be fuller and perhaps different as a result of its juxtaposition and dialogue within the canonical shape of the Twelve. J. Nogalski takes this further, arguing that the shape and meaning of the Book of the Twelve arises from an intertextuality between the constituent parts constructed around quotations, allusions, catchwords, motifs and framing devices.

2.2.2. Reader-response Intertexuality. With canonical intertextuality, the locus of meaning is objectively contained within the canonical text (i.e., there is a meaning put there by its ultimate author for the modern reader to draw out). In contrast, Reader-response intertextuality argues that the reader is the final arbiter of meaning. Readers do not draw out the objective "original meaning(s)" of the canonical text; they subjectively create meaning by the juxtaposition of texts. According to K. Nielsen, in this type of intertextuality it is "the reader and the tradition of which he or she is part which single out the intertexts" (Nielsen, 18-19). Meaning is not objectively "in" the text (or "in" the canon), but instead arises in the mind of the modern reader.

An example of reader-response intertextuality is M. Love's book *The Evasive Text,* an examination of Zechariah 1—8 that is "heavily influenced by theories of intertextuality, reader-response criticism and Bakhtin" and explicitly eschews diachronic questions of historical priority and dependence (see Love, 36, 38-39).

3. Issues of Intertextuality in the Prophets.

3.1. Methodology.

3.1.1. Establishing a Connection between Texts. For all forms of intertextuality, there needs to be a basis for establishing a connection between texts. This is true even in a reader-response approach, because it is necessary to explain why two particular texts should be brought into dialogue with each other.

One of the key methodological issues is whether the connection must be established on the basis of "verbal repetition" between the texts, or whether a connection might be established based only on shared "thematic threads" or "traditions." Nurmela argues that the only objective evidence of textual reuse is to be found in "verbal repetition" of rare words or expressions (Nurmela, 27). A similar approach is taken by R. Schultz. In his contribution to a volume entitled *Thematic Threads in the Book of the Twelve,* Schultz argues (somewhat ironically, given the title of the book) that a method based on "thematic allusions" is too vague, and that "verbal parallels that offer a more extensive textual basis for positing an intentional interrelationship is a more viable approach" (Schultz, 28).

However, this strict methodological approach is in tension with the notion of intertextuality as defined above. Intertextuality recognizes the rich textual web created by the interconnections between multiple texts and expects that texts will transform and adapt other texts in the process of reuse. This "intertextual play" may result in the erasure of the exact verbal connections required by a method based on "verbal repetition." An intertextual approach requires that we recognize a much broader range of textual interplay.

Some examples of approaches to establishing connections include the following:

- Mason examines "inner-biblical exegesis" in Zechariah 9—14, recognizing intertexts both on the basis of *verbal and thematic connections.*
- Willey argues for a connection between Isaiah 52:8-10 and Psalm 98:1-4, based on *sequence of consecutive words* (Willey, 120-25). This primary allusion provides the basis for establishing secondary echoes in the surrounding context.
- Sommer uses a methodology based on a *substantial shared vocabulary* (not necessarily consecutive) and repeated stylistic traits. (For an example of this approach applied to Jeremiah 31:7-9 and Isaiah 35:4-10, see Sommer 1996a, 170).
- Nielsen uses a method based on *markers* (in the sense defined by Riffaterre) that point to another text.
- G. Hepner argues for an intertextual method that recognizes *verbal resonances* such as Hebrew partial homonyms based on two or more shared consonants, anagrams, numerical resonances and other word play.
- Some scholars argue for an intertextual connection based on a *shared rhetorical structure.* For example, M. Floyd argues that "Zech. 9-11 recapitulates the distinctive rhetorical structure of Zech. 1-8" in order that it might offer an intertextual reinterpretation of the earlier passage (Floyd, 242).
- Stead argues for intertextual connections based on *sustained allusions* (i.e., the repeated references to another "background" passage that stretch across multiple passages in Zech 1—8) (Stead 2008).

These examples demonstrate that there is a

wide variety of ways in which to establish a connection between texts.

3.1.2. Directionality. For diachronic intertextuality, there is a subsequent methodo-logical step to be undertaken once a connection between two texts has been established. This next step is to seek to establish the "directionality" between the two texts. This is often a complex question because of the many uncertainties surrounding the dating of biblical texts.

J. Leonard proposes six questions to help determine the direction of allusions: (1) Does one text claim to draw on another? (2) Are there elements in the texts that help to fix their dates? (3) Is one text capable of producing the other? (4) Does one text assume the other? (5) Does one text show a general pattern of dependence on other texts? (6) Are there rhetorical patterns in the texts that suggest that one text has used the other in an exegetically significant way? (Leonard, 258).

3.2. Result: What Does Intertextuality Do to a Text?

3.2.1. (Re)Interpretation, Not Exegesis. Intertextuality in the prophets is most often not "exegesis" in the proper sense of that word, in that the reason for quoting earlier texts is not in order to give the meaning of that text in its original context.

Intertextuality transforms the meaning of an older text by the very fact of its reapplication and recontextualization in a new literary and historical context. There are myriad ways in which this transformation may take place, including but not limited to the categories identified above in Fishbane's analysis: extension, spiritualization, nationalization, reappropriation, demythologizing, rhetorical inversion, subversion, rhetorical reworking, revision, reapplication, reinterpretation and reuse in a mantic anthology.

3.2.2. Radical Indeterminacy of Meaning? T. Beal argues that intertextuality must lead to a radical indeterminacy of meaning. "Every text—as an intersection of other textual surfaces—suggests an indeterminate surplus of meaningful possibilities. Interpretation is always a production of meaning from that surplus (Beal, 31). Beal's approach is based on the poststructural semiotics of Barthes, in which any text is a "tissue of quotations drawn from the innumerable centres of culture"

(Barthes 1977, 146). However, as Beal notes, the "innumerable centres of culture" cannot be analyzed, and so, as a matter of expediency, readers must limit the infinite possibilities of a text in order to arrive at an interpretation, and that they do so based on their own ideology. "Movement from the indeterminate 'general text' to particular practices of intertextual reading demands that one ask about the ideological limits, or 'strategies of containment', that make interpretation possible" (Beal, 28). In short, the intertextual nature of all texts leads to multiple interpretations of all texts, and readers choose their preferred interpretation on ideological grounds.

Stead tests the claim that intertextuality leads to a plurality of meaning by examining the intertexts of Zechariah 5:5-11 and comes to the opposite conclusion (Stead 2009, 188-218). Zechariah 5:5-11 is clearly a text formed through the "intersection of other textual surfaces" (to quote Beal), but far from creating an indeterminate surplus of meaning, the intersection of these other texts has the effect of narrowing down the interpretive possibilities. When Zechariah 5:5-11 is read in absolute isolation, these seven verses could bear a wide range of meanings, but when read against its intertexts, this passage has a more limited range of meanings. The intertextual nature of Zechariah 5:5-11 leads, not (as per Beal) to a radical indeterminacy of meaning, but rather to a more determinate meaning.

3.3. Intertextuality as a Genre of Prophetic Literature.
Floyd argues that the Hebrew term *maśśāʾ* is a technical one that "means something like 'prophetic reinterpretation of a previous revelation'" (Floyd, 238). It is debatable whether the term *maśśāʾ* functions as a genre label in this way (see Boda), but it does seem that there is a distinct form of prophecy that functions by way of prophetic reinterpretation of a previous revelation. Fishbane calls this a "mantic anthology." A good example of this occurs in Zechariah 9—14.

However, this does not necessarily imply that there is "transformation from prophecy to exegesis during the second temple period" (Sommer 1996a, 47). Zechariah 9—14 is an intertextual reappropriation of previous revelation, but at the same time it is a genuine revelatory "new" word that (paradoxically) comes via a reiteration and reapplication of the written words of other prophets.

3.4. Relationship to Other Approaches.
K. Schmid has offered an insightful analysis of the relationship between innerbiblical interpretation (*innerbiblische Schriftauslegung*) and the tradition history, redaction history and reception history of a text.

4. Conclusion.
Intertextuality provides insights into the relationship between texts that are helpful for guiding readers into a deeper understanding of the prophets of the Hebrew Bible. Properly understood, *intertextuality* is an umbrella term that encompasses both synchronic and diachronic concerns, because the authors of the prophetic literature in the Bible engaged in a dialogue with other texts when writing, and their texts continue to dialogue with other texts in the wider canon of Scripture. Intertextuality alerts us to the transformations that occur in the reuse and recontextualization of a text in a new literary and historical context.

See also CANONICAL CRITICISM; EDITORIAL/REDACTION CRITICISM; FORM CRITICISM; HERMENEUTICS; FORMATION OF THE PROPHETIC BOOKS; RHETORICAL CRITICISM; WRITING AND PROPHECY.

BIBLIOGRAPHY. **R. Barthes,** *Image, Music, Text,* trans. S. Heath (London: Fontana, 1977); idem, "Theory of the Text," in *Untying the Text: A Post-Structuralist Reader,* ed. R. Young (Boston: Routledge & Kegan Paul, 1981) 31-47; **T. K. Beal,** "Ideology and Intertextuality: Surplus of Meaning and Controlling the Means of Production," in *Reading between Texts: Intertexuality and the Hebrew Bible,* ed. D. N. Fewell (Louisville: Westminster/John Knox, 1992) 27-39; **M. J. Boda,** "Freeing the Burden of Prophecy: *Maśśāʾ* and the Legitimacy of Prophecy in Zech 9–14," *Bib* 87 (2006): 338-57; **J. Clayton and E. Rothstein,** eds., *Influence and Intertextuality in Literary History* (Madison: University of Wisconsin Press, 1991); **J. Day,** "Inner-Biblical Interpretation in the Prophets," in *The Place Is Too Small for Us: The Israelite Prophets in Recent Scholarship,* ed. R. P. Gordon (Winona Lake, IN: Eisenbrauns, 1995) 230-46; **U. Eco,** *Semiotics and the Philosophy of Language* (London: Macmillan, 1984); idem, *The Open Work,* trans. A. Cacogni (Cambridge, MA: Harvard University Press, 1989); **L. M. Eslinger,** "Inner-Biblical Exegesis and Inner-Biblical Allusion: The Question of Category," *VT* 42 (1992) 47-58; **M. A. Fishbane,** *Biblical Interpretation in Ancient Israel* (Oxford: Clarendon Press, 1985); idem, *The Garments of Torah: Essays in Biblical Hermeneutics* (ISBL; Bloomington: Indiana University Press, 1989); idem, "Inner-Biblical Exegesis," in *Hebrew Bible, Old Testament: The History of Its Interpretation,* ed. M. Sæbø (Göttingen: Vandenhoeck & Ruprecht, 1996) 33-48; idem, "Types of Biblical Intertextuality," in *Congress Volume: Oslo 1988,* ed. A. Lemaire and M. Sæbø (Leiden: E. J. Brill, 2000) 39-44; **M. H. Floyd,** "Deutero-Zechariah and Types of Intertextuality," in *Bringing Out the Treasure: Inner Biblical Allusion in Zechariah 9-14,* ed. M. J. Boda and M. H. Floyd (JSOTSup 370; London: Sheffield Academic Press, 2003) 225-44; **G. Hepner,** "Verbal Resonance in the Bible and Intertextuality," *JSOT* 96 (2001) 3-27; **J. T. Hibbard,** *Intertextuality in Isaiah 24-27: The Reuse and Evocation of Earlier Texts and Traditions* (FAT 2/16; Tübingen: Mohr Siebeck, 2006); **W. Iser,** "Indeterminacy and the Reader's Response," in *Aspects of Narrative: Selected Papers from the English Institute,* ed. J. H. Miller (New York: Columbia University Press, 1971) 2-45; **J. Kristeva,** *Desire in Language: A Semiotic Approach to Literature and Art* (Oxford: Blackwell, 1980); **K. J. A. Larkin,** *The Eschatology of Second Zechariah: A Study of the Formation of a Mantological Wisdom Anthology* (CBET 6; Kampen: Kok Pharos, 1994); **J. M. Leonard,** "Identifying Inner-Biblical Allusions: Psalm 78 as a Test Case," *JBL* 127 (2008) 241–65; **B. M. Levinson,** "The Phenomenon of Rewriting within the Hebrew Bible: A Bibliographic Essay on 'Inner-Biblical Exegesis' in the History of Scholarship," in *Legal Revision and Religious Renewal in Ancient Israel,* ed. B. M. Levinson (Cambridge: Cambridge University Press, 2008) 95-182; **M. C. Love,** *The Evasive Text: Zechariah 1-8 and the Frustrated Reader* (JSOTSup 296; Sheffield: Sheffield Academic, 1999); **R. A. Mason,** "The Use of Earlier Biblical Material in Zechariah 9-14: A Study in Inner Biblical Exegesis," in *Bringing Out the Treasure: Inner Biblical Allusion in Zechariah 9-14,* ed. M. J. Boda and M. H. Floyd (JSOTSup 370; London: Sheffield Academic, 2003) 1-208; **K. Nielsen,** "Intertextuality and Hebrew Bible," in *Congress Volume: Oslo 1988,* ed. A. Lemaire and M. Sæbø (Leiden: E. J. Brill, 2000) 17-31; **J. D. Nogalski,** "Intertextuality and the Twelve," in *Forming Prophetic Literature: Essays on Isaiah and the Twelve in Honor of John D. W. Watts*, ed. J. W. Watts and P. R. House (JSOTSup 235; Sheffield: Sheffield Academic, 1996) 102-24; **R. Nurmela**, *Prophets in Dialogue: Inner-Biblical Allusions in Zechariah 1-8 and 9-14* (Åbo: Åbo Akademi University Press, 1996); **M. Riffaterre**, *Semiotics of Poetry* (Advances in Semiotics; Bloomington: Indiana University Press, 1978); **K. Schmid**, "Innerbiblische Schriftauslegung: Aspekte der Forschungsgeschichte," in *Schriftauslegung in Der Schrift: Festschrift für Odil Hannes Steck zum seinem 65. Geburtstag*, ed. R. G. Kratz, T. Kruger and K. Schmid (BZAW 300; Berlin: de Gruyter, 2000) 1-22; **R. L. Schultz**, "The Ties That Bind: Intertextuality, the Identification of Verbal Parallels, and Reading Strategies in the Book of the Twelve," in *Thematic Threads in the Book of the Twelve*, ed. P. L. Redditt and A. Schart (BZAW 325; Berlin: de Gruyter, 2003) 27-45; **B. D. Sommer**, "Allusions and Illusions: The Unity of the Book of Isaiah in Light of Deutero-Isaiah's Use of the Prophetic Tradition," in *New Visions of Isaiah*, ed. R. F. Melugin and M. A. Sweeney (JSOTSup 214; Sheffield: Sheffield Academic, 1996a) 156-87; idem, "Exegesis, Allusion and Intertextuality in the Hebrew Bible: A Response to Lyle Eslinger," *VT* 46 (1996b) 479-89; idem, *A Prophet Reads Scripture: Allusion in Isaiah 40-66* (Stanford, CA: Stanford University Press, 1998); **M. R. Stead**, "Sustained Allusion in Zechariah 1-2," in *Tradition in Transition: Haggai and Zechariah 1-8 in the Trajectory of Hebrew Theology*, ed. M. J. Boda and M. H. Floyd (LHBOTS 475; New York: T & T Clark, 2008) 144-70; idem, *The Intertextuality of Zechariah 1-8* (LHBOTS 506; New York: T & T Clark, 2009); **P. K. Tull**, "Intertextuality and the Hebrew Scriptures," *CurBS* 8 (2000) 59-90; **K. W. Weyde**, 'Inner-Biblical Interpretation: Methodological Reflections on the Relationship between Texts in the Hebrew Bible," *SEÅ* 70 (2005) 287-300; **P. T. Willey**, *Remember the Former Things: The Recollection of Previous Texts in Second Isaiah* (SBLDS 161; Atlanta: Scholars Press, 1997).

M. R. Stead

ISAIAH: BOOK OF

Isaiah was a prophet who ministered in Judah in the last third of the eighth century BC (approximately 735-700 BC). The book records his sayings from that period but also includes a lot of material that relates to later times. Some believe that the same prophet was responsible for authorship of the whole book, but most scholars think that it was written by several authors over a long period of time. Recent work has emphasized, however, that this does not prevent study of the book as a whole and discussion of its teaching as a unity of some sort. In the NT, Isaiah is the most frequently cited of all the Prophetic Books, and a number of passages, whether messianic or not, have featured prominently in Christian liturgy and teaching, as well as in wider cultural works of art, literature and music.

1. Structure and Content
2. Survey of Scholarship on Composition
3. The Text of the Book of Isaiah
4. Two Major Theological Themes
5. King and Messiah

1. Structure and Content.
The book of Isaiah is long and, at first sight, bewildering in its variety. The following is a somewhat rough and abbreviated outline that may help with initial orientation.

1.1. Introduction. Isaiah 1 serves as an introduction to the book, not in the sense that it includes a summary of the whole (note, e.g., that there is nothing here about kingship), but rather that it mirrors the shape of the book and so invites a responsive reading. The nation is criticized for its defection from following the Lord and threatened with even worse punishment; the survival of even a remnant is already a mark of God's grace (Is 1:2-9; cf. Is 2—39). Despite severe disjuncture between religious practice and ethics, there is an offer of full *forgiveness still open to those who are willing to respond (Is 1:10-20; cf. Is 40—55). This response is anticipated at the individual level rather than at the full national level, and those who reject it will be judged severely (Is 1:21-31; cf. Is 56—66).

1.2. Programmatic Statement. Isaiah 2—12 seems to contain a wide variety of different types of material, but it encapsulates many of the major themes that will recur. Following another introductory heading (Is 2:1), it puts forward a *vision of how things will be one day, with Zion exalted and all the *nations streaming in and out in order to learn of God's ways, the outcome of which will be world *peace (Is

2:2-4). However, "the house of Jacob" falls far short of the ideal required for the fulfilment of this vision (Is 2:5-6), and much of the remainder of the book is devoted to addressing this problem. Most of Isaiah 2—5 amplifies and condemns the nature of the people's sin and failure, though Isaiah 4:2-6 keeps the vision alive with a glimpse of what *Zion could and will be.

Isaiah 6 marks something of a fresh start with Isaiah's vision of the exaltation of the Lord as king and warrior, his highly ambiguous, though threatening, commission of Isaiah as his spokesperson, and a solemn warning of the judgment that will come before there is any hope of restoration. In a mixture of third- and first-person material, Isaiah 7—8 then shows the outworking of this commission in the specific context of the Syro-Ephraimite crisis (see Israelite History), while Isaiah 9:1-7 issues a reminder that God can reverse his punitive acts of judgment and use a Davidic descendant to initiate his rule of *justice, righteousness and peace. Isaiah 9:8—10:34 generally renews the threats of judgment on both the northern kingdom of Israel and the southern kingdom of Judah at the hands of the Assyrians, whereas Isaiah 11 again affirms the ideal of righteousness and peace that God will bring through his appointed king. Isaiah 12 rounds off this section with an anticipatory hymn of praise—a structural feature of Isaiah 40—55 as well, the language of Isaiah 12 being also familiar from there.

1.3. Oracles Concerning the Nations. Isaiah 13:1 has a heading that consciously balances that of Isaiah 2:1. Bearing the introductory vision in mind, Isaiah 13—23 is largely concerned with foreign nations, both those that were active in the region of Judah during Isaiah's own lifetime and others that became prominent only later. There are two exceptions: one concerns Jerusalem (apparently) at the end of Isaiah's ministry (Is 22), and the other is a short prose account of his actions during the revolt of Ashdod that helps to bind the two previous chapters (Cush and Egypt) together. While this material keeps the international dimension of the prophecy in mind in relation to Isaiah's own time, Isaiah 24—27 (often called the "Isaiah Apocalypse") transposes these concerns on to a more timeless and universal scale (see Sweeney 1988). As with the original vision, the shape of the book thus encourages reflec-

tion on the truths propounded beyond the narrow historical context of Isaiah's own lifetime.

1.4. Headlong to Disaster. About twenty years after the fall of the northern kingdom of Israel (see Is 28:1-6), most of Isaiah 28—39 charts the course of Judah's history through to an almost equally serious catastrophe in the outcome of the revolt of King Hezekiah against the Assyrians and Sennacherib's punitive invasion in 701 BC. Scathing condemnations of Judah's policies at this time are included, though there are also smaller passages interspersed that remind the reader that this is not God's last word. Isaiah 36—39 then recounts the course of Sennacherib's invasion in a manner closely parallel with 2 Kings 18—20. Although the outcome is a miraculous deliverance for Jerusalem, the last word is not hopeful, in that the story of the Babylonian envoys points forward to eventual *exile there (Is 39:6-7), so setting the scene for the following major section of the book. Before these narratives, Isaiah 34 again universalizes the word of judgment (it is not confined to Judah, therefore), while Isaiah 35 contrasts sharply by sketching the joy and praise that will be offered when God restores his people; the talk of the ransomed of the Lord returning and coming to Zion again strongly anticipates the next major section of the book, so that the chapter functions in a manner similar to Isaiah 12.

1.5. "Comfort My People!" Isaiah 40—55 breathes a significantly different atmosphere from the bulk of what has preceded. Although, as we have seen, there are some small anticipations, now the message is this: forget the former things, and look to the new thing that God is doing. Cyrus, the coming Persian king who is named as God's messiah (Is 44:28; 45:1), is coming to take over oppressive Babylon (Is 41:2-4; 43:14-15; 45:1-7; 46—47) and to set in motion the ingathering of the dispersed people of Israel from there as well as from all four corners of the earth. The prophet's message throughout Isaiah 40—48, therefore, is meant to encourage the people to respond in faith in place of their current despair (e.g., Is 40:27). They may believe God's promise because of his power shown as creator, his superiority to the idols of the peoples (as seen in a series of courtroom-like trials), and because he controls the destiny of the nations.

Although the audience in Isaiah 49—55 seems to be largely the same, the tone of the writing is significantly different. The style is more intimate, with the people addressed now more as Zion, though the reassuring note and the expectation of joy remain.

This transition in style is mirrored in the transition in the role of the famous servant figure (for a messianic reading, see 5 below). In Isaiah 42:1-4 the servant was clearly Israel in some shape or form (see, e.g., the close similarities with Is 41:8-10), presented in royal guise as the one through whom God would bring justice to the nations. In Isaiah 49:1-6 this remains the final goal (see Is 49:1, 6), but the path to its realization has become more complex. The servant remains Israel (Is 49:3), but he now has first to restore the tribes of Jacob as a prior step in his mission. And what that will cost is spelled out in Isaiah 52:13—53:12, where the suffering is undertaken on behalf of "my people" (Is 53:8) but will astound and lead to a complete change of heart on the part of nations and kings (Is 52:13-15; 53:12; note how this may pick up on the witness of Is 40:5 and elsewhere).

1.6. The Reordering of a Godly Society. In many ways the last eleven chapters of the book (Is 56—66) are the most confusing. It may help to observe that Isaiah 60—62 is closest in thought to Isaiah 40—55, but now the standpoint seems to have switched back to the Jerusalem community. Prior to that there are passages apparently explaining why the promised deliverance has not turned out to be so glorious as had been hoped, and following it there is a long prayer of lament (Is 63:7—64:12) that complains again at the delay, to which the bulk of Isaiah 65—66 may be seen as the divine response. As part of these moves there is the start of a shift to a more individualized rhetoric. The community is divided between the righteous and the wicked, dependent upon repentance, so that the distinction between Israel and the nations begins to be transformed into a distinction between those of Israel and the nations who respond to God's call vis-à-vis those of either group who do not. Thus, at the start of the section (Is 56:1-8) and at the end (Is 66:18-24) we find introductory and concluding passages that show a remarkable universality about the potential of God's salvation, even though not all, by any means, avail themselves of it. In this way, the book concludes on a similar note to the end of the first, introductory chapter.

2. Survey of Scholarship on Composition.

The preceding outline of the book has revealed a remarkable diversity of topics discussed and of historical situations presupposed by the author or authors of the various parts. Conservative scholars believe that all of this can be accommodated under the banner of predictive prophecy; probably late in his life, when Isaiah realized that judgment was inevitable for the present dispensation, he was guided by God to foresee the eventual deliverance and restoration, including, for instance, the name of the Persian monarch Cyrus. It is often claimed that the NT references, which, it is thought, associate Isaiah with passages cited from the second half of the book, are conclusive in this argument. The majority of scholars, including many evangelicals, however, think that the evidence is better explained by the hypothesis that the book had more than one author. The hypotheses that have been advanced over the years differ considerably from one another, however, as the following highly selective and compressed survey will demonstrate.

2.1. Before 1892. Toward the end of the eighteenth century, earlier adumbrations by the medieval Jewish commentator Ibn Ezra (see Simon) were picked up by J. B. Koppe, J. C. Döderlein and, especially influentially, J. G. Eichhorn (see the survey in Vincent) to the effect that the second half of the book (from Is 40 on) was not written by Isaiah of Jerusalem in the eighth century BC but rather by an unknown prophet of the sixth century BC who directed his oracles toward the Judean exiles in Babylon. This view spread rapidly in the nineteenth century, so that although during those decades the most important work on Isaiah related to textual criticism and philology, the division of the book between two authors became something of a consensus position, attracting even the eventual agreement of the otherwise conservative F. Delitzsch in the fourth and final edition of his commentary.

2.2. Bernhard Duhm. In 1892 Duhm published the first edition of his commentary, which rapidly established itself as a classic. This is generally best known for two significant hypotheses, though a third is also of importance. First, Duhm argued for a third division of the book, following Isaiah 55, so that it now became common to speak of Proto-, Deutero- and Trito-Isaiah (Is 1—39; 40—55; 56—66). He demonstrated that just as Isaiah 40—55 presupposed a setting in the Babylonian exile, so Isaiah 56—66 presupposed a later situation back in the partially restored Jerusalem. Although Duhm himself did not hold this further opinion, it came to be widely believed that Deutero-Isaiah should be located in Babylon during the exile and Trito-Isaiah in Jerusalem at some time following the return from exile early in the Persian period.

Second, Duhm was the first to isolate as a separate composition the four so-called Servant Songs (see Servant of Yahweh) in the second half of the book (Is 42:1-4; 49:1-6; 50:4-9; 52:13—53:12). He maintained that the presentation of this servant was so at variance with the faithless servant of the surrounding chapters that they could not have been held together in the mind of a single author. He thought that they had a quite separate origin, and that they were copied into conveniently blank spaces or margins in the manuscript of the larger book. Their present context therefore was not significant. This proposal has had a major bearing on many interpretations of these cardinal passages ever since, for it was considered even by conservative evangelicals somehow to give warrant to expounding them in isolation from their present literary setting.

Third, Duhm did not accept that all of Isaiah 1—39 should be attributed to Isaiah of Jerusalem. Rather, he sought to press the evidence for different sections within these chapters as indicative of material of diverse origin, some of which (such as Is 24—27) certainly was very much later than Isaiah (and, indeed, later than some parts in the second half of the book as well). Because this third aspect of Duhm's commentary was not so startlingly original as the first two, it has not attracted the attention that they have. Nevertheless, it contributed strongly to the growing tide of opinion that the first half of the book was written by several authors, stretching over several hundreds of years.

2.3. The Decades Following Duhm. As the influence of Duhm's major conclusions spread, it became common during much of the twentieth century to treat the various parts of the book in more or less complete isolation from one another. Books of introduction to the Bible had separate chapters on Isaiah of Jerusalem and Deutero-Isaiah, for instance, and these could be separated from each other if the treatment was chronological. Similarly, many commentary series assigned the different parts of the book to different commentators, and monographic studies focused their attention exclusively on one section or another. Scholarly trends in regard to each section differed starkly from one another.

2.3.1. Isaiah 1—39. Opinions regarding the composition of this part of the book have diverged more widely than any other, so that any summary is bound to be inadequate. Only a few significant trends can be mentioned.

The general tendency in the decades following Duhm was to find ever more divisions within these chapters. While it was relatively uncontroversial to ascribe the Isaiah Apocalypse (Is 24—27) to a late (and sometimes very late) period, this trend was quickly followed with regard to a number of the other oracles against the nations (e.g., the oracle against Babylon in Is 13—14 could not be earlier than the neo-Babylonian period, coinciding with the exile). In addition, Isaiah 35 obviously belonged closely with Isaiah 40—55 (note that Is 35:10 is more or less identical with Is 51:11), and Isaiah 34 went along with it. Isaiah 33 was also often seen as non-Isaianic, so that the end of the prophet Isaiah's own composition was found somewhere in the course of Isaiah 32.

A similar stripping off of material also characterized much of the opening chapters of the book. As we have already seen, parts of Isaiah 1 are close to the final chapters of the book and generally were thought to have been written at the same time. Isaiah 4:2-6 was more or less universally ascribed to an author in a late postexilic time, where several of its images find their closest parallels. Oracles of unconditional hope tended also to be denied to Isaiah of Jerusalem on the understanding that his ministry was primarily "negative" (see Is 6:9-10); this applied especially to the "messianic" passages in Isaiah 9:1-6; 11:1-9, but equally, the end of Isaiah 11 and especially Isaiah 12 were related closely with the work of Deutero-Isaiah. The same sort of conclusion was also drawn with regard to some of the more hopeful material in Isaiah 28—32. A standard English commentary such as that of G. Gray (covering Is 1—27 only) gives a fair and balanced discussion of these issues. What was noticeably missing, however, was serious exegetical attention to much of the material that was considered "later" or "secondary." There was an atmosphere in which early was considered best, or most important, so that little attention was given to how or why the larger work developed as it did. Moreover, virtually nobody writing during those decades considered how these chapters related to the second half of the book.

One significant and influential counter-theory, however, was that of K. Budde, who advanced the case that Isaiah 6:1—9:6 was entirely written by the prophet himself as what has come to be called the "Isaiah Memoir." While most of the theory and certainly the designation were more or less universally adopted, it is astonishing to find that within this Budde included material that in other respects certainly should have been considered "later," such as the last part of Isaiah 7, and equally that he lumped together the third-person narrative in Isaiah 7:1-17 and the first-person accounts in Isaiah 6 and Isaiah 8. This had serious consequences for the understanding of Isaiah 7 in particular that only recently have begun to be unraveled.

2.3.2. Isaiah 40—55. By complete contrast with the treatment of Isaiah 1—39, scholars varied very little in their conviction that Isaiah 40—55 should be ascribed to the work of a great prophet in the Babylonian exile. Exceptions were made only for the Servant Songs and some of the anti-idol polemical passages (e.g., Is 40:19-20; 41:6-7; 44:9-20). Progress in research on these chapters was concentrated more on the increasingly sophisticated application of *form criticism, a method that detected comparable literary shapes between various passages that enabled them to be classified as trial speeches, oracles of salvation, disputations and so on. This had positive benefits: the otherwise rolling lyrical poetry could be divided into intelligible passages, and a meaningful social setting could be found for each type in a manner that led to a deeper appreciation of the rhetoric and encouraging argument of the prophet. This whole trend reached its climax in the commentary by C. Westermann, who both summarized and advanced research in this particular regard. It will have been in connection with the interpretation of the Servant Songs that opinions remained most widely divided.

2.3.3. Isaiah 56—66. Despite Duhm's breakthrough in connection with the last part of Isa-

iah, very few scholars after him found in these chapters the work of a single author. K. Elliger, as well as several Israeli scholars, with whom in this respect C. Torrey was in agreement, sought to uphold the authorial unity of the whole of Isaiah 40—66. The majority, however, considered that the diversity of material and viewpoint was indicative of the work of more than one writer working over an undefined period of time. If a majority viewpoint emerged, it will have been that again best represented in Westermann's commentary (see too Smith), in which Isaiah 60—62 is regarded as the earliest part, closely in succession to the views of Deutero-Isaiah. A sense of disillusion set in, however, when these promises appeared not to be being fulfilled in their entirety (see Is 58 for a clear example), and so the surrounding chapters came to be added in order to make clear what the conditions were that needed to be met as a first step. The decidedly universalist material at the start and close of the section might have been the final level of addition.

2.4. The Most Recent Trends. The last thirty years or so have witnessed several significant developments on many of these topics; although from one perspective they seem to be moving in opposite directions, there is an element of coherence that might permit the development of a new consensus. The key, it appears, is the increasingly sophisticated application of redaction criticism to the book in all its parts and as a whole (*see* Editorial/Redaction Criticism).

2.4.1. Isaiah 1—39. As far as the first part of the book is concerned, a significant development was initiated by H. Barth, who in 1977 argued in detail that many of the passages that had been regarded simply as random additions could be understood together as a single redaction in the reign of Josiah, the time that saw the sudden decline and eventual demise of the Assyrian Empire. Barth's proposal was adopted (with minor variations) by many leading commentators such as R. Clements, M. Sweeney and J. Vermeylen (who had reached many of the same conclusions independently). A similar, though less far-reaching, proposal was to find evidence for a redactional layer that related to the fall of Jerusalem to the Babylonians and the exile of many of the people (e.g., Clements 1980b). The significance of such proposals was to demonstrate that earlier work had overlooked historical levels of coherence within the book; that is, its literary growth was not random or haphazard, but rather at certain key points in the nation's history, leading religious thinkers returned to the valued work of their predecessors in order to find ways of continuing to apply their teaching to the changing circumstances.

Another way in which this same development was advanced concerned the prose narratives about Isaiah (Is 7:1-17; 20; 36—39). These are told in the third person and thus were unlikely to have been written by the prophet himself. Furthermore, they have a number of significant points of connection between them (see, e.g., Conrad, 38-40) indicating that they may have been derived from a single source; parts were also used, of course, in the composition of the books of Kings. While they include good historical memory, the question of the present positioning in the book is fertile ground for redaction criticism; for instance, Isaiah 7:1-17 applies the "hardening" saying of Isaiah 6:9-10 to the individual person of the king, whereas Isaiah 8 does so to the people as a whole; Isaiah 20 served to bind together the two previous chapters relating to Cush and Egypt, and Isaiah 36—39 draws out the consequences of all the preceding judgment oracles while at the same time pointing forward to the second part of the book. It remains a challenge to the interpreter, however, to hold together the generally positive presentation of Hezekiah in these chapters with the harsh criticism of what has to have been his own policies in some of the preceding chapters (Is 28—31).

2.4.2. Isaiah 40—55. In recent decades a strange division has opened up between German-speaking and English-speaking scholars with regard to the composition of these chapters. Whereas generally the latter have tended to continue to hold to the essential unity of authorship (although, following the lead of H. Barstad, there has been some debate about whether the author should be located in Babylon or Judah), the former have moved toward a much more complicated presentation. In many monographs, as well as now in some commentaries, the material is thought to have developed in multiple phases. An initial core may have gone through as many as five or six subsequent stages of expansion, the result being that it is not really meaningful to talk of Deutero-

Isaiah any more, at least if by that a single author is implied. The theories inevitably differ somewhat one from another, so that in earlier years it was difficult to know how to evaluate them. More recently, however, they have been brought together into a fine synthesis by R. Albertz, so that one can now begin at least to see the forest from the trees in this regard.

Two points may be made about this particular development, which many people find puzzling when first encountered. First, there is certainly a division of some sort within Isaiah 40—55 following Isaiah 48. After Isaiah 48 there are no more trial scenes or anti-idol polemic; there is no more reference to the fall of Babylon; there is no further reference or allusion to Cyrus; Zion is addressed in a far more extended manner than previously; finally, Isaiah 48:22 obviously marks the end of a section, as a comparison with Isaiah 57:21 makes clear, and Isaiah 49:1-6 (the second Servant Song) is itself a passage that speaks of transition. To the extent that these new theories make us sensitive to the differences between the parts of Deutero-Isaiah, they should be welcomed, even if we do not accept all of their conclusions.

Second, as we will see shortly, some of this detection of redactional layering is due to the consequence of reading these chapters not in isolation, as had been the previous tendency, but rather within the context of the book of Isaiah as a whole; the detection of some connections with earlier or later passages obliged some scholars to seek a redactional explanation, not least because they still held to the likelihood that the core of these chapters began its life independently of the remainder of the book.

2.4.3. Isaiah 56—66. Work on these chapters has apparently been less dramatic because it effectively continues the kinds of development just described. That is to say, on the one hand, there is greater openness to finding more layers within the text than was previously entertained, and on the other hand, there is an increasing tendency to associate this with the development of the book as a whole. Regardless of opinions about the origins of Isaiah 40—55, most scholars are agreed that Isaiah 56—66 was not written in isolation from what precedes. Thus, one's understanding of the growth of the earlier parts of the book is likely to affect how one envisages the process in these closing chapters as well.

2.4.4. The Book of Isaiah as a Whole. This survey of recent developments in scholarship with regard to the various parts of the book must be put in subservience, as it were, to the most dramatic change of opinion in recent decades: the rediscovery of the book's essential unity. For most scholars, this is not what might be identified as a unity of authorship; instead, it is an acknowledgment that the various parts of the book developed not in isolation from one another but rather as part of a dynamic, and to some extent integrated, process of growth. In this, multiple examples of apparent literary dependence of one passage upon another and of the use of clauses and phrases (such as "the Holy One of Israel") that are rare or nonexistent elsewhere in the OT have been major contributory factors.

I have offered a detailed survey of the origins of this development elsewhere, crediting the work of numerous scholars (Williamson 1994, 1-18). There remains an important distinction, however, between those who conceive the unity as being seen only in the relatively late welding together of originally separate compositions (so prominently O. Steck with his pupils and followers) and those, such as myself, who believe that the later parts of the book were written in the first place only in order to carry forward the earlier parts that were at those authors' disposal. Thus, I sought to demonstrate that Isaiah 40—55 was directly influenced by an earlier form of Isaiah 1—39, that its author envisaged himself as proclaiming the deliverance that Isaiah had so long anticipated (see especially Is 8:16-18; 30:8 for evidence that this was specifically written down with an eye to the future), and that he edited the first part of the work specifically so that the two parts could be read together as a pair in relation to the end of the Babylonian exile (see, e.g., the role and position of Is 12, and the positioning of the oracle against Babylon as first among the oracles against the nations). Most recently, J. Stromberg has taken this suggestion forward to find a similar sort of process at work in relation to Isaiah 56—66 and the remainder of the book.

2.5. Some Conclusions. The view is sometimes expressed that there is so much diversity of scholarly opinion that none of it can be of any solid worth. This is a mistake. On the one hand, biblical scholars do not disagree any more than do other people on other issues in all walks of life; what counts is not so much the answers that are proposed as the fact that all the scholars, in careful consideration of the material at hand, come up with related questions. On the other hand, there is a developing agreement with regard to Isaiah that a pathway through the book's undoubted complexities is probably best sought in terms of literary history insofar as that can be traced by the observance of how one passage may be dependent in some way upon another. Where does this lead us, and what are its consequences for the ultimately more important task of interpretation?

First, I do not find the idea of unity of authorship to be either plausible or necessary. Despite frequent claims to the contrary by conservative scholars, this conclusion has nothing to do with belief or not in the power of predictive prophecy; after all, there is still predictive prophecy included in all parts of the book even on the most radical of critical positions. The issue turns rather on three considerations. (1) The setting presupposed by different parts of the book varies considerably. Much of Isaiah 40—55, for instance, takes its standpoint with those who have suffered judgment in the past and should now be anticipating deliverance; what sense would that make in the eighth century BC? If a concept of divine inspiration lies behind the view that all of this material was written at that earlier date, it would mean that God did not speak in a way that was intelligible to its audience at the time of delivery, so that this flies in the face of Christian understandings of the word of God, seen ultimately in incarnation. (2) The messages of the different parts of the book are so diverse that they cannot be understood as other than accompanying historical change. If all of them were delivered and considered together in the eighth century BC, they would be contradictory; it is only as they are related to different periods that the underlying unity becomes meaningful. Thus, to deny the probability that the book grew over a considerable period of time is to empty it of a major hermeneutical key. (3) The NT references do not alter this conclusion, since the use in those contexts of "Isaiah" may be perfectly well understood as a reference to the book, not the author. The only passage where the prophet himself is involved in action rather than as speaker or author in the argument is at John 12:41 ("Isaiah said this because he saw his glory and spoke about him" [NRSV]), and there the citation from Isaiah 6 poses no difficulty.

Second, even though the results of redaction criticism as outlined above may differ between scholars, there are three major underlying gains for interpretation in the newer approaches adopted over the last twenty or thirty years. (1) It is unusual now to find material simply dismissed as "late" or "additional." Regardless of quite when or by whom a verse or passage was added, the first question nowadays is to ask after the rationale of this addition at just this point in the text. In other words, redaction criticism makes commentators and preachers more aware of the depth in the text and drives them to probe that creatively rather than to try to underplay its significance. (2) Redaction criticism has opened up in principle the legitimacy of interpreting one part of the book in the light of the whole. As will be illustrated below, many themes are treated in complementary ways in the different parts of the book, the variety being due to the differing historical circumstances. At any given time, expositors today may believe that it is necessary to stress one aspect or another—for instance, severe critique of hypocrisy, or the liberating message of sin forgiven and an open pathway into the future. However, the book will always bring balancing features into play that need also to be included—for instance, the changing impact of *repentance in humility in the first case, and the fact that there is no cheap *forgiveness in the second. (3) Because redaction criticism works primarily through the detection and evaluation of literary associations across many passages, it deflects the commentator's attention from too heavy a preoccupation with the precise historical dating of any saying (a quest that usually cannot be answered with any certainty because we lack so much of the necessary data) and focuses attention instead on an interpretation of the text that we have and with which we can deal more securely. After a brief look at the state of the text of Isaiah, we will move on to consider some of the major theological themes in the book in the light of these conclusions.

3. The Text of the Book of Isaiah.

The position with regard to the Hebrew *text of the book of Isaiah is not as complicated as in the case of many others, such as Jeremiah. Most versions of the printed Hebrew Bible, on which English and other translations are based, are a copy of a manuscript dating from 1008 or 1009 and now housed in the Russian National Library in Saint Petersburg.

Uniquely, a more-or-less complete copy of Isaiah has been preserved among the *Dead Sea Scrolls, dating from the first pre-Christian century (i.e., over a millennium earlier than anything that was previously available). In addition, substantial parts remain in another manuscript, also found in Cave 1 when the scrolls were first discovered in the late 1940s. For an edition of both scrolls, see Ulrich and Flint. In addition, fragments (often very small) of some eighteen further manuscripts of Isaiah (or at least parts of it) were found in Cave 4, and they too have now been published (Ulrich et al.).

The Cave 4 fragments and 1QIsa[b] are quite similar to the later traditional MT (although without the vocalization, of course). In the case of 1QIsa[a], however, there are many more variants. The overwhelming majority of these are of a linguistic nature (e.g., there is evidence of influence from Aramaic) or due to variations in spelling. In a major study, E. Kutscher concluded that the scroll was textually inferior to the MT, and although he may have pressed his case too far, generally he was correct. It therefore is clear that all the new evidence confirms that there is only a single textual tradition with regard to the book of Isaiah, so that each attested variant should be evaluated on its merits, not according to some other wider textual hypothesis. Nonetheless, there are a few passages where these recently discovered older manuscripts probably preserve more ancient readings, and these are usually adopted in modern translations; in the RSV there are just under twenty such readings adopted (though most readers remain unaware of the fact, which indicates that they are not of major import).

Among the ancient translations that predate the medieval manuscript, the same broadly conservative conclusion is also mostly justified. The Greek rendering (the LXX), however, raises particular questions of its own, and these are important because the translation was undertaken even earlier than the time of the DSS. It often seems to be a relatively free rendering, and this sometimes can make it difficult to know whether it is a rendering of the Hebrew text as we know it or whether it attests some variant reading. This translation is the subject of much debate in its own right, there being a sharp difference of opinion over whether, for all its freedom, its renderings are to be accounted for as an attempt to translate the text alone or whether the translator has also introduced significant theological or sociological interpretations of his own (for a survey of opinions, see Troxel). Whichever of these two positions is correct, it is agreed that the LXX also generally attests the form of the Hebrew text as we know it, and that only occasionally may it be cited as evidence for superior readings.

While all these considerations mean that the text of Isaiah is a continuing subject of lively debate, their bearing on the general reader is strictly limited. We may be confident that the text of the book is relatively secure.

There remain a number of elements in the vocabulary of the book whose meaning is not precisely known (especially in the realms of technical botany, clothing and the like). Sometimes, discoveries of inscriptions or parallels in related languages shed light on these problems, but readers need to be aware of the tentative nature of many such proposals.

4. Two Major Theological Themes.

Even in a relatively lengthy dictionary article such as the present one, it is impossible to present a full survey of all the teaching of the book in each of its parts. In the following I will outline two of the major distinctive elements that straddle the book as a whole—one on the nature of God, the other on human response—in order to illustrate the importance of the recent rediscovery of the book's unity for responsible exegesis. (Other important themes could equally well have been chosen, such as *Zion [on which, see Maier] or the development and reversal of the "hardening" saying of Is 6:9-10 [on which, see Uhlig].) At the end, I will add a separate section on the messianic passages, for which the book is especially well known.

4.1. God.

4.1.1. God as "High and Lifted Up." Few would doubt that Isaiah's call or commissioning (it is not quite clear which it is) as recorded in Isaiah 6 was a foundational experience for the prophet, just as its recorded version in writing has become for the development of the book as a whole. Its vocabulary and themes are con-

stantly cited or alluded to elsewhere, and of course its influence on later theology and liturgy is pervasive.

It starts with a vision of God in all his royal majesty (he is called "the king" in Is 6:5), and in Isaiah 6:1 the words "high and lifted up" appear. Grammatically, it is not quite clear whether these words apply directly here to God or whether they instead qualify the throne on which he is sitting. Either way, however, as we will see shortly, they came in the course of time to be understood as referring to God.

From this opening statement, a number of other characteristic phrases and words may be seen to take their natural place. The use of the "holiness" word group in relation to God is prominent (see further below). "Glory" is another favorite term in the book, and it takes its place alongside "holy" as early as Isaiah 6:3 in the praise of the seraphim in the Trisagion (the proclamation that begins "Holy, holy, holy"). From there the language ripples out in several different directions. Another characteristic title for God is "the LORD of hosts" (again, starting from Is 6:5), the "hosts" in this context almost certainly being the heavenly armies of the divine king. This too adds to the impression of all-powerful and completely dominating divine power.

Appreciation of this exalted majesty of God undoubtedly was a dominating consideration for Isaiah in his theological worldview. He has a strong sense of hierarchy and a consequent appreciation that it is important for each part of the created order to know its place. At the simplest level, therefore, anything else that claims a "high and lifted up" position is doomed to destruction because it manifests hubris in the face of the only truly exalted one, God himself. Thus, the several occurrences of these words with relation to trees, mountains, towers and the like in Isaiah 2:12-17 are sufficient to explain without further justification why the Lord of hosts has a day against them, "against all that is proud and lofty, against all that is lifted up and high."

The same principle then explains Isaiah's theology in relation to Assyria, for instance. As long as Assyria acts in judgment even against Judah, it is regarded as God's minister, as "the rod of my anger, the staff of my fury! Against a godless nation I send him" (Is 10:5-6). But as soon as the Assyrians exceed their God-given brief and start to act in arrogant independence (Is 10:7-14), their own fate is sealed (Is 10:15-19), for this again is a clear example of hubris. This pattern we find repeated elsewhere.

This theology translates downwards, we may also note in passing, into Isaiah's understanding of the proper ordering of society. There are aspects of this that some today might well find inappropriate or distasteful, though it should be remembered in partial mitigation that Isaiah has an equally strong sense that those higher up the ladder have correspondingly larger responsibilities to care for those lower down. Nevertheless, it is helpful to appreciate the theology on which some of these more challenging passages, such as Isaiah 3, are based.

If this brief characterization of God in the first part of the book is correct, then it is of more than passing interest to see how it is handled later on, not least because of the ways, as we have noted, one part of the book often is balanced in important ways by another. The most striking way into this is the use of the same vocabulary in reference to God (and where, indeed, "high and lifted up" has actually become a divine title) in Isaiah 57:15: "For thus says the high and lofty one who inhabits eternity, whose name is Holy: I dwell in the high and holy place, and also with those who are contrite and humble in spirit, to revive the spirit of the humble, and to revive the heart of the contrite" (NRSV). The majesty of God as recapitulated from the first part of the book is here shown not to make him necessarily remote, as we might otherwise suppose. Rather, when God's majesty encounters people of a suitably contrasting disposition, he is said to dwell with them quite as much as in the high and holy place. The same sentiment exactly is echoed in Isaiah 66:1-2, which concludes, "But this is the one to whom I will look, to the humble and contrite in spirit, who trembles at my word" (NRSV).

This balancing between the parts of the book could be developed further in this regard, of course, but it serves as a reminder once again of the need to consider each individual part of the book in the light of the whole. On this occasion, there is just one further dimension that should be added here, for this same language recurs at the start of the fourth of the Servant Songs, at Isaiah 52:13: "See, my servant shall prosper; he shall be exalted and lifted up,

and shall be very high" (NRSV). This is a remarkable statement of how the servant will share the status and designation that previously we had thought was reserved exclusively for God. It comes in the introduction to a passage of extended reflection on rejection and suffering and anticipates (as is not unusual in Hebrew narrative) the outcome of the sequence of events that is to follow (cf. Is 53:12, which brings us back to the same point as this opening). Of the many insights that this affords, let it suffice here to state the obvious: when God finds an attitude of acceptance of his will in the service of others, no matter what the cost, he is prepared against all expectation to share the highest honors with his servants.

4.1.2. "The Holy One of Israel." A comparable, though slightly more complex, pattern may be traced with regard to the distinctive divine title "the Holy One of Israel." This occurs twenty-five times in Isaiah, and there are a few similar related expressions in addition. This sometimes has mistakenly been cited as evidence of unity of authorship; however, its usage is more interesting than that (for the following, see Williamson 2001).

It is probable (in view of Ps 71:22; 78:41; 89:18) that this title was in infrequent use in the Jerusalem cult. Isaiah's experience of the thrice-holy God (Is 6:3) may have led him to make use of it, even though the title itself does not occur in that chapter. On normal critical grounds, some five occurrences may be ascribed to him, mostly from the later part of his ministry. In these cases, as Isaiah 6 might lead us to expect, God's holiness stands in contrast with Judah's faithlessness, so that the title is used in connection with coming judgment. In this, Isaiah will have been turning cultic expectations on their head: the God whom the psalms led the people to believe would fight on their behalf turns out, in his sovereignty, to be the one who is planning their judgment for sin.

In the second part of the book, however, the exact opposite situation obtains. The judgment now is pictured as past, and the prophet seeks to turn his people's attention forward to the creatively new work that God is about to do. As part of that, the familiar title, which has come to be seen as threatening, is turned again to announce that the free and sovereign Lord is able to work as vigorously and surprisingly in grace as he had in judgment; all thirteen examples of the usage there are uniform in this regard. This therefore opens the reader up to a new appreciation of the rich character of God, who is not bound by institution or routine but rather is free to respond to his people's situations in ways that constantly take them unawares and ultimately, so far as this book proclaims, in grace.

Finally, we should note that while some of these later positive uses are reflected in what most scholars regard as positive redactional passages in Isaiah 1—39, the title drops almost completely from use thereafter. There are only two occurrences in Isaiah 56—66, one of which (Is 60:9) is merely a citation of Isaiah 55:5, and the other of which (Is 60.14) may be an echo of Isaiah 12:6. It then does not occur at all in the later material such as Isaiah 24—27; 34—35. Careful attention to the literary contexts of the title's use thus opens up an illuminating theology in this particular regard.

4.2. Justice and Righteousness. In common with some other parts of the OT, as well as elsewhere in the ancient Near East, the first half of the book of Isaiah stresses the need for *"justice and righteousness" in various spheres of life. There are some dozen occurrences of this word pair. Such language is not in common use today, and thus it requires some explanation.

By observing uses in context, including topics with which these values are contrasted, we soon learn that this goes far beyond just the administration of the criminal legal system (though that is included). It speaks instead of the need for probity, including compassion, in all walks of social and political life; one scholar has even gone so far as to gloss it with the phrase *"social justice." This may have taken very different forms in antiquity than it does today, but the general area is one of obviously continuing need at various levels of local, national and international life.

According to Isaiah's presentation, these qualities used to be characteristic of Zion in what he portrays as the golden era of Davidic rule, even though things have declined seriously since (Is 1:21-23). He concludes his parable of the vineyard by asserting that God still looks for these qualities in the present time, but instead he finds only their opposite: bloodshed and the cry of oppression (Is 5:7, with the clever use of word play). However, he is confident that they will once again characterize the restored Zion of the future, as pictorially God as builder of the new city declares, "I will make justice the line, and righteousness the plummet" (Is 28:17 NRSV). Their importance is underlined still further by the fact that they should be the concern of the ideal king (Is 32:1) and indeed will be of the royal child whose birth is announced in Isaiah 9:6-7. Many other passages could be cited where these words either occur together or on their own to demonstrate how central a concern this was to Isaiah and how the perversion of justice and righteousness was a significant cause of the judgment that he anticipated.

When we turn to the next part of the book, however, we find a remarkable contrast. To be sure, there are some elements of continuity (e.g., in Is 42:1-4, though the words "justice" and "righteousness" do not appear in tandem at any point in Isaiah 40—55), but more commonly we find "righteousness" singled out and used in a very different way. It appears several times in parallel with the word for *"salvation," so that whereas in Isaiah 1—39 it was something that persons in positions of responsibility had to do or perform, now it becomes part of the gracious deliverance and provision by God. There are those, indeed, who understandably would translate it as "victory" or "deliverance" in these chapters; examples include Isaiah 41:10; 45:8; 46:13; 51:5, 6, 8.

Finally, and remarkably, we find that these two apparently contrasting uses are brought into relationship in the twofold use of the word at the very start of the third section of the book, Isaiah 56:1: "Keep justice, and do righteousness, for soon my salvation will come, and my deliverance be revealed" (RSV) (see Rendtorff). Here the parallel form familiar from Isaiah 1—39 reappears in the first line as an urgent imperative, whereas in the following lines "righteousness" (the rendering of the RSV, which I have cited, is "deliverance") is used in parallel with "salvation," as in Isaiah 40—55, as indicative of God's imminent deliverance and as motivation to obey the command of the first line. This theologically rich intertwining of the two preceding sections of the book is then taken up and developed in various ways in the concluding chapters.

The foregoing remarks are only the sketchiest outline of a topic of central importance to the book. The striking balance introduced in Isaiah 56:1 needs constantly to be kept in mind, however. In some situations it may be necessary to focus on the practice of justice and righteousness and so to concentrate on one or more of the relevant passages in the first half of the book. It would be a mistake, however, to leave the matter there, for there is also a rich source of encouragement from reflection on God's correspondingly salvific righteousness. Conversely, the need may be for the dispirited to be comforted by the good news of God's deliverance as joyfully proclaimed in so much of the second part of the book, but here too it would be unbalanced so to concentrate on that without any indication that God looks for a response in gratitude in the treatment of others. The recovery of the sense of the book's unity thus brings balance to our understanding of its teaching with regard to human response.

5. King and Messiah.

Isaiah has several classical *messianic prophecies that feature regularly in most church lectionaries. They raise many exegetical problems, however, so that a few words of guidance here may be helpful. Included prominently among these passages (though there are a few others that are less well known) are Isaiah 7:14; 9:1-7; 11:1-9; 42:1-4; 49:1-6; 52:13—53:12; 61:1-4. (For the following, see more fully Williamson 1998.)

In terms of a traditional Christian reading of these passages, there are two main dangers. First, often they are applied so directly to Jesus that they are treated in willful disregard of their present immediate context in Isaiah. The bits that fit the NT tend to be pulled out with no attempt to relate them to other things that are equally prominent in the passage under consideration. Second, there is a tendency to stress so emphatically that Jesus has fulfilled these prophecies that they are emptied of any other content, including matters that should be prominent in our exegesis.

The first point to notice is that the emphasis falls more on the task that the figure is to perform than on the identity of the figure in question. In Isaiah 9:6-7, for instance, the whole drive of the prophecy is that the child has been given in order to establish and uphold the kingdom "with justice and with righteousness," so that this fits closely with the theme that we surveyed briefly in the preceding section. We can well imagine that such hopes would have attended the birth of any

royal child in ancient Judah; surely, this new prospective king will improve the social circumstances of the kingdom over the present state of affairs. The focus in Isaiah 11 turns out, upon inspection, to be not so very different. It is also immediately in line with the proverbial saying of Isaiah 32:1: "A king should reign in the interests of righteousness, and princes rule for the furtherance of justice."

The case of the Immanuel prophecy in Isaiah 7:14 is different. So far as its immediate context is concerned, the child in question clearly is to be born in the immediate future, as the close link with the promise of deliverance from the threat of the invading Syro-Ephraimite coalition makes clear in the two following verses. Furthermore, there is no direct statement as to the identity of the child's mother. The three main views are (1) he is another child of the prophet, as with the children in Isaiah 7:8; 8:1-4 (see too Is 8:18); (2) he is in some way a member of the royal household, perhaps even a child of King Ahaz, as the several references to the Davidic house in Isaiah 7:1-17 might lead one to suppose; (3) he is no specific child, but generically just any children who are born to Judean mothers in the very near future. Even if we prefer the second option (which I regard as marginally the most probable), this does not make it a long-term messianic prophecy as usually understood. The messianic interpretation is familiar from the citation in Matthew 1:22, of course. The legitimacy of that is not a question of historical exegesis of the text as it stands in Isaiah (where equally the mother of the child is not specifically identified as a virgin, though the word in question does not rule out such an interpretation either); rather, it needs to be justified through the path of the history of interpretation and the manner of the citation of the OT in the NT (a topic that runs beyond the parameters of the present article).

When we turn to the second half of the book, we find that the political conditions have changed completely, and that the royal hopes of the first half of the book are turned now to the community of God's people in relation to the nations (see Is 55:3). The essential task remains, however: three times it is stressed in Isaiah 42:1-4 that this new "servant king," clearly identified in context as Israel/Jacob (see the similar language used of Israel in Is 41:8-13 as of the unnamed servant in Is 42:1-4), will "bring forth justice to the nations." The relation of the servant and the nations is also the dominant topic in the second Servant Song (Is 49:1-6), while in the third (Is 52:13—53:12) it is also prominent, as the opening and closing verses indicate. As with the anticipated king in the first half of the book, therefore, the main point to grasp is that the figure portrayed whom we now read in messianic terms is defined by his or their role in relation to justice and peace brought to others (in Israel to start with and then internationally) (for sensible guidance on the controversial question of whether the prophet should be characterized as a nationalist or a universalist, see Van Winkle).

At Isaiah 54:17 we have the only reference in Isaiah 40—55 to the servants (plural) of the Lord, and again in this verse the familiar pair of "justice and righteousness" appears, albeit in a varied form: they are promised that they will be vindicated against any who rise up against them in judgment (the same word as "justice"), while equally their vindication ("righteousness") is guaranteed by the Lord. As others have noted (e.g., Jeppesen; Beuken 1990; Blenkinsopp 1997), this verse forms a bridge into the final section of the book, where, as we saw in our introductory survey, there is a more individualized portrayal of the community of God, and where correspondingly the servants of the Lord are always plural—a collection of faithful people rather than a community regarded as a single entity. Thus, in terms of a messianic reading, the focus moves once again under the pressure of changing national and social conditions away from the exilic community regarded in royal terms as the bearer of promise and hope for the nations toward a world in which individuals are responsible for their own condition before God and consequently as a witness to his concern for social well-being.

In these changed circumstances the people are beginning to wonder why all the great promises do not seem to have been realized in the spectacular fashion that they perhaps had hoped for. Nevertheless, the figure in Isaiah 61:1-3 recapitulates many of the characteristics of the earlier messianic passages and emphasizes again that he will come to proclaim deliverance for the oppressed, which was an integral element of justice as envisaged in this book. He seems to gather up into himself many of the tasks that had previously been identified separately, and in that way its use by Jesus at the start of his ministry (Lk 4:16-21) may be regarded as supremely appropriate.

This brief sketch suggests that these are passages that indicate God's purpose for a broken nation and a distressed world. That nation and that world move through all sorts of different circumstances, but the vision remains constant. When Jesus came, he lived in a situation that again was not directly envisaged in Isaiah: an artisan living under oppressive foreign occupation. Christians believe that in that very situation he demonstrated to perfection what it means to inaugurate justice under the constrained political circumstances within which he had to operate. His concern for the outcast, his care for the suffering, and his love for the unloved are part of that work, and supremely, of course, his journey to the cross and his death there fulfilled the work of reconciliation between humanity and God in a way that even surpasses what had previously been envisaged.

This does not, however, exhaust those prophecies. We should not understand their fulfilment in Christ in such a way that we do not realize that the tasks posed for the kings and servants of antiquity remain open and necessary still in the modern world. Justice, righteousness and peace at all levels, from international relations all the way down to those at the bottom of the social heap in our own neighborhoods, have not yet been fully realized. To hear these passages read during Advent or in Holy Week is not to encourage a smug feeling that all that has been taken care of by Christ; rather, it is to remind us that as imitators of him, we are challenged to implement these same costly and tiring values in our own changed circumstances.

See also ISAIAH: HISTORY OF INTERPRETATION; PROPHETS IN THE NEW TESTAMENT; SERVANT OF YAHWEH; ZION.

BIBLIOGRAPHY. *Commentaries:* **W. A. M. Beuken,** *Jesaja 1–12, 13–27* and *28–39* (3 vols; HThKAT; Freiburg: Herder, 2003-2010); **J. Blenkinsopp,** *Isaiah: A New Translation with Introduction and Commentary* (3 vols; AB 19, 19A, 19B; New York: Doubleday, 2000-2003); **R. E. Clements,** *Isaiah 1-39* (NCB; Grand Rapids: Eerdmans, 1980a); **F. Delitzsch,** *Biblical Commentary on the Prophecies of Isaiah* (Edinburgh: T & T Clark, 1894); **B. Duhm,** *Das Buch Jesaia* (HKAT 3/1;

Göttingen: Vandenhoeck & Ruprecht, 1892); **J. Goldingay,** *Isaiah* (IBC; Peabody: Hendrickson, 2001); idem, *The Message of Isaiah 40-55: A Literary-Theological Commentary* (London: T & T Clark International, 2005); **J. Goldingay and D. Payne,** *A Critical and Exegetical Commentary on Isaiah 40-55* (2 vols; ICC; London: T & T Clark, 2006); **G. Gray,** *A Critical and Exegetical Commentary on the Book of Isaiah I-XXVII* (ICC; Edinburgh: T & T Clark, 1912); **J. N. Oswalt,** *The Book of Isaiah: Chapters 1-39* and *Chapters 40-66* (2 vols; NICOT; Grand Rapids: Eerdmans; 1986-1998); **C. Westermann,** *Isaiah 40-66: A Commentary* (OTL; London: SCM, 1969); **R. N. Whybray,** *Isaiah 40-66* (NCB; London: Oliphants, 1975). **H. Wildberger,** *Isaiah 1–12, 13–27* and *28–39* (3 vols; Continental Commentary; Minneapolis: Fortress, 1991-2002); *Studies:* **R. Albertz,** *Israel in Exile: The History and Literature of the Sixth Century B.C.E.,* (SBL 3; Atlanta: Society of Biblical Literature, 2003); **H. Barstad,** *The Babylonian Captivity of the Book of Isaiah: "Exilic" Judah and the Provenance of Isaiah 40-55* (Oslo: Novus Forlag, 1997); **H. Barth,** *Die Jesaja-Worte in der Josiazeit: Israel und Assur als Thema einer produktiven Neuinterpretation der Jesajaüberlieferung* (WMANT 48; Neukirchen-Vluyn: Neukirchener Verlag, 1977); **J. Barton,** *Isaiah 1-39* (OTG; Sheffield: Sheffield Academic, 1995); **W. A. M. Beuken,** "The Main Theme of Trito-Isaiah: 'The Servants of YHWH,'" *JSOT* 47 (1990) 67-87; **J. Blenkinsopp,** "The Servant and the Servants in Isaiah and the Formation of the Book," in *Writing and Reading the Scroll of Isaiah: Studies of an Interpretive Tradition,* ed. C. C. Broyles and C. A. Evans (2 vols.; VTSup 70/1, 70/2; Leiden: E. J. Brill, 1997) 1:155-75; **C. C. Broyles and C. A. Evans,** eds., *Writing and Reading the Scroll of Isaiah: Studies of an Interpretive Tradition* (2 vols; VTSup 70/1, 70/2; Leiden: E. J. Brill, 1997); **K. Budde,** *Jesajas Erleben: Eine gemeinverständliche Auslegung der Denkschrift des Propheten (Kap. 6,1-9,6)* (BCW; Gotha: Leopold Klotz, 1928); **R. E. Clements**, "The Prophecies of Isaiah and the Fall of Jerusalem in 587 B.C.," *VT* 30 (1980b) 421-36; **E. W. Conrad,** *Reading Isaiah* (OBT; Minneapolis: Fortress, 1991); **K. Elliger,** *Die Einheit des Tritojesaja, Jesaia 56-66* (BWANT 45; Stuttgart: Kohlhammer, 1928); **G. I. Emmerson,** *Isaiah 56-66* (OTG; Sheffield: JSOT, 1992); **P. Flint and E. Ulrich**, *Qumran Cave 1. II: The Isaiah Scrolls* (DJD 32; Oxford: Clarendon, 2010);

D. G. Firth and H. G. M. Williamson, eds., *Interpreting Isaiah: Issues and Approaches* (Downers Grove, IL: IVP Academic, 2009); **K. Jeppesen,** "From 'You, My Servant' to 'The Hand of the Lord Is with My Servants,'" *SJOT* (1990) 113-29; **E. Y. Kutscher,** *The Language and Linguistic Background of the Isaiah Scroll (1QIsaᵃ)* (STDJ 6; Leiden: E. J. Brill, 1974); **C. M. Maier,** *Daughter Zion, Mother Zion: Gender, Space, and the Sacred in Ancient Israel* (Minneapolis: Fortress, 2008); **R. Rendtorff,** *Canon and Theology: Overtures to an Old Testament Theology,* (Edinburgh: T & T Clark, 1994); **U. Simon,** "Ibn Ezra between Medievalism and Modernism: The Case of Isaiah xl-lxvi," in *Congress Volume: Salamanca 1983,* ed. J. Emerton (VTSup 36; Leiden: E. J. Brill, 1985) 257-71; **P. A. Smith,** *Rhetoric and Redaction in Trito-Isaiah: The Structure, Growth and Authorship of Isaiah 56-66* (VTSup 62; Leiden: E. J. Brill, 1995); **O. H. Steck,** *Studien zu Tritojesaja* (BZAW 203; Berlin: de Gruyter, 1991); **J. Stromberg,** *An Introduction to the Study of Isaiah* (London: T & T Clark, 2011); idem, *Isaiah After Exile: The Author of Third Isaiah as Reader and Redactor of the Book* (OTM; Oxford: Oxford University Press, 2011); **M. A. Sweeney,** "Textual Citations in Isaiah 24-27: Toward an Understanding of the Redactional Function of Chapters 24-27 in the Book of Isaiah," *JBL* 107 (1988) 39-52; idem, *Isaiah 1-39: With an Introduction to Prophetic Literature* (FOTL 16; Grand Rapids: Eerdmans, 1996); **C. C. Torrey,** *The Second Isaiah: A New Interpretation* (Edinburgh: T & T Clark, 1928); **R. L. Troxel,** *LXX-Isaiah as Translation and Interpretation: The Strategies of the Translator of the Septuagint of Isaiah* (JSJSup 124; Leiden: E. J. Brill, 2008); **T. Uhlig,** *The Theme of Hardening in the Book of Isaiah: An Analysis of Communicative Action* (FAT 2/39; Tübingen: Mohr Siebeck, 2009); **E. Ulrich et al.,** *Qumran Cave 4, X: The Prophets* (DJD 15; Oxford: Clarendon Press, 1997); **D. W. Van Winkle,** "The Relationship of the Nations to Yahweh and to Israel in Isaiah xl-lv," *VT* 35 (1985) 446-58; **J. Vermeylen,** *Du prophète Isaïe à l'apocalyptique: Isaïe, I-XXXV, miroir d'un demi-millénaire d'expérience religieuse en Israël* (2 vols.; EBib; Paris: Gabalda, 1977-1978); **J. M. Vincent,** *Studien zur literarischen Eigenart und zur geistigen Heimat von Jesaja, Kap. 40-55* (BBET 5; Frankfurt: Lang, 1977); **H. G. M. Williamson,** *The Book Called Isaiah: Deutero-Isaiah's Role in Composition and Redaction* (Oxford: Clarendon Press, 1994); idem, *Variations on a Theme:*

King, Messiah and Servant in the Book of Isaiah
(Carlisle: Paternoster, 1998); idem, "Isaiah and
the Holy One of Israel," in *Biblical Hebrew, Biblical Texts: Essays in Memory of Michael P. Weitzman*,
ed. A. Rapoport-Albert and G. Greenberg
(JSOTSup 333; London: Sheffield Academic,
2001) 22-38.

H. G. M. Williamson

ISAIAH: HISTORY OF INTERPRETATION

Isaiah held a prominent place within ancient
Israel, Judaism and Christianity and continues to hold widespread influence in Judaism
and Christianity today. This popularity is due
in part to the scale and scope of Isaiah's vision. Isaiah is the only major prophet to mirror the Book of the *Twelve by addressing
preexilic, exilic and postexilic concerns (*see*
Israelite History). Isaiah's importance for
early Christians cannot be overstated, as evidenced not only by the numerous NT quotations and allusions to the prophetic book, but
also demonstrated by the fact that several NT
books possess an Isaianic narrative or rhetorical structure. The Gospel of Mark opens with
a conflated reference from Exodus 23:20; Isaiah 40:3; Malachi 3:1 and then attributes the
entire quotation solely to Isaiah, demonstrating the prominent role that Isaiah played in
the author's mind. Isaiah was held in high regard in early Christianity because Jews in this
period similarly valued the prophetic book.
Ben Sira describes Isaiah as "great and trustworthy in his visions" (Sir 48:22) and as having "revealed what was to occur to the end of
time, and the hidden things before they happened" (Sir 48:25). The interpretation of Isaiah became a key point of debate between
Jews and Christians, and christological and
ecclesiological interpretations of Isaiah became a means to distinguish the claims of
Christianity over and against forms of Judaism. Early Christians read Isaiah as a "fifth
Gospel" (Sawyer 1996), and it is this view that
dominated Christian reception of Isaiah. In
the twentieth and twenty-first centuries Isaiah has been influential for Zionism, global
peace and ecological movements, and various
apocalyptic visionaries. In biblical scholarship Isaiah has proven to be a flashpoint for
theological debate as well as fertile ground to
explore new interpretive methods.

1. Second Temple Judaism and Early
   Christianity
2. Patristic Era
3. Medieval and Reformation Periods
4. Modern Times

1. Second Temple Judaism and Early Christianity.

1.1. Postexilic Canonical Writings. In addition
to Isaiah being reinterpreted through its own
canonical editorial process (*see* Isaiah: Book of),
writers in the postexilic period interpreted
their present and future circumstances in light
of Isaiah's prophecy. Although Ezra 1:1 identifies Cyrus's edict as a fulfillment of Jeremiah's
prophecy, it appears that the source actually is
Isaianic. In Isaiah 41—45 Cyrus is pronounced
Yahweh's shepherd and anointed one who will
rebuild Jerusalem. The announcement "Yahweh stirred up [*hē'îr*] the spirit of King Cyrus of
Persia" (Ezra 1:1) fulfills Isaiah's prophecy that
Yahweh will "stir up" (*hē'îr*) the Persian conqueror to release Israel and restore it to its
homeland (Is 41:2, 25; 45:13). Given Zechariah
1—8's appreciation for the "earlier prophets"
(Zech 1:4; 7:7, 12), it is unsurprising that Zechariah draws extensively from Isaiah in addition
to other Prophetic Books. M. A. Sweeney has
even suggested that the rendering of the prophet's name as "Zechariah ben Berechiah ben
Iddo" was a deliberate attempt to equate him
with Zechariah ben Jeberechiah, witness to Maher-shalal-hash-baz in Isaiah 8:2. Among the
numerous citations of Isaiah 12—14 in Zechariah 1—2, the verse Zechariah 1:11c, "the whole
earth remains at peace," contains a deliberate
allusion to Isaiah 14:7a, "the whole earth is at
rest and quiet," and suggests that Persia's defeat
of *Babylon was viewed as a fulfillment of Isaiah's prophecy. Yahweh's commitment to "again
comfort Zion and choose Jerusalem" (Zech
1:17) recalls Isaiah 14:1, "Yahweh will have compassion on Jacob and will again choose Israel,"
and reactivates the promises of "comfort" and
"choosing" in Isaiah 40—55. Zechariah 1—8's
extensive use of Isaiah 54 in Zechariah 1:12-14;
7:9-14 demonstrates that the author viewed his
generation to be the children of the once barren Lady *Zion. The allusions in Daniel 12:1-4
to Isaiah 4:3; 8:16; 26:19; 29:11; 33:2; 52:13; 53:11;
66:24 demonstrate that the angel possesses an
authoritative interpretation of Isaiah's prophecy of the eschaton. Daniel 12:2, "Many of those

who sleep in the dust of the earth shall awake," echoes Isaiah 26:19, "O dwellers in the dust, awake and sing for joy," and together both passages make the strongest case for bodily resurrection in the OT. Daniel 12:4, "Keep the words secret and seal the scroll," recalls Isaiah 29:11, "The prophecy of all of this has become for you like the words of a sealed scroll," Isaiah 8:16, "Seal the teaching among my disciples," and Isaiah 24:16, "My secret is with me, my secret is with me." These texts demonstrate that the author of Daniel viewed Isaiah as an apocalyptic work. In Daniel 11:33-35 a community described as "wise" (cf. Is 52:13) suffers on behalf of the "many" (cf. Is 52:14-15; 53:11-12), and in Daniel 12:3 the wise "make many righteous" (cf. Is 53:11). It appears that Daniel possesses the first collective interpretation for the *Servant of Yahweh of Isaiah 53.

1.2. Septuagint Isaiah. Since reception involves interpretation, any investigation into the history of interpretation of Isaiah requires attention to matters of translation. The translator(s) of LXX Isaiah is likely situated in Alexandria near the middle of the second century BC. Scholars generally assume that the *Vorlage* of LXX Isaiah does not differ much from the MT. Such was the view of scholars working before the findings at Qumran, and the discovery of the scrolls has not altered this position. When LXX Isaiah and 1QIsa[a] do diverge from the MT, they oftentimes mutually do so, and they infrequently share readings in common against the MT (*see* Text and Textual Criticism). "Free" translations as well as literal renderings of the Hebrew original coexist in LXX Isaiah, and it is important to acknowledge that at points the LXX Isaiah translator was working with a Hebrew text different from the proto-MT. Since modern scholars do not have access to the Hebrew *Vorlage* of LXX Isaiah, the reconstruction of the Hebrew text and the investigation into the translator's methods ought to be viewed dialectically. What does seem clear is that the author was primarily interested in translating the Hebrew text into readable Koine Greek.

Several instances where LXX Isaiah differs from the MT are due to the translator's inadequate knowledge of the Hebrew text. In Isaiah 7:4 it appears the translator mistook *rĕṣîn* for *rāṣôn* ("favor"), so rather than "because of the anger of Rezin," the LXX reads "when my

fierce anger comes, I will heal again." In other cases the translator finds the Hebrew text puzzling or objectionable and renders the Greek in a manner suitable to his understanding. In Isaiah 26:15 the translator appears to have understood *qaṣwê-ʾāreṣ* ("ends of the earth") as *qĕṣînê-ʾāreṣ* ("rulers of the earth") and interpreted the increase of the nation as a divine judgment. So rather than read as in the MT, "You have increased the nation, O LORD, you have increased the nation; you are glorified; you have enlarged all the borders of the land," the LXX reads, "Increase evils on them, O Lord; increase evils on the rulers of the earth."

LXX Isaiah reflects the social, historical and cultural context of Alexandrian Hellenistic Judaism. An example of this influence is found in Isaiah 59:5, where the Greek translator interpreted the "viper" as a "basilik." S. E. Porter and B. W. R. Pearson point out that the notion of a mythical lizard is a later development, and that the term *basiliskos* is a diminutive of *basileus*, used to refer to an Egyptian cobra. It appears here the translator used terms appropriate to his own Egyptian cultural milieu. In addition, it seems the LXX Pentateuch and other LXX texts were at his disposal and influenced his thinking and writing. In LXX Isaiah 3:25 the phrase is added "and your most beautiful son, whom you love" before the MT's "Your men shall fall by the sword and your warriors in battle." D. A. Baer suggests that this reference to a singular "your most beautiful [*kallistos*] son, whom you love [*agapas*]" is derived from the description of Isaac in LXX Genesis 22:2: "your son, the beloved one, whom you love." Both *kal los* and *agapaō* describe Jacob in Psalm 47:5, and in Isaiah 41:8 Yahweh declares that he has "loved" Israel, Jacob and the seed of Abraham. Baer believes that the translator read features of these texts back into Isaiah 3:25 so that this verse represents an "exegetical nationalization," a manner of interpretation in which Hellenistic Jews privileged their destiny over that of Gentiles.

I. L. Seeligmann advanced LXX Isaiah studies by suggesting that the text does not merely reflect the idiosyncrasies of the individual translator, but rather functions as a communal document of "Jewish-Alexandrian Theology." He believes that the paraphrastic elements of the text reflect "the translator's notion that the period in which he lived was to be time for the fulfilment of ancient prophecies, and of his efforts to contemporize the old biblical text and revive it by inspiring it with the religious conceptions of a new age" (Seeligmann, 128). Seeligmann believes that the translator was a theologian who regarded the Diaspora in Egypt, a community to which he belonged, as the rightful recipients of Isaiah's promised *salvation. Accordingly, the scholar's task is to determine the theological motivations behind the differences between the MT and LXX Isaiah. He then postulates that some of the variance between texts was the result of the translator's own actualizing interpretations of the Hebrew. The MT of Isaiah 11:16 prophesies of an eschatological highway from Assyria for the remnant of God's people, yet in LXX Isaiah the passage for the remnant instead originates in Egypt. In another eschatological highway text, Isaiah 19:25, Yahweh pronounces in the MT, "Blessed be Egypt my people and Assyria the work of my hands, and Israel my inheritance." In LXX Isaiah, however, the blessing falls solely on the Jewish remnant in Egypt and reads, "Blessed be my people that are in Egypt and among the Assyrians, even Israel my heritage."

A. van der Kooij develops Seeligmann's thesis even further by reading LXX Isaiah as a coherent work. He employs what he identifies as a contextual approach whereby he analyzes the differences between the MT and the LXX not merely at the word level, but also at the scope of whole pericopes or chapters. In doing so, the contextual approach investigates whether the Greek text is coherent. For van der Kooij, LXX Isaiah represents a distinct genre in which the prophecy of Isaiah is understood to be fulfilled in the time of the translator. He observes that the Hebrew word for *sōpēr* in LXX Isaiah 33:18 is translated as *hoi grammatikoi*, the only instance of this term in the LXX. He believes that the translator viewed himself as among these scribes who understood themselves to be interpreters of prophecy in the manner of Daniel 11—12, the Teacher of Righteousness in 1QpHab, and Isaiah in Sirach 48:24-25. When van der Kooij analyzes Isaiah 23 according to his contextual method, he finds that the Greek text differs from the MT and forms a meaningful and coherent text syntactically, stylistically and semantically. Whereas the MT speaks about the destruction of Tyre, LXX Isaiah describes

the destruction of Carthage with serious consequences to Tyre. Van der Kooij believes that the vision was written by a member of the high priestly family of the Oniads in response to the destruction of Carthage by the Romans in 146 BC, the Parthian invasion of Babylon, and Tyre's involvement in the Hellenization of Jerusalem. He classifies LXX Isaiah 23 as an eschatological oracle containing *vaticinium ex eventu* prophecies meant to help people overcome national crises.

Baer characterizes the translator of LXX as a preacher whose purpose is to produce a contemporizing exposition with minimal violence to the details of the Hebrew text. The translator consistently changes third-person verbal forms into first- and second-person forms and imperatives that better suit his homiletical aims. His interpretive practices develop into the forms seen in the Targumim, midrashim and the Talmud. Baer describes the translator as a biblical theologian of sorts who ameliorates anthropomorphic and anthropopathic descriptions of God and other texts that would trouble Jewish sensibilities. He also observes a nationalistic bias that privileges Jews over Gentiles in a manner that is absent in the Hebrew text. Whereas the MT of Third Isaiah (Is 56—66) describes an intra-Jewish communal debate, the Greek text focuses on the relationship between Jews and Gentiles. In LXX Isaiah 66:14 the translator glosses *'ăbādîm* not with the more typical *douloi* or *paides*, but instead with *sebomenoi*, a word used nowhere else in LXX Isaiah for *'ebed* and that functioned as a semitechnical term for Gentile God-fearers in the Greco-Roman era. By doing so, LXX Isaiah affords Gentile worshipers second-class status in the eschatological Jerusalem. In addition, LXX appears to minimize judgments against Israel found in the MT. Baer observes that in LXX Isaiah 3:17 the violence of judgment against the daughters of Zion is softened, and in Isaiah 10:22 exile is foreshortened. In Isaiah 6:12 the Greek adds the phrase "after these things" and translates "abandonment" in the MT with "those who have been left." So whereas the MT describes Israel experiencing the judgment of exile, "until the LORD sends people far away, and abandonment increases in the midst of the land," LXX Isaiah describes a postexilic situation where "after these things [the desolation of exile], God will send people [oppressors] far away, and those who have been left will be multiplied in the land."

R. L. Troxel does not believe that the LXX Isaiah translator viewed himself among the *grammatikoi* (Is 33:18) and is skeptical of attempts to describe a method or theology in his work. Troxel's translator is situated among the literati of the Jewish Hellenistic world and influenced by the likes of the LXX Pentateuch translators, as well as Aristarchus and the other scribes in the Alexandrian Museum. His translator possesses no exegetical method or actualizing tendency, but rather works in an ad hoc fashion to produce a translation intelligible for his audience. R. F. de Sousa similarly doubts the existence of a consistent and systematic "theology of the LXX" in his analysis of purported eschatological and messianic texts in LXX Isaiah 1-12. Since LXX studies are a developing discipline, it appears that continued work is required to determine the extent to which the LXX Isaiah translator intentionally interpreted the Hebrew text for his theological purposes.

1.3. Qumran. Clearly, Isaiah held a special place within the Qumran community (*see* Dead Sea Scrolls). Its twenty-one copies make it the third most copied book, behind Psalms and Deuteronomy, and its six pesherim are the most numerous of the commentaries. Within the sectarian writings, Jeremiah is cited four times, Ezekiel four times, but Isaiah is cited at least twenty-three times. Interestingly, no commentaries of Jeremiah or Ezekiel have been found, and whereas rewritten forms of these two major prophets were found at Qumran, such is not the case for Isaiah and the Twelve. These findings indicate a close relationship between Isaiah and the Twelve and also suggest that Isaiah gained authoritative status at an earlier stage than did other books, given its stable text tradition. Based upon paleography, the biblical and pesherim texts have been dated from about 100 BC to the middle of the first century AD.

Working with a three-line gap between chapter 33 and chapter 34 in 1QIsaᵃ and orthographic peculiarities to each half, W. H. Brownlee was the first to suggest that Isaiah ought to be bisected into two scrolls, the first composed of chapters 1-33, the second of chapters 34-66. He then proposed that this division reflected an ancient understanding of the literary structure of the book, and that each half was comprised of seven parallel sections written by two different scribes. C. A. Evans would go on to further develop Brownlee's thesis. G. J. Brooke observes that several copies of Isaiah from Cave 4 contain only portions from chapters 1-33, while several other texts contain portions only from chapters 34-66. These findings call into question the traditional critical divisions of First Isaiah (Is 1—39), Second Isaiah (Is 40—55), Third Isaiah (Is 56—66).

Brooke classifies the interpretation of Isaiah at Qumran under the following types: legal uses, eschatological uses, poetic uses and exhortatory uses. Although legal texts such as the *Temple Scroll* make little use of prophetic texts, in certain cases they employ prophetic writings as a basis for their legal presentation or as support for a particular position. Regarding eschatological uses, the authors of the scrolls believed that the prophets had spoken predictively about them and their contemporary situation. They believed that eschatological blessings and curses were currently being fulfilled in their community and to their contemporaries as demonstrated in their exegesis. The Qumran writers incorporated words from Isaiah into their poetic or liturgical texts, and in doing so they formed new anthological compositions. In homiletical texts the authors employed passages from Isaiah to encourage particular patterns of behavior or understanding in the audience.

"Pesher" has been defined as "a form of biblical interpretation peculiar to Qumran, in which biblical poetic/prophetic texts are applied to postbiblical historical/eschatological settings through various literary techniques in order to substantiate a theological conviction pertaining to divine reward and punishment" (Berrin, 110). The Qumran authors believed that their inspired interpretation or prophecy came about through the agency of the Holy Spirit (1QS VIII, 13-16), but they did not articulate a theory of inspiration. They assumed that God dictated a hidden message to the original prophet that was to be revealed in the eschaton. The author of the Habakkuk pesher describes this process: "God told Habbakuk to write down what would happen to the final generation, but did not make known to him the consummation of the end time" (1QpHab VII, 1-2). Following the citation of Isaiah 5:9-10, the pesher reads, "The eschatological interpretation of the text concerns the punishment of the land by means of sword and famine. This will happen at the time when punishment is visited on the land" (4Q162 II, 1-2). The citation formula "the eschatological interpretation of the text" is unique to Isaiah pesherim and occurs frequently. J. Blenkinsopp observes that the "visitation of the land/earth" is synonymous with the final judgment, and in the *Damascus Document* the final judgment is prefigured in the Babylonian exile as "the first visitation." Taken together, "exile and end time are the two poles around which the thinking of the Qumran sectarians revolves" (Blenkinsopp, 110).

Given the Qumranians' propensity for Isaianic titles and their adoption of exile and eschatology as conceptual foci for the community, it is unsurprising that Isaiah 40:3 functioned as a core text in the *Rule of the Community*, and "the way" functioned as a semitechnical term for their religious life. The members viewed themselves as "the elect of the way" (1QS IX, 17-18) and "the perfect of the way" (1QS VIII, 10, 18, 21; IX, 5) and saw recidivists as those "who deviate from the way" (CD-A I, 13; II, 6). The *Rule of the Community* quotes Isaiah 40:3, "Prepare in the wilderness the way of the LORD, make straight in the desert a highway for our God," as the justification to separate from "sinful men" and migrate to the wilderness. In addition, it defines the "way" as "This is the study of the law which he commanded by the hand of Moses, that they may do according to all that has been revealed from age to age, and as the prophets have revealed by his Holy Spirit" (1QS VIII, 15-16). It goes on to state that they are to continue on this "way" in the wilderness "according to the determination of the appointed time" (1QS IX, 18) when the Righteous Teacher reveals all the mysteries of the prophets. Since the community underwent a process of reform during which it became less hierarchical and more egalitarian, Brooke believes that Isaiah 40 initially functioned metaphorically for the study of the *law with the imminent eschatological expectation of Yahweh's advent. At a subsequent stage the exhortation to "prepare a way in the wilderness" began to carry a literal force, and a later generation interpreted the passage as a command to move into the Judean wilderness.

1.4. New Testament. With some six hundred instances of quotations, paraphrases, allusions or echoes, Isaiah is the single most referenced work in the NT (*see* Prophets in the New Testament). It appears that Jesus' own use of Isaiah in his preaching and teaching led to its prominence in early Christianity. Certainly all depictions of Jesus' teaching are mediated through the evangelists, yet it is noteworthy that within the Synoptic Gospels Jesus quotes or alludes to Isaiah on twenty occasions. In addition, the Gospel writers associate significant aspects of Jesus' life and ministry as a fulfillment of Isaiah's prophecy: his birth, baptism, healing miracles, parables, passion, resurrection, prayer, preaching, mission, salvation and forgiveness. Because of these correspondences, it appears that Jesus himself understood his vocation and ministry in terms of Isaiah. C. A. Evans observes that one of the principal texts that summarizes Jesus' gospel preaching of repentance, Mark 1:14-15, possesses a striking resemblance to the Aramaic version of Isaiah 52:7. Aramaic Isaiah 52:7 reads, "proclaiming good tidings ... 'The kingdom of your God is revealed,'" and Mark 1:14-15 says, "proclaiming the good tidings ... 'The kingdom of God is at hand!'" The theme of gospel and the lexeme *bśr* play a prominent role in Isaiah 40—55, occurring five times (Is 40:9; 41:27; 52:7; 60:6; 61:1). Although it is debated, Jesus' identification with the "suffering servant" of Isaiah apparently originated with him rather than the apostles. Mark's record of Jesus' statements regarding his own suffering and death on behalf of many (Mk 9:12; 10:45; 14:24) fits linguistically and conceptually with the description of the servant in Isaiah 50:6; 53:3-12.

In a manner similar to the Qumran community, early Christians appealed to Isaiah 40:3 as indication that they were preparing the way in the wilderness for the eschatological return of Yahweh to Zion. For Mark, the gospel of Jesus Christ is thoroughly Isaianic, as is evidenced in his introduction: "The beginning of the good news of Jesus Christ, the Son of God. As it is written in the prophet Isaiah" (Mk 1:1-2a). Isaiah's concept of the way of the Lord/new exodus has been deemed the locus classicus (Marcus) or the *Weltanschauung* (Watts) for Mark, and the hermeneutical lens (Pao) or framing discourse (Litwak) for Luke. As such, it is an ideologically shaped schema of Israel's history that functions as a hermeneutical organizing principle for the gospel as well as a controlling paradigm for the lives of early Christians. The quotation of Isaiah 40:3 by Mark functions in an iconic manner and suggests that the inauguration of Israel's eschatological comfort began with the appearance of John the Baptist and Jesus in the wilderness. Included in this prophetic expectation are Israel's deliverance from the oppression of foreigners and the exiles' subsequent return to Jerusalem. According to Mark, Jesus' journey to Jerusalem fulfills, at least in part, Isaiah's eschatological expectations of the way of the Lord. Jesus' travel to Jerusalem along the "way" in Mark is no ordinary journey. In Mark 10:32-34 a technical term for festal ascents to the holy city, *anabainō*, is used to describe Jesus' "going up" on the "way" to Jerusalem, where he will suffer and be killed. Jesus' miraculous healings of the blind, deaf and lame are not unrelated miracles, but rather are characteristic of the eschatological way announced by Isaiah (Is 35:1-7; 42:10-16). In particular, Jesus' healing of a lame man through the pronouncement of forgiveness of sin (Mark 2:1-12) corresponds not only to the pivotal declaration of forgiveness in Isaiah 40:2, but also to Isaiah 33:23-24, the only text in the OT where lameness and forgiveness of sin are explicitly connected.

Prominent themes in Isaiah 40—55 become the organizing principles for both volumes of the Lukan writings, so the quotation of Isaiah 40:3-5 in Luke 3:4-6 not only introduces the Gospel of Luke but also serves to unify Luke and Acts as a continuous work. Luke's use of "the consolation of Israel" (Lk 2:25) testifies to the comfort that initiates Isaiah's salvation program (Is 40:1). In addition to Luke 3:4-6, the texts of Luke 1:17; 2:30; Acts 13:23-26; 28:28 share allusions to Isaiah 40:3-5. In a manner similar to Mark, Jesus' way in Luke 9:52; 10:1, which refer to the journey to Jerusalem, have in view the eschatological return of Yahweh to Zion announced in Isaiah. D. W. Pao observes that the "way" terminology in Acts is rooted in Isaiah 40:3-5 and functions in polemical contexts to distinguish the identity of the true people of God. For the early Christians, the "way" is a means to define themselves in distinction to the dominant culture in a manner similar to the Qumran community. In Acts 9:2 the term functions to identify those who separate themselves from the synagogue. In Acts 22:3-21 the "way" serves to distinguish Paul as the legiti-

mate heir of the ancestral traditions as opposed to those who do not belong to this "way." In Acts 13:10 a person who opposes Christians is someone who makes "crooked the straight paths of the Lord," an obvious allusion to Isaiah 40:3. Luke's quotation of Isaiah 61:1-2, the announcement of a new age of salvation that includes the Gentiles, is supported by the overall narrative of Luke 4:16-30. In this passage the identity of the people of God is a major concern, as well as in Acts 10:35-38, which again evokes Isaiah 61:1. Later, in Luke 24:44-49, the Isaianic program introduced in Luke 4:16-30 is advanced a step further with the introduction of the theme of the inclusion of Gentiles. Pao sees Isaiah 32:15; 49:6, texts signifying the coming of the Spirit in the new exodus, as the backdrop for Acts 1:8. The conversion of the Ethiopian eunuch in Acts 8:26-40 corresponds to the inclusion of the outcasts in Isaiah 56:3-5 and is another fulfillment of the new exodus. Acts 13:46-47 inserts the quotation of Isaiah 49:6 strategically within the narrative to highlight the connection between the themes of rejection by the Jews and offer of salvation to the Gentiles. Acts 28:26-28 contains an explicit quotation of Isaiah 6:9-10 as well as an echo of Isaiah 40:5, "salvation of our God." Taken together, the two Isaianic references in Acts 28:26-28 highlight the inclusive and exclusive nature of the church. The citation of Isaiah 6:9-10 signifies that only the remnant will participate in Yahweh's announcement of salvation, and the reference to Isaiah 40:5 recalls the universal scope of salvation that includes Gentiles.

With fifteen citations and some twelve allusions to Isaiah, the book of Romans, particularly Romans 9—11, demonstrates Paul's sustained interest in the book of Isaiah. Given these numerous references, it appears that Paul, like Mark and Luke, interpreted large sections of Isaiah, along with other books such as Deuteronomy, as proclaiming Yahweh's eschatological redemption of the world begun through Israel. Both J. R. Wagner and R. B. Hays believe that the cumulative effect of his references to Isaiah in Romans demonstrates that in Isaiah 40—55 Paul sees a prefiguration of his own apostolic mission to the Gentiles as well as the rejection of the of gospel by the Jews. Whereas in its original context Isaiah 65:1-2 refers to Yahweh's relentless pursuit of a faithless Israel, Paul reinterprets this passage as a prophecy of both Gentile salvation and Israel's obduracy. In Romans 10:20 Paul inserts the phrase "And Isaiah dares to say" prior to quoting Isaiah 65:1a, "I have been found by those who did not seek me; I have shown myself to those who did not ask for me," as a means of redirecting the original prophecy to now speak of Gentile salvation. In Romans 10:21 he prefaces his citation of Isaiah 65:2a, "All day long I have held out my hands to a disobedient and contrary people," with "But to Israel he says" in order to sharply distinguish this text as speaking solely of Jews. It appears that his self-understanding as the herald of Isaiah's gospel (Rom 10:15; cf. Is 52:7) and his missionary theology provided the hermeneutical justification for Paul to interpret Isaiah in this fashion. In a similar manner, it appears the redemptive drama of Isaiah 40—66 serves as the figural representation of the portrayal of Christ in 2 Corinthians 5:14-21 and Paul's apostolic ministry in 2 Corinthians 6:1-10. Commentators have observed that "servants" function as the main theme of Isaiah 54—66, initiated through the work of the servant in Isaiah 53, who through his suffering produces many offspring (Is 53:10) and makes many righteous (Is 53:11). M. Gignilliat believes that Paul's quotation of Isaiah 49:8 in 2 Corinthians 6:2, "At an acceptable time I have listened to you, and on a day of salvation I have helped you," serves as the hermeneutical key that initiates the redemptive drama of Isaiah 40—66. Viewed in this manner, Christ's reconciling work described in 2 Corinthians 5:14-21 ought to be understood through the poetry of Isaiah 53, and the new creation in 2 Corinthians 5:17 as alluding to the "new things" of Isaiah 43:18-19. Paul's claim in 2 Corinthians 6:4 to be among the "servants of God" demonstrates his self-understanding as a servant of the servant in the pattern of Isaiah 53—66.

2. Patristic Era.

From the earliest days of Christianity, Isaiah was perceived as the "fifth Gospel" (Sawyer 1996). Augustine recalls the occasion when he asked his spiritual mentor what he should read. Bishop Ambrose told him "to read the prophet Isaiah, I think because more clearly than others he foretold the gospel and the calling of the Gentiles" (*Conf.* 9.5.13). The church fathers viewed Isaiah alongside the four evangelists in proclaiming the good news of Jesus to the world. This view is articulated by Jerome, who believed that Isaiah contained all the sacred mysteries of Jesus. Jerome wrote, "I will propose that Isaiah is not only a prophet but also an evangelist and an apostle. Isaiah spoke about both himself and the other evangelists in this way" (*Comm. Isa.*, prologue 18-24). So extensively did the passages from Isaiah prefigure the events of Jesus' life that an early medieval writer, Isidore of Seville, recounted the entire Gospel narrative through the words of Isaiah.

For the early patristic authors such as Justin Martyr and Clement of Rome, the OT had yet to surface as a theological problem and was viewed as the received sacred Scriptures of the church. These fathers stand in close proximity to the NT authors, so when Clement refers to "scripture" or "it is written," he cites OT texts far more often than the words of Jesus. The fathers recognized that these books were not merely documents from the past, but rather living testimonies that continued to speak about events in their day. Since the NT authors cited Isaiah so frequently, the fathers followed suit and similarly adopted it as the most beloved, esteemed and quoted prophet. Initially, Isaiah as a "fifth Gospel" antedated the other four, but as the Gospels, Pauline Epistles and other apostolic writers were elevated to a canonical status, Isaiah and the other OT books were relocated from their status as shared Scripture with Jews to their distinct role as Christian Scripture. In this new context the unity of the Bible became an article of faith, and patristic exegesis reflects this new doctrinal commitment. Two principles generally governed their interpretation. First, they believed that the Bible was a single, integrated book, and that the best approach was to interpret one passage in light of another. The NT and the full revelation of God in Jesus Christ served as the lens to interpret the OT. Second, OT texts contained two basic levels of meaning: a literal or historical meaning, and a deeper spiritual meaning.

Nevertheless, patristic authors believed the literal sense to be as much a part of Scripture as the spiritual sense. Yet because the church fathers often were engaged in anti-Jewish polemic, oftentimes the literal sense became associated with the unbelief of the Jews, and the spiritual sense distinguished Christian faith. A primary concern for early Christians was to demonstrate that they were the heirs of the OT, and spiritual exegesis became a means of doing so. One of the reasons why Isaiah was so popular for early Christians was its popularity within ancient Judaism. The exegesis of Isaiah proved to be a key point of debate between the early Christians and their Jewish contemporaries. Justin cites Isaiah more than any other biblical text, including Psalms and the Gospels, in his *Dialogue with Trypho*. He goes on to interpret Isaiah's harsh judgments against ancient Israel as denunciations against the Jews of his day for rejecting Christ. Ultimately, what distinguished early Christian exegesis from Jewish exegesis was not a particular hermeneutical method but rather a particular hermeneutical event. Early Christians interpreted Isaiah as fulfilled in the life of Jesus and the ministry of the church, whereas Jews understood the prophecy to refer to the reestablishment of a Jewish kingdom in the land of Israel. Varying interpretations of Isaiah 23 demonstrate this difference. Van der Kooij observes that patristic exegetes interpreted Isaiah 23 as fulfilled in two eras: the first (Is 23:1-14) in the sixth century BC, and the second, particularly Isaiah 23:18, in the Christian era. LXX Isaiah, however, interprets Isaiah 23:1-14 as being fulfilled in the time of the translator, and Isaiah 23:15-18 as yet to be fulfilled.

Isaiah as Christian Scripture was read by the church fathers in Greek, Jerome being the sole exception. By the time Jerome attempted to recover the Hebrew text, the church had been reading LXX Isaiah for almost four hundred years and possessed little to no knowledge of the Hebrew language, the Hebrew text of Isaiah, or any of the exegetical traditions based on the Hebrew text. Origen and Jerome were aware that the Hebrew text for Isaiah 7:14 contained the word ʿalmâ ("young woman"), whereas the Greek text uses *parthenos* ("virgin"). Origen writes, "If a Jew should ingeniously explain it away by saying that it is not written, 'Behold, a virgin,' but 'behold, a young woman,' we should reply to him that the word ʿalmah . . . also occurs, so they say, in Deuteronomy applied to a virgin" (*Cels.* 132.168-172). Apparently, Origen was completely dependent on hearsay in this case, since the passage that he quotes from, Deuteronomy 22:23-26, lacks the word ʿalmâ. Jerome does not appeal to Ori-

gen's faulty argument but rather cites an instance in Genesis 24:43 where ʿalmâ refers to Rebecca and demonstrates that the text speaks of a virgin. Cyril, who was aware of Jerome's writings, completely ignores his discussion of the Hebrew and simply assumes the Greek text to be authoritative. Theodoret rejects the Greek translations by Aquila, Theodotion and Symmachus in favor of LXX Isaiah because the former translate the term as "young woman" rather than "virgin." In doing so, he privileges the authority of LXX Isaiah on the basis that its testimony of seventy is greater than that of three. Theodoret argues that since LXX Isaiah was translated prior to the incarnation, it is more reliable than the translation of the three, who possessed both the means to falsify the text, since they lived after Jesus, and the motivation to do so, since they were Jews.

J. D. Cassel demonstrates that patristic interpreters employed the methods of their classical education in their exegesis of biblical texts. The Greco-Roman education system was a three-tiered system that involved learning basic reading skills in Greek and Latin, grammatical skills necessary to understand the meaning of texts and their ethical implications, and the techniques of textual criticism to properly read corrupted texts. Cassel finds that it was the second stage of this education that influenced patristic authors most, since its textbooks took the form of commentaries that proceeded seriatim through the text, word by word and line by line. Origen, who possessed a strong classical education, was among the first Christians to employ these principles in the study of the Bible. His examination of Scripture in the classical commentary form was adopted by other exegetes and became among the most popular forms of early Christian scholarship, as is evidenced by the commentaries on Isaiah by John Chrysostom, Origen (although no longer extant), Eusebius of Caesarea, Jerome, Cyril of Alexandria and Theodoret of Cyrus. Cyril, in his commentary on Isaiah, clarifies tropes, historical aspects of the text, etymologies and analogies, and he reflects the classical grammarian's belief that the proper interpretation of texts required the understanding of the references to history, geography, agriculture, philosophy and science. Nevertheless, C. Kannengiesser observes that their education did not adequately prepare them to engage in literal exegesis. Instances of fanciful etymology and numerology occur in their writings, as well as geographical and historical errors. Since patristic interpretation involved not only the literal sense but also the spiritual, exegesis involved a process of moving from the *gramma* and *historia* to the *dianoia*.

What may be perceived by modern interpreters as idiosyncratic exegesis must be understood within the shared beliefs and practices of the church. For patristic exegetes, Jesus was the Alpha and the Omega, the first and the last, so he brought about the unity of Scripture and served as the key to proper interpretation. Since John 12:41 states that Isaiah "saw his [Christ's] glory and spoke about him," Cyril interprets Isaiah 6:1-13 as a prediction of Christ's incarnation and ministry and of the destruction of the temple in AD 70. In addition, he interprets the threefold repetition of "holy" as representative of Nicene trinitarian theology, and the coal pressed to Isaiah's lips as a symbol for Christ and atonement theology. Just as Isaiah 53 was virtually universally understood as a reference to the passion of Christ, the early church interpreted the march from Edom by the bloodied and vengeful warrior in Isaiah 63 as a reference to the ascended *Christus victor*. The early church also saw in Isaiah validation that the *pax Romana* represented the triumph of Christianity over Judaism. Even though the MT possesses the same preposition ʿal in Isaiah 1:1; 2:1, LXX Isaiah introduces the vision in Isaiah 1:1 as one "against" (*kata*) Judah and Jerusalem, and the one in Isaiah 2:1 as "concerning" (*peri*) Judah and Jerusalem. Cyril believes that Isaiah 1 refers solely to the historical Jerusalem and Judea, while Isaiah 2:1-4 speaks of the church. He, along with Eusebius of Caesarea, goes on to interpret the passage as fulfilled in the political stability provided to the church through Roman conquest.

3. Medieval and Reformation Periods.

The creative appropriation of the combined OT and NT canon by Christian interpreters represented the most important event in the history of Christianity for the first five centuries. Interpreters of the Latin and Byzantine Middle Ages would, by and large, continue to use and develop patristic modes of interpretation. Not until the Renaissance and Reformation would hermeneutical models be challenged and new ones

proposed. For this reason, the focus here will be on John Calvin, an important figure in the history of interpretation, because he engaged patristic, medieval, Renaissance and Reformation interests in his exegesis.

Medieval exegesis was by no means monolithic, as it drew upon the fathers, who displayed great diversity in regard to hermeneutical method. Calvin chose within the medieval tradition the more literal interpretation represented by Thomas Aquinas and Nicholas of Lyra. For Thomas, the literal meaning is to be gauged by the intentions of the divine author, as well as by the intentions and the stylistic characteristics of the human writer. Nicholas went on to uniquely propose a "double literal sense," such that for the first time in literature a NT reading of an OT passage was granted the label "literal." Thus, Calvin inherited an interpretive tradition that saw no conflict between the historical and the theological. He recognized that the Scriptures were written by human authors and therefore employed human methods to ascertain the plain sense of the text.

Although he speaks of the dictation of the Scriptures by the Holy Spirit, Calvin rejects a dictation theory of inspiration and acknowledges that biblical books were composed and edited. In the preface to his commentary on Isaiah Calvin admits his own difficulty understanding the composition of the book. He goes on to suggest a process whereby the prophets wrote down abstracts of their preaching and left them at the temple gates for public viewing. These summaries later were edited by the priesthood into prophetic books. Yet in this whole process, from the oral speech of the prophet to the final form of the book, Calvin never allows for the words of the prophet to be corrupted in any way, even if transmitted by fallible men. He writes, "That these writings have come down to us through the agency of the Priests, whose duty it was to transmit the prophecies to posterity, (though the Priests were often the bitterest enemies of the Prophets), is a remarkable instance of the providence of God" (*Commentary on Isaiah*, preface). It seems that for Calvin, his belief in Isaianic authorship derives not from critical analysis of Isaiah, but rather according to a larger theological framework. Since sacred Scripture contains the very words of God, it is a unique document, so it is natural to assume that its interpretation would also be unique. In his comments on the word "vision" in Isaiah 1:1 Calvin makes clear that he believes that the contents of all sixty-six chapters of Isaiah are the revealed and inspired words of God to the eighth-century BC prophet and therefore certain in doctrine.

Unlike other Protestant Reformers, such as Luther and Oecolampadius, who focused on the christological fulfillment of Isaiah's prophecies to the virtual exclusion of the original historical context, Calvin's exegesis of Isaiah was predominantly ecclesiocentric rather than christocentric. His main concerns were theological and pastoral. He maintained that the text first refers to the historical return from exile, second to the advent of Christ and the church era, and third to the culmination of history in the eschaton. Viewed in this manner, the literal meaning embraces God's past dealings with Israel, Christ's present work in the church, and God's future kingdom, without collapsing these three into a spiritualized interpretation. In Calvin's interpretation of Isaiah 40:1 we see him drawing an application for Israel as well as for the church. He recognizes that this prophecy was not completely fulfilled in the return from Babylon and ought not to be limited to one single period. The NT's claim that Jesus' ministry fulfilled this prophecy (Mk 1:3; Lk 3:4-6) does not nullify its original application, but rather provides greater clarity to it. He observed that consolation to a persecuted people was what united exilic Israel with the Geneva of his day. Calvin writes, "And this prophecy must be of so much the greater importance to us, because it addresses us in direct terms; for, although it may be a spiritual application on what goes before, so as to be doctrine common to both the Jews and to us, yet, as he leaves the Jews of that age, and addresses posterity down to the end of the world, it appears to belong more especially to us" (*Commentary on Isaiah* 40:1). What is striking is that for Calvin, the indirect and spiritual application of the passage is for exilic Israel, and the direct and literal application of this text is for the church. Given that the Scriptures were intended to serve as a theological witness to posterity, direct application of OT texts to the church became for Calvin none other than the literal interpretation of a passage from a transhistorical perspective. Passages that condemned the people of Judah were interpreted

as admonitions to the church to repent of its sins, and the references to Cyrus the Persian conqueror served as the basis for Calvin to appeal to Edward VI to act politically on behalf of the Protestant church.

4. Modern Times.
Modern interpretation of Isaiah has largely focused on issues of composition and aesthetics, and at times these foci have not simply run parallel to each other but instead have intersected in fresh ways. Even before B. Duhm's influential 1892 commentary, interpreters had suggested that not all of the prophecy was written by Isaiah ben Amoz. The Babylonian Talmud identifies "the assembly of Hezekiah and his colleagues" (*b. B. Bat.* 14b-15a) as the authors of the book, and Abraham ibn Ezra's remarks, written in the twelfth century AD, may be interpreted as to suggest a belief in non-Isaianic authorship for the last section of the book. It appears that J. C. Döderlein in 1775 was the first to suggest that Isaiah 40—66 was written by an exilic poet who, he believed, was also named "Isaiah ben Amoz." J. G. Eichhorn, in his introduction to the OT (1780-1783) distinguishes between authentic and inauthentic materials and reconstructs the historical person of Isaiah to be distinct from the character of Isaiah portrayed in the narratives. W. Gesenius, in his 1821 commentary, treated Isaiah 40—66 in a separate volume and attributed these texts to a "Pseudo-Isaiah"; by doing so, he initiated a process by which these chapters would be associated with the exilic prophetic individual now called "Deutero-Isaiah."

R. Lowth's study of Hebrew poetry and his 1778 translation of Isaiah with notes made a huge impact in Britain and Germany. His groundbreaking work to set biblical poetry in verse form, his genre distinctions particularly with regard to editorial superscriptions, his subdivisions of chapters into smaller units, critical notes on the text, and focus on the sublime had enormous influence on Isaianic scholarship. J. B. Koppe's notes on Lowth's commentary were highly regarded and were of great use to Gesenius. Lowth's attention to the sublime and his characterization of prophets as poets had a great impact on Herder, who in turn influenced H. Gunkel with his romanticism. Under this influence, H. Ewald attempted to distinguish authentic prophecy as spoken words and inauthentic prophecy as written words. Duhm set forth a summative explanation of the redaction of Isaiah, much in the manner that his contemporary J. Wellhausen did for the Pentateuch. Duhm's rationale for setting Isaiah 56—66 apart from Isaiah 40—55 was based upon his observation that the former was a more corrupt text, full of glosses and additions, less poetically refined, and degenerated into a prosaic nature. In addition, his romanticism and bias against the law influenced his decision to separate out Isaiah 56—66, which contained numerous cultic references. Just as Wellhausen dated the Priestly source to the postexilic period, Duhm designated Isaiah 56—66 as a distinct "Trito-Isaiah" dated to the same period for many of the same reasons. Conservative scholars such as J. A. Alexander in the nineteenth century and E. J. Young in the twentieth century continued to defend Isaianic authorship and read Isaiah as a prophecy of Christ, but their works largely were ignored by critical scholarship.

Form critics continued the nineteenth-century legacy of dividing the book of Isaiah into the smallest units possible. It appears that *form-critical study of Isaiah began with H. Gressman's 1914 work on Isaiah 40—55, in which he identified various prophetic genres, including promises, threats and exhortations, and also nonprophetic genres. J. Begrich advanced form-critical studies by identifying the genre that he named the "priestly salvation oracle." This was an oracular genre spoken in cultic settings by priests as a direct address, and it included the exhortation "Fear not." In North America, form-critical study of Isaiah by and large evolved into rhetorical critical analysis due to the influence of J. Muilenburg. He believed that a literary revolution took place in ancient Israel toward the end of the seventh century BC in which genres of various works were fused together such that precise genre distinctions could no longer be made. The units of analysis no longer were short passages, but rather lengthy poems consisting of several strophes. Muilenburg influenced scholars to regain a sense of the literary dimensions of Isaiah, not for the purposes of determining its *Sitz im Leben*, but rather analyzing Isaiah as a literary product. His contribution is clearly evident in the works of two influential Isaianic scholars, C. Westermann and R. Melugin.

Toward the end of the twentieth century, scholars began to revisit the issue of unity and probe synchronic and diachronic issues, with particular attention to the final form of the book. P. R. Ackroyd, B. S. Childs and R. E. Clements began to reread Isaiah 1—39 in light of the whole of the prophetic book. Ackroyd observed that Isaiah 36—39 served as bridge between Isaiah 1—35 and Isaiah 40—55, Clements noted how the author of Isaiah 40—55 consciously developed the themes of blindness and deafness in Isaiah 6, and Childs suggested that the mention of "former things" in Isaiah 40—55 was in reference to Isaiah 1—39. H. Williamson, in *The Book Called Isaiah*, offered the most sustained argument that Isaiah 40—55 never circulated independently of Isaiah 1—39 (*see* Isaiah: Book of). He argued that an anonymous prophet wrote Isaiah 40—55 to intentionally supplement the prophecies of Isaiah ben Amoz and, in doing so, wrote portions of Isaiah 1—39 and redacted this material. The Formation of Isaiah Study Group formed in 1991 under the assumption that the book of Isaiah achieved its present form due to intentional literary and theological decisions. Some participants, such as M. Sweeney, explored issues of unity on redactional grounds, while others, such as E. Conrad, approached the topic through literary methods. The synchronic and diachronic study of Isaiah informed, and was informed by, similar inquiries into the formation of the Book of the *Twelve. Childs and C. Seitz pressed the theological implications of Isaiah as a canonical text. They assert that texts within Isaiah were dehistoricized and arranged such that the final form of the book itself is a theological statement. In their view, interpretation ought to focus not on recovering a text's original setting but rather on investigating the theological purpose of a text within the prophetic book and the Christian canon (*see* Canonical Criticism). Investigations into precritical readings of Isaiah have blossomed partly in response to Childs's theological concerns and also because of growing interest in ecclesial interpretations at large.

The growing interest in synchronic and *literary readings, coupled with a growing awareness of the social context of ancient writers and modern interpreters, has influenced various reader-response interpretations of Isaiah. The wide variety of these synchronic approaches can be seen in Conrad's attempt to identify semiotic codes embedded with the text, P. Miscall's reading of Isaiah's poetry as imagistic and polysemous, and K. P. Darr's recovery of feminine themes within the book (*see* Women and Female Imagery). Concerning this last point, it is striking that even though Daughter Zion is of equal importance with the Servant of Yahweh within Isaiah, focus on the latter has by far dominated biblical inquiry. As more evangelicals have embraced multiauthorship views toward the book, other evangelical scholars, such as J. Oswalt and R. Schultz, have responded by defending traditional views of authorship. In Germany, scholars such as O. Steck have continued to pursue diachronic questions through redactional analysis, dating more and more of the material throughout the book of Isaiah to the Hellenistic period.

See also DEAD SEA SCROLLS; FEMINIST INTERPRETATION; FORM CRITICISM; HERMENEUTICS; ISAIAH: BOOK OF; LITERARY APPROACHES; PROPHECY AND ESCHATOLOGY IN CHRISTIAN THEOLOGY; PROPHETS IN THE NEW TESTAMENT; REDACTION/EDITORIAL CRITICISM; SERVANT OF YAHWEH; SOCIAL-SCIENTIFIC APPROACHES.

BIBLIOGRAPHY. **P. R. Ackroyd**, *"Isaiah 36-39: Structure and Function,"* in *Von Kanaan bis Kerala: Festschrift für Prof. Mag. Dr. Dr. J. P. M. van der Ploeg O.P. zur Vollendung des siebzigsten Lebensjahres am 4. Juli 1979*, ed. W. C. Delsman et al. (AOAT 211; Kevelaer: Butzon & Bercker; Neukirchen-Vluyn: Neukirchener Verlag, 1982) 3-21; **J. A. Alexander**, *The Earlier and Later Prophecies of Isaiah* (2 vols.; New York: Wiley & Putnam, 1846-1847); **D. A. Baer**, *When We All Go Home: Translation and Theology in LXX Isaiah 56-66* (JSOTSup 318; Sheffield: Sheffield Academic, 2001); idem, *"'It's All About Us!' Nationalistic Exegesis in the Greek Isaiah (Chapters 1-12),"* in *"As Those Who Are Taught": The Interpretation of Isaiah from the LXX to the SBL*, ed. C. M. McGinnis and P. K. Tull (SBLSymS 27; Atlanta: Society of Biblical Literature, 2006) 27-47; **J. Begrich**, *Studien zu Deuterojesaja* (BWANT 77; Stuttgart: Kohlhammer, 1938); **W. H. Bellinger and W. R. Farmer**, eds., *Jesus and the Suffering Servant: Isaiah 53 and Christian Origins* (Harrisburg, PA: Trinity Press International, 1998); **S. Berrin**, *"Qumran Pesharim,"* in *Biblical Interpretation at Qumran*, ed. M. Henze (Grand Rapids: Eerdmans, 2005) 110-33; **J. Blenkinsopp**, *Opening the Sealed Book: Interpretations of Isaiah in Late Antiquity* (Grand Rapids: Eerdmans, 2006); **M. J. Boda and M. H. Floyd,** eds., *Traditions in Transition: Haggai and Zechariah 1-8 in the Trajectory of Hebrew Theology* (LHBOTS 475; New York: T & T Clark, 2008); **G. J. Brooke**, *"Isaiah 40:3 and the Wilderness Community,"* in *New Qumran Texts and Studies: Proceedings of the First Meeting of the International Organization for Qumran Studies, Paris, 1992*, ed. G. J. Brooke and F. García Martínez (STDJ 15; Leiden: E. J. Brill, 1994) 117-32; **D. Brown,** *Vir Trilinguis: A Study in the Biblical Exegesis of Saint Jerome* (Kampen: Kok Pharos, 1992); **W. H. Brownlee**, *"The Servant of the Lord in the Qumran Scrolls I,"* *BASOR* 132 (1953) 8-15; idem, *The Meaning of the Qumran Scrolls for the Bible* (New York: Oxford University Press, 1964); **C. C. Broyles and C. A. Evans**, eds., *Writing and Reading the Scroll of Isaiah: Studies of an Interpretive Tradition* (2 vols.; VTSup 70; Leiden: Brill, 1997); **J. D. Cassell**, *"Patristic Interpretation of Isaiah,"* in *"As Those Who Are Taught": The Interpretation of Isaiah from the LXX to the SBL*, ed. C. M. McGinnis and P. K. Tull (SBLSymS 27; Atlanta: Society of Biblical Literature, 2006) 145-69; **J. H. Charlesworth**, *"Intertextuality: Isaiah 40.3 and the Serek Ha-Yahad,"* in *The Quest for Context and Meaning: Studies in Biblical Intertextuality in Honor of James A. Sanders*, eds. C. A. Evans and S. Talmon (BIS 28; Leiden: E. J. Brill, 1997) 197-224; **B. S. Childs**, *Introduction to the Old Testament as Scripture* (Philadelphia: Fortress, 1979); idem, *The Struggle to Understand Isaiah as Christian Scripture* (Grand Rapids: Eerdmans, 2004); **R. E. Clements,** *Old Testament Prophecy: From Oracles to Canon* (Louisville: Westminster/John Knox, 1996); **J. J. Collins,** *A Commentary on the Book of Daniel* (Hermeneia; Minneapolis: Fortress, 1993); **Cyril of Alexandria,** *Commentary on Isaiah: Chapters 1-14*, trans. R. C. Hill (Brookline, MA: Holy Cross Orthodox, 2008); **K. P. Darr,** *Isaiah's Vision and the Family of God* (Louisville: Westminster/John Knox, 1994); **R. Davidson,** *"The Imagery of Isaiah 40:6-8 in Tradition and Interpretation,"* in *The Quest for Context and Meaning: Studies in Biblical Intertextuality in Honor of James A. Sanders*, eds. C. A. Evans and S. Talmon (BIS 28; Leiden: E. J. Brill, 1997) 37-55; **J. D. Dawson,** *Christian Figural Reading and the Fashioning of Identity* (Berkeley: University of California Press, 2002); **H. de Lubac,** *Medieval Exegesis*, 1: *The Four Senses of Scripture* (Grand Rapids: Eerdmans, 1998);

R. F. de Sousa, *Eschatology and Messianism in LXX Isaiah 1-12* (LHBOTS 516; New York: T & T Clark, 2010); B. Duhm, *Das Buch Jesaia* (HKAT 111/1; Göttingen: Vandenhoeck & Ruprecht, 1892); M. W. Elliott, ed., *Isaiah 40-66* (ACCS 11; Downers Grove, IL: InterVarsity Press, 2007); C. A. Evans, "From Gospel to Gospel: The Function of Isaiah in the New Testament," in *Writing and Reading the Scroll of Isaiah: Studies of an Interpretive Tradition*, ed. C. C. Broyles and C. A. Evans (2 vols.; VTSup 70; Leiden: E. J. Brill, 1997) 2:651-92; idem, "On the Unity and Parallel Structure of Isaiah," *VT* 38 (1988) 129-47; A. J. Everson and H. C. P. Kim, eds., *The Desert Will Bloom: Poetic Visions in Isaiah* (SBLAIL 4; Atlanta: Society of Biblical Literature, 2009); D. G. Firth and H. G. M. Williamson, eds., *Interpreting Isaiah: Issues and Approaches* (Downers Grove, IL: IVP Academic, 2009); M. Gignilliat, *Paul and Isaiah's Servants: Paul's Theological Reading of Isaiah 40-66 in 2 Corinthians 5.14-6.10* (LNTS 330; London: T & T Clark, 2007); J. Goldingay, *Daniel* (WBC 30; Waco, TX: Word, 1989); H. Gressman, *Die literarische Analyse Deuterojesajas*, *ZAW* 34 (1914) 254-97; P. D. Hanson, *The Dawn of Apocalyptic: The Historical and Sociological Roots of Jewish Apocalyptic Eschatology* (Philadelphia: Fortress, 1979); R. B. Hays, *The Conversion of the Imagination: Paul as Interpreter of Israel's Scriptures* (Grand Rapids: Eerdmans, 2005); R. W. Holder, *John Calvin and the Grounding of Interpretation: Calvin's First Commentaries* (SHCT 127; Leiden: E. J. Brill, 2006); M. J. Hollerich, *Eusebius of Caesarea's Commentary on Isaiah: Christian Exegesis in the Age of Constantine* (Oxford: Clarendon Press, 1999); B. Janowski and P. Stuhlmacher, eds., *The Suffering Servant: Isaiah 53 in Jewish and Christian Sources* (Grand Rapids: Eerdmans, 2004); C. Kannengiesser, *Handbook of Patristic Exegesis: The Bible in Ancient Christianity* (2 vols.; BAC 1; Leiden: E. J. Brill, 2004); Y. Kaufman, *The Babylonian Captivity and Deutero-Isaiah* (New York: Union of American Hebrew Congregations, 1970); B. H. Lim, *The "Way of the Lord" in the Book of Isaiah* (LHBOTS 522; London: T & T Clark, 2010); K. D. Litwak, *Echoes of Scripture in Luke-Acts: Telling the History of God's People Intertextually* (JSNTSup 282; London: T & T Clark, 2005); J. Marcus, *The Way of the Lord: Christological Exegesis of the Old Testament in the Gospel of Mark* (Louisville: Westminster/John Knox, 1992); S. A. McKinion, ed., *Isaiah 1-39* (ACCS 10; Downers Grove, IL: InterVarsity Press, 2004); S. Moyise and M. J. J. Menken, eds., *Isaiah in the New Testament* (NTSI; London: T & T Clark, 2005); J. Muilenburg, "The Book of Isaiah: Chapters 40-66," *IB* 5:381-773; K. M. O'Connor, "'Speak Tenderly to Jerusalem': Second Isaiah's Reception and Use of Daughter Zion," *PSB* 20 (1999) 281-94; T. H. Olbricht, "Isaiah at Princeton One Hundred Fifty Years Ago and Now: Joseph Addison Alexander (1809-1860) and J. J. M. Roberts (1939-)," in *David and Zion: Biblical Studies in Honor of J. J. M. Roberts*, ed. B. F. Batto and K. L. Roberts (Winona Lake, IN: Eisenbrauns, 2004) 387-403; J. N. Oswalt, *The Book of Isaiah* (2 vols.; NICOT; Grand Rapids: Eerdmans, 1986-1998); R. R. Ottley, *The Book of Isaiah According to the Septuagint (Codex Alexandrinus)* (2 vols.; Cambridge: Cambridge University Press, 1904-1906); D. W. Pao, *Acts and the Isaianic New Exodus* (WUNT 130; Tübingen: Mohr Siebeck, 2000); S. E. Porter and B. W. R. Pearson, "Isaiah through Greek Eyes: The Septuagint of Isaiah," in *Writing and Reading the Scroll of Isaiah: Studies of an Interpretive Tradition*, ed. C. C. Broyles and C. A. Evans (2 vols.; VTSup 70/1-2; Leiden: E. J. Brill, 1997) 2:531-46; D. L. Puckett, *John Calvin's Exegesis of the Old Testament* (Louisville: Westminster/John Knox, 1995); J. F. A. Sawyer, "Daughter of Zion and Servant of the Lord in Isaiah: A Comparison," *JSOT* 44 (1989) 89-107; idem, *The Fifth Gospel: Isaiah in the History of Christianity* (Cambridge: Cambridge University Press, 1996); B. Schramm, *The Opponents of Third Isaiah: Reconstructing the Cultic History of the Restoration* (JSOTSup 193; Sheffield: JSOT, 1995); R. L. Schultz, "How Many Isaiahs Were There and What Does It Matter? Prophetic Inspiration in Recent Evangelical Scholarship," in *Evangelicals and Scripture: Tradition, Authority and Hermeneutics*, ed. V. Bacote, L. C. Miguélez and D. L. Okholm (Downers Grove, IL: InterVarsity Press, 2004) 150-70; I. L. Seeligmann, *The Septuagint Version of Isaiah and Cognate Studies*, ed. R. Hanhart and H. Spieckermann (FAT 40; Tübingen: Mohr Siebeck, 2004); C. R. Seitz, "Isaiah, Book of (First Isaiah)," *ABD* 3:472-88; idem, "Isaiah, Book of (Third Isaiah)," *ABD* 3:501-7; idem, *Prophecy and Hermeneutics: Toward a New Introduction to the Prophets* (Grand Rapids: Baker Academic, 2007); M. R. Stead, *The Intertextuality of Zechariah 1-8* (LHBOTS 506; New York:

T & T Clark, 2009); **O. H. Steck,** *The Prophetic Books and Their Theological Witness* (St. Louis: Chalice, 2000); **M. A. Sweeney,** *The Twelve Prophets* (2 vols.; Berit Olam; Collegeville, MN: Liturgical, 2000); **R. L. Troxel,** *LXX-Isaiah as Translation and Interpretation: The Strategies of the Translator of the Septuagint and Isaiah* (JSJSup 124; Leiden: E. J. Brill, 2008); **A. van der Kooij,** *The Oracle of Tyre: The Septuagint of Isaiah XXIII as Version and Vision* (VTSup 71; Leiden: E. J. Brill, 1998); **J. R. Wagner,** *Heralds of Good News: Isaiah and Paul in Concert in the Letter to the Romans* (NovTSup 101; Leiden: E. J. Brill, 2002); **R. E. Watts,** *Isaiah's New Exodus and Mark* (WUNT 2/88; Tübingen: Mohr Siebeck, 1997); **P. Wilcox,** "Calvin as Commentator on the Prophets," in *Calvin and the Bible*, ed. D. K. McKim (Cambridge: Cambridge University Press, 2006) 107-30; **R. L. Wilken et al.,** *Isaiah: Interpreted by Early Christian and Medieval Commentators* (Grand Rapids: Eerdmans, 2007); **E. J. Young,** *The Book of Isaiah* (3 vols.; NICOT; Grand Rapids: Eerdmans, 1965-1972); **J. Ziegler,** *Untersuchungen zur Septuaginta des Buches Isaias* (ATA 12/3; Münster: Ashendorffschen Verlagsbuchhandlung, 1934).

B. H. Lim

ISAIAH SCROLL. *See* DEAD SEA SCROLLS.

ISRAEL

The word *Israel* occurs frequently in the writing prophets, as elsewhere in the OT, both alone and in compound constructions. Yet it is used with a variety of distinct and different meanings, depending upon context. These range from designating the historical individual from whom the nation traced its identity, to the nation itself in the different configurations that constituted it at different points of its history, to a particular geographical location, to a future entity that God promised to bring into existence. This article looks first at the semantic range of the word *Israel* across the prophets (the categories may be compared with the similar list in Scatolini, 6-13), then at what this reveals about the prophetic conception of Israel and how these prophetic ideas find their development and fulfillment in the NT.

    1. The Semantic Range of "Israel" in the Prophets
    2. The Prophetic Conception of Israel

1. The Semantic Range of "Israel" in the Prophets.

1.1. Israel as the Original Ancestor of the People. To begin with, "Israel" can denote Jacob, the eponymous ancestor of the people. In Isaiah 63:16 the name occurs in parallel with "Abraham," referring to the patriarchs from whom the people came. In Hosea 12:12 it appears as the other name of Jacob, recalling the patriarch's journey from the promised land to a time of exile in Paddan Aram. Not all of the occurrences of the name in parallel with Jacob have to do with the original patriarch: in Isaiah the two names often are combined to denote the present people of God (e.g., Is 42:24) and the future people of God (e.g., Is 27:6). Yet the frequent occurrence of the formulae such as the "children of Israel" (*bĕnê yiśrāʾēl*) and the "house of Israel" (*bêt yiśrāʾēl*) reflects a sense that common ancestry from Jacob/Israel is the glue that binds the people together.

1.2. Israel as the People of God Delivered Out of Egypt. The prophets often recounted the early history of their nation, when Israel came out of Egypt and wandered in the *wilderness. That experience formed a pattern and analogy for later generations, demonstrating the Lord's power (Jer 32:20; Amos 3:1), communicating his love and his presence (Hos 11:10; 12:9), revealing his prophetic word (Hos 12:13) and giving them his law (Mal 4:4). Yet both in the past and in the present, the prophets noted, Israel often had rebelled against that experience of God's grace and in consequence faced severe judgment (Jer 2:5; Ezek 20:8).

1.3. Israel as the Tribal League/Alliance That Predated the Monarchy. References to premonarchic Israel after the wilderness period are sparse in the prophets. However, Jeremiah 7 recalls the false confidence that Israel placed in Shiloh, the home of the ark of the covenant in Samuel's day, and the subsequent exposure of this hope as futile. This forms a rebuke to the people of God in his own day who have a similarly misplaced confidence based on the presence of God in their midst in the temple in Jerusalem. Just as the Lord abandoned Shiloh to destruction, so Jerusalem will share the same fate.

1.4. Israel as a United Monarchy. The theme of Israel as a united community is one to which the prophets refer repeatedly. Although all of the writing prophets lived after the division of the kingdom into two separate parts, Israel and

Judah, they often reminded the people that it was not so in the beginning. The two kingdoms are viewed as the constituent parts of one larger reality: they are "the two kingdoms of Israel" (Is 8:14), or the single rebellious "house of Israel and Judah" (Ezek 9:9). The two historical entities are the common realm over which the Lord promised that David's descendants would reign forever, and whose God he would be forever (Jer 33:17; Mic 5:2). For that reason, the Lord can be referred to as "the God of Israel," "the King of Israel" or "the Holy One of Israel" (Is 1:4; 44:6; Jer 7:3; Ezek 8:4). These epithets always have Israel in view as a single, united nation (Kratz, 106), even when the surrounding context distinguishes clearly between "Israel" and "Judah" as separate entities (e.g., Jer 51:5). There can only be one Israel in relation to God.

1.5. Israel as the Northern Part of the Kingdom. As we have noted, the historical reality with which the prophets lived was of a divided Israel, in which the northern part inherited the name "Israel." The prophets accepted this attribution without dispute, referring to the king of the northern kingdom as the "king of Israel" (Is 7:1; Jer 41:9; Hos 1:1). The formulae "children of Israel" (*běnê yiśrāʾēl*) and "house of Israel" (*bêt yiśrāʾēl*) can also be used somewhat anachronistically to denote the inhabitants of the separate northern kingdom, alongside the designations "children of Judah" and "house of Judah" to denote the inhabitants of the southern kingdom (e.g., Jer 32:30; 31:31). The prophets sometimes also refer to this northern kingdom more distinctively as "Ephraim" (Is 7:2; Hos 5:3; Zech 9:13) or "Joseph" (Ezek 37:16; Amos 5:6), reflecting the identity of the largest of the northern tribes. Yet when Amos was accused of being a foreigner from Judah, meddling in the affairs of the northern kingdom, he justified his right to speak there by the fact that it is "Israel" and therefore the territory of their common Lord (Amos 7:15) (Harvey, 108).

1.6. Israel as the Southern Part of the Kingdom. Because both north and south were part of the single kingdom of Israel, the unique nation that belonged to the Lord, the southern kingdom of Judah could also be referred to as "Israel." Isaiah's message was directed to Judah at a time when the northern kingdom of Israel was a hostile political power (Is 7:1), yet the Lord addressed those Judeans, whose capital city had been left isolated by judgment, as "my people, Israel" (Is 1:3; cf. Is 5:3) (Harvey, 162). Writing after the fall of the northern kingdom, Jeremiah spoke of the Lord's plan in the future to bring a nation from afar against the house of Israel (Jer 5:15), which in context can only mean Judah (cf. Jer 18). Likewise, Ezekiel's prophecies speak of "Israel" when it is clear that the southern kingdom is in view (Ezek 2:3; 8:12). In fact, Ezekiel uses "Israel" far more often (185x) than "Judah" (15x), even though his audience was primarily made up of exiled Judeans (Zimmerli 1958, 76-77).

1.7. Israel as Judeans Exiled to Babylon. The community of Judeans who were exiled to Babylon immediately before and after the fall of Jerusalem in 586 BC could also be described as "Israel," indicating the prophets' recognition that these were the true heirs of the title "people of God." This is the group repeatedly addressed as "Jacob/Israel" in Isaiah 40—66, as "the people of Israel" in Jeremiah 16:15 (cf. Jer 46:27) and as "the house of Israel" in Ezekiel 11:15 (cf. Ezek 28:25; 37:11; 43:10). In some cases the exiles represented a broader community of God's people, including those scattered by the *exile of the northern kingdom in 722 BC (Is 49:6; Jer 31:1-8; Ezek 37:21; Obad 1:20). The continued existence of Israel in the form of this exiled community was a significant fulfillment of God's promise to maintain a people for himself until the time when the Lord would bring his people home in a new *exodus from many lands (Is 11:12-16; Ezek 11:15-17). A remnant of both northern and southern kingdoms would return and be reunited once again in their homeland (Ezek 37:16-22).

1.8. Israel as the Judeans Who Returned during the Persian Period. Given this confident anticipation of a return from exile, it is not surprising that the title "Israel" was claimed by those who returned to Judah during the Persian period (Ezra 2:2). In the prophets, this identification is clearest in the headings of oracles given to Zechariah and Malachi ("The word of the LORD concerning Israel" [Zech 12:1; Mal 1:1]). In addition, the sin of the postexilic inhabitants of Judah in intermarrying with foreigners is considered to have been done "in Israel" (Mal 2:11), although in this case the language may simply reflect a frozen ancient idiom for any serious crime (see Deut 22:21; Josh 7:15).

1.9. Israel as a Geographical Location. Given how frequently the formula "land of X" (*ʾereṣ X*) occurs with other names as a geographical location in the prophets, it is perhaps surprising how rarely it is used to designate Israel as a place. "The land of Egypt" is especially common (e.g., Is 11:16), but "the land of Assyria" and "the land of the Chaldeans [= Babylon]" also occur with some regularity (e.g., Is 27:13; Jer 25:12). Closer at hand, there are references to "the land of Edom" (Is 34:6) and "the land of Moab" (Jer 48:24), as well as individual tribal areas—for example, "the land of Zebulun and the land of Naphtali" (Is 9:1), "the land of Judah" (Is 26:1) and "the land of Benjamin" (Jer 1:1). Yet in the prophets, the phrase "the land of Israel" (*'ereṣ yiśrā'ēl*) occurs only in Ezekiel 27:17; 40:2; 47:18. Of all of the prophets, Ezekiel is the only one to use "Israel" regularly as a geographical term; he normally does so by using the phrase *'admat yiśrā'ēl* ("the soil/land of Israel"), which occurs fifteen times in his writings. He also uses the geographical phrases "mountains of Israel" (*hārê yiśrā'ēl* [15x]) and "border of Israel" (*gĕbûl yiśrā'ēl* [2x]). Apart from Ezekiel, the only use of Israel in the prophets to denote a geographical location is Malachi 1:5, which declares that the Lord's greatness extends beyond the border of Israel (*gĕbûl yiśrā'ēl*).

1.10. Israel as a Future Eschatological Reality Yet to Be Constituted. The prophets were convinced that the past and present realities did not exhaust God's purposes for his people. For that reason, "Israel" often appears in the prophets as the designator of a future reality, a renewed and restored people who would be regathered to their former homeland (Ezek 37:21; Zech 9:1) (Zimmerli 1983, 563). This new Israel would finally fulfill the Lord's original purposes in calling a people for himself, which was to create a holy nation and a kingdom of priests (Ex 19:6). Although nothing like that had been seen before, during or after the exile, the Lord had promised that in the future there would be such a dramatic transformation in the people's hearts and lives that an entirely new "Israel" would appear. It would take its place alongside Egypt and Assyria among God's former enemies who had now become his friends (Is 19:24-25). The fruitfulness of this new Israel would mean blessing for the entire world (Is 27:6), just as God had promised when he first called Abraham (Gen 12:1-3).

2. The Prophetic Conception of Israel.

2.1. The Origins and History of Israel. The prophets certainly are aware of the OT traditions concerning the history of the world before Abraham. The Lord created all things in the beginning (Is 40:12-28), including the first human beings in the garden of Eden, who then rebelled against him (Ezek 28:12-17; Hos 6:7 [?]). Ezekiel uses the foundational images of protohistory (storm, spirit, living creatures, firmament and rainbow) to remind his hearers of an originally good creation that was overwhelmingly destroyed because of human sin but still received hope in the shape of the rainbow of God's compassion in the midst of the storm (Ezek 1). For Ezekiel, this story provided an analogy for Israel's (= Judah's) present condition and hope for their future. Although the nation in its present form was doomed, and even a Noah could not save it (Ezek 14:14), the presence of the rainbow around the throne (Ezek 1:28) pointed to a new beginning that could be appropriated only on the far side of the destructive storm of God's judgment.

In the prophets, however, Israel's story more often begins with God's calling of Abraham. Abraham and Sarah were the physical and spiritual parents of the people of Israel (Is 51:2). The Lord called Abraham and redeemed him out of Babylon (Is 29:22); Israel, as a historic individual (Jacob) and as a nation, is descended from this "friend of God" (Is 41:8). As a result, they cannot be rejected utterly by God, in spite of their long history of sin (Jer 33:26; Mic 7:20). The parallel between God's electing grace shown to Jacob as an individual and his electing grace shown to the nation is the foundational demonstration of God's love for his people (Mal 1:2-7). It is this grace that preserved them through judgment that distinguishes them from their closest neighbor state, Esau/Edom, and all other nations. When the other nations were judged, their fall would be full and final, without hope for the future, but Israel must be preserved.

Israel is constituted as a nation by their descent from this historical individual, as the use of the common terms "children of Israel" and "house of Israel" demonstrate. Yet membership in the community of Israel is not merely a matter of genetic relationship: not all of those who are physically descended from Abraham are truly "Israel." For example, those who remained in the ruins of Judah after its destruction by Nebuchadnezzar might claim ownership of the Abrahamic promise, but by their actions they proved that they were not Abraham's true heirs (Ezek 33:24-29). Being part of Israel is not merely a matter of physical descent from Jacob, any more than it is conveyed simply by bearing the physical sign of circumcision (Jer 4:4) or by living in the city where God promised to dwell (Jer 7). Abraham's children must follow in his faith-filled footsteps if their calling and inheritance is to be a *blessing and not a curse.

Equally paradigmatic for the prophets is Israel's early experience of being delivered through the exodus out of Egypt, followed by a lengthy time of wilderness wandering. This past experience of exodus sometimes forms a paradigm for their future deliverance from exile in other countries (Is 11:16; Jer 16:14-15). At times, the initial community of Israel is depicted as having been pure and wholly devoted to the Lord, before subsequently falling into spiritual decay (Jer 2:3; Hos 9:10), while on other occasions, it is described as having been corrupt and going astray from the very beginning (Jer 32:21, 30; Ezek 20:5-8) (Wong, 214). Either way, there is no doubt in the minds of the prophets that the present Israel cannot stand before God in its own righteousness. They are corrupt and rebellious children (Is 1:2), an adulterous wife who has been unfaithful to her Lord (Hos 1—3). They have broken the Lord's *covenant, as did their fathers before them (Jer 11:2-8).

This heritage of unfaithfulness belongs equally to both northern and southern kingdoms: "Israel" and "Judah" are two twisted sisters from the same family (Jer 3:8; cf. Ezek 16; 23); they are two unfaithful households that have rebelled against their master (Jer 13:11; 32:30; Mic 1:5), and each will face its own fitting punishment of *destruction and exile (Ezek 4:4-6; Zech 1:19). That destruction mirrors the fate of the wilderness generation before them, who were similarly judged and destroyed by God's *wrath (Ezek 20:36). The Lord cannot dwell in the midst of such an unholy people; since they have defiled his chosen dwelling place in Jerusalem, he will abandon it, leaving it at the mercy of their *Babylonian enemies (Ezek 8—11).

2.2. Israel's Future. Yet the destruction of Israel that was first anticipated and then realized in the days of the prophets could not be the end of the story, any more than it could have been when their fathers were similarly judged for their unfaithfulness in the wilderness (Ezek 20:13). Because the Lord had attached his name to Israel when he called them, becoming the "God of Israel," the nation would necessarily have to be restored, lest that holy name be profaned among the nations (Ezek 20:14). Even though Israel (in all of its manifestations) repeatedly broke the covenant, and received the punishment that they deserved for their sins (Jer 11:10; 34:18), nonetheless, the Lord would remain faithful and remember his covenant with them. The promises made at Mount Sinai ultimately had to be fulfilled (Jer 33:20-21; Ezek 16:60). In addition, the Lord is a merciful and gracious God (Exod 34:6-7), who had compassion on his straying people (Is 14:1; Jer 12:15; Hos 11:8-9).

That meant that in the days to come, the Lord would restore the two nations of Israel and Judah into a single, reunited body comprising all of the clans of Israel (Jer 31:1; 33:7; Zech 8:13). This reunited community, made up of those from the former northern and southern kingdoms, would submit to a single king, a new David (Ezek 37:16-22; Hos 3:5). They would then repossess the land that had been promised to Abraham. Yet this hope, which is prominent in Zechariah 9—10, is threatened by the people's rejection of the good shepherd that the Lord provided for them (Zech 11:8). The people would be handed over for a time to worthless shepherds, resulting in a disunity completely reversing the sign act of Ezekiel 37. However, the Lord's final word is one of judgment on the worthless shepherd, which leaves open the hope of a restored reunion (Zech 11:17).

The severing of the tie between people and land caused by the exile provided the stimulus for the extension of the name "Israel" from the people to the land itself in the book of Ezekiel. However, the borders of this restored land of "Israel" would not correspond to the accidents of the historical past: the Transjordanian portion settled by the two and a half tribes before the promised land proper was conquered (Num 32) no longer featured as part of Ezekiel's description. Meanwhile, the tribal areas themselves were rearranged into equal portions aligned along the sacred east-west axis of the temple, rather than returning to the patchwork of tribal areas that belonged to Israel's previous history (Ezek 47). Significantly, the central holy city in Ezekiel's vision, which adjoins (but does not encompass) the area of the temple, is likewise disconnected from past history. It is now renamed "The LORD Is There" rather than "Jerusalem," and it occupies a location significantly to the north of the historical site of Jerusalem.

These substantial transformations show that what is at stake in this revised description of "Israel" is not merely a return to the status quo ante. Instead, the prophet Ezekiel is illustrating in geographical imagery the same kind of theological transformation that he earlier pictured in architectural terms in his description of the new *temple (Ezek 40—42) and in legislative terms in his description of the new *liturgy (Ezek 44—45) (Duguid, 549). The fact that upon their return the exiles did not seek to implement Ezekiel's description of the new Israel, even where that would have been possible, shows that they understood his description of the restored land to have spiritual rather than literal significance.

The most important transformation to take place affecting this new Israel of God would be their spiritual transformation into a new people, whose old rebellious and unresponsive hearts of stone would be transformed into new hearts of flesh through a new covenant (Jer 31:31-33). This new people would be changed by an outpouring of God's *Spirit (Ezek 36:22-28). They would be ashamed of all of their past unfaithfulness (Ezek 16:61; 20:43) and would be acceptable to God, a pleasing aroma before him (Ezek 20:40-41). The people who had been rejected by the Lord because of their sins and sent into captivity in Babylon would be redeemed by the Lord. The Lord would once again address them as "my people," for their hard service would be over and their sins fully paid for (Is 40:1-2). The new Israel would become the Lord's servant, the messenger of his good news. Although they were small and weak, the Lord would use them to be a light for the Gentiles, bringing freedom from bondage and healing to all nations, ultimately even to the ends of the earth (Is 42:6, 10).

This anticipated transformation suggests that the regular and distinctive paralleling of the names "Jacob" and "Israel" in Isaiah 40—

66 is not coincidental but rather connects back to the patriarchal narratives (Kratz, 112). Jacob himself received the new name "Israel" after his life-changing encounter with God at Peniel. It was a representation and testimony to the transformation that God had accomplished in his heart. Yet in addition to his new name, he continued to bear his old name, "Jacob" ("deceiver"), which aptly described his old nature. Jacob/Israel was *simul justus et peccator*, at the same time justified and a sinner. So too the postexilic Israel that Isaiah addressed would be at the same time renewed by God, restored to a new relationship with him, but also a struggling and weak people who needed continual exhortation to pursue obedience as well as constant encouragement to trust in God's faithful love for them.

In other words, the new Israel depicted in Isaiah 40—48 is not yet the new Israel that can fulfill the terms of the Sinai covenant and thus bring about the blessings promised by that covenant. Another, better Israel is yet required. This explains why even though the *servant in Isaiah 40—48 clearly represents Israel, the servant in Isaiah 49 is distinct from and more than Israel (Goldingay, 124-29). He both is identified with Israel (Is 49:3) and has a ministry to Israel (Is 49:5). This servant is entrusted with a mission like that of Isaiah himself in Isaiah 6, where the prophet's personal experience of *repentance and cleansing formed a paradigm for the people as a whole. Here too in Isaiah 49—66 the servant takes Israel's place, doing what Israel was unable to do and in that way bringing light and *justice not only to Israel itself but also to the nations (Is 49:6). Unlike historical Israel, which repeatedly rebelled against God and suffered for its own disobedience, the prophetic figure of the servant would be obedient, suffering in silence for Israel's sins and looking forward in hope to the day of his final vindication.

2.3. The Israel of the Prophets and the New Testament. This suffering servant "Israel" takes flesh in the NT in the person of Jesus Christ. From the moment of his birth, he began to re-enact Israel's history, going down to Egypt with his parents so that he too could be the son whom God called out of Egypt (Mt 2:15, quoting Hos 11:1) (Kynes). As Israel passed through the Red Sea, Jesus passed through the waters of baptism (Mt 3) before being led out into the wilderness (Mt 4). There Jesus faced the same temptations that had exposed Israel's rebellious heart (Ezek 20), yet he resisted each one perfectly. As Jesus began his public ministry, he read aloud Isaiah 61:1-2 and declared that the Scripture had been fulfilled in their presence (Lk 4:18-19): he himself was the Isaianic servant upon whom God's Spirit rested. On the Mount of Transfiguration Jesus met the archetypal prophets, Moses and Elijah, to discuss his exodus (*hē exodos autou*), which he was to accomplish in Jerusalem (Lk 9:31). As the new Israel, Jesus perfectly fulfilled the demands of the law: indeed he is the goal (*telos*) for which the law exists (Rom 10:4). The new covenant that Jeremiah anticipated has now been established in his blood (Lk 22:20). Jesus himself is the chosen holy one of God, who fulfills God's original purpose for humanity and submits perfectly to his heavenly Father, thereby personally embodying the new Israel for which the prophets looked.

Since Jesus Christ himself is the new Israel, it follows that all those who are united to him by faith are incorporated into this new community of believers, the Israel of God (Gal 6:16). He is the vine, the classic image for Israel in the prophets (e.g., Is 5), and his followers are incorporated into the new Israel as they become his branches. Because Christ is the living cornerstone of God's house, all those who trust in him and are joined to him thereby become living stones in that house (1 Pet 2:4-5) and can be described in terminology that the OT exclusively used of Israel: believers are "a chosen race, a royal priesthood, a holy nation, a people for his possession that you may proclaim the excellencies of him who called out of darkness into his marvelous light. Once you were not a people, but now you are God's people; once you had not received mercy but now you have received mercy" (1 Pet 2:9-10, alluding to Ex 19:6; Is 9:2; 43:20-21; Hos 2:23) (Beale and Carson, 1030-31). In the new covenant that has been established through Christ the promises of a new heart with the law written upon it that were first addressed to "the house of Israel" and "the house of Judah" now become the inheritance of the church (Heb 8).

Thus, being part of this new covenant Israel is not a matter of physical descent from Abraham, but rather of sharing Abraham's repentance and faith (Lk 3:8). As a result, this new people of God includes Jews and Gentiles together on an equal footing (Gal 3:28), as both are grafted into the new olive tree, Christ/Israel (Rom 11:17-24). That does not mean that God has forgotten his promises to those physically descended from Abraham. By no means (Rom 11:1)! But not everyone descended physically from Israel is part of the new Israel that Christ embodies (Rom 9:6). Indeed, this Israel of God has now expanded to encompass the ends of the earth, as Isaiah anticipated. Before Jesus' ascension into heaven, he answered the disciples' question of whether he was going to restore the kingdom to Israel at this time by sending them out as his witnesses in Jerusalem, Judea, Samaria (the former northern kingdom of Israel) and to the ends of the earth (Acts 1:6-8). This is how the restoration of the single kingdom of Israel under a new David, promised in the OT prophets, is accomplished under the new covenant. It comes as the gospel is preached to members of the former northern and southern kingdoms, together with the Gentiles, who are then incorporated into the new people of God, united as one through faith in Christ (Is 2:2-4; 19:25; 49:6; Zech 14:16-20).

In the book of Revelation John heard the full and perfect number of God's people, individually counted and securely sealed as belonging to God, described as a people totaling 144,000 made up of the twelve tribes of Israel (Rev 7:4-8). Yet when he looked and saw, he discovered that the same group has become an innumerable crowd from every nation, tribe, people and language worshiping the Lamb (Rev 7:9-12) (Beale, 418). They are two descriptions of the same single people of God who have been granted access to the heavenly new Jerusalem, the eternal city of God, a city that itself shows us the vision of Ezekiel 40—48 refracted through the lens of fulfillment in Christ (Rev 21—22). Although the enemies of God's people, represented by Gog, will assault God's people in one last battle, they cannot triumph against them, for the Lamb will fight for them and win the final victory (Rev 20:7-10; cf. Ezek 38—39). The Lord's bride, another image repeatedly used in the OT prophets for Israel (e.g., Ezek 16; Hos 1—3), is the church, who has now been beautifully adorned for her husband (Rev 21:2). In spite of her repeated unfaithfulness, she is clothed in pure linen, without spot or defect (Rev 19:8), finally fitted to stand at her husband's side and dwell with him forever. In that day, God's original purpose and plan for Israel—to have a united, holy, devoted people belonging to himself—will finally and fully be fulfilled.

See also ISRAELITE HISTORY; NATIONS; SERVANT OF YAHWEH.

BIBLIOGRAPHY. **G. K. Beale**, *The Book of Revelation: A Commentary on the Greek Text* (NIGTC; Grand Rapids, Eerdmans, 1999); **G. K. Beale and D. A. Carson**, eds., *Commentary on the New Testament Use of the Old Testament* (Grand Rapids: Baker Academic, 2007); **E. Ben Zvi**, "Inclusion in and Exclusion from Israel as Conveyed by the Use of the Term 'Israel' in Post-Monarchic Biblical Texts," in *The Pitcher Is Broken: Memorial Essays for Gösta W. Ahlström*, ed. E. W. Holloway and L. K. Handy (JSOTSup 190; Sheffield: Sheffield Academic, 1995) 95-149; **R. B. Coote**, "The Meaning of the Name *Israel*," *HTR* 65 (1972) 137-42; **G. A. Danell**, *Studies in the Name Israel in the Old Testament* (Uppsala: Appelbergs, 1946); **P. R. Davies**, *In Search of "Ancient Israel"* (JSOTSup 148: Sheffield: JSOT, 1992); **I. M. Duguid**, *Ezekiel* (NIVAC; Grand Rapids: Zondervan, 1999); **J. Goldingay**, *God's Prophet, God's Servant: A Study in Jeremiah and Isaiah 40-55* (Carlisle: Paternoster, 1984); **G. Harvey**, *The True Israel: Uses of the Names Jew, Hebrew and Israel in Ancient Jewish and Early Christian Literature* (Boston: Brill Academic, 2001); **R. G. Kratz**, "Israel in the Book of Isaiah," *JSOT* 31 (2006) 103-28; **W. Kynes**, *A Christology of Solidarity: Jesus as the Representative of His People in Matthew* (Lanham, MD: University Press of America, 1991); **J. R. Linville**, *Israel in the Book of Kings: The Past as a Project of Social Identity* (JSOTSup 272; Sheffield: Sheffield Academic, 1998); **L. Rost**, *Israel bei den Propheten* (BWANT 4/19; Stuttgart: Kohlhammer, 1937); **S. S. Scatolini**, "On the Elusiveness and Malleability of 'Israel,'" *JHScr* 6.7 (2006) <http://www.arts.ualberta.ca/JHS/Articles/article_57.pdf>; **H. G. M. Williamson**, "The Concept of Israel in Transition," in *The World of Ancient Israel: Sociological, Anthropological and Political Perspectives; Essays by Members of the Society for Old Testament Study*, ed. R. E. Clements (Cambridge: Cambridge University Press, 1989) 141-60; **K. L. Wong**, "Profanation/Sanctification and the Past, Present and Future of Israel in the Book of Ezekiel," *JSOT* 28 (2003) 210-39; **W. Zimmerli**, "Israel im Buche Ezechiel," *VT* 8

(1958) 75-90; idem, *Ezekiel 2: A Commentary on the Book of the Prophet Ezekiel, Chapters 25-48*, trans. J. D. Martin, ed. P. D. Hanson and L. J. Greenspoon (Hermeneia; Philadelphia: Fortress, 1983). I. M. Duguid

ISRAELITE HISTORY

The portion of Israelite history most relevant to the Major and the Minor Prophets (including Daniel) extends from the mid-eighth century BC to the mid-second century BC. In terms of Israel and Judah, the period stretches from the reigns of Jeroboam II of Israel (788-748 BC [all dates for Israel and Judah follow Hayes and Hooker; Egyptian chronology follows Kitchen, *ABD* 2.322-31]) and Uzziah of Judah (785-760 BC) to the period of Greek (Seleucid) dominance over Jerusalem (c. 165 BC). In terms of wider ancient Near Eastern history, the time span overlaps all the major historical periods in the Iron Age: the Assyrian period (c. 900-609 BC), Babylonian period (c. 605-539 BC), Persian period (c. 539-333 BC) and Hellenistic period (c. 333-64 BC)—a time span often designated in terms of the biblical story of Israel as including the preexilic, exilic and postexilic, or Second Temple, periods. The available prophetic materials cluster around several eras within these periods: 750-700 BC (Amos, Hosea, Is 1—39, Micah, Jonah?), 640-570 BC (Jeremiah, Zephaniah, Nahum, Habakkuk, Ezekiel, Obadiah, Daniel?), 539-450 BC (Is 40—66, Haggai, Zechariah, Jonah? Joel? Malachi) and 190-160 BC (Daniel?). The Prophetic Books have played a significant, though often circular, role in study of these eras, with historical reconstructions being used to interpret the prophetic texts, even as the prophetic texts were used as sources for those historical reconstructions.

1. Preliminary Issues
2. Assyria, Israel and Judah Prior to the Mid-Eighth Century BC
3. The Assyrian Period (750-609 BC)
4. The Babylonian Period (605-539 BC)
5. The Persian Period (539-333 BC)
6. The Hellenistic Period (333-64 BC)

1. Preliminary Issues.

1.1. Sources. The relevant sources for the periods of Israelite history related to the Prophetic Books include biblical texts and extrabiblical data, the latter including epigraphical and archaeological discoveries. The type and availability of these sources, however, vary widely among the different historical periods, and their nature and usefulness are matters of ongoing debate.

1.1.1. Biblical Sources. The relevant biblical sources vary in quantity, type and coverage. The principal historiographical writings (1-2 Kings, 1-2 Chronicles, Ezra, Nehemiah; see also 1-2 Maccabees) are driven primarily by theological interests, prioritizing the concern to explain why the Israelites and Judeans experienced destruction and exile. For the Assyrian and Babylonian periods, the OT Historical Books contain two overlapping accounts of Israelite and Judean history: 1 Kings 16—2 Kings 25; 2 Chronicles 17—36. The Kings account is generally considered as part of the Deuteronomistic History, a larger historiographical composition. Some evidence suggests that a first edition of this work originated in the latter part of the Assyrian period, perhaps as early as the time of Hezekiah (Campbell, 209; Weinfeld) or Josiah (Cross, 274-89; Nelson), although it is clear that the composition continued to be supplemented in various ways throughout the Babylonian and Persian periods. The Chronicles account postdates that of Kings, originating perhaps in the sixth century BC but more likely stemming from later with even later revision and supplementation. The biblical compositions themselves attribute some of their material to earlier sources such as the Book of the Annals of the Kings of Israel/Judah (see 2 Kings 15:11; 16:19). The existence, nature and contents of these sources remain uncertain; yet such references represent the biblical writers' consciousness of their own selectivity in the material presented. Additionally, at least some of the speeches attributed to certain writing prophets belong to the Assyrian and Babylonian periods (Is 1—55, Jeremiah, Ezekiel, Hosea, Amos, Obadiah, Micah, Nahum, Habakkuk, Zephaniah), even if the final forms of their books come from a later era. In the view of most modern historians, the prophets are thought to have addressed the situations of their day, aiming to persuade their audience to certain beliefs and actions (see Kelle 2006); hence, their oracles may supplement the materials in the Historical Books by providing indirect information about Israelite and Judean political workings, as well as a more thorough picture of domestic, social and religious affairs (Miller and Hayes, 244). The books also include narratives that often contain historiographical materials, some of which overlap with materials in 1-2 Kings (e.g., Is 36—39; Jer 39; 52).

For the Persian period, the main historiographical biblical sources appear in the books of 2 Chronicles (esp. 2 Chron 36), Ezra and Nehemiah, which tell the story of the return from exile and the rebuilding of Jerusalem and its temple from the late sixth to mid-fifth centuries BC. Additionally, various references and date formulas associate texts from Haggai, Zechariah and Malachi with situations concerning Jerusalem in the Persian period, and a number of other biblical compositions (e.g., the Pentateuch, certain psalms) underwent final stages of editing and compilation during this era. These texts may reveal information concerning political, social and religious affairs in the sixth and fifth centuries BC, but their range of vision is limited almost entirely to the area of Jerusalem and the time between the mid-500s and mid-400s BC. Moreover, a number of unsettled issues complicate the evaluation of the biblical sources for this era, including uncertainty about when books such as Ezra and Nehemiah were compiled, what sources were used in their compilation, and how reliable were those sources.

For the Hellenistic period, the primary biblical material is limited to the book of Daniel, which is commonly seen as achieving its final form in the mid-second century BC, with its earliest roots perhaps in the sixth century BC. The most relevant texts are the visions in Daniel 7—12, but as is the case with other prophetic books, the potential data provided by these texts remains only indirect, often shrouded in figurative language and apocalyptic symbols. The primary historiographical material appears in the books of 1-2 Maccabees, which the Protestant canon places in the Apocrypha. Together, these distinct works, extant only in Greek and with some overlap between them, present a history of events from the beginnings of Seleucid rule in Judah to the death of the Jewish leader Simon (c. 180-135 BC), concentrating on the principal figures and events of the Maccabean Revolt (167-164 BC). The historical reliability of these compositions remains vexed, however, and scholars avoid generalizations and evaluate each episode on a case-by-case basis (Greenspoon, 342).

1.1.2. Archaeological and Extrabiblical Textual Sources. Archaeological remains from Israel, Judah and elsewhere are important insofar as they provide direct, unmediated evidence. Even so, these sources require interpretation because they often lack specific references to people and events. The nature and use of archaeology has shifted in recent decades from a preoccupation with major urban centers and political events to an increased interest in data related to the everyday life of ordinary people in the ancient world (see Binford). These changes have gone hand in hand with more extensive use of comparative sociological and anthropological models.

For the Assyrian and Babylonian periods, important archaeological data have come from evidence at Israelite and Judean sites such as Samaria, Jezreel, Jerusalem and Lachish. These sites have yielded data pertaining to architecture (city gates, walls, etc.), pottery styles and destruction layers. Similarly, excavations at non-Israelite sites throughout the territories of Assyria and Babylonia (e.g., Nineveh, Ashur, Dur-Sharrukin, Babylon) have yielded insights into the workings of the empires and the daily life of local peoples. Archaeological analysis of the area of Judah and Jerusalem in the Persian period (often designated as Iron Age III) remains particularly complex, as the material record does not clearly distinguish Persian-period Judean society and structures from those that existed in the preceding eras (see Stern 1982). Only a few Judean sites from the first part of the Persian period (c. 539-450 BC, known as the Persian I period) provide significant archaeological data, with most major Persian-period sites dating from the years between 450 and 333 BC (the Persian II period) (Carter, 116-17; Kessler, 131).

Some extrabiblical texts from the areas of ancient Israel and Judah have been discovered during the excavations of various locales. With the possible exception of the Siloam Tunnel inscription, these are not royal inscriptions and annals or king lists and chronicles such as one finds in Assyria and Babylonia. Rather, these sources tend to be local and occasional documents such as ostraca, seals and seal impressions, as well as various Hebrew inscriptions and letters, which commonly deal with domestic and economic matters (see Davies). The nature of these items makes them useful for specific questions but limits their significance for broader historical reconstruction.

A large amount of textual evidence from outside of Israel is available for the Assyrian and Babylonian periods. The most important textual data is the corpus of royal inscriptions from Assyria, Babylonia and Egypt. These texts often provide historians with non-Israelite perspectives on events and dates that are mentioned in the Bible (Cogan 1998, 243). The Assyrian Eponym Chronicles, or "*limmu*-lists," for example, preserve a year-by-year account in which each year is named after a key Assyrian official (Akk *limmu*, *līmu[m]*) and records some condition or event that transpired that year, or the location of the army at the end of the year. Assyrian royal annals also report the accomplishments of various kings and display inscriptions record military achievements, often engraved on stone statues of the victorious ruler. This corpus of royal inscriptions contains a number of specific references to rulers and events in Israel and Judah during the Assyrian period. Alongside these official records stand letters, judicial records, administrative documents and religious texts from all areas of the Assyrian Empire. Of special note here are vassal treaties (e.g., the vassal treaties of Esarhaddon from the seventh century BC), which offer a number of insights into the relationship between Assyria and its western vassals such as Israel and Judah. The Babylonian Chronicles, a partial chronological record that provides a year-by-year account of the king's major military actions with minimal editorial bias, constitute the primary source from Babylonia (Grayson 1975). Extant portions of the Chronicles cover the periods from 626-623 BC, 616-594 BC and 557-538 BC. Sources from Egypt during the Assyrian and Babylonian periods often are few and focused on internal political happenings, although some inscriptions recount Egyptian movements into Syria-Palestine (Cogan 1998, 244; Kitchen 1986; Spalinger). The smaller kingdoms in the immediate vicinity of Israel and Judah also provide some relevant textual sources. Two of the most important are the Mesha Inscription, or Moabite Stone (*ANET* 320; *COS* 2.23:137-38), a stela set up by Mesha, king of Moab, in the ninth century BC that refers to Omri of Israel, and the Tel Dan Inscription

(*COS* 2.39:161-62), an Aramaic text apparently erected by Hazael, a ninth-century BC king of Aram-Damascus, which mentions kings of both "Israel" and the "House of David," although the proper reading of the inscription has been heavily debated (see Athas; *COS* 2.39:162n11).

A variety of extrabiblical textual sources exists from the Persian Empire. These texts are of various types, languages (Akkadian, Aramaic, Egyptian, Elamite) and provenance, but only a limited number of them bear directly on affairs in Judah after 539 BC. Critical among texts of the Persian era are royal inscriptions, including portions of the Babylonian Chronicles, the Nabonidus Chronicles, the Cyrus Cylinder (*ANET* 315-16; *COS* 2.124:314-16) and the Behistun Inscription, as well as various domestic and economic records, such as the archive of the Murashu business firm (c. 464-404 BC) (see Grabbe 1992; 2004). These Persian sources may be supplemented by a variety of bullae and cylinder seals from the area of Judah that preserve the names of governors of the province of Yehud in the Persian period (see Avigad). Earlier assessments tended to accept relatively uncritically the favorable presentation of the Persian rulers offered by these inscriptions, especially in contrast with the seemingly militaristic character of the Assyrian and Babylonian Empires (Leith, 285). Scholarly assessment has changed as historians have taken the pro-Persian bias and self-serving nature of the source materials more seriously, revealing a fuller picture of the militaristic and violent actions taken by the Persians when deemed necessary to the empire's goals.

In the later Persian period and especially in the Hellenistic period, some classical writings, including the works of Herodotus, the fifth-century BC Greek historian, and Josephus, the first-century AD Jewish historian, offer important information on earlier events and circumstances in the Assyrian and Babylonian periods, as well. Classical Greek writings (e.g., Thucydides, Xenophon) provide some of the most extensive narrative sources for the Persian period and following, especially due to the increasing interaction of the Persians and the Greeks after the mid-sixth century BC. Even so, the extensively pro-Greek perspective of these writings means that scholars must evaluate their historical reliability on a case-by-case basis in conjunction with other available evidence.

1.2. The Nature and Use of Biblical and Extrabiblical Sources. Over the last two decades the study of Israelite history has fostered increased and vigorous debate in contemporary scholarship (see Moore and Kelle; Long). How one understands the nature, reliability and usefulness of the biblical texts, extrabiblical inscriptions and archaeological remains, not to mention the interrelationship of these materials, is now hotly debated and often dictates the way one reconstructs Israelite history in its various periods (see Moore 2006a; Grabbe 2007; Lemche).

Since the 1970s there has been a growing trend in scholarship to consider the biblical texts as literary and ideological constructs that can be used only cautiously, if at all, as a historical source for ancient Israel. In the 1990s especially the discipline of Israelite history focused almost exclusively on methodological, theoretical and philosophical debates, some of which questioned whether the entire enterprise of the study of Israelite history was seriously flawed. Currently, three primary approaches can be identified:

The maximalist position: The overall storyline of Genesis through 2 Kings is predominantly historically accurate, and the biblical texts constitute an important reliable source for Israelite and Judean history in the Iron Age.

The minimalist position: The character and late date of the biblical texts render them too problematic to be used even selectively as evidence for most of Israel's past. The biblical literature is better understood as an artifact from the Persian or Hellenistic periods, although it reveals little direct information about the critical happenings in those eras. Furthermore, contrary to the impression gained from the OT, the kingdoms of Israel and Judah were modest kingdoms of minimal historical importance throughout most of the Iron Age.

A middle position: Portions of the OT, especially in the Historical Books and the prophetic literature, preserve some historical information that can be used after critical analysis and in conjunction with other available evidence.

The general trend in present scholarship has been to assign the origins of more and more of the materials in the OT to the exilic and postexilic periods (post-586 BC), thus placing them at some remove from the events that they describe relating to the Iron Age kingdoms of Israel and Judah. The typical, but not necessarily foregone (see Provan, Long and Longman), conclusion that follows from this trend is that the biblical materials are less important for historical investigation than the contemporaneous extrabiblical textual and artifactual sources, which at times yield differing or conflicting historical information. Clearly, the biblical texts are a mixture of reportage and interpretation and contain elements (ancient perspectives, visionary reports, folk traditions) that make them difficult to use as historical sources by modern historiographical standards (see Miller and Hayes, 70-79). But the same considerations attend to archaeological and extrabiblical textual sources, the latter also being literary, ideological and theological formulations whose biased and selective character does not permit them to be used uncritically (Grayson 1992, 734; Cogan 1998, 244). Historians, then, must take up specific issues and sources on a case-by-case basis and attend to the importance of clarity and consistency in method. Any reconstruction should make full use of all available data, particularly looking for points at which various sources converge, while at the same time taking account of the literary, theological and even ideological nature of the sources involved (see Kelle 2007, 8-11).

The recent debates in the field of Israelite history have had a direct impact on the question of whether and how the OT Prophetic Books in particular should be used as historical sources. The relevant questions include whether the Prophetic Books can be considered "history" or "historical," what specific types of information about the past one can find in the Prophetic Books and how such information should be used in historical reconstruction, and how the prophetic corpus might aid in writing about Israel's past in ways that go beyond the typical political history (Moore 2006b, 23).

On the one hand, the Prophetic Books contain various historical features that connect the prophetic words to particular events and circumstances. The most evident historical features occur in historiographical narratives that appear in a few of the Prophetic Books, some of which overlap texts in 1-2 Kings (e.g., Is 36—39; Jer 39; 52). At least three other types of specific information about the past appear in the prophetic texts: (1) superscriptions, although the

references found in such texts are often general in nature; (2) imagery that seemingly alludes to historical events (e.g., Is 1:7-9; Hos 5:8—6:6) but often remains ambiguous; (3) incidental (or nonintentional) information regarding domestic life, religious practices and socioeconomic realities (Moore 2006b, 25-27). Considered as a whole, a number of texts in prophetic books such as Hosea and Amos offer particular renderings of history and seem to indicate a historical consciousness that lies at the heart of prophetic theology (e.g., Hos 1—3; 11:1-4; 12; Amos 2:9-11). On the other hand, the features just described do not qualify the Prophetic Books as "history" in the same way that one thinks of a composition that was intended to record significant happenings for future generations. Furthermore, the Prophetic Books share characteristics that present lingering difficulties for their use as historical sources. These include a mixture of the original words of the prophet and the later additions of editors, as well as the symbolic and theological nature of the books' portrayals of historical situations (see Cogan 1998, 243-48). Scholars typically have concluded that the study of Hebrew prophecy can play a supporting role to the study of Israelite history, if one balances these factors.

Recent decades have seen challenges to the usefulness of the Prophetic Books as historical sources. At one level, these challenges point to the composite and literary nature of the Prophetic Books, developed through multiple stages over a lengthy period of time and dominated by poetic and metaphorical language that often remains vague (see Kelle 2005, 5-7; Melugin; Ben Zvi 1996). Even more recently, challenges have placed greater emphasis upon the macrogenre of the prophetic writings as "authoritative prophetic books," ultimately compiled in the Persian period as a way to educate the postmonarchic literati by associating authoritative teachings with prophetic personages and messages of the past (Ben Zvi 2005; 2006). Hence, the function of these books is not historical but rather social, ideological and didactic, and any historical information relates primarily, if not solely, to what the book's final form reveals about its Persian-period authors, audiences and circumstances. The present forms of the Prophetic Books, it is argued, intentionally dehistoricize and deconcretize specific texts, associating the prophet's words only with general time periods (as reflected in the superscriptions), in order to create a lasting application and authority for their message (Ben Zvi 2006).

These recent developments call for theoretical and methodological precision in the use of the prophetic texts as historical sources. Given the complexities involved, any examination of the prophetic texts should take account of their poetic and metaphorical character, as well as the compositional process that produced the authoritative books preserved in the OT canon. Even so, the historicizing references in several books, which explicitly associate some speeches and visions with very narrow historical circumstances (e.g., Is 6:1; 36:1; Hag 1:1; 2:1), and the apparent similarity of prophetic discourse to rhetoric and oratory, which interacts closely with shared rhetorical-historical situations, suggests that the Prophetic Books can be used alongside other sources in the service of historical reconstruction (see Kelle 2006).

1.3. Social History. Traditionally, reconstructions of Israel's past have focused on the political history of persons and events with large-scale social impact (kings, wars, governments, etc.). Many of the prophets' speeches, however, concern domestic, economic and religious aspects of daily life and society in ancient Israel and Judah, especially as they decry personal and societal practices such as the exploitation of peasant farmers, disparity in access to resources, and royal consolidation of land and wealth. These aspects of the prophetic literature fit well with the growing interest in a larger-scale approach to history and a deeper appreciation of social history that emerged in the second half of the twentieth century (see Moore and Kelle). This type of study avoids too narrow a preoccupation with events and examines social changes over a long period of time, with attention to environment, climate, geography and the experiences of common people in ancient society (see Kessler). Social history, which began to find a significant place in works on Israel's past in the 1980s (see Coote and Whitelam), brings together a variety of evidence—texts, artifacts, demography, sociological and anthropological models—to explore such things as systems of material production, relationships between landed gentry and peasants, shifts in economic systems (e.g., from a subsistence agrarian economy to a tribute-based economy) and differing types of societies (e.g., kinship/tribal societies versus stratified class societies). Given the prominence of social concerns in the prophetic literature, an outline of Israelite/Judean political history like the one given here should also give attention to significant elements of social history in the periods under consideration (*see* Social-Scientific Approaches).

2. Assyria, Israel and Judah Prior to the Mid-Eighth Century BC.

By the mid-eighth century BC—the period in which Israelite history becomes most directly relevant for the Prophetic Books—the Assyrian Empire had held sway over the ancient Near East for more than one hundred years. The rise of Assyria was a gradual process that began in the preceding centuries as various emperors developed bureaucratic, imperial and military systems that allowed them to expand control westward (Grayson 1992, 741-42). By the mid-ninth century BC, Shalmaneser III (858-824 BC) solidified Assyrian power and dominance by conducting annual military campaigns and asserting control over territories in northern and southern Syria (see Hallo, 37).

According to the biblical story, much had already occurred in Israel's history: Israel's ancestors had journeyed throughout Mesopotamia, the Israelites had experienced an exodus from Egypt and settlement in the land of Canaan, and David and Solomon had reigned from Jerusalem over a united Israel. The Prophetic Books contain allusions and references, both direct and indirect, to events in these earlier eras (e.g., Jacob [Hos 12]; Moses, Miriam and the exodus [Mic 6:4]; entrance into the land [Mic 6:5]; David [Ezek 37:24-25]). However, the immediate backdrop for the historical periods relevant to the writing prophets was the time of the Omride and Jehu dynasties in the northern kingdom and their concomitant rulers in the south (879-748 BC) (see 1 Kings 16—2 Kings 8; 2 Chron 17—20). The biblical texts concerning the Omrides (Omri, Ahab, Ahaziah, Jehoram) focus almost exclusively on the issue of religious apostasy and the royal house's propagation of Baal worship. The only achievements noted for Omri and Ahab are the founding of Samaria (1 Kings 16:24) and various building projects (1 Kings 22:39). By contrast, the available extrabiblical evidence suggests that the reigns of Omri and Ahab saw significant developments for Israel in both the domestic and geopolitical arenas (see Kelle 2007, 29-33). Archaeology attests building activities at cities such as Samaria, Megiddo, Hazor and Jezreel (Campbell, 220). Other biblical and extrabiblical textual data suggests that the Omrides, while often in conflict with the kingdom of Aram-Damascus, cooperated with and, at times, established dominance over neighboring kingdoms, such as Phoenicia, Edom and Moab (see 1 Kings 16:31; 22:47; the Mesha Inscription). Ahab (868-854 BC) appears to have reduced Judah to a subservient, if not vassal, status and the Assyrian Monolith Inscription of Shalmaneser III depicts Ahab as part of a coalition of western kingdoms, perhaps even as the dominant partner to some of them, which opposed Assyrian expansion in 853 BC (see Kelle 2007, 32-37).

After the death of Ahab, Israel's long-time regional rival Aram-Damascus experienced a resurgence with the ascension of Hazael to the throne (see Grayson 1996, 118). Against this backdrop, 2 Kings 8—10 and 2 Chronicles 22 describe Jehu's assassination of Jehoram of Israel and Ahaziah of Judah and usurpation of the throne in Samaria. The historical details, including the identities of the kings involved and the agents responsible, remain unclear, as the Tel Dan Inscription, a memorial stela of a ninth-century Aramean king (probably Hazael), seems to reflect these events but differs in its details from the biblical presentation. Probably the most significant event of the years of Jehu's rule came in 841 BC, when Jehu paid tribute to Shalmaneser III as a vassal and voluntarily submitted to Assyrian sovereignty (as recorded on Shalmaneser III's Black Obelisk; see *ANEP*, nos. 351-55). Jehu's pro-Assyrian alignment would be Israel's (and seemingly Judah's) dominant political posture for nearly a century and during that time Israel's fortunes would be constantly affected by the struggle for power between Assyria and regional entities such as Aram-Damascus. The tension between pro- and anti-Assyrian sentiments, as well as questions concerning Israel's and Judah's involvement in alliances and rebellions, constitute the focus for some of the oracles of the eighth-century prophets (e.g., Is 7:1-9; 8:5-8; Hos 7:11; 8:9).

3. The Assyrian Period (750-609 BC).

The several centuries of Assyrian rule over the ancient Near East, especially the height of Assyrian power from the mid-eighth to late seventh centuries BC, form the ostensible backdrop for the prophetic messages of *Hosea, *Amos, *Jonah, *Micah, *Nahum and *Zephaniah, as well as portions of *Isaiah 1—39 and *Jeremiah.

3.1. The Resurgence of Israel and Judah: The Reigns of Jeroboam II of Israel (788-748 BC) and Uzziah and Jotham of Judah (785-744 BC). After several years of regional dominance by Aram-Damascus in Syria-Palestine, an Assyrian resurgence and return to active campaigning in the west near the end of the ninth century BC inaugurated a period of national restoration and prosperity in Israel and Judah that would last for nearly fifty years. As loyal Assyrian vassals, Israel and, presumably, Judah benefited from a strong Assyrian presence in the region. The bulk of the reigns of Jeroboam II in Israel (788-748 BC) and Uzziah (785-760 BC) and Jotham (759-744 BC) in Judah witnessed this revitalization. Although the Deuteronomistic History, with its focus upon religious matters, devotes only seven verses to Jeroboam II (2 Kings 14:23-29), even the biblical texts hint at major accomplishments during this period. Second Kings 14:25 says that Jeroboam II expanded (or "restored") the border of Israel northward to the Beqa' valley and southward to the Dead Sea, expansions likely to have been made at the expense of Damascus and Hamath. While some of the biblical claims are not historically substantiated and may be exaggerated (e.g., 2 Kings 14:28; 2 Chron 26:6), archaeological discoveries, such as larger quantities of luxury items (e.g., ivory inlays; see Amos 6:4), and extrabiblical texts, such as the Samarian Ostraca (shipment receipts from eighth-century Samaria), witness to increased prosperity in this era.

When examined from the perspective of social history, this overall resurgence carried some negative consequences (see Kessler). The prosperity of the time seems to have produced dramatic changes in the social structure, likely stretching back to developments under the Omrides and giving rise to an economically stratified society characterized by the emergence of an economic elite that increasingly controlled major land estates meted out by the royal government (see Campbell, 234-35). Israel underwent a transition from a family-based agrarian and subsistence economy, where farmers retained most of their surplus, to a tribute-based economy, centralized in the royal administration in order to meet the demands created by political alliances, vassal tribute and commercial trade (see Kelle 2007, 64-66). In this tribute-based economy, surpluses were funneled to local rulers/elites (patrons) who did not distribute them to farmers, while the royal government created estates through land grants and consolidation and forced local farmers to plant cash crops (grain, wine, oil) that could be used for trade and tribute. As a result, Israel developed more fully toward an "ancient class society," characterized by conflicting groups with oppositional social and economic interests and increasing disparity in access to resources (Kessler, 108-10). Prophetic books such as Isaiah, Amos, and Micah provide a different perspective on the "boom" experienced in Israel during the time of Jeroboam II, voicing apparent objections to these realities of a society divided by economic class (Amos 2:6-8; 4:1; 5:10-12) with resources concentrated in the hands of an aristocratic few (Is 5:8; Mic 2:1-2).

3.2. The Syro-Ephraimitic War (734-731 BC). The prosperity of the major part of Jeroboam II's reign did not last (see Hayes and Hooker, 53-54; contrast Soggin, 229). As long as Assyria maintained a strong presence in the west, its loyal vassals like Israel and, presumably, Judah reaped the benefits of renewed stabilization. Assyria, however, fell into decline during the reigns of Adad-nirari III's successors (c. 780-750 BC; Hallo, 44), and Aram-Damascus began to reassert its influence. Both Assyrian and biblical texts attest the emergence of Rezin as the new king of Damascus, who became the dominant political force in the region after 750 BC (see Tadmor, 187). Second Kings 15:37 and 16:5 suggest that Rezin encroached upon Israelite territory already during the final years of Jeroboam II, and Amos's prophetic oracle against Damascus in Amos 1:3-5, which describes a Syrian invasion of Galilee, may date from this time (c. 750 BC).

The circumstances throughout the ancient Near East changed dramatically in 745 BC, however, when Tiglath-pileser III took the throne of Assyria. He immediately undertook a series of campaigns designed to reassert control over the full extent of the empire (see Tadmor). Given Aram-Damascus's newfound power, As-

syria's resurgence further destabilized relations among kingdoms in the west, especially for long-standing pro-Assyrian vassal kingdoms such as Israel and Judah. Additionally, the resurgence brought Assyria into conflict with Egypt. The Twenty-fifth (Kushite/Ethiopian) Dynasty from Napata in present-day Sudan was attempting at this time to subjugate the Egyptian Delta and to extend its influence into southern Syria-Palestine (Miller and Hayes, 232-33; Spalinger, 358-59; Kitchen 1986, 358-98). These Egyptian maneuverings likely provided some of the impetus for renewed rebellions against Assyrian authority in Syria-Palestine. The combination of all of these factors must have produced turmoil in Samaria over where to place the kingdom's loyalty. 2 Kings 15—17 briefly notes that after the death of Jeroboam II four kings (Zechariah, Shallum, Menahem, Pekahiah) reigned in rapid succession, with three of the four being assassinated after brief reigns, and one (Menahem) achieving a longer reign as a result of loyal submission to Tiglath-pileser III (Tadmor, 69, 89, 107; 2 Kings 15:19-20). Judah under Jotham (759-744 BC) and Ahaz (743-728 BC) remained more stable but still suffered the effects of Rezin's ascendant Damascus (see 2 Kings 15:37).

The tension between the ascendancy of Aram-Damascus and the resurgence of Assyria reached a peak in the years immediately preceding 734 BC. Although Rezin of Damascus is recorded as paying tribute to Tigalth-pileser as early as 738 BC (see Tadmor, 55)—perhaps nominal payments designed to appease—Rezin was simultaneously building a widespread, anti-Assyrian coalition in the west. Pekah of Israel apparently played a key part in these developments, although the chronology of his reign is difficult to establish. Sometime around 734 BC Pekah, probably with Rezin's support, assassinated Pekahiah and seized the throne in Samaria (2 Kings 15:25), but he may have been active as a rival king in league with Rezin and his anti-Assyrian movement as early as the time of Jeroboam II (see 2 Kings 15:27, 37; Hos 5:5 [Kelle 2007, 42]). These actions brought the northern kingdom into an apparent coalition of rebellious states opposing Assyria's hegemony and precipitated a conflict between Damascus, Israel and Judah referred to as the "Syro-Ephraimitic War" (734-731 BC).

Upon Pekah's accession, for the first time in

over a century, Judah under Ahaz refused to follow the northern kingdom's lead and pursued an independent course (for another perspective on the nature of this conflict, see Tomes; Oded). Several biblical texts—most notably Isaiah 7:1-17—indicate that Rezin and Pekah besieged Ahaz in Jerusalem in order to replace him with a ruler who would cooperate with the coalition (see also 2 Kings 16:1-18; 2 Chron 28:1-25). Other prophetic oracles may also preserve theological interpretations of this course of events (e.g., Hos 2:1-23; 5:8—6:6; see Kelle 2005). It is not possible to work out the precise timing and sequence of these events (see Irvine, 95-109), but the attack failed. Tiglath-pileser III moved his forces down the Mediterranean coast beginning in 734-733 BC, subduing the kingdoms that were in open rebellion and ultimately besieging and capturing Damascus in 733-731 BC. The Deuteronomistic History explains the Assyrian intervention by claiming that Ahaz sent a "bribe" to Tiglath-pileser (2 Kings 16:8; but cf. Is 7), but Assyrian texts record a payment by Ahaz in 733 in terms of a typical tribute given after the Assyrians were already in the area (see Tadmor, 171; Irvine, 107-108). In any case, the Assyrians did not move against Pekah of Israel during this campaign. Rather, a rebellion broke out in Israel led by Hoshea in the late 730s BC. Apparently after Tiglath-pileser had left the area, Hoshea captured Samaria, deposed Pekah, and sent tribute to the Assyrian king (2 Kings 15:30; see also Hos 1:10—2:23).

3.3. The Fall of Israel (730-720 BC). Tiglath-pileser III died on campaign in 727 BC. Either just before or immediately upon his death, rebellion broke out in the west, and Tiglath-pileser's son and successor Shalmaneser V extended his father's campaign in that direction. These events inaugurated a protracted period of antagonism between Israel and Assyria that led to the end of the northern kingdom's existence as a political entity by 720 BC. The events and chronology of this period, however, are extremely complex and remain debated. The primary biblical text for this era, 2 Kings 17:1-6, provides several pieces of information that are difficult to correlate and seems to condense multiple events into a succinct theological explanation that attributes the fall of Israel to divine punishment for the abandonment of Yahweh. For example, 2 Kings 17:4 highlights a

rebellion by Hoshea during the beginning years of Shalmaneser V's reign in which Hoshea appealed for help to "King So" of Egypt, whose identity remains in dispute (see Redford, 346-47; Spalinger, 359; Kitchen 1986, 374-75). Likewise, the Assyrian texts are unclear concerning which king conquered Samaria and when. Although there are no surviving inscriptions of Shalmaneser V, the Babylonian Chronicles attribute a capture of Samaria to him sometime prior to the year 722 BC (see Grayson 1975, 10; Kelle 2002, 662; contra Younger, 466). Several Assyrian inscriptions of his successor, Sargon II, however, claim that he captured Samaria sometime around 720 BC as part of a campaign against Hamath (see *COS* 2.118A: 293-94; 2.118D: 295-96; 2.118E: 296-97). Scholars have explained the confusing biblical and extrabiblical references to the capture of Samaria in numerous ways, with proposals ranging from one destruction claimed by two different kings to as many as four separate captures under various circumstances (cf. Younger; Becking; Hayes and Kuan; see the references to political turmoil in Hos 8—13).

Whatever the precise course of events, Sargon II imposed lasting provincial status upon the northern kingdom in 720 BC. An Assyrian governor assumed control of the area, a significant number of the population were deported, and foreign peoples were forcibly relocated into their place (2 Kings 17:6, 24). Sargon himself claims to have captured over 27,000 Israelites and there are archaeological indications of destruction at northern cities such as Tirzah, Shechem, and Samaria (Campbell, 239). One by-product of this destruction may have been the flight of portions of the north's population to the south, perhaps bringing some of their traditions with them. This migration could perhaps explain the preservation of textual traditions with northern origins, possibly including those that later became the book of Hosea. It would be a mistake to assume, however, that the territory and population of the former northern kingdom ceased to be of any significance for the remainder of the Iron Age. Recent studies have increasingly concluded that the destruction and population transfers of the late eighth century BC were localized and temporary in their effects, and there was an ongoing presence in the area of a people with ethnic and religious continuity to their predecessors in the northern kingdom (Tappy; Knoppers).

3.4. The Reign of Hezekiah of Judah (727-699 BC).

3.4.1. Initial Expansion under Assyria (720-714 BC). Hezekiah inherited the throne in Judah (2 Kings 18:1) at the beginning of the turbulent years that led to the final destruction of the northern kingdom (c. 730-720 BC). It does not appear, however, that Judah became involved in the anti-Assyrian rebellions that marked this period. Biblical texts make no mention of Hezekiah in this regard, and the scattered references to Judah in Assyrian texts before 712 BC record a Judean tribute payment and give no indication of rebellious activity (see Dalley, 388). One Assyrian letter thought to date to about 715 BC may even mention a contingent of Judean troops fighting alongside Assyrian troops in Urartu (Dalley, 388).

Assyrian kings frequently rewarded kingdoms that remained loyal in the midst of nearby rebellions by giving them expanded territory taken from rebels. While the primary biblical materials about Hezekiah (2 Kings 18—20; 2 Chron 29—32; Is 36—39) focus on religious reforms, the period immediately after the fall of the northern kingdom (720-714 BC) was a time of political ascendancy and expansion for Judah within the Assyrian system, perhaps due to Hezekiah's consistent loyalty. Archaeological evidence from Jerusalem and its environs indicates the emergence of new settlements and the expansion of the capital city to nearly three times its previous size (Cogan 1998, 246; Finkelstein and Silberman, 243). Also in this time, Sargon II opened a cooperative trade relationship with the Egyptian rulers in the Nile Delta (against the Ethiopians of the Twenty-Fifth Dynasty) and expanded the border of Assyrian territory in the southwestern corner of the empire further south of Gaza to the Wadi el-'Arish, events perhaps reflected in the hopeful oracle concerning Egypt in Isaiah 19 (see *COS* 2.1118D:296; Kitchen 1986, 375-76; Spalinger, 359). Coincidentally, 2 Kings 18:8 says that Hezekiah also expanded Judean territory as far as Gaza. Taken together, these indications raise the possibility that the years between 720 and 714 BC represent the height of Judean power, as Judah at least bordered the territory that was the primary area of Assyria's expansion and perhaps received Sargon II's appointment to supervise this vicinity.

3.4.2. The Ashdod Revolt (714-712 BC). The biblical texts that describe Hezekiah's reign jump immediately from his accession and reforms to his confrontation with the Assyrian king Sennacherib in 701 BC. Assyrian inscriptions, however, point to Judah's participation in an earlier anti-Assyrian revolt. Sargon II's annals and other inscriptions report that a rebellion broke out in Syria-Palestine in 714 BC while the emperor was occupied in Urartu (*COS* 2.118A:293; 2.118E:296; 2.118F:297). This revolt, led by the usurper Yamani of Ashdod, included other kingdoms such as Philistia, Edom and Moab (see *ANET* 287). The rebels appealed for help, at least according to the Assyrian accounts, to an Egyptian Pharaoh, probably the Ethiopian Shabako (716-702 BC), who had invaded the delta in 715 BC (Kitchen 1986, 380; Spalinger, 359). Inspiration may also have come from Babylon, where Merodach-baladan had wrested control away from Assyria near the beginning of Sargon II's reign in 721 BC. Sometime in either 712 or 711 BC (Sargon's annals and prisms do not match) the Assyrians moved west to put down the Ashdod revolt. Yamani fled to Egypt, where the Egyptian king turned him over to Assyria (see *COS* 2.118J:300), and Sargon made Ashdod into a province.

The OT Historical Books make no mention of the Ashdod revolt. One of Sargon's inscriptions, however, specifically lists Judah as a participant (see *ANET* 287), yet curiously does not name Hezekiah. Given the fact that Hezekiah had remained loyal to Assyria for more than a decade, and apparently reaped political and economic benefits as a result, it is difficult to imagine how and why he would have become involved. The Prophetic Books, which contain the Bible's only explicit witness to these events, may suggest a possible explanation. The prophetic narrative in Isaiah 20 refers to the affair but does not state directly that Judah was involved. Yet, several elements of the biblical presentation of Hezekiah's reign that are placed by Kings, Chronicles and Isaiah in the later context of Sennacherib's invasion in 701 BC seem to fit better with the earlier Ashdod revolt. For instance, 2 Kings 18:13 and Isaiah 36:1 identify Hezekiah's "fourteenth year" as the time of Sennacherib's invasion in 701 BC. If this reference is not an indication of the need to down-date Hezekiah's accession or posit some kind of co-regency, Hezekiah's fourteenth year would be not 701 BC but 714 BC, a date that corresponds nicely with the Ashdod revolt (cf. 2 Kings 18:10's equation of the fall of Samaria in 722 BC with Hezekiah's sixth year). Likewise, the story of Hezekiah's life-threatening illness, which 2 Kings 20, 2 Chronicles 32 and Isaiah 38 place in the context of 701 BC, promises Hezekiah fifteen additional years of rule (2 Kings 20:6), a reference that makes more sense if these years are added to his fourteenth year (see 2 Kings 18:2, which assigns Hezekiah's reign a total of twenty-nine years).

Given the failure of the Assyrian texts to name Hezekiah, the likely dating of the king's life-threatening illness to around 714 BC, if correct, suggests the possibility that Hezekiah became incapacitated and turned the leadership of the kingdom over to his chief officials, who in turn threw Judah's lot in with Yamani. The prophetic oracle in Isaiah 22, which occurs in a broader context that references the Ashdod revolt (Is 20:1), may provide a fuller picture, as the prophet condemns Shebna, called the "master of the household" (Is 22:15; see also Jotham in 2 Kings 15:5) (see Goldberg). There is conflicting evidence as to the results of Judah's participation and Assyrian reprisals. Sargon's annals refer only to the capture and provincialization of Ashdod, but some evidence may be construed as reporting the destruction of certain Judean territories (e.g., Azekah [see *COS* 2.119D:304-305; Goldberg]). In any case, Hezekiah, perhaps after recovering and reversing his officials' actions, remained on the throne but surely lost the favored status and expanded territory that he had possessed.

3.4.3. Sennacherib's Invasion of Judah (701 BC). In 705 BC Sargon II died on the battlefield in Anatolia, and rebellions broke out throughout the empire. The new Assyrian ruler, Sennacherib (704-681 BC), struggled to subdue revolts in the east throughout his first few years. In the west, Hezekiah, perhaps motivated by the Assyrian reprisals taken against his kingdom in 712-711 BC, became the ringleader of a rebellion that included Sidon, Ekron and Ashkelon (see *COS* 2.119B:302-303; Gallagher, 255). Textual and archaeological evidence indicates that Hezekiah undertook a series of preparations in anticipation of his revolt and Assyria's reactions (Vaughn). These preparations focused on military organization, supply and defense (e.g., 2 Chron 32:5-6) (Finkelstein and Silberman,

255-57). Perhaps most noteworthy were the construction of a new segment of the city wall around Jerusalem (the so-called Broad Wall), as well as the Siloam Tunnel, cut through the rock to bring water into Jerusalem and bearing an inscription that describes the digging process (see Cogan 1998, 250; contrast Dalley), and the use of numerous storage jars stamped with the seal *lmlk* ("belonging to the king"), found primarily in the southwestern corner of Judah and serving apparently as a system for shipping supplies.

Sennacherib's response came in 701 BC. This invasion is the most well-documented event in Judean history, with numerous biblical and extrabiblical texts, as well as archaeological remains, witnessing to the affair. As a result, the general course of events is clear (see Gallagher). After putting down the revolts in the east, Sennacherib moved down the Mediterranean coast, captured cities in Phoenicia and Philistia, and turned back an Egyptian force at Eltekeh. He then directed his forces against Judah. Sennacherib's inscriptions attest to the massive destruction that he inflicted upon Judean territory (perhaps described in Is 1:7-9; Mic 1:8-16). He claims to have captured forty-six fortified cities and deported 200,150 people (but see De Odorico). Archaeological remains demonstrate that the Judean city of Lachish suffered the most extensive damage, and a wall relief in Sennacherib's palace in Nineveh gives a graphic depiction of the battle for the city.

What remains unclear, however, is the precise course of events involved in the final outcome of the invasion, specifically concerning Jerusalem. The biblical account in 2 Kings 18—19 (paralleled in 2 Chron 32; Is 36—37) consists of several different traditions that have now been combined, providing varying descriptions that cannot easily be reconciled (see Evans; Gallagher, 145): (1) Hezekiah's surrender and payment of tribute (2 Kings 18:13-16); (2) Sennacherib's withdrawal under threat from elsewhere (2 Kings 19:7, 9a, 36-37; Is 36:2—37:9a, 37-38); (3) Yahweh's miraculous killing of 185,000 Assyrians in a single night (2 Kings 19:9b-35; Is 37:9b-36). Numerous attempts have been made to untangle these references and establish their connections with Assyrian and other extrabiblical texts (e.g., comparisons with Herodotus, *Hist.* 2.141). Due to the confusing nature of the sources, it seems likely that the specific details of the affair will remain unclear. Even so, the available evidence points to the interpretation that Hezekiah submitted and paid tribute to Assyria, but for some reason, Sennacherib relented from the siege without taking Jerusalem and allowed Hezekiah to remain on the throne (see Dalley). Still, the land of Judah as a whole was decimated by the invasion. Along with the destroyed cities and deported peoples, Sennacherib redistributed parts of Judean territory into the control of Philistine kingdoms such as Ashdod and Ekron (Cogan 1998, 252).

3.5. Judah as an Assyrian Vassal: The Reign of Manasseh (698-644 BC). The corpus of OT prophetic literature attributes no surviving prophetic voices to the years from around 700 to 640 BC, a period that covers the reigns of Manasseh (698-644 BC) and Amon (643-642 BC), as well as the first part of the reign of Josiah (641-610 BC). Even the accounts of Manasseh and Amon in the OT Historical Books (2 Kings 21; 2 Chron 33) are sparse, largely passing over the first half of the seventh century BC except to theologize about the kings' apostate practices. Manasseh inherited a Judean kingdom in dire straits after the events of 701 BC. Surveys of sites in the Shephelah indicate that 85 percent of the eighth-century BC settlements were abandoned and not reoccupied in the seventh century BC (Faust). These historical realities, especially when combined with the biblical presentations, yield the impression that Judah under Manasseh was merely a marginal and depressed Assyrian vassal. Historians throughout the twentieth century often have followed this impression and downplayed any importance of Manasseh's time (e.g., Provan, Long and Longman, 274-75). Recent works, however, have pointed to other evidence that suggests significant domestic and economic recovery took place under Manasseh. Archaeological evidence from throughout the whole of Manasseh's time suggests a recovery that featured rebuilding in Jerusalem, expansion into other areas, and participation in the commerce of the Assyrian Empire, leading some current scholars to conclude that the time of Manasseh was, in fact, the peak of settlement and development in the history of the southern kingdom (e.g., Faust).

In the wider context, during Manasseh's reign the Assyrian Empire reached the height of its power under Esarhaddon and Ashurbanipal, and some later prophetic texts contain allusions to events that took place in these years. This power was especially marked by a series of offensive campaigns against Egypt (679, 673, 671, 669-668 BC), culminating with Ashurbanipal's capture of Memphis and destruction of Thebes in 664 BC (see the retrospective reference to the destruction of Thebes [called "No-amon"] in Nah 3:8) (see Kitchen 1986, 394). In the course of these events, Manasseh is mentioned only in passing in Assyrian texts as a loyal vassal who provided building materials to Esarhaddon and contributed troops to Ashurbanipal's invasion of Egypt in 668 BC (*ANET* 291, 294; but cf. 2 Chron 33:10-17, whose historicity remains disputed). Yet, perhaps the most important facet of these years for the study of the prophetic literature is religious. As noted above, the biblical texts demonize Manasseh by telling how he sponsored apostate and idolatrous forms of worship (2 Kings 21:1-9), practices that may be reflected in the criticisms of prophets from later periods (e.g., Zeph 1:4-6). Some interpreters attribute these developments to an Assyrian imposition of their religious practices on vassals such as Manasseh (Spieckermann), but others have maintained that typical Assyrian imperial relations do not support this conclusion (McKay; Cogan 1974). It is more likely that Manasseh's propagation of unorthodox worship, while probably reflecting Assyrian influence, was a voluntary syncretism that also revived older religious practices from the time before Hezekiah's reforms.

3.6. The End of the Assyrian Empire: The Reign of Josiah (641-610 BC). When Josiah ascended the Judean throne in 641 BC, Assyria had entered a downward spiral from which it would not recover. Throughout the second half of Ashurbanipal's reign, Assyria became increasingly involved with conflicts to the north and firm control over other parts of the empire began to slip away. By the mid-620s BC, Nabopolassar had wrested Babylon from Assyrian control, and the Babylonian Chronicles indicate that he had complete control of Babylonia by 616 BC, actively engaging in military conflict against Assyria (see Grayson 1975). Throughout the period of Assyria's decline, Egypt benefited the most. Ashurbanipal's capture of Thebes in 664 BC had brought an end to the anti-Assyrian Twenty-Fifth (Kushite) Dynasty and given control of Egypt to the Twenty-Sixth Dynasty, ruled from Sais, reestablishing the cooperative relationship between Assyria and Egypt that had existed in the time of Sargon II (Miller and Hayes 446; Kitchen 1992, 325). During the long reign of Pharaoh Psammetichus I (664-610 BC), Egypt, as an Assyrian ally, played an ever-increasing role in the control of Syria-Palestine that filled the void created by Assyrian withdrawal, a role attested in the frequent references to Egypt in books such as Jeremiah.

This course of events forms the background against which 2 Kings 22—23 and 2 Chronicles 34—35 depict Josiah as Judah's most righteous king. Josiah is said to have carried out an extensive religious reform that reversed the apostate practices of Manasseh by centralizing worship in Jerusalem and destroying all outlying sanctuaries, including some in the territory of the former northern kingdom (2 Kings 23:15-20). Although the accounts in Kings and Chronicles do not align precisely (cf. 2 Kings 23:4-20; 2 Chron 34:3-7), both attribute the impetus for Josiah's actions to the discovery of a "book of the law" in the temple. The exact nature and significance of this event, attested only in the biblical narratives, remain disputed. The scholarly consensus since the early nineteenth century has identified Josiah's law book with some form of the book of Deuteronomy, but debate continues over whether it was an ancient work that was "found" in the temple, a seventh-century BC document that was composed then to support Josiah's reforms, or some combination thereof.

The thoroughgoing positive judgment of Josiah in the OT Historical Books has led some scholars to propose that an edition of the Deuteronomistic History was first produced during his reign (Cross). Interpreters have also viewed Josiah's reign as a generative time for parts of the prophetic literature. The superscriptions of the books of Jeremiah and Zephaniah, for example, place some of the preaching of both prophets in the reign of Josiah, although neither book seems to mention Josiah's reform. Additionally, similarities in superscriptions and other elements lead some scholars to conclude that an initial collection of books that would later grow into the Book of the Twelve (the Minor Prophets) was first produced during Josiah's time and under Deuteronomistic influences (Nogalski).

The combination of the biblical presentation with evidence for Assyrian decline leads many contemporary interpreters to consider Josiah's reign as a period of renewed political freedom and territorial expansion, even constituting, in the minds of some, the greatest period of autonomy that Judah had experienced since the time of David (e.g., Bright, 316; Soggin, 257; Sweeney). Josiah, it is suggested, was able to annex territories in the former northern kingdom and establish Judean dominance over the bulk of Syria-Palestine. This interpretation rests especially on the biblical texts, but proponents also marshal extrabiblical evidence, including Hebrew inscriptions from Mesad Hashavyahu (a small fortress on the Mediterranean coast), the construction of a seventh-century fort at Megiddo, and the fortification of some important southern cities such as Arad and Kadesh-Barnea. In recent years, however, new scholarly assessments, especially concerning the role of Egypt, conclude that the archaeological evidence does not clearly indicate that fortifications like that at Mesad Hashavyahu were Judean, and that several texts and artifacts from throughout Syria-Palestine indicate that Egypt, under the Twenty-Sixth (Saite) Dynasty, came to play the dominant role in the region during this era (see Na'aman 1991; Finkelstein and Silberman, 348-53; Redford, 430-69). These reassessments point to the conclusion that Judah likely was subservient to Egypt throughout most of Josiah's reign, especially its latter portions. If accurate, this situation accords well with the events depicted by the biblical sources concerning the end of Josiah's rule. The biblical accounts in 2 Kings 23:29-30; 2 Chronicles 35:20-24; Jeremiah 22:10-12 are exceedingly vague and difficult to reconcile; hence, the debate over the historical reconstruction remains unsettled. However, the biblical accounts place Josiah's unexpected death at the hands of the Egyptians in the context of the clashes between Egypt and Babylonia in the waning days of Assyrian vitality (c. 610 BC) and assign the decisive power in deposing and appointing Judean kings after Josiah's death to the Egyptian Pharaoh Neco II (610-595 BC).

The events in Judah parallel the developments that led to the final collapse of the Assyrian Empire and the transition to Babylonian dominance in Syria-Palestine and beyond (see

Arnold, 87-93; Brinkman). In 614 BC the Medes captured the city of Ashur and formed an alliance with Nabopolossar of Babylonia. In 612 BC the new alliance destroyed the Assyrian capital Nineveh, an event celebrated as divine judgment in the book of Nahum. Sometime in 610 BC Pharaoh Neco II marched northward through Syria-Palestine, killing Josiah on the way (2 Kings 23:29), to join forces with the Assyrians at Haran. Through a series of attacks and counterattacks, the Babylonians and the Medes defeated the opposing Assyrian-Egyptian force. The Egyptians, for their part, withdrew southward and maintained nominal control for the time being over southern Syria-Palestine. The Assyrians, however, would never again play a role in the politics of the ancient Near East or the life of Judah. For the next half-century the southern kingdom's fate would be intertwined with the two powers of Babylonia and Egypt.

4. The Babylonian Period (605-539 BC).

The period of Babylonian dominance over the ancient Near East between the late seventh and mid-sixth centuries BC forms the ostensible backdrop for the prophetic books of *Obadiah and *Habakkuk, as well as portions of *Isaiah 40—55, *Jeremiah, *Ezekiel and *Daniel.

4.1. The Establishment of Babylonian Dominance (605-601 BC). In the years immediately following Assyria's demise, Babylonia (under Nabopolossar [625-605 BC]) and Egypt vied for dominance over the western territories in Syria-Palestine (see Arnold, 89-91; Vanderhooft, 23-33). The decisive turning point came in 605 BC, when the Babylonian crown prince Nebuchadnezzar II (alternatively, "Nebuchadrezzar" [see Jer 39:1]) defeated the forces of Pharaoh Neco II at Carchemish. Both the Babylonian Chronicles (see Grayson 1975, 99) and Jeremiah's oracle against Egypt in Jeremiah 46:1-12 point to this as a decisive victory that drove the Egyptians out of Syria-Palestine and established Babylonian control of the region down to the border of Egypt south of Philistia. During the following period of 605-601 BC, Nebuchadnezzar, who ascended to the Babylonian throne shortly after the battle of Carchemish, marched throughout Syria-Palestine in an effort to consolidate power and establish the many smaller kingdoms in the area as Babylonian vassals.

The early years of the reign of King Jehoiakim in Judah (608-598 BC) unfolded against this background. His rule provides the context for much of the material in the book of Jeremiah, and the prophet is almost always at odds with the king's foreign policy. As one who had been placed on the throne by the Egyptians (2 Kings 23:34-35), Jehoiakim, like other local rulers in the area, faced the choice of maintaining loyalty to Egypt or capitulating to the new Babylonian emperor. The biblical materials give the impression of a tense and divisive situation in Judah, and Jeremiah in particular depicts this reign as marked by misguided policies and unjust practices (e.g., Jer 22:13-19; 26:1-24). The book of Habakkuk also preserves some of the angst present in Judah at the time. The decisive moment seems to have come in 604 BC, when, the Babylonian Chronicles report, Nebuchadnezzar destroyed the coastal city of Ashkelon (see Grayson 1975, 100). Archaeological evidence not only confirms this report but also attests to further destructions at other Philistine cities. These Babylonian successes likely provided the impetus for Jehoiakim to switch his loyalty to the Babylonians, though surely not without significant reservation (note the fast in Jerusalem in Jer 36:9) (Arnold, 92-93; Vanderhooft, 90-99).

Only a few years later, however, the Babylonians apparently made the fateful decision that they could not allow Egypt to remain autonomous. Hence, late in 601 BC Nebuchadnezzar invaded Egypt. The Babylonian Chronicles, in their characteristically unbiased style, reported that the Babylonians were repelled, and Nebuchadnezzar returned to Babylon for the duration of the following year (see Grayson 1975, 101). This defeat allowed Pharaoh Neco II to advance northward into Syria-Palestine, possibly conquering Gaza (see Jer 47:1). Babylonia's perceived weakness, along with Egypt's apparent resurgence, seemingly led Jehoiakim of Judah to enter into open rebellion against Nebuchadnezzar sometime around 600 BC (see 2 Kings 24:1).

4.2. The Fall of Judah: The Reigns of Jehoiakim, Jehoiachin and Zedekiah (601-586 BC). The precise course of events in Judah following Nebuchadnezzar's defeat in Egypt in 601 BC is difficult to establish. The account in 2 Kings 24 is highly telescoped, but various passages set in the time of Jehoiakim in the book of Jeremiah may provide a somewhat fuller picture (e.g., Jer 22:13-23; 25; 26; 35). Throughout these texts, Jeremiah is a forceful advocate for submission to the Babylonians, casting rebellion as an act of disobedience to the divine will. The Babylonian response to the rebellion in the west began in late November or early December 598 BC, when Nebuchadnezzar led the main army out of Akkad toward the specific target of Jerusalem. Although no details of this campaign are known, 2 Kings 24:2 states that forces from the Chaldeans, Arameans, Moabites and Ammonites, perhaps auxiliary forces in the service of Nebuchadnezzar, moved against Judean territory. Collections of Hebrew ostraca discovered at the fortified Judean city of Arad preserve correspondence that may be related to Judean military preparations and allude to Edomite advances into the Negeb at this time (see Obadiah).

Differing biblical traditions exist concerning the fate of Jehoiakim (cf. 2 Kings 24:6; 2 Chron 36:6), but it seems likely that he died in office before Nebuchadnezzar's forces arrived in Jerusalem. Both biblical and extrabiblical accounts suggest that Jehoiakim's eighteen-year-old son, Jehoiachin, inherited his father's royal throne and ill-advised rebellion (2 Kings 24:6-8). The combined evidence fits a scenario in which Jehoiachin surrendered without a battle when Nebuchadnezzar finally reached Jerusalem (see 2 Kings 24:12). The Babylonian Chronicle for the year in question preserves the precise date of Jerusalem's capture as March 15/16, 597 BC (see Grayson 1975, 102). Perhaps because Jehoiachin was not personally responsible for the revolt and offered immediate submission, Nebuchadnezzar did not destroy Jerusalem or provincialize Judah on this occasion. Rather, he exiled Jehoiachin and deported members of the royal family, aristocracy, soldiers, artisans and religious leaders, including the priest-turned-prophet Ezekiel (see Ezek 1:1-3). The precise number of deportees, as well as its relationship to the size of the population as a whole, remain unclear. Yet, probably in an effort to maintain stability in a region so near to the troublesome Egyptians, Nebuchadnezzar left Jerusalem's ruling dynasty intact by installing Zedekiah, Jehoiachin's twenty-one-year-old uncle, on the throne as a Babylonian vassal.

The limited sources for Zedekiah's reign render precise historical reconstruction diffi-

cult. The Babylonian Chronicles are not extant for these years, and archaeological data remains mostly indirect. The primary biblical account in 2 Kings 24—25 (cf. Jer 39; 52) skips from the beginning to the end of Zedekiah's reign and narrates only the final stages of the events, with a focus limited to Jerusalem. Other biblical materials, however, provide more potential information, especially the books of Jeremiah, who is pictured as preaching in Jerusalem and interacting with Zedekiah in various ways, and Ezekiel, who is portrayed as one of the exiles deported from Jerusalem in 597 BC. Both prophets consistently advocate submission to the Babylonians, and Jeremiah's royal encounters in particular (Jer 37—44) show the conflict among multiple factions and perspectives (pro-Babylonian, anti-Babylonian) in Jerusalem at the time (Cogan 1998, 262).

Based almost entirely on the biblical depictions, most historians conclude that Zedekiah initiated a rebellion against Babylonia in conjunction with an Egyptian resurgence in the late 590s BC (see Miller and Hayes, 473; Provan, Long and Longman, 279-80). Zedekiah apparently hosted a council in Jerusalem with officials from Edom, Moab, Ammon, Tyre and Sidon in order to coordinate a regional revolt against Babylonia, an event known only from Jeremiah 27:3. The exact timing of the council remains debated (cf. Miller and Hayes, 469; Soggin, 250), but this initial revolt evidently never materialized. Perhaps the reference in Jeremiah 51:59 to Zedekiah's being compelled to appear before Nebuchadnezzar in Babylon reflects the emperor's response to this initial sedition. Whatever the case, in 592 BC the new Pharaoh Psammetichus II (595-589 BC), who had succeeded Neco II shortly after Zedekiah came to the throne, won a decisive victory over Nubia (Ethiopia) and subsequently embarked on a victory tour of Syria-Palestine, an event recorded in an Egyptian priestly composition (Rylands IX Papyrus) (see Grabbe 2007, 209). Possibly inspired by this Egyptian resurgence, Zedekiah withheld annual tribute and entered into open rebellion against Babylonia in the late 590s or early 580s BC.

Both biblical and extrabiblical texts offer snapshots of discrete events in the course of what happened next. Hebrew ostraca, for instance, note that a Judean royal official was dispatched to Egypt, likely to negotiate for sup-

411

Ishmael originally Jewish?

port. Perhaps more significantly, the totality of evidence for Babylonian actions over the following years suggests that the resurgent Egyptian threat and the quickly renewed western rebellion led Nebuchadnezzar to alter his earlier policy of maintaining stability in the region, which had resulted in the survival of Jerusalem and the Davidic dynasty after Jehoiachin's surrender in 597 BC. Nebuchadnezzar apparently decided henceforth to deal with rebellious vassals by removing the current ruling line, relocating the kingdom's capital city, and ruling the territory more directly (see Lipschits). Thus, in the late fall of 589 BC Nebuchadnezzar set out for Jerusalem, soon placing the city under an extended siege. As part of this campaign, the Babylonians inflicted serious devastation on a number of Judean towns. Messages on ostraca from the fortified city of Lachish, for example, most likely testify to the soldiers' inability to receive communications from another town that has presumably fallen (*COS* 3.42:78-81; see Jer 34:6-7). Some evidence also points to Edom's aggression against Judean territory, especially in the area of the southern Negeb desert (see the condemnations of Edom in Obad and Ps 137:7). At some point during the siege of Jerusalem, the Babylonian army temporarily withdrew to turn back an Egyptian force that had entered Syria-Palestine under the new Pharaoh Apries (Hophra) (589-570 BC) (see Jer 37:1-10) and thereafter reconstituted the siege.

Biblical texts indicate that the siege of Jerusalem that had begun in January 587 BC concluded eighteen months later in July 586 BC, although the lack of a surviving Babylonian Chronicle makes these dates imprecise, perhaps off by as much as a year (Arnold, 95). In any case, the biblical texts (2 Kings 25; Jer 39; 52) recount that Zedekiah and a military escort attempted to flee toward the Transjordan but were captured and brought to Nebuchadnezzar at Riblah. There, perhaps in keeping with the stipulated punishments of his vassal treaty, Zedekiah's sons were executed, his eyes were put out, and he was deported to Babylonia in chains. One month after the city's capture, Nebuzaradan, captain of the Babylonian royal guard, razed Jerusalem, burning the temple, palace and houses, dismantling the city's walls (see Jer 39:9-10; 52:12-26), and exiling a significant number of the population to Babylonia.

4.3. Judah under Gedaliah and the Babylonian Exile (586-539 BC). Immediately after, or perhaps even during, the siege of Jerusalem, the Babylonians established a new administrative capital for Judah at Mizpah and placed Gedaliah, a non-Davidic royal official, in authority there (2 Kings 25:22-26; Jer 40:5—41:3). These events provide the background for some of the final stories about the prophet Jeremiah (Jer 39:11—43:13), but only indirect evidence from a few seals and archaeological data from the city of Mizpah are available for comparison. The available evidence suggests a few things clearly: (1) the Babylonians reorganized the government of Judah by removing the Davidic family from power and relocating the administrative capital; (2) Gedaliah governed alongside a Babylonian garrison stationed in Mizpah and gathered remaining Judeans around himself for a time; (3) Gedaliah subsequently was assassinated by Ishmael, a member of the Davidic family, perhaps with the support of the Ammonites, and his government collapsed; (4) after the assassination, army officers from Mizpah took a number of Judeans, including the prophet Jeremiah, and fled to Egypt because they feared Babylonian reprisals. Beyond this general course of events, however, much remains uncertain. Scholars debate Gedaliah's exact status as a ruler—whether he was installed as a non-Davidic king of what was still considered to be a semi-independent vassal kingdom, or merely as a governor of a directly ruled imperial province (cf. Soggin, 255; Miller and Hayes, 483). Also uncertain is the timing of Gedaliah's assassination depicted in the biblical texts (2 Kings 25:25; Jer 41:2-3), which provide the month but not the year of the event (e.g., Jer 52:30 mentions a third Babylonian deportation from Judah in Nebuchadnezzar's twenty-third year [581 BC]) (see Cogan 1998, 268; Miller and Hayes, 486).

In any event, the end of Gedaliah's government in Mizpah marked the beginning of what has come to be known as the "exilic period" (c. 586-539 BC). Other than the brief reference to the first capture of Jerusalem (597 BC) in the Babylonian Chronicles, only the biblical texts offer information on the number of Judean exiles, and these sources do not agree in the numbers that they provide. The book of 2 Kings, for instance, mentions two deportations, with several numbers of deportees whose referents are

Isaiah 40?

not clear: (1) a deportation of ten thousand or more people in Nebuchadnezzar's eighth year (597 BC) (2 Kings 24:12, 14-16); (2) a deportation of an unspecified number in Nebuchadnezzar's nineteenth year (586 BC) (2 Kings 25:8, 11). The book of Jeremiah reports three deportations, featuring different numbers and dates (cf. Jer 52:28, 29, 30). Historians offer a variety of interpretations of this data, often harmonizing the figures or assuming some exaggeration, but the conflicting data resists any firm conclusions on the number of deportations and deportees (see Albertz, 74-80; Miller and Hayes, 478-97).

Whatever the number, historians typically have focused on the nature and conditions of life in exile for those who were deported to Babylonia, although other deportations resulted in Judean exiles also living in places such as Egypt (see Jer 43—44 and, later, the Elephantine texts). Historians mostly have proceeded by combining biblical, especially prophetic, texts (e.g., Is 40—55; Jer 29; Ezek 1-24) with indirect extrabiblical references, relying heavily on analogy, inference and extrapolation. Several cuneiform sources, such as records prescribing rations for King Jehoiachin and his sons, tablets mentioning a "city of Judah" near Babylon, and later texts from the Nippur area associated with the Murashu business firm—receipts from a mid-fifth century BC business firm's real estate and commercial activities that refer to the participation of persons with Jewish names (ANET 308; Cardascia; Stolper)—have generated the common interpretation that the deported Judeans did not experience undue subjugation or persecution but rather maintained their basic communal identity and had a reasonable level of participation in the social and economic life of the empire. In this view, the group of Babylonian exiles numbered in the tens of thousands, and the majority settled in dilapidated areas as a type of somewhat free immigrant community of land tenants (see Albertz, 99-101; Cogan 1998, 270). In the last two decades, however, new evaluations of the evidence and new constructions of life among the Babylonian exiles have emerged (see Smith-Christopher; Moore and Kelle). These reconsiderations stress that most of the data used to support the common interpretation is only indirect, limited or geographically and chronologically removed from the Babylo-

nian deportees. By examining biblical references to suffering and bondage (e.g., Is 40—55; Lamentations) and, especially, by employing insights from sociological, anthropological and psychological studies of refugees and displaced populations, some recent interpreters conclude that the Judean experience of exile was a severe and traumatic personal, social and psychological event, constituting a crisis that forced the deportees into destabilizing recalibrations of their communal and theological understandings, some of which are reflected in the prophetic texts such as Ezekiel and Isaiah 40—55 (see Kelle 2009).

The constitution and character of life in the land of Judah after 586 BC has also received attention in recent years and presently affords no consensus. The most directly relevant OT texts (2 Kings 25:8-9; 2 Chron 36:17-21; Jer 52:12-34) claim that the Babylonians essentially emptied the land of all but a meager group of the poorest inhabitants, thus implying that all significant elements of Judean life shifted to Babylonia. The majority of scholarly treatments before the 1990s (see Bright, 344; Soggin, 92), as well as some more recent ones (e.g., Stern 2001), supplemented this biblical picture with archaeological evidence of destruction at major urban centers (Lachish, Azekah, Ramet Rahel) and posited that although the territory of Judah was surely not devoid of all inhabitants and towns, Judah suffered a high degree of devastation that left a sixth-century BC gap in meaningful social, cultural and political activity. This gap left the area and its people without any significance for the future development of Judah's life and faith. In recent years, however, several interpreters have revisited the archaeological data in particular and proposed a different reconstruction with several elements (see Barstad; Lipschits): (1) the Babylonian destruction in Judah was limited to certain major urban centers (especially Jerusalem and its environs), while other areas were less, if at all, affected (especially Mizpah and its environs); (2) the deportees constituted only a small group of political and social elites, and the majority of the population remained in the land, especially in the areas north of Jerusalem and the Judean hills; (3) cultural, societal and religious activity continued in Judah, with substantial continuity to what was there before 586 BC. These conclusions rest primarily upon new interpretations of the archaeological data for levels of continued occupation and settlement patterns, especially surface surveys and demographic studies. Overall, the ongoing investigation of life in Judah after 586 BC is a lively archaeological debate, with archaeologists offering different interpretations of the same evidence.

5. The Persian Period (539-333 BC).

The period of Persian dominance over the ancient Near East between the mid-sixth and late fourth centuries BC forms the ostensible backdrop for the prophetic materials of *Isaiah 40—66, *Haggai, *Zechariah and *Malachi, perhaps also being the time of origin for the books of *Joel and *Jonah. In terms of the biblical presentation, this era signals the end of the Babylonian exile by relating the return of various members of the exilic community, the rebuilding of the temple and city in Jerusalem, and the establishment of the Persian province of Yehud in part of the former territory of the kingdom of Judah. The biblical depiction, however, leaves much untold, as significant Jewish communities continued to exist in places such as Babylonia and Egypt throughout the remainder of the Persian and Hellenistic periods (see Kessler, 151-52).

In addition to the biblical books of Ezra, Nehemiah, Haggai and Zechariah, archaeology and social-science modeling have helped flesh out the overall picture of these centuries. Still, the nature of the available sources constitutes a particularly complex issue for this period, and current scholarly approaches remain in flux (see Moore and Kelle). The biblical texts likely preserve some accurate information about the postexilic era, but they offer detailed data about only a limited group of people (the immigrants to Jerusalem from Babylonia) and a narrow geographical area (Jerusalem and its immediate environs). Moreover, the biblical texts relate only to a few years scattered throughout the period (c. 520-450 BC) and only in an episodic fashion, with a sometimes unclear chronology. A number of unanswered questions about the biblical sources, including when the books of Ezra and Nehemiah were compiled, what sources their authors used, and how reliable those sources were, further complicate the issue (see Briant; Grabbe 2004). Extrabiblical texts related to events in Judah are rare, and archaeological evidence from the Persian period is just beginning to come to light in significant ways, although the majority of what has been uncovered and analyzed does not come from the area of Judah. Hence, even archaeological evidence for matters such as the size and population of Jerusalem during these years remains heavily contested.

5.1. The Rise of Persia Before 539 BC. The OT Prophetic Books contain no voices that relate explicitly to the time between the final visions of Ezekiel (c. 571 BC) and the poetry of Isaiah 40—55 (c. 539 BC), the era that marked the transition from Babylonian to Persian power. Very little is known of Persian history before 550 BC, when the small Indo-European kingdom in the area of ancient Susa began expanding under Cyrus II (the Great) (see Leith). After winning victories over the Medes and Lydians, the Persians moved against the Babylonians. The Babylonian emperor at the time was Nabonidus (556-539 BC), a usurper whose reign was characterized by internal strife. For reasons that are not fully known, Nabonidus installed his son Belshazzar as regent in Babylon three years after his accession and led the army into northwest Arabia, where he stayed for ten years at Teima, five hundred miles from Babylon (Arnold, 101-3). These actions may have been religiously motivated, as Nabonidus sponsored the worship of the moon-god, Sîn, who had a cult center in the Syrian city of Haran and whose worship put the emperor at odds with the dominant cult of the god Marduk in Babylon (Cogan 1998, 273). Alternatively, Nabonidus's sojourn may have been strategic, perhaps an attempt to establish a control base for the Arabian caravan routes (see Arnold, 103). Whatever the case, extrabiblical texts (e.g., the Prayer of Nabonidus, found among the DSS) indicate that legends grew up around the emperor casting his actions as the result of a madness brought upon him by divine means. The stories of Nebuchadnezzar's madness and exile in Daniel 4, whose broader context also contains a reference to Belshazzar's rule in Babylon (Dan 5:1), are considered by most scholars to be adaptations of the traditions originally associated with Nabonidus (see Collins, 216-21).

Nabonidus's extended absence from his capital city and royal duties eroded Babylonian power abroad and led to unrest at home. In 539 BC, the Babylonian Chronicles record that the Persians defeated the Babylonian army in

Opis, and that Cyrus subsequently gained control of the city of Babylon without a fight. The OT prophetic texts preserve positive evaluations of Cyrus and these accomplishments. The collection of poems in Isaiah 40—55, for example, which reflects the circumstances around 539 BC, describes Cyrus as Yahweh's "anointed" (lit., "messiah" [Is 45:1]), whom Yahweh will use to bring about a deliverance from exile in the vein of a second exodus (e.g., Is 43:1-13). Over the next two centuries, the textual and archaeological data reveal a significant distinction relevant to Judah and the Judeans between the early and later Persian periods, known as the Persian I (c. 539-450 BC) and Persian II (c. 450-333 BC) periods (see Carter). Prior to the mid-fifth century BC, Persian emperors such as Darius remained focused on the north and west and paid little attention to the area of Syria-Palestine. The postexilic prophetic books about whose dating we can be reasonably certain relate only to the early Persian period: Isaiah 40—55 reflects the beginning of Persian rule in 539 BC, Haggai, Zechariah and Isaiah 56—66 relate to the time around the rebuilding of the temple in 520-515 BC, and Malachi likely dates to the situation in Jerusalem around 500 BC. Important material development and strategic significance came to the area of Syria-Palestine only in the Persian II period (c. 450 BC; i.e., the time of the biblical figures of Ezra and Nehemiah), when there is evidence for the establishment of new political and social structures and an increase in building projects and seal and coin production. The population of Jerusalem before 450 BC, for instance, likely consisted of only about five hundred people, but this number seems to have grown to more than one thousand in the following years (note the prophetic calls to repopulate Jerusalem in the late 500s BC [e.g., Zech 8:4-8]) (Leith, 289-90).

5.2. The Early Persian Period (539-450 BC). During the time between Cyrus's capture of Babylon in 539 BC and the completion of the Jerusalem temple in 515 BC, Judah existed as a subprovince called "Yehud" in the fifth satrapy of the Persian Empire, called "Abar Nahara" ("Across the River"), which consisted of Syria-Palestine and Cyprus (Leith, 286). Few details of Persian administration are known, however, and the question of how Yehud related to the subprovince of Samaria, ruled by several gen-erations of the Sanballat family, remains debated (see Grabbe 1992, 2004; Briant). Additionally, although scholars disagree over the precise borders of Yehud at various times in the Persian period, the evidence from lists in the biblical texts (e.g., Ezra 2:1-63; Neh 3:2-32; 7:5-65; 12:1-26) and Judean seals and coins points to a much smaller community around Jerusalem than in the Assyrian and Babylonian periods (see Carter; Lipschits). From the sociohistorical perspective, postexilic Yehud also differed from its preexilic predecessors. The Persians deviated from the deportation policies of the Assyrians and Babylonians, granting limited autonomy to their provinces, allowing formerly deported populations to return home, and possibly supporting the revitalization of local religious temples and practices. For Yehud, an area located on the fringes of Persian territory and attention (at least prior to c. 450 BC), these developments produced a "provincial society" characterized by some sense of restoration and religious identity but also by a lack of full autonomy under the constraints of imperial governors, taxation requirements and difficult economic conditions (Kessler, 153-55).

In keeping with these general characteristics, the biblical texts (2 Chron 36:22-23; Ezra 1:1-4; 6:3-5) identify the beginning of the return from exile with Cyrus's decree that Yahweh had commissioned him to let the Judean exiles return to Jerusalem and rebuild the temple. The Rassam Cylinder (or Cyrus Cylinder) (*ANET* 316; *COS* 2.1214:314-16), a cuneiform inscription in which Cyrus describes his similar allowances for Babylonians and the worship of the god Marduk, has traditionally been understood as indicating that such actions were not a special favor bestowed upon the Jews but rather are representative of Persian policies more generally. In recent years scholars have more adequately assessed these policies not as indicators of the benevolence of the Persian emperors but as means to create loyal vassals and reestablish areas of the empire as sources for economic and material goods (see Hoglund). Even so, questions concerning the details and extent of the return to Jerusalem remain vexed (see Miller and Hayes, 511). Ezra 2 and Nehemiah 7 claim to present lists of returnees, with the former naming about fifty thousand persons, but doubts remain regarding how many waves of return are included, the times from which the lists come, and the level of their authenticity. The initial return was likely small, and the relevant biblical texts as a whole give the impression of a return that unfolded in several phases, with different leaders at different times.

Ezra 1 and Ezra 5 attribute the first phase of the return to Sheshbazzar, a Persian-appointed governor, in 538 BC. This phase accomplished the laying of the new temple's foundation (but cf. Ezra 3:10). The work, however, apparently stopped, a circumstance that the OT attributes to opposition from the local population who had remained in the land throughout the sixth century BC (Ezra 4—5) (see Leith, 277-98). From the perspective of the biblical texts, the conflict was primarily about defining the identity of the true community of Israel, with texts such as Ezra and Nehemiah later making the ethnically exclusive argument that only the returnees constitute the legitimate Jewish community (see the conflict over mixed marriages in Ezra 10; Neh 13). From a broader perspective, conflict among groups in Yehud likely included economic and political struggles over control of Jerusalem, with its temple and resources. Earlier scholarly proposals to define postexilic Yehud specifically as a "citizen-temple community" in which a restricted group of privileged citizens formed a closed community around the temple (Weinberg) have not found continued support, but these political and economic aspects certainly supplement the religious factors emphasized by the biblical sources (Kessler, 135).

According to the biblical texts, the work stoppage on the temple's construction provided the context for the next phase of return (Ezra 3—6) and the preaching of the prophets Haggai and Zechariah (c. 520 BC). Scholars traditionally have reconstructed this phase as taking place under the leadership of Zerubbabel, a Persian-appointed governor apparently from the Davidic line (but see Miller and Hayes, 518), and Joshua, the high priest who governed Yehud as a "diarchy" of cooperative political and religious authority (see Zech 4:6b-10a; 6:9-15) (Kessler, 140-41). The traditional notion of such a diarchy, however, has been challenged more recently (see Boda; Rooke). Haggai and Zechariah proclaimed Yahweh's involvement with Zerubbabel and Joshua and attempted to convince the people of the divine calling to finish the work on the temple. This era corresponds with the beginning of the reign of Darius I (522-486 BC). After the death of Cambyses, civil war erupted in the empire, and eventually Darius secured the throne, perhaps as a usurper (Briant, 107-14). Darius was forced to respond to revolts that broke out across the empire, and these events resulted in significant changes in the imperial structure and operations. Sometime after securing the throne, Darius reorganized the empire into twenty satrapies and developed systems of roads, currency and communication (Leith, 292-93). He also sponsored the creation of a notable inscription at Behistun, offering a biased account of his early years and perhaps indicating the promulgation of law codes as a means of local control. The completion of the work on the Jerusalem temple accomplished by Zerubbabel and Joshua in 515 BC should be viewed against the context of Darius's more direct interest in the local affairs of his territories. Moreover, the widespread unrest and significant changes in the empire likely provide the backdrop for Haggai and Zechariah, especially some of their more apocalyptic predictions and imagery (Berquist, 65-73). Against this background, the laudatory language about Zerubbabel in Haggai and Zechariah (e.g. Hag 2:20-23) perhaps reflects a growing messianic expectation that was attached to him as a member of the Davidic line, possibly expressing local hopes that he might reestablish an independent kingdom in Judah. Zerubbabel, however, suddenly disappears without explanation from the biblical account. Perhaps these two elements are related and Darius removed Zerubbabel from power sometime after the completion of the temple to stem the growing tide of messianism in the Jerusalem community.

5.3. The Late Persian Period (450-333 BC). Neither the OT nor extrabiblical literature provides any direct information on events in Yehud between the rebuilding of the temple in 515 BC and the work of Ezra and Nehemiah after 458 BC—the rest of the Persian I period (for potential incidental data, see Ezra 4:6-23; 6:7). In Persian imperial history this era overlapped the reigns of Darius I (522-486 BC), Xerxes (486-465 BC) and Artaxerxes I (465-424 BC). The lack of source material may suggest a period of relative stability in the region, but archaeological data indicates that sites in Yehud were more limited and less prosperous than those elsewhere in the area (Leith, 303). This situation provides the likely background for the prophetic material in Isaiah 56—66 and Malachi. These prophets allude to social and economic struggles of the Jerusalem community in the years immediately after the completion of the temple (c. 515-500 BC). They interpret hardships such as drought, community division and lack of resources (e.g., Mal 3:10-11) as results of the people's unfaithfulness to Yahweh and as motivations for the community to aspire to a new level of ritual and ethical diligence.

As noted above, the strategic and material importance of the area of Syria-Palestine changed significantly from the Persian I to Persian II periods. The impetus for change began around 460 BC with the outbreak of a major revolt in Egypt during the early years of Artaxerxes I, a rebellion that featured hostile Greek activity in Egypt and elsewhere (see Leith, 304-5). As a result, the area of Syria-Palestine and the province of Yehud became vital to Persian security, which in turn led to increased imperial involvement and administration. Since the time of Isaiah 56—66 and Malachi (c. 500 BC) is the last period that is directly relevant for the prophetic literature until the mid-second century BC (the oracles in Zech 9—14 may date to later periods, but their apocalyptic nature makes them cryptic), the course of Israelite history in the remainder of the Persian period (c. 450-333 BC) will not be discussed here. However, the new material situation and increased strategic significance for Yehud in the Persian II period likely provide the context for interpreting the Bible's depictions of Ezra and Nehemiah, traditionally dated to 458 BC and 445 BC, respectively. The activities of Ezra and Nehemiah perhaps should be understood from the Persian perspective as part of the renewed imperial efforts to establish secure administration and refortify important cities in the areas close to Egypt. The scholarly study of this era continues to flourish (see Moore and Kelle), and reconstructions must deal with a host of complicated issues, such as the historical reliability and proper sequence of Ezra and Nehemiah and their roles as priest and governor, the socioeconomic composition and conditions of Yehud at this time and its relationship to the empire and other regional entities, and the ethnic and religious concerns addressed in the biblical texts (see Miller and Hayes, 529;

Grabbe 1992; 2004).

Subsequent to these years, virtually no historical information has survived on the history of the Jerusalem community from the time after Nehemiah's second term as governor to the rise of the Greeks under Alexander the Great in the mid-300s BC, even though the general contours of Persian history are well known in this era. By 333 BC, Alexander and his Greek and Macedonian forces had achieved successes against the last Persian emperor, Darius III (336-330 BC), winning a decisive victory at Issus, and by 332 BC the region of Judea had come under Alexander's control (Leith, 314; Levine, 231).

6. The Hellenistic Period (333-64 BC).

The period of Greek dominance over the ancient world lasted nearly three centuries, but only one era of that period constitutes the probable background of an OT prophetic book. Although the happenings described in the book of Daniel are set against the ostensible backdrop of the sixth-century BC Babylonian exile in the courts of Babylonian, Median and Persian kings, scholars since at least the eighteenth century have widely recognized that the visions in Daniel 7—12 relate most closely to circumstances under the Seleucid kings who controlled Syria-Palestine in the years after 190 BC. More specifically, the visions seem to focus on the time of the Maccabean Revolt in Jerusalem, relating explicitly, even if symbolically, to the period between the decrees concerning Jerusalem by Antiochus IV Epiphanes in 167 BC and the reclaiming of the temple by the Maccabees in 164 BC (Greenspoon, 341). For many modern interpreters, the dramatic circumstances involved in this era provide the best context for understanding the production of the whole book of *Daniel as well, at least in its present form (see Collins). While the stories in Daniel 1—6 may be older, and perhaps formed a collection even before the Maccabean period, the book's apparent lack of familiarity with some historical details of the Babylonian period and overwhelming preoccupation with the significance of events under the Greek emperors are most easily explained if the author (or final editor) was living in the mid-second century BC.

The Greek dominance that reached a flashpoint in Jerusalem in the mid-second century BC had begun when Alexander the Great (356-323 BC) arrived in the east in 333 BC after consolidating power in Greece over the preceding two decades (see Greenspoon; Hayes and Mandell). He conquered Judea in 332 BC, but he died suddenly about a decade later (323 BC). Upon Alexander's death, his generals struggled over succession and territory, and the area of Judea initially came under the rule of Ptolemy and his successors, whose government center was at Alexandria in Egypt. While under the control of the Ptolemies, Judea and other territories north of Egypt seemingly enjoyed a period of relative self-rule under the leadership of local high priests and officials, with little Greek intervention (Greenspoon, 319). In time, however, Judea's geographical location between the Ptolemies and the Seleucids—the other major Hellenistic power that had succeeded Alexander and was centered in Antioch in Syria— made the area an important site of conflict (Levine, 232). The territories of Syria-Palestine passed from Ptolemaic to Seleucid control during the reign of the Seleucid emperor Antiochus III (c. 200 BC), a ruler who initially continued the generally positive relations with Jerusalem's local leadership.

The series of dramatic events commonly associated with the book of Daniel began about twenty-five years later when Antiochus IV Epiphanes came to the Seleucid throne (c. 175 BC). Already during the preceding years, several factors had set the stage for the conflicts that would occur in Jerusalem. First, at nearly the same time that the Seleucids gained control of Syria-Palestine (c. 200 BC), the Romans began to extend their power into the Mediterranean and soon scored a decisive victory over Greek forces in Asia Minor (190 BC) (Hayes and Mandell, 46). As a result, Seleucid emperors, even while exerting their own power over local populations in Syria-Palestine, had to exist under Roman hegemony, a situation that they may not have willingly acknowledged or accepted. This hegemony included Roman demands for significant payment from the Seleucid kings, which often exceeded their normal resources and drove them to extract funds from local temples in their territories (Greenspoon, 324).

A second, perhaps even more significant, factor in the years leading up to hostilities under Antiochus IV was the cultural aspect of Greek ascendancy. The expansion of Greek dominance brought with it the spread of "Hellenism," a "complex of cultural, economic, philosophical, and social factors" that represented the dissemination of the Greek way of life throughout the Mediterranean region (Greenspoon, 317). The area of Judea, once relatively isolated, began to encounter cultural and religious institutions, ideas and practices that offered assimilation into the dominant culture of the Hellenistic world. Predictably, these cultural developments elicited differing, even conflicting, reactions among groups within Judaism, divisions that produced an increasingly fractious and polarized Jewish society during the first part of the second century BC. The third factor that set the stage for the conflicts that would emerge in Jerusalem was, to some extent, an outgrowth of these varied reactions to the assimilative pressures of Hellenism. The early decades of the second century BC were characterized by ever-increasing rivalry and discord among prominent families in Jerusalem's religious leadership, especially the two main families, the Tobiads and Oniads, who often vied for control of the high priestly office in the Jerusalem temple (see Hayes and Mandell, 1-2, 47). Conflicts among such families, as well as numerous other groups and factions, were not only political and religious but also socioeconomic, as upper-class, elite families struggled to secure power over the resources represented by the city of Jerusalem and its temple (Kessler, 162).

The general course of events under Antiochus IV Epiphanes between 175 and 164 BC is well established, although many of the details remain obscure (see Kessler, 159). In the years leading up to and including Antiochus's accession, various figures in Jerusalem vied for the high priesthood, often representing different reactions to the pressures of assimilation to Hellenism and frequently bribing their way into office by promising to make increased funds available to the Seleucid emperor. Around 175 BC, Jason, the brother of the current high priest Onias III, bribed Antiochus IV for the high priesthood, marking the turning point after which the Greek emperor would often intervene directly in the city's religious and political leadership (Greenspoon, 326). Jason embraced Jewish assimilation into Hellenism and established in Jerusalem a Greek-style "gymnasium," a social institution for the physical and intellectual training of Greek citizens (Levine, 237). Just a few years later (c. 170 BC), Jason was deposed when Menelaus bribed Antiochus IV for appointment to the high priesthood. At home, Menelaus, who did not come from the traditional Oniad family of Jerusalem high priests, may have been a polarizing figure, as the Jewish population became increasingly divided between those who embraced Seleucid rule and Jerusalem's increasing Hellenism and those who remained more traditional in the face of such cultural modernizations. The former high priest Onias III, perhaps a figurehead for resistance, was murdered in these years, apparently at Menelaus's direction (see Dan 9:26). Menelaus also experienced increased economic conflict with both his Seleucid overlords and his own population, as his promises of significant payments to the emperor led to increased use of temple resources and local taxation (Greenspoon, 327).

In the broader geopolitical context, the turning point for Jerusalem came in 169 BC, when Antiochus IV came to Jerusalem and took large amounts of gold and silver from the temple on his way home from a victorious campaign against the Ptolemies in Egypt. About a year later (c. 168 BC), Antiochus again invaded Egypt. On the brink of victory, however, the Romans exerted their hegemony, ordering Antiochus to leave Egypt, perhaps in a state of humiliation at the sudden reminder of his ultimate subservience. Although the connections, if any, between the events remain unclear, chaos broke out in Jerusalem around this same time, as the former high priest Jason led a small force into the city in an attempt to displace Menelaus. These occurrences touched off a series of events over the next year that resulted in Menelaus's power being secured in Jerusalem but led to direct hostility between the Jews and their Seleucid rulers (see Greenspoon, 328). Sources such as Daniel 7—12 and 1-2 Maccabees allow for a secure reconstruction of only the general outline of events, which included the removal of Jerusalem's defensive walls, the establishment of a citadel in the city that housed soldiers and officials loyal to the Seleucids, and an increase in taxation. Most importantly, at some point Antiochus IV effectively outlawed, perhaps through a royal edict (see 1 Macc 1:41-51; 2 Macc 6:1-11; but see Hayes and Mandell, 66-67), Jewish religious practices and traditions such as Sabbath and circumcision. The Jerusalem temple became a worship site for the Greek god Zeus Olympius, complete with an altar to Zeus and statues of Greek gods (Greenspoon, 328). According to ancient Jewish sources (1 Macc 1:54-57; Josephus, *Ant.* 12.253), these events reached their negative climax in the month of Kislev (December) 167 BC, when a pig was sacrificed on the altar of burnt offerings in the temple, an act described in Daniel as the "abomination that desolates" (Dan 9:27; see also Dan 11:31; 12:11; 1 Macc 1:54).

Within this general course of events, however, much remains unclear, including who primarily initiated these developments and how various Jewish groups in Jerusalem and elsewhere responded to them. Jewish participation and reactions resist simplification, as some Jews probably supported Antiochus and Menelaus, embracing Hellenism and adapting religious practices in ways perhaps seen by them as faithful to Judaism (see Levine, 239; Greenspoon, 328-29). Scholars especially grapple with the possible motives for Antiochus's hostile actions against Jerusalem and the Jewish religion (see Gruen). Although some ancient legends preserve stories of the king's madness, most interpreters suggest a political and economic motive whereby Antiochus sought to extend his influence after his humiliation in Egypt and, especially, to gather the money and resources demanded by the Romans (Bringmann). In this scenario, the Seleucid king precipitated the turmoil in Jerusalem, and the Jews reacted violently to this oppression. Equally plausible, however, is that the motive for Antiochus's actions lies with the Hellenizing Jewish leaders themselves, especially in the conflict between Menelaus and Jason, who perhaps sought out the king's aggressive intervention for their own purposes (cf. Bickerman; Tcherikover). The hostilities in Jerusalem, then, were not a reaction to the king's actions but rather the catalyst for them, actions that should be understood as a response to the chaos already unfolding in Judea.

Whatever the details, the events in Jerusalem around 167 BC generated an opposition movement that took root in the town of Modein under the leadership of the priest Mattathias and his five sons (see 1 Macc 2:1-68; 3:1—9:22; 2 Macc 8:1—13:26) (Greenspoon, 331). By 164 BC, this Maccabean Revolt, later led by one of Mattathias's sons, Judah or Judas, also called "Maccabeus" (perhaps meaning "hammer" [but see Levine, 239]), drove the Seleucids to a partial compromise (the so-called Peace of Lysias) that allowed the resumption of some Jewish practices but maintained Menelaus's authority and Greek control of the temple. The revolt scored its most significant victory when the Maccabeans regained control of the Jerusalem temple and purified it for renewed ritual use. Jewish tradition dates this event, which became the basis for the Hanukkah ("rededication") holiday, to 25 Kislev 164 BC, exactly three years to the month after the sacrifice of a pig on the temple's altar (1 Macc 4:52) (Greenspoon, 332). Although the conflict between Jews and Greeks would continue, the events of the Maccabean Revolt constitute the last era of Israelite history that is directly relevant to the OT Prophetic Books. Antiochus IV died in battle in the east in November or early December 164 BC (see Hayes and Mandell, 73), not long after the rededication of the temple by the Maccabeans. Neither of these significant events appears explicitly in the book of Daniel (cf. Dan 11:40-45), however, perhaps indicating that the book was completed in the fall of 164 BC, as the writer sought guidance through the political, social, and religious confusion of his day.

See also BABYLON; EXILE; ISRAEL; FORMATION OF THE PROPHETIC BOOKS; PROPHECY AND SOCIETY; PROPHECY, HISTORY OF.

BIBLIOGRAPHY. **R. Albertz,** *Israel in Exile: The History and Literature of the Sixth Century B.C.E.* (SBL 3; Atlanta: Society of Biblical Literature, 2003); **B. T. Arnold,** *Who Were the Babylonians?* (SBLABS 10; Atlanta: Society of Biblical Literature, 2004); **G. Athas,** *The Tel Dan Inscription: A Reappraisal and New Interpretation* (JSOTSup 360; Sheffield: Sheffield Academic, 2003); **N. Avigad,** *Bullae and Seals from a Post-Exilic Judean Archive* (Qedem 4; Jerusalem: Institute of Archaeology, the Hebrew University of Jerusalem, 1976); **H. M. Barstad,** *The Myth of the Empty Land: A Study in the History and Archaeology of Judah during the "Exilic" Period* (SO 28; Oslo: Scandinavian University Press, 1996); **B. Becking,** *The Fall of Samaria: An Historical and Archaeological Study* (SHCANE 2; Leiden: E. J. Brill, 1992); **E. Ben Zvi,** "Studying Prophetic Texts against Their Original Backgrounds: Pre-Ordained Scripts and Alternative Horizons of Research," in *Prophets and Paradigms: Essays in Honor of Gene M. Tucker,* ed. S. Reid (JSOTSup 229; Sheffield: Sheffield Academic, 1996) 125-35; idem, *Hosea* (FOTL 21A; Grand Rapids: Eerdmans, 2005); idem, "De-Historicizing and Historicizing Tendencies in the Twelve Prophetic Books: A Case Study of the Heuristic Value of a Historically Anchored Systemic Approach to the Corpus of Prophetic Literature," in *Israel's Prophets and Israel's Past: Essays on the Relationship of Prophetic Texts and Israelite History in Honor of John H. Hayes,* ed. B. E. Kelle and M. B. Moore (LHBOTS 446; New York: T & T Clark, 2006) 37-56; **J. L. Berquist,** *Judaism in Persia's Shadow: A Social and Historical Approach* (Minneapolis: Fortress, 1995); **E. J. Bickerman,** *The God of the Maccabees: Studies on the Meaning and Origin of the Maccabean Revolt* (SJLA 32; Leiden: E. J. Brill, 1979); **L. R. Binford,** *An Archaeological Perspective* (Studies in Archaeology; New York: Seminar Press, 1972); **M. J. Boda,** "Oil, Crowns and Thrones: Prophet, Priest and King in Zechariah 1:7-6:15," *JHScr* 3.10 (2001) <http://www.arts.ualberta.ca/JHS/Articles/article_22.htm>; **P. Briant,** *From Cyrus to Alexander: A History of the Persian Period* (Winona Lake, IN: Eisenbrauns, 2002); **J. Bright,** *A History of Israel* (4th ed.; Louisville: Westminster/John Knox, 2000); **K. Bringmann,** *Hellenistische Reform und Religionsverfolgung in Judäa: Ein Untersuchung zur jüdisch-hellenistischen Geschichte (175-163 v. Chr.)* (Abhandlungen der Akademie der Wissenschaften in Göttingen, Philologisch-historische Klasse 3; Göttingen: Vandenhoeck & Ruprecht, 1983); **J. A. Brinkman,** *Prelude to Empire: Babylonian Society and Politics, 747-626 B.C.* (OPBF 7; Philadelphia: University Museum, 1984); **E. Campbell Jr.,** "A Land Divided: Judah and Israel from the Death of Solomon to the Fall of Samaria," in *The Oxford History of the Biblical World,* ed. M. Coogan (Oxford: Oxford University Press, 1998) 206-41; **G. Cardascia,** *Les archives des Murašû* (Paris: Imprimerie Nationale, 1951); **C. E. Carter,** *The Emergence of Yehud in the Persian Period: A Social and Demographic Study* (JSOTSup 294; Sheffield: Sheffield Academic, 1999); **J. J. Collins,** *Daniel* (Hermeneia; Minneapolis: Fortress, 1993); **M. D. Coogan,** *Imperialism and Religion: Assyria, Judah, and Israel in the Eighth and Seventh Centuries B.C.* (SBLMS 19; Missoula, MT: Scholars Press, 1974); idem, "Into Exile: From the Assyrian Conquest of Israel to the Fall of Babylon" in *The*

Oxford History of the Biblical World, ed. M. Coogan (Oxford: Oxford University Press, 1998) 244-75; **R. B. Coote and K. W. Whitelam**, *The Emergence of Early Israel in Historical Perspective* (SWBA 5; Sheffield: Almond, 1987); **F. M. Cross**, *Canaanite Myth and Hebrew Epic: Essays in the History of the Religion of Israel* (Cambridge: Harvard University Press, 1973); **S. Dalley**, "Recent Evidence from Assyrian Sources for Judaean History from Uzziah to Manasseh," *JSOT* 28 (2004) 387-401; **G. I. Davies**, *Ancient Hebrew Inscriptions: Corpus and Concordance* (2 vols.; Cambridge: Cambridge University Press, 1991-2004); **M. De Odorico**, *The Use of Numbers and Quantifications in the Assyrian Royal Inscriptions* (SAAS 3; Helsinki: University of Helsinki Press, 1995); **P. S. Evans**, *The Invasion of Sennacherib in the Book of Kings: A Source-Critical and Rhetorical Study of 2 Kings 18—19* (VTSup 125; Leiden: E. J. Brill, 2009); **A. Faust**, "Settlement and Demography in Seventh-Century Judah and the Extent and Intensity of Sennacherib's Campaign," *PEQ* 140 (2008) 168-94; **I. Finkelstein and N. A. Silberman**, *The Bible Unearthed: Archaeology's New Vision of Ancient Israel and the Origin of Its Sacred Texts* (New York: Free Press, 2001); **W. R. Gallagher**, *Sennacherib's Campaign to Judah: New Studies* (SHCANE 18; Leiden: E. J. Brill, 1999); **J. Goldberg**, "Two Assyrian Campaigns Against Hezekiah and Later Eighth Century Biblical Chronology," *Bib* 80 (1999) 360-90; **L. L. Grabbe**, *Judaism from Cyrus to Hadrian* (2 vols.; Minneapolis: Fortress, 1992); idem, *A History of the Jews and Judaism in the Second Temple Period*, 1: *Yehud: A History of the Persian Province of Judah* (London: T & T Clark, 2004); idem, *Ancient Israel: What Do We Know and How Do We Know It?* (London: T & T Clark, 2007); **A. K. Grayson**, "Mesopotamia, History of (Assyria)," *ABD* 4:732-55; idem, *Assyrian and Babylonian Chronicles* (TCS 5; Locust Valley, NY: J. J. Augustine, 1975); idem, *Assyrian Rulers of the Early First Millennium BC II (858-745 BC)* (RIMA 3; Toronto: University of Toronto Press, 1996); **L. J. Greenspoon**, "Between Alexandria and Antioch: Jews and Judaism in the Hellenistic Period," in *The Oxford History of the Biblical World*, ed. M. Coogan (Oxford: Oxford University Press, 1998) 317-51; **E. S. Gruen**, "Hellenism and Persecution: Antiochus IV and the Jews," in *Hellenistic History and Culture*, ed. P. Green (Berkeley: University of California Press, 1993) 238-74; **W. W. Hallo**, "From Qar-

qar to Carchemish: Assyria and Israel in the Light of New Discoveries," *BA* 23 (1960) 34-61; **J. H. Hayes and P. K. Hooker**, *A New Chronology for the Kings of Israel and Judah and Its Implications for Biblical History and Literature* (Atlanta: John Knox, 1988); **J. H. Hayes and J. K. Kuan**, "The Final Years of Samaria (730-720 BC)," *Bib* 72 (1991) 153-81; **J. H. Hayes and S. R. Mandell**, *The Jewish People in Classical Antiquity from Alexander to Bar Kochba* (Louisville: Westminster/John Knox, 1998); **K. G. Hoglund**, *Achaemenid Imperial Administration in Syria-Palestine and the Missions of Ezra and Nehemiah* (SBLDS 125; Atlanta: Scholars Press, 1992); **S. A. Irvine**, *Isaiah, Ahaz, and the Syro-Ephraimtic Crisis* (SBLDS 123; Atlanta: Scholars Press, 1990); **B. E. Kelle**, "What's in a Name? Neo-Assyrian Designations for the Northern Kingdom and Their Implications for Israelite History and Biblical Interpretation," *JBL* 121 (2002) 639-66; idem, *Hosea 2: Metaphor and Rhetoric in Historical Perspective* (SBLAB 20; Atlanta: Society of Biblical Literature, 2005); idem, "Ancient Israelite Prophets and Greek Political Orators: Analogies for the Prophets and Their Implications for Historical Reconstruction," in *Israel's Prophets and Israel's Past: Essays on the Relationship of Prophetic Texts and Israelite History in Honor of John H. Hayes*, ed. B. E. Kelle and M. B. Moore (LHBOTS 446; New York: T & T Clark, 2006) 57-82; idem, *Ancient Israel at War 853-586 BC* (Essential Histories 67; Oxford: Osprey, 2007); idem, "Dealing with the Trauma of Defeat: The Rhetoric of the Devastation and Rejuvenation of Nature in Ezekiel," *JBL* 128 (2009) 469-90; **R. Kessler**, *The Social History of Ancient Israel: An Introduction* (Minneapolis: Fortress, 2008); **K. A. Kitchen**, "Egypt, History of (Chronology)," *ABD* 2:321-31; idem, *The Third Intermediate Period in Egypt (1100-650 B.C.)* (2nd ed.; Warminster: Aris & Phillips, 1986); **G. N. Knoppers**, "In Search of Post-Exilic Israel: Samaria after the Fall of the Northern Kingdom," in *In Search of Pre-Exilic Israel: Proceedings of the Oxford Old Testament Seminar*, ed. J. Day (JSOTSup 406; London: T & T Clark, 2004) 150-80; **M. J. W. Leith**, "Israel among the Nations: The Persian Period," in *The Oxford History of the Biblical World*, ed. M. Coogan (Oxford: Oxford University Press, 1998) 276-316; **N. P. Lemche**, *The Old Testament Between Theology and History: A Critical Survey* (Louisville: Westminster/John Knox, 2008); **L. I. Levine**, "The Age of Hellenism:

Alexander the Great and the Rise and Fall of the Hasmonean Kingdom," in *Ancient Israel: From Abraham to the Roman Destruction of the Temple*, ed. H. Shanks (rev. ed.; Upper Saddle River, NJ: Prentice-Hall, 1999) 231-64; **O. Lipschits,** *The Fall and Rise of Jerusalem: Judah under Babylonian Rule* (Winona Lake, IN: Eisenbrauns, 2005); **O. Lipschits and J. Blenkinsopp,** eds., *Judah and the Judeans in the Neo-Babylonian Period* (Winona Lake, IN: Eisenbrauns, 2003); **O. Lipschits and M. Oeming,** eds., *Judah and the Judeans in the Persian Period* (Winona Lake, IN: Eisenbrauns, 2006); **V. P. Long,** ed., *Israel's Past in Present Research: Essays on Ancient Israelite Historiography* (SBTS 7; Winona Lake, IN: Einsebrauns, 1999); **J. W. McKay,** *Religion in Judah under the Assyrians, 732-609 BC* (SBT 26; Naperville, IL: Allenson, 1973); **R. Melugin,** "Prophetic Books and the Problem of Historical Reconstruction," in *Prophets and Paradigms: Essays in Honor of Gene M. Tucker,* ed. S. Reid (JSOTSup 229; Sheffield: Sheffield Academic, 1996) 63-78; **J. M. Miller and J. H. Hayes,** *A History of Ancient Israel and Judah* (2nd ed.; Louisville: Westminster/John Knox, 2006); **M. B. Moore,** *Philosophy and Practice in Writing a History of Ancient Israel* (LHBOTS 437; New York: T & T Clark, 2006a); idem, "Writing Israel's History Using the Prophetic Books," in *Israel's Prophets and Israel's Past: Essays on the Relationship of Prophetic Texts and Israelite History in Honor of John H. Hayes,* ed. B. E. Kelle and M. B. Moore (LHBOTS 446; New York: T & T Clark, 2006b) 23-36; **M. B. Moore and B. E. Kelle,** *Biblical History and Israel's Past: The Changing Study of the Bible and History* (Grand Rapids: Eerdmans, 2010); **N. Na'aman,** "The Kingdom of Judah under Josiah," *TA* 18 (1991) 3-71; **R. D. Nelson,** *The Double Redaction of the Deuteronomistic History* (JSOTSup 18; Sheffield: JSOT, 1981); **J. Nogalski,** *Literary Precursors to the Book of the Twelve* (BZAW 217; Berlin: de Gruyter, 1993); **B. Oded,** "The Historical Background of the Syro-Ephraimitic War Reconsidered," *CBQ* 34 (1972) 153-65; **I. W. Provan, V. P. Long and T. Longman III,** *A Biblical History of Israel* (Louisville: Westminster/John Knox, 2003); **D. B. Redford,** *Egypt, Canaan, and Israel in Ancient Times* (Princeton, NJ: Princeton University Press,

1992); **D. W. Rooke,** *Zadok's Heirs: The Role and Development of the High Priesthood in Ancient Israel* (OTM; Oxford: Oxford University Press, 2000); **D. L. Smith-Christopher,** *A Biblical Theology of Exile* (OBT; Minneapolis: Fortress, 2002); **J. A. Soggin,** *An Introduction to the History of Israel and Judah* (2nd ed.; Valley Forge, PA: Trinity Press International, 1993); **A. Spalinger,** "Egypt, History of (3rd Intermediate-Saite Period [Dyn 21-26])," *ABD* 2:353-64; **H. Spieckermann,** *Juda unter Assur in der Sargonidenzeit* (FRLANT 129; Göttingen: Vandenhoeck & Ruprecht, 1982); **E. Stern,** *Material Culture of the Land of the Bible in the Persian Period, 538-332 BC* (Jerusalem: Israel Exploration Society, 1982); idem, *Archaeology of the Land of the Bible,* 2: *The Assyrian, Babylonian, and Persian Periods, 732-332 BCE* (New York: Doubleday, 2001); **M. W. Stolper,** *Entrepeneurs and Empire: The Murašû Archive, the Murašû Firm, and the Persian Rule in Babylonia* (Uitgaven van het Nederlands Historisch-Archaeologisch Instituut te Istanbul 54; Leiden: Nederlands Historisch-Archaeologisch Instituut te Istanbul, 1985); **M. A. Sweeney,** *King Josiah of Judah: The Lost Messiah of Israel* (Oxford: Oxford University Press, 2001); **H. Tadmor,** *The Inscriptions of Tiglath-pileser III King of Assyria* (Jerusalem: Israel Academy of Sciences and Humanities, 1994); **R. E. Tappy,** *The Archaeology of Israelite Samaria,* 1: *The Eighth-Century BCE* (HSS 50; Winona Lake, IN: Eisenbrauns, 2001); **V. Tcherikover,** *Hellenistic Civilization and the Jews* (Philadelphia: Jewish Publication Society of America, 1959); **R. Tomes,** "The Reason for the Syro-Ephraimitic War," *JSOT* 59 (1993) 55-71; **D. Vanderhooft,** *The Neo-Babylonian Empire and Babylon in the Latter Prophets* (HSM 59; Atlanta: Scholars Press, 1999); **A. G. Vaughn,** *Theology, History, and Archaeology in the Chronicler's Account of Hezekiah* (SBLABS 4; Atlanta: Scholars Press, 1999); **J. Weinberg,** *The Citizen-Temple Community,* trans. D. Smith-Christopher (JSOTSup 151; Sheffield: JSOT, 1992); **M. Weinfeld,** *Deuteronomy and the Deuteronomistic School* (Oxford: Clarendon Press, 1972); **K. L. Younger,** "The Fall of Samaria in Light of Recent Research," *CBQ* 61 (1999) 461-82. B. E. Kelle

J, K

JEREMIAH: BOOK OF

This major book of classical prophecy gives an edited presentation of the message and import of the prophet Jeremiah. To this end, it uses poetic and prose oracles, accounts of *visions and symbolic actions (*see* Sign Acts), prophetic *laments and providentially interpreted historical narratives. It evidently originated among Judean exiles in Babylon by employing texts and traditions relating to Jeremiah's prophetic ministry. It was intended as a theological explanation of the downfall of Judah and subsequent *exile and also as an encouragement to maintain hope for restoration to God's favor and to the *land.

1. Literary Survey
2. Historical Framework
3. Basic Structure
4. Smaller Divisions
5. Prominent Genres
6. Some Elements of Hope
7. The Septuagint of Jeremiah
8. The Masoretic Text
9. Theology
10. Purpose

1. Literary Survey.

This long and complex book calls for an initial overview before it is examined in detail.

1.1. A Horizontal Perspective. The double thrust of imminent doom and eventual hope that runs through the book gives the impression of a rollercoaster ride. In an uneven succession of contrasting vantage points, readers are alarmingly taken down long tracks of despair, but at times they are lifted up to heights of hope.

1.1.1. Jeremiah 1; 52. The first and last chapters, which function as prologue and epilogue for the book, cogently embody this double feature of despair and hope. Jeremiah 1:10, in an account of the prophet's call and commissioning, summarizes his messages with a lengthy series of verbs of destruction and a pair of verbs of reconstruction. Jeremiah 52 uses the different exilic experiences of the last two kings of Judah as long and short enacted parables of the nation's past and present doom and future restoration.

1.1.2. Jeremiah 2—10. The book in its present form has been roughly divided into thirds. Jeremiah 10 marks the close of the first part. Its dominant portion, Jeremiah 10:1-16, consists of a triumphant hymn that contrasts omnipotent Yahweh with the ineffectual images of the Babylonian gods, who ultimately must perish. The preceding material in Jeremiah 2—9 is largely a series of oracles of judgment looking ahead to the fall of Jerusalem and subsequent exile. However, it also contains anticipations of post-judgment hope, in Jeremiah 3:12-18 and in the reassuring postscripts in Jeremiah 4:27; 5:10, 18 that judgment will not be total.

1.1.3. Jeremiah 11—33. The hopeful notes struck in the closing four chapters follow a long run of negative material. Yet, its negativity is interrupted by messages of a positive aftermath, notably in Jeremiah 12:14-17; 16:14-21; 23:5-8; 27:10-14.

1.1.4. Jeremiah 34—51. The oracles against the nations in Jeremiah 46—51 amount to virtual oracles of salvation for God's own people, and four of them conclude with brief affirmations of restoration for the nations. Long as this collection of oracles is, it caps the even longer series of grim narratives in Jeremiah 34—45. Once more the book looks round the corner of military defeat, interpreted in terms of divine judgment, toward prospects of eventual hope.

1.2. A Vertical Perspective. Readers of the

English text of Jeremiah must appreciate that the present book of Jeremiah is like a stately home that has been added to and updated. The evidence lies in the old Greek version, the Septuagint (LXX), and in the fragments of Hebrew manuscripts found at Qumran that match it. They jointly attest an earlier, shorter Hebrew edition of the book than the standard Hebrew text, the Masoretic Text (MT), which is also represented at Qumran in a proto-Masoretic form and has become the canonical text (*see* Text and Textual Criticism).

1.2.1. The Structure of the Earlier Text. This text already reflects to a large extent the shape it would eventually take in the later development. It does, however, predominantly display a bipartite, negative structure in which poetic messages of doom and Jeremiah's laments over his persecution in Jeremiah 2—25 are paralleled by prose narratives of Jeremiah's persecution and increasing disaster for Jerusalem and Judah in Jeremiah 26—45. Understandably, the poetic oracles of doom for the nations were squeezed into Jeremiah 25, in accord with that chapter's international flavor. Yet, the earlier text already contains the poetic and positive Jeremiah 30—31 in the second part of the book, appropriately placed next to the story of Jeremiah's symbolic action of territorial hope in Jeremiah 32. In fact, a minor focus on hope is a pervading feature of this text.

1.2.2. The Structure of the Later Text. The text perpetuated in the MT has created a structural shape for the book that gives a larger role to its positive content. It mainly does so by moving the oracles against the nations to the close of the book, before the epilogue, thus establishing a literary parallel to Jeremiah 10 and Jeremiah 30—33. Other new features develop this change. The positive ending to the Elam oracle in Jeremiah 49:39 has been complemented with similar additions to three other oracles at Jeremiah 46:26b; 48:47; 49:6. Moreover, the parallel structuring has been enhanced by repeating in Jeremiah 30:10-11 the oracle of salvation for Israel at Jeremiah 46:27-28. Already in the earlier text the hymn of Jeremiah 10:12-16 had been reused in Jeremiah 51:15-19. The later text has built upon the positive pointers present in its predecessor and given them a greater role.

2. Historical Framework.

There are a number of pathways and recurring landmarks that must be explored to explain the book of Jeremiah adequately in its own terms. The book urges us to begin with history.

2.1. The Superscription. The superscription in Jeremiah 1:1-3 summarizes Jeremiah's ministry as extending from the thirteenth year of Josiah's reign over Judah via Jehoiakim's reign as far as the eleventh year of Zedekiah's (i.e., from 627 to 586 BC). There is obvious shorthand here that presupposes that readers can expand it with some basic historical knowledge of their own. This long period encompasses the downfall of the Assyrian Empire, in which Judah was a vassal kingdom, and its replacement by the Babylonian Empire (*see* Israelite History). The sole mention of the climactic event of "the captivity of Jerusalem" evokes the momentous end of a nation clustered round the twin nuclei of Yahwistic worship and Davidic monarchy that were located in the capital.

2.2. Historical Sequencing. The initial superscription launches a loose chronological framework, largely by means of a series of references to Judean kings. These are lacking from Jeremiah 1:4 to Jeremiah 20, apart from the reference in Jeremiah 3:6 to Josiah's reign, though Jeremiah 2—6 contains material that belongs to the early period of Jeremiah's prophesying. Although Jeremiah 21:1-2 jumps to the attack on Jerusalem late in Zedekiah's reign by the Babylonian king Nebuchadnezzar, the following series of royal oracles progresses in order from Josiah's short-lived successor Jehoahaz ("Shallum" [Jer 22:11]) to Jehoiakim (Jer 22:18) and his brief successor Jehoiachin ("Coniah" [Jer 22:24]), while Jeremiah 23:6 alludes to Zedekiah by the name "The LORD is my righteousness." Jeremiah 24 also relates to Zedekiah's reign in referring to Jehoiachin's exile in 597 BC as having already occurred (Jer 24:1; cf. Jer 24:8). Jeremiah 25 steps back to the fourth year of Jehoiakim's reign in its review of Jeremiah's twenty-three years of prophesying since 627 BC. Jeremiah 26 stays in Jehoiakim's reign but moves back to his accession year (Jer 26:1). Jeremiah 28 goes on to Zedekiah's accession year (Jer 28:1; the chronological reference in the MT's addition at Jer 27:1 is dubious). Jeremiah 32 progresses to his tenth year (Jer 32:1), where Jeremiah 34 also seems to belong (Jer 34:1). The next two chapters revert to Jehoiakim's reign, to an unspecified portion (Jer 35:1) and then to his fourth and fifth years (Jer

36:1, 9). From Jeremiah 37 to Jeremiah 39 incidents in Zedekiah's fateful last years of Babylonian siege and conquest are narrated (see Jer 37:5; 39:1). Jeremiah 40—44 recounts postwar events, probably up to 582 BC, though Jeremiah 45 briefly reverts to Jehoiakim's fourth year (Jer 45:1). The relatively independent section of oracles against the nations in Jeremiah 46—51 has comparatively few royal references. It does mention in sequence Jehoiakim's fourth year (Jer 46:2) and Zedekiah's accession year (Jer 49:34) and fourth year (Jer 51:59). The historical appendix to the book in Jeremiah 52 singles out the siege of Jerusalem from Zedekiah's ninth to eleventh years (Jer 52:4-5) and its immediate aftermath and then leaps ahead to the exiled King Jehoiachin's thirty-fifth regnal year (i.e., 561 BC). Despite its deviations, the book exhibits substantial evidence of chronological progression as a structural element.

2.3. Two Significant Periods. In both its chronological unfolding and tangential deviations, the book highlights two periods. The more important of the two is the siege and fall of Jerusalem in 588-586 BC. Although Jeremiah 40-44 extend Jeremiah's prophesying beyond that period, there is good reason for the superscription to stop at 586 BC: much of the book's concern belongs to that period both by prediction and in actuality. The other period is Jehoiakim's fourth year. In Jeremiah 25; (35-)36; 45 this time marker is dramatically allowed to disturb the sequencing. Jeremiah 46:2 explains it in terms of Nebuchadnezzar's defeat of the Egyptian army at Carchemish in north Syria (605 BC). It was a watershed event, spelling the final downfall of the old Assyrian Empire by the defeat of Assyria's recent ally Egypt and so the passing of Syria-Palestine into the new Babylonian Empire (cf. 2 Kings 24:7). It meant validating identification for Jeremiah's anonymous premonitions in his earlier, doom-laden "foe from the north" oracles (Jer 4:5-8; 6:1-8, 22-23; 15:12; cf. Jer 1:13-15; 4:15-17; 5:15-17) and so marked the beginning of the end for Judah. In fact, while "the king of Babylon" is first mentioned as the future conqueror of Judah in the literary ordering at Jeremiah 20:4 in an undated passage, the earliest chronological mention of him is at Jeremiah 36:29 in Jehoiakim's fifth year (the references to him in Jer 25, set in Jehoiakim's fourth year, have been introduced in the MT). The focus on two reigns parallels the highlighting of the reigns of Ahaz and Hezekiah in Isaiah 1—39 at Isaiah 7—8; 36—39. However, the book of Jeremiah gives much more coverage to the historical role of the prophet, tracing both reactions of rejection to his message of doom and the outworking of that message.

3. Basic Structure.
Although the book of Jeremiah in its present form reflects a subsequent editorial history that must take the evidence of the LXX and the MT into account (see 7 and 8 below), the eventual additions and other changes have not upset the main presentation in a radical way. For the most part, its basic structure, along with superscriptions, assignments of historical settings and arrangements of material, features early elements of the book. If the chapters of Jeremiah 46—51, which are variously placed in the LXX and the MT, are left out of consideration for now, the book falls into two halves, Jeremiah 2—25 and Jeremiah 26—45, with a prophetic prologue in Jeremiah 1 and a historical epilogue in Jeremiah 52. The first half largely consists of oracles and laments about the coming destruction of Judah and Jerusalem and is mostly undated. The second half mainly features a series of dated biographical narratives relating to Jeremiah in which that destruction is gradually worked out in a historical context of rejection of the prophet and his prophetic messages.

4. Smaller Divisions.
4.1. Literary Blocks. A largely systematic effort has been made in the book to demarcate blocks of material by means of initial oracle reception headings, "A message that Jeremiah received from Yahweh" or, less often, "What Jeremiah received as Yahweh's message" (see Neumann). The headings appear in this role at Jeremiah 1:2; 11:1; 14:1; 18:1; 21:1; 25:1; 30:1; 32:1; 34:1; 40:1. One might have expected such signals elsewhere: at Jeremiah 7:1, where the MT has added it; Jeremiah 26:1, where an oracle reception statement, "this message came from Yahweh," appears instead; Jeremiah 37:1; and Jeremiah 46:1, where the MT has constructed a heading out of the earlier relative clause in Jeremiah 25:13. On the other hand, headings also occur at times within evident blocks, at Jeremiah 34:8; 35:1; 44:1; 45:1 and erratically within Jeremiah 46—51.

4.2. Compositions. Blocks of material appear to fall into groups of compositions, which in turn are arrangements of units, either oracular units set together in a batch or episodes in a larger narrative. For example, the block made up of Jeremiah 21—24 has combined two separate collections of oracular units, a royal collection (Jer 21:11—23:8) and one attacking Jeremiah's prophetic rivals (Jer 23:9-40). They have been editorially set in a frame, Jeremiah 21:1-10 and Jeremiah 24:1-10. The consequent block has been split into six compositions: Jeremiah 21:1-22:9, which has a key word "fire"; Jeremiah 22:10-30, which features three consecutive reigns; Jeremiah 23:1-8, which gives a positive perspective after earlier negative ones; Jeremiah 23:9-40, a series of poetic denunciations of false prophets; Jeremiah 23:25-40, a pair of prose denunciations; and Jeremiah 24:1-10, a closing oracle vision report. In Jeremiah 22:6 a separate unit has been stitched to the previous one by the conjunction "for." This editorial device for continuity in terms of elucidation is often used (e.g., Jer 2:20; 4:3, 15; 10:21; 25:15; 30:12). In the narrative block of Jeremiah 34—36, the three chapters represent compositions that incriminatingly demonstrate step by step the rejection of the whole range of divine revelation, given first in an old Torah tradition, then in the legitimate, long-standing prophetic movement that Jeremiah inherited (cf. Jer 28:8), and finally in his own oracles of disaster. The next narrative block, Jeremiah 37—39, reverts to the historical context of Jeremiah 34 with which the previous block commenced. It announces the general rejection of Yahweh's messages through Jeremiah at the beginning (Jer 37:1-2) and the catastrophe entailed by that rejection at the end (Jer 39:1-10). In between, narratives intertwine the mistreatment of Yahweh's messenger and the rejection of the messages; the so-called confessions of Jeremiah earlier in the book have a similar function (see 5.7 below). The pace of the block is set by Jeremiah's loss of freedom. Broached in Jeremiah 37:4, it is used as a structural marker at the close of episodes (Jer 37:16, 21; 38:13, 28; cf. Jer 39:14). The recurring motif serves as a "code": "The prophet, the word of God, was put away and not heard" (Holt, 164). The imprisonment of Jeremiah, like Herod's incarceration of John the Baptist (Lk 3:19-20), was the final proof of opposition to God. One can agree with much of W. McKane's elaboration of

a rolling corpus underlying the book (McKane 1986, l-lxxxiii), but D. Jones has fairly criticized his cardinal view of uncontrolled, haphazard growth on the grounds that it "overlooks the design in the putting together and assembly of originally independent oral units" (Jones, 27).

4.3. Prose Sermons. Organically linked with the arrangement in literary blocks is the presence of so-called prose sermons, which are regularly used to inaugurate blocks, though they also appear elsewhere in the book. L. Stulman has analyzed them, carefully differentiating between the evidence for them in the LXX and the later MT (Stulman 1986). They have solidly literary features: the use of stereotyped formulations, often but by no means always taken from Deuteronomy and the Deuteronomistic History, and quotations from these and other OT books. The sermons appear in Jeremiah 7:1—8:3; 11:1-14; 14:11-16; 18:7-12; 21:5-9; 22:1-5; 25:3-12; 26:3-6; 30:3, 8-9; 32:29-41; 34:8-22; 40:2-3; 44:2-10, 20-23. Prose sermonic language is also a sporadic mark of prose oracles elsewhere (e.g., within Jer 17:19-27; 32:17-25; 35:13-17). In some cases a prose sermon evidently has been constructed out of a particular earlier oracle, while in other cases it summarizes Jeremiah's perspectives in an adjacent text or elsewhere in the book. In Jeremiah 44 this literary form is employed to give a final summary of his message. The prose sermons appear to be versions of his message written for a later generation. They are "not the firsthand voice of the prophet, but a voice filtered through memory and tradition" (Rosenberg, 188). Their use of distinctive vocabulary outside the main Deuteronomistic tradition (see Bright, 25-27) seems to indicate that they stand on the fringe of that tradition, though strongly influenced by its style and perspectives.

5. Dominant Genres.

The book of Jeremiah has used a variety of genres to communicate its message. Recognition of these cultural conventions in a particular text helps readers to engage with it by fostering expectations about its particular function and flow.

5.1. Oracles of Disaster. Such oracles, both in poetry and prose, make up most of the book. Many of them preface the announcement of disaster with a reason for it, while the announcement usually appears in the double form of a divine intervention in the human situation and the dire repercussions of that intervention. A simple example occurs in the mixed prose and poetry of Jeremiah 11:21-23: "Concerning the men from Anathoth who have designs on your life. . . . Look, I am going to deal with them. Their young men will die by the sword, their sons and daughters will die of famine, and they will have no survivors." The reason sometimes has its blameworthiness accentuated by a contrast motif, as in Jeremiah 2:21: "Yet it was I who planted you as a red grape vine, wholly from true seed." In Jeremiah 2:1-3 a whole unit is devoted to a contrast motif, as a preface to subsequent descriptions of the degeneration of God's people and consequent divine reprisals. The beginning of the oracle of disaster may be expanded by attention-grabbing features, such as questions, as in Jeremiah 2:23; 5:7; 8:4-5; 18:13-14, or imperatives, as in Jeremiah 3:2; 5:10, 20-21; 7:21; 22:20.

The whole oracle or only its announcement is frequently introduced by a quotation formula of the type "Here is what Yahweh said," indicating that the prophet is proclaiming the divine word. At times these formulas are used in what appears on other grounds to be editorial contexts, so that they represent not Jeremiah's speaking to his constituency but literary elaboration for the book's hearers or readers, legitimating what follows as divinely inspired and treating its textual nature as a means of public transmission (Jer 3:16; 12:14; 24:5, 8; 26:2; 30:2; 32:36; 33:10, 12). The formulas similarly appear in material added in the MT, at Jeremiah 33:14, 17, 20, 25. Unless this phenomenon is to be regarded as purely literary, readers are meant to consider the editors either as prophets in their own right or citing later prophetic oracles. Another type of quotation formula, "declared Yahweh," can also mark the opening of divine speech, though it follows the first phrase or clause. More often it is used to signal the end of a unit or section. The MT frequently adds it for delimitation purposes.

Other, more general introductory formulas are the oracle reception heading and the oracle reception statement (see 4.1 above). A recurring peculiarity of the book, one that has perplexed readers and commentators alike in their failure to recognize it, is that introductory oracular formulas of various kinds can have an advance, anticipatory role, alerting the reader

to a divine oracle to be cited later in the passage (Allen 2008a, 5). They occur at Jeremiah 9:17; 14:1, 17; 17:5; 25:1; 30:5; 31:2, 10, 15; 32:1, 14; 40:1; 45:2; 48:40; 50:33. For instance, the heading for the composition of Jeremiah 14:1-16 announces the oracle in Jeremiah 14:10, while the heading to the next composition in Jeremiah 14:17 looks beyond the first unit of Jeremiah 14:17-22 to the oracular units in Jeremiah 15:1-4 and 15:4-9.

5.2. Disputations. A disputation with the basic elements of a thesis, dispute and counterthesis has been discovered in other prophetic books (Murray). There are a strikingly large number of them in Jeremiah, and recognition of them yields exegetical insights. They appear in Jeremiah 2:23-25; 3:1-5; 8:8-9; 18:6; 28:2-4, 6-9, 14; 33:23-26; 37:9-10; 42:13-18; 44:1-30; 45:3-5a; 48:14-17 (Allen 2008b). They are combined with oracles of disaster, widening their perspective by citing an opposing viewpoint and arguing against it. In Jeremiah 8:8-9, for instance, the disputation acts as a bridge, underscoring reasons for coming disaster and already moving over to announce a form the disaster was to take: "How can you say, 'We are wise because we have in our possession Yahweh's torah'? In fact, look, it has been transformed into a falsehood by the false pen of scribes. The 'wise' will be humiliated, defeated and captured. Look, Yahweh's message they have rejected—so what kind of wisdom can they have?" The disputation is over wisdom. The people's attitude cited at the outset is a thesis that is incorporated into the dispute, while the final line is the counterthesis. The disputed thesis and the counterthesis match in their contemptuous questions and echo of "wise" by "wisdom." The two-pronged development of the dispute is marked by the repetition of "look."

In Jeremiah 28 the narrative of the confrontation between Hananiah and Jeremiah as rival prophets of Yahweh is enhanced by proceeding on the lines of a disputation that moves from speech to speech in a developing plot. Hananiah engages in a symbolic action, which Jeremiah opposes by launching another genre, a disputation. His interruption of Hananiah's attempt to move from interpretation to action in Jeremiah 28:6-9 represents a dispute that downgrades his rival's divinely attributed speech in Jeremiah 28:2-4 to a thesis that must be challenged. The counterthesis appears within a divine speech, at Jeremiah

28:14. The direct speech before and after Jeremiah 28:14 rounds off the dispute. The MT has recognized the symmetry of thesis and counterthesis in Jeremiah 28:2-4 and Jeremiah 28:14 by adding "Almighty, Israel's God" to "Yahweh" in their initial quotation formulas, while leaving the other formulas in Jeremiah 28:13 and Jeremiah 28:16 unexpanded.

5.3. *Proclamations of Salvation.* Hananiah's prophetic speech in Jeremiah 28:2-4 is actually a proclamation of salvation. In principle, this genre is a happy counterpart to the announcement of punishment in the oracle of disaster, but it occurs much less often in the book. It follows the same pattern of divine intention and human consequences, but now in positive terms. Examples are especially abundant in the block of Jeremiah 30—31, including Jeremiah 30:18-22; 31:4-6, 8-9, 31-34.

5.4. *Symbolic Actions.* Hananiah's speech was meant to introduce the performance of his symbolic action in Jeremiah 28:10. The rest of the symbolic actions (*see* Sign Acts) in the book are performed by Jeremiah or under his auspices (see Friebel). Reports of symbolic actions typically are written in the first person and generally consist of three parts: divine command, prophetic performance in public, and divine interpretation, which takes the form of an announcement of disaster or a proclamation of salvation. Such actions were carried out by prophets as a dramatic means of reinforcing the divine message.

5.4.1. Jeremiah 13:1-11. This action, which involves the spoiling of a linen sash, lacks a public performance, so that the communication lies solely in the written report. It warns of coming ruin for Judah and Jerusalem, despite their prestigious tradition.

5.4.2. Jeremiah 16:1-9. This report, which also lacks the element of prophetic performance, relates to a series of symbolic actions that represent a refraining from normal activities: marriage, funeral observances and attending the marriages of others. By these means Jeremiah was to be a witness to the coming disaster that would sweep aside such cultural norms.

5.4.3. Jeremiah 19:1-13. The breaking of a jug basically enacts before a selected group of witnesses the imminent destruction of Jerusalem because of the pagan worship carried on there. The performance of the action is not reported, though Jeremiah 19:14 assumes it.

5.4.4. Jeremiah 27—28. The prophetic conflict between Jeremiah and his prophetic rivals involves symbolic actions. He is commanded to make six wooden yokes, wear one, and distribute the rest to foreign delegates who had come to Jerusalem to plan secession from Babylonian hegemony. The message was that under God, Babylonian control of the west would end no time soon, and so submission was the only constructive option. A statement of the performance of the action is lacking, but Jeremiah 28:10 presupposes that Jeremiah was wearing his yoke. Hananiah's counteraction of breaking the yoke has a positive purpose, and so the divine interpretation features a proclamation of salvation. The rare lack of the element of a precise divine command to engage in it, for which the specially formulated Jeremiah 51:59-64 provides the only parallel in the book, appears to sound a warning to readers, who earlier have read in Jeremiah 27:2-3 such an instruction for Jeremiah's own action, not to take it at face value.

5.4.5. Jeremiah 32:6-15. This positive symbolic action is discussed in 6.4 below. The initial element of a divine command is rhetorically delayed until it is reported in Jeremiah 32:25.

5.4.6. Jeremiah 35:1-19. The symbolic action of offering wine to the teetotal Rechabites, who predictably refuse it as contrary to their traditional principles, is used to contrast the failure of Judah to comply with God's long-term prophetic revelation.

5.4.7. Jeremiah 43:8-13. In Tahpanhes, an Egyptian frontier town, Jeremiah receives a divine command to engage in a symbolic action in the presence of some of the Judean refugees who have brought him there, and to proclaim its meaning in an announcement of disaster. The report of its performance is not given, presumably to keep the focus on the interpretation. The action predicted the extension of Babylon's power to Egypt. Unfortunately, the role of the stones in the action is not clear. Were the stones to be buried to mark the spot where Nebuchadnezzar's throne was to be set (NRSV, NIV)? Or, covered with a mortar skim, were they to form a dais for the throne (REB, NJPS)?

5.4.8. Jeremiah 51:59-64. Elsewhere in the book Yahweh has commissioned Jeremiah to perform a symbolic action. In this case, however, Jeremiah delegates somebody else, who will be present at the place designated for the action. Nevertheless, the assignment of the task of sinking in the Euphrates a scroll containing oracles against Babylon as a forecast of Babylon's own doom evidently goes back to Yahweh's own command, as the divine "I" in Jeremiah 51:64 intimates. In this commissioning report, Jeremiah functions as the intermediary of the divine command, and there is no room for mention of the performance.

5.5. Visions. A prophetic *vision is one of the vehicles of communication between Yahweh and the prophet. There are seven reports of visions in the book, all of them autobiographical, as personal reports of private experiences. Most of them are oracle visions, in which a visionary experience provides the occasion for an oracular utterance. Most of them also involve natural sights to which Yahweh draws Jeremiah's attention and attaches symbolic meanings.

5.5.1 Jeremiah 1:11-12. This report supplements the call and commissioning report in Jeremiah 1:4-10 and functions as a confirmatory sign. The attention-drawing question-and-answer format is a standard one in vision reports (cf. Jer 24:1-3; Amos 7:7-9). Here it involves word play in that the Hebrew for "almond" sounds like the verb "to be alert" (cf. Amos 8:1-2), so that the point of the question is to make Jeremiah pronounce the word as a clue to the meaning. Yahweh promises ("I am going to be alert"; cf. KJV: "I will hasten") providential alertness over fulfilling the messages given now in principle to the prophet and to be individually given in the future.

5.5.2. Jeremiah 1:13-19. This vision report has the more usual role in prophetic literature of leading into an explanatory oracle. It appears to launch a fresh commissioning that presupposes a period of prophetic ministry. The overlap of Jeremiah 1:18-19 with Yahweh's answer to the prophet's lament in Jeremiah 15:20, along with the repetition of "from the north" in Jeremiah 15:12, suggests that a later situation is in view (see Lundbom 1995). Now the imagery features a metaphor that uses a key word, as in Amos 7:7. Yahweh calls Jeremiah's attention to a cooking pot happening to slip in a particular direction on the stones round the fire and interprets the incident in terms of military invasion from the north against the apostate people of Judah. Jeremiah is given reassuring and challenging exhortations to maintain his ministry. This report of catastrophe for Judah introduces the main theme of the book.

5.5.3. Jeremiah 4:19-31. Three reports of visions are clustered in Jeremiah 4:19-22, 23-28, 31. All of these visions feature Jeremiah's psychic perception of dramatic scenes of future destruction. The first two conclude with divine oracles and involve the whole country (Jer 5:20, 27). The initial report has both auditory and visual aspects of battle scenes, for which the closing oracle supplies the reason. The second one gives a vivid description of total devastation, which an oracle explains that Yahweh is to bring about. The third report, at the end of the unit of Jeremiah 4:29-31, is both auditory and visual like the first, but it envisions Jerusalem's coming destruction as a woman in her death throes.

5.5.4. Jeremiah 24. This vision report, like the ones in Jeremiah 1:11-19, features Yahweh's drawing attention to a scene, an answered question, and a closing oracle in Jeremiah 24:4-10, which from Jeremiah 24:6 onwards is pervaded with prose sermonic language that elaborates its importance. Because two opposing entities are involved, the oracle combines a proclamation of salvation and an announcement of disaster. The reported scene features two baskets of figs placed as firstfruits in the temple area and awaiting a priestly decisions about their acceptability. They are interpreted in terms of good or bad prospects for the deported Jehoiachin and the reigning Zedekiah and their associates respectively (see 6.3 below).

5.5.5. Jeremiah 38:21-23. This report lacks an oracle. Divine agency is indicated by the introductory "this is the message Yahweh caused me to see," so that the report itself conveys the message. The visionary and auditory vision report is part of a longer speech that the prophet addresses to Zedekiah. It communicates a potential preview of the royal harem being captured and singing a taunt song about the king's desertion.

5.6. Dirges. One would expect to find expressions of grief in a book largely devoted to the downfall of Jerusalem and Judah. One way it is expressed in the OT is in terms of a dirge or lamentation that, along with nonvocal mourning rituals, was primarily associated with death but could be extended to other experiences of disaster. In the brief form of a cry "Alas!" a dirge features literally in the divine denial of a proper funeral for Jehoiakim (Jer 22:18-19) and forecast of an honorable one for Zedekiah (Jer 34:5). But mainly in the book such lamentation is associated more widely with the great disaster to come. Whereas prayer *laments brought a crisis to Yahweh for help, as in the communal and individual laments in the Psalter, the dirge accepted the inevitability of a crisis as a lost cause. However, in Jeremiah 30:15, Rachel's postjudgment dirge over her exiled children receives a positive divine answer in Jeremiah 30:16-17, as if to a lament—something that the matriarch never imagined to be possible. Occasionally a form or tone of a dirge is employed simply to convey the magnitude of the disaster in view. This appears to be the case in Jeremiah 30:7, with its initial "Alas" and in Jeremiah 47:2 (cf. Jer 47:5), where wailing is described as a reaction to coming invasion. In Jeremiah 48:31-32, 36, in the course of a passage borrowed from Isaiah 16:7-11, the intense sympathy of the speaker similarly appears to be an emotional means of registering the overwhelming nature of Moab's fate.

5.6.1. Anticipatory Dirges. In the place of oracles of disaster or in order to reinforce them, Jeremiah sometimes announces future calamity by calling on the Judean community to anticipate it by engaging in national mourning. Thus, in Jeremiah 4:5-8 there is a summons to mourn coming enemy invasion, which is despairingly interpreted in terms of Yahweh's inevitable wrath. A similar call is issued in Jeremiah 6:26, to mourn "as if for an only son," in reaction to the invading foe from the north. The prose sermon in Jeremiah 7 picks up this summons in a snatch of poetry and explains it in terms of Yahweh's rejection of "a generation that deserves his wrath" (Jer 7:29). On a broader canvas, the kings of foreign nations are urged to mourn in advance over inevitable invasion (Jer 25:34-35). A particular example occurs in Jeremiah 49:3, where in Rabbah, the capital of Ammon, its womenfolk or satellite villages are summoned to engage in mourning for the coming exile of their god and priests.

5.6.2. Dirges and Laments Polarized. The genre of prayer lament stays in the field of grief but goes a giant step further by turning to God for help. In Jeremiah 8:18—9:1 the people's lament is strikingly mingled with Jeremiah's own heartfelt mourning in the mood of a funeral lamentation that grieves hopelessly over inexorable coming disaster. His tone is like Jesus' weeping over Jerusalem's inevitable fall in Luke 19:41-44. The prophet was tragically aware that the people's prayer would go unanswered. This bitter truth is made clear in a pair of similar passages within the compositions of Jeremiah 14:1-16; 14:17—15:9. In Jeremiah 14:7-9 a communal lament over a drought features such psalm lament elements as acknowledgment of sins, petitions to Yahweh for help, and also accusing quotations that turn the lament into a strident complaint (see 5.7.6 below), accusing Yahweh of lack of covenant commitment and of failing to intervene in power. The sequel in Jeremiah 14:10, 11-12 reports divine rejections of the community's appeal. Jeremiah 14:17-18 records Jeremiah's acute reaction to a military disaster in the tones of a dirge. Over against his despairing reaction is set the people's optimistic prayer lament, which contains the proper elements of a description of the crisis, acknowledgment of sins, petitions and a backing affirmation of faith. Of the two parties, the prophet had read the divine mind correctly, His response anticipates the divine no of Jeremiah 15:1-4, which Jeremiah 15:5-9 reinforces. Mention may also be made of Jeremiah 10:19-20, 23-25, where only portions of a prayer lament appear, but they are set in a context of disaster that no such lament can avert. A collective first-person speaker engages in a lament that moves with formal propriety from description of crisis to affirmation of faith and petition. But the lament is spoken in vain and receives no answer. Jeremiah himself was a theological realist who knew that judgment had to come, and so only a dirge was appropriate as an expression of anticipatory grief. Likewise, in response to the recital of Jeremiah's oracles of doom, the narrator was disappointed that the hearers did not resort to the dirge-related behavior of tearing their clothes (Jer 36:24).

5.6.3. Mocking Dirges. A dirge can be used in a tone of mockery to celebrate the justice of well-deserved punishment. In Jeremiah 38:22 a dirge functions as a taunt song that describes the desertion of Zedekiah's erstwhile supporters. It uses the 3 + 2 meter often associated with a poetic dirge. All the other examples in the book occur in Jeremiah 48; 50, in the oracles against Moab and Babylon. In Jeremiah 48:1-2 the cry "Alas" is combined with a report of the loss of Moab's glorious past. Such reversal is typical of a dirge. In a call to lamentation in

Jeremiah 48:17 an even more typical usage occurs, the combination of "How" and a note of reversal (cf. 2 Sam 1:19, 25, 27). Some of these elements recur in the lamentation of Jeremiah 48:39. In Jeremiah 48:46, a passage added in the MT from Numbers 21:29, an ironical use of "Alas" turns Moab's downfall into a matter of exultation. Jeremiah 50:23 features the same combination of "How" and reversal of fortunes that appeared in Jeremiah 48:17, while in Jeremiah 50:27b "Alas" launches a mock lamentation over Babylon's leaders.

5.7. Jeremiah's Laments. Interspersed in Jeremiah 11—20 is a series of eight laments, cries for God's help that Jeremiah utters in anguish. "There is no compelling reason not to place them within the prophet's ministry" (Smith, xviii). They are traditionally known as "confessions," though neither confession of sinning nor confession of divine praise characterizes them. They are in one respect like Augustine's spiritual biography, called *Confessions*, in that they feature the inner life of the prophet, and so the label has stuck. However, they reveal little biographical information about the prophet, only specifying a home village setting for the first lament (Jer 11:21, 23) and family conflict for the second (Jer 12:6). The narrative of Jeremiah's public punishment in Jeremiah 20:1-6 that precedes the seventh lament is intended merely as a typical example of how the prophet was persecuted rather than as the actual background of the lament. The other five laments lack any biographical context. What, then, is their purpose? Jeremiah functions in these laments as "the paradigmatic illustration of the degree of total national rejection of the message of the prophets" (Clements, 114). So they are meant to show the lengths to which Judah's rejection of Yahweh, who had commissioned Jeremiah, went and to be a measure of that rejection. God's people rejected both the divine messages given through Jeremiah and the prophetic messenger. As the poster boy for the people's rejection of God, the prophet went through gut-wrenching experiences that he could not stand. The laments are his cries of pain, his garden of Gethsemane experience, corresponding to the anguished prayer of Jesus, "Abba, Father, for you all things are possible. Remove this cup from me" (Mk 14:36). They also parallel Jesus' cry of dereliction on the cross, "My God, my God, why have you forsaken me?" (Mk 15:34).

His laments reflect the tradition of individual laments in the Psalter, adapted to express the prophetic aspect of Jeremiah's own suffering (Baumgartner).

It is important to perceive the literary contexts in which the laments have been placed. Presumably, they once formed a distinct collection, but now they have been dovetailed in pairs or singly into Jeremiah 11—20. The first four make up two pairs and have divine answers appended (Jer 11:18-23; 12:1-6; 15:10-14, 15-21), while the last two (Jer 20:7-13, 14-18) are also placed together. The fifth and sixth (Jer 17:14-18; 18:19-23) stand by themselves. The laments form constituent parts of three blocks of material, Jeremiah 11—13; 14—17; 18—20. They have been positioned with care. The first pair appears near the beginning of the first block, the second pair and the fifth lament come at the close of the first and second halves of the second block, while the sixth and the last two similarly close the twin compositions of the third block. These arrangements indicate the compositional importance of the laments.

5.7.1. Jeremiah 11:18-12:6. In the first block of five compositions, the initial pair of laments makes up a second composition that follows the first, Jeremiah 11:1-17. While the first composition deplores the breaking of the Torah covenant, this second one features Jeremiah as exemplar of the rejection of prophecy. The slighting of the double divine revelation of Torah and prophecy, which develops a joint motif of Jeremiah's prophesying in Jeremiah 6:16-17 and of the prose sermon of Jeremiah 7 at Jeremiah 7:22-27, constitutes a powerful indictment of Judah.

5.7.2. Jeremiah 15:10-21. Relatively early in the second block, Jeremiah 14—17, this pair of answered laments forms a third composition that presents the people's rejection of the prophet as Yahweh's agent ("for your sake" [Jer 15:15]). Jeremiah's own laments have been woven into the block's issue of the prophet's dirges versus the people's laments (see 5.6.2 above). His answered prayers contrast with the people's unanswered prayers in the first two compositions, Jeremiah 14:1-16; 14:17—15:5. Yahweh had in turn "rejected" the people, as they feared (Jer 14:19). Prophet and people stood respectively on either side of a great divide, for or against Yahweh and headed for deliverance or doom.

5.7.3. Jeremiah 17:14-18. The lament near the

close of the block is the first unit of a two-unit composition, Jeremiah 17:14-27. The two units share the phrase "the word of the LORD" (Jer 17:15, 20). The lament bemoans the belittling of the prophetic message, while the next unit, Jeremiah 17:19-27, supplies an illustration of that message, which features neglect of the Torah principle of Sabbath observance. Once more, both Torah and prophecy were rejected.

5.7.4. Jeremiah 18:19-23. In the third block, Jeremiah 18—20, the sixth lament closes the first of two compositions, Jeremiah 18:1-23; 19:1-20:18. It makes up most of its third unit, Jeremiah 18:18-23, and reflects the community's rejection of Yahweh via the prophet's rejection. Ironically, Jeremiah is demonized, from the community's warped perspective, as the enemy of not only priestly Torah but also prophetic revelation and sapiential instruction, and so needing to be silenced (Jer 18:18). At the center of the overall block, in Jeremiah 19:15, stands an interpretive divine statement that sheds light back onto this lament and forward to the final pair in Jeremiah 20:7-18. It grounds coming national punishment in the refusal to listen to Yahweh's prophetic messages. The statement follows an indictment of pagan worship, the worship of "other gods" (Jer 19:4), implicitly in defiance of the Torah. Again Yahweh's double revelation had been ominously rejected.

5.7.5. Jeremiah 20:7-18. This final pair of laments comes on the heels of a narrative that illustrates refusal to listen to Yahweh's prophetic messages by persecuting Jeremiah as Yahweh's messenger (Jer 20:1-6). The former of the pair, in Jeremiah 20:7-13, mirrors in graphic and emotional terms the personal anguish such rejection brought to Jeremiah, while it also broaches the vindication that the eventual fulfillment of his message would bring. The second of the two, in Jeremiah 20:14-18, underlines the overall theme of rejection by portraying the nadir of suffering to which the prophet descended. So it also constitutes further justification for the overall message of divine retribution.

5.7.6. Complaint Elements. A striking feature of Jeremiah's laments is that they adopt at times the shriller form of a complaint against Yahweh. Scholars often use lament and complaint interchangeably in Psalms study, but a good case can be made for reserving the latter term for a subtype of prayer lament in the psalms that combines its appeals for help with charges against God (see Broyles). It goes beyond the persuasive arguments for help used in an ordinary lament and employs accusatory arguments against God. Grief and anger are attested psychological companions; accordingly, at times the prophet's laments turn not merely against his human opponents but against Yahweh. Complaint elements appear in four of the eight prayer laments of Jeremiah: the bewildered and challenging questions "Why?" in Jeremiah 12:1; 15:18a; 20:18, the question "How long?" in Jeremiah 12:4 that presupposes endurance strained beyond reasonable limits, and direct accusations of God in Jeremiah 15:18b for failing to help Jeremiah and in Jeremiah 20:7 for actively siding with his persecutors. Such elements stay within the bounds of traditional faith according to the OT. They are an honest measure of the horrendous stress that the prophet suffered.

6. Some Elements of Hope.

The dominant message of the book is the interpretation of Judah's downfall through military defeat and exile in terms of a theology of *retribution for religious and moral failings. There is a replay of this scenario in Jeremiah 40—44, where survivors in the homeland waste their opportunity to claim the prophet's positive offer to live in Judah subject to Babylonian rule (Jer 27:11), for which Jeremiah himself became a role model (Jer 40:2b-3; cf. Jer 40:9, 15, which echo Jer 27:15; 42:10-12). Nevertheless, hope beyond judgment does play a minor but real part in the overall book, grounded in the prophet's own divinely guided expectations.

6.1. "To Build and to Plant." This element in the account of the prophetic call and first commissioning of Jeremiah at Jeremiah 1:10 within Jeremiah 1:4-12 posits from the start a postjudgment promise for Judah and for other nations. The promise aligns with material in Jeremiah 2—6, in which Hosea's influence on the prophet is evident. Hosea's message looked beyond the northern kingdom's destruction to expectations of eventual renewal and restoration. Jeremiah became the heir of this positive tradition, though readers are not told when this privately revealed element was promulgated. The phrase "to build and to plant" is a programmatic fanfare for two themes of the book. First, it is echoed in postjudgment promises to God's people in Jeremiah 24:6; 31:28; 42:10, and more generally announces the positive future for Judah or for Israel and Judah developed later in the book. Second, it is applied to the nations, tentatively in Jeremiah 12:17; 18:9. More generally, again, it prepares for their eventual worship in Jerusalem in Jeremiah 3:17, potential blessing in Jeremiah 4:2, and their own categorical affirmation of faith in Jeremiah 16:19-21, as well as the individual restoration of Elam's fortunes in Jeremiah 49:39 and, in the MT, of those of Egypt, Moab and Ammon in Jeremiah 46:26; 48:47; 49:6.

6.2. Jeremiah 3:12-14. Even more closely attuned to Hosea's precedent is a pair of oracles in Jeremiah 3:12-14 addressed by Jeremiah to nondeported members of the former northern kingdom. In the former oracle the invitation to them to return to Yahweh's favor, denied to Judah in Jeremiah 3:1-5, serves contextually as a snub to reinforce Judah's guilt. The latter oracle has been blended with a wider positive invitation to Judah in Jeremiah 3:15-18, evidently at an editorial stage that presupposes the experience of judgment as lying in the past, but it carries its own prophetic authority ("says the LORD" [Jer 3:16]).

6.3. "Seventy Years." In the block of Jeremiah 26—29 the issue of true versus false prophecy comes to the fore. The crucial issue was whether Judah's final downfall, prophesied by Jeremiah but denied by his optimistic rivals, would occur, and accordingly how long the deportation of King Jehoiakim and leading citizens after the Babylonian attack on Jerusalem in 597 BC would last. The issue had already been broached in Jeremiah 24 by means of the vision of good and bad figs, whereby bad prospects for the post-597 BC regime in Judah are declared and reinforced by the promise of good prospects for those already deported. The only path to eventual salvation was an experience of judgment. In Jeremiah 26—29 the issue is raised again in a context of prophetic dispute. It comes to a head in the claim of Jeremiah's archrival that restoration would occur by two years' time (Jer 28:3-4, 11; cf. Jer 27:16, which the MT has clarified by adding "soon"). In Jeremiah's letter to the deportees in Jeremiah 29, his denial takes the impressionistic form of a premonition of "seventy years" of ex-

ile (Jer 29:10); the denial is now presented as a hopeful feature for those who are prepared to accept the divine sentence of judgment. In the summarizing prose sermon in Jeremiah 25, the double-edged nature of this premonition concerning the future of God's people is spelled out, negatively (Jer 25:11) and positively (Jer 25:12).

6.4. Purchase of Ancestral Land. Jeremiah 32:6-15 contains an account of the only positive symbolic action in the book, apart from Hananiah's in Jeremiah 28. At an earlier stage of the book's development, the chapter, which encompasses Jeremiah's prayer and Yahweh's response, probably capped the intimations of hope in Jeremiah 26—29. During the final siege of Jerusalem, Jeremiah, under detention in the palace grounds, is approached by a relative with a request that he act as a redeemer, the next of kin responsible for buying back land sold outside the family as a result of personal financial stringency (cf. Lev 25:25-28, 48-49). In this case, a preemptive intervention is requested to avoid such a sale. The incident and the drawing up of legal documents are given prophetic value by means of divine revelations reported in Jeremiah 32:6-7, 15. It all becomes a striking expression of eventual hope for the future of God's people in the land.

6.5. Jeremiah 30—31. This literary block picks up and amplifies the intimations of hope in recent chapters and paves the way for Jeremiah's positive symbolic declaration in Jeremiah 32. Probably its position reflects the insertion of the contents of a separate scroll that was part of the Jeremianic tradition. Its nucleus is a series of Jeremiah's early oracles envisioning the return of exiles of the northern kingdom of Israel (Jer 31:2-6, 15-17, 18-20), which are supplemented with a medley of prophetic oracles of hope that appear to be later than Jeremiah's time. In its present setting the block now defines what was to happen after the seventy years of Jeremiah 29:10. The first of the block's compositions, in Jeremiah 30:1—31:1, blatantly matches three times Yahweh's past punishment of the covenant people (Jer 30:5-7, 12-15, 23-24) with their future restoration (Jer 30:8-9 [the MT has added Jer 30:10-11 from Jer 46:27-28], 16-17, 18-21 [supplemented in the MT with Jer 30:22]; 31:1). The God who treated them negatively in the past was as surely to do so positively in the future. Jeremiah 30:23-24 has reused an oracle of the prophet that appears in Jeremiah 23:19-20, and the two earlier negative oracles are evidently his also. The second composition, in Jeremiah 31:2-26, is concerned with resettlement in the land, while the block's third and final composition, in Jeremiah 31:27-40, offers a series of assurances about the future security of the reunited peoples of Judah and Israel, including the promise of a new covenant in Jeremiah 31:31-34 (see 9.5 below).

6.6. The Oracles Against the Nations. These are placed in Jeremiah 46—51 in the MT and in the middle of Jeremiah 25 in the LXX (Jer 25:14—31:33 in LXX editions). Aspects of them will require discussion later (see 7 and 8 below); here their positive role is in view. Collections of oracles against foreign nations are not uncommon in the Prophetic Books, notably in Isaiah 13—23; Ezekiel 25—32. They are a rhetorical mode of communicating to God's own people, even when they address other nations. They have this role in the book of Jeremiah despite the prophet's direct contact with foreign delegates in Jerusalem in Zedekiah's accession year, according to Jeremiah 27. This collection celebrates Yahweh as the Lord of the nations who uses for divine ends the imperial power of Babylon, which is unwittingly subservient to Israel's God. Most of the foreign oracles in Jeremiah 46—49 can be attributed to Jeremiah. Individual oracles have been blended into a collection intended for Judeans living late in the exilic period. An opportunity has been taken to enlarge an earlier collection. Notably, material from elsewhere in the OT has been added in the Moabite anthology of Jeremiah 48:28-47. The Babylonian material in Jeremiah 50:1—51:58 reflects a late exilic setting in its present form, though a nucleus feasibly goes back to Jeremiah, including the pro-Babylonian poem in Jeremiah 51:20-23 (see Bellis, 148-49). The foreign oracles, which are a series of proclamations of disaster, are ultimately vehicles of hope for Judah. They function as a red traffic light that means a green light for Judah in the cross street. Their role as implicit pronouncements of salvation for Yahweh's own people is intermittently confirmed by featuring Israel as a counterpart to the other nations. An oracle of salvation for Israel is appended to the Egyptian material (Jer 46:27-28 [LXX 26:27-28]). Moab's destruction was to be a reprisal for mocking Israel (Jer 48:27 [LXX 31:27]). Am-

mon's seizing Israelite territory would result in Israel's regaining it (Jer 49:1-2 [LXX 30:17-18]). In the first of the two Babylonian compositions, its disaster is set alongside repatriation for Israel and Judah (Jer 50:4-5, 19, 28 [LXX 27:4-5, 19, 28]), and in the second composition alongside the vindication of God's people (Jer 51:24, 35-36, 50-51 [LXX 28:24, 35-36, 50-51]). Nor is God's people to be the only beneficiary. In the LXX the negative oracle against Elam, which is listed first in that edition, is concluded with a sudden note of reversal, a postjudgment promise of restoration (Jer 25:19 [MT 49:39]). The MT appears to assume that the promise is paradigmatic for other nations, since in its different ordering it not only keeps it at the end of the Elam oracle but also adds such promises to the key oracles against Egypt, Moab and Ammon (Jer 46:26b; 48:47a; 49:6).

7. The Septuagint of Jeremiah.
The complexity of the book of Jeremiah may be gauged from the phenomenon of the LXX. It has a vital role in this book beyond its usual function of being a text-critical witness to an early form of the Hebrew text current in Egypt, from which it was translated between 250 and 150 BC. It represents a literary edition of the book, in the sense of a distinct redactional stage, from which the later edition attested in the MT was developed (see Tov 1985). It has a shorter text than that of the MT by about one-eighth. It lacks certain passages and a large number of individual words and phrases that appear in the later edition. It also places the oracles against the nations (Jer 46—51 in the MT) in the middle of Jeremiah 25 and lists the oracles in a different order.

7.1. The Diversity of Qumran Discoveries. Both editions are represented in Hebrew texts found at Qumran. Fragments of scrolls found in Cave 4, 4Q71 and 4Q72a (both from the first half of the second century BC), attest, though in a scanty way, a short text closely related to that underlying the LXX. Examples of a proto-Masoretic, longer text form of the text have also surfaced, mostly from the same cave: 2Q13 (early first century AD), 4Q70 (early second century BC) and 4Q72 (end of first century BC) (see Baillet 1962; Tov 1997; 2001, 319-27). So the issue is "not a *veritas graeca* over against a *veritas hebraica*, but two *veritates hebraicae*" (de Waard, xxii).

7.2. The Placing of the Oracles Against the

Nations. The most striking feature of the edition of the Hebrew text that underlies the LXX is that the oracles in Jeremiah 46—51 of the MT are placed in the middle of Jeremiah 25. The new location is secondary because it interferes with the system of compositional units that is integral to the book. This system has been restored in the MT by its closely related three units of Jeremiah 25:1-14, 15-29, 30-38. The location in the LXX is to be explained by the insertion of an independent scroll of foreign oracles that belonged to the Jeremian tradition. Jeremiah 25:13 was added to prepare for the insertion by introducing "this book" or scroll. The editor reasonably judged that the best place for this important material was within the only part of the overall book that dealt with the nations, Jeremiah 25, and alongside the listing of nations that appears in Jeremiah 25:18-26, which itself was an insertion, made separately and retained in the MT, that breaks the connection between Jeremiah 25:17 and Jeremiah 25:27.

7.3. The Order of the Nations. In the LXX the order is Elam, Egypt, Babylon, Philistines, Edom, Ammon, Arab tribes, Aramaeans and Moab. The MT order is Egypt, Philistines, Moab, Ammon, Edom, Aramaeans, Arab tribes, Elam and Babylon. The priority of Elam is enhanced in the LXX by paradigmatically attaching to it a promise of restoration that the MT has retained and extended (see 6.6 above). Logical justification for the LXX ordering is difficult to find, apart from the placing of Babylon next to Egypt, its fellow world power. The Babylonian material (LXX Jer 27—28; MT Jer 50—51) was originally written on its own scroll, according to Jeremiah 51:60. It is nearly as large as the size of the oracles against the other nations put together. The decision to incorporate it relatively early in the listing of the other scroll was doubtless influenced by another factor, that the editorial value of the combined oracles stated in the preparatory Jeremiah 25:13 was to corroborate the fall of Babylon, to which it makes an oblique reference, and this is what the Babylonian material is all about.

8. The Masoretic Text.

The MT of Jeremiah represents further editing of the text represented in the LXX and in most of the Hebrew texts found at Qumran. It places the oracles against the nations near the end of the book and has made a great number of mainly small, but occasionally larger, additions

(the translation in L. Allen's 2008 commentary has italicized the evident additions so that they are easily recognizable). This later edition clearly treated the earlier one as a work in progress and sought to improve it in a number of ways. Because the Masoretes adopted this later edition, it received official recognition as canonical. Christian circles, apart from the Greek Orthodox Church, also have so recognized it. E. Tov has classified the changes found in the MT under six categories: text arrangement, additions of headings to oracles, repetitions of sections, additions of new verses and sections, additions of new details, and changes in content (Tov 1985). He has also characterized these features in terms of exegetical clarification. They make a significant contribution to the book, often demonstrating insight into the text. The LXX edition appears to be an adaptation of an earlier one, as the insertion of the oracles against the nations in Jeremiah 25 indicates, so that the MT represents a third edition, if it was carried out as a single piece of work. Enough time must have elapsed between the second and third editions for the second to become established. By the turn of the era, both were known, as the Qumran evidence indicates, although their respective origins were obviously earlier than the earliest extant texts. The dating of the proto-Masoretic edition cannot be ascertained, though the addition of Jeremiah 33:14-26 in the MT has affinity in its pairing of royal and priestly rulers with an early postexilic convention (cf. Hag 1:1; Zech 4). Moreover, its addition of patronymics in Jeremiah 29:21 and of Baruch's job description in Jeremiah 36:26, 32 indicates knowledge of old traditions. The additions continue to use prose sermonic language, borrowing it from sermons already found in the book (Tov 2008, 413-14, 416).

8.1. The Oracles Against the Nations. In the edition adopted by the MT, these oracles have been moved to the back of the book. Evidence is not lacking that the LXX placement, editorial though it was, was an intermediate stage that the MT presupposes. First, Jeremiah 25:13, with its reference to the following scroll of oracles, was left awkwardly isolated. Second, the relative clause that closes Jeremiah 25:13 was made to do double duty by also adapting it as a heading for Jeremiah 46:1, which the MT has added. Third, it also added Jeremiah 25:14 as a stopgap statement that loosely summed up the oracles and specifically alluded to the fall of Babylon by echoing Jeremiah 50:29, 41; it also added "wrongdoing" to Jeremiah 25:12 from Jeremiah 51:6.

8.1.1. The Placement of the Oracles. The oracles have a positive value, primarily by contrasting the nations' fate explicitly and implicitly with Judah's fortune and secondarily by the addition of promises of postjudgment restoration to three more of the nations (see 6.6 above). As such, the oracles were placed at the close of the book to form an exuberant expression of future hope as part of the structural pattern reflected in the MT edition (see 8.2 below).

8.1.2. The Order of the Oracles. The ordering in the MT is quite different from that in the LXX (see 7.3 above). If the LXX order is taken as the primary one, it is not difficult to explain most of the differences. Although an early placement of Babylon suited the immediate context, as Jeremiah 25:13 testifies, it was no longer applicable in its new context. In fact, from the standpoint of future expectation, Jeremiah 25:12, vague though it is in its LXX form, indicates that the fall of Babylon celebrated in the Babylonian material was to come after Babylon's conquest of the other nations attested both in Jeremiah 25:8, 11 and in the oracles pertaining to those nations. After Babylon was duly put at the end, Elam was set before it for both geographical and chronological reasons. Chronology also appears to have played a role in the overall ordering. The Elam oracle belonged to Zedekiah's accession year (LXX Jer 25:20; MT Jer 49:34). Egypt was associated with Jehoiakim's fourth year (LXX Jer 26:2; MT Jer 46:2), and Babylon with Zedekiah's fourth year (LXX Jer 28:59; MT Jer 51:59). Respect for the historical framework of the book in terms of Judean reigns (see 2.2 above) probably constrained the editor behind the MT to reorder the oracles accordingly, so that Elam preceded Babylon and both had to come after Egypt. Then the definition of Jehoiakim's fourth year in terms of the capture of Carchemish (LXX Jer 26:2; MT Jer 46:2)—one of the two historical events most significant for the book (see 2.3 above)—guaranteed Egypt its pride of place. Moreover, beginning with Egypt now dovetails with the focus on Egypt in Jeremiah 42—44 (LXX 49—51), while the dating in Jeremiah 46:2 nicely coincides with that in Jeremiah 45:1

(LXX 51:31). Philistia was left as Egypt's minor neighbor in an overall block of Jeremiah 46:1—47:7. The Moabite material was feasibly put next as a second block (Jer 48) because it was the largest of the remaining oracular pieces. Why was Ammon put at the head of a third block, which it formed with the remaining four oracles that now included Elam? Special importance seems to have been attached to Ammon and also to Egypt and Moab. Only in their cases has the MT added promises of restoration at the close of their oracles, to match the preexisting one attached to the Elam oracle (see 6.6 above). Furthermore, only in the oracles of Egypt, Moab and Ammon does Yahweh's own people feature as a counterweight to these punishable nations (see 6.6 above).

8.2. The Masoretic Macrostructure. The Prophetic Books attest a pattern of moving beyond a major theme of divine judgment to a minor but very significant theme of *salvation that was to follow that judgment (Clements, 191-202). This pattern can sometimes take the form of a structural series, as in the book of Hosea, where each of three literary complexes, Hosea 1—3; 4—11; 12—14, ends on a positive note. There is evidence of sequential patterning in the book of Jeremiah at an early stage. The historical epilogue, Jeremiah 52, in both the LXX and the MT uses 2 Kings 24—25 to cap a long account of Zedekiah's fate with a short account of the rise in Jehoiachin's fortunes as a token of hope. On a small scale, Jeremiah's threefold negative role "to uproot and tear down and destroy" in the prologue of Jeremiah 1 has been matched with a hopeful pair, "to build and plant" (Jer 1:10). Jeremiah 10, in the shorter version attested in the LXX, contains a hymn to Yahweh that maintains Yahweh's superiority to Babylon's images and so predicts their downfall (Jer 10:12-16, especially Jer 10:15). It is significant that in the common text of the LXX and the MT Jeremiah 10:12-16 reappears (MT Jer 51:15-19; LXX Jer 28:15-19) as an expression of hope. The insertion of Jeremiah 30—31 in the common text has developed the sketches of a postjudgment positive future in Jeremiah 26—29 and earlier, bolstered Jeremiah's positive symbolic action in Jeremiah 32 and encouraged its sequel in Jeremiah 33:1-13.

The edition of the book in the MT has made consistent efforts to boost this positive perspective. At times it is done with subtlety. In the epilogue Zedekiah's "bad" behavior is added in the MT at Jeremiah 52:2-3 to contrast with the "good" treatment of Jehoiachin in Jeremiah 52:32 and so suggest the good and bad prospects of the two kings presented in Jeremiah 24. In the prologue the addition of "and demolish" in Jeremiah 1:10 draws further attention to the contrasted long and short series of verbs. More blatantly, the movement of the oracles against the nations to Jeremiah 46—51 has brought a hopeful finale to the book, both explicit and implicit. The addition of Jeremiah 33:14-26 has magnified the salvific complex of Jeremiah 30-33; so too did the copying of the oracle of salvation of Jeremiah 46:27-28 in Jeremiah 30:10-11. As for Jeremiah 10, the hymn to Yahweh's power in Jeremiah 10:12-16 was enlarged by supplementing it with Jeremiah 10:4-8, 10, which spelled doom for other "nations," the key word of the new section. All these changes indicate a refinement of the book's structure. Destruction and eventual reconstruction are now clearly celebrated three times over, in Jeremiah 2—9; 10, in Jeremiah 11—29; 30—33, and in Jeremiah 34—45; 46—51. The duplication of Jeremiah 10:12-16 in Jeremiah 51:15-19, noted above, now enhances the sectional parallelism. The whole book in its present form echoes the pattern of Jeremiah 1:10 and of Jeremiah 52. The earlier arrangement in blocks, compositions and units has been retained, but it has been overlaid with a new focus that, as in the book of Hosea, crowns each third of the book with a message of hope that transcends its relative brevity with a climactic force. What has been lost is the clearcut division of the book into two halves, the oracular Jeremiah 2—25 and the narrative Jeremiah 26—45, which in the LXX edition had been preserved by incorporating the oracles against the nations near the close of the oracular material. In the new configuration, each of the three conclusions gathers up earlier anticipations in a crescendo of future triumph. The MT form of the text has completed an earlier process by adding to, repeating and rearranging what it inherited.

9. Theology.

The canonical Prophetic Books cluster around a political crisis: the threat and reality of Assyrian and Babylonian domination, resistance to which led to increasing loss of national independence and eventual exile for the divided kingdoms. The books, including Jeremiah (cf. Jer 28:8), reflect an antiestablishment tradition that gave a theological interpretation to the crisis. Five components of the tradition are Israel's initial receipt of covenant grace, its obligation of an appropriate lifestyle and worship, its irresponsibility, its consequent rejection at God's hands, and yet the promise of renewal from God (Allen 1992). What follows here is a sketch of how the book of Jeremiah displays and develops these theological components.

9.1. Israel's Receipt of Covenant Grace. Yahweh's fundamental commitment to Israel as a *covenant nation is summed up in the traditional complex of saving events, from the exodus from Egypt to the occupation of the land (Jer 2:2-3, 6-7; 11:4-5; 16:14; 23:7; 31:2, 32).

9.2. Israel's Obligation. A corresponding commitment for Israel is presented in "the terms of the covenant" at Jeremiah 11:3-5, with reference to the Torah. The Torah tradition is virtually defined as a series of ethical sanctions in Jeremiah 22:3, to which religious ones are added in Jeremiah 7:9. The sanctions are summed up as "the age-old paths" (Jer 6:16; 18:15) and as the moral principles of *"justice" (Jer 5:1; 7:5) and "trustworthiness" (Jer 5:1, 3; 7:28; 9:3).

9.3. Israel's Irresponsibility. Failure to live up to the covenant standards is portrayed as chronic (Jer 2:20; 3:25; 22:21; 32:30-31), deepseated (Jer 5:3: 13:23; 17:1) and coming to a head in Jeremiah's period (Jer 3:11; 7:26; 16:12). Both social injustice (Jer 9:2-8; 22:13-17) and pagan worship (Jer 2:6-32; 7:30-31) were rife. Supremely, the Davidic monarchy failed in its mandate as a responsible divine agency (Jer 13:18; 21:11—23:2). The situation was exacerbated by popular complacency caused by "false" prophets who insisted on God's unconditional blessing and positive intervention (Jer 6:12-14; 23:9-32; 27:14-18; 28:1-4; 29:24-32). The people's regular rejection of God's true prophets, after rejection of the divine Torah, only increased their guilt (Jer 6:16-19; 7:22-26). Their rejection of Jeremiah, the last of Judah's preexilic prophets, was their crowning *sin (Jer 25:3-7). Jeremiah 34—36 sets out this threefold rejection in sequence (see 4.2 above). In turn, Jeremiah's maltreatment as prophetic messenger is elaborated in his series of laments and in the persecution narratives as the most incriminating evidence of Judah's opposition to its God (see 4.2 and 5.7 above).

9.4. Israel's Rejection by God. Jeremiah was expressly forbidden to engage in the normal prophetic task of interceding on the people's behalf (Jer 7:16; 11:14; cf. 15:1). Moreover, Yahweh removed the covenantal "peace, steadfast love, and compassion" that usually protected them (Jer 16:5). Jeremiah's premonitions of a foe from the north eventually crystallized into Nebuchadnezzar's devastating campaigns and deportations (see 2.3 above), as his prophesying turned inexorably into fulfillment. Such vehement *warfare was a measure of divine anger, in a radical reprisal provoked by Judah's aberrations (Jer 4:5-8; 7:18-20; 21:3-7; 32:28-32, 37; 52:3). The fire of such anger would last "forever" (Jer 17:4). From another perspective, Israel incurred the curse envisioned in the Torah (Jer 11:1-8).

9.5. Israel's Coming Renewal. Jeremiah stands in the tradition of *Hosea that embraced post-judgment hope, and so the merited "forever" of Jeremiah 17:4 is transcended. "Everlasting love" (Jer 31:3) will trump the divine hatred in Jeremiah 12:8 (cf. Hos 9:15; 11:8-9). The prophet's early oracles were positive ones addressed to residents of the old northern kingdom (see 6.2 and 6.5 above), while his symbolic action of redeeming land in Benjamin gloriously challenged the southern kingdom's crisis (see 6.4 above). His very commissioning incorporates a positive future for both Judah and other nations that becomes programmatic for the book (see 6.1 above). That future embraces the revival of Israel's traditional institutions, the Davidic monarchy (Jer 23:5-6) and, alongside it, the Levitical priesthood in the MT's addition at Jeremiah 33:14-22.

This subsection (complementing 6 above) will focus on the proclamation of salvation in Jeremiah 31:31-34, which, beyond its intrinsic significance, has an important role in the NT, notably at 1 Corinthians 11:25 and in the discussion of the quotations at Hebrews 8:8-12; 10:16-17. The NT claims the inauguration of this new covenant and looks forward to its consummation.

9.5.1. A Promise for Israel and Judah. "The house of Israel and the house of Judah" (Jer 31:31) refer to the old political entities, which together make up the theocratic entity of "the house of Israel" in Jeremiah 31:33. The breadth of the promise, embraced also by Ezekiel (Ezek 37:15-23), is consonant with Jeremiah's early oracles and with the literary context (Jer 30:3, 31:1, 18, 27).

9.5.2. Old and New Covenants. The newness develops the "new thing" in Jeremiah 31:22 concerning Israel's spiritual commitment to Yahweh. From a larger perspective, the passage provides a God-given solution to the problems of a broken covenant and a rejected Torah expressed in the prose sermon of Jeremiah 11:1-14. So it complements the promise in Jeremiah 16:14-15; 23:7-8 of a fresh exodus from exile and the Diaspora to a renewed occupation of the land. The proclamation draws a formal contrast between the old covenant and its human breakdown and divine judgment, on the one hand, and its new counterpart and divine undergirding, on the other hand. Despite God's fatherly care, Israel broke the old covenant, and so "I had to show myself their master, says the LORD" (Jer 31:32 NAB). The proclamation looks beyond the completion of that period of reprisal, the radical judgment that occupies most of the book ("after those days" [Jer 31:33; cf. Jer 30:24]).

9.5.3. New Obedience to God's Torah. Here is the essentially new element of the promise. Covenant and Torah are intimately related, as in Jeremiah 11, where "the terms of the covenant" refer to the Torah. Yahweh will do a work of spiritual engineering whereby the Torah is internalized (cf. the "new heart" in Ezek 36:26). The human "heart," as seat of the will, is no longer to be beset by stubbornness, as in Jeremiah 11:8 (and seven other times in Jeremiah). The Torah's requirements will be met by an instinctive response to internal cues rather than to merely external ones. Accordingly, the mutuality of the divine-human covenant will be assured, while at the human level both priestly teaching and family instruction will be rendered obsolete.

9.5.4. Divine Forgiveness. The book of Jeremiah refers to *forgiveness more than any other prophetic book. Here God promises to formally wipe the moral slate clean (cf. Jer 33:8; 50:20). Amnesty is to be the precursor to the new covenantal relationship, once the punishment stated in Jeremiah 31:32 has run its course (cf. Is 40:2; 55:6-7). Formerly, forgiveness was not possible, since reprisal for sinning was regularly deemed necessary (Jer 5:1, 7, 9). In Jeremiah 36:3, as in Isaiah 55:6-7, repentance is a precondition of God's forgiveness. However, in Jeremiah 31:34, as in Jeremiah 31:33, focus is placed on the divine initiative.

10. Purpose.

The book of Jeremiah is like the four Gospels, each of which addresses the particular needs of its constituency and is the product of a generation later than the scenes that it narrates, taking over and faithfully developing oral and written records. Jeremiah still looks forward to the downfall of the Babylonian Empire in 539 BC, while its later oracles read like those of Second Isaiah. The perspective of the book encourages a search for some guiding statements that take a general look back at Jeremiah's period and/or appear to belong to the later time frame of the book's constituency.

10.1. Telling Why. Four similar passages punctuate the first half of the book. They occur with some regularity, in Jeremiah 5:19; 9:12-16; 16:10-13; 22:8-9. They have the same question-and-answer format that looks back to Jeremiah's oracles of disaster as already fulfilled. They ask why the disaster, including the exile in three cases, has happened and supply the same reason: divine retribution for pagan worship. All of them are written in prose sermonic style; indeed, the same format occurs in Deuteronomy 29:24-28 and 1 Kings 9:8-9. The prose passages are interspersed among the long series of poetic oracles of disaster and patiently explain to the book's readers the necessity of such drastic measures. In the second half of the book there is a counterpart in Jeremiah 32:21-23, 29b-35, a pair of editorial passages designed to answer Zedekiah's own question "Why?" in Jeremiah 32:3 (see Fretheim, 454).

10.2. Hermeneutical Asides. A short aside seems to occur in the course of Jeremiah 2:31, the appeal "You members of this generation, consider Yahweh's message." The prose appeal set in a poetic context sounds like a homiletical call for hearers of the text to take Jeremiah 2:29-30 seriously, in case they too repudiated divine authority. The Hebrew verb rendered "consider" has been borrowed from appeals in Jeremiah 2:10, 19, 23, which suggests that those too should find contemporary listening ears. A longer call occurs in Jeremiah 9:23-24 in the form of a general exhortation. The call to

"know" Yahweh follows Jeremiah's accusation in Jeremiah 9:3, 6 that preexilic Judah's propensity to falsehood, untrustworthiness and deception revealed that they neither knew nor acknowledged their God. From the accusation, which has occurred earlier in the book (Jer 4:22; 5:4; 8:7), is extrapolated a positive spirituality of knowing God that probably has Jeremiah 22:15-16 also in view and certainly echoes virtues valued earlier in the book (Jer 2:2; 4:2; 5:1-5; 7:5; 8:7).

10.3. Babylonian Religion Decried. Not far from the previous example, the direct exhortations in Jeremiah 10:2, 5b not to be intimidated by astrological divination or pagan worship of *idols seem to be addressed to Judean exiles in Babylon, implicitly urging them not to abandon their ancestral faith. The exhortations are accompanied in the intervening verses by a satirical polemic in the Second Isaiah tradition. It is not surprising that the following hymn in Jeremiah 10:12-16, which explicitly contrasts Yahweh and divine images, is reused at Jeremiah 51:15-19 in a Babylonian context, as that seems to be the setting of both passages in Jeremiah 10.

10.4. Contemporary Warnings. The proverb-like generalities that mark most of Jeremiah 17:5-13 leave behind the description of preexilic sinning and its punishment in Jeremiah 17:1-4 and speak of sinning in different terms. The alternatives of curse and blessing in Jeremiah 17:5-8 counsel trust in Yahweh instead of humans. Their reference to the "heart" echoes Jeremiah 17:1 and updates the message. So does the next saying in Jeremiah 17:9-10, which warns of divine punishment for the heart so prone to wickedness. Jeremiah 17:11 names ill-gotten wealth as an example of such sin, while Jeremiah 17:12-13 reiterates the punishment awaiting all those who currently forsake the true God, Yahweh.

10.5. A Trajectory of Hope. Despite the prevalence of messages of doom in the book of Jeremiah, an insistence on postjudgment hope is an essential element. It is difficult to discern at what developmental stage expressions of hope have been grafted into the book when they appear in the common text of the LXX and the MT, since the book itself was written from a post-586 BC perspective. A staccato note can afford a clue to literary adaptation, such as Elam's sudden, unelaborated restoration, extended to three other nations in the MT (see 6.6 above). Another case is the flagrant interruption of announcements of disaster with postjudgment cries of "No, not complete disaster" in Jeremiah 4:27; 5:10, 18, cries that receive their warrant from the late exilic oracle in Jeremiah 46:27-28, to which the MT gives greater prominence by adding it in Jeremiah 30:10-11. As indicated earlier, the common text contains a number of editorial intimations of hope that faithfully develop Jeremiah's own vision of Yahweh's will to build and plant after the necessary work of destruction, while the MT has fostered the process further. The completed book never fails to look ahead to the joy that will come in the morning, after the weeping of the night (cf. Ps 30:5). Its readers are meant both to take its grim history to heart and to hold on to its hope.

See also BABYLON; COVENANT; EXILE; FORMATION OF THE PROPHETIC BOOKS; ISRAELITE HISTORY; JEREMIAH: HISTORY OF INTERPRETATION; LAMENT, MOURNING; LAMENTATIONS, BOOK OF; RETRIBUTION; SIGN ACTS.

BIBLIOGRAPHY. *Commentaries:* **L. C. Allen,** *Jeremiah: A Commentary* (OTL; Louisville: Westminster/John Knox, 2008a); **W. Brueggemann,** *A Commentary on Jeremiah: Exile and Homecoming* (Grand Rapids: Eerdmans, 1998); **P. C. Craigie, P. H. Kelley and J. F. Drinkard Jr.,** *Jeremiah 1-25* (WBC 26; Dallas: Word, 1991); **T. E. Fretheim,** *Jeremiah* (SHBC; Macon, GA: Smith & Helwys, 2002); **W. L. Holladay,** *Jeremiah: A Commentary on the Book of the Prophet Jeremiah* (2 vols.; Hermeneia; Philadelphia: Fortress, 1986-1989); **D. R. Jones,** *Jeremiah* (NCBC; Grand Rapids: Eerdmans, 1992); **G. L. Keown, P. J. Scalise and T. G. Smothers,** *Jeremiah 26-52* (WBC 27; Dallas: Word, 1995); **J. R. Lundbom,** *Jeremiah 1-20* (AB 21A; New York: Doubleday, 1999); idem, *Jeremiah 21-36* (AB 21B; New York: Doubleday, 2004); idem, *Jeremiah 37-52* (AB 21C; New York: Doubleday, 2004); **W. McKane,** *Jeremiah I-XXV* (ICC; Edinburgh: T & T Clark, 1986); idem, *Jeremiah XXVI-LII* (ICC; Edinburgh: T & T Clark, 1996). *Studies:* **L. C. Allen,** "Images of Israel: The People of God in the Prophets," in *Studies in Old Testament Prophecy: Historical and Contemporary Images of God and God's People,* ed. R. L. Hubbard Jr., R. K. Johnston and R. P. Meye (Dallas: Word, 1992) 149-68; idem, "Disputations in the Book of Jeremiah," *PRSt* 35 (2008b) 135-46; **M. Baillet,** *Les "petites grottes" de Qumran* (DJD 3; Oxford: Clarendon Press, 1962) 62-69; **W. Baumgartner,** *Jeremiah's Poems of Lament,* trans. D. Orton (HTIBS 7; Sheffield: Almond, 1988); **A. O. Bellis,** *The Structure and Composition of Jeremiah 50:2-51:58* (Lewiston, NY: Mellen Biblical, 1995); **J. Bright,** "The Date of the Prose Sermons of Jeremiah," *JBL* 70 (1951) 15-35; **C. C. Broyles,** *The Conflict of Faith and Experience in the Psalms: A Form-Critical and Theological Study* (JSOTSup 52; Sheffield: JSOT, 1989); **W. Brueggemann,** *The Theology of the Book of Jeremiah* (OTT; Cambridge: Cambridge University Press, 2007); **R. E. Clements,** *Old Testament Prophecy: From Oracles to Canon* (Louisville: Westminster/John Knox, 1996); **J. de Waard,** *A Handbook on Jeremiah* (Winona Lake, IN: Eisenbrauns, 2003); **A. R. Diamond,** *The Confessions of Jeremiah in Context: Scenes of Prophetic Drama* (JSOTSup 45; Sheffield: JSOT, 1987); **K. G. Friebel,** *Jeremiah's and Ezekiel's Sign-Acts: Rhetorical Nonverbal Communications* (JSOTSup 283; Sheffield: Sheffield Academic, 1999); **E. K. Holt,** "The Potent Word of God: Remarks on the Composition of Jeremiah 37-44," in *Troubling Jeremiah,* ed. A. Diamond, K. O'Connor and L. Stulman (JSOTSup 260; Sheffield: Sheffield Academic Press, 1999) 161-70; **J. G. Janzen,** *Studies in the Text of Jeremiah* (HSM 6; Cambridge, MA: Harvard University Press, 1973); **J. R. Lundbom,** "Jeremiah 15,15-21 and the Call of Jeremiah," *SJOT* 9 (1995) 143-55; **J. G. McConville,** *Judgment and Promise: An Interpretation of the Book of Jeremiah* (Winona Lake, IN: Eisenbrauns, 1993); **D. J. Murray,** "The Rhetoric of Disputation: Reexamination of a Prophetic Genre," *JSOT* 38 (1987) 95-121; **P. K. D. Neumann,** "Das Wort das geschehen ist ...: Zum Problem der Wortempfangsterminologie in Jer. I-XXV," *VT* 23 (1973) 171-217; **K. M. O'Connor,** *The Confessions of Jeremiah: Their Interpretation and Role in Jeremiah 1-25* (SBLDS 94, Atlanta: Scholars Press, 1987); **J. Rosenberg,** "Jeremiah and Ezekiel," in *The Literary Guide to the Bible,* ed. R. Alter and F. Kermode (Cambridge, MA; Belknap, 1987) 184-206; **C. R. Seitz,** *Theology in Conflict: Reactions to the Exile in the Book of Jeremiah* (BZAW 176; Berlin: de Gruyter, 1989); **M. S. Smith,** *The Laments of Jeremiah and Their Contexts: A Literary and Redactional Study of Jeremiah 11-20* (SBLMS 42; Atlanta: Scholars Press, 1990); **L. Stulman,** *The Prose Sermons of the Book of Jeremiah: A Redescription of the Correspondences with

Deuteronomistic Literature in the Light of Recent Text-Critical Research (SBLDS 83; Atlanta: Scholars Press, 1986); idem, *Order amid Chaos: Jeremiah as Symbolic Tapestry* (BibSem 57; Sheffield: Sheffield Academic, 1998); **E. Tov**, "The Literary History of the Book of Jeremiah in the Light of Its Textual History," in *Empirical Models for Biblical Criticism*, ed. J. H. Tigay (Philadelphia: University of Pennsylvania Press, 1985) 211-37; idem, "Jeremiah," in *Qumran Cave 4, X: The Prophets*, ed. E. Ulrich et al. (DJD 15; Oxford: Clarendon Press, 1997) 145-207; idem, *Textual Criticism of the Hebrew Bible* (2nd ed.; Minneapolis: Fortress, 2001); idem, *Hebrew Bible, Greek Bible and Qumran: Collected Essays* (TSAJ 121; Tübingen: Mohr Siebeck, 2008).

L. C. Allen

JEREMIAH: HISTORY OF INTERPRETATION

The book of *Jeremiah's extensive biographical sections, the prophet's lamentations over persecution and rejection, his accusations regarding systemic failure, the tragic circumstances of the fall of Jerusalem, the *exile of Judah to *Babylon, and the prophecy of a new *covenant—all of these mark the book's impact on history. Its extensive protests against *idolatry and injustice eventually gave rise in Western society to the term *jeremiad*, which refers to a sustained complaint or bitter lament against perceived unrighteousness.

    1. Postexilic Judaism
    2. Rabbinic Judaism
    3. New Testament
    4. Church Fathers
    5. Reformation and Renaissance
    6. Modern Interpretations

1. Postexilic Judaism.

There are two aspects of Jeremiah reflected in the Chronicler's presentation of Judah's final decades before the exile. These are perhaps the earliest explicit interpretations of Jeremiah outside the book bearing his name, depending on the dating of the reference in Daniel 9:2. Jeremiah is credited with composing laments for Josiah, compositions that later were taken up and performed by singers in remembrance of the king (2 Chron 35:25; cf. 1 Esdr 1:32; Josephus, *Ant.* 10.5). In the final chapter (2 Chron 36:17-23; cf. Ezra 1:1) he is named as a representative of prophets sent by God to warn Judah of impending doom. This picks up a strand in the canonical book (e.g., Jer 7:25; 25:4; 28:8). Judah's exile in Babylon, a resulting Sabbath rest for the land, and the subsequent Persian decree allowing a return to Jerusalem are described as fulfilling Jeremiah's prophecies. These latter items do interpret major claims in the book about exile and future restoration, although there is nothing explicit in Jeremiah about the land of Judah enjoying Sabbath rest. Perhaps the prediction of seventy years for the exile, a multiple of a seven-year Sabbatical cycle, is interpreted by the Chronicler in light of the Sabbath instructions in Leviticus 25 and, more particularly, the explicit statement in Leviticus 26:34-35 that the land would have a Sabbath rest during the period of exile. Laments for Josiah are not part of the book of Jeremiah either, and while curious, the report nevertheless reflects a part of the book's impact: lamentation was a constituent part of the prophet's testimony (e.g., Jer 15:15-21; 20:7-12). The canonical book of Lamentations, which should not be confused with the laments for Josiah, was widely associated with Jeremiah in antiquity and is explicitly attributed to him in Greek translation (LXX Lam 1:1). From at least the Hellenistic period onward, Jeremiah's prophetic work has been linked to the lamentations offered for Josiah, Jerusalem and the people of Israel.

In Daniel 9 there is a prayer confessing Israel's sins and acknowledging the judgment that fell upon Jerusalem. Daniel's prayer is prompted in part by the prophecy of Jeremiah that a seventy-year period of judgment (Jer 25:11)—that is, exile—must be fulfilled for the devastation of the city and is set at the beginning of Persian rule over Babylon.

Some interpreters have proposed that the figure of the Suffering *Servant in Isaiah 52:13—53:12 is modeled on Jeremiah's persecution as a prophet and the tradition of his public rejection. Both figures, for example, are compared to a lamb led to slaughter (Jer 11:19; Is 53:7). If the portrait in Deutero-Isaiah is drawn with the Jeremiah tradition in mind, it is likely the earliest interpretation of Jeremiah outside of the prophetic book bearing his name. From a slightly later period, Jeremiah is likely one of the instructive models for the prophecy of *Zechariah (see Zech 1:1-6; 7:1-11) and a source for some innerbiblical allusions in Zechariah 9—14.

There are compositions in Greek and other languages that interpret Jeremiah for Judaism (and early Christianity). Sirach, a book widely read among Jews and Christians in antiquity, associates Jeremiah's prophecies with Judah's last kings and Jerusalem's destruction (Sir 49:4-7). The prophet's persecution and his themes of tearing down and building up are noted, citing elements announced in Jeremiah 1 and developed elsewhere in the prophetic book. His association with Josiah, a relatively minor element in the book of Jeremiah, is described in 1 Esdras (1 Esdr 1:28-33), following the tradition of the Chronicler. The Letter of Jeremiah takes its cue from Jeremiah 29 and presents the prophet writing to those soon to be taken into exile. A later Greek collection entitled *Paraleipomena of Jeremiah* (= *4 Baruch*) contains a number of things circulating about Jeremiah and Baruch, including the tradition that both men were in Babylon for a time. Also among its (late) traditions is the claim that Jeremiah was stoned to death (*4 Bar.* 9:31; cf. *Liv. Pro.* 2:1). Its redaction extended into the second century AD and shows evidence of a Christian hand at work.

The book of 2 Maccabees cites three traditions about Jeremiah from otherwise unknown "records" (2 Macc 2:1-8; 15:12-16). The first is that Jeremiah exhorted those about to be deported to take some of the sacred fire from Jerusalem with them and not to forget God's commandments. The second is that Jeremiah received a divine oracle to hide the tent (tabernacle), the ark of the covenant, and the altar of incense in a cave at the mountain where Moses ascended to see God's "inheritance," so that these things would not fall into the hands of the Babylonians. In the third, the high priest Onias sees a vision of a venerable Jeremiah, who is described as someone who loved Israel and prays for the people. This last item has Jeremiah in a postmortem role of prayer—a most interesting role in itself and a reversal of one aspect of his earthly ministry, where he was forbidden to pray for his contemporaries (Jer 7:16; 11:14).

There are also texts associated with Jeremiah's secretary. The most widely known is the book of Baruch, which also has the prophet's companion writing from Babylon. And there are others testifying to his impact: *2 Baruch* is preserved in Syriac; *3 Baruch* is in Greek; in its Greek form *4 Baruch* is also part of the *Paraleipomena of Jeremiah* (the Ethiopic version has the heading "The rest of the words of Baruch").

The DSS contain Hebrew fragments of several scrolls of Jeremiah (see 6.6. below), as well as other small fragments that are collected together because they mention Jeremiah or Baruch. These latter fragments could be evidence of an otherwise unknown document in Judaism interpreting the life of Jeremiah or additional evidence for the expanding Jeremiah tradition reflected in texts such as 2 Maccabees, Baruch, and *Paraleipomena of Jeremiah*. Some interpreters (see Brooke) have hypothesized a "Jeremiah Apocryphon" to account for them. Such a document, if it can be shown to exist, should not be confused with the Coptic *Apocryphon of Jeremiah* (Kuhn), which contains several (late) stories about the prophet.

The six centuries after Jeremiah's death saw the development of a large variety of texts and traditions about him and Baruch, all in addition to the formation of two primary forms of a prophetic book (Hebrew, Greek). These things are evidence for both the resilience and the significance of Jeremiah for Judaism (and early Christianity). Nothing similar developed for either Isaiah or Ezekiel, the two prophetic scrolls comparable in size to Jeremiah. The expanding literary traditions about Jeremiah have more in common with those that developed around *Daniel and Ezra.

2. Rabbinic Judaism.
The Hebrew text of Jeremiah was a constituent source for rabbinic Judaism and its construction of Jewish life. J. Neusner has collected most of the talmudic and midrashic references for comparison. Biographical traditions, for example, hold that Jeremiah was a descendant of Rahab, the prostitute from Jericho, as was Baruch, and that he was also related to Huldah the prophetess (*b. Meg.* 14b; *Pesiq. Rab Kah.* 13:5, 12). Josiah consulted Huldah about the scroll discovered in temple repair (see 2 Kings 22:8-20) because Jeremiah was gone for a time to bring back the ten tribes of Israel.

Jeremiah's prophetic credentials were such that he predicted the destruction of the first as well as the second temple (*y. Naz. 5:3*). Not only did Jeremiah predict the Babylonian exile, but also his book provides evidence that God went into exile with his people to Elam (cf. Jer 49:38; *Lam. Rab.* 53:1). The Babylonian Talmud also preserves a tradition that Jeremiah was the first in order of the "latter prophets" (*b. B. Bat.* 14b), to be followed by Ezekiel and Isaiah. The rabbis knew that Jeremiah does not come first chronologically, but they argue the principle that Jeremiah speaks throughout of destruction and should go after 2 Kings, the last of the Former Prophets, which also ends with the destruction of Jerusalem. Destruction is thereby joined to destruction. They posit, furthermore, that Ezekiel starts with destruction and ends with consolation, and Isaiah, which comes next, is all about consolation. Likely such an explanation of Jeremiah's place among prophetic scrolls tries to make sense of an inherited tradition among the rabbis; if so, the tradition did not prevail, as Isaiah became first among the Latter Prophets in medieval codices and in printed versions of the Hebrew Bible. Nevertheless, the tradition is a precursor to modern questions regarding the placement and sequencing of biblical books. It also represents a fundamental impact of the book. Jeremiah predicted the destruction of Jerusalem, and that came to pass. He became the prophet of destruction, even though the book of Ezekiel is every bit as uncompromising on Judah and Jerusalem's demise at the hands of the Babylonians.

The rabbis also inherited the tradition that Jeremiah was the author of several types of lamentations, and they developed their own perspectives on it. For example, Jehoiakim was told that Jeremiah had composed a book of lamentations, which the king promptly rejected (*y. Moʾ ed Qat.* 3:1-2). This offers a distinct take on the account in Jeremiah 36, where the king cuts off pieces of a scroll of the prophet's oracles. Some also took this to mean that Jeremiah had composed the book of Lamentations before the fall of Jerusalem, making Jehoiakim even more culpable for rejecting it. According to another tradition, not only did Jeremiah lament and weep, but also God wept at the failures of his people and the destruction of Jerusalem (*Lam. Rab.* 24:2; 50:2).

The book of Jeremiah played a role in determining Jewish halakah. One example comes in the discussions regarding divorce and remarriage, where Jeremiah 3:1-2 is cited in the application of Deuteronomy 24:1-4 (*Sipre Deut.* 213:1).

3. New Testament.

The influence of Jeremiah can be seen in several places in the NT. Matthew, for example, cites the book or refers to the prophet three times (Mt 2:17; 16:14; 27:9), though the last reference actually quotes Zechariah 11:12-13 and only alludes to texts in Jeremiah. The first reference comes in the context of Herod's murder of children in Bethlehem. "Rachel weeping" (cf. Jer 31:15) is understood as a prophecy fulfilled in the people's lamenting for the slain children. A later Jewish tradition identifies a tomb for Rachel near Bethlehem. The Gospel writer may have known such a tradition; however, the biblical account of Rachel's death on the way to Ephrath is explicated with a reference to Bethlehem (Gen 35:19-20), and this alone may have prompted his typological connection with Rachel's sorrow for her children.

The reference in Matthew 16:14 proposes "Jeremiah" as one of several prophetic models for Jesus. The Synoptic parallels to this text (Mk 8:28; Luke 9:19) do not refer explicitly to Jeremiah, which raises the question whether Jeremiah was of special significance for the writer of Matthew. M. Knowles has proposed a number of allusions to Jeremiah in Matthew, and that the traditions of Jeremiah as a rejected prophet and his announcement of Jerusalem's destruction have influenced the Matthean portrayal of Jesus. Similarly, reflecting on the reference in Matthew 16:14, D. Law concludes, "It is precisely the richness of the theological ideas associated with Jeremiah—new covenant, suffering, rejection by Israel, prophecies of judgement—that make Jeremiah such a useful tool for conveying insights concerning the meaning and significance of Jesus, the messiah" (Law, 301).

Jeremiah is the only book in the OT to refer to a "new covenant" (Jer 31:31) that God will make with Israel and Judah, although there are other prophetic texts that approximate the term and what it represents (Ezek 37:26; Hos 2:18-20; perhaps also Is 55:3). The text in Jeremiah 31:31-34 contrasts the Mosaic covenant mediated at Mount Sinai, which Israel and Judah broke, with a new covenant that God will institute in the future, a covenant that will internalize divine instruction and be based on God's resolve to forgive his people and remember their sin no more. The Sinai covenant had been ratified with blood sacrifice (Ex 24:3-8). Thus, references to the "blood of the new covenant" in Luke 22:20 and 1 Corinthians 11:25 and the combining of "new covenant" and "sprinkled blood" in Hebrews 12:24 (cf. Heb 8:8, 13; 9:15) link Jeremiah's prophecy of a new covenant with the foundational events of Christianity. The Pauline contrast in 2 Corinthians 3:4-18 between ministries of death and life, represented by Moses and Christ respectively, also equates the Christian faith with a "new covenant" (2 Cor 3:6) derived from the Holy Spirit.

4. Church Fathers.

The church fathers used the term "new covenant" initially as a reference to the Christian faith as prefigured in prophecy. Correspondingly, the "old covenant" could refer to a collection of authoritative writings preserved by Jews (cf. Melito of Sardis) or to Judaism bereft of the proper interpretation of those documents (*Epistle of Barnabas*; Justin Martyr). Jeremiah thus was seen as a prophet of righteousness under the old covenant and a herald of the Gospel that he predicted in the new covenant. At the end of the second century AD the term "new covenant" (Lat *novum testamentum*) begins to be used not only to describe what Christ instituted, but also to indicate authoritative texts written by apostles and their disciples giving expression to the Christian message. Eventually the term "New Testament," mediated through early Christian writings and church councils, is the heading for the Christian texts collected with the OT to form a Christian Bible. Even so, Jeremiah is not extensively quoted in the post-Nicene fathers. Isaiah, for example, is more popular. Nevertheless, the Greek, Latin and Syriac versions of Jeremiah were a resource for expositors (Wenthe), and the medieval European tradition included Jeremiah in its glossing of texts for ecclesiastical usage. Jerome was the one Christian commentator of his day to make comments on the Hebrew text (Graves).

5. Reformation and Renaissance.

With the Reformation and Renaissance in Europe came renewed attention to the historical sense of OT texts and, in varying degrees, to the Hebrew version. Martin Luther's assessment of Jeremiah is an early example. He interpreted the harsh language against Judah and Jerusalem as God's historical judgment on a stiff-necked people when left to their own devices. In his treatise "The Jews and Their Lies" he quotes the judgmental language of Jeremiah as if it could apply to the Jews of his day. Jeremiah's prophecies of future transformation (Jer 30—33) prefigured the grace brought by Christ. John Calvin begins his lectures on Jeremiah with a survey of the historical events that led to the Babylonian siege of Jerusalem, and he follows Luther and others in presenting Jeremiah as a preacher of righteousness and one who announced the gospel of Christ in the form of a new covenant.

Perhaps the two best-known visual interpretations of Jeremiah in Western civilization are those of Michelangelo and Rembrandt. Michelangelo's fresco (c. 1512) in the Sistine Chapel has a seated, somber Jeremiah holding his head in his right hand, perhaps in response to Jerusalem's destruction. Rembrandt's portrayal of Jeremiah is one of his early works (1630). It has the prophet sitting forlornly outside of Jerusalem, with his head propped up by his left hand, grieving that his prophecy of the city's destruction came true. His elbow rests on a bound *Bibel*, an anachronistic touch but symbolic of the prophet's task of proclaiming the word of the Lord. Light plays off the stones behind Jeremiah, reflecting the light of the city burning from the Babylonian torch. On the left margin, quite small and backgrounded, is King Zedekiah, hands to his eyes. Zedekiah is also grieving the fulfillment of Jeremiah's prophecy, and the covering of his eyes reminds the viewer that the king was blinded by the Babylonians.

6. Modern Interpretations.

Modern interpretations of Jeremiah have been influenced by the confessional lines of interpretation from the past, by historical questions that emerged in the Reformation and Renaissance, and by subsequent critical theories of knowledge emerging from the Enlightenment. The genesis and production of the Jeremiah book were tasks to be reconstructed by historical and literary analysis.

6.1. Bernhard Duhm. Building on the conclusion that the law in Israel developed later than the early prophets, Duhm produced a critical study of the book in 1901 that attributed some 280 verses of poetry to Jeremiah, an innovative individualist, and the rest of the book, including all the prose portions, to Baruch and later redactors. It is a watershed in the modern study of the book. Duhm reacted strongly against the redactors, concluding that they were theological legalists, and that they combined poetry and prose materials in a haphazard way. The structure of the book as a whole remains a topic under discussion among interpreters, and no consensus has yet developed to account for it. This may be because the compilers followed what can be described as an additive style, being more concerned to collect oracles and accounts and paying less attention to an overall structure for the completed task.

6.2. Sigmund Mowinckel. Mowinckel built on the work of Duhm and others, proposing in 1914 that editors used three major sources in compiling the book. Source A is poetic oracles. Source B is a narrative source containing mostly biographical material, of which there is more in Jeremiah than in any other prophetic text. Source C is also prose material, mostly speeches in Deuteronomic style. His basic categories have been widely used ever since, even when modified in particulars. In the last four decades, studies of the book's composition have given more attention to redactional matters and the concerns that drove editorial activity (*see* Editorial/Redaction Criticism).

6.3. John Skinner and George Adam Smith. Two influential works in English were first published a year apart from one another, the first by John Skinner (1922) and the second by George Adam Smith (1923). Both follow Duhm's general lead in seeing the prophet as a poet and individualist, though neither denigrated the book's editors as did Duhm. Both books also expand on earlier public lectures, presenting a historically reconstructed figure of Jeremiah that might then be understood in modern terms and religious sensibilities. The emphasis is on the figure of the prophet and his experience of God in times of crisis, using particularly the psychological clues discerned from his laments. Smith's seventh chapter is "The Story of His Soul," while Skinner's eleventh chapter is "The Prophet and His Inner Life." The figure that they reconstruct and then interpret is Jeremiah the individualist, drawn to God in spite of being rejected by his contemporaries, who in his direct dependence on God revealed the dangers of nationalism inherent in temple and state. Skinner finds that Jeremiah possessed an "instinctive and universal sense of the divine in which he recognized the permanent essence of religion" (Skinner, 219). The "cradle of individual religion" came to birth in his person (Skinner, 224). Smith, for his part, describes Jeremiah as the "likest to Christ of all the prophets" (G. Smith, 7), the "first in Israel to realize the independence of the single self in religion," and the "supreme example under the Old Covenant of the sacrifice of that self for others" (G. Smith, 341). Both authors interpret the proclamation of the "new covenant" as the high-water mark of the prophet's work. Skinner writes, "It is the announcement of a new and final stage in the manifestation of God's purpose of redemption. . . . It must have been written by Jeremiah, and is rightly regarded as his most noteworthy contribution to the ideal religion of the future" (Skinner, 332-33). Elsewhere he describes the new covenant as "one of the profoundest anticipations of the perfect religion that the Old Testament contains" (Skinner, 330). Smith says simply that it is "a prophecy of Christianity which has hardly its equal in the Old Testament" (G. Smith, 380).

6.4. Poetry, Laments and Form Criticism. The poetic oracles were the foundation for reconstructing Jeremiah's individual religious experience by such scholars as Duhm, Smith and Skinner, but the developing form-critical analysis of texts pioneered by H. Gunkel questioned this approach (*see* Form Criticism). Poetry and prose employed recognized genres of speech, and thus the emphasis fell on their setting in life and public role rather than, in the first instance, their being a clue to the experience of the author. An early example of this approach applied to Jeremiah was W. Baumgartner's 1916 study of the prophet's laments, which demonstrated formal characteristics in common with laments in the Psalter. Baumgartner himself did not deny that Jeremiah's laments were his own, but eventually form-critical analysis would lead some scholars away from an analysis of the personal life of Jeremiah (and other prophetic figures) to an investigation of representative forms of expression in the book, even those employing "first person" speech (see Reventlow). One direction of this research is to discard the historical figure altogether in favor of a literarily constructed "persona" (Polk).

The connection between Jeremiah's personal or inner life and the formulaic expressions of complaint in the book is an issue that remains under debate in modern scholarship. G. von Rad, for example, stood in the tradition that the laments or "confessions" were central to the interpretation of the prophet, seeing in them the combination of inherited poetic forms of lament and the prophet's own struggle with the press of the prophetic office and the rejection of his message by contemporaries. In theological terms, von Rad sees the prophet confronting an abyss where God seems hidden and where the prophet walks a "via dolorosa" and "stations of the cross" (von Rad, 36, 206-7) and finally casts himself into the hands of a mysterious God without a resolution of his predicament. Here one sees von Rad's typological hermeneutic at work, as the tradition of a suffering prophet is reframed in light of Christ's "passion" (von Rad, 274). In recent scholarship, the interpretive task has dealt not just with the formal properties of the laments themselves, but also with the literary and redactional questions of their role in the book (Ittmann; Diamond; M. Smith; Kiss). Recent interpreters have reopened a line of approach from the classical rabbis, asking whether Jeremiah's book represents God as well as the prophet in pain over the failure of the people (Bak; Fretheim). There is interest also in reading the lamentations as a form of protest against perceived injustice and putting the book of Lamentations in dialogue with the prophetic critique of people and city in the prophets, including Jeremiah (Lee and Mandolfo; Mandolfo).

6.5. Deuteronomy and Jeremiah. The third quarter of the twentieth century brought to the foreground the question of the relationship between Deuteronomy and the book of Jeremiah. At one level, it is a classical question, given the similarity of expressions between them. It was commonly recognized that portions of the prose tradition in Jeremiah had terminology similar to what was commonly called "Deuteronomic vocabulary." Scholars such as Duhm, Skinner and Smith had raised the question of Jeremiah's relationship to the reform efforts of Josiah, with its impetus in the discovery of a Book of the Law (2 Kings 22—23), a book that many concluded was an early form of Deuteronomy produced by a reforming element. The greater the emphasis on Jeremiah the individualist, however, the less some of his interpreters felt that the prophet could have supported the encapsulation of divine revelation in the legal form of a book such as Deuteronomy. If certain passages in the book of Jeremiah suggested otherwise (e.g., Jer 11:1-8), it was the work of

editors or a phase that Jeremiah outgrew. The new element in relating the two books came in response to M. Noth's influential 1943 study of what he called the "Deuteronomistic History," with Deuteronomy understood as the initial work in a literary scheme that continued in Joshua, Judges, 1-2 Samuel and 1-2 Kings, all of which were edited during the Babylonian exile. The question then became this: were Jeremiah and Baruch influenced by the language of the Deuteronomistic editor(s) responsible for compiling this history from Moses to Judah's exile, or did members of a Deuteronomistic school also pull together disparate materials to then compose a book of Jeremiah? On the one hand, H. Weippert and W. Holladay gave primacy in varying degrees to the figures of Jeremiah and Baruch, even if certain forms of expressions were similar to Deuteronomistic vocabulary. On the other hand, P. Hyatt, W. Thiel and E. Nicholson gave primacy to Deuteronomistic editing or authorship in the prose speeches and significant parts of the biographical narratives. This meant that the redacted book of Jeremiah and the Deuteronomistic History were produced in similar circles. The theological rationale for their production was a response to the experience of exile.

Among modern scholars, one still sees the historical question raised regarding Jeremiah's relationship to Josiah's reform and the production of the book of Deuteronomy. The work of M. Leuchter links Jeremiah to scribal circles like the family of Shaphan and to the reforming work that they undertook in Judah.

In another recent study, C. Maier has proposed that a major thrust of the redacted book is to present Jeremiah as a teacher of Torah. She distinguishes that presentation from what might be discerned about the historical Jeremiah. There is a sense that segments of modern interpretation have come almost full circle from Duhm, who recognized the importance of Torah piety in the editorial layers of the book but essentially dismissed it as the work of legalists. Maier follows scholars who seek to identify the concerns of those who compiled the portrait of the prophet and to pay attention to that portrait in its final form.

6.6. The Texts of Jeremiah. Textual analysis of Jeremiah entered a new phase with the discovery of the DSS in 1947 (Tov 1985; 1997; Barthélemy). It has been recognized at least since Jerome that there were differences between the Greek and Hebrew manuscript traditions of Jeremiah. There is difference in the order of subsections, and the LXX is approximately one-eighth shorter overall. It is essentially the prose texts in the Hebrew that are longer than their Greek counterparts, particularly with introductory and concluding formulas (Janzen; Parke-Taylor). The fragments from six different scrolls, dating approximately 125 BC-AD 50, are evidence for a prolonged period of transmission in Hebrew of more than one textual tradition. A fragment from Cave 4 (4Q71) preserves a Hebrew text more in line with its LXX counterpart, while two other fragments from the same cave (4Q70; 4Q72) are closer to what became the MT. On the one hand, the fragments provide evidence for a Hebrew tradition underlying at least parts of the LXX tradition, even when it departs from the MT; on the other hand, they provide evidence that written forms of the Jeremiah book were in editorial development well into the postexilic period. This last matter has made the dating of redactional layers in the book an extremely complicated matter (Stipp).

6.7. Recent Scholarship. In recent decades, large commentaries and surveys of research provide inviting fare for the student of Jeremiah. One set (the three-volume Word Biblical Commentary) has multiple authors. W. McKane, W. Holladay and J. Lundbom, have each produced multivolume commentaries on their own. McKane sees the production of the book of Jeremiah as a long, complicated process, which at one point he characterizes as a "rolling corpus" (McKane, 1:li). Holladay, on the other hand, places much of the book's production in the lifetime of the prophet and Baruch. He is one of several modern scholars who prefer to the see the beginning of Jeremiah's public ministry at a date later than the thirteenth year of Josiah (Jer 1:1). Lundbom's work is sensitive to poetic and rhetorical analysis of the text, and he is more sanguine than McKane at identifying settings in Jeremiah's own lifetime. These authors interact with a wide range of scholarship in presenting their views. R. Carroll's large, one-volume commentary takes an agnostic approach to questions of historical connection between the book and the prophetic figure. Carroll sees the book as comprising various traditions seeking to come to grips with the impact of the exile.

S. Herrmann authored a volume that rehearses scholarship devoted to the book and concentrates on nineteenth- and twentieth-century interpretations. Essays edited by L. Perdue and B. Kovacs and by A. Curtis and T. Römer, and survey articles by R. Carroll and C. Carroll provide good cross-sections of studies related to the book.

There are trends underway in scholarship whose influence will be determined by the future. Commentaries, particularly in English, currently give less attention to matters of source analysis or the genetic stages of the book's production than was done earlier in the twentieth century. Some of this is due to the emphasis of B. Childs and others on the final form of a book as the object of theological analysis (*see* Canonical Criticism), and some of it to the literary conviction that a book's present form has its own integrity. One also sees employment of reading strategies that use a more dialogic approach and/or one that emphasizes the response of readers to the text (cf. surveys by R. Carroll and C. Carroll). Theories of *intertextuality, theme and metaphor (Lalleman-de Winkel, Bourguet; Shields) also contribute to the emphasis on literary analysis.

Archaeological research on ancient Israel has illumined several aspects of Jeremiah (King). One aspect is the connection between public figures (officials) in the book and the still-growing corpus of Semitic inscriptions from the seventh and sixth centuries BC (Mykytiuk). There are now probable connections with such figures as Gemariah (Jer 36:10), Gedaliah (Jer 40:7), Baalis (Jer 40:14), Seriah (Jer 51:59) and Jerahmeel (Jer 36:26). Clay bullae with the name of Baruch son of Neriah have also come to light, but their authenticity is questionable.

See also EXILE; JEREMIAH: BOOK OF.

BIBLIOGRAPHY. **D. H. Bak,** *Klagender Gott, klagende Menschen: Studien zur Klage im Jeremiabuch* (BZAW 193; Berlin: de Gruyter, 1990); **D. Barthélemy,** *Critique textuelle de l'Ancien Testament 2: Isaïe, Jérémie, Lamentations* (OBO 50/2; Fribourg: Éditions Universitaires, 1986); **W. Baumgartner,** *Die Klagegedichte des Jeremia und die Klagepsalmen* (BZAW 32; Giessen: Töpelmann, 1916); **D. Bourguet,** *Des metaphores de Jérémie* (EB 9; Paris: Gabalda, 1987); **G. J. Brooke,** "The Book of Jeremiah and Its Reception in the Qumran Scrolls," in *The Book of Jeremiah and Its*

Reception, ed. A. H. W. Curtis and T. Römer (BETL 128; Leuven: Leuven University Press, 1997) 183-205; **C. Carroll,** "Another Dodecade: A Dialectic Model of the Decentered Universe of Jeremiah Studies 1996-2008," *CurBS* 8.2 (2010) 162-82; **R. Carroll,** *Jeremiah: A Commentary* (OTL; Louisville: Westminster/John Knox, 1986); idem, "Surplus Meaning and the Conflict of Interpretation: A Dodecade of Jeremiah Studies (1984-95)," *CurBS* 4 (1996) 115-59; idem, "Century's End: Jeremiah Studies at the Beginning of the Third Millennium," *CurBS* 8 (2000) 18-58; **A. H. W. Curtis and T. Römer,** eds., *The Book of Jeremiah and Its Reception* (BETL 128; Leuven: Leuven University Press, 1997) 183-205; **A. R. P. Diamond,** *The Confessions of Jeremiah in Context: Scenes of a Prophetic Drama* (JSOTSup 45; Sheffield: Sheffield Academic, 1987); **B. Duhm,** *Das Buch Jeremia* (HKC 11; Tübingen: Mohr, 1901); **T. E. Fretheim,** *Jeremiah* (SHBC; Macon, GA: Smith & Helwys, 2002); **M. Graves,** *Jerome's Hebrew Philology: A Study Based on His Commentary on Jeremiah* (VCSup 90; Leiden: E. J. Brill, 2007); **S. Herrmann,** *Jeremia: Der Prophet und das Buch* (EdF 271; Darmstadt: Wissenschaftliche Buchgesellschaft, 1990); **W. L. Holladay,** *Jeremiah* (2 vols.; Hermeneia; Philadelphia: Fortress, 1986-1989); **J. P. Hyatt,** "The Deuteronomic Edition of Jeremiah," in *A Prophet to the Nations: Essays in Jeremiah Studies,* ed. L. Perdue and B. Kovacs (Winona Lake, IN: Eisenbrauns, 1984) 247-67; **N. Ittmann,** *Die Konfessionen Jeremias: Ihre Bedeutung für die Verkündigung des Propheten* (WMANT 54; Neukirchen-Vluyn: Neukirchener Verlag, 1981); **J. G. Janzen,** *Studies in the Text of Jeremiah* (HMS 6; Cambridge: Harvard University Press, 1973); **P. J. King,** *Jeremiah: An Archaeological Companion* (Louisville: Westminster/John Knox, 1993); **J. Kiss,** *Die Klage Gottes und des Propheten: Ihre Rolle in der Komposition und Redaktion von Jer 11-12, 14-15 und 18* (WMANT 99; Neukirchen-Vluyn: Neukirchener Verlag, 2003); **M. Knowles,** *Jeremiah in Matthew's Gospel: The Rejected Prophet Motif in Matthaean Redaction* (JSNTSup 68; Sheffield: Sheffield Academic, 1993); **K. H. Kuhn,** "A Coptic Jeremiah Apocryphon," *Le Muséon* 83 (1970) 95-135, 291-350; **H. Lalleman-de Winkel,** *Jeremiah in Prophetic Tradition: An Examination of the Book of Jeremiah in the Light of Israel's Prophetic Traditions* (CBET 26; Leuven: Peeters, 2000); **D. R. Law,** "Matthew's Enigmatic Reference to Jeremiah in Mt 16,14," in *The Book of Jeremiah and Its Reception,* ed. A. H. Curtis and T. Römer (BETL 128; Leuven: Leuven University Press, 1997) 277-302; **N. C. Lee and C. Mandolfo,** eds., *Lamentations in Ancient and Contemporary Cultural Contexts* (SBLSymS 43; Atlanta: Society of Biblical Literature, 2008); **M. Leuchter,** *Josiah's Reform and Jeremiah's Scroll: Historical Calamity and Prophetic Response* (HBM 6; Sheffield: Sheffield Phoenix, 2006); **J. R. Lundbom,** *Jeremiah* (3 vols; AB 21A, 21B, 21C; New Haven: Yale University Press; New York: Doubleday, 1999-2004); **C. Maier,** *Jeremia als Lehrer der Torah* (FRLANT 196; Göttingen: Vandenhoeck & Ruprecht, 2002); **C. Mandolfo,** *Daughter Zion Talks Back to the Prophets: A Dialogic Theology of the Book of Lamentations* (SBLSS 58; Atlanta: Society of Biblical Literature, 2007); **W. McKane,** *A Critical and Exegetical Commentary on Jeremiah* (2 vols.; Edinburgh: T & T Clark, 1986-1996); **S. Mowinckel,** *Zur Komposition des Buches Jeremia* (Oslo: Jacob Dybwad, 1914); **L. Mykytiuk,** *Identifying Biblical Persons in Northwest Semitic Inscriptions of 1200-539 B.C.E.* (SBLAB 12; Atlanta: Society of Biblical Literature, 2004); **J. Neusner,** *Jeremiah in Talmud and Midrash: A Source Book* (Lanham, MD: University Press of America, 2006); **E. W. Nicholson,** *Preaching to the Exiles: A Study of the Prose Tradition in the Book of Jeremiah* (Oxford: Blackwell, 1970); **M. Noth,** *Überlieferungsgeschichtliche Studien 1: Die sammelnden und bearbeitenden Geschichtswerke im Alten Testament* (Halle: Niemeyer, 1943); translation of section 2 in *The Deuteronomistic History* (JSOTSup 15; Sheffield: Sheffield Academic, 1981); **G. Parke-Taylor,** *The Formation of the Book of Jeremiah: Doublets and Recurring Phrases* (SBLMS 51; Atlanta: Society of Biblical Literature, 2000); **L. Perdue and B. Kovacs,** eds., *A Prophet to the Nations: Essays in Jeremiah Studies* (Winona Lake, IN: Eisenbrauns, 1984); **T. Polk,** *The Prophetic Persona: Jeremiah and the Language of the Self* (JSOT 32; Sheffield: Sheffield Academic, 1984); **H. G. Reventlow,** *Liturgie und Prophetisches Ich bei Jeremia* (Gütersloh: Mohn, 1963); **M. Schreiber,** *The Man Who Knew God: Decoding Jeremiah* (Lanham, MD: Lexington Books, 2008); **M. E. Shields,** *Circumscribing the Prostitute: The Rhetoric of Intertextuality, Metaphor and Gender in Jeremiah 3.1-4.4* (London: T & T Clark, 2004); **J. Skinner,** *Prophecy and Religion: Studies in the Life of Jeremiah* (Cambridge: University Press, 1922); **G. A. Smith,** *Jeremiah: The Baird Lectures for 1922* (London: Hodder &

Stoughton, 1923); **M. S. Smith,** *The Laments of Jeremiah and Their Contexts: A Literary and Redactional Study of Jeremiah 11-20* (SBLMS 42; Atlanta: Scholars Press, 1990); **H.-J. Stipp,** *Das masoretische und alexandrinische Sondergut des Jeremiabuches: Textgeschichtlicher Rang, Eigenarten, Triebkräfte* (OBO 136; Freiburg: Universitäts Verlag; Göttingen: Vandenhoeck & Ruprecht, 1994); **W. Thiel,** *Die deuteronomistische Redaktion von Jeremia 1-25* (WMANT 41; Neukirchen-Vluyn: Neukirchener Verlag, 1973); idem, *Die deuteronomistische Redaktion von Jeremia 26-52* (WMANT 52; Neukirchen-Vluyn: Neukirchener Verlag, 1981); **E. Tov,** "The Literary History of the Book of Jeremiah in the Light of Its Textual History," in *Empirical Models for Biblical Criticism,* ed. J. H. Tigay (Philadelphia: University of Pennsylvania Press, 1985) 211-37; idem, "Jeremiah" in *Qumran Cave 4, X: The Prophets,* ed. E. Ulrich et al. (DJD 15; Oxford: Clarendon Press, 1997) 145-207; **G. von Rad,** *Old Testament Theology,* Volume 2: *The Theology of Israel's Prophetic Traditions* (New York: Harper & Row, 1965); **H. Weippert,** *Die Prosareden des Jeremiabuches* (BZAW 132; Berlin: de Gruyter, 1973); **D. O. Wenthe,** ed., *Jeremiah, Lamentations* (ACCS 12; Downers Grove, IL: InterVarsity Press, 2009). J. A. Dearman

JOEL, BOOK OF

Joel is the second book in the *Book of the Twelve, the Minor Prophets. The occasion for this book was a locust plague that so severely devastated the land and its crops that the survival of the people, their livestock and even of local wildlife seemed in doubt. The date of the book's composition is disputed. Few scholars claim an elaborate compositional or redactional history for Joel; it is widely regarded as single, unified work. The chapter and verse division of the Hebrew text differs slightly from that of the English. The English of Joel 2:28-32 corresponds to Joel 3:1-5 in the Hebrew, and the English Joel 3:1-21 corresponds to the Hebrew Joel 4:1-21. There is one important problem in the interpretation of the text. Although it is widely agreed that Joel 1 describes the great locust plague, the meaning of Joel 2:1-11 is a matter of debate. Interpreters are divided over whether this passage continues the description of the locusts from Joel 1 or, instead, it predicts an invasion by a human army. In addition, the account of the pouring out of the

Spirit (Joel 2:28-32 [MT 3:1-5]) is of particular interest to Christian readers because Peter cites it in full at Acts 2:17-21.

1. Author and Composition History
2. The Text
3. Place and Date of Composition
4. Structure
5. Issues in Interpretation

1. Author and Composition History.

1.1. Author. Joel son of Pethuel, the stated author of the book (Joel 1:1), is not mentioned in any other biblical text, and the book of Joel itself lacks any meaningful biographical information about the man. Everything about him (the era in which he lived, his social status, his tribal membership and ancestral home, specific details of his life story) is either lost or must be inferred from his book. The dates to which one assigns his life depend upon the date one assigns to the composition of the book (see 3.2 below).

One distinctive interpretation, however, combines interpretation of the book with specific inferences about the prophet. It claims that he was a cultic prophet; that is, he was attached to the Jerusalem temple and participated in its ritual by means of ceremonially acted out prophecies. A. Kapelrud, for example, compares the prophecy of the Spirit (Joel 2:28-32 [MT 3:1-5]) to Zechariah 12:10, where Yahweh promises to pour out a spirit of grace on the people when they look upon "the one whom they pierced." He argues that the *Zechariah text refers to a cultic object called the "pierced one," and that the people performed ritual dirges before it. He concludes that in Joel, similarly, the promise of the coming of the Spirit is associated with ecstatic ritual. G. Ahlström argues that Joel used his position as a temple prophet to resist a revival of Baalism there, while G. Ogden claims that Joel led the nation in a liturgy of *lament over foreign invasions.

Against these interpretations, it is true that Joel calls upon the people to mourn at the temple (Joel 2:15), but this is hardly distinctive and by no means marks him as a member of the temple personnel. Kapelrud's interpretation depends on a dubious analysis of Zechariah 12:10, and Ahlström's interpretation is seriously undermined by the fact that Joel never refers to Baal. Ogden, quite eccentrically, concludes that the locusts of Joel 1 are a metaphor only.

1.2. Unity. A number of scholars have attempted to discern various sources behind Joel. An older view is that Joel 1:1—2:27 (MT 1—2) is a work distinct from Joel 2:28—3:21 (MT 3—4). J. Bewer detects a number of interpolations and argues that references to the Day of Yahweh are secondary. On the other hand, scholars such as R. Pfeiffer and W. Prinsloo are impressed with marks of the unity of the book, and this remains the most common position. The most significant argument against the unity of the book is that the locusts of Joel 1:1—2:27 disappear in Joel 2:28—3:21, but this argument is considerably weakened if one recognizes that the northern army in Joel 2:1-11, 20 is composed of soldiers and not locusts (see 4.1 below); so interpreted, these passages represent a strong conceptual link to the judgment on the armies of the *nations in Joel 3 (MT 4). Also, the interlocking structure of the book (see 4.2 below) suggests that it is a unity.

2. The Text.

2.1. Stylistic and Rhetorical Issues. Joel is written in standard biblical Hebrew. It is not marked by linguistic anomalies, and, as Ahlström has shown, it does not have Aramaisms that would indicate a late date of composition. It employs rhetorical devices that are common to biblical Hebrew, including hendiadys ("great and dreadful" at Joel 2:31 [MT 3:4]), merism ("sons and daughters" at Joel 2:28 [MT 3:1]), rhetorical questions (Joel 3:4 [MT 4:4]), repetition for emphasis (*hămônîm hămônîm*, "Throngs! Throngs!" at Joel 3:14 [MT 4:14]), consonance (*ûkěšōd mišadday*, "like destruction from Shaddai," at Joel 1:15) and assonance (*hōbîš tîrôš*, "grain has dried up," at Joel 1:10). (For further examples, see Crenshaw; Thompson; Myers; Marcus.)

2.2. Text-critical Issues. The MT of Joel is very clean, and with few exceptions there is little evidence of textual corruption. The LXX reading of Joel 3:11 (MT 4:11) is preferred by L. Allen over the MT. The Hebrew text of Joel 1:17 is extraordinarily difficult, and Joel 3:21 (MT 4:21) probably should be emended in agreement with the LXX (*see* Text and Textual Criticism).

3. Place and Date of Composition.

3.1. The Location of the Events of Joel. The book evidently was written in Jerusalem. Joel calls for the trumpet to sound in *Zion (Joel 2:1, 15) and speaks of reviving Jerusalem and Judah (Joel 3:1 [MT 4:1]; see also Joel 3:16 [MT 4:16]). There is no indication that the book comes from any other location.

3.2. The Date of Joel: Evaluating the Data and Arguments. Many scholars date Joel to the postexilic period, although some interpreters set it in the ninth century BC, treating it as the earliest book of prophecy (*see* Israelite History). Arguments regarding this issue are as follows.

1. Some argue that the book refers to no kings (contrast, e.g., Is 1:1; Jer 1:2; Hos 1:1), and therefore it was written during the postexilic era. But even postexilic books often date themselves by reference to kings—Persian kings (e.g., Ezra 1:1; Hag 1:1; Zech 1:1). As such, the lack of any synchronism to the reign of a king is insignificant.

2. Some argue that priests and elders are the authorities in the city, and therefore the book is postexilic. But the priests are not addressed as men with governing authority; they are mentioned only with respect to their ritual duties (Joel 1:9; 2:17). The "elders" of Joel 1:2 are, literally, old men; they are not governing elders. Therefore, these references are inconsequential for the date of the book.

3. The book several times mentions Jerusalem (e.g., Joel 2:32) but never alludes to the northern kingdom. Joel speaks of "Israel" at Joel 3:2 (MT 4:2), not as a separate state but as part of a unity that includes Judah (Joel 3:1 [MT 4:1]), analogous to what one sees in late preexilic texts (Jer 31:31) and in postexilic texts (Neh 12:47). This implies that Joel was written after the fall of Samaria (722 BC).

4. Jerusalem has walls at the time of writing (Joel 2:7), and therefore the book is either preexilic or was written after the reforms of Nehemiah. It is doubtful that Joel would have spoken of walls had they been the rubble of the early postexilic period (Neh 2:13).

5. The temple exists and has a functioning priesthood (Joel 1:9; 2:17). If the temple were a burned-out ruin, as it was in the exilic period, the lack of grain for a grain offering (Joel 1:9) would have been the least of its problems. Therefore, the book is either preexilic or written after the rebuilding of the temple.

6. In the order of the Book of the Twelve (the Minor Prophets), Joel falls between Hosea and Amos, two of the earliest writing prophets. This could imply that Joel is very early, but

while it is generally true that earlier prophets are near the head of the list in the Twelve (Hosea, Amos, Jonah, Micah) and that later prophets are at the end (Haggai, Zechariah, Malachi), this is not invariable. Obadiah stands between Amos and Jonah in the Hebrew canon, but it is almost certainly exilic in origin. In the LXX, represented by Codices Vaticanus and Alexandrinus, Joel is between Micah and Obadiah. Furthermore, the scribes who placed the books of the Twelve in their current MT order may have been motivated by considerations other than chronology. In particular, Joel may be in its present position because the similarity between Joel 3:16 (MT 4:16) and Amos 1:2 creates a link between the two books. Both verses speak of Yahweh roaring from Zion. Perhaps the framers of the canon had no idea when Joel was written, and thus they used this catchphrase as the best basis for positioning the book in the canon.

7. Joel 3:1-2 (MT 4:1-2) speaks of a restoration of Jerusalem and Israel and also refers to a regathering of exiles. This does not contradict evidence indicating that Jerusalem had walls and a functioning temple, but it does imply that the city's fortunes were at a low point relative to other nations. This could apply equally either to the late preexilic or to the postexilic period. The exiles appear to be more closely linked to "Israel" (Joel 3:2) than to Judah (Joel 3:1), suggesting that the prophecy dates from the period after the fall of Samaria to Assyria but before the fall of Jerusalem to Babylon.

8. Joel 1:14 calls upon "all the inhabitants of the land" to gather at the temple. This indicates that the population is small and concentrated around Jerusalem. This could apply either to the late preexilic period or the postexilic period.

9. Some, such as M. Treves, argue that Joel cites other OT books and is therefore later than the books that it cites. But it is difficult to prove that one book is citing another; both may be using a common expression. Also, even if direct citation appears to be present, it is not necessarily obvious which book came first. For example, Joel 3:18 (MT 4:18) is similar to Amos 9:13, but it is not clear that one is citing the other, or if so, who is citing whom. Two texts in Joel, however, are especially worthy of note. First, Joel 2:32 (MT 3:5) is almost identical to Obadiah 17 ("but in Mount Zion there shall be a group of survivors"), except that Joel, apart from also having

"in Jerusalem," has the words "as Yahweh has said." This could indicate that Joel is citing Obadiah. On the other hand, Joel could be rephrasing Isaiah 37:31-32. Second, Joel 3:10 (MT 4:10) has "beat your plowshares into swords." This is the reverse of Isaiah 4:2 (and Mic 4:3), "and they shall beat their swords into plowshares." Our familiarity with Isaiah's version causes us to assume that it is the original, but this is actually unlikely. It is more probable that "beat your plowshares into swords" is an ancient rallying cry meant to mobilize a community for war. This is precisely how it is used in Joel. It appears that Isaiah and Micah reverse this common idiom in order to illustrate the peacefulness of the eschatological age. Joel, by contrast, seems to preserve the original idiom. But the language has no bearing on the date of Joel.

10. Joel 3:6 (MT 4:6) assails the Phoenicians and Philistines for selling Israelites as slaves to the Greeks. For some, this alone is enough to show that Joel is postexilic. However, the notion that the Greeks were unknown to peoples throughout the Near East in the eighth or seventh century BC is absurd. What is significant, however, is that in Joel Greece is perceived to be far from Israel. Perception of distance is, to a great degree, psychological. After the failed Persian invasion of Greece, Greek mercenaries and colonists became a familiar sight in Egypt and the Near East, and after Alexander's conquests they were ubiquitous. In such a situation, familiarity with Greeks and frequent interchange with the Greek homeland would have made Greece seem fairly near. Prior to that, when encounters with Greeks were more limited, Greece would have seemed far away. Also, J. Myers points out that the Greeks underwent a major economic expansion from the eighth to sixth centuries BC when they imported numerous slaves. Joel 3:6 (MT 4:6), implying that Greece was in the market for slaves but was perceived to be distant, suggests a late preexilic date.

11. Joel 3:4 (MT 4:4) refers to conflicts with the Phoenicians and Philistines, and Joel 3:19 (MT 4:19) implies enmity with Egypt and Edom. A number of scholars have tried to use this information to date Joel, but with widely conflicting results. Bewer takes Joel 3:4 (MT 4:4) to be evidence that Joel was written in the reign of Artaxerxes III Ochus and between the years 352 and 348 BC. By contrast, G. Archer

indicates that the combination of enemies described in Joel requires for the book a date no later than around 800 BC, the end of the reign of Joash of Judah. Both claims are unfounded; there is not nearly enough evidence from the passing references to these enemies in Joel to create a synchronism. The conflicts that Joel describes seem to be relatively small incidents now lost to us. Joel gives us an accumulation of grievances, not a particular moment in history. In short, the list of enemies is of no value in dating the book.

12. Joel 3:11 (MT 4:11) calls on Yahweh to send down his warriors, and this could reflect the advanced angelology of the postexilic era. But the language hardly implies the extravagant theology of angels that we see in the pseudepigraphal texts. Angelic armies are already implied in the ancient title "Yahweh of hosts," making Joel 3:11 (MT 4:11) unexceptional. In addition, the Targum, Syriac, LXX and Vulgate have a variety of readings here, but they have no reference to angels.

In light of all the evidence taken together, Joel could come from Jerusalem after Nehemiah. But based on the implication that Israel (not Judah) is scattered and on the perception of Greece as a distant land, a late preexilic date, perhaps in the seventh century BC, is preferable.

4. Structure.
Joel is best understood to be composed of two interlocking chiastic structures. The first chiasmus, as the following interpretation of Joel 2:1-11 implies, is based upon the typological linkage between the locust plague and the northern invader. Both cause great destruction, and in the end both are destroyed. A middle, transitional element is at Joel 2:11-19, a call to repentance. This act of turning back to God is thus structurally the pivot point that leads into the reversal of the earlier calamities.

(A) Punishment: locusts (Joel 1:2-20)
  (B) Punishment: northern army
    (Joel 2:1-11)
    (C) Transition: repentance
      (Joel 2:12-19)
  (B') Grace: northern army destroyed
    (Joel 2:20)
(A') Grace: rain poured out to heal land
  (Joel 2:21-27)

The second chiasmus contains the destruction of the northern army (Joel 2:20) and the healing of the land (Joel 2:21-27) from the first chiasmus, creating the interlocking structure.

(A) Northern army destroyed (Joel 2:20)
  (B) Rain poured out to heal land
    (Joel 2:21-27)
  (B') Spirit poured out to heal people
    (Joel 2:28-32 [MT 3:1-5])
(A') Judgment on Gentile armies
  (Joel 3:1-21 [MT 4:1-21])

The theological significance to this structure is that the gift of the Spirit and the final judgment on the nations are anticipated respectively by the healing of the land and destruction of the northern army.

5. Issues in Interpretation.
5.1. Joel 2:1-11: Locusts or Soldiers? Joel 1 self-evidently concerns a locust plague, notwithstanding the opinion of some that the locusts are a metaphorical representation of the Babylonian army (Stuart). But the topic of Joel 2:1-11 is debated. Some take it to be a continuation from Joel 1 of the lament over the locusts, while others argue that it is a prophetic announcement of a future (human) army that will invade the land. This issue, moreover, is critically important for coming to terms with the structure and message of the book.

Since we have an account of a locust plague in Joel 1, and since Joel 2:21-27 describes the healing of the land after a locust plague, context appears to favor the locust interpretation for all of Joel 1:1—2:27. Specific details of Joel 2:1-11 that can be read as metaphoric references to locusts include that they leave the land looking as though it had been scorched in a fire (Joel 2:3), that they seem to look like horses (Joel 2:4 [interpreters note the similarity between a locust and a horse's head]), and that they sound like cavalry or a raging fire (Joel 2:5). Also, the point that the invaders in Joel 2 are said to be "like" soldiers (Joel 2:7) suggests that in fact they are not soldiers.

As persuasive as this may appear, however, it is better to see the enemy of Joel 2:1-11 as a human army and not as locusts. First, the fact that the language is reminiscent of a locust plague is not surprising; the locusts are a type for the human army that is to come. Thus, the way they denude the land, the similarity between locusts and horses, and the terrible noise they make are intentionally included. What was true of the locusts will be true of the coming army, albeit in a manner more terrible. The reader is supposed to catch the sensible connection between the sight and sound of the coming enemy army and of the recent locust plague. In addition, the fact that the invaders in Joel 2:1-11 are "like" soldiers does not mean that they are actually something other than soldiers. The particle here translated as "like" (Heb kĕ) sometimes means more than that; it describes the fulfillment of an ideal. It is analogous to an English expression such as "He always acts like a man." Here the speaker does not mean that the subject only seems like a man and is not really one; rather, the subject is an actual man who fulfills the ideal of a man. A close parallel is in Ezekiel 26:10, which says of a future invader that he will "enter your gates like [kĕ] men entering a breached city," when what they will be is in fact men entering a breached city. So also in Joel 2:4 the invading force is not locusts that are "like" cavalry; they are mounted soldiers who spread panic as only a well-trained cavalry can. But there are several other compelling reasons for taking Joel 2:1-11 to refer to a human army.

First, Joel 1 is dominated by verbs in the perfect (qatal) form, but Joel 2:1-11 is dominated by verbs in the imperfect (yiqtol) form. While it is true that we cannot simply equate the Hebrew perfect with past tense and the imperfect with the future tense, those are the default meanings of the inflections, and the shift from the one to the other cannot be accidental. There are some perfect verbs in Joel 2:1-11, but these are descriptive (Joel 2:3 "before him, fire consumes ['ākĕlâ]"). But the perfect verbs of Joel 1 plainly refer to the past (Joel 1:19: "fire has consumed ['ākĕlâ] the pastures of the wilderness"). Similarly, the imperfect verbs that appear in Joel 1 describe a response to what has just come (Joel 1:19: "to you, Yahweh, I will make my cry ['eqrā']"), but the imperfects of Joel 2:1-11 speak of the future deeds of the enemy (Joel 2:7: "like warriors they shall run [yĕruṣûn]; like men of war they shall climb [ya'ălû] the wall"). The implication is that Joel 1 is in the past, but Joel 2:1-11 is in the future.

Second, the people fight the invaders in Joel 2:1-11 in a manner not appropriate to dealing with locusts. Joel 2:8b can be translated, "Through weapons they plunge; they do not break off [the attack]." People try to fight back this invader with spears, arrows and swords; this is something no one would do with locusts. The Hebrew word used here (šelaḥ) means "weapons" and especially "projectiles" (as at Neh 4:17 [MT 4:11]; 4:23 [MT 4:17]; 2 Chron 23:10; 32:5). Contrary to J. Crenshaw, who bizarrely imagines a swarm of locusts entering Jerusalem via the Siloam Tunnel, it does not refer to the Pool of Siloam.

Third, the goal of the invaders in Joel 2:1-11 is incompatible with a locust plague. They scale the city walls and run along them, and at the climactic moment they burst into the private homes inside the city (Joel 2:9). While there is no doubt that in a locust plague some locusts would get upon the walls and some would enter houses, that is a fairly inconsequential matter. A locust plague does its damage out in the fields, not inside the city. But when an army has taken the walls and has entered houses where women and children have taken shelter, the city has fallen and all is lost.

Fourth, the invader in Joel 2:1-11 is called "northerner" at Joel 2:20. This designation is not possible for a locust plague. In ancient times, as now, locust plagues formed in the horn of Africa and flew north across the Red Sea and toward the Arabian Peninsula, but if wind currents were from the east, they made their way northward toward Israel. That is, locusts always came up from the south and never from the north. By contrast, the great enemies of Israel and Judah (Syria, Assyria, Babylon) entered the land from the north (see Jer 1:14-15; 4:6; 6:1, 22; 10:22; Ezek 23:24; 38:6).

Fifth, the reversal of the locust plague in Joel 2:21-27 is concerned only with the events of Joel 1 and not with Joel 2:1-11. The healing of the land is introduced in Joel 2:21, with a sequence of specific acts of restoration taking up Joel 2:22-27. Table 1 demonstrates how the disasters from Joel 1 are reversed when God restores the land. The sequence in Joel 2:21-27 is also in the reverse order from what we see in Joel 1. But the important point is this: in Joel 2:22-27 the whole description of the locust event comes from Joel 1, with nothing from Joel 2:1-11. This indicates that the prophet does not regard the material from the latter text as an account of a locust plague.

Tell people about locusts *for generations* (Joel 1:2-3)	People *never again* so shamed (Joel 2:26-27)
Four locust swarms eat everything (Joel 1:4)	Restoration from the *four locust swarms* (Joel 2:25)
Wine and oil fail (Joel 1:5, 10)	*Wine and oil* restored (Joel 2:24)
Grain depleted; *granaries* ruined (Joel 1:10-11, 17)	*Grain* restored and *threshing floors* full (Joel 2:24)
Land is *parched* (Joel 1:12, 17)	*Rains* come upon *land* (Joel 2:23)
Trees stripped bare (Joel 1:12, 19)	*Trees* bear fruit (Joel 2:22)
Animals dying (Joel 1:18, 20)	*Animals* have pasture (Joel 2:22)

Table 1. Disaster and Restoration in Joel 1—2

In conclusion, context favors seeing the invader in Joel 2:1-11 as a human army, not as locusts. The invader in Joel 2:1-11 is the northerner, a human enemy that is the typological counterpart of the locusts and whose destruction is anticipated in Joel 2:20. The locust devastation that is reversed in Joel 2:21-27 relates only to Joel 1.

5.2. The Day of Yahweh in Joel. The common thread that links the whole of Joel together is the theme of the Day of Yahweh (see Day of the Lord). While lamenting the locust plague, Joel 1:15 says, "The day of Yahweh is upon us!" Describing the invasion by the northern army, Joel 2:11 says, "For the day of Yahweh is great and very frightening." In the aftermath of the people's repentance, Joel 2:18 speaks of Yahweh as "jealous" for his land and "compassionate" for his people, and he moves to give them salvation and to show that he is among them (Joel 2:27). In Joel 2:28-32 (MT 3:1-5) the pouring out of the Spirit is declared to be "the day of Yahweh," replete with signs in heaven, such as the moon turning to blood (Joel 2:31 [MT 3:4]). Finally, the great judgment on all the nations in the valley of Jehoshaphat is also described in terms of the Day of Yahweh: the sun, moon and stars are darkened (Joel 3:15 [MT 4:15]). In short, every major event of Joel, whether it be for Israel's punishment or deliverance, either is explicitly called "the day of Yahweh" or is described in terms befitting that day.

The interpretation of so many and varied events as the Day of Yahweh in Joel is of consequence. First, it warns us that we must be careful about supposing that the Day of Yahweh is strictly an aspect of the divine *warfare ideology. In Joel, the event with the strongest and most explicit use of Day of Yahweh language is the pouring out of the Spirit, and it is difficult to see Yahweh as a warrior in that event. In addition, we tend to conceive of the Day of Yahweh as an act of judgment, but plainly it is an act of salvation in the healing of the land in Joel 2:21-27 as well as in the gift of the Spirit in Joel 2:28-32 (MT 3:1-5). Even the judgment on the nations in Joel 3 (MT 4) is also salvation for *Zion, where "Yahweh is a fortress for his people" (Joel 3:16).

Joel's use of the Day of Yahweh motif is most important, however, for demonstrating how the prophets conceived of their messages. For Joel, the Day of Yahweh is not a single event in the future; that is, in contrast to how we may perceive it, that day is not simply the last judgment. The Day of Yahweh may be something as localized as a locust plague affecting the hill country of Judah, or it may be an eschatological event of grace, such as the pouring out of the Spirit. It may be a judgment upon Israel—even an event as calamitous as the fall of Jerusalem—or it may be a saving event for Israel. For Joel, the Day of Yahweh is a moment at which God decisively acts to judge or to save, perhaps after a long period of apparent inactivity. Every event, from the locust plague to the last judgment, is a milestone in the history of salvation. As a model of prophetic hermeneutics, this tells us that the prophets did not simply issue discrete predictions about things to come. Rather, they spoke of an ideal or type, such as the Day of Yahweh, and saw all the individual manifestations of that ideal as integrally tied together by the common type that they fulfilled. Great events of the distant or eschatological future are anticipated by smaller, more localized fulfillments of the same ideal within the historical present. The prophets rarely spoke of the great events of the future without at the same time speaking of events of their own time that fulfilled the same typological theme.

5.3. Joel 2:28-32 and the Day of Pentecost. Joel raises a number of theological issues of importance to the church. The locust plague in Joel 1 invites the reader to consider matters related to theodicy; in particular, one may reflect upon this passage against the backdrop of the tsunamis, earthquakes and storms that continue to cause massive destruction and loss of life in our time. Also, the passages of woe and disaster for Israel (Joel 1:1—2:11) shift to promises of salvation after the call for repentance at Joel 2:12-19. This suggests the pivotal role of repentance in bringing about redemption. Above all, however, Christians naturally want to understand Peter's claim in Acts 2:14-21 that the events of Pentecost fulfilled Joel 2:28-32 (MT 3:1-5).

Several points may help us to understand how Joel relates to Acts 2. First, as detailed above, the gift of the Spirit is understood in Joel to be a great fulfillment of the ideal of the Day of Yahweh. Second, Acts goes out of its way to inform us that the people in the temple area who saw that event were from many different nations and spoke many languages (Acts 2:6-11). Although almost all of these people were Jewish, they foreshadow the movement of the gospel to the nations, a theme that dominates Acts and fulfills the promise that the nations would stream to Zion (Is 2:1-4). These considerations indicate that at Pentecost the eschatological age had begun.

In addition, Joel describes the coming of the Spirit as a "pouring out" (Joel 2:28 [MT 3:1]), as though the Spirit were a liquid. This peculiar language links the gift of the Spirit to the healing rains of Joel 2:23. Furthermore, the occasion for prophecy of Joel was a locust plague that devoured all of Judah's crops, and because of that catastrophe Joel urged the people to come to the temple and lament (Joel 2:12-17). Pentecost, we must remember, was an agricultural thanksgiving holiday; it came at the end of the spring grain harvest that officially began with Passover. How appropriate, then, that the Spirit should be "poured out" in the temple, where lamentation over famine had once rang out. The spiritual antitype to the healing rains of Joel 2:23 came on a day of harvest celebration, Pentecost Sunday (*see* Prophets in the New Testament).

See also BOOK OF THE TWELVE; DAY OF THE LORD; WARFARE AND DIVINE WARFARE.

BIBLIOGRAPHY. **G. W. Ahlström,** *Joel and the Temple Cult of Jerusalem* (VTSup 21; Leiden: E. J. Brill, 1971); **L. C. Allen,** *The Books of Joel, Obadiah, Jonah, and Micah* (NICOT; Grand Rapids: Eerdmans, 1976); **G. L. Archer,** *A Survey of Old Testament Introduction* (Chicago: Moody, 1974); **J. L. Crenshaw,** *Joel* (AB 24C; New York: Doubleday, 1995); **D. A. Garrett,** *Hosea, Joel* (NAC 19A; Nashville: Broadman & Holman, 1997); **A. S. Kapelrud,** *Joel Studies* (Uppsala: Almqvist & Wiksells, 1948); **D. Marcus,** "Nonrecurring Doublets in Joel," *CBQ* 56 (1994) 56-57, 65-66; **J. M. Myers,** "Some Considerations Bearing on the Date of Joel," *ZAW* 74 (1962) 177-95; **G. S. Ogden,** "Joel 4 and Prophetic Responses to National Laments," *JSOT* 26 (1983) 97-106; **R. Pfeiffer,** *Introduction to the Old Testament* (New York: Harper, 1941); **W. S. Prinsloo,** "The Unity of the Book of Joel," *ZAW* 104 (1992) 66-81; **J. M. P. Smith, W. H. Ward and J. A. Bewer,** *A Critical and Exegetical Commentary on Micah, Zephaniah, Nahum, Habakkuk, Obadiah and Joel* (ICC 24; New York: Charles Scribner's Sons, 1911); **D. K. Stuart,** *Hosea-Jonah* (WBC 31; Waco, TX: Word, 1987); **J. A. Thompson,** "Repetition in the Prophecy of Joel," in *On Language, Culture, and Religion: In Honor of Eugene A. Nida,* ed. M. Black and W. A. Smalley (The Hague: Mouton, 1974); **M. Treves,** "The Date of Joel," *VT* 7 (1957) 149-56; **W. VanGemeren,** "Joel," in *Theological Interpretation of the Old Testament: A Book-by-Book Survey,* ed. K. J. Vanhoozer (Grand Rapids: Baker Academic, 2005).   D. A. Garrett

JONAH, BOOK OF

The book of Jonah is unusual among the prophets because it recounts a story about the prophet himself rather than mainly preserving the words that he preached. Typically, the OT Prophetic Books do the latter; they provide little or no biographical information about the prophet whose name they bear, but they do preserve the text of the message that he was inspired to preach. In the case of Jonah, only five Hebrew words that he preached to the people of Assyria are preserved, those that are translate as "Forty days from now Nineveh will be overthrown" (Jon 3:4). The remainder of the book records a story about Jonah, in which he speaks often but not mainly as a prophet preaching to the audience to whom God sends him. Rather, the book describes his actions and words in connection with an assignment that he found difficult to accept from the Lord: to preach to an enemy nation (Assyria) with the attendant possibility that they would respond in such a way as to be shown mercy by God, an outcome that Jonah was determined to resist.

Other biblical stories tell about prophets who also took on difficult assignments. For example, Exodus 3—5 (and much of Ex 3—15) details Moses' challenge to serve God in a hostile Egypt, and parts of Jeremiah describe that prophet's woes encountered trying to convince the Israelites to accede to Babylonian conquest as God's will. To cite another example, several portions of Daniel contain accounts of Daniel's trials at the hands of the Babylonians and Persians. Jonah is thus not unique in containing biography of a prophet and his trials, but of the Prophetic Books, none other is so dominantly biographical and so minimally reflective of a prophet's preached words. Accordingly, the reader gets the message of the book mainly by evaluating what happened to Jonah and what he did in response rather than by analyzing what God told Jonah to say.

Jonah is one of the Bible's best-known characters. Even strangers to most biblical content have heard about Jonah and the "whale." Yet outside of the short book that bears his name, Jonah is mentioned in the OT only once (2 Kings 14:25), relative to his prophetic role in the reclaiming of traditional lands by northern Israel in the reign of Jeroboam II (793-753 BC). He is identified there as being from Gath-Hepher, a small city in Zebulun (probably modern Khirbet ez-Zurra, about three miles northeast of Nazareth).

Jonah's name means "dove" or "pigeon" in Hebrew, one of many biblical names taken from animals and not symbolic in any way of Jonah's character (Stuart, *ISBE* 3:483-88). The book of Jonah indicates that Jonah was, like many Israelites in his day, an ardent nationalist, pro-Israel, antiforeign, and particularly anti-Assyrian (cf. Nahum, esp. Nah 3:19). The book also describes him as a dedicated, disciplined, strong-willed prophet, a poet, and a person capable of being peevish and stubborn, even against God's will.

But these personal traits of the prophet Jonah are learned only as the book progresses. At the outset, nothing is known to the reader or revealed by the introductory words of the book other than the barest facts: he is the son of someone named "Amittai" (of whom nothing otherwise is known); he is a prophet; God has called him to preach to Nineveh. The reader is not required to know much about Jonah's background to appreciate the story. His age, marital status,

family size, upbringing, past career, friendships, special skills and prior prophecies (without 2 Kings 14:25 we would not even know that there were any) are not mentioned. Thus, his past and future are not essential to the book's development. His story, for a period of time that took just a few weeks of his life, is the focus.

1. Structure and Content
2. Date and Setting
3. Canonization
4. Form and Style
5. Unity and Integrity Vis-à-Vis the Psalm of Jonah
6. Historicity
7. Sources and Authorship
8. Text
9. Message and Purpose

1. Structure and Content.

Jonah tells about a northern Israelite prophet, the story containing descriptions of his and others' actions, conversations that he had with others and with God, a poem of thanksgiving that he prayed after being delivered from drowning by a divinely appointed fish, the response to his message by the king and people of Nineveh, and an object lesson about caring for others taught to him by God via the growth and death of a plant. There are some slight differences between the Hebrew text and the English versions in verse numbering and boundaries in the first two chapters, but the content is the same.

The book begins with a brief superscription identifying Jonah, followed by the account of his attempt to run from an assignment from God to preach God's grace to the people of Nineveh, a task that he finds odious (Jon 1). But he cannot outrun an omnipresent, omnipotent God, and he ends up being thrown out of a ship and facing death by drowning in the Mediterranean Sea. But God has other plans for him and appoints a fish to swallow Jonah, who then eloquently thanks God for deliverance via a psalm of thanksgiving: he is in a fish, but he is alive (Jon 2)! After being disgorged by the fish and reaching Nineveh, he preaches a chance to repent, and the king and people of Nineveh respond with genuine *repentance, not to be confused with conversion to Judaism, which is not what his message is about (Jon 3). The final chapter of the book describes Jonah's vigil to see if, as he hoped, Nineveh would be destroyed for its *sins, and his bitter disappointment that it was not. The book ends with God's comparing Jonah's concern for a plant that gave him shade with God's concern for people and animals—life forms far more important than plants. It is not clear that Jonah gets the point that he too should be concerned for everyone, even his enemies, but the alert reader cannot miss that point and will learn an important lesson from Jonah's error (Jon 4).

2. Date and Setting.

Opinions as to the composition of the book fall within wide boundaries (ca. 750-250 BC) because there are no clear indicators within the book of the date of its writing. Four considerations are sometimes advanced as relevant to the dating: (1) the supposed Aramaisms in the language, such as běšellēmî ("on whose account?" [Jon 1:7]) and běšellî ("on my account" [Jon 1:12]); (2) the supposed dependence of certain motifs or theological considerations on the book of Jeremiah; (3) some putative verbal connections with Joel 2; (4) the supposedly erroneous identification of Nineveh as the actual royal capital of Assyria in Jonah's time.

With regard to Aramaisms, these have increasingly disappeared from scholarly debate, being replaced by Northwest Semitisms because many words previously identified as Aramaisms have turned up in early Northwest Semitic texts and Ugaritic texts, which cannot be later than 1200 BC, and the questionable arguments from silence on which such identifications were once made can now be dismissed as spurious. Indeed, none of the total of seven Aramaisms variously identified in the book fits for certain the criteria necessary to constitute a genuine Aramaism (so Loretz).

As to the possible dependence of Jonah on Jeremiah, the evidence is both minimal and ambiguous. The book of Jonah reminds its audience that God is willing to adjust his plans for a nation according to that nation's attitudes and actions before him, a concept expressed propositionally in Jeremiah 18:7-8. But similarity of concepts is not dependency of concepts, and it is more cogently attributable to the univocal nature of divine revelation throughout the Scripture than to a borrowing from Jeremiah on the part of the book of Jonah. For that matter, if Jonah actually prophesied during the first half of the eighth century BC, as 2 Kings

14:25 taken at face value affirms, and Jeremiah during the last third of the seventh century BC and beginning of the sixth, it would be historically more probable that if any sort of borrowing occurred, it was by Jeremiah from Jonah, not the other way around.

The connections of Jonah and Joel must be evaluated in much the same way, though here the issue centers only on the sharing of two virtually exact wordings (part of Jon 3:9 and Joel 2:14; part of Jon 4:2 and Joel 2:13), and it is not clear which prophet would be quoting from which, if any quoting in fact occurs (for the argument that Joel quotes from Jonah, see Magonet, 77-79). Both could have drawn upon a common source for their similar wordings.

Regarding the fourth consideration, Nineveh as the capital of Assyria during Jonah's time, see 6 below.

3. Canonization.

K. Budde suggested that Jonah was included among the Minor Prophets mainly to bring their number to twelve (see Twelve, Book of the). Some have speculated that Jonah is a midrash on one or another of the prophets. E. König opined that Jonah is a midrash on Obadiah 1; R. Coote, on Amos; and others, on Joel 2:13-14. But the degree to which Jonah functions as a midrash to any of these three books has not been easy for scholars to perceive, hence the wide disagreements among them.

It can be just as cogently argued that the placement of Jonah among the prophets resulted from a simple combination of its length, date and subject. Self-contained and brief, it fit easily with the so-called Latter Prophets in a way that the similar Elisha-Elijah stories, except if they were somehow stripped from their context and perhaps condensed, could not easily do. Early in date, at least in Jewish tradition, and quite defensibly in fact, it was sufficiently early that it was not relegated to the Writings (as was, for example, Daniel, a book later joined with the prophets in the Septuagintal, Latin and subsequent canonical orderings but not in Jewish tradition). Its subject matter was in part the call and preaching of a prophet, a concern not entirely removed in some aspects from a book such as Haggai or even Amos (see Amos 7). It is useful to remember that Jonah is atypical of the Prophetic Books primarily in regard to quantity; in regard to quality (i.e., categories rather than percentages), there is little in Jonah that is not represented to some degree elsewhere in the prophetic corpus. Its size, of course, is what makes it a *minor* (from the Latin for "smaller") prophetic book.

4. Form and Style.

4.1. Form. Jonah is a prophetic narrative, paralleling in some ways the prophetic narratives in the books of Kings, but with the prophet portrayed in a distinctly negative light as one whose approach to fulfilling God's call is incorrect. Whereas Elijah, for example, was a prophet who powerfully proclaimed the word of God against great odds (1 Kings 18—19), Jonah was a prophet who ran from God's word when its implications were unpleasant to him.

All biblical narratives are didactic to one degree or another, but in the case of Jonah the narrator has carefully shaped the story for an obviously didactic purpose. There is, in fact, a flashback (Jon 4:5-11) and even a brief "flash forward" (Jon 1:16) in the book. Large blocks of time are passed over rapidly (the long trip from Palestine to Nineveh), while brief moments (Jonah's *prayer in Jon 2; the conversation between God and Jonah in Jon 4) are given detailed attention. The focus can shift from Jonah onto others (to the sailors in Jon 1; to the Ninevites, including the king, in Jon 3) and back to Jonah again, and so on. Such narrative techniques build to the didactic purpose of the book, which is fully unveiled in the divine speeches in Jonah 4 (see Jon 4:4, 10-11). Thus, the book of Jonah may be described not simply as a prophetic narrative, but as a didactic prophetic narrative.

Additionally, Jonah is sensational literature. The book intends to arouse the imagination and emotion of the audience (the storm at sea, the fish story, the plant story, etc). In this sense, Jonah resembles the accounts in the early chapters of Daniel and the miracle stories in the accounts of Elisha's ministry (mainly in 2 Kings 2—7). This does not mean, however, that it is less than fully historical.

As sensational, didactic, prophetic narrative, the book shares features with those genres of literature known as parable and allegory, but it is neither of these. Parables are brief (not four chapters long), normally containing a single scene or two, make comparison to people or things outside the story who are the real focus,

and end with a punch line that draws the hearer up short as it teaches a lesson, the reader hopefully seeing a personally relevant truth in the story. And parables have anonymous figures as their characters. The book of Jonah borders on some of these characteristics but manifests none of them exactly. Moreover, parables are obviously fictional. That is, they are illustrative narrative rather than historical narrative. Jonah is by no means obviously fictional.

Nor is Jonah an allegory. An allegory is an extended analogy, sometimes including extended metaphors, in which the meaning of the story is found in concepts and actions outside the story to which the story points analogically. It would be an unusual allegory indeed that waited to the end (the fourth chapter in the case of Jonah) to reveal the point of its hero's actions. Allegories are distinctly constructed so as to point beyond themselves at each stage. The figures in an allegory are patently symbolic and fictional, and the audience must realize this at once if the allegory is to be effective. Jonah does not fit this pattern either.

Jonah is also not midrash, even though, as noted above, some scholars have suggested that it should be understood this way. Midrash functions as commentary upon particular biblical texts and may include illustration as well as propositional explanation. Midrash is didactic, but by no means is all didactic literature, including narrative, to be identified as midrashic. For Jonah to be convincingly identified as a midrash, it would need to be demonstrated that the story was composed to serve as an illustrative explanation of something taught elsewhere in the OT. Not only can this never be done convincingly in light of the lack of data relevant to the task, but also it would be virtually the reverse of a typical late Jewish midrash. The early midrashim that we do know about are characterized by analytical discussion of stories, laws or other "primary" material. By its nature, Jonah appears far more likely to be not a midrash but rather primary material itself.

4.2. Style. Relatively simple vocabulary prevails throughout the book, something to be expected if the narrator did not wish the didactic impact of the story to be missed at any point owing to an overly complex style. Two vocabulary words have been selected by the narrator and used at various points in the story, each according to two aspects of their wide ranges of meaning: *gādôl* ("great," etc.) and *ra*ᶜ ("bad," etc.). Capitalizing upon two nuances of each of these words is an effective unifying device, providing diversity (in meaning) while at the same time maintaining consistency (in form).

The adjective *gādôl* ("great") appears fourteen times. It has the meaning "great" or "large" (in size or extent) eight times (Jon 1:4 [2x], 10, 12, 16, 17 [2:1 MT]; 4:1, 6). In addition, it has the meaning "important" (or, according to one's translation preference, "key, chief, major") six times (Jon 1:2; 3:2, 3, 5, 7; 4:11) either in reference to the "important" city of Nineveh or the "important" people in the city (i.e., its nobles or leaders). It is significant for the understanding of the story to see that the emphasis placed on Nineveh is not primarily in terms of its physical size but rather its importance to God. The reference to Nineveh's population in Jonah 4:11 notwithstanding, the basic issue goes beyond Nineveh's sheer bulk to its intrinsic value to God.

This value becomes evident partly in the usage of *ra*ᶜ in the book. The word is used, in connection with Nineveh, to describe the troubles the city is having, not merely its *evil ways. To fail to recognize this sense of *ra*ᶜ is to fail to see, for example, an early (Jon 1:2) adumbration of God's compassionate concern for the city. God is as concerned about Nineveh's miseries as he is angry at its evils, and the book's audience did not have to wait until the end of Jonah 3 to gain a sense of that fact.

In total, the word *ra*ᶜ appears nine times in the book. In only two instances does it mean "evil," as the adjective (Jon 3:8, 10). In the other seven occurrences it is a noun, and it means "trouble" or a close synonym—for example, "disaster, misery, difficulty, harm," depending on translation preference (Jon 1:2, 7, 8; 3:10; 4:1, 2, 6). The problems of the Assyrians in Nineveh move God to commission Jonah to preach there. The divine names vary ("Yahweh," "Elohim," "ha-Elohim," "Yahweh-Elohim"), for the most part according to who is addressing the deity (generally, the pagans use "Elohim," and Jonah uses "Yahweh," as might be expected), and the exceptions to this pattern are not easily explained according to any didactic motif (for a contrary view, see Magonet, 33-38).

As sensational didactic historical narrative, Jonah shares a certain style with the Elijah-Eli-sha stories, the stories in the early chapters of Daniel, parts of Ruth and Esther and other OT portions as well (e.g., Ex 4:24-26; Num 12; Judg 14—16). This style wins an audience's attention by its vividness. In spite of its selectivity, the style does not represent exaggeration or literary degradation. Jonah is not a sentimental story, nor is it a humorous one. It is told without embellishment but with an emphasis on engaging the imagination. When a hearer or reader can visualize a scene at each point, the impact of a story is always strong. Jonah is quite "scenic" in this sense, so much so that J. Watts divides the story according to its shifting "scenes."

5. Unity and Integrity Vis-à-Vis the Psalm of Jonah.

The psalm in Jonah 2:2-9 (2:3-10 MT) has been the only part of the book seriously considered an interpolation. From time to time the psalm has been judged a later addition, usually on one or more of the following three grounds: (1) it may be excised without disrupting the story; (2) it is inappropriate, being a thanksgiving psalm when a *lament is called for; (3) it does not relate smoothly to the rest of the story in style, vocabulary, theology or overall impact.

Each of these objections to the appropriateness of the psalm raises questions. The ability to excise part of a literary work without doing damage to the remainder depends entirely on how one analyzes both the excision and the remainder of the text. An ability to excise does not equal, at any rate, a warrant to excise. Few stories contain segments so essential to the flow of the whole that an excision would render the remainder incoherent. Excisability is, in fact, never a legitimate indication of actual lack of integrity in a literary work. In the case of the psalm of Jonah, the same principle applies. However, it applies more easily when the psalm is wrongly interpreted relative to its relationship to the rest of the book. Should not the psalm be a lament rather than an expression of thanksgiving? B. Anderson originally stated the case typically: "The psalm is obviously out of place in its present context. In the belly of a 'fish' a cry for help (i.e., a lament) would be appropriate, but not a thanksgiving for deliverance already experienced!" (Anderson, 105). The trouble with this view is, of course, that the fish is precisely a vehicle of rescue in the story. Once Jonah is inside the belly of the fish, he has been delivered from drowning, as his conversation with the sailors in Jonah 1 makes clear (he tells them how to kill him in order to get rid of the storm, and drowning at sea is the method of killing him). A lament psalm would have been appropriate only while he was still sinking down into the Mediterranean. But by the time Jonah 2 arrives in the book, he has already experienced deliverance via the fish that God appointed to save him from drowning, and a thanksgiving psalm is the only sort of psalm fully appropriate to his situation then.

It is in the area of theology and applicational impact that the psalm, upon careful examination, turns out to be genuinely integral—nonexcisable—within the context of the overall message of the book. The full case has been argued convincingly by G. Landes, whose lengthy argument may be summarized briefly as follows. First, divine deliverance is a central theme in Jonah, and the psalm vividly advances this theme. Second, without the psalm, Jonah's attitude of gratefulness for his own deliverance is nowhere noted explicitly. It cannot then later serve as a contrast to his resentment at the deliverance of Nineveh. Third, when the component parts of the psalm are analyzed in detail, it becomes clear that "the psalm as it now stands is in the proper position, of an appropriate type, and agrees quite harmoniously with the situation of Jonah in the narrative, both in terms of his physical and psychological portrayal" (Landes, 30). Without the psalm, the story would be impoverished, leaving the reader with the impression of a more consistent, principled Jonah than the inspired narrator intends to convey.

6. Historicity.

One can appreciate the story of Jonah whether or not it represents actual historical events. The answer to the key question "What right do you have to be angry?" (Jon 4:4, 9) would still be "None!" even if the account were fictional. But the issue of historicity has important implications. If the events in the book actually happened, then the audience's existential identification with the characters and circumstances is invariably heightened. People act more surely upon what they believe to be true in fact than upon what they merely consider likely in theory.

It is important to note that there is ample evidence to support the historicity of the book,

and surprisingly little to undermine it. The style, as noted above, is neutral to the question of historical accuracy; sensationalism can never be equivocated with a lack of factuality. A true story may be told in a host of ways, from dull to sensational, as may a false story, as may a fictional story. As to the improbability of the general repentance in Nineveh described in Jonah 3, this must now be tempered by the recognition that our historical evidence preserves the fact that things were not going well for the Ninevites at approximately the time Jonah served as a prophet (toward the end of the first half of the eighth century BC). Military and diplomatic losses internationally were coupled with famine and popular uprisings domestically during the time of Ashur-dan III (773-756 BC), the king most likely to be the monarch described in Jonah 3. In addition, both an earthquake and an eclipse, dreaded major omens to the highly superstitious Assyrians, were experienced concurrently to other problems occurring at that time. A weak monarch reeling from domestic and international turmoil could well have welcomed the chance to solidify his acceptance among a suspicious populace, already set on edge by the prevailing problems, via the sort of royal proclamation preserved in Jonah 3:7-9.

The idea that Nineveh could not have had a "king" is a problem often raised against the historical accuracy of the book. The assumption that the phrase "king of Nineveh" (*melek nînwê*) in Jonah 3:6 reflects both a lack of understanding of the Assyrian Empire (so that it is analogous to speaking of "the king of London" [Neil, 966]) and a befuddled historical memory (since Nineveh could not have been the capital of Assyria in Jonah's time, according to the Assyrian records themselves) has been a central objection to the book's historicity. The reply to this objection requires an appreciation of two facts: (1) "king of Nineveh" is a simple, comprehensible phrase in the context of the book; (2) it is entirely possible that an Assyrian king would be present in Nineveh early in the eighth century BC whether or not Nineveh was technically the capital (the concept of a national capital being mainly a modern notion, at any rate) of the Assyrian Empire.

Regarding the first problem, it was common for a king to be designated by only one city within the region he ruled. For example, in Deuteronomy 1:4; 3:2; 4:46 Sihon is called "king of the Amorites," but in Deuteronomy 2:24, 26, 30 Sihon is called "king of Heshbon." Similarly, Jabin is called "king of Canaan/the Canaanites" in Judges 4:2, 23, 24, but "king of Hazor" in Judges 4:17. In other words, a king could be associated with a capital or main city within his empire, as well as with the empire itself (see, e.g., 2 Sam 8:5; 1 Kings 11:23, where Hadadezer's kingship is associated with "Zobah" even though his control extended considerably further). An especially close parallel to "king of Nineveh" is found in 1 Kings 21:1, where Ahab is called "king of Samaria" (*melek šōmĕrôn*), in contrast to "king of Israel," the title used for him routinely elsewhere. If Ahab can be called "king of Samaria," surely there can be no valid objection to Ashur-dan III (or whoever was the king who responded to Jonah's preaching) being called "king of Nineveh" in Jonah 3:6.

But, second, how could there be a king in Nineveh in Jonah's time? Did not Nineveh become the actual capital of the Assyrian Empire only in the time of Sennacherib (705-682 BC), as is commonly alleged? In fact, Nineveh may well have been at least an alternate capital, if not the capital of Assyria throughout much of the first half of the eighth century BC. We know, for example, that Shalmaneser I (1275-1246 BC) began an expansion of the city, and that by the time of Tiglath-Pileser I (1114-1076 BC), Nineveh had become an alternative royal residence to both Ashur and Calah. Thereafter, a palace of some sort appears to have been established in the city and used by various kings, including Ashurnasirpal II (883-859 BC) before Jonah's time, and Sargon II (722-705 BC) after Jonah's time. It therefore is likely that Nineveh functioned as a royal residence, even if not the capital technically, during most of the eighth century BC (see Thompson and Hutchinson; Parrot). Our knowledge of the affairs of the weak kings of Assyria between the latter years of Adad-nirari III (811-784 BC) and Tiglath-Pileser III (745-728 BC) is spotty. It is probable, however, that each of these kings (Shalmaneser IV [783-774 BC], Ashur-dan III [773-756 BC] and Ashur-nirari V [755-746 BC]) ruled at least part of the time from Nineveh. Ashur-dan III shifted his residence at least once, and possibly more. Thus, regardless of whether the ancient Assyrians thought of capitals in the same way that moderns do, it is clear that Nineveh, because of its size and wealth, became de facto the chief city of the Neo-Assyrian Empire and host to royalty during much of that period. There is therefore nothing in the phrase "king of Nineveh" in Jonah 3:6 that can be falsified historically.

The actions of the king and of the people of Nineveh in response to Jonah's preaching there as described in Jonah 3 can be appreciated in light of the relative weakness of the Assyrians during the first half of the eighth century BC. Prior to the accession to the throne by Tiglath-Pileser III in 745 BC, the Assyrian Empire was teetering politically, especially in international diplomatic-military influence. One reason for this was the fairly constant military encroachment by the neighboring nations of Aram (to the northeast) and Urartu (to the northwest, a kingdom centered around Lake Van in the Armenian highlands). The Assyrian Eponym Chronicle is an important source for understanding Assyrian weakness and the attendant problems experienced by the people of Assyria at this time. G. Roux describes the situation bluntly: "for thirty-six years (781-745 BC) Assyria was practically paralysed" (Roux, 274). After the death of the Assyrian king Adad-Nirari III (810-783 BC) and before the ascendancy of the empire builder Tiglath-Pileser III (745-727 BC), Assyria endured nearly four decades of turmoil. Kings were weak, the nation was disunited and provincial in its governance, and individual cities bore more significance as centers of economic and political power than did the country as a whole. During these years, as W. Hallo points out, "even the central provinces maintained only a tenuous loyalty to Assyria, for the various governors ruled in virtual independence" (Hallo and Simpson, 131). Thus, the wording of Jonah 3:7 ("By the decree of the king and his nobles") is given attention by commentators such as F. Page, citing the work of P. Lawrence and A. Grayson, noting that "the precarious position of the king may have necessitated his acknowledging in his decree the power and influence of surrounding provincial governors" (Page, 205).

7. Sources and Authorship.

As a vehicle for divine revelation, the narrator of the book would hardly have been dependent exclusively on human sources for the details of the story. Yet from a human point of view, virtually all the data from which the story is constructed could have been supplied by two sources: Jonah and at least one of the sailors mentioned in Jonah 1. Any of the sailors, whose ship eventually returned to safety, would have been an adequate source for information on what happened while Jonah was asleep (Jon 1:5) and after he was thrown overboard (Jon 1:15, 16). Every other detail used in the book could have come from Jonah himself, who had ample opportunity to observe and inquire about, in and around Nineveh, those events that he himself may not have actually witnessed (e.g., the king's actions in Jon 3:6, if in fact Jonah did not appear in person before the king).

Jonah's travel to Nineveh is somewhat paralleled by the missions of Elijah to Sidon and Elisha to Syria. Jonah may have traveled farther than those prophets, but certainly he did not travel uniquely—except, of course, for his unusual mode of travel through part of the Mediterranean. Travel to deliver a divine message is also characteristic of the paradigm OT prophet, Moses, who went from Midian to Egypt on a comparably dangerous assignment to confront a royal enemy at the head of a great hostile nation. Further, all four of these prophets' stories include a rather large concentration of miracles, in light of which the story of Jonah is not so unusual as is sometimes thought.

From a technical point of view, the book of Jonah is sufficiently unified in theme and style (on the psalm in Jon 2, see 5 above and 9.2 below) in a manner suggesting a single narrator. Earlier attempts such to argue that Jonah had a history of composite authorship and/or editing (e.g., Böhme; Köhler; Winckler; Schmidt) relied almost exclusively on evolutionistic literary theories rather than hard data.

Of the narrator, however, we know little. On the basis of the use of *hāyâ* ("to be") in the past tense in describing Nineveh in Jonah 3:3, the assumption sometimes has been made that the narrator wrote after 612 BC, after Nineveh fell to the Babylonians and was destroyed. This dating depends upon taking the sentence in question to read, in essence, "Nineveh was a city ..."; that is, it is a city no longer from the perspective of the narrator and his or her audience. However, if the sentence is understood to describe Nineveh's importance to God's plan at that time—"Nineveh was a city important to God" (*gĕdôlâ lē'lōhîm*)—then the relative distance of the narrator from the story is impossible to fix with certainty. Depending on how one takes

one or two wordings, the book could be the product of a contemporary of Jonah (or Jonah himself [see below]), someone writing within a short time after the death of Jonah, or of a considerably later time when the importance of the story for its message was especially welcome and/or needed. Besides this, the Hebrew narrative style calls for the past tense generally in this sort of story about a prophet regardless of proximity to the events. Thus, the importance of the past tense of *hāyâ* in Jonah 3:3 is easily overrated and potentially misleading.

Could the narrator have been Jonah himself? Though possible, this usually is thought unlikely in a story so critical of Jonah's hypocrisy, ending with a description of his almost childish stubbornness against the point that God makes via the object lesson of the plant. But time and God's influence on any person's outlook can change even a stubborn attitude. It is conceivable that a contrite Jonah might eventually admit that he had been entirely wrong in his former attitudes and actions. Does he not learn in the process of events that disobedience to God's commands is futile? If the events described in the book are true, could not Jonah have been changed into a more willing and humble vehicle for God's will, and have swallowed his pride and written the account that we now read in the little book that bears his name? By way of parallel, the NT Gospels display a variety of indicators that they are the product of eyewitnesses (Bauckham), yet they are remarkable for their blunt portrayal of the disciples as being well worthy of Jesus' frequent criticisms for their lack of faith and judgment and their seeming inability to "connect the dots" of the teachings that he gave them (e.g., Mt 8:26; 14:31; 16:8; Lk 24:44-45; Jn 14:19). Somewhat comparably, Paul in his own writings strongly bemoans his former status as a persecutor of the church and one who trusted in legal obedience for salvation. Similarly, Moses does not paint a glowing picture of himself, his popularity and his leadership skills at several key points in the Pentateuch, and Amos acknowledges the rejection of his preaching in the north via reporting highly critical comments of himself (Amos 7). Similarly, Jeremiah describes his personal discouragement and despondency as well as the frequent rejection of his preaching in various points in the book that bears his name.

By no means does this sort of argument

prove that Jonah was the author of the book of Jonah. Nothing in the book demands that Jonah be the author, and nothing in Jonah's story would automatically be enhanced if Jonah could somehow be proved to have written it or to have been the informant for the person who did. However, the fact that he might have written it does serve to suggest that arguments that assume that the book must have been written long after the life of the prophet described therein, let alone arguments that assume that the book is merely fictional, are less cogent than has often been thought.

8. Text.

The text of Jonah is well preserved. Variants are few and do not display any sort of fixed pattern. Even the Targum is only mildly expansionistic, in contrast to its substantial tendency toward commentary and explanation in other books of the Minor Prophets. The quality of the text means that careful linguistic analysis can be undertaken with confidence in any wording under analysis. For example, the translation of the last few words of Jonah 1:2 should be "their trouble is of concern to me," a translation that gives a very different impression to the reader from the usual "their evil has come up before me" or the like, and that is essential for understanding why Jonah tried to escape his divine assignment to preach in Nineveh. It presumably was easier for ancient scribes to preserve the text of an easy-to-follow mostly prose story like that of Jonah more accurately over the centuries, as compared to poetry or more complex prose narratives.

9. Message and Purpose.

9.1. Basic Message. On one level, the message of Jonah is simply "Do not be like Jonah." Jonah gladly receives deliverance and blessing (via the fish, which is not a punishment but rather a means of rescue), yet he stubbornly refuses to see his enemies, the Assyrians, receive the same. But the story also emphasizes the character and power of God. God's servants can neither oppose him and succeed nor expect him to be unfaithful to his own character of patience, forgiveness and eagerness to forestay harm. The book, in other words, is about Jonah's hatred of his enemies, but it is especially also about God's compassion on his. What happens to Nineveh and to Jonah happens precisely because of what God is like. Thus, the audience of the book is

invited implicitly to revise their understanding of what God is like, if indeed they have shared Jonah's selfish views about how God should want to handle the Assyrians.

In ancient Judaism the book served as a bulwark against the narrow particularism that allowed Jews to think that they alone were worthy of God's blessing. To a more modern reader, the message may be seen in light of Jesus' own teaching about forgiveness: it is the sinners, not the righteous, who most often may recognize their need for forgiveness and do something about it (Jon 3:5-10; Mt 12:41; cf. Lk 15:10). No one should oppose God's mercy in receiving sinners into the kingdom.

At one time it was popular to assume that Jonah was written as a kind of universalistic treatise against the supposedly rigid, narrow reformist views of Ezra and Nehemiah. This view rightly lost favor on two accounts. First, the book is hardly universalistic. The book nowhere implies that the Ninevites somehow became, as it were, God's chosen nation by reason of their occasion of repentance at Jonah's preaching, or even that their repentance was anything like an actual conversion to Yahwism and the Mosaic covenant. Second, the predominant concerns of Ezra and Nehemiah were the restoration of pentateuchal *worship practices, the security of Jerusalem, the elimination of foreign influences and the prevention of mixed marriages. The fact that Jonah addresses none of these topics, even indirectly, means that it probably would never have occurred to the ancient Jews of the mid-fifth century BC that Jonah somehow was an attack on Ezra and Nehemiah. The double question in Jonah 4:4, 9, "What right do you have to be angry?" (*hahêṭēb hārâ lāk*), is a key to the book's central message. The climax of the story comes here, when God challenges Jonah to recognize how wrong he has been in his bitter nationalism, and how right God has been to show compassion toward the plight of the Assyrians in Nineveh. The person who resents the mercy of God to his or her enemies shows enmity to God's purposes and discontinuity with God's thinking. Every reader must reflect on the questions that God asks, including the final, specific, "Should I not spare Nineveh?" (Jon 4:11). Anyone who replies, "Why is that such an important question?" has not understood the message. Anyone who replies, "No!" has not believed it.

9.2. The Message of the Book Passage by Passage.
The first passage (Jon 1:1-3) describes Jonah's rebellion against God's call. He wants to avoid being part of the means by which God will show compassion to Israel's enemy, Assyria (specifically its capital, Nineveh), because he understands God's words, as best translated from the Hebrew, to mean "Speak against it because their trouble [not 'evil'] is of concern to me." In other words, God has announced that he intends to consider showing mercy to the Assyrians, and Jonah wants none of it. This frames Jonah's further actions in the book.

The next passage (Jon 1:4-16) shows that God, not Jonah, is in charge everywhere, and that Jonah cannot run from God in spite of his hope to do so. Jonah is a flawed prophet whose theology was not always correct. He seems to have believed, as many ancient pagans did, that a god's influence was limited mainly to the locale of the worshipers. But in fact, the book shows that the true God is omnipresent and omnipotent, controlling even the weather (which most ancients would have thought to be the province of a separate weather god). Jonah 1:16 is a sort of coda revealing a follow-up fact: even the pagan sailors got the point that Yahweh was to be feared and his word to be obeyed. Seeing Jonah prohibited from fleeing God by a severe storm gave them a very clear idea of who was in charge.

In the next passage (Jon 1:17—2:10) Jonah prays from inside a fish that God designates to swallow him. This is not punishment but rather rescue, as Jonah's psalm (Jon 2:2-9) shows, since as a psalm of thanksgiving it clearly indicates by its very nature his understanding that he has been spared, not condemned. His eloquent gratitude for God's mercy to him, a sinner, provides an unmistakable contrast to his later resentment at God's mercy to the people of Nineveh, also sinners.

A second beginning of sorts is described in the next passage (Jon 3:1-3a). Now Jonah obeyed and went to Nineveh, however reluctantly or resentfully. Then follows a passage describing the eager repentance of the people of Nineveh (Jon 3:3b-10), including the key words "on the first day." In the ancient world a visit by a dignitary to a foreign country normally required three days: the first to arrive and present one's credentials and purpose, the second to conduct business, and the third for a proper conclusion and send-off. But the people of Nineveh could not wait for the second and third days; they jumped at the chance to repent on the first day, as soon as they knew why Jonah had come to them. From king to animals, they formally displayed an attitude of mourning for their sins and asked Jonah's great God for forgiveness. This was not conversion to the God of the Bible, but it was real repentance by people whose problems (the Assyrians were economically in distress and under attack from enemies at this time in history) made them realize their need of divine help.

In the final passage (Jon 4:1-11) God teaches Jonah about anger and compassion. Jonah immediately becomes angry that Nineveh is spared, but God is slow to anger, as Jonah in fact knew all along (Jon 4:2-3). Jonah is so angry at the grace that his enemy, Nineveh/Assyria, has received that he wants to die. But he has no right to be angry (Jon 4:4). God, however, has every right to be slow to anger—that is, merciful and forgiving—as Jonah 4:5-11 illustrates: God controls nature once again, this time not a fish but a plant, in such a way that Jonah begins to love that plant because it gave him shade from the blazing sun of Mesopotamia. God then reminds Jonah, via appeal to the commonsense hierarchy of life (plants, animals, humans), that if Jonah loved a plant and wanted it spared, it should be obvious, a fortiori, that God loves animals and people and desires that they be spared. Such should always be the attitude of God's people: why seek the consequence of someone's sin if that person's repentance could instead result in God's favor?

9.3. The Special Importance of Jonah 4:2 and of Jonah 4 in General. By including in the story Jonah's admission of the fact that he had fled from God because he knew that God is compassionate, the narrator effectively silences all speculation about Jonah's motives. "What is God really like?" is thus a much more important question in this book than the question "What was Jonah really like?" God is a God of grace, of whom it is hopeless—indeed, hypocritical—to expect a display of grace only to his own people. It was God's grace that Jonah resented so violently—except, of course, when he was the recipient.

Jonah's famous confession (Jon 4:2) extols divine grace and does not restrict to any person or group God's forgiveness and willingness to reconsider bringing harm. Jonah, from the moment he first heard God's call to preach repentance to the Ninevites, had made up his mind that Nineveh ought to be destroyed. God had a better idea.

Prophetic books do not necessarily come to a climactic resolution in a final chapter. Some do not end with a resolution at all. For example, the final chapter in Jeremiah describes the desolation of Judah and Jerusalem and the exile of its leading people, and it concludes with the modestly positive but otherwise historically minor note that the last legitimate king of Judah, Jehoiachin (who reigned briefly in 598 BC), had been shown mercy by a relatively obscure Babylonian king, Evil-Merodach (Babylonian *Awil-marduk*).

Jonah, on the other hand, ends with the whole point of the story in Jonah 4: God wants to show mercy to all, if they will respond to his offer of grace. His special love for Israel does not mean that he has no plan for or interest in other *nations. The chapter vividly and dramatically shows Jonah arguing for his own interests (even for a plant that gave him shade) against God, who, from a much more authoritative position, of course, teaches Jonah that his attitude should include mercy toward the interests of other people, people such as the Ninevites, whom he should have been glad to see come to repentance at his preaching.

See also REPENTANCE; TWELVE, BOOK OF THE.

BIBLIOGRAPHY. *Commentaries*: L. C. Allen, *The Books of Joel, Obadiah, Jonah, and Micah* (NICOT; Grand Rapids: Eerdmans, 1994); D. W. Baker, T. D. Alexander and B. K. Waltke, *Obadiah, Jonah, Micah* (TOTC; Downers Grove, IL: InterVarsity Press, 1988); J. Baldwin, "Jonah," in *The Minor Prophets: An Exegetical and Expository Commentary*, 2: *Obadiah, Jonah, Micah, Nahum, and Habakkuk*, ed. T. McComiskey (Grand Rapids: Baker, 1992) 543-90; J. K. Bruckner, *Jonah, Nahum, Habakkuk, Zephaniah* (NIVAC; Grand Rapids: Zondervan, 2004); T. Butler and M. Anders, *Hosea, Joel, Amos, Obadiah, Jonah, Micah* (HOTC; Nashville: Broadman & Holman, 2005); P. Cary, *Jonah* (BTCB; Grand Rapids: Brazos, 2008); T. Fretheim, *The Message of Jonah: A Theological Commentary* (Minneapolis: Augsburg, 1977); J. Limburg, *Jonah: A Commentary* (Norwich: SCM, 1993); J. Nogalski, *Hosea—Jonah* (SHBC 18A; Macon, GA: Smyth & Helwys, 2011); F. S. Page and B. K. Smith, *Amos, Obadiah, Jonah* (NAC; Nashville: Broadman & Holman, 1995); J. Sasson, *Jonah* (Yale Anchor Bible Commentary; New Haven: Yale University Press, 1995); D. Stuart, *Hosea—Jonah* (WBC 31; Waco, TX: Word, 1987); J. D. W. Watts, *The Books of Joel, Obadiah, Jonah, Nahum, Habakkuk and Zephaniah* (CBC; Cambridge: Cambridge University Press, 1975) 72-97; H. W. Wolff, *Obadiah and Jonah: A Commentary*, trans. M. Kohl (Minneapolis: Augsburg, 1986). *Studies*: S. Abramsky, "About Casting Lots in Order to Catch a Sinner," *Beth Mikra* 26 (1981) 231-66; T. D. Alexander, "Jonah and Genre," *TynBul* 36 (1985) 35-39; B. W. Anderson, *Out of the Depths: The Psalms Speak for Us Today* (Philadelphia: Westminster, 1974); M. E. Andrew, "Gattung and Intention of the Book of Jonah," *Orita* 1 (1967) 13-18, 75-85; R. Bauckham, *Jesus and the Eyewitnesses: The Gospels as Eyewitness Testimony* (Grand Rapids: Eerdmans, 2006); E. J. Bickerman, "Les deux erreurs du prophète Jonas," *RHPR* 45 (1965) 232-64; W. Böhme, "Die Komposition des Buches Jonah," *ZAW* 7 (1887) 224-84; K. Budde, "Vermutungen zum Midrasch des Buches der Könige," *ZAW* 12 (1892) 37-151, esp. 40-43; M. Burrows, "The Literary Category of the Book of Jonah," in *Translating and Understanding the Old Testament: Essays in Honor of Herbert Gordon May*, ed. H. T. Frank and W. L. Reed (New York: Harper, 1980) 80-107; B. S. Childs, "Jonah: A Study in Old Testament Hermeneutics," *SJT* 11 (1958) 53-61; R. Clements, "The Purpose of the Book of Jonah," in *Congress Volume: Edinburgh, 1974* (VTSup 28; Leiden: E. J. Brill, 1975) 16-28; A. D. Cohen, "The Tragedy of Jonah," *Judaism* 21 (1972) 164-75; R. Coote, *Amos among the Prophets: Composition and Theology* (Philadelphia: Fortress, 1981); F. M. Cross Jr., "Studies in the Structure of Hebrew Verse: The Prosody of the Psalm of Jonah," in *The Quest for the Kingdom of God: Studies in Honor of George E. Mendenhall*, ed. H. B. Huffmon et al. (Winona Lake, IN: Eisenbrauns, 1983) 158-67; G. I. Davies, "The Uses of רעע Qal and the Meaning of Jonah IV:1," *VT* 27 (1977) 105-10; G. Elata-Alster and R. Salmon, "Eastward and Westward: The Movement of Prophecy and History in the Book of Jonah," *Dor le Dor* 13 (1984) 16-27; B. D. Estelle, *Salvation through Judgment and Mercy: The Gospel According to Jonah* (Phillipsburg, NJ: P & R, 2005); J. H. Eybers, "The

Purpose of the Book of Jonah," *ThEv* 4 (1971) 211-22; **S. Ferguson,** *Man Overboard! The Story of Jonah* (Edinburgh: Banner of Truth, 2008); **K. Galling,** "Der Weg der Phöniker nach Tarsis," *ZDPV* 88 (1972) 1-18, 140-81; **J. J. Gluck,** "A Linguistic Criterion of the Book of Jonah," *OuTWP* 10 (1967) 34-41; **S. Goodhart,** "Prophecy, Sacrifice and Repentance in the Book of Jonah," *Semeia* 33 (1985) 43-63; **A. K. Grayson,** "Assyria: Ashur-Dan II to Ashur-Nirari V (934-745 B.C.)," in *Cambridge Ancient Histories*, 3.1: *The Prehistory of the Balkans; the Middle East and the Aegean World, Tenth to Eighth Centuries B.C.* (Cambridge: Cambridge University Press, 1982) 238-81; **W. W. Hallo and W. K. Simpson,** *The Ancient Near East: A History* (2nd ed.; New York: Holt, Rinehart & Winston, 1997); **O. Kaiser,** "Wirklichkeit, Möglichkeit und Vorurteil: Ein Beitrag zum Verstandnis des Buches Jona," *EvT* 33 (1973) 91-103; **K. Köhler,** "The Original Form of the Book of Jonah," *TR* 16 (1897) 139-44; **E. König,** "Jonah," in *A Dictionary of the Bible*, ed. J. Hastings (Honolulu: University Press of the Pacific, 2004 [1899]) 2:744-53; **G. M. Landes,** "The Kerygma of the Book of Jonah: The Contextual Interpretation of the Jonah Psalm," *Int* 21 (1967) 3-31; **P. J. N. Lawrence,** "Assyrian Nobles and the Book of Jonah," *TynBul* 37 (1986) 121-32; **J. Lindblom,** "Lot-Casting in the OT," *VT* 12 (1962) 164-78; **O. Loretz,** "Herkunft und Sinn der Jonaerzählung," *BZ* 5 (1961) 19-22; **J. Magonet,** *Form and Meaning: Studies in Literary Techniques in the Book of Jonah* (BLS 8; Sheffield: Almond, 1983); **W. Neil,** "Jonah," *IDB* 2:964-67; **A. Parrot,** "Ninive und das AT," *BibAr* 1 (1955) 111-69; idem, *Nineveh and the Old Testament*, trans. B. E. Hooke (London: SCM, 1955); **G. Roux,** *Ancient Iraq* (London: Allen & Unwin, 1964); **H. Schmidt,** "Die Komposition des Buches Jona," *ZAW* 25 (1905) 285-310; **J. H. Stek,** "The Message of the Book of Jonah," *CTJ* 4 (1969) 23-50; **D. Stuart,** "Names, Proper," *ISBE* 3:483-88; **R. C. Thompson and R. W. Hutchinson,** *A Century of Exploration at Nineveh* (London: Lusac, 1929); **W. D. Tucker Jr.,** *Jonah: A Handbook on the Hebrew Text* (Waco, TX: Baylor University Press, 2006); **R. D. Wilson,** "The Authenticity of Jonah," *PTR* 16 (1918) 280-98, 430-56; **H. Winckler,** "Zum Buche Jona," *AoF* 2.2 (1900) 260-65; **D. J. Wiseman,** "Jonah's Nineveh," *TynBul* 30 (1979) 29-51.

D. Stuart

JOY. *See* LAMENT, MOURNING.

JUDGE, GOD AS. *See* GOD.

JUDGMENT. *See* BLESSINGS AND CURSES; DAY OF THE LORD; DESTRUCTION; ESCHATOLOGY; EXILE; RETRIBUTION; SUFFERING; WRATH.

JUSTICE, RIGHTEOUSNESS

The interrelated concepts of justice and righteousness inform the exhortations and encouragement communicated by the biblical prophets as they act as intermediaries between God, king and covenant people. The terms *mišpāṭ* ("justice") and *ṣedeq, ṣĕdāqâ, ṣaddîq* ("righteousness," "righteous one") are found individually, as word pairs and as concatenations with other significant terms, such as *ʿāśâ* ("to do"), throughout the prophetic literature of the OT. Although justice and righteousness often are characterized as legal terms, an overview of the terms as used within the Prophetic Books indicates that these concepts are indicative of God's expectations for his people with regard to every aspect of society. These terms are used with reference not only to legal matters, but also to the royal court, aspects of *worship, and community well-being.

1. The Vocabulary of Justice and Righteousness
2. Literary Use of "Justice" and "Righteousness" in the Old Testament Prophets
3. Rhetoric and Reality

1. The Vocabulary of Justice and Righteousness.

1.1. Definitions. The Hebrew term *mišpāṭ* ("justice") is found in all of the Major Prophets and several of the Minor Prophets, including Hosea, Joel, Amos, Micah, Habakkuk, Zephaniah, Zechariah and Malachi. Most frequently *mišpāṭ* is translated as "justice," although the semantic range includes concepts of judging and judgment, rules and ruling, and being just and right. The term *mišpāṭ* is used to describe legal situations, particularly when found in parallel construction with the forensic root *dyn* ("to judge," "judgment") in verses such as Jeremiah 5:28; Isaiah 3:13-14. It is also used to evaluate and critique social and economic relationships within the *covenant community (Is 1:11-17; Jer 22:3, 15-16; Amos 5:21-24; Mic 6:6-8).

Hebrew terms derived from the root *ṣdq* are also found throughout the Prophetic Books. These terms include the noun forms *ṣedeq* and *ṣĕdāqâ* ("righteousness") and the substantival adjective *ṣaddîq* ("righteous one"). The substantival form "righteous one" can refer to God (Is 24:16; Jer 12:1; Zeph 3:5), society (Is 53:11 [when the servant is understood to be Israel]) and individual humans (Is 26:7; Ezek 3:20; Amos 5:12; Hab 2:4). The use of this term to refer both to God and to his people highlights the relational nature of righteousness: even as God is righteous, so his people are to be righteous. Additionally, even as God is the arbiter of justice, so his people are to exhibit justice in their relationships with one another. This is especially important for kings and leaders because the consequences of their behavior devolve upon their subjects (Jer 22:3; Ezek 45:9) (see Leadership).

1.2. Syntax. In OT prophetic texts the terms *mišpāṭ* ("justice") and *ṣedeq*, *ṣĕdāqâ* and *ṣaddîq* ("righteousness," "righteous one") appear individually, as word pairs and in concatenation with other terms. When *mišpāṭ* and *ṣedeq/ṣĕdāqâ* appear as a word pair, they form a particularly significant hendiadys pertaining to the right ordering of society within God's covenant community (Weinfeld, 228). In texts such as Hosea 2:21-22; Isaiah 16:5; Jeremiah 9:24 "justice" and "righteousness" are grouped with other significant terms, creating still greater rhetorical impact. In Hosea 2:21 God's promise of a future relationship with Israel is stated in a marital metaphor that contains the word pair "righteousness and justice" followed by the word pair "goodness and mercy" and the single term "faithfulness." Isaiah 16:5 describes the characteristics of a future leader who will sit on a throne characterized by "goodness," "faithfulness," "justice" and "righteousness." In Jeremiah 9:23-24 God discloses himself as one who acts with "kindness," "justice" and "righteousness" in the world. In these verses "goodness" and "kindness" are used to translate the Hebrew term *ḥesed*, which is associated with covenant love and loyalty. The term acts as a linguistic echo of the covenant relationship between God and his people.

2. Literary Use of "Justice" and "Righteousness" in the Old Testament Prophets.

A literary-rhetorical approach to prophetic literature is effective because prophetic speech is persuasive speech: the message of the prophet is that of an intermediary between God and his people. Because prophetic speech and its literary presentation are intended to persuade a given audience, the speakers and writers use a variety of genres, such as prose, poetry and discursive speech, in crafting their message. They use various figures of speech, such as metaphor, simile and repetition. Conceptual metaphor is often present: ideas such as "God is judge," which assigns an array of knowledge regarding the law court to the relationship between God and his people, run through the texts. These techniques are used in the prophetic text to highlight the importance of justice and righteousness for a community called by God.

2.1. Rhetorical Use of "Justice" and "Righteousness" in the Major Prophets. It is well recognized that the canonical texts of Isaiah, Jeremiah, Ezekiel and Daniel exhibit a multilayered composition history (Carroll, 38) (see Formation of the Prophetic Books). The presence of multiple speech situations in each of these books adds complexity to interpreting the texts. A variety of voices resonate within each text, including those of the prophets themselves and those of subsequent editors. Those receiving the message of the prophets and editors include both the original audience and those to whom the texts were presented in later contexts. Voices cajole, criticize and comfort the hearers as the call to do justice and to be righteous echoes from situation to situation.

2.1.1. Justice and Righteousness in Isaiah. The interwoven themes of justice and righteousness are most prevalent in the book of Isaiah, as evidenced by the use of both terms throughout the book. In his discussion of the Isaiah text, J. Goldingay notes that "justice" and "right" (the same Hebrew term that is translated as "righteousness") permeate the entire text (Goldingay, 9). The prophet's call to "keep justice and do righteousness" at Isaiah 56:1 introduces the third major section of the book. It combines the interests of the first section (Is 1—39), which emphasizes Israel's role in seeking and maintaining righteousness, and the second section (Is 40—55), which emphasizes God's role as the just and righteous one. In Isaiah 41:2 the nominal term *ṣedeq* might also convey the sense of "victor" (so the NRSV): the one whom God calls to administer justice will surely be victorious. The conditional clause in Isaiah 56:1, "for soon my salvation will come, and my deliverance will be revealed," highlights the relational nature of justice and righteousness for a people who are to seek after these qualities and their just and righteous God. For the book of Isaiah, justice and righteousness are rhetorically significant from the perspective of the text as a whole.

The book of Isaiah contains both poetry and prose, but references to justice and righteousness cluster in sections that scan as poetry. This is significant for those who see poetry as representative of the original words of the prophet, as it implies that doing justice and being righteousness are important concerns both for the prophet and for the original audience. Because the themes run throughout the book, it follows that these issues were of continuing concern for later audiences as well. The subject matter of the references varies: there are accusations, such as the discussion of inappropriate worship at Isaiah 1:12-17 (cf. Is 1:21; 5:7; 59:8); descriptions of the identity and actions of God (Is 5:16; 30:18; 40:14; 51:4); and indications of future restoration (Is 1:27; 28:6-7; 32:1, 16; 33:5; 56:1). In Isaiah 9:7 there is a discussion of the distant future that includes a description of the one who will sit on the throne of David: "His authority shall grow continually, and there shall be endless peace for the throne of David and his kingdom. He will establish it and uphold it with justice and with righteousness from this time onward and forevermore" (see also Is 16:3, 5). There is an explanation of the role of the servant in Isaiah 42:1, 3-4 as one who is to "bring forth" justice to the nations and to "establish" justice on the earth. Isaiah's confession on behalf of the people repeatedly mentions the failure to maintain justice and righteousness according to covenant expectations (Is 59:9-11, 15). The role of doing justice and being righteous within the themes of accusation, restoration and future faithful leadership through the line of David permeate the message of Isaiah.

The role of doing justice and being righteous finds its way from the book of Isaiah to the NT by way of direct quotations, allusions and echoes of some of these verses. In Matthew 12:18-21 the Gospel writer quotes Isaiah 42:1-4 to support the idea that Jesus' retreat from confrontation with the Pharisees was done in fulfillment of this passage (Williamson, 143). In Luke 1:32-33 the words of the angel Gabriel to Mary, "the Lord God will give to him the throne of his ancestor David," are an echo of Isaiah 9:7. Quotations, allusions and echoes are important for linking the theology of the OT with that of the NT.

Given the frequent references to justice and righteousness in the poetic texts of Isaiah, it is somewhat surprising to note the paucity of literary features such as metaphor, simile and repetition used to elaborate upon these concepts. Since the terms often are presented in a straightforward manner, conceptual metaphor (an understanding taken from cognitive linguistics) is a fruitful way to explore the use of these terms in prophetic text. While conceptual metaphor often underlies instances of literary metaphor, conceptual metaphor may also be observed in narrative text and ordinary speech as well. Simply stated, conceptual metaphor involves "understanding one conceptual domain in terms of another conceptual domain" (Kövecses, 4). Two conceptual domains are involved: the "*source domain*" provides metaphorical expressions that are used to understand information in the "*target domain*." Conceptual metaphor comprises nonlinguistic concepts that underlie specific instances of linguistic expression. These may include concepts such as SOCIETY IS A PERSON and SOCIETY IS A PLANT (conventionally indicated by small capital letters). In each of these examples, "society" is the target domain, while "person" and "plant" are source domains. Conceptual metaphor plays upon the way things work in the world: plants are sown, they flourish, they bear fruit and they wither away; people grow, they behave in certain ways, and they have familiar characteristics.

The "society is a person" and "society is a plant" conceptual metaphors are at work in the Isaiah text. Isaiah 1:21 reads, "How the faithful city has become a harlot, she that was full of justice! Righteousness lodged in her, but now murderers (RSV). In this accusation the city is characterized as a harlot. The underlying conceptual metaphor, "society is a person," encourages the reader to understand all of society in terms of a person of questionable and undesirable moral standing. Without naming names, the inhabitants of the city are critiqued and found wanting due to the lack of justice practiced therein. The conceptual metaphor "society is a plant" underlies the Song of the Vineyard in Isaiah 5:1-7. Here, the people are understood in terms of a carefully planted and tended vine (see Floral Imagery). It is only at the point of harvest that the owner of the vineyard discovers that the vine has produced an unexpected type of fruit. In the normal course of plant growth a given type of plant can be counted upon to produce a normal crop, hence the element of surprise when the grapes turn out to be wild rather than domesticated. God's disappointment with the situation is clear in Isaiah 5:7: "For the vineyard of the LORD of hosts is the house of Israel, and the people of Judah are his pleasant planting; he expected justice, but saw bloodshed; righteousness, but heard a cry!" (NRSV). This verse also contains a notable word play with the Hebrew terms for "justice/bloodshed" and "righteousness/cry." While the Hebrew word play tends to become muted in translation, the "society is a plant" conceptual metaphor works well cross-linguistically: something unexpected and undesirable has taken place.

2.1.2. Justice and Righteousness in Jeremiah. The themes of justice and righteousness are prevalent in the book of Jeremiah. The book reflects the language and thought of Deuteronomy and is particularly concerned with the consequences of the broken covenant, which leads to God's judgment upon the Judah and Jerusalem (Deut 28). While the call to turn from false worship and injustice and to return to right relationship with God is heard throughout the book, the specifics of what it means to do justice and to be righteous are more fully addressed in the first part of the book. The terms *mišpāṭ* ("justice") and *ṣedeq* and *ṣĕdāqâ* ("righteousness") are clustered in Jeremiah 2—25, the first of four major sections, which contains poems and sermons against Jerusalem and Judah. The details of what it means to do justice are elaborated upon in the prophet's instructions to the king of Judah at Jeremiah 22:3, where he states, "Act with justice and righteousness, and deliver from the hand of the oppressor anyone who has been robbed. And do no wrong or violence to the alien, the orphan, and the widow, or shed innocent blood in this place" (NRSV). The terms are used more sparsely in the following three sections. The second section, Jeremiah 26—36, comprises narratives about Jeremiah and discussion of future restoration. In this section the term *mišpāṭ* is used to describe two legal matters concerning Jeremiah. At Jeremiah 26:10 the priests and prophets declare that Jeremiah deserves "the sentence of death" because he had prophesied against the temple. At Jeremiah 32:7-8 Jeremiah receives a request from his cousin Hanamel, who asks Jeremiah to use his right of redemption to buy the field at Anathoth. The term *mišpāṭ* is used only once in the third section, Jeremiah 37—45, when King Nebuchadnezzar passes sentence on King Zedekiah (Jer 39:5). In the fourth section, Jeremiah 46—51, the term *mišpāṭ* is translated as "judgment" at Jeremiah 48:21, 47; 51:9. Thus, although the themes of justice and righteousness are significant for a large portion of the book, they are not rhetorically significant for shaping the whole of the text.

The terms "justice" and "righteousness" are found across genres in the book of Jeremiah, evenly divided between prose and poetry. Some of the clearest statements regarding what doing justice entails are found in the prose of Jeremiah's Temple Sermon in Jeremiah 7:1-15. In this section Jeremiah states, "If you truly amend your ways and your doings, if you truly act justly one with another, if you do not oppress the alien, the fatherless or the widow, or shed innocent blood in this place, and if you do not go after other gods . . ." (Jer 7:5-6 NRSV). Positively stated, these are the behaviors that God expects of his people.

As in the book of Isaiah, the references to justice and righteousness in Jeremiah are relatively unadorned with literary features such as metaphor, simile and repetition. The "people are plants" conceptual metaphor is present in the description of the righteous Branch in Jeremiah 23:5; 33:15, where a future king is described in terms of a flourishing plant or tree. In both verses this king "shall execute justice and righteousness in the land." This is a particularly poignant in Jeremiah 23, where the first four verses contain a woe oracle directed against the sheep-scattering bad shepherds who have led the people into disaster.

2.1.3. Justice and Righteousness in Ezekiel. The themes of justice and righteousness are significant for the book of Ezekiel. T. Renz, who takes a rhetorical approach to the book, explains that the overarching aim of the book is "to establish a specific type of community by promoting certain values" (Renz, 59). In this book Ezekiel is speaking to an audience already in *exile. For this audience, the option of doing justice as a means of staving off God's judgment is no longer possible. Rather, it is imperative that the community discovers the means for addressing issues of *sin and judgment in a context that is bereft of *land, status, city, *temple and king (Joyce, 17). For the exiles, choosing righteousness is seen to be the correct response to fall of Jerusalem.

The terms "justice" and "righteousness" appear in rhetorically significant clusters in the various sections of Ezekiel. Ezekiel 1—24 is written in a forensic tone and seeks to explain the judgment on Judah and Jerusalem to the exilic community in Babylon. In this section the issue of righteousness first appears within Ezekiel's call account, where Ezekiel is given the somber task of warning the people. This is stated in life-and-death terms: "If the righteous turn from their righteousness and commit iniquity . . . , they shall die" (Ezek 3:20 NRSV). In Ezekiel 18 the prophet uses a case law format to explore what it means to "do what is lawful and right." The phrase is repeated at Ezekiel 18:5, 19, 21, 27. Ezekiel 18:5 begins, "If a man is righteous and does what is lawful and right. . . ." This is followed by a detailed list in Ezekiel 18:7-8: no idol worship, integrity regarding a neighbor's wife and ritual purity with regard to approaching a woman, not oppressing others, no robbery, taking care of the hungry and poor, not charging interest, not committing iniquity, executing justice in court, following God's statutes and ordinances. At Ezekiel 18:9 God declares that this man will live. An unrighteous son who does all of these things is introduced at Ezekiel 18:10. He will die because of his choices. His son, seeing his father's fate, chooses the righteous way and lives. This section often is seen as a statement of individual responsibility regarding sin and judgment, but P. Joyce rightly points out that the arguments appear in a corporate context, where the sin and punishment of the nation are in view (Joyce, 25). Ezekiel uses both repetition and the "God is judge" conceptual metaphor in Ezekiel 18. As a result, argumentation in this chapter is memorable and effective.

The theme of righteousness is also important for the last half of the book. The theme of righteousness is absent in the oracles against the *nations in Ezekiel 25—32, but it reappears

in Ezekiel 33. This chapter acts as a hinge between the first part of the book and Ezekiel 34—48, which is written in a political tone and describes a future restoration of Jerusalem.

2.1.4. Justice and Righteousness in Daniel. The theme of righteousness is important to the book of Daniel, although *ṣedeq* is not a rhetorically overarching term in the text. There is a marked shift in genre between court legends in Daniel 1—6 and apocalyptic visions in Daniel 7—12. In the first section Daniel's position as an advisor in the royal court in Babylon is in view. At Daniel 4:27 Daniel interprets King Nebuchadnezzar's dream and urges him, "Break off your sins by practicing righteousness, and your iniquities by showing mercy to the oppressed" (RSV), in order to avoid the consequences of the king's ominous dream in Daniel 4:7-14. In the second section the issue of righteousness arises in the context of Daniel's prayer in Daniel 9:1-27, in which Daniel explores the seventy weeks of punishment first described in Jeremiah 25:11-12. Daniel's confession is based upon the presuppositions of covenant obligations, and the issue of righteousness is a thematic thread running through the whole section. In Daniel 9:4-14 he acknowledges that God is faithful even though the people have sinned and failed to keep the covenant (Dan 9:7, 9:18). Daniel's prayer is perhaps one of the clearest articulations within the prophetic corpus of the consequences of breach of covenant.

2.2. Rhetorical Use of "Justice" and "Righteousness" in the Minor Prophets. The themes of justice and righteousness are important to several of the Minor Prophets. The terms "righteousness" and "justice" appear in seven of the twelve books, including Hosea, Amos, Micah, Habakkuk, Zephaniah, Zechariah and Malachi. With the exception of Zechariah, which contains only the term "righteousness" (Zech 8:8), the terms are used individually in each book at least once in each book. Hosea, Amos and Habakkuk each use the word pair "justice and righteousness," which emphasizes the right ordering of society within the covenant community. The most significant rhetorical units that utilize these terms are Hosea 2:19-20, which is an announcement of future restoration for Israel; Amos 5:1—6:14, which is an extended judgment oracle against Israel; and Micah 3:1-12, which is a reflection of failed leadership that led to the fall of Jerusalem. Thus, although the terms are not used as overarching ordering devices for the final form of these texts, they are rhetorically significant for smaller units of text.

Conceptual metaphor is a powerful way to highlight the issues of justice and righteousness in Hosea. The "society is a person" metaphor governs Hosea 2, where Israel is presented as a harlot. After a thorough discussion of "wife" Israel's unfaithfulness and a vivid description of her upcoming punishment in Hosea 2:2-15, there is an abrupt shift to an announcement of restoration in Hosea 2:16-23. Highlights of the restoration include God's promise of a new covenant and his intention to betroth himself to Israel "in righteousness and in justice, in steadfast love and mercy" (Hos 2:19-20). The "society is a plant" metaphor is evident in Hosea 10:12, where the people are instructed, "Sow for yourselves righteousness; reap steadfast love."

3. Rhetoric and Reality.

The preceding literary and rhetorical discussion demonstrates that the nature of justice and righteousness was seen as multifaceted, and the expectation for just and righteous behavior was rooted firmly in the realities of Israel's religious, political and social life. The prophets explore the multifaceted nature of justice and righteousness at the cosmological and human levels: in comparison to humankind, "the LORD of hosts is exalted by justice, and the Holy God shows himself holy by righteousness" (Is 5:16 NRSV [cf. Is 30:18]). The Creator, God himself, is the model and origination point both for being just and righteous and for acting with justice and righteousness. By extension, God's people, who were called to be holy as God is holy, were expected to conduct themselves with justice and righteousness in all spheres of life.

For the Israelites, proper worship and effective community leadership were the expected manifestations of a flourishing relationship between God and his people. However, this was not always the case. In many instances failure to uphold the standards set forth elsewhere in Scripture gave grounds for God's just judgment. In one of his earliest oracles Jeremiah details the interrelated nature of failures on the human level, with God stating, "The priests did not say, 'Where is the LORD?' Those who handle the law did not know me; the rulers transgressed against me; the prophets prophesied by Baal, and went after things that do not profit" (Jer 2:8 NRSV).

Oftentimes what is known from the prophets about justice in the social sphere is defined not in positive terms but rather by descriptions of social injustice: Isaiah, Jeremiah, Ezekiel and Amos decry those who would oppress the poor and neglect the widow and orphan (Is 1:17; Jer 22:3; Ezek 18; Amos 5:4-8). By implication, true *social justice would include speaking for the poor and caring for the widow and orphan. These actions were the purview of king and leader in the first instance. Failures on the part of king and leader would constitute grounds for God's judgment on king, leader and people alike. With the heavy losses of land, king and temple during the Babylonian period, these failures also gave rise to the hope of a future leader who would lead with righteousness and justice (Is 9:7; 42:1; Jer 23:5; 33:15). For Christians, this expectation was met in the life and ministry of Jesus Christ. With regard to Jesus, Luke 1:32 states, "He will be great, and will be called the Son of the Most High, and the Lord God will give to him the throne of his ancestor David" (NRSV). Matthew 12:18-20 identifies Jesus as the servant in Isaiah 42:1, part of whose task is to proclaim justice to the nations.

Justice and righteousness are highly important for the message of the biblical prophets. A just and righteous God asks nothing less than that his people do justice and be righteous, as Micah 6:8 states: "He has told you, O mortal, what is good; and what does the LORD require of you but to do justice, and to love kindness, and to walk humbly with your God?"

See also COVENANT; ETHICS; SOCIAL JUSTICE.

BIBLIOGRAPHY. H. V. Bennett, "Justice, OT," NIDB 3:476-77; J. Blenkinsopp, *A History of Prophecy in Israel* (Louisville: Westminster/John Knox, 1996); R. P. Carroll, *Jeremiah: A Commentary* (OTL; Philadelphia: Westminster, 1986); N. deClaissé-Walford, "Righteousness in the OT," NIDB 4:818-23; J. Goldingay, *Isaiah* (NIBCOT; Peabody, MA: Hendrickson, 2001); P. Joyce, *Ezekiel: A Commentary* (LHBOTS 482; London: T & T Clark, 2009); Z. Kövecses, *Metaphor: A Practical Introduction* (Oxford: Oxford University Press, 2002); T. Leclerc, *Yahweh Is Exalted in Justice: Solidarity and Conflict in Isaiah* (Minneapolis: Fortress, 2001); J. R. Lundbom, *Jeremiah 1-20: A New Translation with Introduction and Commentary* (AB 21; New York: Doubleday, 1999); J. L. Mays, *Amos: A Commentary* (OTL; London: SCM, 1969);

M. Nissinen, ed., *Prophecy in Its Ancient Near Eastern Context: Mesopotamian, Biblical, and Arabian Perspectives* (SBLSymS 13; Atlanta: Society of Biblical Literature, 2000); **T. Renz,** *The Rhetorical Function of the Book of Ezekiel* (VTSup 76; Leiden: E. J. Brill, 1999); **J. J. Scullion,** "Righteousness (OT)," ABD 5:724-36; **M. Weinfeld,** "'Justice and Righteousness'—וצדקה משפט—The Expression and Its Meaning," in *Justice and Righteousness: Biblical Themes and Their Influence,* ed. H. G. Reventlow and Y. Hoffman (JSOTSup 137; Sheffield: JSOT, 1992) 228-46; **H. G. M. Williamson,** *Variations on a Theme: King, Messiah and Servant in the Book of Isaiah* (Carlisle: Paternoster, 1998).   E. R. Hayes

KINGS OF ISRAEL AND JUDAH. *See* Israelite History.

L

LAMENT, MOURNING

The Prophetic Books are filled with language, imagery and forms related to the expression of lament and mourning. This is a reflection of the dominant negative tone of the prophets as they address a community threatened with or experiencing the discipline and judgment of Yahweh. On the one hand, these cries reflect the oral genesis of prophecy, evidence of the original interaction between prophet and people; on the other hand, these cries play a key role in the literary shaping of the prophetic material as books (see Sweeney and Ben Zvi; Ben Zvi and Floyd) (*see* Form Criticism). Both of these dimensions are highlighted in this article, which focuses on the role of lament within the prophets (for the Book of Lamentations, *see* Lamentations, Book of).

1. Lament and Mourning in the Prophets as Oral Artifact
2. Lament and Mourning in the Prophets as Literary Device
3. Comfort and Joy as Response to Lament

1. Lament and Mourning in the Prophets as Oral Artifact.

S. Olyan identified four distinct types of mourning activity represented in biblical texts: mourning for the dead, petitionary mourning, either penitential (e.g., Ezra 9—10; Joel 1—2) or non-penitential (e.g., 1 Sam 1; Ezra 8:21-23; 2 Chron 20:1-19), nonpetitionary mourning (2 Sam 13:19; Ezek 27:28-36; Esther 6:12), and mourning over a skin disease (Lev 13:45-46). Another type not mentioned by Olyan is mourning over the destruction of a city (see Dobbs-Allsopp). All of these types of mourning, except mourning over a skin disease, appear within the OT Prophetic Books. In some cases mourning forms and rituals inform the vocabulary and imagery of smaller

sections of a prophetic pericope, and in other cases one can discern specific forms related to these purposes (for a list of vocabulary typically associated with these mourning forms and activity, see Ferris, 109; for broader ancient Near Eastern evidence, see Ferris; Anderson, 60-82; Pham, 16-24; Dobbs-Allsopp; Bouzard 1997; 2004).

The most common forms are related to mourning for the dead (funeral dirge), petitionary mourning (communal and individual lament), and mourning over the destruction of a city (city lament) (Westermann 1991, 202-3; 1994), although the distinction between these various forms is not always clear (Olyan, 19-25; Pham, 23). The dirge is a "composition whose verbal content indicates that it was composed in honor of a deceased person sometimes eulogizing the individual, sometimes merely bewailing the loss" (Ferris, 11). It can be uttered by either an individual or a community (2 Sam 1:17-27; 3:33-34). Mourning included visible rites such as loud weeping and wailing, tearing clothes, self-mutilation, shaving the head and beard, fasting, and placing dirt on the head, but it could be followed by a period of silence, and then by voices of comfort (Anderson; Pham, 16-35; Olyan). The ritual mourning period lasted for a portion of a day (2 Sam 1:12), a single day (2 Sam 3:35), seven days (Gen 50:10; 1 Sam 31:13) or thirty days (Num 20:20; Deut 34:8) (Olyan, 27). Some have suggested that the woe oracle may also have been associated at some point with mourning for the dead (Janzen; Ferris, 76), although this has been challenged (Roberts, 118; Shipp, 47). The lament is a "composition whose verbal content indicates that it was composed to be used by and/or on behalf of a community [/individual] to express both complaint, and sorrow and grief over some perceived calamity, physical or cultural, which had befallen or was about to befall them and to appeal to God for deliverance" (Ferris, 10). Laments appear in the Psalter, where they possess a regular pattern of elements (Westermann 1981, 165-213). Such laments can be expressed by an individual or a group of people, and in many cases they were accompanied by particular ritual acts similar to mourning rites, including fasting, shaving hair, tearing clothes, wounding oneself, weeping, throwing dirt on the head (e.g., Neh 1:4; 9:1-5; Jer 41:4-9). The city lament, which appears to have developed from the dirge, was a lament form used as part of ceremonies accompanying the refounding and restoration of sanctuaries destroyed by war throughout the ancient Near East (Ferris; Westermann 1994; Dobbs-Allsopp; Bouzard 1997; 2004).

The importance of these various mourning forms to prophetic revelation is showcased in the fact that the scroll that Ezekiel is commanded to consume at his commissioning had written on its front and back "lamentations, mourning and woe" (Ezek 2:10). Not surprisingly, then, dirge, lament and city lament forms appear throughout the OT prophetic corpus. At times the form of funeral dirges is used by prophets to declare judgment over a nation or leader (see Shipp, 47-66). Typical elements of prophetic judgment speeches that utilize dirges in the prophetic corpus include a call to hear, followed by the funeral song (dirge) proper, then a messenger formula followed a prediction of judgment (e.g., Is 14:13-21; Ezek 19:1-14; 26:17-18; 27:32; Amos 5:1-3). By introducing their predictions of judgment with a funeral dirge, the prophets were emphasizing the seriousness and even at times the hopelessness of the people's predicament. Evidence of more complex mourning rituals involving mourner and divine messenger has been identified in passages such as Isaiah 51:9—52:2 (Pham, 148-89). In Ezekiel 24:15-18 the prohibition of mourning (the death of Ezekiel's wife) is symbolic of the severity of the judgment about to befall Israel. In Zechariah 12:10-14 the prophet looks to a day when the people will mourn over the death of one they have killed, here most likely a reference to their penitential remorse over their past treatment of Yahweh.

In other cases the form of lament can be discerned in the prophetic literature. At times the prophet uses lament in order to express judgment (e.g., Mic 1:8-9). In other instances the prophet responds to the present lament of the people experiencing judgment (e.g., Mic 4:9) or describes the future lament of people as a response to judgment (e.g., Mic 2:4). In certain cases there is evidence of a structure that reflects a communal liturgy in which the prophet played a key role (Boda 2001). For instance, Jeremiah 14:1—15:4 contains a repeated *liturgical structure that entailed a prophetic description of the calamitous conditions, a communal lament, a prophet-deity dialogue (including a prophetic approach to the deity asking for an answer to the lament followed by an answer from the deity). A similar structure has been discerned in passages such as Isaiah 56:9—59:15a; 63:7—66:17; Hosea 14:2-9. While in Jeremiah 14:1—15:4 the answer from the deity is negative (declaring judgment on the nation), the answer in Joel 1—2 is positive. Individual laments also appear throughout the prophetic corpus. At times it is the prophets themselves who express their lament to God over the painful predicament in which they find themselves as they seek to express warning and judgment to their rebellious generation (see Is 6:11; Jer 4:10, 19-21; 8:18—9:1; 11:18-23; 12:1-6; 15:10-14, 15-21; 17:14-18; 18:18-23; 20:7-13, 14-18). The prophet Habakkuk expresses his lament to Yahweh as he questions divine justice (e.g., Hab 1:2-4, 12-17). At times, individuals representing the prophet's audience or within the prophet's audience express individual lament to Yahweh (e.g., Is 40:27b; 49:14b; Jer 31:15, 18-19).

While there is some controversy over the extent to which the book of *Lamentations reflects the Mesopotamian city lament form, F. W. Dobbs-Allsopp has identified the "city-lament mode" to greater and lesser degrees within both the OT oracles against the *nations (e.g., Is 15:1—16:14; 23:1-14; 47:1-15; Jer 48:1-47; 50:1—51:58; Zeph 2:13-15) and the OT oracles against Judah and Israel (e.g., Jer 4—6; 8—10; Mic 1:2-16). It is not surprising to find the influence of such a mourning form in the OT prophetic corpus, considering the greater focus placed in prophetic literature on warnings over impending judgment of *sin that would lead to destruction of the city and state.

These various form critical observations provide insight into the original oral character of biblical prophecy, evidence of God's word interacting with a community experiencing the disciplinary pain of Yahweh.

2. Lament and Mourning in the Prophets as Literary Device.

The forms of mourning identified above now function within the literary works of the OT Prophetic Books, where they play new roles in the final form of the text (Boda 2012). In a few cases these forms play key roles in the highest structural level of the texts. For instance, lament appears at two crucial junctures within Isaiah 40—55 (Westermann 1969, 28, 218-19; Baltzer, 82, 319; Oswalt, 303). After the initial prophetic commissioning in Isaiah 40:1-11 and a disputation series in Isaiah 40:12-26 that raises the major challenges to the exilic community's faith (the power of foreign nations and their deities), the prophet employs the *rhetorical device of apostrophe by citing the lament of his audience Jacob/Israel in Isaiah 40:27: "My way is concealed from Yahweh. The justice I deserve is ignored by my God." A second lament appears at Isaiah 49:14 as for the first time in Isaiah 40—55 the figure of *Zion/Jerusalem speaks: "Yahweh has abandoned me, Yahweh has forgotten me." These two figures who lament at these two junctures in this section of Isaiah (the male servant Jacob/Israel, the female daughter Zion/Jerusalem) are the same audiences addressed in the sections that follow their respective lament in Isaiah 40—55. Thus, Israel/Jacob is addressed in Isaiah 40:27; 41:8, 14; 43:1, 22; 44:1-2, 21; 45:4, 19; 46:3; 48:1, 12; 49:3, and Jerusalem/Zion in Isaiah 49:14; 51:16-17; 52:1-2, 7, 9. The prophetic address in Isaiah 40:27—49:13 is directed mainly at servant Jacob/Israel, who eventually emerges in Isaiah 49:1-13 from exile in Babylon (Is 47—48; see Is 48:20). The address shifts in Isaiah 49:14—54:17 to daughter Zion/Jerusalem, who in the concluding piece in Isaiah 54 breaks forth in joyful shouts in response to Yahweh's victory through the *servant (Is 52—53). This evidence highlights the key role that laments play in the literary structure of Isaiah 40—55, setting in motion the prophetic message by identifying the implicit audience of the various sections and introducing the foundational challenges that the prophet must address.

Another example of this literary role can be seen at the core of the book of Jeremiah, a book with the greatest concentration of lament forms among the prophets. At the center of Jeremiah 11—20 lies a double lament liturgy through which the community expresses its lament to Yahweh through the prophet with the hope of receiving a positive message of salvation (Jer 14:1—15:4). The people's cry appears in Jeremiah 14:7-9, 19-22, employing the classic elements of lament, including the question "Why?" (Jer 14:9, 19), the imperative request (Jer 14:9, 21) and motivations based on the severity of the situation (Jer 14:3-6, 19) as well as God's character and past action (Jer 14:8, 21-22). In both liturgies there are also penitential elements (admission of sin [Jer 14:7, 20]), a minor feature within the lament tradition. The prophetic response, however, is not what the community hoped for, as Yahweh points out the people's apostasy (Jer 14:10) and justifies his pronouncement of judgment, which includes prohibition of intercession by the people (Jer 14:12) and the prophet (Jer 14:11; 15:1) alike. Surrounding this tragic double lament liturgy in Jeremiah 14:1—15:4, however, is a series of laments expressed by the prophet appearing in Jeremiah 11:18-23; 12:1-6; 15:10-14, 15-21; 17:14-18; 18:18-23; 20:7-13, 14-18 (see Diamond, 24). The prophetic laments in the first half of Jeremiah 11—20 are distinct from those in second half, with each of the former (Jer 11:18-23; 12:1-6; 15:10-14, 15-21) followed by a response from God, but each of the latter (Jer 17:14-18; 18:18-23; 20:7-13, 14-18) lacking a divine response (von Rad, 88-99; Skinner, 208-14). In addition, there is a progression in the laments as the prophet moves from confident trust to frustrated concern over divine *justice. The key transition point in this sequence occurs in Jeremiah 15, showcased especially in the lament in Jeremiah 15:15-21, the final lament to which Yahweh responds and in which Yahweh calls the prophet to repent from uttering worthless words as the people do. After this point Yahweh no longer replies to the prophet's cries, and this occurs at the same point that Yahweh has rejected once and for all the people's lament to him (Jer 14:1—15:4) (see Diamond, 77-78).

The book of Joel begins with a complex invitation to the nation to assemble for a day of fasting and lament due to a natural disaster (Wolff, 9; Stuart, 239, 244). Various audiences are addressed in Joel 1:2-14, each invited to mourn over the present predicament of the nation. In Joel 1:13-14 the prophet exhorts the priests who were responsible for coordinating the day of fasting and lament to gird themselves, lament and spend the night in sackcloth as the first step toward consecrating a fast, proclaiming a solemn assembly and gathering those addressed throughout Joel 1:2-12. Joel 1:15-20 then cites the lament to be used to cry out to Yahweh for help in the present crisis. What follows in Joel 2, however, reveals the literary role played by invitation to lament in Joel 1 (on the literary character of Joel, see Ogden 1983, 97). After the invitation to Jerusalem for a day of fasting and lament, it is revealed in Joel 2:1-11 that the present predicament is but a harbinger of a greater disaster in which Yahweh threatens to destroy Israel. Thus, the invitation to lament turns into an invitation to repent in Joel 2:12-17. Once again a form related to lament is used strategically within the literary structure of one of the Prophetic Books.

These three examples highlight the way lament, either within a stock form-critical unit (the prophetic liturgy, invitation to lament) or a rhetorical device (apostrophe), functions rhetorically within the macrostructure of a prophetic section. The language of lament and dirge is also used to develop key metaphors within prophetic literature—for example, the depiction of the mourning earth (Hayes). The ubiquitous mourning forms, vocabulary and images throughout prophetic literature function in their own respective literary units to a lesser or greater degree.

3. Comfort and Joy as Response to Lament.
While the language of lament and mourning appears often in the forms and rhetoric of OT prophecy, at times contrasting expressions also appear. Thus, while the invitation to lament occurs throughout the Prophetic Books (e.g., Jer 9:17-22; Joel 1:8) (Westermann 1991, 7), the summons to joy also is found (e.g., Is 12:6; Zeph 3:14-15) (Crüsemann, 55-65). Both G. Anderson and X. Pham have noted the importance of comfort in mourning rituals within the OT, obtained by participating in visible mourning rites and by remaining silent for a period, and also given through speech to the mourner (Anderson, 84-85; Pham, 27-35). It therefore is not surprising that comfort is a common motif within the Prophetic Books, especially in relation to the announcement of salvation or a new era in redemptive history. Thus, the message of Isaiah to the exilic community opens with "Comfort, comfort my people" (Is 40:1), and

the role of the servant figure at the heart of Isaiah 56—66 is "to comfort all those who mourn, to provide for those mourning over Zion, giving them a garland in place of ashes, the oil of gladness in place of mourning, the mantle of praise in place of a spirit of fainting" (Is 61:2-3). Similarly, Jeremiah looks to a day of comfort when mourning will be transformed into gladness, and sorrow into joy (Jer 31:13). Although the prophets are dominated by the forms, vocabulary and images of mourning and lament, comfort and joy remain as their ultimate hope.

See also EXILE; LAMENTATIONS, BOOK OF; PRAYER; SUFFERING.

BIBLIOGRAPHY. **G. A. Anderson,** *A Time to Mourn, a Time to Dance: The Expression of Grief and Joy in Israelite Religion* (University Park: Pennsylvania State University Press, 1991); **K. Baltzer,** *Deutero-Isaiah: A Commentary on Isaiah 40-55* (Hermeneia; Minneapolis: Fortress, 2001); **E. Ben Zvi and M. H. Floyd,** eds., *Writings and Speech in Israelite Prophecy and Ancient Near Eastern Prophecy* (SBLSymS 10; Atlanta: Society of Biblical Literature, 2000); **M. J. Boda,** "From Complaint to Contrition: Peering through the Liturgical Window of Jer 14,1-15,4," *ZAW* 113 (2001) 186-97; idem, "'Uttering Precious Rather Than Worthless Words': Divine Patience and Impatience with Lament in Isaiah and Jeremiah," in *Why? ... How Long? Studies on Voice(s) of Lamentation Rooted in Biblical Hebrew Poetry,* ed. M. J. Boda, C. Dempsey and L. Snow Flesher (LHBOTS 552; London: Continuum, 2012); **W. C. Bouzard Jr.,** *We Have Heard with Our Ears, O God: Sources of the Communal Laments in the Psalms* (SBLDS 159; Atlanta: Scholars Press, 1997); idem, "Doves in the Windows: Isaiah 60:8 in Light of Ancient Mesopotamian Lament Traditions," in *David and Zion: Biblical Studies in Honor of J. J. M. Roberts,* ed. B. F. Batto and K. L. Roberts (Winona Lake, IN: Eisenbrauns, 2004) 307-17; **F. Crüsemann,** *Studien zur Formgeschichte von Hymnus und Danklied in Israel* (WMANT 32; Neukirchen-Vluyn: Neukirchener Verlag, 1969); **A. R. Diamond,** *The Confessions of Jeremiah in Context: Scenes of Prophetic Drama* (JSOTSup 46; Sheffield: JSOT, 1987); **F. W. Dobbs-Allsopp,** *Weep, O Daughter of Zion: A Study of the City-Lament in the Hebrew Bible* (BibOr 44; Roma: Editrice Pontificio Istituto Biblico, 1993); **P. W. Ferris,** *The Genre of Communal Lament in the Bible and the Ancient Near East* (SBLDS 127; Atlanta: Scholars Press, 1992);

K. M. Hayes, *The Earth Mourns: Prophetic Metaphor and Oral Aesthetic* (SBLAB 8; Atlanta: Society of Biblical Literature: 2002); **W. Janzen,** *Mourning Cry and Woe Oracle* (BZAW 125; Berlin: de Gruyter, 1972); **G. S. Ogden,** "Joel 4 and Prophetic Responses to National Laments," *JSOT* 26 (1983) 97-106; **S. M. Olyan,** *Biblical Mourning: Ritual and Social Dimensions* (Oxford: Oxford University Press, 2004); **J. Oswalt,** *The Book of Isaiah, Chapters 40-66* (NICOT; Grand Rapids: Eerdmans, 1997); **X. H. T. Pham,** *Mourning in the Ancient Near East and the Hebrew Bible* (JSOTSup 302; Sheffield: Sheffield Academic, 1999); **J. J. M. Roberts,** *Nahum, Habakkuk, and Zephaniah: A Commentary* (OTL; Louisville: Westminster/John Knox, 1991); **R. M. Shipp,** *Of Dead Kings and Dirges: Myth and Meaning in Isaiah 14:4b-21* (SBLAB 11; Atlanta: Society of Biblical Literature, 2002); **J. Skinner,** *Prophecy and Religion: Studies in the Life of Jeremiah* (Cambridge: Cambridge University Press, 1951); **D. K. Stuart,** *Hosea-Jonah* (WBC 31; Waco, TX: Word, 1987); **M. A. Sweeney and E. Ben Zvi,** eds., *The Changing Face of Form Criticism for the Twenty-First Century* (Grand Rapids: Eerdmans, 2003); **G. von Rad,** "The Confessions of Jeremiah," in *Theodicy in the Old Testament,* ed. J. L. Crenshaw (IRT 4; Philadelphia: Fortress, 1983) 88-99; **C. Westermann,** *Isaiah 40-66: A Commentary* (OTL; London: SCM, 1969); idem, *Praise and Lament in the Psalms* (Atlanta: John Knox, 1981); idem, *Basic Forms of Prophetic Speech,* trans. H. C. White (Louisville: Westminster/John Knox, 1991); idem, *Lamentations: Issues and Interpretation* (Minneapolis: Fortress, 1994); **H. W. Wolff,** *Joel and Amos: A Commentary on the Books of the Prophets Joel and Amos,* trans. S. D. McBride (Hermeneia; Philadelphia: Fortress, 1977). M. J. Boda

LAMENTATIONS, BOOK OF

The book of Lamentations offers a window into the struggle of the people of God in the wake of the fall of Jerusalem and demise of the kingdom of Judah. The book presents a series of poems that express the grief of the community using language, imagery, forms and theology in line with Hebrew traditions of mourning and *suffering. The struggle expressed in these poems is communicated through contrasting voices: female and male, individual and corporate, bitter and penitent, suppliant and prophetic. The book attempts through the acrostic style in Lamentations 1—4 to articulate exhaustively the pain of the fall of Jerusalem and provides through the elaborate and copious third poem a way forward through a penitential response to Yahweh's grace. In the end, however, these goals are frustrated by the endurance of suffering, which in the final pericope leads to the abandonment of the acrostic pattern and to the erratic swings between confidence in Yahweh's sovereignty and uncertainty over Yahweh's grace.

1. Authorship and History
2. Genre and Setting
3. Literary Features and Structure
4. Content of Each Poem
5. Theological Traditions and Themes
6. Canon

1. Authorship and History.

1.1. Authorship. One of the oldest interpretations of the book of Lamentations is represented by the Jewish Greek translation of the book, and this translation identifies Jeremiah as the composer of at least the first of, if not all, the laments in the book with the addition of the preface: "And it was after Israel had gone into *exile and Jerusalem had been laid waste that Jeremiah sat weeping and composed this lament concerning Jerusalem, saying. . . ." This connection to Jeremiah may have been suggested by the Chronicler's note in 2 Chronicles 35:25 that Jeremiah composed laments for Josiah, but the note in Chronicles says nothing about laments related to the fall of Jerusalem. The connection between the prophet and the book of Lamentations usually is based on the number of literary connections that have been identified between books of Lamentations and Jeremiah (see 6.1 below). However, many have questioned this conclusion, noting that the perspective and ideology of some of the sections of Lamentations stand in tension with the message of a prophet who consistently predicted and justified God's punishment of Judah (cf. Lam 4:17-20 with Jer 2:18; 37:5-10; Lam 1:10 with Jer 26:4-6).

While there is plenty of evidence within the book of Jeremiah itself that the prophet could shift from one perspective to another (note the laments of Jeremiah throughout Jer 11—20), probably the greatest challenge to Jeremianic authorship for Lamentations is found in the dominant structuring device throughout the book: the acrostic. Similar to Psalms 9—10 and Psalm 119, four of the five chapters in Lamentations are written as an acrostic, which means that each verse (Lam 1—2; 4), or series of verses (Lam 3), begins with a successive letter of the Hebrew alphabet (twenty-two letters). Lamentations 5 contains twenty-two verses but is not written in acrostic. The order of the alphabet in these poems, however, is not identical. Lamentations 1 contains the traditional order of the Hebrew alphabet, where the sixteenth and seventeenth letters are ordered ʿayin/pê. In contrast, Lamentations 2—4 contains the order pê/ʿayin. Evidence from ancient abecedaries reveals that both arrangements of the alphabet were acceptable in Israel, but it is difficult to imagine a single person using two different orders of something as basic as an alphabet. This suggests that there is not a single genius behind these compositions, but rather they represent poems used in a common liturgical setting over a period of time.

1.2. Date. This, however, does not mean that the book is unrelated to the prophet Jeremiah and the period in which he lived. Despite the assertion of some (e.g., Provan 1990, 130-43; 1991, 11-12) that the book cannot be set accurately into a particular historical context, most scholars agree that the book reflects the conditions of the final years of the kingdom of Judah in the sixth century BC. In this period Judah experienced the destruction of its city and temple, the exile of its king and upper class, and the massacre of its population (*see* Israelite History). Although the vivid poetry in Lamentations may merely reflect the genius of an imaginative poet and probably shows that these poems were composed by trained liturgists, there is no reason to deny that this vividness arose from the personal observation of the poet(s) or that liturgists could compose authentic expressions of pain for the community (*contra* Westermann, 100-101). F. W. Dobbs-Allsopp places Lamentations in the period of 586-520 BC based on linguistic evidence as well as intertextual connections to Isaiah 40—55 (Dobbs-Allsopp 1998). Additionally, some discern within the book a voice that echoes the voice of Jeremiah or at least the book that bears his name (see 6.1 below), evidence that suggests that the connection of this book to the prophet Jeremiah in the Greek tradition may be legitimate.

Although most scholars place these compositions in the period immediately after the fall of the kingdom of Judah in 587/6 BC (see Westermann, 54-55, 104-5), there has been disagreement over the chronological order of the individual poems that now comprise Lamentations. For instance, S. Gurewicz argued for the order Lamentations 3; 2; 4; 1; 5; R. Gordis for the order Lamentations 2/4; 3; 1/5; and R. Brandscheidt for the order Lamentations 2; 1; 5; 4; 3. Many have argued that Lamentations 5 is the latest of the compositions (see Lee) because of its employment of temporal references such as "forever" (nēṣaḥ) and "so long" (lĕʾōrek yāmîm), but such evidence is not that helpful because expressions such as these are not only stereotypical in liturgical compositions (see Pss 9:19; 10:11; 23:6; 44:24; 93:5) but also relative to the composer's perspective. Additionally, the reference to the "sins of the ancestors" in Lamentations 5:7, which to some suggests a later generation looking back on the generation at the fall of Jerusalem, is not a secure argument because such appeals are evident in compositions arising in the last decade before the fall of Judah (cf. Jer 31:29; Ezek 18:2). The dominant perspective of the poems is that of life in the land in the wake of the fall of Jerusalem rather than life in exile, suggesting that it arose among those who had remained in the land after the fall of the city (although there is some interest in the plight of exiles in Lam 4:15 and especially in Lam 4:22).

2. Genre and Setting.
The placement of Lamentations among the five Megillot (scrolls) secured its role at the enduring commemoration of the destruction of the Second Temple on the ninth day of Ab in AD 70. This connection to the destruction of the temple probably was seen as appropriate in a later era because of a much earlier precedent in the life of the Jewish community. The link between this book and the demise of the temple and state has informed scholarly discussion over the genre and liturgical setting of the poems in the book.

2.1. Genre. H. Gunkel saw the various poems as examples of either the funeral dirge (Lam 1; 2; 4), individual lament (Lam 3) or communal lament (Lam 5).

2.1.1. Funeral Dirge. After Gunkel, some focused on the funeral dirge as the key form that underlies the poems found in Lamentations (see Jahnow; Lee). Examples of actual funeral dirges are found in 2 Samuel 1:17-27; 3:33-34; Jeremiah 9:16-21; 38:22, with forms modified for poetic use as short prophetic sayings (Is 1:21-23; Jer 9:10, 17-22; Ezek 26:17-18; Amos 5:2) or as popular sayings (Is 14:4-21; 23:1-14; Ezek 19:1-9, 10-14; 27:2-36; 28:11-19; 32:12-16) (see Westermann, 6). The influence of the funeral dirge is usually associated with Lamentations 1; 2; 4.

The employment of female voices and female personification at various points in Lamentations also suggests the funeral dirge form, since in ancient cultures (including Israel) dirges and laments often were chanted by *women, some of whom engaged in mourning rites as a vocation (2 Chron 35:25; Is 22:12; Jer 7:9; 9:17; Ezek 32:16 [for ancient Near Eastern evidence, see Block, 210]). In ancient societies premature death was most often associated with males, especially in relation to *war. Furthermore, males were older than their female marriage partners and, as in modern societies, typically preceded their mates to the grave. This explains why widows and the fatherless were regularly identified as the most vulnerable within ancient cultures and why women were concerned to bear a son to protect their interests later in life (see Ruth 4; 1 Sam 1). Thus, the most common occasion for funeral dirges was defeat in war (e.g., 2 Sam 1:17-27). Its counterpart probably was the "call to joy" (*Aufruf zur Freude*), a form associated with victory in war and usually elicited from women (Is 12:4-6; 54:1; Hos 9:1; Joel 2:21-24; Zeph 3:14; Zech 2:10; 9:9 [see Crüsemann, 55-65]). Interestingly, this form is addressed to "Daughter Zion" in Zephaniah 3:14; Zechariah 2:10; 9:9 and to a female inhabitant of *Zion in Isaiah 12:6, and it is employed in a satirical way in Lamentations 4:21-22.

2.1.2. Lament. Others, however, have questioned the extent of the funeral dirge's influence on Lamentations (see Westermann, 6-11). For these scholars, the lament forms of the Psalter dominate the book, with elements from both individual and communal lament evident throughout Lamentations. As C. Westermann noted, these forms dominate Lamentations 3; 5, but they are also present throughout the other poems.

2.1.3. Mesopotamian City Dirge. Beginning with the suggestion by S. Kramer (see Dobbs-Allsopp 1993, 2-10; Lee, 37n163) that Mesopotamian laments over ruined cities and their sanctuaries were the foundation for the poems in Lamentations, the majority of scholars have highlighted close connections between these two forms (see, e.g., Kraus; Gwaltney; Gottwald 1962; Hillers; Ferris; Westermann; Dobbs-Allsopp 1993; 2002; Bouzard; Morrow). These Mesopotamian forms were used as part of ceremonies accompanying the refounding and restoration of sanctuaries destroyed by war (see Boda 2006; Boda and Novotny). The Mesopotamian forms link the destruction of a key city and/or its sanctuary to a decision made in the divine assembly and resulting in the abandonment of the sanctuary by its gods. The destruction is carried out by the god Enlil through a human enemy. In the Mesopotamian laments usually the city's patron goddess challenges this decision of the assembly and laments the demise of city and sanctuary (see Dobbs-Allsopp 1993; 2002).

2.1.4. Form. F. W. Dobbs-Allsopp has identified key connections between these Mesopotamian dirges and the book of Lamentations but is careful to note that Lamentations is a "thorough translation and adaptation" of the genre put to a different use (Dobbs-Allsopp 2002, 9). Unlike the Mesopotamian laments, Lamentations employs typical Hebrew poetic devices, clearly identifies the culpability of the people, replaces the destructive god Enlil with Yahweh and the weeping goddess with the personified city of Jerusalem (Daughter Zion), and avoids any mention of the return of Yahweh or restoration of the temple and city (Dobbs-Allsopp 2002). Therefore, in the view of these researchers, the Mesopotamian city dirges may have provided a precedent for some of the elements found in Lamentations, but even so, there is evidence that the form has undergone significant changes and may only echo a general tradition of lamenting over the destruction of a city and sanctuary. This evidence, along with the fact that the Mesopotamian city dirges typically incorporated lament prayers, could explain why other traditional Hebrew forms, including the funeral dirge (cf. 2 Sam 1:17-27 with Lam 1:1-11, 17; 2:1-12; 3:48-51; 4:1-6) and the individual (Lam 1:12-16, 18-22; 2:20-22) and communal (Lam 3:40-47; 5) lament can also be identified within Lamentations (see Gunkel; Westermann). Of the five poems, only Lamentations 1; 2; 4 usually are seen as reflecting strongly the genre of the city dirge, with Lamentations 3 dominated by individual lament with some communal lament, and Lamentations 5 comprising a communal lament.

Although it is possible that all three form traditions (funeral dirge, individual lament, communal lament) have informed the book of Lamentations (see O'Connor, 10-11), there may be another way to explain the connections at least to the tradition of the Mesopotamian city dirge. The use of a goddess to express the predicament of the city and sanctuary within the tradition of the Mesopotamian city dirge suggests that it has been influenced by the ubiquitous phenomenon of female mourning rites in ancient societies. Therefore, it is likely that the ancient Mesopotamian liturgists envisioned a *divine council akin to human society, with a female figure crying out against the merciless acts of a male-dominated divine council as she mourned the loss of the city and sanctuary. Motifs shared by the city dirges in Mesopotamia and the poems in Lamentations, therefore, can be attributed to female mourning rituals that ancient societies shared in common.

2.2. Setting. Even if a link can be established between the Mesopotamian city dirges and the poems in the book of Lamentations, the absence of any reference to the rebuilding of the sanctuary and the return of the deity shows clearly that the setting in which the poems in Lamentations arose is different from the ceremonies related to temple refoundation that gave rise to the Mesopotamian city dirges (see Dobbs-Allsopp 2002; *contra* Gwaltney). The fixation with the events surrounding the fall and destruction of the city and its aftermath in Lamentations suggests that the setting of the poems is most likely the series of days of fasting that arose immediately after the fall of Jerusalem. Evidence for mourning rites associated with the destroyed sanctuary and possibly also the fallen state is found in Jeremiah 41:4-9. There, eighty men from Shechem, Shiloh and Samaria, displaying rites associated with mourning (shaved beards, torn clothes, self-inflicted wounds, weeping), are depicted in the seventh month as on their way to "the house of Yahweh" with grain offerings and incense. While this evidence comes from the beginning of the Babylonian exilic period, Zechariah 7—8 speaks of the practice of four fasts during the "seventy years" of the exile, fasts that took place in the fourth, fifth, seventh and tenth months (Zech 7:5; 8:19). That these fasts were related at least to the temple in Jerusalem (as Jer 41) is suggested by the fact that a delegation from Bethel approaches the priests and prophets of "the house of the LORD Almighty" (Zech 7:3) to determine whether they should now come to an end with the second temple nearing completion. Some have suggested that the four fasts were related to a complex of four key events related to the fall of the Judean kingdom (Wellhausen, 103-7; Ackroyd, 207n122): tenth month (588 BC), the siege of Jerusalem began (2 Kings 25:1; Jer 39:1); fourth month (587 BC), Jerusalem's walls were breached, and leadership fled (2 Kings 25:3-7; Jer 39:1-10; 52:6-11); fifth month, Jerusalem was destroyed (2 Kings 25:8-12; Jer 52:12-16); seventh month, Gedaliah was assassinated (2 Kings 25:25-26; Jer 41:1-3). Since the delegation from Bethel in Zechariah 7 originally only asked about one fast (fifth month [Zech 7:3]), which was expanded first to two fasts (fifth, seventh months) in Zechariah 7:5 and later to four fasts (fourth, fifth, seventh, tenth months) in Zechariah 8:19, it is possible that these fasts reflect a diversity of rites observed by different communities within the land and possibly also in exile.

Other compositions that may have arisen in this liturgical setting are now found in the Psalter (Pss 44; 60; 74; 79; 83; 106; 123; 137) as well as in narrative books describing the practice of penitential *prayer in the Persian period (Ezra 9; Neh 1; 9; Dan 9). That the same context is suggested for both laments and penitential prayers, the latter coming to dominate the liturgical expression of the Persian period community, is bolstered by close literary and ideological connections that have been established between the book of Lamentations and this tradition of penitential prayer (see Boda 2008). Close associations also between Lamentations 3 and the prophetic lament liturgy in Jeremiah 14:1—15:4 (which most likely occurred during the reign of Zedekiah, last king of Judah) suggests a common liturgical setting for prayers of lament and penitence throughout the sixth century BC.

3. Literary Features and Structure.
Observations on the original setting of the in-

dividual compositions provide some insights into the historical circumstances that gave rise to these compositions as well as the basic building blocks of the individual poems. However, such insights need to be supplemented by analysis of the final canonical shape of these originally independent prayers. This involves paying attention to key rhetorical features employed throughout the collection (*see* Rhetorical Criticism).

3.1. Personification. One regular rhetorical feature is personification, usually related to the city of Jerusalem, but also to its gates, walls, roads and surrounding kingdom. By personifying these physical structures and regions, the composers were able to vividly describe the pain and express the heart cry of the people. There is a sense that the poets send out God's "precious" Zion to intercede for them, hoping that she may have greater success to gain Yahweh's ear (see Lanahan, 43-45; Heim; on the image "Daughter of Zion/Jerusalem," see Dearman 2009; Floyd 2008, 2012).

3.2. Voice. Another rhetorical feature has been highlighted especially in the work of N. Lee, who analyzes the modulating voices throughout the book (although see Westermann, 65, 139-40). Lee identifies the two dominant voices in Lamentations with two voices that can be discerned in the book of Jeremiah: Jeremiah the prophet and a female poet voicing personified Jerusalem's pain (called "Jerusalem's poet"). This dialogue, which Lee traces back to "different poetic singers who performed their composed songs in response to one another" (Lee, 42), is prominent in Lamentations 1; 2; 4. The female perspective of Lamentations 5 (cf. Lam 5:14b with Lam 5:15a) and links to the earlier cries of personified Jerusalem (cf. Lam 5:17 with Lam 1:13, 22; Lam 5:17 with Lam 4:17) suggest that the communal lament of Lamentations 5 has taken over the role of the personified Jerusalem (Lee, 196).

Lee's study, building on the earlier work of W. Lanahan on Lamentations and especially of C. Mandolfo (2002) on biblical laments, highlights the importance of sensitivity to the various voices that appear throughout the book (see also Miller 2001; Mandolfo 2007; Conway 2012; Boda, forthcoming). No two poems are alike in the structuring of the voices. One needs to be alert to the impact that employing

various voices has on the reading of the poem. W. Kaiser picks this up in his analysis of Lamentations 1 when he notes, "It would appear that emotional and psychological progress is realized in this poem as it moves from a more distant, descriptive 3rd-person reporting in verses 1-11 to a more personal, private 1st-person speech in verses 12-22" (Kaiser, 44). The poem begins with an external point of view, observing the pain of the personified city, only to give voice to the suffering woman, who discloses her inner turmoil. In Lamentations 3 this inner turmoil is presented from the outset and is expressed not by the city personified as a woman but rather by a suffering man (warrior?). The interplay of various voices provides more opportunities to express and experience the pain of the crisis.

3.3. Acrostic. A third key rhetorical feature in Lamentations is the acrostic that structures four of the five poems (Lam 1—4). This literary device appears at several points in the OT (Pss 9—10; 25; 34; 119; 145; Prov 31:10-31; Nah 1) as well as in other Semitic literature, including Akkadian, Ugaritic and Paleo-Canaanite (see Westermann, 98-100; O'Connor, 12). Several purposes have been offered to explain the use of acrostics, including fulfilling magical rites, aiding memorization of poems, emphasizing completeness, or producing aesthetically pleasing literature (Westermann, 98-100; O'Connor). Although there may be multiple purposes behind the use of acrostics, most likely they communicate that the poem expresses totality, and in the case of Lamentations both the total devastating effect of the destruction and the total expression of the pain of those who experienced it.

3.4. Structure. The uniqueness of each poem's acrostic pattern in Lamentations 1—4 shows that each poem in the book has its own integrity. Nevertheless, some have questioned whether the book merely represents an anthology of poems or instead was designed as an integrated collection. Although recognizing independence for each poem, J. Renkema (1988; 1998), for instance, argues for a collection united by connections between equivalent letter stanzas in the four poems (e.g., elements in stanza ʾālep in Lam 1 may be found in stanza ʾālep in Lam 2, 3 or 4). Although some examples seem to support his view, the evidence is not consistent across all stanzas in all poems.

D. Reimer draws on modern grief theory in order to trace the thematic structure of Lamentations, concluding that the book moves through the stages of isolation (Lam 1), anger (Lam 2), bargaining (Lam 3), depression (Lam 4) and acceptance (Lam 5). Reimer is careful to admit that these themes are only "dominant" in their respective poems, but these various stages appear at various points in all the poems—a point that led earlier scholars to abandon such psychological theory as a basis for structural analysis (see Moore; Joyce). Especially difficult to this structure is Reimer's identification of the final poem with its conclusion vacillating between confident hope and embittered lament.

The fact that Lamentations 3 has not only the longest poem but also the most complicated acrostic brings rhetorical focus onto this poem within the collection. The reader should take note of the message of this central poem (see Morrow, 112), which represents the height of rhetorical artistry and so also, as K. O'Connor has said, functions as "the book's most important chapter, the book's theological heart" (O'Connor, 13). This central poem points to a theological solution to the present suffering, one that accentuates Yahweh's grace and justice (Lam 3:1-40). This solution, however, is seriously challenged in the remainder of the book, first in the central poem itself (Lam 3:41-66) and then in the two poems in Lamentations 4—5. This latter is emphasized recently by I. Provan (1991), Dobbs-Allsopp (1997) and T. Linafelt, who remind readers that the book does not end with Lamentations 3:40. The final two chapters contain poems shorter than Lamentations 1—3, with Lamentations 5, although containing twenty-two verse units as the first four poems, abandoning the acrostic pattern. This suggests that Lamentations 5 signals the end of this completeness—something made clear in its painful and dialectal conclusion. As O'Connor has argued, Lamentations 4—5 "move back to themes of grief, anger, and despair, and smother hope like a blanket over fire" (O'Connor, 13-14). Therefore, the overall flow of the book of Lamentations suggests an honest struggle in the midst of the darkness of the exile, even if it foreshadows the dominant solution that will be adopted within the community in the wake of the exile (cf. Ezra 9; Neh 1; 9; Dan 9) (see Boda 2008).

4. Content of Each Poem.

4.1. Lamentations 1.

1:1-9a	Third-person description of Zion's suffering
1:9b	First-person singular cry of Zion to Yahweh
1:10-11a	Third-person description of Zion addressed to Yahweh and Zion
1:11b	First-person singular cry of Zion to Yahweh
1:12-16	First-person singular cry of Zion to onlookers (the nations?)
1:17	Third-person description of Zion's suffering and its cause
1:18-19	First-person singular cry of Zion to the nations about Yahweh's innocence and Zion's rebellion
1:20-22	First-person singular cry of Zion to Yahweh about the nations' guilt (malediction)

The first poem in the collection draws the reader in to view the pain of personified Zion from an external vantage point through third-person speech (Lam 1:1-11). At the outset no attribution of guilt is given; the reader is allowed to experience the shocking pain before realizing in Lamentations 1:5 and again in Lamentations 1:8-9 that Zion's sins lie behind this suffering. This first section introduces a key emphasis of this poem—the solitude of the city, first seen in the opening declaration that she is "deserted" (Lam 1:1) and then in the refrain in Lamentations 1:2, 9: "there is none to comfort her." At two points in Lamentations 1:1-11 the voice of the suffering city emerges, both consisting of cries for Yahweh to look upon her affliction (Lam 1:9b, 11b). The detachment of the first half of the poem is soon lost in the second half as Lamentations 1:12-16 shifts to the first-person voice of the city as she pleads with those who pass by. Zion echoes the themes already introduced in the third-person section, admitting her sins and repeating the refrain of solitude in Lamentations 1:16, "no one is near to comfort me," already encountered in Lamentations 1:2, 9. For a moment in Lamentations 1:17 the perspective shifts to the external with a short third-person description of Zion that again reminds the reader that "there is no one to comfort her." But then the poem plunges back into the bitter first-person pain of Zion that carries the poem to its conclusion (Lam 1:18-22). In this concluding section

Zion first speaks to the nations about Yahweh ("Listen, all you peoples" [Lam 1:18-19]), admitting that her suffering was caused by her rebellion; Yahweh was innocent. Her speech then engages Yahweh directly, expressing her distress, admitting her culpability, but also highlighting the pain that the nations have inflicted upon her (Lam 1:20-22). Here again the refrain emerges in Lamentations 1:21, now expressed in first-person speech by Zion herself: "There is no one to comfort me." This section calls for vengeance upon those who have treated Zion so brutally, suggesting that although the discipline was deserved, the nations have violated God's justice in their actions.

4.2. Lamentations 2.

2:1-10   Third-person description of the suffering of Zion and Judah

2:11-12   First-person singular lament over Zion's suffering

2:13-19   First-person singular address to Zion

2:20-22   First-person singular lament of Zion to Yahweh

The second poem begins, as did the first poem, with a detached third-person description of the pain (Lam 2:1-10) focusing on the city (Daughter Zion) and kingdom (Daughter Judah) as women. The final verse in this section (Lam 2:10) describes rites connected to mourning and lament (sit on ground in silence, sprinkle dust on heads, put on sackcloth, bow heads to ground), and this introduces the first-person voice that emerges in Lamentations 2:11-12, the voice of one who weeps while observing the pain of the people. In Lamentations 2:13-19 this or another first-person voice turns and addresses Daughter Zion directly, highlighting the city's suffering, attacking the false prophets, and identifying the defeat of the enemy as the planned judgment of Yahweh. As in Lamentations 2:10, so Lamentations 2:18-19 depicts the rites of mourning and lament of the people and even encourages such rites from the "walls of Daughter Zion" (Lam 2:18-19). In response to this invitation a voice of prayer addresses Yahweh directly to conclude the poem in Lamentations 2:20-22. In the first poem Daughter Zion asked onlookers this searching question: "Is any suffering like my suffering that was inflicted on me, that the LORD brought on me in the day of his fierce anger?" (Lam 1:12). In this second poem Daughter Zion addresses this to God directly: "Whom have you ever treated like this?" (Lam 2:20).

4.3. Lamentations 3.

3:1-20   First-person singular lament over God's judgment on the male poet

3:21-24   First-person singular transition to hope

3:25-39   Application of the poet's experience to all people

3:40   First-person plural cohortative invitation

3:41-47   First-person plural communal response

3:48-51   First-person singular lament over God's judgment on the people

3:52-66   First-person singular thanksgiving and request (malediction)

The third poem begins with the expression of a "man" (geber [Lam 3:1]) who has experienced suffering at the hand of God (Lam 3:1-17) and explains to the reader how he moved from despair (Lam 3:18-20) to hope (Lam 3:21-24). This situation is then applied universally to anyone who experiences similar circumstances (Lam 3:25-39)—a presentation that prompts an invitation to the entire community to examine their ways and return to God (Lam 3:40). A response to this invitation by the people comes in Lamentations 3:41-47, and this response appears to reject the observation in Lamentations 3:39 that no one has a right to complain against God. This communal complaint argues that although they have admitted their sin, God has not responded to them (Lam 3:41-47). Furthermore, a first-person common singular voice follows in Lamentations 3:48-51, weeping over the despicable state of the city-community, and functions as a transition to a closing individual prayer in Lamentations 3:52-66, which contains both thanksgiving and request.

The source of hope for the afflicted man (Lam 3:1-20) in Lamentations 3 is clearly his consideration of the gracious character of God in Lamentations 3:21-33. Here the composer uses the breadth of Hebrew lexical stock of "grace," including "covenant loyalty" (ḥesed [Lam 3:22, 32]), "compassions" (raḥămîm [Lam 3:22, 32]), "faithfulness" (ʾĕmûnâ [Lam 3:23]), "goodness" (ṭôb [Lam 3:25, 26, 27]) and "salvation" (tĕšûʿâ [Lam 3:26]). In light of such grace, the poet encourages the people to wait (qwh [Lam 3:25]), seek (drš [Lam 3:25]), wait silently (*yḥl* Hiphil + *dûmām* [Lam 3:26]), bear the yoke (*nśʾ* + *ʿōl* [Lam 3:27]), sit alone (*yšb* + *bādād* [Lam 3:28]), be silent (*dāmam* [Lam 3:28]), put one's mouth in the dust (*ntn* + *beʿāpār pîhû* [Lam 3:29]), give one's cheek to the smiter (*ntn* + *lĕmakkēhû lehî* [Lam 3:30]) and be filled with reproach (*śbʿ* + *bĕḥerpâ* [Lam 3:30]). Such actions describe the posture of passively accepting the discipline of God but also of awaiting God's deliverance.

All of this leads to a presentation of the *justice of God in Lamentations 3:33-38, teaching that God "does not afflict with delight" (Lam 3:33) but rather disciplines because of *sin (Lam 3:37-38). In light of this, there is no room for complaint when being punished for one's sins (Lam 3:39). Thus, in this central poem it is a consideration of the grace of God that is to prompt an acceptance of the discipline of God and a refusal to complain in light of one's culpability. It is this that leads to the key penitential invitation in Lamentations 3:40. Nevertheless, the frustration of the people comes out in Lamentations 3:41-47 as they declare that they admit their sins (Lam 3:41), and yet God has not pardoned, and they continue to live in their suffering. The repetition of the term "destruction" (*šeber*) in Lamentations 3:47-48 shows that the first-person common singular voice (possibly the same one that began the poem in Lam 3:1-20) feels this frustration of the people (Lam 3:48, 51) and is committed to interceding for the people (Lam 3:49) until Yahweh looks upon their suffering (Lam 3:50). This same voice closes off the poem with a prayer of request for himself as well. In this closing prayer the poet calls for God's justice and vengeance on his enemies (Lam 3:59-66) based on his own past experience of God's *salvation (Lam 3:52-58).

4.4. Lamentations 4.

4:1-10	First-person singular description of the need of the people
4:11-16	Third-person description of the need of the people
4:17-20	First-person plural lament over disaster
4:21-22	Second-person prophetic announcement of judgment and salvation

The fourth poem begins in Lamentations 4:1-10 with a first-person description of the need of the people (note "my" in Lam 4:3, 6, 10), focusing especially on the common fate of those considered most (children) and least (princes) vulnerable. In this section the focus is on the deplorable circumstances rather than on the cause of the crisis. With Lamentations 4:11-16 the poem shifts into a third-person description of the need, now identifying the cause as Yahweh's fierce anger against the sins of prophets and priests (Lam 4:13). In Lamentations 4:17-20 a first-person plural voice, possibly the voice of the prophets and priests who now "grope through the streets as if they were blind" (see Lam 4:14), emerges. This voice articulates the failure of both international allies (Lam 4:17) and national leadership (Lam 4:20) to rescue them in their time of need. The poem ends (Lam 4:21-22) with what appears to be a prophetic announcement of judgment and salvation, declaring a curse against the rival Daughter Edom, who takes pleasure in their demise, and promising Daughter Zion that her punishment will one day end.

4.5. Lamentations 5.

5:1	Request: call for Yahweh's attention
5:2-18	Lamenting the predicament, admitting guilt
5:19	Motivation for God to act
5:20	Questions (borderline accusations)
5:21	Request: call for Yahweh's action
5:22	Motivation for God to act

What is immediately noticeable about the final poem in the book is that even though it consists of twenty-two units, it is not an alphabetic acrostic, as are the other four. There are other points of divergence. It is the shortest of all the poems and the most consistent, employing a first-person plural voice throughout. The poem contains the elements typical of the communal laments of the Psalter, with the depiction of the predicament (Lam 5:2-5, 8a, 9-16a, 17-18), the assignment of the cause of the predicament (Lam 5:6-7, 8b, 16b, 20, 22), the motivations for help (Lam 5:19, 21) and the request for help (Lam 5:1, 21). In the prayer of Lamentations 5 there is no denying that the cause of the predicament is traced to the sin of the people: both in the previous generation (Lam 5:6-7) and (most likely) in the present generation (Lam 5:16b). However, the questions of Lamentations 5:20 ("Why do you always forget us? Why do you forsake us so long?") and the suggestion of Lamentations 5:22 ("unless you have utterly rejected us and are angry with us beyond measure") imply that the endurance of the predicament is God's responsibility. What is missing is blame directed at the enemies, which dominates much of the earlier poems in Lamentations. The request forms a bracket around the entire poem with three imperatives for God's attention in Lamentations 5:1 ("remember . . . look . . . see") and two imperatives for God's action in Lamentations 5:21. The community longs for God to cause them to return to God in *covenant relationship, a return that has both physical and spiritual dimensions, and to renew their community's experience to the glory days of the past. The final stanza of Lamentations 5 brings the book as a whole to an awkward end, vacillating as it does back and forth between the postures of hope (Lam 5:19, 21) and frustration (Lam 5:20, 22). It is not surprising in the darkness of the exile that the book ends without acrostic style and with the declaration of frustration. As T. Linafelt has argued, "The book is left opening out into the emptiness of God's nonresponse. By leaving a conditional statement dangling, the final verse leaves open the future of the ones lamenting" (Linafelt, 60).

5. Theological Traditions and Themes.

5.1. Suffering and Redemption. Taken as a whole, these diverse poems provide theological resources for suffering and salvation (see Kaiser). The present pain is identified as a loss of rest (Lam 1:3) and inheritance (Lam 5:2), an absence of comfort (Lam 1:2, 9, 16b, 17a, 21) and especially a loss of covenant relationship with Yahweh through the loss of the religious structures that sustained this relationship (Lam 2:1, 6, 7, 9c). This pain has affected all levels of society (rich/poor, male/female, young/old), all aspects of society (physical, social, spiritual) and even ongoing generations of society (past and present).

The poems express the reason for pain in various ways. At times the frustrated voice of the poets suggest that this pain, or at least its enduring quality, is purposeless, the result of an angry God whose wrath will never be satisfied (Lam 5:20, 22). At many places it is clearly seen as discipline for sin (Lam 1:5, 8-9, 14, 18, 20; 2:14; 3:39-42), even though the amount of suffering seems to be disproportionate to the

sin of the people, pain at a level unknown to humanity (Lam 1:12; 2:20). Lamentations 3:40 suggests that there is a purifying role as the people speak of examining and testing their ways. Of course, the cause of the pain often is linked to the wiles of enemies taking advantage of the people's plight (Lam 1:21-22; 2:16; 3:52-66; 4:21-22; 5:2, 8), even if this opportunity was provided by Yahweh's legitimate judgment (Lam 1:15, 17; 2:17; 4:13).

The cause of the suffering is linked to the three classic reasons found in the biblical lament tradition: self, enemy, Yahweh. The various poems consistently identify the supplicants as responsible for their own pain due to their rebellion against God. The enemies often become the subject of the lament. Yahweh is regularly identified as playing an active role in the suffering that has been experienced, but this is carefully nuanced with the qualification that this action was justified because of the sins of the community.

The request in the various prayers is dominated by calls for Yahweh (e.g., Lam 1:11, 20; 2:20-21) or passing nations (e.g., Lam 1:12, 18, 21) to give attention to the need of the people, for God to uphold their cause (Lam 3:59), and for God to wreak vengeance on their enemies (Lam 1:22; 3:64-66; 4:21-22). At times voices describe or exhort the people or city to cry out to Yahweh (Lam 2:18, 19), to call for relief (Lam 3:55-56), to confess and *repent of their sin (Lam 3:40-42), to wait upon Yahweh by submitting to the suffering (Lam 3:19-30), even though at other times such cries are considered rejected by Yahweh (Lam 3:8). In Lamentations 5 the request becomes far more explicit and practical, calling at the outset (Lam 5:1) for Yahweh to give attention to their past circumstances and their present disgrace, and at the end (Lam 5:21) for Yahweh to restore their relationship with him and renew their life as in "days of old."

Strategies for surviving the present pain appear at various places in the poems. Key is accepting culpability for this suffering—that is, admitting one's sins and even the sins of former generations (Lam 5:7, 16) and absolving Yahweh of any wrongdoing (Lam 1:16). At a couple of places Yahweh's character is highlighted as essential for living through the pain. In Lamentations 3:19-39 the poet encourages a submissive posture toward the suffering, one demanded by the culpability of the sufferer. In this section the poet clings to the gracious character of Yahweh, and it is this that gives him hope. Additionally, it is Yahweh's sovereignty over the affairs of the world that infuses meaning into the present discipline (Lam 3:34-38). In Lamentations 5:19 the community clings to the eternal and sovereign character of Yahweh. Surviving the pain, however, will mean not just a theological reorientation but also a spiritual reorientation, one that involves crying out to God (Lam 2:18-19), a cry that ultimately involves not complaint (Lam 3:39) but rather self-examination, repentance and confession (Lam 3:40-42).

5.2. Zion, Retribution and the Character of Yahweh. One cannot miss the central role that *Zion theology plays in the book of Lamentations (see Albrektson, 219-30; Ackroyd, 46; Renkema 1998, 44-45). This theology was foundational to Judah's kingdom and thus was emphasized by royal circles and the priestly groups that the monarchy supported. The first move that David made as king of the united tribes was to shift his capital from Hebron, which lay in the heart of Judah's tribal territory, to Jerusalem, which lay on the northern border, which Judah shared with Benjamin and was a city without traditional attachment to any tribe. This shift helped David control the northern tribes, uniting the nation geographically at Jerusalem and personally in the Judahite king. The connection between the name "Zion" and Jerusalem is uncertain, but it appears that it predates David's arrival in the city, a part of which was called "the fortress of Zion" (2 Sam 5:7; 1 Chron 11:5). Another dimension of Davidic kingship also appears to be associated with the pre-Davidic Jerusalemite tradition, that of Melchizedek's priestly kingship (cf. Gen 14:18-19 with Ps 110). As various psalms reveal (Pss 2; 46; 48; 76; 84; 87; 122; 137), the Zion tradition depicted Jerusalem as the place of God's dwelling and seat of his rule over all the earth, replacing and exceeding the Canaanite seat of divine rule on Mount Zaphon. So exalted was this city that it is seen as invincible, secure from any attack of the enemy—a belief that led to an emphasis on the inviolability of Zion, lulling the people into a false confidence based on God's past choice of Jerusalem and its sanctuary. The prophets will confront this royal ideology, predicting that Zion would be de-

stroyed (Jer 26:18-19; cf. Jer 7:1-15; Mic 3:12) and its sanctuary abandoned by Yahweh (Ezek 10) because of the rebellious behavior of the people. It is understandable, then, why the Zion tradition is expressed so strongly in the book of Lamentations as the people struggle with the promises related to the city of Jerusalem and its sanctuary. In the book it is the Zion tradition that is associated with the most bitter of lament and pain.

Combined with this Zion theology, however, is a strong *retribution theology that has been informed by the Deuteronomistic and prophetic traditions and accepts that the fall of Jerusalem has been caused by the covenantal rebellion of the people against Yahweh (see Brandscheidt; Gottwald 1962, 66, 70; Albrektson, 230-37; Ackroyd, 46; Hawtrey, 78). Thus, even when the lament is most bitter, there is always an admission of the culpability of the people.

However, the greatest hope in the book is not related either to the election theology of Zion or to Deuteronomistic or prophetic retribution theology; rather, it is only with the abandonment of Zion theology in the central chapter that one is shown the way forward for the community. In place of Zion theology is the key grace tradition (Lam 3:21-33), linked especially to the ancient rehearsal of Yahweh's "name" found in Exodus 34:6-7 (cf. Num 14:18; Ps 86). This fixation on the "character creed" is followed immediately in Lamentations 3:33-39 with a theology of divine discipline closely allied with Deuteronomistic and possibly wisdom theology (see Gottwald 1962, 71-72), which reminds the people that God does not "afflict with delight" (Lam 3:33) or approve of injustice (Lam 3:34-36) but rather dispenses discipline because of sin (Lam 3:37-38). Instead of complaint (Lam 3:39), the people are encouraged to examine their ways and turn back to God and confess their sins (Lam 3:40). This solution is informed by the agenda set out in several key earlier texts (Lev 26:40-41; Deut 30:1-4; 1 Kings 8:46-51), even though these texts look to the exilic community and Lamentations looks to the community left behind in the land (see Boda 2008).

The book of Lamentations showcases the theological struggle of a people living in the wake of the greatest crisis in their history. In it we observe the intersection of several key theological streams that rose to prominence in the closing moments of the kingdom of Judah. As the central poem and conclusion to the book make clear, the theological struggle would remain unresolved in the short run.

6. Canon.

6.1. Lamentations and the Old Testament.
The Hebrew Jewish canonical traditions generally placed Lamentations among the Ketubim (Writings), the third and final section of the canonical books, as one of the five Megillot (scrolls) to be read at the major festivals (Ruth, Song of Songs, Ecclesiastes, Lamentations, Esther). In this way, Lamentations is read in terms of the enduring worship rhythms of the Jewish community in the postexilic period. In contrast, the Greek Jewish canonical traditions placed Lamentations between Jeremiah and Ezekiel—that is, among the Prophets. As noted above, this connection to Jeremiah is reflected in the preface to the book of Lamentations provided in the Greek tradition, which identifies the lament that follows as arising from Jeremiah in response to the exile of the community and destruction of Jerusalem. There is, however, internal evidence for a connection between the book of Lamentations and Jeremiah (cf. Lam 2:14 with Jer 5:31; Lam 2:22 with Jer 6:25; Lam 3:14 with Jer 20:7; Lam 3:15, 19 with Jer 9:14; 23:15; Lam 3:48-51 with Jer 14:17; Lam 3:53 with Jer 38:6; Lam 4:17 with Jer 2:36) (see Morrow, 110-11). This connection to Jeremiah, as well as to other Prophetic Books (esp. Is 40—55), has received particular attention in recent scholarship (e.g., Lee; O'Connor; Boase; Mandolfo 2007; Boda, Dempsey and Snow Flesher). The connections between Lamentations and the prophets, however, have not led to the conclusion that Jeremiah was responsible for the book of Lamentations, although Lamentations 3 appears to be the closest to the Jeremianic tradition (see Boda 2008), but rather that the book of Lamentations offers a response from the perspective of an abused Daughter of Zion to the earlier prophetic tradition that set in motion the suffering catalogued in the book of Lamentations (e.g., Jeremiah) or sought to express hope beyond the suffering (e.g., Is 40—55). In the book of Lamentations the Daughter of Zion gets to talk back to prophet and deity alike.

6.2. Lamentations and the New Testament.
Lamentations is not the final word on the Jewish community in Jerusalem. The fasts with their laments and penitential prayers at the temple site would be replaced by the renewal of the festal calendar with the reconstruction of the second temple in the late sixth century BC. But Zion would never regain the glory of the preexilic era, and the dominance of the penitential prayer tradition after the exile is testimony to the fact that the people longed for more. This longing can be discerned among that cast of faithful characters who appear in the temple courts early in the Gospel of Luke (Zechariah and Elizabeth, Simeon and Anna, Joseph and Mary) as they await the *Messiah and identify him in Jesus. This Jesus would enter into his people's suffering in a land still under foreign occupation. He would express his pain over and compassion for Jerusalem and yet predict its downfall (Lk 13:34-35). Like Lamentations 3, his message would be focused on God's gracious invitation to repentance. He would even cry out in lament to God ("My God, my God, why have you forsaken me?" [Mt 27:46; Mk 15:34]) on that hill outside of Zion as he hung dying for the sins of his people and those of the whole world. It is interesting to see how the Zion traditions are resurrected in the NT to describe the new experience of grace for the people of God in Jesus Christ, who functions in the order of Melchizedek, as these traditions are transferred to the "heavenly Jerusalem," which is both a present reality (Heb 7:1—9:28; 12:22-23) and a future hope (Rev 21) (see Fuller Dow).

See also JEREMIAH: BOOK OF; LAMENT, MOURNING; SUFFERING; ZION.

BIBLIOGRAPHY. *Commentaries*: **A. Berlin,** *Lamentations* (OTL; Louisville: Westminster/ John Knox, 2002); **D. I. Block,** *The Book of Ezekiel: Chapters 25-28* (NICOT; Grand Rapids: Eerdmans, 1998); **J. A. Dearman,** *Jeremiah and Lamentations* (NIVAC; Grand Rapids: Zondervan, 2002); **F. W. Dobbs-Allsopp,** *Lamentations* (IBC; Louisville: Westminster/John Knox, 2002); **D. R. Hillers,** *Lamentations* (2nd ed.; AB 7A; Garden City, NY: Doubleday, 1992); **P. R. House,** "Lamentations," in *Song of Songs, Lamentations,* by D. Garrett and P. R. House (WBC 23B; Dallas: Word, 2004) 267-473; **H.-J. Kraus,** *Klagelieder (Threni)* (3rd ed.; BKAT 20; Neukirchen-Vluyn: Neukirchener Verlag, 1968); **I. W. Provan,** *Lamentations* (NCBC; Grand Rapids: Eerdmans, 1991); **J. Renkema,** *Lamentations* (HCOT; Leuven: Peeters, 1998). *Studies*: **P. R. Ackroyd,** *Exile and Restoration: A Study of Hebrew Thought of the Sixth Century B.C.*

(OTL; Philadelphia: Westminster, 1968); **B. Albrektson,** *Studies in the Text and Theology of the Book of Lamentations, with a Critical Edition of the Peshitta Text* (STL 21; Lund: Gleerup, 1963); **E. Boase,** *The Fulfilment of Doom? The Dialogic Interaction between the Book of Lamentations and the Pre-Exilic/Early Exilic Prophetic Literature* (LHBOTS 437; New York: T & T Clark, 2006); **M. J. Boda,** "From Dystopia to Myopia: Utopian (Re)visions in Haggai and Zechariah 1-8," in *Utopia and Dystopia in Prophetic Literature,* ed. E. Ben Zvi (PFES 92; Helsinki: Finnish Exegetical Society; Göttingen: Vandenhoeck & Ruprecht, 2006) 211-49; idem, "The Priceless Gain of Penitence: From Communal Lament to Penitential Prayer in the 'Exilic' Liturgy of Israel," in *Lamentations in Ancient and Contemporary Contexts,* ed. N. C. Lee and C. Mandolfo (SBLSymS 43; Atlanta: Society of Biblical Literature, 2008) 81-101; idem, "'Varied and Resplendent Riches': Exploring the Breadth and Depth of Worship in the Psalter," in *Rediscovering Worship: Past, Present, Future,* ed. S. E. Porter (MNTS; Eugene, OR: Wipf & Stock, forthcoming); **M. J. Boda, C. Dempsey and L. Snow Flesher,** eds., *Daughter Zion: Her Portrait, Her Response* (SBLAIL; Atlanta: Society of Biblical Literature, 2012); **M. J. Boda and J. R. Novotny,** eds., *From the Foundations to the Crenellations: Essays on Temple Building in the Ancient Near East and Hebrew Bible* (AOAT 366; Münster: Ugarit-Verlag, 2010); **W. C. Bouzard,** *We Have Heard with Our Ears, O God: Sources of the Communal Laments in the Psalms* (SBLDS 159; Atlanta: Scholars Press, 1997); **R. Brandscheidt,** *Gotteszorn und Menschenleid: Die Gerichtsklage des leidenden Gerechten in Klgl 3* (TThSt 41; Trier: Paulinus-Verlag, 1983); **M. L. Conway,** "Daughter Zion: Metaphor and Dialogue in the Book of Lamentations," in *Daughter Zion: Her Portrait, Her Response,* ed. M. J. Boda, C. Dempsey and L. Snow Flesher (SBLAIL; Atlanta: Society of Biblical Literature, 2012); **F. Crüsemann,** *Studien zur Formgeschichte von Hymnus und Danklied in Israel* (WMANT 32; Neukirchen-Vluyn: Neukirchener Verlag, 1969); **J. A. Dearman,** "Daughter Zion and Her Place in God's Household," *HBT* 31 (2009) 144-59; **F. W. Dobbs-Allsopp,** *Weep, O Daughter of Zion: A Study of the City-Lament Genre in the Hebrew Bible* (BibOr 44; Rome: Editrice Pontificio Istituto Biblico, 1993); idem, "Tragedy, Tradition, and Theology in the Book of Lamentations," *JSOT* 74 (1997) 29-60; idem,

"Linguistic Evidence for the Date of Lamentations," *JANESCU* 26 (1998) 1-36; **P. W. Ferris,** *The Genre of Communal Lament in the Bible and the Ancient Near East* (SBLDS 127; Atlanta: Scholars Press, 1992); **M. H. Floyd,** "Welcome Back, Daughter of Zion!" *CBQ* 70 (2008) 484-504; idem, "The Daughter of Zion Goes Fishing in Heaven," in *Daughter Zion: Her Portrait, Her Response,* ed. M. J. Boda, C. Dempsey and L. Snow Flesher (SBLAIL; Atlanta: Society of Biblical Literature, 2012); **L. K. Fuller Dow,** *Images of Zion: Biblical Antecedents for the New Jerusalem* (NTM 26; Sheffield, England: Sheffield Phoenix, 2010); **R. Gordis,** *The Song of Songs and Lamentations: A Study, Modern Translation and Commentary* (rev. ed.; New York: Ktav, 1974); **N. K. Gottwald,** "Lamentations," *Int* 9 (1955) 320-38; idem, *Studies in the Book of Lamentations* (rev. ed.; SBT 14; London: SCM, 1962); **H. Gunkel,** *Einleitung in die Psalmen: Die Gattungen der religiösen Lyrik Israels* (HKAT; Göttingen: Vandenhoeck & Ruprecht, 1933); **S. B. Gurewicz,** "The Problem of Lamentations 3," *ABR* 8 (1960) 19-23; **W. C. Gwaltney Jr.,** "The Biblical Book of Lamentations in the Context of Near Eastern Lament Literature," in *Scripture in Context II: More Essays on the Comparative Method,* ed. W. W. Hallo, J. C. Moyer and L. G. Perdue (Winona Lake, IN: Eisenbrauns, 1983) 191-211; **K. Hawtrey,** "The Exile as a Crisis for Cultic Religion: Lamentations and Ezekiel," *RTR* 52 (1993) 74-83; **H. Heater,** "Structure and Meaning in Lamentations," *BSac* 149 (1992) 304-15; **K. M. Heim,** "The Personification of Jerusalem and the Drama of Her Bereavement in Lamentations," in *Zion, City of Our God,* ed. R. S. Hess and G. J. Wenham (Grand Rapids: Eerdmans, 1999) 129-69; **H. Jahnow,** *Das hebräische Leichenlied im Rahmen der Völkerdichtung* (BZAW 36; Giessen: Töpelmann, 1923); **P. Joyce,** "Lamentations and the Grief Process: A Psychological Reading," *BibInt* 1 (1993) 304-20; **W. C. Kaiser Jr.,** *A Biblical Approach to Personal Suffering* (Chicago: Moody, 1982); **S. N. Kramer,** *Lamentation over the Destruction of Ur* (AS 12; Chicago: University of Chicago Press, 1940); **W. F. Lanahan,** "The Speaking Voice in the Book of Lamentations," *JBL* 93 (1974) 41-49; **N. C. Lee,** *The Singers of Lamentations: Communities under Siege, from Ur to Jerusalem to Sarajevo* (BIS 60; Leiden: E. J. Brill, 2002); **T. Linafelt,** *Surviving Lamentations: Catastrophe, Lament, and Protest in the Afterlife of a*

Biblical Book (Chicago: University of Chicago Press, 2000); **C. Mandolfo,** *God in the Dock: Dialogic Tension in the Psalms of Lament* (JSOTSup 357; London: Sheffield Academic, 2002); idem, *Daughter Zion Talks Back to the Prophets: A Dialogic Theology of the Book of Lamentations* (SBLSS 58; Atlanta: Society of Biblical Literature, 2007); **C. W. Miller,** "Reading Voices: Personification, Dialogism, and the Reader of Lamentations 1," *BibInt* 9 (2001) 393–408; idem, "The Book of Lamentations in Recent Research," *CBR* 1 (2002) 9-29; **M. S. Moore,** "Human Suffering in Lamentations," *RB* 90 (1983) 534-55; **W. S. Morrow,** *Protest against God: The Eclipse of a Biblical Tradition* (HBM 4; Sheffield: Sheffield Phoenix, 2006); **K. M. O'Connor,** *Lamentations and the Tears of the World* (Maryknoll, NY: Orbis, 2002); **I. W. Provan,** "Reading Texts against an Historical Background: The Case of Lamentations 1," *SJOT* 1 (1990) 130-43; **D. J. Reimer,** "Good Grief? A Psychological Reading of Lamentations," *ZAW* 114 (2002) 542-59; **J. Renkema,** "The Literary Structure of Lamentations (I-IV)," in *The Structural Analysis of Biblical and Canaanite Poetry,* ed. W. van der Meer and J. C. de Moor (JSOTSup 74; Sheffield: JSOT, 1988) 294-396; **J. Wellhausen,** *Prolegomena zur Geschichte Israels* (6th ed.; Berlin: Reimer, 1905); C. **Westermann,** *Lamentations: Issues and Interpretation* (Minneapolis: Fortress, 1994).

M. J. Boda

LAND

The theological importance of land in the Prophets, as in the rest of the OT, cannot be overemphasized. However, it is difficult to generalize across the prophetic tradition because variations of emphasis can be detected, reflecting different authorial and editorial perspectives and changing historical contexts. The preexilic and exilic prophets are most clearly concerned with the land of Israel and the events leading up to the *exile and hoped-for restoration. The postexilic prophets, although writing from a perspective after the exiles' return to their land, have different concerns and preoccupations. Of all the prophets, Jeremiah is most vocal on the subject of land, whether physical, political or theological, for which reason he is described as "the poet of the land par excellence" (Brueggemann, 101).

1. Words and Meanings
2. Politics, Geography, Economics and Ecology
3. Theological Themes

1. Words and Meanings.

Two Hebrew words are used to denote "land" in the biblical prophets, *'ereṣ* and *'ădāmâ*. Of these, by far the most frequent is *'ereṣ*, which is found over nine hundred times compared with only seventy-five uses of *'ădāmâ*. The range of meanings for both *'ereṣ* and *'ădāmâ*, though very wide, falls broadly into three overlapping categories: (1) denoting the whole earth or world (in the case of *'ereṣ* sometimes paired with "the heavens" [e.g., Is 1:2]); (2) describing a land mass, whether territory in general or a particular land or country, in the latter case often with its name (e.g., "land of Egypt" [Jer 44:12]) or a possessive pronoun (e.g., "your land" [Is 2:7]); (3) referring to the soil or to land as a portion of ground (e.g., Amos 2:7). The meaning (and thus translation) of the Hebrew usually can be determined by the characteristics noted above and by the context, but there are numerous instances of ambiguity. The fluidity in the terms and their referents undoubtedly reflects the narrower geographical horizons of the ancient world and the much closer overlap in biblical thought between ideas of cosmic space and territory. This article focuses on the range of meanings in the second and third categories listed above. Across the Prophetic Books both *'ereṣ* and *'ădāmâ* are most often used within the second category—that is, to denote land or territory, whether general or specific. More than six hundred occurrences of *'ereṣ* and fifty of *'ădāmâ* fall into this category.

2. Politics, Geography, Economics and Ecology.

Land in any time period or place has enormous importance for a range of complex and often interlinked reasons. Both local and national landscapes have economic, political, environmental and cultural significance, as well as physical characteristics. All these issues feature in the writings of the biblical prophets, who are aware of the social, environmental and military importance of land as well as its theological potential.

2.1. Politics. Political negotiation and military struggles over land form an important part of the history of Israel and Judah, and many of the prophets deal directly or indirectly with matters of diplomacy and *warfare. The three main clusters of prophetic activity represented by the Prophetic Books center on key political events concerning the overpowering, loss and restoration of the promised land (see 3 below): (1) the eighth-century BC threat from Assyria and last stages of the northern kingdom, Israel, culminating in its destruction in 722 BC (Hosea, Amos, First Isaiah, Micah); (2) the Babylonian invasion and conquest of the southern kingdom, Judah, in 587 BC and the exile in Babylon (Jeremiah, Ezekiel, Obadiah, Habakkuk, Zephaniah, Second Isaiah); (3) the return from exile and rebuilding of Judah and Jerusalem from the late sixth century BC onwards (Third Isaiah, Haggai, Zechariah, Malachi) (*see* Israelite History). Three books fall outside this categorization: Joel lacks any historical markers that locate it in a particular time frame, although it graphically depicts the turmoil of warfare and an invading army; Nahum comprises a judgment oracle against the Babylonian city Nineveh; Jonah is a story about the *repentance of that same city.

The preexilic and exilic prophets highlight the inextricable link between Israel's and Judah's faithful obedience to God and the political security of their land, and this theme is explored by N. Habel in his analysis of land ideology in the book of Jeremiah (Habel). Military defeat and exile are held up as the consequence of rebellion against the Lord (Is 1:19-20; Jer 25:7-9; Ezek 12:2-3), and conquering armies and rulers are regarded as acting at the behest of the Lord (Is 5:26-30; Jer 5:15-17; 25:8-9; Amos 6:14; Hab 1:6). Conversely, the conquest of Babylon by the Persian emperor Cyrus, which paves the way for the return of the exiles to Judah, is also seen as God's action (Is 45:1-3). Attempts by individual prophets to shape political and military policy take the form of direct confrontations with the king (Is 7:1-17; 37:5-13; Jer 37:17-21) and of oracles warning against forming alliances with the surrounding *nations instead of trusting in the Lord's power and care (Is 30:1-3; Jer 2:17-18; Ezek 17:15-21; Hos 7:11-12; 12:1).

2.2. Geography. The prophets demonstrate considerable awareness of geographical and topographical features of the land, both of Israel itself and of its neighbors. The location of surrounding nations is identified (sometimes inaccurately) according to points of the compass (Is 9:11-12; Mic 7:12). Knowledge of particular geophysical events, such as the annual inundation of the Nile floodplains upon which Egyptian agriculture depended, is used to graphic effect (Is 19:5-10; Amos 8:8; 9:5). *Mountains and valleys, rivers and deserts (*see* Wilderness, Desert) form part of the prophetic vocabulary, and the prophets clearly are keen observers of their surroundings. Many references to such features, although undoubtedly informed by their geophysical characteristics, take the form of stylized and/or metaphorical descriptions—for example, the mountain of the Lord (Is 2:2-4; Mic 4:1-3; Zech 8:3), natural elements accompanying divine theophany (Hab 3:8-10), and disaster coming "from the north" in Jeremiah (Jer 1:14-15, and a further sixteen times; see also Ezek 23:24).

2.3. Economics. The political significance of land is matched by its importance as a natural resource, with key crops such as grapes and olives being valuable export commodities in ancient Israel. The importance of vines and viticulture in prophetic material, especially Isaiah (e.g., Is 5:1-7; 27:2-5), can be accounted for by the ease of cultivating vineyards in the soil conditions and topography of the hill slopes of Israel, in contrast to the salinated floodplains of the Mesopotamian and Nile Deltas. This makes the production of grapes and wine in the land of Israel a potentially lucrative source of income and may account for the Babylonians permitting the resumption of agriculture in Judah under Gedaliah the governor (Jer 40:9-12). The prophets demonstrate knowledge of agricultural practice in their oracles (Is 17:6; 24:13; Ezek 17:5-8) and awareness of the need for wisdom in farming methods (Is 28:23-29). The distinction, and sometimes conflict, between agricultural and pastoral concerns is well represented, with the outcome of political defeat being depicted as the incursion of cattle and sheep into cities and their agricultural hinterlands (Is 7:23-25; 32:14).

2.4. Ecology. The prophets show great awareness of, and concern for, the interconnection between human populations and their environments (Marlow 2009). This connection is part of a three-way relationship, between God, the people and the land. When God is honored and obeyed, the land flourishes, as do its inhabitants. When God is put to one side, the land is desolate and unfruitful. The close interdependence between people and environment that informs prophetic oracles is partly a result of the economic and practical factors mentioned above; the prophets themselves, as much as their audiences, depend on the land for survival. The climatic conditions of ancient Israel, whereby short wet winters are followed by exceptionally hot and dry summers, make for a precarious existence for human beings and livestock, and drought is an ever-present fear (Jer 14:1-6). Conversely, a raging torrent over hard, sun-baked soil results in flash flooding that can destroy crops and livestock in a moment (Is 28:2; Jer 47:2).

Prophetic concern with the relationship between people and landscape also reflects the prophets' keen observation of their surroundings as they draw on the natural world for a rich range of metaphors and similes. This is particularly true of Hosea, who "clothes the thoughts of each succeeding sentence in new imagery" (Wolff 1974, xxiv) (see, e.g., Hos 11:10-11). Wild *animals such as the lions and bears that roamed the ancient Near East represent both a literal threat to human beings (Jer 5:6; Amos 3:4, 8) and a graphic metaphorical picture of judgment (Jer 49:19; Amos 5:18-19). Warfare and enemy invasion have an immediate and catastrophic effect on the land. The destruction of habitation and the depopulation of human settlements are followed, as one might expect, by the colonization of ruined buildings by a variety of wild animals (Is 13:20-22; 34:13-15). Although undoubtedly devastating for the human populations concerned, it is part of the creatures' God-given right of possession and happens at his volition (Is 34:16-17). The natural scavenging instinct of creatures such as vultures and jackals, with which the prophets were familiar, undoubtedly informs oracles that describe the destruction of a nation by means of "the birds of the air and the wild animals of the land" (Jer 15:3 [cf. Ezek 39:4]). The destroying power of a plague of locusts paints a graphic picture of a forthcoming, yet unspecified, enemy invasion (Joel 1:4-7; 2:2-5).

The political, economic and ecological importance of land is explored by E. Davis in her agrarian reading of the OT in dialogue with contemporary agrarian authors such as W. Berry. She discusses the warnings of preexilic prophets such as Amos against the aggressive and acquisitive centralized agrarian policies of his day and draws comparison with today's tendency to value economic growth at the expense of land care that she sees demonstrated in much contemporary large-scale agribusiness.

3. Theological Themes.

W. Brueggemann's description of the ancient Israelite story as land gift, land possession and land loss provides a helpful framework for exploring land theology in the prophets (Brueggemann, xvii). To this may be added land restoration as a key concern, even if one that is rather ambiguous and elusive, and the notion of the land mourning and rejoicing as a powerful and significant theological theme.

3.1. Land Gift. The notion of land as a gift from God is expressed in a variety of forms. The prophets frequently refer back to Israel's historical traditions to remind the people of God's gracious dealings with them in the past, to call them to account for their current behavior, and to offer hope based on collective memories. Although Abraham, Isaac and Jacob rarely are mentioned by name in connection with land in the prophets, the prose sections of Jeremiah record over fifteen times that the land was given by God to the ancestors (e.g., Jer 7:7; 11:4; 24:10), as does Ezekiel (20:42, and a further three times). Closely associated with this is the concept of the land as the Lord's most beautiful inheritance or heritage (naḥălâ) (Jer 3:18-19), which the children of Israel have defiled (Jer 2:7; 16:18), and which they will forfeit on account of their actions (Jer 17:4). Ezekiel's *temple vision speaks of the restoration of that inheritance (Ezek 47:13-14; 48:29; see also Zech 2:12). A separate strand in the prophets emphasizes the Lord's deliverance of Israel from the land of Egypt, the land of their captivity. This historical recollection forms part of the prophetic repertoire when passing judgment (Amos 3:1-2) or calling for repentance (Hos 13:4; Mic 6:4), in laments over the present wickedness of the exiles (Ezek 20:5-10) and in confessions of sin (Dan 9:15).

3.2. Land Possession. In general terms, Isaiah, Jeremiah and Ezekiel use the expression "the land of the living" to denote being alive, in contrast to being consigned to the underworld, or Sheol (Is 38:11; Jer 11:19; Ezek 26:20). More specifically, Israel's dwelling in the land is depicted metaphorically by the prophets as being planted by the Lord as a choice vine (Is 5:1-7; Jer 2:21; Ezek 17; see also Hos 9:13), but which has incurred his wrath (Jer 11:16-17) and will be uprooted from the land in which it were planted (Jer 12:14-17; 45:4; see also Jer 1:10). The return from exile is depicted in similar vein as a replanting of Israel by the Lord (Is 60:21; Jer 24:6; Amos 9:15).

The land itself is described as beautiful (ṣĕbî [Jer 3:19; Ezek 20:6, 15; Dan 11:16]), pleasant, (ḥemed [Jer 3:19; see also Is 27:2]) and glorious (kābôd [Is 10:18; Ezek 20:6, 15]). It is a land flowing with milk and honey (Jer 11:5; 32:22), likened to the garden of Eden (Joel 2:3), and one in which a variety of plants and animals abound (see 4 below). The land is implicitly viewed as holy, by association with the holiness of Mount Zion (Is 57:13; Jer 31:23; Ezek 20:40). The presence of the glory of the Lord that Isaiah encounters in his temple vision fills the whole land (Is 6:1-3), and its human inhabitants unsuccessfully look to the land to conceal them from his presence (Is 2:10-21; cf. Amos 9:3).

3.3. Land Loss. The preexilic and exilic prophets are clear that Israel's right to remain in the land is dependent upon their faithfulness to the Lord (Is 1:19), and the impending military defeat and exile are attributed to a number of specific factors, including unfaithfulness to God, neglect of *social justice, and hypocrisy. Hosea uses a carefully constructed metaphor in which marital fidelity and the welfare of the land are combined to condemn the northern kingdom, Israel, for worshiping Canaanite gods (Hos 2:1-13) (see Marlow 2009, 166-72), a theme picked up by Jeremiah some 150 years later (Jer 2:2-3; 3:1-5). The outcome will be a return to the instability and precarious existence of their previous lives before settlement in the promised land (Hos 12:12) or being scattered among the nations as God turns his back on them (Jer 18:15-17). The land is described as polluted or defiled by the sins of its inhabitants, who have ignored God's *laws and statutes (Is 24:5), pursued other gods (Jer 2:23-24; 3:2, 9) and set up idols (Jer 16:18; Ezek 36:18).

Amos, First Isaiah and Micah speak out against the hypocrisy of devout religious observance while the basic, God-given principles of *justice and righteousness are being ignored (Is 1:12-17; Amos 5:21-24; 8:4-7; Mic 6:6-12). Such exploitation of the poor by the complacent and decadent elite in society provokes the prophets' condemnation (Is 3:13-15) and results in God's judgment on the people and their exile from the land (Is 5:11-14; Amos 6:4-7). This judgment on the sin of the inhabitants has physical consequences for the land itself, including the loss of fertility (Is 5:7-10; Mic 6:13-15), *destruction by flood and earthquake (Amos 5:6-9; 8:7-10) and desertification and drought (Jer 9:10-12) (see Marlow 2010, 106-13).

It is a misconception that following the exile to Babylon the land of Judah was completely destroyed and depopulated. Despite prophetic hyperbole such as Jeremiah 13:19 and descriptions of the exile that suggest that only some of the poorest were left behind (2 Kings 25:8-12), both biblical (Jer 40:9-12) and extrabiblical (see Middlemas) evidence supports the view that the land continued to be inhabited and farmed. Significant theological themes in Second Isaiah such as Zion-Jerusalem (Is 52:1-3, 7-10) may refer to the inhabitants of "templeless" Judah rather than the Babylonian exilic community as commonly assumed (Tiemeyer). The presence of a continuing population in Judah also accounts for some of the hostility experienced by those returning from exile (Ezra 4:1-6).

3.4. Land Restoration. The return from exile and restoration of the land are hinted at by some of the prophets and are the focus of extensive visionary descriptions in others. Although the oracles of salvation in preexilic prophets such as Amos (Amos 9:11-15) and Hosea (Hos 2:18-23) may reflect a later editor's desire to moderate the harsh and unequivocal judgement oracles of earlier prophets, the view of source critics that these must necessarily be postexilic additions is unsatisfactory and takes no account of the allusive and unspecific content of these texts. The hope and optimism that characterize these exilic messages of deliverance and restoration often are without specific historical marker, a notable exception being Second Isaiah's description of the Persian king Cyrus as the one anointed by the Lord to deliver Israel (Is 45:1-4).

A number of powerful images and ideas are evoked as the prophets announce *salvation and the end of exile. It is couched as the renewal of Israel's *marriage to the Lord (Is 54:5;

Hos 2:16-17), a new *covenant (Jer 31:31-34; Ezek 34:25-31; 37:26; Hos 2:18) and restoration of the Davidic throne (Jer 33:14-22; Ezek 34:23-24; Amos 9:11-12). The three-way interconnection noted above (see 2.4) can be seen in the fact that, for the prophets, renewal of the relationship between God and his people also involves the well-being of the land, not just its political significance. As well as the Lord comforting his people (Is 40:1-2; 49:13) and forgiving them (Is 4:4; Jer 33:8; Ezek 36:23-28), the land itself will be restored to its former fertility (Ezek 36:29-30; Hos 2:21-22). Renewal of the land is couched in exaggerated language as "dripping with sweet wine" (Joel 3:18; Amos 9:13) and a return to its Eden-like state (Ezek 36:34-36). In the prophet Isaiah's vision of a future idyllic existence the relationships between human beings and wild animals will be harmonious instead of hostile (Is 11:6-9; 65:25). By far the most extensive picture of restoration from exile is Ezekiel's vision of the restored temple (Ezek 40—44), which encompasses not only the temple itself and its ritual practices but also an idyllic picture of the flourishing and healing of the land (Ezek 47:7-12).

3.5. Land Mourning and Rejoicing. The land fails or flourishes according to the sins of the people that live in it. This is depicted in graphic terms as the sorrow and delight of the natural world at the breaking and re-forming of the relationship between God and his people (*see* Lament, Mourning). The prophets make good use of the ambiguous meaning of the Hebrew root ʾābal ("to mourn, dry up") (see Hayes) to depict the land in personal terms, mourning and desolate as a result of Israel's sinfulness (Jer 12:4, 11; 23:10; Joel 1:10). The sequence of cause and effect is particularly clear in Hosea 4, in which the inhabitants of the land (i.e., Israel) have neglected God's laws (Hos 4:1). This results not only in the breakdown of human society, in which stealing, adultery and murder become rife (Hos 4:2), but also in the mourning and desolation of the physical land and its inhabitants, both human and animal (Hos 4:3). This prophetic insistence that human sinfulness has consequences for the natural world is particularly pertinent in the light of the serious environmental issues facing the world today (Marlow 2008).

The land is also able to praise God alongside its human inhabitants. Isaiah's depiction of restoration of the land includes the rejoicing and blossoming of the desert alongside the salvation and healing of Israel (Is 35:1-2; see also Joel 2:21). The impending return from exile is a reason for all to sing a "new song" of praise to the Lord—land and sea, mountains and forests, town and desert (Is 42:10-11; 44:23; see also Is 51:3). The message of hope that the prophets present is grounded in their view of the land as a good gift from the Lord that has been destroyed because of human disobedience to God but that will be walked upon again with joy.

See also ANIMAL IMAGERY; COSMOLOGY; CREATION THEOLOGY; EXILE; EXODUS IMAGERY; FLORAL IMAGERY; MOUNTAIN IMAGERY; WILDERNESS, DESERT.

BIBLIOGRAPHY. **W. Brueggemann,** *The Land: Place as Gift, Promise, and Challenge in Biblical Faith* (Minneapolis: Fortress, 2002); **E. Davis,** *Scripture, Culture, and Agriculture: An Agrarian Reading of the Bible* (Cambridge: Cambridge University Press, 2009); **N. Habel,** *The Land Is Mine: Six Biblical Land Ideologies* (OBT; Minneapolis: Fortress, 1995); **K. M. Hayes,** *The Earth Mourns: Prophetic Metaphor and Oral Aesthetic* (SBLAB 8; Atlanta: Society of Biblical Literature, 2002); **H. Marlow,** *The Earth Is the Lord's: A Biblical Response to Environmental Issues* (Cambridge: Grove Books, 2008); idem, *Biblical Prophets and Contemporary Environmental Ethics: Re-reading Amos, Hosea and First Isaiah* (Oxford: Oxford University Press, 2009); idem, "Justice for Whom? Social and Environmental Ethics and the Hebrew Prophets," in *Ethical and Unethical in the Old Testament: God and Humans in Dialogue,* ed. K. J. Dell (LHBOTS 528; London: T & T Clark, 2010) 103-21; **J. Middlemas,** *The Troubles of Templeless Judah* (OTM; Oxford: Oxford University Press, 2005); **L.-S. Tiemeyer,** *For the Comfort of Zion: The Geographical and Theological Location of Isaiah 40-55* (VTSup 139; Leiden: E. J. Brill, 2011); **H. W. Wolff,** *Hosea: A Commentary on the Book of the Prophet Hosea,* trans. G. Stansell, ed. P. D. Hanson (Hermeneia; Philadelphia: Fortress, 1974).

H. F. Marlow

LATE PERSIAN PERIOD. *See* ISRAELITE HISTORY.

LAW

The great medieval Jewish philosopher Maimonides insightfully highlighted an important aspect of divine law that is central to the messages of the biblical prophets: at its heart, law is teleologically oriented. That is, God gives laws so that people might be wise, theologically and generally, and so that humanity might flourish and prosper (Novak, 92-121). The prophets encouraged Israel to live in accordance with God's instructions, and they brought messages of judgment when these standards were not met. The prophets appealed to many different sources to discern divine law: human moral consensus, Deuteronomistic traditions, oracles and visions, and, very occasionally, Sinai. Surprisingly, the prophets very rarely appeal to Sinai in order to highlight Israel's breach of law. This article provides a summary of the prophets' engagement with law as well as the relationship of the legal corpus in the Pentateuch to the Prophetic Books. Then, a prophetic theology of law is given that attempts to take into account the way in which the prophets viewed and rhetorically employed law.

1. Law in the Prophets
2. Relationship of the Pentateuch and the Prophets
3. A Prophetic Theology of Law

1. Law in the Prophets.

This section summarizes the ways in which the prophets viewed and integrated law into their messages. There are several words that can refer to legal documents, traditions or concepts: *tôrâ* ("law, instruction,"), *ḥuqqâ* ("stipulation"), *ʿēdût* ("testimony"), *mišpaṭ* ("judgment") and *dāʿat* ("knowledge").

1.1. Law in Isaiah. The book of Isaiah opens with the prophet denouncing economic and social oppression (Rendtorff, 170). The leaders of the nation traded justice for a bribe and exploited the most vulnerable members of society (Is 1:17, 23). Within this warning the leaders are encouraged to "listen to Yahweh's message [*dĕbar-yhwh*]" and to "give ear to our God's instruction [*tôrat ʾĕlōhênû*]" (Is 1:10). Although Isaiah describes his teaching as *tôrâ*, T. Lescow believes that he did not mean to equate his message with previously received Torah; rather, Isaiah employed this term for polemical effect (Lescow, 372-73). Since "our God's instruction" is parallel to "Yahweh's message," it likely refers to the contemporary message of the prophet rather than previously revealed Scripture.

Tôrâ also appears in the book's second mes-

sage (*dābār*). The prophet describes a future day in which the *temple of Yahweh will reach global prominence (Is 2:2). The Gentile nations will stream to it in order to learn (*yrh*) from *tôrâ* how to live in peace (Is 2:3). While the Jerusalem temple is pictured as the storehouse for *tôrâ*, as individuals learn from and internalize it, *tôrâ* flows out from *Zion (*miṣṣîôn tēṣēʾ tôrâ*) when they go back to their homelands (Is 2:3). At this time, disputes will be settled amicably, and instead of preparing for war, people will devote their energies to agricultural production (Is 2:4). *Tôrâ* not only teaches people outwardly but also seemingly transforms them into a new kind of humanity that pursues a godly way of life instead of the path of violence and oppression (Is 2:5). M. A. Sweeney outlines traditional views that see a parallel between *tôrâ* in this passage and that in the Pentateuch (Sweeney, 50-52). Just as the law was given on Mount Sinai in the first exodus, so in the return from Babylon *tôrâ* will proceed from Mount Zion (for application of this to Is 1:10 as well, see Fischer, 24-36). While this is a valuable observation from a canonical perspective, it should be noted that there is no explicit mention of the exodus or Sinai traditions in the Isaiah passages themselves.

Isaiah faced opposition in his day, and he encouraged his disciples to carry on his teaching, "Bind up teaching [*tĕʿûdâ*], seal instruction [*tôrâ*] among my students" (Is 8:16). He said that a time would come when people will seek instruction not from the prophets but instead from ancestral gods and the dead (Is 8:19). Yet, disciples who previously received *tôrâ* from Isaiah would remember that this had been foretold and take comfort in the fact that people who seek wisdom from unauthorized sources "will have no dawn" (Is 8:20 NRSV). This passage may imply that both oral and written dimensions were involved in the prophetic educational process (Carr, 143-44). Therefore, *tôrâ* was not merely something to "give an ear to" (Is 1:10) but also to write down and preserve.

Isaiah 24:5 contains a similar theme as Isaiah 5. The verses leading up to Isaiah 24:5 describe God as "about to empty the earth, devastate her, and turn her face into a heap of rubble" (Is 24:1). No one will be spared from this judgment—from priest to layperson, owner to slave, creditor to debtor (Is 24:2). The inhabitants of the earth have "transgressed instructions [*tôrōt*], overturned prescriptions [*ḥōq*], broken the eternal covenant" (Is 24:5). This is the only time in the MT of Isaiah in which *tôrâ* appears in the plural; however, the Greek tradition translates this as a singular. In any case, since *tôrōt* and the terms of the covenant have been breached, the earth will be consumed by a curse [*ʾālâ*]" (Is 24:6) (*see* Blessings and Curses).

While the book of Isaiah, along with most other OT texts, presents *tôrâ* as a divine gift to Israel, it does not picture *tôrâ* as Israel's exclusive possession. Instead, one way in which Yahweh intended for the knowledge of God's upright character (*ṣedeq*) to spread was by expanding and making more prominent *tôrâ* among the *nations (Is 42:21; the LXX has *ainesis* ["praise"] in place of *tôrâ*, likely the result of confusing the similarly shaped letters ד in *tôdâ* ["praise"] and ר in *tôrâ*). Yahweh desired Israel to accomplish this through obedience and adherence to divine law, but instead they were unwilling to walk in God's ways (Is 42:24). God therefore handed the people over to looters and foreign captors, which temporarily stunted the spread of *tôrâ* (Is 42:22-24). The clearest passage within the Isaianic corpus that reflects these concepts is Isaiah 51:4: "Pay attention to me, my people! My nation, give ear to me! For *tôrâ* will go out from me, my decision will be a light for peoples." Some argue that Mosaic *tôrâ* is in view here (e.g., Koenig, 356-57), but the imagery of light used in connection with correction/instruction was quite common throughout the ancient world because many cultures regarded the sun-god Shamash as the god of justice (Smith), and ancient readers likely would have understand the use of this imagery in Isaiah as a similarly broad trope.

In fact, nowhere in the book of Isaiah is *tôrâ* directly linked to Sinai or the Pentateuch in particular (nonetheless, R. E. Clements maintains that all of First Isaiah's uses of *tôrâ* refer to the inchoate "law-book of Moses" [Clements 2007, 70]). Reflecting upon all of the uses of *tôrâ* within Isaiah, Sweeney defines *tôrâ* as "the teaching of YHWH, expressed by the prophet, which stands as the norm for proper conduct by both Israel and the nations, and which stands as the norm for order in the created world" (Sweeney, 63). Accordingly, we should view Isaianic law as having a universal rather than particular scope and application. In some ways, this is similar to the perspectives seen in other

ancient Near Eastern texts, as in the Akkadian "Shamash Hymn," in which the sun-god is described as watching everything that happens and concomitantly is all-wise. In response to this belief the hymn proclaims, "The whole of mankind bows to you, / Shamash, the universe longs for your light" (Lambert, 128-29). Yet, for the Israelite prophets, Yahweh takes on the attributes and functions that the Mesopotamians ascribe to Shamash.

The biblical writers approached law more broadly than is typically the case within the Anglo-Saxon legal tradition (Renz, 77). For instance, the first oracle of what is commonly referred to as Deutero-Isaiah recounts God's greatness in creating the world. Isaiah 40:14 asks the rhetorical question "Whom did he consult, and who showed him discernment, and who taught him in the laws of nature [*ʾōraḥ mišpāṭ*] and taught him knowledge [*daʿat*] and made known to him the way of discernment [*derek tĕbûnôt*]?" This passage refers not to forensic legal stipulations but rather to the patterns and formations of the universe.

1.2. Law in Jeremiah. In Jeremiah 2 the prophet delivers an oracle against Israel in which Yahweh accuses the people of God of unfaithfulness. He recounts God's saving acts in bringing the people up out of Egypt and into the land. However, the leaders spurned God, and the prophet outlines the infidelity of three groups in particular along with their offense: the priests (the "graspers of the law" [*tōpĕśê hattôrâ*]) did not actually know (*ydʿ*) God, the civil leaders (*rōʿîm*) rebelled against God, and the prophets prophesied for Baal (Jer 2:8). It is noteworthy that the priests are criticized not for having failed to read or remember *tôrâ* but rather for not knowing God. It seems that even the OT, or at least this prophet, saw *tôrâ* as living and active and not merely as dead letters. In other words, since the priests did not know God, who, as we saw in the discussion of Isaiah, was the very source of *tôrâ*, they had no hope of knowing God's instruction even though they grasped it in their hands. In a slightly different triad later in the book, the people maintain that Jeremiah's public voice must be silenced, and that doing so will have no effect on national leadership, for "*tôrâ* will not disappear from a priest, nor council from a sage, nor a message from a prophet" (Jer 18:18). Again, *tôrâ* is seen as being within the purview of the priestly caste.

In contrast to Jeremiah 2; 18, which seem to imply that the priests were mere preservers of *tôrâ*, Jeremiah 8:8 indicates that *tôrâ* was intentionally manipulated by (priestly?) scribes (*sōpĕrîm*): "How can you say, 'We are wise' and 'Yahweh's Torah is with us'? In actuality, the lying stylus of scribes fashions it into a lie." According to T. E. Fretheim, the scribes are not accused of rewriting *tôrâ* and destroying the previous versions; rather, it is their interpretation of the law that is at issue. Specifically, the scribes promulgate the message of "peace" and complacency alongside the (false) prophets. Fretheim ably describes this situation: "Their 'soft' use of the law never convicts anyone, never moves people to ask, 'What have I done?' (v. 6). They find ways of using the law to conceal the real problem rather than to reveal it" (Fretheim 2002, 150). On the other hand, J. W. Rogerson believes that "the most natural sense of the passage is that those who claim to be wise, perhaps to belong to a class of learned interpreters, are mistaken, because that on which they base their interpretations is flawed. . . . The wise men may not be aware of this, in which case the insidious effects of the corruption are even worse" (Rogerson, 114).

The scribes were supposed to preserve *tôrâ* because it contained the words (Jer 6:19) and even the voice (Jer 9:13; 32:23) of God, and it was given to guide the way of life of God's people (Jer 26:4; 44:10). The prophet compares the apostasy of his own day to that of their ancestors as they failed to keep *tôrâ* and instead followed after other gods. Yet, the contemporary stubbornness of heart is more egregious than the sins of previous generations (Jer 16:11-12). In line with Deuteronomic theology, since the people have rejected the teachings and commands of God, they will be expelled from the land (Jer 16:13; 44:23). However, this period of judgment will not last forever; there will be a day when God will restore the people, just as they were previously brought up from Egypt (Jer 16:14-15). At this time Yahweh will make a covenant with the "house of Israel" in which he will place (*ntn*) his *tôrâ* inside them (*bĕqirbām*) and inscribe (*ktb*) it upon their heart ('*al-libbām*) (Jer 31:33). Theoretically, according to Deuteronomy 6:5, this should already have been the case, yet Jeremiah seems to have thought that more work was necessary.

Jeremiah 44:23 is another text conveying Deuteronomic theology, and it is the only place where the word '*ēdût* ("testimony") appears in the prophets, although it is fairly frequently used elsewhere: "Because you burned incense and sinned against Yahweh and did not obey Yahweh, and because you did not follow his teaching [*tōrātô*], his stipulations [*ḥuqqōtāyw*], and his exhortations ['*ēdĕwōtāyw*], therefore this disaster has befallen you, as is still the case."

1.3. Law in Ezekiel. As with other prophets, Ezekiel employs a three-part trope (Greenberg, 156) differentiating the various mediums of divine revelation to the appropriate offices: visions belong to prophets, *tôrâ* belongs to priests and wisdom belongs to elders (Ezek 7:26). In this account God will enact judgment upon the people by removing all three types of revelation from their midst. In Ezekiel 22:26 the prophet describes the behavior of the priests as "criminally violating my *tôrâ*" (*ḥāmĕsû tôrātî*) and subsequently lists what this entailed: profaning holy things, not maintaining the difference between impurity and purity, and not teaching (*hôdî'û*) about the Sabbaths. Ezekiel 43:12; 44:5 use *tôrâ* to designate the architectural designs, maintenance and procedures governing the Jerusalem temple. One of the violations of this law that Ezekiel highlights is that foreigners are brought into the temple and, even more, the priests have outsourced the care of holy objects to them (Ezek 44:5-9) (see Zimmerli, 448, 453-55). Toward the end of this chapter the prophet says that the day is coming when the Zadokite priests will properly keep these regulations, in particular, the Sabbaths and festivals (*mô'ădîm*) (Ezek 44:24).

In Ezekiel 20:11 God says that after the Israelites were brought out of Egypt and into the wilderness, "I gave to them my statutes [*ḥuqqôtay*] and made known to them my regulations [*mišpāṭay*] which humanity should do and live by." Ezekiel 20:12 specifies the Sabbath as a sign that would remind the people that Yahweh was the one who consecrated (*qdš*) them. Many commentators assume that Ezekiel refers here to the tradition relating the giving of the law at Sinai (e.g., Fishbane, 138), and while this is likely the case, we should note in passing that there is no explicit mention of Moses, Sinai or the Decalogue. Ezekiel also contains an extensive section commonly known as the Temple Vision (Ezek 40:1—48:35), in which he gives detailed instructions regarding the restoration of the building and activities of the Jerusalem temple. Yet, the details that Ezekiel gives, including terminology, furnishings, offerings for the first month, liturgical calendar, Levitical territory and laws of inheritance, differ in many respects from pentateuchal stipulations (Blenkinsopp 1990, 195). These differences were thought to be so significant that at times the canonicity of Ezekiel was somewhat in doubt (*b. Šabb.* 13b), and they have prompted a contemporary commentator to observe, "These and other differences challenge the fundamental prophetic law of noncontradiction; true prophecy must agree with Mosaic revelation (Deut. 18:15-18)" (Block, 500).

1.4. Law in the Twelve. Hosea proclaims that God was so frustrated with Israel as to bring a legal dispute against them: "Listen to the message of Yahweh, O Israelites, for Yahweh has a lawsuit [*rîb*] against the inhabitants of the land because there is no faithfulness or loyalty or knowledge [*daʿat*] of God in the land" (Hos 4:1). The prophet also condemns the dishonest nature of society: "So they conclude agreements and make covenants with false oaths, and justice [*mišpāṭ*] degenerates into poison weeds, breaking out on the furrows of the fields" (Hos 10:4 njps). Similarly, Amos addresses Israel as those who "turn justice [*mišpāṭ*] into wormwood and discard righteousness [*ṣĕdāqâ*] to the ground" because they extract onerous payments from the poor and they take bribes at the expense of justice for the needy (Amos 5:7).

Habbakuk opens with an observation that the efficacy of *tôrâ* is blunted (*pwg*) when people commit violent acts and corrupt justice (Hab 1:4). By implication, *tôrâ* is powerful only when people comply with it. Zephaniah announces the judgment of God against the people because of a catalog of sins that includes priests who do violence (*hms*) to *tôrâ* because they profane what is holy (Zeph 3:4). Haggai also centers his use of *tôrâ* upon purity laws (Hag 2:11) and uses the analogy of food becoming unclean when it touches profane provisions to describe the nation as unclean because they have not finished rebuilding the temple (Hag 2:10-19).

Zechariah 5:1-4 recounts the prophet's vision in which he saw a flying scroll with a list of names detailing those who had stolen or lied.

The scroll likely represents law and justice that flow out from the temple (Tiemeyer, 143). The lone positive use of *tôrâ* within the Twelve appears in Micah 4:2, in which *tôrâ* is used along with the word (*dĕbar*) of Yahweh that proceeds from Zion. A day will come when the nations will joyously stream to the holy mountain to receive this divine teaching and in order to settle disputes in a peaceful manner as God (through the priests who mediate and apply *tôrâ*) judges them (Mic 4:3).

Most scholars believe that two appendices were added to the book of Malachi: Malachi 4:4 (MT 3:22) and Malachi 4:5-6 (MT 3:23-24). It is likely that the appendices originally were intended to bring only the book of Malachi to a close, but during the process of compiling the Twelve it was felt that they would also provide an appropriate ending to the entire prophetic corpus (Chapman, 131-46). The first appendix reaffirms the complimentary relationship of the Pentateuch and prophets with the imperative "Remember the instruction [*tôrâ*] of Moses my servant whom I charged in Horeb with statutes [*huqqîm*] and regulations [*mišpāṭîm*] for all Israel." The second appendix describes the future return of Elijah, which many see as a way of including the former prophets into this scheme.

2. Relationship of the Pentateuch and the Prophets.

Perhaps the most curious issue surrounding law in the prophets is the absence of features concomitant with and even essential to law within other sections of Scripture. For instance, the narrative that recounts Moses receiving the law, most prominently distilled in the Decalogue, from God at Mount Sinai is in many ways the most important event within the Pentateuch. Accordingly, Sinai is so closely associated with law that J. D. Levenson states, "The experience of Sinai, whatever its historical basis, was perceived as so overwhelming, so charged with meaning, that Israel could not imagine that any truth or commandment from God could have been absent from Sinai" (Levenson, 18-19). Yet, from a cursory reading of the biblical prophets it seems that Sinai was far less significant for them.

Within Jewish and Christian literature it is common for writers to use *tôrâ* to refer to the Pentateuch as a whole. However, the prophets hardly ever used the term in this way. Within the last few centuries of biblical scholarship it has been a matter of debate whether the Pentateuch as it exists in the so-called canonical forms of the LXX and the MT was around when the biblical prophets were active. Some scholars believe that the prophets worked with the Pentateuch as a whole (Sailhamer, 484), while other scholars think that the majority of the prophets and their early editors were familiar with the Deuteronomistic school but Priestly sections were added later in the compositional process (Otto). Classic examples illustrating this are the theological similarities between Jeremiah and the Deuteronomistic History (Brueggemann, 143-46; Maier), on the one hand, and the remarkable absence of Moses and the Sinai tradition in all but a handful of passages in the prophets, on the other. The latter phenomenon contains two elements worthy of further consideration.

2.1. Moses in the Prophets. Moses is the person most intimately associated with law within the Pentateuch and in Jewish and Christian interpretation. Yet, his presence within the prophets is scant. His name appears in the prophets only five times in the MT. Isaiah 63:11-12 recalls the salvation of God at the parting of the sea. Most translations of Isaiah 63:11 render the first line of the poetic arrangement similar to "Then his people recalled the days of old, the days of Moses and his people," yet the second half, which includes "the days of Moses and his people," is likely a later insertion, since the Greek tradition does not translate this. However, Moses does legitimately appear in Isaiah 63:12 as the one through whom God worked to part the sea. This passage goes on to give praise to God for the care and deliverance of Israel, yet no mention is made of Sinai and the giving of law to Moses.

In Jeremiah 15:1 Yahweh gives the prophet a blistering oracle to pass on to the people in which God says, "Even if Moses and Samuel were to stand before me, my heart would not go out to this people. Send them away from my presence! Let them go!" (NIV). This oracle merely relates the significant intercessory role of Moses and Samuel, and no specific mention is made of the traditions surrounding their lives and ministries or Moses' reception of *tôrâ* (Choi, 200-201).

Micah 6:4 mentions Moses along with Aaron and Miriam as the leaders whom God sent to the people as they came up from Egypt. The prophet also mentions the opposition from Balak king of Moab and from Balaam the seer, but again explicit mention of Sinai and Torah are completely absent. Nonetheless, some have seen the three individuals in this verse as representing different facets of life: Moses represents law, Aaron the priesthood, and Miriam prophecy (Kessler, 264). Furthermore, in the remainder of the chapter Micah does go on to briefly mention aspects of cultic sacrifice and economic dishonesty. B. K. Waltke believes that the inclusion of Moses here in Micah is "a strong argument for the antiquity and authenticity of the biblical traditions ascribed to Moses" (Waltke, 377). Yet, since many believe that this passage has a more Deuteronomic than Priestly tone (Mays, 130), the question concerning which of "the biblical traditions" were available to Micah is still in play.

2.2. The Decalogue in the Prophets. As we saw above, the prophets do not explicitly connect *tôrâ* to Moses. Furthermore, and perhaps even more striking, the prophets mention only once the theophany at Sinai and the giving of the Decalogue (Mal 4:4). We might be inclined to skip over this as inconsequential were it not for the fact that the Sinai event "constitutes the most salient religious event of the wilderness sojourn" (Aaron, 143). From a literary perspective, the only pentateuchal event comparable to the Sinai theophany is the deliverance of the Israelites through the Red/Reed Sea and the destruction of Pharaoh's army. No single event within the Pentateuch receives more treatment than Sinai (the specific event is narrated in Ex 19—20; 24; 32—34; also in Deut 5—6; 9—10), except perhaps the plague narrative (Ex 7—13) (the Joseph story is a narrative composed of multiple scenes and events that stretched over many years).

The themes of exodus and law naturally go together. It is only after Yahweh has delivered the people from slavery that he can then grant them freedom within the bounds of divine instruction. The prologue of the Decalogue makes this link explicit with God's statement "I am Yahweh, your deity who brought you out from the land of Egypt, from a house of slaves" (Ex 20:2; Deut 5:6). References to the exodus often appear within the prophets (e.g., Is 40:3; 43:2, 19-21; 51:9-11; 52:4-5; Hos 2:14-15), yet clear links to the Decalogue are few and far between, if they exist at all.

B. S. Childs thought that "at times certain prophets virtually cite the text of the Decalogue" (Childs, 64), yet an examination of the two texts that he cites, Hosea 4:2 and Jeremiah 7:9, does not lead to such an optimistic conclusion. Additionally, A. Rofé believes that Hosea quotes the opening formula of the Decalogue in 12:10; 13:4 (Rofé, 394). However, these references are oblique and might be better explained as literary tropes. It is true that *intertextuality in extrabiblical ancient Near Eastern oracles was subtle and proper nouns were not often used; nonetheless, Mesopotamian prophets quoted or adapted some of the most prominent and characteristic phrases of the literature to which they alluded in order to make a literary link clear (Halton). The biblical prophets did not function this way with respect to the Decalogue or to the Sinai tradition (aside from a few echoes in Is 4:2-6; 25:1-9 [Fischer, 24-36], and possibly the understanding expressed in the Talmud that Ezekiel "annulled" divine teaching within the Decalogue [Levinson, 63]), yet their references to the exodus from Egypt and the parting of the sea are unmistakable and fairly frequent (for a discussion of methodologies relating to OT intertextuality, see Hays). Furthermore, a reference to the Decalogue and/or Sinai would lend tremendous support to the rhetorical goals of the prophets as they judged the people for their sins and called them to repentance. Yet, instead of reminding the people of the Sinai event and their obligation to live according to the stipulations in the Decalogue, the prophets more often appealed to Yahweh's law found within the norms of "human moral consensus" (Barton, 61).

3. A Prophetic Theology of Law.

R. E. Clements argues that while many of the prophets predate the Pentateuch from a canonical perspective, the prophets are dependent upon it to provide the background for their critique of Israel (Clements 1978, 123-25). Yet, as we have seen above, the prophets seldom refer to the most central elements within the Pentateuch to provide a basis for their understanding of law. Therefore, it seems that Clements must appeal to the placement of the prophets within the second section of the tripartite division of the Jewish canon to show dependence upon the Pentateuch. Yet, this alone does not lead to the conclusion that books in the latter part of the canon are dependent upon former books either from a literary or theological dimension. Traditionally, Job is seen as reflecting a very early period, from the time of Abraham or even before; however, its placement in the last section of the Jewish canon, the Writings, did not imply that it was dependent on the Pentateuch, since in much of ancient Jewish interpretation Job was seen as predating Moses (Dell, 7-8). Accordingly, a "canonically" informed theological reflection need not imagine that the prophets were reading from complete Torah scrolls and should instead attempt to discern the actual method of the prophets themselves rather than construct a secondary "canonical" schema.

Instead of an appeal to Sinaitic Torah, the prophets appear to refer to a broad, pre-Sinai conception of law that is reflected in Genesis 26:5: "[All this will come to pass] because Abraham heard my voice and he kept my injunction [$mišmart\hat{\imath}$], my commands [$miṣw\bar{o}tay$], my statutes [$ḥuqq\hat{o}tay$], and my laws [$t\hat{o}r\bar{o}t\bar{a}y$]" (we should keep in mind that Genesis could have been, and probably was, reworked in light of the Sinai tradition). Even elements that seem central to Sinaitic revelation, within the narrative world of the Hebrew Scriptures, actually have roots going back to primeval stories in Genesis (e.g., Sabbath in Gen 1, the temple as a reflection of the creation of the world [Balentine, 136-41], and clean and unclean animals in the account of Noah). Since these concepts are more closely related to and spelled out in greater detail within the Sinai tradition, from a historical perspective we could view them as anachronistic interpolations of the Priestly and/or Holiness schools. But, from a theological perspective, as Fretheim points out, the Genesis 26 passage "is no simple anachronistic reference to the law given at Sinai" (Fretheim 2003, 186). We could extend this observation to the other Genesis accounts as well.

Within Genesis law is linked to creation (Schmid, 104-5). Along these lines, we could view the prophets as bypassing the Sinai tradition in favor of highlighting a more fundamental breach—a breach of the created order and, concomitantly, humanity's relationship with God. For the biblical prophets, law is not an abstract concept but rather is the very character and nature of God that God embedded into the fabric of the universe. As A. Heschel puts it, "Crime is not a violation of a law, but a sin against the living God" (Heschel, 217).

This perspective gains further footing when viewed alongside the theme of creation and new creation that is repeated throughout the Jewish and Christian Scriptures. The Bible recapitulates the sequence of creation, de-creation and re-creation starting with Eden, expulsion from the garden, and Eve giving birth to two sons; a cycle or two later we read of the flood that obliterated the distinction between the waters and dry land, the preservation of the new human (Noah), and creation starts anew as the waters recede (Blenkinsopp 2011, 155-70), and so on until the exodus and the people of God receive another start in Canaan; in a sense, this is an act of re-creation, a new crop of humans (the old ones having died in the wilderness) are brought to the Eden-like land. The giving of the law at Sinai was a contextually conditioned guide to accompany this new creation (Sweeney). From a theological perspective, the prophets skip over Sinai and tap into an *Ur*-tradition of law in order to admonish the nation to repent and hopefully avoid the coming de-creation (the exile) or to look back to the recent experience of de-creation (again, the exile) in order to avoid another iteration of this cycle. As Fretheim explains, "God's creation is at stake in Israel's behaviors, not simply their more specific relationship with God" (Fretheim 2005, 165).

This perhaps leads to the message concerning law that the prophets most urgently sought to convey: embracing divine law leads to *peace and life, while rejection of it leads to *destruction and violence (see Is 2—5). Divine law fosters human flourishing and a harmonious relationship with God. According to the diversity of prophetic witness, God's law is found in many forms: Siniatic revelation, Deuteronomistic reflections, prophetic oracles and *visions, the natural world, and human moral consensus. While the prophets warn that turning aside from this path will lead to de-creation, the penitent can take comfort that re-creation is just around the corner.

See also BLESSINGS AND CURSES; COVENANT; ETHICS; PROPHECY AND TRADITION.

BIBLIOGRAPHY. **D. H. Aaron,** *Etched in Stone: The Emergence of the Decalogue* (New York: T & T Clark, 2006); **S. E. Balentine,** *The Torah's Vision of Worship* (OBT; Minneapolis: Fortress, 1999); **J. Barton,** *Ethics and the Old Testament* (London: SCM, 1998); **J. Blenkinsopp,** *Ezekiel* (IBC; Louisville: John Knox, 1990); idem, *Creation, Un-Creation, Re-Creation: A Discursive Commentary on Genesis 1-11* (London: Continuum, 2011); **D. I. Block,** *The Book of Ezekiel: Chapters 25-48* (NICOT; Grand Rapids: Eerdmans, 1998); **W. Brueggemann,** *The Theology of the Book of Jeremiah* (OTT; Cambridge: Cambridge University Press, 2007); **D. M. Carr,** *Writing on the Tablet of the Heart: Origins of Scripture and Literature* (Oxford: Oxford University Press, 2005); **S. B. Chapman,** *The Law and the Prophets: A Study in Old Testament Canon Formation* (FAT 27; Tübingen: Mohr Siebeck, 2000); **B. S. Childs,** *Old Testament Theology in a Canonical Context* (Minneapolis: Fortress, 1989); **J. H. Choi,** *Traditions at Odds: The Reception of the Pentateuch in Biblical and Second Temple Period Literature* (LHBOTS 518; New York: T & T Clark, 2010); **R. E. Clements,** *Old Testament Theology: A Fresh Approach* (London: Marshall, Morgan & Scott, 1978); idem, "The Meaning of תורה in Isaiah 1-39," in *Reading the Law: Studies in Honour of Gordon J. Wenham,* ed. J. G. McConville and K. Möller (LHBOTS 461; London: T & T Clark, 2007) 59-72; **K. J. Dell,** *The Book of Job as Sceptical Literature* (BZAW 197; Berlin: de Gruyer, 1991); **I. Fischer,** *Tora für Israel, Tora für die Völker: Das Konzept des Jesajabuches* (SBS 164; Stuttgart: Katholisches Bibelwerk, 1995); **M. Fishbane,** *Haftarot: The Traditional Hebrew Text with the New JPS Translation* (Philadelphia: Jewish Publication Society, 2002); **T. E. Fretheim,** *Jeremiah* (SHBC; Macon, GA: Smyth & Helwys, 2002); idem, "Law in the Service of Life: A Dynamic Understanding of Law in Deuteronomy," in *A God So Near: Essays on Old Testament Theology in Honor of Patrick D. Miller,* ed. B. A. Strawn and N. R. Bowen (Winona Lake, IN: Eisenbrauns, 2003) 183-200; idem, *God and World in the Old Testament: A Relational Theology of Creation* (Nashville: Abingdon, 2005); **M. Greenberg,** *Ezekiel 1-20: A New Translation with Introduction and Commentary* (AB 22; Garden City, NY: Doubleday, 1983); **J. Goldingay and D. Payne,** *Isaiah 40-55* (2 vols.; ICC; London: T & T Clark, 2007); **C. Halton,** "Allusions to the Stream of Tradition in Neo-Assyrian Oracles," *ANES* 45 (2009) 50-61; **C. B. Hays,** "Echoes of the Ancient Near East? Intertextuality and Comparative Study of the Old Testament," in *The Word Leaps the Gap: Essays on Scripture and Theology in Honor of Richard B. Hays*, ed. J. R. Wagner, C. K. Rowe and A. K. Grieb (Grand Rapids: Eerdmans, 2008); **A. J. Heschel,** *The Prophets*, vol. 1 (New York: Harper & Row, 1962); **R. Kessler,** *Micha* (2nd ed.; HTKAT; Freiburg: Herder, 2000); **J. Koenig,** *L'Herméneutique analogique du Judaïsme antique d'après les témoins textuels d'Isaïe* (VTSup 33; Leiden: E. J. Brill, 1982); **W. G. Lambert,** *Babylonian Wisdom Literature* (Oxford: Clarendon Press, 1960); **T. Lescow,** "Die dreistufige Tora Beobachtungen zu einer Form," *ZAW* 82 (1970) 362-79; **J. D. Levenson,** *Sinai and Zion: An Entry into the Jewish Bible* (Minneapolis: Winston Press, 1985) **B. M. Levinson,** *Legal Revision and Religious Renewal in Ancient Israel* (Cambridge: Cambridge University Press, 2008); **F. G. López and H.-J. Fabry,** "תּוֹרָה" *TDOT* 15:609-46; **C. Maier,** *Jeremia als Lehrer der Tora: Soziale Gebote des Deuteronomiums in Fortschreibungen des Jeremiabuches* (FRLANT 196; Göttingen: Vandenhoeck & Ruprecht, 2002); **J. L. Mays,** *Micah* (OTL; Philadelphia: Westminster, 1976); **C. Nihan,** " 'Moses and the Prophets': Deuteronomy 18 and the Emergence of the Pentateuch as Torah," *SEÅ* 75 (2010) 21-55; **D. Novak,** *Natural Law in Judaism* (Cambridge: Cambridge University Press, 1998); **E. Otto,** "Scribal Scholarship in the Formation of Torah and Prophets," in *The Pentateuch as Torah: New Models for Understanding Its Promulgation and Acceptance*, ed. G. N. Knoppers and B. M. Levinson (Winona Lake, IN: Eisenbrauns, 2007) 171-84; **R. Rendtorff,** *The Canonical Hebrew Bible: A Theology of the Old Testament*, trans. D. E. Orton (TBS 7; Leiden: Deo, 2005); **T. Renz,** "Torah in the Minor Prophets," in *Reading the Law: Studies in Honour of Gordon J. Wenham*, ed. J. G. McConville and K. Möller (LHBOTS 461; London: T & T Clark, 2007) 73-94; **A. Rofé,** *Introduction to the Literature of the Hebrew Bible*, trans. H. N. Bock and J. H. Seeligmann (JBS 9; Jerusalem: Simor, 2009); **J. W. Rogerson,** *A Theology of the Old Testament: Cultural Memory, Communication, and Being Human* (Minneapolis: Fortress, 2010); **J. H. Sailhamer,** *The Meaning of the Pentateuch: Revelation, Composition, and Interpretation* (Downers Grove, IL: IVP Academic, 2009); **H. H. Schmid,** "Creation, Righteousness and Salvation: 'Creation Theology' as the Broad Horizon of Biblical Theology," in *Cre-ation in the Old Testament*, ed. B. W. Anderson (IRT 6; Philadelphia: Fortress, 1984); **M. J. Selman,** "Law," *DOTP* 497-515; **D. Smith,** "A Ritual Incantation-prayer against Ghost-induced Illness: Shamash 73," in *Reading Akkadian Prayers and Hymns: An Introduction*, ed. A. Lenzi (SBLANEM 1; Atlanta: Society of Biblical Literature, 2011); **M. A. Sweeney,** "The Book of Isaiah as Prophetic Torah," in *New Visions of Isaiah*, ed. R. F. Melugin and M. A. Sweeney (JSOTSup 214; Sheffield: Sheffield Academic Press, 1996) 50-67; **L.-S. Tiemeyer,** *Priestly Rites and Prophetic Rage: Post-Exilic Prophetic Critique of the Priesthood* (FAT 2/19; Tübingen: Mohr Siebeck, 2002); **B. K. Waltke,** *A Commentary on Micah* (Grand Rapids: Eerdmans, 2007); H. G. M. Williamson, *Isaiah 1-5* (ICC; London: T & T Clark, 2006); **W. Zimmerli,** *Ezekiel 2: A Commentary on the Book of the Prophet Ezekiel, Chapters 25-48*, trans. J. D. Martin, ed. P. D. Hanson and L. J. Greenspoon (Hermeneia; Minneapolis: Fortress, 1983). J. C. Halton

LEADERSHIP

The OT describes a range of leadership positions within Israel's society. As the prophets interact with different aspects of their society, they inevitably engage with these leaders. The authority of these leaders is recognized by the prophets, though they are aware that holding an office does not necessarily indicate actual leadership. The prophets expect their leadership to lead the nation to a more faithful walk with Yahweh. Leaders who fail to do this are rebuked by the prophets.

1. Leadership Terms
2. Assessments of Leadership in the Prophets
3. Integrated Perspectives

1. Leadership Terms.

There are a range of terms in the OT related to this subject, though no one summary term is equivalent to the English word *leadership* (for a summation of the main terms in this field, see *NIDOTTE* 5:117, though it does not include religious leaders in this domain). Rather, the focus tends to be on the specific leadership role that is fulfilled, though the semantic range of these terms can overlap. For instance, both *dîn* and *šōpēṭ* can refer to a judge as someone who decides legal questions, though both can also refer to governance or administration more generally. In this latter sense, their meaning relates to ʾādôn ("lord"), which can also be a synonym for melek ('king'), though ʾādôn is perhaps the broadest term. Nevertheless, even from this brief survey it becomes apparent that anyone searching for leadership terms in English needs to be aware that a range of Hebrew terms may lie behind any one term in English, and conversely, any one Hebrew term may be translated in a range of different ways, depending upon the emphasis in the particular text.

Although these terms overlap in meaning, it is possible to identify two principal areas of leadership, each of which is reflected at various points in the prophets, though this typology is more a tool of analysis than something on which the prophets consciously reflect. Leadership terms may be used with reference to rule (including administration and military command) or religious action, but they often cut across these fields, and it is not always possible to limit any one occurrence to only one category. For example, a king was at various times a ruler, someone who participated in specifically religious activities, someone responsible for administration (such as hearing legal complaints) and also a military commander. Approaching leadership through these subcategories can be helpful because it recognizes the OT's concern with the function that a leader fulfills at any point; and even staying with the example of the king, it is generally the case that only one or two of these aspects is emphasized at any one point. On the other hand, this typology is not one that the prophets formally develop, and we will also see points where an integrated approach is more helpful.

A consistent theme that emerges is that all forms of leadership exist under Yahweh's greater rule. Leaders are required to lead the people to an authentic practice of faith in Yahweh and to model this in their own actions. Thus, leadership is concerned both with what leaders do and their character. Leaders who fail may be removed by Yahweh and replaced by another. The removal of Eli from the priesthood and Saul from the throne in 1 Samuel therefore are paradigmatic for the prophets, as they demonstrate Yahweh's authority over all forms of leadership, while David and Moses provide the dominant human model of faithful leadership.

2. Assessments of Leadership in the Prophets.

2.1. Rulership. A collection of terms is related to the theme of rule, so that to a certain extent terms associated with judicial or military matters can be subsumed under them. Among the most important of these are melek ("king"), ʾādôn ("lord"), nāgîd ("ruler, leader"), nāśîʾ ("chief, king"), peḥâ ("governor"), śar ("prince, official") and zāqēn ("elder"), though others come into this subcategory at various points, including priests. It is clear even from these, however, that rulers may function in different ways, and the type of leadership offered may vary from local expressions (chiefs, elders) through to that associated with the nation as a whole (king, prince), though the distinctions between these types of rule are not absolute. Likewise, when considering rulers, we will also see that their rule is at various points focused on civil administration or military command, so that they become the model for all other leaders in these areas. An important theme for kings is that they are also often characterized as shepherds, something that draws on both a common motif across the ancient Near East and also the presentation of David as a shepherd in 1 Samuel 16—17 (see Laniak, 42-74).

The prophets approve such leaders whom they believe lead the people to serve Yahweh faithfully, while the failure to do so leads to prophetic condemnation. A clear example of this can be seen in Jeremiah's message to Josiah's sons in Jeremiah 22:11-30, though this passage needs to be seen in the wider context established for it in Jeremiah 21:11-22:10. In Jeremiah 21:11-14 the prophet announces Yahweh's word to David's house, though a specific king is clearly intended. The dynasty as a whole is summoned to execute justice and work for the needs of the weak because the failure to do so would result in Yahweh's judgment (Jer 21:11-12), judgment modeled in his promised actions against Jerusalem in Jeremiah 21:13-14. It is this background that enables the prophet to summon the Davidic dynasty to practice justice, while assuring it of Yahweh's judgment should it fail (Jer 22:1-9). Because of this, Jeremiah is able to announce Yahweh's judgment on Shallum (better known as Jehoahaz [Jer 22:11-17]), Jehoiakim (Jer 22:18-23, though Jer 22:20-23 is concerned with the effect of judgment on Jerusalem) and Coniah (better known as Jehoiachin [Jer 22:24-

30]). Each is judged as inadequate, and in the case of Shallum it is specifically indicated that he has sought his own wealth rather than justice for his people. In this, he is specifically contrasted with Josiah (Jer 22:15-16), who is assessed positively because he did execute justice and righteousness, thus forging a close link between the leader's actions and character. The close association between rulers and their people shows that they can bring blessing to them by establishing justice, but they incur judgment by failing to do so. Jeremiah accepts that kings can be positive, but he also is aware of the dangers that they pose.

The potential and threat of rulers can also be seen in Isaiah. In Isaiah 7:3-9 Ahaz is challenged to trust Yahweh in the face of the threat from an alliance between Syria and Ephraim against Judah, and in Isaiah 7:10-11 he was even offered the chance to ask for a sign from Yahweh in confirmation. His failure to do so results in the famous "Immanuel" prophecy (Is 7:12-17), along with the assurance of an attack by Assyria instead. By contrast, when confronted by the Assyrians, Hezekiah trusted in Yahweh and led the people to do so, bringing a stinging rebuke from the Rabshakeh (Is 36:4-10), though in a telling irony his words do point to the truth (see Briggs, 121-22). Faced with evidence that seemed contrary to faith, Hezekiah demonstrated the faith that Ahaz did not and thus provided appropriate leadership for his people. A similar struggle to be faithful is evident in the stories of Jeremiah's encounters with Zedekiah (Jer 37—38), where Zedekiah seemingly wanted to follow Jeremiah's advice but ultimately was unable to do so because of his fear of others (Jer 38:19). Since Jeremiah has then to negotiate with the other officials, it is clear that they exercised the real leadership at the time, even though Zedekiah was in office. Similarly, it was the intervention of Ebed-Melech that saw Jeremiah removed from a cistern where he was held (Jer 38:7-13) after Zedekiah confessed that he could not act against the wishes of his officials (Jer 38:5), so it was Ebed-Melech who actually offered leadership.

Kings were not the only figures who could be assessed in this way. In Isaiah 3:13-15 we read of a court case initiated by Yahweh against the princes (*śar*) and elders (*zāqēn*) of the people because not only had they failed to bring forth justice for the people, but in fact they were the ones responsible for the oppression of the poor. These terms refer here to a broader pattern of leadership than kings alone but make clear that all forms of rule are a responsibility, not a privilege.

This pattern continues into the postexilic period. At the center of a series of visions concerning the situation of the community, Zechariah 3—4 records visions concerned with the high priest Jeshua and the governor Zerubbabel. These men provided joint leadership for the community, though both seem to have faced significant opposition, perhaps because Zerubbabel was a descendant of David but did not bring about a restoration of the monarchy. Nevertheless, Zechariah insists that Yahweh was working through them both. In the case of Jeshua this is symbolized by a change of his clothes (Zech 3:4-5), while Zerubbabel was assured that the presence of Yahweh's *Spirit was sufficient to overcome opposition (Zech 4:6-7) and see the new *temple completed (Zech 4:8-10). If Zechariah 4:11-14 refers to them as the "sons of oil" ("anointed ones" in most English translations), then the sense of the vision would be that just as the oil from an olive tree is part of Yahweh's agricultural blessing for his people, so these two leaders are a blessing, even if this is not recognized by all (similarly Redditt 1995, 68; for an alternative view, see Boda). Leadership that sought to lead the people to worship was regarded as a blessing, but in Zechariah 9—14 we encounter a number of passages referring to shepherds that clearly are critical of them. Like much of Zechariah 9—14, the interpretation of these passages is disputed, but such a high concentration of "shepherd" and "flock" language indicates that leadership is a crucial concern in these chapters (see O'Kennedy), while the fact that the shepherds are never identified means that they are best taken as leaders in general (Redditt 1989, 631). Yahweh remains the good shepherd for the people (Zech 10:3), but at the same time he condemns those shepherds who fail to protect their people (Zech 11:17). Jeshua and Zerubbabel could be commended because their leadership reflected Yahweh's concerns, even though they lacked public support. But leaders who fail to do this, even if publicly recognized, stand under Yahweh's judgment. Zechariah thus continues to develop themes developed by earlier prophets in commending rule that is committed to Yahweh while condemning that which undermines the well-being of the community. That rule, and especially kingship, could provide appropriate leadership is reflected in the messianic hope, though there it is a transformed leadership that understands the priority of Yahweh's rule (e.g., Is 11:1-11).

2.2. Religious Leaders. References to religious leaders are less common than to rulers but are still relatively frequent. We are not concerned only with priests here, since prophets and the wise can also provide leadership. Although it is a quotation from his adversaries, Jeremiah 18:18 indicates that each of these exercised some form of leadership, and Jeremiah himself does not seem to dissent from the understanding of their roles, even if he would not accept their conclusion that leadership and instruction would continue even if Jeremiah were to be removed. Indeed, it is not impossible that priests, the wise and prophets were central figures among Jeremiah's opponents (similarly Thompson, 440). What is clear, however, is that teaching was central to each of these forms of religious leadership. For the priests, this was concerned with the *tôrâ*, which here is best understood as "instruction" rather than simply "law" (Hutton, 138), whereas for the wise it was "counsel" and for the prophet the "word." Each was recognizable because their teaching came in a different mode, but they provide leadership through their teaching, and their particular leadership role can be recognized by the mode of that teaching. In the case of priests, there was the additional element of their association with worship, but although this is sometimes mentioned and clearly contributes to them being viewed as leaders, the main focus of the prophets is on their teaching.

Priests can be viewed by the prophets as reliable figures, though before the exile this tends to occur in reference to isolated actions rather than in their wider role (Is 8:2; Jer 37:3). We do not find positive portrayals of the wise, and the prophets who are mentioned in the prophetic literature usually are presented as false (e.g., Hananiah in Jer 28). However, in Haggai and Zechariah we see a more positive portrayal, in part because of their support for the high priest Jeshua (e.g., Hag 1:14), but also because of the expectation that priests would provide appropriate teaching in response to the people's questions (Hag 2:10-13; Zech 7:3). The impor-

tance of Jeshua's role as high priest is stressed in Zechariah 6:11-13, where he not only shares leadership with a mysterious figure known as "the Branch," but also shares "counsel" with this figure, thus uniting priestly teaching with wisdom. In Joel 1:13; 2:17 we find a point where the priests' role in leading worship is important in leading the nation's repentance, suggesting that although they were implicated in the situation that led to the nation's distress, they were still able to fulfill their role.

It is, however, more common to find the prophets criticizing religious leaders for their failures. This is invariably the case with the wise (e.g., Is 3:3; 5:21; 29:14; Jer 8:8-9) and usually true of prophets (e.g., Mic 3:5-7), but it is also frequently true of the priests. Thus, in Isaiah 28:7-13 the teaching of prophet and priest is contrasted with Yahweh's justice, parodying their instruction as drunken ramblings. Similarly, in Jeremiah 2:8 we find the failures of the priests and prophets linked (here also with kings) for failing to provide proper instruction to prevent the people from turning from Yahweh. It is this failure in teaching that leads to Yahweh's judgment on priest, prophet and elder (in terms of counsel, so wisdom is the issue) in Ezekiel 7:26, while in Micah 3:11 it is the fact that the teaching of priest and prophet is sold that leads to their judgment (cf. Zeph 3:4). In spite of the possibilities for priests hinted at in Haggai and Zechariah, Malachi points to their continued shortcomings, especially their failure in instruction (Mal 2:1-9) (see Tate, 401). The contention of Hosea 4:4-14, that the people reflect their religious leaders (see Lundbom, 67-68), is thus a common one across the prophets.

In spite of the religious leaders' failures, the prophets anticipate the inclusion of them in Israel's restoration. Thus, the national restoration portrayed in Jeremiah 31:7-14 particularly mentions the priests among those who will experience Yahweh's bounty. Likewise, in Jeremiah 33:17-22 the priests are mentioned along with the descendant of David as those who are central to Yahweh's process of restoration. But it is in Ezekiel 40—48 that the importance of the priests in the program of restoration is particularly highlighted. Although critical scholarship has often sought to trace various layers within this text, a case for its general unity can still be made (McConville, 13-17; Greenberg, 181-89) from which a reasonably unified picture emerges, even if issues such as the relationship between the Zadokites and Levites cannot be resolved here. Ezekiel does not legislate for priests so much as assume that they will be central to any restoration of worship. As such, space is made for them in the temple and *land (Ezek 40:44-47; 42:13-14; 45:4; 48:10-14), and worship practices are assumed to involve them (Ezek 43:19-27; 44:15, 29-31; 45:18-20; 46:2, 19-20). More importantly, their teaching function is specifically reinstated so that they not only instruct the people on matters of practice but also act as judges and so demonstrate how the law applies (Ezek 44:23-24). Ezekiel thus anticipates a restored religious leadership, but its restoration is shaped by the law. In Isaiah 61:6; 66:21 we may have something that goes beyond this in that future priests are not restricted to Levites and Zadokites, though their role appears to be similar. That is, although religious leaders fulfill several roles, teaching continues to be central, but that teaching already has its content defined in the law.

3. Integrated Perspectives.

Although I have separated out these areas of leadership for the purposes of analysis, the reality is that they were woven together such that although we can identify the different functions that were fulfilled, all forms were interrelated. That leadership could be viewed collectively is apparent from passages that link various forms of leadership, the clearest example of which occurs in Micah 3. Both Micah 3:1 and Micah 3:9 address the "heads of Jacob," who are then accused by Micah of a failure to establish justice. One could therefore imagine that Micah's concern is with rulers, and to the extent that he focuses on the corruption of the judicial system, this is correct. But in Micah 3:5-8 the prophets who preach in return for payment are highlighted, the concern being that such prophets have become one with the government and therefore no longer critique the abuses perpetrated by the nation's leadership. Micah does not deny their status as prophets, but contrasts their concern with payment with his own empowerment by the Spirit so that he might declare the nation's transgression, a transgression that must be judged because of its absence of justice. Likewise, although Micah 3:9-10 addresses government abuses, Micah

again notes that the prophets divine for money while adding that the priests teach for money while claiming Yahweh's presence. Rulers are meant to establish Yahweh's principles in the life of the community, and religious leadership was meant to teach what that was. The two are meant to complement one another even as they retain a degree of independence so that each could critique the other. The various functions of leadership are here integrated with one another because they had collectively failed to develop a community that reflected Yahweh's purposes. This is why Yahweh's judgment had to come. Nevertheless, the failure of those leaders was not the last word, which is why Micah 4:9 insists that the absence of king and counselor is not the end, for Yahweh is Israel's ultimate leader, which is also why all leaders are accountable to him.

See also PROPHECY, HISTORY OF; PROPHECY AND SOCIETY.

BIBLIOGRAPHY. **R. Abba,** "Priests and Levites in Ezekiel," *VT* 28 (1978) 1-9; **M. J. Boda,** "Oil, Crowns and Thrones: Prophet, Priest and King in Zechariah 1:7-6:15," *JHScr* 3.10 (2001) <http://www.arts.ualberta.ca/JHS/Articles/article_22.pdf>; **R. S. Briggs,** *The Virtuous Reader: Old Testament Narrative and Interpretive Virtue* (Grand Rapids: Baker Academic, 2010); **M. Greenberg,** "The Design and Themes of Ezekiel's Program of Restoration," *Int* 38 (1984) 181-208; **R. R. Hutton,** *Charisma and Authority in Israelite Society* (Minneapolis: Fortress, 1994); **T. S. Laniak,** *Shepherds after My Own Heart: Pastoral Traditions and Leadership in the Bible* (Downers Grove, IL: InterVarsity Press, 2006); **J. R. Lundbom,** "Contentious Priests and Contentious People in Hosea iv 1-10," *VT* 36 (1986) 52-70; **J. G. McConville,** "Priests and Levites in Ezekiel: A Crux in the Interpretation of Israel's History," *TynBul* 34 (1983) 3-31; **D. F. O'Kennedy,** "The Shepherd Imagery in Zechariah 9-14," *OTE* 22.2 (2009) 404-21; **P. L. Redditt,** "Israel's Shepherds: Hope and Pessimism in Zechariah 9-14," *CBQ* 51 (1989) 631-42; idem, *Haggai, Zechariah, Malachi* (NCBC; Grand Rapids: Eerdmans, 1995); **M. E. Tate,** "Questions for Priests and People in Malachi 1:2-2:16," *RevExp* 84 (1987) 391-407; **J. A. Thompson,** *The Book of Jeremiah* (NICOT; Grand Rapids: Eerdmans, 1980).
D. G. Firth

LIFE AFTER DEATH. *See* AFTERLIFE.

LITERACY. *See* WRITING AND PROPHECY.

LITERARY APPROACHES

The Bible, an enduring written work of undisputed social power, has always held a primary place in the canon of Western Literature. As such, this article could explore the multiple ways in which the prophets, as participants in the Bible's literary canon, have been read as literature through history. That is a worthy and encompassing pursuit, but the aim of this article is more modest. It explores an approach to the prophetic texts that arose in the 1970s and 1980s and self-consciously and critically engages the final form of the prophets as coherent literary works.

Reading the prophets in this way is part of a trend in broader biblical scholarship. The publication of J. Muilenburg's 1968 Society of Biblical Literature presidential address, "Form Criticism and Beyond," observed the need for, and hastened the proliferation of, methodologies that "moved beyond" historical-critical paradigms and focused on narrative shaping and aesthetics, and on rhetorical affect. In subsequent years, methodologies such as rhetorical, narrative, reader-response and structural were appropriated to explore the biblical text, including the prophets.

Historical-critical methodologies view the prophets as charismatic figures whose genuine oracular utterances are preserved in the books of their name together with the accretions of subsequent traditions. Historical-criticism pursues the *ipsissima verba* of the prophets. Its intent is wholly historical: unearthing the historical prophet, his words, and the compositional history by which those words grew into the present text.

Literary approaches to the prophets seriously engage the final form of the biblical books. While attention to diachronic, historical questions at times informs the investigation, its focus remains upon the final form of the text as an appropriate locus of study in which prophetic books yield evidence of intentional literary shaping and a coherent message.

Some of the literary methods and concerns explored in this article apply equally to each of the books of Isaiah, Jeremiah, Ezekiel, Daniel and the Twelve Prophets; others are more narrowly applied. The literature is, of course, extensive; each prophetic book could be treated separately. This article, then, is intentionally a survey, drawing selectively for illustrative purposes from research on the entire prophetic corpus.

1. Literary Unity
2. Textual Poetics
3. Theology, Canon and Scripture
4. Future Directions

1. Literary Unity.

The eschewal of historical questions and the consideration of the final form as a unified whole is one of the primary hallmarks of a literary approach to the prophets. This remains, explicitly or implicitly, part of all literary approaches, and though a commitment to investigate the text as received may be a priori, it is affirmed by a variety of signifiers that point to the Prophetic Books' character as unified literary works.

For instance, a literary approach to the book of *Isaiah moves beyond the historical-critical consensus of the existence of First, Second and Third Isaiah to explore issues of verbal, thematic and theological unity in the final form. R. Rendtorff's 1993 essay (published originally in German, 1991) demonstrates this new approach, noting such unifying factors. Continuing prolific work by the guild has strengthened the idea of Isaianic unity. Unifiers such as those explored by Rendtorff, and others such as structure, metaphors, *intertextualities and the impact of Isaiah's canonical and scriptural character (see essays in Melugin and Sweeney; Watts and House; Hauser) question the viability of a continuing commitment to a tripartite reading of the book.

Similar work moves *Jeremiah studies from a historical-critical investigation of sources A, B and C to consideration of the work's literary unity. Elements such as consistent themes, the place of key chapters within the structure, and even the unifying force of the prophetic persona that pervades the whole support the intentionally literary nature of the work. Such studies reveal "the contours of an overall plan and a theology that keeps the canonical book together, so that those who listen carefully will hear its message" (Kessler, xii).

*Ezekiel too is now approached with a commitment to viewing its literary form as a unified whole. Thus, M. Greenberg's 1983 commentary, while not naive regarding authorial unity, argues for the book's essential character as a "product of art and intelligent design . . . [shaped by] Ezekiel, if not the very words of Ezekiel himself" and engages the rhetorical purposes of such artful design (Greenberg, 26). Similarly, D. Block's two-volume commentary attends to the book's literary nature, apparent in its unifying framework (Block, 1:23-39).

The unity movement does not pass over the Book of the *Twelve, which early modern research considered only as an anthology of separate books. P. House argues that the collection, united by genre, structure and theme, and a discernible comedic plot, is intentionally presented as a unified work (House 1990). Further evidence of synchronic readings is apparent in M. Sweeney's two-volume work on the Twelve in which he primarily attends, without ignoring diachronic considerations, to synchronic considerations.

Finally, even such a dichotomized book as *Daniel (with its divide between narrative and apocalyptic prophecy and its use of two languages [Dan 2–7, in Aramaic, is enclosed by Dan 1; 8—12, in Hebrew]) can be considered in literary categories. Thus, recent commentaries witness to the influence of literary studies, note structural and theological unities, and demonstrate a commitment to engage the book in its final form (e.g., Goldingay).

Unified literary readings do not necessarily presuppose wholesale affirmation of the books as the *ipsissima verba* of historical prophets. Although the books may be so construed, the prophet might also be construed as an implied persona garnered from the finished product and created by the redactional work of disciples and/or redactors. Then, too, the historical or redacted prophet may also virtually be erased from the interpretive process, and the inscribed message freed from any such historical or redactional moorings. But pointedly in each case, historical-critical consideration is no longer the sole, or even the reigning, paradigm. Fresh, critical literary engagement with the work argues that in order to properly hear the prophetic message, it must be heard primarily as presented, as a literary whole.

Several methods of investigation, as noted above, are used to support the unified character of Prophetic Books. Some of these methods are also applied to reveal the literary character of a smaller section or to connect a prophetic book to others works within the canon of Scripture. To these varied methods we now turn.

2. Textual Poetics.

Textual poetics are the constituent ingredients of a literary work; working together, a text's poetics form literature. Poetics is not the process of interpretation, but it is an exploration of the building blocks of literature and of how those building blocks are assembled. An investigation of literary approaches to the prophets necessarily requires an investigation of poetics, and although many categories could be pursued (e.g., irony, characterization, perspective, chiastic structures) here, the categories of narrative plot and unifying structure, intertextuality, and metaphor provide an entry into the central poetics of the prophets.

2.1. Narrative Plot and Unifying Structure. Plot and structure are necessities of a literary work, and a few examples will show the importance of these elements within a literary approach to the prophets. C. Seitz's assessment of Isaiah's overall structure breaks down its tripartite divisions (Seitz 1988; 1990). He notes that as one moves from First to Second to Third Isaiah, no clear indication is given that redactional boundaries are crossed. Further, a superscription is found as the book opens but not also at the start of Second or Third Isaiah, contrary to what one might expect of a redacted composite. Finally, he notes that the book has only one commissioning narrative (Is 6), and that Isaiah 40, rather than providing a second commissioning narrative to open Second Isaiah, is structured to serve as a reactivation of the message of Isaiah 1—39 for a new audience—the audience to whom the whole book is addressed. Seitz's arguments for structural unity within the book have been favorably received and extended.

Similarly, structuring the book of Jeremiah in its canonical form is undertaken while acknowledging its complex literary composition. Offerings by A. J. O. van der Wal, L. Stuhlman and M. Kessler in a 2004 collection of essays (Kessler) provide three different approaches to structuring the book; the variations attest not only to the book's complexity, but also to the rapidly moving field of Jeremiah scholarship, which has yet to arrive at consensus.

Van der Wal's structure falls just short of a true synchronic reading, as he leaves Jeremiah

52 outside the structure as a later redacted piece. Stuhlman and Kessler, however, though each provides a different structure, use a truly synchronous reading of the whole book. Interestingly, each also describes Jeremiah in terms of its storyline or plot. For Kessler, that plot begins in Jeremiah 1 with Yahweh as Lord of Judah and the nations and is retrospectively addressed in Jeremiah 25 as the prophetic message is summarized while also proleptically presenting Babylon's doom. Finally, that prolepsis is fulfilled in Jeremiah 52. Stuhlman's plot presents a two-part drama focusing on the prophetic persona of Jeremiah. In the drama Jeremiah's fall into hopelessness and rise into seasoned endurance reflects Judah's own destiny.

Isaiah too can be conceived as a literary drama with plot, characters and scenes. J. D. W. Watts's commentary presents Isaiah 1—33 as a drama in six scenes whose plot centers on the relationship between Yahweh and Israel. The plot extends via a prologue (Is 1—4) and epilogue (Is 62—66) to draw in Jerusalem and the temple. The complication in the drama is Israel's sin, which calls for Israel's condemnation. As the plot unfolds, several solutions to absolve Israel are presented (Is 7—64), until Yahweh presents his decision in the final chapters. Throughout, Watts treats Isaiah as a coherent and synchronous whole.

A final example reveals how the exploration of plot has marked literary approaches to the prophets. P. House, working with the final form of the Book of the Twelve, argues that its arrangement is an intentional presentation of a U-shaped comedic plot in which the protagonist (here, *Israel) descends to the depths (*exile) before rising once again to restoration (fully experienced only in the future) (House 1990, 111-62). House traces a plot that includes expected elements such as an introduction (Hosea, Joel), complication (Amos, Obadiah, Jonah, Micah), crisis (Nahum, Habakkuk), falling action (Zephaniah) and resolution (Haggai, Zechariah, Malachi). House's argument urges that the Book of the Twelve be read as one book, a unified, synchronic account of Israel's relationship with Yahweh. Though not undisputed (see the diverse opinions in Ben Zvi and Nogalski), House's reading of a unified plot demonstrates the application of this literary identifier to the prophetic works.

2.2. Intertextuality. Appropriate definitions for *intertextuality* are debated. Here, a summation provided by J. Nogalski provides a framework for discussion and includes the following four categories: quotations (the reuse of a phrase, sentence or paragraph), allusions (a word or words eliciting recollection of another text for a specific purpose), catchwords (a quotation or allusion often found at the seams of text and used to form connections across textual units) and motifs and themes (devices, often present across a large corpus, used to reveal the unique emphases of that specific work) (Nogalski 1996). A further category of intertextuality that takes up the extensive reuse of biblical texts within a prophetic work is also examined. Consideration of the prophets as literature draws attention to these forms of intertextuality, revealing the artfulness of the literary work in its final form. Again, questions of compositional history may be an extended part of such consideration, but they are not its necessary focus.

2.2.1. Allusions, Quotations, Catchwords, Motifs and Themes. A prime example of extensive intertextuality is traced in Rendtorff's 1993 work mentioned above, which argues for the unified character of the book of Isaiah. Several examples of Rendtorff's findings are mentioned here to illustrate the literary power of intertextuality.

Rendtorff traces the occurrences of the word *comfort* throughout Isaiah and its service to the motif of Yahweh's comfort granted to various groups, including his people, *Zion and all who mourn. He is careful to acknowledge that comfort is highlighted throughout the corpus, and he particularly notes its presence in key chapters, such as Isaiah 12; 40; 51; 66. Similarly, he traces the use of the phrase "the glory of Yahweh," significantly present in each of the three sections of Isaiah. His essay reveals that other intertextualities span the book's three sections, but often they cluster in key chapters (such as Is 6; 12; 40; 51; 66). Though found throughout the book, Rendtorff particularly marks their presence in Isaiah 40, which Rendtorff counts as a central chapter, uniting and thematicizing the whole book.

Rendtorff also considers certain themes and motifs in the book, noting their consistent presence, but also the ways in which these themes and motifs develop and change as Isaiah progresses. So, for instance, the theme of Zion or Jerusalem is present in Isaiah 1—39 but is not fully developed. In the second part of Isaiah it is richly developed as a personification and is a central theme. The theme continues in the third section of Isaiah but is less widely dispersed, being concentrated in Isaiah 60—62; 65—66. As in the intertextualities of "comfort" and "the glory of Yahweh," Rendtorff notes the coalescing of this motif in key chapters (Is 1; 12; 35; 40) that provides a unifying thematic skeleton across Isaiah.

Rendtorff also considers the motif of *righteousness, noting its presence in Isaiah as a theological concept. In the first section of Isaiah it appears in relation to human behavior, while its usage in the second section of Isaiah reveals the character of Yahweh's actions. Finally, in the third section of Isaiah the two stand in reciprocal relationship: Yahweh's righteousness calls for human righteousness. As Isaiah draws toward its close, it is Israel's *salvation that will bring about Israel's righteousness.

Rather than the themes and motifs calling for a dissection of Isaiah into purported earlier traditions, Rendtorff allows that they hold the book together. The medium of intertextuality adds to the coherent message of Isaiah, issuing a powerful call for Israel to abandon sin and to embrace Yahweh's salvation.

The study of theme is also apparent in literary approaches to the Twelve. Particularly, the theme of the *Day of Yahweh is traced to suggest an intentional theological unity (Rendtorff 2000). This reading argues for an inclusio marked by the term the "day of Yahweh" in Joel 2:11 and Malachi 4:5, within which the Day of Yahweh finds expression in almost every book. The theme is built through various related terms that, if the Twelve are read sequentially and in light of Joel's concern with the Day of Yahweh, are likewise seen to refer to the same day. Yet, while the theme unites the books, it does not present a monochromatic picture of that day. As the Day of Yahweh first presented in Joel encompasses "different . . . and divergent" perspectives (Rendtorff 2000, 80), so such difference is echoed throughout the remainder of the Twelve.

The intertextual phenomenon of catchwords is particularly pertinent in literary readings of the Twelve. Assuming that the Twelve are intentionally redacted to be read as one book with chronological, thematic and plot progression, Nogalski points to the presence of catchwords that stand most often at the seams of the books (i.e., at significant junctures and at the beginnings and endings of books), appear often to be redactionally inserted, and serve to connect both adjacent and nonadjacent books (Nogalski 1993; 1996). So, for instance, Amos 1:2 takes up Joel 3:16, while Obadiah 4 reuses verses that close Amos (Amos 9:2-4). The catchwords may also develop as a juxtaposition that ties into overarching themes within the Book of the Twelve. Thus, Hosea 14:7 utilizes agricultural words such as "vine," "wine" and "grain" promised to the "inhabitants" in their future. By contrast, Joel 1:2-20 presents the "inhabitants" facing present agricultural disaster that involves the "vine," "wine" and "grain." The juxtaposition thus highlights overarching themes of loss through judgment and of future restoration. Further, Nogalski argues that these catchword motifs reappear throughout the corpus at significant junctures (thus, the agricultural images reappear in Hab 3:17; Hag 2:16-19; Zech 8:12; Mal 3:10-11).

2.2.2. Reuse of Biblical Traditions. Intertextuality is also apparent in the use within prophetic texts of pentateuchal traditions. While the direction and nature of such reliance remains debated, scholarship has successfully compared the intertexts as synchronous readings. In each instance it is the intertextual juxtaposition of an evoked past to the constraints of a new present that garners powerful theological commentary.

An extensive example of such intertexts is found in Ezekiel's use of pentateuchal traditions, particularly in the historical overviews of Ezekiel 20; 23 (see McKeating; Patton; Levitt Kohn). Ezekiel's historical overview shows a similar unfolding of events such as is found in Deuteronomy 1—11 and related in Deuteronomistic texts such as Joshua 24; 1 Kings 8. It is, however, a highly selective, negative reading of Israel's past. The retelling appears as a response to the events of exile and anticipates a new exodus—not now from Egypt, but from Babylon.

Ezekiel's historical retelling conspicuously absents Moses as a character. Yet, C. Patton argues that the "no good laws" of Ezekiel 20 prepare for the giving of a new law that evokes Moses' lawgiver role, a law found in Ezekiel 40—48. H. McKeating also connects these chapters with the figure of Moses. He cites a narrative framework that reflects Moses' life and shows that Ezekiel 40—48 is concerned with laws that in the Pentateuch attach to Moses: regulations regarding temple worship, priestly service, land allocation and conduct of leadership. R. Levitt Kohn also sees in the character of Ezekiel a life of a second Moses, taking on the Mosaic roles of prophet, priest and legislator.

By pursuing the intertextual relations between the Pentateuch and Ezekiel, the literary creativity of the prophetic text is unveiled. Reusing familiar traditions, Ezekiel reframes them in new literary contexts. In these new contexts intertextual echoes provide theological commentary that is more than the sum of its parts.

2.3. Metaphor. Given the deep emotion expressed by the prophets, Israel and even Yahweh surrounding covenant failure and the possibility of (and eventual actuality of) exile, it is not surprising that metaphor, which stirs emotion in such multivalanced ways, is so common in the Prophetic Books. The abundant supply of literary metaphors is explored in scholarship in a variety of ways.

R. Melugin reads Isaiah 1 synchronically, showing how the metaphor of Yahweh's trial of his foolish sons is juxtaposed to that of the punishment and restoration of Yahweh's faithless bride. The juxtaposition of the two metaphors forms a mosaic picture of Israel's past, present and future. Melugin traces the metaphors' message throughout the entire book, not by flattening all subsequent metaphors to woodenly conform to those in Isaiah 1, but instead by exploring the evocative ways in which each articulates with those in Isaiah 1. The unifying mosaic of metaphors imaginatively evokes the judgment and restoration of Israel.

The troubling, extended metaphors in Ezekiel 16; 23 provide rich resources for literary study (similar studies also engage the feminine images in Jer 2—5 [see Weems]). J. Galambush examines the metaphorization in Ezekiel of cities as woman and wife, plumbing both its nature and function and bringing expertise from the fields of feminism and semiotics. To the study of the metaphor she adds a study of the depiction of the city of Jerusalem elsewhere in Ezekiel, noting that it too takes up images of female sexuality and defilement. Ultimately, Galambush concludes that the extended metaphors in Ezekiel 16; 23, together with the depiction of Jerusalem in feminine terms elsewhere in the book, builds a picture of city-as-woman

so defiled and abominable that it can no longer serve as a viable image for the future restored city. Instead, the restored Jerusalem in Ezekiel 40—48 is depicted as an inviolable fortress.

Galambush explores the meaning of metaphor for its contribution to the essential meaning of the whole prophetic work. Other studies of metaphor ask not so much after the metaphor's contribution to the meaning of the whole book; rather, a metaphor within a specific passage is explored as to its rhetorical effect upon both ancient and modern audiences. Thus, F. van Dijk-Hemmes applies feminist insights and the study of pornography to the metaphor in Ezekiel 23, and C. Newsom explores the rhetorical effect of metaphor in Ezekiel's oracles against Tyre.

3. Theology, Canon and Scripture.

Literary approaches to the prophets work out of a commitment to the unified nature of the prophetic texts and attempt to hear them in their final form. The attention to the prophets' final form aligns literary approaches to the prophets quite naturally with questions of theology, canon and Scripture, each of which similarly turns to the final form of the text as the locus of inquiry.

3.1. Theological Readings. With the locus of study moved from the history behind the text to the text itself, it is inescapable that the major character within those texts—Yahweh, the God of Israel—becomes a central focus of study.

Certainly, any of the approaches discussed above can lead to questions of theology. Thus, the structure of the Twelve, plotted from sinfulness through judgment to restoration, evokes reflection upon the character of Yahweh, who is instrumental to the plot's progression. Tracing the structure of Jeremiah through the lens of the prophet's own life, which moves from despair to endurance, calls for reflection upon Yahweh. For instance, what is Yahweh's role in the midst of Jeremiah's complaints, and what does this role reveal about God? Or, as one considers the theme of righteousness as it develops in Isaiah, what does this theme reveal about Yahweh's priorities and purposes in salvation? The sometimes shocking metaphor of the city as a woman calls for deep (even troubling) reflection upon the God whose city Jerusalem is, and the indeterminacy of metaphor in Hosea speaks of God, but in ways that both conceal and reveal (Landy 2001). Whether the theological reading arises as a corollary to the data revealed through literary study or becomes the intentional purpose of a literary approach (so, e.g., House 2000), theological reflection is an expected outcome of literary approaches.

3.2. Canonical Readings. In 1979, B. S. Childs's *Introduction to the Old Testament as Scripture* introduced a canon-oriented interpretive stance. This stance, in attending to the final or canonical form of the text, is also literary in its orientation. His work on Isaiah in that volume, given the preponderance of historical-critical inquiry at that time, especially reveals the newness of canon-oriented interpretation (*see* Canonical Criticism). Exploring the canonical setting of the three sections of Isaiah, Childs does not deny the value of historical-critical inquiry. However, he moves well beyond this by attention to the literary, canonical form of the text. He argues that so-called First, Second and Third Isaiah lose historical particularity once set into their canonical form. The canonical setting requires the sections to be heard in light of the whole, and, under the influence of Isaiah 40—66, the whole finds an eschatological meaning.

Many interpreters, working with the categories described above under "Literary Unity" and "Textual Poetics" may also work with a canonical orientation, and canonical orientations generally are attuned to literary categories within the text. More recently, Seitz, working with a canonical understanding of one Book of the Twelve, seeks to build a conceptual hermeneutic for canonical reading. He argues that such reading is not ahistorical but truly historical, as "final canonical form is also a piece of history, belonging to decisions made in the past about how an ancient prophetic witness is finally to be heard" (Seitz 2007, 233). His argument, aligning canonical reading with historical processes, is important because it addresses a disjunction. The disjunction arises through the different foci of historical criticism (diachronic) and literary approaches (synchronic), which too often pit one against the other as the appropriate method to engage the biblical text. Seitz's work attempts to incorporate both stances, acknowledging the interpretive value of each yet still holding the canon as the final locus of interpretation.

3.3. Scriptural Readings: Reception by a Hearing Community. Since this article began with a nod to the social power of the Bible through history, it seems appropriate to end the discussion in a similar place. Once the final literary form of the prophets is examined, it is not long before one asks how those writings are heard by communities ancient and modern. An exploration of a text's hearing communities may include investigation of how ancient audiences heard metaphors (e.g., the metaphorical presentation of Jerusalem as Yahweh's wife), or it may explore the reception of the Twelve by literati in postexilic Yehud (Ben Zvi).

But hearing the prophets as literature also involves present-day communities for whom the prophets are Scripture. Such hearing, working in the heritage of historical criticism and the critical engagement of literary approaches over thirty years, should not be naïve. Thus, Melugin's 1996 essay stands in an anthology of twelve essays that critically engage literary readings of Isaiah. Of those twelve essays, five explore the reception of the text, two of them from an explicitly scriptural perspective. That Melugin introduces the volume and is himself a prolific contributor to critical study of the prophets as literature suggests that his reflections on Isaiah as Scripture themselves have passed through a critical framework.

Melugin's article unfolds various figurative constructs in Isaiah that together form an allusive mosaic (see 2.3 above). He spends much of the article simply explaining the constructs and how they articulate one to the other. But his concluding paragraphs reveal his commitment to make his literary explanation subservient to the reading of the prophets as Scripture. He notes, "The most basic purposes for the use of Scripture in communities of faith, I believe, should be performative; the community's most sacred texts should be powerful agents for judgment and healing. Explanation should be supportive rather than primary" (Melugin, 302). His exploration of prophetic tropes reveals a "construction of a symbolic world in which a community may hear and respond to God" (Melugin, 303).

As Melugin draws to a conclusion, he recognizes that his own generation's application of literary approaches is indelibly marked by the concerns, scholarly locations and conventions of that generation. By that token, present-day literary reading of Isaiah as Scripture will likely differ from those of ancient Israel (and, indeed, every successive generation). But the commitment to reading the texts as Scripture engages one in a "centuries-old community which employs Isaiah (and other scriptures) to shape its experience of God as judge and savior" (Melugin, 303).

4. Future Directions.

Scholarly investigation of the prophets as literature, begun in the 1970s, has not yet run its course or ushered in a successor. As further study on literary approaches to the prophets proceeds, I suggest briefly three areas for further fruitful engagement.

First, Isaiah studies have garnered a lion's share of the attention of literary approaches, but as indicated in 1.1 above, none of the prophetic corpus remains unaddressed. Yet, there remains ample room to increase the literary study of Isaiah, Jeremiah, Ezekiel, Daniel and the Twelve. For instance, the search for coherence in Jeremiah studies can be described as being in "ferment" (see Kessler, ix), and much work is needed to bring scholarly consensus to such ferment. Another area for further work is Daniel. Although there are several commentaries that utilize literary insights, further work can address the possibility of engaging the highly dichotomized book as a unified literary work.

Second, critical engagement around key issues must continue. Basic questions such as the nature of intertextuality and how to determine its intentionality remain open for investigation. How does scholarship speak with certainty to whether intertextuality is merely in the eye of the reader, or, indeed, can scholarship do so at all? And, given attention to the receptor as a genuine location of meaning, are such questions the ones to be asked?

Another key issue that continues to face ongoing debate is the nature of the Book of the Twelve. Is it rightly read as an anthology, or as one book? If one book, do such readings apply literary methods too liberally, finding "coherence" in words or themes that are simply standard within the prophetic genre? That a consensus can be achieved is doubtful, but perhaps the ongoing debate will serve to sharpen each approach.

Third, Seitz's work (see 3.2 above) suggests a possibility of rapprochement between diachronic and synchronic studies. Conversation regarding the place of each in scholarly engagement will continue, with the hope that the insights of both can be critically integrated. Seitz's work moves in this direction, and there are hopeful signs elsewhere that the divide between the two schools can be bridged.

Such directions in scholarship are inevitable, given the current field. But it is also assured that the prophetic works—in their grand scope, in their literary expertise, in their emotive expanse—will simply continue to delight, engage and trouble readers. Good literature remains just that, and the prophets exemplify the genre.

See also CANONICAL CRITICISM; EDITORIAL/REDACTION CRITICISM; FORMATION OF THE PROPHETIC BOOKS; HERMENEUTICS; INTERTEXTUALITY AND INNERBIBLICAL INTERPRETATION; PERFORMANCE CRITICISM; RHETORICAL CRITICISM.

BIBLIOGRAPHY. **E. Ben Zvi,** "Is the Twelve Hypothesis Likely from an Ancient Reader's Perspective?" in *Two Sides of a Coin: Juxtaposing Views on Interpreting the Book of the Twelve/the Twelve Prophetic Books,* ed. T. Römer (AG 201; Piscataway, NJ: Gorgias Press, 2009) 47-96; **E. Ben Zvi and J. D. Nogalski,** *Two Sides of a Coin: Juxtaposing Views on Interpreting the Book of the Twelve/the Twelve Prophetic Books,* ed. T. Römer (AG 201; Piscataway, NJ: Gorgias Press, 2009); **D. I. Block,** *The Book of Ezekiel* (2 vols.; NICOT; Grand Rapids: Eerdmans 1997-1998); **B. S. Childs,** *An Introduction to the Old Testament as Scripture* (Minneapolis: Fortress, 1979); **E. Conrad,** *Reading Isaiah* (Minneapolis: Fortress, 1991); **J. Galambush,** *Jerusalem in the Book of Ezekiel: The City as Yahweh's Wife* (SBLDS 130; Atlanta: Scholars Press, 1992); **J. Goldingay,** *Daniel* (WBC 30; Dallas: Word, 1989); **M. Greenberg,** *Ezekiel 1-20: A New Translation with Introduction and Commentary* (AB 22; Garden City, NY: Doubleday, 1983); **A. J. Hauser,** ed., *Recent Research on the Major Prophets* (RRBS 1; Sheffield: Sheffield Phoenix Press, 2008); **P. House,** *The Unity of the Twelve* (JSOTSup 97; Sheffield: Almond, 1990); idem, "The Character of God in the Book of the Twelve," in *Reading and Hearing the Book of the Twelve,* ed. J. D. Nogalski and M. A. Sweeney (SBLSymS 15; Atlanta: Society of Biblical Literature, 2000) 125-45; **M. Kessler,** ed., *Reading the Book of Jeremiah: A Search for Coherence* (Winona Lake, IN: Eisenbrauns, 2004); **F. Landy,** *Hosea* (RNBC; Sheffield: Sheffield Academic Press, 1995); idem, "In the Wilderness of Speech: Problems of Metaphor in Hosea," in *Beauty and the Enigma: And Other Essays on the Hebrew Bible* (JSOTSup 312; Sheffield: Sheffield Academic Press, 2001) 273-97; **R. Levitt Kohn,** *A New*

Heart and a New Soul: Ezekiel, the Exile and the Torah (JSOTSup 358; Sheffield: Sheffield Academic Press, 2002); **H. McKeating,** "Ezekiel the 'Prophet Like Moses'?" *JSOT* 61 (1994) 97-109; **R. F. Melugin,** "Figurative Speech and the Reading of Isaiah 1," in *New Visions of Isaiah,* ed. R. F. Melugin and M. A. Sweeney (JSOTSup 214; Sheffield: Sheffield Academic Press, 1996) 282-305; **R. F. Melugin and M. A. Sweeney,** eds., *New Visions of Isaiah* (JSOTSup 214; Sheffield: Sheffield Academic Press, 1996); **J. Muilenburg,** "Form Criticism and Beyond," *JBL* 88 (1969) 1-18; **C. Newsom,** "A Maker of Metaphors—Ezekiel's Oracles against Tyre," *Int* 38 (1984) 151-64; **J. D. Nogalski,** *Literary Precursors to the Book of the Twelve* (BZAW 217; Berlin: de Gruyter, 1993); idem, "Intertextuality and the Twelve," in *Forming Prophetic Literature: Essays on Isaiah and the Twelve in Honor of John D. W. Watts,* ed. J. W. Watts and P. House (JSOTSup 235; Sheffield: Sheffield Academic Press, 1996) 102-24; **C. Patton,** "'I Myself Gave Them Laws That Were Not Good': Ezekiel 20 and the Exodus Traditions," *JSOT* 69 (1996) 73-90; **P. Quinn-Miscall,** *Reading Isaiah: Poetry and Vision* (Louisville: Wesminster/John Knox, 2001); **R. Rendtorff,** "The Composition of the Book of Isaiah," in *Canon and Theology: Overtures to an Old Testament Theology* (Minneapolis: Fortress, 1993) 146-69; idem, "How to Read the Book of the Twelve as a Theological Unity," in *Reading and Hearing the Book of the Twelve,* ed. J. D. Nogalski and M. A. Sweeney (SBLSymS 15; Atlanta: Society of Biblical Literature, 2000); **C. R. Seitz,** "Isaiah 1-66: Making Sense of the Whole," in *Reading and Preaching the Book of Isaiah,* ed. C. R. Seitz (Philadelphia: Fortress, 1988) 105-26; idem, "The Divine Council: Temporal Transition and New Prophecy in the Book of Isaiah," *JBL* 109 (1990) 229-47; idem, *Prophecy and Hermeneutics: Toward a New Introduction to the Prophets* (Grand Rapids: Baker Academic, 2007); **M. A. Sweeney,** *The Twelve Prophets* (2 vols; Berit Olam; Collegeville, MN: Liturgical Press, 2000); **F. van Dijk-Hemmes,** "The Metaphorization of Woman in Prophetic Speech: An Analysis of Ezekiel XXIII," *VT* 43 (1993) 162-70; **J. D. W. Watts,** *Isaiah 1-33* (rev. ed.; WBC 24; Nashville: Thomas Nelson, 2005); **J. W. Watts and P. R. House,** eds., *Forming Prophetic Literature: Essays on Isaiah and the Twelve in Honor of John D. W. Watts* (JSOTSup 235; Sheffield: Sheffield Academic Press, 1996);

R. Weems, *Battered Love: Marriage, Sex and Violence in the Hebrew Prophets* (OBT; Minneapolis: Fortress Press, 1995). L. Wray Beal

LITERARY UNITY. *See* LITERARY APPROACHES.

LITURGY AND CULT

Investigation of the relationship between canonical prophets and the *worship practices of ancient Israel involves a variety of issues. One must first examine the cultic function of prophets within the wider context of the OT and the *ancient Near East. From this background, questions emerge regarding how canonical prophets addressed the cult and to what extent if any their contributions to worship have been preserved in the Prophetic Books. The writing prophets can easily be misunderstood as being antiritualistic, but consideration of their broader message indicates that they were deeply concerned that the cult function properly, and their *visions often portray a vibrant and promising future for *temple worship. The presence of liturgical elements within the prophets is difficult to validate; nevertheless, a number of passages likely preserve records of liturgical performance.

1. Definitions
2. Prophecy and Cult in the Ancient Near East
3. Old Testament Cultic Prophecy
4. Opposition to the Cult
5. Support of the Cult
6. Contribution to Liturgy
7. Conclusion

1. Definitions.

"Prophecy," properly speaking, is a divine message intuitively received by a human agent for transmission to a third party. The intuitive aspect of this definition is important to differentiate prophecy from forms of deductive *divination that were also related at times to worship and sacrifice, such as the use of Urim and Thummim or, common in Mesopotamia, extispicy. Deductive divination involved binary answers (yes or no) to consultations of the deity, but prophecy involved direct speech by the deity through the human agent. While a binary response to an inquiry may be indistinguishable from prophecy at the literary level (e.g., 2 Sam 5:23-24), generally the length of the message and the use of formal, prophetic speech introductions identifies a message as prophetic.

The "cult" is understood to be any setting of worship, whether an official institutional site, such as a royally sponsored temple (1 Kings 5:3; 12:28-31; Amos 7:13), a temporary altar or shrine (1 Sam 10:8; 1 Kings 3:2, 4; 18:30) or a private household (Judg 17:1-13). "Liturgy" pertains to words and actions performed by cultic officials or laity in the course of worship. While priests and prophets sometimes were listed as separate functionaries in the OT (Is 28:7; Jer 14:18; 18:18; Mic 3:11), the social identity of a prophetic intermediary could be priest, Levite or lay person, and any of these could function in relation to the cult in official or unofficial capacities (2 Chron 20:14; 1 Sam 1:1, 20 with 3:1, 20; 10:11; Jer 20:6; Ezek 1:3; Amos 7:14).

2. Prophecy and Cult in the Ancient Near East.

Most of what is known about prophecy in the ancient Near East stems from royal or temple records, whether administrative archives or monumental inscriptions. Because these texts were selected for preservation by institutional interest, they are by nature pro-temple and predominantly pro-royal. The sources portray a very active role of prophets in cultic affairs in Mesopotamia. There is also evidence of divine speech delivered in the royal cult of Egypt. Extrabiblical prophetic texts from Zakkur in Syria as well as Deir ʿAllah and Amman in the Transjordan may be related to cultic activity. The following discussion is important to show that the phenomenon of cultic prophecy was deeply imbedded within the culture of the ancient Near East and resulted in written records. As such, it raises the expectation, a priori, that prophets engaged in service of the cult in Israel as well, and that their writings preserve liturgical elements.

2.1. Mesopotamia.

2.1.1. Mari and Eshnunna. Although prophecy existed in Mesopotamia prior to the Old Babylonian period, the archive of Zimri-Lim discovered at Mari preserves the most extensive collection of texts related to prophecy in the second millennium BC. Royal correspondence, recording the words of prophets, frequently refers to oracles originating in temple settings, and often these reports concern commands from a deity regarding cultic affairs (Huffmon, 48-56). This comports with the command from the king, reported in one letter: "Write to me whatever oracle is delivered in the temple of God and which you hear" (ARM 26 196; Nissinen, Seow and Ritner, 27). An example of one such report states, "In the temple of Ḫišamitum, a prophet called Isi-aḫu arose and said" (ARM 26 195; Nissinen, Seow and Ritner, 26). Some of these divine messages offer instruction or mild rebuke to the king regarding his cultic duties (e.g., A. 1121 + A. 2731; ARM 26 194, 206, 215, 220, 221; see Nissinen, Seow and Ritner, 17-21, 24-25, 38-39, 49-50, 54-55, 55-56). A particularly informative document, the "Ritual of Ishtar," describes a liturgy in which various participants, including musicians and prophets, are mentioned (A. 3165; A. 1249b + S. 142 75 + M. [unnumbered]; Nissinen, Seow and Ritner, 80-83). The musicians are directed to perform alternate tunes, depending on whether or not the prophet is "inspired" to speak at a fixed point in the liturgy.

Contemporary with the Mari sources are two prophetic texts from Eshnunna that likely derived from the temple archive, indicating the presence of cult prophets in that city (FLP 1674 and 2064; Nissinen, Seow and Ritner, 94-95). A later, Middle Assyrian text, which specifies food rations for prophets among the temple personnel, suggests that cult prophecy was not restricted to the Mari period of the second millennium (VAT 17999; Nissinen, Seow and Ritner, 185).

2.1.2. Nineveh and Babylon. Unlike the Mari archive, which reports prophetic speech and activity within administrative correspondence, texts from Assurbanipal's library in Nineveh preserve direct scribal records of prophetic speech. Although prophets were active outside of temple contexts, the messages that were preserved originated largely from prophets and prophetesses closely associated with the cult of Ishtar, hailing from cities with major Ishtar temples (Nissinen 2000, 95-102). One of the prophecies itself contains a colophon identifying the prophetess as a temple votaress (SAA 9 1.7; Nissinen, Seow and Ritner, 108). The substance of these prophecies is chiefly *salvation oracles in response to inquiry and lament by the king or the king's mother (Hilber 2005, 62-69). For example, in one oracle Ishtar responds to the king's mother, "Since you implored me" (SAA 9 1.8; Nissinen, Seow and Ritner, 109). A unique text (SAA 3 13) closely related in substance to one prophetic oracle (SAA 9 9) is formulated as a lament-response dialogue in the temple between the god Nabu and the king Assurbanipal (Hilber 2005, 70-74). In a few places the deity demands increased cultic support from the king (SAA 9 2.3 ii 24-27; 3.5 iii 26-27; Nissinen, Seow and Ritner, 113-14, 122-24).

Other texts reinforce this portrait of cult prophecy. Prophets were active participants in the Akitu festival, the substitute king ritual, and the ritual of Ishtar and Dumuzi, all involving cultic activity (SAA 3 34, 35; SAA 10 352; SAA 13 37; K 2001; Nissinen, Seow and Ritner, 151-52, 164-68, 175-77). A priest's letter placing a cultic demand on the king cites a prophecy originating explicitly in the Assur temple (SAA 13 37; Nissinen, Seow and Ritner, 167-68); another letter from a temple official contains a report of prophetic rebuke to the king for a cultic misdeed (SAA 13 144; Nissinen, Seow and Ritner, 169). Not all prophetic address to the king concerning cultic affairs was admonitory. Assurbanipal claims to have received authorization for temple restoration from prophets (Assurbanipal Prism T ii 7-24; Nissinen, Seow and Ritner, 143-44). Finally, the mention of prophets among temple personnel in various lexical lists (SAA 12 69; *MSL* 12 4.212, 4.222, 6.2; Nissinen, Seow and Ritner, 166-67, 186-88) further supports the assertion that prophetesses and prophets were established servants in temple liturgy during Neo-Assyrian times.

Evidence of cult prophecy exists for the Neo-Babylonian and Late Babylonian periods as well. A temple offering list includes a prophet along with the high priest (OCuT 1 20-21; Nissinen, Seow and Ritner, 192-93), and prophetic speech comprised part of the liturgy for the Akitu festival (*RAcc* 129-146; Nissinen, Seow and Ritner, 195-96).

2.2. Egypt. A consensus prevails that prophecy did not exist in Egypt. The texts usually consulted, which contain foretelling and social admonition, are actually a form of wisdom literature not derived from divine messenger speech (e.g., Prophecies of Nerferti). While the assessment of these texts is correct, a class of Egyptian texts has been overlooked in discussions on Egyptian prophecy (Hilber 2011). These royal inscriptions record first-person divine speech that is framed with introductory speech formulas and was delivered to the king in a cultic setting. Hatshepsut's and Horemheb's coronation rituals set the pattern for suc-

ceeding kings from the New Kingdom onwards. Both sources record divine speeches to the king, but Hatshepsut's inscription contains a particularly enlightening report of the proceedings: the ritual priests "proclaimed her royal names, for the god caused that it should be in their hearts to make her names according to the form with which he had made them before" (Breasted, §§229-30, 239). Even if fictive in the case of Hatshepsut's unorthodox ascension, this report probably corresponds with actual custom in order to portray a credible coronation. Horemheb's reliefs describe the god coming forth from the temple to meet him and declaring his divine sonship. Texts accompanying Tutankhamen's Opet festival set divine address to the king in the context of reliefs depicting ritual procession, presentation of offerings, dancing and records of human speeches and songs celebrating the event. Perhaps the best examples of royal cultic prophecy are in temple dedication inscriptions of Thutmosis III and Amenophis III, featuring triumph hymns spoken by Amun to the king, some of which were preserved at the Station of the King in the temple where the king stood for cultic ritual. These texts were adapted for the next five hundred years in royal reliefs depicting sword conferral by the god to the king (Kitchen, §§28, 29, 64). Therefore, it seems likely that priests functioned prophetically in the royal cult of Egypt.

2.3. Levant. From Iron Age Levant a salvation oracle delivered in response to royal lament is preserved on a stela from Zakkur in Syria, and an announcement of victory has survived from the former capital of the Ammonite kingdom. Although a temple setting cannot be proven for these texts, it seems likely that cultic ritual was involved. Also from the Transjordan is the Balaam oracle found at Deir ʿAllah, probably in what was a sanctuary (Nissinen, Seow and Ritner, 202-12).

3. Old Testament Cultic Prophecy.

3.1. Cult Prophetic Activity. Among the many scholars who advocated for extensive involvement by OT prophets in the cult, S. Mowinckel and A. Johnson stand out. Their primary evidence is as follows: (1) prophets were active at festivals and cultic sites (1 Sam 3:21; 10:5; 19:19-24; 1 Kings 18:16-39; 19:10; 2 Kings 2:3; 4:22-25, 38); (2) there was a close association between prophets and priests (Is 28:7; Jer 6:13; 8:10;

14:18; Lam 2:20; 4:13; Mic 3:11; Zech 7:3); (3) Jeremiah and Ezekiel are of priestly descent (Jer 1:1; Ezek 1:3); (4) the book of Jeremiah describes his ministry in the temple and relates his ministry to priests and other prophets who were there (Jer 23:11; 26:7; 27:16; 29:26; 35:4); (5) in addition to the prophetic ministry of the Levites (1 Chron 25:1), there is an extended description of the intercessory role of a Levite who prophesies in response to a royal lament (2 Chron 20:5, 14).

This proposal never attained full consensus, and prominent voices have expressed skepticism regarding the existence of cult prophets. H. Gunkel, for example, observed that the conjunction of prophets and priest was not cultic, since other texts of a similar nature include other functionaries as well who are not cultic figures (Jer 4:9; 8:1; 18:18; Mic 3:11). The presence of prophets at a cultic site does not establish their cultic duties. Rather, they may be present simply because of their desire, as pious individuals, to be present, or if they spoke prophetically, it was only because a cultic site would assure them of an audience, and the message need not be related to the cult. A text such as Jeremiah 29:26 merely suggests that priests were responsible to lock up antagonistic prophets such as Jeremiah. The priestly descent of Jeremiah is problematic (1 Kings 2:26-27 shows that his family was cut off from priestly duty), and Ezekiel's call came after exile from the temple.

Although many of the texts advanced in support of cult prophetism do not bear up under examination, several passages remain strong witnesses to this phenomenon. The Shunammite's desire to seek Elisha at a shrine on a day other than a feast day (2 Kings 4:23) suggests both that he resided there and was active on holy days. The fact that the prophets descending from the high place were still prophesying (1 Sam 10:5) indicates that they assumed this role in worship at the site. Most clear is the function of prophets alongside priests in the temple, since their "wickedness in the temple" is equated with their prophetic words (Jer 23:11, 14, 34-40). In this regard, Jeremiah 20:1-6 serves as a reminder that an overlap between priests and lay prophets is likely, but in either case, the prophetic voice was heard in the cult. The reference in Jeremiah 29:26 to sanctioning "every" maniac gives the impression that this occurrence was common. Indeed, the likelihood that some prophets lived in the temple, and therefore were part of the institutional staff, is not easy to disregard in the light of Jeremiah 35:4. At a minimum, Chronicles attests to cultic prophecy in the postexilic period, but also in the preexilic period, if the Chronicler's sources are historically credible.

The question of the nature of the cultic prophecy described in 1 Chronicles 25:1-3 remains. Were some Levitical singers recipients of oracles in the usual sense of prophecy, were they merely described as "prophesying" only by analogy to early traditions linking prophecy with music (e.g., 2 Kings 3:15), or does this text witness to a broader sense of "prophecy" that existed in both the preexilic and postexilic temples in which prophetic speech could take various forms? However one conceives of this phenomenon in 1 Chronicles 25, it does not preclude the ministry of prophets serving liturgically in the periods of the first and the second temples.

3.2. Psalms. One of the debates between Mowinckel and Gunkel regarding cult prophecy was whether or not actual prophetic speech is preserved in the book of Psalms. Mowinckel argued that certain psalms originated from cultic prophets, but Gunkel maintained that psalms appearing to contain prophetic speech are merely poetic imitation of prophetic style. Given the evidence just described, that prophets not only participated in worship but also were in some cases part of institutional temple staff, and that cult prophecy is deeply embedded in the culture of worship throughout the ancient Near East, it is most likely that some psalms preserve actual prophetic speech (Hilber 2005). Recent studies that attend to the rhetorical function of divine speech in the psalms might support Gunkel's contention that such speech is only a poetic device. However, examples of the process from oral prophecy to written liturgical text in both Mesopotamia and Egypt make the theory of cult prophecy more likely, since rhetorical function does not necessarily preclude prophetic origin. Thus, prophetic speech preserved in the psalms reinforces interpretations that some canonical prophetic texts preserve liturgical material.

4. Opposition to the Cult.

The capacity of prophets to critique cultic practice appears for the first time in the historical record with the oracle of the man of God against Jeroboam's illicit altar at Bethel (1 Kings 13:1-5). Following this, the prophet Ahijah directed an oracle against the house of Jeroboam, specifically because he sponsored idolatrous worship in conjunction with it (1 Kings 14:1-16). Numerous passages in the writing prophets criticize the cult in Israel and Judah, and debate has emerged over whether the prophets were opposed to the cult in principle or were only critical of cultic malpractice and disregard for ethical duty. Inseparably related to this question is the antagonism between prophet and priest characterized by some scholars as inherent in the relationship.

4.1. Anticultic or Reformist? Much of late nineteenth-century scholarship viewed preexilic prophets as ethical revolutionaries who opposed the ritualism of the cult and mocked its religious efficacy. Only in exile did the institution of the cult and priesthood gain a foothold in the prophetic tradition through the writing of Ezekiel. Opinion swung away from this consensus during the twentieth century toward a model in which prophets opposed only hypocritical ritual that disregarded ethical demands, and writing prophets came to be viewed more closely with the cult (Gordon, 9-12). Along with this paradigm change, the older position was criticized as the product of nineteenth-century liberal Protestantism, specifically the combination of enlightenment humanism and anti-Jewish (and anti-Catholic) sentiment (Zevit). Nevertheless, some recent contributors to the debate, working outside of nineteenth-century presuppositions, still advocate a polarization between prophet and cult.

Numerous texts in the writing prophets demean the value of ritual offerings (e.g., Is 1:10-17; Jer 6:20; 7:21-26; Hos 6:6; Amos 5:21-24; Mic 6:6-8) and even circumcision (Jer 4:4; 9:24-25). R. Hendel writes, "Although many scholars in recent years have attempted to read these passages as something other than rejection of ritual, . . . these scholarly attempts do not do justice to the texts" (Hendel, 190-91). Hendel draws upon the contributions of social theorists Max Weber and Mary Douglas, who suggest that there is a natural conflict in cultures between religious functionaries who claim legitimacy based upon their hereditary rights and tradition (priests) and those whose social

authority stems from acceptance of their personal call as mediators of divine revelation (prophets). At the foundation of this conflict are differing cosmological understandings as to whether or not ritual is efficacious. Furthermore, Hendel argues that the prophet binds together history and ethics (e.g., Mic 6), whereas the priest links them together with ritual (Lev 19). So in priestly theology, ritual is inextricably connected to the ethical, with sacrificial procedures purifying human pollution from the sanctuary. Prophets deny this efficacy.

Advocating a similar position, J. Barton uses Douglas's theory to counter the claim that prophets would have to step outside their culture altogether in order to maintain such a thoroughly antiritualistic stance. He grants that some prophets may have thought only festive indulgence or hypocritical worship to be unfitting, but since several texts (e.g., Jer 7:22; Amos 5:25) appear strictly antiritualistic, nineteenth-century scholars who polarized prophet and cult were essentially right, in spite of their unjustified presuppositions.

In general response to these arguments, evidence suggests that preexilic, classical prophets held a positive view of the cult when it functioned in its prescribed manner. The report of Isaiah's call (Is 6), whether an experience while in the temple complex or only a vision with temple imagery, would be incongruent for a prophet whose position was uncompromisingly anticultic. His encouragement to Hezekiah in the face of Sennacherib's invasion was a positive response to the king's temple lament (Is 37). Z. Zevit observes that both Isaiah (Is 2:2-3) and Micah (Mic 4:1-2) envisioned the cult as a magnet to attract the nations, and Jeremiah spoke encouraging words *in the temple*: "Make good your ways and your deeds, and I will cause you to dwell in this place" (Jer 7:3 [although, in light of Jer 7:7, it must be admitted that "this place" may not refer specifically to the temple]) (Zevit, 208). More pertinent is Jeremiah's promise that Sabbath obedience would result in an abundance of temple offerings (Jer 17:24-26; 33:10-11, 18). Even if, as some commentators maintain, these are not words from the prophet Jeremiah, the author saw no incongruence between Jeremiah's *covenantal theology and procultic sentiments. Isaiah's future vision also depicts outcasts and Gentile nations gathering to the sanctuary with lavish *sacrifices (Is

517

56:4-7; 57:13; 60:7, 13; cf. Zephaniah [see 4.2.6 below]). These are hardly appropriate visions if prophets were in principle opposed to ritual.

Furthermore, several psalms contain rhetoric that elevates a right attitude and ethical life over ritual (Ps 40:6; 50:8-15; 51:16-17; 69:30-31). Although this rhetoric is not antagonistic, as in the case of the prophets, it demonstrates a similar hierarchy of values commonly used to mitigate the anticultic rhetoric of the prophets. In addition to these psalms, M. Weinfeld points to wisdom texts, both Israelite (Prov 15:8; 21:3, 27; 28:9) and Egyptian (Weinfeld, 190-93). For example, the Instruction of Merikare exhorts, "More acceptable is a loaf [offering] of the upright than the ox of the wrongdoer" (Weinfeld, 190). Thus, the common interpretation that prophets opposed only unorthodox or hypocritical cultic activity is intrinsically reasonable when viewed in the broader cultural context.

Social theory illustrating that religious functionaries polarize over ritual only suggests that such is possible, but nothing in the OT necessitates conflicting theologies between prophets and priests. L.-S. Tiemeyer provides a valuable treatise on the relationship between prophets and priests, demonstrating that prophets opposed only priestly malpractice. In fact, within highly ritualistic cultures, "prophetic" and "priestly" functions can cohere in the same individual (e.g., shamans). There is evidence of "professional competition" for prestige between prophetic and priestly functionaries in Mesopotamia, but their activities were not viewed as intrinsically antithetical.

J. Jeremias carefully nuances the supposed dichotomy between "anticult" writing prophets and "peace prophets" of the cult. He argues that all prophets potentially participated in the cult, challenging the people to orthodox worship and ethical practice but also interceding for the welfare of the people. Some misused the latter role and were called to account (cf. Jeremiah [see 4.2.2 below]), and their liability for failure to announce judgment implies that it was their responsibility to do so (Jeremias, 6-9). Those prophets who announced a message of national doom found themselves isolated from the institutional cult. The preservation of this message in the writing prophets was due to the national relevance and historical vindication of their burden (Jeremias, 195-99).

4.2. Unorthodox Cultic Practices. The propensity of Israelites throughout their history and from all strata of society to engage in unorthodox forms of worship is well attested in the biblical record. For this reason more than any other, Yahweh sent the prophets (2 Kings 17:13). Section 2 above summarizes the role of Mesopotamian prophets in advocating for cultic reform, specifically when the king was neglectful of his duties in this regard. However, nothing in the broader ancient Near East resembles the exclusive devotion of OT prophets to one God and his cult (see Gordon, 86). Indeed, the same Mesopotamian prophet could speak in the name of several deities (e.g., SAA 9 1.4), a phenomenon in stark contrast to the preaching of biblical prophets.

4.2.1. Isaiah. The criticism of cultic unorthodoxy in Isaiah 56—66 (Is 57:1-10; 65:1-12; 66:1-6, 17) is complicated in the scholarly literature by a debate concerning the social setting and identity of the prophet's opponents. One common proposal (e.g., Hanson) suggests that during the exile and the early postexilic period conflict arose in the Judean community regarding the manner by which Yahweh would restore his people. On one side, "realistic" theocrats contended for a political solution through a Persian-sponsored temple community led by Zadokite priests. However, a movement of "visionaries" opposed this hierarchy. This antitheocratic group drew upon earlier prophetic ideals and argued that the prophetic function of Yahweh's servant had been subsumed collectively in the entire community. Representing this latter position, Isaiah 56—66 stands in direct opposition to the Zadokites and pro-temple theology as advocated in Ezekiel 40—48, Haggai and Zechariah.

This hypothesis has been questioned from several angles (for a summary, see Tiemeyer, 10-13), but the most relevant consideration for this essay concerns the proposed polarization between Isaiah 56—66 and temple theocracy (e.g., Ezra, Haggai, Zechariah). Tiemeyer argues that Zechariah (Zech 3:1-10; 6:9-15) and Haggai (Hag 2:10-14) also criticize the priesthood (cf. Mal 1:6—3:5). The difference is that Isaiah 56—66 calls not just for radical cleansing, but for the destruction of corrupt priests. Thus, all prophets speak with the same voice, condemning a corrupt priesthood. The theology that God's presence transcends earthly habitation (Is 66:1-6) does not deny the validity of the cult either (Ezek 40—48; Haggai; cf. 1 Kings 8:27); rather, it subordinates cultic ritual (Is 66:3) to right attitude and obedient behavior (Is 66:2b) that is free from syncretism (Is 66:17) (Schramm, 162-68).

One may question whether Isaiah 56—66 originated in a postexilic context or instead comprises oracles of Isaiah of Jerusalem. The latter option avoids the doubtful proposal of rank *idolatry in the postexilic Jerusalem temple, which draws no fire from any postexilic prophet. Whatever one's view of the compositional history of the book of Isaiah, disparaging comments and condemnation about cultic practice are best understood in a manner consistent with the positive visions for the cult elsewhere in Isaiah.

4.2.2. Jeremiah. Jeremiah announced that the cult of his day had become so corrupted by syncretism and worship of other gods that offerings were unacceptable and destruction of the temple was imminent (Jer 2:8-13; 6:19-20; 7:9, 16-34; 11:15; 14:10-12; 18:15; 23:10-14, 39). However, he faced strong opposition from cult prophets who proclaimed the inviolability of the temple (Jer 4:10; 6:14; 7:4; 8:11; 14:13; 18:18; 23:16-22; cf. Ezek 13:10, 16), in part through their hermeneutical misuse of earlier tradition (Jer 23:30 [?]; 28:1-11).

Jeremiah 7:22 is particularly difficult because it appears to draw on a tradition that denied any sacrificial cult in early Yahwism (cf. Amos 5:25). Whether such a tradition ever existed is doubtful, and alternative explanations are numerous (see Lundbom, 481-89). Probably, Jeremiah employs an "idiom of exaggerated contrast" whereby "the first of two statements is negated only for the purpose of setting off the second" (Lundbom, 488). In similar fashion, Amos builds on the implied negation in Amos 5:25 to underscore Amos 5:26-27: Israel's cult will accompany them into exile. The illocutionary force of these statements is not about cultic history or sacrifice per se but rather the relative subordination of cultic duty to covenant obedience (cf. Jer 6:19-20; 7:5-7; 9:23-26).

4.2.3. Ezekiel. Addressing Israel in exile (Ezek 3:4-11), Ezekiel undermined the same false notions of temple inviolability attacked by his contemporary Jeremiah in Jerusalem. The vision of Yahweh's glory departing the temple (Ezek 9—11) incorporates a common ancient Near Eastern motif of divine abandonment of a sanctuary immediately before its destruction, in this case prompted by various manifestations of idolatry and uncleanness that defiled God's holiness in the temple (Ezek 5:11; 8:6; for the cause of social violence as well, see Ezek 22—23; 36:18). As with other prophets, this anti-temple message must be balanced with Ezekiel's vision for the sanctuary offerings in the future restoration (Ezek 20:40-41) (see 5.1 below).

4.2.4. Hosea. Hosea derides Israel for manifold covenant violations (Hos 4:1-2), yet his assault on the cult is framed primarily by his abhorrence of Israel's idolatry and their sacrifice at illicit worship sites (Hos 4:11-14; 13:1-4; for announcements against Judah, see Hos 4:15; 5:5, 13; 6:4; 12:2). Cultic officials, both priest and prophet, are culpable (Hos 4:4-6, 9; 5:1; 9:7-8; 10:5), with final rejection evident in exile (Hos 8:11-13; 9:1-6, 15-17), a fate awaiting Jeroboam's calf cult as well (Hos 8:5-6; 10:5-6). Consequently, Israel's cult is a vacuous attempt to meet Yahweh (Hos 5:6), who delights in loyalty more than sacrifice (Hos 6:6). His rebuke is not a condemnation of the institution of the cult or ritual but rather is an exhortation to orthodoxy and orthopraxis.

4.2.5. Amos. Amos's criticism of the cult is primarily directed against worship corrupted by social injustices (see 4.3.3 below). However, one text, Amos 8:14, alludes directly to the defection from covenant stipulations set in motion by Jeroboam, a prime target in the books of Kings (1 Kings 12:28-32; 16:26; 2 Kings 10:29; 17:16; 23:15). The reference to idolatry in Amos 5:25-26 also implies that Amos viewed worship by some of his contemporaries to be idolatrous (see 4.2.2 below).

4.2.6. Zephaniah. Zephaniah attacks Judah's priests and worshipers who have turned to other gods (Zeph 1:4-6). If the phrase *bêt ᵓădōnêhem* ("house of their Lord") in Zephaniah 1:9 refers to Yahweh's temple rather than an aristocrat's estate ("house of their lord"), then priestly violence and pagan ritual are linked directly with the temple. Priestly defilement is clear in Zephaniah 3:4. The unusually frequent use of the "gathering" motif for both judgment and worship (Zeph 1:2; 2:1; 3:8, 18, 20) hints at a possible setting for Zephaniah's speeches as the Feast of Ingathering. While the "gathering" of some on the Day of Yahweh will be for judgment (i.e., *they* will be the sacrificial victims [Zeph 1:7; 2:1]), a remnant will be gathered for restoration in the prophet's "pro-cult" portrait of universal worship by all nations (Zeph 3:9-10, 18-20).

4.2.7. Malachi. Restoration of worship after the exile did not end the need for reform. Although Malachi does not voice the same accusations against idolatry that pervade the preexilic prophets, flirtation with foreign gods surfaces indirectly in his remarks about intermarriage and profanation of the sanctuary (Mal 2:11), a defilement inseparably related to social injustice toward Israelite wives (Mal 2:12-13). The prophet also condemns defilement from inappropriate offerings (Mal 1:6-14) and the withholding of tithes (Mal 3:7-10). Malachi warns that failure to reform will lead to purification of the temple and community by Yahweh's messenger, who will eradicate both cultic corruption and social injustice (Mal 3:1-5).

4.3. Ethics and Cult. M. Nissinen has observed that looking out for the poor and needy was an expected social function of temples in the ancient Near East (Nissinen 2003) (*see* Wealth and Poverty). Therefore, it is not surprising to find the potential among ancient Near Eastern prophets to admonish the king regarding social themes, although this is a minor emphasis in the extant texts. The Israelite cult also provided for the poor (Lev 7:11-21; Ps 22:25-26), adding irony to the need for biblical prophets to implicate the Israelite cult in their criticism of social injustice and ethical failure (*see* Social Justice).

4.3.1. Isaiah. Isaiah lists social injustice as a disqualification for acceptable worship (Is 1:10-17). The fact that Isaiah mentions prayer among the rejected practices (Is 1:15) strongly supports the view that it was not ritual or the cult to which he objected but rather cultic practice without an appropriate attitude and ethical commitment. This interpretation is reinforced in Isaiah 58:1-14 (cf. Is 56:1), where the prophet condemns days of fasting because proper ethical behavior does not match the humility avowed by the fast.

4.3.2. Micah. According to Micah 1:13; 2:1-2; 6:9-12, social elites in Judah had adopted oppressive economic policies similar to those practiced in Israel and spoken against by Amos (Amos 5:11; 6:4; 8:4-6). In this context, Micah 6:6-8 is not an anticultic proclamation but rather an exhortation to the higher calling of justice (cf. Mic 6:9-12).

4.3.3. Amos and Hosea. Amos's polemic against the cultic institutions of the northern kingdom alludes to unorthodox syncretism (Amos 8:14), but his primary accusation implicates cultic centers with the social injustices of Israel's elite. So the end of luxurious homes accompanies cutting off the horns of the altar at Bethel (Amos 3:14-15), symbolizing impotency of sacrifice under such social conditions. Similarly, Yahweh rejects festivals and offerings because of the injustice and hypocrisy associated with them (Amos 5:21-24; 8:4-6). In his satirical invitation to worship at Bethel (Amos 4:1, 4-5 with Amos 5:4-7), the central symbol of Jeroboam's kingdom (Amos 7:9, 13), Amos indicts the whole nation for seeking injustice rather than Yahweh. An accusation against social violence also contributes to demeaning the cult by Amos's contemporary Hosea (Hos 6:6, 9).

4.3.4. Zechariah. Zechariah's interests extend beyond completion of the temple to spiritual restoration of the people (see 5.2 and 6.6 below). The question posed by the delegation from Bethel regarding fasting (Zech 7:3) offered Zechariah an opportunity to instruct the broader community on a ritual matter. Fasting must flow from true repentance and a life of covenant fidelity evidenced by social justice (Zech 7:9-10; 8:16-17) (see Boda 2003a, 399, 405). In this, Zechariah affirms continuity with the cultic theology of earlier prophetic tradition (Zech 7:12), envisioning as well the attraction of Jewish feasts for gathering the nations to Yahweh (Zech 8:18-23; 14:16-21).

5. Support of the Cult.

The prophets always attempted to move the cult toward its ideal function. In this sense, even criticism constitutes cultic support. But continuing the procultic visions of preexilic prophets (see 4.1 above), Ezekiel and postexilic prophets in particular endeavored to restore worship through visions of a new temple community.

5.1. Ezekiel. Regardless of one's view of its compositional history, the book of Ezekiel as a whole, including Ezekiel 40—48, was transmitted by the ancient community as a prophetic contribution relevant to temple cult. Ezekiel addresses the important question of the place of the temple after the exile. No longer would Yahweh be a "sanctuary" in a diminished way as during the exile (Ezek 11:16). Concomitant with Israel's spiritual revival, Yahweh would restore his holy presence in the midst of his people for all time (Ezek 37:27-28; 39:29). Expanding this theology, Ezekiel appends his vision for the temple (Ezek 40—48), closing the book with a re-naming of Jerusalem, "Yahweh is there."

Ezekiel's vision complements the balance evident in the rest of the prophetic tradition, both "visionary" and "priestly," "dream" and "reality" (*contra* Hanson; see Joyce, 147-48). In the new temple, the glory's departure is reversed (Ezek 43:4). The temple once again becomes the cosmic center of creation, from which emanates a river, giving life to the most desolate places (Ezek 40:2; 47:8-9). Nations are welcome to reside with Israel within the temple's sanctified hinterlands (Ezek 45:3; 47:21-23; 48:12), yet maintaining graded holiness (Ezek 24:20). Although the sacrificial system is lavish and efficacious (Ezek 43:27), Ezekiel's description leaves the temple "empty" of furnishings, perhaps to focus on a strikingly anthropomorphic divine presence, which replaces the ark (Ezek 43:7; cf. Jer 3:16-17) (Joyce, 150-53). Not only would Ezekiel's vision have offered theological support to postexilic cultic initiatives, but also it had practical application for Ezekiel's contemporaries to move them to repentance from their idolatrous ways (Ezek 43:10-12).

5.2. Haggai and Zechariah. Political and socioeconomic difficulties hindered the postexilic community from following through on temple construction, so Haggai and Zechariah lent their prophetic voices to move the community forward (Ezra 4:24—5:2; 6:14; similarly, this entire narrative of the return and rebuilding of the temple commences by reference to the prophecy of Jeremiah in Ezra 1:1). Haggai urged that the solution to economic fruitlessness was responsible action (Hag 1:2-11; 2:18-19), promising a day when their warrior God (Hag 2:6) would bring the wealth of nations to their humble temple (Hag 2:7-9) (*see* Warfare and Divine Warfare). Zechariah, on his part, echoed the political sentiments of Haggai (Hag 2:21-23), advancing Zerubbabel for his support of the temple (Zech 4:6-10) and endorsing Joshua as high priest (Zech 3:1-10; 6:9-15). Zechariah's oracles (and perhaps visions) are closely related to temple construction (Zech 1:16; 2:10-13; 4:9; 6:14-15) (see 6.6 below).

6. Contribution to Liturgy.
If one accepts that OT prophets in both the pre-

exilic and postexilic periods promoted ethical piety and orthodox practices in worship, then it is natural to expect that they not only spoke critically when necessary for cultic reform but also contributed in a constructive manner toward its liturgy. As noted above, ancient Near Eastern prophets contributed in various ways to the liturgy of their respective cults. The presence of prophetic speech in Psalms 12; 60 (cf. Pss 75; 82; 85) also suggests a role for prophets in liturgical intercession. Even Gunkel admitted that many features of psalms were influenced by patterns of prophetic speech (Gunkel, 286-87). When the issue is examined from the side of the Prophetic Books, the difficulty is determining what texts might preserve liturgy. Did a prophet merely utilize a speech form similar to what one might find in the cult, or was the performance setting for a particular prophetic discourse actually cultic? The following discussion focuses on texts for which there is evidence of liturgical performance in the prophet's speech.

6.1. Isaiah. Isaiah is replete with oracles that conform to hymnic patterns (e.g., Is 12:1-6; 25:1-5; 26:1-6; 42:10-13; 49:13; 54:1-3). Salvation oracles in Isaiah 40—48, with their "fear not" formula, self-identification of the Deity ("I am Yahweh") and recollection of previous prophecy, find some of their closest correspondence, form-critically, to cultic prophecy from Assyria (e.g., SAA 9 1.1; 1.4; 1.6; 2.5; Nissinen, Seow and Ritner, 102-16; Weippert). Yet there is no certainty that these Isaianic oracles functioned liturgically.

Two passages containing penitential lament (Is 59:1-21; 63:7—64:12) are frequently proposed as liturgies, stemming from observations that hold true regardless of one's dating of the texts. Isaiah 59:1-20 exhibits a prophetic accusation (Is 59:1-8), with corporate lament and confession (Is 59:9-15a) followed by divine response (Is 59:15b-20) (Werline, 36-41). Most commentators separate Isaiah 59:21 from Isaiah 59:15b-20, but this detracts from the liturgical pattern. The first-person divine speech in Isaiah 59:21 caps the third-person report of Yahweh's intent to intervene, which strengthens the function of Isaiah 59:15b-20 as divine response in a liturgical dialogue (cf. the change to first person in Ps 12:5; 60:6-8; Joel 2:18-20). Commentators note that the abrupt shift to the theme of covenant and the mission of the servant (singular "you") recalls Isaiah 42:6; 49:8; 54:10; 55:3.

Closer to the pattern of communal psalms is Isaiah 63:7—64:12 (cf. Pss 44; 78; 106). These texts incorporate lament with a rehearsal of national salvation history and in some cases highlight the failure of the people as the cause for their lamentable situation. Like Isaiah 59:1-20, Isaiah 63:7—64:12 features confession (Is 64:4-7) and petition for Yahweh's intervention as a warrior (Is 64:1-3; cf. Is 63:1-6), but the element of petition is more explicit (Is 63:15—64:5, 8-10 [see Werline, 41-44]). Conspicuously absent from Isaiah 63:7—64:12, but present in Isaiah 59:1-21 and other communal laments, is an oracle of assurance (Bautch, 40).

6.2. Jeremiah. The fact that Yahweh forbids Jeremiah to intercede for the people (Jer 7:16; 11:11 with 14) implies that he would customarily do so (cf. the communal "we" in Jer 3:22-25). Jeremiah's "confessions" with divine response offer evidence of prophetic liturgy (Jer 10—20 [divine dialogue]). Other instances in Jeremiah describe his involvement as a mediator with divine response to inquiry from the community, but not intercessory lament (Jer 21:2; 37:3; 42:2; cf. Jer 26:1-8, where the prophet's words on a fast day call the people to repentance, but they do not constitute intercession). M. Boda argues that the occurrence of this theme in Jeremiah 14:1—15:4 suggests a communal ceremony in which the prophet responds to a lament offered by a representative of the people (Boda 2001). While R. Werline stresses Jeremiah 29:10-14 as showing a shift toward penitential prayer drawing on Deuteronomy 4:25; 30:1-4 (Werline 29-30), Boda notes similarities between Jeremiah 14:1—15:4 and Leviticus 26 to demonstrate how Jeremiah infused priestly theology into the prayer tradition of the people. So one sees in Jeremiah a prophetically authorized transition in emphasis toward national penitential prayer over the classical pattern of complaint, an emphasis represented in exilic and postexilic prayers such as Psalm 106; Ezra 9; Nehemiah 1; 9; Daniel 9.

6.3. Daniel. The emphasis on penitential themes described in the preceding section is clearly evident in the prayer of Daniel 9. The prayer follows no thorough outline, although the general thrust moves from opening praise (Dan 9:4) through confession and acknowledgment of God's just judgment (Dan 9:5-14) to petition for forgiveness (Dan 9:15-19). It displays all the themes that have been associated with penitential form (Boda 2006a): the central attribute is repentance, drawing on both Deuteronomic (Dan 9:13; cf. Deut 30:1-2 [šûb]) and Priestly (Dan 9:4, 7, 20; cf. Lev 26:39-40 [hitwaddâ, māʿal]) terminology for confessing guilt associated with exile. Failure to heed the prophet's warnings (Dan 9:6, 10) also rings a Deuteronomistic note (cf. 2 Kings 17:13). The concern for guilt is coupled with Jeremiah's seventy weeks (Dan 9:2), which Daniel's *angelic interpreter takes up in response to the prayer as he relates the solution to exile with Levitical remedies for sin (Dan 9:24; cf. Lev 16:21; 26:18, 21, 24, 28). Intergenerational sin links the continuous failure of Israel with the consequence of exile (Dan 9:5-6, 8; cf. Lev 26:39). Conversely, complaint in these prayers is replaced with creedal confession of God's great attributes and acknowledgment of his righteous judgment (Dan 9:4, 7). The people are characterized as a remnant whose *exile by the nations cuts them off from their identity with the land (Dan 9:7, 16-17). Yet they are rooted in the traditions of the *law and *covenant (Dan 9:4-5, 11-13, 15, 19). Though not necessarily related to a cultic setting, Daniel's prayer is intimately concerned with a crisis in the cult.

6.4. Joel. The book of Joel bears marks of a liturgical origin. In the face of national calamity, Joel summons the people to gather for lament and fasting at the temple (Joel 1:13-14; 2:15-17a), calling for repentance, concomitant to sincere shows of lament (Joel 2:12-13a). After the summons, Joel presents a liturgical sample of the lament (Joel 1:15-20). An oracle of salvation follows (Joel 2:19b-27), recording the divine response. The oracle is reported with narrative introduction (Joel 2:18-19a [cf. ESV; NET; NRSV; NIV]), taking a viewpoint after all these events had run their course (preferable to the future-tense translations of the NASB, which disregards the normal past-time function of the preterite verbs). It is possible that Joel only adopts liturgical forms and so does not reflect actual events (Ogden, 97). But even if this were the case, the book preserves the type of contribution that might be expected from prophets serving in the cult: a liturgical pattern of summons, lament and prophetic response. G. Ogden suggests that Joel 2:28—3:21 records further divine response to the *prayers of the prophet, reflecting motifs common to many psalms of communal lament.

6.5. Habakkuk. There is nothing to adjudicate whether or not the prayers and oracles in Habakkuk 1—2 were performed in a cultic setting. The prayers are complaint in form, but they could be either communal (with representative "I") or purely individual. Habakkuk 3, on the other hand, bears a superscription (authorship with musical notation) and postscript (designation with further musical notation) indicating its cultic function. All four elements appear together in the superscription of Psalm 6:1, and three appear in other psalms (e.g., Ps 8:1; 12:1; 22:1; 53:1; 61:1; 62:1). Psalm 102 bears the same classification, "prayer."

Of further interest regarding the liturgical use of Habakkuk 3 are David's song (2 Sam 22:1-51) and Hezekiah's poem (Is 38:9-20). The former song functions to commemorate David's experience of Yahweh's deliverance over a critical period of life (2 Sam 22:1). Hezekiah's poetic memoir (Is 38:9) captures his reflections on Yahweh's deliverance for future temple music (Is 38:20). In a similar manner, Habakkuk 3 offers a theological reflection of the prophet's dialogue with Yahweh in the first two chapters: Habakkuk rests in the terrifying, sovereign power of the Divine Warrior to judge the wicked and vindicate the righteous.

6.6. Haggai and Zechariah. Boda argues that temple reconstruction rituals from the ancient Near East influenced the structure of Haggai as a book (decision [Hag 1], preparation [Hag 2:1-9], foundation laying [Hag 2:10-23]) (Boda 2006b). Although this order would reflect the natural course of events for any such project, Haggai could preserve words used in the actual rituals. Zechariah's visions in Zechariah 1:7—6:15 are also possibly united around the theme of temple foundation (Zech 1:16; 2:10-11; 4:9; 6:15) in a way that reflects ancient Mesopotamian rituals for temple restoration, suggesting a liturgical background for Zechariah 1—6 (Halpern). However, some of these parallels are speculative, and parts of the visions could simply be alluding to temple foundation imagery without constituting a liturgy as a whole. Other concerns are also evident in the text, such as the theme of *repentance in the narrative frames of Zechariah 1:1-6; 7:1—8:23, which leads Boda to propose a setting in postexilic penitential rituals (Boda 2003b). But even this theme is subordinate to Zechariah's support for temple restoration (Zech 8:9, 18-23). So al-

though Zechariah probably ministered in liturgical settings, direct associations between these cultic messages and passages from the book of Zechariah are difficult to establish.

7. Conclusion.

Throughout the ancient Near East, prophets were concerned with the cult, often contributing to temple service. In the OT, the most conspicuous role was criticism, reflecting the prophetic passion to reform the worship of ancient Israel. This concern reverberates throughout preexilic and postexilic prophetic writings. The only discernible change is not in the prophetic phenomena, but rather in a theological shift in response to different religious challenges. Preexilic prophets called for reform but in the end announced complete destruction of the cult as the only solution toward a future glorious restoration. But the messages of exilic and postexilic prophets concerned the restoration of proper temple worship. In both periods there is evidence that prophets actively contributed to the liturgy, interceding on behalf of the people with lament, penitence and divine response.

See also ANCIENT NEAR EASTERN PROPHECY; PRAYER; PROPHECY, HISTORY OF; SACRIFICE AND ATONEMENT; TEMPLE; WORSHIP.

BIBLIOGRAPHY. **J. Barton,** "The Prophets and the Cult," in *Temple and Worship in Biblical Israel,* ed. J. Day (LHBOTS 422; London: T & T Clark International, 2005) 111-22; **R. J. Bautch,** *Developments in Genre between Post-Exilic Penitential Prayers and the Psalms of Communal Lament* (SBLAB 7; Atlanta: Society of Biblical Literature, 2003); **M. J. Boda,** "From Complaint to Contrition: Peering through the Liturgical Window of Jer 14,1-15,4," *ZAW* 113 (2001) 186-97; idem, "From Facts to Feasts: The Literary Function of Zechariah 7-8," *CBQ* 65 (2003a) 390-407; idem, "Zechariah: Master Mason or Penitential Prophet?" in *Yahwism after the Exile: Perspectives on Israelite Religion in the Persian Period,* ed. R. Albertz and B. Becking (STR 5; Assen: Van Gorcum, 2003b) 49-69; idem, "Confession as Theological Expression: Ideological Origins of Penitential Prayer," in *Seeking the Favor of God,* 1: *The Origins of Penitential Prayer in Second Temple Judaism,* ed. M. J. Boda, D. K. Falk and R. A. Werline (SBLEJL 21; Atlanta: Society of Biblical Literature, 2006a) 21-50; idem, "From Dystopia to Myopia: Utopian (Re)Visions in Haggai and Zechariah 1-8," in *Utopia* and Dystopia in Prophetic Literature, ed. E. Ben Zvi (PFES 92; Helsinki: Finnish Exegetical Society; Göttingen: Vandenhoeck & Ruprecht, 2006b) 210-48; **J. H. Breasted,** *Ancient Records of Egypt II* (Chicago: University of Chicago Press, 1906); **R. P. Gordon,** "A Story of Two Paradigm Shifts," in *The Place Is Too Small for Us: The Israelite Prophets in Recent Scholarship,* ed. R. P. Gordon (Winona Lake, IN: Eisenbrauns, 1995) 3-26; **H. Gunkel,** *Introduction to Psalms: The Genres of the Religious Lyric of Israel,* completed by J. Begrich, trans. J. D. Nogalski (Macon, GA: Mercer University Press, 1998 [1933]); **B. Halpern,** "The Ritual Background of Zechariah's Temple Song," *CBQ* 40 (1978) 167-90; **P. D. Hanson,** *The Dawn of Apocalyptic: The Historical and Sociological Roots of Jewish Apocalyptic Eschatology* (Philadelphia: Fortress, 1975); **R. S. Hendel,** "Prophets, Priests, and the Efficacy of Ritual," in *Pomegranates and Golden Bells: Studies in Biblical, Jewish, and Near Eastern Ritual, Law and Literature in Honor of Jacob Milgrom,* ed. D. P. Wright, D. N. Freedman and A. Hurvitz (Winona Lake, IN: Eisenbrauns, 1995) 185-98; **J. W. Hilber,** *Cultic Prophecy in the Psalms* (BZAW 352; Berlin: de Gruyter, 2005); idem, "Prophetic Speech in the Egyptian Royal Cult," in *On Stone and Scroll: Essays in Honour of Graham Ivor Davies,* ed. J. K. Aitken, K. J. Dell, and B. A. Mastin (BZAW 420; Berlin: Walter de Gruyter, 2011) 39-53; **H. B. Huffmon,** "A Company of Prophets: Mari, Assyria, Israel," in *Prophecy in Its Ancient Near Eastern Context: Mesopotamian, Biblical, and Arabian Perspectives,* ed. M. Nissinen (SBLSymS 13; Atlanta: Society of Biblical Literature, 2000) 47-70; **J. Jeremias,** *Kultprophetie und Gerichtsverkündigung in der späten Königzeit Israels* (WMANT 35; Neukirchen-Vluyn: Neukirchener Verlag, 1970); **A. R. Johnson,** *The Cultic Prophet in Ancient Israel* (2nd ed.; Cardiff: University of Wales Press, 1962); **P. M. Joyce,** "Temple and Worship in Ezekiel 40-48," in *Temple and Worship in Biblical Israel,* ed. J. Day (LHBOTS 422; London: T & T Clark International, 2005) 145-63; **K. A. Kitchen,** *Poetry of Ancient Egypt* (Documenta Mundi, Aegyptiaca 1; Jonsered: Paul

Åströms, 1999); **J. R. Lundbom,** *Jeremiah 1-20: A New Translation with introduction and Commentary* (AB 21A; New York: Doubleday, 1999); **S. Mowinckel,** *The Psalms in Israel's Worship,* trans. D. R. Ap-Thomas (2 vols.; Oxford: Blackwell, 1962); **M. Nissinen,** "The Socioreligious Role of the Neo-Assyrian Prophets," in *Prophecy in Its Ancient Near Eastern Context: Mesopotamian, Biblical, and Arabian Perspectives,* ed. M. Nissinen (SBLSymS 13; Atlanta: Society of Biblical Literature, 2000) 89-114; idem, "Das kritische Potential in der altorientalischen Prophetie," in *Propheten in Mari, Assyrien und Israel,* ed. M. Köckert and M. Nissinen (FRLANT 201; Göttingen: Vandenhoeck & Ruprecht, 2003) 1-32; **M. Nissinen, C. L. Seow and R. K. Ritner,** *Prophets and Prophecy in the Ancient Near East* (SBLWAW 12; Atlanta: Society of Biblical Literature, 2003); **G. S. Ogden,** "Joel 4 and Prophetic Responses to National Laments," *JSOT* 26 (1983) 97-106; **B. Schramm,** *The Opponents of Third Isaiah: Reconstructing the Cultic History of the Restoration* (JSOTSup 193; Sheffield: Sheffield Academic Press, 1995); **L.-S. Tiemeyer,** *Priestly Rites and Prophetic Rage: Post-Exilic Prophetic Critique of the Priesthood* (FAT 2/19; Tübingen: Mohr Siebeck, 2006); **M. Weinfeld,** "Ancient Near Eastern Patterns in Prophetic Literature," *VT* 27 (1979) 178-95; **M. Weippert,** "'Ich bin Jahwe'-'Ich bin Ishtar von Arbela': Deuterojesaja im Lichte der neuassyrischen Prophetie," in *Prophetie und Psalmen: Festschrift für Klaus Seybold zum 65. Geburtstag,* ed. B. Huwyler, H.-P. Mathys and B. Weber (AOAT 280; Münster: Ugarit-Verlag, 2001) 31-59; **R. A. Werline,** *Penitential Prayer in Second Temple Judaism: The Development of a Religious Institution* (SBLEJL 13; Atlanta: Scholars Press, 1998); **Z. Zevit,** "The Prophet versus Priest Antagonism Hypothesis: Its History and Origin," in *The Priests in the Latter Prophets: The Portrayal of Priests, Prophets and Other Religious Specialists in the Latter Prophets,* ed. L. L. Grabbe and A. O. Bellis (JSOTSup 408; London: T & T Clark International, 2004) 189-217.

J. W. Hilber

LORD GOD. *See* GOD.

M

MAGIC. *See* DIVINATION, MAGIC.

MALACHI, BOOK OF

The book of Malachi is the last of the twelve Minor Prophets and is the final book of the OT in most English versions of the Bible. The prophet Malachi preached to a diverse audience. His sermons were directed to the disillusioned, the cynical, the callous, the dishonest, the apathetic, the doubting, the skeptical and the outright wicked in postexilic Judah. Yet, as a sensitive pastor, Malachi offered the "valentine" of God's love to a disheartened people. As a lofty theologian, he instructed the people in a basic doctrinal catechism, highlighting the nature of God as universal king, faithful suzerain and righteous judge. As Yahweh's stern prophet, Malachi rebuked corrupt priests and warned of the coming day of God's judgment. As spiritual guide, he exhorted his audience to a more sincere life of *worship and challenged the people to live out the ethical standards of the Mosaic *covenant. Most important, Malachi was Yahweh's messenger and his essential message to Israel was profoundly simple: "'I have always loved you,' said the LORD" (Mal 1:2).

The prophet's references to the messenger who prepares the *Day of the Lord, along with the Lord's sudden appearance in his *temple (Mal 3:1) and the coming of the prophet Elijah, build a natural bridge to the NT (Mal 4:5; cf. Mt 11:10, 14; 17:10-12; Mk 1:2; 9:11-13; Lk 7:27). The message of Malachi is always relevant to the life of the church, with its emphasis on proper worship, priestly (i.e., pastoral) *leadership, *marriage and divorce, and matters of *social justice.

1. Author
2. Date and Occasion of Writing
3. Structure
4. Text and Versification
5. Malachi Among the Twelve Prophets
6. Literary Style
7. Audience
8. Message
9. Theological Concerns
10. Imagery in Malachi

1. Author.

The book is silent on the issue of authorship, although it is assumed that the prophetic-word formula ("The word of the LORD to Israel through Malachi" [Mal 1:1]) signifies that Malachi penned his own oracles. Based on the translation of Malachi 1:1 in the LXX ("by the hand of his messenger"), some scholars have taken "Malachi" to be a title for an anonymous prophet, perhaps a play on words with Malachi 3:1, "my messenger" (Heb *mal'ākî*). The fact that "Malachi" stands as a unique proper noun in the OT should not disqualify its use as a personal name, since both Habakkuk and Jonah are also exceptional among the names of the Hebrew prophets. The name "Malachi" may be translated "my messenger" or "my angel," and it serves as a fitting name for a prophet of God. The name "Malachi" also fits a pattern of other Hebrew names ending in *i*, such as "Beeri" (Hos 1:1) and "Zichri" (Ex 6:21).

The Bible records no biographical information for Malachi. His inclusion among the OT prophets both identifies Malachi as spokesperson for God and verifies his commission as a divine messenger. Malachi's sermons display a strong interest in the temple, priesthood and *sacrificial system of worship. Although he may have been a priest, he seems to speak as an outside observer of that system. Later Jewish tradition includes Malachi, along with Haggai and Zechariah, as members of the Great Synagogue (*b. B. Bat.* 15a). According to this tradition, this assembly of Jewish prophets, elders and teachers was instrumental in the collection, preservation and transmission of the Hebrew Scriptures and Jewish religious traditions during the time of transition between the end of the biblical era and the beginning of the rabbinic period of Jewish history.

2. Date and Occasion of Writing.

Typically, the book of Malachi is dated around 450 to 430 BC. It often is assumed that Malachi was a contemporary of Ezra and Nehemiah because the prophet addresses the same religious concerns and social ills confronted by these two postexilic reformers. For example, Malachi denounces a lax and corrupt priesthood (Mal 1:6—2:9), mixed marriages and divorce (Mal 2:10-16), liturgical decay, including neglect of the tithe (Mal 3:8-12), and social injustice (Mal 3:5)—the same abuses corrected during the ministries of Ezra and Nehemiah (cf. Ezra 9:1-15; Neh 5:1-13; 12:30, 44-47; Neh 13:4-31).

A careful study of the language of Malachi's oracles, however, reveals that the Hebrew text of the book has great affinity to the books of Haggai and Zechariah (see Hill, 395-400). Socioeconomic and political analysis of Persian-period Judah also suggest chronological ties between the three postexilic prophets (*see* Israelite History). For example, the Haggai-Zechariah-Malachi corpus acknowledges the leadership of a (presumably Persian appointed) "governor" (Hag 1:1; Mal 1:8; cf. Zech 4), a functioning second temple in Jerusalem (Hag 1:14; Zech 7:1-3; Mal 1:10-14), and generally an era of economic decline and spiritual malaise (Hag 1:5-6; Zech 8:12-13; Mal 3:8-12, 14-15). In fact, E. Meyers and C. Meyers note that the social setting for the language of power, the lack of reference to any royal social context (in Zech 9—14 and Malachi), and the Persian activities in response to the problems with Greece and Egypt that reduced the potential for provincial autonomy in Judah make the most sense against the backdrop of the early fifth century BC (Meyers and Meyers, 16-32). On the basis of this evidence, it seems more likely that Malachi was a slightly later contemporary of these two postexilic prophets of the second temple. He probably was preaching in Jerusalem sometime between 500 and 475 BC. It is even possible that the battle between the Persians and Greeks at Mara-

thon (c. 490 BC) was the occasion that prompted Malachi's message. Given Malachi's report of the destruction of Edom (Mal 1:3-5) and his references to the "nations" (Mal 1:11, 14), the prophet may have interpreted that titanic struggle between east and west as at least a partial fulfillment of Haggai's prediction that God was about "to shake the heavens and earth" and "overthrow royal thrones" (Hag 2:21-22).

Malachi addressed Jews in the recently formed province of Judah (formally Yehud) in the Persian satrapy of Eber-Nahara during the reign of King Darius I (522-486 BC). His audience included expatriates resettled in Judah and the descendants of those Hebrews who survived the Babylonian sack of Jerusalem but were not deported to Mesopotamia.

The edict of Cyrus the Great issued in 538 BC serves as the historical background for the ministries of the postexilic prophets Haggai, Zechariah and Malachi. The decree permitted conquered people groups who had been deported to Mesopotamia by the Babylonians to return to their native lands. The royal edict is associated by some scholars with the clay barrel known as the Cyrus Cylinder, discovered in the late nineteenth century. In it Cyrus also issued decrees permitting other captive people groups to return to their homelands. The edict cited in 2 Chronicles 36:23 and repeated in Ezra 1:1-4 is presumably such a directive. The first wave of emigrants to Jerusalem numbered 42,360, along with 7,337 servants (Ezra 2:64-65).

These emigrants were led back by Sheshbazzar, a prince of Judah and the first governor of the restoration community in postexilic Judah (Ezra 1:5-11). The foundation for a new temple was laid during the early stages of his administration, sometime in 538 or 537 BC (Ezra 5:16). The meager project was soon abandoned, however, and the construction site lay neglected for two decades. The promising start quickly faded amidst the stark reality of Persian domination and the problems of mere survival among the competing provinces of the satrapy. Not until the preaching of the prophets Haggai and Zechariah (520-518 BC) did the initiative to rebuild the Jerusalem temple resume (cf. Hag 1:14). The second temple was completed in March of 515 BC (Ezra 6:15). The second temple was erected under the auspices of the Persian king Darius I, and the monies granted for the rebuilding probably took the form of "tax rebates" from the Persian royal treasury.

Politically, Judah struggled for identity amidst a sea of hostile neighboring satrapy provinces. The office of provincial governor was still in its infancy, and the provincial bureaucracy was in an embryonic stage of development. Any deference shown to Judah by the Persian overlords, religious or otherwise, was largely a matter of political pragmatism, since the Persian army needed a base of operations for the conquest and control of Egypt.

Religiously, the second *temple had been completed, but it paled in comparison to its Solomonic predecessor (Ezra 3; Hag 2:1-9). Temple worship was in a sorry state, as worshipers cheated God in their sacrifices and tithes. The priesthood was also in need of reform, as the ministry of the apathetic priests was actually leading people into sin, not out of it. The hopes raised by Haggai and Zechariah for a revival of the Davidic dynasty rooted in the figure of Zerubbabel (Hag 2:20-23; Zech. 3; 6:9-15) seem to have disappeared by the time of Malachi. The priests and the Levites were the "powerbrokers" when he preached to Judah.

Socially, Malachi confronts a population given to religious cynicism and political skepticism. The disillusionment of the postexilic Jewish community was prompted by several theological misunderstandings, including the expectations for wealth that Haggai had promised once the second temple was rebuilt (Hag 2:7, 18-19), the restoration of the Davidic covenant predicted by Ezekiel (Ezek 34:13, 23-24), and the implementation of Jeremiah's "new covenant" (Jer 31:23, 31-33). In the minds of many in Malachi's audience, God had failed his people.

3. Structure.

Most biblical interpreters divide the book of Malachi into six oracles or disputations (see the outline below), although other divisions are suggested (e.g., P. Verhoef breaks Mal 1:6—2:9 into two pericopes [Mal 1:6-14; 2:1-9] and counts seven oracles [Verhoef, 162], while W. Kaiser identifies five oracles by combining Mal 2:1-9 with Mal 2:10-16, and Mal 2:17—3:5 with Mal 3:6-12 into single pericopes [Kaiser, 17]).

The book roughly follows the general pattern of prophetic literature, including an indictment (Mal 1:2—2:17 [often outlining specific covenant violations]), the threat of divine

judgment (Mal 3:1-5), instruction (Mal 3:6-12 [usually including a call to repentance]) and the aftermath (Mal 3:13-4:3 [including an affirmation of future hope or the promise of deliverance]). Beyond this, however, the overall structure and organization of these literary units has proven more difficult to assess. For instance, J. Smith regards Malachi as a well-planned and harmonious book (J. Smith, 3), while J. Baldwin finds no particular literary structure in the book and considers the work a haphazard treatment of topics (Baldwin, 214). Still others view Malachi's oracles as heavily redacted composite speeches created as a literary device for didactic purposes (so Redditt, 152-55) or fashioned merely as a literary "bookend" for the twelve Minor Prophets (so Nogalski, 211) (see Book of the Twelve).

A middle ground between the somewhat loose structure of the book observed by Baldwin and the highly edited structure of Malachi's speeches proposed by Redditt and Nogalski is preferred. Attempts to discern structure in the collection of oracles by relating the prophet's sermons to more formal structural analysis and overarching theological ideas have merit. One method, the structuralist approach, highlights keyword links that join sections within a pericope or join one pericope to another (e.g., McKenzie and Wallace, 558-60; they document covenant terminology connecting the oracles of Mal 1:6—3:12 with the idea of covenant presumed in God's election of Israel in Mal 1:2-5). Such an approach affirms that the oracles are linked by covenant ideas and terms and suggests that the first oracle, God's election of Israel (Mal 1:2-5), is a prologue or introduction that informs the rest of the oracles (Hill, 34; cf. Verhoef, 179-84, loosely arranging Malachi's oracles after the pattern of the suzerain treaty, with Mal 1:2-5 functioning as the historical prologue).

Attempts to connect Malachi's disputations to formal treaty structure (so Verhoef) or the covenant-lawsuit pattern (the so-called rîb pattern) are useful for emphasizing the covenant theme of the book, but they strain to compress all the data into the precise literary form (e.g., O'Brien 1990, 63-64). In either case, the prophet's tone and style are confrontational, similar to the reasoned and forceful argumentation typical of a courtroom setting (see Achtemeier, 172).

Additionally, E. Clendenen's *rhetorical analysis of Malachi proves helpful in assessing the thematic structure of the book (Taylor and Clendenen, 221-22). He identifies the prophet's oracles as a hortatory discourse type of persuasive speech that possesses no definite order (like the more careful notational structure of narrative). Malachi's oracles are in keeping with prophetic speech that may be both repetitive and recursive (or overlapping). This accounts for the covenant context and pervasive legal tone of the oracles and helps to explain the inverted or chiastic structure of the prophet's message, arranged accordingly (see Dorsey, 323):

(A) Yahweh, who loves (Mal 1:2-5)
(B) priests who have cheated God
    (Mal 1:6-14)
(C) Levi's covenant in the past (Mal 2:1-9)
(D) [the focal point] the call to faithfulness
    (Mal 2:10-16)
(C') the future messenger of the covenant
    (Mal 2:17—3:6)
(B') people who have robbed God
    (Mal 3:7-12)
(A') Yahweh rewards the righteous
    (Mal 3:13—4:3 [MT 3:13-21])

This reading of Malachi assumes the traditional division of the book into six hortatory disputations framed by a superscription (Mal 1:1) and a double appendix (Mal 4:4-6 [MT 3:22-24]):

Superscription: Malachi, Yahweh's
    messenger (Mal 1:1)
First Disputation: Yahweh's love for Israel
    (Mal 1:2-5)
Second Disputation: Indictment of corrupt
    priesthood (Mal 1:6—2:9)
Third Disputation: Indictment of faithless
    people (Mal 2:10-16)
Fourth Disputation: Yahweh's coming
    messenger of justice and judgment (Mal
    2:17—3:5)
Fifth Disputation: The Call to Serve
    Yahweh (Mal 3:6-12)
Sixth Disputation: The Coming Day of
    Judgment (Mal 3:13—4:3 [MT 3:13-21])
Appendices (Mal 4:4-6):
Challenge to obey the law of Moses (Mal
    4:4 [MT 3:22])
Elijah and the Day of Yahweh (Mal 4:5-6
    [MT 3:23-24])

4. Text and Versification.

The Hebrew text (MT) of Malachi is in a very good state of preservation (see Text and Textual Criticism). Portions of the book of Malachi are attested by fragments of the DSS, including Malachi 1:13-14 and parts of Malachi 2:10—4:6 (MT 2:10—3:24). Preliminary study of these fragments reveals that portions of these manuscripts (4Q76) agree with the LXX against the MT (see Fuller). Two verses in the MT of Malachi are especially difficult to interpret (Mal 2:15, 16), due both to textual corruption and grammatical anomaly. Baldwin has suggested that the text at this point has "suffered perhaps at the hands of scribes who took exception to its teaching" (Baldwin, 240).

The versification of the MT differs from the versification of English Bibles at the conclusion of the book of Malachi. The Hebrew Bible orders the last six verses of the book (Mal 4:1-6) as a continuation of Malachi 3 (MT = 3:19-24).

5. Malachi Among the Twelve Prophets.

The ancient Hebrew and Greek manuscript traditions reveal that most or all of the twelve Minor Prophets often were written on a single scroll (although scribal practice does not explicitly indicate that these books were considered a literary unity). This has led some scholars to postulate that the twelve Minor Prophets are a "book" (often called the *Book of the Twelve), a collection of prophetic books organized into a unified composition with discernible literary structure and plot movement (see House). At the very least, it may be possible to regard the twelve Minor Prophets as a scroll unified by the prophetic genre with an implied narrative and a central theme (or themes? [see Gottwald; Petersen 2000]). D. Petersen identifies the prophetic concept of the Day of the Lord as the dominant theme of the Minor Prophets (Petersen 2000, 9-10). T. Collins recognizes several principal themes in the Book of the Twelve, including covenant election, fidelity and infidelity, fertility and infertility, turning and returning, God's justice and God's mercy, God's kingship, the temple, and nations as enemies and nations as allies (Collins, 65). Additionally, the Book of the Twelve is framed by the prophetic call to repentance (employing similar phraseology). Notably, the first two books (Hos 6:1; 7:10; 14:1-2; Joel 2:12-14) and the last two books of the collection (Zech 1:3-4; Mal 3:7) admonish the Hebrews to turn back to God and restore faithful covenant relationship with him.

The books of Haggai, Zechariah and Malachi form a distinct subcollection or literary corpus within the Book of the Twelve. All three prophets belong to the Persian period of early postexilic Hebrew history and are unified by literary device (e.g., the rhetorical question and the repetition of prophetic speech formulas) and theological themes (God's sovereignty over the nations, God's faithfulness to his covenant promises, *repentance, temple worship, eschatological judgment and *blessing).

Like Zechariah 9—11; 12—14, the book of Malachi is prefaced by the compound title that includes the genre classification term "oracle" (Heb *maśśā'*) and the prophetic-word formula "the word of the LORD" (Heb *dĕbar yhwh*). The relationship of the three *maśśā'* oracles is a point of scholarly discussion. The headings do provide a basic literary framework for Zechariah 9—14 and Malachi and may indicate the activity of an editor group responsible for bringing Haggai-Zechariah-Malachi into their canonical arrangement (Meyers and Meyers, 90-91; on the literary integrity of the three oracles, cf. Childs, 490-91). The combination of the two expressions is a distinctive feature of late biblical prophecy (Meyers and Meyers, 91). The term *maśśā'* means "oracle" or "burden" in the sense of a pronouncement of prophetic judgment and invests the prophet's message with both divine authority and a certain sense of urgency.

The Haggai-Zechariah-Malachi corpus sometimes is described as a narrative profile of postexilic Jerusalem recounting the spiritual history of the Hebrew restoration community. For example, R. Pierce understands the record of the postexilic prophets more negatively as one of covenant failure, since Malachi ends where Haggai begins, with a religious community in disarray (Pierce 1984b, 411). Conversely, others interpret the spiritual history of the restoration community as recorded in the Haggai-Zechariah-Malachi corpus more positively as the account of repentance and worship renewal prompting the return of the community to proper relationship with the Lord God (e.g., Schneider, 143-49; House, 96-109). The closing verses (Mal 4:4-6) may serve double duty as both appendices to the book and perhaps to the entire OT prophetic corpus. These additions, with their appeal to the ideal figures of Moses and Elijah, tie the oracles of Malachi (and the Book of the Twelve) to the larger collections of the Torah and the Latter Prophets in the OT canon.

6. Literary Style.

Like Haggai and Zechariah, the speeches of Malachi are essentially prose summaries in the third person. The speeches of Malachi are formally classified as belonging to the genre "oracular prose." The messages are "oracular" in nature because they represent authoritative prophetic speech motivated or inspired by God himself. By "prose" is meant that the literary texture of Malachi is a blend of prosaic and rhetorical features approaching poetic discourse but distinctive of prophetic style. This kind of prophetic speech often is characterized by formulaic language. Examples of these stylized expressions in Malachi include the prophetic-word formula ("the message that the LORD gave" [Mal 1:1]), the messenger formula ("said the LORD Almighty" [e.g., Mal 1:8, 14; 2:4]), the self-introduction formula ("I am the LORD" [Mal 3:6)] and the call-to-repentance formula ("return to me" [Mal 3:7]).

The discourse units in Malachi may be broadly categorized as judgment speeches because they accuse, indict and pronounce judgment on the audience (*see* Form Criticism). The prophet's style is also argumentative, whether understood more generally as disputation speeches (e.g., Baldwin, 213-14; Glazier-McDonald, 20-21) or identified narrowly as a covenant lawsuit format (e.g., O'Brien 1990, 63-64). More precisely, the literary form of Malachi's oracles may be linked to both Westermann's "legal procedure" (or trial speech) and the "disputation" as a subset of the legal-procedure speech form (Westermann, 169-76). The disputation speech pits the prophet of God against his audience in confrontational dialogue. It is possible that the origin of the disputation format in Malachi should be traced to a source deeper than the rhetorical style of the writer. For instance, J. Adamson suggests that the prophetic speech form of charge and countercharge exchanged between prophet and audience may have been rooted in the heated cries of hecklers protesting and questioning the prophet's sermons when he first preached his message on the street corners (Adamson, 805). Typically, in Malachi the disputation features these elements: (1) a truth claim declared by the prophet; (2) a hypothetical refutation on the part of the audience in the form of a question; (3) the prophet's answer to the audience rebuttal by restating his initial premise; (4) the presentation of additional supporting evidence.

The desired outcome in both covenant-lawsuit and disputation speeches "is to leave the opponent devoid of further argumentation and resigned to the divine decision" (Patterson, 303). The disputation developed as an alternative form of prophetic speech because the people were unresponsive to the more conventional oracular speech. This rhetorical-question-and-disputation format gave rise to the dialogical method of exposition peculiar to the later rabbinic schools of Judaism (cf. the teaching method of Jesus in Mt 5:21, 27: "You have heard that it was said . . . , but I say unto you . . .").

7. Audience.

Malachi's first oracle (Mal 1:2-5) is addressed generally to the Hebrew community living in postexilic Jerusalem and environs. The prophet's second (Mal 1:6-2:9) oracle is aimed specifically at the priests and Levites serving in the second temple. The final four oracles (including the call to repentance [Mal 3:6-12]) of Malachi's prophecy are once again directed broadly to the inhabitants of postexilic Judah (Mal 2:10-16; 2:17—3:5; 3:6-12; 3:13—4:3), although the Levites are specifically mentioned again in the fourth oracle or disputation (cf. Mal 3:3-4). The righteous Hebrews within the restoration community are singled out and contrasted with the wicked in the final oracle (see Mal 3:16-18).

8. Message.

The message of Malachi is all about "getting things right." The thrust of Malachi's preaching may be placed under the umbrella theme "covenant," specifically the covenant of Jacob (i.e., the patriarchs [Mal 1:2]), the covenant of Levi (Mal 2:4-5, an obscure reference, perhaps an allusion to the covenant made with Phinehas in Num 25:10-13), the covenant of marriage (Mal 2:14) and the covenant of Moses (Mal 4:4). The essential idea of covenant is that of an agreement or treaty that establishes a relationship between parties with attendant obligations and responsibilities. It is not surprising, then, that three of Malachi's disputations deal with

right relationships. The prophetic messenger also works on the premise that proper knowledge of God and his covenant is essential to maintaining these right relationships.

First, the prophet calls the people back to a right understanding of who God is as Israel's father, suzerain and covenant maker (Mal 1:2-5). Next he admonishes the priests and the people to return to the practice of right worship by participating in the temple sacrifices with honesty and integrity (Mal 1:6—2:9). The prophet addresses the issue of right relationships in marriage by decrying divorce and encouraging loyalty on the part of spouses (Mal 2:10-16). Right relationships must extend to the community at large in attitudes and behavior that promote honesty because God is just (Mal 2:17—3:5). The honesty foundational to social justice must also motivate right giving to God because he is gracious and generous in his response to those who are faithful (Mal 3:6-12). Finally, Malachi summons his audience to right relationship with God because he is faithful to his word and desires genuine worship (Mal 3:13—4:3). Interestingly, a pervasive subtheme in the book is honesty, as three of the six disputations urge the people of postexilic Judah to embrace this virtue.

9. Theological Concerns.

The book of Malachi is primarily a theology proper, a treatise on the nature and character of God (see VanGemeren, 204-8). The prophet reminds his audience that their Lord is "father" of Israel (Mal 1:6), as well as "master" and "king" (Mal 1:6, 14). Wary of the extremes of familiarity and formality, Malachi is careful to present a balanced picture of the Lord Almighty. God is sovereign over both the nations (Mal 1:3-5, 11, 14) and Israel as his elect nation or "special treasure" (Mal 1:2; 3:17). Yet his love for Israel (Mal 1:2) does not preclude divine testing and even judgment for the sake of purifying his people (Mal 3:2-3).

Malachi's knowledge of and identification with Israel's covenant tradition place his book in the mainstream of OT theology. The prophet recognized God as both the maker and keeper of covenant with Israel (Mal 1:2; 2:10), and he understood the status of Israel as "adopted child" by virtue of that covenant relationship (Mal 1:6). The conditional nature of Yahweh's covenant placed a premium upon Israel's obedience to the treaty stipulations and the necessity of repentance for a breach of the covenant relationship (Mal 3:7, 16-18). The threat of divine judgment against Israel is rooted in God's unchanging nature (Mal 3:6) (see God). This is not so much a metaphysical statement about God's immutability, a theological commentary on the nature of his being, as it is an affirmation that God is eternally faithful to his covenant initiatives (cf. Ex 6:5; Lev 26:40-42; Ps 111:9; Jer 31:20) (see Baker, 288-89). Malachi acknowledged that Israel's relationship with the Lord demanded both "vertical" and "horizontal" responsibilities in the form of proper *worship (Mal 1:10-14) (see Mallone, 43-59) and *social justice (Mal 3:5) (see Baker, 275-80).

Perhaps more troublesome for Malachi's audience is the sobering reality that the Mosaic covenant is still operative. The prophet maintains that the stipulations of God's Sinai treaty established with Israel after the exodus from Egypt, with its attendant *blessings and curses, has currency for postexilic Judah. This raises theological questions for Malachi's audience at two levels. If the Mosaic covenant is still in effect, "Where is the God of justice?" (Mal 2:17). Malachi's audience alleges that the retribution principle of the Sinai covenant has been revoked because the righteous were not experiencing divine blessing, and all the while the wicked appeared to be thriving (Mal 3:14-15). Implicit in this charge of divine injustice is the perception that postexilic Judah still languished under the "corporate curse" of the *law of Moses due to the disobedience of other (or even previous?) members of the Hebrew community. The pious Jews of the restoration community were clamoring for the "new covenant" paradigm of Jeremiah (Jer 31:31-34). Under the umbrella of this covenant relationship the righteous would no longer be held hostage to the covenant misbehavior of an earlier constituency. Rather, individuals were now to be held accountable for their own sins (Jer 31:29-30; Ezek 18:2-4). Malachi's sermons, and the responses of his audience, reflect the tension for the people of God living between these two theological realities as the old covenant slowly makes way for the new covenant (cf. Mt 9:14-17; Lk 22:20).

Malachi preaches a lofty doctrine of *marriage as companionship with the spouse of one's youth (Mal 2:14) and parenting as a shared responsibility (Mal 2:15). The prophet calls attention to the sacred nature of the husband-wife

relationship by placing the covenant of marriage (Mal 2:14) within the context of the covenant between God and Israel (Mal 2:10) (see Hugenberger, 27-47). This explains his censure of easy divorce and the exhortation to remain loyal to one's marriage vows (Mal 2:16). Malachi's teaching anticipates the more rigid instruction of Jesus and Paul on divorce (cf. Mt 19:11; 1 Cor 7:1-16). In context, the prophet's prescriptive treatment of divorce may reflect the "exclusivist" tendencies of postexilic Judaism to reestablish the ethnic purity of Israel diluted by intermarriage (cf. Ezra 9; Neh. 13:23-31).

Malachi's *eschatology conforms to the conventional prophetic paradigm of threat and promise. Like Zechariah, Malachi pictures divine judgment as both punishment for sin and a call to repentance (Mal 3:7). The goal of God's judgment is purification and especially the restoration of acceptable worship on the part of the faithful of Israel (Mal 3:3-4). The NT understands that the "messenger" or forerunner who prepares the way for the Lord's epiphany at his temple was realized (at least in part) in the ministry of John the Baptist (Mal 3:1; 4:5-6; cf. Mt 11:14). John's ministry affirms that divine judgment entails both purification of the righteous and punishment of the wicked (Lk 3:4-9). Malachi does make an original contribution to OT eschatology with his reference to the "scroll of remembrance," in which the names of the righteous are recorded (Mal 3:16; cf. Dan 12:1; Rev 20:12). Malachi, and thus the OT, ends with an admonition to obey the teachings of the Mosaic covenant, an exhortation to look expectantly to the future for the coming Day of the Lord, and a warning to maintain covenant faithfulness across the generations, punctuated with the threat of divine curse (see Johnston, 262).

10. Imagery in Malachi.

At one level, the Bible is a product of the historical and cultural environment from which it emerges, and the book of Malachi is no exception. The prophet makes reference to images and symbols well known in his day. An understanding of the background and context of these word pictures enhances the significance of Malachi's message to his audience. A few of the more striking examples are noted below.

The "refiner's fire" and the "fuller's soap" are powerful images depicting the purifying effects of divine judgment (Mal 3:2). The word for "soap" (Heb *bōrît*) describes an alkaline salt or soda powder derived from the iceplant (found in Mesopotamia but not Syro-Palestine) and used as a laundry detergent in the ancient world. There is some question as to whether the prophet makes reference here to two common trades in the biblical world, the smelter and the fuller or launderer, or whether the expression should be understood against the backdrop of a two-stage metallurgy process of smelting and purifying crude lead by using potash as a reagent in separating the dross from the precious metal. The word picture of the alkali soap applied for the cleansing of sin in postexilic Judah is unique to Malachi in the OT. The passage advances the sober reminder that the judgment associated with the Day of the Lord is meant for both the righteous and the wicked.

Malachi makes reference to a symbolic "book [or scroll] of remembrance" (Mal 3:16), and this heavenly register may have its earthly counterpart in the Persian "book of records" (Esther 6:1). The idea of heavenly tablets kept by deities upon which were recorded the deeds and destinies of individuals and nations extends from Sumerian to talmudic times. The idea of a "heavenly book of life" is known elsewhere in the OT (cf. Ex 32:32-33; Ps 69:28; Dan 12:1). These heavenly books become symbols of divine judgment in Daniel 7:10; 10:21; 12:4. Such texts may provide the OT background for the books opened at the great white throne judgment in Revelation (Rev 20:11-15).

Malachi appeals to the metaphor of a furnace in his forecast of a coming day when God will destroy the arrogant and the wicked (Mal 4:1 [MT 3:19]). The "furnace" (Heb *tannûr*) refers to a fixed or portable beehive shaped earthenware oven or stove used especially for baking bread. For the prophet, it becomes a frightening symbol of divine judgment likening the Day of the Lord to an oven that incinerates those who oppose God (cf. Ps 21:9 [MT 21:10]).

The best-known image in Malachi is the celestial figure of "the sun of righteousness" rising "with healing in its wings" (Mal 4:2 [MT 3:20]). The sun is a symbol for God in Psalm 84:11, but "the sun of righteousness" probably is an adaptation of the winged sun-disc icon of Persian art. In ancient Mesopotamia the winged sun-disc icon was widely used and represented the guardianship of the deity for the king. Malachi applies the solar epithet to God as the deity who will truly provide blessing and protection for those people overshadowed by his wings. As early as Hippolytus, Christian interpreters have understood the word picture as a messianic title fulfilled in Jesus Christ (see Ferreiro, 307-11).

See also COVENANT; DAY OF THE LORD; TEMPLE; TWELVE, BOOK OF THE.

BIBLIOGRAPHY. *Commentaries:* E. Achtemeier, *Nahum-Malachi* (IBC; Atlanta: John Knox, 1986); J. T. H. Adamson, "Malachi," in *The New Bible Commentary*, ed. D. Guthrie et al. (3rd ed.; Grand Rapids: Eerdmans, 1970) 804-9; D. Baker, *Joel, Obadiah, Malachi* (NIVAC; Grand Rapids: Zondervan, 2006); J. G. Baldwin, *Haggai, Zechariah, Malachi* (TOTC; Downers Grove, IL: InterVarsity Press, 1972); K. Cathcart and R. Gordon, *The Targum of the Minor Prophets* (The Aramaic Bible 14; Wilmington, DE: Michael Glazier, 1989); D. Clark and H. Hatton, *A Handbook on Haggai, Zechariah, and Malachi* (UBS Handbook Series; New York: United Bible Societies, 2002); P. C. Craigie, *Twelve Prophets, 2: Micah, Nahum, Habakkuk, Zephaniah, Haggai, Zechariah, and Malachi* (DSBS 2; Philadelphia: Westminster, 1985); A. Ferreiro, ed., *The Twelve Prophets* (ACCS 14; Downers Grove, IL: InterVarsity Press, 2003); A. E. Hill, *Malachi* (AB 25D: New York: Doubleday, 1998); W. C. Kaiser Jr., *Malachi: God's Unchanging Love* (Grand Rapids: Baker, 1984); R. Mason, *The Books of Haggai, Zechariah, and Malachi* (CBC; Cambridge: Cambridge University Press, 1977); C. Mendoza, "Malachi," in *Global Bible Commentary*, ed. D. Patte (Nashville: Abingdon, 2004) 325-28; J. M. O'Brien, *Nahum, Habakkuk, Zephaniah, Haggai, Zechariah, Malachi* (AOTC; Nashville: Abingdon, 2004); D. Petersen, *Zechariah 9-14 and Malachi* (OTL; Louisville: Westminster/ John Knox, 1995); P. L. Redditt, *Haggai, Zechariah, and Malachi* (NCBC; London: Marshall Pickering, 1995); P. J. Scalise, "Malachi," in *The IVP Women's Bible Commentary*, eds. C. C. Kroeger and M. J. Evans (Downers Grove, IL: InterVarsity Press, 2002) 500-507; E. M. Schuller, "The Book of Malachi," *NIB* 7:843-77; J. M. P. Smith, *A Critical and Exegetical Commentary on Haggai, Zechariah, Malachi and Jonah* (ICC; Edinburgh: T & T Clark, 1912); R. L. Smith, *Micah-Malachi* (WBC 32; Waco, TX: Word, 1984); D. Stuart, "Malachi," in *The Minor Prophets: An Exegetical and Expository Commentary, 3: Zephaniah Haggai, Zechariah, and Malachi*, ed. T. McComiskey

(Grand Rapids: Baker, 1998) 1245-96; **R. A. Taylor and E. R. Clendenen**, *Haggai, Malachi* (NAC; Nashville: Broadman & Holman, 2004); **P. A. Verhoef**, *The Books of Haggai and Malachi* (NICOT; Grand Rapids: Eerdmans, 1987); **J. H. Walton, V. Matthews and M. Chavalas**, "Malachi," in *Bible Background Commentary: Old Testament* (Downers Grove, IL: InterVarsity Press, 2000) 810-11; **H. M. Wolf**, *Haggai and Malachi* (EBC; Chicago: Moody, 1976); **Y. Yilpet**, "Malachi," in *The Africa Bible Commentary*, ed. T. Adeyemo (Grand Rapids: Zondervan, 2006) 1093-98. *Studies:* **J. L. Berquist**, *Judaism in Persia's Shadow: A Social and Historical Approach* (Minneapolis: Fortress, 1995); **B. S. Childs**, *Introduction to the Old Testament as Scripture* (Philadelphia: Fortress, 1979); **T. Collins**, "The Scroll of the Twelve," in *The Mantle of Elijah: The Redaction Criticism on the Prophetical Books* (BibSem 20; Sheffield: JSOT, 1993) 59-103; **D. A. Dorsey**, *The Literary Structure of the Old Testament: A Commentary on Genesis-Malachi* (Grand Rapids: Baker, 1999); **J. A. Fischer**, "Notes on the Literary Form and Message of Malachi," *CBQ* 34 (1972) 315-20; **R. E. Fuller**, "Text-Critical Problems in Malachi 2:10-16," *JBL* 110 (1991) 47-57; **D. E. Garland**, "A Biblical View of Divorce," *RevExp* (1987) 419-32; **B. Glazier-McDonald**, *Malachi: The Divine Messenger* (SBLDS 98: Atlanta: Scholars Press, 1987); **N. K. Gottwald**, "Tragedy and Comedy in the Latter Prophets," *Semeia* 32 (1985) 83-96; **P. R. House**, *The Unity of the Twelve* (JSOTSup 97; Sheffield: Almond, 1990); **G. P. Hugenberger**, *Marriage as a Covenant: Biblical Law and Ethics as Developed from Malachi* (Grand Rapids: Baker, 1998); **P. S. Johnston**, "Malachi," *NDBT* 260-62; **R. Klein**, "A Valentine for Those Who Fear Yahweh: The Book of Malachi," *CurTM* 13 (1986) 143-52; **G. Mallone**, *Furnace of Renewal: A Vision for the Church* (Downers Grove, IL: InterVarsity Press, 1981); **H. Marks**, "The Twelve Prophets," in *The Literary Guide to the Bible*, ed. R. Alter and F. Kermode (Cambridge, MA: Belknap, 1987) 207-33; **R. Mason**, "Theology of Malachi," *NIDOTTE* 4:927-29; **S. L. McKenzie and H. W. Wallace**, "Covenant Themes in Malachi," *CBQ* 45 (1983) 549-63; **E. Meyers and C. Meyers**, *Zechariah 9-14* (AB 25C: New York: Doubleday, 1993); **J. Nogalski**, *Redactional Processes in the Book of the Twelve* (BZAW 218; Berlin: de Gruyter, 1993); **J. M. O'Brien**, *Priest and Levite in Malachi* (SBLDS 121; Atlanta: Scholars Press, 1990); **R. D. Patterson**, "Old Testament Prophecy," in *A Complete Literary Guide to the Bible*, ed. L. Ryken and T. Longman III (Grand Rapids: Baker, 1993) 296-309; **D. L. Petersen**, "A Book of the Twelve?" in *Reading and Hearing the Book of the Twelve*, ed. J. Nogalski and M. Sweeney (SBLSymS 15; Atlanta: Society of Biblical Literature, 2000) 3-10; **R. W. Pierce**, "Literary Connectors and a Haggai-Zechariah-Malachi Corpus," *JETS* 27 (1984a) 277-89; idem, "A Thematic Development of the Haggai-Zechariah-Malachi Corpus," *JETS* 27 (1984b) 401-11; **D. A. Schneider**, "The Unity of the Book of the Twelve" (Ph.D. diss., Yale University, 1979); **W. A. VanGemeren**, *Interpreting the Prophetic Word* (Grand Rapids: Zondervan, 1990); **J. D. W. Watts**, "Introduction to the Book of Malachi," *RevExp* 84 (1987) 373-81; **C. R. Wells**, "The Subtle Crisis of Secularism: Preaching the Burden of Israel," *CTR* 2.1 (1987) 39-61; **C. Westermann**, *Basic Forms of Prophetic Speech*, trans. H. White (Louisville: Westminster/John Knox, 1991). A. E. Hill

MANTIC WISDOM. *See* APOCALYPTICISM, APOCALYPTIC LITERATURE.

MARI, PROPHECY AT. *See* ANCIENT NEAR EASTERN PROPHECY.

MARRIAGE AND DIVORCE

The prophets do not set out to describe practices and institutions such as marriage and divorce for their audiences. Instead, they address marriage and divorce in Israel both as social realities and as a metaphor for the relationship between Yahweh and Israel.

J. J. Pilch states that Hebrew does not have a single unambiguous word for "marriage" (the verb *bʿl* is translated in some versions as "to marry," but other versions translate it as "to be[come] a husband"). Marriage is conveyed in the prophets with language similar to that found in the Pentateuch: *lqh* ("to take" a woman/wife [Ezek 44:22; cf. Gen 19:14]), *bʿl* ("to marry, be[come] lord" [Is 54:1; 62:4, 5; cf. Gen 20:3]), *ntn* ("to give" a woman/wife [Jer 29:6; Dan 11:7; cf. Ex 2:21]).

Hebrew also lacks a single unambiguous term for "wife." The word *ʾiššâ* can mean "woman," "wife" or "female animal." The word *ʾiššâ* conveys "wife" when it combines with certain words or when it is set in the context of certain social descriptions mentioned in the accompanying paragraphs. "Wife" is conveyed in the prophets with language similar to the Pentateuch: wife forsaken (Is 54:6), wife of youth (Jer 3:1), wife of a neighbor (Jer 5:8; cf. Ex 20:17), take a wife (Jer 16:2; cf. Gen 24:7), adulterous wife (Ezek 16:32), my wife (Ezek 24:18; cf. Gen 20:11), wife of your covenant (Mal 2:14).

The absence of unambiguous technical terms for "marriage" and "wife" does not suggest, however, that the institution or practice of marriage did not exist. Nor does it imply that there was no way of talking specifically about marriage, wives or husbands. Hebrew possesses many terms reflecting the practice of marriage: "husband," "concubine," "son-in-law," "daughter-in-law," "father-in-law" and "mother-in-law." It also possesses many terms denoting what happens when marriage is violated or broken: "adultery," "divorce decree" and "prostitution."

Marriage is a significant institution in ancient Israel. Isaiah, Jeremiah, Ezekiel, Daniel, Hosea, Joel, Zechariah and Malachi deal with marriage in some form or fashion. It would be helpful for us to know how a wedding was conducted, how marriage was commonly lived out, and how divorce was worked out, but none of the prophets offer specific descriptions. For the most part, they assume that their audience is aware of these institutions and practices. The prophets engage both marriage and divorce as practices to be addressed and as metaphors designed to illustrate the sacred nature of the relationship between Israel and Yahweh. The prophets offer only glimpses of marriage and divorce, so at best we have only pieces of a much larger puzzle. It is clear that marriage in the time of the prophets shares a family likeness to practices described throughout the rest of the OT.

1. The Practice of Marriage in Israel
2. The Practice of Divorce in Israel
3. Marriage, Divorce and Remarriage as a Metaphor
4. Marriage and Divorce

1. The Practice of Marriage in Israel.

M. D. Carroll R. notes that the prophets do not attempt to legislate family law as in the Pentateuch, nor do they attempt to produce narratives of marriage as in Genesis or Samuel or reflections on marriage like those preserved in various wisdom texts. In the Prophets marriage is predominantly used as a metaphor for the re-

lationship between Yahweh and Israel. *Feminist scholars such as R. J. Weems and A. Brenner, following the lead of other traditional scholars, have taken the words of Hosea 1—3 and Ezekiel 16; 23 as literal descriptions of actual marriage practices. This leads these feminist scholars to condemn the culture, the prophets and the God of these texts as misogynistic. Other scholars, such as P. L. Day and Carroll R., have urged caution in reading the rhetoric of these prophets as literal descriptions of marital practices. When reading powerful texts such as Hosea and Ezekiel, one needs to focus on their powerful use of metaphor in the rhetoric that they employ (Stienstra). Day illustrates this point by asking about the contemporary phrase "to nurse a tree." This metaphor communicates neither the medical practices of nursing nor the way a mother feeds her newborn child. Day's illustration shows us that caution needs to be exercised in reading the Prophets for glimpses of the practice of marriage and divorce in Israel. If we are attentive to this caution, we may still be able to infer some understanding of marriage and divorce practices as described in prophetic texts.

1.1. Marriage Ceremony. It appears that some of the figurative usages of marriage seem to disclose the actual practices and conventions of marriage. As noted above, it is not easy to discern when this is so, but the following seem to give us glimpses of marriage in the times of the prophets. Not surprisingly, weddings were meant to be memorable events where both the bridegroom and the bride dressed for the occasion. The groom was decked in garland, and the bride in special clothing and jewels (Is 61:10; Jer 2:32). The wedding was meant to be a time of rejoicing (Is 62:5; Jer 25:10), singing (Jer 33:11) and *worship of the Lord (Jer 33:11). The bride was known for her devotion (Jer 2:2). A wedding was a time of joy for the community, and the absence of this community event would be felt (Jer 7:34).

1.2. Marriage Benefits (Singleness and Widowhood). It is clear that singleness of any state for a woman was not seen or experienced as a benefit. Both Isaiah and Jeremiah remind and plead for the people to defend widows (Is 1:7, 23; Jer 7:6; 16:9; 22:3), since some viewed widows as vulnerable and some viewed them as prey (Is 10:2). In dangerous times, it appears that women preferred a polygamous marriage to being single (Is 4:1). Although marriage offered security to a woman, it did not create invulnerability to war and conquest (Jer 6:11-12; 8:10; 14:6). Marriage could stay intact in times of *warfare, but couples could go into exile (Jer 38:23). Like all wars, the war and conquest in Jeremiah's day multiplied the number of widows (Jer 15:8; 18:21). Wives in Jeremiah's day experienced famine, pestilence and war, which meant that their children were vulnerable to suffering and early death. Wives were not, however, merely passive recipients of what came along; sometimes they too were active in committing crimes and worshiping other gods (Jer 44:9, 15).

Oddly, Jeremiah tells the people to see that exile will not bring an end to the nation, so he encourages the exiles to marry, to take wives for their sons, and to give their daughters to be wives (Jer 29:6). They are to settle there and grow their families.

1.3. Personal Life of the Prophets and Marriage. We are told of the marital status of four of the prophets. Isaiah was married to a prophetess, and they had children together (Is 7:3; 8:3). Jeremiah is commanded by the Lord not to take a wife and not to have children (Jer 16:2). Ezekiel is told that his wife is going to die, and that he is not to mourn (Ezek 24:16) (D. Lipton takes a minority position and believes that Ezekiel was not forbidden to mourn her after her death, but he was to refrain from petitioning on her behalf before her death). Hosea is commanded to marry a wife of whoredom (Hos 1:2).

1.4. Violations of Marriage. Infidelity was practiced by husbands (Jer 5:8) and by wives (Jer 3:20). The practice of adultery was prevalent enough to make it into various lists of prophetic rebuke (Jer 7:9; 23:10, 14; 29:23).

2. The Practice of Divorce in Israel.
The prophets take up the language of divorce as it is used in the Torah (*see* Law). Ezekiel utilizes the same terminology for divorce that appears in Leviticus and Numbers: *grš*, which often means "to drive out." Isaiah, Jeremiah and Malachi use the language of Deuteronomy: *šlḥ*, which often means "to send out." While it is possible that the two words refer to different practices, it is more likely that the words are just different terms used by each community in Israel (with Leviticus and Numbers referring to

the priestly community and Deuteronomy referring to the community at large).

Ezekiel's discussion of divorce focuses on the qualifications of a Levitical priest who is allowed to serve in the future sanctuary. He echoes the words of Leviticus as he addresses the life and practices of Levitical priests. A Levitical priest is not allowed to take a divorced (*gĕrûšâ*) woman as a wife and be eligible for service in the sanctuary.

In Malachi 2:14-16 we hear Yahweh making it clear that he hates divorce (in particular he hates the divorce of Judeans from Judeans). Instead, he expects faithfulness to the wife of one's youth. It appears that in Malachi divorce itself can be the act of faithlessness (for an alternative view, M. Zehner argues that this passage is linked to Malachi 2:10-12, and that Malachi is addressing more specifically the time and situation of Ezra and Nehemiah where Israelite men were divorcing their first wife, who is Jewish, and marrying foreign women). In addition to Deuteronomy, Malachi also seems to be arguing that the people of Israel are to uphold marriage as a gift of God at creation (Gen 1:27; 2:22-24) (Perdue). Isaiah and Jeremiah also speak of the practice of divorce found in Deuteronomy. In Deuteronomy 24:1-4 we learn that if a man is displeased with the woman whom he takes in marriage, he may write her a certificate of divorce, place it in her hand, and send her out. Isaiah speaks of the practice of using a divorce decree (Is 50:1). Although Jeremiah uses the same term as Isaiah for a divorce decree, Jeremiah has a fuller description that parallels that of Deuteronomy 24:1-4. In Jeremiah 3:1 a man sends his wife away; a little later, in Jeremiah 3:8, Yahweh tells Jeremiah that he gave Israel a certificate of divorce for her unfaithfulness. This legal document, or "quitclaim" (as P. J. Scalise calls it), functions as proof of the divorce for the divorced women. We are told by Malachi that Yahweh hates divorce (Mal 2:16), but we note that Yahweh speaks of "divorcing" Israel (Jer 3:8) and Judah (Is 50:1).

3. Marriage, Divorce and Remarriage as a Metaphor
Although the metaphors of marriage and divorce are utilized by the prophets, no prophet uses the images of marriage in a monolithic way.

In line with what is mentioned above, it

should be noted that Ezekiel and Hosea have been viewed as "pornoprophets" by some feminist scholars. Although these texts of Scripture have traditionally been accepted, many feminist scholars have worked to show them to be objectionable (Weems and Brenner are among scholars who represent this position). Day states that both traditional and feminist scholars mistakenly agree that the descriptions of the treatment of the women in Ezekiel and Hosea are based on actual practices in the ancient Near East. Day, however, offers a corrective reading that assumes that since Ezekiel uses the metaphor extensively, there is no need to assume that these practices described actually occurred. Nor is there much support from ancient Near Eastern literature to indicate that these were actual practices. Carroll R. joins Day in offering a helpful critique of such readings. Both Day and Carroll R. make clear that what we assume about the practices deeply impacts our readings of the prophets.

3.1. Isaiah. The image of the bride in Isaiah functions in messages of hope to God's people. This is seen in Isaiah 49:18, where the image makes clear that the days of devastation will turn into days of blessing, and in Isaiah 60, with the image of a bride who is clothed lavishly by her husband.

In Isaiah 50 Isaiah contends that Yahweh has been faithful, but Israel has not. In this chapter Yahweh asks the question, "Where is your bill of divorce?" The question should elicit the answer "It does not exist," since Yahweh did not leave or send them away; rather they reaped the consequences of their sins. Israel has been unfaithful. Yet through it all Yahweh faithfully keeps coming back for them (Is 50:2), and they do not respond to his overtures. However, in Isaiah 54 we see the opposite. Here it is Yahweh who left Israel for a period, so that she was like a widow, but now he has returned. He will gather Israel, who is like a wife forsaken, and give her everlasting love. The metaphors are not reified or fixed; instead, the author feels free to move in different directions with them.

3.2. Jeremiah. Jeremiah feels free to identify Judah as a whore (Jer 2:20), an incompetent bride (Jer 2:32), a wayward wife (Jer 2:33) and a murderously oppressive woman (Jer 2:34). In Jeremiah 3 the metaphors switch throughout the chapter. Judah is a wayward bride who acts like an assertive whore, but she tries to return

to Yahweh as a daughter who asks her father to take her back. Yahweh sees through the insincerity of Israel and states that false sister Judah should have learned a lesson from wayward sister Israel's experience. Israel becomes less guilty when viewed in the light of Judah's actions, so the prophet is told to offer an invitation to the north (where the remnant of Israel live) to return to Yahweh. In Jeremiah 31:32 Yahweh, after offering great hope, reminds them that although they broke their covenant with him as their husband, he will make a new covenant with them.

3.3. Ezekiel. As mentioned above, Ezekiel 16; 23 have generated great controversy among readers, commentators and the church. In Ezekiel 16 Yahweh speaks of Jerusalem as a woman whom he has taken for his wife. She turns out to be wantonly unfaithful. Yahweh describes in vivid sexual metaphors how she will be punished. In Ezekiel 23 the word of the Lord speaks of Yahweh having two wives, Oholah (Israel) and Oholibah (Judah), both of whom are unfaithful. Oholah became unfaithful first. She was delivered to her lovers (Assyria), who uncovered her nakedness and killed her. Oholibah had the opportunity to learn from her sister's demise, but instead she becomes more corrupt. Again Ezekiel uses vivid sexual metaphors to describe how this wife of Yahweh will be punished. Weems and Brenner are representative of scholars who take these descriptions as evidence of an abusive and misogynistic patriarchal society. Both Day and Carroll R. argue that the focus of the metaphor is on the relationship of Israel and Yahweh. If we take Day's position, we find that the texts are powerful metaphorical pieces that point to the oncoming destruction of a people who have been unfaithful to their covenant with Yahweh.

3.4. Hosea. Various questions have emerged on the relationship of Hosea 1—2, told in the third person, and Hosea 3, told in the first person. These questions deal with the chronology of events, the identity of the woman, the historical nature of Hosea's wife, and the call of Hosea. Is the woman in Hosea 3 Gomer or another wife? Do the accounts in Hosea 1 and Hosea 3 offer parallel accounts of the marital history of Hosea or accounts that supplement one another? Are these historical referential accounts, or are they figurative? Did Hosea know that Gomer was a whore before he married her, or did he discover this after he had married her?

J. A. Dearman, with reference to H. H. Rowley, argues that a plain reading shows that the woman in all three chapters is Gomer, that the stories supplement each other, and that they are told in a chronological fashion. While acknowledging the possibility that the command "to marry a whore" is a retrospective view of the prophet, again Dearman argues that the plain reading of Hosea 1 assumes Hosea's obedience to the commands of Yahweh. The call of Hosea is to marry a wife of whoredom and to have children of whoredom.

The names of the children cause us to wonder if the children are actually Hosea's or are the result of Gomer's unfaithfulness. In Hosea 2 it seems that Hosea is a violated husband who wants to take his anger out on his wife, but then we realize that it is Yahweh who is the violated one (Hos 2:8). It is at this point that we are no longer sure how much access or clarity we have to the historical Hosea. D. J. A. Clines points out that Yahweh makes one threat (Hos 2:3-5), and then the next threat (Hos 2:6-13), and then the threats turn empty. Yahweh switches course and promises to come after them with love (Hos 2:14-23). Hosea 3 gives us a cloudy glimpse into Hosea's life, but even in this chapter the point is not Hosea or his wife, but rather Yahweh disciplining Israel.

4. Marriage and Divorce.
Marriage was a significant institution in ancient Israel. Divorce was a major disruption of this practice. The prophets expected marriage to be honored and to last. They have no positive words for the brokenness of divorce. Marriage and divorce provided a metaphor to describe the relationship between Yahweh and Israel. Unfortunately, Israel only provides reasons for the dissolution of their relationship, and God responds sometimes with judgment and ultimately with hope.

See also COVENANT; FEMINIST INTERPRETATION; HOSEA, BOOK OF; PROPHECY AND SOCIETY; WOMEN AND FEMALE IMAGERY.

BIBLIOGRAPHY. **A. Brenner,** "Pornoprophetics Revisited: Some Additional Reflections," *JSOT* 70 (1996) 63-86; **M. D. Carroll R.,** "Family in the Prophetic Literature," in *Family in the Bible: Exploring Customs, Culture, and Context*, ed. R. S. Hess and M. D. Carroll R. (Grand Rapids: Baker Academic, 2003) 100-122; **D. J. A. Clines,** "Hosea 2: Structure and Interpretation," in *Studia Biblica 1978: Sixth International Congress on Biblical Studies, Oxford 3-7 April 1978*, 1: *Papers on Old Testament and Related Themes*, ed. E. A. Livingstone (JSOTSup 11; Sheffield: JSOT, 1979-1980) 83-103. **P. L. Day,** "Adulterous Jerusalem's Imagined Demise: Death of a Metaphor in Ezekiel XVI," *VT* 50 (2000) 286-309; idem, "The Bitch Had It Coming to Her: Rhetoric and Interpretation in Ezekiel 16," *BibInt* 8 (2000) 232-54; **J. A. Dearman,** *The Book of Hosea* (NICOT; Grand Rapids: Eerdmans, 2010); **D. Lipton,** "Early Mourning? Petitionary Versus Posthumous Ritual in Ezekiel XXIV," *VT* 56 (2006) 185-202; **L. G. Perdue,** "The Israelite and Early Jewish Family," in *Families in Ancient Israel*, by L. G. Perdue et al. (Louisville: Westminster/John Knox, 1997) 163-222; **J. J. Pilch,** "Marriage," *TBT* 40 (2002) 314-19; idem, "Adultery," *TBT* 41 (2003) 117-22; **H. H. Rowley,** "The Marriage of Hosea," *BJRL* 39 (1956-1957) 200-233; **P. J. Scalise,** "Scrolling through Jeremiah: Written Documents as a Reader's Guide to the Book of Jeremiah," *RevExp* 101 (2004) 201-25; **N. Stienstra,** *Yhwh Is the Husband of His People: Analysis of a Biblical Metaphor with Special Reference to Translation* (Kampen: Kok Pharos, 1993); **R. J. Weems,** *Battered Love: Marriage, Sex, and Violence in the Hebrew Prophets* (OBT; Minneapolis: Fortress, 1995); **M. Zehner,** "A Fresh Look at Malachi II 13-16," *VT* 53 (2003) 224-59.
T. C. Parker

MASORETIC TEXT. *See* TEXT, TEXTUAL CRITICISM.

MESSIAH
Originally referring primarily to someone anointed by Yahweh into a specific role as a prophet, priest or (especially) king, the term *messiah* is also applied more widely to cover a hoped for redeemer figure who emerges in the OT and whom Christians affirm finds fulfillment in Jesus. Intertestamental texts (e.g., *T. Sim.* 7:1-2) seem to expect a priestly savior as well as a royal one, while the Qumran community may have anticipated a prophetic messiah too (1QS IX, 9-11; 1Q28a II, 11-21 [cf. Jn 1:19-28]). If we accept the wider definition in the NT, then a range of titles could also be considered, such as "Servant of Yahweh" or "Son of Man." Since these other titles are considered

elsewhere in this volume, the focus in the present article is restricted to a royal figure associated with the promise to David, though royal themes are also evident in the other titles.

1. Terminology and Hermeneutical Issues
2. The Influence of the Davidic Covenant
3. Perspectives within the Prophets

1. Terminology and Hermeneutical Issues.
The English word *messiah* is based on the Hebrew *māšîaḥ*, an adjective related to a verb (*mšh*) meaning "to anoint" or "to cover with oil." The verb does not necessarily have a technical sense related to messianism. For example, in Amos 6:6 those who "anoint themselves with the finest oils" refers to the excesses of the wealthy who are unconcerned with the needs of the poor, and four times the verb *mšh* refers to wafers spread with oil (Ex 29:2; Lev 2:4; 7:12; Num 6:15). However, the most common use is to mark something or someone initiated into a role by Yahweh. Hence, individuals called by Yahweh to a specific task could be anointed by smearing them with oil. When Aaron and his sons were initiated into their priestly ministry, they were anointed (Ex 28:41; 29:7), as also was the tabernacle and its equipment (Ex 29:36; 30:26). Similarly, Elisha's anointing (1 Kings 19:16) was to initiate his prophetic ministry. However, anointing is most commonly to designate someone as Yahweh's appointed king, such as Saul (1 Sam 9:16; 10:1), David (1 Sam 16:13), Solomon (1 Kings 1:34) or Jehu (1 Kings 19:16; 2 Kings 9:3). This is not restricted to Israelite kings, as Elijah was directed to anoint Hazael as king of Aram (1 Kings 19:15), and the only occurrence of *māšîaḥ* in Isaiah (Is 45:1) refers to the Persian king Cyrus. Anointing did not necessarily indicate Yahweh's choice of someone as king, but rather could point to popular acceptance of someone as king (Judg 9:15; 2 Kings 11:12).

Consideration of the terminology indicates that we cannot simply look up all occurrences of *māšîaḥ* (or its cognate verb) and understand the hope of messiah within the prophets. Indeed, *māšîaḥ* occurs infrequently in the prophets, and apart from Isaiah 45:1 it is found only in Habakkuk 3:13, while in Daniel it occurs only twice (Dan 9:25-26). None of these passages is quoted in the NT, and the passing allusion to Daniel 9:26 in Luke 21:24 does not directly address the question of the Messiah. The verb *mšh* is similarly infrequent, and often it

lacks any overt messianic overtones. This does not mean there is no messianic consciousness in the prophets, but it does suggest that the messianic hope is not found through a simple word study. This, therefore, raises an important hermeneutical issue about how to identify those texts that can properly be considered messianic. Some, such as W. Kaiser, have argued that the prophets consciously anticipate the Messiah in a range of texts, and therefore those texts that the NT cites were messianic in intention (Kaiser, 13-35). But even allowing for Kaiser's concept of "corporate solidarity," in which the Messiah can be seen in the form of either an individual or the nation, it is difficult to see that a text such as Hosea 11:1 (cited in Mt 2:15) is intentionally messianic, and in any case one must inquire as to what Matthew means by claiming that this text was "fulfilled" in Jesus' return from Egypt. As P. Jenson has argued, there is a range of ways in which prophecy can be understood, and this must be acknowledged in how we read prophetic texts (Jenson, 190-204). Hence (with McConville, 13), we should see that there are connections between these texts, but these emerge through the process of reading texts against developing circumstances and seeing new significance in them.

There is a two-way movement between the OT and the NT in their final form (Sailhamer, 18, 22), where the OT expresses a hope for deliverance and restoration that is relevant to its own historical context. We can consider as "messianic" those that express this hope through a royal figure (though without excluding priestly and prophetic elements) who brings redemption. It is important that there be some reference to a central redeemer figure if we are to distinguish messianic texts from those that are more generally eschatological. The NT shows us one way in which the messianic hope was understood, seeing connections that might not have been immediately apparent but are either expressed directly or are latent within the OT. The NT interprets a range of texts as messianic but does not exhaust those that are significant for this theme. Although the term *māšîaḥ* is rare within the prophets and is never used in them with the technical sense of "messiah," we can acknowledge that through those passages that point to a redeemer, it provides the theological impetus that led to a more developed messianism.

2. The Influence of the Davidic Covenant.

Because the messianic hope within the OT as a whole draws so strongly on royal themes, we must briefly consider the basis of this. The covenant with David recorded in 2 Samuel 7:1-17 is foundational (see Clements, 12), and is drawn on in a variety of ways throughout the OT (see Schniedewind). D. Hubbard has summarized some of the ways in which this covenant contributed to messianic thought through its restatement of the promises to Abraham and pivotal place within the books of Samuel and the Former Prophets generally (Hubbard, 39-42). Through this, the Davidic hope not only shaped the proclamation of many of the prophets but also contributed to the understanding of figures such as the Servant of Yahweh, who, though not strictly Davidic, is presented in themes that draw on Davidic kingship. Although most scholars date the final edition of the books of Samuel to the period of the exile, it is arguable that knowledge of the promise became widespread much earlier so that prophets from the eighth century BC were able to draw on it. That David's successors failed to live up to the terms of the promise seems to have spurred the prophets to look toward an idealized future Davidide who would fulfill the terms of the promise (e.g., Jer 23:5-6). Of particular importance was that David's dynasty would hold the kingdom in perpetuity (2 Sam 7:13) so that his throne would be secure (2 Sam 7:16). The exile triggered reflection on how this promise could be fulfilled in the absence of a Davidic monarch, but rather than rejecting the Davidic hope, this was then expressed in specifically eschatological terms (e.g., Ezek 37:24-28). This was not the point at which such thinking was initiated; rather, it was an extension of a thought process that already reached back into Israel's history (*see DOTHB*, Kings and Kingship).

The influence of the Davidic covenant also explains why some themes are so important within the messianic texts of the OT. It was particularly important that kings in the ancient Near East provide both security and justice for their people. Whether from external or internal pressures, it was the task of the king to protect their people from oppression. Yahweh is seen as Israel's king within much of the OT, providing such security for his people (e.g., Ps 99:1-4), but it is equally the case that Yahweh achieves his rule through the Davidic monarch (Ps 72), who could also be understood as Yahweh's son (Ps 2:7). Hence, themes of *justice and *peace are particularly prominent in the messianic hope in the prophets, extending the traditional role of the king into an eschatological renewal. There is also is an interplay between the messianic figure and Yahweh's own work as these themes are extended into an eschatological renewal that is to be initiated through the Messiah.

3. Perspectives within the Prophets.

In examining specific texts within the prophets, it is possible to survey the central passages within any given book (as does H. G. M. Williamson for Isaiah, M. Boda for Haggai, Zechariah and Malachi [Boda, 45-74], and W. Kaiser across the collection [Kaiser, 136-230]), but there is also value in highlighting the central themes that emerge across the collection as a whole. The danger in such an approach is that a distinctive text might be overlooked, but it does stress the fact that there is a significant unity in how the messianic hope develops across the collection as a whole. The themes considered here emerge from the discussion of the influence of the Davidic covenant, though it should be noted that most texts draw on several of them. Some passages, therefore, will be discussed under more than one heading as we appreciate the multicolored nature of the messianic hope. An important motif that emerges through this is that the messianic hope is placed within the context of Yahweh's work for his people, so that Yahweh remains the savior of his people, though the Davidic figure to which the prophets refer is one through whom he will bring this salvation.

3.1. Restored/Renewed Davidic Kingship. A crucial element in the messianic understanding of the prophets focused on the continuation of the reign of David, and in particular on a representative of David's family who would provide a reign consistent with Yahweh's promise to David. Such a king's reign would be truly consistent with Yahweh's reign. This pattern is also consistent with the theology of kingship outlined in Deuteronomy 17:14-20, where the king's central task was to read the Torah (possibly Deuteronomy itself) and so fear Yahweh by living out the Torah. This theme is explored also in the books of Samuel, which interpret kingship as one manifestation of Yahweh's reign, though emphasizing that human kings always stand under Yahweh's authority (Firth, 43-45). Even before the exile we begin to see texts that anticipate a Davidic king who will truly reign on Yahweh's behalf, though it is also true that the exile triggered further reflection on how Israel could experience such a king. Consistently, as the prophets reflect on this theme, they stress that Yahweh is the one who brings restoration to and through Davidic kingship. Yahweh remains as the nation's savior, but the future king is integral to his purposes. Thus, in Zechariah 9:9-10 the coming king is clearly patterned on David and is said to come and initiate a reign of peace, but this is achieved only because of what Yahweh does first. The royal hope is founded in Yahweh's activity, some of which he may bring about through his king.

One of the earliest expressions of this hope occurs in Hosea 3:4-5. Assuming that this is an authentic oracle of Hosea's (for the issues, see Davies, 97-98, though he regards the reference to David as an exilic addition), we may need to date it fairly late in his ministry, perhaps into the 720s BC, but still before the fall of Samaria in 722/21 BC. As the only northern prophet (Amos was slightly earlier, but most likely from Judah though active in the north), Hosea is an important witness about how the Davidic monarchy was understood. The oracle occurs as the conclusion to a passage where Hosea is again to love an adulteress woman, a prophetic sign act that also points to Yahweh's love for his people. Israel will experience many years without a king (cf. Hos 7:16; 10:3, 7; 13:10-11), which in the north meant various dynasties not descended from David, but there would come a point when they would again seek Yahweh and David their king and so experience Yahweh's goodness. The timing of this is not made clear, merely occurring "afterward" and "in the latter days" (Hos 3:5), but that such a Davidic hope was held out is both a critique of the various dynasties of the north and early evidence that even though the north had rejected the reign of David (1 Kings 12:16-20), his line was understood as providing the appropriate direction for the nation. Like Amos 9:11-15, this effectively presumes a reunification of the people of God within the framework of the promise to David, but that Hosea refers to "David" and not

the current Judean king suggests that Hosea is looking toward an ideal descendant of David. For Hosea, the future of the people of God was under a renewed Davidic ruler.

Although Hosea speaks of such a king from the perspective of an anticipated *exile of the northern kingdom, his language appears to be taken up in Jeremiah 30:9 and applied to Judah's exile as well. This passage comes from when there was no longer a descendant of David ruling in Jerusalem. It promises that Yahweh would overcome the nation that then ruled Judah and raise up David their king for them. Jeremiah thus subtly updates Hosea's language, emphasizing that it was Yahweh who would restore David's line.

Though disputed by some (for details, see Boda, 52-53), a similar theme seems to emerge in Haggai 2:20-23. Living after the exile, Haggai appears to reflect on Jeremiah 22:24, where Coniah (better known as Jehoiachin) had been rejected, described as a "signet ring" that Yahweh would remove. For Haggai, the question would be whether there could be a future for the line of David now that Judah was ruled by the Persians. By describing Zerubbabel, Jehoiachin's grandson, as a "signet ring" chosen by Yahweh (Hag 2:23), he shows that the promise to David continued in spite of the enduring absence of a Davidic king. The absence of a Davidic king therefore was not an impediment to the continuation of the promise, though it is still Yahweh's reign that is preeminent.

Reflection on the Davidic hope is also apparent in several passages in Isaiah (Williamson, 30-72). This royal hope is an important feature of Isaiah 1—35. It is notable that Isaiah 40—66 has different emphases, though this does not mean that these chapters lack messianic awareness. Isaiah 9:1-7 thus celebrates the birth of a child who will bear the responsibility of government, but who will specifically hold David's throne (Is 9:7). The identity of this child is not made clear, but though the titles given to him in Isaiah 9:6 may be conventional, they also point to one who transcends any existing ruler. The child is not seen as a redeemer himself; rather, it is Yahweh's zeal that will accomplish it, though the child will indeed bring about Yahweh's justice. Something similar can be noted in Isaiah 11:1-5, which anticipates a future ruler from the "stump of Jesse" (Is 11:1). The reference to Jesse probably is a means of looking beyond any existing descendant of David, though it is especially important in highlighting that this is a renewed Davidic line where the king has Yahweh's Spirit rest upon him, thus also stressing that what the king does is actually what Yahweh does. Similarly, the king mentioned in Isaiah 16:4b-5 is said to be active only after oppression is ended, again assuming that Yahweh is the savior for his people, but that he expresses his salvation through his king.

We have already noted Jeremiah 30:9 on this theme, but this passage is also related to Jeremiah 23:1-6. Here, the prophet criticizes other shepherds who have failed God's people. Indeed, they have scattered Yahweh's people, but he will bring them back and give them shepherds who will properly care for them. Within this pattern of leadership, Yahweh promises to raise a righteous "Branch" (see also Zech 3:8, 6:12) for David to rule as king. The name given to this king, "Yahweh is our righteousness," puns "Zedekiah," indicating that Jeremiah here looks beyond David's current descendants for an ideal descendant. This considers kingship in the context of other rulers, a theme also evident in Isaiah 32:1-8, but which again points to the king as Yahweh's gift for his restored people rather than the king being the savior figure. Daniel 9:24-27 could be understood along similar lines, but the interpretation of the figure mentioned there is disputed, and it might not refer to an individual messianic figure (Meadowcroft, 430-32, 440-46). This hope continues to be articulated after the exile as the prophets wrestle with the political structures imposed by Persia, and though David is not directly named, it is evident in texts such as Zechariah 6:9-15.

3.2. Justice and Righteousness. Because the restoration that is to come will be Yahweh's work and the king will reign on his behalf, the expectation is that the king will enact Yahweh's will for his people, a will expressed in the practice of *justice and righteousness. In so doing, the king truly represents Yahweh to his people.

This theme is particularly important in Isaiah 11:1-9; 16:4b-5. Isaiah 11:1-9 is a description of the work of a shoot from the stump of Jesse, probably extending the metaphor of the forest from Isaiah 10:33-34, where Yahweh brings down human powers that have opposed him, thus emphasizing that the work of the king takes place within a context established for him by Yahweh. That we see here a renewed Davidic

kingship is apparent from the reference to the *Spirit of Yahweh in Isaiah 11:1-2. It is the endowment of the Spirit that enables the king in Isaiah 11:3-5 to practice justice and righteousness for his people, judging not by what he sees but with equity for the poor while bringing down the wicked. This is precisely what Yahweh is said to have done in Isaiah 10:33-34, so the king thus continues Yahweh's work, though it is extended beyond bringing down those powers opposed to Yahweh to also establish justice for all the earth. Similarly, in Isaiah 9:7 the king is said to establish justice and righteousness as part of the increase of his government, especially as the mechanism by which his throne is established, though again it is the zeal of Yahweh that will bring this about. The element of "counsel," which was important in Isaiah 11:2, reemerges in Isaiah 16:3, where an unnamed figure is also directed to give counsel and grant justice. The question of who is speaking at various points in Isaiah 16:1-5 is much contested (see Childs, 131-32), but if we understand it as a dialogue between representatives of Moab and Jerusalem, then Isaiah 16:1-2 could be a request by Jerusalem that Moab sue for peace to which the Moabites respond asking for counsel in Isaiah 16:3-4a. Isaiah 16:4b-5 would then explain a future hope for all, in light of the victory that Yahweh will bring, which would include justice for all through a Davidic king. The Moabites thus are pictured seeking justice and, along with Jerusalem, discover it comes through a renewed Davidic king. If Isaiah 11:10 also refers to a Davidic king (so Stromberg) to whom the nations will come, then Isaiah 16:5 provides a specific illustration of this, while also suggesting that Isaiah 11:4 refers to equity for the poor of the earth as a whole and not just the land of Israel.

The king's role in expressing Yahweh's justice and righteousness is also emphasized in two passages in Jeremiah. In Jeremiah 23:1-6 the coming Davidic king is contrasted with the "shepherds" who have destroyed the people (Jer 23:1), though this king is placed within the context of the renewal of leadership that Yahweh will bring (Jer 23:4). Expressing themes similar to Isaiah 11:3-5, the promise is that Yahweh would raise up a Davidic king who would execute justice and righteousness, though here the land discussed is the land of Israel. Again, this is a renewed Davidic king, the renewal being demonstrated in the play on the name of Zedekiah in the promised king's name, emphasizing Yahweh as the source of righteousness. These themes are further developed in Jeremiah 33:14-26. Although textually problematic (the whole passage is not in the LXX), it has significant text-linguistic links with the whole of Jeremiah 30-33 (Rata, 82-85), suggesting there are good reasons for considering it as genuinely from Jeremiah, though given its emphasis on the continuity of the Davidic covenant (Jer 33:17, 25-26), it probably is from early in the exile. The passage also refers to a perpetual covenant with the Levites (Jer 33:18), a theme that may lie behind Paul's description of Christian ministry in Romans 15:14-29. It thus was necessary to affirm during the exile that the nation's hope for righteousness and justice lay with Yahweh fulfilling his promise to David (Jer 33:15-16). Although Jerusalem rather than the king is here called "Yahweh is our righteousness" (Jer 33:16), this seems to be an outcome of the justice wrought by the Davidic king, something earlier attributed to Josiah (Jer 22:15) but that here takes on an eschatological cast.

3.3. Security. The hope of security for the people of God is closely linked to that of justice and righteousness and also flows from the fact that Yahweh is the savior. The promise of the king is then for one who rules within the context of the salvation that Yahweh has established, though in Isaiah 7:10-17 it is Ahab's failure to understand this that leads to the promise of Immanuel, so that even where the Davidic kings fail, Yahweh continues to provide his people with security symbolized in the child. It is the presence of Yahweh that brings security, and indeed Yahweh's presence is vital for all these themes. However, where the theme of justice and righteousness tends to reflect on how the people of God experience the king's reign, the theme of security is concerned with how they relate to other peoples. It is clear that both these themes depend upon and shed light on one another.

The element of security is particularly emphasized in Isaiah 9:1-7. If the passage is intended to be announced by a herald to Galilee as a result of Tiglath-pileser's conquest of the region in 734-32 BC (so Tate, 416), then this is an authentic message from Isaiah that expects a renewal of the Davidic kingdom for both the north and the south, though this should not be tied too closely to any one Davidic king, since the king's reign is "from this time forth and forevermore" (Is 9:7), though this figure is never actually called "king." That is, whatever specific elements were anticipated within the tumultuous period at the end of the northern kingdom, Isaiah looks beyond them to announce that Yahweh will bring in his reign through his king, with the oracle as a whole perhaps based upon an enthronement ritual. From this perspective, it anticipates not only the nation's joy at the defeat of the enemy but also a king whose throne names point to his status as one who reigns under Yahweh to bring peace. The king who brings justice to his people also ensures their security and prosperity (šālôm), though only because Yahweh ensures it. Something similar can be said for Jeremiah 23:6, where the promised Davidic king will be central to the security of both Israel and Judah, though again this security is ultimately provided by Yahweh, with the king as the means by which this is delivered, something that here stands in contrast to the abject condition of Judah relative to Babylon under Zedekiah.

The impact of the Assyrians is evident also in Micah 5:1-6, where it seems that several different oracles have been woven together to highlight how Yahweh would deliver his people and the role of an anticipated ruler in this. Here, Jerusalem appears to be besieged, most likely by Sennacherib in 701 BC, so that (as with Jer 23:6 a century later) the word of hope offered here emerges out of a period of extreme national distress. Like Isaiah 9:1-6, Micah refrains from calling the Davidic figure described here "king," but the reference to Bethlehem as the place of origin for this figure (Mic 5:2) clearly points to David, while the language of military success has royal overtones. These links with David also suggest that the description of the ruler as "from of old" (Mic 5:2) refers back to the origin of the Davidic dynasty. In the context of the nation being given up (reading Mic 5:3 as "one shall give them up"), the ruler is pictured as the point to which the nation returns. The ruler's task is to shepherd the people, a royal image, though he does so in Yahweh's strength, and so he brings security not only for his people but also to the ends of the earth and so delivers the nation not only from the invading Assyrians but also from "Nimrod," a reference to Babylon (Mic 5:6), though here

Babylon is subservient to Assyria. Again, confronted by external pressure, the prophet looks to Yahweh to bring deliverance but understands that deliverance to come through a Davidic figure who also brings security.

That the security brought by the Davidic king is subservient to Yahweh's is emphasized in Ezekiel 37:24-28. In a wider discussion of the return from exile and renewal of covenant, Ezekiel anticipates the nation being restored under David, who will be "prince forever," though he is also described as king. This is clearly more than the historical David, but although David reigns, it is Yahweh who brings security for them such that they can multiply, because Yahweh dwells with them.

3.4. Restored Creation. Besides providing security from enemies, the prophets anticipate a restoration of *creation that is associated with the restored Davidic figure. This goes beyond the absence of warfare and sees a restoration to the harmony of creation noted in Genesis 1—2. A clear example of this can be seen in Isaiah 11:6–9. Within the context of the Davidic references in Isaiah 11:1, 10, the text anticipates a restoration of harmony so that hunter and prey live in peaceful coexistence, with Jerusalem as the central example of this (Is 11:9). It is never stated that the king will initiate this restoration, but it is clearly linked to his reign of justice in Isaiah 11:4-5 and thus to Yahweh's Spirit. That this is so is evident from the fact that these themes are also taken up in Isaiah 65:17 in terms of Yahweh's eschatological work and without reference to a royal figure. But since the king's role is to do Yahweh's work, it is simply the case that in Isaiah 65:17 the prophet points to the ultimate source of this restoration rather than the king as Yahweh's agent. It is striking that both Isaiah 11:9 and Isaiah 65:17 emphasize the universal knowledge of Yahweh so that this knowledge, in part evidenced by the king's demonstration of justice, provides a reference point for understanding creation's restoration.

A more detailed expression of this theme occurs in Ezekiel 34:17-31. The passage occurs within the context of Ezekiel's prophecy against the nation's "shepherds" (Ezek 34:1-16). Ezekiel appears to draw on Jeremiah 23:1-7, which critiques Judah's earlier kings before anticipating the righteous reign of a Davidic king. Ezekiel here criticizes Israel's earlier kings for failing their people and not bringing them back to

Yahweh. Ezekiel goes further, insisting that Yahweh would judge between the sheep yet also bring back his flock so that they would no longer be prey and would have Yahweh's servant David as "prince" (Ezek 34:23-24). Yahweh would save his people, but the Davidic figure would continue his reign. This reign would be marked by a covenant of peace (Ezek 34:25), where wild beasts would be banished, the land would receive adequate rain and there would be abundant harvests, as well as security from foes. Ezekiel thus makes explicit the link between the security associated with the king and the restoration of creation. Like Isaiah, however, Ezekiel links this to the knowledge of Yahweh, with the text twice declaring that this was so the people would know Yahweh (Ezek 34:27, 30). The abundance of covenant language here also suggests a close link with Jeremiah's new covenant (Jer 31:31-34), but Ezekiel's emphases highlight the close association of this hope with the Davidic king.

3.5. Promise of the Spirit. A final theme to note is the association of the royal figure with the *Spirit of Yahweh. In the OT, reference to the Spirit frequently is a means of pointing to Yahweh's empowering presence and not to a nascent Trinitarian theology, though it is consistent with the latter. The idea of a Spirit-empowered ruler goes back to Saul's anointing (1 Sam 10:9-16), but it is especially important because of David's experience in 1 Samuel 16:13. This provides the paradigm for the anticipated Davidic ruler. The experience of the Spirit is especially clear in Isaiah 11:1-3, where the endowment of the king enables him to live in a close relationship with Yahweh and is crucial to the king's ability to exercise Yahweh's justice and bring security. Ezekiel 37 also brings together the theme of Spirit and king, so that it is Yahweh's breath/wind/Spirit (*rûaḥ*) who brings life back to the dry bones of Israel (Ezek 37:4-14) while also anticipating the just rule of a Davidic king (Ezek 37:24). Although the king's experience of the Spirit is not specific here, being part of the nation's experience, it is clear that the reign of the king is still dependent upon the work of the Spirit. Again, this emphasizes the fact that the king's role is to reign faithfully under Yahweh, and it is the enabling of the Spirit that permits this.

See also DANIEL: BOOK OF; PROPHECY AND ESCHATOLOGY IN CHRISTIAN THEOLOGY; PROPH-

ETS IN THE NEW TESTAMENT; SALVATION, DE-
LIVERANCE; SERVANT OF YAHWEH.

BIBLIOGRAPHY. **D. I. Block,** "Bringing Back
David: Ezekiel's Messianic Hope," in *The Lord's
Anointed: Interpretation of Old Testament Messianic
Texts,* ed. P. E. Satterthwaite, R. S. Hess and G.
J. Wenham (Grand Rapids: Baker, 1995), 167-
88; idem, "My Servant David: Ancient Israel's
Vision of the Messiah," in *Israel's Messiah in the
Bible and the Dead Sea Scrolls,* ed. R. S. Hess and
M. D. Carroll R. (Grand Rapids: Baker Aca-
demic, 2003) 17-56; **M. J. Boda,** "Figuring the
Future: The Prophets and the Messiah," in *The
Messiah in the Old and New Testaments,* ed. S. Por-
ter (Grand Rapids: Eerdmans, 2007) 35-74;
B. S. Childs, *Isaiah* (OTL; Louisville: Westmin-
ster/John Knox, 2001); **R. E. Clements,** "The
Messianic Hope in the Old Testament," *JSOT*
43 (1990) 3-19; **A. Y. Collins and J. J. Collins,**
*King and Messiah as Son of God: Divine, Human
and Angelic Messianic Figures in Biblical and Related Literature* (Grand Rapids: Eerdmans,
2008); **G. I. Davies,** *Hosea* (NCBC; Grand
Rapids: Eerdmans, 1992); **D. G. Firth,** *1 and 2
Samuel* (ApOTC 8; Nottingham: Apollos,
2009); **D. A. Hubbard,** "Hope in the Old Testament," *TynBul* 34 (1983) 33-60; **P. P. Jenson,**
"Models of Prophetic Prediction and Matthew's Quotation of Micah 5:2," in *The Lord's
Anointed: Interpretation of Old Testament Messianic Texts,* ed. P. E. Satterthwaite, R. S. Hess
and G. J. Wenham (Grand Rapids: Baker,
1995) 189-212; **W. C. Kaiser Jr.,** *The Messiah in
the Old Testament* (Grand Rapids: Zondervan,
1995); **J. G. McConville,** "Messianic Interpretation of the Old Testament in Modern Context,"
in *The Lord's Anointed: Interpretation of Old Testament Messianic Texts,* ed. P. E. Satterthwaite, R.
S. Hess and G. J. Wenham (Grand Rapids:
Baker, 1995) 1-18; **T. Meadowcroft,** "Exploring
the Dismal Swamp: The Identity of the
Anointed One in Daniel 9:24-27," *JBL* 120
(2001) 429-49; **T. Rata,** *The Covenant Motif in
Jeremiah's Book of Comfort: Textual and Intertextual
Studies of Jeremiah 30-33* (SBL 105; New York: Peter Lang, 2007); **J. H. Sailhamer,** "The Messiah
and the Hebrew Bible," *JETS* 44 (2001) 5-23;
D. Schibler, "Messianism and Messianic Prophecy in Isaiah 1-12 and 28-33," in *The Lord's
Anointed: Interpretation of Old Testament Messianic Texts,* ed. P. E. Satterthwaite, R. S. Hess
and G. J. Wenham (Grand Rapids: Baker,
1995) 87-104; **W. M Schniedewind,** *Society and*

*the Promise to David: The Reception History of 2
Samuel 7:1-17* (Oxford: Oxford University Press,
1999); **R. Schultz,** "The King in the Book of
Isaiah," in *The Lord's Anointed: Interpretation of
Old Testament Messianic Texts,* ed. P. E. Satterth-
waite, R. S. Hess and G. J. Wenham (Grand
Rapids: Baker, 1995) 141-66; **J. Stromberg,**
"The 'Root of Jesse' in Isaiah 11:10: Postexilic
Judah or Postexilic Davidic King?" *JBL* 127
(2008) 655-69; **M. E. Tate,** "King and Messiah
in Isaiah of Jerusalem," *RevExp* 65 (1965) 409-
21; **H. G. M. Williamson,** *Variations on a Theme:
King, Messiah and Servant in the Book of Isaiah*
(Carlisle: Paternoster, 1998).   D. G. Firth

METAPHOR. *See* LITERARY APPROACHES.

MICAH, BOOK OF

The prophet Micah is known only from his
book and from the allusion to him in Jeremiah
26:18-19, the most remarkable reference to a
prophet by another prophet in the Hebrew Bible. His name is a contraction of *mikā᾿ēl,* "Who
is like God?" (see Mic 7:18), or possibly *mikāyĕhû,*
"Who is like Yahweh?" (as Micaiah, 1 Kings
22:8; the form of the name in Jer 26:18 MT is
close to the latter). The heading of the book, its
content (e.g., Mic 1:10-16) and the Jeremiah allusion all point to Micah's having worked at
least in the time of King Hezekiah, and therefore against the background of Assyrian aggression, first against the northern kingdom of
Israel, then against Judah (*see* Israelite History).
This makes him roughly a contemporary of Isaiah, also a southern prophet (cf. Is 1:1). As with
Isaiah, Micah's message bears significantly
upon Judah and Jerusalem, or *Zion. Indeed,
one of the striking features of the book of Micah is that it shares with Isaiah the important
oracle about the pilgrimage of the nations to
Zion (Mic 4:1-4; cf. Is 2:2-4).

The book of Micah stands sixth in the Book
of the *Twelve in the MT form, but third in the
LXX (after Hosea and Amos). Perhaps surprisingly, it is the first of the Twelve to turn the
spotlight of prophetic criticism directly on Judah and Jerusalem (since Hosea and Amos are
spoken mainly to the northern kingdom, Joel
contains hardly any criticism of its addressees,
Obadiah is a salvation oracle, and Jonah has no
obvious political setting). Micah's realization
that even the Jerusalem *temple was not immune to divine punishment (Mic 3:12) is one of

the most important theological affirmations of the book and made its mark upon the prophetic canon, as is shown by the citation of this prophecy in Jeremiah 26:18. His message is designed to avoid the worst disaster by turning people from their *sins. He is remembered as having been successful in this, at least as far as Jerusalem was concerned, in Jeremiah 26:18-19. The deliverance of Jerusalem is recorded in 2 Kings 18—19 and Isaiah 36—37.

1. Date, Setting and Composition
2. Structure and Outline
3. Major Themes
4. Micah in the Canon

1. Date, Setting and Composition.

1.1. Date and Historical Context. The prophecy of Micah is located by its superscription (Mic 1:1) in the kingdom of Judah in the latter half of the eighth century BC. As well as Hezekiah (725 or 715-687 BC), it also mentions Jotham (742-735 BC) and Ahaz (735-715 BC). These dates span the fall of the northern kingdom (722 BC) and the crisis of Sennacherib's attack on Judah in 701 BC. Scholars differ on the dating of Hezekiah's reign, some adopting an earlier chronology for him, which puts his accession at 727 or 725 BC (see Anderson and Freedman, xviii). In that case, there would be no clear evidence of Micah having worked earlier than that king. It is not possible to identify particular sayings that go back as far as Jotham's reign, though equally one cannot exclude this. As the book does not afford clear evidence of this sort, it is possible that the dating of Micah's ministry to the reigns of the kings named may function to locate him broadly in a period of history. For E. Ben Zvi the information in the superscription corresponds to the shape of the past in the imagination of the community for whom the book was written, rather than necessarily to strict factual accuracy (Ben Zvi, 18).

Micah's home town was Moresheth, probably Moresheth-Gath, not to be confused with Philistine Gath mentioned in Micah 1:10 (see Andersen and Freedman, 110, for a discussion). It was probably a fortified city in the Shephelah, the low hills west of Jerusalem, bordering on Philistine country. The places named in Micah 1:10-16, therefore, must have been familiar to him. And assuming that he did in fact minister in the period of rising Assyrian dominance and

aggression, he will have felt acutely the danger to his homeland, which reached its height in 701 BC. An oracle such as Micah 5:2-6 [MT 5:1-5] appears to come from a time when the Assyrian invasion of Judah was a threat that had not yet been realized (esp. Mic 5:5-6 [MT 5:4-5]; see Cook, 114).

1.2. Composition. Because certain passages seem to presuppose an *exile, it is usually held by commentators that the book contains additions to the words of Micah. It is common to date Micah 4:1-4 to a postexilic period, for example (but see below). Indeed, there is a tendency to find genuine words of Micah in chapters 1—3 and additions from later times in chapters 4—7. Micah 7:11-20, for example, seems to presuppose an exile and also has some similarities with Isaiah 40—55. Ben Zvi points to the reference to *Babylon in Micah 4:10, which would be anachronistic in the eighth century, and other references to exile and the return of exiles (e.g., Mic 2:4, 10, 12-13; Ben Zvi, 9). E. Achtemeier concludes that Micah's words were "incorporated into a Micah book that found its final form sometime after 515 BC" (Achtemeier, 290). Some modern studies attempt to reconstruct the composition histories of specific parts of the book. J. Jeremias does this for Micah 7:8-20 in an excursus. J. A. Wagenaar traces the growth of Micah 2—5 through five stages, beginning with a handful of sayings he considers authentic to Micah in chapters 2—3, then finding levels of material from the period after the fall of Jerusalem in 587 BC, originating in circles around Jeremiah; a late exilic layer associated with Ezekiel, featuring a redactional organization of oracles of judgment and hope; a postexilic strand including Micah 4:1-5, with its vision of the nations' pilgrimage to Jerusalem; and a fifth stage in which the book as a whole was formed, at some time in the fifth or fourth centuries BC (Wagenaar, 317-26). C. S. Shaw, in contrast, noting the kind of approach exemplified by Wagenaar, offers a response to this, finding settings for speeches throughout the book in preexilic times (Shaw, 1-22). The issue, as often with the prophetic books, is how far the process of the book's composition can be traced with any confidence.

The cases of Micah 3:12 and 4:1-4 raise this issue in particular ways. First, the memory of Micah 3:12 in Jeremiah 26:18 has led scholars to ask how such a memory might have been preserved. Did the elders who remembered Micah in Jeremiah's day know the text in written form? The elders do not seem to be quoting a book. Rather, they know more about Micah than is written in the book. (They know that Hezekiah did not kill him, a fact that we do not know from any other biblical source). It may be that the sayings of Micah were passed on in more than one form, perhaps both oral and written. The oracles may have been attached at one time to stories about the prophet, of the sort that we find in Amos 7 and Hosea 1—3. If so, it seems as if only some of these have been preserved as the sayings of the prophets became fixed into the book forms that we now know. (See Andersen and Freedman, 111-16, for more detailed discussion).

Second, Micah 4:1-4 raises a similar question. How did it come about that two almost identical oracles could find their way into two different prophetic books? The main options, all espoused in the modern critical era, are: (1) The saying originated with one of the prophets, and was taken over by the other (or it has been introduced into the other's book by redactors); (2) The saying was already known to both; (3) The oracle is original to neither prophet but was introduced into both books by later redactors (see Hillers, 52, for a brief account).

The last of these options is often adopted, because the thought in the passage is similar to Second Isaiah, and because it is supposed that eschatological sayings are likely to be postexilic. R. Mason puts it thus:

It is . . . idle to ask whether 4:1-4 (= Isa 2:2-4) is "originally" by either Isaiah or Micah. It is by neither; but its presence in both books shows how the prophetic collections were treated in order to make them relevant to later generations (Mason, 49).

The placement of Micah 4:1-4 immediately after Micah 3:9-12, reversing the words of judgment there point by point, Mason thinks is the work of postexilic editors who are convinced that the time of judgment is past and the time of salvation has come.

This point about the structure of Micah 3:9—4:4 is perfectly valid. However, each of the other possibilities above can be taken seriously too. Of these, it is simplest to suppose that the oracle was taken over by one prophet from the other. There is no reason to think this might not have been considered legitimate (a similar duplication occurs in Obadiah 1-7 and Jer 49:9-10). And, as Andersen and Freedman point out, neither the language nor the ideas in the passage are demonstrably postexilic (Andersen and Freedman, 424). On the basis of a detailed comparison of the textual differences between the two, they cautiously favor the view that Micah is the original (Andersen and Freedman, 423). B. Waltke comes to the same conclusion (Waltke 1988, 170-75; 2009, 213-29). J. Blenkinsopp leans to a likelier original setting in Isaiah, while noting the extreme difficulty of deciding the issue (Blenkinsopp, 190). Ben Zvi draws attention to the range of opinions that have been advanced, without adopting any, but rather observes that the essential point is that in its context here it is entirely "Mican," in the sense that "it is integral to the book, it fits its broader (textual) environment, and that it clearly communicates a sense of coherence within the larger set of readings in chs. 4-5 and with its preceding unit" (Ben Zvi, 102).

Like the case of Micah 3:12, this text also suggests that prophetic oracles had an existence apart from the books in which they found a place. Oracles were collected into books in a way that is not fully known to us. This unique occurrence of the same oracle in two books gives some indirect evidence of the process. It is an instance of an oracle that was presumably originally associated with one prophet being included also in the book of another, albeit integrated carefully into that book's discourse and themes. This was hardly accidental, since in both Isaiah and Micah it has a function in the structure and theology of that book (*see* Formation of the Prophetic Books).

2. Structure and Outline.

Commentators vary considerably in their attempts to break Micah down into satisfactory subsections. M. Jacobs finds that commentators have divided the book into between two and six sections (Jacobs, 60). It is common, however, to divide it into three: either Micah 1—2; 3—5; 6—7 (Smith, 8; cf. Allen, 257-61) or Micah 1—3; 4—5; 6—7 (Andersen and Freedman, 7; Mason, 13-14). Sometimes Micah 7:18-20 is considered a separate concluding section (e.g., Ben Zvi, 4). The former threefold division may be seen to produce a pattern in which each section consists of a judgment passage—followed by an assurance of salvation (Mic 1:1—2:11 and 2:12-13; 3:1-12 and 4:1—5:15; and 6:1—7:7 and 7:8-20 (Achtemeier, 288; see also Hillers, 8). The latter can yield a slightly different structure: Micah 1—3 (judgment); 4—5 (hope); 6—7 (judgment and hope). Differences like this can depend on how a particular passage is interpreted. For example, Micah 2:12-13 has been read either as an oracle of salvation or of judgment, or it has even been moved to a different point in the book because it is seen as out of place (Jacobs, 83-84, 193). Ben Zvi's five- or six-fold division, namely, Micah 1:1 (Superscription); Micah 1:2—2:13; 3:1-12; 4:1—5:14; 6:1—7:17; 7:18-20 (Conclusion), has the effect of heightening the significance of Micah 3, with its explanation of the fall of Jerusalem in terms of misguided leadership (Mic 3—4).

2.1. Structure. No structure of Micah is perfect or commands agreement. In the outline of the book's structure that follows, I follow the first pattern given above:

Micah 1:1—2:13: Witnessing the just judgment on Samaria and Judah—but a gathering.
Micah 3:1—5:15 [MT 5:14]: Zion condemned—but redeemed!
Micah 6:1—7:20: Controversy and lament—but pardon!

2.2. Outline.
2.2.1. Micah 1:1—2:13: Witnessing the Just Judgment on Samaria and Judah—But a Gathering.
Micah 1:2. Micah's words begin with an appeal to the *nations to witness God's judgment (cf. Deut 32:1). This affirms that the whole earth belongs to him (cf. Ps 24:1). Curiously, the judgment is directed "against you," that is, the nations themselves. The point seems to be that in God's judgment on his own people all the nations are somehow involved. This fits with the vision in Micah 4:1-4, where the nations come to a restored Zion to see Yahweh there. Yet in other texts they are clearly under his judgment (Mic 7:16-17; cf. Mic 4:11-12).

Micah thinks of God as speaking "from his holy temple," that is, in Jerusalem (cf. Amos 1:2). Yet Jerusalem and Judah themselves are accused and under threat from invasion by an enemy as a punishment from God. Zion-Jerusalem appears elsewhere in the book under the banners of both judgment and *salvation (see 3.4 below).

Micah 1:3-16. The background is the Assyrian attacks in the late eighth century, including the fall of Samaria (the northern kingdom) in 722 BC and the destruction of many of the cities of Judah by Sennacherib in 701 BC (*see* Israelite History). There is an oracle against Samaria in Micah 1:6-7. Then attention turns to Jerusalem in Micah 1:10-16, as the enemy closes in by a western route. This could be the attack recorded in 2 Kings 18:13-16, which forced King Hezekiah to pay tribute. But there is not enough detail to make this certain, and it could come from a time before the fall of Samaria (Andersen and Freedman, 113).

As a cause of the judgment the religious sins of the people are emphasized, and the same prostitution metaphor is used as in Hosea (Mic 1:7). Micah is depicted as suffering personally because of the burden of his message in a way that is reminiscent of the later Jeremiah (Mic 1:8-9; cf. Jer 8:22—9:3 [MT 9:2]; see also Jer 30:12).

Micah 2:1-11. Micah takes further the reason for God's judgment, now mainly oppression of the poor. The powerful are accused of ruthless greed as well as pride (like Is 2) and falsehood (like Jer 9) (*see* Social Justice). God's judgment meets the sin point by point: the powerful rob others of their "inheritance" (as Ahab robbed Naboth, 1 Kings 21); so God will destroy the "inheritance" that is Israel itself (Mic 2:4: a different Hebrew word from Mic 2:2, yet close in meaning. The two are used in parallel in Deut. 18:1). Micah 2:6-11 shows Micah in a kind of dialogue with opponents, who apparently argue that judgment will not come (Mic 2:6; see Jacobs, 113-14). This is similar to Jeremiah's dispute with "false prophets" (Jer 23; 28). The motif of "falsehood" is also echoed in Jeremiah (Mic 2:11; cf. Jer 9:3 [MT 9:2]).

Micah 2:12-13. The theme of "gathering" is surprising after Micah 2:1-11 (some put it after Micah 4:7). But we find words of salvation coming at early stages in other prophetic books, before the full message of doom has been unfolded (e.g., Hos 1—3; Is 2:2-4; Jer 3:12-18). The imagery itself is hard to pin down. But the passage is part of the pattern of alternation of judgment and salvation sayings (see 2 above).

Scholars have commented on the odd sequence of metaphors in these verses. The "gathering in" to the safety of a sheepfold in Micah 2:12 is hard to relate to the "breaking out" in Micah 2:13. Is it the same shepherd-image, or is the picture now a military one? And does it relate to the "breaking out" of a siege, or more generally to God's rule in a future time? The difficulty of interpreting individual sayings of this sort is one reason why it is hard to establish settings for prophetic passages. (Contrast the comments of Smith, 28-29, and Hillers, 39.)

2.2.2. Micah 3:1—5:15 (MT 5:14): Zion Condemned—But Redeemed!

Micah 3:1-12. "Heads," "rulers," "prophets," "seers," "diviners" and "priests" come under attack here, that is, all who exercise power. They are accused of savage oppression. When the poor are denied the justice they should receive from those in authority, it is as good as committing the worst kind of violence against them (Mic 3:2-3). (For denial of justice in the courts, see also Amos 5:7, 15).

As a result, Zion itself stands under judgment (Mic 3:12). This was shocking to those who believed that Yahweh dwelt in the temple in Jerusalem, and would not abandon his people (Mic 3:11). It is the first full frontal attack on Jerusalem and the temple in the Book of the Twelve, and it comes from a prophet who began with Yahweh speaking "from his holy temple" (Mic 1:2). Micah is addressing the hard question about the nature of Yahweh's relationship with Israel. The ancient *covenant with David involved a promise that David's son Solomon would build a temple for Yahweh and that the dynasty thus established would last "forever" (2 Sam 7:13). Micah plays his part in working out how this promise related to historical events, and also to the covenantal strain that emphasized the need for the chosen people to pursue justice. His words are quoted a century later in defence of Jeremiah, who made a similar prophecy to this (Jer. 26:16-19, cf. vv. 2-6).

Micah 4:1-13. The theme changes abruptly again to salvation. Micah 4:1-4 is very similar to Isaiah 2:2-4. Micah looks beyond the present crisis to a time when nations shall come to Jerusalem to learn the *tôrâ* ("law" or "instruction") of Yahweh, and there will be peace between them. (This *tôrâ* does not necessarily equate with the Torah of Moses, as in the canonical form of the Pentateuch, but rather to the ongoing teaching of Yahweh's words, as mediated by both prophets and priests) (*see* Law). In Micah

the passage makes a stark contrast with Micah 3, especially Micah 3:9-12. In R. Mason's words, this is "no coincidence." The condemnation in Micah 3:9-12 "is followed immediately by a promise that this judgment will be reversed in every particular" (Mason, 49).

Micah 4:5 sounds a change in direction, where the nations are still worshiping their own gods. The continuation (Mic 4:6-13) is in contrast to the vision of nations at peace, for now the image is of the people of Zion rescued from exile in Babylon, and their conquerors defeated. Micah 4:13 contrasts with Micah 4:3. The picture is of a *"remnant" (Mic 4:7) returning after exile. The thought here is a little like that of Isaiah 40—55.

Micah 5:1-15 (MT 4:14—5:14). Micah 5:1 is obscure, but it seems to refer to a siege in which the ruler of Judah is humiliated (Achtemeier, 338). This image is immediately reversed with a prophecy of a future ruler (Mic 5:2-4 [MT 5:1-3]). The word "king" is avoided here, yet the reference to Bethlehem makes us think of David, the son of Jesse from Bethlehem (1 Sam 16:1, 18; cf. Gen 35:19). The shepherd metaphor was widely used for kings in the OT and in the ancient Near East (Jer 23:1-6; Ezek 34), and it also evokes memories of the shepherd David. The historic line of kings will come to an end, but God will raise up a new king. This will be after a period of *suffering (Mic 5:3 [MT 5:2], probably referring to the exile). The ruler who is proclaimed here will be a true shepherd, who will feed his flock and bring peace. (For peace as a feature of the messianic kingdom, see also Is 9:7 [MT 9:6]).

The restoration of Judah (or its "remnant," Mic 5:7 [MT 5:6]) will mean that it will prevail over the nations that had oppressed it (Mic 4:5-9 [MT 4:4-8]). Micah 5:10-15 is a direct word of judgment against those nations.

2.2.3. Micah 6:1—7:20: Controversy and Lament—But Pardon!

Micah 6:1-5. The final section of the prophecy turns back to judgment. It opens with a saying in the familiar style that is found in other prophetic texts (cf. Hos 4:1-10; Is 3:13-15; Jer 2:4-13). The form is sometimes called the controversy, or lawsuit, pattern, because of the dominant word here in Micah 6:1-2 (*rîb*). It is better termed a "covenant accusation." It is not a rigid form, but used freely by the prophet (Andersen and Freedman, 510-11). Yahweh recalls the *exodus from Egypt itself, and Israel's leaders whom he appointed (cf. Amos 2:9-10). He then mentions Balaam, a sort of opposite of Moses. Together they stand for true and false prophecy. The Balaam incident shows that God was determined to save Israel, and that he could not be stopped by any other power (in this case an enchanter's spell, Num 22—24). "Shittim to Gilgal" is the last stage of Israel's journey to the promised land. Shittim was a place where Israel sinned (Num 25:1), so here too God hints that he brought them to the land even in spite of their sin. He argues for these reasons that they should have kept faith with him.

The covenant accusation has often been thought to have a special form with a legal or cultic background. Micah 6:1-4 may be compared with Psalm 50, which is said to be a fuller example of the form. (Important treatments are found in Huffmon; Clements 1965; Nielsen; Cook, 75-76. See also Andersen and Freedman, 508-11, for a cautious review of this approach to *rîb* texts, in which they argue that the prophets used traditions freely, rather than reproducing rigid forms.) The specific covenantal background of the *rîb* has been questioned, in line with the tendency in scholarship to date the fully developed conditional form of covenant to the Deuteronomic movement, which is later than the eighth-century prophets (Clements 1975).

Micah 6:6-8. Micah poses questions rhetorically as if from would-be worshipers. Yet the tone is ironic, and the way the questions are asked suggests the answers: "Will the LORD be pleased with thousands of rams?"—of course not! The thought behind these questions is the same one that we find in Hosea 6:6; Amos 5:21-24, as well as Psalms 40:6 [MT 40:7]; 50:7-15. The point is that the formalities of worship are nothing in themselves.

Micah's summary of true religion (Mic 6:8), in contrast, is famous. It does not consist in any kind of religious performance. Instead, it stresses doing justice (*mišpāṭ*, like Amos 5:24), showing "kindness" (*ḥesed*, like Hos 6:6), and it adds a touch of Micah's own, a humble walk with God. "Walking," together with the associated "ways" and "paths," is a common OT metaphor for the moral life or the life lived with God, already used by Micah in 4:2 (cf. Pss 23:3; 25:4, 9-10; and Brown, 31-53). There is a further echo of Micah's language in Deuteronomy

10:12-13. Micah 6:8 implies that the people had enough knowledge already to know what true religion was. The form of address, "O mortal" (NRSV, that is, "man," in the sense of "human being," *'ādām*) suggests that human beings in general have a knowledge of God's basic commands and are subject to them.

Micah 6:9-16. A renewed accusation of injustice leads to a threat of "desolation" (Mic 6:13, 16; cf. Jer 19:8). Other threatened punishments have an ironic ring about them (like Hag 1:6) that remind of the "futility curses" of Deuteronomy (Mic 6:14-15; cf. Deut 28:38-44).

Micah 7:1-7. The last accusation in the book is a *lament, in which Micah again expresses his own anguish at the falsehood in the land (Mic 7:1, 7; cf. Mic 1:8; Jer 8:22—9:9 [MT 9:8]). In doing so he gives a glimpse of the prophet's faithfulness and his rejection of his people's sin (cf. Hos 9:14). (This strand in prophetic thinking reaches its height in Jeremiah's so-called Confessions; e.g., Jer 11:18-23; 12:1-6; 15:15-21.) His attitude of "waiting" for the LORD is exemplary for a people who look for deliverance (Mic 7:7; cf. Hab 2:1-4).

Micah 7:8-20. The final turn in the book is again to *salvation. The voice in Micah 7:8-10 appears to come from one who is in exile but who knows that deliverance will come. Return from exile is assured (Mic 7:11-13). A prayer for Yahweh to "shepherd" his people (Mic 7:14) echoes the "shepherding" of the messianic ruler (Mic 5:4 [MT 5:3]). The nations who opposed Israel shall be brought low (Mic 7:15-17; cf. Is 2:9-10). Yet there is a hint of them turning to the LORD (Mic 7:17). Here again there are similarities to Isaiah 40—55, which also had visions of salvation for the nations, or at least their recognition that Yahweh is God (Is 49:22-26; Achtemeier, 290). But the passage must also be understood within the structure of Micah. In Micah 1:2 the nations' "seeing" was a witness to judgment on Israel; now they witness God's salvation of his people. They in turn are judged but turn to Yahweh for salvation.

The book closes (Mic 7:18-20) with a praise to Yahweh. The rhetorical question, "Who is a god like you?" (Mic 7:18), is a play on Micah's name (see the preamble, above). The uniqueness of Yahweh, also a major theme of Isaiah 40—55, is in his willingness to forgive and show compassion. This theological high point in the book puts Micah close to Hosea (Hos 11:8-11).

3. Major Themes.

The book of Micah, like other prophetic books, seeks to understand the destiny of *Israel in the light of both Israel's theological heritage and its historical experience of adversity and judgment. The elements of the book's theology are the familiar themes of sin and judgment, exile from land and the hope of salvation. The way in which these are considered to arise in the book varies with the critical approaches taken. Thus, in the strongly *redactional method espoused by Wagenaar, he finds a progressive theologizing of judgment and salvation, beginning with words of judgment directed against oppressive landholders, and developing through to a rationalization of God's dealings with Israel through the Babylonian exile and restoration from it. In contrast, for example, Cook's analysis embeds much of the discourse of Micah in what he calls the "Sinai theology," which had ancient sources and which fed ultimately into the Deuteronomic stream.

In another modern trend, there is attention to the *rhetorical form of the language in the book (Shaw, Jacobs). Jacobs examines the relationship between hope and judgment as part of her search for coherence in the book's discourse, and aims to make sense of both the individual parts and of the relationship between coherence within the parts and that of the book as a whole. Her reading is set against the background of a history that goes beyond the time of Micah to the exile, but is distinct from the older redactional method in its understanding of the text's coherence.

Finally, mention should be made of E. Runions, who brings a cultural criticism to bear on critical attempts to establish coherence, showing how cultural assumptions and images affect perceptions of problems and resolutions. In critical dialogue with Shaw (191-97), Runions draws attention, for example, to the case of feminized cities of Samaria and Jerusalem, which are readily cast respectively in the roles of contagious prostitute and "damsel in distress" rescued by a male hero. Her reading resists unities and solutions that she regards as unduly and unwittingly influenced by the reader's ideology (see Feminist Interpretation).

The question of how much the prophets were inheritors of theological tradition and how much the books that bear their names contribute and testify to the development of the theology of the OT remains contested (see Prophecy and Tradition). For example, some form of belief in Yahweh's election of Israel is evidently implied in Micah 6:1-5, an instance of the so-called lawsuit pattern, or rîb (as noted above, see Huffmon; Cook, 75-76). But how much can be concluded from this about what form of election theology Micah knew is not obvious and depends on how one evaluates a whole range of evidence both within Micah and elsewhere. However, in highlighting theological emphases in the book, it will be useful to start with five topics identified by Cook, who sees Micah as heir to Israel's "Sinai theology." Cook organizes the book's theology around the basic notion of Israel's tenancy of the land.

3.1. Election. The people of Israel are Yahweh's "elected vassals" (Cook, 71). The central evidence for this is the lawsuit in Micah 6:1-5 and its continuation in Micah 6:6-8. God's controversy (rîb) with his people depends on an assumption that they owed him something (Mic 6:1-2). That obligation is traced here to his deliverance of their ancestors from slavery in Egypt (Ex 19:4-6; 20:2). The phrase "my people" itself (Mic 6:3) has echoes in the exodus narrative (Ex 3:7; 5:1), and the allusion to the Balaam story (Num 22—24) also points to the Pentateuchal traditions of exodus and progress toward the land. Cook finds several linguistic echoes of the exodus narrative in Micah's words, and for him it is significant that Israel's obligation to Yahweh is grounded here in the Sinai tradition of the exodus rather than in the concepts of covenant associated with David or Zion (Cook, 75-76).

3.2. Land as Inheritance. The people possess the *land by inheritance. In Micah 2:1-5, 6-11, Micah's accusation of the oppressive landowners is based in the notion that ordinary Israelites, as families and kinship groups, had a stake in the land as an inheritance (naḥălâ, as frequently in Deuteronomy, e.g. Deut 4:21; Cook, 81-82). For ordinary people, such a stake in the land meant in practice their security to enjoy a place to dwell without threat from powerful neighbors (Mic 2:9). Micah is opposing the progressive annexation of land and property in Israel by a powerful elite, who were in effect clients of the increasingly centralized royal establishment, at the expense of the traditional family lineages of Israel. This analysis of Micah's social critique goes back to A. Alt and is adopted, with variations, by J. A. Dearman (45-48; cf. Cook, 81-84). The point of theological importance is that Micah has a specific theological view of land possession in Israel that attributes the benefits of Israel's inheritance of the land to the people as a whole and according to their families. To assert rights to land by virtue of overwhelming *wealth or power was therefore a violation of Israel's status as heirs to a land given by Yahweh (to put it in Deuteronomic terms), and an offence against justice and against Yahweh.

3.3. Yahweh Alone. If the people are "vassals" who hold the land as a fiefdom from Yahweh, Israel's loyalty is to Yahweh alone, or to keep the metaphor, he is the true owner of the land and its sole "landlord" (cf. Lev 25:23). The unique claim of Yahweh on Israel is expressed in Micah 1:2-7, in terms which bring the southern Micah very close to the northern Hosea (esp. in Mic 1:7; cf. Hos 2:2-13 [MT 2:4-15]; Cook, 92-93; Allen, 273). The insistence on separation from other gods continues in Micah 5:10-15, in a passage sometimes thought to be later than Micah because of its Deuteronomic overtones (Mic 5:12-14, cf. Deut 7:5; 16:21; 18:9-14). However, the thought is anticipated in Micah 1:2-7 and has echoes elsewhere in the preexilic prophets (Hos 13:2).

3.4. Conditional Possession. As we saw, the lawsuit pattern in Micah 6:1-5 was an indication of obligations that came with elect status. The continuation of that passage in Micah 6:6-8 is one of the best-known texts in the prophets, expressing the fundamental requirement of Israel, that they "do justice" (*mišpāṭ*), and "love kindness" (*ḥesed*), and "walk humbly with your God." Micah has this in common with other preexilic prophets, who also strongly insist on the futility of formal *worship apart from a deep commitment to loving and doing what is right (cf. Is 1:10-17; Hos 6:6) (*see* Liturgy and Cult). The mirror opposite of loving what is right is in Micah 2:1-2, with its echo of the tenth commandment (Ex 20:17) and its understanding of the relationship between desire and the action, in this case for evil. The criticism of worship severed from *ethics need not be taken as a repudiation of sacrificial worship in itself, however, but rather as part of an expression of the nature of Yahweh worship in its full dimensions.

Other passages also point to conditionality in Israel's relationship with Yahweh and its enjoyment of the benefits of the land. Micah 6:14-15 consists of so-called futility curses, where all attempts to secure well-being are frustrated (*see* Blessings and Curses). The passage is reminiscent of the covenant curses in Deuteronomy 28:38-40 (Cook, 100-101), and in a similar way strikes an ironic chord in the context of the belief that Yahweh has given his people the land for their good, a central tenet of Deuteronomy's covenantal theology. But the most remarkable instance of Micah's conditional theology is his awareness that not even Jerusalem with its temple carries a permanent guarantee of Yahweh's favor (Mic 3:9-12; Cook, 102-3). The logic of this passage is very similar to that of Jeremiah's famous "temple sermon" (Jer 7:3-15; also in Jer 26:2-6). It is in the context of that sermon that some of the elders of Judah recall this saying of Micah, and recognize that a word spoken against the Jerusalem temple might indeed be a *word of God. The debate that followed that sermon, as recorded in Jeremiah 26, exposes the issues that attend the preaching of both prophets. Sections of the audience of Jeremiah evidently think that Jeremiah has in effect blasphemed by daring to utter a word against the temple (Jer 26:7-11), but others recognize that this cannot be so, citing the older prophecy of Micah and its vindication in the sparing of Jerusalem (Jer 26:16-19). (The reference is to the miraculous deliverance of the city from the siege laid to it by Sennacherib's Assyrian forces in 701 BC; 2 Kings 18—19; Is 36—37.) At stake is the nature of the covenant. There is evidence, from Jeremiah 26 and elsewhere, of a belief that Jerusalem and its temple would always be protected from destruction by Yahweh on the grounds that it was his chosen dwelling place (e.g., Ps 46; Is 31:4-5). The word of Micah testifies to an understanding, long before the temple actually fell, that Yahweh's commitment to Israel did not separate the promise of continuance from his requirement both of loyalty to him and of the practice of justice in the land. The latter suggests affinities with Sinai traditions rather than those of Zion (cf. Mic 3:11 with Ex 23:8; Deut 16:18-19; see Cook, 104).

3.5. Just Rule. The question of Jerusalem also raises that of the nature of rule in Israel, since there is a close connection in Israel's traditions between the Jerusalem temple and the Davidic royal house (2 Sam 7; Ps 132). Micah's attitude to this is not entirely clear. The crucial text is

Micah 5:2-6 [MT 5:1-5], a traditionally messianic passage heralding a ruler from Bethlehem Ephrathah. The prophecy uses royal language ("shepherding," Mic 5:4), and the vision of a reign of *peace has certain echoes of the Davidic prophecy in Isaiah 9:5-6. On one view, Micah here refers to none other than King Hezekiah (Shaw, 222-23). This is plausible because Hezekiah is remembered in 2 Kings 18—19 as a righteous king who averted a national disaster by his prayer and trust in Yahweh. The passage may be taken quite differently, however, because it avoids the term "king" (*melek*), preferring the more general "ruler" (*môšēl*). Bethlehem too may be thought to stand in opposition to Jerusalem, representing the traditional clans of Judah in contrast to the ruling classes around the king in the capital. On this view the predicted ruler is actually contrasted with Hezekiah, because of the (equally valid) memory that in his day Judah had in fact been overrun by the Assyrians (Cook, 118). This debate is hard to resolve. There is some danger of unnecessarily polarizing, as between Davidic and non-Davidic, centralizing and locally based authority. But it can be said that the text holds out the hope of a victorious ruler, who may be called "messianic," and whose reign of peace must be understood to stand in contrast to all self-serving, overweening power, whether Israelite or foreign (*see* Messiah).

One narrative illustration of the kind of power Micah rejects is provided by King Ahab, from a century before. Ahab craves the property of his neighbour Naboth, and egged on by his wife Jezebel, Ahab allows the man to be conspired against and murdered, and then takes his chance to get what he wanted (1 Kings 21:1-16). The story corresponds to several of the themes we have observed: the desire for a just ruler, the concern for justice in the way in which property is held, and the dangerous relationship between the craving of the heart and murderous action.

3.6. The Prophecy as a Whole. The Book of Micah, like other prophetic books, is diverse in form and expression. Some of this diversity consists in the prophet's use of a range of types of speech to create rhetorical effects. He vividly portrays people leaving towns in his home region to go into exile (Mic 1:10-16). He accuses people of *sin with great insight (Mic 2:1-2), and sometimes with savage imagery (Mic 3:1-3) or irony (Mic 2:11). He thinks the unthinkable, that Zion itself should be razed to the ground, as if there had never been a city there (Mic 3:12). He appeals to reason, with his "covenant accusation" (Mic 4:1-4). He conducts rhetorical "dialogues" with his hearers in order to arrest attention and then drive home a point (Mic 6:6-8). And he utters a lament (Mic 7:1-7). Like Jeremiah's "confessions," this lament no doubt reflects his own anguish at the terrible message he is proclaiming, but it is also part of his proclamation. His grief over sin is at the same time an accusation of sin. Yet the factor of personal lamentation is a powerfully persuasive device. It also says something important about the role and influence of the prophet—to be one who embodies and reminds of the true path of covenant obedience. The message of Micah cannot be evaluated apart from a recognition of the prophet's personal investment in proclaiming God's word and his desire to see judgment averted.

The message itself, as we have seen, has notes of accusation and coming judgment on one hand and of the hope of salvation on the other. It stands as a testimony not just to fluctuating hopes and fears as the fortunes of Israel and Judah change, but to theological reflection on how the God of Israel can come to his people in judgment, and yet still be found to be the source of future hope. One recent treatment of this theme is that of Jacobs. She argues that hope and judgment may be "aspects of the same reality" (Jacobs, 219). A reading of the book of Micah points to the reality of hope, not in the sense of an unrealistic belief that adversity, or judgment, can simply be avoided; rather, "Hope may also be constituted in the awareness of the character of God," as in Micah 7:18-20 (Jacobs, 220). This is a hope that can reckon with the reality of judgment, but believe, on the grounds of God's character and historic commitment to Israel, that judgment may not be the end (Jacobs, 221).

The balance of possible effects of the prophecy on an audience may change, however, with new situations. People who have had to endure the terrors and losses at the hands of both Assyrians and Babylonians may need to be encouraged to hope in God for restoration and salvation, while those who have been restored to temple and land after exile may need to go on hearing the words of judgment in order to keep it from falling back into false trust—a big part of the problem Micah (and others) addressed in the first place. However, the salvation oracles also continue to be needed, for even after the temple was rebuilt, the community had trying times when God's promises seemed to have been only partially fulfilled. Mason compares postexilic Micah with Chronicles:

So, after the exile, the faith of the people was stimulated by a renewal of the prophetic promises of old, but with a pastoral call to the community to keep the faith during the present time of waiting (Mason, 50).

4. Micah in the Canon.

Micah's significance in the canon has much to do with the book's attitude to Jerusalem and kingship. Its record of Micah's word of warning against presumption on Yahweh's favor on the grounds of Israel's possession of the temple (Mic 3:9-12) took an important place in the witness of the prophetic canon with its preservation in the Book of Jeremiah (Jer 26:18-19). Micah's word therefore grasps the problem that comes to expression not only throughout the prophetic books, but also other parts of the OT canon, especially the books of Samuel and Kings, and the Psalms, namely in what way might the ancient covenant of Yahweh with Israel be considered still to stand, in the light of his judgment on them, with its climax in the destruction of the temple? Micah's influence on Jeremiah in particular presumably stems from this, but goes further, as shown by Andersen and Freedman (27; drawing on Cha), who find numerous echoes of Micah in Jeremiah, for example: Micah 1:8 (Jer 4:8); Micah 1:9, 14 (Jer 15:18); Micah 1:10, 16 (Jer 6:26; 7:29); Micah 2:4 (Jer 9:18); Micah 3:5 (Jer 6:14); Micah 3:11-12 (Jer 7:4-15); Micah 4:9-10 (Jer 4:31; 6:24); Micah 7:1-2 (Jer 5:1); Micah 7:5-6 (Jer 9:4-5 [MT 9:3-4]).

Paradoxically, Micah also contains one of the OT's most memorable prophecies of a glorious future for Zion-Jerusalem, in its vision of the nations' pilgrimage (Mic 4:1-4). While it is the Book of Isaiah that exhibits the most elaborate and profound reflection on the theme of Zion, Micah nevertheless contributed to the theological thinking whereby the symbolism of Jerusalem could be sustained through and beyond the loss of the temple in 587 BC and given eschato-

logical significance in the hope of an ultimate inclusion of the nations in God's salvation.

Finally, Micah's prophecy about a ruler from Bethlehem is quoted in Matthew 2:3, in answer to Herod's question, prompted by that of the magi, as to where the Messiah was to be born. The birth of Jesus in Bethlehem has an echo of David's origins there, and forms part of Matthew's demonstration of Jesus' fulfilment of messianic prophecy. At the same time, it fits well with Micah's concept of the ideal ruler, who is distinguished from self-serving power, now in the form of King Herod. Micah anticipates a kingdom of peace extending to the ends of the earth, and this is now proclaimed with the coming of the Messiah Jesus (*see* Prophets in the New Testament).

See also ISAIAH: BOOK OF; MESSIAH; REMNANT; TEMPLE; TWELVE, BOOK OF THE; ZION.

BIBLIOGRAPHY. *Commentaries*: E. Achtemeier, *Minor Prophets I* (NIBC; Peabody: Hendrickson, 1996); L. C. Allen, *The Books of Joel, Obadiah, Jonah and Micah* (NICOT; Grand Rapids: Eerdmans, 1976); F. I. Andersen and D. N. Freedman, *Micah* (AB; New York: Doubleday, 2000); E. Ben Zvi *Micah* (FOTL XXIB; Grand Rapids: Eerdmans, 2000); D. R. Hillers, *Micah* (Hermeneia; Philadelphia: Fortress, 1984); J. Jeremias, *Die Propheten Joel, Obadja, Jona, Micha* (ATD 24,3; Göttingen: Vandenhoeck & Ruprecht, 2007); J. L. Mays, *Micah* (OTL; Philadelphia: Westminster, 1976); W. McKane, *Micah*, (Edinburgh: T. & T. Clark, 1998); D. Simundsen, *Hosea, Joel, Amos, Obadiah, Jonah, Micah* (AOTC; Nashville: Abingdon, 2005); R. L. Smith, *Micah-Malachi* (WBC; Waco: Word, 1984); B. Waltke, "Micah," in D. W. Baker, T. D. Alexander and B. Waltke, *Obadiah, Jonah and Micah* (TOTC; Leicester: Inter-Varsity Press, 1988) 135-207; idem, *A Commentary on Micah* (Grand Rapids: Eerdmans, 2009); H. W. Wolff, *Micah* (Hermeneia; Minneapolis: Augsburg Fortress, 1990). *Studies*: J. Blenkinsopp, *Isaiah 1-39* (AB 19; New York: Doubleday, 2000); W. P. Brown, *Seeing the Psalms: Theology of Metaphor* (Louisville: Westminster/John Knox, 2002); J. H. Cha, *Micha und Jeremiah* (BBB 107; Weinheim; Beltz Athenäum, 1996); R. E. Clements, *Prophecy and Covenant* (SBT 43; London: SCM, 1965); idem, *Prophecy and Tradition* (Oxford: Blackwell, 1975); M. Cogan and H. Tadmor, *II Kings* (AB; New York: Doubleday, 1988); S. L. Cook, *The Social Roots of Biblical Yahwism* (SBL 8; Atlanta: Society of Biblical Literature, 2004); **J. A. Dearman,** *Property Rights in the Eighth Century Prophets* (SBL Diss, 106; Atlanta: Scholars Press, 1988); **H. B. Huffmon,** "The Covenant Lawsuit in the Prophets," *JBL* 78 (1959) 285-95; **M. Jacobs,** *The Conceptual Coherence of the Book of Micah* (JSOTSup 322; Sheffield: Sheffield Academic, 2001); **R. Mason,** *Micah, Nahum, Obadiah* (OTG; Sheffield: JSOT, 1991); **J. G. Millar,** *Now Choose Life: Theology and Ethics in Deuteronomy* (Leicester: Inter-Varsity Press, 1998); **K. Nielsen,** *Yahweh as Prosecutor and Judge* (JSOTSup; Sheffield: JSOT, 1978); **E. Runions,** *Changing Subjects: Gender, Nation and Future in Micah* (Sheffield: Sheffield Academic, 2001); **C. S. Shaw,** *The Speeches of Micah: a Rhetorical-Historical Analysis* (JSOTSup 145; Sheffield: JSOT, 1993); **J. A. Wagenaar,** *Judgement and Salvation: the Composition and redaction of Micah 2-5* (VTSup 85; Leiden: Brill, 2001). J. G. McConville

MILLENNIALISM. *See* Prophecy and Eschatology in Christian Theology.

MINOR PROPHETS. *See* Twelve, Book of the.

MONOTHEISM. *See* God.

MOSAIC COVENANT. *See* Covenant.

MOUNTAIN IMAGERY

Mountains and hills are poignant figures of speech in the prophets. The imagery is multivalent, bringing to mind the land, divine presence, idolatry, future blessing and so forth. To appreciate the function of mountains as figures of speech, one must be sensitive to how the prophets used poetic imagery.

The primary Hebrew terms were *har* ("mountain") and *gibʿâ* ("hill"). The words appear in parallel poetic lines, suggesting that the domains of meaning overlap. English versions usually translate *gibʿâ* as "hill," but *har* is glossed as "hill" or "mountain." The NIV, for example, translates *har* as "hill," "hill country" or "hillside" approximately one-third of the time and as "mount," "mountain" or "mountain top" approximately two-thirds of the time. Both *har* and *gibʿâ* are used as figures of speech.

1. The Culture of Mountains
2. Mountains as Figures of Speech
3. Mountains as Images of Deity

4. Mountains as Images of Criticizing and Energizing
5. Interpreting Mountain Imagery

1. The Culture of Mountains.
In order to understand what mountains signified, we begin by reviewing the significance of mountains for the Israelites.

In Palestine, mountains and *wilderness are the two most prominent geographical features. At almost any location, one is either on a mountain or can see a mountain. In contrast to the barrenness and disarray of deserts, mountains suggested abundance and stability (Ps 65:12-13; Prov 8:25). But mountains could also be obstacles and places of danger.

Mountains carried special meaning throughout the ancient world. Various ancient Near Eastern sources attest to mountains as the primary sources of commodities. Timber, stone and marble came from mountains; gold, silver and copper were mined in mountains (Waldman). Streams flowed from mountains (Jer 18:14). Pasture was found in mountains and valleys. Cedars from the mountains of Lebanon were especially renowned (1 Kings 5:6, 10; Hag 1:8).

Mountains came to be places of religious power, the intersection of heaven and earth (Ex 19:18; 24:17). Since the holy presence seemed to be geographical rather than personal or communal, the most sacred space was on the highest mountains (Eliade, 41-46). People went to mountains to *worship and to make requests of the gods (Is 30:29; Jer 17:26).

Similar to Mount Olympus, whose summit was the residence of the Greek gods, Mount Zaphon in northern Syria was home to the Canaanite god Baal-Hadad (cf. Is 14:13). Victory celebrations and banqueting of the gods occurred frequently on Baal's mount. The mountain acquired cosmic significance, for the gods met there and made decisions that affected the whole cosmos (Clifford, 57-79, 97, 192) (*see* Divine Council).

From early in the history of the Israelites, mountains were the loci of pivotal encounters with Yahweh, as Abraham, Moses, Joshua, Elijah and others experienced (Gen 22:9-12; cf. Ex 3:1-4:17; 17:6-7; Deut 32:48-50; Josh 8:30-35; 1 Kings 18:30-39; 2 Chron 3:1). God became closely identified with mountains: "Yahweh is a god of the mountains" (1 Kings 20:28). Mountains became holy ground (Ex 19:12-13a, 23b).

In the Gospels, mountains continued to be featured places of divine events, such as when two prophets, Moses and Elijah, appeared on the mount where Jesus was transfigured (Mt 17:1-13; Mk 9:2-13; Lk 9:28-36).

For several centuries Mount Sinai was *the* mountain of the Israelites, and for good reason. There, Yahweh revealed himself to Moses as never before, turning the mountain into a volcano (Ex 19:18-19), adding decrees to the *covenant and ratifying it (Ex 19:5-8; 34:10-14), inscribing the Ten Commandments on stone tablets, permitting Moses to see his back (Ex 33:23), venting his anger when the desert wanderers worshiped a golden calf, and affecting Moses so much that his face was terrifyingly radiant (Ex 34:29-30). Although Sinai is rarely referred to by name in the prophets (Paran [Hab 3:3]; Horeb [Mal 4:4]), the *law of Moses and the covenant relationship provided the underlying framework of the prophetic ministry. The objective was to rescue the people from a return to Egypt (Deut 28:68; Jer 43:7; 44:12; Hos 8:13; 9:3) and to bring them back to Sinai and its covenant.

When the ark of the covenant was placed in the holy of holies, Mount *Zion became the holiest of mountains. Yahweh manifesting his presence in a *temple on a high place precisely fit Israelite expectations of their God. In contrast to Sinai, which kept the people at bay (Ex 19:12-13, 21-24), the temple mount welcomed pilgrims (Songs of Ascent [Pss 120—134]).

Remarkably, a psalmist and a prophet, employing poetic license, described Mount Zion as if it were Zaphon: "the city of our God, his holy mountain . . . Mount Zion, the peaks of Zaphon" (Ps 48:1-2 [cf. Is 14:13]). It probably is too much to conclude, however, that "the application to Zion of the name of Baal's mountain suggests a large degree of continuity between Israel and Canaan" (Levenson, 1099).

In the OT Wisdom literature, mountains and hills evoked images of antiquity, stability, refuge, provision and primeval order (VanGemeren, 481-82). But mountains could also signify *wrath, as in the quaking of mountains on the *Day of the Lord (Ps 18:7), or redemption, as in the skipping of mountains on the day of deliverance (Ps 114:4).

2. Mountains as Figures of Speech.

Given the prominence of mountains in Palestine and given the importance of events and people associated with mountains, it is not surprising that mountains became a prophetic mode of apprehension and a rhetorical device. If the prophets wanted to refer to the land, mountains were their image of choice. If they wanted to refer to the people, they could do so via mountains. With poetic license and imagination, the prophets gave mountains meaning far beyond literal, geographical phenomena.

2.1. Metonymy. The land was central to Israelite religion, and mountains became a figure of speech for the *land of the covenant: "I will crush the Assyrian in my land, and I will trample him on my mountains" (Is 14:25a [cf. Is 25:10; 37:32; 57:13; 65:9; Ezek 19:9; 35:12; 37:22]); "I will weep and wail for the mountains" (Jer 9:10a). Mountains could figure the land of Edom (Obad 8-9; Mal 1:3) or Assyria (Nah 3:18). Mountains were also metonymy for the people of Israel: "O mountains of Israel, hear the word of the LORD" (Ezek 36:1 [cf. Ezek 36: 4, 6, 8; 6:2-3; 7:7; 39:2]).

The most frequent referent for the image of mountain or hill was the Temple Mount in Jerusalem. The site was referred to with essentially synonymous designations: "the mountain of the LORD's temple," "Mount Zion," "the mount of the daughter of Jerusalem," "the hill of Jerusalem," "the high mountain of Israel," "my mountain," "my holy hill" and "the mountain of the sovereign LORD" (Is 2:2; 8:18; 10:32; 60:14; Jer 17:3; 31:23; Ezek 20:40; Zeph 3:11; Zech 8:3).

By metonymy and synecdoche, the referent for mountain could shift from the Temple Mount to the city as a whole, to the ruling authority in Jerusalem, to the inhabitants of Jerusalem, and to God's kingdom (Is 2:2; 10:12; 16:1; 29:8; 31:4; 37:32; Dan 2:35, 44-45). For an even more imaginative referent, note in the NT: "You have come to Zion, the mountain and city of the living God, the heavenly Jerusalem . . . the church of the firstborn" (Heb 12:22-23).

2.2. Personification. Mournful music or the absence of music envisaged dark times of judgment (Ezek 26:13; Amos 8:3, 10); however, the opposite was true in times of hope: mountains were called on to sing joyfully (Is 44:23; 49:13; 55:12). Mountains were also summoned into court for jury duty: though the people of Israel failed to recognize their guilt, inanimate mountains would understand the case that Yahweh had against the people (Mic 6:1-2).

2.3. Apostrophe. The Lord speaks through Ezekiel: "Hear, O mountains of Israel, . . . I am bringing a sword against you" (Ezek 6:3 [cf. Ezek 35:3, 15; 36:1, 4, 6, 8]). Also, "I am against you, O destroying mountain" (Jer 51:25 [cf. Hos 10:8; Mic 6:2; Zech 4:7]).

2.4. Meiosis. By diminishing the importance of towering mountains and high hills— "the haughtiness will be humiliated"—Isaiah magnifies the Lord: "he alone will be exalted" (Is 2:12-18, 22). Similarly, "Though the mountains be shaken and the hills be removed, yet my unfailing love for you will not be shaken" (Is 54:10 NIV).

2.5. Metaphor. Mountains could be images of prominence and proclamation. A flag displayed on a mountain was a metaphor for a summons to battle (Is 18:3). On the other hand, a flag on a mountain could suggest a scene of forlornness, being left to flap aimlessly in the wind (Is 30:17). Making an announcement from a mountain portrayed communicating news far and wide (Is 40:9). A summons for people to assemble on a mountain was a metaphor for viewing events taking place in the land (Amos 3:9).

Mountains also signified protection and provision: "I will bring back the flock of Israel to their pasture, and they will graze on Mount Carmel, in Bashan, on the hills of Ephraim, and in Gilead; their hunger shall be satisfied" (Jer 50:19). However, the sense of protection and safety could be deceiving (Jer 49:16; Amos 6:1).

Mountains could denote prestige and power. God denounced Sennacherib's prideful claim that he had ascended to the tops of the mountains (Is 37:24). Nebuchadnezzar was described as a conqueror: "He will be as imposing as Mount Tabor is among the mountains, as Mount Carmel is against the backdrop of the sea" (Jer 46:18 NET).

Sometimes mountains were images with negative overtones. Describing the despair of the people, God referred to them as lost sheep roaming the mountains (Jer 50:6; Ezek 34:6; Nah 3:18). Enemies were pictured as coming from mountains: "With a noise like that of chariots they leap over the mountaintops, like a crackling fire consuming stubble, like a mighty army drawn up for battle. At the sight of them, nations are in anguish; every face turns pale" (Joel 2:5-6 NIV [cf. Is 13:4; Jer 4:15]). Mountains were metaphors for obstacles, and leveling them portrayed paving the way for a deliverer (Is 40:4; 45:2; 49:11).

2.6. Allegory. Ezekiel offers an extended description of Assyria as a cedar tree growing on a mountain. It was majestic in beauty, yet God cast it aside: "Foreigners from ruthless nations cut it down and left it on the mountains" (Ezek 31:12a [cf. Is 5:1-7]).

3. Mountains as Images for Deity.

Because mountains brought to mind prominence, prestige and power, they were ready images of kingliness. Jeremiah refers to the Babylonian king as a mountain (Jer 51:25). The king of Babylon claimed, "I will raise my throne above the stars of God; I will sit enthroned on the mount of assembly, on the utmost heights of the sacred mountain. I will ascend above the tops of the clouds; I will make myself like the Most High" (Is 14:13b-14 NIV). Regarding the king of Tyre, "You were on the holy mountain of God and you walked among the stones of fire" (Ezek 28:14). In poetic language, the prophets pictured these kings with semidivine status.

Regarding Yahweh, his mountain is said to be holy and the home of righteousness (Jer 31:23; cf. Is 11:9). "Jerusalem will be called the city of faithfulness, and the mountain of the LORD of hosts will be called the holy mountain" (Zech 8:3). "You who forsake Yahweh and forget my holy mountain . . . I will destine for the sword" (Is 65:11-12a [cf. Zeph 3:11]).

Mountains became influential images of divine presence. The Temple Mount became "the place of the name of Yahweh Almighty" (Is 18:7), an enduring theophany. It was God's home and throne (Is 8:18; 25:10; cf. Ezek 11:23), and he would reign there in glory (Is 24:23; Mic 4:7). "Zion with its temple was the symbol and sacrament of the presence of the living, life-creating God" (Keel, 112). But disobedience to the covenant relationship could jeopardize God's presence on the mountain. Ezekiel observed Yahweh abandoning the mountain of his temple: "The glory of the LORD ascended from the midst of the city and stood on the mountain to the east" (Ezek 11:22 [cf. Ezek 10:18]).

God's immensity and incomparability were underscored by the prophets' imaginative scenes of how mountains respond when Yahweh appears. Like peons before a potentate, mountains tremble, writhe and even disappear in the presence of the divine (Is 64:1, 3; Mic 1:4; Nah 1:5; Hab 3:10). Habakkuk says, "The ancient mountains disintegrate; the primeval hills are flattened" (Hab 3:6 NET). Indeed, God is higher than these mountains, for he created them (Amos 4:13). Isaiah raised a provocative question: "Can anyone weigh one of God's mountains?" (Is 40:12). The prophetic imagery makes a compelling statement: while mountains were of the highest magnitude in human consciousness, God's greatness surpasses everything.

4. Mountains as Images of Criticizing and Energizing.

Adopting the paradigm that prophetic imagination fundamentally entails criticizing and energizing (Brueggemann, 3), we find that mountain imagery was common in both aspects of the prophets' endeavor to dismantle the dominant consciousness and to nurture an alternative worldview.

4.1. Criticizing. In contrast to mountains as images of divine presence, mountains could be images in relation to *idolatry. Using the illicit love of prostitution as metonymy for the illicit love of idolatry, Israel is portrayed as a prostitute lying on every mountain with her lovers (Is 57:7; 65:7; Jer 2:20; 3:6; Ezek 20:28; 22:9; Hos 4:13; 10:8). "Do the cool waters from those distant mountains ever cease to flow? Yet my people have forgotten me and offered sacrifices to worthless idols!" (Jer 18:14b-15a NET [cf. Is 65:11]). "So I will pull your skirt up over your face and expose you to shame like a disgraced adulteress! People of Jerusalem, I have seen your adulterous worship. . . . I have seen your disgusting acts of worship on the hills throughout the countryside" (Jer 13:26-27 NET [cf. Jer 17:2; Ezek 18:6, 11, 15]).

In order to help hearers gain a sense of God's disappointment with the chosen people and with the surrounding nations, the prophets used imagery involving mountains. While today we might say that the world was turned upside down, the prophets said that the mountains were quaking, the hills were swaying, and the earth had returned to the primeval state of being formless and void (Jer 4:23-24). The prophets said the people were like chaff blown by the wind across the hills (Is 17:13). They announced that the people would become prey for the birds of the mountains (Is 18:6). "I will

strew your flesh on the mountains" (Ezek 32:5-6 NRSV [cf. Ezek 35:8]). "The slain will be left to rot, the stench from the corpses will be everywhere, and the mountains will be drenched with blood" (Is 34:3).

Mountains were specifically pictured as bearing the brunt of God's wrath. They will shudder in the face of his burning anger (Is 5:25; Jer 4:24; Nah 1:5). God will send a sword against the mountains (Ezek 6:3; cf. Ezek 7:7). They will become a wasteland without inhabitant, and no one will pass through them (Ezek 33:28-29; 35:3, 15; cf. Is 32:14; Hag 1:11). They will be overturned (Ezek 38:20). "Zion will be plowed like a field, Jerusalem will become a heap of rubble, the temple hill a mound overgrown with thickets" (Mic 3:12 NIV [cf. Jer 26:18]). "I will make you a threshing sledge, sharp, new, and having teeth; you shall thresh the mountains and crush them, and you shall make the hills like chaff" (Is 41:15 NRSV [cf. Is 27:12]). Possibly addressing Babylon, God declares, "I am against you, O destroying mountain. . . . I will stretch out my hand against you, roll you off the cliffs, and make you a burnedout mountain" (Jer 51:25 NIV). "What are you, O great mountain? Before Zerubbabel you shall become a plain" (Zech 4:7 NRSV). God's frustration with the marital infidelity in the covenant relationship reaches a climax when he stunningly announces, "My mountain . . . and all your treasures I will give away as plunder" (Jer 17:3 NIV).

4.2. Energizing. In contrast to mountains suffering under the weight of God's wrath, they became the focus of future blessings. "How beautiful upon the mountains are the feet of the messenger who announces peace, . . . who says to Zion, 'Your God reigns'" (Is 52:7 NRSV [cf. Nah 1:15]). God will restore Israel to the mountains in the same way one might plant a tender sprig on a high and lofty mountain (Jer 50:19; Ezek 17:22-23; 20:40; 34:13-14; 36:8). The prophets imagined streams of water, wine and milk flowing freely on mountains—preferred beverages on the preferred landscape (Is 30:25; Joel 3:17-18; Amos 9:13). They imagined an abundant banquet of meat and wine being held on Mount Zion for all the nations (Is 25:6-7) and animals not harming or destroying on the holy mountain (Is 11:9; 65:25). "Every valley shall be lifted up, and every mountain and hill be made low; the uneven ground shall become level, and the rough places a plain" (Is 40:4 NRSV [cf. Is 49:11]). "The mountains and the hills before you shall burst into song, and all the trees of the field will clap their hands" (Is 55:12b NRSV [cf. Is 42:11]). God and the exiles will return to Mount Zion, and he will establish his kingdom and rule over the remnant (Dan 2:35, 44-45; Joel 2:32; Obad 1:21; Mic 4:6-7; Zech 8:3). Opposite to the language of criticizing, in which God announced that he would give away his mountain, now he says, "Whoever takes refuge in me will inherit the land and possess my holy mountain" (Is 57:13 NIV [cf. Is 65:9]).

5. Interpreting Mountain Imagery.
The prophets used the imagery of mountains in various ways, and in many cases the imagery was not limited to a single, specific meaning. This is not disconcerting, for it is the nature of poetry. The poet's imagery of mountains could express ideas better than words, allowing hearers to experience a concept, not necessarily to perceive precise information. While it was impossible in the ancient world to put into words all that mountains did to the Israelites' minds and emotions, it would be even less possible today. In some cases, the language of the prophets may be almost too intense and vivid for modern readers' ears. As L. A. Schökel seminally commented, "What has been written with imagination, must also be read with imagination, provided the individual has imagination and it is in working order" (Schökel, 104).

Examples of prophetic imagery that especially require imagination to grasp pertain to energizing figures of speech. Sometimes we simply have to let imagery stand in its audacity without disembodying it by exegesis: "On that day the mountains shall drip sweet wine, the hills shall flow with milk, and all the stream beds of Judah shall flow with water" (Joel 3:18a NRSV [cf. Amos 9:13b]).

An energizing theme occurring in a variety of passages involves the mountain of Yahweh being raised above other hills and nations streaming to it (Is 2:2-3; 60:3; Mic 4:1-2; Zech 8:22). Distant people, tall, smooth-skinned, and strange of speech, will bring gifts (Is 18:7). God will bring the foreigners to his mountain who have become God-fearers (Is 56:6-7). Israelites who were perishing in Assyria and exiled in Egypt will return to the mountain and wor-

ship (Is 27:13; Jer 31:6, 12; Mic 7:12). Horses, chariots, wagons, mules and camels will bring pilgrims to the mountain (Is 66:20).

The Israelites were accustomed to making pilgrimages up to Jerusalem, and in their thinking, the hill of God was the greatest mountain on earth. Geographically speaking, Mount Zion sat in the shadow of the Mount of Olives to the east and was not the highest hill in Jerusalem or in Palestine, much less in the world. But because God dwelled there, it was the mountain of all mountains, standing stronger and taller than all others and commanding the respect of all people. According to Psalm 48:2, it was beautiful in its loftiness. The act of worship of going up to the mountain was a means of exalting the name of the Lord.

So when Isaiah proclaims, "Nations shall come to your light, and kings to the brightness of your dawn" (Is 60:3 NRSV), we may not know fully what that means, but we do know that the function of the imagery is acclamation: God's preeminence and universal rule are being pictured as if the whole world will come and bow at the mountain. It was a call to the errant Israelites to come back to the mountain, to celebrate God's return to his mountain, and to worship the God of the mountain.

See also ANIMAL IMAGERY; FLORAL IMAGERY; LAND; WILDERNESS, DESERT; ZION.

BIBLIOGRAPHY. **W. Brueggemann,** *The Prophetic Imagination* (2nd ed.; Minneapolis: Fortress, 2001); **R. J. Clifford,** *The Cosmic Mountain in Canaan and the Old Testament* (Cambridge, MA: Harvard University Press, 1972); **R. L. Cohn,** "Mountains and Mount Zion," *Judaism* 26 (1977) 97-115; **M. Eliade,** *Images and Symbols: Studies in Religious Symbolism,* trans. P. Mairet (London: Harvill, 1961) 41-46; **L. J. Hoppe,** *The Holy City: Jerusalem in the Theology of the Old Testament* (Collegeville, MN: Liturgical Press, 2000); **O. Keel,** *The Symbolism of the Biblical World: Ancient Near Eastern Iconography and the Book of Psalms* (Winona Lake, IN: Eisenbrauns, 1997); **J. D. Levenson,** "Zion Traditions," *ABD* 6:1098-1102; **W. J. T. Mitchell,** "Image," in *The New Princeton Encyclopedia of Poetry and Poetics,* ed. A. Preminger and T. V. F. Brogan (Princeton, NJ: Princeton University Press, 1993); **D. B. Sandy,** *Plowshares and Pruning Hooks: Rethinking the Language of Biblical Prophecy and Apocalyptic* (Downers Grove, IL: InterVarsity Press, 2002); **L. A. Schökel,** *A Manual of*

Hebrew Poetics (SubBi 11; Rome: Editrice Pontificio Istituto Biblico, 1988); **M. Selman,** *"har,"* *NIDOTTE* 1:1051-55; **W. A. VanGemeren,** "Mountain Imagery," *DOTWPW* 481-83; **N. M. Waldman,** "The Wealth of Mountain and Sea: The Background of a Biblical Image," *JQR* 71 (1981) 176-80.
D. B. Sandy

MOURNING. *See* DEATH.

N

NAHUM, BOOK OF

In the Protestant canon, the prophecy of Nahum is the thirty-fourth book, and the seventh book of those known as the Minor Prophets. It offers a strong warning to Nineveh (cf. *Jonah), which was for a period the capital of the Assyrian Empire, the nation that had controlled Israel and Judah since the mid-eighth century BC. It had destroyed the northern nation of Israel and its capital, Samaria, in 722 BC, leaving the tribes of Judah under its subjection. Assyria itself fell to Babylon in 612 BC, bringing to fruition Nahum's warnings.

1. Historical and Geographical Background
2. Composition and Literary Craft
3. Content
4. Theological themes

1. Historical and Geographical Background.

Understanding the prophecy of Nahum depends on knowing its particular setting in time and place, since without this understanding, Israel and its God appear harsh and vengeful. Lying athwart the major trade routes between Egypt and Africa to its southwest and Asia Minor, Syria and Mesopotamia to its north and east, Israel encountered the movement of foreign troops from among the Egyptians, Hittites, Syrians, Assyrians and *Babylonians as they campaigned one against the other. Israel also suffered periods of occupation by several of these regional superpowers.

Assyria had influence in Israel during the mid-ninth century BC under Shalmaneser III (858-824 BC) and wielded imperial power more strongly over both Israel and Judah a century later, defeating the northern kingdom of Israel in 722 BC, taking many into exile from there (2

Kings 17), while also threatening Judah in the south (2 Kings 18:17—19:37) (*see* Israelite History). During this period of Assyrian strength, Nineveh, the object of Nahum's prophecy, became its capital city. It was not Assyrian imperialism per se that was problematic to Nahum, but rather the cruelty with which it was wedded (see Nineveh as "the city of blood" [Nah 3:1]). Sennacherib, the Assyrian king who invaded Judah in 701 BC (2 Kings 18:13; 2 Chron 32:1-19; Is 36:1-22), recorded his siege of Lachish in carved reliefs on his palace walls in Nineveh. Included are depictions of flaying and impaling some of the captives, just one example of the physical atrocities committed by Assyria upon those they conquered. Many surviving captives were exiled, with heavy annual tribute levied on those remaining. Such brutality terrorized Assyria's enemies and angered Judah's God (Nah 1:2-6).

2. Composition and Literary Craft.

Nahum's prophecy lacks explicit reference to kings' reigns that could aid in dating its composition. A date range is discernible, however. It must have been written after the destruction of the Egyptian city No-Amon/Thebes (modern Karnak or Luxor) in 663 BC, which is referred to in the past (Nah 3:8-10), yet before the fall of Nineveh to the Babylonians in 612 BC, since this event is what is being anticipated in the prophecy. With the death of Ashurbanipal in 631 BC, Assyria's power started to wane, with its great armies (Nah 1:12) starting to fade away (Nah 3:13), so the prophecy could be associated with this pivotal death.

Some regard the book as a compilation of numerous, originally separate oracles. The work of K. Spronk, showing an overarching structure and the interplay between various parts of the book, supports compositional unity in its present canonical form (Spronk, 3-5). The composition exhibits fine literary craft, mixing numerous literary genres and various poetic devices. The book begins with a hymn (Nah 1:2-8), has a vision of a court scene (Nah 1:12—2:2) and contains a dirge (Nah 3:1). Some suggest a partial acrostic, with successive sections beginning with successive letters of the Hebrew alphabet (Nah 1:3-7). There is clear use of metaphor (Nah 1:10, 13; 2:11-13; 3:4-7, 13) and simile (Nah 2:7; 3:12, 15-17) as well as irony (Nah 3:1, 14). Some of these devices show their power in oral/aural presentation, while others, such as the chiasm in the last two chapters of the book (Spronk, 5), come through more clearly in written form (see Literary Approaches).

3. Content.

3.1. Heading (Nah 1:1). This prophecy is doubly identified as an "oracle" and a "book." The former is a verbal message often, though not exclusively, referring to non-Israelites (cf. Is 13:1; 15:1; 17:1; 19:1; 21:1, 11, 13; 23:1; Zech 9:1), here Nineveh, the Assyrian capital city. On the east bank of the Tigris River about six hundred miles upstream from the Persian Gulf, it is the site of the modern city of Mosul. The "book" is a written document, indicating that the importance of the material goes beyond a simple oral presentation to its enscripturation, making it available to a wider audience. The heading also identifies the means of revelation, a "vision," and its recipient, Nahum. The name "Nahum," meaning "comforted," shares its root with "Menaham," ("one who comforts" [2 Kings 15:14]) and "Nehemiah" ("Yahweh has comforted"). The location of Nahum's hometown, Elkosh, is uncertain.

3.2. Hymn Describing Yahweh (Nah 1:2-11). Hymns praise God for several of his attributes and actions. They regularly mention those that would be considered positive toward those in a good relationship with him (e.g., Nah 1:7; cf. Ps 145), though attributes such as *wrath and vengeance toward opponents of himself and his people are also worthy to be praised, as they are here (see also Ex 34:6-7, which mixes vengeance and blessing, though emphasizing the latter). Being jealous, God brooks no rivals (Josh 24:19-20), but against those who unjustly harm his faithful lover, Judah, he brings vengeful wrath, repaying the wrongdoers (Deut

32:41). The hymnic introduction to Nahum's prophecy is theologically significant, indicating that the following words, which could be seen as simply the oppressed angrily lashing out from their physical *suffering, are driven by the very character of *God, who both cares and is just, reacting to their suffering from the essence of his being. He is also powerful, controlling not only human enemies but also the forces of nature (Nah 1:3-6). The hymn is not satisfied with simple objective description, but becomes much more personal, closing by confronting Nineveh directly as the "you" facing God's wrath (Nah 1:11).

3.3. Oracle of Two Verdicts (Nah 1:12—2:2). God addresses the two sides, both addressed as *women by way of feminine grammatical forms (see Nah 3:1-7), in subsequent oracles, alternating second- and third-person pronouns ("you/them") to distinguish addressee and subject, first providing hope to Judah (Nah 1:12-13, 15) and then judgment to Nineveh (Nah 1:14, 16-2:2). Each party's identity, only implicit in the original (which uses "you"), is made explicit with them being named in some translations (Nah 1:12, 14 [e.g., NIV, MESSAGE]). God acknowledges that Judah's affliction was from his hand, but now it will cease, bondage turning to freedom. Affliction's cause is unspecified here, though Isaiah specifically identifies Assyria as God's means for punishing Judah for turning away from him like any pagan, godless nation (Is 10:5-11). Isaiah there contends that Assyria's excesses in carrying out God's ordained punishment of his people causes Assyria's downfall, which could also be the cause for chastisement here, though the reason is not explicit. Punishment of the oppressor is good news for Judah (Nah 1:15; cf. Is 52:7) because this diminution will allow Judah again to flourish (Jer 27:22). Historically, the one coming against Assyria (Nah 2:1) was Babylon, to which Assyria fell in 612 BC. Theologically, it is God who is behind Babylon's actions, as the author indicates by using the term "attacker" (NRSV: "shatterer"), used elsewhere of Yahweh (2 Sam 22:15; Hab 3:14; Zech 13:7).

3.4. Increasing Confrontation (Nah 2:2-13). The brutal attack upon Assyria is described in vivid color, particularly red, for which the Hebrew word is a play on "blood" (2 Kings 3:22). This and other oracles of destruction in the prophecy anticipate the impending onslaught of Babylon, with Nineveh's fall to these southern neighbors in 612 BC. Some suggest that the description is so vivid that it must have been written after having actually been witnessed by the author. The argument is not compelling, however, since rare was the generation from that period that did not have firsthand contact with such conflict on some scale.

The oracle follows a chronological progression of battle: the blazing attack (Nah 2:3-4) met by a hurried defense (Nah 2:5), which proves ineffective (Nah 2:6-8), with the city defenseless and open to pillage (Nah 2:9-10). Nineveh's former ferocity, expressed in metaphors of wild, ravening beasts, is remembered and mocked (Nah 2:11-12), with God claiming ultimate victory, picking up numerous themes and concepts from the previous verses, making the punishment appropriate to those who suffer it (Nah 2:13). Those who took exiles suffered the same fate (Nah 2:7).

3.5. "Woe, Bloody City" (Nah 3:1-7). Nineveh will experience mourning due to shocking depredations that will befall the city. The Assyrian king Ashurbanipal records his actions against a captured city in a royal inscription: "I captured many soldiers alive. The rest I burnt. . . . I built a pile of live (men and) heads before their gate. . . . I burnt their adolescent boys and girls" (Millard, 159). Bloody anguish afflicted on others will be repaid, the plunderer plundered (Nah 3:1), the attacker attacked (Nah 3:2) and the slaughterer slaughtered (Nah 3:3). Brisk, clipped sentences conjure up the swift enemy attack. Nineveh is metaphorically compared to two women operating on the margins of society: the prostitute and the witch (cf. 2 Kings 9:22; Is 57:3). A prostitute, whose seduction and enticements degrade all parties, will herself be degraded, and a witch, whose sorceries force others to her will, will herself be overpowered. The head of the world's most powerful empire of the period, to which people had flocked in awe at its power and in supplication for its favors, will now be shunned by these same people due to its great ruin. The lack of "comfort" (Heb root *nhm*) plays on the prophet's name, "Nahum," meaning "comforted."

3.6. A Satire Against Might (Nah 3:8-13). Nineveh, in its egotistical self-elevation, is called to compare itself to No-Amon/Thebes, also an imperial capital city, of Egypt during the Middle and New Kingdoms. It later became a religious center for the worship of Amon, the remains of whose temples are still visible in Luxor and Karnak. Located on the east bank of the Nile some five hundred miles south of the Mediterranean, Thebes could rely neither upon water barriers nor neighboring allies, Cush (Ethiopia [Zeph 2:12]), Put (Gen 10:6) and Libya (2 Chron 12:3) for salvation from the Assyrian onslaught under Ashurbanipal, to whom the city succumbed in 663 BC. Ironically, Thebes' captors, those who perpetrated upon the city war crimes of infanticide, dispossession and slavery, themselves will suffer in similar ways. Nineveh's mighty armies and strong defenses will prove futile, might becoming like the "weaker sex," and strength made vulnerable because defenses are left open.

3.7. Useless Preparations (Nah 3:14-19). Nineveh is called to a fool's errand, preparing for a siege from which there will be no escape. Enclosing oneself for protection of necessity closes out the water supply needed to supply a city, so storage in anticipation is called for, as is hasty reworking of defenses that might have fallen to ruin (Nah 3:14). From the fire of God's wrath (Nah 1:6) and the approaching assault there will be no escape. The metaphor of the swarming and devouring locust/grasshopper (see Joel 1:2-12; 2:1-11) is given a dual focus. On the one hand, the overwhelming, swarming enemy will pick them clean (Nah 3:15). On the other hand, among their own number are merchants who would be expected to provision the city and military personnel who would be expected to protect it; both will vanish, without trace or help against the encroaching enemy.

The prophet finally directly addresses the Assyrian ruler, whose capital city, Nineveh, is on the verge of collapse. Even those charged with the care of the people are instead careless, leaving the sheep in their charge to wander defenseless (Nah 3:18). The wound of the Assyrian Empire is now mortal, a matter of woe for them (Nah 3:1) but an occasion for rejoicing and applause (see Is 55:12) for those who have felt the empire's cruelty. God is finally vindicated; the jealous keeper and defender of his people (1:2) brings justice.

4. Theological Themes.

4.1. The Nature of God. Nahum's *God is called "Yahweh" (rendered in English Bibles as "LORD") thirteen times in the course of the book. The only true "name" of God, it indicates a covenant intimacy, promising aid to God's people (Nah 1:7; 2:2), but judgment on those who oppose him (Nah 1:2 [3x], 3 [2x], 9, 11, 12, 14; 2:13; 3:5), a dichotomy spelled out in Nahum 1:7. His role in bringing vengeance against his opponents is reiterated by Paul (Rom 12:19). He is thus not capricious but instead deliberate in his responses, showing justice in both blessing and cursing. In light of this, though it is not spelled out in so many words in the prophecy itself, the fact that Yahweh had in the past "afflicted" his people would indicate that they had turned against him, but now they were restored upon returning to him.

Yahweh is depicted in masculine images, such as a general leading his troops who defeat the mighty enemy, a foil to the other masculine player, the Assyrian king, whose followers are ineffective (Nah 3:18).

4.2. The Nations. God exercises control over all peoples, not just Judah (*see* Nations). The two superpowers of the period, Egypt and Assyria, though seemingly all-powerful to those who faced them, were swiftly dispatched by Judah's God. He was able to use as his instrument to this end the Babylonians, who, though not named in the prophecy, are the anticipated conquerors of Assyria. Being foreign is not itself the cause for punishment, however, but rather opposition to God and his servants. God's previous actions against Judah are proof of this, and their restoration upon repentance would suggest that blessing could befall even Israel's enemies if they too would turn to Israel's God, as it did to the same Ninevites when they responded to Jonah's warnings (Jon 3:6-10).

See also TWELVE, BOOK OF THE.

BIBLIOGRAPHY. E. A. Achtemeier, *Nahum-Malachi* (IBC; Atlanta: John Knox, 1986); C. E. Armerding, "Nahum," in *The Expositor's Bible Commentary*, 7: *Daniel-Malachi*, ed. F. E. Gaebelein (Grand Rapids: Zondervan, 1985) 447-89; **D. W. Baker**, *Nahum, Habakkuk, Zephaniah* (TOTC; Downers Grove, IL: InterVarsity Press, 1988); **J. Bruckner**, *Jonah, Nahum, Habakkuk, Zephaniah* (NIVAC; Grand Rapids: Zondervan, 2004); **D. L. Christensen**, *Nahum: A New Translation with Introduction and Commentary* (AB 24F; New Haven: Yale University Press, 2009); **T. Longman III**, "Nahum," in *The Minor Prophets: An Exegetical and Expository Commentary*, 2: *Obadiah, Jonah, Micah, Nahum, and Ha-* *bakkuk*, ed. T. E. McComiskey (Grand Rapids: Baker, 1993) 765-829; **A. R. Millard**, "Nahum," in *Zondervan Illustrated Bible Backgrounds Commentary*, ed. J. H. Walton (5 vols.; Grand Rapids: Zondervan, 2009) 5:148-63; **T. C. Mitchell**, "Judah Until the Fall of Jerusalem (*c.* 700-586 B.C.)," *CAH²* 3/2.371-409; **J. M. O'Brien**, *Nahum* (RNBC; London: Sheffield Academic, 2002); **J. J. M. Roberts**, *Nahum, Habakkuk, and Zephaniah* (OTL; Louisville: Westminster/John Knox, 1991); **K. Spronk**, *Nahum* (HCOT; Kampen: Kok Pharos, 1997). D. W. Baker

NARRATIVE PLOT. *See* LITERARY APPROACHES.

NATIONS

This article focuses on countries or people groups that are considered foreign from the perspective of Israel and Judah. Much of the prophetic literature of the OT deals with foreign nations, but attitudes toward them are far from uniform. On the one hand, very many individual prophetic oracles pronounce judgment against foreign nations, and the books of Nahum and Obadiah are devoted entirely to the denunciation of Assyria and Edom, respectively; on the other hand, other prophetic statements speak very highly of foreigners, especially during the period following the return from *exile. In any case, it is clear that prophets very rarely viewed Israel in isolation from events that were unfolding on the international scene. Rather, the prophetic literature most often reflects the assumption that Yahweh's activity held implications at home as well as abroad.

1. Terminology
2. Specific Nations
3. Oracles About Foreign Nations
4. Universalism, Monotheism and Isaiah 40—55

1. Terminology.

Two Hebrew terms are used most often in reference to foreign nations in the OT. The word *gôy* ("nation" [often expressed in the pl., *gôyim*]) tends to be understood in the political sense, while *'am* ("people" [pl., *'ammîm*]) is generally understood as an expression of kinship. Thus, for example, Yahweh significantly instructs Hosea to name his son *lō' 'ammî*, meaning "not my people" (Hos 1:9).

Other terms are used with less frequency.

Within the prophetic literature, nearly all occurrences of *lĕ'ummîm* are limited to the book of Isaiah, and the term frequently appears alongside words that have similar meanings, such as *gôyim* (Is 34:1; 43:9), *'ammîm* (Is 51:4; Jer 51:58; Hab 2:13), *'ādām* ("humanity" [Is 43:4]) and *'îyyîm* ("coastlands" [Is 41:1; 49:1]). While *'îyyîm* is very often translated as "coastlands," on some occasions it can refer more generally to distant lands (e.g., Is 42:4, 10; 66:19; Jer 31:10). All occurrences of this word in the Prophetic Books are concentrated within Isaiah, Jeremiah and Ezekiel, with only two exceptions (Dan 11:18; Zeph 2:11). The word *tēbēl* ("world") appears predominantly in late prophetic literature (e.g., Is 24:4; 26:9, 18, 27:6; 66:19), and often it refers to the inhabitants of the world in a far-reaching, universalistic sense (Fabry and van Meeteren, 559, 561-62).

2. Specific Nations.

It is not possible here to detail all of the foreign entities mentioned in the prophetic literature, but several are addressed on a recurring basis. The coastal cities of Tyre and Sidon are frequently mentioned (e.g., Is 23; Jer 47:4; Ezek 26—28; Joel 3:4; Amos 1:9-10; Zech 9:2-3), as are Ammon (Jer 49:1-6; Ezek 21:28-32; 25:1-7; Amos 1:13-15; Zeph 2:8-9), Moab (Is 15—16; Jer 48; Ezek 25:8-11; Amos 2:1-3; Zeph 2:8-9) and the cities of Philistia (Is 14:28-32; Jer 47:1-7; Ezek 25:15-17; Joel 3:4; Amos 1:6-8; Zeph 2:4-5; Zech 9:5-8). Edom is often remembered for its apparent complicity with *Babylon in the destruction of Jerusalem (Is 34:5-15; Jer 49:7-22; Ezek 25:12-17; Obad 1-21; cf. Ps 137:7; Lam 4:21-22).

Among foreign nations, Assyria, Babylonia and Egypt are especially prominent. The book of Nahum, which is devoted entirely to judgment against Assyria, details some of the Assyrian atrocities (e.g., Nah 3:1-4). Also, the prophet Hosea may be referring to Israel's temptation to align with Egypt against Assyria when he describes Israel as a "dove, silly and without sense" (Hos 7:11 NRSV). Another key episode involving Assyria comes from the Judean king Hezekiah's interaction with Sennacherib's forces at the time of the siege of Jerusalem in 701 BC (Is 36—37). Although Assyria had surrounded Jerusalem and defeat seemed inevitable, the angel of Yahweh struck down the Assyrian troops overnight and Jerusalem was miraculously spared.

After the Neo-Babylonian Empire replaced Assyria as Judah's main military threat, the long reign of Nebuchadnezzar II (605-562 BC) brought about the destruction of Jerusalem and the *temple by 586 BC. Texts such as Jeremiah 27:1-17 suggest that there was considerable disagreement about the most appropriate stance toward Babylon, with Jeremiah advancing the unpopular opinion that Judah would be best served by submission to Babylon. Jeremiah even advises the exiles to pray for the city of their captivity (Jer 29:1-7). All the same, those prophets who witnessed the subsequent fall of Babylon were inclined to view this turn of events as no less than the hand of God at work to deliver the people of Israel (Is 13:1—14:23; 44:24—45:8; Jer 50—51; Zech 2:6-8).

Egypt is best remembered in the OT as Israel's former taskmaster when the Hebrew people were enslaved in the land (e.g., Is 52:3-4). Yahweh's deliverance of his people from the land of Egypt serves as the basis for the covenant at Sinai (Ex 20:2), which adds a theological dimension to Israel's relationship with Egypt. Thus, in Hosea 11:1-4, for example, Yahweh compares his deliverance of Israel to raising a young child (cf. Hos 2:15; 13:4; Amos 3:1; Mic 6:4). However, Israel's inclination to turn to Egypt for assistance (Hos 7:11, 16; 12:1) was tantamount to a rejection of Yahweh's covenant. The anticipated result of such action is a return to captivity (Hos 8:13; 9:3).

The book of Isaiah similarly admonishes King Hezekiah of Judah against alliances with Egypt in the face of the Assyrian threat during the late eighth century BC. As the Assyrian commander puts it, Egypt will prove to be an unreliable ally, a broken reed that will only pierce the hand of anyone who leans on it (Is 36:6, 9). Despite their horses and military strength, the Egyptians are merely human, and so such plans are doomed to failure (Is 30:1-5; 31:1-3). More than a century after the reign of Hezekiah, Jeremiah and Ezekiel similarly denounced King Zedekiah's inclination to turn to Egypt in rebellion against his treaty obligations with Babylon, just prior to the fall of Jerusalem (Jer 37:1-9; Ezek 17:1-21).

3. Oracles About Foreign Nations.

3.1. Origins. Nearly all of the Prophetic Books contain a collection of oracles about foreign nations, but their origin is not immediately obvious (Hayes 1968). It is entirely possible that oracles directed against other nations constitute some of the earliest types of prophecy in Israel (Gottwald, 49). This is supported by comparison with prophetic sayings against foreign nations in ancient Near Eastern literature dating to the beginning of the second millennium B.C., including the Sumerian "Curse of Agade" (*ANET* 646-51; Cooper) and several Egyptian execration texts (*ANET* 328-29; Bentzen). In both cases, the utterances are given within the context of warfare, presumably to bring about a favorable outcome. Likewise, a number of texts found at Mari, also from the first part of the second millennium BC, contain messages from various prophetic figures to Zimrilim, the king of Mari. One such letter, possibly written in association with a military conflict, is addressed to Zimrilim but condemns Babylon directly (ARM 13.23; Malamat, 214-19; Hayes 1967). This is not unlike many oracles about foreign nations in the Bible, which directly address other nations even though they may not have ever received them.

In the OT, Balaam is portrayed as a mercenary prophetic figure who is recruited by Balak, the king of Moab, to curse Israel so as to bring about its defeat, in a role similar to the prophetic figures of the ancient Near East. This view of a prophet who performs duties for the royal court is also similar to that of later prophets, such as Isaiah ben Amoz (e.g., Is 7; 36—39). On this basis, the Balaam account is often thought to be an early representative of the prophetic role in international affairs.

Many other early representations of Hebrew prophecy take place on the battlefield (e.g., 1 Sam 15:2-3; 1 Kings 20:26-30; 2 Kings 13:14-19), which may indicate that oracles concerning foreign nations initially developed within the context of holy *warfare (von Rad, 94-114; Miller; Cross). If so, the pronouncement of judgment against Israel's enemies would be perceived as a confirmation of Yahweh's presence and assistance in military victory, with an implicit blessing for Israel (see Christensen). However, even if the prophetic denunciation of foreign enemies developed out of the context of early warfare, it is difficult to be certain that the later foreign nations oracles, such as those collected in the books of Isaiah, Jeremiah and Ezekiel, have been directly influenced by "holy war" traditions. These collections exhibit broad diversity in form, content and purpose, and they do not always pronounce judgment against foreign nations.

In addition to warfare, Israel's *worship may also have influenced the development of oracles about foreign nations. In Psalm 60:6-8, for example, God responds to a cry of distress by announcing the destruction of other nations. Similarly, Lamentations 4:21-22 correlates the alleviation of Yahweh's punishment of *Zion with judgment against Edom. Such oracles may reflect the context of the royal court, although other cultic settings have also been suggested (see Hayes 1968, 87-92). Despite these possibilities, it is most likely that a variety of circumstances have contributed to the development of oracles concerning foreign nations. Furthermore, their origins cannot be determined with certainty from the extant collections in the Bible.

Alongside the prevailing view that oracles about foreign nations developed from the context of warfare, it is commonly assumed that such oracles—often called "oracles against the nations"—imply a message of *salvation for Israel (Westermann, 204-5). This is undoubtedly true in some cases, but a proclamation of judgment against a foreign nation does not necessarily convey salvation for Israel (Hamborg). The Egypt oracles in Isaiah, for example, seem to denounce military dependency on Egypt against the Assyrian threat (Is 19:1-4; 30:1-5; 31:1-3; cf. Is 18:1-2, 4-6, concerning Cush). These oracles predict the downfall of Egypt as evidence of its inadequacy as an ally (cf. Is 36:6-9). In at least one case, the oracle conveys judgment against Judah for its dependency on Egypt: "When the LORD stretches out his hand, the helper will stumble, and the one helped will fall, and they will all perish together" (Is 31:3 NRSV). Similarly, the oracle at Isaiah 14:28-32 ostensibly warns the people of Philistia that the Assyrian oppression is not yet over, but one can assume that the warning is ultimately intended for the Judeans. Since Philistia was not involved in the oppression of Judah at that time, a word of judgment should not be taken as a message of salvation for Judah. To be sure, an oracle announcing the downfall of Babylon, for example, can be understood to imply the salvation and restoration of Judah (e.g., Is 13:1—14:23; Jer 50:1—51:58). But it cannot always be said that an oracle against a foreign nation conveys good news for Israel or Judah.

In sum, it seems that a variety of circumstances may have prompted oracles about foreign nations oracles. In any event, such oracles are best understood in terms of their implications for Israel or Judah rather than simply in reference to the foreign nations themselves.

3.2. Collections of Nations Oracles. One interesting dimension of oracles about foreign nations is that while isolated examples can be found (e.g., Is 10:5-19; 30:6-7), they often are grouped together into collections (e.g, Is 13—23; Jer 46—51; Ezek 25—32; Amos 1:1—2:3). In addition to any organizational or thematic aim, a particular collection may also serve a rhetorical function. For example, the book of Amos employs an element of surprise by pronouncing judgment against several foreign nations before finally pointing the finger of accusation at Israel, beginning at Amos 2:6 (the oracle against Judah at Amos 2:4-5 is often viewed as a later insertion, in which case the rhetorical effect would still apply). Ezekiel's oracles against Tyre (Ezek 26—28), followed by several concerning Egypt (Ezek 29—32), clearly are taken out of chronological order, but the present arrangement seems to support the belief that Nebuchadnezzar's attack against Tyre was a prelude to Egypt's downfall (cf. Ezek 29:17-20).

At the same time, any deliberate initial arrangement of a collection of oracles is likely to be obscured by expansion or reorganization of the collection over time. In the book of Ezekiel, for example, the oracles against Egypt (Ezek 29—32) disrupt the otherwise clockwise geographic arrangement of oracles addressed to Judah's neighbors in Ezekiel 25—28. Also, the current form of the collection at Isaiah 13—23 contains several oracles with a uniform *maśśāʾ* title ("oracle concerning . . . "), which are disrupted by several non-*maśśāʾ* oracles (Cook, 25-47). Moreover, some collections of foreign nations oracles now include oracles directed against Israel or Judah (e.g., Is 22:1-11; Amos 2:4-5, 6-8). Thus, it is reasonable to suppose that the aims and sensibilities regarding the assembly of oracles into collections have likely changed over the course of the development of the literature.

By way of summary, it may be safe to say that oracles about other nations play such a prominent role in the prophetic literature because they ultimately concern Israel and Judah.

Above all, the rich deposit of oracles regarding foreign nations witnesses to belief in the sovereignty of Yahweh, who is not simply the God of the Israelites, but is Lord of all nations. This conviction often reinforces the prophetic message in light of unfolding international circumstances. Thus, the anticipation of defeat at the hands of a political enemy might be interpreted as divine judgment against misdeeds (e.g., Jer 44:2-6) rather than as evidence of Yahweh's impotence. By contrast, the downfall of an enemy can be interpreted as an indication of divine favor and vindication against the injustice of Judah's oppressors (e.g., Is 14:24-27).

4. Universalism, Monotheism and Isaiah 40—55.

With regard to international affairs, the prophetic literature provides some of the best examples in the OT of the development of the theme of universalism. Within the context of the present discussion, "universalism" does not refer to "Christian universalism," the notion that all of humanity will eventually be reconciled to God. Rather, the concept of universalism in the OT begins with the belief that Yahweh is not the God of the Israelites only, but is sovereign over all nations. For example, Zephaniah 2:11 declares, "The LORD will be terrible against them; he will shrivel all the gods of the earth, and to him shall bow down, each in its place, all the coasts and islands of the nations" (NRSV). Similarly, the call of Jeremiah as a "prophet to the nations" (Jer 1:5) seems to imply from the outset that the message of the book has a global significance. Often, the universalistic vision includes a pilgrimage to Jerusalem, as in Zechariah 8:22: "Many peoples and strong nations shall come to seek the LORD of hosts in Jerusalem, and to entreat the favor of the LORD" (NRSV [cf. Is 2:2-4 // Mic 4:1-3; Is 60:1-3; 66:18-21; Zech 14:16-19]).

Isaiah 40—55 seems to be especially interested in the theme of the nations of the world acknowledging the sovereignty of Israel's God. Not only will the nations observe what Yahweh has done for Israel (Is 41:4; 42:11-12; 49:7), but also Israel will be a "light to the nations" (Is 42:6; 49:6). The meaning of this phrase has been much debated, especially as it potentially relates to foreign nations. It often has been interpreted in reference to the conversion of foreigners (e.g., Blenkinsopp), although an alternative view is that the "nations" are understood as dispersed Israelites (e.g., Hollenberg). In any case, the primary interest in Isaiah 40—55 seems not to be in the salvation of foreign nations for their own sake, but rather in the universal exaltation of Yahweh as the God who reigns over all nations (e.g., Is 52:10; cf. Mic 1:11) (see Kaminsky and Stewart). By contrast, Luke 2:32 echoes this reference in a way that refers to the conversion of Gentiles.

This universalistic perspective in Isaiah 40—55 often is accompanied by explicit expressions of monotheism, which may indicate an important shift in Israel's view of Yahweh (see God). While the entire OT unequivocally prohibits the worship of foreign deities, much of the literature presupposes their existence (Ex 20:2-3; Deut 5:6-7; cf. Jer 16:13; 25:6; Mic 4:5). The ancient Song of the Sea asks, "Who is like you, Yahweh, among the gods?" (Ex 15:11 [cf. Ex 18:11; 23:32-33]), and in Psalm 82 God brings other deities to trial for their injustice. By contrast, Isaiah 40—55 frequently asserts that there are no other gods besides Yahweh (Is 44:8; 45:5, 14-23; cf. Jer 5:7; 16:20).

This emphasis on monotheism may help to explain differing viewpoints toward the nations in Isaiah 40—55 and elsewhere. Some texts, such as Isaiah 49:23, envision foreign nations in subservience to Israel: "Faces to the ground, [kings and queens] will bow down to you and lick the dust of your feet" (cf. Is 49:26; 51:22-23; 60:11-12, 14; Mic 7:16-17). Although they are bowing to Israel, this verse goes on to state that the outcome will be Israel's acknowledgment of Yahweh's sovereignty. As this example illustrates, the concern is not simply for the welfare of foreign nations, but mainly for the recognition of the greatness of God.

At the same time, other texts envision foreign nations living in peaceful harmony with each other and with Israel. Some of these are especially noteworthy for their positive portrayal of former enemies and oppressors of Israel. This is especially true for Egypt and Assyria, traditionally viewed among Israel's greatest enemies (e.g., Is 7:18; 10:24; 52:4; Jer 2:36; Hos 11:5; Zech 10:11). Despite this, Isaiah 19:23-25 envisions Egypt and Assyria worshiping together with Israel (cf. Mic 7:12), and the book of Jonah also deals favorably with the subject of Assyria as the recipients of God's mercy. Additionally, Isaiah 56:3-8 speaks specifically of the inclusion of foreigners in the worship of Yahweh.

Attitudes toward foreign nations seem equally diverse outside of the book of Isaiah, including the literature of the postexilic period, although the date of such texts is often disputed. Zechariah 9:1-8 denounces several foreign entities, but Zechariah 9:7b remarkably asserts Philistia as a "remnant for our God" (NRSV), just like one of the clans of Judah (cf. Amos 1:8). Also, Joel 3:1-15 speaks of Tyre, Sidon and Philistia being sold into the hands of the Judeans. The prophet even calls for a reversal of Isaiah 2:4; Micah 4:3, so that plowshares are beaten into swords, and pruning hooks are made into spears. In another example of opposing viewpoints, Zechariah 14:1-5 envisions an apocalyptic day of Yahweh's coming when the nations will be summoned to do battle against Jerusalem, but then Yahweh will fight against these nations (Zech 14:3), and Jerusalem will ultimately remain secure (Zech 14:10-11). Finally, Malachi 1:2-5 exhibits a strong sense of nationalism, with particularly harsh words against Edom, but by contrast, Malachi 1:11 emphasizes the purity of worship among the nations, where Yahweh's name is revered (also Mal 1:14). This statement could be interpreted to refer to the worship of Diaspora Jews who were scattered abroad, but one need look no further than the book of Jonah to find a clear instance of foreign worshipers of Yahweh (e.g., Jon 1:16; 3:5-10).

See also BABYLON; EXILE; ISRAEL; ISRAELITE HISTORY; WARFARE AND DIVINE WARFARE; ZION.

BIBLIOGRAPHY. **A. Bentzen,** "The Ritual Background of Amos i 2-ii 16," *OtSt* 8 (1950) 85-99; **J. Blenkinsopp,** "Second Isaiah—Prophet of Universalism," *JSOT* 41 (1988) 83-103; **D. L. Christensen,** *Prophecy and War in Ancient Israel: Studies in the Oracles against the Nations in Old Testament Prophecy* (Berkeley, CA: BIBAL Press, 1989); **P. M. Cook,** *A Sign and a Wonder: The Redactional Formation of Isaiah 18-20* (VTSup 147; Leiden: E. J. Brill, 2011); **J. S. Cooper,** *The Curse of Agade* (JHNES; Baltimore: Johns Hopkins University Press, 1983); **F. M. Cross,** "The Divine Warrior in Israel's Early Cult," in *Biblical Motifs: Origins and Transformations,* ed. A. Altmann (Cambridge, MA: Harvard University Press, 1966) 11-30; **H. J. Fabry and N. van Meeteren,** "תֵּבֵל," *TDOT* 15:557-64; **N. K. Gottwald,** *All the Kingdoms of the Earth: Is-*

raelite Prophecy and International Relations in the Ancient Near East (New York: Harper & Row, 1964); **G. R. Hamborg,** "Reasons for Judgement in the Oracles against the Nations of the Prophet Isaiah," *VT* 31 (1981) 145-59; **J. H. Hayes,** "Prophetism at Mari and Old Testament Parallels," *AThR* 49 (1967) 397-409; idem, "The Usage of Oracles against Foreign Nations in Ancient Israel," *JBL* 87 (1968) 81-92; **D. E. Hollenberg,** "Nationalism and 'The Nations' in Isaiah XL-LV," *VT* 19 (1969) 23-36; **J. S. Kaminsky and A. Stewart,** "God of All the World: Universalism and Developing Monotheism in Isaiah 40-66," *HTR* 99 (2006) 139-63; **A. Malamat,** "Prophetic Revelations in New Documents from Mari and the Bible," *Volume du congrès, Genève 1965*, ed. O. Eissfeldt (VTSup 15; Leiden: E. J. Brill, 1966) 207-27; **P. D. Miller,** "The Divine Council and the Prophetic Call to War," *VT* 18 (1968) 100-107; **G. von Rad,** *Holy War in Ancient Israel,* trans. and ed. M. J. Dawn (Grand Rapids: Eerdmans, 1991); **C. Westermann,** *Basic Forms of Prophetic Speech,* trans. H. C. White (Louisville: Westminster/John Knox, 1991).

P. M. Cook

NEW COVENANT. *See* COVENANT.

NEW EXODUS. *See* EXODUS IMAGERY.

NEW TESTAMENT. *See* PROPHETS IN THE NEW TESTAMENT.

NIGHT VISIONS. *See* ZECHARIAH, BOOK OF.

NONWRITING PROPHETS. *See* PROPHECY, HISTORY OF.

O

OBADIAH, BOOK OF

Obadiah, the smallest book of the OT, consisting of a mere twenty-one verses, focuses on the prophesied destruction of Edom following that country's aggressive acts toward Jerusalem during a time of Israelite national calamity. Along with *Jonah and *Nahum's prophecy against Nineveh, Obadiah is the only book in the OT whose primary subject matter concerns a foreign nation. Despite its brevity, the book contains important theological messages about the relationship between God and the *nations, the significance of Jerusalem, the *Day of Yahweh, and God's commitment to his people. Obadiah also raises questions about the role that the *canon plays in the overall interpretation of individual books, in particular how Obadiah's position within the collection of the Book of the *Twelve influences its reading.

1. Author
2. Historical Setting and Canonical Location
3. Content
4. Interpretation

1. Author.

Although the size and subject matter of the book of Obadiah have played a part in its partial neglect, the fact that it is a self-contained work has ensured that it has not lacked for contentious attention. Debates about the book reach as far back as Jerome, and many have long noted that "its difficulty is in inverse proportion to its length" (Mason, 87). One reason for this is the lack of authorial identity. Unlike other prophetic books, Obadiah's superscript (Obad 1:1a) is particularly sparse, noting nothing about the background of the prophet, the name of his father, the current king, or even his hometown (cf. Joel 1:1; Hab 1:1; Nah 1:1; Mal

1:1). The name "Obadiah" (Heb ʿōbadyâ) derives from the participial form of ʿābad and means "one who worships/serves Yahweh." This varies slightly from the LXX *Abdias* and Vulgate *Abdia* pronunciation, which probably is based on the Hebrew noun form ʿebed and means "the servant of Yahweh." Because "Obadiah" is a common name, denoting twelve different people spread across different periods of OT history, it is unlikely that the name is symbolic or allegorical, as many suggest for "Malachi," though this is a possibility. The most famous Obadiah (Heb ʿōbadyāhû) was King Ahab's palace chamberlain (1 Kings 18:1-15) and a believer in Yahweh who hid a hundred of Yahweh's prophets from Ahab's and Jezebel's persecution. The Babylonian Talmud (*b. Sanh.* 39b) identifies this northern Obadiah as the one responsible for the prophecy that bears his name, though there is nothing in the story that indicates that this Obadiah was a prophet. This traditional identification has generally been rejected by modern scholars.

2. Historical Setting and Canonical Location.

2.1. Historical Setting. Israel's relationship with Edom is long and full of conflict, which allows Obadiah a wide range of possible historical settings. Edom is one of the first enemies that Israel encountered following the exodus events, when Edom's army prevented Israel from passing through their country on the way to Canaan (Num 20:14-21). Later, David was able to subjugate them (2 Sam 8:13-14), though the situation did not last (2 Kings 8:20), and Israel/Judah maintained various levels of control over Edom (2 Kings 3; 14:7) and the port city of Elath (2 Kings 14:22; cf. 2 Kings 16:6) throughout the period of the monarchy. During the postexilic period, Edom became associated with the burning of the *temple at the time of the Babylonian destruction of Jerusalem (Ps 137:7; 1 Esdr 4:45; cf. Lam 4:22; Ezek 25:12-14; 35:5-15), though Chronicles, Kings and Jeremiah are silent on the issue. Edom later occupied the Negev following the Nabatean invasion of their homeland in the fourth/third century BC.

Because of this continued conflict, the suggested dates for Obadiah span almost five hundred years and are generally relegated to a few specific biblical events (Raabe, 49-51): (1) The early ninth-century BC setting of Ahab's chamberlain Obadiah. This connection is sometimes expanded to include a possible Edomite invasion during the time of Jehoshaphat (2 Chron 20). (2) Edom's revolt against Jehoram king of Judah c. 845 BC (2 Kings 8:21-22). It is argued that this revolt should be understood in connection with the joint Philistine/Arab invasion mentioned in 2 Chronicles 21:16-17, thus implying a Philistine/Arab identity for Obadiah's "strangers/foreigners" (Obad 11). (3) The Edomite capture of Elath from Judah c. 735 BC during the reign of Ahaz (2 Kings 16:6). The parallel account in 2 Chronicles 28:17-18 mentions a simultaneous Edomite/Philistine invasion of Judah, when Edom "carried off prisoners." (4) A date close to the time of Malachi and Nehemiah, c. 450 BC. It is argued that both Obadiah (Obad 1-7) and Malachi (Mal 1:2-7) frame their prophecies as depictions of past events: the Nabatean invasion, destruction and occupation of the traditional Edomite homeland. (5) Sometime during the *exile. Luther and Calvin, among others, associate Obadiah with Edomite aggression during and soon after the fall of Jerusalem in 587/6 BC.

2.2. Canonical Context. The decision to read Obadiah as an individual work or as part of the collection of the Book of the Twelve can influence the implied historical setting of the book. When read on its own, Obadiah's language and subject matter parallels Jeremiah 49 and Psalm 137, which may hint at a postexilic setting. Additionally, although the text does not demand it, Obadiah's descriptive language of destruction and exile fits comfortably within the context of the years following the traumatic events of 587/6 BC and Edom's historical developments with the Nabateans. Furthermore, the destruction of the temple is such a significant event that even if Obadiah referred to some older Edomite atrocity that occurred centuries before, the book could be reinterpreted to fit the later setting. However, Obadiah's canonical location within the MT order of the Book of the Twelve implies a more symbolic and possibly much earlier reading in which the descriptions of destruction and exile could fit the general context of any of the aforementioned points in Israelite history. Such a reading recognizes the loose chronological organization to the MT canonical order (Sweeney 2000a), and that Obadiah is positioned in the eighth-century BC block (Hosea through Micah) between two historical eighth-century BC prophets Amos and Jonah. Because the LXX order of the Book of the Twelve does not follow this pattern, it seems possible that the MT editors understood Obadiah according to the traditional identification of the ninth-century BC figure.

Obadiah's position within the canon is far from random. In the English and MT orders of the Book of the Twelve, Obadiah follows Joel and Amos, both of which contain their own calls for Edom's destruction (Joel 3:19; Amos 1:11-12; 9:12). While Amos first mentions Edom within a small "oracles against the nations" setting, it is his use in Amos 9:12 that probably influenced Obadiah's final position. Amos 9:11-15 is a restoration section that looks forward to the reestablishment of the Davidic monarchy (Amos 9:11), the return of the exiles (Amos 9:14), Israel's possession of the nations in general (Amos 9:12b) and the "remnant of Edom" specifically (Amos 9:12a). When the Book of the Twelve is considered as a collection, Amos's call for Edom's possession serves as an introduction to Obadiah's own calls for destruction and possession. In this way, it becomes possible to understand the book of Obadiah as a detailed expansion of Amos 9:12. In the LXX, Obadiah is preceded by Joel, not Amos, a situation that is partially explained by the LXX's translation "men" (*anthrōpōn*) for the MT's "Edom" in Amos 9:12 (Jones). The LXX's Joel-Obadiah order instead highlights Joel's own call for the conquest of Edom (Joel 3:19), as well as the restoration of *Zion (Joel 2:32; Obad 17).

2.3. Parallels with Jeremiah 49. Obadiah shares obvious parallels with Jeremiah 49:7-22. The use of similar vocabulary and imagery between the two passages, particularly Obadiah 1-4 and Jeremiah 49:14-16 (cf. Obad 5 with Jer 49:9, and Obad 16 with Jer 49:12), is evident and has raised questions of authorial dependency that have yet to be resolved. While some have found various levels of influence (Nogalski, 61-74; Niehaus, 500-502; Renkema, 38; Sweeney 2000b, 282-85), others have argued that both prophets borrowed from independent sources (Allen, 132-33; Ben Zvi, 99-109).

Despite the similarities, some differences are notable. Jeremiah's oracle concerning Edom takes place within the broader context of the oracles against the nations (Jer 46—51), in which Edom is just one of a number of nations to receive a message of prophetic doom. This is similar to Amos's prophecies against Edom (Amos 1:11-12) and the surrounding nations (Amos 1—2) that precede Obadiah canonically. While it is possible to argue that Obadiah functions in a comparable manner within the context of the wider Book of the Twelve, taken on its own, Obadiah is a self-contained prophecy against Edom that later expands to include judgment against the nations as a whole (Obad 15-16). Because of this, the scope of Obadiah with its progression from Edom to the nations diverges from Jeremiah 49:7-22, which never turns away from its singular message of doom regarding Edom.

3. Content.

There is no universal agreement on the outline or organization of Obadiah. Often, a distinction is made between the poetry (Obad 1-18) and prose (Obad 19-21) sections, but this is not always reflected in the English translations (cf. NIV, REB). Internally, it is possible to use Yahweh's three speeches (Obad 1-4, 5-7, 8-18) and the phrases "Thus says the Lord Yahweh" (Obad 1), "declares Yahweh" (Obad 4, 8) and "For Yahweh has spoken" (Obad 18) to locate four main sections (Obad 1-4, 5-7, 8-18, and 19-21, which is a prophetic expansion) within the book. In terms of subject matter, however, the core of the book hinges on Obadiah 15 and the results of Yahweh's intervention on the Day of Yahweh, when he moves from calling for Edom's destruction (Obad 1b-14) to punishing Edom and the nations (Obad 15-16) and restoring Israel (Obad 17-21).

  I. Introduction (Obad 1a)
 II. The Call for Edom's Destruction
      (Obad 1b-14)
      A. Announcement of Destruction
         (Obad 1b-4)
      B. Description of Destruction
         (Obad 5-9)
      C. Reasons for Destruction (Obad
         10-14)
III. The Occasion for Edom's
      Destruction: the Day of Yahweh
      (Obad 15-21)
      A. Day of Punishment for the
         Nations and for Edom (Obad
         15-18)
      B. Day of Restoration and
         Occupation (Obad 19-21)

The structure of Obadiah 15 has long been questioned. Some argue that the verse should be inverted (Barton; cf. Ben Zvi) because Obadiah 15b serves as a more appropriate conclusion for Obadiah 1-14 and the description of Edom's despicable acts, while Obadiah 15a serves as a better introduction to the broader discussion of the judgment of the nations that follows in Obadiah 16. Whether or not this is the case, it is in Obadiah 15 that the prophet transitions from recounting a historical situation and the actions of Edom at a time of national calamity (Obad 10-14) to speaking of an eschatological future wherein the offending nations are repaid for their deeds according to *lex talionis* (Obad 15b) (*see* Retribution), Zion is made safe (Obad 17, 21), the exiles are returned (Obad 20) and Edom is possessed by Israel (Obad 18-19, 21).

Following the introductory superscript, Obadiah begins his message with a summons to all nations to rise up and attack Edom. Obadiah 2-4 is rich in imagery that alludes to the height and rugged geography of the Edomite homeland. It is from this "height" and the false sense of security that it implies that Yahweh concludes with the promise of an ironic reversal to "bring you down" (Obad 5). Following the announcement, the totality of the destruction that faces Edom is described with the vivid metaphors of robbers and grape pickers (Obad 5) and is reinforced by the destruction of Edom's wise men (Obad 8) and complete slaughter of its warriors (Obad 9). Indeed, nothing will be left (Obad 6). The implication that this judgment will be the result of treachery by former friends and allies (Obad 7) is especially painful. Obadiah 10-14 depicts the results of actual historical events, though when these descriptions are examined closely, specific details prove elusive. The main charge against Edom is the "violence" (ḥāmās) committed against his "brother" Jacob (Obad 10). The other charges include passively allowing foreigners to sack Jerusalem (Obad 11), rejoicing in Jerusalem's destruction (Obad 12, 13b), marching through the gates (Obad 13a), taking their wealth (Obad 13c) and killing/handing over Israelite fugitives (Obad 14). Most noteworthy is that there is no specific mention of any action against the temple, which gives some support for the possibility that Obadiah, or the original source behind the prophecy, is older than the exile and was only later reinterpreted in light of the temple's destruction.

The constant use of "day" and "day of disaster/calamity/distress" saturates Obadiah 11-14 and prepares the reader for the dramatic reversal of the Day of Yahweh in Obadiah 15. Following Yahweh's intervention and the humbling of the nations (Obad 16), a renewed Israel/Mount Zion (Obad 17-18, 21) is contrasted with the utter destruction of the house/mountains of Esau (Obad 18-19, 21). In Obadiah 19-21, the terrible situation of Israel's day of calamity is gone, and the exiles will return to possess Esau (Obad 19, 21), the Negev (Obad 20) and the land of the Philistines (Obad 19). The book ends with the declarative statement that "the kingdom will be Yahweh's."

4. Interpretation.

The choice of interpretation once again depends on the decision to read Obadiah as an independent work or as part of the Book of the Twelve, and though such readings emphasize different theological aspects, they are not contradictory. When read on its own, Obadiah reflects the similar concerns of other passages that depict the destruction of Edom found throughout the OT (Is 21:11-12; 34; Jer 49:7-22; Ezek 25:12-14; 35; Joel 3:19-21; Amos 1:11-12; 9:12; Mal 1:2-5). It has long been noted that Edom receives an inordinate amount of attention from the biblical prophets, though the reasons for this are not clear. For such a small nation, Edom appears no more hostile than any of the smaller kingdoms that surround Israel, and yet Obadiah is an entire book devoted to its destruction, a distinction given only to the su-

perpower Assyria in Nahum. Such emphasis seems to reflect a historical tension between Edom and Israel that arose following the destruction of Jerusalem. From the viewpoint of Israel during the period of the exile, Edom had something to do with the destruction of Jerusalem and possibly the temple, or at least did not come to Israel's aid during this destruction. Once Israel was weakened and in exile, Edom took advantage of his "brother" and moved into the Negev and occupied traditional Israelite territory. It is possible that such actions struck at the theological heart of Israel's special relationship with Yahweh (Assis) and contradicted Israel's belief that Yahweh chose Israel over Esau (Mal 1:2-5; cf. Gen 25:19-34).

From Israel's exilic/postexilic viewpoint, and in light of these historical circumstances, was *Israel really Yahweh's chosen people, or was it Esau/Edom? Did Israel's sin cause Yahweh to abandon his people? Did Jerusalem's destruction and Edom's occupation of the land mirror Israel's destruction and occupation of Canaan under Joshua? Had Yahweh revoked his promise to Israel? Obadiah reassures Israel of Yahweh's faithfulness and provides answers to these questions by describing a fast-approaching day of reversal in which Yahweh will set things right and judge both Edom and the nations. Edom in particular will be held accountable for its actions and will be destroyed; and Mount Zion, not the mountains of Esau, will be restored. The people of Israel not only will return to their own land, but also will actually occupy Edom. Such a prophecy certainly would have reassured an Israelite group that was struggling to understand their situation and Yahweh's actions in the years following the Babylonian destruction.

When Obadiah is read as part of the collection of the Book of the Twelve, however, the book takes on a more symbolic meaning and emphasizes Yahweh's broader plan and purpose for the nations as a whole. The ultimate aim of his actions is to bring about their eventual repentance and inclusion into the eschatological kingdom of Zion (Mic 4:1-5). In the Book of the Twelve as a whole, Joel is the first to specifically introduce the concept of the Day of Yahweh (Joel 1:15). In Joel, the Day of Yahweh comes first against Israel (Joel 2:11) before the arrival of an eschatological age (Joel 2:28-32) in which Yahweh turns his attention toward the judgment of the nations (Joel 3:1-

21) and *lex talionis* (Joel 3:4, 7). This division in the Day of Yahweh between Israel and the nations is realized in Amos and Obadiah, as Amos discusses the Day of Yahweh against Israel (Amos 5:18-20), and Obadiah outlines its implications for the nations (specifically Obad 15-21). In this reading, Edom, one of Israel's oldest enemies, becomes a symbol for all of Israel's traditional enemies. The destruction that faces Edom is therefore symbolic of the judgment that will face all nations that oppose Yahweh and his people.

Within the collection of the Twelve, Obadiah's message of absolute judgment, however, is quickly mitigated by Jonah's offer of grace. In the balance between Obadiah and Jonah, the broader picture of Yahweh's dealings with the nations is made evident. When Obadiah is read in light of Jonah, Obadiah's dreadful judgment that awaits all nations is not a foregone conclusion, and the opportunity for repentance remains. However, when Jonah is read in light of Obadiah, Jonah's message of grace toward the nations cannot be understood as a type of universalism. This nuanced balance of judgment and grace prepares the way for a new eschatological age (Mic 3:12—4:5) when a destroyed Zion is rebuilt, the nations are peacefully incorporated into Jerusalem, and the implements of war are no longer needed (Mic 4:3). That Nahum's message of Assyrian destruction has been separated from Jonah in the MT and is located immediately after Micah serves to reemphasize the seriousness of Obadiah's judgment and shows that Yahweh's requirement for inclusion and national repentance is a continual necessity, not a one-time act. Finally, the concern for the fate of Edom specifically and the nations generally is such an important theme that it is repeated in Malachi (Mal 1:2-5), the Twelve's concluding book.

See also DAY OF THE LORD; NATIONS; TWELVE, BOOK OF THE; ZION.

BIBLIOGRAPHY. **L. C. Allen,** *The Books of* *Joel, Obadiah, Jonah, and Micah* (NICOT; Grand Rapids: Eerdmans, 1976); **E. Assis,** "Why Edom? On the Hostility Towards Jacob's Brother in Prophetic Sources" *VT* 56 (2006) 1-20; **J. R. Bartlett,** *Edom and the Edomites* (JSOTSup 77; Sheffield: JSOT Press, 1989); **J. Barton,** *Joel and Obadiah* (OTL; Louisville: Westminster/John Knox, 2001); **E. Ben Zvi,** *A Historical-Critical Study of the Book of Obadiah* (BZAW 242; Berlin: de Gruyter, 1996); **B. Dicou,** *Edom, Israel's Brother and Antagonist: The Role of Edom in Biblical Prophecy and Story* (JSOTSup 169; Sheffield: Sheffield Academic Press, 1994); **B. A. Jones,** *The Formation of the Book of the Twelve: A Study in Text and Canon* (SBLDS 149; Atlanta: Scholars Press, 1995); **R. Mason,** *Micah, Nahum, Obadiah* (OTG; Sheffield: JSOT Press, 1991); **J. Niehaus,** "Obadiah," in *The Minor Prophets: An Exegetical and Expository Commentary*, 2: *Obadiah, Jonah, Micah, Nahum, and Habakkuk*, ed. T. E. McComiskey (Grand Rapids: Baker, 1993) 495-541; **J. D. Nogalski,** *Redactional Processes in the Book of the Twelve* (BZAW 218; Berlin: de Gruyter, 1993); **P. R. Raabe,** *Obadiah* (AB 24D; New York: Doubleday, 1996); **J. Renkema,** *Obadiah* (HCOT; Leuven: Peeters, 2003); **D. Stuart,** *Hosea-Jonah* (WBC 31; Waco, TX: Word, 1987); **M. A. Sweeney,** "Sequence and Interpretation in the Book of the Twelve," in *Reading and Hearing the Book of the Twelve*, ed. J. D. Nogalski and M. A. Sweeney (SBLSymS 15; Atlanta: Society of Biblical Literature, 2000a) 49-64; idem, *The Twelve Prophets*, 1: *Hosea, Joel, Amos, Obadiah, Jonah* (Berit Olam; Collegeville, MN: Liturgical Press, 2000b). J. LeCureux

ORACLES AGAINST THE NATIONS. *See* NATIONS.

ORAL TRANSMISSION. *See* WRITING AND PROPHECY.

P, Q

PATRIARCHY. *See* Feminist Interpretation.

PEACE, REST

Peace and rest are closely interconnected ideas in the Prophetic Books. When depicting current social and political realities, they refer to a state of existence characterized by security and prosperity. They also play an important role in the prophetic description of the future. In such passages rest and peace are an integral part of Yahweh's eschatological gift of *salvation. Finally, they are used by the prophets to explore various aspects of the human response to God—that is, belief in his power and obedience to his will.

    1. The Vocabulary of Rest and Peace
    2. Rest, Peace and War
    3. The Eschatological Vision of Rest and Peace
    4. The Prince of Peace
    5. Rest and Peace as a Call to Trust and Obedience

1. The Vocabulary of Rest and Peace.

There are a number of Hebrew words related to the notion of rest and peace: *šqṭ*, "to be at rest, be peaceful and quiet" (*šeqeṭ*, "peace"); *nwḥ*, "to settle, repose, wait" (*měnûḥâ, mānôaḥ*, "resting place, rest"; *naḥat*, "rest, calmness"); *rgʿ*, "to come to rest, be quiet" (*margôaʿ, margēʿâ*, "rest, resting place"); *šʾn*, "to be at ease, be untroubled" (*šaʾǎnān*, "carefree, undisturbed"); *šlh*, "to be quiet, at ease" (*šālēw*, "undisturbed, secure, prosperous"; *šalwâ*, "security, prosperity"). The motifs of safety (*beṭaḥ*, from *bṭḥ*, "to trust"; *ʾěmet*, "firmness, trustworthiness") and healing (*rpʾ*) play an important role in prophetic descriptions of peace. The Hebrew word traditionally translated as "peace" is *šālôm*. It denotes wholeness, harmony, well-being and more specifically

wealth, physical health, security, a state of satisfaction and ease, relationships of friendliness and communion (Stendebach, 17-20). In some passages it comes close in meaning to "salvation" (*yěšûʿâ*).

2. Rest, Peace and War.

"Peace" (*šālôm*) is used in a political sense to describe absence of war and bondage (Is 39:8 [parallel to *ʾěmet*, "security"]; Jer 14:13) and the resulting state of general well-being (Jer 29:7) and safety (*beṭaḥ* in Ezek 34:25, 27, 28; *šalwâ* in Jer 22:21). Sword, famine and oppression deprive people of *šālôm* (Jer 8:15; 14:19b [here in parallel to *ṭôb*, "good," and *marpēʾ*, "healing"]; 12:12; Ezek 7:25) and rest (*rgʿ* in Jer 50:33-34; *nwḥ* and *šqṭ* in Is 14:7; 23:12). In the book of Jeremiah the term *šālôm* comes up often in the context of polemic against the prophets of peace (Jer 4:10; 6:14; 8:11; 14:13 [together with *ʾěmet*]; Jer 23:17 [contrasted with *rāʿâ*, "calamity"]; Jer 28:9; cf. Ezek 13:10, 16) who apparently promised security and restoration of Judah's well-being, possibly on the basis of a belief in Zion's inviolability (Sisson, 430-33, 437-38). Similar polemic is reflected in Micah 3:5, where false prophets are criticized for proclaiming messages of well-being and prosperity (*šālôm*) to all who pay them (see also 1 Kings 22).

    The promise of a life of security and peace becomes prominent in prophetic texts during and after the exile. Return from exile will lead to a life of tranquility (*šqṭ*), quietness (*šʾn* in Jer 30:10; 46:27) and safety (*beṭaḥ* in Ezek 28:26) free from the oppression of enemies and from the fear of new invasions. The rest of the redeemed remnant is portrayed with the help of the image of a grazing flock (Zeph 2:7; 3:13). In the postexilic situation the promise of peace (*šālôm*, parallel in Jer 33:9 to *ṭôbâ*, "good") involves restoration (*ʾărûkâ*), rebuilding of the nation, healing (*marpēʾ*) the wounds of war and enjoying a life of joy, praise and forgiveness (Jer 33:6-9).

3. The Eschatological Vision of Rest and Peace.

The Babylonian *exile forms the background of the message of peace in Isaiah 49—55, but the rich imagery of these chapters transcends the confines of their original historical situation and points toward "a new exodus, a fundamental new salvific event described in the categories of creation" (Stendebach, 35). *Zion's *šālôm* is based on the establishment of God's royal rule (Is 52:7), manifestation of his glory (*kābôd* [Is 40:5]) and the arrival of his presence in the city (Is 40:3-11) as its true king. It begins with the announcement of Yahweh's victory or salvation (*yĕšûʿâ*) over the oppressor (Is 52:1-7) and the destruction of the power of evil (Is 51:9-11) and culminates in the restoration of the city, where peace (*šālôm*) abounds (Is 54:13), whose walls are made of precious stones (Is 54:11-12) and whose enemies are powerless (Is 54:14-17). This new age of security, prosperity, mercy and fruitfulness is compared to the renewal of creation after the flood (Is 54:9) and is confirmed by a "covenant of peace" (*bĕrît šālôm*) (Is 54:10; cf. Ezek 34:25, 37:26; also Hos 2:18-23) (see Batto, 188-92). This covenant indicates Yahweh's commitment to restore the relationship not only between his people and himself but also between humanity and the cosmos at large (Goldingay, 443-45), thus rebuilding the primeval harmony of the created order (Batto). Isaiah 55:12-13 concludes this part of the book with the promise that Zion's children will be led back to her in joy (*śimḥâ*) and peace (*šālôm*), picking up the theme of departure (from Babylon) from Isaiah 52:11-12. The exodus imagery of Isaiah 52:11-12, however, gives way here to a more extravagant description of the journey from slavery to freedom. Nature is personified and transformed to celebrate the deliverance of God's people. Peace stems from God who is a creator, redeemer and warrior, and describes the reality of life of fullness and joy in his royal presence when evil is defeated and creation is renewed.

A picture of universal peace, including not just *Israel but all the *nations of the world, is further developed in Isaiah 2:2-4 (= Mic 4:1-3).

Although there might be some differences between Isaiah and Micah in the way Israel's relationship to the nations is envisaged during the age of peace (Sweeney), it is clear that this would be a time of complete cessation of war (cf. Hos 2:18, see also 4 below; Wolff, 115-16), the establishment of God's worldwide royal rule and the elevation of Mount Zion as a universal center of *worship. Connection between temple and peace (*šālôm*) is also present in Haggai 2:1-9 (see the link between rest and temple in 2 Sam 7:1-2, 9-10). Here the gift of peace is the climax of a restoration process that includes the shaking of the cosmos and the nations and the confirmation of God's presence among his people by filling the temple with glory (*kābôd*) (building on Ex 24:15-16; 40:34-35; 1 Kings 8:10-11) (see Assis, 593-94). In Haggai 2:5, 9, like in Isaiah 32:15, 17 (on which, see next paragraph), the giving of *šālôm* is related to the presence/pouring out of Yahweh's spirit (*rûaḥ*) on the community. This connection with temple and the spirit of Yahweh underlines the fact that true peace is not the outcome of human efforts but rather stems from God and comes only as a result of God's indwelling among people.

As in the Deuteronomistic literature (see Roth), the giving of rest (*nwḥ*) is sometimes connected in prophetic texts to the fulfillment of God's promises and the gift of the land after the exodus (Is 63:14). When rest is portrayed as something in the future, it depicts God's eschatological gift of salvation and renewal (Is 32:15-20). The primary force that brings about this reality is the pouring out of the spirit (Is 32:15 [spirit and rest are connected also in Is 63:14]). As a result, the *wilderness is transformed into an orchard, suggesting the notion of fertility and agricultural abundance (peace involves prosperity also in Is 60:11, 16-17). The product of this transformation in Isaiah 32:18 is the establishment of a "habitation of peace" (*nĕwēh šālôm*), "secure dwellings" (*miškĕnôt mibṭaḥîm*) and "undisturbed resting places" (*mĕnûḥôt šaʾănannôt*) for God's people. Peace (*šālôm*), tranquility (*šqṭ*) and security (*beṭaḥ*) are explicitly described as the result of righteousness (*ṣĕdāqâ*) dwelling among the community (Is 32:17 [for the close connection between righteousness and peace, see also Is 9:7; 48:18; 60:17]) (*see* Justice, Righteousness). *Chaos, manifested in *sin and devastation (Is 32:9-14), is removed from nature and society and substituted by peace, understood as flourishing of the natural world and proper exercise of human authority (Goldingay, 443). This connection not just with absence of military threat but also with fertility and justice points to a meaning of peace as part of the divinely created cosmic, life-sustaining order (Steck, 55-59) disrupted by human sin and reestablished by Yahweh in the new age.

4. The Prince of Peace.

The connection between peace and righteousness is also stressed in the description of the royal figure in Isaiah 9:1-7. The oracle begins with the promise that God will bring glory, light and joy to people who walk in humiliation, darkness and anguish. This is achieved through putting an end to foreign dominion and an end to war itself (Is 9:4-5). An important step in this development is the birth or enthronement of a new Davidic ruler, the "Prince of Peace" (*śar šālôm*) (*see* Messiah). Of the four titles of the child in Isaiah 9:6, this last one seems to be especially significant because the notion of everlasting peace (*šālôm 'ên qēṣ*) is picked up and developed in the following verse. In light of the context, "peace" must refer to absence of war and the freedom from oppression and may be an alternative way of expressing the "rest from the enemies" theme in the original Davidic oracle in 2 Samuel 7. However, peace involves more than that. It is a necessary precondition for the establishment of the throne and kingdom of David with justice (*mišpāṭ*) and righteousness (*ṣēdāqâ*). It is indispensable to a life of joy, stability and order, which the king raised by Yahweh will be instrumental in establishing (Williamson, 40-42). Although historically this oracle might reflect the period of Assyria's oppression of Israel and Judah, within its present literary and canonical context it acquires an added eschatological meaning. This is confirmed by Isaiah 11:6-9, where the new Davidic ruler (the shoot from the stump of Jesse—i.e., the second David [Is 11:1]) brings peace to the whole of creation lifting the Edenic curse, transforming the innate destructive instincts of the animal world and creating harmony and security.

Peace (*šālôm*) is one of the fruits of the suffering of Yahweh's *servant in Isaiah 53. It stands here in parallel to the healing (*rp'*) of wounds (see also Is 38:17; 57:18-19; Jer 6:14; 8:15; 33:6) and *forgiveness of transgressions

(Is 53:4-5) and describes a condition of both physical and spiritual wholeness achieved through harmonious relationship with God and the removal of sin. "Healing is a wide-ranging image for God putting things right where they were wrong" (Goldingay, 377), and so here both healing and peace must be equivalent in meaning to "salvation." Undoubtedly, the most striking feature of this passage is the proclamation that this peace is achieved for the speakers through the suffering that the servant undertook on their behalf. Therefore, even to a greater extent than the Prince of Peace in Isaiah 9:1-7, the Suffering Servant is instrumental in achieving the eschatological vision of restoration and peace described in Isaiah 52—55. The achievement, however, comes not through the use of power or the rule of righteousness but rather through suffering for others.

Two other prophetic texts connect the idea of peace with the figure of an earthly ruler. In Zechariah 9:9-10 we see the Davidic king appearing after Yahweh has reincorporated the neighbors of Israel into what might be a reestablishment of the Davidic empire (Zech 9:1-7). Much like Isaiah 9:1-7, the figure of the king is subordinated to and overshadowed by the power of God and is connected to the ideas of righteousness, end of war and an offer of peace (*šālôm*), not just to Israel but to all the nations. This may be interpreted to mean freedom for Judah from foreign oppression, but it could also encompass the idea of just order and state of general well-being for all nations (Stendebach, 40).

The figure of a ruler (*môšēl*) providing victory and security appears also in Micah 5:2-6. This is a second David, who comes, like the first David, from Bethlehem of Ephrathah (Mic 5:2). The main focus of the oracle, in Micah 5:4, is his power and ability to deliver his people from the enemies. By the power of Yahweh he will "shepherd" (*r'h*, "to feed, protect, rule") the nation and will enable it to dwell in security (*yšb* [the notion of security is either implied in the verb or has fallen out of the text]). The opening phrase of Micah 5:5, *wĕhāyâ zeh šalôm*, often is rendered "He will be the One of Peace" and is taken as a messianic title, similar to the "Prince of Peace," which sums up the king's achievements and significance. However, the translation of the phrase and its relationship to the immediate context are disputed (it can alternatively be translated "and this will be our peace" and related to what follows).

5. Rest and Peace as a Call to Trust and Obedience.

Rest and peace are not only a gift from God; they can be used to express an appropriate human response to God (note "to walk in peace [šālôm]" with God [Mal 2:6; cf. Is 27:5]). Sometimes a state of rest is a reflection of an attitude of trust in Yahweh. In Isaiah 30:15 Judah is reproached for having rejected repentance (šûbâ), calm (naḥat), quietness (šqṭ) and trust (biṭḥâ), which would have resulted in victory (yšʿ) and power (gĕbûrâ). This verse is commonly believed to come from the time of Hezekiah's rebellion against Sennacherib (705-701 BC), in which case the rest and quietness would mean refraining from rebellion against Assyria and from seeking Egypt's help. This is confirmed by the following verse, which contrasts rest and trust in Yahweh to riding on horses (i.e., engaging in military activities). Similar is the situation in which Isaiah confronts King Ahaz with the command to be calm (šqṭ) when facing the challenge of northern Israel and Damascus during the Syro-Ephramite war (Is 7:4). This is not so much a call to political inactivity as an encouragement to believe (ʾmn) in Yahweh (Is 7:9) and to have confidence in his power to help. Ahaz's fear and his reliance on Assyria's assistance are expressions of his unbelief. The more general point is that on certain occasions human action may imply reliance on one's own strength and rejection of God's plans. In such situations rest, refraining from activity and waiting on God to intervene, is faith demonstrated in practice.

In other situations, however, being at ease can imply an attitude of complacency and therefore is condemned as sinful. This is the case with the leadership of Jerusalem and Samaria whose life of luxury betrays their arrogance and lack of concern for the welfare of their people. Being at ease (šaʾănān) and feeling secure (bṭḥ) results in indifference to the challenge of the prophetic message (Amos 6:1; cf. Zeph 1:12). The ease (šaʾănān) and security (bṭḥ) of the daughters of Zion in Isaiah 32:9-11 are in stark contrast to the ease (cf. the "untroubled resting places" [mĕnûḥôt šaʾănannôt] in Is 32:18) and security (beṭaḥ [Is 32:17]; cf the "secure dwellings" [miškĕnôt mibṭaḥîm] in Is 32:18) given by Yahweh to his people later on in the same passage. Sodom is also condemned

for living a life of prosperity ("excess of food"), security (šalwâ) and ease (šqṭ) without any concern for the poor (Ezek 16:49).

Obedience to God's commandments leads to a life of harmony and peace. In Zechariah people are called to render "judgment of peace" (mišpaṭ šālôm) (Zech 8:16) and to "love truth [ʾĕmet] and peace [šālôm]" (Zech 8:19). The context shows that this involves striving to promote society where justice is practiced, where harmony and integrity characterize relationships, and where there is a passionate concern for the poor and the helpless (taking into account the parallel calls in Zech 7:9-10). In contrast, the wicked do not practice justice (mišpāṭ), and so they do not know the way of peace (šālôm) (Is 59:8). Consequently, there is no šālôm for them (Is 48:22; cf. Jer 30:5), and they are "are unable to rest [šqṭ]" (Is 57:20-21). They will experience neither the redemption of the new exodus promised to Jacob (Is 48:20-21) nor the healing (rpʾ) and peace (šālôm) given by God to his people (Is 57:18-19). Only those who trust (bṭḥ) in the Lord will find peace (šālôm), even in the midst of chaos and battle (Is 26:3), and those who are obedient to God's will and commandments will find rest (margôaʿ) in the face of the difficulties and challenges of life (Jer 6:16).

See also FORGIVENESS; JUSTICE, RIGHTEOUSNESS; SALVATION, DELIVERANCE; WARFARE AND DIVINE WARFARE.

BIBLIOGRAPHY. E. Assis, "A Disputed Temple (Hag 2,1-9)," *ZAW* 120 (2008) 582-96; P. A. Baker, "Rest, Peace," *DOTP* 687-691; B. F. Batto, "The Covenant of Peace: A Neglected Ancient Near Eastern Motif," *CBQ* 49 (1987) 187-211; J. Goldingay, *Old Testament Theology, 2: Israel's Faith* (Downers Grove, IL: IVP Academic, 2006); H. Preuss, "נוח," *TDOT* 9:277-86; W. Roth, "The Deuteronomic Rest Theology: A Redaction-Critical Study," *BR* 21 (1976) 5-14; J. P. Sisson, "Jeremiah and the Jerusalem Conception of Peace," *JBL* 105 (1986) 429-42; O. H. Steck, "The Jerusalem Conceptions of Peace and Their Development in the Prophets of Ancient Israel," in *The Meaning of Peace: Biblical Studies*, ed. P. B. Yoder and W. M. Swartley (Louisville: Westminister/John Knox, 1992) 49-68; F. J. Stendebach, "שלום," *TDOT* 15:13-49; M. A. Sweeney, "Micah's Debate with Isaiah," *JSOT* 93 (2001) 111-24; H. G. M. Williamson, *Variations on a Theme:*

King, Messiah and Servant in the Book of Isaiah (Carlisle: Paternoster, 1998); **H. H. Wolff,** "Swords into Plowshares: Misuse of a Word of Prophecy?" in *The Meaning of Peace: Biblical Studies*, ed. P. B. Yoder and W. M. Swartley (Louisville: Westminister/John Knox, 1992) 110-26.   T. S. Hadjiev

PERFORMANCE CRITICISM

Performance criticism is a critical methodology used to analyze the way in which repeatable and socially recognizable events (e.g., theater, parade, graduation, political inauguration) use specific techniques to powerfully express social values and themes. The application of the methodology to the prophetic literature of the Old Testament is based on the premise that select portions of the OT are literary variations of originally oral compositions presented or recited before live audiences. "Thus says the LORD" and "Hear the word of the LORD" are two common introductions found throughout the Hebrew prophets that, in many important ways, symbolize the whole of the prophetic enterprise. Both phrases imply the oral delivery of an identifiable, repeatable message to an audience. Both phrases announce a performance.

Embedded in the prophetic literature of the OT are echoes of the prophetic performance, only now layered over and sometimes co-opted by a scribal performance. The media transferability (from oral to written or vice versa) of performative structures, conventions and characteristics results in the ghosting or echo of those original performances in the written form the material has now assumed within the pages of the biblical text. Performance criticism, applied to the Hebrew prophets, is designed to elucidate performance dynamics and the manner in which the prophetic performance was captured and reused in a scribal presentation.

1. Performance as Event
2. Performance Criticism and Its Relation to Other Methodologies
3. Performance Criticism's Building Blocks
4. Application to the Prophets of the OT

1. Performance as Event.

Performances are events that occur in a variety of forms and are not limited to stage or formal theater. Yet, in whatever venue presented, performance utilizes recognizable conventions and structures that are used to facilitate communi-

cation. Performative events (e.g., prophesying, singing, sermonizing, debating, memorializing) have left their mark on portions of the biblical text. And just as a playwright's script can give clues to the nature and event of the performance, so too select portions of the biblical text are imbued with communicative conventions and structures that are particularly susceptible to analysis by performance criticism. Performance criticism is concerned with identifying, describing and analyzing a performative event in which there is the presentation of character and event by actors using formal patterns that might include movement, gesture, costume and speech in order to create a shared imagined reality between actor and spectator.

Performance can be a particular type of orality, and so the first step in determining the applicability of performance criticism to a literary text (biblical or otherwise) is detecting the clues of orality that remain in the literary text. Those clues include the language of immediacy, dialogue, spontaneity and "face-to-face" constructions that employ a denser number of verbs when compared to more distant and formal linguistic characteristics common in literary texts. These linguistic characteristics point us to a way of organizing thought, orally conceived and orally presented, that is distinct from the organization of thought commonly expressed in written texts. Oral presentations follow conventions of composition, content, structure and style just as distinct as those characteristic of literary works. And just as literary works can be categorized into groupings, so too oral presentations can be classified into different types of orality.

One type of oral presentation is performance and is identifiable by the particular performative mode of thought in which performances were conveyed and characteristics of which still reside embedded in the written literature. A performative mode of thought is a way of thinking that engages both the cognitive and imaginative aspects of thought to conceive of reality not in propositions, but in actions and being. Similar to the notion of dramatic imagination, a performative mode of thought is the shared imaginative space of performance where the performer/presenter and the spectator meet. That shared imaginative space of performance often is used as a means of examining social conflict and crises, as well as an imaginative vision for social unity and conflict resolution. Prophetic performances are reiterated behaviors addressing periods of crisis or uncertainty that accompany individual or cultural transitions, often presenting an imagined resolution.

2. Performance Criticism and Its Relation to Other Methodologies.

Performance criticism takes its place alongside the methodologies within the historical-critical approach. As applied to the OT, performance criticism, in conjunction with *form criticism, *rhetorical criticism and, to some degree, narrative criticism, provide multiple lenses through which to see and understand better the dynamics of communication at work in particular texts, especially those texts with oral presentations at their origin. In some important ways, analysis done using performance criticism is similar to the types of discussions that take place in both form-critical and rhetorical-critical investigations. The major difference, however, between performance criticism and form or rhetorical criticism is that, as usually conducted, form and rhetorical criticisms are literary criticisms of structures, types or literary genres and the social settings in which they were used, whereas performance criticism focuses on the event or the dynamic complex of action of a performance and the social settings in which those events occurred. Performance criticism shares with rhetorical criticism an interest in the presumed audience of either the performed or literary material. Within this array of methodologies, performance criticism offers its own unique contribution. Whereas form criticism may identify legends, epics, hymnic types and the like, and rhetorical criticism focuses on the stylistic features of prose and poetry (again literary types) that help make the composition persuasive and influential, performance criticism considers movement, voice, costume, dialogue, activity and the way events play out in performative episodes built upon particular act-schemes.

Performance criticism is also linked to cognitive studies. Cognition, it is suggested, is itself an embodied action that contributes to the enactment of the surrounding world, helping to create that world and give it meaning on both the page and in the body. Performance, whether traditionally theatrical or not, mirrors this process of "embodied action," or our ability to represent what we perceive through some kind of embodied enactment: preaching, prophesying,

oration, narration, singing and so on. The relationship between the performed and the real is at the heart of the prophetic experience.

3. Performance Criticism's Building Blocks.

As with other critical methodologies, there are several core principles that help to give performance criticism its shape and unique contribution. Below are brief descriptions of the more central concepts that have particularly useful applicability to the OT. This list by no means exhausts the possibilities; it simply creates a framework for understanding a performance-critical approach.

3.1. Medium Transferability. Medium transferability is the ability of communication conventions and structures to transfer between an oral and a written medium. Although not unique to a performance-critical analysis alone, the medium transferability of performative material is important for the application of performance criticism to the biblical text. Performative material is media transferable in two ways. First, performance is not a specific genre or form, such as play or mime, but is an event that occurs in a variety of forms. School graduations, sermons and political speeches are just as performative as are parades, plays and operas. Performative dynamics apply to all. Those performative dynamics were hard at work particularly in those parts of the OT tradition that began as oral presentation. Those performance dynamics helped to form the bundle of conventions enabling communication. A transference, of sorts, occurs when conventions used expressly for recognizable formal performance are transferred to events not formally performance (graduations, sermons, etc.).

There is a second manner in which medium transferability applies to the performance criticism of the OT. The echo of those performance conventions remains present in the text of the OT. Just as a playwright's script gives clues about the actual performance of the play, so too clues of oral presentation and performance remain embedded in the OT. The oral presentations that became the literary text of the OT follow conventions just as formal as those in the literary text. In fact, an appreciation of those performance conventions can help explain certain characteristics of the literary text. The manner in which performance conventions are media transferable (oral to written) allows for their continued presence in the pages of the OT.

Prophetic performers delivered speeches and other live presentations, the text of some now appearing in the prophetic literature. But, in the prophetic literature the text of the prophetic speech is recontextualized into the written drama now presented by the scribe. The media transference of the prophetic performance into a literary text causes the prophetic actor of the oral performance to become a prophetic character in the scribal performance of the literary text. The prophetic performance is past. The prophetic performer is gone. What remains are texts in which the prophetic actor lives on as a prophetic character in the drama fashioned by the scribe. With the transformation of prophetic actor into prophetic character, control over the prophetic message transfers from the prophet to the scribe.

3.2. Act-scheme. An act-scheme is the structural organization of the performance event. Dramatic structure is governed by a socially dynamic process of selection and feedback resulting in recognizable literary and performance structures that are shared by both performers and spectators. Act-schemes generally fall into one or more categories, such as acts of glorification, acts of illusion, acts of skill and acts of re-creation. Under these larger categories one may find specific articulations: parades, tragedies and comedies, gladiatorial combats and circuses, and reenactments. Each of these, in turn, relies on units of performed activity, the way prophetic literature ultimately relies on someone engaging in the act of prophesying. A simple example of an act of re-creation appears in 1 Kings 22, where Zedekiah sought to signify a military victory by donning horns of iron to perform before the kings of Judah and Israel. Prophetic oracles, visions and narratives often are constructed to form extended series of act-schemes. The dialogues early in Habakkuk or the narrative of domestic intrigue in Hosea are examples of act-schemes giving structure to performances. Act-schemes are the building blocks out of which a performance is formed. The logic applied to the structure and sequencing of the act-schemes is as recognizable as the logic that governs sentences and paragraphs in plot formation of a literary text. Patterns of repetition and variation of themes created by the act-scheme structure can be found in some portions of the biblical literature. Each of the visions in the series spanning Amos 7—8 has its own integrity, but together they form a progression of acts leading to a climax and resolution.

3.3. Audience, Act, Actor. The relationship between the audience and the act (the thing witnessed) is a critical component to performance criticism. As content and structure (act-scheme) come to life in performance, a dynamic exchange occurs between the act and the audience. Shapes, sounds, colors, movements, words, intonations, images—all swirl before the audience, giving the audience something to respond to. This something is both real and imagined. It is the place, in performance, where the audience unites with the performance by identification with shared or conflicting values and belief. This connection is most often brought about by the actor/presenter, whose human presence makes the event possible. The performer transcends the ordinary and real by calling the spectator into the realm of the imagined action of the performance. The transformation of a spectator into an audience occurs when performer and spectator meet in that imagined realm of performance. This meeting between audience and actor, in the place of performance, constitutes the powerful moment of transformation seen in the audience response formula during the temple dedication performance (2 Chron 7:3). Likewise, the rhetorical questions scattered throughout the prophetic oracles have the effect of creating an audience by drawing the spectator into the performance space. The anticipated and repeated audience response of "Lo! Lo!" (Heb for "No! No!") to the rhetorical questions of Amos 6:12 becomes a moment of self-incrimination as the prophetic performer skillfully uses the audience's own implied response to drive home his social judgment (the "Lo Debar" phrase of Amos 6:13). The same skill is apparent in the oracles against foreign *nations in Amos 1—2. Here, the prophetic performer wins a hearing before a hostile Israelite audience by first pronouncing judgment on surrounding people groups in a fashion that his immediate audience would have found quite appealing. Audience formation is, therefore, a major component of performance and performance criticism. This notion of audience formation is similar to the concerns of reader-response analysis and rhetorical criticism of literature. In that the audience formation dynamics are found in events, the echo of which resides in select portions of literature, the patterns and conventions examined by performance criticism are not the same as those analyzed by rhetorical criticism.

3.4. Iconic Presentation, Dialectic Presentation. Content and structure (act-scheme), dynamically shaped through performance (act-audience relationship), are interchanges of either iconic or dialectic modes of presentation. These two modes of presentation are perhaps the most crucial concepts to the development of a performance-critical approach to the Bible. Understanding iconic and dialectic modes of presentations is essential to moving outside of the literary frame and into the realm of performance. Iconic modes of presentation stress being, while dialectic modes of presentation stress becoming. Iconic modes of presentation tend to present, celebrate and reify who we are, while dialectic modes of presentation stress conflict, tension and change. Under the iconic mode of presentation, a variety of celebratory forms and genres have emerged: parades, exhibitions, processions, promenades, demonstrations, pageants, liturgical celebrations and so on. Dialectic modes tend to be those forms and genres more closely associated with specific theater and drama traditions: tragedies, comedies, dramas, musicals and operas.

The two modes of presentation are not impermeable and often exist side by side or share performance events. The iconic can contain the dialectic, and vice versa. For example, in the midst of a military parade, a clearly iconic form of presentation, a small battle can be staged that brings about the demise of the enemy, suggesting the dialectical conflict and tension of achieving victory. The ways in which iconic and dialectic modes of presentation take form, or are manifest from age to age, are determined by the same social, religious, political and economic forces that shape so many other aspects of culture. Both modes can be found in the prophetic literature. Amos 7:10-14 presents a concise dialectic mode stressing the becoming of the tension between the prophet and the religious elite of Israel that gives power and force to the being of moral tension found in the iconic oracles of the same book (Amos 1—6). This technique of forcefully counterpositioning iconic and dialectic is scattered throughout the OT, illustrated clearly by songs found in prose contexts. The exodus narrative

leading up to Exodus 15 tells a story, a becoming, that unfolds with the plot of the story. That becoming is interrupted by the song in Exodus 15, which stresses the being of those singing the song. In the singing of the song, the singers adopt the story as their own. The same is true of Deborah's song in Judges 5, and this juxtaposition of becoming and being helps explain the anachronistic or conflicting details between the songs and the prose.

3.5. Explicit and Implicit Activity. Explicit and implicit activity are patterns of activity (movement, behavior) embedded in many parts of the OT. Singing, prophesying, preaching, teaching, arguing and debating are examples of some of the explicit activities that form the basis of various performative patterns. Wherever explicit activity (such as prophesying or singing) is present, a series of implicit questions must be asked. How did the prophet prophesy? Where was the prophet standing? How was the prophet's voice altered in tone or pitch? When and where did the prophet move, gesture? We may not be able to definitively answer all these questions, but they provide a way into the oral and performed world of the Bible, which can impact our understanding of the text. They are questions that seek to draw out the nature of the activity (natural/artificial, real/virtual) embedded in the text. Often, clues to that implicit activity remain in the literary variation of the performance. For example, in the introduction to a series of oracles in Amos 1:2 the prophetic performance begins, "The LORD roars from Zion." It is unimaginable that this introduction was given in anything but the most powerful and intimidating tone of voice, in both volume and pitch. This implied performed activity, although still attested, loses its force of presence in the literary rendition. Clues to implied activity, like stage directions in a script, are still present in the biblical prophetic text.

3.6. Project. The project of a character is the concrete focal point of the character's energy. The project includes the character's intention and the activities or manners in which that intention is pursued. In fulfilling a project, a character meets with resistance, and tension is formed. The tension provides to the audience varying degrees of intensity that facilitate the audience's participation in the imagined space of shared values or beliefs intended by the performer. The series of visions in Amos 7—8, interrupted by the prophetic narrative of Amos 7:10-14, provides a good illustration of the varied levels of intensity employed to develop the prophetic character's project. Here the project is the announcement of punishment on Israel while maintaining empathetic identification with Israel. The threat of punishment ebbs and flows, drawing the audience ever deeper into the performance, while the resistance and tension in pursuing the project are given concrete dialectic expression in the conflict with Amaziah. The manner in which the project is given form in the act-schemes of the performance follows socially recognized conventions—conventions that may not be the same as those giving shape to literature. The media transference of the performed act-scheme into literature may account for the problematic duplications, inconsistencies and awkward transitions that sometimes occur in the prophetic literature. Here, in Amos 7, it explains the insertion of the prophetic narrative interrupting the vision sequence.

4. Application to the Prophets of the OT.

4.1. Preclassical Prophets. Moses and Miriam, both remembered as prophetic personages, perform songs—that is, iconic presentations—intended to help shape Israel's communal memory and identity. The extended story of Samuel interweaves the projects of Samuel, Eli and the Lord, changing the trajectory of Samuel and establishing an origin story for the Davidic monarchy. The oracles of Balaam (both in the biblical text and the Deir ʿAlla texts) provide evidence of the performative mode of thought that, through prophetic embodiment, sought to bring together the real and imagined into moments of cultural transition, both within Israelite lore and without. The stories of Elijah and Elisha are replete with the recounting of acted-out events giving life and power to the message of the prophets.

4.2. Classical Prophets. The literature of the classical prophets in the OT has long been appreciated for its poetic elegance. The material flows majestically and abounds with signals, clues and explicit references to its original oral delivery. That oral quality has provided the springboard for performance-critical analysis. The literature of the classical prophets, most obviously the prophetic oracles and other recorded speech events, has provided a fertile field for performance-critical analysis resulting in a deeper understanding of the relationship between actor, character and audience as developed within the literature. Hosea, Jeremiah, Ezekiel, Zephaniah, Isaiah and Amos have been considered through performance-critical analyses. For example, the oracles against the foreign nations of Amos 1:3—2:6 yield a rich understanding when considered through the performative concepts of explicit and implicit activity, iconic and dialectic modes of presentation, and project, resistance and tension. The oracles are, in performance-critical terms, the dialogue of an unfolding drama in which the actor (Amos) assumes a character (prophet of the Lord) in order to create a shared reality with the spectator in which the God of Israel invokes a shared identity of ethical obligation upon the audience.

Performance criticism is not limited to the speech events included in the prophetic literature. Hosea and Jonah are susceptible to new investigation as dramatic performances utilizing structures of act-schemes in the development of project. The mixture of narrative, oracle and prayer provide a balance of iconic and dialectic presentation that is especially powerful in creating a shared space between performer and audience.

In addition to providing a lens by which to view portions of the prophetic literature, performance criticism offers new suggestions concerning the social dynamics that produced the prophetic literature. The assumption of a smooth transition between the charismatic oration of the prophet and the scribal recording by the disciple has been challenged as a greater appreciation of the tension between performance event and written description or "script" suggests that the prophetic literature itself is a result of a social power struggle in which the prophetic performer lost control of the message, and prophecy came to an end. By some, at least, prophecy itself is viewed suspiciously (Zech 13:1-6). In the trajectory that led to the Hebrew prophetic literature, the Hebrew prophets leave their role of actor to become characters, given life in the presentation of another actor: the scribe with pen in hand.

See also CONVERSATION ANALYSIS; FORM CRITICISM; HERMENEUTICS; RHETORICAL CRITICISM; SIGN ACTS.

BIBLIOGRAPHY. **K. Baltzer,** *Deutero-Isaiah: A Commentary on Isaiah 40-55,* trans. M. Kohl

(Hermeneia; Minneapolis: Fortress, 1999); **E. Ben Zvi and M. Floyd,** eds., *Writings and Speech in Israelite and Near Eastern Prophecy* (SBLSymS 10; Atlanta: Society of Biblical Literature, 2000); **B. Beckerman,** *Dynamics of Drama: Theory and Method of Analysis* (New York: Drama Book Specialists, 1979); idem, *Theatrical Presentation: Performer, Audience, Act,* ed. G. B. Beckerman and W. Coco (New York: Routledge, 1990); **M. Carlson,** *Performance: A Critical Introduction* (New York: Routledge, 1996); **W. Doan and T. Giles,** *Prophets, Performance and Power: Performance Criticism of the Hebrew Bible* (New York: T & T Clark, 2005); idem, *Twice Used Songs: Performance Criticism of the Songs of Ancient Israel* (Peabody, MA: Hendrickson, 2008); **P. House,** *Zephaniah: A Prophetic Drama* (JSOT-Sup 69; Sheffield: Almond, 1989); **S. Levy,** *The Bible as Theatre* (Brighton: Sussex Academic Press, 2002); **S. Niditch,** *Oral World and Written Word: Ancient Israelite Literature* (Louisville: Westminster/John Knox, 1996); **E. Rozik,** *The Roots of Theatre: Rethinking Ritual and Other Theories of Origin* (Iowa City: University of Iowa Press, 2002); **R. Schechner,** *Between Theater and Anthropology* (Philadelphia: University of Pennsylvania Press, 1985); **Y. Sherwood,** "Prophetic Performance Art," *Bible and Critical Theory* 2.1 (2006) 1-4; **D. Stacey,** *Prophetic Drama in the Old Testament,* (London: Epworth, 1990). T. Giles

PERSIAN PERIOD. *See* ISRAELITE HISTORY.

PESHER INTERPRETATION. *See* DEAD SEA SCROLLS.

PLANT IMAGERY. *See* FLORAL IMAGERY.

POETIC JUSTICE. *See* RETRIBUTION.

POETRY. *See* HEBREW LANGUAGE.

POST-EXILIC PROPHECY. *See* HAGGAI, BOOK OF; PROPHECY, HISTORY OF; ZECHARIAH, BOOK OF.

POVERTY. *See* WEALTH AND POVERTY.

PRAYER

In one important sense, prayer is understood as talking with *God. However, this description would include much of the process of divine revelation to and through those called by God to be his spokespersons—the prophets. Thus,

we find many examples of the prophets talking with God in their vocational role.

More narrowly, one may look at prayer as the personal engagement with God that may include confession and *repentance, reflection and thanksgiving, praise and *worship, petition and intercession, and so on. Prayer is personal conversation with God, either individually or corporately—what S. Balentine calls "the drama of divine-human dialogue."

The English verb "pray" derives from the Latin *precor,* meaning "to beg, entreat, implore, plead." However, the practice of prayer in the OT in general and in the Prophetic Books in particular gives evidence of a much broader semantic range. For the prophets, "to pray" encompasses both various aspects of conversation with God and aspects of petition to God.

While a wide variety of individuals are presented as praying in the OT, the prophet often is presented in the role of praying for the welfare of the people. The priesthood was focused on cultic worship, while the prophet was the one who interceded in prayer (Johnson 1962, 58-60; 1979, 3, 68), Moses, Samuel, Elijah and Jeremiah being prime examples (see 6 below).

1. Terminology of Prayer
2. Basis of Prayer
3. Antecedents of Prayer
4. Types of Prayer
5. Auxiliaries of Prayer
6. Prophet as Intercessor

1. Terminology of Prayer.

The more common terms used in the OT for "prayer" are *tĕpillâ* (77x; 17x in the Prophetic Books [e.g., Is 1:15; 37:4; 56:7]) and the cognate verb *pll* Hithpael (e.g., Jer 29:12; 42:4), "to advocate, intercede." But other terms are used as well: *ʿātar,* "to plead, entreat" (e.g., Is 19:22); *ḥānan,* "to implore compassion" (e.g., Hos 12:4 [MT 12:5]; cf. Is 33:2); *qārāʾ,* "to call" upon God (e.g., 2 Sam 22:7; Ps 17:6; Jon 1:14); *zāʿaq,* "to cry out" (e.g., Ezek 11:13; Joel 1:14); *šwʿ* Piel, "to call for help" (e.g., Is 58:9; Jon 2:2 [MT 2:3]); *dāraš,* "to seek" God (Amos 5:4); and *šāʾal,* "to inquire, beg" (e.g., Is 7:11; Ezek 21:26; Jon 4:7). (For a helpful summary of the various forms of prayer found outside the Psalter, see Boda, 806-9.)

2. Basis of Prayer.

In the OT the basis of a conversation between persons or a people, on the one hand, and the supremely sovereign God of creation and history, on the other, is the *covenant relationship that God initiated by grace (see Deut 4:37; 7:6-8; 9:4-6; 10:15; Is 43:4; Jer 31:3). It is on the basis of this covenant that people are "known" by God as "my people" (e.g., Is 19:18-25; Hos 1:9-11) and they "know" God as "my God" (e.g., Hos 2:19-23). Thus, many of the recorded conversations demonstrate being grounded in the covenant and covenant expectations—for example, Hezekiah's plea that God would "remember" (Is 38:3) how Hezekiah had faithfully lived in light of the Shema (Deut 6:4-9) and Jeremiah's various wrestlings with God (Jer 11—20) as set against the consolation of covenant surety in Jeremiah 30—33 (esp. Jer 30:2, 22; 31:2-3, 31-34; 32:37-42; 33:3, 6-9, 14-18, 19-22, 25-26).

3. Antecedents of Prayer.

Examples of prayer in the period of the prophets reflect the influence of the five books of Moses—the Torah.

In their prayer conversations with God, Abraham and Sarah are challenged by Yahweh, "Is anything too difficult for Yahweh?" (Gen 18:14). Jeremiah picks up on this theme when he prays to Yahweh, "O Lord Yahweh! Look, it is you who made heaven and earth by your great power and by your outstretched arm! Nothing is too hard for you!" (Jer 32:17). Modeled after the intercessory roles of Abraham (Gen 18:23-32) and Moses (Ex 32:11-14; Deut 9:26), Jeremiah prays, "O great and mighty God" and rehearses key themes of the Torah narrative (Jer 32:17-22). And Yahweh replies, "Look here! I am Yahweh—God of all flesh—is anything too hard for me?" (Jer 32:27).

Anchored in the covenant promises to Abraham, Isaac, Jacob and David, Daniel prays in *exile too, "O Lord, the great and awesome God who maintains the covenant and steadfast love," as he confesses breach of covenant on the part of the covenant community (Dan 9:4). Similarly, in the setting of the public reading of Torah the Levites pray to the God of creation and of history and of covenant, "So now, our God, the great, the mighty and awesome God who keeps covenant and loyal love . . . " (Neh 9:32).

These examples reflect Moses' reference to Yahweh as "God of gods and Lord of lords, the great, the mighty, the awesome God" of the covenant (Deut 10:17). In the face of Israel's rebel-lion, Moses engages in candid dialogue with the Lord in Numbers 14:11-35, standing in, as it were, between Israel and the Lord, and pleads that the Lord's "great power" and integrity (promise) (Num 14:17) be demonstrated by the Lord graciously being "slow to anger and abounding in steadfast love, forgiving iniquity and transgression" (cf. Ex 34:6-7) while holding the unrepentant accountable.

Beyond the Torah, the Psalter provides examples of prayer that can be seen reflected in a number of the prayers in the prophets (e.g., Jer 10:23-25 [cf. Ps 6:1; 38:1; 79:6-7]; Jer 17:12-18 [cf. Ps 54:1; 60:5; 88:15; 35:4, 8, 26]). W. Holladay notes that P. Bonnard argued that Jeremiah influenced thirty-three of the Psalms, but J. Bright concluded that Jeremiah was influenced by the psalmists. Holladay concludes that there is little reason not to think that influence may have been exerted in both ways (Holladay, 245-46). In the aftermath of his painful confrontation with the chief priest (Jer 20:1-6), Jeremiah prays and laments, "For I hear whispering of many, 'Terror on every side!'" (Jer 20:10a), which echoes verbatim the line in the lament attributed to David in Ps 31:13.

4. Types of Prayer.

There are two main sorts of prayers exhibited in the prophets: (1) talking to God or conversation; (2) asking God for something or petition (Miller, 32-38).

Types of conversational prayer include reflection on God, his attributes and works; consecration to God; expressions of thanksgiving, adoration and praise. Types of petitionary prayer include confession and penitence, supplication, and intercession. Complaints or *laments include both talking to God and petitioning God for relief. Individual believers talked with God directly in a variety of settings and circumstances. But prayer was also an integral part of public worship, so that one of the designations of the *temple in Jerusalem was the "house of prayer" (e.g., Is 56:7; Jer 7:11; 32:16-25; Jon 2:2-9; Dan 9:3-19).

4.1. Reflection. In spite of the vicissitudes of life and fearful threats, prayers of the prophets demonstrate a conviction that, by his grace, Yahweh is the one-of-a-kind savior (e.g., Is 12:1-6). Even though God has cause to be angry, the believer reflects on God's grace to turn his anger away: "Look! God is my salvation [yĕšûʿâ]; I will trust and not fear, because my strength and my might is Yahweh God!" (Is 12:2).

The prophet Isaiah speaks with God, addressing him as an "everlasting rock" (Is 26:4) and the "upright one" (Is 26:7). And Jeremiah reflects on God and declares, "There is no one like you, O Yahweh! You are great, and great is your name in power! Who would not be afraid of you, O king of the nations, because it is your due! For among all the nations' sages and in all their kingdoms there is no one like you!" (Jer 10:6-7). Again, in Jeremiah 16:19-20 the prophet reflects on the uniqueness of God. And Daniel reflects on God's attributes: "O Lord, the great and awesome God who maintains the covenant and steadfast love with those who love him and who pay attention to his instructions" (Dan 9:4).

4.2. Consecration. The strong sense of being set apart to God is seen in the dialogue between the believer and God. As Isaiah is gripped by an awareness of God's "otherness," he is keenly aware of his personal need to be consecrated to God (Is 6:5). And to God's cleansing act and invitation to now take up a mission, the one forgiven and purified responds, "Here I am, send me!" (Is 6:8). Jeremiah 1:4-10 presents a dialogue between the prophet and God that focuses on consecration. Here, the claim is that God "consecrated" Jeremiah before he was even born, which consecration is bolstered by the affirmation "I am with you"—Emmanuel theology.

4.3. Thanksgiving. In the Prophetic Books are examples of the grateful spirit evidenced in the Psalter. As in the Psalter, so in the prophets, prayers of thanksgiving may be retrospective and also prospective. Isaiah, anticipating God's making all things right, anticipates a prayer of thanksgiving: "I will thank you, Yahweh, for though you were angry with me, your anger turned away, and you comforted me. Look! God is my salvation, I will trust and not fear. . . . Give thanks to Yahweh, call on his name; among the nations give exposure to his deeds; cause them to remember that his name is exalted" (Is 12:1, 4). Even under threat of death, Daniel challenges his compatriots, "Blessed be the name of God forever and ever. . . . To you, O God of my fathers, I give thanks and praise" (Dan 2:20, 23).

4.4. Adoration and Praise. Attributing worth to God, who alone deserves true worship, is a significant theme in the prophets (e.g., Is 2; 5:16; 12:1-6; 33:5; 42:9-13; 63:6-8; Jer 17:12; 20:12-14; 33:8-10). Praise and adoration are themes of prophetic prayers. For example, Isaiah 25:1-12 begins with a prayer song in exaltation of God: "O Yahweh, you are my God; I will exalt you, I will praise your name because you have done marvelous things, plans made long ago with perfect faithfulness" (Is 25:1). In the context of Daniel's thanksgiving just mentioned, he expresses adoration and praise: "Wisdom and might belong to him [God]. It is he who changes times and seasons; he removes kings and raises kings up; he gives wisdom to the sages and knowledge to those who have understanding. It is he who reveals what is profoundly obscure; he knows what is in the dark, and light dwells with him" (Dan 2:20-22).

One important corollary to the themes of adoration and praise is the theme of God's reputation. The motivation for answering the prayer with grace is for the sake of God's good name. So, for example, Jeremiah prays for God to respond in grace in spite of Judah's sin: "Though our sins testify against us, O Yahweh, act for the sake of your own reputation" (Jer 14:7); "Do not reject us, for the sake of your own reputation; do not dishonor your glorious throne; remember and do not revoke your covenant" (Jer 14:21).

4.5. Confession and Penitence. From the Torah through the former prophets and especially in the Psalter the significance of a contrite and pure heart is highlighted. It is worth noting how the prophets, rather than wagging their finger at their audience, personally identify with their community in confessing and asking forgiveness. Perhaps the most striking example of prophetic identification with a people under judgment is found in Daniel 9, where Daniel confesses with, not for, his people: "We have sinned and done wrong and acted wickedly and revolted, even removing your instructions and your justice. And we would not listen to your servants the prophets who spoke in your name to our kings, our princes, to our fathers and to all the people of the land. . . . To us, O Lord, belongs humiliation just as this day—to the men of Judah, to the residents of Jerusalem and to all Israel, those who are near and those far away in all the countries to which you have driven them because of the infidelity that they committed against you" (Dan 9:5-7). And in

Jeremiah 10:23-25 the prophet gives voice to the penitent confession of his flock: "Discipline me, O Yahweh, but with justice, not out of your anger, lest you bring me to nothing" (Jer 10:24).

4.6. Supplication. Earnest requests may be personal or vicarious. Deeply discouraged, Jeremiah pleads on his own behalf, "O Yahweh, heal me and I will be healed; save me and I will be saved, for you are my praise. . . . Do not be a terror to me; you are my refuge in the day of disaster. Let my persecutors be put to shame; do not let me be shamed" (Jer 17:14-18). And in Jeremiah 32 he pleads for understanding and wisdom. On the other hand, Isaiah 33:1-6 is an example of supplication on behalf of the community: "O Yahweh, be gracious to us; in you we hope! Be our strength every morning, our salvation in the time of trouble" (Is 33:2).

4.7. Intercession. In the face of Sennacherib's slander of Yahweh, Hezekiah intercedes for the sake of Yahweh's reputation, "so all the kingdoms of the earth will know that you alone are Yahweh" (Is 37:20). In 1 Kings 13:6 King Jeroboam asks the prophet from Judah, "Please appease the face of the LORD your God" on his behalf. Jeremiah reminds his audience that Hezekiah feared the Lord, and that he "appeased the face of the LORD, so the LORD changed his mind" (Jer 26:19). In Zechariah 7 the citizens of Bethel send emissaries to ask the priests and prophets to "appease the face of the LORD." Daniel, in his intercessory prayer, indicates that "appeasing the face of the LORD" involves "repentance from guiltiness," on the one hand, and "understanding [God's] truth," on the other (Dan 9:13) (see 6 below).

4.8. Lament. The prophets, following their brothers and sisters in the faith, prayed personal or individual laments. Rather than grousing about God behind his back, as it were, they candidly approached God directly with their complaint. For example, having recounted the evidence of Yahweh's steadfast love and grace in the past as he redeemed his people in order to establish for himself "a glorious name," Isaiah foresees a time when, although the exile has formally ended, God will seem distant and disinterested. Against this setting, the prophet gives voice in Isaiah 63:15—64:12 to the people's prayer of lament that their hearts had become hard, and begging that an intimate faith relationship be restored.

After an episode in Jeremiah's ministry that was particularly physically painful, emotionally humiliating and spiritually draining (Jer 20:1-6), Jeremiah confronts God directly in lamentation (Jer 20:7-13). The laments in Jeremiah, in keeping with the laments found in the Psalter, indicate that believers were not reticent to express their disappointments and to present, unvarnished, their complaints, even accusations. And God is not offended by the candor. And, as is typical of these lament prayers, in the process of laying it all out on the table before the God of the universe, the supplicant gains perspective that fosters confidence of faith. And then the hurting complainant confesses: "But Yahweh is with me like a dreaded warrior; therefore, my persecutors will be tripped up, they will not succeed. They will be deeply shamed because they will have failed with an everlasting humiliation that will never be forgotten. O LORD of the whole world, who examines the righteous, who sees heart and mind, let me see your retribution on them, because it is to you that I have disclosed my complaint! You all, sing to Yahweh! Praise Yahweh, you all! For he has rescued the life of the needy from the hand of evildoers!" (Jer 20:11-13). The conclusion: God, the "accused," is indeed trustworthy after all!

5. Auxiliaries of Prayer.

5.1. Body Language. In addition to the verbal expressions of prayer, supplicants often expressed themselves by body language. For example, the supplicants may humbly kneel before God (e.g., Dan 6:10) or fall on their face (e.g., Ezek 9:8; 11:13). They may imploringly raise their hands (e.g., Jer 4:31; Lam 1:17; 2:19; 3:41).

5.2. Fasting. Fasting may accompany prayer as an aspect of expressing grief and lament or of contrition and penance or of supplication, such as Daniel does: "I turned my face to the Lord God, seeking him in prayer and pleas for compassion with fasting, sackcloth and ashes. And I prayed to the LORD my God and confessed" (Dan 9:2-4 [cf. Joel 1:14; Jon 3:4-6]).

6. Prophet as Intercessor.

There is a sense in which the role of the prophet in Israel paralleled the role of the priest. In the case of the latter, the role was as sacerdotal mediator. In the case of the former, the role was communicative: speaking on God's behalf to the people and interceding with God on the people's behalf (Samuel [2 Sam 12:19, 23; 15:11]; Isaiah [2 Kings 19:1-7]; Jeremiah [Jer 7:16; 37:3; 42:2, 4, 20]; Ezekiel [Ezek 9:8; 11:13]; Amos [Amos 7:2, 5]) (see von Rad 1965, 2:51). This role filled by Moses and Samuel is contrasted with how the people's intransigence rendered ineffectual Jeremiah's exercise of the normative role (e.g., Jer 7:16; 11:14; 14:11; 15:1-4).

This role played out by the prophets during the Israelite monarchy is foreshadowed by the intercession earlier of prophets such as Abraham (e.g., Gen 18:16-33; 20:7) and Moses (e.g., Ex 32:11-14; Num 11:1-3), who "stood in the breach" between God and people (Ps 106:23). Intercession is a significant element of the prophetic ministries of Samuel (e.g., 1 Sam 7:5; 12:19, 23) and Elijah (e.g., 1 Kings 18:36-39). The prophet Isaiah's intercessory role can be seen in vignettes such as Sennacherib's siege of Judah (2 Kings 19:1-7; Is 37:1-7).

See also LAMENT, MOURNING; LITURGY AND CULT; REPENTANCE; WORSHIP.

BIBLIOGRAPHY. **S. E. Balentine,** *Prayer in the Hebrew Bible: The Drama of Divine-Human Dialogue* (OBT; Minneapolis: Fortress, 1993); **M. Boda,** "Prayer," *DOTHB* 806-11; **W. Brueggemann,** *The Psalms and the Life of Faith,* ed. P. D. Miller (Minneapolis: Fortress, 1995); idem, *Great Prayers of the Old Testament* (Louisville: Westminster/John Knox, 2008); **R. E. Clements,** *In Spirit and in Truth: Insights from Biblical Prayer* (Atlanta: John Knox, 1985); **A. Diamond,** *The Confessions of Jeremiah in Context: Scenes of Prophetic Drama* (JSOTSup 45; Sheffield: JSOT, 1987); **P. W. Ferris Jr.,** *The Genre of Communal Lament in the Bible and the Ancient Near East* (SBLDS 127; Atlanta: Scholars Press, 1992); **M. Greenberg,** "On the Refinement of the Conception of Prayer in Hebrew Scriptures," *AJSR* 1 (1976) 57-92; idem, *Biblical Prose Prayer: As a Window to the Popular Religion of Ancient Israel* (Berkeley: University of California Press, 1983); **W. L. Holladay,** "Indications of Jeremiah's Psalter." *JBL* 121 (2002) 245-61; **A. R. Johnson,** *The Cultic Prophet in Ancient Israel* (2nd ed.; Cardiff: University of Wales Press, 1962); idem, *The Cultic Prophet and Israel's Psalmody* (Cardiff: University of Wales, 1979); **P. D. Miller,** *They Cried to the Lord: The Form and Theology of Biblical Prayer* (Minneapolis: Fortress, 1994); **K. M. O'Connor,** *The Confessions of Jeremiah: Their Interpretation and Role in Chapters 1-25* (SBLDS 94; Atlanta: Scholars Press, 1988); **A. Rhodes,** "Israel's Prophets as Intercessors," in *Scripture in History and Theology: Essays in Honor of J. Coert Rylaarsdam,* ed. A. L. Merrill and T. W. Overholt (Pittsburgh: Pickwick, 1977) 107-28; **G. von Rad,** *Old Testament Theology,* trans. D. M. G. Stalker (2 vols.; Louisville: Westminster/John Knox, 1965); idem, "Confessions of Jeremiah," in *A Prophet to the Nations: Essays in Jeremiah Studies,* ed. L. G. Perdue and B. W. Kovacs (Winona Lake, IN: Eisenbrauns, 1984) 339-48; **C. Westerman,** *Praise and Lament in the Psalms,* trans. K. R. Crim and R. N. Soulen (Atlanta: John Knox, 1981). P. W. Ferris Jr.

PRESENCE OF GOD. *See* DIVINE PRESENCE.

PRIESTLY COVENANT. *See* COVENANT.

PROPHECY, HISTORY OF

Prophets and prophetesses in the OT were spokespersons for God who announced God's will or intentions for people, or predicted the future, or did both. The noun *prophecy* designates the contents of those utterances, and the verb *prophesy* designates the actions involved in receiving and delivering the divine messages. Prophesying in ancient Israel varied from actions performed by persons of diverse occupations to the actions of recognized functionaries associated with prophetic groups and/or with temples and royal houses. Israelite prophecy, moreover, had a history, which can be traced at least partially. In tracing that history, this article will situate prophecy within the context of the *canon and of ancient *Israel and then follow its development in the OT.

1. Prophets and the Canon
2. Prophets, Prophetesses and Their Relationships to Other Groups in Ancient Israel
3. Nonwriting and Writing Prophets
4. Scribes and Editors
5. Eighth-Century BC Prophets
6. Seventh-Century BC Prophets
7. Sixth-Century BC Prophets Down to the Fall of Jerusalem
8. Fifth- and Fourth-Century BC Prophets
9. Daniel
10. Conclusion: An End of Prophecy?

1. Prophets and the Canon.

The three divisions of the Jewish canon are Torah (Law), Nebiim (Prophets) and Ketubim

(Writings). In this structure, the *Law stands at the heart of the revelation; the Prophets and the Writings surround and elaborate the Law but do not contradict it. The Prophets themselves are divided into two groups: Former (Joshua, Judges, Samuel, Kings) and Latter (Isaiah, Jeremiah, Ezekiel, Book of the Twelve). The Christian canon, following the divisions of the LXX, differs in that it has a fivefold structure: the books of law, history (containing among other things the Former Prophets), poetry, the Major Prophets and the Minor Prophets. Its structure is temporal: past (Pentateuch and history books), present (poetic books) and future (prophetic books). The Major Prophets are Isaiah, Jeremiah, Lamentations, Ezekiel and Daniel; the Minor Prophets are (in the same order as the Book of the *Twelve in the Hebrew canon) Hosea, Joel, Amos, Obadiah, Jonah, Micah, Nahum, Habakkuk, Zephaniah, Haggai, Zechariah and Malachi. The order of the first six books, or collections, within the Twelve in LXX, by contrast, is Hosea, Amos, Micah, Joel, Obadiah and Jonah. That order leaves together the eighth-century BC collections Hosea, Amos and Micah, whereas the MT intersperses them with three others. It is neither necessary nor possible to say which order is primary. Each serves its own purpose. One manuscript among the *Dead Sea Scrolls, 4QXIIa, places Jonah last, but M. A. Sweeney suggests that the people of Qumran arranged the order of biblical books to suit their own needs (Sweeney 1:xxviin37).

The canonical sequence of "the Law and the Prophets" goes back at least to the time of the writing of Malachi 4:4-6 (MT 3:22-24), which refers to the lawgiver Moses and the prophet Elijah. These references suggest that the Pentateuch and the prophetic corpus (both Former and Latter Prophets), and probably including the Twelve as a whole, was seen as constituting a line of inspired writings. The date of Malachi 4:4-6 is debated, but it cannot be earlier than the writing of Malachi, traditionally placed in the mid-fifth century BC, nor later than about the beginning of the second century BC (Schmid, 207). The rabbinic writing *Pirqe 'Abot* describes the relationship between Torah and Nebiim as follows: "Moses received Torah from Sinai and delivered it to the elders, the elders to the prophets, and the prophets delivered it to the men of the Great Assembly." In other words, the proph-

ets bridged the gap between the revelation at Sinai to Moses and the rabbis (Blenkinsopp, 24). Even so, that distinction is too neat; the pentateuchal texts themselves speak occasionally of prophets, and the Prophetic Books quote and allude to the Pentateuch. Prophets, moreover, were not unique to Israel. They flourished also in ancient Egypt, Mesopotamia and Mari, beginning before the patriarchal period, in fact (see Ancient Near Eastern Prophecy).

2. Prophets, Prophetesses and Their Relationships to Other Groups in Ancient Israel.

An old saying goes, "No one lives in a vacuum, let alone prophesies in one." Even the messages of a prophet or prophetess are contextualized by their own experiences and thought processes, the language they use, the world they try to interpret, and the audience(s) to or for whom they speak and with whom they otherwise interact. It is useful, therefore, to survey the terms and phrases used in the HB to designate people who seem to have fallen under the general heading of "prophet."

2.1. Major Terms Denoting Prophets. The most important term for such intermediaries in the OT is *nābî'*. The word is used about four hundred times, and the verb *nābā'* ("to prophesy") over one hundred times, frequently in connection with someone delivering a message. The noun *nābî'* appears especially frequently in 1—2 Samuel, 1—2 Kings, Jeremiah and Ezekiel, often in connection with someone delivering a message. It is thus consistent with the conclusion that prophets modeled their phrase "Thus says Yahweh" after the style of messengers of kings, and that their action was comparable to the practice of earlier prophets at Mari (Westermann, 98-128). The term could be used even in connection with someone deemed a false prophet (note esp. 1 Kings 22:22).

Two other titles also deserve mention here. One is *hōzeh*, usually translated as "seer," which is used more than a dozen times. It derives from the verb *hāzâ*, meaning "to see," and typically designates something a prophet "saw," perhaps a *vision. Numbers 24:4 uses the term in connection with Balaam's third oracle, in which he blessed Israel, to the dismay of Balak, and Numbers 24:16 employs it in Balaam's fourth oracle, in which he predicts Balak's demise. Ezekiel 13:16, 23 use the verb in a context where what the "prophets of Israel" saw (namely, a peaceful future) was wrong. The second title, *rō'eh*, designates someone that today might be called a "diviner," one who could discover things that were hidden (*see* Divination, Magic). The term is used famously in 1 Samuel 9:9, where Saul's servant suggests that they consult Samuel to help find the missing donkeys that the two men were seeking. The narrator observes that the one who was formerly called a *rō'eh* was now called a *nābi'*. In other words, terms fell in and out of favor with various traditions and writers in the OT and overlapped in meaning.

2.2. Other Titles Denoting Prophets. The three aforementioned terms were by no means the only ways by which the OT denoted and described prophets. Samuel is called a "man of God" in 1 Samuel 9:6-10, and Elisha is also in 2 Kings 5:8, 14-15. God says to Amos that God never does anything to punish people without first divulging the divine intentions to them through God's "servants the prophets" (Amos 3:7). In addition, a prophet is compared to a sentinel (Jer 6:17), a watchman (Ezek 3:16-21; 33:1-9), a lookout (Is 21:6) and a refiner (Jer 6:27-30). The OT also speaks of groups of prophets—for example, the band or company of prophets around Samuel (1 Sam 10:5, 10; 19:20), and the one that accompanied Elijah at the time of his ascension (2 Kings 2:3-15).

2.3. Cultic and Noncultic Prophets. The distinction that scholars sometimes make between official (or cultic) and unofficial (or noncultic) prophets helps differentiate prophets at times, but care must be taken with such terms. Anthropologists note that all prophets depend on a group of followers to validate their experience or message. That validation can also be withdrawn by the group that gives it (Wilson, 56). Even prophets attached to a palace or a temple must maintain the confidence of those to whom they deliver their message.

The prophets of the OT constitute a mixed group. In a famous confrontation with a priest at the temple in Bethel, Amos denied that he was a prophet or even a son of (i.e., an apprentice to) a prophet (Amos 7:14). He apparently meant he was not attached to any temple or prophetic guild. Likewise, Micah is nowhere termed a prophet in the book bearing his name, and the only place that book mentions prophets is in a derisive attack against (false?) prophets

(Mic 2:11). Still, Jeremiah 26:18 explicitly identifies Micah as a prophet. There a crowd witnessing the arrest of Jeremiah recalls that the prophet Micah of Moresheth made charges like Jeremiah's against Jerusalem, and that members of his audience repented and were spared destruction by God. Other OT prophets, by contrast, do appear to have been closely associated with temples. For example, Isaiah appears to have been connected to the temple in Jerusalem, and Haggai and Zechariah championed the building of the second temple.

2.4. Prophets and Prophetesses. Most of those who prophesied in the OT were men, but four texts speak of prophetesses. Judges 4:4 says that Deborah, a prophetess, was a judge in Israel who sat under a palm tree between Ramah and Bethel to hear cases. She also took the initiative in summoning Barak and directing him to take his troops to Mount Tabor and prepare for battle against Sisera. In that narrative, of course, Jael, the wife of Heber the Kenite, killed the defeated and fleeing Sisera in her tent, where she had bidden him to take refuge. That sequence of events is without parallel in the OT for the roles played by women. Still, prophetesses are mentioned three other places. 2 Kings 22:14-20 narrates an incident when Hilkiah (the high preist), Ahikam (the son of Shaphan and a key figure in the restoration of the temple and reading of the law under Josiah), Achbor (the son of a man named Micaiah) and Asaiah (otherwise unknown) went to the prophetess Huldah to ask what action to take with regard to the requirements concerning the temple found in the newly discovered law code (most likely Deuteronomy). In view of the prominence of at least the first two men named, she must have had a high reputation for discerning that which was hidden. Nehemiah 6:14 includes a prophetess, Noadiah, along with Tobiah, Sanballat and other people who wished to scare Nehemiah away from the task of repairing the walls of Jerusalem. Finally, Isaiah 8:3 mentions a prophetess who was the wife of Isaiah and conceived the child named "Maher-shalal-hash-baz" (meaning "the spoil speeds, the prey hastens"). It is not clear whether bearing the child was her only prophetic act. The slim number of prophetesses mentioned probably reflects male domination in ancient Israel, but that they are mentioned gives evidence that some women did prophesy. There is no way, however, to assess their number.

2.5. Prophets and Other Groups. Prophets were not the only identifiable groups in ancient Israel. Others with whom prophets interacted included priests, kings, the wise and the populace at large. It will be useful to survey the relationship of prophets with each.

2.5.1. The Relationship Between Prophets and Priests. The relationship between these two groups is especially important for at least two reasons. First, the Major Prophets Jeremiah and Ezekiel seem to have been priests themselves, and the report of Isaiah's "*call vision" is set inside the *temple, suggesting at least that he was attached to the temple as a prophet. Among the Minor Prophets, Joel 1:1—2:17, with its twofold call for people to repent at the altar, reads like sentiments from the lips of an official at the temple (Redditt 1986, 231-33). The book of Habakkuk ends with a "prayer," complete with the name of a tune to accompany the prayer when sung. Almost surely it was a temple hymn (Hab 3:1-19). Haggai and Zechariah 1—8 have as their main concern the rebuilding of the temple in Jerusalem, and Malachi reads like a dispute between priestly groups (Redditt 1994, 251-54).

2.5.2. The Relationship Between Prophets and Kings. No relationship, perhaps, was chancier than the relationship between a prophet and his king. In an uncertain world, some kings wished to avail themselves of a person whom they trusted to be in touch with God. Illustrations abound. (1) Samuel at one point chose and anointed Saul to be king (1 Sam 9:1—10:16), though later he turned against Saul. Even on the last night of his life, however, the king attempted to consult the dead prophet by means of a séance (1 Sam 28:3-25) and went to his fate fully aware he would die in battle. (2) Nathan was a prophet in the court of David, and he remained such even when he chastised David for his actions in regard to Bathsheba and her husband (2 Sam 12:1-15; see the heading of Ps 51). (3) King Ahab consulted his prophets about a proposed attack against the king of Aram at Ramath-gilead. Prophets for hire, they assured him that his proposed attack would be successful. King Jehoshaphat of Judah was suspicious of such unanimity and asked for another opinion. After lying at first, Micaiah ben Imlah relayed God's message, namely that God had put a "lying spirit in the mouth" of all the prophets of Ahab. So warned

and wearing a disguise, Ahab launched an attack and in a case of mistaken identity was killed anyway (1 Kings 22:1-40). (4) Isaiah seems to have had access to the temple and the palace, and he gave advice. (5) The prophet Jeremiah, by contrast, suffered at the hands of several monarchs, though he managed to outlast them all in Jerusalem.

2.5.3. The Relationship Between Prophets and the Teachers of Wisdom. The prophets receive no mention in the Wisdom literature of the OT: Job, Proverbs and Ecclesiastes (*see* Prophecy and Wisdom). J. L. Crenshaw addresses this issue, resisting what he called "pan-sapientialism" among twentieth-century scholars who saw wisdom influence on Genesis 1—11; 37—50, Deuteronomy, Ruth, 2 Samuel 9—20 + 1 Kings 1—2, Psalms, Micah and Jonah. One can concede that prophets and wise men faced some of the same problems without concluding that one stream drew from another. Still, Crenshaw saw one passage, Jeremiah 17:5-11, that seemed to him to resemble "The Instruction of Amen-em-opet." The similarities led him to the conclusion that the author clearly knew the Egyptian text. Still, Crenshaw understood the passage to condemn any pretense to possess knowledge of the divine mystery. "Precisely because the human intellect is perverse, claims like these cannot be trusted" (Crenshaw, 82). In view of Crenshaw's argument, one is wise to downplay suggestions of direct wisdom influence on the OT prophets.

In the apocalyptic book of Daniel, however, the book's hero not only interprets the dreams of Nebuchadnezzar and Belshazzar and the writing on the wall, but also sees visions that require an angelic interpreter. Neither the ability to interpret the dreams of others (like Joseph) nor to see visions (like Amos, Isaiah and other prophets) is sufficient in the end. Ultimately, in Daniel the mysteries of God require an angelic interpreter to explain them.

2.5.4. The Relationship Between Prophets and the People at Large. Many, though by no means all, of the prophets' messages and actions were aimed at kings, priests and other leaders, and those messages and actions generated quite diverse reactions. Some texts, however, describe interactions between prophets and the general population. According to 1 Kings 17:8-24, God directed Elijah to go to the town of Zarephath, where the prophet performed a miracle for a widow by causing her meal jar to rejuvenate daily. Then Elijah resuscitated her dead son. In 2 Kings 4:8-37 a similar resuscitation is reported of Elisha, who also saw to the restoration of a woman's land to her when she returned after living elsewhere for seven years (2 Kings 8:1-6). These narratives are reported, however, to enhance the reputation of the prophets rather than to illuminate relations between prophets and the people at large.

Reports about other prophets, however, suggest that people both knew them and in some cases even remembered them after their death. The most obvious example concerns Micah, who condemned the wealthy for their mistreatment of the poor (see Mic 2:1-11) (see Wealth and Poverty). Jeremiah 26 reports that people remembered Micah and quoted his words a century or so later when Jeremiah was arrested. Several other prophets demanded fair treatment of the poor and not simply correctly following ritual (see Is 1:21-26; 5:8; 10:1-4; Jer 22:13-17; Amos 4:1-3; Mic 6:8). Others focused on the collective *sins of the whole nation, especially in connection with the worship of other gods. Zechariah made it clear that preexilic people had failed to show justice, kindness and mercy to the poor (Zech 7:8-14). Trito-Isaiah painted a verbal picture of the future Judah, which would have a place for all sorts of people: the foreigner, the eunuch, the outcasts of Israel (Is 56:3-8), and the oppressed, the brokenhearted, the captives (Is 61:1-6). The people must have felt a wide range of emotions toward the prophets: anger over their criticism, gratitude for being defended, fear over the predicted future, and even the conviction that the prophets were wrong. Still, some, maybe most, of the people wanted a word from God, especially when they were in distress. Prophets of all stripes filled that need.

3. Nonwriting and Writing Prophets.

The idea that there were "nonwriting" and "writing" prophets is a distinction brought about at least partly through the process of *canonization. For readers of the OT who know of the collections gathered under the names Isaiah, Jeremiah and Ezekiel and the so-called Minor Prophets, the people called "prophets" are broadly characterized by their words. In the Pentateuch and Former Prophets, however, the prophets are largely discussed through their actions. To be sure, accounts of

their deeds may include short sayings. Still, the existence of a book like Amos, which describes only one episode in the prophet's life (see Amos 7:10-17), or Hosea, which contains only two prose narratives (whose relationship to the message is not explained), not to mention books such as Micah, Nahum, Habakkuk and Zephaniah (which contain only sayings of the prophets), all point to a basic difference in the conceptions of those prophets. Simply put, a number of prophets, and especially early prophets, are known more for what they did (note Elijah, Elisha, Jonah), while others, especially later ones, are known more or even exclusively for what they said. Due to the variations, it is useful to see the categories "writing prophets" and "nonwriting prophets" as forming not a polarity but a continuum along which to position the variety of prophets in the OT.

3.1. Nonwriting Prophets. Major nonwriting prophets included Balaam and various unnamed prophets in Deuteronomy as well as Samuel, Nathan, Elijah and Elisha. Numbers 22:1—24:25 is a carefully and humorously crafted narrative designed to ridicule Balak the king of Moab for his attempt to thwart the actions of God in guiding Israel to Canaan. It also, however, involves a delightful spoof on prophets, at least on Balaam, a "seer" for hire whose donkey could see what he could not: a menacing angel barring the road as he was en route as a prophet for hire to pronounce a curse on the people of Israel.

The discussion of prophets in Deuteronomy is carefully nuanced. Like the rest of Deuteronomy, its literary setting is east of the Jordan River in the land of Moab, where Moses delivers a sermon for the generation about to enter Canaan. The concern of the book is to reveal afresh for that generation the laws revealed earlier on Mount Sinai and thus to remind all future generations of their obligations in Canaan. Deuteronomy 13:1-5 warns against following prophets who divined by interpreting dreams, and Deuteronomy 18:21-22 offers two criteria for determining whether a prophet is genuine. First, a prophet must speak in the name of Yahweh (and not some other god), and second, what the prophet predicts must come to pass. How, though, was one to know what to do if prophets speaking in the name of Yahweh disagreed and one could not wait to see which prophet was correct? In such a case, Jeremiah counsels following the prophet predicting misfortune rather than good times (Jer 28:8-9), until, that is, the prediction of good comes true.

The depiction of the late eleventh-century BC figure Samuel as a prophet offers a different perspective. Samuel is depicted also as a priest, a kingmaker, an adviser to King Saul and a traveling judge. In other words, the narratives about Samuel do not reflect a situation in which Samuel held but one office. One might speak instead of various roles played by Samuel, one of which was prophet or seer, in connection with which he headed a group of apprentices called a "band of prophets." They were deemed useful for discerning hidden information—for example, the location of the lost donkeys belonging to Saul's father, Kish (1 Sam 9:1-14). Seances, however, were ruled off limits for legitimate prophets, their use being left to witches (see 1 Sam 28:3-25).

Nathan (early tenth century BC) is portrayed as a prophet at the side of David as an adviser. It was he who delivered to David the message that the king was not to build a temple for God; the tabernacle would suffice (2 Sam 7:8-11). David's son Solomon would build the new temple. The text is widely viewed by scholars as apologetic, but the issue here is its portrayal of Nathan's role as a prophetic adviser to the king. Nathan also seized the right of royal review by calling David to account for his adultery with Bathsheba (2 Sam 12:1-15).

Finally, mention should be made of Elijah and Elisha (mid-to-late ninth century BC), about whom 1-2 Kings has much to say. Elijah headed a band or school of prophets, and Elisha, one of his pupils, succeeded him. Elijah is shown predicting the future (e.g., 1 Kings 17:1-7), performing miracles (1 Kings 17:8-24), defeating the priests of Baal in a contest of rainmaking (1 Kings 18:40), predicting the death of Ahab (1 Kings 21:17-29) and ascending into heaven without dying (2 Kings 2:1-12). His roles combine wonder worker, adviser to the king, and defender of Yahwism. The same can be said for his successor, Elisha (2 Kings 2:19-25; 4:1—5:19; 6:1-7; 8:1-6). Like Samuel, he anointed a king, Jehu (2 Kings 9:13), but he also delivered the news to Hazael of Damascus that his king, Ben-hadad, would die and counseled Hazael to lie about the seriousness of Ben-hadad's condition (2 Kings 8:7-15).

Although these figures are dated from the late eleventh to the late ninth centuries BC, many scholars set the time of the writing of these accounts later (see Schmid, 69-72). Ultimately, the accounts were utilized by the so-called Deuteronomistic Historian or School, which seems to have flourished at least by the reign of Josiah (640-609 BC), and which probably continued until after the fall of Jerusalem (586 BC), perhaps as late as the elevation of the Judean king Jehoiachin in exile in 560 BC (see 2 Kings 25:27-30). While the accounts of these prophets may have been shaped by the Deuteronomic scribes, they may have utilized older traditions without significant distortions.

3.2. Writing Prophets. By far the larger percentage of prophetic sayings, however, was amassed in extended collections (the Major and the Minor Prophets) under the names of particular prophets. Only Jonah is an exception. His message is summarized thus: "In forty more days Nineveh will be destroyed" (Jon 3:4). Many scholars think most of those collections grew over time and contain sayings and other information from different periods and from different persons. More will be said about them below, but here it is important to notice the change in Israelite/Judean society in the mid-eighth century BC. Simply stated, public writing in the form of public inscriptions blossomed. K. Schmid (69-72) provides information from archaeological digs about that increase. From the tenth century there are only four; from the ninth, 18; from the first half of the eighth, 16; from the last half of the eighth, 129; from the first half of the seventh, 50; from the last half of the seventh, 52; and from the beginning of the sixth, 65. In other words, the explosion of public documents coincided with the rise of the "writing prophets." That was surely no accident (*see* Writing and Prophecy).

Many of the Prophetic Books provide a date of some sort in their superscription and/or refer to events datable from ancient records from Egypt, Assyria, Babylon, Persia or Greece. The starting place for dating a prophet and the work bearing his name is such data. These data provide only a starting place, however, because some (maybe all) the books contain sayings that appear to address later periods than the one in which the titular prophet lived. One good example from the early prophet Amos is the ending of the book. No careful reader can fail to notice that Amos 1:1—9:10 contains only threats, warnings and predictions of doom. Amos 9:11-15, by contrast, is entirely positive. Could Amos have looked past the imminent doom to a brighter day? Of course. Is that what happened? Many scholars think not. Amos 9:11 quotes God as promising, "On that day I will raise up the fallen tent of David." Most likely the reference to the fallen state of the Davidic monarchy indicates that the author of Amos 9:11-15 is looking *back* at the fall of the Davidic dynasty in 586 BC and *predicting* its future renewal, along with that of Israel (Amos 9:15, which, by the way, is reminiscent of Jer 1:10).

Thus, a second way to arrive at the date for a passage or a collection is to determine from what one knows of the history of ancient Israel and the surrounding ancient Near East a plausible time at which particular traditions might be especially meaningful (*see* Israelite History). The book of Isaiah, for example, seems—to many scholars—to have grown over a significant period of time stretching from the eighth to the sixth centuries BC or later. For example, O. H. Steck argues that Isaiah 1—55 + Isaiah 60—62 reached its basic form in the Persian period, but that numerous passages within those chapters plus Isaiah 56—59 and Isaiah 62—66 were added in three basic expansions during the Greek period, concluding around 253 BC.

3.3. Ascriptions of the Title "Prophet" to Pentateuchal Figures. Before leaving this topic, it would be helpful to look briefly at the Pentateuch. There, the ancient figures Abraham, Moses and Aaron are called prophets, and Miriam (Moses' sister) is called a "prophetess" (Ex 15:20). In such cases, readers need to recognize that the terms are being applied retroactively and descriptively. That is, these figures at times played roles later generations saw as prophetic. An example may be found in Numbers 11:16-30. At God's instruction, Moses took seventy of the elders of Israel to the tent of meeting to receive a portion of his "spirit" (or "charisma"). This spirit would allow them to bear part of Moses' burden, so a good modern term to describe them might be "deputies." Two elders who remained in the camp while Moses and the others were gone began prophesying when the spirit rested on them. Word of their conduct reached the tent, causing Joshua, who reacted jealously, to implore Moses to stop them. Moses declined, saying, "If only all Yahweh's people

were prophets" (Num 11:29). That is, Moses wished all the people of Israel would heed and spread God's commands.

Numbers 12:6-8, however, seems different. It is a later narrative calculated to emphasize the superiority of the commands of God to and through Moses over the sayings of prophets. It presupposes clashes between the law as propagated and passed down and more laissez-faire prophets, and it attempts to reign in the influence of the latter. Whether those verses had in view any prophets included among the Nebiim remains an open question.

4. Scribes and Editors.

If the record of prophecy in Israel underwent a profound change beginning in the eighth century BC in connection with the rise of public writing, one of the causes lay with the availability of scribes to write down messages and to collect, arrange and preserve them. For the most part people labored unknown and behind the scenes. Is it possible that some of the prophets (e.g., the temple prophet Isaiah) were literate? Yes, though literacy rates in the ancient world were so low the likelihood is not high, and a high degree of literacy was necessary to craft that work or others. With regard to Jeremiah, the answer seems to be affirmative. Jeremiah 51:59-64 records an event in which Jeremiah himself "wrote in a scroll all the things that would come upon Babylon" and gave the scroll to a man named Seriah to carry to Babylon. Regardless of the circumstances behind those verses, they clearly indicate that Jeremiah was literate, though the book bearing his name gives ample evidence that he used the scribe Baruch to write it down. Is it likely, however, the shepherd/farmer Amos was literate? Not really. In any case, the Prophetic Books almost never record the prophets as writing, and sooner or later their words and descriptions of their deeds passed into the hand of scribes.

The manuscripts themselves then took on a life of their own. Whether the scribes responsible for the creation of the manuscripts belonged to one or more schools is a matter of speculation. The major exception is the book of Jeremiah, the prose in which is so similar to that of Deuteronomy through Kings as to make it probable that Jeremiah's scribe(s) belonged to or had been trained by Deuteronomists.

A brief review of the work of scribes in the Latter Prophets is in order. Scholars often suppose that the book of Isaiah underwent a period of growth from the eighth to sixth centuries BC at least. Narratives about Isaiah appear in Isaiah 7:1—9:1, and Isaiah 36—39 is substantially the same as 2 Kings 18:13, 17—20:19, from which it was likely taken and to which it added the prayer in Isa 38:9-20 and a brief narrative of Isaiah's healing the king. No scribe, however, is named in the entire book of Isaiah. In the case of Jeremiah, as mentioned, Baruch seems to have recorded the sayings of the prophet (see Jer 36:1-32; 45:1) in addition to recording a transaction for him (Jer 32:12-16). It is difficult to judge how much of the extensive prose material is from Baruch.

It is possible that Ezekiel wrote (or employed someone to write) some of his messages, perhaps with the intention that Ezekiel or someone read them aloud. Regardless, the hand of a redactor is obvious in the elaborate dating system attached to a number of Ezekiel's messages. That the dating system is secondary is clear from the opening three verses. Ezekiel 1:1 is written in the first-person singular and appears to be original. Ezekiel 1:2-3, written in the third person, restates the date, employing the dating system used for a number of other messages scattered through the book (see Ezek 8:1; 20:1; 24:1; 26:1; 29:1; 30:20; 31:1; 32:1, 17; 33:21; 40:1). It appears, then, as if the dates were used as a redactional device (arrangement in chronological order), overridden only in the final version of the book by the familiar scheme of doom against Judah and Jerusalem (in Ezek 1—24), doom against foreign nations (in Ezek 25—32) and hope (in Ezek 33—48) (*see* Redaction/Editorial Criticism).

Finally, the Book of the *Twelve appears to have undergone its own history, roughly parallel to that of Isaiah. A number of scholars have proposed a process that began with edited collections of the sayings of Amos and Hosea in Israel plus Micah and Zephaniah in Judah, a so-called Book of the Four. Haggai and Zechariah 1—8 underwent an obvious common redaction with unique, dated introductions to the sayings of the two prophets. On the prior existence of those two collections there is widespread agreement. In addition, D. L. Christensen has argued that Nahum and Habakkuk were edited together as well, creating a chiasmus (Christensen, 193):

(A) Hymn of theophany (Nah 1)
   (B) Taunt song against Nineveh
      (Nah 2—3)
      (X) The problem of theodicy
         (Hab 1)
   (B') Taunt song against the
      "wicked one" (Hab 2)
(A') Hymn of theophany (Hab 3)

Eventually, three other prophetic collections (Joel, Obadiah, Malachi), plus the narrative about Jonah, were added, creating the Twelve. The debate about the nature of that creation has not yet reached a resolution. (Redditt 2003, 1-26, summarizes the discussion. Nogalski and Zvi 2009 articulate the pros and cons in more depth.)

5. Eighth-Century BC Prophets.

The earliest of the writing prophets (Amos, Hosea, Isaiah, Micah) flourished in the eighth century BC. The superscription (or heading) dates Amos's ministry during the reigns of Uzziah of Judah (ca. 783-742 BC) and Jeroboam son of Joash of Israel (ca. 786-746 BC). Those kings provided political stability for Judah and Israel at a time when the Assyrian emperors displayed little interest in sending armies there to demand tribute. As noted above, public writing blossomed, proof of a rising class of scribes. Hosea flourished during the reigns of Uzziah, Jotham, Ahaz and Hezekiah, kings of the south, and Jeroboam of the north.

Unfortunately, there is a problem in determining the dates of Jotham, Ahaz and Hezekiah. Uzziah (also called "Azariah") died in 743/2 BC, but he was leprous much of his reign. His successors were Jotham (said to have reigned sixteen years), Ahaz (sixteen years), and Hezekiah (twenty-nine years), for a total of sixty-one years—that is, until 682 BC. Added together, however, the numbers are somewhat off, since according to Assyrian annals, the Assyrian king Sennacherib invaded Judah in 701 BC, while 2 Kings 18:13 ascribes that invasion to the fourteenth year of Hezekiah, which would be about 697 BC, using its chronology. Hezekiah then suffered a serious illness that threatened his life, after which Hezekiah is said to have lived and reigned fifteen more years (2 Kings 20:6). Moreover, Hezekiah's successor, Manasseh, is said to have taken the throne when he was twelve, and his reign is said to have lasted fifty-five years. It ended in 642 BC. The numbers add up only if Manasseh served as a co-regent with his father over a period, perhaps the last fifteen years, and both kings were ascribed the years of their co-regency.

The fact that a northern prophet is dated in terms of kings of the north *and* the south suggests that the words of Hosea were carried south, perhaps after the fall of Samaria in 723 BC. In any case, the books of Amos (see Amos 9:11-15, but also Amos 2:4-5) and Hosea (in fourteen different verses spread throughout the book) direct their message to Judah as well. Since Amos was from the Judean city of Tekoa and was ordered to leave by the priest Amaziah (Amos 7:12-13), readers should not be surprised if that work took its written shape in Judah. Moreover, the flight of persons in Israel south to Judah when the Assyrians crushed Israel provides a ready explanation for the words of Hosea, though not necessarily the prophet himself, to have traveled there too.

5.1. Amos and Hosea. In any case, the words of the prophets, not their deeds, now stand front and center in the prophetic movement. The book of Amos relates one incident in that prophet's life (Amos 7:10-17), and the book of Hosea relates two accounts of the prophet's home life, but only one (Hos 3:1-3) is written in the first person. The actions of the prophets were of far less importance than the words ascribed to them. Moreover, the words give evidence, even in Hosea and Amos, of sometimes addressing audiences later than the careers of the two. Critical scholars have long argued that Hosea, Amos and indeed all the collections in the Latter Prophets grew over time as later tradition bearers kept the ancient words alive by stripping them of much of their specificity concerning their time and place of origin and by adding words of later prophets (including their own words) to update them.

5.2. Isaiah. If a process of collecting, preserving and expanding the words of prophets was true in connection with Amos and Hosea, the process also stood behind the collection ascribed to Isaiah. In his case, of course, there are more narratives. First, there was a collection of narratives that some scholars consider to have been the original part of the book: a first-person account of his calling as a prophet (Is 6:1-13), a third-person narrative about an audience he had with King Ahaz (Is 7:1-25), a first-person narrative of a prophetic sign (Is 8:1-4), a first-person narrative about Isaiah's reception of instructions from God (Is 8:11-15) and a concluding instruction (apparently to Isaiah's disciples) to write down what he had told them (Is 8:16-22). Some of these prose accounts appear to be composite in nature, but they do seem to include early words and actions of Isaiah. Second, another biographical account appears in Isaiah 20:1-6, describing a prophetic sign acted out by Isaiah and explaining it. Third, the final narrative appears in Isaiah 36—39, all but Isaiah 38:9-20 of which was taken from 2 Kings 18:13, 17—20:19. (The borrowing almost surely did not go the other way; the literary style is that of Kings.)

This episode, by the way, marks the last place in Samuel-Kings that speaks of a named prophet. 2 Kings 23:17-18 does mention an anonymous "prophet who came of Samaria," whose tomb King Josiah ordered to be left undisturbed. The Chronicler, for his part, mentions a prophet only once. 2 Chronicles 34:22 mentions "Huldah the prophet, the *wife* of Shallum son of Tokhath," whom Josiah consulted. She confirmed that threats against Judah and Jerusalem contained in Deuteronomy would come to pass, though after the death of Josiah. If the actions of prophets were important to those responsible for the Former Prophets in their present form, they nevertheless left the words of the Latter Prophets to their own scribes.

The rest of Isaiah 1—39 is taken up by a rich collection of diverse literary genres, often so devoid of names and historical allusions as to become almost timeless. Scholars vary in their judgment about how many and which of these messages originated with Isaiah. Isaiah 19 will illustrate the difficulty of determining a date. It refers to Egypt, predicting its overthrow, but the conqueror is not named. Even if, therefore, the passage originated with Isaiah in the Assyrian period, one can no longer be certain of that. It would fit equally well during the Babylonian period. O. Kaiser's analysis of Isaiah 1—39 (Kaiser, ix-xii) may be taken as an example of mid-to-late twentieth-century scholars concerning the growth of Isaiah 1—39. The preponderance of authentic sayings appeared in Isaiah 1—12; 28—31. The so-called Isaiah Apocalypse (Is 24—27) and the passage contrasting Israel and Moab (Is 34—35) join Isaiah 36—39 as whole sections added to the growing corpus, with the oracles against the foreign nations being added as late as the turn from the fourth to the third centuries BC. B. S. Childs reacted against that kind of splintering of the text and argued instead for a canonical reading (Childs, 3-8). Still, he did not deny that the text was composite. What remains clear, moreover, is that the sayings ascribed to Isaiah grew exponentially. That process seems to have continued through the exile and beyond (see 7.4 below).

5.3. Micah. The last of the four famous prophets from the eighth century BC is Micah. Almost nothing is known about him personally except that he lived in the small town of Moresheth near the Philistine city of Gath, to which it would have been economically tied. Micah's criticism of the urban elite (in Samaria, Jerusalem, Lachish and elsewhere) seems understandable against the background of a man whose town and perhaps his own fortunes were adversely affected by the control ancient cities could hold over the "daughter" villages around them (see Mic 1:1-7; 2:1-11; 3:1-12). Juxtaposed to those verses, however, are pictures of peace and future prosperity (see Mic 4:1-8) and God's future blessing (Mic 7:11-20), including a reunion of Israel and Judah and the *restitution* of the Davidic king (Mic 5:2-5; MT 5:1-4) (Redditt 2008, 69-73). Parts of Micah, therefore, looked back on the fall of Jerusalem, so the book of Micah did not reach its final form until at least the exilic period.

6. Seventh-Century BC Prophets.

The seventh century BC saw the rise of more "writing" prophets: Nahum, Habakkuk and Zephaniah. Three other prophetic books appear prior to them in the LXX Twelve: Joel, Obadiah and Jonah. Those same three appear interspersed among Hosea, Amos and Micah in order of the first half of the MT Twelve: Hosea, Joel, Amos, Obadiah, Jonah and Micah. Either way, canonically, Joel, Obadiah and Jonah appear before Nahum, Habakkuk and Zephaniah in what perhaps was intended as chronological order. Consequently, though Joel and Jonah are often dated later, they will be treated first in what follows. Obadiah looks back on the fall of Jerusalem, so it will be treated with prophets of the sixth-century BC.

6.1. Joel and Jonah. The book of Joel is devoid of allusions to Israelite, Judean, Mesopotamian and/or Egyptian figures who might be used to determine an approximate date for the prophet. Hence, Joel has been dated anywhere from the ninth to the third centuries. The book is a classic example of having been shorn of historical allusions (or, perhaps, written without them) so that it speaks to many ages and peoples. The first half of the book (Joel 1:2—2:17) threatens *destruction on Jerusalem and surrounding rural Judah, while the second half describes (as a past action) God turning in jealousy toward God's people and *blessing them. As a result, all God's people (male and female, old and young, owner and slave) will receive the charisma of prophecy, the nations will gather for battle against Judah, and God will defeat them.

Jonah is the sole book among the Latter Prophets that is substantially prose. It does contain a song of thanksgiving for God's rescuing the singer from the clutches of death, but that song comes while Jonah is still inside the fish. Perhaps the song was sung in anticipation of God's rescuing Jonah, but the text does not say so. The book contains only the gist of Jonah's message to Nineveh: "There are forty more days until Nineveh is overthrown." Scholars have sometimes suggested, plausibly, that the book of Jonah was included to bring the number of Minor Prophets to a dozen. That suggestion also recognizes implicitly that the book was written in the postexilic period despite its place in the Twelve. Its genre also is debated, except that it is a narrative.

The book's setting is the city of Nineveh at the peak of its power. The name of its hero perhaps was taken from the eighth-century BC prophet Jonah the son of Amittai, mentioned in 2 Kings 14:25. If so, the statement in Jonah 3:6-9 that the king of Assyria dwelled in Nineveh was anachronistic, since Nineveh became the capital during the reign of Sennacherib (r. 704-681 BC). Regardless, in contending that God wanted to spare the cruel Assyrians, the book itself articulated an openness to foreigners not always seen among the prophets.

6.2. Nahum, Habakkuk, Zephaniah. There is good evidence that Nahum and Habakkuk were redacted together, forming an inclusion device that opened and closed with a song of theophany (Nah 1:1-8 and Hab 3:1-19), surrounding taunts (Nah 2—3 and Hab 2:6-20), with the issue of theodicy standing in the middle (see the argument in 4 above). Placing the three prophets in apparent chronological order would have required dividing the redacted pair and placing Zephaniah between them. Nahum, with its prediction of the fall of Assyria (which occurred in 605), came earliest chronologically. Habakkuk itself may have undergone several stages of growth, but as it stands, one of its key emphases is the power of Babylon to exact its will on Judah (Hab 1:6-11). It does not, however, anticipate the fall of Jerusalem (in 586). Zephaniah opens with God's hyperbolic threat to destroy everything on the face of the earth (Zeph 1:2—2:15), including Judah and Jerusalem, but it closes, as it now stands, with thirteen verses (Zeph 3:1-13) that castigate Jerusalem for its sinfulness and seven (Zeph 3:14-20) that anticipate God's *forgiveness of the sins of the city and the return of the exiles. Its conclusion appears, therefore, to have been shaped to lead into the postexilic words of Haggai and Zechariah.

7. Sixth-Century BC Prophets Down to the Fall of Jerusalem.

The sixth century BC witnessed the careers of Jeremiah, Obadiah, Ezekiel, Haggai and Zechariah, not to mention redactional additions to earlier prophetic collections, especially Isaiah 40—66. Many scholars argue that Jeremiah's career began as early as 626 BC, the thirteenth year of the reign of Josiah (see Jer 1:2), but it is difficult to date passages in the book earlier than the reign of Jehoiakim, specifically the fall of Assyria to Babylon in 605 BC (Hyatt, 779-780). In any case, since the overwhelming percentage of his messages related to the early sixth century BC, he will be treated here as the first of the sixth-century prophets. The background of all these books was the rise and fall of the *Babylonian Empire and its replacement by the Persian Empire. The Babylonian Empire did not last as long as either the Assyrian or the Persian, flourishing only in the years 605-539 BC, but it burst on the scene under the powerful Nebuchadnezzar (d. 562 BC). It lasted just over two decades after his death, until its powerful neighbor to the east (Persia) took it over.

7.1. Jeremiah. In addition to prose and poetic sermons attributed to Jeremiah, the book bearing his name also contains narratives and reflections concerning the career of Jeremiah, the condition of Judah before and during the exile, and the nature of prophecy itself. The book bears testimony that Jeremiah was literate (Jer 51:60), but the style of the prose sections of the book resembles closely the style of Deuteronomy. Was that perhaps an "official" style used by many scribes? Prophets who proclaimed bad times or punishment for wrong conduct were often ignored and at times even challenged by their hearers, a fate that befell Jeremiah. He was at various times arrested, tried and sentenced for what he said or did (see Jer 26:10-24; 37:11-21; 38:1-13). He was even threatened with death by the people of his own village, Anathoth (Jer 11:18-23). At the end of his career he was seized by the assassins of Gedaliah and taken to Egypt (Jer 43:1-7). Nevertheless, Judean kings and others who opposed what he said still sought out his counsel.

What was his message? Simply stated, he predicted the fall of Jerusalem and Judah for the sinfulness of their people, in particular their *idolatry. That message seemed to his audience to be unfounded, so wherein lay the dispute? They apparently recognized Yahweh as God, but not as the sole God in Judah, the only God to be worshiped (cf. Ezek 8:1-18, which lists various gods worshiped in Jerusalem itself in the years leading up to the fall of the city). Foreigners, of course, would have worshiped their own gods, but various prophets charge both Israel and Judah with worshiping other gods than Yahweh. Those gods would have been traditional divinities, and perhaps the people saw them as inferior to Yahweh but not without the ability to help in a time of need. Other Judeans may have found it expedient to worship the gods of the major powers. Jeremiah 2:11 appears to have rejected them all: "Has a nation changed its gods, even though they are no gods?" The people, of course, would have denied that they had abandoned God at all. Jeremiah, however, quoted God's condemnatory rejoinder: "But my people have changed their glory for something that does not profit" (Jer 2:11).

These two lines from Jeremiah require further theological exploration. If monotheism is defined as belief in the existence of one *God only, combined with the denial of the existence of all other gods, Jeremiah qualifies as a monotheist. Usually, scholars say that Deutero-Isaiah was the first monotheist, and a monotheist he was (see Is 45:18-19; 46:8-13), but Jeremiah seems to have been the first in the OT.

The book of Jeremiah also contains remark-

Yahweh Servant of

able language about the future of God's covenant with Judah. It set forth a new covenant, one that is explicitly contrasted with the old covenant given by God to Moses on Mount Sinai (Jer 31:31-34). First, the old *covenant was breakable; Israel had proved that over and over. The new covenant would be unbreakable. Second, the old covenant was external, written on stone, but the new covenant would be internal, written on the heart. Third, the old covenant had been mediated through Moses, but the new covenant would be mediated by God directly to the people, whether individually or collectively.

7.2. Lamentations and Obadiah. In the OT *Lamentations appears among the Writings, but both the LXX and the Christian Bible place it directly after Jeremiah. It appears to be a collection of five *laments over the fall of Jerusalem rather than a collection of prophetic sayings, and it is anonymous. If the prophet Jeremiah anticipated the fall of Jerusalem, Lamentations reacted to it (see, e.g., Lam 1). It did so, moreover, out of deep fear that God had permanently destroyed the city (see esp. Lam 5:20-22), which possibility is denied, however, in Lamentations 3:31-33. It also mourned the end of the monarchy (Lam 4:20), but it says nothing explicit about the misery of the people in the surrounding countryside and their losses. Obadiah, by contrast, is angry about the role of Edom, Judah's nearest kinsmen, during the destruction of the city, and predicts that the treachery of its people will rebound against them (Obad 1-14). By contrast, God will restore Judah (Obad 15-21). Lamentations and Obadiah, then, articulate the most disparate views in the OT for the future of Jerusalem.

7.3. Ezekiel. Very little of Ezekiel is written in poetry (but see Ezek 7:1-9a, 10-19, 21-27 as one of several exceptions), often considered a hallmark of authentic prophecies. Instead, much of the book is presented as prose narratives of visions (e.g., Ezek 1—3; 8—11; 37—48). It has even been suggested that Ezekiel was written down for public reading by Ezekiel, and some scholars think its repetitive style is the result of a long process of growth. Regardless, it is a lengthy work explaining the fall of Jerusalem to the Babylonians (Ezek 1—34) and predicting a new covenant between God and Judah (Ezek 34:25). It also anticipates God's defeat of the king and kingdom of Babylon (represented by

Gog and Magog in Ezek 38—39), followed by the restitution of the land of the twelve tribes of Israel (Ezek 40—48), beginning with the prediction of the restitution of the temple and the Zadokite priesthood. The book also envisions a new Davidic king (Ezek 34:22-24), also referred to as a "prince" (Ezek 37:25; 44:3; 45:7; 46:16-18; 48:21-22), as someone lower in prestige than the priests. Because of its visionary style and extended and obscure symbolism, it is sometimes considered a precursor to apocalypses, though not an apocalypse itself.

7.4. Deutero-Isaiah and Trito-Isaiah. Isaiah 40 marks a change to a more positive view of the future of Israel than the one found for the most part in Isaiah 1—39. Isaiah 40—55 address exiles in Babylon and promises that Yahweh, the only God, would bring them back home. The exile was their punishment for worshiping other gods, and they had paid double what their sins deserved (Is 40:2). Moreover, God would use the Persian conqueror Cyrus as an instrument for punishing Babylon (Is 44:24—45:8). The chapters often speak of God's servant(s), and no consensus about his identity exists among scholars. One of the most carefully argued views is that of J. Blenkinsopp, who thinks that the servant in Isaiah 44:1-4 is Cyrus, while the servant in the remaining occurrences of the word in Isaiah 40—48 is Jacob, the ancestor of the people of Israel (Blenkinsopp 78, 118-19). In the Suffering Servant passages of Isaiah 49—55, however, the servant is a prophet predestined by God for a mission before birth (Is 49:1), who lived his early life under the providence of God (Is 53:2a), who was equipped for a mission involving prophetic speech and instruction (Is 49:2; 50:4), and who received divinely revealed knowledge and guidance (Is 50:4b). His mission was directed both to Israel and to the nations (Is 49:5-6). A sense of foreboding about him gives way to an assurance of vindication (Is 50:7-9), but opposition increases, resulting in his death (Is 53:7-12). Deutero-Isaiah was mediated by the disciples of that prophet. Christian thought, of course, has often identified the servant as Jesus, a view based on the NT writers' interpretation of Isaiah, however, not on the book of Isaiah itself (*see* Servant of Yahweh).

Blenkinsopp argues further that Isaiah 40—55 was mediated by the disciples of Deutero-Isaiah, and that Isaiah 60—62, the oldest part of Trito-Isaiah, shows close affinity with Deutero-Isaiah (Blenkinsopp, 77-78). All of these chapters, moreover, betray influence by the Deuteronomistic school (see esp. Is 48:17-19; 58:1-14). Prophecy was becoming much less oral and much more literary. Strongly eschatological, but not *apocalyptic (Blenkinsopp, 88-89), the chapters promise a better future for penitent Judeans through God's grace (Is 59), the rebuilding of ruined Jerusalem (Is 61:1-7), its preservation by God (Is 65:6-16) and vengeance on Edom (Is 63:1-6), all dependent on the people's true *worship of God (Is 66:1-5).

7.5. Haggai and Zechariah 1—8. As mentioned earlier, these two books underwent a common redaction, with sections introduced by a phrase unique to them: "In the X year of King Darius, in the Y month, on the Z day of the month." Haggai fastened his hope for the future on the rebuilding of the temple and the restitution of the monarchy under the Davidide Zerubbabel (which restitution, obviously, never occurred). Zechariah 1:7—6:15 consists of a series of eight visions and two exhortations (Zech 2:6-13; 6:9-15). The visions reveal God's future plans for the Judean community, and the exhortations urge people to take up the demands inherent in those visions. Zechariah 7—8 opens (Zech 7:1-3) with a question about the necessity of fasting for the temple after it was rebuilt, and the chapters close (Zech 8:18-19) stating that those fasts plus two others will be turned into feasts. In between stands a variety of passages addressing the postexilic community.

8. Fifth- and Fourth-Century BC Prophets.
The last two collections within the Book of the Twelve are Zechariah 9—14 and Malachi. Critical scholars typically separate Zechariah 9—14 from Zechariah 1—8, though some of them adopt the strategy of reading Zechariah 7—14 as a unified collection (see Conrad, 16-22), and B. G. Curtis argues that Zechariah himself wrote the whole book within about twenty years (Curtis, 1-23). R. F. Person, by contrast, argues that Zechariah 10—14 possibly derived from the Deuteronomic school responsible for Jeremiah (Person, 205). Zechariah 9 does seem to fit well around the turn of the sixth to fifth century BC, but no further hope for a king appears in Zechariah 10—14. Indeed, in Zechariah 11 the primary focus is on excoriating the ruling families in Jerusalem. Zechariah 14 anticipates

no new David, but the reign of God in Jerusalem. Many scholars think that Zechariah 13:2-6 announces the end of prophecy in Judah, but it does not. Rather, it condemns false prophets for deceiving people, but the struggle between false and true prophets had been a recurring them in the OT. Malachi is no less discontent with priests of his day. He charged them with the worst offense of all for religious leaders: insincerity and indifference in carrying out the duties of their office.

Malachi does end, however, with Malachi 4:4-6, a passage usually considered secondary, though B. Glazier-McDonald argues that the verses are authentic to Malachi (Glazier-McDonald, 243-52). The verses mention both Moses and Elijah. Moses had been mentioned only once before in the Book of the Twelve, in Micah 6:4, where he is listed with Aaron and Miriam as a hero of the exodus. Elijah had not been mentioned at all. In fact, Elijah is mentioned nowhere else in the Latter Prophets. Why, then, are these two men suddenly mentioned at the end of Malachi? The best answer seems to be that the verses look back to the Law (represented by Moses) and the Prophets (represented by the earlier prophet Elijah) and form a fitting conclusion to the first two parts of the Hebrew canon: the Law and the Prophets.

9. Daniel.
The book of Daniel is, technically speaking, an *apocalypse, not a prophetic book. An apocalypse "is a genre of revelatory literature with a narrative framework, in which a revelation is mediated by an otherworldly being to a human recipient, disclosing a transcendent reality which is both temporal, insofar as it envisages eschatological salvation, and spatial insofar as it invokes another temporal world" (J. J. Collins, 9). Moreover, that revelation is "intended to interpret present, earthly circumstances in light of the supernatural world and of the future, and to influence both the understanding and the behavior of the audience by means of divine authority" (A. Yarbro Collins, 7). The LXX and the Christian canon, nevertheless, placed Daniel among the Prophets. Hence, it will be treated here. In addition, modern scholars have often treated apocalyptic literature as "the child of prophecy," and no doubt it drew upon prophetic books. Its structure, in which a revelatory being communicates with a human

and explains what the human had seen, is evidenced as early as Zechariah 1—6. Some, even much of its subject matter, drew upon prophetic literature too, so its inclusion in the present article seems justified.

The issue of history stands front and center in the book of Daniel. For one thing, the book includes five revelations that survey a sweep of time: Daniel 2:31-35 (interpreted by Daniel in Dan 2:37-45); Daniel 7:2-14 (interpreted by an angel in Dan 7:23-27); Daniel 8:3-14 (interpreted by an angel in Dan 8:20-26); Daniel 9:24-27 (a revelation from Gabriel); and Daniel 11:2—12:3 (the last vision of Daniel). In those visions, Daniel sees strange beasts or receives coded information about the end of the time of evil and the institution of God's new kingdom on earth. The images are vague enough that readers of the Bible for centuries have seen their own history anticipated in the visions of Daniel. It is quite likely, however, that those visions anticipated the end of the Babylonian Empire (Dan 2:37-38) as well as the Median, Persian and Greek Empires (Dan 8:20-21), and the phrase "the transgression that makes desolate" (Dan 8:13) referred to the actions of Antiochus IV Epiphanes when he defiled the temple in Jerusalem in 167 BC (see 1 Macc 1:41-61).

Traditional scholars often date the book during and at the end of the exile, but critical scholars typically calculate the date of the book of Daniel around 164 BC, based on a few misstatements of history. First, the book dates Nebuchadnezzar's initial defeat of Jerusalem in the third year of Jehoiakim, 606 BC, though that defeat did not occur until after the end of Jehoiakim's reign in 598 BC and the three-month reign of Jehoiachin, according to 2 Kings 23:36—24:17. Second, Daniel 11:40-45 depicts the death of Antiochus as occurring in Palestine, when in fact he died in Persia. Still, the seer behind the book about Daniel predicted correctly the death of the tyrant. Scholars often argue, therefore, that the author's presentation of events down close to Antiochus's death actually constitutes a recitation of history, but his prediction of the king's death was genuine prophecy.

A third alleged error, however, probably is not an error at all but instead a deliberate reinterpretation of an inherited symbol. The sequence of the four nations in Daniel 7—Babylon, Media, Persia, Greece—is said to have derived from an original Mesopotamian scheme listing Assyria, Media and Persia, later supplemented by Greece. The seer behind Daniel 7 used the available figure but reinterpreted the first animal (the lion) as Babylon, not Assyria. He did so for obvious reasons. The first was that his narrative was set in Babylon, and the second was that Babylon, not Assyria, had proved to be the deadly nemesis of Judah. The book of Daniel, moreover, employs that reinterpretation already in Daniel 2, where again the first of the four world empires is Babylon in the person of Nebuchadnezzar.

10. Conclusion: An End of Prophecy?

Psalm 74:9 bewails the destruction of Jerusalem by Nebuchadnezzar and the lack of any prophets therein. No one, therefore, could tell people how long the desolation of the city would last. The verse is haunting because it makes manifest the hopelessness of exilic Jerusalem and the people of Judah. The reality as seen in this study, of course, is that early in the exile Jeremiah still flourished (at least until after the death of Gedaliah [see Jer 43—44]), though many in Judah still refused to listen. In addition, Ezekiel was active in Babylon, Isaiah 40—55 addressed the conditions of exile and promised its end, and Isaiah 56—66, Haggai, Zechariah, Malachi and a number of anonymous prophets continued both orally and in writing to function as prophets. Daniel too was called a prophet, though modern scholars would consider the book apocalyptic and a product of the second century BC in its present form. Still, this ongoing flow of prophetic voices, however obscure the prophetic writers may have been behind the identities of well-known names, shows that prophecy did not so much die as become transformed. Christian readers will recall that according to the Gospels, the birth of Christianity was accompanied by prophetic activity, which continued on. One has reason to say, then, that prophetic activity did not die in the postexilic period. The emphasis on earlier prophets was part of a process that valued the received traditions—prophetic and otherwise—as the surest guide to understanding and pleasing God. An old text in the hands of a later exegete (e.g., a prophet's disciple or a rabbi) could be as timely and prophetic (broadly conceived) as anything that Isaiah said.

See also ANCIENT NEAR EASTERN PROPHECY;

APOCALYPTICISM, APOCALYPTIC LITERATURE; CALL/COMMISSION NARRATIVES; ISRAELITE HISTORY; FORM CRITICISM; FORMATION OF THE PROPHETIC BOOKS; PROPHECY AND SOCIETY; PROPHECY AND TRADITION; REDACTION/EDITORIAL CRITICISM; WRITING AND PROPHECY.

BIBLIOGRAPHY. **E. Ben Zvi and J. D. Nogalski,** *Two Sides of a Coin: Juxtaposing Views of Interpreting the Book of the Twelve/the Twelve Prophetic Books* (Piscataway, NJ: Gorgias, 2009); **J. Blenkinsopp,** *A History of Prophecy in Israel: From the Settlement in the Land to the Hellenistic Period* (Philadelphia: Westminster, 1983); idem, *Isaiah 40-55* (AB 19A; New York: Doubleday, 2000); idem, *Isaiah 56-66* (AB 19B; New York: Doubleday, 2003); **B. S. Childs,** *Isaiah* (OTL; Louisville: Westminster, 2001); **D. L. Christensen,** "The Book of Nahum," in *Forming Prophetic Literature: Essays on Isaiah and the Twelve in Honor of John D. W. Watts,* ed. J. W. Watts and P. R. House (JSOTSup 235; Sheffield: Sheffield Academic, 1996) 187-94; **A. Y. Collins,** "Introduction," *Semeia* 36 (1986) 1-9; **J. J. Collins,** "Introduction: Towards the Morphology of a Genre," *Semeia* 14 (1979) 1-20; **E. W. Conrad,** *Zechariah* (RNBC; Sheffield: Sheffield Academic, 1999); **J. L. Crenshaw,** "Deceitful Minds and Theological Dogma," in *Prophets, Sages, and Poets* (St. Louis: Chalice, 2006) 73-82; **B. G. Curtis,** *Up the Steep and Stony Road; The Book of Zechariah in Social Location Trajectory Analysis* (SBLAB 25; Atlanta: Society of Biblical Literature, 2006); **B. Glazier-McDonald,** *Malachi: The Divine Messenger* (SBLDS 98; Atlanta: Scholars Press, 1987); **J. P. Hyatt,** "Introduction and Exegesis of the Book of Jeremiah," *IB* 5:775-1142; **O. Kaiser,** *Isaiah 13-39: A Commentary,* trans. R. A. Wilson (OTL; Philadelphia: Westminster, 1974); **J. D. Nogalski,** *Literary Precursors to the Book of the Twelve* (BZAW 217; Berlin: de Gruyter, 1993); idem, *Redactional Processes in the Book of the Twelve* (BZAW 218; Berlin: de Gruyter, 1993); **R. F. Person,** *Second Zechariah and the Deuteronomic School* (JSOTSup 167; Sheffield: Sheffield Academic, 1993); **P. L. Redditt,** "The Book of Joel and Peripheral Prophecy," *CBQ* 48 (1986) 225-40; idem, "The Book of Malachi in Its Social Setting," *CBQ* 56 (1994) 240-55; idem, "The Formation of the Book of the Twelve," in *Thematic Threads in the Book of the Twelve,* ed. P. L. Redditt and A. Schart (BZAW 325; Berlin: de Gruyter, 2003) 1-26; idem, "The King in Haggai—Zechariah 1-8 and the Book of the Twelve," in *Tradition in Transition: Haggai and Zechariah 1-8 in the Trajectory of Hebrew Theology,* ed. M. Boda and M. Floyd (LHBOTS 475; London: T & T Clark, 2008) 56-82; **K. Schmid,** *Literaturgeschichte des Alten Testaments: Eine Einführung* (Darmstadt: Wissenschaftliche Buchgesellschaft, 2008); **O. H. Steck,** *Der Abschluss der Prophetie im Alten Testament* (BTSt 17; Neukirchen-Vluyn: Neukirchener Verlag, 1991); **M. A. Sweeney,** *The Twelve Prophets* (2 vols.; Berit Olam; Collegeville, MN: Liturgical Press, 2000); **C. Westermann,** *Basic Forms of Prophetic Speech,* trans. H. C. White (Philadelphia: Westminster, 1967); **R. R. Wilson,** *Prophecy and Society in Ancient Israel* (Philadelphia: Fortress, 1980); **A. Yarbro Collins,** "Introduction," *Semeia* 36 (1986) 1-9.
P. L. Redditt

PROPHECY AND ESCHATOLOGY IN CHRISTIAN THEOLOGY

For many Christian theologians and NT scholars, the field of eschatology is a critical, even foundational, component of Christian theology. The influential twentieth-century theologian J. Moltmann, for example, writes, "Eschatology cannot be only a part of Christian doctrine. Rather, the eschatological outlook is characteristic of all Christian proclamation, of every Christian existence and of the whole Church" (Moltmann 1967, 16). While not all scholars maintain that eschatology is as all-encompassing as Moltmann does, most acknowledge that eschatology is an important doctrine in the Christian faith. The goal of this article is to address the manner in which OT prophecy relates to the larger field of Christian theology, especially in regard to the various different schools of eschatological understanding within Christian theology.

1. Definition of Eschatology
2. Eschatology and Old Testament Scholarship
3. Primary Elements in the Old Testament Prophetic View of the Future
4. Interpretive Challenges
5. Theological Interpretive Systems and the Old Testament Prophets

1. Definition of Eschatology.

The word *eschatology* is derived from the Greek word *eschatos* ("last"), and thus in a very narrow sense it refers to the study of "last things," "final things," or even the "end of things."

G. Thomas provides a helpful qualification, suggesting that eschatology is not so much about "last things" as it is about "ultimate things" (Thomas, 55). Eschatology is a study of how God's purpose and direction for history are revealed in Scripture. It is a study not of how the world ends or how time ends but rather of how the story ends—how God brings the biblical story to a climactic end (Hays, 78).

2. Eschatology and Old Testament Scholarship.

Contemporary OT scholarship remains divided on several basic issues relating to eschatology, even including the basic definition given above. Much of the diversity stems from the issues connected to the relationship between prophetic literature and apocalyptic literature. Indeed, eschatology is at heart of the complex issue of determining the relationship between prophecy and apocalyptic (see Apocalypticism, Apocalyptic Literature). On one end of the spectrum is the approach that defines eschatology narrowly, limiting it to concepts associated with a future but ahistorical radical transformation of the cosmos. Thus, almost by definition they locate OT eschatology squarely within apocalyptic literature and see little evidence of eschatology within the "this-world" emphasis of prophetic literature. On the other end of the spectrum, as described in the definition given above, is the understanding that eschatology is intertwined with the future hope proclaimed by the OT prophets, the time when God's actions in history climax into a spectacular and ultimate restoration. Thus, this view maintains that eschatology is the broader theological field that draws on both prophetic literature and apocalyptic literature (see Boda, 39-43; Arnold, 23-39).

Another central issue within OT scholarship that spawns diversity is that of messianic prophecy. Most Christian theologians and NT scholars would argue that the life, death, resurrection and return of Jesus Christ (i.e., the OT *Messiah) stand at the heart of eschatology. OT scholarship, on the other hand, is highly divided on this issue. In summarizing the history of this division, R. Clements writes, "The conservative and critical paths of interpretation became widely divergent, so much so that by the end of the nineteenth century the more critical expositions of biblical prophecy had al-

most entirely lost interest in the question of its messianic significance" (Clements, 19). At issue is the relationship between the OT and the NT, as well as the relationship between the church and the synagogue. Within the broad academy of OT scholarship there is no consensus on how to interact with Christian theology, or even if such interaction is a valid endeavor. Few critical studies on the OT prophets produced in the last hundred years even address the messianic connection to the NT, much less the connection to the broader field of Christian eschatology. Most of the recent serious studies of messianism in the OT and its connection to Christ in the NT have been conducted by conservative/evangelical scholars and generally fall into two groups. Either they tend to have an apologetic tone, seeking to persuade the academy that the study of messianism is indeed a valid field of critical study (e.g., McConville), or they simply embrace the conservative/evangelical presupposition that Jesus is the Messiah of the OT, thus addressing only the conservative/evangelical community (Hess and Carroll R.). If messianism itself is a questionably valid issue for critical scholarship, it is no surprise that most recent critical works on the OT prophets reflect very little interest in how the message of the prophets connects to Christian theology, especially eschatology.

There are, of course, exceptions. D. Gowan devotes an entire book to the topic of eschatology in the OT, and he cautiously and briefly explores how some of the central themes of the prophetic hope are continued and developed within later Christian (and Jewish) tradition. But in general, in order to find a good discussion on how the OT prophets relate to Christian eschatology, one must look to conservative/evangelical scholars (see esp. Goldingay, 350-516).

3. Primary Elements in the Old Testament Prophetic View of the Future.

Most of the material in the OT prophets deals with issues and events of their day and time (e.g., covenant violation; idolatry; injustice; call to repentance; warnings of judgment, especially brought about by the Assyrians and Babylonians). G. Fee and D. Stuart observe, "Less than 2 percent of OT prophecy is messianic. Less than 5 percent specifically describes the new-covenant age. Less than 1 percent concerns events yet to come in our time" (Fee and Stuart,

182). These estimates probably are low, yet for Christians seeking to formulate Christian theology regarding the kingdom of God and the unfolding of God's plan for the future, even one percent (still a lot of text!) is very important.

Gowan distills the core of the prophets' special hope for the future (i.e., eschatology) to three basic transformations: (1) God will transform the human person by providing a new spirit and heart; (2) God will transform human society, especially seen in the restoration of Israel and focused on the reemergence of Jerusalem/Zion (this includes a righteous king who will replace the present evil times with justice); (3) God will transform nature itself into a "new creation," abolishing hunger forever (Gowan, 2-3). Preferring the term "hope" over the term "eschatology," J. Goldingay nonetheless stresses the centrality of eschatology/hope to the Christian faith (Goldingay, 350-51). His discussion of the OT prophetic hope, much more thorough and extensive than Gowan's, is organized into ninety-four category headings, including such significant topics as "Yhwh's Longstanding Purpose," "Yhwh's Holiness," "Yhwh's Reign," "Fortunes Restored," "A Greater Exodus," "A United People," "A Permanent Covenant" and "Where Breath/Wind/Spirit Is Poured Out" (Goldingay, 350-516).

For a brief overview, this article has synthesized the major components of OT prophecy relating to eschatology into six central categories: the historical pattern, the covenants, the restoration of Israel, the nations, the Day of Yahweh and the postexilic clarification.

3.1. The Historical Pattern. Much of the OT prophetic material is set in the context of either the Assyrian invasion of Israel or the *Babylonian invasion of Judah. Drawing primarily from Deuteronomy, the prophets announce judgment on Israel and Judah for abandoning Yahweh and his law. The future prophetic aspects of the prophets come in this context, as the prophets look beyond the terrible destruction brought on by the Assyrians and Babylonians to a new, glorious restoration. Many of the terms and concepts used by the prophets to describe the wonderful time of blessing in the future are exact reversals of the terms and concepts used for judgment. For example, practically all of the blessings promised in Jeremiah 30—33 are reversals of the judgments proclaimed in Jeremiah 1—29 (e.g., sickness to

healing; scattering to gathering; weeping to joy; uprooting to planting; destruction of Jerusalem to rebuilding Jerusalem; harlot to virgin) (Hays, 175). In striving to understand these images of future restoration (healing, gathering, joy, planting, rebuilding, virgin, etc.) and to relate them to NT eschatology, it is important to keep their negative (historical) counterparts of judgment in view.

The NT parallels the OT prophets in the sense that NT eschatological texts likewise proclaim the coming reign of Christ within a context of coming judgment upon unbelieving Israel (e.g., Mk 13), following the OT prophetic pattern.

3.2. The Covenants. Israel's covenants are deeply imbedded into the OT prophetic message. The prophets proclaim judgment on Israel and Judah because they have seriously violated the *covenant that Yahweh made with them at Sinai. Yet when the prophets look hopefully toward the new glorious restoration, they base much of that hope on the promises/covenants that God made with David (promise of king) and Abraham (promise of land, descendants, blessings on nations) (e.g., Is 2:2-4; 9:7; 41:8-13; 51:1-6; 55:3; Jer 3:14-18; 16:14-15; 23:5-8; 30:9; 33:14-26; Ezek 34:23-24; 37:24; Hos 3:5; Amos 9:11; Mic 7:20; Zech 8:12-23). Jeremiah goes even further, declaring that God will inaugurate a "new covenant," one that will work better than the old covenant made at Sinai (Jer 31:30-34) (Goldingay, 382-84, 431-33, 486-90; Hays, 62-69). The NT continues this understanding of the covenants, clearly presenting Jesus Christ as the fulfillment of the Abrahamic and Davidic covenants as well as the one who inaugurates the new covenant.

3.3. The Restoration of Israel. A central feature of the OT prophets is that they look beyond the terrible judgment and destruction that the Assyrians and Babylonians will bring, and they describe a wonderful time of glorious restoration for Israel (merged with Judah, Jerusalem, Zion, etc.) (e.g., Is 11:10-16; 49:8-26; 54:1-17; 60:1-22; Jer 30—33; Ezek 40—48; Amos 9:11-15; Mic 4:1-8). This restoration will be brought about by the coming of a glorious and righteous Davidic king who will rule with power, justice and compassion. As mentioned above, all of the terrible images of destruction are reversed in this spectacular picture of hope: rebuilt city, regathered people, peace, safety, justice, population increase, planting and harvesting, joy, proper worship of God, deliverance of the poor, forgiveness, experiencing the presence of God, establishment of the new covenant, and so forth. This is the most central feature of the OT prophets' view of the future. Even images of "new creation" (Is 65:17-25) are set within the context of a restored *Israel (and rebuilt Jerusalem [note Is 65:18-19]).

Recently, J. Levenson has argued that the theme of resurrection is likewise integrally connected to the restoration of Israel. The concept of resurrection is a critical component of NT eschatology, but most scholars maintain that the concept is absent (or faint at best) in the OT prophetic literature, appearing only very late in the OT along with the rise of apocalypticism (e.g., Dan 12:2). Levenson, however, maintains that prophetic books such as Isaiah, Jeremiah and Ezekiel contain intimations and implications pointing to the tight connection between resurrection of individuals and the restoration of Israel.

NT eschatology connects to most of the OT prophetic imagery regarding the restoration of Israel, especially the establishment of a powerful and just Davidic king and a rebuilt Jerusalem. However, the nature of this connection, especially in regard to whether the reference is literal, symbolic or a mixture, is highly debated (see 4.3 below).

3.4. The Nations. The prophets proclaim judgment on the *nations, just as they proclaim judgment on Israel and Judah. Likewise, as the prophets describe the future regathering and deliverance of Israel and Judah, they often include the nations, depicting them as streaming to Jerusalem to *worship God in truth (e.g., Is 2:2-4; 11:10-12; 18:7; 56:6-8; 66:18; Jer 3:17-18; Mic 4:1-3). At the heart of this feature of the prophetic picture is Genesis 12:3 and the promise that in Abraham all nations of the world would be blessed. In the NT the nations (or Gentiles) move from the prophetic periphery to center stage.

3.5. The Day of Yahweh. The OT prophets frequently speak of the time of God's dramatic intervention into human history as the "Day of Yahweh" (e.g., Is 13:6, 9; 30:3; Ezek 30:3; Joel 2:31; 3:14; Obad 15; Zeph 1:7-18) (*see* Day of the Lord). They use this term when describing both God's judgment and his deliverance. Likewise, in the prophetic literature the "Day of

Yahweh" can refer to "near view" (i.e., imminent) events such as the Babylonian invasion, as well as future ("far view") events such as the restoration and regathering of Israel. Numerous other similar terms such as "the day" or "that day" are also used by the prophets in the same sense (e.g., Is 2:2, 11, 17; 4:2; 12:1; 34:8; Ezek 30:2-3; Hos 2:16-21; Joel 1:15; Amos 9:11; Zeph 1:9-10, 15).

The NT writers use this term ("day of the Lord") often to refer to the second coming of Christ. Likewise, they use similar terms such as "that day," "those days," and "the day of our Lord Jesus" as synonyms for "the day of the Lord."

3.6. Postexilic Clarification. The postexilic prophets (Haggai, Zechariah, Malachi), along with Ezra-Nehemiah, play an important role in that they testify to the fact that the return of the exiles back to the land under the leadership of Zerubbabel, Ezra and Nehemiah did not fulfill the great promises of restoration made by the preexilic prophets. This return was perhaps a start, or a glimpse, of the coming restoration (e.g., Hag 2:1-9; Zech 8:1-23; Mal 3:6-18), but the continued mention of Persian kings throughout the postexilic literature was a strong reminder that Israel did not have a Davidic king on the throne, a central component of the glorious restoration described by Isaiah, Jeremiah and the rest of the preexilic prophets (Hag 1:1; 2:10; Zech 1:1, 7; 7:1).

Similarly, several NT scholars recently have noted that in the first century AD the "still in exile" thinking was an important strand of theological thought among the Jews and thus played an important role in NT eschatology (e.g., Wright 1992, 243, 268-71). Furthermore, one of the interests in recent NT scholarship has been to explore the interaction between the NT writers and Roman rule. This interaction bears similarity at several points to the frequent mention of the Persian Kings in the postexilic OT writers.

4. Interpretive Challenges.

Even among evangelical scholars there is widespread disagreement regarding how to appropriate the future promises of the OT prophets into a broader, biblical Christian eschatology. The absence of a consensus approach is not surprising because OT prophecy, especially the predictive components of OT prophecy, can be extremely complex. For example, in order to gain insight into just how OT predictive prophecy finds fulfillment, D. B. Sandy examined prophecies within the former prophets (Joshua through 2 Kings) that were made and declared as fulfilled within this corpus. From this prediction/fulfillment within the OT he made the following observations. OT prophecies may (1) have a measure of uncertainty about fulfillment; (2) be inherently translucent; (3) give incomplete or enigmatic information; (4) employ stereotypical language; (5) conceal long spans of time; (6) predict something that does not happen as expected; (7) be given in poetic verse; (8) be fulfilled transparently (Sandy, 129-54). Without doubt, OT prophetic passages that look to the future confront interpreters with numerous *hermeneutical challenges. The major challenges include poetry and figurative language; the phenomenon of "near view/far view" imagery; the nature of the future kingdom; the relationship between Israel and the church; the *land; and conditional prophecy.

4.1. Poetry and Figurative Language. Much of the prophetic material in the OT is written in poetry and is characterized by parallelism and the extensive use of figurative language. Likewise, even in the prose sections figures of speech abound. The prophets paint a picture of the glorious future restoration using colorful imagery. A major challenge for interpreters in connecting these images to NT texts on eschatology is determining what these images mean. Is the prophetic picture of the future (often couched in figurative language) to be understood literally, symbolically, both, or somewhere in between? This is a very complex question. For example, Isaiah looks to the future and proclaims, "The wolf will live with the lamb, the leopard will lie down with the goat" (Is 11:6 NIV). Clearly, these are figures of speech, but how should they be understood? Taken rather literally (but still understanding "wolf" and "lamb" figuratively to represent a wider category of animals), this might refer to the future transformation of nature in which peace reigns supreme, even to the extent that carnivores will no longer hunt other animals (*see* Animal Imagery). Or is Isaiah perhaps using these images to refer to political enemies? That is, do "wolf" and "lamb" refer to nations? Clearly, Isaiah is proclaiming that the future restoration will be characterized by peace, but is he referring to the end of war or to the end of carnivores?

Looking to the NT does not necessarily clarify whether one should lean toward the literal side or the symbolic side in interpreting OT prophetic texts. Some OT prophecies are fulfilled quite literally (e.g., Jesus actually was born in the literal town of Bethlehem, in fulfillment of Mic 5:2). Many others are symbolic and quite complex, as is the NT citation and usage of these prophecies (Beale and Carson, xxiii-xxviii).

The decision of whether to approach the OT prophetic promise of the future as primarily literal or as primarily symbolic is a watershed decision in connecting these promises into Christian eschatology.

4.2. Near View/Far View. Another complication in interpreting the OT prophetic view of the future is that as the prophets paint the picture of the future, they do not always distinguish clearly between the near future (e.g., the imminent Babylonian invasion) and events in the far or even farther future (e.g., return of the exiles, the first coming of Christ, the final coming of Christ). The prophets seem to go back and forth from near future events to far future events and then back to near future events. Indeed, often their images seem to be quite fluid in regard to time. A similar situation occurs in the NT in regard to the "already/not yet" aspects of the kingdom of God (Beasley-Murray; Kreitzer). Indeed, there appears to be a connection between the "near view/far view" of the OT prophets and the "already/not yet" NT presentation of the kingdom.

4.3. The Nature of the Future Kingdom. The prophets paint a picture of a glorious restoration in which a Davidic king sits on the throne in Jerusalem, ruling with justice over the world, as the nations stream into the city to worship Yahweh alongside regathered Israel. The interpretive challenge here relates both to the "near view/far view" issue as well as the "literal versus symbolic" issue in figurative/poetic language. How much of this prophetic picture was fulfilled by the first coming of Christ, and how much remains future? If some aspects are still future, how are they to be understood, and how literal are they? Some interpreters maintain that Jesus will return and literally reign from a throne in Jerusalem. Others view the reign of Christ in a symbolic fashion, arguing that he reigns even now over his kingdom and among his people. Some interpreters see almost total *land?*

fulfillment in the first coming of Christ, others stress a millennial kingdom, while yet others posit that much of the fulfillment will come in the final new heavens, new earth and new Jerusalem described in Revelation 21—22.

4.4. Israel and the Church. This issue is tightly intertwined with one's understanding of the nature of the future kingdom as well as one's approach to the "literal versus symbolic" challenge of figurative language. The OT prophets describe the future blessings of God and the new kingdom of God in terms of restored *Israel. They do not mention the church. In the NT, however, the church quickly becomes a central entity in the unfolding of God's plan. How does the OT prophetic picture of restored Israel relate to the NT church? This also is a watershed issue in Christian eschatology. Do Israel and the church remain totally separate? That is, will the prophecies about Israel be literally fulfilled in the future by the nation of Israel? Or does the church replace Israel and thus fulfill these prophecies symbolically? Or is there some kind of mixture whereby the two are combined into a broad category of "people of God," sometimes identical and sometimes separate?

4.5. The Land. A closely related interpretive challenge is in regard to the many prophetic promises about "the *land." In much of the OT (from Abraham to Ezra-Nehemiah) the land plays a very important theological role and is mentioned repeatedly. As W. Brueggemann observes, "Land is a central, if not *the central theme* of biblical faith" (Brueggemann, 3). Whereas almost all other prophetic themes carry over into the NT, the land as a theological theme disappears from the NT almost completely. What should Christian theologians do with the OT prophecy about the land? Does the NT "spiritualize" or "redefine" the land, shifting the source of divine blessing from "life in Canaan" to "life in Christ" (Waltke, 560)? Or does the silence of the NT regarding the land imply that the OT prophetic trajectory of the land should be carried directly into NT eschatology in a literal fashion even though the NT rarely mentions it?

4.6. Conditional Prophecy. In Jeremiah 18:7-10 Yahweh declares that what will actually happen in the future depends on how people respond to the prophetic word. Thus, the prophets imply rather strongly that often there is a conditional component to the fulfillment

of their prophecies. The story of Jonah provides another clear example: the impending judgment that he proclaimed on Nineveh was averted due to the repentance of the Ninevites. The possibility of conditionality in OT prophecy should suggest some tentativeness and caution against absolute certainty when one tries to explain exactly how these prophecies will be fulfilled in the future.

5. Theological Interpretive Systems and the Old Testament Prophets.
Eschatology is a more prominent feature in the NT than in the OT; thus, most theologians lean heavily on NT texts for shaping their doctrine of eschatology. Central to the discussion in the NT is the nature of the kingdom of God and the thousand-year reign of the coming righteous king described in Revelation 20:1-6 (referred to as the "millennial kingdom"). There is no consensus, even among theologians who otherwise have similar approaches to Scripture (such as evangelicals). Thus, several systems or approaches to Christian eschatology are popular today, and these differing systems likewise interpret OT prophecy in differing ways, particularly in regard to the interpretive challenges discussed above. The four major eschatological systems are amillennialism, premillennialism (with several variations), postmillennialism and eclectic (for overviews of these systems, see Pate; Grenz; Bock).

5.1. Amillennialism. The amillennial view tends to stress the symbolic and figurative nature of prophecy. Amillennialists interpret Revelation 20 figuratively as describing a spiritual kingdom of Christ's reign in the present. They adhere to the "already/not yet" understanding of the kingdom (the kingdom is here, but not yet complete), but they see the completion as occurring when Christ comes at the end of the age, followed immediately by a general resurrection, the last judgment, and the eternal state. According to amillennialism, there will not be a literal earthly millennial kingdom. Thus, amillennialists interpret much of OT prophecy figuratively and symbolically. Typically, they maintain that all of the OT prophecies about the restoration of Israel are fulfilled in the church, which in essence replaces Israel. Many of these prophecies, they argue, were fulfilled at the first coming of Christ. The rest of these prophecies will be fulfilled symbolically at the final coming of Christ and in the eternal state.

5.2. Premillennialism. The premillennial view tends to interpret prophecy (both NT and OT) more literally than amillennialism. The prefix *pre* means "before," indicating that premillennialists believe that Christ will return before the millennial kingdom. Indeed, Christ will establish the millennial kingdom, and it is within this millennial kingdom that many of the OT prophecies about Israel and the nations will be fulfilled. Within premillennialism are three major subgroups: classic dispensational premillennialism, progressive dispensational premillennialism and historic premillennialism. These three views can be placed on a spectrum, classified as to how literally or how symbolically they interpret prophecy. Classic dispensational premillennialism is the most literal in its approach, and historic premillennialism is the least literal (although still fairly literal). The progressive dispensational premillennial view lies in the middle.

5.2.1. Classic Dispensational Premillennialism. Dispensationalists believe that God deals with people differently throughout history, and that these different "administrations" or "dispensations" are identifiable as eras of biblical history. Of the three premillennial views, classic dispensationalism is the most literal in its interpretation of prophecy. In regard to OT prophecy, classic dispensationalists maintain a sharp and clear distinction between Israel and the church. Thus, they underscore that the new covenant in Jeremiah 31:31-33 was made with Israel and Judah, not the church (which enjoys the benefits of this covenant but is not a recipient of it). They interpret the OT prophecies about the future restoration of Israel in as literal a manner as possible, including the restoration of the temple and the worship system (as described in Ezekiel). In classic dispensational premillennialism many of the OT prophecies about the restoration of Israel will take place during the millennial kingdom.

5.2.2. Progressive Dispensational Premillennialism. Toward the end of the twentieth century a significant segment of dispensational premillennialists moved away from some aspects of classic dispensationalism, developing a modified view now known as progressive dispensationalism. This system still leans toward a literal view of prophecy, but its adherents give more attention to the figurative aspect and complexities of prophecy than classic dispensationalists do. At the heart of the progressive dispensational movement is the "already/not yet" understanding of the kingdom. This view argues that Christ did indeed inaugurate the kingdom of God at his first coming (the "already"), but that he will not consummate or establish fully the kingdom of God until he returns and reigns over his millennial kingdom (the "not yet"). Thus, progressive dispensational premillennialists maintain that some OT prophecies about the kingdom were partially fulfilled by the first coming of Christ, but that many of them still await fulfillment in the millennial kingdom. Progressive dispensational premillennialists likewise maintain a distinction between Israel and the NT church, but they do not tend to see this difference as universally present in the OT prophetic material. While views vary to some extent, some within progressive dispensationalism argue that Israel and the church are "mostly separate," but that some promises made to Israel are at least "partially" fulfilled in the church. On the other hand, progressive dispensationalists agree with classic dispensationalists in maintaining that there will be a future restoration for national (literal) Israel.

5.2.3. Historic Premillennialism. Similar to the other premillennial systems, the historic premillennial system posits that Christ will return to earth and establish a literal millennial kingdom. This view derives its name ("historic") from seeking to connect to the millennial views of the early church fathers (i.e., the "historic" millennial view). Historic premillennialism tends to be less literal than the dispensational premillennial views but not completely symbolic like amillennialism. Like the progressive dispensationalists, the historic premillennialists understand the kingdom of God according to the concept of "already/not yet." Thus, they maintain that while Christ did indeed inaugurate the kingdom at his first coming, the ultimate consummation of the kingdom, along with fulfillment of many OT prophecies, will come through the future millennial kingdom. Unlike the dispensational premillennialists, the historic premillennialists do not maintain a sharp distinction between Israel and the church. Most historical premillennialists understand the church to be the "true Israel," thus fulfilling many of the promises made to

Israel. Likewise, although many historical premillennialists recognize the possibility of many Jews converting to Christianity at the end of the age, they do not generally see a unique role for the literal nation of Israel.

5.3. Postmillennialism.

5.3.1. Classic Postmillennialism. In the term *postmillennial*, the prefix *post* means "after" and is used to indicate the view that Christ will return in glory after the millennial reign. Postmillennialists, however, understand the millennial reign quite differently than the premillennialists do. Classic postmillennialism maintains that through the proclamation of the gospel and through the general progress of "Christian" civilization, the majority of people in this present age will come to saving faith, thus ushering in a "kingdom-like" era (the millennium) in which the prophecies about *righteousness, peace and prosperity will be fulfilled. Some postmillennialists view the ushering in of the kingdom as a gradual development that includes all of church history. Postmillennialism was very popular within the English-speaking church at the end of the nineteenth century and the beginning of the twentieth, but its optimistic view of ushering in the kingdom of peace was largely shattered in the twentieth century by the two world wars and the Holocaust. Today, postmillennialism in its classic formulation is very much a minority view, especially in comparison with amillennialism and premillennialism.

5.3.2. Modern (Preterit) Postmillennialism. In recent years many NT scholars and Christian theologians have underscored the importance of the destruction of Jerusalem in AD 70 for interpreting NT prophecy (e.g., Wright 1996). This same conclusion has led a group of others to a radically different understanding of the kingdom of God. Preteritism (and its related system, Christian reconstructionism/theonomic postmillennialism), argues that the parousia (coming) of Christ to judge the world and to establish his kingdom actually happened in AD 70 at the fall of Jerusalem (and through other associated events). This view interprets the fulfillment of central NT texts such as the Olivet discourse (Mt 24; Mk 13; Lk 21) and Revelation 1—20 as a past event ("preterit" means "past") through which the kingdom began. Christian reconstructionism/theonomic postmillennialism posits that as the kingdom is ush-

ered in, there will be a gradual return to the OT norms of civil justice through missions, evangelism and education. Furthermore, modern postmillennialists believe that the vast majority of the world's population will convert to Christ through the proclamation of the gospel (Gentry, 13-25; Pate, 55-73).

In regard to OT prophecies, modern postmillennialists take a symbolic approach, interpreting Israel as representing the people of God (i.e., the church). Likewise, the OT images of the nations of the world streaming to Jerusalem to worship God are viewed as a picture of world evangelism, as the peoples of the world stream into the church to find salvation (Gentry, 36-38).

5.4. The Eclectic View.

In recent years J. Duvall, followed by C. Pate, has put forward a hybrid view dubbed simply "eclectic" (Duvall, 288-94; Pate, 129). Pate, for example, acknowledges that the fall of Jerusalem played an important role in the fulfillment of prophecy (the emphasis of preterist postmillennialism), but he also embraces the "already/not yet" nature of the kingdom and wants to stress the presence of the kingdom here today (similar to amillennialism). On the other hand, he still sees a future climax of the kingdom in the millennium and thus retains a premillennial view of Revelation 20 (Pate, 129-31). Although Duvall appears to be one of the first to use the actual term "eclectic" for this approach, this mixture of views is not unique to him or Pate. D. Bloesch held a similar position, labeling it "historical-symbolic" (Bloesch, 111). In fact, under the "already/not yet" umbrella there appears to be a place on the spectrum where premillennialism overlaps to some degree with amillennialism, and the eclectic view appears to describe this part of the spectrum. In this regard, R. Moore argues that the near consensus view among evangelicals regarding the "already/not yet" feature of the kingdom of God stretches across the line between premillennialism and amillennialism and thus provides common ground for understanding eschatology and its implications for the church today.

Those advocating the "eclectic" view have not yet developed a thoroughgoing approach to OT prophecy. In all likelihood, those holding this view will maintain a cautious, nondogmatic mixture of literal and symbolic interpretations, probably similar to the historical premillennial position.

5.5. Other Views and Trends. In his books *Theology of Hope* and *The Coming of God*, Jürgen Moltmann, an influential Christian theologian of the latter half of the twentieth century, espouses a millennial view that does not quite fit into any of the mainline positions described above, although perhaps it could be considered another "eclectic" view. Placing a strong emphasis on Christian hope, as well as on the OT prophetic themes of social justice and new creation, Moltmann's millennial view combines aspects of traditional postmillennialism and premillennialism "in order to construct a socio-dynamic view of the future that heralds justice and peace for the whole creation" (Bloesch, 106 [see also the discussion and critique in Bauckham 1997, 261-77]). Moltmann posits that Christ will indeed come and establish his kingdom in a visible way, but Moltmann consciously shifts the focus from the future to the implications that this hope creates in the life of the church now. Eschatology, Moltmann argues, includes both aspects.

Numerous other theological systems (e.g., liberation theology, feminist theology, ecological theology, postcolonial theology, black theology), reflecting a wide range of approaches to Scripture, likewise shift much of their discussion regarding eschatology from the future to the present. Many of these approaches developed and are being articulated out of a context of sociopolitical oppression, suffering and marginalization. Thus, the OT prophetic vision of social justice, often along with the prophetic image of a new creation, frequently plays a foundational role in their formulation of eschatology, even amid frequent skepticism among some of those holding these views regarding personal immortality or the final triumph of good over evil (Ruether, 334-39; Westhelle, 311-23). For discussions of these views, see Schwarz, 152-72; Pate 97-128.

Evewn in recent eschatological discussions among evangelicals there has been a growing concern to project the relevance of eschatological faith back into the praxis of the church. This is particularly true in the area of ecology, where the OT promise of a new creation, expanded by Paul in Galatians 6:15; 2 Corinthians 5:17, is being connected both to the future new creation and to "creation care" or "creation stewardship" in the here and now (e.g., Moo, 39-60).

See also APOCALYPTICISM, APOCALYPTIC LITERATURE; CANONICAL CRITICISM; ESCHATOLOGY; FEMINIST INTERPRETATION; HERMENEUTICS; MESSIAH; PROPHETS IN THE NEW TESTAMENT.

BIBLIOGRAPHY. **B. T. Arnold**, "Old Testament Eschatology and the Rise of Apocalypticism," in *The Oxford Handbook of Eschatology*, ed. J. L. Walls (Oxford: Oxford University Press, 2008) 23-39; **R. Bauckham**, "Must Christian Eschatology be Millenarian? A Response to Jürgen Moltmann," in *Eschatology in Bible and Theology: Evangelical Essays at the Dawn of a New Millennium*, ed. K. E. Brower and M. W. Elliot (Downers Grove, IL: InterVarsity Press, 1997) 263-78; **R. Bauckham and T. Hart**, *Hope against Hope: Christian Eschatology at the Turn of the Millennium* (Grand Rapids: Eerdmans, 1999); **G. K. Beale and D. A. Carson**, eds., *Commentary on the New Testament Use of the Old Testament* (Grand Rapids: Baker Academic, 2007); **G. R. Beasley-Murray**, *Jesus and the Kingdom of God* (Grand Rapids: Eerdmans, 1986); **D. G. Bloesch**, *The Last Things: Resurrection, Judgment, Glory* (Downers Grove, IL: InterVarsity Press, 2004); **D. L. Bock**, ed., *Three Views on the Millennium and Beyond* (Grand Rapids: Zondervan, 1999); **M. J. Boda**, "Figuring the Future: The Prophets and Messiah," in *The Messiah in the Old and New Testaments*, ed. S. E. Porter (Grand Rapids: Eerdmans, 2007) 35-74; **K. E. Brower and M. W. Elliot,** eds., *Eschatology in Bible and Theology: Evangelical Essays at the Dawn of a New Millennium* (Downers Grove, IL: InterVarsity Press, 1997); **W. Brueggemann**, *The Land: Place as Gift, Promise, and Challenge in Biblical Faith* (2nd ed.; OBT; Minneapolis: Fortress, 2002); **R. E. Clements**, *Old Testament Prophecy: From Oracles to Canon* (Louisville: Westminster/ John Knox, 1996); **W. J. Dumbrell**, *The Search for Order: Biblical Eschatology in Focus* (Eugene, OR: Wipf & Stock, 2001); **J. S. Duvall**, "New Testament—Revelation," in *Grasping God's Word: A Hands-On Approach to Reading, Interpreting, and Applying the Bible*, by J. S. Duvall and J. D. Hays (Grand Rapids: Zondervan, 2005) 282-301; **G. D. Fee and D. Stuart**, *How to Read the Bible for All Its Worth* (Grand Rapids: Zondervan, 2003); **K. L. Gentry**, "Postmillennialism," in *Three Views on the Millennium and Beyond*, ed. D. L. Bock (Grand Rapids: Zondervan, 1999) 11-57; **J. Goldingay**, *Old Testament Theology*, 2: *Israel's Faith* (Downers Grove, IL: IVP Academic, 2006); **D. E. Gowan**, *Eschatology in the Old Testament (2nd ed.; Edinburgh: T & T Clark, 2000); **S. J. Grenz,** *The Millennial Maze: Sorting Out Evangelical Options* (Downers Grove, IL: InterVarsity Press, 1992); **J. D. Hays,** *The Message of the Prophets: A Survey of the Prophetic and Apocalyptic Books of the Old Testament* (Grand Rapids: Zondervan, 2010); **J. D. Hays, J. S. Duvall and C. M. Pate,** *Dictionary of Biblical Prophecy and End Times* (Grand Rapids: Zondervan, 2007); **R. S. Hess and M. D. Carroll R.,** eds., *Israel's Messiah in the Bible and the Dead Sea Scrolls* (Grand Rapids: Baker Academic, 2003); **L. J. Kreitzer,** "Kingdom of God/Christ," *DPL* 524-26; **J. D. Levenson,** *Resurrection and the Restoration of Israel: The Ultimate Victory of the God of Life* (New Haven: Yale University Press, 2006); **J. G. McConville,** "Messianic Interpretation of the Old Testament in Modern Context," in *The Lord's Anointed: Interpretation of Old Testament Messianic Texts,* ed. P. E. Satterthwaite, R. S. Hess and G. J. Wenham (TynHS; Carlisle: Paternoster; Grand Rapids: Baker, 1995) 1-18; **J. Moltmann,** *Theology of Hope: On the Ground and Implications of a Christian Eschatology* (New York: Harper & Row, 1967); idem, *The Coming of God: Christian Eschatology,* trans. M. Kohl (London: SCM, 1996); **D. J. Moo,** "Creation and New Creation," *BBR* 20 (2010) 39-60; **R. D. Moore,** *The Kingdom of Christ: The New Evangelical Perspective* (Wheaton, IL: Crossway, 2004); **C. M. Pate,** *What Does the Future Hold? Exploring Various Views on the End Times* (Grand Rapids: Baker Academic, 2010); **O. P. Robertson,** *The Christ of the Prophets* (Phillipsburg, NJ: P & R, 2004); **R. R. Ruether,** "Eschatology in Christian Feminist Theologies," in *The Oxford Handbook of Eschatology,* ed. J. L. Walls (Oxford: Oxford University Press, 2008) 328-42; **D. B. Sandy,** *Plowshares and Pruning Hooks: Rethinking the Language of Biblical Prophecy and Apocalyptic* (Downers Grove, IL: InterVarsity Press, 2002); **H. Schwarz,** *Eschatology* (Grand Rapids: Eerdmans, 2000); **G. J. Thomas,** "A Holy God among a Holy People in a Holy Place: The Enduring Eschatological Hope," in *Eschatology in Bible and Theology: Evangelical Essays at the Dawn of a New Millennium,* ed. K. E. Brower and M. W. Elliot (Downers Grove, IL: InterVarsity Press, 1997) 53-69; **J. L. Walls,** ed., *The Oxford Handbook of Eschatology* (Oxford: Oxford University Press, 2008); **B. K. Waltke, with C. Yu,** *An Old Testament Theology: A Canonical and Thematic Approach* (Grand Rapids: Zondervan, 2007); **V. Westhelle,** "Liberation Theology: A Latitudinal Perspective," in *The Oxford Handbook of Eschatology,* ed. J. L. Walls (Oxford: Oxford University Press, 2008) 311-27; **N. T. Wright,** *The New Testament and the People of God* (Minneapolis: Fortress, 1992); idem, *Jesus and the Victory of God* (Minneapolis: Fortress, 1996).   J. D. Hays

PROPHECY AND PSYCHOLOGY

For well over a century and a half biblical scholars have authored treatments on the relationship between prophecy and psychology (see, e.g., Delitzsch [1st ed. 1855]; Foster; Beck [German original, 1843]; Kurtz; Kaplan 1908; 1919; Fletcher; Povah). The connection is due, on the one hand, to the nature of psychology itself, which is the study of the relationship between mental processes and behavior, including, but not limited to, matters of personhood and selfhood, consciousness and the will. (Since psychology has many branches, including experimental, clinical, social, developmental, etc., one must be careful about speaking of "psychology as a whole"; it is best to be clear whenever possible about the specific branch of psychology that one is speaking of when referring to the discipline.) It is also due, on the other hand, to the nature of the prophets themselves, several of whom manifest characteristics that have struck many readers as extraordinary if not abnormal and pathological. Until relatively recently, however, the psychological study of biblical prophecy (as well as other parts of the Bible) has been in bad repute. This is the unfortunate result of several factors, one of which is terminological, another of which is misunderstanding between the disciplines of psychology and biblical studies, especially the misunderstanding of psychology by biblical scholars. An antagonistic relationship need no longer obtain, since both disciplines have changed, with the study of psychology now far developed beyond Freud and Jung (foundational though they remain), let alone pre-Freudian days (see Mitchell and Black), and the study of the Bible now enlarged far beyond historical-critical research only (especially as that was practiced in particularly staid and unimaginative modes).

The sea changes evident in the study of psychology, in particular, should impact studies of "prophecy and psychology," though realization of such changes has come too slowly to biblical scholars, who have, again until fairly recently, either eschewed (contemporary) psychological approaches or offered only "older" style analyses à la Freud and Jung (for overviews, see Bucher; Rollins, *DBInt* 2:337-41; 1999; Kille 2001; Rollins and Kille). The present article reviews the history of the study of prophecy and psychology before focusing attention on the psychological *affect* of the prophets themselves as described in the biblical text, the psychological effect of the prophets on their audiences, and finally the psychology of God according to the prophets.

1. The Prophets and the "Old (Biblical) Psychology"
2. The Prophets and the "New (Modern) Psychology"
3. The Psychological *Affect* of the Prophets (The Psychology of the Prophets *Themselves*)
4. The Psychological *Effect* of the Prophets (The Psychology of the Prophets' *Audience*)
5. The Psychology of God (According to the Prophets)

1. The Prophets and the "Old (Biblical) Psychology."

Already in the first edition of his *System of Biblical Psychology* (1855), F. Delitzsch spoke of "the immensely wide range of psychological literature" available to him (Delitzsch, ix). He begins his work proper by writing, "Biblical psychology is no science of yesterday. It is one of the oldest sciences of the church" (Delitzsch, 3), and he traces that "science" as far back as the second and third centuries AD via a work by Melito of Sardis (d. ca. AD 180) entitled "Concerning the Soul and the Body and the Mind," and via Tertullian's (d. ca. AD 220) treatise "On the Soul." These works, like Delitzsch's own and others from this era of scholarship, study the notion of the "soul" (Gk *psychē*; cf. Heb *nepeš*) in Scripture—where it appears, what it means, how it relates to other aspects of the human being mentioned by the biblical authors (often divided by Testament [see Fletcher]), and so forth. These sorts of studies, from classical antiquity up through the early-twentieth century, might be termed the "old (biblical) psychology," since the beginning of modern psychology customarily is dated to 1879, the year when W. Wundt established a laboratory in Leipzig for experimental research (Rollins and Kille, 4). The first major breakthroughs of Freud and his colleagues and pupils followed only a few decades later (see 2 below).

In this "old" era, the concept of "biblical psychology" was closely aligned with biblical theology, on the one hand, and with the classical topics of dogmatic/systematic theology, on the other hand. So, one finds in these works treatments of the nature and states of the soul (creation, life, death) along with the doctrine of the resurrection, sometimes with extensive interaction with systematic theological works of the day (see Foster; Delitzsch; cf. Rollins, *DBInt* 2:338).

Two further aspects of research in this period should be noted. First, it was not uncommon for many writers working within this older paradigm to move quickly and easily from discussing the "soul" to discussing the specific personalities or personality traits of specific biblical personages; hence, studies of "the prophetic mind" (Kaplan 1908; 1919; cf. Scott) or "prophetic spirit" (Kurtz) are not uncommon. Second, studies of prophecy and psychology in the late nineteenth and early twentieth centuries often referenced comparable psychological phenomena in other parts of the world, whether those were of ancient or modern vintage (e.g., Delitzsch; Kaplan 1908). Both of these aspects had direct impact on the studies that followed. The study of prophetic "personalities" would be severely critiqued in historical-critical circles (see 2 below). The comparative bent, however, has been widely employed in subsequent study of the prophets, though not always with psychological interest (see, e.g., Widengren, 94-120; Lindblom; cf. Wilson 1980; Overholt 1986; 1989). Among other things, the comparative work raises large questions regarding what, if anything, is psychologically "universal" and what is or is not culturally distinctive. One must also constantly worry about cultural difference, temporal distance, and the constant threat of reductionism (Miell, 571; cf. Gunkel 1924a, 366).

2. The Prophets and the "New (Modern) Psychology."

Psychology changed forever and entered the modern period with the work of S. Freud (1856-1939) and C. Jung (1875-1961). The first psychoanalytic essay was written by Freud and J. Breuer, a Viennese internist, in 1893. Their coauthored *Studies in Hysteria* (1895) served to inaugurate the modern discipline of psychology (Mitchell and Black, 3-4). Although Freud was not the first to "discover" or mention the unconscious, he was the first to "excavate" it in such fashion and to such an extent, and his theories regarding (1) the structure of the psyche (especially id, ego, superego), (2) the therapeutic techniques of free association, transference and dream interpretation and (3) sexual development (especially the Oedipus complex) and instinctual drives (especially repetition compulsion, the pleasure principle and the death instinct) are widely known (see Mitchell and Black, 1-22).

Also well known is the early, acrimonious split between Freud and Jung. Generally speaking, Jung was far more open to the role of religion than was Freud, and so Jung's work was more easily (and directly, if not immediately) adapted by scholars in religion and the Bible (see, e.g., Povah; Rollins 1983; DBInt 2:339; Kille 2004). Jung's contributions include his work on symbolism and the collective unconscious, both of which were utilized in subsequent work on the prophets. F. Haeussermann's 1932 book, for example, notably subtitled "An Investigation of the Psychology of Prophetic Experience," discusses both the individual and collective unconscious (Haeussermann, 41-42) and is especially concerned with Yahweh's work in its different symbolic forms (die Gestalt des Symbols), including water, fire, light, snakes, mother/father, king, and so forth (Haeussermann, 28-102).

Despite Freud's aversion to many religious matters, his work also often engages religion and religious issues (notably in his "trilogy" on religion: Freud 1939, 1950; 1989 [see Rollins 1999]). Regardless, his understanding of the psyche and the instinctual drives, particularly the sexual drives, was quickly picked up by scholars of literature. This was due in part to the fact that Freud himself illustrated his work via literary characters. The Oedipus complex above all, of course, derives from Sophocles' play Oedipus Rex, but Shakespeare's Hamlet is another favorite example of the oedipal complex at work in literature (see, famously, Jones 1949 [original, 1910]; Holland, Kugler and Grimaud, 998). Freudian readings were thus received into literary-critical studies of the mid-twentieth century (Guerin et al., 152-81; Barry, 96-108), though not always appreciatively (Holland, Kugler and Grimaud, 998; Guerin et al., 153-54; Rashkow, DBInt 2:335-36), and eventu-

ally they found their way into biblical studies as well, including the study of prophecy proper (see the early work of Povah; and the later work of Halperin on Ezekiel). The same was true for Jungian approaches to literature (see Holland, Kugler and Grimaud, 1000). Notably, some of this work was done by psychologists, not biblical scholars (Fingert; Cohen; Nussbaum).

Psychology, however, is no monolithic discipline. Indeed, contemporary psychology—even just one of its branches, such as clinical psychology—is like any other field: highly fractious, marked by many different and competing schools of thought, even if there is considerable overlap and agreement among many of these (see Brueggemann 2009). In a word, then, "classical" Freudian readings and Jungian readings—whether of Hamlet or Ezekiel, however insightful these might be—are now severely dated, especially in light of the fact that today even the "Freudians" are significantly post-Freud, and Jungians are few and far between. Advances in both empirical and clinical psychology have moved the discussion far from the id, ego and superego, and far from the collective unconscious. So, again, although the work of Freud and Jung remains foundational on many levels (Freud more so than Jung), that work has been further developed and superseded by theorists and clinicians working in self, object relations and relational psychology. This listing does not include still "larger" psychological subjects, such as group- or social-psychological investigations (see Buss; Wilson 1980; Overholt 1989). Nor does it mention the fastest-growing area of psychology: brain research, including neuropsychology and cognitive science. Advances in these areas have confirmed long-held beliefs of psychology such as the existence of the unconscious (what cognitive scientists call the "cognitive unconscious") and certain aspects of learning theory (e.g., the discovery of mirror neurons, which helps to explain why we learn through imitation behavior). Another rapidly growing area, also finding major support via brain research, is in attachment theory, which studies how human infants attach to their caregivers (parents) and develop affect regulation and relational patterns that prove to be fairly consistent throughout the lifespan. Attachment theory is thus becoming an important lens through which to understand psychopathology and therapeutic efficacy. Finally, newer understandings of human motivation (e.g., moving from Freud's instinctual drives to the drive for human relations via object relations psychology) has opened new vistas for understanding religious experience as well (see Brueggemann 2009).

An obvious point that should nevertheless be stressed is that these developments in psychology indicate that psychological approaches to biblical prophecy need not be condemned because of problems with Freud (or Jung). To put it differently, many of the critiques of "prophecy and psychology" simply no longer apply because they often concern only the "new psychology" of Freud, which is now, in turn, quite old (W. Brueggemann observes that "these studies make for interesting reading, but seldom . . . do they illuminate the text," and that much in them strikes the reader as "self-indulgent and misleading" [Brueggemann 2009, 228]).

The substance of these criticisms typically came from the historical-critical tradition of biblical study. Once a book like Amos, for example, was deemed the end result of a long process of composition, editing and transmitting—with multiple, typically anonymous hands playing a part in the process—gone was the possibility of psychoanalyzing Amos. Which Amos would one psychoanalyze: the eighth-century BC prophet or his disciples and redactors? What Amos? Was there a real person by that name responsible for the book as opposed to, say, "Amos" being a nom de plume or literary creation (see Jobling 2004, 204-5)? Historical criticism's interest in the world behind the text, coupled with arguments from form, source, tradition and redaction criticism (among others), effectively eliminated most biblical personas from direct "analysis" (in the technical psychoanalytic sense). As J. Lindblom puts it, "Literary documents from so remote a time cannot yield much to the psycho-analyst" (Lindblom, 219); or as P. M. Joyce says, "It must be concluded that we can know next to nothing of Amos's own personality, let alone his psychology" (Joyce 2011, 108). The same position marked biblical theological approaches, which until recently often proceeded lockstep with historical-critical research. Biblical theology too, that is, "put psychological considerations into the background" (Barr, 171). The work of W C. Klein may be taken as exemplary. In his 1956 monograph *The Psychological Pattern of Old Testament Prophecy* he concludes that none of the main trends of then-contemporary psychology is useful in illuminating the OT prophets and vice versa—again, mostly because of historical-critical considerations such as temporal distance (but see further 3 below).

What, then, might explain the recent revival of interest in psychology and the Bible more generally, and psychology and the prophets more specifically, both of which are so contrary to this council of despair (for a major turning point, see Grant)? One factor surely is the explosion of research in psychological circles, much of it empirical, which has demonstrated the validity of this discipline and the accuracy of its insights; subsequently, psychology, along with its main tenets and conclusions, has been widely adopted both intellectually and culturally. Unfortunately, this progress in the study of psychology has taken place so quickly and its (sub)disciplines are so complex that "the application of these methods demands special qualifications which cannot reasonably be expected of a Biblical exegete" (Lindblom, 219; cf. Klein, v; Brueggemann 2009). It is not surprising, then, that most exegetes and biblical studies as a whole have proven incapable of "keeping up"; hence, knowledge of the newer trends and developments in psychology, let alone their application, has lagged significantly behind. Happily, that has begun to change due to the careful work of several scholars, most notably D. A. Kille (Kille 2001) and W. G. Rollins (Rollins 1999; see also Rollins and Kille; Ellens and Rollins).

Already mentioned earlier is a second important factor explaining the recent revival of interest in the Bible and psychology: the gradual inclusion of other, nonexclusively historical-critical approaches in biblical studies. Many of these approaches derived from the study of literature, which had both influenced early Freudian theories (see above) and quickly adopted psychological insights. Although this development is positive, when it combined with the problems besetting the first one, the unfortunate result has been a plethora of works from the side of biblical studies that are overly beholden to outmoded Freudian (and Jungian) perspectives.

Other important items relating to the rapprochement of psychology and biblical studies that should be mentioned include the close tying together of the study of literature, language and psychology as evidenced in, for instance, the work of J. Lacan, much of which views psychotherapy as a kind of textual analysis (see his "Seminar on 'The Purloined Letter,'" in Lacan, 6-48 [cf. Barry, 108-18]), or in the field of psycholinguistics. In fact, Lacan and others have argued that the unconscious is structured like a language so that literature, properly interpreted, can be used to illustrate "the major concepts of . . . psychology" (Rashkow 2000, 153 [cf. Barry, 111]). Perhaps most important is the widely held belief in the unconscious itself. If such exists—and it is the sine qua non of most modern psychology and established by recent studies in cognitive science and neuropsychology—then it is everywhere operative: now and in the past; in this culture and in every other culture; in the authors of texts, in the texts themselves, and in any and all subsequent interpreters of the texts (see Sherman; Johnson; Clines and Exum, 18; Rashkow, *DBInt* 2:335; Jobling 2004, 206; Joyce 2011, esp. 114-16). Finally, just as there is no one psychological school of thought, it is important to stress that there is no (and should be no) one psychology of the prophets. As D. K. Miell observes, "After rigorous empirical testing, psychology . . . [has been shown to] yield non-obvious and counter-intuitive insights into . . . fundamental aspects of individual and social behavior . . . [so] one would expect them to throw new light on the biblical text" (Miell, 572). We will have to reckon, then, with many different "psychologies," each of which may be productive in the study of the several different prophets, prophetic books, prophetic traditions, and so on (see Ellens and Rollins). The remainder of this article highlights a few ways that research has proceeded and how it may proceed in the future.

3. The Psychological *Affect* of the Prophets (The Psychology of the Prophets *Themselves*).

In light of the developments recounted above, gone are the days when one could confidently state that "the average prophet was tall, spare, and nervous" (Klein, 75) or remark that the prophets were "not ordinary . . . but strong enthusiastic personalities . . . of powerful passionate nature . . . young men, with blood still warm . . . men of religion, in whom faith burned, not with a cheerful homely glow, but with mighty destroying flame" (Gunkel 1924b, 25), men "in whom two things met—powerful religious excitation, which threw them into amaze, and noble religious thoughts which took entire possession of them" (Gunkel 1924b, 24) (In another place, Gunkel speaks of Jeremiah as "a man of tender nature, much too soft for his frightful vocation, suffering bitterly in having to do battle with his people, indeed, even with members of his own family" [Gunkel 2001, 118]). We must begin more generally when it comes to the psychological affect of the prophets.

Several different terms are used to describe prophets and/or prophecy in the OT, and each occurs numerous times (*rō'eh* ["seer"], *nābî'* ["prophet"], *ḥōzeh* ["visionary"], *'îš-'ĕlōhîm* ["man of God"]). Apart from a few brief references to prophets or prophecy in the Pentateuch (Gen 20:7 [of Abraham]; Ex 7:1 [of Aaron]; Ex 15:20 [of Miriam]; Deut 34:10 [of Moses]; note also Num 11:24-30 [of the seventy elders, including Eldad and Medad]; Num 12:6; Deut 13:1-5; 18:15-22), our first extensive information about prophets is provided in Samuel and Kings (cf. the mention of an anonymous prophet in Judg 6:7-10, a passage that seems out of place and is missing in 4Q49). Here we hear of several prophets by name, including Samuel (1 Sam 3:20), Gad (1 Sam 22:5) and Nathan (2 Sam 7:2), and also learn that at different points in Israel's history prophets were called by different terms ("prophet" versus "seer" [1 Sam 9:9]). Still, many of these passages are rather innocuous. To be sure, prophets can "see" things—something about the future, what will happen, which way to go, or where lost donkeys are to be located (see 1 Sam 9:6, 15-17, 20; cf. 1 Sam 9:27—10:8)—but most of these texts do not present prophets behaving "abnormally."

The narrative about the "band of prophets" (NRSV) in 1 Samuel 10 changes all that. Here we hear of a group of prophets who, when coming from a shrine and accompanied by music (which may be related to trance inducement [see Wilson 1979, 332; Gunkel 1924a, 359-60]), are said to be "in a prophetic frenzy" (1 Sam 10:5). Saul is said to be possessed by the Lord's spirit, caught up in the prophetic frenzy as well, and "turned into a different person" (1 Sam 10:6), though apparently this frenzy is short-lived (1 Sam 10:13). Those who observed it, however, wondered if Saul too was a prophet (1 Sam 10:11-12). A similar, though less positive, story is found in 1 Samuel 19:18-24 (see Wilson 1979, 334-35; Gunkel 1924a, 364).

There, three sets of Saul's servants are caught up in prophetic frenzy, which prevents them from seizing David. Finally, Saul himself is similarly incapacitated and ends up lying naked before Samuel. These two narratives, though in tension on several points (Wilson 1979, 333)—for example, with regard to the origin of the proverb "Is Saul also among the prophets?"—are fascinating because they give tantalizing glimpses into the ecstatic states that at least some prophets (or types of prophets) experienced. Moreover, although abnormality is certainly a culturally defined datum (see Van Nuys, 245; Klein, 5), both narratives indicate that the audience also viewed them as atypical in some fashion. At the very least, the texts reflect awareness that Saul's participation in prophetic activity was unusual.

Attempts to correlate types of prophetic activity (especially ecstatic frenzy) with particular terms used for the prophets have been largely unsuccessful. It does seems clear that two of the main terms used for prophets speak to their ability to "see" ($r^{\circ}h$, hzh) things. Numbers 12:6 indicates that *visions and dreams are given to prophets by God (or not given [see 1 Sam 28:6])—a point that the writing prophets confirm via the vision reports recounted there (e.g., Amos 7:1-9; 8:1-3; Ezek 1—2). Direct divine revelation via a vision or dream would count as abnormal behavior for many, if not most, modern people, and despite the widespread phenomena of ancient prophecy, the fact that most people were not prophets (cf. Num 11:29) indicates that the same probably held true for antiquity. Hosea 9:7 is especially intriguing in this regard when it states that "the prophet is a fool, the man of the spirit is mad [měšuggāʿ]" (cf. 2 Kings 9:11; Jer 29:26; see Widengren 96, 113). At this point it is instructive to note that one of the main terms for prophets in Akkadian is maḫḫû(m)/muḫḫû(m), which is derived from the verb "to rave, become frenzied, act crazy" (maḫû). It is sometimes posited that the main Hebrew verb "to prophesy" (nbʾ), which often occurs in the reflexive-reciprocal stem (Hithpael), has similar valence (see Wilson 1979, 330-36; Parker; Heschel, 505-6). This is debated, but what is incontrovertible is that the Hithpael of nbʾ is used to describe Saul's madness in 1 Samuel 18:10.

Abnormal prophetic psychology may be signaled not only by the experience of vision and dreams or by ecstatic frenzy/trance/speech (a heavily debated point [see Parker; Wilson 1979; Petersen 1981]), but also by other aspects, especially certain behaviors. The prophetic *sign acts are especially important in this regard (Friebel), and the most famous prophet, psychologically speaking, is far and away Ezekiel (Klostermann; Gunkel 1924a, 363-64; Broome; Koch, 92-93; Halperin; see also Wiener [on Elijah]; Fingert and Lacocque/Lacocque 1990 [on Jonah]). In 1877 A. Klostermann diagnosed Ezekiel as suffering from the psychiatric disorder catalepsy. E. C. Broome later argued (1946) that the cumulative effect of the data—especially the claim that Ezekiel was mute for seven years (Ezek 3:22-27; 24:25-27; 33:21-22) and the notice that he laid for 390 days on his left side and then forty days on his right side (Ezek 4:4-6)—indicated that this prophet was a paranoid schizophrenic, with periods of catatonia, hallucinations, delusions of persecution and grandeur, narcissistic-masochistic conflict and withdrawal/anxiety, some of which were directly related to certain Freudian stages (especially the oral and anal). For Broome, Ezekiel was "a true psychotic," though this was unrecognized in Ezekiel's day, and he was merely seen as an ecstatic (Broome, 291; for critique, see Cassem; for a defense, see Halperin).

This diagnosis of Ezekiel, clearly in the "old psychological" mode, was given fullest expression in a 1993 study by D. J. Halperin, who, among other things, traced the prophet's condition back to childhood sexual abuse. Few scholars have followed Halperin's lead, with many, though not all (see Jobling 1995; 2004; Smith-Christopher 1999; cf. Cassem; Heschel, 508-9), of the criticisms coming from historical-critical quarters that questioned the validity of analysis of dead individuals who, moreover, may be literary creations, to some degree, or who at least are presented in literary works as opposed to, say, direct interview, (auto)biography, and so forth (see 2 above). In the "new psychological" mode several scholars have profitably studied Ezekiel—both the prophet and especially the book (see 4 below)—in the light of trauma theory, whether that is literature about trauma and trauma survivors or the actual diagnostics of posttraumatic stress disorder (PTSD) (see Smith-Christopher 2002; Garber 2004; 2005; Bowen; cf. Morrow [on Second Isaiah]).

Several things should be noted in concluding this section on the psychological affect of the prophets themselves. First, behavior every bit as bizarre as what one finds in the OT prophets is attested elsewhere in the ancient Near East. For example, in an Akkadian letter found at Mari a prophet (*muḫḫum*) of the god Dagan is said to have devoured (*akālum*) a lamb raw in front of the city gate, adding "A devouring [*ukultum*] will take place" (Nissinen, 38). This document conjoins a strange prophetic sign act with oracular content, connected via a rhetorical device (word play), in a complex that is quite similar to what one finds in the OT. Indeed, the oracular content with literary troping indicates that even the most egregiously "abnormal" prophetic acts or words were in service to a larger communicative agenda. So, with reference to Jeremiah's and Ezekiel's sign acts, K. G. Friebel makes the case that they are intentionally chosen nonverbal behaviors designed to communicate specific messages to an audience. They are thus evidence not of the prophets' abnormality, but rather of their high skill as communicators and rhetors.

Second, although the historical-critical concerns are quite valid—the prophets are, after all, long dead and gone—one should not rule out completely the possibility of psychohistory, especially if that is carefully and appropriately done. Psychohistory (analysis of dead individuals, even literary characters, or a synthesis of the two: analysis of literary characters so as to analyze dead authors) has a long history stretching back to Freud (who analyzed Leonardo da Vinci [Freud 1961]) and continues to be practiced (A. Miller 2006; cf. Stiebert [on Ezekiel's wife]). E. H. Erikson famously analyzed Luther (Erikson 1993) and Ghandi (Erikson 1969), and others have done the same with Jesus (Capps 2000) or with important figures in religion and psychology (Capps 1997; cf. James). To be sure, not all of this work is well received, and many psychologists would disparage psychohistorical approaches by highlighting their real limitations (the critique here is not far different from the historical-critical concerns noted in 2 above). Still, psychohistorical works continue to be produced, and the biographical genre itself typically traffics in psychohistorical arenas (see Breger). Even more importantly it should be noted that, to some degree at least, the shift in recent work from the psychological

study of the prophetic individual to the prophetic book (see below and, further, 4 below) is still very much within the realm of psychohistory. It simply relocates the subject (psyche) that is being interpreted. An important point here is a neuroscientific one: the human brain has changed very little for thousands of years, which means that we can compare ancient brains, "which were not directly studied, with modern ones, which have been probed and catalogued in normal, injured, and surgical conditions" (Shantz, 108 [see further O'Shea; more generally, Joyce 2011, 112, on Troeltsch's historical principle of analogy]).

Third, even if many of the prophetic literary forms (e.g., call narrative, prophetic lawsuit) are conventional, this need not be understood as negating the psychological significance of the form in question for the prophet or the prophet's audience. The basic form-critical insight, after all, is that there is a life experience or event (*Sitz im Leben*) behind the literary form. Moreover, formal conventionality need not be indication that the form itself is not "abnormal" or unusual in some sense, at least by modern standards. Anthropological evidence indicates that even trance behavior is often quite rational and understandable by those witnessing it, and that "traditional prophetic speech forms are in reality simply manifestations of stereotypical prophetic possession behavior" (Wilson 1979, 329).

Fourth, even those who would eschew psychological analysis of specific prophetic individuals or personalities have, of late, not shied away from thinking about the psychological dynamics of the prophetic book (see, e.g., Clines and Exum, 18; Garber 2004; 2005; Bowen). Such approaches are less interested in diagnosing the prophet Ezekiel as having PTSD as they are interested in speaking of the book of Ezekiel as an example of literature that reflects the traumatic experience of *exile and is a way the exilic community coped with that trauma (see further 4 below). This is an acceptable move, but is not in the least bit a nonpsychological one. As already indicated, at most it simply shifts the subject from the psychology of the prophetic individual to the psychology of the prophetic audience/prophet's community. But this move (and the latter subjects) is no less hampered, historical-critically speaking, than the former subject (the prophetic individual) when it comes to data suitable for psychological study. That is to say that just as the prophetic individual is long dead and gone, so is the original audience and the vast majority of subsequent audiences. Or, to reverse the formulation: the data that would permit a scholar to speak of the psychology of a prophetic book could equally well be applied to the psychology of a prophetic individual, assuming that one existed. Here the point is that when critics speak of the effect of literature on a reader or (only slightly less overtly) speak of the rhetorical purpose or function of a unit, even without mention of author or receiver, they are very much making psychological statements (see Holland, Kugler and Grimaud, 997). Indeed, it could be said that "[a]ll crit[icism] is in a sense psych[ological] crit[icism], since all crit[icism] and theory proceed from assumptions about the psychology of humans who make or experience or are portrayed in lit[erature]" (Holland, Kugler and Grimaud, 997; cf. Guerin et al., 153).

Fifth, a major subtext in the discussion of the psychology of prophetic affect has been whether or not the prophet's ideas can be trusted if they stem from someone who is neurotic or psychotic (see Widengren, 119; Van Nuys; Cassem; Wilson 1979). Is the cogency of the prophet and the message affected if the prophet is, in fact, pathological? Scholars have been at pains to say no. So, for example, K. Koch contends that "at no point do Ezekiel's mental powers appear to be in any way clouded" (Koch, 92), and earlier Broome wrote that "even in paranoia . . . the patient's powers of observation, intellect, and native shrewdness are frequently unimpaired" (Broome, 290). Broome's conclusion is thus that Ezekiel's "religious significance is by no means impaired by our diagnosis of a paranoic condition, as William James convincingly argued in the case of other great spiritual leaders" (Broome, 292; see James). Such remarks are clearly reacting against those who would say that ecstasy is irrational in some way. These comments are also engaged with the legacy of, among others, G. Hölscher, who claimed that all Israelite prophets were ecstatic (see Gunkel 1924a, 358-59, 427-29; Widengren, 97). R. R. Wilson points out that scholars have responded to Hölscher in several different ways, one of which is to deny the ecstatic experience altogether (Wilson 1979). But Koch is certainly right: "Our modern rational way of looking at

things may protest as it likes: the parapsychological riddle of prophetic clairvoyance can only be eliminated from this writing [i.e., Ezekiel] at the cost of an exegetical act of violence" (Koch, 94). One must beware, in other words, of a kind of "unintentional linguistic reductionism" wherein all that biblical scholars care about is "textuality" or "rationality" at the expense of religious experience and the embodiment of knowing (Shantz, 208-9). Texts such as Jeremiah 4:19; 23:9, among many others, simply will not permit complete elimination of elements of ecstasy from at least some ancient Israelite prophecy, though all of that was of one piece and so it must be carefully nuanced or filleted appropriately (Wilson 1979; Petersen 1981). Whatever the case, K. Van Nuys is not alone in arguing that what he calls the "creative reorganization of experience" ultimately enhances the greatness of the prophets, and he notes that in modern times madness and genius often have been linked (Van Nuys, 244-46; cf. Heschel, 498-523; see also Jamison). Furthermore, the fact that abnormal affect, ecstasy, spirit-possession, trance, and so forth do not automatically translate into deviant pathology is demonstrated by both anthropological data and neuroscientific studies. The former indicate that even trance behavior is often fully controlled (rational?) and completely understandable to observers (Wilson 1979). The latter reveal that "religious ecstasy . . . is a means of coming to know as well as the source of some of the content of what is known" (Shantz, 205). The fact that the prophets were not pathological or considered to be so by others (at least not always), regardless of their often unusual affect, speech and deeds, receives further and perhaps definitive support by the obvious (psychological) effect that the prophets apparently had on their audiences—a point to which we now turn.

4. The Psychological *Effect* of the Prophets (The Psychology of the Prophets' *Audience*).

The Mari letter mentioned above includes the notice that the bizarre act of eating the lamb raw and delivering the associated oracle was not done in private, but was rather done "in the assembly of the elders" (Nissinen, 38). This information is explicitly noted for the king, the letter's addressee, indicating that the public nature of the oracle was both significant and possibly worrisome. Again, then, as already noted above, even the "abnormal" aspects of prophecy had an audience in view that was affected by things prophetic. Prophetic things, that is, had (and still do have) rhetorical force and function (Friebel; Lundbom). So, for example, after God forbids Ezekiel to *conduct* mourning rituals after the death of his wife (Ezek 24:15-17), the prophet states, "So I *spoke* to the people in the morning" (Ezek 24:18a).

There can be little doubt that audiences were often troubled by the prophetic word or deed. In Ezekiel 24, when the prophet does what he is commanded the morning after his wife's death, the people ask, "Will you not tell us what these things mean for us, that you are acting this way?" (Ezek 24:18). Here the audience appears to be disturbed. At other times, the prophets seem to have elicited anger from their audiences; at yet other times, indifference.

A possible explanation for different audience reactions also raises a crucial aspect of audience psychology: audiences enable and support (or not) prophetic activity (see Wilson 1979; 1980; Petersen 1981; Overholt 1986; 1989). As T. W. Overholt remarks, "In the case of a social process like prophecy no performance at all can take place—and, consequently, no players (in this case, prophets) can be identified—apart from a conceptual program in the collective consciousness of a society. Such a program allows a given performance to be recognized and therefore authorizes it" (Overholt, 150). So, in Ezekiel 24:18 the audience assumes that Ezekiel's bizarre behavior after the death of his wife means something *for them.* Or, in Ezekiel 8:1 (similarly Ezek 14:1; 20:1-3), before Ezekiel's vision of the desecrated *temple and the departure of God's glory, we hear that "the elders of Judah" were sitting before him, evidently waiting for prophetic insight, though probably not of the kind that they received! Authorization of a prophet allows the prophet "to be" a prophet and requires the audience to attend to the prophetic word. Nonauthorization means that the prophetic word will be ignored and/or the prophet will be viewed as irrelevant, if not, in some cases, completely insane (Wilson 1979, 333n25, 334-35, 337; cf. Heschel, xxv-xxvii).

At least two different prophetic audiences (with respective psychologies) should be distinguished. The first is the original, ancient audience (as reflected in the literature itself); the second audience, which in truth is legion, is comprised of all subsequent readers/listeners. The prophets' affect, words and deeds influence these different audiences and their psychologies differently. Part of that is the result of historical distance: ancient audiences, even if not contemporary with a particular prophet, were more accustomed to the prophetic milieu than many (though certainly not all) modern audiences, especially in the industrialized West (Wilson 1979; 1980). What is inescapable, regardless, is that psychological effects are taking place in the working of the literature itself, in both its writing and its reading: "Consciousness is continually being imagined (imaged, in-formed) by the metaphors in the very text it is writing or reading" (Holland, Kugler and Grimaud, 1000; cf. Clines and Exum, 18; Rashkow, *DBInt* 2:336; Rollins, *DBInt* 2:339).

A noteworthy development in this regard is the recent interest in what might be identified as the psychodynamics of prophetic books, as opposed to prophetic individuals. The book of Ezekiel as trauma literature has already been mentioned in this regard above (see 3 above). Such approaches often are portrayed as primarily literary-critical in orientation (Garber 2004, 222; 2005, 44; Bowen, xviii), and this seems to function as a way to evade some of the real historical problems besetting old psychological approaches if not psychohistory more broadly. While that is understandable, even laudable to some degree, we have already noted that these approaches are not, in fact, nonpsychological, and that every interpretive act is to some degree irreducibly psychological insofar as it involves the psyche of the individual interpreter. Indeed, it is somewhat ironic, as D. Jobling has noted, that the problems facing psychological approaches to the Bible are due not only to its nature as ancient literature, but also to its nature as sacred (canonical) literature, which means, among other things, that the Bible has been heavily "curated" (Jobling 2004, 204). Primacy should be given to social psychology, then, because many psyches have contributed to the composition, transmission and preservation of canonical literature. The irony is that while such curation complicates direct psychological analysis, the very canonical nature of the sacred literature simultaneously lends psychological credibility to the text at hand (Jobling 2004, 205; cf. Bowen, xix). As abnormal as Ezekiel (the prophet and the book) may be, it is apparently instructive "for us."

In the case of Ezekiel and/as trauma literature, the book becomes a way of witnessing to a trauma that cannot be fully grasped, whether by the ancient community or by subsequent ones. This testimony "helps the community reexperience the event of their catastrophe" (Garber 2004, 223). While this is a painful and difficult process, it also seems to be the case that "the only way for the audience of Ezekiel to appreciate the magnificence of the resurrection that occurs in Chapter 37 is to travel through the haunting images of death in the first twenty-four chapters, in a sense reexperiencing the trauma of Jerusalem's destruction in each reading" (Garber 2004, 228). According to Wilson, then, "Interpreters must explore the possibility that the aberrant characteristics of the book are not primarily the result of the prophet's 'abnormal' personality . . . but are themselves part of the message which the prophet and his disciples sought to deliver to concrete Israelite communities facing specific theological and social problems" (Wilson 1984, 119).

Of course the psychological effect of the prophets' words and metaphors may not always be salutary (e.g., on problematic marriage metaphors and sexual violence in the prophets, see Weems; Sherwood): the effect may be pathogenic as well as therapeutic. Either way, the precise effect of the prophets has as much, if not far more, to do with audience psychology as it does with the texts themselves ("Many texts . . . are powerfully shaped by assumptions that no one involved in the production of the text was consciously making" [Jobling 2004, 206]). In other words, to attribute possible pathogenesis to the text (or author) may be to commit the intentional fallacy and underestimate the agency of the receiving audience for good or for ill. According to Jobling, "It is meaningless to psychoanalyze some historical 'Ezekiel'; even if we managed to diagnose him we could not heal him or make him understand. Any understanding or healing that happens through our work as psychocritics of the Bible must be of *our* world, and of ourselves" (Jobling 2004, 207). To be sure, reckoning with traumatic aspects or deleterious, pathogenic outcomes may be part of any such healing process.

5. The Psychology of God (According to the Prophets).

Finally, one might ask about the psychology of *God according to the prophets. They did, after all, claim to speak for God and often did so using first-person speech forms. This would seem to have at least some bearing on the prophetic self-consciousness (Gunkel 1924a, 431-32; 1924b, 29; Scott; Heschel), but it is also the case that this was common messenger speech in antiquity. If the prophets are understood primarily as intermediaries between the divine and human realms (Petersen 2002), how does what they say for and about God relate to psychology?

This is, obviously, a large topic. Here there is space only to highlight three important points: (1) the God of the prophets is one who is prone to *wrath and judgment; (2) the God of the prophets is also one who is prone to *forgiveness and *mercy; (3) the God of the prophets is both of these things at one and the same time (at least according to the prophets' divine psychology writ large on the canonical level). What can be said about these three points, especially the interrelation of the first two, which is encapsulated in the third?

Perhaps both the first and the last thing that should be said is that the God of the prophets is, psychologically speaking, complex. The texts witness to "Yahweh's rich, unsettled interior life" (Brueggemann 1997, 328), one that cannot be simplistically reduced to either wrath or mercy. Rather, God's self, according to the prophets, is no less complex, even multiple, as are human selves. That the divine self is complex and highly variegated should come as no surprise, since we have comparable knowledge about our own selves (see Cooper-White; Gunkel comments, "What . . . [the prophets] conceive their God to be, overwhelming in His anger and in His love, they themselves are—all temperamental, at full tension" [Gunkel 1924a, 427]). Among other things, then, the complex psychology of God means that one cannot reduce the deity to just one or another quality but instead must reckon with multiple temperaments, "at full tension," and, armed with that knowledge, read prophetic theology accordingly.

The second thing that should be said is that when it comes to wrath/judgment and forgiveness/mercy, God's complex self is not equally divided in some sort of 50/50 split or paralyzed between the two options as if in a state of catatonic schizophrenia. To be sure, God's actions (and thus, inferentially, the internal divine psyche), according to the prophets (and all of Scripture for that matter), can often seem to be inconsistent if not downright capricious. But that need not be viewed as all bad: such "inconsistency" demonstrates, among other things, God's freedom to be God, and that freedom can translate into God's free extension of mercy, even to those deemed beyond the pale (so Jer 18:7-10; Jon 3:10; see Cooper; P. Miller 2004).

This is not to sugarcoat portraits of divine wrath in the prophets. God's anger and judgment are a large part of the prophetic message (Heschel, 359). Passages such as Ezekiel 5:13-17 (and they are legion) can create a "picture of God as cruel and unbending, as jealous and vindictive," leaving "the hearers of the word disturbed" (P. Miller 2004, 270)—certainly a very real and very negative psychological outcome. And yet such disturbance may have been part and parcel of the intended prophetic message, a shrewd though still troubling rhetorical device to arrest audience attention. It must be stressed again, however, that God's wrath is only one part of God's complex psyche in the prophets. Texts such as Jeremiah 9:24 (and they too are legion) highlight God's acts of "steadfast love, justice, and righteousness" because, as God says, "In these things I delight."

God's wrath and judgment must somehow be reconciled and correlated with God's concern for justice and righteousness. It appears that the former is produced by human sin—the failure to manifest justice and righteousness (cf. Is 5:1-7; Amos 5:21-24); divine judgment often is presented in direct contrast with and in equal measure to human *sin (see P. Miller 1982). This means that one must reckon not with a *Deus irae* (God of wrath) but rather with the *ira Dei* (wrath of God). God's wrath is instrumental, intended to bring about a result: *repentance and reform. In linguistic terms, God's wrath is not stative (such that God *is* angry, ontologically or dispositionally, especially not always) but rather is transitive, which means that it takes an object (God is angry *about something*). But when the object of wrath is tended to—the offending sin or circumstance removed—the wrath disappears as well (see Heschel, 358-92).

Such a "best case" portrayal of God's wrath still acknowledges anger in the divine psyche but sees it as an anthropomorphism (or anthropopathism) that is best understood vis-à-vis human wickedness. It is thus a way to account for God's wrath and punishment—a kind of theodicy, as it were (P. Miller 2004, 271-72; Heschel, 358-82). One should be careful not to overdo such a theodicy—the difficult texts are still there, and they are often ferocious—but other texts deserve equal attention if one wishes to capture the full range of the divine self in the prophets. Jeremiah 14:11, for example, seems to give the sense that "God is afraid for Jeremiah to pray for the people because the Lord knows there is an inclination within the heart of God to be moved to mercy by the prayers of the prophets" (P. Miller 2004, 274). Then there is Jeremiah 15:6, which states that God is "weary of relenting," apparently indicating "that such relenting is the operative tendency, enough so as to wear out God because circumstances, that is, the people's sin and stubbornness, bring such [divine] change of mind into play so often" (P. Miller 2004, 275-76).

In sum, then, "The wrath and judgment of God are . . . marked by considerable ambivalence and resistance on God's part" (P. Miller 2004, 276). Thus, divine wrath and judgment are never simplistic but rather are "the outcome of a complex process of divine wrestling, anguish, attempted overtures to the people, calls for repentance, warnings that keep the door open, and the like" (P. Miller 2004, 276). Note that this complexity highlights only the pole of God's wrath, and one must not forget the pole of God's mercy; but again, these poles are not perfectly balanced or divided. Rather, the prophetic texts writ large suggest that "the Lord's bent toward compassion is a part of what it means to be God, not just an option among other possibilities. . . . Reticence to wrath in favor of compassion is what it means to be the Lord" (P. Miller 2004, 276). In the words of Isaiah 54:7-8, "For a brief moment I abandoned you, but with great compassion I will gather you. In overflowing wrath for a moment I hid my face from you but with everlasting love I will have compassion on you, says the LORD, your Redeemer" (NRSV). Judgment, then, "does not come easily for the Lord of Israel," and it "is no less unsettling for God than it is for those who view [or experience] it" (P. Miller 2004, 277) (or as Heschel says, "The wrath of God is a lamentation" [Heschel, 365]). Surely these are important aspects of God's psychology according to the prophets.

Indeed, P. D. Miller argues that the very reason so much judgment prophecy is preserved in the OT is to make the case for the importance of "justice and compassion over wrath and anger, to make the point that again and again the people went their own way, did not do the will of the Lord, said no when reproved, continued in their sinful ways when specifically called to obedience by the prophets" (P. Miller 2004, 279). Ultimately, then, Miller sees God's judgment as "a part of renewing and reshaping a people for God's own way" (P. Miller 2004, 281). Even so negative an affect as anger thus has a positive, salutary effect.

Again, however, let it be stressed that the divine psychology is both complex and complicated in the prophets. Even if God's wrath is instrumental, it is nevertheless wrath and it belongs to God. But then again there is the divine mercy and love (cf. Hos 11:1-9). So, "The Lord is long-suffering, compassionate, loving, and faithful, but He is also demanding, insistent, terrible, and dangerous" (Heschel, 366), and vice versa. How these sentiments, their interrelation and correlation, can, do, will and/or should affect contemporary readers (just the latest audience with attendant psychology/psychologies) are large questions indeed. It must suffice to say that (1) these elements of the divine psychology will indeed affect readers because the reading process is psychologically charged; and (2) they will affect readers differently precisely because of different readerly psychologies. This, no doubt, is what leads so many readers to focus on only one or the other aspect of God's psyche according to the prophets. While that may be expected psychologically speaking, the texts as a whole resist such splitting off and recommend (re)integration, as difficult as that is. So, any position that writes off the difficult parts of the prophets (or the prophets as a whole precisely because they are difficult) in favor of some sort of univocal, overly simplistic and altogether syrupy sweet interpretation of God and God's ways in the world—whether that is motivated by concern for human psychological benefit or not—is seriously misguided if not, in fact, unhealthy. In the opinion of one early church writer, such a position is even heretical (see Tertullian, *Marc.* 1.25-26; cf. Heschel, 383-92).

See also SOCIAL-SCIENTIFIC APPROACHES; VISIONS, PROPHETIC; WRATH.

BIBLIOGRAPHY. **J. Barr,** *The Concept of Biblical Theology: An Old Testament Perspective* (Minneapolis: Fortress, 1999); **P. Barry,** *Beginning Theory: An Introduction to Literary and Cultural Theory* (2nd ed.; Manchester: Manchester University Press, 2002); **J. T. Beck,** *Outlines of Biblical Psychology,* trans. J. Bonar (Edinburgh: T & T Clark, 1877); **N. R. Bowen,** *Ezekiel* (AOTC; Nashville: Abingdon, 2010); **L. Breger,** *Freud: Darkness in the Midst of Vision* (New York: John Wiley & Sons, 2000); **E. C. Broome,** "Ezekiel's Abnormal Personality," *JBL* 65 (1946) 277-92; **W. Brueggemann,** *Theology of the Old Testament: Testimony, Dispute, Advocacy* (Minneapolis: Fortress, 1997); idem, "Psychological Criticism: Exploring the Self in the Text," in *Method Matters: Essays on the Interpretation of the Hebrew Bible in Honor of David L. Petersen,* ed. J. M. LeMon and K. H. Richards (SBLRBS 56; Atlanta: Society of Biblical Literature, 2009) 213-32; **A. A. Bucher,** *Bibel-Psychologie: Psychologische Zugänge zu biblischen Texten* (Stuttgart: Kohlhammer, 1992); **M. J. Buss,** "The Social Psychology of Prophecy," in *Prophecy: Essays Presented to Georg Fohrer on His Sixty-Fifth Birthday, 6 September 1980,* ed. J. A. Emerton (BZAW 150; Berlin: de Gruyter, 1980) 1-11; **D. Capps,** *Men, Religion, and Melancholia: James, Otto, Jung, and Erikson* (New Haven: Yale University Press, 1997); idem, *Jesus: A Psychological Biography* (St. Louis: Chalice, 2000); **N. H. Cassem,** "Ezekiel's Psychotic Personality: Reservations on the Use of the Couch for Biblical Authors," in *The Word in the World: Essays in Honor of Frederick L. Moriarty, S. J.,* ed. R. J. Clifford and G. W. MacRae (Cambridge, MA: Weston College Press, 1973) 59-70; **D. J. A. Clines and J. C. Exum,** "The New Literary Criticism," in *The New Literary Criticism and the Hebrew Bible,* ed. J. C. Exum and D. J. A. Clines (JSOTSup 143; Sheffield: JSOT Press, 1993) 11-25; **S. Cohen,** "The Ontogenesis of Prophetic Behavior: A Study in Creative Conscience Formation," *Psychoanalytic Review* 49 (1962) 100-122; **A. Cooper,** "In Praise of Divine Caprice: The Significance of the Book of Jonah," in *Among the Prophets: Language, Image and Structure in the Prophetic Writings,* ed. P. R. Davies and D. J. A. Clines (JSOTSup 144; Sheffield: Sheffield Academic Press, 1993) 144-63; **P. Cooper-White,** *Many Voices: Pastoral Psychotherapy in Relational and Theological Perspective*

(Minneapolis: Fortress, 2007); **F. Delitzsch,** *A System of Biblical Psychology,* trans. R. E. Wallis (2nd ed.; Edinburgh: T & T Clark, 1869); **J. H. Ellens and W. G. Rollins,** *Psychology and the Bible: A New Way to Read the Scriptures* (4 vols.; Westport, CT: Praeger, 2004); **E. H. Erikson,** *Ghandi's Truth: On the Origins of Militant Nonviolence* (New York: W. W. Norton, 1969); idem, *Young Man Luther: A Study in Psychoanalysis and History* (New York: W. W. Norton, 1993 [1958]); **H. H. Fingert,** "Psychoanalytic Study of the Minor Prophet, Jonah," *Psychoanalytic Review* 41 (1954) 55-65; **M. S. Fletcher,** *The Psychology of the New Testament* (London: Hodder & Stoughton, 1912); **J. L. Foster,** *Biblical Psychology in Four Parts* (London: Longmans, Green, 1875); **S. Freud,** *Moses and Monotheism,* trans. K. Jones (New York: Vintage, 1939 [1937]); idem, *Totem and Taboo,* trans. J. Strachey (New York: W. W. Norton, 1950 [1912-1913]); idem, *Leonardo da Vinci and a Memory of His Childhood,* trans. J. Strachey (New York: W. W. Norton, 1961 [1910]); idem, *The Future of an Illusion,* trans. J. Strachey (New York: W. W. Norton, 1989 [1927]); **K. G. Friebel,** *Jeremiah's and Ezekiel's Sign-Acts: Rhetorical Nonverbal Communication* (JSOTSup 283; Sheffield: Sheffield Academic Press, 1999); **D. G. Garber Jr.,** "Traumatizing Ezekiel, the Exilic Prophet," in *Psychology and the Bible: A New Way to Read the Scriptures, 2: From Genesis to Apocalyptic Vision,* ed. J. H. Ellens and W. G. Rollins (Westport, CT: Praeger, 2004) 215-35; idem, "Trauma, History, and Survival in Ezekiel 1-24" (Ph.D. diss., Emory University, 2005); **F. C. Grant,** "Psychological Study of the Bible," in *Religions in Antiquity: Essays in Memory of Erwin Ramsdell Goodenough,* ed. J. Neusner (SHR 14; Leiden: E. J. Brill, 1968) 107-24; **W. L. Guerin et al.,** *A Handbook of Critical Approaches to Literature* (5th ed.; New York: Oxford University Press, 2005); **H. Gunkel,** "The Secret Experiences of the Prophets," *Expositor* 1 (1924a) 356-66, 427-33; *Expositor* 2 (1924b) 23-32; idem, "The Prophets: Oral and Written," in *Water for a Thirsty Land: Israelite Literature and Religion,* ed. K. C. Hanson (Minneapolis: Fortress, 2001) 85-133; **F. Haeussermann,** *Wortempfang und Symbol in der alttestamentlichen Prophetie: Eine Untersuchung zur Psychologie des prophetischen Erlebnisses* (BZAW 58; Giessen: Töpelmann, 1932); **D. J. Halperin,** *Seeking Ezekiel: Text and Psychology* (University Park, PA: Pennsylvania State University Press, 1993); **A. J. Heschel,** *The*

Prophets (New York: Perennial, 2001 [1962]); **N. N. Holland, P. K. Kugler and M. Grimaud,** "Psychological Criticism," in *The New Princeton Encyclopedia of Poetry and Poetics,* ed. A. Preminger and T. V. G. Brogan (Princeton, NJ: Princeton University Press, 1993) 997-1002; **G. Hölscher,** *Die Profeten: Untersuchungen zur Religionsgeschichte Israels* (Leipzig: Hinrichs, 1914); **W. James,** *The Varieties of Religious Experience: A Study in Human Nature* (New York: Simon & Schuster, 2004 [1902]); **K. R. Jamison,** *Touched with Fire: Manic-Depressive Illness and the Artistic Temperament* (New York: Free Press, 1993); **D. Jobling,** review of *Seeking Ezekiel: Text and Psychology,* by David J. Halperin, *Religion* 25 (1995) 392-94; idem, "An Adequate Psychological Approach to the Book of Ezekiel," in *Psychology and the Bible: A New Way to Read the Scriptures, 2: From Genesis to Apocalyptic Vision,* ed. J. H. Ellens and W. G. Rollins (Westport, CT: Praeger, 2004) 203-13; **C. B. Johnson,** *The Psychology of Biblical Interpretation* (Grand Rapids: Zondervan, 1983); **E. Jones,** *Hamlet and Oedipus* (Garden City, NY: Doubleday, 1949), originally published as "The Oedipus-Complex as an Explanation of Hamlet's Mystery: A Study in Motive," *American Journal of Psychology* 21 (1910) 72-113; **P. M. Joyce,** "The Prophets and Psychological Interpretation," in *Prophecy and the Prophets in Ancient Israel: Proceedings of the Oxford Old Testament Seminar,* ed. J. Day (LHBOTS 531; New York: T & T Clark, 2010) 133-48; idem, "The Book of Amos and Psychological Interpretation," in *Aspects of Amos: Exegesis and Interpretation,* ed. A. Hagedorn and A. Mein (LHBOTS 536; New York: Continuum, 2011) 105-16; **J. H. Kaplan,** *Psychology of Prophecy: A Study of the Prophetic Mind as Manifested by the Ancient Hebrew Prophets* (Philadelphia: Julius H. Greenstone, 1908); idem, *The Mind of the Prophet* (Cincinnati: A. J. Eggers, 1919); **D. A. Kille,** *Psychological Biblical Criticism* (GBS; Minneapolis: Fortress, 2001); idem, "The Day of the LORD from a Jungian Perspective: Amos 5:18-20," in *Psychology and the Bible: A New Way to Read the Scriptures, 2: From Genesis to Apocalyptic Vision,* ed. J. H. Ellens and W. G. Rollins (Westport, CT: Praeger, 2004) 267-76; **W. C. Klein,** *The Psychological Pattern of Old Testament Prophecy* (Evanston, IL: Seabury-Western Theological Seminary, 1956); **A. Klostermann,** "Ezechiel: Ein Beitrag zu besserer Würdigung seiner Person und seiner Schrift," *TSK* 50 (1877) 391-439; **K. Koch,** *The*

Prophets, 2: *The Babylonian and Persian Periods*, trans. M. Knohl (Philadelphia: Fortress, 1984); **R. Kurtz,** *Zur Psychologie der vorexilischen Prophetie in Israel* (Possneck: Feigenspan, 1904); **J. Lacan,** *Écrits: The First Complete Edition in English,* trans. B. Fink (New York: W. W. Norton, 2006); **A. Lacocque and P.-E. Lacocque,** *Jonah: A Psycho-Religious Approach to the Prophet* (Columbia: University of South Carolina Press, 1990); **J. Lindblom,** *Prophecy in Ancient Israel* (Philadelphia: Fortress, 1962); **J. R. Lundbom,** *Jeremiah: A Study in Ancient Hebrew Rhetoric* (Winona Lake, IN: Eisenbrauns, 1997); **D. K. Miell,** "Psychological Interpretation," in *The SCM Dictionary of Biblical Interpretation,* ed. R. J. Coggins and J. L. Houlden (London: SCM, 1990) 671-72; **A. Miller,** *The Body Never Lies: The Lingering Effects of Hurtful Parenting,* trans. A. Jenkins (New York: W. W. Norton, 2006 [2004]); **P. D. Miller Jr.,** *Sin and Judgment in the Prophets: A Stylistic and Theological Analysis* (SBLMS 27; Chico, CA: Scholars Press, 1982); idem, "'Slow to Anger': The God of the Prophets," in *The Way of the Lord: Essays in Old Testament Theology* (FAT 39; Tübingen: Mohr Siebeck, 2004) 269-85; **S. A. Mitchell and M. J. Black,** *Freud and Beyond: A History of Modern Psychoanalytic Thought* (New York: Basic Books, 1995); **W. Morrow,** "Post-Traumatic Stress Disorder and Vicarious Atonement in the Second Isaiah," in *Psychology and the Bible: A New Way to Read the Scriptures,* 1: *From Freud to Kohut,* ed. J. H. Ellens and W. G. Rollins (Westport, CT: Praeger, 2004) 168-83; **M. Nissinen,** *Prophets and Prophecy in the Ancient Near East* (SBLWAW 12; Atlanta: Society of Biblical Literature, 2003); **K. Nussbaum,** "Abnormal Mental Phenomena in the Prophets," *Journal of Religion and Health* 13 (1974) 194-200; **M. O'Shea,** *The Brain: A Very Short Introduction* (Oxford: Oxford University Press, 2005); **T. W. Overholt,** *Prophecy in Cross-Cultural Perspective: A Sourcebook for Biblical Researchers* (SBLSBS 17; Atlanta: Scholars Press, 1986); idem, *Channels of Prophecy: The Social Dynamics of Prophetic Activity* (Minneapolis: Fortress, 1989); **S. B. Parker,** "Possession Trance and Prophecy in Pre-exilic Israel," *VT* 28 (1978) 271-85; **D. L. Petersen,** *The Roles of Israel's Prophets* (JSOTSup 17; Sheffield: JSOT Press, 1981); idem, *The Prophetic Literature: An Introduction* (Louisville: Westminster John Knox, 2002); **J. W. Povah,** *The New Psychology and the Hebrew Prophets* (London: Longmans, Green, 1925);

I. Rashkow, "Psychoanalytic Interpretation," *DBInt* 2:335-37; idem, "Lacan," in *Handbook of Postmodern Biblical Interpretation,* ed. A. K. M. Adam (St. Louis: Chalice, 2000) 151-53; **W. G. Rollins,** "Psychology and Biblical Studies," *DBInt* 2:337-41; idem, *Jung and the Bible* (Atlanta: John Knox, 1983); idem, *Soul and Psyche: The Bible in Psychological Perspective* (Minneapolis: Fortress, 1999); **W. G. Rollins and D. A. Kille,** eds., *Psychological Insight into the Bible: Texts and Readings* (Grand Rapids: Eerdmans, 2007); **R. B. Y. Scott,** "Isaiah XXI 1-10: The Inside of a Prophet's Mind," *VT* 2 (1952) 278-82; **C. Shantz,** *Paul in Ecstasy: The Neurobiology of the Apostle's Life and Thought* (Cambridge: Cambridge University Press, 2009); **M. H. Sherman,** "Biblical Commentary as a Psychoanalytic Defense," *Modern Psychoanalysis* 27 (2002) 243-61; **Y. Sherwood,** *The Prostitute and the Prophet: Hosea's Marriage in Literary-Theoretical Perspective* (JSOTSup 212; Sheffield: Sheffield Academic Press, 1996); **D. L. Smith-Christopher,** "Ezekiel on Fanon's Couch: A Postcolonial Dialogue with David Halperin's *Seeking Ezekiel,*" in *Peace and Justice Shall Embrace: Power and Theopolitics in the Bible; Essays in Honor of Millard Lind,* ed. T. Grimsrud and L. L. Johns (Telford, PA: Pandora, 1999) 108-44; idem, *A Biblical Theology of Exile* (OBT; Minneapolis: Fortress, 2002); **J. Stiebert,** *The Exile and the Prophet's Wife: Historic Events and Marginal Perspectives* (Interfaces; Collegeville, MN: Liturgical Press, 2005); **K. Van Nuys,** "Evaluating the Pathological in Prophetic Experience (Particularly in Ezekiel)," *JBR* 21 (1953) 244-51; **R. J. Weems,** *Battered Love: Marriage, Sex, and Violence in the Hebrew Prophets* (OBT; Minneapolis: Fortress, 1995); **G. Widengren,** *Literary and Psychological Aspects of the Hebrew Prophets* (UUÅ 10; Uppsala: Lundequistska Bokhandeln, 1948); **A. Wiener,** *The Prophet Elijah in the Development of Judaism: A Depth-Psychological Study* (London: Routledge & Kegan Paul, 1978); **R. R. Wilson,** "Prophecy and Ecstasy: A Reexamination," *JBL* 98 (1979) 321-37; idem, *Prophecy and Society in Ancient Israel* (Philadelphia: Fortress, 1980); idem, "Prophecy in Crisis: The Call of Ezekiel," *Int* 38 (1984): 117-30.

B. A. Strawn and B. D. Strawn

PROPHECY AND SOCIETY

Israelite society was centered on adherence to the collective obligations of kinship ties, a sense of *honor and shame that governed behavior and speech, a social and economic strategy of reciprocity, and a firm recognition of divine presence in their lives. These social principles are common to other peoples in the ancient Near East, and what set the Israelites apart from other nations was the *covenant with Yahweh and the intricate legal system (*see* Law) that developed to quantify its meaning and obligations. Social order initially was maintained through local and later through national authority figures and by the force of public opinion that overtly or subliminally served as a check on the actions of each member of the community (Crook, 598-99). The social, economic and political forces that gradually transformed Israel from a loosely affiliated group of tribes centered on extended houses and clans into a nation and then into a remnant striving to survive in the midst of international empires are chronicled in what has survived of their recorded history and in the poetic traditions of the prophets (Peckham, 1-12). To understand how these events shaped the nation, it is necessary to explore how the prophets fit into the social mix in each of Israel's historic periods, and not just focus on their message in times of crisis.

1. Historical and Social Context
2. The Role of the Prophet
3. Prophetic Message
4. Enacted Prophecy
5. References to Everyday Life
6. Conclusion

1. Historical and Social Context.

Within the social context of the world of the ancient Near East, ancient Israel developed a sense of identity based on the exodus event and reinforced by a set of legal codes keyed to the establishment of a covenant with their God, Yahweh. For most of their history, the majority of Israelites lived in small agricultural villages that governed themselves through consensus in the gate court with the assistance of their local elders (Willis, 8-13). The local system of governance was superseded to some extent by the establishment of the monarchy and the growth of its bureaucratic extensions that were designed to collect taxes from the villages, draft men into the military and co-opt others into the corvée to complete capital projects (1 Sam 8:11-18). However, it should be understood that law codes and political developments do not completely answer the question of governance,

and it should be expected that there were social expectations regarding behavior that remained uncodified while still being enforced in informal ways (McNutt, 175). The transition from tribal structure to a chiefdom occurs in the time of Saul and David and to a bureaucratic state starting with Solomon. These social transformations placed stress on Israelite society and led to the evolution of its legal and social system in order to meet these new challenges without entirely dispensing with concepts such as tribal identity and kinship and also a sense of place associated with particular regions of the country (Levinson, 3-6).

Although the monarchy helped to solidify the concept of national identity, it also removed a level of local autonomy and contributed to the process of cultural borrowing that took place as Israel and Judah became subject to the hegemony of either Egypt or the various Mesopotamian empires over the centuries. Still, the social values that had been developed during the premonarchic period and that continued to be invoked throughout the nation's history provided a continuing ideological underpinning for their community. With that in mind, this article explores how the message of the Hebrew prophets reflects both the shifting social context and the cultural ideology of ancient Israel as it evolved from the time of the monarchy into the postexilic period (*see* Israelite History).

2. The Role of the Prophet.

Belief in a covenantal relationship and service to the deity helped to shape and influence the lives of the ancient Israelites, although it must be noted that there is a distinction to be made between Israelite religion and the theology found in the received text (Hess, 16-17). There was also a basic difference in focus between the northern and southern kingdoms once the division occurred, since Jerusalem contained the *temple of Solomon and was heralded by the Deuteronomistic tradition as the site where God's name dwelled. The shrines at Dan and Bethel in the north, along with the continued use of high places, allowed for a more diverse set of religious rituals and beliefs. In both kingdoms, however, devotion to Yahweh included identification with sacred space and sacred objects, the formulation of religious practices and rituals, and the development of a corps of religious practitioners, priests and prophets. These individuals were social reflections of the people's need to interact with the divine, and they had the important role in society of serving as intermediaries and spokespersons for God. Priests functioned as officiants in local or national shrines and temples and thus were associated with maintaining the status quo as members of the elite. They performed sacrifices that were designed to recognize God's power and give thanks for the blessings of the covenant.

Prophets, in their capacity as spokespersons for Yahweh, operated independently of the cult centers, although some of them were also priests (see Prophecy, History of). There are echoes of liturgic themes and language in the message of many of the exilic and postexilic prophetic figures (esp. Ezekiel, Haggai, Malachi), but they also function as critics rather than as exponents of the cultic community (Murray, 202-3). They are associated with the centers of power (Samuel anoints both Saul and David as king), but they generally maintain their independence when it comes to their message. While some, like Nathan in David's time, served as court prophets and royal advisers, they were not bound to an official political regime or the protection of the king's position in the face of civil and covenant violations (2 Sam 12:1-15). It was this independence that gave the prophets the singular opportunity to transcend power structures and labels (see Amos 7:14) and to serve as social critics when the necessity arose. It may also explain why both men and women are called as prophets, while priests are exclusively male.

Having a distinctive role within society also raises certain expectations for these individuals. While that means speaking for the deity and occasionally interceding for the people (Amos 7:2-3), the social and political character of the times often determines the message. Shifting power structures and social realities may leave prophets on the margins of society, dependent upon the aid and goodwill of their own support groups, as with Elijah and Elisha (Wilson, 76-83), or a prophet, such as Isaiah, may be able to speak on the same social level with a king and demand a hearing, if not the compliance of the monarch (Pleins, 222-23). The problem with expectations for the power and effectiveness of the intermediary prophets is that the words spoken in the name of the De-

ity may not match the hopes or the expectations of the audience (Petersen, 93-94). As a result, the prophet may be cheered when announcing the defeat of Israel's enemies (Amos 1:3—2:5) or provide comfort and reassurance that God's wrath has an end and the nation will be restored (Is 40:1-2; Joel 3:1-3). However, prophets would receive a much chillier reception when the message reminds the people of their own covenantal failings (Hos 8:4-6; Mic 6:9-16) or exhorts them to return to compliance with the law (Jer 7:3-7).

2.1. Spokesperson for the Deity. The cultures of the ancient Near East included a class of diviners whose role was to determine through a variety of means the will of the gods (Grabbe, 119-20). In ancient Israel there are occasions when inquiries were made by casting lots (Num 27:21) or by some other mechanical means of *divination, as with Joseph's divining cup (Gen 44:5). In other instances (Judg 1:1; 20:18) the narrative suggests that some means of divination may have been employed without specifically describing the means of questioning the deity.

When it became necessary to seek divine direction without engaging in extispicy or other physical means of detection, prophets were called on to interpret dreams (Jer 23:28), pray for guidance or simply open themselves up to divinely inspired direction (Balaam in Num 22:38). This role that distinguishes them from cultic personnel or diviners dependent upon omen texts and physical examination of phenomena points to their task as divine intermediaries. Their identity as prophet would have been a recognized fact in their community (Overholt, 11). That is made clear by the very explicit method of determining who is a true prophet (Deut 18:15-22): the prophet must speak in the name of the Lord, and what the prophet says must prove to be true (see True and False Prophecy).

Still, some of the court prophets become associated too closely with the establishment and thus are more likely to promote the current administration and the status quo (note Ahab's four hundred court prophets in 1 Kings 22:6). However, not all court prophets are so quick to please their employer. Nathan, for instance, is not constrained from criticizing King David for his unjust behavior and adultery with Bathsheba (2 Sam 12:1-15).

On those occasions when prophets are consulted by high officials, the most common questions involve whether to go to war (1 Kings 22:5-8) or whether God will protect the people in a crisis (Jer 37:4-10). Because the assumption is that disease and other calamities are inflicted by God, prophets sometimes are consulted on matters of health (Elisha in 2 Kings 5:1-19). Their authority as conduits for divine response also led to questions on the authenticity of documents (Huldah in 2 Kings 22:13-20) or even of the statements made by other prophets (1 Kings 22; Jer 28).

2.2. Prophets and the Covenant. Since the ancient *covenantal relationship between Yahweh and the people of Israel is such a distinctive characteristic of the society, it is not surprising that one of the Israelite prophets plays on the people's obligation to their God and the legal stipulations and traditions of the covenant (Kapelrud, 180-81). After all, there would be no need for them to be called as prophets or for them to remind the people of their covenantal obligation if there has been no violation of its basic character. Rulers of an unjust society who are indifferent to the plight of the poor, who pervert the courts for their own gain (see Amos 4:1; 5:7, 10-11), fly in the face of the legal tradition of righteous behavior first outlined in the covenant code (Ex 22:20-26; 23:1-3, 6-9), which has as much to do with social values as it does with the *law (Mays, 66). For the prophets, it is the reality of injustice and the spirit of the law rather than specific legal injunctions that are paramount (Phillips, 221-23). The rich may well use their influence and apparently legal means to displace the poor from their land or cheat a widow in the courts, but that may still be condemned as oppression and unrighteousness (Is 1:21-23; Mic 2:1-5) (*see* Wealth and Poverty; Social Justice).

The perception that many prophets operated on the periphery of society, as "voices in the wilderness," does fit individuals such as Elijah and Elisha (1 Kings 18; 21:17-29; 2 Kings 6) (Wilson, 72-73). But their calls for religious reform (i.e., a return to Yahweh worship) and an end to the idolatrous practices of Ahab's administration still contain within them the same message found in other prophetic literature: a return to compliance with the covenant, an end to all forms of *idolatry, and a commitment to seek Yahweh alone for help in times of crises. What all of the prophets share, whether they are classic outsiders like Elijah and Micaiah or members of the cultic establishment like *Isaiah and *Ezekiel, is an effort to get those in authority or the agents of change to recognize their failings with respect to the covenant and the very principle of justice. That in turn sets up confrontations in which both prophet and powerbroker attempt to manage their own emotions and those of the people (Goffman, 110).

Furthermore, since most of the prophets speak during times of national crisis, their message tends to center on (1) a theodicy explaining why the nation was being punished by their God (see Is 5:1-7; Ezek 8); (2) a reassurance that a righteous remnant would survive to rebuild the nation and restore the people's relationship with God (Is 10:22-23; Jer 50:17-20). In responding to these crises, all of the prophets exercised their power as the monarchs' loyal opposition. Such a sociologically important role, independent of human power structures, brought them repeatedly to challenge the diplomatic policies of the state that had derailed the people's dependence on Yahweh (Lang, 63-68; Matthews and Benjamin 1993, 214). For instance, it is clear in Isaiah's approach to national identity that the very idea of nationhood is based on the sovereign covenantal relationship with Yahweh, the conditions of that compact, and the need for explicit and total loyalty to the will of God (Hanson, 217). In the process of delivering their message, the prophets also championed the cause of the weak in society and reminded the nation's leaders of their primary duty to serve and protect the people and to recognize God's role in maintaining the well-being of the nation.

Even after the monarchy ended and the people had been forced into *exile, the prophets continue to use the covenant as the basis for their exhortations. In that sense, the covenant forms a social glue or compass point that holds the people together, provides them with a form of identity, and draws them back to the promise of land and children that had brought Abraham to the promised land (Is 42:5-9; 49:8-21). Then, on their return from exile, the prophets continue to draw on earlier traditions of the covenant and its obligations to challenge the people to remain obedient to Yahweh (Mal 2:10-12) and to recognize the saving power of Yahweh (Zech 9:11-13).

3. Prophetic Message.

It is a basic axiom that no society can escape anarchy and dissolution if it chooses to ignore the established tenets of law and accepted social order. These legal principles and commonly recognized rules of social interaction develop over time and evolve to meet changing social situations and growing complexities in political structure and economic activity. In this way, things such as property rights, marriage contracts, personal honor and safety, liability issues, judicial practices and sexual norms (e.g., incest taboos) are maintained and upheld. Some, such as the determination of honorable and shameful actions, can be enforced through the court of public opinion. Others require the intervention of authority figures or their delegates. However, when a society experiences tensions, both internal and external, these basic social values and legal guarantees can break down. When that happened in ancient Israel, prophets arose to champion a return to adherence to the covenant made with Yahweh and to the law that further defined that relationship and social bond.

3.1. Social Values. Although what we know about prophets and prophetic pronouncements in ancient Israel is based solely on what has come down to us in the biblical text (Nissinen, 153-55), it is still possible to filter this material (whether it consists of the original words of the prophets themselves or of the scribal culture that edited the message into its written form) in such a way as to identify basic social values that mattered to and helped to govern social interaction in that ancient society (Wilson, 16-18). There is enough consistency in the message of each of the prophets to indicate that certain social expectations were present that resonated with the community when they were expressed by these prophetic figures, and there is no greater principle than justice in their vocabulary (see Is 1:17; Amos 5:15).

In other words, the prophets did not invent new social values or attempt to initiate a social revolution based on divine revelation. Instead, their goal, the very reason why prophets continuously appear in ancient Israel and Judah, is to defend an already existing social system, embodied in the covenant, against rampant innovation and cultural assimilation. Their very purpose is to defend the covenant between God and the "chosen people" against cultural assaults and the continuous desire to worship other gods as these two tiny nations struggled to maintain their identity amidst a maelstrom of encroaching Mesopotamian and Egyptian hegemonic overtures in the period 850-550 BC. In the course of fast-moving political events, it is clear that prophets represented continuity with previous tradition and decried unwarranted change or accommodation to the wider culture of the ancient Near East. They employed a variety of methods to convey their message in such a way as to override the temptations of assimilation and acculturation that were being voiced continuously by neighboring nations and foreign powers and call on the people to "return" (Heb *šûb*) to their devotion to the covenant (Is 31:6; Joel 2:13). Of course, a certain amount of adaptation would have been necessary among the returned community of Yehud to accommodate to life under the rule of the Persians. Once the temple is restored (515 BC), some prophets, such as Joel, speak from a cultic perspective with emphasis on the regularized cultic functions of the *temple community and *Zion theology (Cook, 189-92).

3.2. Relationship to the Law. If the assumption can be made that the Hebrew prophets represent and voice genuine aspects of their society and social context, then their message can be used to analyze and reconstruct that ancient society. As noted above, that places the prophets in the position of defending and advocating for a just society and revolves on the principles of righteous behavior and ethical leadership. In addition to the Decalogue (Ex 20:1-17) and the various law codes, one place to start in examining the essence of covenant and the law is Deuteronomy 10:12-22. In this passage the Deuteronomist exhorts the Israelites to right behavior by first noting that Yahweh is a God who (1) is "not partial and takes no bribe"; (2) "executes justice for the orphan and the widow"; (3) "loves the strangers, providing them with food and clothing" (Deut 10:17-18). They are reminded to worship Yahweh alone among the gods of the nations and to "swear by his name" (Deut 10:20).

Working with a fairly coherent, preexistent and straightforward set of legal principles and social values such as this, it becomes the task of the prophets to champion these elements of basic social ethics and to set aside those things that either mask or contradict them. For example, Amos condemns the wealthy landowners who abuse their day laborers by refusing to return their cloaks at the end of the workday and leave them to shiver through the night (Amos 2:8; cf. Ex 22:26-27). Not only does his statement echo a legal principle advocating a just society, but also it speaks to basic human compassion for the poor (see Is 3:14-15) (Mays, 68). In a similar vein, there are many instances in prophetic pronouncements in which a statement is made citing a basic social value, but in a negative context. Thus, in Isaiah 1:23 the prophet charges that "everyone loves a bribe," while that practice is prohibited in Exodus 23:8, "for a bribe blinds the officials," and Deuteronomy 16:19 notes that "a bribe blinds of the eye of the wise." Conversely, the prophet applauds those who "wave away a bribe" and uphold the basic social value of maintaining justice for all (Is 33:15).

In several cases, a prophet expands on simple statements of law and proper behavior and provides a formal bill of particulars indicting Israel for failure to comply with the terms of the covenant as outlined in a Deuteronomistic recitation of the Decalogue and the ancillary law codes and as evidence of the people's rejection of Yahweh as their God (Phillips, 229). Perhaps the most spectacular of these indictments is found in a staged performance by Jeremiah in his so-called temple sermon, delivered before the gate of the Jerusalem temple during the early reign of King Jehoiakim (c. 604 BC). Having chosen a venue (sacred space) that would give him maximum exposure for his message, Jeremiah harangues a festival day crowd with emphasis on two important points. First, he targets the belief that the physical presence of God's temple ensures that Jerusalem will never be destroyed. This myth of inviolability had been growing since the time of Hezekiah when the Assyrians had failed to capture Jerusalem. It had been reinforced by the reforms instituted by Josiah, which centralized sacrificial and festival practices in Jerusalem as the place that God had chosen "as a dwelling for his name" (Deut 14:23; 16:2; 26:2). Second, Jeremiah makes the point that only strict obedience to the covenant and to the stipulations of the Ten Commandments will prevent Yahweh's abandonment of the unfaithful people of Judah and Jerusalem to their destruction.

The framework for this message consists of two opposing slogans. Jeremiah warns the assembled crowd, "Amend your ways and your doings" (Jer 7:3, 5), if they expect God to continue to dwell in their midst. He then parodies the threefold popular liturgic chant "the temple of the LORD" (Jer 7:4). It apparently served both as a common ritual utterance and a religious slogan designed to reassure the people of Yahweh's protection. As a ritual formula, it may have been used to protect people as they entered the temple. Now as the people push forward toward the temple's entrance, Jeremiah mocks their slogan and declares that no chant will cast a protective spell over them. This building can be called the "temple of the LORD" only if the people obey the covenant and treat each other in a fair and just manner.

To reinforce his argument, Jeremiah points to the now ruined shrine at Shiloh, about twenty miles north of Jerusalem, as an example of a sacred site that has been abandoned by God. Although it had once served as the seat of Yahweh worship (1 Sam 1—4), the unfaithfulness of Eli's sons and their corruption of the cult (1 Sam 2:12-17) had given God cause to allow it to be destroyed. That charge echoes Jeremiah's indictment of the Jerusalemite cult community for abandoning Deuteronomic principles of sole adherence to Yahweh (Wilson, 246). No amount of ritual performance or sacrificial offerings could save them or that place (1 Sam 3:11-14) because, without due respect for Yahweh's covenant, it constituted "hollow" worship (Is 1:11; Amos 5:21-24).

Like Micah (Mic 6:6-8) in the previous century, Jeremiah negates the effectiveness of rote ritual behavior that also does not reinforce the desire to obey Yahweh's covenant (Jer 7:23). This declaration, that sacrifice is worthless without the abiding love (Heb *hesed*) for Yahweh and the covenant, is a familiar prophetic theme. It is also found in the tension-filled confrontation between Samuel and Saul over the king's failure to complete the *herem* (holy war) against the Amalekites (1 Sam 15:22-23) and in Hosea's poignant charge against the non-Levitical priests in Israel: "For I desire steadfast love [*hesed*] and not sacrifice, the knowledge of God rather than burnt offerings" (Hos 6:6).

For this reason, the people of Jerusalem cannot expect the temple's presence alone to save them, despite previous occasions when the city had been spared (see Is 37:1-13). It is misguided to freely violate every law and then blithely call on Yahweh's name, expecting forgiveness and protection. Jeremiah assures them that Yahweh is not blind (Jer 7:11b), and that God will abandon them just as he left the people of the northern kingdom to their fate (Jer 7:15; see also Ezek 10).

Another quite systematic example of a prophetic indictment is found in Ezekiel 22:7-12. This passage contains an extensive and comprehensive list of violations that encompass a wide range of legal pronouncements (Block 1997, 709-10). With each charge the prophet points to a contemporary practice that violates the covenant and in fact does violence to the law (Harland, 113). In so doing, he intentionally references the legal codes that are intended to buttress the relationship with their God. Some items on his list are familiar: abusing the orphan and widow, taking bribes, committing adultery and engaging in idolatry. All together, these charges represent several items found in the Decalogue as well as a number of specific injunctions contained in the Holiness Code (Lev 17–26) that deal with incest taboos. This list suggests that aspects of Israelite society had broken down, allowing previously prohibited or unthinkable acts to take place. The prophet's role as social arbiter thus comes into play as he makes it clear that a society that feeds on itself, abusing its members and preying on the innocent, cannot survive.

Of course, the idea of a world turned upside down is a common feature of ancient Near Eastern wisdom literature and is generally composed during periods of stress or political transition. Examples of this genre include the Middle Kingdom Egyptian "Tale of the Eloquent Peasant" and the eighth-century BC Babylonian dialogue between a sufferer and a friend (Matthews and Benjamin 2006, 230-44). In each case, the author decries the breakdown of social values and exhorts those in authority to take the steps necessary to restore justice and equilibrium to the community. However, Ezekiel goes so far as to say that the only way to remove the uncleanness associated with the shedding of blood and idolatry is the destruction of the coming fall of Jerusalem, that "bloody city" (Renz, 87).

4. Enacted Prophecy.

Another way in which the prophets and their message reflect Israelite society is found in the performance of enacted dramas or street theater (*see* Sign Acts). Their gestures or symbolic acts not only demonstrate how effective nonverbal communication can be, but also indicate a number of social values held by the community. Thus, Isaiah's three-year-long "naked circuit" makes it clear to his audience that they too will be stripped of their freedom, dignity and possessions if they engage in a revolt against the Assyrians (Is 20:2-4). He presents them with his own shame as a reflection of what awaits those who fail to listen to God's message and instead trust in alliances with other nations (Stiebert, 48). In a similar way, when God restricts Jeremiah's ability to engage in the normal range of human emotions (joy or sorrow), the prophet's failure to marry, have children or attend the funerals of his parents causes his neighbors to ask why and thus gives him the opening to warn them of the coming crisis for Judah and Jerusalem (Jer 16:1-13). And, when it becomes clear that the city of Jerusalem will fall to the Babylonians in 587 BC, Jeremiah takes the symbolic step of redeeming a field to keep the land in his extended family (Jer 32:1-15). In this way, the prophet uses a common economic transaction, including witnessed copies of the agreement, to demonstrate that there will be an end to the exile and a return to the land of promise. Reassurance comes from the use of the familiar even though the people are in the midst of a crisis that will transform their lives.

One more example that graphically illustrates the value of prophetic gestures is found in Ezekiel 4:4-8. Here Ezekiel engages in a pantomime or prophetic symbolic action, lying on his left side for 390 days and then on his right side for forty days to signal the number of years of the kingdoms' exile. This kind of staged event (see also the procession and execration ritual in Jer 19) functions as an extra physical prop to represent the message and to elicit questions or a reaction from the audience. Ezekiel is also instructed to prophesy against Jerusalem "with bared arm." Presumably, this means that he raised his arm above his head, which caused his robe to slip off his arm. It is also likely that he is employing a gesture of command typically used by military leaders (note God's "outstretched arm" [Deut 5:5; 7:19; 11:2; 26:8; 1 Kings 8:42; 2 Kings 17:36]) or when God's "bared arm" indicates divine action against the nations (Is 52:10).

5. References to Everyday Life.

In order to have an impact on the audience (either in the prophets' own day or in the time of the editors of their prophetic materials), prophetic speech had to contain images and metaphors that would ring true to their cultural ear. Speaking on their level about activities or items with which the audience was familiar added greater impact to the message and insured understandability. Only in the case of some of the later *apocalyptic literature is the meaning shaded in more complex imagery (see the visions in *Zechariah that require a divine interpreter). Therefore, an examination of these references, many of which are agricultural, provides an additional means of recreating ancient Israelite society.

5.1. Agricultural References. In the Mediterranean climate of the Middle East, rain in its season (Jer 5:24) brings life to the fields in spring and autumn and insures a good harvest. However, the many gods worshiped in this region that are said to bring rain or the dew provide competition to the Israelite's Yahweh. Thus, the prophets try to make the case that their God both provides the rain and can withhold it. The idyllic image in Isaiah 30:23-26 contains God's promise of the "rain for the seed with which you sow the ground." A more frightening picture is found in Amos 4:7, in which the prophet points out that God can "send rain on one city, and send no rain on another city." Similarly, Haggai uses famine and want to warn the returned exiles to note that they "have sown much and harvest little" (Hag 1:6) because God's temple has not been rebuilt.

The field and the threshing floor provide a common and quite useful setting for prophetic speech. A farmer would be quick to answer Isaiah's question, "Do those who plow for sowing plow continuously?" (Is 28:24), or Amos's sarcastic query, "Does one plow the sea with oxen?" (Amos 6:12), with an amused "No!" Having gotten their attention, the prophet could go on to make his analogy with God's teachings that prevent such useless and wasteful behavior. In a similar manner, Micah warns the disobedient Israelites that their plans that exclude giving thanks or recognition to God will leave them in a situation in which they "shall sow, but not reap" (Mic 6:15).

Once the harvest is ready and the people rejoice at the prospect of a return on their labors (Is 9:3), the prophets can use this activity to make their point. In some cases, these efforts resulted in disappointment, as in Isaiah's vineyard song, in which the grape harvest proves to be useless and sour (Is 5:1-7). Such a poor crop provided a ready metaphor for a nation that had not turned out the way God had hoped it would. Also using an agricultural allusion to describe an imminent crisis, Hosea warns the endangered people of the southern kingdom, "For you also, O Judah, a harvest is appointed" (Hos 6:11). In a later period, Joel uses the concept of harvest to envision a battle in which God will direct the armies of Israel to "put in the sickle, for the harvest is ripe" (Joel 3:13) and utterly destroy the enemy nations just as a field is cleared of its grain (Barton, 103-4).

The activity on the threshing floor creates a vivid picture for those who have spent long hours working there to process their grain. On these open sites with the aid of prevailing wind gusts, the people would deposit their harvested grain (Job 5:26) and crush the stocks of wheat and barley with sledges pulled by teams of oxen (2 Sam 24:22). Then large wooden forks were used to cast the grain into the air so that the lighter chaff will be carried away and the heavier grain could be swept up and sieved to remove stones and other objects (Is 30:24; Amos 9:9). This familiar set of steps in processing the grain and readying it for use gives fertile ground to the prophets as they exhort the people. Jeremiah, for instance, can transfer the act of winnowing into God's efforts to indicate to the people that he is displeased with their violations of the covenant. Using a dual metaphor of judgment in the gate court and separating the wheat from the useless chaff, the prophet describes how God has "winnowed them with a winnowing fork in the gates of the land," and yet "they did not turn from their ways (Jer 15:7). In contrast, Second Isaiah gives hope to a people who have experienced the exile and now look forward to taking revenge on their enemies. He assures them that God "will make of you a threshing sledge, sharp, new, and having teeth" and promises that they "shall winnow them and the wind shall carry them away" (Is 41:15-16).

Of course, produce from the fields, vineyards and fruit trees finds its way into prophetic speech as well. Amos can liken the people of Israel to "summer fruit" that looks delicious when picked and contains the promise of the last sweet taste before the fall and winter rains, but that also is quick to spoil and become rotten (Amos 8:1-2). Jeremiah's vision of the two baskets of figs gives him the occasion to once again provide a theodicy of exile by pointing out how the people are like good figs (the exiles of Judah) whom the Lord will eventually return to their land, and the bad figs (Zedekiah, his advisers, etc.), "so bad they cannot be eaten," who will become a curse and a taunt "in all the places I shall drive them" (Jer 24:1-10) (*see* Floral Imagery).

5.2. References to Tools and Occupations. While many of the people in the villages engaged in pottery making and weaving, in the towns there were specialists whose skills were worth watching. Recognizing this and playing off the desire to share in the creative process, even as spectators, Jeremiah uses the potter at his wheel as the basis for one of the best examples of the remnant theme (Jer 18:1-11). In this way, the people of Jerusalem are warned that the divine potter may well become dissatisfied with the clay in his hands and, seeing that the vessel he is shaping is spoiled, stop the wheel and begin again after mashing it down before beginning again. Using references to workers common to their society, Isaiah portrays the economic disaster that God will cause to befall Egypt, listing a variety of occupations that will be affected, including fishermen, flax workers, carders and weavers whose livelihood will be destroyed (Is 19:5-10).

Construction projects were a continuous form of activity in the villages and towns of ancient Israel. Walls had to be rebuilt or strengthened on houses and around cities. Additions were made to personal dwellings as extended families grew, and the rich were able at times to construct fine new homes (Amos 3:15) and tombs (Is 22:16). The builders' tools as well as the construction process found their way into prophetic speech and once again give us insight into everyday life in that ancient society. So we find in Zechariah 2:1 a reference to a surveyor's tool, a measuring line, which was used to measure the width and length of Jerusalem in preparation for rebuilding its walls. But the prophet enjoins the people not to proceed, because God intended to place a "wall of fire" around the city to provide divine protection. In another, more judgmental example, Amos describes God as a mason constructing a wall using a plumb line, a tool ordinarily used to keep the rows of stone straight and true (Amos 7:7-9). However, in this instance it is Israel's fidelity to the covenant that is being measured, and it is found to be off center due to Israel's idolatry and use of local high places.

In another case, Second Isaiah condemns the use of idols while providing an interesting recital of the methods in which artisans create them (Is 44:12-17). He describes the ironsmith at the forge shaping the metal with a hammer, and the carpenter who meticulously measures a piece of wood with line and stylus, while pointing out how comical it is to use a portion of the wood for the reversed idol and the rest to bake his bread. Jeremiah also creates a metaphor using a hammer ordinarily used to break up stones and likens it to the strength and effect of God's word (Jer 23:29).

5.3. References to Social Institutions. To truly plumb the depths of a society, it is necessary to explore its social institutions, such as marriage customs, inheritance laws and mourning rituals. As members of that society, the prophets recognized how important these social dimensions were and wove them into their message. Through their many references to basic social interaction and the analogies that they drew with them, we gain a better understanding of matters that are at the heart of everyday life in ancient Israel.

5.3.1. Marriage Customs. The institution of *marriage is intended to bind families together through contract and association, produce heirs for the family's estate, and perpetuate the memory-linked story of the shared experiences. The prophets understood this and used marriage customs as a way of demonstrating the nation's bond with Yahweh. Thus, it is quite easy for the prophets to describe the joy of the bride and bridegroom on their wedding day and compare it to the joy that God takes in the faithful of the nation (Is 62:5). They can also call on the exiles to maintain a sense of normalcy while in a foreign land by marrying and giving their children in marriage with the hope that they eventually will return to Israel (Jer 29:6).

Before the exile, however, marriage is used quite effectively by several of the prophets to demonstrate the breach that had formed between the people and God. Hosea's extended marriage metaphor plays on the infidelity of his wife, Gomer, as an analogy with Israel's idolatry and unfaithfulness to Yahweh (Hos 1—2). What is clear in this case is that although the husband/God had provided the expected items to sustain his wife/Israel (water, bread, wool, flax, wine, oil [Hos 2:5, 9]), she went after other lovers/gods, and he chose to publicly humiliate her and then divorce her (Hos 2:9-13). Even with such provocation, the end of the story is the effort to bring her/Israel back into the marriage/covenant by offering her the chance to renounce her lovers/gods and once again swear totally devotion to Hosea/Yahweh (Hos 2:14-23). Ezekiel uses a similar situation, although in his case the marriage is preceded by the efforts of an adoptive parent; however, the result is the same: blatant idolatry and ungrateful infidelity (Ezek 16). Such antisocial behavior cannot be countenanced, and the punishment takes the form of reciprocal action: stripping the woman of her finery and property and leaving her to be stoned and cut by the mob (Ezek 16:38-41). When, like Gomer, the wife is restored, it adds to her shame and is designed to both prevent a recurrence and demonstrate God's care for the covenant even when it is undeserved (Ezek 16:53-63). Since the prophets do employ a certain amount of poetic license in describing these exaggerated and violent actions to further demonstrating God's passion for the people and the covenant, they should not be considered a model for behavior in every marriage situation (Carroll R., 120).

5.3.2. Inheritance Laws. There is a long-standing tradition in ancient Israel that ties each family's identity as members of the covenantal community to the portion of the promised land that they will hold in perpetuity (note the systematic division of the land by Joshua following the conquest [Josh 13—21]) (Myers, 19). That is at the heart of Naboth's argument when he refuses to allow King Ahab to purchase his vineyard, proclaiming, "I will not give you my ancestral inheritance" (1 Kings 21:1-4) (Mays, 63). After allowing his wife, Jezebel, to arrange the judicial murder of Naboth and his family, Elijah confronts Ahab as the king is greedily stepping off his new property. The prophet's curse encompasses Ahab's "selling himself" (i.e., abandoning his role as the champion of the law for personal gain) and threatens him with a shameful death without burial and the extinction of his dynasty. The irony of the situation is that Ahab's family loses their own claim to rule and to their inheritance as kings when Naboth's inheritance rights are stolen from him.

Perhaps in response to the injustice done to Naboth and to other abuses by the kings, Ezekiel pronounces a series of regulations intended to prevent the exploitation of land owners while upholding inheritance rights within a family (Ezek 46:16-18) (Block 1998, 678-79). In this case, the prophet proclaims that a "prince" may divide up his estate, including lands, among his sons, and they will hold that inheritance as their possession. However, under no circumstances may the prince seize the lands of his subjects or evict them from their property (see the prohibitions against cheating neighbors in Lev 25:13-17). The object here is to prevent monarchs or rich landowners from taking advantage of the poor or intimidating them into the sale of their land and thus depriving future generations of their inheritance. Such a position once again marks the prophet as the guardian of social justice and economic fair dealing within the community.

5.3.3. Mourning Practices. Mourning often took the form of physical gestures as well as crying and moaning by the bereaved (King and Stager, 372-73). For a set period of time (Is 60:20) the mourners fasted (Joel 2:12), and they tore their clothing or replaced it with sackcloth (Jer 6:26; 41:5) while their hair was disarrayed and covered with dust and ashes (Ezek 27:30). Although some of these practices, such as the use of professional mourners (Jer 9:16-17), seem to be staged as expected behavior in their society, others are clearly a way of venting uncontrollable grief. When such deep emotions are involved, there is an opportunity to draw analogies, and the prophets took advantage to call on the people to mourn the fate of the exiles (Mic 1:16) or to acknowledge their culpability in the face of God's punishment (Jer 25:34). There is also the chance, as Joel indicates, to use a common mourning ritual and transform it into a physical gesture of repentance and self-examination: "Rend your hearts and not your clothing" (Joel 2:13).

6. Conclusion.

The prophets were a manifestation of ancient Israelite society serving as intermediaries between the people and Yahweh and defending tradition (*see* Prophecy and Tradition) against the political and economic forces that threatened righteousness and *justice. They served the purpose of voicing social criticism in the face of judicial and economic abuse of the poor and the powerless, and they continuously reminded the people of their obligations under the covenant with Yahweh. Despite physical and verbal abuse by authorities with a vested interest in silencing them (Jer 20:1-6; Amos 7:10-17) and their own self-doubts (Jer 20:7-18), they functioned as the conscience of the nation in very trying situations. While carrying out this task, they did not set themselves apart from their audience, but instead used aspects of their social world that were easily understood by the people to illustrate their message. Their efforts may have provided some comfort to those who chose to listen, and now they give us a glimpse of the society that they tried so hard to caution and preserve.

See also COVENANT; ETHICS; HONOR AND SHAME; LAW; PROPHECY AND TRADITION; SOCIAL ETHICS; SOCIAL-SCIENTIFIC APPROACHES; WEALTH AND POVERTY.

BIBLIOGRAPHY. **J. Barton,** *Joel and Obadiah* (OTL; Louisville: Westminster/John Knox, 2001); **D. I. Block,** *The Book of Ezekiel: Chapters 1-24* (NICOT; Grand Rapids: Eerdmans, 1997); idem, *The Book of Ezekiel: Chapters 25-48* (NICOT; Grand Rapids: Eerdmans, 1998). **M. D. Carroll R.** "Family in the Prophetic Literature," in *Family in the Bible: Exploring Customs, Culture, and Context,* ed. R. S. Hess and M. D. Carroll R. (Grand Rapids: Baker Academic, 2003), 100-122; **S. L. Cook,** *Prophecy and Apocalypticism: The Postexilic Social Setting* (Minneapolis: Fortress, 1995); **Z. Crook,** "Honor, Shame, and Social Status Revisited," *JBL* 128 (2009) 591-611; **E. Goffman,** *Interaction Ritual: Essays in Face-to-Face Behavior* (Garden City, NY: Anchor Books, 1967); **L. L. Grabbe,** *Priests, Prophets, Diviners, Sages: A Socio-Historical Study of Religious Specialists in Ancient Israel* (Valley Forge, PA: Trinity Press International, 1995); **P. D. Hanson,** "Covenant and Politics," in *Constituting the Community: Studies on the Polity of Ancient Israel in Honor of S. Dean McBride, Jr.,* ed. J. Strong and S. Tuell (Winona Lake, IN: Eisenbrauns, 2005) 205-233; **P. J. Harland,** "What Kind of 'Violence' in Ezekiel 22?" *ExpTim* 108.4 (1997) 111-14; **R. S. Hess,** *Israelite Religions: An Archaeological and Biblical Survey* (Grand Rapids: Baker Academic, 2007); **A. S. Kapelrud,** "The Prophets and the Covenant," in *In the Shelter of Elyon: Essays on Ancient Palestinian Life and Literature in Honor of G. W. Ahlström,* ed. W. B. Barrick and J. R. Spencer (JSOTSup 31; Sheffield: JSOT Press, 1984) 175-83; **P. J. King and L. E. Stager,** *Life in Biblical Israel* (LAI; Louisville: Westminster/John Knox, 2001); **B. Lang,** "What Is a Prophet?" in *Monotheism and the Prophetic Minority: An Essay in Biblical History and Sociology* (SWBA 1; Sheffield: Almond, 1983) 60-91; **B. M. Levinson,** *Deuteronomy and the Hermeneutics of Legal Innovation* (New York: Oxford University Press, 1997); **V. H. Matthews and D. C. Benjamin,** *Social World of Ancient Israel, 1250-587 BCE* (Peabody, MA: Hendrickson, 1993); idem, *Old Testament Parallels: Laws and Stories from the Ancient Near East* (3rd ed.; Mahwah, NJ: Paulist Press, 2006); **J. L. Mays,** "Justice: Perspectives from the Prophetic Tradition," in *Constituting the Community: Studies on the Polity of Ancient Israel in Honor of S. Dean McBride, Jr.,* ed. J. T. Strong and S. S. Tuell (Winona Lake, IN: Eisenbrauns, 2005) 57-71; **P. M. McNutt,** *Reconstructing the Society of Ancient Israel* (Louisville: Westminster/John Knox, 1999); **R. Murray,** "Prophecy and the Cult," in *Israel's Prophetic Tradition: Essays in Honour of Peter R. Ackroyd,* ed. R. Coggins et al. (Cambridge: Cambridge University Press, 1982) 200-216; **C. Myers,** "The Family in Early Israel," in *Families in Ancient Israel,* by L. G. Perdue et al. (Louisville: Westminster/John Knox, 1997) 1-47; **M. Nissinen,** "How Prophecy Became Literature," *SJOT* 19 (2005) 153-72; **T. W. Overholt,** *Prophecy in Cross-Cultural Perspective: A Sourcebook for Biblical Researchers* (SBLSBS 17; Atlanta: Scholars Press, 1986); **B. Peckham,** *History and Prophecy: The Development of Late Judean Literary Traditions* (New York: Doubleday, 1993); **D. L. Petersen,** *The Roles of Israel's Prophets* (JSOTSup 17; Sheffield: JSOT Press, 1981); **A. Phillips,** "Prophecy and Law," in *Israel's Prophetic Tradition: Essays in Honour of Peter R. Ackroyd,* ed. R. Coggins et al. (Cambridge: Cambridge University Press, 1982) 217-32; **J. D. Pleins,** *The Social Visions of the Hebrew Bible: A Theological Introduction* (Louisville: Westminster/John Knox, 2001); **T. Renz,** *The Rhetorical Function of the Book of Ezekiel* (VTSup 76; Leiden: E. J. Brill, 1999); **J. Stiebert,** *The Construction of Shame in the Hebrew Bible: The Prophetic Contribution* (JSOTSup 346; Sheffield:

Sheffield Academic Press, 2002); **T. M. Willis,** *The Elders of the City: A Study of the Elders-Laws in Deuteronomy* (SBLMS 55; Atlanta: Society of Biblical Literature, 2001); **R. R. Wilson,** *Prophecy and Society in Ancient Israel* (Philadelphia: Fortress, 1980).   V. H. Matthews

PROPHECY AND TRADITION

The relationship between the OT prophets and tradition is somewhat Janus-like, facing two ways. There is the issue of what traditions the prophets themselves inherited that may have influenced the style and presentation of their work and, to some extent, the content of their message. But there is also the tradition to which they themselves gave rise, testimony to which we have in the books bearing their names and also, occasionally, in other writings. Precision in the study of both aspects of the topic is difficult because we are given very little hard evidence of the nature of prophecy before the appearance of the eighth-century BC prophets, and although we may be fairly confident that even where individual prophets did commit their words to writing, those writings have gone through long and extensive processes of editing, additions and shaping after their time; separating original words from editorial additions is by no means an exact science.

    1. Prophetic Tradition Before the Eighth
       Century BC
    2. Eighth-Century BC Prophecy in Israel
    3. Eighth-Century BC Prophecy in Judah
    4. Seventh-Century BC Prophecy
    5. Exilic Prophecy
    6. Postexilic Prophecy

1. Prophetic Tradition Before the Eighth Century BC.

The activity of prophets is widely attested throughout the ancient Near East (*see* Ancient Near Eastern Prophecy). Prophets were attached to sanctuaries and also to the royal courts. For example, from Mari we have a prophetic declaration to a king promising him victory if he obeys the god Adad (*ANET* 625), in much the same way the Deuteronomistic History records prophets warning Judean and Israelite kings, as when, for example, Elijah threatens Ahab (1 Kings 21:20-23). Such prophets can serve the interests of those in power, as when the king of Moab hired Balaam to pronounce a curse against Israel because he had a reputation for effective "oracles" (Num 22:6). Groups of charismatic prophets like those mentioned in 1 Samuel 10:5-13; 19:18-24 may well have been attached to religious sanctuaries. Gradually, individual figures begin to emerge in the story such as Samuel, Elijah, Elisha, Nathan and Gad, remembered for their deeds (sometimes of miraculous nature [e.g., 2 Kings 4:32-37]) as well as their words, which were also often said to have effective power (e.g., 1 Kings 18:36-39). Already in the challenge of some of these individual figures to those in power we hear the ethical emphasis later associated with those prophets who have left books in their name, as in Nathan's challenge to David over his sin with Bathsheba (2 Sam 11—12). The earlier prophets used some of the literary formulae and devices to be found in the later prophetic books (e.g., Nathan's "Thus said the LORD" in 2 Sam 12:7 and his use of the literary device of the parable in 1 Sam 12:1-6).

Of course, we must remember that the picture of prophecy recorded in the Deuteronomistic History is strongly influenced by that movement's belief in God's control of history through the prophetic word. This they demonstrate by the prophet's prior announcement of what will happen and the subsequent event as that word's "fulfillment" (e.g., 1 Kings 2:27), and there are strong indications in the Prophetic Books that they have been edited in similar circles. But it seems safe to assume that the phenomenon of OT canonical prophecy did not spring suddenly from heaven, but rather inherited a continuing prophetic tradition that flourished from much earlier times.

2. Eighth-Century BC Prophecy in Israel.

*Amos, although from Judah in the south, prophesied in the northern kingdom of Israel during the reign of Jeroboam II. It was a brief period of security and prosperity, at least for some, for Amos denounces the extremely wealthy who have achieved their gains by exploiting the poor. The main tradition that he seems to have inherited is that of God's special relationship with Israel, whom he has chosen (Amos 3:2) and brought from slavery in Egypt to their present land (Amos 3:1; 9:7). Scholars nowadays are wary of speaking as confidently as once they did of a developed *covenant theology by this time (see e.g., Perlitt; Nicholson), but these individual elements of the tradition to which Amos alludes must have formed the basis of the later, more developed Deuteronomistic covenant theology. But Amos mercilessly turns these traditions on their head. His opening series of oracles against surrounding *nations (see Barton), in which he accuses them of excessive cruelty in time of war, no doubt would have brought comfort to his Israelite hearers. But such comfort was shattered by his final oracle against Israel itself (Amos 2:6-8), uttered in exactly the same form as the others with the same charge of excessive cruelty. But the enormity of Israel's sin is that in their case the cruelty was exercised against their own people. Similarly, their comforting belief that they were special because of God's favor toward them in their history is also swept away by the claim that while God had indeed brought them out of Egypt to their present *land, God had equally been involved in the movements of nations such as the Philistines and the Arameans (Amos 9:7).

But just as Amos dealt radically with the traditions that he inherited, it is clear from the book that bears his name that he himself gave rise to a tradition process. There are indications that it was finally edited in the southern kingdom of Judah. The oracle against Judah (Amos 2:2-5), clearly intrusive in its present position, suggests later tradents urging Judeans to learn the lessons that Amos taught, lessons reinforced by the subsequent conquest of Israel by Assyria. Indeed, one suspects that for later editors, the fact that what a prophet predicted came to pass guaranteed his authentic, divine commission. This certainly was the view of the Deuteronomists, who usually are thought to have had a major influence on the editing of the prophetic books (Deut 18:22). Further, the rather happier conclusion to the book in Amos 9:11-15, in strange contrast to the apparent totality of judgment threatened earlier, may well have picked up on concerns from the prophet for the oppressed poor in the community and translated them into exilic hopes for the future restoration of the Davidic monarchy and the future of "the house of Jacob" (Amos 9:8, 11-15).

*Hosea, who also prophesied in the northern kingdom of Israel in the eighth century BC, inherited similar traditions to those of Amos. He depicts God's gracious deliverance of his people from Egypt in the picture of loving parent caring for a child (Hos 11:1-4; cf. Hos 13:4-6). But he also accuses them of repeated unfaithfulness to Yahweh, although he concentrates more on their religious apostasy in adopting the rites of the Canaanite fertility religions (e.g., Hos 13:1-3). There are, however, also accusations of social and moral *sins in the manner of Amos (e.g., Hos 4:1-3, a passage that seems closely to parallel the Ten Commandments [cf. Ex 20:3-17; Deut 5:7-21]). Neither the king nor the religious leaders escape fierce criticism (e.g., Hos 4:4-6; 5:1-2; 8:4). But it is above all for their religious apostasy that the northern kingdom is threatened with a judgment that includes loss of the land whose fertility they have sought in vain from the Canaanite gods, and whose security they have sought to ensure by foreign alliances (Hos 7:11-13).

It is true that there is some ambivalence in the book about the totality and finality of judgment, with God alternately pleading with them like a lover (Hos 2:14-23), confessing that a parent cannot bear to lose a child so loved (Hos 11:8-9), while the book, as with the finally edited edition of so many of the Prophetic Books, ends with a promise of final deliverance (Hos 14:4-9), though probably this should be read as dependent upon their acting on the words of repentance that precede it (Hos 14:1-3). So, while Hosea may not be quite as total in his picture of judgment as Amos appears to be, there can be no doubt that he challenges the received traditions of the north in a thoroughly radical and subversive way.

But, again, Hosea is a prophet who seems to have left a very strong tradition process in his wake. Many scholars have pointed out the strong similarities between the theology of Hosea (and, to some extent, of Amos), with its insistence that total and undivided loyalty to Yahweh alone is the vital condition of experiencing the divine blessing, and the theology of Deuteronomy and what is known as the Deuteronomistic movement (see Nicholson). In Amos and Hosea there is not, of course, the insistence that loyal worship of Yahweh can be conducted only at the one, central sanctuary in Jerusalem that is found in Deuteronomy, for although they roundly condemn what goes on at Bethel, Gilgal and other shrines, they do so because the conduct of their devotees does not match the words of their worship, not because they are worshiping at the wrong places. Further, there can be little doubt that the close relationship between the eighth-century BC prophets and Deuteronomy is not a one-way process. As already suggested, there is no doubt that the Deuteronomists edited the final versions of the Prophetic Books. But to have influenced so significantly such an important movement in the southern kingdom of Judah is no small tribute to the tradition that these prophets inspired.

3. Eighth-Century BC Prophecy in Judah.

Scholars have long believed that the record of the ministry of "Isaiah of Jerusalem," as he has been known, is to be found mainly in *Isaiah 1—39. Isaiah 40—55 is widely held to have come from the period of the exile, while many believe Isaiah 56—66 to be postexilic. Even within Isaiah 1—39 there is usually thought to be some later material, and the usual questions about just what may have come originally from the prophet and what from later hands that face us in all the Prophetic Books are unusually acute and much debated here. What is evident is that the prophet is steeped in the traditions of the southern kingdom of Judah: Jerusalem with its sacred *temple is God's dwelling place on earth, and the Davidic dynasty is divinely appointed. He is as severe in his judgments on society in Judah, however, as Amos and Hosea were in theirs against the northern kingdom. The corruption and oppression that the people tolerate and promote make their scrupulous *worship invalid in God's eyes (Is 1:15-17). Where God had looked for the fruits of justice and righteousness in the tenderly nurtured "vine" of the nation, he found only bloodshed and the cry of the oppressed (see Is 5:1-7, where there is play between the Hebrew words mišpāṭ ["justice"] and mišpāḥ ["bloodshed"], which, similar in sound, convey wildly opposed qualities). For all this God will judge his people, although there is a strangely ambivalent note in what the threats will mean (as there was with Hosea). According to Isaiah 1:21-26, God will come in judgment against all that is corrupt in Jerusalem, and yet this judgment turns out to result in a refining process that will lead to renewal. In much the same way, Isaiah 17:12-14 pictures the onrush of the threatening floods of chaos against the city, in much the same terms as some psalms (e.g., Ps 46:1-7; 93:3-4), but then God suddenly asserts power over the

chaos waters as in the act of creation (cf. Gen 1:6-13). So Isaiah certainly is influenced by the tradition, found also in many psalms, that God dwells in Jerusalem and, at the last, will defend it against all comers. And these chapters of the book of Isaiah also reiterate the belief found in many of the royal psalms that God has chosen the Davidic dynasty, and, even if there were to be a break in the historical line of its descent, in the future it will be restored (Is 11:1-10).

There is great emphasis in these chapters on the place of *faith, in the sense of a quiet trust in God and the divine power to act and deliver his people. He calls on Ahaz to "have faith" in a time of severe national threat (Is 7:9). He denounces trust in alliances with foreign powers, calling instead for utter reliance on Yahweh (Is 30:15). Perhaps this is the link between his threats of judgment but also hope of a divinely wrought renewal of the community on the other side of that judgment. But there can be no doubt that it is this aspect of Isaiah's teaching that has influenced the tradition process that he initiated, especially with the great hopes of renewal beyond defeat and exile found in Isaiah 40—55; 56—66 and among the postexilic prophets.

*Micah's criticisms of Judean society are often very close to Isaiah's (the almost verbatim agreement of Is 2:2-4 and Mic 4:1-4 is, however, probably due to later editing). But there are close thematic similarities, as between Isaiah 5:11-12 and Micah 2:1-2. Religious and secular leaders, who should have served and promoted the people's interests, have instead been their oppressors (Mic 3:1-3). Ominously, in these verses it is the poor and oppressed who, alone, are described by God as "my people." Micah is much more devastating in his picture of judgment than Isaiah was, announcing that the holy city of Jerusalem would be totally destroyed (Mic 3:12). It was as such a prophet of judgment that Micah was remembered, and he is the only canonical OT prophet who is mentioned by name outside his book. Jeremiah 26:17-19 actually cites Micah 3:12, thus showing one thread of the tradition that the eighth-century BC prophets such as Micah instituted, as their threats provided keys for interpreting the disasters of 586 BC in terms of faith and theodicy. The greater hope for national renewal expressed at the end of the book (Mic 7:7-20) may express the hopes of that later time for restoration beyond exile, but even so, they might be based on Micah's own hopes for some purpose of God for the oppressed who are described as "my people."

Thus, taken together, the eighth-century BC prophets of Israel and Judah initiate a tradition by which later disasters could be interpreted in terms of faith and a hope in God's ultimate purpose could be maintained.

4. Seventh-Century BC Prophecy.

The book of *Jeremiah is the towering example of seventh-century BC prophecy. Much of the recorded early preaching of the prophet shows strongly the influence of Hosea, accusing the people in just the same way of religious apostasy in turning to other gods, and attacking similar kinds of social abuse and injustice that are seen to flow from that. Much of this would reflect the conditions that were said to give rise to King Josiah's reforms, described in 2 Kings 24—25, a reform organizing worship in the central sanctuary of Jerusalem made possible by the decline of Assyrian power. As we have seen, the influence of the northern prophets was also strongly evident in the emergence and development of the Deuteronomistic movement, and it is perhaps no coincidence that the book of Jeremiah in its final form shows strong Deuteronomistic influence, particularly in the prose sermons attributed to the prophet (e.g., Jer 7:1-15). We should view this process of Deuteronomistic editing and shaping as part of the process by which the words of individual prophets were remembered, treasured and reissued to show their relevance for later times. There is no need to think that the figure of Jeremiah is wholly a later, Deuteronomistic construction (with Carroll), but it does reveal the tendency of later editors to portray prophets as "preachers of Torah" (see Clements). Both the prose sermons and the poetic oracles threaten the people with destruction at the hands of a "foe from the north" (e.g., Jer 1:14-16), although the book also has strong elements of hopes of a future made possible by the divine renewal (e.g., the new covenant promise of Jer 31:31-34), but such action will take place only on the other side of the judgment that will befall in the destruction and loss of land, city, temple and kingdom.

As the complex state of recent scholarly interpretation reveals (for a summary, see Schmidt), it is probably impossible with confidence to distinguish between original words and deeds of the historical figure Jeremiah and the very strongly Deuteronomistic form in which so many different forms of literary genre are brought together in the present book (of which the differences between the two extant versions, the Hebrew and the Greek, show how open the prophetic tradition could continue to be). But, in facing the utterly transforming events of 597 and 586 BC, interpreting them in terms of faith and offering hopes of a future beyond the catastrophe, it is difficult to exaggerate the significance of the continuing tradition to which the seventh-century BC prophet Jeremiah gave rise. Nor did its influence end with the emergence of the postexilic community in Judah, as the strong influence of the book in the NT, particularly its concept of a "new covenant" (e.g., Mk 14:24), reveals.

5. Exilic Prophecy.

It is difficult to imagine what a completely devastating event the final destruction of Jerusalem at the hands of Nebuchadnezzar, king of *Babylon, must have been for the people of Judah, with the city that God had promised would last forever (e.g., Ps 48:8) destroyed, and the Davidic king, representative of a dynasty God had also said would last forever (e.g., Ps. 89:19-37), forcibly removed into exile. We know very little of the fortunes either of those taken into exile or those remaining in Judah, but two outstanding prophetic voices speak from that time.

*Ezekiel is said to have been a priest (Ezek 1:3) who was taken to Babylon among the first exiles. He seems to have been a figure of some standing, consulted more than once by the elders of the community (e.g., Ezek 8:1). The opening vision of Ezekiel 1:1—32:11 shows him also being commissioned as a prophet. The form and content of his prophecy appear strangely new, with its mysterious *visions, his apparently being transported by the *Spirit to different scenes and his strange symbolic prophetic actions (e.g., Ezek 4—5). However, there is more continuity with earlier prophetic tradition than might appear. The themes of the book's message, of judgment against Judah (Ezek 4:1—24:27) and against foreign nations (Ezek 25:1—32:32) and of hopes of a future restoration (Ezek 33:1—48:35), reveal a structure similar to other prophetic books. Ezekiel's *sign acts and his being transported by the Spirit recall the earliest of Israel's prophetic traditions of Elijah and Elisha. The prediction of the end about to come upon the land (Ezek 7:2-3) recalls Amos 8:2, while Isaiah's imagery of the smelting of Israel (Is 1:22-25) is echoed in Ezek 22:17-22. But the strongest parallels are with the book of Jeremiah (as some time ago noted by J. W. Miller). Among many that could be cited is Ezekiel's vision of the threat to Judah as "coming from the north" (Ezek 1:4; cf. Jer 1:13). Ezekiel is directed to "eat the scroll"— that is, to assimilate it fully—taking up the picture of Jeremiah 15:16, while Ezekiel 34 enlarges on Jeremiah's theme of God as Israel's shepherd (Jer 23:1-8). Thus, Ezekiel is pictured as taking up many of the themes of earlier Israelite prophecy and maintaining their continuing validity by finding in them the reasons for the historical calamity and holding out their promises for future fulfillment. These words of hope for the future also continue some of the themes found in Jeremiah, particularly that of the renewal of human hearts (Jer 31:31-34; cf. Ezek 36:26-27). Yet there are distinctive elements in Ezekiel, not least a strong emphasis on divine sovereignty. God acts, apparently, not for the sake of the people but rather for the divine reputation (e.g., Ezek 36:22-32). The verses show that this is by no means indicative of lack of divine compassion, but that God must be shown as the supreme power, authority and disposer of destiny. At a time when other nations and their gods appeared to be having things all their own way, it may be that this was an emphasis needed to bring hope to the despairing exiles. They are also encouraged by a strong reassurance that, neither as individuals nor collectively, are they bound by past actions and guilt (e.g., Ezek 18:1-32). It is not too late, nor is their condition so hopeless, as to rob their repentance of significance.

The final section of the book echoes the vision of the defiling of the *temple in Ezekiel 8—11, with its poignant picture of the departure of God's "glory" from the sanctuary (Ezek 8:18), by detailing the dimensions and details of the temple to be restored in the future and the glorious reentry of God into it (Ezek 43:1-4). This certainly was to be a tradition that was taken over by the postexilic prophets, with their encouragement to the returned exiles to rebuild the temple.

Isaiah 40—55 seems to reflect an exilic situation, and for this reason traditional critical scholarship has assigned them to an unnamed prophet, later than Isaiah, usually referred to as Second Isaiah. More recently, however, there has been much greater attention paid to the structure of the book as a whole (see, e.g., Williamson). H. G. M. Williamson argues that these chapters are an "exposition" of Isaiah 1—39. Certainly the prominence given to Zion in them reflect the strongly Jerusalem-centered themes of Isaiah 1—39, since Zion symbolizes the community whom God is going to redeem and renew (e.g., Is 51:1-3, 11). Yet these chapters also draw on other mainstream traditions, of creation (Is 40:12, 21f.) and, above all, of the *exodus tradition. Now that the people have suffered for their sins, God is going to reverse their punishment and bring them back from exile, thus effecting a second exodus in their history far transcending the first (e.g., Is 43:14-21). There is allusion also to the patriarchal traditions (e.g., Is 51:1-2) and even to the ancient creation myth of God's overcoming of the *chaos monster in order to bring about the order of *creation (e.g., Is 51:9-11), an allusion found in the creation account of Genesis 1, where the Hebrew word for the watery chaos that existed before creation, *tĕhôm* (Gen 1:2), is etymologically related to the name of the chaos monster Tiamat in the Babylonian creation story (see Day).

There is also a mention of the David tradition in these chapters (Is 55:3-5), but in a somewhat startlingly new way. Several times in the passages promising hope in Ezekiel 33:1—39:29 a restoration of the Davidic dynasty is explicitly predicted (e.g., Ezek 37:24-28). However, this is not so explicit in Ezekiel 40—48, where there is much more talk of the priestly orders, and the civil leader is, perhaps significantly, given the title of "prince" rather than "king" (e.g., Ezek 45:7-9) and is pointedly reminded not to repeat the oppression of the people as their preexilic forerunners had done. But Isaiah 55:3-5 goes further. Here, it is the whole restored community being addressed, and the covenant with David is being democratized; that is, it is no longer with him and his line alone, but with the people as a whole who will inherit the Davidic kings' role in God's purposes for the world.

So, while these chapters draw on a range of

earlier Israelite traditions, there is a creatively new element to be found as well. Not only are the destruction of Jerusalem and the exile of king and people given the already familiar interpretation of being God's judgment for the nation's sin, but also there is some attempt to give a theological meaning to the whole process, not least in the four passages that relate to God's "servant" (Is 42:1-4; 49:1-6; 50:4-9; 52:13—53:12) (*see* Servant of Yahweh). As with all poetry, they are rich in symbolic significance and can be legitimately interpreted at many levels, but the actual identification of Israel with the "servant" (Is 41:8-10) should not be ignored. The last of the passages, in particular, says that their sufferings will not have been in vain. Although these sufferings were just punishment for sin (the "innocence" of the servant in Isaiah 53 is in relation to the nations who oppressed Israel, who are the speakers here), they will be the means by which these other nations come to acknowledge God (Is 53:10-11). By virtue of God's divine *redemption and restoration of Israel, all nations will come to acknowledge that the God of Israel is the only true God, whose power extends over all nations and all creation. Such a bold, creative, even daring interpretation of the calamities of the exile is a striking tribute to the power of OT prophecy to inherit and reverence older traditions, but not to be so bound by them that it cannot create powerful, far-reaching new traditions of its own.

6. Postexilic Prophecy.

It is a remarkable testimony to the continuity and resilience of the phenomenon of prophecy in Israel that in the quite new situation of the emergence of postexilic Yehud under Persian rule, with no temple and no Davidic king on the throne, prophets emerged who both built on the great traditions of the past and renewed and reinterpreted them to inspire the faith and energize the life of the restored community. First among them was *Haggai, who addresses the conditions of physical hardship and poverty of the people and the daunting task of rebuilding that confronts them (Hag 1:4-7). He draws on the *Zion and temple traditions of the preexilic period. The temple is Yahweh's "house" and so an essential feature of the life of the community. Haggai urges them to rebuild it, whatever the cost in materials and

to other, more self-centered interests, and he assures them that when Yahweh dwells among them again, the temple will be filled with "glory" (Hag 2:7, using *kābôd*, the technical name for the glory that signifies God's presence [cf. 1 Kings 8:11]). There, God will rule again over all the earth so that the treasure of all peoples will again flow toward it, so enriching the whole community (Hag 2:4-11). This emphasis on the saving presence of God echoes both the Zion traditions (Ps 46:4-7, 9-11) and the exodus tradition (Hag 2:5; cf. Ex 13:21-22) and also takes up Ezekiel's forceful use of the same promise of God's return to the new temple (Ezek 43:4).

If a postexilic prophet such as Haggai draws so much on the Zion tradition, a legitimate question would be "How does he treat the David tradition?" The book envisages a joint leadership between Zerubbabel (a Babylonian name) as governor and Joshua as high priest. According to the Chronicler, Zerubbabel was a grandson of King Jehoiachin (1 Chron 3:17-19) and thus a descendant of the Davidic line. The two leaders are described as being empowered by God to lead in the enterprise of rebuilding the temple (Hag 1:12; 2:4-6), but a final oracle in the book (Hag 2:20-23) suggests a future, greater honor for Zerubbabel, using a term, "signet ring," used by Jeremiah of King Jehoiachin (Jer 22:24). This would suggest that some kind of messianic hope for a political restoration of the Davidic line was still held by some after the exile.

The book describes an enthusiastic response by leaders and people to the prophet's call (Hag 1:12-15) in terms that recollect the tradition of the willing response of the people to the call of Moses to build the tabernacle in the wilderness (Ex 35:29; 36:2-7). Thus, by reasserting the continuing relevance of their preexilic traditions and hopes, postexilic prophecy assures the restored community of its continuing identity as those who inherit all the earlier promises of God.

*Zechariah 1—8 contains the message of a prophet claimed by the dates given throughout to be a contemporary of Haggai. These chapters consist of a series of eight "visions of the night" (Zech 1:7—6:15), the "vision" being a form familiar from earlier prophecy, especially Ezekiel (visions form approximately one-third of the book of Ezekiel). They may suggest the idea of the prophet as "watchman," looking out for the first signs of the dawn of God's new actions (e.g., Is 21:8-9; Ezek 3:17; Hab 2:1-3). Those in Zechariah take the form of a description of the vision, the prophet's request to know its meaning, followed by an explanation given by an angel. The form may suggest that Zechariah is the divinely appointed watchman commissioned by God to report the first signs of deliverance and salvation after the exile.

The message of the visions is a renewal of the hopes for Jerusalem so strongly expressed by Isaiah 40—55 and Ezekiel. Judah has paid the price for its sins, and now God is going to restore Judah, and the city and temple will be rebuilt (Zerubbabel is specifically named as the one who will achieve this [Zech 4:9]). Thus, as with Haggai, the tradition of exilic prophecy is strongly reinforced, in both its promises and its literary forms.

There are apparently conflicting pictures of the type of rule that will be exercised. Zechariah 4:12-13 suggests a joint rule between Zerubbabel and Joshua much as Haggai does. On the other hand, in Zechariah 6:9-14, an obscure and difficult passage, it appears as though Joshua is crowned as high priest in promise of the coming of "the Branch" (a messianic term [cf. Is 11:1-5]) who "shall build the temple." Either this is from an earlier stage, before Zerubbabel's return from Babylon, or it is a recognition that any messianic hopes that attached to him were disappointed, and later tradents saw the continuing priestly line of postexilic Yehud as a guarantor that the former promises concerning a ruler of the Davidic line would be fulfilled some time in the future (see Mason 1990, 210-12).

A similar role of later tradition in the shaping of the prophetic tradition may well be found in Zechariah 7—8. In addition to reinforcing the promises of the prophet concerning God's purposes for Jerusalem and the temple to those who grow impatient with the lack of signs of it (the objection being expressed in Zech 7:1-3, and the prophet's answer in Zech 8:18-19), the prophet is portrayed as preaching the kind of general ethical teaching of the preexilic prophets on the nature of true cultic worship (Zech 7:4-7) and the need for ethical conduct (Zech 7:8-14), preaching that is backed by appeal to the tradition of the preexilic prophets (Zech 7:7, 12). In this way the tradition, while holding on to the eschatological promises of these postexilic prophets, also represents them as authentic teachers of Torah for the continuing community by which, until the promises are fulfilled, their lives are to be governed.

Zechariah 9—14, although undoubtedly later (though difficult to date with any precision), deserves to be mentioned here. Zechariah 9—14 often has been assigned more to the genre of apocalyptic than to that of prophecy, but, like all the so-called *apocalyptic sections of the OT, these chapters draw strongly on prophetic tradition, seeking to reinforce the certainty of the fulfillment of the prophetic promises, even if that fulfillment is now cast into a more distant and unspecified future. These later chapters of the book certainly draw much from the Zechariah tradition (see Mason 1976) and hence may suitably be mentioned here, but they also draw from a much wider tradition, and especially from Second Isaiah (Is 40—55). One instance must suffice. In Zechariah 9:9-10 Zion is called upon to rejoice because of the coming of its king. He is said to be "triumphant" (ṣaddîq, which basically means "righteous" but can also carry the sense of "righteousness vindicated"), "victorious" (nôšāʿ, which is a passive form of the verb "to save, deliver" but can also be translated as "bearing salvation") and "humble" (ʿānî, which can mean either "humble" or "afflicted"), and he is described as "speaking" (or "commanding") "peace" (šālôm) to the nations. All four of these attributes of the coming king are found in the royal psalms describing the reigning king of the Davidic dynasty. But, interestingly, all four also occur in the so-called Servant Songs of Isaiah 40—55 (Is 42:1-4; 49:1-6; 50:4-9; 52:13—53:12). In Isaiah 50:8 the servant says, "He who pronounces me righteous is near"; in Isaiah 49:6 God says to the servant, "I will give you as a light to the nations that my salvation may reach to the ends of the earth"; in Isaiah 53:4 it is said of the servant, "Yet we accounted him stricken, struck down by God and afflicted"; and, finally, in Isaiah 53:5 it is said, "The chastisement of our peace was upon him."

If this represents later prophetic tradition reinterpreting of older hopes of the reappearance of a Davidic king, it would also reflect another modification of tradition in Second Isaiah whereby he appears to "democratize" the historic Davidic royal dynasty as now finding its embodiment in the whole nation and mission of Israel (Is 53:3-5). Zechariah 9—14 would then endorse the earlier prophet's belief that the *sufferings Israel had endured, and from which God had already delivered them and would yet more fully and triumphantly deliver them in the future, were the price that the "servant" paid for being the means of revealing God's power and grace to the world. But, not only would that be a remarkably creative reinterpretation of received tradition; it also was to have a powerful and creative shaping force on subsequent tradition, when the Christian community found in it a means of explaining why Jesus, whom they claimed was the promised "messiah," should nevertheless have suffered humiliation and a shameful death (it is, perhaps, no coincidence that Zech 9—14 is one of the most frequently quoted Old Testament texts in the New).

A similar picture emerges in the book of *Malachi (the name means "my messenger"). It comprises a series of questions and answers between the prophet and his hearers, either as a rhetorical device or, perhaps, in echo of what some have called "the Disputation" (see Westermann, 210). Here the prophet appears very much in the role of expounder of Torah (see Law), on the nature of true *sacrifice, on mixed *marriages with those of other races, on the proper payment of tithes—all matters, it seems, that fall particularly within the role of the priest. Indeed, the priesthood is highly idealized (Mal 2:4-7), with special emphasis on his role as "teacher of Torah" in Malachi 2:6-7, the only place in the OT where the priest is called "the messenger of the LORD." Yet the book also holds out the fulfillment of the *eschatological promises of the prophets (Mal 3:1-5; 4:1-3), and those who have grown cynical about this are strongly condemned, and their fate is contrasted with those who remain faithful (Mal 3:13-18).

It is, perhaps, fitting that this last prophetic book of the OT, even while stressing the certain fulfillment of the prophetic promises for the future, should end with a reference to the past traditions on which it rested and from which it sprang. Some have suggested that Malachi 4:4-6 was intended as a conclusion to the whole prophetic section of the Hebrew canon. Certainly the reference both to Moses the lawgiver and Elijah the prophet reminds

us of the traditions on which the prophets drew, the way they were remembered and portrayed by later tradition, and the tradition that they inspired of a strongly held flame of hope for God's divine intervention in the future, a flame that neither the passing of time nor repeated delays and disappointments could ever finally extinguish.

See also COVENANT; ETHICS; EXODUS IMAGERY; INTERTEXTUALITY AND INNERBIBLICAL INTERPRETATION; ISRAEL; LAW; PROPHECY, HISTORY OF; PROPHECY AND WISDOM; SACRIFICE AND ATONEMENT; SOCIAL JUSTICE; TEMPLE; WILDERNESS, DESERT; ZION.

BIBLIOGRAPHY. J. Barton, Amos's Oracles against the Nations: A Study of Amos 1.3-2.5 (SOTSMS 6; Cambridge: Cambridge University Press, 1980); R. P. Carroll, Jeremiah (OTG; Sheffield, Sheffield Academic, 1989); R. E. Clements, Prophecy and Tradition (GPT; Oxford: Blackwell, 1975); J. Day, God's Conflict with the Dragon and the Sea: Echoes of a Canaanite Myth in the Old Testament (UCOP 35; Cambridge: Cambridge University Press, 1985); R. A. Mason, "The Use of Earlier Biblical Material in Zechariah IX-XIV: A Study in Inner Biblical Exegesis" (Ph.D. diss., University of London, 1973), published in M. J. Boda and M. H. Floyd, eds., Bringing Out the Treasure: Inner Biblical Allusion in Zechariah 9-14 (JSOTSup 370; London, Sheffield Acadamic, 2003) 1-208; idem, "The Relation of Zech. 9-14 to Proto-Zechariah," ZAW 88 (1976) 227-39; idem, Preaching the Tradition: Homily and Hermeneutics after the Exile; Based on the "Addresses" in Chronicles, the "Speeches" in the Book of Ezra and Nehemiah, and the Post-exilic Prophetic Books (Cambridge: Cambridge University Press, 1990); J. W. Miller, Das Verhältnis Jeremias und Hesekiels sprachlich und theologisch Untersucht, mit besonderer Berücksichtigung der Prosareden Jeremias (Assen: Van Gorcum, 1955); E. W. Nicholson, God and His People: Covenant and Theology in the Old Testament (Oxford: Oxford University Press, 1986); L. Perlitt, Bundestheologie im Alten Testament (WMANT 36; Neukirchen-Vluyn: Neukirchener Verlag, 1969); W. H. Schmidt, Das Buch Jeremia: Kapitel 1-20 (ATD 20; Göttingen: Vandenhoeck & Ruprecht, 2007); C. Westermann, Basic Forms of Prophetic Speech (London: Lutterworth, 1967); H. G. M. Williamson, The Book Called Isaiah: Deutero-Isaiah's Role in Composition and Redaction (Oxford: Clarendon Press, 1994).

R. A. Mason

PROPHECY AND WISDOM

Prophecy and wisdom are presented in the OT as two significant aspects of life in ancient Israel. They are depicted as both complementing one another and conflicting with one another, and are described positively only when they are founded on the *law of God. This article examines various aspects of the relationship between prophecy and wisdom.

1. Definitions
2. Wisdom and Prophecy
3. Literary Features of Wisdom and Prophecy
4. The Relationship Between Prophets and Sages
5. Conclusion

1. Definitions.

1.1. Wisdom. The broad semantic range of the Hebrew term *ḥokmâ* ("wisdom") presents some difficulties in the attempt to define wisdom precisely, let alone its relationship to prophecy (see Whybray, 181-83). The term itself refers to any form of skill: "all those skilled in some trait or profession possess wisdom of a sort: the craftsman, the potter, the builder, the farmer" (Grabbe, 162-63). Kings were given wisdom by God in order to rule (e.g., Deut 34:9; 1 Kings 3:12; 5:26; Is 11:2); others were given wisdom for specific tasks, such as the skill required by Bezalel to construct the tabernacle (Ex 31:1-5). Wisdom also appears in different guises: proverbial wisdom (as found in much of Proverbs); mantic wisdom, involving divination and largely confined to foreign sages; or speculative wisdom, such as that found in much of Ecclesiastes. So although Daniel is declared to be wise, his wisdom rests, at least in part, on direct revelation from God (Dan 2; cf. Joseph in Gen 40—41). Thus Daniel's wisdom has more in common with prophecy than it does with the speculative wisdom of Qohelet.

Further complicating the tasks of defining wisdom and understanding's relationship with prophecy is the evolution of wisdom through history. R. Whybray (195) noted, "[That] wisdom ideas or theology underwent great changes during the OT period . . . is obvious. . . . There are tremendous theological differences between the older elements in Proverbs and the later ones, between Proverbs and Job, between Job and Ecclesiastes." Beyond this, the speculative wisdom of Ecclesiastes seems to have given way to a form of wisdom that found its basis in the law by the time of Ben Sira (see Sir 24:23), and the evolution did not stop here, for later wisdom texts suggest further development (see Aitken, 181-93).

These vagaries should not, however, obscure the fact that the bulk of the biblical treatment of wisdom and its interaction with prophecy is focused on the intellectual aspects of wisdom, as noted by L. Grabbe (179): "There is a special sense in which wisdom was applied to intellectual characteristics, especially those gained or developed by formal learning, education, and study." The task of these sages is well described by J. Crenshaw (1993, 6): "The sages . . . insisted on the intellect's capacity to assure the good life by word and deed. By using their intellectual gifts the sages hoped to steer their lives safely into harbor, avoiding hazards that brought catastrophes to fools." Moreover, outside of the Wisdom literature, references to the wise frequently focus on their role as royal advisors in Israel and beyond. Thus, when considering the relationship between wisdom and prophecy, the biblical text concentrates on the intellectual stream of wisdom frequently manifest in advisors who sought to influence the course of government.

1.2. Prophecy. The literary records of prophecy preserved in the OT are somewhat more uniform than the wider phenomenon of prophecy in ancient Israel appears to have been. The existence of bands of prophets pronouncing ecstatic utterances (e.g., 1 Sam 10:9-12) and indications of the existence of institutionalized prophets (e.g., 2 Kings 6:1; Amos 7:14) reflect aspects of prophecy that are largely unrepresented among the prophetic books. Precisely how these prophets operated is not entirely clear, and because of the very limited information on them and their activities, any informed discussion of prophecy and wisdom must confine itself to the form of prophecy recorded extensively in the biblical text itself (*see* Prophecy, History of).

Consequently, for the purposes of this article, the definition of a prophet by Grabbe (107) is sufficient: "The common denominator . . . is that the prophet is a mediator who claims to receive messages direct from a divinity, by various means, and communicates these messages to recipients." It thus follows that a prophecy is the message received and transmitted by the prophet.

2. Wisdom and Prophecy.

Wisdom and prophecy are depicted both favorably and unfavorably in the OT. False prophecy is prophecy not arising from the *God of Israel; false wisdom is wisdom that is not founded in the fear of Yahweh. True prophecy reflects God's desire for his people and so reflects his will as revealed in the law. True wisdom is defined within the law as obedience to the law (see Deut 4:5-6). It is this link to the law that is the touchstone for both wisdom and prophecy, and against which they are each assessed by the biblical authors.

The fundamental difference between wisdom and prophecy lies in the nature of wisdom as a skill or the ability to live well, whereas prophecy conveys direct and specific information from God addressing a particular situation. As such, although the intellectual acumen that constitutes some examples of divinely given wisdom—that of Solomon, for instance— may be said to come from God, there is no implicit guarantee that the results of the application of wisdom also carry divine authority (see Scott, 11). Solomon is a prime example of this distinction, for in spite of the divine origin of his wisdom, he employed it to make strategic alliances through marriage and subsequently introduced *idolatry into the very center of the kingdom. Unlike the prophets, whose words often are presented as direct quotations of God's words to them, the sages' insights are their own even if the intellectual capacity for reaching their conclusions was God-given.

Consequently, the authority of the sage differs fundamentally from that of the prophet: "[That] priest and prophet were regarded as speaking with divine authority is clear. It is less certain that the same can be said of the 'counsel' of the wise man and the elders" (Scott, 3). The criticism of this distinction by B. Gemser (208-19), arguing that "counsel" ('ēṣâ) is presented as bearing equal authority to the word of the prophet (cf. Crenshaw 1971, 119), requires significant qualification. Gemser correctly notes that this counsel derives its authority from its relationship with the Torah; however, he fails to account adequately for either the evolution of wisdom through history or the frequent assertions within the OT text that the wisdom of the sages had become disconnected from the law and thus had lost its authority (cf., e.g., Is 5:21; 19:11-12; 47:10; see

Shields, 7-19). Where wisdom derives from and expounds God's revealed instruction and calls for an obedience to those instructions founded in the fear of Yahweh (see Deut 4:6), it is favorably depicted in the OT. Wisdom that ignores God's word—that of Qohelet or of Job's counselors, for instance—is condemned.

3. Literary Features of Wisdom and Prophecy.

Scholars have recognized that the various types of literature present in the OT are frequently characterized by specific literary forms (see Form Criticism). The proverb, for example, is generally recognized as a feature of wisdom. It is therefore significant to note instances where forms typically associated with one genre occur in literature of another genre. The appearance of wisdom forms in prophecy or of prophetic forms in wisdom is often construed as revealing something of the relationship between wisdom and prophecy.

3.1. Prophetic Features in Wisdom Literature.

3.1.1. Proverbs. Both Agur and King Lemuel label their sayings as *maśśāʾ* (Prov 30:1; 31:1; [traditionally, "oracle," but *HALOT* suggests "pronouncement," while others prefer "burden"]). As a description of speech, this term is elsewhere exclusively associated with prophecy (e.g., Is 13:1; 14:28; 15:1; 17:1; 19:1; 21:1, 11, 13; 22:1; 23:1; 30:6; Ezek 12:10; Nah 1:1; Hab 1:1; Zech 9:1; 12:1; Mal 1:1). In fact, so anomalous does its use in Proverbs appear to some scholars and translators that they understand the word to be a place name rather than as a claim that the words that follow are in any way akin to a prophetic pronouncement (see *HALOT*; cf. Gen 25:14; 1 Chron 1:30; Ps 120:5).

B. Waltke (81-82) claims, however, that the use of the term here affirms the inspired status of the utterances of the sages, and that the wisdom recorded in Proverbs is founded not merely on intellectual analysis of the natural and social world but rather on special divine revelation. The only other use of *maśśāʾ* in the Wisdom literature (Job 7:20) clearly does not include the notion of revelation, but the fact that Proverbs 30:1 also uses the term *nĕʾum*, which *HALOT* describes as "an almost completely fixed technical expression introducing prophetic oracles," strengthens Waltke's case.

However, there are grounds for caution before claiming too much based on the use of these terms alone. In spite of Agur's and Lemuel's use of this distinctively prophetic language to introduce their words, the form and content of those words remains distinct from the prophetic utterances elsewhere associated with these terms. Furthermore, these terms are not explicitly applied to all of Proverbs, let alone all the Wisdom literature, and if the use of these terms in Proverbs 30:1; 31:1 is intended to ascribe to the words of these sages prophetic authority, it is quite clear from the perspective of Job and Ecclesiastes that this ascription cannot be extended to all wisdom, for both these works denounce human wisdom and contrast it with direct revelation from God.

3.1.2. Job. The book of Job, which records God's direct intervention and speech to Job and his counselors, has long been recognized as reflecting some degree of prophetic influence. For example, Crenshaw (1971, 108) argued that "the continuity between Job and prophecy cannot be denied" (cf. Snaith, 33).

Job represents an interesting blurring of wisdom and prophecy, but one that ultimately undermines the wisdom presented by the human sages, Job's "friends" (cf. Job 5:13; 12:17; 38:2). Unlike Proverbs, which contains material that balances the tendency to read its wisdom as endorsing a purely retributive understanding of the world (e.g., Prov 10:2; 16:8, 19; 17:1; 19:1, 22; 22:1; 28:6), the book of Job does not resort to wisdom to counter the arguments of Job's acquaintances. Rather, the ultimate corrective to their wisdom comes in direct special revelation from God (see Job 38—42), a mode more akin to prophecy than wisdom. In thus resorting to special revelation rather than wisdom, together with the expression of wisdom's limitations (Job 28), the book highlights wisdom's inadequacies and the ultimate role that prophecy plays in understanding the world in which we live.

3.1.3. Ecclesiastes. One portion of the words of the epilogue to Ecclesiastes (Eccles 12:11-12a) is often understood to affirm the divine origin of the biblical Wisdom literature. The basis for this understanding is the apparent assertion that the words of the wise are given by the one shepherd, widely understood as a reference to God. This understanding is reflected in most modern English translations. For example, the ESV reads, "The words of the wise are like goads, and like nails firmly fixed are the collected sayings; they are given by one Shepherd. My son, beware of anything beyond these." G. Ogden (210) endorses this interpretation of the passage, stating that the epilogist, in writing these words, is "claiming that the observation-reflection method typical of the sage . . . qualifies as a method by which the divine will and purpose may be ascertained. This then gives the sage's words an authority as revelation, as scripture."

There are, however, a number of significant problems with this understanding of the epilogue to Qohelet's words (see Shields, 69-92). The identification of the "one shepherd" as God is dubious. When God is described as a shepherd elsewhere, the identification is always explicit and unambiguous, and since others are described as shepherds of the people (e.g., Ezek 34:23, which uses the phrase *rōʿeh eḥād* ["one shepherd"], found in Eccles 12:11), if the shepherd here is to be understood metaphorically, then it is not immediately clear how that identification ought to be made. Further, these words claim far more than most would be happy to affirm, for they do not restrict the assertion made regarding the words of the sages to the words of Qohelet, nor even to the canonical Wisdom literature, but simply to all the words of the wise, without qualification. Yet few would claim that all words from all sages have a divine origin.

Instead, it is better to read these words of the epilogue as a warning against the wisdom of the sages rather than an endorsement of it. As such, they can be translated thus: "The words of the wise are like goads, and like cattle-prods are [the words of] the masters of collections, those which are used by a lone shepherd. In addition to these things, my son, beware of making many texts. . . . " As a lone shepherd must employ painful goads to direct his flock, so the wise use their words to manipulate and coerce their students. Furthermore, warns the epilogue, beware of being consumed by the literary activities typical of the sages, for such tasks are pointless.

If these words do not affirm the divine origin of the wisdom of the sages, then there is little to indicate any prophetic influence in the book of Ecclesiastes. Qohelet reaches his conclusions without ever appealing to special divine revelation; indeed, it may well be that he actively repudiates any notion that such information can ever be reliably discerned and distances himself from any who would claim to have access to such information (see 4.2 below).

3.2. Wisdom in the Prophets. The prophetic books of the OT occasionally employ wisdom language and forms, as R. Scott (4) notes: "Isaiah and Jeremiah scorn the wise men of their time, yet they themselves adopt some of the language, forms, and ideas of the wisdom teachers." J. Lindblom (201-2) identifies a number of instances of wisdom forms used in prophetic literature (e.g., Is 5; 10:15; 28; Hos 7:4-5; Amos 3:3-6; 6:12), together with prophetic use of aphorisms (e.g., Jer 31:29; Ezek 18:2 [although both in reference to aphorisms that will no longer be used]; also Is 65:8; Jer 8:4; 13:12; 15:12; 23:28; 49:24; Ezek 11:3; 16:44). He further identifies rhetorical questions with a specific didactic intent that resembles wisdom utterances (e.g., Is 10:15; Jer 23:28; Ezek 15:2-8; Amos 3:3-8; 6:12; 9:7; Mal 1:6; 2:14-15, 17; 3:7-8, 13-14).

The appearance of such wisdom forms within the Prophetic Books has prompted a number of explanations from scholars. In the mid-twentieth century some such as J. Fichtner suggested that they indicated that these prophets were once numbered among the sages. Others suggest that the broad distribution of wisdom material throughout the OT can be attributed to the activities of scribal sages who were responsible for the compilation and transmission of the texts preserved as the OT, and that the wisdom forms embedded in the text can be traced, at least in some instances, to their hands. For example, R. Van Leeuwen (1993, 49) suggests that "the end-redaction of the *Tanakh* as a whole was the work of scribal sages who were forerunners of Ben Sira."

Both of these explanations are founded on uncertain presuppositions. No prophet ever claims to have been previously counted among the sages, and so to suggest that several of them were is based entirely on a speculative assessment of the significance of wisdom forms among their words (see Lindblom, 197; Van Leeuwen 1990, 297-98).

Similarly, the suggestion that wisdom language and forms can be attributed to later editorial work by scribes imposing their own agenda upon the text, though impossible to exclude in every instance, is founded on no manuscript evidence and supposes that the use of wisdom language either would have been inappropriate for the prophet or does not cohere with the work's message. Yet, if some wisdom originated in the home and so was shared in by most of the population—as seems likely, given the subject matter—then it would hardly be surprising that wisdom forms and language should be found throughout the OT. Furthermore, if the observation by M. Sato (142) that "to *propheticize* non-prophetic genres of speech, is in itself a characteristic of prophetic-inspiratory dynamism" is correct, then the presence of wisdom forms and language in the prophetic books ought to be even less in need of special explanation.

Identification of wisdom language in the Prophets is also complicated somewhat by wisdom's frequent use of examples from everyday life. In spite of the tendency of some scholars to see in such illustrations dependence of the prophet upon the wise, such connections are almost always unwarranted by the evidence, for to make such a claim ascribes to the sages a monopoly on using common language for their ends. As Crenshaw (1969, 134) says, "The mere use of wisdom phraseology by a prophet does not make him a sage, for his meaning may be completely alien to wisdom thinking" (see also Murphy, 104; Reventlow, 381-82).

3.2.1. Isaiah. Isaiah contains a number of passages that employ wisdom language and forms (e.g., Is 5:21; 29:13-16). The prominence of wisdom themes in Isaiah led Fichtner to argue that Isaiah was once a sage who had turned against the wise upon recognition that their wisdom had departed from its roots in the law (cf. Is 6:9-10). Few scholars go so far as Fichtner, recognizing the degree of speculation involved in so identifying Isaiah with the wise, but a number of scholars (e.g., Whedbee; Jensen) do nonetheless acknowledge the significance of wisdom language for Isaiah, particularly when addressing those who claim to be wise (cf. Is 10:13; 19:11-12; 44:25; 47:10).

J. Whedbee helpfully suggested some means to limit speculation as to the extent of Isaiah's dependence upon wisdom by proposing that the identification of influence ought to be restricted to those sections where there is a conjunction between wisdom form and content, pointing to the parables of Isaiah 1:2-3; 5:1-7; 28:23-28, the proverbial material in Isaiah 10:15; 29:15-16, and the "summary appraisals" in Isaiah 14:26; 28:29.

Van Leeuwen (1990, 299) argues that Isaiah's criticism of the sages reflects that of Proverbs itself: "That Isaiah used the wisdom of Proverbs to attack courtly wisdom probably means that the sages were not true to their own wisdom, or that there were conflicting factions in the court, some of which, at certain times in his lengthy career, Isaiah attacked. Unfortunately, the limited data leave uncertainty in these matters" (cf. Collins, 10). This note of caution is certainly warranted, for even the claim that Isaiah used the wisdom of Proverbs is speculative.

The presence of such material in Isaiah, however, has not convinced more careful scholars that Isaiah has been significantly influenced by the wisdom movement (see Whybray; Crenshaw). In light of the apparent ubiquity of wisdom in some form at all levels of society, it seems likely that Isaiah at least shared some degree of familiarity with wisdom and so could employ wisdom forms and language to his own ends without having to have ever himself been a sage.

3.2.2. Jeremiah and Ezekiel. Jeremiah and Ezekiel share with Isaiah their general disdain for the sages while occasionally adopting wisdom forms and language. The book of Jeremiah, in particular, recounts details of the prophet's conflict with royal advisers when seeking to guide foreign-policy response to Nebuchadnezzar (although see Jeremiah's letter to the exiles in Jer 29, at which point Zedekiah would appear to have been in agreement with his advice [see McKane 1995, 150]).

Both Jeremiah and Ezekiel employ aphorisms, perhaps most famously Ezekiel 18:2 (cf. Jer 31:29-30): "Fathers have eaten sour grapes, but the teeth of the sons have been dulled." This aphorism bears all the hallmarks of a wisdom saying, but it is quoted by the prophets to refute its teaching, for they wish to make the opposite point. Jeremiah goes so far as to offer an amended version of the proverb: "Every person who eats the sour grapes, his teeth will be dulled" (Jer 31:30). Thus, although both Jeremiah and Ezekiel employ wisdom language, they self-consciously do so in order to undermine the sages. We will examine this conflict in more detail later (see 4.1 below).

3.2.3. Hosea. The extent of Hosea's acquaintance with wisdom is not entirely clear. Hosea does draw on the natural world for some metaphors (cf. Hos 9:10, 13, 16; 10:1; 14:6; 4:16; 8:7;

10:4; see Macintosh, 129), as the sages also frequently did, but this alone is not sufficient basis for claiming any significant interaction with the sages on Hosea's part. Likewise, although his use of aphorisms does suggest at least some passing familiarity with wisdom, given the likely ubiquity of wisdom in some of its forms, this cannot be construed as indicative of any special connection to more formal wisdom or the sages who promoted it (Macintosh, 125).

Nonetheless, the final verse of Hosea does stand out for its appeal to wisdom: "Whoever is wise, let him discern these things. Whoever is discerning, let him know them. For the ways of Yahweh are straight, and the righteous walk in them, but those who are disloyal stumble in them" (Hos 14:9). Van Leeuwen (1993, 36-39) sees this final verse as evidence of the activity of a scribal redactor shaping the Book of the Twelve to function as a theodicy and overlaying the prophetic material with a decidedly wisdom agenda. However, the appeal made in this verse is not wholly foreign to Hosea, who has referred to those without wisdom (Hos 13:13) and to those without understanding (Hos 4:14). As such, this closing appeal, although clearly couched in wisdom terms, reflects the prophet's own concerns and need not be read as evidence of later redaction.

3.2.4. Amos. Numerous features of Amos have prompted scholars to identify links with wisdom of one form or another: his use of sayings introduced by sequential cardinal numbers (Amos 1—2 [see Lindblom, 202; although, the connection of these with wisdom has been refuted by Soggin, 120-21]), theological emphases, special vocabulary and rhetorical devices (such as the "woe" sayings). Although these have prompted some to speculate about Amos's links to the sages, these do not make a compelling case for any close association, as J. Soggin (120) has noted: "[A] biblical author . . . writes in his own style, and uses particular devices for expressing himself. In our case, these could incidentally have been borrowed from wisdom. But such a stylistic analogy does not turn a writing into a text dependent upon wisdom" (cf. Crenshaw 1969, 134; Whybray, 188).

3.2.5. Jonah, Habakkuk, Malachi. Any unequivocal connection with wisdom in the remaining Minor Prophets is difficult to establish. Some have suggested that Jonah and Habakkuk are in some way connected with wisdom because both are understood to address the problem of theodicy on some level (see Crenshaw 1998, 29; Gowan). Furthermore, some scholars suggest that Jonah is a *māšāl* ("proverb" [although, the Hebrew term describes a more diverse range of literary forms than does the English "proverb," including "parable"]) and as such is of a form more at home among the sages than the prophets (Landes; Crenshaw 1998, 29). The appearance of disputations, particularly in Malachi, has prompted some to suggest wisdom influence also in that book. Yet the appeals to such features overlook the significant differences between the prophetic use of disputation and those found elsewhere (see Crenshaw 1969, 134). In the end, it is difficult to claim any more than a conscious borrowing of wisdom language and forms by the prophets, who turned these facets of wisdom to their own ends and employed them in the service of their own prophetic, not sagacious, message.

4. The Relationship Between Prophets and Sages.

Any discussion of the nature of the relationship between sages and prophets turns not only on the definition of wisdom and prophecy but also on the identity of the sages and prophets themselves. Whybray, for example, has argued that there never was, in ancient Israel, a class of specialists known as "the wise," and so the notion of conflict between prophets and the wise "falls to the ground" (Whybray, 193). Most scholars, however, think that Whybray goes too far in totally rejecting the existence of an identifiable class of wisdom professionals (e.g., Blenkinsopp, 11; Shields, 43-45).

There is evidence that both prophets and sages occupied positions in the royal courts of Israel and other nations, testifying to their "specialist" status (e.g., 2 Sam 24:11; cf. 2 Sam 16:23). Aside from official court positions, there are also reports of prophets seeking to influence the decisions made by the king. As such, they would have found themselves competing with royal counselors whose advice would have been founded more on principles of wisdom than immediate divine revelation (see 2 Chron 25:14-24; and perhaps the ultimate example is 1 Kings 11:29-39, where the prophet Ahijah opposes Solomon himself).

In light of the competing interest of prophets and sages in the royal court, it is unsurprising to find indications throughout the OT of enmity between the two groups. W. McKane (1965, 48), for one, concluded that "there was constant tension between [prophets and sages] since the wise men did not permit themselves the luxury of religious or ethical assumptions, their task being to advise the king on matters of statecraft."

4.1. Prophets' Attitudes Toward the Sages. The prophets whose words have been recorded in the OT clearly did not have high regard for the sages. Van Leeuwen (1990, 306) notes that "the sages (*ḥkmym*) explicitly mentioned in the prophetic texts are almost always opponents of the prophets. Such wise men, as domestic or foreign royal courtiers, stand opposed to the prophets with regard to justice and political guidance. These sages are not false per se but only as they forget the human limits of wisdom (according to the criteria from Proverbs) and defy the word of Yahweh's messengers" (cf. Scott, 3; McKane 1995, 142; 1965, 65-91; Dunn, 7).

Although it has been common to identify this conflict as arising out of the distinction between "sacred" prophecy and "secular" wisdom (e.g., McKane 1965), the reality appears somewhat more nuanced than is reflected in this disjunction. Wisdom cannot be depicted in monolithic terms, and the criticisms leveled against the sages by the prophets reflect warnings already present within the book of Proverbs (see Van Leeuwen 1990, 300). As such, the prophets are critical of those who deviate from the law, including priests and other prophets, not merely those who employed a form of wisdom that neglected God's revealed will. So their condemnation is not reserved merely for the royal advisers but rather is directed at all in leadership roles who would flout God's law.

4.1.1. Isaiah. Isaiah's antagonism toward the wise is readily apparent in many passages (e.g., Is 5:21; 19:11-12; 29:14; 40:20; 44:25; 47:10). Of these, Isaiah 19:11-12 is particularly significant because of the explicit link that it makes between wisdom and the counselors who functioned in the royal court: "The princes of Zoan are nothing but fools; the wisdom of the advisors [y*ʿ*ṣ] of Pharaoh is stupid advice [*ʿēṣâ*]. How can you say to Pharaoh, 'I am one of the sages, a son of kings of old'? So where are your sages who can tell you and who know what General Yahweh has planned [y*ʿ*ṣ] against Egypt?" Isaiah notes that the diplomatic plans (*ʿēṣâ* [cf.

Is 30:1-5; 31:1-3]) of the royal counselors consistently elevated human wisdom over Yahweh's plan, and so their plans would be thwarted (cf. Prov 19:21; 21:30-31; see Van Leeuwen 1990, 302). For Isaiah, true wisdom lies with God alone, and those who are truly wise derive their wisdom from him. This is apparent in the descriptions of the ideal coming ruler (Is 9:6; 11:1-9; cf. Is 33:6).

4.1.2. Jeremiah. One characteristic of Jeremiah is the frequent opposition that he faces as he seeks to fulfill his commission to speak God's word to God's people. This opposition sometimes comes from the wise or those described as advisers (see Jer 18:18-23 [particularly note v. 23, which refers to the plans of his opponents using the plural of *ʿēṣâ*]), although Jeremiah faced opposition from all quarters, including from other prophets. Jeremiah in turn announced God's opposition to the sages and advisers of his day, as can be seen in numerous passages (e.g., Jer 4:22; 8:8-9; 18:18; 49:7; 50:35; 51:57). As with Isaiah, the only wisdom viewed positively by Jeremiah was God's own wisdom (see Jer 10:12; 51:15).

4.1.3. Ezekiel. Ezekiel has less to say about sages or advisers than does either Isaiah or Jeremiah, but all that he says is negative. The most exalted wisdom language is reserved for the ruler of Tyre (Ezek 28), who stands in opposition to God and whose wisdom and other virtues are thus ultimately abhorrent. Aside from this, Ezekiel only makes brief mention of those who give evil advice: "The Spirit lifted me and brought me to the eastern gate of the House of Yahweh, which faces eastward. There were twenty-five men at the entrance to the gate, and among them were Yaʾazaniah son of Azzur and Pelatiahu son of Benaiahu, leaders of the people. Then he said to me, 'Son of man, these are the men who plot iniquity and who advise [yʿṣ] evil advice [ʿēṣâ] in this city'" (Ezek 11:1-2 [cf. Ezek 7:26]).

4.1.4. Summary. The prophets unequivocally condemn the sages and their wisdom for their departure from true wisdom, which was founded in obedience to God's law—a feature of wisdom reflected in Proverbs but absent from the sages, whom the prophets opposed. This condemnation, however, does not extend to all wisdom, for they recognized that true wisdom comes from God and is expressed in obedience to him. Furthermore, although the

prophetic condemnation of the sages is unrelenting, it is not exclusively directed at the sages, for the prophets are also critical of priests and even other prophets.

4.2. Sages' Attitudes Toward the Prophets. There appears to be little direct information regarding the attitude of the sages toward the prophets in the OT (see Scott, 3). Proverbs 29:18 could be a reference to the prophets, as it contains one of the few words frequently associated with prophecy (*ḥāzôn* ["vision"]) to be found in the Wisdom literature: "When there is no vision, the people are unchecked, but the one who keeps the law, he is happy." The parallelism of the aphorism links vision (*ḥāzôn*) with keeping the law (*tôrâ*) and reveals approval for both vision and obedience to the law. Proverbs 30:1; 31:1 (see 3.1.1 above) also use language more commonly associated with prophecy (and found nowhere else in the Wisdom literature of the OT). These passages, however, reveal little of the sages' attitude toward prophets or prophecy, except perhaps to indicate that some sages sought to attribute to their words an authority on par with those of the prophets.

In light of the scathing assessment of wisdom and the wise recorded in the prophets outlined above (and, indeed, throughout the remainder of the OT [see Shields, 7-20]), it might be expected that the Wisdom writings may reflect some enmity directed back toward the prophets. There is no sign of this in Proverbs, but there may be some echoes of such enmity among the words of Qohelet recorded in Ecclesiastes.

Aside from reaching conclusions that placed Qohelet in direct contradiction to the prophets (e.g., Eccles 1:10; cf. Eccles 3:14-15, where he claims that there is nothing new, whereas the prophets consistently taught that God was about to do something new [cf. Is 42:9; 43:19]), some of his words may represent a direct attack on the prophets and other religious officials in ancient Israel. In Ecclesiastes 8:5b-7 Qohelet says: "[Regarding the] appropriate time and a just outcome, a wise heart knows that for every matter there is an appropriate time and a just outcome, . . . that no one knows what will happen; and that when something will happen no one can tell." Here and elsewhere (cf. Eccles 3:22; 6:10-12) Qohelet affirms that no one knows what will take place in the future, whereas the prophets consistently announce the impending arrival of God's judgment or other events.

In Ecclesiastes 5:1-7 Qohelet condemns those who utter many words in God's house. Although the reference is somewhat ambiguous, it could be that those who spoke many words in God's house were either priests or prophets. Given that Qohelet also makes reference twice in this passage to dreams, and that dreams in the OT are frequently modes of divine revelation (e.g., Gen 20:3; Num 12:6; 1 Sam 28:6), it is quite possible that he directs his words at the prophets who expounded their visions in the precincts of the temple.

Finally, Qohelet may have sought to belittle prophecy by seeking to imply wisdom's superiority, at least in some ways. For example, prophets were known to announce the destruction of entire cities (e.g., Jer 26 [see McKane 1995, 144-45]; Mic 3:12). Qohelet, on the other hand, presents a parabolic tale of a small, relatively defenseless town faced with destruction that could have been saved had the rulers of that town listened to a poor sage (Eccles 9:14-15). Although prophets may have announced destruction, a sage could offer salvation in the face of overwhelming odds.

5. Conclusion.

True prophecy and wisdom are rooted in exposition and application of God's law to God's people. Prophecy proclaimed divine application, whereas wisdom appealed to the human intellect shaped and guided by the fear of Yahweh. In this form both shared the same authority and goal. Furthermore, wisdom's reach extended through all levels of society, such that prophets could readily employ the stylistic characteristics of wisdom when expounding their message. Yet the sages in Israel consistently departed from this ideal and found themselves in conflict with the prophets, who pronounced God's condemnation of the wise.

See also APOCALYPTICISM, APOCALYPTIC LITERATURE; CREATION THEOLOGY; DANIEL: BOOK OF; LAW.

BIBLIOGRAPHY. **J. K. Aitken,** "Apocalyptic, Revelation and Early Jewish Wisdom Literature," in *New Heaven and New Earth: Prophecy and the Millennium; Essays in Honor of Anthony Gelston,* ed. P. J. Harland and C. T. R. Hayward (VTSup 77; Leiden: E. J. Brill) 181-93; **J. Blenkinsopp,** *Sage, Priest, Prophet: Religious and Intellectual Leadership in Ancient Israel,* ed. D. A. Knight (LAI; Louisville: Westminster/John Knox, 1995); **J. J. Collins,** "Proverbial Wisdom and the Yahwist Vision," *Semeia* 17 (1980) 1-17; **J. L. Crenshaw,** "Method in Determining Wisdom Influence in 'Historical' Literature," *JBL* 88 (1969) 129-42; idem, *Prophetic Conflict: Its Effect on Israelite Religion* (BZAW 124; New York: de Gruyter, 1971); idem, "The Concept of God in Old Testament Wisdom," in *In Search of Wisdom: Essays in Memory of John G. Gammie,* ed. L. G. Perdue et al. (Louisville: Westminster/John Knox, 1993) 1-18; idem, *Old Testament Wisdom: An Introduction* (rev. ed.; Louisville: Westminster/John Knox, 1998); **J. D. G. Dunn,** "Biblical Concepts of Revelation," in *Divine Revelation,* ed. P. Avis (Grand Rapids: Eerdmans, 1997) 1-22; **J. Fichtner,** "Isaiah among the Wise," in *Studies in Ancient Israelite Wisdom,* ed. J. L. Crenshaw (New York: KTAV, 1976) 429-38; **B. Gemser,** "The Spiritual Structure of Biblical Aphoristic Wisdom: A Review of Recent Standpoints and Theories," in *Studies in Ancient Israelite Wisdom,* ed. J. L. Crenshaw (New York: KTAV, 1976) 208-19; **D. Gowan,** "Habakkuk and Wisdom," *Perspective* 9 (1968) 157-66; **L. L. Grabbe,** *Priests, Prophets, Diviners, Sages: A Socio-Historical Study of Religious Specialists in Ancient Israel* (Valley Forge, PA: Trinity Press International, 1995); **J. Jenson,** *The Use of* Tôrâ *by Isaiah: His Debate with the Wisdom Tradition* (CBQMS, vol. 3; Washington, DC: Catholic Biblical Association of America, 1973); **G. M. Landes,** "Jonah: A *Māšāl?*" in *Israelite Wisdom: Theological and Literary Essays in Honor of Samuel Terrien,* ed. J. G. Gammie et al. (Missoula, MT: Scholars Press for Union Theological Seminary, 1978) 137-58; **J. Lindblom,** "Wisdom in the Old Testament Prophets," in *Wisdom in Israel and in the Ancient Near East: Presented to Professor Harold Henry Rowley in Celebration of His Sixty-Fifth Birthday, 24 March 1955,* ed. M. Noth and D. W. Thomas (VTSup 3; Leiden: E. J. Brill, 1955) 192-204; **A. A. Macintosh,** "Hosea and the Wisdom Tradition: Dependence and Independence," in *Wisdom in Ancient Israel,* ed. J. Day, R. P. Gordon and H. G. M. Williamson (Cambridge: Cambridge University Press, 1995) 124-41; **W. McKane,** *Prophets and Wise Men* (SBT 44; London: SCM, 1965); idem, "Jeremiah and the Wise," in *Wisdom in Ancient Israel,* ed. J. Day, R. P. Gordon and H. G. M. Williamson (Cambridge: Cambridge University Press, 1995) 142-51; **R. E. Murphy,** "Assumptions and Problems in Old Testament Wisdom Research" *CBQ* 29 (1967) 407-18; **G. Ogden,** *Qoheleth* (RNBC; Sheffield: JSOT, 1987); **H. G. Reventlow,** "Participial Formulations: Lawsuit, Not Wisdom—A Study in Prophetic Language," in *Texts, Temples, and Traditions: A Tribute to Menahem Haran,* ed. M. V. Fox et al. (Winona Lake, IN: Eisenbrauns, 1996) 375-82; **M. Sato,** "Wisdom Statements in the Sphere of Prophecy," in *Gospel behind the Gospels: Current Studies on Q,* ed. R. A. Piper (NovTSup 75; Leiden: E. J. Brill; 1995); **R. B. Y. Scott,** "Priesthood, Prophecy, Wisdom, and the Knowledge of God," *JBL* 80 (1961) 1-15; **M. A. Shields,** *The End of Wisdom: A Reappraisal of the Historical and Canonical Function of Ecclesiastes* (Winona Lake, IN: Eisenbrauns, 2006); **N. H. Snaith,** *The Book of Job: Its Origin and Purpose* (London: SCM, 1968); **J. A. Soggin,** "Amos and Wisdom," in *Wisdom in Ancient Israel,* ed. J. Day et al. (Cambridge: Cambridge University Press, 1995) 119-23; **R. C. Van Leeuwen,** "The Sage in the Prophetic Literature" in *The Sage in Israel and the Ancient Near East,* ed. J. G. Gammie and L. G. Perdue (Winona Lake, IN: Eisenbrauns, 1990) 295-306; idem, "Scribal Wisdom and Theodicy in the Book of the Twelve," in *In Search of Wisdom: Essays in Memory of John G. Gammie,* ed. L. G. Perdue et al. (Louisville: Westminster/John Knox, 1993) 31-49; **B. K. Waltke,** *The Book of Proverbs: Chapters 1-15* (NICOT; Grand Rapids: Eerdmans, 2004); **J. W. Whedbee,** *Isaiah and Wisdom* (Nashville: Abingdon, 1971); **R. N. Whybray,** "Prophecy and Wisdom," in *Israel's Prophetic Tradition: Essays in Honor of Peter R. Ackroyd,* ed. R. Coggins, A. Phillips and M. Knibb (Cambridge: Cambridge University Press, 1982) 181-99.

M. A. Shields

PROPHETIC VISIONS. *See* VISIONS, PROPHETIC.

PROPHETS IN THE NEW TESTAMENT

The OT prophets are used in a variety of ways in the NT. The most obvious is direct quotation, and the overwhelming favorite in this regard is Isaiah. According to the fourth edition of the United Bible Societies' *Greek New Testament,* the NT quotes sixty-five different verses of Isaiah, compared with only six verses from each of Jeremiah, Hosea and Zechariah, five from Joel and Amos, three from Ezekiel, Ha-

bakkuk and Malachi, and one each from Daniel, Jonah and Haggai. It is no wonder that Isaiah has sometimes been designated as the "Fifth Gospel" (Sawyer). On the other hand, if we compare the United Bible Societies' list of "allusions and verbal parallels," we find a rather different story. Isaiah is still on top, with around 210, but the figures for Ezekiel (130), Jeremiah (95) and Daniel (70) are more comparable. Indeed, if we were interested in the concentration of allusions taken from a particular book, Daniel would be the winner (followed by Joel).

This raises an important question about the relative importance of quotations, allusions and themes. For example, in Mark's Gospel (generally thought to be the earliest), if we focus on explicit quotation, then Jesus identified with the "rejected but precious stone" of Psalm 118:22-23 (Mk 12:10-11), the "smitten shepherd" of Zechariah 13:7 (Mk 14:27) and the "forsaken sufferer" of Psalm 22:1 (Mk 15:34), but he did not identify with the "suffering servant" of Isaiah 53 (Hooker), however "obvious" that identification has seemed to later Christians. On the other hand, scholars such as J. Marcus and R. Watts have argued that Mark's opening quotation of Isaiah 40:3 ("Prepare the way of the Lord") sets the scene for understanding Jesus' ministry as a fulfillment of Isaiah's promise of a new *exodus (Is 40—55). In support, they note that there are explicit quotations of Isaiah in Mark 4:12; 7:6-7; 11:17, and the teaching on discipleship in Mark 8—10 focuses on following Jesus "on the way" (Mk 8:3, 27; 9:33, 34; 10:52), a reference back to "the way" of Isaiah 40:3. In the light of this Isaiah background, it could be argued that when Jesus says that he will give his life as a "ransom for many" (Mk 10:45), and that his blood will be "poured out for many" (Mk 14:24), he is referring to Isaiah 53:11-12, despite the fact that there are only a few words in common: "The righteous one, my servant, shall make *many* righteous, and he shall bear their iniquities. Therefore I will allot him a portion with the great, and he shall divide the spoil with the strong; because he *poured out* himself to death, and was numbered with the transgressors; yet he bore the sin of *many,* and made intercession for the transgressors" (Is 53:11-12) (*see* Servant of Yahweh).

Whatever view one takes on this debate, it is clear that Isaiah deserves pride of place, and thus it is the starting point for this article, followed by shorter sections on Jeremiah, Ezekiel, Daniel and the Book of the Twelve.

1. Isaiah
2. Jeremiah
3. Ezekiel
4. Daniel
5. The Book of the Twelve
6. Conclusion

1. Isaiah.

It may come as a surprise that the majority of the sixty-five verses of Isaiah quoted in the NT are applied not to Jesus but rather to the identity of the people of God (R. Hays therefore calls it "ecclesiological" rather than "christological" interpretation). For Paul, the central issue is the inclusion of the Gentiles, and he assumes that the salvation oracles in Isaiah refer to the church, while the judgment oracles refer to Israel's current unbelief. An important exception to this occurs in Romans 11, where the promise that God will redeem "those in Jacob who turn from transgression" (Is 59:20-21) is taken as evidence that Israel's current unbelief cannot be permanent, since God's word is irrevocable (Rom 11:26-27).

1.1. Israel's Blindness and Unbelief. Following his vision of God in the temple, Isaiah is told to preach to a people whose eyes and ears are closed and whose minds are dull (Is 6:9-10). This is quoted in the Gospels to explain why outsiders cannot understand Jesus' parables (Mt 13:13-14; Mk 4:12; Lk 8:10) or why the crowds are not responding to his "signs" (Jn 12:40). Luke's use is particularly interesting because he includes only the phrase "looking they may not perceive, and listening they may not understand" in the Gospel passage but has Paul give the quotation in full at the end of the book of Acts, followed by the statement "Let it be known to you then that this salvation of God has been sent to the Gentiles; they will listen" (Acts 28:28). Whatever Jesus may have originally said, Luke thinks that the text also applies to the rejection of Paul's preaching, with the positive consequence that the Gentiles will be more receptive.

Because the people are blind, they stumble and fall. There are several sayings in the Gospels about stumbling (Mt 18:8-9; Jn 11:9-10), but they are not linked with Scripture. However, Jesus is said to have identified with the "rejected stone" of Psalm 118:22-23, and this

probably is what led the early church to Isaiah 8:14 ("He will become a sanctuary, a stone one strikes against; for both houses of Israel he will become a rock one stumbles over"). The author of 1 Peter understands the text to apply to anyone who does not believe in Jesus (1 Pet 2:8), but Paul applies it more specifically to unbelieving Israel (Rom 9:33).

Isaiah 29 is also an important text for explaining Israel's unbelief. Both Matthew and Mark record Jesus accusing the Pharisees of hypocrisy by quoting the LXX of Isaiah 29:13: "This people honors me with their lips, but their hearts are far from me; in vain do they worship me, teaching human precepts as doctrines" (Mk 7:6-7). Since the Hebrew text says nothing about teaching doctrines but reads, "their worship of me is a human commandment learned by rote" (NRSV), some scholars deduce that Jesus could not have said this. Others suggest that Mark has simply replaced whatever Jesus originally said with the words of the LXX for the benefit of his Greek-speaking readers. Whichever is correct, Paul finds in the same chapter of Isaiah a statement that can be applied to Israel's present unbelief ("God gave them a sluggish spirit, eyes that would not see and ears that would not hear, down to this very day" [Rom 11:8, citing Is 29:10]), as well as the more general proposition that God destroys "the wisdom of the wise" and thwarts the "the discernment of the discerning" (1 Cor 1:19, citing Is 29:14).

1.2. Inclusion of the Gentiles. Although the inclusion of the Gentiles ("nations") is present in Isaiah, it certainly is not its major theme. However, in the NT it is one of the most important topics to be discussed. Thus, Matthew understands the promise of better times for the "land of Zebulun and the land of Naphatali" (cf. Is 9:1-2) to be fulfilled when Jesus settles in Galilee, no doubt prompted by the expression "Galilee of the nations" (Mt 4:15-16). Mark has Jesus accusing the temple authorities of making the temple a "den of robbers" (cf. Jer 7:11), whereas it should be a "house of prayer for all the nations" (Mk 11:17, citing Is 56:7). But the key text is Isaiah 49:6, where the mission of the servant is to be a "light to the nations" so that God's salvation "may reach to the end of the earth." The verse is alluded to in Luke 2:32 and Acts 26:23 (and perhaps the "light of the world" sayings in John), where it is applied to Jesus, but it is explicitly quoted in Acts 13:47, where it is applied to Paul. This might explain why Paul never explicitly applies Isaiah 53 to Jesus; he thinks of himself as the servant (Gal 1:15, alluding to Is 49:1) who brings the gospel message to the Gentiles (Rom 15:20-21, quoting Is 52:15).

The inclusion of the Gentiles forced the early church to wrestle with the question of whether they should be required to be circumcised and keep the law (Acts 15). Paul's arguments focus on the Abraham narratives, but he also finds support in verses that speak of "faith." The key text is Habakkuk 2:4, but he also draws on Isaiah 28:16; 65:1-2. Isaiah 8:14 speaks of a "stone" that causes people to stumble, but Isaiah 28:16 speaks positively of a "precious cornerstone" in which one can trust. Paul and the author of 1 Peter bring the two texts together (the link is already present in Is 8:14 LXX, which begins "and if you trust in him") to show that unbelief leads to destruction, but faith or trust leads to salvation (Rom 9:33; 1 Pet 2:6).

Paul's use of Isaiah 65:1-2 in Romans 10:20-21 is somewhat controversial. The text indicts Israel for walking in ways that are not good, neither seeking God nor calling on his name. The pathos is expressed in the words "I held out my hands all day long to a rebellious people." However, Paul splits the passage so that the first verse applies to Gentiles ("I have been found by those who did not seek me; I have shown myself to those who did not ask for me"), while the "rebellious" clause is specifically applied to unbelieving Israel ("But of Israel he says"). Some regard this as quite arbitrary, but J. Wagner defends it on two grounds (Wagner, 205-17). First, there clearly is a tension between the two verses: Isaiah 65:1 speaks of God being found by those who were not seeking, but Isaiah 65:2 suggests that God's offer was refused. This is somewhat alleviated by the NRSV ("I was ready to be sought . . . to be found"), but the NIV preserves the tension ("I revealed myself . . . I was found"). Second, although the overall sense makes it clear that both verses are talking about Israel, they do in fact use different words for "people," one of which the LXX translates as *ethnos*, Paul's usual word (in the plural) for referring to Gentiles.

In Paul's quotation of Isaiah 11:10 in Romans 15:12, the particular rendering of the LXX plays an even greater role. According to the Hebrew text, Isaiah 11:10 says, "On that day the root of Jesse shall stand as a signal to the peoples; the nations shall inquire of him, and his dwelling shall be glorious." In this case, Paul does not play on the difference between "peoples" and "nations" but follows the LXX rendering of the verb for "inquire" (Heb *dāraš*) with *elpizō* ("to hope"). He is thus able to support the inclusion of the Gentiles with a text that reads, "The root of Jesse shall come, he who rises to rule the Gentiles; in him shall the Gentiles hope" (Rom 15:12).

1.3. Redeemer Figures Applied to Jesus. It is not clear how the various "redeemer" figures in Isaiah are related. Isaiah 9 speaks of a future Davidic king who will establish justice and righteousness on earth and will be called "Wonderful Counselor, Mighty God, Everlasting Father, Prince of Peace" (Is 9:6). Despite the familiarity of this verse from Christmas liturgies, it is never applied to Jesus in the NT (Lk 1:32 comes closest). Establishing justice is also central to the servant's role in Isaiah 42:1-4, but this is somewhat different from the figure in Isaiah 53, who had "no form or majesty that we should look at him" (Is 53:2) and was "despised and rejected" (Is 53:3). Talk of victory is muted ("Out of his anguish he shall see light; he shall find satisfaction through his knowledge" [Is 53:11a]), although his suffering is said to benefit others (Is 53:5, 11b-12). A further figure is described in Isaiah 61, who is anointed with the Spirit (like the servant in Is 42) and whose mission is to bring good news to the oppressed and announce the vengeance of God (Is 61:1-2). What does the NT make of these various figures?

1.3.1. Jesus as Anointed Prophet. If Jesus saw himself fulfilling any of these figures, most scholars think that the anointed prophet of Isaiah 61 is the most likely one. Indeed, Luke has Jesus reading this very passage in the synagogue and declaring, "Today this scripture has been fulfilled in your hearing" (Lk 4:21). There are problems with accepting this at face value, since the reading not only follows the LXX by speaking of "recovery of sight to the blind" instead of "release to the captives," but also incorporates a snippet of Isaiah 58:6 ("let the oppressed go free"). It is therefore highly unlikely that Jesus could have read from a Hebrew scroll that said what Luke reports. C. Kimble's answer is that Luke has combined the reading with the sermon that would have followed, deducing that Jesus saw himself not only as the herald of salvation from Isaiah 61:1-2, but also as the agent who would bring it about from Isaiah 58:6 (Kimble, 110).

Alternatively, Luke may have deduced that Jesus must have read/preached from this passage at some point in his ministry, since he clearly alludes to it in his reply to John the Baptist. John wants to know whether Jesus is "the one who is to come, or are we to wait for another?" (Lk 7:22). Jesus' reply combines phrases from Isaiah 29:18 ("the blind receive their sight"), Isaiah 35:5-6 ("the lame walk . . . the deaf hear"), Isaiah 26:19 ("the dead are raised") and Isaiah 61:1 ("the poor have good news brought to them"). Although some of these phrases could come from other texts (e.g., Ps 146:8), it does suggest that Jesus associated the messianic signs with the anointed prophet in Isaiah 61 (*see* Messiah).

1.3.2. Jesus as Suffering Servant. Although it has been questioned whether Jesus specifically identified with the figure in Isaiah 53, the chapter is quoted in Matthew 8:17; Luke 22:37; John 12:38; Acts 8:32-33; Romans 10:16; 1 Peter 2:22-25. However, only in thwe last text is it explicitly used to explain the meaning of Jesus' death. As table 1 shows, the author of 1 Peter has skillfully taken phrases from Isaiah 53:4, 5, 6, 7, 9, 12 and woven them into his own salvific statement.

Isaiah 53:4, 5, 6, 7, 9, 12	1 Peter 2:22-25
(A) surely he has borne our infirmities (B) upon him was the punishment that made us whole, and by his bruises we are healed (C) all we like sheep have gone astray (D) he was oppressed, and he was afflicted, yet he did not open his mouth	(E) He committed no sin, and no deceit was found in his mouth. (D) When he was abused, he did not return abuse; when he suffered, he did not threaten; (F) but he entrusted himself [*paradidōmi*] to the one who judges justly.
(E) he had done no violence, and there was no deceit in his mouth (F) he poured out [*paradidōmi*] himself to death (G) he bore the sin of many	(A, G) He himself bore our sins in his body on the cross, so that, free from sin, we might live for righteousness; (B) by his wounds you have been healed. (C) For you were going astray like sheep, but now you have returned to the shepherd and guardian of your souls.

Table 1. Isaiah 53 and 1 Peter 2

Acts 8:32-33 belongs to the passage where Philip meets a court official returning home to Ethiopia after worshiping in Jerusalem. The man is in his chariot reading from Isaiah 53 and wishes to know whether Isaiah is referring to himself or someone else. We are not told Philip's answer, but the text gives a summary statement that "starting with this scripture, he proclaimed to him the good news about Jesus" (Acts 8:35). This could mean that Philip showed the man how Isaiah 53 applied to Jesus, but equally it could mean that he moved from this passage to other passages in order to proclaim the gospel to him. The summary statement in Luke 24:44 ("everything written about me in the law of Moses, the prophets, and the psalms must be fulfilled") perhaps favors the latter.

Both John and Romans quote Isaiah 53:1 ("Who has believed our message?" [NIV]) in support of Israel's unbelief, but it is not related to Jesus' death. Matthew follows the Hebrew text of Isaiah 53:4 ("he has borne our infirmities and carried our diseases") to support Jesus' healing ministry, whereas 1 Peter follows the LXX ("he himself bore our sins"). This leaves Luke 22:37, where Jesus tells the disciples that he will be "counted among the lawless," four words that appear to come from Isaiah 53:12. However, there is no indication that Jesus is instructing the disciples about the theological meaning of his death; he is simply indicating that like the servant, he will die an ignominious death.

1.4. An Isaianic Framework? As we noted above, some scholars believe that the influence of Isaiah in the NT is not simply through quotation and allusion but provides an overarching framework for understanding the entire salvation event. Thus, D. Pao notes that Isaiah 40 acts as a prologue to the themes of Isaiah 40—55: release from captivity, proclamation of the word of God, conquest of enemies, giving of the Spirit, and God teaching his people. He suggests that all of these themes are found in Luke-Acts, and that this, along with the evidence of the explicit quotations (Lk 3:4-5; 4:18-19; 8:10; 19:46; 22:37; Acts 8:32-33; 13:34, 47; 28:26-27), shows that Luke understands the entire Christ event as a fulfillment of Isaiah's "new exodus" theme. On the other hand, P. Mallen thinks that the "dual mission of the servant" offers a better framework, since it can explain Luke's emphasis on Gentiles (which is present in the "new exodus" theme but hardly prominent), as well as the fact that the servant imagery is applied both to Jesus and to his followers. This mirrors the oscillation between individual and corporate characteristics in Isaiah's servant figure. K. Litwak agrees that Isaiah is an important influence but denies that it is being used as a framework; the psalms, for example, are just as important.

2. Jeremiah.

We have already noted the snippet of Jeremiah 7:11 ("den of robbers") that is included in Jesus' accusation against the temple authorities. It is possible that this is nothing more than a colorful phrase, but the chapter is concerned with those who think that the temple will protect them from judgment (Jer 7:4). If they amend their ways, God promises to dwell with them (Jer 7:3, 7), and it is possible that Jesus wishes to evoke this background. According to T. Berkley, Paul draws on Jeremiah 7:9 ("Will you steal, murder, commit adultery, swear falsely, make offerings to Baal, and go after other gods that you have not known?") when he indicts Jewish teachers of hypocrisy in Romans 2:17-23. Paul also draws on Jeremiah 9:24 to exhort the Corinthians to boast not in their own accomplishments but only in the Lord (1 Cor 1:31; 2 Cor 10:17). The reference is highly abbreviated ("Let the one who boasts, boast in the Lord"), whereas Jeremiah 9:24 says, "Do not let the wise boast in their wisdom, do not let the mighty boast in their might, do not let the wealthy boast in their wealth; but let those who boast boast in this, that they understand and know me, that I am the LORD."

The most significant use of Jeremiah in the NT is the "new *covenant" passage of Jeremiah 31, where God indicts Israel for breaking the covenant and promises a time when the *law will be written "on their hearts" (Jer 31:33) and their sins and iniquities will be forgiven (Jer 31:34). This probably lies behind the language of "new covenant" in the Paul/Luke version of the Last Supper (1 Cor 11:25; Lk 22:20) and texts such as 2 Corinthians 3:6 ("who has made us competent to be ministers of a new covenant") and Romans 11:27 ("and this is my covenant with them, when I take away their sins"). However, only in Hebrews 8:8-12; 10:16-17 is the passage explicitly quoted, the former being the longest quota-

tion in the NT (131 Greek words). The author of Hebrews does not immediately explain the relevance of the quotation, except to say that talk of a "new covenant" implies that the previous one is "obsolete" (Heb 8:13). What he wants to say is that this promised forgiveness comes through the sacrificial death of Christ, but before he can do that, he needs to establish that "without the shedding of blood there is no forgiveness of sins" (Heb 9:22), and that "it is impossible for the blood of bulls and goats to take away sins" (Heb 10:4). Having done that, he then can assert that Christ has "offered for all time a single sacrifice for sins" (Heb 10:12), and so the prophecy of Jeremiah 31 has been fulfilled.

3. Ezekiel.

There are brief quotations of Ezekiel in 2 Corinthians 6:16-17, and the "good shepherd" discourse in John 10 owes something to Ezekiel 34, but the extensive use of Ezekiel in the book of Revelation is what stands out. Over half of the 130 or so allusions to Ezekiel in the NT are from Revelation, and many scholars have observed how a number of the visionary descriptions occur in the same order in both books (see table 2).

Ezekiel	Allusions	Revelation
1	God on his throne; multi-faced creatures; "full of eyes"	4
9—10	Saints protected by a seal; burning coals hurled to the earth	7—8
16; 23	Harlot city left desolate and naked; destroyed by fire	17
26—27	Lament over the fallen city; list of luxury imports; people throw dust on their heads; music heard no more	18
37—48	Dry bones come to life; battle with Gog of Magog; new Jerusalem; river of life; tree with healing leaves	20—22

Table 2. Ezekiel Allusions in Revelation

M. Goulder attempted to put the two books into a one-to-one correspondence, but there are too many exceptions for that to be plausible. Nevertheless, there is good evidence to suggest that John's final vision of the new Jerusalem has been substantially modeled on Ezekiel, though with some interesting modifications. G. K. Beale is more impressed with the parallels and argues that Revelation 20—22 represents the true fulfillment of Ezekiel, but other scholars are more inclined to speak of John's transformation of Ezekiel (see table 3).

Ezekiel		Revelation	
37:10	Revival of dry bones	20:4	*Saints* come to life
37:21	Israel reunited under Davidic king	20:4	*Saints* rule with Christ *for one thousand years*
38:2-16	Gog of Magog roused for battle	20:8	Gog *and* Magog roused for battle
38:22	Gog of Magog destroyed by fire	20:9	Gog *and* Magog destroyed by fire
39:4	Birds invited to gorge on corpses	*19:21*	Birds invited to gorge on corpses
40:2	Ezekiel transported in spirit to high mountain	21:10	John transported in spirit to high mountain
40:5	Angel measures the temple	21:15	Angel measures the *city*
43:2	Temple full of the glory of God	21:23	*City* is full of the glory of God
47:12	Trees of life provide leaves for healing	22:1-2	*Tree* of life provides leaves for healing *of the nations*
48:30-34	Three gates on each side of city bearing the names of the twelve tribes	21:12-13	Three gates on each side of city bearing the names of the twelve tribes

Table 3. Ezekiel and Revelation 20–22

4. Daniel.

Discussion of the use of Daniel in the NT has focused on the way the Gospel writers present Jesus as speaking about a "son of man" who comes "in/with clouds" in "power and glory" (Mk 13:26; 14:62 pars.). On its own, one would assume that Jesus is speaking about someone else, but since he frequently has referred to himself as "son of man," most scholars think this is a self-reference. But with what meaning? Traditionally, it has been taken as a reference to his "second coming," but this clearly is not Daniel's meaning, since the figure is coming to God, not from God (Dan 7:13-14). So either the Gospels (or Jesus) are substantially changing the meaning of Daniel or the traditional interpretation is incorrect. N. T. Wright is one scholar who has championed the latter, arguing that the text is not to be taken literally, as if Jesus needed a mode of transport to get from heaven to earth; it is a metaphor (Wright, 510-19). What the visionary language of Daniel is claiming is that the persecuted saints will be vindicated (Dan 7:18), and that is what Jesus is claiming for himself.

The other major use of Daniel in the NT is in Revelation. The book opens with the statement that a "revelation" of "what must soon take place" has been given to John, and this is generally recognized as an allusion to Daniel 2:28: "There is a God in heaven who reveals mysteries, and he has disclosed to King Nebuchadnezzar what will happen at the end of days." The particular Greek phrase for "what will happen" (*ha dei genesthai*) occurs at pivotal points in Revelation (Rev 1:1, 19; 4:1; 22:6) and clearly is important to John. The "son of man" text (Dan 7:13) is quoted in Revelation 1:7, but the chapter has also supplied images for John's vision of the risen Christ (Rev 1:12-18), God on his throne (Rev 4—5), the beast that rises from the sea, which combines the traits of Daniel's four beasts (Rev 13:1-10) and the final judgment scene (Rev 20:11-12).

5. The Book of the Twelve.

It is likely that the NT authors saw the twelve Minor Prophets as a single book (the Book of the *Twelve), though Hosea, Joel and Jonah are mentioned by name. There are significant quotations from Joel (Acts 2:17-21; Rom 10:13), Amos (Acts 7:42-43; 15:16-17) and Malachi (Mk 1:2; Mt 11:10; Lk 7:27), but here I will restrict comments to Zechariah, Hosea and Habakkuk.

5.1. Zechariah. A case can be made that Jesus had Zechariah 9:9 in mind when he chose to ride into Jerusalem on a donkey (made explicit in Mt 21:5; Jn 12:15), and that he saw the desertion by his disciples in the light of Zechariah 13:7 (Mk 14:27). This appears to have led the early church to see much of Jesus' passion in the light of Zechariah 9—14. Thus, Matthew suggests that the betrayal of Jesus for thirty pieces of silver fulfills Zechariah 11:12-13, even though the reference to Jeremiah ("potter's field") is a little confusing (Mt 27:9-10). John sees the onlookers at the crucifixion as a fulfillment of Zechariah 12:10 ("look on the one whom they have pierced" [Jn 19:37]), a text that also appears in Matthew 24:30; Revelation 1:7. What is interesting about these two references is that both of them combine the Zechariah reference with Daniel's "son of man" text. Some argue that it is precisely Jesus' combination of the texts in Matthew 24:30 that led to the other developments, but since it is not found in Mark's version of the same text (Mk 13:26), others think that it is part of the same tendency to align more and more of Jesus' passion with Zechariah 9—14.

5.2. Hosea. There are six quotations from Hosea in the NT. Hosea 1:10 and Hosea 2:23 are combined in Romans 9:25-26 to show that God can change "not my people" into "my people." Hosea is referring to the unification of Israel, but Paul understands the text as a reference to the inclusion of the Gentiles, perhaps because the idolatrous Israelites had effectively become like Gentiles. He also draws on Hosea 13:14 in 1 Corinthians 15:55 to argue that death has been defeated through Christ's resurrection. This is some distance from Hosea's meaning, and it may be that the quotation that precedes it (Is 25:8) is the supporting text and the words from Hosea are used to fill out the meaning. There are three quotations in the Gospels: the reference to Jesus's departure and return from Egypt (Mt 2:15, quoting Hos 11:1); the priority of mercy over *sacrifice (Mt 9:13; 12:7, quoting Hos 6:6); and the severity of times to come (Lk 23:30, quoting Hos 10:8; cf. Rev 6:16). It has also been argued that the most likely text behind Paul's statement that Christ's resurrection on the third day is according to Scripture (1 Cor 15:3) is Hosea 6:2 ("After two days he will revive us; on the third day he will raise us up, that we may live before him"). However, the contexts are very different, and it is more likely that Paul is referring to the general theme of vindication in Scripture rather than a specific text.

5.3. Habakkuk. Habakkuk 1:5 is quoted in Acts 13:41, and Habakkuk 2:3-4 in Hebrews 10:37-38, but it is the use of Habakkuk 2:4 by Paul that has attracted most attention. In particular, Paul follows the quotation of Habakkuk 2:4 in Galatians 3:11 with the assertion that "the law does not rest on faith," which suggests that he understands the prophet's reference to "faithfulness" as "faith in Christ" rather than obedience to the law. This raises the question of whether Paul has simply imposed his doctrine of justification on the ancient text. F. Watson thinks not, arguing that the "faithfulness" required of Habakkuk is because the vision concerns the end and awaits an inspired interpreter (Watson, 127-64). Paul sees himself as that interpreter and can now offer the clarity that was denied to Habakkuk. However, when Paul quotes the text in Romans 1:17, it is immediately followed by a long section on the importance of obeying the law (Rom 1:18-2:29). R. Hays argues that Romans is not primarily about salvation (justification of the sinner) but rather theodicy (justification of God's ways), and this is why Paul quotes the Habakkuk text; it is the locus classicus for the theme in the OT (Hays, 34-44). Watson, however, thinks that the argument of Romans is basically the same as Galatians, the critique of obeying the law coming later in Romans 3.

6. Conclusion.

It is evident that the OT prophets are used in a variety of ways in the NT. It has often been assumed that this is to show that Jesus is the fulfillment of the prophets. However, relatively few texts are directly applied to him. The majority of texts are applied to the events that followed, particularly the birth of the church, the inclusion of the Gentiles, the present unbelief of Israel and future salvation. Of course, all these events are dependent on the life, death and resurrection of Jesus, and so it is not incorrect to describe it as "christological" or "messianic" interpretation. However, it is precisely because the NT authors discovered that the prophets "spoke" to so many of their concerns that such headings can be misleading. Paul can even suggest that Isaiah 28:11-12 ("with stammering lip and with alien tongue he will speak to this people") is directly relevant to the issue of speaking in tongues (1 Cor 14:21). And 2 Timothy 3:16 is often quoted in discussions about the inspiration of Scripture, but the thrust of the passage is primarily about function and offers a good summary of the use of the prophets in the NT: "All scripture is inspired by God and is *useful* for teaching, for reproof, for correction, and for training in righteousness, so that everyone who belongs to God may be proficient, equipped for every good work."

See also DANIEL: HISTORY OF INTERPRETATION; EZEKIEL: HISTORY OF INTERPRETATION; HERMENEUTICS; ISAIAH: HISTORY OF INTERPRETATION; JEREMIAH: HISTORY OF INTERPRETATION; MESSIAH; SERVANT OF YAHWEH; TWELVE, BOOK OF THE: HISTORY OF INTERPRETATION.

BIBLIOGRAPHY. **G. K. Beale,** *The New Temple: The Temple and the Church's Mission; A Biblical Theology of the Dwelling Place of God* (Downers Grove, IL: InterVarsity Press, 2004); **G. K. Beale and D. A. Carson,** eds., *Commentary on the New Testament Use of the Old Testament* (Grand Rapids: Baker Academic, 2007); **T. W. Berkley,** *From a Broken Covenant to Circumcision of the Heart. Pauline Intertextual Exegesis in Romans 2:17-29* (SBLDS 175; Atlanta: Society of Biblical Literature, 2000); **M. D. Goulder,** "The Apocalypse as an Annual Cycle of Prophecies," *NTS* 27 (1981) 342-67; **R. B. Hays,** *Echoes of Scripture in the Letters of Paul* (New Haven: Yale University Press, 1989); **M. D. Hooker,** *Jesus the Servant: The Influence of the Servant Concept of Deutero-Isaiah in the New Testament* (London: SPCK, 1959); **C. Kimble,** *Jesus' Exposition of the Old Testament in Luke* (JSNTSup 94; Sheffield: Sheffield Academic Press, 1995); **K. D. Litwak,** *Echoes of Scripture in Luke-Acts. Telling the History of God's People Intertextually* (JSNTSup 282; London: T & T Clark, 2005); **P. Mallen,** *The Reading and Transformation of Isaiah in Luke-Acts* (LNTS 367; London: T & T Clark, 2008); **J. Marcus,** *The Way of the Lord: Christological Exegesis of the Old Testament in the Gospel of Mark* (Louisville: Westminster/John Knox, 1992); **M. J. J. Menken and S. Moyise,** eds., *The Minor Prophets in the New Testament* (LNTS 377; London: T & T Clark, 2009); **S. Moyise,** *Paul and Scripture: Studying the New Testament Use of the Old Testament* (Grand Rapids: Baker Academic, 2010); **S. Moyise and M. J. J. Menken,** eds., *Isaiah in the New Testament* (London: T & T Clark, 2005); **D. W. Pao,** *Acts and the Isaianic New Exodus* (Grand Rapids: Baker Academic, 2002); **J. F. A. Sawyer,** *The Fifth Gospel: Isaiah in the History of Christianity* (Cambridge: Cambridge University Press, 1996); **J. R. Wagner,** *Heralds of the Good News: Isaiah and Paul "In Concert" in the Letter to the Romans* (NovTSup 101; Leiden: E. J. Brill, 2002); **F. Watson,** *Paul and the Hermeneutics of Faith* (London: T & T Clark, 2004); **R. E. Watts,** *Isaiah's New Exodus and Mark* (WUNT 2/88; Tübingen: Mohr Siebeck, 1997); **N. T. Wright,** *Christian Origins and the Question of God, 2: Jesus and the Victory of God* (London: SPCK; Minneapolis: Fortress, 1996).

S. Moyise

PSYCHOLOGY. *See* PROPHECY AND PSYCHOLOGY.

PUNISHMENT. *See* RETRIBUTION; WRATH.

QUMRAN. *See* DEAD SEA SCROLLS.

R

RECORDING OF PROPHECY. *See* WRITING AND PROPHECY.

REDACTION CRITICISM. *See* EDITORIAL/REDACTION CRITICISM.

REDEEMER, GOD AS. *See* GOD.

RELIGIOUS LEADERS. *See* LEADERSHIP.

REMARRIAGE. *See* MARRIAGE, DIVORCE.

REMNANT

The prophetic writings of the eighth through fourth centuries BC portray descriptions of historical events in which the future existence of a distinct ethnic and geopolitical people named *"Israel" was often in question (e.g., aggression and destruction of Samaria and the northern kingdom in 734 BC and 722 BC, the threat against Jerusalem in 701 BC, and subsequent incursions against and deportations of Judeans in 605, 597, 586 and 581 BC) (*see* Israelite History). As the threat of either slavery or pogrom from other surrounding nations such as the Neo-Assyrian, Neo-Babylonian and Persian Empires was continually in the purview of the northern and southern kingdoms, the prophetic figures associated with Israel and Judah interpreted the concept of "remnant" both in negative and positive manners. There are five Hebrew lexemes that provide a semantic range associated with a "remnant theology" (ʾhr [*NIDOTTE* 1:360-62; *TDOT* 1:207-12]; ytr [*NIDOTTE* 2:571-74; *TDOT* 6:482-91]; plt [*NIDOTTE* 3:621-26; *TDOT* 11:551-66]; śrd [*NIDOTTE* 3:1271-72; *TDOT* 14:215-18]; šʾr [*NIDOTTE* 4:11-17; *TDOT* 14:272-86]); the corresponding Greek lexemes in the LXX are *leimma, hypoleimma, loipos* and *kataloipos*. Beyond the lexical material, the idea of a remnant

people can also be adduced through conceptual developments. The conceptualization of a people who are "left behind" has multiple connotative values that may range from positive or negative to suprahistorical or eschatological. The concept of remnant is directly associated with the various historical events that caused those in Israel and Judah to reinterpret who they were as a people of Yahweh.

Depending on the approach taken, theological or strictly historical, the answer to the question of how the understanding of "remnant" originated and developed will differ accordingly. Concerning the former, the first explicit occurrence of the remnant motif is found in Genesis 7:23: "He [God] wiped out everything that was on the face of the ground, from humanity and animals to creeping things and birds of the sky. They were wiped away from the earth. Only Noah was left [*wayyiššāʾer*], and those with him in the ark" (see Elliott, 723). Since this is the first appearance of the remnant motif in the canon of the HB set in the context of the primeval flood story, it is curious that the first literary occurrence of this topos in the ancient Near East is found in another Sumerian flood story from the third millennium (*ANET* 42-44). Although the observation that this idea occurs early in the "biblical history" of Israel demonstrates its importance to the metanarrative of a more comprehensive biblical theology of "remnant groups" (Rendtorff, 265-79), our concern will be with the prophetic literature and how this literary corpus takes up the remnant topos as a response to the various historical events that shaped the history and self-identity of Israel/Judah.

1. The Historical Question of Origins
2. Remnant in the Prophetic Literature of the Neo-Assyrian Era

1. The Historical Question of Origins.

The variety of adaptations of the remnant theme in ancient Near Eastern literature (see Hasel 1980, 50-134) suggests that the concept derived from the practical concern that a people might survive a natural threat such as disease or drought or a social threat such as war or civil strife (Hasel, *ISBE* 5:130). Further, this topos is present in Egyptian mythological texts (e.g., "Book of the Cow of Heaven" [*ANET* 10-11; *COS* 1.24:36-37]) and Mesopotamian king lists (e.g., Sumerian King List [*ANET* 265-69]). The Akkadian creation story *Enuma Elish* (*ANET* 60-72, 501-3; *COS* 1.111:390-402) features a remnant people as well as the Syria-Palestine creation story Baal and Anath Cycle (*ANET* 129-42; *COS* 1.86:241-74). The remnant motif is also found in the Hittite "Plague Prayers" of King Muršili II (*ANET* 394-96; *COS* 1.60:156-60). These primary texts are just a sampling, and the remnant motif spans West Semitic and Mesopotamian literature genres, including hymns, myths, epics, prayers and annals. Although the Neo-Assyrian Empire employed the motif as a propagandistic military tactic to terrify conquered peoples (see Müller and Preuss; Carena), this use is a later specification of the concept as seen in the eighth-century BC prophets (Amos, Isaiah, Micah) after it was already well ingrained in the conceptual and literary milieu of the ancient Near East. The widespread dissemination across all types of *Gattung* suggests that the concept arose from the quite mundane desire for humanity's survival and existence when life was jeopardized by natural threats. G. Hasel suggests that the remnant concept can be either "historical" or "eschatological," but this may be slightly reductionistic, and, strictly speaking, the pervasive concern of the writing prophets was not so much for the eschaton as for the return from Babylonian exile. Instead, we can observe in the literature, whether in the OT or greater ancient Near Eastern context, that the survival of a remnant people was viewed both as looking back to physical harm or national disaster and looking forward to a future hope of national existence and identity. Therefore, the notion of remnant evinced a dimension of discontinuity whereby a people were kept for or from judgment and a dimension of continuity whereby a people were kept for *salvation.

2. Remnant in the Prophetic Literature of the Neo-Assyrian Era.

From the first and earliest instances where the remnant motif is employed in the prophetic literature, the purpose is clear: Yahweh has spared a people from judgment and destruction. The idea refers to a people who have survived either foreign or domestic threats, whether war, famine or pestilence. Amos and Isaiah support this purpose.

2.1. Amos. As with the motif of the Day of Yahweh in Amos 5:18-20, the Judean prophet to northern Israel has anything but positive pronouncements to the people. The concept of a remnant theology is pervasive in the book of Amos, but to Amos's audience this notion only signifies a people who escape destruction from the aggressive Assyrian armies, where an initial deportation occurred in 734 BC and was then fully realized in 722/21 BC. The first mention of the remnant motif occurs in the oracles against the nations (Amos 1:2—2:16). As the prophet proclaims Yahweh's judgment over the surrounding enemies of Israel and Judah, even the "remnant" (*šĕʾērît*) of the Philistines will be destroyed (Amos 1:8). The same is said for Israel, where Yahweh will allow only a few people to remain for a time (Amos 3:12; 5:3) before he eventually sends the sword and serpent to kill any who have escaped the first round of judgment (Amos 9:1-4). Yahweh will make sure that there is no "escapee" (*plṭ*) from the northern kingdom to make up a surviving remnant. This use of the remnant motif corresponds with the Neo-Assyrian war annals, where a conquered and displaced people were left alive so that they might be a sign of judgment for other nations. As Yahweh "shakes" Israel and the other nations, not one "pebble" will fall to the ground (Amos 9:9-10). Thus, the final form of Amos marks out Joseph/Ephraim (i.e., northern Israel) for death, but a remnant from the house of Jacob (i.e., southern Judah) will continue in covenant relationship. The prophet's use of the remnant topos is diverse and innovative. He negates the preconceptions of those in Bethel (cf. Amos 7:10-17), and he sets forth a hope for a remnant people of Yahweh as exclusive to those who align themselves with the reconstitution of the "booth of David" (*sukkat dāwîd*) in Jerusalem (Amos 9:11-15). The diverse appropriations in the book of Amos provide a conceptual richness that both antedates and influences subsequent prophetic traditions (see Hasel 1980, 173-215).

2.2. Isaiah. The characteristics of the remnant motif in Isaiah 1—39 differ from those in Isaiah 40—66, largely due to issues regarding composition, audience and historical concerns. From the outset of the book, Daughter *Zion has already suffered from war and brutality (Is 1:7-8), and the surviving community recognizes that it is only due to Yahweh's mercy that anyone from Judah is still alive (Is 1:9). Although only a few remain (*hôtîr lānû śārîd*), this motif of the "left over" people contributes to the literary plotline of the book of Isaiah.

The "remnant" people of Yahweh are set against the historical backdrop of Assyrian hegemony and recurring aggression, principally under the reigns of Ahaz and Hezekiah. The initial image regarding the remnant motif is that of a tenth of a people who survive divine judgment, and they serve as the "holy seed" (*zeraʿ qōdeš*) who will repopulate the land (Is 6:13). In Isaiah 7 the prophet's son, Shear-jashub (*šĕʾār yāšûb*), is a sign both to Ahaz and to Isaiah himself that King Rezin of Aram and King Pekah of Israel will turn back to their own countries as "fire stumps" that are all but extinguished. In this way, the eldest son of the prophet Isaiah serves as a "living sign" that Yahweh will provide victory over Judah's northern aggressors. In Isaiah 10 there is a further development of this eponym. Now Yahweh declares that a "remnant will return" (*šĕʾār yāšûb*) in the context not of Judah's defeated enemies but rather of Judah's continued existence by means of a people who will survive the destruction that Yahweh has determined for the southern kingdom (Is 10:20-23). The only hope of national existence from the defeat of first the Neo-Assyrian armies and then the Neo-Babylonian armies is that Yahweh keeps a "remnant of Jacob." Although this remnant people will be dispersed among the surrounding nations (Is 11:11-12), Yahweh will provide for their return to the land. This hope, however, is not given to the surrounding nations and their remnant people (Is 16:14; 17:1-6; 21:16-17).

The chief contribution that Isaiah evinces for the remnant motif is its depiction in terms of agrarian and horticultural imagery. Some scholars see this interpretive expansion as having taken place post-586 BC (*TDOT* 14:279-80). This development is provided in a number of texts (Is 4:2-3; 11:1, 10; 17:6; 37:31-32). In this manner, the conceptualization of a remnant people for Yahweh is associated with the "root" (*šōreš*), "shoot" (*gēzaʿ, nēṣer*) and "branch" (*ṣemaḥ, ḥōṭer*) of a tree. It is difficult to determine whether the origin of this metaphor is drawn from the ancient Near Eastern notion of a cosmic tree, where the root, shoot and branch represent the three-tiered cosmos, or from a divine or royal figure that symbolizes the source of earthly fertility. For Isaiah, the locus of this people is Mount Zion (Is 37:31-32), which then brings together the motifs of the cosmic tree coming out of the cosmic mountain. In other prophetic texts such as Joel 2:32; Haggai 1:12, 14, a remnant is identified by those who are faithful to Yahweh in Mount Zion (i.e., Jerusalem). This observation implies that the expectation of a remnant people in the prophetic literature is directly linked to those who are loyal to the *worship of Yahweh in his Jerusalem sanctuary.

In the latter literary unit of Isaiah 40—66 little lexical and thematic attention is given to the remnant theme (Is 44:17; 46:3; 49:21). However, when the concept does surface, it applies to the "survivors of the nations" (*pĕlîṭê haggôyim*) that Yahweh calls to worship (Is 45:20-22). Although the lexical terms do not occur often in this latter part of the book, the concept is there and is enforced by the theme of new exodus in Isaiah 40—55, and an exilic audience is in view that is reminded of the remnant expectations in Isaiah 1—39. The idea of a new or second exodus suggests a salvific or redemptive divine act for the benefit of a remnant people, this time leaving Babylonia. This motif has been readily observed, for example, in Isaiah 40:1-11; 48:17-22, where Yahweh leads his people out of Babylonia and into the land of Israel. In addition to the preservation and deliverance of a people, the motif of a second exodus is associated with a renewed creation (Is 51:3). Both of these events—the preservation of a people and the restoration of creation—find their locus at Mount Zion (see Anderson).

2.3. Micah. The prophet Micah had just witnessed the Neo-Assyrian conquest of the northern kingdom in 722/21 BC, and this aggressive empire was set to besiege Jerusalem in the closing years of the eighth century BC. Regardless of whether the remnant theme is due to a postexilic editing, the book of Micah gives this concept a strong theological import. Two perspectives are in view in Micah. On the one hand, the gathering of Yahweh's people will occur when a sign act is observed whereby a woman will give birth to a child. This event will mark the period when the "remainder" (*yeter*) of the child's brothers will return to and constitute Israel (Mic 5:3). In response to the birth of this child, Yahweh will gather together a nation from this exiled remnant (Mic 2:12; 4:6-7; 5:7-8). The "remnant [*šĕʾērît*] of Jacob" is described as "dew" that comes from Yahweh (Mic 5:7) and as a "lion" that is fierce and overpowering (Mic 5:8). In this poetic imagery the remnant topos is given a diverse collocation that allows the concept of remnant to intimate both permanence and retribution. As reflected in the prophets such as Amos and Isaiah, Mount Zion (i.e., Jerusalem) is the locus of this remnant people (Mic 4:7). A parallel interest is given in other prophetic books where the "escapees" (*pĕlêṭâ*) take refuge at Yahweh's earthly sanctuary (Joel 2:32; Obad 17).

3. Remnant in the Prophetic Literature of the Neo-Babylonian Era.

Once Neo-Assyrian armies exiled northern Israelites and Neo-Babylonians armies exiled southern Judeans, the Prophetic Books reaccommodate the remnant motif to provide hope for a deported and displaced people. Among the Book of the Twelve, Micah (see 2.3 above) and Zephaniah contribute to this development, and then Jeremiah and Ezekiel provide complementary perspectives for how the prophets envision this future hope.

3.1. Zephaniah. There are three instances of the remnant motif concerning Yahweh's people in Zephaniah (Zeph 2:7, 9; 3:13). This book is set in the historical context of King Josiah of Judah (Zeph 1:1), and so the reader is aware that Judah is at the cusp of Babylonian deportation. Just four years after the death of Josiah in 605 BC, Nebuchadnezzar already exercised control over Judah and began to deport Judeans

(cf. Dan 1:1-3). Moreover, in the final order of the Book of the Twelve, Zephaniah is positioned as the last book before the Babylonian exile, while the subsequent book of Haggai takes up the concerns of the remnant which has returned to Jerusalem.

In Zephaniah 2:7 the very regions where Nebuchadnezzar has complete hegemony (i.e., the coastal area of Ashkelon) are where Yahweh will restore the influence and control of the "remnant [*šĕʾērît*] of the house of Judah." The same idea is conveyed in Zephaniah 2:9, where Yahweh's "remnant" (*šĕʾērît*) will control not only Cisjordan but also Transjordan areas, including Ammon and Moab. The third occurrence of this topos is in Zephaniah 3:13, where the "remnant [*šĕʾērît*] of Israel" is returned by Yahweh to the land, and the people are characterized by the removal of sin and deceit from their midst. The writer of Zephaniah portrays the "remnant" of the impending exile as those who will have control over the very areas where the Neo-Babylonian Empire was conquering territory, and they will be a purified and holy people for Yahweh. The descriptions correspond to the overall theme that Yahweh will "remove" (*swr*) a prideful people and that he will "leave" (*šʾr*) a humble people (Zeph 3:11-12). But first, Yahweh must remove the "remnant [*šĕʾār*] of Baal" from the land (Zeph 1:4).

3.2. Jeremiah. Jeremiah follows a similar line to that of Amos, with the notion of a "remnant" people largely being a description of disdain. The root *šʾr* is used often (42x), but the root *glh* is what signifies that the community who would become the postexilic remnant people of Yahweh (*NIDOTTE* 4:16). With a few passages, however, the idea of a "remnant" is still a positive notion (cf. Jer 23:3; 31:7 [*šĕʾērît*]; Jer 39:9 [*yeter*]; Jer 43:5-6; 50:20) For Jeremiah, the "remnant" is destroyed by Yahweh, but the "exiled" are preserved in Babylon to secure a future generation who will return to the land (Jer 28:4; 52:28-30). The "escapees" (*plṭ*) and "survivors" (*śrd*) of the Babylonian invasion will die if they stay in Judah or seek refuge in Egypt (Jer 42:17; 44:14). The book of Jeremiah abounds in metaphor, and this is no different with the remnant theme. It is the "good figs" that are preserved in exile, while the "bad figs" are a rotten remnant that will die in Jerusalem or Egypt (Jer 24:5-10). The "good figs" are actually the Golah community in Babylonia, who are beneficiaries of Yahweh's favor and promise of return (Jer 29:4-14). W. L. Holladay notes that this reversal of remnant expectation takes language from Jeremiah's initial call in Jeremiah 1:10 (Holladay, 141). Yahweh sets the prophet "to build" (*bānâ*) and "to plant" (*nāṭaʿ*), and then Yahweh decides to "build" and "plant" the exiles in Babylonia (Jer 24:6) and commands the Golah community to "build houses" and "plant gardens" in exile (Jer 29:5). This interesting turn for Jeremiah identifies the Golah with the remnant people who will repatriate Israel in a later generation (Clements, 281-82). Although the concern for a remnant people is central to Jeremiah, it is not a positive term for anyone who remained in Judah or Egypt.

3.3. Ezekiel. On two occasions the priest Ezekiel, who served as a prophet during the exile, cries out to Yahweh to relent from killing the "remnant [*šěʾērît*] of Israel" (Ezek 9:8; 11:13). These accounts clearly note that Ezekiel understands the remnant to be the sole hope for the continuation of the Judean people. The oracles of Ezekiel employ the idea of a remnant people who initially would be associated with the Golah community in Babylonia and later with a Golah community that would repopulate Jerusalem in the postexilic period. The presence of Yahweh continues only with those who are in Babylon (Ezek 11:16), while any other alleged remnant will indeed be abandoned and scattered "to every wind"— that is, throughout the earth (Ezek 5:10 [*šěʾērît*]; Ezek 17:21 [*hanniš'ārîm*]). Other than an enigmatic "mark" (*tāw*) on the forehead of those who are still loyal to Yahweh in Jerusalem (Ezek 9:4), which separates them from being killed by Yahweh's agents of judgment (Ezek 9:6), remnant terminology is sparse in Ezekiel, which is the very prophetic tradition in which it should be most expected. These observations point to the possibility that a thoroughgoing theology of remnant was formulated in Persian Yehud after the Golah community had already returned to Jerusalem.

4. Remnant in the Prophetic Literature of the Persian Era.

4.1. Haggai and Zechariah. Haggai and Zechariah display the remnant motif and are set in the context of postexilic Persian Yehud. The references to a surviving or remnant people are exclusive to the Golah community that

has returned from the Babylonian exile (Hag 1:12, 14; 2:2, 3; Zech 8:6, 11-12) (L. V. Meyer, 671). In this respect, the idea of a remnant people serves as the "bridge concept" between previous generations who have been judged and destroyed by Yahweh and future generations who will be a community prepared for the messianic age (Elliott, 724). As the remnant community set out to build the second temple under the shadow of the Persian Empire, the self-designated remnant saw itself as the true people of Yahweh over and against those who would not take up the task of rebuilding Yahweh's sanctuary in Jerusalem (Hag 1:12, 14). Not only did this Golah remnant rebuild the Jerusalem *temple cult (Hag 1:8), but also they alone had obeyed Torah and consequently received Yahweh's covenantal blessings (*NIDOTTE* 4:17). In addition, this Golah community was imbued with the spirit of Yahweh. For Haggai's audience, only those who have the spirit are designated as the remnant of Israel (cf. Hag 1:12, 14). Further, only the remnant (*šěʾērît*) of the former people will experience the full restoration of Jerusalem (Zech 6:15; 8:7-8) and the subsequent effect on agricultural prosperity and fecundity over the entire land (Zech 8:11-12). The expectation for a remnant people in Zechariah 9—14 encompasses both those who are Gentiles (Zech 9:7) and those who are Judeans (Zech 13:7-9). This accords well with the expectation that concludes Zechariah where only those nations who worship Yahweh at the annual autumn Feast of Booths in Jerusalem will be spared drought and plague, which again identifies the remnant of Yahweh as those who support the Yahweh's sanctuary at Mount Zion.

4.2. Malachi. The last book of the Twelve has one reference to the remnant topos. As with Haggai and Zechariah, the postexilic designation of the remnant having the spirit of Yahweh is also noted in Malachi. Only those who have the "remnant of the spirit" (*šěʾār rûah*) have not betrayed Yahweh through cultic and social rebellion (Mal 2:15).

5. Remnant in the Literature of the Greek and Roman Eras.

5.1. Developments in Qumran, Intertestamental and New Testament Literature. Foreign religious and political entities in Judea grew more oppressive against those who sought to keep Torah and hold fast to the Second Temple cultus during the last two centuries BC. Manuscripts at Khirbet Qumran provide an understanding of the remnant motif that associates the notion with survivors from historical, physical threats (1Q33 I, 6; IV, 2) as well as the self-understanding of those who composed this "sectarian" literature (1Q33 I, 3; XIII, 8; XIV, 8; 4Q393 3, 7). For the sectarians, keeping Torah was prerequisite to being within the remnant community (1Q33 XIII, 8; XIV, 8-9). After rehearsing Israelite history at the beginning of the *Damascus Document* (CD-A I—III), the writer connects the surviving remnant from this historical overview with those who have covenanter identity (CD-A III, 21—IV, 4). Among the Qumran documents, these *Zadokite Documents* are most revealing of the sectarian's self-designation with Yahweh's remnant (Collins, 288-92).

Even in the pseudepigraphal literature this group distinguished itself as Yahweh's remnant in light of having undergone intense persecution (4 Ezra 7:27; 8:26-28). Moreover, it is those who survive physical threats and who continue in works and faith who will be the eschatological remnant and will be returned to the land (4 Ezra 9:7-9). The agrarian motif is taken up in *1 Enoch*, where the "remnant" is the seed for a new people (*1 En.* 83:8; cf. *Apoc. Ab.* 29:17). As mentioned in a number of the prophetic traditions, the locus of the remnant people is expected to be Mount Zion (*2 Bar.* 40:1-2). Appearances of the remnant topos in the NT are relatively sparse (cf. Mt 22:14; Lk 12:32; Rev 11:13), but there is a conceptual reality of exile for the Jewish people, which is enlivened with the ministries of John the Baptist and Jesus. The apostle Paul provides a sustained treatment of the remnant motif in Romans 9—11.

5.2. Exile in the First Century AD Since the remnant motif is exhibited in literature as late as the first century BC, it may be inferred that some Jewish groups still considered themselves to be in an exilic state (cf. Tob 13:5, 13; 14:5; Sir 36:10; 2 Macc 2:7, 18; *Pss. Sol.* 8:28). E. P. Sanders argues that a removal of foreign presence in the land and the restoration of the twelve tribes were focal points to a postbiblical remnant understanding (Sanders, 95-98). Evans notes that Jesus' ministry of preaching and providing signs and wonders exhibited an exilic awareness (Evans, 91-100). Taking this evidence into account, N. T. Wright maintains that a first-century AD Jew would answer positively, "We are in exile," when asked by a fellow Jew, "Where are we?" In this manner, the exile/restoration nexus with that of a remnant people provides for a remnant theology that moves beyond that of the Babylonian exile and significantly influences the social and literary developments among NT writers (see the essays in Scott).

6. Conclusion.
The "escapees" (*plṭ*) and "survivors" (*śrd*) of the successive invasions and deportations by the Neo-Assyrian Empire in the late eighth century BC and the Neo-Babylonian Empire in the early sixth century BC struggled with a continual theological resignification of their remnant status. The development of the remnant motif can be seen in the prophetic literature whereby certain historical events brought about the need to reassess theologically the nature and identity of Israel (*TDOT* 14:278-79). In a sense, remnant terminology became a *de facto* mark of identity for those loyal to Torah and the centralization of the second temple in fifth-century BC Yehud. In later Jewish traditions, various groups aligned themselves with this remnant designation where each understood itself to be the *šĕʾērît* of Yahweh. However, after AD 70 the Pharisees became the dominant and authoritative group in Judaism and believed that all Israel constituted the remnant and would be saved for the coming world. Again, agrarian metaphor was applied to the remnant motif, but this time within an eschatological perspective: "All Israel will have a portion in the world to come, for it is written: 'Your people are all righteous; they shall inherit the land forever, the branch of my planting, the work of my hands, that I may be glorified'" (*b. Sanh.* 90a).

See also EXILE; DAY OF THE LORD; ISRAEL; ISRAELITE HISTORY; TEMPLE.

Bibliography. **B. W. Anderson,** "Exodus Typology in Second Isaiah," in *Israel's Prophetic Heritage: Essays in Honor of James Muilenburg,* ed. B. W. Anderson and W. Harrelson (London: SCM, 1962) 177-95; **O. Carena,** *Il resto di Israele: Studio storico-comparativo delle iscrizioni reali assire e dei testi profetici sul tema del resto* (RivBSup 13; Bologna: Edizioni Dehoniane, 1985); **R. E. Clements,** "שָׁאַר," *TDOT* 14:272-86; **J. J. Collins,** *Beyond the Qumran Community: The Sectarian Movement of the Dead Sea Scrolls* (Grand

Rapids: Eerdmans, 2009); **K. H. Cuffey,** "Remnant, Redactor, and Biblical Theologian: A Comparative Study of Coherence in Micah and the Twelve," in *Reading and Hearing the Book of the Twelve,* ed. J. D. Nogalski and M. A. Sweeney (SBLSymS 15; Atlanta: Society of Biblical Literature, 2000) 185-208; **M. A. Elliot,** *The Survivors of Israel: A Reconsideration of the Theology of Pre-Christian Judaism* (Grand Rapids: Eerdmans, 2000); **M. W. Elliott,** "Remnant," *NDBT* 723-26; **C. A. Evans,** "Jesus and the Continuing Exile of Israel," in *Jesus and the Restoration of Israel: A Critical Assessment of N. T. Wright's "Jesus and the Victory of God,"*ed. C. C. Newman (Downers Grove, IL: InterVarsity Press, 1999) 77-100; **G. Hasel,** "Remnant," *ISBE* 5:130-34; idem, *The Remnant: The History and Theology of the Remnant Idea from Genesis to Isaiah* (3rd ed.; AUMSR 5; Berrien Springs, MI: Andrews University Press, 1980); **J. Hausmann,** *Israels Rest: Studien zum Selbstverständnis der nachexilischen Gemeinde* (BWANT 124; Stuttgart: Kohlhammer, 1987); **W. L. Holladay,** *Jeremiah 2: Chapters 26-52* (Hermeneia; Minneapolis: Fortress, 1989) **S. Japhet,** "The Concept of the 'Remnant' in the Restoration Period: On the Vocabulary of Self-Definition," in *Manna fällt auch heute noch: Beiträge zur Geschichte und Theologie des Alten, Ersten Testaments; Festschrift für Erich Zenger,* ed. F.-L. Hossfeld and L. Schwienhorst-Schönberger (HBS 44; Freiburg: Herder, 2004) 340-61; **S. McKnight,** *A New Vision for Israel: The Teachings of Jesus in National Context* (Grand Rapids: Eerdmans, 1999); **B. F. Meyer,** *The Aims of Jesus* (London: SCM, 1999); **L. V. Meyer,** "Remnant," *ABD* 5:669-71; **W. E. L. Müller and H. D. Preuss,** *Die Vorstellung vom Rest im Alten Testament* (2nd ed.; Neukirchen-Vluyn: Neukirchener Verlag, 1973); **R. Rendtorff,** "Israels 'Rest': Unabgeschlossene Überlegungen zu einem schwierigen Thema der alttestamentlichen Theologie," in *Verbindungslinien: Festschrift für Werner H. Schmidt zum 65. Geburtstag,* ed. A. Graupner, H. Delkurt and A. B. Ernst (Neukirchen-Vluyn: Neukirchener Verlag, 2000) 265-79; **E. P. Sanders,** *Jesus and Judaism* (Philadelphia: Fortress, 1985); **J. M. Scott,** ed., *Exile: Old Testament, Jewish, and Christian Perspectives* (JSJSup 56; Leiden: E. J. Brill, 1997); idem., *Restoration: Old Testament, Jewish, and Christian Perspectives* (JSJSup 72; Leiden: E. J. Brill, 2001); **M. A. Sweeney,** *The Twelve Prophets* (2 vols.; Berit Olam; Collegeville, MN: Liturgical Press, 2000); **N. T. Wright,** *The New Testament and the People of God* (Minneapolis: Fortress, 1992).

D. M. Morgan

REPENTANCE

Repentance refers to the human experience of turning away from attitudes and activities opposed to God and his ways and turning to God and his ways. It is expressed through a breadth of vocabulary, images and themes. Within the OT repentance can refer to human experiences that involve a human's affections, voice and/or behavior. While repentance often has been considered one of the hallmarks of the prophetic movement and corpus, the Prophetic Books of the OT highlight the ultimate failure of this agenda, at least as a human act. This article investigates the presentation of repentance within Isaiah, Jeremiah, Lamentations, Ezekiel, Daniel and the Book of the Twelve (see further Milgrom 1990; Dempsey; Krašovec; Boda 2009, 190-356, 452-71).

1. Isaiah
2. Jeremiah
3. Lamentations
4. Ezekiel
5. Daniel
6. The Book of the Twelve
7. Canon

1. Isaiah.

The introductory pericope of the book of Isaiah (Is 1) highlights two major strategies for dealing with *sin within the community, the first in Isaiah 1:2-20, focusing on the human response of repentance, what B. Childs called the "radical reversal" (Childs, 20), in which the community in both its inner affections and outer behavior (Is 1:19-20) turns from doing *evil to doing good (Is 1:16-17); and the second in Isaiah 1:21-31, focusing on the divine response of refining, in which Yahweh purges the community from the impurities of rebellion through a drastic act of discipline. The placement of repentance first suggests that this is the preferred strategy, but the second strategy is the ultimate outcome of the people in the first major section in Isaiah (Is 6—39). This reality is made clear from the outset of Isaiah 6—39 in the commissioning narrative of Isaiah 6. One can discern an ideal prophetic process underlying Isaiah 6:9-10 that entailed revelation (seeing, hearing), reception (understanding, perceiving with hearts), response (turning) and restoration (healing)— that is, one in which repentance was a key component. However, God's commission to Isaiah undermines this prophetic process, as God commissions Isaiah to dull the people's organs for receiving revelation so that they would be unable to repent and find healing (Boda 2009, 195-97; *contra* Wong, 213-33). The verses that follow in Isaiah 6:11-13 describe a drastic refining work of Yahweh that will result in the production of "holy seed" out of the ashes of the mighty forest that once was Israel and Judah. Repentance in Isaiah 7—39 is especially related to the issue of Judah's trust, an emphasis made clear by the crises experienced by a father (Ahaz) and son (Hezekiah) who are called to rely on Yahweh for protection (Oswalt, 55, 629-30; Conrad, 34-51; Seitz, 195-96).

Throughout Isaiah 28—33 the community is enticed to place its trust in religious (other gods [Is 28:15, 18]), political (other nations [Is 30:1; 31:1-3]) and economic (social injustice [Is 30:12-14]) resources rather than Yahweh. Repentance entails turning from these objects of trust to Yahweh (e.g., Is 28:16; 30:15, 18; 31:1, 6-7). This repentance, however, must not entail merely empty words (Is 29:13); it must include a deep engagement of the inner affections (Is 29:13) and a shift in behavior (Is 33:13, 16). While the Hezekiah narrative in Isaiah 36—38 showcases the kind of trust that Yahweh was demanding, the final scene in Isaiah 39 reveals Hezekiah's ultimate failure, which would lead to the drastic refining foreshadowed in Isaiah 6:11-13 (cf. Is 39:5-8). The name of one of Isaiah's sons, "Shear-jashub," meaning "a remnant will return" (Is 7:3; cf. Is 8:18), provides hope for the remnant that will emerge from the discipline envisioned in Isaiah 6. Not only does this *remnant return in a physical sense to the *land, but also this remnant returns by trusting in Yahweh rather than the *nations (Is 10:20-21) (Clements, 115; Webb, 72).

The drastic discipline of *exile clearly underlies the second major section of Isaiah (Is 40—55), a section addressing the exilic community. It soon becomes apparent, however, that the strategy of refinement has been unsuccessful as the community remains a deaf and blind servant (Is 42:18; 43:8; cf. Is 6). The answer in Isaiah 43:1 is a new act of divine grace by which Yahweh blots out the transgressions of the people (Is 43:8, 14, 25) and then invites the community to repent (Is 44:21-22). This is a key development in Isaiah's vision of repentance, as grace precedes repentance (Goldingay, 256). This same order can be discerned also in the concluding section of Isaiah 40—55. It is after the revelation of Yahweh's gracious act of *salvation for his people in Isaiah 52—53 that the community is invited "to participate in a renewal covenant" (Oswalt, 10) in Isaiah 55. This renewal uses the imagery of food, as the community is invited to enjoy a delicious and satisfying banquet without cost rather than its present diet. That repentance lies at the heart of this renewal is made explicit in its closing chapter (Is 55:6-7), which calls the community to seek and call on Yahweh while forsaking its present behavior and thoughts and turning to Yahweh.

The final section of Isaiah (Is 56—66) reveals enduring challenges within a community living in the wake of early returns from exile (see Is 56:8)—that is, in the early Persian period. Isaiah 58 highlights a community involved in fasting rituals, possibly reflecting penitential rites that emerged in the wake of the fall of Jerusalem and continued well after the Babylonian period. The prophet attacks these fasting rituals as merely external ritual and words without a true seeking of God reflected in repentance in behavior (Is 58:6-7). This theme of repentance is repeated in the prophetic liturgy of Isaiah 59, which depicts a community confessing their sins (Is 59:12-13) and repenting from rebellion (Is 59:20). This penitential community is promised God's spirit (Is 59:21). The prayer in Isaiah 63:7—64:12 often has been connected with the tradition of penitential *prayer, especially in light of its admission of sin (Is 64:5-8). In contrast to later exemplars of this tradition (Ezra 9; Neh 1; 9; Dan 9), this prayer blames God for the enduring apostasy of the people (Is 63:17). For this reason, the prophetic response to this prayer in Isaiah 65—66 is not positive, as God reminds the audience that he was the *covenant party who had been reaching out to them (Gärtner; Boda 2012).

The book of Isaiah thus reflects varying perspectives on repentance, moving between repentance as a prophetic agenda to avert judgment (Is 1; 7—38), to the abandonment of repentance as an agenda in judgment (Is 6), to repentance as an agenda prompted by God's new act of salvation (Is 40—55), to repentance as once again a prophetic agenda (Is 56—66).

2. Jeremiah.

A similar prophetic process to that underlying Isaiah 6:9-10 can be discerned throughout Jeremiah, especially showcased in passages such as Jeremiah 18:1-17; 25:3-11 and entailing three basic elements: divine word, human response, divine response. The ideal is a human response in which the community turns away from evil and turns to God, even though the norm in Jeremiah is a community that continued to do evil or turned away from God to do evil. Essential to ideal penitential human response in Jeremiah is "listening" (*qšb, nṭh, ʾzn, šmʿ*), not surprising in light of the emphasis on the divine word as the first key step in the prophetic process. At the core of the vocabulary of human response lie words related to change, especially *šwb*, but also *nḥm* Niphal and *pnh* (see Holladay; Thompson, 76-81; Ossom-Batsa; Shields, 41). Jeremiah showcases the twofold process involved in repentance: turning from evil behavior and turning to appropriate behavior (Jer 18:11; 26:3, 13; 35:15). There is a "repentance," however, in which the people turn from God to sin, and for this the prophet Jeremiah again uses the root *šwb* (e.g., Jer 3:10), but also *swr* (e.g., Jer 5:23), *ymr* (e.g., Jer 2:11) and *šnh* Piel (e.g., Jer 2:36). Echoing the dominant root *šwb*, the community is described with the pejorative terms "apostate" (*mĕšûbâ* [e.g., Jer 2:19]) and "rebellious" (*šôbāb* [e.g., Jer 3:14]).

In Jeremiah repentance is described on three levels. First, at times repentance entails speech, whether calling on God (Jer 29:12, 13; 36:7) or admitting culpability (Jer 3:13; 8:6). Second, repentance is regularly associated with a change in behavior, especially putting away *idolatry and acting justly (e.g., Jer 4:1-2; 7:3-6). Third, in some cases repentance is described in terms of the deep engagement of the affections of the heart (e.g., Jer 3:10; 24:7), which starkly contrasts repentance that is merely deception (Jer 3:10).

The dominant motivation for repentance in the book of Jeremiah is the threat of judgment (e.g., Jer 4:4; 36:3). However, at times a more positive strategy is used as the prophet points to God's promised *blessing and salvation (e.g., Jer 11:4) or the opportunity for renewal of covenant relationship (e.g., Jer 7:23).

The book of Jeremiah reveals a shift in the agenda of repentance. In Jeremiah 2:1—4:4 the prophet calls the community to a repentance that involves inner affections, verbal expressions and practical actions. As the book progresses, however, one can discern a major crisis in the prophetic process (see Paterson). The people's lack of response ultimately leads to Yahweh shutting down the prophetic process and with it removing the opportunity for the people to repent, seen especially in the attempted penitential liturgy in Jeremiah 14:1—15:4, which concludes with Yahweh demanding that Jeremiah no longer seek him on behalf of the people (Dempsey). The prophet becomes intertwined with his people as even he is told to repent (Jer 15:19) and loses access to God's voice in relation to his own predicament (Jer 17:14-18; 18:18-23; 20:7-13; 20:14-18) (Diamond, 77-78; Boda 2012).

The demise of penitence depicted in Jeremiah 1—25, however, is not the end of the book, and Jeremiah 26—52 provides future hope for the community to deal with its sin. Jeremiah 29:12-13 articulates a future penitential agenda that includes calling on Yahweh, coming and praying to him, seeking and searching for him with all one's heart. What will make this possible has been foreshadowed in Jeremiah 24:7 and clarified in Jeremiah 31:27-40; 32:37-41 as the prophet promises the gift of a new covenant with a new heart upon which the law of God will be written and the fear of God will be placed. Thus, repentance and avoidance of apostasy are secured in the end only by an internal, divine work (Raitt 1977, 175-84; Dempsey) based on God's declaration of forgiveness (Jer 31:34; 33:8). Thus, as J. Unterman has noted, the prophet most closely connected with the call to repentance ultimately "abandons the principle of free will and the attendant demand for repentance" (Unterman 1987, 177).

3. Lamentations.

One can discern at various points in the book of Lamentations a penitential agenda (see Boda 2008). Admission of culpability is explicitly stated in Lamentations 1:8 ("Jerusalem sinned greatly"); 1:17 ("I have rebelled against his command"); 1:22 ("all my transgressions"); 4:6 ("the iniquity of the daughter of my people"); 4:13 ("the sins of her prophets, the iniquities of her priests"); 4:22 ("your iniquity"); 5:7 ("our fathers sinned"); 5:16 ("we have sinned"). While at times Yahweh's actions are justified (e.g., Lam 1:18), the general message is that the punishment that has befallen Jerusalem exceeds the crimes committed (e.g., Lam 1:12; 2:13, 20). At the center of the book, however, lies an invitation to repentance. First, the grace of Yahweh is rehearsed in Lamentations 3:21-33, focusing on the full breadth of the Hebrew lexical stock for God's care for his people. This prompts a rehearsal of the justice of God in Lamentations 3:33-38, revealing that Yahweh "does not afflict with delight" (Lam 3:33) but rather disciplines because of sin (Lam 3:37-38). This leads to the invitation to repentance in Lamentations 3:40: "Let us examine and probe our ways, and let us return to the LORD." While the response that follows (Lam 3:41-47) does admit sin (Lam 3:41), it expresses the frustration of the people that although they have confessed their sin, God has not pardoned, as they continue to suffer. The remainder of the book of Lamentations returns to the tone of the first two chapters, expressing the deep pain and frustration of the people while admitting culpability.

The book of Lamentations thus showcases the frustration of penitential rhythms for the community living in the wake of the destruction of Jerusalem. Its placement among the prophets within the Greek traditions brings it into conversation with the prophets whose works emphasize the theme of repentance. On the one side, Lamentations contrasts the prophets in its rejection of the penitential invitation of Lamentations 3:40; on the other side, Lamentations echoes the crisis in penitential traditions evidenced in the Prophetic Books. While the answer of Lamentations appears to be a combination of frustration and *faith (Lam 5:19-22), the prophets at times look to a new era of transformation initiated and accomplished by Yahweh himself.

4. Ezekiel.

The penitential process identified above in Isaiah and Jeremiah can be discerned also in the book of Ezekiel, especially in Ezekiel 2—3; 18; 33, where the people's response to the prophetic warning is articulated clearly. Key vocabulary used for penitential response involves not only turning (*šwb* [e.g., Ezek 3:19]), but also listening/obeying (*šmʿ* [e.g., Ezek 2:5, 7; 3:6, 11), acting (*šmr*, *ʿśh*, *hlk* [e.g., Ezek 18:5]), keeping holy (*qdš* Piel [e.g., Ezek 20:20]) and clean (*ṭhr* Piel [Ezek 24:13]), and separating oneself (*nzr* [Ezek 14:7]).

Ezekiel's prophetic commission in Ezekiel 1—3 does emphasize the necessity of repentance for averting judgment, but there is a dominant tone of skepticism over the people's ability to respond. This skepticism dominates the chapters that follow in Ezekiel 4—33, suggesting that the fate of Jerusalem is sealed. The role of repentance in this section of Ezekiel has been controversial. Calls to repentance do appear in Ezekiel 1—33 (see Ezek 2—3; 14:6; 18:30-32; 33), and these have been treated in various ways from later redactional insertions (e.g., Zimmerli, 205), to "an interesting and authentic interlude" between Ezekiel's judgment and salvation phases of preaching (Raitt 1971, 49), to rhetorical flourishes to justify God's punishment (Fishbane, 147-48; Joyce, 50-60), to stimulation to prompt admission of guilt (Kaminsky, 166). The problem with these approaches is that they assume that repentance here is related to the impending judgment on Jerusalem/Judah. It appears, however, that Ezekiel's audience is the exilic community rather than the community in Jerusalem/Judah (Fishbane, 147-48), and that the penitential calls in Ezekiel 1—32 are directed to the exilic community from which will emerge a purified remnant (Matties). Ezekiel, like Jeremiah, was denied an intercessory role for the city (Ezek 3:24-27; 24:26-27; 33:21-22) (see Wilson; Block, 255; Odell, 106).

The tone of the book of Ezekiel shifts considerably after the message of the fall of Jerusalem reaches the prophet in Ezekiel 33 (Ezek 33:21-22). It is not surprising that this event is preceded by a reiteration of the Ezekiel's initial calling (Ezek 33:1-20) and the importance of repentance. The themes of salvation and restoration dominate the chapters that follow (Ezek 34—48). A key component of this vision of restoration is a spiritual renewal that will see restoration in the relationship between Yahweh and the people and renewal in their hearts. The core of this renewal is remembering and loathing sin (Ezek 36:31; cf. Ezek 6:9; 20:43) and experiencing shame over one's past behavior (Ezek 36:32; cf. Ezek 16:60-63), acts that follow God's gracious acts toward his people (see Ezek 16:60, 62). Loathing of past sin will be accompanied by changes in behavior (Ezek 37:23-24; cf. Ezek 11:18-20). Such internal and external signs of repentance will be enabled by a divine operation of deep inner transformation as Yahweh takes away their heart of stone to give them a single heart, new heart, new spirit, heart of flesh, and divine spirit (Ezek 11:19; 36:26-27; 37:14; 39:29) (Dempsey). One cannot miss the deep contrast between this vision of repentance and that found in Ezekiel 18:30b-32, where the people are called to repent and get for themselves a new heart and a new spirit.

5. Daniel.
Repentance is associated with three groups of people in the book of Daniel. First, the emperors in Daniel 1—6 are at times exhorted to repent. Daniel tells King Nebuchadnezzar to avoid the punishment of God by destroying his sins through righteous and merciful treatment of the poor (Dan 4:27) and even after punishment to experience restoration by acknowledging the sovereignty of the Most High (Dan 4:26, 32, 34b, 37). Second, Daniel is presented as an exemplar penitential figure as he prays a penitential prayer to Yahweh (Werline 1998; 2007; Boda 1999; 2008; Venter). Such a prayer is based on the theological and liturgical foundations of Leviticus 26; Deuteronomy 30; 1 Kings 8; Jeremiah 25; 29. Daniel is depicted as discerning from Jeremiah that the time of exile was coming to an end (Jer 25:11-12; 29:10) and so prayed in line with the agenda laid out in Leviticus 26:39-40; Deuteronomy 30:1-3; 1 Kings 8. Similar prayers are found in Ezra 9; Nehemiah 1; 9; Psalm 106. This verbal penitential act contrasts the prayer found in Isaiah 63:7—64:12 and the book of Lamentations not only by admitting the culpability of the community due to their sins and those of their ancestors, but also by justifying Yahweh for the judgment that befell the nation. Daniel prays this on behalf of his people and city Jerusalem with hope that the state of destruction would come to an end. Daniel is clear that the gracious response of Yahweh is dependent upon human response, since Daniel 9:4-5 refers to "those who love him and keep his commandments," and Daniel 9:13 describes those who seek God's face by "turning from their iniquity and giving attention to his truth." The divine response to this penitential act, however, is disappointing as Gabriel announces in Daniel 9:24 that the expected seventy-year limit to the destruction of Jerusalem would increase sevenfold in order to deal with sin. This suggests that although Daniel may express repentance, the community that he represents continues to struggle with sin.

Daniel thus showcases repentance as a normative activity both for pagans (emperor) and the covenant community (Daniel). However, the ineffectiveness of Daniel's prayer suggests the failure of repentance (Venter, 37), an emphasis echoed in the Prophetic Books.

6. The Book of the Twelve (Minor Prophets).
The book of Zechariah begins by highlighting the importance of repentance to the message of the prophets (Zech 1:3-4). By referring to the "earlier prophets," Zechariah 1:4 brings into view the earlier prophets found in the Book of the Twelve, but by citing vocabulary reminiscent of Jeremiah, it brings into view the broader prophetic corpus. The cry of repentance can be discerned throughout the Book of the Twelve (Unterman 1982; Collins, 59-87; Smothers; Van Leeuwen; Rendtorff 1998; 2000; Watts; House; Boda 2011). Hosea, Amos and Micah, the eighth-century BC prophets in the collection, call the people to repentance (Hos 2:2-4, 7; 5:4; 6:1-3; 7:10, 16; 11:5; 12:6; 14:1-2; Amos 4:6-11; 5:4-6, 14-15; Mic 6:6-8). However, each of them highlights the inability and insincerity of the nation to respond to these calls (Hos 2:7-8; 5:4; 6:1-4; 7:10, 14, 16; 8:1-3; 11:5, 7; 12:11—13:16; Amos 4:6-13; Mic 6:1-16 (Smothers). These books focus on certain future judgment (Hos 2:9-13; 5:8-14; 11:5-6; 12:14; 13:16; Amos 1—2; 8:1—9:10; Mic 1—3; 7:1-10) and at times on a future divine unilateral initiative to restore the people (Hos 2:14-23; 3:1-3; 14:4-7; Amos 9:11-15; Mic 2:12-13; 4-5; 7:11-13). At times, this future judgment or salvation prompts repentance and confession (Hos 3:4-5; 5:15; 6:1-3; 14:1-7; Mic 7:16-20). These perspectives on repentance have led to divergent conclusions on the role of repentance within these books, from treating repentance as restricted to the future (e.g., Stuart, 7-8 [on Hosea]) to treating it as a present demand to avert judgment (e.g., Sweeney, 1:26-27 [on Hosea]). By juxtaposing the message of repentance with depictions of the people's rejection of the message, these prophets undermine the efficacy of repentance.

However, Joel and Jonah, the two Prophetic Books that have been placed in proximity to these eighth-century BC prophets, contrast the message of Hosea, Amos and Micah by showcasing positive responses to the message of repentance using similar vocabulary (Joel 1:13-14; 2:11-16; Jon 3:5-10). Key to repentance in Joel and Jonah is the revelation of Yahweh found in Exodus 34:6-7, where Yahweh declares himself to be "gracious and compassionate, slow to anger, abounding in covenant faithfulness" (cf. Joel 2:13; Jon 4:2). Repentance thus is closely linked to the grace of Yahweh, even though the threat of God's judgment plays a key role (see Joel 2:11; Jon 3:4). The message of repentance disappears in the second phase of the Book of the Twelve, signaled by the reflection on the revelation of Yahweh from Exodus 34:6-7 at the outset of the book of Nahum (Nah 1:2-3). While Jonah's message prompted repentance among the Ninevites, Nahum declares an irreversible announcement of judgment upon Nineveh. This tone of judgment without an opportunity for repentance to turn away *wrath continues into Habakkuk and Zephaniah, even though there are encouragements for penitential response for the remnant that will survive the judgment (e.g., Hab 2:4b; 3:16; Zeph 2:1-3 [see also Ezekiel in 4 above]). Haggai, however, signals the beginning of the final phase of the Book of the Twelve and with it a renewal of the call to repentance. Haggai's vision of repentance is focused on the restoration of the temple, but with Zechariah this expands to include repentance from immoral and ungodly behavior (Hag 1:4), related in Zechariah 7—8 especially to social injustice (see Zech 5) (Boda 2003). Amidst the warnings of salvation and judgment in Zechariah 9—14 one finds the depiction of a community receiving "a spirit of favor and pleading for favor"—that is, a spirit that prompts a penitential mourning over what the community has done to Yahweh (Zech 12:10-14). This is reminiscent of the hoped-for "spirit" declared by Ezekiel (see 4 above). Repentance is also of key importance to the message of Malachi, as this final prophet of the Twelve confronts the priests and community of his day. That summary message of the earlier prophets found in Zechariah 1:3 is repeated in Malachi 3:7, revealing that human penitential response is an enduring priority of the prophets, even if it will take "the day of his coming" to produce the ideal community (Mal 3:1-2).

The echo of the penitential message "Return to me, and I will return to you" (Zech 1:3; Mal 3:7) in these concluding chapters of the prophetic corpus emphasizes the relational priority in the message of repentance among the prophets. Repentance is first and foremost a return to a relationship with a personal God who longs to enjoy covenant fellowship with his people. That this has implications for behavior is made clear in the surrounding texts (Zech 1:4; Mal 1—2), but this kind of repentance makes sense only within the context of relationship.

7. Canon.

Clearly, repentance is a key theme in the prophetic traditions of the OT. This theme can be discerned within this tradition from its origins. This agenda of repentance is not limited, however, to the Prophetic Books of the OT, but also can be discerned in the priestly traditions (e.g., Lev 26 [Milgrom 1975; 1990]), the Deuteronomic traditions (e.g., Deut 4:25-31; 30:1-10; 1 Kings 8 [Boda 2006]), the liturgical traditions (e.g., Pss 51; 106 [Boda 2009, 395-451]) and the narrative traditions of the Persian period (e.g., 2 Chron 7:14; Ezra 9; Neh 1; 9 [Kelly; Werline 1998]). However, the theme is developed most extensively in the prophetic traditions, and although repentance is never fully abandoned, its limitations as a human act are showcased most vividly. The legacy of this great penitential project can be discerned in the NT (Nave; Boda and Smith), beginning with the messages of John the Baptist (e.g., Mt 3:2) and of Jesus (e.g., Mt 4:17), and then those who proclaimed the gospel (Lk 24:47; Acts 2:38, 3:19; 5:31; 20:21). Repentance is both a gracious divine gift based on the mercy of God (Acts 5:31; Rom 2:4) and a human response that prompts God's gracious response (1 Jn 1:9).

See also EVIL; FORGIVENESS; LAMENT, MOURNING; PRAYER; SIN, SINNERS.

BIBLIOGRAPHY. **D. I. Block,** *The Book of Ezekiel: Chapters 1-24* (NICOT; Grand Rapids: Eerdmans, 1997); **M. J. Boda,** *Praying the Tradition: The Origin and Use of Tradition in Nehemiah 9* (BZAW 277; Berlin: de Gruyter, 1999); idem, "Zechariah: Master Mason or Penitential Prophet?" in *Yahwism after the Exile: Perspectives on Israelite Religion in the Persian Era,* ed. R. Albertz and B. Becking (STR 5; Assen: Van Gorcum, 2003) 49-69; idem, "Confession as Theological Expression: Ideological Origins of Penitential Prayer," in *Seeking the Favor of God, 1: The Origin of Penitential Prayer in Second Temple*

Judaism, ed. M. J. Boda, D. K. Falk and R. A. Werline (SBLEJL 21; Atlanta: Society of Biblical Literature, 2006) 21-51; idem, "The Priceless Gain of Penitence: From Communal Lament to Penitential Prayer in the 'Exilic' Liturgy of Israel," in *Lamentations in Ancient and Contemporary Contexts*, ed. N. C. Lee and C. Mandolfo (SBLSymS 43; Atlanta: Society of Biblical Literature, 2008) 81-101; idem, *A Severe Mercy: Sin and Its Remedy in the Old Testament* (Siphrut 1; Winona Lake, IN: Eisenbrauns, 2009); idem, "Penitential Innovations in the Book of the Twelve," in *On Stone and Scroll: A Festschrift for Graham Davies*, ed. B. A. Mastin, K. J. Dell and J. K. Aitken (BZAW 420; Berlin: de Gruyter, 2011) 291-308; idem, "'Uttering Precious Rather Than Worthless Words': Divine Patience and Impatience with Lament in Isaiah and Jeremiah," in *Lament: Israel's Cry to God*, ed. M. J. Boda, C. Dempsey and L. Snow Flesher (LHBOTS; London: Continuum, 2012); **M. J. Boda and G. T. Smith**, eds., *Repentance in Christian Theology* (Collegeville, MN: Liturgical Press, 2006); **M. J. Boda, D. K. Falk and R. A. Werline**, eds., *Seeking the Favor of God—Volume 1: The Origin of Penitential Prayer in Second Temple Judaism* (SBLEJL 1; Atlanta/ Leiden: Society of Biblical Literature/Brill, 2006); **B. S. Childs**, *Isaiah* (OTL; Louisville: Westminster/John Knox, 2001); **R. E. Clements**, *Isaiah 1-39* (NCBC; Grand Rapids: Eerdmans, 1980); **T. Collins**, *The Mantle of Elijah: The Redaction Criticism of the Prophetical Books* (BibSem 20; Sheffield: JSOT, 1993); **E. W. Conrad**, *Reading Isaiah* (OBT 27; Minneapolis: Fortress, 1991); **C. J. Dempsey**, "'Turn Back, O People:' Repentance in the Latter Prophets," in *Repentance in Christian Theology*, ed. M. J. Boda and G. T. Smith (Collegeville, MN: Liturgical, 2006) 47-66; **A. R. Diamond**, *The Confessions of Jeremiah in Context: Scenes of Prophetic Drama* (JSOTSup 46; Sheffield: JSOT, 1987); **M. Fishbane**, "Sin and Judgment in the Prophecies of Ezekiel," *Int* 38 (1984) 131-50; **J. Gärtner**, "'. . . Why Do You Let Us Stray from Your Paths . . . ' (Isa 63:17): The Concept of Guilt in the Communal Lament in Isa 63:7-64:11," in *Seeking the Favor of God*, 1: *The Origin of Penitential Prayer in Second Temple Judaism*, ed. M. J. Boda, D. K. Falk and R. A. Werline (SBLEJL 21; Atlanta: Society of Biblical Literature, 2006) 145-63; **J. Goldingay**, *Isaiah* (NIBC; Peabody, MA: Hendrickson, 2001); **W. L. Holladay**, *The Root*

Šûbh in the Old Testament: With Particular Reference to Its Usages in Covenantal Contexts (Leiden: E. J. Brill, 1958); **P. R. House**, "Endings as New Beginnings: Returning to the Lord, the Day of the Lord, and Renewal in the Book of the Twelve," in *Thematic Threads in the Book of the Twelve*, ed. P. L. Redditt and A. Schart (BZAW 325; Berlin: de Gruyter, 2003) 313-38; **P. M. Joyce**, *Divine Initiative and Human Response in Ezekiel* (JSOTSup 51; Sheffield: JSOT, 1989); **J. S. Kaminsky**, *Corporate Responsibility in the Hebrew Bible* (JSOTSup 196; Sheffield: Sheffield Academic, 1995); **B. E. Kelly**, *Retribution and Eschatology in Chronicles* (JSOTSup 211; Sheffield: Sheffield Academic Press, 1996); **J. Krašovec**, *Reward, Punishment, and Forgiveness: The Thinking and Beliefs of Ancient Israel in the Light of Greek and Modern Views* (VTSup 78; Leiden: E. J. Brill, 1999); **G. Matties**, *Ezekiel 18 and the Rhetoric of Moral Discourse* (SBLDS 126; Atlanta: Scholars Press, 1990); **J. Milgrom**, "Priestly Doctrine of Repentance," *RB* 82 (1975) 186-205; idem, "Excursus: Repentance in the Torah and the Prophets," in *Numbers* (JPSTC; Philadelphia: Jewish Publication Society, 1990) 396-98; **G. D. Nave Jr.**, *The Role and Function of Repentance in Luke-Acts* (SBLAB 4; Leiden: E. J. Brill, 2002); **M. S. Odell**, *Ezekiel* (SHBC; Macon, GA: Smyth & Helwys, 2006); **G. Ossom-Batsa**, "The Theological Significance of the Root of *SWB* in Jeremiah," *AUSS* 39 (2001) 223-32; **J. Oswalt**, *The Book of Isaiah: Chapters 1-39* (NICOT; Grand Rapids: Eerdmans, 1986); **R. M. Paterson**, "Repentance or Judgment: The Construction and Purpose of Jeremiah 2-6," *ExpTim* 96 (1985) 199-203; **T. M. Raitt**, "Prophetic Summons to Repentance," *ZAW* 83 (1971) 30-49; idem, *A Theology of Exile: Judgment/Deliverance in Jeremiah and Ezekiel* (Philadelphia: Fortress, 1977); **R. Rendtorff**, "Alas for the Day! The 'Day of the Lord' in the Book of the Twelve," in *God in the Fray: A Tribute to Walter Brueggemann*, ed. T. Linafelt and T. K. Beal (Minneapolis: Fortress, 1998) 186-97; idem, "How to Read the Book of the Twelve as a Theological Unity," in *Reading and Hearing the Book of the Twelve*, ed. J. D. Nogalski and M. A. Sweeney (SBLSymS 15; Atlanta: Society of Biblical Literature, 2000) 75-87; **C. R. Seitz**, *Zion's Final Destiny: The Development of the Book of Isaiah—A Reassessment of Isaiah 36-39* (Minneapolis: Fortress, 1991); **M. E. Shields**, "Circumcision of the Prostitute: Gender, Sexuality, and the Call to Repentance in Jeremiah 3:1-4:4," *BibInt* 3 (1995) 61-74; **T. G. Smothers,** "Preaching and Praying Repentance in Hosea," *RevExp* 90 (1993) 239-46; **D. K. Stuart,** *Hosea-Jonah* (WBC 31; Waco, TX: Word, 1987); **M. A. Sweeney,** *The Twelve Prophets* (2 vols; Berit Olam; Collegeville, MN: Liturgical, 2000); **J. A. Thompson,** *The Book of Jeremiah* (NICOT; Grand Rapids: Eerdmans, 1980); **J. Unterman,** "Repentance and Redemption in Hosea," *SBLSP* 21 (1982) 541-50; idem, *From Repentance to Redemption: Jeremiah's Thought in Transition* (JSOTSup 54; Sheffield: JSOT, 1987); **R. C. Van Leeuwen,** "Scribal Wisdom and Theodicy in the Book of the Twelve," in *In Search of Wisdom: Essays in Memory of John G. Gammie,* ed. L. G. Perdue, B. B. Scott and W. J. Wiseman (Louisville: Westminister/ John Knox, 1993) 31-50; **P. M. Venter,** "A Penitential Prayer in Apocalyptic Garb," in *Seeking the Favor of God,* 2: *The Development of Penitential Prayer in Second Temple Judaism,* ed. M. J. Boda, D. K. Falk and R. A. Werline (SBLEJL 22; Atlanta: Society of Biblical Literature, 2007) 33-49; **J. D. W. Watts,** "A Frame for the Book of the Twelve: Hosea 1-3 and Malachi," in *Reading and Hearing the Book of the Twelve,* ed. J. D. Nogalski and M. A. Sweeney (SBLSymS 15; Atlanta: Society of Biblical Literature, 2000) 209-17; **B. G. Webb,** *The Message of Isaiah: On Eagles' Wings* (BST; Downers Grove, IL: InterVarsity Press, 1997); **R. A. Werline,** *Penitential Prayer in Second Temple Judaism: The Development of a Religious Institution* (SBLEJL 13; Atlanta: Scholars Press, 1998); idem, "Prayer, Politics and Social Vision in Daniel 9," in *Seeking the Favor of God,* 2: *The Development of Penitential Prayer in Second Temple Judaism,* ed. M. J. Boda, D. K. Falk and R. A. Werline (SBLEJL 22; Atlanta: Society of Biblical Literature, 2007) 17-32; **R. R. Wilson,** "An Interpretation of Ezekiel's Dumbness," *VT* 22 (1972) 91-104; **G. C. I. Wong,** *The Road to Peace: Pastoral Reflections on Isaiah 1-12* (Singapore: Genesis, 2009); **W. Zimmerli,** *Ezekiel 1: A Commentary on the Book of the Prophet Ezekiel, Chapters 1-24,* trans. R. E. Clements, ed. F. M. Cross, K. Baltzer and L. J. Greenspoon (Hermeneia; Philadelphia: Fortress, 1979).

M. J. Boda

REST. *See* PEACE, REST.

RESTORATION. *See* CREATION THEOLOGY; ESCHATOLOGY; EXILE; EXODUS IMAGERY; LAND; REMNANT; SALVATION, DELIVERANCE; TEMPLE; ZION.

RESURRECTION. *See* AFTERLIFE.

RETRIBUTION

Retribution is a corollary of divine *justice. If God is indeed just, then he will punish or reward people according to their actions, whether individually or corporately. As the etymology of the term *retribution* suggests, God "pays back" to humans what their actions deserve (Towner, 203; Wong, 2). In the prophetic literature, as in contemporary English usage, the notion of retribution is usually associated with judgment, though the idea of reward is also attested on rare occasions.

1. The Language of Retribution
2. The Rhetoric of Poetic Justice
3. Examples of Divine Retribution in Prophetic Texts
4. The Dynamics of Retribution

1. The Language of Retribution.
The prophets express the concept of retribution with a variety of words and phrases. The most common of these are as follows.

1.1. The Verb šāpaṭ ("to Judge") and the Related Noun mišpāṭ ("Justice"). Isaiah uses the verb form only twice of God as judge (Is 33:22; 66:16) but employs the related noun seven times (Is 3:14; 4:4; 5:16; 26:8-9; 30:18; 34:5). Isaiah 30:18 characterizes the Lord as a just God.

Jeremiah uses the verb three times of divine judgment (Jer 2:35; 11:20; 25:31) and the noun seven times (Jer 1:16; 4:12; 10:24; 30:11; 46:28; 48:47; 51:9). Jeremiah 11:20 is important to the theme of retribution because it affirms that the Lord judges "righteously" (*ṣedeq*) as he examines thoughts and motives carefully. This judgment is closely associated with divine vengeance (*nĕqāmâ* [see 1.3. below]). In Jeremiah 10:24 the prophet asks the Lord to implement his discipline "in justice" (i.e., "in just measure"), not "in anger." As one would expect if a judicial concept of retribution is assumed, this suggests that a principle of justice and fairness be employed, in contrast to a mere outpouring of anger. This same idea of "just measure" appears in Jeremiah 30:11, where it stands in contrast to allowing wrongdoing to go unpunished (see also Jer 46:28).

Ezekiel uses the verb seventeen times of divine judgment (Ezek 7:3, 8, 27; 11:10-11; 16:38; 17:20; 18:30; 20:35-36; 33:20; 34:17, 20, 22; 35:11; 36:19; 38:22) and the noun twice (Ezek 5:8; 39:21). Five times the verb is collocated with "according to one's ways" (Ezek 7:3, 8; 18:30; 33:20; 36:19), indicating a direct correspondence between the people's actions and the divine response, as one would expect if the principle of retribution is assumed (Wong, 239-42). Ezekiel 33:20 is instructive because the Lord pronounces his intention to judge each one "according to his ways" in response to the charge that he (Heb *derek ʾădōnāy* ["the way of the Lord"]) is unjust. Ezekiel 18:30 gives insight into the relationship between divine intervention and human responsibility. After announcing his intention to judge each one "according to his ways," the Lord urges the people to *repent, because otherwise their "iniquity will become to them [*yihyeh lākem*] their stumbling block." The Lord will clearly intervene ("I will judge you"), but from another perspective it is the people's sin that brings them to ruin because it prompts divine intervention. Divine sovereignty and human responsibility are held in delicate balance.

The verb is used only once of divine judgment in the Book of the Twelve (Joel 3:2), and the noun seven times (Hos. 5:1, 11; 6:5; Mic 7:9; Hab 1:12; Zeph 3:15; Mal 3:5). Hosea 6:5 is enlightening because the instrument of the Lord's judgment is identified as his word, spoken by the prophets. In this passage judgment is not something that works itself out in a purely mechanistic or even providential manner; it is initiated by the prophetic word, which sets judgment in motion. Habakkuk 1:12 indicates that the instrument of judgment, the Chaldeans, was ordained by the Lord, emphasizing once more the divine initiation of punishment.

1.2. The verb šillam ("to Repay"). Isaiah, Jeremiah and Joel use the verb *šillam* ("to repay") to express the concept of divine retribution. This use of the verb appears to be rooted in the law. In Exodus 21:33—22:14 it is used of making full restitution for something stolen or destroyed. In Isaiah 59:18 the prophet announces that the Lord "will repay his enemies according to their actions." According to Isaiah 65:6-7, the Lord "will repay upon their lap their iniquities and their fathers' iniquities." The Lord speaks of measuring or meting out (*mādad*) "their former actions upon their lap." The language indicates that the judgment will be commensurate with the sins committed, and that the Lord himself will intervene to bring retribution. Speaking through Jeremiah, the Lord warns that he "will repay" his idolatrous people "double" for their iniquity and sin (Jer 16:18). In Jeremiah 25:14 the Lord declares that he will repay the Chaldeans "according to what they have done and according to the work of their hands" (cf. Jer 50:29). Although the majority of cases pertain to judgment (see also Is 66:6; Jer 51:6, 24, 56), the verb is used on two occasions to describe how the Lord will repay his repentant people with renewed blessing (Is 57:18; Joel 2:25). In Jeremiah 32:18 the verb is used of judgment, but this is an aspect of the broader principle that the Lord repays all people according to their actions, whether good or evil (Jer 32:19) (Krašovec, 47).

1.3. The Verb nāqam ("to Avenge") and the Related Nouns nāqām, něqāmâ ("Vengeance"). These terms suggest that the Lord has been offended (see Is 1:24) and that his vengeance constitutes retribution (see Vannoy, 1145-46). In Isaiah 34:8 the Lord's "day of vengeance" is associated with his "year of repayment" (*šillūmîm*). Vengeance is equated with "recompense" (*gěmûl*) in Isaiah 35:4. In addition to Isaiah (see also Is 47:3; 59:17; 61:2; 63:4), the concept appears in Jeremiah (Jer 5:9, 29; 9:9; 11:20; 15:15; 20:12; 46:10; 50:15; 51:6, 11, 36), Ezekiel (Ezek 24:8; 25:14, 17), and the Twelve (Mic 5:15; Nah 1:2). In Jeremiah 11:20 divine vengeance is the outworking of the Lord's righteous judgment. When the Lord's vengeance is implemented against Babylon, the prophet urges the instruments of divine judgment to "do to her as she has done" (Jer 50:15). In Jeremiah 51:6 vengeance is associated with the ideas of "recompense" (*gěmûl* [cf. Is 35:4]) and repayment, while in Jeremiah 51:36 it appears to have a legal connotation.

1.4. The Collocation pāqad ʿal ("to Visit Upon") = "to Punish"). G. André understands this expression to mean "to pronounce judgment upon" (André, 57-58). In many cases, the object of judgment simply follows the preposition in the verbal expression (Is 10:12; 24:21; Jer 9:24; 11:22; 21:14; 23:34; 27:8; 29:32; 30:20; 44:13, 29; 46:25; 50:18 [ʾel is used here, not ʿal]; 51:44, 47, 52; Hos 4:14; 12:2; Zeph 1:8-9, 12; Zech 10:3). Jeremiah 21:14, where "according to the fruit of your deeds" is added, is particularly instructive because it suggests that judgment will correspond to the effects ("fruit") of the royal court's deeds. In this regard, several passages assert that divine judgment operates according to this principle (Jer 17:10; 32:19), including both reward (Is 3:10) and punishment (Mic 7:13).

Less common are cases where the verbal idiom takes the form "visit iniquity/sin upon a person/place." In these cases the sin boomerangs, as it were, back upon the wrongdoer. The punishment implemented by the Lord is viewed as a direct consequence of the sinful action. For example, in Isaiah 13:11 the Lord declares that he will "visit upon the earth wrongdoing and upon the wicked their iniquity." In all of these instances divine intervention is highlighted (see also Is 26:21; Jer 23:2; 25:12; 36:31; Amos 3:2, 14). The idiom is used differently in Hosea, where the object of the verb is "his ways" (Hos 4:9) or the specific sin involved (Hos 1:4 [the bloodshed perpetrated in Jezreel]; Hos 2:13 [idolatrous worship of the Baal idols]).

A related noun pĕquddâ ("punishment") is also used of divine judgment, always modifying "time," "day" or "year" (Is 10:3; Jer 8:12; 10:15; 11:23; 23:12; 46:21; 48:44; 50:27; 51:18; Hos 9:7; Mic 7:4).

1.5. The verb šûb ("to Return"). One of the clearest expressions of the concept of retribution occurs in Obadiah 15, where the prophet warns, "As you have done, it will be done to you. Your deeds will return on your head." The first statement has a talionic ("eye for an eye") flavor, while the second pictures sin rebounding on the evildoer. The Hiphil form of the verb is more common; here the Lord makes evil actions "return to" (Hos 4:9; 12:2, 14) or "turn back on the head of" (Joel 3:4, 7) the evildoer. The notion of evil deeds returning upon the head of the perpetrator is talionic (Raabe, 665).

2. The Rhetoric of Poetic Justice.

In addition to the terminology discussed above, which directly states the principle of divine retribution, the prophets express the concept in more subtle ways. They use a variety of literary devices to demonstrate that the punishment fits the crime and therefore constitutes appropriate and just payment for the sin(s) committed. P. Miller has developed a detailed taxonomy of these rhetorical techniques (Miller, 111-19). Three of the most common and significant are as follows.

2.1. Verbal Repetition Is Used to Correlate the Sin and the Punishment. The prophets often use the same word to describe both the sin and the punishment. Through this verbal correspondence they draw attention to the fact that the punishment fits the crime. The sin receives an appropriate and just divine response.

For example, in Isaiah 1:4 the prophet laments that sinful Israel has become alienated (nāzōrû, from zûr, "to be foreign") from the Lord. As a result, the Lord (see Is 1:9) has judged the nation, allowing foreigners (zārîm) to invade and devour the land (Is 1:7) (Chisholm 1987, 51). In Isaiah 5:20 the prophet pronounces a woe upon those who confuse darkness (what is morally wrong [cf. Is 5:20a]) and light (what is morally right). He then announces (Is 5:30) that the coming judgment will turn light (security and prosperity) into darkness (death and destruction). Those who had caused moral darkness to descend on Judah would experience the darkness of divine judgment when the Assyrian army, summoned by the Lord (Is 5:26), swept through the land (Chisholm 1986, 54).

Jeremiah and Ezekiel also employ this device. For example, in Jeremiah 30:16 the Lord declares that those who "devoured" his people will themselves be "devoured." They had "plundered" Israel; they would in turn become "plunder." In Ezekiel 5:8 the Lord announces that he will bring "judgments" (mišpātîm) upon his people because they have disregarded his "ordinances" (mišpātîm) and followed the "customs" (mišpātîm) of the nations (Ezek 5:7) (Wong, 202). In Ezekiel 36:6-7 the Lord informs his people that the nations that have caused them to "bear reproach" will in turn "bear reproach." As Miller observes, the language "is clearly talionic" (Miller, 74).

One also finds this rhetorical technique in the Book of the Twelve. For example, in Hosea 4:6 the Lord informs the sinful priests, "Because you have rejected knowledge, I will reject you from serving as my priest; because you have forgotten the law of your God, I will forget your children." As Miller states, the prophet "announces a judgment against the priesthood which point for point matches the sin it has committed"; his language "underscores heavily the character of the priestly sin and declares an appropriate justice" (Miller, 14). In Micah 2:3 the Lord announces that he is "planning calamity" (the collocation is *ḥāšab rā'â*) against those who are "planning" wicked schemes and already working out in their minds how they will implement "evil" (*rā'*) (Mic 2:1). More specifically, these sinners are devising plans to rob their victims of their property (Mic 2:2), and the Lord's corresponding plan in turn takes from the sinners what they had stolen (Mic 2:4-5). As Miller points out, "The effect of Yahweh's scheme will be the same as the effects of their nocturnal schemes. Those whose sin was the greedy and oppressive seizing of houses and fields belonging to others will be punished by having their own fields portioned out among others"; he adds, "What is clear is that the judgment is wrought by God and is like the sin. It is not pictured as a consequence of the sin except by Yahweh's decision to punish the wicked deeds. The judgment corresponds to the sin but becomes a consequence of it only as Yahweh determines that" (Miller, 30-31).

Sometimes verbal repetition creates an intertextual link between distinct speeches. For example, in Hosea 7:13 the Lord pronounces woe upon the people because they have ignored him and "wandered" (*nādĕdû*, from *nādad*, "to wander") from him. In a later speech the prophet announces that the Lord will reject them, forcing them to be "wanderers" (*nōdĕdîm*) among the nations (Hos 9:17) (Chisholm 1987, 47).

On occasion, the correlation between sin and punishment is conceptual, not verbally exact. For example, in Isaiah 5 the prophet pronounces a woe upon those who carouse at sumptuous feasts (Is 5:11-12). Ironically, these sinners will die of hunger in exile (Is 5:13) and become the main course at Sheol's banquet (Is 5:13-14). Only sheep will be left to eat in the ruins of the banqueting halls (Is 5:17) (Chisholm 1986, 52).

2.2. The Instrument or Location of Sin Becomes the Object of Punishment.

In Hosea 10:1 we read how Israel, as they prospered, constructed idolatrous altars and pillars. In response, the Lord would break the altars and destroy the pillars. The judgment in this case targets the instrument of Israel's disloyalty. Miller explains that the correspondence between the sin and its punishment "illumines the inner relationship between human offense and the divine response of justice" (Miller, 19).

In Amos 5:5 the location of Israel's sin becomes the target of divine judgment. The prophet urges the sinful people not to go to Gilgal, for "Gilgal will surely go into exile." The prophet utilizes sound play to suggest that the town's destiny is already inherent in its name (*haggilgal gālōh yigleh*). Similarly, in Hosea 12:11 the Lord states that he will turn the altars of Gilgal into ruins (*gallîm*).

2.3. Sinners Are Deprived of What Their Sin Acquired.

Micah 2:1-5, discussed above, provides a vivid example of this. Those who had stolen fields from their victims would be deprived of those same fields. Similarly, Isaiah pronounces a woe upon those who had accumulated houses and vineyards at the expense of the oppressed (Is 5:8), for the houses would be reduced to uninhabited ruins and the vineyards would yield almost nothing (Is 5:9-10; cf. Amos 5:11).

3. Examples of Divine Retribution in Prophetic Texts.

The principle of divine retribution permeates the judgment oracles of the prophetic literature. It is especially prominent in the oracles against the nations, but God's covenantal people, Israel, are by no means exempt from it.

3.1. Isaiah's Vision of Cosmic Retribution.

Isaiah 13—23 contains a series of oracles against the nations, followed by the so-called Little Apolcalypse (Is 24—27), which describes an outpouring of divine judgment upon the entire earth in conjunction with the inauguration of God's kingdom on Zion (Is 24:23; 25:6-8). In the very first oracle, which has a strong cosmic flavor, the Lord announces his agenda: "I will punish the world for its evil, the wicked for their sins" (Is 13:11). In the Little Apocalypse it becomes apparent that the context for this judgment is covenantal, for the people of the earth have violated "the everlasting covenant" made between them and God. They have "defiled" the earth beneath them (Is 24:5) by shedding human blood indiscriminately (Is 26:21). The Lord will intervene (Is 24:1), activating the covenant curses (Is 24:6), reactualizing the Noahic flood (Is 24:18) and subduing his cosmic enemies (Is 24:21-23; 27:1).

3.2. Jeremiah's Oracle against Babylon.

Jeremiah's prophecies, at least as arranged in the Hebrew Bible, conclude with a series of judgment oracles against various nations (Jer 46—51). The list culminates with a lengthy oracle against *Babylon, the nation that destroyed God's temple in Jerusalem. Throughout the oracle the Lord declares in the first person his intention to intervene and personally judge the Babylonians (see Jer 50:9, 18, 24, 31-32, 44; 51:1-2, 14, 24-25, 36, 39-40, 44, 52-53, 57). The language of retribution (surveyed above) permeates this oracle. The Lord's "judgment" (Jer 51:9) is designed to "punish" Babylon (Jer 50:18, 27; 51:18, 44, 47, 52). It constitutes divine "vengeance" (Jer 50:15; 51:6, 11, 36) and "repays" Babylon for its deeds (Jer 50:29; 51:6, 24, 56).

3.3. Amos's Oracles against the Nations. Amos likewise announces judgment against a series of nations (Israel and Judah included) that have "rebelled" (*pāšaʿ*) against the Lord's covenantal authority (The precise meaning of the expression "I will not cause it/him to return" is uncertain. The pronominal object may refer to the Lord's decree of judgment, his anger, or the specific nation addressed, viewed as a subject state ["I will not take him back," i.e., "I will not reinstate him to the status of covenant partner"].) In each case, following the formal accusation, the Lord announces his direct intervention in judgment, which begins (with the exception of the eighth oracle, directed against Israel) with the Lord setting fire to the object of his anger (Amos 1:4, 7, 10, 12, 14; 2:2, 5). The language makes it clear that retribution is judicial in nature (the announcement of judgment follows the stereotypical introduction, "because of three crimes, even four") and involves direct divine intervention. None of the crimes mentioned is inherently incendiary; it is the Lord who sets the fire.

3.4. The Punishment of Jerusalem in Isaiah 40—55. In Isaiah 40 the Lord proclaims a message of comfort to personified Jerusalem (Is 40:1), announcing that he is ready to return to her, bringing her exiled people home with him (Is 40:9-11). In Isaiah 40:2 he informs Jerusalem that her time of *warfare is over, and that she has "received from the hand of the LORD double for all her sins" (cf. Is 51:19). The concept of double restitution, though known in the law, probably is hyperbolic in this case, emphasizing that Jerusalem has indeed "done her time." Her sins caused her suffering and prompted the Lord to divorce her (Is 50:1). The Lord's interventional punishment is especially apparent in Isaiah 51:17-23, where he speaks of forcing Jerusalem to drink from the cup of his wrath (Is 51:17, 22; cf. Jer 25:15, 17, 28; 49:12;

51:7; Ezek 23:31-33; Obad 15-16; Hab 2:15-16). In Jeremiah 25:13-17, 28-29; Obadiah 15-16; Habakkuk 2:15-17 the image of drinking the cup of the Lord's judgment is directly associated with the concept of divine retribution.

4. The Dynamics of Retribution.
Should we view the concept of divine retribution strictly in judicial terms, where God intervenes and punishes or rewards human actions? Or should we opt for a providential model in which consequences are built into actions? Over the past six decades scholars have debated this issue.

4.1. Klaus Koch's Thesis. In 1955 Koch offered a provocative challenge to the traditional view of retribution. Prior to this, God was viewed as a judge who implemented rewards and punishment within a covenantal context (see Chapman, 175-79). But Koch, appealing to evidence in the Wisdom literature, Hosea and Psalms, argued that retribution should not be understood in a strictly judicial sense. Instead, human actions have "built-in consequences." God, operating providentially, oversees "the connection between actions and destiny, hurries it along, and 'completes' it when necessary" (Koch 1983, 64). Scholars have interacted extensively with Koch's thesis, which has come to be known as the "act-consequence" or "dynamistic" model (for surveys, see Chapman, 179-82; Gammie, 1-5; Kaminsky, 22-29; Krašovec, 82; Wong 3-25). Some refer to indirect (the act-consequence model) and direct (the judicial model) retribution. J. Barton suggested that indirect retribution be viewed in terms of natural law.

As noted above, Koch drew heavily on the Wisdom literature in developing his thesis. Yet he also utilized texts from Hosea where consequences are viewed as the natural fruit or harvest of sinful actions (see esp. Hos 7:2; 8:4-7; 10:12-13) (Koch 1983, 64-69). In subsequent discussion other passages have emerged as evidence for the act-consequence model (see esp. Is 3:9-11; Jer 2:5, 19).

4.2. Critiques of Koch's Thesis. Miller examines these texts carefully and offers a detailed critique of Koch's thesis. He shows that one must not make a false dichotomy between act-consequence and divine involvement. In one sense, sinners' deeds result in their demise (see Jer 2:19), but in another sense, the Lord is the one who brings about their demise. This "interaction of the divine activity and the fate-effecting deed" is especially apparent in Jeremiah 6:19; 14:16 (Miller, 126-27; see also Scalise, 97-98). Miller points out that "a sizable number of judgment speeches do not suggest an internal relationship between the deed and its consequence"; in many instances "the reliance on wordplay creates a correlation that cannot be viewed as inherent in the deed. It is created or revealed only by the poetic style of the prophet" (Miller, 134). He argues that similarity between sin and punishment "does not necessarily point to a cause and effect relationship. There is no inherent reason why consequences should be like the deeds that flow from them" (Miller, 134) (see also McConville, 31). Indeed, "the emphasis upon correspondence appears to point to something other than the mechanism of cause and effect. It points rather to a concept of *retributive justice*" (Miller, 134).

K. Wong's study of retribution in Ezekiel demonstrates that Koch's act-consequence model is inadequate. The "act-consequence connection is governed by a juridical understanding, particularly by the covenant" (Wong, 246). This "requires an external agent to serve as the judge who deliberates on what should happen to the actor according to some agreed norms" (Wong, 250). Likewise, M. Fishbane states that Ezekiel's "persistent theme of divine judgment of Jerusalem (and Judea) for her sins makes it clear that the punishment to come is the personal justice of Israel's covenant God, not simply the working out of some impersonal principle of natural balance or retribution" (Fishbane, 148).

See also DAY OF YAHWEH; EXILE; FORGIVENESS; JUSTICE, RIGHTEOUSNESS; SACRIFICE AND ATONEMENT; SIN, SINNERS; WRATH.

BIBLIOGRAPHY. **G. André,** "פָּקַד," *TDOT* 12:50-63; **J. Barton,** "Natural Law and Poetic Justice in the Old Testament," *JTS* 30 (1979) 1-14; **S. B. Chapman,** "Reading the Bible as Witness: Divine Retribution in the Old Testament," *PRSt* 31 (2004) 171-90; **R. B. Chisholm Jr.,** "Structure, Style, and the Prophetic Message: An Analysis of Isaiah 5:8-30," *BSac* 143 (1986) 46-60; idem, "Wordplay in the Eighth-Century Prophets," *BSac* 144 (1987) 44-52; **M. Fishbane,** "Sin and Judgment in the Prophecies of Ezekiel," *Int* 38 (1984) 131-50; **J. G. Gammie,** "The Theology of Retribution in the Book of Deuteronomy," *CBQ* 32 (1970) 1-12; **J. S. Kaminsky,** *Corporate Responsibility in the Hebrew Bible* (JSOTSup196; Sheffield: Sheffield Academic, 1995); **B. E. Kelly,** *Retribution and Eschatology in Chronicles* (JSOTSup211; Sheffield: Sheffield Academic, 1996); **K. Koch,** "Gibt es ein Vergeltungsdogma im Alten Testament," *ZTK* 52 (1955) 1-42; ET, "Is There a Doctrine of Retribution in the Old Testament?" in *Theodicy in the Old Testament,* ed. J. Crenshaw (IRT 4; Philadelphia: Fortress, 1983) 57-87; **J. Krašovec,** "Is There a Doctrine of 'Collective Retribution' in The Hebrew Bible?" *HUCA* 65 (1994) 35-89; **H. G. May,** "Individual Responsibility and Retribution," *HUCA* 32 (1961) 107-20; **J. G. McConville,** "The Judgment of God in the Old Testament," *ExAud* 20 (2004) 25-42; **P. D. Miller Jr.,** *Sin and Judgment in the Prophets: A Stylistic and Theological Analysis* (SBLMS 27; Chico, CA: Scholars Press, 1982); **H. G. L. Peels,** *The Vengeance of God: The Meaning of the Root NQM and the Function of the NQM-Texts in the Context of Divine Revelation in the Old Testament* (OTS 31; Leiden: E. J. Brill, 1995); **P. R. Raabe,** "The Particularizing of Universal Judgment in Prophetic Discourse," *CBQ* 64 (2002) 652-74; **P. J. Scalise,** "Justice and Judgment in the Book of Jeremiah: Discerning the Boundaries of God's Wrath," *ExAud* 20 (2004) 89-105; **W. S. Towner,** "Retributional Theology in the Apocalyptic Setting," *USQR* 26 (1971) 203-14; **G. M. Tucker,** "Sin and 'Judgment' in the Prophets," in *Problems in Biblical Theology: Essays in Honor of Rolf Knierim,* ed. H. Sun and K. Eades (Grand Rapids: Eerdmans, 1997) 373-88; **J. R. Vannoy,** "Retribution: Theology of," *NIDOTTE* 4:1140-49; **K. L. Wong,** *The Idea of Retribution in the Book of Ezekiel* (VTSup 87; Leiden: E. J. Brill, 2001).

R. B. Chisholm Jr.

REVEALER, GOD AS. *See* GOD.

RHETORICAL CRITICISM

Rhetorical criticism is a method of interpretation that focuses upon the *literary and persuasive characteristics of the biblical text. It seeks to understand the message of prophetic texts, focusing on elements including structure, organization and persuasive techniques. It is also interested in the response of the audience to the prophetic proclamation. This article traces the development of rhetorical criticism as an interpretive method, focusing on prophetic literature. It also considers issues pertaining to the development of rhetorical criticism while suggesting trajectories for its continued use.

1. Introduction.

Rhetorical criticism is an extremely valuable tool for interpreting prophetic literature. Rhetorical criticism is practiced across the *canon, but it has a particularly strong resonance with prophetic literature and its attempt to persuasively communicate messages from Yahweh. Rhetorical criticism focuses on the means of persuasion that the prophets employ to gain a hearing and to convince their audiences to respond appropriately. This concern with persuasion is what tightly links prophetic literature and rhetorical-critical study. Prophetic literature is a "rhetorical *tour de force*" that takes the unfolding story of Israel and arranges it so that it represents the logical outcome of Israel's relationship with Yahweh (Barton, 52). The rhetorical nature of prophetic literature is revealed further in the apt claim that "by any definition prophecy is rhetoric. The prophets were concerned with persuasion and they are indeed persuasive" (Fox, 4). Rhetorical criticism provides a well-suited approach to consider the ways in which the prophets attempted to persuade their audiences.

The identification of prophetic literature as fertile ground for rhetorical criticism has led to considerable diversity on the subject. Different approaches to the prophetic text continue to claim the title of rhetorical criticism. The origin of this discipline, the issues with which it continues to wrestle, and its potential future trajectories are worth considering in greater detail.

2. Origins.

The inaugural incarnation of rhetorical criticism in the OT typically is attributed to J. Muilenburg's presidential address to the Society of Biblical Literature in 1968. In this address, entitled "Form Criticism and Beyond," Muilenburg encourages biblical scholars to consider approaching the text in a fashion that appreciates its literary character and uniqueness. He calls for scholars to pay attention to the various literary devices and structural strategies that give the text its artistic qualities and claims that "rhetorical criticism" is an appropriate name for this approach. He intends for this approach to move beyond identifying the text's generic elements, which was the principal interest of *form criticism, toward appreciating each text's individual compositional strategies and literary character. As potential outcomes of rhetorical criticism, Muilenburg suggests, such studies could uncover the delimitation of literary units, the identification of major motifs, and the discovery of points of climax within the text. While he acknowledges the continued importance of form criticism, he views the move toward rhetorical criticism as the next step in better appreciating the uniqueness of individual biblical texts. For example, Muilenburg considers the form of a lawsuit oracle in Deuteronomy 32 and Micah 6:1-8, suggesting that while both passages share form-critical features, their distinct approaches to the form make them worthy of closer, individual study.

Essentially, Muilenburg's construction of rhetorical criticism establishes a relationship with form criticism where each can check the excesses of the other. While form criticism may not be sensitive to the unique literary features of a text, rhetorical criticism runs the risk of focusing too narrowly and missing the function of other similar texts in shaping the audience's understanding (Tull 2003, 327-28). Rhetorical criticism as conceived by Muilenburg thus establishes a useful tension between the formal characteristics of a text and the creativity with which it is constructed. Muilenburg's vision of rhetorical criticism marks a significant moment in biblical interpretation because it calls interpreters to a very close reading of the text, urging them to devote significant scrutiny to its literary devices and aesthetic qualities.

3. Growth of the Discipline.

From its foundation in Muilenburg's article, rhetorical criticism grew and expanded in scope and influence in studies of the OT. This process gave rise to two issues that require significant reflection. The first involves considering precisely what it is that makes a study "rhetorical," while the second requires determining the position that rhetorical criticism should take in the discussion of diachronic and synchronic approaches to the text. Both issues deserve further discussion here.

3.1. Descriptive and Persuasive Rhetoric. Following Muilenburg's point of departure, it is evident that rhetorical criticism as applied to the OT categorizes a wide range of studies. Essentially, rhetorical-critical studies proceed down one of two paths, which P. Trible helpfully categorizes as rhetorical criticism either as "the art of composition" or as the "art of persuasion" (Trible, 32). The former follows mostly closely in the tradition of Muilenburg. This species of rhetorical criticism explores the literary and structural devices found in a passage. It is interested in detecting poetic devices such as chiasmus, inclusio or merismus within a particular text. It focuses primarily on the final form of the text, allowing the interpreter to concentrate on an aesthetic evaluation of its qualities. In this fashion, rhetorical criticism bears a strong resemblance to aesthetic or stylistic analysis as it focuses on the text's use of literary devices as an end in itself. A. Hauser's survey essay of rhetorical criticism in the OT from the mid-1990s focuses primarily on studies of this nature, notably mentioning the work of Alter, Berlin, Bar-Efrat and Sternberg, which continues to set the standards for stylistic analysis of prosaic and poetic texts in the OT. Such studies successfully bring out the creative qualities and intricate patterning found in prophetic texts, which is a worthy legacy for this stream of rhetorical criticism.

As scholars put forward studies that fit into the rubric of rhetorical criticism as the "art of composition," others began to call into question whether these studies actually merited the title of "rhetorical." This reflects an impulse to look behind Muilenburg and recapture the classical understanding of rhetoric as the study of a speaker's (or text's) persuasive artistry. Whereas Muilenburg's understanding of rhetorical criticism derives from the perceived excesses of form criticism, this focus on persuasion looks back to classical conceptions of rhetoric (Howard, 103). One of the strongest calls for a correction in the aims of rhetorical criticism comes from W. Wuellner, who refers to rhetorical criticism in Muilenburg's formulation as "rhetoric restrained," or "the Babylonian captivity of rhetoric reduced to stylistics" (Wuellner, 453). In its place, Wuellner calls for rhetorical criticism to move toward studies that

consider the persuasive appeal of biblical texts and how this impacts the communities that read them. Through this appeal, he aims to return rhetorical criticism to what he understands as its classical definition: a study of finding the means of persuasion within a given discourse. This supplies the foundation for the second branch of rhetorical criticism, categorized as the "art of persuasion."

Although Wuellner's appeal primarily focuses on NT studies, it has a significant impact on rhetorical criticism as practiced in the OT. This is evident in the realization that the role of the rhetorical critic is both to analyze the literary features of the text and to articulate its impact of upon its audience (Hauser, 14). In this way, rhetorical criticism can focus on how texts function as persuasive discourse (Howard, 102-3). This orientation toward persuasion links rhetorical criticism to the broader field of rhetorical studies that is developing from applying classical rhetorical paradigms to a more universal understanding of the art of persuasion. In this way, rhetorical criticism of the OT can move beyond merely cataloging lists of rhetorical or literary devices. Instead, it can consider more broadly all the means of persuasion that OT texts bring to bear upon their audiences.

The preceding considerations provide the groundwork for the movement of rhetorical criticism from its focus on the "art of composition" to the "art of persuasion." This vein of rhetorical criticism in the OT has grown alongside of NT rhetorical approaches that dialogue with classical Greco-Roman oratory, referring back to works on the topic such as Aristotle's. Overall, it has been less visible in OT studies due to valid concerns of the viability of using Greco-Roman rhetorical categories with Hebrew texts. However, there are many scholars of the OT who have latched onto the idea of persuasive rhetoric as a universal phenomenon and thus applicable to the OT. In the realm of prophetic literature, Y. Gitay has been the most prominent to employ classical categories of rhetoric in conversation with the biblical text. He uses Aristotle's definition of rhetoric as the discovery of the available means of persuasion in a given discourse as well as Aristotle's fivefold division of the tasks of rhetoric as the foundation for much of his work on Isaiah (see Gitay, 34-45).

Recent developments in the broader discipline of rhetorical studies also influence the study of OT texts. The twentieth century witnessed the rise of studies that develop the universal nature of rhetoric and its means of persuasion. Such approaches claim that rhetoric is available in any area where people are addressed in order to put forward social action or to gain adherence to a particular proposition. By emphasizing the universal qualities of rhetoric, these types of approaches have the potential to bypass the concerns of importing foreign categories into the study of an OT text. C. Perelman and L. Olbrechts-Tyteca put forward a massive study of elements of argumentation along these lines, calling their approach the "new rhetoric." They explore the discursive techniques that can be used to increase adherence to the propositions put forward for evaluation. Their study explicitly focuses on persuasive elements in a wide variety of literary texts, including novels and sermons. Their study also moves beyond the political topics emphasized in Aristotelian rhetoric to a more universal conception of situations in which argumentation is employed. Bringing their work into the OT, Gitay again makes use of their description of the order in which arguments should be presented to gain maximum adherence. The "new rhetoric" thus has influenced the development of rhetorical studies of OT prophetic texts.

On a slightly different track, the literary theorist K. Burke develops a dramatistic theory of rhetorical analysis based on determining the relative significance of five categories within different units of a rhetorical piece. These categories include act, agent, agency, purpose and scene. He argues that in this "pentadic" analysis the ratio between the two most prominent categories within each unit will demonstrate how the rhetor is attempting to be persuasive. Pentadic analysis appears in the study of OT prophetic literature concerning prophetic passages related the Day of Yahweh (see LaRocca-Pitts). This provides a means of tracing the development of the rhetorical functions related to the Day of Yahweh in prophetic literature (*see* Day of the Lord).

This survey of the development of rhetorical criticism in the OT suggests that rhetorical criticism as the art of persuasion is a worthwhile avenue through which to pursue studies of prophetic texts. The prophets speak to their audiences and attempt to persuade them to respond to their message. There is room for studies that

are concerned with the art of composition and seek to articulate the literary skill and structure found within the biblical text, but studies that take the next step and consider it in terms of its persuasive impact offer intriguing possibilities for broadening our understanding.

3.2. Synchronic and Diachronic Orientations. Another significant issue related to rhetorical criticism is its temporal orientation to the texts that it examines. This issue gains added impetus as scholars pursue rhetorical-critical studies that focus on the art of persuasion. If it is possible to assert that a text is persuasive, it then appears to require an audience upon whom one can say that the text had a persuasive effect. This requires considering whether a rhetorical-critical approach should focus on the final form of the text, which conceivably represents the fullest articulation of the text's persuasive potential, or whether it should work alongside diachronically oriented methods in order to determine the original utterances of the prophet and consider how these would have affected the text's original audience.

Essentially, the development of rhetorical criticism in prophetic literature takes place alongside an ongoing shift in orientation that scholars bring to the text. Biblical scholarship has been dominated by diachronic approaches that studied biblical texts in order to better understand the "world behind the text." These approaches work from the perspective that texts have complex prehistories, and that one of the scholar's tasks is to isolate and locate each stage of textual development. In response, literary approaches to the text reflect a desire to move beyond the study of the "world behind the text" and to appreciate the literary qualities inherent in the text itself ("world of the text"). However, scholars also continue to pursue the "world behind the text." Rhetorical criticism of prophetic literature developed in this scholarly atmosphere. Consequently, one of the key questions related to rhetorical criticism is whether its focus ought to be synchronic or diachronic. Unsurprisingly, there are a variety of perspectives to consider.

There is an understandable tendency to view rhetorical criticism as a primarily synchronic approach. This relates to the origin of rhetorical criticism in Muilenburg's proposal. Muilenburg's concern with the literary shape of the text and its use of stylistic devices is most consistent with synchronic studies of the final form of the text. While such studies do not necessarily dispute the idea of the text's growth and redaction, they do not appear well suited to address such issues. Accordingly, while practitioners may acknowledge the existence of diachronic concerns in rhetorical-critical studies, the primary purpose of such projects is to focus on a synchronic reading of the text. M. Kessler even proposes that rhetorical criticism ought to be categorized as "the leading candidate for synchronic criticism" (Kessler, 14). He makes this explicit in a methodological proposal that contains nine separate elements. Two of these (authorship; setting) set up a general diachronic background for the study, but the remaining seven elements (whole piece; medium: Gattung; stance; form: structure; style; metastyle; ratio) are synchronic in focus and are given much greater significance in his articulation of his approach (Kessler, 9). In this type of analysis the synchronic nature of rhetorical criticism is dominant, although concerns related to the diachronic development of the text are not completely eliminated.

Many practitioners of rhetorical criticism, however, would not wish for their work to deal only with the final form of the text, with little concern for its growth and development. It is possible to suggest a more nuanced relationship between the diachronic and synchronic concerns of rhetorical criticism. For example, G. Kennedy proposes that rhetorical criticism can bridge the gap between diachronic and synchronic approaches such as form and literary criticisms by considering the text "as we have it," and how such a text would be received by an audience of "near contemporaries" (Kennedy, 3-4). In prophetic studies, T. Renz constructs rhetorical analyses in accordance with an understanding of redactional layering within the text, thus basing his reading on previous diachronic results (Renz, 5-8). In this way, it may be possible to trace the persuasive potential of prophetic proclamation about its original audience if the work devoted to uncovering the text's redactional history is secure.

The relationship between rhetorical criticism and synchrony/diachrony attains further complexity when rhetorical criticism claims that its efforts can affect the results of diachronically oriented approaches. This is most notable in K. Möller's attempt to speak to the synchronic/diachronic balance. Essentially, Möller takes another step beyond Renz and argues that rhetorical-critical studies can challenge the results of diachronic criticisms when they discover literary seamlessness within a text that may render unnecessary theories of complex redaction and secondary additions (Möller, 5-10). Consequently, rhetorical criticism is not necessarily reliant on the observations of source and redaction criticism to delineate the boundaries of the persuasive potential of prophetic proclamations. Rhetorical criticism, according to this view, can exist in between synchronic and diachronic approaches, appropriating concerns from both sides, but it need not rely solely on the results of previous diachronic analysis as its foundation. It can offer results that affect both the synchronic and the diachronic understandings of the text.

As a result of these issues, rhetorical criticism as the "art of persuasion" demonstrates significant variation as a method of studying the OT. It is a discipline capable of supporting different presuppositions concerning the development of the text, and adherents of both diachronic and synchronic approaches to the text incorporate it into their studies. However, it is more prevalent among those who favor the literary integrity of the text and work with its final form. Further, some adherents of this discipline have sought to bring the analysis forward so that the texts in question can be studied in situations far removed from their original location. In doing so, rhetorical criticism thus appears to function as a bridge discipline in a greater sense than that envisioned by Kennedy. Möller claims that one of rhetorical criticism's strengths is its potential to combine the three primary foci of interpretation: the author ("the world behind the text"), the discourse ("the world of the text") and the reader ("the world in front of the text"). Not all rhetorical studies will examine all three foci, but the potential to offer a well-rounded view of a text lends promise to the future of rhetorical criticism.

4. Model.

The broad scope of what rhetorical criticism can study means that there are many different possible models. One model, however, is worth considering in greater detail. It is derived from Kennedy's NT model of rhetoric, but it has been used effectively to study prophetic literature (see Möller on Amos; Shaw on Micah; Renz on Ezekiel). This model consists of five steps. The first is to determine the rhetorical units of the text, or to break the text into its composite oracles for analysis. The second step is to describe the rhetorical situation of the text, which involves placing the text into its social, historical and literary context in order to describe how the prophetic text is responding to this situation. The third step is to consider the rhetorical genre of the text, which determines the basic approach to persuasion that the text will adopt. Texts are classified as (1) judicial, which involves making judgments on persons or events; (2) deliberative, which invites consideration of future actions; or (3) epideictic, which aims to reinforce certain values or beliefs. The fourth step is to consider the text's rhetorical strategy, which is where the interpreter can discuss all the literary and stylistic devices that the text employs to heighten the persuasive punch of its message. The fifth and final step is to consider the rhetorical effectiveness of the text, which provides the interpreter with an opportunity to look back over the preceding steps and determine how well a prophetic oracle spoke into a given situation and what effect it could have achieved.

This model is useful because it articulates an interpretive procedure that is easy to follow but also is adaptable to the concerns of individual texts. This is most noticeable in the categories of rhetorical situation and rhetorical effectiveness. It is impossible to completely get behind the world of the text and capture its rhetorical situation perfectly, which provides the interpreter with latitude to consider the most relevant elements. If information concerning the social and historical circumstances is lacking, the interpreter can focus on the literary situation of the oracle within a prophetic book, considering how it contributes to the argument of the whole book. Rhetorical effectiveness is not often described within the text, so the interpreter has the freedom to consider what its effect should have been, or perhaps to even consider the continuing effectiveness of the prophetic text upon different audiences. This model provides a useful point of departure for appreciating how rhetorical criticism can contribute to the study of prophetic literature.

5. Recent Developments.

This section surveys some of the recent developments in the field of rhetorical criticism. It shows how rhetorical criticism incorporates insights from related methodologies and uses them to more clearly articulate the persuasive appeal of prophetic language. This brief survey also demonstrates the continued vibrancy of rhetorical criticism in its study of prophetic literature.

5.1. Rhetorical Criticism and Speech-Act Theory. Rhetorical criticism successfully incorporates the insights of speech-act theory. Popularized by J. Searle and J. Austin, speech-act theory emphasizes the performative quality of language. Speech-act theory argues that words are not simply reflections of reality; instead, they can evoke new states of being. Speech-act theory employs the categories of locution (the words themselves), illocution (the actions they perform) and perlocution (the effects of the illocutionary actions) to describe what functions language can perform. The idea that words have a performative purpose is highly useful in classifying the ways in which language can be used, and it offers the possibility of new insight for the study of prophetic literature.

Speech-act theory has a natural parallel with rhetorical criticism in prophetic literature. The concepts of illocution and perlocution provide ways of examining what the prophets were trying to do in their oracles and what effect these might achieve on their audiences. This approach coincides with the concern for identifying the persuasive effect of prophetic literature, which is at the heart of rhetorical criticism. One useful example is to look at what speech-act theory might reveal about the persuasive intent of oracles of woe and doom in prophetic literature. There appears to be space between the locutionary and the illocutionary intentions of such oracles, where the prophet appears to be doing more than simply announcing the fixed reality of divine judgment. One suggestion to explain this is that the illocutionary force of the oracle of doom is intended to motivate return and repentance to Yahweh (cf. Jer 18:1-12). Thus, illocutionary act of proclaiming doom and destruction may well reflect an attempt to provoke a response of penitence.

Jonah 3 provides a fascinating test case. Jonah proclaims a succinct oracle of doom that leaves no hope for averting the prophesied fate. Nineveh, however, responds with penitence, and so Yahweh spares the city. In this instance it would appear that Jonah's words (locution) perform the act of initializing divine judgment (illocution) that provokes a powerful response from the audience of the prophetic oracle (perlocution). This illocutionary act and its perlocutionary response are active even in spite of Jonah's wishes (see Eagleton, 233). Whether the audience adopts the proper perlocutionary response to an oracle of woe and doom is an open question, but it does not eliminate the illocutionary force of the prophetic proclamation (Houston, 76). This brief example demonstrates the usefulness of using the insights of speech-act theory in a rhetorical-critical study of a prophetic oracle.

5.2. Rhetorical Criticism and "Interested" Methodologies. Another significant development in rhetorical-critical studies is its link to methodologies that try to uncover the diverse interests of the text. This reflects the continuing impact of rhetorical criticism as the "art of persuasion," since if it is persuasive, its effects on its audiences ought to be considered. This coincides with the development of the postmodern mentality that denies the possibility of proclaiming objective truth. Such methodologies seek to discover the embedded interests of the text, its audience and even of the practitioners of rhetorical criticism in order to better understand the means of persuasion being employed. There is warrant for this development in rhetorical criticism because it also important to consider the role of the interpreter in the persuasive potential of a prophetic text. Rhetorical criticism from this perspective cannot make the claim that it is objectively seeking the truth about a text's persuasive potential. Instead, the way in which the interpreter presents the text's rhetoric has persuasive force itself. P. Tull aptly summarizes this perspective, asserting that "the very practice we are analyzing, we are also ourselves exercising, since any stance that an interpreter takes concerning the text is by nature a rhetorical stance" (Tull 1999, 163).

The consideration of "interests" in rhetorical criticism opens up two primary interpretive trajectories. First, it provides an opportunity for "suspicious" readings of the text to flourish, where the interpreter deliberately reads against the grain of what would appear to be the persuasive intention of the prophetic text. This approach refuses to cede the normative voice to the prophetic text; rather, it seeks to undermine the prophetic text's privileged position and provide a reading from an alternative perspective (Clines). Other alternative perspectives could include feminist readings that challenge some of the highly charged sexual imagery found in prophetic texts, and liberationist readings that see prophetic rhetoric as a tool for crying out on behalf of the poor and oppressed. While such readings will hold differing opinions on the normative nature of prophetic literature, they share the perspective that its persuasive power speaks beyond the ancient text and can be used to affect other reading and hearing audiences.

Second, it is also possible to apply the idea of the "interested interpretation" to readings of the text that accept it as normative. According to this approach, interpreters place themselves within the audience of those whom the rhetorical power of the prophetic oracle can persuade. This is not done passively based on a simplistic reading of the text; rather, it is an active choice by the interpreters to situate themselves in this manner. This helps to reveal the persuasive potential of the prophetic text because "the interpreter can only *receive* truth from a text if he or she is willing to entertain the possibility of its being true" (Patrick, 77). Essentially, this approach argues that one can more comprehensively consider the prophetic text's persuasive potential if one reads the text as someone whom it could affect and persuade. It provides a useful counterweight to "suspicious" readings of prophetic texts and suggests that their persuasive potential can have beneficial effects beyond the boundaries of the original hearers and readers.

5.3. Rhetorical Criticism and Discourse Analysis. Rhetorical criticism also overlaps with emerging field of discourse analysis and its concerns with the composition of the text. Essentially, engaging in discourse-related studies helps to identify the boundaries of a prophetic text, the internal bonds of cohesion, and the way in which it builds to points of climax (Wendland, 26). It permits the interpreter to consider the way in which the prophetic text constructs its argument through the precise construction of its language, noting, for example, how variations in expected word order reveal points of potential climax within the text (van der Merwe and Wendland). This information is helpful in determining the persuasive power of a prophetic passage because it helps the interpreter to identify the manner in which the text constructs its argument. Discourse analysis is also concerned with the macrostructural arrangement of the biblical text, which is useful because it can provide the rhetorical critic with the means of placing the persuasive intention of a particular oracle within the broader strategy of the entire book. The field of discourse analysis is continuing to expand, which should provide opportunities to consider how it aids rhetorical critics in better understanding the composition of the text and how this contributes to its persuasive power.

6. Conclusion.

The term *rhetorical criticism* encompasses a wide range of models and methods that continue to have a significant voice in the study of prophetic literature. The focus of rhetorical criticism on the persuasive potential of the text resonates powerfully with the nature of prophetic proclamation. Rhetorical criticism has the capacity to help its practitioners to appreciate the aesthetic qualities of the text and to consider the various ways in which it can be persuasive. It allows the interpreter to articulate the text's use of imagery and literary devices while considering how these affect their audiences. Rhetorical criticism can consider the persuasive potential of the text on both its original audience and the audiences that continue to read it. The prophets spoke persuasively to their ancient audience, and as such texts continue to be celebrated and studied, it is important to consider how they affect contemporary audiences. The flexible nature of rhetorical criticism provides the foundation for continued use in studying prophetic literature.

See also CONVERSATION ANALYSIS; EDITORIAL/REDACTION CRITICISM; FORM CRITICISM; LITERARY APPROACHES; PERFORMANCE CRITICISM.

BIBLIOGRAPHY. **J. Barton,** "History and Rhetoric in the Prophets," in *The Bible as Rhetoric: Studies in Biblical Persuasion and Credibility,* ed. Martin Warner (London: Routledge, 1990) 51-64; **D. J. A. Clines,** "Metacommentating Amos," in *Interested Parties: The Ideology of Writers and Readers of the Hebrew Bible* (JSOTSup 205; Sheffield: Sheffield Academic Press, 1995) 76-93; **T. Eagleton,** "J. L. Austin and the Book of Jonah," in *The Book and the Text: The Bible and Liter-*ary Theory, ed. R. M. Schwartz (Oxford: Blackwell, 1990) 231-36; **M. V. Fox,** "The Rhetorical of Ezekiel's Vision of the Valley of the Bones," *HUCA* 51 (1980) 1-15; **Y. Gitay,** *Prophecy and Persuasion: A Study of Isaiah 40-48* (FTL 14; Bonn: Lingustica Biblica, 1981); **A. J. Hauser,** "Comments on Selected Works in the Bibliography," in *Rhetorical Criticism of the Bible: A Comprehensive Bibliography with Notes on History and Method,* ed. A. J. Hauser and D. F. Watson (BIS 4; Leiden: E. J. Brill, 1994) 14-20; **A. J. Hauser and D. F. Watson,** *Rhetorical Criticism of the Bible: A Comprehensive Bibliography with Notes on History and Method* (BIS 4; Leiden: E. J. Brill, 1994); **W. Houston,** "What Did the Prophets Think They Were Doing? Speech Acts and Prophetic Discourse in the Old Testament," *BibInt* 1 (1993) 167-88; **D. M. Howard Jr.,** "Rhetorical Criticism in Old Testament Studies," *BBR* 4 (1994) 87-104; **G. A. Kennedy,** *New Testament Interpretation through Rhetorical Criticism* (Chapel Hill: University of North Carolina Press, 1984); **M. Kessler,** "A Methodological Setting for Rhetorical Criticism," in *Art and Meaning: Rhetoric in Biblical Literature,* ed. D. J. A. Clines, D. M. Gunn and A. J. Hauser (JSOTSup 19; Sheffield: JSOT Press, 1982) 1-19; **M. A. LaRocca-Pitts,** *The Day of Yahweh: The Use and Development of Yahweh's Motive on That Day as a Rhetorical Strategy by the Hebrew Prophets* (Saarbrücken: VDM Verlag, 2003); **K. Möller,** *A Prophet in Debate: The Rhetoric of Persuasion in the Book of Amos* (JSOTSup 372; London: Sheffield Academic Press, 2003); **J. Muilenburg,** "Form Criticism and Beyond," *JBL* 88 (1969) 1-18; **D. Patrick, with A. Scult,** "Rhetoric and Ideology: A Debate within Biblical Scholarship over the Import of Persuasion," in *The Rhetorical Interpretation of Scripture: Essays from the 1995 London Conference,* ed. S. E. Porter and T. H. Olbricht (JSOTSup 146; Sheffield: Sheffield Academic Press, 1997) 63-93; **C. Perelman and L. Olbrechts-Tyteca,** *The New Rhetoric: A Treatise on Argumentation,* trans. J. Wilkinson and P. Weaver (Notre Dame, IN: University of Notre Dame Press, 1969); **T. Renz,** *The Rhetorical Function of the Book of Ezekiel* (VTSup 76; Leiden: E. J. Brill, 1999); **C. S. Shaw,** *The Speeches of Micah: A Rhetorical-Historical Analysis* (JSOTSup 145; Sheffield: JSOT Press, 1993); **P. Trible,** *Rhetorical Criticism: Context, Method, and the Book of Jonah* (Minneapolis: Fortress, 1994); **P. K. Tull,** "Rhetorical Criticism and Intertextuality," in *To Each Its Own Meaning: An Introduction to Biblical Criti-*

cisms and Their Application, ed. S. R. Haynes and S. L. McKenzie (rev. ed.; Louisville: Westminster/John Knox, 1999) 156-82; idem, "Rhetorical Criticism and Beyond in Second Isaiah," in *The Changing Face of Form Criticism for the Twenty-First Century,* ed. M. A. Sweeney and E. Ben Zvi (Grand Rapids: Eerdmans, 2003) 326-34; **C. H. J. van der Merwe and E. Wendland,** "Marked Word Order in the Book of Joel" *JNSL* 36 (2010) 109-30; **E. Wendland,** *The Discourse Analysis of Hebrew Prophetic Literature* (MBPS 40; Lewiston, NY: Mellen, 1995); **W. Wuellner,** "Where Is Rhetorical Criticism Taking Us?" *CBQ* 49 (1987) 448-63.   J. D. Barker

RICH, RICHES. *See* WEALTH AND POVERTY.

RIGHTEOUSNESS. *See* JUSTICE, RIGHTEOUSNESS.

RULERSHIP. *See* LEADERSHIP.

S

SACRED MOUNTAIN. *See* COSMOLOGY.

SACRIFICE AND ATONEMENT

Perspectives of the OT Prophetic Books regarding sacrifice and atonement have aroused vigorous debate among modern scholars. The former tendency to interpret preexilic prophetic critiques as rejecting all sacrifice, thereby sharply contradicting the Pentateuch (e.g., Wellhausen, 422-23, 425), is now largely replaced by more nuanced approaches. These recognize that prophets before, during and after the Babylonian *exile invalidated various kinds of ritual practice but not the efficacy of sacrifices properly performed by loyal people at the authorized temple in Jerusalem. Their opposition was aimed at cultic abuse through practices such as pagan rituals or pagan elements in syncretistic *worship of the Lord, sacrifice at illegitimate northern Israelite cult sites, and sacrifices by unrepentant, disloyal people.

1. Positive or Neutral Prophetic Recognition of Sacrifice
2. Negative Prophetic Views of Sacrifice
3. Atonement with or without Sacrifice
4. Relationship Between Prophets and the Pentateuch

1. Positive or Neutral Prophetic Recognition of Sacrifice.

Sacrifices are ritual offerings to deities that serve as instruments for various kinds of relational interaction. Prophets, some of whom belonged to priestly families (Jer 1:1; Ezek 1:3), recognized that sacrificial worship was important in the lives of their people. They knew categories of sacrifice prescribed in the Pentateuch and could view them positively (e.g., Jer 17:26; 33:11; 33:18; Ezek 43:27; cf. Lev 1-7). This section considers positive or neutral prophetic references to sacrifice.

1.1. Positive References to Sacrifice in Narratives. In the book of Jonah a sacrifice by non-Israelite mariners (Jon 1:16) and the prophet's promise of a sacrifice (Jon 2:9) are positive expressions of belief in the Lord. After the temple in Jerusalem was destroyed, the fact that eighty men planned to present (nonanimal) grain offerings and incense at its site (Jer 41:5) shows the enduring centrality of this place of sacrifice for worship. Likewise, Daniel prayed from Babylon toward Jerusalem even while the temple lay in ruins (Dan 6:10; cf. 1 Kings 8:29, 30, 35).

In response to Daniel's prayer of confession and intercession for his exiled people, who had violated God's covenant and thereby incurred its curse (Dan 9:3-20; cf. Lev 26:40-41), the angel Gabriel flew to him about the time when the evening offering would have been performed (Dan 9:21; cf. Ex 29:38-42; Num 28:1-8) had the temple not been destroyed. The timing (cf. Ezra 9:4-10:1) implies that God heard his petition as if in response to a sacrifice (cf. Ps 141:2). So the concept of sacrifice for the benefit of faulty people was still valid. But the Lord could provide the same atoning benefit in answer to *prayer when they confessed or were humbled so that they made amends for (Qal of 2-*rṣh*) their culpability (Lev 26:41, 43), just as a sacrifice would be acceptable (Niphal of 1-*rṣh*) to him on their behalf (Lev 1:4).

1.2. Sacrificial Language in Metaphor or Simile. Such usage implies the existence of literal sacrificial practice, without which its force would have been lost on the original audience. Several prophets employed the term *zebaḥ* ("sacrifice") metaphorically (with neutral implications for literal practice) to portray the Lord's future destruction of his human enemies (Is 34:5-7; Jer 46:10; Ezek 39:17-20; Zeph 1:7-8). The word lent itself to such usage because the verb *zbḥ* means "to slaughter," and the offerer of a *zebaḥ* ate from it and could share it with others (Lev 7:15-21; 1 Sam 9:13; cf. Zeph 1:7-8). Thus, the Lord's sword would "devour" (Jer 46:10), and he would share his "sacrifice," the corpses, with birds and *animals (Ezek 39:17-19). An Israelite was forbidden to consume fat or blood (Lev 7:23-27), but the Lord's sword and wild creatures would devour the fat and blood of his enemies (Is 34:6; Ezek 39:17-19). In Isaiah 34:5-7 the human victims of such a "sacrifice," referred to as sacrificial animals, belong to the Lord as a *ḥerem* ("banned thing") devoted to sacral destruction (cf. Lev 27:28-29; Josh 6:17-18, 21).

Isaiah 66:20 predicts that Gentiles would bring God a gift (*minḥâ*), namely, dispersed Jews, whom they would assist in returning to the Lord's place of worship. Isaiah positively likens the gift to an acceptable grain offering (also *minḥâ*) brought by an Israelite, implying that the Lord would be pleased with it.

1.3. Restoration and Reform of Sacrifice. If the preexilic prophets had invalidated all sacrifice, Isaiah 43:22-24a would be strange. Here God disapproves of ungrateful people who were not offering him sacrifices because they had grown weary of him. Their attitude was unjustified because he had not burdened them with ritual requirements; rather, they had burdened him with their sins, which he still offered to wipe out (Is 43:24b-25).

Several prophets predicted a better time after the Babylonian exile, when sacrificial worship would be restored (e.g., Is 60:7; Jer 33:11, 18; Zeph 3:10). If they did not regard sacrifice as worthwhile, they would not have seen the need for its continuation in the future.

The most elaborate prophecy of restoration is that of Ezekiel, whose vision of a new, transformed *temple is accompanied by detailed ritual instructions (Ezek 40—48). Many aspects of this temple's infrastructure and procedures correspond to those of the wilderness tabernacle (Ex 25—31; 35—40; Lev 1—9; 16; 23; Num 28—29) and the first temple (1 Kings 6—8; 2 Chron 3—8). But there are also significant differences, such as Ezekiel denying laypersons access to the area of the altar or slaughter of their own sacrifices (Ezek 40:32-47; 44:11, 15-19; contrast Lev 1:3-5), purgation of Ezekiel's temple in the first month (Ezek 45:18-20; cf. Lev 16 [Day of Atonement in the seventh month]), and a special role

for a "prince" (e.g., Ezek 44:3; 45:17, 22-25; 46:2). Most strikingly, Ezekiel's temple is surrounded by a far more extensive holy area, including inner and outer courtyards with gates (Ezek 40; 42; 45-46; 48; cf. Ex 27; 1 Kings 6; 2 Chron 4), in order to protect its sacred domain from profanation and encroachment by impurities (Ezek 43:7-12; 44:5-9). The temple complex was never built, but Ezekiel's vision points to the need for purer sacrificial worship, a holy community and permanent divine presence after the exile (Kasher).

After the exile, the prophets Haggai and Zechariah supported construction of the second temple (Ezra 5:1-2; 6:14; Hag 1-2; Zech 1:16; 4:9-10; 6:11-15; 8:3, 9). Like Ezekiel, postexilic prophets were concerned with purity. Malachi looked forward to a "messenger of the covenant" who would purify the Levites, so that they would present offerings in righteousness that would please the Lord (Mal 3:1-4). Zechariah also foresaw a time of reform when all cooking pots in Jerusalem and Judah would be holy to the Lord, so that sacrificial meat (of well-being offerings [Lev 7:15-16; cf. 1 Sam 2:12-14]) could be boiled in them, and there would no longer be merchants in the temple (Zech 14:21; cf. Mk 11:15-17; Jn 2:14-16).

Some prophecies of restoration include universalism. Non-Israelite peoples would worship the Lord through valid sacrifices, whether in Egypt (Is 19:19-22) or Jerusalem (Is 56:6-8). Malachi cites widespread Gentile worship of the Lord, by the offering of incense and the presentation of a pure offering (*minḥâ*), as already occurring during the Second Temple period (Mal 1:11).

2. Negative Prophetic Views of Sacrifice.
2.1. Pagan Rituals.
2.1.1. Sacrifices by Non-Israelites to Deities Other Than the Lord. Not surprisingly, Jeremiah condemns pagan ritual worship practiced by Moabites (Jer 48:35). Habakkuk protests that God allows the Chaldeans to destroy peoples like catching fish in a net, so that they joyfully offer sacrifices to their "net" (Hab 1:14-16). Here the net represents their military system, which apparently they regard as divine (cf. Dan 11:38). Whether the Chaldeans literally performed such sacrifices or not, they failed to acknowledge the true God (cf. Is 10:5-14 of Assyria).

2.1.2. Pagan Ritual Activities Performed by Israelites. The preexilic prophets arraigned the national communities of Judah and Israel before God, presenting a lurid litany of pagan ritual practices that the chosen people were perpetrating in rebellion against their covenant Lord, who had forbidden them to have relations with other deities or to engage in *idolatry (Ex 20:3-6). Such illegitimate activities provoked him to anger (Jer 7:18; 32:29; 44:3, 8).

Apostates were burning sacrifices in service to other gods (Jer 1:16; 19:4; 44:3, 5, 8, 15 [by women]), such as Baal(s) (Jer 7:9; 11:17; Hos 2:13), and bowing to worship idols (Jer 1:16) or the "host of heaven" (Zeph 1:5). Their illicit rituals were performed on mountains or high hills, under leafy trees or in gardens, on bricks, or with "sacred" prostitutes (Is 57:3, 7; 65:3; Ezek 20:28; Hos 4:13-14; 11:2; 13:2), or on roofs of houses to the entire "host of heaven" (Jer 19:13; cf. Zeph 1:5) or to Baal (Jer 32:29). They were burning incense (Ezek 8:11), including to Baal(s) (Jer 11:12-13; Hos 2:13), pouring out drink offerings (Is 57:6; Jer 7:18; 19:13; 32:29; Ezek 20:28), presenting grain offerings (Is 57:6), burning sacrificial cakes to the "queen of heaven" and pouring out libations to her (Jer 7:18 [all family members participating]; Jer 44:17-19, 25). Worse, some were slaughtering children (Is 57:5) and burning their children as burnt offerings to Baal at high places of that deity (Jer 19:5).

Undoubtedly, many who engaged in pagan worship also participated in worship of the Lord. Zephaniah condemns those who bow down to and swear by both the Lord and other gods (Zeph 1:5). Even the Lord's temple in Jerusalem was not immune from pagan practices (Ezek 8; cf. 2 Kings 21:4-5, 7; Jer 7:30; 32:34).

In Jeremiah 17:1-2 metaphorically engraving the Judahites' sin (ḥaṭṭāʾt), including pagan practices, "on the tablet of their hearts and on the horns of their altars" alludes to the purification offering (also ḥaṭṭāʾt) in a way that reveals profound understanding of this sacrifice as prescribed in the Pentateuch. There, daubing purification offering blood on the horns of the Lord's incense altar or of his outer altar contributes to removal of sin from the (penitent) offerer, a prerequisite to divine forgiveness (e.g., Lev 4:18, 20, 25-26). In a second, corporate stage on the Day of Atonement, applications of special purification offering blood purge the sanctuary, including its altars, from pollution resulting from human evils (Ex 30:10; Lev 16:16, 18-19) (Gane, 106-43, 230-41, 267-84). Even though the Judahites' egregious sins had reached their altars, the fact that the sins were still etched on their hearts showed that they had not benefited from expiation. So their faults belonged to the category of inexpiable rebellious transgressions that automatically (not through purification offerings [cf. Lev 6:27-28]) defiled the sanctuary from a distance, and for which the offender was condemned to terminal punishment (cf. Lev 20:3; Num 15:30-31; 19:13, 20) (Gane, 144-81, 202-13). To make matters even worse, the horns belonged to "their" illegitimate altars (Jer 17:1), not the Lord's altar. So expiation was impossible, and they would suffer the divine judgment of exile (Jer 17:3-4).

2.2. Sacrifice at Northern Israelite Cult Sites. Emphases of the prophets varied according to the nature of their audiences and their relationships to the trajectory of events. Those who addressed northern Israel were especially opposed to syncretistic, idolatrous worship of the Lord at cult sites that he had not authorized, where no sacrifices could be acceptable (e.g., Hos 4:15—5:4; 8:5-6, 13; cf. 1 Kings 12-13) (see Ahlström, 120). Use of illegitimate altars to expiate for sin only increased it (Hos 8:11-12).

In Amos 5 God rejects "your festivals," sacrifices, and even songs and harp music (Amos 5:21-23). Repeated second-person pronouns ("your") focus attention on the offerers: it is the worship of these people that God refuses to accept, not all sacrifice, singing and harp music per se. When they worship at unauthorized cult sites, they fail to seek him (Amos 5:4-6), and they have abandoned justice and righteousness (Amos 5:7, 10-15, 24).

In apparent contrast to unacceptable contemporary sacrifices (Amos 5:22), Amos 5:25 asks whether Israel brought sacrifices (pl. of zebaḥ) and offerings (minḥâ) to the Lord during the forty years in the wilderness. If the expected answer is no, as a number of scholars have assumed, this would seem to contradict the Pentateuch (e.g., Ex 24:5-6; 40:29; Lev 9). But the Hebrew syntax of the question emphasizes the objects: "Were sacrifices and offerings what you brought me?" In context, this could be taken to mean "Is that all you brought me, or did you also bring corresponding justice and righteousness?" (cf. Amos 5:24). The answer would be "No, that was not all. . . . Yes, we also

. . . " (for yes to a rhetorical question, cf. 1 Sam 2:27) (Lucas, 61-62). So whereas the ancestors brought acceptable sacrifices to the Lord before entering the promised land, their descendants would carry their idols into exile, where they would continue to worship other gods outside the land (Amos 5:26-27 [cf. NJPS]) (Andersen and Freedman, 531-37, 542-44).

2.3. Sacrifices Offered to the Lord at Jerusalem by Disloyal People. To both northern Israel and Judah, Hosea reiterated the relative values of obedient loyalty to God and sacrifice that Samuel had stated to Saul (1 Sam 15:22), but more starkly: the Lord wanted faithfulness and not sacrifice, and knowledge of God more than (comparative preposition *min* [cf. NKJV]) burnt offerings (Hos 6:6). Given that Hosea foresaw that the Israelites would again seek the Lord along with a Davidic king (Hos 1:7; 3:5), it seems clear that he did not mean to invalidate all sacrificial worship at the authorized temple in Jerusalem. His point was that loyalty was the essential element of a positive relationship with God, so that without loyalty, even proper sacrifices could not atone.

According to Isaiah, God refused to accept sacrifices, incense, sacred times and even prayers (Is 1:15) because his people had rebelled against him and persisted in doing evil, especially sins of social injustice (Is 1:2-4, 10, 15-23) (*see* Social Justice). The objection was not to the idea of sacrifices atoning for repentant sinners, but to rituals of particular unrepentant people: "your sacrifices" (Is 1:11, 12, 14, 15). It was not assemblies in general that the Lord could not stand, but their assemblies with iniquity; it was not all prayer that he refused to acknowledge, but prayer made with hands full of bloodguilt (Is 1:13, 15). What he desired was moral cleansing and justice, which rituals could not replace (Is 1:16-17; cf. Ps 40:6-8; Mic 6:6-8).

For Isaiah, loyalty was essential to the divine-human relationship (Is 1:2-4), which was based on divine grace (Is 40:16 [no burnt offering was sufficient]). So no religious activity performed outside the framework of loyalty could serve as a valid expression of that relationship. Later, in Isaiah 66:3-4, worship by those who did evil rather than listening to God was as unacceptable as murder, offering impure animals, or idolatry. Because sacrifices signified aspects of relationship, acceptance or rejection of the rituals and their offerers went together. If God rejected one, he also rejected the other. Jeremiah agreed: incense, sacrifices, fasting and crying out to the Lord were unacceptable to him and therefore unable to avert disaster, since the people had spurned his teaching and broken his covenant (Jer 6:19-20; 11:3-17; 14:10-12).

Jeremiah 7:1-20 counters the presumption that the Lord's temple in Jerusalem provided safety to Judahites who were breaking his commandments, as if cult could substitute for morality. Then the Lord jarringly commands the people to eat the flesh of their burnt offerings along with their sacrifices (Jer 7:21). All flesh from burnt offerings was consumed in the altar fire for the Lord (Lev 1); it was never eaten by a human being, even a priest. So telling the Judahites to eat it along with their "sacrifices" (pl. of *zebaḥ*), from which they were permitted to eat (Lev 7:15-16), means that God rejected the burnt offerings as his because the offerers were disloyal to him (cf. Jer 7:22-31).

The divine assertion in Jeremiah 7:22-23 that God had commanded the Israelites to obey him at the time of the exodus but did not then speak to them regarding/because of burnt offerings and sacrifices (*zebah*) appears to contradict the Pentateuch (e.g., Ex 12; 20:24; 23:18; 29:28, 38-42; Lev 1; 3; 6—7; Num 28:6). However, Jeremiah could be referring to the fact that God's first proclamations at Sinai called Israel to covenant obedience (Ex 19:3-6; 20:1-17 [the Decalogue]) but did not specify requirements for the cultic system, which were presented in detail (e.g., Ex 25—31) only after ratification of the covenant (Ex 24). This order implies that obedience was more important than ritual practices (Thompson, 287-88). Alternatively, the prophet may be using hyperbole to emphasize the same relative priority (cf. 1 Sam 15:22). The possibility that Jeremiah's statement was limited to individual, voluntary burnt offerings and sacrifices (Lev 1; 3) (Milgrom, 273-75) is unlikely because the prophet was addressing presumption regarding the temple system as a whole (Jer 7:7:2-14) (see Klawans, 81-82).

Prophetic rejection of sacrifice tended to be more limited and specific during the Second Temple period. In Haggai 2:10-14 the Lord deploys an analogy to vividly express the importance of completing construction of his temple. If a person contaminated by contact with a corpse touched food, it became ritually impure.

Similarly, because the returnees to Judah had been "impure," so was everything they touched, including what they offered—that is, sacrifices at the reconstructed altar (cf. Ezra 3:1-6). The following verses (Hag 2:15-19) imply the cause of the people's "impurity," which had made everything they did unacceptable to God and consequently doomed to failure: they had sinfully neglected to build the Lord's house (cf. Hag 1).

Sometime after the second temple was built, a problem arose when people thought they could get away with offering defective sacrificial victims (Mal 1:8, 13-14), which were disqualified according to Leviticus 22:17-25. God took sacrifices personally as tokens of attitudes toward him. So when he rejected a sacrifice, the individual who presumed to bring it was out of favor with him (Mal 1:8-9; cf. Gen 4:3, 5-7), and he would accept no gift from that one; the doors of the temple may as well be kept shut and the altar fire left unlit (Mal 1:10)! Pure (i.e., proper) sacrifices honored his reputation (Mal 1:11), but those who brought improper offerings scorned his name (Mal 1:6-7, 12).

Animals obtained by robbery also were disqualified (Mal 1:13). Not only did they cost their offerers nothing (cf. 2 Sam 24:24), they were not legally owned and therefore could not be legitimately offered. Moreover, a sacrifice gained by breaking God's command against robbery (Lev 19:13) added insult to him on top of the initial crime. J. Klawans argues that other prophetic critiques included concern for ownership in a broader sense: sacrificial material from wealth gained by dishonesty and economic exploitation was disqualified because it did not legitimately belong to the offerers. So ethics and ritual were integrally connected (e.g., Is 61:8 NJPS; cf. Amos 2:6, 8) (Klawans, 84-89, 91).

In Malachi 2, as in preexilic prophecies, offerers are disqualified due to moral/ethical sin, in this case divorce (Mal 2:13-16). The sanction against intermarriage with pagans was even more severe: such an individual would be "cut off," so that he would not even have anyone (in his line of descendants; on "cut off," cf. Gane, 201) to bring an offering to the Lord (Mal 2:11-12 [see NJPS]).

2.4. Cessation of Cultic Systems. The preexilic prophets did not call for reform of sacrificial procedures; they pronounced doom on the ritual systems of Israel and Judah. There was never hope for the northern cults because they were illegitimate from the start. The northern Israelites were going into exile, where they would have no opportunity to offer sacrifices acceptable to the Lord (Hos 9:1-5), and they would long remain without ability to worship any deity (Hos 3:3-4).

Continuation of the first temple in Jerusalem was conditioned on return to loyalty (e.g., Jer 17:21-27; 26:1-19). But Ezekiel witnessed the departure of God's presence from his house due to breakdown of his nation's relationship with the Lord, as especially indicated by idolatry at the temple (Ezek 8—11; cf. Ezek 5:11; Lev 20:3 [idolatry also automatically defiles the sanctuary from a distance]). This implied that God had abandoned the temple and its entire sacrificial system to its fate (cf. Ezek 24:21, 25), pending establishment of a new temple, to which he would return (Ezek 40—48).

Joel prophesied interruption of rituals at the (first or second) temple due to a locust plague so devastating that there would not even be enough grain or drink for offerings (Joel 1:9, 13). Restoration was contingent on human repentance and divine mercy (Joel 2:12-14).

In Daniel 9 one who would strengthen a covenant with many for one "week" would make sacrifice (*zebaḥ*) and offering (*minḥâ*) cease in the middle of that "week"—that is, the last of seventy weeks of years (cf. Sabbatical cycles in Lev 25:1-8) following the decree to restore Jerusalem after the Babylonian exile (Dan 9:24-27). During the last "week" coincides with the time when the Anointed One (Messiah) is "cut off" (Dan 9:25-26 [after 7 + 62 weeks of years]). So it appears that the Messiah would bring an end to the sacrificial system (cf. Mt 27:51), after which the temple would be destroyed (Dan 9:26b, 27b). In the NT, the end of the need for an earthly ritual system involving animal sacrifices (including the temple system of Ezek 40—48, even though it was not implemented) coincides with Christ's once-for-all sacrifice of himself and inauguration of his priestly ministry in God's heavenly temple (e.g., Heb 7—10).

3. Atonement with or without Sacrifice.

Atonement is reconciliation with the deity, whether through sacrifices or not. The Hebrew verb traditionally rendered "to atone" is *kipper* (Piel of *kpr*), which denotes removal/expiation of an impediment to the divine-human relationship, whether it is caused by sin or physical ritual impurity (e.g., Lev 4:26; 12:7) (Gane, 191-95). The prophets employ *kipper* in several ways. Ezekiel's usage in the context of the ideal temple is similar to that of pentateuchal ritual law: various sacrifices expiate for the people (Ezek 45:15, 17 [cf. Lev. 23:37; Num 28—29; note expiatory efficacy for the sacrifice of well-being in Ezek 45:15, 17, as in 1 Sam 3:14]), purification offering blood cleanses the altar at its initial authorization (Ezek 43:18-26; cf. Lev 8:15), and such blood annually purges the temple from inadvertent sins committed by members of the covenant community (Ezek 45:18-20; cf. Lev 16 [but also removing rebellious sins in Lev 16:16]).

Animal sacrifice is not the only means of expiation. In Isaiah's temple vision, the prophet's sin is removed when a seraph touches his lips with a burning coal from the altar (Is 6:6-7). In Isaiah 27:9 expiation comes through reformation resulting from repentance: destruction of (unauthorized) altars and (pagan) sacred poles. Isaiah 53 points beyond animal sacrifice to the substitutionary death of God's suffering servant as a means for removing guilt (*'āšām* [Is 53:10]). In this sense his death functions like an expiatory reparation offering (also *'āšām* [Lev 5:16, 18; 6:6-7], but outside the ritual system (see Janowski).

In Ezekiel 16:63 the Lord mercifully promises to expiate (*kipper*) for the people of Jerusalem, without mention of how it is accomplished. Similarly, Daniel 9:24 does not state how conclusive expiation (*kipper*) for the iniquity (*'āwōn*) of the Jewish people would be achieved by the end of seventy weeks of years, although it appears that the Messiah could play a role in this (cf. Dan 9:25-27). Direct divine removal of guilt is expressed elsewhere by other terms, such as the Qal of *mḥh* ("to wipe out" [Is 43:25; 44:22]), Piel of *ṭhr* ("to purify" [Jer 33:8]) and Qal of *nś'* +*'āwōn* ("to bear culpability" [Is 33:24; Hos 14:2; Mic 7:18]). Some interpreters take Isaiah 40:2 to mean that God accepts the suffering of exile as expiatory (e.g., NJPS; cf. NASB, NJB, NKJV). But here the culpability of personified Jerusalem is paid for (Niphal of 2-*rṣh*) simply because she has completed her term of punishment (cf. NIV, NRSV).

Divine mercy can be withheld by refusal to grant expiation (*kipper*) for iniquity (Is 22:14; Jer 18:23) or prevention (*kipper*) of disaster (Is 47:11). In Isaiah 28:18 *kipper* refers to annul-

ment of a protective covenant with death, leaving presumptuous people exposed to disaster.

4. Relationship Between Prophets and the Pentateuch.

Pentateuchal and prophetic attestations of sacrifices are radically different. Pentateuchal ritual law provides systematic instructions to institute and regulate sacrificial worship officiated by priests, but only the vision of the priest-prophet Ezekiel (Ezek 40—48) is comparable in the prophetic corpus. Elsewhere, the prophets do not even directly mention reparation and purification offerings (see only Is 53:10; Jer 17:1, respectively), perhaps because the scope of these mandatory expiatory sacrifices was mostly limited to unintentional sins and/or cases of sacrilege (Lev 4:1—6:7) that were not significant concerns for them.

Agendas of prophets diverged from those of priests, who administered details of the ritual system and gained their livelihood from it. Prophets lacked such vested interest in the cult. Rather, they viewed it from outside priestly circles and were mainly concerned with effects of their people's ethical and ritual choices (including departures from strict monotheism) on the divine-human covenant relationship (e.g., Is 24:5; 55:3; Jer 22:9; 31:31-34; Ezek 16:8, 59-62). Not surprisingly, opposition of prophets to sacrifices that they regarded as unacceptable to the Lord aroused the ire of some priests (and cultic prophets), who were protective of their institutions and entitlements (e.g., Jer 26; Amos 7).

Prophets invalidated sacrifices for several reasons, but there is no solid evidence for outright rejection of all sacrifice by any prophet (*contra* Hendel, 190, 196; Barton, 120-21), although Daniel predicted eventual cessation of sacrifice at the second temple (Dan 9:27). "If the prophets had really meant that sacrifice under all circumstances was evil, they would not have needed to bring condemnation of the lives of men into association with their denunciation of the sacrifices" (Rowley, 343).

Where teachings of the Pentateuch and the prophets overlap, they agree on core concepts. For example: (1) The Lord was in voluntary residence at the sanctuary/temple, which meant that he could come or go (Ex 40:34-35; Jer 7:3, 7; Ezek 10—11). (2) Obedience to God, doing justice, and heartfelt loyalty are essential for the divine-human relationship, with no dichotomy between inner experience and outward practice (e.g., Lev 19; 26; Deut 6; Mic 6:8). (3) Ritual and ethics are linked (e.g., Lev 6:1-7 [sacrificial expiation for ethical sin]; Is 61:8 NJPS). (4) Sins committed by priests and prophets, who represent God to their people, are especially grave (Lev 4:3-12; 10:1-3; Num 20:10-13; Is 28:7; Jer 6:13; 8:10; 14:18; 23:11). (5) God can directly grant atonement, without mention of a need for animal sacrifice (Ex 34:7; Is 6:6-7; 27:9; Jer 33:8; Ezek 16:63; Hos 14:2; Mic 7:18; cf. Ex 32:30; Num 14:19-20). (6) An acceptable sacrifice is a genuine expression by a person loyal to God (e.g., Lev 1—5 [assumed]; Jon 1—2), but a person who despises God's word and defiantly breaks one of his commandments is terminally condemned and therefore barred from receiving the benefit of sacrificial expiation (e.g., Num 15:30-31; Jer 17:1-4). (7) Among the covenant curses, the Lord will reject sacrifices from idolatrous rebels and will destroy them along with their cult sites, idols and cities (Lev 26:30-31; cf. Prov 15:8; 21:27). Much of the prophetic indictment consists of implicit or explicit application of the covenant curses (Lev 26; Deut 27—28) to people of their times (explicitly in Jer 11:1-17).

Scholarly views regarding the original authorship, redaction and dating of the pentateuchal ritual texts and how they relate to other parts of the Pentateuch vary widely. So the chronological relationship between those texts and the classical prophets is a matter of complicated dispute. However, there are indications that at least the original authorship of the pentateuchal texts preceded the preexilic prophetic writings. For example: (1) The prophets remembered the Israelite wilderness experience, when the covenant and pentateuchal laws were given (according to Exodus through Deuteronomy, through the prophet Moses), as the time of their ancestors (Jer 7:22-23; 11:3-5; 31:32; Amos 5:25). (2) The prophets made literary allusions to pentateuchal law, including ritual law (e.g., Jer 11:1-17; 17:1) (see above; Fishbane, 292-317), but the Pentateuch contains no allusions to the prophetic writings. (3) Comparison between the pentateuchal language of the so-called Priestly source (P), which includes ritual law, and that of Ezekiel has indicated that the former belonged to an earlier stage of Hebrew (Hurvitz, 150-51, 154-55).

Whether the prophets interacted with those who formed the pentateuchal ritual texts at some stage(s) of their development (including editing) or not, conceptual differences between pentateuchal ritual and prophetic ethics do not seem sufficiently qualitative or clear-cut to support the conclusion that they represent two opposed trajectories of religious thought. Nor do such differences provide an adequate basis to reconstruct diachronic development from the prophets to the Pentateuch or vice versa (see Klawans, 75-76, 97; Averbeck, 728-29). In any case, if the pentateuchal and prophetic authors had lived at the same time, it appears that they would have gotten along with each other quite well.

See also FORGIVENESS; LITURGY AND CULT; SIN, SINNERS; TEMPLE; WORSHIP.

BIBLIOGRAPHY. **G. W. Ahlström**, "Some Remarks on Prophets and Cult," in *Transitions in Biblical Scholarship*, ed. J. C. Rylaarsdam (ED 6; Chicago: University of Chicago Press, 1968) 113-29; **F. I. Andersen and D. N. Freedman**, *Amos: A New Translation with Introduction and Commentary* (AB 24A; New York: Doubleday, 1989); **R. E. Averbeck**, "Sacrifices and Offerings," *DOTP* 706-33; **J. Barton**, "The Prophets and the Cult," in *Temple and Worship in Biblical Israel*, ed. J. Day (LHBOTS 422; London: T & T Clark, 2005) 111-22; **J. Chinitz**, "Were the Prophets Opposed to Sacrifice?" *JBQ* 36 (2008) 73-80; **M. Fishbane**, *Biblical Interpretation in Ancient Israel* (Oxford: Clarendon Press, 1985); **R. Gane**, *Cult and Character: Purification Offerings, Day of Atonement, and Theodicy* (Winona Lake, IN: Eisenbrauns, 2005); **R. S. Hendel**, "Prophets, Priests, and the Efficacy of Ritual," in *Pomegranates and Golden Bells: Studies in Biblical, Jewish, and Near Eastern Ritual, Law, and Literature in Honor of Jacob Milgrom*, ed. D. P. Wright, D. N. Freedman and A. Hurvitz (Winona Lake, IN: Eisenbrauns, 1995) 185-98; **A. Hurvitz**, *A Linguistic Study of the Relationship between the Priestly Source and the Book of Ezekiel: A New Approach to an Old Problem* (CahRB 20; Paris: Gabalda, 1982); **B. Janowski**, "He Bore Our Sins: Isaiah 53 and the Drama of Taking Another's Place," in *The Suffering Servant: Isaiah 53 in Jewish and Christian Sources*, ed. B. Janowski and P. Stuhlmacher (Grand Rapids: Eerdmans, 2004) 48-74; **R. Kasher**, "Anthropomorphism, Holiness and Cult: A New Look at Ezekiel 40-48," *ZAW* 110 (1998) 192-208; **J. Klawans**, *Purity, Sac-*

rifice, and the Temple: Symbolism and Supersessionism in the Study of Ancient Judaism (Oxford: Oxford University Press, 2006); **B. A. Levine,** "An
Essay on Prophetic Attitudes Toward Temple
and Cult in Biblical Israel," in *Minhah le-Nahum:
Biblical and Other Studies Presented to Nahum M.
Sarna in Honour of His 70th Birthday,* ed. M. Brettler and M. Fishbane (JSOTSup 154; Sheffield:
JSOT Press, 1993) 202-25; **E. C. Lucas,** "Sacrifice in the Prophets," in *Sacrifice in the Bible,* ed.
R. T. Beckwith and M. J. Selman (Grand Rapids: Baker, 1995) 59-74; **J. Milgrom,** "Concerning Jeremiah's Repudiation of Sacrifice," *ZAW*
89 (1977) 273-75; **H. H. Rowley,** "Ritual and
the Hebrew Prophets," *JSS* 1 (1956) 338-60;
J. A. Thompson, *The Book of Jeremiah* (NICOT;
Grand Rapids: Eerdmans, 1980); **J. Wellhausen,**
Prolegomena to the History of Israel (SPRTS; Atlanta: Scholars Press, 1994 [1885]).

R. E. Gane

SAGES. *See* PROPHECY AND WISDOM.

SALVATION, DELIVERANCE

Some argue that the concept of salvation/de-
liverance is the unifying plot of the Bible (see
Ryken, Wilhoit and Longman, 752). This divine rescue found its paradigm in the deliverance of God's people from Egypt, persisted
with military victories over enemies, and eventually was articulated in *worship literature.
Building on theological, historical and cultic
themes such as these, the understanding of salvation in the Prophetic Books continues to
find expression. God is still the one, the only
one, who accomplishes salvation for his people, but they are rescued from even higher
powers, those of God's *wrath and their own
*sin, and delivered to an even greater end, that
of eternal salvation.

1. Language of Salvation and Deliverance
2. Agent of Salvation and Deliverance
3. Nature of Salvation and Deliverance
4. Conclusion

1. Language of Salvation and Deliverance.
G. B. Stevens notes that "in the Old Testament
the idea of salvation was the subject of a long
development, and is therefore many-sided"
(Stevens, 19). Language, in the form of vocabulary, stories, images and literary parallels, demonstrates how full and complex the concept really is.

1.1. Vocabulary. The two most typical Hebrew roots for salvation are *yšʿ* ("to deliver" or
"to save" [Hiphil]) and *nṣl* ("to snatch away" or
"to deliver" [Hiphil]), the former being found
in its verbal form fifty-six times, and the latter
sixty-five times. The verb *yšʿ* implies bringing
help to people in trouble ("deliverance unto"),
while *nṣl* implies the snatching away or freeing
from distress ("deliverance from"). Typically,
God is the subject of both verbs.

Related to *yšʿ* are the nouns *yēšaʿ, yēšûʿâ, tēšûʿâ,*
each of which can be translated "salvation" or
"deliverance." The word *môšîaʿ,* usually translated as "savior" or "deliverer," rounds out the
salvation language related to *yšʿ* and is a Hiphil
participle. Although the majority of the occurrences of these terms do not appear in the Prophetic Books, they serve to fill in the depiction
of salvation/deliverance in this portion of the
HB. Also noteworthy is the fact that many
proper names in the OT can be traced back to
the verbal root *yšʿ.* The names of the prophets
Isaiah and Hosea are two of the more prominent examples. "Isaiah" means "salvation of
Yahweh" or "Yahweh is salvation," and "Hosea"
is an abbreviated form of "Yahweh is salvation."

Of course, oracles of salvation and various
descriptions of deliverance do not necessarily
contain this typical language of salvation.
Many other Hebrew terms are used by the
prophets to refer to saving deeds. They include
but are not limited to: *šzb* ("to rescue") and *mlt*
("to rescue"), *gʾl* ("to redeem"), *ʿzr* ("to help")
and *brk* ("to bless"). C. Westermann observes
that the noun *šālôm* occurs often in oracles of
salvation and can mean both *"peace" and
"salvation," the latter of which he defines as
the restoration of a whole relationship with
God. "Never does [*šālôm*] mean simply the cessation of war, and never does it mean only the
relationship of an individual to God, that is,
. . . 'peace with God'. . . . We cannot have peace
without the restoration of a true relationship
with God and all that belongs to it. . . . It is not
possible to have the 'peace with God' that is
announced here without the effect of that
peace on the rest of life and on the life of men
and women in community" (Westermann
1991, 272).

Further demonstrating the complexity and
richness of the concept, Westermann even suggests that the expression "fear not" in Isaiah
44:2 represents the central point of the pas-

sage, which is the assurance of salvation (Westermann 1969, 134). "The only way by which Israel can learn that she is God's servant, chosen by him, and give practical effect to her status, is for her to accept the assurance of salvation now being addressed to the nation" (Westermann 1969, 135).

1.2. Story Reviews. The depiction of salvation in the prophetic literature goes beyond mere vocabulary. J. R. Middleton and M. J. Gorman put it well: "Beneath the OT's use of explicit salvation language lies a coherent worldview in which the exodus from Egyptian bondage, followed by entry into the promised land, forms the most important paradigm or model" (Middleton and Gorman, 45) (*see* Exodus Imagery). Furthermore, the exodus "constitutes the sociopolitical deliverance of a community from a real, concrete situation of oppression . . . [and thus] resists any 'spiritualizing' of salvation, keeping it firmly rooted in life in this world" (Middleton and Gorman, 46). T. E. Fretheim, however, warns of two dangers: either collapsing salvation into a political theology or neglecting the spiritual dimension of salvation altogether. Nevertheless, he can say, "This ought not detract from the biblically-based point that God's saving activity also has to do with deliverance from oppressive social, economic, and political realities" (Fretheim 1993, 367). The continuation of the story of salvation thus captures all aspects of human existence: from history to community to political affairs and daily life.

Recollection of the exodus event and subsequent wilderness wandering can make up an integral part of a prophetic argument. Jeremiah 2, for example, contains a full description of the saving action of the Lord and the unfortunate response of his people, only to conclude, "Therefore I bring charges against you" (Jer 2:9 [all biblical quotations are NIV]). In the same way, Ezekiel 20 is the prophet's answer to the elders of Israel who inquire of the Lord. The divine response, "As surely as I live, I will not let you inquire of me" (Ezek 20:3), is defended with a lengthy account of bringing their ancestors out of Egypt (e.g., Ezek 20:6, 10, 17) and of their detestable practices that followed shortly thereafter (e.g., Ezek 20:8, 13, 21). And in Jeremiah 32, when the prophet is commanded to buy a field in Judah almost immediately before its destruction, part of the basis for his obedi-

ence is God's prior saving acts. The prophet prays, "You brought your people Israel out of Egypt with signs and wonders, by a mighty hand and an outstretched arm and with great terror. You gave them this land you had sworn to give their ancestors" (Jer 32:21-22).

Not to be overlooked amidst the lengthy story reviews are the brief historical reminders of the exodus that punctuate many of the prophets' words as modifiers. For example, frequent mention is made of the God "who brought [his] people out of Egypt with a mighty hand" (Dan 9:15 [see also Hos 12:9; Amos 2:10; Mic 6:4]) and of Israel's ancestors who were taken by the hand out of Egypt (e.g., Jer 7:25; 31:32). The historical event is also used as a kind of time stamp by which the audiences can orient themselves: "As in the days when you came out of Egypt, I will show them my wonders" (Mic 7:15 [see also Is 11:16; Jer 34:13; Hag 2:5]).

The exodus event was never far from the minds of the prophets or their audiences, and, according to Fretheim, it would have prompted them to consider the saving act of God in the future: the return of the exiles. "The 'old' exodus event no longer stands on its own as a redemptive and cosmic event; indeed, it is sharply reduced in importance compared to the new" (Fretheim 2005, 192). The Lord says, "Forget the former things; do not dwell on the past. See, I am doing a new thing!" (Is 43:18-19a [see also Is 42:9; 48:3, 6; Jer 16:14-15]). Westermann, however, balances that thought by thinking that it would be "very strange" if the exodus were to be forgotten and obliterated by the new thing to come (Westermann 1969, 127). In either case, this story of salvation from the past has a profound impact on the prophets' understanding of future salvation.

1.3. Images. Throughout the OT, the Hebrew language effectively describes more abstract concepts, such as salvation, using concrete images. Salvation/deliverance in the Prophetic Books is no exception. When God determines to work deliverance on his own, he dons the helmet of salvation (Is 59:16-17). Even the prophet himself has been clothed with garments of salvation (Is 61:10). From the wells of salvation water will be joyfully drawn, and thirst therefore will be quenched (Is 12:3). In response to the rain of righteousness, salvation will spring up like plants (Is 45:8). Salvation is also depicted as the walls of a city (e.g., Is 26:1;

cf. Jer 1:18-19; 15:20). Speaking of the glory of *Zion and the end of violence and destruction there, Isaiah says, "You will call your walls Salvation and your gates Praise" (Is 60:18). Isaiah later describes Zion's salvation as a blazing torch (Is 62:1).

1.3.1. The Arm of God. One of the more frequently used images and parallel expressions for salvation is "the arm of God," which, of course, is equated with and often translated as his strength (e.g., Is 33:2; 51:5). The arm is also depicted, more particularly, as the agent of salvation (e.g., Is 59:16; 63:5). Using a simple chiastic structure, Isaiah says, "The LORD will lay bare his holy arm in the sight of all the nations, and all the ends of the earth will see the salvation of our God" (Is 52:10).

1.3.2. The Shepherd of the Sheep. A frequent image in the OT is that of the sheep and its shepherd. The prophet Ezekiel uses this image quite fully in Ezekiel 34 to depict salvation (see also Jer 23:1-8). As the chapter begins, it is clear that the human shepherds have failed, and that God saves or rescues the flock from them, taking over the ineffective caretakers' responsibilities from them (Ezek 34:1-10). In Ezekiel 34:11-16 salvation is then described in terms of the good that a shepherd will do for his sheep; among other things, he will "rescue them from all the places where they were scattered" (Ezek 34:12). The sheep of the flock, however, will be judged as well and eventually brought under the care of one shepherd, the servant David (Ezek 34:17-24). In the final verses of the chapter God describes the new covenant of peace for his flock (Ezek 34:25-31): "They will know that I am the LORD, when I break the bars of their yoke and rescue them from the hands of those who enslaved them" (Ezek 34:27).

1.4. Relation to Righteousness. Helping to fill out this picture of salvation in the prophets is its relationship to the concept of "righteousness" (ṣedeq, ṣĕdāqâ). On many occasions the salvation of God is set in literary parallel with his righteousness (e.g., Is 46:13; 56:1; 61:10), sometimes complemented by concrete images. For instance, adding to the image of God's own arm working salvation is the parallel expression "his own righteousness sustained him" (Is 59:16) (*see* Justice, Righteousness). To accomplish this act of deliverance, the next verse says, God dons the complementary divine armor of the helmet of salvation and the breastplate of righteousness (Is 59:17). As Zion's salvation is like a blazing torch, so will Zion's righteousness shine like the dawn (Is 62:1). The rain of righteousness will produce a growth of salvation and more righteousness (Is 45:8).

These relatively simple poetic parallels hint at the complexity of salvation as a theological concept. Stevens notes that national salvation, which is not merely political, and real moral righteousness go hand in hand, so that righteousness accompanies salvation and gives to it its deeper meanings (Stevens, 20). One sees this in Isaiah 51, where in the space of four verses salvation is compared to righteousness three different times (Is 51:5, 6, 8), portraying the universality and eternity of God's righteous salvation. In the first reference righteousness and salvation are described as being on their way to the nations, so that salvation is what God does, and righteousness is the quality of that which fills it (see Motyer, 405-6). "The saving work satisfies every standard of the Lord's righteous nature, meets every legal claim and discharges every debt before the eternal law. . . . In a way that fully satisfies absolute *righteousness* there will be *salvation*, an end of divine wrath, an entrance by faith upon divine comfort, strength and joy" (Motyer, 405). The latter two references (Is 51:6, 8) highlight the eternity of righteous salvation that will not fade or flee. "Salvation's durability is in its constitution" (Motyer, 406).

N. H. Snaith goes one step further and relates righteousness and salvation to the doctrine of holiness, making sure that neither holiness nor righteousness is regarded as a mere ethical concept. "Just as religion is more than ethics, so holiness should be regarded as being more than awefulness plus moral perfection. It should be regarded as involving Salvation to at least an equal extent as Righteousness. God is Saviour at least as surely as He is Judge" (Snaith, 79). He continues, "Righteousness is the visible effect of this nearness of God in the affairs of this world . . . and is in fact a personal relationship at root. It is because Righteousness involves Salvation. . . . Without [this nearness and personal activity of the unique, holy God] there could never be any connection between Holiness, Righteousness, and Salvation. . . . Unless the three were inextricably involved, the Holy God could never be the Saviour" (Snaith, 80).

Snaith makes his case primarily using the

text of Second Isaiah. "No prophet has insisted more certainly upon the nearness of God to His people Israel, and to His saving activity on their behalf" (Snaith, 80). This is seen, as Snaith notes, in the two characteristic epithets that Second Isaiah uses for God: "redeemer" (e.g., Is 41:14; 43:14; 47:4; 48:17) and "savior" (e.g., 43:3, 11; 45:15, 21; 49:26) (Snaith, 85-87). Snaith concludes his argument saying that "in Second-Isaiah the word *tsedeq-tsedaqah* (righteousness) has come to mean 'salvation.' The Righteousness of God shows itself in his saving work. Whilst the ethical content must by no means be neglected, . . . in the Prophets . . . the salvation *motif* steadily becomes supreme" (Snaith, 92). And in Second Isaiah the "idea of Salvation is everywhere dominant" (Snaith, 92).

1.5. Relation to Creation. Like the concept of righteousness, the doctrine of *creation can contribute to one's understanding of salvation/deliverance. G. von Rad says that creation is "a magnificent foil for the message of salvation, which thus appears the more powerful and the more worthy of confidence" (quoted in Fretheim 2005, 189). Touching on the complementary roles of creator and redeemer, Isaiah 44:24 describes the Lord as "your Redeemer, who formed you in the womb . . . who has made all things." "God's saving action upon his chosen people as proclaimed by himself was, [as] it were, an island within the mighty universe of God's work as creator. It is therefore no accident that the combination, Israel's creator and her redeemer, most of all occurs in the promises of salvation (43.1, 15; 44.2; 44.21, 24; 54.5; also 45.11; 51.13)" (Westermann 1969, 25).

While the relationship between creation and salvation is often based on the power of God that enables him to create and to save, Fretheim and H. H. Schmid champion the more involved connections between the two concepts. Fretheim notes, "God's redemptive work does not put an end to God's creative work; God's work as Creator continues through and beyond such historical redemptive actions. . . . The objective of God's work in *redemption* is to free people to be what they were *created* to be, the effect of which is named *salvation*" (Fretheim 2005, 10). But Fretheim is careful not to equate creation and salvation. Speaking in particular of Second Isaiah, he regards the redemptive work of God as a special dimension of his activity as creator (Fretheim 2005, 11).

And then looking ahead to God's cosmic and universal goal, all the while making sure to distinguish between redemption and salvation, he says that "God's redemption is a means to a new creation, and salvation will be the key characteristic of that new reality" (Fretheim 2005, 12) (see also Fretheim 2005, 191-92).

Schmid expounds another aspect in the relationship between creation and salvation, especially as it relates to an ancient Near Eastern view of creation. He first explains the connection of act and consequence: "Whoever does what is right conforms to the created order . . . and hence stands under the blessing. Whoever acts wrongly must in some special way bear the consequences of this deed and thus stands under the curse" (Schmid, 106). Implicating the latter is the preoccupation of the prophets. "The circumstances in which the prophets appeared, the radical consistency of their indictment of the people, and the deadly earnestness with which they demand righteousness and justice comprise a specifically Israelite phenomenon quite without any ancient Near Eastern parallels; nevertheless the substance of their proclamation, the horizon and even the logic thereof, is that of the general Near Eastern view of the order of creation" (Schmid, 106-7).

Bringing the concepts of creation, salvation and righteousness together, Schmid says, "In those cases . . . where salvation (*Heil*) is described with the concept of *ṣĕdāqâ* [e.g., Is 45:8, 23f; 46:12f; 51:6, 8] . . . 'righteousness' is not understood narrowly as a legal matter, but as a universal world order, as comprehensive salvation. Here too the basic structure of the prophetic message corresponds essentially with the ancient Near Eastern view of creation" (Schmid, 107). Creation theology need not take a secondary position to soteriology, as it too often does, but is rather, as Schmid calls it, "the broad horizon of biblical theology" (Schmid, 102).

2. Agent of Salvation and Deliverance.

2.1. The Incomparability of God. In the Prophetic Books great pains are taken to portray God not just as the typical agent of salvation for his people, but as the only agent of salvation and hence as the Savior. In God's accusation against Israel he frequently notes Israel's persistent appeal to that which cannot save: idols, other gods, humans. Sometimes mention of God's salvation is not made directly, but the implication in those instances is that only he could save. Even if a human instrument is somehow involved in the act of salvation, God is still to be given sole credit. Several passages highlight that there is none besides God who saves (e.g., Is 45:21-22; 59:15-16), and therefore that he alone can claim the designation "Savior" (e.g., Is 43:3; 49:26; 63:8-9; Hos 13:4; Mic 7:7).

In Isaiah 43, for example, God proves himself to his people and concludes, "I, even I, am the LORD, and apart from me there is no savior" (Is 43:11). God is insistent on proving himself as the singular deliverer of his people. In Isaiah 47 God castigates *Babylon, who mocks him by taking his words for herself: "I am, and there is none besides me" (Is 47:8, 10). God does not tolerate such arrogance, and of Babylon's beloved astrologers he pronounces, "There is not one that can save you" (Is 47:15).

Habakkuk 1 records the complaint of one prophet who boldly questions God, "How long, O LORD, must I . . . cry out to you, 'Violence!' but you do not save?" (Hab 1:2). Yet even Habakkuk eventually acknowledges God as the author of salvation when, in the midst of trouble, he says, "I will be joyful in God my Savior" (Hab 3:18). In another prayer God's anger for sin is acknowledged as the speakers ask rhetorically, "How then can we be saved?" (Is 64:5), thus implying that God is the only one to deliver them.

2.1.1. In Relation to Idols. A technique often used by the prophets to demonstrate the incomparability of God's salvation is to contrast it with the inability of others to save. Idols, for one, are unable to deliver (e.g., Is 57:13). In Isaiah 44 God almost humorously describes the situation. A person carves an idol and prays to it, saying, "Save me" (Is 44:17), but "such a person feeds on ashes; a deluded heart misleads him; he cannot save himself, or say, 'Is not this thing in my right hand a lie?'" (Is 44:20). In Isaiah 45 the conclusion is reached: "Truly you are a God who has been hiding himself, the God and Savior of Israel. All the makers of idols will be put to shame and disgraced. . . . But Israel will be saved by the LORD" (Is 45:15-17).

2.1.2. In Relation to Other Gods. Often used interchangeably with the idols are the gods identified with them, and neither are they able to save (e.g., Is 45:20; 46:5-7; Jer 2:26-28; 11:12).

In Isaiah 36—37 Sennacherib himself, king of Assyria, ironically acknowledges that gods are not able to deliver their lands, but he misapplies the rule to the God of Jerusalem when he says, "Do not let Hezekiah mislead you when he says, 'The LORD will deliver us.' Have the gods of any nation ever delivered their lands from the hand of the king of Assyria? . . . How then can the LORD deliver Jerusalem from my hand?" (Is 36:18, 20). Referring to the king of Assyria, God defends his unique ability to save: "He will not enter this city. . . . I will defend this city and save it" (Is 37:33, 35).

Foreign rulers are also known, however, to acknowledge positively the unique ability of the God of Israel to save. As recorded in the book of Daniel, edicts were announced that made it mandatory to bow down to other gods. Men such as Shadrach, Meshach, Abednego and Daniel himself refused to do so and were punished. Nebuchadnezzar, king of Babylon, after witnessing how God kept Shadrach, Meshach and Abednego from harm in the fiery furnace, decreed that no people of any nation or language should say anything against the God of Israel, "for no other god can save in this way" (Dan 3:29). King Darius spoke similarly in a later context: "I issue a decree that in every part of my kingdom people must fear and reverence the God of Daniel. . . . He rescues and he saves. . . . He has rescued Daniel from the power of the lions" (Dan 6:26-27).

2.1.3. In Relation to Humans. Along with idols and other gods, human salvation cannot compare to that of God. Specifically, astrologers, as mentioned above, cannot save the people or even themselves (Is 47:13-14); the king cannot save his people (Hos 13:10); one nation cannot save another (Is 20: 5-6; Lam 4:17; Hos 14:3); and Judah is certainly not able to save itself (Is 26:18). Likewise, the possessions of humans—silver and gold—cannot save (Ezek 7:19; Zeph 1:18). In Hosea 1:7 God claims that he will save the house of Judah, yet this he will not do through human instruments such as "by bow, sword or battle, or by horses and horsemen"; instead, he will save by himself (cf. Jer 14:9).

Ezekiel 14:12-20, however, appears to suggest that at least three men—Noah, Daniel and Job—could hypothetically save themselves by their righteousness (Ezek 14:13, 20). But also this illustration serves the broader point that even these three great men of faith could not save the nation or their own sons and daughters.

2.2. The Instrument of the Messiah. Prophetic references that traditionally are understood as being messianic address the topic of deliverance by speaking of God's instrument of salvation, the coming *Messiah. Jeremiah makes reference to the "righteous Branch," in whose days Judah will be saved (Jer 23:5-6). Micah introduces a ruler from Bethlehem (Mic 5:2) who will, most immediately, deliver God's people from the Assyrians (Mic 5:6). Zechariah announces the coming of Zion's king, righteous and having salvation (Zech 9:9).

Also, the character referred to as the *"Servant of Yahweh" in Isaiah is the one who brings the salvation of God (Is 49:6 [lit., "to be" the salvation of God]). Although the typical vocabulary of deliverance is not found in Isaiah 42, the Servant of Yahweh is the one who will establish *justice (Is 42:1, 3, 4) and who will "free the captives from prison" and "release from the dungeon those who sit in darkness" (Is 42:7).

M. de Jonge observes that the messianic prophecies "announce a decisive and lasting change in the plight of the people, brought about by God. War will end, peace and plenty will be restored, Israel and Judah will be reunited, people in Exile will return; salvation has worldwide dimensions" (de Jonge, 781).

2.3. The Role of the Prophet. Although the prophet (*nābî'*) is in no way the agent or even instrument of salvation, his role as messenger to the people is crucial and deserves consideration, since he is one who speaks in the name of God. "Divine inspiration was what made a person a prophet, and what caused the prophet to speak out, and what made others listen to the prophet as a legitimate spokesperson for the divine" (Schmitt, 482). The evidence of this inspiration is the messenger formula. The most common formula is "thus says the LORD," and it indicates that the prophet is authorized by God to pronounce the message (be it of salvation or judgment). Even when the formula is not used consistently, "it is clear from the message itself that an oracle of salvation is commissioned by God" (Westermann 1991, 253). Other formulas include "on that day" and "days are coming."

2.3.1. The Oracle of Salvation. Especially, though not exclusively, the prophet conveys the message of deliverance with the oracle (*maśśā'*) of salvation. Although "oracle" often is used generically to refer to any prophetic speech,

maśśā' (which can also be translated "burden") more precisely designates a type of speech used by ancient Israelite prophets (Weis, 28). R. D. Weis suggests that translating *maśśā'* as "prophetic exposition of divine revelation" is preferable to "oracle" (Weis, 28). He furthermore notes that mostly before the exile, the genre of *maśśā'* represented the product of a prophetic encounter with God, communicating how God is at work and how the audience should respond, but that later examples of the genre refer to revelations previously communicated, giving insight into the future rather than direction for action (Weis, 28-29).

Narrowing the broader genre and surveying only oracles of salvation in the prophetic literature, Westermann makes three observations. First, an oracle can be addressed to an individual (sometimes representing a whole family) or a community (mostly Israel and then later the remnant). Second, the length of time between announcement and fulfillment of that oracle varies, usually being short for an oracle addressed to an individual and longer for those directed to a community. Third, regarding the content of an oracle, there is a distinction, expressed in the forms of the oracle, between God's activity in deliverance and the state of well-being, both of which constitute God's saving activity. Many oracles of salvation, however, consist only of the proclamation of deliverance, which reflects a fixed pattern: distress, cry for help, cry heard, deliverance (Westermann 1991, 14-16).

Westermann also helpfully categorizes the oracles of salvation based on their structure and content. He observes that the majority are found in collections of oracles (as in Second Isaiah, Jeremiah, Ezekiel, Third Isaiah, Micah and Zephaniah), while others are found in reports of situations in which oracles were given (only in Isaiah, Jeremiah and, perhaps, Ezekiel, and in the Historical Books). Westermann further subdivides the former into groups: a major group (Group 1) and three secondary groups (Westermann 1991, 15).

The oracles of Group 1, Westermann notes, follow the pattern of Second Isaiah (see also Is 1:1-17; Mic 2:12-13; Nah 1:15—2:2; Zeph 3:18-20). "First, the salvation announced for Israel is open to the people of all nations [cf. Group 2]. ... Second, ... the regaining of political power and influence is not proclaimed. That was not a part of the salvation that was being announced" (Westermann 1991, 66). The oracles of Group 2 are mostly short and supplementary and always have two parts, which proclaim the destruction of Israel's enemies and salvation for Israel (e.g., Is 14:24-27; Joel 2:18-20; Obad 15-17). The oracles of Group 3 are conditional proclamations of salvation (e.g., Jer 3:6-18; Hos 3:2-5). Finally, the oracles of Group 4 combine the message of salvation with the fates of the pious and the wicked (e.g., Is 33:14-15; Amos 9:8-10) (Westermann 1991, 17-18). Westermann notes, "It is especially striking that in all the prophetic books there are only these four groups and none of the groups is found only in one or two of the books" (Westermann 1991, 17).

2.3.2. Second Isaiah. Although reference has been made above, the distinctive nature of Second Isaiah is worth noting in greater detail. As described by Westermann, the "message as contained in chapters 40-55 is, as a whole, a proclamation of salvation, a situation not duplicated in any other prophetic book. The reason for this is that the proclamation is concentrated on a single event, the liberation of Israel from Babylonian captivity. A further difference is that here we do not have individual oracles one after another. . . . Rather we have a coherent whole consisting of various literary forms" (Westermann 1991, 39). Westermann identifies at least seven of these literary forms, all of which express salvation: the oracle (or promise) of salvation, which is the most typical form (e.g., Is 41:8-13, 14-16); the proclamation of salvation, which speaks of future events (e.g., Is 41:17-20); praise language (e.g., Is 40:12-31); aggressive polemics against foreign nations and gods (e.g., Is 41:1-5, 21-29); polemics against Israel (e.g., Is 43:22-28); songs or cries of exultation (e.g., Is 42:10-13); and the Servant Songs (e.g., Is 42:1-4) (Westermann 1969, 11-21).

3. Nature of Salvation and Deliverance.

3.1. Scope. While the threats of enemies are ever present in the Prophetic Books, the scope of God's salvation is broadened to include deliverance from the threats of the people's own sin and, somewhat ironically, of God's *wrath. First, the people's own sin has been alluded to above: creating and worshiping idols and looking to other humans or nations for their salvation. Thus, the people's trust in that which cannot save represents the very sin from which they need to be saved. Looking to the future, God speaks of his covenant people in Ezekiel 37: "They will no longer defile themselves with their idols and vile images or with any of their offenses, for I will save them from all their sinful backsliding, and I will cleanse them. They will be my people, and I will be their God" (Ezek 37:23 [see also Ezek 36:29]).

Second, God's wrath, often described by the prophets in terms of the dreaded *Day of the Lord, will ultimately be a day of deliverance for his people. In the emphatic words of Joel, "Everyone who calls on the name of the LORD will be saved; for on Mount Zion and in Jerusalem there will be deliverance, as the LORD has said, among the survivors whom the LORD calls" (Joel 2:32). Zephaniah 1, as well, describes in vivid detail the Day of the Lord, when God will stretch out his hand against all who live in Jerusalem (Zeph 1:4), saying, "Neither their silver nor their gold will be able to save them on the day of the LORD's wrath" (Zeph 1:18). But the closing declaration of God to Jerusalem is this: "The LORD your God is with you, the Mighty Warrior who saves" (Zeph 3:17).

3.2. Duration. Whereas historical deliverance of God's people from their enemies is short-lived and temporary, the prophets develop the eschatological dimension of divine salvation: it is everlasting (e.g., Is 45:17). In Isaiah 51 God speaks of this eternal salvation for Zion. God says that although heaven and earth will pass away, "My salvation will last forever, my righteousness will never fail" (Is 51:6). And again he says, "My salvation [will last] through all generations" (Is 51:8). Likely speaking eschatologically of "that day" (e.g., Zeph 3:11) and after pronouncing that he is mighty to save (Zeph 3:17), God says, "At that time I will deal with all who oppressed you; I will rescue the lame; I will gather the exiles. . . . I will give you honor and praise among all the peoples of the earth" (Zeph 3:19-20).

3.3. Recipients. Related to the notion of God's everlasting salvation is the idea that it is reserved not just for the remnant of Israel, or even all of Israel (e.g., Amos 3:12); some prophetic passages suggest that foreigners may also be the recipients of divine attention that can lead to divine salvation (e.g., Is 45:22; 56:1-3). Speaking to his servant, whether individual or corporate, God says, "It is too small a thing for you to be my servant to restore the tribes of Jacob and bring back those of Israel I have kept. I will also make you a light for the Gentiles, that my salvation may reach to the ends of the earth" (Is 49:6 [see also Is 49:22-23]).

A particular example of the salvation of foreigners, though perhaps more short-term than long-lasting, comes in the book of Jonah when God shows compassion for Nineveh. In response to Nineveh's repentance, God did not bring destruction on the city and its inhabitants (Jon 3). Although the typical language of salvation is not found in this chapter, it is ironic that Jonah, the happy recipient of a unique divine deliverance through the means of a fish (Jon 1:17), was not pleased with this particular foreign recipient of God's deliverance. The book of Jonah well illustrates the truth of the prophet Jonah's own confession from inside the fish, "Salvation comes from the LORD" (Jon 2:9), even if the prophet is angered when this divine deliverance is applied to a foreign city.

3.4. Reason. Salvation in the Prophetic Books often is portrayed as a means to an end. Of course, the reason for deliverance, especially from human oppressors, is practical: life can continue, privately and nationally. Yet more than that, the prophets highlight that salvation, be it from one's enemies, from one's own sin, or from God's righteous wrath, is for the sake of foreign nations and for the sake of God's own people, that all might know God. Salvation is even for the sake of God himself. Alluding to all three reasons for salvation and referring to the recently mentioned illustration of the recipients of salvation, C. F. Keil notes that God's direction for Jonah to preach to the foreign city was not for her conversion but "to give His people Israel a practical proof that He was the God of the heathen also, and could prepare for Himself even among them a people of His possession" (Keil, 277).

3.4.1. For the Sake of Foreigners. First, divine deliverance comes to the people of God, or even to foreign nations, so that the ends of the earth will know God (e.g., Is 52:10). Hezekiah himself acknowledges this when he prays for God to save his people from the king of Assyria: "Now, LORD our God, deliver us from his hand, so that all kingdoms on earth may know that you, LORD, are the only God" (Is 37:20). In an oracle concerning Egypt the prophet Isaiah says, "It will be a sign and witness to the LORD

Almighty in the land of Egypt. When they cry out to the LORD because of their oppressors, he will send them a savior and defender, and he will rescue them. So the LORD will make himself known to the Egyptians" (Is 19:20-21).

Narrowing the focus even further and demonstrating that not all within the community of Israel are to be counted among God's people, in Ezekiel 13 God speaks to the daughters who "prophesy out of their own imagination" (Ezek 13:17): "I will tear off your veils and save my people from your hands. . . . Then you will know that I am the LORD. . . . And because you encouraged the wicked not to turn from their evil ways and so save their lives, . . . I will save my people from your hands. And then you will know that I am the LORD" (Ezek 13:21-23).

3.4.2. For the Sake of God's People. Likewise, God saves his people so that they themselves will come to know him and not fear. To that end, the themes of salvation and of the divine presence sometimes are coupled. This is seen often in the book of Jeremiah and comes first of all for the benefit of the prophet himself. Knowing that his message would not always be received favorably among the nations, God says to Jeremiah, "Do not be afraid of them, for I am with you and will rescue you" (Jer 1:8 [see also Jer 1:19; 15:20]). God speaks similar words to a broader audience, his people in exile, reassuring them of their eventual restoration: "Do not be afraid of the king of Babylon. . . . For I am with you and will save you and deliver you from his hands" (Jer 42:11 [see also Jer 30:11; Zeph 3:17]). "Salvation . . . witnesses to the active presence of God among his people and with his leaders" (Hartley, 416).

3.4.3. For God's Own Sake. Finally, salvation is for God's sake—that is, for the sake of his holy name (e.g., Ezek 36:22-32; cf. Is 43:25; Jer 14:7-9; Dan 9:15-19). In response to Hezekiah's prayer mentioned above, God answers, "I will defend this city and save it, for my sake and for the sake of David my servant" (Is 37:35). And in Ezekiel 20 God refers to the paradigmatic act of deliverance, the deliverance from Egypt (e.g., Ezek 20:5-6), when defending his own name or reputation. Responding to his people's rebellion, he says, "But for the sake of my name, I brought them out of Egypt. I did it to keep my name from being profaned in the eyes of the nations among whom they lived and in whose sight I had revealed myself to the Israelites. Therefore I led them out of Egypt and brought them into the wilderness" (Ezek 20:9-10 [cf. Ezek 20:14, 22, 44]).

4. Conclusion.

The theme of salvation, expressed in rich and varied language and communicated by the prophet with the oracle, occupies a prominent place in the Prophetic Books. Only God can save, and he will do so how, when, for whom, and for whatever reason he pleases. "The saving deed then is determinative for the nature of each generation's relationship with Yahweh, and its proclamation inspires the faith to establish and to maintain the relationship (cf. Is 52:7)" (Hartley, 416).

See also BLESSINGS AND CURSES; DAY OF THE LORD; DESTRUCTION; ESCHATOLOGY; EXODUS IMAGERY; JUSTICE, RIGHTEOUSNESS; MESSIAH; NATIONS; PEACE, REST; REMNANT; RETRIBUTION; WRATH.

BIBLIOGRAPHY. **U. Bergmann,** "נצל," *TLOT* 2:760-62; **M. de Jonge,** "Messiah," *ABD* 4:777-88; **J. S. Feinberg,** "Salvation in the Old Testament," in *Tradition and Testament: Essays in Honor of Charles Lee Feinberg* (Chicago: Moody, 1981) 39-77; **T. E. Fretheim,** "Salvation in the Bible vs. Salvation in the Church," *WW* 13 (1993) 363-72; idem, *God and World in the Old Testament: A Relational Theology of Creation* (Nashville: Abingdon, 2005); **J. E. Hartley,** "ישׁע," *TWOT* 1:414-16; **R. L. Hubbard Jr.,** "ישׁע," *NIDOTTE* 2:556-62; idem, "נצל," *NIDOTTE* 3:141-47; **C. F. Keil,** "Jonah," K&D 10:253-282 **J. R. Middleton and M. J. Gorman,** "Salvation," *NIDB* 5:45-61; **J. A. Motyer,** *The Prophecy of Isaiah: An Introduction and Commentary* (Downers Grove, IL: InterVarsity Press, 1993); **G. G. O'Collins,** "Salvation," *ABD* 5:907-14; **L. Ryken, J. C. Wilhoit and T. Longman III,** eds., "Salvation," in *Dictionary of Biblical Imagery* (Downers Grove, IL: InterVarsity Press, 1998), 752-56; **H. H. Schmid,** "Creation, Righteousness, and Salvation: 'Creation Theology as the Broad Horizon of Biblical Theology," in *Creation in the Old Testament,* ed. B. W. Anderson (IRT 6; Philadelphia: Fortress, 1984) 102-17; **J. J. Schmitt,** "Prophecy (Preexilic Hebrew)," *ABD* 5:482-89; **N. H. Snaith,** *The Distinctive Ideas of the Old Testament* (New York: Schocken, 1969); **G. B. Stevens,** *The Christian Doctrine of Salvation* (New York: Charles Scribner's Sons, 1917); **F. Stolz,** "ישׁע," *TLOT* 2:584-87; **R. D. Weis,** "Oracle," *ABD* 5:28-29; **C. Wes-**termann, *Isaiah 40-66: A Commentary,* trans. D. M. G. Stalker (OTL; Philadelphia: Westminster, 1969); idem, *Prophetic Oracles of Salvation in the Old Testament* (Louisville: Westminster/John Knox, 1991). J. C. Moeller

SANCTUARY. See TEMPLE.

SCRIBES. See PROPHECY, HISTORY OF; WRITING AND PROPHECY.

SEPTUAGINT OF BOOK OF THE TWELVE. See TWELVE, BOOK OF: HISTORY OF INTERPRETATION.

SEPTUAGINT OF ISAIAH. See ISAIAH: HISTORY OF INTERPRETATION.

SEPTUAGINT OF JEREMIAH. See JEREMIAH: BOOK OF; TEXT AND TEXTUAL CRITICISM.

SERAPHIM. See ANGELS, MESSENGERS, HEAVENLY BEINGS.

SERVANT OF YAHWEH

The phrase "servant of Yahweh" occurs only once in the Prophetic Books, in Isaiah 42:19; most OT occurrences of the phrase come in Joshua, where it is a description of Moses. But the expressions "my servant," "your servant" and "his servant," with the pronoun referring to Yahweh, come a number of times in the Prophetic Books. The use of these expressions in Isaiah 40—55 has been a subject of close study, particularly because some references are particularly significant in the NT and are also difficult to interpret in their OT context.

1. Occurrences
2. The Unidentified Servant of Yahweh in Isaiah 42:1-4; 52:13—53:12
3. The Unidentified Servant of Yahweh: New Testament References
4. The Servant Songs

1. Occurrences.

In the Prophetic Books, the first person whom Yahweh designates as "my servant" is Isaiah himself (Is 20:3), the second is a Judean political leader, Eliakim (Is 22:20), and the third is David (Is 37:35; cf. Jer 33:21-22, 26; Ezek 34:23-24; 37:24-25). The description then becomes transferred to Israel as a whole (Is 41:8-9; 43:10; 44:1-2, 21; 45:4; 48:20; 49:3; cf. Jer 30:10; 46:27-28). This transfer has a background in the description of Israel's ancestor, the individual Jacob, as "my servant" (Ezek 28:25; 37:25). In some other passages Yahweh's servant is not identified (Is 42:1, 19; 44:26; 49:5-6; 50:10; 52:13; 53:11). In yet other passages Yahweh's servants (plural) refer to the Israelites corporately or to faithful Israelites (Is 54:17; 56:6; 63:17; 65:8-9, 13-15; 66:11; Dan 3:26, 28). Elsewhere, Yahweh's servants are the prophets (Jer 7:25; 25:4; 26:5; 29:19; 35:15; 44:4; Ezek 38:17; Dan 9:6, 10; Amos 3:7; Zech 1:6).

In Jeremiah, Nebuchadnezzar is "my servant" (Jer 25:9; 27:6; 43:10). Elsewhere, Moses is Yahweh's servant (Dan 9:11; Mal 4:4), as are Daniel (Dan 6:20; 9:17), Zerubbabel (Hag 2:23) and the unnamed "Branch" (Zech 3:8), a new growth from the felled Davidic tree. Zerubbabel himself was such a new growth, and here Zechariah may denote him by "the Branch" as one who represents an embodiment of God's faithfulness to David. Alternatively, the Branch's not being named may reflect the awareness that Zerubbabel's leadership was short-lived, and that he never became king (see Israelite History). "The Branch" then refers to a future Davidic ruler whom God will one day send—a *"Messiah," to use the later term.

The Hebrew word 'ebed ('ăbad in the *Aramaic passages in Daniel) denotes a person such as Abraham's servant in Genesis 24, who is in a committed relationship with a master. This relationship involves a commitment on the servant's part to do whatever the master requires and a commitment on the master's part to protect and provide for the servant. In addition, a servant's relationship with a master means the servant can represent the master and have full power to act on the master's behalf and with the master's authority. The servant's words and acts have the same weight as the master's. These considerations apply in varying ways when the prophets describe someone as Yahweh's servant. Moses' or Isaiah's being Yahweh's servant means that people must pay heed to their words; the same applies to the description of the prophets in general as Yahweh's servants. Ignoring the servant's words means risking the wrath of the master. Something similar is true of Nebuchadnezzar, God's agent in bringing trouble on Judah; the Judahites must submit to him because he is Yahweh's servant. Jacob, David or Zerubbabel is Yahweh's servant (along with "the Branch," if that is not Zerubbabel);

this means that Yahweh is committed to them, fulfilled promises to them, and will do so again. Eliakim's being Yahweh's servant means that Yahweh is committed to him rather than to the person who will be displaced in his favor.

This understanding of masters and servants is also background to the description of Israel as "my servant." It is an aspect of the way positions occupied by individuals such as David can be applied to the people as a whole. Yahweh chose David as servant and thereby put him in a position of honor and security. Yahweh has done the same to *Israel as a whole, in a way that reflects Israel's being the descendants of Yahweh's servant Jacob. In the context of *exile, when Israel feels like a worm and has grounds for seeing itself as cast off by Yahweh because of its waywardness, Yahweh assures it that it actually has the exalted status that Jacob and David had as Yahweh's chosen servant. Yahweh has not rejected it (Is 41.8-9; cf. Is 44:1-2; Jer 30:10; 46:27-28). Yahweh's faithfulness to Israel as servant will be expressed in restoring it, and it is a basis for appealing to Israel to return to Yahweh (Is 44:21-22). It is for the sake of Israel as Yahweh's servant that Yahweh is summoning Cyrus to be the means of putting Babylon down and restoring Israel (Is 45.4; cf. Is 48:20). David acted as a witness to Yahweh's deity and power by carving out his empire; now the people as a whole will function as witnesses to Yahweh's acts in restoring it, and in this way they will function as Yahweh's servant (Is 43.10; 55:3-5). Thus, it is Yahweh's intent that through Israel Yahweh's attractiveness should be demonstrated (Is 49:3).

2. The Unidentified Servant of Yahweh in Isaiah 42:1-4; 52:13—53:12.

The central focus of study in connection with the phrase "servant of Yahweh" has been several passages in Isaiah where the servant is not identified, especially Isaiah 42:1-4; 52:13—53:12 (Is 42:5-9 can be seen as an extension of the first passage). Both might be called *"visions," though the term applies more strictly to Isaiah 52:13—53:12 than to Isaiah 42:1-4. Both passages might also be called "job descriptions." Both include words and phrases that are difficult to interpret, which complicates issues raised by the servant's anonymity. The appropriateness of calling them "visions" derives initially from the fact that the prophet (or rather, Yahweh) begins by pointing to the servant, as if he is someone who can be seen: "There is my servant" (Is 42:1); "There, my servant will act with insight" (Is 52:13). Both passages utilize the form of a declaration such as a prophet might make at a king's coronation, in which the prophet proclaims what the king would or should do, what his achievements would be, and/or what God would bring about through him. The servant's designation is thus analogous to that of a king. By implication, the designation lays an agenda before the king; it presents a challenge to him.

In Isaiah 42:1-4 the role of "my servant" relates to the *nations, and key to it is the idea of bringing out *mišpāṭ* to them or establishing *mišpāṭ* among them (*see* Justice, Righteousness). The word *mišpāṭ* is hard to translate into English. It often is translated as "justice," but the older translation "judgment" is nearer its meaning, though without the negative connotations that often attach to that word. *Mišpāṭ* denotes the exercise of power or authority or the capacity to make decisions. Ideally, this will be an expression of justice, though this is not always so. "Government" comes near to the word's meaning. Isaiah 40:14 asked, rhetorically, who taught Yahweh the way of *mišpāṭ*, the way to make decisions about how to create the world or how to run the world. In Isaiah 40:27 Israel asked what had happened to its own *mišpāṭ*, to the exercise of governmental power by Yahweh on its behalf in the world. Isaiah 42:1-4 declares that the servant's role will be to see that such *mišpāṭ* reaches the nations. While this might mean that Yahweh's servant is the means of implementing Yahweh's rule there, in the last of its three occurrences in these four verses *mišpāṭ* is paralleled by *tôrâ* ("teaching"). This rather suggests that the servant's role is to instruct the nations, to enable them to see how Yahweh has been exercising authority in the world, specifically in the rise of the Persians, who are overthrowing the Babylonian Empire. The term "nations" often refers to the empire itself, and this may be so here; or it may refer to other peoples who, like the Judahites, will benefit from the fall of Babylon. In the following verses (Is 42:5-9), similar ideas are expressed in different ways as the prophecy follows the form of a commission addressed to a person such as a king, rather than a statement about the king. It declares that the person addressed (it is the context that suggests that this is Yahweh's ser-

vant) has been appointed as "a covenant of the people, a light of the nations." The servant is the embodiment of what it means to be in a covenant with Yahweh and thus models this for people in general and thereby brings illumination and blessing to the nations.

Isaiah 52:13—53:12 likewise adapts the form of a declaration about a king, though reworking it more radically. One mark of its poetic nature is the way it is structured as a chiasm. It begins and ends with words from Yahweh (Is 52:13-15; 53:11b-12). Inside these words of Yahweh are the introductions and conclusions of a group that speaks about Yahweh's servant (Is 53:1, 10-11a). Inside this frame, in turn, are the group's actual reflections (Is 53:2-9), with their key insight at the center (Is 53:4-6). The poem as a whole describes Yahweh's servant as one who has been attacked and taken near to death, perhaps to actual death. Yahweh affirms that he will be restored and recognized by people. In the vision Yahweh and the prophet stand at a point where the attacks are past but the restoration future, though this does not establish where things are in real time outside the vision. As in Isaiah 42:1-9, Yahweh's words speak of his significance for the nations, which will be astonished at what they hear about him. In the main part of the vision, the group that recognizes him describes how they came to do so. He was someone who had gone through humiliation, rejection and pain, and they had assumed that this was because of wrong that he had done. They had come to realize that actually he had gone through his affliction as a result of identifying with them in the suffering that came to them, which in their case was indeed caused by their wrongdoing, and also as a result of the ministry that he had exercised to them. He had been willing to go through this experience because doing so could bring them well-being (*šālôm*). It could do so because he was prepared in accordance with Yahweh's own purpose to make his obedient suffering a kind of offering to Yahweh that could make compensation for their disobedience (an *ʾāšām*, a restitution offering). The key factor in their coming to this new understanding of his affliction was the silent, accepting way he put up with it.

3. The Unidentified Servant of Yahweh: New Testament References.

The account of the servant's vocation and significance in Isaiah 42:1-9 and Isaiah 52:13—53:12 is very different from the significance that attaches to being Yahweh's servant in passages such as those that explicitly identify Israel or Isaiah or Nebuchadnezzar or some other person as Yahweh's servant. In Christian tradition it was customary from NT times to take the two passages to refer to Jesus. Thus, Matthew 12:18-21 quotes the whole of Isaiah 42:1-4 and declares that Jesus' healing ministry "fulfilled" it. The NT quotes many individual verses from Isaiah 52:13—53:12 and sees them embodied in aspects of the Christ event. In Matthew 8:17 Yahweh's taking up people's infirmities (Is 53:4) is "fulfilled" in Jesus' healing ministry. 1 Peter 2:22 looks at Jesus' suffering in light of the way Isaiah 53:9 describes Yahweh's servant as suffering without being led into sin or deceit; 1 Peter 2:24-25 utilizes further phrases from Isaiah 53:4-6. In Luke 22:37 Jesus speaks of a "fulfillment" in him of the words in Isaiah 53:1 about Yahweh's servant being counted with the transgressors. John 12:38 sees people's failure to believe in Jesus as "fulfilling" the rhetorical question "Who has believed our message?" (Is 53:1; see also Rom 10:16). In Romans 15:21 Paul looks at his preaching of Jesus around the Mediterranean in light of the declaration that nations and kings would see and understand things that they had never heard of (Is 52:15). Beyond such actual quotations, the picture of Yahweh's servant in Isaiah 42:1-4 and Isaiah 52:13—53:12 is of more pervasive influence in the NT, especially in connection with an understanding of Jesus' death. Thus, until the nineteenth century, Christian understanding of the passages simply assumed that they referred to Jesus.

The rise of critical interpretation of Scripture brought a sea change in the interpretation of these passages from Isaiah. The nature of critical interpretation is to question the church's tradition of interpretation, to seek to start from scratch in interpreting passages, and to ask what they meant to their authors and original hearers. In that context, people would not take Isaiah 42:1-4 as a prophecy of the Messiah's healing ministry, nor would they take Isaiah 52:13—53:12 as an anticipatory account of a crucifixion.

When the NT uses these passages, it starts from Jesus and the knowledge that he is Savior and Lord, and it looks back at the Scriptures (i.e., the OT) for help in understanding what that means. In particular, the first Christians

needed help in understanding the surprising fact that the Messiah had been executed. The NT was not preoccupied with proving that Jesus was the Messiah. Its writers and the people for whom it was written knew that Jesus was the Messiah; they did not need to be convinced of this. Instead, they were concerned with knowing more clearly what it meant to call Jesus "Messiah," "Savior" and "Lord" and with understanding puzzling facts about Jesus. Isaiah 52:13—53:12 gave crucial help in that connection. Like any reading of Scripture that starts from the questions of later readers, this use of Isaiah was concerned not with understanding the text in its own right but rather with seeing how it answered these questions. Arguably, critical interpretation did the same thing; it started from different questions, but its quest for the text's original historical meaning was believed to correspond more to the text's own agenda.

4. The Servant Songs.

Critical study thus sought to work out afresh the detailed exegesis of these two difficult passages and also asked whom they describe, not assuming that they describe Jesus. The context in which it considered them in this connection was their setting in Isaiah 40—55 understood against the background of the exile, instead of their setting in the story of Jesus. Yet the collocation of the descriptions of an unnamed servant of Yahweh with the references to Israel as Yahweh's servant in the chapters either side of Isaiah 42 deepened the mystery of whom they referred to. Could Yahweh's servant as portrayed in Isaiah 42:1-4 and Isaiah 52:13—53:12 be the same person as Yahweh's servant in those other passages in the context? It seemed implausible to see Israel as Yahweh's servant in Isaiah 42:1-4, where Yahweh's servant does not cry out in distress (the verb is similar to the one used of Israel crying out under oppression in Egypt) and does not snap off bent reeds or snuff out flickering candles. In the context of the exile, Israel itself is a bent reed and flickering candle and is crying out again as it did in Egypt. In Isaiah 52:13—53:12 Yahweh's servant is suffering as a result of his identification with the wrongdoing of other people and as a result of his ministry to them, and suffering without protest. In the context of the exile, Israel has been suffering as a result of its own wrongdoing, and it is now protesting at Yahweh's long-

term abandonment of it.

In subsequent discussion of the tension in the portrayal of Yahweh's servant in these varying ways, a key role has been played by a theory put forward by Bernhard Duhm in his epoch-making commentary on Isaiah, first published in 1892. One of his key theses was that these two passages, along with Isaiah 49:1-6 and Isaiah 50:4-9 plus Isaiah 50:10-11, were not original parts of Isaiah 40—55 but rather were a separate group of poems inserted later into the text. This then would explain the different understanding of Yahweh's servant expressed in these four passages. In light of Duhm's work, it came to be regular convention to refer to these four poems as the "servant songs," even on the part of people who would not share Duhm's critical views.

Separating the four poems from their context in Isaiah 40—55 solved one problem but created another. The problem that it solved was the need to relate the four poems to that context; at one level, interpreters no longer had to reconcile the portrait of Yahweh's servant in these four passages with the portrait elsewhere in the chapters. The problem that it created was the question of whom the four passages did refer to. This question dominated study of Isaiah 40—55 during the twentieth century.

Acts 8 tells of a man reading Isaiah 53 and wondering about its significance. He asks the evangelist Philip whether the prophet is talking about himself or about someone else. Beginning from this passage, Philip tells him the good news about Jesus. Along with the explicit identification of Israel as Yahweh's servant elsewhere in Isaiah 40—55, this discussion provides a framework for discussing possible answers to the question of who is Yahweh's servant in the four passages.

4.1. The Servant's Identity: The Messiah? First, a usual Jewish and Christian view is that it is the Messiah (so, e.g., Oswalt, 108). Partly if not entirely in reaction to Christian stress on the passages in this connection, this view became less common among Jews, who emphasized weaknesses in the Christian claim that the four passages prophesied Jesus. Whereas Matthew 12:18-21 says that Jesus' healing ministry "fulfilled" Isaiah 42:1-4, it did so only in a loose sense. The NT's only actual quotation from the first-person testimonies in Isaiah 49:1-6 or Isaiah 50:4-11 makes a connection with Paul and Barnabas, not

with Jesus (see Acts 13:47). While some aspects of Jesus' significance correspond to aspects of Isaiah 52:13—53:12, Jews point out, for instance, that this vision does not suggest crucifixion, that Jesus did not stay silent under sufferings, was not allocated a grave with the wicked, did not have offspring, and did not live a long life (see Outreach Judaism). Whereas it became customary for Christians to use passages such as Isaiah 52:13—53:12 apologetically, as a means of proving that Jesus was the Messiah, we have noted that the NT uses such passages theologically and parenetically rather than apologetically. It uses them, that is, not to prove something but rather to help believers understand what it means for Jesus to be their Lord and Savior, and to help them understand the nature of the life of discipleship to which they are called (see esp. 1 Pet 2:22-25). If passages such as Isaiah 52:13—53:12 are not prophesies of the Messiah, this does not make it inappropriate for Christians to see Jesus as the supreme embodiment of the vision of Yahweh's servant, but it does require a different way of articulating that point.

The NT helps us in two other ways to understand the connection between these passages and Jesus. When the Ethiopian asks whether Isaiah 53 is about the prophet or someone else, Acts does not report that Philip simply says, "It is about the Messiah" or "It is about Jesus." Rather, it reports that Philip started from this passage and told the man the good news about Jesus. This is a rather more allusive statement; it suggests a less direct way of understanding the relationship between the passage and Jesus. Indeed, it corresponds to the way I have suggested that the NT uses the passage. It does not treat it as an anticipatory video of the crucifixion. Rather, starting from specific facts about Jesus such as his silence under attack or people's failure to believe in him, it goes back to Isaiah 53 to enable us to see these facts not as mere accidents but as part of a broader picture of the achievement of God's purpose.

The other way the NT helps us is by Matthew's use of the Greek verb plēroō, translated "fulfill," which often appears in the NT in such connections. In Christian parlance, "fulfill" is a quasi-technical term in connection with the idea that God made concrete revelations about the future, which then come about as announced. But the verb plēroō is not by nature a technical term. It is the ordinary Greek word for "fill." In contexts such as this, it suggests something like "fill up" or "fill out" as easily as "fulfill." When Paul speaks of love as the "fulfilling" of the law, he does not mean that if you love, you will obey the law. He that means you will do the kind of thing that the law was aiming at. As there is an indirect relationship between the law and what Christians do when they live by the Spirit, there is an indirect relationship between prophecy and what happens in NT times. The fulfillment fills out the prophecy as it fills out the law; it takes it in new directions, ignores parts of it and reshapes others, and assimilates it to a new agenda.

4.2. The Servant's Identity: Some Other Individual? During the century following the publication of Duhm's commentary, many suggestions were made for the identity of Yahweh's servant in Duhm's "servant songs." C. North surveyed the theories propounded over the first half of this period (although North's book is now over fifty years old, it reports quite enough theories to satisfy most investigators). For a number of these, the starting point could be the identification of this servant in other passages of Scripture, noted above. Moses, for instance, undertook aspects of the role described, and he experienced suffering as a consequence of being Yahweh's servant. The same might have been true of Zerubbabel. E. Sellin suggested that Zerubbabel was enthroned as king in Judah and then executed by the Persians. Isaiah 52:13—53:12 would then link with this. Zerubbabel had a son called "Meshullam" (1 Chron 3:19), a name meaning something like "one in a covenant of well-being." The word *měšullām* comes with that meaning in Isaiah 42:19 as a description of Yahweh's servant, and J. L. Palache suggested that the verse actually refers to this Meshullam (about whom nothing else is known) and identified him as Yahweh's servant.

While no one has suggested that Nebuchadnezzar is Yahweh's servant in Isaiah 40—55, the notion that Yahweh's servant is a non-Israelite king opens up the possibility that it is Cyrus the Persian leader, the equivalent figure to Nebuchadnezzar in the time to which Isaiah 40—55 speaks (so Watts, 643-61; Blenkinsopp, 76-77, at least in connection with Is 42:1-9). He certainly is identified as Yahweh's "anointed" (*měšîaḥ*) in Isaiah 45:1.

4.3. The Servant's Identity: The Prophet? Whereas Isaiah 42:1-4 and Isaiah 52:13—53:12 speak of Yahweh's servant in the third person, Isaiah 49:1-6 and Isaiah 50:4-9 are first-person testimonies in which someone speaks like a prophet. This fits the description of Isaiah ben Amoz and of prophets in general as Yahweh's servants. R. N. Whybray's comment is apposite: "In view of the fact that in the prophetical books generally the subject of speeches in the first person singular, when it is not Yahweh and not otherwise indicated, is normally the prophet himself, it is remarkable that this identification should have been contested in this case by so many commentators" (Whybray, 135).

The implication is that these two passages describe the ministry of the anonymous prophet whose work lies behind Isaiah 40—55. In Isaiah 49:1-6 the prophet speaks of being summoned by Yahweh before birth, as happened to Jeremiah, and of being designated "my servant." Isaiah 49:3 goes on to speak of Yahweh designating the prophet as "Israel, in whom I will display my attractiveness," and then of commissioning a ministry to bring Israel back to Yahweh. The reference to Israel as both the identity of the speaker and as the object of the speaker's ministry is an issue for any view of Yahweh's servant's identity; the designation implies a call to embody what Israel was supposed to be, on an interim basis until Israel itself is brought back to Yahweh. The testimony goes on to describe the prophet's lack of success but then speaks of Yahweh giving a larger task to the prophet: to be the means whereby Yahweh's deliverance comes to be known to the ends of the earth. The further testimony in Isaiah 50:4-9 then describes the prophet's experience of opposition and certainty of vindication. It is only in the supplementary verses of Isaiah 50:10-11 that the speaker in Isaiah 50:4-9 is explicitly identified as Yahweh's servant.

Along with other scholars, Whybray takes the view that Isaiah 42:1-4 and Isaiah 52:13—53:12 also refer to the prophet, though one could pursue his initial logic and suggest that, as it is natural to take the use of first-person speech to indicate that the prophet speaks, so it is natural to take third-person speech to indicate that the passage refers to someone else.

This raises the question of whether all four of Duhm's "servant songs" need denote the same person. Many people are designated Yahweh's servant within the OT as a whole; why should this not be so within Isaiah 40—55?

There is a related question. The problem with the twentieth-century quest for the identity of Yahweh's servant was that it was far too fruitful, as there was no way of arguing for or against many of the theories. This was the problem that Duhm created. Isolating the four "servant songs" from their context in Isaiah 40—55 makes it impossible to identify Yahweh's servant. Thus, T. Mettinger suggests, as in the title of his book, that it is time to say *Farewell to the Servants Songs*. The fact that they are no more or no less songs than other parts of Isaiah 40—55 is one supporting argument. Going back to reading the "songs" in their context more likely opens up the possibility of progress in interpreting them.

4.4. The Servant's Identity: Israel? This takes us back to Israel as Yahweh's servant, the explicit identification in Isaiah 41:8-9 and the usual modern Jewish view regarding all the passages about Yahweh's servant. When Isaiah 42:1-4 follows on from Isaiah 41:8-9 in making further statements about Yahweh's servant, it is natural to assume that the term refers to the same entity. Isaiah 42:1-4 describes Israel's task as being Yahweh's servant. We noted that the relationship between a master and a servant is one of mutual commitment between the two parties. Isaiah 41:8-9 and Isaiah 42:1-4 represent the two directions of this commitment. But in itself, Isaiah 42:1-4 then describes not a person but rather a role. Its exegesis "must not be controlled by the question, 'Who is this servant of God?'" for it neither tells nor intends to tell us that (Westermann, 93). "The question of the identity of the servant is not raised; attention is restricted to what he is to do" (Motyer, 318). Isaiah 41 has told us that Israel is Yahweh's servant, and Isaiah 42:1-4 goes on to describe what that will involve. The problem is that we know that this servant cannot fulfill this role. Our assumption is confirmed in Isaiah 42:18-25, the sole passage where the actual phrase "Yahweh's servant" occurs, and where the servant is described as being deaf and blind. In this sense, we might see Yahweh's servant in Isaiah 42:1-4 as "the ideal Israel." Isaiah 43—48 confirms that Israel itself nevertheless still has this status and ultimately this vocation, but in the meantime it needs to have the servant role fulfilled toward it. It is in this connection and in this sense that the prophet is to embody

what it means to be Israel, to bring Israel itself back to God. Insofar as one can speak of the remnant of Israel as fulfilling the role of Yahweh's servant, it is the prophet who is the remnant of Israel; the broader remnant would be the people who respond to the challenge to identify with Yahweh's servant (Is 50:10-11). The task of bringing Israel back to Yahweh and being a light to the nations is then systematically described in Isaiah 52:13—53:12. In my view, it makes sense to see this as a further description of the prophet's vocation. Its application to Jesus then involves a typological interpretation of it.

In terms of the meaning of Isaiah 40—55, then, there is thus truth both in the view that Israel is Yahweh's servant and in the view that the prophet is Yahweh's servant. Outside of the context of Isaiah 40—55, Christians know that Jesus is the supreme embodiment of the servant vision, and in this sense there is truth in the view that the Messiah is Yahweh's servant. Yet passages such as 1 Peter 2 indicate that the NT also expects the job description or vision of Yahweh's servant to be one that the church fulfills. Isaiah 52:13—53:12 is not fulfilled in the person of Jesus in a way that then means that it has no further implications. The vision of Yahweh's servant is one to be fulfilled again and again. It has been fulfilled by the Jewish people as well as by the church. By its own nature, the vision seeks to draw its readers into fulfilling it (Clines, 63-64).

See also ISAIAH: BOOK OF; ISAIAH: HISTORY OF INTERPRETATION; MESSIAH; PROPHETS IN THE NEW TESTAMENT.

BIBLIOGRAPHY. **W. H. Bellinger and W. R. Farmer,** eds., *Jesus and the Suffering Servant: Isaiah 53 and Christian Origins* (Harrisburg, PA: Trinity Press, 1998); **J. Blenkinsopp,** *Isaiah 40-55: A New Translation with Introduction and Commentary* (AB 19A; New York: Doubleday, 2002); **D. J. A. Clines,** *I, He, We and They: A Literary Approach to Isaiah 53* (JSOTSup 1; Sheffield: JSOT, 1976); **S. R. Driver and A. Neubauer,** The *"Suffering Servant" of Isaiah, according to the Jewish Interpreters* (Eugene, OR: Wipf & Stock, 1999 [1969]); **B. Duhm,** *Das Buch Jesaia* (HKAT 3/1; Göttingen: Vandenhoeck & Ruprecht, 1892); **J. Goldingay,** *The Message of Isaiah 40-55: A Literary-Theological Commentary* (London: T & T Clark, 2005); **B. Janowski and P. Stuhlmacher,** eds., *The Suffering Servant: Isaiah 53 in Jewish* and Christian Sources, trans. D. Bailey (Grand Rapids: Eerdmans, 2004); **T. N. D. Mettinger,** A Farewell to the Servant Songs: A Critical Examination of an Exegetical Axiom (ScrMin; Lund: Gleerup, 1983); **J. A. Motyer,** The Prophecy of Isaiah (Leicester: Inter-Varsity Press, 1993); **C. R. North,** The Suffering Servant in Deutero-Isaiah: An Historical and Critical Study (2nd ed.; London: Oxford University Press, 1956); **J. N. Oswalt,** The Book of Isaiah: Chapters 40-66 (NICOT; Grand Rapids: Eerdmans, 1998); **Outreach Judaism,** "Who Is God's Suffering Servant? The Rabbinic Interpretation of Isaiah 53," http://www.outreachjudaism.org/uploads/pdf%5CRabbinic%20Interpretation%20Isaiah%2053_Suffering%20Servant.pdf; **J. L. Palache,** The 'Ebed-Jahveh Enigma in Pseudo-Isaiah: A New Point of View (Amsterdam: Hertzberger, 1934); **E. Sellin,** Serubbabel: Ein Beitrag zur Geschichte der messianischen Erwartung und der Entstehung des Judentums (Leipzig: Deichert, 1898); **J. D. W. Watts,** Isaiah 34-66 (rev. ed.; Nashville: Thomas Nelson, 2005); **C. Westermann,** Isaiah 40-66: A Commentary, trans. D. Stalker (OTL; Philadelphia: Westminster, 1969); **R. N. Whybray,** Isaiah 40-66 (NCBC; Grand Rapids: Eerdmans, 1981).

— J. Goldingay

SERVANT SONGS. See ISAIAH: BOOK OF; SERVANT OF YAHWEH.

SEVENTY SEVENS. See DANIEL: BOOK OF.

SEVENTY YEARS. See JEREMIAH, BOOK OF.

SEXUAL IMAGERY. See FEMINIST INTERPRETATION; HOSEA, BOOK OF.

SHAME. See HONOR AND SHAME.

SHEPHERD, GOD AS. See GOD.

SIGN ACTS

The biblical prophets had available the full spectrum of verbal and nonverbal elements of communication as they proclaimed their messages. It can be assumed that the prophets used a wide range of nonverbal components, such as body movements, gestures and facial expressions, to emphasize points of their messages. The written records have preserved very few references of such, probably due to the inherent theological and ideological nature of the preserved text, which was concerned almost solely with the content of the messages rather than with how the messages were delivered. Thus, nonverbal elements were reported in the text only when they bore the message content (see Performance Criticism).

1. Definition of "Sign Acts"
2. The Literary Form "Report of a Sign Act"
3. Summary of the Sign Acts and Their Meanings
4. Characteristics of the Sign Acts
5. Type of Encoding
6. Actual Performance
7. Hermeneutical Paradigms for Understanding the Sign Acts

1. Definition of "Sign Acts."
Sign acts are nonverbal actions and objects intentionally employed by the prophets so that message content was communicated through them to the audiences.

Sign acts, therefore, do not refer to noncommunication activities—for example, Isaiah's going to a location to deliver an oracle (Is 7:3) or Jeremiah's writing the message on a scroll (Jer 36:2). Also, sign acts do not encompass actions that the prophets did in *visions—for example, Ezekiel's eating the scroll (Ezek 2:8-3:3). A further differentiation must be made between an intentionally performed sign act and the prophetic interpretation of an action performed by another person, where there was no intent to communicate a specifiable message—for example, Jeremiah's observing the potter (Jer 18:1-11) and Samuel's interpreting Saul's tearing of his robe (1 Sam 15:27-29). Another distinction must be made between sign acts and rhetorical commands that are figures of speech not intended to be carried out. That category includes, for example, the commands to Ezekiel to "set his face" (Ezek 6:2; 13:17) and to do cooking activities (Ezek 24:3-14); those to Jeremiah to take the cup of *wrath to the nations to drink (Jer 25:15-29) and to go through the streets (Jer 5:1); and the ones to Zechariah to be a shepherd (Zech 11:4-17). Some suggest that actions may have accompanied other verbalized messages, such as Ezekiel performing some type of "sword dance" (Ezek 21:8-17). However, when the text never specifies that actions were performed, it is unwise to include those hypothetical possibilities in the discussion of sign acts.

2. The Literary Form "Report of a Sign Act."

Sign acts are recounted through the literary form "report of a sign act." This distinct literary form has two primary components: the divine command to the prophet to perform the specified action, and the interpretation of the sign act.

Frequently, a report will also include other subsidiary elements or motifs, such as an account of the prophet performing the commanded action, a statement indicating the presence of eyewitnesses, a promise or declaration that the event depicted by the action would come to pass, and an explicit statement of the simile relationship between the sign and its referent.

3. Summary of the Sign Acts and Their Meanings.

Reports of sign acts occur in the prophetic books of Isaiah, Jeremiah, Ezekiel, Hosea and Zechariah:

- Isaiah 20:1-4: Isaiah goes naked for three years to represent the people of Cush and Egypt being led away naked as captives by the Assyrians.

- Jeremiah 13:1-11: Jeremiah buys, wears and buries, by the River Perat, a waist sash to illustrate the people's initial closeness to God and their subsequent deterioration.

- Jeremiah 16:1-9: Jeremiah does not marry or attend funerals or feasts, representing the people's future decimation, such that they would be devoid of family members and occasions of ritual mourning and festivity.

- Jeremiah 19:1-13: Jeremiah shatters an earthenware jar, demonstrating that God will shatter Jerusalem.

- Jeremiah 27: Jeremiah wears a yoke to advise Judah to continue its submission to Babylon. In response, Hananiah (cf. Jer 28:10-11) breaks the yoke to symbolize the divine breaking of the Babylonians' rule.

- Jeremiah 32: Jeremiah purchases a parcel of land to signify that, in the future, fields would once again be bought and sold by the Judahites.

- Jeremiah 35: Jeremiah offers wine to the Rechabites, who refuse to drink it out of commitment to their ancestral oath. Their faithfulness is then verbally contrasted with the Judahites' failure to keep their covenant with God.

- Jeremiah 43:8-13: In Tahpanes, Egypt, Jeremiah buries a stone to indicate that the king of Babylon would invade Egypt and construct a throne on that very location.

- Jeremiah 51:59-64: Jeremiah sends with Seraiah a scroll to Babylon, which is thrown into the Euphrates to signify the demise of Babylon.

- Ezekiel 3:24-27; 24:25-27; 33:21-22: Ezekiel remains speechless from the time of his calling as a prophet until he receives the news that Jerusalem has fallen.

- Ezekiel 4—5: Ezekiel performs multiple actions revolving around a brick with "Jerusalem" inscribed on it. He lays siege to the city, sets an iron griddle next to it, and sets his face against the griddle; he lies on his left side for 390 days and then on his right side for forty days to symbolize the bearing of the people's iniquities; he consumes both rationed portions of food and water to represent the scarcity of food during the siege; he bakes his bread on dung to symbolize the unclean food of the *exile; he shaves off his hair, divides it into three portions, and then, to show the threefold fate of the inhabitants of Jerusalem, burns one third upon the model siege, chops up another third with his sword, and scatters the last third to the wind and chases after it with the sword.

- Ezekiel 6:11-12: Ezekiel claps his hands and cries "Ah!" to display God's indignation over the people's wicked practices.

- Ezekiel 12:1-16: Ezekiel prepares a bag, digs a hole in the wall of his house, places the bag upon his shoulder, exits through the hole with his eyes covered, and departs from the city to represent the people of Jerusalem going off into exile.

- Ezekiel 12:17-20: Ezekiel eats and drinks with trembling to show the Jerusalemites' emotional distress during the Babylonian invasion.

- Ezekiel 21:6-7: Ezekiel groans to demonstrate the people's response to the news of God's impending judgment.

- Ezekiel 21:8-17: Ezekiel cries out and strikes his thigh to depict the people's gestures of grief. Later, he claps his hands to show the divine indignation toward the people.

- Ezekiel 21:18-23: Ezekiel sets up a signpost to show the ways the king of Babylon might take in his march against the west.

- Ezekiel 24:15-24: Ezekiel refrains from weeping or performing the normal mourning rituals at his wife's death to illustrate how the people should respond to the news of the fall of Jerusalem.

- Ezekiel 37:15-28: Ezekiel joins two pieces of wood to signify the reunification of Israel and Judah.

- Hosea 1:2-9: Hosea takes a wife of harlotry, symbolizing God's relationship to his people.

- Hosea 3: Hosea buys back his wife to symbolize God's taking back and restoring his wayward people.

- Zechariah 6:9-15: Zechariah makes a crown and places it on the high priest Joshua to show God's crowning of the person who will rebuild the temple.

In addition to these accounts in the Prophetic Books, there are three in the Historical Books (1 Kings 11:29-37; 1 Kings 22:11 // 2 Chron 18:10; 2 Kings 13:14-19) and one in the NT (Acts 21:10-11).

4. Characteristics of the Sign Acts.
There are several general characteristics of prophetic sign acts:

- They often coordinated gestures, movements or actions with objects.

- Only in a few cases were the sign acts nonverbal paralanguage—for example, Ezekiel's interjection, "Ah!" (Ezek 6:11; 21:15) and his groaning and wailing (Ezek 21:6, 12).

- Since nonverbal communication is inherently ambiguous, the sign acts were coupled with verbal proclamations, which either gave the meaning of the actions or complemented them by giving additional information that was not part of the nonverbal depiction.

- In the temporal sequencing, many of the nonverbal actions were performed first, followed by the verbal interpretation, or were concurrent with the accompanying verbal pronouncements.

- The connection between the prophetic action (the sign) and its meaning (the referent) often was that of a simile: "Just as the prophet has done, so it has or will be or should be done" (see Is 20:3; Jer 13:9-11; 19:11-12; 28:11; 51:64; Ezek 4:13; 12:11; 24:22-24; Hos 3:1).

- In the simile comparison, the prophet could take on the role of either the people or God. In the role of the people, the prophet portrayed the people's past, present or future behavior ("So the audience has done, is doing, or will do"). Ezekiel eats rationed portions of food (Ezek 4:9-11) to show the people's eating of limited quantities of food during the siege of Jerusalem. He eats and drinks with severe trembling (Ezek 12:17-20) to show the people's frightened response to the Babylonian invasion. Isaiah depicts how the people of Cush and Egypt would be led away naked into captivity (Is 20).

Besides depicting actual behavioral responses, some of the sign acts exemplified commended responses ("So the audience should do"). Jeremiah wore the yoke to advise the people of the type of response that God was advocating them to take (Jer 27).

When in the role of God, the prophet depicted how God was acting toward the people, who often were signified through the artifact.

Jeremiah shattered the jar, showing that God would destroy Jerusalem (Jer 19:10-11). Jeremiah wore the linen waist sash to signify God's binding the people close to himself. Just as Jeremiah removed it and buried it, so God would remove his people into exile (Jer 13:1-11).

5. Type of Encoding.

With respect to sign-referent relationship, the prophetic sign acts were encoded in two ways:

(1) Representational (or iconic) sign acts had a close resemblance between the sign and the referent, such that the nonverbal act looked like what it signified. For example, Ezekiel's miniature siege of Jerusalem (Ezek 4:1-2) replicated the event. Ezekiel's eating mixed grains and drinking water in rationed portions (Ezek 4:9-11) looked just like the eating habits of the Jerusalemites during the siege. Ezekiel's leaving the city with a bag slung over his shoulder (Ezek 12:6) looked visually like a person going into exile. Isaiah's going naked (Is 20:2-3) looked like the captives being led away naked. Jeremiah's land purchase (Jer 32:9-12) resembled precisely the future legal transactions involved in buying fields. Zechariah's crown and act of crowning (Zech 6:11) looked precisely like a coronation.

(2) Figurative (or symbolic) sign acts were arbitrarily coded in such a way that there was no visual resemblance between the sign and its referent. For example, the people or nation was figuratively symbolized through a waist sash (Jer 13:1-11), an earthenware jug (Jer 19), a scroll (Jer 51:59-64), hair (Ezek 5:1-4), two pieces of wood (Ezek 37:15-28) and a woman taken in marriage (Hos 1; 3). The divine disposition was portrayed through an iron griddle (Ezek 4:3). Bread baked on dung symbolized the uncleanness of the food eaten in exile (Ezek 4:12). Lying on one's side was a figurative depiction of bearing iniquity (Ezek 4:4, 6). The concept of submission was figuratively depicted through wearing a yoke (Jer 27).

In a number of cases the total message was communicated through figurative and representational actions and artifacts being coordinated together. For example, in Ezekiel 4—5 the representational model city (= Jerusalem) (Ezek 4:1-2) was combined with the figurative iron griddle (= divine disposition) (Ezek 4:3), along with the figurative lying on the sides (= bearing iniquity) (Ezek 4:4-6) and the repre-

sentational rationed food (= siege food) (Ezek 4:9-11), and the figuratively depicted unclean food (= exile food) (Ezek 4:12). The figuratively encoded hair (= people) was cut up with the sword, representational of military slaughter, and burned with fire, representational of the conflagration of Jerusalem (Ezek 5:1-4).

6. Actual Performance.

The actual performance of some of the sign acts has been questioned on various grounds. It has been suggested that some would have been incapable of being performed, or that some exceed the boundaries of moral decency or violate prescribed religious practices, or that some are too unaesthetic in nature. For some of the sign acts, it has been suggested that they were too subtle, either in their performance, so that they would not have been noticed, or in their meaning, so that they would not have been understood. It has been argued that the rhetorical impact of telling about an action obviates the necessity of the audience having to see a live performance of it. Based on those objections, the accounts of sign acts are viewed as literary fictions of events that did not actually occur or were accounts of visionary experiences.

Contrary to that perspective, the literary accounts themselves describe the sign acts as things the prophets actually did. First, several of the accounts include statements that the prophets carried out the actions (Is 20:2; Jer 13:2, 5, 7; 32:9-14; 35:3-5; Ezek 12:7; 24:18; 33:22; Hos 1:3; 3:2). Second, some of the narratives refer to the presence of eyewitnesses (Jer 19:1, 10; 32:12; 43:9; Ezek 4:12; 12:3-7; 21:6; 24:27; 33:22; 37:20). Third, verbal audience responses are sometimes recounted, which indicates the presence of audiences who then inquired about what they had just seen (Ezek 12:9; 21:7; 24:19; 37:18). Fourth, some of the sign acts are designated as "signs" (ʾôt, môpēt [Is 20:3; Ezek 4:3; 12:6, 11; 24:24, 27]). The primary characteristic of those Hebrew terms is that of a visually observable phenomenon. Fifth, the imperatives that command the nonverbal sign acts are verbs of "doing." Thus, they are distinct from commands to verbally prophesy, which are verbs of speaking (such as "speak," "call out," "say," "prophesy"). Sixth, the literary form "report of a sign act" and the language used to command the actions are quite different from the reports of visions and the distinctive language associated with the apprehension of visions (such as "look," "see," "behold").

These accumulative arguments suggest that the reader is to view the actions as actually haven taken place, and that they were, under divine directive, intentionally and publicly performed by the prophets.

7. Hermeneutical Paradigms for Understanding the Sign Acts.

The prophetic sign acts have been analyzed from several varied perspectives to explain both the relationship between the sign acts and the real events that they portrayed and the purpose and function of the nonverbal actions as prophetic proclamation.

7.1. Inherently Efficacious. The perspective of inherent efficaciousness views the performances of sign acts as causally setting the depicted events in motion, which would then inevitably occur. An underlying presupposition is that the actions' effectiveness was an inherent quality within the actions themselves, and thus the sign acts are comparable to sympathetic magic or the power of the spoken word (Amsler; Bowker; Fohrer; Fraser; Matheney; Pilch; Robinson). With respect to the connection between prophetic sign acts and sympathetic magic, the sign acts are viewed as originating out of sympathetic magic, but as employed by the Israelite prophets, they had, to varying degrees, overcome or transformed the incompatible magical metaphysical and functional presuppositions and ideology. The ideology transformation was such that the sympathetic magic perception that the power to produce results was inherent in the act itself or in the properly executed technical ritual was altered so that within the prophetic perspective the efficaciousness of the sign acts was derived from and guaranteed by God.

Frequently the sign acts' inherent efficaciousness is viewed as being equivalent to the power of the spoken word, which posits that the word was viewed as a substantive entity, which, once spoken, would assuredly come to pass. It is suggested then that nonverbal communication must have the same type of, or even greater, efficaciousness in bringing about the resultant fulfillment.

Another assumption of this approach is that the sign acts were always predictive and portrayed future events. However, some of them were not future-oriented. Rather, they depicted past or present events. Hosea's marriage (Hos 1:2) depicted the past and current state of the covenant relationship. Similarly, Jeremiah's wearing of the waist sash (Jer 13:1-2) depicted the people's past closeness to God (Jer 13:11), which contrasted radically with the future spoiled condition of the people (Jer 13:7-10). Jeremiah's wearing of the yoke (Jer 27) depicted the people's current subjugation to the Babylonians under which they were to remain.

Besides some of the sign acts not depicting future events, the assumption of an inherent efficaciousness, based either on some type of link with sympathetic magic or the power of the word, has been challenged along several other lines. Anthropological and sociological studies challenge the presupposition that Israelite culture must have had a magical worldview out of which the sign acts would have derived (Lang). The concept that the ancient Israelites believed in the efficacious power of the word has been challenged with the argument that words are to be viewed as performatives (Hutton; Thiselton), whose ability to "do" things is related to the speaker and the occasion of the speech rather than being an inherent metaphysical quality.

7.2. Prophetic Drama. The perspective of prophetic drama views the sign acts as expressing reality rather than causing it (Stacey). The divine will, as a single entity, has many different modes of expression, consisting of not only the event or fulfillment itself but also the verbal oracle that speaks of it and the sign act that nonverbally depicts it. The dramatic expression of the divine will through the sign acts was only a window through which the divine reality was perceived. Within this paradigm, the communicative and persuasive aspects of the sign acts are relegated to a secondary function, even to the point that audiences need not have been present if the sign acts were actually performed. Likewise, whether the action was performed or whether it was merely a literary construct is of no real significance when understanding it as an expression of the divine will.

Whereas this explanation seeks to elucidate the metaphysical relationship between the depicted event (referent) and the depiction (sign), it does little to explain the purpose and functional aspects of the prophetic sign acts as to why they were performed or why they were addressed to particular audiences.

7.3. Acts of Power. A sociological approach to understanding the prophetic sign acts is viewing them as acts of power or prophetic actions (Overholt; McKnight). This perspective seeks to determine how the actions functioned within the context of the social interaction between the prophets and their audiences, specifically with respect to legitimating and authenticating the prophets' authority as intermediaries. The sociological category "acts of power" encompasses all actions that inform of the prophets' status. So, along with sign acts, acts of power include performances of miracles and all actions done in the role of prophet, many of which did not intentionally communicate specifiable message content.

Although that paradigm gives insight as to how the actions functioned within the social context of the prophet and audience interaction, it does not deal with the sign acts' primary communicative and rhetorical functions, with respect either to the meanings of specific messages or to the reason for communicating the particular messages within a particular context. Rather, the sociological paradigm deals with a secondary aspect of the sign acts of how identity as a prophet was attributed.

7.4. Street Theater. Street theater is public performance by individuals that employs dramatic, unexpected and unconventional methods as they seek to attract the audience's attention so that they will listen to and be persuaded of messages to which they would normally be unreceptive. Frequently street theater is associated with political propaganda (Lang). One such example is Nikita Khrushchev's banging his shoe on the table at the United Nations in 1960. The focus of the comparison with the prophetic sign acts is that of their public and persuasive purpose.

Although emphasizing the persuasive aspect of the prophetic sign acts, this paradigm fails to make technical distinctions between various actions with respect to their type, encoding or primary functions. For example, Khrushchev's action was an intrinsically encoded action (i.e., the act and the referent were the same) that displayed his personal anger, whereas the prophetic sign acts were representationally and figuratively encoded actions that were separate and distinct entities

from the events or emotions that they referenced. Khrushchev's action functioned primarily in an interactive sense to gain attention, whereas the prophetic sign acts, although interactive, were primarily communicative as they sought to communicate specifiable messages in simile form.

7.5. Rhetorical Nonverbal Communication. This interdisciplinary approach seeks to explain the sign acts' various types, functions and purposes using definitions from the fields of both nonverbal communication and rhetoric (Friebel). The intentional purpose and function of the prophetic sign acts were to communicate specific messages through the nonverbal elements and to persuade the audiences through a wide range of rhetorical strategies. As rhetorical communication, there are similarities between the sign acts and verbal prophecy. Beyond just prediction, both gave advice of what action to take, warned of the consequences of behaviors, or indicted for sin. For example, Jeremiah's wearing the yoke (Jer 27) functioned in an advisory way as to how Judah should respond to the current Babylonian rule. Jeremiah's offering wine to the Rechabites (Jer 35) produced a demonstration of their covenant faithfulness, which he then used, in a contrastive manner, to indict the Judahites for their ongoing unfaithfulness in their covenant relationship with God. Even if predictive, some of the sign acts can be viewed as warnings that conveyed divine intention and conviction, but not necessarily an inevitable happening (see the sign act in Acts 21:10-11), as with contingent verbalized predictions. Whereas the nonverbal sign acts served communicative and rhetorical functions similar to those of verbalized prophecies, the key distinction was the channels (nonverbal versus verbal) through which the communication took place.

See also Ancient Near Eastern Prophecy; Performance Criticism; Prophecy, History of; Rhetorical Criticism.

Bibliography. S. Amsler, *Les actes des prophètes* (EsBib 9; Geneva: Labor et Fides, 1985); J. W. Bowker, "Prophetic Action and Sacramental Form," in *Studia evangelica*, 3.2: *The New Testament Message*, ed. F. Cross (TU 88; Berlin: Akademie-Verlag, 1964) 129-37; G. Fohrer, "Die Gattung der Berichte über symbolische Handlungen der Propheten," *ZAW* 64 (1952) 101-20; idem, *Die symbolischen Handlungen der Propheten*

(2nd ed.; ATANT 54; Zürich: Zwingli Verlag, 1968); **E. R. Fraser,** "Symbolic Acts of the Prophets," *StBT* 4 (1974) 45-53; **K. G. Friebel,** *Jeremiah's and Ezekiel's Sign-Acts: Rhetorical Nonverbal Communication* (JSOTSup 283; Sheffield: Sheffield Academic Press, 1999); idem, "Hermeneutical Paradigm for Interpreting Prophetic Sign-Acts," *Did* 12 (2001) 25-45; **R. R. Hutton,** "Magic or Street-Theater? The Power of the Prophetic Word," *ZAW* 107 (1995) 247-60; **B. Lang,** "Prophetie, prophetische Zeichenhandlung und Politik in Israel," *TQ* 161 (1981) 275-80; idem, "Street Theater, Raising the Dead, and the Zoroastrian Connection in Ezekiel's Prophecy," in *Ezekiel and His Book: Textual and Literary Criticism and Their Interrelation,* ed. J. Lust (BETL 74; Leuven: Leuven University Press, 1986) 297-316; **M. P. Matheney Jr.,** "Interpretation of Hebrew Prophetic Symbolic Act," *Enc* 29 (1968) 256-67; **S. McKnight,** "Jesus and Prophetic Action," *BBR* 10 (2000) 197-232; **T. W. Overholt,** "Seeing Is Believing: The Social Setting of Prophetic Acts of Power," *JSOT* 23 (1982) 3-31; **J. Pilch,** "Jeremiah and Symbolism: A Social Science Approach," *TBT* 19 (1981) 105-11; **H. W. Robinson,** "Hebrew Sacrifice and Prophetic Symbolism," *JTS* 43 (1942) 129-39; **W. D. Stacey,** *Prophetic Drama in the Old Testament.* (London: Epworth, 1990); **A. Swidler,** "Prophets and Symbolic Acts Today," *TBT* 19 (1981) 182-87; **A. C. Thiselton,** "The Supposed Power of Words in the Biblical Writings," *JTS* 25 (1974) 283-99.   K. G. Friebel

SIN, SINNERS

One key dimension of the role of the prophet was to confront the people of *Israel and the *nations of the world with their sin, and so it is not surprising that the theme of sin dominates the prophetic corpus. This dominance can be demonstrated by the ubiquity and breadth of vocabulary and images related to sin in the Prophetic Books and the development of the theme of sin throughout the individual Prophetic Books. Sin is here defined as a violation in thought, word or deed against another party (divine, human, creation) that breaks a divinely ordered norm (Boda, 11).

    1. Words Related to Sin and Sinners
    2. Images Related to Sin and Sinners
    3. Sin and Sinners
    4. Acts and Motivations Related to Sin
    5. Dealing with Sin and Sinners

1. Words Related to Sin and Sinners.

The prophets regularly employ the roots and their cognates most commonly associated with sin throughout the OT, including: *ʾšm* (Qal: "be guilty," Hos 4:15; Ezek 25:12; *ʾāšām:* "guilt," Jer 51:5; *ʾašĕmâ:* "guilt," Amos 8:14), *ḥṭʾ* (Qal: "do wrong, sin," Is 1:4; Hiphil: "mislead into sin," Jer 32:35; *ḥēṭʾ:* "sin," Is 1:18; *ḥaṭṭāʾ:* "sinful," Is 1:28; *ḥaṭṭāʾâ:* "sin," Is 5:18; *ḥaṭṭāʾt:* "sin," Jer 36:3), *pšʿ* (Qal: "rebel," Hos 8:1; *pešaʿ:* Ezek 18:30, "sin"), *ʿwn* (*ʿāôn:* "sin," Hos 5:5; "guilt," Hos 7:1; *ʿŏnâ:* "sin," Hos 10:10), *ršʿ* (Qal: "be evil," Dan 9:15; Hiphil: "do wrong," Dan 9:5; "declare guilty," Is 50:9; *rāšāʿ:* "guilty," Is 5:23; "guilty, wicked person," Ezek 3:18-19; *rešaʿ:* "wickedness," Is 58:4; *rišʿâ:* "offence," Ezek 18:27) and *rʿʿ* (Qal: "be evil," Is 59:15; Hiphil: "do evil," Zeph 1:12; *raʿ:* "bad, evil," Jer 8:3; *roʿa:* "evil, wickedness," Hos 9:15; *rāʿâ:* "evil, wickedness," Jer 11:15; *mēraʿ:* "evil deed," Dan 11:27; *mērēʿa:* "evildoer," Is 1:4), *ʿāwâ* (Qal: "do wrong," Dan 9:5; Hiphil: "do wrong," Jer 9:4; *ʿāwel:* "wrong," Ezek 3:20), *ʿwl* (Piel: "do evil, act wrongfully," Is 26:10; *ʿawāl:* "evil, unjust one," Zeph 3:5; *ʿawĕlâ:* "wickedness, injustice," Is 59:3; *ʿalĕwâ:* "evil, wickedness," Hos 10:9); and *mʿl* (Qal: "violate one's legal obligations," Ezek 20:27; *maʿal:* "disloyalty, infidelity," Ezek 14:13).

It is commonplace in OT scholarship to provide a specific nuance for many of these words, for example, defining the root *ḥṭʾ* as "missing the mark" (in light of the use of this root in Judg 20:16) or the root *ʿwn* as "to be crooked" or *pšʿ* as "to rebel" (2 Kings 3:5) or "to breach a relationship" (cf. Martens). However, the ubiquity of these terms in a variety of contexts that do not evidence these meanings suggests otherwise (see Knierim 229-35). Too close attention to this dominant vocabulary also deflects attention from the breadth of vocabulary and imagery used to designate sin in the Prophetic Books, including: *ʾāwen* ("sin, injustice," Hos 6:8); *bzh* (Qal: "despise," Mal 1:6); *bĕlîyaʿal* ("wickedness, evil person," Nah 1:11); *znḥ* (Qal: "reject," Hos 8:3, 5); *znh* (Qal: "commit fornication," Jer 3:6; *zĕnûnîm:* "fornication," Ezek 23:11; *zĕnût:* "fornication," Jer 3:2; *tazĕnût:* "fornication," Ezek 23:7); *ḥnp* (Qal: "be desecrated," Is 24:5; Hiphil: "defile," Jer 3:2; *ḥānēp,* "godless, ungodly," Is 10:6; *ḥānēp:* "ungodly person," Is 9:17 [MT 16]; *ḥōnep:* "wickedness," Is 32:6; *ḥănupâ:* "wickedness," Jer 23:15); *yāʾal* (Niphal:

"turn out to be a fool," Jer 5:4); *kātam* (Niphal: "be defiled/morally unclean," Jer 2:22); *m'n* (Piel: "refuse," Zech 7:11; *mā'ēn*: "refusing," Jer 38:21; *mē'ēn*: "disobeying," Jer 13:10); *m's* (Qal: "reject," Hos 4:6); *mrd* (Qal: "rebel," Ezek 2:3); *mrh* (Qal: "be rebellious," Jer 5:23; Hiphil: "behave rebelliously," Ezek 5:6; *mĕrî*: "rebellious," Ezek 2:5); *n'p* (Qal: "commit adultery," Jer 3:9; Piel: "commit adultery," Ezek 23:37; *ni'up*: "adultery," Jer 13:27; *na'ăpûp*: "adultery," Hos 2:4); *n's* (Qal: "spurn," Jer 33:24; Piel: "spurn," Is 1:4; *ne'āṣâ*: "blasphemy," Ezek 35:12); *nû'a* (Qal: "wander," Jer 14:10); *'br* (Qal: "overstep, contravene," Dan 9:11); *'zb* (Qal: "abandon," Jer 1:16); *'ml* (*'āmāl*: "harm," Hab 1:13); *swg* (Niphal: "prove faithless," Jer 38:22); *swr* (Qal: "turn aside," Jer 5:23; *sārâ*: "apostasy," Is 1:5); *srr* (Qal: "be stubborn," Is 1:23; *sar*: "stubborn ones, revolters," Jer 6:28); *sût* (Hiphil: "mislead, incite," Jer 38:22); *šwb* (Qal: "apostatize," Jer 3:19; *šôbāb*: "backsliding," Is 57:17; *šôbēb*: "backsliding," Mic 2:4; *mĕšûbâ*: "backsliding," Jer 2:19). This breadth of vocabulary reveals the multifaceted nature of the description of the sin of the prophets' audiences.

2. Images Related to Sin and Sinners.

Not only is the vocabulary of the prophets dominated by the theme of sin, but so also is its imagery (see especially Goldingay 2:254-349). Many of these images are drawn from the world of nature, both animate and inanimate. *Animal imagery related to sin and sinners is connected with the snake (hatching eggs, Is 59:5), spider (weaving webs, Is 59:5), camel (running aimlessly, Jer 2:23), donkey (in heat, Jer 2:24), lion (ravenous, Jer 2:30; Ezek 22:25), horse (charging into battle, Jer 8:6; neighing, 50:11), cow (untrained calf, Jer 31:18; threshing, Jer 50:11; of Bashan, Amos 4:1; stubborn, Hos 4:16), wolf (tearing prey, Ezek 22:27), sheep (gone astray, Is 53:6), goat (goring, Dan 8:4), partridge (hatching eggs not its own, Jer 17:11), ostrich (cruel, Lam 4:3) and dove (silly, without sense, Hos 7:11). These images are dominated by depictions of the violent and uncontrollable behavior of animals, whether domesticated or not. Connections to fertility and web-weaving suggest the spread of evil.

Botanical features (*see* Floral Imagery) like the flower (fading, Is 28:1; 40:6-8), grass (withering, Is 40:6-8), chaff (blown away from the threshing floor, Hos 13:3), leaf (wither, Is 64:6), oak (whose leaf fades away, Is 1:30), garden (without water, Is 1:30), grape (rotten, Is 5:2, 4), plant and vine (foreign species, Is 17:10; Jer 2:21), straw (trodden down in manure, Is 25:10), fig (rotten, Jer 24:8) and thorn (tangled, Nah 1:10) are used at other times to designate sin and sinners. These features often point to the ephemeral nature of sinful humanity, but also to the inappropriate fit of the sinful before Yahweh.

Various inanimate basic elements in nature, such as fire (burning forests, Is 9:18), water (rumbling, Is 17:12-13), cloud/mist/dew (wiped out, Is 44:22; Hos 13:3), wind (blows away, Is 64:6), smoke (blown away from a chimney, Hos 13:3), dung (on the ground, Jer 25:33) and ashes (trampled underfoot, Mal 4:3), are also employed as images for sin and sinners. These images emphasize the power of sin (fire, water), but also its ephemeral (cloud/mist/dew, wind, smoke) and worthless (dung, ashes) nature.

In other cases agricultural features such as a scarecrow (idols as mute, Jer 10:5), fallow ground (in need of breaking up to sow righteousness, Hos 10:12), a vineyard (producing worthless grapes signifying evil, Is 5:1-7) and a shepherd (feeding himself as a self act, Ezek 34:2) are employed to describe sin and sinners.

Sin and sinners are related in the Prophets to various human manufactured items, such as a cistern (broken, Jer 2:16), a cord/rope (to drag iniquity, Is 5:18), liquor (diluted, Is 1:22), attire (unclean skirt, Lam 1:9; unclean garments, Zech 3:3-4), an earthen jar (valueless in contrast to fine gold, Lam 4:2), a rod (Ezek 7:11), an oven (smoldering, Hos 7:6), metal (silver becomes dross, Is 1:22; bronze, tin, iron, Ezek 22:18-19), cake (not turned, Hos 7:8), bow (deceitful, Hos 7:16), and traps and nets (Hos 5:1; snare of a bird catcher, 9:8). Each of these images has its own nuance.

Various types of humans are used to designate sin and especially sinners, including a son (rebellious, Is 1:2; 30:1; 57:4; Ezek 2:4), a daughter (arrogant and seductive, Is 3:16; trusting in her treasures, Jer 49:4), a woman (pregnant, Is 26:18; figurine, Zech 5:7-8), a wife (adulterous, Ezek 16:32), a harlot (Is 1:21; 23:16-18; Jer 2:16; Ezek 6:9; 23:3-21; 43:9; Hos 2:2-7; 4:10-15; 5:4; 6:10; 9:1; Nah 3:4), a drunkard (the earth staggering under transgression, Is 24:20), a swimmer (spreading hands, Is 25:11). Finally, human social groupings, especially the household (Ezek 2:5, 6, 8; 24:3) and the city (Sodom, Lam 4:6; the tyrannical city, Zeph 3:1; the bloody city, Nah 3:1), are also employed to designate sinners.

This lexical and imagistic data alone highlights sin as a major motif within prophetic literature, a dominant interest for this tradition commissioned by Yahweh to call the people to fidelity in relationship with both God and humanity. The many passages in which these words and images appear provide the best insight into the prophetic viewpoint on sin and sinners.

3. Sin and Sinners.

3.1. Isaiah. Isaiah focuses considerable attention on sin and sinners, offering insights into God's revelation to the nation over more than two centuries. Noting how the book begins and ends by focusing on the rebellion of the people (*pš^c*; Is 1:2; 66:24), Oswalt (38) concludes: "Above all else, sin is rebellion for Isaiah" (cf. Is 24:20; 27:4; 10x in Is 40—55; 6x in Is 56—59), and "this rebellion is an expression of human pride" (cf. Is 2:17; 9:9; 13:11; see also Nysse, who notes Is 48:8 as well). The problem of sin in the book of Isaiah is largely understood through the lens of trust, that is, the people's shortcomings are described in terms of their lack of trust in Yahweh. Thus throughout Isaiah 28—33 the leaders and people fall into the trap of trusting in human religious (Is 28:15-19), economic (Is 30:12-14) and political (Is 30:1; 31:1-3) resources. This theme of trust continues into Isaiah 40—55. Isaiah 40:12-31 reveals that the people are struggling to trust in Yahweh before the might of the nations and the allure of their *idols. Thus the people are tempted to trust in idols (Is 42:17). The final section of the book, Isaiah 56—66, reveals the enduring struggle of the community with sin (esp. Is 56:9—59:15; 63:7—66:17). Here the emphasis is on *justice and righteousness (56:1; 59:14), with the contrast between unjust behavior and fasting rituals in Isaiah 58 highlighting the dysfunction of the community.

3.2. Jeremiah. Jeremiah played a key role in the closing moments of the kingdom of Judah, delivering a message of judgment that would seal its fate. The book that bears his name consistently highlights the sin of the people (see Thompson, 110-12; Eldridge 322-25), focusing particularly on the people's propensity to *worship false gods, which compromised their rela-

tionship with Yahweh (e.g., Jer 2:7), and to engage in personal and social sins, which destroyed their relationships with one another (e.g., Jer 7:5, 8). Such acts were "not just casual or habitual breaches but a basic attitude (2:22; 5:3, 5; 36:7), even though not natural since nations don't forsake their gods (2:10, 11), leopards their spots or Ethiopians their skin (13:23)" (Thompson 110-12; on this unnaturalness see Eldridge, 322). Sin is described in terms of negative behaviors, including idolatry, injustice, adultery and murder, but also in terms of the affections of the heart, as the people are accused of acting in the stubbornness of their evil hearts (Jer 7:24; 11:8; 13:10; 16:12; 18:12).

3.3. Lamentations. There is admission of sin in the book of Lamentations (Lam 1:5, 8-9, 14, 18, 20, 22; 2:14; 3:39-42; 4:6, 13, 22; 5:7, 16), but few details are provided as to the specific sins that were committed, besides the more general references to rebelling against Yahweh (Lam 1:20; 3:42) and his command (Lam 1:18), allusions to inappropriate lovers, possibly other nations or their gods (Lam 1:19), and comparative evil (greater than Sodom in Lam 4:6). Sin is connected with the prophets and priests (Lam 4:13), as well as with former generations (Lam 5:7).

3.4. Ezekiel. The sins identified in Ezekiel echo those attacked by earlier prophets, that is, both social sins (Ezek 34) and the sins of idolatry and apostasy (Ezek 8; see McKeating 85-91; Goldingay 2:256; Fishbane [134] speaks of "the people's civil and cultic sins"). What distinguishes Ezekiel, however, is thus not as much in sins identified, although at times he focuses on priestly offenses like Sabbath breaking and purity violations, but rather "in consistently designating the sins of the people as profanation and impurity" (Wong 120; von Rad II:224), especially using terms like abomination (*tô^cēbâ*; e.g., Ezek 6:9; 11:21; 18:24; 43:8), profaning (*ḥālal*; e.g., Ezek 20:16), impurity (*ṭm^ʾ* Piel; e.g., Ezek 5:11; 36:17; 43:7-8), unfaithfulness (*ma^cal*; e.g., Ezek 14:13; 18:24; 39:23); (McKeating 87; Wong 133; Goldingay 2:256). Commissioning narratives such as Ezekiel 1—3 focus on the rebellion (*měrî*) of the people (e.g., Ezek 2:5), while other key passages leverage imagery drawn from the violation of the marital covenant (Ezek 16, 17, 20) or vassal treaty (Ezek 12, 17; Wong 246-54) to describe the sin of the people.

3.5. Daniel. Sin within the first major section of Daniel (Dan 1—6) is associated with non-Judahites, that is, the emperors and their officials. Emphasis is placed on the sin of the emperors throughout these chapters, especially focusing on the pride of Nebuchadnezzar and Belshazzar, who fail to acknowledge Yahweh's sovereignty (Dan 4—5). The second major section of Daniel (Dan 7—12) continues this emphasis on the sin of the kingdoms of the earth, the source of great oppression against the faithful community. The fact that these kingdoms arise from the "sea" (Dan 7:3) suggests that they are of evil origin. Their oppression involves violation of orthodox worship as they eliminate daily sacrifice, destroy the holy city and sanctuary, and institute illicit worship (Dan 8:11-12; 9:26-27). Sin is evident in this section among the members of the Jewish community, hypocrites who forsake and violate the covenant (Dan 11:30-34). Embedded within this section is the important prayer of Daniel (Dan 9), which confesses the sins of the nation, seeking to bring an end to exile according to the agenda of Deuteronomy 28, Leviticus 26:39-40 and 1 Kings 8. Daniel is honest about the sin of his nation, employing the full breadth of vocabulary available to him (e.g., Dan 9:5, 15, 16) and identifying the various groups whose behavior violated Yahweh's instructions (Dan 9:5-8).

3.6. Book of the Twelve. Within the Book of the Twelve Hosea's presentation of sin is notably dominated by the metaphor of the unfaithfulness of Israel as the wife of Yahweh.

> Such a metaphor is appropriate in part because of the similarity of the marriage relationship to the covenant relationship. Harlotry as going after lovers outside of and in violation of the relationship of undivided loyalty between husband and wife vividly uncovers the nature of Israel's sin. (Miller, 7)

This marital unfaithfulness points in particular to the community's involvement in illicit cult activity (Hos 4:4-19; 6:1-6; 8:4-6, 11-13; 9:1; 10:1-8; 13:1-3) which has resulted "in the dissolution of her personal relationship with her God, who has given himself to her in personal acts of love throughout the course of her history" (Wolff 1974, xxvii). The list of sins in Hosea 4:1-3 reveals that the prophet is also concerned with violations against fellow Israelites,

focusing on both sins of omission ("there is no truth or faithfulness or knowledge of God in the land") as well as those of commission ("swearing, deception, murder, stealing and adultery"; see Miller, 10). Offenses that compromise Israel's relationship with Yahweh and their fellow Israelites are both related to the key theme in Hosea of "the knowledge of God," whether that means knowing Yahweh as the one who has provided for them in the past (Hos 2:8; 11:3) or knowing Yahweh's requirements for relationships with one another (Hos 4:1; Davies, 22-24).

Many have noted the lack of mention of any sin in the book of Joel, although the necessity of the call to a day of repentance suggests some violation, as does the use of a term like drunkard in Joel 1:5 (see Boda, 305n35).

Amos emphasizes Israel's abuse of one another, displayed especially in their manipulation of the courts and accumulation of *wealth (Wolff 1977, 104; Miller, 21). As Hubbard (111) has noted,

> their crimes would fill an out-sized police-blotter: enslaving their countrymen for petty debts (2:6; 8:6), perverting justice for the disadvantaged (2:7-8; 5:10, 12, 15), practicing incest (2:7?), exacting harsh taxes (2:8; 3:10; 5:11), throttling the prophets who would condemn such deeds (2:12; 3:8; 7:12-13), maintaining an extravagant life-style at the expense of the poor (4:1; 6:1-6).

Amos focuses at points on dysfunctions in their worship practices, especially noting the lack of attention to justice and righteousness in their festal gatherings (e.g., Amos 5:24; see Bailey, 81-82).

Obadiah focuses attention on the sin of a foreign nation (Edom) and their "exploitation" of Judah in its destruction in the early sixth century BC (Allen 138). Their sin lies in "standing aloof" (Obad 11), "gloating" and "boasting" over Judah's calamity (Obad 12, 13), finally entering the city and looting its wealth (Obad 13) and even slaughtering and imprisoning its survivors (Obad 14). This sin is simply described as "violence" (ḥāmās) in Obadiah 10.

While the mission given to Jonah highlights the sin of a foreign city (Nineveh), few details are provided as to the nature of the sin, and the emphasis is clearly placed on the rebellion of the prophet himself (Jon 1) and, in the end, his lack of alignment with the deep values of Yahweh for humanity (Jon 4).

While Micah begins with an accusation against the religious sins of the two kingdoms of Israel and Judah (Mic 1:5), the emphasis in the book is on the "fierce condemnation of injustices arising from the economic and social policies of the privileged classes in Israel," thus showing that "religion and ethics [are] inseparable" (Ex 20:1-17; Jenson, 100). Throughout the book the theology of land is key, as inheritances are seized from the vulnerable within society (e.g., Mic 2:2) by the elite classes (including leaders, priests, prophets and judges, see Mic 2:1-5; 3:5, 11).

With Nahum the focus returns to that found in Obadiah, that is, on a foreign nation, this time the Assyrians. This nation is called Yahweh's enemy (Nahum 1:8) who plotted evil (Nahum 1:11), "a wicked counselor" (Nahum 1:11) and "a wicked one" (Nahum 1:15). Its capital city Nineveh is tagged as "the bloody city, completely full of lies and pillage" (Nahum 3:1).

The fundamental problem in the book of Habakkuk revolves around the issue of sin as the prophet expresses frustration over the behavior of humanity in his generation. The prophet laments over the violence, iniquity, wickedness, destruction, strife and contention (Hab 1:2-3) he observes among the wicked who "surround" the righteous by abusing the administration of justice (Hab 1:4). While the answer to this predicament is linked to Yahweh raising up the Babylonians (Hab 1:5-11), the Babylonians themselves are not above such wicked patterns (Hab 1:12-17), which prompts further frustration for the prophet as he dialogues with Yahweh.

Zephaniah "combines criticism of cultic apostasy with indignation against the social injustice by which the rich and powerful exploit the poor" (Mason, 55) by identifying the involvement of Judah and Jerusalem in illicit cult and revelatory practices (Zeph 1:4-6, 9) as well as unjust acts (Zeph 1:9, 13, 18). Attention is also placed on the nations, first for their arrogant treatment of the people of God (Zeph 2:8, 10), as well as their arrogant self-reliance (Zeph 2:15). Jerusalem receives considerable treatment, identified as rebellious, defiled, tyrannical, whose leaders have done violence to the law by not practicing justice (Zeph 3:1-5). The arrogance associated with the nations in Zephaniah 2 is also evident among those who live in Jerusalem (Zeph 3:11).

In Haggai sin is defined largely by misplaced priorities related to the reconstruction of the temple in Jerusalem.

Zechariah, however, expands the focus considerably from the outset (Zech 1:1-6), broadening the agenda to include injustices perpetrated by earlier imperial powers (Zech 1:18-21; 2:6-9), uncleanness related to the disciplinary destruction of Jerusalem (Zech 3), and especially unjust behavior (Zech 5:1-4; 7:4-14; 8:16-17) and idolatrous practice (Zech 5:5-11) within the restoration community. Problems with idolatry and attendant false prophecy can also be discerned in the latter sections of Zechariah (Zech 10:1-2; 13:1-6).

Malachi closes the Book of the Twelve by focusing on the sins of both priest and people in the restoration community in Jerusalem. Malachi's attack echoes the earlier concerns of the prophets, focusing on violations in worship as well as ethics. The priests are upbraided for defiling the altar by permitting the use of unacceptable *sacrifices (Mal 1:6-14) and then for showing partiality by favoring the powerful in their legal rulings at the temple (Mal 2:1-9). The people, complicit in both of these previous offenses, are also attacked for divorcing their wives in favor of women from the imperial elite (Mal 2:10-16).

4. Acts and Motivations Related to Sin.
These many prophetic traditions share much in common, not only vocabulary and imagery but also descriptions of the sin of the community throughout over three centuries of prophetic activity. C. Dempsey has traced some of the key common trends. Sinful acts identified by the prophets include:

Excessive land appropriation (Is 5:8), the perversion of justice (Is 5:20), self-centeredness (Is 58:3a), oppression of laborers (Is 58:3b), infidelity and disloyalty (Hos 4:1), swearing, lying, murder, stealing, adultery (Hos 4:2), false prophecy (Mic 3:3-5), political and religious depravity and arrogance (Mic 3:9-11), social injustices of every sort (Amos 8:4-6), idolatry (Mic 1:7; Ezek 6:4, etc.), apostasy (Jer 2:19), among other transgressions. A people guilty of having broken covenant relationship, they have refused to turn back to God (Jer 5:1;

Is 9:13) despite the prophets' preaching and pleas. (Dempsey, 49)

Such acts, however, are regularly traced by the prophets to the inner motivations of the people:

Namely, a false, devious, perverse, stubborn, rebellious, and proud heart (see, e.g., Hos 10:2; 13:6; Jer 5:23; 17:9; 49:16; Ezek 28:7; Obad 1:3). Into its heart Israel has taken its idols (Ezek 14:4). Thus, the people's hearts have not remained one with the heart of their God; they have fallen out of covenant relationship with their God and consequently, right relationship with all other people as well. (Dempsey, 49)

The enduring prophetic witness to the sinful actions and motivations of humanity, however, is not included in the canon as merely a record of past failures, but is accompanied by a record of prophetic revelation designed to transform the community and deal with its sin.

5. Dealing with Sin and Sinners.

The opening chapter of Isaiah reveals the propensity of the community to deal with their sin through attention to cultic activity (cf. Hos 8:11-13) (see Liturgy and Cult). This key chapter lays out the two fundamental agendas within the prophets for dealing with sin (see Boda, 191-93, 220). Isaiah 1:2-20 showcases the prophet confronting the people with their sin (Is 1:2-15) and calling them to *repent from their evil behavior (Is 1:16-17) so that they may avoid divine punishment and enjoy God's blessing (Is 1:18-20). In contrast, Isaiah 1:21-31 reveals Yahweh's plan to purify the people by turning his hand against them (Is 1:25). The outcome in both cases is a purified people who walk in obedience to Yahweh, but the process by which this is accomplished is radically different. These two agendas can be discerned throughout the Prophetic Books, evidence of God's passionate pursuit of a holy community. However, the Prophetic Books also highlight the ultimate failure of these two agendas, as the penitential cries of the prophets largely fall on deaf (or deafened) ears (Boda, 354-55), and even a community purified through discipline falls back into sin (Is 40—66; Zech 7—14; Mal).

Nevertheless, there is another agenda for dealing with sin in the Prophets, especially evi-

dent in the books of Jeremiah and Ezekiel. In these two books, tracing the prophetic word spoken into the community that experienced the annihilation of the kingdom of Judah, one can discern a similar development near the end of the two books (possibly also Is 59:20-21 in Isaiah and Zech 12:10-14 in the Book of the Twelve; Boda, 356). Whereas the agendas of repentance and purification are clearly developed in both books, both provide a vision of renewal that shifts from human response to a divine gracious and transformative initiative. This vision of renewal looks to a unilateral gracious initiative of Yahweh to forgive his people and grant them an inner renewal that would enable them to avoid sin and walk faithfully before God and humanity (Jer 24:6-7; 31:33-34; 32:37-44; Ezek 11:19; 36:26-27; 37:14; 39:26).

See also EVIL; FORGIVENESS; IDOLS, IDOLATRY, GODS; REPENTANCE; SACRIFICE AND ATONEMENT; SOCIAL JUSTICE; SUFFERING.

BIBLIOGRAPHY. **L. C. Allen,** *The Books of Joel, Obadiah, Jonah, and Micah* (NICOT; Grand Rapids: Eerdmans, 1976); **D. W. Bailey,** "Theological Themes in the Prophecy of Amos," *TE* 52 Fall (1995) 79-85; **M. J. Boda,** *A Severe Mercy: Sin and Its Remedy in the Old Testament* (Siphrut 1; Winona Lake, IN: Eisenbrauns, 2009); **G. I. Davies,** *Hosea* (OTG; Sheffield: Sheffield Academic, 1993); **C. J. Dempsey,** "'Turn Back, O People:' Repentance in the Latter Prophets," in *Repentance in Christian Theology,* ed. M. J. Boda and G. T. Smith (Collegeville, MN: Liturgical Press, 2006) 47-66; **V. J. Eldridge,** "Jeremiah, Prophet of Judgment," *RevExp* 78 (1981) 319-30; **M. Fishbane,** "Sin and Judgment in the Prophecies of Ezekiel," *Int* 38 (1984) 131-50; **J. Goldingay,** *Old Testament Theology, Vol. 2: Israel's Faith* (Downers Grove, IL: IVP Academic, 2006); **D. A. Hubbard,** *Joel and Amos: An Introduction and Commentary* (TOTC; Leicester, England/Downers Grove, IL: InterVarsity Press, 1989); **P. P. Jenson,** *Obadiah, Jonah, Micah: A Theological Commentary* (LHBOTS; New York: T & T Clark, 2008); **R. Knierim,** *Die Hauptbegriffe für Sünde im Alten Testament* (Gütersloh: Gerd Mohn, 1965); **E. A. Martens,** "Sin, Guilt," in *DOTP,* ed. T. D. Alexander and D. W. Baker (Downers Grove, IL: IVP Academic, 2003) 764-78; **H. McKeating,** *Ezekiel* (OTG; Sheffield: Sheffield Academic: JSOT, 1993); **P. D. Miller,** *Sin and Judgment in the Prophets: A Stylistic and Theological Analysis* (SBLMS 27; Chico, CA.:

Scholars Press, 1982); **J. Oswalt**, *The Book of Isaiah, Chapters 1-39* (NICOT; Grand Rapids: Eerdmans, 1986); **R. Nysse**, "Rebels from Beginning to End," *WW* 19 (1999) 161-70; **J. A. Thompson**, *The Book of Jeremiah* (NICOT; Grand Rapids: Eerdmans, 1980); **G. von Rad**, *Old Testament Theology* (Edinburgh: Oliver and Boyd, 1962); **H. W. Wolff**, *Hosea* (Hermeneia; Philadelphia: Fortress, 1974); idem, *Joel and Amos: A Commentary on the Books of the Prophets Joel and Amos* (Hermeneia; Philadelphia: Fortress, 1977); **K. L. Wong**, *The Idea of Retribution in the Book of Ezekiel* (VTSup; Leiden: Brill, 2001).   M. J. Boda

SOCIAL INSTITUTIONS. *See* PROPHECY AND SOCIETY.

SOCIAL JUSTICE

A significant first step in understanding the Israelite prophets' approach to social justice lies in appreciating the cultural distance that separates the world of ancient Israel from contemporary Western society. Much more so than is the case in many parts of the world today, Israel was a socially and economically stratified society, patriarchal, with fixed gender roles. It would be wrong, therefore, to impose on it a concept of social justice that has emerged in Western industrialized liberal democracies only in the past century. It is also helpful to distinguish between justice in general and social justice in particular. The need for *justice is a basic requirement of civil societies, ancient or modern. The *covenant stipulations of Exodus through Deuteronomy that preserve what remains of ancient Israelite jurisprudence presuppose a basic system of morality and justice that was essential to the functioning of Israelite society. Within this framework, those in authority were expected to judge fairly. For the purposes of this article, "social justice" refers principally to the issues of justice as they relate to the most vulnerable members of Israelite society.

Although social justice might primarily be concerned with oppression and denial of justice at the level of human relationships, the failure to act justly in this way could have ramifications that extended far beyond the level of society itself. In Israel and the ancient Near East injustice was thought to have potential consequences for *creation as a whole. At Ugarit, for example, the Aqhat myth describes how the murder of the man Aqhat by proxies of

the goddess Anat results in drought and the ruin of crops (*COS* 1.103:351-52). Similarly, in Genesis the *sin of Adam and Eve results in an earth that easily yields thorns and thistles but produces food only with great human toil (Gen 3:18-19). Later, after Cain kills his brother, Abel, the blood of the murdered brother cries out to God from the ground. Thereafter, the earth refuses to respond to Cain, forcing him to become a wanderer (Gen 4:10-12; cf. Hos 4:2-3). For the nation of Israel as a whole, a refusal to follow God's laws could so defile the *land that it might "vomit" Israel out as it had its previous inhabitants (Lev 18:24-28). All of this suggests that the created order itself could be affected by human misdeeds and acts of injustice (Rom 8:22) (see Taylor, 21-22).

As a consequence of the above, part of following God's covenant law and acting justly meant attending to the needs of the land and creation as a whole. When the Israelites were besieging an enemy city, they were forbidden from felling the city's fruit trees, since to do so would be to harm a noncombatant even as it would deprive the army of a source of food (Deut 20:19-20). Just as humans were to enjoy the rest of the Sabbath, so too the land was to enjoy its Sabbatical year (Lev 25:2-7). According to the writer of Chronicles, a failure to observe the needs of the land resulted in the total number of years of the *exile (2 Chron 36:21; cf. Lev 26:34-35). Within the postexilic community of Yehud, the Sabbath for the land was given renewed attention (Neh 10:31).

Israel had specific moral obligations as part of its covenant with Yahweh, but this did not mean that the nations were without a responsibility to practice justice. This idea is clearly expressed in the primeval narrative of Genesis 1—11. There, it is human beings as a race who are created to be in relationship with God and who suffer alienation from him when they rebel (Gen 1:27-31; 2:7-8, 16-25; 3:8-24). The image of God, which all humans share, places a specific moral obligation on all humans in the form of the universal prohibition against murder (Gen 1:27; 9:6). Here too, human wickedness has ruinous consequences for creation (Gen 6:11) and prompts God to judge the peoples of the earth by flood and start anew through Noah and his family (Gen 6:1—9:19). The responsibility of the nations to practice justice is also conveyed in the patriarchal narratives of Genesis 12—50. In the case of Sodom and Gomorrah, for example, God descends from heaven in response to reports of human misdeeds and responds in judgment against people who are not in covenant relationship with him (Gen 18:20-21). This same idea appears in prophetic literature. The prophetic mandates given to Jonah (Jon 1:2) and Jeremiah (Jer 1:5, 10; 25:15-31) to announce divine judgment over foreign nations represent cases in which the God of Israel imposes a standard of justice over nations other than Israel. The responsibility of the nations to practice justice is also forcefully articulated in the oracles against the nations found in the books of Amos (Amos 1:3—2:3) and Jeremiah (Jer 46—49). Here Yahweh condemns the nations for acts of violence and oppression even in cases where his covenant people are not counted among the victims (e.g., Amos 1:9-10).

Even as the nations are accountable before God, however, so too are they given the opportunity to experience redemption that results in an experience of God's justice. Through the promise first made to Abram, Israel plays a mediating role in this enterprise with the goal being that "all peoples on earth will be blessed through you [Abram and his descendants]" (Gen 12:2-3). The mediatory character of Israel's role in relation to the world is made plain in its identity as "a kingdom of priests and a holy nation" (Ex 19:6) (see 2 below). Israel's election to such a role constitutes a national mandate that is repeated at several points in the book of Isaiah. Of Israel, Yahweh declares, "Here is my servant, whom I uphold, my chosen one in whom I delight; I will put my Spirit on him and he will bring justice to the nations" (Is 42:1 [cf. Mt 12:18]). The law given to and practiced by Israel will produce justice and will eventually lead the nations toward God: "The law will go out from me; my justice will become a light to the nations" (Is 51:4). In the postexilic era the prophets envision a future date in which all nations will respond to God's invitation and will stream to Jerusalem to learn his ways (e.g., Mic 4:2; Zech 8:20-23).

The need to experience justice in the present was a vital concern in ancient Israel. The limited understanding of life after death that prevailed in Israel during the preexilic period presumably made the issue of justice in the present a matter of pressing concern (Eccles 3:20; 8:14; 9:2-5) (see Wellhausen, 469; Rauschenbusch, 17-18). It is clear from the OT

and cognate literature that Israel and its Canaanite neighbors believed that life continued beyond the grave, but this future life was regarded as a dismal, shadowy subsistence that was a pale reflection of life on earth. Those who had died were separated from the land of the living and from God's care (Ps 6:5; 88:5; Is 53:8) and occupied a realm in which the righteous and the wicked lived together as they had on earth (Gen 37:35; Job 21:13; 24:19; Ps 89:48; Eccles 3:20; 9:2; Is 14:9-11) (see Johnston, 69-85). In the OT era this place was one of continued, but diminished, existence where the prospect of judgment and reward was far from certain. The uncertainty surrounding what happened beyond the grave greatly increased the concern that justice be done in this life and accounts for the urgency typical of the individual complaint psalms (e.g., Pss 10; 13; 22) and the frustration of both Job and the teacher in the book of Ecclesiastes (Job 21:5-13; Eccles 4:1-3; 7:15; 8:14; 9:1-10; cf. COS 1.151-54:485-95). The unknowable character of life after death also explains the importance placed on the king as the one responsible for maintaining justice in the present and the angry prophetic action when this responsibility was not adequately realized.

1. Terms Related to Justice
2. Social Justice as Covenant Obligation
3. Social Justice as a Royal Responsibility
4. Social Justice in Prophetic Literature
5. Conclusion

1. Terms Related to Justice.
The concept of justice is found throughout the OT in widely varying genres. In prophetic literature a concern with justice is frequently, though by no means exclusively, expressed by use of the parallel word pair *mišpāṭ* ("justice, judgment" [145x; 425x in the MT]) and *ṣĕdāqâ* ("righteousness" [76x; 159x in the MT]) (Weinfeld, 25-44). The term *ḥesed* ("loving-kindness, mercy, loyalty") appears as a component of justice in Jeremiah 9:24, where it is used in conjunction with *mišpāṭ* and *ṣĕdāqâ* as characteristics exercised by God (cf. Ps 33:5). Elsewhere, love of *ḥesed* is counted along with righteousness and humility as a quality that should characterize the person of God (Mic 6:8). Other important concepts related to social justice are *'ĕmet* ("truth" [e.g., Ps 89:14; Is 59:14; Ezek 18:8; Zech 8:16]), *'emûnâ* ("faithfulness" [e.g., 1 Sam 26:23; Ps 40:10; 143:1; Is 59:4; Jer 5:1]), and

raḥămîm ("mercy, compassion" [e.g., Ps 119:156; Hos 2:19; Zech 7:9]). In a negative sense, injustice is often indicated by use of the terms *ʿāwel* ("perversity, injustice" [e.g., Ezek 18:8; 28:18; 35:15]) and *rešaʿ* ("wickedness" injustice" [e.g., Is 58:6; Mic 6:10-11]), as well as *raʿ* ("evil" [e.g., Is 33:15-16; 59:15; Amos 5:15]).

Social justice is frequently in view when the aforementioned terms are used in conjunction with a range of nouns associated with vulnerable or marginalized individuals or groups, including *ʾalmānâ* ("widow"), *yātôm* ("orphan"), *gēr* ("sojourner, alien, refugee"), *ʿānî* ("poor, afflicted"), *ʾebyôn* ("needy, oppressed") and *dal* ("weak, helpless"). Individuals included in these categories were those who fell outside the social support system of land ownership, family and/ or patriarchy that served ancient Israel. In the language of today, such individuals could be described as facing "systemic discrimination," since their very identity left them outside of the "systems" that existed to protect those living in Israel. As a consequence, individuals such as the *ʾalmānâ*, *yātôm*, and *gēr* came under the special care of Yahweh, his surrogate the king, and were to be cared for as a covenant obligation by the people at large. Such attention was necessary, given the realities of life in ancient Israel, where warfare, disease and famine ensured that widows, orphans and refugees were always present.

Persons such as widows, orphans and sojourners were the most easily ignored and exploited in society and least able to respond should their rights be denied. Although the vulnerable position of the poor merited the close attention of those in authority, it did not mean that they were to receive favoritism in legal proceedings, since this would constitute a miscarriage of justice (Ex 23:3; Lev 19:15). Rather, the obligation of the king and the judge was to ensure that the vulnerable were granted equal access to justice (Ex 23:6). In all of its dealings, Israel was to follow Yahweh's example and act with *ḥesed* ("faithfulness" [Hos 6:6; Mic 6:8; Zech 7:9]), *ʾĕmet* ("truth" [Ezek 18:8; Zech 7:9; 8:16]), and *mîšôr* ("fairness" [Ps 67:4; Is 11:4]).

2. Social Justice as a Covenant Obligation.

For the prophets, social justice was not a theological abstraction or a passive activity; it was a way of being rooted in Israel's covenant identity, one that had consequences for how the nation lived and ordered its life. Within Israelite society, values and hence behavior were governed by roles and responsibilities laid out in the covenant that bound members of society to each other and to God. In entering into covenant with Yahweh at Sinai (Ex 19), Israel took on a priestly role in relation to the world. In declaring that Israel would be for him "a kingdom of priests and a holy nation" (Ex 19:6), Yahweh identified the entire nation as an intermediary between himself and the world in the same way that Israel's priests were intermediaries between individual worshipers and Yahweh. This covenant identity tasked Israel with the responsibility of living in a way that reflected Yahweh's character to the nations (Wright 2004, 62-65). The Torah given at Sinai served to order society, but also it ensured that Israel adopted values and behaviors that allowed them to remain in Yahweh's presence and accurately reflect his character to the nations. A foundational principle for Israel in both regards is embodied in Yahweh's oft-repeated admonition that Israel "be holy to me because I, the LORD, am holy" (Lev 20:26 NIV; also Lev 11:44-45; 19:2; 20:7; 21:6). The fact that Israel's concept of social justice was grounded in the Sinai covenant has convinced some scholars that in their concern for justice the prophets were not radical innovators but rather theological conservatives. T. Fretheim concludes, "Unless these social concerns of the prophets were reasonably well known by their audiences, . . . their message would have been obscure, even unintelligible" (Fretheim, 159-60 [cf. Brueggemann, 15-27]).

The covenant stipulations found in Exodus through Deuteronomy provided the instruction that allowed Israel to reflect God's character in specific ways. Yahweh's commitment to social justice, for example, is embodied in the command "You shall not wrong or oppress a resident alien [*gēr*], for you were aliens in the land of Egypt. You shall not abuse any widow [*ʾalmānâ*] or orphan [*yātôm*]. If you do abuse them, when they cry out to me, I will surely heed their cry" (Ex 22:21-23 NRSV [cf. Lev 19:33-34; Deut 10:17-18; 24:17, 19-21; 26:12-13; 27:19]). The alien (better, "sojourner" or "refugee"), the widow and the orphan were among those who did not benefit from the normal societal protections enjoyed by most Israelites. The widow and orphan, for example, did not enjoy the social and physical protection afforded by a husband or father in a society that was structured along patriarchal lines. In the order of inheritance given as a legal precedent in the case of Zelophehad's daughters, for example, the widow is conspicuously absent (Num 27:8-11). Although the experience of Naomi suggests that inheritance by a widow and the subsequent sale of property to provide income was not impossible (Ruth 4:3), it is clear that the redemption of property was concerned primarily with retaining family ownership and not with supporting widows (Lev 25:23-28). Similarly, although levirate marriage served the function of providing for a widow, its fundamental role was to ensure an heir for her deceased husband (Deut 25:5-10; cf. Gen 38:8-10). Also lacking the protection offered by property and clan relationships were refugees or sojourners (*gēr*), non-Israelites who had left the land of their birth (often due to war, famine or some other calamity [e.g., Gen 12:10; 27:42-45; Ruth 1:1; 1 Sam 21:10; Jer 43:1-7]). Without the resources of land or family, economic options were severely limited. Although some might possibly enter royal service (e.g., Doeg the Edomite [1 Sam 21:7]; Uriah the Hittite [2 Sam 11; 1 Chron 11:41]), the fate of most sojourners was the life of the day laborer (Deut 24:14-15) or slave (Lev 25:45).

Widows and orphans were particularly at risk of losing the familial holdings that helped ensure economic stability. For refugees forced to relinquish ancestral property in favor of the relative safety of a foreign country, acquiring new agricultural land would have been economically and culturally difficult. As a result, these groups were given particular rights intended to keep them from starvation. Israelites were not to charge interest on loans or sell food at profit to their fellow Israelites who had fallen into poverty (Lev 25:35-38) (*see* Wealth and Poverty). During the various grain harvests, the crops on the edges and corners of the field were left ungathered so that the poor could reap there. Similarly, the fruit that fell from the olive tree or grapevine was to be left for the poor to gather (Lev 19:9-10; 23:22; Deut 24:19-21; Ruth 2). In addition, every third year the agricultural tithe was to be shared among these marginalized people and the Levites (Deut 14:28-29; 26:12). These rudimentary benefits, of course, depended on the magnanimity of the average Israelite. In the book of Ruth, Boaz's instruction to his reapers (Ruth 2:15) and his warning to Ruth (Ruth 2:8-9) imply that some Israelites were reluctant to cooperate with the poor who sought to exercise these rights. The sojourner was particularly vulnerable to the vigilantism that could arise if involved in a case of manslaughter. For this reason, the sojourner was granted the right to access the cities of refuge along with native Israelites (Num 35:15).

A significant aspect of Israel's commitment to social justice was the year of Jubilee (*yôbēl* [Lev 25:13-17]). This event occurred every fifty years as a moment of economic equalization for all Israelites. Land that had been sold because of financial distress was returned to its original owners, and Israelites who had been forced into indentured servitude were freed (Lev 25:39-43). Although scholars disagree over whether the Jubilee year was actually practiced or was solely a theoretical ideal, there is ample evidence in the ancient Near East for the remission of debts and freeing of prisoners when a king ascended the throne. Even so, there is no clear parallel to the sacral or cyclical character of the Israelite institution of the Jubilee year (Epsztein, 133-34; Wright 1995, 197-212; Weinfeld, 140-78).

3. Social Justice as a Royal Responsibility.
In Israel, as elsewhere in the ancient world, the administration of justice was a royal responsibility that was exercised by virtue of the monarch's connection with the divine realm. In Egypt the Pharaoh was understood to be the incarnation of the god Horus with responsibility for upholding *maat*, the standard of divine "truth" or "justice" without which society could not function. In the late third-millennium BC Sumerian law code of Ur-Nammu, the king boasts that he dispensed justice with equity: "I did not deliver the orphan to the rich. I did not deliver the widow to the mighty. I did not deliver the man with but one shekel to the man with one mina [i.e., sixty shekels]. I did not deliver the man with but one sheep to the man with one ox" (*COS* 2.153:409). In the law code instituted by Hammurabi of Babylon (1792-1750 BC), the gods Anu and Enlil are said to have elevated the king to the throne with the responsibility to "make justice prevail in the land, to abolish the wicked and the evil, [and] to prevent the strong from oppressing the weak" (*COS* 2.131:336). In Egypt Pharaoh was thought to be divine, while in Babylon the monarch was a human called to kingship by the

god Marduk and was favored by him. In both cases, these relationships made the ruler responsible for administering laws that were entrusted to the king by the gods.

As Yahweh's adopted son (Ps 2:6-7), the Israelite king functioned as an earthly agent of the divine being and so bore special responsibility for ensuring that justice was carried out. Such responsibilities are the subject of Psalm 72, where royal attention to them is associated with long life and prosperity. In the OT the example of the king as Yahweh's agent of justice is set by David (Weinfeld, 46-48). Following closely on Yahweh's royal promise to David and his house, 2 Samuel 8:15 notes, "David reigned over Israel, doing what was just [*mišpāṭ*] and right [*ṣĕdāqâ*] for all his people" (NIV). In the subsequent narrative the author provides an example of how David rules in a manner that extends justice to the most vulnerable. By seeking out Mephibosheth and bringing him to court (2 Sam 8:1-13), David extends protection to one who was doubly disadvantaged. As a direct descendant of Saul, Mephibosheth might well have been considered a potential rival to David. Additionally, as a person with a significant physical disability from a now-decimated clan, the son of Jonathan had limited economic and social prospects. In extending "kindness" (*hesed*) to Mephibosheth (2 Sam 9:1), David clearly establishes himself as one who rules with a view to caring for the vulnerable. Later, the prophets will build on David's reputation as they look forward to a future king whose coming reign would restore justice (Jer 23:5-6).

It is the basic need to provide justice that informs Solomon's request for wisdom (1 Kings 3:9), and it is his demonstrated ability in this regard that earns him the admiration both of his people (1 Kings 3:28) and the visiting Queen of Sheba (1 Kings 10:9). The failure of the king to establish justice or, worse, to actively pervert justice was a violation of the monarch's fundamental obligation to both God and subjects. It is no surprise, therefore, that when Absalom seeks to undermine his father David's credibility as ruler, he does so by questioning the latter's commitment to maintaining justice in the land (2 Sam 15:1-4). In the case of David's adultery with Bathsheba (2 Sam 11), the severity of the king's infraction is multiplied not only by the murder-by-proxy of Bathsheba's husband, Uriah, but also by the fact that as a resident non-Israelite (i.e., *gēr*), Uriah was one whose welfare was to be a matter of special concern to Yahweh's agent, the king. Not surprisingly, David's actions in this case earn him a thorough excoriation from the lips of the prophet Nathan (2 Sam 12:1-15). The role of the king in maintaining justice and the interest of Yahwistic prophets in ensuring that this duty was carried out were also characteristics of the northern monarchy. There, Ahab's complicity in the judicial murder of the landowner Naboth shows the king, as one charged with maintaining justice, to be actively perverting it (2 Kings 21:8-19). This act is especially grievous because for the Israelites, land was a trust and inheritance from Yahweh and a sign that they were participants in covenant promise (Gen 12:7; Josh 13—19) (Mays 1983, 10-11). Through the mouth of the prophet Micaiah, Yahweh pronounces a sentence of death upon the Israelite monarch, a judgment carried out in poetic fashion by a lying spirit to parallel the lying witnesses earlier employed against Naboth (2 Kings 22:19-23) (Irwin, 59-62).

In the end, the royal need to maintain on earth the behavior and values of Yahweh is best summed up by the maxim offered by Jeremiah in the closing days of the Judean monarchy: "'But let him who boasts boast about this: that he understands and knows me, that I am the LORD, who exercises kindness, justice and righteousness on earth, for in these I delight,' declares the LORD" (Jer 9:24).

4. Social Justice in Prophetic Literature.

During the latter part of the nineteenth century, scholars such as B. Duhm and J. Wellhausen emphasized the individualism and spiritual vitality of the prophets, particularly over against what they perceived to be the institutionalism, legalism and ritualism of the priestly cult. In the years that followed, an increasing number of interpreters came to understand the prophets as independent-minded figures who preached an "ethical monotheism" that represented the pinnacle of Israelite religion (Dearman, 132; Wilson, 3-4; Wellhausen, 398-99, 473-75). For many, the prophets were understood to be reformers whose interest was in bringing about social change. This understanding of the prophets resonated well with the concerns of what later would become known as the Social Gospel movement. In the

America of the late nineteenth-century, many scholars, clergy and theologians were increasingly concerned by the human toll exacted by unfettered capitalism and the ineffectiveness of a pietistic church in addressing such injustice. A prominent spokesperson for this movement was the German-American pastor and church historian Walter Rauschenbusch (d. 1918). According to Rauschenbusch, the great impediment to social equality and justice in ancient Israel was the nobility whose extravagant lifestyle was maintained at the expense of the poor. In this context, the role of the prophets was to give voice to the needs of the agrarian poor and demand justice from the urban social elite (Rauschenbusch, 3-16). Driven in part by this prophetic impulse, the Social Gospel movement became socially and politically active in an effort to move American society toward what it saw as a Christian ideal.

The Social Gospel movement was optimistic concerning the human capacity to respond to the prophetic message and consequently was hopeful with regard to the social change that was possible. Against this background, World War I, with its attendant horrors, was a profoundly disillusioning experience for many in the movement. Despite this, the view of the prophets as agents of social change that the movement espoused continued to influence the agenda of American liberal Protestantism throughout the remainder of the twentieth century.

The priority of social transformation at the expense of personal conversion was one feature of the Social Gospel movement that kept many conservative Protestants in North America from embracing its agenda. Although many theological conservatives were active in social work, such efforts often were tied to evangelism rather than to any prophetic imperative. With regard to the role of the prophets, many theological conservatives, particularly at the popular level, continued to be influenced by the dispensationalism that had begun in the early nineteenth century with the teaching of J. N. Darby. As a consequence, much of the interest that North American conservative Protestants showed in the prophets revolved around messianic prediction and end-times speculation rather than issues of social justice.

The understanding of the prophets as promoters of social justice that undergirded the Social Gospel movement has been echoed more recently in the work of W. Brueggemann. Brueggemann argues that the prophets promoted the values of the alternative community founded by Moses and stood in stark opposition to the monarchy, an institution that he regards as the primary source of injustice in ancient Israelite society (Brueggemann, 28-61; cf. Mendenhall). Such a view of the prophets, however, oversimplifies both their message and place in ancient Israel. While it is obvious that the preexilic prophets did oppose the kings of Judah and Israel, even to the extent of facilitating the removal of individual monarchs (e.g., 1 Kings 19:16), nowhere do we read that they promoted political revolution with the goal of replacing monarchy as a governing institution. Rather, as J. Dearman observes, prophetic critique includes passages that exhort the king and other passages that outline the king's social responsibilities (e.g., Is 9:1-6; Jer 21:11-12; 22:1-5; cf. Ps 72; 132:11-18) (Dearman, 141-43).

An additional corrective to this older view of the prophets as class-conscious advocates for social justice has been offered by J. Pleins, who uses a comparative approach to highlight the range of social locations out of which ancient prophets operated as well as the connections that often existed between prophets and royal institutions (Pleins, 219-23). Pleins also shows how the composition and the shaping of prophetic works in the exilic and postexilic eras make it difficult to maintain a view of the prophets that sees them solely as ones interested in social justice and opposing the elite. With regard to the book of Isaiah, for example, Pleins notes how in the context of the exile, the term *'ānî* ("poor") comes to be applied to the nation as a whole, including its most elite citizens. This shift in the final form of the book makes it clear that the prophetic enterprise cannot be reduced to the simple opposition of advocates of social justice railing against the abuses of the wealthy (Pleins, 251, 264-70).

As noted above, in ancient Israel maintaining social justice was an inescapable royal duty (Ps 72). Even so, responsibility to protect the vulnerable extended beyond the king to become the obligation of every Israelite; when justice was not done, both felt the wrath of the prophets (Is 1:17; Jer 7:6; 22:3; Ezek 22:7; Zech 7:10). Depending on their context, the prophets vary between demanding justice in the present and seeing it as something to be brought about by an eschatological *messiah figure. In general, in preexilic contexts condemnation for failing to do justice falls upon ruler and ruled in equal measure. With the fall of Jerusalem and the dissolution of the monarchy, however, the king no longer existed to function as an agent of Yahweh's justice. Thus, in exilic and postexilic contexts the prophets often look to an eschatological Davidic ruler as the one whom Yahweh eventually will send to restore justice.

4.1. Amos. Nowhere in the OT is the issue of social justice a more focused matter of concern than in the book of Amos. In this short collection of oracles, a Judean pastoralist from Tekoa crosses over to the kingdom of Israel to deliver Yahweh's message of condemnation. The reign of Jeroboam II of Israel (793/92-753 BC) that forms the backdrop to Amos's ministry was a period of political, military and economic success. For most of Jeroboam's reign, the world power that was Assyria had been weakened by internal strife—a state of affairs that left regional powers such as Israel and Judah free to pursue their own interests. In cooperation with Uzziah (792/91-740/39 BC) of Judah, Jeroboam II had seized this opportunity to create wealth on a scale unseen since the days of the united monarchy. Such economic success, however, was achieved on the backs of the poor, and this earned the Israelite king the condemnation of the prophet.

The final form of the book of Amos is skillfully constructed to condemn the northern monarchy for its abuse of the vulnerable. The series of oracles against the nations with which the book begins assails various foreign powers for acts of oppression such as violence (Amos 1:3, 11, 13; 2:1) and slavery (Amos 1:6, 9). The seventh oracle, targeted against Judah, condemns Israel's southern neighbor for failing to obey the law (*tôrâ*) of Yahweh (Amos 2:4). The effect of these oracles and of Israel's nodding assent to them was to lure Israel into self-condemnation. In this way, Amos's audience is unable to deflect the accusation of oppression when the prophet's words are turned against them. The list of abuses catalogued in Amos 2:6-8 shows how the people of Israel had enriched themselves by their oppression of the poor. The latter were forced into indentured servitude for miniscule degrees of indebtedness (Amos 2:6b) while at the same time being denied access to the courts (Amos 2:7a). Once forced into servitude, the young girls (*na'ărâ*) were sexually abused by both master and son (Amos 2:7b; cf. Ex 21:8). Garments taken as collateral for loans and wine given as fines were misappropriated and used for drunken carousing (Amos 2:8; cf. Ex 22:26-27). The reference in this section to the destruction of the Amorites (i.e., Canaanites) and the liberation of Israel from Egypt is an ominous reminder to these abusers that Yahweh has a history of deposing oppressors and extending mercy to the oppressed (Amos 2:9-10).

The extent to which a culture of oppression had taken root in Israel is illustrated in Amos's condemnation of the women of Samaria (Amos 4:1-3). By characterizing these women as "cows" (*pārâ*), the prophet likens them to an animal that, unlike an ox, is not primarily a beast of burden, but one that exists to become fat (Gen 41:2). In parallel condemnations, Amos accuses these women of oppressing the poor and crushing the needy while demanding that their husbands wait on them (Amos 4:1). In the first instance, the prophet condemns the women for ignoring the fundamental covenant obligation to protect the needy and see that they received just treatment (Deut 15:7-18; 24:15; Lev 25:35-43). In the second instance, he condemns them for overturning the patriarchal social order that was the mechanism by which most Israelites were protected. For both of these crimes, the women of Samaria are sentenced to the fate of capture and exile that was the most severe of the covenant curses (Lev 26:17, 25, 33).

In what some regard as the focal point of the book (Jeremias, 83-85), Amos castigates Israel for having turned "justice into something bitter" and "thrown righteousness to the ground" (Amos 5:7a). This Israel has done by oppressing the poor, then denying them justice at the city gate, where disputes were settled (Amos 5:10-12). In such a situation, where the powerful are free to abuse and then bribe their way out of accountability, those with legitimate grievances are imperiled. In such times, the prophet ironically remarks, the "wisest" course of action is to remain silent, foregoing justice in favor of the security that comes with anonymity (Amos 5:13).

In Amos 5:18-20 the prophet describes how Israel's oppression of the poor will bring upon it the Day of Yahweh. What was originally considered a hopeful possibility—the arrival of

Yahweh and the imposition of his authority—has, in light of Israel's abuses, become a terrifying prospect. In the first of two woe speeches, the prophet likens the Day of Yahweh to a time when there will be no escape from deadly animals, an allusion to the covenant curse in which wild animals take over the land (Amos 5:19; cf. Lev 26:22). In the second woe speech, the ultimate covenant curse of exile is directly invoked (Amos 6:7; cf. Lev 26:33).

In what have become the most memorable words of his prophecy, Amos identifies the quality that should characterize true justice: "Let justice [*mišpāṭ*] roll on like a river, righteousness [*ṣĕdāqâ*] like a never-failing stream!" (Amos 5:24 NIV). For justice to exist, it cannot be like the wadi or brook that runs full in winter but is reduced to an empty, cracked stream bed by the heat of the summer. For there to be justice, it must be like the stream that flows throughout the year (*nahal 'êtān*), constant and dependable.

4.2. Hosea. A close contemporary of Amos, and another figure who preached to the northern kingdom, was the prophet Hosea. Although best known as one who condemned the north for its idolatry, this prophet also strongly attacked the nation for its disregard for justice (see Nardoni, 104-6). For the prophet, idolatry and injustice are connected in that both flow from a rejection of Yahweh (Hos 1—2). While the rejection of Yahweh results most visibly in the idolatry that the prophet sees everywhere and vociferously condemns, it also creates a moral vacuum in which injustice flourishes. A recurring theme in the book, therefore, is the connection between Israel's disinterest in knowing God and the growth of injustice in the land (see Mays 1969, 63-64). In Hosea 4:1 the prophet assesses the situation by declaring, "There is no faithfulness ['ĕmet], no love [*ḥesed*], no acknowledgment of God [*da'at 'ĕlohîm*] in the land" (NIV). The rejection of these values along with the searching after God by which they are found has resulted in a society in which they have been replaced by injustice: "Oath making, lying, murder, stealing, and adultery—they burst out so that bloodshed follows on bloodshed" (Hos 4:2). All of the foregoing elements represent the fundamentals necessary for just human relationships; in their absence, anarchy prevails. Ultimately, this lack of knowledge (*da'at*) leads to destruction (Hos 4:6). National ruin, however, will not be God's

final word. At the outset of the book the prophet uses the language of betrothal to describe how as a suitor he will bring Israel reengagement gifts of "righteousness"(*ṣedeq*), "justice" (*mišpāṭ*) and "lovingkindness" (*ḥesed*) and draw the nation into a relationship in which they will truly know (*yd'*) him (Hos 2:19-20) (see Achtemeier, 27-29; Taylor, 19-20).

Throughout the book it is clear that the people of Israel long to experience the bounty conveyed in the covenant blessings, but they are unwilling to do anything substantive to merit those blessings. In response to this mindset, God exhorts the people to do the spiritual and moral work that is the prerequisite of such blessing: "Sow for yourselves righteousness [*ṣĕdāqâ*], reap the fruit of unfailing love [*ḥesed*], and break up your unplowed ground; for it is time to seek the LORD, until he comes and showers righteousness on you" (Hos 10:12 NIV). The people of both kingdoms, however, assume that their crimes can be covered over by a superficial acknowledgment of God that will compel him to forgive and restore (Hos 6:1-3). The frustration that God feels toward this way of thinking is clearly evident: "What can I do with you, Ephraim? What can I do with you, Judah? Your love [*ḥesed*] is like the morning mist, like the early dew that disappears" (Hos 6:4 NIV). In what is perhaps the best-known verse in the book, the prophet declares that God does not want from his people empty ritual intended to conjure up his favor; what God desires is that his people truly practice *ḥesed* and sincerely desire to know him (*da'at 'ĕlohîm*) (Hos 6:6).

In the case of the northern kingdom, however, deceit has become part of the fabric of daily life and, not surprisingly, has left its practitioners self-deceived. In the evidentiary portion of a divine lawsuit the prophet observes, "A trader, in whose hands are false balances, he loves to oppress. Ephraim has said, 'Ah, I am rich, I have gained wealth for myself; in all of my gain no offense has been found in me that would be sin'" (Hos 12:7-8 NRSV) (see Stuart, 184-97). Faced with this, the prophet draws from the story of Jacob to show how God took a grasping and deceitful outcast and changed him into the father of the nation. Building on this example, God exhorts the people, "Return to your God; maintain love [*ḥesed*] and justice [*mišpāṭ*], and wait for your God always" (Hos 12:6 NIV). Israel's self-deception prevents such a return, however, and at the close of the lawsuit Yahweh announces that the nation will not avoid punishment for its sins (Hos 12:14).

At various points in the book, Hosea points the finger at those whose lapses have permitted the rise of injustice. The priests charged with teaching Israel the knowledge of God are the first to be condemned (Hos 4:4-19); they, and prophets along with them, have failed in their responsibilities (Hos 4:5). Rather than opposing the people's sin, the priests seized upon the opportunity to profit from it (Hos 4:8). Rather than acting to protect the people, they became predators who waited undetected until pouncing upon the unsuspecting (Hos 6:9). Similarly condemned is the royal establishment, whose fundamental role was to ensure that justice was carried out. Far from being a moral example or advocate of justice, however, the royal house has been on the same moral wavelength as the most corrupt in society (Hosea 7:1b-3). By rejecting Yahweh and embracing corruption, though, the kings sow the seeds of their own destruction; some are betrayed and killed by conspiring princes, while others who have rejected God are killed in battle (Hosea 7:7, 16).

4.3. Micah. At about the same time that Amos and Hosea delivered their condemnations of the northern kingdom, another prophet rose to speak against both Israel and Judah. Much of Micah's denunciation is related to the idolatry prevalent in both kingdoms, but a significant subtheme is Yahweh's displeasure over his people's abuse of the vulnerable. The prophet depicts his audience as obsessed with injustice. Ingenious abuses are planned out at night and quickly put into action at first light. Through fraudulent means these persons seize the houses and fields of their neighbors (Mic 2:1-2).

Micah identifies those who should be Israel's source of justice—its leadership—as being its worst oppressors (Mic 3:1). The image of cannibalism that the prophet invokes paints a picture of a leadership devouring the nation that it is charged with protecting and perhaps alludes to a covenant curse (Mic 3:2-3; cf. Lev 26:29). Such leaders cannot expect the assistance of Yahweh when they themselves are imperiled (Mic 3:4). These rulers, who should be the nation's source of justice (*mišpāṭ*), have no sense of it and have actually developed an inverted morality in which they hate good (*ṭôb*) and love evil (*rāʿ*). Consequently, they are a study in contradic-

tions: they have perverted justice, what is "straight" or "right" (*yāšār*) they have made "crooked" or "false" (*ʿqš*), while Zion, Yahweh's holy hill, they have expanded through bloodshed (Mic 3:9-10). Finally, they have accepted bribes when judging cases (Mic 3:11; 7:3). As a consequence of this behavior, Jerusalem will succumb to the covenant curse of destruction of city and sanctuary (Mic 3:12; cf. Lev 26:31). If the human leaders have failed, however, Micah nonetheless looks forward to a future date when Yahweh himself will restore Zion and make it a place where justice will be dispensed not only for Israel, but also for the nations (Mic 4:1-3).

In Micah 6:4-5 Yahweh reviews the mighty acts that he performed to rescue and bless Israel and enhance his own reputation in the world. By contrast, Israel's acts have ruined God's reputation. In light of this, Israel's solution—more numerous and extravagant sacrifices (Mic 6:6-7)—is feeble and misses the point. What God suggests (Mic 6:8) and what Israel needs is a spiritual rehabilitation that makes them people who can accurately reflect God's character to the world. By adjuring his people "to act justly and to love mercy and to walk humbly with your God" (Mic 6:8), Yahweh draws attention to the fact that the exercise of justice must always be accompanied by an attitude of humility that recognizes the authority of Yahweh and the relationship of humans to it.

When it comes to doing evil, both ruler (*śar*) and judge (*šōpēṭ*) are well practiced (Mic 7:3). As in Amos, the injustice rampant in Israel and condemned by Micah will merit a divine visitation. The day of Yahweh's coming will be one of hope for those who have been wronged (Mic 7:4, 7; cf. Amos 5:18).

4.4. Isaiah. During the second half of the eighth century BC, the prophet Isaiah carried the message of Yahweh to the city of Jerusalem. The consensus among the majority of scholars is that in its present form, the book of Isaiah contains the message of this preexilic prophet along with voices from the exilic and postexilic eras (Childs, 1-7; McConville, 1-11). In the final shaping of the book, these voices unite to proclaim Yahweh as the "Holy One of Israel" and the only one in whom Israel should place its trust.

The book of Isaiah begins with the familiar prophetic condemnation of Israel's tendency to favor religious ritual over the principled and faithful living that puts covenant values into practice (Is 1:10-31; cf. Hos 6:1-6; Amos 4:1-5; 5:4-15, 21-24; Mic 6:6-8; Zech 7:4-10). In the introduction to the book Yahweh declares, "Stop bringing meaningless offerings! Your incense is detestable to me. New Moons, Sabbaths and convocations—I cannot bear your worthless assemblies" (Is 1:13 NIV). Instead, Israel needs to practice a religion characterized by a commitment to justice: "Stop doing wrong. Learn to do right; seek justice [*mišpaṭ*]. Defend the oppressed [*ḥāmôṣ*]. Take up the cause of the fatherless [*yātôm*]; plead the case of the widow [*'almānâ*]" (Is 1:16b-17 NIV). Although all Israel is culpable, they have been led in their sin by the dereliction of their rulers: "Your rulers are rebels, partners with thieves; they all love bribes and chase after gifts. They do not defend the cause of the fatherless; the widow's case does not come before them" (Is 1:23 NIV [cf. Is 3:14]). The result of this is that Jerusalem has gone from being a city inhabited by justice to one populated by murderers. If allowed to persist, this situation will force Yahweh to purge the city before restoring it as a place of righteousness (Is 1:21, 24-27; 3:1-15).

Israel's self-absorbed behavior has negative consequences for Yahweh's reputation as the "Holy One of Israel." If Yahweh's representative in the world will not practice justice, then it will be exiled, and Yahweh himself will initiate justice in a way that enhances, not harms, his reputation: "People are bowed down, everyone is brought low, and the eyes of the haughty are humbled. But the LORD of hosts is exalted by justice, and the Holy God shows himself holy by righteousness" (Is 5:15-16 NRSV). Those in authority who drink while accepting bribes and denying justice to the righteous will be consumed as Yahweh summons agents of judgment from afar (Is 5:22-23, 26-30).

Following the chastening of military defeat and subjugation, one of the ways in which Yahweh might restore justice to Zion is through the ascension of a king whose rule will bring justice after the manner of his ancestor David (Is 9; 2 Sam 8:15). The titles and hyperbole found in this passage have suggested to many that a messianic figure is in view. In a royal psalm that might have been a standard hymn heralding the birth of a Judean crown prince, the prophet celebrates the birth, contemporaneously or in the future, of one who would "reign on David's throne and over his kingdom, establishing and upholding it with justice and righteousness from that time on and forever" (Is 9:7 NIV) (Seitz, 86; cf. Sweeney, 178-79, 182-83). If the leaders of Israel have failed in their responsibility to ensure that justice is done, then Yahweh in his "zeal" or "jealousy" (*qin'â* [Is 9:7c]) can raise up a ruler who will be faithful to his assigned responsibilities.

In Isaiah 11 a royal figure once again stands at the center of a chapter focusing on the arrival of justice. Here, however, the picture drawn goes beyond that of the Davidic king who will rule over Israel in righteousness. The fact that this figure comes from the "stump" and "roots" of Jesse (Is 11:1) implies that the Davidic house has fallen and points to a date after 586 BC. A date after 538 BC is suggested by the fact that with the arrival of this figure, Yahweh will initiate a "second" return from exile that will focus on the tribes taken away by Assyria (Is 11:11, 16) (Clements, 121-22; cf. Oswalt 1986, 277-84; Seitz, 96-98). The royal figure depicted here is a superhuman being of eschatological character, one endowed with multiple manifestations of God's spirit and issuing words of judgment to cosmic effect (Is 11:2-4). The justice inaugurated by his advent and rule will extend not only to Israel, but also to the world as a whole (Is 11:4, 9).

This movement from the expectations regarding justice that were placed on a newborn crown prince or the ascension of a king in the present to the hope of future intervention by a messianic figure is understandable, given developments in Israelite history. With the destruction of the institutions of temple and palace that came in 586 BC, Judah was bereft of the forces that had been most directly responsible for communicating the need for justice and for ensuring that it was carried out. In addition, the exile and the ever-diminishing hope that the monarchy would be reinstituted meant that the prophets could no longer point to the ascension of a new king as the one who would restore justice. In this context, the responsibility toward justice that had been embodied by the Davidic king was now projected upon an eschatological figure who one day would come to reign on David's throne with a Yahweh-imbued commitment to righteousness.

According to the prophet, this figure will be so infused with the spirit of Yahweh that he will not need to use his senses of sight and hearing to render judgments (Is 11:1-3). Rather, this person will offer judgments to the needy from an innate sense of righteousness and justice (Is 11:4a). For the wicked, the judgments that proceed from his mouth will bring destruction (Is 11:4b). For the faithful, the new era of covenant peace and blessing that this figure will inaugurate is depicted in the image of peaceful coexistence between animals that once had been in the relationship of predator and prey (Is 11:6-9; cf. Lev 26:6b). The work of this figure will result in a second return of Israel and Judah to the land, undoing the ultimate covenant curse of exile (Lev 26:33; Deut 28:64-68) and restoring the ultimate covenant blessing of living at peace in the land (Lev 26:7-13; Deut 28:3-14).

The rulers of Judah are condemned once again in Isaiah 28. Through chiasm (A, B, C, B', A'), the prophet highlights the connection between false worship and the perpetration of injustice. The rulers of Jerusalem, the prophet says, have made [A] a "covenant with death" (bĕrît + māwet) and an "agreement with Sheol" (šĕʾôl + ḥōzeh) (Is 28:15a) and boast that they are immune from the "surging flood" (šôṭ + šôṭēp + ʿābar) (Is 28:15b) because they have taken refuge in [B] a "lie" (kāzāb) and something "false" (šeqer) (Is 28:15c); to this boast, Yahweh replies that he will [B'] make "justice" (mišpāṭ) and "righteousness" (ṣĕdāqā) (Is 28:17) the standard by which everything is measured, and that [A'] hail will sweep away their refuge and the "surging flood" (šôṭ + šôṭēp + ʿābar) (Is 28:18) their hiding place so that the "covenant with death" (bĕrît + māwet) and "agreement with Sheol" (šĕʾôl + ḥāzût) (Is 28:18) is annulled. The result of this arrangement is to focus attention on [C] Isaiah 28:16: "See, I lay a stone in Zion, a tested stone, a precious cornerstone for a sure foundation; the one who trusts will never be dismayed." The emphasis here repeats a major theme of the book: Yahweh is the only one whom Judah should trust; to replace Yahweh with another deity is to remove Israel's basis for justice and *ethics (Is 28:16).

In Isaiah 32 two or perhaps three oracles are brought together to address the need for justice (Oswalt 1986, 583-84; cf. Childs, 236). The first of these (Is 32:1-8) paints a picture of a time to come when king and princes will reign justly. The example set by the leadership will filter down to ordinary Israelites who will be a refuge (Is 32:1-2). Scholars differ on the setting of this passage, but the initial reference to king and princes, as well as the subsequent critique of the "noble" (nādîb [Is 32:5]) implies that it is preexilic (Clements, 259). The advent of righteous leadership will bring to an end the rule of a so-called noble class that has perpetrated evil, ignoring the plight of the hungry, depriving the thirsty of water, and subverting justice in order to deny the poor (ʿānî) and the needy (ʾebyôn) (Is 32:6-7). Contrasting with this picture of a future when men will act to protect others is a present in which women seem utterly indifferent to the culture of injustice they inhabit. This group lives as though they are under the covenant blessings of abundant grape harvest (bāṣîr) and assured security (bṭḥ) (Is 32:9-10; cf. Lev 26:3-6a), even though such blessing is undeserved. Such moral disorientation and complacency in the face of injustice will lead to the covenant curses of depletion of abundance, loss of physical security, and the ruin of the city (Is 32:9-14; cf. Lev 26:20, 31a). In place of this situation, Yahweh will pour out his spirit on all Israel in order to bring justice, righteousness and security to the people (Is 32:15-20). This blessing and security will take place not in the verdant hill country or within the walls of Jerusalem, but rather in the arid "wilderness" (midbār), a miraculous prospect that confirms Yahweh to be the one worthy of Israel's trust. Through these oracles the writer makes the point that while rulers bear primary responsibility for the existence of injustice, ordinary citizens share culpability when they live and move in such a culture as if it were "normal." When such a darkly symbiotic relationship exists, an outpouring of the divine Spirit is necessary to sweep away the old and replace it with something new.

Isaiah 33:1-6 comprises a declaration of woe against the power (likely Assyria) that is oppressing the nation and a community lament in which the prophet cries out to Yahweh for deliverance. Although the nations have plundered the land, they themselves will be plundered (Is 33:4). Interestingly, the development that will remove the threat from Israel is the arrival of Yahweh not as an avenging force, but as a source of justice: "He will fill Zion with justice and righteousness. He will be the sure foundation for your times, a rich store of salvation and wisdom and knowledge; the fear of the LORD is the key to this treasure" (Is 33:5b-6 NIV). Security and covenant blessing cannot be enjoyed apart from a return to justice. As in the previous chapter, it will be an act of divine intervention that will achieve this.

In Isaiah 42, a passage that most scholars hold to be exilic, Yahweh identifies the "servant" (*'ebed*) whom he will use to bring justice to the nations. At first unnamed, this figure, it soon becomes clear, is the nation of Israel itself (Is 42:5-9; 49:1-7; cf. 51:1-8). Some see messianic overtones in the passage (e.g., Oswalt 1998, 108), but the basic task of being a conduit for Yahweh's aims in the world is entirely in keeping with both the promise given to Abraham (Gen 12:1-3) and Israel's covenantally rooted, intermediary role as a kingdom of priests (Ex 19:6).

Israel will not accomplish this task on its own, however. As is noted elsewhere in the book (e.g., Is 11:1-3; 32:15-20), an infusion of Yahweh's Spirit will transform and equip Yahweh's servant Israel in preparation for its task. Elsewhere in the OT, such an infusion of Yahweh's Spirit can be not just an equipping, but also a compelling, force (e.g., 1 Sam 10:9-11; 1 Kings 22:19-23; Is 37:7). Israel will bring justice not through coercion or force of arms, but rather through a faithful determination that will eventually see the nations accept its teaching (*tôrâ*) (Is 42:2-4). As Israel undertakes this task, it can be assured of Yahweh's guiding presence (Is 42:6). The once-blind Israel (Is 6:9) will become a light to the nations, freeing them from blindness and giving them liberty (Is 42:7). All of this Yahweh can do because as creator of heaven, earth and all life, he has authority over the nations (Is 42:5).

This passage reminds an exilic Israel that Yahweh has given meaning to their existence even when they are not in the land of promise. Even when in exile among the nations, Israel has a role given by Yahweh that is in perfect conformity with the promises given to them at Sinai. Furthermore, it is clear from this passage that Yahweh's authority is universal, and that the standards of justice that Yahweh has long demanded of his people Israel will one day be required of all nations.

The theme of Yahweh's justice being made available to others is taken up in Isaiah 56. Based on its placement in the book (Is 56—66) and on Isaiah 56:8 in particular, most scholars see this passage as arising during the postexilic period, a time during which the returning exiles struggled to reestablish a foothold in Judah and fend off opposition from a hostile local population (Ezra 4; Neh 4; 6:1-14). The need to preserve the religious integrity of this fledgling community and avoid assimilation to the surrounding populace led its leaders to reject intermarriage with outsiders (Ezra 9—10; Neh 9:2a; 13:23-30). As a corrective to this, the writer of Isaiah 56 reminds the postexilic audience that Yahweh accepts the foreigner who chooses to be faithful to him. That even eunuchs, technically excluded from worship in the temple (Lev 21:18-20; Deut 23:1), receive such acceptance shows that Yahweh's interest is in caring for any vulnerable outsider who turns to him (Is 56:4-7). This passage reminds the community that social justice is not complete if it consists solely of arm's-length charity. Here, social justice is depicted as having the relational component of full acceptance into the community of faith. As the one who gathers exiles from afar, Yahweh is one who cares for the outcast and is prepared to challenge Israel with who that might be (Is 56:8).

The disconnect between religious practice and ethics criticized so thoroughly in Isaiah 1 comes to the fore once again in Isaiah 58. In what most scholars regard as a postexilic oracle, Yahweh complains that his people clamor to know his ways, receive just decisions and have him present—all of this despite the fact that they are rebellious (Is 58:1-2). When the people point to their fasting, Yahweh counters that even while engaging in this religious observance, they continue to abuse their workers (Is 58:3-4). The result is their need to adopt a new kind of "fasting," an observance that includes freeing those who have been enslaved (Is 58:6), offering food, shelter and clothing to the poor (*'ānî*), and caring for family (Is 58:7). Only if such "authentic" religious observance takes place will the fortunes of the people change and Yahweh begin to respond to their cries for help (Is 58:9). Once this takes place, Yahweh will reinvigorate the people so that they will be able to rebuild the ruined walls of the city (Is 58:11-12).

In Isaiah 59 the writer laments how the sin of the people has separated them from Yahweh and how no one seems interested in pursuing justice (*ṣedeq* [Is 59:4]). Yahweh is quite able to rescue (Is 59:1), but the sin of the people is a behavior that cannot lead to the covenant blessing of peace (Is 59:8; cf. Lev 26:6a). The sin of the people has kept justice always out of reach (Is 59:9, 12-14). Surveying the situation and seeing that there was no one willing to carry out justice, Yahweh determines to intervene and arms himself for battle. The successful conclusion of this action brings the restoration of covenant blessing and testimony. The nations will be punished, and from east to west they will fear God's name (Is 59:18-19). The final verse sees Yahweh returning triumphantly to Zion (Is 59:20).

4.5. Jeremiah. Much of the book of Jeremiah condemns the people of Jerusalem for their idolatry, but also the prophet charges them with practicing injustice. In an allusion that compares Judah's practice of injustice to that of Sodom and Gomorrah, the prophet is commanded to go through the city to see if he can "find but one person who deals honestly [lit., 'does justice'; *ōśeh mišpāt̄*] and seeks the truth" (Jer 5:1). Judah's sin is something that the prophet tentatively attributes to a simple lack of understanding (Jer 5:3-4). Consequently, he goes to their leaders (*haggĕddōlîm*) only to discover that they too had consciously rejected Yahweh's teaching (Jer 5:5). With both leaders and people rejecting God's teaching and correction, the result is a land turned over to wild animals (Jer 5:6; cf. Lev 26:22) and vineyards that are ruined (Jer 5:10; cf. Deut 28:30b, 39; Lev 26:5).

Later in the same chapter Yahweh issues a proclamation that exposes the obvious culture of injustice that has taken root in Judah. Even though it is clear that Yahweh has cosmic authority, restraining the chaotic power symbolized by the sea, the people of Judah have chosen to ignore his dictates (Jer 5:22-23). As a result, Yahweh has withheld the rain and the harvest that it produces (Jer 5:24-25; cf. Amos 4:7-8). Even so, the people have continued to practice injustice with callous premeditation. The image of the fowler is used to describe the manner in which the wicked lie in wait to snare human victims. Victimizing others, they have become fat and sleek (Jer 5:26-28a). They refuse to plead the cause of the orphan (*yātôm*), with the result that the orphan has no chance of prospering; they refuse to extend justice to the needy (*'ebyôn*) (Jer 5:28).

This situation of injustice is allowed to continue in part because the prophets, whose task it is to hold the nation to account for how it is following the terms of the covenant, have prophesied lies (Jer 5:31; also Jer 6:13-14; 8:10-11; 14:14-16). In other words, the prophets have pronounced covenant blessing where covenant curse is actually called for. The priests, who comprise the other group that might intervene to ensure justice, behave in the same way. This situation of officially sanctioned injustice is something that the people "love." The rhetorical question that follows, "But what will you do in the end?" (Jer 5:31b NIV), concludes the section on an ominous note. The final shaping of the book answers this question with the command "Flee!" which introduces the prediction of attack that is the preoccupation of the subsequent chapter (Jer 6:1). The description in this same chapter of Yahweh's intent to attack his own people (Jer 6:2-5) likewise answers the rhetorical question of Jeremiah 5:29.

The theme of rampant injustice enabled by lies continues in the well-known temple speech of Jeremiah 7. Here, the prophet takes up position at the entrance to Judah's house of worship and harangues the passing supplicants with stinging rebuke. The temple in Jerusalem was thought of as the earthly dwelling place of Yahweh—a belief reflected in the fact that the word for "house" (*bayît*) can also mean "temple." By Jeremiah's time, however, the people of Jerusalem had come to think of the temple in Jerusalem as a talisman that would guarantee their deliverance. Thus, even as the Babylonian army was threatening Jerusalem, the people were clinging to the mistaken belief that the presence of Yahweh's temple would render them invulnerable. The prophet bluntly counters this notion: "Will you steal and murder, commit adultery and perjury, burn incense to Baal and follow other gods you have not known, and then come and stand before me in this house, which bears my Name, and say, 'We are safe'—safe to do all these detestable things?" (Jer 7:9-10 NIV). In short, Judah had deluded itself into believing that there is no such thing as cause and effect, that they could ignore the covenant requirement of justice and still lay hold of the covenant blessing of security (see Lev 26:5b-6a; Deut 28:7). The one hope that Jeremiah offers to this self-deluded people is a radical encounter with reality that sees them change their ways: "If you really change your ways and your actions and deal with each other justly, if you do not oppress the foreigner, the fatherless or the widow and do not shed innocent blood in this place, and if you do not follow other gods to your own harm, then I will let you live in this place" (Jer 7:5-7 NIV).

The twin elements of a delinquent and deluded leadership come together in Jeremiah 21:12-14 and the chapter following. In a short initial oracle apparently addressed to King Zedekiah (597-586 BC) (cf. Jer 21:1), the prophet addresses the royal administration and commands its members to be true to their responsibility to maintain justice: "Administer justice [mîšpāt] every morning; rescue from the hand of his oppressor the one who has been robbed" (Jer 21:12 NIV). Despite abdicating its responsibility to protect the vulnerable, this royal family—and all Jerusalem with it—nonetheless feels secure in its fortified location atop the city of David (Jer 21:13) (Holladay 1986, 577-78). This same theme is taken up in a further oracle delivered at the palace gate (Jer 22:1-5). The command to pay special attention to the plight of the sojourner, the orphan and the widow (Jer 22:3) is intended to remind the royal family of their duty as Yahweh's agents, and the emphasis in both oracles of the ruling family's association with "David" (Jer 21:12a; 22:2, 4) recalls the dynasty's founder as an outstanding example in this regard (see 2 Sam 8:15).

To drive home the point, Jeremiah reviews recent history to demonstrate how Yahweh has already begun to judge the royal family. He begins by declaring that Shallum (Jehoahaz) (609 BC), son of Josiah, deposed and taken captive by Pharaoh Neco II (609-593 BC) after a rule of only three months, will die in captivity (Jer 22:11-12; cf. 2 Kings 23:31-35). The prophet then turns his attention to Shallum's successor, Jehoiakim (609-598 BC). In a woe speech (Jer 22:13-17), the prophet condemns this monarch for violating the royal responsibility to bring justice by pressing the people into forced labor to build a spacious new palace, and this during a time of crisis. Jehoiakim's behavior contrasts sharply with that of his late father, Josiah, who, in the spirit of David, "did what was just and righteous" ('śh + mišpāt + šĕdāqâ [Jer 22:15b; cf. 2 Sam 8:15). As punishment for enslaving his own people, Jehoiakim will have his security torn from him; his allies will disappear, and he himself will die and his corpse be disposed of

as if it were that of a donkey (Jer 22:18-23). Even King Jehoiachin (598-597 BC), whom Jeremiah and Ezekiel treat favorably for having been the only one of Josiah's sons to heed the prophetic word to submit to Babylon (Jer 27:1-15; cf. 2 Kings 24:12), will die in exile.

A new declaration of woe (Jer 23:1) summarizes the situation. The sons of Josiah, shepherds who are charged with protecting Yahweh's flock, have by their oppression and injustice ended up scattering it. The term for "scatter" (pwṣ) used here is the one used in Deuteronomy of the scattering that occurs when sin leads to the covenant curse of exile (Deut 4:27; 28:64; cf. Deut 30:3). Since the royal house of Judah has failed to maintain justice, Yahweh declares that in the future he will act in a new way. The flock that his negligent agents have scattered, Yahweh himself will gather and restore. At that future date, Yahweh himself will choose a member of David's line who will reign in the spirit of David to bring justice and restore covenant blessing: "'The days are coming,' declares the LORD, 'when I will raise up to David a righteous [ṣaddîq] Branch, a King who will reign wisely and do what is just [mišpāt] and right [ṣĕdāqâ] in the land. In his days Judah will be saved and Israel will live in safety'" (Jer 23:5-6a NIV [cf. Jer 33:15-16]). The idea that this new Davidic king is one chosen by Yahweh is in marked contrast with the fact that two of the final Judean kings had been chosen by foreign earthly powers: Jehoiakim by Pharaoh Neco II (609-593 BC) (2 Kings 23:34) and Zedekiah by Nebuchadnezzar II (605-562 BC) (2 Kings 24:17). Chosen by Yahweh, this figure will unfailingly act as Yahweh's agent of justice, as is evidenced by his very name: "The LORD Our Righteousness" (Jer 23:6b). The name of this future king (yhwh ṣidqēnû) is an obvious play on the name of Zedekiah, Judah's final king and the monarch with which this sequence of oracles began in Jeremiah 22:1 (cf. Jer 21:1, 11; 33:15-16).

The failure of both monarch and people to maintain justice is dramatically illustrated in the dying days of the kingdom of Judah (Jer 34:8-22). With the army of the Babylonian king Nebuchadnezzar II (605-562 BC) surrounding Jerusalem, King Zedekiah (597-586 BC) of Judah leads the people to free all Israelite slaves, in an act that some have seen as the observance of the Sabbatical year (Jer 34:14-15) (Carroll, 645) or the Jubilee year (Weinfeld, 13). Accompanied by his officials, subjects, and members of the priestly class, the king enters into a covenant before Yahweh and pledges to release those Israelites who were under enslavement. Perhaps emboldened by a temporary withdrawal of the Babylonian army (Jer 34:21-22), Zedekiah reverses his commitment and, soon after the pledge is made, allows the reenslavement of those so recently liberated (Jer 34:11). The consequence of violating the covenant and abrogating his responsibility to ensure justice earns Zedekiah the stinging rebuke of the prophet Jeremiah and the imposition of covenant curses of sword, plague, famine and ultimate military defeat (Jer 34:17-22).

4.6. Zechariah. In the book of Zechariah the prophet's vision of a massive, flying scroll emphasizes the importance of the covenant law that was to ground the postexilic community and the dire consequences that would result should the people ignore its requirements (Zech 5:1-4) (Boda, 290-302). The two crimes that the angel singles out, theft and perjury, have the potential to destroy a closely knit community because theft represents a fundamental betrayal of personal relationships, and perjury carries with it the intent to pervert justice. At their core, both crimes represent a failure to love one's neighbor (cf. Lev 19:11-18). It is not surprising, then, that the prophet encourages his audience to practice relationships consistent with covenant justice: "Administer true justice; show mercy and compassion to one another. Do not oppress the widow or the fatherless, the foreigner or the poor" (Zech 7:9-10 NIV). This command had been given a generation earlier, and the error of ignoring it had resulted in the exile of Israel by Yahweh (Zech 7:11-13). Now it is repeated in the hopes that the return to covenant justice will initiate a concomitant return of divine blessing and presence (Zech 7:4-10; 8:1-8). When this happens, Jerusalem will become known as the "City of Truth" ('îr-hā'ĕmet), and Zion known as the "Holy Mountain" (Zech 8:3). Yahweh's presence and the justice lived out by the inhabitants of Jerusalem will attract the attention of the nations that will come to Zion to seek Yahweh's favor (Zech 8:14-23). With this, Israel will at last fulfill the promise given to Abraham that he and his descendants would be a blessing to the entire world (Zech 8:13; cf. Gen 12:1-3).

5. Conclusion.

The emphasis on social justice that so often is a concern of the prophets is rooted in the Sinai covenant and as such constitutes a central aspect of Israel's identity. Israel's practice of social justice is important for the prophets because it is consistent with God's character, something that Israel's covenant identity required them to imitate. When Israel failed to act justly, they were misrepresenting Yahweh's character to the nations. In such a situation the covenant curses were applied with an increasing degree of severity until Israel either reformed its ways or was silenced through exile. Throughout the preexilic era the enthronement of a new king, or even the birth of a crown prince, brought with it fresh hope that justice would be upheld. Where Israelite kings were unwilling to act as Yahweh's agents of justice or where they had been chosen and installed by a foreign power, Yahweh sometimes vowed to "raise up" another from the line of David who would ensure justice for the vulnerable. With the disappearance of the monarchy after 586 BC, the royal responsibility for justice sometimes was embodied in a messianic figure whom Yahweh would one day bring to liberate his people and rule over them with justice. The future intervention of this figure will also have the effect of extending Yahweh's rule of justice to the nations as a whole, bringing to fullness the claims of authority implicit in the various oracles against the nations (e.g., Jer 46—49; Amos 1:3—2:3) and fulfilling the promise made to Abraham (Gen 12:1-3).

See also COVENANT; ETHICS; JUSTICE, RIGHTEOUSNESS; LAW; PROPHECY AND SOCIETY; WEALTH AND POVERTY.

BIBLIOGRAPHY. **E. Achtemeier,** *Minor Prophets I* (NIBCOT 17; Peabody, MA: Hendrickson, 1996); **S. Bendor,** *The Social Structure of Ancient Israel: The Institution of the Family (Beit 'Ab) from the Settlement to the End of the Monarchy* (JerBS 7; Jerusalem: Simor, 1996); **M. J. Boda,** *Haggai, Zechariah* (NIVAC; Grand Rapids: Zondervan, 2004); **W. Brueggemann,** *The Prophetic Imagination* (Philadelphia: Fortress, 1978); **R. P. Carroll,** *Jeremiah: A Commentary* (OTL; Philadelphia: Westminster, 1986); **B. S. Childs,** *Isaiah: A Commentary* (OTL; Louisville: Westminster/John Knox, 2001); **R. E. Clements,** *Isaiah 1-39* (NCBC; Grand Rapids: Eerdmans, 1980); **J. A. Dearman,**

"Hebrew Prophecy and Social Criticism: Some Observations for Perspective," *PRSt* 9 (1982) 131-43; **L. Epsztein,** *Social Justice in the Ancient Near East and the People of the Bible* (London: SCM, 1986); **T. E. Fretheim,** "The Prophets and Social Justice: A Conservative Agenda," *WW* 28.2 (2008) 159-68; **W. L. Holladay,** *Jeremiah 1: A Commentary on the Book of the Prophet Jeremiah, Chapters 1-25* (Hermeneia; Philadelphia: Fortress, 1986); idem, *Jeremiah 2: A Commentary on the Book of the Prophet Jeremiah, Chapters 26-52* (Hermeneia; Philadelphia: Fortress, 1989); **B. P. Irwin,** "Yahweh's Suspension of Free Will in the Old Testament: Divine Immorality or Sign-Act?" *TynBul* 54 (2003) 55-62; **J. Jeremias,** *Amos: A Commentary* (OTL; Louisville: Westminster/John Knox, 1998); **P. S. Johnston,** *Shades of Sheol: Death and Afterlife in the Old Testament* (Downers Grove, IL; InterVarsity Press, 2002); **B. V. Malchow,** *Social Justice in the Hebrew Bible: What Is New and What Is Old* (Collegeville, MN: Liturgical Press, 1996); **J. L. Mays,** *Hosea: A Commentary* (OTL; Philadelphia: Westminster, 1969); idem, "Justice: Perspectives from the Prophetic Tradition," *Int* 37 (1983) 5-17; **J. G. McConville,** *A Guide to the Prophets* (EOT; Downers Grove, IL: InterVarsity Press, 2002); **G. E. Mendenhall,** "The Monarchy," *Int* 29 (1975) 155-70; **E. Nardoni,** *Rise Up, O Judge: A Study of Justice in the Biblical World* (Peabody, MA: Hendrickson, 2004); **J. N. Oswalt,** *The Book of Isaiah: Chapters 1-39* (NICOT; Grand Rapids: Eerdmans, 1986); idem, *The Book of Isaiah: Chapters 40-66* (NICOT; Grand Rapids: Eerdmans, 1998); **J. D. Pleins,** *The Social Visions of the Hebrew Bible: A Theological Introduction* (Louisville: Westminster/John Knox, 2001); **W. Rauschenbusch,** *Christianity and the Social Crisis* (New York: Macmillan, 1907); **C. R. Seitz,** *Isaiah 1-39* (IBC; Louisville: Westminster/John Knox, 1993); **D. Stuart,** *Hosea-Jonah* (WBC 31; Waco, TX: Word, 1987); **M. A. Sweeney,** *Isaiah 1-39: With an Introduction to Prophetic Literature* (FOTL 16; Grand Rapids: Eerdmans, 1996); **J. G. Taylor,** "Hosea," in *Zondervan Illustrated Bible Backgrounds Commentary,* ed. J. Walton (5 vols.; Grand Rapids: Zondervan, 2009) 5:2-41; **M. Weinfeld,** *Social Justice in Ancient Israel and in the Ancient Near East* (2nd ed.; Jerusalem: Magnes; Philadelphia: Fortress, 2000); **J. Wellhausen,** *Prolegomena to the History of Ancient Israel, with a Reprint of the Article Israel from the Encyclopaedia Britan-*

nica, ed. A. Menzies (New York: Meridian, 1957 [1885]); **R. R. Wilson,** *Prophecy and Society in Ancient Israel* (Philadelphia: Fortress, 1980); **C. J. H. Wright,** *Walking in the Ways of the Lord: The Ethical Authority of the Old Testament* (Downers Grove, IL: InterVarsity Press, 1995); idem, *Old Testament Ethics for the People of God* (rev. ed.; Downers Grove, IL: InterVarsity Press, 2004).

B. P. Irwin

SOCIAL-SCIENTIFIC APPROACHES

The history of attempts to apply sociological, anthropological and psychological insights to the study of the OT and to the world of ancient Israel is a long one. Pioneering studies appear in the last quarter of the eighteenth century, when Europeans began to travel to the Middle East and to compare those cultural realities to scenes and behaviors depicted in the biblical text. Others have reviewed this history in detail, so there is no need to replicate that work here. These surveys demonstrate the increasing sophistication of these approaches over time, as biblical scholars explored a variety of social-science theories and employed them with greater skill (Rogerson; Wilson 1984; Mayes; Overholt 1996; Carter 1999; *DOTHB* 905-21; Kessler).

The goal has been to reconstruct the world portrayed in the text, as well as to understand the context within which the text may have been produced. Social-scientific theory often is combined with archaeological data, literary studies and critical biblical research. It is not uncommon for social-science research in the Prophetic Books to have a moral thrust, as it has taken as its task to identify their underlying message of justice and look for its contemporary relevance.

1. Methodological Considerations
2. Early Approaches
3. Recent Developments
4. Future Directions

1. Methodological Considerations.

Social-science study of the prophetic literature is characterized by multiple approaches. The breadth of these efforts can prove daunting, but several taxonomies of the kinds of methods that have been applied to these texts can serve as practical heuristic categories to sort out viewpoints and interests.

One way to classify approaches is to follow the primary tracks within macrosociology that privilege social dynamics and define in large measure the theoretical orientation of inquiry. These are of two broad types (Mayes). Conflict models, as the label suggests, concentrate on the struggles between individuals or groups within society to achieve their respective ends. A context's distinct distribution of influence, wealth and power, as well as the roles of competing ideologies, commands attention. Recognizing causal relationships for these vectors and the changes over time are key. These studies are a legacy of K. Marx and M. Weber, although these two giants in the history of the field and their heirs would not agree on, for instance, the level of impact of the means of production and labor, the part played by human subjectivity, and the relationship of religion and the world of ideas to a society's infrastructure. Marxist approaches prefer a more cultural materialist tact, which accords great warrant to concrete economic matters, environmental factors and the use of natural resources.

Structural functionalism, which is traced to E. Durkheim, emphasizes instead a society's core institutions, traditions and rituals—their interconnections, purposes and authority—and the stability and cohesion that they engender. The collective consciousness and shared representations of a society take precedence over the individual. Other disciplines, such as cultural anthropology and phenomenology, which focus on meaning systems and how these shape human identity and how people organize themselves, create symbolic worlds and evaluate behaviors, display similar concerns. Such approaches have been critiqued as idealist, but at their best they couple these genuine, more subjective realities with tangible social conditions and conflicts.

Second, social-science approaches can be grouped according to the perspective of the research. This can be deemed as either emic or etic, a distinction rooted in linguistics (Headland, Pike and Harris). Emics prioritizes the "native point of view"; that is, it observes and explains phenomena according to categories that the actors under study would consider appropriate and meaningful. Etic accounts, on the other hand, are defined by the framework of the observer. These standpoints are not necessarily mutually exclusive, but methodological clarity demands awareness of differences in outlook, values and assessment.

A third set of helpful distinctions comes from the French historian F. Braudel of the *Annales* school of sociology. Here, the object of study is specified. To begin with, research can concentrate on *l'histoire événementielle*, on specific events or discrete historical moments. A second focus is the *conjecture*, which is not limited to a specific item but rather looks at developments over longer periods of time, like decades. The *longue durée* is interdisciplinary research into social institutions, structures and patterns over still longer time frames. In addition to the more common tools of sociological research, the *longue durée* takes into account other wide-ranging concerns, such as the impact of geographic location, climate, demographic patterns, ideologies and technological advances within the complex rhythms and trajectories of civilizations. The kinds of societal and environmental conditions, which are the target of the *conjecture* and the *longue durée*, are by their nature generic and enduring and facilitate comparative study. Similar structures and patterns in multiple contexts across cultures and eras offer a degree of certainty for seeking analogies with ancient Israel and the prophetic text.

Perhaps one could add another dimension to Braudel's three. It could be called *l'histoire constitutive*. These would be those constituent realities that appear in every society across time, such as the abiding conditions of charity and oppression, and of fair treatment and injustice that manifest themselves in diverse ways in particular contexts. These deeper moral issues are the primary concern of many prophetic texts and permit them to continue to be an important voice across the centuries (Carroll R. 1992, 156-62).

Fourth, research requires clarity in the formulation of sociological models. W. G. Runciman delineates four tasks that need to be distinguished but are commonly confused (cf. Carroll R. 1992, 36-47). The first is reportage. This is the attentive portrayal of the object of research, which clearly distinguishes the native point of view from that of the investigator. The second step is explanation, which is the proposal of a plausible, testable account for this state of affairs. Care must be taken to not misrepresent the data, and there must be an awareness of evidence that could refute the proposal and of the possibility of alternative hypotheses. A third point is description. This is not the same as reportage. In Runciman's terminology, description refers to engaging the reportage and explanation with the worldview of the researcher and of the agents under study in such a way that each would consider the findings to be comprehensive and authentic. Incompleteness and oversimplification are shortcomings to be avoided at this stage. The final step is evaluation, the value judgment to be placed on the object of research. Again, the assessment of the investigator and of the agents under study should be distinguished. Every effort must be made not to allow an inappropriate agenda to misconstrue the work. This prudent and rigorous procedure can safeguard the quality of research.

These various means of analyzing social-science research of the prophetic literature are useful guides for its appraisal and appropriation. Nevertheless, all approaches have inherent limitations, and it is common for introductory texts to voice caution. First, researchers wrestle with the problem of the availability of data. The amount of information provided by archaeology continues to grow, but this always will be partial because of the inescapable challenges related to excavations. These include limited access to certain areas and the destruction or displacement of evidence over millennia. The fact that scholars disagree over the significance of the evidence reveals, too, that some speculation is unavoidable.

A second problem concerns expertise in the application of the social sciences, the degree of acquaintance with relevant theories and the academic literature. Studies conducted by biblical scholars can suffer from an appeal to dated ideas, unawareness of the latest research, or the unconscious influence of scholars' presuppositions. The history of the utilization of the social sciences to interpret the OT is replete with examples of such shortcomings, from the early attempts by pioneers such as W. R. Smith in the 1880s, to scholars in the mid-twentieth century such R. de Vaux, to some of more recent vintage (Rogerson; Herion).

A third issue concerns the reliability of the biblical text for sociohistorical reconstructions.

The wide differences in opinion range from the suspicious attitude of the "minimalist" position to those with greater confidence in the trustworthiness of the text's descriptions. This sometimes acrimonious debate shows little sign of resolution (McNutt, 1-32; Kessler, 24-32). One way forward may be to reconfigure how these texts should be perceived. Perhaps they can be appreciated as ethnographic reports, accounts that naturally have biases and limited purview but still present adequately the contours of the society that they depict (Carroll R. 2000; cf. Overholt 1996, 1-23).

One of the more negative voices regarding the employment of the social sciences to understand prophecy is that of R. P. Carroll (Carroll 1989). He categorizes the inevitable obstacles that biblical scholars face under three headings: data, definition, analysis. The first is based on his conviction that the biblical texts are not trustworthy representations of ancient realities. The problem of definition is that the HB, he says, does not present a uniform picture of prophets and prophecy, and so attempts at definitive, consistent reconstruction are problematic. The last critique is that efforts to apply the social sciences often are simplistic and overly accepting of the texts' presentation of the prophets and their world. This assessment is overly pessimistic. It is indeed profitable to appeal to the social sciences, as long as studies keep in mind the aforementioned caveats and appreciate the tentative nature of the enterprise.

Some within faith communities view social-science approaches with misgiving (Carter 1999). The unease is that the uniqueness of the people of Israel as presented in the OT will be lost. In other words, parallels with other contexts, both ancient and modern, and social-science explanations will reduce what is found in the Bible to common human socioreligious ideas and practices. There also is the fear that some scholars involved in this research have as their goal to undermine Christian faith. In response, it is important to appreciate the value of this research in illuminating the particulars and messages of biblical passages; they supplement purely textual approaches and deepen in fresh ways classical background studies. A more constructive view recognizes that social-science approaches lead to greater understanding, which is foundational for an informed faith.

2. Early Approaches.

Studies from the late nineteenth century to the mid-twentieth century that appealed to the social sciences can be divided into three categories. These should be considered not as sequential foci of study, but rather as areas of research among which, of course, there are overlaps.

2.1. Socioeconomic and Religious Critique. One of the important achievements of nineteenth-century OT scholarship, articulated so powerfully by J. Wellhausen and that held sway for many decades, was the reformulation of the relationship between the prophets and the law. Instead of functioning to condemn their audience for failure to obey the *law's demands, these spokespersons for God were presented as predating the promulgation of the law codes and as preachers of a pure faith divorced from the rituals that stifle direct communion with God and disorient moral life. Once the law was dated late and interpreted (in negative fashion) as the precursor to Judaism, the prophets were separated from any possible moorings in the law. They were envisioned as champions of ethical monotheism, and the social critiques in the Prophetic Books (especially those of the eighth-century BC) were taken as the high point of Israelite religion.

Working within a conflict view, L. Wallis contended that much of the blame for the ills denounced by the prophets targeted the growing class stratification that accompanied the rise of monarchy. Israel began to experience conflicts endemic to urban life, such as tensions deriving from financial and power disparities and the emergence of debt, along with the land loss suffered by debtors and the unjust accumulation of property by the privileged. In Wallis's view, the prophets were the voice of the rural peasantry against the urban elites. Over time, he believed, the perspective of the prophets expanded beyond the rural-versus-urban dichotomy to include moral issues within the cities as well. This facile bifurcation of a simpler, more ethical rural community (*Gemeinschaft*) as opposed to an urban, bureaucratic, hierarchical society (*Gesellschaft*) is a position that continues to find adherents.

2.2. The Prophet in Context. The reconstruction by sociologist M. Weber of the rise of prophecy was complex and multifaceted, but its influence was enduring. Even though he discussed the ecstatic character of prophetic personalities and experience (Weber 1952), his primary impact lay elsewhere. To begin with, he located prophecy within a discussion about the nature of religious authority (Weber 1964). Utilizing his concept of "ideal types," which are theoretical constructs to help decipher social realities, Weber classified the prophets as individuals of charismatic authority, in contradistinction to the more rational, bureaucratic legal and traditional hierarchical kinds (cf. Emmet; Berger). These individuals are believed to have exceptional capacities that derive from a unique call, which legitimates their mission and message before their followers and the broader society.

Another important aspect of Weber's work was his reconstruction of the prophets' social roles and context (Weber 1952). He connected the origins of prophetism with the concept of Yahweh as a war deity of a people bound by *covenant. At the beginning of Israel's history the "nebiim," as Weber called them, had as one of their primary functions to accompany the peasant tribes' militia in war. This responsibility changed with the establishment of the monarchy and a professional army. Eventually those prophets, who were independent of royal circles and the professional prophets, stood against the religious and sociopolitical corruption of the monarchy. They championed early Yahwistic ethical norms in defense of those who had been taken advantage of, and they looked to the people's nomadic existence as God's ideal. These spokespersons, Weber maintained, often were "genteel intellectuals" supported by wealthy, pious families and Levites. Their words were a moral indictment, however, not a charge for revolution; they offered no alternative sociopolitical program. He classified them as "aesthetic," as opposed to "mystic," prophets because ethical demands were so central to their work.

There also was interest in the social location of the prophets and their messages on the part of those working in biblical studies. A crucial component of *form criticism was identifying the hypothetical *Sitz im Leben* ("setting in life") or situation where prophetic genres, especially at the oral stage of development, arose. Today, form critics have a greater appreciation of the complexity of the social, historical and literary settings of these forms, but discovery of those social contexts occupied much of the attention of early form critics. The various types of prophetic speech, such as judgment oracles, announcements of salvation, the messenger formula, woe oracles and the lawsuit, were assigned to a variety of *Sitze im Leben*, such as the cult, legal institutions, or wisdom and royal circles. An interpretation that held sway for many years located the prophets in the cult. Based on certain psalms, prophetic texts and comparative Mesopotamian data, S. Mowinckel, A. R. Johnson, A. Haldar and others argued that certain genres were grounded in religious rituals, and that some of the prophets, even among the writing prophets (especially Ezekiel, Haggai, Zechariah, Joel), were temple functionaries (*see* Liturgy and Cult). Nevertheless, although these studies had sociological interests, they did not apply social-science methods.

2.3. Psychological Approaches. In 1855 OT scholar F. Delitzsch published the first edition of *A System of Biblical Psychology*, in which he explored the relationship between the soul and the body and what it means to be human. This work was based almost solely on the biblical text, although Delitzsch did engage to some degree the nascent field of psychology. The prophets and the prophetic literature, however, were not central to his task (*see* Prophecy and Psychology).

The primary area of research in this period that did center on the prophets investigated the religious experience and the nature of self-consciousness in the reception of revelation from God. Some of what is described in the OT seems at quite a distance from clear-headed ethical preachers and thoughtful theologians! G. Hölscher shifted attention from the prophets' religious ideas to their behaviors and social settings and attempted to understand the ecstasy passages (e.g., 1 Sam 10:5; 2 Kings 3:15) through the lens of psychology (see Lindblom; Clements, 66-69). Hölscher connected these to mantic prophecy, which is induced by music and characterized by trance, that in his historical scheme had been absorbed from Israel's Canaanite neighbors. A scene in the Egyptian Wen-Amon text (c. 1100 BC) seemed to offer an ancient parallel (*COS* 1.41). In time, this bizarre activity was replaced by the moral messages of the writing prophets, although those experiences of heightened awareness and strange actions are still visible in Ezekiel.

Using the psychology of religion, J. Lindblom surveyed a series of accounts of ecstatics from different parts of the globe and diverse time periods in order to compare them with the OT prophets. A common denominator was the experience of an atypical mental state in which they felt overwhelmed by the deity and called to speak divine messages. This experience was characterized by abnormal behavior and an altered state of the body and mind. Like Hölscher, Lindlom related these incidents to the earlier prophets and less to the classical prophets, although they too had *visions, auditory experiences and uncommon sensations (e.g., Is 6; Jer 15:16; 20:7-9; 23:9; Amos 7). Once again, Ezekiel was the exceptional case. Lindblom related aspects of his call to aphasia and neurotic paralysis (see Ezek 3—4; cf. Dan. 7:15; 8:27; 10:8, 16).

Psychological theory also was beginning to be utilized to analyze individual prophets. A pioneer article in the field was E. Broome's argument that Ezekiel was a paranoid schizophrenic. Broome suggested that within the book of Ezekiel there was evidence of the prophet in a catatonic state and exemplifying fantasies of castration and sexual regression, as well as delusions of persecution and greatness.

3. Recent Developments.
The last few decades have witnessed an increase, a "second wave" of research some suggest, in the use of the social sciences (Wilson 2009). It is characterized by greater diversity and increased sophistication, even as it continues the trajectories of earlier work. The sheer abundance of material allows for only a representative survey.

3.1. Socioeconomic and Religious Critique. One of the most fruitful areas of study has been the analysis of the social, economic and political composition of the monarchies in Israel and Judah. Scholars have employed a variety of social-science approaches to try to identify and explain the mechanisms of oppression that are denounced in the prophetic literature and the socioeconomic and class crises that generated these inequalities. These books do not offer formal sociological analyses; their descriptions are general and impressionistic. The rhetoric is strident and expressive of moral indignation. Social-science research attempts to reconstruct the realities that motivated these enduringly powerful messages.

B. Lang appeals to "rent capitalism," a form of mercantilism, to explain the exploitation described in Amos. According to this hypothesis, Israel was largely a peasant society, and the life of the peasantry was precarious. In that part of the world these small farmers were at the mercy of adverse climatic conditions and crop failures. The socioeconomic system compounded these difficulties. Formerly self-sufficient rural peasants increasingly became dependent on urban merchants, moneylenders and self-indulgent absentee landowners, and were at the mercy of tax demands beyond their means (Amos 3:15; 4:1; 5:11; 6:4-6; 8:4-5). Many would have lost their land in this web of contrary conditions. Separated from the ownership of their land, they fell into debt to pay for seed and sustenance and eventually were forced into debt slavery (Amos 2:6; 8:6). For these violations of Yahweh's moral order, the prophet announced an imminent, inescapable judgment on Israel.

J. D. Pleins combines historical critical analysis and social-science studies to reconstruct the ethical views of the entire Hebrew Bible. His discussion of the Prophetic Books occupies four substantive chapters. In his exposition of the material in Isaiah, Pleins presents the ethical convictions of Isaiah 1—35, which demand national justice and international judgment in tension with a proclamation of hope for restoration centered in *Zion, and attempts to demonstrate how they anticipate Isaiah 40—66. To unpack the concrete elements of the prophetic critique in the earlier chapters, Pleins turns to the "rent capitalism" model to explain the change from the early premonarchic land distribution system to latifundialization (Is 5:8-10). He adds that legal abuse and the incorporation of Canaanite values and personnel, which would have occurred at the taking of Jerusalem centuries before by David, created the cancerous climate condemned by the prophet. Later redactors among the returnees from the *exile co-opted that message for themselves; now the elite are depicted as the victims of empire and had the hard task of restarting national life, although the original ethical message is not totally obscured (Is 58).

This same process of muting the original prophetic voice, Pleins argues, is present in other texts. While prophets had words uniquely pertinent to their contexts, the kind of social critique exemplified by Amos and Isaiah would have been a common thread. Later redactors subverted this clarion call for justice. Two cases in point are the books of Jeremiah and Micah. In the former, subsequent layers of prose commentaries and covenant theological emphases soften and redirect the prophetic message; in the case of Micah (here Pleins bases his analysis on the work of I. J. Mosala), the radical original message is distorted by a very different ideology, which centers on the renewal of Zion.

A more sophisticated sociological analysis of the tensions within ancient Israel has roots in the Marxist model of the "Asiatic mode of production." N. K. Gottwald has done much of the pioneer work in its application to biblical studies, although he has preferred other labels, such as "tributary mode of production," or simply discussed the socioeconomic realities of a centralized state without alluding to that terminology (Gottwald 1993a; 1993b; 2001). In ancient Israel it would have had three features: the principal owner of the land was the state; society was made up largely of self-sufficient agrarian villages of multifamily households; and the centralized state had the power to extract the surplus value from the production of these villages through the collection of taxes, which supported the lifestyles of the ruling class and funded (and led to conscription for) public works. Other state functionaries, such as administrators, military leaders, merchants and priests, would have benefited from this arrangement. The prophets decried the violation of the values of the more equitable founding communitarian mode of production of Israel's earlier history. Gottwald claims that the prophets, at their best, unmasked the false consciousness of the powerful and pointed to a more emancipatory perspective (Gottwald 1991; 1996).

In a series of publications M. L. Chaney has argued that a "command economy" controlled by the crown and urban elites arose in eighth-century BC Judah and Israel (Chaney 1993; 1999; 2006). This economic development arose with the growth of international trade, regional specialization and intensification of crops for export (see 2 Chron. 26:10), and the centralization of productive land into latifundia. Evidence for these realities includes the Samaria ostraca, *lmlk* seal impressions, an increase in the number of olive oil presses, new technology for production and storage, and population growth. Extensive critical analysis of Isaiah 5:1-7 and Micah 6:9-15 reveals prophetic anger at injustices suffered by subsistence farmers and the vulnerable. D. N. Premnath has expanded upon these ideas in a full-length book.

M. J. M. Coomber turns to the insights of cultural-evolutionary theory as an alternative to the proposal of Chaney and Premnath. His is a multidimensional approach that is neither linear nor simplistic. It includes within its purview, for instance, the impact of environmental factors and religious and cultural values and thus can allow for greater complexity in social arrangements and attitudes. He uses the agrarian society of present-day Tunisia and its entrance into the global economy as a case study to illuminate the prophetic critique (in particular, Is 5:8-10; Mic 2:1-2) of the new economic conditions of the Assyrian Empire's presence and influence. A cluster of realities ignited censure. These were social (intensification of existing social hierarchies and violation of traditional patronage roles), economic (injustice by various perpetrators, including judges, political elites and their collaborators) and religious (some religious elites attacked changes because it affected their income; others balked at the loss of traditional religious influence).

W. R. Domeris questions the common view that the rise of the monarchy was the primary culprit for the oppression denounced in the HB. He, like some recent scholars, believes that material that has been attributed to the preexilic period actually belongs to a Persian context. On the basis of the lower chronology of the Israelite monarchy, Domeris proposes that the northern kingdom did not become a full-fledged state until the ninth century BC and Judah not until the eighth, and that both remained essentially peasant societies until the Persian period. Exploitation of the peasantry during the divided monarchy was caused by several factors. There were the pressures of tributary obligations to the Assyrian and Babylonian Empires. Internally, in addition to perennial environmental challenges, peasants suffered the asymmetrical distribution of power between rural dwellers and urban dwellers and the abuse of the obligations of reciprocal patronage. These conditions, along with exploitation through rents, taxation, forced labor, debt bondage and an unfair judicial system, were denounced by the prophets. With the postexilic era came a market economy, and in its train followed the emergence of large-scale peasant debt and latifundialization. Like many social-science models, Domeris's theory of Israel's social and economic history relies on studies of modern peasant societies (see Lenski).

W. J. Houston offers yet another perspective. After a detailed survey of several explanatory models, Houston claims that patron-client relationships offer the best insights into the social realities of the prophetic literature (Houston 2008; cf. Simkins). These relationships are personal, hierarchical and reciprocal. In these kinds of societies expectations are that a more powerful individual provide lower-placed persons sustenance and protection in exchange for loyalty and perhaps labor. Houston's contention is that what is decried by the prophets is the violation of these arrangements, and that patrons at all levels—from members of prominent families of local villages to urban elites and the royalty—oppressed the unfortunate through various mechanisms at their disposal, such as unfair credit practices, foreclosures and crippling taxation. In a more recent publication (Houston 2010), he proposes that prophetic accusations dealt primarily with injustice in the capital cities and other urban centers. Archaeological data suggest that villages were able to maintain some semblance of economic independence and stability—this in contrast to the working assumption of most sociological models that social stratification was generalized, and that the rural peasants were the particular victims of oppression.

These studies exhibit a general sympathy for the prophetic censure of injustice. Ideological criticism, however, now questions that social critique (see Bible and Culture Collective, *The Postmodern Bible*). It casts suspicion on interpretive strategies that might mask contemporary unequal power relations; it also reads "against the grain" of biblical texts to uncover the potentially problematic ideology of their producers that has been canonized. These readings resist the Bible and subvert its unquestioned authority in order to offer what is thought to be a more transformative engagement between it and modern audiences.

In the past, some liberation theologians appealed to the early Marx's assessment of true religion as one that should oppose oppression. For instance, J. P. Miranda argued that the authentic prophetic call of interhuman justice was to be found in a critical reconstruction of the prophets' original message, which had been obscured over time by the additions of later redactors and avoided by biblical interpreters. In other words, the true prophetic voice was exemplary, a champion for the poor. This positive view, however, is questioned by several scholars who appeal to Marxist literary theory, especially the work of T. Eagleton and F. Jameson. Although several, such as Pleins, compare and contrast the perspectives of redactional layers, ideological critics ground their views more self-consciously in sociology of literature research.

In his materialist reading of Micah, I. J. Mosala divides the book into A, B, C stages of production. Only the first directly represents the class interests of the oppressed as over against the powerful (Mic 1:10-16; 2:1-5, 8-9; 3:8-12; 5:9-14; 6:9-15). R. Boer contends that in fact the message of the prophets (Is 5:1-7 is his case study) is full of contradictions (Boer 2003; cf. Houston 2008). Although they did denounce abuses, their advocacy of justice sought to preserve the inherently unfair socioeconomic arrangements of the existing class system. What is worse, he suggests, these texts reveal that Yahweh ultimately is the source and creator of these conflicting affairs and expectations. Ideological suspicion of the Bible in the end has become theological criticism.

3.2. The Prophet in Context. Efforts to locate the prophets within ancient Israel continue, but a significant shift is that these individuals are no longer viewed as solitary outsiders but rather as those with a support group and following. This change has been pursued in several ways. D. L. Petersen assembles a matrix of various sources of data to reconstruct the complex context of the prophets, both socially and geographically. He appeals to role theory to distinguish various levels of prophetic involvement in society and to explain the skills and expectations required for each task (cf. Buss). This information is coordinated with assorted biblical labels for prophets to argue that the northern and southern kingdoms referred to the different types of prophets in diverse ways. A third dimension to his presentation refers to the work of the anthropologist I. M. Lewis.

Lewis's categories of peripheral and central prophets are useful for charting the prophets' degree of interaction with and support by the ruling social groups and institutions. This classification could clarify their connection (or opposition) to the prevailing religious symbolic universe and political ideologies.

R. R. Wilson's extensive study begins with a comprehensive survey of prophetic phenomena in contemporary societies and the ancient Near East. Based on broad anthropological research, he prefers the term "intermediary" to "prophet" as more methodologically precise. Wilson discusses in detail central and peripheral intermediaries in regards to their calling, social validation, functions and support groups. Using this information as well as biblical data, such as the titles assigned to these spokespersons and speech forms, Wilson assigns the prophetic figures in OT narratives and the Prophetic Books to either the Ephraimite or Judean streams of traditions and places them on a central-peripheral social continuum.

T. W. Overholt also looks to anthropological research, but his primary concern is to investigate the dynamics of the communicative act between an intermediary and the deity and between the intermediary and the audience. Foundational to his comparisons with the biblical material are reports of several Native American experiences and prophets, such as the Ghost Dance of 1890 and Handsome Lake. From them Overholt gleans the importance of culturally defined patterns of expectations regarding the content of prophetic messages, acts of power, and the workings of feedback and audience acknowledgment to acquire social legitimation. All of this is fruitfully applied to several passages, including the exchange between the prophet Amos and Amaziah at the Bethel sanctuary in Amos 7:10-17.

Some continue to pursue comparative possibilities with other cultures to clarify the behavior and messages of the prophets (e.g., Grabbe). Methodological variety, however, characterizes the field. D. L. Smith, for instance, uses communication theory and the sociology of knowledge to explain the sociopolitical rhetoric of the critiques in the Prophetic Books and of their visions of an alternative future world. G. Ramírez employs a group/grid anthropological model to propose that the prophet Amos best fits within an "enclavist cultural" type, which represents peripheral groups that oppose the violation of values by a society's hierarchical structure.

Efforts to explore the general social context of the prophets clearly have a long history and are sure to continue. Recently, research has taken a different turn to concentrate on a particular chronological context, more specifically the exilic and postexilic periods as the arenas in which prophetic literature was produced. An earlier view is exemplified by P. D. Hanson, who understands the milieu of *apocalyticism to be the conflict between various factions within postexilic community of Persian Yehud. In his view, marginalized prophetic visionaries and their sympathizers among the Levitical priests produced Third Isaiah (Is 56—66) and Zechariah 9—14. These texts reflect their view of the faithful, the world and its future in very different terms than does the hierarchical Zadokite priestly party of Jerusalem, whose perspective lies behind Ezekiel, Haggai, Zechariah 1—8 and Joel (cf. Brueggemann).

S. L. Cook has criticized this "conventicle" model, which is based on deprivation theory, as reducing the setting of millennial groups to the disenfranchised and oppressed. In fact, he says, these groups can represent a range of social classes and interests, galvanized by a predisposition to an imminent climactic end of their present situation. Cook suggests that Ezekiel, Zechariah 1—8; 9—14 and Joel come from different conservative central priestly groups, functioning in diverse times and settings, and that it is an error to posit their source as sharply opposed circles within the Jewish community. For his part, Gottwald appeals to materialist literary theory to argue that Isaiah 40—55 represents the ideology of descendants of exiled former Jerusalem officials in Babylon who see themselves, on the one hand, as called to preserve their distinctive faith in Yahweh over against the allure of that foreign culture and, on the other hand, as uniquely qualified by their suffering and heritage to head the restoration of Judah and its religion with the aid and approval of Cyrus, the Persian king (Gottwald 1992).

D. L. Smith-Christopher approaches exilic and postexilic texts from quite a dissimilar perspective. He contends that to understand the mindset of the displaced communities in exile, as well as that of the returnees, it is helpful to seek insights from sociological studies of groups that have migrated, whether by force or by free will, in the contemporary world (cf. D. L. Smith). This research explores how such displaced communities handle challenges of identity as a minority people and develop survival mechanisms. Three such strategies are applied to prophetic texts: Jeremiah's letter to the exiles is read as a competing tactic to Hananiah's regarding the nature and goals of exilic existence (Jer 29), Isaiah's Suffering Servant as an illustration of a "diaspora novella" representing the powerlessness of a minority community, and the exhortations of Haggai as a reflection of the concerns of a community that seeks to reestablish itself. In a more recent work Smith-Christopher turns to trauma studies of refugee communities and diasporic theology to probe the language of Ezekiel and Lamentations. K. M. O'Connor appeals to his work to probe the passionate, sometimes even violent, language of the personae in the book of Jeremiah. God, the prophet and the people desperately wrestle with the horrific circumstances and aftermath of the Babylonian invasion and try to give voice to their misgivings, despair, anger and hope.

A growing number of scholars assign the production of the Prophetic Books (along with much of the OT) to a guild of scribal elites in Persian Yehud (Edelman and Ben Zvi). These literati reworked earlier prophetic stories and oracles and created new material in the name and authority of these earlier spokespersons for God in order to communicate their own sociopolitical convictions. The harsh denunciations now found in this literature, which audiences would have connected to the ministry of those prophets, served as an avenue to attack the societal ills or imperial policies contemporary to those later redactors. This perspective has not established a consistent well-orbed, or "thick," social-science framework. An exception is the work of L. K. Handy on the book of Jonah. He proposes that its author was a scribe of Yehud's elite who created this imaginary literary world to express the centrality of the temple in Jerusalem and sovereignty of Yahweh over the Persian Empire, which is represented by Nineveh.

Lastly, another approach to cultural location sheds light on the rural setting of ancient Palestine within which the prophets lived, which often is quite foreign to modern audiences, who can be largely urban and educated. The imagery of that world lies behind many of the descriptions, metaphors and analogies that appear in the prophetic literature. D. C. Hopkins appeals to ethnographic work in Palestine to explain activities of agricultural labor and the numerous matters related to the care of fruit trees and the processing of their products that appear in multiple texts. E. F. Davis turns to contemporary work in agrarian theory to cite four areas that find an echo in the OT: the commitment to the primacy of the land, an appreciation of the wisdom woven into the natural order, the material concreteness of human existence, and the transcendent value of the land for the community as a sign of God's covenant. As does Hopkins, Davis cites agricultural activities, which are scattered throughout the Prophetic Books and include, among others, plowing (Amos 6:12; Mic 3:12), harvesting (Jer 40:10; 48:33; 50:16) and threshing (Is 28:27). In the aboricultural sphere there is mention of, for example, gathering (Jer 24:2; Amos 8:1) and the harvest of fruit and olives (Is 24:13; Mic 7:1). This agrarian way of thinking, Davis contends, is manifest in the language pictures in the prophets' messages. They speak of the yoke of oppression (Is 9:4; 47:6; Jer 27:11), reaping what was sown (Hos 8:7), experiencing the harvest of God's judgment (Is 17:5-6; Joel 3:13), the threshing of a people in war (Amos 1:3) and the pruning of the wicked (Is 18:5). Likewise, the hope of a future *peace is expressed in agricultural imagery (Amos 9:13-15; Mic 4:3-4; Zech 3:10).

3.3. Psychological Approaches. Dialogue between the disciplines of biblical studies and the wide range of theories of psychology has a long history but has increased in breadth and sophistication over the last two decades (Kille; Ellens and Rollins; Joyce). Studies have tried to uncover issues of the unconscious that may lie behind the production of texts or to analyze the psychology of their characters (see Prophecy and Psychology).

Among the Prophetic Books, the two that have garnered the most attention are Ezekiel and Jonah. For example, the psyche of Ezekiel has long proven to be fertile ground for Freudian psychoanalysis. D. J. Halperin argues that the prophet's behavior and the book's imagery suggest a troubled childhood of rejection by his mother and abuse by a dominant male, while the descriptions in Ezekiel 8:7-12 and the shocking allegories in Ezekiel 16 and Ezekiel 23 reveal a revulsion of female sexuality. These troubling characteristics should raise questions, he believes, regarding the book's authority and usefulness. Halperin's interpretation of passages has been questioned, as have his efforts to reconstruct the psychological makeup of a person from snippets drawn from an ancient text. E. F. Edinger, on the other hand, uses a Jungian lens to analyze the prophet. J. J. Pilch proposes that the opening chapters are best understood as an altered state of consciousness experience, while D. Jobling proposes that the prophet's concern for purity and orderliness reflects anal-retentive symptoms.

Jonah has attracted several Jungian readings. A Lacocque and M. A. Corey mine the narrative for what they consider to its symbolic potential. They contend that the book reflects the difficult process of the self's journey toward individuation, that condition of wholeness where the ego overcomes barriers and is reconciled to the shadow self. Their Jungian archetypes include Jonah as the ego, the sea as the anger of the unconscious, the ship's hold as the deep reality of repression, and the flight from Nineveh as the effort to avoid facing the dark side of our person.

In this increasingly therapeutic age, it is not surprising that psychological research has been utilized to engage the prophets in multiple ways. While many studies, such as those cited for Ezekiel and Jonah, focus on the possible emotional composition of the prophets, psychological approaches have gone in other directions as well. For example, R. P. Carroll uses the social psychological theory of cognitive dissonance to look at a number of prophetic texts, especially from the book of Isaiah (Carroll 1979). Carroll explores what he perceives were the hermeneutical techniques within the prophetic literature to resolve the failures of predictions and to comprehend the interplay between contingencies related to human behavior and decisions and divine sovereignty in connection with those predictions. D. G. Garber, in turn, employs literary trauma theory (particularly those arising from experiences of the bombing of Hiroshima) to explain Ezekiel's vivid imagery.

W. G. Rollins helpfully sets forth a wide

range of topics in need of future research. His list includes the conscious and unconscious factors at work in the writing of biblical literature and in the interpretative process, the archetypical nature and power of biblical material, the psychodynamics inherent within texts, the psychoanalysis of biblical characters, the presence today of biblically related religious phenomena (e.g., conversion, glossolalia, dreams, demonic possession), the salutary and constructive impact of the Bible on individuals and communities over time, and the greater integration of psychology with the study of biblical psychology and anthropology.

3.4. Gender. Social-science research has been brought to bear on prophetic texts by *feminist scholars. Comparative ethnography has been applied by feminist scholars to explore the roles and behavior of women within the religious world of ancient Israel. Anthropological sensibilities have helped broaden interest in biblical studies beyond possible female participation in official clerical positions and cultic ceremonies, which are the primary interest of the biblical material, to include gender-specific practices within that complex religious culture. Research into the economic and religious roles of women in households and village communities of traditional agricultural societies is shedding new light on biblical texts.

P. A. Bird, for instance, demonstrates that women's actions that are reported in the OT are principally an extension of female domestic roles. Snapshots appearing in the prophetic literature include the baking of raisin cakes for the Queen of Heaven (Jer 7:17-18; 44:15-25) and weeping for Tammuz (Ezek 8:14). Cooking and mourning, for the most part, were understood as tasks for women. C. Meyers presents an array of ritual behaviors usually exclusive to women that would have been connected especially to childbearing and the raising of children. These very well could have been designed to assure fertility, a safe pregnancy, delivery and lactation. Some customs, such as the washing of newborns and rubbing them with salt (Ezek 16:4-5), and the existence of female religious professionals, such as midwives, sorceresses (Is 57:3) and diviners (Ezek 13:17-23), are still evident in that part of the Mediterranean today (*see* Divination, Magic). On the basis of these comparative studies, Meyers has argued that the status and function of women within the complex peasant households and local societies of ancient Israel, which were largely domestically focused, were more significant than many suppose.

Working from the perspective of the shift from a redistributive village economy to the rise of a command economy and latifundialization with the advent of the monarchy, A. A. Keefe redefines Hosea's tropes. The woman and her sexuality are explained as symbols for productive land; the relationships with other lovers in the book's opening chapters represent the commercial ventures and political arrangements of Israel's elite with surrounding states. The prophet denounced the official cult that legitimated this systemic injustice, not the fertility beliefs of the people. G. Yee utilizes ideological criticism and various social sciences to read OT texts. She discusses the regulation of sexuality and agricultural modes of production in her interpretation of Hosea and appropriates trauma research to the message of Ezekiel.

4. Future Directions.

The expectation is that the application of social-science research into the study of prophetic literature will continue within the broad categories that have characterized this work for over a century—socioeconomic and religious critique, the context of the prophets, and psychological approaches—even as scholars probe new areas or pursue greater precision in older studies. Interest in matters related to gender, of course, will continue.

A newer voice that is becoming more prominent is that of postcolonial criticism (Sugirtharajah). Like ideological criticism and certain strands of feminism, it moves beyond a critique of oppressive interpretations to an analysis of what are deemed unacceptable attitudes within the Bible, yet its concerns lie with the colonial perspectives, such as nationalism and ethnicity, embedded in the text. Its critique of liberation theologies is that they privilege the Bible, the Christian tradition and institutions, whose monopolistic roles in the history of the Third World sometimes have been problematic. By nature, it is multidisciplinary. A related area, diaspora research, increasingly is important among minority scholars, who find multiple parallels between the biblical material and, for instance, immigrant experiences (Lee Cuéllar).

The social sciences have provided more precision in the interpretation of textual particulars. These approaches have explained customs, religious rituals, and sociopolitical and economic structures and dynamics, all of which have added greater realism to multiple passages in the HB. This concreteness allows for the better visualization of the OT and, where suitable, its appropriation for ethical reflection. Nevertheless, the caveats mentioned earlier (i.e., the problem of the availability of data, the inadequate grasp of theory, the challenges of historical reconstruction) should encourage scholars to be careful in positing hypotheses and to avoid grandiose claims. A certain degree of speculation is unavoidable, and models are subject to revision or replacement by more viable constructs. The history of social-science research in OT studies attests to both the variety and the tenuousness of these proposals. Nevertheless, the opportunity to better grasp the context and message of the prophets makes these efforts worthwhile.

See also Feminist Interpretation; Form Criticism; Liturgy and Cult; Prophecy and Psychology; Prophecy and Society; Social Justice; Visions, Prophetic; Wealth and Poverty.

Bibliography. **P. L. Berger,** "Charisma and Religious Innovation: The Social Location of Israelite Prophecy," *American Sociological Review* 28 (1963) 940-50; **Bible and Culture Collective,** *The Postmodern Bible* (New Haven: Yale University Press, 1995); **P. A. Bird,** "Notes of Gender and Religious Ritual in Ancient Israel," in *To Break Every Yoke: Essays in Honor of Marvin L. Chaney,* ed. R. B. Coote and N. K. Gottwald (SWBA 2/3; Sheffield: Sheffield Phoenix Press, 2007) 221-33; **R. Boer,** *Marxist Criticism of the Bible* (London: Sheffield Academic Press, 2003); idem, "Twenty-five Years of Marxist Biblical Criticism," *CBR* 5 (2007) 298-321; **F. Braudel,** *On History* (Chicago: University Of Chicago Press, 1980); **E. C. Broome Jr.,** "Ezekiel's Abnormal Personality," *JBL* 65 (1946) 277-92; **W. Brueggemann,** "Trajectories in Old Testament Literature and the Sociology of Israel," *JBL* 98 (1979) 161-85; **M. J. Buss,** "The Social Psychology of Prophecy" in *Prophecy: Essays Presented to Georg Fohrer on His Sixty-fifth Birthday, 6 September 1980,* ed. J. A. Emerton (BZAW 150; Berlin: de Gruyter, 1980) 1-11; **R. P. Carroll,** *When Prophecy Failed: Cognitive Dissonance in the Prophetic Traditions of the Old Testament* (New York: Seabury, 1979); idem, "Prophecy and Society," in *The World of Ancient Israel: Sociological, Anthropological, and Political Perspectives; Essays by Members of the Society for Old Testament Study,* ed. R. E. Clements (Cambridge: Cambridge University Press, 1989) 203-25; **M. D. Carroll R.,** *Contexts for Amos: Prophetic Poetics in Latin American Perspective* (JSOTSup 132; Sheffield: Sheffield Academic Press, 1992); idem, "Re-examining 'Popular Religion': Issues of Definition and Sources—Insights from Interpretive Anthropology," in *Rethinking Contexts, Rereading Texts: Contributions from the Social Sciences to Biblical Interpretation,* ed. M. D. Carroll R. (JSOTSup 299; Sheffield: Sheffield Academic Press, 2000) 146-67; **C. E. Carter,** "Opening Windows onto Biblical Worlds: Applying the Social Sciences to Hebrew Scripture," in *The Face of Old Testament Studies: A Survey of Contemporary Approaches,* ed. D. W. Baker and B. T. Arnold (Grand Rapids: Baker, 1999) 421-51; idem, "Social-Scientific Approaches," *DOTHB* 905-21; **M. L. Chaney,** "Bitter Bounty: The Dynamics of Political Economy Critiqued by the Eighth-Century Prophets," in *The Bible and Liberation: Political and Social Hermeneutics,* ed. N. K. Gottwald and R. A. Horsley (Maryknoll, NY: Orbis, 1993) 250-63; idem, "Whose Sour Grapes? The Addressees of Isaiah 5:1-7 in the Light of Political Economy," *Semeia* 87 (1999) 105-22; idem, "Micah—Models Do Matter: Political Economy and Micah 6:9-15," in *Ancient Israel: The Old Testament in Its Social Context,* ed. P. F. Esler (Minneapolis: Fortress, 2006) 145-60; **R. E. Clements,** *A Century of Old Testament Study* (rev. ed.; Cambridge: Lutterworth, 1983); **S. L. Cook,** *Prophecy and Apocalyptic: The Postexilic Social Setting* (Minneapolis: Fortress, 1995); **M. J. M. Coomber,** *Re-Reading the Prophets through Corporate Globalization: A Cultural-Evolutionary Approach to Understanding Economic Injustice in the Hebrew Bible* (Piscataway, NJ: Gorgias, 2010); **M. A. Corey,** *Job, Jonah, and the Unconscious: A Psychological Interpretation of Evil and Spiritual Growth in the Old Testament* (Lanham, MD: University Press of America, 1995); **E. F. Davis,** *Scripture, Culture, and Agriculture: An Agrarian Reading of the Bible* (New York: Cambridge University Press, 2009); **R. de Vaux,** *Ancient Israel,* trans. J. McHugh (2 vols.; New York: McGraw-Hill, 1965); **W. R. Domeris,** *Touching the Heart of*

God: The Social Reconstruction of Poverty among Biblical Peasants (LHBOTS 466; New York: T & T Clark, 2007); **T. Eagleton,** *The Function of Criticism: From "The Spectator" to Post-Structuralism* (London: Verso, 1984); **D. V. Edelman and E. Ben Zvi,** eds., *The Production of Prophecy: Constructing Prophecy and Prophets in Yehud* (London: Equinox, 2009); **E. F. Edinger,** *Ego and the Self: The Old Testament Prophets* (Toronto: Inner City Books, 2000); **J. H. Ellens and W. G. Rollins,** eds., *Psychology and the Bible: A New Way to Read the Scriptures, 2: From Genesis to Apocalyptic Vision* (Westport, CT: Praeger, 2004); **D. Emmet,** "Prophets and Their Societies," *Journal of the Royal Anthropological Society* 86, no. 1 (1956) 13-23; **P. F. Esler,** ed., *Ancient Israel: The Old Testament and Its Social Context* (Minneapolis: Fortress, 2006); **D. G. Garber Jr.,** "Traumatizing Ezekiel, the Exilic Prophet," in *Psychology and the Bible: A New Way to Read the Scriptures, 2: From Genesis to Apocalyptic Vision,* ed. J. H. Ellens and W. G. Rollins (Westport, CT: Praeger, 2004) 215-35; **N. K. Gottwald,** "The Biblical Prophetic Critique of Political Economy: Its Ground and Import," in *God and Capitalism: A Prophetic Critique of Market Economy,* ed. J. M. Thomas and V. Visick (Madison, WI: A-R Editions, 1991) 11-29; idem, "Social Class and Ideology in Isaiah 40-55," *Semeia* 59 (1992) 43-57; idem, "A Hypothesis about Social Class in Monarchic Israel in the Light of Contemporary Studies of Social Class and Social Stratification," in *The Hebrew Bible in Its Social World and in Ours* (SBLSS; Atlanta: Scholars Press, 1993a) 139-64; idem, "Social Class as an Analytical and Hermeneutical Category in Biblical Studies," *JBL* 112 (1993b) 3-22; idem, "Ideology and Ideologies in Israelite Prophecy," in *Prophets and Paradigms: Essays in Honor of Gene M. Tucker,* ed. S. B. Reid (JSOTSup 229; Sheffield: Sheffield Academic Press, 1996) 136-49; idem, *The Politics of Ancient Israel* (LAI; Louisville: Westminster/John Knox, 2001); **L. L. Grabbe,** "Shaman, Preacher, or Spiritual Medium: The Israelite Prophet in the Light of Anthropological Models," in *Prophecy and Prophets in Ancient Israel: Proceedings of the Oxford Old Testament Seminar,* ed. J. Day (LHBOTS 531; New York: T & T Clark, 2010) 117-32; **A. Haldar,** *Associations of Cult Prophets among the Ancient Semites,* trans. H. S. Harvey (Uppsala: Almquist & Wiksell, 1945); **D. J. Halperin,** *Seeking Ezekiel: Text and Psychology* (University Park: Pennsylvania State

University Press, 1993); **L. K. Handy,** *Jonah's World: Social Science and the Reading of Prophetic Story* (London: Equinox, 2007); **P. D. Hanson,** *The Dawn of Apocalyptic: The Historical and Sociological Roots of Jewish Apocalyptic Eschatology* (Philadelphia: Fortress, 1979); **T. N. Headland, K. L. Pike and M. Harris,** eds., *Emics and Etics: The Insider/Outsider Debate* (Frontiers of Anthropology 7; Newbury Park, CA: Sage, 1990); **G. A. Herion,** "The Impact of Modern and Social Science Assumptions on the Reconstruction of Israelite History," *JSOT* 34 (1986) 3-33; **D. C. Hopkins,** "'All Sorts of Field Work': Agricultural Labor in Ancient Palestine," in *To Break Every Yoke: Essays in Honor of Marvin L. Chaney,* ed. R. B. Coote and N. K. Gottwald (SWBA 2/3; Sheffield: Sheffield Phoenix Press, 2007) 149-72; **W. J. Houston,** *Contending for Justice: Ideologies and Theologies of Social Justice in the Old Testament* (rev. ed.; JSOTSup 428; London: T & T Clark, 2008); idem, "Exit the Oppressed Peasant? Rethinking the Background of Social Criticism in the Prophets," in *Prophecy and Prophets in Ancient Israel: Proceedings of the Oxford Old Testament Seminar,* ed. J. Day (LHBOTS 531; New York: T & T Clark, 2010) 101-16; **F. Jameson,** *The Political Unconscious: Narrative as a Socially Symbolic Act* (London: Methuen, 1981); **D. Jobling,** "An Adequate Psychological Approach to the Book of Ezekiel," in *Psychology and the Bible: A New Way to Read the Scriptures, 2: From Genesis to Apocalyptic Vision,* ed. J. H. Ellens and W. G. Rollins (Westport, CT: Praeger, 2004) 203-13; **A. R. Johnson,** *The Cultic Prophet in Ancient Israel* (2nd ed.; Cardiff: University of Wales Press, 1962); **P. M. Joyce,** "The Prophets and Psychological Interpretation," in *Prophecy and Prophets in Ancient Israel: Proceedings of the Oxford Old Testament Seminar,* ed. J. Day (LHBOTS 531; New York: T & T Clark, 2010) 133-48; **A. A. Keefe,** *Woman's Body and Social Body in Hosea* (JSOTSup 338; London: Sheffield Academic Press, 2001); **R. Kessler,** *The Social History of Ancient Israel: An Introduction,* trans. L. M. Maloney (Minneapolis: Fortress, 2008); **D. A. Kille,** *Psychological Biblical Criticism* (GBS; Minneapolis: Fortress, 2001); **A. Lacocque,** "A Psychological Approach to the Book of Jonah," in *Psychology and the Bible: A New Way to Read the Scriptures, 2: From Genesis to Apocalyptic Vision,* ed. J. H. Ellens and W. G. Rollins (Westport, CT: Praeger, 2004) 83-91; **B. Lang,** "The Social Organization of Peasant Poverty in Biblical Israel," in *Monotheism and the Prophetic Minority: An Essay in Biblical History and Sociology* (SWBA 1; Sheffield: Almond, 1983) 114-27; **G. Lee Cuéllar,** *Voices of Marginality: Exile and Return in Second Isaiah 40-55 and the Mexican Immigrant Experience* (AUS 7/21; New York: Peter Lang, 2008); **G. E. Lenski,** *Power and Privilege: A Theory of Social Stratification* (rev. ed; Chapel Hill: University of North Carolina Press, 1984); **I. M. Lewis,** *Ecstatic Religion* (Baltimore: Penguin, 1971); **J. Lindblom,** *Prophecy in Ancient Israel* (Oxford: Blackwell, 1962); **A. D. H. Mayes,** *The Old Testament in Sociological Perspective* (London: Pickering, 1989); **P. McNutt,** *Reconstructing the Society of Ancient Israel* (LAI; Louisville: Westminster/ John Knox, 1999); **C. Meyers,** *Discovering Eve: Ancient Israelite Women in Context* (New York; Oxford University Press, 1988); idem, *Household and Holiness: The Religious Culture of Israelite Women* (Minneapolis: Fortress, 2005); **J. P. Miranda,** *Marx and the Bible: A Critique of the Philosophy of Oppression*, trans. J. Eagleson (Maryknoll, NY: Orbis, 1974); **S. Mowinckel,** *The Psalms in Israel's Worship*, trans. D. R. Ap-Thomas (2 vols. in 1; Nashville: Abingdon, 1962); **K. M. O'Connor,** "Reclaiming Jeremiah's Violence," in *Aesthetics of Violence in the Prophets*, ed. J. M. O'Brien and C. Franke (LHBOTS 517; New York: T & T Clark, 2010) 37-49; **T. W. Overholt,** *Channels of Prophecy: The Social Dynamics of Prophetic Activity* (Minneapolis: Fortress, 1989); idem, *Cultural Anthropology and the Old Testament* (GBS; Minneapolis: Fortress, 1996); **D. L. Petersen,** *The Roles of Israel's Prophets* (JSOTSup 17; Sheffield: JSOT Press, 1981); **J. J. Pilch,** "Ezekiel—An Altered State of Consciousness Experience," in *Ancient Israel: The Old Testament in Its Social Context*, ed. P. F. Esler (Minneapolis: Fortress, 2006) 208-22; **J. D. Pleins,** *The Social Visions of the Hebrew Bible: A Theological Introduction* (Louisville: Westminster/John Knox, 2001); **D. N. Premnath,** *Eighth Century Prophets: A Social Analysis* (St. Louis: Chalice Press, 2003); **G. Ramírez,** "The Social Location of the Prophet Amos in Light of the Group/Grid Cultural Anthropological Model," in *Prophets and Paradigms: Essays in Honor of Gene M. Tucker*, ed. S. B. Reid (JSOTSup 229; Sheffield: Sheffield Academic Press, 1996) 136-49; **J. W. Rogerson,** *Anthropology and the Old Testament* (BibSem; Sheffield: JSOT Press, 1984); **W. G. Rollins,** "The Bible and Psychology: New Directions in Biblical Scholarship," *Pastoral Psychology* 45,

no. 3 (1997) 163-79; **W. G. Runciman,** *A Treatise on Social Theory, 1: The Methodology of Social Theory* (Cambridge: Cambridge University Press, 1983); **R. A. Simkins,** "Patronage and the Political Economy of Monarchic Israel," *Semeia* 87 (1999) 123-44; **D. L. Smith,** *The Religion of the Landless: The Social Context of the Babylonian Exile* (Bloomington, IN: Meyer-Stone, 1989); **G. V. Smith,** *The Prophets as Preachers: An Introduction to the Hebrew Prophets* (Nashville: Broadman & Holman, 1994); **W. R. Smith,** *Lectures on the Religion of the Semites, First Series: Fundamental Institutions* (London: Adam & Charles Black 1889); **D. L. Smith-Christopher,** *A Biblical Theology of Exile* (OBT; Minneapolis: Fortress, 2002); **R. S. Sugirtharajah,** *The Bible and the Third World: Precolonial, Colonial, and Postcolonial Encounters* (Cambridge: Cambridge University Press, 2001); **L. Wallis,** "Sociological Significance of the Bible," *American Journal of Sociology* 12, no. 4 (1907) 532-52; **M. Weber,** *Ancient Judaism*, trans. and ed. H. H. Gerth and D. Martindale (Glencoe, IL: Free Press, 1952); idem, *The Theory of Social and Economic Organization*, trans. A. R. Anderson and T. Parsons (New York: Free Press, 1964); **R. R. Wilson,** *Prophecy and Society in Ancient Israel* (Philadelphia: Fortress, 1980); idem, *Sociological Approaches to the Old Testament* (GBS; Philadelphia: Fortress, 1984); idem, "Reflections on Social Science Criticism," in *Method Matters: Essays on the Interpretation of the Hebrew Bible in Honor of David L. Petersen*, ed. J. M. LeMon and K. H. Richards (SBLRBS 56; Atlanta: Society of Biblical Literature, 2009) 505-22; **G. Yee,** *Poor Banished Children of Eve: Woman as Evil in the Hebrew Bible* (Minneapolis: Fortress, 2003).

M. D. Carroll R.

SOCIETY. *See* PROPHECY AND SOCIETY.

SON OF MAN. *See* DANIEL: BOOK OF.

SORCERY. *See* DIVINATION, MAGIC.

SOVEREIGN, GOD AS. *See* GOD.

SPIRIT OF YAHWEH

The majority of references to the Spirit of Yahweh in the OT occur in the prophetic literature from the exilic period and after. In total, the term *rûaḥ* is used 389 times in the OT, including eleven instances in the *Aramaic chapters of Daniel (Even-Shoshan, 1063-66). The term *rûaḥ* is applied to God in approximately 107 references. This number includes the phrase "Spirit of Yahweh" (*rûaḥ yhwh*), which occurs twenty-seven times, and "Spirit of God" (*rûaḥ ʾĕlōhîm*), which appears fifteen times in Hebrew and five times in Aramaic. Due to the prominence of "Spirit" [*rûaḥ*] references in many OT contexts, this article provides a brief synopsis of this term in the Pentateuch, the Former Prophets and the Writings.

The immediate context of *rûaḥ* usually indicates whether the term refers to a human anthropological function (approximately 167 occurrences) or a wind (approximately 115 times). Yet, within these contexts there may be a wide and complex range of meanings to indicate "mind," "breath," "heart," "air" or similar terms (Tengström, 373-79; Hildebrandt, 1-27). When the term refers to a human function, it is used in an anthropological or psychological sense. A primary connotation of *rûaḥ* in relation to humankind is its function as the animating principle of life. Due to the importance of context for the meaning of Hebrew words, the interpretation of *rûaḥ* in regard to humankind, God or wind is at times tentative. Moreover, the question often arises whether the Spirit of Yahweh in the OT is understood as an actual person or hypostasis. Systematic theologians debate this matter extensively (for a good synopsis, see Berkhof, 87, 95-97). A biblical analysis indicates that the OT authors advance in their understanding of the Spirit of Yahweh's roles, function and pervasive activities. This is evident from the increase of references to the *rûaḥ*, which intensify during Israel's history to the exilic period. References grow in quantity as well as in the range of meaning in relation to the Spirit's functions in creation, the life of Israel as a nation, leadership roles and prophecy. This development in the understanding of the *rûaḥ*, which typically indicates the powerful presence of God to effect the divine will, may be seen in two examples. In Psalm 51 the psalmist refers to the *rûaḥ* four times to show how the *rûaḥ* interacts with humankind through interpersonal ways. In one reference the psalmist uses the epithet "Holy Spirit" to express the plea that God would not remove his presence from his life. A similar reference is made in regard to the nation of Israel where the "Holy Spirit" is grieved by the nation's response. There is no doubt that

in Isaiah 63:10-11 this term refers to the presence of God in an active role in Israel's life.

1. The Spirit of God in the Pentateuch
2. The Spirit of Yahweh in the Former Prophets
3. The Spirit in the Writings
4. The Spirit of Yahweh in the Latter Prophets

1. The Spirit of God in the Pentateuch.

The OT begins with the phrase *rûaḥ ʾĕlōhîm* to feature the work of the Spirit of God in creation (Gen 1:2). This reference presents the presence and activity of God in bringing forth the created world through the agency of the word and the Spirit (Hildebrandt, 28-66; Tengström, 385). The theme of creation in the OT rests on the conception that the Spirit of God brings order out of chaos. What God commands in regard to the created world, the Spirit shapes into reality (Ps 33:6; Is 40:13). Furthermore, humankind is created and animated by the breath of God (Gen 6:17). The *rûaḥ* may also refer to a variety of human dispositions (Gen 26:35; 41:8; 45:27; Ex 6:9; Num 14:24). Often the translation of *rûaḥ* as "wind" indicates an instrumental usage by God to accomplish a divine purpose (Ex 10:13, 19). The *rûaḥ* causes the floodwaters to recede (Gen 8:1); the wind from God also brings the plague of locusts over the land of Egypt (Ex 10:23) and parts the Reed Sea (Ex 14:21) to provide Israel with an escape route. This intervention from Yahweh is also recorded in the Song of the Sea, where "the blast [*rûaḥ*] of your nostrils" (Ex 15:8) and "you blew with your *rûaḥ* "(Ex 15:10) describe the agency whereby Israel is delivered from Egypt. After this exceptional event, Israel is established as a nation in a covenantal relationship with Yahweh (Hildebrandt, 67-72).

In addition to these foundational concepts, the Pentateuch also presents a number of references to God's influence in providing leadership skills to specific individuals. The first instance of this phenomenon occurs when Pharaoh recognizes a special endowment of wisdom in Joseph, who also has the ability to interpret dreams. Joseph's unique ability is attributed to the *rûaḥ ʾĕlōhîm*, whose presence earns Joseph the leadership position as vizier of Egypt (Gen 41:6). Moreover, similar expressions are made in reference to practical leadership qualities or skills as given by the Spirit for a particular task. Those involved in the tabernacle construction and the making of sacred garments are given "wisdom" (*ḥokmâ*), which gives them the special abilities for their tasks (Ex 28:3). Specifically, Bezalel is "filled" (*mālē'*) with the *rûaḥ 'ĕlōhîm* (Ex 31:3; 35:31), which not only provides the ability and knowledge for work in all kinds of crafts, but also gives Bezalel and Oholiab the ability to teach others their skills (Ex 35:34; cf. Ex 36:1-2).

Another aspect introduced in the Pentateuch regarding the influence of the *rûaḥ* for leadership in Israel involves prophecy. An extraordinary experience occurs with seventy elders who "prophesy" when the *rûaḥ* comes upon them (Num 11). These elders are not designated as prophets. The term *nābî'* ("prophet") does appear fourteen times in the Pentateuch, in reference to Abraham (Gen 20:7), Aaron (Ex 7:1) and the paradigmatic Moses (Deut 34:10-12). The biblical evidence that Moses gave leadership by the *rûaḥ yhwh* is implicit for the most part in the Pentateuch, but it is made explicit in Numbers 11 and in Isaiah 63. Moses was instructed by Yahweh to call seventy officials and leaders together. "Then the LORD came down in the cloud and spoke to him, and took some of the Spirit that was on him and put it on the seventy elders. And as soon as the Spirit rested on them, they prophesied. But they did not continue doing it" (Num 11:25 ESV). Implicitly, the *rûaḥ* that is understood to be on Moses is now distributed among the seventy elders. This narrative provides some background to Moses' role as God's exemplary prophet (Deut 18:15-18), mediator and intercessor for the nation (Ex 33:12-16; Num 11:1; 12:13; 14:16-19). In this context Moses expresses the programmatic desire that Yahweh should put the *rûaḥ* on all of his people (Num 11:29).

Joshua was among the seventy who experienced Spirit reception and prophetic utterance (Num 11). As for wisdom, Joshua is identified as being filled with the *rûaḥ ḥokmâ* for leadership. Moses placed his hands on Joshua (Deut 34:9) to commission him, and with the *rûaḥ* Joshua was enabled to lead Israel in the conquest of Canaan (cf. Num 27:18). In another instance, the coming of the *rûaḥ* on the enigmatic Balaam also results in the activity of prophecy. When the *rûaḥ 'ĕlōhîm* comes upon him, he is inspired with two oracles (Num 24:2-24). The consequences of Balaam's prophecies indicate features normally associated with the "later"

prophets of Yahweh. His "inspired" oracles have extensive future implications for Israel.

2. The Spirit of Yahweh in the Former Prophets.

The concepts introduced in the Pentateuch take considerable shape or development in the literature of the Former Prophets. In the book of Judges there are seven references to the *rûaḥ yhwh* (Judg 3:10; 6:34; 11:29; 13:25; 14:6, 19; 15:14). In each occurrence the phrase indicates a special provision from the Lord to four individual leaders who are enabled by the Spirit of Yahweh to accomplish deliverance from oppressors. In each case there are violations to the covenantal relationship that have led to Israel's oppression. When Israel cries out for deliverance, the Spirit of Yahweh comes upon Othniel, Gideon, Jephtah and Samson at different times "to effectuate Yahweh's salvation of His covenant people" (Martin, 22). In Judges the use of *rûaḥ yhwh* features the covenantal relationship with Israel and the Lord's intention to bless his chosen people. This emphasis continues into the period of the monarchy, where the *rûaḥ* comes upon Saul and David to enable their leadership in Israel (1 Sam 10; 16). In addition to the undergirding of leadership functions, the prophetic element initiated in Numbers 11 continues to develop. For Israel's first king, the coming of the *rûaḥ yhwh/'ĕlōhîm* causes Saul to prophesy (1 Sam 10:6, 10; 11:6; 19:20, 23). The nature of this "ecstatic" outburst is an external manifestation of prophesying that serves as a public indicator of Spirit reception to authorize Saul as the designated leader. The rejection of Saul as king is made complete when the *rûaḥ yhwh* departs from him (1 Sam 16:14). The *rûaḥ* that gave Saul authority and power to conquer the enemy is now replaced by the evil *rûaḥ*, which is characterized by mental anguish, fear and depression. This experience for Saul introduces elements of ecstatic prophecy that sometimes leads to behavioral aberrations (1 Sam 19:20-24) and conflict between prophets (1 Kings 13; 18:28-29; 22:10-28) (see Hildebrandt, 159-62, 179-87).

After Saul is rejected as king, David is elected by Yahweh (1 Sam 16:1-12) and anointed by Samuel. Consequent to his anointing, "the *rûaḥ yhwh* rushes upon David from that time onward" (1 Sam 16:13). This act of anointing symbolizes the Spirit's endowment on the king, who is authorized and enabled to carry out leadership duties in Israel. At the end of his reign as king, David attributes his successes to the *rûaḥ* on him (2 Sam 22) and claims prophetic inspiration: "The Spirit of the Lord spoke through me, his word was on my tongue" (2 Sam 23:2). Furthermore, the *rûaḥ yhwh* is shown to be active in the Elijah and Elisha narratives (1 Kings 18:12; 2 Kings 2:16), which explains some of the unique miracles and transfer motif in these episodes. These prophets led the fight against apostasy in the nation. When Elijah is taken away by the Spirit of Yahweh (1 Kings 18:12; cf. 2 Kings 2:16), his prophetic authority is transferred to Elisha (see Hildebrandt, 174-79).

3. The Spirit in the Writings.

References to the activity of the *rûaḥ* are limited in the Writings, but there are several commentaries on concepts initiated in the Pentateuch. God breathes life into his creation and thereby animates, renews and sustains the cyclical patterns that bring life and fertility to each generation of humankind (Job 26:13; 32:8; 33:4; Ps 104:30; 147:18). Wisdom in the proverbs emanates from God and may be compared to a spring that is poured out, as in Proverbs 1:23: "I will pour out my *rûaḥ* to you." Wisdom is like a charismatic gift of the Spirit that may be poured out like an anointing oil or in the sense of revitalizing God's people (Is 44:3). Furthermore, the continued presence of God with his people is evident. Providential care and guidance are given by the *rûaḥ* (Ps 33:4-9; 139:7; 143:10). After his sin with Bathsheba, David fears for the loss of the *rûaḥ*, which he knew would debilitate him as king. David pleads with God to not take the Holy Spirit from him (Ps 51:11). In 1-2 Chronicles the Levitical priests give prophetic leadership to the community. Inspired speech often is connected to the *rûaḥ* coming upon the priests (1 Chron 12:18). The Spirit of prophecy continues to be as vital in the exilic period as it was during the monarchy (2 Chron 15:1, 8; 18:23; 20:14; 24:20). The Chronicler names more than twenty-four of these prophets! Two notable summaries are made by Nehemiah. This first one provides a historical review of Yahweh's dealings with Israel that highlights the preservation and guidance of the nation by Yahweh's Spirit. "Because of your great compassion you did not abandon them in the wilderness. By day the pillar of cloud did not fail to guide them on their path, nor the pillar of fire by night to shine on the way they were to take. You gave your good Spirit to instruct them. You did not withhold your manna from their mouths, and you gave them water for their thirst. For forty years you sustained them in the wilderness; they lacked nothing, their clothes did not wear out nor did their feet become swollen" (Neh 9:19-21 NIV). Nehemiah also notes the role of the prophetic word: "For many years you were patient with them. By your Spirit you warned them through your prophets. Yet they paid no attention, so you gave them into the hands of the neighboring peoples" (Neh 9:30 NIV). Yahweh gave his "good *rûaḥ* to instruct them," to provide for them, and to sustain them on their journey. The nature of their instruction came through the prophets, who were endowed with the Spirit, but not often were they receptive to the prophetic word.

4. The Spirit of Yahweh in the Latter Prophets.

The word *rûaḥ* does not appear in all of the Prophetic Books (it is not used in Obadiah, Nahum, Zephaniah). When it is employed, it has a variety of connotations, from wind to breath to the presence of Yahweh. In Daniel *rûaḥ* occurs fifteen times, including eleven in the Aramaic chapters. It occurs infrequently in Hosea (7x), Amos (1x), Jonah (2x), Micah (3x), Habakuk (2x), Haggai (4x), Zechariah (9x), Malachi (2x). Jeremiah (18x) uses it mainly in reference to the wind as God's instrument of judgment. In the absence of Spirit references in these prophets there is more of an emphasis on the word of Yahweh. However, the occurrence of *rûaḥ* with a developed theological significance intensifies during the exile and postexilic period, where *rûaḥ* appears often in Isaiah (51x) and in Ezekiel (52x). Although Joel only refers to the *rûaḥ* twice (Joel 2:28-29 [3:1-2 MT]), it deserves emphasis as a "theologically important statement concerning the outpouring of the spirit at the eschaton" (Tengström, 373). In this section, the discussion will mainly concern the occurrences of *rûaḥ* that denote an influence among God's people (judgment and restoration) and the *rûaḥ* in prophecy and in the leadership of individuals.

4.1. The Spirit of Yahweh and Israel: Judgment and Restoration. The prophetic literature serves as a record of God's dealings with Israel according to the covenant established at Mount Sinai (Ex 19). The prophets present their messages of judgment for *covenant breach and often use the word *rûaḥ* to indicate God's *wrath that may come upon his people like a "scorching breath." Furthermore, Isaiah uses the epithet "the Holy Spirit" to personalize the divine grief that is caused when Israel breaks the covenantal agreement (Is 63:10). This is evident in the indictment of Isaiah 1, which proclaims a perverted cultus and Israel's broken relationship with God. However, the sins of Israel will be dealt with through a process of cleansing and judgment. "The LORD will wash away the filth of the women of Zion; he will cleanse the bloodstains from Jerusalem by a *rûaḥ* of judgment and a *rûaḥ* of fire" (Is 4:4). The word *mišpāṭ*, used several times here, is a legal term for "right judgment" in the sense of a judicial decision rendered by the intervention of Yahweh. A cultic purifying is implied that brings individuals and the community into a right relationship with Yahweh. In the prophetic literature this procedure of judgment and cleansing is the prerequisite to Yahweh's "pouring out of the Spirit" on his people (Is 32:15; 44:3; Ezek 39:29). In Isaiah 4:4 the sins of Israel will be cleansed by Yahweh's purifying work through his *rûaḥ*. This concept is developed further in Isaiah. "See, the Name of the LORD comes from afar, with burning anger and dense clouds of smoke; his lips are full of wrath, and his tongue is a consuming fire" (Is 30:27). The breath (*rûaḥ*) of the Lord is likened to a stream of sulfur (Is 30:33), and the wrath of God may be poured out in fiery anger (Ezek 21:31; 22:31). When the breath of Yahweh blows, the grass withers and the flower fades (Is 40:7). In these passages the opposite effect of God's beneficence, which is often "poured out" on his people through the Spirit, is experienced. In this sense, God comes like a consuming fire that burns, refines and, on occasion, destroys.

The prophet Isaiah also uses this metaphor to declare God's judgment on the enemies of Israel, who are punished by a "scorching wind [*rûaḥ*]" (Is 11:15; cf. Is 27:8; 30:28; 33:11; 40:7; Hos 13:15). This may refer to the hot east sirocco or metaphorically to a foreign power. In these passages the presence of God is manifested in a theophany that not only destroys the enemies of Israel but also purifies the nation

through a mitigated punishment (cf. 2 Kings 17:17b-18). This is God's manifested power of judgment, sometimes for Israel's foes, but at times also turned upon his people (Goldingay 1997, 13). Isaiah also prophesies that God's judgment will be meted out by "the branch from Jesse," who will exercise judgment by the Spirit (Is 11:15). Through his intervention the remnant will be restored.

An illustration of Israel's covenantal breach occurs in Isaiah 30:1: "'Woe to the obstinate children,' declares the LORD, 'to those who carry out plans that are not mine, forming an alliance, but not by my Spirit [*rûaḥ*], heaping sin upon sin.'" This oracle is given during the time of revolt led by Hezekiah against Sennacherib (703-701 BC) (see Kaiser, 283-85). Rather than turning to Yahweh for security, the leaders turned to Egypt for protection even though Egypt was also weak and in need of assistance. The prophetic rebuke specifically addresses the leaders who devised their plans apart from the direction and oracle of Yahweh (cf. Jer 37:17-21; 38:14-28). Instead of consulting "my *rûaḥ*," the leaders contrived an alliance with Egypt and ratified it according to their plans and wisdom. Another passage sets forth the antithesis between trust in God and trust in humanity: "But the Egyptians are mere mortals and not God; their horses are flesh and not spirit [*rûaḥ*]" (Is 31:3). The difference in the nature of God and flesh, and the strength of God and flesh, are here distinguished (cf. Ezek 28:2, 9; Hos 11:9) to indicate the necessity for dependence on God and the Spirit. In an oracle of judgment for Edom, God's actions are illustrated in the way he can intervene: "For it is his mouth that has given the order, and his Spirit [*rûaḥ*] will gather them together" (Is 34:16). The frequent connection between the spoken word and the *rûaḥ* that will carry it out is clear in this passage.

Isaiah 63 is a reflection on Yahweh's vengeance as well as his deeds accomplished on behalf of Israel. It takes the form of a community lament, however, because God's gracious acts for the chosen people were met with rebellion rather than praise and adoration. The consequence of their sin was due to their poor response to Yahweh's blessings. Isaiah records the lament: "Yet they rebelled and grieved his Holy Spirit. So he turned against them as their enemy, and he himself fought against them" (Is

63:10). The result of their transgression was that they "grieved his Holy Spirit," indicating the sorrowful response of the *rûaḥ* due to the consequence of Israel's failure to acknowledge the one who "brought them through the sea" and who it was that set "the Holy Spirit" among them to guide and deliver them: "Then his people recalled the days of old, the days of Moses and his people—where is he who brought them through the sea, with the shepherd of his flock? Where is he who set his Spirit of holiness among them, who sent his glorious arm of power to be at Moses' right hand, who divided the waters before them, to gain for himself everlasting renown, who led them through the depths?" (Is 63:11-13a NIV). This passage marks an important step toward the use of "Spirit" "in relation to God in which each and all of his acts can be attributed to his Spirit or to God's Holy Spirit" (Westermann, 389). The community of faith recognizes the miracle of the *exodus and the resulting "rest" as the provision of Yahweh by his *rûaḥ* (Is 63:14). They now lament their improper response, which grieved the *rûaḥ* and caused their punishment. Moreover, they realize that restoration may be affected by the renewed work of the Spirit on their behalf.

4.2. The Spirit of Yahweh and the Messianic Servant. In the Former Prophets several kings were anointed for their royal roles. This act symbolized the presence of the *rûaḥ yhwh* to prove the authority and provide abilities for the role of "judge" or "king." The term "anoint" gives rise to the concept of the messiah (1 Sam 10:1-2; 16:13; 2 Sam 5:2; 6:21) and indicates the special relationship of the anointed one to Yahweh. Anointing is a sacramental sign that confers authority to act and is tied closely to the bestowal of *rûaḥ* for enablement. The externally flowing oil represented the internal reality of the Spirit's filling. The four main messianic qualities connected to kingship and anointing are (1) the election of an individual; (2) anointing by priest or prophet; (3) Spirit endowment; (4) the public demonstration of the gift in bringing about victory over enemies (Knierim, 114-15).

This is the background to some of the messianic concepts presented in the book of Isaiah. The prophet presents some of the characteristics of the ruler whom Yahweh will raise up (Is 11:1-2). The charismatic endowment of the *rûaḥ* that characterizes his rule is emphasized by the fourfold use of *rûaḥ* in this passage. The *rûaḥ*

yhwh will "rest" upon him and qualify him for his task. This term for "rest" (*nûaḥ*) is reminiscent of the Spirit resting on the elders (Num 11:25-26) and on Elisha (2 Kings 2:15). The first two qualities given by the Spirit are "wisdom" (skill necessary for the application of knowledge) and "understanding" (discernment necessary for proper administrative functions). The king also receives the *rûaḥ* of "counsel" to assist him with the intellectual ability and volition required to make correct judgments. The *rûaḥ* is the motivating power of the king's rule that bestows the necessary leadership virtues characteristic of ideal kingship. He receives the *rûaḥ* of "knowledge" indicative of an intimate relationship with Yahweh (*see* Messiah).

This ideal ruler will mete out judicial pronouncements with righteousness and justice. It is probable that Isaiah 11:1-9 brings the military charisma of the judges and the judicial charisma of the king together. Thus, the wisdom of Solomon for judicial administration (1 Kings 15:23; 16:5, 27; 2 Kings 18:20) and the martial charisma of Saul and David are merged to include the two main functions of the messianic role (Mettinger, 249). His reign is characterized by wisdom and compassion through which all may find help (Is 11:3-5). Some of these concepts are also presented in Isaiah 9:6-7, where a son is born to reign on David's throne.

Several texts stand out in the book of Isaiah that usually are referred to as the Servant Songs (Is 42:1-9; 49:1-13; 50:4-11; 52:13—53:12), but Isaiah 61:1-3 should also be included in this category (*see* Servant of Yahweh). It is mainly in Isaiah 40—55 that the prophet focuses attention on the servant of Yahweh. The significant themes reiterated in these chapters include the investiture of the *rûaḥ* (Is 42:1), the proclaiming of good news (Is 40:9; 41:27; 52:7) and various acts of mercy (Is 42:5-9). In Isaiah 40—42 the *rûaḥ* has a central role for the exiles. Yahweh has not left them and assures them that he has chosen a servant (*'ebed*) through whom salvation will come (Is 41:8-10). In Isaiah 42:1 the *'ebed* is Yahweh's chosen one, whom he will uphold for the task entrusted to him. The relationship between Yahweh and the chosen servant is intimate, as expressed by the term "delight." It is by Yahweh's power and presence (*rûaḥ*) that the success of the servant's mission is assured. The promise of the *rûaḥ* comes before the extent of his service is presented. His task, characterized by *justice (*mišpāṭ*) and righteousness, has far-reaching consequences for the nations. As a central term of the text, *mišpāṭ* is the characteristic feature of the servant's role (cf. Is 9:6; Jer 21:11). The descendant of David on whom Yahweh's breath will rest is given wisdom, understanding, counsel, might and recognition (all qualities relevant in Is 40—42) to enable him to decide for the poor and weak of the earth with right and faithfulness (Goldingay 2005, 154).

The coming of the Spirit on the servant will be evident by his character and in the way he serves others. His calm, quiet disposition and the manner of his service contrast with that of the soldier (Is 42:2). Through the *rûaḥ* he takes care to represent the helpless and brings forth justice in "truth" (Is 42:2-3). He is kept faithful to his role, and regardless of the consequences, justice will be established. In his law (*tôrâ*) the islands will place their hope and trust. The scope of the servant's task is broadened from that of a focus on the nations to a universal ministry (Is 42:4; cf. Is 2:13). The task is further elaborated on in Isaiah 42:6-7, where the servant will be made a "covenant for the people." Through the servant Yahweh will effectively transform others. The servant will be a covenant pledge for the world because he embodies the covenant and perpetuates it for Israel (Dumbrell, 192-94). This far-reaching ministry is made possible by the Spirit-endowed servant.

A further consequence of the servant's ministry is to open blind eyes, to liberate prisoners from dungeons, and to free prisoners who dwell in darkness. The subject of the infinitives in the Hebrew text is not as immediately evident in Isaiah 42:7 as in Isaiah 61:1-3. Both texts proclaim the salvation and spiritual illumination to come. They will be liberated from their captivity through the work of the anointed servant of the Lord, who announces, "The *rûaḥ yhwh* is upon me" (Is 61:1). The words in the prophet's mouth are characteristic of the Davidic king whom Yahweh raises up as the royal servant. The authority of the proclaimed message and the actions carried out by the servant are attributed to the inspiration and power given by the Spirit. This reaffirms that restoration and order will yet be realized through the work of the servant, whose twofold task is marked by the *rûaḥ*. The first task involves the proclamation of "good news to the poor," of "freedom for the captives" and of "release from darkness for the prisoners." He is to proclaim "the year of the LORD's favor and the day of vengeance." The second task involves several activities. He is sent to "bind up the broken-hearted," to "comfort all who mourn," to "provide for those who grieve," and to bestow on them "a crown of beauty," "the oil of gladness" and "a garment of praise." The servant is endowed with the Spirit for this broad program of restoration. The exiles are not to abandon hope, but instead look for the deliverer whom Yahweh has chosen and equipped to address the present and future concerns of the community.

4.3. The Spirit of Yahweh and Israel: Covenantal Restoration. The threat of judgment that the prophets presented "by the word of the LORD" came to pass on Israel as well as on their enemies. This was not the last word, however, for intermingled with the word of judgment came words of hope for restoration. During the exilic period the prophets grew in their understanding of the *rûaḥ yhwh*. They applied the necessity of the Spirit's involvement for new life and transformation in the people as well as in nature. The reality of the *rûaḥ yhwh* with Israel revitalized expectations of restoration to their land (Sklba, 1-3). The prophets not only gave adequate reasons for the exile of God's people, but they also spoke of a new beginning and a return to Israel. In order to experience the restoration and renewal prophesied, however, the people were called to respond in repentance, faith and covenant loyalty (Hildebrandt, 91-103).

The hope for restoration and all that it implied is particularly evident in Isaiah 40—55, which presents vivid images of the restoration longed for. There will be fertility and an abundance of water in the land (Is 40; 41:17-20; 49:19-26). The people of God will be reestablished in a covenantal relationship with Yahweh (Is 55:3-5; 45:9-23). Cities will be rebuilt and repopulated, and God's blessings will abound (Is 44:24-28). The content of Isaiah 32 refers to a future time when renewal within the nation will take place by the coming of the *rûaḥ*. Renewal will not come until "the *rûaḥ* is poured upon us from on high." The phrase "from on high" refers to the heavenly abode of Yahweh, from where the Spirit of God descends (cf. Is 57:15; Jer 25:30). Verbs that refer to the *rûaḥ* as being "poured out" are frequent in prophetic literature (Is 32:15; 44:3; Ezek 39:29; Joel 2:28-

29 [3:1-2 MT]). They portray metaphorically the blessings brought by the Spirit just as the rain brings about the fructification and fertility of the earth. The coming of the Spirit, which will change the character and nature of the people, indicates a new attitude to the lordship and rule of God. "For I will pour water on the thirsty land, and streams on the dry ground; I will pour my Spirit [*rûaḥ*] on your offspring, and my blessing on your descendants" (Is 44:3 NIV). In this process the prophetic word inspired by the *rûaḥ* will have a primary role in the covenant renewal (cf. Is 59:21).

Ezekiel, who prophesied during the years 593-571 BC, presents a similar message after a period of time when many prophets avoided the term *rûaḥ* (notably Jeremiah). Ezekiel emphasizes Yahweh's work in the exilic community to vindicate his name (Ezek 36:20-23) and cleanse his people by a new creative act that would restore the people to a covenant relationship with God (Zimmerli, 568). The essence of the "new thing" that God would do concerned the persistent sin of Israel that defiled the land. The problem was Israel's apparent inability to fulfill the command of obedience and faithfulness to the covenant bond (Ezek 2:3-8; 15—16). Now Yahweh will intervene: "I will give you a new heart and put a new spirit [*rûaḥ*] in you; I will remove from you your heart of stone and give you a heart of flesh. And I will put my Spirit [*rûaḥ*] in you and move you to follow my decrees and be careful to keep my laws" (Ezek 36:26-27 NIV [cf. Ezek 11:19; 18:31; 37:14]). The Spirit of Yahweh "transforms" the human spirit to motivate a new and favorable response to the covenant.

The terms employed in these passages are reminiscent of Jeremiah 31:31-34, which signifies the internalization of religion by way of the "new thing" that Yahweh was ready to do (North, 236-37). Although the new covenant indicates new features such as the universal knowledge of God (Jer 31:34), universal peace, security, prosperity and possession of the Spirit (Is 4:2; Jer 32:41; Ezek 34:25-27; 37:26; Hos 2:18; Joel 2:32), it is not new in the sense of "better." It was new in the sense that Yahweh was prepared to put the *law in the hearts of the people, enabling them to live in accordance with the covenant obligations through the power of the *rûaḥ*. The goal of Yahweh's actions was to bring about a new attitude toward him whereby the covenantal reality of "I will be their God, and they will be my people" is experienced as originally intended (Jer 7:11; 11:4; 24:7; 30:22; 31:1, 34; Ezek 36:28).

The intervention of Yahweh in the circumstances of God's people involved gathering the people to their own land (Ezek 36:24), purifying and cleansing them from defilement (Ezek 36:35), and replacing the "heart of stone" with a "new heart" and a "new spirit." The intent of this is clearest in Ezekiel 36:27, which indicates that Yahweh's Spirit would be given in order to motivate the recipients to follow his decrees and keep his laws. Yahweh would actively participate in human obedience and as a result vindicate his name (Ezek 36:36). Moreover, the personal knowledge and presence of God, which often were limited to the priests and prophets, would be made available to all of God's people.

A metaphor of Israel's restoration is presented in Ezekiel 37, where the term *rûaḥ* appears ten times. The vision of the valley of bones is structured in two sections, beginning with a vision (Ezek 37:1-10) and ending with the interpretation (Ezek 37:11-14). The question put to the prophet is whether the bones can come to life. His answer indicates the thrust of the whole passage: only God knows whether the nation can be restored to their former glory, which depends on the coming of the Spirit. The term *rûaḥ* in Ezekiel 37:5, 6, 8, 10 is closely related to the "breath of life" given to all human beings, apart from which existence is impossible. The prophet features the renewing of the covenant relationship to show a development from the "life spirit" (Ezek 37:1-8) to Yahweh's Spirit (Ezek 37:9-14). Yahweh's purifying and sanctifying work prepares them to receive Yahweh's spirit (Launderville 2007, 141).

Yahweh declares, "I will put my Spirit [*rûaḥ*] in you and you will live, and I will settle you in your own land" (Ezek 37:14). The purpose of this event is to make clear to Israel that God is the one who brings to fulfillment the divine promises and thereby vindicates his name. The emphasis of the passage is on the supernatural, life-giving power of Yahweh, who alone can renew and restore the nation back to life in their land. This idea is reiterated in Ezekiel 39:29, where Yahweh will reveal himself by gathering the exiles and by "pouring out" his *rûaḥ* on the house of Israel. "I will no longer hide my face from them, for I will pour out my Spirit [*rûaḥ*] on the house of Israel, declares the Sovereign LORD." Despite future threats against the nation, Yahweh pledges to bless and abide with Israel to give new life in the land as a symbol of his presence. "Ezekiel proclaimed that Yahweh would make the Israelites into authentic symbols of him by placing his Spirit in them. This participation in Yahweh's reality would enable them in their bodily existence to proclaim Yahweh's sovereign power. Israel's exile would be replaced by a return to a land that would enjoy abundant fertility. But most of all, the presence of Yahweh's Spirit in the Israelites would enable them to be obedient and thus to send a true picture of what Yahweh was like through their collective existence" (Launderville 2007, 381).

A similar message is presented in the book of Joel, which consists of a judgment oracle (Joel 1:1—2:12) followed by an oracle of *salvation (Joel 2:18—3:21). At the heart of the book is the passage concerning God's eschatological promise: "And afterward I will pour out my Spirit [*rûaḥ*] on all people" (Joel 2:28). This phrase is a transition from the oracles of judgment to a message of hope and promise for a more distant time (Wolff, 65). It is then that Yahweh will "pour out" (*šāpak*) the *rûaḥ* on "all flesh" (cf. Ezek 39:29; Zech 12:10). The *rûaḥ* is poured out in this context by God to convey his immediate presence to the recipients, which provides a new and vibrant relationship with God. A refreshing, revitalizing work is implied. "The pouring out of God's spirit upon flesh means the establishment of new, vigorous life through God's unreserved giving of himself" (Wolff, 65). "The promise of the spirit of Yahweh functions here as the guarantee of the fulfillment of his promises, especially the promise of the knowledge of Yahweh" (McQueen, 40). This announcement is as revolutionary as the "new heart" and "new spirit" prophesied in Jeremiah 31:33-34 and in Ezekiel 36:26-27.

Yahweh's action in pouring out the Spirit has extensive effects. "I will pour out my Spirit on all people. Your sons and daughters will prophesy, your old men will dream dreams, your young men will see visions. Even on my servants, both men and women, I will pour out my Spirit in those days" (Joel 2:28-29). The thrust of the passage indicates that the coming transformation brought about by the *rûaḥ* will radically change social conditions in the community. All people will be privileged possessors of the Spirit, not just the prophets. In fact, both sons and daughters will function as prophets. All people will have access to the words of Yahweh and to communion with him. Social status will no longer be a criterion for Spirit reception. The programmatic desire of Moses is here affirmed and moved a step closer to fulfillment: "Would that all Yahweh's people were prophets" (Num 11:29 [cf. Ex 19:3-6]). The charismatic endowment of the gift is extended to the whole community (see Tyra, 49-50).

The oracles of Haggai in 520 BC address Zerubbabel the governor and Joshua the high priest of Judah. After the edict of Cyrus (ca. 538 BC), a number of exiles returned to Judah under the leadership of Sheshbazzar (Ezra 1:11), Ezra (ca. 458 BC) and Nehemiah (ca. 445 BC). Although these oracles are primarily addressed to the leaders of Judah, they are also for the whole community, which was distressed by the opposition to their temple building and discouraged by the poor harvest (Hag 1:3-12; cf. Ezra 5:14-16).

To encourage the returnees, Haggai's message affirms the presence of Yahweh with them (Hag 1:13; 2:5, 14). Yahweh also takes an active part in motivating the leaders and people alike. When he acts, he moves upon the human spirit to effect his purposes. Yahweh "stirred up" the *rûaḥ* of Zerubbabel, Joshua and the remnant to motivate and inspire God's people to complete the house of the Lord.

In Haggai 2:5 it is the *rûaḥ yhwh* that is with the remnant to encourage and assure them. They are reminded that as Yahweh was with the people throughout the exodus events, so now he abides with them (cf. Ex 29:45). The emphasis in Haggai on the presence of God is connected to the *temple, which was the symbol of God dwelling among the people (*see* Divine Presence). It is the place from where the divine blessing and *shalom* issue. The remnant is assured of Yahweh's continued presence by the *rûaḥ* among them that encourages them to complete the work of temple building. A similar emphasis is made by a contemporary of Haggai. Zechariah's prophecy shows concern for the temple building, the community and the new age. His oracle addresses the anointed leaders, who need strength for their work. The word of the Lord to the governor is, "Not by might nor by power, but by my Spirit [*rûaḥ*]"

(Zech 4:6). The completion of the temple construction cannot be accomplished by human strength alone. The *rûaḥ yhwh* will grant the necessary resources to enable the remnant in their building of the temple.

4.4. The Spirit of Yahweh in Prophecy. The importance of prophecy in Israel is clearly evident from the large corpus of prophetic literature in the OT. Moreover, the prominent leadership provided by prophets is noted from the Pentateuch through to the Writings. A foundational understanding in this literature is that prophecy is inspired by the Spirit of Yahweh (see Flattery, 93-111). The *rûaḥ* comes upon the prophet to commission and provide divinely inspired oracles. This is illustrated in Isaiah 48:16, where the prophet says, "And now the Sovereign LORD has sent me, with his Spirit." And Yahweh says, "I foretold the former things long ago, my mouth announced them and I made them known; then suddenly I acted, and they came to pass" (Is 48:3). This is the particular work of the Spirit that inspires the prophetic word and then brings it into reality. The prophet is conscious of the Spirit's presence with him and is confident of the authority that he possesses in his prophetic ministry. From the exemplary prophetic leadership of Moses, who was empowered to perform "awesome deeds" (Deut 34:12), to Elijah, Isaiah, Ezekiel and many others, the Spirit of Yahweh enabled their ministry.

Usually, prophets receive a "call" to ministry (Ex 3; 1 Sam 3; Is 6; Jer 1). Ezekiel has one of the more dramatic call experiences, where the *rûaḥ* is very active in communicating the presence and glory of God (Launderville 2004, 361). Not only so, but also the Spirit of Yahweh transports Ezekiel and "lifts him up" (Ezek 8:3; 11:1, 24; 43:5) to show him visions and revelation of the prophetic word. The prophet claims to receive the divine message and inspiration when "the Spirit entered into me" (Ezek 2:2; 3:24). The prophet Micah exudes a similar confidence in Yahweh's power and inspiration. "But as for me, I am filled with power, with the Spirit of the LORD [*rûaḥ yhwh*], and with justice and might, to declare to Jacob his transgression, to Israel his sin" (Mic 3:8). Micah is full of "power" to bring Yahweh's message. He is sustained by the Spirit to stand in the midst of opposition and courageously proclaim the word of the Lord to a rebellious people. "The empowering Spirit of Yahweh confers on Micah everything the opposing religious leader's lack, all that had made them credible religious authorities in the first place, such as revelations, special knowledge, and insight into the future" (Wessels, 42).

This level of empowerment is necessary because the prophets not only were ridiculed and ignored but also persecuted and killed. Zechariah also faced this problem. In summary of the response of the populace to the prophets, Yahweh says, "But they refused to pay attention; stubbornly they turned their backs and covered their ears. They made their hearts as hard as flint and would not listen to the law or to the words that the LORD Almighty had sent by his Spirit through the earlier prophets. So the LORD Almighty was very angry" (Zech 7:11-12 NIV).

Yahweh extends his grace and *forgiveness to Israel through the message of hope in Isaiah 59, which is a reflection by the community on their past sins of apostasy, deceit and injustice. In this passage the prophet assures and encourages the disheartened community: "'As for me, this is my covenant with them,' says the LORD. 'My Spirit [*rûaḥ*], who is on you, and my words that I have put in your mouth will not depart from your mouth, or from the mouths of your children, or from the mouths of their descendants from this time on and forever'" (Is 59:21). This prophecy points to the expectation of the realization of the prophetic word for all Israel. The word and the *rûaḥ* operate together and assert the reality that the covenant promises will be fulfilled from generation to generation in the experience of God's people (Is 42:6; 49:8; 54:10; 55:3; 61:8). The word is an assurance that the *rûaḥ* will not depart from the people. Here the prophetic charisma is connected with anointing, which is "metaphorical, conveying the idea of full and permanent authorization to carry out the prophet's God-given assignment" (Blenkinsopp, 223). It is a prophetic assignment that includes speaking as well as action. This brief summary of the Spirit's role in prophecy features the positive elements of Yahweh's inspiration of the prophets. However, the veracity of the prophetic word is an issue that requires testing and validation, which often leads to prophetic conflicts (1 Kings 22:19-23; Is 19:13-14; 29:9-10) (see Hildebrandt, 182-86; Hamori).

See also DIVINE PRESENCE; GOD.

BIBLIOGRAPHY. **R. Albertz and C. Westermann**, "רוח, Geist," *THAT* 2:726-53; **L. Berkhof,**

Systematic Theology (Grand Rapids: Eerdmans, 1939); **J. Blenkinsopp,** *Isaiah 56-66: A New Translation with Introduction and Commentary* (AB 19C; New York: Doubleday, 2003); **W. J. Dumbrell,** *Covenant and Creation: A Theology of the Old Testament Covenants* (Nashville: Thomas Nelson, 1984); **W. Eichrodt,** *Theology of the Old Testament,* vol. 2, trans. J. A. Baker (OTL; Philadelphia: Westminster, 1967); **A. Even-Shoshan,** ed., *A New Concordance of the Old Testament* (Jerusalem: Kiryat Sepher, 1983); **G. M. Flattery,** *A Biblical Theology of the Holy Spirit: Old Testament* (Springfield, MO: Global University, 2009); **J. Goldingay,** "The Breath of Yahweh Scorching, Confounding, Anointing: The Message of Isaiah 40-42," *JPT* 11 (1997) 3-34; idem, *The Message of Isaiah 40-55: A Literary-Theological Commentary* (London: T & T Clark, 2005); **E. J. Hamori,** "The Spirit of Falsehood," *CBQ* 72 (2010) 15-30; **W. Hildebrandt,** *An Old Testament Theology of the Spirit of God* (Peabody, MA: Hendrickson, 1995); **O. Kaiser,** *Isaiah 13-39: A Commentary,* trans. R. A. Wilson (OTL; Philadelphia: Westminster, 1974); **R. Knierim,** "Die Messianologie des Ersten Buch Samuel," *EvT* 30 (1970) 113-33; **D. F. Launderville,** "Ezekiel's Throne-Chariot Vision: Spiritualizing the Model of Divine Royal Rule," *CBQ* 66 (2004) 361-77; idem, *Spirit and Reason: The Embodied Character of Ezekiel's Symbolic Thinking* (Waco, TX: Baylor University Press, 2007); **L. R. Martin,** "Power to Save!? The Role of the Spirit of the Lord in the Book of Judges," *JPT* 16 (2008) 21-50; **L. R. McQueen,** *Joel and the Spirit: The Cry of a Prophetic Hermeneutic* (JPTSup 8; Sheffield: Sheffield Academic Press, 1995); **T. N. D. Mettinger,** *King and Messiah: The Civil and Sacral Legitimation of the Israelite Kings* (ConBNT 8; Lund: Gleerup, 1976); **R. North,** "חָדָשׁ," *TDOT* 4:236-39; **R. J. Sklba,** "'Until the Spirit from On High Is Poured Out on Us' (Isa 32:14): Reflections on the Role of the Spirit in Exile," *CBQ* 46 (1984) 1-17; **S. Tengström,** "רוּחַ," *TDOT* 13:365-96; **G. Tyra,** *The Holy Spirit in Mission: Prophetic Speech and Action in Christian Witness* (Downers Grove, IL: IVP Academic, 2011); **W. J. Wessels,** "Empowered by the Spirit of Yahweh: A Study of Micah 3:8," *JBPR* 1 (2009) 33-47; **C. Westermann,** *Isaiah 40-66,* trans. D. M. G. Stalker; (OTL; Philadelphia: Westminster, 1969); **H. W. Wolff,** *Joel and Amos: A Commentary on the Books of the Prophets Joel and Amos,* trans. W. Janzen, S. D. McBride Jr. and C. A. Muenchow, ed. S. D. McBride Jr. (Hermeneia; Philadelphia: Fortress, 1977); **W. Zimmerli,** *Ezekiel 2: A Commentary on the Book of the Prophet Ezekiel, Chapters 25-48,* trans. J. D. Martin, ed. P. D. Hanson with L. J. Greenspoon (Hermeneia; Philadelphia: Fortress, 1983).

W. Hildebrandt

SUFFERING

Suffering in the modern world is readily associated with experiences that sometimes overlap one another—physical, emotional or psychological pain. However experienced, pain and suffering often are inseparable (Swenson, 1-13). This point holds true in the ancient world as well, and particularly for the Prophetic Books of the OT. No single word exhausts the concept of suffering in this corpus. A constellation of terms, idioms and metaphors depicts this experience that, for the prophets, remains no respecter of persons. Both Israel and the nations suffer. Moreover, the created order bears the marks of suffering. And the prophets provocatively suggest that God himself suffers on account of his people and world. Each of these will be taken in turn in this article.

1. Suffering and Theodicy
2. Language of Suffering
3. Survey of Research
4. Causes of Suffering
5. Responses to Suffering
6. The End of Suffering
7. Conclusion

1. Suffering and Theodicy.

This article centers on the topic of suffering in the prophets rather than a broader discussion of theodicy. Of course, the two are related, but the latter often is understood as a philosophical attempt to explain *evil and suffering within the purposes of God. That particular approach arrives late in the eighteenth century from G. Leibniz. He combined the Greek terms *theos* ("God") and *dikē* ("justice") to create a neologism: *theodicy.* This term was used to describe his attempt to philosophically explain the relationship between God, evil and suffering (Laato and de Moor, 1-23). If understood in that way, the prophets cannot be said to provide such a response, not least because it is framed outside of biblical categories.

However, if by "theodicy" one intends various attempts to understand God's actions in the world in particular ways and at particular times, especially in the light of perceived evil and suffering, then this corpus does provide such material. Suffering and theodicy are related even if not explained with a kind of philosophical-systematic logical precision (for more on this, see 6 below).

2. The Language of Suffering.

The Prophetic Books identify suffering with a myriad of terms, but prominent among them are the verbs *'sm* and *ns'* accompanied with specific language describing pain or *sin. But these expressions tell only a portion of the story. Images and metaphors abound in the prophets that prominently depict pain at individual, communal and even cosmic levels. Some notable ones are the mourning *land (Is 24:4; 33:9; Jer 4:28; 12:4, 11; 23:10; Hos 4:3; Amos 1:2), the incurable wound (Jer 6:7-14; 8:21; 10:19; 14:17; 15:18; 30:12; Hos 5:13; Mic 1:8-10; Nah 3:19), bereavement and mourning (city personified [Is 3:26; Jer 31:15]; people [Jer 6:26]; *creation [Is 24:1-20]); divine violence (Jer 20:7; Ezek 16; 23) and, of course, the Suffering *Servant (Is 40—55; esp. Is 53; cf. Is 61:1-3).

3. Survey of Research.

At present, no work specifically addresses the question of suffering in the prophets, even though research on the related field of theodicy abounds (see Laato and de Moor, 1-23; Crenshaw 2005). Yet it is possible to outline a general scholarly narrative on suffering used to negotiate its trajectory in the prophetic material. This traditional narrative, by and large, is organized along developmental lines in the history of Israel's religion.

In the early stages of Israel's religion the Hebrews viewed the world mechanistically and personally. As such, both God and world remain comprehensible and generally followed certain rules. If one sinned against God, then what one got in return was judgment for sin, which was a specific kind of suffering (*see* Retribution). The converse, of course, was true as well: obedience brought blessing from God. Other ancient Near Eastern peoples may have attributed suffering (either individual or corporate) to fitful or strange moods of the gods, but because of the constancy of Israel's God, the Hebrews' suffering could be attributed to divine judgment against sin (Gerstenberger and Schrage, 15-20).

This "retribution and reward" approach to suffering informed the Israelite prophetic imagination. The prophets during the monarchical period serve as "*covenant enforcers" who reminded God's people that judgment follows upon sin. God's people are called to repentance in order to avert or shorten the experience of judgment and suffering (von Rad, 54). The fall of the northern kingdom in 722 BC reinforced this point for those who remained in Judah, reminding the Judahites of the necessity of obedience to God.

This notion was bolstered, it is argued, throughout the monarchical period until Josiah's death in 609 BC at the battle of Carchemish. Josiah, the great reformer who had served God so faithfully, died, and the people of God were threatened with *exile. This trauma of exile became a reality, but it was only one in a series of tragic and painful events: the deportation of the Judahite elite (597 BC), the siege and destruction of Jerusalem (587 BC) and a final military blow to the region in 582 BC. In this period the prophetic voices questioned the veracity of "retribution and reward" theology (Peake, 4-11). The (Deuteronomic) faith advocated by Josiah and his reforms became a problem for explaining the suffering that God's people experienced (Gottwald, 47-62). So, Habakkuk and Jeremiah begin to raise the issue of the undeserved suffering. In their writings, God's ways become a kind of "dark riddle" in the face of pious faith that is enduring undeserved pain (Peake, 11).

The issue of righteous suffering takes a turn in the exilic prophets, especially in the visions of Isaiah 40—55 and Zechariah. God's people indeed suffered because of sin, as Jeremiah and Ezekiel hold, but only for a little while (Zech 1—2). Further, suffering was understood as a means to bear witness to God's ways in the world (Is 42:1-4). In the final analysis, however, God's people would be restored back to their land in *Zion; present suffering is not final. This great hope is then taken up in the prophecies of Haggai and Zechariah in restoration and return. And as God's ways thereby are vindicated, the exilic prophetic voices give meaning to suffering in the midst of confusion and pain (Heschel, 145-58).

In the later stages of prophetic thinking on suffering, God's people had to wrestle with the fact that the return to God's land was not as grandiose as Israel might have imagined. They still bore the weight of an occupying force in their land, and the exigencies of the return brought new challenges to God's people. The response to these new demands is found in the growing prophetic testimonies of *apocalyptic and *eschatological hope for God's people as seen in, for example, Isaiah 24—27; 56—66; Zechariah 9—14; and later, Daniel (Blenkinsopp, 212-39; Sawyer, 102-4). These texts proclaim God's ultimate vindication of his people and his purposes in the world in a future hope. In the "last days" divine vindication will be on display for all nations to see. Further, the righteous will suffer no more, but the wicked will receive their just punishment. Although late in Israel's history, the developing apocalyptic hope provides a (future) perspective of God's ways in the midst of ongoing strife and pain.

This rather tidy historical approach to suffering in the prophets has broken apart in the past few decades, and indeed it was never quite established from the start. The prophetic texts did not overly lend themselves to this developmental view without significant modification through historical reconstruction of the materials. Further, the prophetic voices themselves present nagging questions of righteous suffering as well as retributive suffering throughout the early and late periods of the history of Israel. Hosea, for one, bears the marks of a righteous sufferer from the early days of Israel's monarchy prior to the fall of the northern kingdom. And as A. Peake noted a century ago, one of Jeremiah's distinctive contributions lay in his unique participation with Judah in suffering despite his faithfulness to Yahweh (Peake, 11-16). Still, as a figure, he symbolizes the state of his very nation: imprisoned, under threat and facing the impending judgment of God through exile (McConville, 61-78). In this way he perhaps bears the suffering of his people in himself (Fretheim, 156-66).

Still, some of the main lines of this historical reconstruction remain. Apocalyptic prophecy as a particular response to suffering is still regarded as a late innovation in prophetic thinking (Blenkinsopp, 212-39). Many still visage the hope on display in Isaiah 40—55 and Zechariah 1—2 as a kind of "answer" to the prophetic confusion concerning suffering in the exilic period (Willey, 105-261; Maier, 161-88). And finally, the "retribution and reward" view of early Israelite prophecy is still upheld, with various modifications (see Krašovec). But divergence in the scholarship underscores the fact that the complexities within the prophetic texts problematize overly simplistic schematizations or historical reconstructions.

Recent scholarship moves beyond the purely diachronic reconstructions of prophetic thought (Nissinen). These attempts to negotiate and explain the reality of suffering in the prophetic material have ranged widely in approach. During the late twentieth and early twenty-first centuries, research on Ezekiel and Jeremiah draws upon the insights of *psychological analyses to explain the suffering on display in these books (Joyce; Ellens and Rollins, 141-294; Smith-Christopher, 75-104). One notes also an increase in feminist and postcolonial readings on the prophets that explore suffering from the perspective of the marginalized and read against oppressive ideologies latent or explicit in the biblical text (Mandolfo, 29-54, 79-119; Yee, 81-134; Baumann, 85-222). Finally, narrative and ideological readings have been employed on Jeremiah, Isaiah and Ezekiel to suggest that "crime and punishment" views of suffering in these books may be construed otherwise (Mills; O'Brien).

Along with these ideological and psychological approaches, synchronic explorations on the biblical material explore the responses to suffering in the OT. J. Crenshaw sees five kinds of prophetic attitudes on theodicy and, thereby, suffering: personal affront at God's acts, questioning God's character, explaining historical events through relationship between God and Israel, restorative suffering, understanding suffering through the divine order of creation (Crenshaw 2003). Both M. Thompson and W. McWilliams discover a variety of sources of suffering in the prophetic material and a number of responses to pain in them. Finally, it is appropriate to mention theological accounts of suffering have that been marshalled from the prophetic material (Gowan; Berrigan). In these works the prophets give voice to suffering but also a resolution to the same in and through the work of God through Israel.

4. Causes of Suffering.

Even though the prophetic texts present a variety of causes of suffering, two primary ones stand out: sin and enemies. *Sin is a major cause of suffering for Israel, the nations, the created world and even God himself. Enemies create suffering from within and without Israel. Other causes of suffering will be addressed as well at the end of this section, but these are distinctive and should not be put on the same level as suffering that comes as a result of sin or enemy action.

4.1. Sin.

4.1.1. The Sins of Israel. God is connected to suffering in the prophetic corpus, particularly through his punishment for sin, both for Israel and the nations. For Israel, God as the one who deals with sin becomes evident in Isaiah 3, where God's judgment draws the haughty people of Jerusalem to shame and mourning in the face of disaster. Instead of finery, in divine judgment God's people will wear "sackcloth"; instead of pleasantness, they will experience "rottenness," "baldness" and the "branding" of exile (Is 3:18-24). "Your men shall fall by the sword, and your mighty men in battle. And her gates shall lament and mourn; empty, she shall sit upon the ground" (Is 3:25-26). This theme of mourning over God's judgment is taken up across the corpus of Isaiah (Is 22:12), Jeremiah (Jer 12:11; 14:2), Ezekiel (Ezek 2:10) and the Minor Prophets (Amos 5:16; 8:1-10).

Isaiah's Song of the Vineyard and the succeeding woe oracles in Isaiah 5 illustrate in lucid detail the pain that Israel's sin creates. God plants a vineyard and expects it to produce good grapes of "justice" and "righteousness," only to watch his beloved vineyard produce "wild grapes" of "injustice" and an "outcry" (Is 5:7). Israel's sin brings God pain, and the woe oracles that follow the song (Is 5:8, 11, 18, 20, 21, 22) detail Israel's various legal breaches, which were summarized by the rubric "injustice" and "outcry" in Isaiah 5:7. As such, the woes belong with the song and should be interpreted in light of it. These comprise the substance for the metaphor of "wild grapes": improper land development, drunkenness/self-indulgence, pervasive lying and sin, and disregard for God's plans. All are transgressions that, in turn, bring the land to ruin. In response, God will punish the sinful people for their iniquity (Is 5:5-6). Despite his work to nurture Israel into producing good fruit, his beloved people have spurned his care and produced sin. This, in turn, pains God. His statement in Isaiah 5:4 is anguished: "What more could I do for my vineyard that I have not done in it?"

As the foregoing example reveals, sin is not just an abstract concept in the prophets; it is something actually done among God's people that brings forth suffering and pain. Amos's proclamation of judgment against Israel and Judah horrifically presents a society governed by lies, corruption, cruelty, neglect and sexual perversion that leaves the vulnerable abused and suffering (Amos 2:4-8). Jeremiah too decries his people for their treachery, tainted wealth, crimes, inability to administer justice and lack of care for the vulnerable in society (Jer 5:27-28; cf. Jer 6:28-30). Sin surely brings about divine punishment, but it also creates a society where suffering and oppression become the norm.

The sins of Israel's leaders in particular become a source of pain for the populace writ large, as evidenced by the critique in Micah 3:1-3 (cf. Amos 8:4-8). The sins of the leaders "tear the skin off" of God's people, leaving them mutilated. Isaiah identifies the suffering of God's people from sin as a kind of "sickness" in Isaiah 1:5-6. It is real and present, even if the people do not recognize it. And when one interprets the enemies of Habakkuk 1:1-4 as God's wicked people, then there is a kind of "violence" and "devastation" that brings the prophet to cry out to God in pain, "How long have I cried for help, but you do not listen?" (Hab 1:2).

4.1.2. Sin and the Suffering of Creation. Sin also causes creation itself to mourn. Recent research insightfully delineates the "mourning earth" metaphor in the prophets as testimony to the power of sin as a source of pain (Hayes). "How long will the earth mourn, and the grass of every field wither? From the evil of those who dwell in it, the beasts and birds are swept away" (Jer 12:4). Other texts in the prophetic corpus describe the suffering land (Is 24:1-20; 33:7-9; Jer 4:23-28; 12:1-4, 7-13; 23:9-12; Hos 4:1-3; Joel 1:5-20; Amos 1:2). The metaphor delineates a close relationship between human sin and a broken world. Sin does not just affect the human condition; it infects the created order so that it "mourns" and suffers over its demise.

4.1.3. Divine Suffering. Finally, it is important to note that *God suffers because of his people's sin (as in Is 5:4, noted above). T. Fretheim extensively explores this point and suggests that God suffers with, and for, his people (Fretheim, 107-48). First, God suffers because of the people's rejection of him (Is 1:2-3; 54:6; 63:7-10;

65:1-2; Jer 2; 15:5-9; 18:13-15; Hos 9—11; 13:4-6). The so-called divine laments in the prophetic corpus speak to this reality in a distinctive manner (Jer 9:9; 12:7-12; 15:5-9; 48:29-33; Ezek 27:3-11, 26-36). In these texts God suffers pain at human sin against him, which then leads him to enforce judgment against it (see Long; Smith). Second, God suffers with those who are suffering (Is 15:5; 16:9-11; Jer 9:10, 17-18; 12:7; 31:20; 48:30-36). In these texts God mourns with the mourning, hurts with the hurting, and thereby identifies with suffering from the "inside." A. Heschel in particular outlines the notion of God suffering with peoples in his magisterial work on the prophets. Finally, God suffers for humanity (Is 43:23-24; 48:9; 57:11; Jer 15:6; Ezek 20:21-22; 24:12; Mal 2:17). In these texts God becomes "weary" of restraining his judgment against the rebellious. The point in these texts is that God suffers on account of the peoples' sins and delays judgment. In so doing, he suffers for the sins of humanity. And although God's patience gives way to judgment, punishing a rebellious people (see Fretheim, 138-48), still God's move toward redemption and reconciliation is sure, so that the suffering of God and Israel is caught up in divine restoration and healing: "I will heal their backsliding; I will love them freely. For my anger is turned away from him" (Hos 14:4). This account of God suffering for people is different from vicarious suffering as exemplified in the Isaianic Suffering Servant (see 5.2. below).

4.2. Enemies.

4.2.1. Enemies from Within. Sin represents only one of the sources of pain; the prophetic corpus reveals that internal and/or external enemies are a major source of suffering. A focus upon enemies comprises what is known as the *Feindklage* in the *lament tradition, and this formal element appears prominently in Habakkuk (but also Jeremiah). In Habakkuk 1:2 the prophet complains to God about the "guilty" who surround the "innocent." These wicked few may be Judahites who oppress the righteous in Habakkuk's day, leaving the prophet pleading to God for help.

A similar theme of enemy threat emerges throughout the book of Jeremiah. The prophet is abused by God's people for declaring the word of the Lord. Jeremiah states that he has become a "laughingstock" among wicked Judahites who will not respond to God's word (Jer

20:7-8; cf. Jer 23:1-22; 26:1-15; 36; 38:1-8; 43:1-7). This complaint comes as a result of Jeremiah's encounter with Pashhur, but, as suggested below (see 4.3.2), it also should be understood as a complaint about his divine calling as well. Still, Jeremiah's suffering derives from God's people: internal strife because of Judahite sin (Jer 20:7-8; 23:1-11), Judahite abuse and rejection (Jer 26:1-15; cf. Amos 7:12); prison (Jer 37:11-21); being cast into a cistern (Jer 38:1-8); and ultimately exile (Jer 43:1-7). All of these experiences of pain come directly from enemies within Israel, God's rebellious people (see Fretheim, 149-66).

4.2.2. Enemies from Without. The pain that comes as a result of divine judgment is real for Israel, but for enemy nations as well. This is evident in the series of oracles against the *nations in the prophetic corpus (Is 13—23; Jer 46—51; Ezek 25—32; Joel 3:9-17; Amos 1—2; Nah 1—2). In their literary contexts, the oracles against the nations are designed to provide encouragement to God's people, but this support is necessary precisely because of the suffering that the nations inflict upon God's people. Because of their violence against his people and for their sins, God enacts judgment against them. Indeed, there is a tacit understanding in some of the prophetic material that even when used by God, the enemy nations go beyond God's intended discipline for Israel and are ripe for God's judgment as a result (Is 10:5-7; Hab 2:4a; Zech 1:14-17).

External threats create pain for Israel. In Habakkuk 1:12-17 the prophet complains that God should not use the Babylonians, who will ruin the earth and destroy God's land. For the prophet, the horror of it all stems from the fact that God is using idolaters to carry out his punishment (Hab 1:15-16). Enemy nations, even if ordained of God, are a source of great suffering (see Heschel, 159-86) because they wreck God's people and land in warfare. Moreover, for Habakkuk, this invading army will maul other defenseless peoples in their march down the Levant (Hab 1:6-17).

Hezekiah's response to the Assyrian army in Isaiah 36—37 illustrates this point as well. When the Assyrians advance to Jerusalem, Hezekiah's message to Isaiah is a prayer for help in a "day of distress, of rebuke, and of disgrace" (Is 37:3). The king is terrified in the face of the Assyrian juggernaut, and this leads him to enact rites of mourning over disaster. Further within Isaiah, the theme of divine comfort in Isaiah 40—55 (e.g., Is 40:1-7; cf. Zech. 1—2) testifies to the pain that enemy invasion and exile produces.

Enemy threat is a significant theme in Joel and Amos. In Joel, "a nation has come up against" God's land whose power lays God's "vine" to waste (Joel 1:6). This attack and threat lead to lamentation and deep sadness (Joel 1:8-12). Further, enemy threat from the nations that surround Israel and Judah comprises the substance of the woe oracles in Amos 1, giving way to judgment speech against them in the text. Although Amos employs this negative experience as a rhetorical strategy to pronounce judgment against Israel and Judah respectively, the vivid memory of the enemies' actions reminds God's people of the suffering that they inflicted.

4.3. Other Causes of Suffering.

4.3.1. Illness. Sickness is a source of suffering in the book of Isaiah. Hezekiah's illness and impending death (Is 38) draw him to prayer, weeping and misery (Is 38:2). There is no explanation or rationale as to the cause of his sickness. It is due neither to sin nor to deliberate divine action. Rather, this illness (and death) may be understood as a stark and terrible reality of life. His mortality is not, then, seen to be a good thing but rather a point of deep suffering, a cause for prayer for deliverance and healing (Is 38:10-20).

4.3.2. Prophetic Burden. The burden of prophetic proclamation comprises a source of pain. This might best be understood as a subset of suffering with God as its ultimate source, but nonetheless it is particularly tied to the experience of the prophet and his call. Perhaps nowhere is this more evident than in the prophecies of Jeremiah. In Jeremiah 20:9 the prophet proclaims that the divine message that he is to preach leaves him wearied and pained. The word of God is like a "burning fire" in Jeremiah's bones, so that he is "weary" from holding it in. The fatigue and suffering that accompany the prophetic task are on display in his so-called confessions (Jer 11:18-12:6; 15:10-21; 17:14-18; 18:18-23; 20:7-13; 20:14-18). In these texts the prophet complains to God about the message that he has been given to preach, God's actions in the world, and the suffering that the prophet himself endures. These prayers highlight the pain and struggle of pro-

claiming God's word in Jeremiah's day. They are intensely confrontational, yet intimate, and they disclose a deep (yet dogged) faith in God. The confessions elucidate what Jeremiah states earlier in Jeremiah 6:11: the burden of proclaiming God's message, particularly a dark message of judgment, leaves Jeremiah "weary" and hurting.

4.3.3. Sign Acts. The suffering of the prophets becomes evident especially through the *sign acts that God commands his seers to perform (see von Rad, 52-53; Lundbom, 208-18). Sign acts are lived-out demonstrations of the prophets' messages that bring a degree of power to the messages themselves. They draw God's people to feel and understand the certainty of the word of the Lord. Many of them are not particularly pleasant, and these are the sign acts that will be explored here (for further discussion, see Lundbom, 208-18; Lindblom, 165-73).

The sign acts of the eighth-century BC prophets illumine suffering in obedience to the Lord. Hosea's tumultuous marriage is a lived-out demonstration of God's tenuous relationship with God's people (Lindblom, 166-69). The strain and pain of both relationships leave the prophet (and God) suffering (e.g., Hos 2:14-15; 9:10-13; 10:11; 13:4-6; cf. Mic 6:3). Likewise, Isaiah suffers for God's word. In Isaiah 7 he is commanded to name his child "Shear-jashub," meaning "a remnant shall return." This name implies the impending doom of destruction and exile, which is heightened both in Isaiah 8, with the naming of Isaiah's second child as "Maher-shalal-hash-baz" (meaning "spoil hastens, plunder quickens"), and in Isaiah 20, when God commands Isaiah to go about the city naked and barefoot as a symbolic message to avoid Israelite allegiance with Egypt. In each of these symbolic actions God's word is brought to bear uniquely in the life of the prophet. The prophet experiences physical discomfort (especially in his nakedness) in order to proclaim the message of the Lord.

Jeremiah's and Ezekiel's sign acts also reveal suffering in obedience to God's word. Jeremiah is forbidden to take a wife or have children in order to proclaim that parents and children would die in Jerusalem (Jer 16:1-4). Accompanying this symbolic action, Jeremiah is forbidden from mourning and feasting in order to heighten God's message concerning the appropriateness of divine judgment (Jer 16:5-9). Jeremiah breaks a pot at the potsherd gate in Jerusalem to reveal the imminence of divine destruction (Jer 19:1-15), and he is commanded to bear a yoke on his neck to proclaim that exile is coming (Jer 27:1-22). Each of these actions is set within the context of Jeremiah enduring pain over the proclamation of God's word (cf. Jer 11:18-12:6; 15:10-21; 17:14-18; 18:18-23; 20:7-13, 14-18). Thus, these sign acts are an extension of the pain that comes from the burden of prophecy.

Ezekiel too employs symbolic actions and suffers because of them. He is commanded to be mute except when speaking God's word (Ezek 3:26-27), he lay paralyzed on his side at the command of God to indicate the sin and punishment of Israel (Ezek 4:4-6), he ate only small amounts of food to symbolize the starvation that accompanies siege (Ezek 4:9-11), he ate unclean food to symbolize the reality of eating in exile (Ezek 4:12-17), he shaved off his hair and beard, burning and scattering it to represent the burning of Jerusalem and scattering of its inhabitants (Ezek 5:1-17). The prophet is also forbidden (like Jeremiah) from mourning over death. But for Ezekiel, the pain is all the greater because he is forbidden from mourning the death of his wife (Ezek 24:15-27). In each of these sign acts God commands the prophet to suffer in various ways in order to proclaim and exemplify the certainty of his divine messages (Friebel, 13-78).

5. Responses to Suffering.

5.1. Complaint. S. Balentine reveals the primacy of complaint *prayer when one is confronted with suffering (Balentine, 118-98). This point holds true in some of the prophetic material. The complaint is a means to negotiate pain and bring it before the heavenly throne in hopes that God will end suffering. As indicated above, Jeremiah holds forth complaints when confronted with suffering—both his own pain over the prophetic burden and the suffering of his people. Likewise, in Habakkuk 1—2 the prophet cries out to God because of rebellion within his own people (Hab 1:1-3), God's use of idolaters to achieve his purposes (Hab 1:12-17), and the attack of the enemy that will destroy the earth (Hab 1:12-17). These prophetic complaints are not faith-less prayers but rather are faith-filled prayer, aware that only God can alleviate these distresses.

5.2. Acceptance. The prophets also accept suffering as a result of sin. The almost Janus-like responses of both Jeremiah and Habakkuk emphasize this point. Although both are quite contentious in their complaints, there comes a point when they accept God's judgment. For both, suffering is accepted. Jeremiah desists from complaint after Jeremiah 20, accepting the reality of judgment. But the acceptance of suffering (even its embrace) is crystallized in Habakkuk's powerful testimony: "I will wait for the day of distress to come, for a people who will attack us" (Hab 3:16).

Yet perhaps the most significant example of accepting suffering appears in the Suffering Servant in the book of Isaiah (for the most comprehensive work to date on this topic, see Janowski and Stuhlmacher). In Isaiah 53:1-12 the servant accepts his suffering on behalf of sinful Israel. He embraces his suffering in two primary ways: at the hands of God's people, and at the hands of God. In the first place, his own people cause him to suffer: he is a "man of sorrows" who knew "sickness," "rejection" and what it was to be "despised" (Is 53:3). His own people disdain him and ignore him: they "did not pay attention to him" (Is 53:3b). Further, God's people (like Job's friends) wrongly relate his suffering to his own sin (Is 53:4), only to find that there was no sin in him at all (Is 53:7-9). He accepts suffering not because of his own sin, but rather because he bears the iniquity of his own people in and through his pain. The notion of vicarious suffering is present here, and the servant of the Lord suffers on behalf of, and bears the sins of, God's people: "he was pierced for our transgressions; crushed for our iniquities" (Is 53:6), "and Yahweh caused our iniquity to fall upon him" (Is 53:7). Because of his work, the sins of God's people are dealt with (Janowski). And further, because of the servant's suffering, the suffering and death of exile might be turned back. Within Isaiah, the servant bears Israel's sin, iniquity and even their diseases (Is 53:4-6; cf. Mt 8:14-17) so that the storm-tossed and comfortless Zion (Is 54:11) will be comforted and restored (Is 54:12-14). This happens precisely because the servant accepts and even embraces his experience of suffering, and then he takes the suffering of Israel upon himself (*see* Servant of Yahweh).

5.3. Repentance. Another response to pain, especially when suffering due to sin, is *repentance. The prophets time and again call for repentance, even if that call is matched by the "hardness" of Israel's hearts or the willfulness of their souls. Still, the suffering caused by sin is meant to draw out repentance. Divine judgment is God's deliberate abandonment of his people due to their sinful ways, and his return to them becomes the comfort that alleviates their suffering. Yet wrapped up with God's return to his people is the return of his people to God. This "return" or "repentance" is a significant response to suffering in the prophets. In Jeremiah 24:7 the prophet calls God's people to repent in the vision of the figs: the return of God to his people is matched with a return in repentance to him (cf. Jer 31; Zech 1:3; 10:9; Mal 3:7). Joel 2:12-13 calls upon God's people to return to him with "all their heart" in the face of foreign invasion. This call for repentance is evident as well in the inclusio of divine abandonment/return to the temple in Ezekiel 8—11; 43:1-12. The temple's restoration is generated in part by human repentance: "Now let them put away their whoring and the corpses of their kings far from me, and I will dwell in the midst of them forever" (Ezek 43:9; cf. Ezek 43:10-11). Isaiah 44:22; 55:7; Zechariah 1:6 call for repentance in the face of the pain of exile. Although repentance is a different response to suffering than complaint or acceptance, the comfort that accompanies it is very real in the prophets.

6. The End of Suffering.

6.1. Isaiah. Distinctive to Isaiah, suffering is defeated in and through the work of the Suffering Servant. In Isaiah 51—52 God presents a picture of comfort in the midst of suffering and judgment. Israel will see the Lord comfort and redeem Zion (Is 51:3; 52:1-7). These actions arrive because of God's appointment of the Suffering Servant (Is 53:1-12), as demonstrated above. The servant will bring glorification instead of humiliation to God's people and ease their pain (Is 61:1-3). Still, this future remains indeed just that, as God's people face the threat of "hardening" throughout the Isaianic corpus, and thereby they face the threat of suffering in the present (see Uhlig).

Further, it is evident that the servant's work will bring comfort and healing not only to Israel, but also to the nations and even creation itself (Is 65). Instead of a rebellious and broken people who oppress their neighbors (as in Is 5), Isaiah's vision is for a renewed humanity and cre-

ated order where justice and righteousness springs up in all the world (Is 27:1-6), where God's instruction is a fountain for all nations, where war is abolished, and where instruments of war are instead refashioned to prepare for the harvest of life-giving food (Is 2:1-5; cf. Mic 4:1-7).

6.2. Jeremiah and Ezekiel. These prophets portray the end of suffering in two different ways. For Jeremiah, it comes for Israel in the form of a new covenant marked by devotion to God, return to God's land, and peace and justice being operative amongst God's people (Jer 30—33). God's people and land will be renewed and will not be "uprooted or overthrown" ever again. In this vision suffering that comes through exile will be a memory but never again a reality (Jer 31:40). In Ezekiel, the experience of Israel's suffering is overcome by the renewed and restored *temple in Ezekiel 40—48. The temple is almost cosmic in size, scope and significance. Indeed, as God's people see this vision of the renewed temple, they discover that after the punishment and suffering of exile God will dwell in the midst of his people forever: "the LORD dwells there" (Ezek 48:35). Jeremiah's new covenant is not the central feature here as much as the presence of God in the midst of the people, dwelling in the temple forever.

6.3. The Minor Prophets. The end of suffering can be understood in the Minor Prophets by observing their presentation of Israel. There, Israel is caught up within a movement of history that becomes meaningful within the purposes of God (see Seitz, 189-219). And it is a history that gives a perspective on suffering. Israel undergoes nothing less than a *death and a resurrection in the Minor Prophets. Although they may suffer and even die in exile, his purposes with them will be achieved: Israel will rise again from exile and death (see Hos 5—6; 11; see also Gowan, 9-16, 38-50). In this, God is affirmed as the life-giving and death-defeating Lord.

For the postexilic group reading or hearing the Minor Prophets as a whole, this message would remind them that God is justified as righteous. Despite all that has happened, God will enact Israel's restoration. This restoration encompasses not just Israel, but all of creation as well (cf. Mic 4), because God is the Lord of creation itself. The recurrence of the language of Exodus 34:6-7 reinforces that while God's judgment is in force, it still remains an extension of the "steadfast love of the LORD," so that his mercy and compassion might be demonstrated (Hos 2:21-23; Joel 2:13-14, 18; Amos 9:9-15; Jon 3:7-10; 4:2; Mic 7:18-20; Nah 1:3; Hab 3:2; Zeph 3:16-20; Zech 1:15-17; 8:8, 13; 10:6). The destructions of the northern and southern kingdoms were justified because of sin, but God in his mercy will restore his people and land, even creation itself, because of his justice and righteousness (Mic 4:1-7). This vision of restoration effectively presents the (future) end of suffering.

Still, a real tension persists. The glorious restoration still stands far off. Notwithstanding real historical returns to the land (as Haggai and Zechariah confirm), in the canonical presentation of the Minor Prophets God's "day" of vindication is pressed forward eschatologically, creating space between the "now" of suffering and the "not yet" of justice and restoration (Mal 3:16—4:6). There remains an existential challenge of waiting and watching for God's future redemption. This "now and not yet" dimension leaves the reader sensing the certainty of God's salvation from suffering and sin. Yet its eschatological focus leaves room both for waiting expectantly for that future hope and for prayer and honest questioning in the meantime (cf. Hab 1; Mic 1:8-9). In light of the future, God's people persevere in pain but still press forward in faith.

7. Conclusion.

Suffering remains a complex feature in the prophets. It is borne by individuals and community, Israel and the nations, creation and even God himself. There are a number of sources and responses to suffering as well. None can be discounted. But the future of suffering is certain: it will be swallowed up by the decisive act of God in the future.

The NT picks up this theme and finds that future resolution to suffering in Christ. As the evangelists and apostles interpreted the life and death of Christ, they found in the OT and in Jesus' teaching the resource to understand the meaning of both Christ's and their own suffering. Christ's suffering deals the death blow to sin and sets the world to rights in an ultimate vindication of God's actions with his creation (Wright, 553-653). The evangelists affirm that as he suffered and died in the manner described in Isaiah 43; 53, the man Jesus took the sin and the suffering of Israel, as well as the world, upon himself. The evangelists' understanding coheres with Jesus' own self-understanding (see Stuhlmacher, 150-53). The victory of God in Christ puts an end to suffering.

Still, the NT affirms that while suffering and death have been dealt a death blow and will finally be defeated at the consummation (drawing upon the images of new creation in Is 65 and of restored Zion in Isaiah and the Minor Prophets), the NT repeats that suffering remains an ever-present reality for the church. Indeed, as L. Jervis maintains, suffering is at the very center of the gospel itself: those who follow Christ will experience pain in their life. Suffering represents the battlefront of Christian growth, a marker of a broken world, and a part what it means to be "in Christ." Still, suffering may be borne in the manner of Christ: "By virtue of our being caught between the time of Christ's resurrection and the time of our own we recognize that we will suffer as we hope for glory" (Jervis, 109). This insight draws attention to the fact that for the NT, suffering can be borne because Christ is victoriously raised (Mt 28; Lk 24; Jn 20—21; Acts 2; Phil 1:19-30) and new creation is assured (Rom 8; Col 3:1-4; Rev 21). Still, suffering should not be sought after: it is a marker that the world is out of joint, waiting to be fully clothed in a new creation in which suffering will no longer be operative. Instead, Christians ought to hope in Christ and bear suffering when it comes, knowing that future glory is assured.

See also BLESSINGS AND CURSES; DEATH; DESTRUCTION; EVIL; EXILE; HONOR AND SHAME; LAMENT; PEACE, REST; RETRIBUTION; SALVATION, DELIVERANCE; SERVANT OF YAHWEH; SIN, SINNERS; WRATH.

BIBLIOGRAPHY. **S. E. Balentine**, *Prayer in the Hebrew Bible: The Drama of Divine-Human Dialogue* (Minneapolis: Fortress, 1993); **G. Baumann,** *Love and Violence: Marriage as Metaphor for the Relationship between YHWH and Israel in the Prophetic Books* (Collegeville, MN: Michael Glazier, 2003); **D. Berrigan,** *Minor Prophets, Major Themes* (Eugene, OR: Wipf & Stock, 2007); **J. Blenkinsopp,** *A History of Prophecy in Israel* (rev. ed.; Louisville: Westminster John Knox, 1996); **J. Crenshaw,** "Theodicy and Prophetic Literature," in *Theodicy in the World of the Bible*, ed. A. Laato and J. C. de Moor (Leiden: E. J. Brill, 2003) 236-55; idem, *Defending God:*

Biblical Responses to the Problem of Evil (Oxford: Oxford University Press, 2005); **J. H. Ellens and W. G. Rollins,** eds., *Psychology and the Bible: A New Way to Read the Bible,* 2: *From Genesis to Apocalyptic Vision* (Westport, CT: Praeger, 2004); **T. E. Fretheim,** *The Suffering of God: An Old Testament Perspective* (OBT; Minneapolis: Augsburg Fortress, 1984); **K. Friebel,** *Jeremiah's and Ezekiel's Sign-Acts: Rhetorical Non-Verbal Communication* (JSOTSup 283; Sheffield: Sheffield Academic Press, 1999); **E. S. Gerstenberger and W. Schrage,** *Suffering,* trans. J. E. Steely (BibEnc; Nashville: Abingdon, 1980); **N. K. Gottwald,** *Studies in the Text of Lamentations* (SBT 14; London: SCM, 1962); **D. E. Gowan,** *Theology of the Prophetic Books: The Death and Resurrection of Israel* (Louisville: Westminster/John Knox, 1998); **K. M. Hayes,** *The Earth Mourns: Prophetic Metaphor and Oral Aesthetic* (SBLAB 8; Boston: Society of Biblical Literature; Leiden: E. J. Brill, 2002); **A. J. Heschel,** *The Prophets: An Introduction,* vol. 1 (New York: Harper & Row, 1969); **B. Janowski,** "He Bore Our Sins: Isaiah 53 and the Drama of Taking Another's Place," in *The Suffering Servant: Isaiah 53 in Jewish and Christian Sources,* ed. B. Janowski and P. Stuhlmacher (Grand Rapids: Eerdmans, 2004) 48-74; **B. Janowski and P. Stuhlmacher,** eds., *The Suffering Servant: Isaiah 53 in Jewish and Christian Sources* (Grand Rapids: Eerdmans, 2004); **L. A. Jervis,** *At the Heart of the Gospel: Suffering in the Earliest Christian Message* (Grand Rapids: Eerdmans, 2007); **P. Joyce,** "The Prophets and Psychological Interpretation," in *Prophecy and Prophets in Ancient Israel,* ed. J. Day (LHBOTS 531; New York: T & T Clark, 2010) 133-50; **J. Krašovec,** *Reward, Punishment, and Forgiveness: The Thinking and Beliefs of Ancient Israel in Light of Greek and Modern Views* (VTSup 78; Leiden: E. J. Brill, 1999); **A. Laato and J. C. de Moor,** eds., *Theodicy in the World of the Bible* (Leiden: E. J. Brill, 2003); **J. Lindblom,** *Prophecy in Ancient Israel* (Philadelphia: Fortress, 1965); **B. O. Long,** "The Divine Funeral Lament," *JBL* 85 (1966) 85-86; **J. R. Lundbom,** *The Hebrew Prophets: An Introduction* (Minneapolis: Fortress, 2010); **C. M. Maier,** *Daughter Zion, Mother Zion: Gender, Space and the Sacred in Ancient Israel* (Minneapolis: Fortress, 2008); **C. Mandolfo,** *Daughter Zion Talks Back to the Prophets: A Dialogic Theology of the Book of Lamentations* (SBLSS 58; Atlanta: Society of Biblical Literature, 2007); **J. G. McConville,** *Judgment and Promise: An Interpretation of the Book of Jeremiah* (Winona Lake, IN: Eisenbrauns, 1993); **W. McWilliams,** *Where Is the God of Justice? Biblical Perspectives on Suffering* (Peabody, MA: Hendrickson, 2005); **M. E. Mills,** *Alterity, Pain, and Suffering in Isaiah, Jeremiah, and Ezekiel* (LHBOTS; London: T & T Clark, 2007); **M. Nissinen,** "The Historical Dilemma of Biblical Prophetic Studies," in *Prophecy in the Book of Jeremiah,* ed. H. M. Barstad and R. G. Kratz (BZAW 388; Berlin: de Gruyter, 2009) 103-20; **J. M. O'Brien,** *Challenging Prophetic Metaphor: Theology and Ideology in the Prophets* (Louisville: Westminster/John Knox, 2008); **A. S. Peake,** *The Problem of Suffering in the Old Testament* (London: Robert Culley, 1904); **J. F. A. Sawyer,** *Prophecy and the Prophets of the Old Testament* (OBS; Oxford: Oxford University Press, 1987); **C. R. Seitz,** *Prophecy and Hermeneutics: Toward a New Introduction to the Prophets* (STI; Grand Rapids: Baker Academic, 2007); **M. S. Smith,** "Jeremiah IX 9: A Divine Lament," *VT* 37 (1987) 97-99; **D. Smith-Christopher,** *A Biblical Theology of Exile* (OBT; Louisville: Westminster/John Knox, 2005); **P. Stuhlmacher,** "Isaiah 53 in the Gospels and Acts," in *The Suffering Servant: Isaiah 53 in Jewish and Christian Sources,* ed. B. Janowski and P. Stuhlmacher (Grand Rapids: Eerdmans, 2004) 147-62; **K. M. Swenson,** *Living Through Pain: Psalms and the Search for Wholeness* (Waco, TX: Baylor University Press, 2005); **M. E. W. Thompson,** *Where Is the God of Justice? The Old Testament and Suffering* (Eugene, OR: Pickwick, 2011); **T. Uhlig,** *The Theme of Hardening in the Book of Isaiah* (FAT 2/39; Tübingen: Mohr Siebeck, 2009); **G. von Rad,** *The Message of the Prophets,* trans. D. M. G. Stalker (London: SCM, 1969); **P. T. Willey,** *Remember the Former Things: The Recollection of Previous Texts in Second Isaiah* (SBLDS 161; Atlanta: Scholars Press, 1997); **N. T. Wright,** *Jesus and the Victory of God* (London: SPCK, 1996); **G. A. Yee,** *Poor Banished Children of Eve: Woman as Evil in the Hebrew Bible* (Minneapolis: Fortress, 2003). H. A. Thomas

SUFFERING SERVANT. *See* SERVANT OF YAHWEH.

SUPERNATURAL BEINGS/CREATURES. *See* ANGELS, MESSENGERS, HEAVENLY BEINGS.

SYRO-EPHRAIMITIC WAR. *See* ISRAELITE HISTORY.

T, U

TEMPLE

The various terms for the temple reflect a fundamental anthropomorphic metaphor: God lives in the temple just as a person lives in a house and a king in a palace. The splendor and character of a house/temple/palace reflects the personality and power of its resident, and so the character of the God of Israel is reflected by the architecture and furniture of the temple and the activities that take place in it. However, the differences between a god and a king also lead to distinctive features. There is no need for a bed or bathroom in the temple (at least for its divine resident), for Yahweh is not defined by sexual differentiation or by human physical needs. Israelite temples have much in common with other temples, but the theological distinctives of belief in Yahweh required adaptation on occasion. What was important was not so much the form and goal of *worship but rather the identity and character of the god to whom worship was offered.

Most of the prophetic texts referring to the temple and its worship are negative. Interpreting these depends on significant assumptions about the development of the history of Israelite religion (McKane; Klawans, 75-100). J. Wellhausen emphasized the Canaanite origin of Israel's worship, allowing paganism easy entry. Setting themselves over against the institutions of temple and priesthood, the prophets were heroic individuals who highlighted the priority of ethical behavior and belief in one God. M. Noth, on the other hand, proposed an early intertribal league with a central sanctuary. The prophets therefore did not see a fundamental contradiction between the temple institution and authentic covenantal behavior summed up in, for example, the Ten Commandments. Prophets are guardians rather than innovators.

Their ultimate goal was to recall the people of Israel to their proper calling and to reform God-given institutions that had been corrupted (Janzen, 155). Prophetic rhetoric employs hyperbole and the radical threat of judgment in order to provoke *repentance. The relative lack of positive statements stems from the fact that the role of the prophets is to address a society that is deeply compromised, and promises for the future are less likely to bring repentance than warnings of judgment.

Some scholars even consider that prophets played a key role in the temple. Cultic prophets answer the requests of supplicants with a word from God, and it is the corruption of this class of prophets that is condemned in Micah 3:5-7 (Johnson, 34). However, the texts in the prophets and the psalms cited to support this view can be interpreted in other ways, and there is no explicit evidence for a significant role for prophets in worship. Scholars also suggest that the temple *liturgy is reflected in some of the forms and vocabulary used by the prophets. The doxologies in Amos (Amos 4:13; 5:8-9; 9:5-6) make use of the so-called hymnic participle (e.g. "the one who forms the mountains" [Amos 4:13]), often found in psalms of praise (e.g., Ps 136). However, it is uncertain how far the prophets creatively adapted or subverted temple forms, or whether these forms were more widely used and indeed may have originated outside a cultic context.

The consensus view is that the prophets do make a contribution to Israel's life, but one that that is different from that of the priests and distinctive (Jer 18:18). The "reform" approach is closer to the truth, even though how much we can know about the early history of Israel and its worship remains fiercely disputed. But the prophets did not simply demand a return to the past. The creative imagination of the prophets sought to move beyond the past to the new. Ongoing institutions such as the temple tend to emphasize the continuity and assured character of *God's presence, whereas the prophets point to a time of crisis and the need to make radical changes. It is not surprising that the fiercest critics of the prophets came from within the temple establishment. Yet, from a canonical perspective, the integration of *ethics and worship is a priestly as much as a prophetic ideal.

1. Terminology of the Temple
2. Eighth-Century BC Prophets
3. Isaiah of Jerusalem
4. Jeremiah
5. Ezekiel
6. Postexilic Prophecy
7. Conclusion

1. Terminology of the Temple.

"Temple" is the normal translation of *hêkāl*, which elsewhere refers to the palace of a king (Is 39:7; Dan 1:4). It is a loanword from the Akkadian *ekallu*, which normally means "palace" and more rarely "temple." The Akkadian is derived ultimately from Sumerian *É.GAL*, which means "large house," whether of a wealthy person, a king or a god. Thus, the temple is also the "house of Yahweh" (*bêt yhwh*), the equivalent to the house of the king (Jer 21:11). God's presence is thus localized in a "place" (*māqôm* [Hos 5:15; Jer 7:12]). To look on the temple (Jon 2:4) and come before Yahweh (Is 37:14) is to encounter the living God. It should be noted, though, that Hosea probably refers to the land of Israel when he refers to the house of Yahweh (Hos 8:1; 9:8, 15). Because God is holy and the temple takes on a corresponding holiness when it is consecrated to him, it is his "sanctuary" (*miqdāš* [Ezek 5:11]) or "holy place" (*qōdeš* [Mal 2:11]). The location of the Jerusalem temple is *Zion, an elevated ridge where the present Temple Mount is found (Zech 8:3). Since in Canaanite thought the gods lived on a mountain, the divine and cosmic significance of the temple as Yahweh's dwelling place is polemically indicated by titles such as "Mount Zion" (*har-ṣîôn* [Is 4:5]) or "my holy mountain" (*har qodšî* [Obad 16]). It often is difficult to know how far references to Jerusalem incorporate the divine presence associated with the temple. In Isaiah 2:3 the poetry sets in parallel mountain of Yahweh, house of the God of Jacob, Zion and Jerusalem.

2. Eighth-Century BC Prophets.

The eighth-century BC prophets know of the Solomonic temple, but few details of its construction and character were relevant for their concerns, which were largely theological and ethical. They were alert to attitudes and behavior that compromised the proper role of the temple in the life of the people. The only legitimate temple is in Zion/Jerusalem, where Yahweh is present to speak and warn (Joel 3:16; Amos 1:2). The prophets frequently condemn worship outside the temple. The high places (*bāmôt*) were traditional Canaanite places of worship (Is 15:2; 16:12), and there was a consistent danger of their becoming the focus of the worship of Baal and other gods (Hos 10:8; cf. Jer 19:5; Ezek 6:3). Both Hosea and Amos attack the northern kings for setting up alternatives to the Jerusalem temple as a means of legitimizing their independent political status. Preeminent among these is Bethel, which is literally the "house of God" and the place where God revealed himself to Jacob (Gen 35:1). Amos's opponent, the high priest Amaziah, insists that it is the "sanctuary [*miqdāš*] of the king" and the "house [i.e., temple] of the kingdom" (Amos 7:13). It has altars for *sacrifice (Amos 3:14; 4:4), priests, and a golden calf that Hosea fiercely condemned as idolatrous (Hos 8:4-5).

For the prophets, false religion is inseparable from immoral behavior. In his condemnation of the northern kingdom, Amos juxtaposes social and economic oppression with drinking wine in the house of God bought with unjust fines (Amos 2:8). The consequences will be defeat and death of the people (Amos 2:13-16) and the destruction of the high places and sanctuaries (Amos 7:9). For Hosea, kindness (*ḥesed*) and a living knowledge of God are more important than sacrifice (Hos 6:6). The lack of such qualities will lead to exile, where the absence of the temple will mean no opportunity to exercise the covenantal privileges of offerings and sacrifices (Amos 9:4). The continuation of the worship of Israel is contingent upon the active pursuit of righteousness, for the object of that worship is "a god of justice" (Is 30:18) (Heschel, 198-200) (see Justice, Righteousness). The continuing existence of "the mountain of the house" is never unconditional (Mic 3:12).

3. Isaiah of Jerusalem.

Isaiah 6 offers a vivid and positive interpretation of temple worship. Some regard it as a vision of Yahweh's temple in heaven, with no necessary connection to what took place in the Solomonic temple. However, the opening mundane note (Is 6:1) and Isaiah's location in Jerusalem (Is 7:3) suggest that the vision is evoked by the earthly temple worship, perhaps on one of the major festivals. In common with ancient Near Eastern ideology, the temple is the link between heaven and earth (Wyatt, 147-82). In worship the barriers between the heavenly and the earthly dwelling of God become transparent. The priestly servants of the temple have as their counterparts the angelic hosts that serve Yahweh, and the antiphonal singing of the Levitical choirs may have inspired Isaiah's account of the praise of the seraphim (Is 6:3). The smoke that filled the temple might reflect the copious use of incense (Is 6:4; cf. 1 Kings 9:25). The throne where Yahweh sits as king is high and lofty (Is 6:1), symbolized by the location of the temple on Mount Zion and by the flight of steps that probably separated the main hall from the innermost room (Monson, 290).

At the same time, the heavenly temple transcends all earthly realities. The size of the heavenly temple far exceeds the impressive but limited size of the Jerusalem temple, and even then it is too small for the incomparably great God of Israel, the hem of whose robes alone fills the space. The uniquely emphatic "Holy, holy, holy!" uttered by the seraphim reflects the most intense presence of Yahweh at the very heart of his heavenly/earthly temple. The holiness of Yahweh's person has to be preserved in its focused fullness, for to see God is to die (Judg 13:22). Isaiah wisely looks no higher than God's lowest clothing, and the smoke provides another protective barrier (cf. Lev 16:12-13). In the light of Israel's aniconic tradition, it is highly unlikely that there was any image or representation of Yahweh in the earthly temple that evoked his appearance. The throne above the cherubim in the innermost room of the temple is empty, for Israel's iconography is linguistic and metaphorical, not physical (Mettinger, 187).

Isaiah's dismay has a moral as well as an ontological basis. Impurity is a ritual category, but it may be caused by moral evil, and such impurity is absolutely incompatible with divine holiness. Isaiah recognizes that he is unclean and so is undone (Is 6:5). Yet a large part of the

temple sacrificial system concerned the purification of sins through the blood of animal sacrifices. Here, unusually, he is purified by a live coal from (presumably) the heavenly incense altar, perhaps reflecting an unknown temple purification ritual.

The presence of God in the temple is the source of life, blessing, forgiveness and protection. When Jerusalem is besieged by the Assyrians, the Rabshakeh ironically misunderstands Hezekiah's removal of the high places and altars (Is 36:7). Hezekiah's godly dismay is represented by his going to the house of Yahweh (Is 37:1). When he receives a letter, he spreads it "before Yahweh" in the temple and then prays for *salvation to the God who is "enthroned above the cherubim" (Is 37:15-16). The pleas of the *prayer do not presume a positive answer, but they receive an assurance of salvation from Isaiah (Is 37:21-35). It was most fitting to pray in the temple, but Hezekiah's answered prayer on his sickbed demonstrates that the temple was not essential for conversing with God (Is 38:2, 5).

4. Jeremiah.
Jeremiah is a priest and had access to parts of the temple (Jer 35:2), but his prophetic ministry takes place outside the temple and is highly critical of the people's attitude toward it. The assurance of God's presence and protection represented by the temple, so vividly demonstrated in the defeat of Sennacherib's armies in the time of Hezekiah, seems to have become an easy assumption over the course of the next century. This is analyzed and contradicted in the great temple sermon of Jeremiah 7 (cf. Jer 26:1-6). Many attribute the account to a Deuteronomistic editor, since it reflects the preaching style of Deuteronomy and its concern to set before the people a stark contrast between Torah obedience and disobedience (Jer 7:23-24). However, the diction is distinctive and could well represent a style of preaching adopted by Jeremiah, among others.

The prophet warns the people against trusting in the "temple of Yahweh, temple of Yahweh, temple of Yahweh" (Jer 7:4). The triple repetition conveys the deterioration of a theology of God's presence in the temple to a "meaningless mantra" (Fretheim, 132) that may be a parody of the thrice holy acclamation of Isaiah 6:3. While the temple remains "my house" (Jer

11:15), this heightens rather than lessens the demand for a corresponding righteousness of life (Jer 7:5-7). Jeremiah undermines the acclaimed holiness of the temple by describing it as a den of robbers (Jer 7:11), yet it is appropriate that it is precisely here that he announces God's word (Jer 7:2; 19:14; 26:2). The real threat of abandonment by God and destruction is proved by the historical example of the Shiloh temple, where the presence of God's name did not prevent judgment on an evil people (Jer 7:12). The people attack Jeremiah for this comparison, perhaps interpreting the destruction of Shiloh in the north as a sign of God's blessing on Jerusalem (Jer 26:9). But the doctrine of election can never trump the demand for upright behavior. Just as blessing on all of life flows from God's presence in his temple among a righteous people, so God's anger on *evil will lead to an equally comprehensive judgment that includes temple, people, *animals and land (Jer 7:20).

Although the moral dimension is primary, the speech also condemns religious practices external to the temple, such as the women making cakes of the Queen of Heaven (Jer 7:18) and the offering of sons and daughters on the high place of Topheth (Jer 7:31). This indicates that Hezekiah and Josiah's programs of centralization of worship in the temple (2 Kings 18; 23) were incomplete and often ineffective. Jeremiah 17:12 is a triple acclamation of praise of the temple, perhaps from a temple hymn or liturgy: "throne of glory, on high from the beginning, place of our sanctuary [miqdāš]." Some regard this as contrary to Jeremiah's critical attitude to the temple, but a reference to the heavenly dwelling of God would provide a strong contrast to the corrupted earthly temple.

Jeremiah, in contrast to Ezekiel, has little interest in the specific features of the temple. The ark, which had disappeared by the time of the exile, will not be remembered or remade (Jer 3:16). The ark was regarded as the footstool of God's throne (2 Kings 19:15; 1 Chron 28:2), but this title is now transferred to Jerusalem (Jer 3:17). The absence of explicit references to a new temple suggests to some that Jeremiah did not regard this as necessary (Clements, 102), a view reinforced by the absence of a number of references to the temple and the cult in the LXX. However, the expectation of a restored temple is implied by the Hebrew text. Jeremiah

33:17-18 describes the sacrifices offered by a restored priesthood, and it is a natural assumption that these would take place in a temple. After the fall of Jerusalem, Jeremiah announces the Lord's vengeance on the Babylonians for destroying the temple (Jer 50:28; 51:11), suggesting a future restoration. A broader consideration is that the general prophetic attitude to the future includes a temple, so that its omission in the shorter form of Jeremiah is perhaps accidental rather than polemical.

5. Ezekiel.

A priest as well as a prophet (Ezek 1:3), Ezekiel has a unique interest in the temple, both in its abuse and in its reconstruction. The defilement of the sanctuary is a catastrophic undermining of the entire structure of holiness that preserved God's presence in the land, and it is given a preliminary statement in Ezekiel 5:11. This is then expounded in Ezekiel 8, which records how Ezekiel is taken by the Spirit from *exile in Babylon to the Jerusalem temple. Four scenarios, which may be drawn from different times and occasions, highlight the depth of Israel's apostasy in the place that is meant to be wholly devoted to Yahweh's. A "statue of jealousy" (sēmel haqqin'â [Ezek 8:3, 5]) is perhaps a symbol of Asherah, the mother-goddess of the Canaanite pantheon. However, M. S. Odell points out that Ezekiel's usual words for *"idol" are not used and so proposes that it is a votive statue, a human figure representing the "zeal" (an alternative translation of "jealousy") of the worshiper (Odell, 104-8). Second the prophet sees a secret room with representations of images prohibited in the second commandment (Ezek 8:10; cf. Deut 5:8-9; see also Deut 4:17-18). They may also depict unclean creatures (Lev 11) that are incompatible with the holiness of the temple. The seventy elders represent the people's apostasy in a travesty of the original *covenant (Ex 24:1-9). Their idolatry complements the third scenario, women worshiping Tammuz, probably a Babylonian fertility god. Finally, twenty-five men are described as bowing towards the sun in the east, literally and metaphorically turning their back on Yahweh. Significantly, these cultic sins are juxtaposed with the social sin of violence (Ezek 8:17). The quality of religion in the temple mirrors and reinforces the quality of moral behavior outside.

It is possible that those involved interpreted

their actions as legitimate forms of Yahweh worship. For example, the sun may have been honored as one of Yahweh's host of heaven rather than as another god or equated with Yahweh. Ezekiel, though, condemns any such assimilation or syncretism. The fourfold account leads to a corresponding four-stage departure of the glory of Yahweh. The *lex talionis* (punishment matching the crime) is even more evident if the journey of Ezekiel 8 is progressively inward, toward the heart of the temple. The "sanctuary" (Ezek 8:6) describes the whole area, while "house of Yahweh" (Ezek 8:14, 16) describes the temple, and the "palace of Yahweh" (Ezek 8:16) refers to the main hall (Block, 1:285). The increasing holiness of these areas toward the innermost most holy room is an architectural reinforcement of the narrative structure that cumulatively portrays comprehensive disobedience of the first commandment (cf. Ex 20:3).

The glory thus retreats from the entrance of the gateway of the inner court (Ezek 8:3) to the threshold of the house (Ezek 9:3), to the entrance of the east gate (Ezek 10:18-19), and finally to the mountain east of the city (Ezek 11:22-23). The presence of Yahweh that manifested itself in glory in the building of the temple (1 Kings 8:11) has withdrawn, and with it any protection of the city and nation from invasion and defeat. Yet this is not a total abandonment, for Yahweh promises that he will be to the exiles a *miqdāš mĕʿaṭ* (Ezek 11:16), an enigmatic phrase referring to time ("a sanctuary for a little while") or quality ("a sanctuary to a limited extent"). It minimizes the importance of the Jerusalem temple, but also hints that the story is not ended. It may refer to forms of access to God possible in exile, such as prayer or the ministry of Ezekiel. The close of the first half of the book announces that Yahweh will profane his sanctuary (Ezek 24:21), anticipating the desecration of the temple by the Babylonians. The temple has become for the Israelites "the pride of your power, the delight of your eyes and the desire of your souls," but the people's trust in the strength, beauty and usefulness of the temple is illusory and must be banished before a better temple can be constructed.

The climax of the prophecies of resurrection, gathering and restoration of the people in Ezekiel 37 is the promise of a sanctuary (*miqdāš*) in the midst of the people (Ezek 37:26, 28) and a dwelling place (*miškān*) over them (Ezek 37:27).

The echoes of the covenant with the ancestors (Ezek 37:26) and with the people at Sinai (Ezek 37:27) emphasize that this is the ultimate fulfillment of God's past promises of presence. This dramatic affirmation then becomes the basis for a vision of a new temple in Ezekiel 40—48. Many see signs of redactional layers in this section, but there is nothing definitely later than the sixth century BC, and the vision can be regarded as a complex unity.

The extensive description of the temple is primarily concerned with the boundaries and practices that maintain the holiness of the temple and guard the presence of Yahweh. Ezekiel is brought to a very high mountain (Ezek 40:2), the traditional home of the gods in Canaanite mythology and the basis for claims about Zion's superiority (cf. Ps 48). It is the polar opposite of the valley of dry bones (Ezek 37:1-14) in Ezekiel's theological geography. Like the tabernacle, the temple consists of a series of divided spaces that communicate increasing holiness. Horizontally there is a square outer court (Ezek 40:17-19) and inner court (Ezek 40:44), where the equality of the sides is possibly a sign of perfection or holiness (Stevenson, 42). The temple itself has three sections: the vestibule (*ʾulām* [Ezek 40:48]), the main hall or nave (*hêkal* [Ezek 41:1]) and the most holy place (*qōdeš haqqŏdāšîm* [Ezek 41:4]). The graded holiness of the whole is reinforced vertically by a series of steps at the entrances of the courts and the temple (Ezek 40:6, 34, 49). The outermost wall has three massive gates. There are none to the west, since the temple and a mysterious building (Ezek 41:12) occupy that side. The military nature of the gates emphasizes the need for a strict separation between the holy and the impure, for Ezekiel has previously shown how the absence of such separation led to the first temple's destruction (Ezek 8—11).

A series of chambers surrounds the outer and inner courtyard, probably places for storage, cooking, and eating. The temple is the dynamic stage for sacrifices and processions. The east gate is where the glory of Yahweh enters the temple (Ezek 43:1-5), reversing the departure described in Ezekiel 8—11. It then remains shut, symbolizing God's permanent presence in the temple. Worshipers must use the other two gates, although the prince is allowed to eat in the east gate, a sign of his rank but also of his limited and defined role in the temple hierarchy. The spaces of the temple, differentiated according to their holiness, are related to the different groups mentioned. The roles of the actors and the restrictions on their movements contribute to the overall goal of ensuring that ordered worship takes place according to the relevant laws. Foreigners and the uncircumcised are barred from entry (Ezek 44:4-8), whereas Levites guard the gates and slaughter the animals for sacrifice brought by the citizens (Ezek 44:10-14). The Zadokite priests alone are responsible for offering the fat and the blood in the main hall (Ezek 44:15-16) because they, unlike the Levites, had proved faithful (Ezek 44:10, 13, 15). Nothing is said about the high priest or holy of holies, perhaps because the potent atonement performed there (see Lev 16) is no longer needed.

The purpose of the temple is to provide access to Yahweh, who is the source of life and blessing in a new Eden (see Gen 2:10). That this is not limited to the center but affects the whole land is symbolized by the stream that flows from the temple and becomes a river of life for all (Ezek 47:1-12). The renewal of the environment is a further result of the return of Yahweh and the restoration of the temple. The temple is also at the center of the city (Ezek 48:21), which is called "Yahweh is there" (Ezek 48:35), a fitting conclusion to the theme of God's presence that is so central to the theology of Ezekiel.

The status of Ezekiel's temple has been much debated. The detailed measurements and laws might indicate a realistic program of restoration aimed at avoiding abuses found in the Solomonic temple. Yet this is not a blueprint for builders (Stevenson), and there are ideal or utopian features, such as the river flowing from the temple (Ezek 47:1-12). Yet the mundane detail also indicates that it is not depicting an eternal heavenly reality, as in Isaiah 6. One suggestion is that it refers to spiritual realities rather than physical possibilities (Block, 2:505), although "spiritual" must not take on an inner or individual nuance that undercuts the material and corporate character of Ezekiel's temple. Another perspective is that Ezekiel presents an extended theological meditation, expressed in a symbolic structure of meaning that transcends the present and provides a critical alternative to the current state of affairs (Blenkinsopp, 199, 237). The vision combines elements of both prophetic and apocalyptic eschatology, but the presentation is located in the present rather than the future: "The vision merges mythic space with historical geography and then situates the prophet in this transformed space" (Odell, 537).

One problematic interpretive trend regards these chapters as a final, definitive solution, whether right or wrong. But prophetic visions are not to be interpreted rigidly; they are statements of intent open to flexible reinterpretation in later, different circumstances. This is what Ezekiel himself is doing in taking up features of the Solomonic temple and the priestly portrayal of the tabernacle but developing them in creative ways that respond to contemporary problems. Ezekiel's map is not reality; it correlates truths about Israel's calling and God's character in ways that acknowledge the deficiencies of the past and pledges hope in a God who promises to dwell once again in the midst of his people. The radical differences of his temple from that of Zerubbabel did not threaten the vision's authenticity, which only became a problem in a later era that read the texts more flatly. In turn, the book of Revelation selectively takes aspects of Ezekiel's temple and integrates them in a vision that incorporates other biblical texts and a grasp of God's radical new revelation in Christ (Rev 21). A common identity in Christ makes internal distinctions within the temple-city unnecessary, all the sacrifices are subsumed under Christ's once-for-all sacrifice, and the greater holiness achieved leads to worship in the three-dimensional perfection of a cubic temple-city (Rev 21:16).

6. Postexilic Prophecy.

The fall of the temple led to a variety of responses to the worship of God in a "templeless age" (Middlemas). These included continued (though limited) worship (Jer 41:5), anguished lamentation focused on the catastrophe of the exile (Lamentations), and assimilation to the religion of the conquerors (the target of Second Isaiah's polemic). But the prophets retain a firm grasp on the sovereignty and purposes of God, who is the source of hope through and beyond judgment. Ezekiel (Ezek 20:40-42) and Second Isaiah (Is 44:28) prepare the people for a return to Jerusalem and the renewed presence of God in the midst of his people.

Ezekiel and others had emphasized that the temple was not necessary for God's continuing presence. It is not surprising that some regarded its rebuilding as a lesser priority, especially in a time of drought and economic hardship (Zech 8:10). However, in 521 BC, sixty-seven years after the destruction of the temple, Haggai accuses the people of neglecting to rebuild the house of the Lord and instead looking to their own houses and well-being (Hag 1:2-4). The "therefore" of Haggai 1:10 highlights the correlation between how the people honor God and how God blesses them (or not). The promise that Yahweh is with them (Hag 1:13) emphasizes that the temple represents but does not exhaust the assured presence of God. When the people lament that the rebuilt temple suffers in comparison to the glory/splendor (*kābôd*) of the Solomonic one (Hag 2:3), Haggai prophesies a shaking of the universe and the nations (Hag 2:5-6) that will fill the temple with a greater glory and bring prosperity/peace (*šālôm* [Hag 2:9]). The temple focuses the returnees' dreams and hopes of a God-given better life, which is anticipated even now in a promise of blessing (Hag 2:19).

Zechariah, Haggai's contemporary, knows that Yahweh has a holy dwelling (*mā'ôn*) in heaven (Zech 2:13), but he looks to the rebuilding of the earthly temple (Zech 1:16; 4:8-10). The vision of the lampstand (Zech 4:1-5) is based on one of the original furnishings of the temple but is freely adapted to highlight the joint significance of king and high priest in the new order. In a related but distinct oracle (Zech 4:6-10), the role of the royal heir, Zerubbabel, is emphasized over that of the high priest in the building and ritual rededication of the temple that his ancestors David and Solomon originally designed and built. The "head stone" of Zechariah 4:7 may be the foundation stone, but D. L. Petersen suggests that it was a "former stone" from the first temple, thereby emphasizing continuity with the temple's previous status and role (Petersen 1974). There are several allusions to the temple in the second part of the book (Zech 9—14). In a difficult verse, the wages of a shepherd are thrown into the house of the Lord (Zech 11:13), possibly reflecting the temple's role as a treasury or bank. The last two verses of the book imaginatively extend a priestly degree of holiness (cf. Ex 39:30; Lev 23:20) to the cooking pots of the temple precincts, the city and even the land (Zech 14:20-21).

The postexilic texts of Isaiah emphasize Yahweh's abiding sanctuary in heaven (Is 57:15), which also allows him to dwell with the humble (Is 63:15). An earthly temple is not essential for access to him. Isaiah 66:1-4 emphasizes the priority of God's temple in heaven, which makes an earthly temple or earthly worship unnecessary and even an abomination. Yet the wider canonical context implies that this is not to be read as an absolute rejection. Israel's material faith ultimately requires the restoration of Jerusalem and Zion (Is 24:23; 66:20), which will include a renewed sanctuary of glory and beauty (Is 60:13) that is a prestigious center of sacrifice (Is 60:7). To earlier prophecies of instruction and justice for the nations (Is 2:3-4) is added a promise that the temple will be a universal house of prayer (Is 56:7).

Whereas Haggai and Zechariah encourage the construction of the temple, Malachi evaluates the ongoing worship in it (Japhet). Like the preexilic prophets, he wishes to reform the abuse of worship. He condemns the priests for imperfect sacrifices that show a lack of honor (*kābôd*) for God (Mal 1:6-10). Wrong attitudes nullify any value to the temple (Mal 1:10), and in ironic contrast, the nations can give Israel lessons in pure offerings (Mal 1:11; cf. Is 19:16, 19; 56:5). Malachi also accuses the people of robbing God by not bringing the fullness of tithes to the temple (Mal 3:8-9). Only reversing this behavior will lift the curse on Israel's crops and bring blessing and honor among the nations (Mal 3:10-12).

Various dates for Joel have been proposed, but its portrait of the temple makes good sense in a postexilic setting. The call to lament assumes a working temple where offerings are brought and priests intercede for the people (Joel 2:15, 17). Joel's vision of the eschatological future includes a temple that will be the source of a fountain of water for the land, a physical and symbolic sign of blessing (Joel 3:18). This provision reverses the disasters announced in Joel 1—2 and flows from God's promise to live in the midst of Israel (Joel 2:27).

7. Conclusion.

The prophets witness to a varied response to the temple, depending on the particular historical, social and moral context of their ministry. The question of the temple is closely bound up with the maintenance and preservation of Yahweh's presence and holiness, which is the source of peace and prosperity. The prophets do not condemn the temple as unnecessary, but they do point out how it can be compromised by idolatrous and unjust behavior. The temple of Solomon is caught up in the judgment announced by the prophets on the people's sinfulness. Its destruction at the exile (587 BC) provides the space for Ezekiel's visionary temple, and a key register for faith in Yahweh was the building of Zerubbabel's temple. This falls far short of what the previous temple stood for, and the prophecies of a renewed temple incomparable in glory and splendor lead to a heightened hope for God's restorative action.

A recurrent assumption is that Yahweh's palace/temple is in heaven (Mic 1:2). This may have a physical counterpart on earth, but the heavenly temple is primary and inviolable; the earthly one a conditional gift. The temple may be a limited earthly and material construct, but it was regarded as an effective, essential and often awesome means of drawing close to God. The omnipresence of God is a relatively superficial affirmation compared with meeting God in a defined space and time. The prophets often apply a hermeneutic of suspicion to the temple, but this is a contextual rather than an absolute standpoint. The temple is a gracious gift of God that has a continuing role (whether in vision or reality) in articulating the practical possibilities of an authentic meeting with God in worship.

But worship is only one dimension of the prophetic conception of the temple. If the temple is properly administered and becomes the holy center of the life of a holy people, then there are personal, national and cosmic consequences. The prophetic vision of the temple as the source of water that flows out to the land is a vivid expression of this belief. When the Lord is present in his temple, then the people will know fertility and blessing, the nations will be instructed into the ways of peace, and the very cosmos will be transformed. The prophetic conception of the temple thus prepares for the coming of Jesus Christ, who is seen as the ultimate focus of God's presence among his people (Eph 2:21-22).

See also LITURGY AND CULT; SACRIFICE AND ATONEMENT; WORSHIP; ZION.

BIBLIOGRAPHY. **G. K. Beale,** *The Temple and the Church's Mission: A Biblical Theology of the Dwelling Place of God* (NSBT; Leicester: Apollos, 2004); **J. Blenkinsopp,** *Ezekiel* (Interpretation; Louisville: Westminster/John Knox, 1990); **D. I. Block,** *The Book of Ezekiel* (2 vols.; NICOT; Grand Rapids: Eerdmans, 1997-1998); **R. E. Clements,** *God and Temple* (Oxford: Blackwell, 1965); **T. E. Fretheim,** *Jeremiah* (SHBC; Macon, GA: Smith & Helwys, 2002); **M. Haran,** *Temples and Temple-Service in Ancient Israel: An Inquiry into Biblical Cult Phenomena and the Historical Setting of the Priestly School* (Oxford: Clarendon Press, 1978); **A. J. Heschel,** *The Prophets* (New York: Jewish Publication Society of America, 1962); **W. Janzen,** *Old Testament Ethics: A Paradigmatic Approach* (Louisville: Westminster/John Knox, 1994); **S. Japhet,** "The Temple in the Restoration Period: Reality and Ideology," *USQR* 44 (1991) 195-251; **A. Johnson,** *The Cultic Prophet and Israel's Psalmody* (Cardiff: University of Wales Press, 1979); **J. Klawans,** *Purity, Sacrifice, and the Temple: Symbolism and Supersessionism in the Study of Ancient Judaism* (Oxford: Oxford University Press, 2006); **W. McKane,** "Prophet and Institution," *ZAW* 94 (1982) 251-66; **T. Meadowcroft,** *Haggai* (RNBC; Sheffield: Sheffield Phoenix, 2006); **T. N. D. Mettinger,** "Israelite Aniconism: Developments and Origins," in *The Image and the Book: Iconic Cults, Aniconism, and the Rise of Book Religion in Israel and the Ancient near East,* ed. K. van der Toorn (CBET 21; Leuven: Peeters, 1997) 173-204; **M. Metzger,** "Himmlische und Irdische Wohnstatt Jahwes," *UF* 2 (1970) 139-58; **J. A. Middlemas,** *The Templeless Age: An Introduction to the History, Literature, and Theology of the "Exile"* (Louisville; London: Westminster/John Knox, 2007); **J. Monson,** "The 'Ain Dara Temple and the Jerusalem Temple," in *Text, Artifact, and Image: Revealing Ancient Israelite Religion,* ed. G. M. Beckman and T. J. Lewis (BJS 346; Providence: Brown Judaic Studies, 2006) 273-99; **M. S. Odell,** *Ezekiel* (SHBC; Macon, GA: Smyth & Helwys, 2005); **D. L. Petersen,** "Zerubbabel and Jerusalem Temple Reconstruction," *CBQ* 36 (1974) 366-72; idem, "The Temple in Persian Period Prophetic Texts," *BTB* 21 (1991) 88-96; **M. Schmidt,** *Prophet und Tempel: Eine Studie zum Problem der Gottesnähe im Alten Testament* (Zollikon-Zürich: Evangelischer Verlag, 1948); **K. R. Stevenson,** *Vision of Transformation: The Territorial Rhetoric of Ezekiel 40-48* (SBLDS 154; Atlanta: Scholars Press, 1996); **H. G. M. Williamson,** "Temple and Worship in Isaiah 6," in *Temple and Worship in Biblical Israel: Proceedings of the Oxford Old Testament*

Seminar, ed. J. Day (LHBOTS 422; London: T & T Clark, 2005) 123-44; **N. Wyatt,** *Space and Time in the Religious Life of the Near East* (BibSem 85; Sheffield: Sheffield Academic Press, 2001). P. P. Jenson

TEN COMMANDMENTS. *See* COVENANT; LAW.

TEXT AND TEXTUAL CRITICISM

This article discusses the Hebrew text of the OT Prophetic Books and the textual criticism and textual problems of those writings. The article also discusses the textual resources available for the study of the text of the Prophetic Books in both Hebrew and Greek, especially the biblical materials available from Qumran and the Judean Desert. Although the textual critic also makes use of the other ancient versions—the Targum (Aramaic), the Peshitta (Syriac), the Vulgate and the Old Latin (Latin)—these versions will not be discussed in this article. As a general rule, the versions just listed, especially the Targum and the Vulgate, tend to stay very close to the traditional text of the Hebrew Bible. To a lesser extent the article also discusses recent theories of the history of the text of the Hebrew Bible as it pertains to the Prophetic Books.

1. General Considerations
2. The Biblical Text at Qumran
3. Textual Resources and Scholarly Tools for the Text of the Prophets

1. General Considerations.

1.1. Textual Criticism. Textual criticism of the Hebrew Bible involves the study of the various textual witnesses and manuscripts of the Bible in order to identify and correct mistakes in the text. As with any text that has been transmitted by hand for a long period of time, the ancient copyists sometimes made mistakes, and those mistakes were not always noticed and corrected. The *Dead Sea Scrolls (DSS) preserve many examples of scribal/copyist mistakes. Many times the mistakes were then corrected by the original scribe or by a later one. Sometimes, however, scribal errors were not noticed, and later scribes continued to copy the mistakes, even when the text no longer made sense. One of the primary goals of the textual criticism of the Hebrew Bible is the detection and correction of ancient scribal mistakes. In order to do that, textual critics make use of every available piece of evidence, particularly ancient biblical manu-

scripts in Hebrew such as the DSS. Textual critics also make use of the ancient translations of the Bible, especially the Greek translation, the Septuagint (LXX), since it is complete and a very early witness to the text of the Hebrew Bible.

It is easy to understand that textual critics make use of ancient Hebrew manuscripts to study the Hebrew text of the Bible. Comparing texts in the same language makes sense. However, we also make use of ancient translations to study the text of the Hebrew Bible, and when we do so, we must first do our best to understand that translation on its own terms. The LXX is an especially important resource for the textual criticism of the Hebrew Bible. We know that it is the earliest translation of the Hebrew text, begun in the third century BC, probably with the Pentateuch, and probably completed for the rest of the Hebrew Bible by the first century BC. The LXX began life as a translation but quickly became the Scriptures for Greek-speaking Jews and later for Christians throughout the Mediterranean world. The LXX became Greek literature. When we use the LXX for the textual criticism of the Hebrew Bible, it is important that we read and understand the entire composition with which we are concerned. It is not enough to read the words of the verse that one is interested in. We must understand the broad context and how the translator worked before we can use the Greek text to correct or reconstruct the Hebrew text. When we use the LXX, we must retranslate it into Hebrew, using knowledge of the techniques of the translator. When we have done this, we produce hypothetical variant forms of the Hebrew text. There is, naturally, greater uncertainty with such reconstructed variants in comparison to ancient Hebrew manuscripts, but we need every piece of evidence that we can secure in order to understand the text better. So even though translated variants from the Greek or another ancient translation are less certain, we use them with due caution in our attempt to correct the text.

In discussing the text and the necessity of the textual criticism of the Hebrew Bible, it is important to clarify assumptions about the text and its history. All textual witnesses, the Hebrew texts as well as the Greek, may have simple scribal mistakes. One of the advantages that the DSS give us is that they preserve many examples of ancient scribal errors and how the scribes corrected their mistakes when they caught them. These mistakes need to be recognized and corrected by the textual critic, but in addition to correcting ancient scribal errors, both accidental and intentional, it is important to recognize where the different witnesses to a composition differ from each other and why.

For example, recognizing how and why the Hebrew and Greek versions of the book of *Jeremiah differ from each other leads us to a new understanding of those witnesses to the text. The Hebrew and Greek versions of Jeremiah are not copies in Hebrew and Greek of the same composition. Scholars now understand that the Hebrew version of Jeremiah, which is the version translated in most English-language Bibles, is actually a revised and slightly expanded version of the book. The Greek version of Jeremiah, however, seems to be a copy of an earlier version of the book that was translated from an older, shorter and differently organized Hebrew copy of Jeremiah. The Hebrew version of Jeremiah became canonical in Judaism and in those varieties of Christianity that used Jerome's Latin translation of Jeremiah, which he based on the Hebrew text. But in Eastern Christianity, wherever the Greek Bible or its daughter translations were used, the older version of the book of Jeremiah remained the canonical form, just as it had been in earliest, Greek-speaking Christianity.

The differences between the Hebrew and Greek versions of the book of Jeremiah represent a clear and obvious example of where the Hebrew and Greek versions of a biblical book can differ from each other. However, differences on a lesser scale exist in many other books of the OT as well. For example, the book of Joshua in the Greek version seems to preserve a shorter, older version of the book than the Hebrew version of Joshua. In addition, the book of *Ezekiel in the Greek version seems to reflect a slightly shorter version of the book than the Hebrew version. The situation in the book of *Daniel is similar, but more complicated. There are two versions of the Greek translation of the book of Daniel, the LXX and a version attributed to Theodotion, which came to dominate in most of the Greek manuscripts of Daniel. The point here is that scholars now recognize that in addition to preserving variant readings, the Greek Bible and the Hebrew manuscripts from Qumran also preserve variant literary editions of books in the Hebrew

Bible. The versions that were chosen to become the canonical forms of some biblical books consistently seem to be later literary editions. The older versions, preserved sometimes in the Greek and Hebrew witnesses to the text, actually preserve older versions of the composition. In other words, the same biblical manuscripts that we use in the textual criticism of the Hebrew Bible also show us the last stages in the literary growth of the biblical text. The comparison of differing editions of a composition is the scholarly practice known as literary criticism, which studies the growth or development of a literary composition.

1.2. The History of the Biblical Text. The Hebrew text of the OT Prophetic Books that most biblical scholars use is based on a single manuscript copied and annotated in the year AD 1009. This is the famous St. Petersburg Codex, formerly known as the Leningrad Codex (B^{19A}). This codex, the oldest complete copy of the Hebrew Bible, is annotated with vocalization, accentual systems and comments on the text collectively known as Masorah in the upper and lower margins of each page as well as in the spaces between columns. The St. Petersburg Codex has been the base text for the most widely used critical edition of the Hebrew text, the *Biblia Hebraica*, since 1937. It is a superb exemplar of the Masoretic Text (MT) of the Hebrew Bible, which is normative in Judaism and has been the basis for most Christian translations of the OT. In the *Biblia Hebraica Quinta* the Masoretic notes to the text are translated, which can provide the student of the text with many useful details. The Minor Prophets volume of *Biblia Hebraica Quinta* was published in 2010. Another very important medieval manuscript of the Hebrew Bible is the Aleppo Codex. This manuscript is slightly older than the St. Petersburg Codex (AD 960) but is, unfortunately, incomplete. The Aleppo Codex is used as the base text, where extant, of the *Hebrew University Bible*. The *Hebrew University Bible* has published volumes for the books of Isaiah, Jeremiah and Ezekiel. The first volume of the Minor Prophets is in preparation at this time.

With the publication of the biblical DSS, scholars now have copies of Hebrew biblical manuscripts that not only provide many variant readings and valuable information for the correction of the text but also allow us to recover the last stages in the composition of some of the biblical books. These manuscripts range in date from c. 275 BC to c. AD 68. All of them are technically "pre-Masoretic" copies of the biblical books without vocalization, accentual systems or Masorah. The biblical manuscripts from the Judean Desert in both Hebrew and Greek also show us the diversity in the text of the developing Bible during the last two centuries BC and the first century AD.

2. The Biblical Text at Qumran.

With the completed publication of the approximately two hundred biblical scrolls from Qumran, the nature of the biblical text known from this collection of manuscripts, which probably represented the library or collection of the Jewish group resident there, has become clearer. It is now evident that the Jewish community at Qumran possessed a collection of biblical and nonbiblical manuscripts that exhibited a great deal of variety in terms of the type of biblical text. Before the discovery of the scrolls, scholars had known of the MT, the LXX and the Samaritan Pentateuch. In a recent study, E. Tov analyzed the biblical scrolls from Qumran and divided them according to their relationships with forms of the OT previously known by scholars. Tov found that approximately 47.1 percent of the biblical manuscripts known from Qumran may be designated as "proto-Masoretic" or "proto-Rabbinic" because they are most closely related to the form of the Hebrew text preserved in the medieval MT. Only 2.5 percent of the Qumran scrolls were most closely related to the Samaritan text of the Pentateuch and are therefore called by some scholars "pre-Samaritan" texts. Another small group of texts, only 3.3 percent of the total, were most closely related to the Hebrew source of the LXX. Finally, 47.1 percent of all biblical manuscripts fall into the category that scholars call "non-aligned" texts. These are biblical scrolls that are independent and therefore do not show any particular affiliation with the known types of text. Of the groups of biblical scrolls from Qumran just mentioned, all except the pre-Samaritan group are known for the Prophetic Books. Especially well-known are the Jeremiah manuscripts from Cave 4 at Qumran 4Q71 and 4Q72a, which are very close to the Hebrew source of the Greek book of Jeremiah, which differs in both length and order of material from the Hebrew book of Jeremiah, as was discussed briefly above.

At Qumran there was remarkable diversity in the text of biblical books, but the two largest groups of biblical manuscripts were the non-aligned group and the proto-Masoretic group. When we look beyond Qumran to biblical manuscripts found at other locations in the Judean Desert and from slightly later in time, the picture begins to change. At other locations, such as Masada and the Wadi Murabbaʿat, the only text type attested among biblical manuscripts is the proto-Masoretic. In other words, as Tov has argued in another study, the proto-Masoretic text type becomes the dominant text type shortly after the first Jewish war against Rome, which ended in AD 73. By that time, and later, all biblical manuscripts in Hebrew from the Judean Desert are of the same textual tradition. These proto-Masoretic texts may be thought of as ancestral to the medieval MT, known from the Aleppo Codex and the St. Petersburg Codex. The proto-Masoretic text type probably was, for the most part, the basis for the Aramaic translations known as the Targum and later still, in the time of Jerome, for the Vulgate. Consequently, the Targum and the Vulgate frequently do not differ dramatically from the MT and therefore seldom contribute much in the study of the problems of the Hebrew text. They are, however, important in the study of the history of the exegesis of the text and its translation. The biblical texts from Qumran and the Judean Desert, regardless of their text type, are important early witnesses to the Hebrew text of the developing Bible and are therefore of first importance for the textual critic. Second in importance for the study of the text is the LXX.

3. Textual Resources and Scholarly Tools for the Text of the Prophets.

3.1. Introduction and Scholarly Resources. In this section I briefly discuss the state of the Hebrew and Greek versions of the text of each of the prophets in the order in which they occur in the Hebrew Bible. I will also mention especially important tools and/or manuscripts for the study of the Prophetic Books. The reader is urged to consult the bibliography, where all the major textual resources are listed. This article is not a textual commentary on the books of the prophets. Therefore, I will not discuss individual difficult passages, but rather present an overview of current scholarly understandings of the text of the Prophetic Books.

The MT of the Prophetic Books is available for all of the prophets in the *Biblia Hebraica Stuttgartensia*, based on the St. Petersburg codex. In the next edition of the *Biblia Hebraica*, the *Biblia Hebraica Quinta*, only the Minor Prophets volume is available. *The Hebrew University Bible*, which is based on the Aleppo Codex, is available for Isaiah, Jeremiah and Ezekiel. The first volume of the Minor Prophets in this important edition is due soon. The Greek text of the prophets is available primarily in the *Göttingen Septuagint* volumes. There are separate volumes for Isaiah, Jeremiah and Ezekiel, and a single volume for the twelve Minor Prophets. There is also an excellent edition of the Greek scroll of the Minor Prophets from Naḥal Ḥever. This is an important manuscript for the study of the Greek text of the Minor Prophets and for the history of the Greek and Hebrew texts of the prophets. In addition, the biblical manuscripts from Qumran are now available in a convenient single volume that presents the Hebrew texts in canonical order along with a listing of textual variants. This volume is based on the publication of these manuscripts in the *Discoveries in the Judaean Desert* series and so makes a consultation of those volumes unnecessary other than for technical work.

3.2. Isaiah. The MT of the book of Isaiah has a large number of *hapax legomena* (words occurring only once in the Bible) and rare words, which can make it very difficult to understand. There are also a number of passages where the text is problematic.

From Qumran we have a total of twenty-one manuscripts of the book of Isaiah. Scholars are fortunate to have the entire scroll of Isaiah from Cave 1 at Qumran, 1QIsaᵃ. This manuscript is the only biblical scroll completely preserved, and it is one of the longest we know of, 7.34 m in length. The scroll was copied by two different scribes between 150 and 120 BC. This means that although 1QIsaᵃ was discovered at Qumran, it was not copied there, since it predates the founding of the settlement. 1QIsaᵃ is available in three editions, including the forthcoming two-volume edition by E. Ulrich and P. Flint. Although 1QIsaᵃ shows thousands of variants from the MT, many of these are orthographic in nature; that is, they consist of spelling differences. Nevertheless, 1QIsaᵃ is extremely important in the study of the text of Isaiah. Also from Cave 1 is 1QIsaᵇ, which is not as well preserved as

1QIsaᵃ and stands closer to the MT in terms of its text. There are eighteen manuscripts of Isaiah from Cave 4 and one manuscript from Cave 5, and while most of these are relatively small, they are potentially important for the study of the text of Isaiah. Finally, there is also a fragment of Isaiah from Murabbaʿat. The LXX of Isaiah, which is thought to date from the mid-second century BC, appears to be a free, even paraphrastic, translation that is also interpretive. It is therefore not as helpful for the reconstruction of the Hebrew text as might be hoped. It is unlikely that the translator had a Hebrew text before him that was radically different from the MT; rather, scholars think that the translator was contemporizing his translation to make it refer to issues and concepts of the translator's own time.

3.3. Jeremiah. As is well known, the MT of Jeremiah differs dramatically from the LXX version of Jeremiah. The Greek text is shorter than the Hebrew by one-sixth (17 percent). The Greek version deviates from the order of some of the chapters in the Hebrew version. For example, most obviously, the prophecies against the nations in Jeremiah 46—52 in the MT are found after Jeremiah 25:13 in the LXX version. In this case, the manuscripts of Jeremiah from Qumran help us to understand why these versions of Jeremiah are different from each other. Two of the five Jeremiah manuscripts from Cave 4 at Qumran, 4Q71 and 4Q72a, correspond to the Greek version of Jeremiah in terms of the arrangement of the content of the book and the length of the book. This correspondence is understood to indicate that it is most likely that the LXX translators of Jeremiah had as their Hebrew source a manuscript very much like 4Q71 and 4Q72a, and that they neither abbreviated their text nor rearranged the content. Tov and others have argued that the pattern of differences between the MT and the LXX most likely indicates that the version found in the MT reflects a revised and expanded version of the form of Jeremiah found in the LXX. In other words, LXX Jeremiah is best understood as an earlier, "first" edition of the book. The version found in the MT is best understood as a "second" edition of the book, which the ancient scribes reorganized and expanded slightly. It is the "second" edition that became normative in Judaism, but the "first" edition was initially, until the time of Jerome, the form of the book used by Greek-speaking Christians, and is still used by Greek-speaking Christians. Although there is some discussion of this model for understanding the textual history of Jeremiah, most scholars find it convincing. In the first volume of his commentary on Jeremiah, W. McKane provides detailed discussion of the textual evidence. He is not entirely convinced by this explanation of the different forms of the text.

3.4. Ezekiel. The situation in the book of Ezekiel is similar to that in Jeremiah, but the differences between the Hebrew version and the Greek version are not so dramatic. The LXX version of Ezekiel preserves a slightly shorter version, by only 4-5 percent. In Ezekiel, unlike Jeremiah, rearrangement of content is not an obvious characteristic of the difference between the two versions. There are recensional differences in Ezekiel 7 only. Although older commentaries usually describe the plusses in the MT text of Ezekiel as "glosses," Tov has argued that they are evidence of recensional differences. The Greek translation of Ezekiel is relatively literal, and this is understood to support the idea of recensional differences. To summarize, the MT text of Ezekiel is thought by some scholars to be a later and slightly longer edition than the LXX version of Ezekiel. Unfortunately, for Ezekiel we do not have the convenient Hebrew manuscript copies from Qumran that support the hypothesis, which we do have for Jeremiah. There are six fragmentary copies of Ezekiel from Qumran and one fragment from Masada.

3.5. Daniel. The book of Daniel is unique in several ways. First, although Daniel is grouped with the Prophetic Books in the Christian canon, most scholars would classify the book of Daniel, or at least Daniel 7—12, as apocalyptic, a genre related to prophecy but quite distinct from it. Apocalyptic writings in the Christian canon are limited to Daniel and the book of Revelation, although parts of Zechariah 9—14 are similar. Second, Daniel is written in a mixture of *Hebrew and *Aramaic. Daniel 1:1—2:4a and Daniel 8:1—12:13 are written in Hebrew; Daniel 2:4b—7:28 is written in Aramaic. Third, as mentioned above, there are two distinct versions of the Greek translation of Daniel. The better-attested version is attributed to an early Christian writer, Theodotion. The less well-attested version is that of the LXX. The LXX translation is

longer than the Hebrew/Aramaic form preserved in the MT and varies from it considerably. The LXX of Daniel arranges the chapters in this order: 1—4; 7; 8; 5; 6; 9—12, a sequence that may go back to the original translation. Although the LXX version of Daniel is longer, it also contains some minuses in comparison to the MT, and the style can be paraphrastic. The version attributed to Theodotion is closer to the MT. This may have been what led to its adoption by the Christian churches, possibly under the influence of Origen. Both the LXX and the Theodotionic versions of Daniel were known to the writers of the NT. The history and relationships among the Greek versions is much debated by scholars and remains unclear. Much work remains to be done, especially on the Greek version assigned to Theodotion. From Qumran we have a total of eight manuscripts of Daniel, some of which are quite fragmentary. All these manuscripts come from the Second Temple period. The Daniel manuscripts from Qumran do not deviate in significant ways from the MT. The shifts between Hebrew and Aramaic and vice versa are preserved in the Daniel manuscripts in agreement with the MT of Daniel. The shorter version of Daniel, preserved in the MT, is also attested in the Qumran manuscripts.

The book of Daniel in its Greek versions has also accrued additions to the story that are not attested in either the manuscripts from Qumran or in the MT.

3.6. The Twelve Minor Prophets. Most scholars assume that the collection of the twelve Minor Prophets was complete by the beginning of the second century BC, based on this reference from Sirach: "May the bones of the Twelve Prophets send forth new life from where they lie, for they comforted the people of Jacob and delivered them with confident hope" (Sir 49:10 NRSV). This may be correct, but it is likely that the Greek collection of the Minor Prophets developed somewhat differently than the Hebrew collection, since the order of the first six books differs between the two collections. The order in the Hebrew texts is Hosea, Joel, Amos, Obadiah, Jonah, Micah. But in the LXX the eighth-century BC prophets are grouped together so that the order is Hosea, Amos, Micah, Joel, Obadiah, Jonah. The LXX of the Minor Prophets is thought by many scholars to be the work of a single translator. In seven of the prophetic books the Greek and the Hebrew texts are quite close to each other. As might be expected, however, where the Hebrew text is difficult or corrupt, as in Hosea or Micah, the Greek text can be quite different from the Hebrew.

The text of the twelve Minor Prophets is known from eight or nine copies from Qumran, seven or eight of which are from Cave 4. The uncertainty in number has to do with one manuscript, 4Q168, which is a fragment of Micah so small that it is uncertain whether it is the remains of a scroll containing at least part of the book of Micah or the remains of a commentary on the book of Micah. Scholars assume that the other manuscripts from Qumran, which are fragmentary and usually do not preserve the transitions between the Prophetic Books, originally contained all twelve Minor Prophets. However, only two of the scrolls from Cave 4, 4Q77 and 4Q82, actually do preserve transitions and thus were likely to be scrolls of the Twelve. One of the two oldest copies of the Minor Prophets from Cave 4 at Qumran, 4Q76, which dates from the middle of the second century BC, also preserves a dramatically different order of the books. The scroll is quite fragmentary, but most of the second and third chapters of the book of Malachi are well preserved. The ending of Malachi is clear on the leather, and so is the fact that on a piece of the following column there was another composition. The editor of the manuscript has reconstructed the meager remains as the beginning of the book of Jonah. This makes sense of the letter remains on the leather, and there are also other fragments of Jonah preserved from 4Q76. If the reconstruction is correct, then we have evidence that the order of the twelve Minor Prophets in the mid-second century BC was not yet set, and that there were at least three different arrangements of the collection in circulation at that time. 4Q76 is one of the oldest manuscripts found at Qumran, and it would have been copied relatively close to the time of the translation of the Minor Prophets into Greek.

This makes one of the other Minor Prophets scrolls from the Judean Desert even more interesting. We are extremely fortunate to have a scroll of the Minor Prophets from Naḥal Ḥever that dates from the last half of the first century BC. This scroll, 8Ḥev 1, is a Greek manuscript. One of the interesting characteristics of this scroll is that although it is in Greek, it preserves the books of the Minor Prophets in

the same order as the Hebrew text, and so, because of its date, it is the earliest evidence for the order of the Minor Prophets that becomes canonical in the MT. In the Naḥal Ḥever scroll the book of Jonah precedes the book of Micah just as it does in the MT. This is especially interesting for a Greek manuscript of the Minor Prophets, and it gives an important indication of the nature of this manuscript. This scroll is not a copy of the LXX; rather, this scroll is a careful revision of the older Greek translation to bring the Greek version closer to the Hebrew text that the reviser had access to. That Hebrew text was not identical to the MT, but it was very close to it. The older Greek translation with which the reviser began was itself not very different from the MT. Nevertheless, the reviser did succeed in correcting the old Greek translation in numerous places where the older Hebrew text, which the original translator used, differed from the MT. The Naḥal Ḥever copy of the twelve Minor Prophets gives us a window into the development of both the Hebrew and the Greek texts of the Bible, which were changing and being repeatedly revised and adapted to each other.

Finally, from Wadi Murabbaʿat we have another copy of the twelve Minor Prophets, this one in Hebrew, which preserves a large amount of material and is close to the MT in its textual type. The Murabbaʿat Minor Prophets scroll, Mur 88, dates to the time of the Bar Kokhba revolt (c. AD 132-135). The Murabbaʿat scroll is a proto-Masoretic text and is evidence for the dominance of that text type in Palestine by the first part of the second century AD.

Although the twelve Minor Prophets seem to have been copied on a single scroll at least as early as the second century BC (4Q76, 4Q77), there is no indication that the individual books of Minor Prophets were ever considered as one composition. The nonbiblical scrolls from Qumran that cite and comment on the Prophetic Books always comment only on individual books from the twelve Minor Prophets. The twelve Minor Prophets are never viewed as a single prophetic work, even though they are copied on a single scroll and therefore treated as a single "book" in terms of the format of the collection. A significant movement has developed among some specialists on the Minor Prophets to approach the collection and interpret it as a single "book" (for a summary and discussion of this approach as well as an opposing view, see Ben Zvi, Nogalski and Römer) (*see* Book of the Twelve).

See also ARAMAIC LANGUAGE; DANIEL, BOOK OF; DEAD SEA SCROLLS; HEBREW LANGUAGE; JEREMIAH, BOOK OF; WRITING AND PROPHECY.

BIBLIOGRAPHY. **E. Ben Zvi, J. Nogalski and T. Römer,** *Two Sides of a Coin: Juxtaposing Views on Interpreting the Book of the Twelve/the Twelve Prophetic Books* (AG 201; Piscataway, NJ: Gorgias Press, 2009); **J. M. Dines,** *The Septuagint,* ed. M. Knibb (London: T & T Clark, 2004); **B. Ego et al.,** eds., *Biblia Qumranica,* 3B: *Minor Prophets* (Leiden: E. J. Brill, 2005); **N. Fernández Marcos,** *The Septuagint in Context: Introduction to the Greek Version of the Bible,* trans. W. Watson (Boston: Brill Academic, 2000); **A. Gelston,** ed., *Biblia Hebraica Quinta: The Twelve Minor Prophets* (Peabody, MA: Hendrickson, 2010); **M. H. Goshen-Gottstein,** ed., *The Book of Isaiah* (Jerusalem: Magnes Press, Hebrew University, 1965); idem, ed., *The Book of Ezekiel* (Jerusalem: Magnes Press, Hebrew University 2004); **S. Jellicoe,** *The Septuagint and Modern Study* (Oxford: Clarendon Press, 1968); **R. Kittel, W. Elliger and W. Rudolph,** eds., *Biblia Hebraica Stuttgartensia* (Stuttgart: Deutsche Bibelgesellschaft, 1997); **R. W. Klein,** *Textual Criticism of the Old Testament: From the Septuagint to Qumran* (Philadelphia: Fortress, 1974); **P. K. McCarter Jr.,** *Textual Criticism: Recovering the Text of the Hebrew Bible* (Philadelphia: Fortress, 1986); **W. McKane,** *A Critical and Exegetical Commentary on Jeremiah,* 1: *Introduction and Commentary on Jeremiah I-XXV* (ICC; Edinburgh: T & T Clark, 1986); **A. Pietersma and B. G. Wright,** eds., *A New English Translation of the Septuagint* (New York: Oxford University Press, 2007); **C. Rabin, S. Talmon and E. Tov,** eds., *The Book of Jeremiah* (Jerusalem: Magnes Press, Hebrew University, 1997); **E. Tov,** *The Greek Minor Prophets Scroll from Nahal Hever (8HevXIIgr)* (rev. ed.; DJD 8; Oxford: Clarendon Press, 1995); idem, *Textual Criticism of the Hebrew Bible* (rev. ed.; Minneapolis: Fortress, 2001); idem, "The Biblical Texts from the Judaean Desert—An Overview and Analysis of the Published Texts," in *The Bible as Book: The Hebrew Bible and the Judaean Desert Discoveries,* ed. E. D. Herbert and E. Tov (London: British Library; New Castle, DE: Oak Knoll Press, 2002) 139-66; idem, "The Text of the Hebrew/Aramaic and Greek Bible Used in the Ancient Synagogues," in *The Ancient Synagogue from Its Origins until 200 C.E.: Papers Presented at an International Conference at Lund University, October 14-17, 2001,* ed. B. Olsson and M. Zetterholm (ConBNT 39; Stockholm: Almqvist & Wiksell, 2003) 237-59; **E. Ulrich,** ed., *Qumran Cave 4, X: The Prophets* (DJD 15; Oxford: Clarendon Press, 1997); idem, "Orthography and Text in 4QDan^a and 4QDan^b and in the Received Masoretic Text," in *The Dead Sea Scrolls and the Origins of the Bible* (Grand Rapids: Eerdmans; Boston: Brill Academic, 1999) 148-62; idem, ed., *The Biblical Qumran Scrolls: Transcriptions and Textual Variants* (VTSup 134; Leiden: E. J. Brill, 2009); **J. Ziegler,** ed., *Isaias* (2nd ed.; Göttingen: Vandenhoeck & Ruprecht, 1967); idem, ed., *Duodecim prophetae* (3rd ed.; Göttingen: Vandenhoeck & Ruprecht, 1984); idem, ed., *Ieremias, Baruch, Threni, Epistula Ieremiae* (2nd ed.; Göttingen: Vandenhoeck & Ruprecht, 1976); **J. Ziegler and D. Fraenkel,** eds., *Ezechiel* (3rd ed.; Göttingen: Vandenhoeck & Ruprecht, 2006). R. E. Fuller

TEXTUAL CRITICISM. *See* TEXT AND TEXTUAL CRITICISM.

TEXTUAL POETICS. *See* LITERARY APPROACHES.

THAT DAY. *See* DAY OF THE LORD.

THEODICY. *See* SUFFERING.

THEOLOGICAL INTERPRETATION. *See* ESCHATOLOGY IN CHRISTIAN THEOLOGY; HERMENEUTICS.

TIME. *See* GOD.

TORAH. *See* LAW.

TRADITION. *See* PROPHECY AND TRADITION.

TRANSMITTING PROPHECY. *See* WRITING AND PROPHECY.

TREES. *See* FLORAL IMAGERY.

TRUE AND FALSE PROPHECY

As long as two or more people have disagreed on anything, the necessity of discerning between true and false claims has been a factor in human relationships. If those disagreements happen between sanctioned or sacred leaders, such as prophets, the stakes are heightened. Depending on the situation and method of discernment, the life of the community and that of the prophet might also hang in the balance. If those disagreements are then canonized within the authoritative Scriptures of a community, the difficulties mount. The OT in general and prophetic literature in particular testify to a wide range of claims and counterclaims among various biblical prophets and other biblical texts and characters that begs for discernment about what is true or false.

At the core of the study of true and false prophecy lie questions of authority and interpretation, not only for original audiences hearing a prophecy for the first time, but also every audience ever since. Can authority be detached from context and use? Can any interpretation claim universal correctness? Whose interests are being legitimated by what ideology? What are the social and political effects of a particular reading? In short, can one distinguish a true prophet from a false prophet? If so, how and by what criteria?

1. Classic Texts in True and False Prophecy
2. Prophet Versus Prophet
3. The Standard Account of the Search for Criteria
4. Canonical Hermeneutics in True and False Prophecy
5. Making Prophecy Come True (An Example)
6. Conclusion

1. Classic Texts in True and False Prophecy.

The Torah (Genesis through Deuteronomy) gathered accounts and issued laws to warn against those who might lead Israel astray. The story of Pharoah's sages and sorcerers challenging the greatest of all prophets, Moses, and losing (Ex 7:8-11) underscores later laws against deceit-prone prophets and others using magic, *divination, witchcraft and necromancy (Lev 19:26; Deut 18:10-11; Num 22:7; Josh 13:22; Jer 14:14; 27:9; 29:8; Ezek 13:6-9; Mic 3:6-7; Zech 10:2). In the shift of generations from those who left Egypt to those who would enter the promised land, Moses is portrayed in the book of Deuteronomy as delivering a constitution of sorts, in which are included specific laws regulating the message and lifestyles of prophets after Moses (Deut 13:11-18; 18:15-22).

The Prophets (Joshua through Micah), as a collection, collate stories in grand historical sweep, telling what went wrong along the way such that Israel ended up being exiled twice, first to Assyria and then to Babylon. This second part of the Hebrew *canon also gathers together, as if exhibits in a court case, the messages of those prophets who had warned of such a tragic outcome. In a sense, a grand argument is being made, after the fact, that God had sent prophets all along the way warning of disaster if the people did not listen. The truth of their message was manifest in it having come to pass. Interwoven into this collection were stories of great prophets such as Samuel, none of whose words failed to come to pass (1 Sam 3:19-20), and accounts of major competitions between prophetic groups that revealed true prophets from false ones (Elijah and Elisha versus Jezebel's prophets [1 Kings 18-22]; Jeremiah versus Hananiah [Jer 27—28]). Late in the prophetic period these claims and counterclaims of prophets seem to have taken a toll such that one prophet sees a day when prophecy itself will cease (Zech 13:1-6a). Such a prophecy projected onto the end of the world raised the stakes, as other prophets countered with their own visions of the end of days, if not the end of prophecy.

2. Prophet Versus Prophet.

The prophets Isaiah and Micah prophesy that the end of the world as they understand it will happen when the nations of the world "beat their swords into plowshares and their spears into pruning hooks" and study *war no more (Is 2:4; Mic 4:3). By contrast, the prophet Joel, in his imagined end-of-the-world scenario, calls on the nations to "beat [their] plowshares into swords and [their] pruning hooks into spears" (Joel 3:10) in order to prepare for an *apocalyptic mother of all battles. Both prophetic utterances quote Yahweh (God) as their source of authority. Readers of Isaiah, Micah and Joel rightfully assume that all are true prophets insofar as their messages have been canonized in sacred Scripture. So, which is it? Will the world end in peaceful resolve or in violent warfare?

In another case among many, Moses, the greatest of all prophets (Deut 34:10), declares that God will punish future descendants for the sins of their ancestors (Ex 34:7b). The prophet Ezekiel, by contrast, says that each person is held accountable for his or her own deeds and will not be punished for the sins of his or her ancestors (Ezek 18:20). So which is it? Are we punished for our parents' sins or not? If we are punished for their sins, what is the justice in that? Who are we to question Moses? On the other hand, Ezekiel seems to do just that.

When the Hebrew Bible was being translated into Greek (the Septuagint), the translators decided that in at least some instances the conflict between prophets was so severe that they simply changed the original text itself. Rather than simply translate the standard Hebrew word for "prophet" (*nābî*), which was used for prophets on both sides of the debate, the translators picked sides and used the Greek term *pseudoprophētēs* ("false prophets") to indicate to the reader their discernment of the matter (Jer 6:13; 26:7, 8, 11, 16; 27:9; 28:1; 29:1, 8; Zech 13:2). Whether or not translators helped separate true prophets from false prophets by means of textual emendation, prophetic conflict would remain a focus of discernment for readers of Scripture down through the ages. By what criteria, then, might a discerning Bible reader decide questions of truth or falsehood provoked by dueling prophetic utterances? Or in the words of God's people in the book of Deuteronomy, "How can we recognize a word that the LORD has spoken?" (Deut 18:21).

3. The Standard Account of the Search for Criteria.

The story of OT research in true and false prophecy is an account of the interplay between the ambiguities of the biblical text itself and the particular biblical scholar's assessment of the nature of prophecy as a whole (Petersen). Early studies focused almost exclusively on the person or personal character and attributes of the prophet (Quell; Mowinckel). So, for example, it was argued that a false prophet could be determined by the prophet's evil intentions or immoral character. Jeremiah charges false prophets with adultery and lying (Jer 23:14). Isaiah adds drunkenness to the list (Is 28:7). Micah accuses false prophets of his day of being motivated by greed (Mic 3:5-7). Such moral criteria were picked up later by Jesus, who said that true and false prophets could be identified "by their fruits" (Mt 7:16). A closer reading of

the biblical data, however, would indicate moral ambiguity in the lives of some noted true prophets: Hosea marries a prostitute at God's bidding (Hos 1:1-2); Isaiah runs naked in public for three years, a scandalous breach of decency (Is 20:2-3; cf. Gen 3:7; 9:21; 2 Sam 6:20); Jeremiah lies to Babylonian princes at King Zedekiah's bidding (Jer 38:14-28); Elisha curses a group of boys who make fun of his baldness, a curse that results in bears mauling forty-two of them (2 Kings 2:23-25). Furthermore, there is no evidence to suggest that Hananiah, the very prophet explicitly labeled a "false prophet" by the Septuagint translators, was, on moral grounds, any less righteous than Jeremiah (Jer 28). And so, it became fairly obvious that a prophet's moral character or person was not necessarily a foolproof gauge of a prophet's claim to truth.

Other scholars focused on the message of the prophet as key to understanding prophecy in general (von Rad, 1972; Westermann). Forms of speech such as Yahweh speeches and salvation or judgment oracles were categorized. Sources of tradition, particular settings, themes of *covenant, holy *war or *wisdom were deemed crucial to understanding a prophecy's meaning. So it was that biblical scholars turned to message-centered criteria for discerning the true prophet from the false prophet. Since Moses was deemed the quintessential true prophet without equal (Deut 34:10-12), his message to the pilgrim wanderers in the exodus and beyond established a baseline set of criteria for determining true prophets from false prophets ever since (Deut 13:1-5; 18:15-21).

According to Deuteronomy 18:18-19, a true prophet speaks "in the name of the LORD," with words put into the prophet's mouth by God. Claim of divine inspiration is central to such a call, a call often reluctantly accepted by the true prophet (Is 6; Jer 1; Ezek 1). The format of such prophetic speech is found throughout prophetic literature under the introductory formula "Thus says the LORD," often labeled a "Yahweh speech" by scholars. But could not anyone seeking validation of his or her prophetic utterance simply attach such an introductory formula to it? Would that necessarily make it true? As if to respond to such a possibility, Moses ups the ante. If a prophet speaks in the name of the Lord, but the prophecy does not come to pass or prove true, then the prophet is false (Deut 18:22). And in order to deter frivolous prophecies, the penalty for false prophecy is death (Deut 18:20). Fulfilled prophecy as a criterion of truth works wonderfully and definitively provided that the time frame for fulfillment is short enough to see it come to pass or not. To the degree that the promised outcome of a prophecy can be shuttled off to some distant indefinite future, its value as evidence of truthfulness is greatly diminished. Furthermore, the criterion of fulfillment is helpful only in cases of predictive prophecy, not in other types of prophecy that simply speak truth to various listening publics.

In other cases, some modern secular prophets or ancient non-Israelite prophets (Num 22—24) have been known to predict quite accurately events that have indeed come to pass (Overholt). Some even conjure omens and offer miraculous signs as proof of their status as true prophets. What then? Moses, in Deuteronomy 13:1-5, warns against taking such miracle-manifesting criteria too seriously, especially in instances where the prophecies lead away from God to the devotion or worship of other gods. Jeremiah warns his community against prophets who prophesy in the name of the Lord (Yahweh) or under the rhetorical banner "the burden of the LORD" and who may even perform miraculous deeds but are false prophets nonetheless because of their loyalty to other gods (Jer 23:13, 27, 37-40). False prophecy is thus linked closely with *idolatry—two sides of the same interpretive coin. More than any other criteria where slippage occurs in the discernment process, Moses (Deuteronomy) and Jeremiah declare that true prophecy always leads to *worship of the one true God.

Messages of hope and well-being or other positive prophecies could be signs of falsehood leading people astray (von Rad, 1933). Positive, affirming messages too often supported the status quo, the establishment, royal prerogatives or Zionist ideology. Even though such prophecies may have had good theological backing, often they were used at the wrong place or time. Jeremiah, for example, uses historical precedent in making his case against Hananiah, whose prophecies were full of optimism and hope. Certainly, Hananiah's prophecy mirrored the hopeful true prophecies of an earlier time (Is 7:4-9; Hos 14:2-9). Jeremiah argues instead that all prophets in preceding generations who were deemed true prophets only ever "prophesied war, famine, and pestilence" (Jer 28:8-9). Prophets who proclaimed, "Peace, peace" when there is no *peace were deemed false by Jeremiah (Jer 6:14). Jesus later uses a similar argument, saying, "Woe to you when all speak well of you, for that is what their ancestors did to the false prophets" (Lk 6:26). Apparently, if a prophet suffered or was despised, and if the prophet prophesied only doom and gloom, then one could assume that the prophecy was true. Of course, such criteria did not account for the many imaginative positive prophecies offered by nearly every true prophet in Scripture (Is 9; 40; 60; Ezek 37; 40—48; Amos 9) or for the possibility that a false prophet might also suffer, be despised and prophesy doom and gloom.

If the message of a prophet did not prove to be altogether sufficient for deciding its truth claims, the study of prophetic literature began to focus on the response of the audience or the *vox populi* (popular voice of the people) as a determinate factor (Crenshaw; Van der Woude). Was a prophet able to persuade others to believe in the truth of the prophecy? In most cases, a certain segment of the population was persuaded, while others were not. As a result, an increased polarization happened between prophets, between people for and against the prophet, resulting in claims and counterclaims ad infinitum. On the one hand, once convinced, true believers rarely were dissuaded by any disconfirming evidence. On the other hand, others began to find prophecy to be inadequate as a source of inspiration or guidance and began to look elsewhere for spiritual direction. Such chaotic polarization led to a deep suspicion of prophecy as a whole (Carroll), which became the impetus for its supposed demise as a phenomenon during the period between the two Testaments.

As if to underscore the difficulties for determining criteria for discerning true from false prophecies, the story in 1 Kings 13 seems to upend all the categories of discernment at once. In the story, a "man of God," a younger prophet made so "by the word of the LORD," predicts a grand reformation under a new king, Josiah, and gives as his proof a sign that the rival altar at Bethel will soon be destroyed. King Jeroboam, no doubt feeling threatened, tries to harm the prophet. In his attempt to do so, the king's hand withers and the altar is destroyed, evidence that seems to validate the "man of God" as a true prophet. The king asks the prophet to restore his hand to full health, which the prophet does. Well and good. The king then invites the "man of God" home for a meal. The prophet declines initially because the Lord had told him not to enter Bethel. The "man of God" leaves. The scene changes to tell of an "old prophet" from Bethel, whose sons tell him about this amazing younger prophet and all he did that day. The old prophet searches after the young prophet and invites him home to Bethel to eat. The young prophet repeats his orders from the Lord that he is not to go to Bethel. The older prophet makes a counterclaim, noting his own prophetic credentials and that, after all, an angel of the Lord came to him telling him to bring the young prophet back to Bethel with him to eat a meal. The young prophet obliges and returns to Bethel with the older prophet. While they are eating, the angel of the Lord comes to the old prophet again, this time telling the old prophet to tell the young prophet that he has disobeyed the Lord by coming back to Bethel. The young prophet then leaves and is killed by lions on the road because of his disobedience. When the old prophet hears the news, he retrieves the body and buries it and declares that the young prophet's prophecies about the fall of Bethel will come to pass, which years later did happen—a noteworthy confirmation indeed. So in this case the old prophet is "false" by the moral criteria of deceiving the young prophet into disobeying, even though the old prophet is "true" by the criteria of being told this by God via the angel of the Lord. The young prophet is "false" by the moral criteria of disobedience and is punished for it, but he is "true" by his prophecies coming true. The old prophet is "true" by moral criteria of hospitality and by the criteria of fulfillment. He confirms the prophecy from the angel of the Lord about the young prophet's disobedience, his restoration and the fall of Bethel.

Clearly, the ambiguous multidimensional possibilities surfacing in this story prompt many questions. Does a false assessment of the historical situation turn a true prophet into a false prophet for that particular historical hour? Is false or true prophecy a permanent state, or can true prophets become false and false true depending on the circumstance? Does a prophet's title, motivation, call or use of right genre automatically deem the prophet true? Were prophets ever completely assured of their own status, or did they walk between certitude and doubt most if not all their days? Are canonical prophets (Isaiah, Jeremiah, Joel, Amos, etc.), by the criteria of being canonized in sacred Scripture, always true in every context, or must critical judgment be passed on them in every context, including their present canonical context and our own? If so, how are such judgments made?

4. Canonical Hermeneutics in True and False Prophecy.

It seems that the decision to determine the truth or falsehood of a prophecy is complex enough that the decisive factor in such determination can never be fixed exclusively on prophetic intention or character or genre or message or theological content or historical hour or audience reception. However, by triangulating or cross-vectoring a number of these factors together, in an accumulating process of sorts, it might be possible to argue for the truth or falsehood of a prophecy in its use across time from its original setting to the present day. By showing how a tradition or prophecy or text was used across time in its various settings within Scripture (innerbiblical exegesis) and its use across time in various postcanonical contexts (comparative midrash), one gets a sense of the range of possible uses and a range of more truthful applications in a variety of settings and situations (Sanders) (see Intertextuality and Innerbiblical Interpretation).

At a basic level, one might simply triangulate the actual historical context (time, place) of the prophet or prophecy with the actual message or content being proclaimed by the prophet with the interpretative slant of the prophet. This has sometimes been called the "hermeneutic triangle." In general, a prophet in biblical literature almost always operates in two modes of interpretation, one of critique, the other of support. Theologically, for the true prophet the universality of God's love critiques narrow particularities, while at the same time God's grace inevitably affirms the unique particularities at the core of human identity— critique and support, two opposing forces held together by God. So it is that almost always a true prophet will do both, if not in a given oracle, then most likely within the scope of the entire work (or prophetic book) of a biblical prophet over time. One can almost always triangulate how a biblical prophet interpreted a particular tradition or text or idea in a particular setting or context. And then, by dynamic analogy, one can identify corresponding contexts in one's own time to apply an identified prophetic text in one of the two dominant hermeneutic modes, to support the situation or to offer constructive criticism. Over time or depending on the context, the most truthful prophetic mode requires one to do both, prophetically critique as necessary and construct positive alternatives as obligatory.

5. Making Prophecy Come True (An Example).

By way of example, let us return to the end-time scenarios of Isaiah (Is 2:2-4) and Joel (Joel 3:9-17). Both are true prophets by dint of their inclusion in the biblical canon. Both claim validation using the "Yahweh speech" form. Both claim to speak for God. Isaiah dreams of a day of universal peace. Joel pines for the day of universal war that will serve as precursor to Yahweh's peaceful reign. Both seek to persuade their audiences to their own version of end-time events. Both used a similar tradition, similar concepts and language about plowshares and swords. Both versions were heard in original contexts and later read at various times as well. By the time of their inclusion into the canon of Scripture, both were known in postexilic times. The Babylonian *exile created a situation in which all prophecy, however unequivocally stated prior to the exile, was now open-ended and contingent. Earlier promises of the inviolability of the *land, monarchy, *temple and community were made contingent by the experience of exile. The exile would forever establish the fact that even unconditionally stated prophetic promises could henceforth be understood as being conditional and might not come to pass. The story of the prophet Jonah only confirms the contingent nature of all biblical prophecy. People might choose to *repent, necessitating a reevaluation of an otherwise straightforward prophetic utterance.

In any case, Isaiah, in his plowshare prophecy, uses a hermeneutic of prophetic critique, arguing against narrow exclusive understandings of a renewed *Israel, welcoming into the fold all nations living in peaceful coexistence. Micah's version of Isaiah's speech (Mic 4:1-5) is even more inclusive. Joel, by contrast, uses a hermeneutic of constitutive support, advocating for the bloody vindication and exclusive particularity of winners (Israel) and losers (the nations of the world).

Today's reader of these two texts reads them side by side in Scripture. The texts await the decision of readers as to what will become of the texts' rhetorical and political fates. The persuasive power of Isaiah and Joel reaches far beyond the historical limits of the Bible, of which Joel and Isaiah are a part. The determining factors, then and now, lie in the ongoing rhetorical power of the ancient and the modern reader to convince his or her audience to accept one reading over another. Which version of the end of the world is true, and which one is false?

It is a disservice to Isaiah and Joel and ethically irresponsible to attempt to harmonize their differences or merge the two into one story, as if both are true in some grand scheme still unknown to us. Nor is it appropriate to mellow the harshness of their differences by positing a temporal gap between them, as if Joel's bloody account prepares the world for Isaiah's peaceable vision. Using the explicit language of Isaiah, Joel rejects Isaiah's peaceful version as ineffective for his own time. Joel's politics precluded Isaiah's. Each prophet believed his point of view and operated under the burden of being accused of uttering falsehoods by those not persuaded. Indeed, the ethic of personal responsibility undertaken by both prophets cannot be underestimated, even if that responsibility sometimes was shuffled into the heavens with the claim that this was Yahweh's word.

The prophet's *rhetoric of persuasion was his own. His use of a Yahweh speech underscores his efforts to persuade. He had to make his case and risk the consequences. The canonical juxtaposition of Isaiah and Joel in Scripture, even when tempered by a history of their use, has sponsored mutually exclusive constructions of the outcome of history.

When it comes to choosing to live by Isaiah 2:2-4 or Joel 3:9-12, today's readers may hesitate to take the same risk that Isaiah and Joel took in declaring their views publicly. Indeed, from the perspective of one reading, the other can rightly be deemed false. In principle, Yahweh can return to *Zion, in accordance with Joel's reconstruction of events, as a violent and exclusive God, or, as Isaiah envisions, Yahweh can return to Zion with Torah in hand and an invitation of inclusion to all nations to join Yahweh there. Yahweh cannot do both, though Yahweh may do neither. In other words, on the surface of things, Yahweh alone appears to be the final arbiter between Joel and Isaiah with regard to their truthful predictions of the destiny of the world. But in fact and effect, we have been given the moral responsibility for making one or the other of these prophecies come true.

The more authoritative one claims these texts to be "the *word of God," the more serious becomes the reading. The problem simply and gravely moves from a literary one to a theological one. Can we so easily shift the moral blame for the outcome of human destiny to God, arguing, as some have, "We cannot do ethics for God"? But we are not so much doing ethics for God as accepting God's way of doing ethics—that is, rising to argue, as did our prophetic forebears, for or against lesser and better ways of living our lives. This is not human hubris. It is merely recognizing the co-creative role that God has given humans to prophesy, in the first place, and then construct a better world accordingly. One honors God in so doing.

The present ethical task is either to advocate for one reading over the other or to read neither. The mutually exclusive claims of these scenarios and the bloody record of history allow no alternative. We today cannot choose to live by both Isaiah's account of human destiny and Joel's. The truth of either Isaiah's version of human destiny or Joel's is not yet decided. We can choose Joel's version as true prophecy to our judgment or Isaiah's to our blessing. What is at stake here is not God, but we ourselves. God will survive another failed prophecy, another exile, another fatal miss. With God there can always be another return, a new creation, an old prophecy resurrected. The question for us in a new millennium has to do with our survival and the quality of the future of our children, to whom we will pass the conflicting traditions of both Joel and Isaiah.

6. Conclusion.
The ambiguity of the criteria for discerning true prophecy from false prophecy within the Bible itself honors a biblical pluralism that must be fully embraced. To say this is at once humbling and demanding. It is humbling to know that for every voice in Scripture, for every interpretation of Scripture, there is likely to be its opposite. It is demanding in that biblical pluralism in no way relieves the reader of Scripture from the responsibility of making judgments of and commitments to specific texts as bearing truth claims for a specific historical hour or time, all the while acutely aware of his or her own potential for false prophecy (mistaken application). Indeed, the Bible's plural nature heightens the responsibility of the reader to "rightly divide the word of truth" to the best of his or her ability. But we are not alone.

There may not be objective criteria that will forever assure us of our use and discernment of Scripture, nor criteria that allow us to decide in advance how best to apply biblical texts for every situation. However, interpreting texts within a confessional community does provide a "stable enough" environment that has an objectifying quality to it. Interpreting texts together, as if invited to do so by God (Is 1:18; 43:9, 26; 50:8), allows us to make reasoned judgments about the truth or falsehood for understanding a particular text or its interpretation for our particular time and place. Of course, such a community must allow for individual prophetic voices to be heard (see 1 Cor 14) in order to ward off groupthink, status quo temptations and spiritual atrophy. In the end, the negotiating of true and false prophecy comes down to simple trust in God's Spirit to inspire the purest of motives, God's grace to forgive failed tests of discernment, and God's strength to again risk interpreting aright.

See also CANONICAL CRITICISM; ESCHATOLOGY; ETHICS; HERMENEUTICS; WORD OF GOD.

BIBLIOGRAPHY. **J. E. Brenneman,** *Canons in Conflict: Negotiating Texts in True and False Prophecy* (Oxford: Oxford University Press, 1997); idem, "Prophets in Conflict: Negotiating Truth in Scripture," in *Peace and Justice Shall Embrace: Power and Theopolitics in the Bible; Essays in Honor of Millard Lind,* ed. T. Grimsrud and L. L. Johns (Kitchener, ON: Pandora; Scottdale, PA: Herald, 1999) 49-63; idem, "Making Prophecy Come True: Human Responsibility for the End of the World," In *Apocalypticism and Millennial-*

ism: Shaping a Believers Church Eschatology for the Twenty-First Century, ed. L. L. Johns (Kitchener, ON: Pandora; Scottdale, PA: Herald, 2000) 21-34; **R. Carroll,** *When Prophecy Failed: Cognitive Dissonances in the Prophetic Traditions of the Old Testament* (London: SCM, 1979); **J. Crenshaw,** *Prophetic Conflict: Its Effect upon Israelite Religion* (BZAW 124; Berlin: de Gruyter, 1971); **L. Festinger, H. W. Reichen and S. Schachter,** *When Prophecy Fails: A Social and Psychological Study of a Modern Group That Predicted the Destruction of the World* (New York: Harper & Row, 1956); **B. O. Long,** "Social Dimensions of Prophetic Conflict," *Semeia* 21 (1981) 31-53; **S. Mowinckel,** *The Spirit and the Word: Prophecy and Tradition in Ancient Israel*, ed. K. C. Hanson (FCBS; Minneapolis: Fortress, 2002 [1922, 1934, 1946]); **T. W. Overholt,** *Channels of Prophecy: The Social Dynamics of Prophetic Activity* (Minneapolis: Fortress, 1989); **D. Petersen,** ed. *Prophecy in Israel: Search for an Identity* (Philadelphia: Fortress, 1987); **G. Quell,** *Wahre und falsche Propheten: Versuch einer Interpretation* (BFCT 48/1; Gütersloh: Bertelsmann, 1952); **J. Reiling,** "The Use of 'Pseudoprophetes' in LXX, Philo and Josephus," *NovT* 13 (1971) 147-56; **J. A. Sanders,** "Hermeneutics," *IDBSup* 402-7; idem, "Hermeneutics in True and False Prophecy," in *Canon and Authority: Essays in Old Testament Religion and Theology*, ed. G. W. Coats and B. O. Long (Philadelphia: Fortress, 1977); idem, *Canon and Community: A Guide to Canonical Criticism* (GBS; Philadelphia: Fortress, 1984); **A. S. Van der Woude,** "Micah in Dispute with the Pseudo-Prophets," *VT* 19 (1969) 244-60; **G. von Rad,** "Die falschen Propheten," *ZAW* 51 (1933) 109-20; idem, *The Message of the Prophets* (New York: Harper & Row, 1972); **C. Westermann,** *Basic Forms of Prophetic Speech*, trans. H. C. White (Philadelphia: Westminster, 1967); **W. Zimmerli,** *The Law and the Prophets: A Study of the Meaning of the Old Testament*, trans. R. E. Clements (Oxford: Blackwell, 1965).

J. E. Brenneman

TWELVE, BOOK OF THE

The Book of the Twelve functions as a collection of twelve individual prophetic works and as a single prophetic book. According to the MT, the twelve prophets include *Hosea, *Joel, *Amos, *Obadiah, *Jonah, *Micah, *Nahum, *Habakkuk, *Zephaniah, *Haggai, *Zechariah and *Malachi. The LXX version presents a different order, including Hosea, Amos, Micah, Joel, Obadiah, Jonah, Nahum, Habakkuk, Zephaniah, Haggai, Zechariah and Malachi, although other sequences also were known in antiquity (Ben Zvi 1996a). The scrolls from the Judean wilderness (*see* Dead Sea Scrolls) generally present the same order as the MT, but one manuscript (4Q76) places Jonah after Malachi (Jones). Each individual work within the Twelve begins with its own superscription or narrative introduction that identifies the prophet and often provides information concerning the historical background of the work, its literary characteristics and its major concerns.

1. Canon, Arrangement, Formation
2. Modern Study
3. The Individual Books

1. Canon, Arrangement, Formation.

The Book of the Twelve is counted as one of the twenty-four books of the Tanak in Judaism and as twelve of the thirty-nine or forty-six books of the OT in Christianity. The book is called *tĕrê ʿāśār* in Jewish tradition, which is Aramaic for "the twelve (prophets)." Early Christian tradition refers to it as *hoi dōdeka prophētai* or *to dōdekaprophēton*, which mean, "the twelve prophets" in Greek. The Latin term *prophetae minores* ("the minor prophets") first appears in early patristic sources, such as Augustine's *City of God*, where it refers only to the relatively small size of the individual prophetic works. The Twelve generally appear as the fourth book of the Latter Prophets in the Tanak (*b. B. Bat.* 14b), but the Talmud also stipulates that only three lines separate the individual books of the Twelve whereas four lines normally separate biblical books (*b. B. Bat.* 13b). Christian canons generally place the Twelve before or after Isaiah, Jeremiah, Ezekiel and Daniel in the prophets of the OT. Although Greek versions of the Christian OT tend to reflect the LXX order noted above, the arrangement varies widely among the manuscripts. With the increasing use of the Vulgate, the Roman Catholic and Protestant Churches sometimes adopt the order found in the MT.

Many interpreters argue that the arrangement of the Book of the Twelve is based on chronological principles, but close examination of the sequence of books in each of the two versions indicates that neither one is arranged according to a chronological scheme (Sweeney

2000, xv-xxix). Both sequences do, however, represent concerns with the punishment of Israel and Judah during the monarchic period and with the restoration of Jerusalem and the *temple in the postexilic period. Both versions begin with Hosea, which metaphorically portrays YHWH as a husband who divorces the bride Israel to portray the disruption of their relationship, and both conclude with Malachi, which states that YHWH hates divorce and calls upon the people to hold firm to the *covenant (*see* Marriage and Divorce). The theme of the *Day of YHWH, a day of punishment for Israel/Judah and the *nations when YHWH's sovereignty is manifested at *Zion, permeates both versions of the Book of the Twelve.

The LXX version presents an initial concern with the punishment of the northern kingdom of Israel, which then provides a model for understanding the experience of Jerusalem/Judah and the nations. Hosea, Amos and Micah each take up the judgment of the northern kingdom as a primary concern, although each also indicates concern with Jerusalem and Judah. Hosea condemns Israel but calls for it to return to YHWH under the rule of a Davidic king. Amos condemns the northern Israelite sanctuary at Bethel and looks forward to the rise of a new Davidic king. Micah compares Israel to Judah and anticipates restoration under a Davidic king after both suffer punishment. Joel then marks a transition within the sequence of books insofar as it focuses on Jerusalem and the threat of attacking nations on the Day of YHWH. Obadiah, Jonah and Nahum follow with specific concerns for YHWH's judgment of the nations. Obadiah relates YHWH's judgment of Edom on the Day of YHWH. Jonah focuses on YHWH's mercy for Nineveh when it repents, and Nahum focuses on YHWH's judgment of Nineveh for its abuse of Israel and defiance of YHWH. Habakkuk, Zephaniah, Haggai and Zechariah then focus on Jerusalem. Habakkuk raises the question of theodicy in asking why YHWH brings the Neo-*Babylonian Empire against Judah. Zephaniah calls for a purge of Jerusalem and Judah on the Day of YHWH. Haggai demands that the people rebuild the Jerusalem *temple in order to realize YHWH's worldwide sovereignty and blessing. Zechariah points to the combat that will engulf the world following the reconstruction of the temple as YHWH's sovereignty is

ultimately recognized by Israel, Judah and the nations at Zion. The book of Malachi concludes with an exhortation to hold to the covenant in anticipation of the Day of YHWH.

The MT presents a very different sequence in which the books concerned with the fate of the northern kingdom of Israel are interspersed among those concerned primarily with Jerusalem and Judah. The resulting sequence emphasizes the fate of Jerusalem from the outset, particularly since the books concerned with northern Israel also signal an ultimate concern with Israel's reunification with Jerusalem/Judah. The MT begins with Hosea and ends with Malachi, so that it too employs the metaphorical portrayal of marriage to depict the tension in the relationship between YHWH and Israel and the concern to call upon the people to maintain the relationship despite suffering of conquest and *exile that they have endured. Although Hosea addresses the fate of northern Israel, its frequent references to Judah and its concern for reunification of Israel and Judah under a Davidic monarch signal its concern with Jerusalem. The placement of Joel ensures that the questions of Jerusalem and the threat posed by the nations will set the agenda for the rest of the sequence. Amos calls for judgment against northern Israel and its reunification with Judah under the rule of a restored Davidic monarchy. Obadiah calls for the punishment of Edom and its submission to Israel at Zion on the Day of YHWH. Jonah tempers Obadiah's message with the contention that YHWH will show mercy to Nineveh when it repents, but later books indicate YHWH's judgment against Nineveh when it oppresses Israel. Micah presupposes that Assyria and later Babylon will be YHWH's agents of punishment against Israel and Judah prior to their restoration around Jerusalem under the rule of a Davidic monarch. The rest of the sequence is identical to that of the LXX version. Nahum celebrates the downfall of the oppressive Nineveh as an example of YHWH's *justice. Habakkuk reassures readers of YHWH's justice by pointing to YHWH's plans to punish the Chaldeans or Neo-Babylonians for their oppression of Judah. Zephaniah calls for a purge of Jerusalem on the Day of YHWH. Haggai calls for the restoration of the temple and the house of David under Zerubbabel. Zechariah outlines the significance of the restoration of the temple, as Israel, Judah, and the nations will ultimately recognize YHWH at the Jerusalem temple. Finally, Malachi calls for its audience to maintain the covenant while waiting for YHWH's manifestation on the Day of YHWH.

The differences in sequence and hermeneutical perspective in the two versions of the Book of the Twelve raise questions concerning the historical formation of each. The LXX form, with its interest in viewing the experience of northern Israel as a model for that of Jerusalem and Judah, appears to reflect the concerns of Judah in the late monarchic, exilic and early postexilic periods, when the nation was attempting to come to grips with the theological significance of the threat posed by Babylon. Such a concern begins in the Josianic reform, when Israel's destruction is understood as YHWH's judgment, which in turn motivates the purification of the temple as a part of a national effort at restoration and rededication to YHWH. With Josiah's death and the realization that Jerusalem and Judah would also suffer at the hands of the Babylonians, the groundwork was laid for the hermeneutical perspective now apparent in the LXX form of the Book of the Twelve. The MT form, with its emphasis on the fate of Jerusalem, appears to reflect the concerns of Judean elements during the Persian period from the time of the rebuilding of the temple through the reforms of Ezra and Nehemiah, who focused on the restoration of Jerusalem as the holy center of Persian-period Judah and the world at large.

Although the two versions of the Book of the Twelve have different sequences that point to differing hermeneutical agendas, both share an *intertextual relationship with the book of Isaiah that points to a very different understanding of the significance of world events for understanding divine purpose (Steck 1991). Like both versions of the Book of the Twelve, Isaiah contends that YHWH brought the nations to punish Israel and Judah for wrongdoing and to reveal YHWH's sovereignty throughout the world. But Isaiah identifies the manifestation of YHWH's sovereignty with the rise of the Persian Empire, particularly the rise of the Persian monarch Cyrus, who is identified as YHWH's messiah and temple builder (Is 44:28; 45:1). It thereby calls upon its audience to accept this state of affairs and to submit to the Persian Empire as the will of YHWH. The Book of the Twelve is very different. Although it too presupposes that YHWH brought the nations to punish Israel and Judah as part of the process by which YHWH's sovereignty is revealed to the world, it calls upon its audience to fight against the nations that oppress Israel/Judah/Jerusalem under the rule of YHWH and the Davidic monarch in order to realize the promised restoration of Jerusalem. Such a scenario is particularly evident when one considers the role of the very famous "swords into plowshares" passage in Isaiah and the Twelve. Isaiah 2:2-4 envisions a scenario of world *peace in which Israel will join the nations in a pilgrimage to Zion to learn YHWH's Torah and to end *war. The Book of the Twelve cites this passage at three points and presents a very different scenario of YHWH's or Israel's warfare against the nations in order to realize this goal. The citation of Isaiah 2:2-4 first appears in Joel 3:10, which calls for the people to beat their plowshares into swords and their pruning hooks into spears to carry out YHWH's judgment against the nations on the Day of YHWH. Micah 4:1-5 cites the passage but states that Israel and the nations will serve their own deities prior to the rise of the Davidic monarch who will subdue the oppressive nations. Zechariah 8:20-23 likewise cites the nations' call to make a pilgrimage to Zion as an introduction to its scenario of YHWH's battle against the nations in Zechariah 9—14 that will result in their recognition of YHWH at the Jerusalem temple. Whereas Isaiah calls for submission to Persia, the Book of the Twelve calls for warfare against the oppressive nations to realize the recognition of YHWH's sovereignty at Zion. Such differences point to debate within the Second Temple period Jewish community, expressed through the writing and redaction of prophetic (and other) literature, concerning its relationship with the Persian Empire.

2. Modern Study.

Modern critical research on the Book of the Twelve begins in the late nineteenth and early twentieth centuries with the work of H. Ewald (Ewald, 73-81) and C. Steuernagel (Steuernagel, 669-72). Ewald employed the superscriptions of the individual books of the Twelve as a basis for explaining the order in which the books entered the collection. He posited that the Book of the Twelve was formed in a three-stage process that began in the seventh century BCE with Joel, Amos, Hosea, Micah, Nahum and Zephaniah. A second stage in the postexilic period saw the additions of Obadiah, Jonah, Habakkuk, Haggai and Zechariah 1—8. A third stage dated to Nehemiah's later years included Zechariah 9—14 and Malachi. Steuernagel posited a seven-stage process of formation that begin in the seventh-century BCE reign of King Josiah ben Amon of Judah and continued through the third century BCE. Steuernagel's stages included (1) Hosea, Micah, Zephaniah; (2) Amos; (3) Haggai, Zechariah 1—8; (4) Nahum 2—3; (5) Habakkuk, Nahum 1; (6) Zechariah 9—14; (7) Joel, Obadiah and Jonah.

K. Budde's 1922 study was the first major redaction-critical study of the individual books that comprise the Book of the Twelve (*see* Editorial/Redaction Criticism). Noting the long-recognized principle that the Book of the Twelve was both a single book and a collection of twelve individual compositions, Budde attempted to explain how such a collection would come together. Budde observed the relative lack of narrative material in the Book of the Twelve when compared to the other prophetic books of Isaiah, Jeremiah and Ezekiel. He argued that the Twelve Prophets were formed in the fourth-third centuries BCE to provide authoritative prophetic Scripture. The final redactors of the Book of the Twelve deliberately excluded narrative material in an effort to eliminate the so-called human material so that the divine word of the Prophets could be presented together with the Torah.

Budde's work was largely dismissed, but it provided the impetus for a 1935 study by R. E. Wolfe, who also attempted to reconstruct the redactional process that formed the Book of the Twelve Prophets. Wolfe applied a source-critical analysis to the Book of the Twelve in an effort to distinguish the authentic prophetic material from later inauthentic additions. He posited a redactional process that extended from the eighth through the third century BCE in which earlier material is expanded and reworked during the course of the book's composition. Wolfe's work has been largely dismissed because of his subjectivity in reconstructing the redactional formation of the Book of the Twelve.

D. Schneider's 1979 dissertation employs a combination of canon-critical and redaction-critical approaches to posit that the present form of the Book of the Twelve is the product of four-stage compositional process. The first stage is an eighth-century BCE collection of Hosea, Amos and Micah as presented in the LXX. The second includes the seventh-century BCE books of Nahum, Habakkuk and Zephaniah, added during the exile by a Josianic reform party. The third is the late exilic collection of Joel, Obadiah and Jonah. And the fourth is the fifth-century BCE collection of Haggai, Zechariah 1—8, Zechariah 9—14 and Malachi.

Contemporary interest in redaction-critical study of the Book of the Twelve appears among a number of scholars who based their work on the redaction- and tradition-critical methodology of O. H. Steck (Steck 1998; see also Steck 1991), who called for an all-encompassing compositional assessment of a work from its earliest layers to its final glosses. P. Weimer's 1985 redaction-critical study of Obadiah identifies six layers of composition. Lexical features of each of these layers correspond to passages in other individual books of the Twelve that he also considers to be the work of later redaction. The result is a redaction-critical model for the composition of the Book of the Twelve as a whole. E. Bosshard's 1987 study points to lexical and thematic parallels between the Book of the Twelve and Isaiah. He identifies major redactional interest in the Day of YHWH tradition and Edom as a symbol of the nations that will be judged by YHWH as part of an overall scenario in which both Israel/Judah and the nations will be judged prior to the restoration of Jerusalem. Such parallels with Isaiah appear in Joel 2:1-11; Obadiah 5-6, 15-21; Zephaniah 2:13-15; 3:14-18. A 1990 study by Bosshard and R. G. Kratz argues for a three-stage process by which Malachi was added as part of the final redaction of the Book of the Twelve and indeed the Prophets as a whole. E. Bosshard-Nepustil's 1997 monograph attempts a detailed explanation of the intertextual relationship between the Book of the Twelve and Isaiah 1—39 by positing an Assyrian-Babylonian layer that appears in passages from Joel, Habakkuk and Zephaniah, beginning in the eighth century BCE and extending through the fall of Jerusalem in 587 BCE. A subsequent Babylonian layer concerned with the significance of Cyrus appears in passages from Joel, Micah, Nahum, Habakkuk, Zephaniah and Zechariah from the late-sixth century BCE.

J. D. Nogalski's two-volume 1993 study employs a combination of catchword associations, thematic associations and redaction-critical arguments to propose a five-stage redaction of the Book of the Twelve. An initial collection of Hosea, Amos, Micah and Zephaniah was edited by Deuteronomistic circles in the sixth century BCE to form the first layer. A second collection including Haggai and Zechariah 1—8 appeared in the sixth century BCE. The two collections were combined and edited in stages through the late-fourth century BCE that included Joel, Obadiah, Nahum, Habakkuk and Malachi. B. M. Zapff's 1997 study attempted to relate the redactional formation of Micah to stages posited by Steck, Bosshard-Nepustil and Nogalski. A. Schart's 1998 monograph builds upon the work of these scholars by positing a six-stage process that begins with an initial layer in Hosea, Amos, Micah and Zephaniah that is expanded in subsequent stages by material in Nahum—Habakkuk, Haggai—Zechariah, Joel—Obadiah, and Jonah and Malachi.

Problems have emerged, however, in critical discussion of the work the Steck school. Critiques by E. Ben Zvi (1996a), B. A. Jones and M. A. Sweeney (2000; 2001) point to a variety of factors that undermine such work and demonstrate the need for analysis of each book within the Twelve. Ben Zvi points to the role that titles, superscriptions and introductions to each of the twelve books play in presenting them as discrete works within the larger framework of the Book of Twelve: each of the books is meant to be read as a distinct literary work within the whole. Both Jones and Ben Zvi point to the unstable structure or sequence of the Book of the Twelve within the ancient manuscript tradition, particularly in the scrolls from the Judean wilderness and the many orders evident in the Greek manuscript tradition and patristic canon lists. The variety of orders undermines catchword arguments that presume the order of the MT as normative. Sweeney's 2000 commentary on the Book of the Twelve points to the hermeneutical significance of the differing sequence of books in the MT and LXX (Codices Vaticanus and Sinaiticus) traditions that emphasize either the fate of Jerusalem (MT) or the fate of northern Israel as an exemplar for the fate of Jerusalem (LXX). Sweeney's 2001 study points

to individual compositional histories for works included in the Book of the Twelve, such as Hosea, Amos, Micah, Zephaniah, Nahum and Habakkuk. J. Wöhrle's massive 2006-2008 study considers the individual compositional histories of each of the books in the Book of the Twelve. He posits a model that begins with Hosea, Amos, Micah and Zephaniah that is combined with the exilic collection of Haggai and Zechariah, and later with Joel. The final stages of composition see the addition of Obadiah, Jonah, Nahum, Habakkuk, Zechariah 9—14 and Malachi.

Collections of studies on the Book of the Twelve appear in edited volumes by J. D. Nogalski and M. A. Sweeney, and by P. L. Reddit and A. Schart. A forthcoming volume based on a 2011 Münster conference, "Perspectives on the Formation of the Book of the Twelve," will be edited by R. Albertz and J. Wöhrle.

The remainder of this article focuses on each of the books that comprise the MT order of the Book of the Twelve.

3. The Individual Books.

3.1. Hosea. The superscription in Hosea 1:1 places Hosea in the reigns of the Israelite monarch Jeroboam ben Joash (786-746 BCE) and the Judean monarchs Uzziah (783-742 BCE), Jotham (742-735 BCE), Ahaz (735-715 BCE) and Hezekiah (715-687 BCE). The reason for the chronological discrepancy between the reigns of the Israelite and Judean kings is not known, although it may be that Hosea was forced to leave Israel for Judah because of his criticism of the dynastic house of Jehu, of which Jeroboam was a member. The period given for Hosea's career was particularly bloody, as four of Israel's last six monarchs were assassinated while Israel veered between a policy of alliance with Assyria and alliance with Aram before finally suffering invasion by the Assyrians. The dynasty of Jehu (842-815 BCE) began in revolt against the house of Omri and shifted Israel's political position from a very troubled alliance with Aram to a far more stable alliance with Assyria that ensured Israel's power and prosperity for the balance of the Jehu dynasty's reign. In the aftermath of Jeroboam's reign, his son Zechariah (746 BCE) was assassinated by Shallum (746 BCE), who sought to break Israel's alliance with Assyria so that it might ally with Aram instead. Shallum in turn was assassinated by Menahem (745-

738 BCE), who returned the nation to its alliance with Assyria. Menahem's son Pekahiah (738-737 BCE) was assassinated by Pekah (738-732 BCE), who broke relations with Assyria once again to ally with Aram. Pekah was killed during the course of the Syro-Ephraimic war, when Assyria invaded Aram and Israel following their attack on Judah in 734-732 BCE. Although Assyria subdued Israel, the country revolted in 724 BCE under the leadership of King Hoshea. The result was the complete destruction of Israel by 722/721 BCE and the deportation of many surviving Israelites.

Based upon Israel's experience of bloodshed and invasion during this period, the book of Hosea addresses the problem of such evil by positing that the nation was suffering punishment because it had abandoned YHWH. By employing his own marriage to Gomer bat Diblaim and the birth of their children as a metaphor for YHWH's relationship with Israel, Hosea draws upon the traditional portrayal of Israel as the bride of YHWH to charge that Gomer/Israel had engaged in harlotry by pursuing other lovers, prompting Hosea/YHWH to punish the wayward bride with divorce. Such a portrayal presupposes Israelite conceptions of pagan Canaanite religious fertility rites and Israel's political relations with Assyria and Egypt. The book does not consider judgment to be the final word, but calls upon its audience to repent and return to YHWH. For Hosea, such a return called for both religious and political action, including a rejection of Canaanite religion and a return to YHWH together with a rejection of Assyria and a return to alliance with Aram, the homeland of the biblical ancestors.

Many interpreters (e.g., H. Wolff 1974; Yee) employ a broadly thematic approach in their assessment of the structure of the book as Hosea 1—3 (narratives concerning Hosea's marriage); Hosea 4—11 (oracles of judgment followed by restoration); Hosea 12—14 (additional oracles of judgment followed by restoration). But close attention to the Hebrew syntax and narrative perspective of the book and the role of *repentance in its presentation indicates a very different structure that is designed to convince its audience to reject alliance with Assyria and to return to YHWH and alliance with Aram (Sweeney 2000). The superscription in Hosea 1:1 introduces the main body of the book in Hosea 1:2—14:8 and the concluding exhortation in Hosea 14:9:

Call for Israel's Return to YHWH (Hos 1:1—14:9)

I. Superscription (Hos 1:1)
II. Body of the book: appeal for Israel's return (Hos 1:2—14:8)
   A. YHWH's instructions to Hosea to marry a harlot and give their children symbolic names (Hos 1:2-11)
   B. Hosea's speeches to Israel (Hos 2:1—14:8)
      1. Hosea's appeal to his children for their mother's return (Hos 2:1—3:5)
      2. YHWH's basic charges against Israel: abandonment of YHWH (Hos 4:1-19)
      3. Specification of YHWH's charges against Israel (Hos 5:1—13:16)
      4. Appeal for Israel's return to YHWH (Hos 14:1-8)
III. Concluding exhortation concerning YHWH's righteousness (Hos 14:9)

Following the superscription, the body of the book appears in Hosea 1:2—14:8. The anonymous narrative in Hosea 1:2-11 introduces this section with a portrayal of YHWH's instructions to Hosea to marry a harlot and to have children with her. This narrative establishes the metaphorical portrayal of YHWH as the husband of the wayward wife Israel in order to illustrate Hosea's understanding of the tension in Israel's relationship with YHWH as a cause for the dangers that Israel faces in its relationship with Assyria. By arguing that Gomer/Israel is acting as a harlot, the prophet contends that the threats posed to Israel are punishment for abandoning YHWH, and that Israel must return to YHWH (and an alliance with Aram) in order to ensure its well-being. The names given to each of the children symbolize the tension. The name "Jezreel," the first son, recalls the site where Jehu overthrew the house of Omri and established his own dynasty (see 2 Kings 9—10). Tension with Aram prompted Jehu and his successors to turn to the Assyrians for support, which provided the basis for Israel's power and prosperity during the Jehu dynasty's reign (see 2 Kings 13—14). The name of the daughter, "Lo Ruhamah," means "no mercy," signifying YHWH's lack of mercy for the purportedly recalcitrant bride. Likewise, the name of the second son, "Lo Ammi," means "not my people," signifying YHWH's willingness to break the relationship.

The book turns to Hosea's own prophetic speeches in Hosea 2:1—14:8. Each subunit begins with an imperative in which the prophet addresses his Israelite audience. The first appears in Hosea 2:1—3:5 with the prophet's appeal to his children for their mother's return. Ultimately, the prophet/YHWH envisions a restoration of the relationship when Israel returns to the wilderness to renew the marriage/covenant as in the days of the exodus from Egypt and the wilderness period when Israel was formed as a nation. The Judean setting for the final composition of the book is evident in Hosea 3:5, which holds that return to YHWH entails northern Israel's return to the house of David.

The second major speech by the prophet appears in Hosea 4:1-19, which lays out YHWH's charges against Israel. The metaphor of marriage gives way as the prophet presents YHWH's charges that Israel has abandoned its covenant. Hosea's statements indicate that the people lack knowledge of YHWH, but the passage also emphasizes a combination of natural images and the legal language of the courtroom to charge that Israel has violated YHWH's commandments. Such an approach presupposes the blessings and curses of legal codes that promise rain, crops and security in the land if the people observe YHWH's commands, and drought, famine and exile if they do not (see Deut 28—30; Lev 26).

The third speech cycle appears in Hosea 5:1—13:16, which takes up specific discussion of the general charges made in Hosea 4. Throughout this passage Hosea and YHWH alternate as speakers. The reader must pay close attention to the use of pronouns and other indicators to determine the identity of each. Hosea begins in Hosea 5:1-7 with an address to the priests, the nation and the king to charge Israel with harlotry or abandonment of YHWH throughout its history. A lengthy speech by YHWH in Hosea 5:8—7:16 emphasizes YHWH's reluctance to accept the people because of their alliances with Egypt and Assyria (Hos 5:13-14; 7:11-12). Hosea 8:1-14 focuses especially on the establishment of illegitimate kings and the golden calves in Samaria as symbols of Is-

rael's rebellion and return to Egypt. Hosea 9:1—13:16 presents an overview of YHWH's relationship with Israel throughout history. YHWH's voice frequently cites episodes of Israel's apostasy to provide background and justification for the current threat. YHWH envisions no end to the relationship and anticipates Israel's repentance. The other motif that holds this section together is the fertility and natural growth of creation, which asserts that YHWH, not Baal, is the creator deity.

Hosea 14:1-8 concludes the prophet's speech to Israel in Hosea 2:1—14:8 with an appeal for Israel's return. This constitutes the rhetorical goal of the book and demonstrates that the prophet's images of judgment are intended to prompt a return by the book's audience rather than to announce irrevocable judgment.

The concluding verse of the book, Hosea 14:9, calls upon readers to recognize YHWH's righteousness.

3.2. Joel. The book of Joel emphasizes the central importance of threats to Jerusalem and its deliverance from the nations on the Day of YHWH. Joel is notoriously difficult to date, since the superscription in Joel 1:1 simply notes Joel ben Pethuel without reference to historical setting. The extensive references to other biblical literature—for example, Exodus 10:1-20, 21-29 (Joel 1—2); Isaiah 13:6 (Joel 1:15); Ezekiel 30:2-3 (Joel 1:15); Amos 1:2; 9:13 (Joel 3:16, 18); Obadiah; Micah 4:1-4 // Isaiah 2:2-4 (Joel 3:10); Zephaniah 1:14-15 (Joel 2:1-2); 2 Chronicles 20:20-26 (Joel 2:28—3:21)—indicate that the book must date to a relatively late period, in the fifth or fourth century BCE (H. Wolff 1977; Crenshaw).

Joel often is perceived to be a protoapocalyptic book. Its portrayal of the portents in heaven and earth on the Day of YHWH—the darkened sun and stars, the moon turned to blood, the pouring out of the divine "spirit" (*rûaḥ* [lit., "wind"]) on all flesh prior to judgment against the nations—suggests an apocalyptic scenario of cosmic disruption. Familiarity with the climate of the land of Israel indicates that this is no cosmic upheaval but rather a description of the very real effects of the so-called east wind or sirocco (Heb "Sharav"; Arab "Khamsin"), a phenomenon like the Santa Ana winds of the American southwest that typically appears in Israel at the transitions between the dry and wet seasons.

The Sharav blows so much dust and dirt that it obscures the sun during the day and gives the moon a reddish cast at night. It threatens crops and people, and therefore it frequently serves as a natural agent of divine action in the HB (e.g., at the Red Sea in Exod 14—15). Insofar as Joel portrays the threat posed by hostile nations to Jerusalem as a locust plague that is defeated by the east wind, the book serves as an enduring assurance of YHWH's pledge of protection for Jerusalem.

Many scholars argue that the original material in Joel 1—2 was expanded by later authors in Joel 3—4 MT, but such claims are based on the purported apocalyptic character of the later chapters. Indeed, the book displays a coherent literary pattern of YHWH's response to national *lamentation at a time of threat. Joel's use of liturgical forms marks him as a figure who stands within priestly circles (*see* Liturgy and Cult). The structure of the book may be portrayed as follows:

YHWH's Response to Judah's Appeals for Relief from Threat (Joel 1:1—3:21)

I.   Superscription (Joel 1:1)
II. Body of the book: YHWH's response to Judah's appeal (Joel 1:2—3:21)
     A. Prophet's call to communal complaint concerning the threat of the locust plague (Joel 1:2-20)
     B. Prophet's call to communal complaint concerning the threat of invasion (Joel 2:1-14)
     C. Prophet's announcement of YHWH's response to protect people from the threat (Joel 2:15—3:21)

Following the superscription in Joel 1:1, the body of the book in Joel 1:2—3:21 is organized to present YHWH's response and reassurance of protection to Judah's complaint concerning the threat posed by the nations, here portrayed as locusts that threaten both crop and city. The initial call for communal complaint by the prophet in Joel 1:2-20 presupposes the typical form and setting of the psalms of complaint or lamentation (e.g., Ps 7), which appeal to YHWH for deliverance at a time of threat. It draws heavily on the Exodus tradition of the locust plague (Ex 10:1-20) to portray the threat against Jerusalem. Such portrayals are typical of the Day of YHWH tradition, which presup-

poses YHWH's role as creator and depicts in natural or cosmic terms (see, e.g., Is 2; 13; 34; Obadiah; Zeph 1).

The prophet's discourse then shifts to the imagery of military invasion with a second call for communal complaint in Joel 2:1-14. Such a shift effectively demonstrates the correlation between the natural and human worlds so frequently articulated in biblical tradition. The prophet announces YHWH's deliverance in Joel 2:15—3:21. YHWH's response culminates in warfare in the Valley of Jehoshaphat against the nations that threaten Jerusalem. The tradition reverses Isaiah's and Micah's calls to turn swords into plowshares (Is 2:2-4; Mic 4:1-5) and recalls Jehoshaphat's victory over the Ammonites and Moabites who threatened Jerusalem in the Valley of Baracah/Blessing (2 Chron 20:20-26). Altogether, Joel upholds the tradition of YHWH's role as the creator who defends Zion from evil.

3.3. Amos. The superscription of Amos indicates that it is set against the background of the rise of the Israelite state under the rule of Jeroboam ben Joash (786-746 BCE) and his Judean vassal, Uzziah ben Amaziah (783-742 BCE). Although northern Israel was powerful during this period, the prophet Amos points to problems in the kingdom that in his estimation will bring about disaster for the state. Amos does not mention the rising power of the Assyrian Empire, although his oracles are set in the period immediately prior to the time of Assyria's westward expansion beginning in 745 BCE. Rather, the reasons for his condemnation of Israel appear to lie in his Judean identity. Amos was a sheepherder and tender of sycamore trees who lived in the Judean town of Tekoa, located south of Jerusalem in the Judean wilderness overlooking the Dead Sea. As a vassal of Israel, Judah was compelled to pay a heavy tribute. Such tribute fell upon the Judean population at large, and Amos appears to have traveled to Bethel, the royal sanctuary of the northern kingdom of Israel, in order to pay a portion of Judah's tribute. Amos points repeatedly to the poverty of his people, who have suffered disasters and yet still have to pay tribute to the north. But Israel was an Assyrian ally during this period and would have been forced to pay tribute to Assyria.

The book of Amos is organized rhetorically to present an argument for the overthrow of the sanctuary at Bethel and an exhortation to seek YHWH. Following the superscription in Amos 1:1 and the associated motto in Amos 1:2, which emphasizes YHWH's association with Zion or Jerusalem, the book begins broadly with a focus on judgment against the nations that surround Israel, and then it narrows its focus to Israel and finally to Bethel, before concluding with a call for the restoration of Davidic rule over all Israel. Although the prophet's oracles emphasize judgment against the northern kingdom, they include calls to seek YHWH (Amos 5:4, 6) to indicate the prophet's ultimate intentions. The structure of the book may be outlined as follows:

Exhortation to Seek YHWH (Amos 1:1—9:15)

I. Introduction (Amos 1:1-2)
    A. Superscription (Amos 1:1)
    B. Motto: YHWH roars from Zion (Amos 1:2)
II. Exhortation proper (Amos 1:3—9:15)
    A. Oracles against the nations (culminating in northern Israel) (Amos 1:3—2:16)
       1. Damascus/Aram (Amos 1:3-5)
       2. Gaza/Philistia (Amos 1:6-8)
       3. Tyre/Phoenicia (Amos 1:9-10)
       4. Edom (Amos 1:11-12)
       5. Ammon (Amos 1:13-15)
       6. Moab (Amos 2:1-3)
       7. Judah (Amos 2:4-5)
       8. Israel (Amos 2:6-16)
    B. Indictment of northern Israel (Amos 3:1—4:13)
    C. Call for repentance of northern Israel (Amos 5:1—6:14)
    D. Amos's vision reports: call for destruction of Bethel and rise of the house of David (Amos 7:1—9:15)

The introduction for the book in Amos 1:1-2 identifies Amos as a sheepherder from the Judean town of Tekoa and notes that his work is placed two years prior to a major earthquake. The motto indicates the prophet's Judean identity, a foundational issue throughout the book, by stating that YHWH roars from Zion/Jerusalem.

The initial oracles against the nations begin the prophet's discourse with a very broad perspective. Although many claim that they represent YHWH's or Amos's universal moral perspective, the nations listed are all Israel's neighbors, and all the events noted stem from their interrelationships with Israel during the ninth century BCE. During that period Aram successfully attacked its ally Israel, and the various nations listed actively supported the move or failed to come to Israel's aid. The rhetorical strategy of the prophet in his indictment of each nation is clear: he condemns each one for its past transgressions against Israel and YHWH and thereby wins over his Israelite audience. Amos then begins to focus on his true target and concludes the sequence with a lengthy diatribe against Israel that highlights its abuses against the poor, in this case, the people of Judah (see Wealth and Poverty).

The second segment of the discourse, Amos 3:1—4:13, focuses specifically on the prophet's charges against the northern kingdom of Israel. He points to signs of coming judgment to claim that YHWH is bringing judgment against the nation as in the past (e.g., Sodom and Gomorrah). The third segment of the discourse, Amos 5:1—6:14, continues to emphasize charges against Israel but couples them with calls for the people to seek YHWH and to reject Bethel and the other northern temples. Overall, Amos envisions the Day of YHWH as a day of YHWH's judgment against Israel (Amos 5:18-20).

The final segment of Amos's discourse appears in his vision reports in Amos 7:1—9:15. The prophet relates the experiences that prompted him to speak his message at the Bethel sanctuary. It is striking that in each case Amos cites an image or an event that would represent a common experience of the ancient Israelite/Judean farmer, but he sees in each an expression of the will of YHWH. He notes the plague of locusts (Amos 7:1-3), a common and recurring threat to ancient (and modern) farmers, that eat the crop and leave little behind after the king's portion of the harvest has been taken. He notes the fires that dry up the deep (Amos 7:4-6), a common occurrence at the end of Israel's dry, summer season. In both cases, he sees them as communications from YHWH and successfully appeals to YHWH to show mercy. The third vision, YHWH holding a plumb line (Amos 7:7-9), again employs a common image of a weighted line used to measure the straightness of a wall. This weighted line was an essential tool in a culture in which house walls were built by hand from stone foundations and mud brick, for an error would quickly result in the collapse of the typical Israelite two-story house. Here it serves as a metaphor for measuring Israel's moral straightness. A brief editorial narrative in Amos 7:10-17 informs the reader of the circumstances of Amos's speech at the Bethel temple, and how he is expelled from Israel for his charges against temple and monarch. The fourth vision, in Amos 8:1-14, employs a pun on Amos's presentation of a basket of summer fruit (*qayiṣ*) at the Bethel sanctuary, which YHWH states represents the end (*qēṣ*) of Israel. The final image in Amos 9:1-10 of YHWH calling for the destruction of the Bethel capitals draws upon the imagery of a temple altar in operation, with the carcasses of sacrificial animals, the knives, the blood, the fire and the smoke, all of which evoke images of destruction. For Amos, such images call for the destruction of the sanctuary itself.

Amos concludes his vision sequence with a call in Amos 9:11-15 for the fallen booth of David. Although many see this as a postexilic addition, it expresses the prophet's Judean viewpoint and hopes for a restoration of Davidic/Judean rule over the north as it was in the days of Solomon (Paul; Sweeney 2000).

3.4. Obadiah. The superscription in Obadiah 1a identifies the book as "the vision of Obadiah." Traditional interpreters identify Obadiah with the ninth-century BCE Israelite official who assisted Elijah (1 Kings 18), but there is no evidence that the present work is to be identified with that official. The dependence of Obadiah 1-7 on Jeremiah 49:7-22 and the explicit references to the exiles of Israel and Jerusalem in Obadiah 19-21 indicate a late exilic or early postexilic dating for the book (Ben Zvi 1996b, 99-109; H. Wolff 1986, 37-42). The body of the book, Obadiah 1b-21, presents an oracular condemnation of Edom for its treachery against Jerusalem. The oracle begins with a prophetic messenger formula in Obadiah 1ba$^{1-5}$, which introduces the prophet's call to punish Edom in Obadiah 1ba$^{6-12}$-7 and the announcement of punishment against Edom in Obadiah 8-21. The structure of the book appears as follows:

Announcement of Judgment Against Edom (Obad 1-21)

I. Superscription (Obad 1a)
II. Oracle concerning the condemnation of Edom (Obad 1b-21)
   A. Prophetic messenger formula (Obad 1ba$^{1-5}$)
   B. Oracle proper (Obad 1ba$^{6-12}$-21)
      1. Call to punish Edom (Obad 1ba$^{6-12}$-7)
      2. Announcement of punishment against Edom (Obad 8-21)

3.5. Jonah. The portrayal of the prophet Jonah draws on 2 Kings 14:25, which presents Jonah ben Amittai as an eighth-century BCE prophet who foresees the greatness of Jeroboam ben Joash's (786-746 BCE) restored kingdom of Israel. There is, nevertheless, no evidence that the book of Jonah presents a historical account of the prophet's life. The narrative makes extensive use of irony, parody and exaggeration—for example, a prophet of YHWH attempts to flee from YHWH; the pagan characters of the narrative acknowledge YHWH; a great fish swallows Jonah, who remains in the fish for three days; YHWH saves Nineveh, which ultimately destroys the northern kingdom of Israel. The book is designed to examine the matter of YHWH's justice and mercy.

Many interpreters maintain that the book poses a conflict between the universalism of YHWH and the particularism of the Jewish community, but such a construction of the issue arises largely from a misreading of the book informed by anti-Jewish stereotypes. Jonah is not a selfish and petulant figure who questions why YHWH's mercy should be shown to Gentiles; rather, he is a prophet who has foreseen the greatness of Jeroboam II, and presumably he also has foreseen that Nineveh, the capital of the Assyrian Empire, will ultimately destroy his own nation in 722/721 BCE, only a few years after Jeroboam's reign. Why should YHWH show mercy to a nation that ultimately will serve such a destructive purpose? Such a question raises the question of YHWH's righteousness and fidelity to the covenant with Israel. Ultimately, the book argues that YHWH responds to repentance with mercy, which has important implications for the exilic or postexilic Judean audience of the book. Repentance brings YHWH's mercy and the possibility of restoration.

The book includes two distinct and yet parallel parts that emphasize the contrast between

Jonah's attempt to flee his initial commission to condemn Nineveh (Jon 1—2) and his frustration over YHWH's mercy when Nineveh repented (Jon 3—4). The structure of the narrative appears as follows:

YHWH's Mercy Toward a Repentant Nineveh (Jon 1:1—4:11)

I. Jonah's attempt to flee from YHWH (Jon 1:1—2:1)
   A. Jonah's attempt to flee YHWH's initial commission (Jon 1:1-3)
   B. Jonah's encounter with the sailors during the storm (Jon 1:4-16)
   C. Jonah's prayer to YHWH from the belly of the fish (Jon 2:1-10)
II. Encounter between YHWH and Jonah concerning YHWH's mercy toward a repentant Nineveh (Jon 3:1—4:11)
   A. YHWH's renewed commission to Jonah and its outcome (Jon 3:1-10)
   B. YHWH's assertion of the right to mercy in encounter with Jonah (Jon 4:1-11)

The two parallel episodes highlight the contrast (and comparisons) between YHWH's two commissions to Jonah. In each half, YHWH commissions Jonah to condemn Nineveh, but something entirely unexpected happens: Jonah, the prophet of YHWH, attempts to flee from the sovereign of the universe (Jon 1—2), and YHWH reverses judgment and grants mercy to Nineveh (Jon 3—4).

The first half of the book, Jonah 1—2, prepares the reader for the primary examination of issues in Jonah 3—4. Jonah 1—2 includes three basic episodes, each of which begins with action by YHWH that serves as the basis for action by the other major protagonists of the narrative. Jonah 1:1-3 presents YHWH's initial commission to Jonah and his unexpected attempt to flee. The absurdity of the situation is highlighted by the portrayal of Jonah's experiences on board ship in Jonah 1:4-16. YHWH brings a storm that threatens to sink the ship. While Jonah sleeps soundly in the hold, the pagan sailors call upon Jonah to pray to YHWH and offer to sacrifice themselves in a futile attempt to stop the storm. They finally and reluctantly accede to Jonah's advice that they throw him into the sea. In Jonah 2:1-11 Jonah finally acknowledges YHWH and prays for mercy, until YHWH prompts the fish to vomit him out onto dry land.

The second half of the book, Jonah 3—4, focuses on the primary questions of YHWH's righteousness and fidelity in relation to the questions of judgment and mercy. In Jonah 3 YHWH commissions Jonah once again to announce judgment against Nineveh. The prophet obeys, and the unexpected happens when Nineveh actually listens and repents. Even the animals of the city repent. Jonah 4 presents Jonah's indignation at YHWH's mercy toward Nineveh and the key examination of the issues posed in the book. Jonah cites the merciful aspects of the formulaic characterization of YHWH from Exodus 34:6-7 and, exasperated at having the message of judgment reversed, demands that YHWH take his life. But such a reversal highlights the purpose of the prophetic judgment speech: it is designed not to serve as irreversible judgment but rather to convince people to change. To illustrate the principle of pity or mercy, YHWH provides a castor bean plant to give Jonah shade and comfort and then sends a worm to destroy it. Despite his sorrow at the loss of the plant, Jonah still contends that he would rather die than give up his anger at YHWH. At this point, YHWH concludes the book by asking Jonah (and the audience of the book) if YHWH should not pity Nineveh, with its one hundred twenty thousand people and many animals, just as Jonah had pitied the plant. The answer to YHWH's rhetorical question is, of course, yes. Such an answer is particularly important to the postexilic Jewish community, which viewed the Babylonian exile as an expression of divine judgment, and the restoration as an expression of divine mercy that resulted from community repentance. Such a portrayal is designed to call for the people to repent and rebuild as exilic and postexilic Judah sought restoration.

3.6. Micah. The superscription attributes the book to Micah the Morashtite, who lived in the days of the Judean kings Jotham (742-735 BCE), Ahaz (735-715 BCE) and Hezekiah (715-687 BCE). Micah's hometown is identified with Moresheth-Gath, a town on the southwestern border of Judah and Philistia, near the Philistine city of Gath. This location is where the Assyrian king Sennacherib concentrated his attack against Judah at the time of Hezekiah's revolt in 701 BCE. It enables readers to understand that Micah was a war refugee who had to flee his home for Jerusalem as the Assyrians advanced. Such a portrayal informs his images of suffering on the part of the people and his anger at the monarchies of Israel and Judah for bringing disaster upon the heads of the people.

Micah appears to have a very different perspective than that of his contemporary Isaiah ben Amoz. Both include nearly identical versions of a famous oracle (Is 2:2-4; Mic 4:1-5) that calls for nations to come to Zion to learn YHWH's Torah and turn their swords into plowshares to bring about world peace, but each book has a very different perspective as to how such an idyllic scenario is to be brought about. Isaiah maintains that YHWH will judge the entire world (Is 2:6-21) and invites Jacob/Israel to join the pilgrimage of the nations to Zion to submit to YHWH (Is 2:5). Ultimately, the book of Isaiah calls for Israel/Judah to submit to punishment by Assyria and Babylon and finally to the rule of Persian monarch Cyrus, who is identified as YHWH's messiah (Is 44:28; 45:1). Whereas Isaiah calls for submission to the rule of the nations, most notably Persia, as the will of YHWH, Micah calls for the overthrow of the oppressive nations and restoration of a righteous Davidic monarch. The reference to the Babylonian exile in Micah 4:10 and the intertextual references to Isaiah 2:2-4; 14:24-27; 2:6-21 in Micah 4:1-5; 5:4, 9-14 indicate that Micah's oracles were edited during the early Second Temple period, when the question of Judah's relationship with the Persian Empire was in question.

Many interpreters follow a diachronic composition-historical model for the structure of the book that posits that Micah's authentic oracles appear in Micah 1—3, and collections of later materials appear in Micah 4—5; 6—7. Close attention to the linguistic structure of the final, synchronic form of the book indicates that Micah's oracles were edited to raise the question of Jerusalem's (or Israel's) future in the aftermath of the Babylonian exile. It begins in typical fashion with the superscription in Micah 1:1, and the balance of the book, Micah 1:2—7:20, is formulated as a prophetic announcement concerning YHWH's future exaltation of Jerusalem at the center of the nations. Micah 1:2-16 begins with a portrayal of YHWH's punishment of Samaria as a paradigm for that of Jerusalem. Micah 2:1—5:14 provides a detailed overview of the process of punishment and restoration for Jerusalem. Micah 6:1-16 appeals to the people of Israel/Judah to return to YHWH as a prelude for this process, and Micah 7:1-20 expresses the prophet's trust that YHWH will act to bring the restoration about once the punishment is complete. The structure may be portrayed as follows:

Announcement of YHWH's Future Exaltation of Jerusalem at the Center of the Nations (Mic 1:1—7:20)

I.   Superscription (Mic 1:1)
II. Announcement of YHWH's exaltation of Jerusalem proper (Mic 1:2—7:20)
     A. YHWH's punishment of Samaria as paradigm for Jerusalem (Mic 1:2-16)
     B. Process of punishment and restoration for Jerusalem: Babylonian exile, new Davidic monarch to punish oppressive nations (Mic 2:1—5:14)
        1. Concerning the process of punishment (Mic 2:1-13)
        2. Concerning YHWH's plans to punish and exalt Jerusalem (Mic 3:1—5:14)
     C. Appeal to Israel/Judah for return to YHWH (Mic 6:1-16)
     D. Liturgical psalm of confidence in YHWH (Mic 7:1-20)

Following the superscription in Micah 1:1, the body of the book is organized to convince the reader that YHWH will act to exalt Jerusalem at the center of the nations after having brought punishment for the erroneous decisions of the kings of Israel and Judah. Micah 1:2-16 begins the sequence with a trial scenario in which the prophet accuses Samaria and Jerusalem of transgression that brought the Assyrians as conquerors against both nations.

The second major component of the book appears in Micah 2:1—5:14, which presents the exile of the northern kingdom as the model and impetus for that of the south in the later Babylonian period. The initial subunit is a woe speech in Micah 2:1-13 that accuses the leadership of Israel with lack of concern for the people, who must flee for their lives while the leaders act as if they were drunk. The prophet then turns to the future of Jerusalem in Micah 3:1—5:14. He begins in Micah 3:1-8 with accusations of injustice and disregard for the welfare of the people in general, and then he turns specifically to Jerusalem in Micah 3:9-5:14. The claim in Micah 3:9-12 that Jerusalem and Zion will be destroyed indicates that, unlike the urbane Isaiah, the rural Micah had no stake in the claims of Davidic or Zion theology that YHWH would protect Jerusalem forever. Micah 4—5 begins with the portrayal of world peace as the nations stream to Zion, but it shifts to the process by which that ideal is achieved when it focuses on the nations that oppressed Israel until YHWH would redeem them in Babylon (Mic 4:10) together with the rise of the Davidic monarch who would defeat the nations and restore the *remnant of Jacob in the midst of the nations.

Micah 6:1-16 appeals to the people for righteous action or observance of YHWH's justice and demands that they not act like the notorious king Ahab ben Omri of Israel (cf. 1 Kings 17-22).

Micah 7:1-20 concludes the book with a liturgical expression of confidence that YHWH will act to realize the plans laid out in the book.

3.7. Nahum. The book of Nahum celebrates the downfall of Nineveh, capital of the Assyrian Empire, which had destroyed northern Israel in 722/721 BCE and oppressed Judah for about a century. The superscription of the book identifies it simply as "the oracle concerning Nineveh" and "the vision of Nahum the Elkoshite." Nineveh fell to a combined force of Babylonians and Medes in 612 BCE, two years after the fall of Assur in 614 BCE and three years prior to the final defeat of the Assyrian army at Haran in 609 BCE The book refers to the fall of Thebes ("No-Amon" [Nah 3:8-10]) to the Assyrians in 663 BCE. Although some scholars attempt to date the book to this period, it appears to represent a precursor for Nineveh's destruction. Nahum 3:8-10 portrays Nineveh as a city surrounded by the waters of the Nile. The Nile did run through the Egyptian city of Thebes, but the portrayal more closely resembles Nineveh, which was protected by moats formed by the Khusur canal that ran through the city. Control of the water in the moats was a decisive factor in the Babylonian/Median conquest of the city.

The portrayal of Nineveh's conquest is a key factor in the rhetorical strategy of the book, which is designed to convince its audience that YHWH is indeed the powerful and just sovereign of all creation who punishes Nineveh for its abusive treatment of other nations. Following the superscription in Nahum 1:1, the body of the book appears as a prophetic *maśśā᾽* ("oracle") in which the prophet attempts to convince his audience to abandon their doubts about YHWH's justice and power to recognize YHWH as the cause of Nineveh's destruction. The prophet employs a form of the disputation speech to challenge the contention of a Judean audience that Assyria's domination of the world showed that YHWH lacks power or righteousness. The prophet attempts to refute the notion that YHWH is powerless by pointing to the fall of Nineveh as an act of YHWH (Sweeney 2000, 419-47). The argument proceeds with an initial masculine-plural address to Judah and Assyria in Nahum 1:2-10 that challenges their low estimation of YHWH's power with a partial acrostic poem in Nahum 1:2-8 and a rhetorical question: "How do you reckon/consider YHWH?" (i.e., "What do you think about YHWH?"). Nahum 1:11—2:1 follows with a feminine-singular address to Judah asserting that the fall of Nineveh and the end of its oppression are an act of YHWH. A key statement is Nahum 1:11, which, read correctly, says, "From you has gone forth wrong thinking about YHWH, worthless counsel." Nahum 2:2—3:19 then concludes the book with a second masculine-singular address to Nineveh and the Assyrian king that again asserts YHWH as the true cause of Nineveh's destruction. The structure of the book appears as follows:

Argument that YHWH is the True Power of the World (Nah 1:1—3:19)

I.   Superscription (Nah 1:1)
II. Oracle proper: refutation of contention that YHWH is powerless (Nah 1:2—3:19)
    A. Address to Judah and Assyria challenging their low estimation of YHWH (Nah 1:2-10)
    B. Address to Judah asserting that the end of Assyrian oppression is an act of YHWH (Nah 1:11—2:1)
    C. Address to Nineveh and the Assyrian king asserting that the fall of Nineveh is an act of YHWH (Nah 2:2—3:19)

3.8. Habakkuk. The book of Habakkuk raises questions concerning YHWH's role in raising the Neo-Babylonian Empire as a threat against Jerusalem and Judah. The two superscriptions for the book (Hab 1:1; 3:1) identify each portion of the book with Habakkuk the prophet. Nevertheless, the portrayal in Habakkuk 1:6 of the rise of the Chaldeans (i.e., the Neo-Babylonian dynasty founded in 625 BCE by Nabopolassar) provides an indication of the historical context. When Nabopolassar's son Nebuchadnezzar defeated Egypt in 605 BCE and took control of Judah, many in Judah saw the Babylonians as foreign oppressors rather than former allies from the days of King Josiah. Habakkuk raises the question as to why YHWH would bring an oppressor against Judah. Although many interpreters argue that Habakkuk's portrayal of the wicked must initially refer to Judeans, the usage of the term throughout the book indicates that it refers to the Babylonians as "the wicked who swallow the righteous" (Hab 1:13; cf. Hab 1:12-17). The portrayal of the Babylonian king as the wicked oppressor who will be destroyed by YHWH (Hab 2:5-20) is opposed to the depiction in Habakkuk 2:4 of "the righteous who shall live by their faith [in YHWH]."

The two-part structure of the book is indicated by the superscriptions in Habakkuk 1:1; 3:1. Habakkuk 1:1—2:20 is a prophetic *maśśā'* ("oracle") that presents a dialogue between Habakkuk and YHWH concerning YHWH's righteousness. Habakkuk laments to YHWH over the oppression of the righteous by the wicked in Habakkuk 1:2-4; YHWH claims to have brought the Chaldeans in Habakkuk 1:5-11; Habakkuk demands to know how YHWH can tolerate such wickedness in Habakkuk 1:12-17; and Habakkuk 2:1-20 portrays YHWH's assurances that the wicked oppressor ultimately will fall. The prayer of Habakkuk in Habakkuk 3:1-19 draws on the imagery of theophany to assert that YHWH will respond to Habakkuk's complaint by destroying the oppressor. The structure of the book appears as follows:

Oracle and Prayer Concerning YHWH's Righteousness (Hab 1:1—3:19)

I. Habakkuk's oracle: dialogue concerning YHWH's righteousness (Hab 1:1—2:20)
   A. Superscription (Hab 1:1)
   B. Oracle proper (Hab 1:2—2:20)
      1. Habakkuk's initial complaint to YHWH concerning oppression of righteous by wicked (Hab 1:2-4)
      2. YHWH's response: YHWH brought the Chaldeans (Hab 1:5-11)
      3. Habakkuk's second complaint: why tolerate evil? (Hab 1:12-17)
      4. Report of YHWH's response: oppressor will fall (Hab 2:1-20)

II. Prayer of Habakkuk: petition for YHWH to act (Hab 3:1-19)
   A. Superscription (Hab 3:1)
   B. Prayer proper: YHWH will act (Hab 3:2-19a)
   C. Instructions for the choirmaster (Hab 3:19b)

3.9. Zephaniah. The superscription for the book of Zephaniah (Zeph 1:1) places it in the reign of King Josiah of Judah (640-609 BCE), who promoted a program of religious reform and national restoration for Judah as the Assyrian Empire declined. Many interpreters argue that Zephaniah has been heavily redacted in the postexilic period to produce a supposed typical three-part structure of the book—punishment against Jerusalem/Israel (Zeph 1:2—2:3); punishment against the nations (Zeph 2:4—3:8); eschatological *salvation for Jerusalem/Israel and the nations (Zeph 3:9-20)—that emphasizes eschatological judgment and salvation of the entire world. But close examination of the literary features of the book indicates that, after the superscription, the body of the book exhibits a two-part structure that reflects the rhetorical effort to convince the people to support Josiah's reform. Zephaniah 1:2-18 announces the coming Day of YHWH (cf. Is 2; 13; 34) as a day of punishment and *sacrifice for those who would adhere to foreign gods. Zephaniah 2:1-3:20 presents an exhortation to seek YHWH—that is, to support Josiah's reform. It is based upon the exhortation in Zephaniah 2:1-3 and the prophet's explanatory address in Zephaniah 2:4-3:20. Zephaniah 2:4 points to the destruction of the Philistine cities as the basic evidence of YHWH's actions, and Zephaniah 2:5-15 and Zephaniah 3:1-20 respectively point to YHWH's actions against selected nations and the projected restoration of Jerusalem as further reason to support the reform. The structure appears as follows:

Exhortation to Seek YHWH (Zeph 1:1—3:20)

I. Superscription (Zeph 1:1)
II. Body of the book: exhortation to seek YHWH (Zeph 1:2—3:20)
   A. Announcement of the Day of YHWH against Baal worshipers (Zeph 1:2-18)
   B. Exhortation to seek YHWH (Zeph 2:1—3:20)

1. Exhortation proper (Zeph 2:1-3)
2. Substantiation: YHWH's actions (Zeph 2:4—3:20)
   a. Basis for exhortation: destruction of Philistine cities (Zeph 2:4)
   b. Punishment of nations (Zeph 2:5-15)
   c. Restoration of Jerusalem (Zeph 3:1-20)

3.10. Haggai. The book of Haggai is set in the second year of the reign of King Darius of Persia (520 BCE) and appears as the prophet's call for the people of Jerusalem to support efforts to rebuild the Jerusalem temple (cf. Ezra 3; 6). Haggai is mentioned together with Zechariah in Ezra 5:1; 6:14 as a prophet who called for the building of the temple at the time that Zerubbabel ben Shealtiel, the grandson of King Jehoiachin of Judah, and Joshua ben Jehozadak, the high priest, returned to Jerusalem to commence the reconstruction efforts. During this period, the Persian Empire was wracked by internal conflict as several major figures fought to gain control of the empire following the death of Cambyses, the son of Cyrus, in 522 BCE. Darius, the son-in-law of Cyrus, ultimately won control of the empire.

The book of Haggai presents a series of oracles, dated to the year 520 BCE, in which the prophet lays out his calls for the rebuilding of the temple and the designation of Zerubbabel as YHWH's regent. Haggai 1:1-15a begins with a narrative concerning the people's compliance with the prophet's first oracle, which calls upon the people to rebuild the temple so that YHWH will provide rain and good harvest. Haggai 1:15b—2:9 presents the prophet's second oracle, concerning the future glory of the new temple, to which the nations will bring gifts to acknowledge YHWH's sovereignty. Haggai 2:10-23 presents two oracles that respectively call upon the people to complete the temple to ensure community purity and announce Zerubbabel as YHWH's signet ring, a metaphor for regent, who will ensure the overthrow of the nations that subjugate Judah. The structure of the book appears as follows:

Oracles About Rebuilding the Temple and Recognition of Zerubbabel as YHWH's Regent (Hag 1:1—2:23)

I. Narrative concerning compliance with YHWH's instruction to build the temple (Hag 1:1-15a)
II. Narrative concerning future glory of the Jerusalem temple (Hag 1:15b—2:9)
III. Narrative concerning purity of land and establishment of Zerubbabel as YHWH's regent (Hag 2:10-23)

3.11. Zechariah. Zechariah presents an account of the visions and the oracles of the prophet Zechariah concerning the significance of the temple's restoration. The book is set in the second and fourth years of the reign of the Persian monarch Darius, 520 and 518 BCE (see Zech 1:1, 7; 7:1). When Darius, the son-in-law of Cyrus, came to the throne following the unexpected death of his brother-in-law Cambyses, Persia was plunged into civil war as several figures attempted to seize control of the empire. Darius had authorized Zerubbabel ben Shealtiel, the grandson of King Jehoiachin of Judah, and the priest Joshua ben Jehozadak to return to Jerusalem in 522 BCE to begin construction of the second temple. The narrative setting of the book therefore coincides roughly with the years of the building of the temple in 520-515 BCE.

Most modern interpreters argue that Zechariah is a composite book like Isaiah insofar as Zechariah 1—8 appears to represents the visions of the prophet Zechariah, whereas Zechariah 9—14 represents a later apocalyptic scenario. Many also argue that Zechariah 9—11 and Zechariah 12—14 are separate compositions that should be designated as Second Zechariah and Third Zechariah. Both of these blocks are designated as a prophetic *maśśā'* ("oracle") in Zechariah 9:1; 12:1. Although past interpreters have dated Zechariah 9—14 to the Hellenistic period, many scholars recognize that those chapters may well date to the Persian period (e.g., Petersen 1995).

A synchronic literary reading of Zechariah shows the literary coherence of the book, particularly when the structural role of the date formulae in Zechariah 1:1, 7; 7:1 are taken into consideration. Whereas the conventional two-part structure of Zechariah 1—8; 9—14 or three-part structure of Zechariah 1—8; 9—11; 12—14 is based on diachronic or historical consideration of the origins of each respective block, the date formulae indicate a two-part structure for the book in which the narrator guides the reader into a presentation of the prophet's eight visions and two major oracles (Sweeney 2000, 561-67; cf. Conrad). Zechariah 1:1-6 presents the introduction to the book with YHWH's initial word to the prophet, and Zechariah 1:7-14:21 presents YHWH's later words to the prophet concerning the visions in Zechariah 1:7-6:15 and the oracles in Zechariah 7:1-14:21. The literary structure for the book appears as follows:

Visions and Oracles About the Significance of the Restoration of Jerusalem (Zech 1:1—14:21)

I. Introduction to the book: YHWH's initial word to Zechariah (Zech 1:1-6)
II. Narrative presentation of YHWH's later words to Zechariah: visions and oracles (Zech 1:7—14:21)
 A. Visions (Zech 1:7—6:15)
  1. Divine horses: YHWH's anger against nations and plan to restore Jerusalem and the temple (Zech 1:7-17)
  2. Four horns: restoration of temple altar; scattering of Israel and punishment of nations (Zech 1:18-21)
  3. City with walls of fire: restoration of Jerusalem (Zech 2:1-13)
  4. Ordination of Joshua ben Jehozadak (Zech 3:1-10)
  5. Menorah and two olive shoots: Zerubbabel and foundation stone (Zech 4:1-14)
  6. Flying scroll: justice for land from the temple (Zech 5:1-4)
  7. Woman in ephah basket: iniquity sent to Shinar/Babylon (Zech 5:5-11)
  8. Four chariots proclaim crowning of Joshua ben Jehozadak (Zech 6:1-15)
 B. Oracles (Zech 7:1—14:21)
  1. Question concerning continued mourning for the temple (Zech 7:1-7)
  2. Answer: YHWH wants rejoicing and righteous action for restoration of the temple (Zech 7:8—14:21)
   a. Call for righteous action (Zech 7:8-14)
   b. Summation of former prophets: call for righteous action (Zech 8:1-17)
   c. Zechariah's report of YHWH's oracles concerning restoration of Zion as holy center for the world (Zech 8:18—14:21)

The introduction to the book (Zech 1:1-6) signals the concern with earlier prophetic tradition by constructing Zechariah's identity in relation to the figure of Zechariah ben Yeberechiah in Isaiah 8:1-4 (cf. the references to Zechariah bar Iddo in Ezra 5:1; 6:14) and by its references to the "former prophets" (Zech 1:4). By referring to the calls for repentance made to the ancestors by the former prophets, the introduction prepares the reader to anticipate the realization of the claims made in the following material.

Zechariah 1:7—6:15 lays out a sequence of the prophet's visions, each of which is based upon his observations of activities connected with the building of the new temple and its preparation to serve as the holy center of creation. The first vision (Zech 1:7-17) draws upon the typical use of horse-mounted messengers by the Persian Empire to portray the four horsemen who announce YHWH's plans to rebuild the temple. The second vision (Zech 1:18-21) draws upon the imagery of workers constructing the four-horned altar for the temple (cf. Ex 27:2) to symbolize the scattering or exile of Israel in all directions and the punishment of all nations that carried out the exile. The third vision (Zech 2:1-13) draws upon the imagery of workers laying out the plans for the reconstruction of the temple and the city to depict Jerusalem as an unwalled, holy city, ringed by fire, much like the Persian holy city of Pasargadae, as a representation of YHWH's presence in the center of the nations. The fourth vision (Zech 3:1-10) portrays the ordination of Joshua ben Jehozadak as high priest for service in the new temple (cf. Ex 28—29; Lev 8—9). The fifth vision (Zech 4:1-14) describes the temple menorah, "candelabrum," flanked by two olive branches to symbolize YHWH's presence and the role of the two anointed figures, the royal Zerubbabel and the priestly Joshua, at the foundation of the new temple. The sixth vision (Zech 5:1-4) employs the image of the flying scroll to symbolize the reading of Torah from the "porch" of the temple as the basis for the holy life of the people. The seventh vision (Zech 5:5-11) portrays the removal of a woman in an ephah basket to Shinar, the site of Babylon, to symbolize the purity of the priests and the offerings made at their ordination. The eighth and final vision (Zech 6:1-15) presents the images of four chariots and the priest

Joshua ben Jehozadak seated on the throne to symbolize the reestablishment of the temple. Many argue that the passage originally had Zerubbabel as the royal figure seated on the throne, particularly since his absence from the temple consecration portrayed in Ezra 6 suggests that the Persians removed him when they concluded that he might attempt to restore Judean independence (cf. Hag 2:20-23).

The narrative account of the transmission of YHWH's word to Zechariah in Zechariah 7:1—14:21 poses a question concerning mourning for the lost temple in Zechariah 7:1-7 and answers the question with a lengthy depiction of rejoicing and righteous action at the restoration of the temple in Zechariah 7:8-14:21. Three subunits, each introduced by the prophetic word transmission formula, lay out YHWH's concerns. Zechariah 7:8-14 begins with an oracle concerning YHWH's call for righteous action that reiterates concern with the reasons for the exile. Zechariah 8:1-17 recalls the earlier words of the prophets to emphasize that restoration will follow the period of punishment. Zechariah 8:18—14:21 calls for joy at the restoration of the temple by portraying how the nations will come to seek YHWH (see Zech 8:18-23). The two major prophetic *maśśā'ôt* ("oracles") in Zechariah 9—11 and Zechariah 12—14 respectively present YHWH's judgment against the shepherds—that is, the three Persian kings Cyrus, Cambyses and Darius, who failed to bring about YHWH's purposes as articulated in Isaiah 40—54 (see esp. Is 44:24—45:1)—and YHWH's judgment against the nations.

3.12. Malachi. Malachi calls for the return of the people to YHWH and rejects the notion of divorce, which had been employed metaphorically to represent the rupture of the relationship between YHWH and Israel at the beginning of the Book of the Twelve in Hosea. Nothing is known of the prophet Malachi. Many suspect that he did not even exist, since the name in Hebrew means simply, "my messenger/angel," and the term does not appear elsewhere in the Bible as a proper name. The book's concern with the neglect of the temple and the marriage of Jewish men to pagan women suggests that it is to be set some time prior to the arrival of Ezra in Jerusalem in the late fifth century or early-fourth century BCE. The literary form of Malachi appears as follows:

Parenetic Address to Priests and People Calling for Proper Reverence for YHWH (Mal 1:1—4:6)

I. Superscription (Mal 1:1)
II. Body of the book: parenetic address proper (Mal 1:2—4:6)
   A. First disputation: YHWH loves the people (Mal 1:2-5)
   B. Second disputation: people and priests have mishandled cultic matters (Mal 1:6—2:16)
   C. Third disputation: justice will be done on the Day of YHWH (Mal 2:17—3:5)
   D. Fourth disputation: call for proper treatment of YHWH's tithes (Mal 3:6-12)
   E. Fifth disputation: YHWH's justice will be realized on the Day of YHWH (Mal 3:13—4:3)
   F. Concluding summation: observe YHWH's Torah (Mal 4:4-6)

Following the superscription (Mal 1:1), the body of the book (Mal 1:2—4:6) appears as a parenetic address to priests and people designed to convince them to provide proper reverence and support for YHWH and the temple. This section includes six disputation speeches that challenge popular perceptions to argue for such adherence to YHWH. Malachi 1:2-5 contends that YHWH loves the people. Malachi 1:6—2:16 argues that both people and priests have mishandled cultic matters. Malachi 2:17—3:5 answers concerns about YHWH's justice to contend that the Day of YHWH's justice is about to arrive. Malachi 3:6-12 calls for the proper treatment of YHWH's tithes. Malachi 3:13—4:3 again asserts that YHWH's justice will be realized on the Day of YHWH. The concluding statements (Mal 4:5-6) sum up the argument by calling for observance of YHWH's Torah and announcing the return of the prophet Elijah prior to the expected Day of YHWH (cf. 2 Kings 2, which contends that Elijah did not die but instead ascended to heaven in a fiery chariot).

See also CANONICAL CRITICISM; EDITORIAL/REDACTION CRITICISM; FORMATION OF THE PROPHETIC BOOKS; INTERTEXTUALITY AND INNERBIBLICAL INTERPRETATION; LITERARY APPROACHES; TWELVE, BOOK OF THE: HISTORY OF INTERPRETATION.

BIBLIOGRAPHY. **F. I. Andersen,** *Habakkuk: A New Translation with Introduction and Commentary* (AB 25; New York: Doubleday, 2001); **F. I. Andersen and D. N. Freedman,** *Hosea: A New Translation with Introduction and Commentary* (AB 24; Garden City, NY: Doubleday, 1980); idem, *Amos: A New Translation with Introduction and Commentary* (AB 24A; New York: Doubleday, 1989); idem, *Micah: A New Translation with Introduction and Commentary* (AB 24E; New York: Doubleday, 2000); **J. Barton,** *Joel and Obadiah: A Commentary* (OTL; Louisville: Westminster/ John Knox, 2001); **E. Ben Zvi,** *A Historical-Critical Study of the Book of Zephaniah* (BZAW 198; Berlin: de Gruyter, 1991); idem, "Twelve Prophetic Books or 'The Twelve': A Few Preliminary Considerations," in *Forming Prophetic Literature: Essays on Isaiah and the Twelve in Honor of J. D. W. Watts,* ed. J. W. Watts and P. R. House (JSOTSup 235; Sheffield: Sheffield Academic Press, 1996a) 125-56; idem, *A Historical-Critical Study of the Book of Obadiah* (BZAW 242; Berlin: de Gruyter, 1996b); **E. Bosshard.** "Beobachtungen zum Zwölfprophetenbuch," *BN* 40 (1987) 30-62; **E. Bosshard-Nepustil,** *Rezeptionen von Jesaja 1-30 im Zwölfprophetenbuch* (OBO 144; Freiburg: Universitätsverlag; Göttingen: Vandenhoeck & Ruprecht, 1997); **E. Bosshard and R. G. Kratz,** "Maleachi im Zwölfprophetenbuch," *BN* 52 (1990) 27-46; **K. Budde,** "Eine folgenschwere Redaktion des Zwölfprophetenbuchs," *ZAW* 39 (1922) 218-29; **E. Conrad,** *Zechariah* (RNBC; Sheffield: Sheffield Academic Press, 1999); **J. L. Crenshaw,** *Joel* (AB 24C; New York: Doubleday, 1995); **H. Ewald,** *Die Propheten des Alten Bundes,* 1: *Jesaja mit den übrigen älteren Propheten* (Göttingen: Vandenhoeck & Ruprecht, 1867); **M. H. Floyd,** *Minor Prophets, Part 2* (FOTL 22; Grand Rapids: Eerdmans, 2000); **B. A. Jones,** *The Formation of the Book of the Twelve: Study in Text and Canon* (SBLDS 149; Atlanta: Scholars Press, 1995); **C. L. Meyers and E. M. Meyers,** *Haggai, Zechariah 1-8: A New Translation with Introduction and Commentary* (AB 25B; Garden City, NY: Doubleday, 1987); idem, *Zechariah 9-14: A New Translation with Introduction and Commentary* (AB 25C; New York: Doubleday, 1993); **J. D. Nogalski,** *Literary Precursors to the Book of the Twelve* (BZAW 117; Berlin: de Gruyter, 1993); idem, *Redactional Processes in the Book of the Twelve* (BZAW 118; Berlin: de Gruyter, 1993); **J. D. Nogalski and M. A. Sweeney,** eds., *Reading and Hearing the Book of the Twelve* (SBLSymS 15; Atlanta: Society of Biblical Literature, 2000); **S. Paul,** *Amos* (Hermeneia. Minneapolis: Fortress, 1991); **D. L. Petersen,** *Haggai and Zechariah 1-8: A Commentary* (OTL; Philadelphia: Westminster, 1984); idem, *Zechariah 9-14 and Malachi: A Commentary* (OTL; Louisville: Westminster/John Knox, 1995); **P. L. Reddit and A. Schart, eds.,** *Thematic Threads in the Book of the Twelve* (BZAW 325; Berlin: de Gruyter, 2003); **J. M. Sasson,** *Jonah: A New Translation with Introduction, Commentary, and Interpretations* (AB 24B; New York: Doubleday, 1990); **A. Schart,** *Die Entstehung des Zwölfprophetenbuch* (BZAW 260; Berlin: de Gruyter, 1998); **D. A. Schneider,** "The Unity of the Book of the Twelve" (Ph.D. diss., Yale University, 1979); **E. Schuller,** "Malachi," *NIB* 7:841-77; **U. Simon,** *Jonah* (JPSBC; Philadelphia: Jewish Publication Society, 1999); **K. Spronk,** *Nahum* (HCOT; Kampen: Kok Pharos, 1997); **O. H. Steck,** *Der Abschluss der Prophetie im Alten Testament: Ein Versuch zur Frage der Vorgeschichte des Kanons* (BTSt 17; Neukirchen-Vluyn: Neukirchener Verlag, 1991); idem, *Old Testament Exegesis: A Guide to Its Methodology,* trans. J. D. Nogalski (SBLRBS 39; Atlanta: Scholars Press, 1998); **C. Steuernagel,** *Lehrbuch in der Einleitung das Alte Testament: Mit einem Anhang über die Apokryphen und Pseudepigraphen* (Tübingen: Mohr Siebeck, 1912); **M. A. Sweeney,** *The Twelve Prophets* (2 vols.; Berit Olam; Collegeville, MN: Liturgical Press, 2000); idem, *King Josiah of Judah: The Lost Messiah of Israel* (Oxford: Oxford University Press, 2001); idem, *Zephaniah* (Hermeneia; Minneapolis: Fortress, 2003); **P. Trible,** "Jonah," *NIB* 7:461-529; **J. Vlaardingerbroek,** *Zephaniah* (HCOT; Leuven: Peeters, 1999); **P. Weimer,** "Obadja: Eine redaktionskritische Analyse," *BN* 27 (1985) 35-99; **J. Wöhrle,** *Die frühen Sammlungen des Zwölfprophetenbuches: Entstehung und Komposition* (BZAW 360; Berlin: de Gruyter, 2006); idem, *Der Abschluss des Zwölfprophetenbuches: Buchübergreifende Redaktionsprozesse in den späten Sammlungen* (BZAW 389; Berlin: de Gruyter, 2008); **R. E. Wolfe,** "The Editing of the Book of the Twelve," *ZAW* 53 (1935) 90-129; **H. W. Wolff,** *Hosea: A Commentary on the Book of the Prophet Hosea,* trans. G. Stansell (Hermeneia; Philadelphia: Fortresss, 1974); idem, *Joel and Amos: A Commentary on the Books of the Prophets Joel and Amos,* trans. W. Janzen, S. D. McBride Jr. and C. A. Muenchow (Hermeneia;

Philadelphia: Fortress, 1977); idem, *Obadiah and Jonah: A Commentary*, trans. M. Kohl (CC; Minneapolis: Augsburg, 1986); idem, *Haggai: A Commentary*, trans. M. Kohl (CC; Minneapolis: Augsburg, 1988); idem, *Micah: A Commentary*, trans. G. Stansell (CC; Minneapolis: Augsburg, 1990); **G. A. Yee,** "Hosea," *NIB* 7:195-297; **B. M. Zapff,** *Redaktionsgeschichtliche Studien zum Michabuch im Kontext des Dodekapropheton* (BZAW 256; Berlin: de Gruyter, 1997).

M. A. Sweeney

TWELVE, BOOK OF THE: HISTORY OF INTERPRETATION

For centuries it was known that the twelve so-called Minor Prophets together formed a single book. This was simply seen as a scribal convention without any implications for the interpretation of the individual writings. However, beginning in the 1990s, the number of studies that treat the Book of the Twelve as a redactional and meaningful entity expanded substantially. Several articles that present a research history to the Book of the Twelve have been published (Nogalski 1993a, 3-12; Schart 1998a; 1998b, 6-21; 2008; Wöhrle 2008, 2-14; also, A. Schart maintains a website that provides a regularly updated bibliography on questions related to the Book of the Twelve: <http://www.uni-due.de/EvangelischeTheologie/twelve-00start.shtml>). In this article only the most important studies will be mentioned.

1. Terminology
2. Hebrew Text Transmission
3. Greek Text Transmission
4. The Sequence of the Writings
5. The Jewish Septuagintal Interpretation of the Book of the Twelve
6. The Christian Greek Old Testament
7. Ancient Interpretations
8. Ancient Christian Commentaries on the Twelve
9. Martin Luther
10. Modern Historical-Critical Approaches
11. Conclusion

1. Terminology.
When dealing with the Book of the Twelve, it is helpful to define some central concepts in a concise way. The "Book of the Twelve Prophets" (or, in short, "Book of the Twelve") shall denote the final edition of the Hebrew original. This is in accordance with the Hebrew text tradition:

In the Codex Leningradensis, the final note after the last verse of Malachi contains the term "the Twelve." In the Babylonian Talmud, the book is called "The Twelve Prophets" (*baba bathra* 14b). In contrast, the expression "the minor prophets," referring to their length, stems from Latin sources ("*prophetae minores*," Augustine, *City of God* 18.29).

The Greek term *Dodekapropheton* is reserved, contrary to general usage, to refer only to the Greek translation of the Book of the Twelve. It is imperative to note that within the Greek tradition an important shift in understanding the Dodekapropheton occurred when the Christian communities appropriated the Dodekapropheton as part of their own canon. In cases where it is relevant to do so, this article distinguishes between the Jewish and the Christian Dodekapropheton.

In what follows, the term "writing" refers to a text attributed to a single author by the scribal tradition. The Book of the Twelve comprises twelve such writings, which are presented as individual compositions, each from a single author, whose name is given. An exception is the writing of Jonah, where the author of the narrative remains anonymous and the prophetic sayings remain seamlessly embedded in the narrative. For our present purpose, the difference between a "writing" and a "book" is that a book was published and disseminated as a self-contained literary unity. In the case of the precursors to the Twelve, it is assumed that different writings were combined in order to be published as one book.

The concept of "author" also has to be defined precisely. A writing has an implied author, to whom the sayings that are presented in the writing are attributed. For example, all sayings in the book of Amos are ascribed to the prophetic figure Amos, who is named in the superscription. However, critical scholarship regards this authorship as fictitious, since many sayings in the book of Amos actually come from later redactors who published their own work under Amos's name. If it is relevant to differentiate between the implied author and the historical person who in most cases stands behind the oldest layer of tradition included in the writing, this article speaks of that historical person as "the historical prophet," leaving aside the question of whether the historical person qualifies as a "prophet" in the sense of the sociology of religion (*see* Prophecy, History of).

2. Hebrew Text Transmission.

The Book of the Twelve as a whole lacks a separate heading. This distinguishes it from the other three Prophetic Books of the Hebrew canon, Isaiah, Jeremiah and Ezekiel. Instead, the Book of the Twelve contains four writings that possess headings that resemble (in the case of Is 1:1 remarkably closely) the headings of the other three Prophetic Books of the Hebrew canon: Hosea 1:1; Amos 1:1; Micah 1:1; Zephaniah 1:1. In this way scribes clearly marked that the Book of the Twelve comes from different authors and different times. Nevertheless, this does not rule out the fact that the Twelve is conceived as one book, just as the Psalter is conceived as one book comprising different collections of psalms and likewise lacks a heading for the book as a whole.

The oldest external evidence for the existence of a Book of the Twelve is found in Sirach 49:10 (ca. 175 BC), where it is stated that "the twelve prophets brought healing to Jacob and helped him with confidence." Since one cannot imagine what kind of motive an author would have to speak of "twelve prophets" unless they had been combined on one scroll, the Book of the Twelve must have existed by the time Sirach wrote his short evaluation.

The oldest extant manuscripts of the Book of the Twelve were discovered in Cave 4, located very close to the Qumran settlement (*see* Dead Sea Scrolls). They clearly demonstrate that the twelve Prophets—Hosea, Joel, Amos, Obadiah, Jonah, Micah, Nahum, Habakkuk, Zephaniah, Haggai, Zechariah, Malachi—were written on a single scroll. The very fragmentary scrolls consistently display a special scribal technique. The separate writings did not always begin at the top of a new column. Instead, between the writings only three empty lines were left in the same column in order to distinguish the individual writings (for the edited manuscripts, including photographs and transcriptions, see Fuller). This writing technique demonstrates that the twelve individual titles were understood neither as separate books nor as a homogenous book like that of Isaiah. The scribes wanted to highlight some new form of unity.

Although the manuscripts were found in the same cave, they come from different times and represent different text types. The oldest manuscript, 4Q76, probably dates to the mid-second century BC, the latest one to the first cen-

tury AD. As with other textual witnesses, some manuscripts should be identified as forerunners of the medieval Masoretic standard text. G. Brooke calls these texts "proto-Masoretic" (4Q77; 4Q81) (Brooke, 32). But there are other textual traditions. One manuscript, 4Q78, is very close to the LXX, but the majority of texts stand on their own ("nonaligned") (4Q76; 4Q80; 4Q82). In another location in the Judean Desert, the Wadi Murabaʿat, a scroll was found that is very close to the Masoretic text type (*see* Text and Textual Criticism).

Within the later Masoretic text tradition, as represented by, for example, Codex Leningradensis, the Masorah at the end of each writing counts the words and verses of this writing (e.g., Malachi: "fifty five verses [pĕsûqîm]"), but at the end of the last writing, Malachi, the Masoretes count in addition the total verses of the book and state that the middle verse of the book is the verse "Zion will be overthrown" (Mic 3:12) (At least this is the case in Codex Leningradensis according to *BHS*. The text edition of *BHQ* [Gelston], however, has only final notes to the individual writings. Nevertheless, in the margin to Mic 3:12 it is noted that this is the middle of the book.) Another Masoretic manuscript, the Aleppo Codex, presents only the total number of verses for the whole of the Book of the Twelve at the end of Malachi (the scanned folio is available for viewing at <http://www.aleppocodex.org>).

3. Greek Text Transmission.

The Book of the Twelve was translated into Greek when significant numbers of communities outside of the land of Israel no longer spoke *Hebrew as their native language and demanded a comprehensible but also reliable and standardized text of this important canonical document. The task probably was carried out by a single translator located in Egypt in the second half of the third century BC. The translator strived very hard to yield a literal, word-for-word translation, and uses the principle that every Hebrew word has a single Greek equivalent throughout the whole book (principle of concordance).

The translation of the Hebrew Book of the Twelve into the Greek language was part of the largest translation project of ancient times, the so-called Septuagint. After the Torah was translated, the Prophetic Books followed, among them, presumably at an early stage, the Book of the Twelve. For the sake of clarity of names, one should designate the Greek version of the Twelve by its Greek name, *Dodekapropheton*. As in other cases the translator used a Hebrew *Vorlage* for this translation that was very close to, but certainly not identical with, the Masoretic text type. In addition, his copy contained some misspellings (e.g., the interchange of some letters) and very few additions. This *Vorlage* was translated as literally as possible. The *Vorlage* certainly was different from the original Jewish LXX, but the *Vorlage* is lost completely and can only be reconstructed. An interesting find was a Greek scroll from Naḥal Ḥever (for the edited scroll, see Barthélemy; Tov). This certainly is not a Christian manuscript, as the name of the God of Israel is written in paleo-Hebrew letters. But how exactly its relation to the original LXX version can be described is still open to discussion. Most influential was the hypothesis by D. Barthélemy: the scroll represents a text type that was secondarily adjusted to the proto-Masoretic Hebrew text of its time. Finally, the Christian communities appropriated the LXX and adopted it in their Greek OT. This stage of the textual development is well attested by comparably well-preserved copies of the text (for an exhaustive description of the manuscript situation, see Ziegler, 7-119). All efforts to reconstruct the original LXX version must start from there. As one can easily imagine, it is notoriously difficult to decide in each individual case whether variants within the Greek text tradition are of Christian origin or were created within the process of translation from the Hebrew.

4. The Sequence of the Writings.

Among the Hebrew manuscripts from the Judean desert there are eight manuscripts from the caves in the vicinity of Qumran and one scroll from the Wadi Murabaʿat. The Masoretic order is well attested in Qumran and in Wadi Murabaʿat. All manuscripts in which the sequence of the writings can be seen on text-external grounds confirm the Masoretic order. There is only one possible exception. In the oldest manuscript, 4Q76 Malachi, the last writing seems to be followed by another one. According to R. Fuller, the very few traces of letters after Malachi belong to Jonah (*see* Text and Textual Criticism). P. Guillaume has questioned his hypothesis, but his arguments are unconvincing. If there were a different sequence, this not only may be evidence for a late inclusion of the book of Jonah into the collection of the Twelve, but also may have some implications for how the narrative of Jonah was understood, at least by one copyist. First, one can say that the preserved sequence was stable; copyists did not accept the variant of 4Q76 but rather followed the later, so-called Masoretic order. According to O. Steck, the narrative of Jonah would serve primary didactic needs in the final position (Steck 1996). Nineveh probably no longer was understood as the historical capital of Assyria but rather as an example for any hearer (or reader) of the prophetic message (Gerhards, 7.2). Jonah could serve as an example to illustrate the proposition in Malachi 3:7 that Yahweh will relent from his punishment as soon as the people heed the prophetic message and repent, exactly as Jonah experienced.

Between the sequence of the writings in the *Dodekapropheton* and that of the MT there is a difference in the sequence of the first six writings. The easiest explanation for this reorganization is that the translator of the original LXX placed Amos and Micah adjacent to Hosea and left the sequence of the remaining writings intact. The reason for this was that he noticed that the superscriptions of these books cohere markedly and evoke the impression that they prophesied at roughly the same time. In addition, only these three prophets directly address Samaria, the capital of northern Israel, whereas the other writings address Judah and Jerusalem.

5. The Jewish Septuagintal Interpretation of the Book of the Twelve.

Since a translation of a text into a different language always implies some form of interpretation, the Jewish LXX version of the Twelve contains the first complete, consistent interpretation of the whole book. The translator had to decide which Greek equivalent represents the sense of the Hebrew expression most accurately for every single word. Besides that, he had to decipher unusual words that he did not have in his lexicon, correct misspellings, and make sense of incomprehensible clauses as much as possible. Although it certainly was the intention of the translator to represent the original meaning of the Hebrew as accurately as possible and to avoid any deliberate change, in fact it was unavoidable that his own interpretation crept into the translation through his attempt to provide the original meaning (for a very good presentation of the LXX of Amos, see Glenny). A few examples may suffice to illustrate the way in which this translational interpretation was achieved.

The translator found the expression *yhwh ṣĕbāʾôt* many times in his Hebrew text. Concerning the Tetragrammaton, he did not keep the name "YHWH," but instead translated the word as *ʾădōnāy*, which was read in the synagogue instead of the name of God, with the Greek word *kyrios* ("Lord"). The Jewish community in Egypt had adopted this Greek title for gods for the designation of YHWH, and the translator followed this usage. In contrast, he dealt differently with the Hebrew word *ṣĕbāʾôt*. One cannot be sure, of course, but there is a good chance that it was the translator who coined the neologism *pantokratōr* as an equivalent to *ṣĕbāʾôt*. Whether the translator had this intention or not, the title *pantokratōr* came to mean "the almighty," which became an important attribute of God's essence.

Hosea 5:2 provides another example of an innovative translation. Here the translator chose the word *paideutēs* ("educator") as a self-designation of God. This title seems to be important for him, because he uses the verb *paideuō* ("to educate") four more times (Hos 7:12, 14, 16; 10:10) (Bons).

A last example comes from Amos 9:11-12. The Hebrew text envisions the rebuilding of the fallen booth of David and his city. In addition, Edom and all the *nations, which are called by God's name, will be brought under Israelite rule. The LXX translator brings in a new tone: "that the remnant of humankind and all the Gentiles upon whom my name is called may earnestly seek me, says the Lord." This new interpretation is based on two different readings of the Hebrew: "humankind" (Heb *ʾādām*) instead of "Edom" (Heb *ʾĕdôm*), and "seek" (Heb *dāraš*) instead of "possess" (Heb *yāraš*). The result is that the picture of the eschatological restitution of Israel differs markedly from that presumed by the Hebrew text. According to the Hebrew text, Israel will possess the foreign nations, whereas in the LXX Israel and the rest of humanity peacefully and jointly seek the Lord.

6. The Christian Greek Old Testament.

The NT authors, although at least some of them presumably were capable of reading and understanding Hebrew, relied on the Jewish Scriptures in their Greek versions. The early Christian communities produced no copies of these Scriptures of their own, but rather used those exemplars common in the synagogues. In some cases it is possible that the Christian authors translated a passage on their own, but this would have happened while bearing the official Greek text in mind. The text of the Greek version would not differ from that of their Jewish home communities. However, the way that the Scriptures were conceived was completely dominated by the conviction that Jesus of Nazareth was the *Messiah of Israel, whom the prophets had proclaimed as coming to save the whole world.

When the Christian communities decided to have a collection of authoritative Scriptures for themselves, apart from that of the Jewish communities, they did so by appropriating the Jewish Scriptures that were part of their own heritage and expanding them by a collection of decidedly Christian writings. The concepts of an "Old Testament" and a "New Testament" came not from the NT authors themselves but rather from later Christian scribes, who combined the Jewish Scriptures and the authoritative Christian writings into one book, comprising two parts.

As D. Trobisch has convincingly argued, it was in this stage that new scribal practices were introduced that made sure that the reader read the OT books according to a Christian hermeneutic. The most important one is the use of the so-called *nomina sacra* ("holy names"). The name of God, *kyrios* in Greek, and the concepts "God" (*theos*), "Christ" (*christos*), and "Jesus" (*Iēsous*) were written only with the first and the last letter of the word with a line above the letters in order to signal the abbreviated writing style. Later, even more *nomina sacra* were written in this style. It is only from this stage of the transmission of the Greek text that extant copies have survived. The reconstruction of the Jewish LXX version must start from and heavily rely on this text. All of the ancient Christian interpreters, from whom commentaries of the Twelve survived, relied on such a text form.

Although it is clear that Christian readers conceived the Book of the Twelve as reflecting a stage of salvation history that culminated in the coming of Jesus Christ, it is remarkable that they only rarely adjusted the text of the prophets to the supposed fulfillment in Christ. Even in passages where the NT authors quote the prophetic texts verbatim, but in a different wording than the LXX version, they very much hesitated to correct the prophetic text on the basis of the NT quotation. An example is the quotation of Amos 9:11-12 in Acts 15:16-17. There, Amos 9:11 obviously differs from the LXX version, whereas Amos 9:12 exactly follows the LXX. The scribes, however, did not eliminate this tension. The Christian scribes obviously did not care so much about the exact match of the wording as long as the sense of the passage referred to Jesus Christ clearly enough.

7. Ancient Interpretations.

7.1. Sirach. In Sirach 49:10 the Twelve are mentioned for the first time. In a long review of the honored men and fathers of Israel that begins in Sirach 44:1, the author summarizes what they contributed to the history of Israel. The author follows the historical sequence, grouping together Hezekiah with Isaiah, and Josiah with Jeremiah, who is followed by Ezekiel. In Sirach 49:10 the Twelve are taken together and a single message is attributed to them, a message of comfort and hope. (The concepts stem from the Greek version. Fortunately, among the Hebrew fragments of Sirach this passage is also attested [Smend; Vattioni; Beentjes]. Although fragmentary, the Hebrew text proves that the Greek version translated this passage very literally.) Since the Twelve consist of prophets who are dated before and after the Babylonian *exile, it is interesting that Sirach places the Twelve before the exile. Their message, however, is presented not as predicting the destruction of Jerusalem as Jeremiah (Sir 49:6), but rather as a message of consolation and hope. This prediction was only partly realized by the rebuilding of the *temple in the period of Zerubbabel and Joshua and the walls of Jerusalem under the leadership of Nehemiah (Sir 49:11-13). Since Micah was famous for having predicted the destruction of the temple on *Zion (Mic 3:12; cf. Jer 26:18), it is noteworthy that Sirach emphasizes the hopeful passages within the Book of the Twelve. This may be explained by a reading strategy that leaves the fulfilled prophecies aside—that is, the doom oracles that were fulfilled by the Babylonian exile—and concentrates on the unfulfilled prophecies that still are relevant for readers after the exile.

7.2. New Testament. Within the NT the Book of the Twelve is cited thirty-three times. This is less than half of the citations of Isaiah (72x), but clearly more than Jeremiah (10x) and Ezekiel (5x). Apparently, the Book of the Twelve contains some ideas that could be related to Jesus Christ and could not be found elsewhere. Most importantly, the prophecy of Amos 9:11-12 was used as a prooftext by James at the apostolic convention in Jerusalem to resolve the conflict between Peter, Barnabas and Paul, on the one hand, who promoted the idea that non-Israelite Christians need not to be circumcised, and their Pharisaic opponents, on the other, who maintained the opposite. It is not totally clear what kind of interpretation James presupposed in his speech (Acts 15:13-21), but it is clear that he thought that the crucifixion and resurrection of Jesus Christ included the foreign nations into Israel in such a way that they did not become Israelites but instead kept their own ethnic identity (*see* Prophets in the New Testament; Schart 2006).

8. Ancient Christian Commentaries on the Twelve.

8.1. Theodore of Mopsuestia. Only a few commentaries on the Book of the Twelve from the ancient church have survived more or less completely. Especially noteworthy is the commentary by Theodore of Mopsuestia (ca. 350-428), who represents the Antiochian school of exegesis. Because Theodore later was banned by the official church, his many commentaries on biblical books were mostly destroyed. Luckily, however, his commentary on the Twelve survived in its entirety in the original Greek (Hill 2004, 2). The commentary presumably stems from around 375. Theodore is rightly praised by modern scholars as a precursor to the historical-critical understanding of the Book of the Twelve, insofar as his preeminent goal is "to bring clarity" or perspicuity (*sapheneia*) to the scriptural text (Hill 2004, 307). He flatly rejects the allegorical approach and tries to understand the prophetic message completely within its original historical situation as intended for the audience at that time. He is very clear that the authors of the OT had no understanding of a trinitarian God; whenever God is referred to as "father" or "spirit," this is not meant in a trinitarian way, as if "father" (i.e., God) is understood as comprising three persons (Hill 2004, 28; Merx, 120). Likewise, Theodore insists that the Israelite prophets foresaw the coming of a worldly king who would restore the nation. This hope was fulfilled by the coming of Zerubbabel. Jesus Christ came in at a later stage of the divine world order, or *oikonomia* (Hill 2004, 25-26).

Only in one case is this distinct: the passage that envisions the pouring out of the *Spirit on all flesh in Joel 2:28-32. Under the influence of Peter's quotation in Acts 2, Theodore insists that "the reality of the account was found to be realized in the time of Christ the Lord" (Hill 2004, 23). In no other case did he find an announcement of Jesus Christ, but rather a completely human and Jewish king, Zerubbabel. A good example is Amos 9:11-12, regarding which Theodore states that the vision of Amos was fulfilled in Zerubbabel, who restored *Israel after the Babylonian destruction (Hill 2004, 172). Only after he had clarified the original meaning does Theodore mention James's application of Amos 9:11-12 in Acts 15, but he does not think that this represents the original meaning but only the apostle's secondary usage of this text. Nevertheless, it is clear to Theodore that James disclosed the true outcome (*ekbasis*), which was not available to the ancient Israelites (Merx, 128).

The copy of the Twelve that Theodore had before him belonged to the text type of the so-called Antiochian text, which differed from the widely accepted Alexandrian text. He does not comment on this different text type. Obviously, he knew that his Greek text was the translation of a Hebrew *Vorlage*, because in rare cases he refers to the Hebrew, whereby in these cases it is clear that he is relying on the expertise of others (Merx, 121-22). Unfortunately, he does not mention their names. As a result, it remains unclear whether he used Jewish sources. Theodore decidedly defends the divine inspiration of the Greek version by referencing the legend about the seventy translators of the LXX that was first attested in the *Letter of Aristeas* and was adopted by Christians, whereby it was inferred that the seventy translated not just the Torah but the entire collection that Christians hold as their Greek OT (Merx, 125).

Interestingly, the sequence of the writings

of the Twelve attested by Theodore followed the Hebrew order and not that of the mainstream Christian codices. The sequence must have been revised by someone in order to match the Hebrew one. Theodore does not comment on this difference in sequence, even if he was aware of it. Apparently, he sees no important difference in meaning between the order of his Greek text and that of the other Greek manuscripts of his time. In any case, we have no comments by him on those differences. Theodore is, however, seriously interested in establishing the historical sequence of the prophets. He tries to identify the historical background of each prophet as best the scarce information of the writings allows. In his introduction to Haggai he establishes the following sequence: Hosea, Joel, Amos and Micah dealt with the ten tribes of northern Israel; Obadiah prophesied against the Edomites at the time of the return; Jonah and Nahum confronted Nineveh; Habakkuk and Zephaniah addressed Judah and Jerusalem and spoke of the Babylonian threat; Haggai is the first to speak after the return from captivity (Hill 2004, 306-7).

The historical background allows him to resolve the famous tension between the portrayals of the Assyrian capital, Nineveh, in the writing of Jonah, on the one hand, and in that of Nahum, on the other. In Jonah the Ninevites respond in a very positive way—they believe in God and turn away from their evil deeds—to the unbelievably brief message, which Theodore conceives only as a short version of what Jonah had really said. In Nahum, however, the prophet confronts Nineveh again in a very harsh way and announces Nineveh's immediate downfall, as if none of the things that the book of Jonah narrates had taken place. Theodore concludes that Nineveh must have returned to its evil behavior. And he sees a pattern of God's behavior in those cases. As in the case of the Egyptian Pharaoh or the Assyrian king Sennacherib, God allows Israel's enemies to attack Israel, but when they overstate their case and try not only to do harm to Israel but also begin "warring against God," God unleashes severe retribution against them (Hill 2004, 246).

8.2. Cyril of Alexandria. Cyril of Alexandria (d. 444) may be chosen as an example of allegorical interpretation. He wrote a commentary on the Twelve in the early years of his episcopate. Cyril certainly was interested in the historical meaning; however, he thinks that a deeper meaning is hidden in many passages, and that the commentator must bring these out. A famous example is the journey of Jonah in the fish. Cyril has no doubt that this event really happened to the historical prophet. However, since Jesus already adopted Jonah as a sign for himself, it is imperative that Jonah's journey is developed at a "spiritual level" (*theōria pneumatikē*) (Hill 2008, 148). That means that it is understood as a shadow of Christ's death and resurrection. What happened to Jonah "describes in shadows, as it were [*hōs en skiais*], the mystery of the incarnation [*oikonomia*] of our Savior as well" (Hill 2008, 148).

A second example is found in the interpretation of Amos 9:11-12. Again Cyril admits that the historical reference (*historia*) to the rebuilding of the "tent of David" is the restoration of the Jews, "when Cyrus released them from captivity" (Hill 2008, 128). However, "the deeper meaning closer to reality [*esōterō kai alēthesteros*] would be in Christ" (Hill 2008, 128). In this sense, the fallen tent refers to the fallen human race suffering from death. The restitution happened when Jesus Christ was resurrected and with him those who believe in him (Hill 2008, 128).

8.3. Jerome. Jerome (ca. 347/348-419) wrote commentaries on all of the writings of the Book of the Twelve between the years 393 and 406 (Höhmann, 41). He was very influential for several reasons. First, he knew Hebrew and was capable of correcting the LXX translation toward the Hebrew version known at his time. Second, he was familiar with Jewish exegesis and consulted it regularly. In so doing, he offered an accurate portrayal of the Jewish interpretation of the shared Scripture and fostered the understanding of the Jewish religion. Third, he compared the different Greek versions (Septuagint, Aquila, Symmachus, Theodotion, the Quinta of Origen's Hexapla). Fourth, writing in Latin, he conveyed the Greek exegetical tradition to the Latin-speaking western half of the Roman Empire. Similar to Cyril, Jerome tried, as best he was able, to establish the historical sense of the text—for example, by using his knowledge of Hebrew and the land of Israel. On the other hand, from Origen he learned to find an allegorical meaning.

Throughout his commentary on Amos, for example, he interprets all statements about Judah and Jerusalem as referring to the church (*ecclesia*), whereas all statements about Samaria or Amaziah or Jeroboam are conceived as referring to the heretics. When commenting on Amos 9:11-12, for example, he states that a Christian reader of this passage must follow the example of the apostles and apply a spiritual reading: the image of the rebuilding of the fallen tent of David refers to the central Jewish cultic place, the synagogue, which was rebuilt through the resurrection of Christ (*resurrectio domini*) as the Christian community (Höhmann, 313 // 481). The phrase "the rest of humankind" (*reliqui hominum*), which is, as Jerome rightly observes, found in the LXX version and not in the Hebrew, refers to those among the Jewish people, who came to believe in Jesus Christ (*qui iudaico populo crediderunt*) (Höhmann, 313 // 481).

9. Martin Luther.
Martin Luther represents an important step in the history of interpretation of the Twelve because he produced very influential translations of the Prophetic Books from the Hebrew into German. In 1532 he published a translation of all of the Prophetic Books (As G. Krause has shown, Luther made use of the translation of the Prophetic Books by L. Hetzer and H. Denck [1527], who translated from the Hebrew. But on the other hand, these two authors had already been influenced by Luther's translation of Hosea for his course work [Krause, 19-61]).

Luther relied neither on the Latin Vulgate, which was the normative Bible version of the medieval period, nor on the Greek version, which had been the normative version of the ancient church. Instead, he relied on the Hebrew text alone. This usage of the Hebrew became a normative principle for all Protestant communities and even influenced scholarly exegesis in the Roman Catholic Church.

Luther did not write a commentary on the Twelve as a whole, but published interpretations of Jonah (1526), Habakkuk (1526) and Zechariah (1527) (for a convenient overview of all sources on Luther's exegesis of the Minor Prophets, see Krause, 1-6). However, while serving as a professor for biblical studies, he did give lectures on all of the Twelve during the years 1524-1526. These lectures were written down by his students, and some of them later were published (the lectures on the Twelve Prophets are collected in WA 13).

In the forewords (*Vorreden*) to his translations Luther gave a rough sketch of his understanding of the Twelve, targeting lay readers of the Bible. He clearly set the prophets within their historical setting and established their historical sequence on the basis of the superscriptions of the books, thereby considering Hosea as the oldest, albeit contemporary with Joel, Amos and Micah. He conceived of the prophetic office (*Amt*) as twofold: on the one hand, the prophets have to preach the law, which results in harsh judgment speeches against their disobedient Jewish fellows; on the other hand, they had to proclaim the gospel, which culminates in the announcement of the coming of Jesus Christ and his kingdom (foreword to Hosea [1545]). In addition, Luther states that at least some of the prophets had to suffer severe persecution from their addressees, who sometimes even went so far as killing the prophets. In this way, they prefigure the fate of Jesus Christ (foreword to Hosea). Luther does not think that the christological interpretation needs an allegorical method. For him, the announcement of Christ is obviously the literal meaning of the prophetic texts (Hermle, 4.1). In fact, Luther does not apply an allegorical methodology at all. When he comes to an interpretation that modern scholars would consider allegorical, he would argue that the historical sense of the text itself is meant in an allegorical way. A good example is the marriage of Hosea in Hosea 1. Since for Luther it is completely unimaginable that God ordered the prophet to take a harlot and have children with her, this action must be understood as a sign enacted (*see* Sign Act) to demonstrate the sin of the people (foreword to Hosea). However, as Krause has noted, Luther significantly reduced the number of passages that he considered as unambiguously speaking about Jesus Christ—for example, Hosea 6:1-3 speaking about the resurrection of Christ, in comparison with his exegetical forebears in the ancient and medieval church (Krause, 365, 369). At the same time, he found some additional texts where the prophets spoke of God's grace and human faith in a way completely in line with the NT (Krause, 364, 380, 383-84).

10. Modern Historical-Critical Approaches.

On the basis of a modern historical-critical approach, F. Delitzsch (1813-1890) discovered the catchword phenomenon that stitches the writings of the Twelve together. Each of the writings, mostly in its first chapter, repeats at least one significant phrase or even verse from the writing immediately before it, in most cases from its last chapter (cf. Hos 14:1 // Joel 2:12; Joel 3:21 // Amos 1:2; Amos 9:12 // Obad 19; Jonah 4:2 // Mic 7:18-19 // Nah 1:2-3; Hab 2:20 // Zeph 1:7). Especially significant is the overlap between Amos 1:2 (Yahweh roaring from Zion) and Joel 3:21 (Delitzsch, 91-93) (the catchword phenomenon later was intensively studied by J. Nogalski [see below]). H. Ewald (1803-1875) used the superscriptions as data for the reconstruction of the redaction history of the collection and proposed the thesis that the six writings Joel, Amos, Hosea, Micah, Nahum, Zephaniah, in this sequence, formed a precursor to the Book of the Twelve (Ewald, 1:74-75). K. Budde (1850-1935) was the first to postulate a *redaction that worked across the different writings. According to him, the redactor eliminated biographical narrative material from the writings in order to give more weight to the *word of God. However, the major breakthrough for understanding the Book of the Twelve as a whole was the Harvard dissertation by R. Wolfe, submitted in 1933 (Wolfe 1933; for a summary of the dissertation, see Wolfe 1935). He elaborated the complicated hypothesis that the different writings were put together by redactors who simultaneously edited several different writings in order to combine them into a single book. Wolfe coined the term "strata hypothesis" and differentiated between thirteen layers that successively worked on four collections: first Amos and Hosea were combined; second, a redactor formed the Book of the Six, comprising the preexilic prophecies (Amos, Hosea, Micah, Nahum, Habakkuk, Zephaniah); third, this book was expanded with the inclusion of Joel, Jonah and Obadiah, thereby forming a Book of the Nine; finally, the Book of the Twelve was formed. Probably because he set out his thesis without serious source-critical arguments, his important contribution was left unheeded for decades.

Research on the Twelve attained new heights after World War II with the outstanding commentaries of H. Wolff (1911-1993) and W. Rudolph (1891-1987), but these commentators concentrated their work on the historical prophets. In his commentary on Hosea, for example, Wolff explained the brevity of many texts by the thesis that they were written hastily by eyewitnesses of the oral communication. He completely ignored the work of Wolfe and analyzed the growth of the writings of the Twelve completely within their individual literary boundaries. B. Childs (1923-2007), in his *Introduction to the Old Testament as Scripture* (1979), shifted the interest away from the historical prophet to the final redaction of the books. (Childs did not address the question of what it might mean for a canonical understanding to take the Book of the Twelve as a whole, but he did supervise D. Schneider's 1979 dissertation on the unity of the Book of the Twelve.) For some reason, the dynamic of the research on the Twelve gained renewed impetus after the breakup of the Soviet Union. In 1990 P. House brought a wind of change to the debate when he examined the literary devices that let the Book of the Twelve appear as a deliberately styled unity. His analysis dealt with the Book of the Twelve as if it were a unified narrative, exploring its genre, structure, plot, characterization and point of view. According to him, the writings were arranged in such a way that the reader faces a thematic development: the first six writings (Hosea, Joel, Amos, Obadiah, Jonah, Micah) concentrate on the sin of Israel; the next three (Nahum, Habakkuk, Zephaniah) depict its punishment; and the last three (Haggai, Zechariah, Malachi) envision its restoration. This study clearly developed the idea of the Twelve as a unified book, but at the same time it completely ignored the redaction-historical dimension of this unity.

The reaction from the redaction-historical side came quickly. In 1991 O. Steck published a study of the interrelation of redactional processes within the book of Isaiah and the Book of the Twelve (Steck 1991). He was aware that his very complicated model of different *Fortschreibungen* ("relectures") was preliminary in several respects, especially because it lacked sound and detailed source-critical examinations of the key passages, as well as well-balanced criteria for determining whether similar passages, even passages that share significant lexemes, belong to the same redactional layer or cite or allude to each other, and if so, in what direction the dependence goes. However, J. Nogalski, who wrote his dissertation under Steck's supervision, brought a widely acknowledged breakthrough. His two volumes on the subject in 1993 began with an extensive study of the catchword phenomenon, already noted by Delitzsch, and on this basis developed an impressive picture of the successive growth of the Book of the Twelve (Nogalski 1993a; 1993b) (*see* Intertextuality and Innerbiblical Interpretation).

Nogalski attributed the most extensive redactional activity to the "Joel-related layer," which made the immediate coming of the *Day of Yahweh the dominant theme of eleven writings. This redaction combined a preexisting "Deuteronomistic corpus" (Hosea, Amos, Micah, Zephaniah) with Nahum, Habakkuk, Haggai, Zechariah 1—8, Joel, Obadiah and Malachi. Subsequently, Jonah and Zechariah 9—14 entered the collection.

Contemporary with Nogalski or inspired by him, a couple of studies appeared in quick succession. The first to follow with a book-length study was A. Schart. In his 1998 book *Die Entstehung des Zwölfprophetenbuchs* he began with an analysis of the openings of the writings. After having differentiated between the different types of beginnings—the different types of superscriptions and the different forms of narrative expositions—he judged that these differences must come from different redactors who successively added more writings to the collection but at the same time reworked the older collection that they had inherited. For the first time since Wolfe, Schart tried to assign every single verse of the Twelve to his six postulated redactional layers. According to him, the collection started with the combination of older versions of Hosea and Amos onto a single scroll in order to present the prophetic message that had foreseen and announced the downfall of northern Israel together with its capital, Samaria. At the next stage he more or less confirmed Nogalski's "Deuteronomistic corpus," for which he preferred the label "D-corpus." He then divided Nogalski's "Joel-related layer" into three layers: a redaction that inserted Nahum and Habakuk; a second redaction that added Haggai, Zechariah and other passages that envisioned a hopeful restoration after the judgment had been executed; and a third redaction that brought in Joel and Obadiah and formed a book comprising ten writings. The final redaction added the satirical narrative about the fate of Jonah and a collection of disputation speeches under the name of Malachi.

J. Wöhrle has offered the most recent study. His two volumes contain an independent source-critical analysis of every writing of the Twelve except for Hosea (Wöhrle 2006; 2008). Wöhrle added a lot of additional evidence to some hypotheses as postulated by Nogalski and followed by others. His study of what he calls the *Vierprophetenbuch* ("Book of the Four Prophets" [Wöhrle picked up the name *Vierprophetenbuch* from Albertz, 164-85]), which is more or less identical with Nogalski's "Deuteronomistic corpus," brilliantly confirms this hypothesis by demonstrating how the redactor of this Book of the Four deliberately alluded to the book of Kings. In addition, there are several new interesting hypotheses—for example, the *Gnadenkorpus*, which is dominated and unified by allusions to the famous definition of God's gracious and compassionate essence in Exodus 34:6-7. Likewise, Wöhrle's proposal to differentiate between three layers that deal with the nations (*Fremdvölker-Korpus I, Fremdvölker-Korpus II, Heil-für-die-Völker-Korpus*) is stimulating. However, these need further evaluation.

11. Conclusion.

Over the past few decades it has been successfully demonstrated that the Book of the Twelve must be conceived as a redaction-historical unity comparable to the other Latter Prophets, but with the marked difference that in the case of the Twelve it is openly stated that the book was composed by different authors. Even the names of the prophets that stand behind the book are explicitly given. The Book of the Twelve presents "the prophets" as a continuous chain of persons throughout history following one another, occasionally overlapping chronologically, and sharing basically the same task and message (*see* Formation of the Prophetic Books). It is of great importance that this chain was not construed as a homogenous growth of knowledge, but rather as one with conflicting positions that can claim equally to have immanent experiences of God's presence and to refer back to the community's normative tradition (*see* Prophecy and Tradition).

Concerning the method in regard to what kinds of evidence can be gathered in order to correlate redactional activities in one writing to those in another, Schart remains fundamental with his reflections on how one can gather evidence for the thesis that Hosea and Amos once were parts of a single book (Schart 1998b, 133-50).

Among the many theses about the redaction history of the Twelve, it is difficult to find some models that are more stable than others, but it seems wise to separate four major stages, no matter how many other layers one is inclined to accept.

The most convincing and broadly accepted thesis is that older versions of Hosea, Amos, Micah and Zephaniah formed a single corpus. The best evidence for this is the system of superscriptions that synchronize every prophet with the contemporary kings of Israel and Judah (*see* Israelite History). It seems as if this system wants to convey the impression that the kings Hezekiah and Josiah responded with their reforms to the message of these prophets. This corpus certainly contains substantial affinities with Deuteronomistic ideas and concepts, but it should not be identified with the editors of the book of Kings. It probably had at least one precursor. The thesis of a scroll that comprised Hosea and Amos is still worth further consideration.

It is self-evident that someone must have combined individual writings into the Book of the Twelve Prophets. This final stage may be called the "final redaction." There is some evidence that Jonah was among the last writings that came into the Twelve.

Between the D-corpus and the final redaction there must have been at least one stage, but probably there were more. One of them implemented the hope of the coming of the eschatological "day of the Lord," which even in the final form characterizes the Book of the Twelve. This eschatological concept permeates the writing of Joel through and through. As a result, it still commends itself that at least one layer of Joel was part of this stage.

Research on the Book of the Twelve must continue in order to find firmer ground. Nevertheless, it seems promising to parallel this research with that in the other Prophetic Books. O. Steck rightly has stressed the fact that the book of Isaiah and the Book of the Twelve are the most similar of the Prophetic Books. E. Bosshard-Nepustil has elaborated this idea in his massive 1997 study *Rezeptionen von Jesaia 1-39 im Zwölfprophetenbuch*. The idea of a parallel and mutual development of the book of Isaiah and the Book of the Twelve needs to be evaluated anew. The results of such undertakings should be expounded for the canonical books and compilations outside the prophets in order to appreciate whether one might be able to find similar redactional processes in their textual backgrounds. The Torah and the process of its development should be considered in light of the studies undertaken regarding the compositional history of the Book of the Twelve.

See also CANONICAL CRITICISM; FORMATION OF THE PROPHETIC BOOKS; INTERTEXTUALITY AND INNERBIBLICAL ALLUSION; REDACTION/EDITORIAL CRITICISM; RHETORICAL CRITICISM; TWELVE, BOOK OF THE (ALSO ARTICLES ON INDIVIDUAL BOOKS IN THE TWELVE).

BIBLIOGRAPHY. **R. Albertz,** *Die Exilszeit: 6. Jahrhundert v. Chr* (BE 7; Stuttgart: Kohlhammer, 2001); **D. Barthélemy,** *Les devanciers d'Aquila: Première publication intégrale du texte des fragments du Dodécaprophéton trouvés dans le désert de Juda, précédée d'une étude sur les traductions et recensions grecques de la Bible réalisées au premier siècle de notre ère sous l'influence du rabbinat palestinien* (VTSup 10; Leiden: E. J. Brill, 1963); **P. C. Beentjes,** *The Book of Ben Sira in Hebrew: A Text Edition of All Extant Hebrew Manuscripts and a Synopsis of All Parallel Hebrew Ben Sira Texts* (VTSup 68; Leiden: E. J. Brill, 2006); **E. Bons,** "Osee, Hosea: Einleitung," in *Septuaginta Deutsch: Erläuterungen und Kommentare zum griechischen Alten Testament, 2: Psalmen bis Daniel,* ed. M. Karrer and W. Kraus (Stuttgart: Deutsche Bibelgesellschaft, 2011) 2287-290; **E. Bosshard-Nepustil,** *Rezeptionen von Jesaia 1-39 im Zwölfprophetenbuch: Untersuchungen zur literarischen Verbindung von Prophetenbüchern in babylonischer und persischer Zeit* (OBO 154; Freiburg: Universitätsverlag; Göttingen: Vandenhoeck & Ruprecht, 1997); **G. J. Brooke,** "The Twelve Minor Prophets and the Dead Sea Scrolls," in *Congress Volume: Leiden 2004,* ed. A. Lemaire (VTSup 109; Leiden: E. J. Brill, 2006) 19-43; **K. Budde,** "Eine folgenschwere Redaktion des Zwölfprophetenbuchs," *ZAW* 39 (1921) 218-29; **B. S. Childs,** *Introduction to the Old Testament as Scripture* (Philadelphia: Fortress, 1979); **F. Delitzsch,** "Wann weissagte Obadja?" *Zeitschrift für die gesammte Lutherische Theologie und Kirche* 12 (1851) 91-102; **H. Ewald,** *Die Propheten des Alten Bundes* (2nd ed.; 3 vols.; Göttingen: Vandenhoeck & Ruprecht, 1867-1868); **R. E. Fuller,** "The Twelve," in *Qumran Cave 4.X: The Prophets,* ed. E. Ulrich et al. (Oxford: Clarendon, 1997) 221-318; **A. Gelston,** *The Twelve Minor Prophets* (BHQ 13; Stuttgart: Deutsche Bibelgesellschaft, 2010); **M. Gerhards,** "Jona/Jonabuch," WiBiLex (2008) <http://www.academic-bible.com/en/nc/wibilex/the-bible-encyclopedia/details/quelle/WIBI/referenz/22740/cache/e212e5897b8b2d42b4eeba4740dd5fab>; **W. E. Glenny,** *Finding Meaning in the Text: Translation Technique and Theology in the Septuagint of Amos* (VTSup 126; Leiden: E. J. Brill, 2009); **P. Guillaume,** "The Unlikely Malachi-Jonah Sequence (4QXIIa)," *JHScr* 7.15 (2007) <http://www.arts.ualberta.ca/JHS/Articles/article_76.pdf>; **S. Hermle,** "Luther, Martin, und das Alte Testament," WiBiLex (2008) <http://www.academic-bible.com/en/nc/wibilex/the-bible-encyclopedia/details/quelle/WIBI/zeichen/l/referenz/25188/cache/549783abdb8e7d50ea33d8124db2e926>; **R. C. Hill,** trans. and ed., *Commentary on the Twelve Prophets: Theodore of Mopsuestia* (FC 108; Washington, DC: Catholic University of America Press, 2004); idem, trans. and ed., *Commentary on the Twelve Prophets: Cyril of Alexandria,* vol. 2 (FC 116; Washington, DC: Catholic University of America Press, 2008); **B. Höhmann,** trans. and ed., *Der Amos-Kommentar des Eusebius Hieronymus: Einleitung, Text, Übersetzung, Kommentar* (Münster: Schüling, 2002); **P. R. House,** *The Unity of the Twelve* (BLS 27; JSOTSup 97; Sheffield: Almond, 1990); **G. Krause,** *Studien zu Luthers Auslegung der Kleinen Propheten* (BHT 33; Tübingen: Mohr, 1962); **A. Merx,** *Die Prophetie des Joel und ihre Ausleger, von den ältesten Zeiten bis zu den Reformatoren: Eine exegetisch-kritische und hermeneutisch-dogmengeschichtliche Studie; Beigegeben ist der äthiopische Text des Joel* (Halle: Verlag der Buchhandlung des Waisenhauses, 1879); **J. Nogalski,** *Literary Precursors to the Book of the Twelve* (BZAW 217; Berlin: de Gruyter, 1993a); idem, *Redactional Processes in the Book of the Twelve* (BZAW 218; Berlin: de Gruyter, 1993b); **A. Schart,** "The Jewish and the Christian Greek Versions of Amos," in *Septuagint Research: Issues and Challenges in the Study of the Greek Jewish Scriptures,* vol. 53, ed. R. Glenn Wooden and Wolfgang Kraus, Septuagint and Cognate Studies (Atlanta: Society of Biblical Literature,

2006), pp. 157-77; idem, "Zur Redaktionsge-schichte des Zwölfprophetenbuchs," *VF* 43.2 (1998a) 13-33; idem, *Die Entstehung des Zwölf-prophetenbuchs: Neubearbeitungen von Amos im Rahmen schriftenübergreifender Redaktionsprozesse* (BZAW 260; Berlin: de Gruyter, 1998b); idem, "Das Zwölfprophetenbuch als redaktionelle Großeinheit," *TLZ* 133 (2008) 227-46; **D. A. Schneider,** "The Unity of the Book of the Twelve" (Ph.D. diss., Yale University Press, 1979); **R. Smend,** *Die Weisheit des Jesus Sirach: He-bräisch und deutsch, mit einem hebräischen Glossar* (Berlin: Reimer, 1906); **O. H. Steck,** *Der Ab-schluß der Prophetie im Alten Testament: Ein Versuch zur Frage der Vorgeschichte des Kanons* (BTSt 17; Neukirchen-Vluyn: Neukirchener Verlag, 1991); idem, "Zur Abfolge Maleachi-Jona in 4Q76 (4QXIIa)," *ZAW* 108 (1996) 249-53; **E. Tov,** *The Greek Minor Prophets Scroll from Nahal Hever (8HevXIIgr)* (DJD 8; Oxford: Clarendon Press, 1990); **D. J. Trobisch,** *Die Endredaktion des Neuen Testaments: Eine Untersuchung zur Entste-hung der christlichen Bibel* (NTOA 31; Freiburg: Universitätsverlag; Göttingen: Vandenhoeck & Ruprecht, 1996); **F. Vattioni,** *Ecclesiastico: Testo ebraico con apparato critico e versioni greca, latina e siriaca* (Pubblicazioni del Seminario di semitis-tica 1; Naples: Instituto orientale di Napoli, 1968); **J. Wöhrle,** *Die frühen Sammlungen des Zwölfprophetenbuches: Entstehung und Komposition* (BZAW 360; Berlin: de Gruyter 2006); idem, *Der Abschluß des Zwölfprophetenbuches: Buchüberg-reifende Redaktionsprozesse in den späten Sammlun-gen* (BZAW 389; Berlin: de Gruyter, 2008); **R. E. Wolfe,** "The Editing of the Book of the Twelve: A Study of Secondary Material in the Minor Prophets" (Ph.D. diss., Harvard Uni-versity, 1933); idem, "The Editing of the Book of the Twelve," *ZAW* 53 (1935) 90-130; **H. W. Wolff,** *Dodekapropheton,* 1: *Hosea* (BKAT 14/1; Neukirchen-Vluyn: Neukirchener Ver-lag, 1961); **J. Ziegler,** *Duodecim prophetae* (3rd ed.; Septuaginta 13; Göttingen: Vanden-hoeck & Ruprecht, 1984). A. Schart

UNDERWORLD. *See* DEATH.

UNFAITHFUL WIFE, GOD'S. *See* FEMINIST INTERPRETATION; HOSEA, BOOK OF; WOMEN AND FEMALE IMAGERY.

UNIFYING STRUCTURE. *See* LITERARY APPROACHES.

UNIVERSALISM. *See* NATIONS.

V

VENGEANCE. *See* RETRIBUTION.

VIOLENCE. *See* FEMINIST INTERPRETATION; WARFARE AND DIVINE WARFARE; WRATH.

VISIONS, PROPHETIC

A prophetic vision is a form of divine revelation that comes by means of a visible or visualized experience. The biblical vocabulary of "vision" (ḥāzôn, marʾâ, etc.) alone is not a reliable guide to the identification of prophetic visions, in that a number of visions do not use this vocabulary, and in other places this vocabulary is used to encompass an extensive range of prophetic experience. Recent attempts to define the genre of the prophetic vision report are more promising, though not without their own difficulties.

1. Prophetic Visions and the Biblical Vocabulary of Visions
2. Defining the Genre
3. Prophetic Visions in the Old Testament

1. Prophetic Visions and the Biblical Vocabulary of Visions.

The biblical vocabulary of "visions" is grouped around two Hebrew roots, ḥāzâ and rāʾâ, both of which mean "to see." From ḥāzâ comes several words for "vision" (ḥāzôn, ḥizzāyôn, ḥăzôt, maḥazeh) and the word ḥōzeh, denoting one who sees a vision. From rāʾâ comes marʾâ ("vision") and rōʾeh ("seer"). There is a high degree of semantic overlap between these two sets of words. For example, Daniel 10:14, 16 use both ḥāzôn and marʾâ to refer to the same vision (cf. 1 Sam 3:1, 15; Is 30:10; Joel 2:28).

A typical use of "vision" vocabulary occurs in 1 Samuel 3:1-21, where the narrator says, "In those days the word of the LORD was rare; there were not many visions [ḥāzôn]" (1 Sam 3:1). As indicated by the parallelism, a vision was a means by which the word of the Lord was revealed. In this case, the visual element is not primary, in that Samuel's "vision" (marʾâ [1 Sam 3:15]) consisted of words spoken to him by the Lord. The final verses of the chapter describe the nexus between prophecy, visions and the word of the Lord: "Samuel was attested as a prophet of the Lord" (1 Sam 3:20) and "The LORD continued to be seen [rāʾâ] at Shiloh, for in Shiloh the LORD revealed himself to Samuel by the word of the LORD" (1 Sam 3:21).

The relationship between visions and prophecy is further described in several key passages. According to 1 Samuel 9:9, "The prophet of today used to be called a seer [rōʾeh]." The mark of true prophecy was that a prophet had received a vision from the Lord: "When a prophet of the LORD is among you, I reveal myself to him in visions [marʾâ]" (Num 12:6). Jeremiah 23 says that false prophets "speak visions [ḥāzôn] from their own minds, not from the mouth of the LORD" (Jer 23:16), whereas the true prophet is the one who has "stood in the council of the LORD to see [rāʾâ] and to hear his word" (Jer 23:18). The mark of the prophet is that the revelation received had come from "the mouth of the LORD," and the prophet had "heard his word."

It is perhaps for this reason that "vision" vocabulary is used to refer to a wide range of prophetic activity, whether or not there is any visual component. The entire book of Isaiah is described as "the vision [ḥāzôn] . . . that Isaiah the prophet saw [ḥāzâ]" (Is 1:1 [cf. 2 Chron 32:32]). Similarly, Nahum 1:1 speaks of "the book of the vision [ḥāzôn] of Nahum," and Habakkuk 1:1 introduces "the oracle that Habakkuk the prophet saw [ḥāzâ]."

It is beyond the scope of this article to canvas the whole range of prophetic activity that is described as either *ḥăzôn* or *marʾâ*. The present enquiry will be limited to "prophetic visions" in which there is a visual component to the revelation.

A typical example of one such vision is found in the opening chapter of the book of Ezekiel. In Ezekiel 1:1 the prophet says, "The heavens were opened and I saw visions [*marʾâ*] of God," and in the subsequent verses he goes on to relate the first of these visions: "And I looked and behold: a windstorm coming out of the north, an immense cloud with flashing lightning and surrounded by brilliant light. The center of the fire looked like glowing metal, and in the fire was what looked like four living creatures" (Ezek 1:4-5a). The book of Ezekiel uses vision vocabulary (*marʾâ*) in Ezekiel 8:1; 40:3; 43:3 to introduce other blocks of vision reports.

However, not every vision is marked by "vision" vocabulary. For example, the vision of the valley of the dry bones (Ezek 37:1-14) uses neither *ḥăzôn* nor *marʾâ*. Likewise, other passages commonly recognized as prophetic visions do not use key terminology. For example, Zechariah's eight night visions are nowhere described in the text as "visions," nor are the visions in Amos 7—9 (although the prophet is described by others in Amos 7:12 as a *ḥōzeh* ["seer"]).

There is semantic overlap between the vocabulary of "visions" and "dreams." Not all dreams are prophetic visions (e.g., Gen 20:3; 31:10, 24; 37:5; 40:5), but a prophetic vision may come by way of a dream (e.g., Dan 7; cf. Zech 4:1, which implies that the preceding vision in Zech 3 occurred during sleep). In a number of places, "visions" and "dreams" are used synonymously: "When a prophet of the LORD is among you, I reveal myself to him in visions [*marʾâ*], I speak to him in dreams [*ḥălôm*]" (Num 12:6); "And it will be like a dream [*ḥălôm*], a vision of the night [*ḥăzôn laylâ*]" (Is 29:7 [cf. Job 4:13; 7:14; 20:8; 33:15]). Furthermore, Joel 2:28 prophesies that in the last days, "Your sons and daughters will prophesy, your old men will dream dreams [*ḥălôm*], your young men will see [*rāʾâ*] visions [*ḥizzāyôn*]."

This brief survey of the biblical vocabulary of "visions" demonstrates that word studies cannot provide a sufficient basis for the identification and analysis of the genre of the prophetic vision, and that another approach is needed to define and analyse the genre.

2. Defining the Genre.

There have been a number of different approaches to the definition of the genre of the prophetic vision. The following four scholars illustrate the diversity of approaches: J. Lindblom categorizes visions based on the differing psychological experience of the prophet; B. Long subdivides visions into three "types" based on "the interconnections between structure, content, and intention" (Long, 354); S. Niditch arranges symbolic visions along an evolutionary chronology of the tradition's historical development; A. Behrens follows a strict form-critical approach.

2.1. Johannes Lindblom (Psychological). In *Prophecy and Ancient Israel*, Lindblom develops a taxonomy of prophetic visions based on the nature and psychology of the prophetic experience (*see* Prophecy and Psychology) with three classifications: ecstatic visions, symbolic perceptions and literary visions.

Lindblom defines an ecstatic vision as a revelation experienced in the form of visual perceptions, as distinct from an audition, which is a revelation experienced in the form of auditory perceptions. The vision is "received in trance or ecstasy, or in a mental state approximating thereto. These perceptions are not caused by any object in the external world, but arise within the soul" (Lindblom, 122). Lindblom subdivides this category into pictorial visions and dramatic visions. In a pictorial vision, the focus of attention is the objects or figures that are seen, such as Amos's visions of locusts consuming the harvest (Amos 7:1-3) and fire devouring the land (Amos 7:4-6). In contrast, the essential element of the dramatic vision is the actions performed by figures that appear in the vision, as seen for example in the vision in Ezekiel 8—11.

In Lindblom's second category, symbolic perception, a real object is seen by means of natural sight but is "conceived of as something particularly significant and interpreted as a symbol of another, higher reality" (Lindblom, 137). Examples of this category are Amos's perception of the basket of ripe fruits (Amos 8:1-2) and Jeremiah's perception of the almond tree (Jer 1:11-12).

Lindblom's final category is the literary vision, in which "a prophet receives an inspiration in the form of a visual creation of the imagination" (Lindblom, 141). The prophet is not "seeing" a vision in an ecstatic state, but rather is "producing" a vision in literary form. Examples of this are the visions in Zechariah 1—2; 6:1-8, which Lindblom argues are "products of the imagination of the prophet, although he was in a state of inspiration" (Lindblom, 145).

Lindblom's categorization is based on the inner psychology of the prophetic experience. However, the biblical texts often do not provide sufficient information to determine what "actually" happened in the mind of the prophet, and the method must rely on a speculative reconstruction of the "original" prophetic experience by supposition, analogy and inference.

2.2. Burke Long (Typology). Building on the earlier work of M. Sister and F. Horst, Long identifies three types of "vision reports." Long's first type is the "oracle vision," marked by a "short report, dominated by question-and-answer dialogue, wherein the visionary image is simple and unidimensional, providing an occasion for oracle" (Long, 357). Examples include Jeremiah 1:11-14; 24:1-1; Amos 7:7-8; 8:1-2; Zechariah 5:1-4.

Long's second type is the "dramatic word vision," marked by "a report which depicts a heavenly scene, or a dramatic action, a situation altogether supramundane taken as a portent presaging a future event in the mundane realm" (Long, 359). Examples include 1 Kings 22:17, 19-22; Isaiah 6; Jeremiah 38:21-22; Ezekiel 9:1-10; Amos 7:1-6; Zechariah 1:8-17.

Long's final type is the "revelatory mysteries vision," marked by "a report whose basic intent is to convey in veiled form, secrets of divine activity and events of the future. Visionary imagery is symbolic, sometimes bizarre, and there is always a pattern of dialogue whose purpose is to decipher its esoteric significance" (Long, 363). Examples include Daniel 8; 10—12; Zechariah 2:3-4; 4:1-14; 5:5-8; and the extrabiblical visions in *2 Baruch* 22—30; 36—37; *3 Baruch*; *4 Ezra* 9:26—10:59; 11—12; 13.

S. Amsler rightly comments that typological approaches such as those of Sister, Horst and Long are based on artificial and overlapping classifications (Amsler, 363n8). These classifications are imposed on, rather than emerge from, the visions.

2.3. Susan Niditch (Tradition History). Ni-

ditch's monograph *The Symbolic Vision in Biblical Tradition* differs from earlier works both because the focus is restricted to "symbolic visions" in particular, and also because it seeks to analyze the diachronic development of this tradition. Niditch identifies twelve "symbolic visions" as participants in one formal tradition and argues that this form has undergone three main stages of development in the biblical tradition.

The first stage, encompassing Amos 7:7-9 (plumb line), Amos 8:1-3 (ripe fruit), Jeremiah 1:11-12 (almond branch), Jeremiah 1:13-19 (boiling pot) and Jeremiah 24 (fig baskets), is characterized by simple form, style and content elements and a metaphorical symbolic usage (i.e., a symbol signifies X).

The second stage encompasses five visions of Zechariah (Zech 5:1-4; 4:1-6a, 10b-14; 2:1-4; 1:7-17; 6:1-8 [listed in order of formal development]) that, Niditch argues, demonstrate important developments in the form of the symbolic vision.

Taken as a group, Zechariah visions VI (scroll), V (menorah), II (horns), I (horse-rider teams), and VIII (horse-chariot teams) reflect other significant trends in the development of the symbolic vision form. One is the movement from the economical-rhetorical style, found in Amos and Jeremiah, to a more clearly prose medium. The lessening of concern with traditional-style repetition and with economy of language, key factors in the earliest stage of the form, is evident in all the Zechariah visions to varying degrees.

Secondly, Zechariah's visions evidence increasing mythologization both in the symbol objects and in the way the symbols are related to their meanings. One might compare the stationary, mundane, non-ritualistic symbol objects of Amos and Jeremiah with the flying scroll of vision VI or the temple paraphernalia of V. The symbols of Zechariah visions II (horns), I (horse-rider) and VIII (horse-chariot) are explained within their own mythic terms; they are not declared a representation of something else. The "symbol = itself" equation in the visions of Zechariah is evidence of genuine mythic mentality. (Niditch, 74)

The third stage encompasses Daniel 7; 8; *2 Baruch* 35—43; 53—76; *4 Ezra* 11:1—12:39; 13:1-53 and demonstrates the symbolic vision form at its baroque and narrative stage.

Niditch's approach argues for an evolving

development in the form of the symbolic vision, but the evolutionary trend for which she argues does not adequately account for all symbolic visions. For example, Niditch describes Zechariah 2:5–9 and Zechariah 5:5–11 as "experiments" that have "strayed off the mainstream of development" (Niditch, 10n22).

2.4. Achim Behrens (Form-Critical). In *Prophetische Visionsschilderungen im Alten Testament*, Behrens offers a form-critical analysis of the genre of the prophetic vision report (*see* Form Criticism). Building on the 1976 dissertation of S. Reimers ("Formgeschichte der profetischen Visionsberichte"), Behrens argues that a prophetic vision report consists of two elements, the vision proper and the subsequent dialogue between the prophet and a heavenly figure, and that each of these elements typically shares a common form.

The vision element begins with the verb *rā'â* ("to see"), usually in the Hiphil, with the Lord as the subject. This is typically followed by *wěhinnēh* ("and behold!"), which introduces a nominal "surprise clause" (*Überraschungssatz*) describing the content of vision.

The dialogue element usually begins with a *wayyiqtol* form of *'āmar* ("to say"), followed by a question if the speaker is the prophet or an imperative if the speaker is a heavenly figure. The dialogue always ends with a final word spoken by the heavenly figure. Table 1 demonstrates this pattern, using Amos 7:1-3:

Vision	verb *rā'â* ("to see")	"This is what the Lord GOD causes me to see [*rā'â* Hiphil]."
	wěhinnēh+ surprise clause	"And behold! [*wěhinnēh*] . . . he was preparing swarms of locusts after the king's share had been harvested and just as the second crop was coming up."
Dialogue	a *wayyiqtol* form of *'āmar* ("to say")	"And when they had finished eating all of the greenery, I cried out [*wā'ōmar*]."
	question / imperative	"Lord GOD, forgive! How can Jacob survive? He is so small!"
	final word	"So the LORD relented. 'This will not happen,' the LORD said."

Table 1. Vision and Dialogue Pattern in Amos 7:1-3

Behrens identifies thirty-one prophetic vision reports and provides a detailed analysis of thirty of them (Amos 7:1-3; 7:4-6; 7:7-8; 8:1-2; 9:1-4; Jer 1:11-12, 13-14; 24:1-10; Isa 6:1-11; Ezek 1:4—2:8; 2:9—3:9; 8:2-6; 8:7-13; 8:14-15; 8:16-18; 9:1-11; 11:17-25; 37:1-14; 43:1-9; Zech 1:7-15; 2:1-4; 2:5-9; 3:1-10; 4:1-14; 5:1-4; 5:5-11; 6:1-8; 1 Kings 22:17; 22:19-22; Dan 8:3-14; 10:5-14; 12:5-7 [listed according to the order of analysis by Behrens]; Ezek 43:1-9 is not included within the scope of his analysis). Behrens finds that these vision reports exhibit a high degree of conformity to the formal pattern described above, while noting some consistent variations (e.g., the vision reports that do not use a *wěhinnēh* surprise clause instead use *rā'â* with the direct object marker [see 1 Kings 22:17, 19; Is 6:1; Amos 9:1; Zech 3:1]).

Behrens concludes that there are two streams of development in the tradition history of the prophetic vision report. The first stream commences with the visions in Amos 7—8, the oldest examples of the genre of the prophetic vision report. The influence of these visions on the developing tradition can be seen in Jeremiah 1:11-14 (word play like Amos 8:1-2) and Jeremiah 24:1 (Hiphil form of *rā'â*). Jeremiah's visions have in turn influenced Ezekiel's vision in Ezekiel 2:9—3:9. The second tradition stream, which has the "throne vision" as a core motif, runs through Isaiah 6; 1 Kings 22:17, 19; Amos 9:1-4 and flows into Ezekiel 1:4—2:8a. Behrens argues that these two streams of tradition coalesce in Ezekiel 1—3, to which the visions in Ezekiel 8—11 add a priestly influence. Both Zechariah and Daniel then make use of this vision form (Behrens, 382-84). Behrens also concludes that there is a gradual and progressive disappearance from the visions of Yahweh, who is replaced by the emergence of intermediary beings (Behrens, 384).

Behrens's work is the most thorough analysis of the form of the prophetic vision report to date, and it advances our understanding in important and helpful ways. However, it also demonstrates the problems inherent with any attempt to use formal criteria alone to define the genre, because these criteria can be, at the same time, both too narrow (excluding some valid prophetic visions) and too broad (including nonvisions). The prophetic vision in Daniel 7 is an example of the first problem.

This chapter is Daniel's report of his vision (*hĕzû*, Aramaic equivalent of *hāzôn*) of four beasts, the Ancient of Days and one like a son of man. In the vision, Daniel asks a heavenly figure for the interpretation of what he sees, which is then given to him. Daniel 7 is manifestly the report of a prophetic vision, but it is not in the form of a prophetic vision report. Behrens describes Daniel 7 as sui generis (Behrens, 317). Exodus 3 provides an example of the opposite problem. God's appearance in the burning bush satisfies all of the formal elements in Behrens's schema. It begins with *rā'â* + *wĕhinnēh* + a nominal surprise clause ("And Moses looked [*rā'â*], and behold [*wĕhinnēh*]: the bush was burning in the fire, but it was not consumed" [Ex 3:2]). It contains a dialogue that begins with a *wayyiqtol* form of *'āmar* and contains both an imperative ("Take off your sandals") and a question ("Who am I, that I should go to Pharaoh?"), and in which the Lord has the final word. The fact that Exodus 3 satisfies all of Behrens's markers of the form suggests that formal criteria alone cannot be relied on to delineate the boundaries of the genre of the prophetic vision.

2.5. The Genre of the Prophetic Vision. We have seen that the genre of the "prophetic vision"/"prophetic vision report" cannot be defined exclusively by any set of formal criteria. What constitutes a prophetic vision must be decided with reference to content, and not merely with reference to form. For the purpose of the analysis that follows, a prophetic vision is a revelation that comes to a prophet by means of a visible or visualised experience.

However, the formal criteria (particularly those identified by Behrens) remain very useful because they identify a "normal" pattern to which a vision will conform to a greater or lesser degree. In the following overview of the prophetic visions in the OT, these formal criteria help to identify the particularities and peculiarities of each vision.

3. Prophetic Visions in the Old Testament.

3.1. Amos 7:1-3; 7:4-6; 7:7-9; 8:1-2; 9:1-4. Amos 7—9 contains five visions, structured as two pairs and a separate final vision. The first four visions are similar in form, with near identical opening ("Thus the Lord GOD/he showed me, and behold"). The fifth vision is shorter, commencing with "I saw."

The first vision (locusts that devour the land [Amos 7:1-3]) and second vision (fire that devours the land [Amos 7:4-6]) are alike in that both record a vision of judgment, the intercession of the prophet Amos, and the announcement that the Lord relents from bringing judgment. The next pair of visions offers no such escape from judgment. In the third vision (a wall tested with a plumb line [Amos 7:7-9]), the Lord declares, "I am setting a plumb line among my people Israel; I will spare them no longer." The ominous refrain "I will spare them no longer" is repeated in the fourth vision (a basket of summer fruit [Amos 8:1-2]). This vision involves a word play that is difficult to capture in English: the prophet sees "summer fruit" (*qāyiṣ*), and the Lord announces that it is "time" (*qēṣ*). The final vision (Amos 9:1-4) reinforces the message of inevitable judgment of the previous two visions. In this vision, Amos sees the Lord standing beside the altar, issuing orders for the destruction of the *temple and judgment on the people, from which "not one will get away, none will escape."

There is continuing debate about the relationship between these five visions and the message of the rest of the book of Amos. There are various explanations of the connections between "vision" and "oracle" generally, the function of the third-person biographical account in Amos 7:10-17, which comes between the third and fourth visions, and the function of the oracles in Amos 8:3-14, which come between the fourth and fifth visions. However, most scholars tend to recognize a tight literary integration of the visions with the wider context of the book, irrespective of any prior oral or literary forms. As J. Watts rightly concludes, "'Vision' and 'word' belong together. The prophet's message cannot be understood apart from those great moments when God revealed his counsel and the prophet was allowed to see eternal meaning in temporal appearance" (Watts, 86).

3.2. 1 Kings 22:17, 19-22. 1 Kings 22 records two visions of the prophet Micaiah. In the first, Micaiah has a vision of "all Israel scattered on the hills like sheep without a shepherd." As the Lord explains, the people are like this "because they have no master" (due to the prophesied death of Ahab).

The second vision recounts Micaiah's vision

of the *divine council, in which he sees "the LORD sitting on his throne with all the host of heaven standing around him on his right and on his left." In this vision, one of the heavenly beings offers to be a lying spirit in the mouth of Ahab's prophets in order to entice Ahab to his death at Ramoth Gilead. According to Jeremiah 23:18, access to the divine council is the mark of all true prophecy: "But which of them has stood in the council of the LORD to see or to hear his word? Who has listened and heard his word?"

3.3. Isaiah 6:1-11. Isaiah 6:1-11 is an example of a prophetic vision that is also the prophet's call/commissioning (on the genre of the call narrative, see Habel). This vision departs from the standard form, in that the direct object marker (rather than *wĕhinnēh*) is used to denote that which was seen. The prophet Isaiah sees a theophanic vision of the Lord in his heavenly temple. The prophet becomes a participant in this visionary scene, as he is first cleansed of his sin and guilt and then volunteers to be sent out to speak a message of judgment on behalf of the Lord. This vision of the "heavenly council" has elements in common with other texts in this setting (e.g., 1 Kings 22:17, 19; Job 1—2; Ps 82; Zech 3:1-10) (see Tidwell, 347-52).

Other prophetic calls similarly occur in the context of a vision. For example, the visions in Jeremiah 1 are embedded in Jeremiah's prophetic call, Ezekiel's call is bound up with the vision complex in Ezekiel 1—3, and the first "night vision" in Zechariah 1:8-17 functions as the call and commissioning of the prophet Zechariah (see Beuken 1967, 239-44).

3.4. Jeremiah 1:11-12; 1:13-14; 4:23-26; 24:1-10; 38:21-23. Jeremiah 1 contains two visions based on a "What do you see?" dialogue, which are similar in form to Amos 7:8; 8:2. The first is a vision of an almond tree (Jer 1:11-12), which, like Amos 8:1-2, depends on word play: the vision of an "almond tree" (*šāqēd*) points to the fact that the Lord is "watching" (*šōqēd*) to see his word fulfilled. The second is a vision of a boiling pot, tilting from the north, which symbolizes destruction coming from the north that is about to be poured out on Judah and Jerusalem.

This same "What do you see?" pattern is used and developed in Jeremiah 24:1-10, in which Jeremiah sees two baskets of figs, one

good and the other bad. After seeing these two baskets, Jeremiah declares "the word of the LORD" that the good figs represent the exiles who have been taken to Babylon, and the bad figs represent those who will remain in the land or go to Egypt. In addition to these three visions in this form, Jeremiah records two other vision experiences. In Jeremiah 4:23-26 the prophet sees a vision of the "de-creation" of the heavens and earth, laid waste by the Lord's anger, and in Jeremiah 38:21-23 he recounts to Zedekiah a vision of the future that the Lord has shown him, in which the women of Jerusalem denounce Zedekiah for his misplaced trust.

Jeremiah's visions (on which, see Zimmerli) are a vital part of the book's message because they highlight one of the book's key themes: the connection between "the word of the LORD" and true prophecy. In Jeremiah 23:28 the Lord declares, "Let the prophet who has a dream [*ḥălôm*] tell his dream, but let the one who has my word speak it faithfully. For what has straw to do with grain?" Some have taken this to mean that in the era of "classical" prophecy prophetic visions and dreams were not recognized as valid. For example, J. Barton quotes this verse and then concludes, "This appears to imply that true revelations from Yahweh do not come in visions or dreams" (Barton, *ABD* 5:493). This cannot be Jeremiah's point, since this would invalidate the prophet's own visions. Rather, Jeremiah's critique of "prophet dreamer" in this verse is part of his wider condemnation of "the prophets." In the book of Jeremiah the "true" prophets are always designated as the Lord's prophets (e.g., "my servants the prophets," "his servants the prophets"). In contrast, the prophets who speak falsehood are always referred to merely as "the prophets." The "prophets" with their dreams in Jeremiah 23:28 are the same as the "prophets" in Jeremiah 23:16, who "speak visions [*ḥāzôn*] from their own hearts, not from the mouth of the LORD." These so-called prophets have not "stood in the council of the LORD to see or to hear his word" (Jer 23:18). Jeremiah 23:28 is not a denunciation of all visions and dreams per se but rather is an attack on the false dreamers. From the outset, the reader knows that Jeremiah is not this type of prophet, since his visions are a revelation from the Lord of the *word of the Lord. This point is underlined by the formula "the word of the LORD was to me, saying," which introduces visions in Jeremiah 1:11, 13; 24:4.

3.5. Ezekiel 1:1—2:8; 2:9—3:9; 8—11; 37:1-14; 40—48, Especially 43:1-9. Ezekiel 1—3 contains a vision complex in two parts. Ezekiel 1:1—2:8 recounts Ezekiel's vision of the four fiery living creatures that support a throne, above which Ezekiel sees "the likeness of the glory of the LORD." The theme of the "glory of the LORD" unites the three main vision complexes of the book (see Ezek 1:28; 3:23; 10:4, 18; 11:23; 43:4-5) and provides a major theological theme of the book: where is the glory of the Lord to be found? As T. Renz notes, this opening vision is foundational for what follows: the dark overtones of the storm and throne room theophany in the vision evokes biblical traditions of judgment that prepare the reader for the message of the first half of the book, and the cherubim chariot stresses the mobility of the Lord that is presupposed by the visions in Ezekiel 8—11 (Renz, 63-64). In Ezekiel 2:9—3:9 the focus shifts to Ezekiel's reception of the word of the Lord, as the prophet is given a scroll inscribed with words of lament and mourning and woe and is commissioned to speak this word to the house of Israel. Ezekiel's positive reception of the word of the Lord stands in stark contrast to the "rebellious house" of Israel.

Ezekiel 8—11 is a single vision composed of several scenes. Ezekiel is transported to Jerusalem, and, as in the first vision, he has a vision of the glory of the Lord enthroned above the living creatures (now identified as cherubim). Ezekiel is shown a worsening progression of "detestable" *idolatry (Ezek 8), which brings judgment on the people of Jerusalem (Ezek 9) and causes the glory of the Lord to depart from his sanctuary (Ezek 10—11). This vision is a graphic announcement of impending judgment on Jerusalem, which will be reiterated by sign act and prophecy in the succeeding chapters.

The remaining visions in the book of Ezekiel are of a new Israel and a transformed society. In Ezekiel 37:1-14 the prophet sees the revivification of the valley of dry bones, representing the restoration of slain house of Israel. Ezekiel 40—48 is a complex of "visions of God" (Ezek 40:2) that unpack the promise of Ezekiel 37:24-28 and in which Ezekiel sees a renewed temple and city. A central part of this vision complex is the vision in Ezekiel 43:1-9, which reverses the effect of Ezekiel 8—11, as Ezekiel sees the glory of the Lord return to the temple. As H. Parunak concludes, "Chaps. 40-48 [emphasize] the restoration of the people to their land and the renewal of their cultus and of the Lord's presence in their midst. The temple tour format of 8-11, including the adapted chariot vision as the bearer of the Lord, are changed from images of judgment to symbols of blessing" (Parunak, 74).

3.6. Zechariah 1:7-15; 2:1-4; 2:5-9; 3:1-10; 4:1-6a + 10b-14; 5:1-4; 5:5-11; 6:1-8. Zechariah 1—6 contains a sequence of eight visions, usually described as Zechariah's "night visions" because they are introduced by the somewhat cryptic words "I saw the night" (Zech 1:8).

The vision sequence in Zechariah 1—6 has inherited its form from multiple sources. There are striking formal connections with Genesis 31:10-12. The phrase in Genesis 31:10 "and I lifted up my eyes and I looked in my dream and behold" provides the formal template for the majority of the night visions, and the otherwise curious departure from form in Zechariah's seventh vision (which begins instead with the imperative "Lift up your eyes and look") follows the pattern of Genesis 31:12.

However, Genesis 31 explains only some elements of the form of Zechariah's visions. Two of the visions in Zechariah 4 and Zechariah 5 use the same "What do you see?" dialogue pattern utilized in Amos and Jeremiah, and as Niditch demonstrates, Zechariah 1—6 draws more widely on the tradition of the symbolic vision from both Amos and Jeremiah. Furthermore, Zechariah's "angelic interpreter" seems to be a development of the man in Ezekiel's vision who interprets the meaning of the visions (see, e.g., Ezek 47:1-12). Also akin to Ezekiel, the visions in Zechariah 1—6 are first-person vision reports (on the nature of Zechariah's vision report, see Tiemeyer).

The "Joshua" vision in Zechariah 3 is different from the other night visions. Rather than drawing on the Amos/Jeremiah tradition, this vision bears striking similarities to scenes of the divine council like Isaiah 6 and 1 Kings 22. The connection with Isaiah 6 is especially strong: both passages denote that which is seen by the prophet using a direct object marker with a participial construction rather than the typical "surprise clause"; both omit the expected "I lifted my eyes and looked"; both have the prophet become a participant in the scene (see Is 6:8; Zech 3:5); both describe a cleansing from sin of an identified historical person. The Joshua vision in Zechariah 3 has been given a different form because it (like Is 6) is not merely a symbolic vision, but also a symbolic act that involves the prophet. The difference in function is marked by a difference in form.

The central theme of Zechariah's eight night visions and interpreting oracles is that the Lord is returning to dwell in the temple in Jerusalem. The visions are concentric, both starting and ending with visions of horses going throughout the earth. There are clear (antithetical) parallels between the first three visions and the last three. In the first three visions the cumulative picture is of the return of the Lord and his people to Jerusalem, centred on the Lord's house. These three visions encourage and enable a movement of God's people toward Jerusalem. In contrast, the final three visions describe those who are "going out" (*yōṣĕʾôt* [Zech 5:3; 5:6; 6:1])—a movement away from Jerusalem in which *sin and iniquity are purged from the land and relocated to Babylon to a "house" to be built for it there. The eight night visions are represented diagrammatically in table 2.

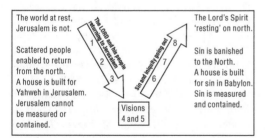

Table 2. The Pattern of Zechariah's Night Visions

These six visions form a frame around two central visions: the fourth vision (Zech 3) about Joshua as the "temple priest" and the fifth vision (Zech 4) about Zerubbabel the "temple builder." These two visions describe the means by which sin is banished and the Lord will return to Zion. As a whole, these eight visions focus on the temple as the means by which the Lord will again dwell in the midst of his people in Jerusalem. The oracles embedded within the night visions and the oracle that concludes the sequence (Zech 6:9-15) work together with the eight night

visions to depict and describe the imminent fulfilment of certain key promises of the "former prophets," especially the *return* of God and his people to Jerusalem (visions one through three), the *restoration* of priesthood, temple and Davidic line (visions four and five + Zech 6:9-15), and the *removal* of sin and idolatry (visions six through eight) (see Stead, 127-32, 185-87, 212-14).

3.7. Daniel 7:2-28; 8:3-14; 10:5-14; 12:5-7. Like the visions the book of Zechariah, the visions in the book of Daniel incorporate both formal elements and motifs from other visions. For example, the visions that begin in Daniel 8:3 and Daniel 10:5 are introduced with the phrase "I lifted up my eyes and looked, and behold," which is typical of Zechariah's night visions. Similarly, the figure described as "a man dressed in linen" (Dan 10:5) is a development of a similar figure in Ezekiel 9:2. However, other parts of Daniel's visions are without parallel. Daniel 7 recounts a vision that came by way of a dream and shares none of the formal markers of a vision as identified by Behrens. All of Daniel's visions are recounted in the first person as vision/dream reports.

The visions in Daniel 7—12 straddle the language divide of the book: *Aramaic (Dan 2:4b—7:28) and *Hebrew (Dan 8—12). Daniel 7 provides a bridge between the court tales of Daniel 1—6 and the succeeding visions in Daniel 8—12. The court tales involve dreams and their interpretations (Dan 2; 4), and Daniel 7 is both dream and vision (see Dan 7:1). This bridging function perhaps explains why Daniel 7 is written in Aramaic, as its language reinforces its connection with Daniel 2—6, whereas its form links it with Daniel 8—12 (see Collins 1977, 17-19).

There is a chiastic arrangement to Daniel 2—7 (Lenglet; Collins 1977, 11-12), with the vision of the four kingdoms in Daniel 7 corresponding to the statue in Nebuchadnezzar's dream in Daniel 2. At the same time, the "symbolic vision" form in Daniel 7 is closely mirrored by Daniel 8 (see Lucas, 32-33, developing Collins 1993, 54-55).

Daniel 7 records a "vision" (Aram *ḥĕzû*) of four beasts that represent four kingdoms. In his dream Daniel sees the fourth beast (kingdom) destroyed by the Ancient of Days, after which one "like a son of man" approaches the Ancient of Days and is given all authority, glory and power. Daniel is disturbed by these visions, so he asks "one of those standing there," who then gives Daniel the interpretation of the dream (Dan 7:17-27).

Like the vision in Daniel 7, Daniel 8 involves a vision and an interpretation given by a heavenly being. As one named "Gabriel" explains (Dan 8:20-21), the twin-horned ram in the vision represents the kings of Media and Persia, and the goat represents the king of Greece. The vision recorded in Daniel 8 is set in the reign of the sacrilegious Belshazzar (Dan 8:1; cf. Dan 5:4), but the content of the vision is addressed to a much later period, when another sacrilegious ruler (Antiochus) would threaten God's people. As J. Goldingay notes, Daniel 8 provides the context for the remaining visions: "The explanation of the symbolic vision in chap. 8 actually explains little, and this prepares the way for the following vision(s). Verse 8:27b thus leads into chaps. 9 and 10-12, which offer further reaffirmation and more explanation of the vision's fundamental perspective. The chapter's connection with the exile (its setting in the reign of the sacrilegious Belshazzar) links with the focus on the question—how long is this exile to last?—that concerns chap. 9. Its epiphany and detailed quasi-prophecies are paralleled on a larger scale by those of chaps. 10-12" (Goldingay, 208). Daniel 10—12 records a vision complex in which a heavenly figure, whom Daniel describes as "a man dressed in linen," outlines for Daniel the "great war" (Dan 10:1) that is to take place between Persia and Greece and their successors, and in particular what the "King of the North" will do to the "beautiful land."

The visions in Daniel 7—12 are the only fully developed examples of *apocalyptic literature in the OT. Some of the apocalyptic features found in these visions include a radical dualism between good and evil, a revelation that is mediated by an otherworldly being to a human recipient, animal and number symbolism and visions of the heavenly realms (see Collins 1979, 21-59). It is important that both the stories and the visions of book of Daniel are read together as providing complementary perspectives rather than opposing viewpoints. As E. Lucas notes, "The apocalyptic worldview of the visions is a development from the worldview of the stories, not a radical departure from it" (Lucas, 314).

See also ANCIENT NEAR EASTERN PROPHECY;

APOCALYPTICISM, APOCALYPTIC LITERATURE; DIVINE COUNCIL; FORM CRITICISM; PROPHECY AND PSYCHOLOGY.

BIBLIOGRAPHY. S. Amsler, "La parole visionnaire des prophètes," *VT* 31 (1981) 359-63; J. Barton, "Postexilic Hebrew Prophecy," *ABD* 5:489-95; idem, *Oracles of God: Perceptions of Ancient Prophecy in Israel after the Exile* (London: Darton, Longman & Todd, 2007); A. Behrens, *Prophetische Visionsschilderungen im Alten Testament: Sprachliche Eigenarten, Funktion und Geschichte einer Gattung* (AOAT 292; Münster: Ugarit-Verlag, 2002); W. A. M. Beuken, *Haggai-Sacharja 1-8: Studien zur Überlieferungsgeschichte der frühnachexilischen Prophetie* (SSN 10; Assen: Van Gorcum, 1967); J. J. Collins, *The Apocalyptic Vision of the Book of Daniel* (HSM 16; Missoula, MT: Scholars Press, 1977); idem, "Introduction: Toward the Morphology of a Genre," *Semeia* 14 (1979) 21-59; idem, *Daniel: A Commentary on the Book of Daniel* (Hermeneia; Minneapolis: Fortress, 1993); J. Goldingay, *Daniel* (WBT; Dallas: Word, 1989); N. Habel, "The Form and Significance of the Call Narratives," *ZAW* 77 (1965) 297–323; A. Lenglet, "La structure littéraire de Daniel 2-7," *Bib* 53 (1972) 169-90; J. Lindblom, *Prophecy in Ancient Israel* (Oxford: Blackwell, 1962); B. O. Long, "Reports of Visions among the Prophets," *JBL* 95 (1976) 353-65; E. C. Lucas, *Daniel* (ApOTC 20; Downers Grove, IL: InterVarsity Press, 2002); J. E. Miller, "Dreams and Prophetic Visions," *Bib* 71 (1990) 401-4; S. Niditch, *The Symbolic Vision in Biblical Tradition* (HSM 30; Chico, CA: Scholars Press, 1983); H. Van Dyke Parunak, "The Literary Architecture of Ezekiel's *MARʾÔT ʾĔLŌHÎM*," *JBL* 99 (1980) 61-74; T. Renz, *The Rhetorical Function of the Book of Ezekiel* (VTSup 76; Leiden: E. J. Brill, 2002); M. Stead, *The Intertextuality of Zechariah 1-8* (LHBOTS 506; London: T & T Clark, 2009); N. Tidwell, "*WĀʾÔMAR* (Zech 3:5) and the Genre of Zechariah's Fourth Vision," *JBL* 94 (1975) 343-55; L.-S. Tiemeyer, "Through a Glass Darkly: Zechariah's Unprocessed Visionary Experience," *VT* 58 (2008) 573-94; J. Watts, *Vision and Prophecy in Amos* (rev. ed.; Macon, GA: Mercer University Press, 1997); W. Zimmerli, "Visionary Experience in Jeremiah," in *Israel's Prophetic Tradition: Essays in Honour of Peter R. Ackroyd*, ed. R. J. Coggins, A. Phillips and M. A. Knibb. (Cambridge: Cambridge University Press, 1982) 95-118.

M. R. Stead

W, X, Y

WARFARE AND DIVINE WARFARE

Divine warfare is a recurrent theme in the prophetic literature of ancient Israel: God combats malevolent forces for and within the nation. Biblical use of the leitmotif reflects Israel's early theological traditions, engagement of other cultures, and victories and defeats.

1. Definition
2. Etiology
3. Ancient Near Eastern Context
4. Representative Texts in the Prophets
5. Theology and Ethics
6. New Testament Appropriation

1. Definition.

A useful starting point in the study of divine warfare is general warfare, which, for purposes of this article, is defined as violent conflict between nations over sovereignty and justice. General warfare is violent and involves the infliction of harm on an adversary, even harm resulting in death. It is also international or intertribal; it is not violence by or against individuals, families or small groups per se unless the social group represents the nation or tribe. In addition, warfare is political. States make war to defend or to gain territory, to secure access to resources, to enforce compliance with treaties, to maintain honor, or to ensure the conduct of internal affairs without external interferences. Wars demonstrate boundaries of control, and they are waged to protect the rights and properties of state and citizenry and to remedy injustices, inhumane conditions and crimes against humanity. The nonpsychological motivations in general warfare are economic and ideological: territorial sovereignty and civil justice.

Divine warfare, which also is violent, international and political, is waged under the aegis of a deity. The deity is envisioned to be a warrior who leads the army, engages the enemy, and protects the favored. Divine warfare is also cosmic: it involves natural and supernatural forces, terrestrial and celestial realms, and primordial, historical and *apocalyptic elements. At stake are not merely the reign of the monarch and safety of the nation, but the honor of the deity and the order of universe. Divine warfare may be defined as violent conflict between a deity and a preternatural, malevolent adversary, or between nation-states fighting under the aegis of patron deities, that demonstrates sovereignty and effects justice. In divine warfare a deity battles an evil antagonist, and in OT prophetic literature it is the God of Israel who assumes the role of warrior and engages adversaries of Israel and the divine order.

2. Etiology.

The idea of divine warfare is related to the outcomes and consequences of battle, which are unpredictable and often unintended. This theory is extrapolated from C. von Clausewitz's seminal work, *On War*, though the volume is not about divine warfare per se. Von Clausewitz defines war as "the continuation of policy by other means" (von Clausewitz, 87). The means to which he refers are violent actions that end lives, damage bodies, displace communities, destroy properties, harm environments and alter identities (Ames 2011). The violence is an extension of political process—"the continuation of policy" (German, *Politik*)—albeit an extreme extension. Warfare is the realpolitik of conflict resolution located on a continuum that devolves from resolution by consensus, to judgment by a third party, to bargaining by the principals, and, if they are intractable, to armed conflict resolved by the army that can inflict and sustain the greatest damage (Morgan; Fox). Might, according to the adage, determines right, though power does not constitute virtue and does not guarantee the outcome of battle. Military strength and strategy are critical factors, but they are not decisive. Von Clausewitz recognized that military campaigns are complex endeavors, and that nontrivial outcomes cannot be predicted with certainty. Victory is contingent upon elements beyond human control (e.g., weather) and is not always determined by the deployment of superior forces and the implementation of sound tactics. The outcomes and even the objectives of war depend on factors that politicians, commanders and citizens can never fully anticipate or manage. This observation suggests an explanation for the prevalence of the divine warfare throughout the ancient Near Eastern world: because the outcome of armed conflict depends on factors beyond human control, victory, when achieved, is attributed to the intervention of a higher power. The deity grants victory, and defeat is attributed to abandonment by the divine patron, typically due to transgression within the community. Thus, the outcome of battle is made contingent upon morality, not strategy.

The sages of ancient Israel recognized unpredictable elements in warfare and acknowledged the limits of human control, and they attributed Israel's victories to Yahweh, *God of Israel. The idea is expressed in the biblical proverb "The horse is made ready for the day of battle, but the victory belongs to the LORD" (Prov 21:31 NRSV). Resources and preparations are necessary but are not sufficient for the day, for God must intervene, and the people must follow God. The OT prophets attributed military achievements to Yahweh (Jer 51:14; Zeph 3:17), reaffirming one of Israel's oldest theological traditions: God is a warrior who fights for the nation (Ex 15:3; Deut 20:4; Judg 15:18).

3. Ancient Near Eastern Context.
Literary traditions and historic conflicts in the ancient Near Eastern world provide a framework for understanding divine warfare in OT prophetic literature.

3.1. Literary Traditions. Ancient Near Eastern literary analogs to the biblical leitmotif are "significant" (Kang, 7). For instance, Assyrian and Israelite prophetic texts abound with oracles assuring that the divine warrior will safeguard the nation and grant victory in a time of war, and those facing the enemy are commanded not to fear (Nissinen, 97-132): "Fear not, Esarhaddon! I will place you between my arm and forearm. In the midst of distress, I will va[nqu]ish the enemies of my king" (SAA 9 2.5 iii 29-32); "Do not fear, for I am with you, do not be afraid, for I am your God; I will strengthen you, I will help you, I will uphold you with my victorious right hand" (Is 41:10 NRSV).

The Sumerian Stela of the Vultures depicts Ningirsu wielding mace and net to conquer an invading army in a dispute over tillable lands. One side of the stela portrays the actions of Ningirsu, the patron deity of the city of Lagash, and the other the actions of Eanatum, the ruler of the city. The design captures the confluence of divine and human realms: the battle is fought by the ruler on earth with outcome determined by the deity in heaven (Lang, 47-48; Hamblin, 55-59).

The epilogue of the Laws of Hammurabi (xlix 18-li 91) is replete with gods whom Hammurabi invokes to destroy anyone who disregards his instructions or defaces his image, and the list includes warrior deities such as Zababa, Nergal and Ishtar. Hammurabi asks that Ishtar "smash his [adversary's] weapon on the field of war and battle, plunge him into confusion and rebellion, strike down his warriors, drench the earth with their blood, make a heap of the corpses of his soldiers upon the plain, and may she [Ishtar] show his soldiers no mercy; as for him, may she deliver him into the hand of his enemies, and may she lead him bound captive to the land of his enemy" (COS 2.131: 353).

The Exaltation of Inanna (iv 29-31) celebrates the military prowess of the goddess, who charges into battle in the guise of a storm—a common motif in divine warfare. The link between storm and battle in the ancient Near Eastern divine warfare motif is prominent in the mythology of the storm-god Baal, who rides the clouds into battle: "Ba'lu (himself) opens up the rift in the clouds, Ba'lu emits his holy voice, Ba'lu makes the thunder roll over and over again. His [holy] voice [causes] the earth [to tremble], [at his thunder] the mountains shake with fear.... The high places of the earth totter. Ba'lu's enemies grasp hold of (the trees of) the forest, Haddu's adversaries (grasp hold of) the flanks of the mountain(s)" (vii 25-37 [COS 1.86: 262-63]).

In the Baal Cycle the storm-god (Baal) defeats the sea-god (Yam) (iv 18-27). The metaphor of the tumultuous sea is a common trope. The armies rise and threaten like raging waters, which the divine warrior either stirs or stills. In ancient Near Eastern creation mythology the divine warrior battles sea monsters and constrains chaotic waters to create the primordial world. In the Creation Epic (iv 1-146) it is Marduk, the champion of Babylon, who defeats and dismembers the sea monster Tiamat to create the new world. The parallel between the creation of the universe and the defeat of the mythological sea monster (also called "Leviathan" and "Rahab") is evident in the Teaching of Merikare: "He made sky and earth for their sake, He subdued the water monster, He made breath for their noses to live" (*COS* 1.35:65, line 131).

Ancient Near Eastern metaphors of storm and sea are woven into biblical references to divine warfare. The God of Israel emerges from the clouds and attacks tumultuous armies, for Israel's divine warrior rules the skies and the seas. Nations that attack Israel are portrayed as raging storms and roaring waters that Yahweh must still (Is 17:12-14). Yahweh rides the clouds into battle (Is 19:1; 28:2; 29:6) and strikes enemies with hail and lightning: "The LORD will cause his majestic voice to be heard and the descending blow of his arm to be seen, in furious anger and a flame of devouring fire, with a cloudburst and tempest and hailstones" (Is 30:30 NRSV [cf. Is 29:6]). Anticipating a coming day of battle, Isaiah draws upon the mythological metaphors of the ancient Near East and declares, "On that day the LORD with his cruel and great and strong sword will punish Leviathan the fleeing serpent, Leviathan the twisting serpent, and he will kill the dragon that is in the sea" (Is 27:1 NRSV [cf. Is 30:7; 51:9-10]).

From the perspective of Israel's prophets, the power that created heaven and earth is the power that governs military conflicts, delivering the people of Israel from other nations and from unrighteous propensities within Israel, for Yahweh created the universe and rules the world with justice.

3.2. Historic Conflicts. Biblical perspectives on divine warfare reflect the embattled histories of Israel and Judah and the implications of victories and defeats.

The exodus from Egypt and the conquest of Canaan demonstrated that Yahweh is a warrior who fights to free the people of Israel and to secure a bountiful land for them. The Song of Moses, which celebrates the freedom of the formerly enslaved Hebrews, declares, "The LORD is a warrior" (Ex 15:3). The historical prologue of Deuteronomy reminded subsequent generations that the Lord formed the nation "by trials, by signs and wonders, by war, by a mighty hand and an outstretched arm, and by terrifying displays of power" (Deut 4:34 NRSV). The book of Joshua applies the "divine warrior" motif to Israel's occupation of Canaan, reporting that no one could turn back the invasion because God fought on the side of the Israelite army (Josh 23:9-10). Because Yahweh fought for the nation, Joshua was able to capture the "whole" land and establish *peace (Josh 11:23). The motif of the divine warrior in the biblical prophets builds upon the *exodus and conquest tradition that Yahweh fights for the nation. In Isaiah, for instance, the nation of Israel is told that it need not fear the Assyrians any more than it feared the Egyptians in the days of Moses, for Yahweh will destroy the empire (Is 10:24-26).

The fall of Samaria to the Assyrians in 721 BC (2 Kings 18:9-12), the fall of Jerusalem to the Babylonians in 586 BC (2 Kings 25:1-20), and the Persian defeat of the Babylonian Empire in 538 BC demonstrated that Yahweh would fight against the unrighteous, even if the unrighteous happened to be the people of Israel and Judah. These conquests also showed that armed forces unleashed by Yahweh must act with restraint, for all nations are subject to judgment for inhumanity borne of hubris. In the book of Isaiah, Yahweh refers to Assyria as "the rod of my anger" and declares, "The club in their hands is my fury" (Is 10:5 NRSV). Yahweh sent the Assyrians against Israel and Judah "to take spoil and seize plunder and to tread down" (Is 10:6b NRSV), but the political objectives of the Assyrians went beyond Yahweh's goal, for the Assyrians intended "to destroy" Israel and Judah (Is 10:7). For this reason, Yahweh intended to "punish the arrogant boasting of the king of Assyria" (Is 10:12b NRSV). The Babylonians, though they served as instruments of divine wrath, would also experience divine wrath due to their excesses: because they plundered, they would be plundered (Hab 2:8). Victories experienced early in the history of Israel and defeats experienced later provide a framework for understanding the dynamics of divine warfare.

4. Representative Texts in the Prophets.

The defining components of divine warfare can be observed in the book of Zephaniah, which inveighs against social corruptions and religious perversions that were condemned by Josiah's reform movement, around 621 BC (Zeph 1:1). The prophet announces a day of judgment that calls for *repentance (Zeph 1:2—3:7) and a day of restoration that will bring celebration (Zeph 3:8-20). Yahweh is portrayed as a warrior who fights against the inhabitants of Jerusalem but who will also fight for the city, restore its exiled inhabitants, and live among them (Zeph 1:4; 3:17-20). First, the prophet envisions violence. Warfare on "the day of the LORD's wrath" (Zeph 1:18; 2:2-3) entails slaughter (with "sacrifice" used metaphorically in the text), pain and destruction (Zeph 1:7-8, 14-16); houses are razed; blood is spilt (Zeph 1:13, 17); and the complacent, who believed that Yahweh would not inflict harm (Zeph 1:12), are shown to be wrong. Second, nations, not individuals, are attacked. These include Judah, the Philistine city-states, Moab, Ammon, Ethiopia and Assyria (Zeph 1:4; 2:4-8, 12-13). Divine warfare, like general warfare, is portrayed as a matter of state, even though individuals endure the consequences. Third, issues of national sovereignty and civil justice are addressed. Warfare is waged because Zephaniah's Judeans had turned from Yahweh to follow foreign gods, including the Canaanite god Baal, the Ammonite god Milcom, and the Philistine god Dagon (Zeph 1:4-6, 9), while government and religious leaders have neglected to observe or enforce the law (Zeph 3:1-4). These acts of disloyalty challenge the sovereignty of Yahweh, who is also angered over instances of "violence and fraud" (Zeph 1:9), and these motivate the prosecution of war. Fourth, war is waged by God. In Zephaniah, Yahweh first discloses the coming onslaught of violence with seven first-person declarations, beginning with the statement "I will utterly sweep away everything from the face of the earth" (Zeph 1:2). The judgement is called the *"day of the LORD" (e.g., Zeph 1:7, 14), and Yahweh is designated a warrior (Zeph 3:17). Fifth, though only Judah and a handful of neighboring countries are named, the conflagration in divine warfare is

extensive and cosmic: "In the fire of his passion the whole earth shall be consumed" (Zeph 1:18b NRSV). The exaggerated language, of course, is poetic and may be hyperbole, but the exaggeration reflects the cosmic dimensions of divine warfare. According to Zephaniah, all earthly inhabitants perish, all earthly gods shrivel, and all nations praise *Zion.

In Isaiah, divine warfare is characterized as royal prerogative, for Yahweh reigns. Yahweh's role as divine warrior is related to his status as righteous sovereign, which is a double-edged sword because Yahweh corrects as well as protects the people of God. Isaiah 6:1-13 portrays Yahweh as a sovereign but offended monarch reigning from a heavenly throne, with royal robe flowing throughout the temple and filling the earth. The monarch sends Isaiah to issue a warning that the people of Israel would not heed "until [their] cities lie waste without inhabitant" (Is 6:11b). Yahweh intends to make war against unrighteous adversaries within and beyond the boundaries of Israel, for divine sovereignty encompasses all peoples. Isaiah 63:1-6 redeploys the symbolism of the royal robe in portraying Yahweh as warrior returning victoriously from Edom (Is 63:2-3). The prophet asks, "Why are your robes red, and your garments like theirs who tread the wine press?" Yahweh replies, ""I have trodden the wine press alone, and from the peoples no one was with me; I trod them in my anger and trampled them in my wrath; their juice spattered on my garments, and stained all my robes" (Is 63:2-3 NRSV).

Yahweh opposes those who oppress Israel—a perspective that informs Isaiah's oracle against Babylon (Is 13:1—14:27). According to the oracle, Yahweh will personally summon an army of warriors (Is 13:2-5), the Medes, who will engage in violent slaughter and overthrow Babylon (Is 13:6-22): "Whoever is found will be thrust through, and whoever is caught will fall by the sword. Their infants will be dashed to pieces before their eyes; their houses will be plundered, and their wives ravished" (Is 13:15-16 NRSV). Thus, the offended sovereign will use organized violence to resolve a conflict that is both international and cosmic, a dispute both between Israel and Babylon and between the God of heaven and the nations of earth: the heavens will dim, and the earth will shake (Is 13:10-13). The oracle envisions exiled Israelites restored to their own land and exalted (Is 14:1-

2) and the fall of Babylon's king as a fall from heaven's heights to Sheol's depths (Is 14:12-20).

In Isaiah 45 the elements of divine warfare appear in Yahweh's speech to Cyrus, the Persian ruler who defeated Babylon. Yahweh directs the army of the ruler against other nations (Is 45:1) and prepares the way (Is 45:2). The ensuing victory demonstrates that Yahweh alone is god (Is 45:3-6), and deliverance rains down from the clouds and springs up from the deep, for the power of Yahweh created the world and brings *salvation (Is 45:8-12, 18-19).

Micah portrays Yahweh emerging from his holy *temple to trample the unrighteous in Israel and Judah (Mic 1:2-7, 10-16; cf. Mic 5:10-15), but God eventually will redeem (Mic 7:18-20). Hosea also envisions Yahweh waging divine war. Yahweh says, "I will come against the wayward people to punish them; and nations shall be gathered against them when they are punished for their double iniquity" (Hos 10:10 NRSV), and the sword falls not only on the men of Samaria, but also on women and children, born and unborn (Hos 13:16). Amos declares that Yahweh will defeat Israel and Judah (Amos 2:4-11), waging war against them as well as other nations guilty of war crimes (Amos 1:3—2:3). Yahweh, however, promises life to those who "seek good and not evil" (Amos 5:14; cf. Amos 9:8).

The theme of divine warfare is prominent in Habakkuk's *prayer (Hab 3), which expresses confidence that God will safeguard the lives of the righteous who exercise faith (Hab 2:4c). The prophet, having learned that God is rallying the warriors of Babylon to punish the unrighteous in Judah (Hab 1:2-11), has also received assurances of God's protection (Hab 2:1-20). One question that troubles Habakkuk is this: How can God use the unrighteous to punish the righteous? (Hab 1:13). Habakkuk's faith is expressed in a concluding prayer, a liturgical *lament, that asks God for mercy in the midst of *wrath (Hab 3:2b). The lament characterizes divine warfare as the onslaught of a storm: lightning flashes and brings death (Hab 3:3b-5, 9a, 11); thunder, winds and water destroy lands and dwellings (Hab 3:6-8, 10); and the wind-borne rider "tramples the sea" (Hab 3:14-15). The warrior God, however, enables the faithful to flee like deer (Hab 3:19).

The prophet Jeremiah also envisions Yahweh as a warrior. For instance, the message that Jeremiah sends to Zedekiah is a speech in which the God of Israel says, "I myself will fight against you" (Jer 21:5a NRSV), and elsewhere Jeremiah portrays Yahweh as the ultimate sovereign who is able to plan and to carry out wars at will (Jer 51:12). Yahweh is the "LORD of hosts," who is able to direct any army (Jer 51:14) and is able to do so because "it is he who made the earth by his power" (Jer 51:15 NRSV). Yahweh said this concerning the army of the Medes: "You are my war club, my weapon of battle: with you I smash nations; with you I destroy kingdoms; with you I smash the horse and its rider; with you I smash the chariot and the charioteer; with you I smash man and woman; with you I smash the old man and the boy; with you I smash the young man and the girl; with you I smash shepherds and their flocks; with you I smash farmers and their teams; with you I smash governors and deputies" (Jer 51:20-23 NRSV).

From the perspective of Israel's prophets, the armies of the nations are weapons in Yahweh's arsenal, but Yahweh the divine warrior also rides into battle with the army. Ezekiel's mysterious lightning storm that threatens from the north, and the wheels within wheels that make a tumultuous sound like an advancing army (Ezek 1:4-28), have glorious Yahweh in their midst (Ezek 1:28; 10:1-22). The vision draws upon the ancient Near Eastern imagery of the war chariot and the divine warrior riding upon the clouds. Visions of war also appear in Daniel, which strongly emphasizes the sovereign and universal reign of God (Dan 4:17, 26; 6:26; 7:27).

According to the prophets, divine warfare was waged for and against the people of God, but it was the experience of war that ultimately challenged and changed popular understandings. Prior to the fall of Samaria and the destruction of Jerusalem, Israel and Judah believed that God protected (Jer 7:8-11). The prophets declared that God also punished—a message challenged by false prophets and rejected by oppressive leaders—but the destruction of Jerusalem confirmed what the prophets had foretold. The restoration of exiles to Judah, however, demonstrated that God did not abandon the people. The Israelites learned that the political objective of divine warfare was related to justice, not citizenship, and the prophets envisioned a future in which war itself, with its many injustices, would be defeated. War, like *death (Hos 13:14), was an enemy to be defeated: "He shall judge between the nations, and shall arbitrate for many peoples; they shall beat their swords into plowshares, and their spears into pruning hooks; nation shall not lift up sword against nation, neither shall they learn war any more" (Is 2:4 NRSV [cf. Mic 4:3]). Divine warfare could be waged against Israel's enemies or against Israel, but ultimately Yahweh the divine warrior would defeat war.

5. Theology and Ethics.

Israel's prophets believed that God is a warrior, and the "centrality of that conviction and its historical, cultic, literary and theological ramifications can hardly be overestimated" (Miller, 1). The characterization of God as a warrior affords hope for deliverance of the downtrodden and stands as a warning to oppressors, and it raises issues that are not merely academic, historical or literary, but are theological and ethical. Focal points are the sovereignty and justice of God and the perpetuation of violence in the pursuit of security, for those who choose to live by the sword are likely to die by the sword (Gen 9:6; Mt 26:52).

5.1. Sovereignty and Justice. Nations engage in warfare to maintain boundaries of sovereignty, and divine warfare expresses the all-encompassing sovereignty of the God of Israel, who directs and defeats antagonistic armies at will. In divine warfare the plans of God cannot be thwarted (Is 14:24-27). In the ancient Near Eastern world the prerogative of the sovereign to wage war to defend or to expand the empire was assumed, not disputed. It is likely that only the details of specific campaigns, their feasibility, logistics and tactics, would have been open to debate, not the pursuit or legitimacy of war itself. Divine warfare, as the designation implies, is an expression of divine will, embodied and expressed on earth by the king of the nation, and the will of the god or goddess would have preempted any substantive debate about the legitimacy of going to war. If the deity commanded war, whether through prophet, priest or monarch, the only choice before the citizenry was obedience or disobedience, though certain categories of people were exempt from fighting (see Deut 20:1-9; 24:5).

Holy war, as G. von Rad has argued, can be viewed as "a cultic phenomenon" (von Rad, 49), with the slaughter of enemy combatants and destruction of property, animals and indi-

viduals captured in battle regarded as offerings sacrificed to Yahweh. The God of Israel was characterized as a warrior who fought in the battle, and warriors were entitled to their share of the spoils (Elgavish). Yahweh led the campaign, and for this reason participation in holy war was construed to be an expression of allegiance and trust, and the Israelite warriors, who followed and were protected by Yahweh, were expected to fight opponents without fear, wholeheartedly embracing the Deuteronomic injunction "Do not lose heart, or be afraid, or panic, or be in dread of them; for it is the LORD your God who goes with you, to fight for you against your enemies, to give you victory" (Deut 20:3b-4 NRSV).

In ancient Israelite religion, however, divine war was not solely an expression of obedience and faith; it was an instrument of justice, "a *legal* judgment of Yahweh made for the purpose of resolving a dispute between Israel and neighboring states" (Good, 387). The judicial nature of divine warfare is evident in the proclamation that the prophet Joel issued to Israel, the nations and Yahweh, a call to arms that characterizes the defeat of nations that are hostile to Israel as an act of divine judgment: "Prepare war, stir up the warriors. Let all the soldiers draw near, let them come up. Beat your plowshares into swords, and your pruning hooks into spears; let the weakling say, 'I am a warrior.' Come quickly, all you nations all around, gather yourselves there. Bring down your warriors, O LORD. Let the nations rouse themselves, and come up to the valley of Jehoshaphat; for there I will sit to judge all the neighboring nations" (Joel 3:9b-12 NRSV).

Divine warfare was waged to effect justice, and the OT prophetic literature portrays the violence of divine warfare to be a measured response to unjust violent acts perpetrated against others and rooted in human arrogance and callousness. According to the prophets, the wars led or prompted by Yahweh purge or requite wickedness and redress grievances and injustices; they remedy wrongs and settle disputes (see Is 59:15-20; Jer 6:1-6; 21:11-12).

The justness of divine warfare, as portrayed in the OT prophets, is rooted in proportionality; that is, divine warfare, though violent, ostensibly inflicts retribution in proportion to the wrongdoing. Obadiah, predicting a time of violent judgment upon the nations that have sought to harm the people of Israel, explicates the principle of proportional justice that is at work in divine warfare. The prophet informs the errant nations, "As you have done, it shall be done to you; your deeds shall return on your own head" (Obad 15 NRSV). The book of Nahum, which celebrates the justness of the destruction of Nineveh and the demise of the Neo-Assyrian Empire (Crouch, 158-73), portrays Yahweh as a patient but powerful judge who is "slow to anger but great in power" and who "will by no means clear the guilty" (Nah 1:2b NRSV). Yahweh's *destruction of the city repays Assyria's aggression against other cities, and the rhetorical question that concludes the book summarizes the rationale: "There is no assuaging your hurt, your wound is mortal. All who hear the news about you clap their hands over you. For who has ever escaped your endless cruelty?" (Nah 3:19 NRSV). The city's suffering, like its cruelty to others, is correspondingly "endless." In divine warfare violence repays violence in equal measure, according to the spirit of the *lex talionis*, a proportional moral calculus that is rooted in Mosaic law codes (Ex 21:23-35; Lev 24:19; Deut 19:19-21) and is echoed in NT texts (Mt 26:52; Rev 13:10). The ancient Israelite ideal of proportional justice, though significantly refined in the prophets (cf. different standards of retribution in Ex 20:5 and Ezek 18:2), is never fully realized in actual combat situations, nor could it be. Although provisions for escaping violence are evident in some instances of divine warfare (see Jer 21:8-10), even just wars are filled with injustices. Warfare inflicts collateral damage that is immediate and lasting, and justice achieved through battle perpetrates its own evils. There are always innocent casualties, and violence begets violence (Mt 26:52).

5.2. Security and the Perpetuation of Violence. Historical accounts and prophetic speeches about divine wars that chasten the righteous and deliver from corruption and oppression have for generations captured the imaginations of readers who turn to the OT prophets for insight, guidance and hope, and the prophetic literature offers these in abundance. Ironically, wars are fought to end wars. *Peace is ostensibly the objective, and the prophets set forth a vision of peace, with "swords beaten into plows." The assurance of a better world that devout readers draw from prophetic visions of divine warfare is powerful, but the hope is bound to violent imagery; the saving acts of God are wed to the harsh realities of war, and the warp and woof of salvation and destruction together form a metanarrative: readers see that deliverance for the righteous often entails the destruction of the wicked. This cannot be excised from a biblical theology of redemption or from the historical realities of justice, for it is embedded in both. Violence, though overtly condemned in some texts, is tacitly endorsed in others, and, unfortunately, the theme of divine warfare has been used to sanction violent activities in modern contexts (Juergensmeyer).

Because Yahweh the divine warrior is righteous and uses violence to establish justice, some will reason, incorrectly, that it is legitimate for humans to engage in violent acts. The violence embedded in biblical texts "cannot be glossed over" (Collins, 19-20) and "should not stand unchallenged" (Fretheim, 22). Empirical studies suggest that exposure to texts that are laden with violent imagery contributes to violence, aggression and decreased sympathy for victims (Berkowitz; Bushman et al.; Fanti et al.).

Of special concern is the desensitization that perpetuates violence against *women, a problem exacerbated by armed conflict (Leatherman). The divine judgments that the prophets typically list are war, famine and pestilence, and they use metaphors of rape, abandonment and humiliation (Gordon and Washington). Hosea, for instance, portrays God as a betrayed husband who abandons an adulterous wife to danger (Hos 2:1-13), and readers are expected to sympathize with the husband—a metaphorical representation of God engaging in divine warfare (Hos 2:1-23). R. Weems notes, "The metaphor of battered wife is admittedly a very risky trope to use to help shed light on questions of God's response to human failures" (Weems, 106; *see* Feminist Interpretation; Exum). In addition, the violent winds of war that Yahweh sends against Israel for rebellion include the slaughter of infants and unborn (Hos 13:14-16).

The theological and ethical dilemmas met at the intersections of the sovereignty of God, the justice of war, and the perpetuation of violence in texts that depict divine warfare are not easily resolved. Awareness of issues and empathy toward victims of violence are essential in understanding the divine warfare leitmotif and in minimizing misappropriations that perpetuate violence.

6. New Testament Appropriation.

The NT appropriates the theme but redirects the violence and largely transforms the prophetic tradition of divine warfare, which the early church interpreted in light of the life, death and resurrection of Jesus, "the Lamb of God who takes away the sin of the world" (Jn 1:29 NRSV). In the NT transformation of the theme, the divine warrior achieves victory by dying rather than killing.

In the book of Revelation the Lamb of God is a warrior who conquers (Rev 17:14) and "in righteousness judges and makes war" (Rev 19:11 NRSV), a warrior who "will tread the wine press of the fury of the wrath of God the Almighty" (Rev 19:15 NRSV). However, the Lamb of God, who brings salvation (Rev 7:10), does not sacrifice the enemy in holy war but is himself the sacrifice. The sword wielded by Jesus in the role of divine warrior is a proclamation of words that are able to destroy maleficent forces and to create a new heaven and earth (Rev 19:15). The apocalyptic imagery of the book of Revelation, which draws from the book of Daniel, does envision real martyrdoms and judgment (though the referent of symbols and extent of metaphorical language remains a matter of debate among contemporary interpreters), but the saints of God are delivered by the sacrificial death of the Lamb and are called to endure persecution, not to attack their oppressors (Rev 12:11). John advises the reader, "If you are to be taken captive, into captivity you go; if you kill with the sword, with the sword you must be killed. Here is a call for the endurance and faith of the saints" (Rev 13:9-10 NRSV). Faith and endurance are rewarded, and the redemption of the saints prompts a new song of praise (Rev 5:9; 14:3), not unlike the victory song of Isaiah 42:10-13.

The Synoptic Gospels identify Jesus as Isaiah's Suffering Servant, who wages war by giving himself to deliver the people of God and to avenge wrongdoing (Is 53:1-12; cf. Mt 8:17). John the Baptist identified Jesus as the divine warrior of whom Isaiah spoke by proclaiming, "Prepare the way of the LORD, make his paths straight" (Is 40:3 NRSV; cf. Mt 3:3; Mk 1:3; Lk 3:4). The warrior and the restored people march to Zion in victory along a highway that is sacred and safe (Is 35:8-10), and Isaiah's war-

rior restores health and wholeness to the people and to creation itself (Is 35:8-10). John the Baptist contrasted the baptism with water that he offered to the baptism of fire—divine war—that would attend the coming of the Lord Jesus (Mt 3:11-12). Moreover, in the Gospel accounts Jesus commands the natural elements and subdues the raging winds and waves (Mt 8:23-27; Mk 4:35-41; Lk 8:22-25), evoking Isaiah's imagery of the divine warrior rebuking the nations, which "roar like the roaring of mighty waters" (Is 17:12; 43:2), and the imagery of the divine warrior delivering the Israelites from Egypt (Is 51:10), wielding the primordial power that created the world (Is 51:15-16). The actions of Jesus recorded in the Gospels echo the motif of the divine warrior who directs and defeats the monstrous forces of the sea (Is 27:1). Similarly, Jesus is the divine warrior whose chariot traverses the clouds (Mt 24:30; Mk 13:26; Lk 21:27; cf. Is 19:1; Dan 7:13). Jesus does provoke conflict (Mt 10:34-36; Lk 12:51-53), but he accepts the fate of death and cautions against the perpetuation of violence (Mt 26:52; Jn 18:11).

The early church reconceptualized participation in divine warfare, though participation in holy war in ancient Israel is honored for its expression of faith (Heb 11:34). The war waged by the church is not a physical struggle but rather a spiritual one, involving cosmic powers (2 Cor 10:3; Eph 6:12; 1 Pet 3:22). Christians are solders (Phil 2:25; Philem 2; 1 Pet 4:1) who endure hardship for the cause (2 Tim 2:3), and their fight is "the good fight of faith" (1 Tim 1:18; 6:12; 2 Tim 4:7). The divine warrior of Isaiah, who is armed for battle to effect justice and to redeem Zion (Is 59:15-20), and those who follow Jesus are also instructed to "put on the whole armor of God" (Eph 6:11 NRSV): truth, righteousness, readiness, faith and salvation (Eph 6:12-17) (see Neufeld).

See also DAY OF THE LORD; DESTRUCTION; EXILE; EXODUS IMAGERY; GOD; PEACE, REST; SALVATION, DELIVERANCE; WRATH.

BIBLIOGRAPHY. **F. R. Ames,** "The Meaning of War: Definitions for the Study of War in Ancient Israelite Literature," in *Writing and Reading War: Rhetoric, Gender, and Ethics in Biblical and Modern Contexts*, ed. B. E. Kelle and F. R. Ames (SBLSymS 42; Atlanta: Society of Biblical Literature, 2008) 19-31; idem, "The Cascading Effects of Exile," in *Interpreting Exile: Displacement and Deportation in Biblical and Mod-*

ern Contexts, ed. B. E. Kelle, F. R. Ames and J. L. Wright (SBLAIL 10; Atlanta: Society of Biblical Literature, 2011) 173-87; **L. Berkowitz,** *Aggression: Its Causes, Consequences, and Control* (New York: McGraw-Hill, 1993); **B. J. Bushman et al.,** "When God Sanctions Killing: Effect of Scriptural Violence on Aggression," *Psychological Science* 18 (2007): 204-7; **C. Carvalho,** "The Beauty of the Bloody God: The Divine Warrior in Prophetic Literature," in *Aesthetics of Violence in the Prophets,* ed. C. Franke and J. M. O'Brien (LHBOTS 517; London: T & T Clark, 2010) 131-52; **J. J. Collins,** "The Zeal of Phinehas: The Bible and the Legitimation of Violence," *JBL* 122 (2003) 3-21; **C. L. Crouch,** *War and Ethics in the Ancient Near East: Military Violence in Light of Cosmology and History* (BZAW 407; Berlin: de Gruyter, 2009); **D. Elgavish,** "The Division of the Spoils of War in the Bible and in the Ancient Near East," *ZABR* 8 (2002) 242-73; **J. C. Exum,** "Prophetic Pornography," in *Plotted, Shot, and Painted: Cultural Representations of Biblical Women* (JSOTSup 215; Sheffield: Sheffield Academic, 1996) 101-28; **K. A. Fanti et al.,** "Desensitization to Media Violence over a Short Period of Time," *Aggressive Behavior* 35 (2009) 179-87; **W. T. R. Fox,** "World Politics as Conflict Resolution," in *International Conflict and Conflict Management: Readings in World Politics,* ed. R. O. Matthews, A. G. Rubinoff and J. G. Stein (Scarborough, ON: Prentice-Hall, 1984) 7-14; **T. E. Fretheim,** "God and Violence in the Old Testament," *WW* 24 (2004) 18-28; **R. M. Good,** "The Just War in Ancient Israel," *JBL* 104 (1985) 385-400; **P. Gordon and H. C. Washington,** "Rape as a Military Metaphor in the Hebrew Bible," in *A Feminist Companion to the Latter Prophets,* ed. A. Brenner (FCB 8; Sheffield: Sheffield Academic, 1995) 308-25; **W. J. Hamblin,** *Warfare in the Ancient Near East to 1600 BC: Holy Warriors at the Dawn of History* (New York: Routledge, 2006); **T. Hiebert,** "Warrior, Divine," *ABD* 6:876-80; **M. Juergensmeyer,** *Terror in the Mind of God: The Global Rise of Religious Violence* (3rd ed.; Comparative Studies in Religion and Society 13; Berkeley: University of California Press, 2001); **S.-M. Kang,** *Divine War in the Old Testament and in the Ancient Near East* (BZAW 177; Berlin: de Gruyter, 1989); **B. E. Kelle,** "An Interdisciplinary Approach to the Exile," in *Interpreting Exile: Displacement and Deportation in Biblical and Modern Contexts,* ed. B. E. Kelle, F. R. Ames and J. L. Wright (SBLAIL 10; At-

lanta: Society of Biblical Literature, 2011) 1-38; idem, *Ancient Israel at War, 853-586 BC* (Essential Histories 67; Oxford: Osprey, 2007); idem, "Warfare Imagery," *DOTWPW* 829-35; **P. Kern,** *Ancient Siege Warfare* (Bloomington: Indiana University Press, 1999); **B. Lang,** *The Hebrew God: Portrait of an Ancient Deity* (New Haven: Yale University Press, 2002); **J. L. Leatherman,** *Sexual Violence and Armed Conflict* (War and Conflict in the Modern World; Malden, MA: Polity, 2011); **T. Longman III and D. G. Reid,** *God Is a Warrior* (SOTBT; Grand Rapids: Zondervan, 1995); **P. D. Miller Jr.,** *The Divine Warrior in Early Israel* (HSM 5; Cambridge, MA: Harvard University Press, 1973); **T. C. Morgan,** "The Concept of War: Its Impact on Research and Policy," *Peace and Change* 15 (1990) 413-41; **T. R. Neufeld,** *"Put on the Armour of God": The Divine Warrior from Isaiah to Ephesians* (JSOTSup 140; Sheffield: Sheffield Academic, 1997); **S. Niditch,** *War in the Hebrew Bible: A Study in the Ethics of Violence* (New York: Oxford University Press, 1993); **M. Nissinen, with C. L. Seow, and R. K. Ritner,** *Prophets and Prophecy in the Ancient Near East,* ed. P. Machinist (SBLWAW 12; Atlanta: Society of Biblical Literature, 2003); **D. G. Reid and T. Longman III,** "When God Declares War," *Christianity Today* (October 28, 1996) 14-21; **M. S. Smith,** *The Early History of God: Yahweh and the Other Deities in Ancient Israel* (San Francisco: Harper & Row, 1990); **R. J. Weems,** *Battered Love: Marriage, Sex, and Violence in the Hebrew Prophets* (OBT; Minneapolis: Fortress, 1995); **C. von Clausewitz,** *On War,* ed. and trans. M. Howard and P. Paret (Princeton, NJ: Princeton University Press, 1976); **G. von Rad,** *Holy War in Ancient Israel,* trans. and ed. M. J. Dawn (Grand Rapids: Eerdmans, 1991).   F. R. Ames

WEALTH AND POVERTY

Socioeconomic motifs cast long shadows over all three sections of the OT. Students of the Pentateuch (Torah) investigate them via sociohistorical (Pleins), socioliterary (Moore 2011) and comparative historical methods (Chelst), while students of the Writings (Ketubim) attend to mythopoeic (Girard), anthropological (Meyers), sociological (Whybray), sociohistorical (Washington) and rhetorical concerns (Sandoval). Similar variety appears in recent studies of Jewish rabbinic (Neusner; Ohrenstein and Gordon), puritan (Murphy) and apocalyptic literature (Gordon). The analysis here focuses on some of the ways in which the poverty-wealth polarity helps to structure and inform the message of the Prophets (Nebiim).

1. Canaanite Critique
2. Assyrian Critique
3. Babylonian Critique
4. Persian Critique

1. Canaanite Critique.

The Hebrew term *kĕnaʿănî* ("Canaanite") etymologically derives from the sphere of economics (translated "trader" in Zech 14:21 RSV, NRSV, ESV, NJPS; "merchant" in Prov 31:24 NIV), and this at least partially explains why the earliest Hebrew prophets so intentionally criticize the Canaanite economies with which they habitually (and satirically) interact (Jemielity, 148-95). One of their most self-contained critiques occurs in the narrative about Nathan's "ewe lamb" parable, a *māšāl* designed to contrast the behavior of a nominally poor man alongside that of an avariciously wealthy man (2 Sam 12:1-4) (Moore 2003, 111-12). Another is Hannah's Song (1 Sam 2:1-10), a lyrical poem praising Yahweh for his ability to control "poverty" (*môrîš*, lit., "[dis]inheritance") as well as "wealth" (*maʿăšîr*) (1 Sam 2:7). Manipulating some of the motifs later picked up in Second Temple texts (*Targum Jonathan, Pseudo-Philo, Gospel of Luke*), this song affirms that Yahweh can both "protect the faithful" and "deal harshly with the self-sufficient" (Cook, 1). Expressed mathematically, it highlights the equation pulsating at the core of the Yahwistic imperative: "creation = acquisition + protection" (Moore 2011, 132, 207, 224).

1.1. Moses. Prophetically shaded portions of the Pentateuch portray Moses as a Hebrew prophet determined to warn his fellow refugees about the seductive temptations that they will soon have to face in the "promised land" of Canaan, especially in the towns already built, barns already stocked, vineyards already planted, and cisterns already dug (Deut 6:10-11) (Weinfeld, 44-57). Tempted by such prefabricated abundance, some will forget Yahweh, the deliverer who rescues them from centuries of slavery, not to mention the provider who sustains them for decades in the wilderness (Deut 8:1-10) (Hardmeier; Moore 2009, 190-94). Some will even begin to imagine that "my power and the might of my own hand have brought me this wealth" (Deut 8:17), when in fact only "Yahweh your God gives you the power to create wealth" (Deut 8:18) (Stansell). The fact that such motifs play so important a role in the Mosaic speeches at the beginning of the Deuteronomistic trajectory of the Nebiim is no accident. These socioeconomic motifs find deep roots in the great literature of Mesopotamia, eventually branching out into the Second Temple literature of the Alexandrians (Philo, *Spec.* 4.176-187), Hasmoneans, Essenes and Nazarenes (Moore 2011, 168-222).

1.2. Elijah. From the mythopoeic epics discovered at Ras Shamra (Ugarit), it is clear that many second-millennium Canaanites worship a deity named *baʿal* ("husband, master, provider"), venerating him as the primary force responsible for providing socioeconomic security to his devotees (*CAT* 1.1-1.4; Handy, 169-79). Against this claim the prophet Elijah lodges several vigorous objections on behalf of his deity, Yahweh, thereby initiating a conflict that eventually leads to a dramatic showdown on Mount Carmel (1 Kings 18:20-46) (Moore 2003, 97-102). Where the Canaanite myths "illustrate the importance attributed to Baal's precipitation" (Smith and Pitard, 15 [see *CAT* 1.16 iii 4-11; 1.19 i 42-46]), Elijah proclaims the Hebrew deity, Yahweh, to be the only true source of fructifying rain. Theologically, this contest covertly alludes to Baal's death and defeat by his sibling brother Mot (Canaanite god of death), thereby contrasting the traditional Canaanite outcome with Yahweh's victory (Hauser and Gregory, 79-82), but socioeconomically it preserves the actions of a Hebrew prophet determined to redefine "success" and "security" within monolatrous, Yahwistic parameters (Beck, 122; Moore 2003, 139-53).

Among the fascinating stories gathered up into the Elijah cycle (1 Kings 17—2 Kings 1) (Coote), the Naboth narrative poignantly illustrates the socioeconomic implications of this conflict by focusing serious attention on the Israelite king Ahab's desire to impose a Baalist definition of "value" (*mĕḥîr*) on his Hebrew neighbors (1 Kings 21:2). To Ahab, the drone-consort of the Baalist princess Jezebel (Walsh, 321), "value" is a variable commodity defined by the fluid ups and downs of the Canaanite marketplace. To Naboth, however, the "value" of "ancestral land" (*naḥălâ*) cannot be so cavalierly negotiated (Peterson; Veerkamp, 112).

Standing up to his "tradesman" king, Naboth stubbornly rejects the materialistic premise that ancestral land is no more valuable than any other kind of land (1 Kings 21:3), and Ahab responds to this rejection of his worldview by subjecting Naboth to the humiliation of a mock trial and public execution (Rand; Moore 2003, 37-44). Central to the Elijah cycle, the Naboth episode eventually concludes with the death of the Baalist king Ahab, followed by the public execution of his princess bride (2 Kings 9:30-37) (Huffmon, 280-82; Moore 2003, 322-31).

1.3. Elisha. Early in the Elisha cycle (2 Kings 2—13) a widowed young mother falls into the ubiquitous, sticky web of socioeconomic debt slavery (2 Kings 4:1-7) (Moore 2011, 228-30), thereby occasioning an opportunity for the prophet Elisha to extend Yahweh's grace. Defenseless and desperate, she cowers before the prospect of having her children sold into slavery by a scoundrel called "the creditor" (*hannōšeh* [2 Kings 4:1]) (Chirichigno, 220; Moore 2003, 139-43), and Elisha responds to this Torah violator by securing for her a miraculous source of income, thereby removing both debt and creditor in one fell swoop (cf. Ex 22:22) (Brodie, 457-62).

Later in the Elisha cycle Elisha's servant Gehazi gets caught in another sticky web: socioeconomic corruption (2 Kings 5:1-27). The textual framework in which this occurs follows the pattern of a typical literary chiasm (Moore 2003, 165):

Naaman's reaction to the Israelite slave
girl's suggestion
The Aramean king's reaction to
Naaman's request
The Israelite king's reaction to the
Aramean king's letter
Naaman's obedience to the
prophetic word
Elisha's reaction to Naaman's gift
Gehazi's reaction to Elisha's reaction
Elisha's reaction to Gehazi's corrupt
behavior

Poised at the center of this chiasm stands Naaman's obedience to the prophetic word, but enveloping the center, Elisha's rejection of Naaman's economic gratitude stands in sharp opposition to Gehazi's attempt to take advantage of it. Thus, although this episode never overtly states the origin of Naaman's leprosy,

Gehazi contracts leprosy for the same reason Miriam does in the wilderness: willful disobedience (Num 12:10) (Moore 1994, 61-72). The problem highlighted in this chiastic text is not just greed. Gehazi's problem looks much like that of Achan, another Hebrew who unsuccessfully tries to test Yahweh's patience (Josh 7:1). Compared to Achan and the Judahite man of God (1 Kings 13:26), in fact, Gehazi's punishment looks rather tame. Occasionally it is appropriate for prophets to accept "gifts" (e.g., Elisha accepts a guest room from the Shunammite [2 Kings 4:10]). Yet prophetic leaders must be careful when it comes to money. Indeed, they must guard their hearts against a plethora of health-and-wealth traps, all having the potential to drag them away from their mission. Sometimes they must say no to innocent-looking invitations, whether from kings (Jeroboam [1 Kings 13:7]), potential employers (Balak [Num 22:18]) (Moore 1990, 97-109) or even colleagues (Ephraimite prophet [1 Kings 13:34]) (Moore 2003, 237-42). Although sometimes bribery is hard to define (Gordon and Miyake, 162), it must be avoided at all costs, not only because it violates Torah (Deut 10:17; 16:19; 27:25), but also because it is but a short step from accepting unsolicited "gifts" to preaching only what well-meaning donors want to hear (Mic 3:5) (Moore 2003, 164-71). Thus, by contrasting Gehazi's greed with Naaman's faith, this episode spotlights a persistent socioeconomic problem afflicting the ancient Hebrew (and indeed, every other) economy (Moore 2011, 225-28).

Another story impacted by the poverty-wealth polarity is the laconic episode of the four lepers (2 Kings 6:24—7:20), a story that, like the one preceding it, communicates its message through a literary chiasm (Moore 2003, 149):

Lepers suffer at city gate
"What have we got to lose?" questions
Testing and discovering the truth
"This is a day of good news!"
Testing and discovering the truth
"What have we got to lose?" questions
Military captain trampled at city gate

Like their cannibalizing sisters (2 Kings 6:28-29), these lepers have come to a place in their lives where they feel they have absolutely nothing left to lose. Forced to the very bottom of the food chain, they suffer as much contempt from "friends" as they do from "enemies." If they go into the besieged city, they most likely will die because no one has any food to give them. If they remain at the city gate, they probably will die because the Syrian siege prohibits anyone from exiting or entering. Thus, their only option is to go out to the Syrian troops and throw themselves on their mercy. From a chiastic perspective, their suffering parallels that endured by the cynical military captain (2 Kings 7:2), except that they eventually turn to hope, whereas he capitulates to despair. Where they ascertain a plan for survival, the captain resigns himself to a "cruel fate."

Further, the utilitarian questions that they ask find a parallel in the utilitarian questions of the Israelite king. Where the lepers learn to ask appropriate questions, however, the king does not. In fact, this king refuses to trust anyone: not his officers or messengers and certainly not a bunch of outcast lepers raving on about "good news" (2 Kings 7:12-13). Paralleling the utilitarian questions of the king with the utilitarian questions of the lepers, this text emphasizes not only that it is important to ask questions, but also that it is important to ask appropriate questions.

The turning point comes not when the lepers discover the treasure abandoned by the Syrians, and not even when the Syrians retreat and the siege abruptly ends. The turning point comes when these suffering Hebrews begin to realize how inappropriate it is to hoard instead of share. Even though their initial reaction is to hoard their newly found treasure, eventually they "come to themselves" and decide to believe that newly discovered treasure must be shared, not hoarded (2 Kings 7:9-10; cf. Matt 13:44) (Moore 2003, 148-50).

1.4. Hosea. Hosea takes this prophetic critique of Baalistic consumerism to a whole new level, manipulating (1) the war-peace polarity to challenge what he perceives to be a defective notion of kingship (Otto, 77-86), as well as (2) the poverty-wealth polarity to criticize the way Israel's leaders blatantly Baalize the Israelite economy. Israel constantly strives to be "rich" (ʿāšar) and "wealthy" (ʾôn), yet even when material gifts are given to them, they deny to Yahweh, the divine giver, the husbandly credit that he so richly deserves (Hos 12:8)

(Stienstra, 127-90). Instead, they credit Baal for their socioeconomic success, relying on false balances and other gimmicks to "oppress" (laʿăšōq) the poor in the process (Hos 12:7; cf. Zech 7:10) (Dearman, 309). Watching Israel play the role of Canaanite "tradesman" (kĕnaʿan [Hos 12:7-8]), Hosea predicts that someday Yahweh will redefine the boundaries of his *covenantal relationship with his children, no matter how fervently they call him "Daddy Baal" (Hos 2:16) (Keefe, 122-24).

2. Assyrian Critique.
Like northern Israel, southern Judah falls into a number of socioeconomic traps laid out by Assyrian soldiers, bureaucrats, diplomats and businessmen (*CAH*[2] 3.2:71-141), creating a situation that inspires Hebrew prophets such as Isaiah to characterize them as "spoil" and "plunder" for eventual foreign consumption (Isa 10:6) (Childs, 78-93).

2.1. Amos. Unlike most Hebrew prophecies, Amos begins with a series of doom oracles against the nations, immediately followed by doom oracles aimed at Judah and Israel (Amos 1:3—2:16). Where the prophet indicts Judah for rejecting Torah, however, he condemns Israel for "selling the righteous for silver" (Amos 2:6). Intratextually he then parallels this sentiment with the phrase "acquire the poor for silver" a few chapters later (Amos 8:6), a parallel heightened by the fact that each of these verbs (*mākar* [Amos 2:6] // *qānâ* [Amos 8:6]) directs attention to the same adjoining colon: "and the needy for a pair of sandals." To ask why this prophet would direct such strong socioeconomic criticism against Israel instead of Judah is to ask why Israel would choose to pursue a life of mindless consumption over compassionate fellowship. Supported by a highly organized system of taxation, Israel's wealthy elite fall headlong into the trap of desiring only comfortable lives for themselves, filled with "palatial private residences, conspicuous consumption, use of luxury items such as fine linen, expensive ornaments, and perfume, and nonproductive recreational activity" (Premnath, 127).

Amos uses such cutting language to criticize this behavior because underneath it he sees Israel abandoning the role of "covenant partner" for that of "godless merchant" (Lang, 482-85). Indicting the royal state officials for blatantly prospering at the poor's expense, Amos predicts that soon these officials will have to explain their entitlement mentality to a much more hostile audience (Amos 3:9-11, 12b-15; 4:1-3; 5:11; 6:1-7) (Jaruzelska, 167). Indicting the Samarian patricians for "acquiring" (*qānâ* [Amos 8:6]) and "crushing" (*rāṣaṣ* [Amos 4:1]) and "uprooting" (*nāṭâ*) the poor (Amos 2:7), Amos predicts that soon their investment portfolio will find itself reduced to a single option: "Prepare to meet your God, O Israel!" (Amos 4:12).

2.2. Isaiah 1—39. Isaiah 5—11 discusses Judah's rebelliousness, Yahweh's decision to use Assyria as a disciplinary tool, Assyria's assault on Yahweh's "vineyard," and Yahweh's desire to root out godless arrogance wherever it exists (Seitz, 480). Judahite patricians pretending to uphold the law in order to collect more "acquisitions" (*ʿāmāl*) will be punished first (Is 10:1) because the socioeconomic hoarding to which they have become addicted so viciously tramples down the hopes and aspirations of the poor (Is 10:2). Indeed, Isaiah predicts that on Yahweh's "day of judgment" many Judahites will frantically scour the hills and caves for a place to hide their ill-gotten "gain" (*kābôd*), but they will not find one (Is 10:3). Where Amos criticizes the "cows of Bashan" for oppressing the poor and crushing the needy (Amos 4:1), Isaiah lays out a tour de force critique of all the personal items cluttering up the closets of Judah's "cows": anklets, headbands, crescents, pendants, bracelets, scarfs, headdresses, armlets, sashes, perfume boxes, amulets, signet rings, nose rings, festal robes, mantles, cloaks, handbags, garments of gauze, linen garments, turbans and veils (Is 3:18-23).

Assyria's role in disciplining Judah will be to play the role of the Yahwistic "rod" (Is 10:5) or, to change the metaphor, the sharp scalpel in the hands of the divine surgeon as he cuts out the cancer of consumerism from Judah's internal organs. The depth of this cancer is measured by the fervency with which Judah's rulers spend their days looking for more and more ways to "engineer oppressive legislation" (Davies, 40) designed to "give themselves a legal foundation to justify their efforts to expand their property," even when the result brings "disaster on their fellow citizens" (Wildberger, 213-14). Such behavior, moreover, is not limited to Israel's leaders; it "extends to the people who look up to them and imitate them, because selfish covetousness is the characteristic of those who think that they have to live out a transitory life in their own strength and so employ every possible means to serve their self-preservation and self-assurance" (Kaiser, 76).

2.3. Micah. Micah sees in Jerusalem a city whose inhabitants "covet fields and seize them," where the homes of the poor are unexpectedly and inappropriately thrown into foreclosure, where the "haughty" laughingly pretend to govern responsibly (Mic 2:2-3). Responding to these injustices, he predicts the coming of a day in which the Judahite economy will dramatically implode, when foreign troops will capture the fields earlier stolen from the poor, when orchards and vineyards will feed not Judah's children but their foreign captors instead (Mic 2:1-5; 6:14-15). After this, however, another day will come when the ignorant will embrace knowledge, when those unjustly imprisoned will receive justice, and when those forced to eat the sour fruits of materialistic corruption will once again experience the sweet solace of socioeconomic security (Mic 4:2-4) (Moore 1993, 320-22).

3. Babylonian Critique.
After the Babylonians take over the Assyrian Empire (*CAH*² 3.2:229-75), and as they plan the Jerusalem invasion, Jeremiah describes the mercenary army gathered together under Nebuchadnezzar's leadership as a "boiling pot" (*sîr nāpûaḥ*) poised to spill over and scald every person unfortunate enough to be standing in his way (Jer 1:13-14) (Reimer, 231-32). From a Hebrew perspective, the main difference between Assyria and Babylon is that where the former falls short in plundering Jerusalem's treasure, the latter does not (Moore 2003, 254-59, 343-50).

3.1. Jeremiah. Celebrating Josiah's kingship as the triumph of Yahwistic *"justice" (*mišpaṭ*) and "righteousness" (*ṣĕdāqâ*) over greed and corruption, Jeremiah condemns the Davidic king Jehoiakim for pretentiously and ridiculously "competing" (*mĕta ăreh* [Jer 22:15]) with other kings for "cedar," manipulating a well-worn metaphor rooted in old Babylonian myths about "sacred cedar forests" (Moore 2011, 43-51). Where Jeremiah aligns this metaphor to the corruption fueled by Jehoiakim's "plunder" (*beṣaʿ* [Jer 22:17]), the Qumranic pesher to Habakkuk uses it to criticize the Jehoiakims of his day (*beṣaʿ* [1QpHab IX, 5]). Where Jeremiah briefly toys with the idea that the poor may be too foolish to understand "Yahweh's way" (Jer 5:4), he soon proclaims rich and poor to be "equally" (*yaḥdāw*) corrupt (Jer 5:5). Often the poverty-wealth polarity impacts Jeremiah's language (note, e.g., the portrayal of Judah as a "partridge hovering over stolen eggs" [Jer 17:11]), but more often than not one finds the metaphorical playfulness of Hosea subsumed by Jeremiah into recurring lists (Jer 9:23) (Overholt; Lalleman-de Winkel, 231-32; Moore 1986, 395-401) and catchphrases (Jer 15:13; 17:3; 20:5), many finding intertextual echos in Isaiah ("wealth of the nations" [Is 60:5; 61:6; 66:12; cf. Zech 14:14]) and Ezekiel ("wealth carried away" [Ezek 29:19; 30:4]). Of particular interest is the fact that Jeremiah manipulates the aforementioned noun in the Naboth narrative (*mĕḥîr*, "value" [1 Kings 21:2]) in repetitive phrases such as "your wealth [*ḥayil*] and your treasure [*ʾôṣār*] I will give as plunder—not for their value [*mĕḥîr*], but in exchange [LXX: *antallagma*] for your sins" (Jer 15:13 [see also Jer 17:3]) (Stuhlman, 17-18).

3.2. Ezekiel. Ezekiel indicts Judah for acting like a criminal gang interested only in shedding blood, defiling women, and "oppressing the poor" (Ezek 18:12), comparing their behavior to the avaricious rapacity of Sodom (Ezek 16:49), the materialistic consumerism of Phoenicia, and the oligarchical covetousness of Egypt (Ezek 27—30). Where Greek writers portray the Phoenicians as "tricky" (*stratēgēma* [Polybius, *Hist.* 3.78.1]), "devious" (*apatēlia* [Homer, *Od.* 14.288]) and "avaricious" (*philochrēmateō* [Josephus, *Ag. Ap.* 1.62]), Ezekiel criticizes them for being "haughty" and "idolatrous" (Ezek 28:5) (Corral 67). Singling out the city of Tyre for "enriching the kings of the earth" with unnecessary, elitist "merchandise" (*maʿărāb* [Ezek 27:33]), he metaphorically warns them that soon they will find themselves "shipwrecked" (*nišberet*), their expensive merchandise thrown into "deep water" (*maʿămaqqê māyim* [Ezek 27:34]) and sunk (cf. Zech 9:4). Survivors of this disaster will attempt to swim away, but dissatisfied business partners will make sure that they drown in their "denigration" (*šaraq* [Ezek 27:36]), and afterwards Yahweh will give Egypt's wealth to the Babylonians as "payment" (*pĕʿullâ*) for engineering this "shipwreck" (Ezek 29:20 [cf. Is 45:14]).

3.3. Habakkuk. Habakkuk frames his prophecy within complementary metaphorical expressions. On land, the Babylonians look like angry real estate brokers more interested in foreclosure than development (Hab 1:5-11). On sea, they act like pirates determined to hook their captives like fresh fish for the marketplace (Hab 1:14-17). Thus, because "the Babylonian worships the tools by which he obtains this abundance as though they were divine," Habakkuk emphasizes the socioeconomic point that "Babylon worships its military power because its military power brings such a high standard of living." Where the Qumranic pesher to Habakkuk applies this critique to its historical context (1QpHab VI, 5-6), the contemporary question is "whether we in our own way deify the means to *our* high standard of living" (Roberts, 104).

3.4. Isaiah 40—66. To Judahites living in Babylonian captivity, an exiled Isaianic disciple predicts that Yahweh will provide for them just as he provided for their wandering ancestors, to the point of making water flow in the desert so that it might miraculously bear fruit (Is 41:17; cf. Ezek 47). Through the reconstructive work of his messiah Cyrus, Yahweh promises to replenish the second temple with the "products" (*yĕgîʿa* [Is 45:14]) of Egypt and the "merchandise" (*sāhar* [Is 45:14]) of Ethiopia. To "fraudulent liturgists" still clinging to the reductionist belief that prayer and fasting alone can restore the temple to its preexilic glory, another Isaianic disciple writes that true fasting involves much more than mere abstention from food; it requires a firm ethical commitment to provide housing for the homeless (Is 58:7) and "refuge" (*māʿôz* [Is 25:4]) for the poor (Creach, 50-73; Brueggemann, 187). Only when ethics and liturgy learn to complement each other will the "wealth of the nations" be available for rescuing Israel from its persistent poverty (Is 60:5, 11; 61:6: 66:12).

4. Persian Critique.

Eventual Hebrew repatriation into the province of Yehud, one of many districts taken over from the Babylonians by the Achaemenid administration of ancient Persia (Berquist), is difficult to understand because of "a decided lack of reliable sources" and the "ideological nature" of the sources in our possession (Carter, 21).

4.1. Haggai. Yet Cyrus's decree (Ezra 1:2-4) inaugurates an era of tremendous change in Hebrew history as refugees of various stripes begin trickling back into the Persian province of Yehud, the old "land of Judah" (Ackroyd, 138-52, 232-56). The *land to which they return, however, suffers the persistent malaise of post-war recession as the earth withholds its "produce" yĕbûl [Hag 1:10]) (Meyers and Meyers, 27). Unlike Zechariah, Haggai explains the factors responsible for creating this recession not in mythological/visionary/oneiromantic categories (Mouton, 24-28) but rather as a measured divine response to the passive-aggressive procrastination permeating the minds of returning refugees. Sixty-seven years have elapsed since the destruction of the temple, and still it lies in ruins (Hag 1:1-15). Thus, while the factors responsible for this reticence can be attributed to ideological (Bedford, 301-10) or socioeconomic concerns (Kessler, 243-56), the prophet castigates his audience for choosing to preoccupy themselves with personal matters instead of temple matters (Hag 1:9). From Haggai's point of view, this is passive-aggressive rebellion, and the primary reason why the land now suffers the ravages of "drought" (ḥōreb [Hag 1:11], a term paralleled elsewhere in the prophetic corpus with the "noise of aliens" and the "song of ruthlessness" [Is 25:5]) (Hanson, 24-25). Where Israel's neighbors exacerbate their troubles, viciously exploiting them to their own advantage (Zech 1:15), Haggai registers great disgust toward the consumerist mentality being imported into Yehud from an alien economy with an alien agenda (Kippenberg, 23, 87).

4.2. Zechariah. However one perceives the connection between the two prophetic books of Haggai and Zechariah (Boda, 392-93; Ben Zvi and Nogalski), Haggai's socioeconomic critique continues on into Zechariah, albeit more symbolically. Referencing the warnings of the "former prophets" at the beginning and end of the night visions laid out in Zechariah 1—6 (Zech 1:4; 7:7, 12), Zechariah warns his audience that Yahweh's *wrath can still cleanse corruption if and when the latter leads to the "exploitation" ('āšaq [Zech 7:10]) of widows, orphans, resident aliens and the desperately poor. Like Haggai, he encourages his audience to recognize that the restoration of the temple is paramount (Zech 6:12-15); otherwise the "desolate land" ('ereṣ nāšammâ) upon which they are trying to eke out a living will never again become "desirable land" ('ereṣ ḥemdâ) (Zech 7:14).

See also ETHICS; HONOR AND SHAME; JUSTICE, RIGHTEOUSNESS; LAND; PEACE, REST; SOCIAL JUSTICE; SUFFERING.

BIBLIOGRAPHY. **P. R. Ackroyd,** *Exile and Restoration: A Study of Hebrew Thought of the Sixth Century B.C.* (OTL; London: SCM, 1968); **M. Beck,** *Elia und die Monolatrie: Ein Beitrag zur religionsgeschichtlichen Rückfrage nach dem vorschriftprophetischen Jahwe-Glauben* (BZAW 281; Berlin: de Gruyter, 1999); **P. R. Bedford,** *Temple Restoration in Early Achaemenid Judah* (JSJSup 65; Leiden: E. J. Brill, 2001); **E. Ben Zvi and J. D. Nogalski,** *Two Sides of a Coin: Juxtaposing Views on Interpreting the Book of the Twelve/the Twelve Prophetic Books* (Piscataway, NJ: Gorgias, 2009); **J. L. Berquist,** "Approaching Yehud," in *Approaching Yehud: New Approaches to the Study of the Persian Period,* ed. J. L. Berquist (SBLSS 50; Atlanta: Society of Biblical Literature, 2007) 1-6; **M. J. Boda,** "From Fasts to Feasts: The Literary Function of Zechariah 7-8," *CBQ* 65 (2003) 390-407; **T. L. Brodie,** "Luke 7:36-50 as an Internalization of 2 Kings 4:1-37: A Study of Luke's Use of Rhetorical Imitation," *Bib* 64 (1983) 457-85; **W. Brueggemann,** *Isaiah 40-66* (WestBC; Louisville: Westminster/John Knox, 1998); **C. E. Carter,** *The Emergence of Yehud in the Persian Period: A Social and Demographic Study* (JSOTSup 294; Sheffield: Academic Press, 1999); **K. R. Chelst,** *Exodus and Emancipation: Biblical and African-American Slavery* (Jerusalem: Urim Publications; New York: Lambda Publishers, 2009); **B. S. Childs,** *Isaiah and the Assyrian Crisis* (SBT 3; London: SCM, 1967); **G. C. Chirichigno,** *Debt-Slavery in Israel and the Ancient Near East* (JSOTSup 141; Sheffield: JSOT Press, 1993); **J. E. Cook,** "The Song of Hannah: Texts and Contexts" (Ph.D. diss., Vanderbilt University, 1989); **R. A. Coote,** ed., *Elijah and Elisha in Socioliterary Perspective* (SBLSS; Atlanta: Scholars Press, 1992); **M. A. Corral,** *Ezekiel's Oracles against Tyre: Historical Reality and Motivations* (BibOr 46; Rome: Editrice Pontificio Istituto Biblico, 2002); **J. F. D. Creach,** *Yahweh as Refuge and the Editing of the Hebrew Psalter* (JSOTSup 217; Sheffield: Sheffield Academic Press, 1996); **A. Davies,** *Double Standards in Isaiah: Re-Evaluating Prophetic Ethics and Social Justice* (BibInt 46; Leiden: E. J. Brill, 2000); **J. A. Dearman,** *The Book of Hosea* (NICOT; Grand Rapids: Eerdmans, 2010); **M. Girard,** *The Psalms: Mirror of the Poor* (Montreal: Médiaspaul, 1996); **B. Gordon,** "Scepticism and Apocalyptic," in *The Economic Problem in Biblical and Patristic Thought* (VCSup 9; Leiden: E. J. Brill, 1989) 33-42; **K. Gordon and M. Miyake**, "Business Approaches to Combating Bribery: A Study of Codes of Conduct," *Journal of Business Ethics* 34 (2001) 161–73; **L. K. Handy**, *Among the Host of Heaven: The Syro-Palestinian Pantheon as Bureaucracy* (Winona Lake, IN: Eisenbrauns, 1994); **K. C. Hanson**, "When the King Crosses the Line: Royal Deviance and Restitution in Levantine Ideologies," *BTB* 26 (1996) 11-25; **C. Hardmeier**, "Wirtschaftliche Prosperität und Gottvergessenheit: Die theologische Dimension wirtschaftlicher Leistungskraft nach Dtn 8," *Leqach* 4 (2004) 15-24; **A. J. Hauser and R. Gregory**, *From Carmel to Horeb: Elijah in Crisis* (JSOTSup 85; Sheffield: Almond, 1990); **H. B. Huffmon**, "Jezebel: the 'Corrosive' Queen," in *From Babel to Babylon: Essays on Biblical History and Literature in Honour of Brian Peckham*, ed. J. R. Wood, J. E. Harvey and M. Leuchter (LHBOTS 455; London: T & T Clark, 2006) 273-84; **I. Jaruzelska**, *Amos and the Officialdom in the Kingdom of Israel: The Socio-Economic Position of the Officials in the Light of the Biblical, the Epigraphic and Archaeological Evidence* (Pozna Wydawnictwo Naukowe Uniwersytetu im. Adama Mickiewicza, 1998); **T. Jemielity**, *Satire and the Hebrew Prophets* (Louisville: Westminster/ John Knox, 1992); **O. Kaiser**, *Isaiah 1-12: A Commentary*, trans. J. Bowden (2nd ed.; OTL; London: SCM, 1983); **A. A. Keefe**, *Woman's Body and the Social Body in Hosea* (JSOTSup 338; London: Sheffield Academic Press, 2001); **J. Kessler**, "Building the Second Temple: Questions of Time, Text, and History in Haggai 1:1-15," *JSOT* 27 (2002) 243-56; **H. G. Kippenberg**, *Religion und Klassenbildung in antiken Judäa: Eine religionssoziologische Studie zum Verhältnis von Tradition und gesellschaftlicher Entwicklung* (SUNT 14; Göttingen: Vandenhoeck & Ruprecht, 1978); **D. Konstan and M. Dillon**, "The Ideology of Aristophanes' *Wealth*," *AJP* 102 (1981) 371-94; **H. Lalleman-de Winkel**, *Jeremiah in Prophetic Tradition: An Examination of the Book of Jeremiah in the Light of Israel's Prophetic Traditions* (CBET 26; Leuven: Peeters, 2000); **B. Lang**, "Sklaven und Unfreie im Buch Amos (2:6; 8:6)," *VT* 31 (1981) 482-88; **C. L. Meyers**, "'Women of the Neighborhood' (Ruth 4:17): Informal Female Networks in Ancient Israel," in *Ruth and Esther: A Feminist Companion to the Bible*, ed. A. Brenner (FCB 3; Sheffield: Sheffield Academic Press, 1999) 110-28; **C. L. Meyers and E. Meyers**, *Zechariah 9-14: A*

New Translation with Introduction and Commentary (AB 25C; New York: Doubleday; New Haven: Yale University Press, 1993); **M. S. Moore**, "Jeremiah's Progressive Paradox," *RB* 93 (1986) 386-414; idem, *The Balaam Traditions: Their Character and Development* (Atlanta: Scholars Press, 1990); idem, "Are Our Wounds Incurable? (Micah 1:9)," in *Today Hear His Voice: The Minor Prophets Speak* (ed. Don Shackelford; Searcy, AR: Harding University Press, 1993) 313-24; idem, *Reconciliation: A Study of Biblical Families in Conflict* (Joplin, MO: College Press, 1994); idem, *Faith under Pressure: A Study of Biblical Leaders in Conflict* (Siloam Springs, AR: Leafwood, 2003); idem, "Numbers," in *The Transforming Word: One-Volume Commentary on the Bible*, ed. M. A. Hamilton (Abilene, TX: ACU Press, 2009) 185-202; *WealthWatch: A Study of Socioeconomic Conflict in the Bible* (Eugene, OR: Pickwick, 2011); **A. Mouton**, *Rêves Hittites: Contribution à une histoire et une anthropologie du rêve en Anatolie ancienne* (CHANE 28; Leiden: E. J. Brill, 2007); **C. M. Murphy**, *Wealth in the Dead Sea Scrolls and in the Qumran Community* (STDJ 40; Leiden: E. J. Brill, 2002); **J. Neusner**, *The Economics of the Mishnah* (Chicago: University of Chicago Press, 1990); **R. A. Ohrenstein and B. Gordon**, *Economic Analysis in Talmudic Literature: Rabbinic Thought in the Light of Modern Economics* (StPB 40; Leiden: E. J. Brill, 1992); **E. Otto**, *Krieg und Frieden in der Hebräischen Bibel und im Alten Orient: Aspekte für eine Friedensordnung in der Moderne* (Stuttgart: Kohlhammer, 1999); **T. W. Overholt**, "Jer 2 and the Problem of Audience Reaction," *CBQ* 41 (1979) 262-73; **E. Peterson**, "Baalism and Yahwism Updated," *ThTo* 29 (1972) 138-43; **J. D. Pleins**, "Law and Justice: The Pentateuch," in *The Social Visions of the Hebrew Bible: A Theological Introduction* (Louisville: Westminster/John Knox, 2001) 41-92; **D. N. Premnath**, "Amos and Hosea: Socio-historical Background and Prophetic Critique," *WW* 28 (2008) 125-32; **H. Rand**, "David and Ahab: A Study of Crime and Punishment," *JBQ* 24 (1996) 90–97; **D. J. Reimer**, "The 'Foe' and the 'North' in Jeremiah," *ZAW* 101 (1989) 223-32; **J. J. M. Roberts**, *Nahum, Habakkuk, and Zephaniah* (OTL; Louisville: Westminster/John Knox, 1991); **T. J. Sandoval**, *The Discourse of Wealth and Poverty in the Book of Proverbs* (BibInt 7; Leiden: E. J. Brill, 2007); **C. R. Seitz**, "Isaiah," *ABD* 3:472-88; **M. S. Smith and W. T. Pitard**, *The Ugaritic Baal Cycle, 2: Introduction with Text, Translation, and Commentary of KTU/CAT 1.3-1.4* (VTSup 114; Leiden: E. J. Brill, 2009); **G. Stansell**,

"How Abraham Became Rich," in *Ancient Israel: The Old Testament in Its Social Context*, ed. P. F. Esler; Minneapolis: Fortress, 2006) 92-110; **N. Stienstra,** *Yhwh is the Husband of His People: Analysis of a Biblical Metaphor with Special Reference to Translation* (Kampen: Kok Pharos, 1994); **L. Stuhlman,** *Order amid Chaos: Jeremiah as Symbolic Tapestry* (BibSem 57; Sheffield: Sheffield Academic Press, 1998); **T. Veerkamp,** *Die Vernichtung des Baal: Auslegung des Königsbücher (1.17-2.11)* (Stuttgart: Alektor, 1981); **J. T. Walsh,** *1 Kings* (Berit Olam; Collegeville, MN: Liturgical Press, 1996); **H. C. Washington,** *Wealth and Poverty in the Instruction of Amenemope and the Hebrew Proverbs* (SBLDS 142; Atlanta: Scholars Press, 1996); **M. Weinfeld,** *Deuteronomy 1-11: A New Translation with Introduction and Commentary* (AB 5; New York: Doubleday, 1991). **R. N. Whybray,** *Wealth and Poverty in the Book of Proverbs* (JSOTSup 99; Sheffield: JSOT Press, 1990); **H. Wildberger,** *Isaiah 1-12: A Commentary*, trans. T. H. Trapp (CC; Minneapolis: Fortress, 1991).   M. S. Moore

WEEKS OF YEARS. *See* DANIEL: BOOK OF.

WIDOWS AND ORPHANS. *See* WOMEN AND FEMALE IMAGERY.

WILDERNESS, DESERT

In the prophetic literature "wilderness" (*midbār*), "dry place" (*'ărābâ, ṣiyyâ*) and "desert" (*yĕšîmôn*) usually represent threatening natural environments beyond the reach of civilization, and as such they provide a setting for divine deliverance and judgment. It is both the place out of which Israel came following the exodus and the potential state to which they will return if they do not follow the commands of the Lord. The intransigence of both Israel and the nations leads to the possibility that each may become a "desolate place" (*šĕmāmâ, horbâ*), the abodes of wild beasts and the world's uncontrolled elements. This risk notwithstanding, the wilderness represents an obstacle to *salvation that can be overcome with divine help, so that it is there that some of God's mightiest acts of salvation may be perceived. Indeed, the Lord provided miraculously for Israel in the wilderness after the *exodus, and the prophetic literature reflects critically on this experience. These reflections on wilderness wandering do little to remove the sense of danger inherent in such

locales, instead heightening it to emphasize the threat that it represents and the great wonder that the Lord might overcome it once again.

1. Wilderness Imagery as General Concept
2. Specific Usages

1. Wilderness Imagery as General Concept.
"Wilderness" (*midbār*) and related words in its semantic field such as "dry place" (*'ărābâ*) and "desolate place" (*šĕmāmâ*) appear throughout the prophetic literature as flexible images in the hands of poets and tradents. Most often, they threaten *destruction and localize divine salvation, and they do so by drawing upon the lived realities of ancient Israel (Talmon 1966). Predominantly a community of subsistence farmers, the Israelites have a strong connection to the *land, and as a result the threat of wilderness was not one from which they were far removed, as drought or famine could ruin cultivated land in a single season (King and Stager). The image of a waterless region replete with sand dunes predominates when many imagine the ancient Near Eastern wilderness, but the land understood as wilderness is often rocky, scarred by torrent valleys and even desert vegetation depending on the exact location. The various wildernesses of the ancient Near East may have consisted of steppe, loess or any number of other less than hospitable environs, but the specific topographical details vary depending on the literary context and prove less important than the general sense that the wilderness is a place beyond human ken, far beyond the controlled environs of civilization. Indeed, the notion of wilderness itself implies contrasting domesticated space (Oelschlager). The imagery is particularly powerful in part because the actual wilderness in Israelite experience was both ubiquitous and near at hand. Characterized by *death, the wilderness threatens those who must travel through it, and ancient Near Eastern iconography imagines the borders of civilization as places where death resides, in part due to the fact that burial grounds were placed there (Keel). Thus, the wilderness was a powerful tool for the prophetic poet, whether the goal of the oracular pronouncement was woe or weal.

1.1. Wilderness as Threat of Judgment. Wilderness usually evokes negative associations, perhaps related to the Israelite experience of wilderness recounted in Exodus through Deuteronomy, and as a result it shows up often in prophetic speech threatening judgment (Talmon, *TDOT* 8:87-118). If Israel fails to heed divine commands to repentance, then they may be returned to a state of wilderness. The wilderness is uninhabited (Is 34:10; Jer 2:6), dark (Is 42:16; Jer 2:31), full of people and things uncontrolled by the surrounding societies (Is 9:3; Jer 9:25), the abode of jackals, ostriches, wild beasts (Is 33:9; 34:11; Jer 9:10-11; 10:22; 12:8-9; Mal 1:3) and even demonic beings (Is 13:21-22; 30:6; 34:8-15). The wilderness represents, then, a general place of death and disorder, and prophetic literature evokes this location to communicate the depth of divine anger and the risk Israel runs if they fail to repent. Jeremiah 4:26 makes the threat explicit: "I looked, and behold, the orchard was wilderness [*hammidbār*], and all its cities had gone to ruin on account of the LORD, on account of his burning anger" (see also Joel 2:3). Micah 1:6 describes the result of such punishment, declaring to Judah that Samaria was "a heap of stones." Hosea ties the fertility of the land to Israelite *worship, so that the cultivated land will be overtaken by the wild, yielding thistle and thorn rather than the fruit of the land, and in so doing, he demonstrates the union of people and land. When the people are punished, so also is the land (Davis; Marlow). Israel must repent, lest the Lord "turn her into a wilderness, and make her like a dry land" (Hos 2:5 [see also Hos 10:8]). In short, the wilderness is the opposite of the "desirable land" promised to and possessed by Israel (Jer 3:19), the future for the nation that rejects divine guidance.

At times the terminology of wilderness in the prophetic literature represents a land not yet cultivated by human hands, but in the prophetic literature it may also connote a state to which the land has returned after a period of civilization. In these cases the prophetic literature often employs the term "desolation" (*šĕmāmâ*), sometimes juxtaposed in biblical parallelism with *midbār* or *ʿărābâ* (e.g., Jer 12:10). Israel stood under the threat that they would become a "place of desolation" (*šĕmāmâ*, sometimes *ḥorbâ*), as in Isaiah 64:9: "Your holy cities have become a wilderness [*midbār*]; Zion has become a wilderness [*midbār*], Jerusalem a desolate place [*šĕmāmâ*]." Such places elicit the pity and fear of nations that observe the wild nature of once-inhabited regions (e.g., Jer 6:8; 9:9). When Jeremiah prophesied that fields would once again be purchased in Judah, he comforted the people by refuting their discouraging words: "The field will again be bought in this land of which you say, 'It is a desolation [*šĕmāmâ*] with neither man nor beast. It is given into the hand of the Chaldeans'" (Jer 32:43). The people believed the land to have returned to its original wild state, but in the future it would once more be parceled out as fields for purchase. A desolate place is like the wilderness insofar as wild beasts pass through it, and there are no inhabitants (Ezek 14:15). Moreover, when the Lord threatens to make the land a "desolation" (*šĕmāmâ*), the land receives the threat, so that both the soil itself and the inhabitants of that territory stand under judgment (e.g., Ezek 15:8). Not only will Israel return to a state of desolation, but also the means by which such desolation might come is from the desert itself, as the "east wind" originates in the desert and scorches cultivated land (see Is 27:8; Ezek 17:10; Hos 13:15). In each of these instances the wilderness symbolizes the potential judgment of the Lord against Israel and the nations, which may receive similar judgment (e.g., Jer 49:13; 50:38; Zeph 2:9). The dangerous threat of the wilderness in their daily lives is used to great poetic effect as the prophets imagine the extension of the chaotic wilderness over the ordered lives of ancient Israelite communities.

1.2. Wilderness as Setting for Refuge and Deliverance. As foreboding as the wilderness is, it sometimes stands for the necessary land used to pasture and feed livestock, so that the loss of these "pastures of wilderness" is significant (Jer 23:10; see also Ps 65:10). Even the Lord mourns when such portions of the land receive punishment (Jer 9:9). The loss of such wilderness occasions the pleas of Joel, who laments twice in Joel 1:19-20 that "fire has devoured the pastures of the wilderness" (see also Amos 1:2). In these contexts the "pastures of the *midbār*" represent the intermediate locales between civilization and the wild, liminal places that exist somewhere between the safety of the village and the danger of the uncontrolled outlying lands (Oelschlager; Talmon, *TDOT* 8:87-118) (see also Joel 2:22 for this phrase, where the "pastures" are restored). On one occasion, the prophet Jeremiah seeks a refuge in the wilderness, a place to leave his people, "for all of them are adulterers, a gathering of cheats" (Jer 9:2). Given the daunting and dangerous nature of the place for which he yearns, the prophet here expresses the depth of his distress, as he believes the people comprise a greater threat to him than the desert. Here his retreat brings to mind Jesus' time in the "wilderness" (*erēmos*). The Spirit leads Jesus to this place, but it is a place where Satan resides and tempts (Mt 4:1-11; Mk 1:12-13). The resonance is even more striking because Jesus understands himself to be a prophet (Lk 4:24).

In other places the threat of wilderness gives way to the full-throated hope for a *remnant (see Is 1:7), a reminder of the potential blossoms that may spring forth if only the people will return to the Lord. Second Isaiah (Is 40—55) provides the most striking instances of this wilderness transformation, sometimes in connection with the specific wilderness separating Israel in *exile from their land, but at other times evoking the more general image of blooming land at home in Israel. "For," as Isaiah 51:3 puts it, "the LORD comforts Zion. He comforts all her waste places [*ḥorbōt*], and will make her wilderness [*midbār*] like Eden, her desert [*ʿărābâ*] like the garden of the LORD." Remembering Zion as a land full of desolate places (*ḥorbōt, midbār, ʿărābâ*), the prophet nevertheless perceives a future beyond that reality when Israel will blossom once more as at creation. The waste and void (*tōhû wābōhû*) of the wilderness will once again become the land of the promise. Unlike the wilderness, the Lord "did not create it [the land] a chaos [*tōhû*]. For dwelling he formed it. In secret I [the LORD] did not speak, in a place, a land of darkness; I did not say to the seed of Jacob, 'In chaos [*tōhû*] seek me'" (Is 45:18-19). A God of order according to both Genesis 1 and Second Isaiah, the Lord continues to create order in wild places (Leal).

1.3. Occasional Uses. Of course, as a poetic symbol the wilderness sometimes functions in the prophetic literature in surprising or unusual ways. One example appears in Jeremiah 17:5-6, where the Lord describes "those who trust in human beings and . . . whose hearts turn away from the LORD": "He shall be like a tree in the Aravah ["dry place," but also a proper name], and he will not see that good is coming. He will live in stone deserts [*ḥărērîm*] in the wilderness, in a salted,

uninhabited land [*ʾereṣ mělēḥâ*]." While this proves true in the literal, historical sense as a result of the Babylonian destruction of Jerusalem, it also communicates the arid nature of the life lived outside the presence of God. Instead of living in the safety of divine company, "in the desert" a person is far from God, under threat from the rest of the world. Also, in Jeremiah 2:31 the Lord asks via the prophet, "Have I become a desert to Israel?" Such a metaphor highlights the contrast between the blessed fruitful land, associated implicitly with the Lord, and that which receives no blessing and yields none. The Lord has been not a wilderness but rather a productive land whose provision to Israel knows no end. These two examples show that wilderness is not always intended as a literal state from which and to which Israel is headed, but that it also symbolizes a dry and difficult state and can even be applied occasionally in the prophetic literature to both human and divine agents (Talmon 1966).

2. Specific Usages.
Particular deserts appear throughout the prophetic literature, especially the "great wilderness" (Num 14:16; Deut 2:7; Judg 11:22) between Egypt and Palestine and the "wilderness of the peoples" (Ezek 20:35) between Palestine and Mesopotamia. A large number of other deserts occur in connection with particular cities or regions, itself a fact that shows the ubiquity of the wilderness and its proximity to settled civilization (e.g., "the wilderness of Moab" [Deut 2:8]). Such specific references move beyond the general threat or setting for salvation and draw upon earlier biblical traditions in their use of wilderness imagery.

2.1. Wilderness Wanderings. As the location of Israel's wilderness wanderings, recounted especially in Numbers, "the great wilderness" between Egypt and Palestine is an especially important place in the imagination of the prophets. Amos 2:10 recalls the events immediately after the exodus succinctly and without much comment: "I brought you up from the land of Egypt, and I led you in the wilderness forty years to possess the land of the Amorite." For Jeremiah, the time of wilderness wandering represents a honeymoon period for Israel: "I remembered concerning you—the steadfast love of your youth, the love of your betrothal period, your following after me in the desert [*midbār*], in a land not sown" (Jer 2:2 [see also

Hos 2:17]). Indeed, in the barren wilderness the Lord cultivated the people: "Holy is Israel to the LORD, the first of his harvest" (Jer 2:3). The utopian vision of this time is remarkably dissonant with the complaint traditions of Exodus and Numbers, but here it is not too difficult to see the prophet's point in his particular memory. Israel was initially faithful but did not persist as the years passed.

Ezekiel, in stark contrast, remembers the time of wandering as a time of immediate betrayal, as in Ezekiel 20:1-26, summed up neatly by Ezekiel 20:13: "The house of Israel rebelled against me in the wilderness." In the wilderness Israel receives God's greatest gift, the statutes, commandments and Sabbaths (Ezek 20:11-12). Nevertheless, two successive generations of Israelites reject the Lord, so that the wilderness becomes the place where the Lord thought to pour out "wrath upon them in the wilderness to put an end to them" but decided against such a course of action so as not to profane his name among the nations (Ezek 20:13, 21). Thus, for Ezekiel, the wilderness becomes the location of rebellion, punishment and forbearance, a microcosm of the divine interaction with humanity over time (Leal). Both prophets engage the wilderness traditions critically, reading Israel's story in fresh ways to condemn Israel for their transgressions against the Lord (see also Hos 13:5-6).

2.2. Weal and Wilderness. In Isaiah the "wilderness of the peoples" between Palestine and Mesopotamia appears as the final obstacle to Israel's return to the promised land. Hearkening back to the wilderness wanderings after the initial exodus from Egypt, here the wilderness is overcome entirely, so that the Lord once again sustains Israel miraculously in the wilderness. Thus, in Isaiah's well-known prophecy of Israelite return the wilderness features prominently: "In the wilderness clear the way of the LORD. Make straight in the desert a highway for our God" (Is 40:3-5 [see also Is 35:5-10]). Here, the Lord domesticates "the wilderness of the peoples" (Ezek 20:35) in particular, overcoming the final obstacle to Israel's return from exile. Elsewhere the desert is personified, a rejoicing agent in the salvific drama rather than an object. Thus, "wilderness and dry land will rejoice and desert shall rejoice and blossom like the crocus" (Is 35:1 [see also Is 42:11]). In this context the land itself is restored, not only imag-

ined as an Israelite thoroughfare. The land, so inextricably intertwined with Israelite experience, here experiences *blessing instead of curse, and all of this takes place "so that they will see and know, consider and understand together, that the hand of the LORD has done this, that the holy one of Israel has created it" (Is 41:20) (on the land as a subject in its own right, see Davis; Marlow).

Hosea 2:14-23 imagines a new future for Israel in which the wilderness will once more be a place of Israelite devotion. Most strikingly here, the land responds to Ephraim's faithfulness by bursting forth with vegetation. Indeed, there will be a "covenant in that day with the beast of the field, with the bird of the heavens, and the creeping things of the soil" (Hos 2:20). Where once these forces represented a great threat to Israelite safety, in the future they will be in covenant relationship with Israel, such that they will be able to "lie down with trust." This new relationship to the wilderness represents not something separate from Israel's devotion to the Lord but instead an integral part of the same, as the subsequent verses demonstrate clearly (Hos 2:21-23; for a similar espousal between Israel and the land, see Is 62:4). This act of covenant with animals representative of the wild demonstrates not something new but rather a return to the Edenic state at the beginning of creation, as the allusions to Genesis 1:20, 24 demonstrate. In the future ordained by God the wilderness need not represent the most fearful place known to Israel; instead, Israel will exist in harmony with it, part of a new covenant with creation, similar to that "with all flesh" in Genesis 9:9-10.

See also DEATH; DESTRUCTION; EXODUS IMAGERY; FLORAL IMAGERY; LAND; MOUNTAIN IMAGERY; SALVATION, DELIVERANCE.

Bibliography. **E. F. Davis**, *Scripture, Culture, and Agriculture: An Agrarian Reading of the Bible* (Cambridge: Cambridge University Press, 2009); **O. Keel**, *The Symbolism of the Biblical World: Ancient Near Eastern Iconography and the Book of Psalms* (Winona Lake, IN: Eisenbrauns, 1997); **P. J. King and L. E. Stager**, *Life in Biblical Israel* (LAI; Louisville: Westminster/John Knox, 2001); **R. B. Leal**, *Wilderness in the Bible: Toward a Theology of Wilderness* (SBL 72; New York: Peter Lang, 2004); **H. Marlow**, *Biblical Prophets and Contemporary Environmental Ethics: Re-Reading Amos, Hosea and First Isaiah* (Oxford: Oxford

University Press, 2009); **M. Oelschlager,** *The Idea of Wilderness: From Prehistory to the Age of Ecology* (New Haven: Yale University Press, 1991); **S. Talmon,** "מִדְבָּר," *TDOT* 8:87-118; idem, "The Desert Motif in the Bible and Qumran Literature," in *Biblical Motifs: Origins and Transformations,* ed. A. Altmann (Cambridge, MA: Harvard University Press, 1966) 31-63.

C. L. Eggleston

WISDOM. *See* PROPHECY AND WISDOM.

WOMEN AND FEMALE IMAGERY

Recent studies on women in the OT favor *literary and *social-scientific approaches. Late twentieth-century biblical scholarship exhibited a rise in interest in women, in social-scientific methodologies, and a greater utilization of literary approaches, including metaphor theory. Sections 1-5 of this article utilize social background and *rhetorical analysis to explore what the prophets have to say about women. The world of Israelite women has been gleaned from critical readings of biblical texts themselves, especially legal texts and stories (e.g., Frymer-Kensky; Perdue et al.; Brenner). Additional information is gleaned from critical use of non-Israelite sources from the ancient Near East (e.g., van der Toorn). Archaeology contributes information about material culture. The biblical books of the prophets add incidental information to this picture, and interpretations of prophetic texts are informed by all these sources.

Sections 6-8 of this article address female imagery in the prophets. Prophetic metaphor is understood through the lens of the social world, historical context and rhetorical strategies. Analysis of biblical metaphor has burgeoned since the 1990s. Scholars in biblical studies, literature, linguistics and philosophy have increasingly come to see metaphor as an integral component of human thought and the construction of meaning. Rather than treating metaphor as a more interesting way of saying what could have been said literally, metaphor is understood to evoke a network of associations and construct a worldview. In Isaiah 13:8, "Pangs and birth-pains will seize them [the Babylonians]" (NRSV), the "tenor" (Babylonians) is informed by the "vehicle" (a woman in labor), but likewise the concept of giving birth is influenced by the tenor of terrified Babylonians (see Dille 2004, chap. 1).

Much of the prophetic corpus is in the form of poetry. As such, it requires reading between the lines and interpreting figurative language.

1. Women's Roles
2. Prophetic Judgments Against Women
3. The Tribulations of Women
4. Women as the Occasion for Men's Sins
5. Specific Women Mentioned
6. Female Imagery for City or Nation
7. Female Imagery for God
8. The Woman in an Ephah Basket

1. Women's Roles.

In Israelite society a woman's two primary roles were wife and mother. In the Prophetic Books references to these roles appear more in metaphor than to women themselves.

1.1. Marriage. Young women were under the authority of their fathers and, upon marriage, came under the authority of their husbands. A man could have more than one wife, but monogamy was increasingly the norm for nonroyals (Blenkinsopp, 64). Most references to marriage in the prophets are metaphorical or symbolic. Hosea is commanded to marry "a wife of whoredom" and marries Gomer (Hos 1:2-3) (see 6.1.1 below). Jeremiah is commanded by God not to get married or have children (Jer 16:2). A single lifestyle went radically against social expectations. As W. Holladay notes, "Celibacy was virtually unknown in Israel," and childlessness "suggests worthlessness" (Holladay, 469). The command to Jeremiah served as a sign of the futility of starting a family in the face of the impending destruction of Jerusalem and widespread death of offspring. The catastrophe is exemplified in God's banishment of "the voice of mirth and the voice of gladness, the voice of the bridegroom and the voice of the bride" (Jer 16:9 NRSV [see also Jer 7:23; 25:10]). But Jeremiah 33:10-11 provides a word of hope for a future when "there shall once more be heard the voice of mirth, and the voice of gladness, the voice of the bridegroom and the voice of the bride" (NRSV). Joel calls for a national fast and beckons even the bridegroom and the bride to join in the solemnity. These examples highlight the time of marriage as one of life's highest joys (Is 61:10), and the abandonment of wedding "mirth" as a sign of great distress.

Despite his own single state, in his letter from Jerusalem to exiles in Babylon Jeremiah encourages them to build houses, to "take wives" for themselves and their sons, and to "give your daughters in marriage," presumably from within the exiled Jewish community (Jer 29:5-6). This was good news in the sense that life can go on in *exile, but bad news in the sense that the exile would not end soon.

We know nothing about Ezekiel's wife except that she accompanied him into exile and died in Babylon. God commands Ezekiel not to weep or observe any normal mourning practices. His abstention from mourning is meant to shock the exiles and serve as a sign that they too will experience profound loss with the destruction of the *temple and loss of their sons and daughters left in Jerusalem. But they are not to mourn (presumably because their own sins brought this about and/or because it is God's will) (Ezek 24:15-27).

The prophet Malachi specifically criticizes the priesthood of postexilic Judah on a number of counts, including divorce and improper *marriage (either their own or for permitting these in Judah). Malachi accuses men of abandoning the wives of their youth, a breach of *covenant (Mal 2:13-16). "Judah" has married "the daughter of a foreign god" (Mal 2:10-12), a reference to marriages to non-Jewish women who become a corrupting influence with their non-Yahwistic religion. B. Glazier-McDonald sees the two charges of divorce and intermarriage as interrelated. In the Persian period many Jewish men, in order to enhance their financial situation and social status, married non-Jewish women from wealthy families. At a time when monogamy had become the common practice, the desire to remarry led a man to divorce the Israelite "wife of your youth." Malachi condemns these practices.

1.2. Childbearing. The event and imagery of childbirth are powerful and are utilized by the Hebrew prophets in their rhetoric. Having many children was a blessing from God. Sons were important for building up the family (daughters left to join their husband's families), and children contributed their labor to agrarian families (Meyers, 27). Barrenness often was interpreted as a sign that God had "closed the womb." The extreme measures portrayed in Genesis to ensure progeny are indicative of this cultural value. Childbirth itself was seen as a dangerous process. Many infants did not survive birth. C. Meyers estimates that in early Israel nearly half of a woman's children

did not survive to age five, and that five to six surviving children was typical. Furthermore, with multiple pregnancies, many women died in childbirth (Meyers, 28).

Loss of children is one of the greatest sorrows. Children and adult offspring died in war or famine, and infant mortality was high. A key component of the ideal age to come is that "no more shall there be in it [Jerusalem] an infant that lives but a few days" (Is 65:20 NRSV). Hosea describes childlessness as a threatened punishment from God for the unfaithfulness of Israel. In Hosea 9:11 he moves backward from birth, to pregnancy, to conception. "Ephraim's glory shall fly away like a bird—no birth, no pregnancy, no conception!" (NRSV). God then threatens, "Even if they bring up children, I will bereave them until no one is left" (Hos 9:12 NRSV). He then pronounces a curse on Israel: "Give them a miscarrying womb and dry breasts . . . Even though they give birth, I will kill the cherished offspring of their womb" (Hos 9:14-16 NRSV).

In connection with specially chosen people, the prophets speak of being formed in the mother's womb and even called or named in the womb (Is 44:2; 49:1, 5; Jer 1:5). This includes Jeremiah, whose wish that he had never been born is meant to shock (Jer 20:14-18; 15:10).

1.3. Women Prophets. Only Isaiah's wife is expressly called a "prophet" in the prophetic corpus (Is 8:1-4). W. Gafney argues that "the prediction, conception, gestation, and delivery of Maher-Shalal-Hash-Baz [is] depicting a joint prophetic undertaking between Isaiah and the Woman-Prophet" (Gafney, 104). Women prophets are mentioned elsewhere in the OT: Deborah in Judges 4—5, Huldah in 2 Kings 14:20, Miriam in Exodus 15:20. Miriam appears in Micah 6:4, where she is listed with Moses, Aaron and the prophet Balaam. Joel 2:28-29 refers to the eschatological age when "your sons and daughters will prophesy," and even "male and female slaves" will receive God's spirit of prophecy. God's spirit of prophecy is "poured out" on women and men alike. Like male prophets, women prophets could be condemned for speaking something other than the word of God (Ezek 13:17) (see 2.2.2 below).

1.4. Lamenting Women. In Israel, as in many cultures, women were official mourners (Meyers, 38). Jeremiah calls for "the mourning women," "the skilled women," to "raise a dirge" to signify doom for Jerusalem (Jer 9:17-22). Jeremiah seems to call on all women to lament: "Hear, O women, the word of the LORD" (Jer 9:20) (*see* Lament, Mourning). (This role for women is reflected in Jeremiah 49:3-5, although the weeping daughters of Rabbah may metaphorically represent the villages around the city of Rabbah [see BDB, 123, meaning 4].)

1.5. Royal Women. Jeremiah's warnings to the kings of Judah include their mothers and wives. The queen mother had a position of importance (the king may have had many wives but had only one mother). Jeremiah warns the king (possibly Jehoiachin) and the queen mother of impending exile (Jer 13:18); he warns that Jehoiachin (Coniah) and his recently widowed mother, Nehushta, will be taken into exile to Babylon (597 BC) (Jer 22:26; see also Jer 29:2). A. Brenner points out that Nehushta is one of only three Israelite/Judahite queen mothers to be called "Lady" (*gĕbîrâ*) (the others are Maacah [1 Kings 15:13; 2 Chron 15:16] and Jezebel [2 Kings 10:13]), but S. Ackerman also includes Athaliah (2 Kings 8:26; 11:1-3, where she is the ruler of Judah) (Ackerman 1993). Brenner argues that the title signifies that these three women had institutional power not granted to other queen mothers, the first two when their sons succeeded the throne while still too young to rule, and Jezebel after the second of her two king sons was killed. This interpretation would suggest that Nehushta had effectively reigned in Judah. Ackerman speculates that the queen mother did have official status, and her duties included "the cult of the goddess Asherah and representative of Asherah devotees" (Ackerman 1993, 401) along with influence in matters of succession. Z. Ben-Barak maintains that she had no official status, while N.-E. A. Andreasen argues that she "held a significant official position superseded only by the king himself" (Andreasen, 180), and Nehushta ruled as co-regent with her son.

Jeremiah warns Jehoiachin's successor, Zedekiah, that when Jerusalem falls to *Babylon, the king's wives and children will be taken captive (Jer 38:23). In Jeremiah 41:10 the daughters of the already captured King Zedekiah are taken captive by the rebel forces of Ishmael. The kings' wives are explicitly included in Jeremiah's list of those who have committed "crimes" against God (Jer 44:9).

Jerusalem's postexilic restoration and triumph is described with reference to foreign queens: "Kings shall be your caregivers, and their royal women your nursing women" (Is 49:23 [cf. Is 60:4]); that is, conquered kings will serve the exiles as childcare workers, and their queens or princesses will be wet nurses.

2. Prophetic Judgments Against Women.

Much of the prophetic material consists of judgments against unfaithfulness. Many of these are directed at the leadership of Israel and Judah. Prophets often addressed the male rulers (e.g., Is 1:10; Jer 1:18; 2:8; Mic 3:1-2, 9-11; Ezek 22:6; Hos 5:10), the priests (male) and the prophets (e.g., Is 28:7; Jer 6:13; 8:10; 14:18, 23:11; Mic 3:11; Zeph 3:4).

Many of the judgments proclaimed against the people of Israel and Judah would have applied to women as well as men. General accusations of infidelity by worship of the Baals or of disregard for the alien, the widow and the orphan would have found women guilty along with the men. Yet often a male audience can be assumed, since men were held more accountable by virtue of being heads of households and in positions of greater social authority and power. Many judgments are, however, gender specific, as in judgments in Jeremiah and Ezekiel of men who "defile" their neighbors' wives (e.g., Jer 5:8; Ezek 18:6). Prophetic judgments targeting women in particular will be reviewed here.

2.1. Eighth-Century BC Prophets.

2.1.1. Amos. Amos's sayings focus on the lack of *social justice in Israel. The poor are sold into debt slavery (Amos 2:6-8), the justice system ("the gate") is corrupted by bribery (Amos 5:12), and the profit motive leads to disdain for the Sabbath and corrupt business practices (Amos 8:5-6). Amos proclaims judgment against the wealthy who care only for themselves (Amos 6:4-6). The prophet explicitly addresses the women of Israel, calling them "you cows of Bashan . . . who oppress the poor, who crush the needy" (Amos 4:1 NRSV). "Cows" is not innately insulting but rather is a reference to their living off the fat of the land. These are the wives or concubines of wealthy men who ask their "lords" to provide for their wants. The women who benefit from the men's corrupt business practices are accountable. Like well-fed cows, they trample the pastureland—that is, those "beneath" them on the economic ladder. Amos predicts their exile from the land, led like cattle with ropes and hooks (see Kleven).

2.1.2. Isaiah of Jerusalem. Isaiah declares judgment against the people of Judah who neglect the widow and orphan (Is 1:23), "do evil" (Is 1:16) and abuse the poor (Is 3:15). The prophet specifically targets the "daughters of Zion" in Isaiah 3:16—4:1 (*see* Zion). They are described as haughty, vain and seductive, adorned with finery, jewelry and perfume. God will take away these emblems of their vanity and give them sackcloth and baldness. In the aftermath of war they will be left without husbands, a condition described as "disgrace" in a culture where a woman needed husband and children to ensure social status (see 3.2 below). But added to this judgment is a promise that the God will have washed away "the filth of the daughters of Zion" (Is 4:4 NRSV). Isaiah 32:9-14 proclaims a judgment against the wealthy, explicitly mentioning "women who are at ease" and "complacent." They will see the desolation of the palace and the city of Jerusalem.

2.1.3. Hosea. Hosea refers to the sins of the men of Israel who are unfaithful to God. "Therefore your daughters play the whore, and your daughters-in-law commit adultery" (Hos 4:13 NRSV). However, God will not punish these. "I will not punish your daughters . . . nor your daughters-in-law . . . for the men themselves go aside with whores" (Hos 4:14 NRSV). God rejects a double standard, as the sins of the women pale in comparison to the sins of the men (see 4 below).

2.2. Seventh- and Sixth-Century BC Prophets.

2.2.1. Jeremiah. The prophet Jeremiah proclaims judgments against the people of Judah for many transgressions (e.g., Jer 7:9-10). Women are explicitly mentioned along with the men and children in connection with worship of the Queen of Heaven (Jer 7:18), a goddess, possibly Babylonian Ishtar, Phoenician Astarte or an Israelite synthesis (Ackerman 1989, 110). Archaeological inscriptional evidence from Kuntillet Ajrud indicates that Canaanite Asherah was worshiped in Israel along with the Israelite God, Yahweh (McCarter).

After the destruction of Jerusalem by Babylon in 586 BC, many Judeans fled to Egypt. Jeremiah proclaimed God's *wrath toward these refugees for worshiping other gods in Egypt (Jer 44:8). Jeremiah 44:9 alludes to "the crimes of your ancestors, of the kings of Judah, of their wives, your own crimes and those of your wives" (NRSV) committed earlier in Judah. The men and women tell Jeremiah, "We will do everything that we have vowed, make offerings to the queen of heaven and pour out libations to her, just as we and our ancestors, our king, and our officials used to do" (Jer 44:17 NRSV) in Judah and Jerusalem. The women argued that as long as they worshiped the Queen of Heaven, things went well. S. Ackerman notes, "This devotion in the face of persecution indicates the worship of the Queen of Heaven was an important part of women's religious expression in the sixth century" (Ackerman 1989, 110). Furthermore, their husbands condoned and participated in this worship (Jer 44:19). It is arguable that women in particular were attracted to the worship of the goddess because they were excluded from many religious functions in the institutional worship of Yahweh (Gruber 1992b).

2.2.2. Ezekiel. Ezekiel also proclaims judgment against the people of Judah for unfaithfulness. Ezekiel 8:14 depicts women at the Jerusalem temple "weeping for Tammuz." Tammuz, or Dumuzi, was a Sumerian-Babylonian fertility god whose death was mourned when the heat of summer dried up the vegetation and whose resurrection from the underworld was celebrated when the winter rains produced the greenery of spring. Only women are mentioned here in relation to the Tammuz ritual, while men are worshiping the sun or the sun god (Ezek 8:16). S. Ackermann sees a connection between this mourning for Tammuz and the cult of the Queen of Heaven in Jeremiah insofar as Ishtar is the goddess who laments for her lover Tammuz (Ackermann 1989, 116; see also Darr 1992, 187).

Ezekiel accuses women false prophets who, like the men condemned a few verses earlier, "prophesy out of their own imagination" (Ezek 13:17 NRSV), accusing them of seeing false visions and practicing *divination (Ezek 13:17-23). They sew bands on wrists and make veils for people. The context suggests that these are magical practices, perhaps meant to ward off evil spirits. Ezekiel further declares God's judgment that they are "putting to death persons who should not die and keeping alive persons who should not live, by your lies to my people." This suggests that the false women prophets have used divination to determine guilt or innocence in criminal cases, resulting in grossly unjust verdicts. W. Gafney speculates whether the rituals of these women were related to pregnancy and childbirth (Gafney, 109).

3. The Tribulations of Women.

3.1. Social Strife. Micah 7 notes how injustice in society has led to strife in the community and the family: "The son treats the father with contempt, the daughter rises up against her mother, the daughter-in-law against her mother-in-law" (Mic 7:6 NRSV). In a healthy and just society there will be harmony between mothers and daughters, and between mothers-in-law and daughters-in-law (living in the same household).

3.2. Widows and Orphans. The phrase "widows and orphans" appears throughout the OT. A better translation of "orphan" is "fatherless," since the term refers to children who may have a mother but have no male provider and protector (Ex 22:24; Lam 5:3). The phrase suggests single mothers and their children who struggle financially without a male provider and are subject to exploitation (Ex 22:22-23; Job 24:21; Ps 94:6). In the Prophets widows and orphans are mentioned with the alien as vulnerable to exploitation and abuse (Jer 7:6; 22:3; Ezek 22:7; Mic 2:9; Zech 7:10; Mal 3:5) and are listed with the poor and the needy (Is 10:2; Jer 5:28; Zech 7:10).

The Hebrew term translated as "widow" does not necessary indicate a woman whose husband is dead, but may refer to a formerly married woman who has lost her male protector and provider (Cohen). The formerly married woman is in a position of social shame (Is 47:8-9; 54:4) because she is vulnerable and lacks access to the social position that a husband would provide. B. Malina observes that in an honor-and-shame society "women not under the tutelage of a male—notably widows and divorced women—are viewed as stripped of female honor . . . sexually predatory, aggressive, 'hot to trot,' hence dangerous. . . . Hence the precarious position of the widow and divorcee" (Malina, 44). A woman derives honor from her status as a wife and a mother. A formerly married woman was especially shamed in the eyes of society. M. Odell comments, "Shame is associated with the dissolation of social bonds [and] . . . can accompany the discovery that one cannot depend on a close social relationship" (Odell, 220) (*see* Honor and Shame).

The practice of social *justice and righteousness is exemplified by defense of the "widow" and "orphan" in Isaiah 1:17: "Rescue the oppressed, defend the orphan, plead for the widow" (NRSV). Those in power, especially the king, have a special obligation to "defend" and protect the widow and the orphan and are judged by their failure to do so (Is 1:23; 10:1-2; Jer 22:3). God will help the orphans and widows (Jer 49:11; cf. Ps 68:5; 146:9; Is 9:17 notes the exception).

3.3. Women and War. In times of war women are explicitly mentioned with men in fleeing the enemy (Jer 48:19), being taken into captivity (Jer 48:46), and seeing their sons and daughters die by sword, famine or disease (Jer 16:3-4). The particular hardships faced by Israelite women in times of war are also mentioned, as are, with a tone of unsavory satisfaction, the hardships of the women of enemy nations. In Jeremiah's judgment against Babylon women and girls, along with men and boys, will be "smashed" by God's judgment (Jer 51:22) (*see* Warfare and Divine Warfare).

In war women are made widows and mourn the loss of their children (Jer 15:8). Jeremiah's judgment against his adversaries in Judah includes "Let their wives become childless and widowed" (Jer 18:21 NRSV). Not only do war widows grieve for their husbands, but also they are left socially and economically vulnerable.

Rape is the particular burden of women in times of war. Isaiah's judgment against Babylon includes the murder of infants and the rape of women (Is 13:16). The wording highlights the distress and shame that this brings to the men who are powerless to protect their wives and children rather than the suffering of the women themselves (see Chapman, 40-44). Amos's judgment against the priest Amaziah focuses on what invasion will mean for Amaziah's wife: "Your wife shall become a prostitute in the city" (Amos 7:17 NRSV).

Pregnant women were vulnerable and perhaps targeted, as they were "ripped open" by enemy soldiers (Hos 13:16; Amos 1:13). Isaiah 37:3 describes the conditions of the siege of Jerusalem by Assyria in 701 BC and its effect on birthing women. Without food coming into the city, "children have come to birth, and there is no strength to bring them forth" (Is 37:3 NRSV). Such a scenario meant death for both mother and child.

Both men and women were subject to being taken captive in war. Nahum portrays how even the slave women of Nineveh taken captive will moan "like doves," beating their breasts (Nah 2:7).

4. Women as the Occasion for Men's Sins.
Numerous times the sinfulness of the men of Israel and Judah is exemplified in their engaging in sex with prostitutes and their "neighbors' wives" (Jer 7:7-8; 29:23; Ezek 33:26; Hos 4:14). The guilt of the men is highlighted. The image of the adulteress or prostitute functions metaphorically in the prophets to signify the unfaithfulness of the people in general (see 6.1 below).

Hosea 4:14 says, "For the men themselves go aside with whores, and sacrifice with temple prostitutes" (NRSV). A number of translations refer to "temple prostitutes" here. The belief that cultic prostitution was characteristic of ancient Near Eastern religion was widespread among twentieth-century scholars (e.g., Mays; Wolff), but that assumption is widely questioned due to lack of clear evidence. M. Gruber comments on the assumption that ancient Near Eastern female cultic functionaries were primarily prostitutes: "Tragically, scholarship suffered from scholars being unable to imagine any cultic role for women in antiquity that did not involve sexual intercourse" (Gruber 1992a, 26). The Hebrew term is qĕdēšôt (sg. qĕdēšâ), which literally means "consecrated women." They are women who had specific functions in relation to a temple or sanctuary and who came to be forbidden after religious reforms. We do not know what they did or why their presence was condemned. Scholarly debate has been extensive. Presumably, their functions came to be associated with alien religious practices (such as divination). The translation "temple prostitutes" is unfortunate because the theory that their function was sexual is only one possibility. P. Bird argues that in Hosea 4:14 the qĕdēšôt are women who had a cultic function that Hosea associates with Baal worship and are paired with prostitutes as a polemical judgment (Bird, 87). Gruber notes that while the Akkadian cognate qadistu "denotes a woman who has been dedicated to the service of a deity" as a cultic singer and a wet nurse (not a prostitute), the Hebrew equivalent in Genesis 38:21-22; Deuteronomy 23:18; Hosea 4:14 indicates a (noncultic) prostitute (Gruber 1992a, 19).

5. Specific Women Mentioned.
In the prophetic corpus individuals mentioned are most often the prophets themselves and the kings. The prophets' other contemporaries are rarely named. However, the prophets sometimes hark back to earlier figures to advance their message. In Isaiah 51:2 Sarah "who bore you" is named as the mother of Israel with Abraham "your father." Rachel, the foremother of the northern tribes of Ephraim, Manasseh and Benjamin, is evoked in Jeremiah 31:15 in a word of hope for the exiled northern tribes. "Rachel is weeping for her children; she refuses to be comforted for her children, because they are no more" (NRSV), but God promises that Rachel's children will return from exile. Miriam is listed in Micah 6:4-5 with Moses, Aaron and Balaam, apparently a list of prophets from the wilderness period.

5.1. Gomer. In Hosea 1—2 Hosea's "wife of whoredom" is both a person and a metaphor along with the "adulteress" of Hosea 3 (Hos 1—3 is discussed in 6.1.1 below).

5.2. The "Young Woman" of the Immanuel Prophecy. In Isaiah 7:7-17 the prophet says, "Look, the young woman is with child and shall bear a son, and shall name him Immanuel" (Is 7:14 NRSV). Judah (the southern kingdom) is under attack from the nations of Israel/Ephraim (the northern kingdom) and Aram/Syria. Isaiah proclaims a sign from God that a child yet to be born will receive the symbolic name "Immanuel" ("God is with us"). The name is a sign that God will deliver Judah from its attackers. Isaiah further adds that by the time the child "knows how to refuse the evil and choose the good" (Is 7:15 NRSV), Judah's enemies will have fallen. Judah withstood the attack, and within twelve years the kingdoms of both Aram and Ephraim had been defeated by Assyria.

When Jewish translators rendered this passage into Greek they translated the term ʿalmâ ("a yet childless young woman"), lacking a precise Greek equivalent, as parthenos, meaning "virgin." The Greek term for "virgin" appears in the Gospel of Matthew in connection with the birth of Jesus. Based on Matthew's quotation (Mt 1:23), Christian tradition has identified the young woman in Isaiah 7 as the Virgin Mary (see Prophets in the New Testament). The identity of the young woman in Isaiah's original context has been variously identified as Isaiah's own wife (Isaiah's sons received symbolic names [Is 7:3; 8:3-4]) (Gottwald), the wife of King Ahaz (Scullion) or even a random young woman whom Isaiah can point to. O. Kaiser interprets it collectively: women will name their sons "Immanuel" in gratitude and praise for the nation's deliverance. The child himself does nothing expressly to deliver Judah from its enemies. Rather, the point is the time period by which the enemies will be defeated: by the time a yet unborn child reaches the age of discernment, the crisis will be over (the prophecy was fulfilled in twelve years).

6. Female Imagery for City or Nation.

In the Hebrew language cities are grammatically feminine, and when a city is personified, it is described as a woman. The female imagery often carries over to the nation. Amos laments over the death of "virgin Israel," who is fallen "with no one to raise her up" (Amos 5:2), signifying Israel's imminent demise if the nation does not repent. Zion or Jerusalem is called a "daughter" a number of times (e.g., Is 1:8; 52:2; Jer 4:31; Mic 1:13; 4:8; Zeph 3:1; Zech 2:7; 9:9). The phrase "virgin daughter" is also used (Is 37:22; Jer 14:17; 18:13; 31:3, 21). Other nations' cities are also referred to as "daughters." The terms often are accompanied by further personification as the daughter-city "despises, scorns, tosses her head" at her enemy (Is 37:21-22); is a captive (Is 52:2); gasps and cries out like a woman in labor (Jer 4:31); is a wounded person (Jer 14:17); is called upon to "return" (Jer 31:21-22); and is one who laments (Joel 1:8). Zephaniah and Zechariah bid Daughter Zion to sing and rejoice at her restoration (Zeph 3:14-20; Zech 2:10-12). Zechariah 9:9-13 calls Zion/Jerusalem "daughter" and calls her citizens her "sons" or "children." Jeremiah proclaims a word of hope that Zion's "incurable wound," guilt and punishment will see God's healing (Jer 30:12-17) and Zion will be rebuilt and dance with joy (Jer 31:4) (the entailments are not explicitly as a woman, but they are a personified "she").

6.1. God's Unfaithful Wife. The people Israel were understood to be in a covenant relationship with their *God. Their God, Yahweh, was a jealous God, with whom they were to have an exclusive relationship, excluding all other gods. The worship of another god thus was seen as infidelity to the covenant relationship. This un-

derstanding is reflected in the marriage metaphor that appears in Hosea, Isaiah, Jeremiah and Ezekiel. Whereas a man could have more than one wife, a wife must be faithful to only one husband. The prophets cast the people Israel in the role of a wife owing exclusive fidelity to God, her husband, who loves her, provides for her, and protects her. The OT speaks of idolatry as the people "prostituting themselves" or "playing the whore" with other gods (e.g., Ezek 43:7; Hos 5:3-4; 6:10; 9:1). This metaphor is used explicitly several times and may be implicit in texts such as Isaiah's claim that Jerusalem, the "faithful city," has "become a whore" (Is 1:21). In recent years scholarly interest in Yahweh's "wife" in Hosea, Jeremiah and Ezekiel has proliferated, but this cannot be fully reviewed here.

6.1.1. Hosea. Hosea's use of the marriage metaphor is the earliest. Hosea is instructed by God to "take a wife of whoredom and have children of whoredom, for the land commits great whoredom" (Hos 1:2 NRSV) (*see* Hosea, Book of). Hosea's symbolic marriage characterizes God's relationship with Israel. "Israel" is masculine, so a more nuanced interpretation identifies the "wife" as either the land (grammatically feminine) of Israel or the capital city (grammatically feminine) of Samaria (Schmitt 1989). Hosea's three children by Gomer receive symbolic names, including "Lo-ruhamah" ("no compassion") and "Lo-ammi" ("not my people"). The last reverses the covenant "I will be your God, and you will be my people." God now proclaims, "You are not my people, and I am not your God" (Hos 1:9). In Hosea 2 the identities of God and Hosea and of Israel and Gomer blur as the husband expresses outrage at the wife's infidelity, threatening to punish her for crediting the nature deities, the Baals, with providing her with the "grain, the wine, and the oil"—that is, all the good produce of the earth. The wronged "husband" will "strip her naked" and "kill her with thirst" (Hos 2:3). He will have no pity on "her" children (Hos 2:4), will "uncover her shame in the sight of her lovers" (Hos 2:10), and then turn and "allure her . . . speak tenderly to her" (Hos 2:14), bringing her out of the land of Canaan back into the wilderness, where she will experience her dependence on him alone as her provider. She will no longer call him "my *ba'al*" ("my master/husband"), but rather "my *'îš*" ("my man/husband," the direct counterpart of the word for "wife," *ʾiššâ*, perhaps highlighting mutuality rather than hierarchy). God will woo his estranged wife, and the children will receive names of compassion and fidelity.

Hosea 3 has Hosea purchasing a woman who is an adulteress as a symbol of Israel's infidelity with other gods. The relationship of Hosea 3 to Hosea 1—2 and whether this also refers to Gomer is contested (see also Hos 8:9; 9:1).

Hosea's depiction of Israel as an unfaithful wife would have conveyed to the men of Israel the level of God's outrage, hurt and sense of betrayal by having them recognize how they themselves would react to an unfaithful wife.

There has been a wide range of interpretations of what is meant by a "woman of whoredom" who subsequently bears "children of whoredom." Suggestions concerning Gomer's identity have included a common prostitute and an ordinary young woman of Israel who is "of whoredom" by virtue of belonging to this unfaithful people. Many scholars have identified Gomer as a woman who participated in Canaanite fertility cults (Wolff, 14-15), but there is little evidence to support that such rites existed (see 4 above).

The first two or three chapters of Hosea traditionally have been interpreted as representing God's love and mercy toward the sinner. However, in recent years critical questions have been raised about the pitfalls of characterizing God as a husband who takes retribution against his wayward wife with the use of violence and shame. D. Setel's 1985 feminist analysis laid the foundation for subsequent critiques of this metaphor. Setel argues that the text objectifies the woman/women, reinforces cultural values of "female passivity and dependence," and justifies spousal abuse (Setel, 92). Setel's essay was a groundbreaking one, raising *hermeneutical questions about how a text not only reflects its own historical social setting, but also continues to construct a worldview and view of women in its reading communities.

Setel's concerns have been taken up by subsequent women scholars such as R. Weems and D. Jacobson, who writes, "The corollary question is what kind of sexuality and marriage are here commended. Are we to value the covenant of marriage above all else in the face of systematic abuse? . . . All right, she is guilty, but should the husband then strip and shame her? Can this metaphor ever really be used compellingly to speak of God's forgiveness and grace? . . . The intent of an author can never itself prevent the real effect of a text in and on a community" (Jacobson 2008a, 195) (for the other side of the argument, see Jacobson 2008b).

There is now a greater appreciation for how metaphors not only illustrate an idea, but also are powerful tools in constructing reality. The critique of the story of Hosea and Gomer is that it constructs a reality in which a husband abusing his wife mirrors divine action. The story resembles the recurring pattern of an abusive marriage in which the husband isolates the wife, shames her, threatens her, and then declares his love (only to repeat the abuse). This is a troublesome and potentially dangerous text if it somehow normalizes (or even divinizes) domestic abuse.

6.1.2. Jeremiah. The image of God's wife appears throughout Jeremiah 2. God says, "I remember the devotion of your youth, your love as a bride" (Jer 2:2 NRSV [see also Jer 2:32]). But, "On every high hill and under every green tree you sprawled and played the whore" (Jer 2:20 NRSV). Unfaithful Jerusalem is like a female animal in heat (Jer 2:23-24). She seeks lovers (Jer 2:25, 33) and, by her example, corrupts even wicked women (Jer 2:33).

In Jeremiah 3 the prophet depicts the two nations of Israel and Judah as the two wives of God. Decades after the fall of the northern kingdom of Israel Jeremiah describes how Israel "played the whore" and did not repent, so God "sent her away with a decree of divorce," signifying the exile of the northern kingdom by Assyria (Jer 3:9). Now her sister, Judah, has also "played the whore," committing adultery with idols (Jer 3:6-10). Jeremiah mixes the husband-wife metaphor and the parent-child metaphor (Jer 3:2-4, 13-14, 19-20), highlighting that both a husband and a father are to be honored. Infidelity and ingratitude dishonor God, who may be compelled to divorce his unfaithful wife and disown his "faithless" children (see also Jer 4:30-31; 10:19-20). Yet God still offers hope of return from exile for Israel. Jeremiah 13:20-27 is addressed to Zion, who will be raped for her sins (Jer 13:22), for her "abominations," "adulteries" and "shameless prostitutions."

A. Diamond and K. O'Connor note that Jeremiah intensifies Hosea's metaphor insofar as "In Hos. 2:7 [MT] she is merely searching for security and fertility, but in Jeremiah raw animal lust drives her (Jer. 2:20-25)" (Diamond and O'Connor, 306-7). Furthermore, the marriage is not restored in Jeremiah. Diamond and O'Connor, with others, echo critiques of Hosea. "Despite the metaphor's sympathetic portrayal of the deity who suffers deeply and longs for his beloved, the metaphor undermines itself by reinforcing cultural images of a punishing unjust God, of punishing unjust husbands, and of wicked independent women" (Diamond and O'Connor, 310).

Jeremiah 31:31-34 uses the marriage metaphor without explicit sexual imagery. God had made a covenant with Israel when they came out of Egypt, "a covenant that they broke, though I had married them" (Jer 31:33 NRSV).

6.1.3. Ezekiel. Ezekiel, writing from exile in Babylon, also depicts Jerusalem as God's wife. Ezekiel 16; 23 convey the outrage and betrayal seen earlier in Hosea, but with the lewd language and violence ratcheted up to a level that some commentators have identified as being pornographic. Ezekiel 16 depicts Jerusalem's Canaanite origins, describing "her" as an abandoned infant girl. God rescued her and "entered into a covenant with you"—that is, married her and adorned her with fine clothing and jewelry. But she "played the whore" and "lavished your whorings on any passer-by" (Ezek 16:15 NRSV). The text goes on to blend descriptions of religious infidelity (making shrines, making idol images, sacrificing or dedicating her "children" to idols) with sexual language, repeatedly referring to her infidelity as acting like a "whore." Jerusalem's "playing the whore" with foreign nations signifies political alliances. Establishing political treaties may have been seen as showing a lack of trust in God to protect them, or, more seriously, it may have involved Judah's acceptance of the gods of their political overlords. Since Judah first was made a vassal of Egypt and shortly thereafter of Babylon (Chaldea), it seems like blaming the victim. To adopt Ezekiel's metaphor, is he calling a rape victim a whore? Perhaps the issue is not the conquest of Judah but rather the degree to which the Judeans embraced the religious rites of their overlords. As a vassal of these nations, Judah had to pay "tribute." "Yet you were not like a whore, because you scorned payment. . . . Gifts are given to all whores; but you have your gifts to your lovers, bribing them

to come to you from all around for your whorings. So you were different from other women in your whorings" (Ezek 16:31-34 NRSV).

God will now gather Jerusalem's "lovers" (nations) and will "uncover your nakedness to them," and she will be judged for adultery. The sentence is death. She will be stripped naked, and a mob will stone her and cut her to pieces (Ezek 16:40). Then God's fury will be "satisfied," and he will be calm and no longer angry. With this final note, God seems to be depicted as a wronged husband whose rage and violence are completely out of control, and only when he had killed his wife will he calm down. L. Day describes Yahweh's behavior in Ezekiel 16 as the typical three-stage pattern repeating of a possessive and jealous batterer: tension building and escalation of irritation and accusations, violent attack, calmness and contrition (Day, 214).

Ezekiel 23 is likewise extreme in its imagery. Samaria (called "Oholah") and Jerusalem (called "Oholibah") are two sisters who "played the whore" in Egypt. F. van Dijk-Hemmes translates Ezekiel 23:3, "'There their breasts were squeezed; There the teats of their maidenhood were pressed' (or, literally: 'There they (masculine; see also v 8) pressed the teats of their maidenhood')" (van Dijk-Hemmes, 167). This early abuse leads to Oholibah's later abuse. "Her harlotry from since (her days in) Egypt she did not give up; For they lay upon/raped her in her youth; And then men pressed the teats of her maidenhood; And they poured out their harlotry upon her" (Ezek 23:8 [trans. van Dijk-Hemmes, 167]). If this is a reference to the exodus story's sojourn in Egypt, it seems, once again, to be blaming the victim. Samaria played the whore with Assyria and its idols until God delivered her into their hands and they killed her. Jerusalem was more corrupt "in her lusting and in her whorings" with Assyrians and with the idols of the Chaldeans (Babylon). The lewdness of this chapter includes descriptions of the huge genitals of her lovers (Ezek 23:20). God will send her lovers against her. They will cut off her nose and ears (Ezek 23:25). Her children will be "devoured by fire" (Ezek 23:25). She will be left naked and be destroyed like Samaria. Further charges are made that Samaria and Jerusalem have offered up their children to idols and defiled the temple. Finally, an assembly will stone them, cut them down, kill their children, and burn their houses (Ezek 23:47). "Thus will I put an end to lewdness in the land, so that all women may take warning and not commit lewdness as you have done," and "you shall know that I am the Lord God" (Ezek 23:48-49 NRSV).

Elsewhere Ezekiel refers to Jerusalem as a city of "filthiness" (Ezek 22:15), "the bloody city" (Ezek 24:7) and a city of "filthy lewdness" that "shall not again be cleansed until I have satisfied my fury upon you" (Ezek 24:13 NRSV). The Israelites' sin is "like the uncleanness of a woman in her menstrual period" (Ezek 36:17 NRSV).

Much speculation has been made about Ezekiel's state of mind in depicting God's judgment with such intense language. The tone says much about the messenger—a temple priest who was torn away from the temple that he loved, marched hundreds of miles into exile, witnessed the death of his wife, and suppressed all mourning (Ezek 24:15-27). Rather than blaming Babylon for his profound losses and displacement, his focus is on those in Jerusalem who, he believes, brought about God's wrath by embracing foreign alliances and religion.

The thorough treatment of these passages by J. Galambush emphasizes the connection between "uncleanness" and the female imagery. For Ezekiel, a temple priest, ritual purity was of utmost concern. Ritual uncleanness was not a condition of sin, but in Ezekiel the sins of the people have rendered the temple unclean (Ezek 8:6). Uncleanness becomes a metaphor for *sin.

F. van Dijk-Hemmes writes, "The androcentric-pornographic character of this metaphorical language must indeed be experienced as extremely humiliating by the male audience forced to imagine itself as being exposed to violating enemies" (van Dijk-Hemmes, 169).

While Ezekiel subsequently writes of God cleansing the people (Ezek 36:25), enlivening the dry bones of Israel (Ezek 37:1-14), and restoring the temple (Ezek 40—47), the female imagery is dropped. Woman/wife Zion is not restored (Galambush).

Feminist critiques of Ezekiel 16; 23 echo those of Hosea and Jeremiah (for a response, see Patton).

6.2. God's Restored Wife. Second Isaiah and Third Isaiah image the restoration of woman *Zion's relationship with God, her husband, and the restoration of children to her. Follow-

ing the destruction of Jerusalem in 586 BC, Isaiah 40—66 proclaims comfort, hope and restoration to Zion/Jerusalem. Second Isaiah begins with words of "comfort" to Jerusalem because "she has served her term . . . her penalty is paid" (Is 40:1 NRSV). Zion is a "herald [fem.] of good tidings" who is to proclaim to the cities of Judah, "Here is your God!" (Is 40:9). Zion says in Isaiah 49:14, "The LORD has forsaken me, my Lord has forgotten me" (cf. Lam 5:20). Then either God responds or Zion continues, asking and answering a rhetorical question: "Can a woman forget her nursing child, or show no compassion for the child of her womb? Even these may forget, yet I will not forget you." While God is a mother who will not forget her children (see 7 below), Zion is also depicted as a mother who is bereft of her children. But she has forgotten her children because when they return to her (the exiles), she does not recognize them (Is 49:19-21). A restored Zion will be "like a bride" (Is 49:18), and her "children" like her bridal ornaments (see Dille 2004, 138-44).

In Isaiah 50:1 God asks, "Where is your mother's bill of divorce with which I put her away?" (NRSV). The implication is that Zion was sent away by her husband, but that there was not a final bill of divorce, leaving open the possibility of reconciliation (Dille 2004, 162-68). In Isaiah 51:17 God calls Zion, "Rouse yourself!" She has lost her "children," but the message now is to arise. "You [fem.] shall drink no more from the bowl of my wrath" (Is 51:22 NRSV). God calls her again to "Awake, awake." Zion is to put on beautiful garments and be freed from captivity (Is 52:1-2).

Perhaps Second Isaiah's most creative description of God's wife, Zion, is in Isaiah 54. In a reversal of Jeremiah 10:19-20, Zion is described as a barren and widowed woman who is promised so many children that she will have to enlarge her "tent" and see abandoned towns reinhabited. "You will forget the shame of your youth, and the disgrace of your widowhood you will remember no more" (Is 54:4 NRSV). The Hebrew word for "youth" here describes a young woman who has not yet borne any children (see also Joel 1:8). Childlessness was regarded as shameful because it was believed to be a sign of God's disfavor. Widowhood is called a "disgrace" (see 3.2 above). If a married man dies childless, his widow is to provide him with a posthumous son through his brother (Deut 25:5-10). This brother-in-law is called a "redeemer" (gō'ēl). Here in Isaiah 54 God will become the husband and "redeemer" (gō'ēl) of the childless widow (Is 54:5). The metaphor is not a perfect fit because the redeemer husband turns out to be the husband who had abandoned her earlier (Is 54:7). But this abandonment was "for a brief moment" (the exile), not permanent. God will now have compassion on Zion and provide her with many children (Dille 2003, 246-47).

With the return of some exiles, the prophet of Third Isaiah speaks of Zion as a mother whose sons and daughters are returning to her (Is 60:1-4). Isaiah 62 is dedicated to God's wife, Zion, who, with exile over, will be vindicated. She is described with both bridal and royal imagery. Rather than being "forsaken" and "desolate," "you shall be called My Delight Is in Her, and your land Married, for the LORD delights in you, and your land shall be married" (Is 62:4 NRSV). In the closing chapter of Isaiah Zion is not explicitly described as God's wife, but rather as a mother delivering her children. Here Zion's children will be nursed "from her consoling breast."

6.3. Personified Zion in Micah. The book of Micah describes "daughter Zion" as a warrior (Mic 4:8—5:1). She is to "writhe and groan . . . like a woman in labor," an expression typically used to describe siege or battle (see 6.4 below). But she will go forth to defeat her enemies. Micah 5:3 may describe either Zion or Bethlehem as "she who is in labor" who will have "brought forth." This birth may represent the coming of a new Davidic ruler (Mic 5:2 [so interpreted in Mt 2:6]) or the city's deliverance from the Assyrian siege.

6.4. Female Imagery for Foreign Cities. Foreign cities and *nations are not depicted in the Bible as the wife of a god, but often they are referred to as "daughters" (Jer 46:11, 24; 48:18; 49:4; 50:42; 51:33; Ezek 32:18; Zech 2:7).

Jeremiah proclaims the fall of Chaldea/Babylon "your mother" and "she who bore you." She will be put to shame. Her walls will be thrown down, and the city will become a wilderness (Jer 50:10-15; see also Jer 51:8-9). In Isaiah 47 Babylon is called "virgin daughter Babylon" and "daughter Chaldea." In this text, written from exile in Babylon, Babylon is portrayed as an aristocratic or royal woman ("noblewoman of kingdoms" [Is 47:5]). She is a woman who engages in the Babylonian "en-chantments," "sorceries" and "consultations" with astrologers (Is 47:12-13). Though confident of her position of power and privilege, she will experience humiliation as she is stripped and forced to work as a slave (Is 47:2-3). She will experience the shame of widowhood and the loss of children (in contrast to Zion in Is 54).

"Virgin daughter Egypt" cannot find healing (Jer 46:11-12). She will have to "pack [her] bags for exile" (Jer 46:19-25). Nineveh (Assyria) is personified as "drunken" (Nah 3:11). Tyre is prostituting herself with "all the kingdoms of the world" (Is 23:14-18). Sidon is a childless woman—a shameful state (Is 23:4).

A city or nation under threat, or even warrior or king, is described as being "like a woman in labor" (or a similar phrase). The phrase describes a physical reaction to great distress associated with words such as "feeble, panic, pain, anguish, sorrows, writhing, limp hands" (Is 13:8; 21:3; 26:17-18; Jer 4:31; 6:24; 22:23; 30:6; 48:41; 49:24; 50:43; Mic 4:9). The context often is that of a city undergoing a current or impending siege from which one must ultimately come forth (or bring forth) or die (see Dille 2004, 52-66).

7. Female Imagery for God.
The God of Israel transcended gender in a way uncharacteristic of the gods and goddesses of the ancient Near East. Orthodox Yahwism did not permit the god to have a feminine consort, eliminating the notion of God as a sexual male. Yet the most common metaphor for God was masculine: God as a king. Nevertheless, the rich poetry of prophetic speech provides a plethora of images for the God of Israel, including female imagery.

The prophets' metaphors and similes ranged from highly conventional (king [Is 6:1]; judge [Mic 6:2]) to unique and even strange (maggots [Hos 5:12]; dew [Hos 14:5]). In between the highly conventional and the anomalous are images such as God as a husband (see above), a potter (Is 64:8), a father (not yet conventional [Is 63:16; 64:8]) and a mother.

7.1. God as a Mother. Second Isaiah (Is 40—55) portrays God as a mother three times. In Isaiah 42:13-14 God cries out like a "man of war" and then cries out "like a woman in labor." God is like both the warrior and the laboring woman in their crying out and who courageously face imminent danger for the sake of the life of another. God's silence seems to compare the exile to the time of gestation. God's people move from darkness into light as a sort of birth into liberation from exile (Is 42:16) (like coming forth from a city after when a siege has ended?) (Dille 2004, chap. 3).

In Isaiah 45:9-10 God is compared to a potter and to a father and a birthing woman. Juxtaposing the potter with the birth parent highlights the role of God as creator, who brings into being the pottery work or the child (Dille 2004, chap. 5).

God is compared to the mother of an infant in Isaiah 49:14-15. Zion is a woman bereft of her children who accuses God of having abandoned and forgotten her. A rhetorical question follows, spoken either by Zion or by God: "Can a woman forget her nursing child, or show no compassion for the child of her womb?" Then it is clearly God who answers, "Even these may forget, yet I will not forget you." God is not only like a mother. In an odd rhetorical twist, the limitations of the metaphor of mother love is acknowledged: "even these may forget." Even mothers have been known to abandon their children, but God will never forget Zion. Isaiah 46:3 has been interpreted as mother imagery, but less persuasively (Loland 2008, chap. 7). God has carried Israel since birth. In Isaiah 66 God is like a mother to Zion and her children, saying, "As a mother comforts her child, so I will comfort you; you shall be comforted in Jerusalem" (Is 66:13 NRSV).

Hosea 11:1-4 appears also to portray God as a mother, but less clearly, since the Hebrew is ambiguous. God speaks of Israel as "my son." Then God either teaches Ephraim to walk, leads Ephraim, or nurses Ephraim. Furthermore, depending on whether one translates 'ol as "yoke" or "infant" God says, "I was . . . like those who lift infants to their cheeks" or "I was like those who ease the yoke on their jaws," continuing, "I bent down to them and fed them" (Hos 11:4). H. Schüngel-Straumann renders it, "I was for them like those who take a nursling to the breast. I bowed down to him in order to give him suck" (Schüngel-Straumann, 195-96). God is either leading Israel, a yoked animal, lifting off its yoke (a metaphor for foreign oppression), and feeding it, or God is caring for a toddler, teaching it to walk, lifting it up and feeding it. The latter reflects the society's expectations of a mother rather than a father. God adds, "I am

God and not a man [ʾîš]" (Hos 11:9), likely contrasting divine compassion with human, but arguably contrasting motherly compassion with that of a man (Schüngel-Straumann).

Other texts portray God as a parent without being explicitly father or mother, such as Isaiah 1:2: "I reared children and brought them up."

7.2. Other Female Imagery for God. Female imagery for God might also include animal imagery. Hosea 13:8 describes God's wrath toward the unfaithful as like that of a mother bear robbed of her cubs. V. Mollenkott, A. Zannoni and J. van Wijk-Bos each provide overviews of female imagery in the Bible, including *animal imagery, with brief discussion. P. Trible includes references to God's "compassion" as female imagery, noting that the Hebrew words for "compassion" (*ruḥāmâ*) and "merciful" (*raḥûm*) are related to the Hebrew word for "womb" (*reḥem*). Trible includes texts such as Hosea 2:21; Isaiah 49:15; 63:15-16; Jeremiah 31:20, the last of which she translates, "Is Ephraim my dear son my darling child? For the more I speak of him, the more I do remember him. Therefore, my womb trembles for him; I will truly show motherly-compassion upon him. Oracle of Yahweh" (Trible, 45).

8. The Woman in an Ephah Basket.
Zechariah 5:5-11 describes one of the prophet's visions of seeing "a woman in an ephah basket." She is "wickedness." Winged women will transport her in the basket to Shinar (Babylon), where they will build a house (temple) for it/her. Many scholars identify the woman as a goddess (Asherah, Anat, Astarte, Ishtar) whose worship is purged from the land (for a list of scholarly sources and proposals, see Edelman, 336-37). Other suggestions are Eve, the unclean land of Judah, the prophets' figurative prostitute, foreign women, and the Samaritans (the last proposed by E. Assis).

See also FEMINIST INTERPRETATION; MARRIAGE AND DIVORCE; PROPHECY AND SOCIETY; SOCIAL-SCIENTIFIC APPROACHES; ZION.

BIBLIOGRAPHY. **S. Ackerman**, "'And the Women Knead Dough': The Worship of the Queen of Heaven in Sixth-Century Judah," in *Gender and Difference in Ancient Israel*," ed. P. L. Day (Minneapolis: Fortress, 1989) 109-24; **S. Ackerman**, "The Queen Mother and the Cult in Ancient Israel," *JBL* 112 (1993) 385-401; **N.-E. A. Andreasen**, "The Role of the Queen

Mother in Israelite Society," *CBQ* 45 (1983) 179-94; **E. Assis,** "Zechariah's Vision of the Ephah (Zech. 5:5-11)," *VT* 60 (2010) 15-32; **Z. Ben-Barak,** "The Status and Right of the *GĔBÎRÂ*," *JBL* 110 (1991) 23-34; **P. Bird,** "'To Play the Harlot': An Inquiry into an Old Testament Metaphor," in *Gender and Difference in Ancient Israel,* ed. P. L. Day (Minneapolis: Fortress, 1986) 75-94; **J. Blenkinsopp,** "The Family in First Temple Israel," in *Families in Ancient Israel,* by L. G. Perdue et al. (FRC; Louisville: Westminster/John Knox, 1997) 48-103; **A. Brenner,** *The Israelite Woman: Social Role ad Literary Type in Biblical Narrative* (BibSem 2; Sheffield: JSOT, 1985); **C. R. Chapman,** *The Gendered Language of Warfare in the Israelite-Assyrian Encounter* (HSM 62; Winona Lake, IN: Eisenbrauns, 2004); **C. Cohen,** "The 'Widowed' City," *JANESCU* 5 (1973) 75-81; **K. P. Darr,** "Ezekiel," in *The Women's Bible Commentary,* ed. C. A. Newsom and S. H. Ringe (Louisville: Westminster/John Knox, 1992) 183-90; idem, *Isaiah's Vision and the Family of God* (LCBI; Louisville: Westminster/John Knox, 1994); **L. Day,** "Rhetoric and Domestic Violence in Ezekiel 16," *BibInt* 8 (2000) 205-30; **A. R. P. Diamond and K. O'Connor,** "Unfaithful Passions: Coding Women Coding Men in Jeremiah 2-3," *BibInt* 4 (1996) 288-310; **S. Dille,** "Honor Restored: Honor, Shame and God as Redeeming Kinsman in Second Isaiah," in *Relating to the Text: Interdisciplinary and Form-Critical Insights on the Bible,* ed. T. J. Sandoval and C. Mandolfo (JSOTSup 384; New York: T & T Clark International, 2003) 232-50; idem, *Mixing Metaphors: God as Mother and Father in Deutero-Isaiah* (JSOTSup 398; New York: T & T Clark International, 2004); **D. Edelman,** "Proving Yahweh Killed His Wife (Zechariah 5:5-11)," *BibInt* 11 (2003) 335-44; **T. Frymer-Kensky,** "Law and Philosophy: The Case of Sex in the Bible," *Semeia* 45 (1989) 89-102; **W. C. Gafney,** *Daughters of Miriam: Women Prophets in Ancient Israel* (Minneapolis: Fortress, 2008); **J. Galambush,** *Jerusalem in the Book of Ezekiel: The City as Yahweh's Wife* (SBLDS 130; Atlanta: Scholars Press, 1992); **B. Glazier-McDonald,** "Malachi," in *The Women's Bible Commentary,* ed. C. A. Newsom and S. H. Ringe (Louisville: Westminster/John Knox, 1992) 232-34; **N. K. Gottwald,** "Immanuel as the Prophet's Son," *VT* 8 (1948) 36-47; **M. I. Gruber,** "The Hebrew *QĔDĒŠÂH* and Her Canaanite and Akkadian Cognates," in *The Motherhood of God and*

Other Studies (SFSHJ 57; Atlanta: Scholars Press, 1992a) 17-48; idem, "The Motherhood of God in Second Isaiah," in *The Motherhood of God and Other Studies* (SFSHJ 57; Atlanta: Scholars Press, 1992b) 3-15; **W. L. Holladay,** *Jeremiah 1: A Commentary on the Book of the Prophet Jeremiah, Chapters 1-25,* ed. P. D. Hanson (Hermeneia; Philadelphia: Fortress, 1986); **D. Jacobson,** "Hosea? No! A Metaphor That Kills," *WW* 28 (2008a) 193, 195; idem, "Hosea? Yes! A God Who Makes Alive," *WW* 28 (2008b) 192, 194; **O. Kaiser,** *Isaiah 1-12: A Commentary,* trans. J. Bowden (OTL; Philadelphia: Westminster, 1972); **T. Kleven,** "A Single Metaphor at Amos 4:1-3," *CBQ* 58 (1996) 215-27; **H. Loland,** *Silent or Salient Gender? The Interpretation of Gendered God-Language in the Hebrew Bible, Exemplified in Isaiah 42, 46 and 49* (FAT 2/32; Tübingen: Mohr Siebeck, 2008); **B. J. Malina,** *The New Testament World: Insights from Cultural Anthropology* (Atlanta: John Knox, 1981); **J. L. Mays,** *Hosea: A Commentary* (OTL; Philadelphia: Westminster, 1969); **P. K. McCarter,** "Aspects of the Religion of the Israelite Monarchy: Biblical and Epigraphic Date," in *Ancient Israelite Religion: Essays in Honor of Frank Moore Cross,* ed. P. D. Miller Jr., P. D. Hanson and S. D. McBride (Philadelphia: Fortress, 1987) 137-55; **C. Meyers,** "The Family in Early Israel," in *Families in Ancient Israel,* by L. G. Perdue et al. (FRC; Louisville: Westminster/John Knox, 1997) 1-47; **V. R. Mollenkott,** *The Divine Feminine: The Biblical Imagery of God as Female* (New York: Crossroad, 1984); **M. S. Odell,** "An Exploratory Study of Shame and Dependence in the Bible and Selected Near Eastern Parallels," in *The Biblical Canon in Comparative Perspective,* ed. K. L. Younger Jr., W. W. Hallo and B. F. Batto (ScrCon 4; Lewiston, NY: Edwin Mellen, 1991) 217-33; **C. L. Patton,** "'Should Our Sister Be Treated Like a Whore?' A Response to Feminist Critiques of Ezekiel 23," in *The Book of Ezekiel: Theological and Anthropological Perspectives,* ed. M. S. Odell and J. T. Strong (SBLSymS 9; Atlanta: Society of Biblical Literature, 2000) 221-38; **J. J. Schmitt,** "The Wife of God in Hosea 2," *BR* 34 (1989) 5-18; **H. Schüngel-Straumann,** "God as Mother in Hosea 11," in *A Feminist Companion to the Latter Prophets,* ed. A. Brenner (FCB 8; Sheffield: Sheffield Academic, 1995) 194-218; **J. J. Scullion,** "Approach to the Understanding of Isaiah 7:10-17," *JBL* 87 (1968) 288-300; **D. T. Setel,** "Prophets and Pornography: Female Sexual Imagery in Hosea," in *Feminist*

Interpretation of the Bible, ed. L. M. Russell (Philadelphia: Westminster, 1985) 86-95; **P. Trible,** *God and the Rhetoric of Sexuality* (OBT; Philadelphia: Fortress, 1978); **K. van der Toorn,** *From Her Cradle to Her Grave: The Role of Religion in the Life of the Israelite and the Babylonian Woman,* trans. S. J. Denning-Bolle (BibSem 23; Sheffield: JSOT, 1994); **F. van Dijk-Hemmes,** "The Metaphorization of Woman in Prophetic Speech: An Analysis of Ezekiel 23," *VT* 42 (1993) 162-70; **J. W. H. van Wijk-Bos,** *Reimagining God: The Case for Scriptural Diversity* (Louisville: Westminster/John Knox, 1995); **R. J. Weems,** *Battered Love: Marriage, Sex, and Violence in the Hebrew Prophets* (OBT; Minneapolis: Fortress, 1995); **H. W. Wolff,** *Hosea: A Commentary on the Book of the Prophet Hosea,* trans. G. Stansell, ed. P. D. Hanson (Hermeneia; Philadelphia: Fortress, 1974); **A. E. Zannoni,** "Feminine Language for God in the Hebrew Scriptures," *Dialogue and Alliance* 2 (1988) 3-15. S. J. Dille

WORD OF GOD

While all Scripture is the word of God, the Prophetic Books perhaps more than any other biblical genre are God's words in that they contain the highest percentage of speech directly attributed to God himself. After discussing relevant terminology, this article examines the method of communication, the context, the mediators, the recipients and the nature of the word as both human and divine.

    1. Terminology
    2. Method of Communication
    3. Context
    4. Mediators
    5. Recipients
    6. Divine Word, Human Word

1. Terminology.

1.1. Words. God speaks to his people frequently, and the text typically uses specific words and phrases to distinguish his speech. A variety of Hebrew words are used in association with divine speech in the Prophetic Books (all occurrences below refer to the Prophetic Books exclusively). Two of the primary words used are the verb *dābar*, "to speak" (almost always in the Piel, *dibbēr*), which appears 289 times (e.g., Is 1:2; Jer 1:16; Ezek 2:1; Dan 9:6; Hos 1:2; Joel 3:8; Amos 3:1; Obad 18; Jon 3:2; Mic 4:4; Hab 2:1; Zech 1:9), and the related noun *dābār*, "word," which appears 448 times (e.g., Is 1:10; Jer 1:2;

Ezek 1:3; Dan 9:2; Hos 1:1; Joel 1:1; Amos 3:1; Jon 1:1; Mic 1:1; Hab 1:1; Zeph 1:1; Zech 1:1; Mal 1:1). The majority of these references occur in the context of divine speech, as will be seen from the discussion below of phrases.

The verb *'āmar*, "to say," is ubiquitous in the Prophetic Books, with 1,411 occurrences. While *'āmar* is also used for human speech (e.g., Is 2:3; Jer 1:6; Ezek 2:4), God is the primary subject of the verb, and it appears in contexts of divine speech in all sixteen of the Prophetic Books (Is 1:11; Jer 1:4; Ezek 2:1; Dan 8:13; Hos 1:2; Joel 2:19; Amos 1:2; Obad 1; Jon 1:1; Mic 2:3; Nah 1:12; Hab 2:2; Zeph 3:7; Hag 1:1; Zech 1:1; Mal 1:2). The two noun forms associated with this verb only appear a few times. The noun *'ēmer*, "speech, word," appears only once to clearly indicate divine speech (Is 41:26; Hab 3:9 is unclear). The noun *'imrâ*, "speech" or "word," appears three times when God speaks (Is 5:24; 28:23; 32:9) and once when Jerusalem speaks (Is 29:4).

The noun *nĕ'ūm*, "utterance, declaration," appears frequently in the Prophetic Books, a total of 355 times (e.g., Is 1:24; Jer 1:8; Ezek 5:11; Hos 2:15; Joel 2:12; Amos 2:11; Obad 4; Mic 4:6; Nah 2:13 [2:14 MT]; Zeph 1:2; Hag 1:9; Zech 1:3; Mal 1:2), with only an additional twenty references elsewhere in the OT. The related verbal root, *nā'am*, "to utter a prophecy," appears only once (Jer 23:31).

The noun *maśśā'*, "oracle," appears twenty-six times, usually to introduce a divine message (e.g., Ezek 12:10; Nah 1:1; Hab 1:1; Zech 9:1; 12:1; Mal 1:1), particularly in the book of Isaiah (e.g., Is 13:1; 14:28; 15:1; 17:1; 19:1; 21:1). Since *maśśā'* can also mean "burden," it is used in Jeremiah 23:33-38 (8x) in an apparent play on words, and English translations are divided, rendering *maśśā'* as either the "burden" (ESV, NRSV) or the "oracle" (NIV, NASB) of Yahweh.

Other words are used less frequently to introduce divine communication in the form or visions or dreams: *ḥāzôn*, "vision" (Is 1:1; Dan 8:1; Hos 12:10; Obad 1; Nah 1:1; Hab 2:2, 2 [although *ḥāzôn* is used also of false visions, as in Jer 14:14; 23:16; Ezek 12:24]); *ḥāzût*, "revelation" (Is 21:2; 29:11); *mar'â*, "vision, appearance" (e.g., Ezek 1:1; 11:24; Dan 8:16; 9:23; 10:1); *ḥălôm*, "dream" (Joel 2:28 [although *ḥălôm* is used also of false dreams, as in Jer 23:32; 27:9; Zech 10:2]); and *ḥēlem*, "dream" (e.g., Dan 2:28; 4:19; 7:1).

1.2. Phrases. Biblical Hebrew has no direct equivalent of quotation marks, so divine speech often is demarcated by a short phrase. Scholars refer to these expressions as "prophetic messenger formulas" (see Greene, 183-90; Schniedewind, 54-57, 60-62). Occasionally, these phrases are spoken explicitly by a prophet in narrative contexts (e.g., Is 37:6, 21; Jer 21:4; Amos 7:17), but in most instances the phrase is simply included in the text without reference to a prophetic mediator (e.g., Is 10:24; 22:15; Jer 2:5; 4:3; Ezek 5:5). After the phrase, the speech itself will then typically use first-person singular pronouns for God ("I," "me," "my"). These phrases take various forms.

The actual Hebrew phrase *dĕbar ʾĕlōhîm*, "word of God," appears infrequently in the OT (e.g., Judg 3:20; 1 Sam 9:27; 1 Chron 17:3; Ps 62:12) and never in the Prophetic Books. However, the closest equivalent to "word of God" is perhaps *dĕbar yhwh*, often translated as "word of the LORD," but more literally as "word of Yahweh." This phrase appears a total of 270 times in the OT, but the majority of these (160) occur in the Prophetic Books (e.g., Is 1:10; Jer 1:2; Ezek 1:3; Dan 9:2; Hos 1:1; Joel 1:1; Amos 3:1; Jon 1:1; Mic 1:1; Zeph 1:1; Hag 1:1; Zech 1:1; Mal 1:1). The phrase appears at the beginning of most of the Prophetic Books, and it is absent from only three books (Obadiah, Nahum, Habakkuk). Variations of these phrases include "the word of the Lord Yahweh" (*dĕbar ʾadōnāy yhwh* [Ezek 6:3; 25:3; 36:4]), "the word of our God" (*dĕbar ʾĕlōhênû* [Is 40:8]) and "the words of the living God" (*dibrê ʾĕlōhîm ḥayyîm* [Jer 23:36]).

The phrase used most frequently in the Prophetic Books to introduce the speech of God is "thus says Yahweh" (*koh ʾāmar yhwh*), which appears 227 times (e.g., Is 8:11; Jer 2:2; Ezek 11:5; Amos 1:3; Mic 2:3; Nah 1:12; Hag 1:5; Zech 1:3; Mal 1:4). The phrase "thus says Lord Yahweh" (*koh ʾāmar ʾadōnāy yhwh*) appears 134 times (e.g., Is 7:7; Jer 7:20; Ezek 2:4; Amos 3:11; Obad 1), the vast majority of them in Ezekiel (122x). The phrase "the word of Yahweh came to" (*wayĕhî/hāyâ dĕbar yhwh ʾel*) appears in various forms over seventy times (e.g., Is 38:4; Jer 1:2; Ezek 3:16; Dan 9:2; Jon 1:1; Hag 1:1; Zech 1:1). The phrase "Yahweh spoke" (*yhwh dibber/dabbēr*) appears fifteen times (Is 1:2, 20; 7:10; 8:5; 22:25; 24:3; 25:8; 40:5; 45:19; 58:14; Jer 13:15; Joel 3:8; Amos 3:7, 8; Obad 18).

The phrase "declares the LORD" (*nĕʾūm yhwh*) appears 257 times in the Prophetic Books. The aforementioned prophetic messenger formulas typically introduce a divine oracle, almost like an opening quotation mark. However, the phrase "declares the LORD" often interrupts (e.g., Is 14:22; Jer 1:15; Ezek 13:7) or concludes an oracle (Is 14:23; Jer 1:8; Amos 1:5; 2:16; Hag 2:9; Zech 8:17), more like a closing quotation mark.

Other words or phrases may be used less frequently to indicate divine speech; however, in many instances Yahweh is clearly speaking even though there are no markers in text to make this explicit. For example, in the book of Habakkuk, after the prophet's original complaint (Hab 1:2-4), Yahweh responds (Hab 1:5-11) without any explicit prophetic messenger formula to either open or close the speech. Textual clues make it clear that the perspective has switched from human to divine. The listener is going to be shocked by the speaker's actions (Hab 1:5), and one of those actions involves the speaker rousing the Chaldeans (Hab 1:6). The prophet's voice reemerges at the end of Yahweh's words: "Are you not of old, Yahweh my God?" (Hab 1:12). Thus, sometimes when explicit divine speech markers are absent, readers must determine from the language and the context when divine speech is being implied by the text.

2. Method of Communication.

2.1. Words. As the preceding discussion has shown, in the Prophetic Books divine communication primarily occurs through words. Yahweh speaks (*dibbēr*), he says (*ʾāmar*) things, he makes a declaration (*nĕʾūm*) or pronounces an oracle (*maśśāʾ*); he expresses himself thorough the word (*dābār*).

Although one might expect that the prophetic mediator would experience the divine word primarily by hearing, this is not the primary method of communication that the text records. The prophet will command the eventual audience to hear the word of God, but in most prophetic books, often at the very beginning the divine word "came" (*hāyâ*) to the prophet (e.g., Is 38:4; Jer 1:2; Ezek 1:3; Dan 9:2; Hos 1:1; Joel 1:1; Mic 1:1; Zeph 1:1; Hag 1:1; Zech 1:1). The phrase "the word of Yahweh came" (*wayĕhî dĕbar yhwh*) appears seventy-three times in the Prophetic Books, concentrated in Jeremiah (21x) and Ezekiel (41x). The verb used, *hāyâ*, often translated as "came," literally means "was" or "became." Since the word appears to be present in some fashion to the prophet, some scholars theorize that these expressions suggest a hypostasis of the word of God as a separate being (see Eichrodt, 2:77; Arnold and Cook, 1000). While it is difficult to argue conclusively for a hypostatization, the divine word appears to tangibly encounter the prophet in such a dramatic manner that it affects not only speech but also behavior.

2.2. Visions. Thus, the word of God comes to the prophet and will eventually be heard by the people, but the prophet also experiences divine communication visually. At the beginning of a divine message Isaiah, Amos and Micah each "saw" (*hāzâ*) the word (Is 2:1; Amos 1:1; Mic 1:1). Prophets not only see words from God; they also "see" (both *hāzâ* and *rāʾâ*) oracles (Is 13:1; Hab 1:1), visions (Is 1:1; Ezek 1:1; 8:4; 43:3; Dan 7:1; 8:2; 10:7, 8) and dreams (Dan 4:5, 9, 18; 7:1). Thus, God communicates his message with multiple senses, not only audibly but also visually (Yahweh also touched the mouths of Isaiah and Jeremiah [Is 6:7; Jer 1:9]; for a Babylonian parallel, see Weinfeld, 180-81). God was not content simply to speak to his prophets; he also wanted to show them the message.

Apart from the vision of the divine throne shown to Isaiah during his call (Is 6:1), most divine visions are clustered in the books of Jeremiah, Ezekiel, Daniel, Amos and Zechariah. Yahweh showed Jeremiah visions of an almond branch and a boiling pot (Jer 1:11-19) and a fig basket (Jer 24:1-2). Yahweh showed Ezekiel visions of a chariot (Ezek 1:4-28), temple abominations (Ezek 8:1—11:25), the valley of dry bones (Ezek 37:1-14) and the restored temple (Ezek 40:1—48:35). Yahweh showed Daniel visions of four beasts (Dan 7:1-14) and a ram and a goat (Dan 8:1-14). Yahweh showed Amos visions of locusts, fire and a plumb line (Amos 7:1-9), summer fruit (Amos 8:1-2) and Yahweh at the altar (Amos 9:1-6). Yahweh showed Zechariah eight visions, involving (1) horsemen (Zech 1:7-11), (2) horns (Zech 1:18-21), (3) a man with measuring line (Zech 2:1-4), (4) Joshua and Satan (Zech 3:1-10), (5) a lampstand and olive trees (Zech 4:1-6), (6) a flying scroll (Zech 5:1-3), (7) a woman in a basket (Zech 5:5-11) and (8) four chariots (Zech 6:1-8). The amazing creativity of Yahweh is revealed by the wide variety of people, animals and

things involved in the visions that he uses to communicate to his people.

The experience of the prophet interacts with the divine *vision, sometimes in surprising ways, to shape the eventual message from God. Amos records in first-person narrative his interaction with Yahweh concerning two visions of judgment, locusts and fire (Amos 7:1-6). With each vision, a strikingly similar process occurs. Yahweh reveals the vision, which has a dramatic effect upon Amos due to the severity of the punishment. And while elsewhere in the book Amos has no qualms about speaking in harsh terms toward the people (e.g., Amos 2:6-7; 3:12-13; 4:1), here in response to the vision he literally begs for mercy because of their weak and helpless condition. Yahweh then relents and declares that the threatened judgment will not happen.

2.3. Dreams. Visions and dreams (*hǎlôm*) often are mentioned together in the OT as a way that God speaks to his people (for a discussion of dreams and visions in prophetic texts from Mari, see Weinfeld, 185-87). However, in some texts dreams are viewed negatively because they can mislead or deceive people. In Genesis dreams are legitimate methods of divine communication, as God speaks through them to Abimelech (Gen 20:3), to Laban (Gen 31:24), to Joseph twice (Gen 37:5, 9) and to Pharaoh, his cupbearer and his baker (Gen 40:5; 41:1). Yahweh declares that he speaks to prophets through both visions and dreams, but these phenomena are contrasted to direct speech, which is what God used to communicate with Moses (Num 12:6-8). Yahweh also states that his people need to be careful to not be led astray by false prophets who perform signs or dream dreams (Deut 13:1-5).

This mixed portrayal of dreams is also seen in prophetic literature. Prophets who dream dreams are contrasted with those who faithfully speak God's word (Jer 23:27-28). God warns his people not to listen to the false prophets and their lying dreams (Jer 23:32; 27:9; 29:8; Zech 10:2). In contrast to these negative perspectives on dreams, Joel describes how God through his spirit will speak prophetically to old men through dreams and to young men through visions (Joel 2:28; cf. Acts 2:17). The most positive portrayal of divine communication by dreams in prophetic literature is seen in the book of Daniel, as Daniel, like Joseph before him (Gen 41:25-32), interprets dreams for a foreign ruler (Dan 2:27-45; 4:1-37).

When God spoke in dreams, the actual message often was obscured, so human interpreters were necessary to clarify and interpret it. In response to Nebuchadnezzar's announcement that all his wise men were to be executed when they could not recall and interpret his dream, Daniel and his three friends prayed for a divine revelation to save their lives (Dan 2:1-18). The mystery of the king's dream (a great statue signifying future empires) was then given to Daniel in a vision from God so that he could relay the hidden meaning to Nebuchadnezzar, who then promoted Daniel (Dan 2:19-48). Thus, the eventual message to the king came via a complicated interaction between God and Daniel involving a forgotten dream, a desperate prayer, a divine vision and a clarifying report.

2.4. Dialogue. While divine messages often involve long speeches, particularly in the midst of visions, there is interaction between the prophet and Yahweh (see discussion of dialogue in Jeremiah in Fretheim 2002, 6). Visions communicate part of God's message to the prophet, but Yahweh often engages in dialogue with the prophet as he reveals the vision, taking and asking questions as part of the process. The vision is thus being used by God to provoke a response or a question. After the throne vision, Yahweh asks Isaiah, "Whom shall I send?" (Is 6:8). Yahweh often interacts with the prophet to be sure that the prophet is seeing accurately. Yahweh (or his messenger) asks an identical question to Jeremiah, Amos and Zechariah: "What do you see?" (Jer 1:11, 13; 24:3; Amos 7:8; 8:2; Zech 4:2; 5:2). After the prophet's brief answer, Yahweh proceeds to explain the vision. After each of the first two visions of judgment shown to Amos, the prophet requests mercy, and Yahweh twice responds that he will relent from the threatened punishment (Amos 7:3, 6). While being shown a series of eight visions, Zechariah discusses their meaning with the divine messenger with whom he is interacting (Zech 1:9, 13; 2:3; 4:1; 5:5; 6:4-5).

The message of the book of Habakkuk centers on a divine-prophetic interaction that reveals a profoundly honest relationship between the prophet and his God. The dialogue between Habakkuk and Yahweh lacks clear speech markers, but it does not lack drama and emotion. While the book begins with the prophet seeing the vision (Hab 1:1), his initial words are complaints and questions about the violence that God made him see (Hab 1:2-4). Yahweh replies that Habakkuk will need to continue to look at violence in the form of the Chaldean army (Hab 1:5-11), which elicits more questions from the prophet about how God's righteous character is not consistent with the wickedness that he is witnessing (Hab 1:12, 13, 17). Habakkuk declares that he will watch and wait (Hab 2:1), and Yahweh answers with another vision calling for more waiting and faithfulness (Hab 2:2-5). The book concludes with the prophet's *prayer of trust and praise, responding to the divine visions and unexpected answers to his questions (Hab 3:1-19).

God's word is therefore not merely monological; it also is dialogical, interrogative and interactive. As God speaks, he questions, listens, responds and engages in dialogue.

3. Context.

When God speaks, his words usually are set within a specific historical context. Some prophetic books are undated, but most situate their message in a specific setting. Typically, the dating of the divine word's arrival was during the reign of one or more rulers, and some of the later prophets mention a specific year, month or day. This historical context usually is mentioned in the first verse or two of the book alongside a claim that the book contains a word, vision or oracle from Yahweh.

Six prophetic books begin with the formula "in the days of King(s) X" (Is 1:1; Jer 1:2; Hos 1:1; Amos 1:1; Mic 1:1; Zeph 1:1). Five books begin by mentioning a specific year (Jer 1:2-3; Ezek 1:1; Dan 1:1; Hag 1:1; Zech 1:1). Six books lack a historical marker in their introduction (Joel, Obadiah, Jonah, Nahum, Habakkuk, Malachi). Divine oracles are also dated to other specific events: the death of Uzziah (Is 6:1), the death of Ahaz (Is 14:28) or two years before the earthquake (Amos 1:1).

Only a couple of northern kings are mentioned by name (e.g., Jeroboam II [Hos 1:1; Amos 1:1], Pekah [Is 7:1]), but far more southern kings are mentioned (e.g., Uzziah [Is 1:1], Jotham [Hos 1:1], Ahaz [Mic 1:1], Hezekiah [Is 1:1], Manasseh [Jer 15:4], Josiah [Jer 1:2], Jehoiakim [Dan 1:1], Zedekiah [Jer 1:3], Jehoiachin [Ezek 1:2]). Several significant foreign rulers are also mentioned in the contexts of divine oracles: Sennacherib of Assyria (Is 37:21-29), Nebuchadnezzar of Babylon (Jer 22:25; 25:9) and Cyrus of Persia (Is 44:28; 45:1). In the Prophetic Books the word of God is a historically grounded, contextualized message.

4. Mediators.

4.1. Prophetic Involvement.
The Prophetic Books are distinct from other OT books in that they consistently mention a specific individual by name in their initial verses and somehow attribute the words contained in the book both to him and to Yahweh (Daniel's attribution appears in the middle [Dan 7:1]). Only four of the twenty-three nonprophetic books of the OT begin with a similar authorial attribution (Nehemiah, Proverbs, Ecclesiastes, Song of Songs). Less than half of the Prophetic Books actually call the eponymous individual a *nābî'* ("prophet" [Is 37:2; Jer 1:5; Ezek 2:5; Hab 1:1; Hag 1:1; Zech 1:1]), but the prophetic designation certainly is warranted because all of them somehow are involved in the communication process. Although Yahweh clearly is the primary partner in the arrangement, the prophet plays a significant role in delivering, shaping and, in some cases, enacting the divine message (see 4.2 below).

Many of the shorter Prophetic Books include no narrative or almost no background about the prophet (Joel, Obadiah, Micah, Nahum, Habakkuk, Zephaniah, Malachi), and thus the prophetic involvement in the process of communicating God's word is deemphasized. However, the majority of the Prophetic Books, all of the longer books and several of the shorter ones, include at least some narrative material (Isaiah, Jeremiah, Ezekiel, Daniel, Hosea, Amos, Jonah, Haggai, Zechariah). The narratives reveal that several of the prophets were resistant to becoming divine messengers. Isaiah and Jeremiah perceive themselves as unworthy initially (Is 6:5; Jer 1:6). Amos declares that he was not a prophet when he was called to prophesy (Amos 7:15). Jonah initially refused to go to the intended audience in Nineveh (Jon 1:3; cf. Jon 4:2). But each of them eventually succeeded on some level in mediating the message despite having to endure hardship and persecution (Jer 1:19; 20:2; Ezek 2:6; Amos 7:10-13).

The prophet who had to endure the most persecution perhaps was Jeremiah, who suffered primarily because of his role as messenger of the word of God. His message involved a word of destruction and judgment against Judah (Jer 1:10, 16), and his ministry embodied this message (see Fretheim 2002, 4-39, 187-202). He was prevented from having a wife and children (Jer 16:1-4), he was imprisoned (Jer 20:2), he was thrown into a cistern (Jer 38:6), and he performed costly acts to symbolize the message (see 4.2 below). Just as the people had rejected Yahweh, they also rejected Jeremiah as mediator of God's word. During Jeremiah's prophetic call Yahweh warned him that the people would fight against him (Jer 1:19), but when the people reject his message and try to kill him, he laments to Yahweh, complaining, questioning and calling down curses upon his enemies (Jer 11:18-20; 12:1-4). Unlike laments in the psalms, which lack a narrative context, Jeremiah's two *laments receive two divine responses (Jer 11:21-23; 12:5-17), giving these so-called confessions a dialogical tone.

4.2. Symbolic Acts.
Perhaps the most significant discomfort of being a messenger involved performing the message in symbolic acts commanded by Yahweh (*see* Sign Acts). The medium literally was the message. Yahweh told the prophet to do something strange and provocative. Either before or after the act was performed, an interpretation of the act was given to explain its significance. Isaiah named his son "The-spoil-speeds-the-prey-hastens" (*mahēr šālāl ḥāš baz* [Is 8:3]) and walked around naked for three years to signify the exile for Egypt and Cush (Is 20:1-6). Hosea married a prostitute to symbolize unfaithful Israel's relationship to Yahweh (Hos 1:2-3) and named his children "No-mercy" (*lō' ruḥāmâ*) and "Not-my-people" (*lō' 'ammî*) (Hos 1:6-9). Both Jeremiah and Ezekiel experienced a series of uncomfortable symbolic acts. The acts of Jeremiah involved a loincloth (Jer 13:1-11), a potter and clay (Jer 18:1-11), a broken pot (Jer 19:1-15), an iron yoke (Jer 27:1-22), a purchased field (Jer 32:6-44) and a stone pile (Jer 43:8-13). Ezekiel portrayed Jerusalem on a brick (Ezek 4:1-3), laid on his side for both 390 and forty days (Ezek 4:4-8), ate exilic rations (Ezek 4:9-17), shaved his head with a sword (Ezek 5:1-12), packed exilic baggage (Ezek 12:1-12), and constructed a map for the invading Babylonians (Ezek 21:18-23).

Although Yahweh's method of communicating primarily involved words, frequently it was not purely verbal, but also visual and dramatic. All of these acts were powerful visual aids signifying, through the costly behavior of the prophetic mediator, God's intended message.

5. Recipients.

In any discussion of who heard the word of God, it first must be acknowledged that except for the prophetic mediators, the text usually does not record whether the intended recipients of the divine message actually received it. With a few exceptions where a response is narrated in the text (e.g., Ahaz [Is 7:10-12], Jehoiakim [Jer 36:1-26], Amaziah the priest [Amos 7:10-11], the people of Nineveh [Jon 3:5]), the divine word comes to the prophet without the text stating that it reached its audience. Obviously, the books were deemed significant enough to record, but it is difficult to discern whether their messages were actually heard or read during the lifetime of the prophet. A variety of intended recipients for the word of God are included in the Prophetic Books, including specific individuals and groups, and more generally the people of God and foreign nations.

5.1. Individuals. The initial recipient of the word of God is, of course, the prophet, but in much of the prophetic literature the focus is not on the prophet but rather on the message. The prophet is in the background, almost absent. However, in a few instances the prophet as an individual becomes a more prominent aspect of the narrative. The book of Jonah is mainly narrative, and although Jonah's message to the people of Nineveh is the backdrop of the story, the focus of the book is the relationship between the prophet and his God, as is seen clearly in their unresolved interaction in the final chapter. Similarly, in the prophetic call narratives of Isaiah, Jeremiah, Ezekiel and Amos (Is 6:1-13; Jer 1:4-19; Ezek 2:1-3:11; Amos 7:14-15 [on call narratives, see Habel, 305-23]), Yahweh is not merely using the prophet as a mouthpiece, since he is saying something specific to the prophet himself in the communication process. For Jeremiah, Ezekiel and Amos, Yahweh wants them to know that he has specifically chosen them, but for Isaiah, Yahweh wants the prophet to volunteer for the task.

Besides prophets, the word of God often is addressed to rulers, both of Judah (e.g., Ahaz [Is 7:3-17], Hezekiah [Is 37:21], Zedekiah [Jer 21:4; 34:2], the sons of Josiah [Jer 22:11-30]) and of foreign empires (e.g., Cyrus of Persia [Is 45:1], Pharaoh [Ezek 30:22], Nebuchadnezzar

of Babylon via dreams [Dan 2; 4]). Other individuals mentioned as recipients of divine messages include Shebna, the steward (Is 22:15); Pashhur, the priest who persecuted Jeremiah (Jer 20:3-4); Shemaiah, the priest and false prophet (Jer 29:24-32); and Baruch, Jeremiah's faithful scribe (Jer 45:1-5). Occasionally, in a word to the people generally, specific individuals are mentioned (e.g., Zerubbabel and Joshua [Hag 2:21]).

5.2. The People of God. The most frequent recipients of God's messages are God's people. Often after the word of God came, the prophetic mediator was told to immediately pass it on to its intended audience: the people of Israel or Judah. Several books mention the primary audience in the initial verse: "Judah" (Is 1:1), "Israel" (Amos 1:1; Mal 1:1), the capital cities "Jerusalem" (Is 1:1; Mic 1:1) and "Samaria" (Mic 1:1). Vocative formulations for these and other locations reappear frequently throughout the Prophetic Books: "O Judah" (Jer 2:28; Hos 6:4), "O Israel" (e.g., Is 40:27; Jer 4:1; Ezek 13:4; Hos 4:15; Amos 4:12; Zeph 3:14), "O Jerusalem" (e.g., Is 40:9; 51:17; Jer 4:14; 6:8), "O Samaria" (Hos 8:5), "O Jacob" (Is 40:27; 43:1; Jer 30:10; Mic 2:12); also the slightly longer dynastic versions: "O house of Israel" (e.g., Jer 3:20; 10:1; Ezek 3:1; Hos 5:1; Amos 5:1, 4), "O house of Judah" (e.g., Zech 8:13), "O house of Jacob" (e.g., Is 2:5; 46:3; 48:1; Jer 2:4; Mic 2:7). Yahweh also speaks to his audience in language reminiscent of the covenant, often calling them "my people" (Is 3:12; 10:24; 26:20; Ezek 37:12, 13; Hos 2:1, 23; Mic 6:3, 5; cf. Ex 6:7).

As the people are being addressed, they often are called to "hear" (*šāmaʿ* in the imperative) the word of God (Is 1:2; Jer 2:4; Ezek 18:25; Hos 4:1; Joel 1:2; Amos 3:1; Mic 1:2; Hag 1:12), although sometimes they refuse to hear it (Is 28:12; Jer 5:21; Ezek 12:2; Zech 1:14; 7:11; Mal 2:2). In Hebrew, hearing someone's voice implies responding to what the speaker is saying, usually involving obedience to the speaker's commands (Jer 7:23; 11:7; Dan 9:11; Zech 6:15).

5.3. Groups. Although God's people generally are the primary audience, subsets of *Israel or Judah are specifically focused upon to receive a message. God speaks to the exiles in Babylon (Jer 29:20; Ezek 3:11) or Judeans residing in Egypt (Jer 44:26). The Rechabites are commanded to break their vows by drinking wine (Jer 35:2). Groups of leaders frequently are targeted in prophetic oracles of judgment: priests (Hos 5:1; Joel 1:13; Mal 1:6; 2:1), elders (Ezek 14:1-5; 20:1, 3; Joel 1:2), the shepherds of Israel (Jer 23:2; Ezek 34:7, 9), false prophets (Ezek 13:1-23; Mic 3:5-8). Occasionally, oracles of hope are directed to groups: the fearful-hearted (Is 35:4), faithful eunuchs (Is 56:4), the poor and those who mourn (Is 61:1-2).

5.4. The Nations. Perhaps more so than in any other OT genre, prophetic literature is concerned with *nations other than Israel and Judah. Yahweh is the God not just of Israel and Judah, but ultimately all peoples and nations. One way that this is emphasized in the Prophetic Books is the inclusion of many oracles against the nations.

Foreign powers are the exclusive focus of two short books, both of which are essentially judgment oracles. The book of Obadiah targets Judah's neighbor Edom (Obad 1), and the book of Nahum targets Nineveh, the capital of Assyria (Nah 1:1). Long sections of other prophetic books contain numerous oracles against the nations, including empires: Babylon (Is 13:1—14:23; Jer 50:1—51:64), Egypt (Is 19:1-25; Jer 46:1-28; Ezek 29:1—32:32), Nineveh (Is 14:24-27; Jon 3:4; Nah 1:1—3:19; Zeph 2:13-15.); and neighbors of Israel and Judah: Ammon (Jer 49:1-6; Ezek 25:1-7; Amos 1:13-15; Zeph 2:8-11), Arabia (Is 21:13-17; Jer 49:28-33), Cush (Is 18:1-7; Zeph 2:12), Damascus (Is 17:1-14; Jer 49:23-27; Amos 1:3-5), Elam (Jer 49:34-39), Edom (Is 21:11-12; Jer 49:7-22; Ezek 25:12-14; Amos 1:11-12), Gaza (Is 14:28-32; Jer 47:1-6; Ezek 25:15-17; Amos 1:6-8; Zeph 2:4-7), Moab (Is 15:1—16:14; Jer 48:1-47; Ezek 25:8-11; Amos 2:1-3; Zeph 2:8-11), Sidon (Ezek 28:20-26), Tyre (Is 23:1-18; Ezek 26:1—28:19; Amos 1:9-10). Although most of these oracles involve judgment on these nations and cities, in Isaiah 19 Yahweh calls Egypt "my people" and Assyria "the work of my hands" (Is 19:25). With the exception of Jonah (Jon 3:4), the texts do not record the delivery of any of these oracles to their intended audience.

In addition to references to specific countries or cities, Yahweh addresses nations more generally. The plural noun "nations" (*gôyim*) appears 104 times in the Prophetic Books, often in contexts where they are being spoke about (e.g., Is 2:2; Jer 1:10; Ezek 5:5; Joel 3:2; Amos 9:12; Obad 15; Mic 5:15; Zeph 2:11; Hag 2:7; Zech 1:15; Mal 3:12), but also in vocative formulations, "O nations" (Is 34:1; Jer 31:10; Joel 3:9).

Thus, the audience of God's word is ultimately God's world, which should be expected because Yahweh's role as creator of the earth is also frequently emphasized by the prophets.

5.5. Creation. In Genesis 1 God creates with his word, so it is not surprising to see creation themes appear as God speaks in the Prophetic Books. To get the attention of his people, God speaks zoomorphically, roaring like a lion (Jer 25:30; Hos 11:10; Amos 1:2; 3:8; Joel 3:16). God's word also impacts nature. When he roars, pastures mourn and mountains wither (Amos 1:2), and the heavens and earth shake (Joel 3:16). When the mouth of Yahweh speaks, valleys are lifted and mountains brought low (Is 40:4-5).

The primary way, however, that God engages nature in the Prophetic Books is by speaking to it directly. The book of Isaiah begins dramatically with Yahweh addressing the heavens and the earth with a call to listen to the indictment against Israel (Is 1:2). Elsewhere God speaks both to the heavens (e.g., Is 44:23; 45:8; 49:13; Jer 2:12) and to the earth (e.g., Is 49:13; Jer 6:19; Mic 1:2). God speaks to the weather, to hailstones (Ezek 13:11) and to the wind (Ezek 37:9). God speaks to geographic features, to mountains generally (Is 44:23; 49:13; Ezek 6:3; 36:1, 4, 8), as well as to mountains specifically, "O destroying mountain" (Jer 51:25), "O great mountain" (Zech 4:7); and he tells the Philistine seacoast that it will become pastureland (Zeph 2:6). God speaks to animals and plants, to cows (Amos 4:1), to horses (Jer 46:9), to cypress and oaks (Zech 11:2), and to the forest of the Negeb (Ezek 20:47). God speaks through Ezekiel even to dry bones, giving them sinew, flesh, skin and breath (Ezek 37:1-14).

Why does God speak to creation? Sometimes there is an obvious connection between the natural feature and the intended human audience. The "cows" of Bashan represent the wealthy women of Samaria (Amos 4:1), and the Philistine seacoast represents the nation of Philistia (Zeph 2:6). In other instances God speaks to heaven and earth as witnesses, since his own people are not listening or obeying (e.g., Is 1:2-4). In all of the language of creation a connection is seen between the natural world and the spiritual world. When God's people have reason to hope, heaven and earth are called in to celebrate alongside them (Is 44:23; 49:13). However, when judgment is coming, nature is affected. Heaven is meant to be appalled by Israel's *idolatry (Jer 2:11-12), and it will tremble at the fierce anger of Yahweh (Is 13:13).

6. Divine Word, Human Word.

The revelation of the word of God in the Prophetic Books is not simply a process in which Yahweh dictates the message to a prophet who then repeats it verbatim to his audience. Yahweh calls his prophets into a human-divine communication partnership that involves not merely preaching the word, but also, among other things, traveling to foreign lands (Jonah), rebuilding the temple (Haggai), confronting rulers (Isaiah, Jeremiah), interpreting visions and dreams (Jeremiah, Ezekiel, Daniel, Amos, Zechariah), and engaging in symbolic acts (Isaiah, Jeremiah, Ezekiel, Hosea).

Yahweh also allows the personalities of the prophet to shape the final message, so that the character and actions of the prophets affect the communication process. While Isaiah is a willing volunteer (Is 6:8), Jonah is rebellious (Jon 1:3; 4:2). When visions of judgment are revealed, Jeremiah apparently submits to the inevitable (Jer 1:11-19), but Amos twice convinces Yahweh to change his mind (Amos 7:1-6). Prophets frequently dialogue with Yahweh and question him about his word and his works (Is 6:11; Jer 12:1, 4; Joel 2:17; Jon 4:2; Mic 6:6-7; Hab 1:2-3, 12). Perhaps most surprisingly, these questions, divine changes and prophet rebellions are recorded and thus are part of the message of these books. The word originates with Yahweh, but he chooses to involve the prophet in the entire communication process, making it a word both divine and human.

See also DIVINATION, MAGIC; FORMATION OF THE PROPHETIC BOOKS; HERMENEUTICS; PROPHECY AND TRADITION; SIGN ACTS; VISIONS, PROPHETIC.

BIBLIOGRAPHY. **B. T. Arnold and P. Cook,** "Word of God," *DOTHB* 999-103; **W. Brueggemann,** "The Prophetic Word of God and History," *Int* 48 (1994) 239-51; **G. W. Buchanan,** "The Word of God and the Apocalyptic Vision," *SBLSP* 14 (1978) 183-92; **W. Eichrodt,** *Theology of the Old Testament* (2 vols.; OTL; Philadelphia: Westminster, 1961-1967); **T. E. Fretheim,** "Word of God," *ABD* 6:961-68; idem, *Jeremiah* (SHBC; Macon, GA: Smyth & Helwys, 2002); **R. P. Gordon,** ed., *"The Place Is Too Small for Us": The Israelite Prophets in Recent Scholarship* (SBTS 5; Winona Lake, IL: Eisenbrauns, 1995); **J. Greene,** *The Role of the Messenger and the Message in the Ancient Near East: Oral and Written Communication in the Ancient Near East; Communicators and Communiqués in Context* (BJS 169; Atlanta: Scholars Press, 1989); **N. Habel,** "The Form and Significance of the Call Narratives," *ZAW* 77 (1965) 297-323; **E. K. Holt,** "Word of Jeremiah—Word of God; Structures of Authority in the Book of Jeremiah," in *Uprooting and Planting: Essays on Jeremiah for Leslie Allen,* ed. J. Goldingay (LHBOTS 459; New York: T & T Clark, 2007) 172-89; **W. Houston,** "What Did the Prophets Think They Were Doing? Speech Acts and Prophetic Discourse in the Old Testament," *BibInt* 1 (1993) 167-88; **W. M. Schniedewind,** *Word of God in Transition: From Prophet to Exegete in the Second Temple Period* (JSOTSup 197; Sheffield: Sheffield Academic Press, 1995); **M. Weinfeld,** "Ancient Near Eastern Patterns in Prophetic Literature," *VT* 27 (1977) 178-95; **C. Westermann,** *Basic Forms of Prophetic Speech,* trans. H. C. White (Philadelphia: Westminster, 1967); idem, *Prophetic Oracles of Salvation in the Old Testament,* trans. K. Crim (Louisville: Westminster/John Knox, 1991); **J. Y. H. Yieh,** "The Use of the Word of God in Second Isaiah: An Investigation of Its Social Functions," *Taiwan Journal of Theology* 10 (1988) 233-53.

D. T. Lamb

WORSHIP

True worship involves reverential acts of submission before the divine Sovereign in response to his gracious revelation of himself and in accordance with his will. Many today perceive OT worship as involving primarily external liturgical acts, in contrast to NT worship, which is perceived as internal and spiritual (cf. Rom 12:1). As we will see, in ancient Israel many did indeed treat worship as cultic acts by which divine favor was won/guaranteed, irrespective of the internal condition of the heart or the conduct of one's life. However, this was precisely the kind of notion the prophets sought to combat. Based on the Torah, particularly the full-bodied worship for which Moses appealed in his valedictory addresses in Deuteronomy, the prophets sought to restore the worship "in spirit and in truth" by reminding the people of Yahweh's grace in rescuing them from the bondage of Egypt and calling them back to the *covenant that Yahweh had established with them. This article tries to recapture the prophetic vision of worship.

1. The Dimensions of True Worship
2. The Nature of True Worship

1. The Dimensions of True Worship.

The multifaceted nature of true Israelite worship is reflected in the rich prophetic vocabulary of worship. Words referring to the notion may be grouped into three broad categories: dispositional, gestural and cultic expressions.

1.1. Dispositional Expressions of Worship.

The fundamental importance of "fear" as a part of acceptable worship is reflected in Deuteronomy 10:12-13: "And now, O Israel, what does Yahweh your God ask of you? Simply this: to fear Yahweh your God; to walk in all his ways; to love him, to serve Yahweh your God with all your heart and with all your being, and to keep the commands and ordinances of Yahweh that I am commanding you today for your own good."

The primary word for "to fear" in the OT is *yārē*'. This word is used in two senses, depending on the nature of the relationship between the parties. In many contexts it speaks of terror or fright in the face of the unknown, whether enemy armies, animals, death and even Yahweh (Jer 5:22; Mic 7:17). The frequent association of this word with others in this semantic field reflects the fearful realities of life in the ancient Near East: *šata'*, "to be dismayed" (Is 41:10, 23); *ḥtt*, Piel, "to be dismayed" (Jer 23:4; 30:10; Ezek 2:6; 3:9); *ḥārad*, "to tremble" (Is 41:5); *'āraṣ*, "to tremble" (Is 2:19, 21; 8:12; 47:12); *ḥûl/ḥîl*, "to writhe in anguish/pain" (Jer 5:22; Zech 9:5); *pāḥad*, "to tremble" (Mic 7:17). The common formula, *'al/lō' tîrā'* ("fear not") spoken by humans or God was intended to reassure frightened persons (e.g., Is 37:6; 40:9). However, where the relationship between the parties was positive, the word *yārē'* also expressed a socially inferior person's reverence, respect and honor toward a superior. Those in covenant relationship to Yahweh need not be frightened in his presence, but this is not a license to be casual. The word *yārē'* expresses appropriate awe of a human subject before the radiance of the divine majesty. Indeed, in a book such as Deuteronomy, where words for "faith" and "believe" are rare (cf. *he'ĕmîn* in Deut 1:32), *yārē'* may be defined as "awed trust" or "trusting/confident awe."

However, reverent awe is not the only disposition associated with worship. Deuteronomy places a great deal of emphasis on love (*'āhab*) for Yahweh as a fundamental attitude (e.g., Deut 6:5; 10:12). Fundamentally, the word expresses covenant commitment demonstrated in actions in the covenant partner's interest. Remarkably, the notion of devotees "loving" their gods surfaces only twice in the prophets, and both in ironically reversed roles. Isaiah 56:6 speaks of foreigners attaching (*nilwâ*) themselves to Yahweh, ministering (*šērēt*) to him, loving (*'āhab*) his name, accepting their status as his servants (*'ăbādîm*), observing the Sabbath, and hanging on tightly (*heḥĕzîq*) to the covenant. Conversely, in Jeremiah 8:2 the prophet accuses Yahweh's own people of demonstrating their love (*'āhab*) for the sun, the moon and all the hosts of heaven by serving (*'ābad*), following after (*hālak 'aḥărê*), inquiring of (*dāraš*) and prostrating (*hištaḥăwâ*) themselves before them.

If true worship is a response to Yahweh's revelation of himself, then, in addition to "fear" and "love," it requires a disposition of trust and belief in him. This is expressed primarily in two words. The word group based on the root *'mn* speaks fundamentally of "confidence, belief," not only in the reality and faithful character of Yahweh, but also in his revelation of himself and his covenantal fidelity to his people (Is 43:10; 49:7; 53:1[?]; Hos 2:20), in contrast to the perfidy of people (Jer 12:6; Mic 7:5). Such confidence to worship is demonstrated dramatically in Jonah 3:5: when the Ninevites heard the divine word that the city would be destroyed in forty days, they believed (*he'ĕmîn*) God, proclaimed a fast and donned sackcloth, to which Yahweh responded by withdrawing his threat (Jon 3:10). The second expression, *bāṭaḥ* ("to have confidence, to be secure") is often used of trust in fortifications, armies or alliances (Is 31:1; 36:4-9; Jer 5:17; 46:25), or of living in secure and peaceful circumstances (*lābeṭaḥ*). This may be the result of divine action (Jer 23:6; Ezek 28:26; 34:25-28; Hos 2:18; cf. Is 33:6) or be the reward for righteousness (Is 32:17), but it may also simply express smugness in one's circumstances (Is 32:9-11; 47:8; Jer 49:31; Amos 6:1; Zeph 2:15). Not surprisingly, the word is also used of trusting in Yahweh for one's security in the face of external threats (Is 12:2; 36:15; 37:10; Jer 39:18; as a synonym of *šā'an*, Niphal, Is 50:10; cf. 10:20; Mic 3:11). However, like *ʾmn*, it is also used of trusting in people's words (Is 59:4; Jer 7:4; 9:4; 13:25; 28:15; 29:31; Mic 7:5), which seals its relevance for the present discussion. False worship involves turning away from Yahweh and trusting in oneself or other people (Jer 17:5-8; Ezek 16:15; 33:13) or idols, which are one's own creation (Is 42:17; Hab 2:18), or even the temple as a symbol of divine presence instead of the divine resident himself (Jer 7:4, 14). Elsewhere, trusting (*bāṭaḥ*) in the name of Yahweh and relying on God are associated with fearing (*yārēʾ*) Yahweh and listening to his voice (Is 50:10), as well as drawing near to God (Zeph 3:2).

1.2. Gestural Expressions of Worship. Any discussion of the gestures of worship in Scripture must begin with the Hebrew word *hištaḥăwâ* (usually rendered in Greek as *proskyneō*). Though traditionally explained as a Hithpael form of *šāḥâ* ("to bow down, to prostrate oneself" [BDB 1005) or *šûaḥ* ("to sink down" [BDB 1001]), in the light of fourteenth/thirteenth-century BC evidence from Ras Shamra/Ugarit, it has been convincingly argued that the word involves a rare Hishtaphel form from a root, *ḥyh/ḥwh*, which links it with the verb "to live." Apparently, the expression refers fundamentally to a gesture (prostration to the ground) by subjects toward superiors by which they declare nonverbally something like "Long live the king" (see Kreuzer; Fretheim). The gesture is also expressed as "falling on one's face" (*nāpal ʿal pānîm* [Ezek 1:28; 3:23; 9:8; 11:13; 43:3], "bowing" (*kāpap* [Is 58:5; Mic 6:6]) or "bending" (*kāraʿ*) the knee (Is 45:23; cf. Ps 95:6), or "prostrating oneself before" an image (*sāgad* [Is 44:15, 17, 19; 46:6]; elsewhere only in the Aramaic portions of Daniel [Dan 2:26; 11x in Dan 3]). Isaiah 49:23 illustrates the nature of the gesture dramatically: "With their faces to the ground they shall bow down (*hištaḥăwâ*) to you, and lick the dust of your feet."

Although *hištaḥăwâ* is usually translated as "to worship," this may be misleading, especially if we assume that "worship" always involves recognition of the superior as deity. In ancient Israel it was customary for people in a relatively lower class to prostrate themselves before other human beings as a gesture of honor and recognition of the latter's higher social standing—for example, Abraham before the people of the land (Gen 23:7, 12), Joseph's brothers before Joseph (Gen 42:6; 43:26, 28), Ruth before Boaz

(Ruth 2:10), David before Jonathan (1 Sam 20:41). Such physical gestures of homage were especially important in royal courts (2 Sam 14:4, 22, 33; 15:5; 16:4). However, our primary concern is sacred/religious prostration. The verb *hištaḥăwâ* often occurs with *ʿābad* ("to serve") in denunciations of apostate and heterodox gestures of homage (Jer 1:16; 8:2; 13:10; 16:11; 22:9), though often it does refer to the proper worship of Yahweh as well (Is 27:13; 66:23; Ezek 46:2-3, 9; Zech 14:16-17).

Of course, prostration is not the only gesture by which people express homage to God. Worship often involves physical postures (lying, sitting, standing) as well as actions performed with the hands (clapping, raising of hands) or the feet (marching in procession, dancing, jumping [for joy]), and so forth. However, these generally are linked to specific kinds of worship (prayer, praise, lament, etc.).

1.3. Ethical Expressions of Worship. As noted above, the verb *hištaḥăwâ* often occurs with *ʿābad* ("to serve"), especially in denunciations of apostate and heterodox gestures of homage. Hebrew *ʿābad* may function as the most general expression for cultic service—Isaiah 19:21 speaks of serving with *sacrifices, offerings and vows (cf. Is 43:23)—but it should not be restricted to actions that in pagan contexts involved the care and feeding of gods to "smooth their faces" (*ḥillâ pānîm* [cf. Jer 26:19; Zech 7:2; 8:21-22; Mal 1:9]) or secure their favor. Fundamentally, *ʿābad* means to work for the agenda and interests of another, usually a superior. With respect to deity, this could involve cultic service, fulfilling a special mission assigned by the divine superior, or simply living in a way that is pleasing to and in accordance with his will. At Sinai, Yahweh formalized the status of those who formerly were slaves (*ʿăbādîm*) to the Egyptians as his vassal (*ʿebed*), and he officially inducted the covenant people into his divine service. In accordance with this role and mission, all citizens were to demonstrate their covenant commitment ("love"), "fear" and subjection to Yahweh by serving him, walking in his ways, and obeying all his commandments (Deut 10:12—11:1). Isaiah 56:6 speaks of foreigners among the ranks of "his servants": they join themselves to Yahweh and minister (*šērēt*) to him, love his name, keep the Sabbath, and hold fast to his covenant. True worship involves all of life dedicated to the service of Yahweh. As we will see, this demands a full-bodied ethical commitment, not only to serving Yahweh, but also to securing the well-being of others, especially the marginalized through righteous conduct as specified in the covenant. This would involve walking in Yahweh's Torah and his ordinances (Jer 44:10) (*see* Law), in his paths (Is 2:3; Jer 6:16) and in his way (Is 30:21; 35:8; Jer 6:16; 7:23); swearing "in truth, justice and righteousness (Jer 4:2); in general obeying Yahweh's voice (Jer 7:3; Hag 1:12); and heeding his commands (Is 48:18). This is worship at its most fundamental and practical level.

Many in the OT bore the title *"servant of Yahweh" (*ʿebed yhwh*). This epithet does not express a menial role; rather, it declares the subjects' privileged and elevated status. Like officials in the courts of kings (*ʿebed hammelek*), servants of Yahweh are called to mission, and their fulfillment of that mission represents their service of worship. Although Israel as a people are portrayed as Yahweh's servants (Is 41:8-9; 44:1-2, 21; 45:4; Jer 30:10; 46:27-28), commissioned to be his light to the nations (Is 42:6; 49:6), this role was also assigned to special classes: prophets (Jer 7:25; 25:4; 26:5; 29:19; 35:15; 44:4; Ezek 38:17; Amos 3:7; Zech 1:6; cf. Dan 9:6, 10), Davidic kings (Is 37:35; Jer 33:21-22; 33:26; Ezek 34:23-24; 37:24-25), the individual servant in Isaiah's "Servant Songs" (whom I take to be a Davidic figure [Is 42:1-4; 49:1-7; 50:4-9; 52:13—53:12]) and even the foreign king Nebuchadnezzar (Jer 25:9; 27:6; 43:10). For Yahweh's servants, worshipful responsibility involved discharging faithfully the duties that he assigned them.

1.4. Liturgical Expressions of Worship. The most important Hebrew expression for liturgical performance is *šērēt* ("to minister, to serve"), whose significance is captured in the LXX preferred rendering, *leitourgeō*, from which we get "liturgy." Like *ʿābad* ("to serve"), fundamentally the verb has to do with service rendered to a superior by a person of lower rank, often as a personal attendant, and may apply directly to "ministry to God." Isaiah 56:6; 61:6 anticipate something like the priesthood of all believers, looking forward to a day when foreigners and lay people will be "priests of Yahweh" (*kōhănê yhwh*) and "ministers of our God" (*měšārĕtê ʾĕlōhênû*). However, of the ninety-seven occurrences of the verb (always in Piel stem), in more than half it functions as a

technical term for cultic service involving particularly the sanctuary (Ezek 42:14; 44:11-19, 27; 45:4-5), the altar (Ezek 44:11, 16; Joel 1:9, 13) and cultic instruments and furniture (Jer 52:18), as well as service as temple guards (Ezek 44:11). From elsewhere we learn that this service also involved music (1 Chron 6:17), the handling of the ark of the covenant (1 Chron 16:4, 37), making petitions, giving thanks, and praising Yahweh (1 Chron 16:4; cf. 2 Chron 5:13-14).

While the noun *kōhēn* ("priest") occurs dozens of times in the prophets, the verb *kihēn* ("to serve, act as priest") occurs only twice. Fundamentally, the root involves mediation between the divine and mundane spheres, but the usage of the verb is more restricted than *ʿābad* and *šērēt*; most references are associated with the office and service of the priest, including his ordination to priestly service (Davies, 86-100). Ezekiel 44:13 uses the expression in the narrow sense of official performance of cultic rituals, in this instance reserved for the sons of Zadok and excluding the Levitical priests. Hosea 4:6 alludes to the priestly task of teaching the Torah of God, a function that is treated in greater detail in Malachi 2:1-9.

Several additional expressions have liturgical implications. Variations of the phrase "to stand before Yahweh" (*ʿāmad lipnê yhwh*) or "to stand in the council of Yahweh" are used of prophets (Jer 15:1; 23:18, 22; cf. Jer 18:20) and Rechabites (Jer 35:19) and in legal contexts (Jer 7:10), although it is also applied to priests and Levites (Zech 3:1; cf. Deut 10:8; 18:7; 1 Kings 8:11; Ps 134:1; 135:2). This idiom derives from the royal court. A person who "stands before the king" is one who has been specially authorized by the king to enter his presence and serve as his courtier (Dan 1:4). To be privy to decisions made in the divine council and to be engaged in this kind of service represent the highest honors imaginable. The expression "to walk before Yahweh" (*hithallēk/hālak lipnê*), also speaks of access to the divine court and being commissioned for official service on Yahweh's behalf. In the prophets this idiom is used only of King Hezekiah (Is 38:3), though elsewhere it is used of other kings (David [1 Kings 3:6; 8:25; 9:4]; Solomon [1 Kings 9:4]) and of Abraham (Gen 17:1; 24:40; 48:15), as well as priests (1 Sam 2:30). The meaning of this expression differs significantly from "to walk with Yahweh" (*hithallēk ʾet*), which expresses general piety (Mic 6:8; Mal 2:6). Finally, we note the idiom "to follow/walk after [a god]" (*hālak ʾaḥărê*), which in the prophets usually bears a negative sense of following illegitimate deities, as illustrated by Jeremiah 8:2: "And they will spread them [the bones of the people of Jerusalem] out to the sun, the moon, and to all the host of heaven, which they have loved, and which they have served, and which they have gone after [*hālēkû ʾaḥărêhem*], and which they have sought, and to which they have prostrated themselves."

In pagan contexts the idiom might have been interpreted literally, reflecting the practice of following images/statues of deities in religious procession. However, in the Hebrew Scriptures the idiom has a pronounced ethical flavor. Texts that speak of "walking after Yahweh" are absent in the prophets, but the correlative expressions in Deuteronomy 13:3-4 flesh out its meaning: "For Yahweh your God is testing you, to know whether you *love* Yahweh your God with all your heart and with all your being. You shall *walk after Yahweh* your God and *fear* him and *keep his commandments* and *listen to his voice*, and you shall *serve* him and *hold fast* to him."

Beyond these general expressions, the prophets speak of the full range of specific liturgical elements of worship, both private and corporate: prayer (noun *tepillâ* [Is 1:15; 37:4; 56:7; Jon 2:8; Hab 3:1]; verb *hitpallēl* [Is 16:12; Jer 29:7]), singing (*zimmēr* [Is 12:5]; *šîr* [Is 26:1; 30:29; 42:10; Jer 20:13; Amos 5:23; 8:10]), lamentation (*qînâ* [Jer 9:20; Ezek 32:16; Amos 8:10]; *ṣûm* [Is 58:3-5; Jer 14:12; 36:6, 9; Joel 1:14; 2:12, 15; Jon 3:5; Zech 7:5; 8:19]), sacrifices and offerings of all sorts (Is 1:11; 19:21), vows (*neder* [Is 19:21; Jon 1:16; Mal 1:14]), festivals (*môʿădîm* [Is 33:20; Ezek 36:38; Hos 2:11; Zech 8:19]), pilgrimages (*ḥag* [Is 30:29; Ezek 45:17; 46:11; Hos 2:11; 9:5; Amos 5:21; Nah 1:15; Zech 14:16-19]), reading the word of Yahweh (Jer 36:6, 13-16) and teaching Torah (Mal 2:6-8).

2. The Nature of True Worship.

Considering the vocabulary used by prophets in connection with worship sets the stage for a closer examination of their disposition toward worship as it was practiced in Israel and as it should have been practiced.

2.1. The Prophetic Disposition Toward Contemporary Worship. As the histories of the northern kingdom of Israel and the southern kingdom of Judah approached their ends in 722 BC and 586 BC, respectively, Yahweh sent his servants the prophets to warn the people of the coming judgment, to denounce them for their rebellious ways, and to call them back to covenant relationship with himself. Based on the evidence of the Prophetic Books, an underlying cause of both nations' demise was the false worship in which the people were engaged. Their worship demanded judgment for two reasons: their spiritual loyalties were divided, and their worship was hypocritical (Ross, 329-39). The biblical records suggest that the former problem was resolved by the exile, but the latter persisted even in the new commonwealth of returned exiles in the sixth-fifth centuries BC.

2.1.1. Worship Directed to the Wrong Deities. The magnitude of this problem in Israel and Judah's waning years is reflected in the broad distribution of rebukes in the Prophetic Books. The number and variety of largely pejorative expressions for these foolish objects of worship reflects the prophets' disposition toward idolatry. *Idols are "the work of human hands" (*maʿăśēh yĕdê ʾādām* [Is 2:8; 37:19; Jer 1:16; 10:3, 9; 25:6-7; 44:8; Hos 14:4; Mic 5:12]), "image" (*ṣelem* [Ezek 7:20; Amos 5:26]), "sculpture" (*pesel* [Is 40:19-20; 42:17; 44:9-17; 45:20; 48:5; Jer 10:14; 51:17; Hab 2:18]; *semel* [Ezek 8:3, 5]; *maśkît* [Ezek 8:12]), "construction, replica" (*tabnît* [Is 44:13; Ezek 8:10]), "molten image" (*nesek* [Is 40:19; 41:29; 44:10; 48:5; Jer 10:14; 51:17]; *māsekâ* [Is 25:7; 30:22; 42:17; Hos 13:2; Nah 1:14; Hab 2:18]), "effigies" (*ʿăṣabbîm* [Is 10:11; 46:1; 48:5; Jer 44:19; 50:2; Hos 4:17; 8:4; 13:2; 14:9; Mic 1:7; Zech 13:2]), "teraphim" (*tĕrāpîm* Ezek 21:21; Hos 3:4; Zech 10:2]), "nonentities, nothings" (*ʾĕlîlîm* [Is 2:8, 18, 20; 10:10, 11; 19:1, 3; 31:7; Hab 2:18]), "nothingness, illusions" (*ʾāwen* [Is 41:29; 66:3; Hos 10:8]), "empty trivialities" (*habĕlê šāwʾ* [Jon 2:9; cf. Jer 18:15]), "vanity" (*hebel* [Jer 2:5; 8:19; 10:8, 15; 14:22, 51:18; Jon 2:9]), "lies" (*kĕzābîm* [Amos 2:4]), "illusions, tricks, lies" (*šeqer* [Is 44:20; Jer 10:14; 16:19; 51:17]), "frightful images" (*ʾêmâ* [Jer 50:38]), "dung pellets" (*gillûlîm* [Jer 50:2; 36x in Ezek 6:4—44:12]), "abhorrent objects" (*šiqquṣîm* [Is 66:3; Jer 4:1; 7:30; 13:27; 16:18; 32:34; Ezek 5:11; 7:20; 11:18, 21; 20:7-8, 30; 37:23]), "abomination" (*tôʿēbâ* [Is 44:19; cf. the worship of foreign gods in Deut 13:14; 17:4]). Jeremiah in particular expresses the heterodox nature of such worship by referring to these objects as "other gods" (*ʾĕlōhîm ʾăḥērîm* [Jer 1:16; 7:18; 19:4, 13; 22:9; 32:29; 44:3, 5, 8, 15]). The worship of other gods was not a problem among other peoples, where gods were perceived to be tolerant of their devotees worshiping other gods (Block 2004). However, with Israel's Yahwistic monotheism (Is 45:5-6, 14, 18, 21-22; 46:9), far from serving the interest of the worshiper, Israelites who worshiped other gods only provoked Yahweh to anger (Jer 7:18; 25:6-7; 32:29-30, 32; 44:8; Ezek 8:17; 16:26), resulting in their own in harm (*raʿ* [Jer 7:6; 25:5-6]).

Hosea paints a picture of pervasive and persistent idolatry in the northern kingdom in the eighth century BC. Israel's going after other gods, specifically using the gifts Yahweh had given her to win the favor of Baal, is portrayed as harlotry. She has abandoned Yahweh her husband in favor of another lover (Hos 2:1-13; 3:3; 4:7-19; 5:3-4; 6:10; 9:1). Isaiah describes a similar situation in Judah at the end of the eighth century BC. With keen insight into the manufacture of idols (see Walker and Dick) and with scathing irony he exposes the folly of pagan worship (Is 44:9-20; 45:16). Despite Josiah's efforts at reform, a century later idolatry persisted; according to Jeremiah, the people had abandoned Yahweh, the fountain of living waters, for cracked cisterns that hold no water (Jer 2:13; 17:13). Picking up Hosea's metaphor of spiritual whoredom, Jeremiah denounces Judah's shameless pursuit of idols (Jer 2:20-25; 3:1-25). Her determination and passion are reflected in the summary statement of Jeremiah 8:2: they "love" (*ʾāhab*), "serve" (*ʿābad*), "follow after" (*hālak ʾaḥārê*), "seek out" (*dāraš*) and "bow down" (*hištaḥăwâ*) in submission and homage before them. Although Micah (Mic 6:7) alludes to child sacrifices, Jeremiah and his contemporary Ezekiel are the first writing prophets to deal with the issue explicitly (Jer 7:31; 19:5; 32:35; Ezek 16:20-21; 20:26; 23:37-39). Whereas in pagan thinking the offering of one's child as a sacrifice to deity was the ultimate expression of piety, in Yahwism this act was the supreme abomination, guaranteed to provoke Yahweh's ire.

Although Ezekiel offers his most forceful denunciation of Judean spiritual infidelity in Ezekiel 16, in Ezekiel 8 he provides the most graphic picture of idolatry as it was practiced in Jerusalem at the beginning of the sixth century BC. Although the visionary nature of his prophetic experience raises questions whether or not we should interpret what he portrays here literally, its rhetorical force depends upon some correspondence with reality. Shockingly, the abominations described are perpetrated by the leaders of the community within the compound of Yahweh's temple. In his visionary tour of the temple Ezekiel recounts four scenes. The first (Ezek 8:3b-6) involves an "idol of passion." The expression "sculpture of the passion" (*sēmel haqqinʾâ* [Ezek 8:5]) reflects Yahweh's disposition toward Israel's worship of other deities. As Israel's husband and covenant lord, his passion is ignited by interference from any gods that might compete for his place in Israel's life. The second (Ezek 8:7-12) involves seventy elders inside a dark room within the sacred temple compound, burning incense to seventy different gods, depicted in creaturely form. They rationalize/justify their worship by complaining of Yahweh's absence and ignorance of their lot/actions. The third (Ezek 8:14) involves women at the north gate of the temple weeping "the Tammuz," perhaps lamenting the death of Yahweh (Block 1997, 295). The fourth (Exek 8:16-17) involves twenty-five men at the doorway of the temple, with their backs to the divine presence and prostrating themselves in submission and homage to the sun. Of course, these actions have no effect on the deities that they are worshiping—after all, they are mere wood and stone, the work of human hands—but they do affect Yahweh, whom they imagine to be absent and blind to their perverse worship (Ezek 8:12). Habakkuk 2:18-19 summarizes well the folly and futility of worship directed to the wrong deities: "What is the use of an idol once its maker has carved it, or a metal image, a teacher of lies? For its maker trusts in his own creation when he makes idols that cannot speak! Woe to him who says to an object of wood, 'Wake up!' Or to a dumb stone, 'Get up!' And this is a teacher? Look! It is plated with gold and silver, and there is no breath at all inside it" (my translation).

2.1.2. Worship of Yahweh Wrongfully Practiced. For all the attention the prophets devote to Israel and Judah's worship of other gods, they actually spend more time denouncing them for the ways in which they worship their own God, Yahweh. The problem seems not to have been the manner in which they performed their rituals, but rather the contradiction between their liturgical practice and their personal lives. They apparently forgot that true worship involves all of life, and that one's everyday ethical conduct determines whether or not one's cultic worship is acceptable to Yahweh. Speaking for Yahweh, Amos gives classic expression to the problem in the northern kingdom in the eighth century BC: "I hate, I reject your festivals, and I take no delight in your solemn assemblies. Even though you offer me your burnt offerings and grain offerings, I will not accept them; and the offerings of well-being of your fatted animals I will not look upon. Remove from me the noise of your songs; I will not listen to the music of your harps. But let justice roll down like waters, and righteousness like an ever-flowing stream" (Amos 5:21-24 [my translation]). This accords with Hosea's assessment regarding both Ephraim and Judah: "Your loyalty [*hesed*] is like morning fog, and like dew it quickly disappears. . . . I desire loyalty [*hesed*], not sacrifice; the knowledge of God, rather than burnt offerings" (Hos 6:4, 6).

Earlier, Yahweh had summarized his case against Israel: fidelity (*ʾĕmet*), loyalty (*hesed*) and the knowledge of God have been replaced by false swearing, dishonesty, murder, theft and adultery; indeed, crime follows upon crime (Hos 4:1b-2). According to Hosea 6:7-11, even the priests were involved in criminal plots. Because of their infidelity, in 722 BC the northern kingdom was destroyed by the Assyrians.

However, hypocritical worship continued in Judah. Isaiah summarizes the problem: "This people draw near with their mouth and they honor me with their lips, but their worship of me is a human commandment learned by rote" (Is 29:13). How this was done is reflected in the scathing indictment that opens the book. Judah is weighed down with sin (*ḥtʾ*), perversion (*ʿāwōn*), evil (*raʿ*) and corruption (*mašḥît*); they have rebelled (*pāšaʿ*) against Yahweh their gracious divine, abandoned (*ʿāzab*) him, treated the Holy One of Israel with contempt (*niʾēṣ*) and turned (*nāzōr*) from him (Is 1:2-4). Since the nation is rotten to the core—like Sodom and Gomorrah (Is 1:5-9)—it is no wonder that Yahweh rejected their cultic charades: "'What use is the multitude of your sacrifices to me?' says Yahweh. 'I have had enough of burnt offerings of rams and the fat of well-fed beasts; I find no pleasure in the blood of bulls, or lambs, or

goats. When you come to appear before me, who asked this of you, this trampling of my courts? Stop bringing futile offerings; incense is an abomination to me. New moon and Sabbath and the calling of assemblies—I cannot stand solemn assemblies with iniquity. Your new moons and your appointed festivals I hate deeply; they have become a burden to me, I can tolerate them no more. When you stretch out your hands, I will hide my eyes from you; even though you multiply your prayers, I will not listen; your hands are full of blood'" (Is 1:11-15 [my translation]). Reminiscent of Psalms 15; 24, Isaiah goes on to describe the prerequisites to acceptable cultic worship: "Wash yourselves; make yourselves clean; remove the evil of your actions from before my eyes; cease to do evil, learn to do good; seek justice, rescue the oppressed, defend the orphan, plead for the widow" (Is 1:16-17).

True and acceptable worship presupposes undivided covenant commitment to Yahweh, as well as covenant commitment to fellow human beings, demonstrated in actions that seek their welfare. When cultic performance is matched by ethical righteousness, Yahweh promises *forgiveness and well-being, but if it is not, the prospect is rejection and judgment by Yahweh (Is 1:18-20).

Isaiah's rural compatriot Micah advocated precisely the same approach: "With what shall I come before Yahweh, and bow myself before God on high? Shall I come before him with burnt offerings, with yearling calves? Will Yahweh take pleasure in thousands of rams, with ten thousands of rivers of oil? Shall I offer my firstborn for my rebellion, the fruit of my body for the sin of my soul? He has declared to you, O human, what is good, and what Yahweh requires of you: doing justice, and loving kindness, and walking humbly with your God" (Mic 6:6-8 [my translation]).

Although Judah survived another century after Isaiah and Micah, the religious situation in Jerusalem remained largely unchanged; if anything, the hypocrisy intensified. In his renowned Temple Sermon (Jer 7:1—8:3), Jeremiah concentrated on the issue of false worship of Yahweh. Taking a position at the gate of the temple, the place of worship par excellence, the prophet reflected deep immersion in the fundamental theology of worship deriving from Israel's knowledge of God, their privilege of *covenant relationship, and the Mosaic exposition of the same in the Torah of Deuteronomy. Mincing no words, he addressed the people's hypocrisy with three critical interrelated points. First, responding to the people's trust in the presence of the temple itself as a guarantee of their security, Jeremiah declared that the physical symbol of divine presence is no substitute for ethical conduct that serves the interest of others and reflects undivided devotion to Yahweh (Jer 7:3-7). Second, with their criminal conduct and their spiritual infidelity, the presence of these worshipers in the temple transforms the building from a sacred residence of Yahweh into a den of robbers (Jer 7:8-11). Third, the ceremonial performance of rituals is no substitute for a life of worship, everyday acts of submission and homage to the divine Sovereign in response to his revelation of himself and in accordance with his will (Jer 7:21-26).

On the surface, Jeremiah's statement concerning sacrifices is shocking: "Thus says the LORD of hosts, the God of Israel: Add your burnt offerings to your sacrifices, and eat the flesh. For in the day that I brought your ancestors out of the land of Egypt, I did not speak to them or command them concerning burnt offerings and sacrifices. But this command I gave them, 'Obey my voice, and I will be your God, and you shall be my people; and walk only in the way that I command you, so that it may be well with you'" (Jer 7:21-23 NRSV). Following J. Wellhausen (see Wellhausen 122-32, 166-76), for a century many have used statements like this to drive a wedge between the perspective of Exodus and Leviticus and that of the prophets. Supposedly, the prophetic emphasis on religion expressed in ethical conduct represents a higher view of religion than cultic expressions. However, it is generally recognized now that this is a false dichotomy. On the one hand, the prophetic statements should be interpreted as hyperbolic rhetoric, attempting to restore balance to the people's views on worship, rather than categorical rejections of cultic worship. On the other hand, the prescriptive pentateuchal texts such as the Book of the Covenant (Ex 20:22—23:19) and the Holiness Code (Lev 17—26) integrate appeals for cultic service with ethical obedience. If anything, Moses' vision of worship in Deuteronomy highlights the ethical dimensions of worship but then frames these exhortations with appeals for proper wor-

ship (Deut 12:1-14; 26:1-15). True worship in response to Yahweh's revelation of himself and in accordance with his will involves both viewing all of life as worship and setting aside special places, times and rituals for the expression of devotion to Yahweh.

The *exile of Israel and Judah represented punishment for their infidelity—their worship of other gods and their failure to match life with cultic performance. The biblical evidence suggests that the first problem was largely resolved by the experience. In postexilic texts references to pagan deities are rare, occurring only in Zechariah 10:2 (*těrāpîm*, "teraphim"); 13:2 (*'ăṣabbîm*, "effigies"). However, problems in the worship of Yahweh resurface. In Haggai, situated within decades of the Judeans' return to Jerusalem, futility in everyday work (Hag 1:5-11) is presented as the consequence of a lack of enthusiasm for worship, particularly the reconstruction of the temple (Hag 1:12-15). But when the project was completed, many remained despondent because the new temple did not match the original in glory, and in any case the glory of Yahweh failed to return to the temple. Haggai sought to inspire the people by pointing them to a future when the glory will return with unprecedented brilliance, and with it will attract the worship of all nations (Hag 2:1-9). In the meantime, the people were to carry on, with the priests assuming their leadership roles (Hag 2:10-19).

Along with Haggai, Zechariah encouraged the people to resume the construction of the temple (cf. Ezra 5:1). As a result, in short order the project was completed and the temple was dedicated (Ezra 6:15-22). While Zechariah 1—6 speaks to the rebuilding of the temple and the reestablishment of the cult, in Zechariah 8 the prophet reminds the people that these cultic achievements may not be divorced from life. In Zechariah 8:16-17 he appeals for truthful speech, righteous judgments in the courts, positive dispositions toward one another, and the repudiation of perjury. The community of faith may have been renewed, but Yahweh's disposition toward ethical fidelity remains the same.

When the last prophet, Malachi, appeared some decades later, problems with worship had intensified. The book that bears his name makes the fundamental issue clear: the people lacked the proper respect/fear for God. The effects of this lack were evident in every aspect of life: the people as a whole were cynical about Yahweh's covenant commitment to them (Mal 1:2-5) and his justice (Mal 2:17), and their cultic worship had degenerated (they treated the altar and their sacrifices with contempt, presenting defiled and unacceptable offerings [Mal 1:6-9, 12-13]; the Levitical priests have despised and abused their office [Mal 2:1-9]; they were bored by the cult [Mal 1:13a]; they were treacherous in the way they fulfilled vows [Mal 1:14]; they were compromising and faithless in their marriages [Mal 2:10-16]; their ethical conduct, especially their disposition toward the marginalized, had degenerated [Mal 3:5]; they were stingy in their contributions to the temple [Mal 3:7-12]; they were perverse in their understanding of covenant relationship [Mal 3:13-15]). Upon those who had no fear of him, Yahweh threatened to come like a refiner's fire to purge out the dross, yielding a community that would bring righteous offerings (Mal 3:1-4). However, Malachi recognized those who feared (yārē') Yahweh; their future would be secure, as Yahweh writes their names in the book of remembrance and treats them as his own special treasure (sĕgullâ) and his son (Mal 3:16-18). Not only would these survive the judgment, but also they would triumph over the wicked (Mal 4:1-3). The solution for this lack of fear is remarkable: a return to the Torah of Moses (Mal 4:4), which accords precisely with Moses' call for the regular reading of the Torah every seven years at the Festival of Booths in order to instill fear of Yahweh that yields obedience and results in life (see Deut 31:9-13). In reading the Torah, people encountered God, were reminded of his past grace, and learned the appropriate response to his grace. Like that of his predecessors, Malachi's view is that God requires full-bodied worship; the fear of Yahweh is expressed not only or even primarily in formal cultic service, but rather in everyday life.

2.3. The Prophetic Vision of Future Worship. It is striking that the prophetic corpus as presently arranged is framed by references to worship: Isaiah 1 reflects the critical situation in the eighth century BC, when the flame of Israel's history and service to Yahweh was about to be extinguished, at least for a while; Malachi reflects the situation when the nation had been revived, at least a portion of it. Obviously, not all the problems were resolved by

the mid-fifth century BC. Apparently, this would not have caught the prophets by surprise, for frequently they provide glimpses into the distant future, when true worship will actually happen in accordance with the will of Yahweh. The clearest pictures of future worship are found in Isaiah and Ezekiel, though Jeremiah, Haggai and Zechariah too offer glimpses into that new world.

What is most remarkable about the vision of future worship in Isaiah is its universality. Hints of this appear early. Echoing Micah 4:1-3, Isaiah 2:2-4 anticipates the day when all nations will stream to *Zion, the mountain of Yahweh, and to the house of the God of Jacob. However, here the focus is not on sacrifices or other cultic rituals; rather, reminiscent of Deuteronomy 4:6-8, the attraction will be the Torah of Yahweh, which they will come to hear that they might walk in his ways. This vision of the nations worshiping with Israel is concretized in Isaiah 19:16-25, which speaks of a world, anchored by Egypt, Assyria and Israel, united in the worship of Yahweh. However, this text makes no reference to Zion. Instead, it speaks of an altar to Yahweh in the heartland of Egypt. Indeed, Isaiah speaks of a reversal of roles: Judah will oppress Egypt, causing them to cry out (sā'aq) to Yahweh (Is 19:20; cf. Ex 2:23), and Yahweh will send them a savior/champion to rescue them. Through his acts of salvation the Egyptians will know Yahweh and will respond to his revelation of himself with the service ('ābad) of sacrifices (zebaḥ) and tribute offerings (minḥâ) and vows (nēder), which they will faithfully keep (Is 19:21). Though it is unstated, the references to a highway linking Egypt, Assyria and Israel that follow may suggest similar worship in Assyria. Remarkably, the oppressors of Israel are transformed and fully integrated into the community of nations worshiping Yahweh.

Isaiah 56 presents a most remarkable image of worship. After an opening salvo on the ethical dimensions of worship (Is 56:1-2), the prophet reassures foreigners and eunuchs who previously had been barred from admission to the assembly (cf. Deut 23:1-6) but who now keep Yahweh's Sabbaths, choose what pleases him, and hold fast to the covenant, that they will be given a permanent place within the temple (Is 56:3-5). Indeed, Yahweh's house will be known as a house of prayer for all peoples; foreigners who join themselves to him will be fully engaged in the cult, ministering (*šērēt*) to him, being covenantally committed (*ʾāhab*, "to love") to the name of Yahweh, functioning as his servants (*ʿăbādîm*), maintaining the sanctity of the Sabbath, holding fast to his covenant, celebrating in Yahweh's house of prayer, and offering acceptable burnt offerings and sacrifices on Yahweh's altar. Indeed, the same God who regathers the dispersed of Israel will gather these worshipers to the temple (Is 56:6-8). The book closes with a scene in the context of the new heavens and the new earth, when Yahweh sends survivors of Israel throughout the world to gather peoples from every tongue and nation and to bring them to the holy mountain Jerusalem that they might see the glory of Yahweh. And they will return with all their vehicles of transport filled with "their brothers" from all the nations as if they were offerings in clean vessels presented to Yahweh. Indeed, he will ordain some of them to serve as priests and Levites.

Whereas Isaiah's images of future worship are scattered throughout the book, Ezekiel's are concentrated in the last nine chapters (Block 1998, 494-746). If Isaiah's vision is remarkable for its universality, then Ezekiel's vision is striking for its parochial nature. Whereas earlier the nations had at least been spectators to what Yahweh was doing (Ezek 30:26; 36:23; 37:28; 38:23), references to the nations (*gôyim*) and the peoples (*ʿammîm*) are missing in Ezekiel 40—48. The closest that Ezekiel comes to this is when he mentions that the new world of worship will include sojourners (*gērîm* [Ezek 47:23]), but they will be considered members of the tribes that occupy the area where they live. In the closing chapters of his book Ezekiel offers a remarkable picture of worship (Joyce), which includes a detailed description of sacred space (Exek 40:1—42:20), instructions for the altar and its consecration (Ezek 43:13-27), a summary of the roles of the sacred personnel, the priests and Levites (Ezek 44:15-31), the plans for a sacred reserve for priestly personnel and the prince (Ezek 45:1-8; 48:8-22), an appeal for righteous exercise of civil *leadership (Ezek 45:9-12), instructions on festivals and offerings (Ezek 45:13-24), a picture of the sanctuary within its environment, with the water flowing out from the temple and transforming the landscape (Ezek 47:1-12), a plan of the tribal territorial allotments (Ezek 47:15—48:7; 48:23-

29) and a schematic plan for an auxiliary city (Ezek 48:30-35). Perhaps most striking of all is Ezekiel's vision of the return of the glory of Yahweh, authenticating this as a replacement for the original temple built by Solomon (Ezek 43:1-9; 44:1-4).

But the question concerning the intention of Ezekiel's worship program remains. Was this a manifesto for worship in a newly constituted nation? If it was, the picture that he paints has many puzzling elements in geography, ritual and personnel: (1) The design of the temple: the text offers many horizontal details, but apart from the series of steps, vertical dimensions are largely lacking, and many details are puzzling. (2) The location of the temple: it is on a high mountain, but which mountain? (3) The territorial allotments: they consist of parallel strips of land running west to east, totally disregarding geography and largely disregarding Israel's history. (4) The river that runs from the temple and fructifies the land: how does this work? (5) The auxiliary city with twelve gates named "YHWH-shammah": what is its function? (6) The sacred reserve: what is its function? (7) The respective roles of the Zadokites and the Levites: what is their relation to the past? (8) The function of sacrifices: were they atoning or merely memorial? (9) The prince (*nāśîʾ*): is he a Davidic figure, and what is his function in the cult? (10) There is an apparent absence of critical features, such as the ark of the covenant. (11) There are contradictions with Mosaic paradigms.

Although the massive *Temple Scroll* composed by the Dead Sea covenanters shortly before the time of Christ displays numerous connections with Ezekiel's plan, and Ezekiel's vision had a profound influence on the imagery of the NT book of Revelation, the description of the temple is not intended as a blueprint for some future building to be constructed with human hands. Nowhere is anyone commanded to build it. The man with the measuring line takes Ezekiel on a tour of an existing structure already made. Indeed, were it not for the present literary location of Ezekiel's Temple Vision, it is doubtful that the eschatological interpretation held by some would ever have arisen.

Ezekiel's salvation oracles have looked forward to the day when (1) the twelve tribes of *Israel would be regathered and returned to their hereditary homeland; (2) the Davidic dynasty would be restored; (3) Yahweh's covenant of peace with Israel would be renewed; (4) Yahweh would establish his permanent residence in their midst. It would have been inconceivable for Ezekiel to envision a full restoration of his people without a literal fulfillment of each of these elements. Nevertheless, in view of the considerations cited above, it seems best to interpret Ezekiel 40—48 ideationally and theologically. The issue for the prophet is not physical geography or cultic ritual, but rather spiritual realities. As in his earlier visions, historical events are described from a theological plane, and the interpreter's focus must remain on the theologically conceptual value of that which is envisioned. At the time of Ezekiel's prophetic inauguration, the sight of Yahweh enthroned above the cherubim had reassured him of his presence even in Babylon among the exiles (Ezek 1:1-28a). His visionary ingestion of the scroll spoke of the importance of accepting the divine message and its incorporation into his own experience (Ezek 1:28b—3:15). The observation of the abominations in the temple and the consequent departure of the divine *kābôd* ("glory") provide theological justification and rationalization for Nebuchadnezzar's razing of Jerusalem (Ezek 8:1—11:25). The vision of the revivified dry bones is not a prophecy of literal individual resurrection but rather a declaration of the certainty of the eventual resuscitation of Israel by a new infusion of breath from Yahweh.

Though more complex and extensive than any of these visions, Ezekiel 40—48 should be interpreted along similar lines. The prophet hereby introduced the theological realities awaiting his own people. Whereas Ezekiel 37:26-27 had spoken of the establishment of Yahweh's permanent residence among his people, following their homecoming, the present vision picks up the theological theme and describes the spiritual reality in concrete terms, employing the familiar cultural idioms of temple, altar, sacrifices, *nāśî'*, and land. In presenting this theological constitution for the new Israel, Yahweh announces the righting of all the old wrongs and the establishment of permanent healthy deity-nation-land relationships. Ezekiel's final vision presents a lofty spiritual ideal: Where God is, there is Zion. Where God is, there is order and the fulfillment of all of his promises. Furthermore, where presence of God is recognized, there is purity and holiness.

See also IDOLS, IDOLATRY, GODS; LITURGY AND CULT; PRAYER; SACRIFICE AND ATONEMENT; TEMPLE; ZION.

BIBLIOGRAPHY. **D. I. Block,** *The Book of Ezekiel Chapters 1-24* (NICOT; Grand Rapids: Eerdmans, 1997); idem, *The Book of Ezekiel: Chapters 25-48* (NICOT; Grand Rapids: Eerdmans, 1998); idem, "Other Religions in Old Testament Theology," in *Biblical Faith and Other Religions: An Evangelical Assessment*, ed. D. W. Baker (Grand Rapids: Kregel, 2004) 43-78; **M. Chyutin,** *Architecture and Utopia in the Temple Era*, trans. R. Flantz (LSTS 58; London: T & T Clark, 2006); **J. A. Davies,** *A Royal Priesthood: Literary and Intertextual Perspectives on the Image of Israel in Exodus 19.6* (JSOTSup 395; London: T & T Clark, 2004); **T. Fretheim,** "חוה," *NIDOTTE* 2:42-44; **A. E. Hill,** *Enter His Courts with Praise: Old Testament Worship for the New Testament Church* (Grand Rapids: Baker, 1993); **J. Jensen,** *Ethical Dimensions of the Prophets* (Collegeville, MN: Liturgical Press, 2006); **P. P. Jenson,** *Graded Holiness: A Key to the Priestly Conception of the World* (JSOTSup 106; Sheffield: JSOT, 1992); **P. M. Joyce,** "Temple and Worship in Ezekiel 40-48," in *Temple and Worship in Biblical Israel: Proceedings of the Oxford Old Testament Seminar*, ed. J. Day (LHBOTS 422; London: T & T Clark, 2005) 145-62; **S. Kreuzer,** "Zur Bedeutung und Etymologie von *hištaḥāwâ/yštḥwy*," *VT* 35 (1985) 39-60; **R. C. Ortlund Jr.,** *Whoredom: God's Unfaithful Wife in Biblical Theology* (NSBT; Grand Rapids: Eerdmans, 1996); **A. R. Ross,** *Recalling the Hope of Glory: Biblical Worship from the Garden to the New Creation* (Grand Rapids: Kregel, 2006); **H. H. Rowley,** *Worship in Ancient Israel: Its Forms and Meanings* (Philadelphia: Fortress, 1967); **K. R. Stevenson,** *Vision of Transformation: The Territorial Rhetoric of Ezekiel 40-48* (SBLDS 154; Atlanta: Scholars Press, 2001); **C. Walker and M. B. Dick,** "The Induction of Cult Image in Ancient Mesopotamia: The Mesopotamian *mīs pî* Ritual," in *Born in Heaven, Made on Earth: The Making of the Cult Image in the Ancient Near East*, ed. M. B. Dick (Winona Lake, IN: Eisenbrauns, 1999) 55-121; **S. Weeks,** "Man-Made Gods? Idolatry in the Old Testament," in *Idolatry: False Worship in the Bible, Early Judaism and Christianity*, ed. S. C. Barton (London: T & T Clark, 2007) 7-21; **J. Wellhausen,** *Israelitische und jüdische Geschichte* (9th ed.;

Berlin: de Gruyter, 1958); **C. J. H. Wright,** *Old Testament Ethics for the People of God* (rev. ed.; Leicester: Inter-Varsity Press, 2004).

D. I. Block

WRATH

Wrath is a strong negative response by *God to human *sin, often leading to expressions of judgment. Although sometimes in the prophetic texts humans display anger, the focus in this article is primarily on divine wrath because the vast majority of prophetic references to anger involve Yahweh. After an overview of scholarship on wrath, this article discusses the terms and metaphors used for wrath in the Prophetic Books. Next, the source and objects of wrath are examined, followed by an investigation of the causes and effects of wrath. Fortunately for *Israel, divine wrath sometimes can be either delayed or avoided, and this is the focus of the final section.

1. Scholarship on Wrath
2. Wrath Terminology
3. Wrath Metaphors
4. The Source and Objects of Wrath
5. The Causes of Wrath
6. The Effects of Wrath
7. Delaying and Avoiding Wrath

1. Scholarship on Wrath.

No scholarly publication that I have encountered has an exclusive focus on wrath in the prophetic corpus. Scholars examine divine wrath in Scripture generally (e.g., Tasker; Hanson; Ashmon), the OT (e.g., Erlandsson; Baloian; Herion; Fretheim 2002) or Isaiah specifically (e.g., Locke). T. E. Fretheim also looks at violence in the Prophetic Books (Fretheim 2004). The closest to an exclusive focus on wrath in prophetic literature is perhaps A. J. Heschel's chapter on the subject of divine wrath in his monograph on the prophets.

B. E. Baloian summarizes his extensive research on divine references in the entire OT in a very useful chart (Baloian, 191-210, chart 2). This article uses the section of Baloian's chart relevant to the prophets in the discussions of objects, causes and effects of divine wrath. But it is necessary to acknowledge beforehand the subjective nature of these categorizations. It often is difficult to determine precisely objects, causes and effects of divine wrath, and a combination of factors frequently is involved. The Prophetic Books include a great deal of poetry,

and the nonlinear nature of the poetic genre means that its message does not translate into a summary chart seamlessly. Despite these concerns, the chart does provide a great deal of helpful information about divine wrath.

2. Wrath Terminology.

2.1. Numerous Terms. Ancient Hebrew included a wide range of nouns and verbs to connote wrath. In the prophets, sixteen words (six verbs and ten nouns) are used for "wrath." These terms primarily appear in contexts of divine, not human, anger. Yahweh often becomes angry in the Prophetic Books. According to Baloian's chart, there are 387 OT texts that mention divine wrath, almost half (176 of 387 = 46%) of which of these appear in the Prophetic Books. (All occurrences listed below refer exclusively to the Prophetic Books.)

2.2. Six Verb-Noun Pairs. Six pairs of verbal roots and their associated nouns are used to connote anger. The verb *ʾānap* ("to be angry") appears only once (Is 12:1), but the associated noun *ʾap* ("anger") appears often (123 times), far more than any other of the other wrath words, occurring in all of the Prophetic Books except for Obadiah, Haggai and Malachi. The word *ʾap* rarely also means "nose" or "nostril" (e.g., Is 2:22; 3:21); in most instances it connotes anger, only occasionally human anger (Is 7:4) and far more frequently divine anger (e.g., Is 5:25 [2x]; 7:4; 9:11, 16, 21; 10:4, 5, 25).

The verb *kāʿas* ("to vex, to provoke to anger") appears nineteen times and is used almost exclusively with God as the one being provoked (Is 65:3; Jer 7:18, 19; 8:19; 11:17; 25:6, 7 [2x]; 32:29, 30, 32; 44:3, 8; Ezek 8:17; 16:26, 42; 20:28; 32:9; Hos 12:14). The noun *kaʿas* ("vexation, provocation") is used only once (Ezek 20:28).

The verb *ḥārâ* ("to burn, to be angry") appears ten times (Is 5:25; 41:11; 45:24; Jer 12:5; 22:15; Hos 8:5; Jon 4:1, 4, 9 [2x]; Hab 3:8; Zech 10:3), but unlike the other verbs discussed in this section, only four repetitions describe the anger of Yahweh (Is 5:25; Hos 8:5; Hab 3:8; Zech 10:3), while five describe humans (primarily Jonah) becoming angry at Yahweh (Is 45:24; Jon 4:1, 4, 9 [2x]). In contrast, all eighteen occurrences of the related noun *ḥārôn* ("burning anger, fury") refer to divine wrath (Is 13:9, 13; Jer 4:8, 26; 12:13; 25:37, 38 [2x]; 30:24; 49:37; 51:45; Ezek 7:12, 14; Hos 11:9; Jon 3:9; Nah 1:6; Zeph 2:2; 3:8).

The verb *qāṣap* ("to be angry") appears thirteen times (Is 8:21; 47:6; 54:9; 57:16, 17 [2x]; 64:5, 9; Jer 37:15; Zech 1:2, 15 [2x]; 8:14), and the noun *qeṣep* ("wrath, anger") appears eleven times (Is 34:2; 54:8; 60:10; Jer 10:10; 21:5; 32:37; 50:13; Hos 10:7; Zech 1:2, 15; 7:12). Among these twenty-four combined references, only two refer to human anger (Is 8:21; Jer 37:15).

The verb *zāʿam* ("to be indignant") appears five times (Is 66:14; Dan 11:30; Mic 6:10; Zech 1:12; Mal 1:4). The noun *zaʿam* ("indignation") appears seventeen times (Is 10:5, 25; 13:5; 26:20; 30:27; Jer 10:10; 15:17; 50:25; Ezek 21:31; 22:24, 31; Dan 8:19; 11:36; Hos 7:16; Nah 1:6; Hab 3:12; Zeph 3:8). Among these combined twenty-two references, only four refer to human anger (Jer 15:17; Dan 11:30, 36; Hos 7:16).

The verb *rāgaz* ("to tremble, to enrage") is typically included in lists of wrath words by scholars (e.g., Baloian; Ashmon), but in the prophets this root usually just means "to tremble" (e.g., Is 13:13; 14:16; 64:1; Joel 2:1; Hab 3:7) or "to shake" (Is 23:11). In only a few instances does it suggest anger or wrath (e.g., Is 37:28, 28; Ezek 16:43). Related noun forms appear once in Hebrew (*rōgez*, "raging" [Hab 3:2]) and once in Aramaic (*rĕgaz*, "rage" [Dan 3:13]) in anger contexts.

2.3. Three Nouns. Three wrath words appear only as nouns and not with their verbal root in the Prophetic Books. The noun *ḥēmâ* ("wrath, rage, heat") appears seventy-five times (e.g., Is 27:4; 34:2; 42:25; Jer 4:4; 6:11; 7:20; Ezek 5:13; 6:12; 7:8; Dan 8:6; Mic 5:15; Nah 1:2; Hab 2:15; Zech 8:2), almost exclusively in contexts describing divine wrath. The related verb *yāḥam* ("to be hot") does not appear in the Prophetic Books.

The noun *ʿebrâ* ("wrath") appears nineteen times (Is 9:19; 10:6; 13:9, 13; 14:6; 16:6; Jer 7:29; 48:30; Ezek 7:19; 21:31; 22:21, 31; 38:19; Hos 5:10; 13:11; Amos 1:11; Hab 3:8; Zeph 1:15, 18). Three of these references refer to wrath of Israel's neighboring nations (Is 16:6 [Moab]; Jer 48:30 [Moab]; Amos 1:11 [Edom]), and the rest refer to divine wrath. The associated verb *ʿābar* ("to infuriate oneself") does not appear in the Prophetic Books.

The noun *zaʿap* ("rage, raging") appears twice in anger contexts (Is 30:30; Mic 7:9), both times describing divine wrath. The related verb *zaʿap* ("vexed") only appears once in the Prophetic Books, but not connoting anger (Dan 1:10).

2.4. Combinations. Often these words are combined, frequently in parallel constructions, to emphasize the severity of Yahweh's wrath (e.g., Is 13:9; Jer 32:31; Ezek 7:8; Hos 11:9) (see also Baloian's chart). For example, we find a verb-noun pattern: "O LORD, for though you were angry [*ʾānap*] with me, your anger [*ʾap*] turned away" (Is 12:1 NRSV); a noun-noun pattern: "Ah, Assyria, the rod of my anger [*ʾap*]—the club in their hands is my fury [*zāʿam*]!" (Is 10:5 NRSV); or a noun-noun-noun pattern: "I myself will fight against you . . . in anger [*ʾap*], in fury [*ḥēmâ*], and in great wrath [*qeṣep*]" (Jer 21:5 NRSV). Other prophetic texts contain three of these wrath words (e.g., Is 5:25; Jer 32:37; Ezek 5:15), and two texts repeat them four times (Ezek 5:13; Zech 8:2).

Thus, divine anger is a major theme in the Prophetic Books, as seen in the literally hundreds of repetitions of the numerous synonyms for "wrath."

3. Wrath Metaphors.

3.1. Day Metaphors. A variety of images and metaphors are used in prophetic descriptions of divine wrath. The prophets Joel and Amos speak of a future "day of Yahweh" (Joel 1:15; 2:1, 11; 3:4; Amos 5:18, 20), which seems to connote judgment and perhaps wrath (*see* Day of the Lord). However, other prophets make an explicit connection between a certain day or a "day of Yahweh" with wrath (Is 13:6, 9; Ezek 7:12; 38:18, 19; Zeph 1:14; 3:8), even specifically a "day of wrath" (Ezek 7:19; Zeph 1:15, 18) or a "day of the anger of Yahweh" (Zeph 2:2-3).

3.2. Nature Metaphors. Images from the realm of nature feature prominently in descriptions of divine wrath. The most common image used for divine wrath is that of fire (Is 5:24-25; 9:19; 30:27, 30; 42:25; 66:15; Jer 4:4; 15:14; 17:4; 21:12; Ezek 21:31; 22:20-21, 31; Nah 1:6; Zeph 1:18; 3:8), which is not surprising, since several of the wrath words imply heat (*ḥēmâ*) or burning (*ḥārâ*, *ḥārôn*). In some texts, divine fire has already gone out in judgment (e.g., Is 5:24-25; Ezek 22:31); in others, the threat of fiery wrath is used to warn people to repent (e.g., Jer 4:4). In at least one of these instances of divine wrath, where there is fire, there is also smoke (Is 30:27). An image that may seem strange to associate with a burning emotion like wrath is that of water, but Hosea uses it to describe how Yahweh's wrath is poured out (Hos 5:10). Less surprising (almost Zeus-like) is the image of a storm to describe divine wrath, which appears in five prophetic texts (Is 30:30; Jer 23:19; 30:23; Ezek 13:11-13; Nah 1:3). Alongside several of these storms of divine wrath, hailstones (reminiscent of the Egyptian plague [Ex 9:22-26]) add to the fury of the tempest (Is 30:30; Ezek 13:11, 13; 38:22). In other texts, earthquakes or trembling mountains contribute to the description of an angry God (Is 5:25; 13:13; Jer 10:10 Nah 1:5).

3.3. Human-implement Metaphors. Four human implements are used in the Prophetic Books to describe divine wrath. Yahweh calls Assyria the "rod" of his wrath (Is 10:5). Yahweh speaks of a "winepress" where he trod peoples in his anger (Is 63:3). In a judgment against Elam, Yahweh declares that he will bring his fierce anger and will send the "sword" after them (Jer. 49:37).

3.4. The Cup of Wrath. The fourth implement, the "cup of wrath," requires a longer discussion because of its prominence both in prophetic literature and in the NT. A. T. Hanson, in his extended discussion of the cup of wrath (Hanson, 27-36), examines parallels from Ugaritic literature where the cup is used as an image of evil destiny, but not necessarily of divine wrath. In the prophets, the "cup" (*kôs*) is strongly associated with divine judgment and divine anger. This image appears in three primary texts where the cup is referred to multiple times in a similar manner (Is 51:17-23; Jer 25:15-29; Ezek 23:31-34) and in several other scattered texts (Jer 49:12; 51:7; Hab 2:16; Zech 12:2). The cup contains the wrath of Yahweh (or the "wine of wrath" [Jer 25:15]) and is held in his hand (Is 51:17, 22, 23; Jer 25:15, 17; 51:7) or specifically his right hand (Hab 2:16). The cup is associated not only with wrath, but also with the effects of judgment that result from his wrath: drunkenness (Is 51:21; Jer 51:7; Ezek 23:33), staggering (Is 51:22), reeling (Zech 12:2), shame (Hab 2:16) and horror and desolation (Ezek 23:33). Jerusalem is often the intended drinker of the cup (Is 51:17; Jer 25:18; Ezek 23:4 [Jerusalem = Oholibah]), but the nations too are supposed to drink from it (Jer 25:15, 17; 51:7). Understandably, the recipients of the cup resist, so they are commanded to drink (Jer 25:28; Ezek 23:32; Hab 2:16). When Yahweh has compassion, he removes the cup (Is 51:22).

The "cup of wrath" image from the Prophetic Books is picked up in several important NT contexts. Although the relevant Gospel texts do not make the connection to divine wrath explicit, the cup that Jesus asks his Father to remove in the garden of Gethsemane would be consistent with the prophetic cup of God's wrath (Mt 26:39; Mk 14:36; Lk 22:42; cf. Jn 18:11). Texts from Revelation, however, make the connection clear, as both the worshipers of the beast and the city of Babylon are given the cup of God's wrath to drink (Rev. 14:10; 16:19).

4. The Source and Objects of Wrath.

4.1. The Source. When anger is expressed in prophetic literature, God usually is the source, and his people usually are the objects. Yahweh expresses his wrath in the context of various divine roles: king (Jer 8:19; 10:10; Ezek 20:33), judge (Ezek 7:3, 8; 16:38) and warrior (Is 42:25; Jer 21:5; 49:37; Ezek 6:12; Hab 3:8). However, with so many of the images used for divine wrath associated with the realm of nature (fire, water, storms, hail, earthquakes), perhaps the primary role that should be attributed to Yahweh in these contexts is that of creator. In this role, the expression of his wrath understandably affects his creation (for discussion of divine roles in OT wrath contexts, see Fretheim 2002, 8-9).

Before a discussion of the objects of divine wrath, a few comments are in order about the nature of divine wrath. Elsewhere in Scripture, wrath can have negative connotations. Fierce anger is cursed (Gen. 49:7), burning anger is repented of (Ex 32:12, 14) and quick anger is foolish (Eccl 7:9). Also, part of the judgment against Edom is that "his anger tore perpetually, and he kept his anger forever" (Amos 1:11). To address this problematic aspect of biblical anger, several scholars describe divine wrath as pathos, not passion (e.g., Heschel, 61-64; Herion, 991, 993; Fretheim 2002, 17). In their understanding, Yahweh's anger is not a spontaneous loss of self-control (passion) but rather a rational, predictable response to sin (pathos). Whereas capricious anger can be condemned, the pathos anger of Yahweh is therefore righteous and legitimate.

4.2. The Objects. God's wrath usually targets his people. According to Baloian's chart, approximately two-thirds (115 of 176 = 65%) of all references to divine anger in the Prophetic

Books have Israel or Judah as the object (on the objects of God's wrath in Scripture generally, see Ashmon, 353; in Isaiah specifically, see Locke, 228-29). One-fourth (44 of 176 = 25%) of these wrath references target "foreign enemies," and the remaining references focus on either an individual (5 of 176 = 3%) or on all people (11 of 176 = 6%). (One of the objects is left blank.)

The prophetic texts mentioning divine wrath refer to the people of Yahweh in a variety of ways, primarily using the national names based on their patriarchal ancestors: Israel (Jer 11:17; Ezek 38:18), Jacob (Is 9:12) and Judah (Jer 4:4; 52:3). Wrath also is directed at "the cities" of Judah generally (Jer 44:6) or specifically the two capital cities, Jerusalem (Jer 32:32; 42:18; 52:3; Dan 9:16) and Samaria (Hos 8:5). Other objects of divine wrath involve familial terminology: "the children" of Israel and/or Judah (Jer 32:30, 32) and "the house" of Israel and/or Judah (Jer 11:17; Ezek 8:17; Zech 10:3). Ironically, Yahweh refers to the objects of his anger as "my people" (Is 47:6; Jer 8:19; 51:45). Similarly, they request an end to his anger based on the fact that they are his people (Is 64:9).

Divine wrath also targets "the nations" generally (Is 34:2; Jer 10:10, 25; 25:15; Mic 5:15; Zeph 3:8; Zech 1:15) or, in the context of a judgment oracle, certain nations specifically: Assyria (Is 10:24-25), Babylon (Is 13:3; Jer 50:13), Elam (Jer 49:37), Edom (Ezek 25:14) and Philistia (Ezek 25:17).

5. The Causes of Wrath.

5.1. Divine Anger Is Provoked. Several scholars (e.g., Eichrodt, 262; Heschel, 69-71; Fretheim 2002, 17) have observed that in the OT wrath is not a permanent aspect of God's character. It does not characterize him in the same way that love, mercy or compassion do, since it is always caused by the sin of humans. In short, anger is provoked (see Ashmon, 350-51). This pattern holds true in the prophets.

5.2. Idolatry and Injustice. The two primary provocations for the wrath of Yahweh in prophetic literature are *idolatry and injustice (see Justice, Righteousness). Baloian's chart lists the causes or "motivations" for divine wrath in the OT. He focuses on two motivations: "rebellion," which he says often involves idolatry, and "oppression," which he defines as excessive human

cruelty. In the prophets, approximately one-fifth of the texts on divine wrath refer only to rebellion as a cause (35 of 176 = 20%), one-fifth refer only to oppression (36 of 176 =21%), and three-fifths of these references mention both rebellion and oppression (103 of 176 = 59%). (One motivation is left blank, and the other listed is "zeal"). In the prophets therefore, the sins of idolatry and oppression almost exclusively are what make God angry. It is difficult to determine which of these two motivations for divine wrath is primary, since they are mentioned with roughly the same frequency, and in the majority of references the two together provoke divine wrath.

The idolatry of Israel and Judah that prompted Yahweh's wrath took a variety of specific forms, including libation offerings to other gods (Jer 7:18), worshiping foreign idols (Jer 8:19), making offerings to Baal (Jer 11:17) and building high places to Baal (Jer 32:32-35). The types of oppression and injustice that provoked God's anger were also diverse, involving, for example, wicked covetousness (Is 57:17), conquering foreign land (Ezek 36:5), shedding the blood of the innocent poor (Jer 2:34-35) and robbing the poor and taking advantage of widows and orphans (Is 10:2-4).

5.3. Relational Anger and Righteous Anger. Thus, the two primary causes of divine wrath in the Prophetic Books could be categorized as relational anger and righteous anger. Relational anger focuses on the "vertical," divine-human relationship. Yahweh is enraged because Israel and Judah are constructing idols and worshiping other gods. His is a jealous wrath because his people who committed to worship him exclusively have given themselves to other lovers. The image of God's people as unfaithful lovers is prominent in the prophets (e.g., Jer 3; Ezek 16, 23; Hos 1—3).

Righteous anger focuses on "horizontal," human-human relationships. Yahweh is angry because humans are mistreating other humans. Just as he had compassion on Israel while they were oppressed in Egypt, so they should have compassion on the weak in their society. Their oppression of their neighbors prompts divine wrath. While Yahweh's relational anger involves the first four of the Ten Commandments, his righteous anger involves the last six commandments (Ex 20:2-17; see also Jer 7:5-9, 18-20).

6. The Effects of Wrath.

6.1. Punishment. The sins that caused Yahweh's wrath resulted in various forms of punishment. Yahweh does not simply simmer with anger; he expresses it in judgment. In the Prophetic Books, wrath can be depicted as synonymous with judgment (e.g., Jer 49:37; Ezek 20:34; Hos 11:9; cf. Mt 3:7; Rom 2:5). Fretheim discusses this wrath-judgment metonymy, noting that wrath usually leads to judgment, but he also values Heschel's perspective that wrath should not be reduced to a synonym for judgment (Fretheim 2002, 11-12; cf. Heschel, 59-60).

While the number of objects and causes of wrath were relatively limited, a much wider variety of possible effects of wrath are mentioned in the prophets. This diversity of effects can be seen in the seventh column of Baloian's chart. The percentages below are only for the 176 references to divine wrath in the Prophetic Books (a few of the categories listed below Baloian does not include).

6.2. Violence and Warfare. The most common types of effects in the prophets involve violence and *warfare: military defeat (76 of 176 = 44% [e.g., Is 5:25; Jer 4:26; Ezek 6:12; Nah 1:6-8]), *death (44 of 176 = 25% [e.g., Is 10:4; Jer 42:18-22; Ezek 6:12]), *destruction (30 of 176 = 17% [e.g., Is 10:25; Jer 10:22-24; Zeph 1:18]), captivity (12 of 176 = 7% [e.g., Is 10:4; Jer 15:14; 17:4]). While Hanson calls the *exile "the great example of the wrath of God" (Hanson, 39), captivity is not mentioned explicitly as often as some of the other military effects. Several texts, however, speak of how God used the two primary exiling empires as instruments of his wrath: Assyria (Is 10:5) and *Babylon (Is 47:5; Jer 25:6-11; 32:29). However, Babylon exceeded its mandate and therefore was also judged (see Fretheim 2002, 24-25).

6.3. Creation. When Yahweh becomes angry, it often affects his creation, so many types of effects involve the natural world: the land made desolate (18 of 176 = 10% [e.g., Is 9:19; Jer 4:26; 12:11-13; Ezek 14:19]), famine (16 of 176 = 9% [e.g., Jer 18:21-23; 21:5-7; 32:36-37; Ezek 5:15-17; 6:12]), plague (9 of 176 = 5% [e.g., Jer 21:5-6; 42:18-22; Ezek 6:12]), earthquakes (3 of 176 = 2% [Is 13:13; Jer 10:10; Ezek 38:19]). As is often the case, many of these natural effects are combined with one another (e.g., Jer 42:18-22) or with some of the military effects (e.g., Jer 32:36-37).

6.4. Divine Abandonment. Although divine abandonment resulting from wrath appears less frequently than military or natural effects, it is perhaps more tragic because it suggests a loss of relationship. God's face is hidden from his people (Is 54:8; Jer 33:5), although the Isaiah 54 text speaks of this separation as temporary and in the past. In the midst of his anger Yahweh informs Ezekiel that he will not be compassionate and will not hear the prayer of his people (Ezek 8:18). Yahweh's wrath leads him to reject and forsake his people, so they are to respond in lamentation (Jer 7:29).

7. Delaying and Avoiding Wrath.

7.1. Delaying Wrath. Most instances of divine wrath in the Prophetic Books result in judgment, but God's expression of wrath can be delayed or even avoided completely. In Yahweh's name revelation to Moses after the incident of the golden calf (Ex 34:6), he describes himself not only as merciful, gracious and abounding in steadfast love, but also as "slow to anger" (’erek ’appayim). This important formulaic description of God's character is repeated elsewhere in the OT (Num 14:18; Neh 9:1; Ps 86:15; 103:8; 145:8), including several times in the Prophetic Books. The book of Joel uses the description of Yahweh as being slow to anger as one incentive for people to repent (Joel 2:13). God's slowness to anger is part of what frustrates Jonah, as he desired destruction for the city of Nineveh (Jon 4:2). While Nahum's oracle does not include the full formula from Exodus, Yahweh is described as "slow to anger" in the context of a description of his wrathful judgment (Nah 1:3).

7.2. Avoiding Wrath. In the prophets, four reasons are given for possibly avoiding the effects of divine wrath: innocence, *prayer, *repentance and compassion (see Fretheim 2002, 18-19; Ashmon, 355.) God's people claim to be innocent, assuming that this condition would lead Yahweh to turn his anger from them, but Yahweh judges them for this false claim (Jer 2:35). Although their assumption may have been warranted, their own guilt prevented God from turning his wrath away from them.

Twice prophets pray that divine wrath be turned away so that others are spared. Jeremiah reminds Yahweh how he interceded for the people to turn away God's wrath, and now they have returned his good with evil by plotting against him (Jer 18:20). Daniel prays that God will turn his wrath away from Jerusalem and forgive its people (Dan 9:16-19).

In several key prophetic texts, if the people repent, Yahweh too will "repent" and turn from his anger. Yahweh commands his people Israel to repent and return to him; otherwise, his wrath will go forth and consume them (Jer 4:1-4). A similar message is given to the people in Joel: if they repent, because Yahweh is slow to anger, he may relent from punishing them (Joel 2:13). In response to Jonah's terse message of destruction, the Ninevites repent, hoping that God will turn from his "fierce anger" (both *ḥārôn* and *ʿap* are used), and God changed his mind about the threatened judgment (Jon 3:3-10).

Ultimately, however, what overcomes divine wrath is divine compassion. Even though Yahweh was angry at Israel, his anger was replaced by a desire to comfort them instead (Is 12:1). Yahweh declares that his anger was temporary, but his love and compassion will be everlasting (Is 54:8). Because Yahweh's compassion grows warm and tender, he will no longer execute his fierce anger, not come in wrath (Hos 11:8-9). Finally, God does not retain his anger forever because he delights in steadfast love and compassion (Mic 7:18-19).

See also DAY OF THE LORD; DEATH; DESTRUCTION; EXILE; FORGIVENESS; GOD; REPENTANCE; RETRIBUTION; WARFARE AND DIVINE WARFARE.

BIBLIOGRAPHY. **S. A. Ashmon,** "The Wrath of God: A Biblical Overview," *ConJ* 31 (2005) 348-58; **B. E. Baloian,** *Anger in the Old Testament* (AmUS 7/99; New York: Peter Lang, 1992); **W. Eichrodt,** "The Wrath of God," in *Theology of the Old Testament,* trans. J. Baker (2 vols.; OTL; London: SCM, 1961-1967) 1:258-69; **S. Erlandsson,** "The Wrath of YHWH," *TynBul* 23 (1972) 111-16; **T. E. Fretheim,** "Theological Reflections on the Wrath of God in the Old Testament," *HBT* 24 (2002) 1-26; idem, "'I Was Only a Little Angry': Divine Violence in the Prophets," *Int* 58 (2004) 365-75; **A. T. Hanson,** *The Wrath of the Lamb* (London: SPCK, 1959); **G. A. Herion,** "Wrath of God (OT)," *ABD* 6:989-96; **A. J. Heschel,** "The Meaning and Mystery of Wrath," in *The Prophets* (2 vols.; New York: Harper & Row, 1962) 2:59-78; **K. Latvus,** *God, Anger and Ideology: The Anger of God in Joshua and Judges in Relation to Deuteronomy and the Priestly Writings* (JSOTSup 279; Sheffield:

Sheffield Academic Press, 1998); **J. W. Locke,** "The Wrath of God in the Book of Isaiah," *ResQ* 35 (1993) 221-33; **W. McKane,** "Poison, Trial by Ordeal and the Cup of Wrath," *VT* 30 (1980) 474-92; **R. V. G. Tasker,** *The Biblical Doctrine of the Wrath of God* (London: Tyndale, 1951).

D. T. Lamb

WRITING AND PROPHECY

Ancient prophecies survive, obviously, only because they were put into writing. Who did this and when and why are long-debated topics in OT study. Most research has been done within the Hebrew books in attempts to uncover a prophet's original words, additions from later generations and editorial activities. Until texts became available from the ancient Near East, there were no points of comparison for such inquiries. With the recovery of "prophecies" written in Mesopotamia, Egypt and the Levant, it is possible to consider the processes of recording Hebrew prophecy in that wider context.

1. Survey of Prophetic Texts from the Ancient Near East
2. Writing Prophecies
3. Implications for the History of Hebrew Prophecy

1. Survey of Prophetic Texts from the Ancient Near East.

1.1. Mesopotamia. Written documents from ancient sites survive haphazardly; they often are damaged, and sometimes their provenance is unknown. Although there are numerous texts to show that divination was practiced from the third millennium BC onward, prophecies are rarer, and reports of messages from a god or goddess often do not explain whether they were received through omen taking or by a prophecy—that is, whether advice was sought from a deity and a response given, or a seer spoke unprovoked. Although one word "prophet" (Akk *maḫḫû*) occurs from about 2300 BC onward, prophetic activities are attested only at two periods and from two places: Old Babylonian Mari and Neo-Assyrian Nineveh (*see* Ancient Near Eastern Prophecy).

1.1.1. Old Babylonian Mari. This is the earliest period that has yielded a great variety of written texts in Babylonian, including hundreds of letters, most coming from the last 150 years of the era, about 1750-1600 BC.

About fifty cuneiform tablets found in the

palace of Mari on the Mid-Euphrates, destroyed by Hammurabi of Babylon around 1760 BC, refer to prophets (usually under the term *āpilum*) or contain their words (Nissinen 2003, 13-77). The majority are letters sent to Zimri-Lim, last king of Mari, by officials in the capital or in other towns; a few were sent to his predecessor. They often are brief, broken and obscure; the longest have fifty or sixty lines. Where they are intelligible, the messages cover a wide range of subjects. Their senders reported them because the prophetic words were addressed to the king or concerned him directly, advising or warning him, encouraging him, or requesting action on behalf of the deity. The reports quote the prophets' words "only to the extent the writers of the letters have considered them worth quoting and bringing to the addressee's knowledge" (Nissinen 2003, 13). In one case, an official wrote a letter to accompany one from a prophet who had asked him to provide a "discreet" scribe to write down the god's message to the king (Nissinen 2003, no. 48; cf. no. 4). The tablets were stored in the palace with hundreds of other letters to the king that survive only because they belonged to the last decades of its life. Had life at Mari continued, they probably would have been jettisoned in a later reign as obsolete; it is unlikely that an archivist would have kept the prediction of the downfall of Hammurabi of Babylon, when it proved to be false (Nissinen 2003, no. 22).

Here we should also note one tablet and a fragment of another written at Eshnunna in northeast Babylonia and contemporary with the Mari archive. These bear messages from the local goddess to a king of Eshnunna assuring him of her support and of success in his reign. Although no prophet is mentioned, the texts are similar to some at Mari and presumably were delivered through prophets (Nissinen 2003, 93-95).

1.1.2. Neo-Assyrian Nineveh. The library of King Ashurbanipal, which lay in the ruins of the palaces at Nineveh destroyed in 612 BC, included eleven tablets bearing prophecies. They are addressed to King Esarhaddon and to his mother, to Ashurbanipal and to the people of Assyria and were associated with Arbela, where the goddess Ishtar had a major temple (Nissinen 2003, 97-132). Seven carry individual messages, some with the names of those who spoke them. One begins, "Word of Ishtar," and an-

other, "Thus says Ishtar," while a third has the name of a "prophetess" (Akk *raggintu*, fem. form of *raggimu*) followed by "This is the word of (the goddess)," and a fourth commences, "Words [concerning the Elam]ites" (Nissinen 2003, nos. 91-93). Different are three other tablets and a piece of a fourth. They display a further stage in recording prophecy, for each holds the texts of several reports, at least nine on the best-preserved examples. Each oracle is separated from the next, and the name and the place of origin of each speaker are given for the messages on two of the tablets: "from the mouth of X from the place Y." On the third tablet a ruled line divides each oracle from the next; only after the final one is the speaker's name given; possibly the speaker was responsible for all the oracles on that tablet. Some of the oracles occupy fifty lines or more, others fewer, and one has only two. These three tablets take their place beside other tablets of similar format, but different content, as archival records, whereas six of the other "prophecy" tablets appear to be reports of oracles either as received in Nineveh or as written there, while the format of one may indicate that it is an archive copy.

In addition to those oracle texts, royal inscriptions boast of communications from the gods, and letters from experts to the kings refer to others, probably obtained by the usual medium of divination, and claims to the gods' support without further detail should be understood in that way. However, a few episodes are more explicit, sometimes quoting a deity's words. In one, Ishtar responded to Ashurbanipal's prayer with an oracle beginning "Fear not," although its mode of delivery is unspecified, and followed it with a dream given to a dream interpreter (Nissinen 2003, no. 101). Study of the oracles reveals a few themes that recur in different combinations and a high literary style (Parpola, LXIV-LXVII).

A different sort of "prophecy text" had become part of the scribal tradition, better denoted as "literary predictive texts" (de Jong Ellis, 156-57). The predictions are not addressed to named rulers but rather take an impersonal form common to omen texts and so could be applied whenever the situation described seemed to fit (*COS* 1.480-83). They forecast reigns of certain lengths in which favorable or unfavorable events would occur, and they name places that would face destruction or elevation. Overall, they are similar to omen texts and, like them, could be open to reinterpretation as circumstances, such as place names, changed.

1.2. Egypt. Ancient Egyptians were aware of prophecy and recorded prophetic words. Alas, none of those survive; there are only references to them in other texts, but they suffice to show that the oracles were written (Kitchen, 386-88). The existence of the "Prophecy of Neferti," a forecast of a successful reign after a period of calamity and social decline, although composed after the events that it describes, exemplifies the concept of written reports of prophetic words (*COS* 1.106-10; see Redford, 163-70).

1.3. The Levant. There are few written records in "alphabetic" script from the Levant that relate to prophecy, yet some are significant for this study.

1.3.1. Zakkur. King Zakkur of Hamath erected a stela in Aramaic about 800 BC to celebrate his triumph over hostile neighbouring kings. In it, he relates how his god Baalshamayn spoke to him "through seers and diviners" (*ḥzyn*, *ʿddyn*) assuring him that he would support him and give him success (*COS* 2.155).

1.3.2. Tell Deir ʿAlla. In 1967 fragments of plaster bearing writing in Aramaic script and a local dialect were unearthed, fallen from the wall of a building of uncertain use at this site, east of the Jordan. After the opening title, "The book of Balaam son of Beor, the man who saw the gods," the text that they carry relates a message of imminent disaster that Balaam had received from the gods, but its fragmentary nature prevents any certain interpretation of many lines (*COS* 2.140-45).

1.3.3. Lachish. Among the Hebrew ostraca found at Lachish and dated to the last days of Judah, letter number 3 is to be noted for its mention at the end of a letter with a prophet's warning "Beware!" (Dobbs-Allsopp et al., 308-14; Ahituv, 62-69).

1.3.4. Horvat ʿUza. An ostracon excavated at the site of a seventh-century BC fortress east of Arad has thirteen lines of partially legible literary Hebrew that refer to future events and may be part of an oracle (Cross 135-37; Dobbs-Allsopp et al., 521-27; Ahituv, 173-77).

2. Writing Prophecies.

2.1. When Were Prophecies Recorded? The evidence from Mari and from Nineveh suggests that the messages were written very soon after the oracles were uttered, or they were reported to someone in authority. The Mari letters often convey a sense of urgency. One letter quotes an oracle given three days before, while other reports were sent on the days the prophets spoke (Nissinen 2003, nos. 23, 30-32). It is impossible to tell how soon after the words originally had been spoken that the oracles on the Nineveh tablets were initially recorded or later collected in groups. In the "Egyptian Prophecy of Neferti" the narrative introduction portrays the king taking a papyrus roll and writing what Neferti said, making an immediate record of what he was told should happen (*COS* 1.107).

2.2. Why Were Prophecies Recorded? At Mari the reason for writing is clear: the tablets were sent by officials who believed that their sovereign should be informed of particular oracles. In the palace the tablets were stored with hundreds of other letters from officials in the archives of the last rulers. Similarly, at Nineveh the tablets containing single oracles may have been stored as messages, like the numerous letters and diviners' reports. The larger tablets containing several oracles are different; for some reason, it was considered necessary to preserve groups of prophecies on each of them. They are unique; no other tablets are known that combine messages in this way at Nineveh, such as letters from one writer or a group of scholars to the king. Nothing implies that these texts might become part of the traditional literature that scribes copied from generation to generation as was the case with the "literary predictive prophecies." When the account of Ishtar's oracle is presented in Ashurbanipal's "annals," it is because its words were realized, as were the words of Baalshamayn Zakkur quoted in his stela. The possibility exists, therefore, that reports of some oracles were preserved in order to discover if their forecasts were correct, for that would give weight to later oracles from the same sources, but that was something that might not become known in the near future. For example, in one oracle, Ishtar promised to Esarhaddon that she would bring King Mugallu of Tabal in Anatolia under control. Although Esarhaddon attacked Mugallu, he was only subjugated several years later, in the reign of Esarhaddon's son Ashurbanipal (Fuchs). Thus, records of prophecies could serve as a means of control on their veracity, and those bearing the names of their speakers would be a means of distinguishing the true prophets from the false, allowing the latter to be disqualified. Writing was the principal means of ensuring that information of any sort was accurately preserved across generations, as the numerous legal deeds attest. In the same way, the written reports could continue to serve as witnesses to the prophets' declarations after they and their audiences were dead (see Nissinen 2000, 248-54).

3. Implications for the History of Hebrew Prophecy.

The evidence from the ancient Near East is unequivocal: prophecies could be written down, and this could occur very soon after they were spoken. Already the practice in the eighteenth century BC at Mari and Eshnunna, it was true in Assyria in the seventh century BC, and it was true in Egypt. Since the cuneiform script and scribal traditions were foreign to preexilic Israel and Judah, comparisons may be considered misleading, although there are several points of similarity. Egyptian scribal practices had influence on Hebrew scribes, as their adoption of the hieratic numerals demonstrates, and the Levantine texts, few though they may be, cannot be separated. Zakkur, who received an oracle of support from Baalshamayn, patently erected his stela in the shrine that he built soon after his neighbors lifted their siege (*COS* 2.155). At what date the vision and forecasts of Balaam commemorated at Deir 'Alla were put into writing is unknown; the exemplar from which the text as copied on to the wall there, with its Egyptian style rubrics, may not have been the first copy, so the date of composition may be placed in the ninth century BC or even earlier (Lemaire, 48).

There has been a widespread attitude of OT scholarship that prophets spoke and their words were remembered in oral tradition for decades or generations before they were committed to writing. This view has to be reconsidered (for discussions of many aspects and various opinions, see the essays in Ben Zvi and Floyd). In its most extreme form, proponents of "oral tradition" suppose a looming crisis, either increasing syncretism or political change, as at the fall of Jerusalem, precipitated the writing of oracles and other texts from fear that the memories might be lost. Nowhere in

the ancient Near East can it be shown that such a crisis caused a surge in committing texts to writing. The fact that texts survive from destruction levels, as did the Lachish letters, is an archaeological accident; in peaceful periods people discarded old documents. Since writing was a specialized craft, the creation of books was a scribal activity, and so, it is assumed, scribes were responsible for creating collections of prophetic sayings, the prophets themselves writing on rare occasions when they could not reach an audience orally; they did not write to preserve their words for the future (van der Toorn, 178-82). Furthermore, scribes were primarily active in palaces and temples, mainly in administrative roles in the former, with some working on diplomatic affairs and royal propaganda, so the latter was the place that provided opportunity for composing books of the words that prophets spoke at the shrines (e.g., Jer 7:1-12; 19:14). Those books would then be deposited in the temple archives (van der Toorn, 86-89).

References to biblical prophets writing their oracles, or having them written, are rare: Isaiah, Jeremiah and Habakkuk are portrayed as writing (Is 8:1; 30:8; Jer 29; 30:2; 36; 51:60-64; Hab 2:2), but this does not imply that it was unusual for them to do so. The production of Jeremiah's scroll, written by Baruch at the prophet's dictation, read, then cut up and burned column by column by Jehoiakim, only to be replaced by a more extensive composition, should not be judged a novelty. Rather, the prophet's dictation to his secretary may reflect a custom reaching back to the first of the "writing prophets," Amos and Hosea, and even earlier to the reigns of David and Solomon, if credit can be given to the notice in 2 Chronicles 9: 29. If scribes wrote down the prophets' words, they could have put them into a recognized literary style and, many scholars would suppose, edited or altered them. Now the way scribes of cuneiform and Egyptian were trained both to copy accurately—something essential for commercial, legal and court matters—and to take letters from dictation might point in the other direction, to ensuring that it was the words spoken that they recorded. The same intent appears in the Mari letter cited above in which a prophet who asked an official for a "discreet" scribe to write down the god's message to the king. Examples of scribal corrections in the

Deir ʿAlla Balaam text and an Aramaic treaty stela from Sefire illustrate the concern for accuracy (Millard 1982, 148-49).

The epigraphic remains from Israel are extensive (see Dobbs-Allsopp et al.; Ahituv), but their nature precludes the preservation of lengthy compositions such as the books of the biblical prophets. This does not mean that there were no long compositions, that prophets could only utter a few words at a time, or only short sayings of two or three lines (see Gunkel, 62-67); the Deir ʿAlla Balaam text testifies to longer creations, for it already existed before the days of Amos and Hosea within, or on the edge of, Israelite territory. The longer texts of all sorts, written on wax-covered writing boards (luḥōt), papyrus or leather scrolls, have perished. Whether or not Amos himself could write, the distribution and the variety of the epigraphic remains imply that he would have had little difficulty finding a scribe wherever he was speaking. When he was in Bethel, the priest reported his words to King Jeroboam, quite possibly in writing, and so the prophet could have used a writer there (Amos 7:10-13). This assumes, however, that only scribes could write, or that those trained as scribes never engaged in other activities. Yet that is unnecessary, for the training, demanding as it may have been, did not preclude other occupations. Any priest, for example, might need to be able to read and perhaps to write in order to perform his duties, although he would not spend all his time doing so. Indeed, if there were rotas for priests, as biblical texts prescribe (1 Chron 24), and those priests not in course were living in and beyond Jerusalem, they could well have turned to other occupations, acting as scribes if required. Jeremiah was a priest who wrote.

In towns where cuneiform was current, archives in private houses contained literary as well as legal and administrative documents and letters. In the seventh century BC in Assyria, at Ashur, priests had houses amid those of other citizens, where they lived and kept all sorts of texts (Millard 2008, 260-61). The recovery of Hebrew ostraca from forts in the south of the country (e.g., Tel Masos, Tel ʿIra, Kadesh-Barnea [see Dobbs-Allsopp et al.; Ahituv]) indicates the presence in small garrisons of at least one man who could read. Professional scribes probably were attached to the administration in major centers where they could serve local needs too and so might write the words of a prophet just as well as the letters of a military officer. The fact that prophets who are told to write or are described as "writing" (see above) are not titled "scribe" does not imply that they could not write or had to employ a secretary (Millard 2010, 112).

The large Nineveh tablets show interest in making collections of oracles, whether spoken by one or more "prophets." In ancient Israel the same practice may be assumed. There, initial records might be kept on ostraca or on writing tablets before being transferred to scrolls that could hold lengthy compositions. The greater length of the books of the Hebrew prophets compared with most of the Assyrian oracles is no objection, since standard scrolls, as known from Egypt, averaging nine to twelve feet in length, could accommodate most of their works (Millard 2010, 112-13).

If it is accepted that Hebrew prophecies may have been written soon after their delivery, the question of access arises. Depositing the only copy in the, or a, temple would restrict readership to temple staff. If, as proposed above, priests might keep books in their houses, then prophets might do so too and be able to read them, or have them read, to their fellow citizens. Once one copy was made, others could be taken from it at the cost of the copyist's time and the materials. The dispatch of messages from individuals in one town in Judah to correspondents in another, as several ostraca witness, allows for the transport of scrolls from one town to another, as Jeremiah is portrayed sending a letter and a scroll of prophecies over a larger distance, from Judah to Babylon (Jer 29; 51:59-64).

Ancient written texts usually presuppose an oral context; they were written in order to be read, sooner or later, and reading was done aloud. Undoubtedly, prophetic words could be remembered by prophets and hearers and repeated to the majority, who could not read. The oral and the written existed side by side. Nevertheless, as colophons on cuneiform tablets may carefully note the origins of their exemplars, or scholars cite established omen collections, while Egyptian scribes refer to old books of prophecy (see above), it is clear that the written form carried authority in Mesopotamia and in Egypt, and so, it may be deduced, it did in Israel and Judah. A prophet might revise and reorganize his oracles, but whether or not his disciples or later followers could alter them or bring them up to date, as often is alleged, remains hypothetical in the absence of early manuscripts. It is noteworthy that Assyrian scholars who found ancient omens relevant to their own times did not rephrase them but rather cited them in their original form and then gave their explanations in the form "place X in the text is now place Y" (Millard 1978, 246-49).

Although the majority of people were illiterate, in most places in Israel and Judah someone who was able to read and write could be found if needed, and such a person would not necessarily be a professional scribe. References to Hebrew prophets writing are few; however, this should not be interpreted to mean that they did not normally write, but simply that the activity only deserved notice when it had special significance. The possibility that their oracles were written soon after they had uttered them deserves more attention than it has received in many commentaries.

See also ANCIENT NEAR EASTERN PROPHECY; EDITORIAL/REDACTION CRITICISM; FORM CRITICICSM; FORMATION OF THE PROPHETIC BOOKS; INTERTEXTUALITY AND INNERBIBLICAL INTERPRETATION; LITERARY APPROACHES.

BIBLIOGRAPHY. **S. Ahituv,** *Echoes from the Past: Hebrew and Cognate Inscriptions from the Biblical Period* (Jerusalem: Carta, 2008); **E. Ben Zvi and M. H. Floyd,** eds, *Writings and Speech in Israelite and Ancient Near Eastern Prophecy* (SBLSymS 10; Atlanta: Society of Biblical Literature, 2000); **F. M. Cross,** *Leaves from an Epigrapher's Notebook: Collected Papers in Hebrew and West Semitic Palaeography and Epigraphy* (Winona Lake, IN: Eisenbrauns, 2003); **M. de Jong Ellis,** "Observations on Mesopotamian Oracles and Prophetic Texts: Literary and Historiographic Considerations," *JCS* 41 (1989) 127-86; **F. W. Dobbs-Allsopp et al.,** eds., *Hebrew Inscriptions: Texts from the Biblical Period of the Monarchy with Concordance* (New Haven: Yale University Press, 2005); **A. Fuchs,** "Mugallu," in *The Prosopography of the Neo-Assyrian Empire,* vol. 2, part 2, ed. H. D. Baker (Helsinki: Neo-Assyrian Text Corpus Project, 2001) 761-62; **H. Gunkel,** "Propheten II.B.," in *Die Religion in Geschichte und Gegenwart: Handwörterbuch für Theologie und Religionswissenschaft,* vol. 4 (2nd ed.; Tübingen: Mohr Siebeck, 1930) 1538-54; ET, "IIB The Israelite Prophecy from the Time of Amos," in *Twentieth Century Theology in the Making,* 1: *Themes of Biblical Theology,* trans. R. A. Wilson, ed. J. Pelikan (London: Fontana, 1969) 48-75; **K. A. Kitchen,** *On the Reliability of the Old Testament* (Grand Rapids: Eerdmans, 2003); **A. Lemaire,** "Les inscriptions sur plâtre de Deir ʿAlla et leur signification historique et culturelle," in *The Balaam Text from Deir ʿAlla Re-evaluated: Proceedings of the International Symposium Held at Leiden, 21-24 August 1989,* ed. J. Hoftijzer and G. van der Kooij (Leiden: E. J. Brill, 1991) 33-57; **A. R. Millard,** "Text and Comment," in *Biblical and Near Eastern Studies in Honor of W. S. LaSor,* ed. G. A. Tuttle (Grand Rapids: Eerdmans, 1978) 245-52; idem, "In Praise of Ancient Scribes," *BA* 45 (1982) 143-53; idem, "Books in Ancient Israel," in *D'Ougarit à Jérusalem: Recuil d'études épigraphiques et archéologiques offert à Pierre Bordreuil,* ed. C. Roche (Paris: de Boccard, 2008) 255-64; idem, "'Take a Large Writing Tablet and Write on It': Isaiah—a Writing Prophet?" in *Genesis, Isaiah and Psalms: A Festschrift to Honour Professor John Emerton for His Eightieth Birthday,* ed. K. J. Dell, G. Davies and Y. V. Koh (VTSup 135; Leiden: E. J. Brill, 2010) 105-17; **M. Nissinen,** "Spoken, Written, Quoted, and Invented: Orality and Writtenness in Ancient Near Eastern Prophecy," in *Writings and Speech in Israelite and Ancient Near Eastern Prophecy,* ed. E. Ben Zvi and M. H. Floyd (SBLSymS 10; Atlanta: Society of Biblical Literature, 2000) 235-71; idem, *Prophets and Prophecy in the Ancient Near East* (SBLWAW 12; Atlanta: Society of Biblical Literature, 2003); **D. B. Redford,** "Scribe and Speaker," in *Writings and Speech in Israelite and Ancient Near Eastern Prophecy,* ed. E. Ben Zvi and M. H. Floyd (SBLSymS 10; Atlanta: Society of Biblical Literature, 2000) 145-218; **K. van der Toorn,** *Scribal Culture and the Making of the Hebrew Bible* (Cambridge, MA: Harvard University Press, 2007).

A. R. Millard

YAHWEH. *See* GOD.

Z

ZECHARIAH, BOOK OF

Zechariah is the penultimate and longest of the twelve books of the Minor Prophets (*see* Twelve, Book of the). It is ascribed to the sixth-century BC prophet Zechariah, son of Berekiah, and contains prophecies addressed to the postexilic Jewish community in Judea. In length it is fractionally shorter than the book of the prophet Daniel of the Major Prophets.

1. Historical Background
2. Main Divisions
3. The Obscurity of the Book
4. The Text
5. Zechariah A (Zech 1—6)
6. Zechariah B (Zech 7—8)
7. Zechariah C (Zech 9—14)
8. Main Themes
9. History of Interpretation

1. Historical Background.

The prophetic ministry of Zechariah overlaps with that of *Haggai, and both prophets are concerned with the rebuilding of the *temple in Jerusalem after the Babylonian *exile (see Ezra 5:1-2). After the decree of the Persian king Cyrus had given the Jews permission to return to their homeland in 538 BC (see 2 Chron 36:22-23; Ezra 1:2-4), an initial contingent of Jews led by Sheshbazzar had undertaken the long trek back to Jerusalem and had begun to reestablish themselves in what was now the Persian province of Yehud (Ezra 1:5-11). They began rebuilding the temple shortly after their return, in 536 BC, but were prevented by local opposition from continuing (Ezra 3—4) (*see* Israelite History). It was sixteen years later, in 520 BC, that Haggai arose to urge the people to take up this task again (Hag 1:12-15). In that same year, while Haggai was still active as a prophet, he was joined in his ministry by his younger contemporary Zechariah. Little is known about Zechariah, beyond the fact that he belonged to a priestly family and seems to have been raised by his grandfather Iddo (compare Zech 1:1, 7 with Ezra 5:1; 6:14).

Other major actors in the postexilic community of Zechariah's day were Joshua the high priest and Zerubbabel the prince, both of whom are mentioned by name in the book of Zechariah. The former was the grandson of Seraiah, the last high priest before the exile, and the latter was the grandson of Jehoiachin, the last king of Judah before the exile, and therefore a direct descendant of David. No doubt for that reason he had been appointed governor of Yehud by his Persian overlords. As the cultic and civic leaders, respectively, of the postexilic community, Joshua and Zerubbabel represented in their persons the institutional continuity with preexilic Israel.

Zechariah's ministry began at a time of great turmoil in the Persian Empire. Cyrus the Great had died in 530 BC, and his son and successor, Cambyses, died unexpectedly in 522 BC The throne was then seized by Darius, who spent the first two years of his reign putting down a series of rebellions throughout the empire. These rebellions and their suppression are recorded in the famous Behistun inscription, which is almost exactly contemporaneous with Zechariah's night visions, and which initially seems hard to reconcile with the horsemen's report that "the whole earth lies quiet and peaceful" (Zech 1:11). Darius successfully put down all the rebellions, and he reigned until his death in 486 BC, shortly after his defeat at the hands of the Greeks at Marathon. Since Zechariah, like Darius, probably was a young man in 520 BC, he may also have lived to hear of this battle and, in general, to be aware of the epic conflict between the Greeks and Persians.

2. Main Divisions.

The book of Zechariah is best thought of as threefold, consisting of the following sections: part A (Zech 1—6), comprising mainly eight visions seen by the prophet in one night; part B (Zech 7—8), consisting largely of exhortations and warnings occasioned by a question about fasting; part C (Zech 9—14), dealing chiefly with the future that God has in store for Jerusalem and his people. Parts A and B are dated (520/519 BC and 516 BC, respectively), but part C is undated. Although since the nineteenth century parts A and B have commonly been grouped together as "Proto-Zechariah," in contrast to part C as "Deutero-Zechariah," there is insufficient warrant for this. Part B stands out as quite distinct in subject and genre from part A, which has led a significant minority of exegetes to group it with part C instead (e.g., Kline; Conrad; Sweeney; Webb). However, since part B is also quite different from part C, it is preferable to reject the binary division of the book altogether and to accept the threefold analysis that has been defended by others (e.g., Feinberg 1976; Bauer; Tidiman).

3. The Obscurity of the Book.

The book of Zechariah is notorious for its obscurity. Although part B consists mainly of relatively straightforward exhortations and admonitions, parts A and C have been the despair of exegetes throughout the history of interpretation. Part A is obscure because it consists largely of dreamlike visions interspersed with apparently unrelated nonvisionary material. Even when the visions are accompanied by an explanation, the explanation itself may be enigmatic (as in Zech 4:14). Part C is difficult to understand because it is composed almost entirely of a kaleidoscope of divine threats and promises regarding the indefinite future of Jerusalem, Israel and the nations, but often having no clearly identifiable referents in actual history. Commentators diverge widely on the question as to when (or whether) these predictions have been or will be fulfilled, or what historical circumstances they reflect. It is not without reason that the church father Jerome called Zechariah *obscurissimus liber* ("a most obscure book"), and that the medieval Jewish commen-

tator Rashi declared that the book of Zechariah would not be understood until the Messiah came. Despite the book's obscurity, however, it contains many messianic predictions that in the light of the NT clearly find their fulfillment in Jesus Christ.

4. The Text.

With the exception of the LXX, the ancient versions generally reflect a proto-Masoretic parent text—a consonantal text that is essentially the same as the MT. In the case of the Peshitta, it needs to be pointed out that its proto-Masoretic character applies primarily to the earliest attested form of the Syriac text, which is not the same as that printed in the Leiden Peshitta. The latter is generally based on later manuscripts, which have incorporated a number of inner-Syriac changes away from the traditional Hebrew text. In the case of the LXX, the Greek of Zechariah (as of the other Minor Prophets) appears to be based on an unreliable Hebrew text (perhaps a single faulty manuscript). Although the LXX occasionally gives a clue to a reading that is superior to the MT (e.g., Zech 1:21 [MT 2:4]; 5:6), this is the exception rather than the rule. In most cases where the LXX reflects a parent Hebrew text that is different from the MT, the latter is to be preferred. Nevertheless, although the MT generally preserves the best recoverable Hebrew text, it is far from perfect. There are a number of places where the MT appears to be garbled (e.g., Zech 2:8 [MT 2:12]; 6:3, 6-7). Although a better Hebrew text sometimes can be restored with some degree of plausibility, it generally is safer to deal with the MT as it has been transmitted and to admit that the text has suffered in transmission. Needless to say, these textual difficulties also contribute to the overall obscurity of the book.

5. Zechariah A (Zech 1—6). This part of Zechariah has three subsections.

5.1. Call to Repentance. The first subsection of Zechariah A (Zech 1:1-6) is a brief opening call to repentance to the postexilic community, reminding them of the terrible consequences of Israel's disobedience in the past. It is not so much an introduction to the book as a whole as the chronologically earliest message that the prophet received (in November-December 520 BC).

5.2. Night Visions and Episodes. The second and largest subsection of Zechariah A (Zech

1:7—6:8) consists of a series of eight night *visions interspersed with a number of nonvisionary passages, which may be called "episodes," and whose connection with the visions themselves is unclear. Although not as tightly structured as has sometimes been suggested, the eight visions form a loosely structured cycle, with the first and last clearly balancing each other, and the middle two focusing on the central concern of restoring the cult (priesthood and temple) in Jerusalem.

5.2.1. First Vision: Riders (Zech 1:7-17). The account of the first vision can be divided into four sections: the vision itself (Zech 1:8), the dialogue that follows (Zech 1:9-10), the expansion of the vision (Zech 1:11-13) and the Lord's assurance (Zech 1:14-17). In the vision itself the prophet sees a man seated on a chestnut horse coming to a halt among myrtle bushes in a shaded garden (not a glen). It is a depiction of God's throne room in heaven that seems to be modeled on its contemporary counterpart on earth in the Persian Empire, the "paradise" or garden palace in the imperial capital of Pasargadae. Behind this rider are other horses of various colors, which turn out to have been on a divinely authorized reconnaissance mission, led by the messenger (or "angel") of the Lord. The horsemen were couriers, heavenly counterparts of the mounted Persian couriers who were a familiar sight near Jerusalem in Zechariah's day, who had been sent out by the Lord to report back to their divine commander on the conditions that prevailed on earth. They report that "the whole earth lies quiet and peaceful," probably an allusion to the prophecy of Isaiah 14:7, which predicts the fall of the king of *Babylon, and which was in the process of being finally fulfilled at the time of the vision (see Wolters 2008). The vision account concludes with the Lord's assurance that he is returning to Jerusalem to reestablish his residence there.

5.2.2. Second Vision: Horns and Craftsmen (Zech 1:18-21 [MT 2:1-4]). Zechariah sees four horns, representing the powers that had scattered God's people to the four winds, and four craftsmen, who as agents of God's judgment destroy the horns in their turn. In Zechariah 1:21 what the craftsmen come to do is best understood as referring to the dehorning of cattle, with the MT slightly emended in light of the LXX to read "to sharpen their blade, in order to gouge out the horns of the nations."

5.2.3. Third Vision: The Surveyor (Zech 2:1-5 [MT 2:5-9]). Zechariah sees a surveyor, measuring line in hand, who is prevented from measuring the dimensions of Jerusalem, apparently because such measuring would needlessly restrict the size of the city. Instead, the Lord declares that he himself, as a dynamic "wall of fire," will define the limits, making room for a multitude of people and animals to live there.

5.2.4. Episode I (Zech 2:6-13 [MT 2:10-17]). This is the first of three interruptions of the vision sequence, sometimes called "oracles" or "epexegeses," which may more appropriately be called "episodes" (compare the *epeisodia* of Greek drama). Episode I consists of an appeal to the Jews who remain in exile to return to Jerusalem. This appeal is likely connected to the turbulent situation in Babylon at the time (519 BC), when a leader claiming to be Nebuchadnezzar was leading a revolt against the Persian hegemony. Tellingly, the Jewish exiles are addressed as *"Zion" (Zech 2:10), tacitly equating God's people, whatever their geographical location, with Jerusalem. Here God's people are also called "the apple of his eye," and anyone who touches them is threatened with judgment (Zech 2:8-9). This exhortation to return is followed by a call to rejoice because the Lord promises once again to take up residence among his people (Zech 2:10). Beyond that, he also declares that in future many nations (*goyîm*) will attach themselves to him and be "my people" (Zech 2:11). The Lord will make a fresh start with his people back in Jerusalem and the "holy land" (Zech 2:12). When all of these things come to pass, Zechariah's status as a true prophet of the Lord will be vindicated (Zech 2:9, 11).

5.2.5. Fourth Vision: The High Priest Reclothed (Zech 3:1-7). Zechariah sees the high priest Joshua, who is stripped of his filthy (Heb *ṣôʾîm*; lit., "excrement-smeared") clothes and dressed in clean garments instead, no doubt representing the acquittal of the high priest as representative of his people, and his reinvestiture in office after the exile. In this dramatic scene, which is unlike the other visions in a number of formal respects, both the Accuser (*śāṭān*) and the "messenger ['angel'] of the LORD" play a role, the one to accuse the obviously guilty Joshua in the court of heaven (Zech 3:1), and the other to stand by (Zech 3:1, 5) and to lay a solemn charge on him to be faithful in his priestly duties (Zech 3:6-7). This charge ends with an enigmatic promise, literally, "then I will give you walkers [*mahlĕkîm*] among these standers" (Zech 3:7b), which leaves unclear (despite the dictionary definition of *mahlĕkîm* as "access") what or who these mysterious "walkers" are. Another active participant is the prophet himself, who interrupts the proceedings to ensure that Joshua also receives the high priest's turban (Zech 3:5). Nevertheless, the central actor is God himself, who silences the Accuser and pronounces the acquittal: "Look, I am absolving you of your guilt, and I am clothing you in spotless robes" (Zech 3:4).

5.2.6. Episode II (Zech 3:8-10). Attached to the fourth vision, but connected to it only by its reference to Joshua, is a further prophecy consisting of three distinct promises: the coming of the messianic servant named "Semah" (Zech 3:8), the removal of the guilt of the land in a single day (Zech 3:9), and the future return, "on that day," of prosperity and peace (Zech 3:10). The Semah of the first promise, foreshadowed by the Israelite priesthood represented by Joshua and his colleagues (which is why they are called "the men of omen"), is reminiscent of the messianic prophecy concerning a coming Semah (*ṣemah*, which means "Shoot," not "Branch") in Jeremiah 23:5; 33:15. The second promise is engraved by the Lord himself on a stone that he places "in front of" Joshua, where the prepositional phrase perhaps is to be understood as much in a chronological or typological sense as in a spatial one. The third promise finally gives an idyllic picture, in traditional terms, of prosperity in an agricultural society.

5.2.7. Fifth Vision: The Menorah and Olive Trees (Incorporating Episode III) (Zech 4:1-14). As though wakened from sleep, Zechariah sees a golden menorah with seven lamps flanked by two olive trees that supply the oil for the lamps (Zech 4:1-3). When the prophet asks what these things represent (Zech 4:4), the answer given by the interpreting messenger (Zech 4:5-6a) is twofold. The first part of the answer turns out to be episode III, full of encouraging words addressed to Zerubbabel (Zech 4:6b-10a). The second part explains that "these seven," apparently referring to the seven lamps of the menorah, are the eyes of the Lord as they scan the world (Zech 4:10b). In a second dialogue with the messenger the prophet now learns that the

two olive trees—more precisely, the two olive-laden "spikes" or branch ends that supply the lamps with oil—are the two "sons of oil" (*bĕnê-hayyiṣhār*), which are said to stand before the Lord of the earth (Zech 4:14).

Although this enigmatic vision is puzzling in many ways, a number of things stand out. The almost violent insertion of episode III, although it does not explicitly refer to the details of the vision and seems to leave the second part of the messenger's explanation hanging in the air, emphatically makes the point that this vision must be understood as a message for Zerubbabel, meant to reassure him that the Spirit of God would enable him to overcome all obstacles to the temple-building project. It is therefore also clear that the *mĕnôrâ* (a word that everywhere else in the OT occurs only in connection with the tabernacle and temple) is a symbol of the temple itself, the holy place where the Lord will again take up residence after the exile. As for the tantalizing phrase "sons of oil" in Zechariah 4:14, this refers in the first instance not to persons but idiomatically to the oil-rich branch ends of the olive trees themselves. There may be a second level of meaning as well, but it is unclear whether on that level it refers to heavenly figures, the prophets Haggai and Zechariah, the contemporary leaders Joshua and Zerubbabel, or some other pair.

5.2.8. Sixth Vision: The Scroll (Zech 5:1-4). Zechariah sees a billboard-sized flying scroll that is identified as "the curse," directed against thieves and perjurers, whose homes it will enter and destroy. The enigmatic Hebrew clause in Zechariah 5:3b is perhaps best rendered, "For everyone who steals has escaped punishment for this—just like that! And everyone who swears (falsely) has escaped punishment for this—just like that!"

5.2.9. Seventh Vision: The Ephah (Zech 5:5-11). Zechariah sees a bushel-sized container (*'êpâ*) containing a female figure, explicitly identified as "Guilt" and "Wickedness," which is picked up by two winged women and flown to a specially prepared shrine in Shinar (i.e., Babylonia). In Zechariah 5:6 the puzzling form *'ênām* (*'ynm*) of the MT, literally "their eye," should be read as *'ăwōnām* (*'wn-m*), meaning "guilt," taking the final letter as an enclitic *mēm*.

5.2.10. Eighth Vision: The Chariots (Zech 6:1-8). Zechariah sees four chariots, drawn by horses of different colors, go out from between two "mountains of bronze" (apparently the gateway of heaven) to different points of the compass on earth. The chariots are identified as "the four winds [*rûḥôt*] of heaven" (Zech 6:5), evoking the image of God riding on the winds like a charioteer. At the same time, the description of this vision also exploits the ambiguity of the word *rûḥôt* (sg. *rûaḥ*), since it can also designate the four points of the compass, as well as the personal "spirits" that are sent out from God's throne room. Furthermore, in the climax of the vision in Zechariah 6:8 there is a further play on the meanings of *rûaḥ* when the Lord states that the northbound horses "cause my *rûaḥ* to rest in the land of the north." Here the reference probably is to the wrath of God being vented on pagan Babylonia. Nevertheless, in the tantalizing ambiguity that so often characterizes the night visions, it is also possible that this phrase has the positive sense "cause my Spirit to rest in the land of the north," which gives the vision an entirely different message. Another puzzling feature of this last vision, at least as preserved in the MT, is that two of the four chariots are said to go north, and one south, but no destination is mentioned for the fourth, giving rise to the suspicion that the text may be in some disarray. In any case, it is clear that this final vision, with its heaven-sent and variously colored horses, is meant as a counterpart to the first vision, ending the vision cycle with a kind of inclusio.

5.3. The Crowning of Joshua and the Coming of Semah (Zech 6:9-15). The third subsection of Zechariah A describes a remarkable coronation scene, accompanied by an enigmatic messianic prophecy (*see* Messiah). Zechariah places a crown, fashioned from gold and silver contributed by a deputation of the Jews still in Babylon, on the head of Joshua the high priest, and simultaneously announces the coming of a royal figure, again called "Semah" ("Shoot"), who will build the temple. This unidentified Semah is not the high priest himself, but rather is someone else who will rule either as or with a priestly figure. In the light of the NT this Shoot can be identified as the king-priest Jesus Christ. The crown placed on Joshua's head is to be preserved in the temple as a reminder of this promise. This section ends, abruptly and suggestively, in a notable example of the literary figure of aposiopesis: "If you really obey the LORD your God, . . . " an echo of the beginning of Deuteronomy 28:1. The reader is expected to mentally supply the unexpressed conclusion of this familiar text, which consists of an extraordinary promise of *blessing. This understood promise also functions as an adumbration of the two remaining parts of the book that now follow.

6. Zechariah B (Zech 7—8).
These chapters, which form a distinct literary unit on their own, stand apart from the rest of Zechariah in that they consist mainly of straightforward ethical exhortations about life in the *covenant, together with the warnings and promises that go with them. These prophetic appeals are framed by the question about fasting that is posed near the beginning of Zechariah 7 (Zech 7:3) and not answered until near the end of Zechariah 8 (Zech 8:18). The question is posed by a delegation from Babylonia, on behalf of Bethel-Sarezer, who inquires of the priests and prophets in Jerusalem whether annual fasts should be continued now that the seventy years of exile were coming to an end. The answer that Zechariah finally gives is that these fasts will be transformed into feasts.

In the intervening material we find urgent appeals to do *justice (Zech 7:9, 8:16), to show kindness and compassion (Zech 7:9), to avoid harshness toward the marginalized or ill-intentioned schemes against others (Zech 7:10), and to speak the truth to one another (Zech 8:16). It is Israel's failure to do these things in the past that has led to the exile. Now, however, especially after the laying of the foundation of the temple, a new era of blessing is dawning (Zech 8:1-15).

Although it is true that the question about fasting near the beginning is balanced by the prophet's answer near the end, there is no clear chiastic pattern that structures these two chapters throughout. The differing claims to the contrary by some scholars (e.g., Baldwin; Butterworth; Tidiman) tend to cancel each other out. What is true, however, is the observation that there are a number of striking verbal parallels between Zechariah 7—8 and the book of Haggai (especially concentrated in Zech 8:9-13). Whether this constitutes evidence for some kind of secondary redactional shaping remains controversial, however.

These chapters conclude with two verses that open up a perspective to the world at large and in this way provide a transition to Zechariah C. After the answer to the initial question about fasting had been given in Zechariah 8:18-19, the prophet concludes with the promise that many Gentiles will in the future join the Jews (or one specific Jew) as they go up to Jerusalem to *worship the Lord. Although this may initially have referred to proselytes who participated in the restored annual pilgrimages to Jerusalem after the exile, it is clear from the perspective of the NT that this prophecy finds an even greater fulfillment in the inclusion of the Gentiles in the church (see Wolters 2006).

7. Zechariah C (Zech 9—14).

Although part C is commonly subdivided into two "oracles," it is in fact not clear that the heading "oracle" in each case is meant to refer to all of the subsequent three chapters. The component parts of these chapters, although all are predictions (promises and threats) of some sort, are of a very heterogeneous character and are not always clearly related to each other. It is too much to say that these chapters are "a haphazard collection of pieces of prophetic tradition strung together by catchwords" (O'Brien, 231), but it is also true that attempts to discern some overall literary pattern in their arrangement (e.g., Lamarche; Kline; Tidiman) have been unsuccessful.

7.1. The First Oracle (Zech 9—11). A new section is signaled by the phrase (to be repeated in Zech 12:1) "An oracle. The word of the LORD." The word for "oracle" (*maśśāʾ*), traditionally translated "burden," here introduces two chapters dealing with judgment on Israel's enemies and deliverance for Israel.

7.1.1. The King of Peace amid War (Zech 9). Although this chapter has its own literary unity, perhaps conforming to the pattern of an ancient "Divine Warrior Hymn" (Hanson), it is also a kind of triptych, with two longer panels that describe the Lord's warfare against Israel's enemies flanking a shorter central panel that announces the coming of a messianic king who will bring an end to warfare.

7.1.1.1. The Lord's Campaign from Syria to Jerusalem (Zech 9:1-8c). In a military campaign that moves from the cities of Syria to the cities of the coast, first of Phoenicia and then of Philistia, the divine warrior defeats these traditional enemies of Israel and then moves again inland to protect Jerusalem (*see* Warfare and Divine Warfare). It often has been pointed out that this trajectory follows closely the campaign of Alexander the Great in 333 BC, which initiated the Hellenistic period of Israel's history. Especially noteworthy is the description of the conquest of Tyre in Zechariah 9:3-4, which seems to correspond to Alexander's famous capture of the island fortress.

7.1.1.2. The Divine Peacemaker (Zech 9:8d-10). In an abrupt departure from the martial theme of the first panel of the triptych, the central panel (beginning with Zech 9:8d: "Yes, now I see with my eyes") envisages the coming of a humble messianic king who will announce peace and destroy the tools of war. In describing the future kingdom of peace the prophet, in Zechariah 9:10, quotes Psalm 72, long regarded in both Jewish and Christian tradition as describing the coming messianic king. A plausible emendation of the MT, supported by all the ancient versions, reads *ûmošiaʿ* instead of *wĕnôšaʿ* in Zechariah 9:9, so that the coming king is described as "righteous and a Savior," which in turn is a probable allusion to Isaiah 45:21, "a righteous God and a Savior," thus implicitly ascribing divinity to the coming king. In the NT Jesus applies this prophecy to himself by deliberately enacting the predicted scenario in his triumphal entry of Jerusalem (Mt 21:1-11 par.).

7.1.1.3. The Lord Wages War Against the Greeks and Promises Prosperity (Zech 9:11-17). In another abrupt change the third panel reverts to the theme of a future divine war and the prosperity that it will introduce. Since it predicts a dramatic military victory of the "sons of Zion" over the "sons of Greece," followed by a period of peace and prosperity, this passage has long been interpreted as a reference to the Maccabean victory over Antiochus IV in 164 BC, which ended the period of Hellenistic overlordship and introduced the Hasmonean phase of Jewish history. This interpretation finds striking support if the "arrow" of the Lord mentioned in Zechariah 9:14 is taken to refer to Halley's Comet, which appeared in the sky over Jerusalem precisely at the time when Antiochus IV unexpectedly died and the Jews recaptured and rededicated the temple (see Wolters 1993).

7.1.2. The Lord Remembers His People (Zech 10). After an initial exhortation to seek prosperity, not from deceitful diviners, but only from the Lord (Zech 10:1-2), the Lord himself speaks words of judgment against Israel's faithless leaders (shepherds), but words of promise to the people (flock) themselves. In an arresting image, he says that he will transform this flock into his magnificent warhorse and will lead them to victory over their enemies (Zech 10:3). He also makes the remarkable promise that he will bring back from foreign lands not only the exiles of Judah, but also those of the erstwhile northern kingdom (designated "Ephraim," and "Joseph"), who had been deported by the Assyrians some two centuries earlier. In another enigmatic passage with messianic overtones (Zech 10:4), he states that out of Judah will come the cornerstone, the peg, the battle bow and "every ruler together."

7.2. Two Curses and Two Shepherds (Zech 11). Whereas the two preceding chapters had given a positive message for Israel, Zechariah 11 is starkly negative with respect to Israel's prospects. It begins and ends with a "curse"—that is, a divine announcement of disaster—against Israel's leaders, and these two curses frame a central section about two shepherds that describes the Lord's determination to break his covenant commitment to Israel. This central section (often called the "shepherd allegory") has the well-deserved reputation of being one of the most difficult pericopes in the entire OT, both exegetically and theologically.

7.2.1. The Forest Curse (Zech 11:1-3). In an artfully constructed initial poem about a devastating forest fire beginning on Mount Lebanon, the reader is initially lulled into believing that the foregoing reassuring announcements of God's judgment against Israel's enemies are continuing, with the tall trees of the forest symbolizing the leadership of Gentile *nations. But in the very last words of the poem, "the pride of the Jordan" (i.e., the lush jungle flanking the Jordan before it empties into the Dead Sea), the rhetorical trap is sprung, and the reader realizes that the divine judgment is now directed against Israel itself and has reached even the restricted area of Yehud, where the postexilic Jewish community had settled.

7.2.2. The Two Shepherds (Zech 11:4-16). After the foregoing ominous beginning this section relates how the Lord commands Zechariah on two separate occasions to play the role of a shepherd to God's flock, a shepherd who in both cases abandons them to their fate. In the case of the first prophetic shepherd impersonation, he is called to tend "the flock destined

for slaughter," and his two staffs, designated "Graciousness" and "Solidarity" (Zech 11:7) and representing respectively God's covenant (Zech 11:10) and the brotherhood between Judah and Israel (Zech 11:14), are deliberately chopped into pieces (Heb *gd^c*) by the prophet-shepherd. Through the actions of this shepherd the Lord announces his intention to pity his people no longer and to hand them over to oppressive overlords (Zech 11:6). It should be noted that the covenant represented by the first staff, designated *bĕrît hā'ammîm* (Zech 11:10), almost certainly refers not to an otherwise unknown covenant with the nations in general, but rather to God's covenant with the nation of Israel. In abandoning his imagined post, the shepherd suggests and receives the substantial sum of thirty shekels of silver as severance pay, which he then contributes to the temple as a votary offering to the Lord. In Zechariah 11:13 the word *'eder* of the MT should be revocalized as the verbal form *'eddor*, and the phrase that it introduces should be translated as "I will vow the weight I am worth, and no longer burden them," representing an uncomplimentary allusion to the worth of a woman compared to that of a man in Leviticus 28. It is this passage that is quoted (and attributed to Jeremiah) in Matthew 27:9, where it is used in a very different context to refer to the thirty pieces of silver paid to Judas. The Lord now calls the prophet to a second shepherd impersonation, explicitly bidding him to be a "foolish shepherd" (*rō'eh 'ĕwilî*) who will neglect and abuse the flock (Zech 11:15-16).

7.2.3. The Shepherd Curse (Zech 11:17). The enigmatic chapter concludes with another curse, this time directed against "the worthless shepherd" (*rō'î hā'ĕlîl*). This designation could refer to either the just-mentioned "foolish shepherd" or to the ruinous prophet-shepherd in both his roles, despite the fact that in both cases the role was played by divine appointment. The curse is pronounced on the shepherd's arm and on his right eye, thereby effectively disabling him from doing his job. Presumably, this means that the future evil leaders whose roles the prophet had enacted are now in turn to be punished by God. The many attempts to identify the enacted shepherds of this chapter with known historical personages have been notably unsuccessful.

7.3. The Second Oracle (Zech 12—14). As in

Zechariah 9:1, a new section is introduced by the words "An oracle. The word of the LORD." The three chapters that follow present an alternation of positive and negative predictions, focusing especially on Jerusalem as the symbol of God's covenant people. These chapters are characterized by the frequent use of the eschatological phrase "on that day," which sounds like a drumbeat on an average of every two or three verses.

7.3.1. Jerusalem's Enemies Destroyed (Zech 12:1-9). The Lord, after identifying himself as the creator of both the universe in general and the human spirit in particular, announces that the nations around Jerusalem will only inflict harm upon themselves (Zech 12:2-3). By God's strength and his active intervention the inhabitants of Jerusalem will defeat their enemies and make their city secure in its place (Zech 12:4-9). There is some suggestion that Jerusalem and Judah (i.e., the Persian province Yehud), although they will fight alongside each other against their common enemy (Zech 12:5-6), will also be in competition with each other to some extent (Zech 12:2), so that the Lord must ensure that the metropolis does not receive more glory than does its hinterland (Zech 12:7). The difficult conclusion of Zechariah 12:2 is best translated as "and it will also be necessary for Judah [to join] the siege of Jerusalem," suggesting that some inhabitants of Judah had been forced by the enemy to be part of the siege of the capital.

7.3.2. Mourning for the Pierced One (Zech 12:10-14). In another abrupt transition, the Lord now turns to a future event affecting Jerusalem that will be of quite a different kind. It will be a dramatic change in the inward affections of its inhabitants, a change associated with the death of someone closely identified with the Lord himself, whom they have killed by "piercing" him. This change is initiated by God pouring out a "spirit of grace and pleas for grace" (Zech 12:10), and it manifests itself in comprehensive national mourning over this pierced one. This mysterious figure, who was interpreted as the Messiah already in early Judaism, is identified in the NT with Jesus Christ (Jn 19:37).

7.3.3. Sin Cleansed (Zech 13:1-6). The scene changes again. "On that day" a cleansing fountain will be opened up for the inhabitants of Jerusalem (Zech 13:1), and the Lord will forcibly remove *idolatry and false prophecy from the land (Zech 13:2). That it is false prophecy, not prophecy in general, that is in view here is clear from the association of "prophets" and "unclean spirit" in Zechariah 13:2. Anyone who has acted as a prophet, if he is not killed by his own parents (Zech 13:3), will now vehemently deny having prophesied (Zech 13:5-6).

7.3.4. The Fate of the Shepherd and the Flock (Zech 13:7-9). In a passage reminiscent of the second curse of Zechariah 11:17, the Lord now calls on his sword to strike someone described as "my shepherd, my associate." As with the mysterious "pierced one" of Zechariah 12:10, there is a close identification between this shepherd and the Lord himself, so that in the NT Jesus could apply this verse to himself (Mt 26:13; Mk 14:27). Not only does the Lord wield his sword against his shepherd-associate, but as the now shepherdless flock scatters, he also attacks their undershepherds (Zech 13:7). It should be noted that the phrase "turn my hand to the *ṣōʿărîm*" (Zech 13:7) does not denote a caring gesture for the little ones of the flock, but instead a threatening gesture against the shepherd lads who assisted in tending the flock. The completely leaderless flock is now subjected to a severe trial: two thirds are to be killed (Zech 13:8), and the remaining third will be tested and purified like silver or gold in a crucible (Zech 13:9a). Only then will the covenant relationship with the surviving remnant be restored (Zech 13:9b).

7.3.5. The Lord Comes and Reigns (Zech 14:1-21). In this final dramatic depiction of the coming *Day of the Lord everything is again focused on Jerusalem. Initially, the Lord allows the nations to attack, plunder and terrorize the city, but then he himself turns against its enemies and performs many miraculous works. In many ways, it seems, the natural order of things will be turned upside down. The regular alternation of night and day will cease, and (according to the most plausible meaning of the difficult phrase in Zech 14:6b) "heavy things will float up." The Lord himself will physically touch down on the Mount of Olives, with the result that it will split in two to form a valley of escape. The surrounding countryside will drop down to the level of the Dead Sea, leaving Jerusalem perched high and safe in its original place. To this Jerusalem the nations of the world will now come to worship the God of the Jews at the annual Feast of Booths. Perhaps most startling of all, in this new Jerusalem the category "Holy to the Lord" will no longer be restricted to the cult; it will be extended to ordinary kitchen utensils and mundane horse tack. No "Canaanite" will be found in the eschatological city.

8. Main Themes.

Despite the obscurity and apparently jumbled character of much of Zechariah, there are broad themes that come through clearly. Among such themes we find the centrality of Jerusalem ("Jerusalem" and "Zion" together occur a total of forty-seven times, quite evenly distributed throughout the book). It is to Jerusalem that the remaining exiles are exhorted to return (Zech 9:12), and it is to Jerusalem that all nations will eventually come to serve Yahweh (Zech 14:16). Other themes are the future inclusion of all nations in Yahweh's covenant (Zech 2:11; 8:20-23), and the continuity with earlier prophecy (throughout the book). As in so many of the prophets, overshadowing all these themes is the emphasis on the sovereignty of *God in both judgment and grace. Terrible judgment is threatened both against the nations at large (Zech 1:21; 2:9; 6:7-8; 9:1-7; 12:3-4, 9; 14:3, 12) and against God's own covenant people (Zech 13:8-9). Particularly chilling is the passage in which God commands the prophet to enact a scenario in which two shepherds are sent to rule over his people, both of whom will abandon and ruin them (Zech 11:4-16). But inexplicable grace is the dominant note. It is not only manifested in the present, as God returns in mercy to his people after the severe punishment of the exile (Zech 1:16-17), but also promised for the future (Zech 8:1-5, 12-13; 9:8, 16-17; 10:6). Especially prominent among these promises of grace are the predictions concerning a coming messianic figure, the Semah or Shoot (Zech 3:8; 6:12-13). In addition, the expectation of a future Davidic king continues to be kept alive. Contrary to some scholarly opinion, this expectation is still clearly present in Zechariah C (see Petterson), and in some ways it resonates with Isaiah's accounts of the Suffering *Servant (Lamarche, 124-47).

9. History of Interpretation.

Much of patristic exegesis—for example, the commentary by Didymus the Blind (fourth-century AD, rediscovered in the mid-twentieth century)—was characterized by an uninhibited allegorical interpretation. The great exception is Didymus's contemporary Theodore of Mopsuestia, who espoused a more literal and historical interpretation. He and a number of Syriac commentators (notably Ephraem Syrus) interpreted the predictions of Zechariah C as referring primarily to the history of Israel before the coming of Christ, especially the time of the Maccabees. Jerome wrote an influential commentary on two levels: one "literal," in which he drew on the Hebrew text and Jewish sources, and one "spiritual," which was heavily dependent on Didymus's allegorical commentary.

Jerome's commentary dominated the interpretation of the Latin West until the time of the Reformation. Early modern interpretation was dominated by Protestant exegetes and by a turn away from allegory toward a philological and historical understanding of the Hebrew text. Nevertheless, it was still characterized by great diversity, especially regarding the historical referents of Zechariah 9—14. Zechariah 14, for example, was taken to refer to the church age (Martin Luther), to the centuries between Zechariah and Christ (John Calvin), to the end times preceding the last judgment (John Oecolampadius), and to the period of the Maccabees (Hugo Grotius). Until the late eighteenth century, there nevertheless was broad agreement that the canonical book of Zechariah was a divinely inspired part of Holy Scripture, spoke the truth about future events, and portrayed the coming Messiah in terms that were fulfilled in Jesus Christ. This also applied to those who, on the basis of Matthew 27:9, ascribed some or all of Zechariah C to Jeremiah.

All of this changed with the rise of modern historical criticism, which began to exclude such confessional commitments from biblical scholarship and to focus on hypotheses of multiple authorship and dating. Zechariah C, for example, was attributed to four or even more different authors and was assigned to dates ranging from the eighth to the second century BC The constituent parts of Zechariah were read with a view to hearing not the voice of God but rather the diversity of human voices, each reflecting its own milieu and agenda and detached from both its immediate and its macrocanonical context. Among confessional interpreters of Scripture in the nineteenth and twentieth centuries, the chief innovations have been the detailed defense of traditional positions (e.g., unity of authorship) against the results of historical criticism, and the rise of a dispensationalist hermeneutic. The latter stressed literal fulfillment of Zechariah's prophecies and thus saw many of these as fulfilled not in the church but rather in a future separate group of converted Jews (so Feinberg).

A remarkable development in the tradition of historical criticism has been the recent trend in dating Zechariah C. After a time (most of the nineteenth century) when this part had been almost unanimously assigned a preexilic date, there followed a period (from about 1880 to 1960) when almost all critical scholars assigned it to the Hellenistic period. Since then, a growing consensus has emerged that Zechariah C should be dated to the early postexilic period (e.g., Lamarche; Hanson; Reventlow; Meyers and Meyers 1993; Petersen 1995; Sweeney; O'Brien; Boda). Thus, there is now widespread agreement that the entire book of Zechariah could have been written within or near the lifetime of the sixth-century BC prophet whose name it bears. As a result, there is currently little distance between the mainstream scholarly consensus and the traditional conservative view that the entire book of Zechariah goes back in all essentials to the prophet Zechariah himself, perhaps to different stages of his life.

Other recent trends in the interpretation of Zechariah are a focus on *literary patterns and on *intertextuality, a new assessment of the relationship of Zechariah to *apocalyptic, and the rise of a modified form of dispensationalism. With the literary turn in biblical studies, the last generation or two of scholars has sought to discern various kinds of *rhetorical structures in the book, such as chiastic patterns structuring the night visions of Zechariah A or all of Zechariah B. Unfortunately, these have not produced a significant scholarly consensus, and a monograph by M. Butterworth on the issue has wisely urged caution. Because Zechariah lived at a time when much of the OT canon was already available, scholars since the nineteenth century (notably E. W. Hengstenberg and B. Stade) have pointed out that he frequently alludes to earlier Scripture. Under the rubric "intertextuality" this emphasis recently has received new impetus, aided by the contemporary possibilities of electronic searching (see, e.g., Stead). Of course, it remains a matter of interpretive judgment to decide whether a verbal parallel between two biblical passages is exegetically significant or merely coincidental. Although all or parts of Zechariah have in the past been described as "apocalyptic," recent discussion of this ambiguous modern category (see esp. Collins) have caused many to conclude that it does not apply to Zechariah at all. Finally, in the dispensationalist camp the rise of "progressive dispensationalism" favors a confessional hermeneutic that does allow for some nonliteral interpretation of prophecy and its partial fulfillment in the church age (Merrill). Alongside these recent trends there continues to be a steady tradition of diachronic analysis that assigns different parts of the book to different redactors and dates, but without forming a critical consensus.

See also DAY OF THE LORD; TWELVE, BOOK OF THE.

BIBLIOGRAPHY. *Commentaries*: J. G. Baldwin, *Haggai, Zechariah, Malachi* (TOTC; Downers Grove, IL: InterVarsity Press, 1972); M. J. Boda, *Haggai, Zechariah* (NIVAC; Grand Rapids: Zondervan, 2004); E. W. Conrad, *Zechariah* (RNBC; Sheffield: Sheffield Academic, 1999); C. L. Feinberg, *The Minor Prophets* (Chicago: Moody, 1976); E. H. Merrill, *Haggai, Zechariah, Malachi: An Exegetical Commentary* (Chicago: Moody, 1994); C. L. Meyers and E. M. Meyers, *Haggai, Zechariah 1-8: A New Translation with Introduction and Commentary* (AB 25B; Garden City, NY: Doubleday, 1987); idem, *Zechariah 9-14: A New Translation with Introduction and Commentary* (AB25C; Garden City, NY: Doubleday, 1993); J. M. O'Brien, *Nahum, Habakkuk, Zephaniah, Haggai, Zechariah, Malachi* (AOTC; Nashville: Abington, 2004); D. L. Petersen, *Haggai and Zechariah 1-8* (OTL; Philadelphia: Westminster, 1984); idem, *Zechariah 9-14 and Malachi* (OTL; Louisville: Westminster/John Knox, 1995); H. G. Reventlow, *Die Propheten Haggai, Sacharja und Maleachi* (ATD 25/2; Göttingen: Vandenhoeck & Ruprecht, 1993); M. A. Sweeney, *The Twelve Prophets, 2: Micah, Nahum, Habakkuk, Zephaniah, Haggai, Zechariah, Malachi* (Berit Olam; Collegeville, MN: Liturgical, 2000); B. Tidiman, *Le livre de Zacharie* (CEB; Vaux-sur-Seine: EDIFAC, 1996); B. G. Webb, *The Message of Zechariah* (BST; Downers Grove, IL: InterVarsity Press, 2003). *Studies*: L. Bauer, *Zeit des zweiten Tempels, Zeit der Gerechtigkeit: Zur sozio-ökonomischen Konzeption im Haggai-Sacharja-Maleachi-Korpus* (BEATAJ 31; Frankfurt: Peter Lang, 1992); **M. Butterworth,** *Structure and the Book of Zechariah* (JSOTSup 130; Sheffield: JSOT, 1992); **J. J. Collins,** ed., *Apocalypse: The Morphology of a Genre* (Semeia 14; Missoula, MT: Scholars Press, 1979); **P. D. Hanson,** *The Dawn of Apocalyptic: The Historical and Sociological Roots of Jewish Apocalyptic* (rev. ed.; Philadelphia: Fortress, 1979); **M. Kline,** *Glory in Our Midst: A Biblical-Theological Reading of Zechariah's Night Visions* (Overland Park, KS: Two Age, 2001); **P. Lamarche,** *Zacharie IX-XIV: Structure littéraire et messianisme* (EBib; Paris: Gabalda, 1961); **A. R. Petterson,** *Behold Your King: The Hope for the House of David in the Book of Zechariah* (LHBOTS 513; New York: T & T Clark International, 2009); **W. H. Rose,** *Zemah and Zerubbabel: Messianic Expectations in the Early Postexilic Period* (JSOTSup 304; Sheffield: Sheffield Academic, 2000); **M. R. Stead,** *The Intertextuality of Zechariah 1-8* (LHBOTS 506; London: T & T Clark, 2009); **A. Wolters,** "Halley's Comet at a Turning Point in Jewish History," *CBQ* 55 (1993) 687-97; idem, "Mission and the Interpretation of Zechariah 8:20-23," in *That the World May Believe: Essays on Mission and Unity in Honour of George Vandervelde*, ed. M. W. Goheen and M. O'Gara (Lanham, MD: University Press of America, 2006) 1-14; idem, "'The Whole Earth Remains at Peace' (Zechariah 1:11): The Problem and an Intertextual Clue," in *Tradition in Transition: Haggai and Zechariah 1-8 in the Trajectory of Hebrew Theology*, ed. M. J. Boda and M. H. Floyd (LHBOTS 475; London: T & T Clark, 2008) 128-43.   A. Wolters

ZEPHANIAH, BOOK OF

The book of Zephaniah contains one of the strongest messages of judgment among the Prophetic Books as it focuses on the impending Day of Yahweh's judgment (*see* Day of the Lord) on the nation of Judah and its ancient Near Eastern neighbors in the late seventh century BC. Alongside this message of judgment, however, is one of *salvation as the prophecies reveal the emergence of a *remnant from the destruction.

1. Date, Setting, Composition
2. Structure
3. Major Themes
4. Zephaniah in Its Canonical Context

1. Date, Setting, Composition.

1.1. Referential Historical Context. The super-

scription that introduces Zephaniah possibly links the prophet to the royal family of Judah (see 2.1 below) and clearly links the prophet to the reign of King Josiah (*see* Israelite History). Josiah reigned in Judah around the years 640-609 BC. Biblical sources evaluate Josiah's reign positively (2 Kings 22:2; 2 Chron 34:2), identifying it as one of the highest points in the post-Solomonic phase of the monarchy (along with Hezekiah, as well as Joash and Jehoshaphat). These sources also agree, however, that the first part of Josiah's reign was not exemplary, with 2 Kings 22:3 focusing on reforms in the eighteenth year of his reign, and 2 Chronicles 34:3 on reforms in his eighth year. In either case, there was a problematic phase in Josiah's reign, one that probably reflects the enduring impact of two previous generations of spiritual decline in Judah, the legacy of Josiah's father, Amon (ca. 641-640 BC), and grandfather Manasseh (ca. 687-641 BC). Thus, the negative message of Zephaniah would fit the early phase of Josiah's reign (e.g., Roberts; Patterson; Berlin), reflecting the urgency after multiple generations of disobedience and the approaching fulfillment of God's warnings to Hezekiah (2 Kings 20:16-19) and Manasseh (2 Kings 21:10-16), which Josiah's reign successfully averted (2 Kings 23:24-27). However, some scholars have suggested later dates. One suggestion has been shortly after the beginning of the reforms by Josiah (in 632 or 622 BC) due to the presence of Deuteronomistic language in Zephaniah (e.g., Vlaardingerbroek; Robertson). Another places the words of this book during the reign of Jehoiakim due to references in Zephaniah 2:8 to Moab and Ammon, which invaded Judah during Jehoiakim's reign (2 Kings 24:2), and to Nineveh, whose fall in 612 BC is mentioned in Zephaniah 2:13-15 (e.g., Hyatt; Williams). This final position is at odds with the superscription in Zephaniah 1:1 and appears to be based on the assumption that the prophecy concerning Nineveh could not have been given prior to its fall.

Some have focused on a particular setting in the life of Judah at which the speeches of the book of Zephaniah were first delivered, arguing that Zephaniah preached these oracles in Jerusalem during a pilgrimage festival such as the Feast of Tabernacles (e.g., Bennett; Goldingay; Kealy).

1.2. Compositional Historical Context. There is a difference, however, between the setting when the words of Zephaniah were first delivered to Judah and Jerusalem and the setting when these words were drawn together into a prophetic book (O'Brien 2007). Many have distinguished material original or attributed to the prophet Zephaniah from supplementary material added by later editors either at the time the original oral speeches of Zephaniah were gathered together for the first time or at a later point after the first edition of the book of Zephaniah (see review in Sweeney 1999). For example, M. Sweeney believes that Zephaniah should be read in terms of the context of the Babylonian *exile, when Judah had been exiled and the *temple destroyed (Sweeney 2003), while M. Széles identifies exilic and postexilic redactions. Discernment of supplementary material has been focused on what were considered contrastive themes (e.g., eschatology/present, universality/particularity, enemy/diaspora) and styles in the book. Views range from those who see the only addition as the superscription in Zephaniah 1:1 (e.g., Baker), to those who see smaller secondary additions (e.g., Holladay: Zeph 1:14-18; 2:10-11, 12, 15a; 3:8b, 10, 13b; Ben Zvi: Zeph 1:2-3; 2:8-11), to those who see major redactional phases (e.g., Redditt: Zeph 1:2-3; 1:7—2:15, then Zeph 1:1, 4-6; 3:1-13, finally Zeph 3:14-20).

The diversity of opinion concerning the compositional development of the book cautions against simplistic or definitive solutions. One must admit that there are some odd shifts in the flow of the book (e.g., Zeph 2:11 to Zeph 2:12), but this may reflect the challenge of drawing together various oral speeches into a literary whole. The text appears to fit in the main the context identified in the superscription, although one can discern a modulation between universal (generic references to all creation/humanity), international (references to specific *nations) and particular (references to Judah, Jerusalem, Israel) contexts. Generally, the international and particular references would fit the audience to which Zephaniah addressed his oracles, while it is possible that the universal references are part of the literary development as Zephaniah's messages were drawn into a collection by himself, his disciples or later tradents. There are also indications at the end of the book that may reflect broader trends related to the development of the Book of the *Twelve as a collection (Nogalski 2000). Thus, the summons

to joy addressed to Daughter *Zion in Zephaniah 3:14-15, which introduces the final section of the book, echoes two key passages in the Haggai-Malachi corpus (Zech 2:10; 9:9-10) that appear to reflect its editorial development. There is a strong possibility then that Zephaniah 3:14-20 was developed as part of a phase in which Haggai-Malachi was brought into a minor prophets collection that eventually became the Book of the Twelve (Boda).

2. Structure.

There have been many proposals for the structure of the book of Zephaniah. A common approach has been to follow what was considered the basic structure of a prophetic book, such as laid out by C. Westermann: (1) judgment speeches to the prophet's own nation; (2) judgment speeches to foreign nations; (3) salvation speeches to the prophet's own nation (Westermann, 95). Thus, for example, J. Roberts identifies Zephaniah 1:2—2:3 as judgment against Judah/Jerusalem, Zephaniah 2:4-15 as judgment against the nations, and Zephaniah 3:1-20 as judgment and deliverance for Jerusalem (cf. Bennett). A creative twist on this approach was suggested by P. House, who claimed that the book is composed in three acts with multiple scenes that unfold a plot from judgment (Day of Yahweh) to words of grace in Zephaniah 3:18-20 (House 1989). However, the traditional tripartite approach has met considerable resistance in recent scholarship (see Sweeney 1991; O'Brien 2007) and has been replaced by approaches that seek for greater sensitivity to the unique flow of thought within Zephaniah as a book (e.g., Ball, who sees in Zeph 2:1-7 the key to the literary components of the book, and Ryou, who discerns a chiastic arrangement). The result has been greater sensitivity to, for instance, the call to gather and seek God in Zephaniah 2:1-3 and its role within the book and the intertwining of judgment and salvation throughout the book.

There are no major disjunctions within the book, although one can discern smaller units. For instance, although one might consider Zephaniah 2:4-15 as a distinct section comprising prophecies directed against the nations, this section is clearly linked to the preceding section by the causal particle kî (Zeph 2:4), which reveals that it provides the motivation at least for "all the humble of the earth" to seek Yahweh

(Zeph 2:3), if not also for the gathered remnant of Judah (Zeph 2:1-2). This section (Zeph 2:4-15) is also linked to the section that follows (Zeph 3:1-7) by the development of the city theme at its conclusion in reference to Nineveh as "exultant city" (Zeph 2:15), which prepares the way for the reference to Jerusalem as "tyrannical city" in Zephaniah 3:1. In addition, the depiction of Jerusalem's sins in Zephaniah 3:1-7 is clearly linked to the material that follows in Zephaniah 3:8-13 through the particle *lākēn* ("therefore"), showing how the attack on Jerusalem sets up the call for the faithful to wait for Yahweh to purge the nation and nations.

Although there are reasons to conclude that the material found in the book of Zephaniah has arisen from diverse settings (see Nogalski 1993), the book in its final form is coherent and cohesive. One can discern a modulation in the book between the universal/international and the particular/national, and this shows an intertwining between the fate of all creation, all nations and Judah and Jerusalem. Thus, the initial depiction of divine judgment in Zephaniah 1:2-6 begins with all of creation in view (Zeph 1:2-3) but then focuses on Judah and Jerusalem (Zeph 1:4-6). The announcement of the imminent Day of Yahweh in Zephaniah 1:7-18 begins by focusing on Jerusalem (Zeph 1:7-13) before broadening to the inhabitants of all the earth (Zeph 1:14-18). It is not surprising then that the call to respond in Zephaniah 2:1-3 addresses both of these audiences: Judah (Zeph 2:1-2) and all the humble of the earth (Zeph 2:3), and that the motivation for accepting these invitations is related to an approaching judgment of the nations that will bring a benefit for the remnant of Judah (Zeph 2:4-15). The same dual modulation of universal/particular and international/national can be discerned in the final chapter of Zephaniah, in which groups emerge from the judgment of Yahweh that are both international (Zeph 3:9) and national (Zeph 3:10-13) in character. Binding all of these passages together is the common motif of "the Day" (Zeph 1:7-10, 14-16, 18; 2:2-3; 3:8), when God's "burning anger" (Zeph 1:15, 18; 2:2-3; 3:8) is unleashed and will produce a purified remnant, over which Yahweh will rejoice.

2.1. Superscription (Zeph 1:1). Zephaniah begins with a superscription that defines the divine and human dimensions of the words in the book that follows. The divine origin of these words is made clear from the outset (the words of Yahweh), but the human agency of Zephaniah is depicted by reference to his social identity (four generations) and historical context (the reign of Josiah). The use of four generations for a prophet is unprecedented in Hebrew tradition and may indicate that Zephaniah himself was of royal lineage traced to King Hezekiah, great-grandfather of Josiah (Berlin, 65; Nogalski 1993, 182-83).

2.2. Depiction of Divine Judgment (Zeph 1:2-6). The initial section of Zephaniah announces judgment by Yahweh, at first universally against the various living components of the created order (Zeph 1:2-3), and then more particularly against Judah and Jerusalem (Zeph 1:4-6). This modulation between the universal and the particular can be discerned throughout Zephaniah.

2.2.1. Judgment on All the Earth (Zeph 1:2-3). Yahweh's announcement of universal judgment is bracketed by statements identified as declarations of Yahweh that refer to the destruction of elements "from the face of the earth," first "all things" (Zeph 1:2) and finally "humanity" (Zeph 1:3c). In Zephaniah 1:3a-b "all things" is defined in terms of the various living beings described in connection with the creation of humanity in Genesis 1:26: human (*ʾādām*), beast (*bĕhēmâ*), bird of the sky (*ʿôp-haššāmayim*), fish of the sea (*dĕgê hayyām*) (cf. Job 12:7-8; contrast Gen 1:28; 9:2; Ps 8:7-8; Ezek 38:20; Hos 4:3). The order of destruction is the reverse of the creation account in Genesis 1. The focus, however, is on humanity, which is repeated at the conclusion of the section after a line that characterizes judged humanity as "evil" (Zeph 1:3c). The totality of the destruction is ominous, although, as the book progresses, there are indications that there will be survivors, a remnant comprising those who turn to Yahweh from Judah and the nations (see comments on Zeph 2—3 below).

2.2.2. Judgment on Judah and Jerusalem (Zeph 1:4-6). Yahweh's first-person announcement of judgment continues into Zephaniah 1:4 as the focus narrows from the earth as a whole to the people of Judah and Jerusalem (Zeph 1:4a). The offenses that have prompted this judgment are listed in Zephaniah 1:4b-6, with this last verse summarizing the basic offense as turning away from following Yahweh and not seeking revelation from Yahweh. The offenses named in Zephaniah 1:4b-5 (idolatry related to Baal, the hosts of heaven and Milcom among clergy and laity alike) are the activities that replaced following and seeking Yahweh. *Idolatry and illicit revelation are commonly connected in the OT (e.g., Zech 13:2), as Israelites sought answers from the heavenly world through illicit means.

2.3. Announcement of the Approaching Day of the Lord (Zeph 1:7-18). The remainder of Zephaniah 1 contains two messages, both of which begin with a declaration that "the day of Yahweh is near" (qārôb yôm yhwh [Zeph 1:7, 14]) (see Day of the Lord). The first message (Zeph 1:7-13) depicts Yahweh's judgment of a particular community who are inhabitants of Jerusalem, while the second message (Zeph 1:14-18) broadens the depiction more universally to encompass "all the earth . . . all the inhabitants of the earth" (Zeph 1:18).

2.3.1. The Approaching Day of the Lord for the Inhabitants of Jerusalem (Zeph 1:7-13). In the first section (Zeph 1:7-13) the day is defined initially in terms of the ritual background of the Day of Yahweh motif—that is, as a festal day of sacrifice (Zeph 1:7b-8)—and judgment is directed at a particular community in Jerusalem. This day, however, will become an opportunity for Yahweh to punish offending elite members of the community who have built fortunes through violence and deceit (Zeph 1:8-9, 13) without regard for accountability to Yahweh (Zeph 1:12). The seriousness of the punishment is suggested by depiction and call to wailing (Zeph 1:10-11) and the revelation that their possessions will be lost and not enjoyed (Zeph 1:13). The call to "silence" (has) often appears in the OT in royal contexts, where it is used to silence (and possibly clear) those gathered around the ruler because he is either moving into or out of the scene (Judg 3:19; Hab 2:20; Zech 2:13 [MT 2:17]; cf. Amos 6:10; Neh 8:11). Here in Zephaniah 1:7 it is used in conjunction with the Day of Yahweh—that is, his appearing among the people in relation to a festal celebration.

2.3.2. The Approaching Day of the Lord for the Inhabitants of All the Earth (Zeph 1:14-18). In the second section (Zeph 1:14-18) the day is defined initially in terms of the military background of the Day of Yahweh motif, seen especially in the use of terms such as "warrior" (Zeph 1:14), "trumpet," "battle cry," "fortified cities" and "high corner towers" (Zeph 1:16) (see Warfare and Divine Warfare). The nearness of the day is emphasized even more at the outset

of this section ("near and coming quickly"), and the day is defined in very strong terms in Zephaniah 1:15 (trouble, distress, destruction, desolation, darkness, gloom, clouds, thick darkness). The reason for this divine judgment is identified as the sin of humanity against Yahweh (Zeph 1:17). The depiction of human components (blood, flesh) in terms of valueless items such as dust and dung emphasizes the divine punishment (Zeph 1:17). The final verse (Zeph 1:18) identifies the characteristics of Yahweh that have been incited by the sin of humanity (his *wrath and jealousy) and reveals the qualitative (complete, terrifying) and quantitative ("all the earth . . . all the inhabitants of the earth") scope of the judgment of this day.

2.4. Responding to the Announcement of the Day of the Lord (Zeph 2:1-15). Following the two judgement sections in Zephaniah 1:2-18, both of which depicted judgment of a universal audience of all the earth and a particular audience of Judah/Jerusalem, Zephaniah 2:1-3 calls these two audiences to respond prior to the day of Yahweh's anger.

2.4.1. Invitation to Judah (Zeph 2:1-2). The first audience addressed is identified as a "nation without shame" (so the Old Greek) or possibly "nation without desire" (so the MT), most likely referring to Judah because a specific and single nation is in view. This audience is invited to "gather," using a verb (qšš) usually associated with inanimate objects such as stubble (Ex 5:7, 12) or wood (Num 15:32-33; 1 Kings 17:10, 12), but here with humans gathering together most likely for a day of seeking Yahweh penitentially (see Joel 1:14-15; cf. 2 Chron 20:4). The group that gathers most likely is the "remnant" (šĕʾērît [Zeph 2:7, 9; 3:13]), "remainder" (yeter [Zeph 2:9]), "the people of the LORD of Hosts" (Zeph 2:10), "the dispersed ones" (pûṣ [Zeph 3:10]) who appear in the rest of Zephaniah.

2.4.2. Invitation to All the Humble of the Earth (Zeph 2:3). The second audience is identified as "all the humble of the earth who have carried out his ordinances," a more universal audience most likely not limited to Judah and Jerusalem (cf. Ps 76:9). The humble are called to "seek" (bqš Piel) three things: Yahweh, righteousness and humility, with the hope ("perhaps") that they will be hidden safely on the day of Yahweh's anger.

2.4.3. Motivation: Judgment on Foreign Nations for the Remnant of Judah (Zeph 2:4-15). The causal particle *kî* at the beginning of Zephaniah 2:4 links Zephaniah 2:4-15 to the "day of Yahweh's anger" referred to at the end of the two invitations in Zephaniah 2:1-2 and Zephaniah 2:3. This day will have serious implications for the nations that surround Israel. The review of nations begins with those traditional enemies of Judah to the west (Philistines [Zeph 2:4-7]) and east (Moab/Ammon [Zeph 2:8-10]). The advantage for Judah's remnant is explicitly noted in relation to the defeat of the Philistines (Zeph 2:7) and the Moabites/Ammonites (Zeph 2:9). The location of the nations in view then shifts further afield, first to those associated with the Mediterranean Sea (Zeph 2:11), then to the Ethiopians (Zeph 2:12), and finally to the Assyrians (Zeph 2:13-15).

2.4.3.1. Judgment on the Philistines (Zeph 2:4-7). Four the five traditional cities of Philistia are mentioned (Gaza, Ashkelon, Ashdod, Ekron), with only Gath left out, a common tradition trend in prophetic lists of the Philistines (cf. Jer 25:20; Amos 1:6-8; Zech 9:5-7) and possibly related to either its early destruction by the Assyrians in 711 BC (cf. Is 20) or the early incorporation of Gath into Israel (cf. 1 Sam 27:1-7; 2 Sam 6:9-12; 15:18-22; 2 Chron 11:5-12). The Philistines were settled along the Mediterranean seacoast of Judah and closely associated in tradition with the Cherethites (Zeph 2:5; cf. Ezek 25:16), most likely a reference to the Cretan origins of the Philistines (Amos 9:7; cf. Deut 2:23; Jer 47:4). The Philistines are also treated as representative of the Canaanites (Zeph 2:5), who here are driven out to give pastureland (Zeph 2:7) to the remnant of Judah.

2.4.3.2. Judgment on the Moabites and Ammonites (Zeph 2:8-10). The focus shifts from west to east of Judah along the Transjordanian Plateau, the traditional lands of Moab and Ammon (as well as further south Edom). The severity of divine judgment is evident in the comparison to Sodom and Gomorrah, which were totally annihilated (cf. Gen 19; Deut 29:23). The cause of this judgment is explicitly identified in Zephaniah 2:10 as their pride, taunting and arrogance against the people of Yahweh. The remnant of Judah will benefit from the defeat of the Moabites and Ammonites by gaining plunder and inheritance (Zeph 2:9).

2.4.3.3. Judgment on the Coastland Nations (Zeph 2:11). Moving further afield, the coastland nations are next in view, most likely a ref-

erence to those people groups to the north and northwest who lived along the Mediterranean Sea, whether on the mainland or island (cf. Gen 10:5; Is 11:11; 20:6; 23:2, 6; 24:15; Jer 2:10; 25:22; 47:4; Ezek 27:6-7). These groups will abandon their gods (depriving them of sacrificial sustenance) and offer obeisance to Yahweh in their own lands.

2.4.3.4. Judgment on the Ethiopians (Zeph 2:12). In a short announcement of judgment Yahweh warns the Ethiopians that they will be killed by Yahweh's sword. As with the Philistines (addressed as Canaan) in Zephaniah 2:5, so the Ethiopians are addressed directly. The Ethiopians, who controlled Egypt at certain points in their history, and the Assyrians, who will follow in Zephaniah 2:13-15, are two key people groups who first butted heads during the Assyrian period (see Is 18:1-7; 20:4, 5; 37:9). It may be that "Ethiopia" is used here as a cipher for "Egypt," as Zephaniah sees the fulfillment of the earlier prophecies of Isaiah against the Egyptian and Assyrian powers of his day.

2.4.3.5. Judgment on the Assyrians (Zeph 2:13-15). The Assyrians are representative of the nations of "the north" (Mesopotamia)—that is, those nations that typically approached Israel and Judah from the north due to the ancient pathways of the Fertile Crescent. The focus shifts almost immediately to the destruction of Nineveh, Assyria's capital city, which fell in 612 BC. Animals, both domestic (flocks, beasts in herds) and wild (pelican, hedgehog, birds), will inhabit this once bustling city, reflective of its utter destruction and desertion (Zeph 2:14). So also the contemptuous reaction of those passing by in Zephaniah 2:15b reflects the desperate condition of Nineveh. The city is described as "the exultant city" whose arrogance ("I am, and there is no one besides me") preceded its fall. This prepares the way for the subsequent pericope, which focuses on another city, Jerusalem, identified as "the tyrannical city," which also will face the judgment of Yahweh.

2.5. Judgment on Jerusalem and Nations Resulting in Purified Peoples and Remnant (Zeph 3:1-20). The final chapter of Zephaniah shifts the attention back on to Jerusalem, beginning with a focus on its sin (Zeph 3:1-7), but then providing hope for the emergence of a purified remnant consisting of both Gentiles and Israelites (Zeph 3:8-13), a message that will prompt the triumphant joy of Zion and Israel and comfort those who grieve over the state of Zion (Zeph 3:14-20).

2.5.1. The Sin of Jerusalem (Zeph 3:1-7). This section begins with the declaration of woe toward Jerusalem, which is described as rebellious, defiled and tyrannical (Zeph 3:1), linked in the following verses to the city's lack of response to and trust in Yahweh (Zeph 3:2) and the illicit actions of the city's inhabitants—princes, judges, prophets, priests (Zeph 3:3-4)—possibly in connection with injustice. The severity of the city's sin is emphasized by the fact that it was committed in a city inhabited by a righteous and just God (Zeph 3:5), and that it continued in a city that had experienced the discipline of God (Zeph 3:6-7).

2.5.2. Hope Through Purifying Judgment on the Nations and Israel (Zeph 3:8-13). Such sin, even after severe divine discipline, may have discouraged the faithful audience called to gather and seek in Zephaniah 2:1-2, but the message of Zephaniah is one of trust as Yahweh fulfills his plans. The collocation "wait for" (*ḥkh* Piel + *l*) can refer to waiting patiently until Yahweh's judgment has passed (Is 8:17) or until Yahweh's salvation comes (Is 64:4 [MT 64:3]); it is closely related to hope and trust (Ps 33:18-22; Hab 2:3-4). Yahweh's plan is to prompt an international crisis ("nations . . . kingdoms," "all the earth") to bring judgment on the sins of cities such as Nineveh and Jerusalem and their respective nations (Zeph 3:8). The reference to Yahweh's burning anger (*ḥărôn ʾap*) reminds the audience of the earlier Day of Yahweh references in Zephaniah 2:1-3. This outpouring of Yahweh's anger will produce a purified group of Gentiles ("peoples" [Zeph 3:9]) and Israelites ("my dispersed ones" [Zeph 3:10]) who will worship Yahweh. The Israelite remnant will undergo even further purging as any remaining proud people will be removed, leaving behind a humble remnant who do no wrong and experience prosperity and security (Zeph 3:11-13).

2.5.3. Joy for Zion and Israel, Comfort for Those Who Grieve (Zeph 3:14-20). The book concludes with an address to *Zion and *Israel, in the form of a summons to joy, which appears regularly throughout the OT to prompt an acknowledgment of a change in fortunes (Is 10:30; 12:6; 23:12; 52:9-10; 54:1; Lam 4:21; Hos 9:1; Joel 2:21-23; Zeph 3:14-15; Zech 2:10; 9:9-10) (Boda). It often is used in relation to a victory in war and is expressed often (as here) by a female voice

rejoicing over the safe return of her warriors. The focus of Zephaniah 3:17 is the victorious warrior-king Yahweh, who reciprocates with his own expressions of joy. Zion is depicted as a city ("daughter Jerusalem") in Zephaniah 3:14-17, 18-20, and then the view shifts to her former inhabitants who grieved over her feasts, probably a reference to that faithful remnant who were exiled from the city yet had distanced themselves from the abuses connected with Jerusalem and its temple (see Zeph 1:4-6, 9; 3:5). Yahweh promises to gather this remnant from "all the earth . . . among all the peoples of the earth" and turn their shame to honor.

3. Major Themes.

3.1. The Day of Yahweh. Zephaniah focuses considerable attention on an approaching day related to Yahweh (see King 1995; Bailey, 396). While at times it is simply called "that day" (Zeph 1:9-10, 15; 3:11, 16) or "the day" (Zeph 2:2), it often is identified as "the day of Yahweh" (Zeph 1:7-8, 14, 18; 2:2-3). This day often is linked to Yahweh's anger and wrath (Zeph 1:15, 18; 2:2-3; 3:8), the implications of which are filled out in the detailed list of attributes linked to the word "day" in Zephaniah 1:15-16: "a day of trouble and distress, a day of destruction and desolation, a day of darkness and gloom, a day of clouds and thick darkness, a day of trumpet and battle cry." Twice in Zephaniah a temporal descriptor is employed as the day is identified as "near" (Zeph 1:7, 14). Two settings are associated with the day in Zephaniah. The first is that of the temple cult as the day is identified as "the day of the Yahweh's sacrifice" (Zeph 1:7-8)— that is, a festal day related to the worship of Yahweh. The second is that of the battlefield as the day is identified as "a day of trumpet and battle cry" (Zeph 1:16). Both of these associations can be observed elsewhere in the OT prophetic corpus. The festal connection is evident in Hosea 9:5, which refers to "the day of the appointed festival, the day of the feast of Yahweh" (cf. Lam 2:22) (see Roberts, 177-78; Sweeney 2000, 115). The battlefield connection is even more common throughout the prophetic corpus (e.g., Is 13:6; Joel 2:11), and at times cosmic imagery is employed as Yahweh's military tactics include the use of or impact on various forces of nature (e.g., Joel 1:15; Amos 5:18, 20). Whether connected with cult or war, the Day of Yahweh tradition points to an approaching destructive action of Yahweh either against Israel or foreign nations. It emphasizes Yahweh's sovereign power as he passionately pursues justice within his creation. At the same time, the coming day is designed to protect and produce a purified remnant. The emphasis on imminence (near and coming very quickly [Zeph 1:14]) functions both as a warning to those who think that Yahweh will not hold them accountable (Zeph 1:12) and as a promise to those who must endure unjust conditions (Zeph 3:8).

3.2. The Remnant of Judah and Israel. Whereas Zephaniah 1 is entirely focused on Yahweh's outpouring of wrath and even is bracketed by declarations of total destruction (Zeph 1:2, 18), Zephaniah 2—3 reveals that a group will survive God's wrath (see Anderson; King 1994; Bailey, 402). It is not by accident that the references to a "remnant" related to Yahweh (contrast "the remnant of Baal," which will be destroyed [Zeph 1:4]) occur in Zephaniah only after the imperatives in Zephaniah 2:1-3, which provide a strategy for Jew (Zeph 2:1-2) and Gentile (Zeph 2:3) to avoid the effects of the day. The surviving Jewish group is called "the remnant of the house of Judah" (Zeph 2:7), "my people" (Zeph 2:8), "the remnant of my people" (Zeph 2:9), "the remainder of my nation" (Zeph 2:9), "the people of Yahweh of hosts" (Zeph 2:10), "my worshipers, my dispersed ones" (Zeph 3:10), "the remnant of Israel" (Zeph 3:13), "those who grieve about the feasts" (Zeph 3:18). They will reap benefits from Yahweh's destruction of the nations, as they plunder and inherit the possessions and territory of their enemies (Zeph 2:7, 9), enjoy prosperity and protection from Yahweh (Zeph 3:13), and are honored among the nations (Zeph 3:19-20). Participation in this group appears to be limited to those who gather themselves to seek Yahweh (Zeph 2:1-2), who wait trustingly upon Yahweh (Zeph 3:8), and who come from the nations to bring offerings (Zeph 3:10). This group is one that will be purified by Yahweh as he removes the proud, leaving behind the humble and lowly who trust in Yahweh and speak and act with integrity (Zeph 3:11-12). There will also be a remnant among the Gentiles, a group identified as "all you humble of the earth who have carried out his ordinances" (Zeph 2:3) and as "the peoples" (Zeph 3:9). Participation in this group appears to be limited to those who seek Yahweh, righteousness and hu-

mility (Zeph 2:3). After the Day of Yahweh, this group is given purified lips by Yahweh so that they may worship him together (Zeph 3:9).

4. Zephaniah in Its Canonical Context.
4.1. Zephaniah and the Prophets. Many have noted a close relationship between the book of Zephaniah and earlier prophetic traditions, especially Isaiah (Bosshard; Bosshard-Nepustil; Steck; Ahn) and Jeremiah (Achtemeier, 62). Others, however, have focused especially on the role that Zephaniah plays in the overall shape of the Book of the Twelve (House 1990; Nogalski 1993; O'Brien 2007). Zephaniah represents the final preexilic prophet who announces the impending and irreversible judgment on Judah and the nations that would begin in the late seventh century BC and continue throughout most of the sixth century BC as first Egypt and then Babylon wrought destruction throughout the Levant. The book, however, also prepares the reader of the Book of the Twelve for the message of Haggai through Malachi, identifying the character of the remnant that would emerge from the judgment, but also providing a theological foundation for both judgment and salvation related to both Jew and Gentile in Haggai-Malachi.

4.2. Zephaniah and the New Testament. While Zephaniah's Day of Yahweh refers to the judgment that befell Israel and the nations in the late seventh and early sixth centuries BC, its articulation of the Day of Yahweh motif would prove important to the enduring prophetic traditions of Judah, showcased in, for instance, the use of the Day of Yahweh motif throughout Zechariah 9—14 and Malachi (Nogalski 2003). The anticipation of an imminent day when Yahweh would appear to judge and save is an essential component of eschatological expectation throughout the NT and the interpretation of the church. Thus, this day is identified as "the day the Son of Man is revealed" (Lk 17:30), "the day of our Lord Jesus (Christ)" (1 Cor 1:8; 5:5; 2 Cor 1:14), "the day of Christ (Jesus)" (Phil 1:6, 10), "the day of the Lord" (1 Thess 5:2; 2 Thess 2:2) and "the day of God" (2 Pet 3:12). The imminence of this coming day is also emphasized in the NT (Lk 21:34; 1 Thess 5:2; 2 Pet 3:10; Rev 3:3; 16:15), as is its severity. The NT also looks to a remnant that will emerge from the events of the coming day, a group depicted in the book of Revelation as composed of people from every tribe and nation (Rev 5:9; 7:9) who, according to Revelation 19—21, will live forever in a new heaven and earth, a new Jerusalem, a new paradise.

See also DAY OF THE LORD; NATIONS; REMNANT; TWELVE, BOOK OF THE; WRATH.

BIBLIOGRAPHY. *Commentaries:* E. R. Achtemeier, *Nahum—Malachi* (IBC; Atlanta: John Knox, 1986); W. Bailey, "Zephaniah," in *Micah, Nahum, Habakkuk, Zephaniah,* by K. L. Barker and W. Bailey (NAC 20; Nashville: Broadman & Holman, 1999); D. W. Baker, *Nahum, Habakkuk, Zephaniah: An Introduction and Commentary* (TOTC; Leicester: Inter-Varsity Press, 1988); A. Berlin, *Zephaniah: A New Translation with Introduction and Commentary* (AB 25A; New York: Doubleday, 1994); J. Bruckner, *Jonah, Nahum, Habakkuk, Zephaniah* (NIVAC; Grand Rapids, Zondervan, 2004); J. Goldingay, "Zephaniah," in *Minor Prophets II,* by J. Goldingay and P. J. Scalise (NIBCOT 18; Peabody, MA: Hendrickson, 2009) 93-134; J. N. B. Heflin, *Nahum, Habakkuk, Zephaniah, and Haggai* (BSCS; Grand Rapids: Zondervan, 1985); J. D. Nogalski, *The Book of the Twelve: Hosea-Jonah* (SHBC; Macon, GA: Smyth & Helwys, 2011); J. M. O'Brien, *Nahum, Habakkuk, Zephaniah, Haggai, Zechariah, Malachi* (AOTC; Nashville: Abingdon, 2004); R. D. Patterson, *Nahum, Habakkuk, Zephaniah* (WEC; Chicago: Moody, 1991); J. J. M. Roberts, *Nahum, Habakkuk, and Zephaniah: A Commentary* (OTL; Louisville: Westminster/John Knox, 1991); O. P. Robertson, *The Books of Nahum, Habakkuk, and Zephaniah* (NICOT; Grand Rapids: Eerdmans, 1990); M. A. Sweeney, *Zephaniah: A Commentary* (Hermeneia; Minneapolis: Fortress, 2003); M. E. Széles, *Wrath and Mercy: A Commentary on the Books of Habakkuk and Zephaniah,* trans. G. A. F. Knight (ITC; Grand Rapids: Eerdmans, 1987); J. Vlaardingerbroek, *Zephaniah* (HCOT; Leuven: Peeters, 1999). *Studies:* J. Ahn, "Zephaniah, a Disciple of Isaiah?" in *Thus Says the Lord: Essays on the Former and Latter Prophets in Honor of Robert R. Wilson,* ed. J. J. Ahn and S. L. Cook (LHBOTS 502; New York: T & T Clark, 2009) 292-307; G. W. Anderson, "The Idea of the Remnant in the Book of Zephaniah," *ASTI* 11 (1977-78) 11-14; I. J. Ball Jr., *A Rhetorical Study of Zephaniah* (Berkeley, CA: BIBAL, 1988); R. A. Bennett, "The Book of Zephaniah: Introduction, Commentary, and Reflections," *NIB* 7:657-704; E. Ben Zvi, *A Historical-Critical Study of the Book of Zephaniah* (BZAW 198; Berlin: de Gruyter, 1991); M. J. Boda, "The Daughter's Joy," in *Daughter Zion: Her Portrait, Her Response,* ed. M. J. Boda, C. Dempsey and L. Snow Flesher (SBLAIL; Atlanta: Society of Biblical Literature, 2012); E. Bosshard, "Beobachtungen Zum Zwölfprophetenbuch," *BN* 40 (1987) 30-62; E. Bosshard-Nepustil, *Rezeptionen von Jesaja 1-39 im Zwölfprophetenbuch: Untersuchungen zur Literarischen Verbindung von Prophetenbüchern in Babylonischer und Persischer Zeit* (OBO 154; Göttingen: Vandenhoeck & Ruprecht, 1997); W. L. Holladay, "Reading Zephaniah with a Concordance: Suggestions for a Redaction History," *JBL* 120 (2001) 671-84; P. R. House, *Zephaniah: A Prophetic Drama* (BLS 16; Sheffield: Almond, 1989); idem, *The Unity of the Twelve* (BLS 27; Sheffield: Almond, 1990); J. P. Hyatt, "The Date and Background of Zephaniah," *JNES* 7 (1948) 25-29; S. P. Kealy, *An Interpretation of the Twelve Minor Prophets of the Hebrew Bible: The Emergence of Eschatology as a Theological Theme* (Lewiston, NY: Edwin Mellen, 2009); G. A. King, "The Remnant in Zephaniah," *BSac* 151 (1994) 414-27; idem, "The Day of the Lord in Zephaniah," *BSac* 152 (1995) 16-32; J. D. Nogalski, *Literary Precursors to the Book of the Twelve* (BZAW 217; Berlin: de Gruyter, 1993); idem, "Zephaniah 3: A Redactional Text for a Developing Corpus," in *Schriftauslegung in Der Schrift: Festschrift für Odil Hannes Steck zu Seinem 65. Geburtstag,* ed. R. G. Kratz, T. Krüger and K. Schmid (BZAW 300; Berlin: de Gruyter, 2000) 207-18; idem, "The Day(s) of Yhwh in the Book of the Twelve," in *Thematic Threads in the Book of the Twelve,* ed. P. L. Redditt and A. Schart (BZAW 325; Berlin: de Gruyter, 2003) 192-213; J. M. O'Brien, "Nahum-Habakkuk-Zephaniah: Reading the 'Former Prophets' in the Persian Period," *Int* 61 (2007) 168-83; P. L. Redditt, *Introduction to the Prophets* (Grand Rapids: Eerdmans, 2008); D. H. Ryou, *Zephaniah's Oracles against the Nations: A Sychronic and Diachronic Study of Zephaniah 2:1-3:8* (BIS 13; Leiden: E. J. Brill, 1995); O. H. Steck, *Der Abschluss der Prophetie im Alten Testament: Ein Versuch zur Frage der Vorgeschichte des Kanons* (BTSt 17; Neukirchen-Vluyn: Neukirchener Verlag, 1991); idem, "Zu Zep 3,9-10," *BZ* (1990) 90-95; M. A. Sweeney, "A Form-Critical Reassessment of the Book of Zephaniah," *CBQ* 53 (1991) 388-408; idem, "Zephaniah: A Paradigm for the Study of the Prophetic Books," *CurBS* 7 (1999) 119-45; idem, *The Twelve*

Prophets, vol. 2 (Berit Olam; Collegeville: MN, Liturgical, 2000); **C. Westermann,** *Basic Forms of Prophetic Speech,* trans. H. C. White (Louisville: Westminster/John Knox, 1991); **D. L. Williams,** "The Date of Zephaniah," *JBL* 82 (1963) 77–88. M. J. Boda

ZION

The term "Zion" (*ṣîyyôn*) is used throughout the OT Prophetic Books (48x in Isaiah, 17x in Jeremiah, 7x in Joel, 2x in Amos, 2x in Obadiah, 7x in Micah, 1x in Zephaniah, 7x in Zechariah). The terminology of "Zion" and related language is far more prevalent in the prophets than in the Pentateuch, Historical Books or even the Writings (with the exception of the Psalter).

"Zion" is the name of the capital city of Jerusalem in the united and divided monarchies of Israel. Originally the term may have been a descriptor for the small hill just between the Kidron and Tyropoean Valleys in Jerusalem. Prior to David's ascendancy to the throne of Israel (c. 1000 BC), the Jebusites controlled this area. Once David conquered the city, Zion/Jerusalem became the locus of the political power for the new king. It culminates in a powerful political and theological symbol as Solomon built the first *temple to Yahweh in this general locale, just north of the former Jebusite city.

In the prophets "Zion" displays a wide semantic range. The term often refers to the geographical location of the Temple Mount, likely due to Zion's close connection to Yahweh's kingship in Zion (Is 4:5; 8:18; 18:7; 24:23; 29:8; 31:4; 37:32; Joel 2:32; Obad 17, 21; Mic. 4:7). Otherwise, it can identify the city itself (Is 2:3; 4:3; 10:12). In other places "Zion" depicts both a city and its inhabitants. In this designation Zion is personified (Is 1:27; 37:22 49:14; Jer 9:19; Joel 2:23; Mic 4:11; Zeph 3:16) as a woman/mother. The epithet "Daughter Zion" is often found in this construction (Is 10:32; 37:22; 52:2; 62:11; Jer 4:31; 6:2, 23; Mic 4:10; Zeph 3:14; Zech 2:10; 9:9; also Lam 1—2; 4:22).

  1. The Zion Tradition
  2. History of Research
  3. Zion and Prophetic Critique
  4. Zion and Prophetic Consolation
  5. Daughter Zion
  6. Conclusion: Zion in Time and Eternity

1. The Zion Tradition.
The term "Zion" (*ṣîyyôn*) first occurs in 2 Samuel 5:7, and this text relates Zion and the Davidic monarchy. Whether it reveals that Zion is a Davidic concept designed to propagate the authority of the monarchy, however, is debated. So too is the role that Yahwistic religion plays in this relationship. There is no doubt, however, that three elements emerge in any discussion of Zion: the city, Yahwistic religion and kingship. The relationship between these constitutes the discussion of what is known as the "Zion tradition" or sometimes called "Zion theology" (Groves).

It is common to identify the central tenets of this tradition as (1) Zion is the peak of Zaphon, the highest mountain; (2) the river of paradise flows from Zion; (3) Yahweh triumphed over the flood of chaos waters at Zion; (4) Yahweh triumphed over the kings and their nations at Zion (Rohland). A final tenet is the pilgrimage of the nations to worship Yahweh in Zion (Wildberger). These tenets have been used to explore Zion theology even in the prophets where Zion is not mentioned (see Renz), but some or all of them appear in Isaiah, Jeremiah, Joel, Micah, Zephaniah and Zechariah. From these elements, scholars arrive at two central conclusions that impinge upon a Zion theology in the prophets: first, God has chosen Zion for his holy abode; second, Zion is protected by God by virtue of his presence there.

It is important to note that this Zion tradition often constitutes cosmic symbolism rather than an overly literal topographical or geographical description in the prophets. Jerusalem is not the highest mountain in the immediate region, much less in the whole of Canaan. Nor is there particularly a river that runs from Zion, although the Gihon Spring seems to be associated with that tenet in particular texts. What is emphasized in the prophets in relation to Zion is God's cosmic rule and authority, particularly dispensed from a particular place, which is Jerusalem. Still, God's rule often exceeds the geographical boundaries of Zion/Jerusalem in the prophets, so that his divine power supersedes any particular localization of its representation.

2. History of Research.
J. Dekker has provided the most extensive and current survey of research on Zion. He rightly notes that scholars had long understood the importance of Zion in the history and theology

of the OT, but E. Rohland's analysis was seminal in that it explored the significance of Israel's election traditions for the eschatological preaching of the prophets. Identification and description of the Zion tradition was a major outcome of his research. Rohland suggested that the tradition originated in Jebusite religious thought. The Jebusites believed that their city was inviolable because their deity was there. Rohland saw latent Zion theology in Jebusite thinking.

But once he captured the Jebusite city, David co-opted and integrated preexisting Jebusite theology into Yahwistic religion for his own political purposes (see von Rad, 1:46-48). By integrating existing Jebusite beliefs concerning the inviolability of the city due to divine election and divine presence, the budding Davidic house could centralize its power and provide a theological rationale for this particular kingship at this particular place against all other rivals.

Scholars thought that the prophets then adapted the Davidic Zion tradition, downplaying the notion that Zion was inviolable and highlighting the notion that Yahweh, as the divine Lord, expected obedience and piety among Zion's inhabitants. Especially Isaiah suggested that Yahweh's presence was not to be taken for granted in the holy city (Is 5:2-20). On this understanding, Zion was indeed God's chosen dwelling place, where he defeats enemies, but this also implies that the inhabitants of Zion must uphold God's standards of *justice and righteousness. Infidelity to Yahweh in Zion leads to a forfeiture of divine protection. Nonetheless, God eventually will provide grace to his holy dwelling and be a refuge for the remaining inhabitants, thwarting the nations that oppose his city and people (see von Rad, 2:158-59). This developmental construal of Zion theology—Jebusite origins, Davidic adoption, prophetic adaptation—influenced a generation.

J. J. M. Roberts critiqued this consensus and argued that Zion theology originated in the Davidic monarchy rather than Jebusite religion (Roberts 1973). David's ascension to the throne provided a sufficient need to develop a theological warrant for his seat of political and religious power in Jerusalem. In Roberts's construal, Zion theology began with (1) Yahweh as the great king of the earth, who (2) has chosen Jerusalem/Zion to exercise his rule, (3)

through his human vice-regent the king of Israel, David (Roberts 1983). So Zion theology celebrated Yahweh's rule and simultaneously justified the Davidic throne and cultic center in Jerusalem. Roberts's construal effectively absorbs Rohland's four other tenets of Zion theology (cosmic mountain, river of paradise, defeat of chaos, defeat of kings) within the aims of the Davidic monarchy. Roberts followed his predecessors in arguing that the prophets effectively critiqued the Zion tradition, particularly in regard to the notion that Zion is impregnable due to its divine election and Yahweh's indwelling presence there. What was required for Yahweh to remain in Zion or return there was the city's faithfulness to him (Roberts 1987).

Not all had been comfortable with either Jebusite or Davidic origins of the Zion tradition. In the 1950s O. Eissfeldt suggested that the origins of Zion actually derive from traditions surrounding the ark of the covenant at Shiloh and the divine title "Yahweh Zebaoth." Only later was this adapted by David and then the prophets. Likewise, H. Gese supposes that the Zion tradition is primarily linked to the ark at Shiloh. In so doing, Gese disassociates the close connection between God's election of David and his election of Zion. In Gese's formulation, divine election of Zion takes precedent because it is here that the divine king rules, and only subsequently through the vice-regent David. The prophets, then, use Zion theology to draw upon the primary denotation of Yahweh's kingship in Zion while they simultaneously critique the secondary connotation that links Zion with Davidic kingship.

B. Ollenburger shifts the focus in research by assessing Zion as a theological symbol rather than strictly as a historical tradition in Israel. Like Eissfeldt and Gese, he thinks that the theological symbol of Zion derives from Shiloh ark tradition, which was then expanded upon in subsequent generations. But he moves away from tradition-historical methods to argue that Zion, in the variety in which it appears in the corpus of the OT, reflects a theological conception that is associated with mythical themes, motifs and cultic forms of speech. The central core for the Zion tradition derives from the premise of the kingship of Yahweh from Zion. As the great king, Yahweh protects and defends his people and their dwelling place, wherever that may be. But likewise, as the divine king,

Yahweh demands that his people place their complete trust in him to secure them against external threats. This is not a prophetic adaptation of the Zion tradition for Ollenburger, but is a theological reflection derived from the reality of Yahweh's kingship inherent within the (early) theological symbol of Zion (so Gese).

Other scholars have limited their research on Zion to particular books, such as Isaiah (Seitz; Dekker). C. Seitz suggests that Zion's destiny is elucidated by the correlation between Hezekiah's sickness and recovery (Is 36—38), Jerusalem's judgment and potential redemption (Is 1—35), and Zion's final destiny explicated in and through return from *exile and the work of the Suffering *Servant (Is 40—66). So Isaiah is concerned to show God's election of Zion as the place where he will dwell in righteousness and justice, but it is a city that bears the sin of its people and thus suffers on their behalf. On this basis, Isaiah presents the city of Jerusalem as a city that is doomed for destruction due to the sins of its people. And yet, although suffering (in exile), Zion awaits God's salvation and redemption, where Zion will once again be identified as the "faithful city" in which all the peoples of the earth will hear God's instruction and delight in a place of joy and *peace (Is 2:2-5).

Other modern research assessed different aspects of Zion. J. Levenson explored the way Zion, with Sinai, becomes a significant entry point to understanding the whole of the Hebrew Bible. In a distinctive Jewish theology, Levenson argues that Zion becomes the symbol that absorbs Israel's experience with God at Sinai and becomes for Israel the center of the world, time and all of reality. As a symbol, it engenders moral obedience to Yahweh and energizes praise to God. Zion is the place where Eden is remembered and revisualized in every successive generation at the temple.

D. Gowan addresses Zion as a significant eschatological symbol in the OT, particularly in and through the prophetic texts of Isaiah, Ezekiel and Jeremiah. From these and other texts, Zion promotes a vision of a transformed and redeemed society, the essence of a transformed human person, a transformed ecology of new heavens and earth, and a distinctive picture of future hope.

Recent feminist research has paid attention to Zion as a gendered metaphor in the proph-

ets. C. Maier has explored at length the ways the OT personifies Zion as a mother and whore in the prophetic texts. The depiction of Zion as a woman, Maier avers, underscores the prophets' rhetorical message of communal demise and degradation. However, it underscores the prophets' rhetorical message of communal restoration as well. So Zion in the prophets is the afflicted whore and redeemed mother. She is the forlorn mother and fertile wife (Is 49:22-23; 50:1; 54:1-3; 60; 66).

Finally, C. Mandolfo has argued that Zion, particularly through the image of Daughter Zion in Lamentations, becomes a resource to challenge the prophets' depiction of Zion as whore in the prophets. Her dialogic theology uses the insights of M. Bakhtin and blends them with the political edge of feminist criticism. In her analysis, Daughter Zion's voice from Lamentations becomes countertestimony against divine sanction of rape and abuse of Zion as depicted in the prophets. For Mandolfo, Zion, particularly Daughter Zion, becomes an ideological and theological form of protest speech (cf. Boase).

3. Zion and Prophetic Critique.
Typical of prophetic speech is a vacillating message of judgment and redemption. This prophetic message often is revealed in the image of Zion. The prophets emphasize that Zion is the place where God the king reigns in justice. Consequently, God's people are called to live in trust of their divine king. On this basis, the inhabitants of Zion/Jerusalem may be critiqued for their lack of fidelity to God.

3.1. Isaiah. Isaiah especially critiques Zion as a place where God's people are faithless to him. Isaiah upbraids the people of Judah and Jerusalem for foreign alliances and a lack of trust in Yahweh (esp. Is 30:1-5; 31:1-3). The rationale behind this critique lay in Yahweh's kingship in Zion. Zion's inhabitants are to be faithful to their divine king, but Israel has become an unfaithful vassal. The inhabitants of Zion ape at righteousness and justice, faithful cultic ritual, and fidelity to Yahweh, but the verdict of God is that the "faithful city" has become an "adulteress" (Is 1:21; cf. Zeph 3:1). As a result, Zion has become the opposite of the chosen place; it has become an "enemy" that God will vanquish through judgment (Is 1:24-25). Zion becomes the object of prophetic critique due to its inhabitants' sins.

Isaiah calls God's people to *repentance and justice (Is 1:27) so that Zion would be saved from *evil that leads to destruction. Whoever trusts in the Lord will be safe in Zion, but those who do not will experience judgment. Isaiah emphasizes the trust necessary for God to reside in Zion (cf. Is 28:16). Those who make God's justice and righteousness their banner for life will be saved (Is 28:14-19).

Yet in Isaiah God's judgment upon Zion is inescapable. The holy city will be reduced to a "hut" (Is 1:8) by the fires of divine wrath. Isaiah's unique use of the title "Ariel" for Jerusalem is employed in judgment contexts (Is 29:2). In essence, God will fight against, rather than on behalf of, Zion because of the people's sin. Yet this judgment will lead to renewal and restoration by the work of the Lord. So Isaiah can say that those who remain after judgment in Zion will be called "holy" (Is 4:3) and a "holy seed" (Is 6:13).

3.2. Jeremiah. Jeremiah's critique of Zion takes a unique form. His well-known temple sermons excoriate the view that God is obligated to protect his people and city because the temple is there. Rather, Jeremiah exemplifies the desolation of Shiloh to illustrate God's commitment to his just rule rather than his obligation to a geographical locale. Holy sites do not enable Yahweh's presence among his people, but holy people do (Jer 7:3-11; 26:1-6). Thus, the Zion theology advocated in Jeremiah reflects a commitment to a divinely chosen site, but only if God's people remain committed to him in that place.

Jeremiah plays upon the possibility of Zion's repentance and return to God, but holds this in tension with Zion's recalcitrance in the face of upcoming judgment from God. Divine judgment that is made clear in Jeremiah's call (Jer 1:10) and various judgment oracles (Jer 4:5—6:30) is held in tension with the authentic offers of restoration: if God's people would repent, he would heal them (Jer 3:12-23; 4:1-4). The judgment oracles that surround this offer of restoration, however, reveal that Zion will not receive divine healing. Instead of receiving God's call for return, Zion will hear the call of war (Jer 4:6). As a result, Zion personified stretches out her hands and languishes in judgment (Jer 4:31).

3.3. Joel and Micah. Joel depicts coming judgment of God against Zion and combines it with "day of the Lord" language typical in the Book of the Twelve (see Rendtorff). God's people in Zion will raise an alarm for coming invasion on the *Day of the Lord, where God will fight against, rather than on behalf of, Zion (Joel 2:1-11). This judgment is due to Israel's (unidentified) lack of fidelity to the Lord. And as a result, Zion will suffer the plague of invasion, and Zion's prosperity will wither in the day of God's judgment. Micah spends more time detailing the various *sins of God's people, including *idolatry, covetousness, oppression, uncleanness, injustice and greed (Mic 1—3). God's people are led by those "who build Zion with blood and Jerusalem with iniquity" (Mic 3:10). As a result, God will wage war against his people, and Zion will be plowed like a field (Mic 3:12).

4. Zion and Prophetic Consolation.

A message of consolation for Zion matches the prophetic critique against Zion in the prophets. God's commitment to his people and place (Zion) funds this vision of consolation so prevalent in the prophets. This shows that the judgment and restoration of Zion are but two aspects of a single divine redemptive movement (see McConville).

4.1. Isaiah. Isaiah's message of judgment is matched with a call for repentance/return and a proclamation of consolation. Isaiah 2—4 concerns the future restoration of Zion, far removed from the egregious sins of the present. This future Zion will be marked by supreme honor among all other locales in the earth (Is 2:2), international pilgrimage for *worship (Is 2:3), and universal instruction of the Lord's ways among all peoples in Zion (Is 2:3) universal justice and eternal peace (Is 2:4). Further, Isaiah reveals that this vision of future Zion will come after a time of judgment for sin (Is 4:4). These themes occur in other Isaianic pictures of Zion's restoration as well (see Is 11; 25—27; 51—56; 60—66).

After divine judgment, Zion reflects divine glory at both Sinai and the tabernacle in the wilderness (Is 4:5-6; cf. Ex 40:34). Zion becomes the place where God's *presence at Sinai is reexperienced for Israel and the nations (Levenson). The possibility of this experience comes through the judgment and restoration of Zion. Only the select few ("remnant") who live through the judgment will experience restoration in Zion (Is 4:4; cf. Is 35:10; 37:32; 62:12).

Isaiah 25—27 gives a particular vision of this renewal, where *death will no longer be operative (Is 25), peace will be the banner of the city (Is 26) and God's vineyard of delight will produce fruit over the face of the world (Is 27). Further, nations will come and worship at the renewed sanctuary in Zion (Is 27:13; cf. Is 2:2-3). Key to Isaiah 25—26 is the vision of the judged yet restored "mountain of God" and "city"—Zion and Jerusalem.

Distinctive to Isaiah, Zion's renewal takes place in and through the work of the Suffering Servant (see Servant of Yahweh), who is God's agent of salvation and power. God's salvific power via the Suffering Servant is part of the larger theological motif of the "arm of the Lord" in Isaiah (Is 30:30, 32; 40:10; 48:14; 51:9; 52:10; 53:1; 62:8). In Isaiah 51—52 God presents a vision of comfort in the face of *suffering, captivity and judgment. The faithful *remnant of Israel will see the Lord comfort (Is 51:3) and redeem Zion (Is 52:1-7). But this restoration will occur because God appoints the Suffering Servant to mediate on behalf of suffering Israel (Is 53:1-12). The Suffering Servant bears Israel's sin and iniquity (Is 53:4-6). Through his suffering, the storm-tossed and not-comforted Zion (Is 54:11) will be comforted and restored (Is 54:12). The Suffering Servant will bring glorification instead of humiliation (Is 61:1-3). At his work, the ruins of Zion will be rebuilt.

The restoration will also incorporate a festal pilgrimage to Zion by the *nations. Zion will be the place where the nations come and worship the Lord (Is 56:6-8), and God's house will be "a house of prayer for all peoples" (Is 56:7; cf. Is 2:3). Zion's restoration will be a beacon to all peoples that renewed Jerusalem is called "The Redeemed of the Lord" and "A City Not Forsaken" (Is 62:12).

4.2. Jeremiah. Zion's restoration is envisioned rather differently in Jeremiah's so-called Book of Consolation (Jer 30—33). Zion is restored not through the Suffering Servant but rather through the unilateral *salvation of God. The Lord inscribes fidelity on the hearts of the people (Jer 31:33). In his salvation, a new covenant will be established, and the city that was forsaken, Zion itself, will be renewed as "sacred to the LORD" and "shall not be uprooted

or overthrown anymore, forever" (Jer 31:40). The theme of safety and security of Zion after judgment permeates Jeremiah 32—33. This is combined with an inward fidelity to the Lord, depicted in God's writing of the law on the hearts of the faithful (Jer 31:33-34). In this divinely orchestrated "restoration of fortunes" (cf. Jer 31:23; 32:44; 33:7, 11, 26), God will instill within Zion fidelity, love and faithfulness not known before in Israel's history. What is called upon for the faithful of God is to await this divinely orchestrated change in penitence, faith and confident expectancy.

4.3. Joel, Micah, Zephaniah, Zechariah. In the face of impending judgment against Zion in the Minor Prophets, an overwhelming vision of consolation is presented as well. Joel juxtaposes its Zion judgment proclamations with salvation oracles in Joel 2:23-32; 3:17-21. In these oracles God comforts and restores Zion's fortunes. Moreover, God will enact judgment against Zion's enemies in the valley of decision (Joel 3:12-16). Through this restoration God will no longer fight against his people and city but rather will dwell in Zion's midst as the divine and just king over creation (Joel 2:27; 3:16, 21). Still, Joel calls its readers to repentance and return in Zion. Instead of a trumpet blast that announces war in Zion (Joel 2:1)', a trumpet blast announces a penitential fast (Joel 2:15-17).

Micah too envisions consolation for Zion. Micah especially understands consolation coming in the "latter days" or "last days," when Zion will be established above all other mountains, and the nations will stream to Zion for worship, instruction, justice and peace (Mic 4:1-5; cf. Is 2:2-5). The vision of Zion's restoration is concomitant with an end to warfare and idolatry, for in Zion the faithful of God will "walk in the name of the LORD our God forever and ever" (Mic 4:5). This picture of consolation also brings healing to the poor, discarded and afflicted. God will redeem them in Zion together, where the divine king will rule over them forever (Mic 4:8-10).

In restoration, Zion will rejoice before God and find refuge in the Lord's renewed city. Zephaniah in particular builds upon Micah's vision of all nations going to Zion to receive God's instruction (Zeph 3:9-10). Purified from sin, "The king of Israel, the LORD," will be in the midst of Daughter Zion (Zeph 3:14-15). Because of his presence, fear and timidity will no longer afflict God's people.

This great reversal from oppression and humiliation to liberation and honor is emphasized especially in Zechariah. The judgment that marked Zion in the past is now repealed by God's love, as Zechariah's refrain reveals: "Thus says the LORD of hosts: I am exceedingly jealous for Jerusalem and for Zion" (Zech 1:14; similarly, Zech 8:2). So Zechariah is a book that proclaims especially Zion's restoration. For Zechariah, as with the other prophets, God's indwelling presence in Zion is concomitant to this restoration (Zech 2:10; 8:3), but Zechariah takes the picture of restoration further: God will establish his righteous yet humble king in the faithful city (Zech 9:9-10; cf. Mic 5:2). The installation of this king in Zion is part and parcel of God's renewal.

5. Daughter Zion.

The epithet "Daughter Zion" (*bat-ṣîyyôn*) appears in the OT, mostly in the Prophetic Books and in Lamentations (in the Prophetic Books: Isaiah 6x; Jeremiah 3x; Micah 4x; Zephaniah 1x; Zechariah 2x). Many scholars understand the title to be a personification of the city of Jerusalem as well as its inhabitants, but some tend to emphasize one or the other.

The reason for the discrepancy arises from the evidence in the prophetic corpus itself. There are instances where emphasis falls on the personification of the city rather than the people in the city. Isaiah 1:8 identifies Daughter Zion as a "besieged city," leading one to think that the term indicates the geographical place of Jerusalem. Further, the phrase "mountain of Daughter Zion" describes the Temple Mount in the midst of the city in Isaiah 16:1 (see Dekker, 269-70). The term also is likely used to describe a geographical locale in Micah 4:8. Still as the term is, at root, a metaphor, we cannot be overly rigid with the classification. So, for instance, Zechariah 2:10 and Zephaniah 3:14 trade upon the restoration of God's people using "Daughter Zion." And when judgment is in view, Micah 4:10 uses "Daughter Zion" to describe God's people going into exile.

Further, some point out that the term functions as a fecund gendered metaphor (*see* Women and Female Imagery). Some of the prophetic texts use the term to present the city as a "mother" whose inhabitants are her children (Maier). In this way, Daughter Zion is a place of security and well-being that nourishes and cares for her inhabitants/children. And the same term can reinforce a sense of loss and abandonment: a mother/Zion who has lost her children/inhabitants in and through the exile (*see* Lamentations, Book of). In these instances, the noun "daughter" represents the "children" of a city who belong to the city of "mother/Zion." The benefit of this view is that it takes seriously the normal syntactical form of a Hebrew construct chain (*bat-ṣîyyôn*) (see Floyd).

In addition to the notion of Daughter Zion as a mother, by using the epithet "daughter," Isaiah and Jeremiah in particular reinforce the notion that Zion is represented as a young marriageable woman. In this gendered metaphor, Daughter Zion is in need of the protection that comes with a husband. Of course, in the OT the protector/husband of Zion is Yahweh. This reinforces the Israelite notion of Yahweh as husband to God's people, and particularly in Zion (Maier).

Rather than press too hard on either the city or the people, it is best to allow individual texts to inform the meaning of the term. When assessed within the prophets, the title "Daughter Zion" is a polyvalent metaphor that is used in complementary but different ways, with emphasis falling sometimes upon the geographical locale of Zion and sometimes upon the inhabitants of Zion. In either case, poetic representation of the Daughter Zion bears interpretative fruit appropriate for each particular context. God's people are always and ever localized within particular places, and the ideal place for them to be is, on the reckoning of the prophets, on God's holy hill in Zion. This is because Zion represents (at least in its eschatological sense) God's people living in God's place under God's rule.

6. Conclusion: Zion in Time and Eternity.

When the prophetic testimony on Zion is taken together, Zion becomes a witness to God's universal dominion in *creation (see Is 60). As a theological symbol, Zion presses the future hope well beyond any former localization in the prophets' presentation of history. Zion, then, absorbs the grandeur of Israel's Sinai theophany into a new vision of God's universal reign in creation (Levenson). Although the Zion tradition may link back to creation theology, in the prophets the vision of "restored Zion" is a picture of creation *redivivus* (Ollenburger; Wildberger; cf. Gese on "Zion Torah"). In this way, for the prophets Zion becomes a rich theological symbol that depicts the reign of God over his creation in time and eternity. Zion becomes a symbol of new creation and redeemed humanity that lives before God without sin, death or pain because God rules in its midst (cf. Is 2:2-4; 65; Mic 4:1-7).

As a theological symbol, Zion reveals God's plan for a future hope. In the Minor Prophets Zion regularly appears as a people/city judged (Amos 1:2; 6:1; Mic 3:12) or saved (Obad 17; Mic 4:1-10) by the activity of God. But in the eschatological future, Zion is the locale where God's kingship will be exercised in creation (Mic 4:7; cf. Pss 95—100). In this way, Zion cannot be relegated for Israel alone. Zion as a symbol intertwines the destiny of Israel with the nations. As those who have been judged and remain, the nations and Israel will find refuge in Zion under the protection of God, the instruction of God, and his appointed king (Mic 4:1-2; Zeph 3:9; Zech 2:10-11; 8:1-23). After purification of sin, Israel and the nations are incorporated into a new humanity—ideal Israel, in Zion (Joel 2:23-32).

Zion in the prophets sets a trajectory that is then received in the NT (see Fuller Dow; Sherwood) (see Prophets in the New Testament). The NT in particular takes a different turn with the concept, for in the OT Yahweh reigns in Zion, whereas the NT interprets the reign of God in Zion christologically. Important to the NT reception of the Zion concept from the OT prophets are Isaiah 28:16; 62:11; Zechariah 9:9. In these texts, the people/city of Zion rejoice over their king who is returning to them to reign (Mt 21:5; Jn 12:15; cf. Zech 9:9; also Is 62:11). In the Gospels, this king is none other than Jesus the Messiah. Further, the Gospels indicate that Zion itself is founded upon Jesus. In this way, both the city and the inhabitants are built into a spiritual house founded upon the "cornerstone" of Zion— that is, Jesus. This is found not least in the Synoptic parable of the wicked tenants (Mt 21:42; Mk 12:10–11; Lk 20:17–18) but also in Romans 9:33 and 1 Peter 2:6. These NT texts draw upon the Zion imagery of Isaiah 28:16 // Ps 118:22 to reinforce the foundation for the church is none other than Christ. So "Zion" refers to the people of God constructed upon the Christ, Zion's cornerstone. This may be understood as a variation on the theme of the pilgrimage of nations seen in Zion ideology. Pilgrimage to Zion is fulfilled in part as both Israel and nations stream to Christ. Further, those who put their faith in "Zion/Christ" will experience ultimate vindication (even despite present suffering): "they will not be put to shame." This point carries thematic parallels to the foundational Zion motif of universal vindication of the righteous and judgment on the wicked at Zion. The NT transforms this ideology by finding its focal point in Jesus.

Finally, "Zion" in the NT seems to indicate the place where both God reigns in and through Christ (cf. Rev 14:1) as well as God's people dwell under his authority forever. This is indeed Zion's final destiny, a point picked up in Revelation 21:1-5, trading upon Isaiah's vision of new heaven and new earth. Here, Zion is filled with God's people (both Israel and the nations [see Sherwood]) under the rule of the appointed king who sits on the throne, Jesus himself. In Zion, Christ makes all things new (Rev 21:5).

See also MOUNTAIN IMAGERY; TEMPLE.

BIBLIOGRAPHY. **E. Boase,** *Fulfilment of Doom? The Dialogic Interaction between the Book of Lamentations and the Pre-exilic/Early Exilic Prophetic Literature* (LHBOTS 437; New York: T & T Clark, 2006) **J. Dekker,** *Zion's Rock-Solid Foundations: An Exegetical Study of the Zion Text in Isaiah 28:16* (OTS 54; Leiden: E. J. Brill, 2007); **O. Eissfeldt,** "Silo und Jerusalem," in *Kleine Schriften III* (Tübingen: Mohr Siebeck, 1966) 417-25; **M. F. Floyd,** "Welcome Back, Daughter of Zion!" *CBQ* 70 (2008) 484-504; **L. K. Fuller Dow,** *Images of Zion: Biblical Antecedents for New Jerusalem* (NTM 26; Sheffield: Sheffield Phoenix Press, 2010); **H. Gese,** *Vom Sinai zum Zion: Alttestamentliche Beiträge zur biblischen Theologie* (BEvT 64; Munich: Kaiser, 1974); **D. E. Gowan,** *Eschatology in the Old Testament* (2nd ed.; Edinburgh: T & T Clark, 2000); **J. A. Groves,** "Zion Traditions," *DOTHB* 1019-25; **J. Levenson,** *Sinai and Zion: An Entry in the Jewish Bible* (New York: Harper & Row, 1985); **C. M. Maier,** *Daughter Zion, Mother Zion: Gender, Space and the Sacred in Ancient Israel* (Minneapolis: Fortress, 2008); **C. Mandolfo,** *Daughter Zion Talks Back to the Prophets: A Dialogic Theology of the Book of Lamentations* (SBLSS 58; Atlanta: Society of Biblical Literature, 2007); **J. G. McConville,** "The Judgment of God in the Old Testament," *ExAud* 20 (2004) 25-42; **B. C. Ollenburger,** *Zion, the City of the Great King: A Theological Symbol of the Jerusalem Cult* (JSOTSup 41; Sheffield:

JSOT Press, 1987); **G. von Rad,** *Old Testament Theology,* trans. D. M. G. Stalker (2 vols.; New York: Harper & Row, 1965); **R. Rendtorff,** "Alas for the Day! The 'Day of the LORD' in the Book of the Twelve," in *God in the Fray: A Tribute to Walter Brueggemann,* ed. T. Linafelt and T. K. Beal (Minneapolis: Fortress, 1998) 186-97; **T. Renz,** "The Use of the Zion Tradition in the Book of Ezekiel," in *Zion: City of Our God,* ed. R. S. Hess and G. J. Wenham (Grand Rapids: Eerdmans, 1999) 77-103; **J. J. M. Roberts,** "The Davidic Origin of the Zion Tradition," *JBL* 92 (1973) 329-44; idem, "Zion in the Theology of the Davidic-Solomonic Empire," in *Studies in the Period of David and Solomon and Other Essays,* ed. T. Ishida (Winona Lake, IN: Eisenbrauns, 1983) 93-108; idem, "Yahweh's Foundation in Zion (Isa 28:6)," *JBL* 106 (1987) 27-45; **E. Rohland,** "Die Bedeutung der Erwählungstradition Israels für die Eschatologie der alttestamentlichen Propheten" (Ph.D. diss., University of Heidelberg, 1956); **C. R. Seitz,** *Zion's Final Destiny: The Development of the Book of Isaiah, a Reassessment of Isaiah 36-39* (Minneapolis: Fortress, 1991); **A. Sherwood,** "The Restoration of Humanity: Temple Cosmology, Worship, and Israel-Nations Unification in Biblical, Second Temple and Pauline Traditions" (Ph.D. diss., University of Durham, 2010); **H. Wildberger,** "Die Völkerwallfahrt zum Zion," *VT* 7 (1957) 62-81.

H. A. Thomas

Scripture Index

Subject Index

abomination, 41, 101, 127, 194, 221, 285, 352, 354, 419, 510, 715, 773, 854, 862, 871-73, 877

abomination of desolation, 41, 127, 285

Abrahamic Covenant, 99, 100, 104

acacia, 250

acrostic, 327, 477, 478, 481-82, 484-85, 561, 800

afterlife, 1-4, 154, 261, 720

agriculture, 9, 29, 106, 134, 189, 192, 198, 201, 249, 250-52, 299, 331, 343, 385, 402-3, 455, 490-91, 494, 503, 509, 575, 624, 630, 660, 662-63, 714, 722, 724, 739, 740, 743-44, 848, 892

Ahaz, 159, 236, 238-39, 288, 319, 326, 341, 375, 404-5, 425, 503, 545, 570, 577, 594-95, 636, 660, 665, 792, 798, 853, 863, 865

Akitu festival, 515

Akkadian, 17, 34, 50, 54, 90, 97, 99, 112-13, 119-20, 166, 201, 294, 310, 313, 400, 481, 495, 615-16, 659, 768, 852

Akkadian prayers, 119

Aleppo Codex, 76, 776-78, 807

Alexander the Great, 56, 115-16, 119, 125, 215, 232, 310, 417-18, 894

allegory, 128, 231-32, 234, 327, 458, 569, 743, 810-13, 895, 897

alliteration, 308

allusion, 1, 4, 7, 15, 79, 85, 94, 121, 123-24, 126, 127, 130-31, 172-74, 179, 183, 189, 205, 212, 222-24, 267, 275, 284, 303-5, 339, 340-42, 357-62, 369, 378, 382-83, 402, 408, 441, 443, 468, 508, 530, 538, 544, 550, 596, 630, 638, 650, 653-55, 691, 715, 726, 731, 773, 815, 846, 891, 894, 895

almonds, 249, 429, 819-20, 823, 862

alphabet, 478, 561

ambiguity, 19, 25-26, 140, 230, 309, 314, 342, 353, 489, 783, 787, 893

Ambrose, 384

amillennialism, 606-8

Ammon, 59, 173, 181, 199, 219, 411, 430, 433-36, 564, 661, 796, 830, 866, 899, 903

Ammonites, 6, 158, 411-12, 795, 903

Amos, Book of, 5-16, 795-97

Anath, 659

ancient Near Eastern background, 16-22, 33-34, 39, 43, 54, 62, 69, 83-84, 89-94, 96-99, 107, 111, 113, 118-19, 126, 152-54, 156, 163, 166, 234, 250, 252, 264, 268, 276, 281-82, 287, 352, 374, 397, 402-4, 410, 414, 473-74, 479, 491, 495, 499, 502, 513-14, 516, 518-21, 523, 536, 539, 548, 554, 565, 593, 616, 624-25, 627, 629, 634, 658-60, 695, 719, 722, 741, 758, 769, 828-29, 831-32, 843, 847, 852, 857, 868, 883, 886, 899

ancient Near Eastern prophecy, 17, 20-21

angel of the Lord/Yahweh, 25-26, 212, 564, 785

angels, 24-26, 28, 104, 117, 122, 125, 163, 228, 452

anger, 107, 133, 140, 173, 183, 188, 212, 222, 225, 254-56, 281, 316, 342, 349, 351, 372, 379, 432, 438, 464, 482-83, 484, 537, 555, 557, 584-86, 591, 618-21, 669, 671, 675, 687, 696, 712, 740, 742-43, 751, 761, 770, 798-99, 803, 823, 829-30, 833, 844, 867, 872, 878-83, 901-4

animals, 7, 15, 29-34, 59, 159, 167, 180-81, 194-95, 216, 243, 288, 298, 456-57, 464, 491-93, 499, 533, 557, 576, 600, 605, 658, 686, 688-91, 714, 725-26, 729, 769-70, 772, 798, 826, 832, 846,

854-55, 858, 862, 866, 868, 873, 891

animals, wild, 30-32, 106, 108, 152, 154, 179, 296, 491, 493, 726, 731

anointed one, 243, 288, 378, 503, 752

anointing, 117-18, 124, 147, 150, 243, 288, 299, 316, 378, 415, 492, 503, 537-38, 590, 592, 652-53, 705, 749, 752-53, 755, 803

anthropology, 70, 87, 337, 399, 402, 413, 617, 734-35, 741, 744, 748, 835

Antiochus Epiphanes, 40-41, 110, 115-19, 124, 127-28, 130-31, 149, 177, 182, 417-20, 600, 826, 894

aphorisms, 645-46, 648

apocalypse, apocalyptic literature, 2, 17, 24-25, 28-30, 33, 36-43, 112-13, 121, 124, 126, 129, 131, 157-59, 166, 178, 215, 232, 310, 322, 325, 378-79, 398, 416-17, 470, 507, 567, 590, 598-600, 602, 630, 640, 759, 772, 779, 782, 794-95, 802, 826-27, 834, 836, 898

Apocalypse of Zephaniah, 124, 131

apocalypticism, 36-37, 113, 131, 604

apostrophe, 475-76

Aquila, 27, 385, 812

Aquinas, 232, 386

Aram, 27, 44, 195, 238, 326, 391, 400, 403-4, 461, 538, 590, 660, 792-93, 796, 825, 852

Aramaic, 16-18, 24, 43-48, 50-51, 54, 110-11, 113-14, 116, 119-21, 124, 145-48, 159, 166, 176-77, 197, 201, 224, 310-13, 371, 382, 400, 450, 457, 507, 701, 747-48, 750, 775, 777, 779, 788, 822, 825, 869, 879, 885, 887

Aram-Damascus, 44, 400, 403-4

architecture, 230, 399, 767

Arm of God, 694

Artaxerxes, 117-18, 416-17, 451

artisans, 57, 198, 200-201, 251-52, 376, 411, 631

Ashurbanipal, 55-56, 408, 560, 562, 884-85

assonance, 450

Assyria, 16-17, 19-21, 24, 31, 41, 44, 45, 53-57, 61, 63-64, 84-85, 97, 99, 100, 102-3, 113, 115-16, 119, 137, 152, 154, 157-58, 160, 173, 179, 180-81, 189, 195, 196, 207, 211-12, 237-39, 245, 251, 268, 273, 276, 280, 285, 287-88, 319, 335-36, 341, 347-49, 368, 372, 380, 393, 397-400, 402-10, 415, 424-25, 437, 451, 453, 455-57, 460-61, 464, 490, 503, 514-15, 521, 536, 543-45, 547, 551, 555-56, 558, 560-65, 567, 572-73, 576-577, 592, 594-97, 600, 603, 635, 637, 658-61, 663, 673, 686, 696, 699, 725, 728-29, 740, 761, 782, 789, 791-95, 797-801, 808, 811, 828-30, 833, 836, 838-39, 851-52, 854-55, 857, 864, 866, 875, 879-84, 886-88, 903

Assyrian period, 19, 53, 154, 397-99, 595, 903

astrology, 160-61

Athanasius, 71

atonement, 169, 253-54, 256, 386, 685, 691, 772

Augustine, 26, 231, 384, 431, 788, 806

authorship, 110, 120, 219, 229, 233, 258, 273, 308, 311, 321, 364, 369, 370, 373, 386-89, 446, 462, 477, 523, 525, 680, 691, 806, 897, 898

Baal, 31, 33, 78, 83-85, 92, 96, 98, 102, 115, 153, 163, 166-67, 210, 236, 341-47, 351-54, 402, 449, 471, 495, 554-55, 592, 654, 659, 661, 673, 687, 731, 768, 794, 801, 828-30, 836, 838, 852, 872, 881, 901, 905

Babylon, 1, 2, 16-17, 19, 21, 31, 34, 40, 44-45, 47, 50-51, 53-60, 70, 83-85, 91-95, 97-98, 100-101, 103,

Article Index